THE OXFORD ENCYCLOPEDIA OF
BUDDHISM

THE OXFORD ENCYCLOPEDIA OF
BUDDHISM

Richard K. Payne
Georgios T. Halkias
EDITORS IN CHIEF

VOLUME 1
A–F

OXFORD
UNIVERSITY PRESS

OXFORD
UNIVERSITY PRESS

Oxford University Press is a department of the University of Oxford. It furthers the University's objective of excellence in research, scholarship, and education by publishing worldwide. Oxford is a registered trade mark of Oxford University Press in the UK and in certain other countries.

Published in the United States of America by Oxford University Press
198 Madison Avenue, New York, NY 10016, United States of America.

Library of Congress Cataloging-in-Publication Data

Names: Payne, Richard K., editor. | Halkias, Georgios, 1967– editor.
Title: The Oxford encyclopedia of Buddhism / Richard K. Payne,
Georgios T. Halkias, Editors in Chief.
Description: New York : Oxford University Press, 2023. |
Includes bibliographical references and index. | Contents: Vol 1 — Vol 2 — Vol 3
Identifiers: LCCN 2023019480 (print) | LCCN 2023019481 (ebook) |
ISBN 9780190256890 (set) | ISBN 9780190605995 (vol. 1 ; hardback) |
ISBN 9780190606008 (vol. 2 ; hardback) | ISBN 9780197746073 (vol. 3 ; hardback) |
ISBN 9780190668433 (ebk)
Subjects: LCSH: Buddhism—Encyclopedias.
Classification: LCC BQ128 .O94 2023 (print) | LCC BQ128 (ebook) |
DDC 294.303—dc23/eng/20230509
LC record available at https://lccn.loc.gov/2023019480
LC ebook record available at https://lccn.loc.gov/2023019481

FSC www.fsc.org MIX Paper from responsible sources FSC® C008955

Sheridan Books, Inc., United States of America

About the *Oxford Research Encyclopedia of Religion*

The Oxford Encyclopedia of Buddhism is published as part of the *Oxford Research Encyclopedia of Religion*, a dynamic and scholarly digital resource. This online collection of overview articles provides in-depth, foundational essays on both core and emerging topics in religion. All articles are commissioned under the editorial leadership of international experts of the highest caliber and are vetted through rigorous peer review. A living reference work, the online publication is updatable and enriched with crosslinking and multimedia features. The essays are intended for scholars, practitioners, and university-level readers, including advanced undergraduates, graduate students, and researchers.

Oxford Research Encyclopedia of Religion
Editor in Chief: John Barton, University of Oxford

Selected print titles from the *Oxford Encyclopedia of Religion* series:

The Oxford Encyclopedia of Martin Luther
Edited by Derek R. Nelson and Paul R. Hinlicky

The Oxford Encyclopedia of Religion in America
Edited by John Corrigan

Contents

List of Articles ix

Thematic and Geographical Outlines xiii

Preface xxi

Introduction xxiii

Acknowledgments xxix

THE OXFORD ENCYCLOPEDIA OF BUDDHISM

Directory of Contributors (vol. 3) 2757

Index (vol. 3) 2765

List of Articles

A

Abhidharmakośabhāṣya (Treasury of Metaphysics with Self-Commentary)
Abhisamayālaṃkāra (Ornament for Clear Realization)
American Buddhism during World War II Imprisonment
Amoghavajra
Art, Architecture, and National Memory-Making
Avalokiteśvara: The Bodhisattva of Compassion

B

Bodhisattvabhūmi (The Bodhisattva Stages)
The Body of the Buddha
The Bön Tradition of Dzogchen
Buddhaghosa
Buddhism and Bioethics
Buddhism and Biography
Buddhism and Globalization
Buddhism and Healing in China
Buddhism and Media
Buddhism and Medicine in India
Buddhism and Medicine in Japan
Buddhism and Medicine in Premodern Japan
Buddhism and Print Culture in China
Buddhism and Shinto
Buddhism and the Environment
Buddhism in Colonial Contexts
Buddhism in Film
Buddhisms in Diaspora: The Canadian Context of Chinese Buddhism
Buddhist Art and Architecture in Tibet
Buddhist Chaplaincy

Buddhist Cosmology
Buddhist Geography and Regionalism
Buddhist Meditation and Contemplation
Buddhist Philosophy as Philosophy
Buddhist Wall Paintings
Buddhist Wizards (*Vidhyadhāra/Weizzā/Weikza*): Contemporary Burma/Myanmar
Buddhist Wizards (*Vidhyadhāra/Weizzā/Weikza*): Origins and History

C

Candrakīrti's Middle Way Philosophy
Canon and Commentary in the Earliest Buddhist Manuscripts
Chan Literature
Chöd: A Tibetan Buddhist Practice

D

D. T. Suzuki: A Biography
D. T. Suzuki: Ideas and Influences
Debate in the Tibetan Tradition
Debate Traditions in Premodern Japan
Domestic Dharma in Japan
Dunhuang Art
Dunhuang Texts
Dzogchen

E

Early History of the Drukpa Kagyü School
Early Modern European Encounters with Buddhism
The Economics of Buddhism
Engaged Buddhism
Epigraphy and the Study of Buddhism: South Asia's Northern Corridor
Esoteric Buddhism in Southeast Asia
Ethics and Buddhism

F

Filial Piety in Chinese Buddhism
Fo Guang Shan
Four Noble Truths
From Manuscript to Print in South and Southeast Asia

G

Gelukpa
Global Buddhism
Global Theravada Buddhism: Asian Foundations
Global Theravada: Transmission beyond Asia
Globalizing Tantric Buddhism
Guardian/Protector Deities in Tibetan Buddhism

H

History of Buddhisms in China: The Nanbeicho Period (Late 4th Century to the Sui Dynasty)
Homa: Tantric Fire Ritual
Hsing Yun
Huineng
Humanistic Buddhism (Rensheng Fojiao 人生佛教 / Renjian Fojiao 人間佛教)

I

Imaging the Buddha in South Asia
The Imamura Families and the Making of American Buddhism
Intention in the Pali Suttas and Abhidharma

J

Japanese Buddhisms in Diaspora
Jātaka
Jebtsundamba Khutugtus of Mongolia

K

The Kadampa: A Formative Movement of Tibetan Buddhism
Kālacakra-Maṇḍala: Symbolism and Construction

L

Longchenpa

M

Madhyamaka
Mahāmudrā in India and Tibet
Mañjuśrī
Maritime Buddhism
Marpa Lotsawa Chökyi Lodrö
Mipam
Monastic Education in Contemporary Asia
Mongolian Buddhism in the Democratic Period
Mongolian Buddhism in the Early 20th Century
Mongolian Buddhism in the Yuan Period
Muslim–Buddhist Relations and Buddhism in Muslim Sources until the Mongol Period

N

Nāgārjuna
Naikan: A Meditation Method and Psychotherapy
Narratives of Buddhist Relics and Images
Nechung: A Tibetan Buddhist Oracle
Nichiren

P

Patronage of Buddhist Monasteries in Eastern India, 600–1300 CE
Perfections (Six and Ten) of Bodhisattvas in Buddhist Literature
The Philosophical Works and Influence of Dignāga and Dharmakīrti
Pilgrimage in Buddhist Tibet
Pilgrimage in China
Practices of Protection in the Pali World
Prajñāpāramitā and Khmer Esoteric Buddhism in the 10th to 13th centuries
Psychological Interpreters of Buddhism
Pure Land Buddhism in Tibetan Contexts

Q

Queering Buddhist Traditions

R

The Reincarnation System in Central Asian Buddhism
Rennyo
Ryōgen

S

The Sangha as an Institution
Śāntideva's Introduction to the Practices of Awakening (*Bodhicaryāvatāra*)
Sarvāstivāda Abhidharma
Secular Buddhism
Sheng Yen
Shingon
The Six Nara Schools
Sōka Gakkai
Southeast Asian Refugees in North America
Sri Lanka's Sinhala Buddhist Guardian Deities: Satara Varan Devi
The Study of Visual Culture in South and Southeast Asian Buddhism

T

Taixu
Tantra and the Tantric Traditions of Hinduism and Buddhism
Tantric Buddhism in Japan: Kukai and Saicho

Tantric Buddhism in Japan: Shingon, Tendai, and the Esotericization of Japanese Buddhisms
Tantric Revival in China
Theravāda Buddhism
Thích Nhất Hạnh in the Context of the Modern Development of Vietnamese Buddhism
Three Turnings of the Wheel of Doctrine (Dharma-Cakra)
Tibetan Book of the Dead (*Bardo Thödol*)
Tibetan Buddhism and the Gesar Epic
Tibetan Buddhist Power Objects
Tibetan Medicine and Its Buddhist Contexts
Tibetan Visionary Buddhism
Transmission of Buddhist Media and Texts
Tri Songdetsen
Tsangpa Gyare (1161–1211), Founder of the Drukpa Kagyü School
Tzu Chi

V

The Vajrakīla Tantras
Vinaya Rules for Monks and Nuns
Visualization/Contemplation Sutras (Guan Jing)

W

Western Buddhism and Race

X

Xuyun

Z

Zhentong (Other-Emptiness)

Thematic and Geographical Outlines

Over its two-and-a-half-millennia-long history Buddhism has developed a profusion of literary sources in several languages, reflecting an astounding variety of lineages, institutions, doctrines, practices, and teachers. As an academic field of study, it is changing and expanding in ways that make the image of a closed and comprehensive encyclopedia a mirage—an ever-enticing, ever-receding goal. Being aware of this, *The Oxford Encyclopedia of Buddhism* seeks to address the current needs of students, researchers, and scholars of Buddhism by surveying the richness of the tradition and the different fields of expertise that have emerged in the 21st century. The volume shows what a research encyclopedia of Buddhism is today: an ongoing organic development of nodes and networks of knowledge; an open-ended project accelerated by technological advancements in the fields of digital information. It inaugurates a promising beginning without a defining end.

The following thematic clusters are intended to facilitate use of this network, giving the user access to entries that may otherwise be difficult to locate in the alphabetic organization of the body of the work itself. As such, it includes well-established categories that the user may be expecting, and ones that are less familiar. As mentioned above, the field is continuously developing, and therefore it does not sort neatly into exclusive categories. Consequently, we have created two outlines—one thematic and one geographic. Additionally, while there are a total of 139 articles constituting this print version, several entries appear under more than one heading. This reflects the overall goal of this research encyclopedia. Rather than presuming to impose some conceptual framework onto the field, our goal has been to represent currently developing topics to facilitate the growth of Buddhist studies.

THEMATIC OUTLINE

ART, ARCHITECTURE, AND SYMBOLIC MOTIFS

Art, Architecture, and National Memory-Making
Buddhist Art and Architecture in Tibet
Buddhism in Film
Buddhist Wall Paintings
Dunhuang Art
Epigraphy and the Study of Buddhism: South Asia's Northern Corridor
From Manuscript to Print in South and Southeast Asia
Imaging the Buddha in South Asia
Kālacakra-Maṇḍala: Symbolism and Construction
Patronage of Buddhist Monasteries in Eastern India, 600–1300 CE
Prajñāpāramitā and Khmer Esoteric Buddhism in the 10th to 13th centuries
The Study of Visual Culture in South and Southeast Asian Buddhism

BUDDHAS, BODHISATTVAS, GUARDIANS, AND DEITIES

Avalokiteśvara: The Bodhisattva of Compassion
The Body of the Buddha
Buddhist Wizards (*Vidhyadhāra/Weizzā/Weikza*): Contemporary Burma/Myanmar
Buddhist Wizards (*Vidhyadhāra/Weizzā/Weikza*): Origins and History
Guardian/Protector Deities in Tibetan Buddhism
Mañjuśrī
Prajñāpāramitā and Khmer Esoteric Buddhism in the 10th to 13th centuries
Sri Lanka's Sinhala Buddhist Guardian Deities: Satara Varan Devi

HISTORICAL AND HISTORIOGRAPHIC STUDIES

Buddhism and Shinto
Buddhism in Colonial Contexts
Buddhisms in Diaspora: The Canadian Context of Chinese Buddhism
Buddhist Geography and Regionalism
Early Modern European Encounters with Buddhism
Global Buddhism
Globalizing Tantric Buddhism
History of Buddhisms in China: The Nanbeicho Period (Late 4th Century to the Sui Dynasty)
Japanese Buddhisms in Diaspora
Maritime Buddhism
Mongolian Buddhism in the Early 20th Century
Mongolian Buddhism in the Democratic Period
Mongolian Buddhism in the Yuan Period
Three Turnings of the Wheel of Doctrine (Dharma-Cakra)

PHILOSOPHICAL AND DOCTRINAL STUDIES

Buddhist Cosmology
Buddhist Philosophy as Philosophy
Dzogchen
Four Noble Truths
Intention in the Pali Suttas and Abhidharma
Madhyamaka
Mahāmudrā in India and Tibet
Perfections (Six and Ten) of Bodhisattvas in Buddhist Literature
The Philosophical Works and Influence of Dignāga and Dharmakīrti
The Reincarnation System in Central Asian Buddhism
Sarvāstivāda Abhidharma
Theravada Buddhism

Three Turnings of the Wheel of Doctrine (Dharma-Cakra)
Vinaya Rules for Monks and Nuns
Zhentong (Other-Emptiness)

RITUALS, CONTEMPLATIVE PRACTICES, AND APPLICATIONS

The Bön Tradition of Dzogchen
Buddhist Chaplaincy
Buddhist Meditation and Contemplation
Chöd: A Tibetan Buddhist Practice
Debate in the Tibetan Tradition
Debate Traditions in Premodern Japan
Dzogchen
Filial Piety in Chinese Buddhism
Homa: Tantric Fire Ritual
Kālacakra-Maṇḍala: Symbolism and Construction
Mahāmudrā in India and Tibet
Naikan: A Meditation Method and Psychotherapy
Nechung: A Tibetan Buddhist Oracle
Pilgrimage in Buddhist Tibet
Pilgrimage in China
Practices of Protection in the Pali World
Śāntideva's Introduction to the Practices of Awakening (*Bodhicaryāvatāra*)
Tibetan Buddhist Power Objects
Tibetan Visionary Buddhism

SCHOOLS, TRADITIONS, AND LINEAGES

The Bön Tradition of Dzogchen
Chan Literature
Chöd: A Tibetan Buddhist Practice
Dzogchen
Early History of the Drukpa Kagyü School
Esoteric Buddhism in Southeast Asia
Fo Guang Shan
Gelukpa
Global Theravada Buddhism: Asian Foundations
Global Theravada: Transmission beyond Asia
Globalizing Tantric Buddhism
Humanistic Buddhism (Rensheng Fojiao 人生佛教 / Renjian Fojiao 人間佛教)
Japanese Buddhisms in Diaspora
Jebtsundamba Khutugtus of Mongolia
The Kadampa: A Formative Movement of Tibetan Buddhism
Mongolian Buddhism in the Democratic Period
Pure Land Buddhism in Tibetan Contexts
Sarvāstivāda Abhidharma
Secular Buddhism
Shingon
The Six Nara Schools
Soka Gakkai
Tantra and the Tantric Traditions of Hinduism and Buddhism
Tantric Buddhism in Japan: Kukai and Saicho
Tantric Buddhism in Japan: Shingon, Tendai, and the Esotericization of Japanese Buddhisms
Tantric Revival in China
Theravada Buddhism
Tibetan Visionary Buddhism
Zhentong (Other-Emptiness)

SOCIAL, CULTURAL, AND INTELLECTUAL ISSUES

American Buddhism during World War II Imprisonment
Art, Architecture, and National Memory-Making
Buddhism and Bioethics
Buddhism and Biography
Buddhism and Globalization
Buddhism and Healing in China
Buddhism and Media

Buddhism and Print Culture in China
Buddhism and the Environment
Buddhism and Medicine in India
Buddhism and Medicine in Japan
Buddhism and Medicine in Premodern Japan
Buddhism in Colonial Contexts
Buddhism in Film
Buddhist Chaplaincy
Buddhist Geography and Regionalism
Muslim–Buddhist Relations and Buddhism in Muslim Sources until the Mongol Period
Domestic Dharma in Japan
The Economics of Buddhism
Engaged Buddhism
Ethics and Buddhism
Monastic Education in Contemporary Asia
Narratives of Buddhist Relics and Images
Patronage of Buddhist Monasteries in Eastern India, 600–1300 CE
Psychological Interpreters of Buddhism
Queering Buddhist Traditions
The Sangha as an Institution
Secular Buddhism
Southeast Asian Refugees in North America
The Study of Visual Culture in South and Southeast Asian Buddhism
Tibetan Medicine and Its Buddhist Contexts
Transmission of Buddhist Media and Texts
Western Buddhism and Race

TEACHERS AND HISTORICAL FIGURES

Amoghavajra
Buddhaghosa
Buddhist Wizards (*Vidhyadhāra/Weizzā/Weikza*): Origins and History
Buddhist Wizards (*Vidhyadhāra/Weizzā/Weikza*): Contemporary Burma/Myanmar
Candrakīrti's Middle Way Philosophy
D. T. Suzuki: A Biography
D. T. Suzuki: Ideas and Influences
Hsing Yun
Huineng
Jebtsundamba Khutugtus of Mongolia
Longchenpa
Marpa Lotsawa Chökyi Lodrö
Mipam
Nāgārjuna
Nichiren
Rennyo
Ryōgen
Taixu
Tantric Buddhism in Japan: Kukai and Saicho
The Body of the Buddha
The Philosophical Works and Influence of Dignāga and Dharmakīrti
The Imamura Families and the Making of American Buddhism
Thích Nhất Hạnh in the Context of the Modern Development of Vietnamese Buddhism
Tri Songdetsen
Tsangpa Gyare (1161–1211), Founder of the Drukpa Kagyü School
Tzu Chi
Xuyun

TEXTS AND PHILOLOGICAL STUDIES

Abhidharmakośabhāṣya (Treasury of Metaphysics with Self-Commentary)
Abhisamayālaṃkāra (Ornament for Clear Realization)
Bodhisattvabhūmi (The Bodhisattva Stages)
Canon and Commentary in the Earliest Buddhist Manuscripts
Chan Literature
Dunhuang Texts
Epigraphy and the Study of Buddhism: South Asia's Northern Corridor
From Manuscript to Print in South and Southeast Asia
Jātaka
The Vajrakīla Tantras
Tibetan Book of the Dead (*Bardo Thödol*)

Tibetan Buddhism and the Gesar Epic
Visualization/Contemplation Sutras (Guan Jing)

GEOGRAPHICAL OUTLINE

EAST ASIA

Amoghavajra
Buddhism and Healing in China
Buddhism and Medicine in Japan
Buddhism and Medicine in Premodern Japan
Buddhism and Print Culture in China
Buddhism and Shinto
Candrakīrti's Middle Way Philosophy
Chan Literature
D. T. Suzuki: A Biography
D. T. Suzuki: Ideas and Influences
Debate Traditions in Premodern Japan
Domestic Dharma in Japan
Filial Piety in Chinese Buddhism
Fo Guang Shan
History of Buddhisms in China: The Nanbeicho Period (Late 4th Century to the Sui Dynasty)
Hsing Yun
Huineng
Humanistic Buddhism (Rensheng Fojiao 人生佛教 / Renjian Fojiao 人間佛教)
Monastic Education in Contemporary Asia
Naikan: A Meditation Method and Psychotherapy
Nichiren
Pilgrimage in China
Rennyo
Ryōgen
Shingon
The Six Nara Schools
Sōka Gakkai
Taixu
Tantric Buddhism in Japan: Kukai and Saicho
Tantric Buddhism in Japan: Shingon, Tendai, and the Esotericization of Japanese Buddhisms
Tantric Revival in China
Thích Nhất Hạnh in the Context of the Modern Development of Vietnamese Buddhism
Tzu Chi
Visualization/Contemplation Sutras (Guan Jing)
Xuyun

EUROPE AND THE AMERICAS

American Buddhism during World War II Imprisonment
Buddhisms in Diaspora: The Canadian Context of Chinese Buddhism
Early Modern European Encounters with Buddhism
Southeast Asian Refugees in North America
The Imamura Families and the Making of American Buddhism
Western Buddhism and Race

INNER ASIA

Abhidharmakośabhāṣya (Treasury of Metaphysics with Self-Commentary)
Abhisamayālaṃkāra (Ornament for Clear Realization)
Bodhisattvabhūmi (The Bodhisattva Stages)
The Bön Tradition of Dzogchen
Buddhist Art and Architecture in Tibet
Buddhist Wall Paintings
Chöd: A Tibetan Buddhist Practice
Debate in the Tibetan Tradition
Dunhuang Art
Dunhuang Texts
Dzogchen
Early History of the Drukpa Kagyü School
Gelukpa
Guardian/Protector Deities in Tibetan Buddhism

Jebtsundamba Khutugtus of Mongolia
Kālacakra-Maṇḍala: Symbolism and Construction
Longchenpa
Mahāmudrā in India and Tibet
Mipam
Monastic Education in Contemporary Asia
Mongolian Buddhism in the Democratic Period
Mongolian Buddhism in the Early 20th Century
Mongolian Buddhism in the Yuan Period
Nechung: A Tibetan Buddhist Oracle
Pilgrimage in Buddhist Tibet
Pure Land Buddhism in Tibetan Contexts
The Sangha as an Institution
Soka Gakkai
The Kadampa: A Formative Movement of Tibetan Buddhism
Marpa Lotsawa Chökyi Lodrö
The Vajrakīla Tantras
Tibetan Book of the Dead (*Bardo Thödol*)
Tibetan Buddhism and the Gesar Epic
Tibetan Buddhist Power Objects
Tibetan Medicine and Its Buddhist Contexts
Tibetan Visionary Buddhism
Tri Songdetsen
Tsangpa Gyare (1161–1211), Founder of the Drukpa Kagyü School
Zhentong (Other-Emptiness)

SOUTH ASIA

Abhidharmakośabhāṣya (Treasury of Metaphysics with Self-Commentary)
Abhisamayālaṃkāra (Ornament for Clear Realization)
Bodhisattvabhūmi (The Bodhisattva Stages)
Buddhaghosa
Buddhism and Medicine in India
Muslim–Buddhist Relations and Buddhism in Muslim Sources until the Mongol Period
Epigraphy and the Study of Buddhism: South Asia's Northern Corridor
Esoteric Buddhism in Southeast Asia
Prajñāpāramitā and Khmer Esoteric Buddhism in the 10th to 13th centuries
From Manuscript to Print in South and Southeast Asia
Imaging the Buddha in South Asia
Jātaka
Kālacakra-Maṇḍala: Symbolism and Construction
Mahāmudrā in India and Tibet
Monastic Education in Contemporary Asia
Nāgārjuna
Patronage of Buddhist Monasteries in Eastern India, 600–1300 CE
Practices of Protection in the Pali World
Sarvāstivāda Abhidharma
Sri Lanka's Sinhala Buddhist Guardian Deities: Satara Varan Devi

SOUTHEAST ASIA

Buddhist Wizards (*Vidhyadhāra/Weizzā/Weikza*): Contemporary Burma/Myanmar
Buddhist Wizards (*Vidhyadhāra/Weizzā/Weikza*): Origins and History
Esoteric Buddhism in Southeast Asia
Prajñāpāramitā and Khmer Esoteric Buddhism in the 10th to 13th centuries
Practices of Protection in the Pali World
The Study of Visual Culture in South and Southeast Asian Buddhism

TRANS-REGIONAL

Art, Architecture, and National Memory-Making
Avalokiteśvara: The Bodhisattva of Compassion
The Body of the Buddha
Buddhism and Bioethics
Buddhism and Biography
Buddhism and Globalization
Buddhism and Media
Buddhism and the Environment

Buddhist Cosmology
Buddhist Geography and Regionalism
Buddhism in Colonial Contexts
Buddhism in Film
Buddhist Chaplaincy
Buddhist Meditation and Contemplation
Buddhist Philosophy as Philosophy
Canon and Commentary in the Earliest Buddhist Manuscripts
The Economics of Buddhism
Engaged Buddhism
Ethics and Buddhism
Four Noble Truths
Global Buddhism
Global Theravada Buddhism: Asian Foundations
Global Theravada: Transmission beyond Asia
Globalizing Tantric Buddhism
Homa: Tantric Fire Ritual
Intention in the Pali Suttas and Abhidharma
Japanese Buddhisms in Diaspora
Madhyamaka
Mañjuśrī
Maritime Buddhism
Nāgārjuna
Narratives of Buddhist Relics and Images
Perfections (Six and Ten) of Bodhisattvas in Buddhist Literature
The Philosophical Works and Influence of Dignāga and Dharmakīrti
Psychological Interpreters of Buddhism
Queering Buddhist Traditions
The Reincarnation System in Central Asian Buddhism
Secular Buddhism
Tantra and the Tantric Traditions of Hinduism and Buddhism
Theravada Buddhism
Three Turnings of the Wheel of Doctrine (Dharma-Cakra)
Transmission of Buddhist Media and Texts
Vinaya Rules for Monks and Nuns

Preface

In my memory, an encyclopedia offered a kind of finality. When I was a student, my school library had an *Encyclopedia Britannica,* to which we were referred as the final word on matters of fact. Later, as a young father, I was so very proud to be able to purchase one to have in our house for my own daughter's use. And in 1987, the *Encyclopedia of Religion* was published under the editorship of the famous Mircea Eliade. Now, the field of religious studies also had its own final statement, one that surpassed the long-outdated Hastings *Encyclopedia of Religion and Ethics.* But then, in 2004, the second edition of the *Encyclopedia of Religion,* now under a different editor, was issued. It still seemed to me to exude an air of finality, despite having come so quickly after the first. And now, as a no longer quite so young scholar, I was proud to have a copy for myself.

But already, by that time, the internet was eroding the sense of there ever being a final encyclopedia. In the world of print, updates were cumbersome—supplementary yearbooks, or complete new editions, were a substantial investment and further eroded the sense that the original was indeed final, and therefore, authoritative—a philological point that seems to elude some Buddhist studies scholars who continue to seek the original.

This, then is a research encyclopedia that does not claim finality. It is, at best, a moment in the field of Buddhist studies, and an uneven one at that. It seeks to be representative and suggestive—but certainly seeks at the same time to avoid the delusion of finality.

Richard K. Payne
Prof. Emeritus, Institute of Buddhist Studies
February 2024

Introduction

BUDDHIST STUDIES: BRIEF HISTORICAL SKETCH

This research encyclopedia is concerned with the contemporary, Western academic study of Buddhism, which begins with the construction of Buddhism as an object of study in the 19th century. That is, conceptualizing Buddhism as a single, continuous entity with a history stretching back over two and a half millennia and extending across multiple cultures and languages. The formation of this modern idea of Buddhism was itself part of the process by which the modern conception of religion was formed.[1] Buddhism came to be treated as one of the world religions (or world's religions, depending on emphasis), while at the same time validating that new way of conceptualizing religion, that is, as an overarching category glossing over a variety of different instantiations located in different times and cultures.[2]

Foundational to the construction of Buddhism as a singular object of study was the publication in 1844 of the *Introduction à l'histoire du Buddhisme indien*[3] by Eugène Burnouf

1 There have been several important studies of the development of the concept of "religion" in the nineteenth century. Particularly important among these is Tomoko Masuzawa, *The Invention of World Religions: Or How European Universalism was Preserved in the Language of Pluralism* (Chicago and London: University of Chicago Press, 2005).

2 See also, Timothy Fitzgerald, *The Ideology of Religious Studies* (New York and Oxford: Oxford University Press, 2000).

3 Eugène Burnouf, *Introduction to the History of Buddhism*, tr. Katia Buffetrille and Donald S. Lopez, Jr. (Chicago and London: University of Chicago Press, 2010).

(1801–1852). Covering the period from its founding through to the late medieval era, this work gave form to Indian Buddhism as a singular object of inquiry. In addition, it did so by focusing on texts—a characteristic of modern Buddhist studies ever since. Starting in the mid-19th century, the idea of there being a set of "world religions" was being developed in European academic circles, and Burnouf's work "played a key role in the creation of Buddhism as a 'world religion,' one that set forth an ancient philosophy that seemed simultaneously most modern."[4] Thus, although itself limited to Indian Buddhism, Burnouf's *Introduction* provided the necessary basis for the creation of the larger conceptual object that Buddhist studies takes as its field of inquiry. Both academically and popularly, Burnouf's *Introduction* established the "historical" Buddha as the founder of Buddhism.[5] In other words, historiographic presumptions based on the model of Christianity created a Buddha whose relation to Buddhism is understood as directly comparable to the sanctified role of Jesus for Christianity.

Given this milieu,[6] Buddhist studies was initially made to fit into the model of biblical studies. Consequently, the methodologies of philology and textual studies, and a focus on doctrines and putatively key doctrinal texts have dominated Buddhist studies since that time. Paradigmatic works for the older conception include publications such as Étienne Lamotte, Le Traité de la *grande vertu de sagesse*, and Gadjin M. Nagao's translation and commentary on the Mahāyānasaṃgraha. This model of scholarship—based on philology as its method, texts as its object of study, and the explication of doctrine as its goal—remains essential and foundational for Buddhist studies.

While the proximate source of this intellectual project lies in the 19th century, the historian Urs App points further back for the roots of our present-day conception of Buddhism and the appropriate methods for its study. According to App, "the systematic study of non-Abrahamic oriental religions and languages by Europeans began in sixteenth-century Japan, and that several key ideas shaping the European discovery of Asian religions in the subsequent centuries have their roots there."[7]

The contemporary study of Buddhism as examined in this volume can be oriented as an "etic" inquiry, that is, intellectual projects that stand outside the object of study. The alternative is an emic perspective, that is, the creation of Buddhism as an object of study from a perspective located *within* the tradition. The scholastic traditions within Buddhism date from a very early period in the history that modern scholarship has constructed for it. The earliest projects of memorizing the teachings, recording them in writing, then organizing them into collections and eventually canons has stretched across that entire history, in every region where Buddhism has been practiced, right up to the present.

One of the scholastic projects examining the tradition as a whole is doxography, also known as "tenet systems" (T. *grub mtha'*).[8] A particularly revealing instance of this emic scholastic genre

4 Donald S. Lopez, Jr., "Introduction to the Translation," in Burnouf, *Introduction to the History of Buddhism*, 1–27, 1.

5 See Thomas Calobrisi, "Beyond Belief: How a French Text on Indian Buddhism Changed American Culture," dissertation, Graduate Theological Union, 2021.

6 Tomoko Masuzawa, The Invention of World Religions: Or, How European Universalism was Preserved in the Language of Pluralism (Chicago: University of Chicago Press, 2005).

7 Urs App, *The Birth of Orientalism* (Philadelphia and Oxford: University of Pennsylvania Press, 2010), 9. See also, Urs App, *The Cult of Emptiness: The Western Discovery of Buddhist Thought and the Invention of Oriental Philosophy* (Rorshchach and Kyoto: University Media, 2012).

8 Jeffrey Hopkins, "The Tibetan Genre of Doxography: Structuring a Worldview," in *Tibetan Literature: Studies in Genre*, José Ignacio Cabezón and Roger R. Jackson, eds., 170–186 (Ithaca, NY: Snow Lion, 1996

is Thuken Losang Chökyi Nyima's *The Crystal Mirror of Philosophical Systems.*[9] The majority of Tibetan tenet system textbooks cover much the same material, and use structurally similar arguments and categories in representing both Buddhist and non-Buddhist Indian religious systems as well as Tibetan developments of Buddhism. Methodologically, Thuken's 18th-century work goes beyond those highly standardized contents by introducing an empirical orientation that opened the work to include not only Bön but also Central Asian and Chinese schools of thought. It is easy to characterize the comparative study of religious systems, including Buddhism, as a European development in the 19th century. However, both App's descriptions of the encounter of Japanese Buddhists and Jesuit missionaries in the 16th century and Thuken's expansion of standard scholastic representations suggest the necessity of engaging more widely and more deeply with the complex intellectual history of conceptualizing Buddhism as a seemingly singular but in fact relational and developmental entity that is the focus of our field of study.

The etic–emic distinction introduced above is, however, a fuzzy one despite the many Buddhist and non-Buddhist theorists who have argued in favor of an epistemology divided by an insider and outsider dualism.[10] Politicized claims that the outsider view is superior because it is more dispassionate and objective are matched by counterclaims that the insider view is superior because it provides experiential understanding. Outside of these polarized debates, some scholars have shown that the distinction leads to pseudo-problems.[11] Although not intending to ignore or substantialize the distinction, we employ it here as a simple yet indicative heuristic device that has contributed to the intellectual course and theorization of Buddhism as an academic field of study.

Several works during the last few decades have examined the social and cultural histories of Buddhist studies, and of religious studies more generally.[12] By at times critically questioning the inherited assumptions of the field, those works have been key to revealing both the neglected and unacknowledged constraints of the field as it had been defined, and the potential value of alternatives for promoting new venues of inquiry and forging pathways to themes, questions, and networks of emerging critical knowledge. This encyclopedia does not attempt to superimpose a metastructure on the field, nor recapitulate the critical aspects of the existing literature on Buddhism. Rather, it provides intuitive access to constructive projects in new areas of evolving interest and to original ways of conceptualizing the critical effect that the foundational works of scholarship have made possible.

THIS RESEARCH ENCYCLOPEDIA: ORIENTATIONS AND APPROACHES

The Oxford Encyclopedia of Buddhism was conceived as the first of its kind research encyclopedia: offering a systematic effort to both identify and give better definition to the ways in which

9 Thuken Losang Chökyi Nyima's *The Crystal Mirror of Philosophical Systems: A Tibetan Study of Asian Religious Thought*, Geshe Lhundub Sopa, tr., Roger Jackson, ed. (Boston: Wisdom Publications, 2009).

10 The very distinction is at times naturalized, see for example N. Ross Reat, "Insiders and Outsiders in the Study of Religious Traditions," *Journal of the American Academy of Religion* LI/3 (1983), 459–476.

11 Jeppe Sinding Jensen, "Revisiting the Insider–Outsider Debate: Dismantling a Pseudo-problem in the Study of Religion," *Method and Theory in the Study of Religion*, 23.1 (2011), 29–47.

12 Exemplary of the former is Donald S. Lopez, Jr., ed. *Curators of the Buddha: The Study of Buddhism Under Colonialism* (Chicago: University of Chicago Press, 1995); of the latter is Timothy Fitzgerald, *The Ideology of Religious Studies* (Oxford and New York: Oxford University Press, 2000).

Buddhist studies is dynamically developing and changing. For decades, scholars have been creatively moving outside the familiar boundaries of academic institutions, examining subjects that were previously not in mainstream disciplines nor considered properly part of Buddhist studies, and employing diverse disciplinary orientations, subject-matters, and methodologies.

Reflecting these innovations, this encyclopedia does not attempt to impose a conceptual architectonic onto the field. Instead, it provides an instructive variety of research articles exemplifying the open-ended nature Buddhist studies, the new subfields of inquiry, and the developing relationships between disciplines that broaden our knowledge of the religion. In other words, it introduces readers to the emerging research and makes available exemplary studies of those new and contemporary directions, rather than presenting the accumulated knowledge accumulated over the two centuries that Western academic Buddhist studies has already existed.

By definition, a research encyclopedia cannot claim to be comprehensive, as was made evident to the editors as the field has continued to change from the time that this project was first formulated up to the present. This print edition is intended as a gateway to the online version, which will expand as the field of Buddhist studies grows across disciplines, and as existing articles are revised and updated. The editors' intent for this volume is to document the current intellectual orientations in the field, highlighting trajectories, issues, and concerns critical to Buddhist studies. This future-facing orientation does not contest the established topical characterizations of the field, which have provided its foundational bases, but rather seeks to enrich the familiar and provide entrée for the unfamiliar through lengthy entries having up-to-date literature review sections.

One of the raisons d'être of this project has been derived from an observation that Buddhist studies is an open-ended discipline, a cross- and interdisciplinary field of inquiry informed by and informing many research areas such as religious studies, cultural studies, history, anthropology, philosophy, economics, political science, sociology, art and architecture, philology, and textual studies, and also contributing to a variety of comparative studies. The idea of a field contrasts with that of a discipline. Disciplines are established by a defined set of theories, methods, and subject matter that delimit content and inquiry. While such limitations give a discipline the focus required to progress along the accepted lines of knowledge formation and preservation, those same limitations foreclose alternatives. Framing Buddhist studies as a field, however, means that we do not see it as having a single focus, method, or a singular subject matter. Fields cover a rich variety of intellectual projects that allow for both independent and interconnected areas of specialized study, diverse methodological approaches, and a florescence of theories. Viewing Buddhist studies as a field does not seek to replace established norms of philology and textual studies, but invites a sharper and more nuanced focus. It is this view gazing toward the future of Buddhist studies that marks this volume as an innovative network of contemporary scholarship and an organically evolving encyclopedia for study and research.

HOW TO USE *THE OXFORD ENCYCLOPEDIA OF BUDDHISM*

The Oxford Encyclopedia of Buddhism is a simultaneous print and online publication. It covers a wide range of foundational and current topics in Buddhist studies with in-depth research articles, averaging 8,000 words, written in English by international experts worldwide. The *Encyclopedia* provides accurate, substantive, and balanced coverage of aspects of the tradition that have typically been neglected or inaccessible—such as regional varieties of Buddhism, Buddhism and gender, economics, tourism, secularization, and globalization—while including equally seminal topics on historiography and the formation of major Buddhist schools, lineages, and traditions; important figures in Buddhist history; the compilation of canons and translation of texts; studies on Buddhist art, philosophy, rituals, and practices; and studies of a comparative nature. Furthermore, each encyclopedia entry provides substantial information on the current state of the field and guides the reader to a succinct representation of existing scholarship, debates and alternative views, and directions for future research.

In this print edition of *The Oxford Encyclopedia of Buddhism* there are 139 entries, nearly over 1.5 million words. The entries selected include ones of general interest, ones with more specialized content, and ones addressing current issues—both intellectual and social. These categories are representative of the depth and breadth of Buddhist academic scholarship, but they are not exhaustive of the ongoing development of the online version.

The online version of *The Oxford Encyclopedia of Buddhism* is part of a larger platform, *The Oxford Research Encyclopedia of Religion* (oxfordre.com/religion). The platform is designed to be easily accessible online from any device, providing the ability to read and download entire articles as PDFs, to cross-reference information, and to search keywords, names, technical terms, and topics of specialized interest. Accessing entries through the online version introduces the reader to a substantial and continuously growing database of the most critical aspects of a given topic in Buddhist studies, a review of major publications, and gaps in scholarship for further research. It also provides the user-reader with the flexibility to interface in the future with inhouse and external digital research tools and databases.

Editors in Chief
Richard K. Payne
Georgios T. Halkias

Acknowledgments

The editors thank the members of our editorial board:

Anne M. Blackburn, Cornell University
Robert Linrothe, Northwestern University
Scott A. Mitchell, Institute of Buddhist Studies
Francesca Tarocco, Ca' Foscari University of Venice and NYU Shanghai
Vesna A. Wallace, University of California, Santa Barbara

Their expertise and willing assistance made it possible to undertake a project of this breadth.

This *Encyclopedia* began several years ago as an online project within the *Oxford Research Encyclopedias* program. Since then, it has benefited from the assistance of many different members of the Oxford University Press staff, all of whom we thank.

In particular, we express our appreciation for the editorial team that guided the transformation of this project from an online one into the print version you now hold:

Robert Repino, Senior Editor
Sarah Yamashita, Project Editor

Development Editors:

Sam Green
Sana Khan
Dylan White
Chandler Carpenter
Marcus Dovigi
Alex Rouch

The editors have taken seriously the status of *The Oxford Encyclopedia of Buddhism* as a research encyclopedia. Rather than a summary of existing knowledge, our goal has been to identify the growing edges of the field of study. Online this *Encyclopedia* continues beyond its physical incarnation, allowing it to grow in new directions as the field of Buddhist studies itself changes and develops. The potential of online development of scholarship was recognized many years ago by Oxford University Press, which under the guidance of Damon Zucca and Ada Brunstein, Publishers, Reference, has made a major commitment to furthering access to important resources for the communities of scholars and educators.

A

ABHIDHARMAKOŚABHĀṢYA (TREASURY OF METAPHYSICS WITH SELF-COMMENTARY)

INTRODUCTION

The *Abhidharmakośabhāṣya* (*Treasury of Higher Knowledge with Self-Commentary*; often abbreviated as *AKBh*) is an influential treatise on early Buddhist doctrine, composed around the end of the 4th century CE by the prominent Indian philosopher Vasubandhu (4th to 5th centuries CE). The work systematically lays down the philosophical views of two key early Buddhist philosophical systems—the Sarvāstivāda (literally "the theory that all [factors] exist") and the Sautrāntika ("followers of the sutras [the buddha's discursive teachings]")—while scrutinizing the stances of other Buddhist and non-Buddhist intellectual circles. Consisting of nine chapters, the *AKBh* delineates the knowledge required for liberation (nirvana) from the cycle of births and deaths by analyzing the various material and mental factors (dharmas) characterizing the non-awakened state of sentient beings, those pure factors by virtue of which liberation is attainable, and the path and practices conducive to this goal.

The Abhidharma genre, to which Vasubandhu's work belongs, aims to achieve two main goals: first, to systematize the buddha's diverse teachings as preserved in the early sutra corpus, and second, to determine thereby the buddha's ultimate doctrines, those doctrines which do not require further explication (*nitārtha*) and which therefore correspond to ultimate reality as it is. To this end, Abhidharma analysis employs exegetical devices as a matter of usual practice, leading to diverging opinions regarding its most essential subject matters. The *AKBh*, in this respect, touches on key doctrinal controversies debated in the Abhidharma literature. Among the contested issues are the existential status of selves (*ātman*) or persons (*pudgala*, *AKBh* IX); the question of whether factors exist in the past and future (*AKBh* V:24–27); the claim that noninformative matter (*avijñapti-rūpa*) is a distinct ultimate factor (*AKBh* IV:4); and the problem of whether latent tendencies are synonymous with active defilements or whether these are two different states (*AKBh* V:2).

In terms of structure, the work is made up of nearly 600 verses—referred to as the *Abhidharmakośakarikā* (*AK*)—and Vasubandhu's prose self-commentary (*bhāṣya*). It is generally accepted by both tradition and modern scholars that the verse portion summarizes the Sarvāstivāda's understanding of the buddha's teachings (and more precisely that of the northern subsect, called the Vaibhāṣika, "followers of the Great Commentary"), while the prose portion critiques components of this interpretation from a Sautrāntika point of view. There are, however, numerous places where the author accedes to Vaibhāṣika doctrines, and some traditional commentators maintain that he did not affiliate himself with one school of thought, but rather proclaimed that which was in accordance with the truth, whether taught by the Vaibhāṣika or by Sautrāntika.[1] At any rate, when Vasubandhu repudiates the Vaibhāṣika standpoint, it is often with respect to the ultimate entities postulated by this school—unnecessarily, according to the Sautrāntika. In cases where the Vaibhāṣika accounts for a phenomenon in this way, the Sautrāntika favors an explication based on causality or temporal processes.

Although historically the *AKBh* constitutes one link in a chain of Abhidharma treatises, it came to the fore and overshadowed its predecessors not long after its composition, becoming the standard reference work for Buddhist scholars studying Abhidharma topics. Thus, it exerted great influence on East Asian traditions, and, once translated into Tibetan, it was accepted as the main representative of this literature in Tibetan Buddhism.

A TEXTUAL HISTORY OF THE *ABHIDHARMAKOŚABHĀṢYA*

The *AKBh* owes much of its structure and thematic organization to a series of manuals composed during earlier stages of the Sarvāstivāda Abhidharma tradition. In particular, Vasubandhu appears to have modeled his composition on works belonging to the Gandhāran *Hṛdaya* (heart or essence) series of treatises. The fundamental stratum in the Abhidharma corpus of the Sarvāstivāda—its Abhidharma-piṭaka—comprises seven scriptures, the chief of which is the *Jñānaprasthāna*, ascribed to Kātyāyanīputra. The school developed in two main directions, corresponding to two geographical areas in which its thought dominated. One subgroup was active in Kashmir and particularly venerated the *Mahāvhibhāṣā*, a voluminous commentary on the *Jñānaprasthāna*, from which this group acquired its appellation, the Vaibhāṣika. A second subgroup of the Sarvāstivāda was concentrated around Bactria and Gandhāra and produced a number of Abhidharma compilations known as the **Abhidharmahṛdaya* (the heart or essence of the Abhidharma), today extant only in their Chinese translations.

The first of these compilations is the **Abhidharmahṛdaya*, ascribed to Dharmaśrī or Dharmaśreṣṭhin (*c.* 200 CE). This text's main innovation lies in the systematization of the doctrine of the Gandhāra subschool and the summarizing of its tenets in the form of verses. The **Abhidharmahṛdaya* also makes reference to the views of other Sarvāstivāda groups. It consists of ten chapters of 250 verses and their commentaries. A commentary on this treatise titled **Abhidharmahṛdaya* or *Abhidharmahṛdayaśāstra* was composed by Upaśānta. This commentary adopts the structure of its root text, including the division into ten chapters, but adds a number of verses, amounting to 249 in total. Upaśānta's work was followed by a third treatise, the **Saṃyuktābhidharmahṛdya* or **Miśrakābhidharmahṛdaya*, which is attributed to Dharmatrāta and is considered to have been composed in the first half of the 4th century.[2] This work adds one chapter to the total of eleven chapters and expands the number of verses to 596, thereby offering a doctrinal elaboration of the first two treatises. The *AKBh*, together with most of the theoretical problems, polemics, and questions it addresses, stems from these three *Hṛdaya* treatises.

Willemen, Dessein, and Cox distinguish between four kinds of texts in Sarvāstivāda Abhidharma literature, each of which exhibits a different degree of development in regard to doctrinal exposition: simple expository texts; texts which adopt more abstract principles of organization; highly polemical works identifying the positions of contending groups; and dialectical expository treatises that summarize the doctrinal position of the philosophical school or subschool to which they belong. According to their analysis, the *Hṛdaya* literature—including the *AKBh*—displays elements of the fourth stage of development.[3]

One figure who played an essential role, albeit chiefly adversarial, in the intellectual development of the *AKBh* is the Vaibhāṣika scholar Saṃghabhadra. According to traditional accounts, after composing the *AK* (verse portion), Vasubandhu sent it to this master, who approved its accuracy and compatibility with the philosophical tenets of the Vaibhāṣika and encouraged the composition of the self-commentary.[4] Having later realized that the commentary was in disagreement with important Sarvāstivāda principles, Saṃghabhadra wrote two treatises of his own with rejoinders to Vasubandhu's Sautrāntika arguments. The two works—the **Nyāyānusāra* (Taisho 1562) and the **Abhidharmasamayapradīpikā* (Taisho 1563)—were translated by Xuanzang and are preserved in their Chinese translations alone.[5]

In the centuries that followed, the *AKBh* was translated from Sanskrit into other Asian languages and, beginning from the 20th century, also into European languages. In premodern times, it was translated into Chinese twice: first between 563 and 567 CE by Paramārtha (Taisho 1559) and a second time between 651 and 654 CE by Xuanzang (Taisho 1558).[6] In the 9th century, the work was translated from Sanskrit into Tibetan by Jinamitra and Ska ba dPal brtegs (*chos mngon pa'i mdzod kyi bshad pa*, Derge 4090). Around the end of the 11th century, a second translation into Tibetan was produced by Smṛtijñānakīrti, but this was not included in the Tibetan Tanjur collection.[7]

Modern scholarship has produced a number of critical editions of the *AK* or *AKBh* in Sanskrit. Described chronologically, it was first edited as part of a critical edition of Yaśomitra's commentary, *Sphuṭārthābhidharmakośavyākhyā* (whose original contains the verse portion of the *AK*), produced by Unrai Wogihara between 1932 and 1936.[8] A decade later, in 1946, V. V. Gokhale edited the verse section of the work based on the then newly found Sanskrit manuscript of the *AKBh*.[9] The standard Sanskrit edition of this text is Prahlad Pradhan's 1967 edition of both the verse and auto-commentary sections of the work.[10] It was followed by a second edition eight years later, which suffers from various mistakes that are not present in the first edition.[11] Finally, Dwarakidas Shastri edited the verse and auto-commentary sections of the *AKBh* alongside Yaśomitra's *Vyākhyā*. This edition appeared in print between 1970 and 1973.[12] Lee (in 2005) provides a critical edition of the ninth chapter of the *AKBh*.[13] In addition to these editions of the Sanskrit text, an important edition of Xuanzang's Chinese translation was prepared by the Japanese scholar-monk Kyokuga Saeki and published in 1886.[14] In this annotated edition, Saeki references Puguang's and Fabao's commentaries and identifies the scholastic affiliation of philosophical positions expressed in the *AKBh*. This edition also includes a translation of the work into Japanese.

Until the 1930s, when a Sanskrit manuscript was found by Rahul Sanskrityayan, the *AKBh* was known only through its Chinese and Tibetan translations. The first translation of the *AKBh* into a European language was made shortly before the finding of the Sanskrit manuscript. This is the monumental French translation by Louis de la Vallée Poussin, which was published between 1923 and 1931.[15] La Vallée Poussin's reading is primarily based on the Chinese version of Xuanzang as elucidated in Saeki's edition, but it relied on other sources for the assessment of the text's meaning. This includes Yaśomitra's Sanskrit commentary, Paramārtha's Chinese translation, and the two extant Tibetan translations.[16] Between 1988 and 1990, La Vallée Poussin's French edition was translated into English by Leo Pruden, and a later translation was produced in 2012 by Gelong Lodrö Sangpo, who also consulted the Sanskrit manuscript and additional secondary literature on the *AKBh*.[17] Also published in 2012 is an English translation from the Tibetan by David Karma Choephel, which includes the root verses and a commentary by the ninth karmapa, Wangchuk Dorje (albeit without Vasubandhu's *bhāṣya*).[18] Finally, an English translation of the *AKBh*, as preserved in the language of Uighur—itself a translation of Xuanzang's Chinese rendering—was undertaken by Masahiro Shōgaito and published in 2014.[19]

Because of its high philosophical value, as well as its relevance to Western philosophical discourses on personal identity, the ninth chapter of the *AKBh* has been separately translated into English several times. Published translations include Theodore Stcherbatsky's 1919 "The Soul Theory of the Buddhists"[20] (from Tibetan), Matthew Kapstein's rendering in his 2001 *Reason's Traces* (from Tibetan, with reference to the Sanskrit text),[21] a translation and modern commentary by James Duerlinger in *Indian Buddhist Theories of Persons*,[22] published in 2003 (from Sanskrit), and Charles Goodman's translation from 2009, which includes the second half of the chapter (from Tibetan).[23]

Modern Japanese scholarship has produced an extensive literature on the *AKBh*, including translations of the text and helpful research tools. Two important translations of the entire work from Chinese (Xuanzang's edition) are Taiken Kimura and Unrai Wogihara's translation from 1920 and Giyū Nishi's translation from 1935.[24] A series of translations from Sanskrit into Japanese offers the most complete translation into a modern language directly rendered from the original Sanskrit. The series includes Hajime Sakurabe's (1969) translation of chapters 1 (on the factors, *dhātu*) and 2 (on the faculties, *indriya*); Susumu Yamaguchi and Issai Funahashi's (1955) translation of chapter 3 (on the world, *loka*); Funahashi's (1987) rendition of chapter 4 (on *karman*); Nobuchiyo Odani and Yoshifumi Honjō's (2007) translation of chapter 5 (on latent dispositions, *anuśaya*); and Sakurabe and Odani's (1999) translation of chapter 6 (on the path and persons, *mārgapudgala*) and (2004) of chapters 7 (on knowledge, *jñāna*) and 8 (on meditative attainments, *samāpatti*).[25] Each of the translations in the series is collated with the respective Tibetan and Chinese translations and, apart from Sakurabe's translation (1969), includes a translation of Yaśomitra's commentary on the respective chapter. The translations are based on Pradhan's critical edition, apart from Yamaguchi and Funahashi's (1955), which relies on the citation of the *AKBh* in Yaśomitra's Sanskrit commentary.

Between 1973 and 1978, Akira Hirakawa, along with a group of scholars, produced a trilingual index of the *AKBh*.[26] Part I of the index follows the order of the Sanskrit terms, with their Chinese and Tibetan equivalents, while Part II follows the order of Chinese terms, offering the Sanskrit equivalent for each. In Part III, the words are indexed according to the Tibetan vocabulary and their Sanskrit original. Another project, which was accomplished in the 2010s as part of the Bauddhakośa series, surveys the seventy-five dharmas of the Sarvāstivāda as enumerated in the *AKBh*. The work provides a Sanskrit–Tibetan–Chinese–English glossary, illustrates each of the terms with examples from the *AKBh* and Yogācāra literature, and links them to other reference works. The printed edition was published in 2018, while an electronic version from 2014 is available online.[27]

THE STRUCTURE AND CONTENT OF THE *ABHIDHARMAKOŚABHĀṢYA*

The *AKBh*, as it has come down to readers, is made up of nine chapters: the specification of factors (*dhātu-nirdeśa*), the specification of faculties (*indriya-nirdeśa*), the specification of the world (*loka-nirdeśa*), the specification of action (*karma-nirdeśa*), the specification of latent dispositions (*anuśaya-nirdeśa*), the specification of paths and persons (*mārgapudgala-nirdeśa*), the specification of the liberating forms of knowledge (*jñāna-nirdeśa*), the specification of attainments (*smāpatti-nirdeśa*), and the refutation of the theory of self (titled *Ātmavāda-pratiṣedha* by Vasubandhu and *Pudgala-viniścaya* in Yaśomitra's commentary). The final chapter is considered to have been composed as an independent treatise and added later as an appendix to the first eight chapters. An indication of this is its distinct form, which, unlike the rest of the *AKBh*, does not develop the philosophical investigation on the basis of root verses, but applies prose only, and Vasubandhu's concluding verses at the end of the eighth chapter of the work. The *AKBh* also deviates from its predecessors in its third chapter on the world, which is absent from earlier Hṛdaya treatises.

Both traditional and modern thinkers have surmised the principle that guides this precise order of chapters. According to the Chinese commentator Puguang, the *AKBh* aims to elucidate the doctrine that all dharmas are without a self. The first two chapters clarify this truth with respect to both pure and impure factors; chapters 3–5 do the same with respect to impure factors, while chapters 6–8 elucidate this principle with reference to pure factors, and the final chapter gives a general explanation of the teaching of no-self.[28] In the *Collection of Records concerning the Tripitaka* (*Chu sanzang ji ji*, Taisho 2145), the 6th-century Chinese translator Jiaojing correlated the order of the **Smayuktābhidharmahṛdaya*, on which the *AKBh* is modeled, with the order of the four noble truths. On this analysis, the first chapter of the *AKBh* on the elements centers on the noble truth of suffering; the second, fourth, and fifth chapters correspond to the noble truth of the origin of suffering; the sixth chapter centers on the noble truth of the cessation of suffering; and the seventh and eighth chapters correspond to the noble truth of the path to the cessation of suffering. Chapters 3 and 9, according to this organizing factor, are additional chapters.[29] Willemen, Dessein, and Cox, building on a scheme drawn up by Funahashi in 1961, propose that the *AKBh* can be divided into three parts.[30] The first—comprising chapters 1 and 2—elaborates on the nature of dharmas; the second—comprising chapters 3 to 5—elucidates the illusional world (or the reasons that beings remain within the cycle of births and deaths); while the third—consisting of chapters 6 to 9—explains the awakened world (or the path that leads sentient beings out of illusion).

In terms of content, the first chapter of the work gives an overview of the variety of conditioned and unconditioned factors (dharmas) that are constitutive of sentient existence. To explain the first of the two categories, Vasubandhu lays out three key models through which conditioned factors are classified. The first is the scheme of the five aggregates (*skandha*). These are the five principal aspects or functions of sentient existence and include the aggregates of matter (*rūpa*), feelings (*vedanā*), cognitions (*saṃjñā*), formations (*saṃskāra*), and consciousness (*vijñāna*). Conditioned factors can also be classified according to the model of the twelve sense spheres (*āyatana*), which consist of the six sense organs (the eye, ear, tongue, nose, body, and mind) and their six corresponding objects (objects of sight, hearing, taste, smell, touch, and the mind), as well as according to the eighteen elements (*dhātu*), which consist of the twelve sense spheres with the addition of the six types of consciousness.[31]

The second chapter presents three related topics, beginning with an exposition of the twenty-two controlling faculties (*indriya*)—elements which exercise control over particular domains of sentient life. The list describes the six sense faculties, the male and female sex faculties, the faculty of life force, five feeling faculties (displeasure, pleasure, dissatisfaction, satisfaction, and equanimity), five spiritual faculties (faith, energy, mindfulness, meditative absorption, and wisdom), and three pure faculties, whose domain is spiritual attainment. The second part of the chapter opens by providing the Vaibhāṣika list of factors, which contains seventy-five entries and is organized according to the five categories of matter (*rūpa*), mind (*citta*), thought concomitants (*caitasika*), conditioned factors dissociated from the mind (*cittaviprayukta*), and unconditioned factors (*asaṃskṛta*).[32] Vasubandhu then goes into a more in-depth examination of the modes of arising of different conditioned factors which come into being simultaneously. This particularly concerns the coexistence of mind moments (*citta*) and the thought concomitants accompanying them. The discussion of simultaneous arising paves the way to the more general topic of causality, wherein the *AKBh* investigates the different types of causes and effects identified by Buddhist and non-Buddhist schools of the time. Vasubandhu recognizes five types of effects: ripened effect (*vipākaphala*), effect of equal outflow (*niṣyandaphala*), effect of disconnection (*visaṃyogaphala*), effect of human action (*puruṣakāraphala*), and effect of dominance (*adhipatiphala*). He also identifies six types of causes: efficient cause (*kāraṇahetu*), coexistent cause (*sahabhūhetu*), homogeneous cause (*sabhāgahetu*), associated cause (*saṃprayuktahetu*), pervasive cause (*sarvatragahetu*), and ripening cause (*vipākahetu*). According to Vasubandhu, all six types of causes are ultimately efficient causes.

In the third chapter, the *AKBh* deals with the universe and the place of sentient beings within it according to Buddhist cosmology. Vasubandhu describes the threefold world in which sentient beings may be born, which comprises the realms of desire (*kāma-dhātu*), fine materiality (*rūpya-dhātu*), and nonmateriality (*arūpya-dhātu*). In light of the significance of transmigration for the reality of non-awakened beings, Vasubandhu elaborates on the planes of existence—particular forms of existence within the three realms—and the intermediate state, in which beings abide from the time of their death until a subsequent rebirth. The doctrine of dependent origination (*pratītya-samutpāda*), with its twelve links, explains the causal manner in which sentient beings take new rebirths and persist in cyclic existence in the absence of an enduring self.[33] Alongside this explanation of the sentient universe, Vasubandhu draws the landscape of the receptacle world (*bhājana-loka*), the physical world that contains sentient existence—Mount Sumeru, which stands at the center of the universe, the continents, oceans, and other mountains—and describes the universe's temporality: its cyclic creation and dissolution.

In the famous passage that opens the fourth chapter, Vasubandhu proclaims that the world of sentient beings results from their actions (*karman*). Thus, this part of the *AKBh* sets out to explicate the metaphysics of action and its results according to Abhidharmic analysis and sutra teachings. The first issue investigated here is the nature of basic action: What is it that counts as the most primitive event which brings about karmic retribution? The debate, primarily revolving around bodily action, places several Buddhist stances in opposition, including the Pudgalavādin view that bodily action is a movement, the Sarvāstivāda claim that it is a shape, and Vasubandhu's own Sautrāntika position that bodily action is an intention (*cetanā*) which has the body as its object. Of the concepts introduced by chapter 4, one pair is particularly significant: informative and noninformative actions. The former refers to any action that can be observed by beings other than the agent, hence revealing the agent's intention, while the latter indicates internal actions accessible to the agent alone. The second category consists of mental action, which either occurs on its own or alongside a physical or verbal action and which is the crucial element in karmic retribution. Other classifications in this chapter shed light on the varieties of actions. The most conspicuous of these is the standard Buddhist catalog of the ten virtuous and nonvirtuous paths of action (*karmapatha*), where the term "path of action" designates the most severe among the constructive and harmful deeds an agent can undertake. The chapter concludes with a list of the various effects that actions bring about. Vasubandhu, however, avoids the topic of the process by which these effects come about, deferring it to the final part of the *AKBh*.

The topic at the heart of the fifth chapter is the nature of proclivities, or latent dispositions (*anuśaya*), referring to mental afflictions (*kleśa*) in their dormant state. Throughout their existence, proclivities remain inactive in the mind, until, under the appropriate causes and conditions, they manifest as active defilements, called "envelopment" (*paryavasthāna*). Their significance for the Buddhist path lies in the principle that defilements motivate the undertaking of *karman*, which perpetuates the existence of sentient beings in samsara. The basic list of proclivities describes six cardinal affects: attachment (*raga*), hostility (*pratigha*), ignorance (*avidyā*), conceit (*māna*), doubt (*vicikitsā*), and afflicted views (*dṛṣṭi*), which, under detailed scrutiny, yields a longer list of secondary proclivities. A central debate in this chapter concerns the nature of proclivities, on which the Sarvāstivāda and the Sautrāntika are divided. As is typically the case in disagreements of this kind, the Sarvāstivādins consider a proclivity to be an ultimately existent factor (dharma) which exhibits its causal efficacy at a particular moment, when it turns into an "envelopment." Therefore, "proclivity" and "envelopment" are two synonyms for a single factor. Vasubandhu, representing the Sautrāntika position, denies the existence of proclivities as ultimate entities and instead explicates them as processes. According to his stance, a proclivity is a force (*śākti*) within the mental stream that retains its momentum over time, giving rise to the manifest affliction when a particular transformation of the stream occurs. Using the terms of his theory of seeds, Vasubandhu likens the proclivity to a seed (*bīja*) whose gradual development results in a fruit (*phala*). The question of the temporal maturation of proclivities leads to a subsequent discussion about the existential status of past and future dharmas, wherein the Sarvāstivāda masters seek to demonstrate their quintessential doctrine that not only present factors, but also past and future factors, exist. The Sautrāntika system, objecting again to the reification of unnecessary ontological entities, rejects this stance.

Moving in the direction of the world of awakened beings, the sixth chapter of the *AKBh* is an account of the stages of the path to liberation from samsara and the attainments of persons who realize it. The stages of the path (or simply, the paths) are explained with respect to the four noble truths. When discussing these essential teachings, Vasubandhu raises and addresses related misgivings, such as the issue of whether pleasant (*sukha*) feeling exists and why the first truth relates only to suffering and not to pleasure as well, even though sentient beings also have experiences of pleasure. It is in this chapter, following the exposition of the truths, that Vasubandhu's stock definition of the conventional and ultimate truths is provided. Under the two headings of calm abiding (*śamatha*) and insight (*vipaṣyanā*), Vasubandhu gives a concise, sometimes critical, exposition of core early Buddhist meditative practices, including the meditation on the loathsomeness of the body, mindfulness of breathing, and the four bases of mindfulness. These meditations belong to the first stage of practice, the path of preparation (*prayogamārga*). Following in order are the path of insight (*darśanamārga*), the path of cultivation (*bhāvanāmārga*), and the path of those beyond training (*aśaikṣamārga*). Persons who have attained direct realizations are situated in one of these three stages. Vasubandhu correlates between the three paths, the level of defilements that are purified in each of them, and the fruits achieved by the practitioners, which are the states of the stream-enterer, once-returner, non-returner, and *arhat*. Another classical explication of the path discussed here is the list of thirty-seven factors that are conducive to awakening (*bodhipakṣikadharma*).

The seventh chapter covers the ten types of knowledge (*jñāna*) enjoyed by beings who reach the levels of spiritual attainments. These are: (a) knowledge of the factors (*dharmajñāna*), whose objects are the four noble truths in the realm of desire; (b) subsequent knowledge (*anvayajñāna*), which cognizes the four noble truths of the form and formless realms; (c) mundane conventional knowledge (*lokasaṃvṛtijñāna*), which comprises impure cognitions of conventional objects; (d) knowledge of the minds of others (*paracittajñāna*), whose object of cognition is the mind moments of other beings; (e) knowledge of suffering (*duḥkhajñāna*), a pure realization of the impermanence, unsatisfactory nature, emptiness, and selflessness of the five aggregates; (f) knowledge of the origin of suffering (*samudayajñāna*), which is the realization of the causal function of the five aggregates; (g) knowledge of the cessation of suffering, whose object is the cessation of the five aggregates; (h) knowledge of the path (*mārgajñāna*), which realizes the liberating function of the five aggregates; (i) knowledge of exhaustion (*kṣayajñāna*), a term that specifically refers to the arhats' knowledge of factors, which is the certainty that the tasks to be accomplished with respect to each of the four truths are being accomplished; and (j) knowledge of non-arising (*anutpādajñāna*), which is, similarly, a title given to subsequent knowledge when the cognizing person is an arhat which indicates the certainty that comes with the realization that the four tasks no longer need to be pursued. The first part of the seventh chapter elaborates on the characteristics of these types of knowledge and the distinction between them, right view (*samyagdṛṣṭi*), and receptivity (*kṣānti*). The latter part deals with the qualities that these forms of knowledge constitute.

Continuing the exposition of spiritual attainments, the eighth chapter focuses on meditative attainments (*samāpatti*). It gives a detailed description of the levels of absorption (*samādhi*), including the qualities of the four meditations (*dhyāna*) connected with the form realm, the four perception spheres (*āyatana*) connected with the formless realm, and the attainment of cessation (*nirodhasamāpatti*). Vasubandhu describes three particular types of *samādhi*: the *samādhi* of emptiness (*śūnyatā*), leading to the realization of the emptiness of the self; the *samādhi* of signlessness (*animitta*), whose object is nirvana, which is free of characteristics; and the *samādhi* of wishlessness (*apraṇihita*), which leads to the aspiration toward no factor whatsoever. Also discussed in this chapter are the practices of the four immeasurables (*apramāṇa* or *brahmavihāra*)—lovingkindness (*maitrī*), compassion (*karuṇā*), joy (*muditā*), and equanimity (*upekṣā*)—and three other frameworks describing attainments of concentration: the eight liberations (*vimukṣa*), the eight perception spheres of mastery (*abhivāyatana*), and the ten perception spheres of totality (*kṛtsnāyatana*). The final section of the chapter offers concluding comments, indicating that this chapter was originally the final one.

The treatise on the negation of the theory of self, which effectively concludes Vasubandhu's magnum opus, mounts a philosophical attack on two notions of individuality. The first is the one held by followers of the Buddhist personalist school (Pudgalavāda, alternatively known as the Vātsīputrīya or the Saṃmitīya), who submit to the existence of a person (*pudgala*) over and above the five aggregates. This person is neither different from nor identical with the aggregates. The second notion is that of the self (*ātman*), which is accepted in some form by all six of the Indian orthodox schools. The chapter opens with arguments from reason and scripture against the Pudgalavādin idea of the person. Particularly, Vasubandhu seeks to show the faults in the school's analogy of fire, which suggests that the relationship between the five aggregates and the person is the sort of reliance that exists between fire and fuel. The latter half of the chapter is dedicated to the non-Buddhist concept of the enduring self. Among other things, Vasubandhu addresses objections formulated by Indian orthodox philosophers, most probably belonging to the Nyāya or Sāṃkhya schools, against the Buddhist rejection of the self. These objections concern the compatibility of the no-self doctrine with commonly observable conventions, such as remembering past experiences, carrying out actions (e.g., walking), and the distinction between individual streams of consciousness.

NOTABLE COMMENTARIES

Due to its thorough, yet refined, presentation of the Sarvāstivāda doctrines, the *AKBh* earned a place of honor in the lineage of Abhidharma manuals and was the subject of numerous commentaries by Indian, Tibetan, and Chinese scholars. Two classical commentaries composed in India are Yaśomitra's 7th-century *Sphuṭārthābhidharmakośavyākhyā*, which is extant in Sanskrit and included in Shastri's edition (mentioned in the section titled "A Textual History of the *Abhidharmakośabhāṣya*") but has not been translated into European languages, and the

Abhidharmakośabhāṣyaṭīkā Tattvārthā by the important 6th-century scholar Sthiramati, extant in its Tibetan translation. Later traditions, particularly the Tibetan, have deemed Yaśomitra's *Vyākhyā* the paramount Indian commentary on the *AKBh.* Two earlier commentaries, which Yaśomitra mentions in his *Vyākhyā* but which have not survived except for a few quotations in Yaśomitra's commentary, were written by Guṇamati and his student Vasumitra, respectively. The *Upāyikā-nāmā Abhidharmakośa-Ṭīkā*, an undated Sanskrit commentary preserved in the Tibetan canon and attributed to the otherwise unknown Śamathadeva, is a collection of canonical quotations that appear in the *AKBh.* The author provides a more complete reference to the textual source from which the quotations are drawn, either by providing a full quotation or by indicating the name of the sutra and the place in which the passage can be found.[34]

Another important commentarial work is Purṇavardhana's *Lakṣaṇāṇusāriṇī* (*Minor Commentary*) from about the 8th century. His exegesis handles selected topics in an abridged manner, but refers to the opinions of other thinkers. Dignāga, a direct student of Vasubandhu, wrote a commentary entitled the *Marmapradīpa.* This is an abridged version of the *AKBh*, in which Dignāga "reproduces word for word the kārikās [verses] and the basic explanations of the *Abhidharmakośa-bhāṣya*," as Mejor observes.[35] Mejor's study of the commentaries preserved in the Tibetan canon is a helpful guide to the history of these works and their authors.

The foundational commentary on the *AKBh* for all schools of Tibetan Buddhism is the *Chos mngon pa'i mdzod kyi tshig le'ur byas pa'i 'grel ba mngon pa'i rgyan* (*The Ornament of Abhidharma*), also known by its abbreviated name *mChims mdzod* (the *mChims Treasury*), by the Tibetan scholar mChims 'jam dpa'i dbyangs (*c.* 1245–1325).[36] This commentary relies to a considerable extent on notes given in the Indian commentaries by Yaśomitra, Sthiramati, and Purṇavardhana. Each of the four Tibetan Buddhist schools has produced commentaries, largely with reference to the *mChims mdzod.* The most common Gelug supplement to the *mChims mdzod* is the *mdzod Tik thar lam gsal byed* (*Illuminating the Path to Liberation*) by the First Dalai Lama, dGe 'dun grub (1391–1474).

In the Kagyu tradition, the commentary *mNgon pa mdzod kyi 'grel pa chos mngon rgya mtsho'i snying po* (*The Essence of the Ocean of Abhidharma*) by the ninth karmapa, Dbang phyug rdo rje (1556–1603), is the standard reference. However, the eighth karmapa, Mi bsyod rdo rje (1507–1554), also wrote an important commentary, namely, *Chos mngon pa'i mdzod kyi 'grel pa rgyas par spros pa grub bde'i dpyid 'jo zhes bya ba glegs bam dang po* (*An Explanation of the Treasury of Abhidharma Called the Essence of the Ocean of Abhidharma, The Words of Those Who Know and Love, Explaining Youthful Play, Opening the Eyes of Dharma, the Chariot of Easy Practice*). The standard Sakya commentary is arguably Rong ston shes bya kun rig's *Shes bya rab gsal* (*Thoroughly Illuminating What Can Be Known*), while in the Nyingma curriculum, a prominent commentary, *Rin po che'i do shal blo gsal dgyes pa'i mgul rgyan* (*Precious Garland, An Ornament of Joyful Understanding*), was composed by 'Ju mi pham.[37]

In the Chinese tradition, the three major commentaries on the *AKBh* were composed by three direct disciples of Xuanzang, who translated the *AKBh* into Chinese: Shentai's commentary, titled *Jushe lun shu*, Puguang's commentary, *Jushe lun ji* (Taisho 1821), and Fabao's commentary, *Jushe lun shu* (Taisho 1822). These commentaries provide valuable information on the ideas found in the *AKBh*, as reflected in La Vallée Poussin's translation. However, modern scholarship has not studied them in their own right.

REVIEW OF LITERATURE

While some modern studies have exclusively directed their attention to the *AKBh*, it is most often the case that the treatise has been examined as part of a broader thematic investigation surveying multiple sources. One of the central issues discussed with respect to the *AKBh* specifically concerns the sectarian position that Vasubandhu took when composing the text. In a series of publications, Robert Kritzer has sought to demonstrate that by the time he composed the *AKBh*, Vasubandhu had already adhered to the tenets of the Yogācāra school.[38] An alternative historical reconstruction advanced by Changhwan Park counters Kritzer's hypothesis, suggesting that the Vasubandhu of the *AKBh* held pre-Yogācāra views, in alignment with the traditional Buddhist account which describes the author of the *AKBh* as a follower of non-Mahāyāna schools.[39] Kritzer's and Park's approach, which inclines toward an intertextual exploration of the *AKBh*'s doctrines, has been adopted by modern scholarship in various other cases.[40]

Studies in the first decades of the 21st century have turned to the *AKBh* in order to obtain a Buddhist perspective on various problems in the philosophy of action. The chapter on *karman*—one of the most comprehensive treatments of the topic in classical Buddhist literature—was analyzed by Johannes Bronkhorst in his investigation of the place of teleology in India's mechanistic theory of *karman* in 2000.[41] Kachru's modern commentary on Vasubandhu's *Viṃśikā* also presents a philosophical examination of the *AKBh*'s action theory.[42] Karin Meyers, who sets out to explore the problem of free will and determinism in the light of South Asian Buddhism, draws substantially on Vasubandhu's treatment of intending (*cetanā*) and action as presented in the chapter on *karman*.[43] Finally, Hanner delineates this chapter's description of the metaphysical mechanism that allows for actions to be undertaken in the absence of an enduring self.[44]

Another research avenue pursued in the literature centers on Indian and Buddhist notions of selfhood and identity. A seminal inquiry into Vasubandhu's critique of the self in the ninth chapter of the *AKBh* is taken by Kapstein as part of his study of personal identity in classical India.[45] Jonardon Ganeri analyzes central arguments concerning the nature of persons formulated by Vasubandhu and his opponents, while comparing them to Western theories of personal identity.[46] The arguments concerning the self have also served as a key source for Mark Siderits's influential reading of the early Buddhist theories of persons developed in various of his works, most prominently in his work in 2003 and 2015.[47] A different thematic and cross-textual investigation, which substantially relies on the second chapter of the *AKBh*, is Alexander von Rospatt's study of the Buddhist doctrine of momentariness.[48]

Being one of the pillars of Vasubandhu's extensive oeuvre, the *AKBh* has played a central role in the lively 20th-century debate regarding Vasubandhu's identity. The question leading this debate has been whether the author of the *AKBh* is the same Vasubandhu who composed the Yogācāra treatises and commentaries. Two important early milestones in this controversy are Frauwallner,[49] who makes the first claim for acknowledging two authors by the name of Vasubandhu, and Jaini's response.[50] In 2015, Gold has attempted to highlight philosophical motifs that indicate a continuity of thought between Vasubandhu's Abhidharma and Yogācāra works.[51]

DIGITAL MATERIALS

The *AKBh* in Sanskrit and its Chinese and Tibetan translations have been digitized and are available online through dedicated websites. The verse portion of the work (that is, the *AK*) was processed by the members of the Sanskrit Buddhist Input Project, which provides a Romanized version of the text, while Hackett and Lusthaus supply a full transliteration of both the verses and the self-commentary. The Chinese Buddhist Electronic Text Association (CBETA) gives Xuanzang's translation in Chinese characters. Digitally scanned images of the Tibetan translation are available through the Buddhist Digital Resource Center (BDRC). Braarvig offers a synoptic edition of the *AKBh*, which includes Vasubandhu's Sanskrit, Xuanzang's and Paramārtha's Chinese translations, and portions of the Tibetan translation. Besides digital versions of the primary text, helpful resources are Potter, with a thorough bibliographical list of philosophical studies of the *AKBh*; Saito et al., which surveys the seventy-five dharmas of the Sarvāstivāda and provides illustrations from the *AKBh* and other Buddhist works; and Korin (Charlie Pokorny), which offers a useful compilation of materials, such as a summary of the *AKBh*'s content and arguments alongside lists of references to secondary literature, both academic and popular, and various online resources (some of which are no longer active).

BDRC (Buddhist Digital Resource Center). "Chos mngon pa mdzod kyi bshad pa" (Abhidharmakośabhāṣya) (https://www.tbrc.org/#!rid=W1KG11694).

Braarvig, Jens, ed. "Vasubandhu: Abhidharmakośabhāṣya." Bibliotheca Polyglota, Thesaurus Literaturae Buddhicae, University of Oslo.

CBETA (Chinese Buddhist Electronic Text Association). "Āpídámó jùshè lùn (Abhidharmakośa)" (https://cbetaonline.dila.edu.tw/en/T1558). Dharma Drum Institute of Liberal Arts.

Hackett, Paul, and Dan Lusthaus, eds. "Vasubandhu: Abhidharmakosa-bhasya. Based on the Editions of P. Pradhan and Dwarikadas Shastri, Swami" (http://gretil.sub.uni-goettingen.de/gretil/1_sanskr/6_sastra/3_phil/buddh/vakobhau.htm). GRETIL—Göttingen Register of Electronic Texts in Indian Languages.

Korin (Charlie Pokorny). "Abhidharmakosa Study: Study Materials" (https://abhidharmakosa.files.wordpress.com/2010/09/kosa-study-materials.pdf). Abhidharma Study Blog: Facing the Dharma.

Members of the Sanskrit Buddhist Input Project. "Vasubandhu: Abhidharmakosa, Karikas Only" (http://gretil.sub.uni-goettingen.de/gretil/1_sanskr/6_sastra/3_phil/buddh/vakobhku.htm). GRETIL—Göttingen Register of Electronic Texts in Indian Languages.

Potter, Karl, ed. "Part I: Texts Whose Authors Can Be Dated, 175.1. *Abhidharmakośa* and *Bhāṣya* Thereon (Sautrāntika) (NCat I, 289–290)" (http://faculty.washington.edu/kpotter/xtxt1.htm). Bibliography of Indian Philosophies, University of Washington.

Saito, Akira et al. "Bukkyō yōgo no teigiteki yōrei shū 仏教用語の定義的用例集 (Buddhist Terminology: A Collection of Definitions and Examples)" (http://www.l.u-tokyo.ac.jp/~b_kosha/html/b_kosha_2014/html/index_75dharma.html). Bauddha Kośa.

FURTHER READING

Anacker, Stefan. "Vasubandhu, His Life and Times." In *Seven Works of Vasubandhu: The Buddhist Psychological Doctor*. Translated by Stefan Anacker, 7–28. Delhi: Motilal Banarsidass, 1984.

Choepel, David Karma, trans. *Jewels from the Treasury: Vasubandhu's* Verses on the Treasury of Abhidharma *and Its Commentary* Youthful Play *by the Ninth Karmapa Wangchuk Dorje*. Woodstock, NY: KTD, 2012.

Coghlan, Ian James, trans. *Ornament of Abhidharma: A Commentary on Vasubandhu's Abhidharmakośa*. Somerville, MA: Wisdom, 2019.

Cox, Collett. *Disputed Dharmas: Early Buddhist Theories on Existence: An Annotated Translation of the Section of Factors Dissociated from Thought from Saṅghabhadra's* Nyāyānusāra. Tokyo: International Institute for Buddhist Studies, 1995.

Dhammajoti, Bhikkhu K. L. *Sarvāstivāda Abhidharma*. 5th rev. ed. Hong Kong: Buddha-Dharma Centre of Hong Kong, 2015.

Dhammajoti, Bhikkhu K. L. "Summary and Discussion of the *Abhidharmakośa-bhāṣya*." In *Abhidharmakośa-Bhāṣya of Vasubandhu: The Treasury of the Abhidharma and Its (Auto) Commentary*. Vol. 1. Translated by Louis de La Vallée Poussin and Gelong Lodrö Sangpo, 1–69. Delhi: Motilal Banarsidass, 2012.

Duerlinger, James. *Indian Buddhist Theories of Persons: Vasubandhu's "Refutation of the Theory of a Self."* London and New York: RoutledgeCurzon, 2003.

Gold, Jonathan. *Paving the Great Way: Vasubandhu's Unifying Buddhist Philosophy*. New York: Columbia University Press, 2015.

Kapstein, Matthew T. *Reason's Traces: Identity and Interpretation in Indian and Tibetan Buddhist Thought*. Studies in Indian and Tibetan Buddhism. Boston: Wisdom, 2001.

Kritzer, Robert. *Vasubandhu and the Yogācārabhūmi: Yogācāra Elements in the Abhidharmakośabhāṣya*. Tokyo: International College for Postgraduate Buddhist Studies, 2005.

La Vallée Poussin, Louis de, and Leo M. Pruden, trans. *Abhidharmakośabhāṣyam of Vasubandhu*. Berkeley, CA: Asian Humanities Press, 1988–1990.

La Vallée Poussin, Louis de, and Gelong Lodrö Sangpo, trans. *Abhidharmakośa-Bhāṣya of Vasubandhu: The Treasury of the Abhidharma and Its (Auto) Commentary*. Delhi: Motilal Banarsidass, 2012.

Takakusu, Junjirō, trans. *The Life of Vasubandhu*. Leiden, The Netherlands: Brill, 1904.

NOTES

1. See Kuala Lumpur Dhammajoti, "Summary and Discussion of the *Abhidharmakośa-bhāṣya*," in Vasubandhu, *Abhidharmakośa-Bhāṣya of Vasubandhu: The Treasury of the Abhidharma and Its (Auto) Commentary*, trans. Louis de la Vallée Poussin and Gelong Lodrö Sangpo (Delhi: Motilal Banarsidass, 2012), 10.
2. See Charles Willemen, Bart Dessein, and Collett Cox, *Sarvāstivāda Buddhist Scholasticism* (Leiden, The Netherlands: Brill, 1998), 255–269; Dhammajoti, "Summary and Discussion," 108–119; and Leo Pruden, "The Abhidharma: The Origins, Growth and Development of a Literary Tradition," in Vasubandhu, *Abhidharmakośabhāṣyam of Vasubandhu*, trans. Louis de la Vallée Poussin and Leo M. Pruden (Berkeley, CA: Asian Humanities Press, 1988–1990), Vol. 1, liii–liv.
3. See Willemen, Dessein, and Cox, *Sarvāstivāda Buddhist Scholasticism*, 18–19. On the history and development of the Abhidharma literature more broadly and the extant Abhidharma treatises, see Ulrich T. Kragh, "The Extant Abhidharma-Literature," *Indian International Journal of Buddhist Studies* 3 (2002): 123–167.
4. On this, as well as on other contemporaneous authors whose work influenced the *AKBh*, see Marek Mejor, *Vasubandhu's Abhidharmakośa and the Commentaries Preserved in the Tanjur* (Stuttgart: Franz Steiner Verlag, 1991), 13–18.
5. On which, see Collett Cox's seminal study, *Disputed Dharmas: Early Buddhist Theories on Existence: An Annotated Translation of the Section of Factors Dissociated from Thought from Saṅghabhadra's* Nyāyānusāra (Tokyo: International Institute for Buddhist Studies, 1995).
6. See Willemen, Dessein, and Cox, *Sarvāstivāda Buddhist Scholasticism*, 272–273.

7. On the transmission of the *AKBh* to Tibet, see Ian James Coghlan, "Translator's Introduction," in *Ornament of Abhidharma: A Commentary on Vasubandhu's Abhidharmakośa*, trans. Ian James Coghlan (Somerville, MA: Wisdom, 2019), 14–18.
8. Yaśomitra, *Sphuṭārthā Abhidharmakośavyākhyā*, ed. Unrai Wogihara (Tokyo: Publishing Association of Abhidharma-Kośa-Vyākhyā, 1932–1936).
9. Vasudeva Vishwanath Gokhale, "The Text of the Abhidharmakośakārikā of Vasubandhu," *Journal of the Bombay Branch of the Royal Asiatic Society* 22 (1946): 73–102.
10. Vasubandhu, *Abhidharma-kośabhāṣya of Vasubandhu*, ed. Prahlad Pradhan (Patna, India: K. P. Jayaswal Research Institute, 1967).
11. Vasubandhu, *Abhidharma-kośabhāṣya of Vasubandhu*, ed. Prahlad Pradhan and Aruna Haldar, was published in 1975 by the same publisher. Electronic texts based primarily on Pradhan's second edition have been published online by the GRETIL project, edited by Paul Hackett and Dan Lusthaus, and by the Bibliotheca Polyglota project, edited by Jens Braarvig, which also offers a helpful synoptic edition that includes the Sanskrit, the two Chinese translations, and, at the time of writing, a limited portion of the Derge edition of the Tibetan translation.
12. Vasubandhu and Yaśomitra, *Abhidharmakoṣa and Bhāṣya of Acharya Vasubandhu with Sphutārthā Commentary of Ācārya Yaśomitra*, ed. Swami Dwarikadas Shastri (Varanasi, India: Bauddha Bharati, 1970–1973).
13. Vasubandhu, *Abhidharmakośabhāṣya of Vasubandhu, Chapter IX: Ātmavādapratiṣedha*, ed. Jong Schoel Lee, with critical notes by Yasunori Ejima, Bibliotheca Indologica Buddhologica 11 (Tokyo: Sankibo Press, 2005).
14. Kyokuga Saeki, *Kandō Abidatsumakusharon* (Kyoto: Hōzōkan, 1978).
15. Vasubandhu, *L'Abhidhramkośa de Vasubandhu*, trans. and annotated Louis de la Vallée Poussin (Paris: Paul Geuthner; Louvain: J. B. Istas, 1923–1931).
16. Pruden, "The Abhidharma," lix.
17. Vasubandhu, *Abhidharmakośabhāṣyam of Vasubandhu*, trans. La Vallée Poussin and Pruden; Vasubandhu, *Abhidharmakośa-Bhāṣya of Vasubandhu*, trans. La Vallée Poussin and Sangpo.
18. Vasubandhu and Wangchuk Dorje, *Jewels from the Treasury: Vasubandhu's* Verses on the Treasury of Abhidharma *and Its Commentary* Youthful Play *by the Ninth Karmapa Wangchuk Dorje*, trans. David Karma Choephel (Woodstock, NY: KTD, 2012).
19. Masahiro Shōgaito, *The Uighur Abhidharmakośabhāṣya: Preserved at the Museum of Ethnography in Stockholm* (Wiesbaden, Germany: Harrassowitz, 2014).
20. Theodore Stcherbatsky, "The Soul Theory of the Buddhists," *Bulletin de l'Academie des Sciences de Russie* 13, no. 12–15 (1919): 823–854 and 13, no. 16–18 (1919): 937–958. Reprinted as Theodore Stcherbatsky, *The Soul Theory of the Buddhists* (Delhi: Bharatiya Vidya Prakashan, 1976), with several further reprints.
21. Matthew T. Kapstein, *Reason's Traces: Identity and Interpretation in Indian and Tibetan Buddhist Thought* (Boston: Wisdom, 2001), 347–374.
22. James Duerlinger, *Indian Buddhist Theories of Persons: Vasubandhu's "Refutation of the Theory of a Self"* (London and New York: RoutledgeCurzon, 2003). An earlier version of this translation was published as James Duerlinger, "Vasubandhu's 'Refutation of the Theory of Selfhood' (Ātmavādapratiṣedha)," *Journal of Indian Philosophy* 17, no. 2 (1989): 129–187. The first half of the translation (the debate with the Pudgalavādins) was also republished as James Duerlinger, "Vasubandhu's Abhidharmakośa: The Critique of the Pudgalavādins' Theory of Persons," in *Buddhist Philosophy: Essential Readings*, ed. William Edelglass and Jay L. Garfield (Oxford: Oxford University Press, 2009), 286–296.
23. Charles Goodman, "Vasubandhu's Abhidharmakośa: The Critique of the Soul," in *Buddhist Philosophy*, ed. Edelglass and Garfield, 297–308.

24. Taiken Kimura and Unrai Wogihara, *Abidatsumakusharon*, Kokuyaku Daizōkyō, Ron-bu, vols. 11–13 (Tokyo: Kokumin Bunko Kankōkai, 1920); Giyū Nishi, *Abidatsumakusharon*, Kokuyaku Issaikyō: Indo senjutsubu, 4th ed., Bidon-bu, vols. 25–26 (Tokyo: Daitō Shuppansha, 1999).
25. Hajime Sakurabe 櫻部建, *Kusharon no kenkyū: Kai, konhon* 俱舎論の研究【界·根品】 (Kyoto: Hōzōkan, 1969); Susumu Yamaguchi 山口益 and Issai Funahashi 舟橋一哉, *Kusharon no genten kaimei: Sekenbon* 俱舎論の原典解明【世間品】 (Kyoto: Hōzōkan, 1955); Issai Funahashi 舟橋一哉, *Kusharon no genten kaimei: Gōbon* 俱舎論の原典解明【業品】 (Kyoto: Hōzōkan, 1987); Nobuchiyo Odani 小谷信千代 and Yoshifumi Honjō 本庄良文, *Kusharon no genten kaimei: Zuiminbon* 俱舎論の原典解明【随眠品】 (Kyoto: Daizō Shuppan, 2007); Hajime Sakurabe 櫻部建 and Nobuchiyo Odani 小谷信千代, *Kusharon no genten kaimei: Genjō bon* 俱舎論の原典解明【賢聖品】 (Kyoto: Hōzōkan, 1999); Sakurabe Hajime 櫻部建, Odani Nobuchiyo 小谷信千代, and Honjō Yoshifumi 本庄良文, *Kusharon no genten kaimei: Chihon, Jōhon* 俱舎論の原典解明【智品·定品】 (Kyoto: Daizō Shuppan, 2004).
26. Akira Hirakawa 平川彰, in collaboration with Shunei Hirai et al., *Index to the Abhidharmakośa-bhāṣyam (P. Pradhan Edition)* (Tokyo: Daizō Shuppan, 1973–1978).
27. Akira Saito 斎藤明 et al., *The Seventy-Five Elements (dharma) of Sarvāstivāda in the Abhidharmakośabhāṣya and Related Works*, Bauddhakośa: A Treasury of Buddhist Terms and Illustrative Sentences 6 (Tokyo: International Institute for Buddhist Studies of the International College for Postgraduate Buddhist Studies, 2018); and Akira Saito 斎藤明 et al. "“Bukkyō yōgo no teigiteki yōrei shū 仏教用語の定義的用例集 (Buddhist Terminology: A Collection of Definitions and Examples)." Bauddha Kośa.
28. See Dhammajoti, "Summary and Discussion," 7–9.
29. See Willemen, Dessein, and Cox, *Sarvāstivāda Buddhist Scholasticism*, 273.
30. Willemen, Dessein, and Cox, *Sarvāstivāda Buddhist Scholasticism*, 274. Issai Funahashi, "Abhidharmakosa-sastra," in *Encyclopedia of Buddhism*, vol. 1, ed. Gunapala Piyasena Malalasekera ([Colombo]: Government of Ceylon, 1961), 59.
31. For a study of this chapter, see Bruce Cameron Hall, *Vasubandhu on "Aggregates, Spheres, and Components": Being Chapter One of the Abhidharmakośa"* (PhD dissertation, Harvard University, 1983).
32. As part of the discussion on conditioned factors dissociated from the mind, Vasubandhu attends to the attainment of cessation. For a study of Vasubandhu's treatment with reference to later commentaries, see Paul Griffiths, "On Being Mindless: The Debate on the Reemergence of Consciousness from the Attainment of Cessation in the Abhidharmakośabhāṣyam and Its Commentaries," *Philosophy East and West* 33, no. 4 (1983): 379–394, and Paul Griffiths, *On Being Mindless: Buddhist Meditation and the Body–Mind Problem* (La Salle, IL: Open Court, 1986).
33. For an exploration of Vasubandhu's explanation of the theory of dependent origination, see Susan Stalker, *A Study of Dependent Origination: Vasubandhu, Buddhaghosa, and the Interpretation of Pratītyasamutpāda* (PhD dissertation, University of Pennsylvania, 1987).
34. An annotated translation of the *Upāyikā-nāmā Abhidharmakośa-Ṭikā* into Japanese is Yoshifumi Honjō 本庄良文, *Kusharon Chū Upāikā No Kenkyū* 俱舎論註ウパーイカーの研究, 2 vols. (Tokyo: Daizō Shuppan 大蔵出版, 2014). Along the same lines, Part I of Hirakawa, with Hirai et al., *Index to the Abhidharmakośa-bhāṣyam*, lists the canonical sources that are explicitly named in the *AKBh* (423–425). Two other resources which offer information on identified canonical passages in Vasubandhu's work are Bhikkhu Pāsādika, ed., *Kanonische Zitate im Abhidharmakośabhāṣya des Vasubandhu*, Sanskrit-Wörterbuch der buddhistischen Texte aus den Turfan-Funden (Göttingen, Germany: Vandenhoeck & Ruprecht, 1989) and Yoshifumi Honjō 本庄良文, *A Table of Āgama-Citations in the Abhidharmakośa and the Abhidharmakoṣpāyikā [sic]* 俱舎論所依阿含全表 (Kyoto: Private publication, 1984).
35. Mejor, *Vasubandhu's Abhidharmakośa*, 76.
36. Translated by Coghlan in *Ornament of Abhidharma*.

37. See Coghlan, "Translator's Introduction," 19–21, for a list of major Tibetan commentaries.
38. Robert Kritzer, *Vasubandhu and the Yogācārabhūmi: Yogācāra Elements in the Abhidharmakośabhāṣya* (Tokyo: International College for Postgraduate Buddhist Studies, 2005); Robert Kritzer, "Quotations Common to the Yogācārabhūmi and the Abhidharmakośa-Bhāsya," *Indogaku Bukkyōgaku kenkyū* 45, no. 1 (1996): 15–20; Robert Kritzer, "Preliminary Report on a Comparison of the *Abhidharmakosabhasya* and the *Yogācārabhūmi*," *Journal of Indian and Buddhist Studies* 49, no. 1 (2000): 8–12; Robert Kritzer, "Sautrāntika in the *Abhidharmakośabhāsya*," *Journal of the International Association of Buddhist Studies* 26, no. 2 (2003): 331–384.
39. Changhwan Park, *Vasubandhu, Śrīlāta, and the Sautrāntika Theory of Seeds*, Wiener Studien zur Tibetologie und Buddhismuskunde 84 (Vienna: Arbeitskreis für Tibetische und Buddhistische Studien, Universität Wien, 2014).
40. See Marek Mejor, "Vasubandhu's *Abhidharmakośa* in Non-Buddhist Philosophical Treatises," in *Buddhist Studies: Papers of the 12th World Sanskrit Conference*, ed. Richard Gombrich and Cristina Scherrer-Schaub (Delhi: Motilal Banarsidass, 2008), 119–150; Johannes Bronkhorst, "Sāṃkhya in the *Abhidharmakośa Bhāṣya*," *Journal of Indian Philosophy* 25, no. 4 (1997): 393–400; and Shoryu Katsura, "Some Cases of Doctrinal Proofs in the Abhidharmakośabhāṣya," *Journal of Indian Philosophy* 31, nos. 1–3 (2003): 105–120.
41. Johannes Bronkhorst, *Karma and Teleology: A Problem and Its Solutions in Indian Philosophy* (Tokyo: International College for Advanced Buddhist Studies, 2000), 67–75. See also Bronkhorst's introductory exposition in *Karma* (Honolulu: University of Hawai'i Press, 2011), 55–88. James Paul McDermott offers a descriptive overview of the chapter in *Development in the Early Buddhist Concept of Kamma/Karma* (New Delhi: Munshiram Manoharlal, 1984), 127–143.
42. Sonam Kachru, *Minds and Worlds: A Philosophical Commentary on the Twenty Verses of Vasubandhu* (PhD dissertation, University of Chicago, 2015), 448–495.
43. Karin Meyers, *Freedom and Self-Control: Free Will in South Asian Buddhism* (PhD dissertation, University of Chicago, 2010). See also Karin Meyers, "Free Persons, Empty Selves: Freedom and Agency in Light of the Two Truths," in *Free Will, Agency and Selfhood in Indian Philosophy*, ed. Matthew R. Dasti and Edwin F. Bryant (Oxford: Oxford University Press, 2014), 41–67; and Karin Meyers, "The Dynamics of Intention, Freedom, and Habituation according to Vasubandhu's *Abhidharmakośabhāṣya*," in *A Mirror Is for Reflection: Understanding Buddhist Ethics*, ed. Jake H. Davis (Oxford: Oxford University Press, 2017), 239–256.
44. Oren Hanner, *Moral Agency under the No-Self Premise: A Comparative Study of Vasubandhu and Derek Parfit* (PhD dissertation, Hamburg University, 2016).
45. Kapstein, *Reason's Traces.*
46. Jonardon Ganeri, *The Concealed Art of the Soul: Theories of Self and Practices of Truth in Indian Ethics and Epistemology* (Oxford: Oxford University Press, 2007).
47. Mark Siderits, *Personal Identity and Buddhist Philosophy: Empty Persons* (Aldershot, UK: Ashgate, 2003); and Mark Siderits, *Personal Identity and Buddhist Philosophy: Empty Persons*, 2nd ed. (Aldershot, UK: Ashgate, 2015).
48. Alexander von Rospatt, *The Buddhist Doctrine of Momentariness: A Survey of the Origins and Early Phase of this Doctrine up to Vasubandhu* (Stuttgart: Franz Steiner Verlag, 1995).
49. Erich Frauwallner, *On the Date of the Buddhist Master of the Law Vasubandhu*, Serie Orientale Roma 3 (Rome: Istituto Italiano per il Medio ed Estremo Oriente, 1951).
50. Padmanabh S. Jaini, "On the Theory of the Two Vasubandhus," *Bulletin of the School of Oriental and African Studies* 21 (1958): 48–53.
51. Jonathan Gold, *Paving the Great Way: Vasubandhu's Unifying Buddhist Philosophy* (New York: Columbia University Press, 2015).

Oren Hanner

ABHISAMAYĀLAṂKĀRA (ORNAMENT FOR CLEAR REALIZATION)

The *Abhisamayālaṃkāra* (*Ornament for Clear Realization*) is an instructional treatise on the Prajñāpāramitā, or Perfect Wisdom, whose authorship is traditionally attributed to Maitreyanātha (*c.* 350 CE). The treatise has 273 stanzas composed in standard Sanskrit. The text contains verses of varying meter and utilizes rare forms of verb tenses, displaying a sophisticated knowledge of Sanskrit by its author.[1] The terse and elliptical language of the text in verse format illustrates its mnemonic function for bodhisattva monks training in Mahayana Buddhist scholasticism amid monastic communities influenced by Prajñāpāramitā. The *Abhisamayālaṃkāra* is unknown in classical East Asian Buddhist traditions; Indian and Tibetan Buddhist traditions ascribe it to Maitreyanātha, who some scholars have assumed was a teacher of the great Indian Buddhist scholar Asaṅga (*c.* 4th century CE), while others believe it was Asaṅga himself who wrote these verses.[2] The Tibetan tradition considers the *Abhisamayālaṃkāra*, along with four other texts, as part of a collection known to the Tibetans as the five texts of Maitreya (*byams gzhung sde lnga*).[3] The work's full title in Sanskrit is *Abhisa mayālaṃkāranāmaprajñāpāramitopadeśāstra*. The term at the beginning of the title, "*abhisamaya*," signifies "comprehensive understanding" or "clear realization," referring to cognitive attainments on the path to buddhahood. *Alaṃkāra* (Ornament) is a literary style that provides an exposition of a topic. The *Abhisamayālaṃkāra* is regarded as an *upadeśaśāstra* (instructional treatise) in that it presents the hidden or concealed meaning (Tibetan *sbas don*, Sanskrit *garbhyārtha*) of the longer Prajñāpāramitā corpus of works. Therefore, the full title may be translated as "An Instructional Treatise on Perfect Wisdom Called 'Ornament for Clear Realization.'"[4]

As a technical treatise, the *Abhisamayālaṃkāra* consists of an encyclopedic table of contents, communicating in an abridged form the instructions, practices, paths, and stages of realization to buddhahood that are mentioned in the Prajñāpāramitā. The primary purpose of the *Abhisamayālaṃkāra* is to describe the stages of the Mahayana path thought by Indian and Tibetan scholars to be implicitly stated in the Prajñāpāramitā, through outlining realizations and practices that bodhisattvas (buddhas-in-training) must achieve in order to attain buddhahood.[5]

The *Abhisamayālaṃkāra* outlines a soteriological system of the entire Mahayana path by either explicitly expressing what is already mentioned in the Prajñāpāramitā, particularly the *Pañcaviṃśatisāhasrikāprajñāpāramitā* (*Perfection of Wisdom in Twenty-Five Thousand Lines*), or superimposing a path schema that is foreign to the scriptures and expressed in abhidharma and Yogācāra terminology. The *Abhisamayālaṃkāra* lays out its system of buddhalogical teachings through fusing together abhidharma catergories and technical terminology found in Yogācāra treatises with content from the Prajñāpāramitā. The use of categories such as the four types of dichotomous conceptualization (*vikalpa*) and the multiple bodies (*kāya*) of a buddha indicate Yogācāra influence on the *Abhisamayālaṃkāra*'s author.[6]

While soteriologically significant, the objectified, codified, and detailed scholastic descriptions of path structures and stages mentioned in the *Abhisamayālaṃkāra*'s accounts of the path do not serve as practical guides to Buddhist practice, nor do they provide details of actual meditation experience.[7] Rather, the descriptions of the path in the *Abhisamayālaṃkāra* serve as an archetypal pattern of the worldview in which liberation is possible for the individual practitioner. Buddhist scholastic accounts of the path are constructs or, as Williams notes, "prescriptive systemizations of scriptural material" that were "compiled by monks of formidable learning who were attempting to systematize and schematize the confused and often conflicting descriptions of practices and stages found scattered throughout the canon."[8] As Dreyfus has noted, the path serves as a structure through which Buddhist traditions will formulate their practices, doctrines, and narratives. In the case of Tibetan Buddhist traditions that study and follow the *Abhisamayālaṃkāra*, "the discussion of the path is central... because it habituates students to the universe in which these narratives make sense, and thus strengthens their religious commitment."[9] Although the descriptions of the path must appear as concrete guides to Buddhist practices for followers of a tradition, Dreyfus argues that this concreteness is itself a reification. The models of the path outlined by texts such as the *Abhisamayālaṃkāra* are mental constructs that serve as maps to influence and support people in their practices.[10] In this manner, the *Abhisamayālaṃkāra* constructs a soteriological worldview that outlines a narrative of progress to buddhahood but does not describe meditative experiences or provide practical guidelines on how to cultivate such experiences. The *Abhisamayālaṃkāra* furnishes "the framework that makes a narrative of spiritual progress possible and introduces an element of closure without which the commitment required by Buddhist practices cannot be sustained."[11]

THE STRUCTURE AND CONTENT OF THE *ABHISAMAYĀLAṂKĀRA*

In terms of general content and structure, the *Abhisamayālaṃkāra* has 273 Sanskrit stanzas within nine chapters that present the concealed meaning (*sbas don*, *garbhyārtha*) of the Prajñāpāramitā sutras. The *Abhisamayālaṃkāra* lays out the same subject matter numerous times, yet with each repetition of the presentation, the subject matter is covered in successively greater detail.[12] The main subject matter of the text is presented five separate times. The (1) homage to Prajñāpāramitā encapsulates the main principles that flow through the whole text. The homage is followed by a restatement of these main principles in (2) a versified table of contents (*Abhisamayālaṃkāra* 1.3–4). These main principles or topics are then slightly expanded and contained in (3) an elucidation of the "body of the text" (*Abhisamayālaṃkāra* 1.5–17). The fourth repetition is the most expansive and consists of (4) a detailed articulation (*Abhisamayālaṃkāra*, 1.18–penultimate) of the paths and stages. Finally, (5) summation verses (*Abhisamayālaṃkāra* 9.1–2) are given that condense the subject matter of the text into three categories: aims (*viṣaya*), practices (*prayoga*), and result (*phala*).

The *Abhisamayālaṃkāra* presents its subject matter in terse verses that are often vague in meaning and difficult to understand without the assistance of a commentary. The text presumes that the reader has a background in Buddhist scholasticism, including a knowledge of abhidharma path structures, categories of mental defilements, meditational attainments, analytical procedures, and cosmology, among other topics. Along these lines, the path systems presented in the *Abhisamayālaṃkāra* are quite complex, with multiple divisions and subdivisions pertaining to each aspect of the path from several angles.

The first repetition of the material occurs in the homage, which embodies in a condensed manner the main doctrines that are found in the *Abhisamayālaṃkāra*. It is the source from which the presentation is derived and contains the overall principles that underline the whole work:

> Homage to the Mother of the Buddha together with *śrāvaka*s and *bodhisattva*s: she who, in the guise of All-knowledge, leads *śrāvaka*s who seek peace to pacification; she who, in the guise of Knowledge of the Paths, causes those who benefit the world to accomplish the welfare of people; [and] possessed of which, Sages teach this all-pervading [dharma] in every aspect.
>
> *yā sarvajñatayā nayaty upaśamaṃ śāntaiṣiṇaḥ śrāvakān yā mārgajñatayā jagaddhitakṛtāṃ lokārthasampādikā /*
>
> *sarvākāram idaṃ vadanti munayo viśvaṃ yayā saṃgatās tasyai śrāvakabodhisattvagaṇino buddhasya mātre namaḥ //*[13]

In this homage, Prajñāpāramitā manifests herself in three forms of omniscience: All-knowledge (*sarvajñatā, thams cad shes pa nyid,* or *vastujñāna, gzhi shes*); Knowledge of the Paths (*mārgajñatā, lam shes*), or Path Omniscience; and Total Omniscience (*sarvākārajñatā, rnam pa thams cad mkhyen pa nyid*). She is glorified as the "Mother" (*mātṛ, yum*) of the śrāvakas (which implicitly include *pratyekabuddhas*), bodhisattvas, and buddhas. The name "Mother" (*mātṛ*) may imply a relationship to "*mātṛkās*," early abhidharma terminological lists that clarified the distinguishing points of the buddha's doctrine that should be known (*jñeya*) or correctly analyzed. Such lists were composed of topics like the four applications of mindfulness, the four right efforts, the seven limbs of enlightenment, and so forth. This term "*mātṛkā*," a secondary formation derived from the ordinary word for "mother" (*mātṛ*), *mātṛkā* (cognate with English "matrix"), is also used figuratively to mean "source" or "origin." The *Abhisamayālaṃkāra* itself may be an early "*mātṛkā*" of the Prajñāpāramitā, serving as a source for the various lists describing paths and stages to full enlightenment.[14]

In the opening verses after the homage, the *Abhisamayālaṃkāra* (1.3–4) states that "the perfection of wisdom is proclaimed through eight subjects: (1) Total Omniscience, (2) Path Omniscience, (3) Empirical Omniscience, (4) Full Realization of All Aspects, (5) Realization that has Attained the Summit, (6) Progressive Realization, (7) Instantaneous Realization, and (8) the Dharma-body."[15] The *Abhisamayālaṃkāra* contains nine chapters, eight of which address each subject in turn. The eight subjects (*padārtha*) of these eight chapters (*adhikāra*) of the *Abhisamayālaṃkāra* correspond to eight clear realizations (*abhisamaya*) that explain the soteriological purport of Prajñāpāramitā.

Total Omniscience or the wisdom of all aspects (Sanskrit, *sarvākārajñatā*, Tibetan, *rnam pa thams cad mkhyen pa nyid*) is regarded as the fundamental wisdom and the central concept of Prajñāpāramitā.[16] For the *Abhisamayālaṃkāra* and its commentaries, Total Omniscience is direct unmediated knowledge that understands reality as it is (Tibetan, *ji lta ba bzhin yod pa*, Sanskrit, *yathāvadbhāvika*) to its fullest possible extent (Tibetan, *ji snyed yod pa*, Sanskrit, *yāvadbhāvikatā*) in all its aspects.[17] The first chapter comprises ten topics within seventy-three verses, which mention the necessary practices that lead to the Total Omniscience of a buddha. These topics include the aspiration for complete awakening (*bodhicittotpāda*), special instructions (*avavāda*), the fourfold limbs of insight (*nirvedhāṅga*), the basis of attainment whose nature is of the *dharmadhātu* (*ādhāraṃ dharmadhātusvabhāvakam*), supports (*ālambana*), purpose (*samuddeśa*), the activity of putting on armor and setting out (*saṃnāhaprasthitikriye*), equipment (*sambhāra*), and emergence (*niryāṇa*). The *Abhisamayālaṃkāra* (1.19–20) lists twenty-two types of aspiration for complete awakening (*bodhicittotpāda*), a list similar to that found in the *Mahāyānasūtrālaṃkāra* (4.15–20), and a topic of great importance in the history of Indo-Tibetan Buddhism.[18] The first chapter (1.23–24) also contains a synopsis of the various types of noble beings (*ārya*), similar to lists in the *Abhidharmakośa* and *Abhidharmasamuccaya*; these became a topic of special exegesis in Tibetan Buddhist monastic education after the 12th century.[19]

The second chapter of the *Abhisamayālaṃkāra*, on the knowledges of all paths (*mārgajñatā*, *lam shes nyid*), or Path Omniscience, discusses eleven topics in thirty-one verses. Path Omniscience in the *Abhisamayālaṃkāra* correlates to three types of path systems that are mastered by bodhisattvas: the paths of śrāvakas, the paths of *pratyekabuddhas*, and the paths of bodhisattvas. A śrāvaka (Tibetan, *nyan thos pa*, "Listener") is a type of individual who has heard or studied the buddha's teachings and who seeks the peace of nirvana through cultivating a direct realization of the nobles' four truths. In the system of *Abhisamayālaṃkāra*, a bodhisattva fixates upon the nobles' four truths (*catvāri āryasatyāni*) with particular emphasis on their sixteen aspects. However, a bodhisattva will cognize the nobles' four truths without perceptually grasping on to their aspects (AA 2.2). This is because even though a bodhisattva recognizes the aspects of disease, calamity, and so forth, he or she does not become attached to these aspects for the purpose of escaping samsara as does a śrāvaka. A *pratyekabuddha* (Tibetan *rang sang gyas*, "Solitary Buddha") is an "individually awakened one" who cognizes the emptiness of external objects through realizing dependent arising but does not thereby attain the full omniscience of a buddha. *Pratyekabuddhas* do not have much compassion and attain their awakening in solitude. Given these distinctions, a *pratyekabuddha* is understood to be superior to a śrāvaka and inferior to a bodhisattva. A *pratyekabuddha* is superior to a śrāvaka through his or her abandonment of the conceptualization of objects but is inferior to a bodhisattva who also eliminates the conceptualization of subjects.

The *Abhisamayālaṃkāra* is primarily a technical digest for the training of bodhisattvas. The bodhisattva (Tibetan, *byang chub sems dpa'*, "buddha-to-be") is an individual who is intent on achieving full buddhahood for the welfare of beings through cultivating wisdom and compassion.[20] The bodhisattva in the *Abhisamayālaṃkāra* is superior in aspiration, abandonment, and realization (AA 1.42). Bodhisattvas are superior in that they aspire for unsurpassable complete awakening (*anuttarasaṃyaksaṃbodhi*), not only for themselves, but for the sake of all other beings. With emphasis on the altruistic intention for the welfare of all sentient beings, one primary distinction from practitioners of other vehicles is that bodhisattvas have great compassion (*mahākaruṇa*) (AA 4.27–28). Bodhisattvas abandon not only the afflictional obscurations (*kleśāvaraṇa*) but also the obstacles that impede complete knowledge (*jñeyāvaraṇa*). The understanding that actuates their abandonment is not just cognition of the essencelessness of the person (*pudgalanairātyma*), but realization of the essencelessness of things (*dharmanairātmya*) through the apprehension of emptiness (śūnyatā) (AA 4.52).

In the course of realizing the two types of essencelessness and abandoning the two types of obscurations, a bodhisattva will travel through ten levels or stages (*daśabhūmi*) (AA 1.47d–1.70). Through the *bodhisattvas*' abandonment of the knowledge obstacles they achieve Total Omniscience (*sarvākārajñatā*), enabling them to help all beings through their achievement of buddhahood.

The *Abhisamayālaṃkāra*'s third chapter describes the qualities of Empirical Omniscience (*vastujñāna, gzhi shes*; literally, "knowledge of bases"), which is a type of knowledge that cognizes empirical objects that are to be abandoned in conditioned existence. In sixteen stanzas, the third chapter makes reference to nine topics that correlate to knowledge that is comprehended by śrāvakas and *pratyekabuddhas*.[21] Empirical Omniscience is mastered by bodhisattvas as well, but bodhisattvas do not cling to the pacifying results of this realization's cognition. That is, bodhisattvas "are not stationed in existence because of wisdom; nor, because of compassion, do they abide in peace" (*prajñayā na bhave sthānaṃ kṛpayā na śame sthitiḥ*, AA 1.10ab). Empirical Omniscience leads śrāvakas, *pratyekabuddhas*, and bodhisattvas to comprehend the entirety of unconditioned and conditioned things (dharmas) found in Buddhist classifications, including the five aggregates (*skandha*), the twelve sense spheres (*āyatana*), and the eighteen sense objects (*dhātu*).

The full realization of all aspects (*sarvākārābhisaṃbodha, rnam rdzogs sbyor ba*), which is the focus of the *Abhisamayālaṃkāra*'s fourth chapter, consists of yogic practices that enable a bodhisattva to gain a cognition of all the 173 modes, or aspects, of the three types of omniscience.[22] This chapter outlines the multiple aspects (*ākāra*) in each of the three knowledges that a bodhisattva masters. This realization also sets forth the special trainings (*prayogā*) that enable a bodhisattva to adopt qualities (*guṇa*) and discard faults (*doṣa*) necessary for acquiring the marks (*lakṣaṇa*) that establish the preparatory factors for liberation (*mokṣabhāgīya*) and the preparatory analytical factors (*nirvedhabhāgīya*). The factors for liberation and preparatory analytical factors constitute the first two paths among the five paths found in the *Abhisamayālaṃkāra*. The final three paths, the paths of seeing (*darśana*), meditation (*bhāvanā*), and the distinctive path (*viśeṣa-mārga*), equivalent to the path of no-more learning (*aśaikṣa-mārga*), are progressively described throughout the remainder of the text. The fourth realization concludes with qualities that a bodhisattva gains through proficiency in the first two paths.

As the bodhisattva progresses to full buddhahood through the cognitive attainments and mental purifications that occur on the paths of preparation, seeing, and cultivation, the paths become irreversible (*avaivartika*) from full buddhahood. The term *irreversible* in this instance generally signifies a point reached in the career of a bodhisattva after which there can be no turning back from the attainment of full buddhahood. The *Abhisamayālaṃkāra* distinguishes three phases of a bodhisattva becoming increasingly endowed with marks and signs of being irreversible: (1) while on the path of preparation cultivating the preparatory analytical factors, (2) while on the path of seeing cognizing eight moments of receptivity and eight moments of knowledge, and (3) while on the path of meditation. As the bodhisattva progresses through these path phases he or she increases cognition of emptiness and thereby turns away from attachment to sensory objects and gains a multitude of moral, ascetic, and even hygienic qualities.[23] The *Abhisamayālaṃkāra* and its commentaries (AA 4.40–43) specify, for example, that the irreversible bodhisattva will abstain from taking life, engaging in theft, or drinking liquor, as well as have clean robes and bodies free from worms. Bodhisattvas who gain these qualities become part of the assembly of irreversible bodhisattvas (*avaivartika bodhisattva saṃgha*) (AA 4.38–4.51), begin to realize the sameness of cyclic existence and nirvana (*saṃsāranirvaṇasamatā*) (AA 4.60), work toward the purification of a buddhafield (*buddhakṣetraviśuddhi*) (AA 4.61), and gain competence in the employment of skillful means (*upāya*) (AA 4.62–63).

The *Abhisamayālaṃkāra*'s fifth clear realization is the summit of full understanding (*mūrdhābhisamaya, rtse sbyor*) or "culminating insight."[24] This *abhisamaya* is composed of forty-two verses outlining eight factors and phases of yogic practices that reach culmination while cognizing emptiness (śūnyatā). The first four factors, signs (*liṅga*), increase (*vivṛddhi*), steadying (*nirūḍhi*), and mental composure (*cittasaṃsthiti*), describe increasingly higher and higher levels of the culminating insight.[25] The fifth and sixth factors, respectively, mark the culminating insight of the path of seeing (*darśanamārga*) and the path of meditation (*bhāvanāmārga*). These two paths are counteragents to four sets of conceptualizations (*caturdhā ca vikalpasya pratipakṣaścaturvidhaḥ*, AA 1.14): two grasped-object conceptualizations (AA 5.5) and two grasper-subject conceptualizations (AA 5.6).[26] The two kinds of grasped-object conceptualizations concern the reification of things that are pursued (*pravṛtti pakṣādhiṣṭhānagrāhyavikalpa, 'jug gzung rtog*) and the reification of things to be relinquished (*nivṛttipakṣādhiṣṭhānagrāhyavikalpa, ldog gzung rtog*). The two kinds of grasper-subject conceptualizations concern substantially existing persons (*pudgaladravya*), which are conceived to be substantially existent (*rdzas 'dzin rtog*), and nominally existing beings (*prajñaptipuruṣa*), which are conceived to imputedly exist (*btags 'dzin rtog*). Comprehensions connected with these four types of concepts, formative in the path of preparation, become the dominant focal point on the Mahayana paths of seeing and cultivation. The last two factors of culminating insight concern how the bodhisattva practices uninterrupted meditative stabilization (*ānantaryasamādhi*) and removes mistaken practices through skillful means.

By reference to thirteen topics in one verse, the sixth chapter defines the gradual full understanding (*anupūrvābhisamaya, mthar gyis sbyor ba*) of the three forms of omniscience.[27] This clear realization of "gradual insight" consists of engaging in the six perfections of bodhisattva practice. The seventh *abhisamaya*, last of the four practices, clarifies the "instantaneous realization" (*ekakṣaṇābhisamaya, skad cig gcig pa'i mngon par rdzogs par byang chub pa*) that occurs at the final moment right before buddhahood. This realization is of four kinds or types (*vidhā, prakāra*), which are outlined in five verses.[28] According to Haribhadra, the first type is the awakening marked by all unpolluted nonmatured dharmas (*avipākānāsravasarvadharma*). The other three are the "perfection of wisdom that arises from the maturation of all bright dharmas" (*vipākadharmatāvasthānāsravasarvadharma*), "that dharmas have no marks" (*alakṣaṇasarvadharma*), and "the non-dual true reality of dharmas" (*advayalakṣaṇasarvadharma*).[29] The seventh realization indicates that the *Abhisamayālaṃkāra* does not only teach gradual stages of realization.

The last subject in the *Abhisamayālaṃkāra*, the result of the path, is the realization of the dharma-body (*dharmakāyābhisamaya, chos sku mngon rtogs pa*) in its multiple aspects. Indian and Tibetan commentators debate about what exactly constitutes the correct interpretation of the multiple aspects of a buddha's embodiment, whether buddhahood has a threefold or fourfold embodiment.[30] A number of Tibetan scholars, following the Indian scholar Haribhadra, will understand these four as (1) the body of dharma (*dharmakāya*), (2) the embodiment of buddhahood in its essence (*svābhāvikakāya*), (3) the embodiment of communal enjoyment (*saṃbhogakāya*), and (4) the limitless forms of awakened manifestation (*nairmāṇikakāya*). The body embodiment of buddhahood in its essence (*svābhāvikakāya*) is constituted by twenty-one undefiled (*nirāsrava*) qualities that have reached complete purity (AA 8.2–6).[31] The embodiment of communal enjoyment (*saṃbhogakāya*) embraces the thirty-two major and eighty minor marks of a great being (AA 8.12–32). The limitless forms of awakened manifestation (*nairmāṇikakāya*) are emanation bodies that impartially work for the benefit of the world, carrying out twenty-seven types of altruistic activities until the end of cyclic existence (AA 8.33–40).[32]

The eight subjects found in the *Abhisamayālaṃkāra* are usually understood in terms of three categories that are mentioned in the final verses of the text's ninth chapter. The first three clear realizations (1–3) are aims or objects (*viṣaya*) to be known by bodhisattvas. The next four realizations (4–7) are practices (*prayoga*) to be cultivated by bodhisattvas in order to cognize the first three realizations. Finally, the dharma-body (*phala*) occurs as a result of the practices that actualize the clear realizations.

INDIAN BUDDHIST COMMENTARIES

A long tradition of commentaries on the *Abhisamayālaṃkāra* developed in India and Tibet. Traditional accounts mention that the great Yogācāra scholar Asaṅga (*c.* 315–390 CE) wrote the *Tattvaviniścaya* and that his half-brother Vasubandhu (fl. 4th century) wrote the *Paddhati*, both commentaries to the *Abhisamayālaṃkāra* that are lost. Ārya Vimuktisena (or Vimuktiṣeṇa, *c.* early 6th century CE) is the author of the earliest extant commentary on the *Abhisamayālaṃkāra*, the *Abhisamayālaṃkāravṛtti*.[33] Ārya Vimuktisena's commentary links the *Abhisamayālaṃkāra* to the *Pañviṃśatisāhasrikā* and serves as the basis for all subsequent Indian and Tibetan commentaries.[34] The next major scholar who comments upon the *Abhisamayālaṃkāra* is Haribhadra, who was active during the reign of Dharmapāla (r. *c.* 770–810). He composed four works related to *Abhisamayālaṃkāra* including the *Abhisamayālaṃkārālokā*, a long explanatory commentary that comments on the *Abhisamayālaṃkārā* in correlation with *Aṣṭasāhasrikāprajñāpāramitā*, and the *Abhisamayālaṃkārakārikāśāstravivṛti*, a short commentary that provides an exposition on the *Abhisamayālaṃkāra* without relying on any Prajñāpāramitā text.[35] The *Abhisamayālaṃkāra-kārikāśāstravivṛti* is the base text for *Abhisamayālaṃkāra* commentaries in the Tibetan tradition. After the works of Ārya Vimuktisena and Haribhadra, another sixteen Indian commentaries on the *Abhisamayālaṃkāra* were composed during the Pāla dynastic era (750–1150 CE) and are preserved in Tibetan translation.[36] Some commentaries are conjoined with a *Prajñāpāramitā* scripture, while others independently comment on the *Abhisamayālaṃkāra* without conjoining to a scripture. Bhadanta Vimuktisena, a student of Ārya Vimuktisena, composed the *Abhisamayālaṃkārakārikāvārttika* (Tôh. no. 3788). Dharmamitra (fl. 800–850 CE) composed the *Abhisamayālaṃkāraprasphuṭapadā* (P 5194), an important subcommentary to Haribhadra's *Vivṛti* that glosses and clarifies Haribhadra's statements on the *Abhisamayālaṃkāra*.[37] Dharmakīrti of Suvarṇadvīpa (fl. 975–1025 CE), known in Tibetan as Serlingpa (*gser gling pa*), "the man from Sumatra Island," composed the *Durbodhālokā*, another subcommentary on Haribhadra's *Vivṛti*. A number of Indian commentaries on the *Abhisamayālaṃkāra* were composed by figures affiliated with Vikramaśīlā during the 11th and 12th centuries. Prajñākaramati (*c.* 950–1000 CE) wrote the *Abhisamayālaṅkāravṛttipiṇḍārtha* (Tôh. no. 3795). Ratnakīrti, a pupil of Jñānaśrīmitra associated with both the Somapuri and Vikramaśīlā monasteries, composed the *Abhisamayālaṅkāravṛttikīrtikalā* (Tōh. no. 3799). Ratnākaraśānti (*c.* 1000 CE) composed the *Abhisamayālaṃkārakārikāvṛttiśuddhamatī* and *Aṣṭasāhasrikā-prajñāpāramitāpañjikāsāratamā*. The *Sāratamā* connects the *Abhisamayālaṃkāra* to the 8,000-verse Prajñāpāramitā from a Yogācāra philosophical perspective.[38] Another well-known scholar from Vikramaśīla Monastery, Abhayākaragupta (fl. 1100 CE), composed the *Aṣṭasāhasrikāprajñāpāramitāvṛttimarmakaumudī* (Tōh. no. 3805), a commentary that connects the *Abhisamayālaṃkāra* with the *Aṣṭasāhasrikāprajñāpāramitā*. Abhayākaragupta's *Munimatālaṃkāra*, of which a complete Sanskrit manuscript has been recovered, is a text that comments on sections of the *Abhisamayālaṃkāra* and has been described by D. S. Ruegg as "one of the last of the major comprehensive treatises of Indian Buddhism."[39]

TIBETAN COMMENTARIES

Tibetan Buddhists have continued the commentarial tradition of the *Abhisamayālaṃkāra* up to the present day. The *Abhisamayālaṃkāra* has "had the most lasting impact of any sūtra commentary [in Tibet]," Schoening notes, serving as a gateway for the study of the *Prajñāpāramitā* by all schools of Tibetan Buddhism as well as being a fundamental text in the contemporary Tibetan Buddhist monastic curriculum.[40] Hundreds of commentaries to the *Abhisamayālaṃkāra* were composed in pre-modern Tibet. The Tibetans translated the root text of the *Abhisamayālaṃkāra* and several of its commentaries in the Imperial period (7th–9th centuries), especially during the reign of Khri-srong lde-btsan (*c.* 740–798).[41] However, the first indigenous commentary was not composed until Rngog lo-tsā-ba blo-ldan shes-rab (1059–1109 CE). Rngog blo-ldan shes-rab translated not only the Haribhadra's *Vivṛti*, but also the *Ālokā*, as well as the *Vṛtti* of Ārya Vimuktisena. Rngog lo-tsā-ba also made a revised translation of the *Abhisamayālaṃkāra* in collaboration with the Indian paṇḍita Go mi 'chi med (Amaragomin). The two principal commentaries Rngog wrote are known as the *Ṭīk chung*, or *Lo tsā ba chen po'i bsdus don* (MHTL no. 11471), and the *Lo tsā ba blo ldan shes rab kyi phar phyin ṭīk chen* (MHTL no. 11470). The *Lo tsā ba chen po'i bsdus don* has only recently become available for study.[42]

The works of Rngog blo-ldan shes-rab are not the only early Tibetan commentaries on the *Abhisamayālaṃkāra* that have recently become available. The dPal-brtsegs Research Centre for Old Tibetan Manuscripts (*Dpal brtsegs bod yig dpe rnying zhib 'jug khang*), based in Lhasa, Tibet, between 2006 and 2015 released 120 volumes of manuscript facsimiles of Tibetan Buddhist scholarly works dating from the 11th to the 14th centuries.[43] Among the commentaries found in these volumes, approximately fifty are related to the Prajñāpāramitā, of which around forty-five are *Abhisamayālaṃkāra* commentaries.[44] Some of the more important commentaries among the manuscripts are Ar byang-chub ye-shes's (11th century) *Mngon rtogs rgyan kyi 'grel ba rnam par 'byed pa* (Volume 2, text 9, pages 91–447), Gro-lung-pa blo-gros 'byung-gnas's (b. 11th century) *Brgyad stong 'grel chen gyi bshad pa* (Volume 3, text 11, pages

579–745), and Khu shes-rab brtson-'grus's (1075–1143) *Shes rab kyi pha rol tu phyin pa'i man ngag gi bstan bcos mngon par rtogs pa'i rgyan gyi 'grel ba'i tshig dang don gsal bar bshad pa* (Volume 10, text 4, pages 15–331).

Among the most highly regarded Tibetan commentaries was that of Gnyal zhig pa 'jam dpal rdo rje (fl. *c.* 1200). He composed a commentary over 500 folios long on Haribhadra's *Vivṛti* called *Theg chen po la 'jug pa* (MHTL no. 11517).[45] This commentary was recently recovered from communist mainland China in the form of a handwritten manuscript that is preserved at the Library of Tibetan Works and Archives in Dharamsala, India.[46] The renowned scholar and historian Bu-ston rin-chen-grub (1290–1364) composed the *Lung gi nye ma,* a commentary on Haribhadra's *Vivṛti.* The Sa skya master Nya dbon kun dga' dpal (1285–1379) was one of the greatest Prajñàpàramità commentators of his era. His *Abhisamayālaṃkāra* commentary, the *Shad sbyar yid kyi mun sel,* was written at Sa skya in 1371 and represents a reformulation of Bu ston's *Lung gi nye ma.* G.yag-ston Sangs-rgyas-dpal (1350–1414), a great master of the Sakya tradition, wrote a number of commentaries on the *Abhisamayālaṃkāra.* His most famous was the eight-volume *Mngon rtogs rgyan 'grel pa rin chen bsam 'phel dbang rgyal* (King of wish-fulfilling jewels). Tsong-kha-pa blo-bzang grag-pa (1357–1419), a famous scholar and founding figure of the Gelukpa (*dge lugs pa*) tradition, wrote the *Legs bshad gser phreng* (*Golden Garland of Eloquence*) in his youth. This work has been translated into English in four volumes.[47] The later Gelukpa (*dge lugs pa*) tradition, up to the present day, follows the interpretation of the *Abhisamayālaṃkāra* found in Rgyal tshab rje dar ma rin chen's (1362/4–1432) *Rnam bshad snying po'i rgyan* (Ornament of the essence). The Sa-skya scholar Rong ston shes bya kun rig (1367–1449), a disciple and successor of G.yag-ston Sangs-rgyas-dpal, also wrote a commentary on the *Vivṛti* of Haribhadra.[48] The Tibetan commentarial tradition on the *Abhisamayālaṃkāra* reached its apex in mid-15th-century Tibet, although individual commentaries are occasionally composed in present-day Tibetan monastic communities. The Tibetan method of exegesis on the *Abhisamayālaṃkāra* allowed for the commentaries to evolve into a tour de force of encyclopedic Buddhist doctrinal knowledge, where even minor topics could be expanded into hundreds of pages and specific topics could develop into separate books or form distinct genre categories within Tibetan Buddhist literature.[49]

CONTROVERSIES AND SUPPLEMENTARY TOPICS IN THE STUDY OF THE *ABHISAMAYĀLAṂKĀRA*

The *Abhisamayālaṃkāra* has prompted a number of supplementary discussions and controversies over the long history of the text's study in both India and Tibet. Discussions and controversies that occurred in India can only be inferred from evidence found among the extant twenty-one Indian commentaries to the *Abhisamayālaṃkāra.* Only a few of these commentaries have been completely translated into English, and even then, we often do not know the full context of what debates and discussions took place in the study and practices related to the *Abhisamayālaṃkāra* in pre-modern India. Despite a number of initial studies, the historical development of Indian, as well as Tibetan, commentarial exegesis on the *Abhisamayālaṃkāra* is unknown. For example, the *Abhisamayālaṃkāra* is usually studied according to eight subjects (*padārtha*), as well as in terms of seventy topics (*don bdun cu,* **artha saptatiḥ*). Is the list of seventy topics an Indian or Tibetan development? Are the same seventy topics listed by commentators? Did the list become standardized, and if so, when? Some scholars claim that the same seventy topics are listed by Ārya Vimuktisena and subsequent commentators.[50] Yet, Tsong-kha-pa blo-bzang grag-pa (1357–1419) explains that the commentaries of Haribhadra are not clear as to exactly what topics count among the seventy and that, further, it is only in the later Pāla-era commentaries of Ratnākaraśānti, in his *Śuddhamatī*, and Ratnakīrti, in his *Kīrtikalā*, that an exact list of seventy topics and their corresponding passages are discussed.[51] So the list of seventy topics appears to be an Indian Buddhist development that was standardized in the later Pāla period, but only further studies will confirm the history of such developments. In brief, an intellectual history of the *Abhisamayālaṃkāra* in India based on the twenty-one commentaries and additional evidence has yet to be written.

Scholarly knowledge on the study and exegesis of the *Abhisamayālaṃkāra* in Tibetan intellectual history is better known, yet there is still a great amount of this literature that needs to be researched, translated, and explained.

A great amount of the current understanding of supplementary discussions and controversies related to the *Abhisamayālaṃkāra* are based on special manuals (*yig cha*) studied in the Tibetan Buddhist monastic colleges among Geluk (*dge lugs*) traditions. A number of these manuals were composed after the 16th century and reflect decades, if not centuries, of analysis and elaboration upon refined subtle points of exegesis related to the *Abhisamayālaṃkāra* primarily based on oral debate. The *Abhisamayālaṃkāra* manuals in the Geluk tradition are established from Tsong-kha-pa blo-bzang grag-pa's *Legs bshad gser phreng* (*Golden Garland of Eloquence*) and his disciple, Rgyal-tshab-rje dar-ma rin-chen's (1362/4–1432) *Rnam bshad snying po'i rgyan* (*Ornament of the Essence*) commentaries in correlation with Haribhadra's *Abhisamayālaṃkārakārikā-śāstravivṛti*. Se-ra rje-btsun chos-kyi rgyal-mtshan (1469–1546) authored the debate manuals for Byes college of Se ra and Byang rtse college of dGa' ldan; the manuals followed by sMad college of Se ra were by mKhas-sgrub bstan-pa dar-rgyas (1493–1568) and Grags-pa bshad-sgrub (1675–1748); those utilized by Shar rtse College of dGa' ldan and Blo gsal gling College of 'Bras spungs were authored by Paṇ-chen bSod-nams grags-pa (1478–1554), and, finally, the manuals used by sGo mang College of 'Bras spungs and bKra shis 'kyil monasteries were written by 'Jam-dbyangs bzhad-pa Ngag-dbang brston-'grus (1648–1721).[52]

Although these manuals have a great amount of subject matter in common, they contain debate on minute points of difference held between monastic collegiate rivals. The points of discussion range from debating whether the purported author of the *Abhisamayālaṃkāra*, which the Tibetan tradition unanimously proclaims to be Maitreya, is a bodhisattva or a buddha, to arcane points in the treatise's final chapters. If fact, a scholar associated with 'Bras spungs Monastery, Ngag-dbang dpal-ldan (b. 1797), composed a manual exclusively devoted to listing and briefly discussing point by point the differences between sGo mang and Blo gsal gling Colleges in the exegesis of the *Abhisamayālaṃkāra*.[53]

The monastic textbooks on the *Abhisamayālaṃkāra* also discuss supplementary topics related to the study of Prajñāpāramitā. For instance, Se-ra rje-btsun chos-kyi rgyal-mtshan discusses in his *Rgyan 'grel spyi don rol mtsho* topics such as the different meanings of nirvana with remnant and without remnant (*lhag bcas lhag med kyi myang 'das*), the manner in which the wheels of dharma are presented (*chos kyi 'khor lo ji ltar bskor ba'i tshul*), and an excursus on conventional and ultimate realities (*kun rdzob bden pa dang don dam bden pa*).[54]

In addition to supplementary topics related to the study of the *Abhisamayālaṃkāra* found within the commentaries and textbooks, the Tibetan scholarly tradition developed supplementary treatises that focused on four subject areas in the study of Prajñāpāramitā (*phar phyin zur bkol bzhi*) correlated with a sequence of four classes (*'dzin grwa*) in the monastic curriculum. The initial course of study (*gzung gsar 'og ma*, "lower level for new students") has the supplementary study of the twenty varieties of the spiritual community (*dge 'dun nyi shu*), the second-level course (*gzung gsar 'gong ma*, "upper level for new students") is supplemented with the study of dependent co-arising (*rten 'brel*), the third-level course (*skabs dang po*, "the first chapter") studies the differences between interpretable and definitive meaning in the interpretation of Buddhist scripture (*drang nges*), and the fourth-level course (*ston mo'i 'dzin grwa*, "course ending with a feast") focuses on the study of the concentrations and formless absorptions (*bsam gzugs*).[55]

Tibetan debate manual authors also developed specialized works treating the study of the *Abhisamayālaṃkāra* in terms of seventy topics (*don bdun cu*, **artha saptatiḥ*). In his study of the seventy topics with Tibetan teachers, the pioneer of the modern study of the *Abhisamayālaṃkāra*, Eugene Obermiller, identified a number of verses that prompted discussion and debate. The *Abhisamayālaṃkāra*'s Chapter 1 (verses 23 and 24) lists the twenty varieties of the spiritual community (*dge 'dun nyi shu*) in relation to the special instructions (*avadāna*) concerning the three jewels of the buddha, the dharma, and Saṃgha. Chapter 1 (verses 48–70) contains an enumeration of the preparation of dharmas (*yongs su sbyong ba*) for the gradual attainment of the ten levels of a bodhisattva. Chapter 1 (verse 71) mentions the equipment of antidotes (*pratipakṣa-saṃbhāra*) to calm subject and object conceptualization (*grāhya-grāhaka-vikalpa*). Chapter 2 (verses 3 and 4) describes the four degrees of path of preparatory analytical factors (*nirvedha-bhāgīya*). Chapter 2 (verses 9 and 10) focuses on the degrees of the path of preparatory analytical factors in the pratyekabuddha path. Chapter 2 (verses 26–27) centers on the conditions for the path of meditation. Chapter 4 (verses 6 and 7) provides the characteristics of the practitioner-vessel for hearing the Prajñāpāramitā. Chapter 4 (verses 55–59) describes the attainment of awakening through the path of meditation and examines the attainment through the purviews of conventional and ultimate realities. Chapter 5 (verse 23) mentions the "Lion's Sport meditative stabilization" (*seng ge rnam par bsgyings pa'i ting nge 'dzin*) where the twelve limbs of dependent-arising (*rten 'brel yang lag bcu gnyis*) are realized in direct and the reverse order. Chapter 5 (verses 35 and 36) concludes "the removal of the conceptualizations on the path of meditation." Finally, Chapter 8 (verses 7–11) provoked discussions on the vision, wisdom, and character of buddhahood. These verses all serve as focal points for ongoing debates about specific topics in the Tibetan study of Prajñāpāramitā.

Influenced by the Geluk tradition's extensive monastic study of the *Abhisamayālaṃkāra* and in consultation with indigenous Tibetan scholars trained in Geluk monastic colleges, modern scholars have examined several of these controversial topics of study. A few examples may be mentioned based on the topic's occurrence in the *Abhisamayālaṃkāra*.

James B. Apple has examined the topic of the "Twenty *Saṃghas*" based on Indian and Tibetan commentaries. As mentioned, the Twenty Varieties of the Saṃgha (*dge 'dun nyis shu*) is a subject derived from Chapter 1 (verses 23 and 24) of the *Abhisamayālaṃkāra* and is considered to be one of most difficult topics to comprehend. The "Twenty *Saṃghas*" refers to an exhaustive list of the stages through which noble beings (*ārya*) may pass in their progress toward enlightenment through various lifetimes in various cosmological realms. The *saṃgha*, as construed in this sense, represents those qualities of an ideal figure that provide structure to the Tibetan Buddhist worldview where soteriological results of the path can take place. The *saṃgha* of noble beings consists of those who have achieved the sixteenth moment of the path of seeing (*darśanamārga, mthong lam*) and who actualize the truth of cessation (*satyanirodha, 'gogs bden*) and the truth of the path (*mārgasatya, lam bden pa*). This typological list of twenty does not provide a description of any one individual's path to enlightenment; rather, it enumerates all of the *possible* stages through which any given individual might pass, depending upon factors such as that individual's cosmological circumstances and the acuity of his faculties. Although the Twenty *Saṃghas* always consists of a list of twenty, various interpretations can lead to various lists of twenty. The lack of regularity in accounting for the list of twenty serves as the basis for varying scholarly accounts and the complexity of the topic.[56]

David Seyfort Ruegg has explored the question of how the unconditioned and undifferentiated dharma-element (*dharmadhātu*) that pervades all reality can be the basis of a variety of spiritual lineages (*gotra*). The *Abhisamayālaṃkāra* mentions the gotra at several places (Chapter 1, verse 5; Chapter 1, verses 38d–39ab), and the commentaries provide an exegesis on the interconnection between the dharma-element and the various spiritual categories. Ruegg has also explored this topic in detail in relation to the question of buddha-nature or the "essence of the Tathāgata" (*tathāgatagarbha*) and the doctrine of One Unique Vehicle (*ekayāna*).[57]

A special course related to the study of the *Abhisamayālaṃkāra* is the study of the concentrations and formless absorptions (*bsam gzugs*). Leah Zahler has studied and analyzed this topic within the Geluk monastic curriculum in several works.[58] This special topic concerns the study of meditation and the meditative states of the four concentrations (*dhyāna, bsam gtan*) and the four formless absorptions (*ārūpyasamāpatti, gzugs med kyi snyoms 'jug*). The Geluk presentation of the topic interconnects the study of the perfections in the *Abhisamayālaṃkāra* with the details on meditative states provided from the Abhidharma literature of the *Abhidharmakośa* and *Abhidharmasamuccaya*. The topic focuses on mapping the concentrations and absorptions to Buddhist cosmological realms and their concomitant mental states within the context of stabilizing meditation (*'jog sgom*) and analytical meditation (*dpyad sgom*) practices. Controversies among the debate manuals are concerned with determining precise definitions for the meditative states and their most soteriological efficacious practice.

As mentioned, Chapter 8 of the *Abhisamayālaṃkāra* provoked discussions on the nature of a buddha and the number of embodiments that constituted buddhahood. A prevalent doctrine upheld by a number of Mahayana traditions was that there exist three bodies of a buddha: *dharmakāya, saṃbhogakāya,* and *nirmāṇakāya*. Some interpreters upheld a fourth body that is found in the exegesis of the *Abhisamayālaṃkara*. John J. Makransky has analyzed this controversy and its interpretation by a majority of Indian and Tibetan commentators of the *Abhisamayālaṃkara*. In brief, the Indian commentator Ārya Vimuktisena held that only three bodies are mentioned in the *Abhisamayālaṃkara*, while the fourth body, the *svābhāvikakāya*, represents the essence of the first three bodies. The Indian scholar Haribhadra enumerated four bodies, with the first three comprising a conditioned basis of a buddha's attainment, and the fourth, unconditioned and related to the *tathāgatagarbha*, as the *svābhāvikakāya*. The distinction between Ārya Vimuktisena and Haribhadra on the enumeration of buddha embodiments encouraged a number of controversies among both Indian and Tibetan commentators.[59]

REVIEW OF LITERATURE

The *Abhisamayālaṃkāra* has been studied by modern scholarship only since the beginning of the 20th century. In broad terms the approach has been to establish reliable editions of the primary texts, furnish translations of these texts, and then explain thematic points of Buddhist doctrine and practice in relation to the *Abhisamayālaṃkāra*. The Russian Indologist Fedore Ippolitorich Shcherbatskoi (Stcherbatsky, 1866–1942) first brought attention to the *Abhisamayālaṃkāra* in a brief article on Yogācāra in 1905.[60] M. P. Masson-Oursel, based on unedited manuscripts of the *Abhisamayālaṃkārālokā* held by Louis de La Vallée Poussin and Sylvain Lévi, published a Sanskrit edition and French translation of an extract of the *Abhisamayālaṃkāra*'s eighth chapter (verses 1–12, 33–40) in his study of the three buddha embodiments (*kāya*).[61] An edition of the base text of the *Abhisamayālaṃkāra* in Sanskrit and Tibetan was first published in 1929 by Stcherbatsky and Eugène Obermiller (1901–1935).[62] Obermiller followed the publication of the base text with pioneering studies—based on consultation with Tibetan scholars and commentaries—that focused on analyzing the doctrines and points of exegesis of Prajñāpāramitā in the *Abhisamayālaṃkāra*. His "The Doctrine of Prajñāpāramitā as Exposed in the Abhisamayālaṃkāra of Maitreya" has not been superseded as an introduction to and summary of the path system of the *Abhisamayālaṃkāra* and its related literature.[63] Obermiller followed this work with a series of fascicles that analyzed each chapter of the *Abhisamayālaṃkāra* with its specific topic, based on the Indian commentaries. The series was unfinished, however, leading up through only Chapter 4.[64] Concurrent with these initial studies, Sanskrit editions of Haribhadra's *Abhisamayālaṃkārālokā*, a work that contains the base text of the *Abhisamayālaṃkāra*, Haribhadra's commentary, and the *Aṣṭasāh asrikāprajñāpāramitā*, was published by the Japanese Buddhologist Unrai Wogihara (1869–1937) and the Italian scholar of Tibetan and the history of Buddhism Giuseppe Tucci (1894–1984).[65] A Sanskrit word-index to the *Abhisamayālaṃkārālokā* was published by Ryūsei Keira and Noboru Ueda in 1998.[66] Kajiyoshi Kōun published a Sanskrit edition and Japanese translation of the *Abhisamayālaṃkāra* in his *Genshi hannyakyō no kenkyū* (1944).[67] The great pioneer of *Prajñāpāramitā* studies, Edward Conze (1904–1979), published the first English translation of the *Abhisamayālaṃkāra*, along with a Sanskrit and Tibetan index (1954).[68] Among Conze's numerous other works related to *Prajñāpāramitā*, his *Large Sutra on Perfect Wisdom* and *The Prajñāpāramitā Literature* contain useful information for the study of the *Abhisamayālaṃkāra*.[69] *The Prajñāpāramitā Literature*, in addition to contextualizing the development of Prajñāpāramitā and its associated works, provides an annotated bibliography on the *Abhisamayālaṃkāra* and all its major commentaries in Sanskrit and Tibetan. After initial editions of Haribhadra's *Ālokā*, an edition of the first chapter of Vimuktisena's *Abhisamayālaṃkāravṛtti* was published, followed by Ratnākaraśānti's *Sāratamā*.[70] Hirofusa Amano (1931–) published a number of studies on Haribhadra's *Abhisamayālaṃkārakārikāśāstravivṛti*, culminating in a complete edition (2000) and Tibetan–Sanskrit index (2005) to the work.[71] An English translation of the first seven chapters of Haribhadra's *Vivṛti* was published by Alexander T. Naughton.[72] In addition to the critical edition of the base text and available Sanskrit commentaries, the *Abhisamayālaṃkāra* and its related literature has been a source in modern scholarship for the analysis of the embodied qualities of buddhahood, issues in the interpretation of *tathāgathagarbha*, and the elucidation of Buddhist categories of noble beings among other topics.[73] Gareth Sparham completed a monumental translation into English of both Vimuktisena's *Abhisamayālaṃkāravṛtti* and Haribhadra's *Abhisamayālaṃkārālokā* in four volumes.[74] Sparham also completed an equally immense translation in English of Tsong-kha-pa's *Golden Garland of Eloquence* followed by the Geluk (*dge lugs*) tradition of Tibetan Buddhism. Karl Brunnhölzl published studies on the *Abhisamayālaṃkārā* and its commentaries as found in the Nyingma (*rnying ma*) and Kagyü (*bka' brgyud*) traditions of Tibetan Buddhism.[75]

FURTHER READING

Apple, James B. *Stairway to Nirvāṇa: A Study of the Twenty Saṃghas Based on the Works of Tsong Kha Pa.* Albany: State University of New York Press, 2008.

Apple, James B. "The Mahāyāna Path of the Bodhisattva in the Ornament for Clear Realization." *Religion Compass* 5, no. 5 (2011): 166–179.

Brunnhölzl, Karl, trans. *Gone Beyond: The Prajñāpāramitā sūtras, the Ornament of Clear Realization, and Its Commentaries in the Tibetan Kagyü Tradition.* 2 vols. Ithaca, NY: Snow Lion, 2011 and 2012.

Brunnhölzl, Karl. *Groundless Paths: The Prajnāpāramitā Sūtras, "The Ornament of Clear Realization," and Its Commentaries in the Tibetan Nyingma Tradition.* Ithaca, NY: Snow Lion, 2012.

Conze, Edward. *Abhisamayālaṅkāra.* Rome: Istituto italiano per il Medio ed Estremo Oriente, 1954.

Conze, Edward. *The Large Sutra on Perfect Wisdom with the Divisions of the Abhisamayālaṅkāra.* Berkeley: University of California Press, 1975.

Conze, Edward. *The Prajñāpāramitā Literature.* 2nd rev. ed. Tokyo: Reiyukai, 1978.

Dreyfus, Georges B. J. *The Sound of Two Hands Clapping: The Education of a Tibetan Buddhist Monk.* A Philip E. Lilienthal Book. Berkeley: University of California Press, 2003.

Makransky, John J. *Buddhahood Embodied: Sources of Controversy in India and Tibet.* Albany: State University of New York Press, 1997.

Obermiller, Eugéne. "The Doctrine of Prajñāpāramitā as Exposed in the Abhisamayālaṃkāra of Maitreya." *Acta Orientalia* 11 (1932): 1–133, 334–354.

Obermiller, Eugéne. *Prajñāpāramitā in Tibetan Buddhism.* Classics India Religion and Philosophy Series 3. Delhi: Classics India Publications, 1988.

Sparham, Gareth, trans. *Abhisamayālaṃkāra with Vṛtti and Ālokā.* 4 vols. Fremont, CA: Jain, 2006–2012.

Sparham, Gareth, trans. *Golden Garland of Eloquence = Legs bshad gser phreng.* 4 vols. Fremont, CA: Jain, 2008–2013.

NOTES

1. David Reigle, "The 'Virtually Unknown' Benedictive Middle in Classical Sanskrit: Two Occurrences in the Buddhist Abhisamayālaṅkāra," *Indo-Iranian Journal* 40, no. 2 (April 1997): 119–123.
2. The question of Maitreyanātha's historicity is too long and complex for the present article. See F. I. Stcherbatsky, "Notes de Littérature Bouddhique: La Littérature Yogàcàra d'après Bouston," *Le Muséon* (1905): 141–155; Giuseppe Tucci, *On Some Aspects of the Doctrines of Maitreyanātha and Asanga* (Calcutta University Readership Lectures, 1930); and Noriaki Hakamaya "Chibetto ni okeru Maitreya

no gohō no kiseki," in *Chibetto no Bukkyō to Shakai*, ed. Yamaguchi Zuihō (Tokyo: Shunjūsha, 1986), 235–268, for discussion on this topic.

3. The "five texts of Maitreya" in the Tibetan traditions are the *Abhisamayālaṃkāra*, *Mahāyānasūtrālaṃkāra*, *Madhyāntavibhaṅga*, *Dharmadharmatā-vibhaṅga*, and the *Uttaratantra*.
4. James B. Apple, *Stairway to Nirvāṇa: A Study of the Twenty Saṃghas Based on the Works of Tsong Kha Pa* (Albany: State University of New York Press, 2008), 48–49.
5. James B. Apple, "The Mahāyāna Path of the Bodhisattva in the Ornament for Clear Realization," *Religion Compass* 5, no. 5 (2011): 166–179.
6. Edward Conze, "Maitreya's Abhisamayâlaṅkâra," *East and West* 5, no. 3 (1954): 196.
7. This paragraph is found in Apple, "The Mahāyāna Path," 166–179.
8. Paul Williams, *Mahāyāna Buddhism: The Doctrinal Foundations* (London: Routledge), 356, note 27; and Robert H. Scharf, "Buddhist Modernism and the Rhetoric of Meditative Experience," *Numen: International Review for the History of Religions* 42, no. 3 (1995): 261–262.
9. Georges B. J. Dreyfus, *The Sound of Two Hands Clapping: The Education of a Tibetan Buddhist Monk*, a Philip E. Lilienthal Book (Berkeley: University of California Press, 2003), 179–180.
10. Dreyfus, *The Sound of Two Hands Clapping*, 181.
11. Georges B. J. Dreyfus, "Tibetan Scholastic Education and the Role of Soteriology," *Journal of the International Association of Buddhist Studies* 20, no. 1 (1997): 62.
12. Gareth Sparham, "Background Material for the First of the Seventy Topics in Maitreyanātha's Abhisamayālaṃkāra," *Journal of the International Association of Buddhist Studies* 10, no. 2 (1987): 142.
13. Kōei Amano, *Abhisamayālaṃkāra-Kārikā-Sāstra-Vivṛti* (Kyoto: Heirakuji-Shoten, 2000), 5.
14. Edward Conze, *The Prajñāpāramitā Literature*, 2nd rev. ed. (Tokyo: Reiyukai, 1978), 13.
15. Apple, *Stairway to Nirvāṇa*, 52.
16. Eugéne Obermiller, *The Doctrine of Prajñā-Pāramitā As Exposed in the Abhisamayālamkāra of Maitreya* (Talent, OR: Canon, 1984), 72–74; and Gareth Sparham, trans. *Abhisamayālaṃkāra with Vṛtti and Ālokā, Volume One: First Abhisamaya* (Fremont, CA: Jain, 2006), 188–190.
17. Ah-yueh Yeh, "A Study of the Theories of yāvad-bhāvikatā and yathāvadbhāvikatā in the Abhidharmasamuccaya," *Journal of the International Association of Buddhist Studies* 7, no. 2 (1984): 185–207.
18. Dorji Wangchuk, *The Resolve to Become a Buddha: A Study of the Bodhicitta Concept in Indo-Tibetan Buddhism* (Tokyo: International Institute for Buddhist Studies of the International College for Postgraduate Buddhist Studies, 2007).
19. Apple, *Stairway to Nirvāṇa*.
20. Apple, "The Mahāyāna Path," 166–179.
21. Sparham, *Abhisamayālaṃkāra*, 51–67, 299–328.
22. Conze, *The Prajñāpāramitā Literature*, 105.
23. Apple, *Stairway to Nirvāṇa*, 65–66.
24. Obermiller, *The Doctrine of Prajñā-Pāramitā*, 79–80.
25. Sparham, *Abhisamayālaṃkāra*, xvi.
26. Sparham, *Abhisamayālaṃkāra*, 12–40.
27. Obermiller, *The Doctrine of Prajñā-Pāramitā*, 81.
28. Brian Galloway, "Sudden Englightenment in the Abhisamayālaṃkāra, the Lalitavistara, and the Śikṣāsamuccaya," *Wiener Zeitschrift für die Kunde Südasiens* 32 (1988): 141–147.
29. Sparham, *Abhisamayālaṃkāra*, xix.
30. John J. Makransky, *Buddhahood Embodied: Sources of Controversy in India and Tibet* (Albany: State University of New York Press, 1997).
31. Hodo Nakamura, "The Classification of the Buddhakāya Theory in the Abhisamayālaṃkāra," *Journal of Indian and Buddhist Studies* (印度学仏教学研究) 58, no. 3 (2010): 82–86.

32. Sparham, *Abhisamayālaṃkāra*, 247–265.
33. English translation Sparham, *Abhisamayālaṃkāra with Vṛtti and Ālokā*, 4 vols. (Fremont, CA: Jain, 2006–2012). Sanskrit edition of first chapter Corrado Pensa, *L'Abhisamayālaṃkāravṛtti di Ārya-Vimuktisena. Primo Abhisamaya, Testo e note critiche* (Rome: Istituto Italiano per il Medio ed Estremo Oriente, 1967).
34. Apple, *Stairway to Nirvāṇa*, 21–36.
35. Gareth Sparham, trans., *Abhisamayālaṃkāra with Vṛtti and Ālokā*. Fourth Abhisamaya, vol. 3 (Fremont, CA: Jain, 2009); and Kōei Amano, *Abhisamayālaṃkāra-kārikā-sāstra-vivṛti: Haribhadra's Commentary on the Abhisamayālaṃkāra-kārikā-śāstra Edited for the First Time from a Sanskrit Manuscript* (Kyōto: Heirakuji-Shoten, 2000).
36. James B. Apple, "Contributions to the Development and Classification of Abhisamayālaṃkāra Literature in Tibet from the Ninth to Fourteenth Century," *Journal of the International Association of Tibetan Studies* no. 5 (December 2009): 1–56.
37. D. Seyfort Ruegg, "The Gotra, Ekayāna and *Tathāgatagarbha*: Theories of the Prajñāpāramitā according to Dharmamitra and Abhayākaragupta," in *Prajñāpāramitā and Related Systems: Studies in Honor of Edward Conze*, eds. L. Lancaster and L. O. Gómez, Berkeley Buddhist Studies Series 1 (Berkeley: University of California Press, 1977), 283–312.
38. Padmanabh S. Jaini, ed., *Sāratamā: A Pañjikā on the Aṣṭasāhasrikā Prajñāpāramitā Sūtra* (Patna: Kashi Prasad Jayaswal Research Institute, 1979).
39. D. S. Ruegg, *The Literature of the Madhyamaka School of Philosophy in India* (Wiesbaden: Harrassowitz, 1981), 115.
40. Jeffrey D. Schoening, "Sūtra Commentaries in Tibetan Translation," in *Tibetan Literature: Studies in Genre*, ed. Lhundup Sopa, José Ignacio Cabezón, and Roger R. Jackson (Ithaca, NY: Snow Lion), 111–124; and Dreyfus, *The Sound of Two Hands Clapping*.
41. Marcelle Lalou, "Les textes bouddhiques au temps du roi Khri-sroṅ-lde-bcan," *Journal Asiatique* 361: 313–353, texts no. 516, 517.
42. rNgog blo ldan shes rab, "rNgog lo tsā ba" (1059–1109). *Lo tsa ba chen po'i bsdus don: A Commentary on the Abhisamayālaṃkāra. Introduction by Blo bzang mkhyen rab rgya mtsho and Dr. David P. Jackson* (Dharamsala: Library of Tibetan Works and Archives, 1993).
43. *The Collected Works of the Kadampas (bka' gdams gsung 'bum), bka' gdams gsung 'bum phyogs bsgrigs thengs dang po* (2006), *gnyis pa* (2007), *gsum pa* (2009), *gzhi pa* (2015). 120 volumes. khreng tu'u/: si khron dpe skrun tshogs pa/si khron mi rigs dpe skrun khang.
44. James B. Apple, "The Transmission of Early Tibetan Prajñāpāramitā Commentaries based on newly uncovered bKa' gdams pa works" (Vancouver, BC: International Association of Tibetan Studies, 2010).
45. Gareth Sparham, "A Note on Gnyal zhig 'Jam pa'i rdo rje, the Author of a Handwritten Sher phyin Commentary from about 1200," *Tibet Journal* 21, no. 1 (1996): 19–29; and Jampa Samten, "Notes on the Late Twelfth or Early Thirteenth Century Commentary on the *Abhisamayālaṃkāra*: A Preliminary Report of a Critical Edition," *Proceedings of the 7th Seminar of the International Association for Tibetan Studies, Vol. I: Tibetan Studies*, ed. Ernst Steinkellner (Vienna: Verlag der Österreichischen Akademie der Wissenschaften, 1997), 831–841.
46. 'Jam-pa'i-rdo-rje, *Mngon par rtogs pa'i rgyan gyi 'grel bshad theg pa chen po la 'jug pa zhes bya ba = An extensive explanation on mngon rtogs rgyan (abhisamayalaṃkāra (sic))* (Dharamsala: Library of Tibetan Works and Archives, 2005).
47. Gareth Sparham, trans., *Golden Garland of Eloquence = Legs bshad gser phreng*, 4 vols. (Fremont, CA: Jain, 2008–2013).
48. David P. Jackson, ed., *Rong-ston on the Prajñāpāramitā Philosophy of the Abhisamayālaṃkāra: His Sub-Commentary on Haribhadra's "Sphuṭārthā: A Facsimile Reproduction of the Earliest Known Blockprint Edition, from an Exemplar Preserved in the Tibet House, New Delhi* (Kyoto: Nagata Bunshodo, 1988).

49. Apple, *Stairway to Nirvāṇa*, 21–46.
50. This seems to be the presumption of Makransky, *Buddhahood Embodied*, 113–114, 129, 141, and 396, note 12.
51. Tsong-kha-pa blo-bzang grags-pa, Sparham, *Golden Garland of Eloquence*, 156.
52. Guy Newland, "Debate Manuals in dGe lugs Monastic Colleges," in *Tibetan Literature: Studies in Genre*, ed. José Ignacio Cabezón and Roger R. Jackson (Ithaca, NY: Snow Lion, 1996), 202–216.
53. Ngag dbang dpal ldan, *Blo gsal gling dang bkra shis sgo man grva tshang gi dbu phar gyi yig cha'i bshad tshul bkod pa blo gsal dga' ston*, *Collected Works*, vol. ga (New Delhi: Guru Deva, 1983), TBRC: 5926.
54. *Bstan bcos mngon par rtogs pa'i rgyan 'grel pa dang bcas pa'i rnam bshad rnam pa gnyis kyi dka' ba'i gnas gsal bar byed pa legs bshad skal bzang klu dbang gi rol mtsho zhes bya ba bzhugs so//.*
55. Eugéne Obermiller, *Analysis of the Abhisamayālaṃkāra* (Fremont, CA: Asian Humanities, 2001), v–vii.
56. Apple, *Stairway to Nirvāṇa*; James B. Apple, *A Stairway Taken by the Lucid: Tsong kha pa's Study of Noble Beings*. Śata-piṭaka Series (New Delhi: Aditya Prakashan, 2013).
57. David Seyfort Ruegg, "Ārya and Bhadanta Vimuktisena on the *gotra*-theory of the Prajñāpāramitā," *Beiträge zur Geistesgeschichte Indiens (Festshrift für Erich Frauwallner), WZKSO* 12–13 (1968/1969): 303–317; and Ruegg, *La théorie du tathāgatagarbha et du gotra: Études sur la sotériologie et la gnoséologie du bouddhisme* (Paris: Ecole française d'Extrême-Orient, 1969).
58. Leah Zahler, *Meditative States in Tibetan Buddhism* (Boston: Wisdom Publications, 1998); Leah Zahler, *Study and Practice of Meditation: Tibetan Interpretations of the Concentrations and Formless Absorptions* (Ithaca, NY: Snow Lion, 2009).
59. Makransky, *Buddhahood Embodied.*
60. Shcherbatskoi, "Notes de littérature bouddhique: La littérature yogācāra d'après Bouston," *Le Museon* 6, no. 1 (1905): 144–155.
61. M. P. Masson-Oursel, "Les trois corps du Bouddha," *Journal Asiatique*, 1, XI série (1913): 581–619, extracts from *Abhisamayālaṃkāra*, chapter 8.1–12, 33–40.
62. Fedore Ippolitorich Stcherbatsky, and E. Obermiller, *Abhisamayālaṅkāra-prājñāparamitā-upadeśa-śāstra: The Work of Bodhisattva Maitreya*, Fasc. I: Introduction, Sanskrit Text and Tibetan Translation (Leningrad, Academy of Sciences of USSR, 1929), XII, 112 (Bibl. Buddh. XXIII, fasc.1).
63. Eugéne Obermiller, "The Doctrine of Prajñāpāramitā as Exposed in the Abhisamayālaṃkāra of Maitreya," *Acta Orientalia* 11 (1932): 1–133, 334–354.
64. Eugéne Obermiller, *Analysis of the Abhisamayālaṃkāra*, Calcutta Oriental Series no. 27 (London: Luzac, 1933, 1936, 1943), published in three fascicles. Reprinted in a single volume by Asian Humanities Press in 2001.
65. Unrai Wogihara, *Abhisamayālaṃkār'ālokā Prajnāpāramitāvyākhyā, Commentary on the Aṣṭasāhasrikā-Prajnāpāramitā by Haribhadra Together with the Text Commented on* (Toyo Bunko, 1932–1935); and Giuseppe Tucci, *The Abhisamayālaṃkārāloka of Haribhadra: Being a Commentary on the Abhisamayālaṃkāra of Maitreyanātha and the Aṣṭasāhasrikāprajñāpāramitā* (Baroda: Oriental Institute, 1932).
66. Ryūsei Keira, and Noboru Ueda, *Sanskrit Word-Index to the Abhisamayālaṃkārālokā Prajnāpāramitāvyākhyā (U. Wogihara Edition) = ogiwara unrai kōteiban genkan shōgonron kōmyō hannya haramitta shaku bongo sōsakuin* ([Place of publication not identified]: [publisher not identified], 1998).
67. Kajiyoshi Kōun, *Genshi hannyakyō no kenkyū* (Tōkyō: Sankibō Busshorin, 1944).
68. Edward Conze, *Abhisamayalaṅkāra: Introduction and Translation from Original Text, with Sanskrit–Tibetan Index*, Serie Orientale Roma, 6 (Rome: Istituto Italiano per il Medio ed Estremo Oriente, 1954).
69. Edward Conze, *The Large Sutra on Perfect Wisdom with the Divisions of the Abhisamayālaṅkāra* (Berkeley and London: University of California Press, 1975); and Conze, *The Prajñāpāramitā Literature.*
70. Corrado Pensa, *L'Abhisamayālaṃkāravṛtti di Ārya-Vimuktisena: Primo Abhisamaya. Testo e note critiche* (Rome: Istituto Italiano per il Medio ed Estremo Oriente, 1967); and P. S. Jaini, *Sāratamā: A Pañjikā on*

the Aṣṭasāhasrikā by Ācārya Ratnākaraśānti, Tibetan Sanskrit Works Series, 18 (Patna: Kashi Prasad Jayaswal Research Institute, 1979).

71. Kōei Hirofusa Amano, "Sanskrit Manuscript of the Abhisamayalaṅkara-vṛtti (in Six Parts)," *Bulletin of the Hijiyama Women's Junior College* 7 (1983): 1–15; *Bulletin of the Faculty of Education of Shimane University* 19 (1985): 124–138; vol. 20 (1986), pp. 67–86; vol. 21 (1987), pp. 39–51; vol. 22 (1988), pp. 10–25; vol. 23 (1989), 1–7; Amano, *Abhisamayālaṃkāra-Kārikā-Sāstra-Vivṛti*; and Amano, *Index to the Abhisamayālaṃkāra-kārikā-śāstra-vivṛti: Tibetan-Sanskrit* (Kyōto: Heirakuji-Shoten, 2005).
72. Alexander T. Naughton, *Classic Mahayana Soteriology: An Annotated Translation of Chapters 1–7 of Haribhadra's Short Commentary on the Abhisamayālaṃkāra* (Otani University Shin Buddhist Comprehensive Research Institute, 1991).
73. Makransky, *Buddhahood Embodied*; Ruegg, *La Théorie du Tathāgatagarbha*; and Apple, *Stairway to Nirvāṇa*.
74. Sparham, *Abhisamayālaṃkāra*.
75. Karl Brunnhölzl, *Groundless Paths: The Prajnāpāramitā Sūtras, "The Ornament of Clear Realization", and Its Commentaries in the Tibetan Nyingma Tradition* (Ithaca, NY: Snow Lion, 2012); and Karl Brunnhölzl, *Gone Beyond: The Prajnāpāramitā Sūtras, The Ornament of Clear Realization, and Its Commentaries in the Tibetan Kagyü Tradition*, 2 vols. (Ithaca, NY: Snow Lion, 2011 and 2012).

James B. Apple

AMERICAN BUDDHISM DURING WORLD WAR II IMPRISONMENT

PREWAR CONTEXT

At the turn of the 20th century, a large number of Japanese migrated to Hawaii and the mainland United States. They came to Hawaii primarily as contract laborers and worked on sugar plantations, while early Japanese migration to the mainland United States consisted of students and laborers. In 1908, based on what was referred to as a "gentleman's agreement," the Japanese government voluntarily restricted the number of Japanese migrants to the United States and Japanese migrants began bringing their families and relatives to America.[1] By 1924, more than 125,000 Japanese and their Hawaii-born children lived in Hawaii. About forty percent of the Japanese immigrants came from Hiroshima and Yamaguchi prefectures,[2] which were known as the stronghold of the Nishi Honganji organization, one of the largest Shin Buddhist denominations of a major Pure Land Buddhist sect, known as Jōdo Shinshū. In the mainland too, the largest numbers of Japanese settlers came from these two prefectures; therefore, members of the Nishi Honganji organization dominated the Buddhist community of Japanese immigrants in North America.

Nishi Honganji was the first Japanese Buddhist organization to set up propagation centers on the Hawaiian Islands and mainland North America. In Hawaii, the Honpa Honganji Mission of Hawaii (HHMH) was established in 1898. The Buddhist Mission of North America (BMNA), its counterpart on the mainland, was formed in the same year in San Francisco. At the beginning of the Japanese migration, Shin Buddhist temples served as town offices in Japanese communities. Shin Buddhist ministers helped Japanese immigrants write letters, send money to Japan, and register newborn babies at the Japanese consulate. They conducted marriage ceremonies, funerals, and memorial services, and mediated disputes. Furthermore, they became teachers at Japanese language schools, which were often built as part of and next to Buddhist temples. By 1924, more than thirty-three Nishi Honganji Buddhist temples had been built on the Hawaiian Islands, while more than twenty Buddhist temples affiliated with BMNA had been built on the West Coast, primarily in California but also in Oregon and Washington. By 1932, the BMNA had built nine more Buddhist temples in those areas and in 1936 founded a Buddhist temple in New York.[3]

In addition to Nishi Honganji, other Japanese Buddhist sects gradually established temples in Hawaii and the mainland United States, and their Buddhist priests also met the mundane, spiritual, and ritual needs of fellow migrants. In the beginning of the Edo period (1603–1867), the Tokugawa shogunate introduced a household registration system in which all Japanese were required by law to become parishioners of Buddhist temples. The government enforced this system to prevent the Japanese people from converting to Christianity. The relationship between a Buddhist temple and its parishioners became inseparable due to the parishioners' needs for funeral rites and memorial services through which they honored their ancestors. This system, known as the *danka* system, "sustained Buddhist temples in Tokugawa Japan more than anything else," to borrow Nam-lin Hur's words.[4] Although the Meiji government took away the privileges of Buddhist organizations, the practice of funerary Buddhism connected to the *danka* system and ancestral veneration remained strong in modern Japan. Japanese migrants continued to observe this long-standing practice in Hawaii and West Coast states, and for the sake of temple members who migrated to those regions, other Japanese Buddhist organizations, such as Jōdoshū, Higashi Honganji (another major Shin Buddhist denomination), the Nichiren, Shingon, and Sōtō Zen, sent their clergy to North America.

While maintaining religious identity and cultural practices associated with Buddhism in Japan, the Nikkei Buddhists Americanized their religion. Japanese Americans as a whole experienced institutional racial discrimination on multiple levels.[5] To refute the public misconception that Buddhism was incompatible with American religious values, Japanese American Buddhists modeled themselves on Protestant Christian churches. They introduced scheduled services on Sunday, used pews, and formed Young Men's and Women's Buddhist Associations.[6] They also adopted Buddhist hymnals compiled by Euro-American Buddhists, which included *gathas* that mimicked Protestant Triumphalism.[7] At the same time, Nikkei Buddhists preserved the core Buddhist practices derived from Japan, such as ancestral worship and confraternity activities, and sustained denominational doctrine. Particularly, Buddhism helped the Nisei to understand who they were and construct their identities as being neither Japanese nor American, but Japanese Americans.[8] While maintaining their cultural heritage, Japanese American Buddhists sought to be accepted by America's mainstream society. Their efforts to make sense of their Buddhist faith and national identity were, however, suddenly disrupted by the outbreak of the Pacific War (1941–1945).

JAPANESE AMERICAN BUDDHIST CLERGY AT THE OUTBREAK OF THE WAR

Immediately after Pearl Harbor was attacked, Nikkei Buddhist leaders strove to demonstrate loyalty to the United States. According to Tetsuden Kashima,

> The Buddhist Mission of North America released a statement to the effect that "the suddenness and the unwarranted and inhuman attack upon the United States of America leaves us, the Buddhists in America, with but one decision: the condemnation of that attack." One duty remained for American Buddhists: "The loyalty to the United States which we have pledged at all times must now be placed into instant action for the defense of the United States of America."[9]

The Issei Buddhists condemned the Japanese navy for attacking Pearl Harbor, purchased US war bonds, and embarked on a campaign for blood donations to the Red Cross. Before the bombing of Pearl Harbor, the more that ethnic Japanese were discriminated against in America, the prouder the Issei became of Imperial Japan, which was seen as the emerging modern nation state in Asia capable of competing with Western powers. After Pearl Harbor, however, the Issei sympathized with the United States where they had settled and raised their children.

Attempts by Japanese Americans to prove loyalty did not, however, assuage war hysteria. There were many instances of so-called hate crimes in the early 21st century against the Nikkei Buddhists. The similarity between the ancient Indian symbol 卍, which Japanese Buddhists had adopted as a Buddhist symbol (called *manji* in Japanese)—and which the Japanese American Buddhists continued to use as emblems for their temples—and the Nazi swastika 卐 caused Nikkei Buddhism to be misunderstood by America's general public and even identified as an ally of Nazi Germany.[10]

According to Duncan Williams, in December 1941 there were about 300 Japanese Buddhist and Shintō priests living primarily in Hawaii and the West Coast states of the United States, such as California and Washington, as well as in Canada. Approximately 250 of them were arrested before the mass incarceration of the rest of people of Japanese ancestry. More than ninety percent of these priests were Issei. Only twelve were Nisei and one was *Sansei* (third generation). About half were Nishi Honganji ministers, but there were substantial numbers of priests from the Shingon, Jōdo, Sōtō, and Nichiren sects, as well as the Higashi Honganji denomination of the Jōdo Shin sect. Also arrested were more than twenty Shintō priests and fewer than twenty ministers of Tenrikyō and Konkōkyō.[11]

Before the Pacific War began, the FBI, the Office of Naval Intelligence, and Canadian intelligence had monitored the leaders of Japanese communities in North America for possible ties to Imperial Japan. The FBI compiled what came to be known as the "ABC" list of would-be arrestees if war began between the United States and Japan. Among the suspected individuals on the list, the FBI classified Buddhist and Shintō priests into the Group A of "known dangerous" aliens, along with Japanese Consulate staff, Japanese language teachers, fishermen, and martial arts instructors, who were subject to immediate arrest. They were considered "likely fifth-column agents." Except for a few Christian leaders in the Japanese community, Japanese Christians were excluded from the Group A list. The intelligence units had concluded that Nikkei Christians were more likely to be Americanized and less loyal to Japan than Nikkei Buddhists.[12]

According to the memoirs of Fujimura Bunyū, then resident priest of Salinas Buddhist Temple affiliated with the Buddhist Mission of North America (BMNA), leaders of Japanese communities in Los Angeles and San Francisco, who had returned to Japan in 1940 for the 2,600th-year celebration of the Imperial Throne, were subject to immediate arrest. They included the owner of a Japanese hotel and the principal of a Japanese language school in San

Francisco, as well as the minister of the Konkōkyō Church and the priest of the Nichiren Buddhist Temple.[13]

Tana Daishō, another Buddhist minister of the BMNA then serving the Japanese community in Lompoc, California, and the author of *A Diary of an Enemy Alien in Santa Fe and Lordsburg Internment* (Jpn, *Santa Fe Rōzubāgu senji tekikokujin yokuryū sho nikki*), known as the *Internment Camp Diary*, described the course of action he took immediately after hearing of the arrest of fellow Japanese:

> December 8, 1941: The First Arrests
>
> At 7 a.m., I received a telephone call informing me that Mr. "T," who had ridden back [from Guadalupe], had been arrested by the FBI immediately upon his return home. As I was still new to this post, I hadn't made a thorough account of all the documents. But I thought that I would most immediately need to deal with all documents related to the Japanese embassy, the Japanese Association, the Women's Association. I put aside the Emperor's photo as my personal property and, aware that I would assume full responsibility for any consequences, I started burning everything. That's when a call came from Mr. "I," warning me to get rid of all the receipts from our donations to the Japanese military. I told him I was dealing with other materials at that moment. . . .
>
> After this, all the children began to arrive at the temple's Japanese-language school, just as usual. I thought that the continuation of the Japanese-language school would be misunderstood by the American officials. So, after telling some folk tales to the first and second year students, we went to the Buddha hall to hold the Jōdō-e ceremony [the celebration of Gautama Siddhartha's Buddhist enlightenment] and a school closing ceremony. I told the students to be good Americans, as the children of Japanese parents, and to keep up their regular attendance at the white people's school.[14]

About three months later, Tana was arrested by the FBI and imprisoned in the Santa Barbara county jail, together with another Japanese Buddhist minister and a Japanese Christian minister.

While many Japanese Buddhist priests voluntarily discarded temple records and documents related to Imperial Japan, somewhat comically Fujimura was ordered by the Salinas chief of police on December 8, 1941, to remove the temple gong, lest the sound be used as a signal to usher the Japanese Imperial naval ships into Monterey Bay. The chief threatened Fujimura, saying he would burn the tower containing the gong if Fujimura did not comply with his order. The demand reflected the hysteria of the Salinas community, which was overly concerned with a Japanese military strike. It was, of course, impossible for the temple gong to be heard in the bay, which was nineteen miles away, and nonsense to think that sounding the temple gong would help Japanese battleships.[15]

Two months later, Fujimura along with two other Buddhists priests who had assisted him in Salinas were arrested. They were the first group of BMNA ministers to be arrested by the FBI. This is how he described it:

> Early in the morning of February 11th, 1942 (February 10th in the United States), to commemorate Empire Day, the anniversary of the day Emperor Jimmu first ascended the Japanese throne, the Japanese Imperial Army took Singapore.

> That same morning, someone knocked softly on the door of our bedroom on the second floor of the Salinas Buddhist Temple. Rubbing the sleep from my eyes, I opened the door to find two men, one in his sixties and the other in his thirties.
>
> "We are from the FBI," the older man said in Japanese, and showed me his badge.
>
> While I was getting dressed, the older man went through all my books, which were, of course, all in Japanese. The younger man carefully checked my clothes.
>
> Reverend and Mrs. Koyo Tamanaha, who were sleeping downstairs, were also awakened. We were then ordered to go to the residence next door, where Reverend Hoshin Fujikado and his family were living.
>
> I noticed over ten policemen keeping close watch over both the front and rear gates of our temple. Perhaps this precaution was taken because they knew Reverend Tamanaha had a fifth-degree black belt in Judo. . . .
>
> Reverends Fujikado, Tamanaha and I were brought to the police station where a group of newspaper photographers were waiting. We were blinded by flashes from their cameras. My wife tells me that I usually have a stern expression, but for some reason, I smiled just as the cameras clicked. . . .
>
> Life Magazine showed a photograph of the gong that had been lowered from its place in the tower, and under it stated that the "three Buddhist priests . . . smiled courteously while being arrested."
>
> Later, when I was sent to Bismark in North Dakota, Mr. Yoshito Fujii told me that a young *nisei* in Seattle saw that photograph and said, "Reverend Fujimura has guts to be able to smile in a situation like that. He is a true Buddhist!"
>
> I was led to wonder how differently the same photograph is perceived by different people.
>
> At any rate, we were imprisoned in the basement of the Salinas jail. Many others were also there, with one exception, all Japanese members of our Salinas Buddhist Temple.[16]

A senior FBI agent, who could speak Japanese, asked Fujimura and Tamanaha many questions to prove his suspicion of their connections to the emperor of Imperial Japan. His questions included, "Are you a spy?" "Did you come to the United States because of orders from the emperor of Japan?" and "How many different denominations are there in the Buddhist teaching?" The FBI agent brought up the fact that Emperor Hirohito and the abbot of Nishi Honganji were cousins and questioned Fujimura if he had received any order from the emperor via the abbot. Further, the agent was suspicious of the activities of Japanese American soldiers and asked Fujimura why the Salinas Buddhist Temple entertained them when they were stationed at Fort Ord. Although Fujimura claimed innocence, he was transported to the San Francisco Detention Station, run by the Immigration and Naturalization Services, detained at its gymnasium with fellow Japanese, and then sent to Bismark Internment Camp in North Dakota.[17]

The majority of Buddhist priests rounded up by the FBI were separated from their families, who were, as result of Executive Order 9066, relocated to fourteen assembly centers and later moved to ten relocation centers operated by the War Relocation Authority (WRA). The vast majority of the Issei Buddhist priests were interned in the detention stations in Santa Fe, New Mexico, run by the Department of Justice (DOJ), while others were interned in camps run by the Immigration and Naturalization Services (INS) or army. As those Buddhist priests were locked up with Japanese and German prisoners of war, they were considered "enemy aliens." After cross-examinations, the Issei Buddhist priests were transferred to either the "family camps" run by the DOJ in Crystal City, Texas, or the WRA's "segregation camp" in Tule Lake, California. The former camp confined those who were considered not harmful to US national security, while the latter camp detained those who were considered dangerous and pro-Japanese and had even expressed wishes to return to Japan.[18]

After the Buddhist priests were forcefully removed from their temples, Euro-American Buddhist priests took care of some of the temples. For instance, Sunya Pratt served as a caretaker of the Tacoma Buddhist Church in Washington. After the Issei and Nisei residents were forced to move to an assembly center named Camp Harmony, Pratt received permission from the local authority to serve the Japanese Buddhists there and conducted Sunday School, until they were relocated to permanent relocation centers.[19] Between 1942 and 1945 the Los Angeles Honpa Honganji board of directors entrusted Julius A. Goldwater with their temple based on "faith built on ten years of association with him."[20] Goldwater provided the Nikkei Buddhists held at the Santa Anita Race Track Assembly Center with materials needed for rituals.[21] Frank B. Udale and Alex S. While took care of the BMNA temples in Northern California.[22]

In Hawaii, Ernest Hunt played a significant role in reopening several of the Shin Buddhist temples closed by the military authorities. He appealed directly to the military governor, General Emmons, for permission to restart Buddhist services, assuring him that he would speak only of religious matters. He and his wife were active in the temple on Makiki Street, Honolulu, and the one in Hilo. He also officiated services at Jikōen, a Shin Buddhist temple founded by Okinawans.[23] Female Nisei Shin Buddhist leaders in Hawaii also administered and took care of ceremonial affairs in their temples during the war.[24]

BUDDHIST PRACTICE IN IMPRISONMENT CAMPS

According to the War Relocation Authority's report on incarcerees' religious affiliations, almost seventy percent of the Issei and about fifty percent of the Nisei were Buddhists, whereas twenty-two percent of the Issei and about thirty percent of the Nisei were Christians.[25] Despite the difference in religious orientations, David Yoo observes that camp religion promoted social service, racial-ethnic solidarity, and religious faith among the imprisoned Japanese Americans.[26]

The Nikkei Buddhists continued to hold Buddhist gatherings in relocation camps. They referred to individual groups in their organizations as "Buddhist churches" to sound more "Christian," i.e., the Heart Mountain Relocation Buddhist Church (Wyoming), the Manzanar Relocation Camp Buddhist Church (California), the Minidoka Relocation Buddhist Church (Idaho), the Poston Relocation Buddhist Church (Arizona), the Topaz Relocation Buddhist Church (Utah), etc. Mess halls and recreational buildings served as the "church" meeting places where Buddhist priests conducted religious services and promoted religious education. The Nisei lay Buddhist members formed *Bussei*, the Young Buddhist Associations (YBA), in these camps.[27] Lester Suzuki, a Japanese American Methodist minister incarcerated in Heart Mountain, recorded the organization of daily Buddhist gatherings:

> By the fall of 1942, the Buddhists conducted Sunday school at five different places, special young people's services and morning services at three different places. On Sunday afternoons they conducted young people's fellowship and afternoon services at three different places. In the evening services were held at three places. On Wednesdays and Fridays they held teaching lectures and studies and lectures for young people and lay people. On Saturdays some regional fellowship groups were held such as the Northwest and Northern California gatherings.[28]

In addition to regular gatherings, the Japanese American Buddhists held annual special services, such as the celebration of the buddha's birthday, *Higan-e* (services during the time of spring and autumn equinoxes) and *Obon* (the celebration of ancestors in summer).

Because the Nikkei Buddhists did not have Buddhist items needed for the services, such as Buddhist statues and altars, they created Buddhist artifacts using whatever they could obtain. In the Bismark Internment Camp, North Dakota, for the celebration of the buddha's birthday, known as Flower Festival (*hanamatsuri* in Japanese), the interned Buddhists carved an image of the buddha from a carrot. In Camp Livingston, Louisiana, a Japanese sculptor carved a statue of Kannon Bodhisattva. He taught sculpture to fellow internees who also constructed a Buddhist altar with candleholders, incense burners, and flower vases.[29] In other camps, Nikkei Buddhists transformed abandoned pieces of wood and spare crate wood into Buddhist statues, altars, and ornaments. A Sōtō Zen priest even made a rosary (*juzu* in Japanese) out of dried peach pits. While confined by barbed wire and under the surveillance of armed guards, the Buddhist incarcerees, guided by the priests, "did their best to bring order to chaos, to create meaning in a seemingly senseless situation," to borrow Williams's words.[30]

In addition to hand-making Buddhist objects, transsectarian Buddhist activities characterized another new development of Japanese American Buddhism during the imprisonment period. Since the War Relocation Authority (WRA) enforced sectarian cooperation within religious categories, such as Protestantism, Catholicism and Buddhism, Buddhist priests of various schools compromised their sectarian practices.[31] Nevertheless, as Duncan Williams puts it, this practice gave the Japanese American Buddhist community a sense of new direction.

> At times, this process involved finding common ground in areas such as chanting "Namu Butsu" (Homage to the Buddha) instead of the various sects' unique chants: "Namu Amida Butsu" (Jōdo Shin); "Namu Daishi Henjō Kongō" (Shingon); and "Namu Myōhō Renge Kyō" (Nichiren). While this phenomenon represented, as Stephen Prothero has suggested, more of an "ecumenism of circumstance"—reflecting the lack of facilities and government categorization for religious worship rather than a conscious choice—this transsectarianism nevertheless reflects an impulse within Japanese American Buddhism, exemplified by priests such as Yemyo Imamura, toward a form of American Buddhism that transcends Japanese sectarian factionalism.[32]

Although unified Buddhism emerged because of the state regulation, it became a symbol of ethno-Buddhist solidarity.

Nagatomi Shinjō, a BMNA minister, represents a figure who actively crossed sectarian Buddhist boundaries. Although not the only Buddhist priest in Manzanar, he was extremely popular. Nagatomi dedicated himself to the Manzanar Social Welfare Division, provided counsel services to individuals and families, circulated newsletters to fellow incarcerees, and officiated at weddings and funerals. Nagatomi seems to have been involved in gatherings of members of the Shingon sect who practiced *goeika,* singing of Buddhist hymns while tinkling a bell,[33] and created a hybrid funerary Buddhist practice for Manzanar incarcerees. Interestingly, he officiated at funeral services for members of the Sōtō sect in which he gave the deceased a posthumous Dharma name associated with Shin Buddhist tradition. Concerning Nagatomi's practice, Williams states, "The importance of maintaining the Japanese custom of ancestral veneration was so strong that sectarian concerns for each family, while normally crucial for the proper performance of the traditional funeral and the selection of the posthumous name, were set aside in this time of crisis. In this way, Buddhism not only provided a spiritual refuge for internees but also served the social function of maintaining family and communal cohesion through ancestral and life-cycle rituals and traditional Japanese festivals and ceremonies."[34] Japanese American Buddhists accepted the transsectarian form of Buddhism out of necessity, which proved to be the most effective way to preserve their culture during their time of imprisonment.

The unified Buddhist services were, however, not without problems. Doctrinal differences persisted, particularly between Shin and Nichiren priests. For instance, in Heart Mountain, the Nikkei Buddhists initially observed the unified services, but Nichiren priests formed their own services, after which the BMNA ministers also held a separate Sunday School and services.[35] In the Lordsburg Army camp, Tana Daishō recorded the awkwardness of sutra chanting during a fall *higan* service, in which a portion of the *Larger Sutra* (one of the sacred texts for Shin Buddhists) was chanted and then a portion of the *Lotus Sutra* (the fundamental sutra for Nichirenists) was recited. Although priests of different sects took turns and led annual Buddhist services, they had to cater to the demand of congregations that had different Buddhist backgrounds and incorporate Buddhist practices other than their own.[36]

How to distribute offertory among clergy was another problem. Some Buddhist priests demanded the distribution be based on the size of sects, while other Buddhist priests insisted on equal distribution. Because Shin Buddhism was the largest Buddhist sect in the Japanese American community, Shin priests held the former position for collecting the larger share and objected to the latter position.[37]

The political inclinations of individual Buddhist priests also prevented transsectarian cooperation. In 1943, the WRA forced the Japanese American inmates to complete a loyalty questionnaire in order to identify who was loyal and who was potentially disloyal, list volunteers for military service, and to allow loyal Nikkei to resettle in the Midwest or the East Coast. In the Jerome Relocation Center in Arkansas, board members of the United Buddhist Church were divided over the issue of loyalty. Among twelve members, three members were found disloyal, which made other members worry that Buddhism could be labeled as a pro-Japanese religion by the WRA. As a result, those three protesters resigned from the United Buddhist Church and established the *Daijō Bukkyō* Church, or the Mahayana Buddhist Church, with three priests and about three hundred people.[38] In other camps, because the Issei and *Kibei Nisei* (literally, "returning Nisei" from Japan) who answered "no" to the loyalty questions were relocated to the Tule Lake segregation camp, the removal of vocal pro-Japan Issei enabled the Nisei Buddhists to become leaders of the Buddhist organizations by "effectively silencing anti-American and anti-Nisei sentiments."[39]

NATIONAL IDENTITY AND AMBIVALENCE OF THE JAPANESE AMERICAN BUDDHISTS

During the period of World War II imprisonment, the Nikkei Buddhists intensified their ambivalent attitudes toward the United States and Japan. These sentiments were not limited to Japanese American Buddhists but experienced by people of Japanese ancestry as a whole; however, as funerals of Nisei soldiers who died on the European front were held in relocation centers, the Nikkei Buddhists had a hard time reconciling their ethno-religious identity and national identity.

The Buddhist Mission of North America (BMNA) speeded up the process of Americanizing its organization. Because the bishop of the BMNA was incarcerated and its central administration was relocated to the Topaz Relocation Center, the Topaz Buddhist Church served as the BMNA headquarters and communicated with its clergy and laity in other camps. In May 1944, the BMNA leaders decided to change the name of their organization from BMNA to the Buddhist Churches of America (BCA) as it sounded more Christian-like, and they transferred its management authority from Issei to Nisei clergy because the Nisei ministers were American citizens. They also replaced the Buddhist symbol of reverse-swastika with that of the wheel of dharma and adopted a new Buddhist hymnal titled *A Book of Ceremonies for Use of Buddhists at Gatherings*, which was created and compiled by the Buddhist Brotherhood of America, led by Julius Goldwater, for the purpose of promoting Buddhism in America in English. The Nisei Buddhists used this service book extensively during the mass incarceration period.[40]

The Nikkei Buddhists also localized their Buddhist identities. For instance, Nyogen Senzaki, a Zen master incarcerated in Heart Mountain, called Heart Mountain the "Mountain of Compassion," because imprisonment gave him more opportunities to practice and promote Buddhism in America.[41] When Buddhist internees from the Oregon Buddhist Church made a Shin Buddhist altar, they modeled it on the shape of Mount Hood in Oregon. Traditionally, the foundation resembled the shape of Mount Sumeru, a mythological mountain in Buddhist cosmology.[42]

While Japanese American Buddhism during World War II acquired a more American look, Issei Buddhist clergy—and for that matter, Issei internees in general—could not sever their emotional connections to Japan. Fujimura Bunyū recalled a shared sentiment among the Issei internees when baseball games between a team of the Japanese prisoners-of-war (members of the Japanese Imperial Navy captured at the Battle of Midway and detained in Camp Livingston) and a team of Japanese internees (who lived most of their lives in the United States) were held.

> Who should we cheer?
>
> If the internee's team won, we could not help feel we had offended the POWs.
>
> If, on the other hand, our internee team lost, there would always be some team players who grumbled that we did not cheer hard enough.
>
> This attitude is difficult to express to non-Japanese. In the United States, everyone has a favorite, and they cheer that team regardless of the repercussions. But for us Japanese, the feeling of *enryo*, of restraint in everything, is still very strong.
>
> At any rate, together with the pleasure of watching the games, I remember the difficulty of deciding which team to cheer for. Perhaps only a Japanese can understand such sentiments. . . .[43]

As Japanese had been educated to respect Japanese Imperial soldiers, it was difficult for the Issei internees to fully support either team.

Tana Daishō's diary represents voices of the Issei internees who initially believed in victory by Imperial Japan. They did not trust news on the progress of battles reported by US media and accepted only the announcements by the Imperial Japanese headquarters. Further, Tana felt the transfers of fellow internees from one camp to another were unnecessary and irrational, as relocations caused the building, destroying, and rebuilding of facilities. He saw the lack of discipline among camp guards as instances of the absence of leadership in the US government, thereby explaining to himself why US armed forces were losing to the Imperial Japanese military. Tana's support of Imperial Japan, however, wavered when he learned of the deaths of Nisei soldiers. He sympathized with fellow Issei internees who had to send their sons to the war front in Italy and hoped for an immediate end to the war.[44]

Unlike their parents, Nisei Buddhists expressed patriotism by serving in the US armed forces. In January 1943, the secretary of war recruited the Nisei to form a special combat regiment made up of Japanese Americans. A large number of Hawaiian Nisei volunteered immediately. The response from mainland Nisei was slow, but about 1,200 Nisei in the relocation centers enlisted. In April 1943, the 442nd Regimental Combat Team was formed, of which the 100th Infantry Battalion headed for Europe. Casualties among the Nisei soldiers were heavy, and selective service was introduced again. According to the War Department, by July 1945, 20,539 Nisei had served in the military, and according to the *Pacific Citizen*, by August 1945, 3,840 Nisei soldiers had been killed.[45] Although it is unknown how many Nisei soldiers were Buddhists, the Young Buddhist Associations that continued to be active in relocation centers supported the 442nd and 100th Combat Regiments, and there are many stories associated with the deaths of Nisei Buddhist soldiers.

Kyōgoku Itsuzō, a BMNA Buddhist minister who served at the Fresno Buddhist Temple before the war, collected stories of Nisei Buddhist soldiers, published a pamphlet titled "The Silver Moon," and dedicated it to them. These stories describe the Buddhist understanding of Nisei servicemen who died in battle:

> A soldier of the 442nd regiment told me: "Once the attack broke out, bombs and shells exploded near the foxhole and a terrible shower of debris poured down into the shelter. Every time the explosion seemed near us we all recited Onembutsu unconsciously, disregarding the hot discussion on the superiority of one's own religion which took place just before the attack of enemy began. Onembutsu, the shortest but deepest form which symbolizes the unity of the savior and one to be saved, was chosen involuntarily."[46]

Placed in life-and-death situations, the nenbutsu, or reciting the name of Amida Buddha, was the last resort for Nisei Buddhist soldiers. For them, the Buddhist teachings, including the impermanence of life and birth in the Pure Land, which they had learned through Sunday school, for the first time became vividly real.

Another story describes the Buddhist awakening of the mother of a Nisei soldier. She could not accept her son's departure to the war front and begged him to change his mind. The son remembered a Buddhist gatha he had learned in Sunday school:

> When we see the silver moon
> Gleaming in the sky,
> We remember
> Still our Lord is nigh;
> By His blessed Law to guide us
> Thru this earthly night
> Our sorrow
> Into joy and light.
>
> The gatha reminded Johnny of the Lord Buddha who was always with him while he did not pay attention to His presence. Johnny thought, we must depend upon His guidance in this grave moment.
>
> Calmly he said, "Mother, are you not a Buddhist?"
>
> "Yes, Johnny," she replied.
>
> "Then, we should not suffer from our destiny. We must live in 'Onembutsu' taking refuge in the Buddha."
>
> The mother, struck with unexpected religious words from her son, said after a few moments: "Well said, Johnny. How ignorant I had been to lament over the things destined to me. It is the fruit of my karma, the law of cause and result, that I should send my son to the front. The fetter of karma is too strong to break with my own power. I must depend upon Buddha who is always with me guiding and protecting this ignorant and miserable woman."
>
> After reciting the Holy Name for a while, she said, "Thank you Johnny. I will never lament and complain hereafter. We are always in the universal and boundless loving-kindness of the Lord Buddha. You advised me to remember Him. . . ."
>
> "Mama, will you make a promise to say 'Namu-Amida-butsu' with gassho remembering me whenever you see the moon? I will do the same while I stay at the front away from you."
>
> "Surely I will promise to do what you ask with pleasure," she said.
>
> They returned to their apartment rejoicing, and they said good-bye in peace when Johnny left the center, each calling the name of the Buddha."[47]

In Kyōgoku's mind, the Buddhist stories about Nisei soldiers served as a perfect example of how Buddhist teachings were understood and practiced during that difficult time.

Kyōgoku analyzed the ethno-cultural background of Nisei soldiers from a Buddhist perspective, which made them heroic in battle. First, he points out the right view of the Nisei soldiers. That is, they correctly understood their circumstances—they were discriminated against by white Americans despite being American citizens—and based on that judgment they made the correct decision. Secondly, the Nisei soldiers were able to transcend life and death because of the Buddhist teaching and religious customs that were derived from Japan, including ancestral worship and memorial services central to each household. The notion of impermanence and the belief that, should they die in battle, their families would honor them by holding Buddhist memorial services made them accept their fate and made them unafraid of dying. Third, the sincerity of Nisei soldiers led them to be loyal to the US government. Kyōgoku concluded that they were practitioners of "straight mind," or *jikishin*, who accepted life as ephemeral and embraced the Japanese perception of nature—cyclic changes of seasons as manifestations of impermanence—associated with the Buddhist teaching.[48]

In his admiration of the Nisei Buddhist soldiers' sacrifices, Kyōgoku—and other Issei Buddhist priests—justified Buddhist participation in war. But just as much of the Nisei's understanding of Japanese culture was superficial and stereotyped,[49] the Issei Buddhist priests' understanding of Buddhism and war was simplistic. Kyōgoku appropriated scriptural Buddhist concepts, such as "sincerity" in the *Larger Sutra* and "sincere mind" in the *Meditation Sutra*—which describe Buddhist followers' attitudes toward Amida Buddha—and applied them to secular contexts to use them as his explanation of the Nisei soldiers' ethics and disciplinary actions. Fujimura Bunyū also described the deaths of Nisei Buddhist soldiers as "truly the Bodhisattva Way in the Buddhist teaching."[50] During the postwar period, Tana Daishō still considered death in action to be an act of giving one's life to one's country, even though he recognized the importance of the Buddhist practice through which "the people live in peace. There is no need for soldiers or weapons,"[51] as stated in the *Larger Sutra*.[52]

On the one hand, the Shin Buddhist teaching of birth in the Pure Land at the time of dying and saying of the nenbutsu helped Nisei Buddhist soldiers overcome the anxiety of death,[53] but on the other hand, Japanese American Buddhists did not reflect on their support of, or participation in, the killing of human beings based on the Buddhist precept of "not killing." For them, Buddhism was not about "not killing," but about the preservation of their families and ethnic values. Buddhist faith was part of ethnic solidarity and patriotic expression. Unlike Buddhist clergy in Japan, Issei Buddhist priests neither used the rhetoric of birth in the Pure Land to promote the war nor formed the wartime theology that the Buddhist organizations in Japan developed during World War II, but in America too, Buddhism was subordinated to patriotism and national ideology.

RESETTLEMENT OF NIKKEI BUDDHISTS AND THE ASSESSMENT OF JAPANESE AMERICAN BUDDHISTS' IMPRISONMENT EXPERIENCES

After March 1943, the War Relocation Authority (WRA) began releasing people of Japanese ancestry from the relocation camps. As its strategy to integrate Japanese Americans into American society, they were dispersed to the Midwest and East Coast states. Between March 1943 and January 1945, when the order to remove Japanese Americans from West Coast states was lifted, approximately 35,000 Japanese Americans left the camps for those regions.[54] Kubose Gyōmei was one of them. After spending two years in Heart Mountain, he moved to Chicago and organized a Buddhist gathering, which became the Buddhist Temple of Chicago in 1944. In addition, the Midwest Buddhist Temple was organized in Chicago in 1944; the Cleveland Buddhist Temple was formed in 1945; and a Buddhist gathering began in New Jersey, which later became the Seabrook Buddhist Temple.[55] Allowing Japanese Americans to disperse to the Midwest and East Coast, therefore, generated the unanticipated consequence of Japanese American Buddhism spreading to those regions.

When the Nikkei returned to the West Coast, Buddhist temples served as temporary shelters, and Japanese American Buddhists strove hard to re-establish themselves in the United States. Through two events, they sought to address "improved race relations between Japanese American

Buddhists and the general public, particularly white Americans," to borrow Michael Masatsugu's words.[56] First, in 1948 the Nisei Buddhist Churches of America (BCA) members organized a Golden Jubilee Festival in San Francisco to celebrate its fiftieth-year anniversary, while honoring the hardships of Issei Buddhists and the sacrifices of the Nisei Buddhist soldiers. As Masatsugu puts it, this event signified "cross-generational ties, loyalty to country, civic inclusion, and aspirations toward the American middle class."[57] Second, a devout Buddhist veteran initiated the campaign for the US army to recognize "B" for Buddhist on dog tags, because during World War II, the army accepted only three religious designations, namely Protestant, Catholic, and Hebrew. A group of Nisei Buddhists also requested authorities of national cemeteries to allow the Buddhist symbol to be engraved on the gravestones of servicemen of the Buddhist faith.[58] According to Duncan Williams, "These two campaigns represent an important legacy of the camps, testing both Japanese American Buddhist loyalty to America and America's loyalty to its Buddhist citizens."[59]

Contrary to the Nikkei Buddhists' efforts to reintegrate themselves into American society, members of the Los Angeles Hompa Hongwanji (LAHH) Buddhist Temple, which is affiliated with the BCA, maintained ethnic space by excluding Julius Goldwater, who had served as the temple caretaker during the incarceration period. Despite his dedication to serve the Nikkei Buddhist internees, the LAHH board of directors sued Goldwater because Goldwater had misappropriated the temple's funds. Although the cause of contention was financial, the lawsuit indicated the underlying tension between Goldwater and Nikkei Buddhists. That is, Goldwater's effort to seek universal Buddhism, which Issei Shin Buddhist clergy supported during the prewar period, was challenged by the board members of Nisei Shin Buddhists who wished to maintain their sectarian affiliation and ethnic identity. The lawsuit led the two parties to terminate their friendship. Goldwater left the LAHH and became a nonsectarian Buddhist teacher in Los Angeles.[60] Unlike Goldwater, however, Sunya Pratt maintained a good relationship with members of the Tacoma Buddhist temple in Seattle until her death in 1986.

Assessment of Japanese American Buddhists' imprisonment experiences varies. In general, their reaction to imprisonment was not as negative as that of the Japanese American Christians. Stephen S. Fugita and Marilyn Fernandez state:

> The contemporary religious orientation of former Japanese American incarcerees is related to differing retrospective views of their World War II incarceration. Specifically, even though Buddhists were more marginalized by the larger society than were Protestants before, during, and immediately after the war, they remember their incarceration as a significantly less negative period in their lives than do Protestants. Moreover, they have a more accommodative and less protest-oriented perspective toward that experience, as indicated by the type of camp leader they currently favor. Finally, Buddhists were somewhat less active than Protestants in the over-decade-long social movement to redress the injustice of their wartime treatment.[61]

For the explanation of their findings, Fugita and Fernandez find the Buddhist worldview of accepting reality as it is and the idea of interdependent human life supported by compassionate acts of others.[62]

Issei Buddhist clergy took the internment as opportunities to study and promote Buddhism further in the United Sates. For Tana Daishō, it was a historical moment of furthering *Bukkyō tōzen*, or the movement of Buddhism moving eastward. Buddhism was introduced from India to East Asia and Japan, and Japanese Buddhism was introduced to Hawaii and the West Coast by Japanese immigrants, and therefore, it should be introduced to eastern parts of the United States.[63] Zen master Nyogen Senzaki held a similar view and called his meditation hall in the Heart Mountain relocation center *Tōzen zenkutsu*, Eastward Meditation Hall, simply because "Wyoming was east of California."[64] In addition, in Santa Fe camp, New Mexico, Tana met Japanese internees from Peru, and because he heard that there had been no Buddhist priest in that country, when they left the camp he arranged for them to take home the pictorial scroll of Amida Buddha and other Buddhist ornaments, which had been worshipped and used by the Nikkei Buddhists in Santa Fe.[65] For Tana, the camp served as a place to gather information from fellow Japanese who had lived in other parts of North and South America, such as Alaska and Peru, and to meet Imperial Japanese prisoners of war from whom he learned about various naval battles between the two countries. Because Tana was separated from his family for the entire duration of imprisonment, internment also gave him opportunities to reflect on his relationships with his wife and children, ministerial duties, and his relationships to fellow ministers and lay members.[66]

While such positive assessments of the imprisonment experienced by Nikkei Buddhists demonstrate both their ambitious and humble attitudes, others witnessed the stagnation of Buddhist practice among Japanese American Buddhists. Goldwater said, "I think many of the Buddhists there had a very shaky foundation in the dharma. . . . It was merely habitual, a point of ethnic pride. When that faith was challenged, the people were bereft; they were set adrift. Once the elegance of their heritage and culture were stripped away, they found themselves to be just ordinary people. They didn't necessarily grow."[67] Tana was also critical of his fellow ministers who busied themselves by playing baseball and mahjong games and neglected their clerical duties.

Further, the Nikkei Buddhist perceptions of white Americans were not always as negative as one may think. In Fort Missoula, Montana, where 633 Japanese had been interned by the end of 1941 and where Ishida Nitten, a bishop of the Nichiren sect, was detained, Issei internees were allowed to make supervised visits outside the camp compound. Once, male Japanese internees from Hawaii strolled through a local cemetery and discovered fifty graves of Japanese who seemed to have worked at railway construction between 1900 and 1909. The gravesites were clean. Later, twenty-four interned Buddhist priests were permitted by the camp commander to perform Buddhist memorial services for the deceased.[68] The story goes on:

> They [the Buddhist priests] burned incense at each grave. Their tears fell, not for the young men who had died without having their dreams realized, but in gratefulness that the town residents had cared for the graves for so many years, and especially now, knowing the ethnic origin of those buried below.
>
> "Those leaders who interned us are Americans," the priest said. "But these Missoula residents are Americans too. These Americans are thoughtful enough to care for graves of unknown people. At home, in Hawaii, some children neglect to clean around their own parents' gravesite. And here are Americans who have kept these Japanese tombstones clean."[69]

This episode does not indicate that Missoulians did not discriminate against Japanese Americans—in fact, they were as hostile to Japanese Americans as other white Americans were—but suggests the diversity of the white Americans' experiences of Nikkei Buddhists and a variation of Japanese American Buddhist experiences vis-à-vis the white American community. As demonstrated by the story of Fort Missoula, Nikkei Buddhist experiences varied from camp to camp and from person to person. By understanding local camp histories and stories of individual lives, the diversity of the Japanese American Buddhists' imprisonment experiences will become clearer.

TOWARD AN UNDERSTANDING OF RELIGION AND RACE IN CONTEMPORARY AMERICA

During the World War II imprisonment period, the US–Japan relationship and domestic sociopolitical conditions that had shaped the contours of Japanese American Buddhism prior to the war became worse. While exclusive American nationalism and an American public intolerant of foreign religions and ethnic minorities had prevented the growth of Nikkei Buddhism, the anti-Japanese public sentiment reached its peak after the bombing of Pearl Harbor, which led the great majority of Japanese Americans to be confined to relocation camps. However, individual commitment, organizational efforts, and ethnic solidarity continued to drive Japanese American Buddhists, who maintained their traditions and formed new practices within barbed wires. At the same time, following the leadership of the Nisei Buddhists, Nikkei Buddhist organizations acquired a more American look. Nisei Buddhist servicemen went to the battlefield and died, contributing to the master narrative of Japanese American history, in which Japanese Americans were accepted by America's general public because of the Nisei soldiers' sacrifices. Although Buddhist experiences during the World War II imprisonment period were specific to Japanese Americans, the Euro-American Buddhists supported and redefined their relationships to the Nikkei Buddhists.

The imprisonment of Japanese American Buddhists also represents the beginning of a new era in the history of American Buddhism. During the resettlement period, Japanese American Buddhists gathered in the Midwest and East Coast and later formed their temples in these regions. During the 1950s and 1960s, Buddhism became popular in the United States primarily because of the Beat generation and Zen boom. The enactment of the 1965 Immigration Act then led other forms of Asian Buddhism to be introduced to America, as more Asian migrants were allowed to enter the United States. As much as Japanese American Buddhism became regionally diverse, forms of American Buddhism became multifarious. Yet, Asian American Buddhists have always dealt with the issues related to their ethno-religious identities, including how to maintain and Americanize their practices at the same time and how to define their boundaries vis-à-vis the Buddhists of different racial and ethnic backgrounds. Furthermore, for Muslim Americans, how to reconcile their religious and national identities has been one of the pressing problems since 9/11. Therefore, the Japanese American Buddhists' incarceration experiences still resonate within American society.

REVIEW OF LITERATURE

While introducing many moving stories of Japanese American Buddhists, Williams analyzes various sociopolitical conditions and misconceptions that led the Nikkei Buddhist priests to be arrested by the FBI; describes vibrant Buddhist lives within and beyond barbed wires; introduces stories of Japanese American Buddhist soldiers serving in the 442nd Regimental Combat Team and the 100th Infantry Battalion, as well as the Military Intelligence Service; and discusses the resettlement of Nikkei Buddhists after World War II. *American Sutra* provides a comprehensive view on the experiences of Japanese American and Euro-American Buddhists during World War II and demonstrates the ways in which a new form of Buddhism emerged in the United States through their efforts to negotiate and redefine their national, religious, and ethnic identities.[70]

This book analyzes the complex processes of imprisonment of persons of Japanese descent. The network of imprisonment was loose and disorganized. Although various institutions (for example, the INS, the War Relocation Authority (WRA), the Department of Justice, and the US Army) participated in imprisonment and worked together, they competed with each other and created conflicts. Kashima mentions the Buddhist experience of internment by translating and citing passages from Tana Daishō's diary.[71]

PRIMARY SOURCES

Tana, Daishō. *Santa Fe Rōzubāgu senji tekikokujin yokuryū sho nikki*. 4 vols. Tokyo: Sankibo busshorin, 1976–1989.

This work is known as the *Internment Camp Diary*. The diary begins on December 7, 1941, when Pearl Harbor was bombed by the Imperial Japanese Navy, which led the FBI to arrest Tana three months later, and ends on March 31, 1946, when he was released by the Department of Justice.

Fujimura, Bunyū. *Though I Be Crushed: The Wartime Experiences of a Buddhist Minister*. Los Angeles: Nembutsu Press, 1985.

This work introduces an Issei Buddhist minister's internment experience. Fujimura was initially interned in an old army camp in Bismark (ND), transferred to Camp Livingston (LA), from there to Santa Fe (NM), and was incarcerated in Poston (AZ).

FURTHER READING

Ama, Michihiro. "A Neglected Diary, A Forgotten Buddhist Couple: Tana Daishō's Internment Camp Diary as a Historical and Literary Text." *Journal of Global Buddhism* 14 (2013): 45–62.

Blankenship, Anne. "Religion and the Japanese American Incarceration." *Religion Compass* 8, no. 10 (2014): 317–325.

Fugita, Stephen, and Marilyn Fernandez. "Religion and Japanese Americans' Views of their World War II Incarceration." *Journal of Asian American Studies* 5, no. 2 (2002): 113–137.

Tetsuden, Kashima. *Judgment without Trial: Japanese American Imprisonment during World War II*. Seattle: University of Washington Press, 2003.

Williams, Duncan R. "Complex Loyalties: Issei Buddhist Ministers during the Wartime Incarceration." *Pacific World* 3, no. 5 (2003): 255–274.

Williams, Duncan R. "From Pearl Harbor to 9/11: Lessons from the Internment of Japanese American Buddhists." In *Nation of Religions: The Politics of Pluralism in Multireligious America*. Edited by Stephen Prothero, 63–78. Chapel Hill: University of North Carolina Press, 2006.

Williams, Duncan R. *American Sutra: Buddhism and the World War II Japanese American Experience*. Cambridge, MA: Harvard University Press, 2019.

Yoo, David K. *Growing Up Nisei: Race, Generation, and Culture among Japanese Americans of California, 1924–49*. Urbana: University of Illinois Press, 2000.

NOTES

1. Yukiko Kimura, *Issei: Japanese Immigrants in Hawaii* (Honolulu: University of Hawai'i Press, 1988), 15.
2. Kimura cites *Hawaii Nihonjin Iminshi: Hawaii Kanyaku Imin 75-nen Kinen* (Honolulu: United Japanese Society of Hawaii, 1964), 314.
3. Michihiro Ama, *Immigrants to the Pure Land: The Modernization, Acculturation, and Globalization of Shin Buddhism, 1898–1941* (Honolulu: University of Hawaii, 2011).
4. Nam-lin Hur, *Death and Social Order in Tokugawa Japan: Buddhism, Anti-Christianity, and the Danka System* (Cambridge, MA: Harvard University Press, 2007), 9.
5. A series of laws enacted on state and national levels undermined the economic and socio-familial bases of the Nikkei community. In 1913, the state of California enacted the Alien Land law, which prohibited the Japanese immigrants from "purchasing agricultural land, and restricted the leasing of such land to three years." Yuji Ichioka, *The Issei: The World of the First Generation of Japanese Immigrants 1885–1924* (New York: Free Press, 1988), 153. In 1922, the US Supreme Court denied a Japanese immigrant's petition for citizenship (Kimura, *Issei*, 18). In the same year, the US congress enacted the Cable Act, according to which "any Nisei woman who married an alien ineligible for citizenship lost her American citizenship by virtue of her marriage" (Ichioka, *First Generation*, 253). Finally, the 1924 Japanese Exclusion Act "prevented immigrants and those who were ineligible for citizenship from being admitted to the U.S." (Kimura, *Issei*, 15).
6. David Yoo, *Growing Up Nisei: Race, Generation, and Culture among Japanese Americans of California, 1924–49* (Urbana: University of Illinois Press, 2000), 44.
7. George J. Tanabe Jr., "Glorious Gathas: Americanization and Japanization in Honganji Hymns," in *Engaged Pure Land Buddhism: Essays in Honor of Professor Alfred Bloom*, ed. Kenneth K. Tanaka and Eishō Nasu (Berkeley, CA: WisdomOcean Publications, 1998), 227.
8. Yoo, *Growing Up Nisei*, 48–54.
9. Kashima, *Buddhism in America: The Social Organization of an Ethnic Religious Institution* (Westport, CT: Greenwood Press, 1977), 48.
10. Duncan R. Williams, "Complex Loyalties: Issei Buddhist Ministers during the Wartime Incarceration," *Pacific World* 3, no. 5 (2003): 255–274.
11. Williams, "Complex Loyalties," 260–263. For the camp experience of Tenrikyō ministers, see Akihiro Yamakura, "The United States—Japanese War and Tenrikyo Ministers in America," in *Issei Buddhism in the Americas*, ed. Duncan R. Williams and Tomoe Moriya (Urbana: University of Illinois Press, 2010), 141–163. For the camp experience of Konkōkyō ministers, see Yoshiaki Fukuda, *My Six Years of Internment: An Issei's Struggle for Justice* (San Francisco: Konko Church of San Francisco, 1990).
12. Peter Irons, *Justice at War* (New York: Oxford University Press, 1982), 22; and Williams, "Complex Loyalties," 256. According to Irons, people in Group B were " 'potentially dangerous' but had not been thoroughly investigated," while people in Group C were monitored because of their "pro-Japanese inclinations and propagandist activities" (Irons, *Justice at War*, 22).
13. Bunyū Fujimura, *Though I Be Crushed* (Los Angeles: Nembutsu Press, 1985), 47.
14. Cited and translated by Williams, "Complex Loyalties," 257–258.
15. Fujimura, *Crushed*, 45.
16. Fujimura, *Crushed*, 51–52.
17. Fujimura, *Crushed*, 54–62.
18. Williams, "Complex Loyalties," 263–265. Tetsuden Kashima categorizes imprisonment camps into ten groups: detention stations operated by the Justice (Immigration and Naturalization Services (INS) and War Departments; internment camps by the Justice (INS) and War Departments; assembly centers by

the War Department; relocation camps by the War Relocation Authority (WRA); isolation and "pro-WRA" centers by the WRA; a segregation center by the WRA and the US Army; a segregation center by the Justice Department; institutions by the WRA; refugee camps by the WRA; and internment hostels by the State Department. Kashima states, "The imprisonment organization was rife with internal competition, lack of coordination, and ad hoc decision making." Tetsuden Kashima, *Judgment without Trial: Japanese American Imprisonment during World War II* (Seattle: University of Washington Press, 2003), 6, 10–11. For the categorizations of "internment," "incarceration," and "imprisonment," see Kashima, pp. 8–9.

19. See Tacoma Buddhist Temple.
20. *Rafu Shimpo*, March 18, 1942, 7. *Issei* temple members were, however, concerned about funeral arrangements without Japanese ministers (*Rafu Shimpo*, March 16, 1942, 3).
21. Kashima, *Buddhism in America*, 53.
22. Eiko Masuyama, *Memories: The Buddhist Church Experience in the Camps 1942–1945*, rev. ed. (unknown publisher, 2004), 141.
23. Ama, *Immigrants to the Pure Land*, chap. 3, n. 104.
24. Ama, *Immigrants to the Pure Land*, 84.
25. Anne Blankenship, "Religion and the Japanese American Incarceration," *Religion Compass* 8, no. 10 (2014): 317–325. The caveat of these data is that, as Blankenship points out, "some incarcerees may have been hesitant to officially affiliate themselves with a religion connected to Japan" (Blankenship, "Japanese American Incarceration," 321). At the same time, Williams states, "The rush to Christian conversion, ironically could be part of a Japanese tradition of subsuming religious identity under political or national identity. But conversions were also born of fear of persecution by neighbors and the government, and *many converts returned to the Buddhist fold during the camp years*" (Duncan R. Williams, "From Pearl Harbor to 9/11: Lessons from the Internment of Japanese American Buddhists," in *Nation of Religions: The Politics of Pluralism in Multireligious America*, ed. Stephen Prothero (Chapel Hill: University of North Carolina Press, 2006), 66.
26. Yoo, *Growing Up Nisei*, 114–123.
27. Williams, "Complex Loyalties," 267.
28. Cited in Masuyama, *Memories*, 21.
29. Fujimura, *Crushed*, 64, 80.
30. Williams, "Complex Loyalties," 266–267.
31. Blankenship, "Japanese American Incarceration," 321.
32. Williams, "Pearl Harbor," 67–68.
33. Masuyama, *Memories*, 35–36.
34. Williams, "Pearl Harbor," 68.
35. Masuyama, *Memories*, 21. In May 1944, however, sectarian services were suspended and Buddhist internees in Heart Mountain resumed observing transsectarian services.
36. Tana Daishō, *Internment Camp Diary*, 4 vols. (Tokyo: Sankibo busshorin, 1976–1989), 2:423–424.
37. Kashima, *Buddhism in America*, 55.
38. Kashima, *Buddhism in America*, 55. Among the loyalty questions, numbers twenty-seven and twenty-eight were controversial, given the fact that most of the Nisei were American citizens: "the first dealt with the respondent's willingness to serve in the armed forces of the United States, and the second, in essence, asked for a renunciation of any allegiance to Japan" (Kashima, *Buddhism in America*, 58).
39. Kashima, *Buddhism in America*, 58–59.
40. Kashima, *Buddhism in America*, 59–61; and Williams, "Pearl Harbor," 69. The preface to *A Book Containing an Order of Ceremonies for Use by Buddhists at Gatherings* is reprinted as "Julius Goldwater, Wartime Buddhist Liturgy (1940s)" in *Asian Religions in America: A Documentary History*, ed. Thomas A. Tweed and Stephen Prothero (New York: Oxford University Press, 1999), 172–177. Initially the WRA allowed the incarcerees to communicate only in English, but because many of the Issei were unable to speak

English, it allowed them to speak the Japanese language. Nevertheless, in order to avoid misunderstanding, the Nikkei Buddhists voluntarily conducted Buddhist services in English (Susan Davis, "Mountain of Compassion: Dharma in American Internment Camps" (Summer 1993): 46–51, 49).

41. Davis, "Mountain," 50.
42. Williams, "Pearl Harbor," 69.
43. Fujimura, *Crushed*, 79.
44. Tana, *Camp Diary*, 1:308, 320–321, 373; 3:421–422.
45. Tamotsu Shibutani, *The Derelicts of Company K: A Sociological Study of Demoralization* (Berkeley: University of California Press, 1978), 39–40, 55, 59, 62.
46. Kyōgoku Ituzō, *The Silver Moon* (May 30, 1949): 10–11. It was "dedicated to Nisei soldiers who sacrificed themselves in defense of their country."
47. Ituzō, *Silver Moon*, 8–9.
48. Kyōgoku Ituzō, "Naniga nisei heishi o kaku yūkan narashimetaka," *Jikishin* 5, no. 2 (July 1949): 4–10.
49. Shibutani states, "Though Americans, the Nisei were also conscious of being part of a proud 'race'—one characterized by high ideals. But their understanding of Japanese values was both imperfect and stereotyped" (Shibutani, *Derelicts*, 25).
50. Fujimura, *Crushed*, 98.
51. Luis O. Gómez, *The Land of Bliss: The Paradise of the Buddha of Measureless Light; Sanskrit and Chinese Versions of the Sukhāvatīvyūha Sutras* (Honolulu: University of Hawai'i Press, 1996), 215.
52. Tana Daishō, *Hotoke no kyōbō* (Kyoto: Hyakkaen, 1972), 466.
53. In his sermon, Fujimura cited the letter of a Nisei Buddhist solider addressed to his mother: "Even if, unfortunately, I fall in battle, I will go to the Buddha's land that I heard about from *sensei* from the time I was a child, so there is nothing for you to worry about. Please give my regards to sensei. And please take good care of yourself. *Sayonara*" (Fujimura, *Crushed*, 99).
54. Yoo, *Growing Up Nisei*, 154.
55. Buddhist Churches of America, ed. *Buddhist Churches of America: A Legacy of the First 100 Years* (San Francisco: Buddhist Churches of America, 1998), 193, 250, 323.
56. Michael K. Masatsugu, "Reorienting the Pure Land: Japanese Americans, the Beats, and the Making of American Buddhism, 1941–1966" (PhD diss., University of California, 2004), 70.
57. Masatsugu, "Reorienting," 67.
58. Masatsugu, "Reorienting," 88–98.
59. Williams, "Pearl Harbor," 71–72.
60. Michihiro Ama, "A Jewish Buddhist Priest: The Curious Case of Julius A. Goldwater and the Hompa Hongwanji Buddhist Temples in 1930–1940s Los Angeles," *Southern California Quarterly* 100, no. 3 (Fall 2018).
61. Stephen S. Fugita and Marilyn Fernandez, "Religion and Japanese Americans' View of their World War II Incarceration," *Journal of Asian American Studies* 5, no. 2 (June 2002), 132.
62. Fugita and Fernandez, "Religion and Japanese Americans," 134.
63. Tana, *Camp Diary*, 1:20.
64. Davis, "Mountain," 50.
65. Tana, *Camp Diary*, 4:806–808.
66. See Michihiro Ama, "A Neglected Diary, A Forgotten Buddhist Couple: Tana Daishō's Internment Camp Diary as a Historical and Literary Text," *Journal of Global Buddhism* 14 (2013): 45–62.
67. Davis, "Mountain," 49.
68. Carol van Valkenburg, *An Alien Place: The Fort Missoula Montana Detention Camp 1941–1944* (Missoula: Pictorial Histories, 2009), 54, 109. Among the list of Japanese internees in Fort Missoula, Nitten Ishida, bishop of Nichiren sect, is found (van Valkenburg, *An Alien Place*, 125).

69. van Valkenburg, *An Alien Place*, 110. Van Valkenburg cites Patsy Sumie Saiki, *Ganbare! An Example of Japanese Spirit* (Honolulu: Kisaku, 1982), 133.
70. Williams, Duncan R. *American Sutra: Buddhism and the World War II Japanese American Experience* (Cambridge, MA: Harvard University Press, 2019, forthcoming).
71. Kashima, Tetsuden. *Judgment without Trial: Japanese American Imprisonment during World War II* (Seattle: University of Washington Press, 2003).

Michihiro Ama

AMOGHAVAJRA

INTRODUCTION AND BIOGRAPHICAL SOURCES

Amoghavajra (*Bukongjin'gang* 不空金剛; 704/705–774 CE) was a Buddhist monk who established and propagated a type of esoteric Buddhism in China during the second half of the 8th century. Amoghavajra typically referred to this esoteric Buddhist teaching as the "Great Teaching of Yoga," the "Teaching of the Diamond Pinnacle," and the "Teaching of the Five Divisions." The most valuable source for constructing Amoghavajra's life is the *Memorials and Edicts of the Venerable Tripiṭaka monk Dabian Zheng Guangzhi, bestowed [with the title] Minister of Works by the court of Emperor Daizong* (*T* 2120; *Daizongchao zeng sikong Dabian Zheng Guangzhi sancang heshang biaozhiji* 代宗朝贈司空大辨正廣智三藏和上表制集; hereafter *Memorials and Edicts*), likely compiled in 795/796 CE. This work consists primarily of correspondence from, to, and concerning Amoghavajra from December of 757 CE until after his death in 774. In addition to the biographical details that emerge from the exchanges between Amoghavajra and his imperial and elite sponsors, the *Memorials and Edicts* also contains Amoghavajra's "Final Testament of the Tripiṭaka Monk" (*T* 2120.844a16-0845a24; *Sanzang heshang yishu* 三藏和上遺書), which includes a brief autobiographical account. Also included in the *Memorials and Edicts* are posthumous biographical sources, the most significant of which for constructing Amoghavajra's life are the *Stele Inscription of the Late Great Worthy, the Commander Ceremonially Equal to the Three Monitoring Offices, the Grand Attendant Chief Minister of the Court of State Ceremonial, and Duke of the Kingdom of Su, Tripiṭaka Da Guangzhi of Xingshan Monastery* (*T* 2120.848b14-849c05; *Da Tang gudade kaifu yitong sansi shi hongluqing Suguo gong Da Xingshansi Da Guangzhi sancang heshang zhi bei* 大唐故大德開府儀同三司試鴻臚卿肅國公大興善寺大廣智三藏和上之碑; hereafter *Stele Inscription*), written by Amoghavajra's monastic disciple Feixi 飛錫 (fl. 742–805 CE), and another stele inscription composed by Yan Ying 嚴郢 (d. 783 CE) for Amoghavajra's memorial cloister in Xingshan Monastery, the *Stele Inscription for the Venerable Tripitka's Cloister* (*T* 2120.860a09-860c08; *Sanzang heshang yuanpei* 三藏和尚當院碑; hereafter *Cloister Inscription*). In addition to these sources for constructing Amoghavajra's life and career, there is also the *Account of Conduct of the Former Great Worthy Bestowed with the Title Minister of Works, Dabian Zheng Guangzhi Trepiṭaka Bukong of the Great Tang* (*T* 2056.292b01-294c09; *Da Tang gudade zeng sikong Dabian Zhengguangzhi Bukong sanzang xingzhuang* 大唐故大德贈司空大辨正廣智不空三藏行狀; hereafter *Account of Conduct*) attributed to Zhaoqian 趙遷 (fl. 776–778 CE) and a stele inscription composed by Quan Deyu 權德輿 (795–818 CE) to accompany the installation of portraits of Amoghavajra and his master, Vajrabodhi (*Jin'gangzhi* 金剛智; 671–741 CE), in Xingshan Monastery 興善寺.[1] Biographical material for Amoghavajra is also included in Yuanzhao's *Zhenyuan Era* (貞元 785–805 CE) *Catalogue of Scriptures* (*T* 2157; *Zhenyuan xinding shijiao mulu* 貞元新定釋教目錄), which intersperses memorials and edicts from and concerning Amoghavajra with biographical narrative (the primary biographical material is found in *T* 2157.881a11-881c20). Representations of Amoghavajra that were produced following the Tang dynasty, such as those found in the *Older Tang History* (*Jiu Tangshu* 舊唐書) and in the *Newer Tang History* (*Xin Tangshu* 新唐書), in Zanning's 贊寧 (919–1001 CE) *Song Dynasty Biographies of Eminent Monks* (*Song gaoseng zhuan* 宋高僧傳; *T*2061) and his *Great Song Dynasty Brief History of the Sangha* (*Da Song seng shilue* 大宋僧史略; *T* 2126), and in the *Comprehensive Records of Buddhas and Patriarchs* (*fozu tongji* 佛祖統記; *T* 2035), for example, are essentially digests of material from Tang dynasty accounts, principally material contained in the *Memorials and Edicts* and particularly the *Stele Inscription* that is incorporated in that source.

BIOGRAPHICAL INFORMATION

The biographical sources concerning Amoghavajra are not in agreement concerning his birthplace or the circumstances that led him to Tang China. The *Stele Inscription* by Feixi describes Amoghavajra as the son of a "north Indian brahman" and states that he traveled with his maternal uncle to China when he was ten years old and arrived in the capital Chang'an at the age of thirteen (*T* 2120.848b19-23). According to this source, Amoghavajra entered monastic life as a novice disciple of Vajrabodhi at the age of thirteen and received full ordination when he was fifteen years old (*T* 2120.848b24-27). As in the *Stele Inscription*, Zhaoqian's *Account of Conduct* states that Amoghavajra was from a northern Indian Brahman family, but adds that Amoghavajra took his mother's surname, Kang 康, an ethnonym traditionally designating peoples from Sogdiana generally and Samarkand specifically (*T* 2056.292b12). This source also describes Amoghavajra as hailing from Xilang Commandery 西良府, identified by Chou Yi-liang as Liangzhou 涼州 in what is now western Gansu Province 甘肅州.[2] Yuanzhao's biographical account of Amoghavajra in the *Zhenyuan Catalogue*, however, states that his family name was unknown, that he was from Sri Lanka, and that he came under Vajrabodhi's tutelage at the age of fourteen when both were in the Southeast Asian kingdom of Dupo (*Dupuo guo* 闍婆國), probably located on the Indonesian island of Java, rather than in Tang China, as described in the *Stele Inscription* (*T* 2157.881a15).

Although the biographical sources are not in agreement concerning Amoghavajra's place of birth, ethnicity, or early life, all available sources affirm that he was a disciple of Vajrabodhi. This is also declared by Amoghavajra in his own self-representations and statements found throughout the *Memorials and Edicts*. Amoghavajra reports that he became a disciple of Vajrabodhi while a youth and that he received partial initiation and training in a teaching he refers to as "yoga" (*yujia* 瑜加) and "secret yoga" (*T* 2120.844a17-18, a20-21). Following the death of his master in 741 CE, Amoghavajra embarked on an ocean voyage to the southern Indic regions. This was likely as part of a diplomatic mission from Emperor Xuanzong 玄宗 (r. 713–756 CE) to the rulers of Sri Lanka and southern India, but for Amoghavajra it resulted in the acquisition of a large cache of scriptures and, according to the *Stele Inscription*, further initiation and training from an Indian master identified as the *ācārya* Samantabhadra (*Puxian azheli* 普賢阿遮梨; *T* 2120.848c09-14). Upon his return to Tang China in 746/747 CE, Amoghavajra is reported to have performed religious services for Emperor Xuanzong before being transferred to the western military command center of Wuwei 武威 at the request of Military Commissioner (*jiedushi* 節度使) Geshu Han 哥舒翰 (699–757 CE) (*T* 2120.848c24-28). There, he is said to have initiated members of the local aristocracy and military elite into esoteric Buddhist practices. At the outbreak of An Lushan's 安盧山 (*c.* 703–757 CE) rebellion in 755 CE, Amoghavajra was recalled to the Tang capital and is described as having performed esoteric Buddhist rites in order to defeat the traitor forces (*T* 2120.848c29-849a03). Over the remaining two decades of his life, Amoghavajra regularly performed religious services for the Tang emperors, first Emperor Suzong 肅宗 (r. 756–762 CE) and then his son and successor, Emperor Daizong 代宗 (r. 762–779 CE). Amoghavajra was the recipient of numerous gifts and honors bestowed by the Tang emperors, and he achieved a pronounced degree of influence in the Tang central government and over the officially sponsored Buddhist complex of the Tang. In the memorial titled "Final Testament of the Tripiṭaka Monk," Amoghavajra summarized his career, highlighting his discipleship under Vajrabodhi, his journey to southern India, his receipt of the *Diamond Pinnacle*, promotion of his esoteric Buddhism, and his service to and the patronage of the Tang emperors.

> In my youth I left home and relied on the master [Vajrabodhi's] instruction, discussing and investigating the Indic texts for more than twenty years. Diligently working day and night, I humbly requested and received [teachings, until my master] then bestowed on me the Yoga Dharma in 4,000 verses. Alas, he became ill and the late master died an old man. Living without anyone to rely on, on whom could I depend to help forward my mission? This is why I journeyed to distant India, crossing the seas and facing danger. Everywhere studying yoga and personally honoring the traces of the Sage, I acquired the 10,000 verse seal of the Dharma Treasury [i.e., the *Diamond Pinnacle*]. I returned to the imperium, practicing conversion at blessed spots. Thus, in one court I served as the master of three generations of emperors. To the lords of men, I exhaustively conferred the secret yoga and transmitted the seal of Dharma. Consequently, since the current Sage [Emperor Daizong] promulgated the teaching, the most profound eighteen assemblies of yoga have been completely established, and the assemblies of the thirty-seven sages are each practiced. (*T* 2120.844a17-26)

Following the restoration of Tang rule in 757 CE, Amoghavajra requested and received imperial permission and sponsorship for a translation project that would occupy the remainder of his life and would constitute a significant element of his legacy. Following Amoghavajra's representations to his imperial sponsors, this translation work was centered on the collection of texts that he brought back from his journey to the southern Indian region in 741–746/747 CE as well as manuscripts that had been previously acquired abroad by Yijing 義淨 (653–713 CE), Śubhakarasiṃha (*Shanwuwei* 善無畏; 637–735 CE), Bodhiruci (*Liuzhi* 流支; fl. 693–727 CE), and Ratnaketu (*Baosheng* 寶生; d.u.) and were then held in monastic libraries in Chang'an 長安 and Luoyang 洛陽 (*T* 2120.828a25-b09, 828c29-828a13). In 771 CE, three years prior to his death, Amoghavajra submitted seventy-one titles in 101 fascicles for inclusion in the imperially approved catalog of Buddhist texts. This collection of texts consisted of translated scriptures and ritual manuals along with commentaries and compendia of his own composition. According to Amoghavajra's memorial that accompanied the texts, this was a heterogenous collection of texts consisting of the "Dharma of the Diamond Pinnacle Yoga" (*jin'gangding yujia famen* 金剛頂瑜伽法門) as well as mainstream Mahāyāna and *dhāraṇī* texts (*T* 2120. 840b01-05). Although Amoghavajra's retranslation of the *Prajñāpāramitā Scripture for Humane Kings Who Protect Their States* (*Renwang huguo banruoboluomi jing* 仁王護國般若波羅蜜經, T 246; hereafter *Humane Kings Scripture*) is perhaps the most well-known product of his translation project, his reference to the "Dharma of the Diamond Pinnacle Yoga" in contradistinction to the other texts provided by Amoghavajra privileges the esoteric Buddhist teaching that he propagated in relation to mainstream *Mahāyāna* scriptures, such as the *Humane Kings*, as well as established *dhāraṇī* traditions.[3] It also foregrounds the central significance of the *Diamond Pinnacle Assembly of all Tathagatas, the Great King of Scriptures* (*Jin'gangding yiqie rulai zhenshishe dacheng xianzheng dajiaowang jing* 金剛頂一切如來真實攝大乘現證大教王經, *T* 865; hereafter *Diamond Pinnacle Scripture*) within his esoteric Buddhism.

Like Amoghavajra's scriptural corpus, the broader scriptural basis of his esoteric Buddhism was also heterogenous. The texts submitted to the court that are evidently of Amoghavajra's own composition are instructive for determining how he conceived of and represented the esoteric Buddhism that he propagated in China, and among the most significant of these original texts in this regard is the *Catalogue of All the Divisions of Dhāraṇī* (*Doubu tuoluoni mu* 都部陀羅尼目; *T* 903). In that text, Amoghavajra summarizes five scriptures that he presents as constituent of the esoteric Buddhist teaching that he promoted: (a) the *Diamond Pinnacle*, which he describes as the fundamental or "root" (*ben* 本) scripture of the teaching, (b) the *Great Attainment of Buddhahood and Supernatural Transformations of Vairocana Scripture* (hereafter *Great Vairocana Scripture*) (*Da piluozhena chengfo shenbian jiachi jing* 大毘盧遮那成佛神變加持經; *T* 848), (c) the *Susiddhikāra Scripture* (*Suxidijieluo jing* 蘇悉地羯囉經; *T* 893), (d) the *Scripture of the Questions of the Lad Subahu* (*Supohu tongzi qingwen jing* 蘇婆呼童子請問經; *T* 895), and (e) the *Recitation and Visualization Secret Methods of the Immovable Honored-One's Trisamaya* (*Dilisanmeiye budong zunshengzhe niansong mimi fa* 底哩三昧耶不動尊聖者念誦祕密法; *T* 1200 and *T* 1201; hereafter *Trisamaya Scripture*). Of these translations, two (the *Diamond Pinnacle* and the *Trisamaya Scripture*) were translated into Chinese by Amoghavajra while the remaining three were Śubhākarasiṃha's products. As such, Amoghavajra's esoteric Buddhism appears to be a teaching that he constructed in China by combining earlier scriptural traditions and subordinating them to his *Diamond Pinnacle Scripture*. Practically, Amoghavajra's esoteric Buddhism was predicated on initiation procedures (Skt. *abhiṣeka*, Chinese *guanding* 灌頂), authorizing both laypeople and monastic Buddhists to engage in efficacious practice. Rudimentary practices appear to have been basically apotropaic, but more advanced rites typically involved the construction of mandalas and fire altars for the purpose of interacting with buddhas, bodhisattvas, and deities and thereby attaining particular outcomes (Skt. *siddhi*). Attendant practices concerning the invocation of and interaction with these supernormal beings regularly involved visualization, *mudrā*, mantra recitation, and the incineration of various materials in a fire altar. Although there is little evidence that the outcomes of Amoghavajra's esoteric Buddhist ritual practice were standardized in either their generalities or their particulars, generally speaking they were of four types: pacification or the quelling of disasters (*xizai* 息災; Skt. *śāntika*), attraction (*jing'ai* 敬愛; Skt. *vaśīkaraṇa*), augmentation (*zengzhang* 增長; Skt. *pauṣṭika*), and subjugation or the elimination of enemies (*xiangfu* 降伏; Skt. *abhicāra*).

Based on the requirement of authorizing initiations that characterized his Buddhism, Amoghavajra's establishment of esoteric Buddhism in China entailed the creation of a discrete lineage of practitioners. By virtue of their complete initiation as *ācārya* by Amoghavajra, these men identified themselves and were recognized by others as possessing and transmitting Amoghavajra's esoteric Buddhism prior to and after his death in 774 CE. Amoghavajra reportedly initiated numerous lay and monastic practitioners into his esoteric Buddhism, requesting and receiving imperial authorization to perform initiation rites in multiple monastic establishments. The *Account of Conduct* attributed to Zhaoqian reports that ten people, who go unnamed, received full initiation from Amoghavajra to become *ācārya* masters of the esoteric teaching, but according to his own report, Amoghavajra only granted eight men full investiture as *ācāryas*. Two of these would-be heirs predeceased him. According to his statement in the "Last Testament of the Tripitaka Monk," the six fully initiated disciples who survived Amoghavajra were Han'guang 含光 (fl. 755–766 CE), Hyech'o 慧超 (fl. 733–780 CE), Huiguo 慧果/惠果 (746–805 CE), Huilang 慧朗 (fl. 774–778 CE), Yuanjiao 元皎 (fl. 755–774 CE), and Juechao 覺超 (fl. 774–778 CE) (*T* 2120.844a28- b03).

In addition to his massive contribution to the East Asian canon, the creation of a Chinese esoteric Buddhism, and the establishment of authorized disciples to carry on that teaching, Amoghavajra's other most significant activity was his oversight and encouragement of the revivification and expansion of the imperial Buddhist complex located at Mount Wutai (*Wutai shan* 五臺山). This project was initiated in June 766 CE, when Amoghavajra requested imperial funds to complete the construction of the Golden Pavilion Monastery (*Jin' ge si* 金閣寺), a project that had begun in 736/737 CE in response to a vision received and reported by Daoyi 道義 (*c.* 713–*c.* 766 CE) (*T* 2120.834a08-b02). Six months after the initial request and its approval, Amoghavajra submitted another memorial requesting funds to refurbish Jade Flower Monastery (*Yuhua si* 玉華寺) at Mount Wutai (*T* 2120.834b17-19). In April of 767 CE, he requested and received permission to ordain monks to fill the monasteries at Wutai and asked that one of his leading disciples, Han'guang, be transferred there in order to perform meritorious service on behalf of the Tang imperium (*T* 2120.835b22-c09). Accordingly, the imperial sponsorship of construction projects and religious performances at Mount Wutai that came at Amoghavajra's behest resulted not only in the restoration of the imperial Buddhist complex at the mountain but also effectively established Wutai as the center of practice for Amoghavajra's esoteric Buddhism.

Titles and Honors. Amoghavajra was the recipient of multiple gifts and titles bestowed by Emperors Suzong and Daizong, honors that contributed to his power in Tang society and indicate his significance and influence in the Tang central government. The most significant of these was the bestowal of the courtesy name Da Guangzhi ("Great Vast Wisdom") and appointment as chief minister of the Court of State Ceremonial (*honglu qing* 鴻臚卿) by Emperor Daizong in 765 CE. With this appointment in the governmental agency charged with overseeing imperially sponsored rites for the benefit of the Tang state and its rulers, among other things, Amoghavajra and his esoteric Buddhism effectively became an official element of the religious complex of the Tang imperium (*T* 2120.832c18-27). Just prior to his death in August 774 CE, Emperor Daizong bestowed Amoghavajra with the prestigious title Commander Unequalled in Honor (*kaifu yitong sansi* 開府儀同三司) and enfeoffed him as the Duke of Su Kingdom (*Suguo gong* 肅國公) with an actual income of three thousand households (*T* 2120.845c23-846a12). Granted in recognition of his decades of service to the Tang, this enfeoffment was more symbolic than actual, given the fact of Amoghavajra's pending death at the time, though it nevertheless indicated the great esteem that Emperor Daizong had for Amoghavajra. Following his death, Emperor Daizong suspended court for three days and sponsored the funeral services. Amoghavajra was formally eulogized by Lady Zhang, mistress of Deng Kingdom (*Dengguo furen Zhangmin* 鄧國夫人張氏, fl. *c.* 710–774 CE; *T* 2120.847b25-c13), by the chief minister of war Li Baoyu 李抱玉 (704–777 CE; *T* 2120.847c25-848a10), by the eunuch official Liu Xianhe 劉仙鶴 (fl. 774 CE; *T* 2120.849c16-23), and by the director of the Secretariat-Chancellery Yuan Zai 元載 (713–777 CE; *T* 2120.849c24-850a09). Relics (Skt. *śarīra*) found among Amoghavajra's cremains were installed in a stupa by imperial command (*T* 2120.850c26-851a08), and Amoghavajra's life and career accomplishments were preserved in the writing of multiple stele inscriptions; the compilation of official correspondence to, from, and concerning him; and the entry of his scriptural corpus into the official Buddhist catalog of scriptures. The esoteric Buddhist teaching that he established in China was also preserved by imperial commands directing that his disciples carry on the teaching (*T* 2120.846c15-20) and that his lineal disciple Huilang assume responsibility for training the next generation of practitioners (*T* 2120.850c12-15).

Legacy. The most significant element of Amoghavajra's legacy was the creation and establishment of esoteric Buddhism as a locally recognized and discrete Buddhist teaching in Tang China. This teaching was identified with a limited group of authorized practitioners who were installed in specific institutions in Tang China. Based on his relationship with Emperor Daizong, Huilang was Amoghavajra's de facto leading heir. He was transferred to Amoghavajra's home monastery, Xingshan Monastery, by imperial decree just before his master's death and replaced Amoghavajra as abbot of Xingshan Monastery following his death (*T* 2120. 859c21-860a03). He also inherited Amoghavajra's relationship with and role vis-à-vis Daizong following Amoghavajra's passing. Huilang was granted an honorific purple robe by the emperor (*T* 2120.851a09-16), in addition to being charged by Emperor Daizong to train future generations of esoteric Buddhists (*T* 2120.850c12-15). Other of Amoghavajra's fully initiated disciples were installed in important centers of Buddhist practice. For example, Juechao was the esoteric practitioner-in-residence at the imperial palace (*T* 2120.854c01-13), and Han'guang was installed at Mount Wutai at Amoghavajra's request (*T* 2120.835b17-835c13). The most well known of Amoghavajra's lineal disciples is probably Huiguo, whose residence was the Qinglong Monastery (*Qinglong si* 青龍寺) in Luoyang 洛陽. Huiguo's fame is principally due to the fact that Kūkai 空海, the recognized founder of the Japanese Shingon 真言 school, claimed to have received full initiation in esoteric Buddhism from Huiguo in 805 CE.[4] As such, the Shingon order of Japanese Buddhism, particularly with its characteristic practices of *abhiṣeka* initiation rites and *homa* (J. *goma*) fire offerings along with its focus on the

Mahāvairocana and *Diamond Pinnacle Scriptures*, may also be justly regarded as part of Amoghavajra's larger legacy in East Asia.

In China, Amoghavajra's legacy also played out in the influence that he exerted in the Tang central government, as his career and role within and vis-à-vis the Tang central government also informed the bureaucratic oversight of religious institutions by the central government for the remainder of the Tang dynasty and influenced the Tang successor states of the Five Dynasties era. While Buddhist practitioners and institutions had been subject to imperial oversight and control for centuries by the second half of the 8th century, as a result of Amoghavajra's influence in the central government and official patronage of him and his esoteric Buddhism, a new office was created in the central bureaucracy in order to facilitate the Tang court's direct management of Buddhist practitioners and institutions. This position was the commissioner of merit and virtue (*gongde shi* 功德使), a post responsible for directly administering institutional Buddhists according to commands issued by the emperor.[5] Incumbents of this post were almost without exception also commanders of imperial troops, reflecting the ascendency of Buddhism as a state-protecting tradition from the second half of the 8th century onward, and it is clear that the emergence of this office in the 770s, its function, and the staffing of the position were largely the result of Amoghavajra's relationship with the Tang court and the institutionalization of roles played by his elite patrons and his disciples vis-à-vis the Tang emperors and the central government. The first historically verifiable commissioner of merit and virtue was Li Yuancong 李元琮 (d. 777 CE), who was simultaneously a commander of imperial troops and one of Amoghavajra's leading patron-disciples. Li Yuancong served as an unofficial go-between for Amoghavajra and Emperor Daizong, and, following Amoghavajra's death in August 774 CE, Li Yuancong's informal role was institutionalized when he was officially designated commissioner of merit and virtue (*T* 2102.851a02, 851a08). The position of commissioner of merit and virtue as the official executor of imperial commands concerning religious practice on behalf of the Tang state persisted well after the death of Li Yuancong. Although Emperor Dezong 德宗 (r. 779–805 CE) eliminated the post of commissioner for the cultivation of merit in 779/780 CE, he reinstituted and expanded it to two commissioners by 789 CE. The position of commissioner of merit and virtue outlasted the Tang dynasty proper, as Zhu Zhen 朱瑱 (r. 913–923 CE), the last emperor of the Later Liang 後梁 (907–923 CE), maintained the post in his government as did Emperor Zhuangzong 莊宗 of the Later Tang 後唐 (r. 923–926 CE).[6] The post was also an element of the Later Jin's 後晉 (936–947 CE) central government.[7]

Amoghavajra's textual legacy was preserved through the incorporation of his textual corpus into the official Chinese Buddhist bibliographies of the Tang and, later, the inclusion of his scriptures, compendia, and commentaries in the Chinese and larger East Asian Buddhist canons. Amoghavajra's textual contribution was first incorporated into existing Chinese bibliography via a section appended to Zhisheng's 智昇 *Kaiyuan [Reign Era] Catalogue of Buddhist Teachings* (*Kaiyuan shijiao lu* 開元釋教錄, *T* 2154) labeled "Catalogue of the Recently Translated Collection of Scriptures, Commentaries, and Visualization and Recitation Ritual Procedures [by the] Great Tang Tripiṭaka [monk] Amogha[vajra]" (*Da Tang Bukongsanzang xinshi zong jing lu ji niansongyiguifa deng mulu* 大唐不空三藏新譯眾經論及念誦儀軌法等目錄, *T* 2154.699c16-700c11). This appendix is effectively a reproduction of the list of titles submitted by Amoghavajra to Daizong in 774 CE, but its inclusion as an appendix to the

Kaiyuan Catalogue marks the official entry of Amoghavajra's textual corpus into the imperial Buddhist scriptural collection of Tang China, which was eventually codified in the production and dissemination of Buddhist canons in the Song dynasty and thereafter. Amoghavajra's career and memory were also preserved in the creation of synoptic Buddhist histories from the Song dynasty onward, the foundational models of which were produced by Zanning 贊寧 at the end of the 11th century. In his *Song Dynasty Biographies of Eminent Monks*, Zanning essentially condenses material drawn from the *Memorials and Edicts*, especially the *Stele Inscription*, to produce a hagiographical representation of Amoghavajra that has informed textual representations of Amoghavajra to the present era. While his account of Amoghavajra in the *Song Dynasty Biographies of Eminent Monks* serves to incorporate him into Chinese hagiographical literature and tropes, Zanning's *Brief History of the Saṃgha* (*seng shiwei* 僧史略; *T* 2126) effectively incorporates his esoteric Buddhism into the longue durée history of Chinese Buddhism. Consequently, Amoghavajra's person and career came to be ossified and preserved in textual representations from the Song dynasty onward, thereby establishing and maintaining his legacy within the larger context of Chinese and East Asian Buddhism.

REVIEW OF LITERATURE

The central question that has informed contemporary scholarship concerning Amoghavajra is how to understand the Buddhism that he presented and promoted in Tang China; the question may be broken into two related ones: was his Buddhism a "sect" or "school" of Chinese Buddhism and did Amoghavajra actively mold Indic Buddhist sources to Sinitic norms and ideals? Chou Yi-lang's translation and study of Zanning's biographical representations of Śubhakarasiṃha (637–735 CE), Vajrabodhi, and Amoghavajra for his 1944 doctoral dissertation, subsequently published in the *Harvard Journal of Asiatic Studies* in 1945 under the title "Tantrism in China," is foundational in English-language scholarship.[8] In addition to effectively establishing Zanning's biographical representations of these men as normative, Chou also presented Śubhakarasiṃha, Vajrabodhi, and Amoghavajra as introducing and representing a "sect" of Buddhism that originated in India and was transmitted to China by these so-called patriarchs. In Chou's work, then, Amoghavajra is understood to have transmitted an Indian form of Buddhism that was recognized as a "sect" or "school." In this regard, Chou was informed by the representations of Amoghavajra and esoteric Buddhism found in previous Japanese scholarship, particularly Ōmura Seiga's *Mikkyō hattatsushi* 密教発達史 (History of the Development of the Esoteric Teaching) and Toganō Shoun's 栂尾祥雲 *Himitsu bukkyō shi* 秘密佛教史 (History of Esoteric Buddhism), that sought to distinguish the "pure Esotericism" (*junmitsu* 純密) transmitted to China by Śubhakarasiṃha, Vajrabodhi, and Amoghavajra from the "mixed" or "miscellaneous Esotericism" (*zōmitsu* 雜密) that is represented by the texts of earlier translators and, problematically, some of the scriptures produced by Śubhakarasiṃha, Vajrabodhi, and Amoghavajra.[9] Chou's historical project, though directed toward India and China, effectively recapitulated an image of Amoghavajra based on Song dynasty sources and a sectarian model of esoteric Buddhism informed by Japanese scholarship.

Amoghavajra and his Buddhism were not generally a subject of interest in Western scholarship again until the late 20th century, when Michel Strickmann began to publish his influential work. Strickmann identified the works of Śubhākarasiṃha, Vajrabodhi, and Amoghavajra as representative of a systematic form of Indian Buddhism that he refers to as "Tantric."[10] Given his interest in the Indian origins of tantric and, in his phrasing, "proto-tantric" Buddhist texts and practice and the popular Chinese appropriation of these materials, Strickmann did not decisively consider the question of whether Amoghavajra's Buddhism was to be understood as a "sect" or "school" of Chinese Buddhism, though he adopts the model inherited ultimately from Zanning in the Song dynasty of grouping Śubhākarasiṃha, Vajrabodhi, and Amoghavajra together as representative of a particular form of Buddhism. However, Strickmann regarded Śubhākarasiṃha and Vajrabodhi as faithful translators or transmitters of Indic material and Amoghavajra as an innovator. Of Amoghavajra and his scriptural corpus, Strickmann says:

> The most curious feature of Amoghavajra's scholarly activity concerns his 167 "translations." Properly speaking, many of these were not translations at all. Instead, they might better be called "adaptations"; essentially, he refurbished them into line with his own terminology and ritual practice. This becomes even more striking in those cases where texts "translated" by Amoghavajra are known to have been written in China centuries earlier, and directly in Chinese. A substantial part of Amoghavajra's output thus comprises revisions of books already known in China, rather than new materials. Among the remaining, a good many cannot be found either in corresponding Sanskrit manuscripts or in Tibetan translation—at least not in the form in which Amoghavajra presents them. Much of what his texts tell us unquestionably goes back to Indian sources; he was clearly working fully within the Tantric Buddhist tradition, but often more as an author or compiler than as a translator in our sense of the term.[11]

Approaching Amoghavajra with reference to a discrete "sect" or "school of Buddhism," either explicitly or implicitly, was problematized by Robert Sharf in his essay "On Esoteric Buddhism in China."[12] Therein, Sharf questions the dominant constructions of "Esoteric Buddhism" and argues that there is little indigenous evidence that esoteric Buddhism was recognized as a distinct teaching of Buddhism in Tang China, arguing that "it was not until the end of the tenth century, well after the eminent Indian masters of the Tang had come and gone, that Chinese commentators began to group certain practices, doctrines, and teachers under the explicit rubric of esotericism."[13] The construction of esoteric Buddhism and, by implicit extension, representations of Amoghavajra that had informed prior scholarship were, in Sharf's view, predicated on the anachronistic projection of Japanese sectarian assumptions onto Tang dynasty historical figures. Consequently, Sharf conjectured that "the teachings of Śubhākarasiṃha and his countrymen were most likely viewed as a powerful new technology for gaining control over supernatural forces rather than as an independent or competing lineage, school, or vehicle."[14]

Richard McBride is among the contemporary scholars who share Sharf's negative response to the question of whether Amoghavajra's Buddhism was understood in the Tang dynasty as a sect or school of Chinese Buddhism. In his 2004 article "Is There Really Esoteric Buddhism?," McBride argues that Amoghavajra did not conceive of the teaching that he propagated as a tradition separate from Mahāyāna Buddhism. Specifically, he argued that Amoghavajra did not use the term "esoteric teaching" (*mijiao* 密教) to indicate anything other than advanced

Mahāyāna.[15] McBride seeks to demonstrate this by first illustrating that authors of earlier periods employed the term *mijiao* to refer to the Great Vehicle Teaching and then providing an example of Amoghavajra deploying the term in a similar manner. He makes a similar argument in his study of *dhāraṇī* and spells in medieval China.[16]

Taking a different approach to the question of whether Amoghavajra's Buddhism was represented and understood to be a distinct school of Buddhism, Charles Orzech has consistently argued in the affirmative. In his early work, Orzech understands the Buddhism presented by Śubhakarasiṃha, Vajrabodhi, and, especially, Amoghavajra as a definable Buddhist tradition that he refers to as "Chen-yen."[17] His fundamental argument is fully elaborated in his *Politics and Transcendent Wisdom*.[18] Therein, Orzech conceives of Chinese esoteric Buddhism as historically and conceptually distinct from the cognate traditions of Indian esoteric Buddhism ("Vajrayāna," as he refers to it in this work) and Japanese Shingon:

> Vajrayāna Buddhism properly speaking is the systematic blending of tantric practices with Buddhist Mahāyāna theology which took place in North India from the eighth century onward. Esoteric Buddhism (*Mijiao*) is usually identified as the system of tantric practice and Mahāyāna theology which took form in China under the leadership of Bukong (Amoghavajra), and it encompasses traditions that draw their lineages from him and other Tang dynasty teachers. *Zhenyan* (Japanese *Shingon*, Sanskrit *Mantra*) is also used to designate this movement. I think this designation is a projection of Japanese sectarian notions on Chinese Esoteric Buddhism . . . Chinese Esoteric Buddhism is further blended with Vajrayāna teachings in the late ninth century through the efforts of the last wave of India Buddhist missionaries and translators, and then in the twelfth century and after by teachings imported by the Mongols.[19]

Regarding the question of whether to understand Amoghavajra as a transmitter of an Indian articulation of Buddhism or as an innovator who crafted an articulation of Buddhism for a Sinitic cultural environment, Orzech understands him to be the latter. In Orzech's view, in his early work, texts and rituals were created in China by Amoghavajra and his immediate Chinese disciples by combining indigenous traditions (specifically those surrounding the Sinitic sage-king) with esoteric Buddhist ritual structure derived from the *Diamond Pinnacle Scripture* to develop rituals specifically for imperial patrons.[20] The essential elements of this approach and model are repeated in Orzech's 2006 article "The 'Great Teaching of Yoga,' the Chinese Appropriation of the Tantras and the Question of Esoteric Buddhism."[21] In part crafted as a response to the critical challenges of Sharf and McBride, with a careful reading of Amoghavajra's works in relation to the Song dynasty constructions of Zanning, Orzech seeks to demonstrate that references to esoteric Buddhism in the Tang dynasty are not entirely predicated on the a priori suppositions of later scholiasts and scholars.[22]

Adopting a position not unrelated to Sharf's negative appraisal, Paul Copp argues that the Buddhist texts and practices presented in China by Śubhākarasiṃha, Vajrabodhi, and Amoghavajra were not understood to have been representative of a distinct Buddhist teaching but were instead received as articulations of precedent *dhāraṇī* spell traditions.[23] Like Sharf, Copp also reads Zanning's Song dynasty representations of Amoghavajra and his Buddhism as evidence that there was not a local, Chinese understanding of esoteric Buddhism as a defined teaching or of Amoghavajra as one of its principal transmitters. Rather, Copp understands Amoghavajra's Buddhism to have been received and understood in terms of established Chinese *dhāraṇī* spell practices.[24]

Adopting a position similar to Orzech's, Geoffrey Goble argues that Amoghavajra's Buddhism was presented and received as a discrete, sectarian form of Buddhism and that it was predicated exclusively on Indian textual and practical sources rather than having been consciously manufactured in order to appeal to a Chinese audience.[25] On the basis of material drawn primarily from the *Memorials and Edicts*, Goble argues that Amoghavajra successfully established his Buddhism as a sectarian tradition on the basis of winning the support of the Tang ruling elite. In his view, the patronage that Amoghavajra enjoyed from the ruling elite resulted in large measure from the appeal of siddhi for the ruling elite and the absence of behavioral prohibitions for lay practitioners of his esoteric Buddhism. The most significant siddhi, in Goble's view, were subjugation siddhi (Sanskrit *abhicāra*), according to which human enemies could be targeted for disease, disaster, and death. This element and application of Amoghavajra's Buddhism was particularly suited to the sociopolitical moment, as the Tang government was seriously threatened at the time by persistent rebellion and invasion. Amoghavajra's Buddhism was employed to counter and eliminate these threats, and their perceived effectiveness led directly to Amoghavajra's elite patronage and official adoption of his Buddhism by the Tang central government.[26]

Open Questions and Areas for Future Research. Aside from what is likely to be an ongoing question concerning how best to understand the presentation and reception of Amoghavajra's Buddhism in China, there remain a number of open questions and areas rich for exploration in future research. What follows are potential avenues of inquiry:

- Robert Sharf has suggested that Chan Buddhism of the late Tang and Song dynasties was informed by certain esoteric Buddhist tropes.[27] What other practices and figures, if any, from Amoghavajra's esoteric Buddhism were incorporated into sectarian and mainstream articulations of Chinese Buddhism from the late Tang onward?
- What is the relationship between Amoghavajra's Buddhism and later esoteric texts, practices, and the figures who produced them in the late Tang and Song? What genealogical relationship, if any, can be found between the texts produced by Amoghavajra and by later translators such as Prajñā 般若 (744–*c.* 810 CE)?[28] Were these later productions understood by historical Chinese exegetes to be related to Amoghavajra's Buddhism?
- Were later tantric texts and practices introduced to China from Tibet and during the Yuan dynasty (1271–1368 CE) understood to be related to the texts and practices associated with Amoghavajra by local exegetes and authors?
- Amoghavajra's esoteric Buddhism was heavily informed by Indic cultural norms (e.g., Vedic fire offerings, Vedic and Puranic deities, Sanskrit spells and terminology transliterated or represented directly in Siddham script, etc.). To what degree, if any, did the relatively large-scale importation of Indic cultural forms into Tang China via Amoghavajra's esoteric Buddhism influence or inform subsequent Chinese cultural forms?

- Particular articulations of Daoism from the Song dynasty onward appear to be informed by esoteric Buddhist practices and figures; for example, the incorporation of *mudrā* in Daoist ritual practice, an emphasis on wrathful terrible deities in Song dynasty Daoist movements, and the Indic deity Mārīcī appropriated as the Daoist Dipper Mother (*Doumu* 斗母). What demonstrable sources, relationships, or patterns of appropriation, if any, can be found between Amoghavajra's esoteric Buddhism and these elements of later Daoism?
- What relationship, if any, is there between Amoghavajra's esoteric Buddhism and esoteric Buddhist praxis in Korea, Japan, Vietnam, and Tibet? What do variations between these different expressions of esoteric Buddhism reveal about local articulations, cultural forms, and sources?
- What relationship, if any, is there between Amoghavajra's esoteric Buddhism and the *ācārya* teaching (*azheli jiao* 阿遮梨教) of the Sinitic Nanzhao kingdom (738–937 CE)? What practical, theoretical, and scriptural relationship, if any, is there between Amoghavajra's esoteric Buddhism and the *ācārya* teaching? Do these constitute entirely different transmissions and local articulations of tantric teachings? If so, what does this reveal about the historical modes and avenues by which Indic tantric materials came to and were incorporated in the Sinitic cultural sphere?
- What relationship, if any, is there between Amoghavajra's esoteric Buddhism and that which is represented by the figure of Liu Benzun 柳本尊 (855–907 CE) commemorated in the Dazu 大足 rock carvings at Boading shan 寶頂山 in Sichuan?[29] As with the questions concerning the *ācārya* teaching of Nanzhao, does Liu Benzun represent an entirely different transmission and local articulation of tantric teachings? If so, what does this reveal about the historical modes and avenues by which Indic tantric materials came to and were incorporated in the Sinitic cultural sphere?
- What role, if any, does Amoghavajra's esoteric Buddhism play in contemporary revival movements in the People's Republic of China, in Taiwan, and in diaspora Chinese communities?

FURTHER READING

Copp, Paul F. *The Body Incantatory: Spells and the Ritual Imagination in Medieval Chinese Buddhism*. New York: Columbia University Press, 2014.

Giebel, Rolf W., trans. *Two Esoteric Sutras: The Adamantine Pinnacle Sutra and the Susiddhikara Sutra*. Berkeley, CA: Numata Center for Buddhist Translation and Research, 2001.

Giebel, Rolf W., trans. *The Vairocanabhisambodhi Sutra*. Berkeley, CA: Numata Center for Buddhist Translation and Research, 2006.

Goble, Geoffrey C. "The Legendary Siege of Anxi: Myth, History, and Truth in Chinese Buddhism." *Pacific World: Journal of the Institute of Buddhist Studies*, third series 15 (Fall 2013): 1–32.

Goble, Geoffrey C. *Chinese Esoteric Buddhism: Amoghavajra, the Ruling Elite, and the Emergence of a Tradition*. New York: Columbia University Press, 2019.

Lehnert, Martin. "Amoghavajra: His Role in and Influence on the Development of Buddhism." In *Esoteric Buddhism and the Tantras in East Asia*. Edited by Charles D. Orzech, Henrik Hjort Sorensen, and Richard Karl Payne, 351–359. Leiden, The Netherlands: Brill, 2011.

McBride, Richard D. "Is There Really Esoteric Buddhism?" *Journal of the International Association of Buddhist Studies* 27, no. 2 (2004): 329–356.

Orzech, Charles D. "The 'Great Teaching of Yoga,' the Chinese Appropriation of the Tantras and the Question of Esoteric Buddhism." *Journal of Chinese Religions* 34, no. 1 (2006): 29–78.

Orzech, Charles D., Henrik Hjort Sorensen, and Richard Karl Payne. *Esoteric Buddhism and the Tantras in East Asia*. Leiden, The Netherlands: Brill, 2011.

Sharf, Robert. *Coming to Terms with Chinese Buddhism*. Honolulu: University of Hawai'i Press, 2002.

NOTES

1. Dong Hao, *Quan Tang wen* (Beijing: Zhonghua shu ju, 1983), Fascicle 506, pp. 19–21.
2. Yi-liang Chou, "Tantrism in China," *Harvard Journal of Asiatic Studies* 8, no. 3/4 (March 1945): 285n1. Reprinted in Richard K. Payne, ed., *Tantric Buddhism in East Asia* (Boston: Wisdom Publications, 2005).
3. Charles D. Orzech, *Politics and Transcendent Wisdom: The Scripture for Humane Kings in the Creation of Chinese Buddhism* (University Park: Pennsylvania State University Press, 1998); and Charles D. Orzech, "The 'Great Teaching of Yoga,' the Chinese Appropriation of the Tantras and the Question of Esoteric Buddhism," *Journal of Chinese Religions* 34, no. 1 (2006): 29–78.
4. Ryūichi Abé, *The Weaving of Mantra: Kūkai and the Construction of Esoteric Discourse* (New York: Columbia University Press, 1999), 120–127.
5. Tsukamoto Zenryū, "Tō chūki irai no chōan no kotokushi," in *Chūgoku chūsei bukkyōshi ronkō*, vol. 3 by Tsukamoto Zenryū (Tokyo: Daitō shuppansha, 1975), 251–284.
6. Wang Qinrou 王欽若, ed., *Cefu yuangui* (冊府元龜) (Beijing: Zhonghu shuju, 1960), fascicle 194, pp. 23b–24a; fascicle 25, pp. 17a–17b.
7. Wang Qinruo, *Cefu Yuangui*, fascicle 52, pp. 19b–20a.
8. Chou, "Tantrism in China."
9. Seigai Ōmura 大付西崖, *Mikkyō hattatsu-shi* (密教発達史), 2 vols. (Tokyo: Bukkyō Kankōkai Zuzōbu, 1918; repr. 1972); and Shoun Toganō, 栂尾祥雲, *Himitsu Bukkyō Shi* (秘密佛教史) (Kyoto: Koyasan Daigaku Mikkyō Bunkaa Kenkyujo, 1982).
10. Michel Strickmann, "Homa in East Asia," in *Agni: The Vedic Ritual of the Fire Altar*, ed. Frits Staal (Berkeley: University of California Press, 1982), 418; and Michel Strickmann, *Chinese Magical Medicine*, ed. Bernard Faure (Stanford, CA: Stanford University Press, 2002), 198.
11. Strickmann, *Chinese Magical Medicine*, 229. See also Michel Strickmann, *Mantras et Mandarins: Le Boudhisme Tantrique en Chine* (Paris: Gallimard, 1996), 80–81.
12. Robert Sharf, "On Esoteric Buddhism in China," in *Coming to Terms with Chinese Buddhism*, by Robert H. Sharf (Honolulu: University of Hawai'i Press, 2002), 263–278.
13. Sharf, "On Esoteric Buddhism," 269.
14. Sharf, "On Esoteric Buddhism," 269.
15. Richard D. McBride, "Is There Really Esoteric Buddhism?," *Journal of the International Association of Buddhist Studies* 27, no. 2 (2004): 350–351.
16. Richard D. McBride, "Dharani and Spells in Medieval Sinitic Buddhism," *Journal of the International Association of Buddhist Studies* 28, no. 1 (2005): 85–114.
17. Charles D. Orzech, "Seeing Chen-Yen Buddhism: Traditional Scholarship and the Vajrayāna in China," *History of Religions* 29, no. 2 (1989): 87–114.
18. Orzech, *Politics and Transcendent Wisdom*.
19. Orzech, *Politics and Transcendent Wisdom*, 135–136.
20. Orzech, *Politics and Transcendent Wisdom*, 170–171.
21. Orzech, " 'Great Teaching of Yoga,' " 29–78.

22. Orzech, " 'Great Teaching of Yoga.' "
23. Paul F. Copp, *The Body Incantatory: Spells and the Ritual Imagination in Medieval Chinese Buddhism* (New York: Columbia University Press, 2014).
24. Copp, *Body Incantatory*, 199–200, 212–218.
25. Geoffrey C. Goble, *Chinese Esoteric Buddhism: Amoghavajra, the Ruling Elite, and the Emergence of a Tradition* (New York: Columbia University Press, 2019).
26. Goble, *Chinese Esoteric Buddhism*.
27. Robert Sharf, "Buddhist Veda and the Rise of Chan," in *Chinese and Tibetan Esoteric Buddhism*, ed. Yael Bentor and Meir Shahar (Leiden, The Netherlands: Brill, 2017), 85–120.
28. Orzech, " 'Great Teaching of Yoga.' "
29. Angela Falco Howard, *Summit of Treasures: Buddhist Cave Art of Dazu, China* (Trumbull, CT: Weatherhill, 2001).

Geoffrey Goble

ART, ARCHITECTURE, AND NATIONAL MEMORY-MAKING

Works of religious art and architecture convey multiple and potentially overlapping meanings that span the spiritual and the sensual, the emotional and the intellectual, the personal and the collective. Scholars of religion and material culture have pointed to the inadequacy of the terms "art" and "artworks" to encompass the variety of social uses of, and social responses to, religious artifacts ("architecture" is less problematic a term, for it denotes built structures that are primarily utilitarian).[1] Depending on the modality of reception enacted by beholders, a buddha image may be approached as a visual aide to meditation, an icon whose apotropaic and soteriological powers can be invoked through prayer, a civic or national symbol, an artifact with archaeological or art historical significance, and an aesthetically pleasing *object d'art*. Social responses to religious artworks—as, indeed, to artworks generally—also include censure and repudiation, of which iconoclasm is the most extreme form, as shown most dramatically by the Taliban blasting in 2001 of the colossal rock-cut buddha images in the Bamiyan valley of Afghanistan.[2] As carriers of multiple meanings and mnemonic associations, works of religious art and architecture are the object of disparate identitarian claims—and occasionally disclaims. For analytical purposes, one can distinguish these claims into confessional, cultural, and political, even though such distinctions are problematic, especially when referred to in historical contexts.

This article reflects on the relation of Buddhist art and architecture to the formation of national cultures and identities in 19th- and 20th-century Asia, focusing in particular on India, Japan, and Thailand. The article highlights the productive tension, most clearly manifest in the built landscape and in designated cultural venues such as temples and museums, between the persistent cultic significance of Buddhist sites and artifacts, and their historical and artistic significance as evidence of individual nations' civilizational achievement. Cult value and exhibition value, as theorized by Walter Benjamin with regard to the history of Western art, are not incompatible or mutually exclusive, for the artwork's aura, intrinsic to its magical and religious origins, survived in its post-Renaissance (or "disenchanted") afterlife as a museum exhibit (though not, for Benjamin, in the era of its technological mass replication).[3] Devotees' habit in Southeast Asia of hanging flower garlands around buddha images not just in temples, but also in state-managed museums and archaeological parks, illustrates the conflation of cult value and exhibition value in the current reception of Buddhist art and architecture.

SACRED OBJECTS BETWEEN IMPERMANENCE AND THE CULT OF TRACES

The modern-day tension between the cultic and exhibition values of Buddhist art redoubles the ambivalent attitude toward objects that is inherent in Buddhism. On the one hand, Buddhism—not unique among religions but with greater doctrinal acumen—promotes an ascetic ideal, exemplified by monastic life, by stressing the ephemerality of both material and mental objects. On the other hand, artifacts—from the portable (relics, icons, amulets, rosaries) to the immovable (reliquaries, temples, rock-carved shrines)—have long had great importance in Buddhist practice as didactic tools and aides to meditation, liturgical implements, and markers of sacred space. The validity of replication in Buddhist visual culture can be appreciated as a strategy to both alleviate cultural anxiety about the physical decay of sacred objects and to multiply their potency via the production of copies.[4] The tension, which for Rambelli "runs through the entire history of Buddhism," between the doctrinal tenets of impermanence (Sanskrit, *anitya*; Pali, *anicca*) and non-attachment (Skt., *naiskramya*; P., *nekkhamma*) on the one hand, and the veneration and replication as well as reconstruction of sacred objects and sites on the other, is crucially mediated by merit-making. This practice, much emphasized in both canonical and extracanonical texts, makes it possible for laypeople to accumulate karmic merit by donating to the monastic community (Skt., *samgha*; P., *sangha*) and also by contributing to the copying of the scriptures and the making of images and reliquaries. The *Lotus Sutra*, one of the most venerated Mahayana texts, encourages the crafting of buddha images in more or less precious materials, even as it affirms that replication of the buddha's words is more meritorious than replication of his image.[5] Copies of the sutras produced in medieval China and Japan possessed, in fact, a distinctive material quality by being written with gold and silver ink on paper, as well as on a variety of materials: silk, tiles, shells, stones, and even—writ large—rock faces.[6]

Veneration of reliquaries, images, and sutras is motivated not only by their function as stand-ins for the buddha, but also by the belief that they possess thaumaturgic properties as objects, not unlike Christian relics and icons.[7] The latter belief stemmed from the initial worship of the historic Buddha Sakyamuni's corporeal remains (Skt., *sarira*; Skt. and P., *dathu*), or what a scholar felicitously termed "the cult of the sacred traces."[8] A trace, both as a physical remnant and as an immaterial sign or mental image (as in Sigmund Freud's notion of mnemic trace), is by nature a mnemonic device—a reminder (i.e., a monument, from the Latin *monumentum*) as much as a remainder (i.e., a relic, from the Latin *reliquia*). Theravadin commentaries composed in Sri Lanka around the middle of the first millennium CE list four classes of sacred remainders, or *cetiya* (a Pali term etymologically related to two cognate verbal roots meaning, respectively, "to remind" and "to construct"): bodily relics and reliquaries; scriptures and inscriptions; objects physically associated to the buddha (alms bowls and footprints, also termed "contact relics"); and representational objects (images and shrines, also termed "commemorative relics").[9] Sacred objects recall the buddha by an association that is either direct (i.e., indexical) or indirect (i.e., iconic). One can accordingly speak with Rambelli, of a Buddhist semiotic system of objects, which "classifies sacred objects on the basis of the modality in which the sacred is produced or manifested in them."[10]

Didactic tools to spread the doctrine as well as physical foci of devotion when considered synchronically, sacred objects have been mobilized by a variety of historical actors, such as monastic chapters, monarchs, and colonial and national governments. The nexus of piety and power is embodied in the Buddhist tradition by the widely emulated figure of the Mauryan Emperor Asoka (r. 268–232 BCE). While historically Asoka memorialized his pious kingship by erecting freestanding pillars (twenty of which are still extant), his biographers instead credited him with building throughout his kingdom 84,000 monumental reliquaries (Skt. *stupa*; P., *thupa*), which enshrined the ashes from the Buddha Sakyamuni's cremation, originally buried according to the tradition under eight stupas (in extracanonical texts, eight and its multiple 84,000 are numerical signs that connote the buddha's infinitude and incommensurability). Notwithstanding the lack of archaeological evidence to support it, the Asoka legend established that in addition to providing for the monastic community, erecting reliquaries is too a means for the accumulation of merit; in fact, an alternative version of the legend recorded in a Sinhalese chronicle states that Asoka erected monasteries, not stupas.[11]

Chinese and Japanese emperors, whose authority was ideologically rooted in local belief systems (Dao and Shintō, respectively) that syncretized variously with Buddhism after its introduction, entertained an ambivalent relationship with Buddhism that oscillated between support and persecution. Accordingly, imperial patronage of Buddhist monasteries and temples was countered by cyclical waves of iconoclasm in both China and Japan.[12] Southeast Asian monarchs, on the other hand, drew legitimacy by being their kingdoms' prime Buddhist patrons, as evidenced by their moniker of "righteous king" (P., *dhammaraja*). This early pattern shaped local notions of political authority lastingly, for the Buddhist legitimation of power has remained a prominent feature of politics in Southeast Asia.[13] Colonial governments made the royal mission of religious patronage their own by substituting knowledge production for merit-making; in so doing, the Buddhist cult of traces was adapted to modern realities. While scholars in metropolitan institutes of learning produced philological editions of the Buddhist canon, scholar-officials in the colonial service conducted surveys and restorations of Buddhist monuments. In places like India, where Buddhism was almost extinguished as a living religion, their activity of architectural restoration had a profound impact on the proto-nationalist imagination. Concurrently, Buddhist artifacts—from small clay tablets to statues and architectural reliefs, often newly excavated by Western archaeologists—came be collected and exhibited in museums that were established both in colonial capitals and in the cities of sovereign Japan and Siam (now Thailand). In the latter countries, cultic artifacts were epistemically reconfigured, in the context of ongoing Buddhist worship, as works of art and fit into art historical periods by pairing history of art and dynastic history; a correspondence was also sought between their aesthetic qualities and the ethnic identity of their putative makers.

The colonial reconstitution of historic Buddhist monuments since the later 19th century may have forced their afterlife as multireligious cultic sites into the scholarly straightjacket of a textual Buddhism that was divorced from actual devotional practice and its material accoutrements; yet it also laid the ground for their successive afterlife as identarian symbols for postcolonial nation-states. This function as national memory sites has been redoubled since the 1970s by inscription on the UNESCO World Heritage List, whereby Buddhist monumental sites have acquired international fame as tourist destinations in addition to their significance as pilgrimage sites.

BUDDHIST SITES BETWEEN SACRED LANDSCAPE AND NATIONAL MEMORIAL LANDSCAPE

Much has been written in recent years on the role of the natural and built landscape in anchoring social memory and collective identities.[14] The sociocultural study of memory, pioneered in the 1930s by Maurice Halbawchs, sees in physical spatial structures and mental spatial images prime catalysts of recollection. Halbawchs based his theory of the collective frameworks of memory on the Holy Land's "legendary topography," which is characterized by the presence of "sacred places [that] commemorate . . . beliefs born perhaps not far from those places and strengthened by taking root in this environment . . . [which] focus most frequently on facts of a supernatural kind."[15] Typified by the occurrence and subsequent commemoration of numinous and historical events, respectively, sacred Buddhist landscape and national memorial landscape in Asian countries share a territory that is marked culturally by sites that are at once foci of cult and of cultural recollection.

Buddhism's legendary topography is anchored in four sites in the Gangetic plains where the life of the Buddha Sakyamuni unfolded: Lumbini, his birthplace; Bodh Gaya, the place of his enlightenment; Sarnath, the place of his first sermon; and Kusinagara, his death place. As early pilgrimage centers, these four locales spatialized the memory of key events in the life of the historic buddha, and thus in the public history of Buddhism. From the second century BCE onward, Lumbini, Bodh Gaya, Sarnath, and Kusinagara were evoked iconically on sculptural reliefs—most famously those of the Great Stupa at Sanchi—in the shape of, respectively, a footprint (Skt. and P., *buddhapada*), a bodhi tree, the wheel of dharma (Skt., *dharmachakra*; P., *dhammachakra*), and a stupa. Besides having an iconic presence within the visual repertoire of early Buddhist art, the four key sites of the sacred Buddhist topography were spatially replicated throughout East and Southeast Asia. Footprints—impressions allegedly made by the buddha during his mythical peregrinations—were fathomed in natural rock formations and also hand-carved, as were *dharmachakra*. Bodhi trees were, like veritable relics, transplanted elsewhere, every sample supposedly stemming from the original tree that had shaded the Buddha Sakyamuni during his meditation sessions at Bodh Gaya, and which became early on the focus of worship. Stupas, which had originated as funerary mounds for northern Indian royalty, became through geographical diffusion, and consequent regional stylistic adaptation, the Buddhist monuments par excellence.[16]

The proliferation of stupas first in India, then in the rest of Asia, signaled the Buddhist assimilation of landscapes that were believed to be inhabited by animistic spirits and chthonic deities; features of the landscape that were worshipped as the abodes of nature spirits (mountain peaks, caves, trees), were wrested away from animistic cults by Buddhist hermits, who established their lodgings there.[17] Memory of those early monastic dwellings later inspired the cutting of shrines in the rock—from Ajanta and Ellora in India to Mogao and Dunhuang in China—that acquired great fame for their lavish painted and sculptural decorations, which were realized as acts of piety.[18] As Paul Mus put it, "the map of the sacred sites of Buddhism, marked by a multitude of stupas, can be superimposed upon the map of local spirits."[19] Buddhism's assimilation of the animistic belief that "the locality is itself a god" (again in Mus's words) underpins the credence that a stupa-enshrined relic bestows its supernatural potency on the host locality. Thus, at the center of the earliest cities founded by the Thais in the

13th and 14th centuries there stood a generically named "monastery of the great relic" (*wat mahathat*). In order to be accorded the privilege to host a buddha relic, a locality must, however, first prove the ability to safeguard it. Buddhist lore in Southeast Asia abounds with narratives of relics that signaled approbation, or conversely disapproval, of the site selected for building a stupa by performing marvels (flying, emitting rays, etc).[20]

A newly built stupa achieved cultic status by claiming lineage from an already revered reliquary, which was evoked through the acquisition of a share of its relics or architectural imitation, according to an aesthetic of replication that applies also to buddha images. Looking up to Sri Lanka as the fountainhead of (Theravada) Buddhism, Thai and Burmese rulers sustained spiritual and mnemonic connections to the island via monastic missions; the importation of duplicates of relics, sutras, and images; and the replication within their kingdoms of famed Lankan monuments and holy sites, such as the gigantic buddha footprint on Mount Sumanata. The replication of topographical and architectural features is a practice not only generative of karmic merit, but also constitutive of cultural memory, which, for Jan Assmann, is intrinsically connected to religion and its textual, ritual, and material forms.[21]

The reliquary tower at Bodh Gaya, pivot of the Mahabodhi temple complex, was imitated in Burma and northern Thailand, and as far as China and Tibet, thanks to the circulation of small-scale models and terracotta plaques impressed with its effigy. While the monumentalization of the Bodh Gaya site began as early as Asoka's time, the Mahabodhi temple might be regarded as "a living record of additions and reconstructions," reflecting continuous veneration, not exclusively Buddhist. The earliest reconstruction occurred probably around the 5th century CE; a railing was added in the 6th century; and a gateway was built in the 8th century during the Buddhist revival promoted by the Pala dynasty.[22] At this time, a branch of the bodhi tree in the Lankan city of Anuradhapura, which had grown from a branch of the Bodh Gaya tree Asoka had reportedly gifted to the Sinhalese king, was brought back to Bodh Gaya in a virtuous cycle of (re-)transplanting across the Buddhist world. Translocal connections are also illustrated by the missions that, from the 11th century onward, the Burmese kings of Bagan, in their role as patrons of Buddhism, sent to Bodh Gaya to repair the Mahabodhi. Firsthand examination by Burmese stonemasons probably inspired the construction of similar monastic complexes in Bagan and Pegu, as well as in Chiangmai, the center of the neighboring northern Thai kingdom of Lanna.[23] The last Burmese mission reached Bodh Gaya as late as 1877, when a rest house for pilgrims was built there. Only a few years later, the Archaeological Survey of India under the direction of Alexander Cunningham initiated the reconstruction of the Mahabodhi reliquary tower. According to the archaeologist Himanshu Prabha Ray, the reconstruction transformed what was a "living" religious site, at which both Buddhists and Hindus worshipped (a devotional ecumenism that contrasted with the view held by orientalist scholars of Buddhism and Hinduism as antagonistic faiths), into a "historic"—and exclusively Buddhist—monument.[24]

Ray's critique resonates implicitly with Pierre Nora's conceptual polarity of *milieux de mémoire*, in which living traditions are part of everyday practice, and *lieux de mémoire*, in which memory is solidified into objects and places (the latter proliferated in Europe during the age of revolutions and industrialization to compensate for the disappearance of the former).[25] Yet while intangible cultural artifacts such as national days and anthems are capable of bonding a community emotionally simply by being performed, physical monuments and cultural repositories such as museums, libraries, and archives can hardly exist without institutional tutelage. The monumentalization of the Mahabodhi temple by the Archaeological Survey of India can be considered as the necessary premise for the postcolonial repossession of Buddhism and its material legacy by postindependence India's first prime minister, Jawaharlal Nehru, as an essential part of Indian national identity and cultural heritage.[26] Enshrined into the very birth of the Republic of India was the political gesture of the repatriation in the late 1940s of Buddhist relics that had been removed some 80 years earlier from the Sanchi stupa to the India Museum (later the Victoria and Albert Museum) in London.[27]

Nehru's authoritative international profile supported the postcolonial repossession of even Indonesia's Buddhist monumental heritage. In 1950, during his state visit to Java, Nehru was taken by President Sukarno on a visit to the 9th-century CE Buddhist monumental complex of Borobudur. During the war of independence against the Dutch that followed the end of the Pacific War, Borobudur lay in an area controlled by the Indonesian republican government, which in 1946 even established an archaeological unit to boost its legitimacy. In 1948, while the anticolonial armed struggle was still ongoing, the Indonesians invited two experts from newly independent India to assess the conditions of Borobudur, which had deteriorated rapidly since the major restoration carried out by Dutch archaeologists in 1907–1911. Against this background, the visit by Nehru and his retinue (which included his daughter and later prime minister, Indira, and the Indian Archaeological Service's director general) evoked not only the remote history of the Indian Ocean's maritime exchanges by which Buddhism had been exported to Southeast Asia, but also a postcolonial scenario of cultural diplomacy fostered by the preservation of Buddhist monuments as an essential part of the national heritage of both India and Indonesia, despite the marginal following enjoyed by Buddhism in the two countries.[28]

Because of the ethnic and religious fault lines around which postcolonial identities formed in South and Southeast Asia, perception of Buddhist monuments as embodiments of national history and cultural identity is not always undisputed, however. Today Borobudur is celebrated primarily as evidence of the grandeur of the pre-Islamic Javanese kingdom of Majapahit as well as a symbol of Indonesia's international status (it was the country's first site to be inscribed on the World Heritage List in 1991 together with the nearby Hindu temple of Prambanan); only secondarily is Borobudur honored as a site sacred to the tiny minority of Indonesian Buddhists. By contrast, the Tooth Relic Temple in the Sri Lankan city of Kandy, also a World Heritage Site, is the main domestic pilgrimage destination as well as the key mnemonic site of Sinhala ethnic identity. Both Borobudur and the Tooth Relic Temple were targeted by iconoclasts—the former in 1985 by unknown hands; the latter in 1989 by the Sri Lankan communist party's military wing, and again, and most gravely, in 1998 by the Tamil Tigers separatist guerrillas. The motivations behind the attacks reflected, however, opposite logics of disavowal. In Muslim-majority Indonesia, the nationalist reclaiming of the pre-Islamic Hindu–Buddhist past and its cultural legacy has been contested by the Islamic intelligentsia since the 1930s; the statement issued in 1985 by the then President Suharto, who blamed the perpetrators as "people who don't feel national pride," indirectly revisited this domestic diatribe.[29] In Sri Lanka, the promotion of an ethno-Buddhist nationalism by the Sinhala majority led to the exclusion of the Tamil Hindu minority from participation in government and the resulting civil war, which lasted from 1983 to 2009. In this context, the Tooth Relic

Temple was arguably targeted as a symbol of Sinhala dominance, which is at once ethnic, religious, and political, rather than specifically as a Buddhist monument (the bombing, which caused also eleven fatalities, was carried out close to the celebrations for the 50th anniversary of Sri Lanka's independence, revealingly organized in Kandy, the island's precolonial royal center, rather than in Colombo, the colonial and now national capital).[30]

BUDDHA IMAGES BETWEEN THE TEMPLE AND THE MUSEUM

The role of museums in forging cultural identities organic to the political construct of the nation-state has been a commonplace in academic literature since the turn of the 1990s. The removal of cultural artifacts from Asia, as well as Africa and Oceania, to museums in (now ex-) imperial metropolises is the crux of the postcolonial critique of Western museology.[31] In her examination of the Western museum's development, from Renaissance princely collection to key cultural institution of the modern state, Carol Duncan likens museums to cultic sites as spaces that are "carefully marked off and culturally designated" for the performance of the "secular ritual of citizenship," which enables visitors "to achieve liminal experience—to move beyond the psychic constrains of mundane existence, step out of time, and attain new, larger perspectives."[32] The typical colonial foundation and postcolonial trajectory of most Asian museums admittedly differ from the European and North American case. Still, Duncan's analogy between museums and temples (whose architecture is often openly evoked by the designers of not only 19th-century museum buildings, but also current exhibits of religious art) as both setting visitors on a ritualized experiential path carries a strong transcultural resonance.[33] Likewise, the argument by Bennet and others that the social and aesthetic disciplining of viewers was the central objective of the museum as a nation-building project, though arguably overstated, strikes an analogy with the disciplinarian dimension of ritual, which affects not only worshippers but the objects of worship as well.[34] As Sharf argues, "If the museum acts to curtail or restrain the power of sacred icons, so too does the temple."[35]

The centrality of image worship throughout the Buddhist world cannot be overstated. Whether images are revered as supernatural entities that can be ritually animated, or as didactic tools (ancient Chinese texts qualify Buddhism as "the teaching of the icons"), their fashioning in a wide range of materials—wood (especially prized varieties such as sandalwood or camphorwood), stone, stucco, clay, bronze—promoted technology and craftsmanship throughout Asia.[36] Sculpting and casting images involve not just manual skills, in fact; sculptors, stonecutters, and carpenters are traditionally required to perform rituals before applying themselves to their task. As is the case also for stupas, lineage matters to the status of buddha images, for every image is ideally a copy of the "original" Sandalwood Image (Japanese Buddhists identify it with a wooden image in Kyoto's Seiryoji Temple, which was imported from China at the end of the 10th century).[37] According to the legend, handed down in both Mahayana and Theravada extracanonical literature, the Sandalwood Image was fashioned on an Indian king's command by thirty-two artisans (one for each of the buddha's unique body marks); once crafted, the image rose up to greet the buddha upon his descent from heaven. The Sandalwood Image's self-revelation as a doppelganger of its living prototype makes the legend instructive on several levels. To start with, it validates image worship and the adoption of anthropomorphism in Buddhist visual culture, which for most scholars followed an earlier "aniconic" phase.[38] It also alludes to the role the artisan's visual memory plays in crafting an image, which must present the correct iconographic traits in order to be identifiable as the buddha, whereas its style, depending on the manual skills of individual artisans as well as on the taste of patrons, may vary.[39] Finally, it accounts for the animation rituals performed in various Buddhist liturgies (typically involving the insertion of relics or relic-like objects inside the image) to make inanimate matter come alive as did the Sandalwood Image.

In the Thai and Lao liturgical traditions, ritual animation is believed to even provide a buddha image with a distinctive personality. But ritual animation is not the sine-qua-non condition for an image to acquire a reputation for being miraculous, for such reputation often arches back to animistic beliefs in animated stones and tree-dwelling spirits, widespread in both East and Southeast Asia, which were supplanted by, or more precisely subsumed under, Buddhism (in Japan, ceremonies are still held to free the spirit of the stone or living tree in which an image is to be carved.[40]). The Phra Kaeo Morakot (the Emerald Buddha in English), the presiding image of the eponymous Bangkok temple, had for centuries enjoyed great veneration in the culturally homogenous region spanning present-day northern Thailand and western Laos. The statuette is actually made of a green variety of jasper that abounds in that region and that, despite its modest value, is regarded as the source of the image's alleged potency, whence its status as the tutelary image of Lao and Thai polities.

The Phra Kaeo's social life, like that of other buddha images of renown, is the subject of chronicles that constitute a distinct genre in the vernacular literatures of East and Southeast Asia.[41] In the formulaic structure of these chronicles, the titular image has its numinous origins in a mythical India and, like the hero of a picaresque novel, must undergo perilous journeys and survive near-fatal accidents before it can reach its final destination. The American art historian A. B. Griswold suggested that the Southeast Asian chronicles of buddha images contain clues of "traditions, or fragments of traditions pieced together, that are much more ancient than the time of compilation and much more ancient than the statues the compilers had in mind."[42] As textualizations by clerics of earlier oral legends about the transfer of Buddhism and associated sacra from South Asia, image chronicles were the medium for, as well as the product of, cultural memory about the translocal Buddhist connections that spiritually charged artifacts embodied. In the sections of the chronicles dealing with more recent times, and hence more factually reliable, the cult image's history is intertwined with the history of the host locality, which the image protected from political and natural upheavals in exchange for the care and protection it was offered by the local community.[43] A palladium's permanence in situ and physical integrity thus stood metonymically for the stability of a kingdom while its seizure and removal foreshadowed subjugation and dynastic collapse.

In both Asia and Europe, the expropriation of palladia from a vanquished polity by the victorious one was an important aspect of ancient and medieval warfare, whereby mutual relationships of domination and subjection were articulated on the political as well as symbolic plane: "Looted images could serve as potent reminders of past humiliations and as the basis for renewed struggle."[44] Such dynamics can again be studied through the Phra Kaeo's biography. After serving as the palladium of the Lao kingdom of Vientiane since its arrival there in the 1560s, in 1780 the Phra Kaeo was captured by the invading Thais, who made it the palladium of their new kingdom, founded in 1782 at Bangkok, where a temple for the image was built adjacent to the royal palace (the rite of the seasonal changing of the Phra

Kaeo's robe is still performed by the Thai sovereign or a representative of his). In the 1820s, after Lao hopes of recovering the Phra Kaeo had waned, the Vientiane ruler had a new jadeite image crafted and placed in a newly built temple. More than simply substituting for the captive Phra Kaeo, the new image served as a reminder of the former's seizure, and thus as a tool for the mobilization of anti-Thai sentiments in view of an ill-fated Lao insurrection that broke out in 1827. Military defeat resulted in the removal of yet more buddha images to Bangkok, including the notorious Phra Bang ("buddha image of little parts"), which is represented in the Thai chronicles as an antagonist of the Phra Kaeo and a harbinger of chaos; the Phra Bang had been previously seized by the Thais and then repatriated as persona non grata in 1783. In 1866, after people in Bangkok blamed a severe drought on the Lao buddha images that had been brought to the city, the court officials convinced King Mongkut to return them to Vientiane on the grounds that they were small and made of cheap materials, hence not worthy of royal patronage.[45]

Several Thai monasteries house collections of buddha images; in Bangkok, Wat Phra Chetuphon and Wat Bowonniwet store images that were brought downriver from Ayutthaya, the former royal capital, after the city was sacked by the Burmese in 1767. One of the latest and largest of these monastery collections was assembled at the turn of the 20th century in the cloister of the newly built Wat Benchamabophit (known in English as the Marble Temple), with the avowed intention of combining devotion and didactics. Fifty statues, both authentic and ad hoc-made replicas, were gathered "for public worship and as models for people to copy when making new images," according to the account by Prince Damrong Rajanubhab, then the minister of the interior and a renowned antiquarian celebrated as "the father of Thai history," who personally assembled the collection.[46] The buddha images in Wat Benchamabophit were displayed according to no particular criterion, for only in the 1920s was an art historical classification outlined by Prince Damrong together with the French scholar George Coedès, during his term as director of the Siamese Archaeological Service (Coedès drafted also a law that for the first time limited the export of antiquities from the kingdom, foregrounding their status as national property). At this juncture, the earlier chronicles of famed icons that spanned the Buddhist world of South and Southeast Asia gave way to a national history of art, which traced the ethnic and territorial origins of antiquities in Thailand as part of the wider nationalist project of mapping its historical landscape.

The Bangkok National Museum was inaugurated in 1926 by assembling the royal collection and artifacts that were kept in temples as well as newly recovered by the Archaeological Service; their exhibition reflected Coedès and Prince Damrong's eightfold art historical periodization encompassing the art and architecture produced before and after the Thais' settlement in the early centuries of the second millennium. Epigraphic records provided the basic chronology of the polities that since the 6th century had ruled over the various regions of what, by the start of the 20th century, had been incorporated into Thailand's national territory; art periods were identified in name and temporal scope with such polities. The kingdom of Sukhothai (*c.* 1240–1370), which by the start of the 19th century had almost entirely vanished from Thai social memory, was recovered from oblivion and lionized as the first independent polity established by the Thais after breaking free of Khmer domination. For Prince Damrong and Coedès, the Sukhothai period marked the apex of the Thai artistic genius, which generated a distinctive "national" style in sculpture and architecture, best represented by the novel iconographic type of the walking buddha image, by adroitly borrowing and adapting Sinhalese and Khmer art. Coedès later wrote that at Sukhothai "between 1250 and 1350, the Siamese were able to develop their own characteristic civilization, institutions and art."[47]

An analogous process had taken place in Japan in the 1890s, during the latter phase of the Meiji Restoration. Here too the epistemic and ideological resignification of Buddhist artifacts into national antiquities involved their selective removal from locations across the archipelago to Tokyo and to the prefecture capitals. The centralization of cultural properties paralleled the administrative centralization of a newly created national space, at once territorial and cultural. To support the mobilization of collective belief in the embryonic nation-state, artifacts that were still the foci of localized cults were converted, by relocation in newly established national museums (like those in Nara, inaugurated in 1895; and in Kyoto, opened in 1897), into expressions of an otherwise abstract national identity, whose prime manifestation was to be found in the spiritually infused aesthetic realm. As later in Thailand, the periodization of Japanese art and the compilation of a canon of masterpieces resulted from the collaboration of a Western scholar, the American Ernest Fenollosa, and his local pupil, Okakura Kakuzo.[48] In the wake of the desecration and demolition of monasteries that followed the imperial proclamation on the separation of Buddhism and Shintō in1872, in 1887 the Meiji authorities tasked Fenollosa with the registration of Buddhist sites and their repositories of cultural artifacts; this mission spearheaded state-driven historic conservation, which was given juridical formulation 10 years later by the Law for the Protection of Ancient Temples and Shrines.

The law of 1897 introduced the category of "national treasure" (*kokuho*), whereby designated shrines and temples were accorded government protection as well as funds for restoration. Among the artifacts designated as national treasures there was a most revered 7th-century wooden image of the Bodhisattva Avalokitesvara, called Kudara Kannon, which was removed from the Horyuji temple to the nearby Nara Museum when this opened in 1895, and then, after being temporarily returned to the temple in 1930, moved again in 1941 to a new building within the vast Horyuji monastic complex. Such "treasure galleries" within temple compounds have promoted the aesthetic and historic appreciation of Buddhist artifacts as representative of the Japanese national spirit. In the most recent Horyuji Treasure Gallery, rebuilt in 1998 in the traditional architectural style, the Kudara Kannon is displayed in the central section, encased in a vitrine like in an ordinary museum, but surrounded by Buddhist paraphernalia, including a donation box; in the gallery's basement, right underneath the image, more liturgical objects are stored. Not visible to visitors, such objects have the apparent function of demarcating an inner sacred space within the gallery's wider space as a site for aesthetic contemplation.[49]

BUDDHIST ART AND ARCHITECTURE BETWEEN PIOUS CARE AND SCIENTIFIC CONSERVATION

The tension between the cult and exhibition values of Buddhist works of art and architecture is redoubled by the tension between conservation-restoration as, on the one hand, a pious activity that generates karmic merit and, on the other hand, as a technical undertaking by national and international agencies responsible for the preservation of cultural heritage. In fact, piety-motivated care and professional conservation in Asia do not form a neat polarity, for restorers have often sought to reach a modus vivendi with the devotional attitude toward sacred artifacts. Despite the doctrinal emphasis on impermanence, preservation and restoration of Buddhist sites and artifacts are attested to in vernacular Buddhist literatures and epigraphic and historical records. A passage in a Thai stone inscription composed in Sukhothai in the late 13th century reports that people, after collecting "old broken statues of the buddha to worship . . . piece[d them] together and repair[ed them] with mortar"; the result were "large, fresh looking and exceedingly beautiful statues." A northern Thai poem written four centuries later likened the dilapidated colossal buddha images of Wat Phra Yuen (whose central reliquary was modeled after the Mahabodhi's) to human beings who, having "completed their passage through samsara . . . achieved nirvana and final release." And the chronicles of the Bangkok era record the construction in the mid-1850s of the Phra Pathom Chedi in Nakhom Pathom (central Thailand) over a ruined stupa, which for King Mongkut was ancient and enshrined a true relic (archaeologists presently date its origins to the mid to later first millennium CE). When the new stupa collapsed soon after its erection, it was again reconstructed; completed in 1870, the massive Phra Pathom Chedi was to be the world's tallest stupa for many years to come.[50]

The sacred status of an image or stupa does not in itself warrant salvaging once decay kicks in; investment of labor and financial resources is directed selectively within the Buddhist devotional economy, which, while acknowledging upkeep and restoration as merit-making activities, nevertheless privileges the construction of new reliquaries in the absence of a concern for the (art) historical value of ruined ones.[51]

Not a mere technical operation, restoration as traditionally practiced aims to reactivate the efficacy of an image or stupa as a potent object, physical integrity being the necessary condition for the inherence in it of the buddha. In Japanese as well as Tibetan Buddhist practice, for example, a buddha image must be temporarily deconsecrated and returned to the status of inanimate matter that preceded its animation before undertaking restoration; once this is completed, the eye-opening ceremony of awakening is performed again to reanimate the image.[52] Here pious care contrasts more sharply with conservation as a technical-scientific procedure handled by professionals that is consistent with the project of institutionalizing a common cultural heritage as the source of, and rallying point for, national identity.

The historic conservation of Buddhist sites by Thailand's Fine Arts Department (FAD) in the 1980s and 1990s exemplifies the attempt to integrate international protocol, cultural nationalism, and devotional practice. In 1985, toward the end of restoration work at the Sukhothai Historical Park in which the seamless integration of missing sculptural and architectural parts had been standard practice, FAD countered mounting academic criticism by amending the Act on Monuments and Antiques (1961). Echoing the 13th-century Sukhothai inscription that records the reparation of buddha images, the amended act negotiated the regulations of the 1964 International Charter for the Conservation of Monuments and Sites (also known as the Venice Charter), which prizes the authenticity of structure and materials. FAD motivated stylistic restoration of "archaeological buildings that are consecrated places well known to the local people" on the grounds that recognizable replacements of missing parts as prescribed by the protocol of scientific conservation "may diminish their values and credibility to people."[53] Far from being of exclusive concern to the heritage professionals, the FAD balancing of international guidelines and local cultural values raises important questions about conservation as an articulation of ideology. On the one hand, conservation of Buddhist "heritage sites" in countries like Thailand, Sri Lanka, and Burma is fraught with political dilemmas and potential ideological manipulations.[54] On the other hand, conservation protocols that claim universal validity are too historically contingent. Though admittedly overrestored by current standards, Sukhothai's Wat Mahathat stops short of the stylistic restoration that was prevalent in Europe in the latter half of the 19th century—exemplified by E. E. Viollet-le-Duc's interventions on French Gothic cathedrals and, in Asia, by the Archaeological Survey of India's integral reconstruction of the Mahabodhi Temple (detailed in the section "Buddhist Sites between Sacred Landscape and National Memorial Landscape").

Thailand, Sri Lanka, and Japan, among other countries in Asia, have promoted the reformulation of architectural authenticity upheld by ICOMOS (International Council of Monuments and Sites), an advisory body to UNESCO, as determined exclusively by the state of conservation of its material fabric. The Nara Document on Authenticity, drawn by ICOMOS in 1994, amends the notion of authenticity upheld under the World Heritage Convention (1972) by taking into account continuity in both use and land occupation of a built site as being integral to its cultural salience.[55] The Nara document takes its name from the Japanese medieval city where it was drafted. In the Nara prefecture lies the forest temple of Horyuji, founded in the 7th century soon after the coming of Buddhism to Japan from China via Korea, and a World Heritage Site. Within the vast temple complex stand timber edifices built according to the bay system of Chinese architecture, the foundational components of which are considered to be among the world's oldest, even though the edifices themselves have been reconstructed multiple times according to the time-honored carpentry technique that is itself part of Japan's intangible cultural heritage (and recognized as such in 2020 even by UNESCO).[56] Conservation practice that is an embodied form of cultural memory can be seen as the *trait d'union* between the sacred landscape animated by nature spirits, reliquaries, and temples, and the historical landscape whose monuments, museums, and archaeological parks testify to the nation's distinctive heritage and identity.

REVIEW OF LITERATURE

The extensive references provided in the endnotes and the additional works recommended in the section "Further Reading" stand in lieu of a comprehensive literature review, which this article's subject matter, straddling fields of scholarship not usually brought together into a consistent analysis, risks making incongruent. This literature review accordingly limits itself to surfacing these diverse fields. The study of Buddhist art and architecture was, until recently, the exclusive province of archaeologists and art historians primarily concerned with authenticating, dating, and classifying artifacts according to criteria of style or provenance. Unlike analogous classificatory labels (e.g., Islamic art), Buddhist art has rarely been treated comprehensively across geographical and historical partitions, but more often as one component of national artistic traditions (e.g., Thai art or Japanese art). The ideological assumptions underlying positivist taxonomies—from racial to museographical—have been questioned since the 1980s by the postcolonial critique of orientalist knowledge. The widening of art history's analytical scope prompted by the new disciplinary fields of visual and material culture studies and heritage studies on the one hand, and the reaction within Buddhist studies against the textual bias of previous scholarship on the other, has produced since the last turn of the century an innovative, anthropologically inflected approach to Buddhist art and architecture, which stresses their primary devotional use and performative function.[57] The study of the cultural dimension of nationalism gained momentum in the 1980s with the publication of seminal works by Anderson, Gellner, and others, which brought into focus the role of symbols, monuments, and civic rituals in the instigation and propagation of nationalist sentiments.[58] "New" museology's alertness to the politics of display compounded this scholarship by documenting the role of museums and heritage sites in the reification and public projection of national cultures and identities.[59] Adding to the scholarship on nationalism as a cultural construct is the historical strain of memory studies best represented by Nora's *Les lieux de mémoire*, a foundational work in the academic field that boomed at the turn of the 1990s.[60] Forays outside the predominant focus of this literature on the modern West are still rare.[61] In particular, there has been little examination as yet of the triangular relationship between religion, political authority, and practices of social remembrance in both the modern and premodern ages.[62]

DIGITAL MATERIALS

Archaeological Survey of India (http://www.asi.nic.in/)
Horyuji Temple (http://www.horyuji.or.jp/)
Thailand: Fine Arts Department (http://www.finearts.go.th/)
UNESCO (http://www.unesco.org/en)

FURTHER READING

ART AND ARCHAEOLOGY

Coomaraswamy, Ananda K. *A History of Indian and Indonesian Art*. London: E. Goldston, 1927.
Faure, Bernard. "The Buddhist Icon and the Modern Gaze." *Critical Enquiry* 24 (1988): 768–813.
Fenollosa, Ernest F. *Epochs of Chinese and Japanese Art: An Outline History of East Asiatic Design*, rev. ed., 2 vols. New York: F. A. Stokes, 1912.
Le May, Reginald. *A Concise History of Buddhist Art in Siam*. Cambridge, UK: Cambridge University Press, 1938.
Leoshko, Janice. *Sacred Traces: British Explorations of Buddhism in South Asia*. Aldershot, UK: Ashgate, 2003.
Mus, Paul. *Barabudur. Esquisse d'une histoire de bouddhisme fondée sur la critique archéologique des texts*. 2 vols. Hanoi, Vietnam: Imprimerie d'Extrême-Orient, 1935. English translation: *Barabudur: Sketch of a History of Buddhism based on Archaeological Criticism of the Texts* (trans. by Alexander W. Macdonald). New Delhi: Indira Gandhi National Center for the Arts, 1998.
Ray, Himanshu Phraba. *Archaeology and Buddhism in South Asia*. London: Routledge, 2017.
Sharf, Robert H., and Sharf, Elizabeth H., eds. *Living Images: Japanese Buddhist Icons in Context*. Stanford, CA: Stanford University Press, 2001.
Snodgrass, Adrian. *The Symbolism of the Stupa*. Ithaca, NY: Southeast Asia Program Publications, Cornell University, 1985.

MUSEOLOGY AND HERITAGE STUDIES

Bloembergen, Marieke, and Eickhoof, Martijn. *The Politics of Heritage in Indonesia: A Cultural History*. Cambridge, UK: Cambridge University Press, 2020.

Byrne, Denis. *Counterheritage: Critical Perspectives on Heritage Conservation in Asia*. London: Routledge, 2014.
Falser, Michael, ed. *Cultural Heritage as Civilizing Mission: From Decay to Recovery*. Cham, Switzerland: Springer International, 2015.
Geary, David. *The Rebirth of Bodh Gaya: Buddhism and the Making of a World Heritage Site*. Seattle: University of Washington Press, 2017.
Guha-Thakurta, Tapati. *Monuments, Objects, Histories: Institutions of Art in Colonial and Postcolonial India*. New York: Columbia University Press, 2004.
Lopez, Donald Jr., ed. *Curators of the Buddha: The Study of Buddhism under Colonialism*. Chicago: University of Chicago Press, 1995.
Mathur, Saloni, and Singh, Kavita, eds. *No Touching, No Spitting, No Praying: The Museum in South Asia*. New Delhi: Routledge, 2015.
Ray, Himanshu Phraba. *The Return of the Buddha: Ancient Symbols for a New Nation*. New Delhi: Routledge, 2014.
Sullivan, Bruce, ed. *Sacred Objects in Secular Spaces: Exhibiting Asian Religions in Museums*. London: Bloomsbury, 2015.

NOTES

1. See David Morgan, ed., *Religion and Material Culture: The Matter of Belief* (London: Routledge, 2010); on Buddhism specifically, see Charles Lachman, "Art," in *Critical Terms for the Study of Buddhism*, ed. Donald Lopez Jr. (Chicago: University of Chicago Press, 2005), 37–55.
2. Finbarr Barry Flood, "Between Cult and Culture: Bamiyan, Islamic Iconoclasm and the Museum," *The Art Bulletin* 84, no. 4 (2002): 642–659.
3. Walter Benjamin, "The Work of Art in the Age of Its Technological Reproducibility: Second Version (1936)," in *Walter Benjamin, Selected Writings*, vol. 3, ed. Howard Eiland and Michael W. Jennings (Cambridge, MA: Harvard University Press, 2002), 101–133.
4. Anne Karlström, "Spiritual Materiality: Heritage Preservation in a Buddhist World?" *Journal of Social Archaeology* 5 (2005): 338–355; Maurizio Peleggi, "The Unbearable Impermanence of Things: Reflections on Buddhism, Cultural Memory and Heritage Conservation," in *Routledge Handbook of Heritage in Asia*, ed. Patrick Daly and Tim Winter (London: Routledge, 2012), 55–68; Hseuh-man Shen, *Authentic Replicas: Buddhist Art in Medieval China* (Honolulu: University of Hawai'i Press, 2019).
5. Ryuichi Abé, "Word," in *Critical Terms for the Study of Buddhism*, ed. Donald S. Lopez Jr. (Chicago: University of Chicago Press, 2005), 304.
6. John Kieschnick, *The Impact of Buddhism on Chinese Material Culture* (Princeton, NJ: Princeton University Press, 2003), 7; Fabio Rambelli, *Buddhist Materiality: A Cultural History of Objects in Japanese Buddhism* (Stanford, CA: Stanford University Press, 2007), 107–108.
7. John Strong, *Relics of the Buddha* (Princeton, NJ: Princeton University Press, 2004); see also David Germano and Kevin Trainor, eds., *Embodying the Dharma: Buddhist Relic Veneration in Asia* (Albany: State University of New York Press, 2004); Robert H. Sharf, "On the Allure of Buddhist Relics," *Representations* 66 (1999): 75–99; Janice Stargardt and Michael Willis, eds., *Relics and Relic Worship in Early Buddhism: India, Afghanistan, Sri Lanka and Burma* (London: British Museum Research Publication, 2018). Scholarship on the cult of Christian relics boomed in the 2010s; see, among others, Charles Freeman, *Holy Bones and Holy Dust: How Relics Shaped the History of Medieval Europe* (New Haven, CT: Yale University Press, 2011); Cynthia Hahn and Holger A. Klein, eds., *Saints and Sacred Matter: The Cult of Relics in Byzantium and Beyond* (Washington, DC: Dumbarton Oaks Research Library, 2015); Robert Wisniewski, *The Beginnings of the Cult of Relics* (Oxford: Oxford University Press, 2019).

8. Nancy Falk, "To Gaze on the Sacred Traces," *History of Religions* 16, no. 4 (1977): 261–293; Strong, in *Relics of the Buddha*, xvi, reports a dictionary's definition of the literal meaning of *dathu* as "a constituent element of essential ingredient," and as such, "not the leftover but the essence that is extracted from the dead, cremated body." As for the Sanskrit term *sarira*, meaning literally "body," Strong subscribes to Schopen's view that when used in the sense of "relic," it takes typically the plural form; see Gregory Schopen, "Relic," in *Critical Terms for Religious Studies*, ed. Mark C. Taylor (Chicago: University of Chicago Press, 1998), 256–268.
9. The Pali terms for the four classes of sacred objects are *dhatucetiya*, *paribhogacetiya*, *uddesikacetiya*, and *dhammacetiya*. This canonical classification is summarized in A. B. Griswold's introduction to Prince Damrong Rajanubhab's *Monuments of the Buddha in Siam*, trans. Sulak Sivaraksa and A. B. Griswold (Bangkok: Siam Society, 1973), which is the translation of the last two chapters of Prince Damrong's book (originally published in 1926 as a memorial volume for his mother's cremation), *Tamnan phraphutta chedi* (Bangkok: Sophon Phiphattanakon, 1926).
10. Rambelli, *Buddhist Materiality*, 65.
11. Strong, *Relics of the Buddha*, chap. 5; see also John Strong, ed. and trans., *The Legend of King Asoka: A Study and Translation of the Asokavadana* (Princeton, NJ: Princeton University Press, 1983).
12. Kieschnick, *The Impact of Buddhism*, 69–80; Fabio Rambelli and Eric Reinders, *Buddhism and Iconoclasm in East Asia: A History* (London: Bloomsbury, 2012); Gregory A. Scott, *Building the Buddhist Revival: Reconstructing Monasteries in Modern China* (Oxford: Oxford University Press, 2020).
13. Bardwell L. Smith, ed., *Religions and Legitimation of Power in Thailand, Laos, and Burma* (Chambersburg, PA: Anima Books, 1978).
14. Ronald A. Luckens-Bull, ed., *Sacred Places and Modern Landscapes: Sacred Geography and Social-religious Transformations in South and Southeast Asia* (Temple: Arizona State University, 2003); Donald M. Stadtner, *Sacred Sites of Burma: Myth and Folklore in an Evolving Spiritual Realm* (Bangkok: River Books, 2011); Donald Swearer, Sommai Premchit, and Phaithoon Dokbuakaew, *Sacred Mountains of Northern Thailand and Their Legends* (Chiangmai, Thailand: Silkworm Books, 2004).
15. Maurice Halbawchs, *On Collective Memory*, ed. and trans. Lewis A. Coser (Chicago: University of Chicago Press, 1992), 199.
16. Adrian Snodgrass, *The Symbolism of the Stupa* (Ithaca, NY: Cornell University Southeast Asia Program Publications, 1985).
17. Richard Cohen, "Naga, Yaksini, Buddha: Local Deities and Local Buddhism at Ajanta," *History of Religions* 37, no. 4 (1998): 360–400.
18. James O. Caswell, *Written and Unwritten: A New History of the Buddhist Caves at Yungang* (Toronto: University of British Columbia Press, 1988); Geri H. Malandra, *Unfolding a Mandala: The Buddhist Caves at Ellora* (Albany: State University of New York Press, 1993); Christopher Munier, *Sacred Rocks and Buddhist Caves of Thailand* (Bangkok: White Lotus, 1998); Pindar Sidisunthorn, Simon Gardner, and Dean Smart, *Caves of Northern Thailand* (Bangkok: River Books, 2006).
19. Paul Mus, *India Seen from the East: Indian and Indigenous Cults in Champa*, ed. and trans. Ian W. Mabbet and David P. Chandler (Melbourne, Australia: Monash University Center for Southeast Asian Studies, 1975), 11.
20. Juliane Schober, "Mapping the Sacred in Theravada Buddhist Southeast Asia," in *Sacred Places and Modern Landscapes*, ed. Lukens-Bull, 16.
21. Jan Assmann, *Religion and Cultural Memory*, trans. Robert Livingstone (Stanford, CA: Stanford University Press, 2006).
22. Himanshu Prabha Ray, "From Multi-religious Sites to Mono-religious Monuments in South Asia," in *Routledge Handbook of Heritage in Asia*, ed. Patrick Daly and Tim Winter (London: Routledge, 2012), 75–76.
23. Robert L. Brown, "Bodhgaya and Southeast Asia," in *Bodhgaya: The Site of Enlightenment*, ed. Janice Leoshko (Mumbai: Marg, 1988), 101–124.

24. Ray, "From Multi-religious Sites to Mono-religious Monuments," 77.
25. Pierre Nora, "Between Memory and History: *Les Lieux de Mémoire*," *Representations* 26 (1989): 7–25.
26. David Geary, "Rebuilding the Navel of the Earth: Buddhist Pilgrimage and Transnational Religious Networks," *Modern Asian Studies* 48, no. 3 (2014): 689, who quotes Nehru's speech at the 1956 celebrations for the twenty-fifth centennial of the buddha's birth.
27. Saloni Mathur, *India by Design: Colonial History and Cultural Display* (Berkeley: University of California Press, 2007), chap. 5; see also Upinder Singh, "Exile and Return: The Reinvention of Buddhism and Buddhist Sites in Modern India," *South Asian Studies* 26, no. 2 (2010): 193–217.
28. Marieke Bloembergen and Martijn Eickhoff, "Save Borobudur! The Moral Dynamics of Heritage Formation in Indonesia across Orders and Borders, 1930s–1980s," in *Cultural Heritage as Civilizing Mission: From Decay to Recovery*, ed. Michael Falser (Cham, Switzerland: Springer International, 2015), 100–102.
29. Jean Gelman Taylor, *Indonesia: Peoples and Histories* (New Haven, CT: Yale University Press), 298–300; Bloembergen and Eickhoff, "Save Borobudur!," 91.
30. Gamini Wijesuriya, "Conserving the Temple of the Tooth Relic, Sri Lanka," *Public Archeology* 1, no. 2 (2001): 99–108.
31. See Tim Barringer and Tom Flynn, eds., *Colonialism and the Object: Empire, Material Culture and the Museum* (London: Routledge, 1998); David Boswell and Jessica Evans, eds., *Representing the Nation: A Reader. Histories, Heritage and Museums* (London: Routledge, 1999); Annie Combes, *Reinventing Africa: Museums, Material Culture, and Popular Imagination in Late Victorian and Edwardian England* (New Haven, CT: Yale University Press, 1994); Nicholas Thomas, *Entangled Objects: Exchange, Material Culture, and Colonialism* (Cambridge, MA: Harvard University Press, 1991).
32. Carole Duncan, *Civilizing Rituals: Inside Public Museums* (London: Routledge, 1995), 10–12. The book developed the initial formulation in C. Duncan, "Art Museums and the Ritual of Citizenship," in *Exhibiting Cultures: The Poetics and Politics of Museum Display*, ed. Ivan Karp and S. D. Lavin (Washington, DC: Smithsonian, 1991), 88–103.
33. Richard H. Davis, *Lives of Indian Images* (Princeton, NJ: Princeton University Press, 1997), 15–18; Yui Suzuki, "Temple as Museum, Buddha as Art: Horyuji's *Kudara Kannon* and Its Great Treasure Repository," *RES: Anthropology and Aesthetics* 52 (2007): 137–138.
34. Tony Bennett, "The Exhibitionary Complex," *New Formations* 4 (1988): 73–102; T. Bennett, *The Birth of the Museum: History, Theory, Politics* (London: Routledge, 1995); Eilean Hooper-Greenhill, "The Museum in the Disciplinary Society," in *Museum Studies in Material Culture*, ed. Susan M. Pearce (Leicester, UK: Leicester University Press, 1989), 61–72.
35. Sharf, "On the Allure of Buddhist Relics," 97.
36. Robert L. Brown, "The Miraculous Buddha Image: Portrait, God, or Object," in *Images, Miracles, and Authority in Asian Religions*, ed. Richard H. Davis (Boulder, CO: Westview Press, 1998), 37–54; Richard Gombrich, "The Consecration of a Buddha Image," *Journal of Asian Studies* 26, no. 1 (1966): 23–36; Donald K. Swearer, *Becoming the Buddha: The Ritual of Image Consecration in Thailand* (Princeton, NJ: Princeton University Press, 2004); quote from Kieschnick, *Impact of Buddhism*, 53.
37. Sharf, "On the Allure of Buddhist Relics," 82–83.
38. The scholarly debate on iconism and aniconism in Buddhist art is long-standing. See the classic essay by Ananda K. Coomaraswamy, "The Origin of the Buddha Image," *Art Bulletin* 9, no. 4 (1927): 287–328; the influential article by Susan L. Huntington, "Early Buddhist Art and the Theory of Aniconism," *Art Journal* 49, no. 4 (1990): 401–408; and the recent, comprehensive study by Robert DeCaroli, *Image Problem: The Origin and Development of the Buddha's Image in Early South Asia* (Seattle: University of Washington Press, 2015).
39. Alexander B. Griswold, *Dated Buddha Images of Northern Siam* (Ascona, Switzerland: Artibus Asiae, 1957).
40. Rambelli, *Buddhist Materiality*, 143, 189–190.

41. The Phra Kaeo image is dealt with in several chronicles, both Buddhist and dynastic; the main one was translated from Lao into English by a French scholar, Camille Notton, *The Chronicle of the Emerald Buddha* (Bangkok: Bangkok Times Press, 1932).
42. Griswold, *Dated Buddha Images*, 43.
43. Maurizio Peleggi, *Monastery, Monument, Museum: Sites and Artifacts of Thai Cultural Memory* (Honolulu: University of Hawai'i Press, 2017), 36–38; cf. Hans Belting, *Likeness and Presence: A History of Images before the Era of Art*, trans. Edmund Jephcott (Chicago: University of Chicago Press, 1994), 14–16, on the analogous case of the tutelary images of Italy's medieval city-states.
44. Davis, *Lives of Indian Images*, 80.
45. Peleggi, *Monastery, Monument, Museum*, 41–43.
46. Prince Damrong Rajanubhab, "Wat Benchamabophit and Its Collection of Images of the Buddha," *Journal of the Siam Society* 22 (1928): 19–28.
47. Maurizio Peleggi, "From Buddhist Icons to National Antiquities: Cultural Nationalism and Colonial Knowledge in the Making of Thailand's History of Art," *Modern Asian Studies* 47, no. 5 (2013): 1520–1548. The quote is from George Coedès, *The Indianized States of Southeast Asia* (1948; 3rd ed. 1964), trans. Susan B. Cowing (Honolulu: East–West Center Press, 1968), 222; see also Maurizio Peleggi, "The Plot of Thai Art History: Buddhist Sculpture and the Myth of National Origins," in *A Sarong for Clio: Essays in the Intellectual and Cultural History of Thailand Inspired by Craig J. Reynolds*, ed. M. Peleggi (Ithaca, NY: Cornell University Southeast Asia Program Publications, 2015), 79–93.
48. Stephen Tanaka, "Imaging History: Inscribing Belief in the Nation," *Journal of Asian Studies* 53, no. 1 (1994), 24–25.
49. Suzuki, "Temple as Museum, Buddha as Art."
50. Peleggi, *Monastery, Monument, Museum*, 26, 65–66.
51. Denis Byrne, "Buddhist Stupa and Thai Social Practice," *World Archaeology* 27, no. 2 (1995): 272.
52. Rambelli, *Buddhist Materiality*, 84; see also Jestün Dragpa Gyaltsen and Yael Bentor, *Clarifying the Meaning of the Arga and Consecration Rituals* (Kathmandu, Nepal: Vajra Books, 2015).
53. Maurizio Peleggi, *The Politics of Ruins and the Business of Nostalgia* (Bangkok: White Lotus), 28–29.
54. Juliane Schober, "Buddhist Just Rule and Burmese National Culture: State Patronage of the Chinese Tooth Relic in Myanma [*sic*]," *History of Religions* 36, no. 3 (1997): 218–243; Wijesuriya, "Conserving the Temple of the Tooth Relic, Sri Lanka."
55. "The Nara Document on Authenticity (1994)" (Nara, Japan: International Council on Monuments and Sites, 1994); "Living with Cultural Heritage: Asia, Perspective at Changing Period," *Proceedings of the Fourteenth Seminar on the Conservation of Asian Cultural Heritage* (Tokyo: National Research Institute for Cultural Properties, 2006); "Asia Conserved: Lessons Learned from the UNESCO Asia-Pacific Awards for Culture Heritage Conservation" (Bangkok: UNESCO, 2007). In 2005, the operational guidelines for assessing the value of nominated sites ("properties" in the Word Heritage Convention lexicon) in the distinct categories of cultural and natural heritage were unified into one set of ten criteria.
56. The World Heritage committee's motivation for the inscription of the "Buddhist Monuments in the Horyuji Area" in the List states that the property, consisting of "48 ancient wooden structures… maintains a good state of preservation… and retains a high level of authenticity in terms of form/design, material/substance, traditions/techniques and location/setting."
57. In addition to the references in this article, see the monographic issue "The Performative Agency of Buddhist Art and Architecture," ed. Michelle C. Wang and Wei-cheng Lin, special issue, *Ars Orientalis* 46 (2016). Frequently cited in this scholarship is the posthumous work by Alfred Gell, *Art and Agency: An Anthropological Theory* (Oxford: Clarendon Press, 1998).
58. Benedict Anderson, *Imagined Communities: Reflections on the Origins and Spread of Nationalism*, 2nd ed. (London: Verso, 1991); Ernest Gellner, *Nations and Nationalism* (Oxford: Blackwell, 1983);

John R. Gillis, ed., *Commemoration and the Politics of National Identity* (Princeton, NJ: Princeton University Press, 1994); Eric J. Hobsbawm and Terence Ranger, eds., *The Invention of Tradition* (Cambridge, UK: Cambridge University Press, 1983); Anthony D. King, *National Identity* (Harmondsworth, UK: Penguin, 1991).
59. In addition to the references cited in endnotes 31, 32, and 34, see also Flora Kaplan, ed., *Museums and the Making of "Ourselves": The Role of Objects in National Identity* (Leicester, UK: Leicester University Press, 1994); Gwendolyn Wright, ed., *The Formation of National Collections of Art and Archaeology* (Washington, DC: National Gallery of Art, 1996). For critical overviews, see the following three essays in Christopher Tilley, Webb Keane, Susanne Kuechler-Fogden, Mike Rowlands, and Patricia Spyer, eds., *Handbook of Material Culture* (London: SAGE, 2006): Beverly Butler, "Heritage and the Present Past," 463–479; Anthony A. Shelton, "Museums and Museum Displays," 480–515; Michael Rowlands and Christopher Tilley, "Monuments and Memorials," 516–533.
60. Pierre Nora, ed., *Realms of Memory: Rethinking the French Past*, trans. Arthur Goldhammer, 3 vols. (New York: Columbia University Press, 1996–1998). This is a partial translation of the original work, comprising three volumes in seven tomes, published in France between 1984 and 1992; for overviews of this literature, see Alon Confino, "Collective Memory and Cultural History: Problem of Method," *American Historical Review* 102, no. 5 (1997): 1386–1403; Paul Connerton, "Cultural Memory," in *Handbook of Material Culture*, ed. Christopher Tilley et al., 315–324; see also the two collections of essays: Mieke Bal, Jonathan Crewe, and Leo Spitzer, eds., *Acts of Memory: Cultural Recall in the Present* (Lebanon, NH: University Press of New England, 1999); Astrid Erll and Ansgar Nünning, eds., *A Companion to Cultural Memory Studies* (Berlin: De Gruyter, 2010).
61. Susan E. Alcock, *Archaeologies of the Greek Past: Landscapes, Monuments, and Memories* (Cambridge, UK: Cambridge University Press, 2002); Karl Galinsky, ed., *Memory in Ancient Rome and Early Christianity* (Oxford: Oxford University Press, 2016).
62. Jan Assmann, *Cultural Memory and Early Civilization: Writing, Remembrance, and Political Imagination*, trans. David H. Wilson (Cambridge, UK: Cambridge University Press, 2011).

Maurizio Peleggi

AVALOKITEŚVARA: THE BODHISATTVA OF COMPASSION

Avalokiteśvara is known by different names in Asia. In China, it is Guanyin (Perceiver of Sounds), shortened from Guanshiyin (Perceiver of the World's Sounds) or Guanzizai (Lord Perceiver). Under Chinese influence, Japanese, Korean, and Vietnamese have also used the same names (Kannon or Kanzeon in Japanese, Kwanse'um in Korean, and Quanam in Vietnamese). He is called Lokeśvara (Lord of the World) in Cambodia and Java; Lokanāntha (Protector of the World) in Burma; Nāth Deviyō in Sri Lanka; and Chenresi (One Who Sees with Eyes) in Tibet.

The different names and identities the bodhisattva assumed reflect the fact that different cultures made different choices in representing him. In Tibet, Sri Lanka, and Southeast Asia, Avalokiteśvara has been very much identified with royalty. But in China and countries having historical and cultural connections with China, such as Japan, Korea, and Vietnam, Guanyin is regarded as the exemplar of wisdom for meditators and as the "Goddess of Mercy," who is particularly kind to women. Although bodhisattvas transcend gender or other worldly distinctions, they, like the buddha, are depicted in scriptures and art as male. But Guanyin underwent a dramatic transformation from male to female in China, an evolution that accounted for why the bodhisattva acquired this nickname.

AVALOKITEŚVARA IN INDIA

Buddhist scholars and art historians do not agree about the exact dates when the cult of Avalokiteśvara appeared in India. Both Marie-Therese de Mallmann and Gregory Schopen put the beginning of the cult in the 5th century.[1] But Nanadana Chutiwongs suggests that literary and iconic data show that Avalokiteśvara appeared in north and northwest India no later than the 2nd century of the Common Era (CE), and by the 5th century, he was already widely worshiped there.[2] The uncertainty about the beginning of the cult of Avalokiteśvara in India is a reflection of the ongoing debates about the origin and early history of Mahāyāna Buddhism. It is not clear when the earliest textual references to the bodhisattva appeared.

Two factors account for the difficulty of a definite dating. One is the lack of devotional narratives datable to a period earlier than the 5th century. The other is because earlier images of Avalokiteśvara do not have inscriptions that provide his identity. However, there is a traditional consensus that he is first mentioned in the *Sukhāvatīvyūha Sutra,* the Mahāvastu and the *Lotus Sutra,* all of which have long been believed to have been written before 300 CE. Moreover, an incomplete triad with Amitābha and Avalokiteśvara to his left was discovered in Taxila, in 1961. It has a Kharoṣṭhī inscription. Based on the script of the inscription, some scholars date the triad to the 2nd century CE. Even though the question of when Avalokiteśvara first appeared in Indian cultic life cannot be settled, all evidence confirms that, by the 5th century, his presence was well attested by contemporary reports. The Chinese pilgrim Faxian, who traveled to Mathurā in about 400 CE, reported that the Mahāyāna monks worshiped Avalokiteśvara by making offerings to his image. By the time Xuanzang traveled in the northwest, during the years 630–645, the cult was firmly established, and he provided eyewitness accounts of Avalokiteśvara images that responded to prayers of devotees from all walks of life, from kings, to monastics, and ordinary people.

AVALOKITEŚVARA IN SOUTH AND SOUTHEAST ASIA

All the Southeast Asian countries, with the exception of Burma, shared the ideology of the cult of the "divine king" (*devarāja*) in which the ruler was identified with a deity, Hindu or Buddhist. The most famous example is the construction of Angkor Wat, one of the largest stone temples in the world, during the 12th and 13th centuries in Cambodia. Angkor Wat was regarded as a dwelling place for deities including the divine kings. The pantheon is a mixture of Hindu and Buddhist deities and the deified kings, exemplified by the Devarāja. The cult of Lokeśvara reached its zenith under Jauyavarman VII (r. 1181–ca. 1218) who built the Bayon temple complex at the center of the royal city Angkor Thom. He made Buddhism the state religion. At the Bayon, there are large towers bearing huge faces that are believed to be images of the deified king in the form of Lokeśvara. Not only the king was identified with the bodhisattva, but his first wife, Queen Jayavajadevi, might also be represented posthumously by a statue usually identified as Tārā, the bodhisattva's attendant.[3]

Similarly, since the 15th century, Avalokiteśvara was worshiped as the guardian deity of the country, by the Ceylonese rulers and the Javanese kings in the pre-Islamic 13th to 15th centuries.[4] In Tibet, Avalokiteśvara is worshipped as the patron deity of the country, and the most famous ruler, King Srong-bstan sgam-po (d. 649) and the Dalai Lama are believed to be the incarnations of Avalokiteśvara.[5] The royal symbolism came quite naturally in a context with no preexisting or competing symbolism. There is, therefore, a common tradition in Asia that Avalokiteśvara is a legitimizing symbol for the royalty.

AVALOKITEŚVARA/GUANYIN IN CHINA

The bodhisattva is not connected with royalty in China. This is because the Chinese royal ideology and symbolism were already established before the introduction of Buddhism in the 1st century CE and thus did not allow similar developments in China. The Chinese emperor received his legitimation through the Mandate of Heaven, which was first formulated in the Zhou dynasty (1122–256 BCE). The Confucian ideology dominated the Chinese understanding of royalty throughout China's imperial history. Although individual rulers might use Buddhist ideas periodically, to legitimize their rules, their efforts were limited and did not last long. For instance, the Northern Wei emperor Wencheng (r. 453–465) had five buddha caves carved at Yungang, each buddha representing a prior emperor, thus symbolizing his desire to create a theocracy. The female Emperor Wu Zetian (r. 684–704) claimed to be Maitreya, and Emperor Qianlong (cr. 1736–1765) claimed to be Manjuśrī Bodhisattva. Except for the late 19th-century Qing Empress Dowager Cixi, who dressed up as Guanyin for amusement and dramatic effect, no ruling emperor claimed to be the incarnation of Guanyin.

The bodhisattva is known in China by two names: Guanyin or Guanshiyin and Guanzizai. These two different names are translations from two different spellings of the bodhisattva. Guanshiyin was the translation for Avalokiteśvara, whereas Guanzizai was the translation for Avalokiteśvara. Avalokiteśvara was used in scriptures coming into China from Kucha, such as those translated by Kumārajīva (344–413) and other Central Asian missionaries, while Avalokiteśvara was found in scriptures originating in India, such as those translated by Xuanzang (600–664), who obtained the texts during his long sojourn there.

There are numerous Buddhist scriptures connected with Guanyin. The bodhisattva appears in more than eighty sutras. This is by no means an exhaustive list, for the esoteric sutras connected with Guanyin alone number eighty-eight, and they occupy 509 pages of the Taisho canon (volume 20), the modern edition of the Chinese Buddhist Tripitaka, printed during 1922–1933 in Japan. The role of Avalokiteśvara varies widely in these sutras, translated from Indic languages into Chinese, ranging from a walk-on bit player of the attending entourage surrounding Śākyamuni Buddha to the leading star of his own grand dramas of universal salvation. The faces of the bodhisattva in canonical scriptures, as in art and other mediums, is thus highly multivocal, multivalent, and multifaceted. The different roles Avalokiteśvara assumes in the scriptures might reflect the increasing importance of his stature in India. On the other hand, they might also reflect different cultic traditions about the bodhisattva. At least three separate and distinct cults can be identified: that of a compassionate savior not bound to a specific place as represented by the *Lotus Sutra*, that of the chief helper of Amitābha Buddha found in the Pure Land sutras, and that of a sage connected with the holy island Potalaka, as seen in the *Avatamsaka Sutra* and some esoteric sutras. The three cultic traditions developed independently.

Prior to the translation of the *Lotus Sutra* in the 3rd century, there was no Chinese deity to compare with Guanyin, who was not only a universal and compassionate savior, but also easily accessible. This sutra was translated into Chinese six times. Of these, the 406 version by Kumārajīva is most famous and followed by all East Asian Buddhists. The gospel of the "Universal Gateway," the twenty-fifth chapter of the sutra, preached a new and democratic way of salvation. The bodhisattva assumes thirty-three forms to deliver people from mortal dangers and lead them to spiritual salvation. There was no specific thing a person had to do to be saved. One did not need to become a scholar learned in scripture, or a paragon of virtue, or a master proficient in meditation. One did not have to follow a special way of life, take up a strange diet, or practice any ritual. The only requirement was to call his name with a sincere and believing heart. This was a new deity who would help anyone in difficulty. There was no discrimination on the basis of status or gender. And the benefits of worshiping him were both spiritual and worldly. Although there were goddesses in China before the appearance of Guanyin, none of them seemed to have enjoyed lasting and continuously active cults. There was thus a religious vacuum in China that Guanyin could conveniently and comfortably fill.

Buddhism thus supplied the necessary symbols and ideals to the host countries. In accommodating itself to the different religious and cultural traditions in the various Asian countries, new and different forms of Buddhism developed. In the case of Sino-Japanese Buddhism, the creation of the Tiantai (Tendai), Huayan (Kegon), Pure Land (Jing tu and Shin), and Chan (Zen) schools are prominent examples. Although the Chinese based their main teachings and practices on some scriptures translated from Indic languages, the specific emphases and formulations reflected the native modes of thought and cultural values. This process of domestication created diversity in the pan-Asian Buddhist tradition. Guanyin's transformation into the compassionate "Goddess of Mercy" in China is an example of this process.

The indigenous sutras also helped to promote and disseminate the belief in Guanyin in China, just as the translated sutras, miracle stories, new images of Guanyin, pilgrimage, and rituals devoted to the bodhisattva did in their different ways. In recent decades, scholars began to re-evaluate the traditional distinction between the sutras translated from Indic languages and those composed in China. Attitudes toward *yijing* ("suspicious scriptures") or *weiing* ("spurious scriptures") have undergone revision. These scriptures are seen as creative attempts to synthesize Buddhist teachings and to adapt them to the Chinese cultural milieu.

Indigenous sutras are closely connected with miracle stories. The origins of two very popular scriptures are good examples. While the *King Kao's Guanshiyin Sutra,* first mentioned in 664, was supposed to result from a miracle, the *Divine Spell of the White-Robed Great Being,* which can be dated to at least the 11th century, promises to create one. The former concerns how a wrongly imprisoned soldier is saved from certain death by execution as a result of his faithful chanting of the sutra, which Guanyin (in the form of a monk) teaches him in a dream. The latter, on the other hand, offers a methodical direction of securing a miracle. Both emphasize the chanting of the text and the dhāraṇī contained therein.

Compilations of miracle stories began in the 4th century, not long after the first translation of the *Lotus Sutra* by Dharmaraksha, in 286. Miracle tales about Guanyin are an important and enduring genre in Chinese Buddhism. They have been collected down the ages and are still being produced and collected today. Miracle tales served as a powerful medium for transforming and domesticating Guanyin. Because the stories related real people's encounters with the bodhisattva in specific times and places, and under critical circumstances, Guanyin was no longer the mythical figure mentioned in the sutras, but rather became a "real presence." Miracles happened to vouch for Guanyin's efficacy (*ling*). They worked because there was the relationship of *ganying* (sympathetic resonance) between the sincere devotee and the bodhisattva. Both concepts have deep cultural roots in China.

Many miracle tales mention images of Guanyin. In the most popular version of the origin myth of *King Gao's Guanshihyin Sutra*, the hero was Sun Jingde, a common soldier who was wrongly sentenced to death. Sun worshiped an icon of Guanyin that he kept in his room. When he managed to finish chanting the sutra that a monk revealed him in a dream one thousand times prior to his beheading, the executioner's knife broke into three sections. Although the executioner changed the knife three times, the same thing happened. When Sun was pardoned and returned to his room, he saw three cuts made by a knife on the neck of the Guanyin image. The implication is clearly that the icon bore the blows of the knife, thus sparing Sun. This was supposed to have happened to him between 534 and 537 CE. Other stories relate similar happenings. Instead of going to a temple to worship Guanyin, these early devotees carried the icons on their bodies as talismans. Since they were worn inside the hair or on top of the crown, they must have been small and light. Indeed, a number of tiny gilt bronze images of Guanyin, some measuring only two centimeters or so, have survived and can be seen in museums. When we view them in the light of such miracle tales, we might speculate that they were small because they were intended to be used as personal talismans. Icons were also sometimes created for such devotional use as a result of miraculous deliverances.

There is a close relationship between the devotees and icons of Guanyin revealed in some early miracle tales. Buddhist art, like all religious art, is intimately connected with the spiritual lives of the faithful. Sculpted and painted images of Guanyin are icons first and foremost, although they can, of course, be appreciated as beautiful objects of art. New forms of Guanyin appearing in devotees' visions of the bodhisattva as contained in some later miracle tales served as effective media for the domestication and transformation of Guanyin. While most early miracle tales refer to Guanyin as a monk when he appears in the dreams or visions of the devotee, the bodhisattva gradually appears either as a "person in white" (*baiyiren*), indicating perhaps his lay status, or as a "woman in white" (*baiyifuren*), indicating her female gender. There is clearly a dialectic relationship between the changing forms of the bodhisattva appearing in the devotees' visions and dreams and the development of new iconographic representations. Changing visions of Guanyin led to new artistic representations of the bodhisattva. Conversely, an image of Guanyin depicted with a new iconography could also predispose the devotees to see him/her in this way in their visions and dreams. What Hu Yinglin (1551–1602), scholar and bibliophile, had to say about this is worth repeating here. In the preface to a collection of fifty-three forms of Guanyin together with eulogies that he compiled, he pointed out that all statues and paintings of Guanyin made in his time depicted the bodhisattva as a woman. He offered an explanation for this: "Because all the Guanyin images nowadays are in the form of a woman, people no longer dream of the bodhisattva as a man. Since people no longer see Guanyin appear in a male form in their dreams, they come to think that the bodhisattva is really a woman. But dreams are produced by the mind and verified by the eye. Since the bodhisattva seen by the eye and thought of by the mind is not male, Guanyin naturally manifests herself as a female in dreams."[6]

Miracle tales about Guanyin provide strong evidence that Guanyin has been worshiped in China by both monastics and laymen and women. In fact, the cult cuts across all social classes. Miracle tale collections were compiled by both monks and literati. The collections included stories about people from diverse walks of life who, for a brief moment, experienced a salvific encounter with Guanyin, and their lives were changed forever. Buddhist sutras glorifying Guanyin received verification from such tales. Scriptural teachings were no longer doctrinal and abstract, but became practical and concrete through the living testimonies of real men and women. At the same time, through their tales about their dreams or visions of Guanyin, the devotees helped to make the bodhisattva take on increasingly Chinese manifestations. The foreign Avalokiteśvara was, in the process, gradually changed into the Chinese Guanyin.

The intimate and dialectical relationship between visions, media, and iconography highlights the role art has played in the cult of Guanyin. Art has indeed been one of the most powerful and effective media through which the Chinese people have come to know Guanyin. It is also through art that one can most clearly detect the bodhisattva's gradual, yet undeniable sexual transformation. Buddhist scriptures always present the bodhisattva as either masculine or asexual. Guanyin usually appears as a monk not only in early miracle stories and in the dreams and visions of the faithful, but wonder-working monks such as Baozhi (425–514) and Zengjie (617–710) are also incarnated as the bodhisattva. The statues of Guanyin in Yüngang, Longmen, and Dunhuang, as well as Guanyin images painted on the frescoes and banners of Dunhuang, like those of the buddhas and bodhisattvas, appear masculine, sometimes wearing a thin mustache that clearly indicates his masculine gender.

The deity underwent a profound and startling transformation beginning sometime during the 10th century, and by the 16th century, Guanyin had become not only completely Chinese but also the most beloved "Goddess of Mercy," a nickname coined by the Jesuit missionaries who were much impressed by the similarities between her iconography and that of the Madonna. Of all the imported Buddhist deities, Guanyin is the only one who has succeeded in becoming a genuine Chinese goddess, so much so that many Chinese, if they are not familiar with Buddhism, are not even aware of her Buddhist origin.

The Chinese created indigenous forms of Guanyin, just as they composed indigenous sutras. In time, several distinctive Chinese forms of Guanyin emerged from the 10th century onward. They are the Water-Moon Guanyin, White-Robed Guanyin, Child-Giving Guanyin, Guanyin of the South Sea, Fish-Basket Guanyin, and Old Mother Guanyin. The creation of new iconographies of Guanyin might be connected with the regional character of Chinese Buddhism and Buddhist art. The new icons were also closely connected with Buddhist theology, ritual, and devotion. The Water-Moon Guanyin was an indigenous iconography that appeared before the White-Robed Guanyin and served as a prototype for the latter. The White-Robed Guanyin gave rise to a cult of fertility in the late Imperial period. With her own indigenous scriptures, rituals, and miracle stories, she came to be known colloquially as the "Child-Giving" Guanyin. Feminization of Avalokiteśvara in China was thus inseparable from the domestication and regionalization of the bodhisattva. The appearance of the Guanyin of the South Sea (Nanhai Guanyin) coincided with the construction of Putuo Island as the Chinese Potolaka, the sacred island home of the bodhisattva described in the *Avatamsaka* and other esoteric sutras. In this iconography Guanyin is always attended by the Dragon Princess and Sudhana on either side and a white parrot hovering over her on the upper right. There is no scriptural basis for such arrangement. Although both the Dragon Princess and Guanyin appear in the *Lotus Sutra* in chapters 12 and 25, respectively, they do not appear together. In the *Avatamsaka Sutra*, Guanyin is the 28th "Good Friend" from whom Sudhana seeks instruction. As for the white parrot, it is not mentioned anywhere in the sutras. Thus, if one follows the traditional way used by art historians who always try to trace each component of a painting or image to its scriptural source, one will not succeed in solving the puzzle. On the other hand, legends, pilgrimage records, and precious volumes about Putuo provide copious and illuminating explanations for such iconography. Similarly, the origin of the Fish Basket and Old Mother Guanyin cannot be found in Buddhist scriptures either. They have to be traced to local legends preserved in drama and precious volumes in the former case, and in the mythology of certain sectarian new religions in the latter case.

The creation of images of Guanyin unauthorized by scriptures is not a unique phenomenon. In cave and cliff sculptures since the early 7th century, we can find Guanyin paired with Dizang (Kṣitigarbha). This pairing is not attested by any scripture. A conventional explanation of why the two bodhisattvas are worshiped together is that, while Guanyin takes care of people when they are alive, Dizang takes care of them after they die. They play different roles in the work of salvation, and the dual worship is the result of a division of labor. The canonical basis of Dizang worship is the *Scripture on the Ten Wheels,* which exists in two versions. The *Great Extended Scripture on the Ten Wheels* (Da fangkuang shilun jing) is an anonymous translation known in north China no later than the 6th century. The *Scripture on Dizang and the Ten Wheels in the Great Mahāyāna Compendium* (Tasheng daji Dizang shilun jing) is a revised translation attributed to the famous monk Xuanzang. There are striking similarities in the depictions of Guanyin and Dizang in these two texts. Dizang, like Guanyin, is very much concerned with saving people from all kinds of problems and also, like Guanyin, is connected with the Pure Land. Since this is the case, instead of a division of labor, the two work jointly on behalf of beings and enable them to achieve these identical goals.

Dizang became exclusively identified as the savior of beings in hell when the *Scripture of Dizang's Original Vow* (Dizang benyuan jing) superseded the *Scripture on Ten Wheels* in popularity. The pairing of the two is therefore due to the new role Dizang came to play. This is a case where indigenous sutras overshadowed esoteric sutras, which presented Guanyin as a savior of beings in hell. The translation of the *Scripture of Dizang's Original Vow* has traditionally been attributed to the 7th-century Khotanese monk Śiksanānda, but it is most likely composed in either Khotan or China. Although it was not introduced into the canon until the Ming, it was definitely already in circulation by the 10th century. The *Scripture of Past Vows* calls upon its reader to recite it for the dying, to relieve their suffering and secure a better rebirth. But a number of esoteric sutras introduced into China several centuries earlier already attributed the power to cure illnesses, to enable a person die a good death, and to save beings from hell to Guanyin when one recites the *dhāraṇīs* revealed by him. One of the earliest such scriptures centering Guanyin as the universal savior is the *Qing Guanyin jing,* translated during 317–420. The chanting of the *dhāraṇīs* revealed therein will save a person from all manner of disasters. If one is faithful and dedicated in chanting the *dhāraṇīs,* he will be able to have a vision of Guanyin while alive and, having been freed from all sins, will not suffer rebirth in the four woeful realms of hell, hungry ghosts, animals, and asuras. Because Guanyin playfully travels in all realms of rebirth, even if a person is so unfortunate as to be born in hell or as a hungry ghost, Guanyin is right there to help him. The bodhisattva is said to suffer in hell in place of the sinner, and by bestowing sweet milk, which issues forth from his fingertips, the hunger and thirst of hungry ghosts are also satisfied. The *Sutra of the Divine dhāraṇī on the Eleven-Headed Guanyin Spoken by the Buddha* (Foshuo Shiyimian Guanyin shenzhou jing), translated in the latter half of the 6th century, is another important example. The sutra calls for a daily routine of bathing in the morning, followed by reciting the *dhāraṇī* 108 times. The result is the gaining of ten rewards in one's present life, including not suffering from any disease and not suffering a sudden death. Moreover, the following four compensations will become one's own: (a) seeing innumerable buddhas before one dies; (b) never falling into hell; (c) not being harmed by any animal; and (d) being reborn in the land of the Buddha Amitāyus.[7] Another group of esoteric scriptures glorifying the Thousand-Handed Guanyin present the bodhisattva as the savior of beings in the six paths including hell. When one recites the *dhāraṇī*, consisting of 84 phrases known as the Great Compassion *Dhāraṇī* (Dabeizhou), one will obtain even more extensive worldly and spiritual benefits than those described above. Because the esoteric Guanyin plays an almost identical role as Dizang, it makes sense that it is either the Eleven-Headed or the Thousand-Handed Guanyin who appears together with Dizang in the Dunhuang banners. This is not a division of labor; rather, they join forces in alleviating the sufferings of beings in hell and enabling them to be reborn in the Pure Land.

The pairing of the two not only appear in the illustrated copies of the *Scripture on the Ten Kings* recovered from Dunhuang, but were evoked together in Buddhist mortuary rituals for the benefit of the dead ancestors. These ritual texts were created from the Song to the Ming dynasties, or the 11th to the 17th centuries. For instance, in the ritual text *Cibei Liang Huang baochan* (Compassionate Precious Penance formulated by Emperor Wu of Liang, preface dated 1138), the presiding priest asks both Dizang and Guanyin to descend to the consecrated space three times. An even more important mortuary ritual, which was created in the 10th century and has remained popular down the ages, is that of feeding hungry ghosts (shishi). Guanyin and Dizang collaborate in the ritual. At the beginning of the ritual, a picture of the hungry ghost Burning Face (Mianjan), the putative originator of the ritual, is placed on the altar facing the assembled monks. When the ritual begins, the Great Compassion *Dhāraṇī* and a hymn praising Guanyin are chanted before the altar. After "fixing the area of the five directions," accompanied by an invocation to five different buddhas, Guanyin is invoked directly. The presiding monk makes a *mudrā* called "Guanyin meditation *mudrā*," through which the celebrant enters into the Guanyin samadhi. Thus identified with Guanyin, the main action of the ritual is performed by Guanyin in the person of the celebrant. The highlight of the ritual arrives when the priest, as Guanyin, makes the mudra of "opening up the gate of hell." He visualizes three red rays emitting from his mouth, hands, and chest, which open up the gates of hell. The three rays represent three powers that can destroy the three categories of sins of the body, speech, and mind committed by beings in hell. At this point in the ritual, Dizang is invoked to lead the dead to come forth, to accept the offerings in response to the call of the chief celebrant. This is accomplished by several *mudrās*. After the invited ghosts are helped to repent by the "*mudrā* of repentance," the presiding monk transforms water into nectar by performing the "mudra of sweet dew." He then enables them to drink it by performing the "*mudrā* of opening up the throat." He visualizes a green lotus held in his left hand, from which "sweet dew" flows out for the ghosts to drink, just as Guanyin is described as doing in the *Kāraṇḍavyūha* the esoteric sutra famous for its six-syllable mantrā "Om Manipadme Hūm."

The two bodhisattvas therefore collaborate in helping people both in life and in death. When and how did they become specialized in only one sphere? The clue can be found in art and temple architecture. An unusual visual example is provided by the pair, seated side by side on separate lotus pedestals, in a small niche attached to the larger Number 1 niche located at Pantuo si in Qiunglai, Sichuan. There is no inscription, but the larger Number 1 niche, which contains the Amitābha triad, is dated 820. There are two groups of smaller figures on relief under the images of the two bodhisattvas. On the right side, beneath Dizang, there are four figures in a flaming rocky landscape, which is clearly meant to represent a vignette of a Buddhist hell. A human head bobs in a large cauldron over a blazing fire and others are being cut by knives. On the left side, beneath Guanyin, four figures are swept up in swirling waves of a rushing river or turbulent sea, praying to Guanyin for help.[8] A more explicit example of how people assign different functions to the two bodhisattvas can be seen in temple architecture. Based on surviving examples of floor plans of temples dated to the Liao and Jin (11th–12th centuries), separate halls dedicated to the four bodhisattvas (Mañjuśrī, Samantabhadra, Guanyin, and Dizang) were built flanking the main buddha hall. The floor plan of Shanhua si in Datong, Shanxi, shows Wenshu Hall (no longer standing) facing Puxian Hall, while Dizang Hall faces Guanyin Hall. But the Guangsheng si, built in the 16th century, retained only the two halls dedicated to Dizang and Guanyin facing each other. Mañjuśrī and Samantabhadra were no longer provided with their own independent halls. This arrangement remains to this day. In many temples today Guanyin Hall faces across from Dizang Hall. The ten kings and scenes of hellish punishments would be depicted in Dizang Hall, while we may find images of Niangniang (Ladies) in Guanyin Hall. With a setup like this, it is clear that worshipers pray to Dizang as savior of hell and to Guanyin as granter of health, fertility, and long life. As Dizang became the sole guardian of beings in hell, Guanyin gave up this part of his original functions and became the chief protector of people in life. The relationship between the pair underwent changes through time. Although there is no scriptural basis for worshiping Guanyin and Dizang together, there is, nevertheless, a logic grounded in the existential needs of the faithful.[9]

There is another example to attest the creation of an indigenous pantheon not based on scriptures. Around the 16th century, Guanyin was provided with an animal mount so that the three great beings (San Dashi) could all ride on their respective animals. Just as Mañjuśrī rides on the lion and Samantabhadra rides on the elephant, Guanyin rides on a mythical animal called *hou*. The artists who created such new forms of Guanyin showed the same freedom as the writers of the indigenous sutras. They tried to present the bodhisattva in a way that would respond to the needs of the faithful. As Dizang came to care for the faithful after they died, Guanyin assumed the role of caring for them during their life. This, of course, is a sharp change for the role Guanyin played in the religion and art of the Pure Land. As the attendant of Amitābha Buddha, Guanyin would welcome the dying to the Pure Land. This was the way the bodhisattva was depicted in the banners from Dunhuang, some of which identified him as the "Bodhisattva Who Leads the Way (Yinlu pusa)."

The indigenization of Guanyin reached completion with the legend of Miaoshan, who came to be seen as the human manifestation of the bodhisattva. We do not know how early the legend began, but the first written record of it was dated 1100, a "life" of Princess Miaoshan written by an official and carved on a stele at the request of the abbot of a temple in Honan, which was a pilgrimage center for Guanyin worship. The legend presents Miaoshan as the third daughter of a king. She is pious from childhood and dedicated to religious cultivation. Unlike her older sisters, she refuses to marry the husband chosen by her father, for which she suffers persecution. However, when the king becomes mortally ill and no medicine can cure him, she offers her eyes and hands to be made into a life-saving potion. Finally, Miaoshan manifests herself as the Thousand-Armed and Thousand-Eyed Guanyin when the royal party led by the king and queen comes to offer thanks as pilgrims. In this famous legend, the bodhisattva is provided with a name, a birthday, a family, and a biography, none of which is found in Buddhist scriptures. Her birthday, the nineteenth day of the second month, has become the most important holy day for the faithful, just as the birthdays of all Chinese gods and goddesses are similarly regarded. Clearly, this transformation fits the Chinese model of divinity. Since the Chinese religion does not posit a sharp distinction between the transcendent and the immanent, human beings can become gods, and gods can appear on earth as human beings. Lao Zi, for instance, was already deified in the second century and was believed to have transformed himself many times to teach people about the Dao. Stories about Daoist immortals, those fabulous beings who straddle the boundary between the human and the divine, serve as another rich resource for such imagination. The legend of Miaoshan anchored Guanyin to China by making her conform to the Chinese model of divinity. It also provided a charter for marriage resistance. Buddhist women could and did follow Miaoshan's example in refusing to get married and carrying out their religious practices, either at home or by joining the sangha.

The cult of Guanyin was created and transmitted in China through various media. Canonical and indigenous scriptures, miracle stories, ritual, and pilgrimage, as well as art and literature, have all contributed to the process. While each medium promoted Guanyin, it transformed the bodhisattva at the same time. Thus, while Guanyin was represented and perceived as a monk prior to and during the Tang dynasty (618–907), the bodhisattva was increasingly feminized and eventually turned into Venerable Mother Guanyin in the Qing (1644–1912). These media, moreover, never existed or functioned in isolation, but constantly interacted and influenced each other. Visions of devotees and pilgrims were reflected in and inspired by the contemporary iconography. Indigenous scriptures, miracle accounts, ritual practices, and popular precious volumes reinforced each other. The development and evolution of the cult was fueled by such dialectical interactions among these media.

Since Avalokiteśvara became a feminine deity only in China and, furthermore, this happened only after the Tang, it is necessary to offer some hypothetical explanations. Instead of seeking the clues in native goddesses, which is inconclusive at best, it has to be examined in the context of new developments in Chinese religions, including Buddhism, since the Song (960–1279). The emergence of the feminine Guanyin must also be studied in the context of new cults of other goddesses, which, not coincidentally, also happened after the Song dynasty. The appearance of the feminine Guanyin in indigenous sutras, art, and miracle stories and the legend of Miaoshan occurred in the 10th to the 12th centuries. It was during these centuries that Neo-Confucianism was established as the official ideology, functioning very much like a state religion. These events did not happen by coincidence, nor were they independent of each other.

The reason that the feminine Guanyin and other new goddesses appeared at this particular time might be connected with the antifeminist stance of established religions, chief of which, undoubtedly, was Neo-Confucianism. This was the hegemonic discourse and ruling ideology of China during the last one thousand years. Neo-Confucianism was a philosophy and a system of political thought, but it was also an ideology sustaining the lineage and family system. In one sense, then, the new goddess cults can be seen as similar responses to this totalistic system of belief and praxis, but in another way, the feminine Guanyin might be viewed as the model and inspiration for the other goddesses. Organized Buddhism and Daoism did not fare much better. Despite the Chan rhetoric of non-duality and the Daoist elevation of the feminine principle, these did not translate into actual institutional support for women. We cannot name any woman who became a prominent Chan master or Daoist priestess.

Having said that the birth of goddesses might have been in response to the overwhelmingly masculine character of the three religions, it is also to be noted that some of these new goddesses did reflect the belief in universal sagehood and enlightenment as espoused by Neo-Confucianism, Buddhism, and Daoism. Just as the emperors Yao and Shun were not born sages, but became so, this apparently was also the case for gods and goddesses. Wang Gen (1483–1540) could salute everyone he met as sages because they were potential sages, if not actual ones. Can we also say that the street was full of bodhisattvas and goddesses?

Did the female Guanyin offer more options to Chinese women? It is often assumed that when a religion provides goddesses to worship, it can empower women. When Avalokiteśvara was transformed into Guanyin, the "Goddess of Mercy," new forms and expressions of religiosity became available to women and men in China. But as long as the traditional stereotypical views about women's pollution or inferiority remained unchallenged, the feminine images of Guanyuin had to be either more or less than real women. They were not and could not be endowed with the characteristics of a real woman. For this reason, the White-Robed Guanyin, though a fertility goddess, is devoid of sexuality. Real women, in the meantime, together with their male countrymen, worshiped Guanyin as the "Child-Giving" Guanyin who saw to it that the family religion would never be disrupted by the lack of a male heir.

AVALOKITEŚVARA IN JAPAN AND TIBET

Avalokiteśvara enjoyed popularity in Japan equal to that in China. There is space to offer only a few examples. Prince Shōtoku (*c.* 573–622), the legendary founder of Japanese Buddhism, was closely identified with the bodhisattva. The famous statue housed in Hōryūji, known as Kuse Kannon, was believed to have been built in conformity to the prince's size. Shinran (1173–1263), the founder of the new Pure Land School, Jōdoshinshū, worshiped Shōtoku as the manifestation of Kannon. Kannon also came to be conceived as feminine by the 12th century in Japan. In a climactic dream that led Shinran to break away from the Pure Land establishment and that initiated married priesthood, Kannon appeared to him and authorized his marriage to the nun Eshinni, who was thought to be the incarnation of Kannon. An important form of Kannon devotion is to go on the pilgrimage circuit to the thirty-three Kannon temples in the western part of the main island of Japan. This has remained very popular down the ages. Images of the thirty-three forms of Kannon are often depicted in a set in Japan. They are primarily feminine and not based on the *Lotus Sutra*, but on Chinese legends.

In Tibet, the Dalai Lama is venerated as the manifestation of the bodhisattva. The six-syllable Buddhist formula *Om Manipadme Hūṃ* is the most important and well-known mantrā associated with Avalokiteśvara, who is Tibet's patron deity. It is carved or painted onto rocks and hills or written on prayer flags. The favorite form of lay devotion is to spin the prayer wheels while chanting the mantrā. Prayer wheels contain printed forms of the mantrā. These refer to the large drums that line the walls outside monasteries; the worshipers turn the drums as they circumambulate. Prayer wheels can also be in the form of small cylinders that individuals hold in their hands and whirl with their wrists. Ordinary Tibetans who are not interested in doctrinal subtlety recite the six-syllable formula in order to achieve rebirth in the Pure Land. For religious practitioners, the mantrā is a form of the name of Avalokiteśvara and the innermost heart of Avalokiteśvara. By chanting the mantrā, one hopes to see Avalokiteśvara and appropriate the bodhisattva's power, enabling one to develop great compassion and achieve liberation.[10]

The various forms that Avalokiteśvara assumes in Buddhist Asia reflect the nature of Buddhism in its long history of encountering various indigenous cultural and religious traditions in the region. For this reason, the bodhisattva is a most eloquent and successful representative of the religion.

REVIEW OF LITERATURE

Existing literature in both Western and Asian languages, as indicated by the following works for further reading, consist roughly of two kinds: art historical and textual. Studies of the iconography of the bodhisattva in different Buddhist regions predominate. Other textual studies discuss the roles and functions of the bodhisattva in Buddhist scriptures. A comprehensive study of Avalokiteśvara in the pan-Buddhist culture is necessary and awaits future scholarly endeavor.

FURTHER READING

Boisselier, Jean. "Precisions sur quelques images Khmeres d'Avalokiteśvara." *Arts Asiatiques* 11, no. 1 (1965): 75–89.

Brough, John. "Amitābha and Avalokiteśvara in an Inscribed Gandhāran Sculpture." *Indologia Tanrinensia* 10 (1982): 65–70.

Bunnag, Jane. "The Way of the Monk and the Way of the World: Buddhism in Thailand, Laos, and Cambodia." In *The World of Buddhism*. Edited by Richard Gombrich, 159–170. London: Thames & Hudson, 1984.

Chutiwongs, Nandana. "The Iconography of Avalokiteśvara in Mainland Southeast Asia." PhD diss., Rijksuniversiteit, Leiden, 1984.

Holt, John C. *Buddha in the Crown: Avalokiteśvara in the Buddhist Traditions of Sri Lanka*. New York: Oxford University Press, 1991.

Jessup, Helen Ibbitson, and Thierry Zephir, eds. *Sculpture of Angkor and Ancient Cambodia Millennium of Glory*. Washington, DC: National Gallery of Art, 1997.

Kapstein, Matthew. "Remarks on the Mana bKa'-'bum and the Cult of Avalokiteśvara in Tibet." In *Tibet Buddhism: Reason and Revelation*. Edited by Steven D. Goodman and Ronald M. Davidson, 57–93. Albany: State University of New York Press, 1992.

Mallmann, Marie-Therese. *Introduction a l'Etude d'Avalokiteśara*. Paris: Annales du Musėe Guimet, 1948.

Schopen, Gregory. "The Inscription on the Kushan Image of Amitābha and the Character of Early Mahāyāna in India." *Journal of the International Association of Buddhist Studies* 10 (1987): 99–138.

Studholme, Alexander. *The Origins of Om Maṇipadme Hūm: A Study of the Kāraṇḍavyūha Sūtra.* Albany: State University of New York Press, 2002.

Suchan, Thomas. "Dynamic Duo: Tang and Song Imagery of Paired Bodhisattvas from Sichuan." Paper presented at the Fourth International Convention of Asian Scholars, Shanghai, China, August 2005.

Yü, Chün-fang. *Kuan-yin: The Chinese Transformation of Avalokiteśvara.* New York: Columbia University Press, 2001.

Yü, Chün-fang, and Yao Chongxin. 2016. "Guanyin and Dizang: The Creation of a Chinese Buddhist Pantheon" *Asitische Studien.*

Zwalf, W., ed. *Buddhism: Art and Faith.* London: British Museum, 1985.

NOTES

1. Marie-Therese de Mallmann, *Introduction a l'Etude d'Avalokiteśara* (Paris: Annales du Musèe Guimet, 1948); Gregory Schopen, "The Inscription on the Kushan Image of Amitābha and the Character of Early Mahāyāna In India," *Journal of the Internaional Association of Buddhist Studies* 10 (1987): 99–138.
2. Nanadana Chutiwongs, "The Iconography of Avalokiteśvara in Mainland Southeast Asia." (PhD diss., Rijksuniversiteit, Leiden, 1984).
3. Helen Ibbitson Jessup and Thierry Zephir, eds. *Sculpture of Angkor and Ancient Cambodia Millennium of Glory* (Washington, DC: National Gallery of Art, 1997) 304; Jane Bunnag, "The Way of the Monk and the Way of the World: Buddhism in Thailand, Laos, and Cambodia," in *The World of Buddhism*, ed. Richard Gombrich (London: Thames & Hudson, 1984) 161; W. Zwalf, ed. *Buddhism: Art and Faith* (London: British Museum, 1985) 176.
4. John C. Holt, *Buddha in the Crown: Avalokiteśvara in the Buddhist Traditions of Sri Lanka* (New York: Oxford University Press, 1991).
5. Matthew Kapstein, "Remarks on the Mana bKa'-'bum and the Cult of Avalokiteśvara in Tibet," in *Tibet Buddhism: Reason and Revelation*, ed. Steven D. Goodman and Ronald M. Davidson (Albany: State University of New York Press, 1992), 57–93.
6. Chün-fang Yü, *Kuan-yin: The Chinese Transformation of Avalokiteśvara* (New York: Columbia University Press, 2001), 194.
7. Chün-fang Yü, *Kuan-yin: The Chinese Transformation of Avalokiteśvara* (New York: Columbia University Press, 2001), 54–55.
8. Thomas Suchan, "Dynamic Duo: Tang and Song Imagery of Paired Bodhisattvas from Sichuan" (paper presented at the Fourth International Convention of Asian Scholars, Shanghai, China, August 2005).
9. Chün-fang Yü and Yao Chongxin, "Guanyin and Dizang: The Creation of a Chinese Buddhist Pantheon," *Asitische Studien*, 2016.
10. Alexander Studholme, *The Origins of Om Maṇipadme Hūm: A Study of the Kāraṇḍavyūha Sūtra* (Albany: State of New York University Press, 2002), 106–108.

Chün-fang Yü

B

BODHISATTVABHŪMI (THE BODHISATTVA STAGES)

THE *BODHISATTVA-BHŪMI*: TITLE AND CONTEXT

The *Bodhisattva-bhūmi* is the fifteenth and largest section of the encyclopedic treatise *Yogācāra-bhūmi-śāstra* (*Treatise of Resources for Yoga Practitioners*), which is one of the most influential texts of the School of Yoga Practitioners (Yogācāra). Yogācāra is one of the two main divisions of Indian Mahāyāna philosophy (the other being Madhyamaka). The term *bhūmi* in both works is sometimes translated as "stage(s)," "level(s)," or "foundation(s)," but in this case, "resources" is probably a more felicitous rendering based on the content and structure of the text.[1] Mahāyāna buddhology contains several presentations of the path to buddhahood divided into *bhūmis*, the most well-known of which is a tenfold list found in, among other sources, the *Ten Stages Discourse* (*Daśabhūmika-sūtra*),[2] but this is not the primary sense in which the term is used in the *Yogācāra-bhūmi* or the *Bodhisattva-bhūmi*.

Bhūmi derives from the Sanskrit root *bhū*, "to be"; it can refer to earth or ground, a place or situation, the floor of a building, the base of a diagram, the extent of an area, as well as a matter or subject. In Mahāyāna literature, it often connotes a basis for something or a foundation on which one relies, as well as a level of accomplishment. Several of these associations are probably in play in the *Bodhisattva-bhūmi*, which contains discussions of a wide range of topics related to bodhisattva conduct and practice, as well as sections detailing *bhūmi* schemas of varying numbers of levels of attainment on the path to buddhahood.

The *Bodhisattva-bhūmi* is the third of a hierarchical series of "*bhūmis*" for specific types of Buddhist practitioners; the prior two are *Resources for Hearers* (*Śrāvaka-bhūmi*) and *Resources for Solitary Realizers* (*Pratyekabuddha-bhūmi*). These two types constitute the divisions of "Hīnayānists" according to Mahāyāna reckonings.

This ordering is not, however, a hierarchy of training; there is no indication that Buddhists should first engage in hearer practices, then become solitary realizers, and finally embark on the Mahāyāna path (although the text does indicate that at least some bodhisattvas begin training as hearers and later convert to Mahāyāna).

The *Bodhisattva-bhūmi* is probably best described as a compendium of resources for bodhisattvas. This sense accords with internal statements in the text itself that describe it as "a summary of the collection of bodhisattva discourses" (*bodhisattva-sūtra-piṭaka-mātṛkā*). The term *mātṛkā* has a range of connotations, including mnemonic formulas used to facilitate memorization of doctrinal material; lists that encapsulate complex ideas; or compendiums that bring together disparate bits of lore. All of these senses can be seen in the *Bodhisattva-bhūmi*, which is replete with lists of various kinds encompassing a wide range of material. In addition, as Gethin has noted, the term *mātṛkā* (Pāli *mātikā*) is etymologically linked with *mātṛ*, the Sanskrit word for mother, and the English word *matrix*. As such, a *mātṛkā* is not primarily "a condensed summary," but rather "the seed from which something grows . . . something creative—something out of which something further evolves. It is . . . pregnant with the Dhamma and able to generate it in all its fullness."[3] Gethin goes on to discuss the term *mātikā-dhara*, "learned in the *mātṛkās*"—that is, a person who is thoroughly familiar with a repertoire of condensed lists and who also "knows how to expand them and draw out expositions from them . . . not simply someone who can spout endless lists of lists learnt by rote, but a person who can improvise and create through the medium of these lists."[4]

These connotations are embedded in the structure of the *Bodhisattva-bhūmi*; its intended audience of aspiring or practicing bodhisattvas is presented with a plethora of lists, and these are then expanded and their implications for practice are revealed. Bodhisattvas are instructed in the meanings behind the lists and how they can be used to explain the dharma to students, as well as the soteriological benefits of the resources contained in the treatise for those intent on pursuing the path to buddhahood. Gethin further notes that Buddhist texts comprised of *mātṛkā* content are generally not intended to be read from beginning to end; rather, various parts can be accessed and studied, their significance drawn out and applied to concrete situations. The *Bodhisattva-bhūmi* presents itself as a guide for the entire bodhisattva path, beginning with the initial aspiration to reorient one's cognitions in accordance with its core principles and then proceeding through ascending levels of profundity of understanding and progressively more effective practice, during which one develops a range of special abilities and insights.

ASIAN-LANGUAGE VERSIONS OF THE *BODHISATTVA-BHŪMI*

The *Bodhisattva-bhūmi* was originally written in Sanskrit and later translated into Chinese and Tibetan (see references). There are several extant Sanskrit manuscripts and two published Sanskrit editions.[5] The former used two Nepalese manuscripts, which Wogihara refers to as the "Cambridge ms." and the "Kyoto ms." based on where they were housed. Dutt based his edition on photographs of a Sanskrit manuscript in Shalu (Zhwa lu) Monastery in Tibet taken by Rāhul Sāṃkṛtyāyana (1893–1963) in 1938 and brought to India, following which they were stored in the K. P. Jayaswal Institute in Patna. There is a consensus among scholars that Wogihara's edition, while it contains some errors, is superior to Dutt's and that the latter contains more textual problems.[6]

Wogihara states that neither manuscript was complete and that "they abound in clerical errors." Both texts had unreadable or missing sections, and so his final version employed both and corrected the remaining errors on the basis of the Tibetan translation. He concluded that the Kyoto manuscript was not only older than the Cambridge recension, but also more corrupt, missing many *tāla* leaf pages (approximately 192) and containing "many lacunae." The entire final chapter ("Anukrama-paṭala") is absent in the Kyoto text. He adds that the Cambridge ms. is missing seven leaves and that many of the extant ones are "greatly damaged at either one or both ends and occasionally illegible with stain or defacement." [7]

Dutt indicates that a number of the photographs on which he based his version were illegible either entirely or in parts. He states that the recension he used corresponds to Wogihara's "Cambridge ms." and that he compared his edition with Wogihara's shortly before publication, but he does not appear to have made any emendations based on this.[8]

The manuscript problems noted by Wogihara and Dutt highlight some of the difficulties faced by contemporary scholars working on incomplete or error-filled sources. One often sees the phrase "Sanskrit original" used uncritically, even by accomplished scholars; the implication is that any Sanskrit manuscript supersedes versions in other languages and represents an earlier and thus more authoritative recension. But most of the extant Sanskrit manuscripts of Buddhist works are Nepalese versions hand-copied from the 15th–17th centuries and are thus the most recent (and often most corrupt) current editions of a particular text. The *tāla* leaves on which Indian Buddhist works were traditionally inscribed tended to become dried and brittle over time, and insects infested libraries and feasted on the volumes they contained. Texts had to be recopied frequently, and scribes had to guess at what was missing, with the result that, over the course of millennia, a given work would become increasingly corrupted. Contemporary editors emend them on the basis of Tibetan or Chinese translations.

Thus, when one refers to "the *Bodhisattva-bhūmi*," there is no single text that corresponds to this title. If there was a treatise of this title composed during the 4th–5th centuries in India, that is long lost; it has been succeeded by innumerable subsequent copies, and it probably circulated throughout areas of the Indian subcontinent in which such literature was studied. It was again copied in various trajectories of recensions before one or more of these was carried to Tibet or China and then translated. There are three versions in the Chinese canon (by Dharmakṣema in 414–421 or 426, by Guṇavarman in 431, and a complete translation of the *Yogācāra-bhūmi* by Xuanzang 玄奘 in 646–648), all of which differ from the others. There is also an undated Tibetan version in the *Translations of Treatises* (*Bstan 'gyur*) section of the Tibetan canon attributed to Prajñāvarma and Ye shes sde. The *Bodhisattva-bhūmi*, like other Indian Buddhist texts, is probably more accurately conceived as a corpus of related literature that may have begun as lore circulating within communities of scholar monks that was brought together in a single work. That treatise, in turn, may have been augmented and edited over time before it reached a more or less settled version that was studied in the great Indian centers of Buddhist learning such as Nālandā and Vikramaśīla. It then became the subject of commentaries and was translated into other Asian languages. The commentaries should also be included within the *Bodhisattva-bhūmi* corpus, along with fragments quoted (or paraphrased) in other Indic works.

THE AUTHOR(S) AND/OR COMPILER(S) OF THE *BODHISATTVA-BHŪMI* AND THE *YOGĀCĀRA-BHŪMI*

In Tibetan tradition, Asaṅga (*c.* 300–350) is credited with authorship of the *Yogācāra-bhūmi*, while Chinese tradition cites the future buddha Maitreya as the author.[9] These differences can be reconciled, however, because according to Tibetan accounts of Asaṅga's life, he traveled to Tuṣita heaven and received instructions from the bodhisattva, one of which was the *Bodhisattva-bhūmi*. Thus, in both Tibet and China, Maitreya is regarded as the ultimate source.

Traditional biographies characterize Asaṅga as a third- (or, in some cases, first-)level bodhisattva. Tāranātha states that, in a previous life, Asaṅga's mother had been a monk who was a devotee of the bodhisattva Avalokiteśvara and that they insulted another monk during a debate, following which Avalokiteśvara predicted that they would have to endure repeated births as a woman until the negative karma of the encounter was eradicated. In one of these lives, she was a Buddhist laywoman named Prasannaśīla, who gave birth to three sons: Asaṅga was the eldest; Vasubandhu, who also became a prominent Buddhist philosopher, was the second; and Viriñcinivatsa was the third. According to Tāranātha, they were conceived as a result of a prayer she made to Avalokiteśvara that she might give birth to boys who would restore Buddhism in India. Tāranātha further reports that Prasannaśīla was a brahman woman of the Kauśika clan, but Asaṅga's father was a *kṣatriya*. The father of her other two sons was a brahman. The family lived in Puruṣapura (Peshawar, Afghanistan, in the early 21st century).[10]

Asaṅga demonstrated an early inclination toward religious practice and as a child would often go into a forest by himself to engage in meditation based on instructions he received from his teacher, Jetāri. Asaṅga was ordained as a monk at an early age and impressed his teachers with his prodigious memory and keen intelligence. Paramārtha states that Asaṅga first studied with teachers of the Sarvāstivāda school and mastered Hīnayāna scriptures under the tutelage of an *arhat* named Piṇḍola. He also read Mahāyāna works, including the Perfection of Wisdom discourses, but he was unable to comprehend them fully. Hoping to rectify this, he received an initiation into the cult of the future buddha Maitreya, following which he engaged in practices intended to facilitate direct communication with the bodhisattva.[11]

Asaṅga left his Hīnayāna teachers and entered meditative retreat in a cave on a mountain named Kukkuṭapāda, where he remained for twelve years. Tāranātha reports that after three years of diligent practice, Asaṅga could see no significant progress, and so he decided to leave the cave. As he passed the entrance, however, he saw that birds flying by the cave had worn smooth the stone above his head; he took this as a sign that he should persevere in his practice.[12]

Three more years of solitary meditation failed to yield a vision of Maitreya, and so Asaṅga again exited his cave. He observed water erosion in rocks outside the cave, which appeared to be another indication that he should not despair. After a total of nine years of practice, however, Asaṅga still had not seen any indication of success in his quest. For a third time, he left the cave and walked along a road toward a nearby town. He came upon a man who showed him some needles he claimed had been fashioned by rubbing cotton on iron: another sign.

Despite the portents and encouragements, he had witnessed and his prodigious efforts in meditation, three more years passed without any indications that Maitreya had responded. Asaṅga abandoned his quest and left the area. After some time, as he approached a town, he saw a dog lying by the side of the road, suffering horribly from an infestation of worms in its flesh. As an aspiring bodhisattva, Asaṅga was filled with compassion for the dog; he also realized that if he removed the worms they would die. But if the situation continued, the dog would die in agony. He decided to cut off some of his own flesh to provide food for the worms, and then he walked to the town to borrow a knife. When he returned to the suffering dog, he raised the knife to cut off part of his arm, but the dog transformed into the glorious form of Maitreya.

Asaṅga's response was somewhat testy: he challenged the bodhisattva, asking why it had taken so long for him to respond to his efforts. Maitreya replied that he had, in fact, been standing beside Asaṅga in the cave from the beginning of his training, but his mental afflictions had prevented Asaṅga from being aware of the bodhisattva's presence. Maitreya then displayed stains on his robe where Asaṅga had unwittingly thrown garbage on him. The act of selfless compassion in which he intended to cut off his own flesh to save a suffering being had elevated Asaṅga's perceptions to a new level, and as a result he could now communicate directly with Maitreya. The two then traveled to Tuṣita heaven, the abode of all incipient buddhas, and during the course of several months, the bodhisattva taught his student five texts that would come to be known as the "Five Treatises of Maitreya," one of which was *Resources for Yoga Practitioners*. These works, along with commentaries by Asaṅga's brother Vasubandhu, would later become foundational sources for the Yogācāra school. According to Buddhist tradition, following his return to India Asaṅga committed the lore imparted by Maitreya to writing. In *Great Tang Records on the Western Regions* (*Da tang xiyu ji* 大唐西域記; T 2087.896b), Xuanzang (602–664) reports that the *Yogācāra-bhūmi* was composed near Ayodhyā in present-dayUttar Pradesh.[13]

MODERN ACADEMIC SCHOLARSHIP ON THE *BODHISATTVA-BHŪMI* AND ITS TEXTUAL HISTORY

The authorship of the *Bodhisattva-bhūmi* and *Yogācāra-bhūmi* has been the subject of a large corpus of published research, mainly by Japanese and German scholars who have taken a text-critical approach and attempted to identify the relative dates of textual and doctrinal strata contained in them. There is currently a broad consensus among academics who have studied the *Yogācāra-bhūmi* in depth that it is not the work of a single author, but rather a compilation of heterogeneous materials from a range of sources. Debates regarding the treatise's authorship have been extensively surveyed and critiqued by Martin Delhey.[14]

Alex Wayman and Mukai Akira followed the traditional attribution of the *Yogācāra-bhūmi* to Asaṅga.[15] Wayman contended that Asaṅga wrote the treatise section by section, much in the order that it has come down to us. His main evidence for this conclusion is the many internal cross-references that direct readers to other sections in which certain ideas are more fully articulated. Hakamaya Noriaki thinks that Asaṅga may have compiled the text but was probably not the author of the entire *Yogācāra-bhūmi*.[16] Noritoshi Aramaki, who was a prominent exponent of the Asaṅga-as-author hypothesis, has been converted to the theory that the treatise is a composite.[17] He states that he now believes that the earliest materials in the *Yogācāra-bhūmi* can be found in a schema of seven bodhisattva stages (*bhūmi*) that preceded the more developed ten-stage model (and other models with varying numbers of stages). In this conception of the path (which differs from what he regards as later and more fully elaborated presentations), bodhisattvas cultivate awareness of the two truths (conventional truths and ultimate truths) in order to eliminate the two hindrances: defiling hindrances (*kleśāvaraṇa*) and cognitive hindrances (*jñeyāvaraṇa*). Progress in these practices gradually leads to buddhahood. Aramaki then asserts that the next stratum of Yogācāra literature consists of meditative practices described in the *Bodhisattva-bhūmi* relating to the "four investigations" (*paryeṣaṇā*) and the four complete knowledges of reality-as-it-is (*yathābhūta-parijñāna*), but he presents these ideas as conclusions without providing detailed textual analysis to back them up.

Schmithausen's work—particularly his investigations of texts and doctrinal development in his monumental study of the foundation consciousness (*ālaya-vijñāna*)[18]—has been enormously influential in the development of a general scholarly consensus that the *Yogācāra-bhūmi* is a composite that incorporates material from various historical strata. He argues that some portions of the *Bodhisattva-bhūmi* are among the earliest extant examples of Yogācāra literature and that the absence of distinctive Yogācāra doctrines (e.g., foundation consciousness) in the text indicates that the tradition developed over time. The fact that discussions of the foundation consciousness and cognition-only (*vijñapti-mātratā*) are absent in the *Bodhisattva-bhūmi* but appear in developed form in the *Discourse Explaining the Thought* (*Saṃdhinirmocana-sūtra*) suggests that the former was composed first.[19] Schmithausen's periodization is based on a comprehensive and detailed study of texts in Sanskrit, Chinese, and Tibetan, and the evidence he adduces supports his conclusions, but they are based on mutually corroborating premises, which cannot themselves be independently verified based on the textual evidence available at this time. For example, a key strategy in his analysis is to relegate less fully articulated statements of the foundation consciousness doctrine to "early" strata, but the *Yogācāra-bhūmi* has numerous internal referents that direct readers to more developed presentations of various doctrines or lists in other parts of the treatise. An alternative hypothesis is that the author(s)/compiler(s) saw no need to expound all the details of ideas that were more fully presented in other parts of the *Yogācāra-bhūmi* and thus make an already massive treatise even larger.

This does not, however, definitively undermine Schmithausen's conclusions because, as a number of scholars have pointed out, the *Yogācāra-bhūmi* contains numerous examples of doctrines that are enumerated or explained differently in various sections. For example, the early parts of the *Bodhisattva-bhūmi* employ the well-known sixfold schema for the perfections (*pāramitā*) that bodhisattvas cultivate on the path to buddhahood, but near the end of the text, a tenfold version appears (which is correlated with the sixfold one). Schmithausen concludes that the *Yogācāra-bhūmi* is a composite of Buddhist lore (both Mahāyāna and Mainstream Buddhist sources) of varying age and provenance that came together over time and that the authors or compilers cannot be identified on the basis of extant materials.[20] Even within sections, disparate sources can be identified through careful comparison with other parts of the text. According to his periodization, there are three primary layers of the *Yogācāra-bhūmi*: (1) parts of the *Basic Resources* (*Maulyo Bhūmayaḥ*), including *Resources for Hearers, Resources for Bodhisattvas*, and the *Compendium of Topics* (*Vastu-saṃgrahaṇī*); (2) the remaining parts of the *Basic Resources*; and (3) the *Compendium of Ascertainments* (*Viniścaya-saṃgrahaṇī*), which contains commentary on earlier parts of the *Yogācāra-bhūmi*, including the *Bodhisattva-bhūmi*.

STRUCTURE AND CONTENTS

The *Bodhisattva-bhūmi* has three main divisions, titled "yoga sections" (*yogasthāna*), which are further subdivided into chapters (*paṭala*). An additional section titled "sequential structure chapter" (*anukrama-paṭala*) that is not part of the text's tripartite format is added at the end. The three *yogasthāna*s are (1) basis (*ādhāra*), (2) subsidiary factors relating to the basis (*ādhārānudharma*), and (3) consummation of the basis (*ādhāra-niṣṭhā*). The text begins with an enumeration of ten primary topics that will be considered sequentially. The first is the subject of the initial *yogasthāna*; #2–5 are discussed in the second *yogasthāna*; and the third *yogasthāna* is concerned with #6–10. The ten topics are (1) the basis for bodhisattva training, (2) attributes (*liṅga*) of bodhisattvas, (3) types (*pakṣa*) of bodhisattvas, (4) superior attitudes (*adhyaśaya*) of bodhisattvas, (5) abodes (*vihāra*), (6) rebirths (*upapatti*), (7) guiding/supporting (*parigraha*) sentient beings, (8) stages (*bhūmi*) of bodhisattva practice, (9) practices (*caryā*), and (10) accession (*pratiṣṭhā*) to buddhahood.

Discussion of the basis begins with predisposition or lineage (*gotra*), which is a precondition for someone to embark on bodhisattva practice. Those who lack the innate inclination to become bodhisattvas are congenitally incapable of generating the altruistic intention to pursue buddhahood for the benefit of other sentient beings (*bodhicitta*), and the text suggests that they will be unable to acquire it in the future. *Gotra* is described as an inherent factor that has been present in the psychophysical continuums of bodhisattvas during the course of innumerable births. It is compared to a seed (*bīja*) that remains in a latent state until the conditions for its manifestation and development are present. Sustained cultivation of good qualities enables bodhisattvas to actualize this potential.

The next two bases require the first; they are (1) the initial inception of the resolve to pursue awakening and (2) the basis for cultivating the factors of awakening (*bodhi-pakṣa*), a group of thirty-seven trainings that are discussed in several parts of the *Bodhisattva-bhūmi*. After an aspiring bodhisattva has developed *bodhicitta*, this serves as a support for subsequent practice. The factors of awakening support their efforts and are the foundation for religious training.

Bodhisattvas are distinguished from hearers and solitary realizers in four ways: (1) bodhisattvas have keen faculties (*tīkṣendriya*)—those of solitary realizers are middling, and hearers have weak faculties; (2) the two Hīnayāna types only pursue the path for their own benefit, while bodhisattvas benefit both themselves and others; (3) bodhisattvas master all fields of knowledge, while hearers and solitary realizers only master certain topics pertinent to their practice; and (4) hearers and solitary realizers attain the respective types of awakening that are the goal of their training, but those who follow the bodhisattva path attain the supreme state: unsurpassed, perfect awakening (*anuttara-saṃyak-saṃbodhi*). This is accomplished by means of a multitude of practices, the most central of which are the six perfections: generosity, ethics, patience, effort, concentration, and wisdom. The text adds that a person who is naturally inclined to pursue such a difficult endeavor for the minimum requisite duration of three countless eons (*asaṃkhyeya-kalpa*) may from time to time be reborn in one of the lower destinies (of animals, hungry spirits, or hell beings), but their sojourns will be brief and relatively less painful than those of other beings who lack their innate goodness. Despite the difficulties they will encounter and the unimaginable length of time required to follow the path to its ultimate destination, those who succeed in developing *bodhicitta* are guaranteed to fulfill their goals. While training must be undertaken by each person individually, a multitude of buddhas and more advanced bodhisattvas will provide assistance and guidance.

Bodhisattvas train in viewing all sentient beings as their mothers or close friends. Everyone is born over and over again in an infinite variety of life situations, and so all have been in every possible relationship with every other transmigrator since beginningless time. One conclusion is that those who are now strangers or enemies were once near and dear, relatives or friends who were loving and kind, or parents and siblings. Becoming fully cognizant of the sufferings they endure, bodhisattvas work tirelessly to aid sentient beings with an unshakeable courage. Bodhisattvas' resolve helps them to sustain two important practices: every day they cultivate the intention to attain buddhahood for the benefit of others, and they also have a daily regimen of doing whatever pragmatic actions can help beings overcome suffering.

The next chapter focuses on the crucial bodhisattva act of generating resolve to attain buddhahood. This marks the inception of the bodhisattva path, following which bodhisattvas cultivate the perfections, motivated by a deep sense of caring or compassion (*karuṇā*) for other beings caught up in the sufferings of cyclic existence (samsara). This has five aspects: (1) its nature (*svabhāva*): it is the initial and essential aspect of bodhisattvas' aspirations; (2) its aspects (*ākāra*): it is expressed as the resolve to attain buddhahood in order to rescue all sentient beings from their sufferings; (3) its objects (*ālambana*): attainment of awakening and sentient beings; (4) its traits (*guṇa*): it is fundamentally good because it embraces all of the qualities that are conducive to awakening; and (5) its excellence (*utkarṣa*): it is the supreme type of aspiration and it leads to the ultimate attainment.

The next chapter discusses how bodhisattvas benefit themselves and others and describes the tension between the two orientations. Bodhisattvas need to recognize when their religious activities are only directed toward their own ends, but they must also avoid solely being concerned with others. When bodhisattvas generate merit through acts of devotion, for example, this helps them progress on the path; the more advanced they become, the greater will be their potential to help others. Their merit will result in future lives in which they have great wealth, excellent health, and physical beauty. These endowments will cause others to naturally seek them out and heed their teachings. These karmic outcomes enable bodhisattvas to benefit beings in ways that would be impossible if they were less well favored. This, in turn, means that bodhisattvas can engage in ever-more-advanced training and thus progress toward buddhahood. The chapter describes a complex dynamic of ways in which the benefits of oneself and others intersect and mutually support each other. One particularly important outcome of this process is that bodhisattvas develop an ability to consciously choose their rebirth situations and so can appear where they are most needed, equipped with the resources required to alleviate suffering and lead others to the peace of nirvana.

A misogynistic thread runs throughout the text, which repeatedly states that men are superior to women and that female births are transcended in the advanced levels of the path. Men are naturally stronger than women, encounter fewer problems and are less prone to illness, and are capable of greater and more effective effort.[21] The text then provides instructions on what techniques will reduce the chances of being reborn as a female; these include regarding maleness as superior and the female body as inferior and saving captive men from being castrated. The resultant merit will increase one's chances of obtaining male bodies in future rebirths.

The fourth chapter, perhaps the most philosophically significant portion of the *Bodhisattvabhūmi,* is titled "The Nature of Reality" (Tattvārtha). It expounds a nominalism that is repeated in several subsequent parts of the treatise. The reality of phenomena has two aspects: (1) their true nature (*bhūtatā*); and (2) their entirety (*sarvatā*). The former is the way things truly exist, and the second refers to their "extent of being" (*yāvad-bhāvikatā*). The text then presents four categories in terms of which "reality" can be understood: (1) in accordance with worldly convention—that is, how ordinary beings conventionally employ language to describe and categorize things; (2) what is determined to be true on the basis of reasoning (*yukti-prasiddha*)—this category encompasses conclusions reached through reliable epistemic instruments (*pramāṇa*) based on direct perception (*pratyakṣa*), that is, the knowledge attained by hearers and solitary realizers, which pertains to the four noble truths (suffering, its cause, its cessation, and the path); (3) knowledge that results from eliminating afflictive hindrances; and (4) knowledge that results from eliminating cognitive hindrances. The fourth type is only found by bodhisattvas and buddhas, who comprehend both the non-self of persons (*pudgala-nairātmya*) and the non-self of phenomena (*dharma-nairātmya*). They understand the inexpressible true nature of phenomena: all things are devoid of intrinsic nature (*svabhāva*). Words and concepts befuddle the perceptions of ordinary beings and lead them to mistake designations for reality.

Those who correctly understand reality as it is know that phenomena are empty of the duality of existence and nonexistence. This is declared to be the middle way (*madhyama-pratipad*) that avoids extremes. Bodhisattvas train, over the course of countless eons, in examining emptiness (*śūnyatādhimokṣa*), gradually deepening their insight. Hearers and solitary realizers, by contrast, seek to escape cyclic existence as quickly as possible and attain the peace of nirvana due to their fear. Bodhisattvas neither seek nirvana nor avoid it because of aversion to the sufferings of samsara. As a result of protracted familiarization with the notion that all phenomena have an inexpressible reality and lack the duality of existence and nonexistence, bodhisattvas overcome all conceptualization and any tendency to equate labels with reality. Instead, they perceive the mere presence of things (*vastu-mātra*), or mere suchness (*tathatā-mātra*). Because phenomena share the same nature, bodhisattvas develop an unshakeable impartiality or equanimity (*upekṣā*). Bodhisattvas who reach this level of awareness eliminate pride and fatigue. They become experts in all fields of knowledge and use their skills to help others overcome doubt.

Transcending acquiescence to ideations within the interrelated complex of mundane linguistic designations plays a key role in this process. Bodhisattvas examine phenomena as they are and understand that words and concepts are mere designations (*prajñapti-mātra*) They lack any essence and do not substantially exist. The text makes a point of rejecting what it characterizes as a nihilistic reading of emptiness, however: it is not a denial of existence tout court, but rather an assertion that there is a mere thing-in-itself that remains when one directly apprehends the ultimate reality (*paramārtha*) of things. This is the basis on which deceptive linguistic conventions are superimposed, but its true nature is inexpressible, only ascertained by bodhisattvas who are adept at meditation and by buddhas. Mahāyānists who mistakenly declare that everything is merely verbal designations are declared to be the "prime nihilists." As Kragh notes, Bhāviveka (*c.* 500–560) understood this to be a critique of Madhyamaka and attempted to rebut it. Bodhisattvas intent on attaining awakening should avoid such people and shun their false doctrines.[22] The correct understanding of emptiness views things as empty of false conceptuality, but "something remains" in this analysis: a non-conceptual, inexpressible reality.

Engagement with words and concepts leads to the proliferation of mistaken ideas, including viewing the transitory collection of the psychophysical personality as "I" and subsequently grasping things regarded as "mine." Bodhisattvas gradually free themselves from false ideation and greed by means of the four thorough knowledges of things as they really are (*yathābhūta-parijñāna*): (1) investigation of names (*nāma-paryeṣaṇā*), through which they understand that names are merely names that rely on other names for their specificity; (2) investigation of things (*vastu-paryeṣaṇā*), which leads to understanding phenomena as they really are, that is, inexpressible and separate from names superimposed on them; (3) investigation of designations of intrinsic nature (*svabhāva-prajñapti-paryeṣaṇā*), which leads to the realization that designations are nothing more than conceptual positings and intrinsic nature is an illusion, like dreams or hallucinations; and (4) investigation of differentiating designations (*viśeṣa-prajñapti-paryeṣaṇā*), by means of which bodhisattvas come to comprehend the thing-in-itself, free from superimposed conceptions. Understood from the perspective of ultimate truth, things are nondual and cannot correctly be posited as either existent or nonexistent. Bodhisattvas who successfully cultivate these analytical exercises free themselves from the ignorance and suffering that result from accepting and acting on false ideations. They also cut off the mental energy that fed the proliferation of false views; this leads to increasingly profound knowledge and understanding, and as a result bodhisattvas also acquire a repertoire of supernatural abilities.

The text then discusses ways in which bodhisattvas work to improve sentient beings and themselves. It begins by stating that only those who already innately possess the requisite predispositions will be able to successfully develop the intention to attain buddhahood and then pursue the path to awakening. Some of the beneficiaries of their care will have hearer proclivities, and others will be inclined toward the solitary-realizer path; bodhisattvas aid them in their endeavors and recognize beings with the superior predispositions required to become bodhisattvas and work to mature their latent abilities. Some beings, however, lack any inclination toward the dharma; bodhisattvas help them engage in meritorious activities that will result in birth in higher realms.

The *Bodhisattva-bhūmi* presents a hierarchy of six stages through which bodhisattvas progress; these are further expounded in the third *yogasthāna*. The text then details how various types of practitioners will make progress (or not) with a dependence on the strength of their proclivities for training and the relative level of effort they put forth. Those of weak faculties and resolve will only attain mediocre results, while those of middling faculties and effort will progress further on their respective paths. The same is true for bodhisattvas, but due to their innate predisposition for the highest goals of the dharma, they will eventually surpass all other practitioners after they put forward the requisite effort and meet the necessary conditions. The first two incalculable eons will be devoted to merit-making activities and cultivation of good qualities. Those who attain "certainty" (*niyata*)—the fourth of the levels outlined in the path—will never again be reborn in the lower realms as a result of negative karma.

Chapter seven of part I is concerned with awakening, the culmination of the bodhisattva path. The attainment of awakening requires two kinds of elimination (*prahāṇa*) and two kinds of knowledge (*jñāna*). The former refers to the elimination of the afflictive hindrances and the cognitive hindrances. The latter are (1) stainless knowledge that is not obstructed by affliction; this results from the complete elimination of the afflictive hindrances; and (2) unobstructed knowledge with respect to all cognitive objects, the result of eradicating the cognitive hindrances. Much of the chapter is concerned with enumerating the ways in which buddhas are superior to all other beings, which includes their perfect bodies, their all-encompassing knowledge, and their flawless conduct.

The chapter concludes with a discussion of how buddhas appear in various world systems. Only one buddha can manifest in a given realm at any particular time, but many bodhisattvas may take rebirth there. The reason for the one buddha rule is because all buddhas possess unlimited power and omniscience, and so a single buddha is able to perform all the necessary dharma activities in a given domain; additional buddhas would be superfluous. In addition, if multiple buddhas were to manifest at one time and place, the beings of that realm would become complacent and would not develop the urgency to practice that results when their buddha appears to die. The chapter concludes with a misogynist statement: buddhas are always male because their practice over the course of three countless eons results in ever more sublime bodies. Long before the attainment of buddhahood, they transcend any possibility of being born in an inferior female form: "women naturally have many mental afflictions and are burdened by inferior wisdom; it is impossible for a person with such a mental continuum . . . to attain complete, unsurpassed awakening."[23]

The *Bodhisattva-bhūmi* then presents several chapters outlining the things bodhisattvas must do in order to fulfill their spiritual potential. These include a range of devotional activities and developing expertise in various fields of knowledge, including logic and grammar. The text then discusses each of the six perfections at length and indicates that they are mutually supportive and not discrete. All are cultivated during the various stages of the path, and when fully developed, they constitute the matrix of good qualities unique to buddhas.

Chapter 15 focuses on the four methods for gathering students (*saṃgraha-vastu*), a topic whose importance for the author(s) is evidenced by the fact that it appears throughout the treatise in a range of contexts. They are (1) giving (*dāna*)—that is, providing students with both material things they need or value and with dharma teachings; (2) affectionate speech (*priya-vāditā*), defined as discourse that appeals to students, that is truthful, sincere, and beneficial, that relates to the dharma, and is meaningful; (3) purposeful activity (*artha-caryā*)—helping those who have listened to the teachings to follow the path, with no thought of profit or loss, concerned only with students' maturation of good qualities; and (4) concordant aims (*samānārthatā*), ensuring that one's actions accord with one's words. The last of these is particularly important: when teachers propound religious and moral principles but act in ways that contradict their words, students will notice and reproach them. This will lead to a loss of faith in the dharma and confidence in the teacher, which, in turn, results in confusion and lessening of enthusiasm for practice. The treatise also advises bodhisattvas to smile and speak politely, avoid harsh or vulgar expressions, and adhere to the norms of social etiquette. Bodhisattvas should also be able to communicate effectively with all sorts of beings, including thieves and murderers, people who are ignorant or who harbor heretical views, and those who are abusive and rude. Bodhisattvas' skillful instructions inspire others and turn them toward the dharma, and their actions demonstrate how the teachings should be put into practice.

Chapter 16 is concerned with "worship, service, and the immeasurables." It details the range of devotional and merit-making activities in which bodhisattvas engage, including venerating the three jewels (buddha, dharma, monastic community), relying on and honoring religious teachers, and various acts of generosity. Bodhisattvas should have unquestioning reverence for teachers; any thoughts (even if justified) that a particular teacher fails to properly uphold monastic discipline, is ugly, of low social status, or has poor communication skills will result in corresponding negative consequences for those who harbor such notions. An attitude of ardent devotion to religious masters helps one acquire the qualities one attributes to them, even if they really are less than ideal exemplars of the Dharma.

The four immeasurables (*apramāṇa*) are attitudes that help Buddhist trainees to develop a positive outlook and avoid negative mental states: (1) lovingkindness (*maitrī*)—wishing that others have happiness and the causes of happiness; (2) caring or compassion (*karuṇā*), which involves caring about the sufferings of sentient beings and caring for them in pragmatic ways to help alleviate their pain; (3) sympathetic joy (*muditā*)—rejoicing in the good fortune of others without any jealousy or rancor; and (4) impartiality (*upekṣā*), an attitude that values all others equally and avoids differentiating some as more dear or beloved than others.

THE SECOND SECTION OF THE *BODHISATTVA-BHŪMI*

Book two is concerned with practice: how bodhisattvas engage in the training outlined in the first section. There is little specificity regarding exactly what sorts of meditative practices Yogācāra bodhisattvas may have employed. As Deleanu has suggested, at the time when the *Bodhisattva-bhūmi* was composed or compiled, the particulars of training may have been imparted orally by masters to students and seldom written down in meditation manuals.[24] The *Bodhisattva-bhūmi* refers to a number of well-known meditative techniques but provides only scanty information on exactly how they were pursued. The first chapter is concerned with the attributes of bodhisattvas: (1) caring, (2) agreeable speech, (3) courage, (4) openhandedness, and (5) the ability to explain profound hidden meanings and intentions. The next chapter states that there are two types of bodhisattvas: householders and monks. In this and other places in the *Bodhisattva-bhūmi*, the latter type is declared to be far superior. Householders are beset by the vicissitudes of family, employment, and social expectations, but monastics are unafflicted by these and so have greater freedom and latitude to work for the benefit of others. Both types, however, share four crucial qualities: (1) the quality of having completed their spiritual activities well, (2) skillfulness, (3) providing assistance to others, and (4) dedication.

THE THIRD SECTION OF THE *BODHISATTVA-BHŪMI*

The final section of the *Bodhisattva-bhūmi* is primarily concerned with the later stages of bodhisattvas' progress and their attainment of buddhahood. It begins with a discussion of how bodhisattvas take rebirth in a variety of situations throughout the universe in order to benefit sentient beings and simultaneously facilitate their own training. This may even include sojourns in hells, but bodhisattvas do this in order to alleviate the torments of their inhabitants and do not experience the same levels of suffering. Bodhisattvas may be born as giant fish during times of famine and willingly donate their bodies to feed the starving. Some manifest as righteous rulers whose reigns are times of peace and prosperity. They may become doctors during epidemics and cure the sick. Some will take birth in communities of brahmans who hold wrong views and skillfully guide them toward the dharma.

In their final births, bodhisattvas perform a standard repertoire of actions that has been followed by all buddhas of the past, and they have bodies that are endowed with the thirty-two "physical characteristics of a great man" (*mahāpuruṣa-lakṣaṇa*) and eighty secondary characteristics (*anuvyañjana*). These include a long and wide tongue that when extruded covers a buddha's face and can be inserted into the earholes, a fist-sized lump on the top of the head (*uṣṇīṣa*), a silver-colored tuft of hair between the eyebrows (*ūrṇā*), webs between the fingers and toes, and a penis covered with a sheath. Universal monarchs (*cakravartin*) also have these features, but they are only fully perfected on the bodies of buddhas. They serve as proof of buddhahood and feature in numerous conversion narratives.[25]

The chapter also describes a variety of ways in which bodhisattvas make contact with sentient beings and then instruct them in the dharma. The following section contains a brief description of the bodhisattva stages and correlates them with thirteen pleasant states that were discussed in book two. This is followed by a list of four types of bodhisattva activity: (1) activities pertaining to the perfections, (2) activities that lead to awakening, (3) activities relating to supra-mundane knowledge, and (4) activities relating to maturation of sentient beings. The final chapters are concerned with 140 unique buddha-qualities.

The final act of the process that was initiated three countless eons in the past begins when bodhisattvas descend from Tuṣita heaven and, after renouncing home life, proceed to the Place of Awakening, where they enter into the vajra-like meditative absorption (*vajropama-samādhi*) and perform the final repertoire of actions characteristic of those who attain awakening. Then as buddhas they will turn the wheel of dharma, establish an order of monks and nuns, and lead countless sentient beings to liberation.

MAIN FEATURES OF THE TEXT

This outline of the *Bodhisattva-bhūmi* can only present some of its main themes and important contributions to Buddhist thought and practice. The treatise is a voluminous work replete with dense lists of material associated both with mainstream Buddhist lore and practice and distinctively Mahāyāna concepts. As Kragh states, the *Yogācāra-bhūmi* was likely "written in a monastic setting and was intended primarily for ordained readers, as suggested by the text's highly scholastic style of writing that would only be intelligible to the well-educated reader who had received a thorough doctrinal training in the monastery."[26] The book was probably not intended to be read from beginning to end, but rather was a compendium of material that might aid yoga practitioners in their religious quests. As its self-description as "a summary of the collection of bodhisattva discourses" suggests, it is not concerned with presenting new or innovative doctrines or critiquing alternative positions; rather, it brings together a disparate conglomeration of lore that probably circulated in circles of Buddhist scholastics, both mainstream and Mahāyāna, from the 2nd to 4th centuries in India.

I. ASIAN LANGUAGE WORKS

SANSKRIT

CHINESE

Maitreya. 414–421 or 426. *Discourse on the Foundations of Bodhisattvas* (*Pusa dichi jing* 菩薩地持經; 10 *juan*). Trans. Dharmakṣema (Tan Wuchen 曇無讖, 385–433). T 1581.30.888a–959.

Maitreya. 431. *Wholesome Morality of Bodhisattvas* (*Pusa shanjie jing* 菩薩善戒經; 9 *juan*). Trans. Guṇavarman (Qiunabamo 求那跋摩, 367–431). T 1582.

TIBETAN

ENGLISH TRANSLATIONS OF THE *BODHISATTVA-BHŪMI*

Engle, Artemus B. *The Bodhisattva Path to Unsurpassed Enlightenment: A Complete Translation of the Bodhisattvabhūmi*. Boulder, CO: Snow Lion Publications, 2016.

Tatz, Mark. *Asaṅga's Chapter of Ethics with the Commentary of Tsong-kha-pa, The Basic Path to Awakening, The Complete Bodhisattva*. Lewiston, NY, and Queenston, Ontario: The Edwin Mellen Press, 1979.

Willis, Janice Dean. *On Knowing Reality: The Tattvārtha Chapter in Asaṅga's Bodhisattvabhūmi*. New York: Columbia University Press, 1979.

CANONICAL COMMENTARIES ON THE *BODHISATTVA-BHŪMI*

Guṇaprabha. *Commentary on Resources for Bodhisattvas* (*Bodhisattvabhūmi-vṛtti*; Tib. *Byang chub sems dpa'i sa'i 'grel pa*). Sde dge #4044, Sems tsam, vol. *'i* (n.d.): 141a1–182a2.

Guṇaprabha. *Commentary on the Bodhisattva Ethics Chapter* (*Bodhisattva-śīlaparivarta-bhāṣya*; Tib. *Byang chub sems dpa'i tshul khrims kyi le'u bshad pa*). Sde dge #4045, Sems tsam, vol. *'i* (n.d.): 182a2–191a2.

Jinaputra. *Explanation of the Bodhisattva Ethics Chapter* (*Bodhisattva-śīlaparivarta-ṭīkā*; Tib. *Byang chub sems dpa'i tshul khrims kyi le'u'i rgya cher 'grel pa*). Sde dge #4046, Sems tsam, vol. *'i*, (n.d.): 191a2–221a7.

Sāgaramegha. *Exposition of Bodhisattva Resources in Resources for Yoga Practitioners* (*Yogācārabhūmau-bodhisattvabhūmi-vyākhyā*; Tib. *Rnal 'byor spyod pa'i sa las byang chub sems dpa'i sa'i rnam par bshad pa*). Sde dge #4047, Sems tsam, vol. *yi* (n.d.): 1b1–338a7.

II. WESTERN LANGUAGE SOURCES

Bendall, Cecil, and Louis de la Vallée Poussin. "*Bodhisattvabhūmi*: Text-book of the Yogācāra School." *Le Muséon*, #24 (1905): 38–52; #25 (1906): 213–230.

Buescher, Hartmut. *The Inception of Yogācāra-Vijñānavāda*. Vienna: Verlag der Österreichischen Akademie der Wissenschaften, 2008.

de Jong, Jan Willem. "Notes on the *Bodhisattvabhūmi*." In *Hinduismus und Buddhismus: Festschrift für Ulrich Schneider*, Edited by Harry Falk, 163–172. Freiburg, Germany: Hedwig Falk, 1987.

Deleanu, Florin. *The Chapter on the Mundane Path (Laukikamārga) in the Śrāvakabhūmi: A Trilingual Edition (Sanskrit, Tibetan, Chinese), Annotated Translation, and Introductory Study* (2 vols.). Tokyo: The International Institute of Buddhist Studies, 2006.

Deleanu, Florin. *Bodhisattvabhūmi*. New York: Oxford University Press; Oxford Bibliographies, 2018: https://www.oxfordbibliographies.com/view/document/obo-9780195393521/obo-9780195393521-0254.xml.

Demiéville, Paul. "Le chapitre de la *Bodhisattvabhūmi* sur la Perfection du Dhyāna." In *Choix d'études bouddhiques*, 300–319. Leiden, The Netherlands: E.J. Brill, 1973.

Hakamaya, Noriaki. "Serving and Served Monks in the *Yogācārabhūmi*." In *The Foundation for Yoga Practitioners: The Buddhist Yogācārabhūmi Treatise and Its Adaptation in India, East Asia, and Tibet*, Edited by Ulrich Timme Kragh, 312–328. Cambridge, MA: Harvard University Press, 2013.

Kajiyama, Yūichi. "Buddhist Cosmology as Presented in the *Yogācārabhūmi*." In *Wisdom, Compassion, and the Search for Understanding: The Buddhist Studies Legacy of Gadjin M. Nagao*, Edited by Jonathan Silk, 183–200. Honolulu: University of Hawaii Press, 2000.

Kragh, Ulrich Timme, ed. *The Foundation for Yoga Practitioners: The Buddhist Yogācārabhūmi Treatise and Its Adaptation in India, East Asia, and Tibet*. Cambridge, MA: Harvard University Press, 2013a.

Kritzer, Robert. *Vasubandhu and the Yogācārabhūmi: Yogācāra Elements in the Abhidharmakośabhāṣya*. Tokyo: International Institute for Buddhist Studies, 2005.

Leumann, Ernst. "Asaṅga's *Bodhisattvabhūmi*, 18.1–4 Nach Wogihara's Ausgabe des Werkes." In *Studia Indo-Iranica*, Edited by Walter Wurst, 21–38. Leipzig, Germany: Otto Harrassowitz, 1931.

Nagao, Gadjin. *Mādhyamika and Yogācāra: A Study of Mahāyāna Philosophies*. New York: State University of New York Press, 1991.

Potter, Karl H., Lambert Schmithausen, and Ronald M. Davidson. "*Yogācārabhūmi* (Asaṅga)." In *Encyclopedia of Indian Philosophies, Vol. 8, Buddhist Philosophy from 100 to 350 A.D.*, Edited by Karl H. Potter, 398–433. Delhi: Motilal Banarsidass, 1999.

Rahder, Johannes. *Daśabhūmisūtra* et *Bodhisattvabhūmi*, Chapitres Vihāra et Bhūmi. Paris-Louvain: Paul Geuthner, 1926. Appendice: 1–28 (ch. II & III).

Roth, Gustav. "Observations on the First Chapter of Asaṅga's *Bodhisattvabhūmi*." *Indologica Taurinensia*, 3–4, no. 3–4 (1977): 403–412; Reprint: *Indian Studies*. Delhi: Sri Satguru Publications, 1986: 109–116.

Sakuma, Hidenori S. *Die Āśrayaparivṛtti-Theorie in der Yogācārabhūmi* (2 vols.). Stuttgart, Germany: Franz Steiner Verlag, 1990.

Schmithausen, Lambert. *Der Nirvāṇa-Abschnitt in der Viniścayasaṃgrahaṇī der Yogācārabhūmi*. Vienna: Österreichische Akademie der Wissenschaften, Philosophische-Historische Klasse, Sitzungsberichte, 264, Band 2. Abhandlung, Veröffentlichungen der Komission für Sprachen Süd- und Ostasiens Heft 8, 1969.

Schmithausen, Lambert. "On the Problem of the Relation of Spiritual Practice and Philosophical Theory in Buddhism." In *German Scholars on India: Contributions to Indian Studies*, vol. II, Edited by Cultural Department, Embassy of the Federal Republic of Germany. Bombay, 1976.

Schmithausen, Lambert. "On Three *Yogācārabhūmi* Passages Mentioning the Three Svabhāvas or Lakṣaṇas." In *Wisdom, Compassion, and the Search for Understanding: The Buddhist Studies Legacy of Gadjin M. Nagao*, Edited by Jonathan Silk, 245–264. Honolulu: University of Hawaii Press, 2000.

Silk, Jonathan. "The Yogācāra Bhikṣu" In *Wisdom, Compassion, and the Search for Understanding: The Buddhist Studies Legacy of Gadjin M. Nagao*, Edited by Jonathan Silk, 265–314. Honolulu: University of Hawaii Press, 2000.

Takahashi, Koichi. "Vastu in the Tattvārtha Section of the *Bodhisattvabhūmi* and the *Viniścayasaṃgrahaṇī*." *Indogaku bukkyōgaku kenkyū* 印度學佛教學研究, 49, no. 2 (2001): 39–41.

Yokoyama, Kōitsu and Hirosawa Takayuki. *Index to the Yogācārabhūmi (Chinese-Sanskrit-Tibetan)* (漢梵蔵対照瑜伽師地論総索引). Tokyo: Sankibo Busshorin, 1996.

Zimmermann, Michael. "The Chapter on Right Conduct in the *Bodhisattvabhūmi*." In *The Foundation for Yoga Practitioners: The Buddhist Yogācārabhūmi Treatise and Its Adaptation in India, East Asia, and Tibet*, Edited by Ulrich Timme Kragh, 872–883. Cambridge, MA: Harvard University Press, 2013.

NOTES

1. See Florin Deleanu, "Buddhist Meditation in the *Bodhisattvabhūmi*: Quest for and Liberation through the Thing-In-Itself," in *The Foundation for Yoga Practitioners: The Buddhist Yogācārabhūmi Treatise and Its Adaptation in India, East Asia, and Tibet*, ed. Ulrich Timme Kragh (Cambridge, MA: Harvard University Press, 2013), 884–919.
2. Anonymous, *Ten Stages Discourse* (*Daśabhūmika-sūtra*; Tib. *Sa bcu'i le'u*), Sde dge #44, *Bka 'gyur*, Phal chen, vol. *kha*: 166a4–283a7.
3. Rupert Gethin, "The *Mātikās*: Memorization, Mindfulness, and the List," in *In the Mirror of Memory: Reflections on Mindfulness and Remembrance in Indian and Tibetan Buddhism*, ed. Janet Gyatso (Albany: State University of New York Press, 1992), 160–161.
4. Gethin, "The *Mātikās*," 161–162.
5. Unrai Wogihara, ed., *Bodhisattvabhūmi: A Statement of the Whole Course of the Bodhisattva (Being Fifteenth Section of Yogācārabhūmi)* (Tokyo: Sanshusha, 1930–1936; rpt: Tokyo: Sankibo Buddhist Book Store, 1971); and Nalinaksha Dutt, ed., *Bodhisattvabhūmiḥ: Being the XVth Section of Asaṅgapada's Yogācārabhūmi* (Patna, India: K.P. Jayaswal Research Institute, 1978).
6. See Martin Delhey, "The *Yogācārabhūmi* Corpus: Sources, Editions, Translations, and Reference Works," in Kragh, *The Foundation for Yoga Practitioners*, 526.
7. Wogihara, *Bodhisattvabhūmi*, 1.
8. Dutt, *Bodhisattvabhūmiḥ*, 3.
9. Asaṅga, *Resources for Bodhisattvas from the Treatise Resources for Yoga Practitioners* (*Yogācārabhūmau-bodhisattvabhūmiḥ*; Tib. *rNal 'byor spyod pa'i sa las byang chub sems dpa'i sa*), trans. Prajñāvarma and Ye shes sde, Sde dge *Bstan 'gyur* #4037, Sems tsam, vol. *wi*: 1b1–213a7; Maitreya, *Treatise on Foundations for Yoga Practitioners* (*Yujia shidi lun* 瑜伽師地論; 100 *juan*), trans. Xuanzang, T 1579.30.279–882, 646–648.
10. Tāranātha, *History of Buddhism in India*, trans. Lama Chimpa and Alaka Chattopadhyaya (Simla: Indian Institute of Advanced Studies, 1970), 155–156.
11. Paramārtha, "The Life of Vasu-bandhu by Paramārtha," trans. Takakusu Jikido, *T'oung Pao*, ser. II, #5 (1904): 269–296.
12. Tāranātha, *History of Buddhism in India*, 156–159.
13. Xuanzang, *Great Tang Records on the Western Regions* (*Da tang xiyu ji* 大唐西域記), T 2087, trans. Samuel Beal (Motilal Banarsidass, 1884); Samuel Beal, trans., *Si-yu-ki—Buddhist Records of the Western World, translated from the Chinese of Hiuen Tsiang (A.D. 629)* (Delhi: Motilal Banarsidass 1884), I, 226.
14. Delhey, "The *Yogācārabhūmi* Corpus," 498–561.
15. Alex Wayman, "Doctrinal Affiliation of the Buddhist Master Asaṅga," in *Amalā Prajñā: Aspects of Buddhist Studies*, B. V. Bapat Volume, ed. N. H. Samtani (Delhi: Indian Books Centre, 1989), 201–221; and Mukai Akira, cited in Lambert Schmithausen, *Ālayavijñāna: On the Origin and the Early Development of a Central Concept of Yogācāra Philosophy* (Tokyo: The International Institute for Buddhist Studies, 1987), 83.
16. Hakamaya Noriaki, cited in Schmithausen, *Ālayavijñāna*, 183.
17. Noritoshi Aramaki, "Notes on the Formation of the *Yogācārabhūmi* Text-Complex," in Kragh, *The Foundation for Yoga Practitioners*, 430.

18. Schmithausen, *Ālayavijñāna*, 1987 .
19. Anonymous, *Discourse Explaining the Thought*, (*Daśabhūmika-sūtra*; Tib. *Sa bcu'i le'u*). Sde dge #44, *bKa' 'gyur*, Phal chen, vol. *kha*: 166a4–283a7.
20. Schmithausen, *Ālayavijñāna*, 14.
21. Wogihara, *Bodhisattvabhūmi*, I.3.6.1.
22. Ulrich Timme Kragh, "The *Yogācārabhūmi* and Its Adaptation: Introductory Essay with a Summary of the Basic Section," in Kragh, *The Foundation for Yoga Practitioners*, 159n325.
23. Wogihara, *Bodhisattvabhūmi*, 94.
24. Deleanu, "Buddhist Meditation in the *Bodhisattvabhūmi* .
25. See John Powers, *A Bull of a Man: Images of Masculinity, Sex, and the Body in Indian Buddhism* (Cambridge, MA: Harvard University Press, 2017), 1–66.
26. Kragh, "The *Yogācārabhūmi* and Its Adaptation," 29.

John Powers

THE BODY OF THE BUDDHA

INTRODUCTION

Buddhism is a religion with thousands of years of history and doctrinal development, and there are few points of doctrine on which there is a clear consensus. Attitudes toward bodies are no exception. On the one hand, from the earliest strata of Buddhist literature there has been a recurring theme of denigration of physical bodies (*kāya*) and a sense that they are the proximate sites of the pervasive suffering (Pāli *dukkha*; Skt. *duḥkha*) that afflicts all beings caught up in cyclic existence (samsara). In Pāli canonical sources, bodies are described as repulsive, as bags of filth containing various disgusting substances such as excrement, urine, saliva, mucus, and blood. Meditators are instructed to take bodies as focal points in their practice and to become fully aware of their foulness. On the other hand, only embodied beings are able to attain the highest levels of the Buddhist path, and the body of a buddha is a topic of fascination in Indic sources, a proof of his past cultivation of merit and wisdom.

Unlike some other Indian religious traditions, Buddhism rejects the notion of an enduring essence or soul that inhabits a succession of bodies. The doctrine of no-self (Pāli *anattā*; Skt. *anātman*) is a fundamental aspect of most Buddhist philosophical schools and a cornerstone of meditation practice. Eliminating the false belief in an enduring soul is a prerequisite for liberation (Pāli *mokkha*; Skt. *mokṣa*) from cyclic existence. In addition, meditations designed to develop mindfulness of the body are regarded in many Buddhist philosophical traditions as important aspects of the path. These techniques, detailed in a number of sources, including the "Foundations of Mindfulness Discourse" ("Satipaṭṭhāna Sutta"; *Majjhima-nikāya* 10), involve visualizing the component parts of the body along with their functions and interactions with each other. Such practices serve to improve awareness of one's own embodiment and of one's environment and reduce attachment to the body and things associated with it. This article will examine some of the contrasting themes in Buddhist discussions of bodies, highlighting the often contradictory ways in which they are presented in (mainly Indian) sources, as well as some of the developments of understandings of bodies in Tibet and East Asia.

BODIES AND KARMA

Buddhist cosmology distinguishes between places where actions have moral consequences, referred to as "karma-sites" (*karma-bhūmi*), and existential situations in which beings lead long and blissful lives but are effectively trapped in heavens and subject to an inevitable trajectory of eventual return to lower realms in which suffering is endemic. The gods of the Formless Realm (*ārūpya-dhātu*), for example, are born without bodies, and they enjoy sublime pleasures and long lives as a result of successfully engaging in meditative practices referred to as the four formless absorptions (*ārūpya-samāpatti*). But eventually their karmic bank accounts will be depleted, and they will be reborn as humans, animals, or other sorts of beings. Their lives as gods are a soteriological dead end because while they reside in the Formless Realm (or other spheres within the expansive cosmology of Indian Buddhism), gods think that their sublime existences will last forever, and so they are unaware of the passage of time or the fact that eventually their celestial sojourns will cease. At the other end of the spectrum are hell realms, whose denizens are born with bodies that are prone to experiencing excruciating torment without any respite. Their lives are unending misery, and because of the pervasiveness of their suffering they can only endure until the karmic debt that resulted in their situation is exhausted, after which they will be reborn in one of the higher realms. But as long as beings—wherever they are situated on the continuum from hells to heavens—continue to be unaware of the realities of cyclic existence, they will make the same misguided choices and will move up or down in accordance with their respective karmas. Their bodies will reflect the actions that led to their births, and they will experience pleasures and sufferings concordant with the karmic trajectories they set in motion in the past (of which most are currently unaware).

Six realms of existence (*gati*) are described in traditional Buddhist sources: (a) hell beings (*naraka*), (b) hungry spirits (Pāli *peta*; Skt. *preta*), (c) animals (*tiryak*), (d) humans (Pāli *manussa*; Skt. *manuṣya*), (e) demigods (*asura*), and (f) gods (*deva*). The human realm is the most desirable situation from the point of view of practice: hell beings and hungry spirits endure so much suffering that they are unable to see the faults that led to their unfortunate situations, and the minds of animals are too clouded to discern the causes and effects of actions. Gods and demigods are caught up in their pleasurable lives, but humans have sufficient intelligence to become aware of how the universe works and the operations of karma. Those who have the resources and time for religious practice can take control of the process of rebirth by engaging in merit-making activities and practicing the sorts of meditation that will lead to improved understanding and mental clarity. Rebirth in a human body, however, is extremely rare: a popular image ("Dutiyachiggaḷayuga-sutta," *Saṃyutta-nikāya* 48.2) compares the chances of birth in the human realm to a blind tortoise that lives at the bottom of the ocean and only surfaces once every hundred years. On top of the ocean, a floating ring bobs on the water, and being born as a human is as likely as the tortoise putting its head through the middle of the ring. This story is used to illustrate the notion of a "precious human birth" and the opportunities it presents.

THE BUDDHA'S PRESENT AND PAST BODIES

Stories of exemplary practitioners who made good use of the brief period of a human (and occasionally nonhuman) life abound in Buddhist sources; some of the most popular of these relate to the Buddha and his path to awakening (*bodhi*). Tales of his past births (Jātaka) describe how he sacrificed parts of his bodies when he was born in animal or human forms, and how in several cases he gave his life for others, resulting in prodigious amounts of merit.[1] A recurring theme in these stories is how the body can function as the site for extraordinary religious activity. Pain is often a core element: the greater the suffering and the more extensive the voluntary injuries the Bodhisattva (future Buddha) inflicted on himself or allowed others to cause, the greater the merit he received as a result. In one popular narrative in which he was Prince Sattva (*Mahāsattva-jātaka*), he comes upon a starving tigress who is about to eat her own children in desperation. His companions decide to search for food for her, but the prince reflects that they may not be able to find any and that if their foraging takes too long she could bring great demerit to herself by killing her progeny. So he decides to jump off a cliff, killing himself in the process. The tigress feasts on his body, and his act of generosity (*dāna*) helps him in his quest to perfect this and other ideal qualities.

In the story of Kṣāntivādin (Pāli Khantivādi; "He Who Professes Patience"; *Jātaka* 313), the Bodhisattva is a wandering ascetic devoted to the cultivation of patience (*kṣānti*). One day he is meditating at the edge of a king's pleasure grove. The king gets drunk and passes out, and his courtesans leave him and wander around the grove in search of diversions. They come across Kṣāntivādin and ask him about his religious practice, in response to which he delivers a discourse on the benefits of patience. The king, meanwhile, wakes up and becomes angry that his entourage has left him alone, so he searches for them. When he finds his harem sitting around an ascetic and listening raptly to his teachings, he confronts Kṣāntivādin and accuses him of being a charlatan. The king asks his name, and he calmly replies: "Kṣāntivādin." The king then strikes the sage, but fails to spark any anger. He then orders one of his soldiers to cut off Kṣāntivādin's hand, but his victim is unperturbed. Every time the king demands that he speak his name, the Bodhisattva says: "I am He Who Professes Patience." After lopping off Kṣāntivādin's remaining limbs, the king orders the soldier to cut off his head, but at no point in the violent encounter does the Bodhisattva waver in the slightest in his calm demeanor. As a result, he perfects one of the matrix of exalted qualities that characterize the mental continuums of buddhas. The physical torment he endures, along with the control required to maintain his mental discipline, are core components of the religious import of the story: only beings with material bodies that are capable of experiencing pain are able to skillfully adapt such situations to their soteriological advantage.

The theme of suffering as a means of supercharging one's practice also appears in Mahāyāna sources. One of the most famous of these is the tale of the self-harming bodhisattva Sadāprarudita, recounted in the *Lotus Sūtra* (*Saddharma-puṇḍarīka-sūtra*), who ingests flammable fluids and sets his body alight as an offering to buddhas. As a result of his actions, he is later born as the bodhisattva Bhaiṣajyarāja, a popular figure in East Asia associated with curing of illness. His actions would probably appear to most modern readers as suicidally insane: he is distraught because he has no money to offer to the Buddha Dharmodgata and decides that if he burns himself alive he will gain great merit and be born in better bodies in the future. He also assumes that Dharmodgata will be impressed by his actions and not appalled: "Dharmodgata will explain the perfection of wisdom and skill in means to me. I will train in them, and as a result I will become a refuge to all beings; and after I have realized full awakening I will acquire a body of golden color, the thirty-two physical characteristics of a great man (*mahāpuruṣa-lakṣaṇa*), the eighty secondary physical characteristics (*anuvyañjana*), the splendor of a halo the rays of which extend to infinitude," along with other exalted qualities.[2] This story is invoked as a model to be emulated by monastics in East Asia, who often burn themselves with incense cones as evidence of their commitment when undertaking monastic vows. It has also been cited by contemporary Tibetans who have self-immolated in protest against Chinese government oppression. They are commonly referred to by other Tibetans admiringly as "bodhisattvas" (*byang chub sems dpa'*) or "heroes" (*dpa' bo*, which is a component of the Tibetan translation of bodhisattva). Their corporal sacrifice is acclaimed as a religiously motivated act that brings great merit.

BODIES AND THE BUDDHIST PATH

During countless past lives, the Buddha gradually perfected such qualities as generosity, patience, ethics, effort, concentration, and wisdom and he was rewarded with better resources, as well as progressively more sublime bodies. Every birth of every being is conditioned by what it did in past lives. Those who are wealthy and powerful are reaping the rewards of meritorious actions, and beauty is also the result of good karma. Those who are poor, crippled, ugly, or prone to illness reflect in their physiques the negative effects of harmful actions. Because the Buddha has attained the pinnacle of embodied existence, his anatomy must proclaim the perfection of his past cultivation of merit and wisdom. The Buddha's body is described as the best of all physical forms, surpassing those of other humans and even gods. The Buddha is the "ultimate man" (*purisottama*; Skt. *puruṣottama*), a superhuman figure who has greater strength and agility than any of his contemporaries, and who early in his life was a sexual athlete who satisfied hundreds of courtesans. People (especially women) who see him remark on his physical beauty.

In the Pāli canon, several discourses (*sutta*; Skt. *sūtra*) are devoted to detailed descriptions of his body, his gait, how he sits and eats, and the impact of his perfect physiognomy on those who witness it. The "Discourse to Cankī," for example, describes the Buddha as "handsome, good looking, graceful, possessing supreme beauty of complexion, with sublime beauty and sublime presence, remarkable to behold" (*Majjhima-nikāya*, II.166–167). The commentary on the *Verses of the Elder Monks* reports that the monk Vakkali, a brahman who was "wise and learned in the Vedas," "witnessed the perfection of the Master's physical form" and joined the monastic order as a result (*Paramattha-dīpanī Theragāthā-aṭṭhakathā*, II.147). Vakkali was so obsessed with observing the Buddha's body, however, that he constantly followed him around and stared at him, which eventually led the Master to request that he stop this behavior. Vakkali complied, but he became depressed: "What is life to me if I cannot see him?" The monk was about to commit suicide, but the Buddha read his mind and realized that this deed would lead to negative karma and undo the progress he had made since joining the order, and so the Buddha "revealed his radiant glory" (i.e., displayed his naked form), as a result of which Vakkali attained an advanced level of insight.

The Buddha's body has three primary narrative purposes in Pāli literature: (a) it serves as an advertisement for the path he teaches, (b) it is a catalyst for conversion, and (c) it convinces skeptics that he really is a buddha, as he and his followers claim. According to Indian Buddhist tradition, shortly after his attainment of awakening, the Buddha decided to begin teaching others what he had discovered. His first sermon was the "Discourse Turning the Wheel of Doctrine" ("Dhamma-cakka-pavattana-sutta"), delivered to five ascetics who had formerly been his companions in an order that emphasized practice of severe austerities as the key to attainment of liberation (*mokkha*; Skt. *mokṣa*). Because he had concluded that severe self-abnegation is a soteriological dead end and ineffective as a means of attaining significant religious goals, when they saw him walking toward Sarnath (near Varanasi in modern-day Uttar Pradesh), the ascetics at first decided to ignore him. But as he approached, they were struck by a profound change in his demeanor: he radiated calm and wisdom, and his physique proclaimed that he had reached the supreme attainment. In spite of themselves, they were compelled to inquire about what he had discovered. After being informed that he had become a buddha, they begged him to teach his doctrine (Dhamma; Skt. dharma). In this and a number of other Pāli sources, his body plays the decisive role in convincing skeptics that he is a buddha. Sometimes words follow and further solidify the initial impression, but in other cases his physical form alone constitutes final proof of his bona fides.

The Buddha's attainments are inscribed on his body: in addition to possessing the best possible human (male) form, his attainment of buddhahood is attested by the "physical characteristics of a great man" (*mahāpurisa-lakkhaṇa*; Skt. *mahāpuruṣa-lakṣaṇa*), which also adorn the bodies of universal monarchs but are uniquely perfect and pronounced on buddhas. These are described at length in various Pāli sources, and an entire *sutta*, the "Discourse on the Physical Characteristics" ("Lakkhaṇa-sutta"; *Dīgha-nikāya* 3), is devoted to this topic. They include a fist-sized lump (*uṣṇīṣa*) on the cranium, a tuft of silver-colored hair a meter in length between the brows (*ūrṇā*), a straight torso, webs between his fingers and toes, legs like an antelope's, a torso and jaw like a cow's, eyelashes like a cow's, hands that reach down to his knees, a penis hidden by a sheath, and a tongue that when extruded can be inserted into each earhole and can cover his forehead. Later texts add a list of eighty "secondary characteristics" (*anuvyañjana*) that include golden-colored fingernails, concealed veins, the gait of a lion or a bull, a rounded body, a slender body, and a perfect male sexual organ. These serve to distinguish the Buddha from other men of lesser attainments, and they are only found on the bodies of "great men." According to Vasubandhu's (ca. late 4th century CE) *Abhidharma-kośa*, each characteristic is the result of past cultivation of one hundred meritorious actions, and Buddhaghosa (*ca.* 5th century) similarly states that each "is produced from its corresponding action" (*Sumaṅgala-vilāsinī*, II.448).

Unlike the archetypal male bodies of contemporary Western societies, the Buddha does not have a muscular, V-shaped torso: his form is slender and lithe, the ideal physique for an archer. He does not have the bulges or indentations associated with weight training; his limbs are rounded, and he has a slight midriff bulge. His skin is so smooth that no dust or dirt can settle on it, and his mouth is delicately shaped, like a *bimba* fruit. This is the sort of anatomy associated with paradigmatic masculinity in ancient India, as attested in both Buddhist and non-Buddhist sources. Features associated with attractive male bodies in Western societies are largely absent in descriptions of the Buddha: in artistic depictions, he has no apparent muscle tone, there are no protruding muscles, and he has flaring hips and rounded facial features, rather than a square jaw and prominent cheekbones. According to Buddhaghosa (*Sumaṅgala-vilāsinī*, II.447), the Buddha has "a fullness of muscles," but they are rounded and not delineated, and no veins or outlines of bones appear on the surface: "in some human beings veins are seen on the surfaces of their hands and feet, bones jut out from the two shoulders and trunk, and they look hideous like human ghosts. Unlike such ill-shaped persons, the great man possesses seven convexities that give his body proper shape and beauty." The Buddha's back is also rounded; there is no indentation at the spine, and no lines of muscle on either side; it "appears like a single golden slab" (*Sumaṅgala-vilāsinī*, II.449). It is difficult to imagine how a man whose body exhibited these features could be regarded as attractive, but Indian Buddhist literature abounds with accounts of the impact of his physique on those fortunate to see him in the flesh, such as the *Extensive Sport*'s (*Lalitavistara*) description of his entry into the town of Rājagṛha to beg for alms. The residents think that he must be Brahmā, Śakra, or another god:

> Crowds of men and women gaze at the man who is like pure gold. His self-mastery is complete; he is marked with the thirty-two physical characteristics. And no one tires of looking at him ... [They ask,] "Who is this being? Never before have we seen one like him; he makes the city radiant with his splendor." Thousands of women, wishing to see the most outstanding of men, leave their houses empty; they stand on the rooftops, in doorways, at windows, and in the streets to gaze at him. The merchants stop doing business; in the houses and in the streets, all drinking and revelry cease, so intent are the people on watching the most remarkable of men. (*Lalitavistara*: 175–176)

THE CULTURAL LOGIC BEHIND THESE TROPES

There is, of course, no way to know what the Buddha actually looked like, or if he really was a handsome, wealthy prince as depicted in Indic sources. The Buddha in this literature is a fictional character whose representation reflects the norms and values of the time. Because the doctrine of karma dictates that those who engage in meritorious activity will be rewarded with progressively more beautiful bodies and abundant resources, the Buddha—the ultimate man, who has reached the pinnacle of embodied existence—must be endowed with the sort of body regarded in ancient India as the supreme manifestation of the human form. The hierarchical caste system places brahmans and *kṣatriyas* (warriors and rulers) in the top positions, and so he must belong to one of them. Men are in the dominant position in this society, and so he must have a male body.

This Buddha is a literary figure whose hagiography probably began during his lifetime and continued after his passing. His unique physiognomy—which would probably appear freakish and ungainly to modern people—was apparently regarded at the time as sublimely beautiful and as a testament to his prodigious efforts during his quest for awakening. It is highly unlikely that any human has actually possessed a body with the "physical characteristics of a great man," and the full elaboration of this odd concatenation of features probably developed well after his death, after living memory of what he actually looked like had faded. Moreover, artists were reluctant to attempt to represent his body in plastic art during and immediately after his lifetime, and so the earliest images are iconic: his presence is indicated by symbols such as a space under the Tree of Awakening (*bodhi-vṛkṣa*) or his footprints, for example. The first images of his physique only began to appear centuries after his passing. Early Indian images from the Gupta Period (ca. mid-3rd century CE–543 CE) and the Pāla Period (750–1174) depict a slender man with a few of the physical characteristics of a great man (presumably because any attempt to create a human form containing all of them would have appeared odd and ungainly, rather than sublimely beautiful).

The Buddha and his followers were operating in a highly competitive religious marketplace in ancient India, with the brahmanical tradition as the most strongly established faction. Many of the stories in which the Buddha's body features involve brahmans who have heard that a buddha has appeared in northern India and seek to verify this claim. In one such narrative ("Brahmāyu-sutta," *Majjhima-nikāya* II.136) the brahman Bramāyu, "a master of the three Vedas" and an expert in the lore of the "great man," decides to travel to where the Buddha is staying and listen to one of his sermons. The Master's words, however, are not regarded as proof of his buddhahood: only verifying that his body displays the thirty-two characteristics of a great man can convince Brahmāyu. Anyone can repeat wise-sounding teachings, but the physical characteristics cannot be faked. Brahmāyu observes the Buddha's body as he speaks and moves and concludes that he possesses thirty of the characteristics, but the brahman is unable to discern whether or not the Buddha has an enormous tongue or a sheathed penis, and so remains unconvinced. He asks, "upon your body, Gotama, is what is normally concealed by a cloth hidden by a sheath, greatest of men?...is your tongue a manly (*narassika*) one? Is your tongue also large?...Please stick it out a bit and cure our doubts." The Buddha assents to Brahmāyu's request, first extruding his tongue and touching the tip into each earhole, and then he covers his forehead with it. Following this, the Buddha uses his magical powers to display his sheathed penis to the entire audience, which proves to everyone that he is in fact a great man.

The lore of the great man is claimed in Pāli texts to be an aspect of brahmanical learning, and this is presumably why brahmans are the interlocutors in stories in which it figures, but T. W. Rhys Davids has noted that "no such list has been found, so far as I know, in those portions of the pre-Buddhistic priestly literature that have survived. And the inference...is that the knowledge is scattered through the Brahmana texts."[3] Some of these features appear in some brahmanical texts, but in the 21st century it is possible to electronically search most of the ancient Indic scriptures in which it might appear, and neither I nor any researcher of whom I am aware has even located a partial list similar to what is presented in Buddhist sources. Buddhaghosa (*Sumaṅgala-vilāsinī* II.448), employing premodern search techniques, came to the same conclusion:

> When the time comes for the birth of a buddha, the Suddhāvāsa Brahmā gods visit the earth in the guise of brahmans and teach humans about their bodily signs as constituting a part of the Vedic learning, so that by this means humans may recognize the Buddha. After his death, this knowledge generally vanishes. That is why it does not exist in the Vedas.

Buddhaghosa adds that the gods impart this knowledge to humans so that they will be able to identify a buddha when he is born and properly revere him, but following his passing there is no longer anyone whose body displays these characteristics and thus no need for the lore to be passed on. As a result, it gradually fades from human memory.

THE BUDDHA'S BODY AS PROOF OF HIS CLAIMS

Indian Buddhist texts describe Śākyamuni Buddha as one among countless buddhas. All sentient beings have the potential to attain awakening if they follow a path similar to his and perfect the same matrix of exalted qualities. Because his soteriological teleology follows an established pattern, beings such as gods and human sages who are aware of the relevant lore know in advance what he will look like and what he will do. All buddhas of the past have enacted the same sequence of great deeds, and all future buddhas will also do so.

This theme begins even before he is born. The *Great Matter* (*Mahāvastu*) reports that during the time his mother carried him in her womb, he resided in a crystal casket, untouched by polluting uterine fluids. His body was tiny but fully formed, and he sat with his legs crossed in a meditative posture. When the time for his birth arrived, he emerged from her left side and his mother experienced no pain, only pleasure. According to several narratives, prior to this event the brahman Asita was informed that a buddha was about to enter the world, someone who would be "a superlative being without comparison, a precious pearl of the health and goodness of the human world... of all beings this one is perfect, this man is the pinnacle, the ultimate, the hero of creatures." Asita then went to see the newborn infant, who was "shining, glowing, and beautiful. It was like seeing molten gold in the hands of a master craftsman as he takes it out of the furnace." The brahman performed a minute inspection of the prince's body and ascertained that it exhibited the physical characteristics of a great man, which led him to declare: "This is the ultimate, this is the perfect man!" (*Sutta-nipāta*: 131–132).

A recurring trope in these texts is that the Buddha was aware of the expected narrative sequence of his life and that each major event was performed for an audience of gods, humans, and other beings who had gathered in anticipation of witnessing his enactment of the physical aspects of buddhahood. As Suzanne Mrozik notes, his corporal perfection was the culmination of countless past lives, during which he sacrificed all or parts of his bodies and cultivated progressively more sublime meditative attainments, accumulating prodigious stores of merit.[4] As a result, he was born with a body on which the physical characteristics of a great man were inscribed, but several accounts make it clear that his body became even more radiant and impressive after his attainment of full awakening in Bodhgaya. People who had seen him previously (and had remarked on his surpassing beauty) noted that his body only attained its full excellence after this event.

THE BUDDHA'S SEX LIFE

Despite the fact that Prince Siddhārtha Gautama would grow up to become a religious leader and found a monastic order that enjoined strict celibacy for its members, during his teens he is commonly depicted as residing in the women's quarters of his father's palace and enjoying sensual pleasures with a large harem of beautiful women. His father, King Śuddhodana, feared that his son might be inclined toward religious pursuits, and so he provided an environment rich in physical enjoyments: sporting activities, archery contests, and alluring women skilled in music and lovemaking. The *Deeds of the Buddha* (*Buddha-carita*) describes the setting: "the women delighted him with their soft voices, enticements, playful intoxications, sweet laughter, curvings of eyebrows and sidelong glances. Then a captive to the women, who were skilled in the arts of love and tireless in sexual pleasure, he did not descend from the palace to the ground, just as one who has won paradise by his merit does not descend to earth from the heavenly abodes" (*Buddha-carita*: 16).

The *Extensive Sport* claims that this was necessary because all past buddhas also had large harems, and part of the narrative sequence of a future buddha's life is a period in the women's quarters during which he engages in prodigious amounts of sexual activity. Behind this is a common notion in ancient Indian sources that celibacy is a core component of the path to liberation, and a voluntary decision to abstain from sex results in great merit and psychic power. But only those who are fully capable of performing sexually can reap such benefits. Moreover, it is important for the story's conceptual logic that the future Buddha fully experience the best of what cyclic existence has to offer, so that when he decides to renounce the world it is not because of misfortune or some inadequacy on his part, but rather a clear-eyed realization that even the best life situations are ultimately unsatisfactory and lead to continued rebirth and suffering. He must also prove that he is a sexual "stallion" who satisfies many women and who is the object of female desire.

Śuddhodana's plan to entice his son to embrace his kingly heritage and the enjoyments it offered hit a snag when others began to question whether or not the boy fulfilled the ideal of a warrior *kṣatriya*. The prince's apparent preference for the company of women led Daṇḍapāṇi, father of the beautiful Yaśodharā, to wonder if such a pampered boy was fit to rule a kingdom and subdue enemies in battle: "It is the custom of our family to give our daughters in marriage only to men skilled in the worldly arts, and your son has grown up in luxury in the palace. If he does not excel in the arts, does not know the rules of fencing or archery or boxing or wrestling, how could I give my daughter to him?" (*Lalita-vistara*: 100).

Siddhārtha rarely engaged in these activities, but training was unnecessary because his physical skills were so extraordinary that he could easily best all his contemporaries. Śuddhodana arranged a contest to which the most outstanding examples of *kṣatriya* manhood were invited, and Siddhārtha easily outshone all of them in "archery, fighting, boxing, cutting, stabbing, speed, and feats of strength, use of elephants, horses, chariots, bows, and spears, and argument" (*Mahāvastu*: II.73–74).

After witnessing this display, Daṇḍapāṇi happily assented to have his daughter marry Siddhārtha. The prince also had a harem of "beautiful, faultless, loving women, with eyes bright as jewels, with large breasts, resplendent white limbs, sparkling gems, firm and fine waists, soft, lovely, and black-colored hair, wearing bright red mantles and cloaks, bracelets of gems and necklaces of pearls, ornaments and rings on their toes, and anklets, and playing music" (*Mahāvastu*: II.147). Several narratives of this period also insert an interesting detail: he engaged in prodigious sexual activity, but he was not really interested. He knew that this was part of the narrative repertoire expected of an incipient buddha, and so he performed his part in the drama. After he had produced a son—which served to fully certify his masculine bona fides—he decided to leave his wife and harem, renounce his royal heritage, and pursue the life of a wandering ascetic seeking liberation. Although he wore coarse robes fashioned from cast-off rags, his body remained supremely attractive; the *Deeds of the Buddha* recounts that when women saw him in monastic garb, they were sexually attracted to him. They "looked up at him with restless eyes, like young deer, as their earrings, swinging back and forth, touched their faces, and their breasts heaved with uninterrupted sighs. [The Bodhisattva], bright as a golden mountain, captured the hearts of the best of women and captivated their ears, limbs, eyes and beings with his voice, touch, beauty and qualities respectively" (*Buddha-carita*: 69). Men were also struck by his physical perfection. When he visited the meditation master Ārāḍa Kālama, the sage exclaimed: "Look at the man who approaches! How beautiful he is!" His disciples responded: "We see him; he is indeed wonderful to behold!" (*Lalitavistara*: 174).

After several years of meditative training with various teachers, Siddhārtha succeeded in attaining advanced states of absorption, but they could not provide release from cyclic existence. He engaged in extreme ascetic practices, fasting for extended periods of time and reducing his sublime body to a state of emaciation, but this too proved incapable of providing the liberation he sought. So he set forth on his own to find the path to cessation, and after six years of meditative training he succeeded in attaining awakening in Bodhgaya. Following this experience, he began his ministry and taught others what he had realized. Many succeeded in becoming *arhat*s, meaning they would attain nirvana after death.

In spite of his achievements, however, he could not overcome the limitations of physical existence. In his later years, he suffered from chronic back pain that was only relieved when he immersed himself in meditative trances. He told his cousin and attendant Ānanda that his body was like an old cart that is held together by cords, and he hinted that the time for his departure from physical existence was imminent. Even the body of a buddha is subject to change, as is true of all material things. His once perfect form had become aged and withered, but some of his transcendent beauty remained. According to an account of his last days, the Buddha called his followers together and displayed his body for them one last time:

> Then the Blessed One took off his upper robe and baring his body said: "Monks, gaze now upon the body of the Thus Gone One! Examine the body of the Thus Gone One! For the sight of a completely awakened buddha is as rare an event as the blossoming of the *uduṃbara* tree." The Buddha then provided instructions regarding disposition of his remains: his corpse should be handled like that of a universal monarch and wrapped in linen, placed in an iron vat filled with oil, and then cremated. The relics left over should be placed in a reliquary mound (*stūpa*) at a crossroads so that in the future people might venerate them and gain merit. ("Mahāparinibbāna-sutta," *Dīgha-nikāya* V.217)

MAHĀYĀNA: BETTER BODIES AND BETTER BUDDHAS

Following the cremation of the Buddha's body and the distribution of relics that remained, Pāli sources report that he passed into final nirvana and thus beyond any possibility of future embodiment. Mahāyāna sutras, however, rewrote the denouement to his story. The Buddha, they declared, did not really die: what people saw was an "emanation body" (*nirmāṇa-kāya*), created as a vehicle for display of the actions expected of a buddha for the benefit of audiences on earth. The Buddha had really become awakened in the distant past and waited until the optimal time to enact the standard narrative sequence of buddhahood for humans and others who might benefit from such a presentation. The events that people took at face value were "skillful means" (*upāya-kauśalya*), didactic sleight of hand (and other parts of his body). Mahāyāna buddhology developed a complex set of explanations for how and why the Buddha engaged in such an elaborate lifelong deception. Had he decided to remain on earth in the body with which he was born for centuries or even millennia (which Mahāyāna texts assured their readers he could easily have done), people would have become complacent and taken him for granted. His death graphically demonstrated the universality of impermanence: even buddhas die (or at least appear to die), and this knowledge prompted his followers to apply themselves to their practice with greater urgency than they would have done had he remained.

In early sources discussing the trope of an immortal buddha who only appeared to die but who in fact merely terminated a simulacrum created as a way of delivering the dharma to audiences incapable of perceiving him as he really was, a distinction is made between emanation bodies and the "dharma body" (*dharma-kāya*). The latter is nonmaterial, and so it is not subject to decay, aging, or death. This complex of ideas provides a doctrinal solution to the problem of having a religious leader born to a human mother with a body composed of matter, which must inevitably succumb to the realities of impermanence and death. This new and improved Buddha possesses a body that surpasses those of the gods, who may live for the duration of a world-age (*kalpa*) but who eventually die and take rebirth in other realms within cyclic existence. It also preserves the essential aspects of the Buddha's standard hagiographies while providing a new twist that helped Buddhists better compete with rival religious orders whose main figures were deities. According to the *Discourse Explaining the Thought* (*Saṃdhinirmocana-sūtra*), the dharma body is the true body of the Buddha (and of all buddhas). It creates various physical (but temporary) manifestations for a range of soteriological purposes. It is the culmination of eons of training by a bodhisattva, during which she or he accumulated vast stores of merit (*puṇya*) and perfected wisdom (*prajñā*) to the highest degree. After completing the final aspects of the tenth bodhisattva level (*bhūmi*), a bodhisattva becomes a buddha and, motivated by compassion guided by an unerring sense of what will be most beneficial to every trainee, embarks on a teaching career as a sage who appears to possess a human (or quasi-human) body for the duration of a human life span: "the great light of exalted wisdom and innumerable emanations appear to sentient beings from the dharma body because it has been established through training in cultivating method and wisdom that observe the immeasurable realm of reality (*dharma-dhātu*)."[5]

The dharma body itself, however, is unchanging. It is the apotheosis of a buddha's training in wisdom and full comprehension of the dharma, which is also eternal and always the same. In the *Discourse Explaining the Thought*, the Buddha provides instructions to Mañjuśrī on the relationship between the dharma body and its manifestations:

> Mañjuśrī, the characteristics of the dharma body of the *tathāgatas* are the well-established transformation of the basis through renunciation, the complete cultivation of the [ten bodhisattva] levels and the [six] perfections (*pāramitā*). Moreover, know that this dharma body has an inconceivable characteristic for two reasons: because it is free from elaborations and free from manifest activity; and because sentient beings very strongly adhere to elaborations and manifest activity.[6]

In other words, the dharma body completely transcends the impermanence and suffering characteristic of cyclic existence, but it creates physical manifestations that accord with the norms of worldly convention. In the *Discourse Explaining the Thought*, the discussion of these two embodiments of buddhas serves to explain how Śākyamuni was able to survive his apparent demise and provides a new narrative in which his cultivation of merit and wisdom during countless past lives resulted in the appearance of a buddha whose teaching career really began in the distant past and will continue into the infinite future. Like all buddhas, he resides in a pure "buddha realm" (*buddhakṣetra*) created by his stores of merit. This is only accessible to advanced practitioners, however, but for their benefit he continues to teach in his Pure Land while simultaneously creating innumerable bodies dispatched to countless realms throughout the universe. The *Discourse Explaining the Thought* only discusses two bodies, but in later Mahāyāna buddhology the doctrine of "three bodies" (*trikāya*) developed. Buddhas also have "enjoyment bodies" (*saṃbhoga-kāya*), composed of subtle energy and not subject to decay like emanation bodies or other phenomena within ordinary cyclic existence. Enjoyment bodies function as the controlling and decision-making nexus of buddhas: the dharma body is essentially inert because it is associated with the unchanging reality of the ultimate truth (*paramārtha*) and the sphere of reality. Emanation bodies are transient, and each only functions for a preordained length of time in a particular situation. Enjoyment bodies are effectively immortal and not subject to old age or death.

MEDITATION AND PHYSICAL PLEASURE

Buddhism is often presented as a tradition that denigrates the body and views sensual pleasure negatively, but arguably the opposite is the case. Buddhism recognizes the pervasiveness of suffering for embodied beings, but its techniques also promise rarified states of bliss that transcend any ordinary delights. In Pāli sources, instructions on how to attain advanced absorptions (*jhāna*; Skt. *dhyāna*) describe in rapturous terms the pleasures of successful meditation:

> With the subsiding of thought and examination, he enters and dwells in the second *jhāna*, which has internal confidence and unification of mind... and has rapture and happiness born of concentration...Just as though there were a lake whose waters welled up from below and it had no inflow from east, west, north, or south, and would not be replenished from time to time by showers of rain, then the cool fount of water welling up in the lake would make the cool water drench, steep, fill, and pervade the lake, so that there would be no part of the whole lake that is not pervaded by cool water; so too, a monk makes the rapture and happiness born of concentration drench, steep, fill, and pervade this body, so that there is no part of his whole body that is not pervaded by the rapture and happiness born of concentration.[7]

Indian and Tibetan tantric traditions also focus on the body as an essential foundation for meditation practice. The tantras contain descriptions of a "subtle body" (*māyā-deha*) roughly contiguous with the physical body in which energies referred to as "winds" (*prāṇa*) and "drops" (*bindu*) circulate through channels. Meditators learn to visualize these components and control the movements of energies, which leads to actualization of blissful mental states, as well as increasing wisdom and attainment of the qualities perfected by buddhas. Even sexual activity is a factor in this practice: during orgasm, coarse levels of mind drop away and more subtle ones manifest, including the most fundamental aspect of consciousness, the "mind of clear light" (*prabhāsvara-citta*). For nonmeditators, this opportunity is wasted, but tantric practitioners learn to harness the mind and the energies of the subtle body in order to directly experience subtle mental states. Through this process, bliss becomes a component of the path, rather than something to be suppressed. Tantric sources claim that such techniques lead to far more rapid progress than is possible through exoteric practices. The final apotheosis of this training is attainment of the "rainbow body" (Tib. *'ja' lus*; Skt. *indracāpa-kāya*), a form composed of pure light and energy, which is often described as arising from the cremated corpse of an adept after death.

CONCLUSION

From its earliest strata, Buddhist literature focuses on the body in a variety of ways. The suffering endemic to embodied beings is a persistent theme, but bodies are also required for those wishing to pursue any of the Buddhist paths. In the "Discourse to Rohitassa" (*Rohitassa-sutta*; *Aṅguttara-nikāya* 4.45), for example, the Buddha dismisses the idea that there is any other possibility: "It is just within this fathom-long body, with its perception and intellect, that there is the cosmos, the origination of the cosmos, the cessation of the cosmos, and the path of practice that leads to the cessation of the cosmos."

As Michael Radich has argued, there is a conceptual trajectory in Buddhist literature that develops the idea that there is something special and unique about the Buddha's embodiment.[8] In Pāli sources, his body is described as the best of all physical forms, the result of his eons of religious practice, but it is still subject to aging and death. Mahāyāna treatises extend the logic of a being who accumulates vast stores of merit on the path to buddhahood motivated by compassion, and the impetus of this ensures that even though he appears to die, he continues to work for the benefit of others, residing in a "pure land" and teaching advanced trainees. Radich discusses sources in which the Buddha is credited with developing an indestructible body that never changes and is not subject to death, referred to as an "adamantine body" (*vajra-kāya*). The notion that the Buddha was able to control the length of his life is found in Pāli sources, which indicate that had he wished he could have remained in the world for an eon or more. Thus the Mahāyāna Buddha—with an infinite life span, who continues to teach under the impetus of the compassion that motivated his long path to awakening—is really a relatively minor conceptual leap. The Mahāyāna Buddha's body is sometimes said to be fashioned from subtle energy, and Radich reports a number of texts that construe it as harder than diamond, and thus impervious to any harm or to the vicissitudes of ordinary existence. In all the sources examined in this article, bodies play a key role as the necessary prerequisites for the training of the Buddhist path, as focal points of meditative scrutiny, and as the reward for successful cultivation of merit and wisdom.

PRIMARY SOURCES

Bhikkhu Bodhi. *In the Buddha's Words: An Anthology of Discourses from the Pali Canon*. Boston: Wisdom Publications, 2005.

Johnston, E. H. (ed.). *Aśvaghoṣa's Buddhacarita, or Acts of the Buddha*. Delhi: Motilal Banarsidass, 1984.

Powers, John (trans.). *Wisdom of Buddha: The Saṃdhinirmocana-sūtra*. Berkeley: Dharma Publishing, 1995.
Rhys Davids, T. W. *Dialogues of the Buddha, Part I*. London: Pali Text Society, 1889.
Vaidya, P. L. (ed.). *Aṣṭasāhasrikā Prajñāpāramitā Sūtra*. Darbhanga: Mithila Institute, 1960.
Vaidya, P. L. (ed.). *Lalitavistara*. Darbhanga: Mithila Institute, 1958.

FURTHER READING

Balkwill, Stephanie. "Why Does a Woman Need to Become a Man in Order to Become a Buddha? Past Investigations, New Leads." *Religion Compass* 12, no. 8 (2018): 1–9. https://doi.org/10.1111/rec3.12270.
Cabezón, José I. *Sexuality in Classical South Asian Buddhism*. Somerville, MA: Wisdom Publications, 2017.
Collins, Steven. "The Body in Theravāda Buddhist Monasticism." In *Religion and the Body*. Edited by Sara Coakley, 185–204. New York: Cambridge University Press, 1997.
Dissanayake, Wimal. "Self and Body in Theravāda Buddhism." In *Self as Body in Asian Theory and Practice*. Edited by Thomas P. Kasulis, Roger T. Ames, and Wimal Dissanayake, 123–145. Albany: State University of New York Press, 1993.
Faure, Bernard. *The Red Thread: Buddhist Approaches to Sexuality*. Princeton, NJ: Princeton University Press, 1998.
Kieschnick, John. *Eminent Monk: Buddhist Ideals in Medieval Chinese Hagiography*. Honolulu: University of Hawaii Press, 1997.
Langenberg, Amy Paris. "Buddhist Blood Taboo: Mary Douglas, Female Impurity, and Classical Indian Buddhism." *Journal of the American Academy of Religion* 84, no. 1 (2016): 157–191.
McClintock, Sara. "Gendered Bodies of Illusion: Finding a Somatic Method in the Ontic Madness of Emptiness." In *Theology: Critical Reflections by Contemporary Buddhist Scholars*. Edited by Roger Jackson and John Makransky, 261–274. Surrey: Curzon Press, 2000.
Mrozik, Suzanne. *Virtuous Bodies: The Physical Dimensions of Morality in Buddhist Ethics*. New York: Oxford University Press, 2007.
Ohnuma, Reiko. *Head, Eyes, Flesh, and Blood: Giving Away the Body in Indian Buddhist Literature*. New York: Columbia University Press, 2006.
Powers, John. *A Bull of a Man: Images of Masculinity, Sex, and the Body in Indian Buddhism*. Cambridge, MA: Harvard University Press, 2009.
Powers, John. "Buddhism and the Body." Oxford Bibliographies, 2017. https://www.oxfordbibliographies.com/view/document/obo-9780195393521/obo-9780195393521-0114.xml.
Radich, Michael. "Immortal Buddhas and Their Indestructible Embodiments: The Advent of the Concept of Vajrakāya." *Journal of the International Association of Buddhist Studies* 34, nos. 1–2 (2012): 227–290.
Tiso, Francis V. *Rainbow Body and Resurrection: Spiritual Attainment, the Dissolution of the Material Body, and the Case of Khenpo A Chö*. Berkeley, CA: North Atlantic Books, 2016.
Williams, Paul. "Some Mahāyāna Buddhist Perspectives on the Body." In *Religion and the Body*. Edited by Sara Coakley, 205–230. New York: Cambridge University Press, 1997.
Wilson, Liz. *Charming Cadavers: Horrific Figurations of the Feminine in Indian Buddhist Hagiographic Literature*. Chicago: University of Chicago Press, 1996.

NOTES

1. For an insightful analysis of this literature, see Reiko Ohnuma, *Head, Eyes, Flesh, and Blood: Giving Away the Body in Indian Buddhist Literature* (New York: Columbia University Press, 2006).

2. P. L. Vaidya, ed., *Aṣṭasāhasrikā Prajñāpāramitā Sūtra* (Darbhanga: Mithila Institute, 1960), 240–241.
3. T. W. Rhys Davids, *Dialogues of the Buddha, Part I* (London: Pali Text Society, 1889), 110.
4. Suzanne Mrozik, *Virtuous Bodies: The Physical Dimensions of Morality in Buddhist Ethics* (New York: Oxford University Press, 2007), 5.
5. John Powers (trans.), *Wisdom of Buddha: The Saṃdhinirmocana-sūtra* (Berkeley: Dharma Publishing, 1995), 305.
6. Powers, *Wisdom of Buddha*, 275.
7. Bhikkhu Bodhi, *In the Buddha's Words: An Anthology of Discourses from the Pali Canon* (Boston: Wisdom Publications, 2005), 251.
8. Michael Radich, "Immortal Buddhas and Their Indestructible Embodiments: The Advent of the Concept of Vajrakāya," *Journal of the International Association of Buddhist Studies* 34, nos. 1–2 (2012): 227–290.

John Powers

THE BÖN TRADITION OF DZOGCHEN

THE TIBETAN TRADITION OF BÖN

The religious system known as Bön (*bon*) has been presented by its adherents as the pre-Buddhist religion of Tibet, spread throughout the high plateaus, long before the advent of Buddhism, in the Land of Snows. The problem that is inevitably raised by this statement is that the Bön religion of these ancient times appears radically different from the later Bön school as it has survived up to the 21st century. Interestingly enough, modern Bönpos are evidently aware of the issue and have coined a presentation of the various "kinds" of Bön that they acknowledge, in order to account for the sometimes striking differences between these diverse forms of Bön. The scheme they have elaborated is threefold and comprises: (a) Old Bön (*bon rnying*), corresponding to the pre-Buddhist beliefs current in Tibet until the 8th–9th centuries (now surviving in some Himalayan villages as well as in the "marches" of the Sino-Tibetan border); (b) Eternal Bön (*g.yung drung bon*), said to be associated with the teachings of the Bön buddha par excellence, Tönpa Shenrab Miwo (Ston pa gshen rab mi bo), and corresponding to the postdynastic form of Bön adopted by absorbing teachings and rituals from the Tibetan Buddhist schools of the day; and (c) New Bön (*bon gsar*), a kind of openly syncretic system retroactively elaborated around typical Bönpo and Buddhist figures of the 8th century, such as Padmasambhava, Vairocana, and Drenpa Namkha (Dran pa nam mkha'). The second form (Eternal Bön) is what is usually defined as Bön in modern literature on the subject.[1]

If one compares Old Bön and Eternal Bön, one cannot but conclude that there is ample evidence showing that postdynastic "modern" Bön has little in common with the Bön tradition as it existed in Tibet in archaic times.[2] What one can assert with relative confidence is that there were some religious beliefs in pre-Buddhist Tibet that were not necessarily styled as "Bön," while being associated with it by later Tibetan historians. These religious beliefs were confronted with Buddhism as the latter became the official religion of the empire during the reign of Emperor Trisong Detsen (Khri srong lde btsan, r. 755–797 CE), and they most certainly absorbed much of this early spread of Buddhism throughout the imperial period and immediately after, during the "time of fragmentation" (*bsil ba'i dus*), when the empire collapsed and a period of civil war, internal conflicts, looting of royal tombs, and so on shattered the last remnants of the centralized empire.

It would seem that during that period of intense troubles, Bön gradually developed a religious system of its own, with a complex organization of rituals, practices, and literary corpuses already in existence by around 1000 CE (and probably slightly prior to that). This field of research is still in its infancy and is definitely in need of deeper investigations conducted into the early literature of Bön, in particular through systematic computerized comparisons of texts with those of the Nyingma tradition and of the nascent Sarma schools. The general consensus is that Bön formed its own image by absorbing religious ideas, philosophical concepts, and yogic practices that one cannot trace back to the Bönpo material available at the time of the empire (as evidenced by the relevant Dunhuang documents, for example). It has absorbed entire philosophical and even hagiographic representations that are specific to Buddhism and reformulated them in order to have them fit, for better or worse, with a rather blurry past to which it is only nominally connected.[3]

Among the corpus of texts that was gradually elaborated around the millennium—through revelations of Termas (*gter ma*), through compositions of original works, and through intense borrowings (for instance of the Prajñāpāramitā literature, which came to actually outnumber the volumes of the Buddhist-related texts)—stands an entire system of thought and practices shared with the Nyingma tradition: Dzogchen (*Rdzogs chen*).[4] It is still very unclear how Bönpos adapted the burgeoning Dzogchen texts from the Nyingma school. Like the latter tradition, they elaborated a whole doxographical and literary structure of texts and practices organized into a system of Nine Vehicles (*theg pa dgu*). Actually, Bönpos have several versions of this system, including an older one following a fivefold scheme known as the "Four Portals and the Treasury as the Fifth" (*sgo bzhi mdzod lnga*).[5] Regardless of the structure that is followed, Dzogchen always stands as the apex of these Vehicles. In fact, a careful study of both Bönpo Sutras (*mdo*) and Tantras (*rgyud*) shows that the vocabulary of Dzogchen has permeated nearly all strata of the Nine Vehicles, including medical texts, with the exception of the apotropaic rituals and practices that are to be found in the lower Vehicles.[6] Thus, it appears—but this would demand a thorough investigation of the Bönpo literature that cannot be conducted with the present tools of research—that Dzogchen concepts are actually present in most of the literature that was borrowed from Buddhism, such as the texts discussing philosophical tenets (*grub mtha'*), tantric rituals, advanced yogic practices, and so forth.[7]

Around the time of the millennium, Bönpos were clearly busy writing back their past and producing a nearly unceasing amount of Treasure texts (*gter ma*), thus creating a totally new school of Tibetan Buddhism with slightly specific traits. First, instead of Śākyamuni, they traced the origin of their lineage back to a buddha named Tönpa Shenrab, supposed to have lived eighteen thousand years ago in a kingdom filled with palaces, gardens, and the like. However, to the best of scholars' current knowledge, there existed no comparable feats of civilization at such an ancient time.[8] Second, they invented a past in which legendary figures play crucial roles in elaborating the teachings of Bön, while not a single trace of these teachings is actually to be found during the imperial period. Third, inspired by the fate of the Nyingma school and their urge for canonicity, they asserted that most of their teachings were first written in other languages, predominantly in the Zhang zhung language, before being translated into Tibetan during the glorious days of the empire.[9] These works were then supposed to have been hidden due to a persecution that, according to postdynastic Bönpo claims, nearly annihilated Bön in central Tibet. There is indeed evidence for establishing Buddhism as a state religion to the detriment of Bön, but there is no proof that Bön existed in such a complex form (with a canon, monasteries, monks, lineages, and so on) at that time. During the imperial period in Tibet (7th to the 9th century, and probably slightly before that), there were indeed priests known as *gshen* or *gshen po*, as well as *bon po* and *bon mo* (for females) who were apparently specialized in particular rituals and practices such as medicine, prognostics, divination, and so on, but there was no seed of what Bön was to become at the end of the period of fragmentation (*bsil ba'i dus*) that followed the demise of the Yarlung dynasty in central Tibet.

During the postdynastic period—and most certainly during the immediate century that preceded the fall of the empire—Bön absorbed teachings from all venues. Through compositions inspired by Buddhist works and through revelations of Treasure texts, Bönpos progressively built up an entire canon, essentially inspired by the various categories of Buddhist teachings available in religious centers around them.[10] Among these doxographical categories, within Sutras (*mdo*) are included texts on monastic discipline (*vinaya*), classical Sutras-like dialogues, and cosmological works of *abhidharmic* nature (*mdzod*) as well as "Stages of the Path" (*lam rim*) texts and a gigantic corpus of Prajñāpāramitā adaptations. As far as Tantras (*sngags*) are concerned, there were important collections centered around specific tutelary deities (*yi dam*), such as the "Five Supreme Citadels" (*Gsas mkhar mchog lnga*) of the Father Tantras (*pha rgyud*), Mother Tantras (*ma rgyud*), and so on.[11] Most of these literary materials can be sourced back to Buddhist texts borrowed and adapted from Nyingma (Rnying ma), Kagyü (Bka' brgyud), Sakya (Sa skya), and Kadam (Bka' gdams) traditions. The borrowings were, of course, not exact copies of the originals but inspired adaptations using a "bön" vocabulary, consisting, for instance, in substituting all occurrences of the term *chos* (dharma, Buddhism) with the word *bon*, creating compounds such as *bon sku* (Absolute Body) instead of *chos sku* (*dharmakāya*), *bon nyid* (Reality) instead of *chos nyid* (*dharmatā*), *bon dbyings* (Absolute Space) instead of *chos dbyings* (*dharmadhātu*), and so on. Owing to the canonical structure and the large amount of Bön works that were produced in this manner, small monasteries or hermitages were built, gradually attracting potential monks and yogic practitioners. Soon, Bönpos had large monastic establishments where they dispensed increasingly complex teachings including those connected to the five major and minor sciences, thus creating an entire cultural tradition that produced some of the most fascinating luminaries in the whole history of Tibet.[12] In the most important monasteries, on the model of the Kadampa system, Bönpos elaborated a curriculum of teachings leading to a *Geshé* (*dge bshes*) degree, often wrongly described by Westerners as the equivalent of a PhD, whereas it is a diploma that sanctions a highly specialized approach to religious practices based on the capacity to memorize and debate a series of compulsory topics taught in the corpus of works studied during a spiritual training lasting in general from nine to fifteen years.[13]

Within this vast corpus of new texts, Dzogchen stands at the apex of the entire Bönpo curriculum, its conceptions pervading most, if not all, Bön teachings. However, it is interesting to note that this central position is not extensively represented in the *Geshé* curriculum, whose main topic is that of the *Myriads* (*'bum*), that is, the vast literature of the Prajñāpāramitā upon which Bön relies for exposing its approach to Madhyamaka (*dbu ma*). In the *Geshé* curriculum and as far as Dzogchen is concerned, monks are essentially taught the topics that are discussed in *The Arcanum* (*Gab pa*) and *The Magic Treasury of the Sky* (*Nam mkha' 'phrul mdzod*), two cycles of teachings that are among the less practice-oriented of all Bön Dzogchen texts.[14] In fact, *The Arcanum* is a very speculative work made up of symbolic repetitive statements that are generally associated in Dzogchen with the Mind Series (*Sems sde*), although it includes numerous images and allegorical verses that have a definite alchemical flavor suggesting its interpretation is in fact not limited to Dzogchen only.[15] *The Magic Treasury of the Sky* is also nearly exclusively speculative and rather looks like a set of Madhyamaka works slightly perfumed with Dzogchen concepts.

The section "What Is the Meaning of Dzogchen?" will explain what Dzogchen actually is for Bönpo devotees, before discussing its literature, the life of some of its most important lineage holders, and its present status in modern Tibet.

WHAT IS THE MEANING OF DZOGCHEN?

In a general sense, Dzogchen (*rdzogs chen*) means "Great (*chen*) Perfection (*rdzogs*)," with "Dzog" referring to that which is already perfect in itself, and "chen" suggesting that this perfection stands above everything and is not an ordinary one. In traditional Bön teachings, Dzogchen is understood to refer to:

1. The entire Ninth Vehicle of Bön, known as the Unsurpassable Vehicle (*bla med theg pa*).
2. The natural state of the mind (*sems nyid kyi gnas lugs*), abiding as the nondifferentiation of emptiness and clarity (*stong gsal dbyer med*).

The literary contents of the Ninth Vehicle is discussed in the section "The Dzogchen Literature of Bön."

As the natural state of the mind, Dzogchen is defined in its experiential aspect in a very special manner that owes nothing to mental proliferations or intellectual analysis but entirely relies on the direct experience of its real nature. This nature is revealed by a qualified master to a qualified disciple during what is designated as the "direct introduction to Awareness" (*rig pa'i ngo sprod*). During that introduction, the master uses special implements (such as a mirror, a crystal, and a peacock's feather) and oral explanations aimed at inducing in the disciple a clear and vivid recognition of his own natural state (*gnas lugs*).[16] For instance, the master holds a crystal in his hand and explains that the natural limpidity of the crystal symbolizes the essence (*ngo bo*) of one's mind (*sems nyid*), its primordial purity (*ka dag*) as well as its original Emptiness (*ye stong*). Then he holds a peacock feather that he places next to the crystal in order to show the arising of five-colored luminous patterns within the crystal. These lights represent the nature (*rang bzhin*) of the mind, its spontaneity (*lhun grub*), and its luminous (*gsal ba*) character.

Based on these symbolic explanations, the receptacle of the direct introduction is then trained in specific practices that are actual methods enabling one to experience both the essence and the nature of the mind. Basically, the practice connected to the essence and emptiness of the mind is known as "cutting-through-rigidity" (*khregs chod*) and essentially relies on contemplative methods such as sky gazing (*nam mkha' ar gtad*). The practice associated with the nature and spontaneity of the mind is known as "passing-over-the-crest" (*thod rgal*) and is centered around yogic key points such as postures, gazes, and a particular style of breathing, as well as specific supports for practice (including the sky, the sun, the moon, and so forth).[17]

There are numerous kinds of direct introductions in the context of Dzogchen teachings, but these have not been carefully studied yet and constitute, therefore, a totally unexplored field of research. For instance, there is a system of yogic direct introductions, known as the "twenty-one direct introductions" (*ngo sprod nyer gcig*), which is quite famous among Dzogchen practitioners, but, except for a few mentions here and there in the nonacademic literature, they have never been studied.[18] Here it should suffice to merely explain that these twenty-one methods are divided into three sets of seven direct introductions, respectively dealing with: (a) seven direct introductions to lights (*'od*) aimed at advanced practitioners, (b) seven direct introductions to wisdom (*ye shes*) aimed at yogis of intermediate capacities, and (c) seven direct introductions to awareness (*rig pa*) aimed at lower practitioners.[19]

There are also more ordinary direct introductions that are common to other systems such as Mahāmudrā and higher tantras. Among them are the direct introductions to the Three Bodies (*sku gsum ngo sprod*) and a more general system of direct introductions to the nature of the mind (*sems kyi ngo sprod*), based on three special methods: (a) introducing perceptions as being the mind (*snang ba sems su ngo sprod pa*), (b) introducing the mind as being empty (*sems stong par ngo sprod pa*), and (c) introducing emptiness as clear-light (*'od gsal*).

THE DZOGCHEN LITERATURE OF BÖN

According to the classics of Dzogchen, the only way to directly experience the nature of the Mind exactly as it abides is by practicing the teachings of the Great Perfection. The philosophical and yogic meditations that one necessarily needs to cultivate in order to concretely engage in this practice are expounded in numerous cycles of instructions within Eternal Bön and New Bön traditions. In a certain sense, one can divide this gigantic corpus of works into two main groups:

1. A set of four cycles of teachings that are officially taught in Menri Monastery, the main monastic establishment of Eternal Bön and the mother-abbey of all monasteries affiliated with Eternal Bön.[20]
2. Individual cycles of teachings belonging to both Eternal Bön and New Bön but, in general, taught individually, outside monastic institutions and often to lay practitioners.

The four cycles of teachings taught in Menri are: (a) the *Oral Transmission of Zhangzhung* (*Zhang zhung snyan rgyud*), (b) the *Instructions on the Primordial A* (*A khrid*), (c) the *Great Expanse of the Supreme Peak of the Great Perfection* (*Rdzogs chen yang rtse klong chen*), and (d) the *Primordial Mind Dispelling Limitations* (*Ye khri mtha' sel*).[21] The first is said to be an uninterrupted oral transmission going back to the primordial Buddha Kuntuzangpo (Kun tu bzang po). The second one is a composition authored by an 11th-century master known as "The Great Noble Hermit" (Dam pa ri khrod pa chen po, 1038–1096). The last two cycles are Treasure revelations (*gter ma*) discovered around the 11th century. The first three of these cycles are also collectively known as "*A-dzok nyen-sum*" (A rdzogs snyan gsum), namely Atri (*A* khrid), Dzogchen Yangtse Longchen (Rdzogs chen Yang rtse klong chen), and Zhangzhung Nyengyü (*Zhang zhung snyan rgyud*).[22]

The *Oral Transmission of Zhangzhung* is the most authoritative cycle of instructions of the entire Bönpo tradition. It is said to go back to archaic times when it was supposedly taught and spread orally in the ancient kingdom of Zhangzhung. Then, in the 8th century, these teachings are said to have been organized according to a fourfold structure, owing to the visionary meetings between Tapihritsa, the twenty-fifth lineage holder of the cycle, and his disciple Gyerpung Nangzher Löpo.[23] The cycle is thus divided into four parts:

1. The general outer sections dealing with the View (*phyi lta ba spyi gcod*), which apparently existed in written form prior to Tapihritsa.[24]
2. The essential instructions of the inner precepts (*nang man ngag dmar khrid*), which were compiled by Nangzher Löpo after his first meeting with Tapihritsa.
3. The secret instructions on seeing awareness in its nakedness (*gsang ba rig pa gcer mthong*), also transmitted by Tapihritsa to Nangzher Löpo.
4. The innermost secret instructions on identifying the natural state (*yang gsang gnas lugs phug chod*).[25]

In general, this single-volume cycle is taught together with its main practice manual, called *The Instructions of the Eternal Victorious One* (*Rgyal ba g.yung drung gi phyag khrid*). This manual is named after its compiler, Bru Gyelwa Yungdrung (Bru Rgyal ba g.yung drung, 1242–1290). Another collection entitled *The Transmission of Experiences* (*Nyams rgyud*) contains the oral instructions given by the successive masters of *The Oral Transmission*, codified into an extended version (*rgyas pa*), an intermediate version (*'bring po*), and a condensed version (*bsdus pa*). Several works associated with *The Oral Transmission* have been published, but there are still numerous historical issues that need to be addressed regarding the study of this cycle, as well as its borrowing of content from other Dzogchen collections (such as the *Bima Nyingthik* of the Nyingma tradition).[26] The teachings associated with this cycle belong to the category of the Precepts Series (*Man ngag sde*).

The system of the *Instructions on the Primordial A* (*A khrid*) is a composition by Dampa Ritröpa Chenpo (1038–1096) based on *The Arcanum* (*Gab pa*) and its eight related texts discovered by Shenchen Luga (996–1035).[27] The reason for this composition is apparently that Dampa Ritröpa had difficulties understanding how to perform the practice of these texts. Therefore, he decided to isolate meditative instructions scattered throughout these works and organize them in a progressive manual of yoga and contemplation. He thus created a system in eight or ten sessions covering preliminaries (*sngon 'gro*) down to the main practice (*dngos gzhi*) dealing with the experience of wisdom, and so on. The main meditative approach specific to this cycle can be classified among the Mind Series (*Sems sde*).

This system was later developed by Dru Gyelwa Yungdrung who expanded it into fifteen sessions, which have since then become the standard manual for the practice of this cycle. Much later, in the 18th century and during the early part of the 20th century, the *Atri* system was further expanded into two cycles: (a) *Pointing at the Essentials* (*Dmar mo mdzub tshugs*) composed by Kündröl Drakpa (Kun grol grags pa, 1700–1769?), and (b) *The Natural Arising of the Three Bodies* (*Sku gsum rang shar*) compiled by Shardza Tashi Gyeltsen (Shar rdza bkra shis rgyal mtshan, 1859–1934). Both new cycles actually integrate numerous practices that were not included in the tradition of Dampa Ritröpa and Dru Gyelwa, to the extent that they can no longer be classified under the Mind Series rubric, but rather among that of the Precepts Series.[28]

The *Great Expanse of the Supreme Peak* is a treasure text (*gter ma*) associated with another cycle of the same nature, entitled *The Trilogy of Proclamations* (*Bsgrags pa skor gsum*), that is, the Proclamation (*bsgrags pa*) of Dzogchen: (a) in the lands of the gods, (b) in the lands of the Nāgas, and (c) in the lands of men. The *Great Expanse* itself is the actual practice manual of the *Trilogy*. It was discovered together with the latter in 1110 CE by Zhötön Ngödrup (Bzhod ston dngos grub, b. 1088) in the Lhodrak region in southern Tibet. The cycle is composed of various categories of texts, but its main topics are the purification of the seeds of the six destinies (*rigs drug gi sa bon*) localized within one's body, sexual practices with an actual female partner, teachings on the intermediate states (*bar do*) of life and death, and special dark retreats (*mun mtshams*) centered upon peculiar visualizations of the Peaceful and Wrathful Deities (*zhi khro*).

The actual collection counts two large volumes that also cover initiation rituals (*dbang chog*), as well as two extensive works respectively dedicated to instructions based on the conventional meaning (*drang don*) of the general Bönpo teachings, and to instructions focused upon the definitive meaning (*nges don*) of the specific precepts of Dzogchen. It also includes various rituals and practices, such as a long-life ritual, a *homa* rite, tantric practices of visualizations and praises dedicated to the three roots (*rtsa gsum*, i.e., the master, the tutelary deity, and the ḍākinīs), and so on. Some studies about the revealer of these teachings have been conducted by Anne-Marie Blondeau, but the analysis of the contents of the actual revelation itself still remains to be done.[29]

The *Primordial Mind Dispelling Limitations* (*Ye khri mtha' sel*) is a single-volume Treasure text (*gter ma*) whose source is not the country of Zhangzhung as for the above-mentioned cycles, but is rather said to be the Buddhist country of India. Indeed, this collection belongs to what is known as the "Bön of India" (*rgya gar gyi bon*), namely teachings that were first taught in India, transmitted in Zhangzhung by Indian Bönpo lineage holders, and then translated into Tibetan before being hidden as Treasure sometime around the late 8th century. This narrative is, of course, essentially mythic since no text associated with Dzogchen—be it of the Nyingma or the Bönpo schools—has ever been found in any Indic languages. However, there are clear links between this cycle and the country of India, starting with the fact that it has borrowed a lot of teachings from the Tibetan Buddhist side of Dzogchen.[30] These borrowings have clearly taken place in the late 13th century since the central Dzogchen text of this cycle—entitled *The Tome on the Explanatory Basis* (*Bshad gzhi mchong*)—is directly borrowed and adapted from the Nyingma text entitled *The Eleven Topics of the Great Perfection* (*Rdzogs chen bcu gcig pa*), a composition of Zhang Nyima Bum (Zhang Nyi ma 'bum, 1158–1213) based on the main Nyingma collection of Dzogchen texts called *The Seventeen Tantras* (*Rgyud bcu bdun*).[31] Given its Buddhist sources of inspiration, the cycle of the *Primordial Mind* should evidently be classified among the Precepts Series (*Man ngag sde*).[32]

The texts and cycles belonging to the second category are, for the most part, Treasure revelations or actual compositions styled as such. If one carefully examines Shardza Rinpoche's *Treasury of Good Sayings* (*Legs bshad mdzod*) and the listing of treasure revelations included therein, one can see that a vast number of Dzogchen individual works and cycles have been lost, or have not surfaced yet from private or monastery libraries.[33] Even though there are about forty Bönpo Dzogchen cycles available, it would be too fastidious to enumerate them. It should suffice to present some of the most famous among them, in chronological order.

The first that ought to be mentioned is the *Oral Transmission known as the Naked Vision of Awareness* (*Snyan rgyud rig pa gcer mthong*) revealed by Bönzhik Khyung-nak (Bon zhig khyung nag, 1103–1183). It is a particularly good example of those Bönpo Dzogchen cycles that stand in between the Mind Series and the Precepts Series while, however, not being explicitly associated with the Expanse Series that is often described as the intermediate category between the two other series. The practice of the cycle revolves around direct introductions (*ngo sprod*) to the nature of the mind and the practice of sky gazing, as well as around yogic exercises based on channels and winds (*rtsa rlung*), and instructions on the various intermediate states (*bar do*).[34]

The second cycle to discuss here is known as the *Golden Needle of the Great Perfection* (*Rdzogs chen gser thur*) and was rediscovered by Bönzhik Yungdrung Lingpa (aka rDo rje gling pa [1346–1405] in the Nyingma tradition). It is a collection of texts compiled in a single volume and is regarded by some to be an abridged version of a much larger cycle known as *The Vast Expanse of the View* (*Lta ba klong yangs*).[35] The *Golden Needle* is entirely focused around the 8th-century figure Drenpa Namkha. It contains an interesting root-tantra (*rtsa rgyud*) in twenty-four chapters as well as individual texts starting with works dedicated to the four initiations (*dbang bzhi*), which inspired later authors such as Shardza Tashi Gyeltsen. The cycle is also famous for his medical instructions, its teachings on the action seal (*las rgya*), and examination of the signs of death (*'Chi ltas*).[36]

The next cycle to be tackled here is the *Refined Gold of the Great Perfection* (*Rdzogs chen gser zhun*), which is a Treasure (*gter ma*) discovered by Tennyi Lingpa (Bstan gnyis gling pa, 1480–1535), who just like Bönzhik Yungdrung Lingpa was both Nyingmapa and Bönpo. His cycle is quite short but contains pith instructions on all practices generally associated with the Precepts Series, namely special preliminaries of Dzogchen, cutting-through-rigidity, passing-over-the-crest, and instructions on postmortem intermediate states. It was regarded by some Bönpos as having been heavily influenced by the Nyingma approach to Dzogchen—which is definitely true since its lineage includes Nyingma figures such as Padmasambhava and his main female disciple Yeshe Tsogyel (Ye shes mtsho rgyal). However, in the late 19th century, the Menri abbot Nyima Tenzin (Nyi ma bstan 'dzin, 1813–1875) carefully examined and practiced the cycle before declaring that it was authentic and should be included in the Bön canon.

The fourth collection to be presented here is known as *Pointing at the Essentials* (*Dmar mo mdzub tshugs*). It consists of a small volume that is regarded by some as a Treasure (*gter ma*) and by others as a composition. The fact is that it is indeed a composition of Kündröl Drakpa (Kun grol grags pa, 1700–1769?) who used the *Instructions on the Primordial A* he had received from his Bön master Yungdrung Tenzin Tsukphü (g.Yung drung bstan 'dzin gtsug phud, late 17th to early 18th century) and combined them with Mahāmudrā and Dzogchen teachings he had received from some of his Kagyü and Nyingma masters. The result is an interesting mix adding a series of instructions that are not found in the original *Atri* set of teachings such as precepts on the emissary (*pho nya*, i.e., sexual yoga), teachings on passing-over-the-crest (*thod rgal*), and so forth. This cycle had a lasting influence on New Bön lineage holders and is still widely taught and practiced.

Except for a few references in academic literature, this cycle has not attracted the interest of Tibetologists and yet constitutes a fascinating topic for research on interactions between Bön and the other schools of Tibetan Buddhism.

Unlike the cycles mentioned above, *The Tantra of the Principles of the Three Bodies* (*Sku gsum don rgyud*) is a single work, discovered in 1885 by Sangngak Ling pa (Gsang sngags gling pa, 1864–1959?). It is in fact included in a mostly ritual cycle, but the *Tantra* itself is a stand-alone of some sort, containing some of the most detailed instructions on Dzogchen practice. In particular, it includes the special guidance instructions that are usually associated with advanced Nyingma Dzogchen teachings, such as: (a) White Guidance (*dkar khrid*), which concentrates mostly on sky gazing (*nam mkha' ar gtad*); (b) Black Guidance (*nag khrid*) dealing with the instructions on dark retreats (*mun mtshams*), a cornerstone of Bönpo Dzogchen; (c) Yellow Guidance (*ser khrid*) concerning practice during the nighttime and gazing at the moon; (d) Red Guidance (*dmar khrid*), which, in this context, is centered around sun-gazing; and (e) Variegated Guidance (*khra khrid*) consisting of a special dark retreat in a house having openings in the four directions. Basing himself on this *Tantra*, Shardza Rinpoche started to elaborate a collection of related texts that he compiled in his *Natural Arising of the Three Bodies* (*Sku gsum rang shar*). This cycle is based on the *Tantra of the Principles of the Three Bodies* whose teachings are combined with those of the most important and authoritative cycles of Dzogchen according to the Menri tradition, and described at the beginning of this section, that is, the *Instructions on the Primordial A*, the *Great Expanse of the Supreme Peak*, the *Oral Transmission of Zhangzhung*, and so forth. The *Natural Arising of the Three Bodies* is now probably the most widespread corpus of Dzogchen teachings among modern Bönpos. Some monasteries have even based their curriculum of practice exclusively on it.

The last corpus of instructions to consider here is the *Treasury of Space and Awareness* (*Dbyings rig mdzod*), which was completed by Shardza Rinpoche in 1909. This text is unlike all the others discussed here: it is a *Treasury* (*mdzod*) modeled on the *Treasury of the Supreme Vehicle* (*Theg mchog mdzod*) and the *Treasury of Topics* (*Tshig don mdzod*) authored by Longchenpa (Klong chen pa, 1308–1364).[37] It is presented as a two-volume encyclopedia of Bönpo Dzogchen and draws heavily on Longchenpa's works, without however mentioning it. It is structured around twenty-one chapters covering the entire system of the Great Perfection: the first volume discusses the base (*gzhi*) of the natural state, including specific topics such as the buddha nature (*sangs rgyas kyi rang bzhin*) present in all sentient beings, the various categories of Dzogchen texts, the four initiations (*dbang bzhi*), the commitments (*dam tshig*) connected with these initiations, the primordial base of the natural state, its epiphany (*gzhi snang*), and so forth. The second volume is dedicated to the path (*lam*) and the fruit (*'bras bu*), dealing with all aspects of the practice of Dzogchen such as the special preliminaries (*khyad par gyi sngon 'gro*) performed in this tradition, teachings on cutting-through-rigidity (*khregs chod*), and secret instructions on daytime and nighttime passing-over-the-crest (*thod rgal*), as well as clarifications on the postmortem intermediate states (*bar do*) and the final obtainment of buddhahood. Given its scope, it has become in modern times one of the most important Dzogchen works ever composed (or revealed) in the Bönpo tradition. Despite that status, it is not taught very often, probably because of the complexity of its contents.[38]

EXTRAORDINARY DZOGCHEN PATRIARCHS OF BÖN

It is evidently subjective to choose a few lineage holders of Bön Dzogchen and briefly discuss their lives, but the individuals discussed in this section have played a crucial role in the development of Bön and its Dzogchen teachings. The following six patriarchs stand as impressive luminaries of the Great Perfection and cover the largest historical spectrum one can think of in terms of Dzogchen, from the 8th to the 20th century.

First of all, one cannot but mention Tapihritsa and Nangzher Löpo (both *c.* 8th century CE) who are the main figures of the *Oral Transmission of Zhangzhung*. Tapihritsa was a yogi who is said to have studied under the guidance of the twenty-fourth lineage holder of this cycle. He reached the ultimate sign of spiritual liberation according to Dzogchen, that is, the Body of the Great Transfer (*'pho ba chen po*), which implies that he actually did not die but reached immortality (*'chi med*), enabling him to appear in any form he chooses. He thus appeared as a young boy to Nangzher Löpo who had developed obstacles in his practice. Tapihritsa teased him at first and eventually transmitted to him highly secret Dzogchen instructions during two decisive meetings.

It is impossible to say whether or not this narrative relies on historical facts. Be it as it may, the story has remained taught to this day and the teachings that were compiled after the meeting of the two masters were to become the most important ones of the entire Bönpo lineage. According to tradition, these works that make up the *Oral Transmission* were not hidden as Treasures (*gter ma*) during supposed or actual persecutions of Bön, but enjoyed a continuous transmission down to the present day.

Nyammé Sherab Gyeltsen (Mnyam med Shes rab rgyal mtshan, 1356–1415) is the founder of the Menri monastery, the most important of all Bönpo monastic establishments. He was a very famous scholar known by all Bönpos of his time, and he even exchanged praises with the Gelukpa hierarch Tsongkhapa (Tshong kha pa, 1357–1419). He has left a large amount of exegetical works organized into a curriculum that has been followed for centuries by most monasteries affiliated with the tradition of Menri. Among these works is a famous commentary on *The Arcanum*, which is a masterpiece of erudition still referred to by Bön masters to this day. Sherab Gyeltsen deeply stressed the gradual approach to the spiritual path of Bön, but he never neglected Dzogchen. Rather, he taught it down to the very day he passed away, teaching from a section of *The Instructions of the Eternal Victorious One* (*Rgyal ba'i phyag khrid*), the main practice manual of the *Oral Transmission of Zhangzhung*.

The next master that ought to be mentioned is the famed New Bön lineage holder named Kündröl Drakpa (Kun grol grags pa, 1700–1769?). He essentially studied and taught in eastern Tibet and received numerous transmissions from a very eccentric younger incarnate lama known as Sangye Lingpa (1705–1735). This master was a syncretist who extensively borrowed from Buddhist sources and elaborated a system of his own, mixing Bön and Nyingma (as well as Kagyü) teachings with great talent. Kündröl Drakpa also contributed a large corpus of works, including several cycles of Dzogchen teachings, such as *Pointing to the Essentials* (*Dmar mo mdzub tshugs*), the *Essential Instructions known as the Thorough Gathering of Contemplation* (*Dmar khrid dgongs pa yongs 'dus*), and so forth. Most of these cycles are compositions, although some are presented as Treasures (*gter ma*). In the most important among these works are detailed instructions on clear-light practice (*'od gsal*), that is, teachings on passing-over-the-crest (*thod rgal*). A complete analysis of his *Collected Works* (in forty-seven volumes) still remains to be done.

One of the most important patriarchs of Bön in modern times was the famed master mentioned several times already: Shardza Tashi Gyeltsen (1859–1934). His spiritual training was guided by two of the most well-known New Bön lineage holders of the late 19th century:

Ratön Tenzin Wangyel (Dbra ston bstan 'dzin dbang rgyal, 1832–1894?) and Dechen Lingpa (Bde chen gling pa, 1833–1893), who both transmitted numerous teachings to him, starting with cycles of Dzogchen instructions. Shardza also studied and followed the Menri tradition and, in particular, the works of Nyammé Sherab Gyeltsen for whom he had an unwavering devotion. Despite being a monk, Shardza chose to leave his monastery to search for a quiet place where he could remain isolated from all kinds of distraction. He found the place he was looking for on the slope of the Shardza Mountains (hence his name, given as a toponymical reference), where he created the hermitage of Dechen Ritrö. Despite some traveling throughout Kham (eastern Tibet) and a couple of trips to central Tibet, Shardza spent most of his life in isolation during which he would divide his time between composition of works and contemplative practices. However, as the years went by, he started to attract disciples seeking a similar hermit-like approach to spiritual life rather than the life of a monk, with all the ritual duties that fall to monastics. Ironically, his hermitage is now one of the most active Bönpo monastic centers of modern Tibet.[39]

BÖN DZOGCHEN IN MODERN TIBET AND IN EXILE

During the first part of the 20th century, Bön Dzogchen has mainly benefited from the teachings and the works authored by Shardza Tashi Gyeltsen, essentially in eastern Tibet. There, numerous masters received his transmissions—directly from him or from his regent (*rgyal tshab*)—and then moved back to their own region to disseminate them. In this manner, the Bönpo Dzogchen tradition of Shardza was, for instance, spread in western Tibet by Jigme Namkha Dorje ('Jigs med nam mkha' rdo rje, 1897–1955) who, in the late 1940s, even went as far as Delhi to have some of Shardza's works printed from manuscript copies. Others diffused these teachings in northern Dolpo where their transmission is still alive.

In a similar way, the Tulkus (*sprul sku*) of the Kündröl line of incarnations have intensely diffused the Dzogchen works of the first Kündröl (Kun grol grags pa), as well as most of his tantric teachings, giving transmissions throughout eastern Tibet. In the most remote valleys close to the Chinese border, these teachings as well as those of other New Bön masters such as Sangye Lingpa were maintained until the dramatic events of the late 1950s.

In central Tibet, the situation did not change much for the Menri tradition where some monks started to voice their concern about the diffusion of New Bön and its Dzogchen lineages since these teachings were eclipsing the cycles generally associated with Menri, and in certain cases completely replacing the original curriculum with newer ones, essentially based on the exegetical works of Shardza Rinpoche. After a while, it would seem that the doctrinal squabbles between the Eternal Bön tradition (represented by the Menri orthodoxy) and the New Bön systems reached their full measure with open criticism expressed by some Menri hierarchs toward New Bön in general and Shardza Rinpoche in particular. In 1925, the latter was summoned by the then Menri abbot Phüntsok Lodrö (Phun tshogs blo gros) to send a copy of his works so that they could be examined by the Menri authority and the abbot himself. Upon examination, the abbot declared them to be perfectly orthodox and even wrote a praise to Shardza and his works. However, the situation did not improve, and the Menri authorities often sent *Geshé* to the eastern region to ensure that the Menri tradition maintained its hegemony. The successors of Phüntsok Lodrö, as well as the Yungdrung Ling authorities, forbade the study and transmission of Shardza's works, while numerous monks from eastern Tibet that had come to complete their *Geshé* degree in Menri actually kept secret their affiliation to the Shardza tradition.

During the invasion of the Chinese Communists in 1959, all the religious traditions of Tibet had to face dramatic events bringing them to the verge of annihilation. However, despite these difficult times—in particular during the Cultural Revolution (文革, 1966–1976)—Tibetans have with great efforts succeeded in preserving their religious and traditional beliefs. Many of them fled into exile, and among them the highly educated hierarchs of the Bönpo school. Some tragically lost their life during their escape from Tibet while some succeeded in reconstructing their monastic tradition in northern India. Among them were two of the most knowledgeable masters of Bön in general and Dzogchen in particular: (a) Yongdzin Sangye Tenzin (1917–1978), and (b) Lopön Tenzin Namdak Rinpoche (b. 1926). Throughout the history of Tibet, Dzogchen teachings had been considered highly secret and were generally taught in private, to individual disciples or at best to a small group of people, scarcely to large crowds. Given the situation in which the Bön tradition was in its exile, the most important lineage holders of Bön decided to hold a repeated divination ritual during which signs appeared, indicating that the protective deities of Dzogchen agreed that the time had come to reveal the teachings more publicly, in order to prevent their disappearance. Decades later, in 1993, Lopön Tenzin Namdak published the abridged translation of a secret manual of Dzogchen practice authored by Shardza Tashi Gyeltsen and entitled *The Heart Drops of Kuntuzangpo* (*Kun bzang snying thig*), which appeared in English under the title *Heart Drops of Dharmakaya*. This was, to the author's knowledge, the first time such a highly secret manual of practice had been issued and made available to the general public. Through this book and his teaching activities around the world, Lopön Tenzin Namdak has thus opened the way to the ongoing publication of numerous works of academic and non-academic nature, greatly enriching a field that was, until this seminal publication, rather uncharted.

PRIMARY SOURCES

KUN GROL GRAGS PA (1700–1769?)

mKha' 'gro dgongs 'dus, Bon gyi brten 'gyur chen mo, vol. 43. 3rd ed. Chengdu, China, n.d.

Dmar khrid dgongs pa yongs 'dus, Bon gyi brten 'gyur chen mo, vol. 78. 3rd ed. Chengdu, China, n.d.

Dmar mo mdzub tshugs, Bon gyi brten 'gyur chen mo, vol. 42. 3rd ed. Chengdu, China, n.d.

RGYAL BA G.YUNG DRUNG, BRU SGOM (1242–1290)

A khrid thun mtshams bco lnga dang cha lag. Delhi, 1967.

Phyag khrid : Zhang zhung snyan rgyud skor and *Snyan rgyud nam mkha' 'phrul mdzod nges skor.* Dolanji, India: Sherab Wangyal, 1972.

Gangs can ti se bon gzhung, Mdo smad rtse zhig g.yung drung bon bstan 'phel rgyas gling, vol. 20. 2009.

Snyan rgyud kyi sngon 'gro rim pa rnams. lythographic ed.; *Bon gyi brten 'gyur chen po*, vol. 138. 3rd ed., Chengdu, Delhi, 1967.
Nyams (sic !) rgyud rgyal ba'i phyag khrid, Triten Norbu Tse. Edited by Ratsa Geshe Tenzin Dargye. 2002.
Nyams rgyud rgyal ba'i phyag khrid, Sangs rgyas g.yung drung bon gyi dpe tshogs, Si khron mi rigs dpe skrun khang. Triten Norbutse Library, 2008.

BSTAN GNYIS GLING PA (1480–1535)

Rdzogs chen gser zhun, *Bon gyi brten 'gyur chen mo*, vol. 301, pp. 1–104. 3rd ed. Chengdu, China, n.d.

BZHOD STON DNGOS GRUB (B. 1088)

Rdzogs chen bsgrags pa skor gsum. Delhi: Tibetan Bonpo Monastic Center, 1973.
Rdzogs pa chen po yang rtse klong chen, vols. 1 and 2. Delhi: Tibetan Bonpo Monastic Center, 1973.

LUNG BON LHA GNYEN (12TH CENTURY)

Rdzogs pa chen po snyan rgyud rin po che nam mkha' 'phrul gyi mdzod chen, *Bon gyi brten 'gyur chen mo*, vol. 129, pp. 567–964. 3rd ed. Chengdu, China, n.d.
Rdzogs chen ye khri dkar po mtha' sel: *sPyi rgyud chen po nam mkha' dkar po ye khri mtha' sel gyi rgyud*. Tibetan Bonpo Monastic Centre, Dolanji, India, *c.* 1985.

SHARDZA TASHI GYELTSEN (BKRA SHIS RGYAL MTSHAN, 1859–1934)

Dbyings rig rin po che'i mdzod, vols. 1–2. Xylographic ed., *Shar rdza bka' 'bum*, Chamdo. *c.* 1990.
Legs bshad rin po che'i mdzod dpyod ldan dga' ba'i char zhes bya ba. In *ib.*, vol. 7, p. 1–549.
Sku gsum rang shar. In *Gangs can ti se bon gzhung*, Mdo smad rtse zhig g.yung drung bon bstan 'phel rgyas gling, vol. 21. 2009.

GSHEN CHEN KLU DGA' (996–1035)

Byang sems gab pa dgu skor, *Bon gyi brten 'gyur chen mo*, vol. 216, pp. 3–192. 3rd ed. Chengdu, China, n.d.

GSANG SNGAGS GLING PA (1864–1959?)

Sku gsum don rgyud: Bla ma sku gsum phur bsgrub las don rgyud bsam 'phel yid bzhin nor bu. In *Bon gyi bKa' 'gyur*, Sgo bzhi mdzod lnga dpe rnying phyogs bsgrigs, Gshen bstan gling, vol. 191, pp. 1–95. Tibet.

COLLECTIONS

Zhang zhung snyan rgyud: *History and Doctrines of Bon-po Niṣpanna-yoga*, Śata-piṭaka Series 73. New Delhi, 1968.

Rdzogs pa chen po zhang zhung snyan rgyud kyi nyams rgyud rgyas 'bring gnyis kyi gsung pod. Kathmandu: Triten Norbutse Monastery, 2002.

SECONDARY LITERATURE

Achard, Jean-Luc. "Bon zhig khyung nag and the *Rig pa gcer mthong* Tradition of rDzogs chen." *Tibet Journal* 23, no. 4 (Winter 1998): 28–57.

Achard, Jean-Luc. "Le Tantra des Vingt-Deux Perles de l'Esprit de Parfaite Pureté—un exemple d'intertextualité entre les traditions Bon po et rNying ma pa." *Cahiers d'Extrême-Asie* 15 (2005): 57–104.

Achard, Jean-Luc. *The Four Lamps.* In collaboration with Lopön Tenzin Namdak Rinpoche. Zhangzhung Nyengyü Studies 3. Munich: Naldjor Institute, 2007.

Achard, Jean-Luc. *Enlightened Rainbows—The Life and Works of Shardza Tashi Gyeltsen.* Leiden, The Netherlands: Brill, 2008.

Cech, Krystyna. "The History, Teaching and Practice of Dialectics according to the Bon Tradition." *Tibet Journal* 11, no. 2 (1986): 3–28.

Karmay, Samten G. *The Treasury of Good Sayings: A Tibetan History of Bon.* London Oriental Series 26. London: Oxford University Press, 1972.

Karmay, Samten G. *A General Introduction to the History and Doctrines of Bon.* Tokyo: Toyo Bunko, 1975.

Karmay, Samten G. *The Arrow and the Spindle: Studies in History, Myths, Rituals and Beliefs in Tibet.* Kathmandu: Mandala Book Point, 1998.

Karmay, Samten G., and Yasuhiko Nagano, eds. *A Catalogue of the New Collection of Bonpo Katen Texts.* Bon Studies 4–5; Senri Ethnological Reports 24–25. Osaka, Japan: National Museum of Ethnology, 2001.

Kværne, Per. "Bonpo Studies: The A Khrid System of Meditation." Pts. 1 and 2. *Kailash* 1, no. 1 (1973): 1–50; 4, no. 4 (1973): 247–332.

Kværne, Per. "The Great Perfection in the Tradition of the Bonpos." In *Early Ch'an in China and Tibet.* Edited by Whalen Lai and Lewis Lancaster, 367–392. Berkeley Buddhist Studies Series 5. Berkeley, CA: Asian Humanities Press, 1983.

Kværne, Per. "The Study of Bon in the West: Past, Present and Future." In *New Horizons in Bon Studies.* Edited by Samten G. Karmay and Yasuhiko Nagano, 7–20. Bon Studies 2. Osaka, Japan: National Museum of Ethnology, 2000.

Martin, Dan, Per Kværne, and Yasuhiko Nagano, eds. *A Catalogue of the Bon Kanjur.* Bon Studies 8; Senri Ethnological Reports 40. Osaka, Japan: National Museum of Ethnology, 2003.

Snellgrove, David L. *The Nine Ways of Bon: Excerpts from Gzi-brjid.* London: Oxford University Press, 1967.

Stein, Rolf A. "Un document ancien relatif aux rites funéraires des bon-po tibétains." *Journal Asiatique* 258 (1970): 155–185.

Stein, Rolf A. "Tibetica Antiqua V: La religion indigène et les bon-po dans les manuscrits de Touen-houang." *Bulletin de l'École Française d'Extrême Orient* 77 (1988): 27–56.

Thondup, Tulku Rinpoche. *Hidden Teachings of Tibet: An Explanation of the Terma Tradition of the Nyingma School of Buddhism.* Edited by Harold Talbott. London: Wisdom Publications, 1986.

FURTHER READING

Achard, Jean-Luc. *Enlightened Rainbows: The Life and Works of Shardza Tashi Gyeltsen.* Leiden, The Netherlands: Brill, 2008.

Baroetto, Giuseppe. *Il libro tibetano dei sei lumi: L'insegnamento zogchen di Tapi Hritsa.* Rome: Astrolabio Ubaldino, 2002.

Clemente, Adriano. "La dottrina rdzogs chen nel ciclo di insegnamenti visionari 'Dran pa gser gdams."' Unpublished diss., Istituto Universitario Orientale, Napoli, 1983.

Clemente, Adriano. *Visionary Encounters and Dzogchen Teachings from the Golden Advice, revealed by Shense Lhaje (Gshen-sras Lha-rje)*. Arcidosso, Italy: Shang Shung Edizione, 1995.

Esler, Dylan. "The Origins and Early History of rDzogs chen." *Tibet Journal* 30, no. 3 (2005): 33–62.

Gyaltsen, Shardza Tashi. *Heart Drops of Dharmakaya: Dzogchen Practice of the Bön Tradition*. Commentary by Lopon Tenzin Namdak. Introduction and bibliographical essay by Per Kværne. Edited by Richard Dixey. Ithaca, NY: Snow Lion, 1993.

Hatchell, Christopher P. *Naked Seeing: The Great Perfection, the Wheel of Time, and Visionary Philosophy in Renaissance Tibet*. New York: Oxford University Press, 2014.

Jurkovic, Ratka. "Prayer to Ta pi hri tsa: A Short Exposition of the Base, the Path and the Fruit in Bon Dzogchen Teachings." *Revue d'Etudes Tibétaines* 16 (April 2008): 5–41.

Karmay, Samten G. *The Great Perfection (rDzogs chen): A Philosophical and Meditative Teaching of Tibetan Buddhism*. 2nd ed. Brill's Tibetan Studies Library 11. Leiden, The Netherlands: Brill, 2007.

Kværne, Per, and Thupten K. Rikey. *The Stages of A-khrid Meditation: Dzogchen Practice of the Bon Tradition (by Bru-sgom Rgyal-ba-g.yung-drung)*. Dharamsala, India: Library of Tibetan Works and Archives, 1996.

Namdak, Lopon Tenzin. *The Main Dzogchen Practices: From the Oral Transmission of the Great Perfection in Zhang zhung*. Edited by Gerd Manusch. Zhang Zhung Nyeng Gyü Manual 3. München: Naljor Institute, 2005.

Reynolds, John Myrdhin. *Practice from the Zhang-zhung Nyan-gyud*. Transmitted orally by Lopon Tenzin Namdak. Transcribed and edited by John Myrdhin Reynolds. Freehold, NJ: Bonpo Translation Project, 1992.

Reynolds, John Myrdhin. *Bonpo Dzogchen Teachings according to Lopon Tenzin Namdak*. Kathmandu: Vajra, 2006.

NOTES

1. See the introduction to David Snellgrove's *The Nine Ways of Bon: Excerpts from Gzi-brjid* (London: Oxford University Press, 1967), which still remains one of the best works discussing the nature of Bön and which briefly introduces some of the key elements associated with this tradition.
2. In most cases, one may refer to it as "monastic Bön" to better figure out how modern Bönpos understand their own identity (on the expression "monastic Bön," see Per Kværne, "The Study of Bon in the West: Past, Present and Future," in *New Horizons in Bon Studies*, ed. Samten G. Karmay and Yasuhiko Nagano, Bon Studies 2 [Osaka, Japan: National Museum of Ethnology, 2000], 17). Calling their own lineage the "Eternal Bon [of those wearing] White Hats" (*zhwa dkar g.yung drung bon*, and other variants of this expression) is a clear hint at how they envision their own religious position compared to "Old Bön," often referred to as the tradition of those wearing black hats (*zhwa nag*), that is, sorcerers, medicine men, diviners, and so forth. One can still see the symbolic presence of these representatives of Old Bön in the performance of specific religious dances (the *zhwa nag tshogs 'cham*), in which monks wearing black hats enact apotropaic deeds definitely associated with the old faith. On Bön dances, see Samten G. Karmay, *The Arrow and the Spindle: Studies in History, Myths, Rituals and Beliefs in Tibet* (Kathmandu: Mandala Book Point, 1998), 190–199.
3. On Bön texts from Dunhuang, see Rolf A. Stein, "Tibetica Antiqua V: La religion indigène et les bon-po dans les manuscrits de Touen-houang," *Bulletin de l'École Française d'Extrême Orient* 77 (1988): 27–56; and Rolf A. Stein, "Un document ancien relatif aux rites funéraires des bon-po tibétains," *Journal Asiatique* 258 (1970): 155–185.
4. Termas are texts or artifacts that are supposed to have been hidden during the 8th century and later revealed by predestined individuals called *tertön* (*gter ston*), that is, treasure revealers. On Termas in general, see Tulku Rinpoche Thondup, *Hidden Teachings of Tibet: An Explanation of the Terma Tradition*

of the Nyingma School of Buddhism, ed. Harold Talbott (London: Wisdom Publications, 1986), passim. For a history of Bön Termas, see Samten G. Karmay, *The Treasury of Good Sayings: A Tibetan History of Bon*, London Oriental Series 26 (London: Oxford University Press, 1972), which contains a partial translation of Shardza Tashi Gyeltsen's (1859–1934) *Legs bshad rin po che'i mdzod*.

5. See Snellgrove, *Nine Ways of Bon*, 16–19.
6. It is most certainly within the concepts shared by these lower Vehicles that one may find obvious traces of influence from Old Bön and rituals going back to the imperial period. To the author's knowledge, no systematic studies have been conducted in this field, which should be an interesting topic for future research.
7. Borrowings of Bön texts by the Nyingmapas is not unknown either. See, for instance, Samten G. Karmay, *The Great Perfection (Rdzogs chen): A Philosophical and Meditative Teaching of Tibetan Buddhism*, 2nd ed., Brill's Tibetan Studies Library 11 (Leiden, The Netherlands: Brill, 2007), 216–223; and Jean-Luc Achard, "Le Tantra des Vingt-Deux Perles de l'Esprit de Parfaite Pureté—un exemple d'intertextualité entre les traditions Bon po et rNying ma pa," *Cahiers d'Extrême-Asie* 15 (2005): passim.
8. In the documents from Dunhuang, Tönpa Shenrab is depicted as a medicine man among other religious specialists, and his "name" may also correspond to a title or a generic moniker rather than to a personal name. Its full form, Tönpa Shenrab Miwoche (ston pa gshen rab mi bo che), "The Revealer (*ston pa*), the Best of Practitioners (*gshen rab*), the Great Man (*mi bo che*)" sounds like a series of epithets of Buddha Śākyamuni himself. One may wonder whether Bönpos are actually worshiping the historical Buddha without knowing it, or without admitting it, owing to the early postimperial stages when they were actively building up historical stratagems to coin their own past so they would not have to acknowledge any debt to the victorious faith. This would certainly explain why Bön, in its "modern," postdynastic form clearly appears as a late school of Tibetan Buddhism.
9. Much like the Bönpos, Nyingmapas were active during the postdynastic period (after *c*. 1000 CE) building up their past around important 8th-century figures. The vast majority of the Nyingma works has been excluded from the constitution of "orthodox" canonical collections of Buddhist scriptures compiled by Sarma hierarchs. This later resulted in the Nyingmapas organizing their own canonical collection such as the *Collection of Ancient Tantras* (*Rnying ma'i rgyud 'bum*), the *Oral Lineage of the Teachings* (*Bka' 'ma*), and so forth.
10. On the Bön Kanjur (*bKa' 'gyur*), see Dan Martin, Per Kværne, and Yasuhiko Nagano, eds., *A Catalogue of the Bon Kanjur*, Bon Studies 8; Senri Ethnological Reports 40 (Osaka, Japan: National Museum of Ethnology, 2003). On the Bön Tengyur (*Brten 'gyur*), see Samten G. Karmay and Yasuhiko Nagano, eds., *A Catalogue of the New Collection of Bonpo Katen Texts*, Bon Studies 4–5; Senri Ethnological Reports 24–25 (Osaka, Japan: National Museum of Ethnology, 2001).
11. On these, see Jean-Luc Achard, *Enlightened Rainbows: The Life and Works of Shardza Tashi Gyeltsen* (Leiden, The Netherlands: Brill, 2008), 149–150.
12. The five major sciences are: arts, medicine, grammar, logic, and the "inner science" (i.e., religious tenets). The five minor sciences are: poetry, etymology, prosody, theater, and astrology.
13. On the training followed by the monks in Menri Monastery, see Krystyna Cech, "The History, Teaching and Practice of Dialectics according to the Bon Tradition," *Tibet Journal* 11, no. 2 (1986): 3–28. On Menri, see note 20 below.
14. See the bibliography in the section "Primary Sources," respectively under Gshen chen Klu dga' and Lung bon Lha gnyen.
15. In his *Treasury of Space and Awareness* (*Dbyings rig mdzod*, vol. 1, p. 63), Shardza Tashi Gyeltsen states that *The Arcanum* actually belongs to the eighth Vehicle (*theg pa brgyad pa*), basing himself on a quote from the *Rtsa rgyud gsang ba bsen thub*, the most authoritative Tantra of the whole Bönpo tradition.
16. In numerous cases, these implements are not used, so the actual "direct introduction" takes the form of an explanation of the nature of the mind, followed by a dialogue—mainly based on maieutic—between the master and the disciple in order to ascertain the latter's accurate understanding.

17. On these practices as performed in Bön, see Jean-Luc Achard, *The Four Lamps*, in collaboration with Lopön Tenzin Namdak Rinpoche, Zhangzhung Nyengyü Studies 3 (Munich: Naldjor Institute, 2007), passim.
18. On these introductions, see Shardza bKra shis rgyal mtshan, *Dbyings rig rin po che'i mdzod*, vol. 2. *Shar rdza bka' 'bum*, 343–345, ed. Xylographic (Chamdo, *c.* 1990).
19. In Dzogchen, practitioners are divided into three categories: (a) those of superior capacities (*dbang po rab*) who reach buddhahood in this life, (b) those of intermediate capacities (*dbang po 'bring*) who reach buddhahood at the time of death, and (c) those of lower capacities (*dbang po tha ma*) who reach buddhahood during postmortem states. Some cycles, such as *Bstan gnyis* Gling pa's *Rdzogs chen gser zhun*, present a different classification, explaining (3rd ed. [Chengdu, China, n.d.], 301:42) that those of superior capacities reach buddhahood (without leaving aggregates behind) during their lifetime; those of intermediate capacities, during the Bardo of Reality (*bon nyid bar do*); and those of inferior capacities, after rebirth in a pure realm. Of course, a yogi knows to which category he belongs only when he reaches the Fruit of the Path (either in this life, at the time of death, or after death).
20. sMan ri monastery was founded in 1404/5 by mNyam med Shes rab rgyal mtshan (1356–1415) after the monastic establishment of Yas ru Dben sa kha was destroyed by a flood. Shes rab rgyal mtshan had the monastery rebuilt (and newly named) in the lower part of the same valley. It was entirely destroyed during the Chinese invasion but was restored again in 1984.
21. The term *khri* in this title is traditionally said to be of Zhang zhung origins and to mean "mind" (*sems*). However, the cycle is supposed to belong to the Bön of India, and it has very little connection to Zhang zhung. Therefore, the author's translation follows the traditional explanation since a better interpretation is not currently available.
22. See Samten G. Karmay, *A General Introduction to the History and Doctrines of Bon* (Tokyo: Toyo Bunko, 1975), 215.
23. For a summary of their life, see "Extraordinary Dzogchen Patriarchs of Bön."
24. This was explicitly admitted by Yongdzin Tenzin Namdak Rinpoche, during a private meeting (Paris, 1994). However, one should not consider that all texts belonging to this section existed prior to Tapihritsa since some are obviously associated with him. This would definitely need further investigation.
25. The root-text of this section is entitled *The Twenty-One Seals* (*Gzer bu nyer gcig*) and encapsulates the entire teachings of the whole cycle, in a verse work accompanied by a commentary attributed to Nangzher Löpo.
26. See Jean-Luc Achard, *The Three Precepts, Zhangzhung Nyengyü Studies*, vol. I (München: Naldjor Institute, 2005); Achard, *Four Lamps*; Jean-Luc Achard, *The Eight Precepts, Zhangzhung Nyengyü Studies*, vol. IV (München: Naldjor Institute, 2010); and Jean-Luc Achard, *The Six Lamps* (Sumène: Editions Khyung-Lung, 2014).
27. Dam pa ri khrod pa chen po, aka Me'u Gongdzö (Rme'u dgongs mdzod/mdzad). These two names are problematic since they are rather descriptive "titles" or designations rather than proper names. The first one means the "Great Noble Hermit" (*dam pa ri khrod pa chen po*) while the second one means the "Treasury of Contemplation" (*dgongs mdzod*) or "Contemplative" (*dgongs mdzad*) from the Me'u (Rme'u) clan. Thus, regarding the name of the founder of this meditative system, the only element that is indicative of who he actually was is simply the fact that he belonged to the Me'u clan. His real name is still unknown.
28. For more about their authors, see the section "Extraordinary Dzogchen Patriarchs of Bön." On *A khrid*, see Per Kværne, "Bonpo Studies: The A Khrid System of Meditation," pts. 1 and 2, *Kailash* 1, no. 1 (1973): 1–50; 4, no. 4 (1973): 247–332; Per Kværne and Thupten K. Rikey, *The Stages of A-Khrid Meditation: Dzogchen Practice of the Bon Tradition (by Bru-sgom Rgyal-ba-g.yung-drung)* (Dharamsala, India: Library of Tibetan Works and Archives, 1996); and Per Kværne, "The Great Perfection in the Tradition of the Bonpos," in *Early Ch'an in China and Tibet*, ed. Whalen Lai and Lewis Lancaster,

Berkeley Buddhist Studies Series 5 (Berkeley, CA: Asian Humanities Press, 1983), passim. See also Jean-Luc Achard, *The Instructions on the Primordial A*, A khrid Studies, vol. I (München: Naldjor Institute, 2008).

29. See the pioneering work of Anne-Marie Blondeau, "Le Révélateur du Maṇi bKa' 'bum était-il bon po?," in *Tibetan and Buddhist Studies commemorating the 200th anniversary of the birth of Alexander Csoma de Körös*, ed. Louis Ligueti, vol. XXIX–I (Budapest: Bibliotheca Orientalis Hungarica, 1986), pp. 77–123. On the contents of the collection, see Samten G. Karmay, *A Catalogue of Bon po Publications* (Tokyo: Toyo Bunko, 1977), 103–105 (no. 55). There exists also an impressive commentarial literature associated with this cycle (see Karmay, *Catalogue of Bon po Publications*, 105–106 [no. 56]).
30. This is also said to come from India or Oḍḍiyāna.
31. This also contains "standard" tantric teachings.
32. This cycle is one of the few Bönpo Dzogchen collections that recognize the classification into three Series (Mind Series, Expanse Series, and Precepts Series), which is widespread among the Nyingmapas and attributed to the 7th-century figure Mañjuśrīmitra; see Lung bon Lha gnyen, *Ye khri mtha' sel*, Dolanji, *c*. 1985, 277. The earliest mention of the three Series seems to be in the *Gsang ba snying thig* literature.
33. As partially translated by Karmay in *The Treasury of Good Sayings*, passim.
34. A detailed history and analysis of this cycle can be found in Jean-Luc Achard, "Bon zhig khyung nag and the *Rig pa gcer mthong* Tradition of Rdzogs chen," *Tibet Journal* 23, no. 4 (Winter 1998): passim. However, to the author's knowledge, not a single text of this collection has ever been translated in any Western language, even in nonacademic publications.
35. Also discovered by Rdo rje gling pa. See Karmay, *Great Perfection*, 218. The cycle is not really comparable to the *lTa ba klong yangs*, in particular because it does not contain instructions on *khregs chod* and *thod rgal*, which are central to the latter.
36. That is, instructions on sexual practices generally known as "instructions on the Great Bliss of the Lower Door" (*'og sgo bde chen la gdams pa*; Bon zhig g.yung drung gling pa, *Rdzogs chen gser thur*, in *Rdzogs chen gser gyi thur ma: A Revealed Cycle of Bon po Rdzogs chen Practice*, Recovered from its Place of Concealment by Bon zhig g.yung drung gling pa, Dolanji, 1977: 345–375).
37. A kind of exhaustive work elaborated around a highly complex structure supplemented with numerous quotations from Dzogchen canonical works.
38. On this text, see Achard, *Enlightened Rainbows*, 117–129.
39. On his life and works, see Achard, *Enlightened Rainbows*, passim.

Jean-Luc Achard

BUDDHAGHOSA

TRADITIONAL BIOGRAPHY

The extant records of Buddhaghosa's life were written several centuries after his death. Chapter 37 of the *Cūlavaṃsa* offers the oldest surviving account of Buddhaghosa's life. It is the *Cūlavaṃsa* upon which the *Buddhaghosuppatti*, the most famous bibliography of him, compiled in the 13th century, was based. Buddhaghosa's life, as described in the *Cūlavaṃsa*, may be summarized as follows.

Buddhaghosa was born to a Brahmin family near the Bodhimaṇḍa in present-day India. He was well versed in the arts and sciences and mastered the three *Vedas*. Once, while wandering about mainland South Asia (Jambudīpa) to engage in debate, he stayed at a certain monastery and ended up lecturing on the niceties of Patañjali's thought. The senior monk at this monastery, Revata, recognizing that Buddhaghosa was an outstanding scholar, explained the Buddha's teaching to him, whereupon the latter joined the Buddhist Order under Revata's tutelage. Because his voice (*ghosa*) was deep like that of the Buddha, people called him Buddhaghosa.

Buddhaghosa wrote the *Ñāṇodaya* first, then the *Atthasālinī*, followed by the *Parittaṭṭhakathā*. Witnessing this display of erudition, Revata urged him to translate into the language of the Magadhans (i.e., Pāli) the commentaries that the elder Mahinda had written in Sinhalese and that had been preserved in Sri Lanka. Buddhaghosa arrived in Sri Lanka during the reign of the king Mahānāma. He went to the Mahāvihāra monastery, where he studied the entirety of the Sinhalese commentaries and the Elders' statements under the elder Saṃghapāla. Realizing that it represented the intention of the Buddha, he asked the monastic community (*saṃgha*) of the Mahāvihāra to show him all their books so that he could write a set of commentaries. In order to test him, the monastic community presented him two verses by which to demonstrate his hermeneutical ability, to which Buddhaghosa responded by writing the *Visuddhimagga* as a commentary on these two verses.

Buddhaghosa then assembled the monks near a bodhi tree on the grounds of the Mahāvihāra to read out the *Visuddhimagga*, yet each time he tried to recite the text, the deities hid his manuscript. When he rewrote it three times without any variations whatsoever between each of the versions, the monks said again and again, "Surely this is Metteya!" and provided Buddhaghosa with the *Tipiṭaka* and its commentaries. While staying in the Ganthākaravihāra, Buddhaghosa translated a subset of the Sinhalese commentaries into the Magadhan language (i.e., Pāli). The teachers of the Theriya school accepted Buddhaghosa's commentaries as if they were canonical texts. Having discharged his duty, Buddhaghosa departed for mainland South Asia (Jambudīpa) to pay homage at the Great Bodhi Tree.

The oldest extant biography of Buddhaghosa is not always consistent with data gleaned from his commentaries and contains some points that are unclear. For example, the *Atthasālinī* was compiled after the *Visuddhimagga* and could not have been written beforehand. In addition, it is unclear whether the *Ñānodaya* and *Parittaṭṭhakathā* are extant or not. On the other hand, the oldest biography depicts Buddhaghosa as the writer of the *Visuddhimagga* and the translator of the commentaries on the *Tipiṭaka*. It also states that the monks of the Mahāvihāra called Buddhaghosa Metteyya and accepted his commentaries as if they were canonical texts. Rather than presenting the historical facts about Buddhaghosa, his biography serves to lend great authority to the Pāli commentaries. In order to learn about Buddhaghosa, therefore, we need to understand the Pāli commentaries attributed to him by the Mahāvihāra school (which this article calls "Buddhaghosa's commentaries").

WORKS AND DATES

According to the colophons in the Pāli manuscripts, Buddhaghosa compiled twelve works: 1. *Visuddhimagga* (*Path to Purification*), and eleven commentaries (*aṭṭhakathā*) on the Pāli canon, which consists of the *Vinayapiṭaka*, the *Suttantapiṭaka*, and the *Abhidhammapiṭaka*. The commentaries on the *Vinayapiṭaka* are 2. *Samantapāsādikā* (*All-Pleasing*), a commentary on the whole of the *Vinayapiṭaka*, and 3. *Kaṅkhāvitaraṇī* (*Overcoming Doubts*), a commentary on the monastic code-named *Pātimokkha* in the *Vinayapiṭaka*.

The commentaries on the *Suttantapiṭaka*, which consists of the five *Nikāyas*, are 4. *Sumaṅgalavilāsinī* (*Splendor of the Highest Blessing*), a commentary on the *Dīghanikāya*; 5. *Papañcasūdanī* (*Clarifier of Proliferation*), a commentary on the *Majjhimanikāya*; 6. *Sāratthappakāsinī* (*Illustrator of Core Meaning*), a commentary on the *Saṃyuttanikāya*; 7. *Manorathapūraṇī* (*Fulfilling Wishes*), a commentary on the *Aṅguttaranikāya*; 8. *Paramatthajotikā* (*Illuminator of the Supreme Truth*), a commentary on the *Suttanipāta* and *Khuddakapātha*, both of which belong to the *Khuddakanikāya*; and 9. *Dhammapadaṭṭhakathā*, a commentary on the *Dhammapada*, which also belongs to the *Khuddakanikāya*.

The commentaries on the *Abhidhammapiṭaka* are 10. *Atthasālinī* (*Expositor*), a commentary on the *Dhammasaṅgani*; 11. *Sammohavinodanī* (*Dispeller of Delusion*), a commentary on the *Vibhaṅga*; and 12. *Pañcappakaraṇaṭṭhakathā* (*Commentary on Five Treatises*), a commentary on the *Dhātukathā*, *Puggalapaññatti*, *Kathāvatthu*, *Yamaka*, and *Paṭṭhāna*. Traditionally, these twelve works were believed to have been composed by Buddhaghosa.

The intertextual relationships present among these texts lead us to the hypothesis that the first of the Pāli commentaries compiled by Buddhaghosa was the *Visuddhimagga*.[1] Among the commentaries on the *Vinayapiṭaka*, the *Samantapāsādikā* and then the *Kaṅkhāvitaraṇī* were compiled after the *Visuddhimagga*, while among the commentaries on the *Suttantapiṭaka*, the *Sumaṅgalavilāsinī* was compiled after the *Visuddhimagga*, followed by the *Papañcasūdanī*, the *Sāratthappakāsinī*, and then probably the *Manorathapūraṇī*.[2] Among these commentaries on the *Suttantapiṭaka*, the *Sāratthappakāsinī* and *Manorathapūraṇī* postdate the *Samantapāsādikā*. As for commentaries on the Abhidhammapiṭaka, the *Atthasālinī* and then the *Sammohavinodanī* were compiled after the *Visuddhimagga*.

According to the colophon of the *Samantapāsādikā*, this commentary was compiled during the 20th and 21st years of the reign of a king bearing the names Sirinivāsa and Siripāla.[3] The Sri Lankan king to whom both of these names were attributed was Mahānāma.[4] As per the *Cūlavaṃsa*, King Mahānāma ruled for twenty-two years.[5] It can also be confirmed in Chinese histories that a king of Sri Lanka (Shiziguo 師子國) called Mahānāma (Mohenan 摩訶南) twice sent embassies to China, first in 428 (Yuanjia 元嘉 5) and later in 435 (Yuanjia 12).[6] In general, it took about one year to travel by sea from Sri Lanka to South China at that time.[7] If he ascended the throne in 427, he would have ruled from 427 to 449, and the year 449 would be the *terminus ante quem* for his reign; If, on the other hand, the year 434 was the final year of his reign, he would have ruled from 412 to 434, and the year 412 would be the *terminus post quem* for his reign. These numbers suggest that Mahānāma ruled for twenty-two years sometime between 412 and 449.[8] Since the composition of the *Samantapāsādikā* began in the 20th year of Mahānāma's reign and ended in his 21st year, it must have been compiled during two years between 433 and 448. The *Visuddhimagga* would have been compiled earlier and the *Sāratthappakāsinī* and *Manorathapūraṇī* compiled later. If these works were composed by the same person—Buddhaghosa, as claimed by tradition—there can be no doubt that they were compiled in the 5th century: around 430s and 440s.

Information about Buddhaghosa's life that can be gleaned from his own writings is extremely limited. In the colophon of the *Manorathapūraṇī*, Buddhaghosa writes that before compiling this commentary he once stayed in Kāñcīpura, a city near modern-day Chennai in today's South India.[9] The colophon possibly means that he merely spent a short time there or that he originally came from southern part of the mainland. In either case, his works do not tell us where he was born, what sort of family he was born into, or where, and under whom, he studied.

SOURCE MATERIALS, AUTHORSHIP, AND SCHOOL AFFILIATION

As he himself stated, Buddhaghosa compiled his works on the basis of various source materials, which can be broadly divided into six types: (a) Pāli canon (*Tipiṭaka*), (b) paracanonical texts, (c) other Pāli commentaries, (d) Sinhalese commentaries, (e) quotations of the doctrinal views held by other schools, and (f) other sources.[10] Among these source materials, the contents of lost texts such as the Sinhalese commentaries can be known only from quotations in the Pāli commentaries.[11]

The views of the compiler(s) of each commentary, whether Buddhaghosa or not, become clear through the stance taken in each commentary toward the *Visuddhimagga*. This is because, unlike the source materials, the *Visuddhimagga* was compiled by Buddhaghosa, and therefore one can see how the compilers of the commentaries situate Buddhaghosa's work.

For example, each of the commentaries on the first four *Nikāya*s begins with a set of prefatory verses, which all start with the formulaic taking of refuge in the Three Jewels, and then state that an old Sinhalese commentary will be translated into Pāli. The prefatory verses next present an outline of the *Visuddhimagga*, after which the compiler himself states that he is the author of the *Visuddhimagga*, that the *Visuddhimagga* is based on the four *Nikāya*s (*Āgama*s), and that any overlapping content will be left to the *Visuddhimagga*.[12] These last three points suggest that the commentaries on the first four *Nikāya*s were compiled as works ancillary to the *Visuddhimagga*.

The *Atthasālinī* and *Sammohavinodanī*, on the other hand, include a foreword and an afterword respectively that cause modern scholars to be skeptical about Buddhaghosa's authorship of these two commentaries.[13] The *Atthasālinī* states in the prefatory verses that the compiler composed the *Visuddhimagga*, but goes on to state that "Buddhaghosa" requested the compiler to organize this commentary.[14] The *Sammohavinodanī* similarly states in the final prefatory verse that it was "written at the request of Buddhaghosa."[15] Oskar von Hinüber writes that Buddhaghosa "composed the *Visuddhimagga* and the commentaries on the first four *Nikāyas*," and is skeptical about his authorship of any other works.[16]

Be that as it may, since all commentaries attributed to Buddhaghosa state that they are based on the traditions of the Mahāvihāra of Sri Lanka, there can be no doubt that they were compiled by monk(s) affiliated with the Mahāvihāra school. This suggests that the Mahāvihāra school assigned the authorial name "Buddhaghosa" to this body of works. In this respect, "Buddhaghosa" was not only a historical figure but also the designation of an authoritative collection of works that were compiled and officially recognized by the Mahāvihāra.[17]

In its historical chronicles consisting of the *Dīpavaṃsa* and *Mahāvaṃsa*, the Mahāvihāra school represented itself as the orthodox successor of the Buddha's teachings preserved by the elders of the councils. These two chronicles refer to the Buddha's teachings recited at the First Council or the school which transmits the orthodox teachings, by the name "Theravāda." In addition, the *Mahāvaṃsa* refers to the orthodox teaching recited at the Third Council as

"Vibhajjavāda." Like these chronicles, Buddhaghosa used the terms *Theriya*, which means "belonging to the elders [in the First Council]," and *Vibhajjavādin* to qualify "dwellers in the Mahāvihāra." Therefore, Buddhaghosa's school (in the sense of a monastic order) may be called the Mahāvihāra school in a narrow sense and the Theriya or Vibhajjavāda in a broad sense.[18]

VISUDDHIMAGGA

The *Visuddhimagga*, the best known of the noncanonical Pāli texts, consists of twenty-three chapters. The entire work is organized around the three steps of gradual progression in the Buddhist path, namely, moral conduct (*sīla*), meditative concentration (*samādhi*), and wisdom (*paññā*). With these three kinds of practice, the *Visuddhimagga* begins and ends with verses urging the reader to attain *nibbāna*.[19] In terms of its great variety of ideas and stories brought together in the exposition of this system of practice, the *Visuddhimagga* also constitutes an outstanding encyclopedia of Buddhism. In the Mahāvihāra tradition, this work is categorized as a commentary (*Aṭṭhakathā*).

In chapter 1, the *Visuddhimagga* explains "moral conduct" for monks, nuns, novices, and the laity from various perspectives—and, unlike Mahāyāna Buddhist texts, does not include what are known as bodhisattva precepts.[20] Next, in chapter 2, thirteen kinds of ascetic practices are explained as forms of practice for perfecting virtues such as having few desires, contentment, and so on to purify one's conduct.

The treatment of practices of "meditative concentration," covering chapters 3 through 11, accounts for more than half of the entire work. In chapter 3, the *Visuddhimagga* explains meditative concentration in general terms and presents forty subjects of meditative concentration (*kammaṭṭhāna*). There follow detailed expositions of these forty: ten devices for meditative concentration (chapters 4–5), ten kinds of foulness as subjects of meditative concentration (chapter 6), ten recollections as subjects of meditative concentration (chapters 7–8), four divine states (chapter 9), four immaterial states (chapter 10), and repulsiveness in nutriment and the four elements (chapter 11). Chapter 11 ends by enumerating five benefits of the practice of meditative concentration and the following chapters explain in detail one of these benefits: the five kinds of special knowledge. Chapter 12 deals with supernormal powers and chapter 13 with the other four kinds of special knowledge.

The remaining chapters, from chapter 14 to chapter 23, articulate practices of "wisdom." The cultivation of wisdom is broadly divided into the "Exposition of the Ground of Wisdom" ("Paññābhūminiddesa") and the "Exposition of the Body of Wisdom" ("Paññāsarīraniddesa"). The former corresponds to chapters 14 through 17 and discusses the five aggregates (chapter 14), the twelve spheres of perception and eighteen elements (chapter 15), the twenty-two faculties and four truths for noble ones (chapter 16), and dependent arising (chapter 17). The "Exposition of the Body of Wisdom" corresponds to chapters 18 through 22 and explains methods for cultivating wisdom in stages. Finally, the benefits of the cultivation of wisdom are explicated in chapter 23.

The *Visuddhimagga* is structured not only around the "three trainings" but also in terms of "seven kinds of purification" expounded in the Pāli canon: (a) "purification of conduct" in chapters 1 and 2, (b) "purification of consciousness" in chapters 3 through 11, (c) "purification of view" in chapter 18, (d) "purification by overcoming doubt" in chapter 19, (e) "purification by knowledge and vision of what is and what is not the path" in chapter 20, (f) "purification by knowledge and vision of the path" in chapter 21, and (g) "purification by knowledge and vision" in chapter 22.[21]

Buddhaghosa rejected both a creator god and monism. He also denied any subjective agent such as *attan* (*ātman* in Sanskrit), instead explaining the process of existence by means of "the way things really are" (*dhamma*). In terms of individual existence, he holds the traditional Buddhist concept of the five factors: (a) physical phenomena (*rūpa*), (b) feelings (*vedanā*), (c) recognition (*saññā*), (d) volitional formations (*saṅkhāra*), and (e) consciousness (*viññāṇa*). In the *Visuddhimagga*, "consciousness" is broken down into three types (wholesome, unwholesome, or indeterminate), or even into a more finely grained set of eighty-nine categories. The type of consciousness (wholesome, unwholesome, indeterminate) is determined by its association with feelings, recognition, and volitional formations. Whereas the five factors that make up the individual are impermanent, Buddhaghosa equated *nibbāna* with the unconditioned (*asaṅkhata*). The Mahāvihāra, to which Buddhaghosa belonged, was unique among the Buddhist schools in that it restricted the "unconditioned" to only *nibbāna*.

In the *Visuddhimagga*, the word *buddha* refers primarily to Gotama Buddha. Unlike Mahāyāna scriptures, there is no mention of buddhas currently residing in other world-realms. But like other monastic orders of South Asian Buddhism, there are references in this text to several buddhas in the past and the Buddha Metteyya in the future.

One of the main sources consulted by Buddhaghosa when composing the *Visuddhimagga* was the *Vimuttimagga* (*The Path to Freedom*), a text similar in content and format composed by Upatissa.[22] The *Vimuttimagga* survives in its entirety only in a Chinese translation by the 5th-century monk Saṅghapāla from Funan in Southeast Asia.[23] There is a Tibetan translation of only the chapter on ascetic practices, and the chapters on wisdom are also quoted in Tibetan translation of an Indian Buddhist text (*Saṃskṛtāsaṃskṛtaviniścaya*).[24]

The *Visuddhimagga* and *Vimuttimagga* are very similar in their organization, the order of their exposition, and the content of their doctrines. In fact, there are many identical passages, as well as numerous distinctive features shared only by these two works. To cite just one representative example, both texts are broken into the same three-pronged conceptual framework of Buddhist practice: (a) conduct, (b) meditative concentration, and (c) wisdom. Each section begins by explaining the respective concept in terms of meaning (*attha*), characteristic (*lakkhaṇa*), function (*rasa*), manifestation (*paccupaṭṭhāna*), proximate cause (*padaṭṭhānāni*), benefits (*ānisaṃsa*), cleansing (*vodāna*), and so forth.[25] This overall structure is not found in any other Buddhist text. Furthermore, there is a passage in the *Visuddhimagga* that criticizes an assertion made by "some," which is also found in the *Vimuttimagga*; Dhammapāla's commentary on the *Visuddhimagga* explains that these critical passages in fact refer to the "*Vimuttimagga*" composed by the Elder "Upatissa." The preceding facts suggest that Buddhaghosa wrote the *Visuddhimagga* on the model of Upatissa's *Vimuttimagga*.

In the *Vimuttimagga*, it is the four truths for noble ones that play the most important role in the cultivation of wisdom, the third stage of practice.[26] In contrast, although Buddhaghosa consulted the *Vimuttimagga*, in the *Visuddhimagga* he adopted the new framework of "threefold thorough understanding" (*tisso pariññā*) and organized practice in the third stage as "observation of impermanent *dhammas*."[27] He restructured the system of practice on the basis of new ideas and in effect removed observation of the four truths for noble ones from the *Visuddhimagga*. Buddhaghosa's redaction contrasts with the path of the Sarvāstivāda, which was the dominant school of Buddhism in mainland India, for whereas the four truths for noble ones constituted the core of the Sarvāstivāda's practice system, Buddhaghosa replaced them with the observation of impermanent *dhammas*.[28]

COMPILING PĀLI COMMENTARIES AND CLOSING PĀLI CANON

Unlike other Buddhist schools, both Mahāvihāra's complete *Tipiṭaka* and its full set of commentaries survive up to the present. Buddhaghosa compiled the bulk of the Pāli commentaries. Unlike the *Visuddhimagga*, the Pāli commentaries follow the structure of the Pāli canon and adopt the format of explicating words and phrases as they appear in the root texts. In his prefaces to the commentaries, Buddhaghosa states that his commentaries are based on older commentaries that were recited by elders at the First Buddhist Council and brought to Sri Lanka and then translated into Sinhalese by Mahinda, the (legendary) founder of the Mahāvihāra. By explaining their provenance in this way, he assigned to the commentaries an authority second only to that of the Pāli canon.

According to the prefaces to the Pāli commentaries, Buddhaghosa translated these texts from Sinhalese into Pāli. At least two reasons can be adduced for rendering the commentaries into Pāli. One of the two was to facilitate its dissemination in mainland South Asia.[29] Since the Mahāvihāra school had by this time advanced into mainland India, this Sri Lankan school needed to compile commentaries in an Indic language rather than in Sinhalese.

The second—and more important—reason for using Pāli was to preserve its position as a sacred language against the increasing cultural hegemony of Sanskrit.[30] As Sheldon Pollock discussed, the "Sanskrit Cosmopolis" had spread widely throughout South and Southeast Asia from the 4th century. In fact, the Sarvāstivāda school and the Mahāyāna had begun to change their scriptural language into Sanskrit for the purpose of more efficient circulation in mainland India. In contrast, the Mahāvihāra school developed what I have termed a "language ideology," which challenged the universality of Sanskrit. The Mahāvihāra school chose the Pāli linguistic medium to authorize the transmission of Buddhist texts.

In the *Visuddhimagga*, Buddhaghosa states that a liberated person acquires an "ability in language" (*niruttipatisambhidā*) pertaining to Pāli. He also calls Pāli (a) "the language of Magadha," (b) "the fundamental language of all beings," and (c) "the language of the Dhamma." These statements underlie his argument that Pāli is (a) the language that the Buddha spoke and (b) the language that was originally spoken by all sentient beings and is therefore (c) the medium best suited to transmitting the Buddhist scriptures.

In fact, Buddhaghosa interprets one passage in the *Vinayapiṭaka* as meaning that the Buddha ordered Buddhist texts to be recited in Pāli, not Sanskrit. Buddhaghosa argued vociferously for this Pāli language ideology throughout his work, calling Pāli "a language suited to the method of [transmitting] sacred texts" and "a language concordant with the method of [transmitting] sacred texts."[31] He also declared to write a commentary in Pāli "following the method of [transmitting] the text [of the *Tipiṭaka*]."[32] These statements indicate that the very act of composing commentaries in Pāli reflected the praxis of the Mahāvihāra's language ideology. The ideology of Pāli in Buddhaghosa's commentaries played an important role in the history of the Mahāvihāra's rejection of Sanskrit-medium scriptural traditions, in contrast to its rival monasteries, the Abhayagirivihāra and Jetavanavihāra, which accepted Sanskrit Buddhist scriptures.[33] As a result, the Mahāvihāra defended the position of Pāli as a sacred language against the totalizing/dominating force of Sanskrit (this is explained in detail in the next section).

At the start of each of his commentaries on the *Tipiṭaka*, Buddhaghosa presents a schema of "the whole of the Buddha's word" (*sabbam pi buddhavacanam*). It is to this schema that K. R. Norman is referring when he writes, "the form of the Theravādin canon, and the texts it comprises, are fixed by the information Buddhaghosa gives."[34] This schema defines the overall structure and scope of the canon by bringing the various categories of scriptures such as the *Tipiṭaka*.[35] Buddhaghosa goes on to explain that the five hundred elders at the First Council "fixed" these conceptual divisions of the canonical corpus.[36] By doing so, he fixed this list of canonical texts (*buddhavacana*: literally, "the Buddha's word") under the authority of the elders at the First Council.[37] As the antonym of "the Buddha's word," Buddhaghosa also supplies the list of heretical texts (*abuddhavacana*: literally, "not the Buddha's word"), which probably includes Mahāyāna scriptures.[38] This approach is in contrast to Buddhist schools in mainland India, such as the Sarvāstivāda and the Mahāsāṅghika, which lacked any fixed and closed list of canonical texts, and therefore accepted the Mahāyāna scriptures.[39]

After Buddhaghosa, the *Mahāvaṃsa*, and the *Cūlavaṃsa*, a series of chronicles compiled in the Mahāvihāra school, criticized the adherents of the Mahāyāna (*Vetulyavāda*, or *Vepullavāda*) and the latter stated that the corpus of Mahāyāna scriptures (*Vepullapiṭaka*) consists of heretical texts (*abuddhavacana*).[40] In addition, the *Sārasaṅgaha*, a Pāli text compiled in Sri Lanka in the 14th century, regards early Mahāyāna scriptures such as the *Ratnakūṭa* and tantric texts, such as the *Māyājālatantra, Mahāsamayatattva, Tattvasaṅgraha, Bhūtaḍāmara, Vajrāmṛta*, and *Cakrasaṃvara*, as heretical.[41]

BUDDHAGHOSA'S LINGUISTIC TURN IN SOUTH AND SOUTHEAST ASIAN HISTORY

The approach to the "buddha's word" in Buddhaghosa's commentaries is completely different from those of the Sarvāstivāda, a Buddhist monastic group that transmitted Sanskrit scriptures in South and Southeast Asia in the following three ways.[42]

First, there is a provision regarding the recitation of Buddhist scriptures in the *Vinaya*s of several monastic groups: at least, the Dharmaguptaka, Mahīśāsaka, Sarvāstivāda, Mūlasarvāstivāda, and the Theriya. According to the interpretation most widely accepted by modern scholars, the Buddha has ordered monks to recite the "buddha's word" not "in the language of the *Veda*s" but "in the language of each region."[43] This interpretation coincides with that of the Dharmaguptaka and Mahīśāsaka *Vinayas*.[44]

The Sarvāstivāda *Vinaya*, however, does not prohibit the recitation of Buddhist scriptures in Sanskrit. The Chinese translation of the Sarvāstivāda *Vinaya* (*Shisong lü* 十誦律) does not include the Buddha's instructions to recite his words in the language of each region.[45] In the Chinese translation of the Mūlasarvāstivāda *Vinaya* (*Genbenshuoyiqieyoubu pinaiye zashi* 根本說一切有部毘奈耶雜事), the Buddha prohibits the recitation of scriptures in the Brahmanical style of recitation but not in Sanskrit.[46] In the Tibetan translation of the

Mūlasarvāstivāda *Vinaya* (*Kṣudrakavastu*), the Buddha states that one should not alter the meter (*sdeb sbyor*), words (*tshig*) or word order (*rim pa*) when reciting the "Buddha's word," but he does not instruct the monks to recite his words "in their own language."[47] Thus, the Sarvāstivāda did not reject the legitimacy of Sanskrit as a language of the Buddhist scriptures, and in this sense, they passively justified its use.

In contrast, in the *Samantapāsādikā* attributed to Buddhaghosa, the relevant passage is taken to mean that monks should recite the "Buddha's word" not in Sanskrit but in Pāli. On the basis of this interpretation, the Mahāvihāra school, unlike the Sarvāstivāda, rejected the transmission of the *Tipiṭaka* in Sanskrit and, unlike the Dharmaguptaka and Mahāśāsika schools, determined that it should be transmitted exclusively in Pāli.

Second, concerning the language spoken by the Buddha, the Sarvāstivāda (Vaibhāṣika) maintained that Gotama Buddha usually preached in the "language of the Āryans" but had the ability to speak in any language. It also argued that the language of the Āryans was the language originally spoken by all beings in the realms of gods, humans, animals, hungry ghosts, and hell. On the other hand, the *Sammohavinodanī* attributed to Buddhaghosa accepts the view, like the Sarvāstivāda, that the language of the Āryans was the language originally spoken by all beings but equates this language with Pāli.[48]

Third, regarding the linguistic ability of noble ones, the Sarvāstivāda (*Mahāvibhāṣā* and **Nyāyānusāriṇī*) and the Mahāyāna Yogācāra school (*Yogācārabhūmi*, *Abhidharmasamuccaya*, and *Mahāyānasūtrālaṃkāra*) took it to mean that a noble one is proficient in the language of each region.[49] This thesis is presumably linked to the Sarvāstivāda assertion that the Buddha taught in the local language of the people to whom he was preaching. In contrast, in the *Visuddhimagga* Buddhaghosa defines the linguistic ability of a noble one as the ability to speak Pāli. He then goes on to quote another view, according to which the linguistic ability of a noble one corresponds to "proficiency in one hundred and one languages," but he continues that "it is to be proficient especially in Māgadhī."[50]

Thus, among the competing approaches to the "Buddha's word" concerning (a) the recitation of Buddhist scriptures, the Sarvāstivāda passively justified their transmission in Sanskrit. Sarvāstivāda discourse on (b) the language spoken by the Buddha and (c) the linguistic ability of noble ones was more or less the same in that it maintained that, when preaching, the Buddha transcended differences among languages. Since these interpretations can be ascertained in Chinese translations of Indian Buddhist texts dating from the 3rd to 5th centuries, they had been established prior to Buddhaghosa. In contrast, Buddhaghosa's commentaries argue, namely, (a) that Buddhist scriptures should be recited not in Sanskrit but in Pāli, (b) that the Buddha spoke in Pāli, and (c) that the linguistic ability of noble ones is tantamount to proficiency in Pāli.

The language ideology of Pāli in Buddhaghosa's commentaries had an impact on language not only in Sri Lanka but also in mainland Southeast Asia. This is because, following Buddhaghosa's commentaries, the Mahāvihāra school maintained the *Tipiṭaka* in Pāli as opposed to the two other schools, Abhayagirivihāra and Jetavanavihāra, on the island that accepted Sanskrit Mahāyāna scriptures. In fact, the Abhayagirivihāra had Sanskrit Mahāyāna scriptures such as the *Karaṇḍamudrā* and *Sarvatathāgatatattvasaṃgraha*.[51] The Jetavanavihāra, another big monastery at Anurādhapura, had a golden manuscript of the *Pañcaviṃśatisāhasrikā Prajñāpāramitā*.[52] In addition, Sanskrit Mahāyāna texts such as the *Ratnakūṭa* (*Kāśyapaparivarta*), Sanskrit Mahāyāna verse such as *Traikāyastotra*, Sanskrit tantric texts such as *Cakrasaṃvara* were also present in Sri Lanka. According to Xuanzang, there were people in Sri Lanka who understood the *Yogācārabhūmi*.[53]

In the 12th century, however, Parakkamabāhu I (r. 1153–1186) unified the three monasteries into one Buddhist *saṃgha*. In the unification process, he defrocked or demoted to the position of novices all the monks of these two monasteries, the Abhayagirivihāra and Jetavanavihāra. The *Cūlavaṃsa* explains that these two monasteries transmitted "the *Vetullapiṭaka* and so on, which are not the Buddha's word," as the "Buddha's word."[54] This process resulted in the disappearance of the Sanskrit Mahāyāna scriptures in Sri Lanka. Thereafter, Sri Lankan Buddhism was reintroduced to mainland Southeast Asia in the 13th to 15th centuries. The timing and nature of these events represented a shift from the Sanskrit cosmopolis to the Pāli cosmopolis.

In the Pāli cosmopolis, the set of the canon and the commentary in Pāli language circulated among Sri Lanka and mainland Southeast Asia on the basis of the language ideology of Pāli, according to which Pāli was the original language of all beings, was the language spoken by Gotama Buddha, and was the only language suitable for transmitting the Buddhist scriptures. Through the recitation, copying, and study of Pāli scriptures, Buddhaghosa's linguistic turn provided a kind of common ground for Buddhism in Sri Lanka and mainland Southeast Asia in that they shared Pāli as a sacred language.

REVIEW OF LITERATURE

Traditionally, Sri Lankan and mainland Southeast Asian monasteries have transmitted the Pāli commentaries, of which the most were Buddhaghosa's works, through oral traditions and manuscripts. It is the 20th century when the editions of the Pāli commentaries were published in Europe and South and Southeast Asia: Pāli Text Society edition (1918–present), the Thai Royal edition (1918–1924), Simon Hewavitarne Bequest Series (1917–1952), The Chaṭṭhasaṅgāyana edition (1957–1968), and so forth.[55] While the *Visuddhimagga*, the *Jātakaṭṭhakathā*, the *Dhammapadaṭṭhakathā*, the *Atthasālinī*, and the *Sammohavinodaṇī* have each English translation(s) in their entirety, the *Samantapāsādikā*, the *Kaṅkhāvitāraṇī*, the *Sumaṅgalavilāsinī*, the *Papañcasūdanī*, the *Paramatthajotikā*, and the *Pañcappakaraṇaṭṭhakathā* have only partial English translations.[56] There is no English translation of other Buddhaghosa's works.

Previous research on the Pāli commentaries can be classified into four significant types. The first type is analysis of the source materials of the Pāli commentaries. E. W. Adikaram and Sodō Mori present an overall picture of these source materials, while Petra Kieffer-Pülz has accomplished a systematic investigation of various source materials quoted in the *Vinaya* commentaries.[57] Moreover, comparative study between the *Vimuttimagga* and the *Visuddhimagga* elucidated that Buddhaghosa compiled the *Visuddhimagga* while referring to the *Vimuttimagga*.[58] The second type is research on questions of authorship. P. V. Bapat and other scholars have pointed out inconsistencies between the *Visuddhimagga* and several Pāli commentaries such as the *Atthasālinī*, proposing the probability that the latter texts are not Buddhaghosa's commentaries.[59] The third type is research on the ideas and characteristics of the Pāli commentaries. Rupert Gethin, Toshiichi Endō and Maria Heim have studied the presentation and development of Buddhist thought in the Pāli commentaries.[60] In addition, Rupert Gethin has published an important finding on Buddhaghosa's school affiliation.[61]

As the fourth type of research, Oskar von Hinüber and Norihisa Baba discussed Buddhaghosa as the compiler.[62] According to the prefaces to them, Buddhaghosa's commentaries are the Pāli translations of Sinhalese commentaries. But Buddhaghosa was no mere translator. For instance, he made use of several source materials and states that he will disregard the meanings of repeatedly occurring words and that he has also adopted interpretations from other commentaries.[63] In other words, insofar as he engaged in editorial work by selectively choosing his source materials, he was no mere translator but a compiler. Therefore, analysis of Buddhaghosa's redaction makes it possible to elucidate what he placed emphasis on. In the future, forthcoming research of Buddhaghosa's works will need not only further philological and philosophical analysis of them, but also historical approaches, such as comparative research of them with mainland Indian Buddhism.

A NOTE ON SOURCES

All page references for Pāli texts in this article are to the Pali Text Society editions.

ABBREVIATIONS

AD—Padmanabh Shrivarma Jaini, ed., *Abhidharmadīpa with Vibhāṣāprabhāvṛtti*. Bhoṭadeśīya saṃskṛtagranthamālā v. 4. Patna: K. P. Jayaswal Research Institute, 1977.

Derge—*Bka' 'gyur sde dge'i par ma (CD-ROM)*, New York: Tibetan Buddhist Resource Center, 2003–2004.

MSA—Sylvain Levi, ed., *Mahāyānasūtrālaṅkāra: Exposé de la Doctrine du Grand Véhicle selon le Système Yogācāra*. Paris: Librarie Honoré Champion, 1907, rep. Kyoto: Rinsen Book Co., 1983.

Peking—Chibetto Daizōkyō Kenkyūkai 西蔵大蔵経研究会, ed., *Eiin Pekin ban Chibetto Daizokyō: Ōtani Daigaku Toshokan-zō* 影印北京版西蔵大蔵経: 大谷大学図書館蔵, Tokyo: Chibetto Daizōkyō Kenkyūkai 西蔵大蔵経研究会, 1955–1961.

T—Junjirō Takakusu and Kaigyoku Watanabe, eds., *Taishō Shinshū Daizōkyō* 大正新脩大蔵経. Tokyo: Daizō Shuppan 大蔵出版, 1924–1934.

PRIMARY SOURCES

Roman editions of Buddhaghosa's texts and their English translations have been published by the Pali Text Society. Other editions are also available in Sri Lankan, Thai, Burmese, and Indian publications. For details on these editions of Buddhaghosa's commentaries, see Sodō Mori, Y. Karunadasa, and Toshiichi Endo, eds., *The Pāli Aṭṭhakathā Correspondence Table* (Pali Text Society, 1994).

DIGITAL MATERIALS

Digital data for the Burmese (Chaṭṭhasaṅgāyana) edition of Pāli texts, including Buddhaghosa's commentaries, can be accessed from this link (https://tipitaka.org).

FURTHER READING

Adikaram, Edward Winifred. *Early History of Buddhism in Ceylon.* Dehiwala, Sri Lanka: Buddhist Cultural Centre, 1946.

An, Yang-Gyu. *The Buddha's Last Days: Buddhagosa's Commentary on the Mahāparinibbāna Sutta.* Oxford: Pali Text Society, 2003.

Baba, Norihisa. *Jōzabu Bukkyō no shisō keisei—Budda kara Buddagōsa e* (上座部仏教の思想形成―ブッダからブッダゴーサへ) [The development of Theravāda Buddhist philosophy: From the Buddha to Buddhaghosa]. Tokyo: Shunjūsha, 2008.

Baba, Norihisa 馬場紀寿. *Bukkyō no Seitō to Itan: Pārikosumoporisu no seiritsu* (仏教の正統と異端パーリ・コスモポリスの成立) [Buddhist Orthodoxy and Heresy: The Birth of Pāli Cosmopolis]. Tokyo: University of Tokyo Press, 2022.

Bodhi, Bhikkhu. *The Discourse on the All-Embracing Net of Views: The Brahmajāla Sutta and its Commentaries.* Kandy, Sri Lanka: Buddhist Publication Society, 1978.

Bodhi, Bhikkhu. *The Discourse on the Fruits of Recluseship: The Sāmaññaphala Sutta and its Commentaries.* Kandy, Sri Lanka: Buddhist Publication Society, 1989.

Bodhi, Bhikkhu. *The Discourse on the Root of Existence: The Mūlapariyāya Sutta and Its Commentaries.* Kandy, Sri Lanka: Buddhist Publication Society, 1980.

Bodhi, Bhikkhu. *The Great Discourse on Causation: The Mahānidāna Sutta and its Commentaries.* Kandy, Sri Lanka: Buddhist Publication Society, 1984.

Endo, Toshiichi. *Studies in Pāli Commentarial Literature: Sources, Controversies and Insights.* Hong Kong: Centre of Buddhist Studies, The University of Hong Kong, 2013.

Gethin, Rupert. *The Buddhist Path to Awakening: A Study of the Bodhi-pakkhiyā Dhammā.* Leiden, The Netherlands, and New York: E. J. Brill, 1992.

Gornall, Alastair, and Aleix Ruiz-Falqués. "Scholars of Premodern Pali Buddhism." *Brill's Encyclopedia of Buddhism Vol. II: Lives.* Edited by Jonathan Silk, Richard Bowring, Vincent Eltschinger, and Michael Radich, 420–436. Leiden, The Netherlands, and Boston: Brill, 2019.

Heim, Maria. *The Forerunner of All Things: Buddhaghosa on Mind, Intention, and Agency.* Oxford and New York: Oxford University Press, 2014.

Heim, Maria. *The Voice of the Buddha: Buddhaghosa on the Immeasurable Words.* Oxford and New York: Oxford University Press, 2018.

Kieffer-Pülz, Petra. *Verlorene Ganthipadas Zum Buddhistischen Ordensrecht: Untersuchungen Zu Den in Der Vajirabuddhitika Zitierten Kommentaren Dhammasiris und Vajirabuddhis,* vols. 1–3. Wiesbaden, Germany: Harrassowitz, 2013. https://www.amazon.co.uk/Verlorene-Ganthipadas-Buddhistischen-Ordensrecht-Vajirabuddhitika/dp/3447065400/ref=sr_1_4?qid=1576231385&refinements=p_27%3APetra+Kieffer-Pulz&s=books&sr=1-4.

Kieffer-Pülz, Petra. "*Vinaya* Commentarial Literature in Pali." In *Brill's Encyclopedia of Buddhism Volume I: Literature and Languages.* Edited by Jonathan Silk, 430–441. Leiden, The Netherlands, and Boston: Brill, 2015.

Law, Bimala Churn. *The Life and Work of Buddhaghosa.* Culcutta: Thacker, Spink, 1923; repr., Delhi: Pilgrims Book, 1999.

Lottermoser, Friedgard. *Quoted Verse Passages in the Works of Buddhaghosa: Contributions towards the Study of the Lost Sīhaḷaṭṭhakathā Literature.* Göttingen, Germany: University of Göttingen,1982.

Malalasekera, Gunapala Piyasena. *The Pāli Literature of Ceylon,* Royal Asiatic Society of Great Britain and Ireland, 1928; repr., Colombo, Sri Lanka: Buddhist Publication Society, 1994.

Mori, Sodō. *Studies of the Pāli Commentaries: A Provisional Collection of Articles.* Niiza, Japan: Self Publication, 1989.

Ñānamoli, Bhikkhu. *The Path of Purification (Visuddhimagga) by Bhadantācariya Buddhaghosa.* Kandy, Sri Lanka: Buddhist Publication Society, 1956.

Ñānamoli, Bhikkhu. rev. Bhikkhu Bodhi. *The Discourse on Right View: The Sammādiṭṭhi Sutta and its Commentariy.* Kandy: Buddhist Publication Society, 1991.

Pind, Ole Holten. "Buddhaghosa–His Works and Scholarly Background." *Bukkyō Kenkyū* [Buddhist Studies] 21 (1992): 135–156.

Pind, Ole Holten. "Pāli Grammar and Grammarians from Buddhaghosa to Vajirabuddhi: A Survey." *Journal of Pāli Text Society* 31 (2012): 57–124.

von Hinüber, Oskar. *A Handbook of Pāli Literature.* Berlin and New York: Walter de Gruyter, 1996.

NOTES

1. Edward Winifred Adikaram, *Early History of Buddhism in Ceylon* (Dehiwala: Buddhist Cultural Centre, 1946); and Sodō Mori 森祖道, *Pāri Bukkyō chūshakubunken no kenkyū: Attakatā no Jōzabuteki yōsō* パーリ仏教注釈文献の研究ーアッタカターの上座部的様相 [A Study of the Pāli Commentaries: Theravādic Aspects of the Aṭṭhakathās] (Tokyo: Sankibō Press, 1984), 92–104.
2. There are no references to the *Sāratthappakāsinī* in the *Manorathapūraṇī*, but judging from the order of the three foregoing works, these commentaries were compiled in the order of the first four *Nikāyas*.
3. *Samantapāsādikā* VII 1415. The Pali Text Society edition has *sirīpāla* (IV 1415), but other versions (Simon Hewavitarane Bequest Series IV 1056, Chaṭṭhasaṅgāyana IV 264) have *siripāla*.
4. On Sirinivāsa, see Nicholas Abeydeera Jayawickrama, *The Inception of Discipline and the Vinaya Nidāna: Being a Translation and Edition of the Bāhiranidāna of Buddhaghosa's Samantapāsādikā, the Vinaya Commentary* (London: Pali Text Society, 1986: xxiv–xxv); and Oskar von Hinüber, *A Handbook of Pāli Literature* (Berlin and New York: Walter de Gruyter, 1996), 102–103. On Siripāla, see Tilak Hettiarachchy, *History of Kingship in Ceylon Up to the Fourth Century AD* (Colombo, Sri Lanka: Lake House, 1972), 63, and Sodō Mori 森祖道, *Pāri Bukkyō chūshakubunken no kenkyū: Attakatā no Jōzabuteki yōsō* パーリ仏教注釈文献の研究ーアッタカターの上座部的様相 [A Study of the Pāli Commentaries: Theravādic Aspects of the Aṭṭhakathās] (Tokyo: Sankibō Press, 1984), 487, 521.
5. *Cūlavaṃsa* Chap. 37, v. 247.
6. *Songshu* 宋書 juan 巻 97, Liezhuan 列傳 57 (Beijing: Zhonghua Shuju 中華書局, 2018), 2616–2617.
7. See Mayuko Kawakami 河上麻由子, *Kodai Ajia Sekai no Taigai Kōshō to Bukkyō* 古代アジア世界の対外交渉と仏教 [Buddhist Missionaries to Bodhisattva Emperors: A Study of the Relationship between China and Surrounding Kingdoms, 400–900] (Tokyo: Yamakawa-Shuppansha Ltd, 2011), 19–20.
8. Wilhelm Geiger surmises that Mahānāma ruled from 409 to 431, but this view need to be emended. See Wilhelm Geiger, *Culture of Ceylon in Mediaeval Times* (Wiesbaden, Germany: O. Harrassowitz, 1960), 224.
9. *Manorathapūraṇī* V 98.
10. Edward Winifred Adikaram, *Early History of Buddhism in Ceylon* (Dehiwala: Buddhist Cultural Centre, 1946).; Sodō Mori 森祖道, *Pāri Bukkyō chūshakubunken no kenkyū: Attakatā no Jōzabuteki yōsō* パーリ仏教注釈文献の研究ーアッタカターの上座部的様相 [A Study of the Pāli Commentaries: Theravādic Aspects of the Aṭṭhakathās] (Tokyo: Sankibō Press, 1984).
11. On the Sīhaḷaṭṭhakathā, see Friedgard Lottermoser, *Quoted Verse Passages in the Works of Buddhaghosa: Contributions towards the Study of the Lost Sīhaḷaṭṭhakathā Literature* (Göttingen, Germany: University of Göttingen, 1982). On the *Andhakaṭṭhakathā*, a source taken up in the *Samantapāsādikā*, see Petra Kieffer-Pülz, "Zitate aus der Andhaka-Aṭṭhakathā in der Samantapāsādikā," in *Studien zur Indologie und Buddhismuskunde. Festgabe des Seminars für Indologie und Buddhismuskunde für Professor Dr. Heinz*

Bechert, ed. Reinold Grünendahl, Jens-Uwe Hartmann, & Petra Kieffer-Pülz (Bonn, Germany: Indica et Tibetica Verlag, 1993), 171–213; Petra Kieffer-Pülz, "Zitate aus der Andhakaṭṭhakathā in den Subkommentaren," *Studien zur Indologie und Iranistik* 27 (2010): 147–235; and Petra Kieffer-Pülz, "Buddhist Nuns in South India as Reflected in the *Andhakaṭṭhakathā* and in Vajrabuddhi's *Anugaṇṭhipada*," *Annual Report of the International Research Institute for Advanced Buddhology at Soka University* 16(2013): 29–46. On Buddhaghosa's Pāli adaptation of a Sanskrit verse, see Ole Holten Pind, "Buddhaghosa—His Works and Scholarly Background," *Bukkyō Kenkyū* [Buddhist Studies] 21(1992): 135–156.

12. *Sumaṅgalavilāsinī* I 2, *Papañcasūdanī* I 2, *Sāratthappakāsinī* I 2, *Manorathapūranī* I 2.
13. For the remaining possibility that the author of the *Atthasālinī* was Buddhaghosa, see Takatsugu Hayashi, "On the Authorship of *Atthasalinī*," *Bukkyō Kenkyū* [Buddhist Studies] 28 (1999): 31–71.
14. *Atthasālinī* 1.18. See also Oskar von Hinüber, *A Handbook of Pāli Literature* (Berlin and New York: Walter de Gruyter, 1996), 151.
15. *Sammohavinodanī* 532.12.
16. Oskar von Hinüber, *A Handbook of Pāli Literature* (Berlin and New York: Walter de Gruyter, 1996), 102–103.
17. As Maria Heim writes, "[t]he name Buddhaghosa has a role, a function, as Michael Foucault puts it, that endows a certain status and authenticity to these texts." See Maria Heim, *The Forerunner of All Things: Buddhaghosa on Mind, Intention, and Agency* (Oxford and New York: Oxford University Press, 2014): 9–10.
18. *Visuddhimagga* 711. 23–24: *Vibhajjavādiseṭṭhānaṃ Theriyānaṃ yasassinaṃ Mahāvihāravāsīnaṃ vaṃsajassa vibhāvino.*
19. *Saṃyuttanikāya* Sagāthavagga Jaṭāsutta (SN I 13).
20. *Visuddhimagga* 15.11–15.20
21. Cf. *Majjhimanikāya* no. 24 Rathavinītasutta. Chapters 14 through 17, which cover "Exposition of the Ground of Wisdom," are not directly related to the steps of practice but deal with the object of the training in wisdom.
22. See Purushottam Vishvanath Bapat, *Vimuttimagga and Visuddhimagga: A Comparative Study* (Poona, India: P.V. Bapat, 1937); and Norihisa Baba 馬場紀寿. *Jōzabu Bukkyō no shisō keisei—Budda kara Buddagōsa e* 上座部仏教の思想形成―ブッダからブッダゴーサへ [The development of Theravāda Buddhist philosophy: From the Buddha to Buddhaghosa] (Tokyo: Shunjūsha, 2008), 89–153.
23. T1648.
24. As many scholars agree, the *Vimuttimagga* was highly probably a work of the Abhayagirivihāra, Mahāvihāra's rival monastery located in Anurādhapura. See Peter Skilling, "Vimuttimagga and Abhayagiri: The Form-Aggregate According to the *Saṃskṛtāsaṃskṛtaviniścaya*," *Journal of the Pali Text Society* 20 (1994): 171–210; Lance Cousins, "The Teachings of the Abhayagiri School," in *How Theravāda Is Theravāda?: Exploding Buddhist Identities*, ed. Peter Skilling, Jason A. Carbine, Claudio Cicuzza, and Santi Pakeekham (Chiang Mai, Thailand: Silkworm Books, 2012), 67–127; and Bhikkhu Anālayo, "The Treatise on the Path to Liberation (解脫道論) and the *Visuddhimagga*," *Fuyan Buddhist Studies* 4 (2009): 1–15. For skepticism on scholars' school affiliation of the *Vimuttimagga*, see Kate Crosby, "History Versus Modern Myth: The Abhayagirivihāra, the *Vimuttimagga* and Yogācāra Meditation," *Journal of Indian Philosophy* 27 (1999): 521–528.
25. Concepts such as "proximate cause," which play an important role in this structure, are peculiar to the *Peṭakopadesa*, a Pāli text transmitted by the Theravāda. This method of explanation is by and large the same in the *Vimuttimagga* (T1648, 32. 400c1–4, 406c23–25, 444c5–6) and *Visuddhimagga* (6. 21–28; 84. 11–18; 436. 12–18).
26. In the *Vimuttimagga*, the development of wisdom begins with observation of the four truths for noble ones (T32, 453c1–454a24). It is also stated that one attains the noble paths by recognizing the four truths.

27. The concept of "threefold thorough understanding" is found in the *Niddesa* and *Paṭisambhidāmagga*, but it was Buddhaghosa who created the system of development of wisdom (*paññābhāvanā*) in the *Visuddhimagga* on the basis of this concept. For his redaction criticism of the *Visuddhimagga*, see Baba, *Jōzabu Bukkyō no shisō keisei*, 89–153.
28. For Sarvāstivāda's system of practice, see Collet Cox, "Attainment through Abandonment: The Sarvāstivādin Path of Removing Defilements," ed. Robert E. Buswell Jr. and Robert M. Gimello (Honolulu: University of Hawaii Press, 1992), 63–105.
29. *Samantapāsādikā* I 2. cf. Oskar von Hinüber, *A Handbook of Pāli Literature* (Berlin and New York: Walter de Gruyter, 1996), 103; Peter Skilling, "Scriptural Authenticity and the Śrāvaka Schools: An Essay towards an Indian Perspective," *The Eastern Buddhist* 41, no. 2 (2010): 1–47.
30. Kate Crosby insists that the origins of the designation "Pāli" as the name of a language lie in the expression *pālibhāsā*, which originally meant "language of texts," then turned into a proper noun in the 12th to 13th centuries, and came to be used as a synonym of "Magadhan." See Kate Crosby, "The Origin of the Language Name Pāli in Medieval Theravāda Literature," *Journal of the Center for Buddhist Studies* 2 (2003): 70–116.
31. *Sumaṅgalavilāsinī* I 1, *Papañcasūdanī* I 1, *Sāratthappakāsinī* I 1–2, *Manorathapūtaṇī* I 2: *bhāsaṃ tantinayānucchavikaṃ* . . . *Atthasālinī* 2: *bhāsan tantinayānugaṃ* . . .
32. *Samantapāsādikā* I 2: *pālinayānurūpaṃ* . . .
33. On the *dhāraṇī* of the *Sarvatathāgatādhṣṭhānahṛdayaguhyadhātukaraṇḍamudrasūtra* from the Abhayagirivihāra, see Gregory Schopen, "The Text on the "Dhāraṇī Stones from Abhayagiriya": A Minor Contribution to the Study of *Mahāyāna* Literature in Ceylon," *Journal of the International Association of Buddhist Studies* 5, no. 1 (1982): 100–108, re., in *Figments and Fragments of Mahyna Buddhism in India* (Honolulu: University of Hawaii Press, 2005), 306–313. On the *dhāraṇī* of the *Sarvatathāgatatattvasaṃgraha* from the Abhayagirivihāra, see Rangama Chandawimala, *Heterodox Buddhism: The School of Abhayagiri* (Colombo, Sri Lanka: Rangama Chandawimala Thero, 2016), 170–192. On the golden manuscript of the *Pañcaviṃśatisāhasrikā Prajñāpāramitā* from the Jetavanavihāra, see Oskar von Hinüber, "Sieben Goldblätter einer *Pañcaviṃśatisāhasrikā Prajñāpāramitā* aus Anurādhapura," *Nachrichten der Akademie der Wissenschaften in Göttingen* 7 (1983): 189–207.
34. Kenneth R. Norman, *Philological Approach to Buddhism* (Lancaster, UK: Pali Text Society, 2006), 191.
35. Steven Collins also says that "by the time of Buddhaghosa the list of texts had come to be fixed." See Steven Collins, "On the Very Idea of the Pali Canon," *Journal of the Pali Text Society* 15 (1990): 108, n. 11.
36. *Samantapāsādikā* I 29.20–29.29; *Sumaṅgalavilāsinī* I 24.3–25.9; *Atthasālinī* 17.19–27.25. However, the *Atthasālinī* does not explain "one taste" or "Dhamma and Vinaya."
37. Immediately after having explained the establishment of the divisions of the "buddha's word," the *Samantapāsādikā*, *Sumaṅgalavilāsinī*, and *Atthasālinī* state that divisions (*pabheda*) within the *Tipiṭaka*, such as summaries (*uddāna*), abridgements (*peyyāla*), and sections (*vagga, nipāta, saṃyutta, paññāsa*), were established by the elders at the First Council, and therefore, the internal structure of the *Tipiṭaka* is also endowed with the authority of the elders of the First Council.
38. *Samantapāsādikā* IV 742–743, *Sāratthappakāsinī* II 201. These lists of the heretical texts include the *Aṅgulimālapiṭaka* and *Rāṣṭrapālagajjita*, which closely resemble the titles of the Mahāyāna scriptures *Aṅgulimālīya* and *Rāṣṭrapālaparipṛcchā* respectively. More importantly, they also include the *Vedalla-/Vepulla-piṭaka*, which are probably the collection of Mahāyāna scriptures, as Seishi Karashima elucidated the *Vedalla/Vepulla* were the older names of the Mahāyāna scriptures. See Seishi Karashima, "Who Composed the Mahāyāna Scriptures?—The Mahāsāṃghikas and the *Vaitulya* Scriptures," *Annual Report of the International Research Institute for Advanced Buddhology at Soka University* 18 (2015): 113–162.
39. See Norihisa Baba, "Fifth Element of the Sūtrapiṭaka," in *Evolution of Scriptures, Formation of Canons: The Buddhist Case*, ed. Orna Almogi (Hamburg, Germany: Department of Indian and Tibetan Studies, Universität Hamburg, 2022), 231–272.

40. *Mahāvaṃsa,* Chap. 36, v. 41. *Cūḷavaṃsa,* Chap. 78, v. 21. On the *Vetulyapiṭaka/Vetullapiṭaka* in the Pāli chronicles, see Baba Norihisa, "Greatness or Heresy? Pāli Discourse on *Vetulla/Vetulya* as the Mahāvihāra's Response to the Mahāyāna," *Transactions of the International Conference of Eastern Studies* 65 (2021): 28–42.
41. *Sārasaṅgaha* 46. See also Nandasena Mudiyanse, *Mahāyāna Monuments in Ceylon* (Colombo, Sri Lanka: M. D. Gunasena and Co. Ltd., 1969), 16–19.
42. On details of this section, see Norihisa Baba 馬場紀寿, *Bukkyō no Seitō to Itan: Pārikosumoporisu no seiritsu* 仏教の正統と異端　パーリ・コスモポリスの成立 [Buddhist Orthodoxy and Heresy: The Birth of Pāli Cosmopolis] (Tokyo: University of Tokyo Press, 2022), 80–85, 111–129.
43. When Pāṇini uses the word *chandasi,* it refers to the Vedas, and the scope of the corresponding grammatical operation is restricted to the Vedas (Thieme 1935, 67ff.). Basing himself on this usage in the study of grammar, Edgerton (1953, 1, n4) states that in the case of Pāṇini *chandas* refers to the Vedic language, while Brough (1980, 463) takes *chandas* to mean "in the manner of the Brahmanical texts" and explains that *chandaso* as used in the *Vinaya* refers to Sanskrit.
44. Dharmaguptaka *Vinaya*: T1428, 22.955a; Mahīśāsaka *Vinaya*: T1421, 22.174b.
45. T1435, 23.274a.
46. 若苾芻作闡陀聲誦經典者、得越法罪。(T1451, 24.232c)
47. *'Dul ba phran tshegs kyi gzhi,* Peking De 69a, Derge Tha 71b: *dge slong gis sangs rgyas kyi gsung rab sdeb sbyor dang|tshig dang|rim pa sbyar nas gdon bar mi bya'o||*. The Mūlasarvāstivāda *Vinaya* does not prohibit the transmission of the "Buddha's word" in the language of each region, stating that it is not a transgression to do so (*'Dul ba phran tshegs kyi gzhi,* Peking De 69a, Derge Tha 71b: *yul gyi nges pa'i tshig dang|skad kyi nges pa'i tshig dang|ljongs kyi nges pa'i tshig yin na ltung ba med do||*).
48. On the relationship of the language ideology between the Sarvāstivāda and the Mahāvihāra, see Norihisa Baba 馬場紀寿, "Jōzabu Daijiha no Pārigo shugi 上座部大寺派のパーリ語主義 [The Language Ideology of Pāli by the Mahāvihāra school]," *Pārigaku Bukkyō Bunkagaku* パーリ学仏教文化学 29 (2015): 33–53.
49. Regarding the linguistic ability of noble ones, the *Mahāvibhāṣā* mentions "words of various regions" (T1545, 27.904a: 諸方言辭), and the **Nyāyānusāriṇī* and *Xianzong lun* 顯宗論 mention "secular and sacred words of various regions" (T1567, 29.751a; T1563, 29.959b: 諸方域俗聖言詞). Regarding the linguistic ability of noble ones, the *Abhidharmasamuccaya* mentions "the language of [each] region" (AS 97: *janapadabhāṣā*), and the *Mahāyānasūtrālaṃkāra* mentions "the language in each region" (MSA 139: *pratyekaṃ janapadeṣu yā bhāṣā*).
50. *Visuddhimagga* 442: *ekasatavohārakusalatā* . . . *Visuddhimagga* 442: *visesena pana Māgadhike kosallaṃ*.
51. Xuanzang 玄奘, who traveled around India in the 7th century, states that there were two branches of the Theriya school in Sri Lanka, whereas the Mahāvihāra rejected the Mahāyāna, at the Abhayagirivihāra both the Mahāyāna and the Hīnayāna were being studied (*Da Tang xiyuji* 大唐西域記 11: T2087, 51.934a).
52. Sri Lankan king Aggabodhi VI (r. 733–772) sent a Sanskrit manuscript of the (probably, *Pañcaviṃśatisāhasrikā-*)*Prajñāpāramitā* to Emperor Xuanzong of Tang (r. 712–756) through Amoghavajra (705–774). See Baba Norihisa, "Greatness or Heresy? Pāli Discourse on the Vetulla/Vetulya as the Mahāvihāra's Response to the Mahāyāna," *Transactions of the International Conference on Eastern Studies* 65 (2021): 28–42.
53. *Daci'ensi sanzang fashi zhuan* 大慈恩寺三藏法師傳 4 (T2053, 50.241a).
54. *Cūlavaṃsa* Chap. 78, v. 21.
55. See Primary Sources.
56. Bhikkhu Ñānamoli trans., *The Path of Purification (Visuddhimagga) by Bhadantācariya Buddhaghosa* (Colombo, Sri Lanka: Semage, 1956; rev. ed., Kandy: Buddhist Publication Society, 1991); Pe Maung Tin, trans., *The Path of Purity: Being a Translation of Buddhaghosa's Visuddhimagga* (London: Pali Text

Society, 1923–1931, repr., 1975); Edward B. Cowell ed., tr., *The Jātaka or Stories of the Buddha's Former Births* (Cambridge: Cambridge University Press, 1895–1907; Oxford: Pali Text Society, repr., 1990).; Eugene W. Burlingame, trans., *Buddhist Legends* (London: Pali Text Society, 1921, repr., 1990–1995); Pe Maung Tin trans., *The Expositor* (London: Pali Text Society, 1920–1921, repr., 1976); Bhikkhu Ñāṇamoli, trans., Lance S. Cousins, Nyanaponika Mahāthera, and Charles M. M. Shaw, rev., *Dispeller of Delusion* (Bristol, UK: Pali Text Society, 1987–1991).; Nicholas Abeydeera Jayawickrama trans., *The Inception of Discipline and the Vinaya Nidāna: Being a Translation and Edition of the Bāhiranidāna of Buddhaghosa's Samantapāsādikā, the Vinaya commentary* (London: Pali Text Society, 1962, repr., 1986); Kenneth R. Norman, Petra Kieffer-Pülz, and William Pruitt, trans., *Overcoming Doubts (Kaṅkhāvitaraṇī), Vol I: The Bhikkhu-Pātimokkha Commentary* (London: Pali Text Society, 2018); Bhikkhu Bodhi, trans., *The Discourse on the All-Embracing Net of Views: The Brahmajāla Sutta and its Commentaries* (Kandy, Sri Lanka: Buddhist Publication Society, 1978); Bhikkhu Bodhi, trans., *The Discourse on the Fruits of Recluseship: The Sāmaññaphala Sutta and its Commentaries* (Kandy, Sri Lanka: Buddhist Publication Society, 1989); Bhikkhu Bodhi, trans., *The Great Discourse on Causation: The Mahānidāna Sutta and its Commentaries* (Kandy, Sri Lanka: Buddhist Publication Society, 1984); An Yang-Gyu trans., *The Buddha's Last Days: Buddhagosa's Commentary on the Mahāparinibbāna Sutta* (Oxford: Pali Text Society, 2003); Bhikkhu Bodhi, trans., *The Discourse on the Root of Existence: The Mūlapariyāya Sutta and its Commentaries* (Kandy, Sri Lanka: Buddhist Publication Society, 1980); Bhikkhu Ñānamoli, trans., Bhikkhu Bodhi, rev., *The Discourse on Right View: The Sammādiṭṭhi Sutta and its Commentariy* (Kandy, Sri Lanka: Buddhist Publication Society, 1991); Bhikkhu Ñāṇamoli, trans., *The Minor Readings and The Illustrator of Ultimate Meaning* (Oxford: Pali Text Society, 1960, repr., 1991); Bhikkhu Ñāṇamoli, trans., *The Suttanipāta: An Ancient Collection of the Buddha's Discourses Together with its Commentaries Paramatthajotikā II and excerpts from the Niddesa* (Oxford: Pali Text Society, 1960, repr., 1991); and Bimala Churun Law, trans., *The Debates Commentary* (London: Pali Text Society, 1940, repr., 1969).

57. See note 15. See also Petra Kieffer-Pülz, "*Vinaya* Commentarial Literature in Pali," in *Brill's Encyclopedia of Buddhism. Volume I: Literature and Languages*, ed. Jonathan A. Silk, Oskar von Hinüber, and Vincent Eltschinger (Leiden, The Netherlands: Brill, 2015), 430–441.
58. For the *Vimuttimagga*, one of the main source materials of the *Visuddhimagga*, see Makoto Nagai, "The Vimutti-magga: The Way to Deliverance: The Chinese Counterpart of the Pāli Visuddhi-magga," *Journal of the Pali Text Society* (1975): 69–80; Purushottam Vishvanath Bapat, *Vimuttimagga and Visuddhimagga: A Comparative Study* (Poona, India: P. V. Bapat, 1937); and Heinz Bechert, "Vimuttimagga and Amatākaravaṇṇanā," in *Āmalā Prajñā: Aspects of Buddhist Studies, Professor P. V. Bapat Felicitation Volume* (Delhi: Sri Satguru Publications, 1989), 11–14. See also Takatsugu Hayashi, "On "*Sopākapañhavyākaraṇa*" in the *Visuddhimagga*," *Bukkyō Kenkyū* [Buddhist Studies] 39 (2011): 1–18.
59. See notes 17, 18, 20, and 21 and Purushottam Vishvanath Bapat and Ranganath Dattatreya Vadekar, *Aṭṭhasālinī: Commentary on Dhammasangaṇi, The First Book of the Abhidhammapiṭaka of the Buddhists of the Theravāda School, for the First Time Critically Edited in Devanāgari Characters* (Poona, India: B.O.R. Institute, 1942), xxxiii–xl. See also Oskar von Hinüber, "The Nigamanas of the *Sumaṅgalavilāsinī* and *the Kaṅkhāvitaranī*," *Journal of the Pali Text Society* 21 (1995): 129–133; and Mahinda Palihawadana, "Buddhaghosa's Comment on Manopubbaṅgamā (A. I. 11) (and Its Significance as Regards the Authorship of the Dhammapada Commentary," *Bukkyō Kenkyū* [Buddhist Studies] 27 (1998): 57–64. There is no mention of Buddhaghosa as the name of the author in the 6th-century Chinese translation of the *Samantapāsādikā*. For the Chinese version, see Purushottam Vishvanath Bapat and Akira Hirakawa, *Shan-Chien-P'i-P'o-Sha, a Chinese Versiton by Saṅghabhadra of Samantapāsādikā, Commentary on Pali Vinaya* (Poona, India: B. O. R. Institute, 1970).
60. Rupert Gethin, *The Buddhist Path to Awakening: A Study of the Bodhi-pakkhiyā Dhammā* (Leiden, The Netherlands, and New York: E.J. Brill, 1992); Toshiichi Endo, *Buddha in Theravāda Buddhism: A Study*

of the Concept of Buddha in the Pali Commentaries (Dehiwala, Sri Lanka: Buddhist Cultural Centre, 1997); Tochiichi Endo, *Studies in Pāli Commentarial Literature: Sources, Controversies and Insights* (Hong Kong: Centre of Buddhist Studies, The University of Hong Kong, 2013); Maria Heim, *The Forerunner of All Things: Buddhaghosa on Mind, Intention, and Agency* (Oxford and New Yok: Oxford University Press, 2014); and Maria Heim, *The Voice of the Buddha: Buddhaghosa on the Immeasurable Words* (Oxford and New Yok: Oxford University Press, 2018). See also Richard Gombrich, "Two Notes on *Visuddhimagga* IX," *Journal of the Pali Text Society* 12 (1988): 169–171; and An Yang-Gyu, "Buddhaghosa's View of the Buddha's Lifespan," *Bukkyō Kenkyū* [Buddhist Studies] 29 (2000): 129–147.

61. For the absence of "Theravāda" as the name of the school to which author belongs in Buddhaghosa's works, see Rupert Gethin, "Was Buddhaghosa a Theravādin? Buddhist Identity in the Pali Commentaries and Chronicles," in *How Theravāda is Theravāda? Exploring Buddhist Identities*, ed. Peter Skilling, Jason A. Caribine, Claudio Cicuzza, and Santi Pakdeekham. (Chiang Mai, Thailand: Silkworm Books, 2012), 1–63.
62. Oskar von Hinüber, "Building the Theravāda Commentaries: Buddhaghosa and Dhammapāla as Authors, Compilers, Redactors, Editors and Critics," *Journal of the International Association of Buddhist Studies* 36/37 (2015): 353–387. See also von Hinüber, *A Handbook of Pāli Literature*(Berlin and New York: Walter de Gruyter, 1996), 100–153.
63. *Sumaṅgalavilāsinī* 1, *Papañcasūdanī* 1, *Sāratthappakāsinī* 2, *Manorathapūraṇī* 2: *hitvā punappunāgataṃ atthaṃ . . . Atthasālinī* 2: *āgamaṭṭhakathāsu pi gahetabbaṃ gahetvāna . . .*

Norihisa Baba

BUDDHISM AND BIOETHICS

BUDDHISM, BIOETHICS, AND BIOMEDICINE

Since the 1980s, numerous publications have been referred to as Buddhist bioethics, that is, as a specifically Buddhist ethical evaluation of decision-making in biomedical therapies and research procedures. Several factors came together to bring bioethics to the attention of Asian Buddhist intellectuals. From the 1980s onward, Japanese and South Korean Buddhists, obviously responding to ethical debates in the biomedically advanced countries, sought to establish bioethical answers from a Buddhist point of view. Some had studied biomedicine or bioethics in the West. Once they saw biomedical therapies surge in their countries, they began to outline how Western bioethics should be modified to solve ethical problems on the basis of Buddhist views such as karma, rebirth, nonviolence, no-self, or compassion (e.g., Pinit Ratanakul in Thailand). From the 1990s onward, Western scholars of Buddhism began to contribute to the field and, among other activities, funded a journal that ushered in studies on issues of Buddhist bioethics (*Journal of Buddhist Ethics*, established 1994). However, despite these developments, the discipline of Buddhist bioethics, understood as a systematic reflection on all ethical, epistemic, anthropological, and social aspects of globalized modern biomedicine, is still in a nascent stage—in contrast to Jewish, Christian, or Muslim bioethics. In order to locate this still-emerging field of Buddhist bioethics as a contemporary form of applied normative ethics, some remarks may be useful on the three topics correlated here: bioethics, biomedicine, and Buddhism.

Most basically, "bioethics" can be defined as the systematic reflection of ethical problems posed by modern biomedicine. Accordingly, bioethics emerged as a response to far-reaching biomedical developments such as artificial reproduction, genetic diagnosis and eugenic treatment, gender transition therapy, human cloning, organ transplantation from brain-dead donors, physician-assisted suicide, and further relevant issues.

Certainly, not all problems discussed in bioethics pertain to modern biomedicine. This is especially true if the latter is understood as clinical practices based on the latest empirical science, most prominently physiological, biological, genetical, pharmacological, and psychological research. Some bioethical questions, such as the legitimacy of euthanasia and physician-assisted suicide, are also dealt with in nonspecialized ethics. In addition, such questions are one of the major concerns of medical ethics (from late antiquity onward), that branch of specialized ethics designed to meet the needs of medical professionals.

Although Buddhist traditions possess a rich corpus of texts that includes a reflection on morals and morality, there is no branch in Buddhist thought that can be seen as a direct equivalent of what in Western philosophy has been developed as ethics. One of the reasons for the absence of ethics as a philosophical and academic discipline is the strong soteriological focus of classical Buddhist thought. Morality, seen as training rules, is part of the personal cultivation practice aimed at liberation. Ethical casuistry, or a systematic discussion of ethical dilemmas, it seems, emerged only in monastic circles discussing the codified moral code (*Vinaya*) for monks and nuns but was very rarely part of philosophical discourse (with the notable exception of some Mahāyāna Buddhist treatises on the ethics of the bodhisattva).[1] The absence of ethics as a systematic enterprise in Buddhism can, moreover, be related to the corresponding absence of pan-Buddhist institutions. After the Buddha entered final liberation, the Buddhist tradition, as is well known, experienced several schisms and developed into two major schools—the Mahāyāna traditions of India, Central Asia, China, Vietnam, Korea, and Japan on the one side, and the Southern Theravāda traditions of South and Southeast Asia on the other. Neither of the different "Buddhisms" as such nor the major traditions including the individual schools are headed by institutions or authorities that were empowered with the function or discursive role to decide on questions of ethics or morality. In contrast to certain religious traditions, in which bioethical decisions are regulated by transnational, faith-based committees of medical doctors, lawyers, and religious specialists, Buddhist traditions have been less ardent to formulate binding dogmatic opinions on bioethics.[2] This irreducible plurality of Buddhist traditions becomes visible in the diversity of ethical evaluation of the latest biomedical technologies and practices among contemporary Buddhist schools.[3] Moreover, it is mirrored in the heated discussion among Western Buddhist scholars on how to conceptualize Buddhist ethics in Western terms. Is Buddhist ethics predominantly a variant of virtue ethics or of utilitarian consequentialism? Or is it impossible to capture the core Buddhist ethical arguments, embedded in karma, salvific efficacy, and other peculiar doctrines, in Western terms? Various scholars emphasized more recently that efforts to construe Buddhist ethics as a single, homogenous theory do harm to the diversity of ethical debates in Buddhism.[4]

However, as a field in which nontrivial, often existential decisions have to be made, ethical orientation is not arbitrary in bioethics but a pivotal, necessary consequence of biomedical innovations. Bioethics is not merely an exchange among experts in ethics but is open to lay input and ethical reflection by family members and health-care professionals at the bedside.

Especially in anthologies on pressing issues such as assisted suicide, brain death and organ donation, or prenatal diagnosis and abortion, Buddhists seem to unify their position. In such contexts, "Buddhist positions," often based on cursory readings of relevant texts on Buddhist ethics and morality, are articulated in a straightforward fashion in order to present them side by side with the answers of other major religious traditions.

Instead of outlining isolated Buddhist answers to bioethical dilemmas, the main part of this article will present the history of Buddhist bioethics in portraits of its major contributors and their works. Thus, this article is not aiming for concrete orthodox action-guides but will instead portray the basic principles that have been suggested so far. The major points of controversy, included in this article, may highlight Buddhist positions in their own right.

FROM BUDDHIST ETHICS TO BUDDHIST BIOETHICS

To a large degree Buddhist bioethics may be described as a certain moral knowledge that the doer of deeds—whether this be a medical professional, family member, or simply an individual—should incorporate and express in their thought, speech, and action. Since reasoning in Buddhist bioethics usually claims to be in line with Buddhist ethics in general, it might be useful to start with a short outline of what this entails.[5] While there is some variety in Buddhist teachings on morality, especially between Theravāda and later Mahāyāna thought, many key aspects are rooted in early Indian Buddhism, particularly in Sūtra literature, Abhidharma scholasticism, and *Vinaya* texts (i.e., the rules for monks and nuns). Firstly, Buddhists subscribe to the ethics of nonviolence (Sanskrit *ahiṃsā*), which includes abstention from intentional killing of all sentient beings. Every act of motivated killing, it is argued, has its foundation in unwholesome intentions, most prominently in greed or attachment, hatred, and delusion (or ignorance, respectively). This holds true even for suicide, which Buddhist ethicists only rarely declare to be permissible.[6] To abstain from the killing of animated beings is, in sum, one of the central moral rules (*śīla*) for monastics as well as for lay Buddhists. Secondly, as a training rule (*śikṣāpada*), nonviolence is based equally on the idea that each sentient being experiences violence as painful and harmful (*Dhammapada*). It is a kind of self-technique aimed at the goal of salvific transformation. Thirdly, Buddhist ethics is less interested in defining the rights of possible victims of violence. It usually takes a much stronger interest in exploring and defining the motives and intentions of the doer of ethically relevant deeds. Buddhist ethics is largely perpetrator-centered and not victim-centered. Ethics is tied to the actor reviewing the moral quality of intentions, motives, and actions, because each is of karmic relevance and therefore decisive for the actor's own salvation. The Sri Lankan professor of Buddhist philosophy P. D. Premasiri emphasized that if "the entire spiritual training is understood as an attempt to transform the moral nature of man," it follows that morality (*śīla*) "can be considered as the beginning of this conscious and deliberate process of self-transformation."[7] This understanding of ethics can be found in a nutshell in verse 183 of the *Dhammapada*: "The omission of all karmically bad [or, all evil], the cultivation of the wholesome, the purification of one's own mind: this is the teaching of the Buddhas."[8] In this spirit, the most prominent systematic outline of Theravāda Buddhism, Buddhagosa's *Visuddhimagga* (*Path of Purification*), explains the training in moral cultivation (Pāli *adhisīla-sikkhā*) to be the first stage of the salvific path.[9] In the same vein, central texts of Mahāyāna Buddhism declare moral cultivation as an indispensable training practice of the bodhisattva, for example the *Lam rim chen mo* (*The Great Treatise on the Stages of the Path to Awakening*) by the famous Tibetan scholar Tsong kha pa.[10] Especially in Mahāyāna Buddhism, the bodhisattva is concerned to generate *karuṇā* (compassion), *maitrī* (empathetic love), and *dāna* (generosity; sometimes even as self-sacrifice) in order to help other sentient beings to overcome suffering. The obvious bioethical significance of the latter will be discussed in the section "Pioneering Scholars of Bioethics and Buddhism: Shōyō Taniguchi and Pinit Ratanakul."

The transition from Buddhist ethics to Western bioethics is, of course, also a question of translation and philosophical terminology. Indian Buddhist texts capture the karmically positive quality of thoughts and actions with different terms. The term *śīla* (moral virtue, morality) has as its literal meaning "custom" or (habitual) "good behavior."[11] Another term, *kuśala*, denotes the positive karmic value and has been translated as "merit," "virtue," "skillful," and "wholesome"; *akuśala* (unwholesome) is used for the opposite, the negative karmic quality.[12] Finally there is the term *puṇya*, which Peter Harvey translates as "a karmically fruitful act" or simply "karmically fruitful," whereas *pāpa* denotes bad actions and intentions—those, again, will have karmically detrimental consequences.[13] These translation differences are far from trivial, because they have their roots in different systems of Western ethics to which the authors adhere.[14] Accordingly, there is an ongoing debate on whether in Western terms Buddhist ethics subscribes to a consequentialist, utilitarian, or virtue ethics approach. While a fourth major approach is deontology, or ethics of duties, obligations, and commandments, in the early 21st century this is less often used to describe Buddhist views and arguments; however, it will become obvious in the following paragraphs that it played a role in some of the attempts to construe modern Buddhist bioethics.[15]

PIONEERING SCHOLARS OF BIOETHICS AND BUDDHISM: SHŌYŌ TANIGUCHI AND PINIT RATANAKUL

Pioneering work on Buddhist bioethics has been done by Shōyō Taniguchi and Pinit Ratanakul. Taniguchi, an American Japanese Buddhist minister living in the United States and affiliated with the *Jōdo-shinshū* (Pure Land school), holds a PhD in Buddhist studies (Graduate Theological Union) and belongs to the first generation of scholars to formulate bioethical guidelines drawn from Pāli Buddhist sources.[16] Subscribing to a modernist claim that Buddhism is "fully capable of presenting a solid and universal approach to contemporary biomedical ethics," her reconstruction focuses on a rather general account of Buddhist doctrines (karma, compassion), which are then applied to bioethical problems such as contraception, abortion, in vitro fertilization, assisted reproductive technology, and suicide, respectively.[17] In contrast to significant contributions on Buddhist bioethics by Western scholars, she emphasized the ethical importance of the illusionary autonomy of the self, the erroneous human self-centeredness, and the ethical impact of an interpretation of the *pratītyasamutpāda* (dependent origination) as the basis on which skillful and unskillful actions play out their invariable effects.[18] Taniguchi used the Buddha's doctrine of dependent origination as a theory of the causation of human suffering, which could be applied to bioethics. "An action in the ethical realm," she argues, "can be discussed and evaluated only when it is put in the context of the interrelatedness of one's own and others' physical and psychological experience."[19] As such, and as the Buddha advised, it is necessary to ask if an action is harmful or skillful to oneself and to others, that is, if it results in *dukkha* (Pāli, unhappiness, stress, anxiety), or in *sukha* for all parties concerned.[20] Taniguchi offered some advice on how Buddhists could resolve bioethical dilemmas, such as how parents should decide when confronted with the diagnosis of their child's Down syndrome, or how to evaluate the explantation and distribution of organs from brain-dead donors. In these situations, she argues on the ground of the classical Buddhist analysis of motives and intentions: if the decision is led by self-centered ruminations, it should be avoided, but if the action is informed by a mindful reasoning, compassion, care, and other skillful intentions, it should be pursued. However, in line with the Buddhist ideal that the reduction of self-centeredness is a broader program, she did not offer a system of bioethical principles of Buddhism. Instead, concrete bioethical problems are analyzed as case studies with the guiding idea of whether or not suffering will arise; a system of Buddhist bioethics, therefore, is only implicitly given. On abortion, for example, she underscores that by taking its life the fetus will suffer, as will the agents who initiate the action. Embryo transplantation, in vitro fertilization, or artificial insemination will all be ethically neutral if these procedures will not cause new suffering.[21] In regard to the discussion on informed consent, and the obligation of medical experts to reveal all information needed for the patient to make an informed decision about possible therapies, Taniguchi argues that from a Buddhist perspective sometimes information itself can be harmful, so that it may not be completely disclosed. In sum, Taniguchi takes the more traditional Buddhist stance here that the overcoming of self-centeredness is usually a longer process of gradual improvement, and individuals' progress toward the goal may differ considerably. While her work offers important insights into how Buddhists, taking a foothold in early Buddhist teachings, may reflect on biomedical ethics, her contributions do not aim to present a contemporary system of Buddhist bioethics.

At about the same time, in the late 1980s, a somewhat more systematic approach to Buddhist bioethics was outlined by Pinit Ratanakul (Mahidol University).[22] Ratanakul, a Thai lay Buddhist, holds a PhD in philosophy (Yale) and was introduced to bioethics by the American philosopher Violette Lindbeck.[23] Participating in national and international debates on bioethics for more than forty years, he became almost an ambassador of Southeast Asian Buddhist bioethics; for example, he served as a representative of the Buddhist traditions in UNESCO hearings prior to the adoption of the *Universal Declaration on Bioethics and Human Rights* (2005).[24] Ratanakul's works include *Bio Ethics: An Introduction to the Ethics of Medicine and Life Sciences*, which not only aims at introducing bioethics into medical education, but also intends to present major Western bioethical approaches and to search bioethical action-guides based in both Western and Thai Buddhist morality.[25]

Reviewing Ratanakul's contributions from 1984 until 2010, one can observe that the Buddhist foundations became increasingly important. In his 1986 monograph Buddhist perspectives were already present, but it was the introduction and an appendix that shed some more light on Buddhist ethics.[26] Similar to Taniguchi's approach, Ratanakul's Buddhist foundation becomes obvious in his explanation on how suffering is generated, namely, by self-centeredness, egoistic craving, greed, lust, hatred, lying, and so forth.[27] In his later development, he went on to propose concrete Buddhist action-guides and discussed examples of moral behavior by Thai Buddhists in medical contexts.

Before moving to Ratanakul's outline of Buddhist bioethics, it is necessary to sketch its Western basis, the standard approach to biomedical ethics, developed by Beauchamp and Childress in their *Principles of Biomedical Ethics*. In this influential work, which was an international success, the authors proposed four guiding principles to be used for resolving ethical problems in the field of biomedicine: (1) respect for autonomy (the right to self-determination); (2) nonmaleficence (one should not harm or exploit patients); (3) beneficence (one should act in accordance with the benefit of patients); and (4) justice (fair allocation, nondiscrimination, and so forth).[28] These guiding principles are declared to be prima facie duties, that is, they are not absolute (in the sense of a strong Kantian deontology) but should be followed unless they conflict with some stronger obligation. Initially Ratanakul accepted these principles, which the authors claimed to be grounded in a "universal common morality."[29] He described his own ethical system as a "mixed-deontological approach."[30] Ratanakul emphasized with William David Ross that bioethical action-guides should not only reflect on future-oriented consequences of any action but should also include the lasting production of "human good." They should include the responsibilities of the past—promises to be kept, the duty of gratitude, the care for grown relationships, etc. In his earliest approach of 1986, therefore, Ratanakul claimed five prima facie duties relevant to bioethics: the duty of fidelity to medicine and to the relationships between health-care professionals and patients, respect for persons and their autonomy, beneficence, nonmaleficence, and justice.[31] Later, Ratanakul modified his account and transformed these duties in order to show how they can be distilled from fundamental Buddhist ethical principles. This move, indeed, is significant for the general process of how a specifically Buddhist bioethics evolved, especially in the Southeast Asian countries, and not only on the level of theory. It does also show how traditional Buddhist values practiced by lay Buddhists are increasingly invoked in medical decision-making.

Ratanakul argued now that there are four duties of Buddhist bioethics:

1. veracity
2. noninjury to life (*ahiṃsā*)
3. justice
4. compassion (*karuṇā*) and lovingkindness[32]

The concept of veracity has been introduced by Ratanakul as a principle in accordance with the early Buddhist ethics of "right speech," which is one of the five training rules for Buddhist laity.[33] This principle, demanding that doctors shall speak truthfully and shall disclose the diagnosis and prognosis, would have the effect that patients develop "strength, will-power, and endurance," even in difficult, life-threatening circumstances.[34] However, as can be seen in Taniguchi's approach, in Mahāyāna Buddhism there is a much stronger acceptance of "noble lies" if they are of help to the patient. This is largely based in the role model of the bodhisattva, who is allowed to use *upāyakauśalya* (skillful means). For example, lying can be justified if it is of help to the patient to overcome existential fear or to achieve mental tranquility. Against such a principle of veracity endorsed by Ratanakul, Robert E. Florida has argued from a Mahāyāna Buddhist perspective with examples of *upāyakauśalya* in the *Lotus Sūtra*.[35] Taniguchi, however, could also show how Pāli Buddhist texts on right speech in the Theravāda Buddhist tradition endorse the idea of nonharmful speech, which she interprets as support for strategies of nondisclosure.[36]

Ratanakul's second principle, *ahiṃsā* (*noninjury*), is certainly a straightforward application of a core Buddhist ethical principle. Ratanakul argues, for example, that according to this principle suicide is not permitted. Similarly, he positions himself against any kind of mercy killing and physician-assisted suicide, stating:

> When a doctor performs what he believes is mercy-killing, actually it is because the pain and suffering of the patient are repugnant to him. It disturbs his mind. . . . Subconsciously he transfers his aversion to the suffering to the one who embodies it.[37]

Significantly, the third principle, justice, has not been replaced by Ratanakul. In countries of the developing world, he argues, impartial treatment and equal distribution are key. While he mentions Buddhist teachings on justice, few details are given. This, and his claim that this principle is exceeded by the ideal of compassion, is less astonishing.[38] Once again, traditionally Buddhist ethics argues from an actor-centered perspective and does not articulate rights of persons nor, in a strong sense, a concept of dignity. Nevertheless, justice and the human rights discourse in general have become increasingly important in modernized Buddhism. Socially engaged Buddhism incorporated ethical ideas of Western humanism and legalism, which is visible in Ratanakul's presentation of Buddhist bioethics, too. At the UNESCO hearing mentioned, in line with engaged Buddhism he declared that the principles of human dignity, human rights, and justice are congruent with Buddhist teachings. However, Ratanakul also pointed out that prioritizing the supremacy of justice, rights, and individual autonomy will lead to "rampant individualism." This will do harm to the Buddhist concept of an all-encompassing "interdependence."[39]

The concept of *karuṇā* (compassion) substitutes the concept of beneficence, as suggested by Beauchamp and Childress. The principle of beneficence, often combined with a Christian understanding of "charity" and "mercy," may be replaced by the principle of compassion, Ratanakul argued, because from the Buddhist perspective "compassion involves both doing all we can to benefit others, to enhance the value of their lives, and to do no harm to them."[40] Compassion may even imply voluntary sacrifice, overriding the ethics of justice and individual rights. Ratanakul combines compassion with another core Buddhist concept, the ideal of *mettā* (lovingkindness), directed not only to humans but to all sentient beings.[41] Increasingly, compassion became the core value, declared to imply beneficence, nonmaleficence, justice, and even "modern concepts of human dignity and human rights."[42] In a contribution on Buddhist monks caring for HIV/AIDS patients, he illustrates the idea as follows:

> Due to their compassion the monks never ostracize HIV/AIDS inflicted people (respect for persons) and treat them equally (justice) with love and care (beneficence) helping them to have meaningful lives to the final days (non-maleficence) and to let go of lives peacefully.[43]

This view of the centrality of compassion, which is a shared conviction of other Asian Buddhist ethicists, especially in the context of palliative care, reflects the ideal of Buddhism's capacity of healing—and also the healing presence of Buddhist teachers. In contrast to the guiding Western view that patients have to be defended against mistreatment by medical professionals, the Thai Buddhist Mano Laohavanich (formerly Bhikkhu Mettānando) argued that Buddhist doctors, mindful of karmic consequences in the case of misbehavior, almost naturally consider themselves as *kalyāṇamitta* (spiritual friends), working compassionately for the best interest of their patients, which will also help to simplify Buddhist bioethics.[44] In other words, in such an idealist view, patient's rights and legal enforcement are second rank to first-person cultivation efforts of health-care providers.

It can be observed that Ratanakul became increasingly interested in outlining a system of Buddhist bioethics that could serve as practical orientation in biomedical dilemmas. As a system, it included elements from Western biomedical ethics and, moreover, what has been termed "Asian values." In his later works, Ratanakul argues that Western "I-self culture" expresses itself in the principle of autonomy, whereas Asian cultures display a "we-self culture." In his search for a Buddhist system of bioethics, Ratanakul seemingly became aware that some of his ethical guidelines were firmly rooted in Thai Theravāda culture, so that to declare his system to be a pan-Buddhist bioethics might prove difficult. The growing importance of East Asian Buddhist perspectives in Ratanakul's work can be seen in his shift from a Theravāda Buddhist interpretation of the *paṭiccasamuppāda* (Sanskrit *pratītyasamutpāda*, dependent origination) as natural law of (karmic) causality toward a Mahāyāna Buddhist interpretation as universal interdependence.[45] This is in line with, for example, ethical views of the Dalai Lama or the Buddhist "Declaration of Interdependence," published in 1995 by Buddhist ethicists. It declared that Buddhism recognizes the "interdependency of all forms of life and the reciprocal obligations which arise from it, such as the duty to repay the kindness of those who in previous lives may have been our parents, relatives and friends."[46] Indeed, other Buddhists have also argued that the perspective of interdependence should be considered as the core contribution of Buddhism in the field of bioethics.[47] But how can this perspective be translated into concrete bioethical action-guides? For Ratanakul, the favored interdependent Asian "we culture" can, for example, be expressed in family consent and similar maxims that limit the individualism of patient autonomy. The Buddhist principle of interdependence, Ratanakul and Scott Stonington argued, "means that doctors, patients and relatives must think about the emotions and interests of all parties involved in a medical decision."[48] One can see in such views how, inspired by the Asian values debate, the view of interdependence becomes a Buddhist counterapproach to the Western concept of individualized autonomy, supported, of course, by the action-guides of nonviolence, compassion, and so forth.

A concrete case of conflict between the ideals of Western and Buddhist bioethical decision-making at the time involved the circumstances of the death of Venerable Buddhadāsa, a prominent monk and prolific Thai Buddhist reformer living in a forest monastery. In 1993, in a state of deteriorating health, he had declared in a living will his wish to die peacefully. Hit by a stroke, he slipped into a coma. His disciples, however, were unsuccessful in preventing doctors at a large hospital in Bangkok from using several artificial means to prolong the life of the eighty-six-year-old monk. Only after intense discussion was life support withdrawn. This case is used by Ratanakul, but also many others such as the Buddhist bioethicist and philosopher Somparn Promta, to illustrate that in Buddhism circumstances may call for nonvoluntary, passive euthanasia in order to die a natural death.[49] Moreover, it was painful for Buddhadāsa's disciples, who according to standard Western bioethics formed a group of nonrelatives with no legitimate voice, to be overridden in their wish that their teacher be disconnected from the respirator.

To summarize this overview on Ratanakul's contributions on Buddhism and bioethics, it should be mentioned that he was not only interested in introducing Theravāda and global Buddhist views on ethics, karma, life, and death but likewise sought to bring regional Thai perspectives into the discourse of ethical problems in biomedical contexts. Ratanakul, however, did not publish more in-depth studies on Buddhist moral views as they are discussed in canonic sources or scholarly commentaries. This could be seen as disadvantage—a shortcoming, however, that the next generation of scholars of Buddhist bioethics such as Damien Keown tried to remedy.

THE CONSOLIDATION OF BUDDHIST BIOETHICS

While in the 1980s bioethics was often construed and practiced as secular applied medical ethics, the 1990s saw a broadening of perspectives. Universalist bioethics approaches became increasingly aware of—and interested in—cultural particularities and religious perspectives. On the one hand, the international debate was transformed, for example, by the fact that many Japanese, including Japanese Buddhists, were reluctant to accept the Harvard committee's criteria of brain death and irreversible coma (1968), resulting in a small number of transplant surgeries in Japan. On the other hand, the widespread introduction of biomedical practices in various Asian countries with considerable Buddhist communities also had the effect that Buddhists were forced to discuss issues such as prenatal sex selection, the rules of distribution of scarce resources, and so forth. In the 1990s, the Human Genome Project was launched and completed. In addition, the first human gene therapies took place. Human embryos were cloned, though not implanted (1993). Dolly the sheep was cloned and born (1996). At that time, in Asian countries biomedical hospitals and research corporations could pursue biomedical research and treatments in an often poorly regulated environment. Some Buddhists were convinced that Buddhism, with its scientific-empirical stance, was far more open to possible biomedical advances (especially on the burning issue of human cloning) than Judeo-Christians could ever be, with their constraints imposed by beliefs in God and the normative dignity of human creation. In 2006, as an aftermath to this debate, spectacular results published by the Korean researcher Wo-suk Hwang—human-cloned blastocysts from a stem cell line—were discredited as fraud. Hwang, who had sought to justify the ethical legitimacy of his research with Buddhist beliefs, had initially enjoyed enthusiastic support by Korean Buddhists, including lay Buddhist organizations and head monks of national orders.[50] In sum, in the 1990s a more heated discussion had started on bioethical problems in their cultural and religious settings; around the millennium this revolved especially around the use of human embryos for research, stem cell therapies, and reproductive cloning.

In the international debate, professor of Buddhist ethics Damien Keown's work *Buddhism and Bioethics* was the first to combine a more detailed attempt to formulate a systematic Buddhist bioethics with Buddhist ethical evaluations of beginning-of-life and end-of-life issues. Like Ratanakul, Keown's work is firmly based on Theravāda Buddhist sources. However, in direct comparison, Keown started initially from the assumption that when well understood, Buddhist ethics—for him essentially a form of virtue ethics—comes to similar conclusions as Western bioethics. Keown suggested that Buddhist bioethics can be deduced from principles that are themselves not articulated in the Buddhist texts but engrained in the normative set of precepts. The three basic goods or fundamental values he arrives at are life, knowledge, and friendship.[51] These goods are indispensable factors in human flourishing. Keown admits that this reconstruction of a positively articulated, ontological value basis of Buddhist ethics is, of course, an innovation. Elsewhere, he argues that Buddhist source texts must be brought "up to date" to become meaningful for contemporary bioethical problems.[52] In contrast to earlier attempts of Buddhist bioethics, Keown aims at uncovering the hidden assumptions of Buddhist ethics and reformulating them in a way that allows one to speak of irreducible values. In other words, he attempted to establish a Buddhist parallel to the Western concept of personhood, rights, and human dignity. To give an example for such a reconstruction: Keown argues that the precept and training rule of noninjury points to the prior, implicit acknowledgment of a fundamental value, life. Life, therefore, has intrinsic value, is intrinsically desirable, and can be looked at, together with the other two values, as good in themselves. Life, as a consequence, assumes a position that is usually filled in Western bioethics by human dignity.[53] In Keown's words, "evidence from Buddhist sources suggests that living beings are worthy of respect simply by virtue of the inherent dignity which is inalienably theirs as living beings."[54] This reconstruction, however, allows one to transform premodern Buddhist ethics with its focus on first-person training and on the intentions of the mind of the actor into a third-person, victim-centered ethics that may provide direct advice for bioethical decision-making. Keown solves the problem that premodern Buddhist texts (e.g., the *Visuddhimagga*, but also texts of Mahāyāna Abhidharma scholastics) distinguish between the moral values of accomplished individuals and of everyday humans by explaining that the source of human dignity in Buddhism is still invariably there. It is "the literally infinite capacity of human nature for participation in goodness"—in other words, the potential to reach buddhahood.[55] Based on this reasoning, Keown argues that human goodness is an equivalent to human dignity in Buddhist thought, and it is the function of human rights to prepare a suitable environment for individuals to gradually realize this potentiality. This innovative and modernist conception of the moral worth of humans almost necessarily calls for modernist readings of other Buddhist doctrines such as karma and rebirth.[56] Equally, the central Buddhist doctrine of *anātman* (selflessness) and the imperative not to identify with the ever-changing categories of the empirical person, the "five categories" (Sanskrit *skandhas*), were somewhat reframed. Not unlike Taniguchi, in his early work Keown saw the teachings of *pratītyasamutpāda* (dependent origination) as relevant to questions of the origination of an individual human being. It explains, for example, the interdependence of body and consciousness described in Buddhist texts on conception. In his later work the idea of interdependence becomes more important, although Keown remains skeptical of attempts to ground moral imperatives directly on (the metaphysics) of interdependence.[57]

Since the 2010s, the global discourse on bioethics has to some extent cooled down again, which also had an appeasing effect on Buddhist bioethics. At the same time, other problems were dealt with, especially ethics of environmental sustainability, anthropogenic climate change, or gender diversity. However, the early 21st century saw no major innovation that immediately stirred a comparable need for ethical orientation. This will probably change as new biomedical innovations gain momentum. Consider, for instance, the new breakthrough technology for genome editing, CRISPR/Cas, which allows humans for the first time to design babies.[58]

REVIEW OF LITERATURE

Damien Keown's works were widely read among Asian Buddhists and Western scholars of bioethics. Together with further approaches to review Buddhist bioethical decision-making in the new millennium (especially noteworthy is Peter Harvey's *Introduction to Buddhist Ethics*), it brought Buddhist bioethics to a certain level of consolidation.[59] However, in the contributions by Ratanakul, Harvey, and Keown, a certain favor for Theravāda perspectives is palpable.

More recent contributions tend to more prominently include perspectives of Tibetan, Chinese, and Japanese Mahāyāna Buddhist ethics. For example, *Into the Jaws of Yama, Lord of Death: Buddhism, Bioethics, and Death* by Karma Lekshe Tsomo, an American Buddhist nun in the Tibetan tradition, adds some distinct Mahāyāna Buddhist perspectives to the discussion of Buddhist bioethics, especially on end-of-life issues. However, it is not her aim to construe a systematic Buddhist bioethics nor to compare or contrast in-depth Western bioethical reasoning. Expanding on Tibetan Buddhist teachings on dying, she raises an issue that is absent in both Western and Theravāda Buddhist bioethics, namely that it takes consciousness a considerable amount of time to retract from the dying body. In addition, in light of the Tibetan teachings of steering the subtle, disembodied consciousness through the *bardo* (intermediate state) in order to prevent a disastrous rebirth, it is not surprising that Tsomo is reluctant to accept Western brain-death criteria as definite.[60] Yet, there is so far no scientific evidence for subtle consciousness, which makes her argument from the Western medical point of view less accessible. These convictions on consciousness surviving brain death and the unique Buddhist practices to cope with death lead her to challenge assumptions that support Western bioethical action-guides—especially those that follow from the belief in an independently existent self.[61] Firmly grounded in Mahāyāna Buddhist views on the bodhisattva, and sympathetic with the latter's more active wish to alleviate the suffering of others, she declares that to donate one's organs is fully congruent with this wish to benefit others. However, it should not be done until after the vital signs have ceased.[62] But to wait for the full absence of those signs of life is barely possible. In most cases, explantations have to be done from brain-dead patients that still show (according to Tibetan Buddhist criteria) vital signs (body heat, heartbeat, etc.), or the presence of subtle consciousness.

Significantly, Keown, who had accepted brain death in earlier publications, became increasingly skeptical of the legitimacy of the removal of liver, heart, or kidneys from brain-dead donors.[63] Other Buddhist ethicists, however, argue that even if a brain-dead person is still alive up to the point when organs are removed and life support is terminated, it can be a beneficial and compassionate act of *dāna* (donation). It is a form of sacrifice, particularly considering the urgent need of the recipient.

This question leads into the heart of what is probably the most important contemporary controversy in Buddhist bioethics. Should killing out of compassion be feasible or not? And finally, how to decide in cases where the donor's intentions are not known, or in principle not obtainable? Almost all Buddhist contributions on the question of euthanasia include respective reflections. Equally, the same basic conflict emerges with embryonic stem cell research—given that Buddhist scholars regard extracorporeal human embryos as actual living beings, which they conclude from certain Buddhist canonic passages on in vivo conception. Buddhist bioethicists such as Somparn Promta suggest that Buddhist ethics may subscribe to a utilitarian form of social ethics: a sacrifice of embryos may be in certain situations considered as legitimate as long as it helps to create therapies for incurable illnesses. Such an "enforced donation," or "mercy killings" in cases of selective abortion or active euthanasia of terminally ill patients, have met with heavy criticism by Ratanakul and scholars working on classical Buddhist Theravāda sources.[64] They argue, in contrast, that early Buddhist ethics follows its most central criterion, the analysis of *cetanā* (the mental intention). If an actor kills, supposedly out of mercy, the intention to kill is basically there (and probably motivated from an additional, unwholesome intention). Rupert Gethin, for that matter, has shown that Abhidharma texts utterly rule out that one kills out of compassion, because "it is considered psychologically impossible to intend to kill someone when motivated by compassion."[65] However, there are still other voices suggesting that there are passages in Buddhaghosa's commentary that support euthanasia (denial of food and medicine in the terminal stage).[66] Among Japanese Buddhist ethicists, and in other countries with Mahāyāna Buddhist schools, there is a continuous debate whether or not intentional killing (of an embryo for higher, compassionate purposes, or euthanasia) may be paralleled to the compassionate bodhisattva who, in some Mahāyāna sources, kills but has to bear the karmic consequences.[67] Exemplary for ethical discourse in the Anglo-Saxon world, Charles Goodman offered a unified consequentialist interpretation of Buddhist ethics with the programmatic title *Consequences of Compassion*.[68]

While there are various strong ties between Buddhism and bioethics, including some book-length treatises on Buddhist bioethics, few scholars are specifically interested in advancing Buddhist bioethics as a discipline. This lacuna is particularly evident if compared to the significant interest in other phenomena, such as the neuroscience of Buddhist meditation or the therapeutic application of mindfulness. Significantly, by the early 21st century many of the book-length treatises on Buddhist bioethics were written by scholars trained in Western bioethics, many of them being Westerners. Understandably, yet unfortunately, contributions on Buddhist bioethics in emic languages rarely enter the international stage, and works in Japanese, Korean, Chinese, Thai, or Sinhala are usually discussed in their respective national environment only.

One can furthermore witness that more recent volumes on Buddhist ethics tend to discuss Buddhist bioethics under the headings of "contemporary issues" or "challenges of modernity." In this arrangement, it seems that modernity (including modern biomedicine and health care) is conceptualized as a secularizing power in modern nation-states, operating as an ally of "biopolitics" (to use a concept of Michel Foucault), and steered primarily by Western bioethics and international regulations. This conglomerate, biomedicine and bioethics, puts pressure on premodern religious and philosophical worldviews. Hence, it is often asked how the concepts of rights, dignity, autonomy, and so on, should be translated into Buddhism.[69] Soraj Hongladarom remarks that for Buddhist bioethics in their particular cultural environment, this will almost necessarily lead to an adoption of the prevailing norms of the international community.[70] Such a top-down approach, often pursued by Western scholars of Buddhism, will likely homogenize specifics of premodern ethical traditions. In the case of Buddhist bioethics, this approach is likely to relativize the ideal of ethics as a moral cultivation practice, preferably excluding the foundational narratives of salvific liberation or downplaying views of a subtle consciousness that is not bound to the body. A systematic approach to Buddhist bioethics by an Asian scholar, exploring in-depth ethical and anthropological ideas from an indigenous Buddhist point of view while addressing the Buddhist world as a whole, is still an enterprise of the future.

DIGITAL MATERIALS

Journal of Buddhist Ethics (http://blogs.dickinson.edu/buddhistethics).

FURTHER READING

Cozort, Daniel, and James Mark Shields, eds. *The Oxford Handbook of Buddhist Ethics*. Oxford: Oxford University Press, 2018.

Davis, Jake H., ed. *A Mirror Is for Reflection: Understanding Buddhist Ethics*. Oxford: Oxford University Press, 2017.

Gethin, Rupert M. L. "Can Killing a Living Being Ever Be an Act of Compassion? The Analysis of the Act of Killing in the Abhidhamma and Pali Commentaries." *Journal of Buddhist Ethics* 11 (2004): 167–202.

Harvey, Peter. *An Introduction to Buddhist Ethics: Foundations, Values, and Issues*. Cambridge, UK: Cambridge University Press, 2000.

Keown, Damien. *Buddhism and Bioethics*, 2nd ed. Houndmills, UK: Palgrave Macmillan, 2001.

Keown, Damien. "Buddhist Ethics: A Critique." In *Buddhism in the Modern World*, edited by David L. McMahan, 215–232. Abingdon, UK: Routledge, 2012.

Keown, Damien, Charles S. Prebish, and Wayne Rollen Husted, eds. *Buddhism and Human Rights*. Richmond, UK: Curzon, 1998.

Ratanakul, Pinit. *Bio Ethics: An Introduction to the Ethics of Medicine and Life Sciences*. Bangkok: Mahidol University, 1986.

Ratanakul, Pinit. *Bioethics and Buddhism*, 2nd ed. Bangkok: Mahidol University, 2004.

Schlieter, Jens. "Some Observations on Buddhist Thoughts on Human Cloning." In *Cross-Cultural Issues in Bioethics: The Example of Human Cloning*, edited by Heiner Roetz, 179–202. Amsterdam: Rodopi, 2006.

Schlieter, Jens. "Endure, Adapt, or Overcome? The Concept of Suffering in Buddhist Bioethics." In *Suffering and Bioethics*, edited by Ronald M. Green, and Nathan J. Palpant, 309–336. New York: Oxford University Press, 2014.

Taniguchi, Shōyō. "Methodology of Buddhist Biomedical Ethics." In *Religious Methods and Resources in Bioethics*, edited by Paul F. Camenisch, 31–65. Dordrecht, The Netherlands: Kluwer, 1994.

Tsomo, Karma Lekshe. *Into the Jaws of Yama, Lord of Death: Buddhism, Bioethics, and Death*. Albany: State University of New York Press, 2006.

NOTES

1. See Damien Keown, "'It's Ethics, Jim, but Not as We Know It': Reflections on the Absence of Moral Philosophy in Buddhism," in *A Mirror Is for Reflection: Understanding Buddhist Ethics*, ed. Jake H. Davis (New York: Oxford University Press, 2017), 17–32.
2. See, as only one example, Marcie Anne Middlebrooks, "Competing 'Originary' Technologies: Human Cloning, Embryonic Stem Cells and Buddhism in South Korea and Beyond" (PhD diss., Cornell University, 2015), 16–18, on the South Korean Buddhist Bioethics Research Committee, who published a large report (2006) in response to the cloning controversy but made it clear that "their book should not be confused with a blanket orthodox stance" (17).
3. See Sīlavādin Meynard Vasen, "Buddhist Ethics Compared to Western Ethics," in *The Oxford Handbook of Buddhist Ethics*, ed. Daniel Cozort and James Mark Shields (Oxford: Oxford University Press, 2018), 317–334.
4. See Maria Heim, *Buddhist Ethics* (Cambridge, UK: Cambridge University Press, 2020), 2–4, with further references.
5. See the discussion in Bob Simpson, "Impossible Gifts: Bodies, Buddhism and Bioethics in Contemporary Sri Lanka," *Journal of the Royal Anthropological Institute* 10, no. 4 (2004): 839–859.
6. However, more recent studies point to a more permissive attitude in canonical sources; see Kanae Kawamoto, "Dialogues Regarding Monastic Suicides: The Acceptance and Observation of Death in the Pāli Sutta," *Bukkyogaku-Kenkyu* 73 (2017): 79–110.

7. Pahalawattage Don Premasiri, "Place of Ethics in Buddhism," in *Encyclopedia of Buddhism*, vol. 5, ed. Gunapala Piyasena Malalasekera et al. (Colombo, Sri Lanka: Government of Sri Lanka, 1990), 144–165.
8. Jens Schlieter's translation; Pāli text in Oskar von Hinüber, and Kenneth Roy Norman, eds., *Dhammapada* (Oxford: Pali Text Society, 1994), v. 183.
9. See Bhikkhu Nyanamoli, trans., *The Path of Purification: Visuddhimagga* (Kandy, Sri Lanka: Buddhist Publication Society, 2011); and on the positioning of moral conduct in the structure of the Visuddhimagga see Helmut Eimer, *Buddhistische Begriffsreihen als Skizzen des Erlösungsweges* (Vienna: Arbeitskreis für Tibetische und Buddhistische Studien, 2006), 145–158.
10. See Alex Wayman, *Ethics of Tibet: Bodhisattva Section of Tsong-kha-pa's Lam rim chen mo* (Albany: State University of New York Press, 1991).
11. See Peter Harvey, *An Introduction to Buddhist Ethics: Foundations, Values, and Issues* (Cambridge, UK: Cambridge University Press, 2000), 66–67.
12. See Barbra R. Clayton, *Moral Theory in Śāntideva's Śikṣāsamuccaya: Cultivating the Fruits of Virtue* (London: Routledge, 2006), 69–72.
13. Harvey, *Buddhist Ethics*, 18.
14. Clayton, *Moral Theory*, 67, argued that translation choices have been "major barriers to any kind of systematic treatment of morality in Indian Buddhism."
15. See, for example, Harvey, *Buddhist Ethics*, 50–51; and Charles Goodman, *Consequences of Compassion: An Interpretation and Defense of Buddhist Ethics* (New York: Oxford University Press, 2009), esp. chap. 11. However, cf. Pahalawattage Don Premasiri, "Moral Evaluation in Early Buddhism: From the Perspective of Western Philosophical Analysis" (PhD diss., University of Hawaii, 1980); and Damien Keown, *The Nature of Buddhist Ethics* (New York: St Martin's Press, 1992), 16, 126–127.
16. See Jens Schlieter, "The Ethical Significance of 'No-Self' (anātman) and Human 'Dignity': Comparative Remarks on Recent Buddhist and Western Bioethical Approaches," in *Life, Body, Person and Self: A Reconsideration of Core Concepts in Bioethics from an Intercultural Perspective*, ed. Stephan Grätzel and Eberhard Guhe (Freiburg, Germany: Alber, 2016), 186–230.
17. Shōyō Taniguchi, "Biomedical Ethics from a Buddhist Perspective," *Pacific World: Journal of the Institute of Buddhist Studies* 3 (1987): 75–83, 75; and Cf. Shōyō Taniguchi, "A Study of Biomedical Ethics from a Buddhist Perspective" (MA thesis, Graduate Theological Union, Institute of Buddhist Studies, 1987), 4–5.
18. Shōyō Taniguchi, "Methodology of Buddhist Biomedical Ethics," in *Religious Methods and Resources in Bioethics*, ed. Paul F. Camenisch (Dordrecht, The Netherlands: Kluwer, 1994), 31–65, 37–47; and Shōyō Taniguchi, "A Systematic Structure of Ethics Founded on Causal Conditionality ('Paticcasamuppāda'): Ethics from the Pali Nikaya Point of View" (PhD diss., Graduate Theological Union, Institute of Buddhist Studies, 1996), 228–230, 276. Pāli *taṇhā* is usually translated as "thirst, desire, or craving." The ethical significance of dependent origination is advocated by Joanna R. Macy, "Dependent Co-Arising: The Distinctiveness of Buddhist Ethics," *Journal of Religious Ethics* 7 (1979): 38–52; and Joanna R. Macy, *Mutual Causality in Buddhism and General Systems Theory* (Albany: State University of New York Press, 1991).
19. Taniguchi, "Methodology," 33.
20. Taniguchi, "Methodology," 51.
21. Taniguchi, "Methodology," 52.
22. Pinit Ratanakul, PhD in philosophy, was the founding director of the College of Religious Studies of Mahidol University, Nontaburi, Bangkok, Thailand.
23. Violette Lindbeck, "Thailand: Buddhism Meets the Western Model," *Hastings Center Report* 14 (1984): 24–26.
24. Ratanakul's suggestions, however, did not find their way into the wording of the UNESCO declaration (emphasizing human dignity, rights, freedoms, and autonomy); see Pinit Ratanakul, "Comments on the

Draft Declaration on Universal Norms on Bioethics," in *Eleventh Session Report*, ed. International Bioethics Committee of UNESCO (Paris: UNESCO, 2004), 3.

25. Pinit Ratanakul, *Bio Ethics: An Introduction to the Ethics of Medicine and Life Sciences* (Bangkok: Mahidol University, 1986); and Pinit Ratanakul, *Bioethics and Buddhism*. (Bangkok: Mahidol University, 2004).
26. Ratanakul, *Bio Ethics*, appendix 3, 305–322.
27. Ratanakul, *Bio Ethics*, 310.
28. See Tom L. Beauchamp and James F. Childress, *Principles of Biomedical Ethics*, 8th ed. (New York: Oxford University Press, 2019), part 2: Moral Principles, 101–300.
29. See Beauchamp and Childress, *Principles*, chap. 10.
30. Ratankul, *Bio Ethics*, 82.
31. Ratankul, *Bio Ethics*, 86.
32. Pinit Ratanakul, "Bioethics in Thailand: The Struggle for Buddhist Solutions," *Journal of Medicine and Philosophy* 13 (1988): 301–312, 301.
33. Ratanakul, "Bioethics in Thailand," 308–309.
34. Ratanakul, "Bioethics in Thailand," 308–309.
35. See Robert E. Florida, "The Lotus Sutra and Health Care Ethics," *Journal of Buddhist Ethics* 5 (1998): 170–189, 173; and Robert E. Florida, "Buddhism and the Four Principles," in *Principles of Health Care Ethics*, ed. Raanan Gillon (Chichester, UK: Wiley, 1994), 105–116.
36. Taniguchi, "Methodology," 53–57.
37. Ratanakul, "Bioethics in Thailand," 310.
38. Ratanakul, "Bioethics in Thailand," 311.
39. Ratanakul, "Comments," 147–150, 149.
40. Ratanakul, "Comments," 149.
41. Pinit Ratanakul, "Buddhism, Prenatal Diagnosis and Human Cloning," in *Bioethics in Asia*, ed. Norio Fujiki, Darryl Macer, Christchurch: Eubios Ethics Institute (2000), 405–407, 407 describes *mettā* as compassion; see also Ratanakul, *Bio Ethics*, chap. 4 and appendix 3.
42. Pinit Ratanakul, "Bioethics in Thailand: An Update," *Asian Bioethics Review* 1, no. 1 (March 2009): 47–53, 47.
43. Pinit Ratanakul, "Bioethics and AIDS in Thailand: A Buddhist Perspective," in *Bioethics in Asia in the 21st Century*, ed. Sang-Yong Song, Young-Mo Koo, and Darryl Macer (Bangkok: Eubios Ethics Institute, 2003), 299–301, 300.
44. Bhikkhu Mettānando, "Buddhist Ethics in the Practice of Medicine," in *Buddhist Ethics and Modern Society: An International Symposium*, ed. Charles Wei-Hsun Fu, Sandra Wawrytko (New York: Greenwood Press, 1991), 195–213, 201–202.
45. Ratanakul, *Bio Ethics*, 305. For Western Buddhist adaptations, see Macy, *Mutual Causality*.
46. Quoted in Damien Keown, ed., *Buddhism and Human Rights* (Richmond: Curzon Press, 1998), 221–222.
47. Ronald Y. Nakasone, "What Can Buddhism Offer Biomedical Ethics?" *Bokkyōgaku Kenkyū* 47 (1991): 1–16, 10. Scott Stonington and Pinit Ratanakul, "Is There a Global Bioethics? End-of-Life in Thailand," *Public Library of Science* 3, no. 10 (2006): e439, holds that because "the concept of interdependence is so central for most Thais, Thailand's bioethical policies may differ dramatically from those found in the West."
48. Stonington and Ratanakul, "Global Bioethics."
49. Pinit Ratanakul, "To Save or Let Go: Thai Buddhist Perspectives on Euthanasia," in *Contemporary Buddhist Ethics*, ed. Damien Keown (Richmond, UK: Curzon, 2000), 169–182; Peter Kaiser, "Medical Professionals and Their Religious Background: Is There an Impact on Therapy: The Case of Buddhadasa Bhikkhu, Thailand," *Curare* 22, no. 2 (1999): 199–207; and Supre Kanjanaphitsarn, "An Analytical

Study of Euthanasia in Buddhism with Special Reference to the Case of Buddhadāsa Bhikkhu's Death," *International Journal of Buddhist Thought and Culture* 21 (2013): 141–154.

50. The most detailed account and discussion of Hwang's research and Buddhism can be found in Middlebrooks, "Competing 'Originary' Technologies." See also Jens Schlieter, "Some Observations on Buddhist Thoughts on Human Cloning," in *Cross-Cultural Issues in Bioethics: The Example of Human Cloning*, ed. Heiner Roetz (Amsterdam: Rodopi, 2006), 179–202.
51. Damien Keown, *Buddhism and Bioethics*, 2nd ed. (Houndmills, UK: Palgrave Macmillan, 2001), 42–43.
52. Keown, *Buddhism and Bioethics*, 74. Keown holds that "the principles underlying Buddhist ethics are rarely made explicit in the sources" (37).
53. Keown, *Buddhism and Bioethics*, 43.
54. Keown, *Buddhism and Bioethics*, 37. Yet, Keown is in other contexts not fully sure "how human dignity is to be grounded in Buddhist doctrine"; see Damien Keown, "Are There Human Rights in Buddhism?," in *Buddhism and Human Rights*, ed. Damien Keown (Richmond: Curzon, 1998), 15–41.
55. Keown, *Buddhism and Bioethics*, 29–30; and Keown, "Human Rights in Buddhism," 34.
56. Keown, *Buddhism and Bioethics*, xiv, 29–32, 47–48, 148.
57. Keown, "Human Rights in Buddhism," 40.
58. See Françoise Baylis, *Altered Inheritance: CRISPR and the Ethics of Human Genome Editing* (Cambridge, MA: Harvard University Press, 2019).
59. Harvey, *Buddhist Ethics*.
60. Karma Lekshe Tsomo, *Into the Jaws of Yama, Lord of Death: Buddhism, Bioethics, and Death* (Albany: State University of New York Press, 2006), 186–187.
61. Tsomo, *Into the Jaws*, 224.
62. Tsomo, *Into the Jaws*, 157–159.
63. Damien Keown, "Buddhism, Brain Death, and Organ Transplantation," *Journal of Buddhist Ethics* 17 (2010): 1–34.
64. Somparn Promta, *Human Cloning and Embryonic Stem Cell Research: A View from Theravāda Buddhist Morality* (Bangkok: ASEAN-EU LEMLIFE Project, 2004), 5–11, 10. Cf., somewhat less permissive, Somparn Promta, "Buddhism and Human Genetic Research," in *Genomics and Bioethics: Interdisciplinary Perspectives, Technologies and Advancements*, ed. Soraj Hongladarom (Hershey, PA: IGI Global, 2011), 1–14.
65. Rupert M. L. Gethin, "Can Killing a Living Being Ever Be an Act of Compassion? The Analysis of the Act of Killing in the Abhidhamma and Pāli Commentaries," *Journal of Buddhist Ethics* 11 (2004): 167–202, 182.
66. See Damien Keown, "On Compassionate Killing and the Abhidhamma's 'Psychological Ethics,"' *Journal of Buddhist Ethics* 23 (2016): 45–82; and Soraj Hongladarom, "Normativity in Buddhism and Its Application in Bioethics," in *Dealing with Bioethical Issues in a Globalized World*, ed. Joris Gielen (Cham, Switzerland: Springer, 2020), 95–113.
67. See Huimin Bhikkhu, "Buddhist Bioethics: The Case of Human Cloning and Embryo Stem Cell Research," *Chung-Hwa Buddhist Journal* 15 (2002): 457–470; and Damien Keown, "Euthanasia," in *The Oxford Handbook of Buddhist Ethics*, ed. Daniel Cozort and James Mark Shields (Oxford: Oxford University Press, 2018), 611–629.
68. Goodman, *Consequences of Compassion*.
69. See, for example, Ellen Y. Zhang, "On Human Rights and Freedom in Bioethics: A Philosophical Inquiry in Light of Buddhism," in *Religious Perspectives on Bioethics and Human Rights*, ed. Joseph Tham, Kai Man Kwan, and Alberto Garcia (Cham, Switzerland: Springer, 2017), 77–89, 88.
70. Hongladarom, "Normativity," 108–109.

Jens Schlieter

BUDDHISM AND BIOGRAPHY

INTRODUCTION

A person unfamiliar with Buddhism might find its venerable biographical tradition an odd phenomenon, since introductory books and courses on this religion tend to stress the doctrine of no-self or *anātman* as one of this religion's foundational tenets. Such a person might even be more surprised by the persistent importance of biographical traditions across the different sociohistorical contexts where Buddhist practitioners can be found. If, for James T. Palmer, "the widespread use of hagiography in early medieval Europe is striking because Europe was not culturally homogeneous in every way," the prevalence of biographical literature about Buddhist saints in the deeply varied contexts of Asia and beyond should cause even more surprise.[1]

The underlying question the article addresses is "what is the function of biographical writing in Buddhism?" The article summarizes scholarship on the various biographical contexts in which Buddhist biographies were written by stating that the narrative form of biography makes the disparate, heterogeneous, occasionally contradictory elements of the Buddhist religion cohere in a given time and place. The textual body of the Buddhist saint becomes the guarantee of (doctrinal, ritual, etc.) coherence, while it also allows for an interlocutor between believer and believed. This argument is mainly indebted to Juliana Schober's conception of biographies as "tools for mapping diverse realities onto one another" and Andrew Quintman's work that extends the body of the Buddhist saint to an understanding of a "body" of literature.[2]

THEORETICAL BACKGROUND

To understand Buddhism and biography, scholarship on literary characters is useful. It is important to be aware that using such scholarship brackets the question of whether or not the people written about in biographical texts have actually existed. In doing so, it departs from a significant amount of scholarship that sought to use Buddhist biographies to reconstruct the lives of the Buddhist saints they purported to describe. Such scholarship was particularly focused on reconstructing the figure of Śākyamuni Buddha himself. Bracketing this concern means following Bernard Faure's suggestion that many Buddhist figures can be studied within a model influenced by French structuralism. In doing so, one pays less attention to the actual "bio"—the historical referent of the biography—and more to the "graphy"—how the narrative portrayal of this person has been adapted to a variety of historical contexts. In the case of the Chan saint Bodhidharma, Faure advocates studying him (it?) as a "textual and religious paradigm."[3]

Like all narrative, biographical writing structures the perception of reality. Starting in the last quarter of the 20th century, many scholars have come to see human life as influenced or even organized by narrative, something often termed the "narrative turn." In the words of one critic, narration and its creation of characters (or "characterization") is "the answer to non-human, a-temporal, and discontinuous chaos."[4] This turn has gained strength in the early 21st century in view of findings in cognitive science, psychology, and related disciplines showing the important role narrative plays in the psychological organization of the self and the reality that this self is considered to experience.[5]

If narration organizes worlds, people relate to these worlds through characters, who among other things function to "establish connections to reality and the life of the audience" and "condense complex contexts and make them tangible."[6] Uri Margolin has provided a detailed overview of the different levels with which readers engage characters. In the first level of such engagement, characters are nothing more than

> a collection of abstract predicates, attributes or intensions held together by an individual constant, i.e., a proper name, but with no specific claim being made and no quantification, hence no existence claim. It is like having a bunch of associated nominal phrases but no sentences to go with them.[7]

Characters are not understood as "persons" at this point, only as a collection of textual propositions tied to a name. At the next level of engagement, characters come to exist as "objects of thought": they are now conceivable entities with an individuality. A third level of engagement is seeing these entities as existing within certain "worlds." The character becomes a sensory entity, who has feelings, a personality, and so on. In the final, fourth, stage, readers begin to involve themselves with the character: they respond (emotionally, morally, intellectually) to the actions of characters: "we ask here not how the reader constructs the narrative world, but rather how the narrative world reconstructs the reader."[8]

This narratological account of literary characters demonstrates that the construction of a character as a person is the action of making coherent, of creating imaginatively, a human being out of data that are not human. These humanized entities that can then go on to shape the daily lives of individuals and societies. This mechanism, of course, mirrors in an uncanny way the Buddhist theory on the creation and continuity of the self on the basis of impermanent *skandhas* that, much like the propositions in a literary text, do not necessarily imply an individual essence.

The ability of characters to make coherent what would otherwise be complex and messy applies to the Buddhist religion as a whole. Narratives surrounding this religion's alleged "founder" quickly became central to fulfilling this role. Whatever the identity of the historical Buddha, his biographical body was in fact a series of narrative interventions that shaped him to fit changing sociohistorical realities. In this respect, Juliana Schober's conception of Buddhist biographies is useful. She sees these texts as

> tools for mapping diverse realities onto one another: local cosmologies are integrated into universal ones; pristine Buddhist ideals and modes of practice are recreated in the present and in the lives of others; the present is explained in terms of causes in past lives; iconic veneration of an absent Buddha allows the community to participate in his continuing biography; and so on.[9]

Biography, with its focus on one individual, allows for the integration or "mapping" of diverse frames of reality onto each other, connecting the local to the universal. As the many essays collected in Schober's volume are at pains to point out, this mapping function allows biography to

> historicize mythic lineages, transform visual reliefs into icons of veneration, contextualize cultural formations and rituals, project local contexts onto universal cosmologies, and provide ritual means to bring Buddhists into the sacred presence of the living Buddha.[10]

Biography thus functions in a staggering amount of ways, ranging from conferring political authority to authorizing ritual activity.

A number of case studies demonstrate how biographical narratives make "Buddhism" coherent in local contexts. A first case is how the historical Buddha Śākyamuni was built up out of various elements in the context of India, Europe, and Japan. A second case is how Chinese Buddhists saints were built up in a similar manner. A third case is the question of how Buddhist biographies can influence individual and communal lives. Finally, an examination of Buddhist autobiographies shows that Buddhist saints, in addition to being shaped by others, also shape their own image.

A note on terminology: there is little point in distinguishing between hagiography (largely fictional, "religious") and biography (historical, scientific). Such a distinction and biography presupposes a value judgment that is unwarranted. Faure, basing himself on Michel de Certeau's work, has argued that

> the biographical process is in most cases only an unconscious duplication of the hagiographical process. Both are characterized by an attitude that I would call "substantialist," in that they consider a personage as some kind of individual entity whose essence is reflected in specific texts-biographical or doctrinal . . . Both share the same obsession with filling the chronological gaps by borrowing from various sources, and both are therefore ideological products.[11]

BUILDING BUDDHAS: THE PROCESS OF ADAPTATION

The Case of Śākyamuni

Śākyamuni in India. In the Western reception of Buddhism, biographies of Śākyamuni played an immense part, and it should be no surprise that immense scholarly efforts have gone toward the study of these narratives. One important achievement of this line of research is Lamotte's description of the distinct layers that compose this biographical corpus.[12] In John Strong's iteration,[13] which fuses some categories and omits some of the chronology that has become problematic to maintain, these are as follows:

1. "Biographical fragments found in canonical texts": generally written in Pāli or Sanskrit, these are episodes of Śākyamuni's life as told in sutras.
2. "Fuller, more autonomous lives of the Buddha": also written in Pāli or Sanskrit, examples include the *Mahāvastu*, the *Buddhacarita*, and the *Lalitavistara*.
3. Later lives of the Buddha in vernacular: examples of this genre are plentiful, and the list of works continues to be added on to. This third category reflects local adaptations of the story, although one might say that the story of Śākyamuni was always already being locally adopted, as Lamotte was very aware.

The "life" of Śākyamuni also must include his previous incarnations, as they were articulated in the so-called *jātaka* stories. Lamotte explains the emergence of these stories (and their popularity around the 2nd century BCE) as acquiescing to a demand of figures people could relate to better than the world-renouncing monks, an argument Strong follows.[14]

The whole growth of narratives around Śākyamuni can be cast as one of gradual adaptation to particular historical contexts. Schober and Alan Sponberg argue that Buddhist biographies base themselves on a limited amount of core themes and narratives, what Sponberg calls "building blocks," and then adapt these building blocks to local preferences.[15] Incidentally, this is something that James Palmer claims is also true for how hagiography functioned in medieval Europe: religious biographies were a "common cultural resource alongside religious texts and the calendar, but one which lent itself to endless adaptation to fit local tastes, circumstances, and political needs."[16] Lamotte himself listed the following motivations for changing or adding to the Buddha's life story:

> the need to justify such-and-such a detail in the tradition, the influence of holy places on the development of the texts, the incidence of religious imagery on the written tradition, the borrowing from outside sources, the claim of regions which were not converted until late that they had been visited by the Buddha and, finally, the desire of the great families to be connected with the Śākyan lineage.[17]

Lamotte's line of thinking carries some of the inheritance of earlier scholarly models that saw the Buddha as a human being on whose person "religious" elements were added over time. It is perhaps better to think of Śākyamuni as always-already changed by local interests including, but not limited to, the various motivations Lamotte lists.

It was only in the beginning of the 21st century that Buddhist scholarship turned its attention to what was in plain sight: the discourse on Śākyamuni's masculinity. Drawing on theories of masculinity as normative discourse, John Powers discovered that, "In Indian Buddhist literature, there is a pervasive concern with bodies—particularly male bodies—and the Buddha's is held up as the highest development of the male physique."[18] The well-known characteristics of this physique (a protuberance on the head, a sheathed penis, very long arms) were repeated again and again in portrayals of the Buddha, and signified his power, good karma, and religious charisma.

Another clear feature of Śākyamuni that was examined in the early 21st century was his humanity. Within the context of the ongoing animal turn in the humanities, Reiko Ohnuma has argued that, "Early Buddhism in India was a profoundly human-centered tradition."[19] As with masculinity, the representation of the human in Buddhism requires a counterpart to define itself against, and the most potent counterpart is the animal. Thus, every animal in Śākyamuni's biography can be seen as "a figure who illuminates the Buddha's character through identification, contrast, or parallelism with an animal 'other.'"[20] Moreover, in an astounding amount of the Pāli *jātaka*, the Buddha appears as an animal who protests against the suffering inflicted on animals by humankind, thus suggesting a countercurrent to the anthropocentrism of doctrinal Buddhism.[21]

Further Transformations of Śākyamuni Europe. The biography of Śākyamuni became the most important narrative in the history of the Western reception of Buddhism. Donald Lopez has suggested that European readings of Śākyamuni are not so different from much older Asian constructions: based on bits and pieces of information, people construct an image of Śākyamuni that reflects their own predilections.[22] Lopez sketches the reception of Śākyamuni as follows: for early travelers to Asia the name Śākyamuni was a collection of heathen idols not necessarily referring to the same entity. For the Roman Catholic missionaries who went to Asia during early modernity, these idols became a myth that they had to understand in order to successfully convert people to Christianity. With British colonial rule over India, the many idols of Śākyamuni were understood to refer to one man, and finally, with the emergence of Buddhist studies and the ability of European scholars to read Asian languages, he became a text.[23] Lopez ends in 1844 with the publication of *Introduction à l'histoire du bouddhisme indien* by Eugène Burnouf, a book where the modern Buddha, as a historical figure and the human "founder" of a world religion, emerged "fully formed." This Buddha has not, Lopez asserts, changed much since then.[24]

What ideologies shaped Burnouf's modern Śākyamuni? As Gregory Schopen has shown, the insistent quest to reconstruct the "real" life of "the Buddha" runs parallel to Protestant quests to discover the real life of Jesus Christ.[25] Characteristic of the latter (and thus also the former) quest was seeing through superstitions such as miracles and magic to get at the "human" Buddha. Once "discovered," this human Buddha was then disseminated by a series of very popular and influential biographies, such as Sir Edwin Arnold's *The Light of Asia* and Hermann Oldenberg's *The Buddha: His Life, his Order, his Doctrine*, both published at the end of the 19th century.[26]

Yet in the 19th century there was a competing vision of Śākyamuni that existed, namely that of those whom Frank Reynolds calls "myth-oriented scholars," who saw Śākyamuni as "a reformer who provided the occasion for the historicization of the solar myth."[27] The tension between this vision and the vision of Śākyamuni as a human being, which Reynolds typifies as that of the "historically oriented philologists," was somewhat resolved in the second half of the 20th century when scholarly consensus coalesced around the idea that Śākyamuni should be understood both as a mythical and a historical person.

What is the contemporary vision of Śākyamuni in the West? Popular interpretations in the early 21st century cast Śākyamuni as a psychologist, a neuroscientist, even a quantum physicist, exemplifying the extent to which Buddhism has become understood as a science and a philosophy rather than a religion. Black practitioners in the United States have seen Śākyamuni as a social reformer who resisted racial prejudice, mirroring B. R. Ambedkar's earlier vision of Śākyamuni as someone resisting the Hindu caste system.[28] Beyond these specific contexts, the Buddha has also become an internet meme synonymous with vague notions of tranquility and well-being.

Further Transformations of Śākyamuni Europe and Japan. The Japanese vision of Śākyamuni provides a very different but related case study. Though Buddhism had been practiced in Japan since the 6th century, due to a variety of historical factors Śākyamuni and his biography had not been very important in the Japanese Buddhist imaginary.[29] As the monastic community had little interest in the portrayal of this figure, his life became the property of dramatists and other commercial writers. According to Micah Auerback, Śākyamuni's life story was "vernacularized," leading to "a Buddha without Buddhism," a Śākyamuni constructed by authors outside of the temples and monasteries.[30]

This changes with the Meiji persecution of Buddhism, which caused Japanese Buddhists to construct a "New Buddhist History" based on scientific methods.[31] It was within this framework that the Buddha's biography became important. These historical narratives differed from the historical records that had preceded them, James Ketelaar argues, in that Buddhist history was to be seen in the context of a general teleology of civilization, a narrative of gradual evolution and perfection. And for this narrative, the historically verified biography of Śākyamuni Buddha and his enlightenment were essential: this narrative "was the transcendent guarantee of Buddhist claims to speak the truth."[32] Suddenly, Japanese Buddhist priests found it necessary to travel to India to encounter Śākyamuni on his birth ground, often with the goals of reconciling Japanese Buddhist factional strife.[33]

The quest to recover the biography of Śākyamuni was all the more necessary since critiques of Buddhism in Japan had shown how the religion was finally logically contradictory, as Tominaga Nakamoto showed even before the Meiji era.[34] Ironically, in Murakami Senshō's 1894 account, the variety of birth dates in scriptural texts, the result of Buddhism's local adaptation to Indian, Chinese, and Japanese contexts, was eliminated to settle on a final date. Ironically, this very process of "dating" the Buddha constitutes a local adaptation of the Buddha's birth date, namely to the contradictory demands of a modernizing Japan.[35] The Japanese rediscovery of Śākyamuni and the evolving European imagination of him both show how the Buddha's body remained a way to adapt Buddhism to local circumstances.

Building Buddhist Biographies in China. How were Buddhist saints built in China? In examining biographical materials produced in China about Indian Buddhist saints, Stuart Young has adapted sociologist Ann Swidler's concept of cultural repertoires to understand how Chinese Buddhist writers constructed three Buddhist saints: Aśvaghoṣa, Nāgārjuna, and Āryadeva.[36] These writers strategically used repertoires of "Indianness" to

> advance a variety of other projects aimed at developing avowedly Indian models of Buddhist sanctity that would integrate and supplant local Chinese religious traditions. In these contexts, the gap between India and China was both negated and exploited, as Chinese authors deliberately foregrounded the patriarchs' Indian identity in order to Buddhicize time-honored Chinese religious repertoires and thus demonstrate the fundamental unity between ancient India and latterday China.[37]

Apart from the incorporation of these saints into Chinese Buddhist lineages (the most commonly studied manner of how Indian Buddhism was made authoritative in China), biographies of these saints also connected China to the Buddhist homeland of India in other ways. Although in the hands of Chinese biographers these Buddhist saints conformed the ideals of Chinese sainthood, their Indianness, Young argues, provided a crucial and flexible element "repertoire element."[38] Young understands the function of Chinese Buddhist biography as an *exemplum*, a rhetorical figure which functions to "create order from an otherwise inchoate jumble of entities, ideas, events, and experiences."[39] He thus interprets the functioning of Buddhist biography much as Schober does: as making coherent what would otherwise be chaotic.

Another important genre were biographies of Chinese "eminent monks" (*gaoseng zhuan*). The first collection was edited by Huijiao (497–554) in 530, with many more such collections to follow (such as Daoxuan's [596–667] *Xu gaoseng zhuan* and Zanning's [919–1001] *Song gaoseng zhuan*). Important in Huijiao's work is his categorization of monks into ten sections that his successors would modify according to historical circumstances in their own collections. These original sections include: "(1) Translators (*yijing*); (2) Exegetes (*yijie*); (3) Divine Wonders (*shenyi*), devoted to wonder-workers; (4) Practitioners of Meditation (*xichan*) . . ." and so on.[40] Though John Kieschnick believes that these divisions are arbitrary, not reflecting any social convention,[41] they can be seen as another attempt to impose patterns on Chinese Buddhist saints, presenting these monks, much as Śākyamuni had been presented in the sutras and biographies, as an ideal model to be emulated. Yet, in mirroring secular histories such as the *Han Shu* or the *Shiji* in recording exact dates and historical data, these biographies were tailored to appeal to political rulers.[42]

With the emergence and eventual dominance of the Chan tradition, biographies of Chan masters started replacing the ecumenical orientation of the earlier *gaoseng* tradition. The speeches, actions, and interactions of such masters were recorded in the so-called "records of sayings" (*yulu*), "transmission of the lamp" (*denglu*), and *gong-an* collections.[43] The genre flourished during the Five Dynasties and Ten Kingdoms period (907–979) going into the Northern Song (960–1127), when numerous collections mapping respective Chan lineages and the masters belonging to them competed in polemical struggles for authority. As Albert Welter has argued for the case of the *Record of Linji*, such biographies catered to the changing tastes of the literati class of powerbrokers in Song China.[44] As a consequence of this, biographical accounts of famous Zen teachers changed significantly over time. In a study of the Chan patriarch Mazu Daoyi (709–788), Mario Poceski shows how the representation of this patriarch shifts from the Tang to the Song dynasty, as Mazu is gradually "zennified": instead of being represented as a thaumaturge and a teacher of Buddhist doctrine, he becomes an iconoclast typical of the encounter dialogue literature.[45]

Biographies of later Chan teachers continued to be shaped by the conventions laid out in the earlier biographical literature. Natasha Heller has demonstrated that the biographical and autobiographical materials of the Yuan dynasty Chan master Zhongfeng Mingben (1263–1323) draw heavily on previous Chan biographical materials to

> crystallize his life around certain narrative modes and themes . . . All parties operated with mental images of a Buddhist monk, and with assumptions about the conduct befitting a Chan master. Mingben's biographies emerge out of this nexus of cultural expectations and historical facts.[46]

This trend of making narrative sense of one's own life through the lives of past eminent monks continued on after the Yuan dynasty, as Jiang Wu has shown in his study of the famous Ming dynasty monk Yinyuan Longqi (1592–1673) and as Stuart Lachs has argued about the 20th-century master Sheng Yen (1931–2009).[47]

How Biographies Organize Buddhist Lives. The growth of the biographical tradition around Śākyamuni and Chinese monks has been described as a process of continuing adaptation. Such adaptations are important, because they allow biographical narratives to continue to exert authority and influence on the way individuals structure their lives, while blocking other possibilities. As Jannidis, Eder, and Schneider note, characters are key in the "construction and dissemination of social stereotypes."[48] In the case of characters in Buddhist biographies, these are "models" for practice, and "mediate between the ideal and the real, the conceptual and the pragmatic."[49] Like Christian saints, Buddhist saints need to be both like ordinary people and beyond them.[50]

Of course, the process of building Buddhist saints and the process of how those narratives influence Buddhist lives is circular. Adaptations influence Buddhists who in turn can go on to author new adaptations. For example, Śākyamuni's biography was deeply influenced by the need to "insert" places that had grown important as pilgrimage sites or that had become Buddhist but were not mentioned in his biography at all.[51] In this respect, Lamotte vividly describes the biographical *Lalitavistara Sūtra* as

> an enlarged—and badly corrected—edition of several pilgrimage guide books placed end to end: the information which it contains often coincides, even down to details of expression, with the words of guides collected at the holy places by Hsüan tsang [Xuanzang] and other pilgrims during their reverent visits.[52]

Lamotte thus casts local pilgrimage guides as inventing new chapters of the Buddha's life to regale their customers. As these stories spread, the holy sites where these events supposedly took place would then come to the attention of even more future pilgrims. Lamotte's fifth and sixth categories of modification to Śākyamuni's biography, namely instances where Śākyamuni is imagined to have paid a visit to regions that he historically could not have visited, and rulers claiming to have descended from Śākyamuni, can similarly be explained: the additions end up conferring legitimacy and power on places far away from Śākyamuni's native soil, thus influencing the lives of many individuals, some of whom will then go on to author new biographies of Śākyamuni.

But Buddhist biographies also determine Buddhist religious ritual and practice. In early Indian Buddhism, Reginald Ray has argued, categories for sainthood prescribed what some Buddhists strove toward.[53] In Song dynasty China, biographies would themselves become the focus of ritual and soteriological practice with Dahui Zonggao's (1089–1163) invention of a new Chan method of meditation. Dahui had students ritually focus on a single phrase of a recorded dialogue (the *huatou*). Such dialogues were excerpted and collected in aforementioned *gongan* collections that prescribed what Chan saints were like.[54]

Another pervasive way practices of representation in biographical materials can regulate lives is how they represent gender. This has served as a fertile point of departure for feminist and gender studies-inspired work. Early scholarly research on this topic, by Caroline Rhys Davids, Mabel Bode, and I. B. Horner, has tended to focus on only two texts: the Pāli Vinaya's restrictions against women and the Therīgātā, a collection of verse authored by Buddhist women.[55] Motivated by a first-wave feminist, suffragist agenda, and under the influence of orientalism and Protestant Buddhism, these scholars portrayed Buddhist women in India as antecedents of themselves. In 1979, Diana Paul shifted the debate by drawing attention to how women were portrayed, thus mirroring the shift to second-wave feminism during the 1960s.[56] A decade later, Liz Wilson dismissed the idea, defended by Paul, that there existed positive portrayals in early Indian Buddhism, claiming that in all texts of early Buddhism women act as passive bodies, "objects of meditation whose sole function in the narratives in which they appear is to lead to the edification of the male subjects who observe them."[57] She argued that such representational practices barred the path of Buddhism to women. And even when they did not, as in the biographies of eminent nuns in India, these nuns are required to "self-objectify" their female bodies as repulsive.[58]

But how effective were these biographies in determining attitudes toward women? For Indian Buddhism, Alice Collett has pointed out that it was not because certain texts said certain things that women were also doing them, an assumption that underlies many early studies on Buddhism and gender. Such studies have, moreover, ignored the fact that early Buddhism has produced and transmitted a comparatively high number of texts authored by or describing women, a fact that in itself should tell us something about the multiplicity of voices in the early Buddhist tradition, rendering any one-sided judgment impossible.[59] Beata Grant and Lori Meeks have argued that this is true in the case of, respectively, 17th-century China and Kamakura Japan. In China, female masters drew on the Linji Chan rhetoric of equality to present themselves as equal to men. In Japan, nuns simply ignored mainstream misogynist ideas and constructed their own Buddhist imaginary based on the biographies of famous Japanese Buddhist noblewomen.[60] Similar to Meeks, but combining textual study with ethnographic fieldwork, Paula Arai has shown how Japanese Soto Zen nuns draw upon biographical portrayals of their forebears to overcome adversity, thus overturning the narrative that sees Buddhist women as powerless victims of patriarchy.[61]

Apart from conditioning attitudes toward sainthood and gender, Buddhist biographies can also have other psychological effects such as healing communal trauma. This is what Charlene Makley and Holly Gayley have suggested in their studies of 20th-century Tibetan Buddhism.[62] Gayley argues that Buddhist biographies functioned as "an alternative to the official account by the [Chinese] state."[63] In this context, notions like karma become "a narrative device, retrospectively asserting interpretive command over events otherwise outside of Tibetan control," and Buddhist leaders become healers in "degenerate" times.[64]

BUDDHIST AUTOBIOGRAPHY IN TIBET AND THE MODERN WEST

The boundary between this biography and autobiography is porous: in the examples of the Chinese masters Zhongben and Yinyuan, it is clear that the masters are authoring visions of themselves. But one could demonstrate this porous border much earlier: if we take at least some of the sutras to contain traces of what Śākyamuni has actually said, then the biographical sections of these texts might very well be said to be autobiographical as well.

The case of Tibet also demonstrates this porosity. Janet Gyatso has noted that the difference between both genres in Tibet is rhetorical: whereas autobiography usually is indifferent toward its subject in tone, biography displays reverence.[65] In a study of the writings of Sera Khandro (1892–1940), a female Tibetan Buddhist teacher who authored both an autobiography and a biography of her teacher, Sarah Jacoby shows that work in autobiographical and feminist studies on relational selfhood is useful to understand the representational position of her research subject.[66] Jacoby understands Khandro's (auto)biographical writing as demonstrating the notion of Buddhist interdependence: her narrative introduces not only her own perspective, but it also ventriloquizes a host of beings, human and supernatural. In narrating the self, Khandro's writing therefore also narrates and makes coherent a whole religious imaginary.

Buddhist autobiographical writing gained more and more prominence during so-called modernity, a period that saw unprecedented social and cultural changes as the result of the eventual worldwide adoption of the capitalist economic system.[67] Resulting from a stress on personal "experience," the 20th and 21st centuries featured an explosion of Buddhist convert life writing, often describing stays in Asian Buddhist environments. Such autobiographical texts often detailed a clash of expectations: what Buddhism is in the minds of such travelers often turns out to be based on misconceptions partially informed by Westernized biographies of Buddhist saints.[68] From the 1990s onwards, autobiographical Buddhist narratives have also flourished via other media, such as blogs and even in virtual worlds such as Second Life.[69] In addition to a focus on Śākyamuni's biography then, a focus on the life writing of Buddhists might thus be seen as a distinctive mark of Buddhism in the West.

REVIEW OF LITERATURE

Overall, scholarship has shifted from using biographies as a means to reconstruct the "real" lives of Buddhist figures (particularly Śākyamuni) to an interest in how biography performs various social and ritual functions. The quest for the details of Śākyamuni's life, which belongs to the former trend, was key to the development of Buddhist studies in the 19th century, and led to a host of new biographies that adapted this figure to become a modern European or American.[70] The major representative figure of this quest was the French scholar André Bareau, whose work minutely compares details in biographical accounts in order to recover the real Buddha.[71] This trend was already waning with the other major francophone figure in the study of Buddhism, Étienne Lamotte, who shifted attention to how Śākyamuni's biography was modified, and the reasons for such alterations.[72]

In the light of criticism such as Gregory Schopen's objection that Buddhist studies projected a Protestant notion of religion onto materials that simply did not have these ideas (such as the primacy of textual materials and the determining influence of the "founder" of a religion), and following the 1970s poststructuralist dismissal of master narratives, scholars started focusing on the performative function of Buddhist biography as a representation worthy of study on its own terms, not on how accurately it conveyed information about a person who may or may not have existed.[73] A paradigm-changing article spurring this shift was Bernard Faure's study of the biographical corpus of the Chan saint Bodhidharma as a "textual and religious paradigm" rather than a series of texts describing a real individual.[74] For Faure, the question of whether Bodhidharma really existed or not, and whether he was really like the texts portrayed him to be, was less interesting than what the portrayal of this saint said about the Chan tradition. Thus, what for 19th-century scholars were "accretions" obscuring a clear view of the Buddhist saint were now seen as interesting in themselves because they allowed one to investigate a greater variety of questions related to the historical evolution of Buddhism.

Under the influence of scholars like Faure, whose ability to read classic Buddhist languages matches his familiarity with ideas and methodologies from continental philosophy and modern "theory," Buddhist studies scholars entered into a fruitful dialogue with other fields. The dialogue with gender studies, for example, allowed scholars to focus on representations of masculinity and femininity in Buddhist biographies, while a debate on Buddhism as an anthropocentric religion is just getting started.[75] Scholars have also gradually moved away from privileging texts as the essence of Buddhism, discovering that there is often a gap between textual representation and reality, and that visual imagery was (and remains) more important for how many Buddhists learn about the lives of their saints.[76] Studies of Buddhist biography have also increasingly been in dialogue with scholarship on medieval Christian saints. The work of Patrick Geary has been particularly influential.[77] Gender-focused studies have also entered into this dialogue, with the attempt to recover lost voices of Buddhist women paralleling the attention given to the lives of medieval Christian nuns.[78] The idea that methodologies developed in non-Buddhist traditions can lead to a richer discussion has also led to edited volumes providing studies of religious biography across Asian traditions.[79]

FURTHER READING

Auerback, Micah L. *A Storied Sage: Canon and Creation in the Making of a Japanese Buddha*. Buddhism and Modernity. Chicago: University of Chicago Press, 2016.

Heine, Steven, and Dale Wright, eds. *Zen Masters*. New York: Oxford University Press, 2010.

Heller, Natasha. *Illusory Abiding: The Cultural Construction of the Chan Monk Zhongfeng Mingben*. Harvard East Asian Monographs 368. Cambridge, MA: Harvard University Asia Center, 2014.

Jacoby, Sarah H. *Love and Liberation: Autobiographical Writings of the Tibetan Buddhist Visionary Sera Khandro*. New York: Columbia University Press, 2014.

Kieschnick, John. *The Eminent Monk: Buddhist Ideals in Medieval Chinese Hagiography*. Studies in East Asian Buddhism 10. Honolulu: University of Hawaiʻi Press, 1997.

Lopez, Donald S. *From Stone to Flesh: A Short History of the Buddha*. Buddhism and Modernity. Chicago: University of Chicago Press, 2013.

Ohnuma, Reiko. *Unfortunate Destiny: Animals in the Indian Buddhist Imagination*. New York: Oxford University Press, 2017.

Quintman, Andrew. *The Yogin and the Madman: Reading the Biographical Corpus of Tibet's Great Saint Milarepa*. New York: Columbia University Press, 2013.

Schober, Juliane. *Sacred Biography in the Buddhist Traditions of South and South-East Asia*. Delhi: Motilal Banarsidass, 2002.

Strong, John S. *The Buddha: A Short Biography*. Oxford: Oneworld, 2001.

Welter, Albert. *The Linji Lu and the Creation of Chan Orthodoxy: The Development of Chan's Records of Sayings Literature*. Oxford: Oxford University Press, 2008.

Young, Stuart H. *Conceiving the Indian Buddhist Patriarchs in China*. Honolulu: University of Hawaii Press, 2015.

NOTES

1. James T. Palmer, *Early Medieval Hagiography*, new ed. (Leeds: Arc Humanities Press, 2018), 4.
2. Juliane Schober, ed., *Sacred Biography in the Buddhist Traditions of South and Southeast Asia* (Honolulu: University of Hawaii Press, 1997); Andrew Quintman, *The Yogin and the Madman: Reading the Biographical Corpus of Tibet's Great Saint Milarepa* (New York: Columbia University Press, 2013).

3. Bernard Faure, "Bodhidharma as Textual and Religious Paradigm," *History of Religions* 25, no. 3 (1986): 190.
4. Michael Bamberg, "Identity and Narration," in *The Living Handbook of Narratology*, ed. Peter Hühn et al. (Hamburg: Hamburg University Press, 2013), 13.
5. Paul John Eakin, *How Our Lives Become Stories: Making Selves*, Cornell Paperbacks (Ithaca, NY: Cornell University Press, 1999).
6. Jens Eder, Fotis Jannidis, and Ralf Schneider, "Introduction," in *Characters in Fictional Worlds* (Berlin and New York: De Gruyter, 2010), 46.
7. Uri Margolin, "From Predicates to People Like Us: Kinds of Readerly Engagement with Literary Characters," in *Characters in Fictional Worlds*, ed. Eder, Jannidis, and Schneider, 403.
8. Margolin, "From Prelates to People Like Us," 410.
9. Schober, *Sacred Biography in the Buddhist Traditions*, ix.
10. Schober, *Sacred Biography in the Buddhist Traditions*, 12.
11. Faure, "Bodhidharma as Textual and Religious Paradigm," 188–189. The work by Michel de Certeau referred to is *The Writing of History*, trans. Tom Conley, European Perspectives (New York: Columbia University Press, 1988). For other discussions of the exchangeability of the two terms regarding the topic of Chinese Buddhism, see John Jorgensen, *Inventing Hui-Neng, the Sixth Patriarch: Hagiography and Biography in Early Ch'an* (Leiden, The Netherlands, and Boston: Brill Academic, 2005), 18; Mario Poceski, *The Records of Mazu and the Making of Classical Chan Literature* (New York: Oxford University Press, 2015), 43.
12. Étienne Lamotte, *History of Indian Buddhism: From the Origins to the Saka Era*, trans. Sarah Webb-Boin, Publications de l'Institut Orientaliste de Louvain 36 (Louvain-la-Neuve: Université Catholique de Louvain, Institut Orientaliste, 1988), 644–684, 718.
13. John S. Strong, *The Buddha: A Short Biography* (Oxford: Oneworld, 2001), 5–6.
14. Lamotte, *History of Indian Buddhism*, 684; Strong, *The Buddha*, 20.
15. Alan Sponberg and Helen Hardacre, eds., *Maitreya: The Future Buddha* (Cambridge, UK, and New York: Cambridge University Press, 1988), 293; Schober, *Sacred Biography in the Buddhist Traditions*, 5.
16. Palmer, *Early Medieval Hagiography*, 3.
17. Lamotte, *History of Indian Buddhism*, 733.
18. John Powers, *A Bull of a Man: Images of Masculinity, Sex, and the Body in Indian Buddhism*, repr. ed. (Cambridge, MA: Harvard University Press, 2009), 9.
19. Reiko Ohnuma, *Unfortunate Destiny: Animals in the Indian Buddhist Imagination* (New York: Oxford University Press, 2017), xiii.
20. Ohnuma, *Unfortunate Destiny*, 97.
21. Ohnuma, *Unfortunate Destiny*, 50.
22. Donald S. Lopez, ed., *Strange Tales of an Oriental Idol: An Anthology of Early European Portrayals of the Buddha* (Chicago: Chicago University Press, 2016), 6–7.
23. Donald S. Lopez, *From Stone to Flesh: A Short History of the Buddha*, Buddhism and Modernity (Chicago: University of Chicago Press, 2013). Matthew Kapstein has contested Lopez's chronology, arguing that the European reception of Buddhism is more complicated than the rather neat schematic outlined by the latter. He also nuances Eugène Burnouf's role as the founder of the historical buddha. Matthew T. Kapstein, "Review of Urs App *The Cult of Emptiness: The Western Discovery of Buddhist Thought and the Invention of Oriental Philosophy*, Donald S. Lopez *From Stone to Flesh: A Short History of the Buddha*," *History of Religions* 54, no. 4 (May 2015): 459–466.
24. Lopez, *From Stone to Flesh*, 3.
25. Gregory Schopen, "Archaeology and Protestant Presuppositions in the Study of Indian Buddhism," *History of Religions* 31, no. 1 (August 1991): 1–23.

26. Sir Edwin Arnold, *The Light of Asia or the Great Renunciation . . .* (Boston: Roberts Brothers, 1890); Hermann Oldenberg, *Buddha: His Life, His Doctrine, His Order* (London: Williams, 1882). I am borrowing Philip Almond's phrasing here: Philip C. Almond, *The British Discovery of Buddhism* (Cambridge, UK: Cambridge University Press, 1988).
27. Frank Reynolds, "The Many Lives of the Buddha," in *The Biographical Process: Studies in the History and Psychology of Religion*, ed. Frank Reynolds and Donald Capps (The Hague: Mouton de Gruyter, 1976), 38.
28. Adeana McNicholl, "Being Buddha, Staying Woke: Racial Formation in Black Buddhist Writing," *Journal of the American Academy of Religion* 86, no. 4 (2018): 883–911; Bhimrao R. Ambedkar, *The Buddha and His Dhamma* (Independently Published, 2019).
29. Micah L. Auerback, *A Storied Sage: Canon and Creation in the Making of a Japanese Buddha*, Buddhism and Modernity (Chicago: University of Chicago Press, 2016).
30. Auerback, *A Storied Sage*, 17.
31. James E. Ketelaar, "The Non-Modern Confronts the Modern: Dating the Buddha in Japan," *History and Theory* 45, no. 4 (December 2006): 66–67.
32. Ketelaar, "The Non-Modern Confronts the Modern," 74.
33. Richard M. Jaffe, *Seeking Sakyamuni: South Asia in the Formation of Modern Japanese Buddhism* (Chicago: University of Chicago Press, 2019).
34. Ketelaar, "The Non-Modern Confronts the Modern," 75.
35. Ketelaar, "The Non-Modern Confronts the Modern," 78.
36. C. Pierce Salguero, "Review of Conceiving the Indian Buddhist Patriarchs in China," *Numen* 63, nos. 5–6 (October 2016): 607–611.
37. Stuart H. Young, *Conceiving the Indian Buddhist Patriarchs in China* (Honolulu: University of Hawaii Press, 2015), 3–4.
38. Young, *Conceiving the Indian Buddhist Patriarchs*, 13.
39. Young, *Conceiving the Indian Buddhist Patriarchs*, 16.
40. John Kieschnick, *The Eminent Monk: Buddhist Ideals in Medieval Chinese Hagiography*, Studies in East Asian Buddhism 10 (Honolulu: University of Hawai'i Press, 1997), 8–9.
41. Kieschnick, *The Eminent Monk*, 14–15.
42. Kieschnick, *The Eminent Monk*, 7–8.
43. On Chan literature, see the eponymous ORE article by Jeffrey Broughton.
44. Albert Welter, *The Linji Lu and the Creation of Chan Orthodoxy: The Development of Chan's Records of Sayings Literature* (Oxford: Oxford University Press, 2008).
45. Poceski, *The Records of Mazu*.
46. Natasha Heller, *Illusory Abiding: The Cultural Construction of the Chan Monk Zhongfeng Mingben*, Harvard East Asian Monographs 368 (Cambridge, MA: Harvard University Asia Center, 2014), 25.
47. Jiang Wu, *Leaving for the Rising Sun: Chinese Zen Master Yinyuan and the Authenticity Crisis in Early Modern East Asia* (New York: Oxford University Press, 2014). Stuart Lachs, "When the Saints Go Marching In: Modern Day Zen Hagiography," Shimanoarchive.com, March 9, 2011.
48. Eder, Jannidis, and Schneider, "Introduction," 57.
49. Schober, *Sacred Biography in the Buddhist Traditions*, 2.
50. Peter Brown, "Enjoying the Saints in Late Antiquity," *Early Medieval Europe* 9 (2000): 16–17.
51. Reynolds, "The Many Lives of the Buddha," 44.
52. Lamotte, *History of Indian Buddhism*, 737.
53. Reginald A. Ray, *Buddhist Saints in India: A Study in Buddhist Values and Orientations* (Oxford: Oxford University Press, 1994), 6.
54. On *koan* and *huatou* practice, see the essays in Steven Heine and Dale S. Wright, eds., *The Koan: Texts and Contexts in Zen Buddhism* (Oxford: Oxford University Press, 2000).

55. Alice Collett, "Buddhism and Gender: Reframing and Refocusing the Debate," *Journal of Feminist Studies in Religion* 22, no. 2 (2006): 55–84.
56. Diana Y. Paul, *Women in Buddhism: Images of the Feminine in the Mahāyāna Tradition* (Berkeley: University of California Press, 1985).
57. Liz Wilson, *Charming Cadavers: Horrific Figurations of the Feminine in Indian Buddhist Hagiographic Literature* (Chicago: University of Chicago Press, 1996), 3.
58. Wilson, *Charming Cadavers*, 13.
59. Collett, "Buddhism and Gender."
60. Beata Grant, *Eminent Nuns: Women Chan Masters of Seventeenth-Century China* (Honolulu: University of Hawaii Press, 2009). Lori Meeks, *Hokkeji and the Reemergence of Female Monastic Orders in Premodern Japan*, 1st ed. (Honolulu: University of Hawaii Press, 2010).
61. Paula Kane Robinson Arai, *Women Living Zen: Japanese Sōtō Buddhist Nuns* (New York: Oxford University Press, 1999).
62. Charlene E. Makley, *The Violence of Liberation: Gender and Tibetan Buddhist Revival in Post-Mao China* (Berkeley: University of California Press, 2007).
63. Holly Gayley, *Love Letters from Golok: A Tantric Couple in Modern Tibet* (New York: Columbia University Press, 2016), 18.
64. Gayley, *Love Letters from Golok*, 19–20.
65. Janet Gyatso, *Apparitions of the Self: The Secret Autobiographies of a Tibetan Visionary* (Princeton, NJ: Princeton University Press, 1998), 102–105.
66. Sarah H. Jacoby, *Love and Liberation: Autobiographical Writings of the Tibetan Buddhist Visionary Sera Khandro* (New York: Columbia University Press, 2014).
67. For important discussions of Buddhist modernity and postmodernity see David L. McMahan, *The Making of Buddhist Modernism* (Oxford and New York: Oxford University Press, 2008); Ann Gleig, *American Dharma: Buddhism Beyond Modernity* (New Haven, CT: Yale University Press, 2019).
68. For an example of an early narrative concerning Japanese Zen, see Janwillem Van de Wetering, *The Empty Mirror: Experiences in a Japanese Zen Monastery*, 1st American ed. (Boston: Houghton Mifflin, 1974). For an example from Thailand, see Tim Ward, *What the Buddha Never Taught* (Berkeley, CA: Celestial Arts, 1993). Studies of autobiographical narrative in the Japanese Zen and Thai Theravāda context, respectively, are the following: Ben Van Overmeire, "Portraying Zen Buddhism in the Twentieth Century: Encounter Dialogues as Frame-Stories in Daisetz Suzuki's Introduction to Zen Buddhism and Janwillem Van de Wetering's The Empty Mirror," *Japan Studies Review* 21 (2017): 3–24. Brooke Schedneck, "Constructions of Buddhism: Autobiographical Moments of Western Monks' Experiences of Thai Monastic Life," *Contemporary Buddhism* 12, no. 2 (November 2011): 327–346.
69. See the edited volume by Gregory Price Grieve and Daniel Veidlinger, eds., *Buddhism, the Internet, and Digital Media: The Pixel in the Lotus* (New York: Routledge, 2014). Grieve's contribution in that volume discusses Second Life, whereas Beverley Foulks McGuire discusses blogs.
70. Almond, *The British Discovery of Buddhism*, 54–79; Thomas A. Tweed, *The American Encounter with Buddhism 1844–1912* (Bloomington: Indiana University Press, 1992).
71. André Bareau, *Recherches Sur La Biographie Du Buddha Dans Les Sūtrapiṭaka et Vinayapiṭaka Anciens: De La Quête de l'éveil à La Conversion de Maudgalyāyana* (Paris: PEFEO, 1963).
72. Lamotte, *History of Indian Buddhism*.
73. Schopen, "Archaeology and Protestant Presuppositions."
74. Faure, "Bodhidharma as Textual and Religious Paradigm."
75. Paul, *Women in Buddhism*; Wilson, *Charming Cadavers*; Powers, *A Bull of a Man*; Ohnuma, *Unfortunate Destiny*.

76. Robert H. Sharf and T. Griffith Foulk, "On the Ritual Use of Ch'an Portraiture in Medieval China," *Cahiers d'Extrême-Asie* 7, no. 1 (1993): 149–219; Donald K. Swearer, *Becoming the Buddha: The Ritual of Image Consecration in Thailand* (Princeton, NJ: Princeton University Press, 2004); James C. Dobbins, *Behold the Buddha: Religious Meanings of Japanese Buddhist Icons* (Honolulu: University of Hawaii Press, 2020).
77. Some examples of Buddhist studies scholarship drawing upon Geary's models are Kurtis R. Schaeffer, *Himalayan Hermitess: The Life of a Tibetan Buddhist Nun* (New York: Oxford University Press, 2004); Jorgensen, *Inventing Hui-Neng, the Sixth Patriarch*; Quintman, *The Yogin and the Madman*. Geary's seminal text here is Patrick J. Geary, *Living with the Dead in the Middle Ages*, 1st ed. (Ithaca, NY: Cornell University Press, 1994). For the limits of Geary's model, see Suzanne M. Bessenger, *Echoes of Enlightenment: The Life and Legacy of Sonam Peldren* (Oxford: Oxford University Press, 2016).
78. Arai, *Women Living Zen*; Grant, *Eminent Nuns*; Meeks, *Hokkeji and the Reemergence of Female Monastic Orders*.
79. For edited volumes surveying religious biography within Asia, see Phyllis Granoff, ed., *Monks and Magicians: Religious Biographies in Asia* (Oakville, NY, and London: Mosaic Press, 1988); Phyllis Granoff and Koichi Shinohara, eds., *Speaking of Monks: Religious Biography in India and China* (New York: Mosaic Press, 1992). For a volume studying biography across disciplinary boundaries, see Reynolds and Capps, eds., *The Biographical Process*.

Ben Van Overmeire

BUDDHISM AND GLOBALIZATION

INTRODUCTION

Buddhism is everywhere. From Tokyo and Bangkok to San Francisco, Paris, and Johannesburg. In monasteries and meditation centers, in bookshops, Buddha Bars and IKEA, in the language and minds of unprecedented numbers of cultures and people. Monks and lamas fly everywhere; some seem always mobile and moving. Meditators shop for retreats around the world, maybe inspired by universal algorithms appealing to digitized involvement, and migrants keep track of transnational relations while recreating their own religious identities abroad. In 2001, Martin Baumann wrote that "Buddhist groups and centres have flourished and multiplied to an extent never before observed during Buddhism's 150 years of dissemination outside of Asia."[1] In recent years, this process has accelerated even further, with "new, indigenized variations of Buddhist forms, practices, and interpretations," and with impact also beyond Buddhism. Buddhists only make up 7 percent of the world population, and Buddhism may even be the only religion not growing in the future, mainly because there are too few young Buddhists to regenerate this "old religion."[2] Religious demography is extremely complex, and notoriously challenging to apply to Asian traditions and Buddhism with their hybrid and creolized traditions, fuzzy "culture religiosity," and more or less religious folk traditions, and it is difficult with statistics to capture the many Western meditators, or sympathizers, performing Buddhism as a cultural narrative. Buddhism may not have been as successful in missionizing and regenerating itself by clear-cut religiosity as Christianity and Islam. However, Buddhism is a missionizing religion. It is a traveling religion, translatable, transportable, and transposable. With its Indian origin and historical dissemination across the globe, this world's oldest religion has truly become global.

GLOBALIZATION

Leaving aside its different trajectories, globalization is generally understood as the transnational and transcultural processes of interchanging ideas, practices, values, and products. Originally used to characterize capitalist societies, the concept encapsulates the worldwide circulation and hybridization of money, goods, and people across borders. The world has thus accordingly been deterritorialized and translocalized, and in a sense diminished into *one place*, not least with the help of new communication technologies, the internet, air travel, and market interests. Until the crises emerging as a result of the COVID-19 pandemic in 2020, international trade and tourism had only seen a slight pause during the previous financial crisis in 2008. Globalization is "the compression of the world," with world citizens having a global consciousness, culturally characterized by continuously elaborating forms of diversity across economic, political, and cultural domains and with new migration patterns of increasing numbers of people.[3] It is almost a Buddhist trope characterizing globalization as "an ever-densening network of interconnections and interdependence."[4]

It could of course be argued that such transnational movements and interconnections have been present throughout history. Before the breakdown of the communist bloc (and the isolationist China) with its apparent acknowledgement of worldwide capitalism, the neoliberal turns could be seen in previous decades. The modernity of the 18th and 19th centuries and the previous Western imperialism were seminal periods expanding the world, as was what Robertson calls the "*take-off period of modern globalization, lasting from about 1870 through to the mid-1920s*."[5] The emerging modern world as a capitalist system giving priority to endless accumulation was closely linked to the 16th century.[6] Viking colonization and trade are archeological signs of globalization, and even putative "Axial" age can be seen as an early representation of proto-global waves.[7] While naturally being related to a long-term perspective, there is, however, a difference of degree concerning both spatiality and temporality. The speed, intensity, and distribution of the elements of globalization are characteristic for, and consequences of, modernity, mainly having explanatory value within the latest decades.[8]

That the concept also carries ideological and political narratives is obvious. Whenever the "supporters" find global evidence of development in trade, wealth, or even common values, the "sceptics" point to uneven development, capitalism's exploitation and historical reminders that all "global elements" were present and more democratically divided before the neoliberal world order.[9] Also a geopolitical bias behind the usage of the term has been criticized. Globalization is often understood as the global implementation of (Western-derived) models of economic and societal systems toward a new world order and a concept celebrating the triumphalism of the West.[10] The responses to such (Western) universalism are thus often inherently part of the globalization process. Roland Robertson termed the localization and relativization of, and resistance to, cultural homogenization "glocalization."[11] As such, the local economy, production, demography, culture, and religion have always had to negotiate, revise, and relativize the demands and narratives of globalization. Postmodern metaphors of hybrids, flows, and interactions with less dichotomic divisions between "them" and "us" are also part of the process. One could claim that "we have never been global," or that globalization has always been everywhere. However, setting aside the obvious ideological interests in the various emic discourses, globalization, as well as pre-global and post-global tendencies (both categories are explored in the sections "Pre-Global Buddhism" and "Post-Global Buddhism"), is undoubtedly a useful analytical concept, both to explore dynamic changes in religion and as a vehicle to transcend traditional Western bias in the study of religion.[12] Also, the study of religion and Buddhism requires a "new agenda for the human sciences in the light of processes of human circulation and the redefinition of the perimeters of societies that are occurring across the entire planet."[13]

RELIGION AND GLOBALIZATION

"Globalized religion" is one domain in which the double-sided expansion and contraction of the world frame the ideas and practices of religions, typically represented by increased and circulating diversity, migration, and hybridity.[14] Religion can be seen both to have been affected by, and also itself constituted, globalization in its cross-cultural interrelations with global networks, transnational human and cultural flows, fluidity, and hybridity. In a way, religions have always "moved, shifted, and interacted with one another around the globe," and as such, "religion has always been global," since it is "related to the global transportation of peoples, and of ideas."[15] Migration, diasporas, transnationalism, and transculturalism all have been part of the dynamics of circulating and traveling religion. Naturally, some contexts and religious transfigurations have historically been more global(ish) than others. Post-axial world religions like Christianity, Islam, and Buddhism have been more prone to universalize their scope and *raison d'être* by traveling and by deculturizing and deparochializing (at least some aspects of) their teachings, practices, and communal belonging. Hellenistic religions were more oriented beyond their local ramifications, and Eastern religions have throughout most of history been marked by diversity. Theosophy, perennialism, New Age, and spirituality are based on translocal traditions, although somewhat influenced by a "Western" gaze.[16] Individual characteristics of global religion are thus not new, but the dimensions and speed of globalization is. Global(ized) religion is potentially everywhere, accessible for everybody, and although often misrecognized as such by its users, also embedded in global economy and commerce. Reality obviously shows that accessibility to the goods of the global world is unevenly distributed, and that global religion has also needed its local revisions and relativizations. Just like the migration, colonialization, and mission of previous periods needed local adaptations, so have the challenges of global religion been indigenized and "glocalized." A process of glocalization can thus be seen as "the ability of religion to mold into the fabric of different communities in ways that connect it intimately with communal and local relations."[17] Syncretism, accommodation, segregation, fundamentalization, and negotiation have been some of the strategies for both the hosts and the guests. Identity essentialism is one particular formation of a deglobalizing strategy, relativizing the mistakes and constraints of globalization. While it can be seen as an inherent possibility of glocalization, the argument for assessing its terminological relevance is its strategic reaction to and undressing of globalization as essentially aparticularized, Western discourse.

Having "a lack of urgency about religious growth" may be a "Buddhist drawback," since endless time for karma to ripen does not encourage proselytization.[18] Buddhism, however, entails several of the characteristics of a prototypical global religion, with webs of "elective affinity" also going back in history as well as to a contemporary Western post-global resistance.

PRE-GLOBAL BUDDHISM

Buddhism was a typical axial religion, in principle universalizing beyond ethnic, cultural, national, and gender boundaries. A purely doctrinal focus on the classical texts may suggest a reading of early Buddhism as being a movement based on social criticism. While there were naturally also social implications of the teachings, the ideas and practices of the early ascetic movement seemed to relate primarily to (socially embedded) existential analyses of a cosmological nature with potential universal relevance: everyone suffers; everyone can follow the road to enlightenment (or better karma). The Sangha accumulated wealth, disseminated its teachings, practices, and cultural imprints through mission and trade, being an institution that had just as much civilizational impact on the Asian sphere as the Christian Church had in Europe.[19] Alexander the Great met Buddhism in the 4th century BC, planting the seeds for later encounters between Buddhism and Western cultures. Emperor Aśoka was instrumental in missionizing Buddhism, having his son Mahinda spread the religion to Ceylon. What Frasch calls "the great translocation" between 800 and 1300, where Buddhism disappeared from India while simultaneously transforming South Asia to a Buddhist region, was a period expanding the already established networks along the Silk Route with its proto-global ramifications.[20] Sectarianism and cultural adaptations were part of the double-sided localization and universalization developments, with Theravāda/Hīnayāna mainly constituting itself as the majority religion, and Mahāyāna in North and East Asia developing more creolized and syncretic forms of religion.[21]

It was not, however, until the 19th century that Buddhism became truly international. This was not least because of the period of Western colonialization, which brought both political and cultural suppression, but also Buddhist reforms and, eventually, what in general terms can be called "modern Buddhism."[22] The new international encounters thus prompted re-evaluation and re-invention of certain sectors of Buddhism. "Protestant Buddhism" was a neo-Buddhist reform movement reacting against (internal religious challenges and) the constraints of the British colonial powers. At the same time, it was also highly inspired by Western culture and religion, both the Protestant Christian emphasis on texts and lay religiosity (hence the term "Protestant Buddhism") and some parallel underpinnings of Theosophical and Perennialist ideas influencing universalizing tendencies in the Buddhist world.[23] Buddhism was invented as a concept in meeting Western colonialism, religion, and scholarship, and it was soon designated as a world religion. The Western trope of Buddhism being a universally applicable way of life combining deep spirituality and scientific thinking has its origin in this period. Buddhism in Ceylon and Japan changed dramatically due to the meeting with the West, as did Buddhism in China, Thailand, Tibet, and other Asian Buddhist countries. Some of these developments had clear nationalist agendas with Buddhism as a legitimate agent in a reverse orientalist and evolutionary scheme, while others reframed their traditions in a universalist paradigm.[24] Given that this period of Buddhist history was also dominated by a capitalist mode of production, a world system of core and peripheral countries, powerful technological advances, and global networks, Cristina Rocha even characterizes it as "thick globalization."[25] It could be argued, however, that it is more relevant to restrict "global" to a later period and characterize—as has also generally been the norm—this period of Buddhist history, with its international relations across East and West, more comprehensively as "modern Buddhism."

GLOBAL BUDDHISM

Martin Baumann, in his influential article on global Buddhism, suggests four distinct developmental stages in Buddhist history: the canonical, the traditional, the modern, and the global.[26] Continuing the general modernization processes of Buddhism, he finds "global" rather than "modern" or "post-modern" to be more inclusive as a spatially more precise concept to represent "the vigorous global dissemination of Buddhist people and institutions that occurred in the late twentieth century."[27] In his analysis of American Buddhism, Scott Mitchell understands modernity as "a collection of rhetorical or hermeneutic strategies."[28] For him, Buddhist modernism thus refers to a set of discourses emerging at the intersection of Western and Asian responses to the modern era. He sees globalization as "the system or means by which these discourses spread across cultures via networks of trade, travel, and telecommunications."[29] Thus, "modernity and colonialism laid the foundation on which our current age of globalization rests," and Buddhism in the United States can be seen as "the result of modernist discourses made possible through the apparatus of globalization."[30]

Global Buddhism can be understood as a specific kind of global religion with its transcultural flows, deterritorialized universality, and centripetal "global religioscape." It is characterized by "transnational and transcontinental flow of Buddhist ideas and practices and the global travel of Buddhist teachers and students."[31] Just like modern Buddhism, the focus on laicization and democratization continues in the global period, whether this means access to meditation techniques, texts, or institutional offices. The process of deculturalization is even more pronounced, since the transnational and transcultural interrelations in principle overrule the logics of localism. In Western contexts, this often means that the traditional Asian Buddhist cosmologies with Gods, heavens, hells, and even ideas about reincarnation are demythologized to neglect what are considered "cultural elements." Universally applicable individual experiences beyond the boundaries of history and culture, however, are typical of globalized discourses and practices. This also fits with "patterns of self-cultivation, administrative structures, dispositions and worldviews that intersect across geographical boundaries, lineage and ethnicity."[32] Such global dynamics have been activated by the centripetal forces where ideas, practices, and institutions have been circulating in an open and interacting world, overcoming isolationist particularism.

Relevant and translatable ideas and practices are necessary for a religion to travel across cultures, countries, and eras. Meditation and karma, interrelated transfigurations of momentary existence, enlightenment, and conscious awareness have been some of the transferable Buddhist elements and "selling points" in contemporary therapy and philosophy of life. Individualization has become global, and so has the global reconfiguration of classical Buddhist values fitting a liberal market in an open exchange society with generously "open hermeneutics" and an accessible universal grammar. But individual actors and networks of important people have also been the building blocks of modern Buddhism, paving the way for global accessibility. Anagarika Dharmapala, D. T. Suzuki, Thich Nhat Hanh, and Dalai Lama were "trailblazers" as principal nodes in the networks of actors paving the way for the spread of Buddhism.[33] Likewise, Tibetan lamas, Zen roshis, and spiritual leaders for new Buddhist groups have been paramount carriers and reformulators of Buddhism. Networks of Buddhist thinkers and missionaries, Western scholars, and spiritually inclined practitioners, such as Theosophists, have been engaged in co-creating modern and global forms of Buddhism.

Internationalization was also the context and aim of the many ecumenic initiatives and organizations. Already the Mahabodhi Society in the late 19th century was instrumental in gathering Buddhists across sectarian divisions, and organizations such as the World Fellowship of Buddhists and, more recently, World Buddhist Forum have continued such endeavors, the proliferation of which is a "significant manifestation of global and transnational forms of Buddhism."[34] Apart from international organizations, regional groups have also flourished, just like individual Buddhist groups have become global, some with higher aspirations for internationalization than others. Soka Gakkai International, Foguang Shan, Tzu Chi Foundation, Dhammakaya, and the Foundation for the Preservation of the Mahāyāna Tradition (FPMT) are some of the most successful groups, sometimes characterized as new religious movements, as opposed to the traditional groups often having more local and national interests. Some transnational groups focus on specific topics (such as education, climate, or meditation), and some initiatives are annually returning activities sponsored by the United Nations.[35]

Interreligious initiatives and transreligious encounters are other examples of initiatives characteristic of modern religion having become globally accessible, sometimes via the international Buddhist organizations. Already the famous Parliament of the World's Religions in Chicago in 1893 was an event with lasting effect, especially for the Buddhist world. Popular culture and mediatized influence in the contemporary world have brought other manifestations of transreligious dialogue, sometimes turning into new, creolized traditions. The largest number of convert Buddhists in America are Jews, hence the acronym JUBU's for the "Jewish Buddhists" who, like the many Christians practicing meditation (or "Christfulness"), or the many young Western Buddhists, being highly eclectic, inclusivist, hybrid, fluid, heterogenous, and flexible, often mix practices and beliefs across (Buddhist and other) religious traditions. When even Dalai Lama says, "don't try to use what you learn from Buddhism to be a better Buddhist; use it to be a better whatever-you-already-are," the symbolic capital of Buddhism as a symbol of world spirituality beyond religious boundaries could not be more pronounced.[36]

Buddhism's positive image was developed over a long historical process going back to the mid-19th century. The global dissemination has since then been made possible not least due to the media revolution supplementing canons and ritual texts with readily accessible images, videos, blogs, homepages, and multidimensional channels of digital communication. Buddhism has spread to the movies; it has been mediatized and popularized. Amazon.com sells popular books on Buddhism for all segments; Buddhist images with their global semiotics are for sale at varieties of shops, and commercials use Buddhism for its recognizable narratives of purity, progress, and happiness. Perhaps the most successful global manifestation of a Buddhist practice having gone "beyond Buddhism" is mindfulness. Meditation has been a key symbol of authentic Buddhism in most of its history, also in the West.[37] But the spiritualization, therapeutization, and secularization of Buddhist meditation in the form of contemporary mindfulness has reached unprecedented global relevance.

GLOCAL BUDDHISM

The question remains: is Buddhism really global? Has the general globalization process truly been embedded and embodied in the lives of living Buddhists around the globe? Has the global homogenization imperative actually reinvigorated the dynamic strings of centripetal forces behind the diversities of Buddhism? Is "global Buddhism" mainly yet another Western narrative, legitimizing a neoliberal market based on Euro-American schemes of cultural and religious patterns also?

First of all, the unilinear narrative of "the West" finding, adapting, transforming, and renewing the "Eastern Buddhism" needs supplementary corrections. Buddhism was never a passive thing to be discovered, and Buddhists were never passive objects or carriers of a religion that was mainly formed by Western intruders. It is important to underline that "Buddhist modernism was created as much in Asia as in the West."[38] Cultures and religions were severely affected by encountering Western modernity, but they were already undergoing changes before and during these encounters. Contemporary Buddhism and spirituality are as much the result of hybrid circulations and negotiated innovations as they are products of the one-way globalization process that is often narrated in and by Western frameworks. " 'Global' does not equal 'West,' for globalization processes of cultural and economic flows have markedly affected all nation-states, be they Asian, African, European, or elsewhere."[39]

However, it may be argued that some forms of Buddhism have never been global. In many places in Asia, Buddhism is very much local and does not carry the same global symbolic capital as in the West. In South Korea, Taiwan, China, Vietnam, and Japan, for instance, any talk of "cool Buddhism" as a signifier of a global brand value may sound rather off the mark for many Buddhists who have been used to seeing Christianity as inherently modern and global—or the newly invented Westernized form of Buddhism as being truly cool.[40]

Global Buddhism is also a phenomenon that is not restricted to Western default values. Buddhism has circulated, been Westernized and vernacularized, exoticized, and domesticized back to Asia in its "global forms," just like it has reached well beyond the traditional hemispheres of "East" and "West," namely Africa, Australia, and South America.[41] Some of these reformed, rearticulated manifestations have celebrated "Westernized" global Buddhism, while others have been critical of it. All, however, have actively responded to, and accommodated locally, the globalized religion. Global Buddhism has also been relativized and indigenized as *glocal Buddhism*.

One particular example of this is in the broad category of "Western Buddhism" and the concept of the "two Buddhisms." This often contested concept has been used to describe the diverse forms of Buddhist practice as seen in the immigrant (or heritage) and convert communities in mainly North America and Europe. It has often been claimed that the immigrant and heritage Buddhists, with their Asian origin as refugees, migrants, or descendants, live and practice a form of Buddhism integrating and preserving elements typical of the lived religion in Asia. The "converts," being those with a Euro-American ethnic origin, mainly use parts of Buddhism compatible with "Western" tropes, typically focusing on meditation and self-development. While the division of the two kinds of Buddhism still seems to have relevance as an explanatory model in many European countries, it has often been criticized in the United States and by American Buddhists.[42] Both the immigrant/heritage Buddhism, the convert Buddhism, and the Buddhist critique of the model are examples of glocalized Buddhist acculturation and reinterpretation, being expressions of globalization's paradoxical combination of "universalization of the particular" and "particularization of the universal."[43]

POST-GLOBAL BUDDHISM

Resistance to Western dominance and hegemonically ascribed rights to define and categorize true religion is nothing new. The 19th-century discovery and invention of other religions was not only a cultural and scholarly landmark, but also a project with a heavy political and ideological agenda. The understandable reactions of Asians (and Buddhists) against Western hegemony and Orientalism have seen a variety of manifestations, some being of a scholarly nature, others being embedded in neo-essentialized culturalism and nationalism. Buddhism has been used as a discourse legitimizing nationalism or even war in Sri Lanka, Myanmar, and Japan, and the anti-Western campaigns usually related to Islamic groups occasionally also pop up in Buddhist discourses, challenging also the combined Westernization–globalization correlation. Factions of reaction and resistance are thus potentially part of all interactional processes, including globalization. Globalization itself is a discourse of power, potentially covering cultural chauvinism.[44] However, apart from the relativization and indigenization of global processes, there seems to be a discourse specifically reacting to, and with visions of going *beyond*, globalization. What could be termed "post-global religion" is characterized by the strategic disruption of existing order, and the articulation of a re-enchanted particularity paradigm favoring the forces of centrifugal dispersion. Post-global sentiments can be seen in the reappearance of religious essentialism, whether based on nation, ethnicity, culture, race, tribe, or territory. It typically favors differentiation and adheres to transgressing or resisting the universalizing, centripetal forces of globalization. This has increasingly been articulated in North American culture wars, where religionization of political, cultural, ethnic, or gender-related identity politics has been turned into sacred authenticity claims.

Such post-global reactions seem also to be present in some (mainly North American) Buddhist discourses. Post-global Buddhism interestingly contextualizes the idea and concept of global Buddhism, yet suggests contours of overcoming and transgressing it to point in a new direction.[45] What constitutes this is twofold: an unveiling of universalized, global Buddhism as basically particularized "white" Buddhism, and an ideological shift beyond such disguised hegemony with recipes for a new diversified Buddhism.

Ann Gleig finds that Martin Baumann's use of "global Buddhism" "is insufficient to capture current developments in North American convert lineages," including the "critical turn" that she has identified in her thorough investigation of American Buddhism.[46] Here, she finds characteristics of what could be called postmodern, critical skepticism toward modern scientific rationalism, universal truth, and human progress.[47] She also links such criticism to discourses of colonialism, suggesting that postcolonial Buddhism designates a new phase of American Buddhism favoring diversity and postsecularity *beyond modernity* (which is the subtitle of her book *American Dharma*).[48] What ties together several of these critical stances is a focus on race. What has been the default understanding of contemporary Western Buddhism in its allegedly authentic and global applicability is actually, the critique goes, a very particular kind of Buddhism, namely a middle- and upper-class, white Buddhism.[49] White lamas and roshis teaching Buddhism do not represent "objective, authentic Buddhism," but are entangled in particularized codes as much as any other "cultural version" of Buddhism. Mindfulness is an illustrative example of such "whitewashing," since "the vast majority of information about mindfulness is disseminated by white people, in media venues controlled by white people, for the primary consumption of white people."[50] Mindfulness has, such as yoga, tantra, and other treasures from the Asian spiritual traditions, been culturally appropriated by white, privileged culture and commercialized by industries playing by the rules of globalization, thus sometimes being derogatively termed "McMindfulness." What Ann Gleig characterizes as American trends *after* Buddhist modernism—postmodern, postcolonial, and postsecular Buddhism—and what I suggest to be designated as "post-global Buddhism" is a "shift in focus from the individual to the collective, the internal to the external."[51] It reflects an emphasis "on an embodied and engaged rather than a transcendent approach to Buddhist practice," and an LGBTQI sangha's "embrace of diversity and intersectionality" reflecting "the wider cultural shift from the modern to postmodern, in which modern liberal goals of assimilation were displaced in favor of a postmodern and postcolonial affirmation of difference"[52] in which "racial diversity and inclusion work replaces a modernist narrative of universalism with a postmodern one of cultural particularity."[53]

The ideals of global Buddhism honouring universal truths, hermeneutical openness, and circular interaction transgressing ethnicity, gender, and nation have thus been exposed as culturally embedded in particularism and dressed in hegemonic garments. Postglobal Buddhism is critical of the grand narratives of (Western) modernity with its rationalism, universalism, and ideals of progress and the centripetal forces of globalization. It envisions itself with new practices, values, identities, and communities based on (gender and) ethnic/racial differentiation. Whether it will spread in space and time or remain limited to a local North American trend is yet to be seen. The re-culturalized differentiation of a new (and thus equally particularized) kind of postglobal Buddhism is, however, an interesting development to be continuously investigated by both scholars of Buddhism and religion.

DISCUSSION OF THE LITERATURE

Global Buddhism has been a concept integrated in much contemporary literature, though not necessarily explained or reflected upon. It has been institutionalized by, especially, the e-journal *Journal of Global Buddhism* and also *Journal of Contemporary Buddhism*, where individual articles cover a broad range of topics related to contemporary and global manifestations of Buddhism. Martin Baumann's article on the developmental stages of Buddhism from 2001 discusses and analyses the concept of "global Buddhism" and has been influential for much scholarship on the topic.[54] The concept of globalization relates to, and sometimes overlaps with, modernity and postmodernity. A work having acquired almost canonical status on Buddhism and modernity is David L. McMahan's *The Making of Buddhist Modernism*, which focuses mainly on historical contexts, while his edited volume on the same topic is a collection of articles with empirically broader perspectives, including an article by Cristina Rocha on globalization.[55] Buddhism in the West has often been identified with the vital ingredients of global Buddhism. Previously having been a minor (and even considered inferior) field, since the beginning of the 20th century it has developed into an independent scholarly field with contributions from scholars of religion, scholars of Buddhism, sociologists, and anthropologists. A major contribution was an anthology on the "Westward dharma," with examples of the dissemination of Buddhism outside Asia.[56] The transfigurations of Buddhism in America have equally been a focus area of research, not least in analyses and discussions of the (contested) concept and model of the "two Buddhisms."[57] In her analyses of the new trends of Buddhism in North America, Ann Gleig finds general critique of what was previously understood as American or even global Buddhism, pointing in new directions with more race, ethnicity, and gender-conscious Buddhist identities—a process termed "post-global Buddhism" by Jørn Borup.[58] Consciousness about not restricting global Buddhism to the West in recent years has made contributions about non-Western Buddhism part of the research on contemporary Buddhism. Local forms of Buddhism around Asian countries have been a traditional field of research for anthropologists, Buddhologists, and scholars of religion, especially the latter including comparative aspects. Michael Jerryson's edited *Handbook of Contemporary Buddhism* is a fine example of a modern handbook covering aspects of Buddhism as a lived religion around the world.[59]

Globalization is a broad concept being covered by various scholarly fields, as can be seen in *The Globalization Reader*. Roland Robertson has covered several of these, while Peter Beyer is one of the influential scholars who has focused on the connections between religion and globalization. Gregory Alles's edited volume is an overview of the study of religion in a global framework. Arjun Appadurai, Manuel A. Vásquez, and Marie Friedmann Marquardt have all theorized the field from anthropological perspectives. Marc Juergensmeyer and Wade Clark Wolf's encyclopedia and Véronique Altglas's four-volume series on the topic provide comprehensive insights into the field, while the review article by Victor Roudometof on globalization provides a well-structured introduction to the field, including references to topics such as transnationalism, spirituality, secularization, and religious studies in general. Several studies have been carried out on globalization and individual religions (e.g., Christianity, Islam, Hinduism, and of course Buddhism) and on topics related to religion (e.g., spirituality, secularization, and diaspora). Books, articles, and occasional special issues of journals investigate such topics. A special issue of the e-journal *Religions* was devoted to the study of glocal religion.

FURTHER READING

Alles, Gregory D., ed. *Religious Studies: A Global View*. London: Routledge, 2008.

Altglas, Veronique, ed. *Religion and Globalization: Critical Concepts in Social Studies*. 4 vols. London: Routledge, 2010.

Appadurai, Arjun. *Modernity at Large: Cultural Dimensions of Globalization*. Minneapolis: University of Minnesota Press, 1996.

Juergensmeyer, Marc, and Wade Clark Wolf, eds. *Encyclopedia of Global Religion*. Thousand Oaks, CA: SAGE Publications, 2011.

Lecher, Frank J., and John Boli, eds. *The Globalization Reader*. Chichester, UK: Wiley Blackwell, 2015.

Religions. Special issue: *Glocal religion*, 9 (10), 2018.

Robertson, Roland, and Jan Aart Stolte, eds. *Encyclopedia of Globalization*. New York: Routledge, 2007.

Vásquez, Manuel A., and Marie Friedmann Marquardt. *Globalizing the Sacred: Religion across the Americas*. New Brunswick, NJ: Rutgers University Press, 2003.

NOTES

1. Martin Baumann, "Global Buddhism: Developmental Periods, Regional Histories, and a New Analytical Perspective," *Journal of Global Buddhism* 2 (2001): 2.

2. Baumann, "Global Buddhism," 2; and Pew Research Center, *The Changing Global Religious Landscape* (April 5, 2017).
3. Roland Robertson, *Globalization: Social Theory and Global Culture* (London: SAGE, 1992), 8.
4. John Tomlinson, *Globalization and Culture* (Chicago: University of Chicago Press, 1992), 2.
5. Robertson, *Globalization*, 59.
6. Immanuel Wallerstein, *World-Systems Analysis: An Introduction* (Durham: Duke University Press, 2004), 23–30.
7. Tamar Hodos, ed., *The Routledge Handbook of Archaeology and Globalization* (London: Routledge, 2017).
8. Ulrich Beck, *Risk Society* (London: SAGE, 1992).
9. On arguments from supporters and skeptics, see Cees J. Hamelink, "The Elusive Concept of Globalisation," *Global Dialogue* 1, no. 1 (1999): 1–9.
10. Mark Rupert, *Ideologies of Globalization: Contending Visions of a New World Order* (London: Taylor & Francis, 2012).
11. Robertson, *Globalization*.
12. Victor Roudometof, "Globalization," in *Handbook of Religion and Society*, ed. David Yamane (New York: Springer, 2016), 508.
13. Lionel Obadia, "Globalisation and New Geographies of Religion: New Regimes in the Movement, Circulation, and Territoriality of Cults and Beliefs," *International Social Science Journal* 63 (2014): 148.
14. On the continuously expanding literature on religion and globalization, see Peter Beyer, *Religion and Globalization* (London: SAGE, 1994); Peter Beyer, *Religions in Global Society* (London: SAGE, 2006); Veronique. Altglas, *Religion and Globalization: Critical Concepts in Social Studies*, 4 vols. (London: Routledge, 2010); and Roudometof, "Globalization," 505–524.
15. Mark Juergensmeyer, "Thinking Globally About Religion," in *The Oxford Handbook of Global Religions*, ed. Mark Juergensmeyer (Oxford: Oxford University Press, 2006), 4, 5.
16. Tomoko Masuzawa, *The Invention of World Religions* (Chicago: University of Chicago Press, 2005) explores the historical and hegemonic basis of the concept of world religions. That modernity and functional differentiation (and in turn the roots of globalization) were indeed also part of non-Western history is argued in, for instance, Ugo Dessi, *The Global Repositioning of Japanese Religions: An Integrated Approach* (London: Routledge, 2017).
17. Roudometof, "Globalization," 518.
18. Joseph Tamney, "Afterword: Modernization, Globalization, and Buddhism," in *North American Buddhists in Social Context*, ed. Paul D. Numrich (Leiden: Brill, 2008), 235.
19. Jørn Borup, "Spiritual Capital and Religious Evolution: Buddhist Values and Transactions in Historical and Contemporary Perspective," *Journal of Global Buddhism* 20 (2019): 49–68.
20. Tilman Frasch, "Buddhist Councils in a Time of Transition: Globalism, Modernity and the Preservation of Textual Traditions," *Contemporary Buddhism* 14, no. 1 (2013): 41.
21. Jørn Borup, "Managing and Negotiating Asian Religious Unities and Diversities," in *The Critical Analysis of Religious Diversity*, ed. Lene Kühle, William Hoverd, and Jørn Borup (Leiden: Brill, 2018), 128–146.
22. David L. McMahan, *The Making of Buddhist Modernism* (Oxford: Oxford University Press, 2008).
23. Gananath Obeyesekere, "Religious Symbolism and Political Change in Ceylon," *Modern Ceylon Studies* 1 (1970): 43–63.
24. On Buddhism, Orientalism, and reverse Orientalism, see Jørn Borup, "Zen and the Art of Inverting Orientalism: Religious Studies and Genealogical Networks," in *New Approaches to the Study of Religion*, ed. Pages Antes, Armin W. Geertz, and Randi R. Warne (Berlin: Verlag de Gruyter, 2004), 451–487. For an example of how Western Orientalist essentializations are used in contemporary Chinese scholarship on Buddhism, see John Powers, "Tibet and China's Orientalists: Knowledge, Power, and the Construction of Minority Identity," *Journal of Global Buddhism* 19 (2018): 1–19.

25. Cristina Rocha, "Buddhism and Globalization," in Buddhism in the Modern World, ed. David McMahan (New York: Routledge, 2012), 289–303.
26. Baumann, "Global Buddhism."
27. Baumann, "Global Buddhism," 6.
28. Scott Mitchell, *Buddhism in America: Global Religion, Local Contexts* (London: Bloomsbury, 2016), 245.
29. Mitchell, *Buddhism in America*, 245.
30. Mitchell, *Buddhism in America*, 240.
31. Baumann, "Global Buddhism," 5.
32. Cameron Warner, "On the Road from Hinduism to Buddhism: Global Buddhism, the Conversion of Nepali Hindus, and What Comes Between," in *Eastspirit: Transnational Spirituality and Religious Circulation in East and West*, ed. Jørn Borup and Marianne Fibiger (Leiden: Brill, 2017), 251.
33. John Harding, "Trailblazers of Global Buddhist Networks," *Contemporary Buddhism* 17, no. 2 (2016): 393–404.
34. Brooke Schedneck, "Buddhist International Organizations," in *The Oxford Handbook of Contemporary Buddhism*, ed. Michael Jerryson (New York: Oxford University Press, 2016), 398.
35. For an overview of international Buddhist groups, see Schedneck, "Buddhist International Organizations"; see Thich Nhat Tu, ed., *Buddhism around the World* (Hanoi: Religion Publisher, 2019), for an example of a United Nations-sponsored project (the United Nations Day of Vesak) and its publication on Buddhism around the World.
36. The often-quoted passage apparently refers to a conversation with the Dalai Lama some years back, quoted also in a feelgood book on Buddhism: Robert Wright, *Why Buddhism is True: The Science and Philosophy of Meditation and Enlightenment* (New York: Simon & Schuster, 2017), xii.
37. David L. McMahan and Erik Braun, eds., *Meditation, Buddhism, and Science* (New York: Oxford University Press, 2017). Even in Pure Land Buddhism, meditation has been used (in Hawaii) as a means to attract non-Asians, see Dessi, *The Global Repositioning of Japanese Religions*, 98–130.
38. Cristina Rocha, "Buddhism and Globalization," in *Buddhism in the Modern World*, ed. David McMahan (New York: Routledge, 2012), 295.
39. Baumann, "Global Buddhism," 5.
40. Some migrant Buddhists have found a "purer" form of global Buddhism in America. Taiwanese immigrants used to see Buddhism in Taiwan as a backward folk religion (Tamney, "Afterword," 234).
41. On Buddhism "coming back" to India in its globalized forms, see Elizabeth Lane Williams-Oerberg, "Young Buddhism: Analyzing Transnational Currents of Religion through 'Youth'," in *Eastspirit*: Transnational Spirituality and Religious Circulation in East and West, ed. Jørn Borup & Marianne Qvortrup Fibiger (Leiden, the Netherlands: Brill, 2017), 255–278; and on Buddhism around the world, see Michael Jerryson, ed. *The Oxford Handbook of Contemporary Buddhism* (Oxford: Oxford University Press, 2017).
42. On the Two Buddhisms model, see Paul Numrich, "Two Buddhisms Further Considered," *Contemporary Buddhism* 4 no. 1 (2003): 55–78; on criticism of the model, see Hickey Wakoh Shannon, "Two Buddhisms, Three Buddhisms, and Racism," *Journal of Global Buddhism* 11 (2010): 1–25.
43. Robertson, *Globalization*, 178.
44. Cultural chauvinism is also one of the underlying discourses in Japanese global Buddhism, as analyzed in Dessi, *The Global Repositioning of Japanese Religions*.
45. Jørn Borup, "Who Owns Religion? Intersectionality, Identity Politics and Cultural Appropriation in Post-Global Buddhism," *Numen* 67, 2-3 (2020): 226–255.
46. Ann Gleig, *American Buddhism After Modernity* (New Haven: Yale University Press, 2019), 285.
47. Gleig, *American Buddhism*, 290.
48. Gleig, *American Buddhism*, 292ff, 298ff.

49. Richard K. Payne, "White-Washing the Buddhisms: Unacknowledged Privilege and the Making of a White-Safe Buddhism," in *Richard K. Payne* (2016, December 12).
50. Jeff Wilson, *Mindful America: The Mutual Transformation of Buddhist Meditation and American Culture* (Oxford: Oxford University Press, 2014), 64.
51. Gleig, *American Buddhism*, 154.
52. Gleig, *American Buddhism*, 5.
53. Gleig, *American Buddhism*, 173.
54. Baumann, "Global Buddhism."
55. McMahan, *The Making of Buddhist Modernism*; David L. McMahan, *Buddhism in the Modern World* (New York: Routledge, 2012); and Cristina Rocha, "Buddhism and Globalization," in *Buddhism in the Modern World*, ed. David McMahan (New York: Routledge, 2012), 289–303.
56. Charles S. Prebish and Martin Baumann, eds., *Westward Dharma. Buddhism beyond Asia* (Berkeley: University of California Press, 2002).
57. Mitchell, *Buddhism in America*; and Paul Numrich, "Two Buddhisms Further Considered," *Contemporary Buddhism* 4, no. 1 (2003): 55–78; and Hickey Wakoh Shannon, "Two Buddhisms, Three Buddhisms, and Racism," *Journal of Global Buddhism* 11 (2010): 1–25.
58. Ann Gleig, *American Buddhism After Modernity* (New Haven, CT: Yale University Press, 2019); and Jørn Borup, "Who Owns Religion?".
59. Michael Jerryson, ed., *The Oxford Handbook of Contemporary Buddhism* (New York: Oxford University Press, 2017).

Jørn Borup

BUDDHISM AND HEALING IN CHINA

BACKGROUND: INDIC VS. CHINESE TRADITIONS OF MEDICINE AND HEALING

Buddhism and healing are closely connected. Some of the earliest scriptures refer to the buddha as the "great king of physicians," and compare him to a doctor who, through the application of his doctrine, removes the poisonous arrows of the three fundamental passions: greed, hatred, and error, and thereby heals them. They also compare the foundational teachings of the four noble truths—(1) suffering; (2) the formation of suffering; (3) the cessation of suffering; (4) the path toward cessation—to the medical process: (1) diagnosis; (2) etiology; (3) therapeutics; and (4) healing.[1] This close connection between Buddhism and healing was not only on the level of analogy. The scriptures also had substantial content on Indian medical concepts and practices, such as the structure of the body, illness, etiology, ritual, and medicinal therapeutics.

The link between Buddhism and medicine played an important role in the transmission of Buddhism to the Sinophone world. Many of the missionaries who brought Buddhism to China were themselves healers or thaumaturges, and their success in healing played an important role in establishing the authority of Buddhism vis-à-vis rival indigenous religio-medical systems. It is important to keep in mind, however, that the medical doctrines and practices that were transmitted to China in piecemeal fashion between the mid-2nd and the 11th centuries CE did not constitute a unitary tradition of "Buddhist medicine." They rather consisted of unconnected, and at times contradictory, bits and pieces of information on the body and healing that stemmed from vastly different genres of texts, traditions, time periods, and geographical regions.[2]

These transmissions led to the first sustained encounter of Indian and Chinese medicine, two highly developed medical traditions with very different outlooks on body and disease. In early China, illness was caused by supernatural agency, by moral transgressions, or by imbalances of bodily and cosmic *qi* 氣, the unitary substance that forms the basis of body and external world. Diseases caused by divinities, demons, ghosts, or ancestors were averted by means of ritual healing—pacifying, warding off, or driving away the offending spirit with sacrifices, exorcisms, incantations, talismans, or by means of negotiation effected by ritual specialists. Sickness due to moral transgressions was remedied by ritual repentance. Depletion of the body's vital *qi*, which left the body vulnerable to the invasion of environmental pathogens, such as wind, cold, or heat, was prevented by jealously guarding one's vitality through the arts of nourishing life (*yangsheng* 養生), consisting of dietetic regimen and yogic exercise, while imbalances of bodily and cosmic *qi* were harmonized by fine-tuning one's bodily essences to the seasonal changes of cosmic *qi*. By safeguarding and nurturing one's bodily *qi* one could live out one's lifespan to the fullest without falling prey to illness or infirmity.[3]

Conceptions of illness causation by supernatural agency and moral transgression in Indian Buddhism differed from those of pre-Buddhist China. Where Chinese might have worried about a disgruntled ancestral spirit, Indian Buddhists feared hungry ghosts; where karmic diseases of Buddhists were occasioned by misdeeds committed in a prior incarnation, Daoists remembered and repented for the sins committed in the present life. By and large, however, the practices of Chinese and Indic Buddhist ritual medicine were compatible enough that they fused into a multitude of hybrid Buddho-Daoist practices. Intense competition for hegemony led to extensive borrowing, and so, as a result, medieval Buddhist and Daoist ritual healing, as well as the hagiographies of Buddhist healers and indigenous thaumaturges, began to look much alike.[4]

Indic and Chinese conceptions of the body were less congenial. Where Chinese imagined the body to consist of precious, unitary *qi*, Indians saw it as an assemblage of mutually conflicting elements, pathogenic body fluids and winds (Skt. *doṣa*), and loathsome, rotting body parts (see section "Physiology and Etiology"). In place of the Chinese ideal of longevity, and a life without disease and the complaints of aging, Buddhism posits the inevitability of suffering sickness, old age, and death. As the *Great Treatise on the Perfection of Wisdom* (Skt. *Mahāprajñāpāramitāśāstra*, Ch. *Da zhi du lun* 大智度論, T. 1509: 131b) puts it:

> The body is never without illness, because it is an assemblage of four great elements (Skt. *mahābhūta*, Ch. 四大) that are naturally at variance and contending with one another. An ulcer is never without pain; it can be ameliorated but not cured by a medicinal unguent. The same is true for the human body: always ill, it demands constant attention; with care it can live, deprived of care it will die.[5]

In such a vision, it is impossible to safeguard the body from disease and decay, because the body itself is composed of pathogenic substances and decaying matter. Chinese translations of Indic bodily structures and processes of illness formation thus used either foreign, "exoticizing" vocabulary to capture the novel Indian ideas, or tapped into the meaning of indigenous medical conceptions that created resonances with existing conceptions of body.[6] In the long run, however, this practice did not give rise to the same extent of hybridity as in the case of ritual healing and hagiography. Even major synthetic creations, such as Zhiyi's 智顗 (538–597) discourse on illness and healing, discuss Indic and Chinese etiologies and healing practices separately, and do not create novel hybrid forms. After the medieval period, Chinese Buddhist monastics reverted to practicing traditional Chinese medicine without recourse to Indic medical ideas (see the section "Influence on Chinese Medicine").

PHYSIOLOGY AND ETIOLOGY

Physiology: Elements and Body Parts. Buddhists understand body and cosmos to be aggregates of separate elements (Skt. *mahābhūta, dhātu,* Ch. *da* 大, *jie* 界). Usually, the number of elements is held to be four: "earth" (Skt. *pṛthivī,* Ch. *tu* 土), "water" (Skt. *ap,* Ch. *shui* 水), "fire" (Skt. *tejas,* Ch. *huo* 火), and "wind" (Skt. *vāta, vāyu,* Ch. *feng* 風). Sometimes the number of elements is augmented to five or six, by adding "space" (Skt. *ākāśa*; Ch. *kong* 空) and "consciousness" (Skt. *vijñāna*; Ch. *shi* 識).[7]

The elements are correlated with specific components of the body (Skt. *dhātu,* Ch. *jie* 界). The earth element is associated with solid body parts; the water element is associated with fluid body parts; the fire element is associated with all that was held to be "hot" (such as digestion, imagined as a process of cooking), and all that is related with motility; the wind element is associated with breathing; the space element with orifices; and the consciousness element with sensory perception. A representative discourse on the discrimination of the six elements can be found in the *Great Jewel Heap Sūtra* (Skt. *Mahāratnakūṭa Sūtra,* Ch. 大寶積經; T. 310: 414).[8]

The components of the body are enumerated in set lists, such as "head-hair, body-hair, nails, teeth, skin, flesh, sinews, bone, kidneys, heart, liver, lungs, large intestines, small intestines, spleen, stomach, faeces, brain and brainstem, tears, sweat, nasal mucus, saliva, pus, blood, sweat, fat, marrow, drool, bile, and urine" (髮, 毛, 爪, 齒, 麁細薄膚, 皮, 肉, 筋, 骨, 心, 腎, 肝, 肺, 大腸, 小腸, 脾, 胃, 摶糞, 腦及腦根, 淚, 汗, 涕, 唾, 膿, 血, 肪, 髓, 涎, 膽, 小便) in the *Sūtra on the Bases of Mindfulness* (Pāli *Satipaṭṭhānasutta* M. 10; *Nianchu jing* 念處經, T. 26: 582b–584b).[9] These lists tend to be found in the context of disquisitions on "impurity meditation" (Skt. *aśubha-bhāvanā*; Ch. *bujingguan* 不淨觀), which instruct monks to contemplate the emptiness, impermanence, and impurity of the physical body. They do so by concentrating on the nine stages of a decomposing corpse (taking as their object of meditation an actual corpse on a charnel ground, or an image of a skeleton), or by visualizing their own bodily components as filthy and repulsive.[10]

Pathogenesis: Elements and Doṣa. The elements of the body are mutually antagonistic, and inherently instable. Famously, they are also compared to four poisonous snakes that are placed in the same basket (the body). According to one theory of illness causation, diseases are caused by imbalanced, or deranged, elements: 101 diseases are caused by deranged earth elements, 101 diseases are caused by deranged water elements, 101 diseases are caused by deranged fire elements, and 101 diseases are caused by deranged wind elements—adding up to the total number of 404 diseases.[11]

According to another theory of illness causation, diseases are caused by the three or four *doṣa* (literally, Skt. *doṣa* means "fault"): wind (Skt. *vāta*; Ch. 風), bile (Skt. *pitta*; Ch. 熱), phlegm (Skt. *ślesman, kapha*; Ch. *tan* 痰), and their "combination" (Skt. *sannipāta*; Ch. *zabing* 雜病, *dengfengbing* 等分病, *zongjibing* 總集病), consisting of a combination of wind, bile, and phlegm. These three or four *doṣa* closely correspond to the three *doṣa* (Skt. *tridoṣa*) of the Āyurvedic classics. In the earliest Pāli Buddhist texts, the *doṣa* exclusively act as pathogens, while in later texts they act both as pathogenic agents and as basic constituents of the body.[12]

It is clear that the ternary scheme of the three *doṣa* (Skt. *tridoṣa*) and the quaternary scheme of the elements were originally independent of each other. They were subsequently connected in the commentarial literature of the *Vibhāṣā* and the *Kośa*, in Mahāyāna sutras, and in native Chinese commentaries through various theories of correspondence between *doṣa* and elements.[13] Out of these, the theory that a *doṣa* emerges as a result of a pathogenic augmentation of its corresponding element (i.e., an augmentation of the fire element causes bile, an augmentation of the wind element causes wind, an augmentation of the earth element causes the "combination" of wind, bile, and phlegm) was commonly adopted in Chinese Buddhist texts.[14]

The Chinese terminology that is used to translate the *doṣa*, especially of bile and phlegm, varies considerably: translations for bile include "yellow" (*huang* 黃), "yellow water" (*huangshui* 黃水), "yellow heat" (*huangre* 黃熱), "yellow phlegm" (*huangtan* 黃痰), and "gall" (*dan* 膽), while translations for phlegm include "cold" (*han* 寒), "cold" (*leng* 冷), "water" (*shui* 水), "lung" (*fei* 肺), and "phlegm" (*tan* 痰).[15] While it is clear that most of these terms correspond rather closely to the terminology of indigenous Chinese medicine, scholars disagree on the reasons for the variations and shifts in the Chinese terminology. Some argue that they reflect an inherent inability of early Chinese translators to grasp the Indic elemental conception of the body. Others think that the variations are due to intentional and strategic translation decisions made by particular individuals with the aim of popularizing Buddhism in China. Yet others have suggested that the shifts reflect the changing meaning of the *doṣa* in India, faithfully rendered into Chinese by translators (these different positions are set forth in "Discussion of the Literature").

Both elements and *doṣa* are distinguished from each other by hot, cold, dry, or wet qualities, and they are associated with corresponding (hot, cold, dry, and wet) seasons and climates. The *Sūtra of Golden Light* (Skt. *Suvarṇaprabhāsottamasūtra*; Ch. *Jinguang mingjing* 金光明經, T. 663.15; T. 664.20; T. 665.24), for example, states that wind illnesses arise in summer, bile illnesses arise in autumn, phlegm illnesses arise in spring, and combination illnesses arise in winter. Consequently, specific diseases can be prevented or treated with medicinal drugs and foods whose flavors counteract or complement the qualities of the respective *doṣa* and season that has caused them. In other words, in spring one should eat astringent, hot, and pungent foods; in summer, one should eat oily, hot, salty, and sour foods; in autumn, one should eat cold, sweet, and oily foods; and in winter, one should eat sour, astringent, oily, and sweet foods.[16] Clarified butter, fresh butter, oil, honey, and molasses, as well as roots, herbs, fruits, salts, and various fats are among the medicinal foods that are most frequently mentioned.[17]

Chinese scriptures that contain these discussions of the elements and *doṣa* are, above all, one chapter from the *Sūtra of Golden Light*;[18] the *Sūtra of Buddhist Medicine Taught by the Buddha* (*Foshuo foyi jing* 佛說佛醫經, T. 793);[19] the *Sūtra on Bathing the Sangha in the Bathhouse* (*Foshuo wenshi xiyu zhongseng jing* 佛說溫室洗浴眾僧經, T. 701; commentaries

T. 1793; T. 2780);[20] relevant passages on the elements and etiology in the *Great Treatise on the Perfection of Wisdom* (T. 1509), and in the *Flower Adornment Sūtra* (Skt. *Avataṃsakasūtra*, Ch. *Dafang guangfo huayan jing* 大方廣佛華嚴經, T. 293: 710–712);[21] and in *Āgama* collections and *Abhidharma* texts.[22]

Embryology. Another group of scriptures that contain a wealth of information on bodily structures are sutras on embryology. These are, most notably, the *Garbhāvakrāntisūtra* (T. 317; T. 310 n. 13 and n.14; T. 1451: 251a14–262a19),[23] the *Abhidharmakośabhāsya* (*Apidamo jushe lun* 阿毘達磨俱舍論, T. 1558, T. 1559),[24] and the *Sūtra on the Difficulty of Repaying the Profound Kindness of Parents Spoken by the Buddha* (*Foshuo fumu enzhong nanbao jing* 佛說父母恩重難報經, P. 3919).[25] These sutras detail the physiological and karmic conditions for conception and provide a week-by-week account of the stages of gestation, culminating in a description of birth. The role of karma in determining all aspects of rebirth, including the physical appearance of the embryo, is also expounded.[26] But the purpose of the narration is not medical. It is to illustrate the suffering and pain of rebirth, and to induce disgust with the cycle of death and rebirth in the reader. Hence the process of birth and gestation is depicted in starkly negative terms.[27] Some scholars have raised the possibility that the conceptions of gestation in these sutras may have influenced the embryological discussions in Chinese medical texts.[28] Others have noted that Indic accounts of gestation emphasize the suffering of the fetus, while Chinese receptions stress the suffering of the mother, thereby promoting filial piety.[29]

Monastic Rules on Nursing, Dietetics, and Hygiene

Vinaya. There is a major discrepancy in the discourse on medical practice in pre-Mahāyāna and Mahāyāna traditions. The Mahāyāna tradition, which dominates in China, includes medicine in the schedule of the five sciences studied at monastic universities, and regards healing as a way to extend compassion toward sentient beings. The pre-Mahāyāna tradition, by contrast, forbids the practice of medicine to the clergy, seeing it as a profession with mundane (Skt. *laukika*; Ch. *shi* 世, *shijian* 世間) instead of supramundane (Skt. *lokottara*; Ch. *chushijian* 出世間, *lishi* 離世, *dushi* 度世) goals.[30] Monks and nuns were, however, allowed to consult lay physicians, and to treat themselves, their colleagues, and their closest kin.[31] Monks, in fact, had a duty to nurse their coreligionists. This is epitomized in an oft-invoked tale from the *Dharmaguptaka vinaya*, which reappears in many other *vinayas* and is quoted in many indigenous Chinese compositions, that recounts how the Buddha comes across a sick monk who is lying in his own excrement. When the Buddha asks who looks after their sick colleague, the monks reply that no one cares for him, because he did not care for other sick monks in the past. Upon hearing this, the Buddha himself attends to the diseased monk, washing him, and arranging his bedding, and admonishes the assembly of monks to always care for the sick, urging that those who would care for the Buddha would also care for the sick.[32]

The *vinayas* (treatises of monastic discipline) describe in detail how a capable sick nurse and a good patient should behave. A capable nurse should be able to concoct medicinal broths, and not be disgusted by the excrements of the patient, while a good patient should be able to bear pain, obey the nurse, and take medications.[33] Monastic disciplinary rules also include guidelines on the kind of medicinal drugs and foods permitted for consumption by monastics, and the type of medical treatments that monks and nuns were permitted to receive. Sick monks were allowed to eat medicinal foods outside of mealtimes, consume forbidden substances (such as alcohol or animal products), and receive massages and minor surgical procedures.[34] Apart from the rules concerning the care of the sick, the *vinayas* also contain detailed rules on everyday hygienic practices, such as bathing, using the toilet, cleaning one's mouth and teeth, and cutting hair and nails.[35]

Daoxuan's Vinaya Commentary. Medieval Chinese *vinaya* commentaries, such as Daoxuan's 道宣 (596–667) *Emended Commentary on Monastic Practices from the Dharmaguptaka Vinaya* (*Sifen lü shanfan bujue xingshi chao* 四分律刪繁補闕行事鈔, T. 1804) and Changlu Zongze's (?–1107?) 長蘆宗賾 *The Rules of Purity in the Chan Monastery* (*Chanyuan qing gui* 禪苑清規, X.111), synthesized and digested information from the many *vinayas* that were circulating in China at the time. They furnish insights into which disciplinary issues were particularly important and meaningful for early medieval Chinese monastics.[36]

Daoxuan's *Emended Commentary* is among the earliest Chinese *vinaya* commentaries. Two of the commentary's chapters, "The Four Types of Medicine That May Be Used By Members of the Monastic Community" (*Siyao shoujing* 四藥受淨)[37] and "Attending to the Sick and Sending Off the Dead" (*Zhanbing songzhong* 瞻病送終),[38] are commentaries on the *Dharmaguptaka vinaya* rules on the types of medicine that are permitted for sick monastics, and on the care of the sick. Daoxuan classifies medicinal drugs into four kinds and explains in great detail which of the monastic dietary rules—such as the prohibitions against consuming alcohol, meat, or pungent foods—can be suspended in the case of illness.[39] He also exhorts the monastic community to look after the sick, referring to the above-mentioned tale from the *Dharmaguptaka vinaya* of the Buddha attending to the sick monk.[40]

Yijing's Account of Indian Monastic Practices. Another treasure trove for information on the rules and customs regarding the practice of medieval medicine and care of the body is furnished by the famous Chinese Buddhist pilgrim to medieval India, Yijing 義淨 (635–713). During his journey, Yijing studied for nine years at the renowned Buddhist university of Nālandā, and he also wrote *A Record of the Inner Law Sent Home from the South Seas* (*Nanhai jigui neifa zhuan* 南海寄歸內法傳, T. 2125).[41] Yijing was particularly interested in medicine—he had even taken up the study of Indian medicine (part of the curriculum at a Mahāyānist university) at some point. Hence, several chapters of his work are concerned with medical theories and practices. Yijing explains Indic conceptions of illness causation, and advocates the medical benefits of cleansing the stomach through purging and fasting, of taking regular baths, and of walking after a meal; he explains proper ways of taking care of one's body such as cleaning the mouth with tooth wood and using a latrine; and he describes Indic medicinal herbs, while harshly critiquing the custom of making medicines from excrement. Yijing's intent was to describe the proper conduct for monks in Indic monasteries so that it could serve as a correction and guidance for the practices of monastics in medieval China. As a result, his account now provides a rare record of both Indian and Chinese medieval medical and hygienic practices.

Ritual Healing and Hagiography

Healing Deities. The Medicine Buddha (Skt. Bhaiṣajyaguru; Ch. Yaoshi fo 藥師佛) is the most important healing deity in China. In his former life, he is said to have made twelve vows to heal those who call out, recite, remember, or hear his name. He is also believed to have the special power to bring back to life those who are on the verge of death. His worship thus promises to alleviate illness and cure suffering. Rituals for the Medicine Buddha, which are set forth in the *Bhaiṣajyaguru* sutras (T. 1331.12; T. 449; T. 450; T. 451), include the construction of altars, images, banners, and lamps, as well as the freeing of captive animals.[42] Some of the later, post-7th-century, versions of these rituals are esoteric, and incorporate the ritual chanting of *dhāraṇī* spells, mantras, and visualizations (T. 451; T. 922–928).[43]

Many aspects of Medicine Buddha worship, such as the importance of lighting lamps—and indeed the predominant association of the Medicine Buddha with healing and longevity itself—are Chinese additions to an Indic cult that had originally centered on the intermediate phase of transition between life and death, and on merit-making for the next life. Chinese Medicine Buddha worship, by contrast, aims at creating good karma for the alleviation of suffering in the here and now.[44]

Other important healing deities in China include the Bodhisattva Medicine King (Skt. *Bhaiṣajyarāja*, Ch. *Yaowang pusa* 藥王菩薩) and his brother Bodhisattva Supreme Healer (Skt. *Bhaiṣajyasamudgata*, Ch. *Yaoshang pusa* 藥上菩薩),[45] the Bodhisattva Avalokiteśvara (*Guanyin pusa* 觀音菩薩), and the Bodhisattva Samantabhadra (*Puxian* 普賢菩薩).[46] From the 7th century onward, many of the healing rituals performed in China were of esoteric or tantric nature. Hence they included the recitation of *dhāraṇī* or healing spells (*zhou* 咒, *shenzhou* 神咒), charms (*zhouyin* 咒印), and *mudrās* or ritual gestures (*yin* 印, *yinxiang* 印相),[47] as well as the use of apotropaic medicinal substances.[48]

Jīvaka Kumārabhṛta. Jīvaka Kumārabhṛta (Ch. Qipo 耆婆, or Qiyu 耆域), "King of Physicians" (*yiwang* 醫王) is the most eminent legendary physician in Buddhist context. Chinese translations of his hagiography, which contain numerous apocryphal interpolations, such as the statement that Jīvaka was born with acupuncture needles (a medical tool unknown in classical India) in his hands. The wondrous cures that are attributed to Jīvaka include trephining a skull and removing worms from the brain; cutting open an abdomen and flipping a misplaced liver; and exchanging the hearts of two patients in a miraculous open-heart surgery.[49]

There are unmistakable resemblances between the cures attributed to Jīvaka, and those attributed to the legendary Chinese physicians Bian Que 扁鵲 and Hua Tuo 華佗.[50] Though doubtless, the cures are fictional, and cannot be taken as a sign of Indian medical influence on China, the resemblances suggest Sino-Indian cross-fertilization. At the very least, the popularity of Jīvaka's biography in China—and the inclusion of some of its elements in the hagiographies of acclaimed Chinese healers—indicate that Indic medical lore was circulating in medieval China. At the same time, the Chinese versions of Jīvaka's hagiography also frame him as an exemplary Chinese physician by including numerous references to Chinese medical terminology and medical concepts.[51]

Eminent Monks: Healers and Thaumaturges. Thaumaturgy, wonderworking, and miraculous cures feature prominently in Huizhao's 慧皎 (497–554) collection of hagiographies of eminent monks, *Lives of Eminent Monks* (*Gaoseng zhuan* 高僧傳, T. 2059).[52] Composed in the well-established Chinese tradition of "anomaly tales" (*zhiguai* 志怪), the collection was popular, and widely used in the proselytization of Buddhism.[53] While healing is not the focus of the collection, many of the monks can be seen to perform spontaneous cures, such as assisting a woman in protracted labor with acupuncture; subduing demons; invoking the support of spirits, bodhisattvas and buddhas; casting spells; and wielding ritual objects in order to vanquish disease.[54] A particularly powerful monk, Zhu Fotudeng 竺佛圖澄, is even reported to have brought a dead person back to life.[55] It appears that an important function of these miracle tales was to demonstrate that Buddhist thaumaturges may be even more potent and successful in controlling the phenomenal world than indigenous experts. As in the case of Jīvaka, it is clear that extensive borrowing between the hagiographies of Daoist healers and Buddhist monks took place.

Important Syntheses

Daoshi's "Suffering of Illness". "The Chapter on the Suffering of Illness" (*Bingku pian* 病苦篇), in the Buddhist encyclopedia *A Grove of Pearls from the Garden of Dharma* (*Fayuan zhulin* 法苑珠林, T. 2122), was particularly important for shaping the Buddhist discourse on medicine and healing in China.[56] It provides a sweeping overview over all aspects of Buddhist healing the encyclopedia's author, Daoshi 道世 (?–683), considered important. It is organized according to the following subtitles: "Quoted Evidence" (*Yinzheng* 引證), summarizing the doctrine of the four elements, seasons, regimen, and causes of disease by means of quotes from the *Sūtra of Buddhist Medicine taught by the Buddha* (T. 793), and the *Great Treatise on the Perfection of Wisdom* (T. 1509); "Nursing the Sick" (*Zhanbing* 瞻病), an overview over *vinaya* rules on caring for sick monastics, complete with a reference to the above-mentioned *Dharmaguptaka vinaya* story of the Buddha's nursing of the sick monk, and Daoxuan's vision of Jetavana; "Therapies" (*Yiyao* 醫藥), a discussion of medicinal drugs and foods according to the principles of *doṣa* and flavors, relying on quotes from the *Sūtra of Golden Light* (T. 663); "Hospice" (*Anzhi* 安置), a section on how to care for the dying drawn from the *Mahāsāṃghika vinaya*; "Collecting the Thoughts" (*Liannian* 斂念), a disquisition on the importance of right thoughts at the moment of death; and "Miracle Tales" (*Ganyingyuan* 感應緣), a collection of tales of supernatural healing sourced from medieval miracle tales and hagiographies.[57]

Zhiyi's Contemplation of the "Objects of Disease". Influential systematizer and Tiantai 天台 patriarch Zhiyi wrote extensively on illness and on healing through meditation. His most substantial treatise on this topic is a chapter on contemplating the "objects of disease" (*binghuan* 病患), part of his *magnum opus*, the *Great Calming and Contemplation* (*Mohe zhiguan* 摩訶止觀, T. 1911).[58] It is complemented by two treatises: *Shorter Treatise on Śamatha and Vipaśyanā* (*Xiuxi zhiguan zuochan fayao* 修習止觀坐禪法要 [*Xiaozhiguan* 小止觀], T. 1915),[59] and *A Step-by-Step Teaching for Understanding Dhyāna-Pāramitā* (*Shi chan boluomi cidi famen* 釋禪波羅蜜次第法門 [次第禪門], T. 1916). In these treatises, Zhiyi draws on both Indic and Chinese etiologies and therapies to elucidate the origins and cures of illness. He explains the causes of sickness with Indic etiologies of the four elements, as well as with Chinese etiologies of the five viscera, with karmic retribution, wrong food, improper meditation habits, demonic infestation, and attacks from Māra. He does not only cite at length from major Mahāyāna scriptures, such as the *Vimalakirti Sūtra* (*Weimojie suo shuo jing* 維摩詰所說經, T. 457; *Weimojie jing*, T. 474; *Shuo wugoucheng jing* 說無垢稱經, T. 476) and the *Great Treatise on the Perfection of Wisdom* (T. 1509), but also from classical Chinese medical treatises, such as the *Classic of the Yellow Emperor* (*Huangdi neijing* 黃帝內經) and the *Classic of Difficult Issues* (*Nanjing* 難經). In terms of healing, he recommends the contemplation of the six breaths (*liu zhong qi* 六種氣)—an indigenous breath-healing practice—side by side with the method of the "twelve respirations" (*shi'er zhong xi* 十二種息)—a reference to an Indic breathing exercise.[60]

Influence on Chinese Medicine. By the time of the Sui and Tang dynasties (581–907), Buddhism had taken deep root in all layers of Chinese society. Consequently, Chinese physicians were well acquainted with Buddhist literature, and Indic concepts found their way into Chinese medicine. Titles referring to Indic medicine, such as "Brahman Medical Formulas" (*Poluomen yaofang* 婆羅門藥方), were housed in imperial libraries and recorded in dynastic histories, while Indic and Buddhist concepts can be found in the writings of eminent Sui and Tang physicians, such as Tao Hongjing 陶弘景 (452–536), Chao Yuanfang 巢元方 (550–630), Wang Tao 王焘(670–755), and Sun Simiao 孫思邈 (581–682).[61] Tanba Yasuyori's 丹波康頼 *Ishimpō* 醫心方 (984), Japan's oldest surviving medical text, also contains much material from Chinese Buddhist sources.[62]

Sun Simiao. A notable example of Buddhist influence in Chinese medicine can be found in the work of the celebrated physician and alchemist Sun Simiao.[63] In *Essential Formulas Worth a Thousand in Gold for Every Emergency* (*Beiji qianjing yaofang* 備急千金要方), Sun refers to the four elements and the 404 diseases,[64] "Indian" (*Tianzhuguo* 天竺国) or "Brahmanic" (*Poluomen* 婆羅門) massage techniques,[65] Buddhist spells, Sanskrit incantations, and foreign drugs.[66] Sun's treatise also includes a celebrated discussion of medical ethics that shows strong Buddhist overtones. It exhorts physicians to extend indiscriminate compassion for all those who are suffering, urges them to refrain from prescribing animal medicines, and advises them to study not only medical treatises, but also the works of Laozi, Zhuangzi, and other Daoist sages, as well as Buddhist scriptures.[67]

Ophthalmology. The influence of Indic medical theory is especially clear in the field of Chinese ophthalmology: India has a long and well-documented tradition of cataract couching, whereas classical Chinese medicine did not know of the procedure. A series of Chinese ophthalmological treatises were composed in the medieval period—*The Indian Classic Discussing the Eye* (*Tianzhu jing lun yan* 天竺經論眼), part of Wang Tao's *Formulary of Secrets and Essentials from the Outer Censor* (*Waitai miyao* 外胎迷藥, 752), *Bodhisattva Nagarjuna's Treatise on the Eyes* (*Longshu pusa yanlun* 龍樹菩薩眼論, early 9th century), and *Nagarjuna's Treatise* (*Longmu zonglun* 籠木總論, late 11th century)—contain clear signs of Indic influence, such as internal references to the four-elements theory. The titles of the works also explicitly refer to India (*Tianzhu* 天竺), and Nagarjuna (Ch. Longshu 龍樹; Longmu 籠木), to whom a chapter on eye diseases in one of the foundational Āyurvedic classics, *The Compendium of Suśṛuta* (Skt. *Suśṛuta saṃhitā*), is attributed.[68] Subsequent Chinese works, such as *Prescriptions Collected by Imperial Favour in the Tai Ping Era* (*Taiping shenghui fang* 太平聖惠方, *juan* 32–33, 992) and the *Essential Subtleties on the Silver Sea* (*Yinhai jingwei* 銀海精微), integrated Indic and Chinese conceptions of the eye.[69]

There are also numerous allusions to cataract couching as a means to lift the veil of ignorance in Buddhist texts. The *Mahāvairocana Sūtra* (*Da piluzhena chengfo shenbian jiachi jing*

大毘盧遮那成佛神變加持經, T. 848), and other tantric texts, describe an initiation ceremony that imitates the procedure of cataract couching by touching the initiand's eyes with a symbolical vajra-wand.[70]

Phlegm. The Chinese concept of phlegm (*tan* 痰) arguably represents the most significant trace of Buddhist influence on Chinese medicine. Absent in the earliest medical classics, Chinese phlegm developed between the 2nd and 6th centuries CE, almost certainly in response to Buddhist translations of the *tridoṣa*. It became one of the most important pathogens in late imperial Chinese medicine, and fundamentally changed the Chinese experience of body and illness through introducing the notion of a pathogenic body fluid into Chinese medical theory.[71]

Buddhist notions continued to influence scholarly physicians after the medieval period. One example is Song physician Chen Yan's 陳言 (1127–1279) association of sovereign fire (*junhuo* 君火) with the heart (*xin* 心), which may represent a borrowing from Buddhism.[72] Another example is the Buddhist elements in the "practice-oriented medicine" of Yu Chang 喻昌 (1585–1664), an influential physician who was also a practicing Chan Buddhist and former monk.[73] We know that during the early Qing many prominent physicians, such as Li Shizhen (1518–1593), Miao Xiyong 繆希雍 (1546–1627), Wang Kentang 王肯堂 (1549–1613), Zhao Xianke 趙獻可 (1573–1664), Li Zhongzi 李中梓 (1588–1655), and Lu Zhiyi 盧之頤 (1598–1664) also practiced Buddhism.[74] At this point, however, Buddhist influence in the work of late imperial Chinese scholarly physicians remains overlooked and understudied—an area of investigation that awaits further study.

Monastic Hospitals and Medical Care for the Laity. Buddhism has played an important role in the history of hospitals in China. Between 701 and 705, the Buddhist empress Wu Zetian 武則天 (624–705) decreed the establishment of hospitals that were to be annexed to Buddhist monasteries. They were financed through the proceeds of so-called "fields of compassion" (*beitian* 悲田), that is, lands that were allocated to the monastery. In 744, the emperor Xuanzong 玄宗 (685–762) decreed that beggars should be housed at these wards at the expense of the state. At the time of the great persecution of Buddhism in 845, the clergy was returned to lay life and monasteries were confiscated, but the hospitals were maintained under secularized administration and recovered by the clergy in subsequent years.[75]

Monastics also provided medical service to the laity by means of home visits by itinerant monks, and in clinics attached to monasteries. One of the best-known examples of the latter is the gynecological clinic run by the monks of the Bamboo Groove Monastery (*Zhulinsi* 竹林寺) of Xiaoshan 蕭山 County in Zhejiang province. The Bamboo Groove monks claim that a mysterious 10th-century visitor to the monastery left behind a medical treatise and recipe collection for women's reproductive illnesses. After these recipes were successfully used by the monks to heal local women, practicing women's medicine became an important part of the monastery's activities and sources of income. By the late Qing dynasty, the monastery laid claim to a lineage of 106 generations of monk healers.[76]

The Bamboo Grove monastery prescriptions are adaptations of well-known formulas from classical Chinese medicine, and there is no indication that they incorporated Indic healing methods or Buddhist ritual technologies. They did, however, benefit from the longstanding association between Buddhism and healing in China, and from a popular custom of women seeking the assistance of Buddhist deities for securing offspring. It has also been suggested that women were particularly attracted to Buddhist healing by dint of its karmic explanations of illness, which conferred agency and offered the possibility of self-healing to women through ritual practice.[77]

MATERIA MEDICA

Indic medicine also influenced Chinese pharmacology. Compared to the foundational pharmacopoeia, *Divine Farmer's Classic of Materia Medica* (*Shennong bencao jing* 神農本草經, 1st–2nd centuries CE) and Tao Hongjing's *Collected Annotations on the Classic of Materia Medica* (*Bencao jing jizhu* 本草經集注), the Tang period pharmacopoeia *Newly Revised Materia Medica* (*Xinxiu bencao* 新修本草, 659) and *Supplement to the Materia Medica* (*Bencao shiyi* 本草拾遺, 739) list 114 new medical substances; furthermore, pharmacopoeia that focused specifically on foreign *materia medica*, such as the no longer extant *Foreign Materia Medica* (*Hu bencao* 胡本草, 7th century), and the *Overseas Materia Medica* (*Haiyao bencao* 海藥本草) (9th–10th centuries) also began to appear.[78] It has been argued that the incorporation of opium poppy into Chinese medical practice during the Song dynasty owed much to the use of this flower in Buddhist monasteries.[79] The rise of the use of excrement-based prescriptions in Chinese medicine may likewise be due to Buddhism.[80]

DISCUSSION OF THE LITERATURE

Just over one decade ago, there was but one comprehensive discussion of Buddhism and healing in Western scholarship, Paul Demiéville's seminal entry on "Byō" ("illness") in an encyclopedia based on the Chinese Buddhist canon, *Hōbōgirin: Dictionnaire encyclopédique du Bouddhisme d'après les sources chinoises et japonaises* (1931),[81] translated into English by Mark Tatz and published as the booklet *Buddhism and Healing: Demiéville's Article "Byō" from Hōbōgirin* (1985).[82] It served as the go-to publication on any aspect of Chinese Buddhism and healing. It was supplemented by three short scholarly articles: Jean Filliozat, "La Médicine Indienne et l'expansion bouddhique en extrême Orient" (1934);[83] Paul U. Unschuld, "The Chinese Reception of Indian Medicine in the First Millennium A.D." (1979);[84] Chen Yinke's pioneering contribution on Indic elements in the figure of Hua Tuo,[85] and Raoul Birnbaum's *The Healing Buddha* (1979)—a work on the ritual and iconography associated with the Medicine Buddha.[86]

There also existed a number of Japanese reference works, Obinata Daijiō 大日方大乘, *Bukkyō igaku no kenkyū* 仏教医学の研究 (Study of Buddhist Medicine, 1965), Fukunaga Katsumi 福永勝美, *Bukkyō igaku jiten, ho yōga* 仏教 医学 事典: 補・ヨーガ (Encyclopedia of Buddhist Medicine with an Appendix on Yoga, 1980), Nihonyanagi Kenji 二本柳賢司, *Bukkyō igaku gaiyō* 佛教医学概要 (Summary of Buddhist Medicine, 1994), and one biographical collection of eminent Chinese Buddhist healers in Chinese, Fu Fang 傅芳and Ni Qing 倪青, *Zhongguo foyi renwu xiaochuan* 中國佛醫人物小傳 (Short Biographies of Chinese Buddhist Medicine Eminent Persons).[87] Chen Ming 陳明, Catherine Despeux, and Michel Strickmann have also contributed significant studies of Buddhism and healing in China.[88]

Around one decade ago, C. Pierce Salguero started to challenge and supplement earlier scholarship in his monograph entitled *Translating Buddhist Medicine in Medieval China* (2014), based on his doctoral dissertation "Buddhist Medicine in Medieval China: Disease, Healing, and the Body in Crosscultural Translation (Second to Eighth Centuries C.E.)" (2010), and later in three edited volumes, *Buddhism and Medicine: An Anthology of Premodern Sources* (2017), *Buddhism and Medicine: An Anthology of Modern and Contemporary Sources* (2020), and *Buddhist Healing in Medieval China and Japan* (2020), one special section on Buddhism and healing in *Asian Medicine* (2017), and well over a dozen scholarly articles.

Earlier scholarship on Buddhism and healing in China, exemplified by Demiéville's "Byō" and Unschuld's "Buddhism and Indian Medicine," was mainly interested in mining the Chinese canon for information on the history of Indic Buddhist healing, and in deciding the question of whether the Chinese Buddhist translation project had imported the seeds of Indo-European "analytical views of body and world" to the Sinophone world. The verdict on the latter was largely negative: mired in correlative thinking and an attributive conception of matter, Chinese translators and translations failed to convey the true meaning of Indic medical concepts, such as the *doṣa*, and therefore the impact of the Indian medical theories on traditional Chinese scholarship remained insignificant.[89]

Throughout his publications, Salguero has challenged this narrative by following a well-established trend in Buddhist studies that shifts the focus to the local reception of Buddhism in China.[90] He argues that individual authors and translators purposely and strategically rendered Indic concepts in ways that made them meaningful and attractive for their Chinese "target audience" as they were competing for clients and prestige in "selling Indian medicine" in a competitive "religio-medical marketplace." Fuzzy translations, in short, were not the result of incomprehension; they were fully intended. Moreover, the reason for the lack of an enduring influence of Indic medical conceptions in China is of a sociohistorical and sociopolitical nature rather than due to inherent incompatibilities between Indic and Chinese medical doctrines.[91]

Salguero has also critiqued earlier scholarship, including that of Demiéville, for downplaying the hybridity and the internal contradictions in Chinese Buddhist medical practices and representing them as a unitary tradition of healing. He blames these "canon-creating practices" for portraying Chinese Buddhism as a homogeneous, unified tradition, and for smoothing over vast doctrinal differences and contradictory positions on medicine and healing.[92] Salguero has further questioned the validity of the categories of religion vs. medicine that are operative in much of the scholarship on Chinese healing.[93] His questioning of the boundaries between medical and religious therapy has initiated further discussions among religious scholars and medical historians.[94]

Salguero, in turn, has been critiqued for its exclusive focus on the Chinese texts and a perplexing failure to consider Indic source materials,[95] as well as for his deployment of the notion of "Buddhist medicine." It is questionable whether the comparatively rudimentary medical content that was recorded and transmitted in Indian Buddhist scriptures is sufficiently different from Āyurveda to merit being considered an independent tradition of "Buddhist medicine," and on par with the complex scholarly traditions of Indian and Chinese medicine.[96] It is also unclear whether historic Buddhists ever considered their medicine to be different from the mainstream Indic medical traditions. In any case—and this is noted by Salguero himself—the notion of "Buddhist medicine" (Ch. *fojiao yixue* 佛教醫學) is a construct of 20th-century Chinese and Japanese Buddhist modernism.[97] As such, it may—or may not—be a useful concept for the historical analysis of Chinese Buddhism and healing.

These criticisms notwithstanding, it is beyond doubt that Salguero's work—particularly his editorial work, bibliographic surveys, and state of the field reviews—has done much to make a wide selection of primary sources available in translation, to render the field of Buddhism and medicine more accessible to non-specialist researchers, and more visible in the field of the history of medicine.[98]

ACKNOWLEDGMENTS

Work on this piece was supported by a GRF grant from the Research Grants Council of the Hong Kong Special Administrative Region, China (12607220) and a start-up grant from Hong Kong Baptist University (RC-SGT2/19-20/SOSC/002).

FURTHER READING

Birnbaum, Raoul. *The Healing Buddha*. Boulder, CO: Shambhala, 1989.

Chen, Ming 陳明. "*Zhuan nü wei nan*: Turning Female to Male, an Indian Influence on Chinese Gynaecology?" *Asian Medicine: Tradition and Modernity* 1, no. 2 (2005): 315–334.

Chen, Ming 陳明. *Zhonggu yiliao yu wailai wenhua* 中古醫療與外來文化. Beijing: Peking University Press, 2013.

Chen, Yunü 陳玉女. "Buddhism and the Medical Treatment of Women in the Ming Dynasty: A Research Note." *Nan Nü* 10 (2008): 279–303.

Demiéville, Paul. "Byō." In *Hōbōgirin* 法寶義林: *Dictionnaire encyclopédique du Bouddhisme d'après les sources chinoises et japonaises*. Vol. 3. Edited by Sylvain Levi, Takakusu Junjirō, and Paul Demiéville, 224–265. Tokyo: Maison Franco-Japonaise, 1937.

Demiéville, Paul. *Buddhism and Healing: Demiéville's Article "Byō" from Hōbōgirin*. Translated by Mark Tatz. Lanham, MD: University Press of America, 1985.

Deshpande, Vijaya, and Fan Ka Wai 范家偉. *Restoring the Dragon's Vision (Nagarjuna and Medieval Chinese Ophtalmology)*. Hong Kong: Chinese Civilisation Centre, City University of Hong Kong, 2012.

Despeux, Catherine. *Médecine, religion et société dans la Chine médiévale: Étude de manuscrits chinois de Dunhuang et de Turfan*. Paris: Collège de France, Institut des Hautes Études Chinoises, 2010.

Despeux, Catherine. "Chinese Medicinal Excrement: Is There a Buddhist Influence on the Use of Animal Excrement-Based Recipes in Medieval China?" *Asian Medicine* 12 (2017): 139–169.

Heirman, Ann, and Mathieu Torck. *A Pure Mind in a Clean Body: Bodily Care in the Buddhist Monasteries of Ancient India and China*. Gent, Belgium: Academia Press, 2012.

Köhle, Natalie. "A Confluence of Humors: Āyurvedic Conceptions of Digestion and the History of Chinese 'Phlegm' (*tan* 痰)." *Journal of the American Oriental Society* 136, no. 3 (2016): 465–493.

Lin, Hsin-yi 林欣儀. *Dealing with Childbirth in Medieval Chinese Buddhism: Discourses and Practices*. PhD dissertation, Columbia University, 2017.

Sakade, Yoshinobu 坂出祥伸. "Sun Simiao et le Bouddhisme." *Kansai Daigaku Bunka Ronshu* 42, no. 1 (1998): 81–98.

Salguero, C. Pierce. "Buddhism and Medicine in East Asian History." *Religion Compass* 8, no. 8 (2014): 239–250.

Salguero, C. Pierce. *Translating Buddhist Medicine in Medieval China*. Philadelphia: University of Pennsylvania Press, 2014.

Salguero, C. Pierce. "Reexamining the Categories and Canons of Chinese Buddhist Healing." *Journal of Chinese Buddhist Studies* 27 (2015): 35–66.

Salguero, C. Pierce. "Healing and/or Salvation? The Relationship between Religion and Medicine in Medieval Chinese Buddhism." Working Paper Series of the HCAS "Multiple Secularities—Beyond the West, Beyond Modernities" No. 4. Leipzig, 2018.

Salguero, C. Pierce. " 'A Missing Link' in the History of Chinese Medicine." *East Asian Science, Technology, and Medicine* 47 (2018): 93–119.

Salguero, C. Pierce. "This Fathom-Long Body: Bodily Materiality and Ascetic Ideology in Medieval Chinese Buddhist Scriptures." *Bulletin of the History of Medicine* 92, no. 2 (2018): 337–360.

Salguero, C. Pierce. *Buddhism and Medicine: An Anthology of Modern and Contemporary Sources.* New York: Columbia University Press, 2020.

Salguero, C. Pierce, ed. *Buddhism and Medicine: An Anthology of Premodern Sources.* New York: Columbia University Press, 2017.

Salguero, C. Pierce, and Andrew Macomber, eds. *Buddhist Healing in Medieval China and Japan.* Honolulu: University of Hawaii Press, 2020.

Scheid, Volker. "The Neglected Role of Buddhism in the Development of Medicine in Late Imperial China Viewed through the Life and Work of Yu Chang 喻昌 (1585–1664)." *Bulletin of the History of Medicine* 94 (2020): 1–28.

Strickmann, Michel. *Chinese Magical Medicine.* Stanford, CA: Stanford University Press, 2002.

Unschuld, Paul U. "The Chinese Reception of Indian Medicine in the First Millen A.D." *Bulletin of the History of Medicine* 53, no. 3 (1979): 329–345.

Wu, Yi-li 吳一立. "The Bamboo Grove Monastery and Popular Gynecology in Late Imperial China." *Late Imperial China* 21, no. 1 (2000): 41–76.

NOTES

1. Paul Demiéville, *Buddhism and Healing: Demiéville's Article "Byō" from Hōbōgirin,* trans. Mark Tatz (Lanham, MD: University Press of America, 1985), 9–17; and Marcus Bingenheimer, "Two *Sutras* on Healing and Healers from the Chinese Canon," in *Buddhism and Medicine: An Anthology of Premodern Sources,* ed. C. Pierce Salguero (New York: Columbia University Press, 2017), 163–169.
2. C. Pierce Salguero, *Translating Buddhist Medicine in Medieval China* (Philadelphia: University of Pennsylvania Press, 2014), 29–66; and Chen Ming 陳明, *Zhonggu yiliao yu wailai wenhua* 中古醫療與外來文化 (Beijing: Peking University Press, 2013).
3. Kuriyama Shigehisa, "Concepts of Disease in East Asia," in *The Cambridge World History of Human Disease,* ed. Kenneth Kiple (Cambridge, UK: Cambridge University Press, 1993), 52–59.
4. Salguero, *Translating Buddhist Medicine,* 121–140; C. Pierce Salguero, "The Buddhist Medicine King in Literary Context: Reconsidering an Early Example of Indian Influence on Chinese Medicine and Surgery," *History of Religions* 48, no. 3 (2009): 183–210; C. Pierce Salguero, " 'A Flock of Ghosts Bursting Forth and Scattering': Healing Narratives in a Sixth-Century Chinese Buddhist Hagiography," *East Asian Science, Technology, & Medicine* 32 (2010): 89–120; Christine Mollier, *Buddhism and Taoism Face to Face: Scripture, Ritual, and Iconographic Exchange in Medieval China* (Honolulu: University of Hawaii Press, 2008); Michel Strickmann, *Chinese Magical Medicine* (Stanford, CA: Stanford University Press, 2002); Edward L. Davis, *Society and the Supernatural in Song China* (Honolulu: University of Hawaii Press, 2001); Robert Ford Campany, *Signs from the Unseen Realm: Buddhist Miracle Tales from Early Medieval China* (Honolulu: University of Hawaii Press, 2012); and Joshua Capitanio, "Sanskrit and Pseudo-Sanskrit Incantations in Daoist Ritual Texts," *History of Religions* 57, no. 4 (2018): 348–405.
5. Demiéville's translation. See *Buddhism and Healing,* 19.
6. Salguero, *Translating Buddhist Medicine,* 67–102; and C. Pierce Salguero, "Mixing Metaphors: Translating the Indian Medical Doctrine Tridoṣa in Chinese Buddhist Sources," *Asian Medicine* 6, no. 1 (2010–2011): 55–74.

7. Demiéville, *Buddhism and Healing*, 73–76; Jyotir Mitra, *A Critical Appraisal of Ayurvedic Material in Buddhist Literature with Special Reference to Tripitaka* (Varanasi, India: Jyotiralok Prakashan, 1985), 40–56; Y. Karunadasa, *The Buddhist Analysis of Matter* (Hong Kong: University of Hong Kong Centre of Buddhist Studies, 2015), 21–36; and Karin Preisendanz, "Mahābhūtas," in *Brill's Encyclopedia of Hinduism*. Vol. 2, *Sacred Texts, Ritual Traditions, Arts, Concepts*, ed. Knut A. Jacobsen, Helene Basu, Angelika Malinar, and Vasudha Narayanan (Leiden, The Netherlands: Brill, 2010), 806–818.
8. For a discussion and partial translation of relevant passages, see C. Pierce Salguero, "This Fathom-Long Body: Bodily Materiality and Ascetic Ideology in Medieval Chinese Buddhist Scriptures," *Bulletin of the History of Medicine* 92, no. 2 (2018): 242–247; Paul U. Unschuld, *Medicine in China: A History of Ideas* (Berkeley and Los Angeles: University of California Press, 2010), 141; and Demiéville, *Buddhism and Healing*, 68–69. See also Fukunaga Katsumi 福永勝美 *Bukkyō igaku jiten* 仏教医学事典 (Tokyo: Yūzankaku, 1990), 37–45.
9. Closely related parallels of this list can be found in other Pāli texts and their Chinese translations. See Eric Matthew Greene, *Of Bones and Buddhas: Contemplations of the Corpse and Its Connections to Purity as Evidenced by 5th Century Chinese Meditation Manuals* (MA thesis, University of California, Berkeley, 2006), 31 n. 92; Salguero, "This Fathom-Long Body," 244; Demiéville, *Buddhism and Healing*, 68–69; Unschuld, *Medicine in China: A History of Ideas*, 141; Fukunaga, *Bukkyō igaku jiten*, 37–45. The lists predate Buddhism and the association of bodily components with the six elements. They go back as far as the Vedas, where they were compiled in the context of sacrifices. Kenneth Zysk, "The Evolution of Anatomical Knowledge in Ancient India, with Special Reference to Cross-Cultural Influences," *Journal of the American Oriental Society* 106 (1986): 689; Reinhold F. G. Müller, "Zur anatomischen Systematik im Yajus," *Sudhoffs Archiv für Geschichte der Medizin und der Naturwissenschaften* 27 (1934): 28; Michael Radich, *The Somatics of Liberation: Ideas about Embodiment in Buddhism from Its Origins to the Fifth Century CE* (PhD dissertation, Harvard University, 2007), 1402, 1405–1407; and Philipp Maas, "The Concept of the Human Body and Disease in Classical Yoga and Āyurveda," *Wiener Zeitschrift für die Kunde Südasiens* 51 (2007–2008): 144 n. 69.
10. For the Chinese context, see Eric Matthew Greene, "Healing Breaths and Rotting Bones: On the Relationship between Buddhist and Chinese Meditation Practices during the Eastern Han and Three Kingdoms Period," *Journal of Chinese Religions* 42, no. 2 (2014): 145–184; Eric Matthew Greene, "Death in a Cave: Meditation, Deathbed Ritual, and Skeletal Imagery at Tape Shotor," *Artibus Asiae* 73, no. 2 (2013): 265–294; Greene, *Of Bones and Buddhas*. For the South Asian context, see K. L. Dhammajoti, "The *Aśubhā* Meditation in the Sarvāstivāda," *Journal of the Center for Buddhist Studies (Sri Lanka)* 7 (2009): 248–295; Stephen Collins, "The Body in Theravāda Buddhist Monasticism," in *Religion and the Body*, ed. Sarah Coakley (Cambridge, UK: Cambridge University Press, 1997), 192–194; and Bhikkhu Anālayo, "Satipaṭṭhāna-sutta," in *Oxford Bibliographies*, March 31, 2016.
11. *Saṃyuktāgama* 雜阿含經 T. 99: 313b–c; T. 205: 503a; *Ekottarikāgama* 增壹阿含經 T. 125: 670a. See Demiéville, *Buddhism and Healing*, 71–73.
12. Hartmut Scharfe, "The Doctrine of the Three Humors in Traditional Indian Medicine and the Alleged Antiquity of Tamil Siddha Medicine," *Journal of the American Oriental Society* 119, no. 4 (1999): 625–629.
13. See details in Demiéville, *Buddhism and Healing*, 71–76.
14. The connection between *doṣa* and elements was not yet made in the earliest Pāli texts. See Kenneth G. Zysk, "Doṣas by the Numbers: Buddhist Contributions to the Origins of the Tridoṣa-theory in Early Indian Medical Literature with Comparisons to Early Greek Theories of the Humours," *History of Science in South Asia* 9 (2021): 1–29.
15. See the table in Endō, Jirō, Nakamura Teruko, Yamaki Hidehiko, Miyamoto Hirokazu 遠藤次郎、中村輝子、八巻英彦、宮本浩和, "Tan no kigen" 痰の起源, *Nihon Ishigaku Zasshi* 39, no. 3 (1993): 335; also found in Natalie Köhle, "A Confluence of Humors: Āyurvedic Conceptions of Digestion and

the History of Chinese 'Phlegm' (*tan* 痰)," *Journal of the American Oriental Society* 136, no. 3 (2016): 475; and Salguero, "Mixing Metaphors," 64–65.

16. A translation of T. 663.15 and T. 665.24 can be found in C. Pierce Salguero, "Understanding the Doṣa: A Summary of the Art of Medicine from the Sūtra of Golden Light," in *Buddhism and Medicine* (2017), ed. Salguero, 30–40; and C. Pierce Salguero, "'On Eliminating Disease': Translations of the Medical Chapter from the Chinese Versions of the *Sutra of Golden* Light," *eJournal of Indian Medicine* 6 (2013): 21–43. See also Demiéville, *Buddhism and Healing*, 72.
17. Demiéville, *Buddhism and Healing*, 69–71.
18. Translated in Salguero, "Understanding the Doṣa"; Salguero, "On Eliminating Disease"; R. E. Emmerick, *The Sūtra of Golden Light* (*Suvarṇaprabhāsottamasūtra*) (Oxford: Pali Text Society, 2004); Prods Oktor Skjaervø, *This Most Excellent Shine of Gold, King of Kings of Sutras: The Khotanese Suvarṇabhāsottamasūtra* (Cambridge, MA: Harvard University Department of Near Eastern Languages and Civilizations, 2004); and Johannes Nobel, "Ein alter medizinischer Sanskrit-Text und seine Deutung," *Journal of the American Oriental Society*, Supplement 11 (1951).
19. Translated in Unschuld, *Medicine in China: A History of Ideas*, 309–314; and Satiranjan Sen, "Two Medical Texts in Chinese Translation," *Visva-Bharati Annals* 1 (1945): 70–95.
20. Translated in C. Pierce Salguero, "Karma in the Bathhouse: The Sūtra on Bathing the Sangha in the Bathhouse," in *Buddhism and Medicine* (2017), ed. Salguero, 84–91. Discussed in Ann Heirman and Mathieu Torck, *A Pure Mind in a Clean Body: Bodily Care in the Buddhist Monasteries of Ancient India and China* (Gent, Belgium: Academia Press, 2012), 33–35.
21. Partially translated in William J. Giddings, "Liberating the Whole World: Sudhana's Meeting with Samantanetra from the Sūtra of the Entry into the Realm of Reality," in *Buddhism and Medicine* (2017), ed. Salguero, 92–102.
22. Demiéville, *Buddhism and Healing*, 69–71.
23. Translated into English in Amy Paris Langenberg, "Fetal Suffering in the Descent into the Womb Sūtra," in *Buddhism and Medicine* (2017), ed. Salguero, 41–48; Robert Kritzer, *Garbhāvakrāntisūtra: The Sūtra on Entry into the Womb* (Tokyo: International Institute for Buddhist Studies, 2014); and into German in Franz Huebotter, *Die Sūtra Über Empfängnis und Embryologie* (Tokyo: Mitteilungen der Deutschen Gesellschaft für Natur- und Völkerkunde Ostasiens, 1932).
24. Translated into French by Louis de la Vallée Poussin, *L'Abhidharmakośa de Vasubandhu*, new ed. Mélanges Chinois et Bouddhiques 16 (Brussels: Institut Belge des Hautes Études Chinoises, 1971), and into English by Leo Pruden, *Abhidharma Kosha Bhashyam*, 4 vols (Berkeley, CA: Asian Humanities Press, 1988–1990). Robert Kritzer, "Childbirth and the Mother's Body in the Abhidharmakośabhāsya and Related Texts," in *Indo tetsugaku bukkyō shisō ron shū: Mikogami Eshō kyōju shōju kinen ronshū* インド哲学佛 教思想論集: 神子上恵生教授頌寿記念論集, ed. Mikogami Eshō 神子上恵生 (Kyoto: Nagatabunshodō, 2004), 1085–1109.
25. Discussed in Jessey Choo, "That 'Fatty Lump': Discourses on the Fetus, Fetal Development, and Filial Piety in China before the Eleventh Century CE," *Nannü* 14, no. 2 (2012): 207 n. 45.
26. See the synoptic discussion of Chinese embryological literature in Anna Andreeva and Dominic Steavu, "Introduction: Backdrops and Parallels to Embryological Discourse and Reproductive Imagery in East Asian Religions," in *Transforming the Void: Embryological Discourse and Reproductive Imagery in East Asian Religion*, ed. Anna Andreeva and Dominic Steavu (Leiden, The Netherlands, and Boston: Brill, 2016), 19–26.
27. Discussed and summarized in Robert Kritzer, "Life in the Womb: Conception and Gestation in Buddhist Scripture and Classical Indian Medical Literature," in *Imagining the Fetus: The Unborn in Myth, Religion, and Culture*, ed. Vanessa R. Sasson and Jane Marie Law (Oxford and New York: Oxford University Press, 2009), 73–89. See also Robert Kritzer, "Semen, Blood, and the Intermediate Existence," *Journal of Indian and Buddhist Studies* 46, no. 2 (1998): 30–36.

28. Li Qinpu 李勤璞, "Yindu qiri zhutailun ji qi zai hanyi de yige biaoxian" 印度七日住胎論及其在漢醫的一個表現, *Zhongyang Yanjiuyuan Lishi Yuyan Yanjiusuo Jikan* 77, nos. 3–4 (2006): 517–590, 729–798; Chen Ming, "*Zhuan nü wei nan*: Turning Female to Male, an Indian Influence on Chinese Gynaecology?" *Asian Medicine: Tradition and Modernity* 1, no. 2 (2005): 315–334; and Chen Ming, "'Shiyue chengtai' yu 'qiri yibian': Yindu taixiang xueshuo de fenglei ji qi dui woguo de yingxiang" "十月成胎" 與 "七日一變": 印度胎相學說的分類及其對我國的影響, *Guoxue Yanjiu* 13 (2004): 33–50. Catherine Despeux draws attentions to Chan Buddhist antecedents of embryological imagery in inner alchemy (*neidan* 內丹) texts. Catherine Despeux, "Symbolic Pregnancy and the Sexual Identity of Taoist Adepts," in *Transforming the Void*, ed. Andreeva and Steavu, 152.
29. Lin Hsin-yi, *Dealing with Childbirth in Medieval Chinese Buddhism: Discourses and Practices* (PhD dissertation, Columbia University, 2017); and Choo, "That 'Fatty Lump,"' 219–221.
30. See C. Pierce Salguero, "Healing and/or Salvation? The Relationship between Religion and Medicine in Medieval Chinese Buddhism," Working Paper Series of the HCAS "Multiple Secularities: Beyond the West, Beyond Modernities" No. 4 (Leipzig, 2018), 9–10, 9 n.13.
31. Demiéville, *Buddhism and Healing*, 35–41.
32. T. 1804, 40: 143a28–b11.
33. Demiéville, *Buddhism and Healing*, 31–35.
34. See Demiéville, *Buddhism and Healing*, 31–41. The landmark study on the medical content of the *vinayas* remains Kenneth Zysk, *Asceticism and Healing in Ancient India: Medicine in the Buddhist Monastery* (Delhi: Motilal Banarsidass, 1998), 95–159. This study is based on the Pāli Vinaya, which was not translated into Chinese. Its contents were available in China in the form of a translation of commentary on the Pāli *Vinaya* (T. 1462). This commentary is available in an English translation by P. V. Bapat and A. Hirakawa, *Shan-chien-p'i-p'o-sha: A Chinese Version by Sanghabhadra of Samantapāsādikā, Commentary on Pali Vinaya* (Pune, India: Bhandarkar Oriental Research Institute, 1970). For translations of excerpts of medical content from other *vinayas* that were translated into Chinese, see C. Pierce Salguero, "Rules on Medicines from the Five-Part *Vinaya* of the Mahīśāsaka School," in *Buddhism and Medicine* (2017), ed. Salguero, 125–129; Jan Jaworski, "La section des remèdes dans le *Vinaya* des Malūśāsaka et dans le *Vinaya* pali," *Rocznik Orjentalistyczny* 5 (1927): 92–101; Robban Toleno, "An Explanation of the Rules on Medicine Excerpted from the *Mahāsāṃghika Vinaya*" (*Mohesengqilü* 摩訶僧祇律, T. 1425), in C. Pierce Salguero, Robban Toleno, William J. Giddings, Joshua Capitanio, and Marcus Bingenheimer, "Medicine in the Chinese Buddhist Canon: Selected Translations," *Asian Medicine* 12 (2017): 281–283; and for a summary on the consumption of alcohol in Chinese monastic settings, see James A. Benn, *Tea in China: A Religious and Cultural History* (Honolulu: University of Hawaii Press, 2015), 55–59.
35. A comprehensive study of the subject of Indian and Chinese monastic bodily care is furnished by Heirman and Torck, *A Pure Mind in a Clean Body*. For translations of excerpts on toilet practices from the *Mūlarsarvāstivāda Vinaya*, the *Emended Commentary on Monastic Practices from the Dharmaguptaka Vinaya*, and the *Imperial Edition of Baizhang's Rule of Purity* (*Chixiu baizhang qinggui* 敕修百丈清規 T. 2025) see Ann Heirman and Mathieu Torck, "Toilet Care in Buddhist Monasteries: Health, Decency, and Ritual," in *Buddhism and Medicine* (2017), ed. Salguero, 137–144; John Kieschnick, "A History of the Bathhouse in Chinese Buddhist Monasteries," in *Belief, Practice and Cultural Adaptation: Papers from the Religious Section of the International Conference on Sinology*, vol. 1, ed. Paul Katz and Liu Shufen 劉淑芬 (Taipei: Academia Sinica, 2013), 107–138. For a translation of the *Sūtra on Bathing the Sangha in the Bathhouse*, see Salguero, "Karma in the Bathhouse."
36. For an overview on the development Chinese monastic regulations, see Yifa, *The Origins of Buddhist Monastic Codes in China: An Annotated Translation and Study of the Chanyuan Qinggui* (Honolulu: University of Hawaii Press, 2002), 3–52.
37. Discussed and partially translated in Jonathan Pettit, "Food and Medicine in the Chinese Vinayas: Daoxuan's *Emended Commentary on Monastic Practices from the Dharmaguptaka vinaya*," in *Buddhism*

and Medicine (2017), ed. Salguero, 130–136. I gratefully acknowledge Marcus Bingenheimer's help with translating the term *shoujing* 受淨 ("to use," "ritually accept"). On the topic of medicine and monastic rules, see the work of Liu Shufen: "Jielü yu yangsheng zhi jian: Tang-Song siyuan zhong de wanyao, ruyao he yaojiu" 戒律與養生之間: 唐宋寺院中的丸藥、乳藥和藥酒, *Bulletin of the Institute of History and Philology* 77 (2006): 357–400; Liu Shufen, "Tang, Song siyuan zhong de cha yu tangyao" 唐、宋寺院中的茶與湯藥, *Yanjing Xuebao* 19 (2006): 67–97; and Liu Shufen, "Chanyuan qinggui zhong suojian de chali yu tangli" 《禪苑清規》中所見的茶禮與湯禮, *Bulletin of the Institute of History and Philology* 78 (2007): 629–670.

38. Discussed and partially translated in Koichi Shinohara, "The Moment of Death in Daoxuan's *Vinaya* Commentary," in *The Buddhist Dead: Practices, Discourses, Representations*, ed. Bryan J. Cuevas and Jacqueline I. Stone (Hawaii: University of Hawaii Press, 2007), 105–133.
39. T. 1804, 40: 117c–119a. Translated in Pettit, "Food and Medicine," 132–135.
40. T. 1804, 40: 143a28–b11; Shinohara, "The Moment of Death," 107–108; and Salguero, *Translating Buddhist Medicine*, 105–109.
41. Li Rongxi, trans., *Buddhist Monastic Traditions of Southern Asia: A Record of the Inner Law Sent Home from the South Seas* (Berkeley, CA: Numata Center for Buddhist Translation and Research, 2000). Takakusu Junjirō, trans., *A Record of the Buddhist Religion as Practised in India and the Malay Archipelago (AD 671–695)* (New Delhi: Munshiram Manoharlal, 1998), originally published in 1896; Christoph Kleine, "Health Care in Indian Monasteries: Selections from Yijing's Record of the Inner Law Sent Home from the Southern Seas," in *Buddhism and Medicine* (2017), ed. Salguero, 145–159 (a translation of chapters 27–29). Discussion in Salguero, *Translating Buddhist Medicine*, 112–116; D. V. S. Reddy, "Glimpses into the Practice and Principles of Medicine in Buddhistic India in the 7th Century A.D. Gleaned from 'The Records of Buddhist Religion' by the Chinese Monk I-Tsing," *Bulletin of the Indian Institute of History and Medicine* 17 (1938): 155–167; and G. A. Liétard, "Le pèlerin bouddhiste choinois I-Tsing et la médecine de l'Inde au VIIe siècle," *Bulletin de la Société FrançAise D'histoire de la Médecine* 1 (1902): 472–487.
42. Discussed in Raoul Birnbaum, *The Healing Buddha* (Boulder, CO: Shambhala, 1989), 84–87; originally published in 1979. Translations of T. 449–451 are found in 149–217. See also the translation of an Indian version of the Bhaiṣajyaguru sutra by Gregory Schopen, "Help for the Sick, the Dying, and the Misbegotten: A Sanskrit Version of the Sūtra of Bhaiṣajyaguru," in *Buddhism and Medicine* (2017), ed. Salguero, 235–251; discussed by Birnbaum, *The Healing Buddha*, 52–76; Raoul Birnbaum, "Chinese Buddhist Traditions of Healing and the Life Cycle," in *Healing and Restoring: Health and Medicine in the World's Religious Traditions*, ed. Lawrence E. Sullivan (New York and London: Macmillan, 1989), 155–160 (also available as appendix to the 1989 edition of Birnbaum, *The Healing Buddha*, 238–263); Kuo Li-ying, *Confession et contrition dans le bouddhisme chinois du Ve au Xe siècle* (Paris: École Française d'Extrême-Orient, 1994), 149–167; and Paul Pelliot, "Le Bhaiṣajyaguru," *Bulletin de l'École Française d'Extrême-Orient* 3 (1903): 33–37.
43. T. 924A, translated by C. Pierce Salguero, "Healing Dhāraṇīs: A Collection of Medieval Spells from the Taishō Tripiṭaka," in *Buddhism and Medicine* (2017), ed. Salguero, 299–301; T. 922 and T. 924A, partially translated by Birnbaum, *The Healing Buddha*, 87–90, and discussed 69–72, 87–90.
44. See especially the argument made by Shi Zhiru, "Lighting Lamps to Prolong Life: Ritual Healing and the Bhaiṣajyaguru Cult in Fifth- and Sixth-Century China," in *Buddhist Healing in Medieval China and Japan*, ed. C. Pierce Salguero and Andrew Macomber (Hawaii: University of Hawaii Press, 2020), 91–117. See also Schopen, "Help for the Sick," 235–236; and Michel Strickmann, "The Consecration Sūtra: A Buddhist Book of Spells," in *Chinese Buddhist Apocrypha*, ed. Robert E. Buswell, Jr. (Honolulu: University of Hawaii Press, 1990), 75–118.
45. *Sūtra on the Contemplation of the Two Bodhisattvas, King of Medicine and Supreme Medicine* (*Foshuo guan yaowang yaoshang erpusa jing* 佛說觀藥王藥上二菩薩經) T. 1161. Translated in Birnbaum, *The*

Healing Buddha, 115–148; *Lotus Sūtra* (*Fahuajing* 法華經) T. 262.23; T. 263.10; T. 264.22, translated in Burton Watson, *The Lotus Sūtra* (New York: Columbia University Press, 1993), 280–289; Leon Hurvitz, *Scripture of the Lotus Blossom of the Fine Dharma (The Lotus Sūtra)* (New York: Columbia University Press, 2009), 269–276; and discussed in Birnbaum, *The Healing Buddha*, 25–51.

46. T. 1059–1060. T. 1059 is translated by Unschuld, *Medicine in China: A History of Ideas*, 314–321; and Sen, "Two Medical Texts," 85–95; T. 1060 is translated by William J. Giddings, "The Sūtra on the Dhāraṇī of the Vast, Complete, and Unobstructed Great Compassion of the Bodhisattva Avalokiteśvara with a Thousand Hands and a Thousand Eyes," in *Buddhism and Medicine* (2017), ed. Salguero, 252–285; and Maria Reis-Habito, *Das Dhāraṇī des grossen Erbarmens des Bodhisattva Avalokiteśvara mit tausend Händen und Augen: Übersetzung und Untersuchung ihrer textlichen Grundlage sowie Erforschung ihres Kultes in China* (Nettetal, Germany: Steyler Verlag, 1993).
47. See especially Strickmann, *Chinese Magical Medicine*. See also the translations in Salguero, "Healing Dhāraṇīs," 292–299; Joshua Capitanio, " 'The Ritual Altar of Kuṇḍalī Vajra for Treating Illnesses' from the Collected Dhāraṇī Sutras," in *Buddhism and Medicine* (2017), ed. Salguero, 314–321; Paul Copp, "Seals of the Bodhisattva: A Buddhist Talismanic Seal Manual from Dunhuang," in *Buddhism and Medicine* (2017), ed. Salguero, 304–313; Prabodh Chandra Bagchi, "New Materials for the Study of the Kumāratantra," *Indian Culture* 7, no. 3 (1941): 269–286; and Prabodh Chandra Bagchi, "A Fragment of the Kāśyapa-saṁhitā in Chinese," in *India and China: A Collection of Essays by Professor Prabodh Chandra Bagchi*, ed. Wang Bangwei and Tansen Sen (London, New York, and Delhi: Anthem Press, 2011), 75–86.
48. Dominic Steavu, "Apotropaic Substances as Medicine in Buddhist Healing Methods: Nāgārjuna's Treatise on the Five Sciences," in *Buddhism and Medicine* (2017), ed. Salguero, 441–453.
49. T. 553; T. 554; T. 1428: 851–854; T. 2121: 166–170. T. 553 has been translated in Edouard Chavannes, *Cinq cents contes et apologues: Extraits du Tripiṭaka chinois et traduits en français*, vol. 3 (Paris: Libraire d'Amerique et d'Orient, 1962), 325–361. Discussed in Salguero, "The Buddhist Medicine King," 183–210; Chen Ming, *Dunhuang chutu huyu yidian "Qipo shu" yanjiu* 敦煌出土胡語. 醫典《耆婆書》研究 (Hong Kong: Xinwenfeng Chuban, 2005); Chen Ming, "Qipo de xingxiang yanbian ji qi zai Dunhuang Tulufan diqude yingxiang" 耆婆的形象演變及其在敦煌吐魯番地區的影響, in *Wenjin xuezhi* 文津學志, Vol. 1, ed. *Guojia tushuguan shanben te cangbu* 國家圖書館善本特藏部 (Beijing: Beijing Tushuguan Chubanshe, 2003), 138–164; Demiéville, *Buddhism and Healing*, 91, 97–98. On the title of "king of physicians" (*yiwang* 醫王), see also Chen Ming and Catherine Despeux, trans., "Le roi des médecins dans les manuscrits médicaux de Dunhuang: un titre indien dans la Chine médiévale," *Études Chinoises* 30 (2011), 141–172. The Pāli recensions of this biography have been analyzed in Zysk, *Asceticism and Healing in Ancient India*, 52–61; and Kenneth G. Zysk, "Studies in Traditional Indian Medicine in the Pāli Canon: Jīvaka and Āyurveda," *Journal of the International Association of Buddhist Studies* 5, no. 1 (1982): 70–86.
50. For references to the biographies of Bian Que and Hua Tuo, see Salguero, "The Buddhist Medicine King," 192–193.
51. See Salguero, "The Buddhist Medicine King," 194–201.
52. See John Kieschnick, "Buddhism: Biographies of Eminent Monks," in *Oxford History of Historical Writing*, ed. Grant Hardy (Oxford: Oxford University Press, 2011), 535–552; John Kieschnick, *The Eminent Monk: Buddhist Ideals in Medieval Chinese Hagiography* (Honolulu: University of Hawaii Press, 1997); Arthur Wright, "Biography and Hagiography: Hui-Chiao's Lives of Eminent Monks," in *Sōritsu nijūgo shūnen kinen ronbunshū* 創立廿五周年記念論文集, ed. Kyōto daigaku jinbun kagaku kenkyūjo hen 京都大學. 人文科學研究所 (Kyoto: Kyōto Daigaku Jinbun Kagaku Kenkyūjo, 1954), 383–432; Arthur F. Wright, "Fo-Tu-Têng: A Biography," *Harvard Journal of Asiatic Studies* 11, nos. 3–4 (1948): 312–371. A Japanese translation of the entire collection is available in Funayama Toru 船山徹, *Kōsō den* 高僧伝, vols. 1–3 (Tokyo: Iwanami Shoten, 2009–2010); and a partial translation is available in French in Robert Shih, *Biographies des Moines Éminents (Kao Seng Tchouan) de Houei-Kiao* (Louvain: Institut Orientaliste, 1968).

53. On anomaly accounts and miracle tales, see Robert Ford Campany, *Strange Writing: Anomaly Accounts in Early Medieval China* (Albany: State University of New York Press, 1996); and Campany, *Signs from the Unseen Realm*; and Robert Ford Campany, "Religious Repertoires and Contestation: A Case Study Based on Buddhist Miracle Tales," *History of Religions* 52, no. 2 (2012): 99–141.
54. C. Pierce Salguero, "'A Flock of Ghosts Bursting Forth and Scattering': Healing Narratives in a Sixth-Century Chinese Buddhist Hagiography," in *Buddhist Healing in Medieval China and Japan*, ed. Salguero and Macomber, 23–56; Salguero, "A Flock of Ghosts Bursting Forth and Scattering," *East Asian Science, Technology, & Medicine*; and Salguero, *Translating Buddhist Medicine*, 133–139; partial translations are available in C. Pierce Salguero, "A Selection of Buddhist Healing Narratives from East Asia," in *Buddhism and Medicine* (2017), ed. Salguero, 205–218.
55. T. 2059: 384b22–24. Wright, "Fo-Tu-Têng," 345–346; Salguero, "A Flock of Ghosts Bursting Forth and Scattering," 36–37.
56. Excerpts of this chapter are translated in Alexander O. Hsu, "Curing/Curating Illness: Selections from the Chapter on the 'Sufferings of Illness' from 'A Grove of Pearls from the Garden of Dharma,'" in *Buddhism and Medicine* (2017), ed. Salguero, 20–29. A similar, but slightly shorter chapter on illness is contained in the *Zhujing yaoji* 諸經要集 (T. 2123), another encyclopedia authored by Daoshi.
57. See the detailed summaries of the contents of this section in Hsu, "Curing/Curating Illness," 21–22; and C. Pierce Salguero, "Reexamining the Categories and Canons of Chinese Buddhist Healing," *Journal of Chinese Buddhist Studies* 27 (2015): 39–43. Three of these miracle tales are translated in Campany, *Signs from the Unseen Realm*, 88–91, 97–98, 132, and in Salguero, "A Selection of Buddhist Healing Narratives," 207–210.
58. Translated in Paul Swanson, *Clear Serenity, Quiet Insight: T'ien-t'ai Chih-i's Mo-ho chih-kuan*, vol. 2 (Honolulu: University of Hawaii Press, 2017), 1322–1363. Discussed by Huang Boyuan 黃柏源, *Zhiyi yixue sixiang zhi yanjiu: yi "Mohe zhiguan" "Guanbing huanjing" wei zhongxin"* 智顗醫學思想之研究以《摩訶止觀》「觀病患境」為中心 (MA thesis, Huafan daxue 華梵大學, 2000); and Yamano Toshirō 山野俊郎, "Tendai Chigi no igaku shisō josetsu" 天台智顗の医学思想序說, *Shinshū SōGō KenkyūJo Kenkyū Kiyō* 3 (1985): 115–142.
59. Available in a critical edition by Sekiguchi Shindai 關口真大, *Tendai shōshikan no kenkyō* 天台小止観の研究 (Tokyo: Sankibō Busshorin, 1954), 356–360. Sekiguchi's edition is considered to be closer to Zhiyi's original than the version in the Taishō canon. Translated in C. Pierce Salguero, "'Treating Illness': Translation of a Chapter from a Medieval Chinese Buddhist Meditation Manual by Zhiyi (538–597)," *Asian Medicine* 7 (2012): 461–473. Salguero's translation is based on Sekiguchi's edition and also reproduces the Chinese from Sekiguchi's critical edition. A translation of T. 1915 is available in Bhikshu Dharmamitra, trans., *The Essentials of Buddhist Meditation: A Classic Śamatha-Vipaśyanā Meditation Manual: The Essentials for Practicing Calming-and-Insight and Dhyāna Meditation, by the Great Tiantai Meditation Master and Exegete: Śramaṇa Zhiyi (Chih-I) (538–597 CE)* (Seattle, WA: Kalavinka Press, 2008), 168–187. Discussed in Salguero, *Translating Buddhist Medicine*, 102–105, and, more extensively, in C. Pierce Salguero, *Buddhist Medicine in Medieval China: Disease, Healing, and the Body in Crosscultural Translation (Second to Eight Centuries C.E.* (PhD dissertation, Johns Hopkins University, 2010), 285–294. See also Demiéville, *Buddhism and Healing*, 80–82, 85; Joshua Capitanio, "Health, Illness, and the Body in Buddhist and Daoist Self-Cultivation," in *Brahman and Dao: Comparative Studies of Indian and Chinese Philosophy and Religion*, ed. Ithamar Theodor and Yao Zhihua (Lanham, MD: Lexington Books, 2013), 181–192; and Dolly Yang, *Prescribing "Guiding and Pulling": The Institutionalisation of Therapeutic Exercise in Sui China (581–618 CE)* (PhD dissertation, University College London, 2018), 256–260.
60. On the six breaths, see Catherine Despeux, "The Six Healing Breaths," in *Daoist Body Cultivation: Traditional Models and Contemporary Practices*, ed. Livia Kohn (Magdalena, NM: Three Pines Press, 2006), 37–67.

61. Salguero, *Translating Buddhist Medicine*, 39–40; Demiéville, *Buddhism and Healing*, 94–97; Jürgen Kovacs and Paul Unschuld, *Essential Subtleties on the Silver Sea: The Yin-hai Jing-wei: A Chinese Classic of Ophtalmology* (Los Angeles: University of California Press, 1998), 29–42.
62. Michael Stanley-Baker and Katja Triplett have touched on the Chinese Buddhist materials in the *Ishimpō*, but a dedicated study of the significance of the *Ishimpō* for the history of Chinese Buddhist healing remains a *desideratum*. Michael Stanley-Baker, "'Indian Massage' from Sun Simiao's Prescriptions Worth a Thousand in Gold," in *Buddhism and Medicine* (2017), ed. Salguero, 533–537; and Katja Triplett, *Buddhism and Medicine in Japan: A Topical Survey (500–1600 CE) of a Complex Relationship* (Berlin: De Gruyter, 2019).
63. Sun Simiao, *Beiji qianjing yaofang* 備急千金要方, *juan* 1, section 1. On Sun Simiao's connections to Buddhism, see Sakade Yoshinobu, "Sun Simiao et le Bouddhisme," *Kansai Daigaku Bunka Ronshu* 42, no. 1 (1998): 81–98; Demiéville, "Byō," 94–96. On the life, work, and medical practice of Sun Simiao, see Liu Yan, *Healing with Poisons: Potent Medicines in Medieval China* (Seattle: University of Washington Press, 2021), 105–24; Sabine Wilms, *Bei ji qian jin yao fang: Essential Prescriptions worth a Thousand in Gold for Every Emergency: Volumes 2–4 on Gynecology* (Portland, OR: Chinese Medicine Database, 2008), 8–15; Paul U. Unschuld, "Der Chinesische "Arzneikönig" Sun Simiao Geschichte–Legende–Ikonographie Zur Plausibilität Naturkundlicher und Übernatürlicher Erklärungsmodelle," *Monumenta Serica* 42 (1994): 217–257; Paul U. Unschuld, *Medicine in China: A History of Ideas*, 150–151; Nathan Sivin, "The Biography of Sun Ssu-Mo: A Historiographic Inquiry," in Nathan Sivin, *Chinese Alchemy: Preliminary Studies*, Harvard Monographs in the History of Science (Cambridge, MA: Harvard University Press, 1968), 81–144; Ang Zou, *The Life of Daoxuan according to Others and his Own Words* (Singapore: Buddhist College of Singapore and Kong Meng San Phor Kark See Monastery, 2019), 35–40; Chen, *Zhonggu yiliao yu wailai wenhua*, 224–277; and Zhu Jianping 朱建平, "Sun Simiao 'Qianjin Fang' zhong de Fojiao yingxiang" 孙思邈《千金方》中的佛教影响, *Zhonghua Yishi Zazhi* 4 (1999): 220–222.
64. *Beiji qianjing yaofang, juan* 1, section 4.
65. *Beiji qianjing yaofang, juan* 27, section 4. Translated in Stanley-Baker, "Indian Massage."
66. See Sakade, "Sun Simiao et le Bouddhisme" for the references to these passages.
67. *Beiji qianjing yaofang, juan* 1, section 2. Translated in Nathan Sivin, "Sun Simiao on Medical Ethics: 'The Perfect Integrity of the Great Physician' from Prescriptions Worth a Thousand in Gold," in *Buddhism and Medicine* (2017), ed. Salguero, 538–542; and in Sakade, "Sun Simiao et le Bouddhisme," 90–91; and Paul U. Unschuld, *Medical Ethics in Imperial China: A Study in Historical Anthropology* (Berkeley: University of California Press, 1979), 24–34. Both Sakade and Sivin stress that Sun's emphasis on showing compassion for all of humanity, rather than restricting it to one's own kin, indicates the Buddhist influence in Sun's treatise.
68. These three ophthalmological treatises have been reproduced and translated in Vijaya Deshpande and Fan Ka Wai, *Restoring the Dragon's Vision (Nagarjuna and Medieval Chinese Ophthalmology)* (Hong Kong: Chinese Civilisation Centre, City University of Hong Kong, 2012), 87–247. See also Fan Ka Wai 范家偉, "Couching for Cataract and Sino-Indian Medical Exchange from the Sixth to the Twelfth Century AD," *Clinical & Experimental Ophtalmology* 33, no. 2 (2005): 188–190; Vijaya Deshpande, "Nagarjuna and Chinese Medicine," *Studia Asiatica* 4–5 (2003): 43–59; Vijaya Deshpande, "Ophthalmic Surgery: A Chapter in the History of Sino-Indian Medical Contact," *Bulletin of the School of Oriental and African Studies* 63, no. 3 (2000): 370–388; Vijaya Deshpande, "Indian Influences on Early Chinese Ophthalmology: Glaucoma as a Case Study," *Bulletin of the School of Oriental and African Studies* 62, no. 2 (1999): 306–322; Kovacs and Unschuld, *Essential Subtleties on the Silver Sea*, 43–46; Unschuld, *Medicine in China: A History of Ideas*, 144–148; and Triplett, *Buddhism and Medicine in Japan*, 80–91.
69. Kovacs and Unschuld, *Essential Subtleties on the Silver Sea*, 44–45.

70. Demiéville, *Buddhism and Healing*, 89–91; and Triplett, *Buddhism and Medicine in Japan*, 73–78.
71. Köhle, "A Confluence of Humors"; Endō Jirō, Nakamura Teruko, Yamaki Hidehiko, and Miyamoto Hirokazu 遠藤次郎、中村輝 子、八巻英彦、宮本浩和, "Tan no kigen"; Natalie Köhle, "Spirit, Sweat, and *Qi*," in *Fluid Matter(s): Flow and Transformation in the History of the Body*, ed. Natalie Köhle and Shigehisa Kuriyama, Asian Studies Monograph Series 14 (Canberra, Australia: ANU Press, 2020), n.p.
72. Suggested by Catherine Despeux, "The System of the Five Circulatory Phases and the Six Seasonal Influences: A Source of Innovation in Medicine under the Song (960–1279)," in *Innovation in Chinese Medicine*, ed. Elisabeth Hsu (Cambridge, UK: Cambridge University Press, 2001), 151.
73. Volker Scheid, "The Neglected Role of Buddhism in the Development of Medicine in Late Imperial China Viewed through the Life and Work of Yu Chang 喻昌 (1585–1664)," *Bulletin of the History of Medicine* 94 (2020): 1–28; Volker Scheid, "Buddhism and Scholarly Medicine in Seventeenth-Century China: Three Prefaces to the Work of Yu Chang (1585–1664)," in *Buddhism and Medicine: An Anthology of Modern and Contemporary Sources*, ed. C. Pierce Salguero (New York: Columbia University Press, 2020), 22–32; Volker Scheid, "Promoting Free Flow in the Networks: Reimagining the Body in Early Modern Suzhou," *History of Science* 56, no. 2 (2017): 154–156; and Shen Junlong 申俊龍, "Cong Yu Jiayan zhi yixue sanshu kan fojiao dui zhongyi de yingxiang" 從喻嘉言之醫學三書看佛教對中醫的影響, *Chung-Hwa Buddhist Studies* 5 (2001): 465–477.
74. See Scheid, "Neglected Role of Buddhism," 6, based on Shi Yongxin 釋永信 and Li Liangsong 李良松, eds., *Zhongguo fojiao yiyao quanshu* 中國佛教醫藥全書 (Beijing: Zhongguo Shudian, 2011).
75. Demiéville, *Buddhism and Healing*, 58–60; Ryōshū Michihata 道端良秀, *Chūgoku Bukkyō to shakai fukushi jigyō* 中國佛教と社會福祉事業 (Kyoto: Hōzōkan, 1967), 178–186; Catherine Despeux, "Chinese Medicinal Excrement: Is There a Buddhist Influence on the Use of Animal Excrement-Based Recipes in Medieval China?" *Asian Medicine* 12 (2017): 151–152; and W. W. Lai, "Chinese Buddhist and Christian Charities: A Comparative History," *Buddhist-Christian Studies* 12 (1992): 9–12. See also Catherine Despeux, "Institutions médicales et thérapeutes à Dunhuang," in *Médicine, religion, et société dans la Chine médiévale: Études de manuscrits de Dunhuang et Turfan*, ed. Catherine Despeux (Paris: Institut des Hautes Etudes Chinoises/Collège de France, 2010), 43–63.
76. Wu Yi-li 吳一立, "The Bamboo Grove Monastery and Popular Gynecology in Late Imperial China," *Late Imperial China* 21, no. 1 (2000): 41–76; and Wu Yi-li, *Reproducing Women: Medicine, Metaphor, and Childbirth in Late Imperial China* (Berkeley: University of California Press, 2010), 54–83.
77. Chen Yunü 陳玉女, "Buddhism and the Medical Treatment of Women in the Ming Dynasty: A Research Note," *Nan Nü* 10 (2008): 279–303.
78. Chen Ming, "The Transmission of Foreign Medicine via the Silk Roads in Medieval China: A Case Study of the *Haiyao bencao*," *Asian Medicine* 3, no. 2 (2007): 244–245; Chen, *Zhonggu yiliao yu wailai wenhua*; Paul U. Unschuld, *Medicine in China: A History of Pharmaceutics* (Berkeley: University of California Press, 1986); and Hu Shiu Ying, "History of the Introduction of Exotic Elements into Traditional Chinese Medicine," *Arnold Arboretum* 71 (1990): 487–526.
79. Jose A. Canton Alvarez, "A Gift from the Buddhist Monastery: The Role of Buddhist Medical Practices in the Assimilation of the Opium Poppy in Chinese Medicine during the Song Dynasty (960–1279)," *Medical History* 63, no. 4 (2019): 475–493.
80. Despeux, "Chinese Medicinal Excrement." See also Dolly Yang and Michael Stanley-Baker, "Dung, Hair, and Mungbeans: Household Remedies in the Longmen Recipes," in *Buddhism and Medicine* (2017), ed. Salguero, 454–477.
81. Demiéville, "Byō," 224–265. On the history of *Hōbōgirin*, see Iyanaga Nobumi, "A History of the Hōbōgirin," *The Eastern Buddhist* 48, no. 1 (2017): 7–22; and Salguero, "Reexamining the Categories."
82. Demiéville, *Buddhism and Healing*. This otherwise immensely useful edition has but one drawback: it only supplies Sanskrit and Pāli version of the scriptural titles, and does not supply characters when discussing Sino-Japanese terminology.

83. Jean Filliozat, "La Médicine Indienne et l'expansion bouddhique en extrême Orient," *Journal Asiatique* 224 (1934): 301–307. An English translation of this article is available as Jean Filliozat, "The Expansion of Indian Medicine Abroad," in *India's Contribution to World Thought and Culture*, ed. Swami Vivekananda and Lokesh Chandra (Chennai, India: Vivekananda Rock Memorial Committee, 1970), 67–70.
84. Paul U. Unschuld, "The Chinese Reception of Indian Medicine in the First Millenium A.D.," *Bulletin of the History of Medicine* 53, no. 3 (1979): 329–345. This article has been reprinted as the chapter "Buddhism and Indian Medicine," in Unschuld, *Medicine in China: A History of Ideas*, 132–153.
85. Chen Yinke 陳寅恪, "San guo zhi 'Cao Chong Hua Tuo zhuan' yu fojiao gushi" ' 三國志曹沖華佗傳與佛教故事, in *Chen Yinke shixue lunwen xuan ji* 陳寅恪史學論文選集 (Shanghai: Guji Chubanshe, 1992), 36–40 (originally published in 1930).
86. Birnbaum, *The Healing Buddha*.
87. Obinata Daijiō, *Bukkyō igaku no kenkyū* (Tokoyo: Kazama Shobō, 1965); Fukunaga Katsumi, *Bukkyō igaku jiten, ho yoga* (Tokoyo: Yūzankaku Shuppan, 1980); Nihonyanagi Kenji, *Bukkyō igaku gaiyō* (Kyoto: Hōzōkan, 1994); and Fu Fang 傅芳 and Ni Qing 倪青, *Zhongguo foyi renwu xiaochuan* 中國佛醫人物小傳 (Xiamen, China: Lujiang Chubanshe, 1996). Cf. the critical discussion of Fukunaga's *Bukkyō igaku jiten* in Salguero, "Reexamining the Categories," 49–51.
88. Chen, *Zhonggu yiliao yu wailai wenhua*; Despeux, *Médecine, religion et société*; Strickmann, *Chinese Magical Medicine*.
89. Unschuld, "The Chinese Reception of Indian Medicine," 344–345; Unschuld, *Medicine in China: A History of Ideas*, 148–153; and Demiéville, *Buddhism and Healing*, 98–99.
90. Well-known examples of this direction are Robert H. Sharf, *Coming to Terms with Chinese Buddhism: A Reading of the Treasure Store Treatise*, Kuroda Institute, Studies in East Asian Buddhism 14 (Honolulu: University of Hawaii Press, 2002); Stephen F. Teiser, *Reinventing the Wheel: Paintings of Rebirth in Medieval Buddhist Temples* (Seattle: University of Washington Press, 2006); and Mollier, *Buddhism and Taoism Face to Face*.
91. Salguero, *Translating Buddhist Medicine*, 145–148.
92. Salguero, "Reexamining the Categories."
93. Salguero, "Healing and/or Salvation?"; Salguero, *Translating Buddhist Medicine*, 146 and *passim*.
94. For related discussions, see Katrin Killinger, Christoph Kleine, and Katja Triplett, "Distinctions and Differentiations between Medicine and Religion," *Asian Medicine* 14 (2019): 233–262; Christoph Kleine and Katja Triplett, "Introduction to Religion and Healing in Japan," *Japanese Religions* 37 (1912): 1–12; Michael Stanley-Baker, "Special Issue: Religion and Science in China: Moving Beyond the 'Two Cultures' Problem," *East Asian Science, Technology, and Medicine* 50 (2019): 9–20; Michael Stanley-Baker, "Daoing Medicine: Practice Theory for Considering Religion and Medicine in Early Imperial China," *East Asian Science, Technology, and Medicine* 50 (2019): 21–66; and Scheid, "Neglected Role of Buddhism."
95. Antonello Palumbo, review of C. Pierce Salguero, *Translating Buddhist Medicine in Medieval China*, Philadelphia: University of Philadelphia Press, 2014, in *Journal of Chinese Religions* 44, no. 2 (2016): 201–204.
96. Janet Gyatso, review of C. Pierce Salguero, *Translating Buddhist Medicine in Medieval China*, Philadelphia: University of Philadelphia Press, 2014, in *Social History of Medicine* 28, no. 3 (2015): 639–641.
97. Salguero, "Reexamining the Categories," 48–51; and Salguero, "Introduction," in *Buddhism and Medicine* (2020), ed. Salguero, xv–xvii.
98. C. Pierce Salguero, " 'A Missing Link' in the History of Chinese Medicine," *East Asian Science, Technology, and Medicine* 47 (2018): 93–119; Salguero, "Buddhism and Medicine in East Asian History," *Religion Compass* 8, no. 8 (2014): 239–250; partially reprinted in the introduction to Salguero and Macomber, eds., *Buddhist Healing in Medieval China and Japan*; and C. Pierce Salguero, "Medicine," in *Oxford Bibliographies Online: Buddhism*, November 24, 2020.

Natalie Köhle

BUDDHISM AND MEDIA

In the years after World War II, as the Japanese American community sought to reestablish itself and raise a new generation of American Buddhists in the aftermath of wartime incarceration, the ritual performance of music during devotional services continued apace. Beginning in the early 20th century, North American Jōdo Shinshū Buddhist communities began adopting a congregational style of worship that included the singing of songs.[1] This song culture developed over the intervening decades, and the songs sung during Sunday morning services came to be called "*gāthās*."[2] Some *gāthās* were traditional and centuries-old Japanese poems set to Western music; others were blatantly appropriated Christian hymns. In the post-war years, new songwriters added to the official and unofficial "canons" of music, and in the 1960s, Jane Imamura and Kimi Hisatsune of Berkeley, California, both contributed a plethora of new Buddhist songs, including the children's song "Buddha Loves You." Not to be confused with the similarly titled Christian hymn, "Jesus Loves Me," Hisatsune's song was about a series of animals "loved" (embraced by the compassion of) Amida Buddha. Hisatsune wrote of her song and its comparison to the Christian hymn:

> The Christian song merely reminds a child that, according to the Bible, "Jesus loves me." It is centered on the child, who in his or her loneliness or frustration may want to look up to a kind, warmhearted intermediary who will save suffering souls from their miseries. . . . The Buddhist song leads one away from an ego-centered concern, or a need for someone to ease one's pain, to a concern for all other living beings—the bird, the puppy, the cat, and the fish as well.[3]

In the early 1980s, hip-hop trio the Beastie Boys began their rise to mainstream popularity. With roots in the New York hardcore punk and rap scenes, the group "explored the unifying threads between hip-hop and punk," recording eight studio albums through 2012, seven of which went platinum, and being inducted into the Rock and Roll Hall of Fame.[4] The Beastie Boys released their fourth studio album, *Ill Communication*, in 1994, a time that has regularly been cited as a period of significant Buddhist development in the United States. Following on the heels of Zen Buddhism's rise to popularity through the avant-garde and Beat Generation through the 1960s counterculture, in 1991 the magazine *Tricycle: The Buddhist Review* was founded and went on to become a major media institution helping to further popularize Buddhism. The Dalai Lama was awarded the Nobel Peace Prize in 1989 and subsequently made several high-profile appearances in the United States. And the humanitarian crisis in Tibet was brought to mainstream American attention in part through public support from actors such as Richard Gere and major motion pictures such as *Seven Years in Tibet* and *Kundun*. At the same time, the Beastie Boys established the Tibetan Freedom Concert series in 1996; the inaugural concert, held in San Francisco, raised over $800,000 and featured a roster of popular musicians such as the Red Hot Chili Peppers and Björk. *Ill Communication* was very much a product of its time, with two tracks reflecting the personal practice of member MCA (Adam Yauch) in the Tibetan-derived Shambhala tradition of Buddhism. The instrumental track "Shambala" (sic) features a sample of the Gyuto monks' famous overtone throat singing; this track is followed by "Bodhisattva Vow" wherein MCA explicitly expresses his Buddhist practice:

Respect to Shantideva and all the others
Who brought down the Dharma for the sisters and brothers
I give thanks for this world as a place to learn
And for this human body that I know I've earned
And my deepest thanks to all sentient beings

Both "Buddha Loves You" and "Bodhisattva Vow" are undeniably Buddhist songs in that they are explicitly about Buddhism or express a particular Buddhist sentiment and were written by self-identified Buddhists. Both are also modern compositions, hybrids if you will, made possible by the convergence of Buddhism and Western musical forms. "Buddha Loves You," however, exists solely in a ritual context, sung by a Buddhist community during a religious service. In this capacity, it functions in a very specific way; its import and meaning are defined by this ritual context and are not easily transferred outside of that context. *Ill Communication*, on the other hand, exists in a pop-cultural and commercial context, reproduced seemingly endlessly on vinyl, cassette tape, CD, and digital mp3 and selling over three million copies.[5] Both songs are examples of Buddhist media; a consideration of their differing contexts and uses draws attention to the issues of genre, ritual, and cultural adaptation and highlights how media studies refocuses Buddhist studies.

Whereas both songs reflect individual or personal religious expressions or sentiments, their distinction is primarily in how they function. One is a religious (ritual) song; the other is commercial. As a religious or ritual song, "Buddha Loves You" functions within a larger liturgical context to do the work of ritual—that is, to mark the boundaries of the communal expression of Buddhist faith within a particular community. As a children's song, it also functions pedagogically to subtly convey Buddhist concepts to younger members of the community. As a commercial song, "Bodhisattva Vow" functions in the context of commercial popmusic more generally, both to sell records as well as to create a shared sense of belonging or affinity among the band's members. As a personal expression of Buddhist faith, it also functions as just that—a means by which an individual Buddhist can articulate what being a Buddhist means for the artist. A focus on Buddhist media, and on the function of media in various contexts—as part of a liturgical service, as personal expression, and so forth—reveals the various ways Buddhism finds expression in the contemporary world, how Buddhism is, and always has been, a lived religion.

The following article is concerned with, first, defining media studies both as field and method, one that has to date been somewhat marginal in the field of Buddhist studies. The hope here is to demonstrate the utility of studying media particularly as it pertains to issues of ritual and practice as well as how media studies may help scholars think through processes of cultural adaptation or change over time. From there various instances of Buddhist media in various contexts and across genres are explored, from the purely religious to the artistic, from film to advertising. Finally, these points are related to the question of authenticity, both in how Buddhists and Buddhist communities define proper media expressions or practices as well as how Buddhist studies as an academic discipline participates in the construction of normative or authentic Buddhist discourses.

Before proceeding, it should be noted that media is necessarily contextual. That is, media does not manifest in a vacuum but is embedded within specific cultural contexts that often shape its meanings and uses. A study of Buddhist media in Japan, say, would therefore need to take into account the particular cultural context of modern Japanese culture and modern Japanese Buddhism, and its conclusions might be wildly different from a study of similar Buddhist media in the United States. To the extent that my own academic interests are rooted in Western cultural contexts, these will be foregrounded in what follows; however, these should not be presumed as normative, and one should fully expect that scholars using a similar approach may come to rather different conclusions should their work focus on Bangkok versus Boston.

DEFINING MEDIA AND MEDIA STUDIES

Media is a culturally located method of communicating ideas and forming identities between persons. Whereas in the vernacular "media" is often a stand-in for either mass media (e.g., news media) or pop-cultural media (e.g., Hollywood films), media studies need not limit its analysis to these spheres and may be as interested in popular culture as folk culture. Indeed, understanding the relationship between media, its creator, and its audience helps to unpack its meanings. As Forbes writes, "high culture is a gourmet meal, folk culture is grandma's casserole, and popular culture is a McDonald's hamburger."[6] These distinctions direct attention, first, to the standards, tastes, and expectations of various media consumers, and second, to the various types of media under consideration. Media studies understands media broadly to refer to both the mass-media Hollywood film as well as media of folk culture, dance, poetry, song, art, and so forth. Moreover, apart from merely describing or defining media in some abstract sense, media studies is concerned explicitly with the processes of mediation—the communication of ideas and formation of identities within groups of persons. As any act of communication—the written or spoken word, images on film, an interpretive dance—may be read as mediated, such analyses are concerned as much with the media itself as with the messages being communicated. For example, the first turning of the wheel of the dharma by the Buddha was itself an instance of (oral) mediation, conveying specific messages and meanings (the four noble truths) from one person (the Buddha) to another (his immediate disciples).

When one compares the media type and message being conveyed in the first turning of the wheel of the dharma with, say, the latest Avengers movie from Marvel Studios, the difference in both media type and message is striking. How media types inform and shape their messages is at the heart of Marshall McLuhan's famous aside that the "media is the message."[7] Since McLuhan made this statement half a century ago, media studies has concerned itself with disclosing the various ways messages are shaped and attenuated by their media forms and the consequences of these media types on the development of culture and individual subjectivities. For example, the Buddha delivering teachings to his disciples can be read as orally transmitted messages that reinforce tribal relationships specifically because of their mode of communication—person to person in small groups. By contrast, broadcast media breaks down small-group connections due to its ability to transmit a single communication to vast audiences. Broadcast media has the ability to create shared identities or *imaginaries*, to borrow from Arjun Appadurai, owing to its ability to easily transcend cultural or political boundaries.[8] At the same time, it can also create cultural hegemony to the extent that such messages are one-way, produced by those in positions of power or authority and disseminated to those who are not. The top-down nature of broadcast media can be destabilized, however, by the Internet and new forms of digital media by virtue of the fact that consumers are simultaneously producers of media messages and content.[9]

Thus, this article takes media studies to be an umbrella term to refer to both studies that take various media forms as their object of study as well as analyses of the messages conveyed through media. As Jeffrey Mahan writes, "there is no religion apart from the process of mediation."[10] That is, religion has always been mediated, and religious persons have always expressed their faith and practice through media. Thus, studies of religion and media overlap with related fields and methodologies that focus on material culture, art, literary studies, and anthropology. Such studies refocus attention from the purely textual or doctrinal aspects of Buddhism toward such things as architecture and icons as well as the rituals in which icons and other types of media are deployed. Thus, a digital version of the *Lotus Sūtra* , say, is merely a continuation of a preexisting practice of copying sutras in Buddhist history more generally. Of course, given the connection between media and its messages, the digital reproduction of a sūtra will invariably change how the text is received, how its message is interpreted.

The actual uses to which media (or in this case, texts) are put draws attention to media's place within religious practice or ritual. Religious ritual is mediated in a variety of ways, through images, iconography, and art; ritual implements such as altars, incense, and offerings; performances of prayers, chanting, and singing; dress, vestments, and robes; and the second-order level of ritual texts and manuals explaining all of the above. Media in these spaces functions, in part, to give shape and meaning to religious practice in some general sense; media also functions to reinforce the boundaries of collective religious belonging, "of creating, maintaining, and re-articulating performative identity."[11] Various uses and types of religious media will be discussed at length in the next section. For now, it is important to note that the ritual deployment of media changes its function and its meaning—and, arguably, mediation in turn changes the meaning of religion.

Whereas media may function within the context of religious ritual or practice to reinforce the boundaries of community or collective identity, media may as often be merely a personal or artistic expression. Richard Seager considers the use of "Dharma images" in and out of Buddhist communities and draws on Mary Douglas's distinction between "condensed symbols" and "diffuse symbols."[12] The former communicate complex ideas that are readily understood within an in-group (a Buddhist community), whereas the latter are more personalized and individual, having arisen within a less-defined social context. "Bodhisattva Vow" may exhibit characteristics of the "diffuse symbol" to the extent that it was composed by an individual Buddhist, not within the context of a sangha but within the context of a recording contract. The song is received by the general public and, therefore, its meanings require "considerable interpretation" as the public are not insiders to the Buddhist community.[13] Nevertheless, within a Buddhist community, the song would likely be readily understood and thus may simultaneously slip into the category of "condensed symbol." Regardless, such studies of Buddhist media outside Buddhist contexts that focus on their personalized meanings allow the researcher entry into the realm of personal expression as well as the ways in which Buddhist ideas have become diffused into the popular imagination.

Thus, media studies reveal how culture crosses both literal and figurative boundaries and can aid scholars in ascertaining the spread and flow of Buddhist culture in the modern global age. Thomas Tweed uses this perspective to great effect in his study of a *gāthā* written at the turn of the 20th century, possibly in San Francisco, possibly by an Irish-born Theravāda monk, and published by Jōdo Shinshū Buddhists in the United States. In locating this *gāthā* within a trans-Pacific Buddhist network, he locates Buddhism within a modern era marked by movements across time and space that "created plural practices, artifacts, and beliefs that were transmitted in entirely new or significantly transformed [Buddhist] institutions."[14] Such (media) artifacts demonstrate the ability of culture to transcend the boundaries of place (back and forth across the Pacific Ocean) as well as Buddhist traditions (Theravāda and Mahāyāna) and ethnic boundaries (cooperative practices or liturgies produced by white converts within a Japanese immigrant tradition).

Thus, whether approached through media studies, as primary texts to be "read," or as exemplars of translocative modern Buddhist culture, media studies are potentially revelatory in their approach, demonstrating the scope of global Buddhism as well as personal subjectivity. The following section discusses some specific examples in more detail.

MEDIA TYPES

Materiality and Ritual: Being Buddhist. Buddhism is mediated. This mediation, as discussed above, comes in the form of all manner of specific media types, though not always recognized as such. Such media may take the recognizable form of texts, but mediation is also found wherever meaning is communicated: in the recitation of texts further nuanced and developed though chanting, ritual, and liturgy; in iconography and art and the rituals related thereto, such as consecration and "eye-opening" ceremonies for images of the Buddha; in place and space where pilgrims travel or in temples where rituals are held; and in all the sights, smells, and senses contained in those spaces.[15] What each of these examples share, of course, is ritual, and it is with ritual and practice that this discussion of Buddhist media and mediation begins.

Ritual texts or manuals have long been research topics in normative Buddhist studies. The study of ritual has been greatly influenced by linguistic analysis, and so studies of Buddhist ritual manuals are more than mere translations; they can also be used to trace the development of rituals across great distances and time.[16] Ritual manuals, as texts, necessarily communicate ideas and are therefore a form of mediation; but the performance of the ritual is itself a form of communication that may also be read as text. Indeed, over the past several decades, Buddhist studies as a field has been enhanced by anthropological and ethnographic studies of Buddhism as a lived religion with ritual and practice at the center of study.

The various objects that populate ritual and practice may also be communicative in nature, and here it is possible to see a crossover between media studies and material culture. Fabio Rambelli notes that " 'being a Buddhist' in contemporary Japan is often signified by the possession of some tokens of Buddhism"—that is, owning or wearing specific Buddhist objects such as rosaries, a home altar, artworks, etc.[17] Such objects communicate meaning; they are visual signifiers to others of one's personal identity or subjective sense of being a Buddhist. Studies that focus on material culture move beyond the textual, doctrinal, or theoretical aspects of the religion and into the realm of Buddhism as lived tradition. Over the past decade, a wealth of scholarship has emerged that focuses on Buddhism in the contemporary world, complicating our understanding of the tradition by taking into account ritual, practice, play, and entertainment as fruitful sites of inquiry.[18]

When deployed within a ritual context, such media functions to reinforce the boundaries of Buddhist or religious belonging.[19] The performance of a weekly communal service in the context of North American Jōdo Shinshū Buddhism functions to clarify and mark the boundaries of both the community and membership within that community. Media elements within that service—songs such as "Buddha Loves You," for example—function to further nuance and clarify the values and meanings of that community or serve as pedagogical tools. Ritual, to borrow from Patricia Campbell, is a means by which individuals perform and embody knowledge about how to be Buddhist.[20]

Media as Personal Expression: Buddhist Ink. "Buddha Loves You" is a liturgical song, deployed within a ritual context and rarely, if ever, performed or sung by an individual or in a commercial context as, say, Christian gospels may be. However, the song was also the composition of an individual, an individual Buddhist, who was expressing a particular orientation toward Buddhist thought or practice. Media as component of ritual and media as personal expression are, of course, not mutually exclusive but merely point to the multivalent purposes or functions media may possess dependent upon context and location.

Thus, whereas Buddhist media may be used within a ritual or practice setting, it is also about the personal, individual, or subjective experience of Buddhism. Consider, for example, the Japanese woodblock artist Munakata Shikō (1903–1975). A prolific artist of oil paintings, calligraphy, and traditional Japanese painting (*yamato-ga*), Munakata appended the phrase "*no saku*" to his woodblock prints, a reference to the Shikoku pilgrimage and the bundles of sticks pilgrims carry with them, leaving a stick at each of the pilgrimage's eighty-eight stages. These sticks—a "condensed symbol" to recall Mary Douglas above—become symbols of the individual's prayers or wish, and Munakata likened his woodblocks to this practice, leaving one behind at each stage of his career like "offering a prayer."[21] In this case, then, the media—the woodblock print—communicates a personal expression of Buddhist faith by an individual artist. This expression is informed by a particular school of Pure Land Buddhism, and in his writings Munakata maintained that religion was not something contained in texts or statues but was something "natural," evoking the Japanese Pure Land concept of *jinen* (naturalness), making "those who are involved in the creative production mere recipients of this religious power."[22] Collapsing the dichotomy of "condensed" and "diffuse" symbols, one can discern from these works a deep conviction on the part of the artist in the Pure Land Buddhist tradition; at the same time, the work stands on its own as an artistic expression and may be approached from a purely aesthetic point of view.

A modern or contemporary corollary—and certainly more diffused in its meaning—to Munakata's personal Buddhistic expression may be the practice of tattooing Buddhist images on one's body to communicate Buddhist sentiments or mark, in a literal sense, one's Buddhist identity. Increasingly popular in Western contexts, and by no means the exclusive purview of self-identified Buddhists, the practice of tattooing a phrase from a sūtra or a mantra or the image of a buddha on one's body has been described as a "body vow," a physical reminder of one's commitment to the Buddhist path.[23] While hardly a universal practice, and certainly not codified or systematized as a "formal" Buddhist practice, Buddhist tattoos can, nevertheless, be read as a form of mediation in that it is a means of conveying particular meanings between persons. In this case, the meanings being communicated are often deeply personal and explicitly

Buddhist in perspective. Moreover, to the extent that such practice may be undertaken by non-Buddhists or done in the problematic context of cultural appropriation, one may also read the practice as the way in which Asian religious icons and ideas are appropriated or absorbed into Western cultural contexts.

However, one needs to be attentive to how varying cultural contexts shape meaning, and this is especially true in the case of Buddhist tattoos. Whereas in Western cultural contexts tattooing may be gaining cultural acceptance, and whereas Western cultural contexts have long appropriated Asian cultural themes to suit non-religious ends, in historically Buddhist Asian contexts this practice may not only be unpracticed, it may also be widely repudiated.[24] Over the past several years, a handful of European tourists have been arrested or deported from Sri Lanka, Myanmar, and elsewhere in Southeast Asia for publicly displaying Buddhist tattoos. In most cases, the tattooed persons self-identified as Buddhist or claimed that they had gotten the tattoos out of religious devotion. Authorities in Buddhist-majority countries generally charged the tourists with knowingly insulting religion or "hurting others' religious feelings."[25] In these contexts, then, the act of tattooing a Buddhist image on one's body is hardly seen as a positive personal expression of faith, but rather a perceived slight or transgression against normative Buddhist or local customs. Thus, media also acts in the service of maintaining the boundaries between in- and out-groups, a concern to which this article will return shortly.

Mass Media Messages: Springtime for Kundun in the Matrix. Munakata's woodblock prints and Kimi Hisatsune's "Buddha Loves You" gesture toward media as personal or artistic expression; modern film is another example of artistic expression, and both film studies and media studies scholars have approached Buddhism in film and Buddhist films from a variety of perspectives. Works such as Ronald Green's *Buddhism Goes to the Movies* take a largely pedagogical approach, using a series of film analyses to discuss broader themes within the study of Buddhism.[26] For example, the Japanese film *Departures* (2008) is used to discus Jōdo Shinshū Buddhism, and the American film *I Heart Huckabees* (2004) is used to illustrate the Buddhist concept of dependent origination. The 2014 volume of the journal *Contemporary Buddhism* was devoted entirely to studies of Buddhism and film. In his contribution, John Whalen-Bridge used a case study of the International Buddhist Film Festival as a means of answering the question, "What is a Buddhist Film?"[27] Christian Feichtinger offers a critical analysis of the *Star Wars* film series as drawing on Buddhist motifs while keeping Buddhism as a distant "other," thus reinforcing orientalist notions of Buddhism and Asian religion generally.[28] Elisabetta Porcu provides a cross-cultural analysis of representations of Zen in both Western and Japanese contexts.[29] And Francisca Cho's close reading of the widely popular Korean film *Spring, Summer, Fall, Winter . . . and Spring* (2003) reflects interest in Buddhism on both sides of the Pacific, nuancing the presumed dichotomy between "East" and "West."[30]

Porcu and Cho remind us that film is hardly a "Western" phenomenon. Vibrant and highly productive film industries exist across Buddhist Asia, competing for audiences alongside Hollywood-produced films. Moreover, film easily transcends markets and geopolitical locations. Kim Kiduk's *Spring, Summer, Fall, Winter . . . and Spring*, for example, has found success as much in Korea as the United States. Whereas one needs to be attentive to how shifting cultural contexts may shape the reception and meaning of any given piece of media, especially film, one also needs to be careful not to reify the distinction between Asian and Western film as if these are mutually isolated categories. Sharon Suh's analysis of *Spring . . .*, for example, well discloses how the film replicates stereotypes of Buddhism as an exotic and otherworldly mystical tradition, a trope easily identified in American-produced films as well.[31]

This is not to say, however, that specifically Western romanticized representations of Buddhism and Buddhists in film have gone ignored by scholars. Indeed, the works of Suh, Jane Iwamura, Eve Mullen, and others note how Western media and film have deployed centuries-old orientalized tropes in their representations of Buddhism and Buddhists. Iwamura has done perhaps the most sustained work on this topic; her critically important *Virtual Orientalism* draws on a decade of work tracing the genealogy of what she terms the icon of the Oriental Monk.[32] Appearing in film and other visual media from the fictional and sinister Fu Man Chu to the affable and approachable (media representation of) the Dalai Lama, she notes how this icon reflects Western interest and anxieties about the Asian "other." In thinking specifically about film, she notes how this icon, as Mr. Miyagi does in *The Karate Kid* (1984), reinforces the orientalist trope that Asian spirituality and wisdom has instrumental value in the West in part because of the decline of authentic Asian culture in its homeland.[33] In Mullen's analysis, *Kundun* and *Seven Years in Tibet* reinforce the "myth of Shangrila" while infantilizing Tibetans and Tibetan Buddhism. In these films we "are shown perfect Tibetan heroes and despicable Chinese villains . . . [Tibetans] portrayed as beatifically smiling, superhuman beings . . . [and Westerners] inevitably depicted as authority figures, heroically rescuing the doomed culture of Tibet."[34] Romantic idealizations of Buddhism need not be positive; they may also reflect the intermingling of Buddhist imagery and Western cultural assumptions. Richard Anderson and David Harper, for example, note how American cultural values—Puritanism, millennialism, militarism, and so forth—have merged with Buddhism in American films to create what they term an "American Militant Buddhism," which argues that violence can be an effective mode of liberation. This theme is best exemplified in the sci-fi action film *The Matrix* (1999), wherein the "enlightened" figure of Neo uses violence to "free the minds" of persons trapped in the illusory virtual reality world, a tactic that often results in the death of the very people he is ostensibly trying to free.[35]

Critics of *The Matrix*—or, rather, those who question the legitimacy of labeling the film "Buddhist"—raise the interrelated issues of genre category and authenticity. That is, first, if there is a genre of "Buddhist film," how is it defined and what may be usefully placed inside or excluded from the category? Second, and by extension, in constructing a category or labeling films thus, one raises the possibility of more or less authentic representation of Buddhism and Buddhists on film. This article will later return to these questions. For now, it is important to note that such representations deployed into mass media communicate specific information about their subjects, often to great effect, and are reproduced and sold on the global market. Regardless of their accuracy or authenticity, they have an effect as they are consumed by worldwide audiences and thus rather than dismissing them as trite or incorrect, researchers (and especially as teachers whose students are invariably impacted by these images) would do well to critically engage such media sources as reflections of cultural understandings—for better or worse—of the Buddhist tradition.

Before turning to the commercial use of Buddhist imagery and icons, a final word on film studies and the work of Cho is due. Cho's recent monograph, *Seeing Like the Buddha*, details a theme she has previously explored—how one might read film as sūtra. Cho links the practice of viewing film to the normative Buddhist practice of visualization through art and icons. "[F]ilm instantiates traditional ways of seeing the Buddha, and thereby becomes the latest artistic technology within a long tradition of cultural practices that have seen art as religion."[36] Such a perspective—a way of seeing film that is more a way of *experiencing* film—brings attention back to the interrelationship between media and practice, a perspective that grounds media fully within Buddhist practice rather than separating it as marginal or secondary to normative Buddhist studies.

Commercialized Buddhisms: Brazilian Bikinis. Iwamura's work on the genealogy of the icon of the Oriental Monk discloses the ways in which media perpetuates a specific image or discourse of Asians and Asian Buddhism. Building on this icon, Scott Mitchell develops a similar icon, the Tranquil Meditator, that is deployed in both films and advertising, in both mass media and Buddhist media.[37] Whereas the Oriental Monk is a vaguely defined Asian or religious figure and points to a range of cultural and spiritual practices, the Tranquil Meditator is specifically Buddhist and points to a particular practice put in service of specific ends. In advertising, this may be the somewhat nebulous "this product will help you relax"; however, in film, the Tranquil Meditator may be an action hero using meditation to prepare for a conflict. Both icons are, in some sense, "diffused symbols" to the extent that they are deployed into the culture at large; at the same time, they may also be read as "condensed symbols" to the extent that they communicate specific ideas about their referents and can be said to be a sort of shorthand for larger (Western) cultural discourses that are hardly lost on the general audience. Such larger discourses include the notion that Asian religions or Buddhism have access to esoteric knowledge that can be used both for heroic quests (e.g., samurai) as well as for general health and well-being (e.g., mindfulness and yoga). When deployed in mass media, the Tranquil Meditator becomes shorthand for a calm repose, a mystified (in Jeff Wilson's sense of the word) serenity reflecting the refined tastes of the consumer.[38]

This larger cultural discourse that equates all things Buddhist (or often just simply Zen) with serenity, calm, and refined taste is used to great effect in Western media to sell all manner of products.[39] Simply placing the word Zen on something signals to the consumer this set of meanings, which may or may not have anything to do with Buddhism or Zen. Shôji Yamada traces the development of this discourse to Eugen Herrigel's 1948 *Zen in the Art of Archery* and links it to both Japanese and Western discourses that spawned a wave of similarly titled "Zen and the art of" works through the late 20th century.[40] The orientalist and romantic notion of a refined ascetic of a Zen style is also referenced by Iwamura in her analysis of fashion magazine representations of D. T. Suzuki in the 1950s and 1960s.[41] And this trend is hardly unique to the United States; Cristina Rocha, in her study of Buddhism in Brazil, notes a type of "Zen aesthetic" propagated among an elite class of Brazilians, Buddhist or otherwise, through fashion and lifestyle magazines. These media representations of Buddhism are critiqued as "fashionable nonsense" in online discussion groups by Buddhists who see both how these representations may help spread the dharma but are doing so in a superficial manner.[42]

Thus, the mediated and especially the commercialized representation of Buddhism represents contested ground within the Buddhist world with products routinely being challenged as, at best, incorrect representations of Buddhism and, at worst, wholly offensive and irredeemable. James Shields discusses this pattern in his study of, among other things, a Victoria's Secret bikini printed with Buddhist images and advertised in the company's typically hyper-sexualized fashion. In online forums, Buddhists in both Asian and Western contexts were offended and outraged over the product, resulting in the company discontinuing sale of the bikini. Buddhist criticism ranged from a postcolonial critique of the assumption that one can appropriate images of the Buddha for commercial sale to a critique of the overt sexuality of the product and its associated advertising. This discourse reflects how Buddhists, "like members of other world religions . . . continue to struggle with issues of sacred representation in an age of consumerism and mechanical reproduction."[43]

Shields is not convinced by Buddhist arguments against the reproduction and sale of Buddhist imagery; however, this article will leave aside the validity of such arguments and instead note that this discourse about the proper use of Buddhist images has emerged within a modern, globalized late-capitalist context. This is to say that as Buddhist images are picked up and redeployed within commercial spaces that, in turn, are globally dispersed, Buddhism itself moves beyond its classically defined boundaries and into non-Buddhist contexts. It should not be surprising, then, that as a result of this process Buddhists are responding by calling into question what constitutes authentic use and representation, a discourse that draws on larger postcolonial discourses around cultural appropriation—"the process by which cultural products (art, music, fashion, and so forth) are removed from their original cultural contexts or communities and selectively and superficially redeployed in another (usually white or Western) cultural context."[44] Thus, it is not simply that Buddhist cultural artifacts or media are moving from one location to another but that one culture is exerting some form of dominance over another. The postcolonial critique calls attention not to the appropriateness of such uses and misuses but to the systems of power that allow for and direct the flow of culture.

Buddhism in the News: The People Versus Tiger Woods. Once deployed into a new cultural context, Buddhism, even as a minority religion, has an impact on culture at large, an impact that is at least partially the result of its deployment and representation in mass media and pop-cultural spaces. Consider, for example, Robert Wuthnow and Wendy Cadge's study, which found that more than half of Americans had had some contact with Buddhists despite the fact that only roughly 1 percent of the population self-identifies as such. Moreover, of those surveyed, 56 percent and 63 percent associated words such as "tolerant" and "peace loving," respectively, with Buddhism; and 30 percent of respondents claimed to have familiarity with Buddhist teachings despite the fact that only 3 percent had spoken with Buddhists regularly about religion or attended a Buddhist temple or center.[45] What accounts for this widespread knowledge and generally positive feeling toward Buddhism and Buddhists despite the minority of self-identified Buddhists in the United States? It would be simplistic to suggest that media representations are singularly responsible for this trend; nevertheless, as Thomas Tweed notes, such representations are generally positive, especially when compared to representation of other minority religions, specifically Islam. In US media, Buddhists are more likely to be depicted as solitary and peaceful meditators whereas Muslims are more likely to be depicted, at best, as masses of persons engaged in ritual (e.g., the Hajj) or, at worst, as terrorists.[46]

Thus, whereas it would be overly reductionist to blame media representations alone for public perceptions of minority groups in the United States, media studies as method can productively direct attention to the political consequences of such representation in mass media spaces. Whereas there have been few sustained studies of Buddhism in US news media, what studies have been conducted reveal that reportage is generally positive. Rick Moore suggests that this is the result of unconscious media biases that employ religious ways of looking at the world and are therefore predisposed to portray religion positively. However, one should note that the media is quick to turn on religion when the story involves perceived religious or ethical lapses, such as when religious leaders are accused of hypocrisy, crimes, or moral failings.[47]

In a sustained analysis of (both mainstream and Buddhist) media representations of professional golfer Tiger Woods, Mitchell notes that the situation is more nuanced than a simplistic "nice Buddhist/bad Muslim" dichotomy. Following revelations of his extramarital affairs, conservative commentators suggested that Woods should convert from Buddhism to Christianity to save his marriage, his soul, and his golf career. Whereas this seemed to be a rare instance of Buddhism being portrayed negatively in the press, a survey of subsequent responses demonstrated that the media cared less about Woods's religious identity and more about pitting (liberal) Buddhism against (conservative) Christianity in a larger American political discourse dominated by ideological division and derision. During his public apology, Woods explicitly claimed a Buddhist identity as a means of redeeming himself; following this statement, news media tended to "fact-check" his description of Buddhism. This fact-checking relied on the testimony of Buddhist studies scholars, suggesting that academics are often called upon to verify the correct representation of Buddhism. "Rather than taking Woods at his word that this is what Buddhism is (or, at the very least, that this is what Buddhism is *for him*) reporters felt the need to reach out to some third party to verify that this is what Buddhism *really* is."[48]

Thus, while media representations of Buddhism communicate specific ideas about the tradition, and whereas these ideas are contested within Buddhist communities as appropriate (or not) or authentic (or not), Buddhist scholars play a role in these debates. Buddhism is mediated, and this mediation plays a role in personal expression and ritual practice; in these spaces, the correct use of a Buddhist artifact is apparent. As Buddhist artifacts and media move beyond the purely ritual and beyond the bounded category of "Buddhism" and into pop-cultural and commercial spaces, this movement becomes critiqued by practitioners and scholars alike. As media communicates information, and as these communications refine and clarify ideas about what is and what is not Buddhism, what is at stake in these discourses is the meaning of the religion itself. It should come as no surprise then that Buddhists have a vested interest in meta-discourses about mediated forms of Buddhism; and scholars should attend to such discourses both for what they reveal about the ongoing development of Buddhism as well as the role scholars play in shaping that discourse.

DISCOURSES OF AUTHENTICITY

Studies of Buddhist media raise the question of genre—what is "Buddhist media" and what makes it "Buddhist"? This genre question can be used as a metaphor for larger Buddhist and scholarly discourses about what constitutes "real" or "authentic" Buddhism, Buddhist practice, or membership within the bounded category of Buddhism. To demonstrate this, one needs to unpack the issue of genre and then discuss how this discourse is applied to fields of practice and study. Finally, this article would urge scholars to think carefully and self-critically about their own roles and locations within these discourses and how their work reinforces and impacts bounded collectives of practicing Buddhists.

To begin, John Whalen-Bridge's contribution to the 2014 volume of *Contemporary Buddhism* raises the question explicitly: what is a Buddhist film?[49] In other words, is there a genre of Buddhist film, and, if so, how is it defined? What films might be included or excluded from the category and upon what criteria? Similarly, the question of genre is taken up in the context of literature by Kimberly Beek in her contribution to *Buddhism beyond Borders*. She argues that there is indeed a genre of "Buddhist fiction" as evidenced by anthologies of notable exemplars as well as secondary literature on the subject. While Beek, here, does not define the genre of Buddhist fiction as much as provide examples of it, elsewhere, and relying on David Duff, she suggests that Buddhist fiction could be said to be work that is either "about or of" Buddhism.[50] A work of fiction that is about Buddhism, foregrounding a Buddhist story or Buddhist character for example, would clearly fit this genre category. So, too, would "indirect" works, such as Charles Johnson's *Middle Passage*, a slave narrative inspired by his Buddhist practice.[51] One may further clarify here that genre categories might not be mutually exclusive. Beek's work juxtaposes Buddhist and Asian American fiction, for example, while acknowledging elements of the former in the latter, thus suggesting that these two genres may overlap as in the case of Amy Tan's *The Kitchen God's Wife*.[52]

Using this as a rough guideline, it may be possible to abstract a general rule that would define "Buddhist media" more generally. This approach benefits from removing authorial intent; that is, one is not limited to saying that Buddhist media is that which is made by a Buddhist, nor is one limited from including work by non-Buddhists that has obvious or inferred Buddhist meaning. However, this guideline has the limitation of being highly subjective. How does one determine if a work is "of Buddhism"? Such an interpretation leaves open the possibility of the critic infusing into the work his or her own biases. The film *Groundhog Day* (1993) is a prime example; widely claimed as a "Buddhist film," the work has no obvious Buddhist themes and its central conceit—that its protagonist must repeat the same day until he grows morally—has been claimed as Christian as well as Buddhist.[53] Nevertheless, the objective here is not to settle the genre debate, but rather to provide a starting point for a larger conversation about genre categories and their implications.

One implication of genre categories is revealed by Ferdinand de Saussure's "differential of signs," wherein he argues that concepts are defined by their relationship to other concepts. "The meaning of the word 'mutton' is defined by exclusion from its neighboring concepts. It is distinguished from references associated with the living animal because there is already a term 'sheep' which has that meaning . . . the meaning of mutton is entirely due to its position in the structure of a larger system of concepts."[54] Put one way, one might recognize "Buddhist media" as a concept because of its relationship to other, related concepts. Put another way, one might also recognize "Buddhist media" for what it is not—namely, *not* Buddhist media. That is, to define the genre category is also to define its opposite. Thus, even if there are overlapping categories, as mentioned before, of Buddhist literature and Asian American literature, these genre categories remain mutually distinct and, in Beek's case, at least partially in contradistinction from the other—e.g., Buddhist fiction is Buddhist in part because it is not Asian American fiction.

One could easily drop the terms "media" or "fiction" or "film" from the above discussion and come to see that Buddhism is itself a defined category, a genre of religion if you will, defined in large part by its relationship and contradistinction from other genres (e.g., Buddhism is Buddhism because it is not Christianity). How one defines "Buddhism"—or membership in the category as a "Buddhist"—is obviously of some debate, and whether intentionally or not, most would probably fall back on the "family resemblance" rule. That is, especially within the academic study of Buddhism, there is the general awareness of the wide diversity of Buddhisms past and present, their variegated responses to some set of "essential" Buddhist postulates, and their endlessly diverse practices and cultural manifestations, most of which bare some familiarity to one another; all of this constitutes some vaguely defined and somewhat internally coherent category of "Buddhism," despite the differences between, say, a Japanese Shingon fire ritual and an individual practicing mindfulness meditation.

Of course, what distinguishes the abstract genre category of "Buddhist media" from the lived category of "Buddhism" is that the latter is just that—a lived category. In other words, the category "Buddhism" is populated by "Buddhists," actual persons who have a perceived stake in clearly defining what it means to be a member of said category. In constructing a genre of Buddhist fiction or film, a scholar or critic is creating a category of things; in constructing a category of Buddhism, however, the scholar or critic is constructing a category of persons. Scholars may do this inadvertently via defining the object of their study; but Buddhists themselves are engaged in the process of (self-)definition. Indeed, it is the purview of Buddhist communities to define what it means to be members of that community, and in several of the previous examples one can see this definitional work at play.

Once a community defines itself, once a community defines what Buddhism is for members of that community, it is, of course, free to "police the borders," so to speak. One can see an example of this in responses to Buddhist tattoos. Whereas in Western cultural contexts tattooing has taken on a specific set of meanings (though certainly not uncontested), this same practice in Sri Lanka, say, has taken on a different set of meanings. In this context, local Buddhist authorities have taken the view that such practices are inappropriate and unbecoming of proper Buddhist behavior and have acted accordingly. Similarly, in response to the commercialization of buddha images or rejection of Zen-as-aesthetics, lines are being drawn between "Buddhist" spaces and "not-Buddhist" spaces and a border-protectionist attitude is levied against those who transgress the line—and those who transgress the line are deemed inauthentic.[55]

Thus, to claim a category of "Buddhism"—and therefore its opposite—is to invite the question of authenticity. Whereas, on the one hand, it may be the purview of a Buddhist community to define what is and what is not Buddhism *for them*, this is complicated by the reality of late modern global culture for two reasons. First, the global flow of culture has made it increasingly easy for Buddhist ideas, products, and images to move in and out of well-defined Buddhist spaces (see the Buddha bikini).[56] Second, the global flow of culture also brings Buddhists into ever-closer proximity with one another. This close proximity means that defining what Buddhism means for them invariably means defining it in contradistinction to some other community of Buddhists.

To illustrate this point, let us return to "Bodhisattva Vow." The song well reflects the movement of Buddhist ideas beyond their traditional contexts and into the realm of commercial popmusic. Further, the song is an expression of an individual Buddhist's understanding of his tradition and thus may be read as an authentic representation of Buddhism either for him (Adam Yauch) or for his particular lineage (Shambhala). However, to the extent that this song reflects normative understandings of Mahāyāna Buddhism—with references to Mahāyāna Buddhist figures and concepts such as Śantideva and bodhisattvas—it would likely not be considered an authentic expression of Buddhism from a Theravāda perspective, regardless of its location within a hip-hop or pop-cultural context. Thus, rather than using the claim of authenticity to authenticate Buddhism writ large, one should be careful to specify the claim of authenticity to a specific lineage or tradition. Buddhism, after all, is hardly monolithic or homogenous.

As evidenced by the discussion of media responses to the Tiger Woods story, media narratives often reinforce this discourse of authenticity. For example, Buddhist media sources dismissed the story and Woods himself as "not really" Buddhist, a clear reference to an undefined category of "Buddhist" from which Woods was excluded.[57] More than merely defining or clarifying a scholarly object of study, such discourses of authenticity work to disenfranchise individuals by means of inclusion or exclusion. Mainstream news sources, on the other hand, concerned themselves with the question or whether or not Woods was *accurately* describing Buddhism, policing the borders of "Buddhism" from the outside as it were. News media were aided in this task by relying on the voice of the scholarly expert. Buddhist scholars were conscripted into this border-protectionist project and asked to check the veracity of what Buddhism "really" is, despite Woods describing what Buddhism is *for him*. Thus, scholars are called upon by media producers to refine the boundaries of the category of Buddhism or Buddhist, and by extension what counts as an authentic member of said category.

The above should not be surprising—that is, in a cultural context where Buddhism is a minority religion, mainstream news sources would seek scholarly opinion to help educate (for lack of a better word) their readers about Buddhism. Moreover, regardless of whether one is asked to define Buddhism in the context of a tabloid-esque sex scandal, one could argue that Buddhist studies scholars have a role-specific obligation (to invoke Thomas Tweed) to define that which they study.[58] And yet, following on the discussion of what constitutes the genres of "Buddhist literature" or "Buddhism," the academic field of "Buddhist studies" itself is subject to the same critique. To invoke the category of "Buddhist studies" is to invoke its opposite—"not-Buddhist studies"—and to engage in the discursive work of boundary construction and maintenance. This work may be explicit, as in the case of a special volume of the *Journal of Global Buddhism* (2008), or it may be implicit, as in a report by Donald Lopez on the state of the field published by the *Canadian Journal of Buddhist Studies*.[59] But to claim that Buddhist scholars are not engaged in field-defining (i.e., boundary-maintaining) work would be naive.[60]

Importantly, this work is neither value neutral nor is it divorced from the lived tradition of Buddhism. As the field of Buddhist studies is defined, so too do scholars define what counts as authentic or appropriate subjects of study. And, in defining appropriate subjects of study, they also define Buddhist communities worthy of academic interest. By extension, those communities that fall outside such academic purview are excluded from the category of "Buddhism" at best and, at worst, are excluded from public knowledge or interest. This is not to say that Buddhist studies, as a field, should be lax and claim that anything and everything should be included in the category of "Buddhism" or accepted as a legitimate subject of inquiry for the field; it is an argument for critical self-reflection to bring awareness to how such choices—intentionally or otherwise—as a field have consequences on a lived tradition of actual persons. Natalie Quli's forthcoming work on this subject is crucial in calling attention not so much to whether or not one should engage in discourses of authenticity but in the ethical implications of such discourses. Deployed within a Buddhist community, the rhetoric of authenticity may disempower or disenfranchise other Buddhists or Buddhist communities. Deployed by scholars, the rhetoric of authenticity has even greater consequences as being not merely polemical but resulting in the silencing or rendering as invisible whole communities or traditions of Buddhism.

REVIEW OF LITERATURE

The study of media and religion covers a lot of ground and, thus, there are multiple theoretical and topical concerns depending on where one looks. An excellent survey of the field is presented by Jeffrey Mahan in his "Religion and Media."[61] Likewise, Bruce Forbes and Mahan's edited volume, *Religion and Popular Culture in America*, provides a solid overview of the field from multiple religious and media perspectives.[62] Buddhist studies, as a separate academic field, has been slow to adopt the concerns or methods of media studies; generally speaking, when it has, scholarship has focused on: representations of Buddhism or Buddhists in specific medias; interpreting media from a Buddhist perspective; or using media generally in the classroom to teach Buddhist topics. Thus, Buddhist studies has been less interested in theoretical concerns or in the various functions media may play, rhetorically or politely, inside and outside Buddhist communities.

Jane Iwamura's excellent *Virtual Orientalism* is a classic in the field, wherein she discusses the ways in which Asians (and Buddhists) have been represented in US media over the course of the 20th century.[63] John Whalen-Bridge and Gary Storhoff have produced a number of edited volumes on Buddhism and literature and Buddhism and film that primarily analyze representations of Buddhism or media from a Buddhist perspective.[64] Gregory Grieve and Daniel Veidlinger extend the study of Buddhist media into digital spaces including online forums, websites, video games, and virtual reality in their edited volume, *Buddhism, the Internet, and Digital Media*.[65] Sharon Suh's *Silver Screen Buddha* does work similar to Iwamura, focusing on filmic representations of Buddhists; she pushes the field forward, however, by including specific engagements with theoretical and Buddhist or theological readings of film in addition to analyses of Buddhist representations.[66]

The related field of material religion, with such works as Fabio Rambelli's *Buddhist Materiality* being a prime example, analyzes cultural products and their meanings directly.[67] Such work points to the interrelationship between material culture and religious meaning-making, identity formation, and ritual practice. Scholars working in media studies have begun to see these linkages, too, as exemplified by Francisca Cho's *Seeing Like the Buddha*.[68] Rather than merely analyzing how a film is or is not Buddhist or in disclosing the Buddhist meaning of a film, Cho's work focuses on how the experience of viewing a film is itself a practice.

The practical use of media and material culture in Buddhist lives leads to the intersection of media studies and ritual studies. Work by Scott Mitchell on the ritual performance of Buddhist songs is a prime example.[69] Moreover, the intersection of media studies, globalization, and modernity is worth pursuing. Thomas Tweed's work is of note here as are more theoretically grounded works by such scholars as Arjun Appadurai, which explore the explicit creation of global imaginaries, shared cultural and mediated experiences that transcend time and place.[70] As media and material culture are necessarily mobile, Buddhist media, practices, meanings, and discourses transcend the bounded categories of place as well as Buddhism itself.

FURTHER READING

Cho, Francisca. *Seeing Like the Buddha: Enlightenment through Film*. Albany, NY: SUNY Press, 2017.

Forbes, Bruce David, and Jeffrey H. Mahan, eds. *Religion and Popular Culture in America*. Berkeley, CA: University of California Press, 2005.

Grieve, Gregory P., and Daniel M. Veidlinger, eds. *Buddhism, the Internet, and Digital Media: The Pixel in the Lotus*. New York: Routledge, 2015.

Iwamura, Jane. *Virtual Orientalism: Asian Religions and American Popular Culture*. New York: Oxford University Press, 2010.

Mahan, Jeffrey H. "Religion and Media." *Religion Compass* 6, no. 1 (2012): 14–25.

Mitchell, Scott A. "Buddhism, Media, and Popular Culture." In *Buddhism in the Modern World*. Edited by David L. McMahan, 305–323. New York: Routledge, 2012.

Mitchell, Scott A. "The Tranquil Meditator: Representing Buddhism and Buddhists in US Popular Media." *Religion Compass* 8, no. 3 (2014): 81–89.

Suh, Sharon A. *Silver Screen Buddha: Buddhism in Asian and Western Film*. London: Bloomsbury Academic, 2015.

Whalen-Bridge, John, and Gary Storhoff, eds. *The Emergence of Buddhist American Literature*. Albany, NY: SUNY Press, 2009.

Whalen-Bridge, John, and Gary Storhoff, eds. *Buddhism and American Cinema*. Albany, NY: SUNY Press, 2014.

NOTES

1. Scott A. Mitchell, "The Ritual Use of Music in US Jōdo Shinshū Buddhist Communities," *Contemporary Buddhism* 15, no. 2 (2014): 1–17; Keiko Wells, "Shin Buddhist Song Lyrics Sung in the United States: Their History and Expressed Buddhist Images (1), 1898–1939," *Tokyo Daigaku Taiheiyō* 2 (2002): 75–99; and Keiko Wells, "Shin Buddhist Song Lyrics Sung in the United States: Their History and Expressed Buddhist Images (2), 1936–2001," *Tokyo Daigaku Taiheiyō* 3 (2003): 41–64.
2. The use of the term "*gāthā*" for "hymn" is clearly idiosyncratic. See Mitchell, "The Ritual Use," 4–5, especially note 2 for the ambivalent use of this term within the community.
3. Quoted in Wells, "Shin Buddhist Song Lyrics (2)," 51.
4. Matt Diehl, "Review: 'Ill Communication,'" *Rolling Stone* (1994). The Beastie Boys were inducted into the Rock and Roll Hall of Fame in April 2012. Within a month, founding member MCA (Adam Yauch) died from cancer; remaining members have stated that they would not perform under the name "Beastie Boys" out of respect for Yauch.
5. See statistics at the Recording Industry Association of America.
6. Bruce David Forbes, "Introduction: Finding Religion in Unexpected Places," in *Religion and Popular Culture in America*, ed. Bruce David Forbes and Jeffrey H. Mahan (Berkeley, CA: University of California Press, 2005), 1–20.
7. Marshall McLuhan, *Understanding Media: The Extensions of Man* (New York: McGraw-Hill, 1964).
8. Arjun Appadurai, *Modernity at Large: Cultural Dimensions of Globalization* (Minneapolis: University of Minnesota Press, 1996), 31.

9. Daniel M. Veidlinger, "Introduction," in *Buddhism, the Internet, and Digital Media: The Pixel in the Lotus*, ed. Gregory P. Grieve and Daniel M. Veidlinger (New York: Routledge, 2015), 1–20.
10. Jeffrey H. Mahan, "Religion and Media," *Religion Compass* 6, no. 1 (2012): 15.
11. Scott A. Mitchell, "The Stories We Tell: The Study and Practice of Jōdo Shinshū Buddhism," *Pacific World: The Journal of the Institute of Buddhist Studies* 3, no. 19 (2017): 81.
12. Richard Seager, "Dharma Images and Identity in American Buddhism," in *Buddhism beyond Borders*, ed. Scott A. Mitchell and Natalie E. F. Quli (Albany, NY: SUNY Press, 2015), 113–124; and cf. Mary Douglas, *Natural Symbols: Explorations in Cosmology* (New York: Routledge, 2003).
13. Seager, "Dharma Images," 114.
14. Thomas A. Tweed, "Tracing Modernity's Flows: Buddhist Currents in the Pacific World," *The Eastern Buddhist* 43, no. 1–2 (2012): 38.
15. See for example Donald K. Swearer, *Becoming the Buddha: The Ritual of Image Consecration in Thailand* (Princeton, NJ: Princeton University Press, 2004).
16. See Richard K. Payne, "Jesus Christ, Tantric Deity: Syntax and Semantics in Ritual Change," in *On Meaning and Mantras: Essays in Honor of Frits Staal*, ed. George Thompson and Richard K. Payne (Berkeley, CA: Institute of Buddhist Studies, 2016), 455–476; and Richard K. Payne and Michael Witzel, *Homa Variations: The Study of Ritual Change across the* Longue Durée (New York: Oxford University Press, 2016).
17. Fabio Rambelli, *Buddhist Materiality: A Cultural History of Objects in Japanese Buddhism* (Stanford: Stanford University Press, 2007), 2.
18. See, for example, Justin T. McDaniel, *Architects of Buddhist Leisure: Socially Disengaged Buddhism in Asia's Museums, Monuments, and Amusement Parks*, Contemporary Buddhism (Honolulu: University of Hawaii Press, 2017); and Jessica Starling's forthcoming work on the role of ritual in the lives of women Jōdo Shinshū Buddhists in Japan is also relevant.
19. Mitchell, "The Ritual Use"; and Mitchell, "The Stories We Tell."
20. Patricia Q. Campbell, *Knowing Body, Moving Mind: Ritualizing and Learning at Two Buddhist Centers* (Oxford and New York: Oxford University Press, 2011).
21. Elisabetta Porcu, "Aesthetics and Art in Modern Pure Land Buddhism," *Japanese Religions* 32, no. 1–2 (2007): 55.
22. Porcu, "Aesthetics and Art," 56.
23. Scott A. Mitchell, "Buddhism, Media, and Popular Culture," in *Buddhism in the Modern World*, ed. David L. McMahan (New York: Routledge, 2012), 305–323. This practice is contested ground, with some claiming that the practice is a form of cultural appropriation or neo-Orientalism. See Mark Hay, "Permanent Buddhism: Buddhist Tattoos," *Tricycle: The Buddhist Review*, May 18, 2016. For more on neo-Orientalism, see Tessa Bartholomeusz, "Spiritual Wealth and Neo-Orientalism," *Journal of Ecumenical Studies* 35, no. 1 (1998): 19–33.
24. On the acceptance and popularity of tattooing generally in the United States, see Gary S. Foster and Richard L. Hummel, "The Commodification of Body Modification: Tattoos and Piercings from Counterculture to Campus," *Quarterly Journal of Ideology* 25, no. 1 (2002): 1–27.
25. Nancy Thompson, "Dharma Connect: Buddha Tattoos—An Homage or a Sign of Disrespect?," *The Interdependence Project*, April 23, 2014; and Rachel Premack, "Advice to Tourists: Don't Sport Your Buddha Tattoo in a Buddhist Country," *The Washington Post*, July 19, 2016.
26. Green, Ronald S. *Buddhism Goes to the Movies: Introduction to Buddhist Thought and Practice* (London: Routledge, 2014).
27. John Whalen-Bridge, "What Is a 'Buddhist Film?,'" *Contemporary Buddhism* 15, no. 1 (2014): 44–80.
28. Christian Feichtinger, "Space Buddhism: The Adoption of Buddhist Motifs in Star Wars," *Contemporary Buddhism* 15, no. 1 (2014): 28–43.

29. Elisabetta Porcu, "Staging Zen Buddhism: Image Creation in Contemporary Films," *Contemporary Buddhism* 15, no. 1 (2014): 81–96.
30. Francisca Cho, "The Transnational Buddhism of *Spring, Summer, Fall, Winter . . . and Spring*," *Contemporary Buddhism* 15, no. 1 (2014): 109–124.
31. Sharon A. Suh, *Silver Screen Buddha: Buddhism in Asian and Western Film* (London: Bloomsbury Academic, 2015), 84–94. Whereas Suh's analysis of the film shows how it relies on the trope of Buddhism-as-otherworldly, her main focus is on the problematic treatment of women in the film (and by extension, Buddhism) as little more than "dangerous mantraps that must be guarded against" (p. 84).
32. Jane Iwamura, *Virtual Orientalism: Asian Religions and American Popular Culture* (New York: Oxford University Press, 2010).
33. Jane Naomi Iwamura, "The Oriental Monk in American Popular Culture," in *Religion and Popular Culture in America*, ed. Bruce David Forbes and Jeffrey H. Mahan (Berkeley, CA: University of California Press, 2005), 25–43.
34. Eve Mullen, "Orientalist Commercializations: Tibetan Buddhism in American Popular Film," *Journal of Religion and Film* 2, no. 2 (1998): 2; see also Donald S. Lopez, *Prisoners of Shangri-La: Tibetan Buddhism and the West* (Chicago: University of Chicago Press, 1998); and Georges Dreyfus, "Are We Prisoners of Shangrila? Orientalism, Nationalism, and the Study of Tibet," *Journal of the International Association of Tibetan Studies* 1 (2005): 1–21.
35. Richard C. Anderson and David A. Harper, "Dying to Be Free: The Emergence of 'American Militant Buddhism' in Popular Culture," in *Buddhism and American Cinema*, ed. John Whalen-Bridge and Gary Storhoff (Albany, NY: SUNY Press, 2014), 133–156.
36. Francisca Cho, *Seeing Like the Buddha: Enlightenment through Film* (Albany, NY: SUNY Press, 2017), 25
37. Scott A. Mitchell, "The Tranquil Meditator: Representing Buddhism and Buddhists in US Popular Media," *Religion Compass* 8, no. 3 (2014): 81–89.
38. Jeff Wilson, *Mindful America: The Mutual Transformation of Buddhist Meditation and American Culture* (New York: Oxford University Press, 2014), 43–74; and Janet Eastman, "Buddhamania: The Religious Symbol as Decoration? It's Complicated," *Los Angeles Times*, June 12, 2008.
39. The practice of using "Buddhism" or "Zen" to sell (non-religious) products is hardly unique to Western cultural contexts. Evidence suggests that traditionally Buddhist countries are beginning to use Buddhism as a marketing device, a subject for future study.
40. Shôji Yamada, *Shots in the Dark: Japan, Zen, and the West* (Chicago: University of Chicago Press, 2009).
41. Iwamura, *Virtual Orientalism*, 26–28.
42. Cristina Rocha, *Zen in Brazil: The Quest for Cosmopolitan Modernity* (Honolulu: University of Hawaii Press, 2006), 148.
43. James Mark Shields, "Sexuality, Blasphemy, and Iconoclasm in the Media Age," in *God in the Details: American Religion in Popular Culture*, ed. Eric Mazur and Kate McCarthy (London: Routledge, 2011), 80–102.
44. Scott A. Mitchell, *Buddhism in America: Global Religion, Local Contexts* (London: Bloomsbury Academic, 2016), 185.
45. Robert Wuthnow and Wendy Cadge, "Buddhists and Buddhism in the United States: The Scope of Influence," *Journal for the Scientific Study of Religion* 43, no. 3 (2004): 363–380.
46. Thomas A. Tweed, "Why Are Buddhists so Nice? Media Representations of Buddhism and Islam in the United States since 1945," *Material Religion* 4, no. 1 (2008): 91–93.
47. Rick Clifton Moore, "Secular Spirituality/Mundane Media: One Newspaper's In-Depth Coverage of Buddhism," *Journal of Media and Religion* 7, no. 4 (2008): 231–255.

48. Scott A. Mitchell, "'Christianity Is for Rubes; Buddhism Is for Actors': U.S. Media Representations of Buddhism in the Wake of the Tiger Woods' Scandal," *Journal of Global Buddhism* 13 (2012): 69, italics in original.
49. Whalen-Bridge, "What Is a 'Buddhist Film?'"
50. Kimberly Beek, "Telling Tales Out of School: The Fiction of Buddhism," in *Buddhism beyond Borders*, ed. Scott A. Mitchell and Natalie E. F. Quli (Albany, NY: SUNY Press, 2015), 125–142; here, Beek states that the genre of Buddhist fiction is defined primarily as fiction with Buddhist themes or characters. See also David Duff, *Modern Genre Theory* (New York: Longman, 2000); and Mitchell, *Buddhism in America*, 182–183.
51. Beek, "Telling Tales Out of School."
52. Beek, "Telling Tales Out of School."
53. Danny Rubin, "Foreword," in *Buddhism and American Cinema*, ed. John Whalen-Bridge and Gary Storhoff (Albany, NY: SUNY Press, 2014), ix–x.
54. See Jason Ānanda Josephson, "When Buddhism Became a 'Religion': Religion and Superstition in the Writings of Inoue Enryō," *Japanese Journal of Religious Studies* 33, no. 1 (2006): 147.
55. Rocha, *Zen in Brazil*, 148.
56. To the extent that the current flow of global culture is the end result of historical colonialism, it is perhaps inevitable that Buddhist ideas, arts, and artifacts are easily removed from their original cultural contexts and appropriated into new cultural spheres; and because of this connection to historical colonialism, it is also inevitable that such movement will be contested.
57. Mitchell, "Christianity Is for Rubes," 73–74.
58. Thomas A. Tweed, *Crossing and Dwelling: A Theory of Religion* (Cambridge, MA: Harvard University Press, 2008), 30ff.
59. Special issue, *Journal of Global Buddhism* (2008); and Donald S. Lopez, "Development in Buddhist Studies, 2015: A Report on the Symposium 'Buddhist Studies Today,'" *Canadian Journal of Buddhist Studies* 11 (2016): 5–36.
60. Lopez makes this boundary-defining work explicit, wherein he notes that the largest question to emerge from a 2015 workshop "was the nature of the boundaries that have long defined the field of Buddhist Studies" and that "[o]ver the course of three days, many of these boundaries were expanded, crossed and blurred." Lopez, "Development in Buddhist Studies," 34.
61. Mahan, "Religion and Media."
62. Bruce David Forbes and Jeffrey H. Mahan, *Religion and Popular Culture in America* (Berkeley, CA: University of California Press, 2005).
63. Iwamura, *Virtual Orientalism*.
64. Gary Storhoff and John Whalen-Bridge, eds., *American Buddhism as a Way of Life* (Albany, NY: SUNY Press, 2010); John Whalen-Bridge and Gary Storhoff, eds., *The Emergence of Buddhist American Literature* (Albany, NY: SUNY Press, 2009); John Whalen-Bridge and Gary Storhoff, eds., *Writing as Enlightenment: Buddhist American Literature into the Twenty-First Century* (Albany, NY: SUNY Press, 2011); and John Whalen-Bridge and Gary Storhoff, eds., *Buddhism and American Cinema* (Albany, NY: SUNY Press, 2014).
65. Gregory P. Grieve and Daniel M. Veidlinger, eds., *Buddhism, the Internet, and Digital Media: The Pixel in the Lotus* (New York: Routledge, 2015).
66. Suh, *Silver Screen Buddha*.
67. Rambelli, *Buddhist Materiality*.
68. Cho, *Seeing Like the Buddha*.
69. Mitchell, "The Ritual Use."
70. Tweed, "Tracing Modernity's Flows"; and Appadurai, *Modernity at Large*.

Scott A. Mitchell

BUDDHISM AND MEDICINE IN INDIA

The earliest records of Buddhist medicine in India can be found in the Pāli canonical and non-canonical sources that shed some light on the Buddhist understanding of health and illness, and on medical treatments utilized in early Buddhist monastic communities. Sanskrit literature of the early and later centuries of the Common Era as well as epigraphic evidence of the 3rd and 4th centuries, which record the names of various wealthy physicians and their family members who made meritorious gifts to the sangha, also provide valuable information on the close relations of the Buddhist tradition and its monastic institutions to medicine and affluent lay physicians.[1] Buddhist medicine in India also had a close connection to the classics of Indian Āyurveda, such as the *Suśruta* and *Caraka Saṃhitās*. The mentions of celebrated expounders of Indian Āyurveda in Buddhist literature, in addition to the names of other medical specialists, is evidence of the familiarity of Buddhist physicians with the Āyurvedic medical system.[2]

From its inception, the Buddhist tradition in India considered the preservation of health to be of great importance. Although it focused primarily on mental training and transformation, it did not neglect physical health. In the *Magandīya Sutta*, the Buddha Śākyamuni himself pointed out the difficulty of achieving the final goal of nirvana with an impaired body. On several occasions recorded in the Pāli canon, the Buddha expressed his view of health as a person's greatest possession and considered it as one of the ten things desirable in the world but difficult to obtain. Similarly, in the *Dhammapada* (ch. 15, v. 204), health is said to be "the highest gain" (*ārogyaparamā lābhā*).[3] In the *Aṅguttara Nikāya* (III.30), one's resistance to illness and one's good digestion are said to be among the five factors that facilitate the monk's effort in Buddhist practice. In the same text, the Buddha counsels monks to reflect in this way: "I am now seldomly ill or afflicted; I possess an even digestion that is neither too cool nor too hot but moderate and suitable for striving. But there will come a time when illness assails this body. Now when one is ill, overcome by illness, it is not easy to attend to the Buddha's teaching; it is not easy to resort to remote lodgings in forests and in jungle groves."[4] A person's perpetual vulnerability to illness is indicated as a consequence of the person's embodiment. In the "Khandhasaṃyutta" section of the *Saṃyutta Nikāya* (III.1), the aged householder Nakulapitā is reminded that it would be foolish for any embodied being to claim to be healthy even for a moment.[5] Similarly, in the Sanskrit *Garbhāvakrāntisūtra*, dated to the early centuries CE, the Buddha speaks of the body's susceptibility to illness in this way: "Nanda, this body becomes an illness; it becomes a tumor; it becomes a thorn."[6]

In several *suttas* of the *Dīgha* and *Anguttara Nikāyas*, the Buddha asserts that everyone, whether a woman or a man, a householder or a *śrāmaṇa*, should often reflect in this way: "I am subject to illness; I am not exempt from illness." The given reason for this way of thinking is to counteract one's infatuation with one's own health (*ārogyamada*). Those infatuated with their health are said to be prone to engage in bodily, verbal, and mental misconduct, but if they often reflect upon their vulnerability to sickness, that infatuation diminishes or completely vanishes.[7] In the *Aṅguttara Nikāya*, the Buddha's advice is to avoid unwholesome lifestyles and non-beneficial things, which obstruct health.[8] In another passage of the same *Nikāya*, while explaining the difference between physical and mental illnesses, the Buddha admits that there are those who claim to enjoy physical health for even up to one hundred and more years; and at the same time, he emphasizes that with the exception of those who are free from mental defilements (*āssava*), it is difficult to find people in the world who can claim to enjoy mental health even for a moment.[9]

The emphasis on maintaining and restoring physical health was also given great importance in the later Indic Mahāyāna tradition, which saw the prolonged life of an altruistic Bodhisattva as profitable for suffering beings. In the context of the yogic Vajrayāna practices, the preservation of health and the body became of paramount importance. This is made explicit in the statement given in the *Kālacakratantra* (ch. 2), in which the tantric adept is instructed to preserve his body for the sake of attaining *siddhis*, since in the absence of the body, neither *siddhis* nor supreme bliss is attainable in this life.[10]

THE BUDDHA ŚĀKYAMUNI AS A PHYSICIAN AND THE DHARMA AS MEDICINE

In the *Questions of King Milinda* (*Milindapañha*), Nāgasena speaks of the buddhadharma as a casket of ambrosial medicine that heals all the diseases of sin. It is said to surpass all of the most powerful medicines in the world, including the antidotes to poison, since it liberates a person from disease, old age, and death, as well as from sins, desires, and karma.[11] In that respect, in the *Milindapañha* and in the *Sela Sutta* of the *Mahāvagga* section of the *Sutta Nipāta*, the Buddha is quoted referring to himself as the "supreme physician," as an "incomparable physician," and as the unexcelled surgeon (*sallakatto anutaro*).[12] In addition to Pāli sources, one finds references to the Buddha as physician and to his dharma as medicine in later Sanskrit sources. In the *Abhidharmakośabhāṣya* (ch. 6), the Buddha is referred to as a physician, the dharma as a remedy, and the sangha as a patient.[13] In the same text (ch. 5), the Buddha is also called "the great physician" (*mahāvaidya*).[14] A similar reference is found in the *Saddharmapuṇḍarīka Sūtra* (ch. 15, v. 21).

The *Mahāvagga* section of the Pāli *Vinaya Piṭaka* describes events in which the Buddha himself acted as a physician, miraculously curing a person or prescribing various treatments and medicines to sick monks. In the *Aṅguttara Nikāya*, one reads about Venerable Girimānanda, who, inflicted by a grave illness, fully recovered while listening to a discourse on ten perceptions presented to him by Ānanda on the Buddha's advice. The ten perceptions that were said to immediately cure Venerable Girimānanda pertain to insight into some of the main Buddhist principles and meditative practices: impermanence, no-self, the foulness of the body, bodily dangers, the abandoning of sensual desires, renunciation, disenchantment with the world, the impermanence of all formations, and mindfulness of breathing.[15] In the *Saṃyutta Nikāya* we find other examples of sick monks recovering from illnesses after receiving teachings on the buddhadharma and an occasion in which the Buddha Śākyamuni himself, having become very sick during his stay in Rājagaha, asked the Venerable Mahācunda to recite the seven factors of awakening (*bodhi-pakkhiyā dhammā*). It is said that after listening to Mahācunda's recitation of the factors of awakening and approving Mahācunda's words, the Buddha recovered from his illness.[16]

Although free from mental defilements, the Buddha himself experienced physical ailments and sought medical help. In the *Mahāvagga* section of the *Saṃyutta Nikāya*, we learn about the Buddha becoming seriously ill and experiencing terrible pains bordering on death while he was residing in Vesālī during the rainy season. The text tells us that despite the severity of those pains, he endured them mindfully and without becoming distressed. He was able to suppress his illness, revitalize his body, and fully recover, as he thought that it would be inappropriate for him to leave for *parinibbāna* without having first addressed his sangha.[17] In another passage of the *Saṃyutta Nikāya*, one encounters Venerable Anuruddha, who also, while gravely ill, endured bodily pains with mental calm. When asked by other monks how it is that his painful bodily sensations do not preoccupy his mind, Anuruddha reveals that this is due to his mind being well established in the four applications of mindfulness (*satyupasthāna*).[18] In the same *Nikāya*, we read about the layman Anāthapiṇḍaka, one of the chief lay followers of the Buddha and a great supporter of the sangha, who, having fallen gravely ill, fully recovered after hearing Sāriputta's words of consolation, which validated Anāthapiṇḍaka's faith in the Three Jewels and his right view and conduct.[19] In another instance, the Buddha instructs a sick lay practitioner named Mahānāma on how a lay devotee should console a sick lay devotee with a fourfold consolation, which resembles that given by Sāriputta to the sick Anāthapiṇḍaka in that it confirms the sick person's faith in the Three Jewels and his unbroken virtues. After the sick lay follower is consoled, he should be asked whether he has abandoned his anxiety about his parents, wife, and children, and his pleasures and desire for heaven. If he expresses his anxiety about any of these, he should be reminded of the inevitability of death and the futility of anxiety.[20]

THE MEDICINE BUDDHA, BHAIṢAJYAGURU

In India, the earliest idea of a divine healer goes back to the *Ṛgveda*, which eulogizes certain deities, such as Aśvins, Varuṇa, Rudra, and Dhvanvantari, for their healing powers. The *Ṛgveda* also speaks of the six Vedic sages (*ṛṣis*) renowned as healers, whose names, together with Dhvanvatari, are also mentioned in the *Milindapañha* and in the *Jātakas*. In the *Bhaiṣajyavaidūryaprabharāja Sūtra*, dedicated to the Medicine Buddha, who presides over the buddha-field (*buddhakṣetra*) of the eastern direction, called Vaidūryanirbhāsa, we learn of his previous twelve aspirations (*praṇidhāna*) to cure diseases, change females into males, dispel the fears of sentient beings, provide them with food/ clothing/ protection, and lead them to his buddha-field and to enlightenment.[21] His body marked with the thirty-two major and eighty minor marks of the Great Man is said to be thoroughly pure like a cat eye's gem (*vaidūrya*). The light of his body, which outshines the light of the sun and the moon, illuminates his entire world system, enabling people to move freely at night. Similar to the Vedic god Dhvanvanatri, he holds a vessel with ambrosia (*amṛta*) in his hand. Those who worship him and recite his name are promised to beget sons, revive the dying, and acquire wealth. In his buddha-field there is no suffering, nor are there women.

The Mahāyāna scriptures also speak of celestial Medicine Bodhisattvas. Two such Bodhisattvas are the brothers Bhaiṣajyarāja and Bhaiṣajyasamudgata, who are mentioned in the earliest segment of the *Saddharmapuṇḍarīka Mahāyāna Sūtra*. According to the *Saddharmapuṇḍarīka Sūtra* (ch. 3), in one of his previous births, the elder of the two brothers, the Bodhisattva Bhaiṣajyarāja, wrapped his body with divine garments, bathed in oil, and burned himself out of his devotion to the Buddha and the *Saddharmapuṇḍarīka Sūtra*. In consequence, his body went on blazing for twelve thousand years, illuminating the worlds.

In the *Kāraṇḍavyūha*, I.15, we encounter the Bodhisattva Bhaiṣajyasena in a vast assembly of Bodhisattvas, listening to the Buddha's teachings, and in the *Saṃghātasūtra Dharmaparyāya* appears the Bodhisattva Mahāsattva Bhaiṣajyasena, who speaks of himself in these words:

I am the medicine of sentient beings.
The best of all medicine,
that I will teach you—
that pacifies all the sicknesses
that has infected sentient beings.[22]

In addition to Bhaiṣajyaguru and the aforementioned Bodhisattvas, Āyurbuddha and Amitāyus Buddha held a central place in granting longevity and protecting the life of a pregnant woman and an infant. The *Āyuḥsādhana, Āyurbuddhānusmṛti, Āyurvardhanīvidhi,* and other practice texts related to these two buddhas contain descriptions of worshiping these two buddhas and performing various rites and *sādhanas* for ensuring one's longevity.

Medicine in the Pāli Vinaya Piṭaka. In the sixth Khandaka of the Mahāvagga, which is dedicated to medicine and medical treatments permissible for sick monks, and in the Cullavagga of the *Vinaya Piṭaka,* one learns of the therapeutic methods and medicinal substances prescribed by the Buddha for the variety of illnesses to which members of the early Buddhist sangha succumbed.[23] Each medical case is presented in a particular formulaic way: after the Buddha himself notices or is told by someone of a medical condition of an individual monk or of a group of monks, he gives a religious discourse prior to offering his medical advice to the sick. In contrast, when rebuking monks for preparing medicine or treating the sick at an inappropriate time or in an inappropriate manner, his rebuke precedes his religious discourse. Several examples given in the Pāli *Vinaya* show that in some cases, the Buddha's initial medical advice failed to bring the desired result for the disease-stricken monks, in which cases he would offer different medical advice that would bring the desired result. The text does not explain for what reason the Buddha's initial advice failed. There is mention of neither the possible role of a monk's karma in unsuccessful treatment nor the Buddha's lack of knowledge of healing.

Numerous examples of disease-stricken monks in the Pāli *Vinaya* suggest that digestive disorders and gastrointestinal problems were the most common ailments of monks and even of the Buddha himself. In the Mahāvagga, one learns of the Buddha becoming troubled with abdominal wind on more than one occasion and finding relief from a *tekaṭula* gruel made with *tila* seeds, rice, and beans, and prepared in the form of a drink.[24] A significant number of medicinal substances and treatments prescribed in the *Mahāvagga* pertain to restoring a healthy digestive system. The five most common types of medicine (*pañcabhesajjāni*) for gastrointestinal ailments, which were also used as ingredients in certain other medicines for other types of ailments, were ghee (*sappi*), fresh butter (*navanīta*), oil (*tela*), honey (*madhu*), and molasses (*phāṇīa*).[25] We learn of sick monks who vomited and became emaciated and yellow in complexion due to suffering from the disease of a "hot season," and being treated with these five medicines on the Buddha's advice. These five substances were also well known for their medicinal properties among the laity, as seen in the story of Venerable Pilindavaccha, who was rewarded with large quantities of ghee, butter, oil, and molasses by local people for his miracle of transforming the king Bimbisāra's residence into a golden palace and thereby saving the lives of a local family of gatekeepers. However, as the supply of medicine became abundant, Pilindavaccha had it distributed among the attending monks; and as their vessels and bags became filled with medicine, rats scattered it all over *vihāras*. The medicine-hoarding monks became the objects of resentment and ridicule in local communities. Hearing about this, the Buddha prohibited that this kind of medicine be stored for longer than a week.[26] In the case of a man who suffered from poor digestion, the ingestion of raw meat was recommended. When a person suffers from indigestion or dysentery, dry, raw meat was to be set on fire. The ashes that fall down from that meat contain an alkaline ingredient that was deemed beneficial as medicine.[27]

Various substances often used as flavor-enhancing spices in cooking were prohibited for healthy monks but allowed as a digestive aids for the sick. These include roots such as turmeric, ginger, orris root (*rhizoma iridis*), ativisa (*Aconitum heterophyllum*), the root of black hellebore (*helleborus nigum*), and the like, which could be prepared as soft, hard, or pulverized. Moreover, astringent decoctions and astringent roots, medicinal leafs, various types of pepper and myrobalans, fruits, different kinds of gums, and salts were all used for digestive problems.[28] In the case of a monk who was troubled by abdominal wind, the usage of decoctions made of oil mixed with strong liquor was prescribed. However, when certain monks poured too much liquor into the oil decoction and became intoxicated, the Buddha no longer permitted that it be used as a drink. However, he allowed its external application as an ointment. For treatments of gastrointestinal sickness that required fatty substances, the fat from animals such as a bear, fish, alligator, pig, or donkey was permitted, but only if prepared and used at the right time. Preparing and consuming animal fat at the wrong time was regarded as a wrong action that results in the monastic *dukkaṭa* offense. Furthermore, any type of surgical treatment of the anal area within a distance of two inches around the anus, such as the lancing of anal fistulas and the like, was prohibited on the grounds that the skin of that area is thin and hard to treat, and a knife difficult to guide. Any such surgery was declared by the Buddha to be a monastic *thulaccaya* offense.[29]

Skin diseases such as scabs, boils, itches, smelly discharges, and the like, and various types of fever were also frequent health problems experienced by monks, and were treated with various medicines. For example, to a senior monk named Belaṭṭhasīsa, who was suffering from thick, oozing scabs that were sticking to his robes, the Buddha prescribed chunam as medicine; and to those having healthy skin he allowed the use of dry dung and clay as a preventive treatment. We also learn of Venerable Sāriputta being relieved of fever by the edible stalks of lotuses, after Mahā Moggallana, seeing Sāriputta in Jetavana grove suffering from fever for some time, departed to Lake Mandākinī, where a *nāga* of the lake provided him with the stalks of lotuses that pacified Sāriputta's fever.[30]

In the case of an occular diseases, the use of eye ointments, such as black collyrium, *rasa* ointment, *sota* ointment, yellow ochre (*geruka*), and soot taken from the flame of a lamp (*kapalla*), were prescribed together with perfumes made of different kinds of sandalwood and fragrant flowers. Sweating by the use of herbs and hot baths mixed with medicinal herbs was prescribed for rheumatism. Larger *ārāmas* contained pools for such use, which were enclosed with fences made of brick, stone, or wood for the sake of privacy and donated to monks. Mustard powder and fumigation were used for sores. Oils were used for blisters on the feet and for wounds, while dung, urine, ashes, and clay were prescribed for snakebites.

The Pāli *Vinaya* also contains examples of various Buddhist lay devotees who procured medicine and assisted sick monks. One such lay devotee was a woman named Suppiyā, who, we are told, having gone to the monks' *ārāma*, went around from *vihāra* to *vihāra*, from one monastic cell to another, asking the resident monks who among them was sick and in need of what.[31]

Dietary and Pharmaceutical Treatments of Digestive Problems in Pāli and Sanskrit Sources. Among all physical ailments, a poorly functioning digestive system seems to be of most concern in Pāli *suttas* and in noncanonical sources. As in the *Vinaya*, here too good digestion is to be maintained with appropriate dietary habits and is to be restored with a proper diet. Moderation in the consumption of food and drink was seen as indispensable for good health and vitality. In the *Saṃyutta Nikāya*, the Buddha tells this to king Pasenadi of Kosala, who was huffing and puffing after eating a bucket-size portion of rice and curries:

> When a man is always mindful,
> Knowing moderation in the food he eats,
> His ailments then diminish:
> He ages slowly, guarding his life.[32]

In the *Bhaddāli Sutta* of the *Majjhima Nikāya*, the Buddha gives these reasons for his good health: "Monks, I eat at a single session. By so doing, I am free from illness and affliction, and I enjoy health, strength, and a comfortable abiding." He further instructs monks to do the same for the sake of health, strength, and comfort.[33] In the *Kīṭāgiri Sutta* of the same *Nikāya*, the Buddha informs the monks in Kāsi who ate their meals at different times, in the evening, the morning, and during the day, "Monks, I abstain from eating at night. By so doing I am free from illness and affliction, and I enjoy health, strength, and a comfortable abiding."[34] In the *Aṅguttara Nikāya*, he expounds the five types of health benefits of eating rice porridge, one of which is a healthy digestive system. Rice porridge is said to still hunger, dispel thirst, settle wind, clean out the bladder, and promote the digestion of the remnants of undigested food.[35] In the *Bodhirājakumāra* and *Kaṇṇakatthala Suttas*, faith in the Buddha's enlightenment is given as another cause of a healthy digestive system. There, the Buddha informs a young prince and the king of Kosala, respectively, that a monk who has faith in the Tathāgata's enlightenment becomes free from illness, has good digestion that is neither too cool nor too hot, and is able to endure the strain of practice.[36]

In the case of dysentery, a mixture of milk, honey, oil, and sugar was recommended.[37] In the *Sumangalavilāsinī*, different kinds of gruels and drinks that function as purgatives are suggested to those suffering from constipation: rice gruel, a gruel of mung, a gruel to which a small amount of oil is added, milk, and a decoction of the ashes of non-husked rice.[38] In the *Dīgha Nikāya* we find other types of purgatives, those for the lower part of the body, those for the upper part of the body, and those for the head.[39] From the *Aṅguttara Nikāya* we learn that purgatives were also given as a preventive medicine to control the excess of wind, bile, and phlegm in the body.

SEASONAL DIETS AND ILLNESSES

In the "Chapter on Healing and Illnesses" of the *Suvarṇaprabhāsottama Sūtra*, a physician by the name of Jatiṃdhara, fully versed in the eight branches of medicine, instructs his son Jalavāhana on the relation between the seasons and illnesses. Food and drink must be consumed in accordance with the six seasons. As the sense faculties and bodily elements change during the change of seasons, various illnesses arise. Illnesses caused by the excess of wind arise during the rainy season, disturbances of bile take place in autumn, disturbances of phlegm occur during the hot season, and the imbalance of the combination of the three humors occurs in winter. Food, drink, and medicine must be administered in accordance with the time, humoral disorder, and person. Thus, fatty, warm, salty, and sour tastes should be administered during the rainy season; in autumn, fatty, sweet, and cold tastes; and in summer, rough, warm, and bitter tastes. Excess of phlegm occurs as soon as one has eaten, excess of bile occurs during digestion, and excess of wind springs up as soon as one has digested. A strengthening medicine is for the imbalance of wind, a purgative for bile disorder, an emetic for phlegm disorder, and a medicine consisting of the three qualities is for imbalances in the combination of the three humors.[40]

The Buddhist medical manuscript from Gandhara known as the *Bower Manuscript*, named after Hamilton Bower, a lieutenant in the British Army who purchased it in 1888, contains an entire chapter dedicated to the medicinal benefits, including digestive ones, of the uses of garlic, and recipes for the preparation of foods with garlic, including the preparation of garlic with various kinds of meat. Brahmins who have traditionally been prohibited from eating garlic are advised to consume milk or milk products from cows that were fed garlic.

SURGERY IN PĀLI SOURCES

The *Jātaka* story of the Buddha's previous birth as a king of Sivi (XV.499) describes the surgical transplant of an eyeball performed on the king Sivikumāra by the surgeon Sīvaka. The surgeon Sīvaka is said to have brushed the king's eye with a strong powder three times until the eyeball moved from the socket and dangled from the tendon. As the blood was trickling from the king's eye socket, Sīvaka took the eyeball with his left hand and cut the tendon with a knife in his right hand. Having done so, he placed the eyeball into the empty socket of a blind *brāhmaṇa*, who was none other than the god Indra in disguise.[41]

In the *Asilakkhaṇa Jātaka* (I.126) we encounter a surgeon who performed a rhino-plastic surgery by affixing an artificial tip to the nose of a *brāhmaṇa* of Benares, who tested a sword made for the king of Benares by a certain smith. When the *brāhmaṇa* pulled out the sword from a sheath that contained some finely ground pepper and sniffed it, the pepper went up his nose and made him sneeze so violently that he slit his nose with the edge of the sword. On the king's request, a surgeon fitted the *brāhmaṇa*'s nose with a false tip that was painted to look like a real nose.[42]

The *Mahāvagga* (VIII.1–36) of the *Vinaya Piṭaka* informs us about a surgery performed by Jīvaka, a personal physician of Bimbisāra, the king of Magadha, and also the Buddha Śākyamuni's personal physician, on a merchant of Rājagaha, who suffered from head ailments caused by worms. Some of the merchant's previous physicians, who could not see both worms that caused the merchant's headaches, had prognosticated that he would die in five days, while others had prognosticated that he would die within seven days. After questioning the sick merchant, Jīvaka tied him to his bed and performed surgery by cutting through the skin, drawing apart the flesh on each side of the merchant's head, and pulling out the two worms, one small and one big, which were about to enter his brain within five or seven days. Jīvaka closed the wounds, stitched the skin, and anointed it with salve. We also learn of Jīvaka performing an intestinal surgery on a son of a merchant of Benares, who suffered from entangled intestines caused due to the game of tumbling, which resulted in his inability to digest any food or drink and in constipation, emaciation, and a yellow complexion. Jīvaka ordered people out of the room, drew a curtain, tied the patient to a pillar, placed his wife in front of him, and then cut through the skin of the belly, drew the twisted intestines out and disentangled them, put the intestines back into the right position, stitched the skin together, and anointed it with salve. In another instance, we read about Jīvaka curing the king Seniya, who suffered from a fistula that stained his garment with blood, for which reason he was not able to appear in public. Due to that, he also experienced sadness, since the women of his court ridiculed him, saying that the king was having his monthly periods and would give birth. Jīvaka applied a layer of ointment to the king's fistula and removed it in one stroke with an instrument called a "nail instrument." In the *Sattigumba Jātaka*, when Devadatta threw a stone, and a splinter struck and injured the Buddha's foot, Jīvaka made his foot well.[43] The *Cullahaṃsa Jātaka* tells the same story, but in a somewhat different version: Jīvaka heals the Buddha's foot by opening the foot with a knife, letting out bad blood, removing the extra flesh, and anointing the wound.[44]

We also find descriptions of other types of surgical procedures in Pāli sources, such as surgery on boils, abscesses, knotty boils, wounds, wounds from a poisonous arrow, and hydroceles. Instead of surgery on hydroceles, the Buddha suggested that a cotton wick or a bamboo tube smeared with oil or an alkaline substance be placed into the rectum of the patient. Pāli literature also sheds light on the different surgical instruments used for various types of surgical interventions, among which are five different types of needles, five types of scissors, twelve types of piercing instruments, cutting instruments, tongs, forceps, small sticks, and so on. In the commentary on the Cullavaga section of the *Vinaya Piṭaka*, it is said that a physician who, ignoring the cause of illness, immediately takes up a surgical instrument, is not a skillful physician.

CLASSIFICATION OF ILLNESSES IN PĀLI AND SANSKRIT SOURCES

Various Buddhist Pāli and Sanskrit sources, contain different classifications of illnesses. Illnesses are most commonly classified into two general categories: physical illnesses and mental illnesses. The *Mahāniddesa* of the *Khudaka Nikāya* lists thirty-five diseases, some of which are diseases of the individual sense faculties.[45] According to the *Sutta Nipāta*, in ancient times humans suffered from only three types of illness: desire (*icchā*), hunger (*anasana*), and senility (*jarā*), but due to the slaughter of animals, these three types of illness proliferated into ninety-eight types of diseases.[46] In the *Aṅguttara Nikāya*, we find a classification of illnesses into forty-nine types narrated in the story of Girimānanda. Some of them are diseases of the eye, internal ear, nose, tongue, body, head, external ear, mouth, and teeth; cough, asthma, catarrh, pyrexia, fever, stomach ache, fainting, dysentery, grips, cholera, leprosy boils, eczema, tuberculosis, epilepsy, ringworm, itches, scabs, chickenpox, scabies, hemorrhage, diabetes, hemorrhoids, cancer, and fistulas; illnesses originating from one of the three humors or from their combination, and illnesses caused by the change of climate, by careless behavior, by assault, and as a result of karma.[47]

In the *Garbhāvakrānti*, the Buddha mentions 404 illnesses, which he groups into four categories: 101 illnesses related to wind disorder, 101 illnesses related to bile disorder, 101 illnesses related to phlegm disorder, and 101 illnesses related to an imbalance in the combination of the three humors.[48] Another passage of the same *sūtra* tells of the Buddhist tradition's familiarity with forty-nine physical illnesses, which to some degree differ from those mentioned in the *Aṅguttara Nikāya*: diseases of the head, eye, ear, nose, teeth, throat, and heart, colds, abscesses, itches, leg sores, leprosy, swellings, eruptions, white leprosy, epilepsy, carbuncles, elephantiasis, fistulas, dropsy, hiccups, vomiting, fissures, diarrhea, contagious fever, intermittent fever, cough, shortness of breath, desiccation, hunger, jaundice, swelling, fat disease, bile disease, erysipelas, fever, daily fever, every-other-day fever, every-third-day fever, every-fourth-day fever, constant fever, fever in the limbs or ribs or heart, and ache in the limbs, in the ribs, in the heart, and in the collar bone.[49]

ETIOLOGY OF ILLNESSES IN PĀLI AND SANSKRIT SOURCES

According to the *Cakkavatisīhanāda Sutta* of the *Dīgha Nikāya*, the gradual deterioration of the lifespan from a time of prosperity to the last days of the *kali-yuga* is a consequence of unethical living: of greed, stealing, lying, killing, and so on.[50] In the *Milindapañha*, when speaking about untimely death, Nāgasena lists eight causes of illness and death: an excess of wind, an excess of bile, an excess of phlegm, the unfavorable combination of these three humors (*dosa*), changes in temperature, inequality of protection, medical treatment, and karma. Death caused by karma is said to be the only timely death.[51] In another passage, Nāgasena gives a somewhat different list of the eight causes of illness: excesses of wind or bile or phlegm, an imbalance of their combination, changes in temperature, inequality of protection, external agency, and karma. According to him, not all diseases are caused by karma, because if this were the case, individual illnesses would lack distinct characteristics by which they can be differentiated from one another. For instance, a disturbance of the wind humor is brought about under the influence of one of these ten factors: cold, heat, hunger, thirst, overeating, standing for a long time, overexertion, walking too fast, medical treatment, and karma. Imbalances of the bile humor are caused by cold, heat, or wrong food, and disturbances of phlegm by cold, heat, food, and drink. One cannot say that all illnesses are caused by karma because, apart from karma, all other causes of disease occur in the present life. A disturbance of one of the three humors or of their combination manifests as an illness with distinctive characteristics that distinguish it from illnesses caused by other factors. Illnesses that arise as the result of karma are said to be fewer in number than those that arise from other causes.[52] With regard to the Buddha Śākyamuni, Nāgasena assures King Milinda that the Buddha's physical pain was never a result of his karma or of an attack through some karmic adversity. Instead, it resulted from the other six aforementioned causes of illness, which could not deprive him of his life.[53] Also, in the *Saṃyutta Nikāya* (IV.230) we find the idea that all of one's painful experiences are due to karma being refuted. The list of types of illness given there corresponds to the previously mentioned eight causes of illness: diseases originating from the disturbance of one of the three humors, from the imbalance of their combination, due to the change of seasons, due to careless behavior, due to assault, and due to karma.[54] However, in the *Cūḷākammavibhanga Sutta* of the *Majjhima Nikāya*, we read that those who abstain from injuring beings with the hand, clod, stick, or knife will possess health in the next life, whereas those who injure beings in the aforementioned ways will be reborn sick.[55] Thus, a connection between a person's previous actions and sickness is made clear here. In the much later Pāli Abhidhamma work, *Abhidhammatthavibhāvinī*, a commentary on Anuruddha's *Compendium of the Topics of Abhidhamma* (*Abhidhammatthasaṅgaha*, the 11th–12th centuries), Sumaṅgala speaks of a "destructive" karma, which interferes with the causes of disease or with the balance of the three humors and thereby obstructs the prolonged activity of a result of another, wholesome karma. He also informs us of a different view, according to which it is an "obstructive" type of karma that brings together the conditions for many diseases and thus interferes with the results of wholesome karmas.[56]

In the *Garbhāvakrāntisūtra*, a different etiology of diseases is given. There the Buddha speaks of 80,000 types of worms that arise in the body a week after one is born. Here we also find a detailed list of the names of those worms and their specific locations in different parts of the body. Feeding on the body day after day throughout one's life, they afflict, torment, weaken, and sicken the body. Therefore the body experiences mental illness, exhaustion, and torment, which even physicians do not know how to cure. Moreover, thirty-two malevolent *graha* demons come to the person, causing insanity and other forms of suffering.[57]

DISEASES CAUSED BY NONHUMAN AGENTS IN PĀLI SOURCES

In the Mahāvagga section of the *Vinaya Piṭaka*, a monk is inflicted by illness caused by a nonhuman entity and is unable to recover despite all the care received from his teacher and his superior. While under the influence of spirit possession, he went to a place where pigs were slaughtered, and he consumed their raw flesh and blood. As the result of this, his illness diminished. The Buddha, having learned this, allowed for the use of raw flesh and blood when a disease is caused by nonhumans.[58] For recovery from a disease inflicted by a nonhuman entity, the *Samantapasādikā* recommends a medicine consisting of the seven ingredients (*sattavidha-odissaṃ*)—flowers of *Bassilia latifolia*, plantain, date, mango, breadfruit, jackfruit, and tamarind—which a patient can take for seven days at any time.[59] In another instance, at a time of famine when monks ate serpents, the serpent king Supassa, having approached the Buddha, warns him of the possible revenge of serpents antagonistic to the buddhadharma that could harm monks on any occasion.[60]

MEDICAL TRAINING AND DIVISIONS OF MEDICAL KNOWLEDGE IN PĀLI AND SANSKRIT SOURCES

The *Milindapañha* tells of the ways in which someone became an apprentice to a physician and what kind of training the apprentice had to undergo in order to become a skillful physician or surgeon. After acquiring a teacher through payment or through service, the apprentice was trained in holding the lancet, in cutting, marking, and piercing with it, in extracting darts, in cleaning and drying wounds, in the application of ointments, and in the administration of various emetics and enemas.[61] When speaking of the past great teachers of medicine who were well versed in medical knowledge, Nāgasena mentions the four types of medical knowledge: the knowledge of the onset of disease and its cause, of the nature and progress of disease, of its cure and treatment, and of cured and uncured disease.[62]

In the *Mūlasarvāstivāda Vinaya*, the Buddha lists the four areas in which a physician should be skilled: disease, the symptoms of disease, the removal of an arisen disease, and the prevention of a disease's reoccurrence after it has been removed.[63]

While medical services were valued in early Buddhism, they were not considered the proper livelihood for monks. In the *Brahmajāla Sutta* of the *Dīgha Nikāya*, we are told that for *śrāmaṇas* who live on the donations of their lay devotees, making a living by practicing medicine in the form of administering emetics, purges, expectorants, or ointments for the ear or eye or nose, performing surgeries, practicing pediatrics, and using balms to counteract the side effects of previous medicine are base arts and wrong means of livelihood.[64] A similar view is also presented in the Pāli *Vinaya*.

Similarly, the *Mūlasarvāstivāda Vinaya* allows for monks competent in medicine to administer sedatives to their lay donors only in the case of emergency, when a physician is unavailable, or in secrecy, without the knowledge of the laity. A monk who would administer medicine to his donor publicly would be guilty of a misdeed. However, the *Vinaya* permits physician monks to administer medicines and to give dietary advice to lay people who seek their consultation.[65]

A PHYSICIAN AND THE "KING OF MEDICINE"

In Pāli literature, the medical profession is listed as one of twenty-one professions, and three types of healers are mentioned: a physician (*bhisaka*), a surgeon (*sallakatta*), and an exorcist (*bhūtavejja*).[66]

In the Pāli tradition, Jīvaka, referred to as a "king of medicine," stands out as the paradigmatic example of a superb physician. He sees medicinal properties in everything he can find in his natural environment, he respects medicinal substances, he cures chronic illnesses that other physicians cannot, and he shows ingenuity. We read in the *Mahāvagga* of the *Vinaya Piṭaka* that while still a student of medicine in Takkasilā (Taxila), Jīvaka was asked by a physician under whom he studied to take a spade and examine a distance of a *yojana* on every side of Taxila and to bring him whatever he saw as devoid of medicinal properties. Having returned empty handed, Jīvaka reported that he could not find anything lacking medicinal properties.[67] As a skilled physician, he successfully treated a laywoman who suffered for seven years from migraines by administering a handful of ghee boiled with various medicines through her nose and out her mouth; he also cured the king Pajjota of Ujjeni from jaundice despite all the previous treatments that the king had received from other physicians who had failed. Jīvaka offered him a drink of boiled ghee. But since the king had an aversion to ghee, Jīvaka boiled the ghee with various medicines to give it the color, smell, and taste of an astringent medicine, which acted as a laxative. Moreover, when on one occasion the Buddha became ill due to a disturbance of the three humors and requested a purgative from Jīvaka, Jīvaka recommended that Ānanda rub the Buddha's body with fat for a few days. After Ānanda did so, Jīvaka thought that it may not be appropriate to give a strong purgative to the Buddha, and therefore he mixed three handfuls of blue lotuses with various medicines and offered them to the Buddha, which were to purge him thirty times. Quickly realizing that the purgative he gave would purge the Buddha's body only twenty-nine times, he advised the Buddha to take a warm bath that would purge him one more time and to abstain from liquid foods. In this way, we are told, he fully restored the Buddha's health.[68]

In contrast to the *Mahāvagga*, in the *Mūlasarvāstivāda Vinaya*, after receiving the title of the "king of physicians" for the third time and prior to becoming a follower of the Buddha, Jīvaka came across as an arrogant man, claiming, "There is no doctor whatsoever who is equal to me. [Just as] I am the foremost among physicians of the body, so too is the Blessed One foremost among physicians of the mind."[69] The Buddha, having noticed Jīvaka's arrogance and his inability to grasp certain truths because of it, showed him the Himālayas and introduced him to numerous medicinal plants, demonstrating the superiority of his knowledge of medicine to that of Jīvaka. Lauding Jīvaka as the one endowed with the four qualities of a physician, who is worthy of a king and suitable to be a king's physician, the Buddha instructs Jīvaka in the Four Noble Truths and makes him his follower.[70]

PATIENTS, CAREGIVERS, AND INFIRMARIES

In the *Aṅguttara Nikāya*, the Buddha speaks of three types of patients: (1) a patient who does not recover from his illness whether or not he or she is given the appropriate food and medicine, (2) a patient who recovers from his illness whether or not he or she receives the appropriate food and medicine, and (3) a patient who recovers only when he or she receives the appropriate food and medicine and has a qualified caregiver. The Buddha further asserts that since there are patients who recover when they are provided with suitable food and medicine, and with a qualified caregiver, therefore other patients must also be assisted in this way.[71] In the same *Nikāya*, the five types of difficult patients and the five types of easy patients are described. A difficult patient is one who does what is harmful, who does not observe moderation in what is beneficial to his health, who does not take his medicine, who does not accurately disclose his symptoms, and who does not report whether his condition is getting better or worse or remains unchanged. In contrast, an easy patient is the one who, in each case, does the opposite of the aforementioned difficult patient. An easy patient also patiently endures painful and harrowing bodily pains, which deplete his vitality.[72]

As for caregivers, an unqualified caregiver is said to be a person who does not know how to prepare medicines, who does not recognize what is beneficial and harmful and hence offers to the patient that which is harmful, who attends to the patient for the sake of material reward and not out of lovingkindness, who feels disgust at having to remove the patient's bodily fluids (feces, urine, vomit, and spittle), and who is unable to encourage, inspire, instruct, or gladden the patient with a dharma talk. In contrast, a qualified caregiver is a knowledgeable person who acts out of lovingkindness and in the ways contrary to those of a bad caregiver.[73]

The story of a monk with dysentery in the Kucchivikavatthu of the *Vinaya* tells of the Buddha Śākyamuni coming across a monk sick with dysentery and lying in his own urine and excrement. Together with his attendant Ānanda, the Buddha proceeds to bathe him. He asks the sick monk and later the community of monks why no one has helped the sick monk. The explanation is that since the sick monk did not do anything for others, no one did anything for him. Thereafter the Buddha addresses the monks, telling them, "If you do not tend to one another, who then will tend to you? Whoever would tend to me, he should tend to the sick . . . If he has a preceptor (*upajjhāya*), the preceptor should attend to him until he recovers. If he has a teacher (*ācāriya*) or a fellow student, they should attend to him until he recovers. And if he does not have any of these, the sangha should attend to him, and whoever does not so will be guilty of *dukkaṭa*."[74]

In the commentary on the *Mahāvagga* section of the *Vinaya Piṭaka*, monks are instructed to assist a sick monk in five ways: to serve the sick monk food, to give him medicine, to serve food to the person who looks after a sick monk, to inquire about the sick monk's health, and, if needed, to serve him and his attendant personally.[75] A sick monk is exempted from receiving exhortation and from the prohibition against eating food at the wrong time, he can have a meal as often as he feels hungry, he is carried on the shoulders of other monks, and he is allowed to eat a ball of honey after his meal. According to the *Cullavagga*, a sick monk is permitted to use an umbrella, to use a stick if he cannot walk, to tie a string to his begging bowl and wear it on his shoulder, and to wear sandals. If he has fallen on the ground due to weakness he should not be asked to get up, he should be given a good bed, he is allowed to use a scrubber if suffering from scabs, he is permitted to eat garlic for abdominal aches, and so on. According to the *Samantapasādikā*, one suffering from a fistula or a similar disease that involves oozing of blood should be given a chamber pot; a monk suffering from excess of phlegm should be given a spitting box; a leper who stains a sitting place should be moved to a leafy cottage, but if a sick monk does not stain a sitting place, he can be given a bed; and monks undergoing a purgative treatment, a nasal wash, or other similar treatment must be provided with a comfortable seat and sleeping accommodations.[76]

Indian Buddhist scriptures give us scarce but valuable information about the nurseries that housed the sick. One was a house of the sick (*gilaṇasāla*), where sick monks dwelled; another was a house of the destitute (*anāthasālā*), where criminals who were punished with mutilation of the limbs, nose, ears, and other bodily parts lay destitute, with pus and blood trickling from wounds covered with flies and worms. According to the *Vibhanga Aṭṭhakathā*, those in a house of the destitute also suffered mentally, experiencing great sadness when seeing the cheerful and colorfully dressed passersby.[77] The *Sumangalavilāsinī* speaks of compassionate people who provided medicine and bandages for those in a house of the destitute.[78] Reference to such houses in Vesali and Rājagaha are found in a number of Pāli commentarial texts.

MEDICINE IN INDIAN VAJRAYĀNA BUDDHISM

In addition to Buddhist *tantras*, a number of medical treatises, such as the *Yogaśataka Jīvasūtra*, *Avabheṣakalpa*, *Āryarājanāmavaṭikā*, *Āryamūlakośamahauṣadhāvalī*, *Rasaratnākāra*, and *Kakṣapuṭa*, which are traditionally attributed to a certain Nāgārjuna, serve as useful sources for the study of the medical knowledge and practices of the later phase of Buddhism in India. Buddhist tantric literature deals with human physiology and the physiological aspects of illness, medicinal formulas, and medical treatments that accord with Āyurveda. But it also informs us of the preparations and usages of alchemical substances, drawings of *yantras* and mandalas, ritual performances, astrological divinations, and applications of protective and healing mantras as additional therapeutic methods. Although the usage of *dhāraṇīs* and mantras for healing purposes was also prescribed in some Mahāyāna treatises, in the Buddhist tantric tradition, they became more profusely applied. Likewise, alchemy and rites of healing were in practice by the time of the emergence of Buddhist *tantras*. The Buddhist tantric preoccupation with the preservation of a *yogī*'s body facilitated the development of yogic methods of rejuvenation, which included various yogic techniques of the manipulation of vital energies (*prāṇas*), the ingestion of life-giving essences extracted from various substances, the ingestion of tonics and elixirs prepared through alchemical processes, and rituals of longevity. According to the Buddhist tradition in general, the optimal lifespan of the individual is said to be one hundred years.

The *Kālacakratantra* (11th century CE), paying close attention to the correspondences between the body and the cosmos, explains the process of bodily deterioration that takes place over the course of one hundred years in this way: the bodily elements undergo a process of maturation that lasts ninety-six years and ten and a half months. For the first thirty-two years and three and a half months, the vital energies (*prāṇa*) in the body are dominated by the quality of *sattva* (luminosity, intelligibility); for the next thirty-two years and three and a half months, the vital energies are dominated by the quality of *rajas* (activity, passion); and for the last thirty-two years and three and a half months, the vital energies are dominated by the quality of *tamas* (darkness, inertia). Over the course of the remaining three years, three fortnights, and three days, the vital energies gradually cease circulating, as the bodily *cakras* begin to collapse. In this way, the vital energies leave the bodily elements, causing their sequential dissolution that results in death. This division of the human lifespan of ninety-six years and ten and a half months is said to correspond to the length of time it takes the eight planets to move through the circle and half of the twenty-seven constellations (*nakṣatra*).[79] As the planets govern certain zodiacal houses as their respective fields, they also preside over the elements carried by the vital energies that circulate through the left and right sides of the body. All physical and mental ailments are ultimately brought into existence by the power of time that is of the nature of death. From the moment of conception in the womb, time, in the form of malefic lunar days, assembles in the joints, knuckles, and other parts of the body due to the efficacy of the elements, and it seizes the person in its merciless grip.

In this tantric system, the elemental nature and medicinal qualities of medicinal plants depend on the time of year in which certain medicinal plants grow and on the geographical areas in which particular medicinal substances are found. Moreover, seasons and geographical areas, in turn, correspond to the nature of particular constellations, planetary positions, and the time of their influence on specific regions of the earth.

The second chapter of the *Kālacakratantra*, the "Chapter on the Individual," contains a long section on medicine, which concerns itself with a variety of illnesses, their causes, and methods of healing that a tantric adept should know.[80] Among various means of the prevention and cure of diseases are offering rites, mantra recitations, drawing of *yantras* and mandalas, and the initiation of a patient into the mandala. All of these are prescribed for dealing with illnesses caused by malevolent entities, and for poisonous snakebites. We find here a detailed list of various types of evil spirits and the illnesses that they cause. Some of them are *yakṣas, grahas, rākṣasas, piśācas,* and evil *nāgas,* who take delight in human blood, as well as *ḍākinīs, rūpikās,* vampire ghouls who feed themselves in cemeteries (*kumbhāṇḍa*), land protectors (*ksetrapāla*), *gaṇapatis, pretas,* goblins, the lords of *ḍākinīs* who cause epilepsy, and *mātṛkās* who seize infants. When appeased with prayers and offerings, they can grant well-being. However, they are not able to ward off death when the symptoms of irrevocable death appear. Therefore, the rites of pacification of these entities should not be performed at that time. Moreover, carrying on the body gems of various colors is considered to be a protection from the aforementioned types of malefic entities. For instance, a gem of the color red, made of substances dominated by the fire element, is believed to prevent evil spirits form possessing a person's body, while a gem made of substances in which the space element is dominant is believed to ward off the casting of an evil eye.[81] At other times, certain herbal medications empowered by mantras are administered to those possessed by malevolent spirits to alleviate the symptoms of their illness. For example, when a pregnant woman suffers from sharp uterine pains caused by malevolent spirits, she is to be given pounded *kuṣṭha, uśīra, kaseru* grass, *tagara*, blue waterlily (*keśara*), and the filament of a lotus with cold water, all of which are consecrated by mantras and *vajras*.

Tantric medicinal mantras are of three general types: protective mantras, supplicatory mantras, and consecratory mantras. In many instances, one mantra performs multiple functions. For instance, in treatments of malignant diseases characterized by fever and joint pains, the single mantra "*oṃ phre vajra*" is said to simultaneously empower medicinal ingredients and to protect the patient's *cakras* in the body.[82] One also finds here references to *haṭha-yoga*, to various yogic postures, and to breathing techniques as therapeutic methods. The *vajra* posture (*vajrāsana*) is recommended for the elimination of backache, the head-stand posture (*śīrṣāsana*) for phlegm-related illness, and the vase technique of breathing (*kumbhaka*) for the alleviation of abdominal ailments, leprosy, and other similar diseases. A patient afflicted by leprosy is advised to practice the *kumbhaka* for a period of six months, in which he should retain seminal fluid during sexual intercourse.[83]

Methods of treatment are chosen based on the symptoms of a disease, the occasions of its occurrence, and the knowledge of its cause. For example, bodily convulsions, sharp ocular pains, a yellowish complexion of the face, arms or legs, a distinctively yellow color of the urine, fever, vomiting, emaciation, and fainting are seen as symptomatic of a disease afflicted upon small children by cruel spirits. In that case, the sick child must be treated with ritual oblation in the mandala. A sick child afflicted by *graha* demons must be bathed in the seven ambrosias (*amṛta*): water, milk, sour milk, ghee, honey, molasses, and fragrant water that have been kept in seven unbaked vessels.[84]

In the case of illnesses caused by other factors, such as disequilibrium of the three humors, external factors, poor hygiene, inadequate diet, and the like, applications of different medicinal herbs are recommended. For instance, the application of slightly warmed *akṣobhya* in the mouth is prescribed for an infection of the mouth; anointing the neck with *karkoṭī, lāṅgalī*, and *indrī* is recommended for the inflammation of the glands in the neck, and so on. Dietary therapy, hydrotherapy, massage, nasal inhalations, fumigation, anointing with oils, and consumption of medicaments are also included in the *Kālacakratantra's* therapeutics. Medicinal substances are chosen and prescribed according to their tastes arising from the elements that constitute them. Each among the five elements and its corresponding taste have their unique, individual efficaciousness. For example, a medicinal substance with a bitter taste, combined with three myrobalans (*kaṭuka*), is said to obliterate disorders of phlegm. Therefore, goat's milk, which has a somewhat bitter taste, when combined with the three myrobalans, is prescribed to those suffering from phlegm-related disorders. Sweet and astringent substances are said to eliminate bile disorders, thus buffalo-cow's milk is given to those suffering from bile-related illnesses; camel's milk, combined with rock salt, becomes alkaline and thereby can cure wind-related disorders. For the treatment of boils, pustules, and similar skin disorders, fumigation with ghee and sea salt wrapped in a cloth and anointing with the sap of the *arka* plant are recommended. For infections of the ear and eye, warm urine is to be applied in the ear and cold urine in the eye. A person suffering from sunstroke must be treated with a decoction made of medicinal herbs, powder, and leaves.

Although the intimate connection between the mind and body has been recognized in Indian Buddhism in general, it was given great significance in Indian Buddhist *tantras*, which contain detailed and intricate accounts of the mutual effects of the body and mind. This is reflected not only in the prescribed Varjayāna religious practices but also in the medical ones. Therefore, practices such as meditation and visualization of tantric deities are often prescribed to *yogīs* as healing practices that accompany the administering of medicine. A *yogī* suffering from throat cancer is advised to abide in meditative concentration (*samādhi*) in order to pacify severe pain. The procedure is described in this way: while practicing *prāṇāyāma*, he is to visualize in his heart *chakra* Viśvamātā, the consort of Kālacakra, appearing as a stainless moon, seated in the *vajra* posture, having one face and two arms, with her hands in the wish-granting gesture and holding a lotus.[85]

REVIEW OF LITERATURE

In comparison to the number of works written on Hindu Āyurveda, literature on Indian Buddhist medicine is remarkably meager. One reason is that Hindu Āyurveda is still in practice. Buddhist medicine that is studied and practiced today in India is primarily Tibetan medicine, which has its roots in Indian Buddhist Āyurveda. Another reason is that many original Sanskrit works that are a valuable resource for the study of Indian Buddhist medicine are no longer extant in Sanskrit but preserved in Tibetan and Chinese translations. So far, there has not been a single, comprehensive, scholarly work on Indian Buddhist medicine produced. The available works tend to focus on a specific subject matter, on particular Buddhist text, or on texts composed within a specific period in the history of Buddhism in India. Secondary sources on Indian Buddhist medicine primarily comprise short articles, small sections within survey volumes, and a very small number of books, most of which are published in India. Moreover, so far, the focus has been on the information provided in Pāli sources and rarely on Sanskrit texts. To my knowledge, Zysk's *Asceticism and Healing in Ancient India: Medicine in the Buddhist Monastery* dedicates one chapter to Buddhist medicine in India in his partial examination of the evolution of classical Indian medicine, and dedicates two chapters to a discussion the *materia medica* and narratives of treatments in the context of early Buddhist monastic medicine, based on Pāli literature. Kritzer's *Garbhāvakāntisūtra: The Sūtra on the Entry into the Womb* is a study and translation from Tibetan of the original Indian Mahāyāna text, which describes the conception, gestation, birth, and sufferings of a newborn child. Although a religious text, the *Garbhāvakāntisūtra* contains certain sections on medical knowledge of embryology, human anatomy, gynecology, and obstetrics. One finds here how medical knowledge of the mentioned areas is utilized to bring the reader to the realization of the First Noble Truth of suffering and to instigate one's desire for a renunciation of the world and escape from cyclic existence. In his article "Life in the Womb: Conception and Gestation in Buddhist Scripture and Classical Indian Medical Literature," Kritzer offers a brief comparative analysis of the views on conception expounded in select Hindu and Jaina religious texts, the

Garbhāvakrāntisūtra and the *Carakasaṃhitā*. In this article he points out not only the main differences among the various theories of conception but also a similarity between these two texts, which take an epigenetic model of fetal development. In the *Science of Medicine and Surgery in Buddhist India*, Talim gives an overview of various types of medicine, including contraceptives, and diseases mentioned in Pāli and Sanskrit sources. The most interesting sections in this book are those describing surgical procedures for eleven types of illnesses, seventy-one surgical instruments, and accompanying illustrations of surgical instruments. In "The Buddhist Tantric Medicine in the *Kālacakratantra*," Wallace addresses theoretical foundations and syncretistic features characteristic of Indian Buddhist tantric medicine as expounded in the *Kālacakratantra*. In "A Convergence of Medical and Astro-Sciences in Indian Tantric Buddhism: A Case of the *Kālacakratantra*," Wallace shows medical applications of astrology in this Indian Buddhist *tantra* and the merging of these two disciplines of Buddhist knowledge. *The Kālacakratantra: The Chapter on the Individual together with the Vimalaprabhā*, translated by Wallace, contains the rich information on the Buddhist tantric understanding of the subtle body, physiology, embryology, anatomy, and therapeutics.

FURTHER READING

The Connected Discourses of the Buddha: A New Translation of the Saṃyutta Nikāya, vols. 1–2. Translated by Bhikkhu Bodhi. Boston: Wisdom Publications, 2000.

Dash, Bhagwan. *Nāgārjuna's Yogasataka*. Dharamsala: Library of Tibetan Works and Archives, 1976.

Ārya Saṅghātasūtra. Translated by Damchö Daian Finnegan. 2006. https://fpmt.org/education/teachings/sutras/sanghata-sutra-in-various-languages.

Bhaiṣajya-Guru-Sūtra (Original Sanskrit Text with Introduction and Commentary). Translated and Commented by F. M. Hassnain and Tokan D. Sumi. New Delhi: Reliance, 1995.

Cullavagga-Parivāra-Aṭṭhakathā. Igatpuri: Vipassana Research Institute, 1998.

The Dhammapada. Translated by John Ross Carter and Mahinda Palihawadana. New York: Oxford University Press, 1988.

Dialogues of the Buddha. Part 1. Translated by T. W. Rhys Davids. Sacred Books of the East 2. London: Routledge and Kegan Paul, 1977.

Garbhāvakrāntisūtra: The Sūtra on Entry into the Womb. Translated by Robert Kritzer. Studia Philologica Buddhica 31. Tokyo: International Institute of Buddhist Studies, 2014.

The Jātaka or Stories of the Buddha's Former Births, vol. 1. Translated by Robert Chalmers. Cambridge, UK: Cambridge University Press, 1895.

The Jātaka or Stories of the Buddha's Former Births, vol. 4. Translated by W. H. D. Rouse. Cambridge, UK: Cambridge University Press, 1901.

The Jātaka or Stories of the Buddha's Former Births, vol. 5. Translated by H. T. Francis. Cambridge, UK: Cambridge University Press, 1905.

Kritzer, Robert. "Life in the Womb: Conception and Gestation in Buddhist Scripture and Classical Indian Medical Literature." In *Imagining the Fetus: The Unborn in Myth, Religion, and Culture*. Edited by Vanessa R. Sasson and Jane Marie Law, 73–91. New York: Oxford University Press, 2009.

The Long Discourses of the Buddha: A Translation of the Dīgha Nikāya. Translated By Maurice Walshe. Boston: Wisdom Publications, 1995.

Lüders, H. "A List of Brahmī Inscriptions from the Earliest Times to About A.D. 400 with the Exception of Those of Aśoka." In *Epigraphica India and Record of the Archaeological Survey of India*, vol. 10. Appendix: 1–212. Calcutta: British India Press, 1909.

Mahāvagga. Bihar: Nava Nalanda Mahavihara Devanagari Pali Gandha Mala, 1959.

The Middle Length Discourses of the Buddha: A Translation of the Majjhima Nikāya. Translated by Bhikkhu Ñānamoli and Bhikkhu Bodhi. Boston: Wisdom Publications, 2001.

Mitra, Jyotir. *A Critical Appraisal of Āyurvedic Material in Buddhist Literature with Special Reference to Tripiṭaka*. Varanasi: Jyotiralok Prakashan, 1985.

Naqvi, Nasim, H. *A Study of Buddhist Medicine and Surgery in Gandhara*. Indian Medical Tradition Series 11. Delhi: Moltial Banarsidass, 2011.

Niddesa I. Mahānidessa, vol. 1. Edited by L. De la Vallée Poussin and E. J. Thomas. London: Pali Text Society, 1916.

The Numerical Discourses of the Buddha: A Translation of the Aṅguttara Nikāya. Translated by Bhikkhu Bodhi. Boston: Wisdom Publications, 2012.

Numerical Discourses of the Buddha: An Anthology of Suttas from the Aṅguttara Nikāya. Translated and Edited by Nyanaponika There and Bhikkhu Bodhi. Walnut Creek: Altamira, 2012.

The Questions of King Milinda. Parts 1–2. Translated by T. W. Rhys Davids. The Sacred Books of the East 35. New York: Dover, 1963.

Saddharmapuṇḍarīka. Edited by P. L. Vaidya. Darbhanga: Mithila Institute, 1960.

Samantapasādika, Vol. 3. Bihar: Nava Nalanda Mahavihara, 1965.

Sumangalavilāsini, Vol. 1. Bihar: Nava Nalanda Mahavira, 1975.

Summary of the Topics of Abhidhamma (Abhidhammatthasaṅgaha) by Anuruddha and the Exposition of the Topics of Abhidhamma (Abhidhammatthavibhāvanī) by Sumaṅgala Being a Commentary to Anuruddha's Summary for the Topcis of Abhidhamma. Translated by R. P. Wijeratne and Rupert Gethin. Oxford: Pali Text Society, 2002.

The Sūtra of the Golden Light (Suvarṇaprabhāsottamasūtra). Translated by R. E. Emmerick. Oxford: Pali Text Society, 2004.

The Sutta-Nipāta. Translated by H. Saddhatissa. London: Curzon, 1985.

Talim, Meena. *Science of Medicine and Surgery in Buddhist India*. Delhi: Buddhist World, 2009.

Vibhanga Aṭṭhakathā. Igatpuri: Vipassana Reasearch Institute, 1998.

Vimalaprabhāṭīkā of Kalki Śrī Puṇḍarīka on Śrī Laghukālacakratantrarāja by Śrī Mañjuśrīyaśa, Vol. 1. Edited by Jagannatha Upadhyaya. Bibliotheca Indo-Tibetica Series 11. Sarnath, Varanasi: Central Institute of Higher Tibetan Studies, 1986.

Vimalaprabhāṭīkā of Kalki Śrī Puṇḍarīka on Śrī Laghukālacakratantrarāja by Śrī Mañjuśrī Yaśas. Vol. 3. Edited by Varjavallabhi Dwivedi and S. S. Bahulkar. Rare Buddhist Texts Series 13. Sarnath, Varanasi: Central Institute of Higher Tibetan Studies, 1994.

Vinaya Texts. Part 1. Translated by T. W. Rhys Davids and Herman Oldenberg. The Sacred Books of the East 13. Delhi: Motilal Banarsidass, 1982.

Vinaya Texts. Part 2. Translated by T. W. Rhys Davids and Herman Oldenberg. The Sacred Books of the East 17. Delhi: Motilal Banarsidass, 1982.

Wallace, Vesna A. "The Buddhist Tantric Medicine in the *Kālacakratantra*." *Pacific World: Journal of the Institute of Buddhist Studies* 11–12 (1995): 155–174.

Wallace, Vesna A. *The Kālacakratantra: The Chapter on the Individual Together with the Vimalaprabhā*. Tanjur Translation Initiative. Treasury of Buddhist Sciences Series. New York: American Institute of Buddhist Studies, co-published with Columbia University's Center for Buddhist Studies and Tibet House, 2004.

Wallace, Vesna. A. "A Convergence of Medical and Astro-Sciences in Indian Tantric Buddhism: A Case of the *Kālacakratantra*." In *Astro-Medicine: Astrology and Medicine, East and West*, 209–222. Edited by Anna Akasoy, Charles Burnett, and Ronit Yoeli-Tlalim. Micrologus' Library 25. Florence, Italy: Sismel Edzioni del Galluzzo, 2008.

Wujastyk, Dominik. "Indian Medicine." In *Companion to Encyclopedia of the History of Medicine*. Edited by W. F. Bynum and Roy Porter, 1:755–781. London: Routledge, 1993.

Zysk, Kenneth G. "Studies in Traditional Indian Medicine in the Pāli Canon: Jīvaka and Āyurveda." *Journal of the International Association of Buddhist Studies* 5, no. 1 (1982): 70–88.

Zysk, Kenneth G. *Asceticism and Healing in Ancient India: Medicine in the Buddhist Monastery*. New York: Oxford University Press, 1991.

NOTES

1. For the content of inscriptions, see Keishō Tsukamoto, *Indo bukkyō himei no kenkyū*, part 1 (Tokyo: Sanhibo Busshorin, 1996), 523; James Burgess, *Report on Buddhist Cave Temples and Their Inscriptions: Being Part of the Result of the Fourth, Fifth, and Sixth Seasons' Operations of the Archeological Survey of Western India: 1876–77, 1877–78, 1878–79* (Varanasi: Indological Book House, 1964), 84, no. 5, plate XLIV; and H. Lüders, "A List of Brahmī Inscriptions from the Earliest Times to About A.D. 400 with the Exception of Those of Aśoka., in *Epigraphica Indica and Record of the Archaeological Survey of India*, 10: Appendix: 1–212 137.1191 (Calcutta: British India, 1909).
2. For instance, the names of Dhanvantari (a teacher of the *Suśruta Saṃhitā*), of his disciples Vetaraṇi and Bhoja, Aṅgirasa (who is mentioned in the *Caraka Saṃhitā*), Nārada (who is referenced in the *Caraka Saṃhitā*), and so on.
3. *The Dhammapada*, trans. John Ross Carter and Mahinda Palihawadana (Oxford: Oxford University Press, 1987), chap. 15, v. 204: 257.
4. *The Numerical Discourses of the Buddha: A Translation of the Aṅguttara Nikāya*, trans. Bhikkhu Bodhi (Boston: Wisdom Publications, 2012), 681, 711, 742, 749.
5. *The Connected Discourses of the Buddha: A New Translation of the Saṃyutta Nikāya*, vol. 1, trans. Bhikkhu Bodhi (Boston: Wisdom Publications, 2000), 853.
6. *Garbhāvakrāntisūtra: The Sūtra on Entry into the Womb*, ed. Robert Kritzer, Studia Philologica Buddhica Series 31 (Tokyo: International Institute for Buddhist Studies, 2014), 87.
7. *The Long Discourses of the Buddha: A Translation of the Dīgha Nikāya*, trans. Maurice Walshe (Boston: Wisdom Publications, 1995), 486; and *The Numerical Discourses of the Buddha: A Translation of the Aṅguttara Nikāya*, trans. Bhikkhu Bodhi (Boston: Wisdom Publications, 2012), 686–687.
8. *The Numerical Discourses of the Buddha: An Anthology of Suttas from the Aṅguttara Nikāya*, trans. Bhikkhu Bodhi (Walnut Creek, CA: AltaMira, 1999), 135; and *The Numerical Discourses of the Buddha: A Translation of the Aṅguttara Nikāya*, trans. Bhikkhu Bodhi (Boston: Wisdom Publications, 2012), 1429.
9. *The Numerical Discourses of the Buddha: A Translation of the Aṅguttara Nikāya*, trans. Bhikkhu Bodhi (Boston: Wisdom Publications, 2012), 522.
10. *Vimalaprabhāṭīkā of Kalki Śrī Puṇḍarīka on Śrī Laghukālacakratantrarāja by Śrī Mañjuśrī*, vol. 1, ed. Jagannatha Upadhyaya. Bibliotheca Indo-Tibetica Series 11 (Sarnath, Varanasis: Central Institute of Higher Tibetan Studies, 1896), chap. 2, v. 107, lines a–b, 228.
11. *The Questions of King Milinda*, vol. 2, trans. Thomas William Rhys Davids. The Sacred Books of the East 36, (1963), IV.5.8: 8, IV.5.10: 10, IV.6.26: 65, V.11: 218, V.12: 219.
12. *The Sutta-Nipāta*, trans. H. Saddhatissa (London: Curzon, 1985), 66.
13. *Abhidharmakośabhāṣyam of Vasubandhu*, vol. 3, trans. Louis de la Vallèe Poussin. (Berkeley, CA: Asian Humanities, 1991), 1033. The Poussin version is in French; the English version was translated by Le M. Pruden.
14. *Saddharmapuṇḍarīka Sūtra*, ed. P. L. Vaidya (Darbhanga: Mithila Institute, 1960), 93.
15. *The Numerical Discourses of the Buddha: An Anthology of Suttas from the Aṅguttara Nikāya*, trans. Bhikkhu Bodhi (Walnut Creek, CA: AltaMira, 1999), 251–253.

16. *The Connected Discourses of the Buddha*, vol. 2, 1582.
17. *The Connected Discourses of the Buddha*, vol. 2, 1636.
18. *The Connected Discourses of the Buddha*, vol. 2, 1757–1758.
19. *The Connected Discourses of the Buddha*, vol. 2, 1816–1820.
20. *The Connected Discourses of the Buddha*, vol. 2, 1834–1836.
21. The *sūtra* is of uncertain date. Its earliest references are found in the *Śatasāhasrikāprajñāpāramitā Sūtra* and in the *Mañjuśrīmūlakalpa*.
22. *Ārya Saṅghātasūtra Dharmaparyāya*, trans. Damchö Daian Finnegan (2006), 95, https://fpmt.org/education/teachings/sutras/sanghata-sutra-in-various-languages.
23. *Vinaya Texts*, part 2, trans. Thomas William Rhys Davids and Herman Oldenberg (Delhi: Motilal Banarsidass, 1982), VI.1.2–VI.40.3: 41–145.
24. In the example given in *Vinaya Texts*, part 2, VI.1.2–VI.17: 68–69, the Buddha rebukes Ānanda for keeping the ingredients for a gruel and cooking it indoors of his own accord and instructs the *monks*, saying, "Whatever is kept indoors, O Monks, or cooked indoors, or cooked of your own accord, is not be eaten." But at the time of food shortages, he gave permission to monks to ignore this prohibition.
25. In the Bhaiṣjyavastu section of the *Sarvastivāda Vinaya*, III.1.3, fresh butter is replaced by sugar molasses (*śarkarā*), and the five medicines are collectively called "*saptāhikāni*," or "allowed for the period of seven days."
26. *Vinaya Texts*, part 2, VI.1.2–VI.14: 55–61.
27. *Mahāvagga*, vol. 1, ed. Jagadīśa Kāśyapa, Nālandā Devanāgarī Pāli Series (Bihar, India: Pāli Publication Board, 1959), 234–235.
28. The mentioned astringent substances are *nimba* (*Azadirachta Indica*), *kuṭaga* (*Wrightia anti-dysenterica*), *pakkava* (a type of a creeper), *nattamāla* (*Pongania Glabra*), etc. Salts include sea salt, black salt, rock salt, red salt.
29. *Vinaya Texts*, part 2, VI.1.2–VI.22: 78–80.
30. *Vinaya Texts*, part 2, VI.1.2–VI.20: 76–77.
31. *Vinaya Texts*, part 2, VI.1.2–VI.23: 80–81.
32. *The Connected Discourses of the Buddha*, vol. 1, 176.
33. *The Middle Length Discourses of the Buddha: A Translation of the Majjhima Nikāya*, trans. Bhikkhu Ñānamoli and Bhikkhu Bodhi (Boston: Wisdom Publications, 2001), 542.
34. *The Middle Length Discourses of the Buddha*, 577–578.
35. *The Numerical Discourses of the Buddha: An Anthology of Suttas from* the *Aṅguttara Nikāya*, 821–822.
36. *The Middle Length Discourses of the Buddha*, 707, 736.
37. *The Majjhima Nikāya*, vol. 1, ed. V. Treckner (Oxford: Pali Text Society, 2000), 378.
38. Buddhaghosa, *Sumangalavilāsinī Dīghanikāya-aṭṭakathā*, vol. 2, ed. Mahesh Tiwari (Nalanda: Nalanda Mahavihara, 1975), 215.
39. *Dīgha Nikāya*, vol. 1, ed. Thomas William Rhys Davids (Oxford: Pali Text Society, 1950), 61.
40. *The Sūtra of Golden Light* (*Suvarṇaprabhāsottamasūtra*), trans. R. E. Emmerick (Oxford: Pali Text Society, 2004), 75–80.
41. *The Jātaka or Stories of the Buddha's Former Births*, vol. 4, trans. W. H. D. Rouse, ed. E. B. Cowell (Cambridge, UK: Cambridge University Press, 1901), 250–256.
42. *The Jātaka or Stories of the Buddha's Former Births*, vol. 1, trans. Robert Chalmers, ed. E. B. Cowell (Cambridge, UK: Cambridge University Press, 1895), 277–280.
43. *The Jātaka or Stories of the Buddha's Former Births*, vol. 4, 267–270.
44. *The Jātaka or Stories of the Buddha's Former Births*, vol. 5, trans. H. T. Frances, ed. E. B. Cowell (Cambridge, UK: Cambridge University Press, 1905), 175–185.
45. *Niddesa I. Mahāniddesa*, vol. 1, ed. H. Milford (London: Pali Text Society, 1916), 13.

46. *The Sutta-Nipāta*, 34, v. 311.
47. *The Numerical Discourses of the Buddha: An Anthology of Suttas from the Aṅguttara Nikāya*, 1412–1413.
48. *Garbhāvakrāntisūtra: The Sūtra on Entry into the Womb*, 86.
49. *Garbhāvakrāntisūtra: The Sūtra on Entry into the Womb*, 86.
50. *The Long Discourses of the Buddha: A Translation of the Dīgha Nikāya*, 395–405.
51. *The Questions of King Milinda*, part 2, IV.8.41: 164, IV.8.44: 168.
52. *The Questions of King Milinda*, part 1, IV.1.62–63: 191–192.
53. *The Questions of King Milinda*, part 1, IV.1.66: 193–194.
54. *The Connected Discourses of the Buddha*, vol. 2, 1279.
55. *The Middle Length Discourses of the Buddha*, 1054.
56. *Summary of the Topics of Abhidhamma (Abhidhammatthasaṅgaha) by Anuruddha and the Exposition of the Topics of Abhidhamma (Abhidhammatthavibhāvanī) by Sumaṅgala Being a Commentary to Summary of the Topics of Abhidhamma*, trans. R. P. Wijeratne and Rupert Gethin, Sacred Books of the Buddhists 50 (Oxford: Pali Text Society, 2002), 173–174.
57. *Garbhāvakrāntisūtra*, trans. Robert Kritzer, Studia Philologica Buddhica 31 (Tokyo: International Institute of Buddhist Studies, 2014), 75–80.
58. *Vinaya Texts*, part 2, VI.1.2–VI.10: 49.
59. Meena Talim, *Science of Medicine and Surgery in Buddhist India* (Delhi: Buddhist World, 2009), 65, 58–59.
60. *Vinaya Texts*, part 2, VI.1.2–VI.23: 86.
61. *The Questions of King Milinda*, part 2, VI.12: 255.
62. *The Questions of King Milinda*, part 2, IV.7.20: 109.
63. Nalinaksha Dutt, ed., *Gilgit Manuscripts* (Srinagar-Kashimir: Calcutta Oriental, 1942), III.2: 45.3.
64. *The Long Discourses of the Buddha: A Translation of the Dīgha Nikāya*, 73. See also *Dialogues of the Buddha*, vol. 1, 25.
65. Paul Demièville, *Buddhism and Healing: Demiville's Article "Byo" from Höbögirin (1937)*, trans. Mark Tatz (Lanham, MD: University Press of America, 1985), 38.
66. *The Milindapañha, Being Dialogues between King Milinda and the Buddhist Sage Nāgasena*, ed. V. Trenckner (London: Williams and Norgate, 1880), I.45. See also Jyotir Mitra, *A Critical Appraisal of Āyurvedic Material in Buddhist Literature with Special Reference to Tripiṭaka* (Varanasi: Jyotiralok Prakashan, 1985), 25.
67. *Vinaya Texts*, part 1, VIII.1.7: 175.
68. *Vinaya Texts*, part 1, 8–33: 175–193.
69. Dutt, III.2: 43.
70. Dutt, III. 44.19–45.2.
71. *The Numerical Discourses of the Buddha: A Translation of the Aṅguttara Nikāya*, 217.
72. *The Numerical Discourses of the Buddha: A Translation of the Aṅguttara Nikāya*, 741–742.
73. *The Numerical Discourses of the Buddha: A Translation of the Aṅguttara Nikāya*, 741–742.
74. *Vinaya Texts*, part 2, VIII.26: 240–243.
75. Buddhaghosa, *Vinayapiṭake Paccitīya Mahāvagga-Aṭṭhakathā* (Igatapuri: Vipaśyanā Viśodhana Vinyāsa, 1998), 56.
76. Buddhaghosa, *Samantapasādikā-nāma Aṭṭhakathā*, vol. 3, ed. Nathmala Ṭāṭiyā (Nalanda: Nava Nālandā Mahāvihāra, 1965), 1306.
77. Buddhaghosa, *Abhidhammapiṭake Sammohavinodinī-nāma Vibhanga-aṭṭhakathā*, Dhammagiri-Pāli-Ganthamālā 126 (Igatapuri: Vipassanā Research Institute, 1998), 98.
78. Buddhaghosa, *Sumangalavilāsinī: Dīghanikāya-aṭṭakathā*, vol. 1, ed. Mahesh Tiwari (Nālandā: Nava Nālandā Mahāvihāra, 1974), 222.
79. *Vimalaprabhāṭīkā of the Kalkī Śrī Puṇḍarīka of Śrī Laghukālacakratantrarāja by Śrī Mañjuśrīyaśa*, vol. 1, ed. Jagannatha Upadhyaya (Sarnath, Varanasi: Central Institute of Higher Tibetan Studies, 1986),

chap. 1, vv. 65, 108–109, lists the moon, the sun, Mars, Jupiter, Venus, Mercury, Saturn, and Ketu as eight planets.

80. *Vimalaprabhāṭīkā of the Kalkī Śrī Puṇḍarīka of Śrī Laghukālacakratantrarāja by Śrī Maṇjuśrīyaśa*, vol. 1, chap. 2, vv. 228–255.
81. *Vimalaprabhāṭīkā of Kalkin Śrīpuṇḍarīka on Śrīlaghukālacakratantrarāja by Śrīmañjuśrīyaśas*, vol. 3, ed. Vrajavallabh Dwivedi and S. S. Bahulkar, Rare Buddhist Texts Research Project (Sarnath, Varanasi: Central Institute of Higher Tibetan Studies, 1994), chap. 5, vv. 187, 128; and *The Vimalaprabhāṭīkā of the Kalkī Śrī Puṇḍarīka of Śrī Laghukālacakratantrarāja by Śrī Maṇjuśrīyaśa*, vol. 1, chap. 2, vv. 154–160, vv. 253–255.
82. *Vimalaprabhāṭīkā of the Kalkī Śrī Puṇḍarīka of Śrī Laghukālacakratantrarāja by Śrī Maṇjuśrīyaśa*, vol. 1, chap. 2, vv. 129: 237.
83. *Vimalaprabhāṭīkā of the Kalkī Śrī Puṇḍarīka of Śrī Laghukālacakratantrarāja by Śrī Maṇjuśrīyaśa*, vol. 1, chap. 2, vv. 129, 127, 122: 233, 237–238.
84. *The Vimalaprabhāṭīkā of the Kalkī Śrī Puṇḍarīka of Śrī Laghukālacakratantrarāja by Śrī Maṇjuśrīyaśa*, vol. 1, chap. 2, vv. 159, 146, and 152: 254–255, 249, 252.
85. The *Vimalaprabhāṭīkā of the Kalkī Śrī Puṇḍarīka of Śrī Laghukālacakratantrarāja by Śrī Maṇjuśrīyaśa*, vol. 1, chap. 2, 128: 237.

Vesna A. Wallace

BUDDHISM AND MEDICINE IN JAPAN

HISTORICAL OVERVIEW

In the 6th century CE, there were heated debates, which escalated to the point of violence, over the acceptance of the Buddhist religion in Japan. Among the rival factions at court, some favored allowing ordination and the establishment of Buddhist temples, while others appeared to have been strictly against worshipping "foreign deities," expressing the fear, according to the early imperial chronicle *Nihon shoki* 日本書紀 (720 CE), that this would incur the wrath of the "national gods." Indeed, after an outbreak of a plague was linked to the worship of the Buddha, the monarch of the newly formed hegemonic state gave in to those who opposed the acceptance of Buddhism: buddha statues were thrown into a canal, temples burned, and the first monastics ordained in Japan, three women, punished. The chronicle reports a subsequent unexplained fire at the palace and outbreaks of epidemic disease, which were interpreted by the afflicted as a punishment for burning the image of the Buddha.

Eventually, Bidatsu 敏達 (r. *c.* 572–585) gave permission for the temple to be rebuilt and the three monastics reinstated to counter the alleged curse of the Buddha. Subsequent rulers of the Yamato dynasty became devout patrons of Buddhism and the religion emerged as a major cultural force in Japan. The link between the well-being of the ruler and their family (and by extension the well-being of the subjects) and Buddhist worship remained a central focus. When the ruler or other members of the elite fell ill, so-called caregiving monks (*kanbyō-sō* 看病僧) were engaged to perform rituals. There are also records of mass ordinations as a pious act dedicated to the recovery of the emperor or empress, as well as dedication inscriptions on Buddhist statuary with supplications for good health. The conviction that the Buddha and the bodhisattvas had superior healing power also found expression in the establishment of temple hospitals and other care facilities and medicinal gardens. Patrons funded the construction of bathhouses at temples for those afflicted with *rai* 癩, usually identified as Hansen's disease, or leprosy, as a good and meritorious deed.

Buddhism is closely interlinked with the history of medicine in Japan because scholar monks, and possibly also nuns, were trained in Chinese-style medicine, which had become the prevalent form of medicine in Japan by the 6th century CE. From about the 8th century onward, Buddhist monastic physicians competed with "secular" court physicians. While court physicians treated members of the ruling and educated elite, Buddhist monastic doctors also treated other members of society. By the end of the 16th century, many doctors that trained in Buddhist temples were ordained only as a formality to obtain their stipends. Ultimately, opposition to this tradition and a change in government led to increasing secularization of the medical profession. In the Edo period (1600–1868), many doctors learned their profession at neo-Confucian academies, and medicine as a family profession evolved to become the dominant form of medical knowledge production and circulation. However, Buddhist temples kept offering cure-all medicines and healing services. Ultimately, a civil law in the reformist Meiji period (1868–1912) led to the legal separation of Buddhism and medicine, so monastics could no longer practice medicine and were forced to either abandon their religious office or to concentrate exclusively on Buddhist matters. In the early 21st century, there are some Japanese Buddhist priests who practice Kampo (*kampō* 漢方), a modern form of Chinese-style medicine.

MEDICINE AND HEALING IN JAPANESE BUDDHIST CONTEXTS

An interesting case is the role of the Indian medical tradition, usually referred to as Āyurveda, in Japan: The practice of Indian medicine with the notable exception of eye surgery remained, in the absence of doctors or healers trained in Āyurvedic practices, almost purely theoretical and known only through Buddhist texts.[1] Still, the identification, purchase, and production of substances used for both medical and ritual purposes mentioned in the translations from Sanskrit Buddhist texts remained a major concern, at least in medieval Japan. Esoteric (or tantric) Buddhism with its elaborate fire-offering ceremonies (*goma* 護摩, from Sanskrit *homa*) involving numerous plant, mineral, and animal substances was especially widely practiced at the time.[2] In general, esoteric Buddhist ceremonies and rituals often centered—and center, since this is a living tradition—on protection from harm including illness and accidents. The ritualists sought the support of various buddhas, bodhisattvas, and deities from the rich esoteric Buddhist pantheon. They engaged in the so-called "three secret practices"—making ritual hand gestures, reciting mantras, and visualizing deities—to unify themselves with the Buddhist deity. The aim was to channel the Buddha's or deity's extraordinary powers, not only for healing illness but also for other this-worldly benefits such as bringing rain and the cessation of calamities.

Ritual activity in esoteric Buddhist traditions was also aimed at attaining the other-worldly, ultimate goal of Buddhist awakening. Esoteric Buddhism shares with other Buddhist traditions in Japan (and elsewhere) that the Buddha, the Awakened One, is regarded as the ultimate physician who not only identified the reasons for sentient beings' suffering but also showed a way to liberate them from suffering forever, or, in other words, provided them with medicine for ultimate healing, or salvation. The Mahāyāna Buddhist tradition in Japan emphasizes the unlimited power of the bodhisattvas, or buddhas-to-be, which alleviate sentient beings' pain and protect them from misfortune. For practitioners, especially monastics, the selfless, wise, and compassionate attitude of the bodhisattva was held to be the ideal norm and guiding moral principle. According to important Buddhist texts, among them the *Brahmā's Net Sūtra* (*Bonmō-kyō* 梵網経), medical activity was not only commendable for a monastic Buddhist but a duty.[3] This precept explains to some extent why monks, and, presumably, nuns in Japan trained in the dominant form of medicine adapted from the Chinese tradition and worked as doctors treating both aristocrats and commoners alike. So far, there is only scant information about female monastics with formal medical training. However, we can assume that nuns treated the medical conditions of other nuns, and that scholar nuns were familiar with the medical texts circulating in the temple networks.

While buddhas and bodhisattvas such as Yakushi Nyorai 薬師如来 (Buddha Bhaiṣajyaguru)—known as the "Medicine Buddha"—and Kannon Bosatsu 観音菩薩 (Bodhisattva Avalokiteśvara) enjoyed—and still enjoy—particular popularity, other deities are less well known.[4] For example, Gozu tennō 牛頭天王 and Shinra Myōjin 新羅明神, protectors from epidemic disease, as well as other deities incorporated into the esoteric Japanese Buddhist pantheon from local traditions in India, China, Korea, and Japan, have all played significant roles at some point in history.[5]

ETIOLOGY AND DIAGNOSIS

According to Buddhist tradition, disease and other misfortunes are caused by one's acts, karma, in this life or past lives, a view that is also fundamental for understanding Buddhist traditions in Japan. Buddhist texts emphasize the need to avoid selfish acts and to lead a morally pure life, not least in order to prevent an accumulation of karmic seeds that would cause misfortune in the future, but they also abound with references to curses and the evil influence of various kinds of nonhuman, supernatural entities that cause sickness and death. However, as the Chinese esoteric Buddhist thinker Zhiyi 智顗 (538–597), regarded as the founder of Tiantai 天台 (Jp. Tendai), expounds in his *Greater* [*Treatise on*] *Śamatha and Vipaśyanā* (*Mohe zhiguan* 摩訶止觀), the disease-causing demons (*ki, oni, mono* 鬼) and evil spirits (*ma* 魔) are, in truth, a person's evil thoughts.[6] Zhiyi listed a total of six causes of illness. Influential monks such as Hōnen 法然 (1133–1212), Eisai (or Yōsai 栄西, 1141–1215), Dōgen 道元 (1200–1253), and Musō Soseki 夢窓疎石 (1275–1351), as well as other medieval thinkers, are known to have studied this treatise and referenced it in their own writings.[7] In this way, the six causes of illness outlined by Zhiyi became an important reference point for premodern scholars in Japan. According to Zhiyi, in addition to demonic and evil spirit (Māra) illnesses, illness can be caused by disharmony of the Four Elements—Fire, Water, Earth, and Wind—a view that is Indian in origin. Insufficient or incorrect nutrition, as well as accumulated karma, can equally cause one to get sick. The treatise also states that doing sitting meditation (*zazen* 座禅) incorrectly can also cause one to feel unwell.[8]

While the Zhiyi's treatise and other authoritative Buddhist texts emphasize the cognitive and emotional nature of demons and evil entities, Buddhist narratives in Japan mention and vividly describe the shape and actions of these supernatural and imaginary creatures in great detail. They seem less like manifestations of evil thoughts but rather have a mind of their own.

To the specially trained or exceptionally gifted, they take on visible shapes and frequently interact with humans. These beings possess women, men, and children alike and strike them with the most terrible diseases. They are also described as attacking domestic animals. The most notorious of these beings are the epidemic demons (*ekiki, ekki* 疫鬼), sometimes also referred to as epidemic deities (*ekishin, ekijin* 疫神). Affliction by demonic forces is part of the law of cause and effect, and so is in principle connected to the Buddhist idea of karmic retribution. Some narratives tell the story of a demon or other "monster" that suffers greatly from having to harm others. They are forced to live their horrifying existence because of misdeeds in their past lives. These frightful entities are thus in need of salvation just like other sentient beings. It is difficult, and perhaps not really necessary, to determine whether these entities are "Buddhist" or not. For much of history, they were thought to be affecting the health of humans and animals alike, and the people affected invited ritual experts to conduct rituals derived from the Buddhist traditions that were often combined with rituals from the Daoist and other, more local, traditions.

Many also believed that illnesses were caused by various kinds of worms (*mushi* 虫). A particularly widespread belief pertained to a group of three worms, the Three Death-bringers, Sanshi 三尸, that reside inside the human body from birth, seek to cause sinful desires, and then record their host's behavior. On the fifty-seventh day of the Chinese sexagenary cycle, the day of the metal monkey (*kōshin* 庚申), the Sanshi ascend to heaven to report their host's bad deeds. The misbehavior reported leads to punishment in the form of the shortening of one's life. However, the vital spirits of the Death-bringers can only leave the body while one is asleep. The ritual of staying awake on the day and night of the metal monkey to prevent the three worms escaping has been and is still held at some Buddhist temples in Japan. It is combined with a ritual centering on Blue-Faced Vajra-yakṣa, Shōmen kongō-yasha 青面金剛夜叉, an esoteric Buddhist deity that protects from the Sanshi.[9] The worms can be killed by cultivating virtue or even by taking medicine.

Chinese-style medicine provided the medical practitioner with ample diagnostic methods such as pulse reading and palpation. Within the framework of Japanese Buddhism, newly imported medical texts during the Song dynasty (960–1279), a period of technological and cultural exchange between China and Japan, led the monastic doctor Kajiwara Shōzen (1265–1337) to fundamentally problematize the notion of karmic illness in his work. While Kajiwara Shōzen did not question Buddhist understanding regarding karmic causes of untreatable diseases, he was aware that the diagnosis of leprosy (*rai*) often led to social stigmatization and further health issues. He argued that because some forms of leprosy could be treated, it was not per se and in all cases a karmic disease caused by evil deeds in the past.[10]

Divination was a further way of determining the cause of one's malady. Expert knowledge in Japan also included guidance derived from the Daoist tradition on avoiding harmful directions of the zodiac, and seeking out more auspicious directions. Elaborate charts circulated in Japan listing correspondences between a cardinal direction and a particular illness, and information on how to counteract the illness.

According to classical Chinese-style medicine, disease was caused by an imbalance in the flow of material energy, *qi* 氣, or *ki* 気 in Japanese. Doctors aimed to determine which factors led to a surplus or a depletion of *ki* in the organ system. One key factor for the stability of one's health was the effect of "wind" (*fū, kaze* 風). Wind could be a dangerous pathogenic agent.

"Wind illness" (*fūbyō* 風病) was a feared malady that featured widely in medical writing. However, the idea of illness being caused by wind was part of general knowledge. Indeed, the modern Japanese phrase for "catching a cold" is "contracting an evil wind," echoing this idea. The fundamental question remains whether "the various diseases come from outside, or [whether] their ultimate cause [is] in the mind," as someone once asked Soshin 祖心 (1588–1675), a lay Zen Buddhist active at the military ruler's court. She answered:

> The various diseases enter from nowhere but break out when the mind has become stagnant inside by [excessive] eating and drinking, and also when Wind from outside has a strong effect on the interior, and also when the Wind itself is very strong. . . . However, until the moment we contract cold *ki* [i.e., a disease caused by cold], it is not painful while the cold is slight. The same thing is also true for the Wind, as long as you think that the Wind is slight. Item: The ultimate cause of disease in the mind is the essential point. Our original mind is free from sickness anyway.[11]

According to Yogacāra philosophy, to which Soshin's teachings relate, insight leads to healing. While philosophical and doctrinal differences created a diverse religious field in Japan, the teaching of the four physical sufferings of birth, old age, sickness, and death, and the four mental sufferings of longing, disgust, disappointment, and fear, remained central to all Buddhist schools.

TREATING PATIENTS

Zhiyi's classification of diseases by their cause guided Japanese Buddhists from various schools including Zen Buddhism in the treatment of patients suffering from the six kinds of illnesses: (a) demonic and (b) evil spirit illnesses were to be treated carefully with spells; physicians could treat (c) the 404 illnesses brought about by the disharmony of the Four Elements as well as (d) illnesses caused by a wrong diet; (e) karmic illness could be treated with the patient's reflection on and repentance of any wrongdoing; (f) correct sitting meditation was the remedy for the malady of meditation.[12] Other classifications differentiated between three main causes—greed, anger, and ignorance; three subordinate causes—Cold, Heat, and Wind, and three resident causes—physical karma, verbal karma, and mental karma.[13] Chinese-style medicine provided a detailed nosology quite different from these classifications. Buddhist monastics were well versed in Chinese-style medical ideas and therapies and apparently had no difficulty combining seemingly quite disparate systems of nosology in order to treat their patients physically as well as soteriologically.

A group of texts commonly referred to as the *Sūtra for the Children* (*Dōji-kyō* 童子経) provided ritualists with means to protect infants from a group of fifteen mostly animal-headed or animal-shaped male and female demons. These demons plagued children and struck them with illness. In particular, Shingon Buddhist monks in Japan conducted rituals based on the *Dhāraṇī for the Protection of All Children* (*Gosho dōji darani-kyō* 護諸童子陀羅尼経), translated by Bodhiruci (fl. 5th/6th century), which is among this group of texts.[14] The sutra provides *dhāraṇīs* (spells) to protect the newborn child from the fifteen demons. According to early medieval Japanese ritual manuals, the ritual was to be repeated regularly as the child grew.[15]

The birth of an aristocratic child in the medieval period involved elaborate preparations: as the time for confinement approached, the birthing room would fill with "midwives, Buddhist ritualists, exorcists, yin-yang diviners, and other specialists who were employed to ensure the safe delivery and postnatal care" of mother and child.[16] Ritualists from the Shingon esoteric Buddhist school conducted rites centering on Mahāmāyūrī #, the "Great Peahen," to protect pregnant empresses, often their own sisters or cousins. Mahāmāyūrī is a female bodhisattva that in China and Japan was often depicted as a wrathful *vidyārāja* (*myōō* 明王, "enlightened king"). *Vidyārāja* are powerful beings that command superhuman knowledge to protect the dharma and the Buddhist ruler. Hāritī (Jp. Karitei 訶利帝), also referred to as "Goddess Demon Mother" (Kishimojin 鬼子母神), a female demon (*yakṣiṇī*) from the Indian pantheon was at the center of aristocratic births, but also became more widely popular outside the aristocracy as a protector of children in childbirth.

Female fertility was a chief concern of Buddhist activities in Japan. Buddhist rituals to increase or cause fertility in women and ease delivery involved empowering *materia medica* used in medicine such as ox bezoars, cow milk, and water.[17] Male fertility was more closely linked with worship of the local gods, but there are some references to involuntary infertility in men in Buddhist texts. Being a *paṇḍaka,* a "defective man," as a monk would theoretically be advantageous as the man would not have any sensation of sexual desire due to physical or psychological "disorders" and would thus more easily keep the precepts and remain "pure." Nevertheless, the ordination rules make clear that *paṇḍaka* were not to be accepted into the order. The precise classification of five different types of *paṇḍaka* in the ancient Indian ordination rules suggests that the classification is based on direct observations, not least in the medical field. In Japan, the relevant passages from the Indian texts were known in Chinese translation, but were seen as something of a curiosity. In the *Lotus Sūtra* (*Hokekyō* or *Hokkekyō* 法華経), which had a great impact on Japanese society and culture, the *paṇḍaka* appears as one of the Ten Troublemakers (*jū nōran* 十惱亂) who were described as not being a good choice for the company of a practitioner as they aroused unwholesome thoughts and thus created spiritual obstacles: here, the *paṇḍaka* is not characterized by his inability to procreate, but by his inability to be sexually aroused. The practitioner who encounters such a man who was freed from the obstacle of sexual desire could become jealous of that man's condition. The Buddha is reported to have prevented a monk from self-castration by instructing the monk that the solution was to cut off the wrong thoughts and not the organ. Nevertheless, individual cases of extreme asceticism in the form of self-castration have been documented in Japan.[18] To overcome the obstacle of sexual desire and transform this emotion into action for the alleviation of the suffering of all living beings, a ritual practice is attested to in medieval Japan that refers to the "sheathed horse penis [of a buddha]" (*meonzō* 馬陰蔵) representing the overcoming of ignorance, which is the origin of suffering. However, this was not a ritual exclusively for men, as one might think, but also for women.[19]

Humans of all ages suffered from physical ailments but also from social ostracization due to impairment such as blindness, loss of limbs, or *rai* (Hansen's disease, leprosy). Old age usually goes hand in hand with a number of maladies and the seeping away of one's strength.[20] Given the limits of what medicine could do in these cases, emphasis was placed on achieving tranquility of mind—at least within social circles that had the means to get council and support from religious experts. Achieving maximum longevity by living a healthy lifestyle, following rules for correct nutrition, sexual hygiene, etc., was still considered an important goal, not least to remain able to progress on the path to liberation for the sake of all beings. Buddhist priests also accompanied the dying and provided palliative care. Depending on the tradition, the dying parishioner or monastic would hold multicolored threads attached to a statue or image of the Buddha Amitābha (Jp. Amida Butsu 阿弥陀仏) and chant the *nenbutsu* 念仏, the "name" of that buddha, concentrating on birth in the Pure Land. Or, if they preferred the teachings of Nichiren 日蓮 (1222–1282), they would chant the *daimoku* 題目, the title of the *Lotus Sūtra*. The central idea in these deathbed rituals was to ensure that the dying could sustain a proper mindset in order to escape the cycle of birth into the Six Realms (*rokudō* 六道).[21] If they were not able to escape, an intermediary being would develop the desire and seek to be born again, according to tradition. The topic of conception and future birth is part of Buddhist embryology which is not a medical teaching as such but describes the path to enlightenment metaphorically using the unborn child's gestation in the womb.[22]

It was not just humans that deserved compassion and medical care. Domestic animals were equally tied to the cycle of birth that torments all sentient beings. Horses and cattle kept in Japan were treated by animal experts and veterinarians. By the 17th century, all cavalrymen knew how to apply a set of five treatments to their horses: moxibustion, acupuncture, medicines, incantations (*juri* 呪理), and magical technology (*jutsuri* 術理).[23] These laymen had religious expert knowledge similar to Buddhist priests.

MONASTIC DOCTORS, HEALERS

Most charismatic monastics used some of the many medical metaphors found in Buddhist sutras and traditional commentaries to elaborate their own teachings at some stage. Some even went beyond metaphors and stated that the Buddha provided medicines in addition to his wise teachings. Apart from the healing rituals, charismatic monastics engaged in medical care using available therapies and medicines. This is evidenced, for example, in a letter from the monk Kūkai 空海 (773–835) to the emperor. In the letter, Kūkai, who is deeply revered as a miracle-working saint and cultural hero, reports on efforts to pray for the emperor's recovery from illness and describes how the prayers had not yet reached the buddhas and deities. In a last effort to heal the patient quickly, Kūkai writes that he has prepared a vial of sacred water and empowered it with prayers of mutual empowerment (*kaji kitō* 加持祈祷) to be taken with medicine.[24] The term *kaji* derives from Sanskrit *adhiṣṭhāna* and means "assistance" from the buddhas.

While healing waters remained a popular cure-all remedy, some monastics creatively combined Buddhistic epistemic ideas with therapeutic methods from Chinese-style medicine to create their own form of medicine. A particularly interesting case is a 12th–13th-century treatise compiled by a number of monks of Onjōji Temple on the treatment of a contagious and often fatal disease called *denshibyō* 伝屍病 (or 伝尸病), translated as "corpse-vector disease." Today, this disease is often identified as tuberculosis. The treatise recommends incorporating moxibustion into a demon-subjugation ritual centering on Blue-Faced Vajra-yakṣa.[25]

Buddhist monastic doctors trained within their monastic institutions and networks. They not only served at the imperial court and at the court of the military rulers and other elite households but also worked in care facilities for public welfare funded by lay patrons. These facilities served as "fields of merit" (*fukuden* 福田, Sk. *puṇya-kṣetra*). Prince regent Shōtoku Taishi 聖徳太子 (574–622) famously opened four such welfare institutions: a dispensary for free medicines (*seyakuin* 施薬院), a hospital, a "field of compassion" (*hiden'in* 悲田院) for the relief of the poor, and a "field of respect" (*kyōden'in* 敬田院) for the elderly. The idea of "fields of merit" also included care for one's parents or teachers as the "field of gratitude" (*onden* 恩田). Some classifications of these fields of merit include care for animals and social action for the common good such as building bridges and roads.

Another well-known founder of welfare institutions was Kōmyō 光明 (659–760), a devout Buddhist empress. She converted her father's residence into a temple, Hokkeji 法華寺. The temple housed a dispensary and a hospital. Kōmyō is renowned for her personal care of "lepers," bathing them and treating their festering wounds, which is elaborated in various legends. After Kōmyō's husband, Emperor Shōmu 聖武天皇 (r. 724–749), died, she donated a collection of crude drugs to Tōdaiji Temple as an offering to Vairocana Buddha. Tōdaiji Temple is an imposing temple in Nara founded by Shōmu and Kōmyō. Some of the collection of drugs, which was kept in the temple's repository, the Shōsōin, has survived.

Monastic physicians such Kitano Yūrin 北野有隣 (d. 1410) considered their practice to be clearly linked to the idea of "fields of merit." Yūrin compiled a medical work with the title *Fields of Merit Formulae* (*Fukudenhō* 福田方, 1363) wishing that his formulae would "save all from the eight kinds of suffering (*hakku* 八苦). Those who will apply these medicines will sow good seeds in the eight fields of merit (*hachi fukuden* 八福田)."[26] The establishment of such public welfare institutions included medicinal gardens. Ninmyō Tennō 仁明天皇 (r. 833–850), for example, built a medicinal garden in Kyoto in the precinct of an existing "field of compassion," a shelter that included a hospital.

While temple precincts continued to have infirmaries and hospices for monastic staff, the tradition of establishing public welfare institutions waned over the centuries. This was changed temporarily by the engagement of several monks involved in the Shingon *vinaya* (Jp. *ritsu* 律) reform movement in the 13th century. Gokurakuji Temple, established by the group in Kamakura, housed not only the traditional Buddhist welfare institutions but also a hospital for those afflicted with *rai* and a shelter for abandoned domestic animals such as horses. The movement focused their attention on marginalized members of society, so-called "nonhumans" (*hinin* 非人), and also attempted to restore female orders. The monk doctor Kajiwara Shōzen, a member of the Shingon Ritsu movement, compiled two significant medical works, the *Book of the Simple Physician* (*Ton'ishō* 頓医抄, *c.* 1304) and the monumental *Myriad Relief Prescriptions* (*Man'anpō* 万安方, 1327).[27] He wrote the *Book of the Simple Physician* in Japanese instead of the usual Chinese. In his comments, he assesses the traditional Buddhist perception and classification of illness, and criticizes, for example, the understanding of *rai* as a karmic illness, arguing that calling all types of *rai* karmic resulted in social stigmatization of the afflicted and even more suffering.[28]

By the late medieval period, Confucian academies such as the Ashikaga gakkō 足利学校 started offering medical training. The Zen Buddhist monk Manase Dōsan 曲直瀬道三 (1507–1594) studied medicine at Ashikaga gakkō but left his order when he started practicing medicine. His motivation is not entirely clear but he remained a devout Buddhist. Jesuit missionary reports claimed that he was baptized but this claim cannot be substantiated.[29] It is probable that there was at least an encounter between the Jesuits and the doctor in Kyoto.

Manase Dōsan had a remarkable career and became the personal physician of a number of powerful members of the elite. Teaching a particular form of Chinese-style medicine, he founded his own academy and left his legacy to his successors who were part of his family.

Apart from the secular and the Buddhist monastic physicians, other healers, equally offered healing services, such as the itinerant *hijiri* 聖 or "saints." Spirit mediums, usually women, cooperated with Buddhist priests in exorcist rituals. Mountain ascetics, *yamabushi* 山伏, or *shugenja* 修験者, belonging to the Japanese religious tradition of Shugendō 修験道 provided ritual and medical healing. They were also known to have collected medicinal herbs from the wild and peddled them in towns and villages.

MEDICINES AND PHARMACOLOGICAL KNOWLEDGE

Monastics involved in healing in Japan were very much concerned with *materia medica* both as ingredients for medicines and as substances used in rituals. The monastic diet was a further area of health and soteriological knowledge circulation and production among Buddhists. Buddhists in Japan were well aware of the Indian origin of their religion and knew about the ordination rules pertaining to the "four supports" (*shie* 四依) for leading a pure life liberated from householders' concerns. The four supports related to clothing, food, shelter, and health. A monk or nun would vow to rely on wearing rags, gathering alms for food, dwelling under a tree, and taking "putrid medicine." The latter was usually interpreted as being made of fermented bovine urine or as being simply discarded medicine. In Japan, this medicine is mentioned in the *vinaya* texts and called *chinkiyaku* 陳棄薬 or *furanyaku* 腐爛薬.[30] However, the ordination rules quote the Buddha as having allowed the monks and nuns to take the Five Medicines (Jp. *goyaku* 五薬), too, usually including appealing types of food such as clarified butter, oil, fresh butter, honey, and raw sugar, to keep healthy in order to be of service to sentient beings. Monastic food and health culture in Japan are connected to the idea of the Five Medicines, and this also had an impact on medicine as practiced in the framework of Buddhist institutions in Japan in general which aimed at "nourishing life" (Ch. *yangsheng*, Jp. *yōjō* 養生). A Buddhist interpretation of such medicines is, for example, found in *The Record on Drinking Tea for Nourishing Life* (*Kissayōjōki* 喫茶養生記, 1211) compiled by Eisai.[31] In his treatise, which is resolutely based in esoteric Buddhist thought, Eisai promoted not only drinking green tea as a medicine but also taking drugs concocted from mulberry, ginger, and other plants to heal various diseases. He found them especially effective against demon-caused ailments.

Health and well-being within the community of monks and nuns was also related to their diet. Traditional monastic food culture today can be enjoyed by everyone but is celebrated as a specialty gourmet cuisine. Some temples offer the multicourse meals called *shōjin ryōri* 精進料理, literally "cooking for spiritual elevation." The dishes are enjoyed in the stark but elegant surrounding of a temple hall as a celebration of time-honored Buddhist vegetarian cooking. Most recipes go back to continental Chinese and Korean Buddhist vegetarian cuisine. Monastery cooks in Japan developed them further using local vegetables and spices and cooking styles. *Shōjin ryōri* was and is served to lay parishioners too on special occasions such as Buddhist celebrations. The cooking only uses plant-based ingredients but the plants must not fall into the group of the "five forbidden pungent roots," *goshin* 五辛 or *gokun* 五葷. The group as a rule includes plants belonging to the onion family (Allioideae) such as leeks, scallions, garlic, onions, and chives. These pungent roots were thought to cause negative emotions and lustful desires that would become obstacles for those who wanted to exert zeal to reach a higher spiritual goal. When reading the sutras out loud, the breath after enjoying such pungent vegetables was thought to chase away the *deva*. The argument that the smell was offensive to heavenly beings and would drive them away is also found in the *Laṅkāvatāra Sūtra* (Jp. *Ryōga-kyō* 楞伽経) in regard to meat preparation and consumption. Intoxicating substances such as liquor were also not part of the monastic cuisine, whereas in the worship of the local gods, *kami* 神, a religious tradition that for most of Japanese history was combined with Buddhism, rice wine was offered to the *kami*. Abstention from consuming meat and liquor remained an important marker of the monastic world until it was *de facto* abolished by civil law in the Meiji period when the state officially allowed monks and nuns to eat meat and drink alcohol.

Animal products and liquor were regarded as *materia medica* and therefore used in some medicines. Chinese-style medicine is well known for its rich pharmaceutical culture, and much effort went into identifying and finding the plants, minerals, and animal parts on which the *materia medica* were based as well as the substances from India named in the Buddhist texts. As most medicines contain parts of plants, the use of plant-based medicines is especially well attested to in Buddhistic medicine in Japan. Apart from sacred water, such as that used by Kūkai for the healing of the emperor's ailment, cure-all medicine made from plants that often had auspicious names, seemed to have been frequently used in the healing of humans and animals alike. The ritualist would empower the plant ingredients with spells, sutra chanting, and prayers to make the medicine effective. Some temples offered cure-all pills.[32] Monastic physicians and other healers administered the medicines uttering mantras of buddhas and bodhisattvas, as for example Kajiwara Shōzen noted in his *Book of the Simple Physician*: If one does not praise the Medicine Buddha, Jīvaka, and the Buddha with a "correct and deep intention" and say the *nenbutsu* wholeheartedly, "placing medicine in the mouth and eliminating the painful ailment is just like [putting] cold water and snow into boiling water. If the chanting is not done as indicated, then the disease will not be cured quickly."[33]

RITUALS

The great range of rituals conducted throughout Japan and over the course of many centuries for protection from calamities including epidemics, the exorcising, quelling, and pacification of hostile and demonic forces as well as the invitation of friendly spirits has formed a vibrant Buddhist culture in Japan. Rituals for healing the physical body and protecting from illness are generally counted as belonging to the class of "worldly" rituals as they aim to promote this-worldly benefits. However, conducting such rituals or sponsoring them was meant to "sow good seeds in a field of merit," and improve the well-being of the suffering sentient beings and thereby uplift society to allow more people to strive for the ultimate, or "other-worldly" goal.

In early Japan, when monarchs such as Genmei Tennō 元明天皇 (r. 707–715) and Genshō Tennō 元正天皇 (r. 715–724) started becoming patrons of Buddhism, a system of state-protecting monasteries and convents was established. Succeeding his grandmother and his aunt as ruler, Shōmu Tennō, together with Empress Kōmyō, created a dual temple system of monasteries and nunneries in all of the provinces of the centralized state that were to protect it by various Buddhist meritorious actions such as copying and reciting the *Sūtra of Golden Light* and the *Lotus Sūtra*.[34] The *Sūtra of Golden Light* was cherished for the chapters on the "Four Deva Kings" that protect the land and for the chapter on "Eliminating Disease" (*Jobyō hon* 除病品) that contains a summary of Indian medical teachings.[35] In it, the Buddha teaches the goddess of the bodhi tree how he, in a previous lifetime, was a physician's son with the name of Jalavāhana. He then tells the story of how Jalavāhana asked his father, a skilled doctor, to pass on his medical secrets so that he, too, could heal "incalculable hundreds of thousands of beings in the kingdom that were afflicted by an epidemic. They were so plagued by their many ailments that they no longer had a happy thought."[36] After becoming a doctor himself, Jalavāhana completely cured all these beings and brought them happiness.

Two of the Seven Parables of the *Lotus Sūtra* (*hokke shichiyu* 法華七喩) deal with medical metaphors: Chapter 5, entitled "The Parable of Medicinal Herbs" (*Yakusō-yu hon* 薬草喩品) likens the dharma—in other texts often referred to as the cure-all Great Medicine (Jp. *daiyaku* 大薬)—to a massive rain shower that nourishes healing plants. These plants represent the *śrāvaka*, pratyekabuddhas, and bodhisattvas. In Chapter 16, "The Lifespan of the Tatāgatha" (*Nyorai jūryō hon* 如来寿量品) the Buddha teaches the parable of the physician who persuades his sons to take his medicine by feigning his death. In this parable, the physician stands for the Buddha, the sons symbolize the human beings suffering from delusion, and the medicine is the path of the One Vehicle (*ichijō* 一乘) expounded in the *Lotus Sūtra*.

Most sutras that provide *dhāraṇī* to cure physical and mental ailments belong to the corpus of esoteric Buddhist sutras.[37] The *dhāraṇī* sutras not only offered ritual specialists and lay Buddhists spells believed to be efficacious but also contained recipes for treating various ailments showing that religious and medical practices were closely interlinked. For example, the *Dhāraṇī Sūtra of the Thousand-Armed and Thousand-Eyed* [*Avalokiteśvara*] (*Senju sengen darani-kyō* 千手千眼陀羅尼経) lists remedies for curing possession by a cat demon, alongside remedies to cure the harm caused by venomous insects, snake bites, and personal intrigue. Sight-related disease, fevers, hearing loss, paralysis, and difficulties in childbirth and other obstacles can, according to the text, be treated by reciting the *dhāraṇī* multiple times while making a particular medicine or when using it.

The bodhisattva Avalokiteśvara, mentioned in several other sutras as well, became a central figure in Japanese Buddhism, not least because of this bodhisattva's acclaimed universal power. Pilgrims and visitors to thirty-three temples that form a circulatory pilgrimage route are said to be able to encounter the bodhisattva at these sacred sites. Some of the temples not only provided a place to worship the bodhisattva and other Buddhist deities but also provided medical services for the pilgrims. Pilgrims also practiced *komori* 籠り, a kind of "incubation ritual" that entailed spending the night at a temple and sleeping close to its sacred image for healing. They hoped to encounter the deity in a dream and receive a remedy from it. Narratives mention pilgrims having visions of the deity during a dream and finding a wonderous medicine on their pillow in the morning. Healing amulets and talismans for protection and healing could be purchased at temples and shrines (and this custom is still in place). Japanese ritualists created a Buddho-Daoist material culture of talismans (*gofu* 護符). These often took the form of paper strips and could either be placed on the afflicted place on the body of the patron-patient or could be dissolved in water and taken as medicine. Sometimes the ritualist burned the seal and administered the ash as medicine.

The medieval period also saw individuals such as Shinran 親鸞 (1173–1263) who held one single Buddhist practice to be sufficient and said that this would render incantations and prayers (*jujutsu kitō* 呪術祈祷) to obtain this-worldly benefits superfluous. Shinran, revered as the founder of True Pure Land Buddhism (Jōdo shinshū 浄土真宗), taught that wholehearted belief in the power of the original vow of the Buddha Amitābha to liberate all beings would naturally free everyone from sickness.[38]

MEDITATION

The umbrella term "meditation" includes a wide spectrum of physical and mental practices. Among meditation techniques that have a link to healing the physical body, correct sitting meditation can heal more than just the "meditation malady." *Śamatha* (Jp. *shi* 止) meditation or "calm abiding" aimed at stopping the flow of mind, one of the seven types of silent meditation, is also thought to have a healing effect. Zhiyi explains in his *Tiantai Shorter [Treatise on] Śamatha and Vipaśyanā* (*Tendai Shōshikan* 天台小止観) that "merely settling one's mind on the location of an illness is enough to cure it" because it has the effect of alleviating negative karma.[39] He also states that *vipaśyanā* (Jp. *kan* 観) or "observation meditation" has health benefits. Here, different kinds of breath or respirations and visualizations are central, as "some teachers say that one who is good at visualization can cure all illnesses. If a person is afflicted with cold, he can visualize within his body a fiery *qi*/*ki* arising and thereby cure it."[40]

Other forms of meditation guide one to focus not on the breath, etc., but on the Buddha's meritorious virtues. The act of continually thinking of the Buddha or concentrating the mind on the Buddha is known as *buddhānusmṛti* in Sanskrit and *nenbutsu* in Japanese. Those who dedicate their whole mind and attention to thinking of the appearance of the Buddha or repeat the Buddha's name, can attain a state of complete absorption, or *samādhi* (Jp. *zanmai* 三昧). A person who enters into this *samādhi*, or merely repeats the name of the Buddha Amitābha (Jp. Amida Butsu 阿弥陀仏), however immoral their life may have been, will acquire the merits of this Buddha and be received into his Pure Land. In Pure Land teachings in Japan, *nenbutsu* mainly refers to the act of uttering Amitābha's name, a practice that became enormously popular. Although saying the *nenbutsu* seems like a prayer, it was not regarded as such, and the practice of prayer (*kitō*) was discouraged: Adherents to the teachings of Shinran stated that patients should take medicine rather than pray.[41] However, the sole emphasis on the *nenbutsu* led to new considerations of how to deal with sickness and dying. The traditional Pure Land Buddhist practice of self-reflection, or self-examination, *mishirabe* 身調べ, proved to be a starting point for modern interpretations and practices.

For example, the pioneering historian of Japanese medicine Fujikawa Yū 富士川游 (1865–1940), who was trained in modern European medicine, also wrote on Buddhist thought. Fujikawa equates true religion with Shinran's teaching of *naikan* 内観, "internal observation," and *jinen hōni* 自然法爾, "naturally occurring as it is."[42] Abandoning the notion of "self-power," compassionate acts arise "naturally and inevitably" (*jinen* 自然). In Pure Land Buddhism, *hōni* 法爾 means occurring through the power of the vow of Amitābha Buddha, the "other-power." Fujikawa admired modern scientific achievements but found them too mechanical and materialistic. He argues that only (true) religion can provide human beings with warmth and emotional strength. To come to an honest and devout subjective attitude, one needs to practice *naikan*. To practice medicine and medical care, Fujikawa continues, one also needs to approach the patient with a compassionate attitude arrived at by having insight into "naturally occurring as it is."

Yoshimoto Ishin 吉本伊信 (1916–1988), a Buddhist priest and prison chaplain, founded "Naikan" in the 1940s as a meditation method and psychotherapy based on the traditional True Pure Land Buddhist form of self-reflective meditation. Naikan as inspired by Yoshimoto has become a worldwide movement.[43]

Contemporary advocates of Buddhism as a medical tradition, such as the Nichiren Buddhist priest and behavioral scientist Kageyama Kyōshun 影山教俊 (b. 1951), seek a revival of East Asian medical traditions as a countermodel to Western medicine. By primarily relying on Zhiyi's meditation treatises, Kageyama propagates Buddhist practice as medicine guaranteeing a healthy life to his Japanese audience, recommending healing prayers and meditation.[44]

REVIEW OF LITERATURE

The field of the study of Buddhism and medicine in Japan includes works from diverse disciplines. The standard works on the history of medicine in Japan by Fujikawa Yū and Hattori Toshirō (1906–1992) stress the role of Buddhism. Both authors appreciate premodern Japanese medicine but advocate modern biomedicine. In his extensive and meticulous work on the history of medicine in Japan, Hattori emphasizes how Japanese medicine was influenced by Buddhist texts from India. He revisits the topic of Buddhism as a cultural force in the development of medicine in a book published in 1968, in which he explores early Indian Buddhist sources to describe what he calls "Śākyamuni's medicine" (*Shaka no igaku* 釈迦の医学).[45] In this book, he attempts to reconstruct the life of the Buddha Śākyamuni in the medical context of the Buddha's time.

The modern term "Buddhist medicine" (*bukkyō igaku* 仏教医学) in book titles indicates that the publications primarily deal with Indian medical ideas and practices.[46] A more recent history of Japanese medicine and healing authored by Sakai Shizu also outlines the role of Buddhism in the historical development of medicine in Japan. Other studies focus more on the evolution of Chinese-style medicine in Japan, de-emphasizing Buddhist actors. Pioneering authors such as Ōtsuka Keisetsu 大塚敬節 (1900–1980), Yakazu Dōmei 矢数道明 (1905–2002), and others, who contributed to modernizing Kampo medicine, tend to depict Buddhist cosmology and the Buddhist worldview as obstacles to the advance toward empirical medicine as espoused by scholars with Confucian leanings.

At the opposite end of the spectrum are the works of Shinmura Taku, especially his 2013 volume dedicated to the history of medical therapeutics in Japanese Buddhism. Shinmura's focus is on ancient and medieval Japan but he also has substantial chapters on early modern Japan and the Meiji period. Healing and medicine also feature in Buddhist folklore studies, established by the historian Gorai Shigeru 五来重 (1908–1993).[47] Historian Nihonyanagi Kenji focuses more on the material medical and religious cultural aspects of the Esoteric Japanese Buddhist tradition.[48] Michel Strickmann introduces and discusses "magical practices" such as spirit possession, demonology, and exorcism in East Asian Buddhism and Daoism with references to Japan in a much-cited volume.[49]

A number of general historical works on Japanese medicine have also been published in European languages. These include contributions to the anthology *Asian Medical Systems: A Comparative Study*, edited by Pierre Huard et al.; Erhard Rosner's handbook *Medizingeschichte Japans*; Mieko Macé's work on the history of medicine and physicians with a focus on the Edo period; and Wolfgang Michel-Zaitsu's history of traditional Japanese medicine.[50] While these valuable works mention the cultural and intellectual role of Buddhism, among other factors, Paul Demiéville's 1937 encyclopedia entry on "sickness" (*byō*) provides a foundation for the study of Asian Buddhism and medicine, including Japan.[51]

The categorization of texts or phenomena as either medicine or religion is a basic theoretical problem in the study of medicine in Japanese Buddhism. To remedy this problem, medical compilations can be searched for religious expressions or religious sources for references to medicine. The question is how to categorize sources that do not fit neatly into either category. The categorization of certain practices as constituting "magic," especially in the context of studying premodern Japan, is a further problem because these practices could be categorized pejoratively as "superstitious" from a modernist viewpoint. Rereading key textual materials, examining pictorial and other materials, and reconsidering Buddhism and medicine as connected fields can help us overcome such unhelpful views and reconstruct past life-worlds in Japan. Some 21st-century studies attempt to grapple with the question of the particular nature of the complex and close relationship between Buddhism and medicine.

Historian of Japanese religions Katja Triplett explored Buddhism in conjunction with medicine in Japan by looking at specific topics such as ophthalmology, the female reproductive body, botany and pharmacognosy, and hippiatry. She also published several studies on the relationship between Buddhism and medicine in Japan.[52] Other topical studies in the emerging field of medicine in Japanese Buddhism include the groundbreaking works by Anna Andreeva, Edward Drott, Andrew Edmund Goble, Benedetta Lomi, Andrew Macomber, Duncan Ryūken Williams, and others.[53]

Charismatic and foundational Buddhist figures in Japan who were involved in healing and medical matters have been the focus of recent publications.[54] The field has also been stimulated by the translation and publishing work of historian and sinologist C. Pierce Salguero, who has discussed key Chinese Buddhist texts that circulated in East Asia, including Japan, and which demonstrate the link between Buddhism and medicine. Lastly, presentations of Buddhism and medicine in modern Japan from a more normative standpoint, such as the work of Kageyama Kyōshun, constitute a fruitful field of academic study that is being developed in the early 21st century.[55]

PRIMARY SOURCES

In addition to medical works published by Buddhist monastic physicians in Japan, doctors used works such as the 10th-century *Essentials of Medicine* (*Ishinpō* 医心方), which quotes from many different sources, among them medical works that are either ascribed to Buddhist authorities, to legendary figures such as the Buddha's personal doctor, Jīvaka, or to East Asian scholar monks.[56] Japanese picture scrolls and other pictorial sources also provide insights into the history of medicine in Japanese Buddhism. A well-known picture scroll is the *Scroll of Illnesses* (*Yamai no sōshi* 病草紙, 12th century) that shows a sufferer of *kakuran* (cholera), someone displaying features of a *futanari* (intersexual), a man suffering from illusions while asleep, and other conditions that can be interpreted as resulting from karmic affliction. Of particular importance are also images of the *Nine Stages of Bodily Decay* (*Kusō-zu* 九相図) of which numerous versions exist from the latter half of the 13th century onward.[57] These images show a corpse decaying in nine defined stages. The imagery goes back to charnel-ground meditation in India, where a meditator sits among corpses and contemplates mortality and the impermanence of the body in all its graphic and sensorial detail. In Japan, the imagery became connected to the overall theme of the evanescence of life and beauty. The images are of medical interest because they often show the decay in realistic anatomical presentations.

DIGITAL MATERIALS

Many of the picture scrolls and other pictorial and textual sources held at the national museums of Japan are digitalized and can be viewed freely online via e-museum (https://emuseum.nich.go.jp).

FURTHER READINGS

Ahn, Juhn. "Malady of Meditation: A Prolegomenon to the Study of Illness and Zen." PhD diss., University of California, Berkeley, 2007.

Andreeva, Anna. "Devising the Esoteric Rituals for Women: Fertility and the Demon Mother in the *Gushi nintai sanshō himitsu hōshū*." In *Women, Rites, and Ritual Objects in Premodern Japan*, edited by Karen Gerhart, 53–88. Leiden, The Netherlands: Brill, 2018.

Birnbaum, Raoul. *The Healing Buddha*. Boulder, CO: Shambhala, 1979.

Demiéville, Paul. *Buddhism and Healing [=Hōbōgirin entry on "Byō,"]*, translated by Mark Tatz. Lanham, MD: University Press of America, 1985.

Drott, Edward "Gods, Buddhas, and Organs: Buddhist Physicians and Theories of Longevity in Early Medieval Japan." *Japanese Journal of Religious Studies* 37, no. 2 (2010): 247–273.

Goble, Andrew Edmund. *Confluences of Medicine in Medieval Japan: Buddhist Healing, Chinese Knowledge, Islamic Formulas, and Wounds of War*. Honolulu: University of Hawaii Press, 2011.

Groner, Paul. "Extreme Asceticism, Medicine and Pure Land Faith in the Life of Shuichi Munō (1683–1719)." *Japanese Religions (Special Issue "Religion and Healing in Japan," edited by Christoph Kleine and Katja Triplett)* 37, no. 1–2 (2012): 39–62.

Killinger, Katrin, Christoph Kleine, and Katja Triplett. "Distinctions and Differentiations between Medicine and Religion." *Asian Medicine (Special Issue "Religion and Medicine," edited by Katrin Killinger, Christoph Kleine, and Katja Triplett)* 14, no. 2 (2019): 275–304. https://doi.org/10.1163/15734218-12341452.

Kleine, Christoph. "Buddhist Monks as Healers in Early and Medieval Japan." *Japanese Religions (Special Issue "Religion and Healing in Japan," edited by Christoph Kleine and Katja Triplett)* 37, no. 1–2 (2012): 13–38.

Lomi, Benedetta. "Dharanis, Talismans, and Straw-Dolls Ritual Choreographies and Healing: Strategies of the Rokujikyōhō in Medieval Japan." *Japanese Journal of Religious Studies* 41, no. 2 (2014): 255–304.

McBride II, Richard "Esoteric Buddhism and Its Relation to Healing and Demonology." In *Esoteric Buddhism and the Tantras in East Asia*, edited by Charles Orzech, Henrik Hjort Sørensen, and Richard Karl Payne, 208–214. Leiden, The Netherlands: Brill, 2011.

Nihonyanagi Kenji 二本柳賢司. "Nihon mikkyō igaku to yakubutsugaku 日本密教医学と薬物学." In *Rekishi no naka no yamai to igaku* 歴史の中の病と医学, edited by Yamada Keiji 山田慶兒 and

Kuriyama Shigehisa 栗山茂久, 545–566. Kyōto, Japan: Kokusai Nihon Bunka Kenkyū Sentā; Shibundō, 1997.

Salguero, C. Pierce, ed. *Buddhism and Medicine: An Anthology of Premodern Sources*. Vol. 1. New York: Columbia University Press, 2017.

Salguero, C. Pierce, ed. *Buddhism and Medicine: An Anthology of Modern and Contemporary Sources*. New York: Columbia University Press, 2019.

Salguero, C. Pierce, and Andrew Macomber, eds. *Buddhist Healing in Medieval China and Japan*. Honolulu: University of Hawaii Press, 2020.

Schrimpf, Monika. "Medical Discourses and Practices in Contemporary Japanese Religions." In *Medicine—Religion—Spirituality: Global Perspectives on Traditional, Complementary, and Alternative Healing*, edited by Dorothea Lüddeckens and Monika Schrimpf, 57–90. Bielefeld, Germany: Transcript Verlag, 2018.

Shinmura Taku 新村拓. *Nihon bukkyō no iryō-shi* 日本仏教の医療史. Tokyo: Hōsei Daigaku Shuppankyoku, 2013.

Strickmann, Michel. *Chinese Magical Medicine*, edited by Bernard Faure. Stanford, CA: Stanford University Press, 2002.

Triplett, Katja. "Pediatric Care and Buddhism in Premodern Japan: A Case of Applied 'Demonology'?" *Asian Medicine (Special Issue "Religion and Medicine," edited by Katrin Killinger, Christoph Kleine, and Katja Triplett)* 14, no. 2 (2019): 313–341. https://doi.org/10.1163/15734218-12341455.

Triplett, Katja. *Buddhism and Medicine in Japan: A Topical Survey (500–1600 CE) of a Complex Relationship*, edited by Gustavo Benavides, Frank Korom, Karen Ruffle, and Kocku von Stuckrad. Vol. 81: *Religion and Society*. Berlin: De Gruyter, 2019.

Triplett, Katja. "Potency by Name? 'Medicine Buddha Plant' and Other Herbs in the Japanese *Scroll of Equine Medicine (Ba'i sōshi emaki,* 1267)." *Himalaya (Special Issue "Approaching Potent Substances in Medicine and Ritual across Asia," edited by Barbara Gerke and Jan van der Valk)* 39, no. 1 (2019): 189–207.

Williams, Duncan Ryūken. *The Other Side of Zen: A Social History of Sōtō Zen Buddhism in Tokugawa Japan*. Princeton, NJ: Princeton University Press, 2005.

Winfield, Pamela. "Curing with *kaji*: Healing and Esoteric Empowerment in Japan." *Japanese Journal of Religious Studies* 32, no. 1 (2005): 107–130.

NOTES

1. Katja Triplett, *Buddhism and Medicine in Japan: A Topical Survey (500–1600 CE) of a Complex Relationship*, ed. Gustavo Benavides, Frank Korom, Karen Ruffle, and Kocku von Stuckrad (Berlin: De Gruyter, 2019), 78–98. For Buddhist medicine in India, see Vesna Wallace, "Buddhist Medicine in India," *Oxford Research Encyclopedia of Religion*, February 26, 2018.
2. See David Gardiner, "Tantric Buddhism in Japan: Kūkai and Saichō," *Oxford Research Encyclopedia of Religion*, December 23, 2019; and David Gardiner, "Tantric Buddhism in Japan: Shingon, Tendai, and the Esotericization of Japanese Buddhisms," *Oxford Research Encyclopedia of Religion*, August 28, 2018.
3. Taishō Shinshū Daizōkyō 大正新修大藏經, ed. Takakusu Junjirō 高楠順次郎 (Tōkyō: Taishō Issaikyō Kankōkai, reprint edition, 1962), vol. 24, no. 1484; and C. Pierce Salguero, "Healing and/or Salvation? The Relationship between Religion and Medicine in Medieval Chinese Buddhism," *Working Paper Series of the HCAS "Multiple Secularities—Beyond the West"* 4 (2018): 17.
4. For more on this bodhisattva, see Chün-fang Yü, "Avalokiteśvara: The Bodhisattva of Compassion," *Oxford Research Encyclopedia of Religion*, August 5, 2016.
5. Sujung Kim, Shinra Myōjin and Buddhist Networks of the East Asian "Mediterranean" (Honolulu: University of Hawaii Press, 2019).
6. *Mohe zhiguan* 摩訶止觀 is pronounced *Maka shikan* in Japan. See Taishō Shinshū Daizōkyō, vol. 46, no. 1911.

7. Taku Shinmura 新村拓, *Nihon bukkyō no iryō-shi* 日本仏教の医療史 (Tokyo: Hōsei Daigaku Shuppankyoku, 2013), 34.
8. Paul Swanson, trans., *Clear Serenity, Quiet Insight: T'ien-T'ai Chih-i's* Mo-Ho Chih-Kuan, 3 vols. (Honolulu: University of Hawaii Press, 2017), 2:1331–1334. See also Juhn Ahn, "Malady of Meditation: A Prolegomenon to the Study of Illness and Zen," PhD diss., University of California, Berkeley, 2007.
9. For a detailed description of the Three Death-bringers (or Three Corpses) translated into English from an early medieval manuscript, see Andrew Macomber, "Moxibustion for Demons: Oral Transmission on Corpse-Vector Disease," in *Buddhism and Medicine: An Anthology of Premodern Sources*, ed. C. Pierce Salguero (New York: Columbia University Press, 2017), 519–522.
10. Andrew Edmund Goble, "Determining Karmic Illness: Kajiwara Shōzen's Treatment of *Rai*/Leprosy in *Book of the Simple Physician*," in Salguero, *Buddhism and Medicine*, 554. For a comprehensive account of Kajiwara Shōzen's work, see Andrew Edmund Goble, *Confluences of Medicine in Medieval Japan: Buddhist Healing, Chinese Knowledge, Islamic Formulas, and Wounds of War* (Honolulu: University of Hawai'i Press, 2011).
11. Quote adapted from Katja Triplett, "On Sickness, Society, and the New Self in Early Edo Japan: Soshin's Dharma Words (Seventeenth Century)," in Salguero, *Buddhism and Medicine*, 18.
12. Swanson, *Clear Serenity, Quiet Insight*, vol. 1–2. See also C. Pierce Salguero, "'Treating Illness': Translation of a Chapter from a Medieval Chinese Buddhist Meditation Manual by Zhiyi (538–597)," *Asian Medicine* 7, no. 2 (2012): 461–473.
13. Edward Drott, "Overcoming Illness with Insight: Kokan Shiren's *Treatise on the Nature of Illness and Its Manifestations*," in Salguero, *Buddhism and Medicine*, 64.
14. Taishō Shinshū Daizōkyō, vol. 19, no. 1028A.
15. Katja Triplett, "Pediatric Care and Buddhism in Premodern Japan: A Case of Applied 'Demonology'?," *Asian Medicine (Special Issue "Religion and Medicine," ed, Katrin Killinger, Christoph Kleine, and Katja Triplett)* 14, no. 2 (2019): 327–329.
16. Triplett, *Buddhism and Medicine in Japan*, 111. For a treatment of the topic in general, see Anna Andreeva, "Childbirth in Aristocratic Households of Heian Japan," *Dynamis* 34, no. 2 (2014): 357–376.
17. Benedetta Lomi, "The Ox-Bezoar Empowerment for Fertility and Safe Childbirth: Selected Readings from the Shingon Ritual Collection," in Salguero, *Buddhism and Medicine*.
18. Paul Groner, "Extreme Asceticism, Medicine and Pure Land Faith in the Life of Shuichi Munō (1683–1719)," *Japanese Religions (Special Issue "Religion and Healing in Japan," ed. Christoph Kleine and Katja Triplett)* 37, no. 1–2: 46–47.
19. Bernard Faure, *The Red Thread: Buddhist Approaches to Sexuality* (Princeton, NJ: Princeton University Press, 1998), 35.
20. For a comprehensive account on the view of old age in Buddhist Japan, see Edward Robertson Drott, *Buddhism and the Transformation of Old Age in Medieval Japan* (Honolulu: University of Hawai'i Press, 2016).
21. Jacqueline Stone, "With the Help of 'Good Friends': Deathbed Ritual Practices in Early Medieval Japan," in *Death and the Afterlife in Japanese Buddhism*, ed. Jacqueline Stone and Mariko Namba Walker (Honolulu: University of Hawai'i Press, 2008), 61–101.
22. Anna Andreeva, "Lost in the Womb: Conception, Reproductive Imagery, and Gender in the Writings and Rituals of Japan's Medieval Holy Men," in *Transforming the Void: Embryological Discourse and Reproductive Imagery in East Asian Religions*, ed. Anna Andreeva and Dominic Steavu (Leiden, The Netherlands: Brill, 2016), 420–478.
23. Triplett, *Buddhism and Medicine in Japan*, 182–183, quoting Shira'i Tsunesaburō 白井恒三郎, *Nihon jūigaku-shi* 日本獣医学史 (Tōkyō: Bun'eidō, [1944] 1979), 47.
24. For an introduction and translation of the letter, see Pamela Winfield, "Esoteric Ritual Remedies: Kūkai's Cures for Emperor Kōnin," in Salguero, *Buddhism and Medicine*, 222–225.

25. For an introduction and translation of the treatise, see Macomber, "Moxibustion for Demons." See also Michel Strickmann, *Chinese Magical Medicine*, ed. Bernard Faure (Stanford, CA: Stanford University Press, 2002), 294–295.
26. Translation adapted from Masamune Atsuo 正宗敦夫, "Fukudenhō Kaidai 福田方解題," in *Yūrin Fukudenhō* 有林福田方, ed. Kitano Yūrin 北野有隣 (Tōkyō: Nihon Koten Zenshū Kankō-Kai, 1936), 1:1; see also Triplett, *Buddhism and Medicine in Japan*, 129.
27. For a comprehensive account of these two key works in the history of Japanese medicine and Buddhism, see Goble, *Confluences of Medicine in Medieval Japan*.
28. Goble, "Determining Karmic Illness," 554.
29. Katja Triplett, "Buddhist Monastic Physicians' Encounters with the Jesuits in Sixteenth- and Seventeenth-Century Japan, as Told from Both Sides," in Salguero, *Buddhism and Medicine*, 6–9.
30. Jasques May, "Chinkiyaku," in *Hōbōgirin: dictionnaire encyclopédique du bouddhisme d'après les sources chinoises et japonaises*, ed. Paul Demiéville (Tokyo: Maison Franco-Japonaise, 1967), 329–335.
31. For a translation of this text into English, see James Benn, *Tea in China: A Religious and Cultural History* (Honolulu: University of Hawai'i Press, 2015), 145–171.
32. Duncan Ryūken Williams, *The Other Side of Zen: A Social History of Sōtō Zen Buddhism in Tokugawa Japan* (Princeton, NJ: Princeton University Press, 2005), 86–102.
33. Goble, "Determining Karmic Illness," 555.
34. See *Konkōmyō-kyō* 金光明経 (*Suvarṇabhāsōttama-sūtra*) in Taishō Shinshū Daizōkyō, vol. 16, no. 665, trans. Yijing 義淨 (635–713); see also *Lotus Flower of the Wonderful Dharma* (*Myōhō renge-kyō* 妙法蓮華経 (*Saddharma-puṇḍarīka-sūtra*) in Taishō Shinshū Daizōkyō, vol. 9, no. 262.
35. C. Pierce Salguero, "'On Eliminating Disease': Translations of the Medical Chapter from the Chinese Versions of the Sūtra of Golden Light," *ejournal of Indian Medicine* 6 (2013): 21–43.
36. C. Pierce Salguero, "Understanding the *Doṣa*: A Summary of the Art of Medicine from the *Sūtra of Golden Light*," in Salguero, *Buddhism and Medicine*, 33.
37. Many appear in Taishō Shinshū Daizōkyō, vol. 20.
38. Shinmura, *Nihon bukkyō no iryō-shi*, 187–188.
39. Taishō Shinshū Daizōkyō, vol. 46, no. 1915. For a recent translation of the full text into English, see Swanson, *Clear Serenity, Quiet Insight*, 3:1659–1757.
40. C. Pierce Salguero, "Healing with Meditation: 'Treating Illness' from Zhiyi's Shorter Treatise on Śamatha and Vipaśyanā," in Salguero, *Buddhism and Medicine*, 386–387, adapted.
41. Shinmura, *Nihon bukkyō no iryō-shi*, 192.
42. Fujikawa Yū 富士川游, *Ijutsu to shūkyō* 医術と宗教 (Tōkyō: Orig. Daiichi Shobō, Repr. Shoshi Shinsui, [1937] 2010).
43. Clark Chilson, "Naikan: A Meditation Method and Psychotherapy," *Oxford Research Encyclopedia of Religion*, April 26, 2018.
44. Monika Schrimpf, "Medical Discourses and Practices in Contemporary Japanese Religions," in *Medicine—Religion—Spirituality Global Perspectives on Traditional, Complementary, and Alternative Healing*, ed. Dorothea Lüddeckens and Monika Schrimpf (Bielefeld, Germany: Transcript Verlag, 2018), 68–69.
45. Hattori Toshiyoshi [Toshirō] 服部敏良, *Bukkyō kyōten o chūshin toshita Shaka no igaku* 仏教経典を中心とした釈迦の医学 (Nagoya, Japan: Reimei Shobōō, [1968] 1982).
46. See, for example, Fukunaga Katsumi 福永勝美, *Bukkyō igaku shōsetsu* 仏教医学詳説 (Tokyo: Yūzankaku, 1972).
47. He edited a volume, for example, that explores the Yakushi Nyorai cult. See Gorai Shigeru 五来重, ed., *Yakushi shinkō* 薬師信仰, Vol. 12: *Minshū shūkyo-shi sōsho* 民衆宗教史叢書 (Tōkyō: Yūzankaku Shuppan, 1986).
48. Nihonyanagi Kenji 二本柳賢司, *Bukkyō igaku gaiyō* 佛教医学概要 (Kyōto, Japan: Hōzōkan, 1994); and Nihonyanagi Kenji 二本柳賢司, "Nihon mikkyō igaku to yakubutsugaku 日本密教医学と薬物学,"

in *Rekishi no naka no yamai to igaku* 歴史の中の病と医学, ed. Yamada Keiji 山田慶兒 and Kuriyama Shigehisa 栗山茂久 (Kyōto, Japan: Kokusai Nihon Bunka Kenkyū Sentā; Shibundō, 1997).
49. Strickmann, *Chinese Magical Medicine.*
50. Pierre Huard, Zensutsu Oya, and Ming Wang, *Asian Medical Systems: A Comparative Study* (Paris: Dacosta, 1974); Erhard Rosner, *Medizingeschichte Japans* (Handbuch der Orientalistik 5, Japan 3.5, Leiden: E.J. Brill, 1989); Mieko Macé, *Médecins et médecine dans l'histoire du Japon: aventures intellectuelles entre la Chine et l'Occident.* (Paris: Les Belles Lettres, 2013); and Wolfgang Michel-Zaitsu, *Traditionelle Medizin in Japan von der Frühzeit bis zur Gegenwart* (München: Kiener Verlag, 2017).
51. The original was published in French 1937; English translation in 1985. See Paul Demiéville, "Byō," in Demiéville, *Hōbōgirin*; and Paul Demiéville, *Buddhism and Healing* [= Hōbōgirin entry on "byō"], trans. Mark Tatz (Lanham, MD: University Press of America, 1985). For an assessment, see, e.g., Triplett, *Buddhism and Medicine in Japan*, 41–43.
52. Triplett, *Buddhism and Medicine in Japan.*
53. See "Further Reading."
54. For instance, on Kajiwara Shōzen, see Andrew Edmund Goble, "Kajiwara Shōzen (1265–1337) and the Medical Silk Road: Chinese and Arabic Influences on Medieval Japanese Medicine," in *Tools of Culture—Japan's Cultural, Intellectual, Medical and Technological Contacts in East Asia, 1000–1500s*, ed. Andrew Edmund Goble, Kenneth Robinson and Haruko Wakabayashi (Ann Arbor, MI: Association for Asian Studies, 2009), 231–257; Goble, *Confluences of Medicine in Medieval Japan*; Goble, "Determining Karmic Illness." On Manase Dōsan, see Takeda kagagaku shinkō zaidan, "Kyōu-shooku henshū 武田科学振興財団杏雨書屋編集," in *Manase Dōsan to kinsei Nihon iryō shakai* 曲直瀬道三と近世日本医療社会 (Tōkyō: Takeda kagagaku shinkō zaidan, 2015). On the monks of the Shingon Ritsu movement Eison (or Eizon 叡尊, 1201–1290) and Ninshō 忍性 (also Ryōkan-bō 良観房, 1217–1303), see David Quinter, *From Outcasts to Emperors: Shingon Ritsu and the Mañjuśrī Cult in Medieval Japan* (Leiden, The Netherlands: Brill, 2015).
55. For example: Kawada Yōichi 川田洋一, ed., *Bukkyō shisō to igaku* 仏教思想と医学 (Tōkyō: Tōyo Tetsugaku Kenkyū-Sho, 1976); Kawada Yōichi 川田洋一, ed., *Bukkyō kango to kanwa kea* 仏教看護と緩和ケア, vol. 3, ed. Kawada Yōichi 川田洋一, Seimei Tetsugaku Nyūmon 生命哲学入門 (Tōkyō: Daisan Bunmei Sha, 2013); and Obinata Daijō 大日方大乗, *Bukkyō igaku no kenkyū* 仏教医学の研究 (Tōkyō: Kasama Shobō, 1965).
56. There are several facsimile editions of the work. See, e.g., Tanba Yasuyori 丹波康頼 and Maki Sachiko 槇佐知子, eds. and trans., *Ishinpō: Maki Sachiko zenshaku seikai* 医心方: 槇佐知子全訳精解, 30 vols. (Tokyo: Chikuma Shobō, 1993–2012).
57. Satomi Yamamoto, "Death and Disease in Medieval Japanese Painting," *Kinjō Gakuin Daigaku ronshū jinbun kagaku hen* 金城学院大学論集人文科学編 6, no. 2 (2010): 81–96.

Katja Triplett

BUDDHISM AND MEDICINE IN PREMODERN JAPAN

BUDDHISM AND MEDICINE IN PREMODERN JAPAN

Medical metaphors and images, along with a general therapeutic orientation, have defined the Buddhist tradition since its beginnings in ancient India. Śākyamuni Buddha was hailed as the "great king of physicians," and his expounding of teachings, known as the dharma, was likened to the dispensation of medicine. The early Buddhist community, or sangha, sought release from all suffering through the ultimate liberation of nirvana, yet Buddhists never ceased to concern themselves with the granular details of bodily and mental suffering, whether illness, disability, or injury. Although Buddhism would undergo dramatic alterations as it spread throughout the world—to South, Central, and East Asia, and more recently to the West—these localized forms were shaped by matters of illness and healing. The study of Buddhism's diverse medical dimensions and its impact on the therapeutic cultures to which Buddhism spread—which for the sake of convenience might be termed "Buddhist medicine"—is now a fast-growing and vibrant subfield of Buddhist studies.

Buddhism's therapeutic dimensions profoundly shaped the history of Japan. As Edward Drott observed, "From the time Buddhism was first introduced to Japan [in the 6th century] up to the point at which the Meiji government instituted German style medical education in 1869, the majority of those involved in the healing arts were Buddhist priests."[1] Buddhist medicine arguably had the greatest impact in the ancient and medieval eras, especially during the Nara (710–794), Heian (794–1185), and Kamakura (1185–1333) periods. Buddhist healers practiced medicine at all levels of society throughout the premodern periods, and the Buddhist imagination of disease found wide and enduring acceptance in Japan. One particularly influential notion was the idea that sickness was the result of unwholesome karma accrued in one's present or past lives. Buddhists presented scriptural justification and anecdotal evidence for this compelling etiology in their narrative tales, letters to lay devotees, and sermons. In the medieval period, the notion of "karmic illness" was at the center of an apparent contradiction: it was used to justify discrimination against the chronically ill, even as it created the possibility for projects aimed at bringing liberation to those same persons. Another idea widely promoted by Buddhists, especially those belonging to esoteric Buddhist lineages, saw illness as the work of malicious demons. The Buddhist image of affliction-causing demons resonated with a firmly rooted imaginary of epidemic gods, who since the ancient period had been held responsible for the frequent outbreaks of contagious disease that ravaged the archipelago.

Buddhists provided for the sick by supplying medical care at special facilities located within their monasteries, including buildings dedicated to the care of the ill and the dying, bathhouses, and adjacent hot springs, some of which would become associated with miraculous stories of bodhisattvas and legendary pilgrims. Throughout history monks and nuns were also called upon to perform therapeutic practices and healing rituals of diverse styles. When deemed effective, these practices enabled Buddhists to earn the trust of patients, whether courtier or commoner. The incorporation of therapeutic and symbolically potent material substances within such practices greatly contributed to the perception of their efficacy, as did the status of the healing monk and the deities by which these substances were empowered. The desire for medicines frequently trumped fears of unpredictable seas and motivated Buddhists to travel to the continent for trade. When trade became unreliable, Buddhists proactively sought out local substitutes in Japan and fashioned new claims for their hitherto overlooked therapeutic powers.

Two prefatory points regarding the terminology, sources, and organization of this article are in order. First, it should be noted that, much like the case in premodern India and China, the term "Buddhist medicine" never functioned as an emic designation in Japan during the eras in question.[2] Although distinct therapeutic systems coexisted with the Buddhist (e.g., the medicine practiced by court physicians [*kusushi* 医師], which was rooted in the corpus of

Chinese medical literature, and that of yin-yang masters [*onmyōji* 陰陽師]), there appears to have been no need to explicitly name the therapeutic dimensions of Buddhism as such. This is hardly surprising given the centrality of medicine to Buddhism since its earliest days. "Buddhist medicine" is thus primarily a scholarly shorthand to demarcate the subject. It remains useful so long as one bears in mind that Buddhist medicine in premodern Japan was never fully systematized or monolithic. Medicine and other conceptual engagements with the body and disease were variably discussed by Buddhists belonging to multiple lineages and sectarian affiliations, as well as by individuals with more idiosyncratic perspectives. Moreover, Buddhists wrote about such issues across a wide range of genres, including hagiographies, didactic tale literature, prescriptive ritual texts, liturgical anthologies, treatises in the style of classical Chinese medical literature, encyclopedic works, letters, and diaries. In practice, Buddhist medicine was performed for diverse objectives, some of which pertained to monastic life and others that were clearly of concern for laypersons; taken together, these objectives did not always align on epistemological or technical levels. Examples include the elimination of physical or mental disease, exorcism of spirits and demons, restoration of the health of the body, restoration of eyesight and hearing, extension of life, resuscitation, treatment of external injury, safe childbirth, and veterinary medicine.

Second, this article is organized into discrete sections on illness and therapeutic practice. It must be acknowledged that this organization reproduces an epistemological distinction often drawn between knowledge and practice, which in turn recalls the divide in modern biomedicine between "research" and "clinical practice." Such artificial divisions, while useful for sorting aspects of the topic thematically, are largely untenable when examining the history of Buddhist medicine in Japan. Like most medical systems, Buddhist medicine in Japan constituted what Charles E. Rosenberg calls an "ecology of knowledge." As he notes, "medical knowledge and practice are always integrated in what can be thought of as ecological – that is, interdependent, dynamic, and interactive – terms."[3] Indeed, one of the most productive ways to learn about what Buddhists *thought* about topics such as disease and the body is to examine prescriptive texts that offer glimpses into what they *did* against disease, since knowledge about disease was more often than not intertwined with practices designed as therapy. In fact, in some cases it seems likely that the transmission and performance of ritual practice shaped the production of knowledge, rather than the other way around. Each section in this survey will thus address aspects of the interaction between knowledge and practice within Buddhist medicine in premodern Japan. The first sections of this article consider Buddhist conceptions of disease, focusing on karmic illness—with special attention to the case of *rai* ("leprosy")—and the imagination of exogenous disease agents, namely plague deities and demons. The next sections discuss aspects of Buddhist therapeutic practice, focusing on healing rituals and the use and acquisition of materia medica.

KARMIC ILLNESS, MERIT, AND THE BODY

Perhaps the most consequential doctrinal notion for the history of Buddhist medicine in Japan was that of karma. Although doctrinal formulations of the concept emphasized that the production of karma was determined by one's intention when performing an act (either wholesome or unwholesome), Buddhist scriptures also stressed the close relationship between past karma and the physical condition of one's body in the present life. Susanne Mrozik aptly calls this "physiomoral discourse," referring to the ways in which Buddhist texts link an ethical perspective grounded in karmic causality to physical manifestations of the body. The paradigmatic and normative example of physiomoral discourse in the Buddhist canon has always been Śākyamuni Buddha, whose marvelously attractive and fragrant body—and in particular his thirty-two major and eighty minor body marks—was seen as the result of his accumulation of merit over countless lifetimes, defined within an ascending trajectory that finally culminated in his attainment of nirvana.[4] Conversely, unwholesome karma produced by less virtuous persons and the enemies of Buddhism was imagined to manifest on their bodies as a foul odor, unattractiveness, and disfigurement. Physiomoral discourse thus provided a conceptual framework for seeing karma as etiology, offering a compelling explanation for why people acquire bodies that get sick, are deformed, or suffer disability or injury in the present life.

Descriptions of karmic etiology can be found throughout major Mahāyāna Buddhist scriptures. An articulation of the idea that widely circulated in East Asia appears in the "Exhortations of the Bodhisattva Samantabhadra" chapter of the *Lotus Sūtra*, which describes what happens to evil persons who slander the holy scripture. Should anyone criticize the scripture, readers are told, "that person in the present age shall get white leprosy"; should anyone make light of it,

> his teeth shall be far apart and decayed, he shall have ugly lips and a flat nose, his arms and legs shall be crooked, his eyes shall be pointed and the pupils out of symmetry, his body shall stink, he shall have sores running pus and blood, his belly shall be watery and his breath short.[5]

Passages like these are not classically "medical" in the sense that the authors were trying to explain disease. Rather, karmic etiology is deployed as a rhetorical strategy to spur readers to protect, worship, and circulate Mahāyāna sutras by warning of what awful physical abnormalities and afflictions befall those who dare do the opposite.

Although the language of such passages may surprise modern readers accustomed to images of more a nonviolent or "peaceful" Buddhism, this evocative discourse, which was understood by readers as orthodox, came to have tremendous persuasive power in Japanese Buddhism from an early period. For example, virtually the same passage from the *Lotus Sūtra* is cited in the *Record of Miraculous Events in Japan* (*Nihon ryōiki* 日本霊異記; 810–824), an early collection of didactic Buddhist narrative tales (*setsuwa* 説話) compiled by the monk Keikai 景戒 (n.d.).[6] The story in which the passage appears describes a man whose mouth is twisted and face distorted after he speaks ill of a woman who piously copies the *Lotus Sūtra*. Other stories in the collection likewise convey the lesson that karma, whether accumulated in a past life or the present one, is the most proximate cause for the acquisition of illness, disability, and injury, ranging from sores all over the body to distorted or oozing body parts, blindness, deafness, and others. The most violent cases of karmic retribution consistently befall those who harm or speak ill of Buddhist monks or laypersons and those who mistreat animals.[7] As William LaFleur has suggested, through the notion of karma, together with the system of cyclical rebirth it undergirds (samsara), Buddhism offered early Japan a "basic map of reality," one that was flexible enough to explain both common and anomalous experiences.[8]

Over time, the compilation of these tales—and their dissemination through preaching—facilitated the wider acceptance of karma as a cognitively satisfying, if sometimes ethically vexing, explanation for sickness.

The notion of karmic etiology was also disseminated in tangible form through its incorporation into visual works of art. Yamamoto Satomi has shown how doctrinal descriptions from the *Lotus Sūtra* and the *Sūtra of Meditation on the True Law* (*Shōbō nenjo kyō* 正法念處經; Chn. *Zhengfa nianchu jing*) guided the visual depiction of illness within illustrated scrolls (*emaki* 絵巻). The *Illustrated Legends of Kokawa Temple* (*Kokawadera engi emaki* 粉河寺縁起絵巻), for example, depicts an ailing woman, the daughter of a wealthy man, whose mysterious affliction has rendered her body covered in scabs. In one scene she is cared for by attendants who cover their noses with their sleeves to avoid the stench, and in another by a Buddhist ascetic who offers healing prayers invoking the bodhisattva Thousand-armed Kannon (Senju Kannon 千手観音). Scholars previously identified the woman's affliction as "leprosy," but Yamamoto reads it more didactically as a karmic affliction owing to the woman's "sin of wealth accumulation."[9] She further suggests that this depiction may also draw upon the famous tale of King Ajase 阿闍世王 (Skt. Ajātaśatru). As told in such scriptures such as the *Mahāparinirvāṇa Sūtra* (Jpn. *Daihatsu nehan kyō* 大般涅槃経), King Ajase was described as an evil man who committed parricide and usurped the kingdom, as a karmic consequence of which he developed foul-smelling scabs all over his body.[10]

The putative founder of the Chinese Tiantai (Jpn. Tendai 天台) school, Zhiyi 智顗 (538–597) was a towering figure in East Asian Buddhism whose writings helped establish "karmic illness" as a discrete illness category. In his *Great [Treatise on] Śamatha and Vipaśyanā* (Chn. *Mohe zhiguan*; Jp. *Makashikan* 摩訶止觀), Zhiyi described six kinds of diseases: (1) discord among the Four Elements (*shidai* 四大: earth, water, fire, wind); (2) unregulated diet; (3) disharmony in sitting meditation; (4) demonic illnesses; (5) *māra* illnesses; and (6) karmic illnesses (Chn. *yebing*; Jp. *gōbyō* 業病).[11] Zhiyi's sixfold nosology circulated in Japan most immediately among monks with a Tendai education, such as Nichiren 日蓮 (1222–1282), who cited the idea in his letters to lay devotees in need of encouragement during bouts of illness. It was also referenced by monk-physician Kajiwara Shōzen 梶原性全 (1265–1337), who, as we shall see, wrestled with karmic etiology from a medical perspective.[12]

One of the reasons Zhiyi's writings on illness came to be so widely influential in Japan was because he was the first to offer a comprehensive and explicit account of the connections between karma and discrete parts of the physical body from which illness arises. According to Zhiyi, murder causes liver and eye diseases, drinking alcohol causes heart and mouth diseases, lustful activities cause kidney and ear diseases, and so on.[13] Succinctly interweaving the notion of karma with Chinese medical understandings of the body and disease in this way, Zhiyi's descriptions reflect the strategies Buddhists in medieval China used to translate Indian Buddhist concepts into compelling new patchworks of medical knowledge.[14] For Zhiyi, an understanding of karma-genic diseases was critical because, within his larger systematic program of meditation, illness experience constituted one field of contemplation adepts must master. As with the other five kinds of disease, Zhiyi prescribed a treatment method specific to karmic illness, instructing adepts to use "the power of contemplation internally while practicing repentance externally."[15] Thus, although karmic illness manifests in physical maladies of the viscera and sense organs, mental exercises to eradicate karma are deemed critical.

A related method for treating karmic illness endorsed throughout East Asian Buddhism and Japan was to apply the Mahāyāna notion of "emptiness" (Skt. *śūnyatā*; Jp. *kū* 空), the potent insight that ultimately all phenomena—including illness—are impermanent, without self or substantiality. The power of emptiness to defang disease was one practical takeaway Buddhists would have gleaned from the *Vimalakīrti Sūtra* (Jpn. *Yuimagyō* 維摩経; Skt. *Vimalakīrti-nirdeśa-sūtra*), a foundational Mahāyāna scripture of considerable importance since the early days of Buddhism in Japan. The scripture centers around a layman named Vimalakīrti, who manifests illness in his own body as a form of "expedient means" (*hōben* 方便) to enlighten the bodhisattvas and arhats who reluctantly visit his sickbed at the Buddha's insistence. Vimalakīrti thus elucidates the ephemerality of all phenomena, including experiences that force their apparent reality upon one's awareness and sense of self as stubbornly as illness.[16] Monks in Japan followed Vimalakīrti's example by translating the insight of emptiness into contemplative therapeutic practice. One example is Kokan Shiren 虎関師錬 (1278–1346), who composed the *Treatise on Illness and Its Manifestations* (*Byōgiron* 病儀論, 1320) by drawing upon his personal experiences with illness. Kokan contends that the diverse signs and symptoms of illness stem from "karma-producing acts," which, under the light of a "subtle form of mindful awareness," can be seen finally to be "empty," leading to the dissipation of affliction.[17] However, owing to the profundity of its teachings on emptiness, many Buddhists in Japan saw the *Vimalakīrti Sūtra* as a potent force in itself. The scripture was thus recited in Japan for its therapeutic value.[18]

The Case of Rai and Its Treatment. However, for many others throughout Japanese history, karma's pathological consequences were not understood to be so easily dissolved in the solvent of emptiness. This is evident in the complicated history of the disease category known as *rai* 癩. In several ways *rai* represents the paragon of karmic illness, and one that instigated a wide range of Buddhist medical activities and discourse during Japan's medieval period. The term *rai* was used for various and sometimes disfiguring skin disorders, including the disease now linked to the bacterium *Mycobacterium leprae*: leprosy. Although numerous scholars writing on the history of *rai* have urged caution in projecting the modern biomedical understanding of leprosy anachronistically on the medieval Japanese notion of *rai* (which in turn drew from Chinese medical texts as well as Buddhist discourses), the term "leprosy" has nevertheless been used to organize studies of *rai* and related diseases in both Chinese and Japanese history.[19] This choice is not entirely indefensible, given the comparably broad usage of the term "leprosy" in medieval Europe.[20] Moreover, both "lepers" in medieval Europe and *rai* sufferers (*raisha* 癩者) in medieval Japan were stigmatized as a result of their condition.[21] It is in light of this historical stigma in Japan that there has been a general preference since the end of World War II for the term "Hansen's disease" (*hansen byō* ハンセン病), after Gerhard Armauer Hansen who discovered *M. leprae*, the mycobacterium that causes leprosy, in 1873.[22]

Issues of terminology and translation aside, the stigmatized status of *rai* sufferers in medieval Japan has posed interpretive problems for scholars of Buddhism in this period. On the one hand, Buddhists contributed to the discrimination of *rai* sufferers by producing and circulating discourses that cast them in a negative light. As the inclusion of "white leprosy" in the *Lotus Sūtra* passage suggests, Mahāyāna scriptures attributed the present pathological condition of *rai* sufferers to the karma of transgressions committed in past lives. In fact, some scriptures singled out *rai* as the worst in that regard. The *Treatise on the Great Perfection of Wisdom* (Chn. *Da zhidu lun* 大智度論) states: "Of the many illnesses, *rai* illness is the most severe. Because of the causes and conditions from transgressions [committed] in previous lifetimes, it is difficult to treat."[23] In Japan, the idea of pathological karmic impurity resonated strongly with the notion of ritual "defilement" (*kegare* 穢れ). A product of indigenous and continental ideas, defilement also encompassed the sense that those who acquired it were transgressors against the realm who were accordingly abhorred by the gods (*kami* 神). A similar status was applied to marginalized persons referred to as *hinin* 非人, literally "nonpersons," a category that included disabled persons and beggars, as well as persons whose occupation involved purifying shrine or temple grounds (*kiyome* 浄), handling corpses, or other tasks associated with polluting substances or spaces.[24]

Despite the hardships such discourses leveled at *rai* sufferers, evidence indicates that Buddhist temples deployed the notion of karmic etiology and related discourses ideologically to leverage authority over tenants living and working on land estates (*shōen* 荘園) in their possession. This is evident in "vow texts" (*kishōmon* 起請文), which were contracts tenants were required to sign. Such contracts warned tenants that, should they break the agreement, they would be punished by the gods and buddhas, fall into hell, or be afflicted by white and black *rai* at the pores of their skin. Kuroda Hideo speculates this discourse would have created considerable unease for tenants, anxieties concentrated at the level of the skin, which was imagined as the very surface of impurity.[25]

On the other hand, some Buddhist monastics—including those who authored vow texts—engaged in philanthropic activities to benefit *rai* sufferers and other destitute and downtrodden members of medieval society. Chōgen 重源 (1121–1206), for example, who happens to be known for the earliest vow texts written by a monk to wave the possibility of white and black *rai* as punishment over signatories, was instrumental in leading the building of as many as sixteen bathhouses for such sufferers.[26] Similar projects were conducted by monks of the Saidaiji 西大寺 order of the Ritsu 律 sect led by Eison 叡尊 (or Eizon, 1201–1290) and his disciple Ninshō 忍性 (1217–1303). Eison is famous for social welfare projects aimed at the salvation of defiled *hinin* and *rai* sufferers, whom he claimed were incarnations of Mañjuśrī (Monju Bosatsu 文殊菩薩). Although these projects would appear consistent with the Mahāyāna ethos of compassion, many have asked how we can reconcile these activities with the fact that Eison also taught that "the chronically ill and chronically poor, the isolated and the abandoned, were responsible for their own karmic conditions, possessors of 'residual sins' in need of repentance."[27] As David Quinter reminds us in his study of Eison and his movement, these claims about the dismal karmic status of such individuals were canonical to the Mahāyāna tradition. For Eison, moreover, they were couched within a broader framework of repentance that applied equally to all seeking to reach buddhahood, not only those who occupied the lowest positions in society.[28]

One treatment prescribed for *rai* sufferers was bathing. Generally speaking, documentary sources such as courtier diaries written in Sino-Japanese (*kanbun nikki* 漢文日記) from the medieval period attest to the frequent use among aristocrats of "hot water therapy" (*tōji* 湯治). This ranged from pouring medicinal or salt water over a diseased part of the body to fully immersing the body and was used for numerous ailments.[29] The hot water therapy thought most efficacious for *rai* sufferers was much more than a strictly physical cleansing of the body. When the bathing facilities were located on the grounds of monasteries, *rai* sufferers who entered the waters were promised an eradication of pathogenic karma as well as the creation of merit ("good karma"). As such, major monasteries in Nara, Kyoto, and Kamakura equipped with bathhouses often opened their doors to *rai* sufferers and others of destitute karmic condition.[30]

Some inspiration for these bathing practices came from hagiographies of important Buddhist monastics. Narratives tell of eminent monks, like the itinerant monk Gyōki 行基 (668–749) in Japan or the famous Chinese pilgrim Xuanzang 玄奘 (602–664), who encounter a "leper" during their travels. The leper requests that the monk cleanse their diseased body. Once the monk has done so—sometimes going so far as to lick the leper's sores at the latter's curious request—and has accordingly proved that their virtue far exceeds any worldly concern with defilement, the leper reveals his true identity as a bodhisattva, often Mañjuśrī, or a buddha, such as the Master of Medicines Buddha (Yakushi Nyorai 薬師如来).

Precedents of monks overcoming physical aversion and caring for *rai* sufferers drew from similar precedents in China.[31] In Japan, as D. Max Moerman has shown, these tales were interwoven into the genre of temple origin stories (*engi* 縁起) and thus served a dual function. On the one hand, in line with the doctrinal etymology of the term *engi*, which refers to the "dependent arising" (Skt. *pratītyasamutpāda*) of conditioned phenomena, such stories guided readers to the Buddhist realization that bodily impurity associated with diseases like *rai* are effects of a discriminating mind caught up in a network of causality. On the other hand, such origin stories also functioned to legitimate temple bathhouses and hot springs associated with temples by telling of virtuous monks who performed miraculous healing and interacted with divinities on site. Moerman's study concentrates on the origin narrative of Onsenji 温泉寺, a temple located at the famous Arima 有馬 hot springs (in today's Kōbe 神戸 city).[32] Throughout the medieval period, bathhouses affiliated with monasteries close to or within cities and hot springs in neighboring provinces became major draws for pilgrims. As Lori Meeks has shown, the bathhouse at Hokkeji 法華寺 in Nara was one such site. Hokkeji circulated its own variation of the legend of the traveling monk bathing the leper in which the monk is replaced with queen-consort Empress Kōmyō 光明皇后 (701–760), who vows to wash with her own hands the first visitor to the bathhouse she establishes. The first visitor to arrive is a leper. After being washed by the initially reluctant Kōmyō, he reveals himself to be the Buddha Ashuku 阿閦仏.[33] The origin story adds that although Kōmyō's original bathhouse no longer remains, Hokkeji uses the same kettle to heat the water for their more recently constructed bathhouse. In this way, while such origin stories for baths and hot springs shared motifs, they were also stylized along locale-specific and sometimes sectarian lines. Duncan Williams, for example, discusses a number of temples and sites associated with Kūkai 空海 (774–835) in particular, the promotion of which drew upon symbolic and ritual imagery specific to Shingon 真言 esoteric Buddhism.[34]

Not everyone in medieval Japan accepted the notion that *rai* was categorically a karmic illness whose treatment necessitated the elimination of karma. Andrew Goble has demonstrated this in his study of Kajiwara Shōzen, a monk-physician who was active at Gokurakuji 極楽寺, a monastery located in Kamakura that boasted an extensive medical facility established under the auspices of Ninshō. Shōzen likely treated hundreds of patients, including sufferers of *rai* for whom Gokurakuji dedicated a lodging facility. Shōzen also authored two major medical works: *Notes of a Simple Physician* (*Ton'ishō* 頓医抄, 1307) and *Myriad Relief Prescriptions*

(*Man'anpō* 万安方, 1327). In his *Notes of a Simple Physician*, Shōzen identified twelve discrete types of *rai*, four of which he considered to be karmic in origin and thus untreatable through conventional means. Shōzen's understanding of *rai* as untreatable echoes sentiments found across contemporaneous literary sources such as the *Tale of the Heike* (*Heike monogatari* 平家物語), courtier diaries, and other medical sources like the *Idanshō* 医談抄 by Koremune Tomotoshi 惟宗具俊 (n.d.).[35] Shōzen prescribed the practice of repentance and the cultivation of good virtue for these intractable cases, thus following orthodox Buddhist methods for karmic illness proposed by Zhiyi long before Shōzen's time. However, Shōzen departed from both precedent and popular views of his time by defining the remaining types of *rai* in largely physicalist terms. In particular, Shōzen proposed that *rai* was caused by "worms" (*mushi* 虫), an interpretation he drew from more recent Song-period medical knowledge transmitted from China. Seeing this redefinition of *rai* as an "intellectual leap," Goble writes, "For Shōzen—well aware of the negative social connotations engendered by *rai* and motivated by the fundamental Buddhist injunction to heal—clinical engagement of *rai* implicitly held out the possibility that it might prove treatable."[36]

THE IMAGINATION OF EXOGENOUS DISEASE AGENTS

Epidemics and Plague Deities. Some of the earliest official historical accounts in Japan suggest that the reception of Buddhism on the archipelago was profoundly shaped by epidemics. According to one record in the *Chronicles of Japan* (*Nihon shoki* 日本書紀, 720) on events of the year 552, the Korean kingdom of Paekche gifted the Japanese court a statue of Śākyamuni Buddha along with ritual implements and sutras. A debate ensued about whether the "foreign god" (*banshin* 蕃神) should be worshipped. The opposition was led by the Mononobe and Nakatomi clans, who protested that worshipping a foreign god would only anger local *kami*. The emperor initially ruled in favor of the pro-worship faction led by the Soga clan, who were permitted to worship the new deity on an experimental basis. Not long after the trial began, a disease ravaged the realm. Blame fell upon the alien god, and its icon was summarily thrown into the Naniwa canal.[37] The tides would later turn once again, however, and the foreign cult would be accepted.

Recorded by officials of the Japanese state, this account, like others in *Chronicles of Japan*, served to legitimate the rulers of the time the text was written and their eventual promotion of Buddhism. The year 552, for example, appears to have been selected deliberately in order to place the arrival of Buddhism in Japan at the precise commencement of the Final Dharma (*mappō* 末法), the third and final age of the Buddhist historical world system. At the same time, the suspicions initially cast toward the foreign religion and its god testify to underlying anxieties held throughout the Nara and preceding periods on the archipelago toward epidemics and the plague deities (*ekijin*/*yakujin* 疫神) thought responsible for their spread throughout the realm. This explains why anti-Buddhist factions succeeded in ascribing an outbreak of pestilence to the recently imported buddha—a view, however, that would soon be displaced by the opposite belief that the Buddha offers relief from epidemics.

By the time the *Chronicles of Japan* was written, the pacification of plague deities was closely interwoven into the affairs of the state. On the annual calendar of rites performed by state institutions, the third month was identified as the beginning of epidemic season. It was imagined that, starting from the third day of the month, plague deities would ride atop flower blossoms that were scattered throughout the land by the wind. Hence, in the third month the Bureau of Divinities (Jingikan 神祇官) conducted the Flower Pacification Ceremony (*chinkasai/hanashizume no matsuri* 鎮花祭), which aimed to placate Ōmiwa 大神 and Sai 狭井, two deities associated with epidemics. (The deity Ōmiwa would continue to be associated with disease and healing well into the medieval period.)[38] Other annual ceremonies for ridding the realm of epidemics, such as the Plague God Festival (Ekijinsai 疫神祭), were performed twice on an annual basis, in the spring and autumn.[39]

Despite the state's attempt to manage plague deities through seasonal observances that largely followed continental procedures, epidemics on the archipelago refused to obey the ritual calendar. William Wayne Farris has dubbed the period 700–1050 the "age of plagues," an era in which Japan saw a steady onslaught of contagious disease outbreaks.[40] Like pestilence deities floating overland on flower petals, microbes carried by persons and domesticated animals entered Japan from the continent where they encountered dense populations lacking immunities. This was one effect of what Farris calls, drawing on William McNeill's *Plagues and Peoples* (1976), Japan's "island epidemiology." Although Japan's distance from the continent provided a certain degree of protection against epidemics, it also meant that when outbreaks did occur they were devastating, and immunities took many centuries to acquire.[41]

Farris notes that the five most frequently reported epidemics in this age of plagues were caused by smallpox, measles, mumps, influenza, and dysentery. Smallpox (*mogasa* 疱瘡) was undoubtedly the most feared. One especially catastrophic smallpox epidemic would in fact precipitate a monumental event in the history of Nara-period Buddhism. The Great Smallpox Epidemic of 735–737 (also known as the Great Tenpyō Epidemic) is, according to Farris, "the earliest well-reported smallpox epidemic in world history."[42] Overall, Farris surmises that the epidemic killed anywhere from 25 to 35 percent of the entire population of Japan at the time, including towering political figures of the Fujiwara family.[43] In the wake of the disaster, Emperor Shōmu 聖武天皇 (r. 724–749), who declared that the responsibility for the epidemic was his, sought the divine assistance of Buddhism. In 743, Shōmu vowed to construct an icon of Vairocana Buddha (Jpn. Rushanabutsu 盧遮那仏), a cosmic buddha who appears in the *Avatamsaka Sūtra* (Jpn. *Kegon kyō* 華厳経), at a scale never before seen in Japan nor indeed throughout most of the Buddhist world.[44] At the expense of the population from which he extracted years of labor, in 749 Shōmu was finally able to create a 14.7-meter-tall bronze icon. Known by tourists today as the Nara Daibutsu 奈良大仏, the icon still stands, as does a Genroku 元禄 era (1688–1703) reconstruction of the Golden Hall of Tōdaiji 東大寺 that houses the statue (more commonly known as the Daibutsuden 大仏殿). The project was completed in 752 with the consecration of the statue, just four years before Shōmu's death.

Shōmu's endeavor to extend his sovereignty over the unseen forces of epidemics through the production of Buddhist icons and temples reflected a growing reliance on Buddhist ritual technologies by Nara-period rulers for managing disease on both collective and individual levels. Far from seeing the Buddha as a bearer of disease, as was once the case just two hundred years earlier when Buddhism arrived, rulers increasingly looked to Buddhist ritual as a means to counter plague deities. One such ritual, a "dharma assembly" (*hōe* 法会) said to have been developed by Rōben 良弁 (689–773) the same year the Vairocana Buddha was consecrated, was the Shunie 修二会. This was performed in the second month of the year at Nigatsudō

二月堂 within the monastic complex of Tōdaiji. Then serving as abbot of Tōdaiji, Rōben would be promoted to the highest clerical office in part owing to his successes as one of Shōmu's "healing meditation masters" (*kanbyō zenji* 看病禅師), an office of priests who personally attended to ailing emperors. The Shunie, popularly known as Omizutori お水取り because of its incorporation of therapeutic waters drawn from the Wakasai well 若狭井, centered around a repentance ritual directed toward the Eleven-Headed Kannon (Jūichimen *keka* 十一面悔過). Because it was already widely understood that karma could generate illness, repentance rituals to eliminate collective karma were seen as effective means of dealing with realm-wide afflictions.[45]

Another repentance ritual that would come to be used against disease was the Yakushi *keka hō* 薬師悔過法, focused on the Master of Medicines Buddha (Yakushi Nyorai 薬師如来; Skt. Bhaiṣajyaguru Tathāgata). One might expect that Yakushi would have been among the first and most frequently called upon during times of epidemics to bring relief to the ailing masses. After all, Yakushi's "original vows" (*hongan* 本願), which are listed in various scriptures associated with him, including the *Original Vows of the Master of Medicines Tathāgata of Lapis Light* (Jpn. *Yakushi rurikō nyorai hongan kudoku kyō* 薬師瑠璃光如来本願功徳経), describe his promise to eliminate illness and extend the life of all sentient beings, among other boons. Yet as Nishio Masahito points out, it was not common to evoke Yakushi for realm-wide protection against epidemics during Japan's era of plagues. Rather, this use appears to be limited to the reign of Emperor Ninmyō 仁明天皇 (r. 833–850).[46] More often, Yakushi was evoked for eliminating illnesses and elongating the lives of the emperor and members of the imperial family. However, it is important to remember that in this early period the karma of the emperor was understood to be intimately tied to the collective karma of society, thus these two functions are not so easily distinguished. As Yui Suzuki writes, "The practice of Yakushi *keka* embodied the emerging belief that, by promoting the health of the emperor, Yakushi would ensure, by extension, the longevity of the country."[47]

Another common ritual sponsored by the state against epidemics was the mass recitation of sutras. Dozens or sometimes even hundreds of monks would be employed to conduct a form of abridged *sūtra* recitation known as "rolling reading" (*tendoku* 転読), in which only select parts of the sutras were chanted. This method was especially useful for concentrating the ritual amplification of the most potent passages within extensive sutras comprising many fascicles. There appears to have existed a general preference for reciting Perfection of Wisdom sutras, including the *Sūtra of the Great Perfect of Wisdom* (*Daihannya kyō* 大般若経), the *Diamond Sūtra* (*Kongō hannya kyō* 金剛般若経) and the *Heart Sūtra* (*Hannya shingyō* 般若心経), which were especially renowned for their efficacy for "eliminating calamity" (*josai* 除災).[48] In this way, although epidemics repeatedly ravaged both the court and the larger population in the Nara period, they also provided occasions for Buddhist monastics to demonstrate the utility of their ritual technologies in the face of national emergencies, a process that led to further entanglement between monasteries and the state.

As Michael Como has observed, the spread of epidemics was an unintended consequence of the creation of capitals that housed dense populations, first at Heijō-kyō 平城京 (Nara) and then Heian-kyō 平安京 (today's Kyoto).[49] As noted by Neil McMullin, "epidemics spread like wildfire in the crowded, filthy conditions of the cities."[50] As a result, Buddhist rituals to expel epidemics would become perennial fixtures of urban life. The most well-known ritual in

Heian-kyō was (and continues to be) the Gion Matsuri 祇園祭. The rite was conducted by the shrine-temple complex known as Gionsha, better known today as Yasaka Shrine 八坂神社. It focused on the "Ox-Head Emperor," Gozu Tennō 牛頭天王, a god likely brought into the capital by yin-yang masters from the nearby Harima province 播磨国. A pestilence deity who was in turn worshipped to placate epidemics, Gozu was representative of the kind of ambivalent god from which people often sought divine intervention in this period. Undergirding the Gion Matsuri was belief in "vengeful spirits" (*goryō* 御霊), the wraiths of departed persons who, owing to the unjust treatment that led to their deaths, return to the world of the living to inflict disaster and disease upon their mortal enemies.[51] Since the earliest cases of vengeful spirits in the Heian period, Buddhist monks provided services such as *sūtra* recitations at *goryōe* 御霊会, assemblies to rid the capital of these dangerous spirits.[52] The Gion Matsuri was one variety of this assembly, and its cultic complex eventually came under the control of the temple Enryakuji 延暦寺, the headquarters of the Sanmon branch of Tendai.[53]

Buddhist involvement in the management of epidemic-causing spirits and gods was justified by a discourse broadly known as "original ground, manifest traces" (*honji suijaku* 本地垂迹), which sought to draw correlations between buddhas and bodhisattvas on the one hand, and kami on the other, whether local or localized. To take just one example from the cult of Gion, Gozu Tennō came to be identified with Yakushi, who was himself at one point the main object of veneration at the Gionsha shrine-temple complex. As the idea gained currency and spread beyond the capital, this pairing gave rise to curious permutations. In the *Gozu tennō shima watari saimon* 牛頭天王島渡り祭文, a 16th-century liturgical text from Tsushima 津島 in Owari province (west Aichi Prefecture), Gozu the pestilence god reveals his true identity as the Master of Medicines Buddha. In an ironic twist, Gozu transforms into a microscopic, contagious affliction that enters Śākyamuni Buddha's body through the latter's fingernail and thereby instigates his death. At one level the tale reimagines the disease-to-death sequence of the Buddha's final nirvana, an event of much significance for the tradition. In its immediate context in late-medieval Japan—when some began to overturn the implicit hierarchy of the *honji-suijaku* paradigm and instead promoted local (or localized) deities over universal Buddhist divinities—this liturgical narrative suggests a reappearance of archaic anxieties about buddhas as epidemic deities, despite the positive reputation buddhas had come to earn since the Nara period by helping the population eliminate pestilence.

The Ox Festival (Ushi Matsuri 牛祭り) is another example of an urban festival for warding off epidemics and numerous ailments caused by demons in the capital. The liturgical text outlines a litany of common diseases addressed by the rite, including acute illness, colds, coughing illness, malaria, swellings, epilepsy, morning sickness, and "corpse-vector disease" (*denshibyō* 傳屍病). The ritual enshrined Matarajin 摩多羅神, a deity the *Peacock Sūtra* (*Kujaku kyō* 孔雀経) claims brings disease to all humankind.[54] Scholars such as Yamamoto Hiroko have classified deities such as Matarajin and Gozu Tennō as *ijin* 異神, "strange deities" who were often imagined as foreign gods that take residence on the Japanese archipelago. Bernard Faure has shown how these strange deities, many of whom were tied thematically to pestilence, constituted an implicit pantheon not adequately captured by the explicit theological binary structure of *honji-suijaku*.[55] Foreign gods had been associated with epidemics in Japan since the ancient period, and these associations informed medieval theology.[56] One example is Shinra Myōjin 神羅明神, another *ijin* who was promoted by monks of the Tendai-Jimon lineage at Onjōji 園城寺 (more commonly known as Miidera 三井寺) and whose name literally means the "Silla God." As Sujung Kim has argued, Shinra Myōjin, often identified with Susanoo, the raging brother of Amaterasu, reflected the long-standing ascription of epidemics to interactions with the Korean peninsula.[57] Indeed, medieval writers linked epidemics such as the Great Smallpox Epidemic of 735–737 to "barbarians" from the Korean peninsula.[58]

Demons and the Final Age. The mid-11th century on saw two apparently contradictory developments surrounding disease and its imagination. On the one hand, as Farris notes, the year 1050 roughly demarcates the end of Japan's "age of plagues" and accordingly the beginning of "declining importance of disease in Japan."[59] Although epidemics continued to strike on occasion, immunities within the population on the archipelago had finally caught up, rendering some of the most infectious killer diseases endemic. The "growing endemicity of disease in the capital" helps to explain why, Farris observes, in 970 the Gion festival "became an annual affair."[60]

On the other hand, it was at roughly this same time that talk about the proliferation of diseases attributed to "demons" (*ki/oni* 鬼, *kishin* 鬼神) rose to a fever pitch. Much overlap had existed between demons and the plague deities of earlier centuries, but the demons of more recent concern were largely defined by Buddhist discourses. For example, some viewed the growing population of disease-provoking demons as a consequence of the arrival of the age of the Final Dharma. As noted previously, writers in earlier centuries in Japan had pinpointed the beginning of the Final Dharma epoch to 552, a year that was conveniently linked to the official introduction of Buddhism to Japan. However, perhaps because of a growing pessimism toward ills specific to their own times—political fragmentation, the rise of warriors, monks taking up arms, and natural disasters—many in the 11th century and afterward began proclaiming that the age of the Final Dharma in fact began five hundred years later, in 1052. As Farris notes, "Ironically, the latter day [i.e., Final Dharma] was believed to begin in 1052, just as the epoch of plagues drew to a close."[61] According to Chinese Buddhist scriptures, such as the *Sūtra on the Annihilation of the Dharma Spoken by the Buddha* (Chn. *Foshuo famiejin jing* 佛說法滅盡經; T. 396), besides the negative influence of this age on Buddhist practice—such as inability to attain awakening, the lack of access to uncorrupted teachings, and the absence of virtuous teachers—one of the unmistakable signs of the Final Dharma was increased numbers of demons, ghosts, animal-spirits, and other strange entities.[62] In Japan, this rhetoric about demonic disease in the age of the Final Dharma appears, for example, in *Record of Nourishing Life by Drinking Tea* (*Kissayōjōki* 喫茶養生記) by Yōsai 栄西 (or Eisai; 1141–1215), which warned that

> in these times, there will be demons and spirits (*kimi mōryō* 鬼魅魍魎) that will send the realm into chaos and antagonize the people, creating manifold diseases for which no medical treatment exists, of which medical knowledge proves ignorant, against which medical formulas provide no salvation.[63]

Besides the notion of the Final Dharma, growing attention to disease-causing demons over the Heian period was closely tied to the rise of esoteric Buddhism and its monastic institutions.

For Michel Strickmann, the prevalence of demonic etiology in Heian Japan was evidence of the unprecedented authority that esoteric priests and their ritual institutions had come to acquire in this period. As he wrote in *Chinese Magical Medicine,*

> It may turn out, upon analysis, that the wave of demonomania that swept over the Japanese aristocracy was to a large extent iatrogenic, produced by the monkish physicians themselves. The dramatic technique of treatment by induced possession may have promoted this diagnostic propensity, vastly increasing the reported attacks by demons. Only an institution of considerable authority and prestige could have so forcefully impressed its view of the world on the upper echelons of society.[64]

In Strickmann's analysis, the surge in cases of spirit possession in Heian Japan constituted a "puzzle" that had long been obscured by the accounts of literary scholars who were apt to see possession rites as heterodox aberrations of a "religious-superstitious Buddhism."[65] For Strickmann, these cases are readily understood when scholars part ways with normative notions of Buddhism as "an enlightened, atheistic religion" and instead turn to the prescriptive literature of esoteric Buddhism translated or composed in China from which the Japanese practices derived. Therapeutic rituals described in the Chinese corpus are rooted firmly in demonology, focused as they typically are on the identification of demons, the transference of these demons into the bodies of mediums, and finally exorcism.[66] Thus, ritual in the esoteric mode staged a martial combat between Buddhist divinities evoked by esoteric priests and malignant demons and spirits. Indeed, monks belonging to esoteric lineages in Japan routinely performed exorcism to eliminate the demons that possessed the bodies of their aristocratic and royal patients.

Although Strickmann's contributions to the study of esoteric Buddhism in Japan are beyond question, his pivoting from reports of spirit possession in Heian-period Japan to Chinese source texts creates the impression that understandings of demonic disease on the ground in Japan were largely derivative, closely following continental precedent. Recent research, however, has sought to grasp the practice of esoteric ritual in Japan in light of the local context of reception, and to do so without recourse to ahistorical notions such as "shamanism" or a timeless Japanese "folk."

Some of this recent research has shed light on the diagnostic categories invoked in cases of spirit possession that occasioned the performance of Buddhist ritual healing. For example, scholars have begun to examine afflictions attributed to "evil *ki*," typically written *jake* 邪気 in courtier diaries and *mononoke* in literary sources. In Chinese medical literature from whence the term may have derived, "evil *ki*" (Chn. *xieqi*) was used broadly to refer to all manner of etiological agents. Some medical historians are of the opinion that the term displaced an etiology of epidemics focused on external demons with a more naturalistic, less agential etiology focused on *qi*.[67] In contrast, in Heian Japan *jake* was unambiguously linked to the demonic, as is evident from the fact that it was frequently invoked to explain cases of spirit possession. Even so, it is evident that the term possessed multiple meanings at any given time and underwent historical development. For instance, it seems first to have referred to the spirits of known deceased individuals. Later in the Heian period, the term was generalized and used without reference to the spirits of specific persons, but this usage did not necessarily displace the earlier meaning. Tsuda Naoshige, for example, saw the initial proliferation of *jake* in the "era of regents" (*sekkan-ki* 摂関期) as closely tied to an increase in political losers produced by what had become an aggressively competitive political system. Fujimoto Katsuyoshi similarly understood *jake* as "vengeful spirits" (*goryō*). Yamada Yūji has observed that whereas vengeful spirits were seen to cause realm-wide mayhem, evil *ki* typically only afflicted individuals who were somehow associated with the deceased when the former were alive. Nonetheless, by the late Heian period, courtiers reported many cases of *jake*-related afflictions in their diaries in which the identity of the spirit is never queried or made the object of diagnostic investigation. Given this multiplicity of referents, one precise nomenclature for the phenomenon of *jake* is unlikely to coalesce. Instead, it is important to examine the Buddhist diagnostic and therapeutic practices within which the evocation of disease-causing spirits was situated.

As research on the character of demonic diseases in Japan advances, one area that is predicted to see greater attention in the scholarship is the representation and iconography of demons in visual sources. Disease-causing demons appear with some frequency in illustrated narrative scrolls (*emaki*) from the medieval period. Perhaps the most iconic depiction comes in the Kamakura-period scroll, *The Miracles of the Kasuga Deity* (*Kasuga gongen genki e* 春日権現験記絵). In this scene, a sick man is depicted vomiting from the raised floor of his home onto the ground below. Two women of the house minister to him, while another individual, likely in the throes of the same affliction, lies bedridden in an adjacent room. Zooming out slightly reveals that the same scene is being observed by a demon, who lurches over, upside-down from the roof, peering into the hut. The demon's body is monstrous, with red skin and a wooden mallet tucked in its loincloth. A strike from a demon's mallet was imagined to cause affliction and death. The underlying story of this scene, given in the narrative text that accompanies the illustration, suggests the demon seeks to do further harm but is kept at bay by the presence inside the home of the *Yuishiki ron* 唯識論, the foundational treatise of the Hossō 法相 (Chn. Faxiang) school. Although such details are specific to the setting of this tale at Kasuga 春日, a shrine associated with the Hossō temple Kōfukuji 興福寺, the features of the disease-causing demon are conventional. Other examples include the hoard of epidemic demons in the *Origins of the Yūzū Nenbutsu* (*Yūzū nenbutsu engi* 融通念仏縁起) and the malaria (*gyakubyō* 瘧病) demon in Kajiwara Shōzen's *Man'anpō*.[68] The *Equine Medicine Book of the Anzai School* (*Anzai-ryū ba'isho* 安西流馬医書) also depicts twelve spirits corresponding to the zodiac, four of whom have patently demonic forms.[69] Overall, illustrating demons in these scrolls offered a compelling way to represent otherwise unseen forces of disease and epidemics and the identifiable agents behind them. Another way to do so was to engage pestilential agents in the performance of ritual practices.

HEALING RITUALS

The preceding sections noted several examples of rites used for healing in ancient Japan, including the recitation of scriptures for quelling epidemics in the realm at large, repentance rites for treating and extending the lives of emperors, and—moving into the medieval period—annual urban ceremonies addressing widespread disease caused by vengeful spirits. The Buddhist ritual repertoire expanded greatly in the mid-Heian period (late 10th century), when monastics began designing rituals to alleviate the illnesses of elite clientele. Much like the increased rhetoric pertaining to the proliferation of demons, the growth of the field of *shuhō* 修法 (or *mishihō*/*mizuhō* 御修法)—rites privately sponsored by aristocrats and members of the imperial family—was tied to the growing dominance of esoteric Buddhist institutions and their modes of practice.[70]

Any consideration of these practices must bear in mind that scholars by and large reject the categorical distinction between "pure esotericism" (*junmitsu* 純密) and "miscellaneous esotericism" (*zōmitsu* 雑密). A product of sectarian scholarship of the early 20th century, this dichotomy suggests that the "pure esotericism" brought to Japan by Kūkai and made the centerpiece of what would become the Shingon sect was utterly different from, and completely displaced, older forms of Nara-period Buddhism. In contrast to the unsystematized, magical, and "this-worldly" focus of "miscellaneous esotericism," Kūkai's transmission was purportedly loftier in its soteriological aims, focused uniquely on "awakening buddhahood in this very body" (*sokushin jōbutsu* 即身成仏). However, now cognizant of the assumptions built into these sectarian claims, more recent research has demonstrated that core elements of esoteric ritual, such as the use of esoteric sutras and mantras, were far from unknown in the earlier Nara period. Moreover, attempts to exploit the power of such techniques for "this-worldly" benefits did not disappear when Kūkai's esotercism appeared on the scene. In fact, a focus on rituals performed for healing demonstrates that practices aimed at this-worldly benefits—which often operated with the notion that the priest had become identical in body to the deity—gained unprecedented importance in Heian-period Buddhism.

Shuhō rituals were typically structured in the form of the *goma* 護摩 (Skt. *homa*) fire ceremony, a ritual with distant roots in early Indian religion.[71] Tantric forms of the fire ceremony, which saw global dissemination in the premodern world, were adapted to a breathtaking array of cultures and contexts.[72] In Japan, the ceremony involved the construction of one or more altars oriented around a central hearth, beyond which the primary deity of veneration (*honzon* 本尊) would be enshrined using an illustrated or sculpted image. A rough schematic of the ritual process is as follows: (a) the officiating priest invites the enshrined deity into the ritual space by making offerings that are thrown into the flames of the hearth (which was itself understood as the fire deity Agni [Jp. Katen 火天]); (b) the priest uses mantras, mudras, and visualization (the three mysteries, *sanmitsu* 三密) to achieve identification with the deity (*sokushin jōbutsu*); and (c) the powers thus acquired are channeled toward the acquisition of this-worldly boons, which differ from one performance to another depending on the requests of the rite's sponsors.

That healing was a commonly sought objective of the performance of these rituals in the Heian period comes across in an edict issued by the Grand Ministry (Daijōkan 太政官) in 901, early in the rising popularity of these practices.[73] The ministry issued the edict to curb the recent sponsorship of esoteric rituals for cursing one's political enemies, but the measure was broadly framed to outlaw the unauthorized employment of altar rituals for personal reasons of any kind. Yet important exemptions were made for therapeutic rites, including normal recitations (*nenzu* 念誦), altar rites, and empowerment (*kaji* 加持) to treat illness. The edict attests to the vital role esoteric rituals had acquired in the lives of those with the means to commission them, and it reveals that the Grand Ministry was willing to permit such personal rites provided they were compassionately aimed at the treatment of patients rather than the cursing of political peers. At the same time, a stipulation in the document that sponsors must first acquire permission before conducting the rites by submitting documents to the appropriate offices betrays a kind of "biopolitics," an attempt by the state to maintain surveillance on practices meant to transform the body.[74]

In subsequent years, however, a surge in the private sponsorship of healing rites would make it unfeasible for the state to keep track of such practices, let alone regulate them. The fragmentation of state power over the Heian period was a major contributing factor. During the era of regents (late 10th to 11th centuries), and even more so during the subsequent era of retired emperors (*insei-ki* 院政期; after the late eleventh century), political power was no longer located in a central state institution but instead diffused over multiple actors and institutions, including emperors, retired emperors, regents, high-ranking aristocrats, warriors, and powerful landowning monasteries. As "public" political actors sought to secure life and lineage, and Buddhists sought to secure patronage, the market for privately commissioned esoteric rites expanded exponentially. This in turn spurred competition between monastic lineages, one result of which was extraordinary ritual innovation. These developments over the mid-Heian period set patterns of ritual practice and the production and transmission of prescriptive liturgical literature that would continue throughout the medieval period.

As might be expected, some healing rituals that became prominent in this period of innovation coalesced around the worship of the Master of Medicines Buddha. One especially important ritual was the Yakushi Ritual of the Seven Buddhas (Shichibutsu Yakushihō 七仏薬師法), conducted frequently by Taimitsu monks.[75] For example, in 1105, Kensen 賢暹, then-abbot of Hosshōji 法性寺, performed the rite to treat an illness of Emperor Horikawa 堀河天皇 (1079–1107). Another divine figure many evoked to treat the ill was the bodhisattva Kannon 観音 (Skt. Avalokiteśvara), whose therapeutic prowess was well established in Japan as early as the *Record of Miraculous Events in Japan*.[76] One notable ritual invoking Kannon was a *goma* ceremony against epidemics based on the *Scripture on the Dhāraṇī for Summoning the Bodhisattva Avalokiteśvara to Eradicate Toxic Harms* (Chn. *Qing Guanshiyin pusa xiaofu duhai tuolunizhou jing* 請観世音菩薩消伏毒害陀羅尼呪経). The scripture describes how a village finds relief from an epidemic when villagers offer a "willow twig and pure water" to Kannon. The fire ceremony that exploited the miraculous willow was transmitted at first primarily by Taimitsu monks, who performed it as early as the year 1156 against a deadly epidemic.[77] (Willow would thus become known for its ability to quell epidemics in Japan, where certain species of willow were native and others imported from the continent at an early date.)[78] As a result, healing continues to be linked with willow branch rites into the present day through the "Empowerment of the Willow" (*yanagi no okaji* 楊枝のお加持) ritual conducted annually on January 15 at Sanjūsangendō temple 三十三間堂 (Renge'ō'in 蓮華王院) in Kyoto.[79] Rituals to other forms of Kannon, such as Nyoirin Kannon 如意輪観音 and Senju Kannon 千手観音, were also commonly used for healing throughout the medieval period. Senju Kannon figures in this capacity, for instance, in the *Illustrated Legends of Kokawa Temple*.

Increased attention also came to be directed toward the less friendly spectrum of the Buddhist pantheon.[80] Rites summoning the wisdom kings (*myōō* 明王; Skt. *vidyārājas*), especially the mandalic configuration of the Five Great Wisdom Kings, garnered immense popularity. As the wrathful emanations of compassionate divinities, these martial guardian deities were seen as uniquely qualified for rituals of "subjugation" (*chōbuku* 調伏; Skt. *ābhicaraka*). A type of fire ceremony performed to eliminate demons and malicious spirits, subjugation was frequently employed against disease in the "age of Final Dharma." Ritualists often called upon all five wisdom kings using the "Five-Altar Rite" (*godanhō* 五壇法), an elaborate ceremony in which the five kings were simultaneously worshipped at their own individual altar, each operated by a different priest—and typically a host of other attending monks necessary to ready the fuel and offerings, clean the altar space, and help keep the fires burning. On some occasions, members of distinct lineages were employed to perform the ritual at the same time in distant locations. For example, during one epidemic, the rite was performed by priests in the center of Heian-kyō at the Shingon'in 真言院 (which had a privileged location within the imperial palace), Ninnaji 仁和寺 in the northwest of the city, Enryakuji atop Mt. Hiei in the northeast, and Onjōji in the neighboring Ōmi 近江 province to the east. The altar for Fudō Myōō 不動明王 was both spatially and symbolically central in any configuration of the Five-Altar Rite and was thus entrusted to the most eminent priests. Ryōgen 良源, a towering abbot (*zasu* 座主) of Enryakuji known for revitalizing the monastic complex on Mt. Hiei, is one priest who operated Fudō's central altar.[81]

The Five-Altar Rite was naturally a lavish and expensive production, the justification for which lies in the logic that the more divinities involved, the greater the chances of prevailing over the demonic agents causing disease. Yet at least in part because not all aristocrats had such means, single-altar rituals gradually became popular as well. This was a key dynamic in what Faure calls the "rise of the *besson* 別尊," in which discrete deities were adopted from mandalas and made the devotional centerpiece of individual cults. Rites were also conducted around wisdom king Kujaku Myōō 孔雀明王 (Skt. Mahāmayūrī). Based on the *Peacock Sūtra* (*Kujaku kyō* 孔雀経), Kujaku rites had a reputation from earlier centuries for reliably pacifying natural disasters. At the height of the era of regents, the Kujaku Myōō rite came to be frequently employed for healing and to ensure safe childbirth (*anzan* 安産).[82] One proponent of the rite was the Shingon monk Shōshin 性信 (1005–1085), who is said to have utilized the ritual successfully to eliminate disease and ensure safe childbirth over a period of roughly twenty years.[83]

The perceived efficacy of these rites was likely enhanced by their extravagant material performance (the fire, fragrant offerings, ritual implements, the scripted gestures and movements of the priest), and in particular the presence of physical icons, illustrations, or statues of the deities with whom the priest communed and eventually merged. As Bernard Faure, Elizabeth Horton Sharf, Robert Sharf, and other scholars have pointed out, these icons were not seen merely as representations of deities or symbolic of their power; rather, they were treated as instantiations, living presences in themselves.[84] This fact holds much significance when considering the use of such icons in the context of healing rites. Mimi Hall Yiengpruksawan has discussed how anxieties about illness among the elite in the Heian period were a major impetus behind the production of religious art.[85] For example, some sculptural icons were created in life-sized proportions to match the body of their ailing donors. One underlying logic behind this precise replication of body size was the belief that compassionate Buddhist deities are ever willing to take the place of the suffering devotee. This idea is expressed in the story of the "substitute body Fudō" (*migawari* Fudō 身代わり不動) told in the *Illustrated Scroll on the Origins of the Crying Fudō* (*Naki Fudō engi emaki* 泣不動縁起絵巻). An alternative to the one-to-one was the logic of the many-to-many. Those with the greatest power and wealth mass-produced icons to create veritable armies of buddhas, bodhisattvas, wisdom kings, and other divinities who would wage battle against the unseen hordes of pestilential demons on their behalf. A famous example is the set of a thousand statues of Senju Kannon installed at the aforementioned Renge'ō'in. This co-production of Taira no Kiyomori 平清盛 (1118–1181) and Goshirakawa 後白河 (1127–1192) was a response to a smallpox epidemic that had struck the previous year.[86] Yiengpruksawan's seminal study encourages us to countenance the ways that art of the early medieval period was not driven primarily by aesthetic motivations—as might be suggested by the incredible artistry of surviving works today—but was often spurred by pervasive fears of invisible legions of malignant demons. This inextricable relationship between art and disease has more recently been examined in the work of scholars such as Yamamoto Satomi and Kasuya Makoto.[87]

Case studies have begun to shed light on important dynamics within innovative healing rituals produced in the medieval period. Benedetta Lomi's examination of the Ritual of the Six-Syllable *Sūtra* (*rokujikyōhō* 六字経法), a ritual recorded in the liturgical anthologies of several Taimitsu and Tōmitsu lineages, is a noteworthy example. The Ritual of the Six-Syllable *Sūtra* was a fire ceremony focused on Rokujiten 六字天, a lesser-known wisdom king considered the divine incarnation of a six-syllable *dhāraṇī* associated with the six forms assumed by Kannon in each of the six realms of transmigration (*rokudō*/*rikidō* 六道). Lomi demonstrates that this ritual offered a comprehensive solution to diverse and seemingly disparate notions of disease agents (evil spirits, the "three foxes," and sorcerers) and defilement (*kegare*). This is showcased in the ritual's incorporation of ritual techniques and actors from outside the orbit of esoteric Buddhism. For example, in the conclusion of the rite, a water-facing boat ceremony, yin-yang masters recited the *Nakatomi harae* 中臣祓 purification formula and used effigies (*hitokata* 人形) to rid the patrons of bodily impurities and disease.[88]

Another example is the Ritual of the Blue-Faced Vajrayakṣa for Expelling Demons and *Māras* (*Shōshiki Daikongō Yasha byaku kima hō* 青色大金剛藥叉辟鬼魔法) developed by monks of the Jimon lineage of Tendai in the late 12th and 13th centuries. As Andrew Macomber has shown, the ritual has several original features, beginning with its worship of Shōmen Kongō 青面金剛, a deity largely unknown in Japan at the time, as well as its focus on eliminating "corpse-vector disease," a wasting disease derived from classical Chinese medical literature. The most distinctive feature of the rite is its adoption and adaption of moxibustion (*kyū* 灸), a Chinese medical modality in which the healer burns dried mugwort on specific locations of the patient's body. Although in preceding centuries moxibustion was more commonly associated with the practice of court physicians, Macomber argues that this healing modality resonated in meaningful ways with symbolic associations of fire central to the imagination of efficacy in esoteric Buddhism, organized as it was around the fire ceremony.[89]

A core component of healing rituals and indeed nearly all forms of esoteric ritual is "empowerment" (*kaji*; Skt. *adhiṣṭhāna*). This refers to the techniques used by the priest to channel the ritual power of invoked divinities through their own person so that it might be directed into the bodies of participants, patrons, or patients, or into material objects used for therapeutic purposes. Pamela Winfield has traced the importance of empowerment for healing back to the contributions of Kūkai, who not only wrote on the topic extensively but also put it into practice in striking ways.[90] On one occasion, Kūkai sent a vial of water he personally empowered to an ailing Emperor Saga 嵯峨天皇 (r. 810–823), an event recorded in a memorial that Kūkai sent along with the consecrated liquid.[91]

Kaji empowerment saw wide deployment owing in part to the ease with which it could be adapted to various ritual scenarios. For example, empowerment procedures were frequently deployed for aristocratic women to ensure safe childbirth and to protect the health of the newborn. As Anna Andreeva has shown through investigations of ritual handbooks preserved at temples in the Kinai 畿内 and Kantō 関東 regions, esoteric monks developed a practice for empowering a fabric sash (*obi* 帯) that was to be wrapped around the body of expectant mother. By empowering an object that was crucial in ceremonial and therapeutic traditions associated with childbirth, esoteric monks carved out a pivotal role for themselves among a panoply of other ritual and medical specialists—yin-yang masters, court physicians, midwives, wetnurses, and other woman relatives permitted into the parturition chamber—who worked jointly to secure the reproductive health of elite women.[92]

This empowerment ritual demonstrates that pregnancy and childbirth were major concerns within a broader, shared field of ritual activity focused on the elimination of disease, the fortification of the body, and the elongation of life. Certain rituals were touted as effective for both healing the body and for safe childbirth, such as the rites focused on Kujaku Myōō. A passage from the *Asabashō* 阿娑縛抄 brings home a similar point about the close relationship between health and childbirth—and the demonic agents that threaten both—in its discussion of the Yakushi Ritual of the Seven Buddhas. The passage promises that women in labor who direct their minds to the Seven Buddhas will give birth to a child with "sharp faculties and clear hearing, few illnesses, and peaceful wellbeing, who will be without non-persons [i.e., demons] trying to snatch their vital energy."[93]

Empowerment procedures also play a central role in *abisha* 阿尾奢, a kind of ritual exorcism that has drawn the attention of numerous Japanese scholars. The Chinese characters for *abisha* (Chn. *aweizhe*) transliterate the Sanskrit term *āveśa*, meaning "spirit possession." As Iyanaga Nobumi 彌永信美 demonstrates, the modified varieties of this ritual format that were practiced in premodern Japan are ultimately rooted in esoteric sutras translated into Chinese and—even more distantly—popular Indian religiosity.[94] Variations of *abisha* prescriptions were preserved in numerous scriptures in Japan, but the most widely practiced forms appear to have been those that focused on Fudō Myōō and those that pertained to the elimination of disease, two foci that often overlap in the ritual literature.

Evidence suggests that the early Tendai monk Enchin 円珍 (814–891) and his group of disciples were among the first to try out the techniques in actual practice. Accordingly, some of the earliest compilations of this material were produced by monks on Mount Hiei. The best-preserved form in which these ritual materials survive today is the *Collection of Ritual Methods* (*Sahō shū* 作法集), a compilation by Jōgen 成賢 (or Seigen; 1162–1231) that contains the teachings of Shōken 勝賢 (1138–1196). Although Jōgen and Shōken were both Shingon monks, one can also find in this text teachings that trace back to oral transmissions attributed to Ennin 円仁 (794–864), another important early Tendai monk. The most relevant section in terms of *abisha* used for healing is the "Procedures of the *genza*" (*Genza sahō* 験者作法). In the Heian and Kamakura periods, *genza* (or *geza/genja*; literally, "efficacious ones") referred primarily to Buddhist practitioners who conducted esoteric-style ritual procedures for therapeutic purposes, including healing, the exorcism of spirits (*jake/mononoke*), and childbirth. *Genza* was a nonsectarian (or non–lineage specific) designation, and one that appears often in the records of aristocrats who sponsored or observed their performance of rituals at court. Still, as Ueno Katsuyuki and Sakō Nobuyuki have noted, monks of the Jimon lineage based on Onjōji appear to have acted in the capacity of *genza* more than monastics of any other major lineage.[95] Tokunaga Seiko speculates the employment of Jimon monks for childbirth and healing rituals at court related to their role as supervisors over pilgrimage routes in the mountains of Kumano (Kumano *sanzan kengyō* 熊野三山検校) in Kii province 紀伊国 (today's Wakayama Prefecture 和歌山県), numinous locations at which Buddhists practiced austerities and cultivated powers that would amplify their ritual potency. The administration of the Kumano pilgrimage routes was by and large overseen by the principal abbot of Onjōji (*chōri* 長吏).[96]

As noted previously, *abisha* rituals constituted a type of exorcism often aimed at expelling disease agents. Koyama Satoko observes that there are two primary types discernible from texts such as the *Collection of Ritual Methods*. Some features are shared between these types, including a set of opening procedures in which the healer achieves identification with the primary object of worship (again, often Fudō Myōō), empowers the patient, and then proceeds to use ritual measures to discern the origin of the disease so that the offending spirit can be cast out from the body of the patient. Importantly, however, one type employs a spirit medium and the other does not. In the ritual requiring the participation of a medium, known as a *yorimashi* 憑座, the ritualist invites a benevolent divinity or set of divinities known as "dharma protectors" (*gohō* 護法) into the body of the medium, and then does the same for the disease-causing spirit. Once the malignant spirit is safely contained within the body of the medium and controlled by the "dharma protector," it no longer afflicts the patient. Ideally the spirit can be coerced into talking in the hopes that the priest can finally convert the spirit to the righteous path of Buddhism from which it has gone astray.[97]

Abisha, which became a predominant ritual form for healing and childbirth in the latter half of the 10th century, greatly impacted how Buddhist healers were imagined in the Heian and Kamakura periods and influenced the subsequent development of ritual therapy in Japan. Dramatic scenes of curative exorcisms appear in such prominent literary works as Murasaki Shikubu's 紫式部 (ca. 973–1014) *Tale of Genji* (*Genji monogatari* 源氏物語)—the sequences involving Rokujō's spirit attacks on Aoi and Murasaki in particular—and Sei no Shōnagon's 清少納言 (b. 966) *The Pillow Book* (*Makura no sōshi* 枕草子).[98] Although there are many differences between these literary accounts and the prescriptive sources upon which actual rituals were based, recent scholarship comparing these sources has validated Strickmann's hypothesis: It is evident that these methods were not "based squarely on primitive shamanistic superstition," as Ivan Morris and other literary scholars suggested, but rather *abisha* procedures, which evidence the influence of the translocal transmission of esoteric Buddhist liturgical literature.[99] Such rituals would be adapted to many new contexts well into the early modern and modern periods. Their impact is most evident in the *yori-gitō* 憑祈祷 performed by *shugenja* 修験者 (*yamabushi* 山伏) of the Shugendō 修験道 tradition, certain lineages of which traced their descent back to the Jimon branch of Tendai. Esoteric influence can also be discerned in the intense exorcisms conducted by monks of the Nichiren-shū 日蓮宗, such as those used for cases of "fox possession" (*kitsunetsuki* 狐憑き), despite their patriarch Nichiren's own disavowal of the esoteric institution in which he was trained.[100]

MATERIA MEDICA

Since the early days of Buddhism in India, Buddhist therapeutic practice incorporated the use of physical substances to be ingested orally, applied to or worn on the body, or used in ritual practice. The turn toward material culture in the study of Buddhism over the past two decades has laid the groundwork for productive consideration of the materiality of Buddhist medicine.[101] New research has given us a better understanding of the varied substances used by Buddhists, the ritual and therapeutic practices in which these substances were utilized, and the Buddhist networks and trade routes through which these substances circulated from one region of the world to another. A perennial theme in this area is the relationship between the two dimensions of materia medica: (a) the collection of substances that were available to Buddhists at any given time and place and (b) the body of knowledge that was constructed around those substances and informed their use in practice.

In the early sangha in ancient India, Śākyamuni Buddha is said to have allowed five basic medicines—ghee (clarified butter), fresh butter, oil, honey, and molasses—but numerous early texts suggest the use of many more. Kenneth Zysk has argued that the Buddhist pharmacopeia, together with medical and anatomical knowledge gleaned partly through practices such as the "contemplation of the corpse," developed within a religious milieu of wandering ascetics (*śramaṇa*), a culture within which the Buddhist Sangha belonged. He further notes that this knowledge would later be absorbed into Āyurveda and given a "Hindu" veneer through associations with the Vedic pantheon.[102] In time, as Buddhism spread along the Silk Roads through Central and East Asia, the number of medicinal materials incorporated into Buddhist healing practices grew dramatically, as did the body of knowledge pertaining to the properties of those materials and the ailments for which their use was indicated. When Buddhism arrived in China in the Han dynasty (206 BCE–221 CE), it was not long before Buddhist pharmacopeias converged with the branch of medicine known in the textual tradition as *bencao* 本草 (Jp. *honzō*). *Bencao* (literally "roots and grasses"), like the term *materia medica*, refers to actual therapeutic substances as well as the written genre in which knowledge about them was inscribed. *Bencao* literature mainly prescribed plant-based substances and formulas, but it also included grains, minerals, and animal-derived substances. (Some later medical writers, like Sun Simiao 孫思邈 [581–682], who was influenced by Buddhist notions of universal compassion, were critical of the medicinal use of animals, which he suggested would negatively impact the karmic status of both physician and patient).[103] Buddhist scriptures translated or produced in China contain references to myriad substances monks and nuns would have acquired on their travels as well as those that were already embedded within the literary medical traditions of China.[104]

It is thus no surprise that when Buddhism was brought to Japan by monks hailing from the Korean peninsula, its scriptures, commentaries, and icons were accompanied by medicines and materia medica literature. Materia medica was mentioned in the oldest surviving record for the transmission of medical texts from the continent to Japan. In the entry for the year 562, during the reign of Emperor Kinmei 欽明天皇 (510–571), the *Newly Compiled Record of Surnames* (*Shinsen shōjiroku* 新撰姓氏録; ca. 799–815) describes how Chisō 智聡, an immigrant arriving in Japan via the Korean peninsula, offered 164 fascicles of works, including the *Illuminated Hall Chart* (*Mingtang tu* 明堂図), a text of much importance for the practices of acupuncture and moxibustion (*shinkyū* 鍼灸), and materia medica. These texts, in the form of updated editions such as the *Newly Revised Materia Medica* (*Xinxiu bencao* 新修本草), would become textbooks for students of the Medical Bureau (Tenyakuryō 典薬寮), and were thus formative for the medical practice of court physicians (*kusushi* 医師) in the Nara and

Heian periods. One of the earliest surviving references to such works, however, is in the writings of Kūkai. Seeking to establish his transmission of esoteric Buddhism, Kūkai drew upon the image of efficacious medical substances found throughout classical materia medica literature to argue for the analogous potency of esoteric ritual technologies like mantra and *dhāraṇī*.[105] This was no fleeting interest on the part of esoteric monks. Buddhist monasteries would come to possess their own copies of such works, some of which are the earliest extant manuscripts known. One famous example is the Kamakura-period copy of *Newly Revised Materia Medica* based on a text dating to 731. The manuscript has been preserved at Ninnaji, a Shingon temple that maintained strong ties to aristocratic and imperial circles and thus had privileged access to medical literature in the possession of physician lineages such as the Tanba 丹波 or Wake 和気.[106]

Equally remarkable is the survival of actual medicinal substances from as early as the Nara period. Sixty different types of medicines were stored in the Shōsōin 正倉院 treasury of Tōdaiji as part of a project carried out by Empress Kōmyō 光明皇后 to preserve the personal items of her recently deceased spouse, Emperor Shōmu 聖武天皇 (701–756), who was responsible for constructing the grand statue of Vairocana Buddha. The Shōsōin housed an incredible range of decorative and practical objects, including musical instruments, robes, furniture, calligraphy, armor and weapons, and ritual implements. (A select number of these objects are exhibited every year at the Nara National Museum, a practice that corresponds to the annual "airing out" of treasures and manuscripts [*mushiboshi* 虫干し, literally "drying out the bugs"] conducted at temples.) Of the sixty medicines that were installed in the collection, as many as thirty-eight are extant, if in dramatically diminished quantities.[107] Scholars have traditionally understood this unique collection of materials, medicines included, in terms of Japan's geographic location at the eastern terminus of the Silk Roads.[108] Indeed, several scientific surveys conducted on the medicines have decisively verified that these specimens were brought from distant regions throughout Eurasia.[109] As Katja Triplett summarizes, "The results reveal that Shōsōin's black pepper was once harvested in western India, the Aleppo wasp galls in northern Persia, the rhubarb in Tibet, the stick lac in northern India on the slopes of the Himalayas, the licorice on the shores of the Yellow River in China, the clove from Sulawesi (Indonesia) and the *hārītakī* fruit in Thailand."[110] This last item, *hārītakī*—also known as chebulic myrobalan (Jpn. *kariroku* 訶梨勒; *Terminalia chebula*)—will be familiar to students of Buddhist healing. It was, for example, one of the fruit medicines permitted for consumption by Śākyamuni. It was also routinely associated with the Master of Medicines Buddha in scriptural and iconographic depictions.[111]

Another perspective from which to understand these medicinal materials is to consider the objectives that motivated their installation in the Shōsōin collection. Fortunately, a catalog of these substances, titled the *Inventory of Medicines* (*Shuju yakuchō* 種々薬帳), was written up at the time of their installation. In addition to enumerating the sixty types of medicines together with notes regarding the amount deposited, the catalog explains the Buddhist-inflected aims of the project.[112] The catalog notes that the medicines were initially kept in the Golden Hall of Tōdaiji, where they were offered to Vairocana. Although not stated, the purpose of doing so was likely to empower the medicines to enhance their potency, just as Kūkai would later empower a vial of water before sending it to an ailing Emperor Saga. Second, the catalog makes clear that these medicines were stored in Shōsōin so that they might benefit those who needed them, if only after such individuals received written permission from the Monastic Office. Although the claim that these medicines would be made available to all cannot be taken at face value—especially given the limited quantities that were deposited—the administrators of the collection did not jealously hoard them. In fact, medicines were supplied to court physicians and Buddhist monks who filed requests, a process that eventually led to the depletion of most (but surprisingly not all) of the medicines. Third, seen in light of the events leading up to the construction of Tōdaiji, one likely aim of the installation of these material medicines was the rectification of the state's medical institutions after the destructive Great Smallpox Epidemic of 735–737. Indeed, in 720, Kōmyō made a vow that formally brought the Seyakuin 施薬院—one of the state's early medical institutions—into the administrative fold of the Office of the Imperial Consort (*kōgō gūshiki* 皇后宮職), an office under Kōmyō's authority. Several of the signatories on the *Inventory of Medicines*, moreover, belonged to Kōmyō's office.

Demand for therapeutic materials like those stored in Shōsōin skyrocketed in the Heian period as esoteric rituals grew in popularity among the aristocracy. This was a consequence of the heavy material toll demanded by the esoteric fire ceremony. Esoteric liturgical texts call for the exorbitant consumption of aromatics (*kō* 香), medicines (*yaku* 薬), grains (*koku* 穀), and minerals (*hō* 宝, literally "treasures"). Unlike icons, altars, ritual implements, and other durable fixtures of ritual that might see dozens or even hundreds of years of use, therapeutic substances served a much more transient role in ritual performance. Together with aromatic oils and specific kinds of wood (e.g., "milkwood," *nyūboku* 乳木), these materials were thrown into the hearth of the fire ceremony as offerings for divine consumption.[113] The precise materials and quantities required depended on the objective of the ritual to be performed, but on the whole, the ritual transformation of such materials in the hearth was seen as vital to securing the efficacy of the rite.

Some scholars have taken the use of these substances as evidence that esoteric ritual was not irrational, uncivilized, or superstitious, contrary to once widely held "orientalist" views toward Tantrism. Taira Masayuki suggests that the incorporation of materia medica into esoteric practice reflects a certain "rationality" (*gōrisei* 合理性) on the part of esoteric monks, who were, by virtue of their use of such substances, engaging with sophisticated medical knowledge imported from continental medical traditions. Another scholar, Nihonyanagi Kenji, examined the relationship between medicines prescribed in liturgical texts for the fire ceremony and those described in the Korean medical classic *Dongui bogam* 東醫寶鑑 (1613). Nihonyanagi's aim is to demonstrate that the use of such substances was not only ritual or symbolic in nature but also utilitarian, since they likely contributed to the rite's salubrious effects. Drawing attention to the proto-scientific and empirical dimensions of esoteric rites, such arguments importantly acknowledge that esoteric priests performed these rites for therapeutic purposes. However, it remains to be shown how, concretely, the burning of substances in the hearth constituted therapeutic effects for patients who were often deliberately isolated from the ritual scene. Although Nihonyanagi notes cases when medicines buried in the ash of the hearth were exhumed and given to patients for consumption, more investigation on this question is needed.

Regardless, it is evident that the use of these medicines in ritual must be grasped in light of the Buddhist engagement with diverse knowledge traditions that enabled them to better articulate the therapeutic efficacy of those practices. The Buddhist study of materia medica knowledge in Japan has in fact left many rich textual sources. For example, the *Kōyōshō* 香要抄, *Kokuruishō* 穀類抄, *Hōyōshō* 宝要抄, and the *Yakushushō* 薬種抄, each compiled by Ken'i 兼意 (1072–1145), a Shingon monk of Mt. Kōya, are veritable clearinghouses of knowledge pertaining to therapeutic aromatics, medicines, grains, and minerals meant for use in ritual. One need only glance at the sundry categories of textual genres these compendia incorporate to appreciate the diverse knowledge traditions that went into the production of Buddhist materia medica knowledge: Buddhist texts, including scriptures (*kyōten* 経典), lexicographies (*ongisho* 音義書), and liturgies; works dealing with "nourishing life" (*yōjō* 養生; Chn. *yangsheng*), some of which might be associated with Daoist traditions; Chinese and Japanese historical and hagiographical sources; old dictionaries (*kojisho* 古辞書) and encyclopedias (*ruisho* 類書); and the compiler Ken'i's own commentary. The bulk of the information comes from Chinese materia medica literature and other classical medical texts, testifying to the availability and consumption of that knowledge among Buddhist monastics.[114]

At the same time, it was often the case that knowledge was *all* that could be accessed because the therapeutic materials were themselves not always at hand. As noted previously, records from the 8th century suggest that medicinal substances were imported to Japan beginning in the 6th century as part of trade and exchange with the continent. These interactions became infrequent after the mid-9th century, only to resume again in earnest following the establishment of the Kamakura capital, which helped instigate a period of relatively stable trade in the mid-13th century.[115] Medical practice involving the use of these substances thus changed significantly in the interim period (the 10th through 12th centuries) when trade failed to keep pace with demand. (It must be remembered, too, that demand was coming not only from monastic quarters but also from aristocrats, who devoted themselves to a robust aromatic culture of cosmetics, perfuming, and recreation, and from court physicians, whose formulas also required these substances.) Monks were thus occasionally forced to locate or cultivate local plants and materials that might serve as functional or symbolic substitutes for those prescribed in esoteric ritual or classical medical texts.[116]

Such botanical negotiations—which are demanded whenever materia medica traditions of one geographic region are transmitted to another—helped to spur a consequential shift for Buddhist medicine in the interim era between periods of active trade. That shift took the form of novel therapeutic programs that reflected a turn away from the extensive pharmacopeia required by the avaricious flames of the *goma* ceremony while remaining indebted to the structures, techniques, and discourse of esoteric ritual. These newer programs concentrated on a small number of substances that could still be acquired via trade or—even better—could be found locally in Japan. The question as to why certain substances were nominated for ritual in this changing milieu has become increasingly important for scholars writing on Buddhist medicine in this period. A few examples shall suffice. Recognized as efficacious in subjugation rites because of its toxicity, poppy seed (*keshi/karashi* 芥子) was one substance that came to prominence over the Heian period. Poppy seeds were made the focus of a ritual centered on Fudō Myōō known as "roasting poppy seeds" (*keshiyaki* 芥子焼). In stark contrast to mainstream fire rituals of the period, poppy seed was the only substance whose consumption in the ritual hearth was prescribed. Yet as Shinmura Taku notes, this practice became one of the most common healing rituals during the Heian period.[117] To get a sense of the rite's popularity, one need only recall the famous exorcism sequence in the *Tale of Genji*, in which Lady Rokujō finds herself permeated with the smell of roasted poppy seeds as a result of the rites performed to subdue her "living spirit" (*ikiryō* 生霊).

Another important therapeutic substance that came to be the focus of specific rites of empowerment was ox bezoar (*goō* 牛黄, literally "ox yellow"). As Lomi has shown, ox bezoar was employed by monks associated with Shingon monasteries, namely Kakuzen 覚禅 (1143–ca. 1213) and Raiyu 頼瑜 (1226–1304), as well as monks of Tendai lineages, to secure safe childbirth for imperial women. Lomi shows that ox bezoar was understood to have therapeutic properties outlined in Chinese medical literature studied in Japan. Another factor contributing to its perceived potency was the fact that it was a precious commodity, the acquisition of which was unpredictable. As Lomi notes, bezoars are "concretions found in the stomach or intestines of animals, generally ruminants," which are "formed due to the lack of proper metabolization of lumps of swallowed hair, seeds, vegetable fibers, and other substances."[118] Thus, specimens of ox bezoar were seen as jewels, a view that elevated the substance beyond therapeutic use and into a symbolic network of potent objects that included "wish-fulfilling jewels" (*nyoi hōju* 如意宝珠; Skt. *cintāmaṇi*) and the sacred relics of buddhas (*busshari* 仏舎利). Lomi's study illuminates how the "social life" of ox bezoar was shaped by a breathtaking variety of discourses and spheres of activity—religious, medical, material, economic, and political.[119]

The most widely discussed case of a Buddhist healing program focused on a small number of therapeutic substances was presented by Yōsai in *Record of Nourishing Life by Drinking Tea* (*Kissayōjōki* 喫茶養生記).[120] In this two-fascicle work, Yōsai promotes the medicinal use of tea (*cha* 茶) and mulberry (*kuwa* 桑), two materials that would have been readily available in Yōsai's time. Because the first fascicle centers around tea, Yōsai's work has long been seen retrospectively as sparking a revival of tea drinking in his time that would eventually culminate in the refined art of the tea ceremony practiced among the elite in the late medieval period. One reason for associating Yōsai with the longer history of the tea ceremony is the fact that he is also credited with importing Rinzai Zen 臨済禅 (Chn. Linji Chan) to Japan from China (which he visited as many as two times), which he purportedly established as a new sect in Japan.

This image of Yōsai has been considerably revised in recent years, however, leading to new readings of his *Record of Nourishing Life by Drinking Tea*. On balance, Yōsai's training and literary output primarily reflect his training as an esoteric monk of the Tendai school. Although it is certain that Yōsai encountered tea drinking among Chan monks in China, tea was also already used in Japan as an offering in the context of esoteric rituals.[121] Tea also had a long history of use as a medicinal substance in Chinese materia medica separate from any ceremonial usage.[122] In his discussion of tea in the *Record of Nourishing Life by Drinking Tea*, Yōsai draws upon parallels between the systems of correlative thinking found in medical literature and esoteric Buddhism. In particular, he claims that the Japanese suffer from various ailments because their diet lacks foods that are bitter, the flavor that is associated with, and thus nourishes, the heart viscus. He recommends that readers drink tea ("external" medicine), a practice to be coupled with a program of visualizing the buddhas that occupy the five viscera ("internal" medicine).

The second fascicle of the *Record of Nourishing Life by Drinking Tea*, which focuses mainly on mulberry, has received far less attention despite the fact that it is characterized by the same general strategy as the first: the promotion of a particular therapeutic substance. Yōsai's contention in this fascicle is that mulberry can be used to expel demons that cause disease because the tree shares an identity with two other plant materials: the "milkwood" of the *goma* fire ceremony; and the bodhi tree (*bodaiju* 菩提樹). Whereas milkwood was a key fuel for subjugation rites used against disease-causing demons, the bodhi tree was famously associated with Śākyamuni's awakening, which was predicated on his conquering of the quintessential demon of Buddhism, King Māra. In this way, Yōsai's rationale for the use of mulberry looks back to the long history of Buddhism's entanglement with special plant substances. At the same time, it illustrates how monastic healers in Japan adjusted their healing programs to navigate shifting circumstances, including the uncertain state of trade and an imagination of disease informed by historical notions such as the age of the Final Dharma.

DISCUSSION OF THE LITERATURE

The recent growth of interest in Buddhism and medicine has spurred the appearance of numerous English-language publications, ranging from in-depth treatments to entry-level anthologies and surveys useful for any scholar or student beginning their study of this topic. Readers would do well to begin with Katja Triplett's *Buddhism and Medicine: A Topical Survey (500–1600 ce) of a Complex Relationship* (2019), the first monograph devoted to the topic in English. Triplett's groundbreaking volume covers a wide range of medical foci, including ophthalmology and the eyes, pregnancy and medical care for the female body, materia medica in the contexts of both trade and local cultivation, and equine medicine, among many other germane subtopics. Besides the important work Triplett's survey does in introducing readers to diverse areas of Buddhism and medicine in Japan, it also offers original analyses on numerous otherwise unexamined manuscripts and sources. Similar in-depth studies of article length can be found in *Buddhism and Healing in Medieval China and Japan* (2020), co-edited by C. Pierce Salguero and Andrew Macomber. This includes Anna Andreeva's examination of the "pregnancy sash," an empowered ritual object used to secure the health of the parturient mother and the unborn child, and Macomber's study of Buddhist forms of moxibustion. Much of the agenda for this more recent research was set by two pioneering works. Originally part of the Hōbōgirin, a monumental encyclopedia of Buddhism, Paul Demiéville's "Byō" (1937; translated into English in 1985) is a classic in the field. Focusing on "Sickness" as one form of suffering in Buddhism, it is exhaustive in its coverage of Buddhism and medicine across Asia, with many sections devoted to premodern Japan. The second is Michel Strickmann's *Chinese Magical Medicine* (2002). Despite its title, Strickmann's posthumously published monograph provides substantial analysis on Buddhist ritual healing and notions of disease in Japan, especially as these were inflected by traditions of tantric Buddhism; the material on Japan is concentrated in the later chapters, "The Genealogy of Spirit Possession" and "Tantrists, Foxes, and Shamans."

Historians of Japan have also made formidable contributions to this area, demonstrating that medical history in Japan cannot neglect the impact of Buddhist medicine. Andrew Goble's study of priest-physician Kajiwara Shōzen in his *Confluences of Medicine in Medieval Japan* (2011), which remains the only monograph to date devoted to the medical history of Japan's medieval period, treats several key aspects of Buddhism's far-reaching influence on that history, ranging from Buddhist monastic networks that facilitated trade, the establishment of medical facilities at temples, and the issue of karmic illness. Karmic illness also figures into

Susan Burns's *Kingdom of the Sick* (2019), a monograph focused on the history of leprosy (*rai*) in Japan.

Although these publications demonstrate that there is now more information in English than ever before on Buddhism and medicine in premodern Japan, any earnest exploration of the topic must also engage with foundational scholarship published in Japanese. The most accessible starting point is Shinmura Taku's *Nihon bukkyō no iryōshi* 日本仏教医療史 (2013), a digest of his more extensive publications discussing Buddhist medicine. Much important information on the history of Buddhist medicine can also be found in the voluminous medical histories by Fujikawa Yū (1868–1940) and Hattori Toshirō (1906–1992). A certain degree of caution is advised when working with Fujikawa and Hattori, however, since both authors rely on normative and—from the perspective of the study of Japanese religious history since the appearance of the research of Kuroda Toshio—outdated views of Buddhism. Both Fujikawa and Hattori tended to see certain forms of Buddhism, particularly esoteric Buddhism, as superstitious in character, and thus a hindrance to the development of proper empirical medicine in ancient and medieval Japan.[123] The influence of this perspective can be seen in early English-language scholarship, such as the article "A Buddhist Prayer against Sickness" by Ilza Veith and Atsumi Minami, though Hattori himself became more sympathetic to Buddhism over time, evident, for example, in his *Shaka no igaku* 釈迦の医学 (1968).[124]

More generally, although the field of medical history (*igakushi* 医学史) in Japan has made great strides in the area of philology and in the transcription and digitization of previously unknown manuscripts and texts (such as the digitization project at Fujikawa Bunko at Kyoto University), Buddhist medicine has yet to emerge as a major subject of inquiry.[125] However, a new generation of religious studies scholars, historians, and literature specialists have produced trailblazing studies that situate Buddhist medicine within a wider range of historical sources, including diaries, tale literature, and illustrated scrolls. These scholars, whose innovative work will shape the direction of future research on Buddhist medicine in premodern Japan, include Ueno Katsuyuki, Oda Etsuyo, Koyama Satoko, Shindō Hiroshi, and Yamamoto Satomi.[126]

PRIMARY SOURCES

The primary texts on which much of the research discussed in this article is based have been made available for the first time in English translation in *Buddhism and Medicine: An Anthology of Premodern Sources* (2017), edited by Salguero. This includes the writings of Buddhist monks such as Kūkai and Kokan Shiren, prescriptive esoteric liturgical literature, and Buddhist figures and therapeutic traditions incorporated into medical works such as the *Ishinpō* 医心方 (984). The collection also contains translations of numerous works from South, Central, and East Asia that are equally critical for understanding the shape Buddhist medicine assumed in Japan.

Researchers with facility in reading premodern Japanese and Chinese works in their original languages will naturally benefit from having a larger number of primary materials by which to expand and deepen their investigation of the topic. Japanese sources on Buddhism and medicine, however, have yet to be collected in the form of curated anthologies. One convenient, if limited, collection of texts pertaining to Buddhism and medicine can be found in the *Zoku gunsho ruijū* 続群書類従 (vol. 31.1).[127] The relevant volume contains three Buddhist materia medica compendia, the *Chōseiryōyōhō* 長生療養方 (1184) by Renki 蓮基, and a treatment manual for corpse-vector disease, together with other works associated with the education of court physicians and the field of wound medicine.[128] Yōsai's *Record of Nourishing Life by Drinking Tea,* arguably the most well-known Buddhist medical text in premodern Japan, can be readily found in Japanese editions as well as English translations.[129] Further exploration of the topic will inevitably require surveying and conducting targeted searches of medical and disease terminology in major collections of Buddhist writings, such as the Taishō canon (*Taishō Shinshū Daizōkyō* 大正新脩大蔵経), as well as gaining familiarity with the collections of materials possessed by temples, universities, and museums throughout Japan, where many unpublished sources pertaining to Buddhism and medicine are preserved.[130]

FURTHER READING

Andreeva, Anna. "Empowering the Pregnancy Sash in Medieval Japan." In *Buddhist Healing in Medieval China and Japan.* Edited by C. Pierce Salguero and Andrew Macomber, 160–193. Honolulu: University of Hawaii Press, 2020.

Drott, Edward R. "Gods, Buddhas, and Organs: Buddhist Physicians and Theories of Longevity in Early Medieval Japan." *Japanese Journal of Religious Studies* 37, no. 2 (2010): 247–273.

Goble, Andrew Edmund. *Confluences of Medicine in Medieval Japan: Buddhist Healing, Chinese Knowledge, Islamic Formulas, and Wounds of War.* Honolulu: University of Hawaii Press, 2011.

Hattori Toshirō 服部敏良. *Heian jidai igakushi no kenkyū* 平安時代医学の研究. Tokyo: Kuwana Bunseidō, 1955.

Hattori Toshirō 服部敏良. *Kamakura jidai igakushi no kenkyū* 鎌倉時代医学史の研究. Tokyo: Yoshikawa Kōbunkan, 1964.

Hattori Toshirō 服部敏良. *Nara jidai igakushi no kenkyū* 奈良時代医学史の研究. Tokyo: Tōkyōdō, 1945.

Hayami Tasuku 速水侑. *Heian kizoku shakai to Bukkyō* 平安貴族社会と仏教. Tokyo: Yoshikawa Kōbunkan, 1975.

Koyama Satoko 小山聡子. *Shinran no shinkō to jujutsu: byōki chiryō to rinjū gyōgi* 親鸞の信仰と呪術—病気治療と臨終行儀. Tokyo: Yoshikawa Kōbunkan, 2013.

Lomi, Benedetta. "Dharanis, Talismans, and Straw Dolls: Ritual Choreographies and Healing Strategies of the Rokujikyōhō in Medieval Japan." *Japanese Journal of Religious Studies* 41, no. 2 (2014): 255–304.

Lomi, Benedetta. "Ox Bezoars and the Materiality of Heian-Period Therapeutics." *Japanese Journal of Religious Studies* 45, no. 2 (2018): 227–268.

Sakō Nobuyuki 酒向伸行. *Hyōrei shinkō no rekishi to minzoku* 憑霊信仰の歴史と民俗. Tokyo: Iwata Shoin, 2013.

Salguero, C. Pierce, ed. *Buddhism and Medicine: An Anthology of Premodern Sources.* New York: Columbia University Press, 2017.

Salguero, C. Pierce, and Andrew Macomber, eds. *Buddhist Healing in Medieval China and Japan.* Honolulu: University of Hawaii Press, 2020.

Shinmura Taku 新村拓. *Nihon bukkyō no iryōshi* 日本仏教の医療史. Tokyo: Hōsei Daigaku Shuppankyoku, 2013.

Shinmura Taku 新村拓. *Nihon iryō shakaishi no kenkyū: kodai chūsei no minshū seikatsu to iryō* 日本医療社会史の研究—古代中世の民衆生活と医療. Tokyo: Hōsei Daigaku Shuppankyoku, 1985.

Strickmann, Michel. *Chinese Magical Medicine*. Edited by Bernard Faure. Stanford, CA: Stanford University Press, 2002.

Suzuki, Yui. *Medicine Master Buddha: The Iconic Worship of Yakushi in Heian Japan*. Leiden, The Netherlands: Brill, 2012.

Triplett, Katja. *Buddhism and Medicine in Japan: A Topical Survey (500–1600 ce) of a Complex Relationship*. Berlin: De Gruyter, 2019.

Ueno Katsuyuki 上野勝之. *Yume to mononoke no seishinshi: Heian kizoku no shinkō sekai* 夢とモノノケの精神史—平安貴族の信仰世界. Kyoto: Kyoto Daigaku Gakujutsu Shuppankai, 2013.

Winfield, Pamela D. "Curing with Kaji: Healing and Esoteric Empowerment in Japan." *Japanese Journal of Religious Studies* 32, no. 1 (2005): 107–130.

Winfield, Pamela D. "Religion and Healing in Pre-Modern Japan." *Religion Compass* 6, no. 11 (2012): 467–479.

NOTES

1. Edward R. Drott, "Gods, Buddhas, and Organs: Buddhist Physicians and Theories of Longevity in Early Medieval Japan," *Japanese Journal of Religious Studies* 37, no. 2 (2010): 249.
2. C. Pierce Salguero, *Translating Buddhist Medicine in Medieval China* (Philadelphia: University of Pennsylvania Press, 2014), 19–21.
3. Charles E. Rosenberg, *Explaining Epidemics and Other Studies in the History of Medicine* (Cambridge, UK: Cambridge University Press, 1992), 6.
4. Mrozik reserves the use of the term "physiomoral discourse" for positive examples and "ascetic discourse" for negative examples; outside of examples where asceticism might be practiced, physiomoral discourse aptly describes both, referring to any linkage between karma and one's physical state; see Susanne Mrozik, *Virtuous Bodies: The Physical Dimensions of Morality in Buddhist Ethics* (Oxford: Oxford University Press, 2007).
5. Leon Hurvitz, *Scripture of the Lotus Blossom of the Fine Dharma* (New York: Columbia University Press, 2009), 336.
6. The full title of this work is *Nihonkoku genpō zen'aku ryōiki* 日本国現報善悪霊異記.
7. Kyoko Motomochi Nakamura, *Miraculous Stories from the Japanese Buddhist Tradition: The Nihon Ryōiki of the Monk Kyōkai* (Cambridge, MA: Harvard University Press, 1973), 248–249. For a recent study of such tales, particularly in relation to blindness, see Mizuguchi Motoki 水口幹記, "'Nihon ryōiki' shosai no mokumō setsuwa wo megutte: Sono 'seijiteki' sokumen nitsuite"『日本霊異記』所載の目盲説話をめぐって—その"政治的"側面について, in *Zenkindai Nihon no byōki chiryō to jujutsu* 前近代日本の病気治療と呪術, ed. Koyama Satoko 小山聡子 (Kyoto: Shibunkaku Shuppan, 2020), 73–107.
8. William R. LaFleur, *The Karma of Words: Buddhism and the Literary Arts in Medieval Japan* (Berkeley: University of California Press, 1983).
9. Yamamoto Satomi 山本聡美, "Illness as Depicted in the Illustrated Legends of Kokawa Temple," *Studies in Japanese Literature and Culture 2: Borders* (2019): 36.
10. Satomi, "Illness as Depicted in the Illustrated Legends of Kokawa Temple," 32–36.
11. T. 1911: 106c23–c25.
12. Andrew Edmund Goble, *Confluences of Medicine in Medieval Japan: Buddhist Healing, Chinese Knowledge, Islamic Formulas, and Wounds of War* (Honolulu: University of Hawai'i Press, 2011), 77–79.
13. *Taishō Shinshū Daizōkyō* 大正新修大藏經, ed. Takakusu Junjirō 高楠順次郎 (Tokyo: Taishō issaikyō kankōkai, reprint edition, 1962), vol. 46, no. 1911: 107c18–26; see also Paul L. Swanson, *Clear Serenity, Quiet Insight: T'ien-t'ai Chih-i's Mo-ho chih-kuan* (Honolulu: University of Hawai'i Press, 2018), vol. 2: 1336.
14. For a discussion of Zhiyi's engagement with Indian and Chinese medicine, see Salguero, *Translating Buddhist Medicine in Medieval China*, 102–105.

15. *Taishō Shinshū Daizōkyō*, ed. Takakusu Junjirō, vol. 46, no. 1911: 108a02–05.
16. Antje Richter, "Teaching from the Sickbed: Ideas of Illness and Healing in the *Vimalakīrti Sūtra* and Their Reception in Medieval Chinese Literature," in *Buddhist Healing in Medieval China and Japan*, ed. C. Pierce Salguero and Andrew Macomber (Honolulu: University of Hawaii Press, 2020), 57–90.
17. Edward R. Drott, "Overcoming Illness with Insight: Kokan Shiren's Treatise on the Nature of Illness and Its Manifestations," in *Buddhism and Medicine: An Anthology of Premodern Sources*, ed. C. Pierce Salguero (New York: Columbia University Press, 2017), 68.
18. Charlotte D. Eubanks, *Miracles of Book and Body: Buddhist Textual Culture and Medieval Japan* (Berkeley: University of California Press, 2011), 81–82.
19. Angela Ki Che Leung, *Leprosy in China: A History* (New York: Columbia University Press, 2009); and Susan L. Burns, *Kingdom of the Sick: A History of Leprosy and Japan* (Honolulu: University of Hawaii Press, 2019).
20. Chimoto Hideshi 千本英史, "'Katai' kō: setsuwa ni okeru raisha no mondai 「かたゐ」考—説話における癩者の問題," *Ōsaka Kyōiku Daigaku Kiyō* 大阪教育大学紀要 36, no. 1 (1987): 35–46.
21. David Quinter, *From Outcasts to Emperors: Shingon Ritsu and the Mañjuśrī Cult in Medieval Japan* (Leiden, The Netherlands: Brill, 2015), 10n1.
22. Burns, *Kingdom of the Sick*, 76.
23. *Taishō Shinshū Daizōkyō*, ed. Takakusu Junjirō, vol. 25, no. 1509: 479a10–12.
24. Thomas Keirstead, "Outcasts Before the Law: Pollution and Purification in Medieval Japan," in *Currents in Medieval Japanese History: Essays in Honor of Jeffrey P. Mass*, ed. Gordon M. Berger, Andrew Edmund Goble, Lorrain F. Harrington, and G. Cameron Hurst III (Los Angeles: Figueroa Press, 2009), 273.
25. Kuroda Hideo 黒田日出男, *Kyōkai no chūsei, shōchō no chūsei* 境界の中世・象徴の中世 (Tokyo: Tōkyō Daigaku Shuppankai, 1986), 233–258; for more on vow texts, see Satō Hiroo 佐藤弘夫, *Kishōmon no seishinshi: chūsei sekai no kami to hotoke* 起請文の精神史: 中世世界の神と仏 (Tokyo: Kōdansha, 2006).
26. Kuroda, *Kyōkai no chūsei, shōchō no chūsei*, 248.
27. Quinter, *From Outcasts to Emperors*, 123.
28. Quinter, *From Outcasts to Emperors*, 123–124.
29. Soga Yoshinari 曽我良成, "Heian, Kamakura-jidai no 'tōji' to onsen ryokō 平安・鎌倉時代の「湯治」と温泉旅行," *Nagoya Gakuin Daigaku Ronshū* 名古屋学院大学論集 21, no. 2 (2010): 68–57.
30. On the baths of monasteries in medieval in Japan, see e.g., Ihara Kesao 井原今朝男, *Shijitsu chūsei bukkyō: ima ni itaru jiin to sōsō no jitsuzō* 史実中世仏教: 今にいたる寺院と葬送の実像 (Tokyo: Kōzansha, 2011), 168–222.
31. Leung, *Leprosy in China*, 69–73.
32. D. Max Moerman, "The Buddha and the Bathwater: Defilement and Enlightenment in the *Onsenji engi*," *Japanese Journal of Religious Studies* 42, no. 1 (2015): 80.
33. Lori Meeks, *Hokkeji and the Reemergence of Female Monasticism in Premodern Japan* (Honolulu: University of Hawaii Press, 2010), 198–200.
34. Duncan Ryūken Williams, "Esoteric Waters: Meritorious Bathing, Kōbō Daishi, and Legends of Hot Spring Foundings," *Matrices and Weavings: Expressions of Shingon Buddhism in Japanese Culture and Society – Bulletin of the Research Institute of Esoteric Buddhist Culture, Special Issue II* (October 2004): 195–216.
35. David T. Bialock, *Eccentric Spaces, Hidden Histories: Narrative, Ritual, and Royal Authority from the* Chronicles of Japan *to* The Tale of the Heike (Stanford, CA: Stanford University Press, 2007), 210–216; and Shinmura Taku 新村拓, *Shi to yamai to kango no shakaishi* 死と病と看護の社会史 (Tokyo: Hōsei Daigaku Shuppankyoku, 1989), 61.
36. Goble, *Confluences of Medicine in Medieval Japan*, 88; for a translation of this section of the *Ton'ishō*, see Andrew Edmund Goble, "Determining Karmic Illness: Kajiwara Shōzen's Treatment of Rai/Leprosy in *Book of the Simple Physician*," in Salguero, *Buddhism and Medicine*, 553–560.

37. W. G. Aston, *Nihongi: Chronicles of Japan from the Earliest Times to A.D. 697* (Rutland, VT: Tuttle, 1972), 2:65–67; and Richard John Bowring, *The Religious Traditions of Japan, 500–1600* (Cambridge, UK: Cambridge University Press, 2005), 15–19.
38. Anna Andreeva, *Assembling Shinto: Buddhist Approaches to Kami Worship in Medieval Japan* (Cambridge, MA: Harvard University Asia Center, 2017), 60–61.
39. Shinmura Taku 新村拓, *Nihon iryō shakaishi no kenkyū: Kodai chūsei no minshū seikatsu to iryō* 日本医療社会史の研究—古代中世の民衆生活と医療 (Tokyo: Hōsei Daigaku Shuppankyoku, 1985), 216.
40. William Wayne Farris, "Diseases of the Premodern Period in Japan," in *The Cambridge World History of Human Disease*, ed. Kenneth Kiple (Cambridge, UK: Cambridge University Press, 1993), 377.
41. Farris, "Diseases of the Premodern Period in Japan," 376.
42. Farris, "Diseases of the Premodern Period in Japan," 378.
43. Farris, "Diseases of the Premodern Period in Japan," 378.
44. Yui Suzuki, *Medicine Master Buddha: The Iconic Worship of Yakushi in Heian Japan* (Leiden, The Netherlands: Brill, 2012), 22–23
45. On Omizutori, see e.g., Hiraoka Jōkai 平岡定海, *Tōdaiji* 東大寺 (Tokyo: Kyōikusha, 1977), 217–242.
46. Nishio Masahito 西尾正仁, *Yakushi shinkō: Gokoku no hotoke kara onsen no hotoke e* 薬師信仰—護国の仏から温泉の仏へ (Tokyo: Iwata Shoin, 2000), 131.
47. Suzuki, *Medicine Master Buddha*, 24.
48. Nishio, *Yakushi shinkō*, 129–131.
49. Michael Como, "Onmyōji, the Earth God and Ghosts in Ancient Japan," *Cahiers d'Extrême-Asie* 21 (2012): 43–62; see also Michael Como, "Horses, Dragons, and Disease in Nara Japan," *Japanese Journal of Religious Studies* 34, no. 2 (2007): 393–415.
50. Neil McMullin, "On Placating the Gods and Pacifying the Populace: The Case of the Gion 'Goryō' Cult," *History of Religions* 27, no. 3 (1988): 273.
51. McMullin, "On Placating the Gods and Pacifying the Populace," 272.
52. Shinmura, *Nihon iryō shakaishi no kenkyū*, 222n3.
53. McMullin, "On Placating the Gods and Pacifying the Populace," 291–293.
54. Helen Hardacre, *Shinto: A History* (New York: Oxford University Press, 2017), 181.
55. Bernard Faure, *Gods of Medieval Japan, Volume 2: Protectors and Predators* (Honolulu: University of Hawaii Press, 2016), 324–327.
56. Como, "Horses, Dragons, and Disease in Nara Japan."
57. Sujung Kim, *Shinra Myōjin and Buddhist Networks of the East Asian "Mediterranean"* (Honolulu: University of Hawaii Press, 2019), 89–99.
58. William Wayne Farris, *Population, Disease, and Land in Early Japan, 645–900* (Cambridge, MA: Harvard University Press, 1985), 54.
59. Farris, "Diseases of the Premodern Period in Japan," 381.
60. Farris, "Diseases of the Premodern Period in Japan," 381.
61. Farris, "Diseases of the Premodern Period in Japan," 381.
62. On this apocryphal scripture, see Michel Strickmann, *Chinese Magical Medicine*, ed. Bernard Faure (Stanford, CA: Stanford University Press, 2002), 58–62.
63. Furuta Shōkin 古田紹欽, *Kissa yōjōki* 喫茶養生記 (Tokyo: Kōdansha, 1994), 204–205.
64. Strickmann, *Chinese Magical Medicine*, 198.
65. Strickmann, *Chinese Magical Medicine*, 197.
66. Strickmann, *Chinese Magical Medicine*; Edward L. Davis, *Society and the Supernatural in Song China* (Honolulu: University of Hawaii Press, 2001); see also Richard D. McBride, "Esoteric Buddhism and Its Relation to Healing and Demonology," in *Esoteric Buddhism and the Tantras in East Asia*, ed. Charles D. Orzech, Henrik Hjort Sørensen, and Richard Karl Payne (Leiden, The Netherlands: Brill, 2011), 208–214.

67. T. J. Hinrichs, "The Catchy Epidemic: Theorization and Its Limits in Han to Song Period Medicine," *East Asian Science, Technology and Medicine*, 41 (2015): 37n77.
68. Shinmura, *Nihon bukkyō no iryōshi*, 31.
69. Katja Triplett, *Buddhism and Medicine in Japan: A Topical Survey (500–1600 ce) of a Complex Relationship* (Berlin: De Gruyter, 2019), 180.
70. The following account relies heavily on the work of Hayami Tasuku, whose monograph provides the most comprehensive picture of the development of esoteric ritual in the Nara and Heian periods; see Hayami Tasuku 速水侑, *Heian kizoku shakai to Bukkyō* 平安貴族社会と仏教 (Tokyo: Yoshikawa Kōbunkan, 1975).
71. On the fire ceremony, see Richard K. Payne, *The Tantric Ritual of Japan: Feeding the Gods, the Shingon Fire Ritual* (New Delhi: International Academy of Indian Culture, 1991); and Robert H. Sharf, "Thinking through Shingon Ritual," *Journal of the International Association of Buddhist Studies* 26, no. 1 (2003): 51–96.
72. Richard K. Payne and Michael Witzel, eds., *Homa Variations: Ritual Change across the Longue Durée* (Oxford: Oxford University Press, 2015).
73. Hayami, *Heian kizoku shakai to Bukkyō*, 33–35.
74. Michel Foucault, *The Birth of Biopolitics: Lectures at the College de France, 1978–1979* (New York: Palgrave Macmillan, 2011).
75. Suzuki, *Medicine Master Buddha*, 103–123.
76. For example, see stories 3.12 ("On a Blind Man Whose Sight Was Restored Owing to His Chanting of the Name of Nichimanishu of the Thousand-Armed Kannon") and 3.34 ("On Gaining an Immediate Cure of a Bad Disease for Being Ordained and Practicing Good") in Nakamura, *Miraculous Stories from the Japanese Buddhist Tradition*, 237–238 and 270–271.
77. This information is found in fascicle 84 of the *Asabashō* 阿娑縛抄, attributed to Shōchō 承澄 (1205–1282); see Suzuki Gakujutsu Zaidan 鈴木学術財団, ed., *Dai Nihon bukkyō zensho* 大日本仏教全書 (1970–1973), 58:231–235.
78. Kinoshita Takeshi 木下武司, *Man'yō shokubutsu shi* 万葉植物文化誌 (Tokyo: Yasaka Shobō, 2010), 558–562.
79. On these topics, see Hayami Tasuku 速水侑, *Kannon shinkō* 観音信仰 (Tokyo: Yuzankaku, 2007), 303–323.
80. Bernard Faure, *Gods of Medieval Japan*.
81. Hayami, *Heian kizoku shakai to Bukkyō*, 89.
82. Hayami, *Heian kizoku shakai to Bukkyō*, 81.
83. Hayami, *Heian kizoku shakai to Bukkyō*, 82.
84. Bernard Faure, "The Buddhist Icon and the Modern Gaze," *Critical Inquiry* 24, no. 3 (1998): 768–813; and Elizabeth Horton Sharf and Robert H. Sharf, eds., *Living Images: Japanese Buddhist Icons in Context* (Stanford, CA: Stanford University Press, 2001).
85. Mimi Hall Yiengpruksawan, "The Visual Ideology of Buddhist Sculpture in the Late Heian Period as Configured by Epidemic and Disease," in *Bukkyō bijutsushi kenkyū ni okeru zuzō to yōshiki* (Tokyo: Kokusai Kōryū Bijutsushi Kenkyūkai, 1996), 69–79.
86. Yiengpruksawan, "The Visual Ideology of Buddhist Sculpture," 72.
87. Kasuya Makoto 加須屋誠, *Shōrōbyōshi no zuzōgaku: Bukkyō setsuwaga wo yomu* 生老病死の図像学—仏教説話画を読む (Tokyo: Chikuma Shobō, 2012); Kasuya Makoto and Yamamoto Satomi 山本聡美, eds., *Yamai no sōshi* 病草紙 (Tokyo: Chūō Kōron Bijutsu Shuppan, 2017); and Yamamoto Satomi, *Chūsei bukkyō kaiga no zuzōshi: Kyōsetsu emaki, rokudōe, kusōzu* 中世仏教絵画の図像誌: 経説絵巻・六道絵・九相図 (Tokyo: Yoshikawa Kōbunkan, 2020).
88. Benedetta Lomi, "Dharanis, Talismans, and Straw Dolls: Ritual Choreographies and Healing Strategies of the Rokujikyōhō in Medieval Japan," *Japanese Journal of Religious Studies* 41, no. 2 (2014): 255–304.

89. Andrew Macomber, "Ritualizing Moxibustion in the Early Medieval Tendai-Jimon Lineage," in Salguero and Macomber, *Buddhist Healing in Medieval China and Japan*, 194–242; see also the translation in Andrew Macomber, "Moxibustion for Demons: Oral Transmission on Corpse-Vector Disease," in Salguero, *Buddhism and Medicine*, 514–530.
90. Pamela D. Winfield, "Curing with Kaji: Healing and Esoteric Empowerment in Japan," *Japanese Journal of Religious Studies* 32, no. 1 (2005): 107–130.
91. Pamela D. Winfield, "Esoteric Ritual Remedies: Kūkai's Cures for Emperor Kōnin," in Salguero, *Buddhism and Medicine*, 222–225.
92. Anna Andreeva, "Empowering the Pregnancy Sash in Medieval Japan," in Salguero and Macomber, *Buddhist Healing in Medieval China and Japan*, 160–193; see also the translation in Anna Andreeva, "Childbirth in Early Medieval Japan: Ritual Economies and Medical Emergencies in *Procedures During the Day of the Royal Consort's Labor*," in Salguero, *Buddhism and Medicine*, 336–350.
93. Suzuki Gakujutsu Zaidan 鈴木学術財団 ed., *Dai Nihon bukkyō zensho, zuzōbu* 大日本仏教全書図像部 (1971), 58:17.
94. Iyanaga Nobumi 彌永信美, "Indo, Chūgoku, Nihon ni okeru hyōrei shinkō wo megutte: Zōmitsu bunken no sekai e no iriguchi toshite" インド、中国、日本における憑霊信仰をめぐって:雑密文献の世界への入り口として, *Nihon koshokyō kenkyūjo kenkyū kiyō* 日本古写経研究所研究紀要 4 (2019): 1–20.
95. Ueno Katsuyuki 上野勝之, *Yume to mononoke no seishinshi: Heian kizoku no shinkō sekai* 夢とモノノケの精神史—平安貴族の信仰世界 (Kyoto: Kyoto Daigaku Gakujutsu Shuppankai, 2013); and Sakō Nobuyuki 酒向伸行, *Hyōrei shinkō no rekishi to minzoku* 憑霊信仰の歴史と民俗 (Tokyo: Iwata Shoin, 2013).
96. Tokunaga Seiko 徳永誓子, "Shugendō seiritsu no shiteki zentei genza no tenkai" 修験道成立の史的前提—験者の展開, *Shirin* 史林 84, no.1 (2001): 96–123.
97. Koyama Satoko 小山聡子, *Mononoke no Nihonshi: Shiryō, yūrei, yōkai no sennnen* もののけの日本史: 死霊、幽霊、妖怪の1000年 (Tokyo: Chūō Kōronsha Shinsha, 2020), 79–104.
98. See e.g., Nancy J. Barnes, "Lady Rokujō's Ghost: Spirit Possession, Buddhism, and Healing in Japanese Literature," *Literature and Medicine* 8, no. 1 (1989): 106–121.
99. Ivan Morris, *The World of the Shining Prince* (London: Penguin, 1969), 149.
100. Strickmann, *Chinese Magical Medicine*, 228–281; and Carmen Blacker, *The Catalpa Bow: A Study of Shamanistic Practices in Japan* (London: Allen & Unwin, 1975).
101. See e.g., John Kieschnick, *The Impact of Buddhism on Chinese Material Culture* (Princeton, NJ: Princeton University Press, 2002); and Fabio Rambelli, *Buddhist Materiality: A Cultural History of Objects in Japanese Buddhism* (Stanford, CA: Stanford University Press, 2007).
102. Kenneth G. Zysk, *Asceticism and Healing in Ancient India: Medicine in the Buddhist Monastery* (New York: Oxford University Press, 1991).
103. Nathan Sivin, "Sun Simiao on Medical Ethics: 'The Perfect Integrity of the Great Physician' from *Prescriptions Worth a Thousand in Gold*," in Salguero, *Buddhism and Medicine*, 538–542.
104. Chen Ming 陳明, *Zhonggu yiliao yu wailai wenhua* 中古医醫療與外来文化 (Beijing: Peking University Press, 2013).
105. Hayami, *Heian kizoku shakai to Bukkyō*, 12; Ryūichi Abé, *The Weaving of Mantra: Kūkai and the Construction of Esoteric Buddhist Discourse* (New York: Columbia University Press, 1999), 58; and Winfield, "Curing with Kaji," 117–118.
106. Kosoto Hiroshi 小曽戸洋, *Chūgoku igaku koten to Nihon: Shoshi to denshō* 中国医学古典と日本—書誌と伝承 (Tokyo: Hanawa Shobō 塙書房, 1996), 189–190.
107. Shibata Shōji 柴田承二, ed., *Zusetsu Shōsōin yakubutsu* 図説正倉院薬物 (Tokyo: Chūō Kōronsha, 2000).

108. See, e.g., Edward H. Schafer, *The Golden Peaches of Samarkand: A Study of T'ang Exotic* (Berkeley: University of California Press, 1963).
109. On these studies, see Yoneda Kaisuke 米田該典, *Shōsōin no kōyaku: Zaishitsu chōsa kara hozon e* 正倉院の香薬: 材質調査から保存へ (Kyoto: Shibunkaku Shuppan, 2015).
110. Triplett, *Buddhism and Medicine in Japan*, 144.
111. Raoul Birnbaum, *The Healing Buddha* (Boulder, CO: Shambhala, 1979), 82–84.
112. Nara Kokuritsu Hakubutsukan 奈良国立博物館, *Shōsō'in ten: Dai 62 kai* 正倉院展—第62回 (Nara, Japan: Nara Kokuritsu Hakubutsukan, 2010), 38–39.
113. On grains and rice in esoteric ritual, see Steven Trenson, "Rice, Relics, and Jewels: The Network and Agency of Rice Grains in Medieval Japanese Esoteric Buddhism," *Japanese Journal of Religious Studies* 45, no. 2 (2018): 269–308.
114. Triplett, *Buddhism and Medicine in Japan*, 145–150; and Andrew Macomber, "Heian kōki ni okeru kōyaku no yoi: 'Kōyōshō' wo chūshin ni" 平安後期における香薬の酔い—『香要抄』を中心に, in *Yoi no bunkashi: Girei kara yamai made* 酔いの文化史—儀礼から病まで, *Ajia yūgaku* アジア遊学, no. 250 (2020), 72–92.
115. Goble, *Confluences of Medicine in Medieval Japan*, 48.
116. Kamikawa Michio 上川通夫, *Nihon chūsei bukkyō to higashi ajia sekai* 日本中世仏教と東アジア世界 (Tokyo: Hanawa Shobō 塙書房, 2012), 135–140.
117. Shinmura, *Nihon iryō shakaishi no kenkyū*, 246–248; and Koyama Satoko 小山聡子, *Shinran no shinkō to jujutsu: Byōki chiryō to rinjū gyōgi* 親鸞の信仰と呪術—病気治療と臨終行儀 (Tokyo: Yoshikawa Kōbunkan, 2013), 22–27.
118. Benedetta Lomi, "Ox Bezoars and the Materiality of Heian-Period Therapeutics," *Japanese Journal of Religious Studies* 45, no. 2 (2018): 228.
119. See also the translations in Benedetta Lomi, "The Ox-Bezoar Empowerment for Fertility and Safe Childbirth: Selected Readings from the Shingon Ritual Collections," in Salguero, *Buddhism and Medicine*, 351–357.
120. On medical dimensions of this work, see Drott, "Gods, Buddhas, and Organs."
121. Yoneda Mariko 米田真理子, "'Kissayōjōki' saidoku: Yōsai ni yoru shuchō no dokusōsei to sono keishō" 『喫茶養生記』再読—栄西による主張の独創性とその継承—, in *Hikaku shisō kara mita Nihon bukkyō* 比較思想から見た日本仏教, ed. Sueki Fumihiko 末木文美士 (Tokyo: Sankibō Busshorinkan, 2015), 55–71.
122. Iwama Machiko 岩間眞知子, *Cha no iyakushi: Chūgoku to Nihon* 茶の医薬史: 中国と日本 (Kyoto: Shibunkaku Shuppan 思文閣出版, 2009).
123. Hattori Toshirō 服部敏良, *Heian jidai igakushi no kenkyū* 平安時代医学の研究 (Tokyo: Kuwana Bunseidō, 1955).
124. Ilza Veith and Atsumi Minami, "A Buddhist Prayer against Sickness," *History of Religions* 5, no. 2 (1966): 239–249.
125. The digital archive of the collection can be accessed at "Fujikawa Bunko 富士川文庫".
126. For the work of Ueno, Koyama, and Yamamoto, see the sources mentioned throughout this article; for Oda and Shindō, see e.g., Shindō Hiroshi 進藤浩司, "Kajiwara Shōzen no igaku shinkō to iryō 梶原性全の医学: 信仰と医療," *Tōkai Bukkyō* 東海仏教 59 (2014): 31–46, and Oda Etsuyo 小田悦代, *Jubaku gohō abishahō: Setsuwa ni miru sō no genriki* 呪縛・護法・阿尾奢法—説話にみる僧の験力 (Tokyo: Iwata Shoin, 2016).
127. Hanawa Hokiichi 塙保己一, ed., *Zoku gunsho ruijū* 続群書類従 (rev. ed.), ed. Ōta Tōshirō, 33 vols. (Tokyo: Zoku Gunsho Ruijū Kanseikai, 1923–1928).
128. On the *Chōseiryōyōhō*, see Drott, "Gods, Buddhas, and Organs."
129. For a transcription and modern Japanese translation of the second edition of the work (*saijibon*, 1214), see Furuta, *Kissa yōjōki*. A translation of this second edition is in James A. Benn, *Tea in China:*

A Religious and Cultural History (Honolulu: University of Hawaii Press, 2016), 145–171. The first edition (*shojibon*, 1211) is translated in Hino Takuya, "The Harmonizing of the Multiple into a Single Flavor (*ichimiwagō* 一味和合) and Buddhist Botany: A Translation of the *Kissa Yōjōki*," *Journal of World Buddhist Cultures* 3 (2020): 62–97.

130. The Taishō canon can be accessed online at the SAT Daizōkyō Text Database.

Andrew Macomber

BUDDHISM AND PRINT CULTURE IN CHINA

BUDDHISM AND PRINT CULTURE IN CHINA: HISTORIOGRAPHIC CONSIDERATIONS

Chinese scholars during the last millennium of imperial times occasionally mentioned printing, largely drawing on official records of the government printing of the Confucian Classics from 932 onwards. Although some scattered references were made to printing in the previous century, almost no mention was made of Buddhist use of woodblock.[1] One premodern writer suggested an earlier date at the end of the 6th century on the basis of a misunderstood Buddhist reference, but this hypothesis did not command much support and his suggestion was definitively eliminated from consideration as a record of printing in the early 20th century.[2] The move toward opening any narrative of the development of Chinese printing with some consideration of its predominantly Buddhist origins depended on two new sources of information: printed Buddhist materials from the 9th century, and apparently earlier among the Dunhuang manuscripts, together with other archaeological finds retrieved from 1900 onward; and accounts of a large number of surviving printed Buddhist *dhāraṇī* in Japan, the production of which was datable by historical records to from around 770. The earliest of these archaeologically retrieved Chinese printed materials turned out to be items that were not designed to be read by human eyes and were of a type that were completely unknown to the transmitted record of Chinese history. The Japanese historical records are also extremely sparse and completely uninterested in the technology involved.

Two factors explain this situation. First, the history of printing technology excited very little interest among traditional scholars, certainly by comparison with the history of papermaking.[3] Second, traditional bibliographical records paid scant attention to Buddhist works. In principle, it seems, translated Buddhist scriptures had since the late 3rd century been listed separately from Chinese works, and from the late 4th century were always recorded within the catalogues devoted to the Buddhist canon. If any Buddhist scriptures appeared in regular library catalogues it was generally because of some special feature such as calligraphy executed by someone famous. Buddhist works composed in China did have a place in traditional Chinese bibliography alongside Daoist religious texts, but perhaps given the existence of catalogues compiled by clergy elsewhere, both were included or excluded in a somewhat haphazard fashion by "mainstream" secular cataloguers, as Japanese scholarship has demonstrated for at least one period.[4] Cumulatively, such a policy affected the recording and perhaps thereby the preservation of Buddhist materials not included in the canon. In any case the nature of the earliest phase of Buddhist printing left no trace in transmitted bibliographic records. This should occasion no surprise, as the earliest references to printed materials in transmitted Chinese sources concern calendars, which would not have been routinely preserved and catalogued by librarians.

BUDDHISM AND THE ORIGINS OF WOODBLOCK PRINTING

The evolution of woodblock printing from the creation of multiple images by means of seals is still a somewhat obscure process. Seals and like vehicles for stamping textual or representational patterns on soft materials such as clay were used by Buddhists in South Asia and beyond and in China by other religious practitioners. The notion of creating images by stamping them on paper first appeared in Daoist sources of about 600 CE, along with the notion of making images out of snow. Stamped buddha images on paper among the Dunhuang manuscripts may date back almost as far, but the earliest textual indication that Buddhists were interested in legitimating for themselves the practices adopted by their Daoist rivals is found in a work by the Chinese pilgrim Yijing 義淨 (635–713) completed in 692, which affirms that he saw the stamping of texts on paper and snowmen in India. He traveled by sea through the tropics, however, so the improbability of the latter assertion makes it probable that his observations, at least insofar as they alleged the use of stamped paper, were written with a polemical purpose.[5]

The earliest date assigned to a printed object from China bearing text—and also manuscript additions—according to the best evidence available in the early 21st century is a *dhāraṇī* recovered by archaeologists in the Xi'an area, which would seem to date to the second half of the 8th century, about the same time as Japanese materials from around 770 that are also *dhāraṇī*.[6] The Chinese example is one of a number of similar texts that were evidently incorporated into funerary procedures for their apotropaic qualities. Such forms of the Buddha's word, which were concentrated in power beyond the point of human intelligibility, promised especially generous benefits to the bearer in this world or the next. Their spiritual value was matched by their brevity, and it would have made sense to manufacture a quantity of these ready-made but customizable *dhāraṇī*. for funerary use. The fact that these printed words were never destined for human readers indicates the perils of attempting to understand Buddhist printing solely in light of the European experience. But the Japanese examples were manufactured and distributed (albeit not very widely) in huge numbers simultaneously, without any overt link to funerals.

Rather, the context indicates a distribution of *dhāraṇī* by a reigning empress in which they functioned as relics of the Buddha (all of Buddha's word possessed this status but again *dhāraṇī* had the advantage of portability combined with potency). The underlying model would then be the distribution of the Buddha's relics by Aśoka, a model also adopted explicitly in the 10th-century distribution of printed *dhāraṇī* by Qian Hongshu 錢弘俶 (929–988, r. 948–978), the king of the state of Wuyue 吳越.[7] Though the use of relics to legitimate imperial rule may be seen earlier in China, under the Sui dynasty and the reigning Empress Wu (r. 684–705), unlike these later cases there is no record at this point of a distribution of relics in textual form. A Chinese printed copy of the same *dhāraṇī* used in Japan, certainly early and perhaps dating to Wu's time, is listed in a Japanese library catalogue but has not been examined by scholars.[8] The possibility that the spread of printed *dhāraṇī* attested to China from the late 8th century may have been originally stimulated by the imperial use of printing technology at the start of the century cannot be proven, but, in light of Yijing's legitimation of printing by a suspect appeal to Indian precedent, it is not impossible.

By the middle of the 9th century printed, small *dhāraṇī* were joined by other forms of printed product. The catalogues of their acquisition by Japanese Buddhist monks who visited China during this period mention reference works such as dictionaries and the image of a tantric deity. Printed calendars are attested by both a textual reference and surviving fragments from Dunhuang, where a number of manuscript copies of reference works include colophons making it clear that they were transcribed from printed originals published in the capital.[9] This rather complicates the interpretation found in many secondary studies of a visiting official's account of printing in Sichuan in the late 9th century: although often construed as evidence for the novelty and hence primacy of printing in that area, the report might better be seen as a comment of the dominance in that region of a form of book production already known in Chang'an but limited there to a part of the book market.[10] It may well be that scribal culture in Sichuan had been affected by foreign invasion in the first half of the 9th century, encouraging a more prominent role for print. Scribal copying costs would have risen where scribes were in short supply, making the initial outlay on carving blocks more attractive. This would have eventually come into play more widely, especially after the dynasty collapsed into chaos, many books were destroyed, and many literate individuals capable of contributing to manuscript production were killed.

This is not to say that Sichuan printing did not influence the publication of Buddhist literature. Colophons from Dunhuang make it clear that in the 10th century a Sichuan edition of the *Diamond Sutra* served as a frequent model for manuscript transcription. It may even be that the famous printed *Diamond Sutra* of 868 from Dunhuang was created in Sichuan, but this is uncertain.[11] What is clear is that Buddhist scribal culture throughout most of China was likely affected by the closure of monasteries and mass laicization that took place in the great Huichang Persecution of 842–846. The 868 sutra ends with a colophon stating that the merit gained from its creation was to be transferred to the benefit of the deceased parents of a certain Wang Jie 王玠. The sutra was part of a multiple set of *Diamond Sutras* created for the same purpose. There are plenty of references to manuscripts of this and other works being copied out a thousand at a time, if not more, so when scribal costs increased due to the need to replace destroyed Buddhist texts Wang Jie was probably opting for something meritorious but not so financially burdensome. But even though the creation of the text was not linked to any stated desire on his part to read it or even put it to some other ritual use, somebody did so, for there is evidence that this book required repairing before it entered the Dunhuang archive.

Another oblique indication exists that restocking monastic libraries was perhaps a necessity after the Huichang Persecution and again late in the century as the Tang dynasty stumbled to its close in a rising tide of rebellion and destruction. A transmitted document known to Chinese scholarship since the 19th century mentions raising funds for a second printing of commentary on the *Vinaya*, apparently in 905 or shortly thereafter.[12] The *Vinaya* and study aids associated with it lie well beyond the karmic economy with which Wang Jie engaged, since they were strictly the business of monks, and limited manuscript circulation within their number would normally have sufficed, so the mention of two consecutive printed editions is a sure sign of some unusual circumstance.[13] Though it is not clear exactly what work of commentary was involved, it would have demanded many more woodblocks than were required for Wang's 868 enterprise, and the same is true for the first collection of Chinese Buddhist poetry to be published in Sichuan in 923.[14]

By contrast, at Dunhuang itself there is very little sign of printing on anything approaching such a large scale, although in 949 the *Diamond Sūtra* was produced locally with government support.[15] More typical of the locality was the production of single sheets, though not so much *dhāraṇī*, even if these continued to be widely manufactured for funerary purposes, as what have been termed "prayer sheets," which combine the depiction of a bodhisattva with an invocation beneath. Some of these latter sheets were also the result of the same government sponsorship, and finds of similar materials produced elsewhere in China at this time also stem from official patronage.[16] Royal patronage was important in the case of the *dhāraṇī* created for Qian Hongshu, and these also bear as a frontispiece illustrations that are much better integrated with the text than those attached to the 868 *Diamond Sūtra*. Qian's capital of Hangzhou was to remain an important place of publication of illustrated Buddhist texts into the 12th century.[17] But his promotion of Buddhist woodblock printing is insignificant next to of that of his eventual overlord, the Song emperor Taizong (r. 976–997). At some point between 984 and 991 the Song ruler sponsored the production of a still partially surviving Buddhist treatise of his own, complete with very finely wrought woodcut illustrations that provide a unique insight into the landscape art of the time.[18] This treatise formed one part of a massive series said to have been printed off some 130,000 blocks: the first edition of the entire Buddhist canon. At this time, the printing of the canon was based in the new imperial capital of Kaifeng, but it was originally started by Taizong's predecessor, the first Song emperor Taizu (r. 960–976) in Sichuan, where an edition of the printed Confucian Classics had already been created.

THE BUDDHIST CANON IN WOODBLOCK

Most historians of Chinese printing, in seeking the background to this colossal endeavor, look no further than the existing expertise in the large-scale creation of woodblocks already evident in Sichuan. But just as the prosperous yet militarily weak ruler Qian Hongshu found it expedient to stress his nonbelligerence in the face of powerful neighbors through his emulation of Aśoka, so too did Taizu have an urgent need to demonstrate in Sichuan in particular his own renunciation of brute force. Taizu's conquering army had exerted an unusual level of violence on the local population, and his generals, for example, had found it expedient to massacre 27,000 surrendered troops in cold blood.[19] No source exists to clarify the motivations for imperial sponsorship, but the dissemination of the Buddhist canon even in later times in East Asia might be seen as still playing the same role as Aśoka's distribution of the Buddha's relics.[20] By contrast, the Daoist Canon, which had no such role, was not edited until the early 11th century and was not printed until well over a century later.[21]

In China both the Buddhist canon and the Daoist canon had a long history in manuscript, with early records of their organization and description by means of comprehensive catalogues stretching back in the Buddhist case to the late 4th century. The reunification of China meant that such catalogues preserve for us precise, normative accounts of the official canon that would have been transcribed at imperial command. No doubt many monasteries that did not benefit from imperial largesse had to make shift with smaller collections, but even in 920 after the chaotic collapse of the Tang dynasty it was possible to find at least one private patron who could sponsor the production of fifteen manuscript copies of a corpus of literature that had swollen to over a thousand titles in over a thousand fascicles.[22] Taizu's canon is generally known as the Kaibao 開寶 canon, after the era name of its inception in 971.[23] But it is important to see that the long life of woodblocks, which kept the entire series in print for a century and a half, meant that a history of revisions and modifications changed somewhat the substance of the edition, even though some blocks may have been used without alteration.[24] It is also important to note that with the inception of these imperial productions Buddhist printing had moved far beyond the crabbed and crowded blocks first used for 8th-century grave goods and continued for commercial reasons by secular printers of the next century. Even the family prestige embodied in Wang Jie's more ample blocks with their added illustrations was surpassed by printing that was clearly designed to be seen and to impress, granted that the demonstration of imperial support for the dissemination of the Buddha's presence in the form of his words still remained more important than securing a wider readership for his scriptures. Additions to the canon during the 11th century in the form of newly translated texts, or works given canonical status by the government, were described by new catalogues, though not all of these have survived. Distribution took place not only within China, but also to the Koreans, Tangut, Vietnamese, Japanese, and Jurchen. The Khitan, chief rival power to the early Song, printed their own woodblock canon that drew on a different manuscript tradition twice, from around 987 on, and though these editions themselves are almost completely lost, they constituted an influence on the rock-cut canon of Fangshan 房山 and on Korean canon production.

The government's direct control over the canon only lasted until 1071, when the blocks, now carrying more than 1,500 different texts, were removed to a major Kaifeng monastery. The next stage in the evolution of the woodblock canon followed soon thereafter, when a monastery in Fujian created its own edition of the canon (*c.* 1080). A rival institution nearby then launched a third edition between 1112 and 1151. There was by this point scope for these private editions to replace the Kaibao original in the territory of the Southern Song, since its blocks were destroyed by the invading Jurchen in 1127; indeed, yet another fresh edition was created in Huzhou 湖州 in Zhejiang between 1126 and 1138. The Jurchen Jin dynasty in 1178 granted recognition to a canon produced by private efforts on their territory in the north, and the blocks of this edition survived the Mongol conquest in the next century and even saw some expansion in its contents. Meanwhile a final Southern Song edition, the Qisha 磧沙 canon, started in 1216 and lived on as a long-term printing project into Mongol times. It reached provisional completion in 1322 and was further developed, despite some losses, well into the Ming. Thus, up to the Mongol reunification the massive enterprise of producing a canon in Chinese had been repeated eight times in what is now China. A further edition had been created in Korea between 1011 and 1029 and was destroyed by the Mongols and replaced between 1236 and 1251. The blocks of this particularly carefully edited canon survive to this day.

Yet in the south of China the impact of the Mongol conquest on Buddhist publishing was not so negative: Hangzhou—Marco Polo's Qinsai—was the home of a new canon published between 1277 and 1290 by a group of lay Buddhists of a type that flourished under Mongol rule. The imperial family included many devout Buddhists, and it has been discovered that around 1332 to 1336 the regime sponsored a lavishly produced canon of its own, though it had little impact. It may, however, suggest that the production of the woodblock canon should have been the responsibility of the emperor, as it was originally. The Ming dynasty from 1399 to 1402 produced a canon in its capital of Nanjing, though the blocks were destroyed by fire by 1407. Undaunted, the Ming between 1413 to 1420 replaced it with a reorganized version of the lost canon. This new compilation was known as the Southern Canon, since after the shift of the Ming capital to Beijing a Northern Canon was produced to the best imperial standards between 1419 and 1440. Despite this ample imperial provision, the rise in Buddhist patronage spurred by the economic progress of the 16th century prompted the planning from 1589 onward of an independent canon designed along the lines of contemporary secular publications in rectangular volumes of folded-over sheets bound by thread. Hitherto the original scrolls pasted together from the block printed sheets of the Kaibao Canon had been replaced by sheets folded "concertina fashion" into longer, thinner rectangles between harder covers, but this format may have seemed somewhat conservative to the late Ming laity.

The vicissitudes of the 17th century certainly delayed progress on this "popular" Jiaxing 嘉興 edition, but even the Manchu conquest did not stop its eventual completion, and indeed the addition of a considerable quantity of supplementary material by 17th-century Buddhist authors, a process of expansion that continued into the 18th century. The tendency of Ming loyalists to enter the Buddhist clergy in the late 17th century perhaps made the Manchu rulers uneasy about the prospect of further volumes drawn from the writings of these erstwhile opponents. As rulers and religious patrons of extensive Buddhist domains beyond the Sinophone world, they soon turned to the production of new woodblock editions in other languages, from 1684 to 1692 and in 1737 in Tibetan and 1717 to 1720 in Mongol. In 1733 a sumptuous new but in form and content somewhat conservative Chinese canon decreed, which was completed in 1738.

By the 17th century however Japanese Buddhists had mastered the financial, organizational, and technical skills necessary for producing the canon in woodblock, and it was they who in the late 19th century pioneered the production of typeset editions. Attempts in China at emulating Japanese success in this field tended to fall short either by failing to achieve the same standards of accuracy or in failing to complete the printing of the very large mass of material involved, given that supplementary materials from China were added to Japanese collections in the 20th century. Photolithography and other facsimile printing techniques have however allowed for the republication of surviving versions of woodblock canons and typeset canons alike. The Zhonghua 中华 edition produced under government sponsorship in Beijing from 1982 onward endeavors to build on this capacity by further adding to a facsimile reprint of the Jin canon. This was supplemented by other facsimile resources: an apparatus of collation notes that draw on a far greater range of evidence than was available to the editors of the most thorough Japanese typeset canon, who worked before the recovery of both the Jin and Qisha canons. But these notes do not seem to have achieved the highest editorial standards.[25] The digitization of the Japanese canon in Taiwan and elsewhere does however offer some scope for the further future consolidation of this vast textual heritage.[26]

THE PUBLISHING OF EXTRACANONICAL BUDDHIST LITERATURE

Indexed modern catalogues of the Chinese Buddhist canons just described cover almost 4,700 titles, though these span some of the 20th-century Japanese editions whose criteria for inclusion were sometimes rather more generous than was traditionally the case in China.

Japanese editions also printed for the first time some texts newly discovered in manuscript at Dunhuang and elsewhere. Traditional Buddhist woodblock canons in Chinese, even including printed supplementary sections, did not far exceed some two thousand titles and generally contained a core of not much more than 1,500 to 1,600. Inclusion in the canon was originally a matter for the imperial authorities, and as in the time of manuscripts some texts could be deliberately excluded. A case in point would be the celebrated *Platform Sūtra* of Huineng, which does not appear in any surviving Song period canon, even though it may have been printed in supplementary series and was only allowed into the main canon during the Ming. By this time an associated work, the *Baolin zhuan* 寶林傳, which had been excluded by all but the Jin canon, had otherwise entirely disappeared in China. The surviving Jin canon edition is only partial, leaving this source as we know it incomplete, even with the help of a further fragment in a Japanese manuscript.[27] Certainly a work might be banned from every woodblock printed canon and yet survive if it was used in everyday ritual contexts that ensured its constant reproduction. The best example of this is *The Scripture on the Ten Kings*, a guide to the torments in store for the wicked in the afterlife that was eventually included in a 20th-century Japanese canon on the basis of a 15th-century Korean print. But such texts were limited in number, and less liturgically important works were much more vulnerable to loss.[28] In general the writings of the Chan tradition in China seem to have been regarded, at least until the Ming, as existing in a separate, noncanonical category, apart from those works of commentary exposition that also circulated outside the canon. Thus, although it is possible to find in modern scholarship examples of studies of the transmission of works from other Chinese Buddhist traditions, Japanese academics affiliated with the Zen school made a particular effort in the 20th century to account for the transmission of their sources, and their results have in some limited cases become known in English.

The findings of this research underline the consequences of exclusion from the canon. A census of surviving Chan texts printed in the Song and Yuan dynasties runs to 135 items; by contrast the number of titles mentioned that do not survive runs to a total of one 179—and this may not be a definitive list.[29] Of the lost titles, only fourteen were ever recorded in any early library catalogue or similar record; the vast majority are only known from references in biographical materials or other nonbibliographical works. One can only conclude that outside the canon a considerable literature existed during this period that entirely escaped bibliographical control. Matters do not seem to have improved in later times. While the Jiaxing canon contains in its supplement about seventy Chan texts in the "Recorded Sayings" (*yulu*) genre that were published during the sixty-year reign of the Kangxi 康熙 emperor (1661–1722) out of its total of about two hundred, the early 20th-century Beijing bookseller Sun Dianqi (1894–1958) noted about one hundred from this period that passed through his hands, of which only about a quarter were identified as having been printed by the publishers of the canon.[30] This again suggests a broader Chan textual production than any conventional bibliography ever hints at. And this literature, at least, did not come into the category of merely ephemeral, popular publication: Chan masters were respected figures who were often considerable poets. By contrast no one felt obliged to mention any example of the sort of single-sheet productions found at Dunhuang, though in Tibet, at least, similar items, which we must surmise were based on Chinese models, seem to have been regularly printed over a span of a thousand years.[31] This apparent drastic undercounting of

Buddhist publications in the secular records hitherto used by book historians poses at least two important questions for the future.

First, it becomes much more difficult to assess the apparent burgeoning of Buddhist publishing in the 20th century. The difficulties that Chinese Buddhists experienced in trying to emulate the modern Japanese compilation of entire canons evidently did not affect less complex ventures. Recent research has on the contrary established that the religious press, and the Buddhist press in particular, built up from impressive beginnings based on revived woodblock publication in the late 19th century to exploit more modern technologies to the full in the Republican era, with dramatic results. One extracanonical Buddhist collection, the writings of Zhou Anshi 周安士 (1656–1739), is said to have sold three million copies during that period, for example.[32] Even the Jinling Scriptural Press, which led the way with its woodblock editions from before the 1911 Revolution, and sustained after 1949 a certain level of permitted publication as a repository of traditional printing skills, is said by the 1980s to have issued more than 200 titles, putting a cumulative total of 800,000 copies of Buddhist works into print.[33] Early 21st-century researchers know much about the organization of Buddhist publishing before 1949.[34] But its historical background remains unclear. Was this a new market, or an old market reached by new technological means? As for Yang Wenhui 楊文會 (1837–1911), the founder of the Jinling Scriptural Press, was his success due to the exploitation of new religious forces or on a restocking of earlier library holdings lost in the indubitably destructive Taiping Rebellion of the mid-19th century? Sun Dianqi's notes suggest a rapid falling off in the production of "Recorded Sayings" after the early 18th century, but this decline may have been specific to that genre, and on less literary materials such as liturgical manuals, for example, he makes no observations at all, though these were certainly produced in new editions in the 19th century. The inclusion of liturgical manuals of any sort in library or other catalogues at any stage of Chinese history seems to have been a particularly problematic and somewhat random process.[35]

ISSUES OF COMPARISON

The problem of the underreporting of Buddhist publications stretches much back further. There is therefore a second question to be addressed that is far from inconsequential. Writers of the broader history of the book, given what we know of the temporal primacy of Chinese printing, even supposing this was not indirectly the ancestor of Gutenberg's invention, have perforce been obliged to take Chinese book production into account in assessing weightier matters such as the comparative availability of readily circulated knowledge in China and the West as a factor in economic development. Early attempts at quantitative comparison were clearly dogged by misunderstandings that gave an exaggerated picture of traditional Chinese book production, including the period of particular interest between the age of Gutenberg and the arrival of new technologies in the 19th century.[36] But the greater availability in English of pioneering accounts of Chinese book history has furnished comparativists with examples of quantitative data that are not well understood.

Counting early modern books is not easy, but those who have done so tend to assume that ratios of known, surviving publications to unknown, lost publications remain constant across cultures, something that has apparently not actually been demonstrated and that plainly depends on identical book collection and recording practices.[37] Traditional book collectors in

China rarely make explicit their criteria for preserving books, but when they did make their criteria explicit then, in at least one instance, it is carefully explained that Buddha's word as embodied in scriptures, which played a key religious role and even in manuscript times were produced in batches of thousands, remained beyond the purview of the cataloguer. How much extracanonical Buddhist material was collected and recorded seems to have depended not on any desire for comprehensiveness, but rather on personal inclination.[38] In the case of many, and probably the majority, of scholarly cataloguers, who tended to be of a neo-Confucian disposition, that inclination, possibly quite unlike the attitudes of the majority of book users, was strongly hostile to Buddhist writings. Modern Chinese bibliographic practice, the ultimate source of information in English used by comparativists, is scarcely better as a starting point for comparison. One apparently extremely thorough census of surviving Ming editions in the People's Republic of China lists the Buddhist canon only once, as a single title, yet it has been noted that it ran to over 1,500 separate works issued over a span of time and published in more than one edition under the Ming dynasty.[39] Its index, for that matter, somewhat improbably lists only four printings of the *Lotus Sūtra* during the Ming; as we shall see, in this case it is possible to find an exemplar from one more edition very easily in London, and in all probability many more editions were produced in monasteries across the land. At present, perhaps, any attempt at comparison might be advised to ignore all European religious literature in comparisons with the Chinese case.

But at least some insight is available into extracanonical Buddhist printing after the Ming and before the onset of new imported technologies. Art historians have identified a number of lavishly illustrated and individually printed texts designed to enhance the prestige of wealthy and often imperially connected patrons, for example.[40] More prosaically, one or two compilations of stories about the workings of Pure Land devotion or of karma are included in series generally designed to provide reading materials for the amusement of the literate, suggesting that Buddhism was not purely a matter for the clergy and their self-declared adherents.[41] Some religious texts deemed heterodox by the authorities, and so suppressed, have for this very reason been much studied by modern scholarship, with the result that a more objective assessment of their validity tends now to accept them as expressions of lay Buddhism that simply failed to win the approval of the elite.[42] In fact some elements from this tradition remain important in local lay ritual performance to this day.[43] Christian missionary book collectors, less discriminating than their learned Chinese contemporaries, but anxious to understand the religious environment that they sought to penetrate, seem to have preserved editions of Buddhist works that might otherwise have been lost, and sometimes afford a valuable glimpse of local, often monastery-based printing, including for instance an exemplar of the fifth Ming *Lotus Sūtra* edition in the earliest missionary-created collection.[44]

Much future work, therefore, will have to done by local researchers in China, since quotidian Buddhist publishing, especially when carried out to serve immediate ritual purposes, appears to have been rather decentralized, unlike the better-known publishing industry that catered to a narrower, more highly educated market. Woodblock printing technology, after all, though it depends on skilled labor, uses no complex machinery and can be carried out anywhere there is room to store blocks, something that was not normally a problem in a traditional Buddhist monastery. Research conducted during Republican times discovered that at least one major monastery that had lost its printing blocks in the Taiping Rebellion was still entirely self-sufficient in printing from woodblock all the basic manuals and disciplinary works that its monks needed; beyond the path of the Taiping armies, yet more substantial woodblock publishing facilities could also be found.[45]

Contemporary Buddhist publishing, by contrast, is better understood within the larger media landscape of a digital age. For decades Chinese Buddhists have been exploiting advances such as the phonograph and the radio.[46] Now the entire Chinese Buddhist canon, as well as many extra-canonical works, are available on the internet. The many issues raised by the long history of Buddhism and printing in China will, one trusts, continue to attract scholarly attention.

REVIEW OF LITERATURE

Buddhism in its relation to print culture is not a category of research in the study of China, either within the history of the book or the history of Buddhism. No overall monograph has been devoted to the topic as such, though some studies of aspects of printing related to Buddhism have appeared. The overall picture is thus uneven, and in some parts is very sketchy. General treatments of the history of the book mention early Buddhist use of woodblock and the creation of the various woodblock canons, whereas histories of Chinese Buddhism tend to mention only the latter. Twentieth-century religious publishing has only recently attracted attention, but scholarship appears to be making rapid progress. The standard work covering the history of paper and printing from the point of view of the history of technology by Tsien naturally touches on Buddhism, but the interpretation of the early evidence in relation to religious ideas has been developed subsequently by T. H. Barrett.[47] On the Canon, the volumes by Jiang Wu and his collaborators, especially the first, have built usefully on the work of Chinese scholars, but for a full account to 2008 of all the scholarship on various aspects of the Buddhist canon, including those based on Chinese texts, the bibliography of Sueki is indispensable.[48] Modern Chinese Buddhist publishing is well-served among other contributions by the work of Gregory Adam Scott, with his Oxford Bibliography entry for the period 1900–1950 a good place to start.[49] Snippets of information about extracanonical Buddhist publishing in imperial China are scattered throughout recent writings on the history of the book, for which the bibliographical essay in the volume edited by Joseph P. McDermott and Peter Burke provides a convenient survey, with a relevant paragraph in its chapter by Cynthia Brokaw, but the history of this quite diverse phenomenon still remains to be written.[50]

PRIMARY SOURCES

The entire corpus of texts included in premodern and modern Buddhist canons is approaching complete digitization by the Chinese Buddhist Electronic Text Association's project based in Taiwan, while other similar projects have also made lesser quantities of material available in the same way.[51] But digitized text tends to obscure important paratextual features of the original works, such as cartouches containing dedications to the emperor. Information from this large body of primary sources needs to be integrated with information from a wide variety of other sources spread over more than a thousand years of history and ranging from casual remarks in anecdotal writing to recent bookseller's catalogues.

FURTHER READING

Barrett, T. H. *From Religious Ideology to Political Expediency in Early Printing: An Aspect of Buddho-Daoist Rivalry*. London: Minnow Press, 2012.

Barrett, T. H. *The Woman Who Discovered Printing*. New Haven: Yale University Press, 2008.

Clart, Philip, and Gregory Adam Scott, eds. *Religious Publishing and Print Culture in Modern China, 1800–2012*. Boston: Walter de Gruyter, 2015.

Katz, Paul R. *Religion in China and Its Modern Fate*. Waltham, MA: Brandeis University Press, 2014.

Kiely, Jan, and J. Brooks Jessup. *Recovering Buddhism in Modern China*. New York: Columbia University Press, 2016.

McDermott, Joseph P., and Peter Burke. *The Book Worlds of East Asia and Europe, 1450–1850: Connections and Comparisons*. Hong Kong: Hong Kong University Press, 2015.

Sueki, Yasuhiro. *Bibliographical Sources for Buddhist Studies from the Viewpoint of Buddhist Philology*. 2nd ed. Tokyo: International Institute for Buddhist Studies, 2008.

Tsien Tsuen-hsuin. *Chemistry and Chemical Technology*. Vol. 5, *Science and Civilisation in China*. Cambridge, U.K.: Cambridge University Press, 1985.

Wu, Jiang, and Lucille Chia, *Spreading Buddha's Word in East Asia: The Formation and Transformation of the Chinese Buddhist Canon* (New York: Columbia University Press, 2016.

Wu, Jiang, and Greg Wilkinson, *Reinventing the Tripitaka: Transformation of the Buddhist Canon in Modern East Asia*. Lanham, MD: Lexington Books, 2017.

NOTES

1. The following account relies on standard works such as Paul Pelliot, *Les débuts de l'imprimerie en Chine* (Paris: Imprimerie Nationale, 1953); and Thomas Francis Carter, *The Invention of Printing in China and its Spread Westward*, rev. L. Carrington Goodrich, 2nd ed. (New York: Ronald Press Company, 1955), for accounts of the traditional historiography of Chinese printing.
2. Carter, *Invention of Printing in China*, 44–45.
3. T. H. Barrett, "The Woman Who Invented Notepaper: Towards a Comparative Historiography of Paper and Print," *Journal of the Royal Asiatic Society*, 3rd ser., 21, no. 2 (2011): 199–210; Jean-Pierre Drège, *Le papier dans la Chine impériale: Origine, fabrication, usages* (Paris: Les Belles Lettres, 2017)—this work constitutes a magisterial collection of translated sources on the history of paper with a lengthy introduction.
4. Timothy H. Barrett, "Ritual in the Library, With Special Reference to Taoism," in *Foundations of Daoist Ritual: A Berlin Symposium*, ed. Florian Reiter (Wiesbaden: Harrassowitz, 2009), 21–22, draws on the work of Aitani Yoshimitsu 合谷佳光 in describing the "perfunctory" treatment of Buddhist works in catalogues of the early Song dynasty.
5. The narrative here and below on early Buddhist printing generally follows T. H. Barrett, *The Woman Who Discovered Printing* (New Haven, CT: Yale University Press, 2008), unless otherwise specified.
6. Paul Copp, *The Body Incantatory: Spells and the Ritual Imagination in Medieval Chinese Buddhism* (New York: Columbia University Press, 2014),235, item 12.
7. John Rosenfield, "Notes on the *Jewel Casket Sutra* in Japan," in *China and Beyond in the Medieval Period: Cultural Crossings and Inter-Regional Connections*, ed. Dorothy C. Wong and Gustav Heldt (New Delhi: Manohar Publishers, 2014), 387–402; Shi Zhenru, "From Bodily Relic to Dharma Relic Stūpa: Chinese Materialisation of the Aśoka Legend in the Wuyue Period," in *India in the Chinese Imagination: Myth, Religion, and Thought*, ed. John Kieschnick and Meir Shahar (Philadelphia: University of Pennsylvania Press, 2014), 85–109.
8. See Peter Kornicki, "The *Hyakumantō darani* and the Origins of Printing in Eighth-Century Japan," *International Journal of Asian Studies* 9 (2012): 50n41.

9. T. H. Barrett, "Transcribed Printer's Colophons at Dunhuang as Evidence for Early Printing," *Journal of Inner Asian Art and Archaeology* 6 (2015): 149–153.
10. Translated in Carter, *Invention of Printing*, 60.
11. Frances Wood and Mark Barnard, *The Diamond Sutra: The Story of the World's Earliest Dated Printed Book* (London: The British Library, 2010), 67, mention Sichuan printing but do not suggest any connection with the 868 scripture.
12. The document has been dated earlier, but see T. H. Barrett, *From Religious Ideology to Political Expediency in Early Printing: An Aspect of Buddho-Daoist Rivalry* (London: Minnow Press, 2012), 78–82.
13. For earlier Buddhist qualms about circulating the *Vinaya* even in manuscript, see Antonello Palumbo, *An Early Chinese Commentary on the Ekottarika-āgama* (Taipei: Dharma Drum Publishing, 2013), 195–204.
14. Barrett, *From Religious Ideology to Political Expediency*, 107–108.
15. See Rong Xinjiang, "Official Life at Dunhuang in the Tenth Century," in *The Silk Road: Trade, Travel, War and Faith*, ed. Susan Whitfield (London: British Library, 2004), 62.
16. See Katherine R. Tsiang, "Buddhist Images and Texts of the Eighth–Tenth Centuries: Typologies of Replication and Representation," in *Esoteric Buddhism at Dunhuang: Rites and Teachings for This Life and Beyond*, ed. Matthew T. Kapstein and Sam van Schaik (Leiden: Brill, 2010), 214–220.
17. Shih-shan Susan Huang, "Early Buddhist Illustrated Prints in Hangzhou," in *Knowledge and Text Production in an Age of Print: China, 900–1400*, ed. Lucille Chia and Hilda De Weerdt (Leiden: Brill, 2011), 135–165.
18. Max Loehr, *Chinese Landscape Woodcuts from an Imperial Commentary to the Tenth-Century Printed Canon* (Cambridge, MA: Belknap Press, 1968).
19. Peter Lorge, "From Warlord to Emperor: Song Taizu's Change of Heart during the Conquest of Shu," *T'oung Pao*, 2nd ser., 91, fasc. 4/5 (2005): 320–346.
20. Compare the discussion in Sem Vermeesch, *The Power of the Buddhas: The Politics of Buddhism During the Koryŏ Dynasty (918–1392)* (Cambridge, MA: Harvard University Press, 2008), 355–360.
21. Piet van der Loon, *Taoist Books in the Libraries of the Sung Period* (London: Ithaca Press, 1984), 29–45.
22. See Barrett, *From Religious Ideology to Political Expediency*, 82–83, where it is pointed out that this patron also had violent crimes to expiate.
23. Unless otherwise indicated, the description of the editions of the woodblock canon, unless otherwise indicated, follows Jiang Wu and Lucille Chia, *Spreading Buddha's Word in East Asia: The Formation and Transformation of the Chinese Buddhist Canon* (New York: Columbia University Press, 2016), especially Appendix 1 on pp. 311–320, which concisely summarizes what is known on this topic.
24. This seems to have been Max Loehr's position, but see Wu and Chia, *Spreading Buddha's Word*, 160–161.
25. Stefano Zacchetti, *In Praise of the Light: A Critical Synoptic Edition with an Annotated Translation of Chapters 1–3 of Dharmarakṣa's Guang zan jing 光讃經, Being the Earliest Chinese Translation of the Larger Prajñāpāramitā* (Tokyo: International Research Institute for Advanced Buddhology, Soka University, 2005), 75; Florin Deleanu, *The Chapter on the Mundane Path (Laukikamārga) in the Śrāvakabhūmi* (Tokyo: International Institute for Buddhist Studies, 2006), 132.
26. Though the work of Jiang and Chia does touch on some modern developments, it is advisable to consult Jiang Wu and Greg Wilkinson, *Reinventing the Tripitaka: Transformation of the Buddhist Canon in Modern East Asia* (Lanham, MD: Lexington Books, 2017).
27. Philip Yampolsky, *The Platform Sutra of the Sixth Patriarch: The Text of the Tun-huang Manuscript* (New York: Columbia University Press, 1967), 47n165, 52, 106.
28. Stephen F. Teiser, *The Scripture on the Ten Kings and the Making of Purgatory in Medieval Chinese Buddhism* (Honolulu: University of Hawaii Press, 1994), 83, 94, 162.
29. Shiina Kōyū 椎名宏雄, *SōGen-ban Zenseki no kenkyū* 宋元禅籍の研究 (Tokyo: Daito shuppansha, 1993), 539–635, which perhaps does not account for all the titles given in surviving Yuan period literary works, as indexed in the late 20th century.

30. These totals are based on a rough count of Sun Dianqi 孫殿起, *Fanshu Ouji* 販書偶記 (Beijing: Zhonghua shuju, 1982), 303–308, and *Fanshu Ouji xubian* 販書偶記續編 (Beijing: Zhonghua shuju, 1980), 193–196.
31. T. H. Barrett, "Pattern Reproduction Possibilities and the Alpha and Omega of Tibetan Printing," in *Tibetan Printing: Comparison, Continuities and Change*, ed. Hildegard Diemberger, Franz-Karl Erhard, and Peter Kornicki (Leiden: Brill, 2016), 560–574.
32. Paul R. Katz, *Religion in China and Its Modern Fate* (Waltham, MA: Brandeis University Press, 2014), 126.
33. See Xiao Dongfa, "Categories, Features and Social Background of the Existing Woodblocks for Printing in China," in *The History and Cultural Heritage of Chinese Calligraphy, Printing and Library Work*, ed. Susan M. Allen, Lin Zuzao, Cheng Xiaolan and Jan Bos (Berlin: De Gruyter, 2010), 80.
34. Note, in addition to Katz, *Religion in China*, the studies collected in Philip Clart and Gregory Adam Scott, eds., *Religious Publishing and Print Culture in Modern China, 1800–2012* (Boston: Walter de Gruyter, 2015), esp. chap. 3; and Jan Kiely and J. Brooks Jessup, *Recovering Buddhism in Modern China* (New York: Columbia University Press, 2016), esp. chap. 3.
35. Barrett, "Ritual in the Library," though concerned with Daoism, describes a situation that also applied to Buddhism.
36. See Endymion Wilkinson, *Chinese History: A New Manual*, 4th ed. (Cambridge MA: Harvard University Press, 2015), 933–936.
37. See for example, E. Buring and J. L. van Zanden, "Charting the 'Rise of the West': Manuscripts and Printed Books in Europe, a Long-Term Perspective from the Sixth through Eighteenth Centuries," *Journal of Economic History* 69, no. 2 (2009), 437; the problem recurs in J. L. van Zanden, *The Long Road to the Industrial Revolution: The European Economy in a Global Perspective, 1000–1800* (Leiden: Brill, 2009), 188. The task of separating out the small segment of the market in China that catered to literati book collectors and then comparing the printing of religious literature in East and West lies as yet in the future.
38. Chao Gongwu 晁公武, *Junzhai dushu zhi* 郡齋讀書志 16, ed. ed. Sun Meng 孫猛 (Shanghai: Shanghai guji chubanshe, 1990), 769. For Chao's work, see Ssu-yü Teng and Knight Biggerstaff, *An Annotated Bibliography of Selected Chinese Reference Works*, 3rd ed. (Cambridge, MA: Harvard University Press, 1971), 15–16.
39. Du Xinfu 杜信孚 and Du Tongfu 杜同書, *Quan Ming fen sheng fen xian ke shu kao* 全明分省分县刻書考 (Beijing: Xianzhuang shuju, 2001), esp. Zongshi 宗室 (Imperial clan) section. This seems to be the only place where the canon, printed several times in the Ming and represented by a number of surviving copies, is mentioned. The first page of the Beijing section likewise lists the Daoist Canon as a single title and the comparative study cited draws indirectly on an earlier and yet more restricted catalogue by Du Xinfu.
40. Craig Clunas and Jessica Harrison-Hall, *Ming: 50 Years that Changed China* (London: British Museum Press, 2014), 214–219.
41. Namely *Nianfo sanmei* 念佛三昧 and *Fojie* 佛解, in *Tanji congshu* 檀几叢書 (1695), *Mingbao lu* 冥報錄, *Xianguo suilu* 現果随錄, *Guobao wenjian lu* 果報聞見錄, in *Shuo ling* 説鈴 (1702 and later editions).
42. Barend J. ter Haar, *Practicing Scripture: A Lay Buddhist Movement in Late Imperial China* (Honolulu: University of Hawaii Press, 2014), argues this case.
43. Stephen Jones, *In Search of the Folk Daoists of North China* (Farnham, U.K.: Ashgate, 2010), 237–261.
44. Andrew C. West, *Catalogue of the Morrison Collection of Chinese Books* (London: School of Oriental and African Studies, 1998), 169–206; note the *Lotus Sūtra* listed on the first of these pages.
45. Johannes Prip-Møller, *Chinese Buddhist Monasteries: Their Plan and Its Function as a Setting for Buddhist Monastic Life* (1937; repr., Hong Kong: Hong Kong University Press, 1967), 52–53, 227–229.
46. Francesca Tarocco, *The Cultural Practices of Modern Chinese Buddhism: Attuning the Dharma* (Abingdon, U.K.: Routledge, 2007), 128–130.

47. Tsien Tsuen-hsuin, *Science and Civilisation in China* (Cambridge, U.K.: Cambridge University Press, 1985).
48. Yasuhiro Sueki, *Bibliographical Sources for Buddhist Studies from the Viewpoint of Buddhist Philology*, 2nd ed. (Tokyo: International Institute for Buddhist Studies, 2008.)
49. Gregory Adam Scott, "Chinese Buddhist Publishing and Print Culture, 1900–1950,"*Oxford Bibliographies.*
50. Joseph P. McDermott and Peter Burke, *The Book Worlds of East Asia and Europe, 1450–1850, Connections and* Comparisons (Hong Kong: Hong Kong University Press, 2015), 192, 327–333.
51. Wu and Chia, *Spreading Buddha's Word in East Asia*, 321–335.

T. H. Barrett

BUDDHISM AND SHINTO

INTRODUCTION

Since its arrival in Japan, Buddhism has interacted in several ways with native cults and beliefs, commonly known today as Shinto. According to received understanding, Shinto (literally, "the way of the [Japanese] gods") is the autochthonous religious tradition of Japan, whose origins date back to the beginning of the Japanese civilization, possibly around the 2nd–4th centuries CE if not even earlier. Its main features are an animistic belief in the sanctity of nature, shamanic practices, ancestor cults, respect for authority and communal value, and a strong capacity to integrate and homogenize foreign elements. Within this received understanding, the history of Japanese Buddhism is as a gradual process of "Japanization," that is, of integration within Shinto beliefs and attitudes. This understanding, however, still broadly circulating in Japan and abroad in textbooks and popular media, has been questioned radically by scholarship in the past few decades, especially in the seminal work by Kuroda Toshio (1926–1991), which has resulted in a very different characterization of Shinto and its relations with Buddhism.

The term *shintō* itself only appears sporadically in ancient texts, and its meaning is still not entirely clear; most likely, it designated not the indigenous religion of Japan but simply local deities in general (as opposed to Buddhism); the pronunciation of the two Chinese characters forming the term (in present-day, *shin* and *tō*) may have been different. In fact, some scholars prefer not to use the term "Shinto" to refer to religious phenomena prior to the 16th century.

Until approximately 150 years ago, Shinto was deeply connected to Japanese Buddhism: Buddhist authors were the first to write doctrines about the Japanese local gods or kami, and most shrines dedicated to the kami used to belong to Buddhist temples or were in fact Buddhist temples themselves dedicated to the kami. This situation of symbiosis was dramatically interrupted in 1868 when the government decided to "separate" Shinto from Buddhism (*shinbutsu bunri*), an operation that resulted in the creation of two separate religions.

Shinto worships spirit-gods called kami (also addressed with honorific forms such as *mikoto, shinmei, myōjin, gongen*, etc.), a wide category of sacred entities that includes natural objects (mountains, waterfalls, stones, the sea, stars), anthropomorphic deities whose deeds are described in myths recorded in the earliest books ever written in Japan, such as *Kojiki*

(712), *Nihon shoki* (720),[1] *Fudoki* and *Man'yōshū* (both mid-8th century) (several of these gods are related to the imperial family, especially the highest deity of the entire pantheon, sun goddess Amaterasu Ōmikami), cultural heroes (warriors, emperors, model citizens, etc.), clan divinities (more or less related to imperial deities through myths and legends), local spirits (often without a name and a clearly defined shape), and even imported deities (from India, Korea, and China).

Today, Shinto is a multiple and diverse tradition, which includes four categories: imperial cults, cults taking place at shrines (*jinja*), folk beliefs, and teachings of several sect organizations. However, it is not clear how these four types of Shinto relate to each other. Imperial cults were codified in laws dating to the 8th century, and further defined in the 10th century. Cults at specific sites, at least in some cases, may originate in an even earlier time, but the earliest permanent buildings dedicated to the kami date from the 8th century. Folk traditions are obviously difficult to date, but many beliefs and festivals existing today in Japan began between the 16th and 18th centuries. In contrast, sectarian Shinto is a relatively recent development from around the mid-19th century, with the formation of new religious organizations that were more or less loosely connected with preexisting teachings about the kami.

Even though today Shinto is considered an independent religious tradition, separate and distinct from Buddhism, this was by no means the situation in premodern times.

HISTORICAL BACKGROUND

The word we read today as *shintō* was, for much of its history, a generic term referring to local deities, either in a Chinese religious context (in which case it was pronounced *shindō*) or in a Buddhist perspective (most likely read *jindō*). In terms of discourses (including histories) about teachings, beliefs, and practices related to the Kami, it is important to distinguish between these two usages. The reading *shintō* seems to have emerged around the 15th century to distinguish discourses about the classical Japanese Kami based on the *Nihon shoki* and other texts from other teachings about deities (either Chinese or Indian).[2] Furthermore, classical and medieval sources tend to distinguish between *jingi* (the Kami worshiped at court) and *jindō/shindō/shintō* (Kami cults based on specific shrine-temples); some sources even add a third category, that of "evil" or heterodox spirits/gods (variously called *jashin, jisshashin, akuryō, shiryō*, etc.), which seem to be related to folk practices and are somehow distinct from the previous two categories.[3]

In any case, Shinto did not designate an established system of religious institutions and their beliefs and rituals until relatively recently. Shinto as an autonomous discourse about the Kami begins with courtier and priest Yoshida Kanetomo (1435–1511). He divided the teachings about the Kami into three groups: one centered on Ise and based on Shingon esoteric Buddhism; one shared by all other shrines and temples in the realm, which was essentially a Buddhist construct that saw the Kami as local and temporal manifestations of buddhas and bodhisattvas; and the Yoshida family's own teachings, which Kanetomo advertised as original and pristine.[4] At the time in which it was formulated, this idea was little more than a marketing strategy to promote the ritual services of the Yoshida House; most shrine-temples in the land had no sense that they were sharing the same discourse about the Kami, and imagery related to the Ise shrines (itself deeply steeped in Buddhism and Chinese thought) was also employed by other institutions (including Hie and Miwa). Undoubtedly, Kanetomo's intervention had crucial consequences: it opened up the possibility to think about the kami as "originally Japanese," an idea that became very important in the Edo period (1600–1868) and ended up affecting the ways we understand the kami even today.

Shinto as an independent and institutionalized religious tradition began only in 1868 with the so-called separation of Kami and buddhas (*shinbutsu bunri*). This forceful separation, carried out upon orders directly emanating from the government, was one of the first acts in the Japanese process of modernization, and amounted to the artificial creation of two separate religious traditions, namely, Shinto and Japanese Buddhism.[5] Subsequently, Shinto developed as directly related to the new Japanese state's policy and ruling imperial ideology, in what is known as "State Shinto" (*kokka shintō*), which was disbanded after the end of World War II.[6]

It is therefore problematic to use anachronistically Shinto as a general term to refer in a unified way to discourses that were perceived as separate at the time. Among the four types of Shinto mentioned, shrine cults and folk beliefs in particular used to be closely related to Buddhism, most recently until the religious policies implemented between 1868 and 1872 forced a separation between them.

MODALITIES OF INTERACTIONS BETWEEN BUDDHISM AND LOCAL CULTS IN JAPAN

The history of the interactions between Buddhism and local cults in Japan begins at the very moment of the official arrival of Buddhism to the archipelago in the mid-6th century, when the Korean kingdom of Baekje (Paekche) sent to Japan as a formal gift a statue of the Buddha, a set of scriptures, and ritual implements. Emperor Kinmei (509–571) of Japan asked the council of clan chiefs to deliberate on whether the new divinity should be worshiped or not. A conflict ensued, opposing the pro-Buddhist faction led by the Soga clan (with ties to the Asian continent) to the anti-Buddhists led by the Mononobe (court ritualists). The former eventually prevailed, and Buddhism was adopted in Japan. Interestingly, the early sources reporting this episode call the statue of the Buddha from Korea the "kami from the foreign lands" (*adashi no kuni no kami*) and the "kami called Buddha" (*butsujin*). The court's decision to adopt Buddhism followed the outburst of epidemics and natural disasters, which the sources attribute to a conflict opposing the local gods to the newcomer Kami Buddha, ending with the triumph of the latter. In other words, the Buddha was understood at the beginning from within the framework of local cults as a new and powerful deity, capable of protecting its worshipers while at the same time cursing its enemies. This understanding of buddhas and bodhisattvas never disappeared, and continued to form one of the bases of premodern Japanese religiosity. It is also interesting to note that Buddhist interactions with local deities proceeded in parallel with the diffusion of Buddhism across Japan. In the mid-8th century, Emperor Shōmu (701–756) ordered the construction of state-supported temples and nunneries in all provinces across the realm (called, respectively, *kokubunji* and *kokubunniji*); at around the same time, aristocratic clans and regional gentry also began to build temples dedicated to local and tutelary kami called *jingūji* or *miyadera* (literally, "Buddhist temple that is a shrine for a kami"). These Buddhist temples for the kami became one of the main aspects of premodern Japanese Buddhism and religiosity in general.

It is possible to identify a number of modalities in the interactions between Buddhism and local deities in Japan, following patterns that seem to be common to most Buddhist cultures. Japanese Kami were subjugated and converted to Buddhism, transformed into dharma protectors, and redefined as local manifestations of buddhas and bodhisattvas; in some cases, local Kami were ignored (for instance, by not mentioning them in written sources), kept strictly separate from Buddhism (as in some imperial gods and at the Grand Shrines of Ise), and even eliminated and forgotten; in other developments, new Kami could be imported from abroad (mostly from the Indian pantheon, but also from Chinese religions and, to a lesser extent, Korean traditions) or created from scratch in Japan.[7] These modalities of interaction are not necessarily stages in a process of historical development in which one stage replaces the previous one, as scholars often maintain, but rather different ways to deal with the sacred that were largely contemporaneous with each other. For example, in the Edo period we encounter all the modes: Kami kept separate and distinct from Buddhist divinities, Kami treated as suffering beings in need of salvation (thus, Buddhist priests chanted sutras and performed ceremonies at shrines affiliated with Buddhist temples specifically for this purpose), Kami envisioned as protectors of Buddhism, Kami as manifest traces of Buddhist entities, and new Kami generated under Buddhist influence. (We cannot discuss the Kami that were ignored and forgotten, but it may be possible to find clues in local accounts about ancient beliefs and rituals that have been lost for centuries, replaced by subsequent strata of religiosities.)

In the first modality, Buddhists envisioned local Kami as dangerous and violent entities, their violence being caused by their deluded condition, from which they could be freed through their conversion to Buddhism. This process tended to happen when itinerant Buddhists monks traveled to remote areas and began to proselytize there. Two stories exemplify this modality well: both describe local Kami as violent entities, a source of calamities to the people, while presenting Buddhism as a pacifying and ordering force.

One day in 763 the Kami of Tado in central Japan manifested itself through an oracle and expressed its desire to convert to Buddhism in order to be freed from its Kami-condition of suffering. A Buddhist temple (*jingūji*) was built in the area where the Kami resided, and special services began to be held for its salvation. This is one of the earliest records of a *jingūji* being built (an earlier, less documented case dates to 716). In this story, the Kami themselves acknowledged the superiority of Buddhism and asked to be saved.

The second story is about a giant tree, believed to be the abode of a Kami, which was felled to the ground because its vast shade area obstructed the development of agriculture. The cut tree rolled down into a river and floated away, carried by the current. Every time it got stranded an epidemic burst out in the area. Eventually, a Buddhist itinerant monk cut it into pieces and with them built three icons of the Bodhisattva Kannon (one of these images is said to be the Kannon at Ishiyamadera temple near Kyoto). In this case, the intervention of Buddhism not only put a stop to epidemics and produced miraculous icons, it also resulted in the material improvement of local people's living conditions through agricultural development.

Both stories describe the Kami as violent but suffering beings that could be saved through their conversion to Buddhism. In the first story, as in many subsequent ones, the Buddhist temple was built not upon order by the central government (as was normally the case at the time), but as a consequence of an autonomous request of a local god—and, one would assume, the local gentry; in this way, Kami were manifestations of local autonomy, and could be used as instruments in attempts by local groups to wrest control of Buddhism away from central government institutions. The second story tells of the autonomous agency of Buddhist individuals and groups who, probably independent from both the central government and the local gentry, spread Buddhism in the provinces through control and incorporation of local gods.

A second modality of interaction envisions newly converted Kami as protectors of the Buddhist dharma and guarantors of the peace and prosperity in their respective locales. These tutelary deities were gradually organized in a hierarchical structure, and by the 12th century we find the deities of twenty-two imperial sponsored shrines at the top,[8] regional shrines at the middle, and village shrines at the bottom.

A third modality involved more subtle hermeneutical moves. Around the 11th–12th centuries, Kami began to be understood as Japanese manifestations (Japanese, *gongen*; Sanskrit, *avatāra*) of buddhas, bodhisattvas, and other deities of the Indian pantheon brought to Japan by Buddhism. The ability to manifest themselves in many forms is a feature of classical Indian gods that was later attributed also to buddhas and bodhisattvas; in Japan, this feature was used to explain the ontological status of the Kami. The theory behind this idea of manifestation was commonly defined as *honji suijaku* or *wakō dōjin* (or their combination, *wakō suijaku*). The term *honji suijaku* (literally, "the original ground and its traces") appears for the first time in an exegesis of the *Lotus Sūtra* by the Chinese Tiantai patriarch Zhiyi (538–597). According to Zhiyi, the first fourteen chapters of the scripture contain the provisional "trace-teaching" of the historical buddha, whereas the final fourteen chapters are the ultimate "original teaching" of the eternal principle of buddhahood. In medieval Japan, *honji suijaku* was employed to mean that "Indian" and "Buddhist" divinities constitute the "original ground" (*honji*) of their manifestations in Japan as Kami (their "traces" or *suijaku*).[9] The expression *wakō dōjin* (literally, "to soften one's radiance and become the same as dust") comes instead from the Daoist classic *Daodejing*, where it refers to the way in which the Dao, the supreme principle of the universe, manifests itself in the world by limiting its power so that it can be understandable to human beings. In this context, the Japanese Kami were the limited ("softened") forms of buddhas and bodhisattvas. The underlying rationale for Buddhist divinities to limit their powers and appear as traces, as explained by several medieval texts, was that the Japanese people were too difficult to convert and too ignorant to understand buddhas and bodhisattvas in their full-fledged forms, and required instead violent and coarse manifestations to guide them to salvation. Other authors, however, took a more cultural relativistic position, and argued that the sacred can take different forms according to cultural and historical context; thus, there was no ontological difference between buddhas and Kami, only superficial distinctions in terms of external appearance and spatio-temporal circumstances.

Another modality of interaction consists in the production of new Kami, either by importing them from abroad or by creating them. Some of the most popular Shinto deities today include Hachiman, Inari, Tenjin, Sannō, Ebisu, Gozu Tennō, Konpira, Benzaiten, Daikokuten—all gods that emerged out of Buddhist temples between the 8th and 14th centuries; until the reforms and persecutions of 1868, worship of these gods was centered at institutions that were either Buddhist temples (Usa Hachimangū in Kyushu, Iwashimizu Hachimangū between Kyoto and Osaka, Tsurugaoka Hachimangū in Kamakura near Kyoto; Tenmangū temples in Kyoto and in Dazaifu in Kyushu; Konpiragū in Shikoku, Ebisu shrine in Sannomiya) or

Kami-shrines controlled and supervised by Buddhist temples (Fushimi Inari, Hie shrine for Sannō, Enoshima Benzaiten, the Suwa shrines). Some of these deities are of foreign origin: Konpira, Benzaiten, and Daikokuten originate from India (their Sanskrit names are, respectively, Kubhera, Sarasvatī, and Mahākāla—the male counterpart of goddess Kālī); in Japan, they developed out of the interactions of tantric Buddhism and local cults. Other gods, such as Sannō and Shinra myōjin, probably derive from mountain deities in China, brought to Japan by Tendai monks. Other deities, such as Hachiman, Inari, and Tenjin (and many more) are hybrids, created within shrine-temple complexes in processes that are not yet fully clear.

A final modality of interaction involves separation, namely, the belief that not all Kami can be assimilated into Buddhism. Thus, we find instances of active isolation of Kami cults from Buddhism (so-called *shinbutsu kakuri*), most notably at some ceremonies that took place at the imperial court and at, more generally, the Ise Shrines, in which Buddhism was considered taboo;[10] the idea that there existed local deities that were not avatars of some Buddhist divinity, as in the case of so-called real Kami (*jisshashin*, *jissha*, or *jitsurui kijin*); but also the existence of critical attitudes toward the cults of the Kami that often culminated in refusals to worship them (so-called *jingi fuhai*).

At the imperial court, the emperor and ritual specialists from selected aristocratic families engaged in archaic ceremonies that were first codified in legal codes (*Jingiryō*) in the early to mid-8th century and that include the yearly *niiname sai* (a fall harvest festival), the *daijōsai* (the enthronement ceremony), and periodic purification rituals such as the *ōharae*. These ceremonies, along with the gods involved in them, collectively known as *jingi* (deities of heaven and earth), were kept strictly separate and distinct from Buddhism. In fact, by the 13th century at least three different sets of ritual were held at court: archaic *jingi* rituals, Buddhist rituals for the protection of the emperor and the state, and Chinese imperial ceremonies (such as the Tensō chifusai ancestors' ceremony).

The idea that some Kami existed that could not be assimilated to Buddhism is based on complex theological arguments. Already by the late 12th and early 13th centuries, the Kami were divided into three categories based on Buddhist original enlightenment (hongaku) thought:[11] (i) Kami of original enlightenment, such as Amaterasu of Ise; (ii) Kami of no-enlightenment (*fukaku*), such as the violent Kami of Izumo shrine; (iii) Kami of acquired enlightenment (*shikaku*), such as Hachiman. Even though this classification was probably devised to enhance the status of the Ise shrines and their deities, the Kami were thought to embody modalities of Buddhist soteriology, and some of them represented a realm of ignorance and violence untouched by Buddhism.[12] This latter point was further developed when authors began to distinguish between "provisional deities" (*gonsha*) and "true deities" (*jissha*). The former refers to the deities of the *honji suijaku* pantheon (and the appellation "provisional" refer to their nature as "traces" of buddhas and bodhisattvas), normally considered benevolent, whereas the latter indicates mostly local divinities that had not yet been integrated within that system and were described as essentially violent and dangerous entities threatening the peace and security of local people. This distinction indicates that in medieval Japan gods still existed that had not been integrated within the Buddhist system; they were described as chaotic forces, much as local deities at the time of the arrival of Buddhism. The Buddhist attitude toward "true deities" was complex. Some authors warned people not to worship them, as they were outside of Buddhism and therefore irrelevant to salvation; others suggested that these deities should be propitiated; still others argued that human beings could not easily tell the difference between one category of deities and the other, and it was thus best to worship them all.

In a sense, the forceful and state-sanctioned persecution of Buddhism and its ensuing separation from Shinto (*shinbutsu bunri*) that occurred at the dawn of modernity in Japan (1868–1871) can also be seen as a special instance of interaction involving distance. At that time, "Buddhist" elements (such as Buddhist-style Kami icons, shrines' architectural elements, Buddhist scriptures offered to the Kami, and so forth) were removed from the shrine-temples and, in many cases, destroyed. "Shinto" elements, on the other hand, were simplified and "normalized." Many local shrines were destroyed; ancestral Kami were substituted with Kami listed in the *Kojiki*, an ancient text that had become the bible of the nativists. Priestly houses that had been in charge of Kami rituals for generations were replaced by state-appointed officers, often followers of the brand of nativism of Hirata Atsutane (1776–1843). Local rituals were replaced by centrally authorized ceremonies that were directly related to a newly created cult of the emperor. People were forced to celebrate new holidays, related to state-sanctioned events. In this way, a new religion, supposedly autochthonous and with roots in a remote past before the arrival of Buddhism, was created and propagated among the people. "Buddhism," on its side, after a few years of prohibition, reorganized itself as unrelated to Shinto and local cults.

A few words regarding the Buddhist temples in charge of Kami worship that characterized the religious field of premodern Japan is in order here, as it is an aspect still not fully understood in its modalities. As previously mentioned, almost all large shrines dedicated to the Kami prior to 1868 were either Buddhist temples or supervised by one. (A significant exception were the two shrines of Ise—which were nonetheless surrounded by more than a hundred Buddhist temples, all removed after 1868; a few other shrines, such as Izumo, became more or less independent of their Buddhist overlords during the Tokugawa period.) These temples functioned in part as full-fledged Buddhist institutions: they were staffed by monks or priests of various ranks with different sectarian and liturgical specializations, carried out Buddhist rituals, and stored canonical scriptures and other commentaries. In addition—and this is what distinguished them from other Buddhist temples without an important Kami component—part of their activities concerned the Kami that was at the center of their worship, a Kami that was understood as a regional avatar of a buddha or a bodhisattva. A relatively extensive literature exists in Japanese about the history and structure of some of these temple-shrine complexes (much less in English), but we a vivid and detailed description of their functioning in real life is lacking. (For an example of a present-day Buddhist temple that has preserved an important Kami component, turn to the Zen temple Myōgonji, commonly known as Toyokawa Inari, in Toyokawa near Nagoya in central Japan, which still worships the fox-like Kami Inari as a variant of Indian tantric goddess ḍākiṇī and a manifestation of the Bodhisattva Kannon.)[13]

ESOTERIC/TANTRIC BUDDHISM AND KAMI CULTS

Various Buddhist traditions in Japan developed their own ways to interact with local gods. For most of them, the kami were either sentient beings in need of salvation or protectors of Buddhism in Japan (the first two modes of interaction outlined). This is particularly evident in the Zen tradition, in which monks traveled throughout Japan to convert and save unruly local gods.[14] The Lotus sects based on the teaching of reformer Nichiren (1222–1282) created a set of thirty gods (*sanjūbanjin*), one for each day of the month, overseeing everyday activities.[15] These sects also promoted devotion to the sun goddess Amaterasu Ōmikami and martial god Hachiman. The Jōdo Shinshū tradition is the exception, as it explicitly disavowed any cult to the kami. However, it is esoteric Buddhism, both in its Tendai and Shingon variants, that played a fundamental role in the Buddhist transformation of the Kami and the development of doctrines and rituals about them. Several schools of Esoteric Buddhist "Shinto" teachings developed at major shrines, such as the Ise Outer Shrine, Hie shrine (controlled by the Tendai temple Enryakuji), and the Shingon temple Ōmiwadera (or Daigorinji). Esoteric Buddhist mandala became conceptual models to represent the sacred space of Kami shrines. In these images (*miya mandara*, literally, "shrine mandalas"), the Kami are represented as both "traces" (*suijaku*), that is, with their earthly forms (as animals or human beings) and "original grounds" (*honji*), that is, buddhas and bodhisattvas.

Tantric discourses about the Kami are generally known as Ryobu Shinto (Shinto of the twofold mandala of Shingon Buddhism) or Shingon Shinto. This was not a sectarian movement, but rather a widespread and polyphonic discourse carried out by various people (mostly Buddhist monks and Kami specialists) at temple-shrine complexes from the 12th until the mid-19th centuries. Recent studies have suggested that tantric (esoteric) Buddhist ideas and representations of deities, originating in India and accumulating elements from East Asian locales, may have contributed in a fundamental way to shape the premodern (and especially, medieval) Japanese understanding of Kami and the modes to interact with them.[16]

Shinto-Buddhist Esoteric teachings were transmitted through numerous initiation rituals, collectively known as *jingi kanjō* or *shintō* (or, perhaps, *jindō*) *kanjō* (literally, "*abhiṣeka* about the *kami*"), modeled on esoteric initiation rituals (*denbō kanjō*), but modified to better represent Kami myths from the *Nihon shoki* and the spatial structure of Kami cult places.[17] The most important among them were *Ama no iwato kanjō* (on the legend of the Heavenly Cavern in which Amaterasu secluded herself plunging the world into darkness), *sanshu jingi kanjō* (on the three imperial regalia), *waka kanjō* (on *waka* classical poetry), and *Reiki kanjō* (on the teachings of the *Reikiki*, an important but elusive Esoteric Buddhist-Shinto text dating to the early 14th century). Variants of these initiations formed the basis for rituals for specific professions (carpenters, merchants, farmers) involving deities of the Buddho-Shinto combinatory universe.[18] Similar initiations were also performed at Tendai temples.

Buddhist priests took pains to study non-Buddhist texts and went through initiation rituals that were often very complicated, time-consuming, and presumably quite expensive. Through those rituals, the initiated became identical with a "Shinto" deity, thus creating a new soteriology that replaced the usual idea of "becoming buddha" (*jōbutsu*) with a form of "becoming *kami*"; all this was related to an awareness of the specificity of Japan as a sacred place. The development of a Tantric discourse on Shinto during the Middle Ages also generated an enormous commentarial activity concerning early Japanese literary texts, such as *Ise monogatari*, *waka* poetry collections, and the *Nihon shoki*.

Ryobu Shinto envisioned that the main deities of the Great Shrines of Ise, Amaterasu and Toyouke, embodied the very essence of dharma-nature (Japanese, *hosshō*; Sanskrit, Dharmatā) and of the cosmic Buddha Mahāvairocana (Japanese, Dainichi Nyorai); this feature gave them an ontological primacy that provoked cosmogonical speculations on the original state of the universe and the primordial godhead. Indeed, to argue that the essence of dharma and the very nature of Dainichi is a Kami at Ise (in fact, two different Kami) opened up a number of problems in Buddhist ontology, cosmology, and soteriology.[19]

Buddhist Shinto texts indicated more or less explicitly that, whereas Buddhism offered a soteriology progressing from ignorance to awakening and as such was still prisoner of a fundamental dualism (one opposing ignorance to enlightenment), doctrines and cults related to the Kami were concerned with the original condition of beings and the universe before the appearance of the first buddha ever—a condition that, they argued, transcended all dualism. For example, the Tendai monk and Kami scholar Jihen (active 1333–1340) claimed that Buddhism was forbidden at the Ise Shrines because it preaches the difference between ignorance and enlightenment and thus defiles the perfect unity of primordial chaos that forms the basis of "Shinto." Another Tendai priest, Sonshun (1451–1514), explicitly advocated the primacy of *kami* over the buddhas, claiming that the Kami belong to a primeval condition of ontological wholeness he identifies with primordial ignorance as original enlightenment (*hongaku*).

This constituted an important twist in the logic of avatars and its impact on the understanding of the Kami, with Buddhist authors arguing that the Kami were in fact the primary, original forms of divine beings, while buddhas and bodhisattvas were local manifestations in India of these originally Japanese beings. This reversal of dominant Buddhist ideas was at the basis of a new Shinto movement, nativist in character, that stressed the superiority of all things Japanese against imported cultural elements. The center of this nativist reversal of the *honji suijaku* paradigm was the Yoshida shrine in Kyoto. Its priest Yoshida Kanetomo (1435–1511) had collected a number of doctrines and rituals about the Kami, mostly related to the then dominant esoteric Buddhism but that also included aspects from Chinese thought, and tried to establish his own tradition by emphasizing, in a paradoxical move, native and non-Buddhist features.[20] Gradually, the Yoshida tradition became the point of reference for nativist thinkers, anti-Buddhists, and Kami priests disgruntled with the Buddhist establishment still dominating their shrines. These were the people and the groups that contributed to constitute a Shinto discourse as distinct from Buddhism during the Edo period in a process whose final stage was the early Meiji separation of Shinto from Buddhism.

PHILOSOPHICAL PROBLEMS WITH BUDDHO-SHINTO RELATIONS

Interactions between Buddhism and Kami (*shinbutsu shūgō*) are commonly understood as discourses related to deities. However, larger cultural issues were influenced by the ways in which Buddhism interacted with local cults; these include subjectivity, cosmology, political ideology, economics, temporal structures, and semiotics. For instance, Allan Grapard has shown that combinatory cults involving Kami and buddhas are not the result of random associations but involve complex semiotic operations: "the associations between divinities of a given cult obeyed linguistically grounded modes of combination such as association, metaphor, palindrome, anagram, and anagogy."[21] This is an extremely productive suggestion that requires further inquiry.

Furthermore, premodern Kami were usually not singular subjectivities, but plural entities that combined historical human beings, deities from various places in Asia, and Buddhist divinities. Hachiman, for example, is both a Kami and a bodhisattva, a king and a holy being: he is the deified aspect of Emperor Ōjin (who reigned in the late 4th to early 5th centuries) and at the same time a Japanese manifestation of the Buddha Amida (Sanskrit, Amithāba). Analogously, the Kami Inari began as an agricultural spirit bringing prosperity, later became the tutelary deity of the Fushimi area near Kyoto, and finally was envisioned as the Japanese manifestation of the Indian ogresses known as *ḍākiṇī* (Japanese, *dakini*). It is represented as an old man, as a white fox, or as a beautiful woman. Thus, in a culture in which buddhas manifest themselves as Kami, and Kami appear in this world as human beings, animals, or natural objects such as trees or mountains; in which there is no center of the self, but a complex set of mental functions and bodily energies; in which reality is not how it is perceived by us but encompasses a number of realms that are beyond our senses and intelligence—where are the boundaries of the "subject"? What are the principles and the forms of legitimization of power? What kind of cycle of exchange between human beings and deities establishes itself that results in the production of value? How can the sacred be represented? These are the philosophical questions posed by the developments of the interactions between Buddhism and Kami in Japan.

BUDDHISM AND LOCAL DEITIES: INDIAN PRECEDENTS

The Buddhist appropriation of local Kami is not a typically Japanese phenomenon: guardian gods and fertility gods are worshiped at Buddhist temples throughout Asia. Monastery gods are perhaps the original forms of adoption of local divinities in a Buddhist context. A central aspect of Buddhism, and one of the key factors in its successful diffusion, is its willingness and ability to interact with preexisting religious traditions. Buddhist canonical sources offer a picture of early Buddhist interest and attention to local cults in India. Archaeological evidence indicates that early Buddhist temples were built on the sites of prehistoric megalithic formations or in nearby areas, suggesting interest in interacting with local cults, including those dedicated to the dead. In general, Buddhism did not attempt to supplant preexisting cults, only to carve for itself a specific cultural space by interacting with these cults in several ways. This resulted in the development of forms of religious syncretism (cults, doctrines, festivals, calendrical rites), but also and especially of specific and original intellectual systems and ritual procedures that would characterize Buddhism and differentiate it from other traditions.

Interactions of Buddhism with local deities have often been described as a concession to the superstitious beliefs of the masses. Buddhist monks would have incorporated some forms of popular beliefs and rituals concerning local deities not because they also accepted them but simply as a skilful means aimed at bringing the unenlightened folks within the Buddhist fold. This view presents at least two obvious problems. On the one hand, the Buddhists involved in establishing relations with local cults appear as opportunists if not outright deceivers, since they were pandering forms of beliefs they did not personally share. On the other hand, commoners involved in local cults appear indiscriminately as superstitious, ignorant folks incapable of understanding the true teachings of the Buddha.

However, recent scholarship has presented a very different picture. For example, Robert DeCaroli writes that "Far from being marginal concessions to the public, spirit-deities played a central role in the development and growth of Buddhism in all of its contexts and in all of its forms." In particular, "Buddhism even in its earliest forms was not simply an otherworldly ideology of transcendence. Parallel to this soteriological concern was a deep investment in mortuary practices and a persistent concern with strategies for coping with spirits and the dead."[22] Thus, the attention dedicated by Buddhist institutions to spirit-deities was not a degeneration from purer, more pristine teachings, but a sign of the Sangha's power toward the supernatural realm and its capacity to generate merit. It is likely that Buddhist interactions with local spirit-deities began with the attempts to come to terms with *yakshas* and *nāgas*, the usual forms of local deities in, respectively, north and south India. It is thus not by chance that references to *yaksha* and *nāga* cults can be found in all cultures in which Buddhism spread.

In addition to their role in the ordering of society (social and cosmic hierarchies, definitions of righteous behavior) and the control over the territory (kingship), local cults are also related to other ideas of cultural identity and definition of subjectivity (souls, spirits, various forms of existence); as such, they enabled Buddhism, originally a translocal religion, to set its roots in foreign localities.

The definition of "local deities" (and local cults in general) in a Buddhist context is not an easy task. In fact, "local deities" is an umbrella-term covering a number of phenomena and entities. Buddhism and Indian religions in general have developed a detailed vocabulary to designate "supernatural" beings, and this terminology cannot always be adequately rendered by English words such as "deity," "god," "spirit," "ghost," "fairy," and "ogre." (Not to mention that these beings cannot even properly be considered "supernatural," given that they exist and operate within the same realm of human beings.) The Sino-Japanese term *hachibushū* (or *tenryū hachibushū*) is an attempt to give a unified classification to various forms of such beings. Systematized and popularized by esoteric Buddhism, this multifarious category includes *devas* (Japanese, *ten*), *nāgas* (*ryū*), *yakṣas* (*yasha*), *gandharvas* (*kendatsuba*), *asuras* (*ashura*), *garudas (karura*), *kinnaras* (*kinnara*), *and mahoragas* (*magoraga*); in addition, we find *rakshasas, pisacas,* and various kinds of ghosts and demonic entities. However, not all local deities were, strictly speaking, "local." Some controlled a very limited territory (the area covered by the shade of the tree, or the lake in which the deity resided); some, such as the Vedic and Brahmanic gods, extended their influence over many world systems and were the objects of widespread cults; others yet were originally regional gods that spread in various parts of the Indian subcontinent. At times, certain local spirit-deities, thanks to their interactions with Buddhism, came to acquire a "translocal" (transnational) character, as in the case of Indian deities worshiped from Southeast Asia to Japan. It may be helpful, thus, to define "local deities" (with "deities" to be understood in the broadest possible sense) as three kinds of nonhuman entities—spirit/deities that were (i) not originally Buddhist (or, outside of India, not originally Indian), (ii) brought elsewhere by Buddhism as part of a larger process of acculturation and that became the objects of local cults, and (iii) produced by the interactions between Buddhism and local traditions.

BUDDHISM AND LOCAL DEITIES: TWO COMPARATIVE CASES

As two examples of possible areas for comparative study, the *nats* cults in Myanmar and the Tibetan Bon religion will be discussed, as a way to shed new light on received understanding of the interactions between Buddhism and Shinto, while at the same time contributing to the clarification of broader issues pertaining to the interactions of local and translocal religious traditions.

Nats *Cults in Myanmar.* *Nats* cults are ancient and multilayered religious formations dedicated to a diverse class of spirit-deities. Scholars debate whether these cults predate the arrival of Buddhism in what is present-day Myanmar around the 5th century CE, or whether they developed under the influence of Buddhism. In any case, the term *nat* itself derives from the Sanskrit *natha*, "lord," and implies that these entities have powers over humans. Based on native typologies, there are several orders of *nats*: the higher *nats*, the lower *nats*, the Thirty-seven *Nats*, and miscellaneous *nats* that do not clearly belong to any of these groups. The higher *nats* are Indian deities (*deva* or *devatā*, Burmese *thewada*) such as Brahma, Indra, and Māra. Buddhist temples usually have a small shrine dedicated to them, but they are not the objects of any particular cult, as they are considered detached from the human world. The lower *nats* are indigenous (at least, non-Indian) entities, normally nature spirits inhabiting specific natural objects and locales, that operate on a territorial basis and in direct relation to individuals and social groups; some protect the house, others are like personal guardian spirits. These lower *nats* are generally considered potentially malevolent and dangerous.

As a separate category situated between higher and lower *nats*, the Thirty-seven *nats* (*thounze khunna min nat*, literally "the thirty-seven chiefs *nats*") refer to a changing group of spirit-deities, rather than a precise numerical indication. Many of these *nats* are in fact angry ghost-like beings, such as people wrongfully sentenced by kings or people who died a tragic death. Through their transformation into *nats*, they escaped the normal Buddhist ritual cycle of merit-transfer and postmortem memorialization and were placed instead in a limbo-like condition as semi-gods capable of influencing people's everyday lives. The beginning of this cult is attributed to King Anawratha (fl. 1017–1059), as part of his religious policies. By introducing Theravāda Buddhism, unrelated to local cults, and by persecuting the religious institutions that had carried out combinatory strategies (the Ari monks), he aimed at simplifying and controlling the religious field, while at the same time securing religious support for his own authority and rule. He did it by emphasizing the traditional Buddhist ideology envisioning the king as an emissary of both Indra and the Buddha, but also by establishing a new state cult dedicated to the Thirty-seven *Nats*, whom he enshrined in the Shwezigon Pagoda in Pagan. This cult was later developed by King Kyanzitta (a former general of Anawratha's) in the second half of the 11th century and King Dhammacetī (r. 1472–1492). It should be noted, however, that while the chief *nats* worshiped by Dhammacedī were defined as "stream-winning gods" (*dewatau sotāpan*), that is, full-fledged Buddhist entities, the Thirty-seven *nats* of Pagan were essentially non-Buddhist deities, and they were believed to take no part in any soteriological project.

Even though the *nats* cults is, structurally at least, similar to aspects of Japanese Shinto, it has never become an autonomous religious tradition but continues to exist in parallel to and in relation with Buddhism. The *nats* have their iconography, cult sites, ceremonies, specialized ritualists, devotees, a body of legends and doctrines (albeit in an unsystematic form). Even though their existence and their activities are generally explained in Buddhist terms, these deities are definitely and consciously non-Buddhist, situated as they are on the margin, if not on the outside, of the Burmese Buddhist cultural system. Thus, we could say that Anawratha and his successors created the Thirty-seven *nats* and sponsored their cult as a way to control the outside of Burmese Buddhism; but in so doing they relativized the center of the system and created two parallel religiosities. In terms of premodern Shinto, *nats* are similar to "real Kami" but also to new deities such as Tenjin, Gozu Tennō, and leaders of peasant revolts worshiped as village Kami.[23]

Tibetan Bon. As is commonly understood, Bon is the Tibetan autochthonous religion, whose existence predates the arrival of Buddhism; more vaguely, it is usually characterized as a form of shamanism and animism. What we know about Bon today is based on texts written after the Buddhist systematic symbiosis with preexisting traditions, and it is not easy to distinguish what is Buddhist and what predates it—a situation similar to our understanding of medieval Shinto. After an initial phase of stern opposition against the adoption of Buddhism (culminating in the anti-Buddhist persecution by King Glan dar ma in 838–842), after which Buddhism disappeared from central Tibet until the 11th century, Buddhism came back and became the dominant religious force of the country; as a consequence, Bon was restructured, and since the late 14th century Bon institutions have been affiliated with th Nyingmapa (e Rñin-ma-pa) order of tantric Buddhism.

The oldest extant history of Bon was written around the late 12th century after the consolidation of the Buddhist supremacy. Bon doctrines, rituals, and monastic organization are clearly indebted to Tibetan Buddhism; deities, however, are different. Bon also developed various cosmogonic myths and genealogies of the gods, which argue that the cosmos began earlier than described in Buddhist texts; the Bon teachings themselves claimed to predate the appearance of the Buddha. In this situation, it is difficult to envision Bon as an unchanged autochthonous tradition from the ancient past. Rather, it is the result of sustained processes of negotiation and symbiosis with Buddhism. In this sense, Ryobu Shinto, but perhaps also Yoshida Shinto seem to show strong structural similarities with Bon: they were parts of the Buddhist establishment but developed themes and rituals in a centrifugal fashion by reworking (re-imagining) ancient religiosity.

Tibetan Buddhism, on its part, was very much involved in efforts to incorporate local elements. For instance, tradition reports that most local deities were defeated by Padmasambhava in the 8th century and subsequently by other Buddhist monks; they were forced to pledge to protect Buddhism from its enemies; in this way, they became protectors of the dharma (Sanskrit, *dharmapāla*; Tibetan, *chos skyong, srung ma, bstan srung*). These protecting deities are divided into two groups: sacred protectors, considered equivalent to buddhas and bodhisattvas; and profane protectors, considered still part of the cycle of samsara. Furthermore, the Anuttara Yoga Tantra tradition considers all deities to be manifestations in this world of the primordial buddha (Ādibuddha), and therefore as sharing with the ultimate essence of reality. We see in this treatment a close parallel to the Japanese medieval situation, in which Kami were variously considered manifestations of buddhas and bodhisattvas, sentient beings in need of salvation, and embodiments of original enlightenment.[24]

BUDDHISM AND LOCAL CULTS BEYOND SHINTO: AN INTERPRETIVE FRAMEWORK

Buddhism has been traditionally understood as a primarily monastic tradition concerned with ultimate salvation. However, a complex cultural system such as Buddhism cannot be simply reduced to a monastic organization, its doctrinal apparatus, and its soteriology, because this would exclude most aspects of Buddhist religiosity throughout history. A very useful way to understand Buddhism as a cultural system has been proposed by Melford Spiro with his positing of three dimensions in Myanmar Buddhism: namely, nibbanic, kammatic, and apotropaic. The nibbanic level refers to the quest for ultimate salvation; historically, this has been the concern of a rather small group of Buddhist practitioners. Kammatic Buddhism refers to the various processes of merit-making and is primarily concerned with improving the material existence in this world (including the next reincarnations) as a means also for spiritual betterment. Finally, apotropaic or magical forms of Buddhism are concerned with securing protection from evil forces and natural disasters—aspects that are commonly, but incorrectly, referred to today as "superstitions."[25]

Spiro's framework can, with opportune modifications, be extended and generalized to Buddhism as a whole. Thus, we have a sphere concerning ultimate salvation (be it extinction into nirvana, deliverance into a Pure Land, or becoming a buddha in the present body), a sphere related to material and spiritual existence in this world envisioned as processes of merit-making, and a sphere of magical operations. It is important to stress that these three spheres are mutually interrelated. Magical protection allows one to lead a more secure life, which can thus be dedicated more easily to merit-making. Merit-making, in turn, is an activity related, more or less directly, to ultimate salvation, which is often envisioned as the final result of the accumulation of good karma. Salvation may also be, at least in part, due to the intervention of "deities" (buddhas, bodhisattvas, and their retinues and manifestations) as a consequence of the performance of magical rituals (this is especially true in tantric Buddhism).

Envisioning Buddhism as a complex mechanism to control interactions among these three spheres allows for a better understanding of the places and roles of local deities. It is clear that interaction with local deities occurs not only in the apotropaic sphere: for instance, merit could be used to deliver local deities from their painful condition of beings prisoners of the cycle of rebirth; as a reward, spirit-deities would protect Buddhist practitioners and facilitate their accumulation of merit and, ultimately, attainment of salvation. Moreover, as we have seen, in premodern Japan soteriological rituals developed involving the *kami* in a Buddhist context: practitioners would "become a Kami" as an intermediate, and easier, step before they could "become buddhas in their body."

To conclude, local cults were not a marginal aspect of Buddhism (especially if compared with meditation and monastic institutions) but a central element in the life of Buddhists since early times. In addition, local cults are not just part of folk religion; they are essential for the ordering of society and the control over the territory and thus have political significance (kingship and power) and are also related to other aspects of culture, including cultural identity; they enabled Buddhism, originally a translocal religion, to set its roots in foreign localities. Moreover, local cults are not just ways to cope with popular superstition and ignorance, given that several of them were based on elite cosmological and ideological constructs (cosmology, ontology, subjectivity, politics, etc.), more or less explicitly developed. They were also ways to define subjectivities (souls, spirits, various forms of existence) and righteous behavior.

REVIEW OF LITERATURE

A critical study of the history of interactions between Buddhism and Shinto begins in the early 20th century, a few decades after their forced separation that marked the beginning of modernity in Japan. However, it is only with Kuroda Toshio that a fuller and deeper picture began to emerge, in a series of seminal works written from around the mid-1970s.[26] Kuroda denied that something called Shinto had always existed in Japan, even predating the introduction of Buddhism, and reconfigured the various forms of medieval Shinto as something deeply intertwined with the dominant Buddhist system (what he called *kenmitsu taisei,* "exo-esoteric system"). Kuroda was deeply influential in Japan and abroad, and many scholars are still working along the path he traced (whether to expand his interpretations or to criticize them). Among the scholars most influenced by him there are Taira Masayuki and Satō Hiroo; Sueki Fumihiko has a more critical stance. More recently, Abe Yasurō and Itō Satoshi, among others, have engaged in a systematic search for medieval texts and in their interpretation, and their work provides a rich and variegated description of medieval Japanese religious mentalities and practices.[27]

Outside Japan, the new historiography of Shinto promoted by Kuroda Toshio is increasingly influential among scholars of religious and intellectual history.[28] Allan Grapard has pioneered new approaches to the study of Shinto cultural history, along lines traced by Kuroda and also Murayama Shūichi (1914–2010), with his work on the relations between Kasuga shrine and Kōfukuji temple in Nara, the origin of the cult to the god Hachiman, and various aspects of medieval Buddhist-Shinto amalgamation phenomena.[29] Another leading expert in the field is Helen Hardacre, with her important work on modern Shinto, on new religions, and, recently, a monumental history of Shinto.[30]

Over the past several years, John Breen and Mark Teeuwen have produced innovative studies of the Shinto tradition, which combine findings by Japanese authors and new critical insights.[31] In addition, a number of new scholars working on the Shinto tradition (and especially, its interactions with Buddhism) has emerged, making the subject one of the most creative and innovative in the field of Japanese religions and Japanese Buddhist studies.

Overall, the attention of scholars oscillates between the exegesis of premodern texts about the interactions of Buddhism with local cults (Shinto), especially about doctrines about the status of the Kami (in their relations to Buddhist divinities), and broader investigations of cultural and intellectual history (themes such as the economy and ideology of Shinto-Buddhist texts and institutions, material culture, rituals, and the diffusion of elite doctrines among the population at large).

FURTHER READING

Aston, W. G. *Nihongi: Chronicles of Japan from the Earliest Times to A.D. 697*. Rutland, VT: C. E. Tuttle, 1972.

Baumer, Christoph. *Bön: Tibet's Ancient Religion*. Turnbull, CT: Weatherhill, 2002.

Bock, Felicia. *Engi-Shiki: Procedures of the Engi Era*. 2 vols. Tokyo: Sophia University, 1970–1972.

Brac de la Perrière, Bénédicte. *Les rituels de possession en Birmanie: Du culte d'état aux cérémonies privées*. Paris: Editions Recherche sur les Civilisations, ADPF, 1989.

Brac de la Perrière, Bénédicte. "The Burmese Nats." *Diogenes* 44, no. 174 (Summer 1996): 45–60.

Breen, John, and Mark Teeuwen. *A New History of Shinto*. London: Wiley-Blackwell, 2010.

DeCaroli, Robert. *Haunting the Buddha: Indian Popular Religions and the Formation of Buddhism*. Oxford: Oxford University Press, 2004.

Grapard, Allan G. "Institution, Ritual, and Ideology: The Twenty-two Shrine-Temple Multiplexes in Heian Japan." *History of Religions* 27, no. 2 (1988): 246–269.

Grapard, Allan G. *The Protocol of the Gods: A Study of the Kasuga Cult in Japanese History*. Berkeley: University of California Press, 1992.
Hardacre, Helen. *Shinto: A History*. London: Oxford University Press, 2017.
Inoue Nobutaka, ed. *Shinto: A Short History*. Translated and adapted by Mark Teeuwen and John Breen. London: Routledge Curzon, 2003.
Itō Satoshi. *Shintō to wa nani ka*. Tokyo: Chūō kōronsha, 2012.
Itō Satoshi, Matsuo Kōichi, Endō Jun, and Mori Mizue, eds. *Shintō* (Nihonshi shōhyakka). Tokyo: Tōkyōdō shuppan, 2002.
Iyanaga Nobumi. *Daikokuten hensō*. Kyoto: Hōzōkan, 2002.
Ketelaar, James. *Of Heretics and Martyrs in Meiji Japan: Buddhism and Its Persecution*. Princeton, NJ: Princeton University Press, 1990.
Kuroda Toshio. *Nihon chūsei no kokka to shūkyō*. Tokyo: Iwanami, 1975.
Kuroda Toshio. *Jisha seiryoku*. Tokyo: Iwanami, 1980.
Kvaerne, Per. *The Bön Religion of Tibet: The Iconography of a Living Tradition*. Boston: Shambhala, 1995.
Matsunaga, Alicia. *The Buddhist Philosophy of Assimilation: The Historical Development of the Honji-Suijaku Theory*. Rutland, VT: Sophia University Press, 1969.
Murayama Shūichi. *Honji suijaku*. Tokyo: Yoshikawa Kōbunkan, 1974.
Murayama Shūichi. *Shūgō shisōshi ronkō*. Tokyo: Hanawa shobō, 1987.
Philippi, Donald L. Kojiki. *Translated with an Introduction and Notes*. Tokyo: University of Tokyo Press, 1968.
Rambelli, Fabio. "Before the First Buddha: Medieval Japanese Cosmogony and the Quest for the Primeval Kami." *Monumenta Nipponica* 64, no. 2 (2009): 235–271.
Scheid, Bernhard. *Der ein und enzige Weg der Götter: Yoshida Kanetomo und die Erfindung des Shinto*. Vienna: Verlag der Österreichischer Akademie der Wissenschaften, 2001.
Spiro, Melford E. *Burmese Supernaturalism*. Englewood Cliffs, NJ: Prentice Hall, 1967.
Spiro, Melford E. *Buddhism and Society: A Great Tradition and Its Burmese Vicissitudes*. Berkeley: University of California Press, 1982.
Tambiah, Stanley J. *Buddhism and the Spirit Cults in North-east Thailand*. Cambridge, UK: Cambridge University Press, 1970.
Tambiah, Stanley J. *World Conqueror and World Renouncer*. Cambridge, UK: Cambridge University Press, 1976.
Teuuwen, Mark. *Watarai Shinto: An Intellectual History of the Outer Shrine in Ise*. Leiden, The Netherlands: Research School CNWS, 1996.
Teeuwen, Mark, and Fabio Rambelli, eds. *Buddhas and Kami in Japan: Honji Suijaku as a Combinatory Paradigm*. London: Routledge, 2003.

NOTES

1. For an English translation of *Nihon shoki* see W. G. Aston, *Nihongi: Chronicles of Japan from the Earliest Times to A.D. 697* (Rutland, VT: C. E. Tuttle, 1972); for *Kojiki*, see Donald L. Philippi, *Kojiki. Translated with an Introduction and Notes* (Tokyo: University of Tokyo Press, 1968).
2. See Mark Teeuwen, "From Jindō to Shintō: A Concept Takes Shape," *Japanese Journal of Religious Studies* 29, nos. 3–4 (2002): 233–263.
3. Fabio Rambelli, "Re-positioning the Gods: 'Medieval Shinto' and the Origins of Non-Buddhist Discourses on the Kami," *Cahiers d'Extrême-Asie* 16 (2006–2007): 305–325.
4. See Allan G. Grapard, "The Shinto of Yoshida Kanetomo," *Monumenta Nipponica* 47, no. 1 (1992): 27–58; Bernhard Scheid, *Der ein und enzige Weg der Götter: Yoshida Kanetomo und die Erfindung des Shinto*

(Vienna: Verlag der Österreichischer Akademie der Wissenschaften, 2001); and Scheid, "Reading the *Yuitsu Shintō myōbō yōshū*: A Modern Exegesis of an Esoteric Shinto Text," in *Shinto: Ways of the Kami*, eds. John Breen and Mark Teeuwen (Honolulu: University of Hawaii Press, 2000), 117–143.

5. See Allan G. Grapard, "Japan's Ignored Cultural Revolution: The Separation of Shinto and Buddhist Divinities in Meiji (*shinbutsu bunri*) and a Case Study: Tōnomine," *History of Religions* 23 (February 1984): 240–265; and James Ketelaar, *Of Heretics and Martyrs in Meiji Japan: Buddhism and Its Persecution* (Princeton, NJ: Princeton University Press, 1990).
6. Helen Hardacre, *Shinto and the State, 1868–1988* (Princeton, NJ: Princeton University Press, 1989).
7. For details, see Mark Teeuwen and Fabio Rambelli, "Introduction: Combinatory Religion and the Honji Suijaku Paradigm in Pre-Modern Japan," in *Buddhas and Kami in Japan:* Honji Suijaku *as a Combinatory Paradigm*, ed. Teeuwen and Rambelli (London: Routledge Curzon, 2003), 1–53.
8. See Allan G. Grapard, "Institution, Ritual, and Ideology: The Twenty-Two Shrine-Temple Multiplexes in Heian Japan," *History of Religions* 27, no. 2 (1988): 246–269
9. Alicia Matsunaga, *The Buddhist Philosophy of Assimilation: The Historical Development of the* Honji-Suijaku *Theory* (Rutland, VT: Sophia University Press, 1969).
10. On this instance of premodern separation (*shinbutsu kakuri*), see Satō Masato, "Shinbutsu kakuri no yōin wo meguru kōsatsu," *Shūkyō kenkyū* 82.2 (2007): 359–383.
11. On the idea of original enlightenment (hongaku) in Japanese Buddhism, see Jacqueline Stone, *Original Enlightenment and the Transformation of Medieval Japanese Buddhism* (Honolulu: University of Hawai'i Press, 1991).
12. On medieval Kami typologies, see Fabio Rambelli, "Before the First Buddha: Medieval Japanese Cosmogony and the Quest for the Primeval Kami," *Monumenta Nipponica* 64, no. 2 (2009): 235–271; and Rambelli, "Re-positioning the Gods."
13. In English, see Allan G. Grapard, *The Protocol of the Gods: A Study of the Kasuga Cult in Japanese History* (Berkeley: University of California Press, 1992); see Steven Heine, "Sōtō Zen and the Inari Cult: Symbiotic and Exorcistic Trends in Buddhist and Folk Religious Amalgamations," *Pacific World* new series, 10 (1994): 75–101.
14. See William Bodiford, "The Enlightenment of Kami and Ghosts: Spirit Ordinations in Japanese Sōtō Zen," *Cahiers d'Extrême-Asie* 7 (1993): 267–282.
15. See Lucia Dolce, "Hokke Shinto: Kami in the Nichiren Tradition," in *Buddhas and Kami in Japan:* Honji Suijaku *as a Combinatory Paradigm*, eds. Teeuwen and Rambelli (London: Routledge Curzon, 2003), 222–254.
16. See Bernard Faure, *The Fluid Pantheon*, 2 vols. (Honolulu: University of Hawai'i Press, 2016).
17. On medieval Shinto, see Itō Satoshi, *Chūsei Tenshō Daijin shinkō no kenkyū* (Kyoto: Hōzōkan, 2011); and Itō, *Shintō no keisei to chūsei shinwa* (Tokyo: Yoshikawa Kōbunkan, 2016).
18. On *shintō kanjō* initiations, see Fabio Rambelli, "The Ritual World of Buddhist 'Shinto': The *Reikiki* and Initiations to Kami-Related Matters (*jingi kanjō*) in Late Medieval and Early-Modern Japan," *Japanese Journal of Religious Studies* 29, nos. 3–4 (2002): 353–385; and Rambelli, "*Honji suijaku* at Work: Religion, Economics, and Ideology in Pre-Modern Japan," in *Buddhas and Kami in Japan:* Honji Suijaku *as a Combinatory Paradigm*, eds. Teeuwen and Rambelli (London: Routledge Curzon, 2003), 255–286.
19. See Itō, *Chūsei Tenshō Daijin shinkō no kenkyū.*
20. See Scheid, *Der ein und enzige Weg der Götter* and "Reading the *Yuitsu Shintō myōbō yōshū*."
21. Grapard, *The Protocol of the Gods*, 82.
22. Robert DeCaroli, *Haunting the Buddha: Indian Popular Religions and the Formation of Buddhism* (Oxford: Oxford University Press, 2004), 187.
23. For a more extended treatment, see Melford E. Spiro, *Burmese Supernaturalism* (Englewood Cliffs, NJ: Prentice Hall, 1967); Bénédicte Brac de la Perrière, *Les rituels de possession en Birmanie: Du culte d'état aux cérémonies privées* (Paris: Editions Recherche sur les Civilisations, ADPF, 1989); and Brac de la Perrière, "The Burmese Nats." *Diogenes* 44, no. 174 (Summer 1996): 45–60.

24. For more details, see Per Kvaerne, *The Bön Religion of Tibet: The Iconography of a Living Tradition* (Boston: Shambhala, 1995); and Christoph Baumer, *Bön: Tibet's Ancient Religion* (Turnbull, CT: Weatherhill, 2002).
25. Melford E. Spiro, *Buddhism and Society: A Great Tradition and Its Burmese Vicissitudes* (Berkeley: University of California Press, 1982).
26. Kuroda Toshio, *Nihon chūsei no kokka to shūkyō* (Tokyo: Iwanami, 1975); *Jisha seiryoku: Mō hitotsu no chūsei shakai* (Tokyo: Iwanami, 1980); and *Nihon chūsei no shakai to shūkyō* (Tokyo: Iwanami, 1990). In English, see "Shinto in the History of Japanese Religions," tran. James Dobbins and Suzanne Gay, *Journal of Japanese Studies* 7, no. 1 (1981): 1–21; and "The Discourse on the 'Land of the Kami' (*Shinkoku*) in Medieval Japan," tran. Fabio Rambelli, *Japanese Journal of Religious Studies* 23.3–4 (1996): 353–385.
27. Taira Masayuki, *Nihon chūsei no shakai to bukkyō* (Tokyo: Hanawa shobō, 1992); Satō Hiroo, *Nihon chūsei no kokka to bukkyō* (Tokyo: Yoshikawa Kōbunkan, 2010) (or 1987); Kami, *hotoke, ōken no chūsei* (Kyoto: Hōzōkan, 1998); *Amaterasu no henbō* (Kyoto: Hōzōkan, 2000); and *How Like a God: Deification in Japanese Religion* (Tokyo: International House of Japan, 2016); by Itō Satoshi, see especially *Chūsei Tenshō Daijin shinkō no kenkyū* (Kyoto: Hōzōkan, 2011); and *Shintō no keisei to chūsei shinwa* (Tokyo: Yoshikawa Kōbunkan, 2016). By Abe Yasurō, see *Chūsei Nihon no shūkyō tekisuto taikei* (Nagoya: Nagoya Daigaku Shuppankai, 2013).
28. An interesting book by Alicia Matsunaga, *The Buddhist Philosophy of Assimilation: The Historical Development of the* Honji-Suijaku *Theory* (Rutland, VT: Sophia University Press, 1969), was not very influential in the field.
29. Murayama Shūichi, *Honji suijaku* (Tokyo: Yoshikawa Kōbunkan, 1974); and *Shūgō shisōshi ronkō* (Tokyo: Hanawa shobō, 1987); By Allan Grapard see, among others, "Japan's Ignored Cultural Revolution" (1984); "Institution, Ritual, and Ideology" (1988); *The Protocol of the Gods: A Study of the Kasuga Cult in Japanese History* (1992); "The Shinto of Yoshida Kanetomo" (1992); and *Mountain Mandalas* (London: Bloomsbury, 2016).
30. Helen Hardacre, *Shinto and the State; Kurozumikyō and the New Religions of Japan* (Princeton, NJ: Princeton University Press, 1986); *Religion and Society in Nineteenth-Century Japan* (Ann Arbor: Center for Japanese Studies, University of Michigan, 2002); and *Shinto: A History* (London: Oxford University Press, 2017).
31. See, among others, Mark Teeuwen, *Watarai Shinto: An Intellectual History of the Outer Shrine in Ise* (Leiden, The Netherlands: Research School CNWS, 1996); John Breen and Mark Teeuwen, eds., *Shinto: Ways of the Kami* (Honolulu: University of Hawai'i Press, 2000); John Breen and Mark Teeuwen, *A New History of Shinto* (London: Wiley-Blackwell, 2010); Mark Teeuwen and Bernhard Scheid, guest editors, "Tracing Shinto in the History of Kami Worship," special issue of the *Japanese Journal of Religious Studies* 29, nos. 3–4 (Fall 2002); and Mark Teeuwen and Fabio Rambelli, eds., *Buddhas and Kami in Japan:* Honji Suijaku *as a Combinatory Paradigm* (London: Routledge Curzon, 2003).

Fabio Rambelli

BUDDHISM AND THE ENVIRONMENT

BUDDHIST ENVIRONMENTS AND THE PROPAGATION OF THE DHARMA IN INDIA

From the very earliest years, and then wherever Buddhism spread in Asia, the lived environment was made meaningful as a Buddhist environment through practices, doctrines, and stories. In the *Mucalinda Sutta*, for example, shortly after his awakening, the Buddha sits in meditation in Uruvelā, by the shore of the Nerañjarā River, under the shade of the Mucalinda tree. An unseasonable storm arises and for seven days the Nāga (serpent spirit) King, Mucalinda, wraps himself around the Buddha and spreads his hood above, protecting the Buddha from cold winds, rain, and insects. When the storm is over, the Nāga King takes on the form of a young man and with palms together pays homage to the Buddha. Numerous Indian Buddhist narratives tell similar stories of monks protected by snakes or dragons. Often, the serpents and dragons are local deities, converted by the monks to Buddhism, who then take on the role of protectors of the monks and, more generally, protectors of Buddhism in their territory.[1] And often, these local deities inhabited pre-Buddhist sacred sites of ritual-ecological practice, places that were already venerated because they were thought to be particularly powerful. Narratives of local deities and spirits of trees, animals, and other natural beings converting to Buddhism and becoming protectors are thus stories of pre-Buddhist environments becoming Buddhist.[2]

Indian places also became Buddhist through association with events in the life of the Buddha or other important Buddhist figures. These sites then became the focus of pilgrimage, frequently marked by pillars, reliquary shrines (stupas), caves, temples, or monasteries. Two pillars, with inscriptions attributed to the 3rd-century-BCE Mauryan emperor Aśoka, mark early sites of Buddhist worship and pilgrimage linked to the Buddha's biography. One was associated with the birthplace of Śākyamuni, the historical Buddha, in what became Lumbinī, in Nepal. The other, also in Nepal, was said to be the site of the reliquary shrine of a previous Buddha, Konākamana. By the time of Aśoka, pilgrimage seems to have been a well-established practice in Indian Buddhism. Some Indian Buddhist texts, such as the *Mahāparinirvāṇa Sūtra*, suggest pilgrimage to four sites important in the life of Śākyamuni: his birthplace, the place of awakening, the place of his first teaching, and the place of his death and final passing into nirvana. Over time, Buddhist traditions came to identify these places of pilgrimage as Lumbinī, Bodh Gāya, Sārnāth, and Kuśinagar.

In addition to these four locations, innumerable other places throughout the early Buddhist heartland, the Middle Ganges region, were associated with the Buddha and became sites of pilgrimage. A number of these sites had stupas said to enshrine the bodily relics of the Buddha. Still more were places where the Buddha was said to have meditated, taught, or marked his presence with a footprint, or where stupas might house his begging bowl or robe. The *Āśokāvadāna*, a 2nd-century-BCE text, includes a pilgrimage narrative in which Aśoka follows a ritual circuit that "maps the Buddha's biography onto the geography of India."[3] Buddhist pilgrimage practices and stupas, pillars, caves, temples, and monasteries made visible the new Indian Buddhist sacred geography.

As missionaries brought Buddhist texts, teachings, and practices to other parts of the Indian subcontinent, these new environments also became Buddhist environments. There is textual and archaeological evidence of numerous Buddhist sites in Gandhāra and Kuṣāṇa, in northwestern India (contemporary Pakistan and Afghanistan); stupas were built in places where relics or objects of the Buddha were said to have been located. There were also sites that became associated with stories from earlier lives of the Buddha. After some years, narratives placed the Buddha himself in Gandhāra and Kuṣāṇa, far from the Middle Ganges, thereby also making these environments Buddhist.[4] Because discourses of the Buddha were understood to be the very embodiment of the Buddha as dharma, Louis O. Gómez writes, scripture "becomes a living relic of the Buddha, so that every place where the text is made known becomes a sacred location, a reliquary, as it were."[5] Thus, as Buddhism spread in the subcontinent and neighboring lands and Buddhists brought discourses and stories that situated the Buddha in new places, these places themselves were transformed into Buddhist environments.

As archaeologists and environmental historians have shown, early Indian Buddhist communities transformed their landscapes in material ways beyond the building of stupas, temples, and monasteries. Their work demonstrates that even in the centuries before the Common Era, many monastic communities were already active in land and water management. Buddhist monastic institutions thus served as repositories of technical and managerial knowledge. At the early Buddhist site of Sanchi, for example, in the Indian state of Madhya Pradesh, archaeologists have found dams almost twenty feet high and forty-six hundred feet long, creating reservoirs just over one square mile.[6] Buddhist water resource systems—including large dams, spillways, sluiceways, and sluice gates—enabled the collection, storage, and distribution of water to irrigate crops. Monks provided engineering and administrative expertise to local people, thereby enabling a transition from subsistence agriculture to the agricultural surplus and patronage networks required to support large monasteries.

Developing complex water systems enabled Buddhist monks to address the immediate needs of local people. Far from transcending the world around them, these monks were socially engaged, providing technologies that helped the surrounding population to live with uncertain drought. In responding to agricultural challenges, they transformed the socioecological environment. And the transformation of the environment led to economic and social changes, including transformations in food culture and land tenure as well as increased population and urbanization. The Buddhist monastic culture that developed in central India was made possible by a predominantly rice-growing economy that itself was predicated on reliable irrigation.[7]

The watery world that resulted from monastic irrigation projects is represented in the plants and animals that appear in early Buddhist relief sculptures, which are often aquatic species (lotus, fish, turtles, and snakes). Julia Shaw suggests that this imagery both reflects the watery environment that produced the resources necessary for Buddhist monuments and symbolizes monastic capacities to live well with the natural world and to diminish the danger and uncertainty of droughts. She characterizes the Buddhist environment created by the water systems as a "hydraulic landscape."[8] Agriculture relied on monastic expertise and was no longer dependent on rain-making cults and the unpredictable serpent deities they propitiated. "Far from negating the eco-*dharma* model," Shaw writes, "the history and chronology of monastic landlordism and the archaeological evidence of the gradual monumentalisation of Buddhist locales in the landscape support the idea of entanglement between monks and their physical and built environment through 'long term relationships of material investment, care and maintenance', the absence of which leads to decay and disrepair."[9] With the decline of Buddhism in central India, dams, sluiceways, and sluice gates at Buddhist sites were not maintained, and diminished irrigation resulted in smaller agrarian production and thus decreased populations at some sites for many centuries.

The relationship between temples, monasteries, irrigation technologies, and agriculture is found in the historical record throughout Buddhist Asia. As Johan Elverskog notes, "systems of wells, tanks, and irrigation are found pretty much everywhere Buddhism became established."[10] Buddhist monks brought irrigation technologies to the oasis towns on the Silk Road, which "played a major role in establishing these cities as bastions of Buddhism in an otherwise inhospitable landscape."[11] Archaeologists and historians have documented this relationship in Burma, Sri Lanka, Tibet, and elsewhere.[12] Some of these projects were massive, with reservoirs covering thousands of acres and holding billions of cubic feet of water. All this water enabled significant increases in rice production, which provided more nutrients than wheat and made possible both a dramatic growth in population and the agricultural surplus necessary to sustain Buddhist monastics who did not themselves do agricultural work. The monastic code eventually contained suggestions for running a granary that could make a profit. In addition to rice and the irrigation technologies on which its production relied, Buddhists also transmitted sugar, cotton, and tea, further transforming socioecological landscapes through agricultural expansion.[13] The agricultural expansion, in turn, made possible increased urbanization, which supported and accompanied the spread of Buddhism in numerous places in Asia.[14] From the early centuries on, then, Buddhism significantly impacted the physical environment and its meaning.

HIMALAYAN AND TIBETAN BUDDHIST ENVIRONMENTS

As Buddhism spread elsewhere in Asia, one can see many of the same dynamics that transformed local landscapes into Buddhist environments in India: local deities and their places were converted; Buddhist structures were built to mark the sacred Buddhist environment; Buddhists brought agricultural technologies that remade local places; stories of buddhas, bodhisattvas, and eminent teachers and practitioners were embedded into the land; even Śākyamuni, the historical Buddha, was said to have meditated and taught across Asia, from Sri Lanka to Tibet and China, marking the environment and its historical past as Buddhist.

According to tradition, when Buddhism was brought to the Tibetan and Himalayan regions, it encountered autochthonous deities and spirits throughout the environment. As with the serpent spirits in India, Buddhist stories tell how these deities and spirits were subdued and converted and became protectors of Buddhism. The most prominent narrative of taming and conversion of a local spirit in Tibet is supposed to have taken place in the 7th century under the leadership of the Tibetan king Songtsen Gampo. When Songtsen Gampo set out to build a temple in Lhasa, local spirits thwarted his attempts. Through divination, Buddhists discovered that the land of Tibet was itself constituted by a great demon, lying on her back, unleashing inauspicious forces and thereby undermining the work of spreading the new religion. According to later stories, guided by geomancy, the Indian tantric adept and teacher Padmasambhava had monasteries, temples, and stupas constructed on the limbs and organs of the demoness—across the vast territory of Tibet, including two sites in contemporary Bhutan—pinning her down and subjugating her wild and destructive energy.[15] The supine demon, tamed and converted, became a protector deity for Buddhism in Tibet.

The story of the supine demon provides an image of the very land of Tibet as it was integrated into a Buddhist framework. Such integration took place throughout the Himalaya regions, where tantric deities and buddhas were thought to permeate the environment. According to oral and textual tradition, there are innumerable minor autochthonous spirits inhabiting the environment. These beings reside in mountains, cliffs, caves, valleys, forests, trees, rocks, cairns, lakes, streams, river bends, confluences of rivers and streams, springs, and other natural features.[16] Himalayan Buddhists employ architectural terms—"castle," "tent," "palace"—to describe these landscape features as the residence of deities and spirits. For Himalayan Buddhists, then, much of the environment is animate and, indeed, the beings who animate the environment are thought to form the very landscape features with which they are associated. Scholars refer to this integration of places and beings into one meaningful whole in the context of tantric Buddhism as the "mandalization" of space, through which the meaning of local environments is determined by the cosmology and practice of tantric Buddhism.

In addition to landscape features regarded as abodes of beings understood in a tantric Buddhist framework, particular places were also understood as powerful based on a prior visitation of a significant Buddhist figure. Such a visitation, typically including meditation, teaching, writing, or performing a miracle, could endow specific entities or larger regions with powerful qualities. Some places were revealed as empowering through the subtle sight of advanced practitioners, who are able to perceive sacred geographies invisible to profane vision. (Sometimes, visionaries discovered whole hidden lands, auspicious places conducive to practice and suitable for refuge.[17]) Reliquary structures, temples, shrines, monasteries, and sky burial sites were often placed in these special places, further creating an environment permeated by Buddhism. Moreover, these places are not just understood as passive receptacles for objects and actions; rather, within this framework, it is the places themselves who are active and agentive beings.

One common way in which Himalayan and Tibetan Buddhists engage places and the particular features of Buddhist environments is through pilgrimage practice. In this context, pilgrimage is an embodied encounter with a living being, the *gnas*, located in a place.[18] Thus, pilgrimage, in Tibetan, is *gnas skor* (going around a *gnas*) or *gnas mjal* (encountering a *gnas*). It involves a variety of mental and physical actions that build relationships with the being who resides at an empowering place. As Toni Huber has noted, these include identifying oneself with the *gnas* through visualization and meditation; "*seeing* (in both the sense of direct encounter (*mjal*) and 'reading' and interpreting landscape, etc.), *touching* (by contacting the place), *positioning* (body in relation to place), *consuming/tasting* (by ingesting place substance), *collecting* (substances of the place), *exchanging* (place substances with personal substances/possessions), *vocalizing* (prayers addressed to the place of specific formulas), and even in some cases *listening* (for sounds produced by the place)."[19] Encountering places in these embodied ways, Tibetan and Himalayan pilgrims experience their bodies as transformed and purified through the energy they receive from the place. In pilgrimage, then, one can see how people and environments are in relationship, interacting with and engaging one another.

This interactive engagement between people and Buddhist environments is manifest in daily life as well as in pilgrimage. Most people who lived in the broad cultural area of Himalayan Buddhism were peasant farmers, nomads, laborers, pastoralists, merchants, traders, or others whose livelihood depended on their environments. Their engagement with the Buddhist environment was generally motivated by mundane concerns: a good harvest, health, fertility, longevity, and wealth. To be successful in one's endeavors, it was necessary to maintain good relations with the deities with whom they shared their environments. This required creating a wholesome "moral climate" by not polluting the dwelling of a deity through unwholesome acts, such as disturbing springs, uprooting plants, hunting in close proximity to the deity, or, in some places, cooking or eating particular kinds of foods.[20] It also required ritual offerings and experts who knew how to make them. For example, Himalayan Buddhists regarded the weather as manifestations of benevolent and malevolent deities. Ritual specialists, monks who were experts in controlling the weather, were required to preserve crops from hail, ensure adequate rainfall, and prevent premature freezing or floods.[21] For many Tibetan and Himalayan Buddhists whose livelihood depended upon good relations with the local spirits, they engaged the environment of their daily activities—and thus their survival—as a Buddhist environment.[22]

EAST ASIAN BUDDHIST ENVIRONMENTS

The history of the propagation of Buddhism in East Asia is also a history of the creation of Buddhist environments. Indian Buddhism spread to China in part through grounding the Buddha himself in Chinese landscapes. Buddhists claimed to find traces of the Buddha, especially footprints and handprints, at sites throughout China, which were interpreted as marks of the Buddha's travels and deeds. Stories of the Buddha's activities in China were mapped onto the landscape, manifesting the very land as Buddhist. Buddhism was also grounded in China through the many classical Chinese Buddhist sources that claimed there had been an earlier propagation of Buddhism in China. China, according to these sources, had converted to Buddhism in an earlier golden age and belonged to the Buddhist empire of Aśoka. These texts suggested that Aśoka—who is said to have established eighty-four thousand Buddhist shrines—had distributed relics in China, which were then "discovered" across the landscape. Some texts go further, mapping stories of earlier buddhas and their deeds in China. With enough faith, one could read the traces of these stories, or find relics and stupas, in the Chinese environment. As James Robson observes, Buddhists in China performed a "colonization of the past," claiming the past as Buddhist as they grounded Buddhism in the soil where relics, stupas, and stories were discovered.[23] As in India and the broader Himalayan region, then, Chinese Buddhists gave new Buddhist meanings to indigenous sacred sites.

One of the characteristic features of East Asian Buddhism is the increased valorization of mountain environments as places of practice and spiritual power. Already in India, mountains were significant in Buddhist traditions. In Indian Buddhist cosmology, for example, it is a mountain, Mount Sumeru, that constitutes the very center of the universe, with seven outer mountain ranges defining the Buddhist world. According to classical sources, the Buddha gave many of the most important Mahāyāna teachings at Vulture Peak (near Rajagriha, India), where he and his followers often resided. Indeed, some sources suggest that the Buddha still resides on Vulture Peak, continuously offering his presence and teaching. Moreover, Indian Buddhists frequently built stupas and monasteries on hills and mountains. And while Buddhism in India is historically intertwined with urbanization, canonical Buddhist texts often recommend practicing in mountains and forests, far from the distractions of social life. Practicing in seclusion was inspired by stories of the Buddha himself and also because it was regarded as particularly conducive to encountering buddhas and bodhisattvas. At the same time, Indian sources often describe Buddhist pure land as flat, suggesting that mountains and hills are imperfect and characteristic of samsara. With Buddhism's spread to East Asia, mountains and their surrounding environments came to take on a much more prominent and positive place in Buddhist thought and practice.

While mountains may have had an ambiguous status in Indian Buddhism, Chinese Buddhists were inspired by Indian sources in the development of a Buddhist environment organized around sacred mountains. Sacred mountains in India, such as Vulture Peak, were even said to have flown to China, literally bringing with them the very sacred ground upon which the Buddha taught. References to the land of the Buddha, and sometimes even the very transplanting of that land, provided an authority that was then strengthened by engagements with local traditions, each of which had their own ideas and practices regarding sacred mountains. As in India and Tibet and the Himalayan regions, in China there are numerous stories of eminent monks taming and converting local spirits, transforming indigenous powerful places into a sacred Buddhist environment. Over time, particular mountains were associated with the presence of buddhas and bodhisattvas. The most well-known of these are: Hiuhua (home of Kṣitigarhba) in Anhui; Putuo (home of Avalokiteśvara) in Zhejiang; Wutai (home of Mañjuśrī) in Shanxi; and Emei (home of Samantabhadra) in Sichuan. At these and at many other mountains, practitioners were understood to be able to encounter and be supported by the presence of awakened beings and protector spirits. Monks and pilgrims traveled to mountain monasteries and hermitages to practice austerities, meditate, and develop supernatural powers. Over time, the character for mountains began to appear in the name of many major monasteries in East Asia, as the monasteries associated themselves with auspicious environments.

In China, sites that were often locally significant became meaningful as part of a larger Buddhist network, as in Tibet and the Himalayan regions, enacting the "mandalization of space." To create a Buddhist environment required "new ways of reading the Chinese natural landscape for Buddhist 'signs.' This process," Robson writes, "involved claiming explicit Buddhist meanings for particularly striking features of the natural landscape . . . it was perceived that the natural landscape could speak a language of its own (engaging all the senses), with special sites marked by particular smells, sounds, or visions."[24] These new ways of reading the natural landscape and valorizing mountains and remote environments were undertaken and accomplished by monks who began to actually live in the mountains and remote environments. In place of an earlier aversion to remote forests and mountains, many Buddhist writers and practitioners now praised these environments as places of practice, places in fact conducive to progress on the Buddhist path.

The new ways of reading the landscape were manifest in the spread of landscape poetry and landscape painting. Painters and poets went to the mountains for spiritual and aesthetic inspiration and often understood their artistic activity as a form of spiritual practice. Buddhist visualization and other meditation practices, as well as ideas of emptiness and the presence of Buddhanature in nonsentient beings, influenced the development of Chinese landscape painting and poetry.[25] Landscape paintings and poems now began to express Buddhist teachings. Consider, for example, this poem by Su Shi (1037–1101), the great Song dynasty poet, calligrapher, essayist, statesman, and Buddhist practitioner:

The murmuring brook is the Buddha's long, broad tongue.
And is not the shapely mountain the body of purity?
Through the night I listen to eighty thousand *gathas*,
When dawn breaks, how will I explain it to others?[26]

Su Shi wrote these lines after sitting through the night by a stream on Mount Lu, one of the prominent sacred mountains in central China, not far from the Yangtze River. They express the poet's awakening experience. According to tradition, there are thirty-two major physical characteristics of a buddha, including a "long, broad tongue." Comparing the sounds of the stream to the tongue of the Buddha, then, in the first line, is to suggest that the sound of the stream is the very teaching, the discourse of the Buddha. Su Shi's awakening is an awakening to the mountain as the body of the Buddha. The "eighty thousand *gathas*" refer to the teachings of the Buddha that reveal a truth that, as the poet suggests in the final line, is itself beyond language. The poet's awakening is an experience of the mountains and waters as the Buddha preaching the buddhadharma.

Su Shi's poem is representative of much landscape painting and poetry as an expression of the synthesis of Buddhism and the Chinese nature cult. It would be a mistake, though, to think that this synthesis, and the corresponding landscape poetry and painting, indicated a wider cultural and political affirmation of the natural world according to contemporary environmentalist sensibilities. As Richard Elvin has pointed out, Chinese perceptions and representations of the environment, as seen in landscape painting and nature poetry, do not necessarily reflect actual environmental history. At some periods, the reverence for nature was expressed most poignantly precisely when forests were being clear-cut, waters dammed, and vast wild animal habitats were being destroyed.[27]

Many of the characteristics of Chinese Buddhist relations to the environment—the mandalization of space, the sacralization of mountains, the appropriation of indigenous sacred sites into a Buddhist framework, the synthesis of aesthetic sensibilities for nature and Buddhist practice, and the association of local environments with India and the Buddha's biography—traveled with Buddhism from China to Japan and Korea.

In Japan, pre-Buddhist Shintō deities were reinterpreted to be buddhas and bodhisattvas who had come from India. They were able to stay in Japan because they were said to have brought their abodes with them, namely, the mountains. Some texts offer precise descriptions and dates for the arrival of sacred mountains flying from India, temporarily alighting in China, and then resting permanently in Japan. These include not just parts of Vulture Peak but also the Pure Land of Avalokiteśvara and the place where the future Buddha, Maitreya, will appear.[28] According to some texts, the very ground of Japan itself was originally Mount Mitra, from the northeastern area of Vulture Peak, which was transported and rose up as the islands of Japan.[29] As Allan Grapard notes, "mandalization of space was a vast historical process which aimed at making all Japan a sacred site: that of the manifestation of the divine in its many forms and the site of the practices leading to the realization of Buddhahood."[30] As in China, then, mountain environments grounded Buddhism in Japan, gathering together the sacred land of India and indigenous traditions and practices to form new environments conducive to becoming a buddha and eventually reinterpreting Japan itself as a Buddhist sacred nation.

In Korea, too, the arrival of Buddhism remapped the environment with new meanings. "This remapping process imposed new significance on the indigenous landscape," Robert Buswell writes, "endowing it with the sacred power of Buddhism."[31] By the 9th century, the Korean peninsula had been reinterpreted according to the universal cosmology of Buddhism together with historical landscapes from India and China. As in China and Japan, there was a colonization of the past. For example, the "meditation stone" of Kāśyapa—the previous

Buddha who predicted that in a future lifetime Śākyamuni would himself attain buddhahood—was discovered and became an important Buddhist site. The remapping of prominent Buddhist sites in Korea—including Vulture Peak and the abodes of buddhas and bodhisattvas—meant that Korean pilgrims no longer had to undertake dangerous journeys to India or China. The Korean Peninsula itself became the land of the Buddha, transforming Korean places into appropriate sites of pilgrimage. It was in part through localizing the universal cosmology of Buddhism in Korean environments that a distinct Korean Buddhist identity developed.[32]

Engaging with local environments as Buddhist was also widespread in Sri Lanka and the Theravāda countries of Southeast Asia, where many of the same phenomena are manifest as in India, Tibet and the Himalayan regions, and East Asia.[33]

BUDDHIST CONCEPTS AND ENVIRONMENTAL ETHICS

Regarding sparsely inhabited environments as conducive to practice; affirming the spiritual significance of particular places; and synthesizing aesthetics, reverence for nature, and spiritual practice inspired the development of Buddhist ritual-ecological practices in Asia and beyond. As with earlier propagations of Buddhism, convert Buddhists and Asian heritage Buddhists outside of Asia have built stupas and other Buddhist structures in the process of mapping new places to be cared for and protected as Buddhist.[34] Some scholars have pointed out that emphasizing that some environments are sacred goes hand in hand with the fact that other environments might be neutral or even polluting. That is, while creating Buddhist environments may be important for Buddhists, and may overlap with some contemporary environmental concerns, it is in fact a very different project from creating a Buddhist environmental ethic. However, in the last decades of the 20th century and the early 21st century, much discussion of Buddhism and the environment focuses on doctrines employed precisely to develop an environmentally friendly green Buddhism. Since the early 1980s, these doctrines have been interpreted in the very contemporary context of the overlapping and escalating environmental challenges of resource depletion, habitat and biodiversity loss, and climate change and other consequences of pollution overload.

Foremost among eco-Buddhist doctrines is dependent origination (*pratītyasamutpāda*), a central teaching across Buddhist traditions that states that everything is dependent on conditions, that nothing arises somehow autonomously or independently. This doctrine is so significant that, according to the *Majjhima Nikāya*, it can stand for the Buddha's teaching as a whole: "One who sees dependent origination sees the Dhamma; one who sees the Dhamma sees dependent origination."[35] Although earlier Buddhist thinkers interpreted dependent origination as being primarily about conditionality, the Chinese Buddhist Huayan school interpreted the idea of dependent origination as a radical and universal interdependence. According to the Huayan interpretation, interdependence is like the Jewel Net of Indra, in which each node reflects all the others. It is not merely that any one phenomenon is dependent upon various conditions; every phenomenon is mutually dependent upon all other phenomena. In developing a Buddhist environmental ethic, many eco-Buddhists have understood the Huayan account of interdependence as articulating something like Aldo Leopold's view of "the land community," the ecological interdependence in which any one plant, animal, or ecosystem is itself interdependent with all the other members of the community. Or, as Joanna

Macy—perhaps the most prominent contemporary Western eco-Buddhist—suggests, the Huayan understanding of interdependence is a form of "deep ecology [that] helps us to recognize our embeddedness in nature, overcoming our alienation from the rest of creation and regaining an attitude of reverence for all life forms."[36]

The Jewel Net of Indra implies a nonanthropocentric view, which for many Western environmental thinkers has been regarded as a defining characteristic of an environmentally appropriate conceptual framework. And there are other ways in which Buddhist thought has been interpreted as a form of nonanthropocentrism. For example, according to Buddhist cosmology, sentient beings transmigrate through six kinds of existence in the realms of humans, animals, gods, demigods, hungry ghosts, and hell beings. This is why there are so many stories of buddhas and bodhisattvas in various animal forms. A badger or crow or salmon or mosquito could have been a human in a previous life and may very well be a human in the next life and may eventually become a buddha. According to Buddhist traditions, there are significant differences between the different realms of existence. Still, eco-Buddhists argue that because sentient beings can migrate across the six realms of existence, humans and beings in other realms all share the same nature as sentient beings. This, they argue, is a nonanthropocentric view, a rejection of what Peter Singer calls "speciesism," the unjustified prioritization of the human in one's thought and practice.

Eco-Buddhists are inspired by another Buddhist doctrine that suggests a form of nonanthropocentrism, namely the Mahāyāna idea of a pure buddhanature, or the seed or womb of a buddha (*tathāgatagarbha*) in all—or for some thinkers, in most—sentient beings, and in some traditions also in nonsentient beings. According to this doctrine, the most fundamental nature of sentient beings is awakened mind, which is of unsurpassed value. Over time, some East Asian Buddhists argued that grasses and trees also possessed buddhanature. And eventually, drawing on the Huayan metaphysics of radical interdependence, some Buddhists argued that all beings, sentient and nonsentient, possessed buddhanature. Here is a passage from Zhanran (711–782), the sixth Tiantai patriarch: "The man whose mind is rounded out to perfection knows full well that Truth is not cut in half and that things do not exist apart from the mind. In the great Assembly of the Lotus, all are present—without divisions. Grass, trees, the soil on which these grow—all have the same kinds of atoms. Some are barely in motion while others make haste along the Path, but they will all in time reach the precious land of Nirvāṇa . . . Who can really maintain that things inanimate lack buddhahood?"[37]

Humans are deluded, Zhanran believes, in thinking that they are exceptional. According to this view, the more awakened one is, the more one recognizes how buddhanature permeates all beings and thus the more one is aware that humans are not radically separate or different from other beings, even nonsentient ones. The idea that the difference between samsara and nirvana is one of perception is one that permeates much of Mahāyāna Buddhism. This understanding of the world as possessing value—indeed, possessing the highest possible value of nirvana—has been interpreted as resonating with an ecologically friendly worldview.

In addition to resources for a nonanthropocentric metaphysics and ontology, eco-Buddhists have also been inspired by Buddhist psychology. The most famous element of Buddhist psychology is that sentient beings, including humans, are persons without selves. That is, there is no substantial soul or essence or spirit behind the phenomena of one's perceptions, volitions, thoughts, feelings, and so on. Rather, humans are, like everything else, impermanent and dependently originated, conditioned by innumerable other phenomena and personal and social habits. Eco-Buddhists, such as Macy, contrast the delusion of a self that is somehow separate from everything else and fragile and constantly in need of defense with an ecological sense of self. Macy interprets Buddhist psychology as offering a compelling understanding of an interconnected, ecological self. The pain people feel for the sufferings of others—human and nonhuman—and for the extinction of other species and the loss of their habitats, all this, according to Macy, is a manifestation of the ways people are fundamentally relational beings.

Buddhist ethics and monastic rules have also offered fertile resources for eco-Buddhists. In Buddhist traditions, there is much analysis and critique of greed and the ways in which it leads to one's own suffering and makes one insensible to the sufferings of others. Greed is also a driver of consumerism, which plays a significant role in pollution overload and resource depletion. Buddhist ethical teachings on the importance of mindfulness, of acting in ways that are responsive to the needs and sufferings of others, and of earning a living in a way that decreases rather than increases suffering lend themselves to an ecologically oriented Buddhism. And Buddhist ideals of universal compassion (*karuṇā*) and lovingkindness (*mettā*) are so expansive as to include care for all sentient beings. Moreover, some monastic rules—such as injunctions against felling trees, polluting waters, and eating certain kinds of meat—have been used to suggest a history of at least some Buddhists acknowledging that Buddhism requires attention to the needs and value of the surrounding environment and its nonhuman inhabitants.

In an age of climate destabilization, when it can feel as if one's individual actions are inconsequential even as everyone's individual actions together are catastrophic, the bodhisattva ideal has proved particularly inspiring for eco-Buddhists. The figure of the bodhisattva, who is committed to working to alleviate the suffering of all sentient beings, is a model for maintaining a commitment of working toward what might feel like an impossible goal through embodying the Buddhist path of ethical action, mindfulness and meditation, and wisdom.[38] "We are all bodhisattvas," Macy writes, "able to recognize and act upon our profound interexistence with all beings."[39] Macy and many other eco-Buddhist teachers and practitioners have reimagined the bodhisattva ideal as an eco-sattva, committed to a path of practicing environmental virtues in a Buddhist framework.

APPROACHES TO BUDDHISM AND THE ENVIRONMENT

Eco-Buddhist interpretations of classical Buddhist ontology, psychology, ethics, and images have been the focus of considerable attention from Buddhist teachers, writers, and practitioners and also scholars in Buddhist studies. To order the vast literature on Buddhism and ecology, some scholars have constructed a taxonomy of different approaches. Donald Swearer, for instance, distinguishes five "suggestive rather than definitive" categories: eco-apologists, eco-critics, eco-constructivists, eco-ethicists, and eco-contextualists.[40]

Eco-apologists, according to Swearer, interpret classical Buddhist doctrines as inherently holistic, nonanthropocentric, and environmentally attuned. And they see in Buddhist ideals of living free from greed and the need to constantly acquire and consume things an appropriate model for an era of pollution overload and resource depletion. This is a widespread view, articulated by prominent Asian Buddhists such as the Dalai Lama, Thich Nhat Hanh, Buddhadāsa Bhikkhu, and Sulak Sivaraksa as well as Macy and many other Western eco-Buddhists.

Eco-critics, Swearer's second category, have charged that eco-Buddhists are projecting contemporary environmental concerns onto a premodern tradition that simply was not asking, or responding to, the kinds of questions raised by the modern ecological crisis. Moreover, some argue, eco-Buddhism is informed by Western monotheism and romantic conceptions of a wild nature that is to be affirmed and appreciated. Eco-critics, often focusing their attention on early Indian Buddhism, argue that Buddhism is very much an anthropocentric tradition, emphasizing individual liberation *from* nature. They point to Buddhist texts that are ambivalent about the value of nature or hostile to wild lands and wild animals. Scholars have observed that while there are indeed plenty of stories of buddhas and bodhisattvas in nonhuman animal form, most Buddhists have regarded nonhuman animal existence as unfortunate and, at best, an opportunity to be reborn as a human. Even if one accepts the ecological interpretation of dependent origination, some scholars have argued that it doesn't provide a basis to distinguish between those beings and phenomena deserving respect and protection (Atlantic salmon and vulnerable people, for example) and those one wants to fight against (injustice and smallpox, for example). In addition, some have argued that the actual environmental history of Buddhism in Asia was far from environmentally benign, as Buddhists played a central role in propagating crops such as cotton, tea, rice, and sugar and the irrigation technologies they require, which resulted in massive increases in agriculture and also urbanization as well as consuming and exploiting natural resources for large Buddhist projects. For eco-critics, such as Ian Harris, eco-Buddhism is a manifestation of a globalized modernity that spreads Western environmental discourse. Eco-Buddhism, according to Harris, contributes to the erosion of distinctive local Buddhist traditions, displacing their ritual-ecological practices with more abstract concepts. According to this line of argument, eco-Buddhism is such a radical form of detraditionalization that it is best understood as a phenomenon of the worldwide postmodern religious marketplace.

Swearer's third category, eco-constructivists, includes those who acknowledge that premodern Buddhist doctrines cannot simply be applied to contemporary contexts. Still, they show that there are singularly Buddhist resources that can inform and inspire contemporary thinking and individual and institutional practice to construct a Buddhist environmental ethic.

Eco-ethicists, according to Swearer, are those who want to emphasize the importance of Buddhist ethical contributions, not just Buddhist ontology and cosmology. In particular, eco-ethicists focus on Buddhist virtues such as humility, self-restraint, equanimity, nonviolence, vigor on the path, and others that, taken together, present an ideal of human flourishing that is both Buddhist and necessary for a life-sustaining society. Eco-ethicists, such as Simon James, then, are interested in developing an environmental virtue ethic.

Eco-contextualists, Swearer's fifth category, emphasize Buddhist thought and practice as embedded in local traditions and communities. While it is informed by the rhetoric of universal eco-Buddhist philosophical ideas, it is equally continuous with classical Buddhist traditions that emphasize the importance of particular places in Buddhist practice. In the 1980s, for example, so-called environmental monks in Thailand began reframing the protection of local forests in the context of Buddhist ethics. Restoring and protecting the forests was directly tied to the well-being of local villagers, whose livelihood depended on the trees, as well as those who lived downstream from the forests and suffered during droughts and in the rainy season, when the forests were no longer absorbing and holding the water. In the late 1980s, some Thai monks started performing rituals in which trees were encircled in saffron robes and ordained, a practice that then spread to other Theravāda countries in Southeast Asia. These culturally specific rituals situated the protection of trees in a familiar Buddhist context that was directly connected to the well-being of a particular place and its human and nonhuman inhabitants.

In addition to tree ordinations, scholars have documented many other localized forms of Buddhist environmental practice and activism both in Asian Buddhist societies and where Buddhism is practiced elsewhere. These include protecting forests, bodies of water, and agricultural areas from large-scale development projects and other harms as well as starting sustainable agricultural projects and conserving land. Sometimes, as with the tree ordinations, classical Buddhist practices have been reimagined and integrated into Buddhist environmental activism. For example, Dhamma Walks (*Dhammayietra*), inspired in part by traditions of pilgrimage, have been used to bring attention to vulnerable ecosystems. According to some scholars, this integration of Buddhist practice and environmental activism informed by Buddhist ideas in specific, community-based actions provides a model for how eco-Buddhism can actually contribute in concrete ways to the transition to a more life-sustaining society. As Seth Devere Clippard proposes, a Buddhist environmental ethic should "grow out of the context in which a specific Buddhist community is addressing specific environmental problems. The response is likely to be a mixture of Buddhist thought, practice, ritual, symbol, and discourse." Such an approach, Clippard argues, will be "a more effective and meaningful Buddhist environmentalism for the reason that it begins with the real suffering of real communities and offers real action in response."[41]

Eco-Buddhism is now integrated into much contemporary Buddhist rhetoric. Many Buddhist institutions understand their efforts toward sustainability, such as committing resources to renewal energy production or producing their food in gardens on-site, to be a form of right action in a time of ecological crisis. Integrating modern environmental practices of land conservation and traditional practices that engage the land, Asian heritage and Western convert Buddhists are creating new sacred Buddhist environments outside of Asia that are being protected. Some Buddhist organizations, and associations of different organizations, have made declarations about Buddhist responses to climate change. And some Buddhist organizations, such as the One Earth Sangha, the Rocky Mountain Ecodharma Retreat Center, Green Sangha, and others understand themselves explicitly as eco-Buddhist. The Sati Center for Buddhist Studies offers a year-long program to train as a Buddhist Eco-Chaplain.[42] In these contexts, Buddhist practice is conceived to include living in ways that are appropriate for and responsive to a time of ecological crisis. This reimagination is articulated succinctly in the revision of the bodhisattva vow, traditionally recited in Zen rituals, by the poets Gary Snyder, Philip Whalen, and Allen Ginsberg:

> Sentient beings are numberless; I vow to save them.
> Consuming desires are endless; I vow to stop them.
> Bio-relations are intricate; I vow to honor them.
> Nature's way is beautiful; I vow to become it.[43]

REVIEW OF LITERATURE

The scholarly field of Buddhism and the environment is relatively recent, beginning—with some exceptions—in the 1960s and 1970s. There is now a vast and diverse literature on

Buddhism and the environment that crosses a variety of disciplines, including archaeology, sociology, anthropology, literary studies, art history, philosophy, pilgrimage studies, psychology, environmental history, place studies, the study of activism, animal studies, and more.

Early in its development, the most influential texts in the field were three edited volumes that gathered the work of Buddhist teachers and scholars: *Dharma Gaia: A Harvest of Essays in Buddhism and Ecology*, edited by Allan Hunt Badiner (1990); *Buddhism and Ecology: The Interconnectedness of Dharma and Deeds*, edited by Mary Evelyn Tucker and Duncan Ryūken Williams (1997); and *Dharma Rain: Sources of Buddhism Environmentalism*, edited by Stephanie Kaza and Kenneth Kraft (2000).[44] Together, these three anthologies engage many of the views and practices of eco-Buddhists; *Buddhism and Ecology* also includes challenges by scholars posing critical questions about the eco-Buddhist project. During the decade when these three anthologies were published, Ian Harris sought to bring some order to the already substantial body of literature by offering "a provisional typology" of approaches to Buddhism and the environment.[45] Ten years later, building on Harris's work, Donald Swearer developed his own taxonomy of approaches to Buddhism and ecology.[46] Christopher Ives has very helpfully made his extensive bibliography on Buddhism and ecology easily accessible, updated through March, 2020, when it included thirty-eight pages of entries.[47] Ives himself has also published a number of essays exploring the resources, challenges, and possibilities of a Buddhist environmental ethic.[48]

While much early work on Buddhism and the environment was focused on philosophical interpretations of classical texts, from the 1990s onward, scholarship on Buddhism and the environment has been very much informed by work in other disciplines and is often itself interdisciplinary. Influenced by the spatial turn in the humanities and social sciences, starting in the 1980s there has been considerable work on Buddhist practice and particular environments, exploring pilgrimage, sacred mountains, Buddhist sacred geography, and the power of place.[49] Associated with this literature on place is scholarship on the relationship between nature, particular environments, and art—especially landscape painting and poetry—in classical Buddhist traditions.[50] Informed by early-21st-century work in animal studies, several scholars have produced significant volumes on animals in Buddhist traditions.[51]

Much excellent scholarly work on Buddhism and the environment explicitly engages historical or contemporary Buddhist environmental practice as well as paying attention to classical texts. Julia Shaw's writings, for example, are rooted in extensive archaeological work she has performed at Indian Buddhist sites. Shaw shows how Buddhist monks were intimately involved in transforming the environment through irrigation systems that reduced suffering by providing increased agricultural yields.[52] Her work demonstrates how archaeological evidence is relevant to debates in Buddhist studies, Anthropocene studies, environmental studies, medical humanities, and environmental history. Developments in environmental history have enabled scholars to raise new questions about the relation between Buddhists and their environments, looking at the actual consumption and exploitation of natural resources that provide a different and helpful approach to the study of Buddhism and the environment.[53]

As part of the turn toward actual environmental practices, scholars have been working to develop a Buddhist environmental ethic that is not based primarily on classical Buddhist metaphysics. Instead, while informed by Buddhist ideas, such an ethic is grounded in the local needs and practices of communities and draws significantly on fieldwork. Seth Devere

Clippard gives an excellent methodological defense of this approach, an approach manifest in Susan Darlington's influential works on tree ordination and other forms of contemporary Buddhist environmentalism.[54]

Another more concrete strand of work on Buddhism and the environment is seen in authors who draw on Buddhist ontology, psychology, ethics, rituals, and images to address contemporary challenges without focusing on specific, localized challenges. Gary Snyder, for example, draws on Buddhist traditions to articulate a vision of living well in one's place, a kind of bioregional practice.[55] Joanna Macy draws on the imagery and concepts of Buddhist traditions to support a contemporary eco-friendly view and concrete practices to help build resilience for activists.[56] And because consumerism and capitalism contribute in significant ways to the ecological crisis, many authors have explored Buddhist resources for relinquishing the grip of consumer culture and capitalist economics.[57]

In the first decades of the 21st century, the study of Buddhism and the environment has continued to grow and diversify. In particular, there has been much more interdisciplinary scholarship as well as work that focuses less on universal ontological ideas from classical Buddhist texts and more on concrete Buddhist engagements with particular environments. Most importantly, in an age of climate destabilization, Buddhists will need to think deeply about how to live in the contemporary world so that Buddhist institutions, communities, and individuals can better realize the Buddhist virtues of non-harming and compassionately and skillfully responding to present and future suffering.

DIGITAL MATERIALS

One Earth Sangha (https://oneearthsangha.org/articles/resources/): This Buddhist organization is devoted to a Buddhist response to the climate crisis.

Yale School of the Environment: This is the Buddhism page from the "Yale Forum on Religion and Ecology (https://fore.yale.edu/World-Religions/Buddhism)," an excellent resource including: an overview essay by Christopher Ives, a bibliography on Buddhism and ecology, statements from Buddhist leaders on Buddhism and ecology, links to eco-Buddhist initiatives, sacred Buddhist texts related to the environment, and links to videos of lectures relevant to Buddhism and ecology.

FURTHER READING

Badiner, Allan Hunt, ed. *Dharma Gaia: A Harvest of Essays in Buddhism and Ecology*. Berkeley, CA: Parallax Press, 1990.

Clippard, Seth Devere. "The Lorax Wears Saffron: Towards a Buddhist Environmentalism." *Journal of Buddhist Ethics* 18 (2011): 214–248.

Darlington, Susan Marie. *The Ordination of a Tree: The Thai Buddhist Environmental Movement*. Albany: State University of New York Press, 2012.

Elverskog, Johan. *The Buddha's Footprint: An Environmental History of Asia*. Philadelphia: University of Pennsylvania Press, 2020.

Harris, Ian. "Getting to Grips with Buddhist Environmentalism: A Provisional Typology." *Journal of Buddhist Ethics* 2 (1995): 173–190.

Huber, Toni. *The Holy Land Reborn: Pilgrimage and the Tibetan Reinvention of Buddhist India.* Chicago: University of Chicago Press, 2008.

Huber, Toni, ed. *Sacred Spaces and Powerful Places in Tibetan Culture: A Collection of Essays.* Dharamsala, India: Library of Tibetan Works and Archives, 1999.

Ives, Christopher. "Resources for Buddhist Environmental Ethics." *Journal of Buddhist Ethics* 20 (2013): 541–571.

Kaza, Stephanie, and Kenneth Kraft, eds. *Dharma Rain: Sources of Buddhist Environmentalism.* Boston: Shambhala Publications, 2000.

Macy, Joanna. *World as Lover, World as Self.* Berkeley, CA: Parallax Press, 1991.

Robson, James. *Power of Place: The Religious Landscape of the Southern Sacred Peak (Nanyue 南嶽) in Medieval China.* Cambridge, MA: Harvard University Press, 2009.

Shaw, Julia. "Early Indian Buddhism, Water and Rice: Collective Responses to Socio-Ecological Stress: Relevance for Global Environmental Discourse and Anthropocene Studies." In *Water Societies and Technologies from the Past and Present.* Edited by Yijie Zhuang and Mark Altaweel, 223–255. London: UCL Press, 2018.

Snyder, Gary. *The Practice of the Wild.* New York: North Point Press, 1990.

Swearer, Donald K. "An Assessment of Buddhist Eco-Philosophy." *Harvard Theological Review* 99, no. 2 (2006): 123–137.

Tucker, Mary Evelyn, and Duncan Ryūken Williams, eds. *Buddhism and Ecology: The Interconnectedness of Dharma and Deeds.* Cambridge, MA: Harvard Divinity School Center for the Study of World Religions, 1997.

NOTES

1. Andrew Rawlinson, "Nāgas and the Magical Cosmology of Buddhism," *Religion* 16 (1986): 135–153.
2. James Robson, "Buddhist Sacred Geography," in *Early Chinse Religion, Part Two: The Period of Division (220–589 AD)*, ed. John Lagerwey and Pengzhi Lü (Leiden, The Netherlands: Brill, 2009), 1383.
3. Toni Huber, *The Holy Land Reborn: Pilgrimage and the Tibetan Reinvention of Buddhist India* (Chicago: University of Chicago Press, 2008), 21.
4. Huber, *Holy Land Reborn*, 24.
5. Louis O. Gómez, "Language: Buddhist Views of Language," in *The Encyclopedia of Religion*, ed. Mircea Eliade (New York: Macmillan, 1987), 5309.
6. Julia Shaw, "Early Indian Buddhism, Water and Rice: Collective Responses to Socio-Ecological Stress: Relevance for Global Environmental Discourse and Anthropocene Studies," in *Water Societies and Technologies from the Past and Present*, ed. Yijie Zhuang and Mark Altaweel (London: UCL Press, 2018), 242.
7. Johan Elverskog, *The Buddha's Footprint: An Environmental History of Asia* (Philadelphia: University of Pennsylvania Press, 2020), 91.
8. Shaw, "Early Indian Buddhism, Water and Rice," 238.
9. Shaw, "Early Indian Buddhism, Water and Rice," 250.
10. Elverskog, *Buddha's Footprint*, 91.
11. Elverskog, *Buddha's Footprint*, 91.
12. Elverskog, *Buddha's Footprint*, 90–96.
13. Elverskog, *Buddha's Footprint*, 96–98.
14. Elverskog, *Buddha's Footprint*, 99–107.
15. For interpretations of this story, see Janet Gyatso, "Down with the Demoness: Reflections on a Feminine Ground in Tibet," in *Feminine Ground: Essays on Women and Tibet*, ed. Janice Dean Willis (Ithaca, NY: Snow Lion, 1987), 33–51; and Martin A. Mills, "Re-assessing the Supine Demoness: Royal Buddhist

Geomancy in the Strong btsan sgam po Mythology," *Journal of the International Association of Tibetan Studies* 3 (2007): 1–47.
16. See Toni Huber, "Putting the *Gnas* Back into *Gnas-skor*: Rethinking Tibetan Pilgrimage Practice," in *Sacred Spaces and Powerful Places in Tibetan Culture: A Collection of Essays*, ed. Toni Huber (Dharamsala, India: Library of Tibetan Works and Archives, 1999), 77–104.
17. Frances Garrett, Elizabeth McDougal, and Geoffrey Samuel, *Hidden Lands in Himalayan Myth and History: Transformations of* sbyas yul *Through Time* (Leiden, The Netherlands: Brill, 2020).
18. Huber, "Putting the *Gnas* Back into *Gnas-skor*," 83.
19. Huber, "Putting the *Gnas* Back into *Gnas-skor*," 88.
20. Elizabeth Allison, "Deity Citadels: Sacred Sites of Bio-Cultural Resistance and Resilience in Bhutan," *Religions* 10 (2019): 10.
21. Toni Huber, "Meteorological Knowledge and Environmental Ideas in Traditional and Modern Societies: The Case of Tibet," *Journal of the Royal Anthropological Institute* 3, no. 3 (1997): 577–597.
22. Karen Gagne, *Caring for Glaciers: Land, Animals, and Humanity in the Himalayas* (Seattle: University of Washington Press, 2019).
23. Robson, "Buddhist Sacred Geography," 1360.
24. Robson, "Buddhist Sacred Geography," 1376.
25. Miranda Shaw, "Buddhist and Taoist Influences on Chinese Landscape Painting," *Journal of the History of Ideas* 49, no. 2 (1988): 183–206.
26. Beate Grant, *Mount Lu Revisited: Buddhism in the Life and Writings of Su Shih* (Honolulu: University of Hawaii Press, 1994), 125.
27. Richard Elvin, *The Retreat of the Elephants: An Environmental History of China* (New Haven, CT: Yale University Press, 2006), xxiii.
28. Allan G. Grapard, "Flying Mountains and Walkers of Emptiness: Toward a Definition of Sacred Space in Japanese Religions," *History of Religions* 21, no. 3 (1982): 218.
29. Grapard, "Flying Mountains and Walkers of Emptiness," 219.
30. Grapard, "Flying Mountains and Walkers of Emptiness," 220.
31. Robert Buswell Jr., "Korean Buddhist Journeys to Lands Worldly and Otherworldly," *Journal of Asian Studies* 68, no. 4 (2009): 1055–1075.
32. Buswell, "Korean Buddhist Journeys to Lands Worldly and Otherworldly," 1055–1075.
33. See, for example, Donald K. Swearer, Sommai Premchit, and Phaithoon Dokbuakaew, *Sacred Mountains of Northern Thailand: And Their Legends* (Chiang Mai, Thailand: Silkworm Books, 2004); John Holt, *Spirits of the Place: Buddhism and Lao Religious Culture* (Honolulu: University of Hawaii Press, 2009); and Alex McKinley, "Plant Persons and Sentient Stones: Human Relativity in Buddhist Philosophies of Nature," forthcoming.
34. See, for example, Sally McAra, *Land of Beautiful Vision: Making a Buddhist Sacred Place in New Zealand* (Honolulu: University of Hawaii Press, 2007).
35. *Majjhima Nikāya* 28, "The Greater Discourse on the Simile of the Elephant's Footprint," trans. Bhikkhu Bodhi, SuttaCentral.
36. William Edelglass, "Joanna Macy: The Ecological Self," in *Buddhist Philosophy: Essential Readings*, ed. William Edelglass and Jay Garfield (New York: Oxford University Press, 2009), 435.
37. William R. Lafleur, "Sattva: Enlightenment for Plants and Trees," in *Dharma Gaia: A Harvest of Essays in Buddhism and Ecology*, ed. Allan Hunt Badiner (Berkeley, CA: Parallax Press, 1990), 137.
38. William Edelglass, "Mindfulness and Moral Transformation: Awakening to Others in Śāntideva's Ethics," in *The Bloomsbury Handbook of Indian Ethics*, ed. Shyam Ranganathan (London: Bloomsbury, 2016), 225–248.
39. Edelglass, "Joanna Macy: The Ecological Self," 434.
40. Donald K. Swearer, "An Assessment of Buddhist Eco-Philosophy," *Harvard Theological Review* 99, no. 2 (2006): 124–125.

41. Seth Devere Clippard, "The Lorax Wears Saffron: Towards a Buddhist Environmentalism," *Journal of Buddhist Ethics* 18 (2011): 242.
42. "Buddhist Eco-Chaplaincy," Sati Center for Buddhist Studies.
43. Stephanie Kaza and Kenneth Kraft, eds., *Dharma Rain: Sources of Buddhist Environmentalism* (Boston: Shambhala, 2000), 444.
44. Allan Hunt Badiner, ed., *Dharma Gaia: A Harvest of Essays in Buddhism and Ecology* (Berkeley, CA: Parallax Press, 1990); Mary Evelyn Tucker and Duncan Ryūken Williams, eds., *Buddhism and Ecology: The Interconnectedness of Dharma and Deeds* (Cambridge, MA: Harvard Divinity School Center for the Study of World Religions, 1997); and Kaza and Kraft, *Dharma Rain*.
45. Ian Harris, "Getting to Grips with Buddhist Environmentalism: A Provisional Typology," *Journal of Buddhist Ethics* 2 (1995): 173–190.
46. Donald K. Swearer, "An Assessment of Buddhist Eco-Philosophy," *Harvard Theological Review* 99, no. 2 (2006): 123–137.
47. Christopher Ives, "Buddhism and Ecology Bibliography," Yale Forum on Religion and Ecology.
48. See especially Christopher Ives, "A Mixed Dharmic Bag: Current Debates about Buddhism and Ecology," in *Routledge Handbook of Religion and Ecology*, ed. Willis Jenkins and Mary Evelyn Tucker (New York: Routledge, 2016), 43–51; Christopher Ives, "Resources for Buddhist Environmental Ethics," *Journal of Buddhist Ethics* 20 (2013): 541–571; and Christopher Ives, "In Search of a Green Dharma: Philosophical Issues in Buddhist Environmental Ethics," in *Destroying Mara Forever: Buddhist Ethics Essays in Honor of Damien Keown*, ed. Charles Prebish and John Powers (Ithaca, NY: Snow Lion, 2009), 165–186.
49. On pilgrimage, see, for example, Huber, *Holy Land Reborn*; on sacred mountains: James Robson, *Power of Place: The Religious Landscape of the Southern Sacred Peak (Nanyue 南嶽) in Medieval China* (Cambridge, MA: Harvard University Press, 2009); Swearer, Premchit, and Dokbuakaew, *Sacred Mountains of Northern Thailand*; on Buddhist sacred geography: James Robson, "Buddhist Sacred Geography," in *Early Chinse Religion, Part Two: The Period of Division (220–589 AD)*, ed. John Lagerwey and Pengzhi Lü (Leiden, The Netherlands: Brill, 2009), 1361–1407; Grapard, "Flying Mountains and Walkers of Emptiness"; Buswell, "Korean Buddhist Journeys to Lands Worldly and Otherworldly"; on the power of place: Holt, *Spirits of the Place*; and Toni Huber, ed., *Sacred Spaces and Powerful Places in Tibetan Culture: A Collection of Essays* (Dharamsala, India: Library of Tibetan Works and Archives, 1999).
50. Miranda Shaw, "Buddhist and Taoist Influences on Chinese Landscape Painting," *Journal of the History of Ideas* 49, no. 2 (1988): 183–206; Jason M. Wirth, *Mountains, Rivers, and the Great Earth: Reading Gary Snyder and Dōgen in an Age of Ecological Crisis* (Albany: State University of New York Press, 2017); Donald K. Swearer, "Principles and Poetry, Places and Stories: The Resources of Buddhist Ecology," *Daedalus* 130, no. 4 (2001): 225–241; and Joseph D. Parker, *Zen Buddhist Landscape Arts of Early Muromachi Japan (1336–1573)* (Albany: State University of New York Press, 1999).
51. Geoffrey Barstow, *Food of Sinful Demons: Meat, Vegetarianism, and the Limits of Buddhism in Tibet* (New York: Columbia University Press, 2018); and Reiko Ohnuma, *Unfortunate Destiny: Animals in the Indian Buddhist Imagination* (New York: Oxford University Press, 2017).
52. See, for instance, Shaw, "Early Indian Buddhism, Water and Rice," 223–255.
53. See, for example, Elverskog, *Buddha's Footprint*.
54. Clippard, "Lorax Wears Saffron," 214–248; Susan Marie Darlington, *The Ordination of a Tree: The Thai Buddhist Environmental Movement* (Albany: State University of New York Press, 2012); Susan M. Darlington, "Buddhist Environmental Imaginaries," in *The Buddhist World*, ed. John Powers (London: Routledge, 2015), 433–452; Susan M. Darlington, "Contemporary Buddhism and Ecology," in *The Oxford Handbook of Contemporary Buddhism*, ed. Michael Jerryson (New York: Oxford University Press, 2017), 487–503; and Susan M. Darlington, "Environmental Buddhism Across Borders," *Journal of Global Buddhism* 19 (2018): 77–93.

55. See, for example, Gary Snyder's essay collection, *The Practice of the Wild* (New York: Farrar, Straus & Giroux, 1990); and his long poem, intended as a sūtra of *Mountains and Rivers Without End* (Berkeley, CA: Counterpoint, 1996).
56. See Joanna Macy, *World as Lover, World as Self* (Berkeley, CA: Parallax Press, 1991); and Joanna Macy and Molly Young Brown, *Coming Back to Life: The Updated Guide to the Work That Reconnects* (Gabriola Island, BC: New Society, 2014).
57. See, for example, Richard K. Payne, ed., *How Much Is Enough? Buddhism, Consumerism, and the Human Environment* (Somerville, MA: Wisdom Publications, 2010); Peter L. Daniels, "Climate Change, Economics, and Buddhism—Part 1: An Integrated Environmental Analysis Framework," *Ecological Economics* 69 (2010): 952–961; and Stephanie Kaza, *Hooked: Buddhist Writings on Greed, Desire, and the Urge to Consume* (Boston: Shambhala, 2005).

William Edelglass

BUDDHISM IN COLONIAL CONTEXTS

DEFINING COLONIALISM IN A BUDDHIST CONTEXT

Overviews of Buddhism and colonialism often begin in the early 16th century and end in the mid-20th century with the independence of polities with significant Buddhist populations such as Korea (1945), Vietnam (1945), Burma (1948), Ceylon (1948), Laos (1949), and Cambodia (1953). In most popular and national histories, these dates have often been seen as the beginning of the postcolonial period, but more nuanced studies show that no act of independence has ever been capable of eradicating the colonial period. Not only did most postcolonial nations maintain the governing technologies of the colonial state but colonial epistemologies had such a profound impact on the societies of both the colonized and colonizer that much of the way humanity conceives of the world today stems from colonial developments. We, are, in other words still living the colonial.[1]

In popular and scholarly consciousness, the term "colonialism" is often reserved for Western European domination in Asia (and Africa), but such a vision is deeply problematic for a number of reasons.[2] First, it is overtly Eurocentric. For not only was the history of modern colonialism across Asia deeply shaped by the advances of Imperial Japan but across the continent as a whole, there were numerous instances of "inner colonialism." From Qing expansion in the west and southwest of China to the Bangkok-based Chakri dynasty's annexation of previously semi-autonomous polities in northern Siam or the Burman conquests, and subsequent Burmanization of minority areas, just prior to and after British colonial rule, Asian states were continually jostling for power within the region.[3] Second, the notion that colonialism is a modern phenomenon is deeply myopic. Although the term has not been widely employed in studies of premodern Asia, colonialism can be more accurately seen as a central facet of human history, as much a part of the Roman conquest of Egypt as it was among the Ottoman Empire of the Turks.[4] A more thorough and systematic overview of Buddhism in colonial contexts would undoubtedly consider a wider range of case studies, drawn from the ancient world and ongoing today.[5] If periodizations of colonialism remain in flux, there is still good reason to focus primarily on the high tide of colonialism in 17th- to 20th-century Asia when European and (later) Japanese powers transformed significant elements of Buddhist history, thought, and practice.

Historians estimate that by the early 20th century, some 50 to 85 percent of the earth's land surfaces were under the nominal control of just a handful of Western powers.[6] While this remarkable statistic obscures much of colonialism's complexities, it also speaks to the profoundly unbalanced nature of the global political economy in the modern world. The European colonization of the globe was already in process by the 16th century and by the mid-1600s, Asian economies were beginning to be restructured in accordance with the four most powerful European colonial powers, Britain, France, Portugal, and the Netherlands. Over the course of the next three centuries, most parts of Asia with significant Buddhist populations came under direct political control of one (or more) European states. Even Thailand, Japan, Nepal, Bhutan, Tibet, and the interiors of China, which maintained their independence (sometimes nominally), were still periodically forced into "unequal treaties" with colonial regimes. By the first quarter of the 20th century, there were three major colonial empires possessing "zones of influence" over regions with significant Buddhist populations: the British in South Asia with a significant maritime presence in Southeast and East Asia at places like Singapore and Hong Kong; the French in mainland Southeast Asia; and the newest imperial power, Japan, with a powerful presence across much of East Asia, including most notably Korea and Taiwan.

With histories of colonialism demonstrating almost innumerable variations in their actual practice and theorization, there is no singular, universally accepted definition that can be used to both describe and explain its various aspects across Buddhist Asia.[7] There are, however, a number of common threads that are helpful in weaving together the wider analysis. The centerpiece of the colonial project is the physical conquest of another people's spaces and territories with an intent to exert control over them via economic, political, intellectual, or military means. At its heart then, colonialism is a system of political domination in which one people's economic, cultural, and intellectual resources are directed to the benefit of another "foreign" people. Many forms of colonialism are also closely tied to imperialism, which in the broadest sense of the term can be defined as the ability of a powerful center to impose its interests via a much grander territorial scale or even globally through the creation and maintenance of trans-colonial empires. If imperialism is defined by domination, colonialism then is defined primarily by the acquisition of territories.[8]

While most of Europe's colonies started as a means to access raw materials and secure their transport to the colonizer's center, they typically adopted different models of political governance and economic structure over time, which in turn gave them varying roles.[9] As colonial governance deepened, colonies also became cultural spaces aimed at representing an image or idea of what the colonizer and their "civilization" symbolized. Within the context of 19th-century European colonization and imperialism, this image was most emphatically marked by the "dual revolutions" of the late 18th century: the industrial transformation of liberal capitalism pioneered in Britain and the democratic nationalist revolution of *liberté, égalité, fraternité* largely confined to France.[10] These dual transformations are seen by many scholars as giving birth to the modern world and to the foundation of "colonial modernity" or "modernity" more widely.[11] Those who accept these terms see them as both a discourse and a condition which was thrust upon Asia as a result of exposure to Western forms of knowledge, growing commercial traffic, new forms of weaponry and technology, and territorially rigid concepts of nation states.[12] In the colonial world of the late 19th and early 20th century, it was often assumed that only the "West" was modern and that as its civilizational program spread to Asia, the colonized would be reshaped according to the imagined attributes of the "modern West."[13]

However, as is well-known, Asian societies, cultures, and religions did not fully adopt imagined Western models. Despite the failure of Western modernization theories as well as the absence of any singular definition of what modernity constitutes—there was no single modernity, only "multiple modernities," as the sociologist Shmuel Eisendstadt put it—Buddhists from across the colonized (and non-colonized) world regularly invoked modernity as a descriptive and analytical tool to interpret Buddhism.[14] While the literature on Buddhist modernity is growing quickly, scholars have identified a series of matrices that underlined the making of most Buddhist modernities.[15] These include the privileging of the rational individual, secularism and laicization, psychologization, democracy and equality, science and empiricism, and social and political engagement.[16] Undoubtedly, these sorts of attributes were central to the imaginings of numerous self-proclaimed Buddhist modernists and reformists, but it is also important to recognize that there were many Buddhists who pushed back against these models, offering "alternative modernities" in acts that can be simultaneously called both counter-modern and modern.[17]

As a system of ideas and practices, colonialism was marked by two major domains. On the one hand, a philosophy of liberalism guided its development. It envisioned a state whose rational rule of law governed the public sphere, enabling economic growth while encouraging individual autonomy and rational self-interest. On the other hand, colonialism moved to systematize and rationalize infrastructures including hygiene, industrial production, communication technologies (like printing presses), and commercial transport. This disciplinary rationalization extended to cultural domains like law, education, and the sciences, including new scientific fields such as ethnography and philology. Thus, the colonized became "beneficiaries" of these domains—the colonizing project was, it bears repeating, typically one of "civilizing subjects." Indeed, as the work of many scholars has shown, there is a deeply paradoxical relationship between liberalism and empire, with the former often serving as the justification for the latter.[18] Although never fixed in time, these ideas and practices were always to some degree serving as a backdrop in the colonial world.

BRITISH EMPIRE IN SOUTH AND SOUTHEAST ASIA

The first sustained colonial interventions in Buddhist lands occurred in the early 16th century when the Portuguese Empire attempted to gain access to Ceylon's (Sri Lanka) cinnamon supply. As Portuguese agents established a growing presence along the coast, the *Padres* of the Catholic Church worked to convince locals of the supremacy of their Savior. The strength of the colonial presence waxed and waned during this early period, but as the works of the elite Sinhala Buddhist poet and later Christian convert, Alagiyavanna Mukaveṭi (1552–*c.* 1625), demonstrate, religious worlds were being deeply challenged.[19] When Portuguese territories in Lanka were lost to the Dutch East India Company with the help of Kandyan armies in 1658, the mountainous interior of the island was still largely independent. The Kandy Kings maintained this status until 1815 when the British East India Company—which had driven out the Dutch in 1796—forced them to sign the Kandyan Convention, formally ceding the entirety of the island to British control.

The British conquest of Ceylon marked just the beginning of the East India Company's (after 1858, Britain's) sustained encounters with Buddhist polities in South Asia. By 1824, Company troops had moved to annex southeast and southwestern Burma, the latter of which included the recently fallen Buddhist kingdom of Arakan—itself a victim of the Burmese Ava Court's imperial expansion in the last decades of the 18th century. Following another military conflict in 1852, Lower Burma (Pegu) was added to the Company's growing list of territories. The final coup d'état, however, occurred in 1885 when British troops entered the city of Mandalay and deposed Thibaw (r. 1878–1885), the last King of Burma's Konbaung dynasty (1772–1885). This marked the high point of British colonial rule with multiple maritime ports across Southeast and East Asia under British control as well as nearly the entirety of mainland South Asia, stretching from what is today Afghanistan through Nepal and Bhutan to the southern tip of India and Sri Lanka under direct or indirect British rule.

India always remained the heart of Britain's imperial enterprise, but apart from Chittagong, Burma (ruled as a province of India from 1885 to 1937), and the upper tracts of the Himalayas in places like Sikkim, Bhutan, Kinnaur, Zanskar, Ladakh, and Spiti, Buddhism had long ceased to be an active part of its religious landscape.[20] While British surveyors and civil servants in India only encountered living Buddhists on the rarest of occasions, they did learn of them as they dug—often literally—into the deep recesses of the subcontinent's history. The British discovery of Buddhism, was, like the wider European "invention" of Buddhism, a centuries-long process that involved scholarly networks linking Asia to Europe, remote monasteries to urban entrepôts, imperial centers to missionary outposts, and Buddhist literati with European savants. Colonialism was central to this process and Buddhology, like its sister disciplines Indology, orientalism, and anthropology, were directly tied to the colonial enterprise.[21]

By the mid-19th century, the deciphering of numerous Indic scripts chiseled into the sides of ancient Buddhist monuments and most importantly, of the Aśokan inscriptions—an act so significant that it has been rightly equated to the deciphering of the Egyptian hieroglyphics[22]—had led to a marked transformation in the way that India's ancient history, and therefore Buddhist history, was understood.[23] Archaeology and epigraphy, however, were not the only new tools in the orientalist's kit. Just as mounds of earth and half-broken images of bodhisattvas could alert archaeologists and art historians to critical junctures in Buddhist history, the ever-growing collection of manuscripts, gathered by antiquarians, merchants, colonial officers, and looters across the continent, also pointed to new horizons. With philology at their side, orientalists took to the study of Buddhist literature, primarily in Sanskrit and Pāli, but also in numerous vernaculars, thereby recovering and often reinventing histories of Buddhist praxis and thought. For the disparate groups in South Asia—Europeans, Indians, Ceylonese, Burmese, Hindus, Buddhists, Muslims, and so on—who associated themselves with organizations like the Asiatic Society (est. 1784), Archaeological Survey of India (est. 1861), and Pāli Text Society (est. 1881), Buddhism came to be seen as an object of knowledge within a wider European taxonomy and liberal secular discourse of "world religions."[24] By the mid- to late 19th century, the leading lights of these organizations had begun to define and imagine Buddhism as a discrete tradition in opposition to the Christianity of the West.

> One a religion of the West, the other of the East; one theistic, the other atheistic; one with a reluctant savior, the other with a savior who proclaimed his superiority from the

moment of his birth; one whose savior is depicted nailed to a cross, the other whose savior is depicted seated cross-legged in meditation.[25]

As a largely scriptural endeavor that supplanted ritual for text, the orientalist understanding of Buddhism, personified by scholars like T. W. Rhys Davids (1843–1922), and his far too often neglected wife, C. A. F. Rhys Davids (1857–1942), came to define Buddhism, in its "original" formation at least, as a rational, scientific teaching based on compassion and kindness.[26] It had, as Donald Lopez puts it, "a complete philosophical and psychological system, based on reason and restraint, opposed to ritual, superstition and sacerdotalism."[27] These were, of course, the very ideas at the root of Europe's own modernity and Victorian Britain's imagined self.[28] Although it is not often acknowledged, Indian scholars—numismatists, epigraphists, archaeologists, and orientalists of the highest caliber—also played a critical role in the refashioning of Buddhism at this time, mastering orientalist disciplines and then using them to pursue their own interests and agendas.[29] The scholarly works of the Bengali savant Rajendralal Mitra (1824–1891), the first "native" president of the Asiatic Society and his student, Haraprasad Shastri (1861–1930), inspired generations of scholars and Buddhists from England and Japan to India and Russia.

Buddhist leaders in colonial Burma and Ceylon were not immune to these ideas and the wider epistemic systems upon which they were founded. From its earliest days, British rule had relied extensively on the assistance of "native agents," and a large body of scholarly monks, lay literati, and other professionals in the Empire had played critical roles in the study of ancient scriptures and inscriptions.[30] Christian missionaries, whose schools, public forums, and vernacular printing presses often reached much further than the colonial state, were also responsible for spreading Western ideas about religious practice, thought, and identity. While the missionary enterprise was only minimally successful in converting the colonial populace, their most enduring impact was arguably in the way their model of religion rendered Buddhist traditions as a bounded entity. Just as in Japan and elsewhere in the colonial world, the dissemination of a liberal secularist discourse about "world religion" became naturalized by Buddhists with the teachings of buddha increasingly imagined and defined as a discrete tradition in contrast to other religious traditions like Christianity, Shintoism, Islam, and Hinduism.[31] As colonial rule deepened, the technologies of the colonial state recognized and enhanced these differences, treating what was essentially a discourse—Buddhism—as a concrete and tangible entity, marked by exclusive individual identities. While government enterprises like the census required individuals to select singular identities, thereby encouraging Buddhists to sharpen and clarify their religious identities, the contested and ultimately ambiguous nature of the term "religion" itself often led to further questions about what constituted "Buddhist religion." In places like Burma, the most dexterous of Buddhists exploited these ambiguities for their own benefit. This is most clearly visible in the early 20th-century legal case which Alicia Turner has termed the "shoe and the shikho."[32] Here, Burmese Buddhists used changing conceptions of religion to not only criticize the British practice of wearing shoes inside pagoda premises as a violation of the state's policy of non-interference in religious affairs but also to resist the state's demands that Burmese students prostrate (*shikho*) to their schoolteachers, an act which they argued was religious in nature and therefore not appropriate in secular classrooms.

Intellectual shifts in how one conceived of Buddhism was one thing, but the colonial state's heavy hand was another. In both Ceylon in 1815 and Burma in 1885, the British dissolved the Buddhist monarchy, thereby stripping the sangha, or monastic body, of the state support upon which it historically relied. As in most Southeast Asian Buddhist polities, Burma's king had possessed both "secular" and "religious" responsibilities, but the British refusal to maintain the king's patronage of the sangha triggered a crisis of authority within the monastic system. When the Burmese sangha's Supreme Patriarch (*thathanabaing*) died in 1895, for instance, the colonial administration refused to appoint a successor for nearly a decade. This not only triggered numerous institutional problems within the monastic education system but was seen by many Burmese as a failure of the British to behave like a righteous Buddhist ruler, since it was the king's responsibility to appoint the new Patriarch.[33] In Ceylon, the British dissolution of the monarchy had a somewhat different impact on monastic politics. Before 1815, the country's political division into low-country maritime and high-country interior regions had placed those monastics in the low country in a rather ambiguous position. Although they took ordination and received their titles and positions from the highland kings of Kandy, they resided in territories administered by colonial authorities where the king's formal authority was null and void. Yet for some, Britain's presence represented something of an opportunity since some low-country monastics and their lay patrons were critical of Kandy's roles in Buddhist affairs, especially in regard to Kandyan discrimination against low-country non-Goyigama men and the Kandyan maintenance of "administrative and ritual structures that favored Kandyan elites."[34] With the collapse of the Kandyan kingdom in 1815, some low-country monks began to reject Kandy's authority outright and in the decades thereafter, the position of the then dominant monastic group, the Siyam Nikāya (est. 1753) was weakened, leading to a power vacuum in which other monastic lineages and elites made efforts to assert or reclaim their influence.[35]

Such events had diverse repercussions across the Bay of Bengal. For scholar monks, like the influential Burmese meditation master Ledi Sayadaw (1846–1923), the perceived decline in monastic learning (*pariyatti sāsana*) wrought by British rule was an issue of grave concern.[36] The only solution to this problem, he contended, was to uproot the whole system and begin making it more widely available among the laity. With the decline of Buddhism deep in Ledi's mind, he embarked on a life of regular travel, founding ad hoc study groups and promoting a simplified *Abhidhamma* system once reserved only for the elite. Ledi put Buddhism "in the hands of all the people," including new audiences, like the youth and women who "had not even the possibility of the same level of access as laymen under the old paradigm."[37] As a writer, he made use of advancements in print technology, by spreading his message through inexpensive and accessible formats while embracing the use of "simple language and an unadorned style."[38] At the center of his teachings was the provocative argument that in order to practice insight meditation (*vipassanā*), one did not have to first enter into the deep states of concentration known as the *jhānas*, but only had to develop the capacity to return again and again to momentary levels of concentration (*khanika-samādhi*). So influential were some of Ledi's writings that they went through print runs of more than ten thousand and in the ensuing decades, Ledi's interpretation of vipassanā on the basis of momentary concentration became part and parcel to the emerging global vipassanā movement.[39]

In Ceylon, religious prestige and power continued as it had prior to colonial rule, but the new power dynamics undoubtedly caused ruptures. Although British policy after 1857 mandated a strict rule of religious non-interference across the Empire, the state regularly sought out religious functionaries for advice on legal and educational issues.[40] At times, this strengthened a new body of typically urban-based monastics, some of who had only minimal or localized influence in pre-colonial settings. Eminent monks, like Hikkaḍuvē Sumaṅgala (1827–1911) of Ceylon's Siyam Nikāya, for instance, worked to reassert the Nikāya's influence across the island at the same time that he corresponded with Buddhist leaders across Asia in the hopes of securing a new patron from the royal courts of Burma or Siam (Thailand). While these dreams never materialized, he was more successful in his institutional capacity as the principal of the state-sponsored Vidyodaya Buddhist College (est. 1873). Here, despite British pressures to introduce more "secular" subjects, monastic curriculums continued to focus on topics of classical Buddhist learning like Pāli and Sanskrit as well as Sinhala, astrology and ayurvedic medicine.[41]

While conversations about the nature of monastic education never faded from the public sphere, the state's creation and expansion of a secular education system also gave rise to new sets of concerns. Although small schools for Buddhist laity had existed prior to colonial rule in both Ceylon and Burma, the British state's desires for a near-universal system of primary education was a novel development. Secular school systems were initially established by Christian missionary societies but after the 1860s, a spectrum of state-supported educational institutions including government and missionary Anglo-vernacular schools began to mushroom across the colonies. Demands for these forms of education were particularly strong among affluent families and local elites who recognized that in an urban colonial economy, socio-economic mobility was closely tied to English-language skills and a Western education. In both Burma and Ceylon, the graduates of these new institutes never formed more than a small proportion of the colonial population, but their access to resources and coveted government jobs allowed them to exercise a disproportionate influence over social, economic and religious affairs. But whether students were educated in Christian missionary schools, which possessed a virtual monopoly in Ceylon, or in Anglo-vernacular government schools—often managed by Christian missionaries nonetheless—there were growing concerns in both Burma and Ceylon about the lack of Buddhist subjects in secular school curriculums.

In 1890s Burma, for instance, the government eventually agreed to support what were known as "Buddhist Anglo-vernacular schools." These institutes included some Buddhist instruction but only as a compartmentalized subject of inquiry, which according to Alicia Turner further solidified the idea of Buddhism as a distinctive religious entity.[42] In Ceylon, these kinds of hybrid institutes were also fast becoming part of the new educational fabric. By the time the American theosophist and famed "White Buddhist" Henry Olcott (1832–1907) arrived in Ceylon in 1880, of more than 1,200 government-sponsored schools, only four were Buddhist.[43] By the time he died in 1907, there were more than 20,000 students attending some two hundred Buddhist schools he had founded.[44] Through his Buddhist Theosophical Society (BTS), Olcott was intent on not only countering Christian influence in the island but making secular education a central part of lay Buddhist life. Olcott's Buddhism, in effect, "became the basic religious ideology of the educated Buddhist bourgeoisie."[45]

Olcott's schools provided instruction in a wide range of secular subjects, but their separate classes in Buddhism, guided by Olcott's textbook, the *Buddhist Catechism*, is what made them unique. First published in Sinhala and English in 1881 and then churned out by the thousands in some twenty languages from Thai and German to Japanese and Tamil, the *Buddhist*

Catechism is an excellent illustration of some of the new ways Buddhism was being imagined in the colonial world. According to the *Catechism*, Buddhism was a rationalized system of ethical and moral thought, fully compatible with modern science and free of the ritual and dogma that Olcott felt had corrupted "original" Buddhism. Despite the text's messy blend of Protestant modernism, metropolitan gentility, academic orientalism, and Western esotericism, several eminent Buddhist monks had "approved" the book's content.[46] Its publication, however, initiated a storm of protest among other monastics. Mohoṭṭivatte Guṇānanda (1823–1890), the polemicist monk and debater often credited with sparking Ceylon's "Buddhist Revival," published his own counter-catechism, the *Bauddha Praśnaya* (Buddhist Questions), presenting "true Buddhism" as a devotional activity based on ritual worship and not on Olcott's "fraudulent" philosophy.[47] The fact that both texts were as popular as they were despised speaks well not only to the diversity of Buddhist views in Ceylon but also to modernity and its discontents.

Olcott's vision of Buddhism and his global travels propagating it had much to do with the wider globalization of Buddhism during the colonial era, but it was his protégé, Anagārika Dharmapāla (1864–1933) who gave it a distinctive touch. Born as Don David Hewavitarane into an elite Sinhala Buddhist family, Dharmapāla was educated by Christian missionaries despite being closely acquainted with many of the island's leading Buddhist clerics. After joining the Theosophical Society and being groomed in Olcott's programs of socioreligious reform, Dharmapāla propagated another self-styled "modern Buddhism" whose grandiose vision of social outreach and this-worldly asceticism was matched only by its confidence in the soteriological path that the Buddha described. Through his Maha Bodhi Society (est. 1891) and influential English-language journal, the *Maha-Bodhi*, originally co-founded with Olcott but by the early 1900s managed to his own devices, Dharmapāla traveled most of Buddhist Asia and the Western world, promoting Buddhism as a solvent to contemporary afflictions and raising funds for his project to revive Buddhism in India and return the Maha Bodhi Temple in Bodh Gaya to Buddhist ownership.[48]

Although the Maha Bodhi Society was one of the most successful Buddhist organizations in the colonial world, it was not alone. By the late 19th century, Buddhist laity—often Western educated—founded and managed dozens of voluntary associations whose formal structures, charitable efforts, and emphasis on socio-educational transformation paralleled other organizations that had become increasingly common across urban South Asia. Most held weekly meetings, study sessions, and regularly scheduled events featuring experts on various Buddhist topics. In Burma, Ceylon, and even in more than a dozen cities in India, Buddhist associations became an important part of urban life, providing new definitions of what it meant to be Buddhist. For the thousands of Buddhists who joined modern associations in Burma, it "offered a democratized and homogenized Buddhist identity that leveled out some of the [existing social] hierarchies."[49] Religious authority was no longer just the providence of royal patrons, ritual specialists, and learned monastics. Some of the most powerful agents were now government clerks, editors, and schoolteachers who could draft an essay and have it printed in a newspaper, knowing that it might be seen by thousands in just a matter of days.

Although many of these organizations were shaped deeply by the cosmopolitan urban cultures in which they thrived, they also marked the growing visibility of an increasingly hard-edged ethno-nationalist religious politics across South Asia, which was itself a wider symptom of the nationalist fever sweeping the early 20th century world. While the relationship between Buddhism and politics is by no means novel, the ways in which Buddhists utilized Buddhist symbols, ideas, and institutions for political ends came to be one of the universal markers of colonial rule. Organizations like the Young Men's Buddhist Association (YMBA), founded in Ceylon in 1898 and then in Rangoon in 1906, became important vehicles of self-expression and organization for Western-educated Buddhists in the early 20th century. Although the organization saw itself as a loyal subject to the British Crown, its popular slogan "To be Burmese is to be Buddhist" was later taken up by political groups, some of whom had anti-colonial objectives. Although it was a Westernized elite who emerged as the primary leaders of the anti-colonial movement, monastics also played a critical role in constructing the nationalist narratives that mobilized the masses against colonial authorities, and as would become increasingly evident in the postcolonial state, against non-Buddhist and/or ethnic minorities.[50]

Some of the first major political protests in Burma, for instance, were led by the globetrotting Arakanese (Rakhine) polyglot and "agitator in yellow robes," U Ottama (1879–1939).[51] By using a combination of print and cross-country tours, Ottama helped convince the country's patriotic youth that not only was the sangha a necessary part of the "nationalist solution" but that political activity was not a violation of the *Vinaya* but in fact a requirement of it. In Ceylon, Dharmapāla helped lay the foundation for the nationalist movement by popularizing the Orientalist argument that texts like the *Mahāvaṃsa* were "authentic" histories of the island nation.[52] By the time of independence, historians, politicians, and monastics alike increasingly interpreted the ancient Pāli chronicle through an ethno-religious and racial lens in which the Sinhalese were seen as a chosen people safeguarding Buddhism against foreign invaders. Colonial archaeology further substantiated Sinhala claims of a once glorious Buddhist civilization that had collapsed due to the pernicious influences of non-Buddhist, non-Sinhala cultures.[53] As the Sinhala-Tamil conflict in post-independence Sri Lanka escalated, *Mahāvaṃsa* histories and ancient ruins like Anuradhapura became firmly cemented in the spatial imagination of Sinhala nationalists who used them to rationalize monastic involvement in political affairs as part of the necessary defense of dhamma.[54] As the walls of colonialism came crumbling down, Buddhism's role in the political landscape had been firmly cemented, as is visible in Prime Minister U Nu's "Buddhist socialism" in 1950s Burma and in Prime Minister S. W. R. D. Bandaranaike's landslide victory in Sri Lanka in 1956 on a platform of "Sinhala-only" as the national language and Buddhism as the state religion.

FRENCH COLONIALISM AND MAINLAND SOUTHEAST ASIA

The French presence in Buddhist parts of mainland Southeast Asia dates to the 17th century when Roman Catholic priests were relatively successful in attracting Vietnamese near Saigon to the Christian mission. However, it was only in the mid-19th century when a resurgent French empire under Napoleon III (r. 1852–1870) established its own colony along the eastern coast of the mainland. Unlike Ceylon or Burma, where the British deposed the Buddhist rulers, French Indochina was governed according to a model similar to what the British employed in India. In Cochin China (southern Vietnam), the populace was under direct French rule while in the remainder of Vietnam as well as in Cambodia and Laos, native monarchs were allowed nominal authority under French protectorates.

For Siam's (Thailand) Bangkok-based Chakri dynasty—what was to be the only Buddhist kingdom in Southeast Asia that remained independent—the French creation of Indochina was of grave concern. In places like Chiang Mai (1899), Lanna (1920), and Nan (1931), all now in Northern Thailand, Siam engaged in a form of internal colonialism by replacing local rulers in what had been previously semi-autonomous Buddhist polities with officials loyal to the new Bangkok bureaucracy (which itself had been recently remodeled on that of the nearby colonial regimes).[55] In one of its most ambitious plans, Bangkok implemented the Sangha Act of 1902, aimed at "unifying" and in effect, controlling, all of the various monastic sects throughout the kingdom's borders. Of special target were those sanghas in the heavily populated regions in the north and northeast where Bangkok's influence was weaker. Paralleling British incursions into northern Burma, Siam's northern encroachments not only triggered a variety of millenarian movements, especially among the Lao of northeastern Siam, but also gave root to an oppositional ethno-nationalist movement led by the charismatic monk Khrūbā Wichai (1878–1939).[56] These late 19th- and early 20th-century efforts by Siam's leaders to expand the orbit of their authority and in turn, further repel European influence, were to have significant influences on the development of Buddhism in French Indochina, particularly in Laos and Cambodia.[57]

In the centuries following the collapse of the Khmer Empire (802–1431), political elites in both Siam and Vietnam gained significant influence over the Cambodian royal court. In 1863, when Cambodia officially became part of the French colonial empire, the recently enthroned Cambodian King Norodom (r. 1860–1904) was already well under the influence of the Bangkok court. Although Norodom was not a deeply religious man, he fulfilled the customary roles of a Buddhist king by supporting the sangha and building temples and resthouses. Prior to becoming King, Norodom had studied in Bangkok under the supervision of royal Thai authorities and even taken temporary ordination in the royal monastic order known as the Dhammayut (Thai, Thammayut), or "those adhering to the Dhamma." Having been founded by Siam's King Mongkut (r. 1851–1868) during his pre-enthronement years as a monastic, the Dhammayut not only laid the foundation for modern Thai Buddhism but inspired those in French Indochina interested in "modernizing" Buddhism. Mongkut's Dhammayut sect had deep interests in matters of scriptural authenticity and drew on a Sinhalese Mahāvihārin recension of the Pāli canon alongside Mon monastic practices that emphasized disciplinary purity.[58] Its stress on rationality and intellectualism over magic and miracles stemmed in part from Mongkut's own conversations with Christian missionaries and Sinhalese monks, but it also had roots in wider reforms triggered by King Rama I (r. 1782–1809).[59] With Norodom's support, several of the highest-ranking monastics in the Dhammayut sect were brought to Cambodia, where they began propagating the idealized and rationalized image of Buddhism that was according to their view, more in adherence to the Dhamma (*Dhammayut*).

The penetration of Siam's Dhammayut order into Cambodian affairs is a reminder that European colonial powers were never hegemonic in their influence, having to regularly contend with competing polities and the long-standing networks of monastic exchange that cut across both Empire and nation. For many monastics in both Laos and Cambodia, the Dhammayut's model of modernity was attractive but for French administrators, its fusion of Buddhism, monarchy and the state was a dangerous cocktail.[60] Although the French had maintained the Buddhist monarchies in Laos and Cambodia, they effectively "destroyed the legitimizing function of myth and religion . . . [and] threw into question the reciprocal relationship between the monarchy and the sangha by relegating Buddhism to a marginal position."[61] Like the British, they established secular education systems for local elites—although in Laos it remained dismal—and the Western-educated intelligentsia arose as the new socioeconomic elite of the region. Only in rural areas where the state's hand did not reach did the sangha maintain its customary roles.

By the early decades of the 20th century, French administrators had become more wary of the Dhammayut's influences in the protectorate and launched a plan to not only mitigate its impact but direct Buddhist energies elsewhere. They began emphasizing the cultural and historical connections between Angkor (mostly in Cambodia) and Luang Phrabang (in Laos), drawing out the "unique" qualities of each kingdom's literature and history. In places like Laos, monks were "guided" away from those monastic centers across the river in Siam and instead toward Cambodia and the Pāli schools the French established at Bassac and Phnom Penh. "This was part of a larger vision," Justin McDaniel writes, "of binding together the peoples of Indochine culturally, educationally, and religiously. It was particularly important for the French to create a history in which Vietnam, Cambodia, and Laos were "naturally" "brothers," to defend against Siam's claims to Cambodia and Laos."[62]

At the heart of this new effort were a set of projects aimed at creating distinctively "Lao" and "Khmer" "national religions" largely modeled after Siam's Dhammayut sect but ingrained with all of the trappings of a "national identity." While the project in Laos took longer to incubate due to the general apathy the French exercised in their governance there, it attained a higher pitch in Cambodia. The institutional center of these projects came from various institutes set up under the auspices of the École Française d'Extrême-Orient (EFEO). Undoubtedly, it is thanks to the EFEO that the Angkorian past was the object of such rich scholarly focus and later became so central to the nationalist imaginings of figures like Sihanouk, no less than Pol Pot. Yet at the same time, the ways in which Siam and Siamese identity were purposely erased from Cambodian history in order to forge a state narrative is striking.[63] Some of the most vivid expressions of this new sense of "Khmerness," in fact came from the "reformed" or "new" *Mahānikāy* sect and its monastic luminaries like Chuon Nath (1883–1969) and Huot Tath (1891–*c.* 1975). Joining Indologists, Buddhologists, and Sanskritists working at the state-sponsored Buddhist Institute (est. 1930) in Phnom Penh, the new Mahānikāy monk-scholars "engineered and oversaw an institutional framework for the documentation and codification of a specifically "Khmer" Buddhist tradition."[64] And yet, as Anne Hansen's important study demonstrates, the Mahānikāy did not simply replicate French Orientalist visions of what a modern Buddhism should look like.[65] Instead, they drew on a wide variety of canonical Pāli sources alongside vernacular materials circulated freely among Buddhist networks across the Theravādin Buddhist world, allowing these sources to hold conversations with French philosophies and practices rather than be dominated by them. The end result was a modern Buddhism that spoke to contemporary Khmer audiences by refocusing attention away from metaphysics and toward more pragmatic issues like monastic discipline and ethical conduct in lay life.

In Cochin China, where Confucian ideals had long dominated elite political life, the French promotion of freedom of religion, which was paraded by the colonial state as a key marker of its progressive modernity and *mission civilisatrice,* resulted in a robust religious scene, one in which the public was confronted with almost any number of religious possibilities. Taking advantage of this "freedom" alongside the state's support for a rationalized Buddhism, scholarly monks from southern and central Vietnam initiated a new modernist language around Buddhism, calling for educational and disciplinary reforms within the sangha.[66] Like their co-patriots in Cambodia, they privileged a text-based Buddhism that stressed self-cultivation and ethics as critical antidotes to the problems facing modern society. Yet unlike Laos or Cambodia, the modernist movement in Vietnam, aided greatly by modern print technologies, was inspired more by contemporary reform movements in China led by the monk Taixu (1880–1947), whose own efforts were giving new shape to the formation of modern Chinese Buddhism.[67] In the last three decades of colonial rule, monks in and around Saigon produced a voluminous and influential body of textual commentaries, periodicals, and devotional works concerning Mahāyāna Pure Land ideals and practices. The vast majority of these works appeared in the Romanized modern alphabet of the Vietnamese language, not in the Chinese script which French authorities had curtailed in an effort to sever Vietnam's ties to its ancient tributary power. This in turn, as Benedict Anderson has argued more widely, gave rise to an imagined community of not Mahāyāna Buddhists with Sinitic roots but of Mahāyāna Buddhists with distinctive Vietnamese histories and cultures.[68]

As everywhere, anti-colonial movements also marked many Buddhist spaces in Indochina with monks playing critical roles throughout the colony. Perhaps the most notable example was the so-called Umbrella War in July 1942 when the French arrest of two Buddhist monks for "preaching nationalist sermons" triggered massive anti-colonial demonstrations across Phnom Penh with thousands of protestors, including some seven hundred monks, pouring into the streets.[69] In Vietnam, the failure of the pre-colonial Confucian leadership to prevent the French takeover provided an opportunity for Buddhists to take on new leadership roles.[70] In Cambodia (and to a lesser degree in Laos), it was the colonial state's creation of the Buddhist Institute and sustained project to create a sense of "Khmerness" vis-à-vis the Siamese that in an ironic, but perhaps predictable outcome, ended up producing the most important architects of Khmer nationalism.[71]

JAPANESE COLONIALISM IN EAST ASIA

In 1940, less than a decade before Vietnam, Laos, and Cambodia gained their independence (1945, 1949, and 1953, respectively), nearly ten thousand soldiers in the Imperial Japanese Army entered Indochina. Although Indochina continued formally as a colony of Vichy France, the region was for all purposes under Japanese control. This in fact represented the last stages of Imperial Japan's 20th-century colonial empire that had in the 1940s been justified by claims of universal benevolence in a "Greater East Asia Co-prosperity Sphere." Having been the target of European and American aggression from the mid-19th century onward, Japanese leaders responded by building their own imperial empire. On paper, the Greater East Asia Co-Prosperity Sphere was a new international order in which Asian countries under the leadership of the Japanese emperor could be free from Western colonialism and domination. In practice, however, Japanese imperialism mirrored Western paradigms, deploying the language of civilizing missions and projecting an image of itself as distinct from its colonial subjects in China, Korea, and Taiwan, despite being "caught in the quandary of non-White, not-quite and yet-alike."[72] From a Buddhist studies perspective, Japanese colonialism is unique because not only were Buddhist populations colonized, particularly in Korea (1910–1945) and Taiwan (1895–1945), but because Japanese Buddhists themselves were active agents in the colonizing process.

The origins of Japanese colonialism can be usefully traced to 1868 when the Tokugawa shogun was overthrown in a bloodless coup, instituting what was known as the Meiji Restoration. At that time, Shinto became the new state religion and Japanese Buddhists, closely connected to the Tokugawa government, were condemned by the new regime for their "antiquated" and "foreign" ideologies. Desperate to gain approval under the new Meiji government, Japanese intellectuals and clerics formulated a "new Buddhism" (*Shin Bukkyō*), one that was seen as relevant to the modernization process that the Meiji government embraced with such force and incredible rapidity. New Buddhism was said to be "socially useful" and to demonstrate this in tangible form, Buddhists took up a variety of social service projects, supported the Meiji Emperor through nation-building activities, and argued that the dharma was not only universal but fully compatible with a modern, scientific world view. As worries about survival in the face of European expansion increasingly gave way to nationalistic calls for imperial maneuvers in the 1880s, Japanese Buddhists, whether "new" "or old" and representing the full spectrum of denominational allegiances, began to support this "mimetic imperialism" with vigor.[73]

When Japan formally colonized Korea in 1910, nearly five hundred years of Confucian rule via the Chosôn dynasty (1392–1910) came to an end. Many Japanese Buddhists saw Korea as a space where they could re-assert their strength and demonstrate their commitment to the Japanese state (*kokutai*) and glory of Great Imperial Japan (*Dai Nihon Teikoku*). Buddhist institutions had suffered immensely under Chosôn rule, and initially, many Korean Buddhists looked to Japanese Buddhists as allies who could help them overcome the discrimination they endured. Even prior to Japan's formal annexation of Korea, multiple Japanese sects from Higashi Honganji and Nishi Honganji to Nichirenshū and Jōdoshū had begun establishing missionary orders across East Asia with Meiji support. From the Meiji perspective, the Buddhist missionaries were vital players in the wider effort to combat Christian influences and foster a pan-Asian Buddhist identity loyal to the emperor.[74]

In the early years of Japanese rule, government regulations were passed in order to "modernize," "reform," and "protect" Buddhist monasteries and properties, hopeful that the new ordinances would not only strengthen the Korean sangha but also curb Christian expansion. Far from being the passive victims who numerous postcolonial histories recall, many Korean Buddhists were strategic in their response to Japanese interventions, seeking alliances with the state and various Buddhists sects in order to protect and expand their own temple properties and social roles.[75] With the passing of the 1911 Temple Ordinance, the Korean Government General became, in effect, the head of all institutionalized forms of Korean Buddhism. The Ordinance made the government directly responsible for the management of all temple life, an act that not only significantly reduced the ability of Buddhist sects (Korean or otherwise) to exercise any degree of autonomy but overhauled existing social hierarchies. The Ordinance and its bylaws also included further "reforms," including the centralization of all monasteries through a single network, the introduction of secular subjects in monastic curriculums, the opening of hundreds of monastic branches aimed at proselytizing among the public, and the encouragement of clerical marriage and meat-eating among monastics.[76]

Although there were numerous Japanese Buddhist sects active in colonial Korea, a brief examination of the Sōtō Zen sect illustrates some of wider Buddhist dynamics involved in Japan's colonization. The Sōtō sect was one of the last Buddhist groups to establish a presence in Korea, only arriving in 1905 but building more than one hundred temples across Korea in the next forty years. According to Nam-lin Hur, these temples carried out three primary tasks.[77] First, they provided ritual services for the Japanese military and the several hundred thousand Japanese civilians who settled in the Korean peninsula between 1876 and 1945.[78] Second, they worked to make Koreans into loyal subjects (*kōminka*) of the imperial state by running Japanese-language schools and teaching them "what Imperial Japan considered desirable with regard to morality, attitude, behavior and practical skills."[79] Third, they worked to pacify the anti-Japanese sentiments both explicit and latent in much of the colonial society. Unlike Korean Christianity, which remained firmly anti-Japanese and held a cherished place for much of the Korean public, Buddhism was seen as a cultural link between Japan and Korea that could be exploited for imperial benefit. Many Korean Buddhists who had been subjected to terrible suppression and humiliation in the Chosôn dynasty eagerly joined hands with Japanese clerics, who not only offered to improve Buddhism's social lot but also provided ample opportunities to enhance their social status.[80]

After the March First Movement of 1919 demanded Korean independence, the response to Buddhist reforms took on more political dimensions. Young clerics—some of whom had studied in Japan—pressed the government to abolish the Ordinance and cease its interference in religious affairs. The famous monastic reformer, Han Yongun (1879–1944), for instance, criticized the close ties between the sangha and the colonial regime, describing it as "Bureaucratic Buddhism" (*kwanje Pulgyo*) and advocating instead a socialist-inspired "Buddhism for the masses" (*minjung Pulgyo*). Han argued that to spread Buddhism among the masses, Buddhists had to "neither abandon human society nor deny close, loving relationships with people. They instead attain enlightenment through defilement and achieve nirvana in the midst of the stream of life and death."[81]

Despite the calls of Han and other clerics to abolish the Japanese reforms, government intervention in the sangha persisted until 1945 when the dropping of atomic bombs on Hiroshima and Nagasaki led to the end of Japanese rule. The legacy of Japanese colonialism in Korea remains deeply politicized, but undoubtedly the most significant and contentious issue concerns the widespread adoption of clerical marriage by Korean Buddhists. This popular practice had already been embraced by the majority of Japanese clerics at the time, who during the Meiji Restoration (1868–1912) began eating meat, drinking alcohol, and marrying, all of which are typically interpreted as being in violation of the *Vinaya* or codes of monastic conduct.[82] This behavior was encouraged on the basis that it was not only pragmatic but that it also lessened the sometimes rigid division between the monastic body and laity. Under Japanese rule, the promotion of marriage and meat-eating among Korean monastics had a profound impact on Korean society with an estimated 80 percent of Korean monasteries having "formally eliminated the restrictions on having wives in residence" by the 1920s.[83]

The Japanese Buddhist missionary presence in colonial Taiwan appears to have been less contested than it was in Korea. After Qing China ceded Taiwan to Japan at the end of the Sino-Japanese War in 1895, Buddhist clerics attached to Japanese armies entered the colony. Paralleling developments in Korea, these chaplain-missionaries came from multiple schools (*shū*) and sects (*ha*) and were initially charged primarily with providing spiritual services to Japanese civilians and troops before attempting to use Buddhism as a bridge between themselves and the people they sought to rule.[84] According to Charles Brewer Jones, missionary success among Buddhist populations in Taiwan was not only minimal but had fewer repercussions than in Korea.[85] Despite the fact that Buddhists in Taiwan were forced into supporting colonial institutions, Jones suspects that because Taiwanese monastics were never pressured to accept clerical marriage or meat-eating, and were able to maintain ordination lineages and networks to the Chinese mainland, fewer ruptures occurred within Taiwanese Buddhist life.

Buddhist involvement in Japanese colonialism was not limited to Korea or Taiwan. As numerous scholars have shown, Zen Buddhists played a critical role in developing the spirit of imperial militarism that characterized much of Japanese national rhetoric during the Fifteen Year War (1930–1945) when Japanese soldiers conquered significant parts of East and Southeast Asia.[86] Buddhist involvement in the war effort was shaped by a number of different forces, including "institutional self-interest, limited knowledge of the suffering the Japanese military was inflicting on other Asians, a traditional closeness to military leaders, indoctrination through the imperial education system, and by extension a good measure of patriotism as fully socialized Japanese citizens."[87] In places like China, where Japanese soldiers torched, pillaged, and raped their way through much of the eastern seaboard between 1937 to 1945, Japanese Buddhists provided ample justifications for state violence. Not all Japanese Buddhists were so supportive but their voices were largely lost in a sea of nationalist aggression.

Just as Korean and Taiwanese Buddhists experienced Japanese imperialism differently, so too did Buddhist communities in China. In the decades prior to the Japanese invasion, Chinese Buddhists were well aware of the transformations that colonial powers were triggering across the Asian world. As their own country suffered from immense political instability and strife, many young monastics began to question not only what was responsible for bringing about this state of affairs but also what could be done to resurrect China's prestige and power. As Rongdao Lai writes, "at a time when the socio-political discourse was dominated by ideas such as democracy, freedom, liberty, equality and republicanism . . . young monks were eager to demonstrate that they, too, were capable of becoming "new monks" for the nation."[88] For figures like Taixu (1890–1947), who eventually emerged as one of the most influential Chinese monastics of the period, China's future rest in "invigorating Buddhism through education" (*jiaoyu xingjiao*), a slogan he coined in response to the popular expression of the day: "saving the nation through education" (*jiayu jiuguo*).[89] Taixu's efforts to revitalize Buddhism were as much informed by global discourses as they were driven by myriad reasons, from long-standing concerns about the negative impact of customary Pure Land devotionalism on Chinese life to deep-seated fears concerning the threat of European and Japanese imperialism. After founding China's first modern Buddhist Studies Academy (*foxueyuan*) in Wuchang in 1922, an institute that shifted learning from being a top-down hierarchical affair to a horizontal relationship that sustained collective identities, Taixu went onto produce a voluminous literature that influenced much of the Sinitic Buddhist world. As his ideas permeated Sinitic spaces across East Asia, the graduates of Wuchang and the other Buddhist Studies Academies that flourished in its wake, began to call themselves "new monks" in opposition to the "conservative" monks who they felt had failed to respond to the needs of the time and defend the nation.[90]

As fears of Japanese aggression grew, even those Buddhist communities in China who had been previously antagonistic to the Republican government and its regular efforts to appropriate Buddhist temple property also began arguing that the future of Buddhism depended on the integrity of the nation.[91] Along with spreading the idea that the sangha's central duty was to protect the nation, they began implementing military training programs for monastics on temple grounds across the country. Although some Chinese monastics like Juzan (1908–1984) organized anti-Japanese guerilla forces, most training programs were organized around ritual prayers and the formation of "sangha rescue teams" (*sengqie jiuhudui*) that would administer medical assistance to the wounded. As the military conflict escalated, Chinese Buddhist intellectuals recognized the conundrum Buddhists were in with the majority of the Buddhist canon clearly advocating a doctrine of non-violence. To resolve this issue, some Chinese Buddhist monastics temporarily renounced their vows, or more commonly, began espousing the idea of "compassionate killing": the idea that the first precept of non-killing would not be broken if a life was taken for the purpose of saving a greater number of lives.[92] In the aftermath of the war, the history of monastic participation in the conflict was strategically used by monastics like Taixu to enhance their reputation among a Chinese public that praised any anti-Japanese effort. As the historian Xue Yu concludes, although the Anti-Japanese War of 1937–1945 left a mass of ruined temples and monuments in its wake, wartime mobilization and the general politicization of the Buddhist community at this time helped spread Buddhism among the wider populace in ways that had not been previously possible.[93]

COMPARISONS AND CONNECTIONS

Viewed from a broad perspective, it becomes clear that changes to Buddhism during the colonial period were linked closely to one another. The most obvious transformation was the emergence of national Buddhisms that rose as colonial empires slowly crumbled in the early 20th century era of "hyperactive nationalism."[94] Although scholars of colonialism have often taken the nation at face value, writing histories of the region according to distinctive and compartmentalized, national "stories," the expansion of imperial power did as much to divide Asia as it did to unite it.[95] While scholars are only beginning to fully understand the extent to which Buddhists were connected to one another at this period, it is now clear that the changes wrought by international commercial interests and new advancements in communication and transportation technologies—namely, steamships, railways, telegraphs, and printing presses—laid the foundation for a new era of global Buddhist connections and networks.[96]

Buddhists from across Asia utilized state connections and new technologies to travel across the Empire, spread the dharma, establish new Buddhist centers, and raise funds for Buddhist projects both at home and abroad. The impetus for their activities often differed. Dharmapāla wished to recover Bodh Gaya for Buddhists while the monk Taixu (1890–1947) wished to make "humanistic Buddhism" (Chinese, *renjian fojiao*) the "meeting place for all races."[97] But they were in some sense drawn together by a shared devotion to the Buddha's teachings, and confidence in the ability of those teachings to alleviate suffering in the modern world. The ever-shifting territorial landscape that accompanied several centuries of imperial aggression also carried Buddhism to new social settings through nearly unparalleled waves of voluntary and involuntary migration.[98] For instance, British control over the Malaysian Peninsula, finalized with the Anglo-Dutch Treaty of 1824, and establishment of Singapore in 1819, enabled Theravāda missionaries to penetrate religious marketplaces previously dominated by Malay Muslims and Chinese Mahāyānists. As major entrepôts in the commercial networks linking British India to the rest of Asia, Singapore, and Penang alongside Java and Sumatra in the Dutch East Indies became key nodes in the modern interaction between Mahāyāna and Theravāda traditions, giving rise to the multi-ethnic, multi-religious, and polyglot populations that form the distinctive cosmopolitan cultures of the Malay Archipelago.[99]

Scholars often invoke Benedict Anderson's "imagined communities" and the role of the printing press in the making of the modern-day nation, but as Christopher Bayly has argued, "the imagined communities of the nineteenth century nation were nowhere near as large as the audiences subject to the huge outflow of printed books, pamphlets, Qurans, Bibles and Buddhist jatakas directed to the faithful. In the Empire of Books, religion trumped all."[100] Buddhism never possessed a monopoly, but in colonial Asia, Buddhist literature was often at the vanguard of the new print culture, even carving out new zones of influence in places like India, Vietnam, and Indonesia, where in the centuries prior to the print revolution, Buddhist treatises had been collecting dust or been lost all together. Across the Sinospheres of East Asia, new publishing houses produced "affordable home editions of sutras, famous monks' treatises, scholarly journals and popular Buddhist themed-magazines" speaking to "a large and translocal imagined community, *a Buddhist public*, which included both Buddhist clerics and lay people sympathetic to and interested in Buddhism beyond the traditional household rituals."[101]

The introduction and near universal adoption of printing presses not only supplanted the manuscript cultures that had characterized much of Asia but also gave rise to new forms of writing and religiosity. Pamphlets, religious tracts, and newspapers were all novel ways to spread knowledge of the dharma. The rise of cheap print, enabled by the invention of lithographic printing in 1804, meant that sponsoring the composition of a Buddhist scripture—an age-old way to generate merit—was suddenly open to a much wider social class. But "printing did not only reflect the tastes of the market," as the historian Nile Green puts it, "it also informed them."[102] In Ceylon, the mass printing of short, simplified liturgical texts on the ritual practice known as *Buddha-vandanā* or buddha veneration transformed what had previously been a small-scale elite practice into a central devotional ritual of lay Buddhist life.[103] Like the Buddha-vandanā texts, the use of commercial printing presses allowed publishers to seek wider audiences, which in turn meant writing for general consumption. Monthly periodicals, like the *Buddhist Review* of the Buddhist Society of Great Britain (est. 1909), Tamil-language *Oru Paisa Tamilan* ("One Penny Tamilan") of the South Indian Buddhist Association (est. 1899), or bilingual Bengali—English *Bauddha-Bandhu* ("Buddhist Friend") of the Chittagong Buddhist Association (est. 1885), reported on Vesak celebrations across the globe, the discovery of long-lost Buddhist monuments in India and new translations of Buddhist scriptures, creating the impression that all Buddhists were united under a single common denominator, part of a larger, broader body of global Buddhists.

Although the power of the colonial regimes always weighed in the background, throughout the colonial period, there was a current of communication, sharing, and borrowing both within and across Asian boundaries. While Mongolian Buddhists under Soviet occupation were brutally persecuted as the Stalinist state took a draconian turn, Buddhists from elsewhere in Asia continued to debate the merits of Marx, forging new Marxist-tinged Buddhist dialectics in places like Japan, China, Korea, and India.[104] Yet it was not just the works of Euro-American thinkers that influenced Asian Buddhist intellectuals. The works of Buddhist notables like Dharmapāla, Shaku Sōen (1860–1919), and Rahul Sankrityayan (1893–1963) were read alongside those of Western Orientalists in cafes in Tokyo, monasteries in Colombo, and rest-houses in Bodh Gaya. Tibetan intellectuals like Gendun Chopel (1903–1951) traveled to India, immersing themselves in transcolonial Buddhist networks and then publishing treatises critical of Tibetan Buddhist geography with the hope of alerting Tibetans to the brave new world that dwelled outside the plateau.[105] In Japan, there was an incredible surge of interest in the Pāli scriptures that southern Buddhists regarded as the purest form of Buddhism but which for centuries had been contemptuously dismissed by Mahāyānists as a "Lesser Vehicle" (*hināyāna*). As the seminal work of Richard Jaffe has shown, Japanese clerics traveled to India and Ceylon to study the Pāli canon and Buddhist doctrines as understood by Indian Orientalists and esteemed Sinhala monks.[106] Some Japanese responded by calling for a return to "original Buddhism" (*genshi bukkyō*) or "fundamental Buddhism" (*kompon bukkyō*) and by the early 1900s, several Japanese had taken ordination in Theravāda lineages. Figures like Shaku Kōzen (1849–1924) embraced Ceylon's Pāli Buddhism as the "purest, truest form of Buddhism," taking full ordination (*upasaṃpadā*) from Hikkaḍuvē in 1890 and returning to Japan to start the "Society for the True Lineage of Śākyamuni" (est. 1893).[107]

Nor was it just colonial powers that transformed the colonized. By blending Western psychology (especially that of William James) with Orientalist thought, the writings of the Japanese intellectual and nationalist D. T. Suzuki (1870–1966) converted much of the Western world to his view that Zen is not a religion but a mystical experience, the "pure unmediated experience of reality and the spontaneous living in harmony with that reality."[108] When the World Parliament of Religions was held in Chicago in 1893, Dharmapāla wowed audiences with his arguments of a scientific Buddhism, gaining the support of the Hawaiian philanthropist Mary Foster (1844–1930), who showed her support by showering the Maha Bodhi Society with tens of thousands of dollars in donations.

Perhaps the most notable reconfiguration of Buddhism that was linked to a much more extensive web of changes across the globe occurred in India. There, the revival of long-distance pilgrimage from across Asia and sustained Orientalist interest led thousands of Indians to the teachings of the Awakened One.[109] At the same time Buddhists from other lands looked to an imagined Buddhist India for inspiration, Indians were seeing their own Buddhist past as a link to the rest of Asia. The Nobel laureate and artist, Rabindranath Tagore (1861–1941), along with his nephew, Abandrinath (1871–1951), the "founder" of the Bengal School of Art, saw Buddhism as a vessel through which to revitalize and redefine contemporary Indian art forms. Through their friendship with the eminent Japanese art historian Okakura Kakuzo (1862–1931), the Tagores began working toward a pan-Asian artistic tradition that blended the shared aspects of "Eastern" spiritual and artistic culture.[110] While most Indian interests in the dharma remained largely academic and nationalistic, the romantic nostalgia for India's Buddhist past and simultaneous "modernity" led some of its national elite to more forceful embraces. The most well-known example was Dr. B. R. Ambedkar (1891–1956), the Dalit leader and chief architect of India's constitution, whose conversion to Buddhism in 1956 along with half a million of his followers was inspired in part by earlier colonial-era conversions among oppressed Indian populaces seeking an escape from caste discrimination.[111] For India's first prime minister and fervent secularist, Jawaharlal Nehru (1889–1964), Buddhism was also an attractive means through which to shape the new nation. Throughout his long political career, Nehru utilized Buddhist symbols and rhetoric to advance the state's foreign and domestic goals, sponsoring regular international celebrations of the Buddha's "birthday" in the name of world peace and parading a new official state regalia flush with Buddhist symbolism.[112] In effect, by Indian independence in 1947, ancient Buddhist sites like Sarnath and Kushinagar, which less than one hundred years prior had been dusty towns more likely to be visited by cattle than monks, were now hosting thousands of international Buddhist pilgrims annually. Bodh Gaya, the site where Buddha Śākyamuni is said to have attained Awakening, would become the center of the "global Buddhist bazaar," and "a vital force in the building [of] a pan-Asian Buddhist identity" and "the global dissemination and exchange of Buddhist ideas, practices, teachers, and institutions."[113] What is no less remarkable than the sheer way in which these ancient sites were transformed into a living reflection of modern global Buddhism is the very fact that these same spaces and their pan-Asian networks gave rise to the very idea of global Buddhism.

REVIEW OF LITERATURE

In recent years, scholars have moved away from, or at the very least begun to interrogate, the utility and meaning of a number of commonly employed binaries used to discuss colonial-era Buddhism, such as traditional and modern, decline and revival, collaborator and patriot. Some of the most substantive debates are those concerning colonialism's role in the making of Buddhist modernism.[114] That discourse itself has often been consumed by the issue of "Protestant Buddhism," or the idea that almost all modern forms of Buddhism are derivative of Protestant models of Christianity introduced to Asian Buddhists by missionaries during the colonial period.[115] Although initially intended to frame new Buddhist movements in British Ceylon, Protestant Buddhism soon became a scholarly shorthand used to characterize (often erroneously) a wide variety of transitional phases and developments in Buddhist cultures across Asia. Despite growing criticism of the expression, Protestant Buddhism and other related expressions such as Buddhist modernism now signify a number of interrelated factors: the enhanced role of lay Buddhists, the decline of monastic power, the increased emphasis on Buddhism's rational characteristics, the privileging of canonical scriptures, and efforts to counter Western influence while simultaneously appropriating Western technologies and epistemological structures.

Many scholars are now calling for a significant revision of the "sea change modernist" discourse. Anne Blackburn, for instance, has challenged the idea that modern Buddhism's scripturalist tendencies are simply products of European or Protestant influences. Using Ceylon's Siyam Nikāya (est. 1753) as a case study, she argues that its promotion of Pāli learning and creation of textual communities mediated via bilingual Pāli-Sinhala commentarial literature (*sutra sannaya*) is evidence of deeper, systemic changes occurring within the sangha on the eve of British colonialism.[116] In a similar vein, several scholars have begun to re-evaluate the formation of the Dhammayut monastic order by King Mongkut (Rama IV), seen by earlier generations as a product of his encounters with Christian missionaries, but now argued by some to be a continuation of rationalizing tendencies triggered generations earlier by King

Rama I (r. 1782–1809).[117] These developments, and many others like them, may in fact be an example of what Charles Hallisey has called "intercultural mimesis," or "occasions where it seems that aspects of a culture of a subjectified people influenced the investigator to represent that culture in a certain manner."[118]

Some scholars have also challenged the wider narrative that sees discourses of reform and rationalism as a totalizing wave that washed over all of Buddhist thought and practice. Like the prominent secularization theorists of the 20th century who wrongly prophesized a 21st-century world where religion would be absent, the notion that Buddhism would emerge from colonialism ritual-free and mirroring secular visions has proved far from true.[119] Anyone who travels extensively through Buddhist Asia today still encounters an enchanted world, where the veneration of relics is thriving and ritual practice remains at the center of not just village life but many urban households. As seen in places like Vietnam, the colonial-era reformist movements that privileged a text-based rational Buddhism had minimal influences on rural populaces who continued to gravitate toward apotropaic practices and the esoteric arts.[120] In other words, the reformist transformation may well have been true for much of the urban bourgeois intelligentsia in the colonial world but it hardly speaks to the socioreligious worlds of the peasant cultivators, laborers, industrial workers, craftsmen, and mid- and low-level government servants at the other ends of the social pyramid. When, or if, scholars turn to the study of these enchanted Buddhist publics, the idea of what it means to be a "modern Buddhist" may become ever more complex and contested. It may be more accurate, then, to see colonialism not as upturning all forms of Buddhism, but rather marking select aspects of it in distinctive ways.[121]

FURTHER READING

GENERAL INTRODUCTIONS TO COLONIALISM

Cooper, Frederick, ed. *Colonialism in Question: Theory, Knowledge, History*. Berkeley: University of California Press, 2005.

Loomba, Ania. *Colonialism/Postcolonialism*. London: Routledge, 1998.

Osterhammel, Jürgen. *Colonialism: A Theoretical Overview*. Translated from the German by Shelley L. Frisch. Princeton, NJ: Markus Wiener, 1997.

GENERAL INTRODUCTIONS TO BUDDHISM IN COLONIAL CONTEXTS

Bechert, Heinz. *Buddhismus, Staat, und Gessellschaft in den Ländern des Theravāda-Buddhismus*, 3 vols. Wiesbaden, Germany: Otto Harrasowitz, 1966–1973.

Borchert, Thomas, ed. *Theravāda Buddhism in Colonial Contexts*. London: Routledge, 2018.

Lopez, Donald, ed. *Curators of the Buddha: The Study of Buddhism under Colonialism*. Chicago: University of Chicago Press, 1995.

STUDIES OF COLONIAL-ERA BUDDHISM IN REGIONAL CONTEXTS

Aloysius, G. *Religion as Emancipatory Identity: A Buddhist Movement among the Tamils under Colonialism*. New Delhi: New Age International, 1997.

Blackburn, Anne. *Buddhist Learning and Textual Practice in Eighteenth Century Lankan Monastic Culture*. Princeton, NJ: Princeton University Press, 2001.

Blackburn, Anne. *Locations of Buddhism: Colonialism and Modernity in Sri Lanka*. Chicago: University of Chicago Press, 2010.
Braun, Erik. *The Birth of Insight: Meditation, Modern Buddhism and the Burmese Monk Ledi Sayadaw*. Chicago: University of Chicago Press, 2013.
Edwards, Penny. *Cambodge: The Cultivation of a Nation, 1860–1945*. Honolulu: University of Hawaii Press, 2007.
Hansen, Anne. *How to Behave: Buddhism and Modernity in Colonial Cambodia, 1860–1930*. Honolulu: University of Hawaii Press, 2007.
Harris, Elizabeth. *Theravāda Buddhism and the British Encounter: Religious, Missionary and Colonial Experience in Nineteenth-Century Sri Lanka*. London: Routledge, 2006.
Jaffe, Richard M. *Seeking Śākyamuni: South Asia in the Formation of Modern Japanese Buddhism*. Chicago: University of Chicago Press, 2019.
Kemper, Steven. *Rescued from the Nation: Anagarika Dharmapāla and the Buddhist World*. Chicago: University of Chicago Press, 2015.
Kim, Hwansoo Ilmee. *Empire of the Dharma: Korean and Japanese Buddhism, 1877–1912*. Cambridge, MA: Harvard University Asia Center, 2013.
Kim, Hwansoo Ilmee. *The Korean Buddhist Empire: A Transnational History, 1910–1945*. Cambridge, MA: Harvard University Asia Center, 2018.
Malagoda, Kitsiri. *Buddhism in Sinhalese Society, 1750–1900: A Study of Religious Revival and Change*. Berkeley: University of California Press, 1976.
McHale, Shawn Frederick. *Print and Power: Confucianism, Communism and Buddhism in the Making of Modern Vietnam*. Honolulu: University of Hawaii Press, 2004.
Ober, Douglas. "Reinventing Buddhism: Conversations and Encounters in Modern India, 1839–1956." PhD diss., University of British Columbia, Vancouver, 2016.
Park, Jin Y., ed. *Makers of Modern Korean Budhism*. Albany: State University of New York Press, 2009.
Prothero, Stephen. *The White Buddhist: The Asian Odyssey of Henry Steel Olcott*. Bloomington: Indiana University Press, 1996.
Turner, Alicia. *Saving Buddhism: The Impermanence of Religion in Colonial Burma*. Honolulu: University of Hawaii Press, 2014.
Victoria, Brian. *Zen at War*. 2nd ed. New York: Rowman and Littlefield, 2006.
Yu, Xue. *Buddhism, War and Nationalism: Chinese Monks in the Struggle against Japanese Aggressions, 1931–1945*. New York: Routledge, 2005.

NOTES

1. Stuart Hall, "When Was 'the Postcolonial'? Thinking at the Limit," in *The Postcolonial Question: Common Skies—Divided Horizons*, eds. Ian Chambers and Lidia Curti (London: Routledge, 1996), 242–260.
2. See Anne McClintock, "The Angel of Progress: Pitfalls of the Term 'Postcolonialism,'" *Social Text* 1, no. 31–32 (1992): 84–98.
3. For Qing China, see Nicola Di Cosmo, "Qing Colonial Administration in Inner Asia," *The International History Review* 20, no. 2 (1998): 287–309; and the introductory essay by Peter C. Perdue, "Comparing Empires: Manchu Colonialism," *The International History Review* 20, no. 2 (1998): 255–262. For an important study that touches on many of these themes within the context of the highlands of mainland Southeast Asia, see James Scott, *The Art of Not Being Governed: An Anarchist History of Upland Southeast Asia* (New Haven, CT: Yale University Press, 2009).
4. For a discussion of colonialism's application in a pre-modern Asian context, see Geoff Wade (ed.), *Asian Expansions: The Historical Experiences of Polity Expansion in Asia* (London: Routledge, 2015).

5. For instance, the relationship between contemporary Tibet and China (to provide just one example) is often said to signify a new reworking of colonial relationships. For discussions of Tibet as an example of "postcolonial colonialism." See Stephen J. Hartnett, "Alternative Modernities, "Postcolonial Colonialism and Contested Imaginings in and of Tibet," in *Imagining China: Rhetorics of Nationalism in an Age of Globalization*, eds. Stephen J. Hartnett, Lisa B. Keränen, and Donovan Conley (East Lansing: Michigan State University Press, 2017), 91–137.
6. The discrepancy between the 50 percent and 85 percent often stems from whether or not the United States and Canada are considered colonial powers. For many historians, the United States was the first postcolonial state, but such an idea must be seen as simply absurd from the perspective of the indigenous populations whose lands were occupied by white settlers. If the United States is removed from this equation, then it must still be recognized that one half of the mainland of earth was under the nominal control of just eight European powers.
7. As Jürgen Osterhammel famously wrote in his *Colonialism: A Theoretical Overview*, translated from the German by Shelley L. Frisch (Princeton, NJ: Markus Wiener, 1997), 4, "colonialism is a phenomenon of colossal vagueness."
8. Osterhammel, *Colonialism*, 21–22.
9. Colonies in the United States, Canada, New Zealand, and Australia, for instance, were in many ways different from those in Asia. In the former regions, white settlers quickly formed a majority of the populace unlike in Asia where settlers never formed more than a small minority, thus providing very different colonial experiences (and possibilities for decolonization). For an excellent overview, see Eric Hobsbawm, *The Age of Empire, 1875–1914* (New York: Vintage Books, 1987), 62–73, and ch. 3 more widely.
10. Eric Hobsbawm, *The Age of Revolution, 1789–1848* (New York: Vintage Books, 1996).
11. See Hyungjung Lee and Younghan Cho, "Introduction: Colonial Modernity and Beyond in East Asian Contexts," *Cultural Studies* 26, no. 5 (2012): 601–616.
12. Hobsbawm, *Age of Empire*, 65–67.
13. Shmuel Eisenstadt, "The Civilizational Dimension of Modernity: Modernity as a Distinct Civilization," *International Sociology* 16, no. 3 (2001): 320–340.
14. Shmuel Eisenstadt, "Multiple Modernities," *Daedalus* 129, no. 1 (2000): 1–29.
15. Despite its rapid growth, several works remain important primers on the subject. David McMahan, *The Making of Buddhist Modernism* (Oxford: Oxford University Press, 2008), provides a formative overview. Pioneering studies include Henri de Lubac's more philosophically-minded exegesis in, *Le rencontre du bouddhisme et de l'Occident* (Paris: Aubier, 1952); and Heinz Bechert's historical-cultural analysis in, *Buddhismus, Staat, und Gesellschaft in den Ländern des Theravāda-Buddhismus*, 3 vols. (Wiesbaden, Germany: Otto Harrasowitz, 1966–1973). Multiple works in the Buddhism and Modernity Series, edited by Donald Lopez and published by the University of Chicago Press have continued to drive the conversation forward (see "Further Readings" at the end of this article for select works). Finally, for an insightful and reflective article on the idea of modernity as a whole within the context of Buddhist studies, see Marilyn Ivy, "Modernity," in *Critical Terms in the Study of Buddhism*, ed. Donald S. Lopez Jr. (Chicago: University of Chicago Press, 2005), 311–328.
16. Of course, while these attributes were increasingly linked to "Buddhist modernity," it does not mean that they were necessarily absent in pre-modern Buddhist traditions. Rationalism and positivism, for instance, were by no means "modern" or "Western" inventions but the creation of formal organizations that measured Buddhism according to these standards were novel developments. For an insightful study of empiricism and rationality in the pre-modern Tibetan Buddhist context, see Janet Gyatso, *Being Human in a Buddhist World: An Intellectual History of Medicine in Early Modern Tibet* (New York: Columbia University Press, 2016).

17. For discussions of the counter-modern in terms of Buddhism, see Matthew King, *Ocean of Milk, Ocean of Blood: A Mongolian Monk in the Ruins of the Qing Empire* (New York: Columbia University Press, 2019). For the argument that even "counter-reformists" are modern in the sense that they are influenced by new trends and adopt new technologies to combat the modern, see Nile Green, *Bombay Islam: The Religious Economy of the West Indian Ocean, 1840–1915* (Oxford: Oxford University Press, 2011).
18. Karuna Mantena, *Alibis of Empire: Henry Maine and the Ends of Liberal Imperialism* (Princeton, NJ: Princeton University Press, 2010). See also the seminal essay, Thomas Metcalf, "Liberalism and Empire," in *Ideologies of the Raj* (Cambridge, UK: Cambridge University Press, 1995), 28–65.
19. Stephen C. Berkwitz, *Buddhist Poetry and Colonialism: Alagiyavanna and the Portuguese in Sri Lanka* (Oxford: Oxford University Press, 2013), 27. See also Alan Strathern, *Kingship and Conversion in Sixteenth-Century Sri Lanka Portuguese Imperialism in a Buddhist Land* (Cambridge, UK: Cambridge University Press, 2007).
20. Our understanding of Buddhism in the Himalayas within the context of scholarly rubrics like "colonial modernity" and "transimperial networks" remains fragmented at best. Some pioneering work, however, includes the latter half of Toni Huber, *The Holy Land Reborn: Pilgrimage and the Tibetan Reinvention of Buddhist India* (Chicago: University of Chicago Press, 2010), 125–376; Sarah Levine and David Gellner, *Rebuilding Buddhism: The Theravāda Movement in Twentieth-Century Nepal* (Cambridge, MA: Harvard University Press, 2007); and *Transcultural Studies* (Special issue), 1 (2016), on global encounters and connected histories in the eastern Himalayas .
21. Undoubtedly, the study of Buddhism became at times inextricably tied to the pursuit of power—the more colonial administrations knew about the people and land they governed the more effective it could be in governing them—but not all research was political (no matter whether it was used for those purposes). For an important critique of the Said-ian thesis of Orientalism, see Thomas Trautmann, *Aryans and British India* (Berkeley: University of California Press, 1997), 18–27. For a more thorough discussion of the discovery of Buddhism, Donald S. Lopez Jr., *From Stone to Flesh: A Short History of the Buddha* (Chicago: University of Chicago Press, 2013).
22. Trautmann, *Aryans and British India*, 137.
23. Upinder Singh, *The Discovery of Ancient India: Early Archaeologists and the Beginnings of Archaeology* (Delhi: Permanent Black, 2004); Nayanjot Lahiri, *Marshalling the Past: Ancient India and Its Modern Histories* (Ranikhet, India: Permanent Black, 2012).
24. On world religions discourse, see Tomoko Masuzawa, *The Invention of World Religions: Or, How European Universalism Was Preserved in the Language of Pluralism* (Chicago: University of Chicago Press, 2005). On the secular-religious discourse more widely, see Talal Asad's seminal works, *Genealogies of Religion: Discipline and Reasons of Power in Christianity and Islam* (Baltimore: Johns Hopkins University Press, 1993), and *Formations of the Secular: Christianity, Islam, Modernity* (Stanford, CA: Stanford University Press, 2003).
25. Donald S. Lopez Jr. and Peggy McCracken, *In Search of the Christian Buddha: How an Asian Sage Became a Medieval Saint* (New York and London: W. W. Norton, 2014), 193–194.
26. Judith Snodgrass, "Defining Modern Buddhism: Mr. and Mrs. Rhys Davids and the Pāli Text Society," *Comparative Studies of South Asia, Africa and the Middle East* 27, no. 1 (2007): 186–202. See also Ananda Wickremeratne, *The Genesis of an Orientalist: Thomas William Rhys Davids and Buddhism in Sri Lanka* (Delhi: Motilal Banrasidass, 1984).
27. Donald S. Lopez Jr., "Introduction," in *Curators of the Buddha: The Study of Buddhism under Colonialism*, ed. Donald S. Lopez Jr. (Chicago: University of Chicago Press, 1995), 6.
28. Philip Almond, *The British Discovery of Buddhism* (Cambridge, UK: Cambridge University Press, 1988).
29. Douglas Ober, "Reinventing Buddhism: Conversations and Encounters in Modern India, 1839–1956," (PhD diss., University of British Columbia, Vancouver, 2016).

30. The Buddhological enterprise, in other words, could not have advanced at the incredible rate it did, without the active aid and assistance of the Empire's "native subjects."
31. For discussions of these issues as applied to Burma, see Alexey Kirichenko, "From Thathanadaw to Theravāda Buddhism: Constructions of Religion and Religious Identity in Nineteenth and Early Twentieth Century Myanmar," in *Casting Faiths: Imperialism and the Transformation of Religion in East and Southeast Asia*, ed. Thomas David Dubois (Basingstoke, UK: Palgrave Macmillan, 2009), 23–39; and Alicia Turner, *Saving Buddhism: The Impermanence of Religion in Colonial Burma* (Honolulu: University of Hawaii Press, 2014). For Japan, see Jason Ananda Josephson, *The Invention of Religion in Japan* (Chicago: University of Chicago Press, 2012).
32. Turner, *Saving Buddhism*, 110–135.
33. Alexey Kirichenko, "The Thathanabaing Project: Monastic Hierarchies and Colonialism in Burma," in *Theravāda Buddhism in Colonial Contexts*, ed. Thomas Borchert, 138–161 (New York: Routledge, 2018).
34. Anne Blackburn, *Locations of Buddhism: Colonialism and Modernity in Sri Lanka* (Chicago: University of Chicago Press, 2010), 10.
35. Kitsiri Malagoda, *Buddhism in Sinhalese Society, 1750–1900: A Study of Religious Revival and Change* (Berkeley: University of California Press, 1976), 73–172.
36. Erik Braun, *The Birth of Insight: Meditation, Modern Buddhism and the Burmese Monk Ledi Sayadaw* (Chicago: University of Chicago Press, 2013).
37. Braun, *Birth of Insight*, 100, 105.
38. Braun, *Birth of Insight*, 91–92.
39. Braun, *Birth of Insight*. See also Brooke Schedneck, *Thailand's International Meditation Centers: Tourism and the Global Commodification of Religious Practices* (London: Routledge, 2015).
40. For studies of Buddhism and law in Burma and Ceylon, see, respectively, Christian Lammerts, *Buddhist Law in Burma: A History of Dhammasattha Texts and Jurisprudence, 1250–1850* (Honolulu: University of Hawaii Press, 2018); Benjamin Schonthal, *Buddhism, Politics and the Limits of Law: The Pyrrhic Constitutionalism of Sri Lanka* (Cambridge, UK: Cambridge University Press, 2016).
41. Blackburn, *Locations of Buddhism*.
42. Turner, *Saving Buddhism*, 45–74.
43. Stephen Prothero, *The White Buddhist: The Asian Odyssey of Henry Steel Olcott*, 2nd ed. (Bloomington: Indiana University Press, 2011), 86.
44. Prothero, *White Buddhist*, 173 and 219fn3.
45. Gananath Obeysekere, quoted in Prothero, *White Buddhist*, 174.
46. On this heady mixture of influences, see Prothero, *White Buddhist*, 101–105. See also Stephen Prothero, "Henry Steel Olcott and 'Protestant Buddhism,"' *Journal of the American Academy of Religion* 63, no. 2 (1995): 281–302, for a wider discussion of the term "Protestant Buddhism" in the context of religious studies and Buddhist studies.
47. Richard Fox Young and Gintora Parana Vidanaga Somaratna, *Vain Debates: The Christian—Buddhist Controversies of Nineteenth Century Ceylon* (Vienna: The De Nobili Research Library, 1996), 206.
48. Steven Kemper, *Rescued from the Nation: Anagarika Dharmapala and the Buddhist World* (Chicago: University of Chicago Press, 2015).
49. Turner, *Saving Buddhism*, 145.
50. For a critical discussion of the colonial-era Buddhist othering of minority groups in Burma via a gendered, racialized, and sexualizd nationalist discourse, see Chie Ikeya, *Refiguring Women, Colonialism and Modernity in Burma* (Honolulu: University of Hawaii Press, 2011). Such exclusionary practices were hardly unique to Burma and were also endemic throughout the Malay peninsula (against non-Malays) and other parts of Southern Asia in places like Ceylon.
51. E. Michael Mendelson, *Sangha and State in Burma: A Study of Monastic Sectarianism and Leadership*, ed. John P. Ferguson (Ithaca and London: Cornell University Press, 1975), 222.

52. Steven Kemper, *The Presence of the Past: Chronicles, Politics and Culture in Sinhala Life* (Ithaca, NY: Cornell University Press, 1991).
53. Elizabeth Nissan, "History in the Making: Anuradhapura and the Sinhala Buddhist Nation," *Social Analysis* 25 (1989): 64–77; Pradeep Jeganathan, "Authorizing History, Ordering Land: The Conquest of Anuradhapura," in *Unmaking the Nation: The Politics of Identity and History in Modern Sri Lanka*, eds. P. Jeganathan and Q. Ismail (Colombo, Sri Lanka: Social Scientists Association, 1995), 106–136; John Rogers, "Historical Images in the British Period," in *Sri Lanka: History and the Roots of Conflict*, ed. Jonathan Spencer (London: Routledge, 1990), 87–106.
54. H. L. Seneviratne, *The Work of Kings: The New Buddhism in Sri Lanka* (Chicago: University of Chicago Press, 1999), 56–188; Kemper, *Presence of the Past.*
55. Charles Keyes, "Buddhism and National Integration in Thailand," *Journal of Asian Studies* 30, no. 3 (1971): 551–567. Similar attempts to exert control over the southern stretches of the peninsula, a predominantly Muslim region, were also made. See Tamara Loos, *Subject Siam: Family, Law and Colonial Modernity in Thailand* (Ithaca, NY: Cornell University Press, 2006).
56. Charles Keyes, "Millennialism, Theravāda Buddhism, and Thai Society," *Journal of Asian Studies* 36, no. 2 (1977): 283–302; Katherine Bowie, "The Saint with Indra's Sword: Khruubaa Srivichai and Buddhist Millenarianism in Northern Thailand," *Comparative Studies in Society and History* 56, no. 3 (2014): 681–713.
57. See also, Justin McDaniel, *Gathering Leaves and Lifting Words: Histories of Buddhist Monastic Education in Laos and Thailand* (Seattle: University of Washington Press, 2008).
58. Anne Hansen, *How to Behave: Buddhism and Modernity in Colonial Cambodia, 1860–1930* (Honolulu: University of Hawaii Press, 2007), 84–85.
59. Hansen, *How to Behave*, 84.
60. Penny Edwards, *Cambodge: The Cultivation of a Nation, 1860–1945* (Honolulu: University of Hawaii Press, 2007), 95–115.
61. Martin Stuart-Fox, *Buddhist Kingdom, Marxist State: The Making of Modern Laos* (Bangkok: White Lotus Press, 1996), 91.
62. McDaniel, *Gathering Leaves*, 45.
63. Edwards, *Cambodge*. For a short, but insightful study that demonstrates this is concrete fashion, see an examination of Cambodian court dancers who purposely downplayed Siamese influences in Sasagawa Hideo, "Post/colonial Discourses on the Cambodian Court Dance," *Southeast Asian Studies* 42, no. 4 (2005): 418–441.
64. Edwards, *Cambodge*, 188.
65. Hansen, *How to Behave*, 120–142.
66. Shawn Frederick McHale, *Print and Power: Confucianism, Communism and Buddhism in the Making of Modern Vietnam* (Honolulu: University of Hawaii Press, 2004), 144–172.
67. Thiên Dô, "The Quest for Enlightenment and Cultural Identity: Buddhism in Contemporary Vietnam," in *Buddhism and Politics in Twentieth Century Asia*, ed. Ian Harris (London and New York: Continuum, 1999), 260. On Taixu, see Donald Pittman, *Toward a Modern Chinese Buddhism: Taixu's Reforms* (Honolulu: University of Hawaii Press, 2001).
68. Benedict Anderson, *Imagined Communities: Reflections on the Origins and Spread of Nationalism* (London: Verso, 1983).
69. Ben Kiernan, *The Pol Pot Regime: Race, Power and Genocide in Cambodia under the Khmer Rouge, 1975–79*, 2nd ed. (New Haven and London: Yale University Press, 2002), 12.
70. Thiên Dô, "Quest for Enlightenment," 260.
71. This included the influential nationalist thinker, Son Ngoc Thanh, the Institute's first secretary, as well as the scholar-monks, Son Ngoc Minh and Tou Samouth, both of whom were founders of the Communist party that gained power in 1979.

72. Lee and Cho, "Introduction: Colonial Modernity and Beyond in East Asian Contexts," 603.
73. On Japanese Buddhist support for these ventures, see Christopher Ives, *Imperial-Way Zen: Ichikawa Hakugen's Critique and Lingering Questions for Buddhist Ethics* (Honolulu: University of Hawaii Press, 2009), 44–50. "Mimetic imperialism" comes from the historian Robert Eskildsen, "Of Civilization and Savages: The Mimetic Imperialism of Japan's 1874 Expedition to Taiwan," *American Historical Review* 107, no. 2 (2002): 388–418. The wider concept of Japanese mimesis of Western powers is explored by Peter Duus, *The Abacus and the Sword: The Japanese Penetration of Korea, 1895–1910* (Berkeley: University of California Press, 1995), 424–438. A more focused study of Japanese intellectual mimesis in terms of Occidentalism, Orientalism, and Buddhism is found in Judith Snodgrass, *Presenting Japanese Buddhism to the West: Orientalism, Occidentalism and the Columbian Exposition* (Chapel Hill: University of North Carolina Press, 2003).
74. Yet sectarian concerns often trumped state agendas and the Japanese government regularly found their efforts to expand sectarian identities (rather than simply "Japanese" ones) to be a nuisance. See Hwansoo Ilmee Kim, *Empire of the Dharma: Korean and Japanese Buddhism, 1877–1912* (Cambridge, MA: Harvard University Asia Center, 2013), ch. 2–4.
75. Kim, *Empire of the Dharma*; see also Hwansoo Ilmee Kim, *The Korean Buddhist Empire: A Transnational History, 1910–1945* (Cambridge, MA: Harvard University Asia Center, 2018).
76. Pori Park, "Korean Buddhist Reforms and Problems in the Adoption of Modernity during the Colonial Period," *Korea Journal* 45, no. 1 (2005): 87–113.
77. Nam-lin Hur, "The Sōtō Sect and Japanese Military Imperialism in Korea," *Japanese Journal of Religious Studies* 26, no. 1–2 (1999): 107–134.
78. By 1945, Korea was home to more than 700,000 Japanese civilians and 300,000 army personnel—nearly all of whom were repatriated to the home islands by the end of 1946. According to Jun Unchida, *Brokers of Empire: Japanese Settler Colonialism in Korea, 1876–1945* (Cambridge, MA: Harvard East Asian Monographs, 2011), 3, this formed one of the largest single colonial communities in the 20th century. Even as early as 1910, more than 170,000 Japanese lived in the Korean peninsula, a product of mass Japanese settlement that began in the 1870s and 1880s.
79. Hur, "Sōtō Sect," 119.
80. Kim, *Empire of the Dharma.*
81. Quoted in Pori Park, "Buddhism in Modern Korea," in *The Wiley Blackwell Companion to East and Inner Asian Buddhism*, ed. Mario Poceski (London: Wiley Blackwell, 2009), 479.
82. Richard M. Jaffe, *Neither Monk nor Layman: Clerical Marriage in Modern Japanese Buddhism* (Princeton, NJ: Princeton University Press, 2001).
83. Robert Buswell, *The Zen Experience* (Princeton, NJ: Princeton University Press, 1992), 29. According to Jeongeun Park, there is ample evidence that many Korean monastics already had children and engaged in meat-eating prior to colonial rule and that it was not the Temple bylaws that increased the rate of meat-eating, married monks so much as it brought the issue to the public for the first time in the history of Korean Buddhism. See Jeongeun Park, "Clerical Marriage and Buddhist Modernity in Early Twentieth Century Korea" (PhD diss., University of British Columbia, Vancouver, 2016).
84. Charles Brewer Jones, *Buddhism in Taiwan: Religion and the State, 1660–1990* (Honolulu: University of Hawaii Press, 1999), 80.
85. Jones, *Buddhism in Taiwan*, 93.
86. For a thorough overview, see Brian Victoria, *Zen at War*, 2nd ed. (Lanham, MD: Rowman & Littlefield, 2006).
87. Ives, *Imperial-Way Zen*, 127.
88. Rongdao Lai, "The Wuchang ideal: Buddhist Education and Identity Production in Republican China," *Studies in Chinese Religions* 3, no. 1 (2017): 63.

89. Lai, "Wuchang Ideal," 55–70. On Taixu more widely, see Pittman, *Toward a Modern Chinese Buddhism.*
90. Lai, "Wuchang Ideal," 56, estimates that between the 1920s and 1940s, Taixu's students had gone onto serve as administrators or teachers in at least fifty other Buddhist academies across China.
91. Xue Yu, *Buddhism, War and Nationalism: Chinese Monks in the Struggle against Japanese Aggressions, 1931–1945* (New York and London: Routledge, 2005), 51–64.
92. Yu, *Buddhism, War and Nationalism,* 45–51.
93. Yu, *Buddhism, War and Nationalism,* 177–196.
94. Christopher Bayly, *The Birth of the Modern World, 1780–1914: Global Connections and Comparisons* (Malden, MA: Blackwell, 2004), 462.
95. Prasenjit Duara, *Rescuing History from the Nation: Questioning Narratives of Modern China* (Chicago: University of Chicago Press, 1995).
96. This area of inquiry remains ripe for future research but since 2012, a number of important conferences have been held on the topic. These include the "Southeast Asia as a Crossroads for Buddhist Exchange: Pioneer European Buddhists and Asian Buddhist networks, 1860–1960" conference at University College Cork, Ireland in 2012; "Bordering the Borderless: Faces of Modern Buddhism in East Asia" at Duke University, in the United States in 2013; "Asian Buddhism: Plural Colonialisms and Plural Modernities," at Kyoto University and Ryukoko University, Japan in 2014 and; "Buddhism in the Global Eye: Beyond East and West," at the University of British Columbia, Canada in 2016. A selection of papers from the Ireland conference was published in the journal *Contemporary Buddhism* 14, no. 1 (2013), as well as in book form as *A Buddhist Crossroads: Pioneer Western Buddhists and Asian Networks, 1860–1960,* eds. Brian Bocking, Phibul Choompolpaisal, Laurence Cox, and Alicia M. Turner (New York: Routledge, 2015).
97. "A World Buddhist Movement," *Maha-Bodhi* 37, no. 7 (1929): 357.
98. According to Sunil S. Amrith, *Crossing the Bay of Bengal: The Furies of Nature and the Fortunes of Migrants* (Cambridge, MA: Harvard University Press, 2015), Southeast Asia, and in particular, the Malaya and Straits Settlements (governed by the British), were home to the largest Indian and Chinese migrant populations in the world for much of the late 19th and early 20th century. Amrith, *Crossing Bay of Bengal,* 104, estimates that between 1840 and 1940 alone, some 28 million people emigrated—often forcibly—from the Indian subcontinent with nearly half of that population going to Burma, Malaya, and the Straits Settlements.
99. Wenxue Zhang, "Interactions between Mahāyāna and Theravāda Buddhism in Colonial Singapore," in *Theravāda Buddhism in Colonial Contexts,* ed. Thomas Borchert (London and New York: Routledge, 2018), 42–58; Jack Meng-Tat Chia, "Neither Mahāyāna Nor Theravāda: Ashin Jinarakkhita and the Indonesian Buddhayāna Movement," *History of Religions* 58, no. 1 (2018): 24–63; Anne M. Blackburn, "Ceylonese Buddhism in Colonial Singapore: New Ritual Spaces and Specialists, 1895–1935," ARI Research Institute Working Paper Series No. 184 (2012), 1–28.
100. Bayly, *Birth of the Modern World,* 333.
101. Adam Yuet Chau, "Transnational Buddhist Activists in the Age of Empires," in *Religious Internationals in the Modern World,* eds. Abigail Green and Vincent Viaene (Basingstoke, UK: Palgrave Macmillan, 2012), 213.
102. Green, *Bombay Islam,* 91.
103. Soorakkulame Pemaratana, "Bringing the Buddha Closer: The Role of Venerating the Buddha in the Modernization of Buddhism in Ceylon" (PhD diss., University of Pittsburgh, Pittsburgh, PA, 2017). Pemaratana, "Bringing the Buddha Closer," 33, estimates that between the late 1880s and early 1900s, a minimum of 22,5000 copies of these booklets were printed for distribution among lay Buddhists.
104. On the early to mid-20th-century Buddhist encounter with Marxist thought, see James Mark Shields, *Against Harmony: Progressive and Radical Buddhism in Modern Japan* (Oxford: Oxford University Press,

2017); Douglas Ober, "Socialism, Russia and India's Revolutionary Dharma," in *Buddhism in the Global Eye: Beyond East and West*, eds. John S. Harding, Victor Sōgen Hori, and Alexander Soucy (London: Bloomsbury Academic, 2020); Xue Yu, "Buddhist Efforts for the Reconciliation of Buddhism and Marxism in the Early Years of the People's Republic of China," in *Recovering Buddhism in Modern China*, eds. Jan Kiely and J. Brooks Jessup (Oxford: Oxford University Press, 2016), 177–215. On Soviet violence against Buddhists in Mongolia, see Christopher Kaplonski, *The Lama Question: Violence, Sovereignty, and Exception in Early Socialist Mongolia* (Honolulu: University of Hawaii Press, 2014).

105. Donald S. Lopez Jr., *Gendun Chopel: Tibet's Modern Visionary* (Boulder, CO: Shambhala, 2018). See also Gendun Chopel, *Grains of Gold: Tales of a Cosmopolitan Traveler*, translated by Thupten Jinpa and Donald S. Lopez Jr. (Chicago: University of Chicago Press, 2014).
106. Richard M. Jaffe, *Seeking Śākyamuni: South Asia in the Formation of Modern Japanese Buddhism* (Chicago: University of Chicago Press, 2019).
107. Richard M. Jaffe, "Seeking Śākyamuni: Travel and the Reconstruction of Japanese Buddhism," *Journal of Japanese Studies* 30 (2004): 87.
108. McMahan, *Making of Buddhist Modernism*, 72.
109. Ober, "Reinventing Buddhism."
110. Rustom Bharucha, *Another Asia: Rabindranath Tagore and Okakura Tenshin* (Oxford: Oxford University Press, 2006).
111. Ober, "Reinventing Buddhism," 237–278.
112. Douglas Ober, "From Buddha Bones to Bo Trees: Nehruvian India, Buddhism, and the poetics of power, 1947–1956," *Modern Asian Studies* (2019): 1–39.
113. David Geary, *The Rebirth of Bodh Gaya: Buddhism and the Making of a World Heritage Site* (Seattle: University of Washington Press, 2017), 44, and 114–146, more widely.
114. McMahan, *Making of Buddhist Modernism.*
115. The argument for Protestant Buddhism was developed in Richard Gombrich and Gananath Obeysekere, *Buddhism Transformed: Religious Change in Sri Lanka* (Princeton, NJ: Princeton University Press, 1998). See also a critical review by John Holt, *Religious Studies Review* 17, no. 4 (1991): 307–312.
116. Anne Blackburn, *Buddhist Learning and Textual Practice in Eighteenth-Century Lankan Monastic Culture* (Princeton, NJ: Princeton University Press, 2001).
117. Hansen, *How to Behave*, 204fn39.
118. Charles Hallisey, "Roads Taken and Not Taken in the Study of Theravāda Buddhism," in *Curators of the Buddha: The Study of Buddhism under Colonialism*, ed. Donald S. Lopez Jr. (Chicago: University of Chicago Press, 1995), 31–62.
119. For an excellent introduction to the secularization thesis and related debates, see Pippa Norris and Ronald Ingelhart, *Sacred and Secular: Religion and Politics Worldwide*, 2nd ed. (Cambridge, U.K.: Cambridge University Press, 2011), 3–32; Jose Casanova, *Public Religions in the Modern World* (Chicago: University of Chicago Press, 1994).
120. Thiên Dô, "Quest for Enlightenment."
121. For a more elaborate discussion of this, see Blackburn, *Locations of Buddhism*, 197–217.

Douglas Ober

BUDDHISM IN FILM

Over 2,600 years ago, the Buddha encouraged his disciples to explore and experience the dharma with his famed phrase, "*ehi passika*," or "come and see" for themselves in order to dispel doubt. The Buddha's invitation and exhortation to come and see demonstrate one of the central Buddhist teachings that in order to understand the dharma, one must first come and explore, engage, and *see* it.[1] It is this emphasis on seeing that plays such a central role in the study of Buddhism and film, for it is through the act of viewing that audience members can develop nuanced understandings of self and other, emptiness, and interdependence. Viewing and seeing into the nature of reality through film are potent ritual activities that give rise to experiential insight. Seeing into the dharma and seeing the world through the dharma have become the cornerstone of what might be called Buddhist ways of looking.

Throughout the Buddhist sutras, references to visualizing the Buddha, various opulent Buddha lands, and seeing oneself as the Buddha abound, for the enlightened gaze allows one to see the origin of suffering, its causes, the ability to free oneself from suffering, and the specific prescription to do so. As primary forms of practice and focus in Buddhist traditions, the gaze and act of seeing are both a physical act and a transformative experience, for by gazing upon the Buddha, visualizing buddha lands, and imaging oneself as a buddha, one hones and re-creates how one sees reality.[2] In so doing, seeing becomes a central Buddhist activity and a distinctly embodied activity precisely because it involves the senses and sense organs. Perspectival shift arises from the act of gazing upon the Buddha through form, which then gives rise to seeing beyond form; in this way, looking also encompasses seeing no-thing in everything and everything in no-thing, or that *form is emptiness and emptiness is form.*[3] In the Heart Sutra, one of the shortest of the Perfection of Wisdom texts, the bodhisattva Avalokiteśvara observes all phenomena as empty of inherent independent existence, and uses his dharmic vision to see beyond form. As modern-day meditational devices, Buddhist films can provide a vision of the dharma and hone our dharmic vision; therefore, film viewing can undoubtedly be approached as a central Buddhist practice.

Over the past quarter century, scholars of Buddhism have shifted their own scholarly gaze upon a new field of study—Buddhism and film because both fields pay significant attention to the religious concept of gaze as opportune occasions for new ways of looking and being looked at. Given the import of the gaze and seeing in Buddhist practice and film spectatorship, the conjoining of Buddhism and film as a field of study seems a natural and generative fit. If Buddhist ways of looking are a sensory and embodied experience, then it certainly lends itself to the study of film as a sensory and bodily experience as the spectator can utilize all the sense organs while gazing upon a screen in a theater. The eyes see the screen and others in the theater; the ears receive cues from the screen through score and dialogue; the nose too is engaged as the ubiquitous scents of food and drink waft through the theater space making contact with the olfactory system. The mouth tastes as it takes in the fountain drinks, the tongue touches the often overly buttery salted snacks on sale in the concession, and the skin of the body makes contact with the theater seat and shifts hither and thither in its attempts to navigate a clear view amongst a sea of audience members. Additionally, the mind constantly processes and engages in the act of perpetual thinking in response to all the external and internal stimuli. Watching a film is an embodied ritualized activity much like Buddhist meditation, which too is an entirely embodied experience. Studies of Buddhism and film suggest that the spectator and the meditator are not so different, for it is in the sitting and the seeing that one gains dharmic insight. Film viewing and Buddhist ritual activities are really not such distant family members: they are closer kin than perhaps previously construed given their family resemblances.

As a relatively new area of study, beginning with the first course offered by Robert Scharf in 2005 entitled "Seeing Through the Screen: Buddhism and Film" (through the UC Berkeley Center for Buddhist Studies) and the establishment of the International Buddhism Film Festival series through the Buddhist Film Foundation in 2003, the subject of Buddhism and film has produced several standalone essays and volumes that address two primary topics: 1) the application of Buddhist themes and philosophical concepts to read and interpret a non-Buddhist film; and 2) the analysis of film to understand something about Buddhist ways of looking and attaining dharmic insight. In her essay "Ethics of Inscrutability: Ontologies of Emptiness in Buddhist film," Lina Verchery cautions against the unintended consequences of these two approaches—essentialism and reductionism in creating criteria about what Buddhism is, and taking depictions of Buddhism as unquestioned actual reflections and representations of some real phenomenon known as Buddhism.[4] The latter rests upon a utilitarian pedagogical approach to film where the film acts as an almost ethnographic glimpse into Buddhism. Thus, film becomes a function to support a particular definition of what Buddhism itself is. Verchery argues for an alternative to these dominant modes of scholarship on Buddhism and film and focuses instead on the *ontologies of emptiness* found in Buddhist films where the film alludes to what is not there, what is conspicuously absent from the screen, and therefore explicitly present. Verchery aims to draw ontologies of emptiness in film into dialogue with Buddhist concepts of emptiness or *śūnyatā* to reveal the consequence of relying solely on the two approaches above, that is, totalizing and utilitarian knowledge.[5] Understanding and interpreting Buddhist films as *ontologies of emptiness* can propel us to recognize that unintelligibility and unreliability of our relative viewpoints are in fact hallmarks of Buddhist ways of seeing and knowing.[6]

The growing number of studies of Buddhism and film ought to give us pause to consider the medium's potential as a new expression of a familiar Buddhist medium—from sutra to sculpture to thangka and mandala and, finally, to film, whose form literally embodies emptiness and expresses the illusory nature of reality as a seamless whole and focus upon which to settle the eyes and transform one's vision. If film can be a ritual implement like a sculpture or a mandala that can proffer new ways to visualize the self and other, then certainly one can make the case that the form itself belongs in the vast collection of ritual implements in the Buddhist world. But how can Buddhist films make us see the dharma and give rise to new ways of looking at self and other? Does a film have to be "Buddhist" in some particularly recognizable and knowable way for dharmic insight, or can any film be used as an example of skillful means and a dharma door to liberation so long as the insight derived from viewing it is dharmic in nature?

There are several skillful tools derived from studies of Buddhism and film that support the argument that indeed a film can elicit dharmic ways of looking. To date, scholars of Buddhism and film have contributed to a growing number of accepted criteria for establishing what makes a Buddhist film while keeping in mind the inherently essentialist effects of this endeavor. Some of the important questions to consider involve examining what makes a Buddhist film Buddhist and what are its primary characteristics. Establishing kinds of questions like the aforementioned are themselves implicated in a process of genre-making which involves methods for inclusion and exclusion, which according to the Buddha can be an inherently flawed approach according to Buddhist non-dualism. The establishment of criteria that define and constitute a Buddhist film lends itself to a multiplicity of interpretations among scholars who are simultaneously involved in naming and constructing a genre and defining a new field of study. Understanding the various methods and approaches to defining what makes a Buddhist film Buddhist enables one to "see" how Buddhist films are themselves instantiations of the multiplicity of interpretations that are central to Buddhist ways of looking.

If Buddhist films are invitations to come and see, they are also opportunities to examine how looking and seeing are expressions of relative truths that point toward ultimate truth and an ontological emptiness that can be gleaned only through form and conventional or relative truth. Each interpretation of a Buddhist film serves as a particularistic perspective that when drawn together become illustrative examples of a central Buddhism—perspectival awareness or the recognition that interpretation is more about the seer than the seen.

WHAT MAKES A BUDDHIST FILM BUDDHIST?

John Whalen-Bridge's comprehensive essay "What Is a 'Buddhist Film'?" offers an excellent entrée into the study of Buddhism and film by establishing some preliminary criteria to elucidate what is meant by this emerging category in Buddhist studies.[7] His method begins by examining films selected for international Buddhist festivals over the past fifteen years that provide opportunities to witness what Wilfred Cantwell Smith considered the "observables" of religion such as rituals and sacred texts in distinction to the more murky concept of faith.[8] Whalen-Bridge distinguishes between "overt" Buddhist films and "draftee" films or those that might not have intentionally expressed Buddhist themes but nonetheless serve as potent sources of living, thinking, and seeing in a Buddhist manner. Here, intentionality of the director, screenwriter, and so on are of little concern. Rather, the film is taken on its own as a meditative piece that can give insight into the nature of the dharma or express a particularly Buddhist perspective. Whalen-Bridge notes that this process of interpreting a non-intentionally Buddhist film qua Buddhist film makes the religion itself more palatable and less exotic to non-Buddhist spectators. One might conjecture then that a Buddhist-themed non-Buddhist film might well be a perfect way to learn how to be a Buddhist.

Whalen-Bridge notes that images of the Buddha, Buddhism, and Buddhist peoples have been on screen outside of Asia since before WWII but that it was not until 1989 that Buddhism became an object of filmic adulation with the awarding of the Nobel Peace Prize to the Dalai Lama. The decade following the Dalai Lama's award ushered in what he designates a "cinematic Buddha Boom," with the release of three films depicting aspects of Tibetan Buddhism and the Dalai Lama such as *Little Buddha* (1994), *Kundun* (1997), and *Seven Years in Tibet* (1997).[9] All three films address the concept of reincarnation of lamas, the Dalai Lama and the plight of the Tibetans, and the "difference" that has come to define Tibetan Buddhist otherness. These films became significant entry points or gateway films for awakening American fascination with all things Tibetan Buddhist, although as Donald S. Lopez argues in *Prisoners of Shangri-La,* Western fascination with Tibetan Buddhism emerged out of the mutually influencing contexts of Orientalism and colonialism, which led to the later exoticization of Tibetan Buddhism.[10] Orientalism rendered Tibetan Buddhists as timeless captives of some more spiritual and idealized past that locked them in sacred timelessness in contradistinction to Western notions of progress and the profane world. Thus, Westerners were compelled to cast themselves as the beneficent saviors of the last few vestiges of all that was sacred in the world, with Tibetans serving as the new remaining holdovers from an ever-dwindling sacred landscape.

Whalen-Bridge also points out that any attempt to define what a Buddhist film is "must consider the 'Buddhist film' in relation to film festival screenings partly because no one really knows what a Buddhist film is."[11] Therefore, if we want to determine what makes a Buddhist film Buddhist, then the criteria established for entry into Buddhist film festivals makes logical sense. An analysis of films collected at twenty-five international Buddhist film festivals from 2003 to 2011 indicates two major thematic differences between the selections—some of the films "foreground imagery, characters, and themes associated with Buddhism" presented alongside those that "are associated with the religion in a more abstract way or which would not be considered outside the context of a Buddhist film festival."[12] These "draftee" films act as veritable tugboats in that they helped usher in or assimilate Buddhist messages to largely non-Buddhist audiences. Films screened at festivals include those made in Buddhist countries where Buddhism was widely recognized as a religion that its viewers are familiar with yet screened for the unfamiliar spectator alongside other more "intelligible" films made in the West that may or may not explicitly address Buddhist themes for general audiences. In addition to the differences between Asian and Western Buddhist film, films screened on the festival circuit are either intentionally Buddhist themed, and ones whose Buddhism may be more obscure and/or "thematically conducive to Buddhist allegorization."[13] Taking a familiar film in the West and providing a Buddhist reading of it renders the Buddhist tradition more knowable in this schema, which Whalen-Bridge contends helps render Asian cultures and religions less peculiar and, by extension, perhaps more palatable and consumable.

If the "thematically conducive to Buddhist allegorization" film helps make Asian religions and cultures more knowable, then, by extension, it follows that the religion and culture rendered intelligible in film has undergone a kind of domestication as well. The theme of Asian domestication is well documented in D. W. Griffith's 1919 *Broken Blossoms*, which served as one of the first introductions of Chinese Buddhism to the West through the character of Cheng Hua, a Buddhist monk with high aspirations to convert the heathens of the West. Upon arrival in the Limehouse district of London, he fails in his civilizing Buddhist mission and winds up a poor shopkeeper in love with a gutter waif of a girl named Lucy, and later a murderer who attempts to avenge her death by shooting her abusive father. This film served as one of the first visual introductions of Asian culture and Buddhism on the silver screen and made Buddhism both somewhat more knowable and yet more foreign and perhaps unassimilable.

Although Whalen-Bridge marks the 1990s as the cinematic Buddhism Boom, certainly film and television have been capitalizing on themes of Buddhist otherness with other earlier films like Frank Capra's *Lost Horizon* (1937), which served as a precursor to the fantasies of Tibetan otherness and timeless captivity found in films like *Kundun* and *Seven Years in Tibet*. Capra's film offers a vision of Tibetan Buddhist utopia in the mysterious mountainous Shangri-La, where its inhabitants never want for anything and live forever, unless they happen to cross over the threshold out of Shangri-La and immediately succumb to sickness, old age, and death (the most obvious signs of dukkha or suffering).

While not exploring film alone, Jane Iwamura's *Virtual Orientalism* introduces a series of popular media forms of Buddhism through the icon of the Oriental Monk constructed out of

Asian difference and exoticization who eventually undergoes a process of racialized abstraction, whereby the Asian identity is taken out of the Buddhist monk and replaced by the image of the lone white male whose own Buddhist meditative (read: martial arts) strength serves as a tonic, salve, and salvific figure of both Asian and Western peoples and cultures.[14] Iwamura situates the mediated image of the Oriental Monk found on the silver screen and television in the context of the arrival of D. T. Suzuki on American soil first in 1893 and later in 1950 for an eight-year stay. Although relatively unknown to Western audiences during his first sojourn, by the time he left in 1958, Suzuki had become for many the icon of Zen Buddhism for Western audiences, an iconic image of Zen difference that shaped the later rise of David Carradine's character, Kwai Chang Caine, in the widely popular *Kung Fu* series. Thus, prior to the cinematic Buddhism boom of the 1990s and Tibetan Buddhism, a Zen boom had already been underway popularized by figures such as D. T. Suzuki, Jack Kerouac, Alan Watts, and of course the biracial Kwai Chang Caine, who served as a "bridge figure" and precursor to the *draftee* film who could make Asian culture and religion more palatable and intelligible to Western audiences.[15] In so doing, Kwai Chang Caine also cast the mold for later martial-arts masters popularized in film such as Mr. Miyagi of *The Karate Kid* films. Like Zen master D. T. Suzuki, Mr. Miyagi reflects a Zen-like antinomianism and unconventional wisdom, but also serves as a surrogate father to the angst-ridden poor and young white man, Daniel, who becomes his apprentice. Mr. Miyagi acts as a bridge figure and Asian surrogate of fatherless American boys like Daniel who come to martial arts out of self-defense but leave all the wiser from having absorbed the wisdom of the master through a master–student relationship.

Iwamura's analysis of the icon of the Oriental Monk and his continued rebirth in virtual Orientalism lays bare larger geopolitical anxieties at the root of Orientalism in its desire to know and therefore contain "the other." Thus, Western films about Buddhism in the Buddhism Boom of the 1990s might also be explored in terms of their own projections of geopolitical angst vis-à-vis US–China relations, and the reincarnation of Orientalism in new forms such as Tibetan Buddhism and the Dalai Lama, which incited great fear among Westerners that Tibet as the last hold of enlightened wisdom was on the verge of mass destruction. In the case of Tibetan Buddhist films, however, it was the Westerner again who could protect the religion from the onslaught of the Chinese military occupation and the subsequent and potentially inevitable demise of all things spiritual from Tibet. The geopolitical investments and spiritual yearnings for the difference that Buddhism represents cannot be abstracted from those films that make it into Buddhist film festivals, for they reflect that selection and popularity of chosen films often say more about the audience in its particular time and place than about the Buddhism of the film itself; hence, a Buddhist film can be one whose theme, form, and content are intentionally Buddhist and those that lend themselves particularly well to a Buddhist interpretation.

Whalen-Bridge's categorization of Buddhist films is nonetheless extremely helpful in urging scholars to consider the following factors in creating a category and genre of Buddhist film: representation, intention, and interpretation. Representation refers to all the Buddhist observables through sight and sound such as Buddhist chanting, an image or images of Buddhists, Buddhist ways of life, temples, and so on. Intention refers to the viewer's own perspective more so than the director's in that non-Buddhist films can "*become* Buddhist" and are, therefore, draftees. It is helpful to reconsider Verchey's point that any film that is seen through a

Buddhist lens or given a Buddhist interpretation may in fact become entangled in processes of reductionism and essentialism with regard to what Buddhism is, but as Whalen-Bridge argues, these kinds of draftee films are intended to do precisely that—render Buddhist difference into something more manageable and intelligible for non-Buddhist audiences. Intention and interpretation are quite interchangeable as well because it is really on the part of the viewers themselves and their own inference that a film is about Buddhism at all. That a non-Buddhist film can be a deep reflection about Buddhist philosophy should of course come as no surprise in Buddhist philosophical circles precisely because the form and derivation of the film and lack of explicit Buddhist reference do not preclude it from becoming an object worthy of giving insight into the buddhadharma. It is like any other skillful means that the Buddha discussed—we simply should not get stuck on the form, the content, or the origin of the film. Instead, it is the nature of the perspectival shift that comes from engaging the film that should be highlighted and given pride of place. Perhaps the Buddha himself would encourage scholars not to get too stuck on these distinctions, which are ultimately empty of inherent characteristics anyway.

Because of the difficulties associated with trying to establish the concrete criteria for Buddhist film, differences that pertain to the very nature of the ultimate emptiness of Buddhist categories, Whalen-Bridges encourages an exploration of the International Buddhist Film Festival (IBFF), whose webpage notes that there are both "Buddhist-themed" films that are included with a Buddhist intention on the part of the makers of the films and more easily recognizable as Buddhist in form, and "Buddhist-inspired" cinema that allows for flexibility of interpretation.[16] Gaetano Maida, the executive director of the Buddhist Film Festival, offers an easy and provocative explanation of what "makes it" as a Buddhist film—those born Buddhist or "Buddhist by birth" and those made Buddhist on the part of the viewers or "Buddhists by conversion."[17] Both approaches, when viewed through the lens Buddhist philosophy, are certainly legitimate types of Buddhism films. Buddhist-themed films, Buddhist-inspired cinema, Buddhist films by birth, and Buddhist films by conversion reflect the Buddha's own teachings of non-attachment to the origins of a particular viewpoint and the significance of the effects of the teachings. Hence, in his famed discussion of a man wounded by a poison arrow, the Buddha reminds his disciple Malunkyaputta that it is ultimately of little value and even more of a hindrance to focus too much on where the arrow came from, who made it, what kind of bow shot the arrow, and so on. Instead, as the Buddha advised, the wounded man should simply remove the poison arrow immediately to end his own suffering.[18] By extension, we might well argue that it really does not matter whether a film is or was Buddhist in intent; the fact that it can be viewed as a means of affecting some kind of perspectival shift in awareness might be more useful or at least practical if arguing the case in Buddhist terms.

SCHOLARLY APPROACHES TO BUDDHISM AND FILM

Given the popularity of Buddhism and film, there are a number of highly creative and popular book-length studies of the subject ranging from Dan Sluyter's *Cinema Nirvana, The Dharma of Star Wars,* and *The Dude and the Zen Master,* to name a few.[19] For the purposes of examining academic approaches to the subject, the most recent books coming from scholarly circles will be discussed: 1. Ronald Green's *Buddhism Goes to the Movies: An Introduction to Buddhist*

Thought and Practice, 2. John Whalen-Bridge and Gary Storhoff's *Buddhism and American Cinema*, 3. Sharon A. Suh's *Silver Screen Buddha: Buddhism in Asian and Western Film*, and 4. Francisca Cho's *Seeing Like the Buddha: Enlightenment Through Film*.[20] These four book-length studies of Buddhism and film are relatively recent publications that reflect the growing interest in this field of study. Each book contributes its own approach to Buddhist films in terms of the definition of Buddhist film, methodology employed, general scope of films covered, and their central argument for conjoining of Buddhism and film as an area worthy of serious scholarly attention.

Ronald Green's *Buddhism Goes to the Movies: An Introduction to Buddhist Thought and Practice* provides an overview of the three main schools of Buddhism (Theravāda, Mahāyāna, and tantric Buddhism) and draws inspiration from the lama-director, Khyentse Norbu, who approaches film as a skillful means through which to question the self, the other, and one's received assumptions about reality. *Buddhism Goes to the Movies* does exactly what its title suggests—it goes to the movies, those that are explicitly Buddhist and those that are Buddhist inspired, to make the case that there are several films that inspire Buddhist ways of looking and knowing. Therefore, *Buddhism Goes to the Movies* proposes that viewing a film in and of itself can be a religious experience; if the film happens to be Buddhist themed or Buddhist inspired, it will inspire a perspectival shift or transformation from one state of knowing to another. Khytense Norbu, an incarnated lama, on the one hand, utilizes film to demystify Buddhism as an otherworldly tradition by highlighting the antics of young monks in Nepal whose main goal is to purchase a television to watch the World Cup in *The Cup* (1999). On the other hand, Norbu also makes films like *Travellers and Magicians* (2003) to highlight the illusory nature of desire and how desire for escape and otherness can backfire and give rise to an appreciation of one's situatedness in the present moment.

Set in the stunning landscape of modern-day Bhutan, *Travellers and Magicians* utilizes the device of frame-tale to illustrate the often fictional and narrated qualities of our own lives. The film presents a tale of a young man's dangerous attachment to and lust for a woman that lead him to conspire to murder her elderly husband. As he hears the old man writhing in pain after ingesting poisonous herbs, the young man is suddenly filled with remorse, and as the camera pans to the tears falling from his eyes, viewers are suddenly awakened from the fantasy of the tale back to the young man's real life. It turns out that the young man was unknowingly ingesting a doctored concoction offered to him by his younger brother, who brought lunch to the man's school each day. The story of the young man deluded by lust is told in snippets by a wise monk to a petty official as they hitchhike to Thimpu. The official wants only to leave the village where he is stationed, catch a bus to Thimpu, and chase his dreams of becoming an apple picker in America. The monk's tale serves as a cautionary story encouraging the petty official to enjoy the sweet fruits of home by showing the official the vagaries of desire, but the film also provides an opportunity to reflect upon the fictive nature of reality by explicitly highlighting the constructed nature of our own realities. Norbu projects our everyday reality as an illusion empty of anything enduring and presents film as a perfect facsimile of the self, for what a viewer sees as a seamless whole of reality presented on screen, in reality, comprises singular shots and scenes woven together into a whole.

Green's study of Buddhism and film introduces readers to both the Buddhist themes found in contemporary cinema and the ways that film can re-visualize Buddhism; thus the encounter appears to be a two-way street, giving neither pride of place. In so doing, *Buddhism Goes to the Movies* introduces the basic teachings of Buddhism found in many Buddhist-themed and Buddhist-inspired films without getting overly caught up in any kind of theoretical arguments for the primacy of one of the other. Instead, his is an interpretive practice aimed at mining films for their Buddhist messages for the edification of the audience.

Each chapter of the book is given to exploring Buddhist teachings in non-Buddhist films such as the Four Noble Truths in *Fight Club* (1999), Buddhist Awakening in *Waking Life* (2001), and Dependent Origination in *I Heart Huckabees* (2004). Interestingly, non-Buddhist films are mined for their Buddhist themes and those that are overtly Buddhist are interpreted as representations of different forms of Buddhism such as Korean Seon, Theravāda Buddhism, Tibetan Buddhism, Shin Buddhism, and Thai Buddhism. In other words, Green's treatment of Asian Buddhist films tends to be more reflective of the ethnographic approach to film where we go to the movies to learn about regional Buddhisms. Asian Buddhist films appear to be more pedagogical and *about* Buddhism, whereas the *draftee* films serve as translators, making Asian Buddhism more intelligible to American audiences through a form familiar to Western audiences. As cultural translators, Western Buddhist films become the necessary tool to ground Buddhism in a recognizable and presumably intelligible manner for Westerners.

Green's primary aim is to introduce readers to the central teachings of Buddhism through studies of Buddhist-themed and Buddhist-inspired films. The book is divided into ten separate chapters, each devoted to a particular Buddhist theme or form of Buddhism found throughout the world. Each chapter opens with a synopsis of the film as well as an overview of the central Buddhist teachings to be gleaned from each film. Asian films such as *Why Has Bodhi-Dharma Left for the East?* (1989), *The Burmese Harp* (1956), *Departures* (2008), *Windhorse* (1998), *Nang Nak* (1999), and *Uncle Boonmee Who Can Recall His Past Lives* (2010) are given their own chapters (minus the last two) and interpreted as films that tell us something about Buddhism and about the regional varieties of Buddhism from which they emerge. Thus, *Why Has Bodhidharma Left for the East?* provides an opportunity to reflect on the nature of reality, one's own attachments, responsibilities to the "world of men," and karma that all transpire in a Korean Buddhist temple. Thus, through Green's reading, the viewer goes to the movie to develop insight into the nature of self and other as well as gets an opportunity to see "firsthand" and up close what Korean Buddhism looks like through the film's depiction of the monastic lives of three monks: an elderly master, a young boy, and a young man who comes to the temple to avoid the suffering of the ordinary world. These Buddhist films become opportunities to imagine what Buddhism looks like on the ground.

Buddhism and American Cinema edited by John Whalen-Bridge and Gary Storhoff provides regional and national boundaries by focusing on Western productions and interpretations of Buddhist films primarily for America moviegoers.[21] Focusing on Hollywood versions of enlightenment on screen, the book is divided into two sections: 1. representation and intention, and 2. allegories of shadow, and light. The first section analyzes four films that contain explicitly Buddhist elements and places each film in the distinct cultural and historical context of the Vietnam War (*Heaven and Earth*) and Tibetan independence (*Little Buddha, Seven Years in Tibet, Kundun,* and *The Cup*). The chapters in section 1 highlight the cultural context of Buddhism, the struggle to define what "authentic" Buddhism might be, and the orientalist tendencies that serve as the backdrop and hidden transcript for much of the Tibetan Buddhist films. The latter section focuses on non-explicitly Buddhist films that nonetheless lend themselves well to a Buddhist reading and, as the authors explain, "many of these films occupy a semiotic 'bardo' space between the films that are intentionally Buddhist (both in terms of representation and thematic/philosophical emphasis) and films that are not about Buddhism but that can be understood from a Buddhist point of view."[22] Films this category include: *Lost in Translation* (2003), *The Matrix* (1999), *Fight Club* (1999), *Star Wars: Episode III* (2005), *The Last Samurai* (2003), *Wall Street* (1987), *Annie Hall* (1977), *Leaving Las Vegas* (1995), *It's a Wonderful Life* (1946), *Jacob's Ladder* (1990), *Donnie Darko* (2001), and *American Beauty* (1999). Each of these American films illustrate Buddhist themes such as impermanence, desire, suffering, liberation, and *bardo*.

Like Green, the authors explore the cultural and historical elements in the more explicitly Buddhist films, and then mine the non-Buddhist films for their Buddhist messages; in this volume, films depicting Asian Buddhism are interpreted for non-Buddhist ends, and non-Buddhist films are explored for their insight into Buddhist thought and practice. In this way, films highlight how we might view Buddhists and how we might view ourselves through a Buddhist lens.

Drawing from the earlier argument set out in his previous essay, Whalen-Bridges makes the case that "Buddhism in popular culture can be overt . . . or it can be inferred," and this distinction is made in this volume as well.[23] As cultural translators, these films render what appears to be the otherness or exoticism of Buddhism into something understandable. The authors note, "[w]hether Buddhist beliefs (about karma or reincarnation) or practices (meditation, especially) have been in the foreground or in the background, it is uncontestable that films, even as they have traded upon the exoticism of Buddhism in the American *imaginaire*, have made Buddhism less exotic than it was previously."[24]

Silver Screen Buddha: Buddhism in Asian and Western Film by Sharon A. Suh provides a comparative analysis of Buddhist-themed films in Asian and Western films to explore how Buddhism, gender, and race have been entangled in the media's projection of the religious tradition.[25] The underlying questions in this book are: How are Buddhists and Buddhism imaged on screen? What aspects of the tradition are normalized, and which are rendered invisible on screen? How do race and gender play into what we see in Buddhist-themed films? And, is there a way to revise what we see on screen to include a more capacious understanding of Buddhist peoples? The book proposes that film is a form of spiritual technology that can be considered a modern-day sutra or text. Seeing film as sutra expands what we understand to be appropriate religious texts and can also help re-imagine the tradition to include those who have been left out of Buddhist texts, both literary and filmic. Thus, the book sees Buddhist film as reflective and constitutive of how we see or do not see Buddhist monks, nuns, the laity, and Asians and Asian Americans. Unlike the previous two works, this book takes a distinctly revisionist approach by re-imagining and re-imaging what Buddhism looks like in the popular imagination both on screen and off.

Silver Screen Buddha begins opens with an analysis of *Broken Blossoms* (1919) and *Lost Horizon* (1947) as exemplars of an orientalist tradition that views Buddhism and Asian as examples of otherness to be both emulated and avoided. The book then moves into a discussion of the antinomian antics of Buddhist monks or quasi-monks in three Zen-themed Western films—*The Big Lebowski* (1998), *Ghost Dog: The Way of the Samurai* (1995), and *Zen Noir*

(2004)—and places them in the long lineage of orientalist and racialized conceptualizations of Asians and Asian Americans as unintelligible or mysterious fonts of wisdom. The book then turns to three Korean directed films, *Spring, Summer, Fall, Winter . . . and Spring* (2003) and *Come, Come, Come Upward* (1989), and *Why Has Bodhidharma Left for the East?* (1989) and offers a feminist reading of each film to reveal the age-old tropes of women as the snares of samsara found in ancient texts and contemporary film, and the opportunity to read against the grain and highlight the roles of women and everyday life as the ground of enlightenment. The book then explores the everyday intimacy, gratitude, and interdependence of Shin Buddhism found in *Departures* (2008) and establishes the possibility of seeing film as *sutra* through an analysis of *Hwa-om-kyung* (Passage to Buddha, 1993), itself explicitly based on the *Gandavyuha Sūtra*. Finally, the book proposes an opportunity to read against the grain by reinterpreting traditionally male centered films such as Samsara (2001) to foreground the other side of Buddhism—that is, the Buddhism of ordinary laywomen that often gets short shrift and little screen time. *Silver Screen Buddha* is both a cultural critique of Buddhism and a reconstructive approach to Buddhism to make space for those voices and faces often absent from the silver screen.

Seeing Like the Buddha. *Seeing Like the Buddha: Enlightenment through Film* by Francisca Cho is the latest arrival in the growing field of Buddhism and film and argues that film can shape not only what one sees on screen, but perhaps more importantly *how* one sees.[26] Cho provides a deep reading of Buddhist philosophical teachings such as emptiness, the three emanation bodies of the Buddha, tathāgathgarba ("embryo of enlightenment") theory, and the phenomenology of the person. The author begins the book with an analysis of films that have an immediately recognizable Buddhist framework and content in films like Kim Kiduk's *Spring, Summer, Fall, Winter . . . and Spring*, which reflects the cycle of samsara, karmic consequences, and buddhanature as standard uddhanature. The book then moves to Buddhist themes of meditative vision, ghosts, karma, and interconnectedness through Nonzee Nimibutr's film, *Nang Nak* (1994), a popular Thai ghost story highlighting both the love between a young wife, Nak, and her husband, Mak. After Mak goes off to war, Nak dies in childbirth and returns as a ghost attempting to resume her domestic life with Mak, who, unbeknownst to him, is rekindling a relationship with a ghost. To protect their reunion, Nak summarily kills those in the village who attempt to awaken Mak to the truth of his wife's ghostly nature. The film concludes with the ghostly form of Mak put to rest by her husband, who has been ordained as a Buddhist monk. Cho categorizes this film as one that offers "visions of emptiness" in its ability to reveal the illusory nature of reality.[27] *Seeing Like the Buddha* extends its emphasis on "visions of emptiness" to Akira Kurosawa's *Rashomon* (1950), which deliberately rejects the "God's-eye" point of view and follows this thread in an examination of Hirokazu Kore'ada's *Maborosi* (1995) about the illusory nature of reality.

The progression of the book is structured to mimic a pilgrim's progress through Borobudor temple in Java. The temple invites pilgrims to enter its space to encounter first images of the Buddha that are explicit renditions of his enlightenment. As the pilgrims progress through the stupa, the representations of enlightenment and wisdom become increasingly less particular and point toward ultimate reality. Once the pilgrims reach the central stupa, they cannot see the Buddha but instead encounter a far wider panoramic perspective of the world. In so doing, the pilgrims see what the Buddha sees and see like the Buddha. The book concludes with an analysis of Terrence Malick's films that reject linearity such as *The Thin Red Line* (1998), *The Tree of Life* (2011), and *To the Wonder* (2013), which fit largely into the category of *draftee* films that, while not explicitly Buddhist, provide opportunities to visualize the self and the world as empty of inherent individual existence. Cho thus constructs her chapters around the visual experiences of pilgrims moving from very explicit narrative depictions of Buddhism to the more obscure utilizing of the blueprint of Borobudor as the books main structure. The reader, like the pilgrim, and the film viewer undergo a perspectival shift and growing awareness of the deeper layers of the buddhadharma until they learn how to see like the Buddha.

The centrality of vision, seeing, and the gaze from the earliest Buddhist sculptures and texts to the present indicate that the Buddhist tradition has continued to evolve in its forms of ritual practice and modes of understanding. Buddhism *in*, *through*, and *as* film serves as one of the latest and most potent forms of skillful means that inspires new understandings of the dharma for its viewers.

REVIEW OF LITERATURE

The study of Buddhism and film is still a relatively new field that has grown tremendously in the area of dedicated scholarly research in the past fifteen years. It has been approached with multiple disciplinary lenses with several contributions from cultural studies, literary studies, film studies, cultural anthropology, theology, religious studies, Buddhist studies, feminist studies, and media studies, to name a few. Several articles on Buddhism and film can be found in the *Journal of Religion and Film* that address films that have an explicitly Buddhist content and context as well as those that are loosely interpreted as Buddhist on the part of the viewer and/or scholar. Most studies of Buddhism and film fall into either of two general camps: those that focus on films that are explicitly recognizable as Buddhist through character, context, and content, and those that focus on films that are not explicitly Buddhist but rather lend themselves to a Buddhist reading. For an excellent overview of essays reflecting these differences, see Almut-Barbara Renger's introductory essay, "Buddhism and Film—Interrelation and Interpenetration: Reflections on an Emerging Field," in the special volume on "Buddhism and Film" in *Contemporary Buddhism*.[28]

For book-length studies of Buddhism and film, see Dan Sluyter's 2005 *Cinema Nirvana: Enlightenment Lessons from the Movies*. Sluyter's book offers a Buddhist analysis of many popular films such as *Snow White and the Seven Dwarves* and *Casablanca*. Matthew Bortolin's *The Dharma of Star Wars* takes up the Buddhist symbolism and philosophy found in the *Star Wars* series.[29] Jane Iwamura's *Virtual Orientalism: Asian Religions and American Popular Culture* provides an excellent detailed analysis of the orientalist context from which many popular images of Buddhism emerged and proliferated in Western media.[30] Ronald Green's *Buddhism Goes to the Movies* offers a wonderful introduction to Buddhist thought and practice through the analysis of specific films that he mines for Buddhist philosophical and religious context.[31] *Buddhism and American Cinema* by John Whalen-Bridge and Gary Storhoff (also published in 2014) focuses on films that are explicitly Buddhist and those that lend themselves to a rich Buddhist interpretation. Sharon A. Suh's 2015 *Silver Screen Buddha: Buddhism in Asian and Western Film* explores the emergence of Buddhism in film and its intersections with race, gender, and lay practice. The most recent book-length contribution to the field of Buddhism and film is Francisca Cho's 2017 *Seeing Like the Buddha: Enlightenment Through Film*, which argues that Buddhist film can inform new ways of seeing like the Buddha. While there have been very rich analyses of Buddhism and film through several different disciplinary approaches, there has yet to be a single volume dedicated to analyzing those most popular Buddhist films that have received the most scholarly attention from a variety of perspectives such as Bae Young-Kyun's 1989 *Why Has Bodhidharma Left for the East* or Kim Ki-Duk's 2003 *Spring, Summer, Fall, Winter . . . and Spring*. Such a volume would contribute greatly to this growing field by drawing perspectival awareness and interpretive differences to the analysis of a single film.

FURTHER READING

Blizek, William L., ed. *Continuum Companion to Religion and Film*. New York: Continuum, 2009.

Bortolin, Matthew. *The Dharma of Star Wars*. Somerville, MA: Wisdom Publications, 2005.

Bridges, Jeff, and Bernie Glassman. *The Dude and the Zen Master*. New York: Blue Rider Press, 2012.

Cho, Francisca. "Imagining Nothing and Imaging Otherness in Buddhist Film." In *Imag(in)ing the Other: Filmic Visions of Community*. Edited by David Jaspers and S. Brent Plate. Atlanta: Scholar's Press, 1999.

Cho, Francisca. *Seeing Like the Buddha: Enlightenment through Film*. Albany: State University of New York Press, 2017.

Green, Ronald. *Buddhism Goes to the Movies*. New York: Routledge, 2014.

Iwamura, Jane. *Virtual Orientalism: Asian Religions in American Popular Culture*. New York: Oxford University Press, 2011.

Jaspers, David and Plate, Brent S., eds. *Imag(in)ing the Other: Filmic Visions of Community*. Atlanta: Scholar's Press, 1999.

Lopez, Donald S., Jr. *Prisoners of Shangri-La: Tibetan Buddhism and the West*. Chicago: University of Chicago Press, 1998.

Lyden, John, ed. *The Routledge Companion to Religion and Film*. Hoboken, NJ: Routledge, 2009.

Plate, Brent S., ed. *Representing Religion in World Cinema: Mythmaking, Culture Making, Filmmaking*. New York: Palgrave/St. Martins, 2003.

Plate, Brent S., ed. *Religion and Film: Cinema and the Re-Creation of the World*. New York: Wallflower Press, 2008.

Schell, Orville. *Virtual Tibet: Searching for Shangri-La from the Himalayas to Hollywood*. New York: Metropolitan Books, 2000.

Suh, Sharon A. *Silver Screen Buddha: Buddhism in Asian and Western Film*. London: Bloomsbury Academic, 2015.

Sluyter, Dan. *Cinema Nirvana: Enlightenment Lessons from the Movies*. New York: Three Rivers Press, 2005.

Whalen-Bridge, John. "What Is a Buddhist Film?," *Contemporary Buddhism* 15, no. 1 (2014): 44–80.

Whalen-Bridge, John, and Gary Storhoff. *Buddhism and American Cinema*. Albany: State University of New York Press, 2014.

Yi, Hyangsoon. "The Real, Anti-real, and Transcendental in Four Korean Buddhist Films." In *Pathways into Korean Language and Culture: Essays in Honor of Young-Key Kim-Renaud*. Edited by Sang-Oak Lee and Gregory K. Iverson. Seoul: Pagijong Press, 2002.

NOTES

1. For a detailed discussion of the Buddhist emphasis on *seeing* rather than mere belief without experience, see Walpola Rahula, *What the Buddha Taught* (New York: Grove Press, 1959), 8–9.

2. Malcolm David Eckel, *To See the Buddha: A Philosopher's Quest for the Meaning of Emptiness* (San Francisco: Harper San Francisco, 1992).
3. Red Pine, *The Heart Sutra: The Womb of the Buddhas* (Berkeley, CA: Counterpoint Press, 2005).
4. Lina Verchery, "Ethics of Inscrutability: Ontologies of Emptiness in Buddhist Film," *Contemporary Buddhism* 15, no. 1 (2014) 145–163.
5. Verchery, "Ethics of Inscrutability," 147.
6. Verchery, "Ethics of Inscrutability," 158.
7. John Whalen-Bridge, "What Is a Buddhist Film?," *Contemporary Buddhism* 15, no. 1 (2014): 44–80.
8. Wilfred Cantwell Smith, *The Meaning and End of Religion* (New York: Fortress Press, 1991).
9. Whalen-Bridge, "What Is a Buddhist Film?," 44.
10. Donald S. Lopez Jr., *Prisoners of Shangri-La: Tibetan Buddhism and the West* (Chicago: University of Chicago Press, 2001).
11. Whalen-Bridges, "What Is a Buddhist Film?," 44.
12. Whalen-Bridge, "What Is a Buddhist Film?," 45.
13. Whalen-Bridge, "What Is a Buddhist Film?," 45.
14. Jane Iwamura, *Virtual Orientalism: Asian Religions and American Popular Culture* (New York: Oxford University Press, 2011).
15. Iwamura, *Virtual Orientalism*, 16.
16. Whalen-Bridge, "What Is a Buddhist Film?," 50.
17. Whalen-Bridge "What Is a Buddhist Film?," 50.
18. Students might find Walpola Rahula's explanation of this story quite valuable. See Rahula, *What the Buddha Taught*, 14–15.
19. Whalen-Bridges, "What Is a Buddhist Film?," 45; Dan Sluyter, *Cinema Nirvana: Enlightenment Lessons from the Movies* (New York: Three Rivers Press, 2005); Jeff Bridges and Bernie Glassman, *The Dude and the Zen Master* (New York: Blue Rider Press, 2012); and Matthew Bortolin, *The Dharma of Star Wars* (Somerville, MA: Wisdom Publications, 2005).
20. Ronald Green, *Buddhism Goes to the Movies: An Introduction to Buddhist Thought and Practice* (New York: Routledge, 2014); John Whalen-Bridge and Gary Storhoff, *Buddhism and American Cinema* (Albany, NY: SUNY, 2014); Sharon A. Suh's *Silver Screen Buddha: Buddhism in Asian and Western Film* (New York: Bloomsbury 2015); and Francisca Cho, *Seeing Like the Buddha: Enlightenment Through Film* (Albany, NY: SUNY, 2017).
21. Whalen-Bridge and Storhoff, *Buddhism and American Cinema*.
22. Whalen-Bridge and Storhoff, *Buddhism and American Cinema*, 8.
23. Whalen-Bridges and Storhoff, *Buddhism and American Cinema*, 1.
24. Whalen-Bridges and Storhoff, *Buddhism and American Cinema*, 3.
25. Sharon A. Suh, *Silver Screen Buddha: Buddhism in Asian and Western Film* (London: Bloomsbury Academic, 2015).
26. Francisca Cho, *Seeing Like the Buddha* (Albany, NY: State University of New York Press, 2017.
27. Cho, *Seeing Like the Buddha*, 23.
28. Almut-Barbara Renger, "Buddhism and Film—Interrelation and Interpenetration: Reflections on an Emerging Research Field," *Contemporary Buddhism* 15, no. 1 (2014): 1–27.
29. Bortolin, *The Dharma of Star Wars*.
30. Iwamura, *Virtual Orientalism*.
31. Green, *Buddhism Goes to the Movies*.

Sharon A. Suh

BUDDHISMS IN DIASPORA: THE CANADIAN CONTEXT OF CHINESE BUDDHISM

CHINESE RELIGIONS IN CANADA: THE 19TH-CENTURY CONTEXT

The origins and development of Chinese Buddhist diaspora communities in Canada are closely linked to sociopolitical factors that shaped immigration policy informed by racist attitudes, and a basic assumption that Canada was for whites only. Substantial reform of immigration policy did not occur until 1967, after which non-European migration began to open the doors to migrants who brought their Buddhist practices and beliefs with them nearly two hundred years after the first Chinese landed on the shores of Canada's west coast.

The presence of Chinese in Canada extends back into the 18th century, although nothing that could be considered a "diaspora" existed at that time. Certainly, no organized religious activity, Buddhist or otherwise, was recorded. The first evidence of Chinese living in Canada is associated with the exploits of John Meares (c. 1756–1809). Having left the Royal Navy, Captain Meares engaged in fur trade with First Nations inhabitants on Canada's west coast. He traded pelts in Guangdong from his base of operations in the Portuguese colony of Macau. It was here early in 1788 that he recruited fifty smiths and carpenters, many of whom were Chinese, in cooperation with the Nootka First Nation, for work on establishing a trading post at Nootka Sound, on what became Vancouver Island. He brought another seventy Chinese from Macau in the following year and expressed his enthusiasm for the quality of their work.[1] It is far from clear what became of this small number of Chinese in the following years, when the Spanish navy confiscated Meares's two ships as part of Spanish efforts to colonize the region. It is nearly certain that these workers from the Pearl River delta region would have brought with them folk religious beliefs and perhaps practices associated with their home counties and villages. Given the frontier nature of the west coast and rudimentary nature of the trading post, it is highly unlikely that any organized institutional Buddhist presence would have existed.

The first significant presence of Chinese migrants in Canada was on the west coast in the mid-19th century, during a time of considerable turmoil in China following the Opium Wars (1839–1842 and 1856–1860). Impoverished Chinese reeling from the social devastation associated with the British opium trade and punitive treaties with the French and British were desperate for opportunities at the same time that the California gold rush began; this was followed by the Fraser River gold rush in British Columbia. Chinese migration, beginning in the mid-19th century, was predominantly of young males brought to the Canada's west coast by the promise of riches by way of the gold rush and later as cheap source of labour for railway construction. The closely-knit familial and clan structures needed to support institutional religious activity were absent. Despite this, family and associated home villages and counties did serve as the ground for religious expression. Altars that included both Buddhist iconography and popular religious figures were core elements constituting shrines or altars in association buildings that served as social support centers.

The beginnings of Canada's first Chinatown, in Victoria on Vancouver Island, can be traced to a handful of wealthy Chinese merchants who arrived by boat in Victoria in 1858. They anticipated the needs of Chinese laborers recruited to pan for gold along the Fraser River. During this initial period, several rough structures were built on Cormorant Street, where the beginnings of Chinatown took shape. By the 1870s, sufficient capital, combined with social solidarity among the Chinese, made possible the construction of a Chinese Methodist Church, a clan association, and a benevolent association. It was also at this time that Canada's first Chinese temple was constructed, Tam Kung Temple (Tangong miao 譚公廟).[2] Tangong is a figure associated with healing and the protection of seafarers. A roadside shrine was set up after a Hakka settler brought a wooden statue of Tangong to Victoria. In 1875 Hakka settlers, pooling their money, rented a house at the corner of Government and Fisgard Streets where the statue was installed. Two Hakka, Tsay Ching and Dong Bang Sang, purchased a small lot on the site of what became 1713 Government Street, and the temple was officially opened on January 21, 1876. The temple continues to function in an Edwardian-era building at the same location on the third floor of the Yen Wo [Hakka] Society Building (Geshu renhe chongzheng hui 客屬人和崇正會).[3] Tam Kung Temple is perhaps best identified as a folk temple, however, as is common with such institutions, Buddhist elements are often present. One of the features of Tam Kung Temple is the inclusion of several large Buddhist parasols (Ch. *san* 傘; Tib. *gdugs*). These are one of eight auspicious symbols (Ch. *babao* 八寶; Tib. *bkra shis rtags brgyad*) originating in India and later incorporated into Tibetan Buddhist iconography. How early and to what extent Buddhist images and objects were incorporated into Tam Kung Temple liturgy and practice is unclear.

The largest wave of early Chinese migration is associated with labour recruitment for construction of the final leg of the Canadian Pacific Railway through British Columbia. Canada's first Chinese settlement in Victoria experienced growth during this period. Between 1880 and 1885, approximately seven thousand laborers arrived in British Columbia, and six new buildings were added to Victoria's Chinatown, including the Chinese Consolidated Benevolent Association (CCBA), constructed in 1885.[4] In addition to office space on the second floor, on the third floor there was a shrine known as the "Palace of the Sages" (Liesheng gong 列聖宮). The shrine still exists but was moved into Victoria's Chinese Public School in 1966. On the altar were Tianhou (天后), Guandi (關帝), Huatuo (華陀, also known as Wuqínxi 五禽戲), and Zhao gongming (趙公明). The shrine was constructed in parts in Guangdong and shipped over to British Columbia where it was assembled. Although there is no record of specifically Buddhist activities at this site, the carvings in the original wooden decorative altar panels include an image of the Bodhisattva Maitreya (Miluo pusa 彌勒菩薩), the Buddha of the future. It would be reasonable to assume that significant dates on the Buddhist calendar, such as the Buddha's birthday and, given the importance of continued ties to the ancestors, the Hungry Ghost Festival (Yunlanpen jie 盂蘭盆節), would have been celebrated. Outside Chinatown's benevolent and clan associations, there is no further evidence of even this modest level of Buddhist activity.

Following completion of the CPR in 1885, a head tax was instituted beginning at $50, followed by increases in 1901 to $100, and 1903 to $500. This punitive entry fee did not dissuade enough Chinese from migrating to Canada, which, despite the onerous fee, remained a place of economic hope for desperate Chinese laborers. In 1923 the Chinese Immigration Act was passed, which effectively barred entry to all but a few exempted classes.[5] Thus, Chinese in Canada were in no position to build religious institutions. Chinese religious activity has always included outdoor ritual performances and festivities. This very public aspect of religious practice combined with traditional architectural features associated with Buddhist temples would have curtailed organized activities during times when the majority European-heritage population was deeply hostile to Chinese migrants. Sequestered away in slums designated as "Chinatowns," the principal concern was for survival and economic supports in a hostile society rather than for building Buddhist institutions that might only inflame racist sentiment. Chinese migrants' personal futures were very uncertain, as they faced systemic racism and economic marginalization, and there was a significant undermining of social stability due to the absence of familial support networks associated, in part, with a pronounced imbalance in the ratio of Chinese males to females.[6] Chinese religious expression has for centuries been deeply related to family networks and clan affiliations, and to a particular geographic locus. None of the social foundations necessary to establish altars and their associated buildings were in place during the first half of the 20th century. Canadian Census records from 1921, just prior to the Chinese Immigration Act, through 1951, four years after the Act was repealed, indicate that the Chinese population in Canada experienced a dramatic 31.7 percent contraction, from a high of 46,519 in 1931 to 32,528 in 1951.[7]

IMMIGRATION REFORM AND THE EMERGENCE OF BUDDHIST INSTITUTIONS

In 1947, after repeal of the Chinese Immigration Act, the Chinese were finally able to vote, though immigration legislation remained deeply racist. During the first decades of the 20th century the Chinese began moving eastward across Canada. While, by 1941, the vast majority lived in Vancouver and Victoria, significant numbers had relocated as far east as Montréal and Toronto. This trend of population concentration, particularly in Vancouver, Montréal, and Toronto, continues to the present. It was not until 1967 that immigrants from Asia were subject to the same requirements as those from Europe. Canada's Liberal government under Prime Minister Pierre Elliott Trudeau (1919–2000) inaugurated the point system, permitting people to qualify for landed immigrant status without reference to their particular country of origin. Prior to 1967, through the postwar period and the 1950s, a number of orders were gradually relaxed and rescinded in council, regulations that had hindered family reunification. Thus, in the decades prior to the 1967 changes to immigration regulations, Chinese families had gradually begun to reunite. This lent a sense of greater stability and shifted perceptions of Canada from that of a temporary home, adopted for the purpose of accruing capital and supporting family across the Pacific, to a potentially permanent home for entire families. By 1967 the Chinese population was finally in a position to turn its attention to supporting cultural beliefs and practices associated with veneration of local deities, reverence for ancestors, and personal cultivation. This included the establishing of Buddhist institutions. This period of emergence and development for Buddhists in Canada coincided with a wave of Chinese migration that originated almost entirely from Hong Kong, with virtually no migrants entering Canada as landed immigrants from the People's Republic of China (PRC). These numbers would not reverse until 1996–2001, with a significant increase from the PRC commencing from 1991–1995.[8]

The roots of the first major Chinese Buddhist temple in Canada, Universal Buddhist Temple (UBT, Shijie fojiaohui 世界佛教會), were established in Vancouver's Chinatown in 1967 with cooperation from the Chinese Benevolent Association. The origins of Universal Buddhist

Temple are associated with a small lay community rather than with a particular lineage or Buddhist teacher. The nucleus of Hong Kong migrants that would become UBT was formed around the figure of Mr. Chao-Chow Lü 呂雒琦 (1899–1982), a Taiwan-based businessman who owned an import-export business. His early background is unclear, though Sichuan was his ancestral home. Members of UBT have suggested it is likely he left China with the Nationalist Party (Guomindang 國民黨) to establish a new life in Taiwan. It was Mr. Lü who provided the principal financial support to rent a space from the Chinese Freemasons at 116 East Pender Street in Vancouver's Chinatown from 1968 until 1977. Acting as UBT's founding president, he had a strong interest in Buddhism and longstanding relationships with lay Buddhist organizations in Hong Kong, the source of many of the first temple members. With considerable volunteer support, the temple space in Chinatown was prepared and opened its doors to the public in 1968. A milestone in the temple's history was the preparation and serving of vegetarian food (*zhai* 齋) to the public. Such events declared to the wider community that the temple was open, prosperous, and well supported by an active membership. During its first nine years of operation the temple membership grew steadily. By 1977 it became necessary to seek a new and more permanent home for the temple outside Chinatown. A vacated church was purchased and converted to the needs of the temple members. Additions and renovations to the structure have been ongoing. The temple continues to function under the direction of a lay board of directors.[9]

Toronto is home to the second-longest-running Chinese Buddhist temple in Canada. Hong Kong monks Ven. Lok To 樂渡 (relocated to New York in 1963), Ven. Sing Hung 性空, and Ven. Shing Cheung 誠祥 founded the Buddhist Association of Canada (Jianada fojiaohui 加拿大佛教会) in 1968 following their trip to see the World Expo in 1967. A small building was purchased in 1968 where Nan Shan (Nanshan 南山) Temple was opened. In 1973 the Association established the Buddhist Association of Canada Cham Shan Temple (Jianada fojiaohui zhanshan jingshe 加拿大佛教会湛山精舍). The main hall located in the Markham, Ontario region, officially opened in 1978. The temple plan and architecture are traditional in form, unlike that of UBT in Vancouver. Money to purchase the site was donated by two devout disciples of Ven. Tan Xu 倓虛, forty-fourth-generation lineage holder of the Tiantai school, and founder of the Cham San Temple in Qingdao, China. Tan Xu is a key figure in the revival and reform of Buddhism in China, which experienced a protracted period of decline through the late Qing (1644–1912) and Republican era. He was responsible for construction and renovation of several temples in China prior to his relocation to Hong Kong in 1949. As with UBT, Cham Shan Temple expanded as its base of support grew; additions of buddha halls were completed in 1984 and 1993. In 1984 another building was purchased nearer to the Dundas- and Spadina-area Chinatown. Two more lots were purchased in North York and Niagra in 1995. Such dramatic expansion is testimony to a high level of financial health and strong membership support.[10]

Apart from these two Buddhist organizations, both with their origins linked to Hong Kong and to Hong Kong immigrants in Canada, there is no clear evidence of other Chinese Buddhist diaspora activities at this level. Chinese immigrants continued to concentrate in Toronto and Vancouver, with a much smaller presence in Montréal and Ottawa. It is no surprise that the earliest development of Chinese Buddhist communities would be in Vancouver and Toronto. During the period immediately following the 1967 immigration reform, development of

Chinese Buddhist temples and associations remained very limited and relied on the capital and Buddhist expertise that followed Hong Kong migration. As the Hong Kong immigrant base was consolidated and deepened, more rapid development of Chinese Buddhist institutions and their associated communities began to take place in the mid- to late 1970s and through the 1980s and 1990s.

GROWTH OF THE CHINESE BUDDHIST DIASPORA, POST-1967

Through the end of the 1960s and into the early 1990s immigration trends continued to see sustained majority migration from Hong Kong, and Chinatowns across Canada continued to be the locus of much cultural activity despite experiencing a steady decline, as newer immigrants no longer had to rely on the socio-economic supports so desperately needed by pre-1967 immigrants.[11] Hong Kong migration to Canada spiked in the early 1980s through the early 1990s due to uncertainties associated with the signing of the Sino-British Joint Declaration, in which Hong Kong was to return to China in 1997. Thus the story of Chinese Buddhists in Canada continued to be linked to Hong Kong and Taiwanese immigrants. Both of these migration source-regions had received an influx of Buddhist teachers and devotees in the years following World War II. The wider narrative, of which these developments are a part, is not simply about local Chinese Canadian immigrant communities developing their own institutions in response to a need for Buddhist ritual and teachings. Instead, the growth of the Chinese Buddhist diaspora resulted in no small part from the proactive efforts of established Buddhist teachers and devoted lay people to transmit the buddhadharma to Canada. As such, these Canadian developments are best seen not as a simple transplanting of beliefs and practices accompanying newcomers from Hong Kong, Taiwan, and the People's Republic of China, but instead Chinese Canadian Buddhist communities were, and continue to be, enmeshed in a global network of organizations. The flow of capital and people, combined with greatly improved transportation and telecommunications infrastructure—including, of course, the ubiquitous media and social networks supported by the Internet—continue to facilitate these developments. Powerful 21st-century social media tools such as WeChat originating in the PRC and WhatsApp in Hong Kong have amplified the ease with which transpacific social bonds and organizational/social activity are generated and sustained.

Several large organizations that have branched out across Canada began their development in the 1980s and 1990s. These include Dharma Realm Buddhist Association (DRBA), with temples in Calgary (est. 1986) and Vancouver (est. 1983); Tzu Chi Buddhist Compassion and Relief Foundation of Canada (est. 1992); and Fo Guang Shan, with its International Buddhist Progress Society in Vancouver (est. 1994) and Fo Guang Shan Temple in Toronto (est. 1997). Fo Guang Shan has also established centers in Ottawa and Montréal. More recently Dharma Drum Mountain was established in Vancouver in 1994, with its permanent practice center opening in 2004. All of these groups are international, and their origins lie outside Canada: DRBA in Canada was launched from its headquarters established in Northern California in 1976, though its beginnings can be traced to earlier developments in Hong Kong. Tzu Chi, Foguang shan, and Dharma Drum all had their origins in Taiwan. A major driving force behind these organizations' aspirations to spread Buddhist teachings is the ideal represented by "humanistic Buddhism" (*renjian fojiao* 人間佛教).

The beginning of this "humanistic" approach to Buddhist teachings is generally traced to Master Taixu 太虛 (1890–1947). Taixu taught Yin Shun 印順, who in turn taught Master Cheng Yen 證嚴, the nun who established Tzu Chi in Taiwan.[12] Another student of Taixu was Dong Chu 東初 (1908–1977), who taught Master Shengyen 聖嚴 (1931–2009), founder of Dharma Drum in Taiwan and centers in New York state and Vancouver. Master Xingyun 星雲, founder of Fo Guang Shan, was inspired by the teachings of Master Taixu and has since become a major representative of humanistic Buddhism. It should be noted that Taixu's student, Yin Shun, also had significant influence on Shengyen and Xingyun. Master Hsuan Hua 宣化 (1918–1995), founder of Dharma Realm Buddhist Association, alone received his teachings through Chan Master Xuyun 虛雲 (1840–1959) and stands as an exception to the more robust enthusiasm for the "scientific" outlook associated with the humanistic Buddhists.[13]

HUMANISTIC BUDDHISM IN CANADA

Humanistic Buddhism, broadly speaking, is an attempt to situate Buddhist activity within the human realm. That is, concerns with demons, spirits of the ancestors, and hungry ghosts, all of which entail associated ritual performance, should recede while concerns with the plight of one's fellow human beings should be foregrounded. Humanistic Buddhism can be understood as a descriptive label, but its deeper currency lies in its normative force.[14] Master Taixu viewed the sangha as deeply misguided due in part to its preoccupation with ritual, particularly that associated with funeral rites, as a means for generating revenues. His rhetorical posture opposed ritual to the "truly spiritual life." This is a sentiment echoed by his disciples including Yin Shun, who accordingly influenced the emergence of humanistic Buddhism in Taiwan.[15] A significant example of both Taixu's and Yin Shun's influence among teachers of subsequent generations is Dharma Drum Mountain founder, Master Shengyen, who lamented the preoccupation of monks in China with the practice of ritual for money and advocated the ideal of the Pure Land as something that should be created here on earth rather than in some transcendent realm.[16]

This language was part of a larger discourse in which a progressive "scientific" and global outlook was considered superior to the regressive path of superstition and an inward-looking and more parochial orientation. This, in turn, was part of a growing national concern with China's inability to defend itself against the imperialist aggression of European states backed by their technological superiority. This theme was taken up by Sun Yat-sen 孫逸仙 (1866–1925) through the first quarter of the 20th century, and later by the Chinese Communist Party with its Marxist-inspired perception of all religious activities and beliefs as "superstition" (*mixin* 迷信) opposed to the progress of China.[17] A strong emphasis on "practical" assistance through a sense of social mission enacted with significant lay contributions and leadership and reduced attention to supernatural forces were also significant elements in Taixu's and Yin Shun's approaches and are found reproduced in the activities of Canadian Buddhist organizations that have followed these ideals.

The most obvious example of this social mission with a pronounced emphasis on lay involvement is represented in the work of the Tzu Chi Buddhist Compassion and Relief Foundation of Canada. In British Columbia alone more than one hundred lay volunteers inspired by the teachings of Master Cheng Yen, the Buddhist nun who founded Tzu Chi in 1966, engage in a host of charitable activities including the running of food banks; language education assistance provided in several secondary schools; work in seniors' residences (thirty-one centers in sixteen cities); meals for hundreds of homeless individuals (72,596 meals in 2017) in cooperation with the Salvation Army; and perhaps best-known, major volunteer efforts directed to providing international disaster relief work.[18] Over a fourteen-year period commencing in 2000, approximately sixteen million dollars was donated to a wide range of charitable societies, hospitals, and educational institutions, and a substantial portion exceeding eight million dollars was applied to disaster relief.[19] Tzu Chi perhaps takes Master Taixu's message deemphasizing the ritual dimensions of Buddhist practice to its furthest point. There are no temples in Canada and no discernible local presence of monastic leaders; instead lay people run the organization from what they call "Service Centres" located in Toronto, Ottawa, Montréal, Calgary, Edmonton, and Vancouver. The intensely service-oriented activities of Taiwan's Tzu Chi Buddhist Compassion and Relief Foundation represent the most extreme example of the focus on non-traditional modes of Buddhist activity. That is, there is a complete absence of Buddhist ritual practice guided by monastics. It is not the case though that humanistic Buddhism entails homogeneity in Canada's Chinese Buddhist diaspora with respect to these ideas.

While all of the groups listed in "Immigration Reform and the Emergence of Buddhist Institutions" and "Growth of the Chinese Buddhist Diaspora, Post-1967" include varying degrees of social-service work undertaken by lay volunteers, they combine this with a significant ritual dimension and formal gatherings in temple settings. In Vancouver for example, Foguang shan holds well-attended chanting sessions in their spacious buddha hall located on the sixth floor of a large modern shopping and office complex in the suburb of Richmond.[20] These include "Grand Offering to Celestial Beings" (Gongfo jaitian 供佛齋天) and "Emperor Liang Repentance Service" (Liangxing fahui 梁皇法會), constituting part of the Hungry Ghost Festival. The branch in Toronto also has a regular weekly schedule of "Dharma services" during which texts are chanted. Outlying locations such as in Waterloo, Ontario, hold these formal services less frequently. Buddhist wedding and funeral services are also offered. Dharma Drum Mountain Buddhist Association, located in its own building in Richmond, hosts weekly chanting services throughout the year. Given the significant levels of attendance, these services appear to be in demand from members of the Chinese Buddhist diaspora. Master Taixu's admonition that the sangha's need for renewal resting partly in a return to the "genuine practice" of the buddhadharma in concert with compassionate service to one's fellow human beings has opened a space for varied interpretations of humanistic Buddhism that permits a modern form of expression in tandem with more "traditional" elements of practice.

An apparent exception to the humanistic Buddhism orientation of most Canadian Chinese Buddhist organizations and temples is True Buddha School (Zhenfo zong 真佛宗), which has locations in twenty-eight countries with eleven locations in eight cities in Canada (Calgary and Edmonton in Alberta, Vancouver and Richmond in British Columbia, Toronto and Scarborough in Ontario, and Laval and Montréal in Quebec). Sheng-yen Lu 勝彥盧 founded True Buddha School in Taiwan in 1975. He claims to be a living buddha (Liansheng huofo 蓮生活佛) trained in Daoist, Buddhist (Vajrayāna, Sūtrayāna), and geomantic arts and to have followed more than twenty teachers. Less formal elements comprising doctrine include geomancy in the form of feng shui and spirit-board divination.[21] Shengyen Lu lives in Taiwan and in Redmond, Washington. When asked during an interview at a Vancouver location about the central teaching of True Buddha School, a monk suggested reading a short verse on the back of a temple booklet that included the final line, "To save Heavenly and worldly beings and those in the nether worlds."[22] Certainly community service is said to be important and is supported by Lotus Light Charity Society (Huanguang gongde hui 華光功德會) established by Sheng-yen Lu, however, elements that Taixu and Yin Shun would have found objectionable are central to the leadership and members of True Buddha School.

CHINESE BUDDHIST DIASPORA IN CANADA: GENERAL CHARACTERISTICS

The Chinese Buddhist diaspora in Canada is heterogeneous. This is due to several factors.

The timing of migration defines diaspora characteristics, as it locates people within a particular context with associated specific motivational elements, political circumstances, and personal capacities to adjust to a new cultural and geographic locus (e.g., economic resources, language ability, educational level). Migrant laborers who left the turmoil and privation of southern China from the late 19th through the early 20th centuries, with virtually no money or education, faced completely different circumstances to those who departed Hong Kong in the 1960s through the 1980s with their expectation of familial and wider kinship support, higher educational levels, and professional skills. Another major factor is English language proficiency. Hong Kong and PRC immigrants have tended to be associated with very different levels of English fluency, with the former tending to fare much better. Language proficiency is also linked to the timing of migration.[23] Furthermore, temple congregations tend to coalesce around the languages with which they are most comfortable, and temple liturgy tends to play a role in determining congregational constitution and can represent a natural resistance to wider participation.

Another major transformation in the Chinese Buddhist diaspora in Canada is the transition between 1996 and 2018, during which Hong Kong migration was eclipsed by PRC migration. Under "visible minority populati on," Canada Census data from 1996 lists 850,160 Chinese. By 2016 this number had increased by nearly one million to 1,769,195. This rapid growth in the PRC immigrant population is concentrated in three major urban centers: Toronto, Montréal, and Vancouver. The result has been steady growth and expansion of sites that cater to Mandarin speakers. An illustrative example in Vancouver is Ling Yen Mountain Temple (Lingyanshan si 靈巖山寺), which has worked for several years on a massive expansion of its facilities to house a significant growth in members. Universal Buddhist Temple and Gold Buddha Monastery in Vancouver have also undergone expansion, as has Avatamsaka Monastery in Calgary.

Language use in Buddhist congregational contexts plays a major role in determining who feels able to participate and who does not. The predominant focus on humanistic Buddhism in Canada, and its disproportionately strong representation by groups from or originating in Taiwan, means that most congregations adopt Mandarin as the principal liturgical language. This is a good match, after the shift in migration commencing in the mid-1990s, for a population that brings Mandarin as its primary language to Canada. This does, however, limit the ability to reach out beyond the cultural horizon defined by language use. Chinese Buddhist community leaders are well aware of this challenge and have varying responses. One obvious solution is to include translation for dharma talks so that, for example, Vietnamese, Cantonese, and English speakers are able to participate. This solution is less effective in the case of liturgy, during which it is impossible to provide simultaneous interpretation. Most temples provide sutras in a format that includes both Chinese characters and a phonetic transliteration so that non-Chinese readers can chant with the group; English translation of the Chinese texts remains relatively rare. This concern with accessibility to liturgy and its unintended demarcation of primary congregational composition is not lost on Chinese Buddhist institutions.

A second challenge with similar consequences to that of the language barrier is a cultural gap between first-generation immigrant Buddhists and individuals of non-Asian heritage or individuals of Asian heritage who have resided in Canada for several generations. Neither group is acculturated to the ceremonial dimensions of Chinese Buddhist praxis normally found in Taiwan, Hong Kong, or the PRC. A response to this challenge has come in the form of what might be called parallel congregations.[24] Both Dharma Drum Mountain and Tung Lin Kok Yuen Canada Society (Jianada donglian jueyuan 加拿大東蓮覺苑), established in Vancouver by Robert H. N. Ho in 1994, have experimented with the idea of providing separate spaces for different constituencies of interest. In the case of Dharma Drum this has included meditation and Buddhist scripture-study classes outside the principal location where Pure Land rites are conducted each week, while Tung Lin Kok Yuen holds similar classes onsite in a space separate from the main buddha hall. Cross-cultural bridges are also built by way of public fairs and festivals that have a less formal or liturgical focus and are more oriented to celebrations through the sharing of food and music, in addition to providing less formal introductions to Buddhist teachings in a setting that is more comfortable for those less familiar with the regular activities associated with Buddhist temples.

A primary defining feature of humanistic Buddhism is its "this-worldly" focus on saving humanity in the "here-and-now" rather than, for example, on post-mortem rebirth in a Pure Land. It is this position that provides the strong missionary drive to take the dharma beyond Asia for the benefit of all humanity. Thus, the Canadian Buddhist diaspora faces a tension between its principal missionary rational or raison d'être and the cultural and linguistic realities that threaten a kind of "two solitudes" with its associated barrier to full realization of the ideals at the core of humanistic Buddhism.

A final feature of the Canadian Buddhist diaspora is its global nature and the associated continual flow of religious personnel, members, capital, and information that characterizes these organizations. The more classic notion of migrants moving to a geographically and culturally new region and adapting to their new circumstances is largely unhelpful in representing and explaining the position of those who lead and participate in Chinese Buddhist intuitions. Integral to self-conceptions of orthodoxy, legitimacy, and identity more generally is an element of resistance to adaptation. Canadian multiculturalism policy originating and evolving since the 1970s, and the Charter of Rights and Freedoms, part of the 1982 Canadian Constitution Act, are viewed as supportive of this position. This does not entail a rejection of broad participation in Canadian society but rather supports that participation in a manner rooted in an authentic Buddhist cultural identity. Participation from this standpoint represents, to members and leaders, a more genuine contribution to the long-standing ideal of the Canadian cultural mosaic.

REVIEW OF LITERATURE

Study of the Chinese Buddhist diaspora in Canada remains in its early stages. There is no single monograph dedicated exclusively to this topic. Instead articles and chapters appear in a handful of books and journals. Book-length works on Buddhism in Canada provide the main source of information on Chinese Buddhists. A relatively early work on Buddhism in Canada, Janet McLellan's *Many Petals of the Lotus: Five Asian Buddhist Communities in Toronto* includes finely detailed ethnographic work and a chapter dedicated to Chinese Buddhists in Toronto.[25] The work engages with themes such as ethnic identity, the role of religion in supporting a process of immigrant adaptation, and how multiculturalism policy has affected Buddhist communities. Books comprised of chapters on different elements constituting the Canadian Buddhist landscape have tended to serve as overviews. Typical of this approach is *Buddhism in Canada*, edited by Bruce Matthews. In the foreword Paul Bramadat observes, "Buddhism in Canada functions first and foremost as a kind of national Buddhist 'map.' In this sense, it is an important step in the study of this tradition in Canada."[26] Bramadat's own book co-edited with David Seljak, titled *Religion and Ethnicity in Canada*, is similar insofar as it provides an overview.[27] The chapters cohere around a central question concerning the adequacy of Canadian responses to increasing ethnic diversity, tied in part to religious expression, in a country that lays claim to a policy of multiculturalism enacted within the nation's legal and constitutional framework. Chinese Buddhists are briefly addressed in Matthieu Boisvert's overview *Buddhists in Canada: Impermanence in a Land of Change*.[28] In Chapter Five, "The Chinese in Canada: Their Unrecognized Religion," David Chuenyan Lai, Jordan Paper, and Li Chuang Paper do not examine Chinese Buddhists specifically, but their work does shed helpful light on the nature of Chinese religiosity.[29]

Two more recent volumes of major importance are those co-edited by John S. Harding, Victor Sōgen Hori, and Alexander Soucy. The first, *Wild Geese: Buddhism in Canada*, grew out of a Canadian Asian Studies Association panel on Buddhism in Canada organized by Harding and Soucy with additional chapters included later.[30] It could be characterized primarily as sociological and anthropological in orientation, though the first section includes articles intended to provide a historical overview. Included is a useful detailed analysis of census categories and data by sociologist Peter Beyer. The opening essay, "How Do We Study Buddhism in Canada?" by Victor Sōgen Hori, reflects on some fundamental methodological concerns.[31] These include how scholars have tried to classify Buddhist adherents in Canada, for example, through the binaries of "immigrant/convert," or "Western/convert" and "Asian/ethnic." The political implications of a term like "ethnic," with its latent hierarchical presumptions, are also subjected to critical evaluation. The topic of Chinese Buddhists in Canada is addressed in three chapters: "The Woodenfish Program: Fo Guang Shan, Canadian Youth, and a New Generation of Buddhist Missionaries" by Lina Verchery; "Globalization and Modern Transformation of Chinese Buddhism in Three Chinese Temples in Eastern Canada" by Tannie Liu; and "The Tzu Chi Merit Society from Taiwan to Canada" by André Laliberté and Manuel Litalien.[32]

The second collection edited by Harding, Hori, and Soucy is *Flowers on the Rock: Local and Global Buddhisms in Canada*.[33] While there is only a single chapter in the book exclusively focused on Chinese Buddhists, it is a vital source for understanding some of the critical methodological questions associated with the study of Buddhism in Canada.[34] This collection examines Buddhist activity in Canada as being closely linked to Buddhist developments globally. At the same time the book aims to recognize the degree to which local developments feed back into the global context; as such it aims beyond a binary analysis, viewing the two aspects as part of a larger whole. The book also expands upon and addresses a "silent paradigm" at work in much of the scholarship on "Buddhism in the West":

> This paradigm assumes that the modernization of Buddhism is equivalent to the Westernization of Buddhism, that Asian culture is a relatively static repository of tradition incapable of innovation or renewal, and that the West will correct the long history of Asian cultural distortion of Buddhism and finally allow the truth of Buddhism to come forth.[35]

The introduction is very helpful in laying bare some of the tacit assumptions beneath the surface of much scholarship on "Buddhism in the West." Three sections look in turn at three binaries: "Asian/Ethnic and Western/Convert," "Traditional and Modern," and "Authentic and Inauthentic Buddhism." All three are described as closely related and mutually implicated. This introductory essay is essential reading for anyone trying to gain a reflexive and wider critical perspective on how Buddhist institutions have been understood in Western countries. This awareness, by extension, lays the groundwork for weakening scholarly reliance on a reductive, essentialist, and hierarchical narrative when examining the movement of Buddhist organizations beyond their Asian geographic contexts. Another significant methodological critique is made by Soucy, who further develops observations he made earlier in *Wild Geese* regarding the problematic assumption that there is a distinctly "Canadian" Buddhism.[36] He questions both the usefulness and validity of this category.

A final source for occasional articles on Chinese Buddhists in Canada is the *Canadian Journal of Buddhist Studies* published by the David See Chai Lam Centre for International Communication at Simon Fraser University.

A useful online source that provides a directory of Buddhist organizations in Canada is the *Sumeru Guide to Canadian Buddhism*.

FURTHER READING

Bramadat, Paul, and David Seljak, eds. *Religion and Ethnicity in Canada*. Toronto: University of Toronto Press, 2005.

Chandler, Stuart. *Establishing a Pure Land on Earth: The Foguang Buddhist Perspective on Modernization and Globalization*. Honolulu: University of Hawai'i Press, 2004.

DeVries, Larry, Don Baker, and Dan Overmyer, eds. *Asian Religions in British Columbia*. Vancouver and Toronto: UBC Press, 2010.

Harding, John S., Victor Sōgen Hori, and Alexander Soucy, eds. *Wild Geese: Buddhism in Canada*. Montréal and Kingston: McGill-Queen's University Press, 2010.

Harding, John S., Victor Sōgen Hori, and Alexander Soucy, eds. *Flowers on the Rock: Local and Global Buddhisms in Canada*. Montréal and Kingston: McGill-Queen's University Press, 2014.

Huang, C. Julia. *Charisma and Compassion: Cheng Yen and the Buddhist Tzu Chi Movement*. Cambridge, MA: Harvard University Press, 2009.

Liu, Tannie. "Globalization and Chinese Buddhism: The Canadian Experience." PhD diss., University of Ottawa, 2005.

Matthews, Bruce, ed. *Buddhism in Canada*. London and New York: Routledge, 2006.

McLellan, Janet. *Many Petals of the Lotus: Five Asian Buddhist Communities in Toronto*. Toronto: University of Toronto Press, 1999.

NOTES

1. For quotations from Meares's personal memoir concerning his impression of the Chinese see Barry M. Gough, *The Northwest Coast: British Navigation, Trade and Discoveries to 1812* (Vancouver: UBC Press, 2011), 97.
2. David Chuenyan Lai, "Victoria Chinatown: The Oldest Surviving Chinatown in Canada 1858–2011," in 加拿大唐人街: 承前啟後, 走進未來 / *Les quartiers chinois du Canada: Passé, présent, vers l'avenir / Canada's Chinatowns: Past, present, and into the future*, ed. David Chuenyan Lai, Paul Crowe, and Jan Walls (Vancouver: David See Chai Lam Centre for International Communication, Simon Fraser University, 2017).
3. In 1912 the Yen Wo Society Building was constructed at 1713 Government Street, Victoria, British Columbia. "Yen Wo Society Building," Canada's Historic Places: A Federal, Provincial and Territorial Collaboration, Parks Canada.
4. "History of Canada's Early Chinese Immigrants," Library and Archives Canada, last modified April 19, 2017.
5. Three classes were exempted in section five of the act: (a) members of the diplomatic corps, (b) children born in Canada, and (c) merchants, as well as foreign students for the duration of their studies.
6. According to the 1921 Canada Census, for example, there were 37,163 Chinese men and 2,424 Chinese women. Quoted in David Chuenyan Lai, *Chinatowns: Towns within Cities in Canada* (Vancouver: UBC Press, 1988), 60.
7. Statistics quoted in Lai, *Chinatowns*, 60.
8. Landed Immigrant Data System, 1980–2001, cited in Don DeVoritz and Shibao Gu, "The Changing Face of Chinese Immigrants in Canada," Discussion Paper 3018 (Bonn: Institute for the Study of Labor, 2007), 10.
9. For further details see Paul Crowe, "Universal Buddhist Temple (世界佛教會): Embracing Myriad Dharmas," *Canadian Journal of Buddhist Studies* 6 (2010): 89–115.
10. Details in this paragraph are largely drawn from Tannie Liu, "Globalization and Chinese Buddhism: The Canadian Experience" (PhD diss., University of Ottawa, 2005), 103–110.
11. Details concerning the heterogeneous and episodic nature of Chinese migrations to Canada are discussed in DeVoritz and Gu, "The Changing Face," 4–5. Lai, *Chinatowns*, 183–272, views the historical trajectory of Canadian Chinatowns as a movement through four stages: "budding" (1858–1870s), "blooming" (1880s–1910s), "withering" (1920s–1970s), and "reviving" (1980s).
12. A detailed account of Cheng Yen and the nature and function of her charismatic authority in maintaining unity and coherence among members of Tzu Chi is C. Julia Huang, *Charisma and Compassion: Cheng Yen and the Buddhist Tzu Chi Movement* (Cambridge, MA: Harvard University Press, 2009).
13. See for example his speech given at the University of British Columbia in Vancouver on February 9, 1985, later published as "人類的未來 (The Future of Humankind)," *Vajra Bodhi Sea: A Monthly Journal of Orthodox Buddhism* (July 2000): 23–26. In this speech he decried the powerful negative impacts of science and technology on modern lives.
14. Marcus Bingenheimer, "Some Remarks on the Usage of Renjian Fojiao 人間佛教 and the Contribution of Venerable Yinshun to Chinese Buddhist Modernism?" in *Development and Practice of Humanitarian*

Buddhism: Interdisciplinary Perspectives, ed. Mutsu Hsu, Jinhua Chen, and Lori Meeks (Hua-lien, Taiwan: Tzuchi University Press, 2012), 142.

15. It should be noted that Yin Shun's position on the problematic notion of supernatural aspects, for example spirits and hungry ghosts, was more strident than that of Xu Yun. Bingenheimer, "Renjian Fojiao," 148.
16. Sheng-yen, *Orthodox Buddhism: A Contemporary Chan Master's Answers to Common Questions*, trans. Douglas Gildow and Otto Chang (Berkeley, CA: North Atlantic Books, 2007), 177–178.
17. Contemporaneous adoption of a similar standpoint, vis-à-vis Hindu traditions, is found, for example, in the views of Rabindranath Tagore (1861–1941) in British colonial India.
18. *Buddhist Tzu Chi Foundation Canada Annual Report 2017*, 6.
19. Gary Ho (Chair of Tzu Chi Foundation Canada), interview with Paul Crowe, September 9, 2006, at the University of British Columbia.
20. A helpful overview of Foguang shan history, its institutional form, and an examination of the political controversy with which it has been associated in Taiwan and the United States is Stuart Chandler, *Establishing a Pure Land on Earth: The Foguang Buddhist Perspective on Modernization and Globalization* (Honolulu: University of Hawaii Press, 2004).
21. For details on the True Buddha School, based on a location in Montréal, see Noah Casey, "The True Buddha School: A Field Research Report on the Chan Hai Lei Zang Temple" (Montréal: Montréal Religious Sites Project, Asian Religion and Ethics Research Unit, McGill University, 2002).
22. Taken from a personal interview at Lotus Light Lei Zang Si Temple, Vancouver, British Columbia, July 26, 2006. The booklet is *True Buddha School: Cultivation and Meditation Booklet* (Vancouver: Lotus Light Lei Zang Si Temple).
23. DeVoritz and Gu, "The Changing Face," 12–14.
24. See Paul Crowe, "Dharma on the Move: Vancouver Buddhist Communities and Multiculturalism," in *Flowers on the Rock: Global and Local Buddhisms in Canada*, ed. John S. Harding, Victor Sōgen Hori, and Alexander Soucy (Montréal and Kingston: McGill-Queen's University Press, 2014), 156–158.
25. Janet McLellan, *Many Petals of the Lotus: Five Asian Buddhist Communities in Toronto* (Toronto: University of Toronto Press, 1999).
26. Bruce Matthews, ed., *Buddhism in Canada* (London and New York: Routledge, 2006), xiv.
27. Paul Bramadat and David Seljak, eds., *Religion and Ethnicity in Canada* (Toronto: University of Toronto Press, 2005).
28. Matthieu Boisvert, "Buddhists in Canada: Impermanence in a Land of Change," in *Religion and Ethnicity in Canada*, ed. Paul Bramadat and David Seljak (Toronto: University of Toronto Press, 2005), 69–88.
29. David Chuenyan Lai, Jordan Paper, and Li Chuang Paper, "The Chinese in Canada: Their Unrecognized Religion," in *Religion and Ethnicity in Canada*, ed. Paul Bramadat and David Seljak (Toronto: University of Toronto Press, 2005), 89–110.
30. John S. Harding, Victor Sōgen Hori, and Alexander Soucy, eds., *Wild Geese: Buddhism in Canada* (Montréal and Kingston: McGill-Queen's University Press, 2010).
31. Victor Sōgen Hori, "How Do We Study Buddhism in Canada?," in *Wild Geese: Buddhism in Canada*, ed. John S. Harding, Victor Sōgen Hori, and Alexander Soucy (Montréal and Kingston: McGill-Queen's University Press, 2010), 12–38.
32. Lina Verchery, "The Woodenfish Program: Fo Guang Shan, Canadian Youth, and a New Generation of Buddhist Missionaries," in *Wild Geese: Buddhism in Canada*, ed. John S. Harding, Victor Sōgen Hori, and Alexander Soucy (Montréal and Kingston: McGill-Queen's University Press, 2010), 210–235; Tannie Liu, "Globalization and Modern Transformation of Chinese Buddhism in Three Chinese Temples in Eastern Canada," in *Wild Geese: Buddhism in Canada*, ed. John S. Harding, Victor Sōgen Hori, and Alexander Soucy (Montréal and Kingston: McGill-Queen's University Press, 2010), 270–294; and

André Laliberté and Manuel Litalien, "The Tzu Chi Merit Society from Taiwan to Canada," in *Wild Geese: Buddhism in Canada*, ed. John S. Harding, Victor Sōgen Hori, and Alexander Soucy (Montréal and Kingston: McGill-Queen's University Press, 2010), 295–320.
33. John S. Harding, Victor Sōgen Hori, and Alexander Soucy, eds., *Flowers on the Rock: Local and Global Buddhisms in Canada* (Montréal and Kingston: McGill-Queen's University Press, 2014).
34. Crowe, "Dharma on the Move," 150–172.
35. Harding, Hori, and Soucy, *Flowers on the Rock*, 4.
36. Alexander Soucy, "Buddhist Globalism and the Search for Canadian Buddhism," in *Flowers on the Rock: Local and Global Buddhisms in Canada*, ed. John S. Harding, Victor Sōgen Hori, and Alexander Soucy (Montréal and Kingston: McGill-Queen's University Press, 2014), 25–52.

Paul Crowe

BUDDHIST ART AND ARCHITECTURE IN TIBET

Geo-cultural Tibet has been the arrival point of artistic expressions that reached it in two periods corresponding to the phases of the spread of Buddhism in the country: the imperial age, from the early 7th to the mid-9th century; and the period during which the clergy gained an increasingly political role, from the 11th to the mid-20th century. Many of the artists and artisans active in Tibet during the former period where foreigners, especially Newars from the Nepal Valley, who in the year 639 started the construction of the Jokhang at Rasa (later Lhasa), fashioned most of the earliest images housed in it, and have been active for Tibetan patrons since. A third period, which has not been the object of systematic research yet, is represented by the reconstruction following the end of the Cultural Revolution in Tibet proper, while elsewhere in geo-cultural Tibet, notably in Ladakh and Bhutan, traditional artists have continued to produce paintings and statues for their monasteries, temples, and shrines.

Buddhist art and architecture reached a peak under the greatest of Tibetan rulers, Tri Songdetsen entire encyclopedia (Tib. Khri Srong lde brtsan, 742–800; ruled 756–797), who adopted Buddhism as the official religion of Tibet. Three of his wives sponsored the construction of the first Buddhist monastery (767–779) to house the earliest monastic community in Tibet: Samye (Tib. Bsam yas, "Inconceivable"; figure 1), in the political and religious heart of the country, between the Yarlung Valley, where the imperial necropolis lies, and Lhasa, the seat of its most important Buddhist temple.

In spite of the fact that Buddhist architecture in geo-cultural Tibet, including Indian and Nepalese Tibet as well as Bhutan, is different from the Indian one, its symbolism is related to Indian Buddhism. In particular, the original plan of Samye, according to Tibetan tradition, was meant to reproduce the Indian cosmogony: the main building at the center symbolizes Mount Meru, the axis of the world; the twelve satellite temples surrounding it conjure up the four main continents facing the cardinal points and the pairs of small continents flanking each main continent; two other temples symbolize the sun and moon; and the wall encircling the monastic compound evokes the chain of mountains surrounding the world. Four large stupas, mound-like architectural structures of Indian origin meant to house Buddhist relics, are placed symmetrically at the corners of the compound.

Figure 1. Samye Monastery (Central Tibet), founded in the 8th century.
Source: Photograph courtesy of Guido Vogliotti.

Tibetan artists and artisans were formed by foreign colleagues, even Kashmiri ones, also during the second phase of the development of Buddhist art in Tibet. Again, the Newar ones, having inherited the northern Indian aesthetics of the Pāla Buddhist dynasty of Bengal and Bihar, and of the following Sena one, played an important role particularly in the monasteries built in Southwest Tibet by the prince-abbots of the monastery of Sakya, who had managed to control the country thanks to the protection of the Yuan dynasty.[1] The weight of Indo-Newar aesthetics on Buddhist art in Tibet was so important that the Tibetan scholar Kongtrul (Tib. Kong sprul, 1813–1899) wrote that, up to the time of the Tibetan painter Menthangpa (Tib. Sman thang pa), the first half of the 15th century, Tibetan painting had been in Newar style.[2] Menthangpa incorporated Chinese features particularly in his landscapes, which added to the earlier adoption of the Chinese style by Tibetan artists in the depiction of some iconographic themes such as those of the Four Great Guardian Kings and of the Sixteen Sthaviras ("Elders"), a group of early disciples of the Buddha chosen by the latter to preserve his teachings according to tradition.

The most sophisticated Buddhist monument in Tibetan art and architecture is the monastic center raised from 1427 to about 1440 by the rulers of Gyantse in Southwest Tibet, where the best painters and sculptors from the region were called to decorate the many temples and chapels in the main monastic building and on the eight floors of the nearby Great Stupa known as Kùmbum (Tib. Sku 'bum, "One Hundred Thousand Images"; figure 2), in which architecture, sculpture, and painting combine in a single encyclopedic, iconographic project

Figure 2. Gyantse Monastery (Southwest Tibet), 15th century.
Source: Photograph courtesy of Ernani Orcorte and CeSMEO.

illustrating the main schools of Indo-Tibetan Buddhism. The control of Tibet, taken in the 17th century by the Fifth Dalai Lama, an eminent scholar as well as a ruthless politician, and thanks to the military support of a Mongol ruler, meant the loss of independence for Southwest Tibet and of other Tibetan regions, but also a renovated artistic activity in the monasteries of his religious order, the Gelukpa (Dge lugs pa, "the School of Virtue"), and in those taken over by it.

The political and cultural symbol of the Dalai Lamas' temporal and religious power was represented by the construction of the two palaces, the Red one (1645–1648) and the White one (1692–1694), built on the Red Hill near Lhasa. The Red Hill came to be known as Potala, a mythical south Indian mountain abode of the Bodhisattva Avalokiteśvara, of whom the Dalai Lamas have been regarded as manifestations. The palatine complex was conceived as both a palace (Tib. *pho-brang*) and a fortress (Tib. *rdzong*), and was built in a strategic position on the model of earlier castles in geo-cultural Tibet. Its construction involved about 7,000 workers and over 1,500 artists and artisans, including 182 Newars, ten Manchurian and Mongolian ones, and seven Chinese.[3]

Being the illustration of thousands of Indian Buddhist texts translated into Tibetan and included in the canonical literature of various schools, religious art in Tibet has been conditioned by iconographic and iconometric rules that have contributed to the conservation of its Buddhist traditions, though painters have enjoyed some freedom in the representation of common people, animals, landscapes, and buildings. Although Tibetan artists have inherited different iconometric traditions affording variations in the proportions of religious images and in spite of the variety of iconographic traditions related to the particular teachings of each Buddhist school, in the course of time there were a progressive standardization of iconometry and a reduction of proportions, especially in the Gelukpa tradition, sometimes making figures a bit stiff (see figure 10).

No major development in Buddhist art and architecture seems to have occurred in Tibet following the establishment of the Manchu protectorate in 1720.

Since the Communist invasion of Tibet, completed in 1959, and the subsequent colonization of the country, Chinese art historians have shown interest in the classification and preservation of what are now termed "Cultural Relics," which is not surprising considering the century-old interest of the Yuan, Ming, and Qing dynasties in Tibetan Buddhism as well as the presence of lamas with Chinese followers in China proper. However, during the period of the so-called Cultural Revolution, most Tibetan monasteries were destroyed by the Red Guards, both Chinese and Tibetan, who invaded the Jokhang in August 1966, damaged it, and set on fire a number of religious texts.

At the time of the Cultural Revolution the metalware of the temples, including roofs, religious emblems, ritual objects, and statues, were taken to foundries to be melted and transformed into ingots. Some were saved from destruction; others were sold and eventually reached the antiquarian market of Hong Kong. Since the fall of the Maoist regime, scores of Tibetan artisans and artists have been involved in the reconstruction and restoration of monasteries and temples in Tibet proper. Indeed, they have never stopped building temples and monasteries, as well as producing religious images and ritual objects elsewhere in geo-cultural Tibet and among the Tibetan diaspora, notably in India and Nepal. Their activity has often been ignored in the West, generally because of common antiquarian prejudices.

Most monasteries have been rebuilt in Tibet by Buddhist communities including a variety of sponsors, as shown by the instances of the monastery of Tsurpu, whose reconstruction started in 1983–1984 on the initiative of a Tibetan lama, thanks to funds collected by the Hawaii-based Tsurpu Foundation, and the monastery of Drango, in eastern Tibet, which was being extensively renovated with funds from the local and regional authorities as well as from local people in the diaspora during the second half of the 1990s. The monastery of Samye and the Potala palace were restored with funds from the central government, since such monuments are regarded as part of the cultural heritage of the People's Republic of China.

ART

Traditional Western approaches to Tibetan art have been largely aesthetic, often more concerned with the style, dating, and iconographic identification of an image than with the motivation as well as purpose lying behind its creation—namely the specific cultural setting in which it originated. Tibetan Buddhist images, mutually isolated when shown outside their original architectural context, ought to be imagined within structured spaces sacred and significant to the people who commissioned and manufactured them. That is particularly true for wall painting, which is actually part of the architectural structure supporting it (figure 4 and see figure 6).

A correct approach to Tibetan art should take into account the Buddhist notion of a religious space within which divine as well human beings are distributed hierarchically, both vertically and horizontally, around an ideal center, starting from the main shrine and temples in which images are found and for which they were commissioned according to criteria reflecting specific aspects of the Buddhist doctrine, to the entrance porch generally painted with the Wheel of Existence, representing the Buddha's vision corresponding to his Enlightenment, and the Four Great Guardian Kings protecting the very doctrine issued from that vision, namely the dharma.

Buddhist art in Tibet has been conditioned by the adoption of mostly Indian iconographic and iconometric traditions, both written and oral, in a religious context in which the divine is primary, while the artist representing it is subordinate, and his creation is an act of devotion, as it has been in Christian art. As a consequence, the value of a Buddhist image is primarily religious and apotropaic, only secondarily aesthetic, which means that, to appreciate it, some Westerners ought to abandon prejudices accumulated since the Renaissance, including an obsession for originality at all costs in spite of the fact that copying was common not only in the Greek, Roman, and Medieval worlds, but even in Renaissance Europe, and has been in icon-painting to this day. Then they would be admitted to an art in which "copying" is implicit in the adoption of iconographic and iconometric rules (see figure 10), and sometimes specifically required by a patron.[4]

Traditional artists, in particular sculptors, are called in Tibetan "deity-makers" (*lha bzo ba*), and the ability of the most famous ones is sometimes celebrated in Tibetan texts and inscriptions mentioning their names. Their role in the illustration and preservation of Buddhism cannot be overstated in a society that was largely illiterate until the past century, and in which reading was a prerogative of the clergy and ruling classes, writing being an ability confined to scribes.

Since religious images represent particular moments in the Buddha's life and in Buddhist history or specific doctrinal aspects of Buddhism including well-defined divine forces, they are bound to follow iconographic conventions expressing a precise symbolism: postures, gestures, attitudes, expressions, attributes, emblems, colors, and mounts as well as the proportions of different deities are given in some of the thousands of Buddhist texts that were carefully translated from Sanskrit into Tibetan starting from the second half of the 8th century. Religious images must be fashioned in conformity with iconographic conventions and iconometric rules, without which they cannot be consecrated and used for the very purpose they have been commissioned for.

Statues should not be regarded as religiously active before being consecrated. For that purpose, they may be filled with prayers and invocations, handwritten or wood-printed on paper rolls, and also with spices, medicinal plants, seeds, clay, sacrificial cakes known as "torma" (Tib. *gtor ma*), precious substances, and even coins, which are stored according to specific criteria within the various sections (head, trunk, legs, and stand) of large seated metal images. In the case of high standing metal statues and large clay ones, they may be introduced into the images through a small "door" at their back. Portable images painted on canvas (Tib. *thang ka*) are framed within cloth, possibly silk and brocade, according to a precise code of proportions, with a central "door" in a different color stitched in the lower section of the frame. Statues and paintings may be accompanied by invocations, prayers, and dedicatory inscriptions, often in verses, chased on the stands of metal images and brush-written on the front or back of painted canvases, where the footprints or handprints of important lamas may be also found. Finally valuable materials, including textiles and jewelry, may be used to dress statues.

Religious images are then ready to be consecrated through appropriate rituals (Tib. *rab gnas*, literally "full abiding") meant to vivify them by calling their spirit to abide in them, implying that they have been fashioned correctly, and sometimes lasting several days. Since no innovation is allowed unless it is specifically requested by a lama, the pleasure that one may feel facing the numberless representations of buddhas, bodhisattvas, goddesses, wrathful and peaceful deities, the complex forms of tantric iconography with its sexual imagery, as well as the kaleidoscopic geometry of mandalas, generally representing a figure at the center of its palace resting on a huge lotus flower, surrounded by a wall of thunderbolts and a ditch of flames, does not depend upon the artist's choice.

Since its beginnings in the 8th century, Buddhist art in Tibet has inherited symbols and motifs from and sometimes through India, as in the case of the lotus flower, which ultimately originated in Eastern Mediterranean countries, or the swastika and acanthus-like scrolls, found in the Greek world, whereas the stylization of clouds, flames, waves, and sometimes, rocks has Chinese origins. Buddhas, bodhisattvas, and tutelary and protecting deities have been depicted mostly in the style of India, the country they derive from, sometimes through its rendition by Newar artists from the Nepal Valley or by Kashmiri artists. The well-known series of sixteen Indian Arhats ("Worthy Ones") known as Sthaviras has been regularly portrayed in Chinese style, while the Four Great Kings protecting the dharma in the cardinal directions display Central Asian features. Trees, flowers, and animals are painted sometimes in Indian style, as in the case of the lotus flower and the Indian sea monster known as *makara*, or sometimes in Chinese style, as in the case of the dragon. The earliest example of stylized lion, found in the imperial necropolis in the Yarlung Valley, has been variously related to Newar, Chinese, Central Asian, and Persian sculpture.[5]

The coexistence of such elements, sometimes amalgamated, sometimes identifiable, allows recognizing an image as specifically Tibetan rather than "Indian" or "Chinese." Indeed, Tibetan aesthetics represent the confluence of different foreign styles of which artists, patrons and scholars in Tibet have been aware over the course of time, well after the great season of Buddhist art had ceased to exist in India itself.[6] In particular, Tibetan historical and hagiographic sources contain references to 15th-, 16th-, or 17th-century patrons who had images fashioned "in the style of India."[7] Copying earlier images and foreign styles has been a traditional and innocent practice in Tibet, as elsewhere, until today.[8]

The main reason for commissioning religious images is to earn merits in order to achieve four kinds of objectives: removing sickness or troubles; obtaining a long and healthy life; creating the conditions necessary to drive a dead relative toward a happy birth; or performing a particular religious practice. The subject of an image is selected in relation to its function: the goddess Tārā will generally be selected in the first case for her ability to save from perils; Amitāyus (figure 3), the transcendent Buddha of "Infinite Life," will be preferred in the second case; Śākyamuni, the historical Buddha, is often chosen in the third case. Some images, such as the scenes illustrating the Wheel of Existence and the episodes from the Buddha's life or previous lives, perform chiefly a didactic role. Others, like the portraits of religious masters, have a special meaning for the latter's disciples.

When present, inscriptions on paintings and statues, generally wishing the final liberation of all sentient beings, may play the role of captions. Besides describing specific figures, they may quote the titles of related religious texts and bear the names of patrons, artists, and even religious masters who oversaw their execution. They hardly ever afford dates, but the names of people mentioned in them may provide at least a *terminus post quem*.

Figure 3. Amitāyus in a Tantric manifestation. Norbu Lingka. Lhasa (Central Tibet), 19th century. *Source*: Photography by Wu Chi and Liu Zhi Gang. (From Erberto Lo Bue. *Tesori del Tibet*. Milan: La Rinascente, 1994: 108, fig. 68.)

Dating Tibetan religious images is complicated by the circumstance that copying has been a normal procedure in traditional Buddhist art and Indian statues of the Pāla-Sena period were copied in Tibet as late as in the 18th century. The quality of an image is not a guarantee, for one may come across fine traditional contemporary images and roughly made ancient ones. In the absence of reliable inscriptions and historical references, dating cannot be based on stylistic analysis alone, which has proved even less reliable since the end of the 1960s, when collecting Tibetan and Himalayan art started to be more fashionable and images aged artificially began to be produced to suit the predominatingly antiquarian tastes of collectors. Unlike those fashioned by the same artists for Buddhist monasteries, temples, and private shrines, including those of the royal family of Bhutan, such images should not be regarded as religious art for the simple reason that they were not produced for religious purposes. Their production has become increasingly sophisticated, to the point of deceiving even specialists, particularly in the case of metal statues fashioned by the most skillful artists of the Nepal Valley who work for Buddhist and Hindu patrons as well as for monasteries and temples not only in the Himalayas, but elsewhere in Buddhist Asia, including Tibet proper, as they had done until the Cultural Revolution. Dating problems for images painted on cloth and carved in wood, including book covers, are not as serious as they are for metal and stone ones, for they may be dated by carbon-14 tests.[9]

Iconography and Iconometry. From a Buddhist viewpoint, a religious image becomes functional only through consecration by appropriate rituals performed by a lama (*bla ma*, Tib. for "guru") and calling the deity to abide in it. The consecration may be refused if the image has not been fashioned correctly. For their work, artists can resort to iconometric drawings affording the iconography and proportions of images as well as to the instructions of a lama, who can base himself on specific texts whose titles and even sections may be mentioned in related inscriptions, for example in the temples and chapels in monastic compounds of Shalu and Gyantse, where the names of lamas having supervised the execution of images may be found. The cubit (Tib. *khru*), or finger (Tib. *sor mo*) of an important devotee may be used as the basic unit of measurement for an image or a building.[10]

Whereas iconography should be understood as the representation of figures according to sets of conventions that are recorded also in the textual tradition, iconometry is a codified system of relative proportions for each class of figures, varying according to the commentarial literature of different tantric texts such as the *Kālacakra* (pron. "Kalachakra"; see figure 6) and *Saṃvarodaya* tantras. Buddhas, tantric tutelary deities with buddha rank (Tib. *'dod-lha, yi dam*), bodhisattvas, guardians of the Buddhist doctrine (dharmapālas), goddesses (Devīs), religious masters, and so forth.[11] Images may portray deities presiding over particular teachings, such as those symbolized by the goddess Prajñāpāramitā ("Perfection of Wisdom," often called Yum chen mo, namely "Great Mother" in Tibetan), or those related to specific tantras translated into Tibetan and found in the canonical collections of Buddhist texts, such as the tutelary deities Vajrabhairava, Hevajra or Saṃvara in their various manifestations.

Given the vastness of Buddhist literature, there cannot be a complete record of all the figures described in the thousands of texts translated into Tibetan and included in the *Bka' 'gyur* and *Bstan 'gyur* canonical collections, nor in the related commentarial literature, nor in the extra-canonical texts (Tib. *gter ma*). Not all deities have been necessarily portrayed, while the

Tibetan pantheon has been subject to a process of accretion because the representation of contemporary religious masters and their specific visions has continued to our times and will be so as long as Buddhism is practiced in Tibet. So none of the iconographic collections put together by scholars may be regarded as exhaustive.

Figures may be portrayed standing, seated, flying, or even lying down, as in the case of the dying buddha, and also under different aspects, peaceful, wrathful, or semi-wrathful, always surrounded by a halo. Their attitudes, attributes, proportions, and colors are dictated by religious texts referring to the thousands of images that evolved in the course of the long history of Buddhism in India before and after its introduction into Tibet. In practice, artists resort to drawings reporting the iconographic and iconometric indications of the figures commissioned to them and related to their patrons' teaching traditions, to other images of the same subject, and, since the 20th century, even to pictures (cf. figures 4 and 8).

Figures generally sit or stand in different postures on stylized Indian lotuses, sometimes on mythical or real animals, or else thrones or simply cushions; and wrathful deities are often represented in militant postures, treading upon enemies of the dharma upon a solar disc supported by a lotus, peaceful deities being generally placed on a lunar disc. In traditional iconography, buddhas and other Buddhist figures may be portrayed with their legs in different sitting postures (Skt. *āsana*) and displaying various gestures (Skt. *mudrā*) with a number of variants, such as the meditation one, with the palms of the hands opened, turned upwards, and lying one above the other, the thumbs touching each other. Gestures may represent important historical moments in the Buddha's life: reaching toward the Earth, or touching it with the right hand over his right leg to call it to witness the moment of his Enlightenment, meaning the establishment of the dharma on it; or the setting into motion of the Wheel of the Dharma (Skt. *dharmacakra*, pron. "dharmachakra"), with both hands raised at the height of the chest, the right turned outwards and the left turned inwards with the forefingers and thumbs touching each other, symbolizing the first sermon delivered by the Buddha after reaching Enlightenment.

Other common gestures are the following: the exposition of the dharma, or reasoning, with the palm of the right hand turned outwards in a vertical position, the thumb and forefinger touching each other; "embracing Wisdom," with the wrists crossed at the height of the chest and the backs of the hands turned outwards, the index and little fingers sometimes stretched out, and the other fingers bent inwards; offering, with the palms joined at the height of the chest; exorcism, with the index and little fingers stretched out, the thumb touching the middle and ring fingers; warning or threatening, with the fist clenched and the forefinger stretched out.

The Buddha's garments vary from the robes worn by Indian ascetics or by the monks of his mendicant order, sometimes made of patches stitched together, to the princely dress of the aristocratic class he belonged to according to his hagiography; in the latter iconography he may wear jewels as well as a crown. Other buddhas, coexisting in space or having lived in previous eras, are generally identifiable thanks to their gestures, postures, and colors.

Figures may also be identified thanks to their specific attributes: the thunderbolt (Tib. *rdo rje*, Skt. *vajra*), a symbol of adamantine strength and purity attributed to Indo-European godly kings from the Indian Indra to the Latin Jupiter; the vase holding the nectar of immortality, an attribute of the Buddha Amitāyus (figure 3) used also for ritual purposes; the jewel, a symbol for spiritual wealth, sometimes tripled to symbolize the Buddha, the dharma, and the

Figure 4. The 14th Dalai Lama. Samye Monastery (Central Tibet), 20th century.
Source: Photograph courtesy of Guido Vogliotti.

monastic community; the disk, originally a weapon used in India until the 19th century, an emblem of the power of the dharma; and the bell, which in esoteric Buddhism became a symbol for transcendent wisdom. In some Indian tantras whose teaching and iconography were adopted in Tibet, the ritual bell came to represent the female coefficient complementary to the *vajra*, conceived both as the male coefficient and the cognitive method aimed at Enlightenment, which may be reached also through ritual sexual union (figure 6).

Figure 5. Mahābodhi Mahāmuni. Gyantse Monastery (Southwest Tibet), 15th century.
Source: Photograph courtesy of Giovanni Da Broi.

Portraits of Indian and Tibetan masters may be caricatured or naturalistic, but they are often simply idealized. They may be represented as part of lineages in relation to the transmission of specific teachings or else in assemblies known as "tsokshing" (Tib. *tshogs zhing*), namely "Field of Accumulation" (of merits), meant to represent the entirety of a teaching transmission. Since the early 20th century pictures have occasionally been used for important

Figure 6. Kālacakra. Spituk Monastery (Ladakh), 20th century.
Source: Photograph courtesy of Paolo Mele.

portraits, as in the case of the Fourteenth Dalai Lama, for the palace built especially for him in the Norbù Lingka park near Lhasa between 1954 and 1956, and in the later 20th-century portrait painted in the upper chapel of the monastery of Samye by the same eastern Tibetan painter, Amdo Jampa, with an inscription describing the Dalai Lama with the title of *ris med*, namely "non-sectarian" (figures 4 and 8).[12]

The variegated complexity of the vast Buddhist pantheon that Tibetans inherited from India is illustrated well in the monastery of Gyantse by the one hundred thousand images found in the chapels and temples of its Great Stupa, illustrating ever more complex iconographic cycles as one proceeds from the lower to the upper stories, housing the tantric manifestations of buddha rank, whereas the chapels on the fourth story house the portraits of the most important masters of the various schools of Buddhism in India and Tibet. The Indian connection in the same monastery is so strong that the chief image in the nearby main monastic building was modelled after the most famous statue of the buddha housed in the holiest Buddhist temple in India, the Mahābodhi, after which its 15th-century Tibetan copy was named (figure 5).[13]

Materials and Techniques. The materials used in Tibetan sculpture are clay and metal, generally brass or copper, hardly ever bronze, and sometimes stone and wood.[14] In clay sculpture, loaves of clay mixed with water are modeled to shape the various elements of the image on a wooden structure surrounded by cloth and paper mixed with animal glue, to which flour may be added. In the case of large clay statues, faggots may surround the wooden structure (figure 7).

Figure 7. Two guardian kings. Dardo Monastery (East Tibet), 1997.
Source: Photograph courtesy of Stella Rigo Righi.

Metal sculpture techniques include casting from permanent molds, lost-wax casting, traditionally from non-permanent molds—a technique of Indian origin commonly used by Newar sculptors for Tibetan patrons to this day (figure 8)—and repoussé, which is also adopted to produce large size images and religious symbols used also in architecture (figure 9).[15]

Whatever the material and technique, metal images and ritual objects are chased, and then the copper ones are generally fire-gilded by the mercury gilding process before being polished.[16] Semiprecious stones may be set in any metal image or ritual object. Faces are usually cold-gilded, and the hair of peaceful figures is traditionally painted with azurite or ultramarine blue pigments, while that of wrathful figures, along with their moustache and beard, is painted with minium.

Painters, who have the advantage of drawing figures on the same surfaces upon which they will work, prepare the dry plaster surface of a wall with kaolin, or else the fine cotton, seldom

Figure 8. Portrait of the 14th Dalai Lama. The wax image, invested with clay, is being checked against a picture. Lalitpur (Nepal Valley), 2004.
Source: Photograph by author.[17]

Figure 9. Coppersmith's workshop. Lhasa (Central Tibet). Craftsmen fashioning Buddhist symbols, 1997.
Source: Photograph courtesy of Guido Vogliotti.

silk, surface of their *thang ka* with a solution of kaolin, animal glue, and water. Then they trace, traditionally with charcoal, sometimes a lead pencil, the iconometric grids of lines upon which they will draw their figures, starting from the main one. In the preparation of *thang kas*, the drawing may be obtained from a woodcut or else with the dusting technique, which is used especially for wall painting. After tracing the drawing, the painter traditionally applies a tempera obtained from pigments mixed with water and animal glue, usually starting from azurite blue and malachite green, other traditional pigments being cinnabar, minium, orpiment, realgar, ochre, gypsum, carbon black, and gold powder. Synthetic colors, notably ultramarine and emerald green, have been used in geo-cultural Tibet since the 19th century, especially in wall painting, which requires large amounts of color (figure 10).[18]

Figure 10. Jokhang Temple. Lhasa (Central Tibet). Colors being applied to drawings, 1997.
Source: Photograph courtesy of Guido Vogliotti.

The use of tempera, both on portable painted scrolls (*thang ka*) and on wall paintings, where the "pastiglia" technique may be used, accounts for their frequently poor state of conservation: scrolls may be rolled up and unrolled according to need; wall paintings are exposed to seepage in an architecture in which roofs are flat. The disadvantages of the tempera technique do not seem to worry Tibetans, who like all other Buddhists believe that the commission of new religious images is useful to accumulate merits in view of a better birth. Although the restoration of religious images and buildings is known in the Tibetan world, a Buddhist canonical text such as the *Kriyāsamgraha* prescribes to throw images beyond repair into water, to burn them or to melt them down.[19] Indeed, in a Buddhist perspective, such images are imperfect, while art has an ephemeral nature. Restoration and conservation—in the modern, technical, and lay sense given to those terms in Western culture—represent a relatively recent phenomenon in Europe itself, where ancient murals in religious buildings were painted over or even destroyed in the course of renovation work until the 19th century. In the traditional Tibetan Buddhist world, commissioning new wall paintings to be painted over old ones has been as acceptable as it was in the traditional Italian Catholic one, in order to acquire merit to their patron.[20]

Mandalas may be fashioned with various materials and techniques: tempera on cloth, on wall, seldom on wood; silk tapestry, following the Chinese tradition of *kesi*; xylography; cast or repoussé metal; and colored sand, the latter being used by specialized monks following a tradition of Indian origin recorded from at least the 8th century.[21] Sand mandalas are destroyed after a ritual ceremony corresponding to a phase of "reabsorption" following that of "production," corresponding to meditation, thus underlining the transience of mental constructions and of their material expressions, which ultimately have a relative value and to which a Buddhist ought not to be attached, "grasping" and "being grasped" being precisely what the Buddha taught to break away from.

ARCHITECTURE

Tibetan religious buildings may be divided into three categories: temples; monasteries; and monuments, including cairns devoted to local deities, prayer walls bearing slabs engraved with religious invocations, and stupas, the earliest aniconic symbol of the Buddha, representing the reliquary mounds housing his remains.[22]

Temples, monasteries, and even stupas may be excavated in the rock, but are generally built with materials, techniques, and structures varying from region to region, depending largely on rainfall and the availability of wood. Plans are characterized by rectangular shapes: they may be square, oblong, or cruciform; curving walls are rare, and the arch is unknown. Materials include dressed stone, sun-dried mud bricks, rammed earth, squared and carved wood, as well as gilded copper and, very seldom, enameled clay for tiles. Technical devices are innumerable and include earthquake-proof contrivances, such as the insertion of wooden "chain" bonds along the length of the masonry.

Stupas and temples are viewed as receptacles or supports (Tib. *rten*) of the Buddha's Spirit, and monasteries in particular are sacred, for they shelter the Three Jewels taken as refuge by devotees: the Buddha's body, as represented by their religious images; the Buddha's speech, namely the dharma as represented by the scriptures preserved in their libraries; and their monastic community, ensuring the transmission of the Buddhist tradition.[23] That is why temples and monasteries—just like stupas and images—are the object of the fundamental Buddhist practice of circumambulation.

Tibetan literature affords several technical texts on arts and crafts, but none comparable to Chinese or Western treatises on architecture: the rules fixing the proportions of images and stupas do not extend to temples and monasteries, and Tibetan architects just follow traditional practices transmitted from master to pupil. Although Tibetan authors do not deal extensively and systematically with architecture, they afford precise rules concerning the choice of the construction site: the erection of an important religious building is always preceded by a close scrutiny of the territory according to the rules established by geomancy, which Tibetan historical sources declare to have been introduced into Tibet by a Chinese princess during the first half of the 7th century.

According to a Tibetan text, the ideal site should have the following requisites: a high mountain at the back; several hills, the confluence of two rivers flowing from the sides, and grassy land with trees at the front; a valley resembling crossed hands below; and an elevation looking like a heap of grains in the middle.[24] Traditionally, Tibetans have regarded their land as the navel of the earth and, likely because of its high seismicity, conceived it as a restless she-demon that had to be tied up by the erection of temples at suitable points of her body before introducing Buddhism during the first half of the 7th century. Thus the Jokhang, the most venerated temple in Tibet, was built on a pond corresponding to her heart after it was filled up with earth and stones.

Before construction starts, the local deities dwelling in the soil ought to be conjured up, propitiated with offerings, and bound by means of appropriate rituals. Then the plan of the building is drawn on the ground with a grid of lines, and the actual construction may start on the auspicious day chosen for its foundation. Repositories holding sacred invocations (Tib. *gzungs gzhug*) are placed under the corners and below or above the pillars at the time of construction. Temples and stupas—just like religious images—acquire their sacredness only after being filled with religious invocations such as mantras written on paper and with precious substances, and after being consecrated by means of an appropriate *rab gnas* ceremony (see "Art" section). The orientation of monasteries varies, the entrance of the main temple at Samye facing east, according to the Indian tradition, that of the Jokhang in Lhasa west, looking toward Nepal, and those of the main monastic building and of the Great Stupa at Gyantse south, toward the holy land of India, as in China. The east-west axis predominates in the religious buildings of the imperial period, whereas the north-south axis is common from the 15th century onwards. The terms "right" and "left" in the descriptions of temples in Tibetan texts correspond to the point of view of the main image looking toward the main entrance and facing the devotee: then the Tibetan "right" corresponds to the beholder's left and the Tibetan "left" to her/his right.

Astrology plays an important role in the construction of a religious building as well as in the making of an important image, as witnessed by historical sources; for instance, in the cases of the Jokhang in Lhasa and of the Mahābodhi statue in the monastery of Gyantse, both built in twelve months according to historical sources, and of the Great Stupa, completed in twelve years in the latter monastic compound, the starting and ending days of construction coinciding with auspicious astral conjunctions, which are also chosen for the *rab gnas* ritual consecration of buildings.

The depth of foundations is generally regarded as irrelevant, since the solidity of the building is traditionally insured by the thickness of its walls and sometimes, on sloping grounds, by buttresses. The masonry of important buildings is often made up of layers of dressed stone alternating with layers of gravel mixed with mortar. Walls, especially when made of mud bricks or rammed earth, may be covered with a layer of plaster of varying thickness, which must be regularly renewed. The outer walls, often tapering upwards, are normally load bearing and support terraced roofs. Their massive look is emphasized by the rarity of windows, often surrounded by a painted decoration having a trapezoidal shape, longer at the bottom than at the top, somehow echoing the inclination of the walls. Parts of the upper stories in later buildings may be framed with a thin paneling of wood, sometimes in conjunction with projecting balconies.

The joists of the floors and roof may be either plain trunks or timbers squared with an adze; they rest on beams supported by vertical wooden columns via brackets. Floors are covered with twigs and beaten earth or with wooden planking. Access from one story to another is provided by ladders or very steep stairs. Terraces are obtained by ramming earth on a layer of gravel; in spite of the draining system, this kind of covering requires regular renewal. Purely ornamental sloping roofs at the top are called "gyapìp" (Tib. *rgya phibs*, literally "Chinese roof"; see for example figure 1); originally made in stone to shelter stone pillars during the imperial period, by the 12th century they had made their appearance above the most sacred temples in the building, with coverings made first of enameled tiles and then of gilded repoussé copper sheets. In the Himalayan areas, with higher rainfall, buildings are protected by a pitched roof supported by a wooden framework.[25]

Early Tibetan Buddhist architecture displays Indian and Central Asian features that are detectable respectively in two of its earliest specimens at Lhasa, one built on a square plan, the other on a rectangular plan: the Jokhang and the Ramoche.[26] The most primitive Buddhist chapel in Tibet generally consists of a single square chamber—with or without a vestibule—whose roof is supported by one or four interior columns; sometimes the rear wall houses a niche for the main statue, which may or may not be surrounded by an ambulatory. The second diffusion of Buddhism, starting from the end of the 10th century, caused an important building activity that lasted for over three hundred years. The new temples and monasteries, such as those at Tabo and Tholing, in West Tibet, and Alchi, in Ladakh, continued to be square, rectangular, and even cruciform, and were erected on flat ground; but from the 13th century onwards, after conflicting interests among competing religious orders brought about wars, monasteries were often conceived as fortresses, sometimes surrounded by walls with turrets, as in the monasteries of Sakya and Gyantse.

In the course of time, some monasteries grew into complex socioeconomic institutions supporting hundreds—sometimes thousands—of inmates, as had been the case for the late Buddhist monastic universities of India. The proportions of temples increased with the addition of a central assembly hall corresponding to the Indian inner courtyard still found in Buddhist Newar architecture, side chapels, a porch in front of the entrance, a courtyard surrounded by one or two orders of arcades in front of the porch, and upper stories covered with terraces topped by lanterns giving light to the assembly hall below and by pavilions covered with Chinese-style roofs. A monastic building may reach several stories in height, including a library and the abbot's apartment with its own chapel and meeting hall, though in the largest monasteries, the abbot generally resides—sometimes with his family—in a separate mansion (Tib. *bla brang*). A few large monasteries are endowed with a special isolated rectangular tower with walls tapering upwards used solely for the purpose of unfolding and displaying huge two-dimensional patchwork *thang ka* images made of various types of cloth stitched together.[27]

Important monasteries progressively abandoned the central plan on a flat surface, whether symbolically ordered as at Samye or conceived as a fortress as at Sakya. They started to be conceived more and more as fortified residences, and their architecture shifted toward a hierarchization of buildings in relation to the number of stories or to their situation on the side or top of a hill.[28] The façades of later buildings—with their play of light and shadow caused by the vertical offsets of the walls following the shape of the elevations upon which they rise—may be related to Tibetan military architecture and to the wars characterizing Tibetan history after monastic orders started vying for supremacy. The visual effectiveness of several monastic buildings in Tibet derives less from the contrast between the simplicity of their massive outer shapes and the sophistication of their inner decorative wealth than from their integration with the surrounding landscape: in spite of their apparently random disposition, monasteries afford an overall impression of harmony because their lines often follow the unevenness of the sites upon which they rise.

The uniformity of walls may be broken by small windows, verandas, porches, and galleries; the tops of buildings are terraced, and the flatness of roofs is emphasized by means of a border formed of tamarisk brushwood (Tib. *spen pad*) cut across evenly, compacted tightly, painted in a brownish red color and placed just below the terraced roof of a building or else crowning the parapet of its terrace. This horizontal component may represent a visual legacy of the firewood branches and fodder piled around the edges of the flat roofs of traditional Tibetan farmhouses. Where branches are absent, they are replaced with a painted band or even a border of enameled clay in a color contrasting with that of the wall below. The horizontality of a building may be emphasized by slabs protecting the top of the parapet walls.

Inner architecture is characterized by pillars—generally square in section, fluted, slightly tapering upwards, and swelling at the top—sometimes carved and supporting a system of capitals, long brackets—made up of a short lower element and of a long upper one—beams, trabeations, joists, and other wooden structures richly carved with stylized designs—hanging foliage, flower patterns, swirling clouds, stylized lions, sometimes human or celestial figures—generally painted in bright colors. Inner walls are painted with cycles of images including various classes of buddhas, bodhisattvas, gods, goddesses, heavenly attendants, as well as historical figures. The inner space is organized around large statues, sometimes stupas, facing the viewer, with appropriate carved and painted wooden furnishings: altars, shelves, side-tables, thrones, benches with tables of various sizes placed at different heights in accordance to a hierarchical order. The outer walls may be whitewashed or—in the case of particularly important buildings—painted in red or yellow, the two sacred colors of Buddhism; those of the monasteries belonging to the religious order of Sakya are painted in bluish grey, with white and red vertical stripes, or else in white, with red and blue stripes.

Functions. Both the inner architecture of the various religious buildings and their arrangement within a monastic compound reflect the activity for which they are meant: liturgy, meditation, and study, other buildings being used as living quarters and related facilities. Individual study takes place inside the monks' dwellings or on the terraced roofs. Except for ritual dances and special rituals, all religious activity takes place inside the assembly hall, where monks perform the liturgy sitting in rows facing each other, parallel to the axis running from the entrance to the main shrine. Other collective activities, such as lectures, debates, and examinations, are generally carried out in the open, often in a courtyard in front of the main assembly hall. Such open spaces are sometimes called after the specific activities for which they are designed: thus the "chöra" (Tib. *chos rwa*, literally "dharma enclosure") is a yard used for religious debates, surrounded by a wall and often planted with trees, whereas the "chamra" (Tib. *'cham rwa*, literally "ritual dance enclosure") is meant for Buddhist ceremonial dances.

The meanings of the terms, sometimes representing the Tibetan translation of Sanskrit ones, recurring more often to designate a monastery and its parts, are significant:

"ling" (Tib. *gling*, literally "continent," "island"), monastic compound, monastery;
"chode" (Tib. *chos sde*), dharma compound, monastery;
"chokhor" (Tib. *chos 'khor*), dharma enclave, monastery;
"gonpa" (Tib. *dgon pa*) monastery, hermitage;
"tsklakhang" (Tib. *gtsug lag khang*, literally "abode of sciences"), chief monastic building;
"lhakhang" (Tib. *lha-khang*, literally "divine abode"), shrine, chapel or temple;
"tsangkhang" (Tib. *gtsang-khang*, literally "pure abode"),[29] main shrine, chapel or temple;
"krlam" (Tib. *skor-lam*, literally "circumambulation path"), outer or inner ambulatory;

"dukhang" (Tib. *'du khang*), meeting hall;
"tsokkhang" (Tib. *tshogs khang*), assembly hall;
"tsokchen" (Tib. *tshogs chen*), main meeting hall;
"khyam" (Tib. *khyams*), courtyard, sometimes surrounded by a colonnade, or assemby hall;
"gonkhang" (Tib. *mgon khang*, literally "abode of the lords"), temple or chapel housing the wrathful deities protecting the monastery;
"wuts" (Tib. *dbu rtse*, literally "top of the head"), topmost part of a monastic building, corresponding sometimes to a squat multistorey tower rising above the "tsangkhang" and including other temples with their ambulatories, and sometimes to the apartments of a religious master;
"shelyekhang" (Tib. *gzhal yas khang*, literally "inestimable abode," in the sense of "celestial palace" or "divine mansion," Skt. *vimāna*), main temple at the top of the "wutsé," sometimes decorated with cycles of painted mandalas.

In spite of the fact that the "tsuklakhang" is often surrounded by ancillary buildings generally added haphazardly in the course of time, such as subsidiary temples with their own assembly hall, storerooms, a huge kitchen and living quarters for monks (either individual dwellings or colleges), Buddhist architecture in Tibet is not a puzzle of heterogeneous elements: it is the expression of the religious needs of a great civilization that—far from disappearing—has survived even outside geo-cultural Tibet: monasteries, temples, and stupas in Tibetan style continue to be built in India, Bhutan, Nepal, China, Mongolia, Europe, the United States, and other countries (see background of figure 9).

Symbolism. Architectural elements may symbolize specific Buddhist concepts. Important monasteries include temples with a threefold entrance symbolizing the three ways leading to liberation: the realization of the unsubstantiality of things; the renunciation of differentiating among various concepts; and the absence of speculation. Symbolism is more apparent in the emblems decorating religious buildings, including roof ornaments such as the Wheel of the Buddhist Dharma (cf. foreground of figure 9) flanked by two deer—a ubiquitous symbol of the earliest "turning of the wheel," namely the first teaching delivered by the Buddha in the "deer park" at Sarnāth—cylindrical victory-banners and stupa-like finials in gilded copper—all of Indian origin—as well as tridents with bunches of yak-hair borrowed from the Mongolian world.

Although the plans of Samye (see figure 1) and few religious buildings in Tibet might be generically interpreted as mandalas, any temple, irrespective of its shape, may be regarded as the mandala of the deity it houses, as witnessed by several wall inscriptions in the Great Stupa of Gyantse calling "mandala" (Tib. *dkyil 'khor*) each of the rectangular chapels in which they are written: a statue portraying the main deity, even if placed not at the center of the chapel, but in an eccentric position against a wall, represents indeed the ideal center (*dkyil*) of a sacred space in which the assembly of attendant figures, including those painted on the walls, represent the surrounding divine retinue (*'khor*).

Of the Buddhist architectural structures that Tibetans imported from India, the richest in symbolic elements is the stupa (Tib. *mchod rten*, literally "support [for] worship"). The essential elements making up a stupa are: the throne, corresponding to its basis; four steps; the "vase" (Tib. *bum pa*), corresponding to the urn containing the Buddha's remains and represented by a circular structure resting on a base; a turret-like pavilion; a spire made up of an odd number of discs (from five to thirteen or more); and an umbrella, generally topped by a finial. According to canonical literature, each of those elements symbolizes important Buddhist concepts.[30] Thus the first step corresponds to the Four Awarenesses, the second to the Four Perfect Renunciations, the third to the Four Miraculous Powers, and the fourth to the Five Faculties. The base supporting the vase symbolizes the Five Powers, the vase itself the seven Concomitances of Awakening or Enlightenment, and the pavilion the Eightfold Path. Each of the first ten discs making up the spire corresponds to a different mystical power, whereas the eleventh, twelfth, and thirteenth symbolize the three supports of the Buddha's particular awareness.[31] The umbrella represents the Buddha's protection and compassion. The same symbolism extends to other architectural and decorative elements, from the stupa's central pole to its finial.

Several sets of stupas are known in the Buddhist tradition in Tibet: the three stupas—sometimes painted respectively in red, white, and blue—representing a triad of particularly important Bodhisattvas (Avalokiteśvara, flanked by Mañjuśrī and Vajrapāṇī); the seven stupas symbolizing the buddhas of the past; and the eight stupas commemorating the great events and miracles in the life of the historical Buddha. The most complex type of stupa belongs to the last set and is called "victorious" with reference to the Buddha's deeds, though in Tibetan literature it is generally known as "tashigomang choten" (Tib. *bkra shis sgo mang mchod rten*), namely "stupa [with] many doors [of] auspiciousness" from the many doors giving access to the chapels and temples opening on the different terraced steps of the building.

The most extraordinary stupa of the "tashigomang" type in Tibet and in the rest of the Buddhist world is the Great Stupa of Gyantse (see figure 2). The doors on its four terraced steps give access to seventy-five chapels and temples in which Buddhist teachings, including the esoteric cycles regarded as particularly important in 15th-century Tibet, are represented symbolically in the cycles of paintings and statues placed in a sequence whose doctrinal complexity increases as the faithful ascend toward the top of the building. The one hundred thousand images actually painted and modeled in the stupa represent the most important and complete structural representation of the Buddhist pantheon preserved to this day. Climbing from one terraced step to another after performing the ritual circumambulation and entering each chapel in the building, the devotee may reach the statue of the primordial Buddha Vajradhara at the top of its central axis, the "Life Pillar" (Tib. *srog shing*) symbolizing the ten Knowledges and inserted also into large-size images such as the Mahābodhi (see figure 5) in the main temple of Gyantse. The Great Stupa of Gyantse is called "City of the Great Liberation" (Tib. *thar pa chen po'i grong khyer*)[32] in the inscriptions on and descriptions of the walls of the vestibules giving access to the stairs and ladders connecting its various levels; it is indeed a visual theological summa that ought to be understood by a learned devotee who, knowing the symbolic meanings of its iconographic programs and of its architecture, may aspire to the boon of liberation from further rebirths.

Even though Tibetan religious art may appear sometimes unnecessarily complicated, and even stiff and formal, it occupies a fundamental role in the history of civilizations, having inherited and preserved most of the Buddhist iconographic traditions of India thanks to the competence of its patrons and artists who, in spite of living in remote areas, have assimilated and preserved the teachings of one of the most sophisticated belief systems in the world: Buddhism.

REVIEW OF LITERATURE

The development of studies in Tibetan art and architecture is relatively recent. Research in the fields of Tibetan history, religion, and art has made considerable progress since the 1930s thanks to Giuseppe Tucci, one of the fathers of modern Tibetology and author of *Indo-Tibetica* and *Tibetan Painted Scrolls*. One of methodological foundations of Tucci's work was that any cultural phenomenon ought to be viewed historically, in its various political, social, religious, literary and artistic components. Tucci was aware of the fact that an isolated image is "almost always an abstraction" and loses much of its symbolic value if it is analyzed individually, out of its religious context and specific iconographic setting. There is no romance in Tucci's work when compared with the picturesque and exotic visions still prompted by Western and even Eastern representations of old and new age Orientalism, for which, also in art historical terms, Tibet continues to be often perceived as a kind of Shangrila.[33]

In spite of the fact that Tucci laid the foundations of modern Tibetology in the field of art history, his methodology—based on the study of original Tibetan and Sanskrit texts—has often been either forgotten or ignored by several "specialists" in the field. Despite the explosion of publications, often catalogues, related to Buddhist art in the last decades, much literature on the subject has been derivative and concerned primarily with issues of iconography and style. That is largely due to the fact that several researchers in Tibetan art are still unable to read inscriptions and historical or hagiographic sources not available in translation, which contain detailed information, including dates and names, in relation to religious images and buildings, and even to artists. Dating in the absence of written or circumstantial evidence often represents a problem, not only because of the impossibility of placing individual paintings and sculptures within a well-documented historical background and a reliable chronological frame, but also because of the artists' fidelity to the same iconographic models, traditional iconometric rules and sometimes even earlier styles.

Furthermore, relatively few authors have endeavored to study Tibetan Buddhist art from the very perspective of the culture from which it originates, which should provide the appropriate starting point: the analysis of a religious image ought to be related to the specific cultural and social environment of the people who have commissioned and produced it. Finally, limited attention has been paid to native classifications of style, Western authors having often invented their own terminology, some presuming that each Tibetan religious school has adopted its own and only style. As a result, despite the publication of *The Place of Provenance. Regional Styles in Tibetan Painting*, one of David Jackson's excellent monographs devoted to Tibetan art, what Gene Smith wrote almost half a century ago still holds partly true: "The pontifications of eminent museologists and art historians regarding the characteristics and dates of the various styles and schools represent nothing but uninformed guesses."[34]

Indeed, since the publication of *Indo-Tibetica* and *Tibetan Painted Scrolls*—the outcome of less than a score of years' work by a single scholar—comparatively few important books on the history of Tibetan art and architecture have appeared. Leaving aside exhibition and museum catalogues as well as conference proceedings, which are inevitably fragmentary, the following must be mentioned in their order of appearance: Heather Karmay Stoddard's *Early Sino-Tibetan Art*, Loden Sherap Dagyab's *Tibetan Religious Art*, Paola Mortari Vergara and Gilles Béguin's *Dimore umane, santuari divini. Origini, sviluppo e diffusione dell'architettura tibetana/Demeures des hommes, sanctuaires des dieux. Sources, développement et rayonnement de l'architecture tibétaine*, Roberto Vitali's *Early Temples of Central Tibet*, Lokesh Chandra's *Buddhist Iconography*, based on Tibetan iconographic collections, Franco Ricca and Erberto Lo Bue's *The Great Stupa of Gyantse. A Complete Tibetan Pantheon of the Fifteenth Century*, Anne Chayet's *Art et Archéologie du Tibet*, including information on Tibetan architecture, David Jackson's *A History of Tibetan Painting: The Great Tibetan Painters and Their Traditions*, the outcome of years of original research in primary sources and a true complement to *Tibetan Painted Scrolls*, *On the Path to Void. Buddhist Art of the Tibetan Realm*, edited by Pratapaditya Pal and containing fourteen articles divided in the three sections of "Architectural Monuments," "Sculpture," and "Painting and Fabric Images," Deborah Klimburg-Salter's *Tabo, a Lamp for the Kingdom. Early Indo-Tibetan Buddhist Art in the Western Himalaya*, with contributions by Christian Luczanits, Luciano Petech, Ernst Steinkeller and Erna Wandl, Amy Heller's *Tibetan Art—Tracing the Development of Spiritual Ideals and Art in Tibet 600–2000 AD*, Christian Luczanits's *Buddhist Sculpture in Clay. Early Western Himalayan Art, late 10th to early 13th centuries*, and *Tibet. Klöster öffnen ihre Schatzkammern*, an exhibition catalogue edited by Jeong-Hee Lee-Kalisch and including important loans from Tibet. Most of them are monographs and only few may be regarded as histories of Tibetan art.[35]

FURTHER READING

Alexander, André. *The Temples of Lhasa: Tibetan Buddhist Architecture from the 7th to the 21st Centuries*. Chicago: Serindia, 2006.

Beer, Robert. *The Encyclopedia of Tibetan Symbols and Motifs*. Boston: Shambala, 1999.

Béguin, Gilles. *Les peintures du bouddhisme tibétain*. Paris: Réunion des Musées Nationaux, 1995.

Bentor, Yael. *Consecration of Images and Stupas in Indo-Tibetan Tantric Buddhism*. Leiden, The Netherlands: E. J. Brill, 1996.

Brauen, Martin. *The Mandala, Sacred Circle in Tibetan Buddhism*. London: Serindia Publications, 1997.

Brauen, Martin (ed.). *The Dalai Lamas. A Visual History*. Zürich, Switzerland: Ethnographic Museum of the University of Zürich, in association with Serindia Publications, 2005.

Debreczeny, Karl, Ian Alsop, David Jackson, and Irmgard Mengele. *The Black Hat Eccentric: Artistic Visions of the Tenth Karmapa*. New York: Rubin Museum of Art, 2012.

Essen, Gerd-Wolfgang, and Tsering Tashi Thingo. *Die Götter des Himalaya*. I. *Systematischer Bestandskatalog*. Munich: Prestel, 1989.

Essen, Gerd-Wolfgang, and Tsering Tashi Thingo. *Die Götter des Himalaya*. II. *Die Götter des Himalaya: Tafelband*. Munich: Prestel, 1989.

Gyatsho, Thubten Legshay. *Gateway to the Temple: Manual of Tibetan Monastic Customs, Art, Building, and Celebrations*. Kathmandu: Ratna Pustak Bhandar, 1979.

Jackson, David. *Patron and Painter: Situ Panchen and the Revival of the Encampment Style*. New York: Rubin Museum of Art, 2009.

Jackson, David. *The Nepalese Legacy in Tibetan Painting*. New York: Rubin Museum of Art, 2010.

Jackson, David, and Christian Luczanits. *Mirror of the Buddha: Early Portraits from Tibet*. New York: Rubin Museum of Art, 2011.

Jackson, David. *The Place of Provenance: Regional Styles in Tibetan Painting*. New York: Rubin Museum of Art, 2012.

Jackson, David, and Janice A. Jackson. *Tibetan Thangka Painting: Methods & Materials*. London: Serindia, 1984

Lo Bue, Erberto. "The *Dharmamaṇḍala-Sūtra* by Buddhaguhya." In *Orientalia Iosephi Tucci Memoriae Dicata*. Edited by Gherardo Gnoli and Lionello Lanciotti, 787–818. Rome: IsMEO, 1987.

Lo Bue, Erberto. *Tesori del Tibet. Bod-kyi dngos-rdzas rin-chen-gyi 'grem-ston. Oggetti d'arte dei Monasteri di Lhasa*. Milan: La Rinascente, 1994.

Lo Bue, Erberto, ed. *Contributions to the History of Tibetan Art*. Special issue, *The Tibet Journal* 27, no. 3–4 (Autumn–Winter 2002).

Lo Bue, Erberto. "Tibetan Aesthetics versus Western Aesthetics in the Appreciation of Religious Art." In *Images of Tibet in the 19th and 20th Centuries*. Vol. 2. Edited by Monica Esposito, 687–704. Paris: École française d'Extrême-Orient, 2008.

Lo Bue, Erberto. "The Condition of Tibetan Monasteries in the 1930s and '40s as Recorded by Giuseppe Tucci." *Marg: A Magazine of the Arts* 67, no. 3 (2016): 66–75;

Lo Bue, Erberto. "Giuseppe Tucci's Remarks on the State of Preservation of Tibetan Monuments in the 1930s and 1940s." October 2015. http://asianart.com/articles/lobue/index.html.

Lo Bue, Erberto, and Franco Ricca. *Gyantse Revisited*. Firenze: Le Lettere, 1990.

Meyer, Fernand. "The Potala Palace of the Dalai Lamas in Lhasa." *Orientations* 17, no. 7 (1987): 14–32.

Oddy, William, and Wladimir Zwalf. *Aspects of Tibetan Metallurgy. British Museum Occasional Papers* 15 (London: British Museum Press, 1981).

Schroeder, Ulrich von. *Indo-Tibetan Bronzes*. Hong Kong: Visual Dharma Publications, 1981.

Schroeder, Ulrich von. *Buddhist Sculptures in Tibet*. Vol. 1. *India and Nepal*. Hong Kong: Visual Dharma Publications, 2001.

Schroeder, Ulrich von. *Buddhist Sculptures in Tibet*. Vol. 2. *Tibet and China*. Hong Kong: Visual Dharma Publications, 2001.

Singer, Jane Casey, and Philip Denwood, eds. *Tibetan Art: Towards a Definition of Style*. London: Laurence King, 1997.

NOTES

1. On the activity of Newar artists, with particular reference to metal sculptors, for Tibetan patrons up to the present, see Erberto Lo Bue, "The Newar Artists of the Nepal Valley: An historical account of their activities in neighbouring areas with particular reference to Tibet," *Oriental Art* 31, no. 3 (1985): 262–277; Lo Bue, "The Artists of the Nepal Valley," *Oriental Art* 31, no. 4 (1985–1986): 409–420; Lo Bue, "Cultural Exchange and Social Interaction between Tibetans and Newars from the Seventh to the Twentieth Century," *International Folklore Review* 6 (1988): 86–114; Lo Bue, "Newar Sculptors and Tibetan Patrons in the 20th Century," ed. Erberto Lo Bue, special issue, *The Tibet Journal* 3/4 (Autumn–Winter 2002): 121–170; and Lo Bue, "Newar Artistic Influence in Tibet and China between the 7th and the 15th Century," in *Tibetan Art Between Past and Present: Studies Dedicated to Luciano Petech. Rivista di Studi Orientali*, ed. Elena de Rossi Filibeck (Pisa, Italy: Fabrizio Serra, 2012): 25–62.
2. On the role played by Newars in Tibetan painting, see David Jackson, *The Nepalese Legacy in Tibetan Painting* (New York: Rubin Museum of Art, 2010).
3. Fernand Meyer, "The Potala Palace of the Dalai Lamas in Lhasa," *Orientations* 17, no. 7 (1987): 17. For the presence of Chinese and Mongolian artists in 14th-century Tibet, see Giuseppe Tucci, *Indo-Tibetica, IV:*

Gyantse ed i suoi monasteri. Part I. *Descrizione generale dei tempi* (Rome: Reale Accademia d'Italia, 1941), 25–26.

4. On this issue, see Erberto Lo Bue, "Tibetan Aesthetics versus Western Aesthetics in the Appreciation of Religious Art." in *Images of Tibet in the 19th and 20th Centuries,* Vol. 2, ed. Monica Esposito (Paris: École française d'Extrême-Orient, 2008), 687–704.
5. Cf. Anne Chayet, *Art et Archéologie du Tibet* (Paris: Picard, 1994), 88; Giuseppe Tucci, *Tibet* (Geneva: Nagel, 1975), 185; and David Snellgrove and Hugh Richardson, *A Cultural History of Tibet* (Boulder: Shambhala, 1995), 54. The treatment of the locks in the mane of this non-Buddhist figure is reminiscent of the hair of statues of Licchavi rulers portrayed in the guise of Garuḍa in front of Vaishnava temples in the Nepal Valley. See for example, Pratapaditya Pal, *The Arts of Nepal,* Vol. 1, *Sculpture* (Leiden, The Netherlands: E. J. Brill, 1974), pl. 98.
6. See for example, Erberto Lo Bue, "Sculptural Styles According to Pema Karpo," in *Tibetan Art: Towards a Definition of Style,* eds. Jane Casey Singer and Philip Denwood (London: Laurence King, 1997), 242–253 and 302–304.
7. See for instance Giuseppe Tucci, *Indo-Tibetica, IV: Gyantse ed i suoi monasteri,* Part II: *Iscrizioni: testo e traduzione.* (Rome: Reale Accademia d'Italia, 1941), 8 and 136; and Tucci, *Tibetan Painted Scrolls,* Vol. 2 (Kyoto: Rinsen, 1980), 663, 5b for a 14th-century silver statue of the goddess Tārā, and p. 669, 55a, for a roof pinnacle raised at the top of a chapel in the monastery of Gyantse. Some examples from the 12th century onwards are described and illustrated in Gilles Béguin, *Dieux et démons de l'Himâlaya* (Paris: Éditions des musées nationaux, 1977), 70–71 and 73, nos. 11, 13, 17, 18, and 19.
8. From the end of the 20th century, when collecting Tibetan art started to become fashionable, fine images began to be produced, notably in the Nepal Valley, to satisfy the collectors' demand. This has created some confusion in the art market and among collectors, scholars, and museum people who have hardly any experience of fieldwork among artists working for temples and monasteries. Buddhist and Hindu statues produced in the Nepal Valley by artists using traditional iconography, materials, and techniques, sometimes on special orders, artificially aged, and sold by dishonest or incompetent dealers to unaware collectors, may be found in antiques shops, auction rooms, art galleries, and Western collections. On this issue, see Erberto Lo Bue. "In memory of Vittorio Chiaudano (1935–1996): 20th-Century Buddhist and Hindu Statues from the Nepal Valley Belonging to the Aniko Collection on Loan to the Victoria and Albert Museum," *The Tibet Journal* 39, no. 2 (2014): 14–22, figures 9–11 and notes 36, 41, 45, 46. The same applies to scrolls including mandalas painted for the tourist market, often not respecting the proper iconography and sometimes aged artificially. Cf. Yael Bentor, "Tibetan Tourist Thangkas in the Kathmandu Valley," *Annals of Tourism Research* 20, no. 1 (New York: Pergamon Press Ltd, 1993): 107–113.
9. Aspects of dating issues are dealt with in Ingrid Kreide-Damani, *Dating Tibetan Art: Essays on the Possibilities and Impossibilities of Chronology from the Lempertz Symposium, Cologne* (Wiesbaden, Germany: Dr. Ludwig Reichert Verlag, 2003). See also Lo Bue. "In memory of Vittorio Chiaudano," 3–35.
10. See for example Tucci, *Indo-Tibetica, IV. Gyantse ed i suoi monasteri,* Part I, 170; and Tucci, *Tibetan Painted Scrolls,* 663, 5b.
11. For the *Kālacakra* and *Saṃvarodaya* tantras, see David Jackson and Janice Jackson, *Tibetan Thangka Painting: Methods & Materials* (London: Serindia, 1984), 144–147; for the buddhas and tantric tutelary deities, see Jackson, *Tibetan Thangka Painting,* 51; and David Snellgrove, *Indo-Tibetan Buddhism: Indian Buddhists and Their Tibetan Successors,* Vol. 1 (Boston: Shambhala, 1987), 189 n. 126.
12. Cf. Alexander Norman, "The 14th Dalai Lama Tenzin Gyatso," in *The Dalai Lamas. A Visual History,* ed. Martin Brauen (Zürich: Ethnographic Museum of the University of Zürich, 2005), 162–171, 170–171, figure 130. For traditional early portrait painting see David Jackson and Christian Luczanits, *Mirror of the Buddha: Early Portraits from Tibet* (New York: Rubin Museum of Art, 2011).

13. See Erberto Lo Bue, "Considerations on the Gtsug lag khang in the Dpal 'khor chos sde of Rgyal rtse," in *The Illuminating Mirror: Tibetan Studies in Honour of Per K. Sørensen on the Occasion of his 65th Birthday*, eds. by Olaf Czaja and Guntram Hazod (Wiesbaden: Dr. Ludwig Reichert Verlag, 2015), 287, 283–302, 596–600. That gilded copper statue, about 4 meters tall, was fashioned by the Tibetan sculptor sKyabs-pa in 1420–1421, while the two statues at his sides were made by the Newar artist Jaya Teja and his assistants; see 'Jigs-med-grags-pa. *rGyal-rtse chos-rgyal-gyi rnam-par-thar-pa dad-pa'i lo-thog dngos-grub-kyi char-'bebs* (Lhasa: Bod-ljongs Mi-dmangs dPe-skrun-khang, 1987), 66, 73.
14. Zinc is preferred to tin in copper alloys used to cast metal images. See for example Paul T. Craddock, "The copper alloys of Tibet and their background," in *Aspects of Tibetan Metallurgy: British Museum Occasional Paper*, No. 15, eds. W. A. Oddy and Wladimir Zwalf (London: British Museum Press, 1981), 26–30.
15. Loden Sherap Dagyab, *Tibetan Religious Art*, Part I: *Texts* (Wiesbaden, Germany: Otto Harrassowitz, 1977), 50.
16. See Erberto Lo Bue, "Mercury-gilding in Traditional Himalayan and Tibetan Sculpture," in *Tibetan Studies: Proceedings of the 7th Seminar of the International Association for Tibetan Studies*, Vol. 2, eds. Helmut Krasser, Michael Torsten Much, Ernst Steinkellner, and Helmut Tauscher (Vienna: Verlag der Österreichischen Akademie der Wissenschaften, 1997), 573–582.
17. The finished statue was published by Alexander Norman. "The 14th Dalai Lama Tenzin Gyatso," in *The Dalai Lamas. A Visual History*, ed. Martin Brauen. Ethnographic Museum of the University of Zürich (Chicago: Serindia Publications, 2005), 162–171, 166, fig. 123. For a traditional portrait of a Tibetan master by a foremost 20th-century Newar sculptor see Lo Bue. "In memory of Vittorio Chiaudano," 7, Fig. 1.
18. See Jackson and Jackson, *Tibetan Thangka Painting*, 79–80.
19. Tadeusz Skorupski, ed., *Kriyāsaṃgraha: Compendium of Buddhist Rituals: An abridged version* (Tring, U.K.: Institute of Buddhist Studies, 2002), 172. When a religious image requires considerable restoration, a special consecration ritual called *arga* is performed, in which the deity abiding in it "is requested to reside temporarily in a specially prepared mirror for the duration of the restoration," from Yael Bentor, *Consecration of Images and Stupas in Indo-Tibetan Tantric Buddhism* (Leiden, The Netherlands: E. J. Brill, 1996), xxi.
20. For the virtual absence of restoration in Tibetan monasteries, see for example Erberto Lo Bue, "The Condition of Tibetan Monasteries in the 1930s and '40s as Recorded by Giuseppe Tucci," in *Marg: A Magazine of the Arts*, 67, no. 3 (2016): 66–75; and Erberto Lo Bue, "Giuseppe Tucci's Remarks on the State of Preservation of Tibetan Monuments in the 1930s and 1940s," October 2015, http://asianart.com/articles/lobue/index.html.
21. Cf. Erberto Lo Bue, "The *Dharmamaṇḍala-Sūtra* by Buddhaguhya," in *Orientalia Iosephi Tucci Memoriae Dicata*, eds. Gherardo Gnoli and Lionello Lanciotti (Rome: IsMEO, 1987), 794–795: "spread coloured powders." Buddhaguhya's text gives a full account of the mandala, including its structure and symbolism.
22. This introductory section is largely drawn from Fernand Meyer and Corneille Jest's contributions to *Dimore umane, santuari divini: Origini, sviluppo e diffusione dell'architettura tibetana/Demeures des hommes, sanctuaires des dieux. Sources, développement et rayonnement de l'architecture tibétaine*, eds. Gilles Béguin, Corneille Jest, Fernand Meyer, and Paola Mortari Vergara (Rome: Università di Roma—Il Bagatto, 1987), 32–68.
23. See for example, Meyer and Jest, "Architettura: funzioni tecniche, sociali, simboliche e religiose"/"Architecture: fonctions techniques, sociales, symboliques et religieuses," in *Dimore umane, santuari divini*, 43–44, 47 n. 27, and 64, 68 n. 27.
24. Meyer and Jest, "Ambiente, materiali e tecniche."/"Milieux, matériaux, et techniques," in *Dimore umane, santuari divini*, 121, 133 n. 8, and 152, 166 n. 8. The section on architecture in this entry is largely drawn from that article.

25. See Meyer and Jest, "Ambiente, materiali e tecniche"/"Milieux, matériaux, et techniques," in *Dimore umane, santuari divini*, 131 and 163.
26. Cf. Chayet, *Art et Archéologie du Tibet*, 144.
27. On other kinds of techniques, including embroidery, appliqué, weaving and printing, used to make Buddhist scrolls see Dagyab, *Tibetan Religious Art*, 24–25, Plates 26–29; 40.
28. See Mortari Vergara Caffarelli, Paola, "Tibet centrale dal X al XV secolo"/"Tibet central du Xème au XVème siècle," and "Tibet occidentale (Ngari) dal sec. XV al XX"/"Tibet occidental (Ngari) du XVème au XXème siècle," and Meyer and Jest, "Architettura: funzioni tecniche, sociali, simboliche e religiose."/"Architecture: fonctions techniques, sociales, symboliques et religieuses," in *Dimore umane, santuari divini*, 299 and 327, 344 and 361, and 32–33 and 52–53.
29. This term may be replaced by *lte-ba*, literally "navel-string," "navel," "center." See 'Jigs-med-grags-pa, *rGyal-rtse chos-rgyal-gyi rnam-par-thar-pa dad-pa'i lo-thog dngos-grub-kyi char-'bebs* (Lhasa: Bod-ljongs Mi-dmangs dPe-skrun-khang, 1987), 82.
30. See for example Tucci. *Indo-Tibetica*, 1: *Mc'od rten e ts'a ts'a nel Tibet indiano e occidentale* (Rome: Reale Accademia d'Italia, 1932), 39–53; and Adrian Snodgrass, *The Symbolism of the* Stupa (Ithaca, NY: Cornell University, 1991).
31. Tucci. *Indo-Tibetica*, 43.
32. See for example, 'Jigs med grags pa, 110.
33. Tucci, *Indo-Tibetica, I: Mc'od rten e ts'a ts'a nel Tibet* (Rome: Reale Accademia d'Italia, 1932); *II. Rin c'en bzan po e la rinascita del buddhismo nel Tibet intorno al mille* (Rome: Reale Accademia d'Italia, 1933); *III. I templi del Tibet occidentale e il loro simbolismo artistico*. Part I, *Spiti e Kunavar* (Rome: Reale Accademia d'Italia, 1935); Part II, *Tsaparang* (Rome: Reale Accademia d'Italia, 1936); *IV, Gyantse ed i suoi monasteri*, Part I, *Descrizione generale dei tempi* (Rome: Reale Accademia d'Italia, 194); Part II. *Iscrizioni: testo e traduzione* (Rome: Reale Accademia d'Italia, 1941); Part III, *Tavole* (Rome: Reale Accademia d'Italia, 1941); English version (New Delhi: Aditya Prakashan, 1988–1989). For painted scrolls, see Tucci. *Tibetan Painted Scrolls. An Artistic and Symbolic Illustration of 172 Tibetan Paintings Preceded by a Survey of the Historical, Artistic, Literary and Religious Development of Tibetan Culture. With an Article of P. Pelliot on a Mongol Edict, the Translation of Historical Documents and an Appendix of Prebuddhistic Ideas of Tibet*, 3 vols. (Rome: La Libreria dello Stato, 1949); Reprint of vols. 1 and 2 (Kyoto: Rinsen, 1980); and see Tucci. *Indo-Tibetica. I. Mc'od rten e ts'a ts'a nel Tibet* (Rome: Reale Accademia d'Italia, 1932), 9.
34. The issue of regional styles is dealt with in David Jackson and Rob Linroth, *The Place of Provenance: Regional Styles in Tibetan Painting* (New York: Rubin Museum of Art, 2012); and in David Jackson, *Painting Traditions of the Drigung Kagyu School* (New York: Rubin Museum of Art, 2015). Cf. Gene Smith, "Introduction," in *Kongtrul's Encyclopaedia of Indo-Tibetan Culture*, ed. Lokesh Chandra (New Delhi: International Academy of Indian Culture, 1970), 52.
35. The few important books on the history of Tibetan art and architecture include: Heather Karmay Stoddard, *Early Sino-Tibetan Art* (Warminster: Aris and Phillips, 1975); Dagyab, *Tibetan Religious Art*; Paola Mortari Vergara and Gilles Béguin, eds., *Dimore umane, santuari divini*, 1987; Roberto Vitali, *Early Temples of Central Tibet* (London: Serindia, 1990); Lokesh Chandra, *Buddhist Iconography* (New Delhi: International Academy of Indian Culture and Aditya Prakashan, 1991); Franco Ricca and Erberto Lo Bue, *The Great Stupa of Gyantse: A Complete Tibetan Pantheon of the Fifteenth Century* (London: Serindia, 1993); Chayet, *Art et Archéologie du Tibet*; David Jackson, *A History of Tibetan Painting: The Great Tibetan Painters and Their Traditions* (Wien: Verlag der Osterreichischen Akademie der Wissenschaften, 1996); Pratapaditya Pal, ed., *On the Path to Void: Buddhist Art of the Tibetan Realm* (Mumbai: Marg Publications, 1996); and *Marg*, 47, no.4 (1996), where the following corrections ought to be made: p. 98, where the caption should read "The Buddha Maitreya, containing the relices of King Rab-brtan-kun-bzang. *Circa* 1442–1443. Gilded copper. Chos rgyal lha khang in the main monastic building.

Photograph: Charles G. Bill"; p. 127, where caption 4 should read: "The Buddha Vairochana. 1422. Gilded copper. Vajradhatu Temple in the main monastic building"; p. 138, line 40, where "east" should replace "southern"; and p. 141, where caption 14 should read: "The Buddha Maitreya, containing the relics of King Rab-brtan-kun-bzang. *Circa* 1442–1443. Gilded copper. Chos-rgyal-lha-khang in the main monastic building"; Deborah Klimburg-Salter, Christian Luczanits, Luciano Petech, Ernst Steinkeller, and Erna Wandl, *Tabo, a Lamp for the Kingdom: Early Indo-Tibetan Buddhist Art in the Western Himalaya* (Milan: Skira, 1997); Amy Heller, *Tibetan Art: Tracing the Development of Spiritual Ideals and Art in Tibet 600–2000 AD* (Milan, Jaca Book: 1999); Christian Luczanits, *Buddhist Sculpture in Clay: Early Western Himalayan Art, Late 10th to Early 13th Centuries* (Chicago: Serindia Publications, 2004); Jeong-Hee Lee-Kalisch, ed., *Tibet: Klöster öffnen ihre Schatzkammern* (Munich: Kulturstiftung Ruhr & Hirmer Verlag, 2006). An articulated, organic, and exhaustive survey of the history of Tibetan art and architecture is still to be written, as implied by Luczanits, "Methodological Comments Regarding Recent Research on Tibetan Art," *Wiener Zeitschrift für die Kunde Südasiens* 45 (2001), 141.

Erberto Lo Bue

BUDDHIST CHAPLAINCY

VIGNETTE: A BUDDHIST CHAPLAIN PROVIDING INTERFAITH CARE IN NORTH AMERICA

In a Catholic hospital in Missouri, an eighty-seven-year-old woman has been admitted from her nursing home after suffering a stroke. The chaplain is called. She checks in on the patient, who is nonresponsive, reads her chart, and speaks with the nurses. The patient is on life support and not expected to recover, but the medical staff are waiting for the arrival of family. The patient is listed as Southern Baptist. The chaplain offers loving compassion to the patient, placing her hand over the patient's hand, and then continues on her rounds.

When she returns later she finds the family, a daughter and son with their spouses and children, with the patient. They greet her warmly and invite her to pray with them for a miracle to heal their mother. They are distressed that the doctor has suggested withdrawing life support. They want to do everything possible to keep their mother alive while they await a miracle from God. The chaplain listens patiently, sits with them through their distress, and prays with them. Then she gently begins to ask about their mother. "What was she like?" The adult daughter and son speak of their mother as a devout woman who attended church every Sunday and sang in the choir until she moved to the nursing home. "What did your mother think might happen after life?" The son describes how she had faith in God and Jesus and believed in heaven. The chaplain wonders aloud carefully, "Isn't that a miracle? To have such strong faith that she'll be called home to God?" The chaplain can see from the daughter's expression that she does not like this suggestion. The medical staff arrive, and their conversation is cut short, but the chaplain promises to return the following day.

When she does return, the daughter catches her outside her mother's room. The chaplain is prepared to be confronted about her comment the other day, but instead the daughter hugs her, thanks her, and asks her to come in and pray with them while the life support is withdrawn. Their mother passes quietly a few hours later and the chaplain remains with the family until their mother's body is removed. After she returns to her office, the chaplain reflects on her own impermanence and her own impending death. She sits a few minutes in meditation, focused on her breathing, and directs thoughts of loving compassion to the family she has just accompanied. Then she makes her chart notes in the patient's file and heads out on her next rounds.

THE FIELD OF BUDDHIST CHAPLAINCY

It may not be immediately obvious from this vignette that the chaplain described is a Buddhist chaplain. In the North American context, a Buddhist chaplain, like other kinds of chaplains, is "a clergyperson or layperson who has been commissioned by a faith group or an organization to provide pastoral services in an institution, organization, or government entity," per *The Dictionary of Pastoral Care and Counseling*.[1] This section describes Buddhist chaplaincy as a professional and academic field and outlines the major forces shaping that field.

It should be noted that there are many communities in which Buddhists are fully engaged in providing spiritual care to their communities, though they may not use the word "chaplain" (or its translation in the local language) or conceive of their activities as spiritual care. In these cases, while spiritual care is being provided, Buddhist chaplaincy, in the professional sense, is not being practiced. In other words, spiritual care can refer to a much broader range of activities related to compassionate care of others. In order to meet the basic definition of chaplaincy, (1) some level of formal training and professional competencies, such as those summarized in this article, are met and (2) spiritual care is provided in an institutional setting other than the religious community, such as a hospital or school. Spiritual care is the primary action of chaplains, but chaplaincy typically refers to a narrower and modern form of spiritual care with specialized training. Additionally, although a chaplain's primary responsibility is usually spiritual care, it can also involve other roles, such as assessment and documentation of careseeker conditions, careseeker advocacy, and mediation ("careseeker" is a generic word for anyone receiving spiritual care from a chaplain, as "patient" is not universally applicable beyond healthcare settings). Professional chaplains, including Buddhist chaplains, study other faith traditions and aim to serve the spiritual needs of all people within their setting (e.g., hospital, hospice, prison, military unit, company). Practically, in North America, this means Buddhist chaplains who are working in hospitals, hospices, the military, prisons, and schools frequently tend to the spiritual needs of Christian and nonreligious careseekers.

Buddhist chaplaincy refers to Buddhists who act as chaplains or Buddhist forms of chaplaincy training.[2] Even though chaplains are usually expected to serve people from any religious background, licensing and training institutions require them to have explored at least one religious tradition more deeply. Most chaplains attend a seminary or other educational program aligned with their personal religious background, but this is not always the case. For instance, a Jain in the United States might train within a Buddhist chaplaincy program or a Buddhist might train in a Presbyterian or nondenominational chaplaincy program.

Jennifer Block, director of the Zen Hospice Project in San Francisco and faculty in various chaplaincy training programs, provides an emic description of the Buddhist form of chaplaincy: "the seeds of Buddhist chaplaincy as a vocation begin with the Buddha," she writes, due to his focus on helping people through the processes of old age, sickness, death, and ultimately liberating living beings from suffering.[3] She asserts that Buddhist chaplains in the early 21st century are continuing this legacy by "accompanying individuals as their awakening and freedom from suffering unfolds."[4] Block succinctly explicates a theoretical underpinning based in non-self, non-clinging, interconnection, and accepting change that enables Buddhist chaplains to perform the basic functions of the profession, including listening, facing suffering, and "encouraging others to discover their own wisdom."[5] Due to its institutional context and inter-religious nature, professional chaplaincy tends toward a more empowering model of reflective self-authored religious belief and practice, rather than a religiously prescriptive model more common within religious communities.

As indicated above, when engaging careseekers, the primary *activity* of Buddhist chaplains (what they do) is usually called pastoral care or spiritual care. Cheryl Giles and Willa Miller, faculty of Harvard Divinity School's Buddhist Ministry Institute, prefer the term "contemplative care" to characterize Buddhist chaplaincy as "care that is informed by rigorous training in a meditative or contemplative tradition."[6] This definition has certain advantages and disadvantages. It distinguishes Buddhist care from other forms of pastoral or spiritual care by emphasizing a practice (meditation) Buddhist chaplains find valuable to their spiritual formation, quality of presence, and emotional regulation.[7] However, it also privileges a particularly Western emphasis on Buddhist meditation as *the* defining practice of *all* Buddhists. This emphasis has been criticized as elite and nonrepresentative of traditional Asian forms of lay practice.[8] This is not to say that Buddhist chaplains should not have a strong meditation practice, only that the definition of their work as "contemplative care" remains an open conversation. For the time being, the terms "pastoral care" or "spiritual care" remain more broadly accepted in the field of chaplaincy and are used interchangeably throughout this article.[9]

Buddhist chaplains find themselves with two primary dialogue partners in their development of the field of Buddhist spiritual care: (a) Christian and other theistic chaplains; and (b) the social sciences, particularly psychology. Howard Clinebell helped define the duties of pastoral care as "ministry of one-to-one and small group relationships to enable healing empowerment and growth to take place within individuals and their relationships. Pastoral care is the broad, inclusive ministry of mutual healing and growth within a congregation and its community, through the life cycle."[10] Clinebell's work naturally focusses on the pastoral needs of Christian congregations, although it is also widely used for chaplaincy in inter-religious settings. Although "pastoral care" is still used by Buddhist chaplains, "spiritual care" is growing more common due to Christian implications from the pastoral analogy (i.e., the "pastor" as "shepherd" to a "flock") alluded to by Clinebell.

A strong affinity between Buddhism and psychology in recent decades, particularly in North America, has developed into a mutually enriching dialogue on chaplaincy practice. This dialogue also reflects an ongoing dialogue between the social sciences and spiritual care more broadly. For example, while his motives and metaphors are Christian, Clinebell also draws liberally from the insights of secular psychology, particularly the practice of "unconditional positive regard" pioneered by Carl Rogers.[11] Buddhist chaplains find affinity with this approach as it relates to equanimity and compassion, or the ability to regard the suffering of all beings equally. Chaplains tend to receive a cursory education in psychology and mental health, especially as it relates to acute cases meriting referral, but focus more on spiritual, religious, and existential caregiving in times of crisis, rather than on long-term care or therapy (although in certain contexts, such as the military and colleges, long-term relationships between chaplains and careseekers are common).

While spiritual care has traditionally been offered by clergy, it is also increasingly the province of trained laypeople. Therefore, rather than refer to the person offering care as a priest, monk, minister, or other member of the clergy, the all-inclusive terms "caregiver" or chaplain are preferable. Likewise, the inverse term "careseeker" refers to the person receiving spiritual or pastoral care. It also clarifies that careseekers are not always and sometimes only rarely fellow Buddhists, especially in North America. In other areas, coreligionist care (i.e., Buddhists caring for Buddhists) is more common.

CORE COMPETENCIES

Existing practices of spiritual care are easily adopted by Buddhist caregivers, including empathy and compassion, listening and responding, prayer and ritual, cultural competency, and reflection for ongoing growth. A survey of what little literature exists on Buddhist spiritual care cannot yet reveal if differences in theoretical understanding have led to quantifiable differences in practice or outcomes. On the whole, variations in technique, approach, and method between Buddhist chaplains and non-Buddhist chaplains appear minor. Differences in these spiritual care practices between Buddhists (as a group) and other caregivers are typically in emphasis and explanation rather than methods or execution. In other words, there are sometimes disagreements on precisely why or how something works but agreement that it works for addressing suffering in situations of crisis and distress.

Collectively, these core competencies contribute to an almost ineffable skill known as "quality of presence" or, in the Christian literature, "ministry of presence." Buddhist chaplains describe this as "just being there," "being present," "fully there," or "showing up." Regardless of how it is described, this practice appears to have three primary components: intention, action, and outcome. The intention is that of goodwill, love or lovingkindness, openheartedness, and "unconditional positive regard" in the Rogerian sense (see the section on Empathy and Compassion).[12] The actions related to being present represent the other core competencies, including listening and responding, prayer and ritual, and other practices. Buddhist chaplains say that when they successfully employ these practices with right intentions, outcomes are positive, often in surprising or counterintuitive ways, such as the vignette demonstrated. Buddhist chaplains report that afterward careseekers say they feel more peaceful, better respected, more emotionally connected, and better able to make sense of their situations. Careseekers express appreciation and gratitude and experience moments of joy and humor. Chaplains also described negative outcomes attributed to times when they failed to be present with careseekers, either due to distraction, anxiety, or fatigue. Moreover, good quality of presence is described as equally beneficial to the chaplain, enabling them to better cope with vicarious suffering, emotional self-regulation, and on-the-job stress.[13] While quality of presence or "being there" may sound passive, it is a surprisingly active and rigorous practice, as the core competencies elucidate.

Empathy and Compassion. Empathy and compassion are similar but not identical skills. Together they constitute right intention and motivate right action for Buddhist chaplains. Right intention seeks to do what is wholesome, beneficial, and skillful, and avoid acting from attachment and greed, aversion and hatred, or ignorance and delusion.[14] In this sense, right intention entails the cultivation of wisdom through self-knowledge and study. Right action entails moral behavior that does that which is beneficial and avoids unwholesome harmful deeds.[15] Both are aspects of the noble eightfold path.[16] Moreover, when present during spiritual care encounters with careseekers, empathy and compassion contribute to a sense of connection beneficial to both careseeker and caregiver. This has been reported by Buddhist chaplains, is explored in the literature on Buddhist chaplaincy, and is broadly affirmed among non-Buddhist chaplains and pastoral care literature (although these sources have somewhat different definitions for empathy and compassion and do not connect them to the Noble Eightfold Path).[17]

Empathy is not the same as compassion, though the two are akin. In some ways, empathy could be considered broader than compassion as it entails understanding and even co-experiencing a broad range of emotions with the careseeker. Compassion, in contrast, is focused on shared suffering and is one of the four divine abodes (*brahmavihāra*). In Buddhism, compassion is balanced by the cultivation of the other three divine abodes, empathetic joy (*muditā*), loving-kindness (*mettā*), and equanimity (*upekṣā*), and should not be cultivated alone, lest one become overwhelmed by suffering. The English word "compassion" derives from the Latin roots meaning "to suffer with," and modern dictionaries describe it as "deep awareness of the suffering of another accompanied by the wish to relieve it."[18] The latter definition is more akin to the Buddhist definition of *karuṇā* (Pāli and Sanskrit), the term translated as "compassion," which lacks the connotation of the shared suffering present in the English term. At the most basic level, people seek to alleviate suffering because it is unpleasant. People seek to alleviate the suffering of others insomuch as empathy entails we share in that suffering. However, *karuṇā*, as an attribute of the Buddha and other enlightened beings, is the deep wish to alleviate suffering and also the act to do so, even if one does not share in the experience of suffering.[19] Buddhist chaplains have explored the roles of empathy and compassion at length, with slightly different emphases depending on their backgrounds.

Robert Chodo Campbell describes compassion as the act of bearing witness, a practice best explored by his teacher, a famous Jewish Buddhist, Roshi Bernie Glassman.[20] "Witnessing" is also referred to in Christian theology, though the Buddhist and Christian conceptions of it are distinct and, based on existing literature, not related. In the Christian tradition, "witnessing" originates in the gospels, which are themselves the testimony of witnesses (the apostles) of Christ's acts. Modern forms of Christian witnessing tend to focus on testimony of God's or Jesus' impact on the life of the witness. The concept of witnessing in Buddhist chaplaincy literature makes no reference to Christian origins or the act of testimony. Rather, Buddhist literature emphasizes being present and seeing reality as it is (a focus of the Zen traditions, in particular), without conceptual filters such as desire, aversion, or delusion. In this sense, it is important to witness but not to testify (share what one has witnessed with others). The knowledge in the careseeker that one has been seen and heard can provide a powerful catharsis.

Many Buddhist authors and the chaplains in a recent qualitative study also emphasize the importance of witnessing suffering with empathy and compassion.[21] Willa Miller emphasizes the caregiver's role as witness and distinguishes it from the more common paradigm of Buddhist clergy as teacher. "To be a witness involves being really present to others, listening to others, developing the capacity to be in skillful relationship. . . . To witness is to be permeable, to be willing to look [at] and listen" to suffering, which is something most people would, understandably, rather not do.[22]

Compassion is critical to the practice of being with suffering and to every stage in the spiritual formation of a Buddhist chaplain, from the earliest stages of self-development, before they even consider becoming a chaplain, to the most advanced stages of spiritual care with suffering careseekers.[23] Kristin Deleo points out that compassion is simple but not easy. It is merely the willingness to be open, aware, and loving but to do so in the presence of illness, aging, death, and dying. She uses contemplative practice as a method for cultivating compassion and includes self-compassion as a necessary component.[24] Deleo describes a common meditation as the foundation of compassion, while other teachers, like Cheryl Giles, provide more detailed and sophisticated methods for cultivating this virtue among Buddhist chaplains.

The vignette described how the Buddhist chaplain at the hospital in Missouri employed compassion with the unresponsive patient, with the patient's distraught family members, and with herself following the death of the patient. She remained present with them through their suffering, witnessed the death of the patient and the family's grief, and witnessed her own reaction to that event through the lens of compassion. Her own empathetic response to the patient and family was likely conditioned from the chaplain's experiences of losing loved ones and working with her own grief. Empathy can elicit deep understanding, yet it can also result in projection (an assumption that another will feel as one felt in a similar situation that does not hold true). Empathy in the face of suffering calls for the use of self-compassion for emotional coping, which the chaplain in the vignette employed.

Listening and Responding. Literature on pastoral care from Christian, Jewish, and Buddhist sources all affirms the basic necessity of skillful listening and responding. Qualitative research with practicing Buddhist chaplains affirms the literature. Barbara Breitman, a Jewish chaplain and clinical social worker, summarizes a common belief of chaplains: "The art of listening is the foundation of all forms of pastoral caregiving."[25] Likewise, the Buddhist authors of *The Arts of Contemplative Care* and *A Thousand Hands* repeatedly reference listening skills and share stories from times they did and did not effectively listen with careseekers.[26] The chaplain in the vignette employed listening skills with the nurses and medical staff, the patient's grief-stricken family, and internal listening skills with herself during and following the encounter.

Miller, an American Buddhist lama in a Tibetan tradition and faculty of the Buddhist Ministry Initiative at Harvard Divinity School, writes that, "Deep listening is a practice of listening with a disciplined, embodied, and compassionate attention that attends to the present moment, the narrative arc of speech, and to the speaker's humanity."[27] She provides three criteria for deep listening: that it be cultivated, attentive, and loving and compassionate. She provides instructions for cultivation, criteria to discern attentiveness, and describes the role of love and compassion and their impact on the outcome of our listening. The chaplain in the vignette employed attentive and compassionate listening and cultivated her conversation with the patient's adult children to elicit important information that would help shape her response wisely.

Qualitative research with practicing Buddhist chaplains affirmed the importance of listening and responding appropriately. Wisdom derived from listening, or *śrutamayīprajñā*, played a particularly important role in their work. First, they cultivated the intention to listen well.

Then they employed listening in two distinct ways: listening to the careseeker and listening to their own responses to the careseeker. They also employed listening with multidisciplinary teammates and clinical pastoral education (CPE) peers and supervisors to gain valuable insight and feedback in relation to specific cases and their work as a whole. Good listening enabled chaplains to be more observant and see complex situations more clearly.

Buddhist chaplains described the outcomes of good listening in particularly Buddhist ways.[28] For example, "They cultivated their ability to listen through all manner of suffering and to remain present, grounded, and emotionally, mentally, and physically healthy without getting 'hooked' or caught up in the careseeker's distress or their own analysis. Wisdom that comes from listening at this stage involves active (even joyful) engagement with the work, while also being nonattached to the outcome."[29] As their spiritual care practice advanced, so too did their ability to listen selflessly to careseekers. Chaplains reported experiences in which their own sense of self faded into the background—though not gone, it was not the focus of the current situation. They manifested "nondual listening" (i.e., without separate subject and object) based in what they perceived as direct experiences of non-self (*anatta* in Pāli). In other words, chaplains reported that because there is no inherent separation between self and other, they were able to be fully present in that moment and listen to the other *as* self and *also* as neither self nor other. Furthermore, they justified this phenomenon not merely as a psychological experience but as a direct experience of reality as "empty" (*śūnyatā*) of inherent existence, per the buddhadharma. This is a difficult idea to explain so briefly. It was difficult to describe even by chaplains who had experienced it. Buddhist literature, particularly a genre of wisdom literature known as *prajñāpāramitā* or the "perfection of wisdom," notes that such experiences are beyond language and concepts and so impossible to describe using language and concepts. However, such experiences are akin to the modern psychological phenomenon of "flow" (whether flow explains experiences of emptiness or the reality of emptiness explains experiences of flow is open to debate), the literary and philosophical ideas of deconstructionism, and the spiritual experience of "transcendence."[30] This served the needs of the careseeker and also protected the chaplain from harm due to vicarious trauma and burnout. At this stage, describing their activity as "listening" seemed inadequate. Instead, chaplains described an experience "beyond words . . . that breaks down all the labels."[31] While listening is a profound practice for Buddhist chaplains, it is interwoven with the ability to respond appropriately.

Daijaku Kinst, a Sōtō Zen priest and faculty at the Institute of Buddhist Studies, titled her chapter in *The Arts of Contemplative Care* "Cultivating an Appropriate Response" and employed the tradition of the Three Prajñās, of which wisdom derived from listening or *śrutamayīprajñā* is the first, followed by wisdom derived from contemplating and practicing, *cintāmayīprajñā* and *bhāvanāmayīprajñā*, respectively. Kinst states that appropriate response is predicated not only on attentive listening but also study in which a chaplain has engaged before providing care. Thus, the chaplain in the vignette relied on her knowledge of Christian traditions gained from study in reframing the family's definition of "miracle" to include an outcome their mother desired, as she learned from listening to their stories about their mother. The miracle proposed (to be with God) was consistent with various branches of Christian theology and therefore an appropriate response in that context. Appropriate topics for study in the buddhadharma, per Kinst, include suffering, emptiness and interdependence, experience, wisdom and compassion, psychology, pastoral care literature broadly, ethics, vows, and awakening. Personal study (or wisdom based on contemplating) then allows the chaplain to articulate an appropriate response.[32] Much of the broader spiritual and pastoral care literature explores various types of appropriate responses, such as reflecting, reframing, or questioning, that are also employed by Buddhist chaplains. Howard Clinebell devotes several chapters to these various types of responses.

Interfaith Understanding, Ritual, and Prayer. The term "ritual" can be understood broadly to include forms of prayer, meditation, poetry, music, contemplation, and patterns of repeatable action. Clinebell notes that such practices are useful to the spiritual caregiver in three ways: (1) for the caregiver's spiritual preparation, (2) when used by the caregiver on behalf of the careseeker, and (3) as things that can be taught to the careseeker for use in spiritual self-care and self-healing. Buddhist chaplains in interreligious settings frequently draw not on Buddhist rituals but on rituals, such as prayer, that are meaningful to their careseekers.

Ritual can be one of the greatest challenges to many chaplains. Buddhist chaplains in the West must not only learn the rituals from their own tradition but also at least basic rituals from other Buddhist traditions and other religions. For example, a Buddhist hospital chaplain may perform an emergency baptism for a baby when Christian clergy could not be summoned quickly after childbirth complications. The chaplain in the vignette participated in rituals of prayer familiar to the family of the patient. Chaplains often learn a range of life transition ceremonies, including those for birth, coming-of-age, marriage, and death. Buddhist chaplains may also learn some of the most basic chants in various traditions and languages to meet these needs. Buddhist chaplains additionally use modern technology to access recorded chants and prayers to comfort careseekers in familiar ways. Many chaplains maintain their own self-compiled books and digital libraries of such resources to deploy at a moment's notice.

Ritual competency includes the ability to shift and adapt rituals to a variety of needs. Prayer styles may sometimes need to adjust to fit a person's medical conditions. An individual, for instance, may not be physically able to prostrate or bow as normal during a traditional ritual. The majority of Buddhist traditions around the world include an act of prostration or bowing as a simple ritual action at the beginning or end of chanting or meditation sessions; some practitioners do many such actions in a row. A full prostration might include getting down on one's knees, with the elbows, hands, and head also touching the floor. However, in a hospital bed, the individual might instead be simply instructed to put their hands together and make a simple bow of the head—ritual actions are adapted to the physical capacity of the careseeker. In the modern era, rituals from different traditions and religions are frequently combined in new ways. Chaplains participate in interfaith ceremonies, which requires the ability to perform rituals in a way that is viewed as inclusive to each tradition represented while not adapting it so far as to appear disrespectful to any particular faith. Possessing a broader theoretical understanding of ritual and the specific desired outcomes of any particular ritual event aid the chaplain in this skill.

Cultural Competencies. Cultural competency refers to the awareness and functioning of caregivers in multicultural environments or among populations different from themselves. Three themes emerge from literature on this topic. First, several authors agree on the need to remain humble, make few or no assumptions, and be prepared to learn about other cultures and people. Second, most authors do advise chaplains to educate themselves to a reasonable extent on the cultural practices of different groups. For example, it was helpful for the chaplain in the vignette to know that she could expect the family, as evangelical Christians, to desire spontaneous prayer rather than recitation of prescribed prayers at the deathbed of their mother. While she cannot assume this is the case for all Christians in that area, it helps her to gain experience in the type of rituals they might expect. Likewise, it would be helpful to know that as a female chaplain, she should not offer to shake hands with an Orthodox Jewish man. This is prohibited in orthodox Judaism and the man might be embarrassed to refuse her. On the other hand, such assumptions should be held lightly as not all members of particular groups adhere to all the groups norms. If the Orthodox Jewish man were to offer to shake her hand first, she should be prepared to do so. Moreover, knowledge of such differences needs to be paired with a genuine respect for those differences. These basic types of cultural competency—humility paired with some basic knowledge—form a foundation for more difficult issues of diversity and inclusion.

The third common theme is the urgent necessity of dealing with various forms of oppression and privilege. Some authors describe how to build bridges between the poor and rich, men and women, and people of different sexual orientations, among others. Cheryl Giles, in *The Arts of Contemplative Care*, points out that efforts to adapt Buddhism to Western culture have often overlooked oppressions and social justice issues.[33] In a racially and ethnically diverse nation still struggling with legacies of colonialism, slavery, and white supremacy like the United States, the Eastern values of community, interdependence, and collaboration meet Western values of individualism, self-interest, and competition. The results of this meeting have not always been positive, and some Buddhist teachings have been employed to reinforce racist and sexist norms rather than liberate society from their oppressions. Buddhist caregivers are still dealing with this legacy. With the rise of the communal-contextual, feminist and womanist, and intercultural paradigms of spiritual care, there is a new focus on the experiences and voices of previously marginalized groups including people of color (POC), women, the poor, LGBTQ+ persons, and members of religious traditions other than Christianity or no religion at all.

Some responses to the pressing needs of oppressed persons and communities are broad and can apply across various communities and types of oppression, such as awareness and education. Other responses are specific to particular types of oppression such as racism, sexism, classism, or homophobia, or to particular communities who experience oppression differently. For example, racism applied to Asians and Asian Americans (i.e., "model minority") is different from the racism experienced by Black and African Americans (i.e., "thugs"). Appropriate caring responses depend greatly on the training, self-awareness, and sociocultural location of the caregiver in relation to the careseeker. They also rely on intersectionality or overlapping patterns of oppression, such as being simultaneously African American, a woman, and a lesbian. Buddhist chaplains in diverse, intercultural communities must undergo all the more training in order to meet the needs of their diverse clientele.

Reflection. Reflection is a skill that supports all of the other competencies. Moreover, reflection is integral to the processes of learning, skill development, spiritual formation, meaning making, the development of wisdom, and emotional coping and regulation.

A recent study of practicing Buddhist chaplains in North America found that they understood reflection in three overlapping ways. First, reflection involves an act of recollection or looking back at a prior encounter or context. Second, reflection enables one to make or find meaning from events or situations. Third, reflection contributes to one's spiritual formation. Reflection can be done in various ways, including as pure thought, emotional awareness and processing, within meditation, through conversation, via writing, or through rereading what one has previously written to reconsider it in light of new knowledge or a different emotional frame.[34] In the vignette, the Buddhist chaplain briefly reflected on her experiences following the death of the patient in order to process her emotions, consider the meaning of death and impermanence within her wider conceptual worldview, and prepare for her next patient visit. She did this via a brief meditation in her office and through writing the patient's chart notes. This is a very simple, but very common, example of reflection in a healthcare setting.

Some Buddhist chaplains find that too much reflection leads to discursiveness or fabrication of meaning for the sake of meaning. Reflection, they warn, can lead one to become attached to particular expectations or outcomes for oneself or careseekers. Concepts can hinder one's ability to see a situation as it is or be present for careseekers in the moment. Some Zen Buddhists have been particularly cautious of too much reflection leading to fabricated interpretations of situations. However, on balance, Buddhist chaplains find a great deal of benefit and utility in the practice of reflection.

There are parallels and distinctions between how Buddhists practice reflection and the skill of "theological reflection" commonly referenced in Christian chaplaincy literature. Both groups emphasize reflection as a process rather than a product. As such, theological reflection is defined as "An activity that enables people of faith to give an account of the values and traditions that underpin their choices and convictions and deepens their understanding."[35] In both cases, reflection enables chaplains to clarify and articulate how they understand the world and act in relation to it. This skill—articulation of meaning—becomes critical in conversations with suffering careseekers struggling to find meaning in their present circumstances. Reflection entails questioning oneself and making connections between ideas.

However, whereas Christian chaplains emphasize the role of reflection as making connections between human life and "divine horizons" or "the nature of God,"Buddhists are more likely to emphasize making connections between cause and effect or between people.[36] Buddhists, including the authors of *The Arts of Contemplative Care,* utilized many methods for reflection similar to Christian methods, including praxis-based and correlation-based methods. They also avoided other methods, such as canonical narrative theology.[37] However, for Buddhists, reflection itself appears to occupy a different context within the dharma than theological reflection does within Christianity. In particular, reflection is described as a process relating to both wisdom (*prajñā*) and meditation, though these relationships cannot be fully explicated here. The major role of meditation and contemplation in reflection (for Buddhists) is not often referenced in Christian literature, by contrast.

Other Competencies. Although this article summarizes the primary competencies, there are many other competencies that Buddhist chaplains develop. Others include self-care and healthy boundaries, use of scriptures and literature in care, spiritual assessment and spiritual care planning, positive use of power or spiritual authority, and working with specific populations or problems, such as: alcoholism and addiction, domestic violence, sexual trauma, chronic illness, aging, family conflict, death and dying, bereavement, mental illness, and natural and man-made disasters.[38] One further area of note unique in emphasis for Buddhist chaplains is the role of meditation or mindfulness.

Deploying mindfulness in service of spiritual care is a common topic among Buddhist (and other) chaplains and allied professions. Already mentioned is the characterization by Giles and Miller of Buddhist chaplains' work as "contemplative care." Several other research projects and publications have recently engaged with this topic. Karthryn Bilotti-Stark conducted a survey of mindfulness practices among Buddhist chaplains and found that mindfulness training supports the spiritual formation of Buddhist chaplains and "may be regarded as a competency in the training of professional chaplains as, while not explicitly stated, a high degree of mindfulness is implied by the Association of Professional Chaplains in its list of competencies."[39] Bilotti-Stark and other authors have identified a potential contribution of Buddhist chaplains to the overall discipline and profession of spiritual care.

Aging, illness, and death are also common topics for Buddhist chaplains. In addition to contributions to the academic literature in this area, chaplains and dharma teachers have published a number of books intended for general audiences, particularly people coping directly with illness, injury, aging, or their own impending death or that of a loved one. Buddhism has always had an affinity for this topic as illness and death are named as primary sources of suffering in the Buddha's first sermon following his enlightenment.[40] Buddhists have since developed a number of sophisticated teachings and contemplative practices to help people come to terms with these forms of human suffering.

While there are many more competencies that are essential for a fully trained Buddhist chaplain, empathy and compassion, listening and responding, interfaith understanding of ritual, cultural competency, reflection, mindfulness, and a Buddhist understanding of aging, illness, and death tend to strongly define the practice of Buddhist chaplaincy.

BUDDHIST CHAPLAINCY AROUND THE WORLD

This section provides an overview of Buddhist chaplaincy by geographic location. Context makes a great deal of difference in the opportunities for education, training, and employment or placement for Buddhist chaplains. Education and training varies from the most formal three-year, accredited, graduate degree programs with clinical internships to short, unaccredited weekend workshops, and in some countries, requirements for monastic training. Paid employment for Buddhist chaplains depends greatly on both location and sector. North America has, by far, the most opportunities for paid employment by both number and sector, with Buddhist chaplains working professionally in hospitals, hospices, palliative care centers, nursing homes, schools and colleges, the military, police forces, emergency response, prisons, social services, and the non-profit sector. This is partly due to the way chaplaincy as a profession is embedded in these sectors and the religiously plural history of North America from the time of colonization. This contributed to an environment where chaplains both have a long history of service (starting with George Washington's Continental Army) and have, to some degree, always provided ecumenical or interfaith spiritual care.[41]

Overall, healthcare is by far the most common setting for Buddhist chaplains. This includes hospices, nursing homes, clinics, and palliative care centers. Buddhist chaplains also provide outpatient services and home visits for palliative, hospice, and bereavement care. Buddhists have been particularly active in hospice care, due to religious teachings on death and dying. While chaplains are most numerous in healthcare, institutionalized chaplaincy may have the longest tradition in the military. Most countries listed in this section have Buddhist chaplains in a few but not all of these sectors, and positions are often volunteer.

There is a correlation between the availability and intensity of educational opportunities and the corresponding availability of professional employment over volunteer placement. Overall, this represents a spectrum of professionalization of Buddhist chaplains from both highly educated and professionally employed to informally trained and volunteer. In Western countries, where Buddhist chaplaincy is more professionalized, Buddhist chaplains are also more likely to provide interfaith care; that is, to serve careseekers who are not themselves Buddhist. In Eastern countries, the correlation is only between training and employment; there does not appear to be a correlation between intensity of training and likelihood of providing interfaith care even in nations (such as South Korea) where Buddhists are also a minority. These differences do not, however, automatically suggest that those with less formal education or paid employment are any less skilled in providing spiritual care, only that opportunities tend to vary greatly worldwide.

Outside of English-speaking countries, there are also linguistic issues in discussing or comparing Buddhist chaplaincy. "Chaplaincy" and "spiritual care" are culturally laden terms that carry influence from originally Christian usage, already complicating their adaptation into Buddhist chaplaincy within English. Translation of words like this into foreign languages—or the lack of a direct translation—causes problems for practitioners in determining what such words really mean for them and for scholars trying to determine what falls within the realm of Buddhist chaplaincy. The movements included within this article each show strong influence from some dimensions of Western chaplaincy because of their efforts to adapt and deal with its originally Christian heritage. Of course, this is not to say that all Buddhist caregiving has Christian roots or heritage. This article's scope, however, is restricted to Buddhist movements and organizations around the world that display at least some clear link to "chaplaincy" as it developed in the West.

North America. Professional chaplains and many volunteer and ministerial chaplains go through extensive training prior to their caregiving work. Board certification and professional employment in North America generally requires the equivalent of three years of full-time, graduate-level coursework. Most chaplains accomplish this through a Master of Divinity program or an extended Master of Arts program.

As of 2018, the United States has three regionally accredited Master of Divinity programs in Buddhist chaplaincy at Naropa University (Boulder, CO), the Institute of Buddhist Studies (in cooperation with the Graduate Theological Union in Berkeley, CA), and University of the West (Rosemead, CA). Maitripa College in Portland, OR, is in the process of seeking regional accreditation for their Master of Divinity program. Some Buddhist chaplains are trained through programs that cater to individuals from multiple traditions, such as Harvard Divinity School (Cambridge, MA) and Claremont School of Theology (Claremont, CA). Emmanuel

College at the University of Toronto recently began an interreligious Master of Pastoral Studies including training for Christian, Jewish, Muslim, Hindu, and Buddhist chaplains, the first program of its kind in Canada.[42] There are several unaccredited yet well-developed Buddhist chaplaincy training programs across the United States as well. Upaya Zen Center (Santa Fe, NM), the New York Zen Center for Contemplative Care (New York, NY), and the Sati Center (San Francisco, CA) are among the most prominent.

Graduate coursework for Buddhist chaplaincy fulfills thirteen areas of training required by the Association for Professional Chaplains (APC) in the United States and the Canadian Association of Spiritual Care.[43] Per the Board of Chaplaincy Certification, these are: (1) religious history, (2) teaching and tenets, (3) sacred texts, (4) morality and ethics, (5) world religions, (6) ethnic and cultural diversity, (7) spiritual care of persons, (8) spiritual counseling, (9) communication, (10) religious education, (11) professional ethics, (12) spiritual leadership, and (13) supervised internship.[44] (Some graduate programs combine certain categories into nine basic areas listed in program descriptions.) These standards broadly match the standards for program content of a Masters of Divinity degree accredited by the Association of Theological Schools.[45] Buddhist training programs consciously adopt this Christian education structure, and literature on Buddhist chaplaincy is still limited, so use of Christian or Jewish source materials is still common in many of the areas.

Beyond coursework, chaplain Board Certification in the United States requires the completion of four units, or 1,200 hours, of Clinical Pastoral Education (CPE) training.[46] CPE is essentially a supervised chaplaincy internship and includes discussion of clinical cases and educational sessions within each program. Many seminary programs for clergy require at least one unit of CPE training and encourage more, even if the student does not intend to become a chaplain. The New York Zen Center for Contemplative Care offers the first and still the only fully accredited CPE program with a Buddhist emphasis.[47] Most Buddhist chaplains complete their CPE requirements in inter-religious programs with non-Buddhist peers and supervisors. A recent dissertation that interviewed thirteen Buddhist chaplains about their CPE experiences found that eleven (85 percent) were the only Buddhist in their cohort and all had a non-Buddhist supervisor.[48] While this study was limited in scope, it matches the common wisdom in the field and anecdotal experience of the authors.

The relative isolation of Buddhist chaplains from one another may be hindering the development of Buddhist spiritual care theory and practice within this Christian-dominant field. Nevertheless, conversations recently began among the APC, the Association for Clinical Pastoral Education (ACPE), and other professional bodies regarding the broadening of chaplaincy standards and training materials to fit more traditions. They resulted in the 2017 elimination of the ordination requirement from the criteria to become a Board Certified Chaplain.[49] A White Paper produced by the Board of Chaplaincy Certification in 2006 otherwise upheld the existing standards as applicable to Buddhists (excepting universal ordination).[50] While Buddhists are fully participating in the profession of chaplaincy in North America, their role in shaping the profession remains limited.

Board certification is commonly expected in healthcare chaplaincy, which includes hospitals, hospices, and other healthcare facilities. Although it is possible to work as a Buddhist chaplain in some areas of healthcare without certification, such positions can be difficult to find. Reverend Madeline Ko-i Bastis was ordained in 1993 through Sōtō Zen's White Plum lineage, and then became the first Buddhist to be board-certified by the APC. Until her death in 2007, she opened many doors in chaplaincy to Buddhists and communicated Buddhist issues in certification to the APC. Since that time, many Buddhist chaplains have been employed within the healthcare networks in North America and several Buddhists also lead CPE training within hospitals. Others have founded key organizations to aid communication between Buddhist chaplains in different areas of health care. Mikel Ryuho Monnett, for example, established the ACPE Buddhist Network and Jon K. Reid started the Buddhist group for the Association for Death Education and Counseling.

Buddhist chaplains are also active in American hospices, including a growing number of Buddhist-founded hospices. The Zen Hospice Project is an end-of-life care organization founded by and run largely by Buddhist chaplains in San Francisco, CA. Maitri Buddhist Home and Hospice, also located in San Francisco, CA, was originally founded particularly to care for people with AIDS, though it expanded its services to help others who are terminally or chronically ill. Other Buddhist care facilities include the Rigpa Fellowship's Spiritual Care for Living and Dying in Santa Cruz, CA; the Project on Being with Dying in Santa Fe, NM; and Maitri Day Health Center in Yonkers, NY. Many Buddhist chaplains receive their introduction to spiritual care in these settings and go on to professional training and employment throughout the healthcare sector.[51]

During World War II, only Christian and Jewish chaplains were allowed within the US military. The Buddhist Missions of North America (the precursor of the Buddhist Churches of America) petitioned the then War Department to commission a Buddhist chaplain, but Buddhism at the time was confused with Japanese state-sponsored Shinto and their request was denied. However, the Buddhist Churches of America (BCA) continued to lead an effort through subsequent decades in approving Buddhism as a faith recognized by the US military and other chaplaincy organizations. Rev. Haruo Yamaoka, the Abbot of the Buddhist Churches of America at the time, lobbied to have the organization granted ecclesiastical endorser status, which would allow approval of chaplains in the military. The request was subsequently approved and the BCA remains the lone Buddhist endorsing organization approved by the US armed forces. The Institute of Heraldry also designed an official Buddhist insignia approved in 1991 to be worn on uniforms for Buddhist chaplains. However, recruiting a Buddhist chaplain would still take time.

Lt. Jeanette Shin became the first Buddhist chaplain in the US military in 2004, when she fulfilled all of the requirements and was commissioned as a Lieutenant Junior Grade (LTJG) in the US Navy Reserves. She went on to the Navy's active-duty service in December 2006. Lt. Thomas Dyer and Lt. Somya Malasri, a former Thai monk, followed shortly thereafter as the first Buddhist chaplains in the US Army in 2008 and 2010, respectively. A number of other Buddhist chaplains have followed in their footsteps in subsequent years, though the total number remains very small at any given time.

Active duty, reserve, guard, or civil air patrol chaplains must have completed each of the following requirements: (1) ecclesiastical endorsement that certifies experience and degree requirements meet the standards of a recognized religious order; (2) two years religious leadership consistent with clergy in applicant's tradition (strongly recommended); (3) US citizenship (no dual citizenship); (4) Bachelor's degree; (5) a graduate degree that includes a minimum of seventy-two semester hours or equivalent from an accredited institution and, of this, no less than thirty-six semester hours must be in theological or ministry and related studies, consistent with the respective religious tradition of the applicant. Endorsers are free to exceed the Department of Defense (DoD) standard per ecclesiastical requirements but cannot go below the minimal DoD requirements, and many endorsers specifically require the Master of Divinity degree.[52] Military chaplaincy sees Buddhist chaplains embedded in a particular battalion, ship, or unit for a standard rotation period (typically four years) to serve as the chaplain to all the military personnel in that group. It is therefore distinct from hospital chaplaincy, as it enables long-term relationships between caregivers and careseekers. The military, therefore, also provides its own training in the form of officer candidate school for chaplains, once the other requirements have been met.

College and university chaplaincy in the United States is similar to military chaplaincy in that it enables long-term relationships between caregivers and careseekers and often works with young adult populations (aged eighteen to twenty-five). College chaplaincy is grounded in departments dedicated to religious or spiritual life on campus. The role of these departments and the models they follow depends a great deal on the institution. Not all institutions have such an office nor do all support the activities of chaplains on campus. Those that do tend to fall into three broad camps, not all of which support Buddhist chaplains. The first type of institution is the religiously founded private school that retains campus chaplains primarily, if not solely, from their own associated religious order. Excepting the small number of Buddhist universities discussed earlier, this frequently precludes Buddhist chaplains. The second type is the large public institution, which tends toward a hands-off approach to religion on campus. While many public institutions do have an office of religious life, they tend to employ a coordinator to liaise with external chaplains assigned to the campus and compensated by their various religious orders. Some large private institutions also use this model. Buddhists have yet to formally participate in this model of campus chaplaincy and do not assign compensated clergy or laypeople to campus ministry. The third type is the large, multi-religious institution that employs chaplains of various backgrounds to tend to the religious and spiritual needs of its community. This model tends to be found only in the most financially secure private institutions. In this case, some universities have hired Buddhist chaplains to serve as staff or even department directors.[53]

In all three instances, Buddhists may also provide spiritual care to college campuses on a voluntary basis; they are more commonly found at larger institutions in coastal or urban areas. Their level of welcome is determined by the orientation of the department and the perceived number and need of Buddhist students on campus. As volunteers, they may be members of the local community, or, more commonly, faculty or staff of the institution employed in another capacity. In either case, their training in the field of chaplaincy, as a profession, is often limited. Most have received training in Buddhist meditation, ritual, and doctrine through their Buddhist community. Those working in higher education may also have some training in student development theory or pedagogy, depending on their discipline. They may also possess a graduate education in religion, philosophy, or education, though rarely a Master of Divinity or equivalent common to professional chaplains in other settings (e.g., hospitals or the military).[54] Their most common activities as volunteers include teaching and leading meditation, advising student clubs, leading rituals (if so trained), and providing spiritual care or mentorship primarily to students.

Chaplains employed by the institution, Buddhists included, tend to have a higher level of professionalization and may also be tasked with providing spiritual care and ethical leadership to the institution as a whole, including faculty and staff, along with other administrative tasks. Professional chaplains are also more likely to provide interfaith care and interreligious programming, whereas volunteer Buddhist chaplains tend to look after the spiritual needs of Buddhist students and staff almost exclusively. There are currently no statistics available on the numbers of Buddhist chaplains, whether volunteer or employed, working in higher education in North America.

In the past two decades, Buddhist engagement in addiction recovery has grown through the publication of many books and the founding of various Buddhist-based addiction recovery programs, such as Refuge Recovery and the Buddhist Recovery Network.[55] In many locations, local temples and sanghas host recovery groups utilizing twelve-step or other recovery models. The Grand Rapids Buddhist Temple (Michigan) is an example of an extensive program for recovery services run by volunteers in spiritual care, though it may not be formal chaplaincy. The temple's program began to have such success as a non-Christian-based option in the city that it expanded to offer different programs on four days per week at two different locations. They re-wrote the "twelve steps" from a Buddhist perspective but invite anyone to participate. Meetings include sūtra readings, *gathas*, and group speaking and feedback sessions, though different days and times have slight differences in programming. One evening places a particular emphasis on the eightfold path and takes inspiration from the book, *Refuge Recovery*, by Noah Levine.[56] Ministers at the temple are also available for more specific and detailed one-on-one meetings.[57]

At least one trained Buddhist chaplain, Joseph Rogers, is working at a Refuge Recovery center in Los Angeles, CA, and there is a growing interest in addiction recovery among chaplains-in-training. Most professional Buddhist chaplains receive a cursory education in addiction and recovery during graduate coursework and many encounter addiction in care-seekers and families in various contexts, even when not working in addiction recovery centers. Many Buddhist prison chaplains often also specifically deal with addiction recovery or lead addiction recovery groups. These chaplains may utilize Mindfulness Based Relapse Prevention methods, which are similar to Mindfulness Based Cognitive Therapy and Mindfulness Based Stress Reduction techniques, or a host of other meditation-based techniques.[58] Addiction recovery is one area where there is significant overlap and dialogue between psychology and medicine, on the one hand, and Buddhist teaching and meditative techniques on the other.

Buddhist prison chaplaincy in the United States has a rather lengthy and influential history compared to its other forms of chaplaincy. Reverend Hogen Fujimoto began an inmate ministry in San Francisco during the early 1960s. A Texas inmate, known as Cruz, then wrote to him requesting his services, leading to a rather pivotal legal case for American prison chaplaincy as a whole (*Cruz v. Beto*). The prison had initially disallowed the inmate's communication. Yet in a case that went to the Supreme Court, they ruled in favor of the inmate in what is one of the foundational cases regarding inmates' religious freedoms. Prisons across the United States still sometimes struggle with cases of religious freedom, which affects the availability of Buddhist chaplains, but on the whole, there is a strong and growing presence of Buddhist chaplains in the prison system.

Most Buddhist prison chaplains in the United States are volunteers, but there are also several professionals. The Federal Bureau of Prisons requires its professional chaplains to have a Master of Divinity or the educational equivalent from a school accredited by the American Theological Schools (ATS), ordination or a similar ecclesiastic recognition, at least two years of experience in spiritual leadership, and the ability to provide services to people from various faith traditions. State system requirements have a variety of slight differences. Of all the Buddhist training programs, only the Institute of Buddhist Studies (as a member school of the Graduate Theological Union) and Harvard Divinity School are ATS accredited, making the requirements sometimes difficult for those seeking a Buddhist-based chaplaincy education.[59]

Volunteer Buddhist prison chaplains do not have nearly as strict requirements and make up one of the more extensive areas of US Buddhist chaplaincy. Numerous organizations have sprouted to help fulfill this work, including Zen Mountain Monastery's National Buddhist Prison Sangha, the Upaya Zen Center's Prison Outreach Program, Kobutsu Malone's Engaged Zen Foundation, Fleet Maull's Prison Dharma Network, and Venerable De Hong's Engaged Buddhist Alliance. Visits from Buddhist prison chaplains have grown in popularity among Buddhist and non-Buddhist inmates alike for their meditation courses.[60]

Buddhist chaplains can be found in other sectors in North America, including police departments, social services, and the nonprofit sector. However, these tend to constitute only a handful of individuals, sometimes one or two, and there is little to no documentation of their work as of this writing. The sectors summarized above tend to be the most common places to find Buddhist chaplains and are also the most familiar with Buddhist chaplains on an institutional basis.

Thailand. Thailand probably has the oldest established form of modern Buddhist chaplaincy, although it has always been primarily limited to the military. It is not known when the position began in the Thai military, but it is thought to date back to the time of King Rama V (r. 1868–1910), who was likely influenced by the chaplains he encountered in the British military. The vast majority of the Thai population is Buddhist, but all military chaplains are Buddhist. The first officially appointed chaplain was Yu Udomslip (1880–?). He was dispatched by King Rama VI (r. 1910–1925) during World War I and then travelled with Thailand's 1,250 soldiers stationed in Europe.[61]

The word now used for chaplain in Thailand is *anusasanachan*. Thailand requires chaplains to have experience as an ordained monk, and because women are excluded from such ranks, they are also excluded from chaplaincy positions. Chaplains must also pass level IX in Pali exams (a high and difficult exam that few monks can pass) or pass level V Pali and graduate from either Mahachulalongkorn University or Mahamakut University, Thailand's two most well-known Buddhist universities.[62] Chaplain candidates must also be citizens of Thailand, have parents who are both citizens of Thailand, be between the ages of twenty-five and thirty-five at the time of their appointment, have a clean criminal record, and pass a physicalexamination.[63]

Chaplains must disrobe before beginning their chaplaincy training, because Thai Buddhist tradition does not allow monks to have extended military contact nor receive wages or hold a gun. Chaplains must participate in the four-week basic training alongside all other military personnel. However, chaplains then complete an extra 525 hours (fifteen-week) course that includes: training in public speaking, how to teach in various settings, boosting morale, basic rites and rituals, and fundamental counseling skills. Chaplains are also bound by a special code of conduct, which resembles Buddhist monastic precepts in many ways. However, as Chaplain Somya Malasri stated, the 21st century has seen the Thai chaplain corps relax some of the rules. For example, the rules prohibit dancing, but chaplains are no longer expected to follow such an ordinance.[64] Despite the fact that all chaplains are Buddhist, they are trained not to proselytize.

The four main duties of Thai military chaplains are: providing dharma talks to soldiers and their families; visiting soldiers in hospitals and prisons; providing guidance to soldiers and their families during difficult times; and educating soldiers and their families in Buddhism, ethics, and morality. Chaplains are present throughout all three divisions of the Thai military: army, navy, and air force. The chaplaincy corps continues to evolve and in May 2018 began to sponsor cooperative training sessions and exchanges with US military chaplains. They are also exploring potential ways to begin incorporating women into their chaplaincy corps.[65]

Vietnam. Vietnamese served as Buddhist chaplains during the Vietnam War. They were requested by soldiers in the Vietnamese Army in 1963, and the request was fulfilled by 1964. In 1968, the military's Buddhist Chaplain Directorate even commissioned a volume on their service by Pham-Quang-Hao, entitled *The Buddhist Chaplain Branch of the Republic of Vietnam Armed Forces*. However, after the end of the war and the departure of the United States, military chaplaincy in Vietnam faded as well. Some of the Buddhist military chaplains, though, escaped to the United States and fulfilled a variety of chaplaincy roles there.[66]

South Korea. The Korean Peninsula has had military chaplains dating back to the Korean War. At first, only Korean Christians joined the military ranks as chaplains. By the Vietnam War, however, Buddhists petitioned the government to become chaplains as well. They referred to the creation of Vietnamese and Thai Buddhist chaplaincy to help further their request.[67] The proposal was approved and Buddhist chaplains began serving around 1968.

Current chaplaincy requirements in Korea are far different from those in the United States or Japan, with less emphasis on postgraduate education and far more emphasis on monastic training. Most Buddhist chaplains declare their intent during their second year of undergraduate school and begin taking courses during their bachelor's degree in psychology and counseling along with classes in Buddhist studies. After graduation, they are expected to be monastics for five years before gaining a chaplaincy post.

Buddhist chaplains make up a significant part of the Korean military chaplain corps but are still a minority within the system. The number of Buddhist chaplains is approximately equal to the Catholic chaplains, but both of these groups together do not equal half the Protestant chaplains. Like other Korean chaplains, Buddhists may rise to the rank of colonel. The contemporary Korean military typically has about six or seven Buddhist chaplains at this highest rank and Buddhist chaplains fill out ranks in the army, navy, and air force. All military chaplains are paid positions and filled almost completely by the Jogye order.[68]

Paid positions for Buddhist chaplains are fairly common through all levels of education in Korea. Many high school Buddhist chaplains are former military chaplains. Nearly all are monastics. (Korean military chaplains, unlike their Thai brethren, do not disrobe during military service.)[69] Requirements differ depending on the job, but graduate degrees in Buddhist studies are common among Buddhist chaplains, some having received doctorates. University chaplains have existed in some capacity for the past century, but the position has evolved over the recent decades to align more with a contemporary professional chaplain model.[70]

Japan. Japan is another example of an area developing systematic training in Buddhist chaplaincy. Some Buddhist care associations began to form in Japan throughout the late 19th and 20th centuries in military, prison, and healthcare chaplaincy, though their participation was either small or short-lived. "Spiritual care" then entered the Japanese vocabulary in 1997, but its practices only began to blossom shortly after the tragic tsunami of 2011. Christian, Buddhist, and Shinto clergy all volunteered in organized efforts to help people deal with the psychological and spiritual consequences of the disaster, but the efforts were led primarily by Buddhists. The brief training programs set up for clergy soon turned into full programs at Buddhist universities across the country, and existing programs were steadily expanded. Within a relatively short period of time, eight university programs across Japan have sprouted to fill a deep social need, along with programs in hospices and other care facilities. Of these eight universities, six are Buddhist universities, one is a public university whose program is led by a Buddhist priest, and one is a Catholic university program.[71]

Licensing for chaplains in Japan only began in 2016, so changes and more formalization are likely in coming years. University education is not required, but CPE programs are compulsory. Compared to North American programs, the ones in Japan are short, due to the lack of professional jobs. Paid opportunities are expanding but still rare, and most chaplains are volunteers. Some CPE programs run a few months in length, but most are less than a week, often occurring over the weekend, so that people with other jobs may participate. Participants often volunteer individually at a hospice or hospital while occasionally travelling to join a CPE meeting for further instruction and reviewing case studies with an instructor. Chaplains who complete the certification process in Japan are sometimes known by a Japanese transliteration of the word chaplain (*chappuren*) but more commonly identified as *rinshōshūkyōshi*, literally meaning "clinical clergy."

The Shingon priest Ōshita Daien is one Buddhist who helped break barriers in Japanese hospitals themselves during the 1990s. He became certified in music therapy and was hired by area clinics as a psychological consultant. After gaining experience, he and a few Japanese Buddhists who trained in chaplaincy programs in the United States helped train others, and an increasing number of hospitals are taking in chaplains or "clinical clergy." The Jōdō Shinshū priest Yozo Taniyama has played an integral role since the 2011 disaster in helping to establish the Society for Interfaith Chaplaincy in Japan, regulate their training, and coordinate work from his department at Tohoku University in Sendai, Japan. The rise of other related organizations like the Japan Association for Buddhist Nursing and Vihara Studies and the Japan Society of Spiritual Care are helping to spread and normalize Buddhist chaplaincy efforts within Japanese healthcare facilities.

Buddhist chaplaincy in Japan is centered almost exclusively on healthcare. Several Buddhist priests began serving hospitals during the 1990s, but only in the 2010s did the practice begin significant expansion. Several Buddhist hospices were also established, especially due to the efforts of the Jōdō Shinshū tradition. Some of the earliest contemporary Buddhist caregiving work in Japan was initiated by Rev. Masahi Tamiya, an Otani branch Jōdō Shinshū priest. He respected the hospice work of Christians in Japan but desired a Buddhist version and coined the term *bihara* (a Japanese rendering of "*vihāra*") as a specifically Buddhist option. *Vihāra* is a Sanskrit word traditionally used to refer to temples in Buddhism but literally means a "place of rest." Furthermore, they were historically also used to house and care for the dying. Tamiya began promoting *bihara* activities as a movement in 1985. The other main branch of Jodo Shinshu then began similar activities the following year. Nichiren Buddhism followed in 1994.[72]

The earliest activities of the movement were simply volunteers in local temples or visiting and supporting others, but in 1993 the first officially certified Buddhist hospice, a non-denominational center, opened in Niigata. A second opened in 2004, sponsored by Rissho Kosei-kai. As of 2010, however, these represented an extremely small portion of the 208 mostly Christian-sponsored licensed hospices in Japan.[73] Considering less than 1 percent of the Japanese population is Christian and most Japanese prefer to have a Buddhist funeral, this is quite an incredible statistical discrepancy. Since 2010, other officially licensed *bihara* have opened in Kyoto and Gifu, among unofficial centers elsewhere in Japan.

Taiwan. Taiwan had numerous Christian hospice programs by the 1990s, but despite having a nearly 80 percent Buddhist population, no Buddhists had developed formal training until the Clinical Buddhist Chaplaincy (CBC) Training Program was founded in 1994.[74] It still took a few years to develop into a viable program but began to receive input from multiple sources. It was started by the Buddhist Lotus Hospice Care Foundation (BLHCF) in cooperation with the Palliative Care Unit of National Taiwan University Hospital. The initial spearhead, Professor Ching-Yu Chen, was joined by Venerable Huimin from Dharma Drum Mountain and they subsequently helped lead CBC for years thereafter. CBC focuses primarily on hospice chaplaincy, calling their work "clinical Buddhism." They define it and summarize its scope as follows: "clinical Buddhism is the contemporary excellence of integrated medicine with the Buddha's teachings for end-of-life care. This work covers six areas: (1) end-of-life suffering, (2) death preparation, (3) life meanings and affirmation, (4) clinical practice of the Buddhadharma, (5) fear of death, and (6) spiritual and life education."[75]

Their training requires 62.5 hours of coursework and 80 hours of internship within a hospice ward. The coursework includes studying the history of hospice work, cancer and other common medical conditions of terminally ill patients, methods to identify psychosocial and spiritual needs, and grief care, as well as an overview of potential ethical and legal issues. After the coursework and internship, candidates must still complete six hundred hours of residency training and a test before they are eligible for certification. Even certified chaplains are required to continue their education thereafter, meeting annually with senior teachers.[76]

Their primary model of patient treatment is based on the four noble truths and follows four stages: "truth-telling," accepting death, experiencing spirituality, and deepening Buddhist practices in preparation for liberation. As of May, 2017, CBC had certified sixty-three chaplains who have served in forty-four different hospices.[77]

United Kingdom. According to the UK Board of Healthcare Chaplaincy (UKBHC), chaplains must "have a qualification relevant to their faith community or belief group and a postgraduate qualification in Healthcare Chaplaincy such as a PG [postgraduate] Certificate in Healthcare Chaplaincy."[78] They list several graduate-level chaplaincy training programs, none specifically for Buddhist chaplains. The only Buddhist chaplaincy training program is a seven-session course (over three days) offered by The Buddhist Society as recently as 2017.[79] Buddhist chaplains can be "accredited" through the UKHBC by presenting a portfolio of evidence documenting experience, training, skills, and knowledge in relation to their seven standards, providing references, and undergoing an interview process. This is not dissimilar from the US process of becoming board certified. Keith Munnings, chairman of the Buddhist Healthcare Chaplaincy Group, the main Buddhist endorsing body in the United Kingdom, notes that while "no one clear entry route and career pathway exists," Buddhist chaplains in the United Kingdom nevertheless "find themselves delivering high quality pastoral services, akin to their paid colleagues, and working to the same professional standards," including both graduate-level education and training from within their particular traditions.[80] Despite this assertion, most Buddhist chaplains in the United Kingdom are volunteers and, as such, their level of training tends to vary broadly based on their individual backgrounds.

Buddhist chaplaincy in the United Kingdom is primarily volunteer across most sectors. The United Kingdom tends to follow a coreligionist model for chaplaincy (i.e., Buddhists caring for Buddhists) rather than the interfaith model (i.e., Buddhist chaplains caring for all) that is more common in the United States. This has resulted in little call for paid positions for Buddhist chaplains within the highest employment sector for spiritual care services, the National Health Service (NHS). Nevertheless, the mandate to provide spiritual care to all who request it has resulted in coordination of care between Buddhist communities and the NHS, according to Munnings.[81]

The first civilian Buddhist chaplain was appointed to the UK military in 2005.[82] This chaplain serves as an advisor to the Ministry of Defense and all three military branches. A 2010 blog noted that they also specifically served the needs of Gurkhas, or soldiers from Nepal serving in the British military, many of whom are Buddhist.[83] Correspondence with Father Paschal Hanrahan in the Royal Army revealed that there are no uniformed and commissioned Buddhist chaplains in the UK military and that UK Buddhist communities have stated a preference for civilian chaplains to serve the needs of UK soldiers, sailors, and airmen.[84] Despite requests, no information was provided as to how one might become a civilian chaplain to the military in the United Kingdom, though Father Hanrahan did indicate that endorsement seemed to be the largest hurdle and that the Ministry of Defense was working to develop review panels for "world religions" chaplains (i.e., non–Church of England).[85]

Buddhist prison chaplaincy in the United Kingdom has been provided by the Angulimala organization for over thirty years. This organization provides a "job description" for Buddhist prison chaplains, training and resources, and liaises with the Ministry of Justice to provide the services of Buddhist chaplains to prisoners who request them.[86] The organization's name, Aṅgulimāla, is taken from a popular scripture in which the Buddha encountered and pacified the mass-murderer Aṅgulimāla (literally meaning "necklace of fingers"), who then became his disciple and was later awakened.[87] This name represents the organization's vision that criminals can transform their minds and deeds and become worthy members of society.

Australia and New Zealand. A Buddhist chaplaincy presence has been slowly manifesting throughout Australia over the past two decades. Buddhist chaplains are still a small minority, and most chaplain positions in Australia are volunteer rather than paid, which might also hinder development. Yet there are a few training programs present in early stages of formation. Australia requires its chaplains to complete a ten-week full-time or twenty-week part-time CPE, along with some coursework at an accredited institution. Sydney and Melbourne both have accredited programs running to facilitate training Buddhist chaplains. Queensland has a training course founded in 2014 and is aiming to develop into an accredited program. Nan Tien Institute in Wollongong is also beginning Australia's first accredited Buddhist ministry program that will include elements of chaplaincy training.

Likewise, in New Zealand, Buddhist chaplaincy is taking root within a society that recognizes the profession, but only began including Buddhists among the ranks of spiritual caregivers in the last decade. Starting in Buddhist hospice centers and expanding to hospitals and nursing homes, around two dozen Buddhist chaplains serve careseekers in New Zealand.[88] There is one local training program for Buddhist chaplains in New Zealand via the Amitābha Hospice Service, which involves three levels of weekend trainings.[89] While invaluable to providing trained hospice volunteers, this falls far short of the standards expected of professional chaplains in New Zealand, which includes graduate-level theological education and supervised CPE.

Australian and New Zealand higher education tends to follow similar approaches to campus chaplaincy as the United States, primarily through the second or third models described in the section on North America, as most universities are large and public. At least one Buddhist is serving in such a post at the Australian National University.[90] Having attended chaplaincy conferences in Australia and with New Zealand chaplains, the structure would not preclude more Buddhists serving in this capacity.

However, in addition to colleges and universities, numerous public primary and secondary schools include multifaith chaplaincy centers in Australia, making school chaplaincy one of the more common forms of chaplaincy to see a Buddhist in Australia. They provide pastoral care services and other forms of spiritual support on campuses, such as leading ceremonies and organizing discussion groups. The Buddhist chaplains and the careseekers they support come from a wide range of cultural and belief backgrounds, requiring chaplains to be open to a diverse range of students, even among the Buddhists.

Other Areas. The ability of the authors to fully investigate Buddhist chaplaincy worldwide was necessarily limited by language barriers. It is likely that Buddhist chaplains are practicing spiritual care throughout the world, including other areas of Asia, Europe, South America, and Africa. This is due in part to a broad diaspora of East and Southeast Asians, particularly ethnic Chinese and Vietnamese, and also due to the growth of Buddhism among non-Asian populations through books, the Internet, and contact with Asian Buddhists.

In these areas, Buddhists are fully engaged in providing spiritual care to their communities, but it is not necessarily chaplaincy in the professional sense of the term. As stated at the beginning of the article, in order to meet the basic definition of chaplaincy, there should be (1) some level of formal training and professional competencies and (2) the spiritual care is provided in an institutional setting other than the religious community, such as a hospital or school. Some locations not covered in this short summary may indeed meet this definition and should be added to this article in the future.

CONCLUSIONS AND TRENDS

Buddhist chaplaincy is a relatively new and rapidly changing movement occurring within a broad spectrum of the Buddhist world. The Christian origins of terms, techniques, and organizational structures continue to influence the ways it develops, yet Buddhist influence and adaptations are also clear. In countries such as England, Australia, Canada, and the United States, where chaplaincy was previously institutionalized, Buddhists are still working their way into the existent systems alongside other non-Christian traditions. The professionalized standards and multifaith emphases within them do not lead to major differences between chaplains of different traditions in most work settings. Yet, even in these countries, Buddhists have their own styles and patterns that they practice for themselves and contribute to the field as a whole. Standards within the profession are changing to accommodate Buddhists and other religions as societies themselves grow more diverse. Moreover, professional associations and institutions began including Buddhist chaplains in those discussions. In Asian countries with larger Buddhist populations and longer Buddhist histories, there are still influences from the terminology and practices that reflect chaplaincy's Christian origins. Nevertheless, the demographic dominance of Buddhism in most of those regions allowed for greater emphasis on traditional forms of Buddhist training, especially as seen in the cases of Thailand and South Korea.

The 21st century is likely to see continued shifts and developments in Buddhist chaplaincy as chaplains from the array of cultures, traditions, and nations correspond through conferences, literature, and other modes of communication. Buddhists continue to wrestle with the language of chaplaincy's Christian inheritance. Buddhists continue to develop their own literature on these topics, which will allow for a more thorough analysis and comparison of Buddhist, Christian, and other approaches to chaplaincy and spiritual care. Legal and policy adjustments continue to affect the professional landscapes. But on the whole, the 21st century seems poised to witness continued growth in this field, in the sheer number of practitioners and the academic research both for and about Buddhist chaplains.

REVIEW OF LITERATURE

Buddhist chaplaincy, especially as a field with professional training, is still very new and developing. Thus, little scholarship exists analyzing its movements. Even literature for Buddhist chaplains to support their training is thin. Buddhist chaplains training in the West rely heavily on Christian materials. Only three books on the topic exist. The first is Cheryl Giles and Willa Miller's 2012 anthology, *The Arts of Contemplative Care: Pioneering Voices in Buddhist Chaplaincy and Pastoral Work*. The authors, mostly faculty, students, and alumni of Harvard Divinity School's (HDS) Buddhist Ministry Program, offer some of the only analyses of Buddhist chaplaincy in the West from academic perspectives, though even this volume is split between emic and etic articles, containing both analysis of different parts of the field along with theological and soteriological chapters that present new theories for chaplains.[91] The second book on the topic is *Benefit Beings!: The Buddhist Guide to Professional Chaplaincy* by Daniel Clarkson Fisher. Originally written as a doctoral dissertation at the same time as *The Arts of Contemplative Care*, it was then self-published one year later, in 2013.[92] This work focuses on an overview of the history and contexts for Buddhist chaplaincy in North America. The third book, *A Thousand Hands: A Guidebook for Caring for Your Buddhist Community*, edited by Nathan Jishin Michon and Daniel Clarkson Fisher, is another anthology and was published in 2016.[93] This book serves as a resource to Buddhist chaplains and covers a variety of skills and topics.

The remainder of the literature in this field consists of chapters within multifaith anthologies, journal articles, and a number of recent dissertations and theses. Two notable chapters include Mikel Monnet's chapter in *Injustice and the Care of Souls* and Daniel Clarkson Fisher's chapter in *Multifaith Views of Spiritual Care*, which are books about spiritual care in general.[94] A 2017 volume entitled *Military Chaplaincy in an Era of Religious Pluralism* included four chapters related to Buddhist military chaplaincy in different parts of the world.[95] Other chapters tend to appear in anthologies with a more topical focus, such as death and dying, prayer, chronic illness, and palliative care, for example. Likewise, journal articles on Buddhist spiritual care often take a topical focus and appear in journals related to medicine, nursing, and, rarely, pastoral care.

A strong secondary literature of topical books written from the Buddhist perspective but aimed at general audiences exists. One such example is *Buddhist Care for the Dying and Bereaved*, edited by Jonathan Watts and Yoshiharu Tomatsu, which is focused specifically on palliative care and grief care and offers chapters on several different areas of the Buddhist world.[96] Several pioneering teachers in the realm of Buddhist chaplaincy, such as Bernie Glassman, Joan Halifax, and Kosho Paley Ellison, while training new generations of Buddhist chaplains, have produced books for general audiences on topics such as death and dying, Zen practice, and other Buddhist teachings. Likewise, there is a host of Buddhist literature on topics relevant to chaplaincy, though not specifically written for chaplains or with advice specifically for caregivers. However, this literature can be useful to Buddhist chaplains and, in the future, will form the much-needed basis for a Buddhist field of "pastoral and spiritual care."

FURTHER READING

Association for Clinical Pastoral Education, Inc. "APCE Standards and Manuals: A Standard for Spiritual Care and Education", 2016, http://www.manula.com/manuals/acpe/acpe-manuals/2016/en/topic/cover-page.

Association of Professional Chaplains. "Common Standards for Professional Chaplaincy". http://www.professionalchaplains.org/files/professional_standards/common_standards/common_standards_professional_chaplaincy.pdf.

Board of Chaplaincy Certification, Inc. "BCCI Certification". http://bcci.professionalchaplains.org/content.asp?pl=25&contentid=25.

Bilotti-Stark, Kathryn. "Compassionate Awareness and Transformation: The Relevancy of Mindfulness Teachings and Practices in Chaplaincy and Spiritual Care." MA diss., Graduate Theological Union, 2012.

Clarke, Stephen. "Kalamitra: A Buddhist Approach to Pastoral Counseling." In *Understanding Pastoral Counseling*. Edited by Elizabeth A. Maynard and Jill L. Snodgrass, 275–289. New York: Springer, 2015.

Ellison, Koshin Paley, and Matt Weingast, eds. *Awake at the Bedside: Contemplative Teachings on Palliative and End-of-Life Care*. Somerville, MA: Wisdom Publications, 2016.

Fisher, Rev. Danny. *Benefit Beings!: The Buddhist Guide to Professional Chaplaincy*. USA: Off the Cushion Books, 2013.

Giles, Cheryl A., and Willa B. Miller, eds. *The Arts of Contemplative Care: Pioneering Voices in Buddhist Chaplaincy and Pastoral Work*. Boston: Wisdom Publications, 2012.

Halifax, Joan. *Being with Dying: Cultivating Compassion and Fearlessness in the Presence of Death*. Boston, MA: Shambhala Publications, Inc., 2008.

Kilts, Thomas. "A Vajrayana Buddhist Perspective on Ministry Training." *The Journal of Pastoral Care & Counseling* 62, no. 3 (Fall 2008): 273–281.

Kramer, Betty J. "Buddhist Perspectives on End-of-Life Care." In *Living with Grief: Spirituality and End-Of-Life Care*. Edited by Kenneth J. Doka and Amy S. Tucci. Washington, DC: Hospice Foundation of America, 2011.

Levine, Noah. *Refuge Recovery: A Buddhist Path to Recovering from Addiction*. San Francisco: HarperOne, 2014.

Malone, Kobutsu. *Prison Chaplaincy Guidelines for Zen Buddhism: A Source Book for Prison Chaplains, Administrators, and Security Personnel*. Sedgewick, ME: Engaged Zen Foundation, 2006.

McGrath, Pam. "Buddhist Spirituality: A Compassionate Perspective on Hospice Care." *Mortality* 3, no. 3 (1998): 251–263.

Michon, Nathan Jishin, and Daniel Fisher, eds. *A Thousand Hands: A Guidebook to Caring for Your Buddhist Community*. Richmond Hill: Sumeru Press, 2016.

Monnett, Mikel. "Developing a Buddhist Approach to Pastoral Care: A Peacemaker's View." In *Injustice and the Care of Souls: Taking Oppression Seriously in Pastoral Care*. Edited by Sheryl A. Kujawa-Holbrook and Karen Brown Montagno, 125–131. Minneapolis: Fortress Press, 2009.

Munnings, Keith, and Madeleine Parkes. "Care of a Buddhist Child and Their Family." In *Multifaith Care for Sick and Dying Children and Their Families: A Multi-Disciplinary Guide*. Edited by Paul Nash, Madeleine Parkes, and Zamir Hussain, 32–54. London: Jessica Kingsley, 2015.

Smith-Penniman, Adele. "Buddhist Resources in Pastoral Care." DMin diss., Andover Newton Theological School, 2006.

Unno, Mark. *Buddhism and Psychotherapy across Cultures: Essays on Theories and Practices*. Somerville, MA: Wisdom Publications, 2006.

Watts, Jonathan S., and Yoshiharu Tomatsu. *Buddhist Care for the Dying and Bereaved*. Boston: Wisdom Publications, 2012.

NOTES

1. Rodney J. Hunter, ed., *The Dictionary of Pastoral Care and Counseling* (Nashville: Abingdon Press, 2005).
2. It should be noted that the terms chaplaincy, spiritual care, and Buddhist chaplaincy do not have an entirely consistent usage, as is normal for developing and changing fields. The definitions provided here represent how the terms are employed a majority of the time as of this writing. But there are instances when "chaplaincy," for example, is used as a direct synonym to spiritual care and, as discussed later in the article, small shifts in meaning that occur when the terms are adapted into different cultures and other languages.
3. Jennifer Block, "Toward a Definition of Buddhist Chaplaincy," in *The Arts of Contemplative Care: Pioneering Voices in Buddhist Chaplaincy and Pastoral Work*, ed. Cheryl A. Giles and Willa B. Miller (Boston: Wisdom Publications, 2012), 3–7.
4. Block, "Toward a Definition," 4.
5. Block, "Toward a Definition," 3–7.
6. Cheryl A. Giles and Willa Miller, eds., *The Arts of Contemplative Care: Pioneering Voices in Buddhist Chaplaincy and Pastoral Work* (Boston: Wisdom Publications, 2012), xvii.
7. Monica Sanford, "The Practice of Dharma Reflection among Buddhist Chaplains: A Qualitative Study of "Theological" Activity among Nontheocentric Spiritual Caregivers" (PhD diss., Claremont School of Theology, 2018), 168–169.

8. David McMahan, *The Making of Buddhist Modernism* (New York: Oxford University Press, 2008), 40.
9. There is little consistency in the application of these terms within the chaplaincy literature, and this article will not attempt to resolve the debate. Pastoral care can sometimes refer to care within congregations but can also be found in reference to care provided within institutions. Spiritual care is becoming more popular, but in some literature also refers exclusively to care provided in healthcare settings. Suffice to say they shall be used interchangeably throughout this article.
10. Howard John Clinebell, *Basic Types of Pastoral Care & Counseling: Resources for the Ministry of Healing and Growth* (Nashville: Abingdon Press, 1984), 25–26.
11. Clinebell, *Basic Types*, 466.
12. For an explanation of unconditional positive regard and the work of Carl Rogers in relation to pastoral care, see Howard Clinebell and Bridget Clare McKeever, *Basic Types of Pastoral Care and Counseling*, 3rd ed. (Nashville: Abingdon, 2011), 466. For evidence of unconditional positive regard in Buddhist chaplains, see Sanford, "The Practice of Dharma Reflection," 177–178.
13. Sanford, "The Practice of Dharma Reflection," 177–179.
14. See Robert E. Buswell Jr. and Donald S. Lopez Jr., eds., *The Princeton Dictionary of Buddhism* (Princeton, NJ: Princeton University Press, 2013), s.v. "samyaksaṃkalpa," 764.
15. Buswell and Lopez, *The Princeton Dictionary of Buddhism*, s.v. "samyakkarmānta," 763.
16. Right Intention and Right Action are two aspects of the Noble Eightfold Path, which makes up the Fourth Noble Truth, the truth of the path to freedom from suffering, generally recognized by all Buddhist traditions as part of the Buddha's first sermon following his enlightenment.
17. See, for example, Sanford, "The Practice of Dharma Reflection," 206–207; Willard W. C. Ashley, "Counseling and Interventions," in *Professional Spiritual & Pastoral Care: A Practical Clergy and Chaplain's Handbook*, ed. Stephen B. Roberts (Woodstock, VT: SkyLight Paths, 2012), 124–130; and Dayle A. Freidman, "Introduction," in *Jewish Pastoral Care: A Practical Handbook from Traditional & Contemporary Sources*, 2nd ed., ed. Dayle A. Freidman (Woodstock, VT: Jewish Lights, 2013), xx; and Clinebell and McKeever, *Basic Types of Pastoral Care*, 100.
18. *The American Heritage(R) Dictionary of the English Language*, 6th ed., s.v. "compassion."
19. This interpretation is not shared among all Buddhist traditions but is an important distinction to make for chaplains. Were chaplains to fully share the suffering of careseekers in their trauma, grief, psychological pain, and physical death, they might quickly become overwhelmed. Good boundaries, physical and psychological, are essential for spiritual care. Furthermore, being unable to empathize with the situation of a careseeker that is beyond one's realm of experience does not prevent one from being able to help them and act with the intention to alleviate suffering.
20. Robert Chodo Campbell, "The Turning of the Dharma Wheel in Its Many Forms," in *The Arts of Contemplative Care: Pioneering Voices of Buddhist Chaplaincy and Pastoral Work*, ed. Cheryl A. Giles and Willa B. Miller (Boston: Wisdom Publications, 2012), 80.
21. Sanford, "The Practice of Dharma Reflection," 269.
22. Willa Miller, "Thus I Have Listened: A Reflection on Listening as Spiritual Care," in *The Arts of Contemplative Care: Pioneering Voices of Buddhist Chaplaincy and Pastoral Work*, ed. Cheryl A. Giles and Willa B. Miller (Boston: Wisdom Publications, 2012), 283.
23. Sanford, "The Practice of Dharma Reflection," 252–272.
24. Kristin Deleo, "Being a Compassionate Presence: The Contemplative Approach to End-of-Life Care," in *The Arts of Contemplative Care: Pioneering Voices of Buddhist Chaplaincy and Pastoral Work*, ed. Cheryl A. Giles and Willa B. Miller (Boston: Wisdom Publications, 2012), 244–251.
25. Barbara Eve Breitman, "Foundations of Jewish Pastoral Care: Skills and Techniques," in *Jewish Pastoral Care: A Practical Handbook from Traditional & Contemporary Sources*, 2nd ed., ed. Dayle A. Freidman (Woodstock, VT: Jewish Lights, 2013), 98–101.

26. Giles and Miller, *The Arts of Contemplative Care*; and Nathan Jishin Michon and Daniel Clarkson Fisher, eds., *A Thousand Hands: A Guidebook to Caring for Your Buddhist Community* (Richmond Hill: Sumeru Press, 2016).
27. Willa B. Miller, "Like an Elephant Pricked by a Thorn: Buddhist Meditation Instructions as a Door to Deep Listening," *Buddhist-Christian Studies* 35 (2015): 15–20.
28. Sanford, "The Practice of Dharma Reflection," 261–263.
29. Sanford, "The Practice of Dharma Reflection," 263.
30. For more on this topic, see the ninth chapter of the *Bodhicaryāvatāra* by Shantideva and the *Aṣṭasāhasrikā Prajñāpāramitā Sūtra* or "Perfection of Wisdom in 8,000 Lines" traditionally ascribed to the Buddha, though most scholars agree it was composed over one thousand years later.
31. Sanford, "The Practice of Dharma Reflection," 269, quoting from Interview 006, June 6, 2017.
32. Daijaku Kinst, "Cultivating an Appropriate Response: Educational Foundations for Buddhist Chaplains and Pastoral Caregivers," in *The Arts of Contemplative Care: Pioneering Voices of Buddhist Chaplaincy and Pastoral Work*, ed. Cheryl A. Giles and Willa B. Miller (Boston: Wisdom Publications, 2012), 9–16.
33. Giles and Miller, *The Arts of Contemplative Care*, 39–52.
34. Sanford, "The Practice of Dharma Reflection," 164–166.
35. Elaine L. Graham, Heather Walton, and Frances Ward, *Theological Reflection: Methods* (London: SCM Press, 2005), 5–6.
36. Graham, Walton, and Ward, *Theological Reflection*, 6.
37. This does not mean that Buddhists do not practice something akin to canonical narrative theology or that all Buddhist reflection is praxis or correlation based. It only means that some of these methods appeared in *The Arts of Contemplative Care* and others did not. As a single anthology, this is an admittedly very limited sample.
38. Many of these common situations are summarized in Michon and Fisher, *A Thousand Hands*, which consists of fifty short chapters providing overviews of various topics and competencies useful to Buddhist chaplains.
39. Kathryn Bilotti-Stark, "Compassionate Awareness and Transformation: The Relevancy of Mindfulness Teachings and Practices in Chaplaincy and Spiritual Care" (MA diss., Graduate Theological Union, 2012), 52–60.
40. Pam McGrath, "Buddhist Spirituality: A Compassionate Perspective on Hospice Care," *Mortality* 3, no. 3 (1998): 256–257.
41. Lee Lawrence and John Brinsfield, "Military Chaplains: A Historian's View from the American Revolution to Iraq". *The Christian Science Monitor*, October 30, 2007.
42. "Master of Pastoral Studies", Emmanuel College of Victoria University in the University of Toronto, 2018.
43. "Certification for Professional Spiritual Care: Common Qualifications and Competencies 2017." Association of Professional Chaplains, 2018.
44. "BCCI Certification Graduate Education Equivalency Worksheet", Board of Chaplaincy Certification Inc., April 13, 2017.
45. "Degree Program Standards", Association of Theological Schools: The Commission on Accrediting, June 2012. It is worth noting that while MDiv in Buddhist chaplaincy programs in North America follow these standards, Buddhist programs and schools are not eligible for accreditation via the Association of Theological Schools, which is an explicitly Christian and Jewish association. Nor are Buddhist programs and schools able to participate in the development or articulation of these standards, which are broadly applied to the profession of chaplaincy as a whole.
46. Association of Professional Chaplains, *Standards for Board Certified Chaplains and Associate Certified Chaplains* (Hoffman Estates, IL: Association of Professional Chaplains, 2016).
47. "ACPE Accredited Centers Directory" ACPE, April 13, 2018.

48. Sanford, "The Practice of Dharma Reflection," 105–106.
49. Buddhists were not the only religious tradition that had trouble meeting this requirement. Quakers, Muslims, humanists, and others all petitioned for its elimination. Association of Professional Chaplains, *Qualifications for Board Certified Chaplains and Associate Certified Chaplains* (Hoffman Estates, IL: Association of Professional Chaplains, 2017).
50. Doug Vardell, *Equivalency Issues for Buddhist Candidates for Board Certification through the Board of Chaplaincy Certification Inc.: A White Paper* (Hoffman Estates, IL: Board of Chaplaincy Certification, 2006). The author (not himself Buddhist) noted, "While these chaplains did not always agree with each other or with my recommendations, they graciously and kindly expressed their reasoning from their understanding and historical perspectives," though the paper did not detail the disagreements mentioned (p. 7).
51. For more information on Buddhist healthcare chaplaincy in the United States, see Danny Fisher, *Benefit Beings!: The Buddhist Guide to Professional Chaplaincy* (Off the Cushion Books, 2013), 41–120.
52. See Fisher, *Benefit Beings!*, 89–120.
53. See Harrison Blum at Emmerson College's Religious & Spiritual Life at Amherst College, and Monica Sanford at Rochester Institute of Technology's Spirituality and Religious Life office.
54. This type of training and education (or lack thereof) for campus chaplains is not unique to Buddhists. Campus chaplaincy among all religions tends to be less professionalized than other settings due to the traditional reluctance of universities to pass judgments on the standards of religious organizations. Instead, universities tend to accept the personnel assigned to them by the religious order, trusting that order has set suitable criteria, especially when these personnel are not employed by the institution. In cases where they are employed directly by the institution, a higher level of education, training, and professionalization is typical.
55. See Refuge Recovery. Accessed April 20, 2018; and Buddhist Recovery Network.
56. Noah Levine, *Refuge Recovery: A Buddhist Path to Recovering from Addiction* (San Francisco: HarperOne, 2014).
57. David Reese, interview with Nathan Jishin Michon, December 14, 2017.
58. "Mindfulness Based Relapse Prevention," Addictive Behaviors Research Center, University of Washington.
59. Buddhist universities are specifically disqualified from ATS accreditation due to the ATS bylaws that specifically include only Christian and Jewish schools for accreditation. See "Bylaws of the Association of Theological Schools," Association of Theological Schools, June 2014.
60. More information on US Buddhist prison chaplaincy is available in Fisher, *Benefit Beings!*, 121–138.
61. Michael Jerryson, "Pluralistic Permutations: The Thai Buddhist Military Chaplaincy," in *Military Chaplaincy in an Era of Religious Pluralism: Military-Religious Nexus in Asia, Europe, and USA*, ed. Torkel Brekke and Vladimir Tokhonov (New Delhi: Oxford, 2017), 153.
62. The 2017 article by Jerryson reported that only 3–5 percent of all Thai monks were able to pass level IX of the Pali exams, making it a very exclusive group. Jerryson, "Pluralistic Permutations," 157.
63. Somya Malasri, phone interview with Nathan Jishin Michon, May 20, 2018.
64. Malasri, phone interview.
65. Aroon Seeda, phone interview with Nathan Jishin Michon, May 20, 2018.
66. Hong Tran, interview with Nathan Jishin Michon, February 1, 2018.
67. Vladimir Tikhonov, "South Korean Military Chaplaincy in the 1950–70s: Religion as Ideology," in *Military Chaplaincy in an Era of Religious Pluralism: Military-Religious Nexus in Asia, Europe, and USA*, ed. Torkel Brekke and Vladimir Tokhonov (New Delhi: Oxford, 2017), 248.
68. Jongmae Park, phone interview with Nathan Jishin Michon, January 29, 2018.
69. This has led to the curious phenomena of a handful of former Thai monks re-ordaining in a Korean order so that they may remain monks and simultaneously serve in the US military as chaplains. This practice is no longer allowed unless the former Thai monk also gains US citizenship, a recent requirement for US military chaplains.

70. Park, phone interview.
71. The eight universities and their affiliation are as follows: Tohoku University (public), Aichigakuin University (Sōtō Zen), Kōyasan University (Shingon), Shuchi-in University (Shingon), Sophia University (Jesuit), Tsurumi University (Sōtō Zen), Musashino University (Jōdō Shinshu), and Ryukoku University (Jōdō Shinshu).
72. Yōzo Taniyama, "The Vihara Movement: Buddhist Chaplaincy and Social Welfare," in *Buddhist Care for the Dying and Bereaved*, ed. Jonathan S. Watts and Yoshiharu Tomatsu (Somerville, MA: Wisdom Publications, 2012), 78.
73. Taniyama, "The Vihara Movement," 78.
74. Jonathan S. Watts and Yoshiharu Tomatsu, "Taiwan: The Development of Indigenous Hospice Care and Clinical Buddhism," in *Buddhist Care for the Dying and Bereaved*, ed. Jonathan S. Watts and Yoshiharu Tomatsu (Somerville, MA: Wisdom Publications, 2012), 113.
75. Watts and Tomatsu, "Taiwan," 115.
76. Rong-Chi Chen, "Clinical Buddhist Chaplaincy Training Program: History of the Development of Taiwan's Clinical Buddhism," *Journal of Scientific Discovery* 1, no. 1 (2017): 3.
77. Chen, "Clinical Buddhist Chaplaincy," 3.
78. "Training & Education," UK Board of Healthcare Chaplaincy.
79. Buddhist Chaplaincy Healthcare Network.
80. Keith Munnings, personal correspondence via email with Monica Sanford, April 5, 2018.
81. Munnings, personal correspondence; and Buddhist Healthcare Chaplaincy Group.
82. BBC News, "Non-Christian Chaplains Appointed," October 19, 2005.
83. Jeanette Yuinen Shin, "UK Buddhist Chaplain to the Gurkas," *Buddhist Military Sangha* (blog), August 6, 2010.
84. Paschal Hanrahan, personal correspondence via email with Monica Sanford, April 6, 2018.
85. Hanrahan, personal correspondence.
86. Angulimala, the Buddhist Prison Chaplaincy.
87. Buswell and Lopez, *The Princeton Dictionary of Buddhism*, s.v. "Aṅgulimālīyasūtra," 46.
88. Ramsey Margolis, "Training Buddhist Chaplains," Secular Buddhism in Aotearoa New Zealand, January 18, 2017.
89. Notification about upcoming training on the Dorje Chang Institute website.
90. "Ven. Alex Bruce," ANU College of Law, Australian National University, Accessed November 28, 2019.
91. Giles and Miller, *The Arts of Contemplative Care*.
92. Fisher, *Benefit Beings!*
93. Michon and Fisher, *A Thousand Hands*. Danny Fisher and Daniel Clarkson Fisher are the same person. Rev. Dr. Fisher changed how he listed his name as an author and editor in later works.
94. Mikel Monnett, "Developing a Buddhist Approach to Pastoral Care: A Peacemaker's View," in *Injustice and the Care of Souls: Taking Oppression Seriously in Pastoral Care*, ed. Sheryl A. Kujawa-Holbrook and Karen Brown Montagno (Minneapolis: Fortress Press, 2009), 125–131; and Danny Fisher, "Three Yanas for Wise Caring: A Buddhist Perspective on Spiritual Care," in *Multifaith Views in Spiritual Care*, ed. Daniel S. Schipani (Kitchener: Pandora Press, 2013), 44–64.
95. Torkel Brekke and Vladimir Tokhonov, eds., *Military Chaplaincy in an Era of Religious Pluralism: Military-Religious Nexus in Asia, Europe, and USA* (New Delhi: Oxford, 2017).
96. Jonathan S. Watts and Yoshiharu Tomatsu, *Buddhist Care for the Dying and Bereaved* (Boston: Wisdom Publications, 2012).

Monica Sanford and Nathan Jishin Michon

BUDDHIST COSMOLOGY

THE PLACE OF COSMOLOGY IN BUDDHISM

Cosmology is fundamental to many aspects of Buddhism. Ideas about the universe form the basis for everything from the ethics of karma to procedures of ritual, structures of art and architecture, stages of meditation, and the final realization of awakening (*bodhi*, or enlightenment). In other words, Buddhist cosmology is not merely a speculative, scholastic endeavor but also a window onto deeply held beliefs and organizing principles that are regularly put into practice in everything from the daily lives of laypeople to the rituals of religious professionals and the political projects of rulers. Because of the way that Buddhism is presented in the modern day, often as a kind of philosophy or ethics divorced from cultural context, its cosmological ideas may seem incidental, but in fact they are foundational.[1]

Another challenge to understanding the significance of Buddhist cosmology is that it is not entirely characterizable in terms of any single system, model, or rational program. Rather, it is a broad domain of discourse about the contents, structures, and processes of the world. As such, within the overarching field of Buddhist cosmology, one can find several different cosmologies (or cosmological systems), such as the mutually contradictory worldviews of the abhidharma and Kālacakra traditions. Despite their conflicting logic and details, however, both may be accepted simultaneously, even by single individuals, as appropriate to different contexts.[2]

Even when authors, artists, ritualists, and patrons seem to be working within the same cosmological system, they often do so in disparate ways and in support of diverse agendas. For example, a tantric practitioner can construct a model of the universe to ritually develop their selfless generosity, while a ruler can build a temple in the shape of the same universe as a sign of personal wealth and authority (see examples of the mandala offering and Samye Monastery in the section "The Greater Relevance of Cosmology in Buddhist Traditions"). Understanding Buddhist cosmology, then, is about apprehending not just a Buddhist view of the world but also the connections of the world to widely varied topics of philosophy, art, and practice. Buddhist cosmological systems explicitly serve as conceptual frameworks for many different aspects of religion and culture.[3]

SOME COMMON FEATURES OF BUDDHIST COSMOLOGY

Given the complexity of Buddhist cosmology and its encompassment of diverse subjects including geography, astronomy, and metaphysics, this short encyclopedia article can only outline some considerations that are essential to understanding its details and significance. The main subject to be addressed is the most straightforward topic of Buddhist cosmology, the physical world as an organized universe. Buddhist views of the world can differ greatly, but there are many key features, terms, and concepts that appear relatively widely, so it is helpful to begin with a brief overview.

Perhaps the most widely known feature of Buddhist cosmology is an enormous mountain called Sumeru (also Meru, Sineru). This mountain sits at the center of a generally flat, disk-shaped world that is filled with oceans, continents, and smaller mountains. Some modern scholars understand Sumeru as an *axis mundi*, a hub of the horizontal cosmos that connects upper realms of heavens with lower realms of hells, but such simplified notions of cosmic structure can obscure the nuanced cosmological thinking of complex traditions.[4] Regardless, Sumeru is generally understood as the largest single object in the world, and as such it frequently serves as a basis for metaphors of enormity and strength.[5] Sumeru also provides dwelling places for many of the most important gods (*deva*) of the South Asian pantheon.

Another key feature of Buddhist worldviews is the island-continent Jambudvīpa, commonly understood as the local human realm. Jambudvīpa can be described quite differently, ranging from an enormous continent encircling Sumeru to, more often, a relatively small island in the far southern periphery of the vast world-ocean. Accounts of Jambudvīpa tend to emphasize the practical geography of rivers, valleys, mountains, and communities in a way that at least partially captures the real landscape of South Asia, where Buddhist cosmology first developed.[6] Jambudvīpa is also the location of the *vajrāsana*, the site where buddhas-to-be sit and become enlightened.[7] Three other major continents lie in the west, north, and east of the cosmos, reflecting a conceptual division of space into four quarters rather than actual continental geography. As descriptions of Jambudvīpa were transmitted across Asia, one natural concern for inhabitants of other regions was how their landscapes could fit into a Buddhist geography described mainly with South Asia in mind.[8]

Surrounding the great, circular ocean is a ring of mountains known as Cakravāla (also Cakravāḍa), which forms the external boundary of the world. The disk-shaped earth that supports all these oceans, continents, and mountains floats atop decreasingly substantial layers of fundamental elements (earth, water, sometimes fire, and wind) that ultimately float in the void of space. Most traditions acknowledge a multiplicity of such single world-systems (*loka-dhātu*), often abutting one another horizontally and sometimes also layered vertically. Groups of thousands, millions, and billions of such worlds play important roles in metaphors for vastness and innumerability. When described in such collections, each world typically has the same basic geographical features, including its own Sumeru, four major continents, great ocean, and so on, making this a generic model for all worlds in Buddhist cosmology.[9] In other cases, however, alternative worlds are described with quite different landscapes to emphasize specific contrasts with this world (see the section "Mahāyāna and East Asia").

Within each single world-system that follows the generic pattern, there are also numerous heavens and hells above and below the relatively flat surface of the world. While the heavens generally rise directly above Sumeru, the hells may descend—depending on the tradition—centrally below Sumeru, peripherally below southern Jambudvīpa, broadly filling all of the elemental layers below the entire cosmos, or even externally in the deltoid interstices between adjacent discoid worlds.[10] Based on these layers above and below the surface of the earth, many cosmological systems also propose vertical divisions of space, most commonly distinguishing the more-or-less geographical realm of the earth, hells, and lower heavens (*kāma-dhātu*, realm of desire) from more ethereal realms of form (*rūpa-dhātu*) and formlessness (*ārūpya-dhātu*) above. Within a single world-system, day and night are caused by the sun's orbit around Sumeru, which temporarily creates the shadow of night for beings dwelling in the peripheral continents (in astronomical terms, a kind of geocentrism). Seasons are caused by changes in the sun's path throughout the year, and the motions of the moon, stars, and planets are also thoroughly examined.[11]

Regardless of the geographical and astronomical details, one of the most important characteristics of Buddhist worldviews is that they are oriented toward understanding not only the physical world but also the types of sentient beings who dwell within it. These are, after all, both the subjects of existence and the patients who receive benefits from the Buddha's teachings. Later expositions of Buddhist cosmology even take pains to articulate that the geography of the world is, in a sense, illusory, and that only the minds who perceive it are important. As such, the geography of the world is perhaps primarily useful for understanding different states of life. Hell realms, for example, are by definition the locations where sentient beings suffer great torments, just as heavens provide beings great pleasure. When alternative world-systems are described, it is generally in service of the characterization of different experiences for beings in those realms.[12]

With this emphasis on the experience of beings in various parts of the cosmos, one of the most famous expressions of Buddhist cosmology is the artistic image of the wheel of existence (*bhava-cakra, samsara-cakra*). Paintings of this subject often adorn the entrances to monasteries as public statements of Buddhist cosmology, an explanation to visitors of the states of life in the world, their causes, and the potential release from suffering offered by the Buddhist path.[13] Such images are diagrams of existence rather than maps of locations, clearly revealing the focus on sentient beings inherent in Buddhist cosmology. These depictions are also among the earliest systematic representations of Buddhist cosmology in the artistic record, with a 5th-century painted version still extant at Ajaṇṭā, India.[14]

KEY HISTORICAL DEVELOPMENTS

Buddhist cosmology is both indelibly connected to South Asia, the birthplace of the religion, and highly adaptable to new contexts, uses, and ways of thinking. Before Buddhism arose, a rich body of cosmological knowledge and speculation already existed in the region. Later, some of the most influential cosmological descriptions of Buddhism were drafted alongside or in contrast to the cosmological descriptions of other religious traditions. As Buddhist cosmology is repeatedly exported to other regions, it remains shaped by principles of the South Asian systems, but it also exhibits great flexibility, changing significantly with the development of new Buddhist traditions and in contact with numerous other religious and scientific perspectives. This section provides an overview of some major historical developments in Buddhist cosmology through several noteworthy traditions, texts, and artworks.

Early Cosmology in Varied Contexts. Sources for Buddhist cosmological thinking originate before the religion itself, dating back even to the earliest source that remains extant from South Asia, the *Ṛg Veda*. In this oral tradition and later text, one finds clear expressions of the organized division of the world into three vertical layers of the earth, atmosphere, and sky and into the four horizontal directions of the compass. Fundamental structures like these remain central to the cosmologies that develop later. Once Buddhist accounts arrive, they build on previous traditions even while distinguishing themselves from other competing cosmological and religious systems of their time. Frequently, these early Buddhist sources do not explicate cosmology as a subject unto itself but rather incorporate cosmological thinking into discussions of other topics. Even such piecemeal descriptions, however, form the basis of later, more systematic thinking about the cosmos as a whole.

The *Āṭānāṭiya Sutta* of the *Dīgha Nikāya*, for example, describes the four quarters of the world (to the east, south, west, and north) in reference to the four divine great kings who guard them and may be entreated to protect the followers of Buddhism.[15] Even the ancient reciters of the *Ṛg Veda* would be familiar with this division of the world into four directions, which is based in part on the importance of the rising and setting of the sun in the east and west. For Buddhists, however, the four great kings also become important symbols of the subservience of worldly deities to the Buddha's teachings, later reappearing frequently as crucial figures of Buddhist ritual, art, and architecture.[16] The division of the world into four geographical quarters is also central to narratives of the ideal Buddhist king, the *cakravartin* (wheel-turning) emperor who righteously conquers the entire world.[17]

Contrasting the very incomplete description of the world contained in the *Āṭānāṭiya Sutta*, a passage from the *Aṅguttara Nikāya* lists more exhaustively the major geographical components of a single world-system, including central Mount Sineru (Sumeru), the continents of the four cardinal directions, the oceans, and the many heavens above. It does so, however, not for the sake of cosmology per se but rather to describe how the Buddha's voice can miraculously carry across a billion such worlds.[18] Such ideas are further elaborated in Mahāyāna traditions, which develop sophisticated descriptions of alternative worlds and the multifarious abilities of buddhas to transcend them.

Revealing another approach to cosmological description, a passage from the *Mahāvastu* details instead the realms of life in this single world as they are experienced by the Buddha's disciple Maudgalyāyana—here as a way of communicating the sufferings of the world and motivating progress along the Buddhist path.[19] Such accounts again become the foundations of numerous other cosmological expressions, such as later Mongolian illustrations of the Buddhist hells and, according to tradition, even the famous imagery of the wheel of existence.[20]

Scholastic Projects. By the 4th to 5th century CE, South Asian descriptions of the cosmos expand greatly in length, scope, detail, and coherence. The Hindu Purāṇas record comprehensive cosmogonies and geographical descriptions in their historical narratives, while Buddhist authors including Vasubandhu and Buddhaghosa characterize relatively complete models of the universe as key parts of their scholastic and soteriological projects. Overall, this is a period of formalization of cosmological ideas from various sources into more-or-less consistent systems that connect even more deeply with other aspects of life, including astral science, ethical theory, and meditative practice.

Vasubandhu's *Abhidharma-kośa-bhāṣyam*, for example, emphasizes the connection of the physical world to the experiences of living beings and the causal processes of karma that underlie suffering and the path to awakening. Since Vasubandhu's text is an encyclopedic accounting of Buddhist scholasticism, it both more deeply integrates cosmology into the wider field of Buddhist knowledge and offers a reference point for many later traditions, sometimes even serving as a standard foundation for monastic curricula.[21]

The world that Vasubandhu described would be familiar to many traditions of Buddhism across Asia.[22] It centers on the enormous mountain Sumeru, which is surrounded by successively smaller ranges of mountains and oceans and eventually the great world-ocean that contains the continents. Jambudvīpa, the largest continent in the southern quadrant, is said to have an essentially triangular shape, much like the Indic subcontinent in which this model of the world was conceived.[23] The three other major continents of Godānīya, Kuru, and Videha lie in the west, north, and east of the circular great ocean, which is ringed by the Cakravāla mountains that mark the boundary of the world. These characteristics, among others, place Vasubandhu's cosmology in direct conflict with other contemporary South Asian cosmologies, such as those described in the Purāṇas, which identify the local human realm much closer to the center of the universe or imagine Jambudvīpa as a circular continent entirely surrounding central Sumeru.[24] Such differences support various other aspects of the Buddhist worldview, such as notions of the rarity of human life and the difficulty of the Buddhist path.

In a separate passage, Vasubandhu also characterized the world as being divided into the three realms of desire, form, and formlessness. The upper heavens are discussed largely in terms of their equivalence to specific mental activities and the philosophical problems posed by beings who live dissociated from material reality.[25] Such correspondences between geographical places and mental conditions allow the cosmic model to serve as an explicit roadmap for meditative development even in a single human life, with the progression of mental states that leads to awakening being seen as equivalent to ascent through the heavens to the highest condition of existence.[26]

Accounts similar to Vasubandhu's are also found in other texts, such as Buddhaghosa's *Vissuddhimagga*, which goes even further in portraying cosmology as intertwined with meditative practice. Its most extensive outline of cosmic geography occurs by way of describing the Buddha's knowledge of the world as a model for meditation and purification.[27] Although it seems likely that Vasubandhu and Buddhaghosa developed their texts based on similar precedents, their motivations and approaches clearly diverged.

Mahāyāna and East Asia. Beginning well before the writings of Vasubandhu and Buddhaghosa, Buddhist cosmological accounts also traveled outside of South Asia. Some sources available from these regions reproduce South Asian descriptions quite faithfully, even recording variations that no longer survive in South Asian languages. The Chinese *Shiji jing* (Sūtra of cosmology), for example, provides detailed elaborations seemingly compiled from South Asian precedents but framed as a sermon by the buddha rather than as a scholastic commentary.[28]

In the early centuries of the common era, Mahāyāna Buddhist ideas developed in South Asia and were quickly transmitted to East Asia, where they continued to evolve. One of the many significant changes of this tradition is a reinterpretation of buddhas as increasingly cosmic and multicosmic figures, beyond mere historical persons. Building on the same models of the world as a circular disk of oceans and continents surrounding central Mount Sumeru, Mahāyāna texts describe diverse buddhas in faraway world-systems with transformed, idyllic geographies and even cosmic buddhas that encompass multiple universes within their own bodies.

A key concept in this context is the buddha-field (*buddhakṣetra*), a world where a buddha currently resides. Because of the passing of the historical buddha from this world, these alternative worlds become desirable for practitioners seeking the direct aid of a fully awakened teacher. The *Akṣobhya-vyūha Sūtra* describes such a distant world called Abhirati, which does not contain the hells or the lower realms or even central Sumeru, representing a simplified landscape better suited to religious practice.[29] The more famous *Longer Sukhāvatī-vyūha Sūtra* develops this logic further, stating that in Amitābha's land of Sukhāvatī, there is no Sumeru, Cakravāla, or even great ocean with continents. The landscape of the entire world is everywhere level and even, signifying the perfect equality of all beings who are born there and the guarantee of their eventual awakening.[30] Similar imagery is also found in the *Saddharmapuṇḍarīka Sūtra* and other texts.[31]

These ideas became incredibly influential, especially in East Asia, launching the traditions of Buddhism known as Pure Land, based on an indigenous Chinese term.[32] Rebirth in the alternative world of Sukhāvatī was widely adopted as a primary goal for religious practice, an easier alternative than enlightenment in this world. Pursuing the implications of this idea, the Chinese commentator Shandao (613–681) wrote the famous "Parable of the White Path" in part to show how Śākyamuni, the historical buddha of this world, can encourage his followers to seek the presence of Amitābha in another.[33] This fundamentally cosmological idea that awakening can be pursued elsewhere is a key factor in the popularization of Pure Land traditions, especially to lay practitioners.[34]

Given the importance of distant lands to religious practice in one's own, Mahāyāna texts also emphasize the visionary revelation of such alternative worlds in the here and now, as occurs through meditation in the *Guan wuliangshoufo jing* (Sūtra on the contemplation of Amitāyus), a text central to Pure Land Buddhism, and through the instruction of an adept teacher in the *Vimalakīrti-nirdeśa*.[35] In the latter, the layman Vimalakīrti miraculously transports the Abhirati buddha-field of Akṣobhya into the palm of his hand.[36] Notably, the description of Abhirati here includes Sumeru, contrasting with the *Akṣobhya-vyūha Sūtra* and confirming that the cosmological descriptions of these worlds are by no means settled. Mural paintings of Vimalakīrti's display in the Mogao Caves at Dunhuang similarly show Abhirati centering on Sumeru, just like this world.[37]

Such supernormal displays that radically shift scale and perspective are another major hallmark of Mahāyāna texts. Suitably awakened individuals can infinitely transform the ordinary perceptions of body, space, and time to demonstrate essential lessons. Descriptions of cosmology in these contexts do not focus so much on geographical distinctions of specific alternative worlds as they do on the power of buddhas (and thus the truth of Buddhism) to encompass all worlds simultaneously. Passages from the primary text of Huayan Buddhism, the *Avataṃsaka Sūtra*, describe the ability of a buddha to fill all worlds with light and contain all worlds within a single pore of his skin.[38] Cosmic Vairocana, the primary buddha of this tradition, both embodies all other buddhas and imbues this same quality of encompassment into his perfected world, which itself contains innumerable other world-systems.[39] Some artistic representations depict other world-systems inside Vairocana's flower-shaped world or on the petals of the lotus on which he sits, as in the monumental image at Tōdai-ji in Nara, Japan.[40] Such representations, along with other key images and metaphors like that of Indra's net, illustrate concepts of interconnection and pervasion that are fundamental to Huayan philosophical analyses.

The final chapter of the *Avataṃsaka*, actually an independent text known as the *Gaṇḍavyūha Sūtra*, combines themes of perfected buddha-fields, visionary experiences, shifting perspectives, and multicosmic worlds in a compelling demonstration of the centrality of cosmology to enlightenment. It describes the pilgrimage of Sudhana to different teachers, many of whom prompt visionary experiences. Toward the end of his journey, Sudhana meets with the Bodhisattvas Maitreya and Samantabhadra, who reveal astounding multicosmic visions that provide culminating insights for Sudhana's awakening.[41] Visual depictions of Sudhana's journey also commonly form parts of complex artistic and architectural statements of cosmology, such as the monument of Borobudur and the main shrine at Tabo.[42]

Tantrism and the Kālacakra. After Mahāyāna Buddhism was exported widely across Asia, new traditions continued to develop in southern Asia, most notably tantric or Vajrayāna Buddhism. Much as Mahāyāna Buddhists reimagined the person of the Buddha as a cosmic rather than historical figure, Vajrayāna Buddhists reinterpreted the process of awakening as similarly cosmological. The 7th-century *Sarva-tathāgata-tattva-saṃgraha*, for example, narrates the enlightenment of the historical Buddha as a journey from Jambudvīpa to the peak of Sumeru, where he is enthroned at the very pinnacle and center of the universe.[43] In doing so, it reaffirms the Buddha's domination of the world-system in cosmological terms, both similar and superior to the *cakravartin*'s conquering of the four quarters.[44] One foundation of tantric practice is the simulation of this cosmic process locally through specific ritual and meditative procedures. Many of these center on specialized diagrams known as mandalas, which can be read simultaneously as images of the palace atop Sumeru, collections of deities invoked for particular ritual goals, procedural guides for edifying mental activities, and more.[45]

Initially, tantric theorization builds on a cosmology similar to that described by Vasubandhu, and indeed his *Abhidharma-kośa* is sometimes cited as an authoritative source. Typically, however, tantric manuals dramatically simplify their presentations of the cosmos, often only mentioning Sumeru, the palace atop the mountain's peak, and the fundamental elements that form the substrata of the world (earth, water, wind, and so on).[46] Initiated practitioners might understand this as a shorthand for the full cosmos in all its complexity, but such simplification also helps correlate the transformations of meditation to human bodies, which are made of the same fundamental elements as the world, and thus clarify how practitioners are purified through ritual.

As tantrism developed, the theorization of such soteriological concerns became considerably more refined, resulting in dramatic reimaginings of the local world-system. One in particular, the Kālacakra tradition developed in the 11th century, revised the entire structure of the universe to reify correlations between the cosmos and body, adopt aspects of other South Asian cosmological systems, and generally represent a changing worldview of the times.[47] Occasionally, this led to self-contradiction, for example, in the simultaneous acceptance of both a greater Jambudvīpa surrounding Sumeru and a lesser Jambudvīpa in the distant southern reaches of the world-ocean. Other changes, such as new correlations between the measurements of the cosmos and the proportions of the human body, allow more significant connections between the macrocosm of the universe and microcosm of the practitioner, enabling Kālacakra proponents to assert that its rituals and meditations are even more effective than those of other systems.[48] Despite the influence of the Kālacakra tradition across Tibetan and Himalayan regions, however, it never entirely replaced other cosmological systems, like that of Vasubandhu's abhidharma. Instead, it exists largely as an alternative suited for specific contexts, especially astronomical calculation and certain ritual programs.

Changing Continuities and Southeast Asia. Despite developments of tantrism across Asia, other cosmological formulations continued to exist and evolve, with many of the earlier sources remaining influential, especially in Southeast Asia. By the 11th or 12th century, Southeast Asian authors also wrote new cosmological treatises with descriptions generally resembling earlier models of abhidharma.[49] The first written in the Thai language was the *Traibhūmi phra ruang* (*Three Worlds According to King Ruang*, also *Traibhūmi-kathā*), a prominent text that introduces Buddhist doctrines and narratives through the framework of cosmology.[50] Another tradition of cosmological treatises, the *Samut phab traibhūmi*, can include lavish illustrations of cosmic geography in place of detailed textual descriptions, with several examples known from the 18th and 19th centuries. Despite continuities with earlier traditions, such objects also evince significant innovation, with some incorporating European imagery and artistic techniques alongside traditional Buddhist concepts.[51] Such intertwining of tradition and innovation is readily apparent in many Southeast Asian cosmological expressions, not only in text and artwork but also in ritual and notions of kingship (see the section "The Greater Relevance of Cosmology in Buddhist Traditions"). Illustrated cosmological manuscripts are also not unique to this region and period, with some Chinese examples dating back a thousand years to the collection found at Dunhuang.[52]

Western Scientific Cosmologies. The later impact of non-Asian cultures, especially their scientific knowledge about the world, prompted significant reevaluations and revisions of Buddhist cosmology, although by no means simply. One obvious complication is the fact that the Europeans who first introduced scientific cosmology to Buddhist regions often did so not to advance scientific progress but to disprove Buddhism and convert the populace to Christianity.[53] In addition, the deep interconnection of Buddhist cosmology with so many aspects of society, ethics, philosophy, ritual, and art means that supplanting even a single cosmological idea can have deep and wide-ranging consequences. Even within Buddhist tradition, the evolution of Mahāyāna and tantric cosmologies was accompanied by revolutions in philosophy and practice as well as debates about those changes. Reactions of Buddhists to imported scientific perspectives, such as heliocentrism and spherical-earth theory, have ranged from rejection to acceptance, with many seeking some kind of negotiation or accommodation.

The Japanese scholar Entsū Fumon (1755–1834), for example, controversially accepted the newly imported scientific data and even developed his own novel theories and methods, but he did so to prove that traditional Buddhist cosmology was correct. He went so far as to use European clockwork mechanisms to simulate the motions of the sun and the moon in his Buddhist model, even as he omitted the crucial heavens and hells because they were irrelevant to the requirements of a physical proof.[54] Ultimately, however, he maintained that the truths of Buddhist scriptures are inherently superior to scientific observations, since they result from the Buddha's divine vision rather than ordinary human perception.[55] Other Japanese thinkers were less quick to defend the absolute authority of received tradition, suggesting that Buddhist cosmology was a product of a particular historical circumstance or that it could be abandoned without affecting the most important teachings of the religion.[56]

In China, some scholars initially sought to defend Buddhism from accusations that it is unscientific by finding support for contemporary scientific interpretations in Buddhist texts, often dramatically reinterpreting the texts in the process. By the 1920s, proponents of modern science realized that Christianity, too, is unscientific, and equally attacked the work of missionaries on those grounds.[57]

The Tibetan scholar Gendün Chöpel (Dge 'dun chos 'phel, 1903–1951), in contrast to Entsū, argued that the traditional Buddhist view of the flat earth is simply wrong, but that it was taught by the Buddha as a skillful method (*upāya*) to engage the people of his time in deeper Buddhist truths, even if the Buddha himself might have known better.[58] The Fourteenth Dalai Lama (b. 1935) has gone even further to reject traditional Buddhist cosmology as outdated, although he maintains that Buddhism still has much to offer modern society.[59] The relationships of Buddhist cosmology with modern science are still very much being negotiated even in the 21st century, especially given the intertwining of cosmology with so many other aspects of Buddhist tradition.

THE GREATER RELEVANCE OF COSMOLOGY IN BUDDHIST TRADITIONS

As is clear even from this brief overview, care must be paid to contextualize Buddhist cosmology not only in terms of historical evidence from texts and objects but also in terms of widely varied concerns of philosophy, meditation, ritual, visual and material culture, and lived experience. Many traditions indicate that understanding cosmology is not only foundational to embarking on the Buddhist path but also that it is part of the final experience of awakening.[60] Furthermore, cosmology cannot be divorced from other fields of knowledge, such as geography, biology, and metaphysics. A few additional examples suffice to show how deeply and broadly cosmology integrates with many diverse aspects of Buddhist culture, including everything from daily personal rituals to theories of divine kingship, plans for architecture, and interfaces between Buddhist and other religious traditions.

One of the most common rituals in the Vajrayāna Buddhist traditions of Nepal, Tibet, and Mongolia is the mandala offering, in which practitioners create a small model of the universe to give to a teacher or deity as a sign of devotion. Aside from encouraging the perfection of generosity (*dāna*), a key Buddhist virtue, this ritual also serves as preliminary to more esoteric practices that depend on the teacher's guidance. While most traditions use the abhidharma cosmology as a framework, it is possible to perform this same ritual with the Kālacakra model, and in any case the details of the offering may change depending on the context of performance. Further, the often-ephemeral objects used to create this offering may not even portray any recognizable cosmological imagery. The most important aspect of this practice is simply the completeness of the offering suggested by conceiving of giving the entire universe.[61]

In contrast, funerals in Thailand often use Buddhist cosmology as a model for the cremation pyres of elite individuals, and by placing the corpse atop Sumeru signify the transition of the deceased to heavenly realms.[62] Lavish expressions, such as the multiple pavilions constructed for the cremation of kings, are signs of wealth to be received, not given away. The process is especially important for traditional rulers, who are understood as divine incarnations who return to heaven upon death.[63] Variations in the designs of these pyres can express highly nuanced political statements, even without altering the underlying cosmological system.[64]

More permanent constructions, such as stūpas, *caityas*, and even monasteries and temples, can sometimes also be understood at least partially to be based on cosmological frameworks. Stūpas, for example, may be laid out with reference to the cardinal directions and have structural features that are interpreted as cosmological, while Vajrayāna *caityas* are actually built on the foundation of tantric mandalas, embodying all that entails.[65] The first monastery built in Tibet, called Samye (Bsam yas, 8th century), has also traditionally been described as exemplifying a cosmic structure, connecting the authority of the king who commissioned it to the larger world and the establishment of a Buddhist lineage in Tibet.[66] In addition, the three levels of the central building have been said to be made in the architectural styles of India, Tibet, and China, signaling a confluence of regional traditions.

Indeed, it is not uncommon for visual and material expressions of Buddhist cosmology to be layered with other, disparate cosmological systems. For example, several murals in the Mogao Caves at Dunhuang freely intermix Buddhist and indigenous Chinese imagery, such as of local divinities and visions of Mount Kunlun.[67] Even single cosmological deities, such as figures who hold the sun and moon near Sumeru, can have complex histories involving multiple religious traditions and reinterpretations.[68] Such cases show that, despite the clear descriptions of cosmological systems collated in texts, the actual understanding and application of cosmological thinking in history is significantly more complex.

REVIEW OF LITERATURE

There are several important theoretical and methodological concerns that shape scholarship on Buddhist cosmology. In the history of religious studies, one of the most influential debates surrounds whether the principles evident in such cosmologies are generally applicable to human thought or are more restricted to local traditions. This conversation is often framed in terms of approaches to structuralism and the work of scholars who see cosmology as a window onto universal principles of humanity.[69] Especially after the mid-20th century, many scholars criticized the oversimplification of diverse traditions that such theorizations encourage, and they opened new avenues for more nuanced and localized investigations.[70]

Among scholars of Buddhism more particularly, cosmology has been readily recognized as noteworthy, but there have also been changes in how the topic has been approached over the years. Perhaps the most significant developments concern whether cosmology is best considered a topic unto itself or a discourse intertwined with other aspects of religion and culture. Especially in the early history of the field, scholars tended to see cosmology more as a topic unto itself, since essential knowledge, categories, and questions were still being outlined.[71] Even in the early days, however, some scholars emphasized the connection of cosmology to other topics, such as social structure, ritual, and the arts.[72] Other accounts have endeavored to summarize major traditions of cosmology in more detail, connecting them to specific historical contexts and developments.[73]

In the late 20th and early 21st centuries, there has been a particular surge in seeing cosmology as deeply intertwined with other subjects, including artistic images, meditative practice, and tantric mandalas.[74] Specialists have also increasingly focused on tracing particular cosmological traditions, adaptations, and innovations across Asia, notably at the confluence of visual and textual cultures, such as in the wheel of existence, tantric objects of the Himalayas, and maps from Japan.[75] As more books, dissertations, and articles continue to appear on subjects related to Buddhist cosmology, it seems likely that future generations of scholars will continue this trend of understanding cosmology as a foundational and nuanced topic in the field of Buddhist studies.

PRIMARY SOURCES

Bodhi, trans. *The Numerical Discourses of the Buddha: A Translation of the Aṅguttara Nikāya*. Boston: Wisdom, 2012.

Buddhaghosa. *The Path of Purification (Visuddhimagga)*. Translated by Ñāṇamoli. Kandy, Sri Lanka: Buddhist Publication Society, 2010.

Cleary, Thomas, trans. *The Flower Ornament Scripture: A Translation of the Avatamsaka Sutra*. 3 vols. Boston: Shambhala, 1984.

Giebel, Rolf W., trans. "The Adamantine Pinnacle." In *Two Esoteric Sutras: The Adamantine Pinnacle Sutra, The Susiddhikara Sutra*. Edited by Rolf. W. Giebel. BDK English Tripiṭaka 29–II, 30–II. Berkeley, CA: Numata Center for Buddhist Translation and Research, 2001.

Gómez, Luis O. *Land of Bliss: The Paradise of the Buddha of Measureless Light: Sanskrit and Chinese Versions of the Sukhāvatīvyūha Sutras*. Honolulu: University of Hawai'i Press, 1996.

Goswami, Bijoya, trans. *Lalitavistara*. Kolkata: Asiatic Society, 2001.

Gyatsho, Tenzin. *Science and Philosophy in the Indian Buddhist Classics: The Physical World*. Edited by Thupten Jinpa. Translated by Ian Coghlan. Somerville, MA: Wisdom Publications, 2017.

Gyatso, Khedrup Norsang. *Ornament of Stainless Light: An Exposition of the Kālacakra Tantra*. Translated by Gavin Kilty. Library of Tibetan Classics. Boston: Wisdom Publications, 2004.

Inagaki, Hisao, and Harold Stewart, trans. *The Three Pure Land Sutras: The Larger Sutra on Amitāyus (Taishō Vol. 12, Number 360), The Sutra on Contemplation of Amitāyus (Taishō Vol. 12 Number 365), The Smaller Sutra on Amitāyus (Taishō Vol. 12, Number 366)*. BDK English Tripiṭaka. Berkeley, CA: Numata Center for Buddhist Translation and Research, 2003.

Jamison, Stephanie W., and Joel P. Brereton, trans. *The Rigveda: The Earliest Religious Poetry of India*. Oxford: Oxford University Press, 2014.

Jones, John J., trans. *The Mahāvastu: Translated from the Buddhist Sanskrit*. 3 vols. London: Luzac, 1952–1956.

Kongtrul, Jamgon. "The Mandala-Offering Which Perfects the Two Accumulations." In *The Torch of Certainty*. Edited by Jamgon Kongtrul. Translated by Judith Hanson, 92–117. Boulder, CO: Shambhala, 1977.

Kubo, Tsugunari, and Akira Yuyama, trans. *The Lotus Sūtra: Translated from the Chinese of Kumārajīva (Taishō, Volume 9, Number 262)*. BDK English Tripiṭaka. Berkeley, CA: Numata Center for Buddhist Translation and Research, 2007.

La Vallée Poussin, Louis de. *Abhidharmakośabhāṣyam*. Translated by Leo M. Pruden. Berkeley, CA: Asian Humanities Press, 1990.

'Phags-pa Blo-gros rgyal-mtshan. *Prince Jiṅ-Gim's Textbook of Tibetan Buddhism: The Śes-Bya Rab-Gsal (Jñeya-Prakāśa)*. Translated by Constance Hoog. Leiden, The Netherlands: E. J. Brill, 1983.

Reynolds, Frank E., and Mani B. Reynolds, trans. *Three Worlds According to King Ruang: A Thai Buddhist Cosmology*. Berkeley: Asian Humanities Press, 1982.

Tayé, Jamgön Kongtrul Lodrö. *The Treasury of Knowledge Book One: Myriad Worlds*. Boulder, CO: Snow Lion, 2003.

Vyāsa. *Puranic Cosmology*. Edited by Danavir Goswami. Kansas City, MO: Rupanuga Vedic College, 2007.

Walshe, Maurice, trans. *The Long Discourses of the Buddha: A Translation of the Dīgha Nikāya*. Boston: Wisdom Publications, 1995.

Watson, Burton, trans. *The Lotus Sūtra*. New York: Columbia University Press, 1993.
Watson, Burton, trans. *The Vimalakirti Sutra*. New York: Columbia University Press, 2000.

FURTHER READING

Brauen, Martin. *Mandala: Sacred Circle in Tibetan Buddhism*. Stuttgart: Arnoldsche Art Publishers, 2009.

Gethin, Rupert. "Cosmology and Meditation: From the Aggañña Sutta to the Mahāyāna." *History of Religions* 36, no. 3 (1997): 183–217.

Gombrich, Richard F. "Ancient Indian Cosmology." In *Ancient Cosmologies*. Edited by Carmen Blacker and Michael Loewe, 110–142. London: Allen and Unwin, 1975.

Howard, Angela Falco. *The Imagery of the Cosmological Buddha*. Studies in South Asian Culture 13. Leiden, The Netherlands: E. J. Brill, 1986.

Huntington, Eric. *Creating the Universe: Depictions of the Cosmos in Himalayan Buddhism*. Seattle: University of Washington Press, 2018.

Kloetzli, Randy. *Buddhist Cosmology: From Single World System to Pure Land*. Delhi: Motilal Banarsidass, 1983.

Lopez, Donald S. "First There Is a Mountain." In *Buddhism & Science: A Guide for the Perplexed*. Edited by Donald S. Lopez, 39–72. Chicago: University of Chicago Press, 2008.

Sadakata, Akira. *Buddhist Cosmology: Philosophy and Origins*. Translated by Gaynor Sekimori. Tokyo: Kosei, 2004.

Sircar, Dineschandra. *Cosmography and Geography in Early Indian Literature*. Calcutta: Indian Studies: Past & Present, 1967.

Skilling, Peter. "Cosmology at the Crossroads: The Harvard Traibhumi Manuscript." In *The Renaissance Princess Lectures: In Honour of Her Royal Highness Princess Maha Chakri Sirindhorn on Her Fifth Cycle Anniversary*, 225–286. Bangkok: Siam Society, 2018.

Teiser, Stephen F. *Reinventing the Wheel: Paintings of Rebirth in Medieval Buddhist Temples*. Seattle: University of Washington Press, 2006.

Wallace, Vesna A. *The Inner Kālacakratantra: A Buddhist Tantric View of the Individual*. Oxford: Oxford University Press, 2001.

RELATED ARTICLES IN THE *OXFORD RESEARCH ENCYCLOPEDIAS*

Megan Bryson, "Buddhist Geography and Regionalism." https://doi.org/10.1093/acrefore/9780199340378.013.626.

David B. Gray, "Tantra and the Tantric Traditions of Hinduism and Buddhism." https://doi.org/10.1093/acrefore/9780199340378.013.59.

Oren Hanner, "Abhidharmakośabhāṣya (Treasury of Metaphysics with Self-Commentary)." https://doi.org/10.1093/acrefore/9780199340378.013.718.

Daniel Veidlinger, "Transmission of Buddhist Media and Texts." https://doi.org/10.1093/acrefore/9780199340378.013.515.

NOTES

1. David L. McMahan, *The Making of Buddhist Modernism* (Oxford: Oxford University Press, 2009), 4–8.
2. Khedrup Norsang Gyatso, *Ornament of Stainless Light: An Exposition of the Kālacakra Tantra*, trans. Gavin Kilty, Library of Tibetan Classics (Boston: Wisdom Publications, 2004), 148–157.

3. See Eric Huntington, *Creating the Universe: Depictions of the Cosmos in Himalayan Buddhism* (Seattle: University of Washington Press, 2018).
4. Compare, for example, Mircea Eliade, *Images and Symbols: Studies in Religious Symbolism*, trans. Philip Mairet (New York: Sheed & Ward, 1961), 27–56, with Huntington, *Creating the Universe*, 45.
5. See, for example, Dharmachakra Translation Committee, trans., *The Play in Full (Lalitavistara)*, 84,000: Translating the Words of the Buddha, 161.
6. Akira Sadakata, *Buddhist Cosmology: Philosophy and Origins*, trans. Gaynor Sekimori (Tokyo: Kosei, 2004), 31–38.
7. Louis de La Vallée Poussin, *Abhidharmakośabhāṣyam*, trans. Leo M. Pruden (Berkeley, CA: Asian Humanities Press, 1990), 2:455.
8. See, for example, Matthew T. Kapstein, "Just Where on Jambudvīpa Are We? New Geographical Knowledge and Old Cosmological Schemes in Eighteenth-Century Tibet," in *Forms of Knowledge in Early Modern Asia: Explorations in the Intellectual History of India and Tibet, 1500–1800*, ed. Sheldon Pollock (Durham, NC: Duke University Press, 2011), 336–364; and D. Max Moerman, "Locating Japan in a Buddhist World," in *Cartographic Japan: A History in Maps*, ed. Kären Wigen, Fumiko Sugimoto, and Cary Karacas (Chicago: University of Chicago Press, 2016), 89–92.
9. See, for example, Dharmachakra, *Play in Full*, 109.
10. La Vallée Poussin, *Abhidharmakośabhāṣyam*, 2:456; Gyatso, *Ornament of Stainless Light*, 81; and Eugène Denis, "La Lokapaññatti et les idées cosmologiques du Bouddhisme ancien" (PhD diss., Université Paris-Sorbonne, 1976), 1:2 (Traduction).
11. See, for example, Philippe Cornu, *Tibetan Astrology*, trans. Hamish Gregor (Boston: Shambhala, 2002); Edward Henning, *Kālacakra and the Tibetan Calendar* (New York: American Institute of Buddhist Studies, 2007); and Brian G. Baumann, *Divine Knowledge: Buddhist Mathematics According to Antoine Mostaert's Manual of Mongolian Astrology and Divination* (Leiden, The Netherlands: Brill Academic, 2008).
12. See, for example, a world defined mainly by fragrance in Burton Watson, trans., *The Vimalakirti Sutra* (New York: Columbia University Press, 2000), 112.
13. See Lhundup Sopa, "The Tibetan 'Wheel of Life': Iconography and Doxography," *Journal of the International Association of Buddhist Studies* 7, no. 1 (1984): 125–145.
14. Stephen F. Teiser, *Reinventing the Wheel: Paintings of Rebirth in Medieval Buddhist Temples* (Seattle: University of Washington Press, 2006), 76–103.
15. Maurice Walshe, trans., *The Long Discourses of the Buddha: A Translation of the Dīgha Nikāya* (Boston: Wisdom Publications, 1995), 471–478.
16. See, for example, Dharmachakra, *Play in Full*, 294; and Thubten Legshay Gyatsho, *Gateway to the Temple: Manual of Tibetan Monastic Customs, Art, Building, and Celebrations* (Kathmandu, Nepal: Ratna Pustak Bhandar, 1979), 50.
17. Walshe, *Long Discourses*, 397–398.
18. Bodhi, trans., *The Numerical Discourses of the Buddha: A Translation of the Aṅguttara Nikāya* (Boston: Wisdom, 2012), 313–314.
19. John J. Jones, trans., *The Mahāvastu: Translated from the Buddhist Sanskrit*, 3 vols. (London: Pali Text Society, 1987), 1:6–29.
20. Karénina Kollmar-Paulenz, "Teaching the Dharma in Pictures: Illustrated Mongolian Books in the Ernst Collection in Switzerland," in *The Arts of Tibetan Painting: Recent Research on Manuscripts, Murals and Thangkas of Tibet, the Himalayas and Mongolia (11th–19th Century)*, ed. Amy Heller, PIATS 2010: Proceedings of the Twelfth Seminar of the International Association for Tibetan Studies, Vancouver, 2010; and Teiser, *Reinventing the Wheel*, 53–56.
21. See, for example, Georges B. J. Dreyfus, *The Sound of Two Hands Clapping: The Education of a Tibetan Buddhist Monk* (Berkeley: University of California Press, 2003), 114.

22. See La Vallée Poussin, *Abhidharmakośabhāṣyam*, 451–456; Vasubandhu and Yaśomitra, *Abhidharmakosam (svopajnabhasyasahitam sphutarthavyakhyopetam ca): The Abhidharmakosa & Bhasya of Acarya Vasubandhu with Sphutartha commentary of Acarya Yasomittra*, ed. Dvārikādās, Bauddha Bharati 5–9 (Varanasi, India: Bauddha Bharati, 1998), 1:506–513.
23. Sadakata, *Buddhist Cosmology*, 31.
24. Dineschandra Sircar, *Cosmography and Geography in Early Indian Literature* (Calcutta: Indian Studies: Past & Present, 1967), 38–51.
25. La Vallée Poussin, *Abhidharmakośabhāṣyam*, 365–370.
26. Rupert Gethin, "Cosmology and Meditation: From the Aggañña-sutta to the Mahāyāna," *History of Religions* 36, no. 3 (1997): 183–217.
27. Buddhaghosa, *The Path of Purification (Visuddhimagga)*, trans. Ñāṇamoli (Kandy, Sri Lanka: Buddhist Publication Society, 2010), 198–201.
28. The text was translated into Chinese in 414 CE. For more information, see Angela Falco Howard, *The Imagery of the Cosmological Buddha*, Studies in South Asian Culture 13 (Leiden, The Netherlands: E. J. Brill, 1986), 6–12, 115–156; and Daniel R. Tuzzeo, "Crafting Cosmologies: Buddhist Cartography and the Spatial Imagination in Medieval China" (PhD diss., Stanford University, 2020), 28, 67–74.
29. Jan Nattier, "The Realm of Akṣobhya: A Missing Piece in the History of Pure Land Buddhism," *Journal of the International Association of Buddhist Studies* 23, no. 1 (2000): 71–102.
30. Luis O. Gómez, *Land of Bliss: The Paradise of the Buddha of Measureless Light: Sanskrit and Chinese Versions of the Sukhāvatīvyūha Sutras* (Honolulu: University of Hawaii Press, 1996), 85–86.
31. Tsugunari Kubo and Akira Yuyama, trans., *The Lotus Sūtra: Translated from the Chinese of Kumārajīva (Taishō, Volume 9, Number 262)*, BDK English Tripiṭaka (Berkeley, CA: Numata Center for Buddhist Translation and Research, 2007), 170.
32. Charles B. Jones, *Chinese Pure Land Buddhism: Understanding a Tradition of Practice*, ed. Richard K. Payne (Honolulu: University of Hawaii Press, 2019), 33.
33. Julian F. Pas, *Visions of Sukhavati: Shan-Tao's Commentary on the Kuan Wu-Liang-Shou-Fo Ching* (Albany: State University of New York Press, 1995), 146–147.
34. Julian F. Pas, "Shan-Tao's Interpretation of the Meditative Vision of Buddha Amitāyus," *History of Religions* 14, no. 2 (1974): 97.
35. Pas, "Shan-Tao's Interpretation," 98; Hisao Inagaki and Harold Stewart, trans., *The Three Pure Land Sutras: The Larger Sutra on Amitāyus (Taishō Vol. 12, Number 360), The Sutra on Contemplation of Amitāyus (Taishō Vol. 12 Number 365), The Smaller Sutra on Amitāyus (Taishō Vol. 12, Number 366)*, BDK English Tripiṭaka (Berkeley, CA: Numata Center for Buddhist Translation and Research, 2003), 63–87.
36. Watson, *Vimalakirti Sutra*, 133–134.
37. See, for example, Eugene Y. Wang, *Shaping the Lotus Sūtra: Buddhist Visual Culture in Medieval China* (Seattle: University of Washington Press, 2005), 308–309.
38. Thomas Cleary, trans., *The Flower Ornament Scripture: A Translation of the Avatamsaka Sutra* (Boston: Shambhala, 1993), 264, 648, 1139.
39. Cleary, *Flower Ornament Scripture*, 213.
40. See, for example, Dorothy Wong, "The Art of *Avataṃsaka* Buddhism at the Courts of Empress Wu and Emperor Shōmu/Empress Kōmyō," in *Avataṃsaka (Huayan, Kegon, Flower Ornament) Buddhism in East Asia: Origins and Adaptation of a Visual Culture*, ed. Robert M. Gimello, Frédéric Girard, and Imre Hamar, Asiatische Forschungen, Band 155, International Huayan Symposium (Wiesbaden, Germany: Harrassowitz Verlag, 2012), 224.
41. David L. McMahan, *Empty Vision: Metaphor and Visionary Imagery in Mahāyāna Buddhism* (London: Routledge Curzon, 2002), 127–130.

42. See, for example, Jan Fontein, *Entering the Dharmadhātu: A Study of the Gandhavyūha Reliefs of Borobudur* (Leiden, The Netherlands: Brill, 2012); Julie A. Gifford, *Buddhist Practice and Visual Culture: The Visual Rhetoric of Borobudur* (London: Routledge, 2011); and Deborah E. Klimburg-Salter, *Tabo: A Lamp for the Kingdom* (New York: Thames & Hudson, 1997), 120–124.
43. Steven Neal Weinberger, "The Significance of Yoga Tantra and the Compendium of Principles (Tattvasaṃgraha Tantra) within Tantric Buddhism in India and Tibet" (PhD diss., University of Virginia, 2003), 56; Dale Allen Todaro, "An Annotated Translation of the *Tattvasamgraha* (Part 1) with an Explanation of the Role of the *Tattvasamgraha* Lineage in the Teachings of Kukai" (PhD diss., Columbia University, 1985), 175–176; and see also Rolf W. Giebel, *Two Esoteric Sutras: The Adamantine Pinnacle Sutra, The Susiddhikara Sutra*, BDK English Tripiṭaka 29–II, 30–II (Berkeley, CA: Numata Center for Buddhist Translation and Research, 2001), 25.
44. See also Ronald M. Davidson, *Indian Esoteric Buddhism: A Social History of the Tantric Movement* (New York: Columbia University Press, 2002), 121.
45. See, for example, Martin Brauen, *Mandala: Sacred Circle in Tibetan Buddhism* (Stuttgart: Arnoldsche Art Publishers, 2009); and Gyatrul Rinpoche, *Generating the Deity*, trans. Sangye Khandro (Ithaca, NY: Snow Lion Publications, 1996), 51–70.
46. See, for example, Tadeusz Skorupski, trans., *The Sarvadurgatipariśodhana Tantra: Elimination of All Evil Destinies* (Delhi: Motilal Banarsidass, 1983), 26–27.
47. John Newman, "Eschatology in the Wheel of Time Tantra," in *Buddhism in Practice*, ed. Donald S. Lopez, Princeton Readings in Religions (Princeton, NJ: Princeton University Press, 1995), 284–289; and see also John Ronald Newman, "The Outer Wheel of Time: Vajrayāna Buddhist Cosmology in the Kālacakra Tantra" (PhD diss., University of Wisconsin–Madison, 1987).
48. Gyatso, *Ornament of Stainless Light*, 89; and Vesna A. Wallace, *The Inner Kālacakratantra: A Buddhist Tantric View of the Individual* (Oxford: Oxford University Press, 2001), 56–104.
49. Oskar von Hinüber, *A Handbook of Pāli Literature* (Berlin: Walter de Gruyter, 1996), 182–185.
50. The exact date of this text is disputed. See, for example, Craig J. Reynolds, "Buddhist Cosmography in Thai History, with Special Reference to Nineteenth-Century Culture Change," *Journal of Asian Studies* 35, no. 2 (1976): 203–220. Frank E. Reynolds and Mani B. Reynolds, trans., *Three Worlds According to King Ruang: A Thai Buddhist Cosmology* (Berkeley: Asian Humanities Press, 1982).
51. Peter Skilling, "Cosmology at the Crossroads: The Harvard Traibhumi Manuscript," in *The Renaissance Princess Lectures: In Honour of Her Royal Highness Princess Maha Chakri Sirindhorn on Her Fifth Cycle Anniversary* (Bangkok: Siam Society, 2018), 225–286.
52. Françoise Wang-Toutain, "Deux diagrammes de cosmologie Bouddhique," in *La fabrique du lisible: La mise en texte des manuscrits de la Chine ancienne et médiévale*, ed. Jean-Pierre Drège (Paris: Collège de France, 2014), 291–308.
53. Donald S. Lopez, "First There Is a Mountain," in *Buddhism & Science: A Guide for the Perplexed*, by Donald S. Lopez (Chicago: University of Chicago Press, 2008), 53.
54. Masahiko Okada, "Vision and Reality: Buddhist Cosmographic Discourse in Nineteenth-Century Japan" (PhD diss., Stanford University, 1997), 5–11.
55. Okada, "Vision and Reality," 43–47, 64, 92–94.
56. See, for examples, Lopez, "First There Is," 47–51.
57. Erik J. Hammerstrom, *The Science of Chinese Buddhism: Early Twentieth-Century Engagements* (New York: Columbia University Press, 2015), 53, 57.
58. Lopez, "First There Is," 58–62.
59. Donald S. Lopez, *The Madman's Middle Way: Reflections on Reality of the Tibetan Monk Gendun Chopel* (Chicago: University of Chicago Press, 2007), 18; Tenzin Gyatsho, *Science and Philosophy in the Indian Buddhist Classics: The Physical World*, ed. Thupten Jinpa, trans. Ian Coghlan (Somerville, MA: Wisdom Publications, 2017), 15; and Tenzin Gyatsho, *The Universe in a Single Atom: The Convergence of Science and Spirituality* (New York: Morgan Road Books, 2005), 3–4.

60. John Strong, *The Legend of King Aśoka: A Study and Translation of the Aśokāvadāna* (Princeton, NJ: Princeton University Press, 1983), 147.
61. Huntington, *Creating the Universe*, 109–167.
62. Rebecca S. Hall, "Materiality and Death: Visual Arts and Northern Thai Funerals," *Journal of Southeast Asian Studies* 46, no. 3 (2015): 357.
63. Supeena Insee Adler and Deborah Wong, "The Funeral of King Rama IX: Mourning and the Thai State," *Asian Music* 50, no. 2 (2019): 127.
64. Lawrence Chua, "A Tale of Two Crematoria: Funeral Architecture and the Politics of Representation in Mid-Twentieth-Century Bangkok," *Journal of the Society of Architectural Historians* 77, no. 3 (September 2018): 319–338.
65. See, for example, Peter Harvey, "The Symbolism of the Early Stūpa," *Journal of the International Association of Buddhist Studies* 7, no. 2 (1984): 81; Kevin Trainor, *Relics, Ritual, and Representation in Buddhism: Rematerializing the Sri Lankan Theravāda Tradition* (Cambridge, UK: Cambridge University Press, 1997), 98–99; Pema Dorjee, *Stūpa and Its Technology: A Tibeto-Buddhist Perspective* (Delhi: Indira Gandhi National Centre for the Arts, 1996), 160; and Alexander von Rospatt, "On the Conception of the Stūpa in Vajrayāna Buddhism: The Example of the Svayambhūcaitya of Kathmandu," *Journal of the Nepal Research Center* 11 (1999): 121–147.
66. Anne Chayet, "Le monastère de bSam-yas: Sources architecturales," *Arts Asiatiques* 43 (1988): 24.
67. See, for example, Satomi Hiyama, "Transmission of the 'World': Sumeru Cosmology as Seen in Central Asian Buddhist Paintings Around 500 AD," *NTM Zeitschrift Für Geschichte Der Wissenschaften, Technik Und Medizin* 28, no. 3 (September 2020): 411–429.
68. Monika Zin, "Cosmological Aspects: Representations of Deities Holding Sun and Moon in Kucha and Beyond," *Rivista Degli Studi Orientali* 92 (2019): 259–285.
69. See, for example, Eliade, *Images and Symbols*, 27–56.
70. For example, Stanley Jeyaraja Tambiah, *Buddhism and the Spirit Cults in North-East Thailand*, Cambridge Studies in Social Anthropology 2 (Cambridge, UK: Cambridge University Press, 1970).
71. Willibald Kirfel, *Die Kosmographie Der Inder* (Bonn, Germany: Schroeder, 1920); William Montgomery McGovern, *A Manual of Buddhist Philosophy* (Lucknow, India: Oriental Reprinters, 1976); and Sircar, *Cosmography and Geography*.
72. Paul Mus, *Barabudur: Esquisse d'une histoire du Bouddhisme fondée sur la critique archéologique des textes*, 2 vols. (Hanoi, Vietnam: Imprimerie d'Extrême-Orient, 1935).
73. Akira Sadakata, *Shumisen to gokuraku* (Tokyo: Kōdansha, 1973); Sadakata, *Buddhist Cosmology*; Randy Kloetzli, "The Teaching of Light: Toward a Mahāyānist Cosmology and Its Placement in Buddhist, Indian, and Extra-Indian Perspectives" (PhD diss., University of Chicago, 1977); and Randy Kloetzli, *Buddhist Cosmology: From Single World System to Pure Land* (Delhi: Motilal Banarsidass, 1983).
74. Howard, *Imagery of the Cosmological Buddha*; Gethin, "Cosmology and Meditation"; and Brauen, *Mandala*.
75. Teiser, *Reinventing the Wheel*; Huntington, *Creating the Universe*; and D. Max Moerman, *The Japanese Buddhist World Map: Religious Vision and the Cartographic Imagination* (Honolulu: University of Hawai'i Press, forthcoming 2021).

Eric Huntington

BUDDHIST GEOGRAPHY AND REGIONALISM

BUDDHIST GEOGRAPHY AND REGIONALISM

Since its birth in India about 2,500 years ago, Buddhism has spread throughout the globe. As Buddhism reached new areas, its followers developed their own regional identities and understandings of Buddhist geography. South Asia, and specifically the sites associated with the historical buddha's life, remained a conceptual center for many Buddhists, but the near disappearance of Buddhism from the subcontinent in the 12th century allowed Buddhists in other regions to overcome their "borderland complexes" and identify sacred Buddhist sites in their own lands.[1] By the 19th and 20th centuries, colonial encounters introduced Buddhism to the West and created categories of national Buddhisms, which led to new visions of Buddhist geography and regionalism.

Prior to the modern period, Buddhism was found almost entirely in Asia, where different traditions developed in the following regions: South Asia, which includes modern-day India, Pakistan, Bangladesh, and Sri Lanka; Southeast Asia, which includes modern-day Cambodia, Thailand, Laos, and Myanmar; East Asia, which includes modern-day China, Taiwan, North and South Korea, Japan, and Vietnam; Central Asia, which include parts of modern-day China, Tajikistan, Kyrgyzstan, and Afghanistan; and the Himalayas, which includes Tibet, Bhutan, and Nepal, and extends (in terms of the form of Buddhism) to Mongolia. Projecting the boundaries of the modern nation-states of China and India onto earlier historical periods is misleading because it creates the false impression that these countries have existed as unified entities with consistent borders throughout history. For example, the territory of the Kitan Liao dynasty (916–1125) now falls within the borders of the PRC, but this does not make Liao Buddhism "Chinese." Kitans drew from the Buddhist sources of the Chinese Song dynasty (960–1279), but maintained their own sense of ethno-cultural distinctiveness, as seen in their creation of a writing system and development of Buddhist doctrines.[2] Similarly, the Gupta Empire (320–550) did not cover the entirety of what is now India, but only the north, and the notion of "Indian" identity did not exist during this period. Therefore, when not indicating specific polities, for the premodern period what is now India will be referred to as the South Asian subcontinent (or just the subcontinent), and what is now China will be referred to as continental East Asia.[3]

Beyond national boundaries, other common regional distinctions include the mapping of Theravāda in Southeast Asia, Mahāyāna in East Asia, and Vajrayāna in the Himalayas, or the mapping of Northern Buddhism as Mahāyāna and Vajrayāna in East Asia and the Himalayas, and Southern Buddhism as Theravāda in Southeast Asia and Sri Lanka. These models have some salience, but the history of Buddhist geography and regionalism reveals that the locations and interactions of different Buddhist traditions are more complex. New models for Buddhist regionalism have moved away from static, bounded spaces to foreground processes of interaction, such as network analyses of trade and transmission routes or areas such as "Maritime Asia" or the "East Asian Mediterranean."

THE GEOGRAPHY OF EARLY BUDDHISM

Sites tied to the Buddha's life were sacred because of their purported contact with the Buddha, but new sites could become sacralized when the Buddha's relics (*śarīra*) were enshrined there in structures known as *stupas* (relic shrines). In this way, sacred Buddhist geography was no longer restricted to the geography of the Buddha's life, but could be created by transferring the Buddha's relics to new locales. The historical Buddha Śākyamuni lived sometime in the 5th to 4th centuries BCE in what is now southern Nepal and northeastern

India. Four sites of major events in his life became pilgrimage destinations: Lumbinī, where he was born; Bodhgayā, where he reached enlightenment; Sārnāth, where he gave his first sermon; and Kuśinagara, where he died. Inscriptions sponsored by the Mauryan king Aśoka in the 3rd century BCE show that pilgrimage to Lumbinī and Bodh Gayā had begun by that time, and that pilgrimage had begun to sites associated with the seven buddhas of the past, as well.[4] The incorporation of locations from past buddhas' lives expanded Buddhist sacred geography, as did the distribution of Śākyamuni's relics. King Aśoka was renowned for his Buddhist devotion and became a paradigm for Buddhist kingship. According to legend, he promoted Buddhism by inserting relics in the 84,000 *stupas* he erected throughout his territory.[5] Though this number is exaggerated, inscriptions with Aśokan edicts do appear as far northwest as modern-day Afghanistan and as far south as Suvarṇagiri in what is now the state of Karnataka.[6] In addition to the legendary Aśokan *stupas*, the *stupas* at the large monastic complex Sāñcī (which may themselves have been tied to Aśoka's project) and Bhārhut offer other examples of early Buddhist reliquaries. Early Buddhists did not limit their relic worship to buddhas, but also enshrined relics of monks and nuns seen as particularly holy.[7] This further expanded the range of Buddhist sacred geography by allowing for *stupas* in regions far from the lives of past buddhas.

Early Buddhists expanded their sacred geography with pilgrimage circuits and *stupa* construction, and they also developed understandings of geography on a cosmological level. Their texts, known as *nikāyas*, divide the cosmos into the three realms of desire, form, and non-form, of which mundane existence occurs in the realm of desire.[8] This realm consists of world discs (*cakravāḍa*) with Mount Sumeru in the center as an axis mundi. Seven rings of mountains and seas encircle Mount Sumeru, and beyond those lie the four continents, which are ringed by a range of iron mountains. Humans inhabit the southern continent of Jambudvīpa, the southern part of which corresponds to the South Asian subcontinent. Eight (or sixteen) hells can be found below the world disc, and six heavens lie above it, with the heavens of the realm of form farther above.[9] Early texts often refer to the thousandfold, two-thousandfold, or three-thousandfold world system, indicating that our world is far from unique. This cosmology purports to be universal, but it is not hard to see that its geography is based on the South Asian subcontinent: Jambudvīpa lies to the south of the Himalayan (snowy) mountains and has a triangular shape.

During Buddhism's first five hundred years, it spread throughout the subcontinent, north into Central Asia, and south into what is now the island of Sri Lanka. The surviving textual and archaeological record is limited, which makes it difficult to ascertain early Buddhists' regional identities. Inscriptions often identify donors by their home region, but do not convey how this relates to the form of Buddhism they follow. However, the different scripts and languages used in early Buddhist manuscripts and inscriptions show that diverse populations had embraced the new religious movement. Early records mainly use Prakrit (written in Brāhmī script) as well as Gāndhārī (written in Kharoṣṭhī script), though two Aśokan edicts were written in Greek and Aramaic. Prakrit and Gāndhārī both came from the northern part of the subcontinent, where Buddhism arose. By the start of the Common Era, Buddhists in Sri Lanka had also begun recording texts in Pāli, which probably came from the western side of the subcontinent. Trade routes connected these areas to other parts of the subcontinent, as well as to Central Asia, which facilitated Buddhism's expansion north and east.

THE EXPANSION OF THE BUDDHIST WORLD

By the 1st century of the Common Era, Buddhism had traveled along the Silk Road into parts of Central Asia, including Kashgar and Khotan, and into the territory of the Han dynasty (206 BCE–221 CE) in continental East Asia. Throughout the 1st millennium of the Common Era, Buddhism expanded even farther. It reached the Korean peninsula as well as Southeast Asia by the 4th century, the Japanese archipelago by the 6th century, and Tibet by the 7th century. This geographical expansion coincided with the developments of new forms of Buddhism, such as the collection of texts and doctrines known as Mahāyāna in the 4th and 5th centuries, and the ritual, textual, and doctrinal systems of tantric Buddhism in the 7th century. These developments, along with the continued innovations in the Pāli-based form of Buddhism known as "Mainstream" Buddhism (or pejoratively as "Hīnayāna"), brought about new geographical models that had profound impacts across the Buddhist world.[10]

The rise of Mahāyāna Buddhism offered doctrinal justifications for a decentered vision in which Buddhists far from South Asia could participate in scriptural production. Though the term "Mahāyāna" is often used for a unified movement starting in the 1st century CE, the term did not gain traction until the 4th or 5th centurie. Even then, it referred less to a cohesive community and more to a set of ideas put forth in texts that identified themselves as Mahāyāna. One of these ideas was that buddhas appear in three kinds of bodies, of which historical buddhas like Śākyamuni are only one kind, the "form body" (*rūpakāya*); the other two kinds of bodies are the "enjoyment body" (*samboghakāya*), like the Buddha Amitābha, who presides over a pure land, and the "dharma body" (*dharmakāya*), which can be conceived as the omnipresent Buddhist teachings themselves.[11] While "form body" buddhas live their final human lives in the same place as Śākyamuni, that is, the northeastern part of the subcontinent, the enjoyment- and dharma-body buddhas are more universal, especially the latter. In addition, some Mahāyāna texts proclaimed that people are inherently buddhas and thus do not need to become enlightened, but rather realize their innate awakening. Having unfettered access to the dharma-body buddha, or one's own innate buddhahood, allows people far in space and time from the historical buddha's life to claim the authority of a buddha's voice, or *buddhavacana*, a key criterion for determining the authenticity of a sutras.[12] In practice, this did not lead to an unquestioning acceptance of all self-proclaimed sutras, as East Asian Buddhists still held that true sutras were written in Sanskrit. However, it opened up possibilities for a decentered view of the Buddhist world.

Mahāyāna ideas spread throughout the Buddhist world, where they coexisted with Mainstream Buddhism. This means the old division between Northern Buddhism (referring to the Mahāyāna of East Asia, Central Asia, and the Himalayas) and Southern Buddhism (referring to the Mainstream Buddhism or Theravāda of Southeast Asia and Sri Lanka) does not accurately represent the relationships among different forms of Buddhism throughout the religion's history. The rise of tantric Buddhism in the 7th century similarly rippled throughout the Buddhist world, including Southeast and East Asia as well as Himalayan and Central Asia. Tantric Buddhism developed in the South Asian subcontinent at the same time as tantric Hinduism, when the fall of the Gupta Empire gave rise to smaller regional polities. Though there are many reasons behind the formation of tantric Buddhism, an important one was that it offered regional rulers a politico-religious ideology through which they could exercise dominion over their territory.[13] The mandala provided a model for visualizing the divine world, but it also offered a geographic model for the political world, with the ruler in the center and his or her domain radiating outward. In the Southeast Asian context, this model has been described as a "galactic polity," an ideal political order that establishes distinct, hierarchical relationships between the core and the periphery (Tambiah).

Many political leaders in these regions embraced Buddhism for its promises of superhuman assistance and empowerment. Court Buddhism tended to emphasize the welfare of the state, creating the impression of regional forms of Buddhism tied to specific polities. Yet the concerns of the court and the concerns of average people were not the same. It is unlikely that most people in the unified Silla Kingdom (668–935) who engaged in Buddhist practices identified as "Silla Buddhists" (let alone "Korean Buddhists") in their daily lives. The regional forms of Buddhism that did develop, such as Chan (better known by its Japanese name Zen), tended to follow linguistic and cultural boundaries rather than political boundaries. Southeast Asian Buddhism drew from South Asian scripts and culture, and existed alongside Hinduism for several centuries. Himalayan Buddhism also drew on South Asian script and the later forms of tantric Buddhism that developed in the subcontinent, though it also encountered Buddhist texts and concepts from East and Southeast Asia as well. East Asian Buddhism used Chinese script and incorporated aspects of Confucianism, Daoism, and indigenous traditions, while also encountering people, texts, and ideas from other Buddhist regions. Of course, South Asian Buddhism continued to develop during this period as well, with Sanskrit displacing Prakrit and Gāndhārī as the main religious language of Buddhist texts, and different regions of the subcontinent and Sri Lanka generating their own distinctive traditions.

When Buddhism entered new regions, it invariably encountered existing ideas of sacred geography, particularly beliefs in divine powers already dwelling within the landscape. Though the specifics varied from place to place, the encounter between Buddhists and advocates for native traditions often involved narratives of conflict, subjugation, and resolution (at least from Buddhist perspectives). For example, Tibetan Buddhism recounts the Indian monk Padmasambhava's defeat of indigenous spirits as a critical moment in his establishment of Buddhism in the region. In Japan, followers of the *kami* reportedly worried that the worship of the Buddha would anger existing deities, but according to legend, Prince Shōtoku (574–622) resolved this tension by worshipping both. In addition to incorporating indigenous spirits into the Buddhist pantheon or recasting them as demons, Buddhists also reinscribed existing sacred sites as Buddhist. Mountains that had been the domains of local deities were reimagined as Buddhist spaces, whether through mandalization, as in Tibet's Mount Tsari and Japan's Mount Koya, or accounts of Buddhist monks subduing snake spirits, as in Mount Song in continental East Asia.

As Buddhism spread, South Asia retained its status as the center of the Buddhist world, but new geographical visions began to challenge its hegemony. For Buddhists in continental East Asia through the Tang dynasty (618–907), the "Western Regions" (Chn. *xiyu*) remained the center of Buddhist geography. For example, the monk Daoxuan (596–667) wrote, "When buddhas appear in the world, they all do so in the Central Province [i.e., India]; they are not born in border towns." He continued by explaining that Central India is the center of the world because at noon there are no shadows, in contrast to the "Han kingdom," namely China.[14] This view challenged indigenous notions of China as the center of the world, as shown in its name "Central Kingdom" (Chn. Zhongguo). The rise of devotion to the Buddha Amitābha in his western Pure Land reinforced the idea of the west as sacred. Tang monks regularly made trips to western lands for the purposes of making pilgrimage to sacred Buddhist sites, collecting texts, and studying with Buddhist masters. However, Buddhists in East Asia also started writing their own sutras and other texts during this time, and began developing their own ritual systems and devotional practices as well. For example, the *Perfection of Wisdom Scripture for Humane Kings to Protect Their States* (*Renwang huguo bore boluomiduo jing*) was probably written during the 5th century under the Northern Wei (386–534), though it was later attributed to the prolific translator Kumārajīva (among others).[15] This shows that even though the Western Regions were a conceptual center, Buddhists in other regions implicitly challenged that position by composing their own sutras.

Buddhists during this period also positioned themselves in the center of the Buddhist world by claiming to have Aśokan pillars or *stupas* in their own regions. Emperor Wu (r. 502–549) of the Liang dynasty (502–557) in continental East Asia identified a *stupa* at Changgan monastery as one of Aśoka's and said that it contained the Buddha's hair and nail relics.[16] Rulers in Japan, Korea, and Southeast Asia made similar claims about Aśokan *stupas* in their territory. Even though these claims are not historically accurate, they show how important it was for Buddhists—especially Buddhist rulers—to overcome their geographical distance from the Buddha's birthplace and the territory of the paradigmatic Buddhist monarch, Aśoka. As Buddhism declined in the South Asian subcontinent and simultaneously grew deeper roots elsewhere, these concerns lessened.

OVERCOMING THE "BORDERLAND COMPLEX"

By the mid-13th century, Buddhism had all but disappeared from the subcontinent due to a variety of factors, including lack of political patronage, insufficient popular support, and the destruction of Buddhist institutions in the conquest leading to the founding of the Delhi Sultanate (1206–1526). South Asian geography remained important as an imagined space for Buddhists in other regions.[17] However, other parts of the Buddhist world increasingly asserted their own claims to be the religious core rather than the periphery.[18] Processes that had already begun in the 1st millennium of the Common Era continued into the 2nd, such as the mandalization of sacred sites and identification of South Asian locales in other regions. In Southeast Asia, the Theravāda Buddhism that had coexisted with Mahāyāna, tantric Buddhism, other forms of Mainstream Buddhism, and Hinduism pushed out these other traditions to become the dominant religion in the region.

Recognizing Aśokan pillars or *stupas* in one's own territory was one strategy for bridging the distance between far-flung Buddhist lands and the Mauryan Empire. Another strategy that appears in Tibet, Japan, and continental East Asia is the claim that mountains flew to these places from the subcontinent.[19] Vulture Peak, the site of many of Śākyamuni's discourses, was said to have landed in Hangzhou in what is now China, and to have landed in Japan as Mount Ōmine. Mount Tsibri was identified as part of a mountain from Bodhgayā that flew to Tibet to cover a noxious lake.[20] On the one hand, such legends reinforce the sacred geography tied to the Buddha's life in the South Asian subcontinent, but on the other hand, they transfer that sacred geography to new places. Mountains that did not fly from South Asia to other regions could also serve as sacred sites. The four Buddhist mountains in continental East Asia were seen as the abodes of four great bodhisattvas, so pilgrims did not need to travel as far to be in the presence of enlightened beings.[21] On the Korean peninsula, the Diamond Mountains (Kŭmgangsan) were seen as the home of the bodhisattva Dharmodgata, who played an important role in the *Flower Garland Sutra* (*Avataṃsaka sūtra*).[22]

In addition to mountains seen as sacred because they flew from India or served as the dwellings of enlightened beings, Japanese Buddhists contributed to the sacralization of mountains by burying texts in them, such as Mount Kimpu and Mount Fuji. This was done for the benefit of the donor and their relatives, but also reinforced the mountain's holiness by making it one with the dharma body. In Tibet, the Nyingma sect identified hidden texts (Tib. *terma*) that past masters buried in the earth for later "treasure discoverers" (Tib. *tertön*) to find.[23] By tying sacred texts to the landscape itself, Buddhists in these regions implicitly claimed sacredness for their own geography.

The Buddhist geography of Southeast Asia included *stupas* for the veneration of relics, encounters with indigenous spirits such as the Burmese *nats*, and claims of connections to King Aśoka. In the 2nd millennium of the Common Era, rulers throughout the region embraced Theravāda Buddhism as a ruling ideology. We see this first in the Burmese kingdom Pagan (11th–13th centuries), then in the Thai kingdom Sukhothai (13th–15th centuries). The court's adoption of Theravāda brought with it the claim to have the orthodox transmission of Buddhism from the Third Buddhist Council in the 3rd century BCE. This meant that some Buddhists in Sri Lanka and Southeast Asia saw themselves as following the original, authentic teachings of the Buddha as recorded in Pāli scriptures. However, mandalic models of ideal Buddhist polities still held sway, and, as in other Buddhist realms, Buddhist sites borrowed the sacrality of indigenous sacred spaces. For example, the capital of Pagan was located close to Mount Popa, an abode of powerful *nats*.[24]

After Buddhism disappeared from the South Asian subcontinent, elite Buddhist monastics in other areas overcame their "borderland complexes" to develop regional forms of Buddhism that claimed their own authority, with often only perfunctory connections to South Asia. Concepts of authority and regionalism changed again with the advent of modernity and its framework of the nation-state.

BUDDHIST REGIONALISM AND MODERNITY

Prior to European colonial expansion and the rise of modernity, which started around the 16th century, Buddhism had already spread in Asia as an imperial religion. Government oversight of monastic institutions gave imperial states an additional channel for extending into the far reaches of their territory. Buddhism also offered justifications for imperial expansion in the form of spreading the dharma to benighted populations, as expressed in literary works such as the Thai *Legend of Queen Cama* and Tibetan epic of Gesar of Ling.[25] European colonial expansion into Asia further spread Buddhism to new areas and changed Buddhists' regional identities. This began in Asia in the 16th century and lasted into the 20th, with continuing repercussions. In addition to the physical violence that colonial powers used to subjugate Asian people, epistemic violence played an important role in colonial projects. This involved imposing the colonizers' worldviews and conceptual frameworks onto the colonized. Colonial expansion occurred as the discourses of modernity became dominant, including the ideals of scientific progress, rationality, and democracy. Developing scientific (or pseudo-scientific) knowledge extended to the humanistic sphere, and religion came to be seen as a universal category found in every society rather than a term denoting Christianity alone. However, Protestant Christianity remained the paradigm around which other religions were reimagined. This meant that religion was seen as a matter of belief in a deity, centered around a scripture, with an ethical-rational core. Politically, the empire gave way to the nation-state, which in theory was unified around a single nationality (or race/ethnicity). As a result, both colonizers and the colonized reenvisioned Buddhism on a Protestant model and in terms of national boundaries, leading to the creation of national Buddhisms.

National Buddhisms. The rise of national Buddhisms becomes apparent in the 19th and 20th centuries. In South Asia, this is clearest in Sri Lanka, where the Portuguese, Dutch, and British established a colonial presence from the 16th to 20th centuries. It was not until the late 19th century that the notion of Buddhism as the national Sinhalese religion took off under the direction of the American theosophist Henry Steel Olcott (1832–1907), who established Buddhist schools and created a Buddhist flag and catechism. Olcott's work inspired the monk Anagārika Dharmapāla (1864–1933), who sought to restore the "original" Buddhism that had been corrupted by colonial regimes and popular practices. As part of this attempt to recover Buddhism's original form, Dharmapāla founded the Mahābodhi Society, which had the mission of reviving sacred Indian Buddhist sites and placing them under Buddhist control. Following Sri Lanka's independence in 1948, fighting between Sinhalese Buddhist nationalists and the Tamil Hindu minority intensified, during which the former claimed that Buddhism was the true religion of the Sinhalese nation.

Myanmar (aka Burma) was under British colonial rule from 1885 to 1947, during which time Buddhist monastic institutions suffered. After independence, however, Buddhism became elevated as the Burmese national religion, which alienated Myanmar's non-Buddhist minority populations. Though the military government that seized power in 1962 initially sought to remove Buddhism from the political sphere, it eventually took control over the monastic community and encouraged Buddhist proselytizing among non-Buddhist populations.[26] In the early 21st century, militant Buddhists in Myanmar have engaged in a series of violent campaigns against the country's Rohingya Muslims, which stems in part from the idea of Burma as a Buddhist nation.

The explicitly political and violent aspects of Buddhist nationalism have also been apparent in Japan, which itself became a colonial power in East Asia from the late 19th century through the end of World War II. Though not all Buddhists in Japan supported their empire's colonial expansion (just as not all Buddhists in Sri Lanka and Myanmar have supported nationalist violence there), many Buddhists did, and in fact argued for Buddhism to play a central role in establishing a pan-Asian empire under the Japanese flag. Buddhists in Japan had to emphasize their Japanese-ness after advocates of State Shinto campaigned against Buddhism on the grounds that it was a foreign religion unsuited to Japan. Figures such as D. T. Suzuki

(1870–1966) argued instead that Buddhism was thoroughly compatible with Japanese culture, and indeed infused in every aspect of it. Suzuki also argued against the prevailing view in Western scholarship that the Mahāyāna Buddhism dominant in East Asia was a corruption of original Indian Buddhism. He claimed instead that Mahāyāna Buddhism in Japan was the religion's highest expression, one that he saw as suited to the "Oriental" (vs. the "Western") mind. People like D. T. Suzuki not only participated in creating the discourse of Japanese Buddhism in Japan, but also spread this idea to other regions and presented national Buddhism as something that had existed throughout Japan's history.

Prior to the 19th century, some Buddhists in East Asia emphasized their regional identities as Chinese, Korean, Japanese, Tangut, and so on, but "Chinese Buddhism" or "Japanese Buddhism" were not common categories. Even though Buddhism in East Asia had regional variations (including *within* single polities), there was also a shared East Asian Buddhist culture that drew from the same traditions, such as Chan, Pure Land, Huayan, and esoteric (or tantric) Buddhism. Yet the political reconfigurations of modernity put national boundaries at the forefront. This meant that, just as D. T. Suzuki and others articulated a national form of Japanese Buddhism, so too did figures in China like Hu Shih (1891–1962) articulate a national form of Chinese Buddhism. Hu Shih was not Buddhist, but he did argue against Suzuki that Chan/Zen was essentially Chinese, as it constituted the victory of rational Chinese humanism over fantastical Indian speculations.[27]

National Buddhisms are not the only kinds of identities Buddhists invoke in their daily lives, nor are they the only ways in which scholars of Buddhism discuss the tradition. Buddhists might identify more broadly as Theravāda, Vajrayāna, or a Mahāyāna tradition like Chan/Zen/Sŏn, or might eschew regional or sectarian identification altogether. However, national Buddhisms have become a widespread category in Buddhist regionalism to the point that their salience throughout history is often assumed, including in the West.

Buddhism's spread beyond Asia through conversion and immigration has strained the categories of national Buddhism to the point that one could also consider using the category transnational Buddhism. When Japanese immigrants bring Zen, Pure Land, and Nichiren Buddhism to Brazil, is it Japanese Buddhism, Brazilian Buddhism, or both? In an increasingly connected world, dividing Buddhism according to region is increasingly difficult, even as nationalism resurges and nation-states continue to police their borders. For example, Tibetan Buddhism has been a transnational movement with the exile of the Dalai Lama and many of his followers after the PRC conquest of Tibet in 1959. Along with the Tibetan population in the PRC, the Tibetan government-in-exile in India and diasporic community throughout the globe have made Tibetan Buddhism a truly global phenomenon.

Online Buddhist communities have also delocalized Buddhist geography, though the language of communication remains a limiting factor for how large the communities can be. Some Buddhist groups even offer virtual pilgrimages for people who are unable to travel to the physical site, whether symbolically visiting *stupas* in the Southwestern United States or hiring a proxy online to make the pilgrimage circuit on Japan's Shikoku Island.

Buddhism in the West. Early trade routes had introduced Buddhism to parts of the ancient Western world prior to the Common Era, but this encounter differed from Buddhism's reintroduction to the West in the modern period. The modern encounter with Buddhism came out of Western colonialism and reframed Buddhism as a religion based on a Protestant model. In addition, the concepts of West and East that underlay this encounter were also products of modernity. In this period, Buddhism's westward transmission involved both people in the West taking an interest in the religion and the immigration of people from Buddhist Asia to Western countries. Both processes changed understandings of Buddhist geography and regionalism.

The Western colonial presence in South and Southeast Asia made Sanskrit and Pāli Buddhist scriptures available to European scholars, who read them in accordance with the values of the Enlightenment and modernity. To these scholars, Buddhism seemed like a rational religion free from theism, the supernatural, and ritual. The discovery that Buddhists in Asia worshiped deities and performed rituals was taken as a sign that the religion (or "philosophy" in some cases) had degenerated over time and must be restored. Mahāyāna and Vajrayāna were seen as the most corrupted, while Theravāda (and Mainstream Buddhism as a whole) was seen as hewing closest to the Buddha's original teachings. This vision of Buddhism made its way back to Asia, where it inspired "rediscoveries" of the Buddha's original teachings, as in the development of humanistic Buddhism in China or the eradication of supernatural elements in Sri Lanka. Monks from China and Japan traveled to India and Sri Lanka looking for ways to restore their own national Buddhist institutions, and Tibetan monks—including the Panchen Lama—made pilgrimages to places like Bodh Gayā as well.[28] Although the practice of making pilgrimages to Indian Buddhist sites was hardly new, modernity and nationalism changed the meaning of pilgrimage by imposing a new framework. In Japan, the perception of monasticism as incompatible with modernity led the government to remove the celibacy requirement for monks in the late 19th century. In this way, Western imaginings of Buddhism shaped regional traditions in Asia as well as nascent Buddhist communities in the West.

In addition to those in the West who embraced a rationalist, non-theistic form of Buddhism, there were those who embraced it for its mystical side. Spiritualism and the occult were quite popular in the Victorian era, and interests in those fields could carry over into Eastern religions, as with the Theosophical Society. While one of its founders, Henry Steel Olcott, understood Buddhism in more rational terms, another founder, Helena Blavatsky (1831–1891), looked to the mystical and magical aspects of Buddhism.[29] This fits with D. T. Suzuki's later characterization of Zen as a product of the mystical East in contrast to the rational West (and, unsurprisingly, Suzuki's wife was a theosophist herself). The construction of the East/West binary led to a Janus-faced image of Buddhism that encompassed both the West's fantasy of itself as rational and its fantasy of the East as mystical.

Buddhism also came to the West as people from Buddhist Asia immigrated in the 19th and 20th centuries, especially to the Americas. As people from China, Japan, and later Southeast Asia made their way to the Americas, they brought Buddhism with them.[30] Because Buddhist immigrants tended not to be high-level monastics or political elites, their Buddhism resembled less the rational Enlightenment Buddhism and more the syncretic religious traditions that Western scholars saw as corrupted. Asian Buddhist immigrants to the Americas faced racial and religious discrimination, such as in the United States with the Chinese Exclusion Act of 1882 and the internment of Japanese American citizens during World War II. However, they still built Buddhist temples, sometimes following Christian models, as with the Japanese Pure Land "Buddhist Churches of America." Tibetan Buddhist organizations have built centers and *stupas* in the Americas and Europe that are modeled on Himalayan examples. These structures, like the monasteries and *stupas* built in Asia, play important roles in expanding Buddhist geography into the West.

REVIEW OF LITERATURE

Scholarship on Buddhist regionalism has recently begun considering alternatives to national Buddhisms, with larger regions (such as East Asia, Southeast Asia, or Maritime Asia) receiving more favor.[31] This has been prompted by the work of figures like Robert Buswell, who has argued against using terms like "Korean Buddhism" anachronistically. An increasingly common approach to this issue has been to focus on networks of interactions rather than bounded spaces.[32] Several edited volumes and a few monographs published in Europe and Asia have pioneered this approach, but it remains to be seen whether it will have long-term effects for how scholars conceive of the Buddhist world.

FURTHER READING

Acri, Andrea, ed. *Esoteric Buddhism in Mediaeval Maritime Asia: Networks of Masters, Texts, Icons*. Singapore: ISEAS Yusof Ishak Institute, 2016.

Blair, Heather. *Real and Imagined: The Peak of Gold in Heian Japan*. Cambridge, MA: Harvard University Asia Center Press, 2015.

Buswell, Robert E., Jr. "Imagining 'Korean Buddhism': The Invention of a National Religious Tradition." In *Nationalism and the Construction of Korean Identity*, eds. Hyung Il Pai and Timothy R. Tangherlini, 73–107. Berkeley: University of California Press, 1998.

DuBois, Thomas David. *Religion and the Making of Modern East Asia*. Cambridge, UK: Cambridge University Press, 2011.

Grapard, Allan G. "Flying Mountains and Walkers of Emptiness: Toward a Definition of Sacred Space in Japanese Religions." *History of Religions* 21, no. 3 (1982): 195–221.

Huber, Toni. *The Cult of Pure Crystal Mountain: Popular Pilgrimage and Visionary Landscape in Southeast Tibet*. New York: Oxford University Press, 1999.

Huber, Toni. *The Holy Land Reborn: Pilgrimage and the Tibetan Reinvention of Buddhist India*. Chicago: University of Chicago Press, 2008.

Kieschnick, John, and Meir Shahar, eds. *India in the Chinese Imagination: Myth, Religion, and Thought*. Philadelphia: University of Pennsylvania Press, 2014.

Lammert, D. Christian, ed. *Buddhist Dynamics in Premodern and Early Modern Southeast Asia*. Singapore: ISEAS, 2015.

Meinert, Carmen, ed. *Transfer of Buddhism Across Central Asian Networks: (7th to 13th Centuries)*. Leiden, The Netherlands: Brill, 2015.

Neelis, Jason E. *Early Buddhist Transmission and Trade Networks: Mobility and Exchange Within and Beyond the Northwestern Borderlands of South Asia*. Leiden, The Netherlands: Brill, 2011.

Prebish, Charles S., and Kenneth K. Tanaka, eds. *The Faces of Buddhism in America*. Berkeley: University of California Press, 1998.

Robson, James. *Power of Place: The Religious Landscape of the Southern Sacred Peak (Nanyue 南嶽) in Medieval China*. Cambridge, MA: Harvard University Asia Center Press, 2009.

Rocha, Cristina. *Zen in Brazil: The Quest for Cosmopolitan Modernity*. Honolulu: University of Hawaii Press, 2006.

Sen, Tansen. *Buddhism, Diplomacy, and Trade: The Realignment of Sino-Indian Relations, 600–1400*. Honolulu: University of Hawaii Press, 2015 [2003].

Sen, Tansen, ed. *Buddhism Across Asia: Networks of Material, Intellectual and Cultural Exchange*. Volume 1. Singapore: ISEAS, 2014.

Strong, John. *The Legend of King Aśoka: A Study and Translation of the Aśokāvadāna*. Princeton, NJ: Princeton University Press, 1983.

Tambiah, Stanley J. *World Conqueror and World Renouncer: A Study of Buddhism and Polity in Thailand against a Historical Background*. Cambridge, UK: Cambridge University Press, 1976.

Victoria, Brian Daizen. *Zen at War*. New York: Weatherhill, 1997.

NOTES

1. Antonino Forte, "Hui-chih (fl. 676–703 A.D.), a Brahmin Born in China," *Estratto da Annali dell'Istituto Universitario Orientate* 45 (1985): 105–134.
2. The Liao developed the concept of Buddhism as the "Perfect Teachings." K. J. Solonin, "Buddhist Connections between the Liao and Xixia: Preliminary Considerations," *Journal of Song-Yuan Studies* 43 (2013): 171–219, esp. 172.
3. The geographers Martin Lewis and Kären Wigen argue for the use of these regional (or area studies) terms over continental or nation-state divisions. Lewis and Wigen, *The Myth of Continents: A Critique of Metageography* (Berkeley: University of California Press, 1997).
4. In Buddhist cosmology, Śākyamuni is the buddha born in the current world cycle, but there were seven buddhas who predated him in their own world cycles, and more buddhas will be born in the future, starting with the next buddha, Maitreya (or Metteya). For the connection between the Aśokan inscriptions and early pilgrimage, see Jason Neelis, *Early Buddhist Transmission and Trade Networks: Mobility and Exchange within and beyond the Northwestern Borderlands of South Asia* (Leiden, The Netherlands: Brill, 2011), 88.
5. John Strong, *The Legend of King Aśoka: A Study and Translation of the Aśokāvadāna* (Princeton, NJ: Princeton University Press, 1983), 109.
6. Jason Neelis, *Early Buddhist Transmission and Trade Networks: Mobility and Exchange within and beyond the Northwestern Borderlands of South Asia* (Leiden, The Netherlands: Brill, 2011), 82.
7. Gregory Schopen, *Bones, Stones, and Buddhist Monks: Collected Papers on the Archaeology, Epigraphy, and Texts of Monastic Buddhism in India* (Honolulu: University of Hawai'i Press, 1997), 178.
8. The *nikāyas*, which are written in the Pāli language, are considered authoritative by Buddhists of the Theravāda tradition.
9. For an overview of this cosmology, see *Abhidharmakośabhāṣyam* of Vasubandhu, vol. 2, translated into French by Louis de La Vallée Poussin, English version by Leo M. Pruden (Berkeley, CA: Asian Humanities Press, 1988–1990), 451–473.
10. Mahāyāna means "Great Vehicle," and Mahāyāna rhetoric labeled other forms of Buddhism "Hinayāna," or "Lesser Vehicle." Because Hinayāna is a pejorative term, scholars of Buddhism increasingly use terms like "Mainstream Buddhism" to indicate that Mahāyāna was an offshoot of this tradition, or "Nikāya Buddhism," which foregrounds the scriptures recognized in this tradition.
11. Two texts from the Yogacāra tradition of Mahāyāna Buddhism, the *Mahāyānasūtralaṃkāra* and *Mahāyānasaṃgraha,* have sections devoted to this system. Paul Williams, *Mahāyāna Buddhism: The Doctrinal Foundations*, 2d ed. (New York: Routledge, 2009), 179.
12. Gregory Schopen, "The Phrase 'sa pṛthivīpradeśaś caityabhūto bhavet' in the 'Vajracchedikā': Notes on the Cult of the Book in Mahāyāna," *Indo-Iranian Studies* 17, no. 3–4 (1975): 147–181, esp. 179. It should also be noted that the rise of Mahāyāna Buddhism entailed a shift in emphasis from oral literature, as

expressed in the term *buddhavacana*, to written literature and what Schopen describes as the "cult of the book."

13. Ronald M. Davidson, *Indian Esoteric Buddhism: A Social History of the Tantric Movement* (New York: Columbia University Press, 2002), 2.
14. Daoxuan, *Guang hongming ji*, in *Taishō shinshū daizōkyō*, eds. Takakasu Junjiro and Watanabe Kaigyoku (Tokyo: Taishō Issaikyō Kankōkai, 1924–1932) no. 2103, 176b10–176b16.
15. Charles D. Orzech, *Politics and Transcendent Wisdom: The* Scripture for Humane Kings *in the Creation of Chinese Buddhism* (University Park: The Pennsylvania State University Press, 1998), 121.
16. Huaiyu Chen, *The Revival of Buddhist Monasticism in Medieval China* (New York: Peter Lang, 2007), 67.
17. Toni Huber, *The Holy Land Reborn: Pilgrimage and the Tibetan Reinvention of Buddhist India* (Chicago: University of Chicago Press, 2008), 16; John Kieschnick and Meir Shahar, eds., *India in the Chinese Imagination: Myth, Religion, and Thought* (Philadelphia: University of Pennsylvania Press, 2014), 1–9.
18. Tansen Sen, *Buddhism, Diplomacy, and Trade: The Realignment of Sino-Indian Relations, 600–1400* (Honolulu: University of Hawaii Press, 2015 [2003]), 143.
19. Toni Huber, *The Holy Land Reborn: Pilgrimage and the Tibetan Reinvention of Buddhist India* (Chicago: University of Chicago Press, 2008), 121; Heather Blair, *Real and Imagined: The Peak of Gold in Heian Japan* (Cambridge, MA: Harvard University Asia Center, 2015), 44.
20. Katia Buffetrille, "One Day the Mountains Will Go Away: Preliminary Remarks on the Flying Mountains of Tibet," in *Reflections of the Mountain: Essays on the History and Social Meaning of the Mountain Cult in Tibet and the Himalaya*, eds. Anne-Marie Blondeau and Ernst Steinkellner (Vienna: Österreichische Akademie der Wissenschaften, 1996), 77–89.
21. James Robson, *Power of Place: The Religious Landscape of the Southern Sacred Peak (Nanyue 南嶽) in Medieval China* (Cambridge, MA: Harvard University Asia Center, 2009), 52–56.
22. Richard D. McBride II, *Domesticating the Dharma: Buddhist Cults and the Hwaŏm Synthesis in Silla Korea* (Honolulu: University of Hawaii Press, 2008), 132.
23. Andreas Doctor, *Tibetan Treasure Literature: Revelation, Tradition, and Accomplishment in Visionary Buddhism* (Ithaca, NY: Snow Lion, 2005).
24. Robert DeCaroli, *Haunting the Buddha: Indian Popular Religions and the Formation of Buddhism* (New York: Oxford University Press, 2004), 153.
25. Donald K. Swearer and Sommai Premchit, *The Legend of Queen Cāma: Bodhiraṃsi's* Cāmadevīvaṃsa, *a Translation and Commentary* (Albany, NY: SUNY Press, 1998); Alexandra David-Neel and Lama Yongden, *The Superhuman Life of Gesar of Ling* (Boston: Shambhala, 2001).
26. Donald K. Swearer, *The Buddhist World of Southeast Asia*, second edition (Albany: State University of New York Press, 2010), 113.
27. Hu Shih, "Ch'an (Zen) Buddhism in China: Its History and Method," *Philosophy East and West* 3, no. 1 (1953): 3–24, 22.
28. Thomas David DuBois, *Religion and the Making of Modern East Asia* (Cambridge, UK: Cambridge University Press, 2011), 181; Toni Huber, *The Holy Land Reborn: Pilgrimage and the Tibetan Reinvention of Buddhist India* (Chicago: University of Chicago Press, 2008), 273.
29. Thomas A. Tweed, *The American Encounter with Buddhism, 1844–1912: Victorian Culture and the Limits of Dissent* (Chapel Hill: University of North Carolina Press, 1992); Philip C. Almond, *The British Discovery of Buddhism* (Cambridge, UK: Cambridge University Press, 1988).
30. Charles S. Prebish and Kenneth K. Tanaka, eds., *The Faces of Buddhism in America* (Berkeley: University of California Press, 1998), 1–10.
31. For example, Sujung Kim adopted Angela Schottenhammer's "East Asian Mediterranean" as a framework for understanding the transmission of a Korean Buddhist deity's cult to Japan. Kim, "Transcending

Locality, Creating Identity: Shinra Myōjin, a Korean Deity in Japan" (PhD diss., Columbia University, 2014), 19.

32. For example, see Andrea Acri, ed., *Esoteric Buddhism in Mediaeval Maritime Asia: Networks of Masters, Texts, Icons* (Singapore: ISEAS Yusof Ishak Institute, 2016); D. Christian Lammert, ed., *Buddhist Dynamics in Premodern and Early Modern Southeast Asia* (Singapore: ISEAS, 2015); Carmen Meinert, ed., *Transfer of Buddhism across Central Asian Networks: (7th to 13th Centuries)* (Leiden, The Netherlands: Brill, 2015); and Tansen Sen, ed., *Buddhism across Asia: Networks of Material, Intellectual and Cultural Exchange*, vol. 1 (Singapore: ISEAS, 2014).

Megan Bryson

BUDDHIST MEDITATION AND CONTEMPLATION

INTRODUCTION

Even before the death at around the age of eighty of the historical Gotama Buddha, probably around 400 BCE, the doctrines and practices associated with his teaching traveled. The traditions that emerged around South and Southeast Asia, in regions known now as Thailand, Cambodia, Myanmar, Laos, and Sri Lanka, are loosely termed South and Southeast Asian, or Theravāda, Buddhism, a term not used until the last two centuries. They are united by a group of texts composed in Pali, a language probably akin to the one used by the Buddha, or even, as has recently been argued, his own.[1] The Pali canon probably contains some elements from the earliest days of the tradition, but some accretions and editing must have occurred in the centuries before writing. South and Southeast Buddhist practices are largely based upon Pali canonical guidelines, though recent research has opened up a large and often unacknowledged variation and creativity within those parameters, particularly in chant, esotericism, and calm (*samatha*) meditations.[2]

Central Asian, or Northern, Buddhism is a development from the form of Buddhism that emerged in India in the first two centuries CE. Principally practiced in Tibet and Mongolia, such Buddhist traditions are part of the Mahāyāna: they were strongly influenced by the efflorescence of new Buddhist meditative texts, often of an inspired and visionary kind, created in India in the period up to the 7th century. Rich symbologies, visualizations, ritual, and an emphasis on the idea of the bodhisattva, the one bound to or for awakening, are key features. The vow to become a bodhisattva is enjoined for many, rather than a few. These traditions use visualizations and, in the Vajrayāna (diamond vehicle), *tantra*, often related to multiple bodhisattvas and their manifold universes; theory systems, linked to meditation, direct the mind toward emptiness (*śunyatā*).

Eastern Buddhism refers to the often related traditions followed by the Chinese, Koreans, Japanese, and many Vietnamese, which, for the most part, also demonstrate the influence of Mahāyāna. Eastern Asia received successive waves of texts and practices from India throughout the first centuries of the first millennium. Highly diverse schools such as Huayan, Chan, Tiantai, and Pure Land represent creative developments in Buddhist practice and theory, evolving in response to these, but also in close connection with often highly sophisticated rituals, philosophies, and practices already flourishing in China. Many Eastern traditions transcend geographical boundaries; some local differentiation is also evident. Chant is especially characteristic of some Eastern schools, particularly of the continuous kind for practice in daily life. Other Eastern schools employ practices with visualizations akin to Central Asian traditions.[3] Texts vary from the richly hyperbolic eloquence and evocation found in Huayan philosophy, to the sparse appeal of the nonverbal and intuitive *gongan/kōans* that characterize Chan/Seon/Zen schools.[4] Such Buddhist meditative and contemplative practice is complex in its diversity and often highly dependent on local conditions and contexts.

MEDITATION AND CONTEMPLATION IN THE EIGHTFOLD PATH

Any study of the practice of meditation in Buddhism must start with the eightfold path and the life story of Gotama Buddha, a paradigm in Buddhism of human meditative development. The Buddha's own account, as it is related in the Pali canon, tells us that after renouncing his royal life, he practiced for several years, trying to find a way of achieving liberation from the cycle of birth, suffering, old age, and death that he saw around him. He tried first to achieve his goal through the practice of two formless meditations, which he later adapted into his own system. The meditation on the sphere of no-thingness and the meditation on the sphere of neither-perception-nor-non-perception were learned from other teachers, according to his own first-person account, quoted in an early sutta (M.36). Although he mastered these, he saw that of themselves they did not lead to liberation. Thus, according to this record of his personal reminiscence, after several years of practicing the extreme austerities advocated by many contemporary ascetics, he recollected a meditation he had found spontaneously as a child, while alone under a rose-apple tree, which he termed the first *jhāna*. This state of unification, he said, is characterized by application of the mind (*vitakka*), exploration of the mind (*vicāra*), joy (*pīti*), happiness (*sukha*), and one-pointedness (*ekaggatā*), a complete sense of unification in no way dependent on the satisfaction of sensory desires. After having practiced self-mortifications for several years, he then, he said, asked himself a question: "Why am I frightened of the happiness that is free from attachment to the senses. What if this meditation might lead to wisdom?" (MN 1.246–7). According to the Pali sutta account, his memory of the relaxed exploration and joy of this state formed the basis for his accepting of food and sitting under the Bodhi tree. Here he practiced four of these *jhāna*s. He does not say that he learned them elsewhere; debate continues as to whether they were his own discovery or, as he would put it, rediscovery, as he claimed that his path was forgotten, not innovative. He then applied his mind to insight. Remembering his own past lives, through many world systems, he became aware of the past existences of other beings too. Beings were born and reborn, in the "beginningless round of existence," according to their karma, so that actions and volitions with clarity and good intent produced good rebirths; those with troubled volition found unhappy rebirths. Seeing these processes allowed him to examine the roots behind this continued cycle of existence and to become free of the corruptions of greed, hate, and delusion binding his mind to continued rebirth. He achieved *bodhi* (awakening). Afterward, prompted by Lord Brahmā, king of the meditative heavens, he decided to teach. He met with his earlier ascetic companions and explained his new realization in terms of four noble truths and the eightfold path, a way to find one's own path to liberation. The four noble truths are in some ways defined by the verb that accompanies each: the noble truth of suffering is to be understood, the noble truth of the craving that leads to suffering is to be abandoned. The noble truth that there is an end to suffering, *nibbāna*, is to be realized. The way to find the realization of this freedom is to be cultivated, or "made to become" (SN 5.420–4). The last element, of what is to be cultivated, is the eightfold path.

The principle behind each element of this path is the middle way, a balanced equipoise between apparently contradictory extremes. Thus, right view is the middle way of "seeing" that does not perceive events with the view that the self continues, or the extreme that it does not. Right intention is the intention that is not colored by hatred, desire, or ignorance. These are both termed "wisdom." Right speech is speaking that does not cause division or harm, right livelihood is a way of life that does not exploit other beings, and right action is that which is suitable for the time. These are termed *sīla*, or morality. Right effort is the putting away of unskillfulness and the cultivation of skillful states of mind. Right mindfulness is the awareness of the four foundations of mindfulness: body, feelings, mind, and "dhammas," or events in the world. Right concentration is the stillness that leads to the meditations. These last three are associated with the balanced development of *samādhi*, concentration.

All these elements are, in the broadest sense, categorized as *bhāvanā*, the "making to become" of the factors that lead to realization. What we call meditation is thus just one element in a path that is conceived and taught as eightfold. All the factors, or "limbs," of the path are interdependent. One cannot arise without some of the others, to a greater or lesser degree: thus, to speak rightly, mindfulness is needed, for instance, as it is needed in all elements of the path. The intention of meditation practice is thus so closely linked to other factors of the path as to be inseparable. The goal of the path is awakening; meditation is one aspect of a number of activities and practices that culminate in this, according to one's temperament and school of practice.

The life story of the Buddha is taken as inspiration, paradigm, an object for meditation itself, and an embodiment of the middle way. The path from the rediscovery of *jhāna*, involving its systematic cultivation until insight is found, is regarded as the classical route to awakening. In meditation, the "evenly tuned" note of the middle way inclines neither to laxness nor tension: it is a poised equipoise amid change and paradoxical conditions. The middle way is felt to steer the practitioner through shifting conditions, requiring the practice of wisdom, meditation, and *sīla*, or virtue.

In Western traditions, a distinction is sometimes made between "meditation" and "contemplation." The first involves discursive thought, such as the exercises of Ignatius Loyola and the *lectio divina*, and the second a largely nonverbal intuition, often accompanied by various degrees of joy, happiness, and equanimity, in the purification of feeling, such as that described by Teresa of Avila and St. John of the Cross. While such a differentiation is not so clear-cut, Buddhist meditations can, to some extent, also be divided between those that involve a strong discursive element, such as the consideration of the attributes of the Buddha, his teaching (dhamma), and his community (sangha), and those where the processes of thinking and verbalization are stilled in states closer to those of contemplation. Overriding all these, and included within them, is the development of mindfulness and wisdom, which may accompany a seated meditation but may also arise at any time, under any circumstance, if the conditioning factors have been cultivated.

MINDFULNESS AND CONCENTRATION: *VIPASSANĀ/VIPAŚYANĀ* AND *SAMATHA/ŚAMATHA*

Mindfulness and Concentration. An ancient pairing within Buddhist texts is that of the factors of mindfulness and concentration. All Buddhist meditation systems in some way attempt to find a workable balance between these two, whatever the sphere of meditation or the object chosen as the means of developing the mind. Thus it is worth looking closely at what these terms mean and how they relate to what are regarded as the two principal strands of Buddhist meditative practice, insight (*vipassanā/vipaśyanā*) and calm (*samatha/śamatha*).

Mindfulness (S. *smṛti*/P. *sati*), derived from the verb *smarati* in Sanskrit, to remember, had previously been applied in Indic traditions to memory of the past and, notably, the memory needed to retain and reproduce long recited texts, the Vedas. The Buddha, however, used it to denote a "remembering" of the events of the present, an encompassing capacity to sustain the mind's attentiveness, interest, and alertness to all the senses, including the mind, also considered a sense in Indic theory. The meaning of memory in the traditional sense is never lost; but, in Buddhism, emphasis is placed on renewal in every moment and the restorative adverting to present events. Traditionally, there are said to be four establishments or domains of mindfulness: body, feeling, mind, and dhammas, or events or phenomena. Complete meditative systems, in highly various ways, include all these, though some may pay more active attention to one domain: some Zen schools pay particular attention to posture, for instance, in the early stages; some calm schools operate primarily on mindfulness of feeling.

Mindfulness is frequently linked in the texts to clear comprehension (P. *sampajañña*), the ability to contextualize and to retain with that awareness a sense of purpose, direction in one's activities, as well as the acquisition of insight into the impermanence of phenomena as they occur. Mindfulness in Buddhism is understood somewhat differently from modern secular definitions.[5] From the evidence of the early texts of the canon and the Buddhist tradition, it is clear this mindfulness was discriminatory, though not judgmental. According to early Buddhist Abhidhamma, ethical factors such as self-respect and lack of recklessness arise at the same time as mindfulness, and, in their presence, unskillful states of mind are avoided. Mindfulness is thus compared to a gatekeeper, who ensures all those that enter a city are vetted, just as all objects that present themselves to the mind and body can be minimally assessed (AN 4.107). Just as past experience and wisdom may influence the discernment of the gatekeeper, so mindfulness discriminates on the basis of recollected events as well as an awareness of present objects of the mind and senses. A post-canonical work, *Questions of King Milinda*, compares mindfulness to the treasurer of a great king, who tells him what reserves of wealth he has, and the advisor of such a king, who suggests to him a judicious course of action on the basis of this. Mindfulness is thus seen as a kind of filtering system that protects the mind from harming itself or others, sustaining a steady alertness that through awareness of objects exercises an essentially moral appreciation and discrimination between events as they arise. In many Buddhist systems, such as the Sārvastavādin, some mindfulness and wisdom are described as being present in all consciousness: it is only right mindfulness and right wisdom that are associated with the discriminatory and "skillful" quality and the capacity to have insight without partiality or taint. Mindfulness can also work proactively, in the direction of attention to objects that have an inherent nature to arouse confidence and peace: such objects affect *how* one is aware as much as the object that awareness includes. In one early text the practice of lovingkindness, for instance, is said to be mindfulness (Sn 151).

Mindfulness has been the subject of considerable study and debate in clinical secular contexts. Buddhist understandings of mindfulness often differ quite deeply from these; debates and dialogue about this subject continue. For in most forms of Buddhism, the extension and cultivation of mindfulness is associated with an inherent or implied ethical discrimination that includes sensitivity not only to one's own mental states, but to those of others, and to the relationship between the two. Some traditions extend traditional techniques for mindfulness according to new perspectives on doctrine, practice, and ethical behavior. Śāntideva, in the "twelve mindfulnesses" he gives to avoid "fruitless waste" in the *Śikṣasamuccaya*, a training manual for novice monks, teaches the extension of mindfulness to the codes of posture and behavior within a monastery.[6] In the Central Asian traditions, with their emphasis on the bodhisattva ideal and the development of awareness of the suffering of all beings, four mindfulnesses are suggested: mindfulness of the teacher, the awakening mind (*bodhicitta*), the body as an expression of the buddha-nature, and the mandala of the world.[7] Mindfulness, in such instances, is perceived as applicable in chosen domains, linked to specific doctrinal demands and ethical needs. Most forms of Buddhist practice involve stated or implicit variations on the four basic foundations of mindfulness: body, feelings, mental states, and dhammas, or phenomena. Although its particular role, area of investigation, and importance in any one meditative system may vary, mindfulness is considered essential in all forms of Buddhist meditative practice.

The relationship of mindfulness to insight is emphasized from early times, when mindfulness with clear comprehension was linked to the development of insight and wisdom. In South and Southeast Asian Theravāda schools this is formulated as insight into impermanence, unsatisfactoriness, and non-self. Central and East Asian traditions articulate the ability to see beyond conventional appearances more as an insight into emptiness (*śunyatā*), whereby the manifold world of conditions and manifestations is seen as entirely void of substance or substantiality. Thus, in the *Bodhicaryāvatāra*, Śāntideva (*c.* 650–750), taking the new emphasis on the interconnectedness of all beings and phenomena, subjects the four foundations of mindfulness to dialectic scrutiny, whereby all four domains cannot be identified as substantial entities and are therefore routes to an insight where they are perceived as inherently empty of substance. His famous insights may be seen as an illustration of changing models in the way mindfulness is seen, understood, and reapplied as part of a doctrinal and practice tradition.[8]

In meditation, the quality said to complement and settle mindfulness is stillness or concentration (*samādhi*), the collectedness of the mind that rests upon a single object. The aspect of concentration is, according to the Abhidhamma/Abhidharma, present in all consciousness. As right concentration, however, it is that unification that is found when the mind comes to rest upon one single, or one complex but restorative, object, whereby the capacity to experience or be distracted by the senses and the hindrances to the mind becomes greatly diminished. In such states, interest and attentiveness allow the arising of joy, happiness, and then equanimity to envelop the body and mind in ever increasing stages of peace and stillness. If the mind is unified on one object, the five hindrances of the mind, known as sense desire or longing for the senses, ill will, sloth and torpor, restlessness and agitation, and doubt, are suppressed. The *jhāna* factors of application of mind, exploring, joy, happiness, and unification or one-pointedness become strong as "limbs" and support one another. The mind then experiences a state termed *jhāna*, whereby unification is sustained within a transformatory experience that stabilizes the mind and brings great peace. According to the Abhidhamma, such a state is also characterized by wisdom (*paññā*) and mindfulness, both of which become more sensitive and active as successive *jhāna*s are cultivated.

The first *jhāna*, practiced by the Buddha as a child and remembered and practiced again at the awakening, is said to be characterized by all five *jhāna* factors and, like subsequent *jhāna*s, arises in "seclusion" from the sense desires. There is bodily experience, of a pervading but undifferentiated kind, that in the absence of any searching for sensory satisfaction unifies the experience of the mind and body. Thus, the bodily experience of the consequent joy and happiness is compared to a bath attendant who moistens soap flakes to make a ball of lather, steeped in moisture.

The second *jhāna* moves beyond thinking about and exploring, and, "accompanied by internal peace, confidence and unification of mind," is suffused with joy and happiness. In this internal silence, joy and happiness become strong; it is possibly comparable to the movement from meditation to contemplation in the Western mystical traditions, whereby an internal silence awakens deeper levels of joy. The experience within the mind and body of these states is compared to a deep lake with waters welling up from below, pervading and drenching the body.

In the third *jhāna*, joy fades away; in the "equanimous, mindful and clearly comprehending" practitioner the factor of happiness becomes strong. The bodily experience of being immersed in this happiness is compared to a lotus pond, with bright lotuses of different colors that grow and flourish beneath the water.

In the fourth *jhāna* the meditator abandons both happiness and sorrow, and there is no pleasant or unpleasant feeling. Rather, filled with equanimity and mindfulness, or the equanimity arising from mindfulness, there is a "purified and translucent mind." The bodily experience of this is not described in terms of water; rather, there has been a kind of emergence to a different level or ground. The practitioner is described as being like a man covered from head to toe with a pure white cloth; in this way there is no part of the body that is not enveloped by the purified and translucent mind.

These states involve the purification of feeling and the development of being, rather than primarily "seeing." Within the terms of the doctrine of dependent arising, they can be said to purify the aspect of feeling, thus preventing the arising of craving. When this work has been done, new possibilities emerge: the fourth *jhāna* is regarded as a major milestone of the Buddhist path. The mind, purified with regard to the aggregate of feeling, is described as "composed, purified, translucent, unblemished, free from stains, malleable and imperturbable" (MN 1.248), and so capable of taking a number of directions, according to temperament and training.

From here, there are a number of options. One can simply progress to the eradication of the defilements and the movement to insight and the four stages of path: stream-enterer, once-returner, never-returner, or arahant. These are the steps by which awakening is described: at the first, doubt is eradicated; at the second and third, various kinds of hindrances, until, at the last, all defilements have been eliminated, including conceit.

Another route is to develop what are known as the *abhiññas*, the higher powers of the mind, described in the *Sāmaññaphala-sutta* (D.2): various miraculous powers such as the ability to change one element to another; the divine ear, able to hear sounds from far away and those emanating from the heavens; the ability to encompass the minds of others; the knowledge of past births; and the divine eye that has the knowledge of the arising and falling away of other beings in differing births. They are often described with two other powers: seeing the four elements in the body, as one might see a string within a jewel, and the ability to conjure up a mind-made body. The last higher power, the end of the sequence, is the eradication of defilements and latent tendencies leading to future rebirths. The development of these higher knowledges is particularly associated with teaching and the bodhisattva route to awakening. Thus, miracles arising as the result of meditative practice are certainly described in most forms of Buddhism. They are carefully contextualized as byproducts, however, rather than goals, and seen as aids in one's capacity to help and encourage others. The Buddha, unlike other religious teachers of the time, largely eschewed the spectacular displays of psychic power apparently considered de rigueur in ancient India. For the most part, features such as the divine eye and the divine ear were used by him and his followers as a means of divining problems in those he taught, and of helping others. These meditations assume different roles in various Buddhist traditions. In some traditions, such as the more secular insight traditions, and some Zen/Chan schools, such skills are not much discussed or emphasized. In Tibetan Buddhism, however, where the power of their proponent, the *mahāsiddha*, is highly valued, a number of psychic feats and challenges are considered a central part of a compassionate bodhisattva path. In one text the Buddha warns of the dangers of higher knowledges but then teaches three: the power to transform elements, the power to divine the minds of others, and, most importantly, the power to teach and to set practitioners on the right direction (D.11).

Yet another route after the fourth *jhāna* is the development of formless meditation. In these meditations, which also came to be called *jhāna*, the very process whereby the mind constructs and builds its world is examined. The first, the sphere of infinite space, explores the infinite field in which objects may arise: it is both defined by, and becomes, its object. The second, the sphere of infinite consciousness, steps back to examine the nature of the mind that experiences an infinite object. The third, the sphere of no-thingness, sees no relationship between subject and object that can be owned or can adhere: no "thing" or "owner" is perceived. Lastly, with the sphere of neither-identification-nor-non-identification, the mind finds a minimal attention at the very threshold of consciousness itself, before any identifying or non-identifying can occur (D.11; D.33; M.77).

The last two were learned by the Buddha before his awakening. In his system they are, however, taught only after the attainment of the first four *jhāna*s. These states are valued in many traditions of Buddhism and regarded as important specialist skills, refining the peace of meditation, loosening any potential attachments to the form meditations, and bringing great peace.

There are a number of debates about the centrality of all these routes and states. Some scholars regard them as supplementary accretions, and not essential to path; others argue that the very frequency with which the *abhiññā*s and the formless meditations are described in accounts of the final stages toward awakening indicate that they test, hone, and prepare the mind for its final goal. They are a marked feature of Central Asian Mahāyāna schools, explained within a different doctrinal framework as aspects of the bodhisattva path. The poet Aśvaghoṣa describes them:

> And just as the goldsmith brings gold to a good state for working into various kinds of ornaments, according to his wishes, so the monk whose mind is purified calms his mind so that it is under his control, and directs it as he wishes, wherever he wishes, with the higher knowledges.[9]

Samatha/Śamatha *and* Vipassanā/Vipaśyanā. The two great strands of meditative practice, central to most forms of Buddhism, could be said to be developments around the balance of mindfulness and concentration. All meditation needs both, but the style and manner of practice can vary greatly. From early times, mindfulness is linked to clear comprehension, and hence to insight. This word, meaning literally "seeing in all directions," is the necessary wisdom, to see the world of changing events and phenomena "as things are," an essential in all forms of Buddhism as the means to awakening.

Recent scholarship has challenged the sometimes monolithic sense of the two traditions of *samatha/śamatha* and *vipassana/vipaśyanā,* with some justification: texts such as the *Ānāpānasati-sutta* (M.118) and the *Mahāsatipaṭṭhāna-sutta* (D.22) suggest rather more a skilled interplay between the two. Their complementary functions suggest that *samatha/śamatha* involves the emotional purification seen through work on feeling, in terms of dependent arising. *Vipassanā/vipaśyanā* describes seeing or knowing, the right view of purification of one's perceptions and opinions whereby the aggregate of identification or perception (*saññā*) is scrutinized; ignorance and volitional activities in dependent arising are key. All well-established schools of meditation in some way address both these features.

The Buddha said there were four paths to awakening: *samatha* first, then *vipassanā; vipassanā* first then *samatha*; both yoked together; and, through "dhamma excitement," a less obviously meditative path based on insight (AN 2.157). The usual pattern for most Buddhist practice has been to *samatha/śamatha* first, to some level of *jhāna,* and then to *vipassanā/vipaśyanā.*[10] In the 19th century, however, in Burma, a movement loosely termed the "insight Burmese method" emerged, which paid particular attention to insight and mindfulness.[11] Teachers of this method have included Mahāsi Sayadaw and U Bha Khin. Some calm practices are usually included too, such as lovingkindness, but *jhāna* is less stressed. This strain of practice was highly influential in the development of many of the techniques and practices in the mindfulness movement and is associated with secular teachers such as Jack Kornfield and Joseph Goldstein.[12] It is particularly popular in America and has also made considerable impact in South and Southeast Asia. Different schools have different approaches to this day, and particular emphases. This differentiation has ancient roots and was described in early texts, appropriately, as the difference between a "wet," calm way and a "dry," insight one.

Most meditation schools teach some form of both. As Kamālaśīla said:

> those who wish to remove all the coverings of illusion should practise *śamatha* and *vipaśyana.* Through the power of *śamatha,* the mind becomes motionless like a lamp in a place where there is no wind. Through *vipaśyanā,* because of "such dharma" the light of true understanding is produced. After that, the entire covering of illusion is eradicated, like the disappearance of darkness with the dawn.[13]

OBJECTS AND TYPES OF MEDITATION

Since early times objects for meditation, and types of meditation practices, have varied. Commentarial stories describe people becoming awakened after seeing the cascades of waterfalls, the movement of a forest fire, or lotus blooms at different stages of bud, growth, and decay. All these manifestations of impermanence can elicit awakening. In stories of a type found throughout the Buddhist world, an activity, such as trying to rub a cloth to make it clean, or testing the readiness of cooking rice, can provide the inherent contradiction or experiential jolt in the cognition of events by which the mind grasps the truth. Accounts of paradoxical or surprise events eliciting awakening are particularly popular in the Chan/Zen/Seon traditions. If we take such accounts as broadly based on traditional practice, such "case histories," found in all Buddhisms, suggest that any object can be the trigger whereby the meditator, having prepared the mind in *jhāna*, frees the mind from the circle of samsara. Impermanence, unsatisfactoriness, and non-self can be seen in anything, if the conditions are right. In all such stories a sense of an intuitive, and sometimes even bodily, apprehension is evident: wisdom is often characterized as nonverbal, arising on the basis of practice, and not based simply on intellectual understanding. These shocks or triggers to awakening are found throughout Buddhisms. The Chinese *gongan*/Japanese *kōan*, for instance, a particularly popular method of Chan and Rinzai Zen schools, is taken as a repetitive puzzle for the mind that, practiced correctly, provides a kind of paradox through which the meditator can break through appearances and logical thought to awakening. Such prompts seem to fuse calm and insight in a way that is appropriate for the meditator at a particular time: in many stories the *gongan/kōan* provide the final condition whereby the practitioner experiences the possibility of the unconditioned.

In order to get to this point, a number of meditations or practices need to be pursued. Such methods of meditation, in ancient times and modern, are many and various. There is no system of classifying the types of meditations and their objects in early texts, although one or two include many (AN 1.39–46; M.77). From the outset of the tradition, however, a loose typology emerged, indicating different types of meditation, often to be pursued in support of one another, with the guidance of a teacher. In the Pali canon, the Buddha chooses particular meditations for individuals and suggests a mix of various practices to combat different tendencies (Ud 34–7). One text suggests that some objects are good antidotes for desire, some for hatred, and some for delusion (Nidd 1.360). In the commentaries of Upatissa and Buddhaghosa, dating from around the 5th to 6th century CE, a system emerges of classifying the objects in ways suggested by the canon. According to Buddhaghosa, there are forty such objects, which he terms "places of work" (*kammaṭṭhāna*; Vism III 104) for the development of *samatha*, or calm. These can broadly be categorized under a few headings, and it will be helpful here to use them as an indicator of some varieties of Buddhist meditative practice. It should be stressed, however, that the system is not universally applied or necessarily consulted. While Buddhism traveled, all kinds of variation in praxis and associated doctrine developed; the forty provide here a helpful guide to some of that range.

One other factor key to a consideration of meditation and its teaching is assessment of temperamental suitability in the assignation of meditation objects to particular people and, in particular, the need for a good friend, teacher, or guru to help in that. Meditation may be a solitary activity, but it can be a group one too; the need to take advice and have friendship with others is a thread in most Buddhisms. Consultation is constantly recommended, implicitly or explicitly, and occasions for asking teachers' advice are also specified.

The Beautiful Object. The first ten involve objects that lead to the four *jhānas*. A device, known as *kasiṇa* (literally, entire or whole), arouses unification and peace: earth, water, fire, air, blue, red, yellow, white, light, and limited space. The common factor among them all is that they are extremely simple and apparently equated with a beauty that brings the mind easily to stillness and unification, if accompanied by the mindfulness exercises suggested in the manuals. Buddhaghosa gives recommendations for the construction of *kasiṇas*, strongly recommending that they are used rather than natural occurrences of the object. Canonical texts suggest a somewhat more fluid understanding: the spheres of transcendence (*abhibhāyatana*) say the "external object" is like the blue, yellow, or red flowers and the white morning star, as well as fine muslin of these colors, thus suggesting such objects were used (MN 2.22-23), as they are in some modern Southeast Asian practice. The *Culasuññatā-Sutta* suggests taking a field of earth, "like a stretched bull's hide," for the first *kasiṇa* (M.121). If commentarial stories, dating from around the 6th century, are taken as realistic indicators, objects are sometimes "created" in some way in the mind's eye or observed in natural surroundings.[14]

Visualized *kasiṇa* practices can be seen as forming the basis of the complex imaginative exercises involving the eidetic faculty, linked to the aural and chant, that characterize the often highly integrated, graduated training systems of many of the Mahāyāna Buddhist traditions. The tantras of Tibetan Buddhism, the complex visualizations of Tientai/Tendai, as well as Eastern and Central Asian systems of meditation based on the notion of a Pure Land, in which a being may take rebirth in the presence of the Buddha of the Western direction, Amitābha, exercise comparable skills: they employ the internal visualization of color, light, space, or the four elements in the mind's eye for the development of calm, and in most cases, through the intimation of emptiness (*unyatā*) at the end, insight as well. For one popular practice, the recitation of the *nianfo* 念佛/*nembutsu*, a rebirth in Sukhāvatī, or a Pure Land, is said to arise through the simple reiteration of the Buddha's name. Through such meditations, control is exercised in the creation, evocation, or, sometimes, invocation of the visualized figure and surroundings, which lie at a midpoint between created and creator, invoked and evoked. For Vajrayāna, a tantric teacher for initiation and guidance is essential.[15] Most involve the visual presence of the Buddha, deities, and bodhisattvas. Techniques to maintain mindfulness are usually sustained throughout, such as a mantra, a chant, or the breath.[16] In most such systems, a complex three-dimensional mandalic space is envisaged; four directions and protective deities are established or invited, gods and attendants support the central figure, and a relationship is made between the power of the visualized figure and the meditator through features such as seed syllables, mantras, and gesture. Visual objects and aural phenomena are dissolved at the end of the practice as the mind experiences emptiness, before ensuring a careful return to the everyday world. Such meditations, in part derived from and employing skills also used in *kasiṇa* practice, are also highly dependent on other meditative techniques, on the theory system whereby the power of the emanation is activated and translated into an assimilable form, and on the often complex features of ritual, offerings, and hand gestures that allow the qualities of the god, goddess, or bodhisattva to be mediated and experienced within the body and mind of the practitioner involved.

The Foul Object. The next set of ten are the meditations on the foul, the stages of decomposition of the corpse (AN 1.42; DhS 263–4; Vism VI). These were apparently particularly characteristic of early Buddhists; to this day monastics conduct group visits to morgues to pursue them.[17] They are, however, considered highly dangerous without close supervision and instruction (Vism VI 52–65). Because the objects are complex, it is possible to progress through them to the first *jhāna*, but not subsequent ones, unless some simple feature such as a color is taken.[18]

Repeated Mindfulnesses. Another ten meditations, also known as calming, are, nonetheless, explicitly linked to the cultivation of mindfulness too. These are the recollections, or literally "repeated mindfulnesses" (*anussatis*). For these, attention and awareness are brought to bear repeatedly on an often complex object. Buddhaghosa says that most do not lead to *jhāna*, with the exception of that of the body and the breath. Such an assertion is challenged, however, throughout many forms of Buddhism, where one or more of these objects constitute a key salvific practice, in some cases capable of taking the mind to *jhāna* and even awakening. Indeed, in most Buddhist traditions variations of these recollections are practiced at all levels of attainment for their capacity to awaken and enliven the mind. Most involve some discursive thought and consideration, but many are said to lead to the suspension of internal verbalization in *jhāna*, and then wisdom. They have been considered from early times ways of ensuring that the mind during the day is healthy and balanced.[19] The Buddha frequently suggests them for laypeople and householders busy with children (AN 1.206–11; AN 5.332–4).

Objects of the Recollections, or Repeated Mindfulnesses:

i) Six recollections
Buddha
Dhamma
Sangha
Morality (*sīla*)
Generosity or letting go (*cāga*)
Devas, or gods, born as the result of good actions and volition in the sense-sphere
ii) Four mindfulnesses:
Death
Body
Breath
Peace

The first six are largely devotional practices, often in various postures, undertaken by the laity and monastics, singly or, often, together. Thus, the recollection of the Buddha, his teaching, and his community is chanted while circumambulating a shrine as a group practice, for instance; the recollection acts of morality, of generosity, and the happiness possible for those that undertake these, represented by the devas, or gods, are inextricably linked in most forms of Buddhism to the chanting, prostrations, ceremonies, and devotional activities that form a central role in so much Buddhist ritual and practice.

This group of practices, in varying mixes, assumed ever growing status and importance within South Asia as an emphasis on devotion grew in the centuries after the Buddha's death. They also assumed immense importance as Buddhism traveled through China, Korea, Japan, Tibet, and Mongolia and interacted in a creative way with the ritual and devotional practices of other regions: schools throughout the first millennium developed practices on the recollection of the internal and external attributes of the Buddha that became, in effect, complete meditation systems. Indeed, it could be argued that many of the developments of what is known as the Mahāyāna can be traced in part to an exploration of the full doctrinal and practice-based implications of the recollection of the Buddha, dhamma, and sangha. With an increased emphasis on the bodhisattva path in the first part of the millennium, the bodily form of the being that enacts the teaching comes to be seen as an embodiment of all possible meditations and all possible paths. Imaginative and visualization exercises that suggested the possibility of infinite bodhisattvas, demonstrating such potential, opened up new fields of meditative exploration that had not been envisaged before. Bodhisattvas enacting the teaching could, in many systems in China, Tibet, Korea, and Japan, be felt to fill countless world systems, and all times. The Visualization Sutras (*Guan wuliang shoufo jing* 觀無量壽佛經 T. 365, vol. 12), popular in 6th-century China, use visual image, body, and breath in highly elaborate, often devotional meditations. In Chinese meditation, walking practices were developed whereby the thirty-two marks of the Buddha, a symbolic means of suggesting the attributes of the fully awakened mind, are imagined as part of one's own body while walking, after devotions, within the meditation hall.[20] These marks, often associated with bodhisattvas as well, are pictured in the meditations associated with Vajrayāna in the Tibetan and Central Asian schools. They are highly regarded in Eastern Buddhism; the Japanese poetic form known as the *waka* was based on the thirty-two marks, and the attributes are characterized in visualizations of Tientai/Tendai meditation.

In such exercises, mindfulness and concentration are unified by the reiteration of a particular object and the bringing of the attention repeatedly to the details of the figure, the path, and the meditation states involved. Wisdom may also be developed on that basis: the impermanence of the manifestations or offerings, the emptiness of the visualized figures allowed to dissolve within the ritual, and insight into the insubstantiality of phenomena may arise, if the meditation is directed toward that.

Until recently, practices associated with these six recollections have tended to be underplayed in assessments of Buddhist meditation. From the 19th century, Westerners influenced by scientific and rationalist interpretations of Buddhist principle concluded that devotional activities such as chant, offering flowers, and prostrations to local deities as well as the Buddha and bodhisattvas were marginal activities for laypeople, without soteriological purpose, and an "impure" Buddhism. Vestigial elements of this remain in the wariness of many toward the ritual "trappings" of particular Buddhist traditions. But such devotions are felt to play a vital role and they are now being more closely examined: indeed, historically, Buddhist practice systems have adapted, integrated, and developed local forms of homage to deities, rituals, and ways of offering, creatively adjusting in a number of ways to different conditions and new cultures.[21] The figure of the Buddha, however, is perceived as having limitless potential:

> the practitioner should first practice calm by settling his mind (*citta*) on the image of the Tathāgata that he has either seen or heard about. He should constantly bring to mind

> this image of the Tathāgata, that shines like heated or smelted gold, endowed with the marks and signs, sitting in the midst of the circle of the retinue of the Buddha, ministering through all kinds of means to the benefit of living beings, and he should generate the aspiration to cultivate the wonderful qualities of the Tathāgata. After calming down states that have arisen with restlessness, he sees, in *jhāna,* the image of the Tathāgata as vividly as if it were in front of him.[22]

Four Mindfulnesses. The next four meditations are usually termed "mindfulnesses": of death, the breath, the body, and peace. Mindfulness of death is the bearing in mind of one's own mortality and is considered useful as an occasional reminder of that; funerary ceremonies in all forms of Buddhism are taken as outlets for grief and also reminders of mortality, with the corpse often on view as a reminder and a meditation object for all. Transference of merit in ceremonies for the deceased are conducted in South and Southeast Asian Buddhism.[23] Tibetan Buddhism in particular has often complex rituals performed by tantric masters to help the dead and act as a reminder. The shock of death is considered a crucial moment for the possibility of awakening.[24]

Mindfulness of body is both an insight and a calm practice, involving awareness of the parts of the different aspects of the body: more general bodily exercises are considered later. Mindfulness of peace is the recollection of states of peace that have occurred, which is considered a restorative application of mindfulness.

Mindfulness of breath has, apparently since ancient times, been one of the principal objects of meditation in all Buddhist traditions. It is the only meditation object Buddhaghosa associates with the sense of touch, it is always present, and it has the capacity to arouse all stages of calm and insight. For a *samatha* breathing mindfulness, appreciation of the breath is refined and developed through feeling and gentle alertness.[25] Sometimes, control is exercised over length of breath, to facilitate the movement between *jhāna*s and, crucially, a safe return to the "normal" breath and one's daily life. When mindfulness and concentration come into balance, a mental image (*nimitta*) arises; this may be used to develop the four *jhāna*s, and then formless states. The emotional resilience aroused by this practice then permits the arising of insight naturally through an awareness that the breath is impermanent, unsatisfactory, and not "owned." An insight school would offer quite different and apparently contradictory instructions, to ignore any images and arouse "letting go" by simply observing, with "bare attention," the rise and fall of the breath on a particular area of the body, such as the abdomen. This allows observation and investigation of the arising and falling away of all physical, mental, and emotional phenomena that occur. Insight methods examine in an analytical manner, with mindfulness of sense impressions and ideas and emotions as they arise, events in the mind and body with the intention of clearing "views" and arousing right seeing. In both methods, mindfulness is developed and becomes strong.

Four meditations follow, known as the divine abidings of lovingkindness, compassion, sympathetic joy, and equanimity. With the object taken as all beings, and wish for their welfare, such meditations may lead to *jhāna*. They are also, however, considered as representing four ways of facing other beings and the world around, and are also recommended as practices in daily life. The *Mettā-Sutta*, for instance, suggests practicing lovingkindness at all times, and in all postures (Sn 143–152). It has been argued that love and compassion were such central elements of early Buddhist practice that their practice was in itself a means of following the Buddhist path to salvation.[26] Indeed, in the Mahāyāna, and thus most forms of Eastern and Central Asian Buddhism, the vow to commit to the welfare of all sentient beings, an undertaking suggested for all, places compassion in particular as having a key role in the practitioner's alignment in meditation and daily life. In these meditation systems, new perspectives on the divine abidings become evident. Perhaps the most famous of these are Śāntideva's words on the exchange of self and others: if all beings are interconnected, as he argues elsewhere in this work, then my suffering is no more important than any other person's; the practice of the divine abidings is perceived in a different way. If all beings suffer as I do:

> Therefore, in the same way that one desires to protect oneself from affliction, grief and the like, so an attitude of protectiveness and of compassion should be practised towards the world.[27]

All forms of Buddhism, however, employ these states. The *Mettā-Sutta*, the *locus classicus* for the practice and celebration of the practice of lovingkindness, is constantly chanted, studied, and recited throughout South and Southeast Asia as providing the fundamental basis of contact with all other beings.

After the four formless meditations, which have been discussed, there are two more: the awareness of the elements in the body, and the repulsiveness of food. Meditative work with the four elements is a marked characteristic of the Southeast Asian Buddhist tradition of *Borān Kamatthān*, whereby, with space, the five elements are associated with the *jhāna* factors; amulets and cloths with yantra designs describing the dynamic balance of the five in meditation are found throughout Southeast Asia.[28] The meditation on food is considered only suitable for monastics, under certain conditions, and is not conducted as a lay practice.

Buddhaghosa's typology is perhaps the most famous attempt to classify meditation objects and routes of practice, but there have been others. Jinul, in Korea, attempting a synthesis of the many different paths and routes available in Eastern Buddhism by the 12th century, undertook a comparable exercise.[29] The list is also not definitive, even in South and Southeast Asian Buddhism, where meditations given in the canon once are not included in the forty: the Buddha apparently sometimes devised particular meditations, and combinations of them, to suit the person or people he was addressing; such a flexibility continues in most traditions of Buddhism to this day.[30]

Other activities are also considered *bhāvanā*. One early text refers to "hearing *dhamma* at the right time, discussion of *dhamma* at the right time, *samatha* at the right time, *vipassanā* at the right time" (AN 2.141). The recitation of texts and listening to them has always been thought important in most forms of Buddhism, as has discussion and debate on aspects of the Buddhist teaching, particularly stressed and formalized in Tibetan traditions. Such activities cannot be isolated from meditation and contemplation. The chanting traditions in particular, whereby the chant or mantra itself becomes the means by which the five *jhāna* factors may be developed, and, from calm, ensure the practitioner experiences insight, are rich, highly differentiated and often core practices in many forms of Buddhism. Chant can be and often is group *bhāvanā*, requiring all the foundations of mindfulness.[31] To chant well, particularly with others, requires alertness to one's own body, feelings, and mind as well as to those of others forming the group, and a sense of the ongoing dhamma, or the fourth foundation, in the memorization and recitation of the chant itself. Again, these elements are felt to include calm and insight. Chanting, as an activity that can be pursued either vocally or subvocally throughout the day, is a core practice in many Eastern schools. Pure Land schools, the Nichiren schools in Japan, and movements such as Soka Gokkai stress the importance of reciting the syllables of specified mantras or chants, particularly associated with the auspicious and salvific features of that school. This can be done out loud, alone or in groups, or as a background internal murmur in one's mind during the day. Doctrinal explanations of such practices vary, but in many cases there is the notion that the storehouse consciousness, *ālayavijñāna*, an underlying substrate of human existence, is gradually purified by the chant, its innate auspiciousness allowing the inherent buddha nature to emerge. In Pure Land traditions, the chant to the Buddha of the Western direction is said to produce rebirth in his heaven. Insight practices can also be applied through chant. In some traditions, such as the Korean Seon schools, investigation of the source of the sound, and an experience of non-self through the act of chant, empty the mind of attachment to the self and are perceived as a means of arousing wisdom.[32]

The Body and Meditation. It is mindfulness of the body, the first of the thirty-seven factors of awakening, however, that is considered the foundational practice in all forms of Buddhism. The Buddha's statement that "in this fathom long body is the arising and ceasing of the world" is applied, in most traditions, also to the care for the health and movement of the body. Extreme asceticism, while sometimes sanctioned, is not usually encouraged. In the earliest texts, the Buddha suggested four postures for meditation: sitting, walking, standing up, and lying down. The very emphasis on such change itself represents the Buddhist position of balance with regard to the body and what is seen as the middle way between the two extremes of excessive sense desire and self-mortification. Thus, awareness of physical movement, mindfulness, and the adoption of a posture suitable for a particular practice are important features influencing and influenced by the meditation itself. As the account of *jhāna* showed, from earliest times the description of meditation states involves description of what happens in the bodily effects of meditation; a suitable posture is needed to experience this. In early texts, the posture is described simply as "suitable, with back straight," in seclusion. The classical pose is the *samādhi* posture, with the feet crossed in full or half-lotus position, hands cupped on lap, right hand over left. Variations include the "Burmese posture," a more relaxed cross-legged position, or the quarter-lotus. The "European posture," seated on a chair, with the back straight and feet firmly placed on the ground, is considered less helpful for *jhāna* practice, but acceptable for many insight methods.

Some significant differences emerge in postural recommendations, dependent on the meditation involved and its particular purpose. Chan/Zen/Seon schools sometimes have specific requirements: the left hand is sometimes placed over the right, with the intent to "let go"; the thumbs are also sometimes raised from the palms to sustain alertness. Some meditators sit astride low stools, or a cushion (J. *zabuton*) specially made for the purpose; the posture adopted may be the hero's pose (S. *virāsana*; J. *seiza*), with shoulders relaxed but the back very straight.

The usual posture for meditation is sitting down; there are only rare instances of standing. Walking practices are used throughout most forms of Buddhism as a complement to sitting.

They are felt to arouse mindfulness internally, externally, and both internally and externally, as the *Satipaṭṭhāna-sutta* (D.22) suggests. Most traditions involve meditative walking, either as a secluded activity or as part of energetic longer exercise, such as the monastic alms round. Such practices support the body for meditation and balance energies aroused in seated meditation. Directed mindful walking practices, such as the observation of the rise, movement, fall, and full contact of each foot as it touches the ground, as well as awareness of bodily adjustments and balance at each stage of each step, are found in many traditions, particularly in South and Southeast Asia. They are often performed on one's own, in an outside area known as a *caṅkamana*, a set walking space. In Chinese Chan/Korean Seon/Japanese Zen traditions a group walking practice around the temple may feature as a way to arouse alertness and awareness of others, the surroundings, and the group, between sitting practices. Bodily activity on routine chores is itself considered a form of practice in these traditions: monasteries often incorporate a specified period of vigorous, alert temple cleaning as part of the daily routine (Japanese *sumu*). Other physical activities, whether walking practices, extended ascetic (Pali *dhutaṅga*) walks, martial arts, Tai Chi, or, in the Central Asian traditions, the practice of continued prostrations, are all felt to arouse the vigor, mindfulness, and strength needed for sustained meditative practice. Such bodily actions are considered to be integral supports for meditation and themselves a form of practice.

A rich language of mudrā, the communication of particular qualities and mental states through gesture and bodily posture, is found throughout Buddhism. In Southeast Asia, each posture of the figure of the Buddha represents a life event and an associated strength: a buddha in the earth-touching gesture, used in the moment when the Buddha defies the god of delusion, Māra, before the awakening, encourages resolve (*adhiṭṭhāna*); the *abhaya mudrā*, with the right palm raised and open, dispels fear.[33] In Chan/Zen meditation, the adoption of a particular posture is particularly stressed as a crucial element in the meditation itself: to assume the posture of a buddha, one participates in that buddhahood.

In Central Asian traditions of practice, mudras or precisely defined bodily gestures provide an emotional vocabulary central to the efficacy of tantric and Vajrayāna meditation. Each one of the senses, for instance, is represented by a bodily gesture during the preliminary offerings; a sophisticated system of precisely differentiated mudras ensures that attentiveness to the body is maintained while the visualization is constructed. During the meditative part of the practice, rosaries, usually with 108 beads, are worked. Finally, after the visualizations have been dissolved into emptiness, gods are invited to leave with words and gesture. Throughout, variation in gesture, visualization, and the final dissolution of all forms into emptiness before a return to the usual world ensure that mindfulness of body, feelings, and mind is both aroused and sustained.[34]

Bodily Devotion. Material attention aids such as prayer wheels and bells are employed in many Buddhist traditions outside the seated practice. All schools of Buddhism suggest that bodily acts of devotion, such as *añjali*s or full prostrations, enact a willingness to let go of pride and rigidity of mind and body through the symbolic release of ego before a shrine. In different schools one's own teacher or, in some traditions, the guru, one's own lineage of teachers, and sometimes bodhisattvas and the arahants are all to be accorded honor. In tantric Vajrayāna meditation, the meditator invokes the guidance of a lama, to be regarded as a buddha; supplicates the

Yidam (deity), whose meditation is to be regarded as supreme; and looks for direction in the community of the *Kandro dakīṇīs* (sky-goers) as well as the usual refuges.[35] Chan/Seon/Zen traditions invoke and pay homage to the full lineage of their teachers.[36] Such bodily practices, often before seated meditation, are regarded as safeguards for the health and balance of the meditator and, on a simply practical level, allow bodily energies to be unconstricted. Types of meditation vary greatly in often significant detail; physical praxis, however, often of a devotional kind, is a key element before and sometimes after the *bhāvanā* involved in seated meditation.

CONCLUSION

The history of Buddhism has traditionally been told within the parameters of a Western preoccupation with orthodoxy and doctrinal differentiation. It is also enacted, however, through the way in which different forms, types of meditation, chanting traditions, visualization practices, and even adjustments in bodily posture are developed in accordance with different understandings and interpretations of the Buddhist path. When seen in this light, the various forms of Buddhism often offer different perspectives, but they employ a comparable complexity of approaches to the care of body, heart, and mind and the particular kinds of attentiveness needed at different times. Thus, to conclude, it will be helpful to look at an example of the way in which features may intermingle in one system. In a session of meditation in a Sōtō Zen temple, after entering, an homage of respect, or a prostration, is given to the Buddha, to the cushion, and then, turning 180 degrees, to those with whom one is about to practice. One sits on the black square (*sutan*) and the cushion (*zafu*), in this tradition, facing the wall. After preliminary chanting, there are thirty minutes of *Zazen*, with the eyes neither open nor shut. Although there is some attention to the breath in early stages, the practice involves "just sitting," allowing the judgmental mind to be suspended and letting all thoughts, feelings, emotions, and ideas arise and fall, in the practice of silent illumination (*shikantaza*). There is then ten minutes of *kinhin*, a directed group walking practice in the area around the temple, followed by another thirty minutes of *Zazen*. A chanting ceremony follows, including the *Heart Sūtra*, and the homage to the lineage of patriarchs. Rice soup (*genmai*) is eaten in the company of others, after a ritual unpacking of the food and chanting. When the ceremony has finished, the practitioners perform *samu*, mindful physical work in the temple.

This brief account shows how elements of the eightfold path are felt to work together in one session; there are careful adjustments in attention in the balancing of needs, the establishment of devotion and respect, an interplay of solitary and communal sitting and walking, calm and insight. Meditation and contemplation are, in most cases, essential for the completion of the eightfold path; their practice, however, is never far from other elements that support and sustain them.

PRIMARY SOURCES

Pali Text Society texts and citations are used with these abbreviations. Volume number is followed by page number (e.g., MN 3.124). All these works, with the exception of the *Mahāniddesa* and the *Visuddhimagga*, may be found at Sutta Central.

AN *Aṅguttaranikāya*
DhS *Dhammasaṅgani*
DN *Dīghanikāya* (cited as D when referring to sutta number, e.g., D.16)
MN *Majjhimanikāya* (cited as M when referring to sutta number, e.g., M.36)
Nidd *Mahāniddesa*
SN *Saṃyuttanikāya*
Sn *Suttanipāta*
Vism *Visuddhimagga*

FURTHER READING

Blofeld, John. *The Tantric Mysticism of Tibet: A Practical Guide*. New York: Dutton, 1970.

Buddhadāsa Bhikkhu. *Mindfulness with Breathing: A Manual for Serious Beginners*. Translated from the Thai by Santikaro Bhikkhu. Bangkok: Evolution/Liberation, 1988.

Buswell, Robert E. *Tracing Back the Radiance: Chinul's Korean Way of Zen*. Honolulu: University of Hawai'i Press, 1988.

Cousins, L. S. "*Samatha-yāna* and *Vipassanā-yāna*." In *Buddhist Studies in Honour of Hammalava Saddhatissa*. Edited by Gatare Dhammapala, et al., 56–68. Nugegoda, Sri Lanka: University of Sri Jayewardenapura, 1984.

Cousins, L. S. "Buddhist *Jhāna*: Its Nature and Attainment According to the Pali Sources." *Religion* 3 (1988): 115–131.

Gethin, Rupert. *Foundations of Buddhism*. Oxford: Oxford University Press, 1998.

Gomez, Luis O. "Meditation." In *Encyclopedia of Buddhism*. Vol. 2. Edited by Robert Buswell, Jr., 520–530. New York: Macmillan, 2004.

Gregory, Peter N., ed. *Traditions of Meditation in Chinese Buddhism*. Kuroda Institute Studies in East Asian Buddhism 4. Honolulu: University of Hawai'i Press, 1986.

Guneratana, Mahathera H. *The Path of Serenity and Insight: An Explanation of the Buddhist Jhānas*. Delhi: Motilal Banarsidass, 1985.

Lopez, Donald S. *Religions of Tibet in Practice*. Princeton, NJ: Princeton University Press, 1997.

Nyanaponika Thera. *The Heart of Buddhist Meditation: A Handbook of Mental Training Based on the Buddha's Way of Mindfulness*. London: Rider, 1962.

Saddhatissa, Ven. *The Buddha's Way*. London: George Allen and Unwin, 1971.

Schaik, Sam van. *The Spirit of Tibetan Buddhism*. New Haven, CT, and London: Yale University Press, 2016.

Schaik, Sam van. *The Spirit of Zen*. New Haven, CT, and London: Yale University Press, 2018.

Shaw, Sarah. *Buddhist Meditation: An Anthology of Texts*. London: Routledge, 2006.

Shaw, Sarah. *Introduction to Buddhist Meditation*. With a chapter on Tibet by Georgios Halkias. London: Routledge, 2009.

Shaw, Sarah. *The Spirit of Buddhist Meditation*. New Haven, CT and London: Yale University Press, 2014.

Suzuki, S. *Zen Mind, Beginners' Mind*. Boulder, CO: Shambhala, 2011.

Tanabe, George T. "Chanting." In *Encyclopedia of Buddhism*. Vol. 1. Edited by Robert Buswell, Jr., 137–139. New York: Macmillan, 2004.

Vajirañāṇa, Mahāthera. *Buddhist Meditation in Theory and Practice*. Kuala Lumpur: Buddhist Missionary Society, 1975.

Yamasaki, Taiko. *Shingon: Japanese Esoteric Buddhism*. Translated by Richard Peterson and Cynthia Peterson. Edited by Yasuyoshi Morimoto and David Kidd. Boston: Shambhala, 1988.

REFERENCES

Beyer, Stephen. *The Cult of Tara: Magic and Ritual in Tibet*. Berkeley, Los Angeles, and London: University of California Press, 1973.

Bizot, François. *Le figuieràcinq branches. Recherches sur le bouddhisme khmer* II, PEFEO CVII. Paris: L'École française d'Extrême-Orient, 1976.

Blofeld, John. *The Tantric Mysticism of Tibet: A Practical Guide*. New York: Dutton, 1970.

Buddhadāsa Bhikkhu. *Mindfulness With Breathing: A Manual for Serious Beginners*. Translated from the Thai by Santikaro Bhikkhu. Bangkok: Evolution/Liberation. 1988.

Buswell, Robert E. *Tracing Back the Radiance: Chinul's Korean Way of Zen*. Kuroda Institute. Honolulu: University of Hawai'i Press, 1981.

Buswell, Robert E. "Chinul's Systematization of Chinese Meditative Techniques in Korean Son Buddhism." In *Traditions of Meditation in Chinese Buddhism*. Edited by P. N. Gregory, 199–242. Kuroda Institute: Studies in East Asian Buddhism 4. Honolulu: University of Hawai'i Press, 1986.

Choompolpaisal, Phibul, and Andrew Skilton. "The Old Meditation (*boran kammatthan*), a Pre-Reform Theravāda Meditation System, From Wat Ratchasittharam: The Pīti Section of the Kammatthan Matchima Baeb Lamdap." *ASEANIE* 33 (2014): 83–116.

Choompolpaisal, Phibul, and Andrew Skilton. "The Ancient Theravāda Meditation System, *Borān Kammaṭṭhāna*: Ānāpānasati in Kammatthan Majjima Baeb Lamdub." *Buddhist Studies Review* 32, no. 2 (2015): 207–229.

Cousins, L. S. "Buddhist *Jhāna*: Its Nature and Attainment According to the Pali Sources." *Religion* 3 (1973): 115–131.

Cousins, L. S. "*Samatha-yāna* and *Vipassanā-yāna*." In *Buddhist Studies in Honour of Hammalava Saddhatissa*. Edited by Gatare Dhammapala, et al., 56–68. Nugegoda, Sri Lanka: University of Sri Jayewardenapura, 1984.

Crosby, Kate. *Traditional Theravāda Meditation and Its Modern-Era Suppression*. Hong Kong: Buddha Dharma Centre of Hong Kong, 2013.

Crosby, Kate, and Andrew Skilton, trans. *The Bodhicaryāvatāra; Śāntideva*. Edited by Paul Williams. Oxford and New York: Oxford University Press, 1996.

Dhammadhāro, Ajahn Lee. *Keeping the Breath in Mind: Lessons in Samādhi*. Translated by Geoffrey DeGraff. Rayong, Thailand: No publisher, n.d. (talks from 1956–1960).

Ferguson, Andy. *Zen's Chinese Heritage: The Masters and Their Teachings*. Expanded edition. Boston: Wisdom, 2011.

Gethin, R. *Foundations of Buddhism*. Oxford: Oxford University Press, 1998.

Gethin, Rupert. "On Some Definitions of Mindfulness." *Contemporary Buddhism* 12, no. 1 (2011): 263–279.

Gombrich, Richard F. *What the Buddha Thought*. London: Equinox, 2009.

Gombrich, Richard F. *Buddhism and Pali*. Oxford: Mud Pie Books, 2018.

Gomez, Luis O. "Meditation." In *Encyclopedia of Buddhism*. Vol. 2. Edited by Robert Buswell Jr., 520–530. New York: Macmillan, 2004.

Goodman, Charles. *The Training Anthology of Śāntideva: A Translation of the Śikṣa-samuccaya*. New York: Oxford University Press, 2016.

Guneratana, Mahathera H. *The Path of Serenity and Insight: An Explanation of the Buddhist Jhānas*. Delhi: Motilal Banarsidass, 1985.

Halkias, Georgios. "Meditation in Tibet." In *Introduction to Buddhist Meditation*. Edited by S. Shaw, 159–186. London: Routledge, 2009.

Harrison, Paul. "*Buddhānusmṛti* in the *Pratyutpanna-Buddha-Saṃmukhāvasthitasamādhi-Sūtra*." *Journal of Indian Philosophy* 6 (1978): 35–57.

Harvey, Peter. "The Dynamics of *Paritta* Chanting in Southern Buddhism." In *Love Divine: Studies in Bhakti and Devotional Mysticism*. Edited by Karel Werner, 53–84. Surrey, UK: Curzon Press, 1993.

Harvey, Peter. *An Introduction to Buddhism: Teachings, History and Practices*. Revised edition. Cambridge, UK: Cambridge University Press, 2013.

Harvey, Peter. "Mindfulness in Theravāda Samatha and Vipassanā Meditations and in Secular Mindfulness." In *Buddhist Foundations of Mindfulness*. Edited by Edo Shonin, William Van Gordon, and Nirbhay N. Singh, 115–137. Cham, Switzerland: Springer, 2015.

Lamrimpa, G. *Śamatha Meditation: Tibetan Teachings on Cultivating Mental Quiescence*. Translated by Alan Wallace. Introduction by H. Sprager. Ithaca, NY: Snow Lion, 1992.

Lopez, Donald. *Religions of Tibet in Practice*. Princeton, NJ: Princeton University Press, 1997.

Matics, K. I. *Gestures of the Buddha*. 4th edition. Bangkok: Chulalongkorn University Press, 2008.

Murphy, Anne. "Mindfulness-Based Therapy in Modern Psychology: Convergence and Divergence From Early Buddhist Thought." *Contemporary Buddhism* 17, no. 2 (2016): 275–325.

Nyanaponika Thera. *The Heart of Buddhist Meditation: A Handbook of Mental Training Based on the Buddha's Way of Mindfulness*. London: Rider, 1962.

Saddhatissa, Ven. *The Buddha's Way*. London: George Allen and Unwin, 1971.

Schaik, Sam van. *The Spirit of Tibetan Buddhism*. New Haven, CT and London: Yale University Press, 2016.

Schaik, Sam van. *The Spirit of Zen*. New Haven, CT and London: Yale University Press, 2018.

Schlütter, Morten. "*Kanhua* Meditation in Chinese Zen." In *Asian Traditions of Meditation*. Edited by Halvor Eifring, 165–184. Honolulu: University of Hawai'i Press, 2016.

Shaw, Sarah. *Buddhist Meditation: An Anthology of Texts*. London: Routledge, 2006.

Shaw, Sarah. *Introduction to Buddhist Meditation*. With a chapter on Tibet by Georgios Halkias. London: Routledge, 2009.

Shaw, Sarah. *The Spirit of Buddhist Meditation*. New Haven, CT and London: Yale University Press, 2014.

Shaw, Sarah. "Meditation Teaching and Suitability: The Depiction of Temperament in Pāli Canonical Text and Commentarial Narrative." In *Asian Traditions of Meditation*. Edited by Halvor Eifring, 122–144. Honolulu: University of Hawai'i Press, 2016.

Shaw, Sarah. *Mindfulness: Where It Comes From and What It Is*. Boulder, CO: Shambhala, 2020.

Shindai, Sekiguchi. "Wonhyo's Calmness and Insight." In *Bukkyo no jissen genre (Buddhist Soteriological Principles)*. Edited by Sekiguchi Shindai, 429–445. Tokyo: Sankibo Busshorin, 1977.

Stevenson, Daniel B. "The Four Kinds of *Samādhi* in Early T'ien-t'ai Budddhism." In *Traditions of Meditation in Chinese Buddhism*. Edited by Peter N. Gregory, 45–97. Kuroda Institute: Studies in East Asian Buddhism 4. Honolulu: University of Hawai'i Press, 1986.

Suzuki, Shunryu. *Zen Mind, Beginners' Mind*. Boulder, CO: Shambhala, 2011.

Swearer, Donald K. *The Buddhist World of Southeast Asia*. New York: State University of New York Press, 2010.

Tanabe, George T. "Chanting." In *Encyclopedia of Buddhism*. Vol. 1. Edited by R. Buswell Jr., 130–137. New York: Macmillan, 2004.

Vajirañāṇa, Mahāthera. *Buddhist Meditation in Theory and Practice*. Kuala Lumpur: Buddhist Missionary Society, 1975.

Yamasaki, Taiko. *Shingon: Japanese Esoteric Buddhism*. Translated by Richard and Cynthia Peterson. Edited by Yasuyoshi Morimoto and David Kidd. Boston: Shambhala, 1988.

NOTES

1. Richard Gombrich, *Buddhism and Pali* (Oxford: Mud Pie Books, 2018).
2. See Phibul Choompolpaisal and Andrew Skilton, "The Old Meditation (*boran kammatthan*), a Pre-Reform Theravāda Meditation System, From Wat Ratchasittharam: The Pīti Section of the Kammatthan Matchima Baeb Lamdap," *ASEANIE* 33 (2014): 83–116; Phibul Choompolpaisal and Andrew Skilton, "The Ancient Theravāda Meditation System, *Borān Kammaṭṭhāna*: Ānāpānasati in Kammatthan Majjima Baeb Lamdub,"

Buddhist Studies Review 32, no. 2 (2015): 207–229; and Kate Crosby, *Traditional Theravāda Meditation and its Modern-Era Suppression* (Hong Kong: Buddha Dharma Centre of Hong Kong, 2013).

3. See, e.g., Taiko Yamasaki, *Shingon: Japanese Esoteric Buddhism*, trans. Richard Peterson and Cynthia Peterson, ed. Yasuyoshi Morimoto and David Kidd (Boston: Shambhala, 1988).
4. See Andy Ferguson, *Zen's Chinese Heritage: The Masters and Their* Teachings, expanded edition (Boston: Wisdom, 2011); Shunryu Suzuki, *Zen Mind, Beginners' Mind* (Boulder, CO: Shambhala, 2011); and Morten Schlütter, "*Kanhua* Meditation in Chinese Zen," in *Asian Traditions of Meditation*, ed. Halvor Eifring (Honolulu: University of Hawai'i Press, 2016), 165–184.
5. See Rupert Gethin, "On Some Definitions of Mindfulness," *Contemporary Buddhism* 12, no. 1 (2011): 263–279; Peter Harvey, "Mindfulness in Theravāda Samatha and Vipassanā Meditations and in Secular Mindfulness," in *Buddhist Foundations of Mindfulness*, ed. Edo Shonin, William Van Gordon, and Nirbhay N. Singh (Cham: Springer, 2015), 115–137; Anne Murphy, "Mindfulness-Based Therapy in Modern Psychology: Convergence and Divergence from Early Buddhist Thought," *Contemporary Buddhism* 17, no. 2 (2016): 275–325; and Sarah Shaw, *Mindfulness: Where It Comes From and What It Is* (Boulder, CO: Shambhala, 2020).
6. See Charles Goodman, *The Training Anthology of Śāntideva: A Translation of the Śikṣa-samuccaya* (New York: Oxford University Press, 2016).
7. "Song of the Four Mindfulnesses," by Kalsang Gyatso, the Seventh Dalai Lama (1708–1757).
8. See Kate Crosby and Andrew Skilton, *The Bodhicaryāvatāra*, ed. Paul Williams (Oxford and New York: Oxford University Press, 1996), 115–132.
9. From *Saundarananda* Canto XV, translated in Sarah Shaw, *Spirit of Buddhist Meditation* (New Haven, CT and London: Yale University Press, 2014), 231.
10. For more discussion of the interplay of calm and insight in varied traditions, see Hammalava Saddhatissa, *The Buddha's Way* (London: George Allen and Unwin, 1971), 74–84; Sekiguchi Shindai, ed., "Wonhyo's Calmness and Insight," in *Bukkyo no jissen genre* (*Buddhist Soteriological Principles*), (Tokyo: Sankibo Busshorin, 1977), 429–445; L. S. Cousins, "*Samatha-yāna* and *Vipassanā-yāna*," in *Buddhist Studies in Honour of Hammalava Saddhatissa*, ed. Gatare Dhammapala, et al. (Nugegoda, Sri Lanka: University of Sri Jayewardenapura, 1984), 56–68; Mahathera Guneratana, *The Path of Serenity and Insight: An Explanation of the Buddhist Jhānas* (Delhi: Motilal Banarsidass, 1985); L. S. Cousins, "The Origins of Insight Meditation," *Buddhist Forum* 4 (1996): 35–58; and Gen Lamrimpa, *Śamatha Meditation: Tibetan Teachings on Cultivating Mental Quiescence*, trans. Alan Wallace, with an introduction by H. Sprager (Ithaca, NY: Snow Lion, 1992).
11. Nyanaponika Thera, *The Heart of Buddhist Meditation: A Handbook of Mental Training Based on the Buddha's Way of Mindfulness* (London: Rider, 1962), 102–107.
12. See Harvey, "Mindfulness," 130–133; and Shaw, *Mindfulness*, 176–183.
13. *Bhāvanākrama* III.1; translated in Shaw, *Spirit of Buddhist Meditation*, 240.
14. For more discussion of this, see Sarah Shaw, "Meditation Teaching and Suitability: The Depiction of Temperament in Pāli Canonical Text and Commentarial Narrative," in *Asian Traditions of Meditation*, ed. Halvor Eifring (Honolulu: University of Hawai'i Press, 2016), 122–125.
15. See Georgios Halkias, "Meditation in Tibet," in *Introduction to Buddhist Meditation*, by S. Shaw (London: Routledge, 2009), 159–186 at 174.
16. Stephen Beyer, *The Cult of Tara: Magic and Ritual in Tibet* (Berkeley, Los Angeles, and London: University of California Press, 1973); Halkias, "Meditation in Tibet"; and Sam van Schaik, *The Spirit of Tibetan Buddhism* (New Haven, CT and London: Yale University Press, 2016), 100–140.
17. See Sarah Shaw, *Buddhist Meditation: An Anthology of Texts* (London: Routledge, 2006): 102–108.
18. Shaw, *Buddhist Meditation*, 104.
19. AN 1.30; and Shaw, *Buddhist Meditation*, 109–162.

20. Daniel B. Stevenson, "The Four Kinds of *Samādhi* in Early T'ien-t'ai Buddhism," in *Traditions of Meditation in Chinese Buddhism*, ed. Peter N. Gregory, Kuroda Institute: Studies in East Asian Buddhism 4 (Honolulu: University of Hawai'i Press, 1986), 45–97.
21. See Paul Harrison, "*Buddhānusmṛti* in the *Pratyutpanna-Buddha-Saṃmukhāvasthitasamādhi-Sūtra*," *Journal of Indian Philosophy* 6 (1978): 35–57; R. E. Buswell, "Chinul's Systematization of Chinese Meditative Techniques in Korean Son Buddhism," in *Traditions of Meditation in Chinese Buddhism*, ed. Peter N. Gregory, Kuroda Institute: Studies in East Asian Buddhism (Honolulu: University of Hawai'i Press, 1986), 199–242; Shaw, *Spirit of Buddhist Meditation*, xv–xvi, 111–139; and Donald Swearer, *The Buddhist World of Southeast Asia* (New York: State University of New York Press, 2010), 3–4.
22. *Bhāvanākrama* III.2, translated in Shaw, *Spirit of Buddhist Meditation*, 241.
23. For discussion of this, see Peter Harvey, "The Dynamics of *Paritta* Chanting in Southern Buddhism," in *Love Divine: Studies in Bhakti and Devotional Mysticism*, ed. Karel Werner (Surrey: Curzon Press, 1993), 53–84.
24. See Halkias, "Meditation in Tibet," 177.
25. See, e.g., Ajahn Lee Dhammadhāro, *Keeping the Breath in Mind: Lessons in Samādhi*, trans. Geoffrey DeGraff (Rayong, Thailand, undated: talks from 1956–1960); Bhikkhu Buddhadāsa, *Mindfulness With Breathing: A Manual for Serious Beginners*, trans. Santikaro Bhikkhu (Bangkok: Evolution/Liberation, 1988), 47–67; and Shaw, *Buddhist Meditation*, 146–158.
26. Richard Gombrich, *What the Buddha Thought* (London: Equinox, 2009), 75–91.
27. *Bodhicaryāvatāra* 8.117, in Crosby and Skilton, *Bodhicaryāvatāra*, 98.
28. See François Bizot, *Le figuier à cinq branches: Recherches sur le bouddhisme khmer* II, PEFEO CVII (Paris, L'École française d'Extrême-Orient, 1976); Sarah Shaw, *Introduction to Buddhist Meditation* (London: Routledge, 2009), 111–139; Crosby, *Traditional Theravāda*, 25, 90–102; and Choompolpaisal and Skilton, "Old Meditation" and "Traditional Theravāda."
29. R. E. Buswell, *Tracing Back the Radiance: Chinul's Korean Way of Zen*, Kuroda Institute (Honolulu: University of Hawai'i Press, 1981); and Buswell, *Chinul's Systematization*, 1986.
30. AN 5.336; MN 1.423; and Shaw, *Buddhist Meditation*, 132, 192.
31. Peter Harvey, *The Dynamics of Paritta Chanting: An Introduction to Buddhism; Teachings, History and Practices*, revised edition (Cambridge, UK: Cambridge University Press, 2013), 243–244; G. T. Tanabe, "Chanting," in *Encyclopedia of Buddhism*, Vol. 1, ed. R. Buswell, Jr. (New York: Macmillan, 2004), 137–139; and Shaw, *Introduction to Buddhist Meditation*, 92–111.
32. Buswell, *Tracing Back*, 1981; and Buswell, *Chinul's Systematization*, 1986.
33. See K. I. Matics, *Gestures of the Buddha*, 4th edition (Bangkok: Chulalongkorn University Press, 2008).
34. John Blofeld, *The Tantric Mysticism of Tibet: A Practical Guide* (New York: Dutton, 1970); Beyer, *Cult of Tara*, 1973; Donald Lopez, *Religions of Tibet in Practice* (Princeton, NJ: Princeton University Press, 1997); Halkias, "Meditation in Tibet"; and van Schaik, *Spirit of Tibetan Buddhism*.
35. Halkias, "Meditation in Tibet," 174.
36. Ferguson, *Zen's Chinese Heritage*; and Sam van Schaik, *The Spirit of Zen* (New Haven, CT and London: Yale University Press 2018), 3–19, and for the power of devotion to the teacher, 100–103.

Sarah Shaw

BUDDHIST PHILOSOPHY AS PHILOSOPHY

CAN BUDDHIST PHILOSOPHY BE INTEGRATED INTO THE CANON?

The term "philosophy" has a long history in Western thought, and it has been used at different times to mean a variety of different sorts of intellectual activity. But the attention should be confined to the term's use in modern academia—to denote philosophy as a scholarly pursuit. So understood, philosophy involves systematic examination of questions in three major areas: metaphysics, or inquiry into the fundamental nature of reality; epistemology, the examination of the nature of knowledge; and value theory or inquiry into the normative dimension, including ethics, metaethics, aesthetics, and political philosophy. But philosophy also has its own distinctive methods, which it uses to address questions in these three general areas. Philosophical investigation involves analysis and argumentation. Philosophical inquiry typically begins with the analysis of the concepts relevant to the inquiry at hand, as a way of clarifying the meanings of the key terms used in discourse concerning those topics. And philosophical inquiry is conducted using the tools of rational argumentation. Thus, much philosophical writing is structured in an argument–objection–reply format. And much philosophical training consists in learning what counts as a good argument and how to formulate objections, whether to a thesis or to an argument given in its support.

This characterization may seem to reveal a Western bias, for it reflects the practice of philosophy as found in departments of philosophy on the European continent and the English-speaking world. But it also applies to the practice of philosophy departments in universities in Asia, Africa, and Latin America. This is no doubt largely a product of the colonialist legacy: the institutions of higher education that were developed in the 19th and 20th centuries in Asia, Africa, and Latin America were commonly built on European models. Still, the widespread adoption of the practice could be taken as evidence against the characterization being biased. This, in any event, is what many members of philosophy departments in Asia, Africa, and Latin America would claim. What may be taken to more clearly suggest bias is not the characterization of the field's areas of inquiry and methods, but the prevailing canon and the agenda associated with that canon. Until quite recently, the works of non-Western authors were simply left out of the philosophy curriculum. One could not be considered educated in philosophy without at least some familiarity with the thought of Plato and Aristotle, but utter ignorance of the work of Dharmakīrti, Kumārila, Confucius, and Hsun-Tzu was no impediment. This in turn shaped what would count as a philosophical problem and what sort of approach to addressing such a problem would be deemed legitimate. For instance, the idea governing most recent work in epistemology, that knowledge is to be understood as justified true belief, can be traced back to Plato. The alternative approach of Indian epistemologists, who sought to understood knowledge by looking at the processes that uniformly cause true cognition, was simply not on the radar of academic philosophers.

Two historical factors contributed to this seeming bias against non-Western philosophy: racism and anti-clericalism. Early modern Europe's initial encounters with classical Indian and Chinese thought were quite positive. The trouble may have begun with Kant, who held that only those of European ancestry were capable of the sort of abstract thought required of philosophers. Less overtly racist attempts to exclude other traditions from the canon have relied on the notion that the term "philosophy" is to be applied only to thoughts and thinkers that belong to a particular historical lineage. But by this criterion, that part of mathematics reliant on place notation cannot be "Western," since the zero is an Indian invention.

Philosophers in the "analytic" tradition prevailing in most English-speaking countries have been less impressed by appeals to ancestry or history. Where dismissiveness toward non-Western philosophy does exist in this community, it has more often been fueled by the conviction that serious philosophical inquiry is not compatible with soteriological concerns. European philosophy may once have been "theology's handmaiden," but the rise of naturalism is thought to require that such relations be severed. This stance of dismissiveness toward thought aligned with spiritual concerns has begun to fade in this century, however, perhaps due in part to the fact that important contributions have been made to analytic metaphysics and epistemology by philosophers whose own religious convictions are well known. What such work has made clear is that religious faith commitments need not stand in the way of engaging in rational argumentation that is open to all. What matters is the strength of the arguments, not the convictions of the author.

Recent years have seen ever more insistent pleas for integrating the canon, and these have begun to bear fruit. Some philosophy departments now offer undergraduate courses in Buddhist philosophy. Meetings of "mainstream" philosophical organizations (such as the Joint Meetings and the annual conferences of the American Philosophical Association) occasionally include papers on Buddhist philosophy. The views of Buddhist philosophers are sometimes discussed in articles in "mainstream" philosophy journals. And there is some reason to believe that this process will continue and grow. What, though, would "integration" actually mean for Buddhist philosophy? More specifically, would it mean that an agenda associated with a historically biased canon is imposed on the Buddhist philosophical tradition, leading perhaps to the loss of specifically Buddhist elements of that tradition? To begin to answer this question further discussion of the nature, history, and role of Buddhist philosophical thought need to be explored.

IS THERE "REAL" PHILOSOPHY IN THE BUDDHIST TRADITION?

As the term "philosophy" is being used here, there is relatively little systematic philosophical thought to be found in the discourses of the Buddha. There are, of course, several arguments for non-self, arguments against the existence of Īśvara, the rudiments of a moral psychology, and considerable theorizing concerning cognitive processes (in connection with a well-developed theory of meditation). But it is with the rise of Abhidharma that full-scale development of philosophical theories begins. One sees in *Kathāvathu*, for instance, records of relatively early disputes over competing interpretations of the Buddha's teachings on topics like the ontological status of persons. One also sees there the development of techniques for rationally adjudicating such disputes when they cannot be settled by appeal to texts deemed authoritative by both parties. These developments lead in time to the full flowering of the Abhidharma movement, with many of the competing schools formed around distinctive theories in metaphysics and epistemology. The Vaibhāṣika school, for instance, is known for its view that past and future entities exist; the Sautrāntika school for the view that external objects are only perceived indirectly; and the Mahāsaṃghika school for the theory that cognitions are reflexive in nature. There is, though, a set of core tenets that all Abhidharma schools accepted: that there is nothing like the self (*ātman/puruṣa*) accepted by the Brahmanical schools; that partite entities such as chariots and persons are not strictly speaking real but instead are merely useful conceptual constructions; that all existing things are momentary; that the ultimately real things (dharmas) have their natures intrinsically. Since these and other tenets commonly accepted by the Abhidharma schools disagree not only with common sense but also with the teachings of the Brahmanical schools, mastery of argumentative skills that depend on norms of rational evaluation became important. Hence the development of a pan-Indian theory of inference, to which Buddhist philosophers like Vasubandhu, Dignāga, and Dharmakīrti made crucial contributions. It was through sustained debate with rival schools, both Buddhist and Brahmanical, that Indian Buddhist philosophy developed its immense body of rigorously argued work.

The development of well-argued defenses of key Buddhist theses such as non-self and impermanence clearly played a role in consolidating and protecting Buddhist institutions in the face of challenges from rival schools and sects. (This may be why the Moghul sacking of the great monastic university of Nālanda hastened the decline of Indian Buddhism.) But philosophy plays a crucial role not only in Buddhism's external relations, but also in the internal matter of Buddhist practice. At the heart of the Buddha's diagnosis of the source of suffering lies the insight that the illusory sense of an "I" is the vital precondition for the arising and perpetuation of existential dread. Extirpating the "I"-sense becomes the core task of those on the Buddhist Path. But this is no easy matter. One may, for instance, find arguments for the nonexistence of a persisting self quite persuasive, yet still feel anger when someone cuts in on the checkout line. One may carefully observe the rise and fall of various mental states, noting how they come and go without any master mental supervisor directing the flow, yet still retain the first-personal stance of seeing these as all states that one is oneself observing. The sense of an "I" that is the subject of one's conscious states and the agent of one's actions seems to run very deep in our conceptual economy. It is not at all obvious how it could be extirpated.

Can philosophy help? It seems unlikely that engaging in philosophy can all by itself bring about the cessation of suffering that is the Buddhist goal. One does occasionally find reference to something called "dry enlightenment"—the attainment of nirvana through intellectual activity alone. But this seems somewhat implausible. Candrakīrti speaks quite scornfully of those who think all one needs to do is refute the self of the philosophers (the *ātman/puruṣa* of the Brahmanical schools). He likens them to someone who, knowing that snakes are nesting in the walls, celebrates the fact that there is no elephant in the house.[1]

It is generally understood that dissipating the "I"-sense requires a great deal of hard work. Much of this work falls under the umbrella term "meditation." This includes the familiar yogic practices of learning to control body, senses, and mind, an ability that in turn enables one to observe one's mental processes in a completely objective fashion. Such observation is then said to provide direct verification of the central teachings of impermanence, non-self, and the ubiquity of suffering. But much of what is found on the "meditation" side of the Path is directed at something else: developing virtues that serve to counteract those vicious habits that perpetuate ignorance. For instance, feeling anger when one has been harmed by the actions of another is obviously based on the presupposition that there is an abiding "I" who serves as locus of the injury. The habit of feeling anger is classified as a vice precisely because it helps perpetuate the "I"-sense, and so perpetuates suffering. Cultivation of the countervailing virtue of forbearance supplants this deep-seated habit, and thus contributes to progress toward cessation of suffering. And, finally, there are meditative practices leading to attainment of various states of altered consciousness, states in which distorting ways of conceptualizing experience are said to fall away. Such altered states are frequently described as the immediate precursors of liberation from suffering.

But can meditation, any more than philosophy, really do the job of extirpating the "I"-sense unassisted? There are several reasons to think that it cannot. Consider the case of the development of virtues like forbearance, compassion, and lovingkindness. It is difficult to learn to feel lovingkindness and not anger when someone has intentionally harmed us. How may one go about learning to do this, and what may motivate one to embark on such a program? Śāntideva provides a good answer to the first question: by deploying the Buddhist reduction of the person to a causal series of impersonal psychophysical elements, one can come to see the infliction of harm as no different from the case of pain caused by excess bile in the digestive tract.[2] As one knows it would be irrational to feel anger toward the bile, so one can come to see anger toward the harm-doer as equally irrational. But for this strategy to work, one must already accept the reductionist account of persons. One does not adopt this stance naturally; what one naturally does is take the stance that deems persons responsible agents and evaluates them and their conduct accordingly. Considerable philosophical theorizing is required before one can come to see the personal stance as no more than a useful shorthand device.

Moreover, why should one embark on the difficult project of "reprogramming" what is taken to be the "natural" responses to insult and injury? Because doing so will improve my rebirth prospects? Improve my chances of attaining liberation? These are self-interested motives. It is, of course, true that if I become more forbearing and compassionate, this may in time reduce the strength of my self-love. So even if my initial motivation was self-interested, the project may in time change my motivational structure—and change it in the direction required for progress on the Buddhist Path. Still, even an initial reliance on self-interested motives—telling the follower that this will give them a better rebirth—makes the Buddhist project appear problematically deceptive. Once again Śāntideva provides an answer. His argument for an obligation to prevent ownerless suffering effectively undermines use of a personal stance to ground reasons for action.[3] The basic idea of the argument is simple: given that neither the self nor the person is ultimately real, and given as well that the ultimate nature of pain is its badness or to-be-prevented-ness, the one ultimate reason for action is to minimize overall pain regardless of when or where it occurs; the rest is just a matter of working out what course of conduct would best achieve this minimizing of (ownerless) suffering. But here once again there is reliance on philosophical rationality. The ownerless suffering argument will make sense only to those who have already come to accept the counterintuitive reduction of the person to a causal series of psychophysical elements. It is difficult to see how such acceptance is to be achieved without relying on reasoned inquiry into the nature of persons.

It is commonly said that the Buddhist Path leads to liberation by helping one attain a personal realization that confirms the Buddha's core teachings. Since non-self is one of those core teachings, it may be thought that one comes to accept the reductionist view of persons through this "personal realization," and that this is something that comes about through meditation. There is a difficulty with this claim, though. Many of the different systems of classical Indian philosophy recognize something called yogic perception: a kind of direct cognition of things that is only available to those who have mastered the techniques of meditation. A Buddhist may claim for instance, that the Nobles (*ārya*s) directly see the karmic connection between actions and their fruits (thereby showing how rebirth is possible in the absence of a self). The problem with appealing to yogic perception to account for belief in non-self is that different schools make different claims about what it is that the yogins "see." The states of altered consciousness that may be attained through meditation can, of course, be quite powerful and persuasive. But what a given yogin takes away from their experience may be shaped by mind-set (for instance, their motives and expectations), setting (such as the institutional context), and background beliefs. The claim that yogic perception is a valid means of knowledge is beset with the problem of confabulation. Buddhist philosophers are well aware of this problem. They are well aware that the contents of a meditational state may be products of the imagination formed in accordance with the teacher's instructions. For this reason, they do not look to such states for confirmation of core teachings. Instead they look to attainment of such states of "personal realization" for their efficacy in bringing about transformation in one's cognitive and affective habits.

If this is indeed the stance of Buddhists toward the role of meditation in their practice, it is easy to see why this would be so. One may fully comprehend the connection between a diet high in refined carbohydrates and the development of type-2 diabetes, and yet not adjust one's own eating habits accordingly—until one sees a beloved uncle lose a leg to diabetes-fueled peripheral artery disease. Where deeply instilled habits are concerned, it can take more direct experience to turn theoretical knowledge into effective action. The personal realization that is said to result in the cessation of suffering may play this role of helping one "get it" in a transformative way. Still, philosophy may be needed in order to ensure that what one "gets" is indeed veridical. This may help explain why the Path is regularly described as consisting of both philosophical theorizing and the practice of meditation.

Of course, there have always been Buddhists who neither meditated nor studied philosophy. In most Buddhist cultures, lay Buddhist practices are understood to play a propaedeutic role: they make it more likely that the lay practitioner will be reborn in circumstances that make the attainment of cessation achievable. The lay Buddhist who gives alms to support the Saṃgha, for instance, may thereby generate the karma that ensures a future life in which they find it far easier to renounce the householder's life and become a monastic. But it is widely held that entry into cessation is attained only through such renunciation. What matter in the end are the practices prescribed for monks and nuns. And these typically include both meditation and philosophy.

The aim of philosophical practice is to work out how things most fundamentally are, strictly speaking. The rationale for including such practice in the Path is based on that idea. It may be objected, however, that philosophical investigation is at best a diversion from, and at worst an impediment to attaining the Buddhist goal of the cessation of suffering. And there are Buddhist voices—indeed voices of Buddhists often classified as philosophers—that can be understood as making precisely this point. Nāgārjuna, for instance, is seen by many as seeking to show that the metaphysical project of looking for the ultimate nature of reality is doomed to fail, and that failure to recognize this can only lead to one's remaining ensnared in the web of conceptual hypostatization. To this it could be replied that while Mādhyamikas like Nāgārjuna do seek to show that the metaphysical enterprises of other Buddhist schools can never get off the ground, they use the tools of philosophical rationality in their efforts. If analysis and argumentation were truly impotent devices, it seems they could never succeed in uncovering this fact about themselves. Perhaps it will be said that Mādhyamikas use the tools of philosophical rationality precisely to demonstrate their impotence and thereby induce the cessation of all philosophical theorizing. But this would be a dangerous strategy for a Buddhist to pursue. To abandon analysis and rational critique leaves one powerless to resist the blandishments of common sense. And the commonsense conception of the world is where the "I"-sense begins. There have certainly been Buddhists who embarked on a project of overthrowing the pretensions of philosophical rationality. But some caution is called for in carrying this out, lest the project end up reinstating an enduring subject of states like anger and craving.

WHAT OBSTACLES STAND IN THE WAY OF INTEGRATION?

Having discussed the place of philosophy in a Buddhist Path, the question of whether the Buddhist philosophical tradition should be incorporated into academic philosophy can be addressed. Here is one way to think about the question. As things currently stand, the works of such Buddhist thinkers as Dharmakīrti, Seng Chao, Buddhaghosa, and Kuiji are more likely to be studied in departments of religious studies and area studies than in philosophy departments. (Just as at one time the works of Plato were the province of classicists and not philosophers.) What might happen if this were reversed, and it were commonly held that a proper understanding of Dignāga required grounding in the tools and techniques of philosophy? Might this enhance understanding of the Buddhist philosophical tradition, or might it instead distort that body of work? That the agenda of the discipline of philosophy is powerfully shaped by its canon is known: the kinds of questions philosophers are expected to grapple with, and the kinds of tools they are expected to use in that grappling, are influenced by the prevailing consensus concerning what count as exemplars of philosophical inquiry. Given that the consensus in the discipline of philosophy as it currently exists has privileged works from the West, what may be lost, and is there anything to be gained, by integrating the Buddhist tradition into the domain of academic philosophy?

Here is an example. When one studies philosophy in the early 21st century, one is sure to encounter a distinction between propositions known *a priori* (known independently of experience, such as that all bachelors are unmarried) and propositions known *a posteriori* (known only through experience, such as that grass is green). One will also encounter a distinction between propositions that are contingently true and propositions that are necessarily true. This latter distinction is often explained in terms of the language of possible worlds.[4] A contingently true proposition is one that holds in this world but not in some other possible worlds, while a necessary truth is one that holds in all possible worlds. Now Buddhist philosophy lacks both of these distinctions. That it lacks the distinction between contingently and necessarily true propositions may be seen from the sorts of examples Buddhist philosophers use to illustrate the concept of a nonexistent object: the horns of a hare, cloth made of turtlehair, but also the son of a barren woman. That neither of the first two exist would be said to be contingently true: there are possible worlds with horned hares and hairy tortoises. That the third does not exist, though, would be said to be necessarily true: there is no possible world in which a barren woman gives birth to a son. But Buddhist philosophers do not distinguish between these two sorts of nonexistents, and the two ways in which statements about them are true. As for the distinction between a priori and a posteriori knowledge, Buddhist philosophers simply do not recognize such a thing as a priori knowledge. For them, everything worthy of the title "knowledge" is empirical in nature. Thus if Dharmakīrti is to be considered a philosopher alongside the likes of Descartes and Davidson, must these distinctions be somehow grafted onto his thought?

What may be a deeper source of resistance to the project of integration is now reached. Philosophers trained along currently prevailing lines of the discipline may well wonder whether work that lacks what they take to be such elementary distinctions as those between *a priori* and *a posteriori*, between *necessarily true* and *possibly true*, can have much to offer to the discipline as it now stands. Scholars of the Buddhist tradition may in turn wonder how distinctions that were not drawn by Buddhist philosophers may be at all relevant to Buddhist projects. There is a way to resolve this seeming standoff, though. What are called for are the services of border-crossers, individuals who are conversant with life on both sides of the (current) border between the two traditions. A border-crosser may, for instance, point out that the absence of a distinction between necessary truth and possible truth in Buddhist philosophy stems from its principled stand in favor of what is known as actualism: the view that all truths about how things may be are grounded in facts about how things actually are. The relation of *grounding* involved here is just the relation that many Buddhist philosophers (specifically those of the Abhidharma schools) claim holds between conventionally true statements and how things ultimately are. The conventional truth of the statement that there is a car in the drive is grounded in how certain of the ultimately real "atoms" (that is, the impartite constituents of ordinary physical objects) are arranged. Possibilities are, according to these same philosophers, imaginative constructions. Hence while statements about possibilities can be conventionally true, they cannot be ultimately true. Since what is of interest to philosophers is how things ultimately are, philosophical systems that make do without drawing distinctions among the alethic modalities are only to be expected. Now those analytic philosophers who champion modal metaphysics—the sort of metaphysics that takes possible worlds seriously—will take issue with this stance (though some analytic metaphysicians now advocate moving on to "post-modal" metaphysics). The point, though, is that Buddhist philosophers pursued a strategy that allowed them to bypass the complexities of modal metaphysics, so the absence of this distinction need not be taken as a deficiency. What the border-crosser can point out is that since Western philosophy and the Buddhist philosophical tradition employ similar tools on a similar set of issues, where there are divergences in strategy, it may be worthwhile to investigate whether there are sound philosophical reasons in favor of one strategy over the other. How did Buddhist philosophers get on without the distinction between the alethic modalities? Is there anything that early-21st-century philosophers may learn from this? The overall point is that the integration of Buddhist philosophy into the academic discipline of philosophy need not result in the complete subordination of the former. When ideas start to flow across a border, change can happen on both sides.

The term "fusion philosophy" was coined with this process in mind. The idea behind a project of fusion philosophy is to find cases where two philosophical traditions employ different approaches to solving a common problem, and investigate whether the approach developed in one tradition may prove useful to the other. Note that the question can be raised in either direction. Are there problems in Buddhist philosophy that may be better handled by bringing in the distinction between the alethic modalities? Are there problems in Western philosophy that may be solved by adopting the actualist stance taken by Buddhist philosophers? The point of fusion philosophy is not to figure out which is the superior tradition. The point is just to try to make progress on solving philosophical problems. Sometimes two heads are better than one.

Genuine border-crossers are relatively rare. In the case of Buddhist–Western fusion philosophy, the skills that are necessary include: mastery of at least several of the relevant languages (Sanskrit, Pāli, Tibetan, classical Chinese, Korean, Japanese), philological skills, knowledge of the history of Buddhist textual traditions, and recognized expertise in at least one core area of Western philosophy. Given that individuals possessing all these skills are rare, progress in fusion projects will depend on cooperation between philologists and philosophers. A few recent missteps—some reflecting a lack of adequate philological grounding, others a lack of familiarity with current work in philosophy—will help show why such teamwork is important:

(1) Indian Buddhist philosophers disagree over the question of the existence of external objects. The Yogācāra school denies that such things exist, while the various Abhidharma schools, as well as some members of the Madhyamaka school, hold that there are mind-independent physical objects. Recently, some Buddhologists have taken to calling the latter position "externalism." This may seem like an apt choice, but philosophers seeking to find out about the Buddhist tradition will find it confusing. In current philosophical parlance, to call a view "externalist" is to say that it claims the status of a subject's state is determined by causes external to them, that is, by factors to which the subject may lack direct access. For instance, externalism about knowledge is the view that whether or not someone knows that *p* depends on how their belief that *p* was caused—something they may be unable to ascertain. The upshot is that for the externalist about knowledge, one may know that *p* without knowing that they know that *p*. Now Yogācāra epistemology is, like that of all other Buddhist schools, externalist in this sense. When I have the experience of seeing a patch of yellow, my experience will count as knowledge only if it was caused in the right way. Of course Yogācāra denies that the experience was caused by my faculty of vision coming in contact with an independently existing yellow object; it says there are no such things. But the experience did have a cause. If that cause was the ripening of the right sort of karmic seed in the storehouse consciousness, then they say the experience is veridical and I have knowledge. But this is something I cannot ascertain just by examining the accessible contents of my mind. This is why a philosopher who is new to the Buddhist tradition would find it confusing to be told that Yogācāra rejects "externalism." They would take this to mean that Yogācāra holds (as Descartes did) that in order to know that *p* one must know that they know that *p*. Buddhologists who wish to communicate their knowledge of Buddhist philosophy to philosophers would do better to call the view that Yogācāra rejects, but other schools accept, "external-world realism," that is, realism about external or mind-independent objects.

(2) The epistemology developed by Dignāga and Dharmakīrti acknowledges two knowledge sources or ways in which knowledge may be produced, perception, and inference. Inference being the domain of logic, modern logicians have wondered how these Buddhist epistemologists may have understood the logic involved in inference. More specifically, they wondered whether this school took the reasoning involved in a good inference to be deductive or inductive, with some scholars advancing the hypothesis that Dignāga used an inductive model while Dharmakīrti replaced this with a deductive model. But this question may be misplaced; it may stem from failure to note the role of epistemological externalism in the project

of Dignāga and Dharmakīrti. What Indian epistemologists in general seek is accounts of the causal conditions that invariably produce veridical cognitive states, states that thus count as knowledge. Arriving at such an account is useful in that it can then be used to guide us toward more responsible epistemic practices.

Here is the stock model of an inference: Suppose I correctly perceive that there is smoke on the hill. Next, I recall that wherever I have perceived smoke I have also perceived fire, as for instance in the kitchen. I then infer that there must be fire on the hill. Does this count as knowledge? Dignāga points out that in order for my reasoning to work, it must be the case that smoke is pervaded by fire—that it is true in all cases at all times that where there is smoke there is also fire. I do have some evidence of pervasion, in my observations of how things have gone in the kitchen. But since I cannot time-travel into the remote past or the future, this pervasion is something I cannot be in a position to be certain of. What I can do is look to see if there are any counterexamples to the claim of pervasion. For instance, what about the white stuff rising off the lake in the morning? There is no fire in the lake, so this may seem to refute the claim of pervasion. But that white stuff is mist, not smoke, so the claim remains unrefuted. If I have done my epistemic duty by gathering evidence for pervasion and looking for countervailing evidence against pervasion, then if it is also true that pervasion does hold universally, I may be said to know that there is fire on the hill. Of course, the evidence I actually possess for pervasion is not airtight, so there is some luck involved in my having knowledge. But for the externalist, epistemic luck is ineliminable. The point of doing epistemology is to improve our odds, so that when we do have knowledge it is not just a lucky guess.

One can see how the inductive vs. deductive question may have arisen. Inductive reasoning is probabilistic, whereas when one reasons in accordance with a deductively valid argument-form, the truth of one's evidence (the premises) guarantees the truth of the conclusion. But the argument-form that both Dignāga and Dharmakīrti have in mind is deductively valid: Everything that is P is Q, *x* is P, therefore *x* is Q. What may have misled scholars is that Dignāga's discussion brings out the fact that one can never obtain all the evidence bearing on the claim of pervasion, while Dharmakīrti's does not. This is, however, neither here nor there, given the externalist paradigm that both employ. Greater clarity about the difference between classical Indian epistemology and how epistemology has generally been done in the modern tradition would have cleared this up.

(3) The tetralemma (*catuṣkoṭi*) is a device for cataloging the available possibilities when it comes to answering some question. It has been used throughout the Buddhist philosophical tradition, beginning with the Buddha's responses to the so-called indeterminate questions. One such question concerns the postmortem fate of the enlightened person. Use of the tetralemma form yields the following possibilities: the enlightened person exists after death; the enlightened person does not exist after death; the enlightened person both exists and does not exist after death; the enlightened person neither exists nor does not exist after death. The Buddha is said to reject each of these four. This is one surprising result. A second surprise is that there should be four possibilities rather than just the first two. Both surprises have led some scholars to suggest that there may be a nonstandard or "deviant" logic at work here. Adherence to such rules of classical logic as noncontradiction and excluded middle rules out the third and fourth lemmas, and negation of all four likewise leads to contradiction. It has thus been suggested that Buddhist philosophers who use this device (particularly

Mādhyamikas) must have at least implicitly accepted a logic that makes room for the possibility of true contradictions without all the dire consequences thought to follow from simultaneously affirming both *p* and not-*p*.

While this hypothesis is interesting, it seems incompatible with what is found in some key texts. The Buddha himself makes clear that his rejection of all four possibilities concerning the enlightened person is based on the fact that all involve the presupposition that there is such a thing as a person (and hence that there can be enlightened persons). Since this presupposition is strictly speaking false (persons being merely conventionally real), the question is analogous to one concerning the ripeness of the mangoes on the tree in my yard. (I live in an apartment.) So no contradiction results from the Buddha's rejection of all four lemmas. As for why there should be four lemmas rather than just two, the device of the tetralemma is used in a variety of different contexts and there may be some variation in how it is understood. But at least in some uses, the third lemma is understood to involve different perspectives—*p* is true from one perspective, not-*p* is true from another perspective—while the fourth asserts that the matter is inexpressible and so cannot be expressed by saying either *p* or not-*p*. There may be other cases where its use is more suggestive of deployment of a nonclassical logic. But the sort of search that may answer this question clearly requires the skills of a scholar with philological training.

WHAT BENEFITS MAY INTEGRATION BRING?

These and similar missteps might have been avoided with greater cooperation between philosophers and philologists. What, though, is the point of embarking on a fusion-philosophical project? More specifically, what may be in it for Buddhologists, and what may philosophers have to gain?

Buddhologists may bristle at the suggestion that there are things they may learn about the Buddhist philosophical tradition from philosophers who are not also philologists. But when it comes to reading texts, philosophy, and philology have slightly different methodological priorities, and this may make a difference in the results obtained. Philologists value consistency: our understanding of a key concept in the text at hand must be consistent with the term's use in other historically related texts. Philosophy values charity: whenever possible, one's interpretation should be guided by the assumption that the author of the text was not stupid. In philosophical texts, stupidity is manifested by propounding theories to which there are clear and powerful objections. And if there is one thing philosophers are good at, it is anticipating the objections that may be raised against a given view. So even when the philosopher lacks all the historical knowledge and hermeneutical skills of the philologist, they may still be positioned to advance interpretations that make more philosophical sense of the text.

Here is an example that illustrates how this can play out. Dharmakīrti is a radical nominalist: he denies not only that there are universals such as *potness*, which is ruled out by the Buddha's claim that everything is impermanent (real universals would have to be permanent); he denies that there are any real similarities as well. If all the things that are called pots do not share a common universal and do not actually resemble one another either, how is it possible to tell a pot from a petunia? Dharmakīrti's answer begins with the claim that all the pots do share something negative, namely their being what is left over when all the things that are non-pots are excluded. The pots are just the things that are not non-pots. This is known as the *apoha* theory because the Sanskrit term *apoha* means "exclusion." As for why the pots may appear to resemble one another, Dharmakīrti explains that utterly dissimilar things may all perform the same function: aspirin, acetaminophen, and ibuprofen all reduce fever. Petunias do not work well as water storage devices. The pots are the things that are left when all the rest is excluded.

This much of the *apoha* theory is attested in Dharmakīrti's writings and the commentaries. The philosopher will point out, though, that there remains what looks to a philosopher like a gaping hole. The theory as so far stated depends on there being causal laws that explain such regularities as that water stays put in a pot. And causal laws involve kinds: that smoke is caused by fire involves the concomitance of *smokeness* and *fireness*. To interpret Dharmakīrti charitably is to assume that he was aware of this gaping hole, and thought he saw a way to fill it. At this point the philosopher may point out that there are two negations in the *apoha* formula "not non-pot": a "not" and a "non-." If these two negations behave differently, it is possible that their combination may succeed in taking us from the particular to the general. Something along these lines is to be found in the work of a much later Indian philosopher, Mathuranātha, but he is a member of a Brahmanical school. So far nothing like this has come to light in the Buddhist *apoha* literature. Still the philosopher would say that it remains an interpretive possibility worth exploring.

Here is another reason that those who value the Buddhist philosophical tradition may want to consider fusion projects. In India, Buddhist philosophizing ended around the 12th century. It continued for some time after that in East Asia, but there it eventually gave over to doxography. What Jan Westerhoff calls the "golden age" of Indian Buddhist philosophy occurred precisely during the period when Buddhists engaged in robust and spirited debate with their Brahmanical and heterodox opponents.[5] This is no mystery: philosophy progresses when prevailing views are challenged. A fusion project promises to take Buddhist philosophy out of the museum diorama and see how it fares when subjected to new challenges. If Buddhist philosophy does play an important part in the Buddhist soteriological project, a fusion project may prove important to the survival of Buddhism under conditions of modernity.

The Buddhist philosophical tradition has by and large rejected physicalism, the view that all existence is physical in nature. But in an age in which the natural sciences play a leading role, physicalism is rapidly coming close to being accepted as common sense. Are there Buddhist resources for challenging this development? Dharmakīrti argued that the mind can change without any accompanying bodily changes, but that is now known to be false. Śāntarakṣita argued that matter is inert or lifeless, but that too turns out to be false. Are there other, better Buddhist arguments against physicalism or can there be? And if not, can there be a recognizably Buddhist system that accepts the physicalist ontology? These are some of the questions that a fusion project may address.

Philosophy on the Western side may likewise benefit from entering into dialogue with another tradition. The guiding assumption behind fusion philosophy is that where two historically separate traditions share a common set of problems, there may be approaches developed in one that would help resolve (or perhaps dissolve) difficulties arising in the other. For instance, Indian epistemologists never adopted the "justified true belief" understanding of knowledge that has dominated Western epistemology since Plato. Because the concept of justification has been central to Western epistemological inquiry, it has proven difficult to jettison the internalist legacy of Cartesian thought. Since Buddhist epistemology has nothing quite like this concept, it offers an interesting alternative to Western models. Similar things may be said about post-modal metaphysics, as well as about the debate between presentism and its critics, which uncannily mirrors the debate between *sarvāstivāda* and its many Buddhist opponents.

There are areas of historical research that would clearly benefit from greater cooperation between philosophers and philologists. Here are some examples:

the formation of Sautrāntika as a distinct school and its conception of the causal relation;
the nature and reach of the four attested formulations of Vaibhāṣika's *sarvāstivāda*;
the role of presentism and actualism in Madhyamaka argumentation;
the Chinese reception of Dignāga as revealed by the commentarial tradition;
the historical transformation of the notion of nonconceptual cognition from early Buddhism, through Abhidharma, to the Mahāyāna schools;
the notion of inexpressibility and the paradoxes arising from its deployment.

But there are also areas of philosophical inquiry where the Buddhist tradition has had relatively little to say. For instance, Western philosophy has a long history of debate around the so-called "free will" issue—the question of whether causal determinism is compatible with holding people morally responsible for their actions. There is likewise virtually nothing in the Buddhist tradition concerning meta-ethics, that part of value theory concerned with what such ethical properties as rightness and wrongness consist in. Those who would like to know what Buddhism could say about such questions would do well to consider using the approach of fusion philosophy to work out answers, for cooperation between philosophers and philologists is clearly called for. (Of course the result may be that the problem is not resolved but dissolved, as some think must happen in the case of the "free will" problem.)

SOME FINAL CAVEATS

The article began with the question of whether the Buddhist intellectual tradition may properly be thought of as belonging to the discipline of philosophy as currently practiced. What was found is that while there are parts of the Buddhist tradition that reject the use of philosophical rationality, there is also much that would fit quite comfortably in the academic philosophy curriculum, and that should be of considerable interest to professional philosophers. Perhaps this should come as no surprise given the role that conceptual analysis and rational argumentation have played historically in Buddhist practice. A common understanding of the Path is that one philosophizes to confirm the Buddha's teachings, one meditates to deepen one's appreciation of those teachings, one philosophizes in order to achieve full understanding of what one finds in meditation, one meditates in order to deepen one's appreciation of that understanding, and so on, in a complicated spiral of reciprocal interaction. On this view, there is much more to Buddhist practice than philosophy, but philosophy plays a crucial role all the same.

Buddhist practitioners may still have cause for concern. A philosopher is someone who is committed to following the argument wherever it leads. To be a Buddhist is, among other things, to hold that the Buddha's insights concerning the nature of sentient existence are fundamentally correct. There is thus some tension here: if the exercise of philosophical rationality leads to the conclusion that some of those insights are wrong, a Buddhist philosopher is confronted with a dilemma. Still, committing to the veracity of the Buddha's claims on the basis of faith alone runs the risk of affirming the "I"-sense, thereby abandoning the Buddhist project. The historical record of Buddhist philosophizing in response to concerted attacks by non-Buddhist opponents should give the practitioner some confidence that following the argument will not force them to choose. But there is no guarantee that the outcome will be to their liking. There is a risk in following the Path understood in this way. But if extirpation of the "I"-sense is indeed central to the Buddhist project, this element of risk may be ineliminable.

PRIMARY SOURCES (WITH TRANSLATIONS)

Abhidharmakośabhāṣyam of Vasubandhu. Edited by Prahlad Pradhan. Patna: Jayaswal Research Institute, 1975.

English translation of Louis de La Vallée Poussin's French translation: *Abhidharmakośabhaṣyam*. Translated by Leo M. Pruden. Berkeley: Asian Humanities Press, 1988.

Duerlinger, James. Trans. "Refutation of the Theory of Selfhood: A Resolution of Questions about Persons," *Journal of Indian Philosophy*, 17 (1989): 137–188.

Śāntideva. *The Bodhicāryāvatāra of Śāntideva with the Commentary Pañjika of Prajñākaramati*. Edited by P. L. Vaidya. Dharbanga: Mithila Institute, 1960.

The Bodhicāryāvatāra. Translated by Kate Crosby and Andrew Skilton. London: Oxford University Press, 1993.

Madhyamakāvatāra of Candrakīrti. Chapter 6, Edited by Xuezhu, Li. Xuezhu, "Madhyamakāvatāra-kārikā Chapter 6," *Journal of Indian Philosophy* 43, (2015): 1–30.

Madhyamakāvatāra. Introduction au Traité du milieu de l'Ācārya Candrakīrti, avec le commentaire de l'auteur, traduit d'après la version tibétaine." Translated by Louis de la Vallée Poussin. Le Muséon 8/3–4, 249–317; 11/3–4, 271–558; 12/4, 236–328.

Mūlamadhyamakakārikā, ed. Raghunath Pandeya as: *The Madhyamakaāstram of Nāgārjuna, with the Commentaries Akutobhayā by Nāgārjuna, Madhyamakavtti by Buddhapālita, Prajñāpradpavtti by Bhāvaviveka, and Prasannapadā by Candrakrti*, Delhi: Motilal Banarsidass, 1988.

Nāgārjuna's Middle Way: Mūlamadhyamakakārikā. Translated by Mark Siderits and Shōryū Katsura. Boston: Wisdom Publications, 2013.

Steinkellner, E., ed. *Dignāga's Pramāṇasamuccaya, Chapter 1: A Hypothetical Reconstruction of the Sanskrit Text with the Help of the Two Tibetan Translations on the Basis of the Hitherto Known Sanskrit Fragments and the Linguistic Materials Gained from Jinendrabuddhi's Ṭīkā*. Vienna: OEAW, 2005.

Hattori Masaaki. *Dignāga on Perception, Being the Pratyakṣapariccheda of Dignāga's Pramāṇasamuccaya from the Sanskrit Fragments and the Tibetan Versions*. Translated and annotated by Masaaki Hattori. Cambridge, MA: Harvard University Press, 1968.

The Pramānavārttikam of Dharmakirti. Edited by Ram Chandra Pandeya. Delhi: Motilal Banarsidass 1989.

Tattvasaṃgraha of Śāntarakṣita. Edited with the Pañjikā (=TSP) by Embar Krishnamacharya. Baroda, India: Oriental Institute, 1984.

The Tattvasaṃgraha of Śāntarakṣita, with the Commentary of Kamalaśīla. Translated by Ganganatha Jha. Delhi: Motilal Banarsidass, 1986.

Vigrahavyāvartanī. In *The dialectical method of Nagarjuna: (Vigrahavyāvartinī)*. Edited by E. H. Johnston and Arnold Kunst. Delhi: Motilal Banarsidass, 2002.

The Dispeller of Disputes: Nagarjuna's Vigrahavyavartani. Translated by Jan Westerhoff, New York: Oxford University Press, 2010.

Viṃśikā of Vasubandhu. In *Materials Toward the Study of Vasubandhu's Viṃśikā*. Translated by Jonathan Silk. Harvard Oriental Series, Vol. 81. Cambridge, MA: Harvard University Press, 2016.

Visuddhimagga of Buddhaghosâcariya. Edited by Henry Clarke Warren. Revised by Dharmananda Kosambi. Cambridge, MA: Harvard University Press, 1950.

The Path of Purification. Translated by Bhikkhu Ñanamoli. Kandy, Sri Lanka: Buddhist Publication Society, 1991.

FURTHER READING

Cowherds, The. *Moonpaths: Ethics and Emptiness*. New York: Oxford University Press, 2015.

Dunne, John D. *Foundations of Dharmakīrti's Philosophy*. Boston: Wisdom Publications, 2004.

Garfield, Jay. *Engaging Buddhism: Why it Matters to Philosophy*. New York: Oxford University Press, 2015.

Eltschinger, Vincent. *Buddhist Epistemology as Apologetics: Studies on the History, Self-Understanding and Dogmatic Foundations of Late Indian Buddhist Philosophy*. Vienna: Verlag der Österreichischen Akademie der Wissenschaften, 2014.

Eltschinger, Vincent. "Philosophical Literature: South Asia." In *Brill's Encyclopedia of Buddhism (I: Literature and Languages)*. Edited by Jonathan Silk, 593–620. Leiden: Brill, 2015.

Frauwallner, Erich. *Studies in Abhidharma Literature and the Origins of Buddhist Philosophical Systems*. Albany: SUNY Press, 1995.

Potter, Karl, ed. *Encyclopedia of Indian Philosophies Volume 8: Buddhist Philosophy from 100 to 350 AD*. Delhi: Motilal Banarsidass, 1999.

Potter, Karl, ed. *Encyclopedia of Indian Philosophies Volume 9: Buddhist Philosophy from 350 to 600 AD*. Delhi: Motilal Banarsidass, 2004.

Potter, Karl, ed. *Encyclopedia of Indian Philosophies Volume 21: Buddhist Philosophy from 600 to 750 AD*. Delhi: Motilal Banarsidass, 2017.

Potter, Karl, ed. *Encyclopedia of Indian Philosophies: Volume 22: Buddhist Philosophy from 750 Onward*. Delhi: Motilal Banarsidass, 2017.

Siderits, Mark. *Buddhism As Philosophy*. Aldershot, UK: Ashgate, 2007.

Stoltz, Jonathan. "Illuminating the Mind: An Introduction to Buddhist Epistemology." In *Buddhist Philosophy for Philosophers*. Edited by Jan Westerhoff. New York: Oxford University Press, 2021.

Tillemans, Tom. *How Do Mādhyamikas Think? and Other Essays on the Buddhist Philosophy of the Middle*. Boston: Wisdom Publications, 2016.

Warder, A. K. *Indian Buddhism*. 2nd rev. ed. Delhi: Motilal Banarsidass, 1980.

Westerhoff, Jan. *The Golden Age of Indian Buddhist Philosophy*. Oxford, UK: Oxford University Press, 2018.

Williams, Paul. *Mahāyāna Buddhism: The Doctrinal Foundations*. London: Routledge, 2009.

NOTES

1. *Madhyamakāvatāra* 6.141
2. *Bodhicāryāvatāra* 6.22–32.

3. *Bodhicāryāvatāra* 8.90–102.
4. A possible world is a maximally consistent way that things may be; things being the way they actually are counts as one of the many possible worlds.
5. See Jan Westerhoff, *The Golden Age of Indian Buddhist Philosophy* (Oxford: Oxford University Press, 2018).

Mark Siderits

BUDDHIST WALL PAINTINGS

INTRODUCTION

Wall painting is integral to the built environment of the Buddhist world. Images of the Buddha and other divinities, appearing both as individual icons and in narrative compositions, began to grace permanent edifices of worship as Buddhism took root in India sometime in the 4th century BCE and then spread across Asia. More than two millennia later, some of the same themes and designs continue to be featured in contemporary structures serving Buddhist communities in the early 21st century. Spanning from antiquity to modernity, Buddhist wall painting is global in its reach. The remarkable adaptability of Buddhism to local culture worldwide naturally gives rise to a multitude of wall painting traditions, each with its distinctive characteristics. On the other hand, these traditions also share certain core features and practices in being part of a wider Buddhist world. At the most fundamental level, Buddhist wall paintings are meant to make abstract doctrines and concepts comprehensible through visual means while promoting key moral lessons to devotees in vivid and memorable ways. They provide donors with an opportunity to express piety and accumulate merit for creating a beautiful home for the Buddha that would enable his followers to follow his footsteps and at the same time impress nonbelievers. Though far from a vehicle of individual expression, the medium of wall painting challenges artists to be innovative with age-old iconographic formulae and compositional schemes in order to make the tradition anew for their own time and place. Indeed, artists from diverse cultures did rise to the occasion by making significant contributions to the world history of wall painting, some redefining the very meaning and purpose of the medium altogether.

The term "wall painting," often in use interchangeably with "mural," refers to works rendered in mineral or organic pigments with binders on vertical wall surfaces that have been prepared with layers of plaster coating on top of the wall's base material, typically made of bricks, stone, clay, wood, straw, or a mixture thereof. The painted images constitute an integral part of the architectural structure, serving as the material and conceptual interfaces between art, society, and the ecosystem that link their viewers to the world they live in and realms in their imagination. The remarkable diversity in architectural context underscores the wide range of viewership and purpose for which Buddhist wall paintings were intended. From freestanding wooden-framed buildings to rock-cut temples created along cliff faces and subterranean deposit chambers, the vast majority of examples from premodern Asia have evolved from the secco or paint-on-dry-plaster methods. This stands in contrast to the Western tradition where the fresco or paint-on-wet-plaster technique has dominated since classical antiquity.

Another salient development was the tremendous range of materials utilized for decorating vertical surfaces. Particularly significant is the use of paper, wood, and textile in lieu of plastered walls as the base support. Across the Himalayas and Inner Asian grasslands, interior decorations for Buddhist temples are often made in woven textiles for hanging against the wall or pillar. In structures built in the 20th century or more recently, paper and cotton are two common materials on which paintings are rendered and then pasted to walls both inside and on the exterior. In addition, paintings are rendered on sliding doors, panel screens, and other portable furniture to complement paintings on plastered wall surfaces nearby, as evident in Buddhist temples or palatial complexes in Japan. While these materials are not wall paintings technically speaking, they do have unmistakable similarities in iconography, style, and function that deserve close examination as related developments.

The heavy concentration of sites with extant materials, some with reliable dates, in the Taklamakan and Gobi Deserts in China is the focus of this article (see map). Drawing on the latest scholarly findings and archaeological discoveries whenever available, this analysis will rely on representative examples to broadly delineate the changes and continuities at major sites in Central Asia and Dunhuang or within a given tradition through time.[1] It will also delve into the function and meaning of murals ascribed by their creators and users by examining the architectural context to which the murals belong. Last but not least, it will account for the artisans who created the murals as much as extant information allows. Unlike the donors who frequently left behind documentation of their actions and intents, most artisans had remained nameless and voiceless. There were also cases in which wall painters were celebrated during their lifetime or made records of their work, but their art was lost forever.

THE KUSHANS AND NEW DEVELOPMENTS IN CENTRAL ASIA

Buddhism, along with other cultural practices from the early Indic world, had spread to the neighboring regions in the 1st millennium CE through the movements of people, animals, and goods within a network of transcontinental routes that came to be known as the Silk Road.[2] As a result, many Buddhist monuments were established by local communities of faith across the Hindu Kush, the Pamirs, and the Tarim Basin. The Kushans played a particularly influential role in facilitating the dissemination. Through a succession of ambitious rulers in the 1st and 2nd centuries CE, the Kushans built an empire that dominated the lands from the Aral Sea eastward through much of Afghanistan, Pakistan, and northern India. The powerful King Kaniṣka (r. *c.* 120–140 CE) was a great patron of Buddhism who followed more or less the footsteps of Aśoka, the most famous Buddhist king in history, by promoting the Buddha's teaching as a state religion across his territories. Under such favorable circumstances, different schools of Buddhism flourished at the empire's center in Gandhara, which corresponds to an area around Peshawar and Taxila in Pakistan, and across northern India as far as Mathura. Likewise, the art and architecture purposely created to facilitate monastic and lay devotional worship at these temples developed in ways not seen before in the subcontinent. The Kushans drew on the artistic language of Hellenism, so deeply rooted in Bactria through centuries of Greek settlements following the conquest by Alexander the Great (d. 323 BCE), to represent the Buddha in anthropomorphic form. Unlike central India where the Buddha tended to be

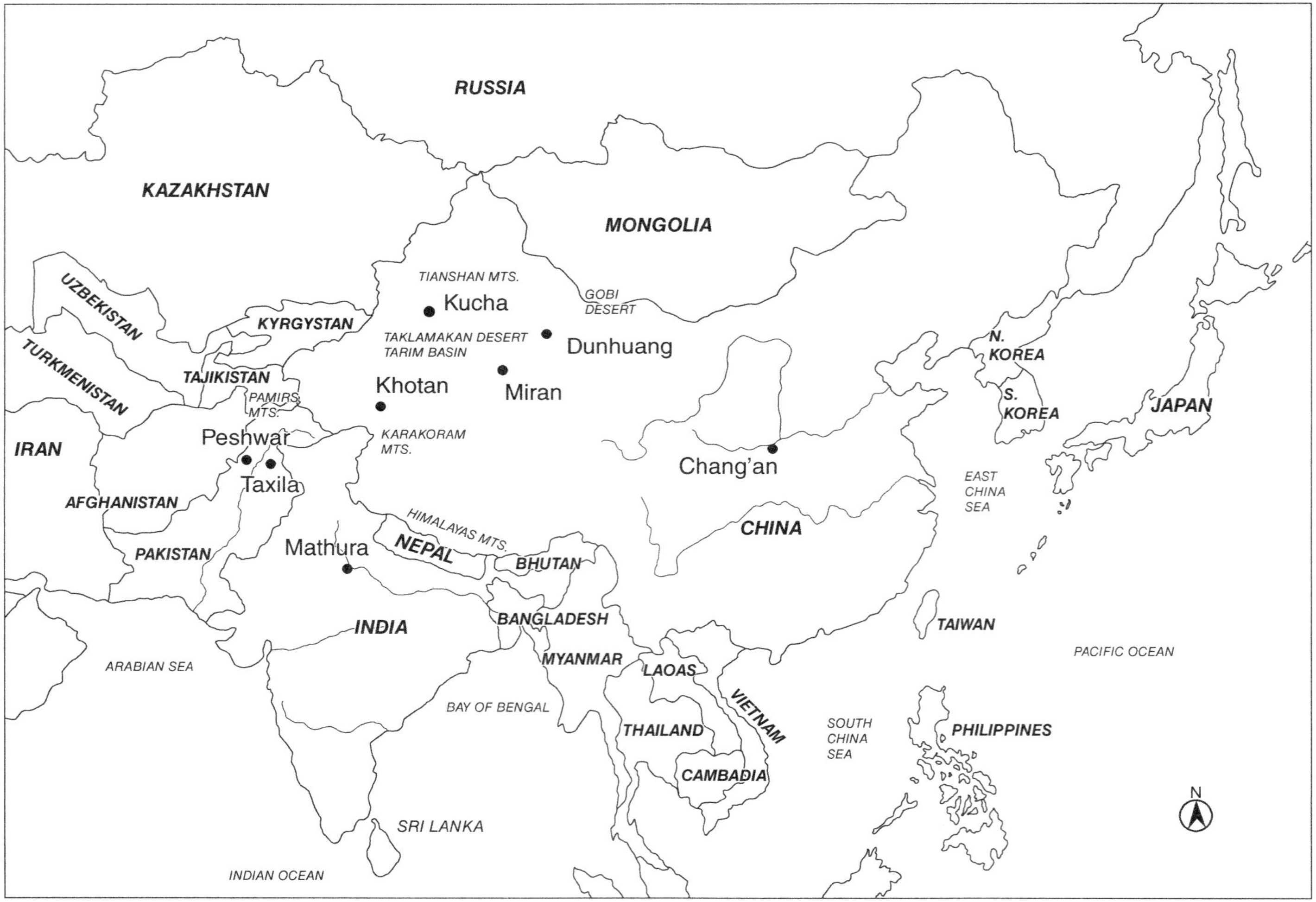

Map 1. Major sites with Buddhist wall paintings. Map by the author.

represented through the use of associative symbols such as an empty throne or a pair of footprints rather than as a human, the Kushan empire marks a turning point at which anthropomorphism would become the dominant mode of representation in Buddhist art across Asia in subsequent times.

In the early 21st century, much of the understanding of the Buddhist art of the Kushans is based on relief carvings and full-bodied sculptures that once filled large monastic complexes such as the one at Takht-i-bahi outside Peshawar. Mural fragments discovered at temple ruins and rock shelters since the 1990s have provided additional information about the practice of wall paintings in Gandhara. Those from Jinnan Wali Dheri in the Taxila Valley are particularly significant in demonstrating a mature painterly tradition in which the three-quarter view of figuration and the skillful use of light and shade to create volume through color were common.[3] The presence of a buddha striking a wheel-turning gesture in one of the fragments points to an iconographic feature indicative of a later phase of development at the monastic site pertaining to the 4th and 5th centuries. The dating would thus put these murals approximately in the same period as the Mahāyāna phase at Ajanta.[4] As for the earlier development in Gandhara, it is necessary to study specimens found in other areas where connections to the style and iconography associated with the Hindu Kush can be established.

It has long been assumed that Buddhism's dissemination across Eurasia followed a unilateral, eastward movement from India to China in a single wave. This simplistic view, first popularized in the 19th century, has been superseded by a more nuanced set of interpretations that call attention to multidirectional traffic across Eurasia as well as additional phases of interactions within different geographical areas. The Tarim Basin provides crucial evidence in support of these new viewpoints. As will be discussed in the next two sections, Buddhist wall paintings from several oasis kingdoms across the Taklamakan Desert, notably in Kroraina and Kucha, flourished at an earlier time than other major Buddhist sites further west, such as Bamiyan in Afghanistan, that shared certain key features in art and architecture.[5] The existence of earlier monuments east of the Pamirs clearly demonstrates that Buddhism and its material culture did, in fact, travel in both eastward and westward directions.

Kroraina and Khotan. The rise of the Sasanian empire in Iran (224–651) in the first quarter of the 3rd century prompted a significant migration of people across the Silk Road region. This coincided with the shift of the Kushan power eastward into the Tarim Basin, where a number of settlements have yielded thousands of ancient documents in Kharoṣṭhī and Sanskrit. Clearly, migrants from the Hindu Kush had moved into that region through the Karakoram Pass and intermingled with native inhabitants.[6] In some of the same settlements, the presence of Chinese documents also reveals that the Chinese state became active across the Tarim Basin in the same period. In this new geopolitical landscape, Kroraina and Khotan along the Southern Silk Road assumed a critical role in facilitating cultural exchange as well as local adaptation of ideas and practices from afar. Wall paintings found at Buddhist temple ruins in both areas are particularly significant. Examples from various locations in Miran, which is believed to have flourished in the 3rd and 4th centuries as an extension of the Kroraina kingdom based at Loulan, provide the clearest evidence of influences from Gandhara and beyond. As exemplified by Shrine V, which took the shape of an enclosed stupa, the murals in the ambulatory path show salient features of Hellenism such as an interest in illusionism by depicting figures in three-quarter view as well as the use of modeling in colors.[7] In the top two registers, the choice of scenes from the Buddha's life story as subject matter and the figuration of the Buddha were based on Gandharan Buddhist iconography and style. A comparison of a fragment depicting the Buddha accompanied by six disciples from Shrine M III (in the National Museum of New Delhi; figure 1) with a relief carving of the Buddha and Vajrapāṇī in the Museum of Asian Art in Berlin shows remarkable similarities in how the Buddha was fashioned as a young male in heavy drapery with large eyes, drooping mustache, and a large bun of hair collected at the top of his head as usnisha.[8] The same iconography appears to have been closely followed in both wall painting and relief sculpture. The Kharoṣṭhī inscription of the painter's name "Tita" found on the south wall of the circumambulatory path in Shrine V further confirms a tie with the Kushans, not ancient Greeks or Romans as previously thought.[9] The use of a meandering garland interspersed with half-length individual figures across the entire bottom register, on the other hand, indicates a certain degree of familiarity with precedents from the Eastern Mediterranean world in the 3rd and 4th centuries in which garlands were utilized in compositions for commemorating the dead.[10]

Artistic influences from Gandhara and other regions are also evident in Khotan, another major center of Buddhism along the Southern Silk Road. The Buddha's teaching was introduced to Khotan sometime in the early 1st century BCE, but it was not until the 3rd century CE that the kingdom became one of the first prominent centers of Buddhism outside the subcontinent.[11] Although a later legend had linked the founding of Khotan to a son of King Aśoka

Figure 1. Wall painting fragment of the Buddha and his disciples, from Shrine III, Miran, 3rd–4th cent. *Source*: Reprinted from Fred Andrews, *Wall paintings from ancient shrines in Central Asia Recovered by Sir Aurel Stein* (London: Oxford University Press, 1948), Plate I: M.III.003.

who was banished from India and then migrated to the Tarim Basin, the discovery of Buddhist texts in Kharoṣṭhī script in Niya, Yotkan, and other sites in the greater Khotan area at least confirms an initial connection to Gandhara.[12] As in the neighboring Kroraina, the dissemination of Buddhism to Khotan coincided with the eastward outreach by the Kushans during the 2nd and 3rd centuries. Yet Khotanese Buddhism would continue to evolve as the kingdom became entangled in military and political conflicts with a succession of ambitious empires that took turns dominating the Silk Road: the Hephthalites in the 6th century and the Western Turks, the Chinese, and the Tibetans in the 7th and 8th centuries. The large group of Sogdian merchants and craftsmen who had settled in Khotan or used it as a base for long-distance travels also played an active role in bringing new ideas and goods in and out of the Tarim Basin. As a result, the material culture that arose out of interactions with such diverse groups of cultures over time was far more complex than anywhere else along the Southern Silk Road.

The early examples of Buddhist wall paintings in Khotan bore telltale connections to the Greco-Bactrian tradition. A set of seven mural fragments depicting celestial dancers from Damago (or Domoko in older publications) provides a tantalizing glimpse into this phase of development.[13] Rendered in mineral paints on straw-filled clay surfaces, these fragments exhibit a uniform painting style and shared design elements, underscoring the likelihood that they once formed part of the same composition. Each fragment features a nude dancer in motion within an arch-like space created by a thick ribbon outlined in red that seems to extend across space in a wavelength (figure 2). The noticeably large eyes outlined in thick black lines and the twisty curls flowing down the two sides of the head are similar to how figures are depicted in mural fragments found in the Yakatoot district in Peshawar City dating to the Kushano-Sasanid period of the 3rd and 5th centuries CE.[14] The use of the garland as a unifying compositional device is evidently similar to the example from Miran Shrine V discussed earlier in this section. Another significant feature shared by some of these mural fragments is a decorative band with illusionistic geometric shapes above the dancer. Interestingly, a nearly identical design is found in a cave temple at Kumtura in Kucha, about 600 kilometers north of Damago.[15] As it turned out, the penchant for incorporating decorative borders like this as part of some larger compositions was pervasive at major cave temple complexes in the Kucha region. The appearance of a nearly identical decorative band at two disparate locales in the Tarim Basin clearly underscores a considerable degree of connections between the two oasis kingdoms. The location of the two sites along the Keriya River network, which once provided a viable path linking the southern and northern routes across the Taklamakan Desert, points to the possibility that artisans with knowledge of the decorative motif were active at both sites.

The Damago area is important for understanding the material culture of later Khotanese Buddhism as well. It was where a significant number of temple complexes from the 7th century and onward once concentrated, as evidenced by architectural remnants and material objects that had surfaced at Khadalik, Balawaste, and Farhad-beg-yailaki. Most mural fragments from these sites represent much greater local adaptation of divergent sources in style and iconography than shown in the earlier works. Iconographic themes central to the Mahāyāna school (including those associated with esoteric teachings) dominated Khotanese Buddhism in this period. Large buddha statues formed the primary subject of worship in the middle of rectilinear temple structures that were designed with circumambulatory paths around them, resembling somewhat the enclosed stupas in Miran. These temple structures were once

Figure 2. Wall painting fragment of a dancer, mineral paints on straw-filled clay surface, 3rd–4th cent. From Damago, Khotan, Xinjiang Autonomous Region, China.
Source: Reprinted from Shanghai bowuguan, ed., *Silu fanxiang: Xinjiang Hetian Damagou fojiao yizhi chutu bihua yishu* (Buddhist vestiges along the silk road: Mural art from the Damago site, Hotan, Xinjiang) (Shanghai: Shanghai Museum, 2014), entry 26, no. 2 on p. 121.

decorated with wall paintings of popular motifs such as the Thousand Buddhas, attendant bodhisattvas, guardian figures, and adoring donor figures. A significant number of mural fragments had been removed by local looters and foreign explorers who visited the sites in the early 20th century and then brought the fragments to Europe.[16] Several of these pieces are in the Los Angeles County Museum of Art, possibly from Balawaste or Khadalik (figure 3). The images were created by the systematic use of preparatory devices such as stencils and templates by professional painters to replicate the same design in different settings. After outlines of figures were traced onto the walls, the individual buddhas were completed with a color scheme of red, white, and black that was strategically applied to the robe, body and head halos, and background so as to create variations within an otherwise repetitive composition. When viewed at a distance, the Thousand Buddhas do appear like wall papers that are interspersed with color blocks in diagonal movements. A similar production method is evident at other sites in Khotan, such as Dandan-Oilik, as well as those further eastward along the Silk Road, such as the Mogao Caves of Dunhuang.

Mahāyāna motifs aside, wall paintings in Khotanese Buddhist temples are also replete with images of local deities or those from other religions that were placed alongside Buddhist ones.

Figure 3. Wall painting fragment of the Thousand Buddhas, paint on gesso over straw-filled clay, 7th–8th cent. From Khotan, Xinjiang Autonomous Region, China.
Source: Los Angeles County Museum of Art, Gift of Nasil M. Heeramneck (M.73.48.144).

Particularly interesting is the pairing of buddhas and Buddhist figures with mounted deities and horsemen. Two such examples were discovered by Chinese archaeologists during excavations conducted at Dandan-Oilik and Topulukdong in Damago in 2002.[17] Dating to about the same time period in the 8th century, both mural fragments show three rows of seated buddhas, possibly representing the Thousand Buddhas motif, filling the upper part of the wall, with a procession of horsemen at the very bottom. In the piece from Dandan-Oilik, two of the horses are covered in spots, which might have been a depiction of Nisean horses, once the most valuable breed from ancient Persia. The possible Iranian connection has led some scholars to identify these horsemen as iconographic conflations with Sogdian deities, whereas others believe that these mounted figures with head halos probably represent pre-Buddhist local gods, as indicated by the black bird flying above each horse and the shallow bowls held by the horsemen.[18] Similar mounted figures were found on a few painted wooden plaques in the British Museum, including one that depicts a horseman in dialogue with the Buddhist protector Vaishravana, who was deemed to be a key figure in the founding of Khotan as a Buddhist kingdom.[19]

Kucha. The British Museum wooden plaque offers an intriguing entry point into a discussion on the art of Kucha. The figural style that its two subjects exemplify—including their unique facial features (arching eyebrows, almond-shaped eyes, curly hair, and drooping mustache) in black and red outlines, bodies captured in distinct poses, extensive use of red and green with highlights in white, and clear articulation of detail in outfits and gear—is also evident in works belonging to what has been labeled the first of three distinct wall painting styles of Kucha.[20] A representation example can be found in Cave 77 at Kizil, from which a number of fragments have been preserved in the Asian Art Museum of Berlin (figure 4). The similarities thus raise questions about the interrelationship between the two oasis kingdoms in the Tarim Basin and their connections to neighboring regions, even though they embraced contrasting forms of Buddhism. From historical records and linguistic evidence, Kucha is known to have had close ties with the Kushans and the more conservative Buddhist schools in

Figure 4. Wall painting fragment of the Vajrapāṇī, paint on plaster and clay, 5th–6th cent. From Cave 77, Kizil, Kucha, Xinjiang Autonomous Region, China.
Source: © Staatliche Museen zu Berlin, Museum für Asiatische Kunst/Sonya Lee.

Gandhara. As noted earlier, the Khotan and Keriya rivers once provided a vital means of transportation for people and goods to circulate between the northern and southern parts of the Tarim Basin. Khotan was an essential stop for travelers from Kucha to cross through the Karakoram Mountains to reach Gandhara as well as for those from the opposite direction to head eastward. Buddhist cave temples in Kucha have preserved a large body of material evidence for understanding the complex exchanges and adaptations that took place during the kingdom's transformation into a major Buddhist center by the 4th century CE.

Kizil. Kizil, located about 70 kilometers northwest of Kucha's capital, is the largest repository of Buddhist wall painting in the Tarim Basin, accounting for about half of the total number of caves in Kucha. Of the nearly 400 units at Kizil (235 numbered and some 150 unnumbered), close to 100 caves are decorated with pictorial images inside.[21] The paintings were mostly religious in nature, embodying key concepts and practices pertaining to the early Buddhist school of the Sarvāstivādins, which flourished in Gandhara under the Kushans and was introduced to Kucha during the empire's expansion into the Tarim Basin during the 2nd and 3rd centuries CE.[22] Followers of this group prized the steadfast observation of moral precepts as well as the practice of meditation both individually and in groups. These two aspects in turn informed the art and architecture of Kizil. Meditation cells (or undecorated, crudely cut spaces in the cliff face that are large enough to accommodate a person seated inside) were abundant across the site; so were central pillar caves, a type of two-chamber unit which was derived from the Indian *chaitya* by incorporating a circumambulating path that links the two, with a front space large enough to accommodate group activities of various sorts and a small, dark chamber in the back.[23] It is inside these central pillar caves that some of most exquisite wall paintings in Kucha are found.

Cave 38 is a classic central pillar cave located in the westernmost section of Kizil. It was carved alongside over forty other units that collectively formed a coherent cluster along the cliff face (figure 5).[24] The cave's relatively well-preserved interior allows for a fuller account of its pictorial program and symbolism. Much of the front chamber is devoted to iconographic motifs related to the historical Buddha Śākyamuni, including *jātakas* and *avadānas* on the ceiling, scenes from the Buddha's life story, and an iconic statue that once occupied the middle of the central wall. In the back chamber, various narrative episodes detailing the Buddha's nirvana are painted on the surrounding walls, plus a large composition featuring the reclining Buddha and those who attended his final moment before entry into extinction. Above the unit's entrance is a large composition that depicts a cross-legged bodhisattva in a paradise full of adoring attendants (figure 6). Based on the wheel-turning hand gesture and cross-legged pose, the central figure has been identified as Maitreya Bodhisattva in Tuṣita Paradise.[25] Taken as a whole, the pictorial program in Cave 38 represents a symbolic passage of time from the present age of the historical Buddha to the future marked by Maitreya's coming, and the Buddha's nirvana marks a crucial moment of transition. The circumambulatory function inherent in the *chaitya* design was skillfully coordinated with the placement of certain pictorial motifs along the viewer's path of viewing, so that they came to experience the transfer of authority from one buddha to another as they walked through the cave. Moreover, the front chamber is decorated largely with preaching scenes and individual conversations that lend themselves to repetition through a shared schematic compositional layout. The seamless array

Figure 5. Exterior of Caves 1–38, Kizil, Kucha, Xinjiang Autonomous Region, China.
Source: Photograph by the author.

of nearly identical scenes thus prompts questions about viewer literacy and participation. The extensive use of abbreviated references to particular stories in Buddhist literature indicates a viewing audience with a high degree of familiarity with these stories and the ability to identify them with a few telling details.[26] While the large size of the chamber clearly points to its utilization by a large group of users, the nature of their activities inside, especially how the cave's users might have made use of pictorial images in ritual or meditational practices, remains unclear.

The Sarvastivadin penchant for meditation has often been cited as an explanation for the depiction of monks meditating before a skull or dead bodies, which represents some of the most extraordinary images from Kucha.[27] Whether or not these images reflect actual practices is difficult to ascertain. Yet other motifs common in Kucha wall painting promoted the tremendous benefits that practitioners might gain through rigorous meditation.[28] The miracles performed by the Buddha at Śrāvastī constitute a case in point.[29] A remarkable presentation of this theme is found inside Cave 123, a central pillar cave with a domed ceiling (figure 7). In the first part of the story, the Buddha emitted fire and water from his body while in the fire samādhi. The shooting flames and spurting water thus can be read as a visual manifestation of the supernatural power that the practitioner would have gained through meditation. In the second part, the Buddha replicated himself in great numbers. The self-multiplication, which is specific to the Sanskrit version of the story and not found in Pali texts, is grandly represented by a stand-

Figure 6. Maitreya Bodhisattva in Tuṣita Paradise, entrance wall, Cave 38, Kizil, Kucha, 5th–6th cent. *Source*: Reprinted from Xinjiang Weiwuer Zizhiqu wenwu guanli weiyuanhui et al., *Kezier shiku* (Kizil caves) Vol. 1. (Beijing: Wenwu chubanshe, 1989), plate 83.

ing buddha enveloped within a large mandorla filled with columns of smaller buddhas in their own mandorlas. This composition in turn is repeated on the opposite walls in the main chamber, further amplifying the spectacular "miracle of double appearances." There is also an abbreviated version of it as represented by a single standing buddha (two on the entrance wall and two in the corridors leading into the back chamber) that is similarly surrounded by smaller buddhas in the head halo and mandorla.

The miracles of Śrāvastī were a popular subject in Gandharan relief sculptures, as attested by the considerable number of extant specimens that depict the crucial scene of the Buddha multiplying himself in a manner similar to the examples in Kizil Cave 123.[30] The existence of

Figure 7. Reconstruction of Kizil Cave 123 in the Museum für Asiatische Kunst, Berlin.
Source: © Staatliche Museen zu Berlin, Museum für Asiatische Kunst/Satomi Hiyama.

iconographic precedents from before the 4th century helps set a *terminus a quo* for the adaptation of this theme in Kucha. The carbon-14 dating performed on the mural fragments from this unit in Germany has yielded the approximate date of 431–533.[31] This is about 100 years earlier than the set of dates, 540–670, obtained by Chinese archaeologists from their own carbon-14 dating in Cave 123 based on straw samples taken from the ceiling of the back chamber.[32] Ironically, the results from China align more closely with the Style II, or Sasanian, phase, to which wall paintings from this cave have been assigned in the German style-based chronology. The art of this later phase is characterized by the extensive use of blue and green and a figural type distinct from that of the so-called Indian model of Style I that was probably introduced through groups from west of the Pamirs, such as the Western Turks and the Sogdians with whom Kucheans had greater interactions after the Kushan migration. In the relative-dating scheme developed by archaeologists in China that relies on grouping of caves *in situ* rather than painting style as the key criterion, Cave 123 purportedly belongs to the fourth and last period of development at Kizil, when nearly half of the caves at the site were created.[33]

The elusiveness in securing a firm date on a single cave temple at Kizil points to the overall difficulty in developing a more nuanced understanding of the history of Kucha wall painting with limited period documentation found at the site. To find additional evidence, it is thus necessary to bring in comparative perspectives by considering the introduction of Chinese artistic elements to Kucha as well as the eastward dissemination of Kuchean styles to Dunhuang and beyond.

DUNHUANG UNDER TANG CHINA

The year 648 marked a watershed in the Chinese engagement with its neighbors in Central Asia, commonly referred to in Chinese records as the Western Regions. The Tang dynasty (618–906) sent its armies to conquer Kucha along with Karashar, thus completing the establishment of the Four Great Garrisons of the Anxi Protectorate. (The other two garrisons, Kashgar and Khotan, became vassals of the Tang court a decade earlier.) This was the first time since the Han dynasty (206 BCE–220 CE) that the Chinese state made such an assertive presence along the Silk Road in order to contend with its chief rivals, the Western Turks and the Tibetans. Amid the power struggles of the 7th century, Kucha and other oasis states in the Tarim Basin struggled to maintain their independence as they came under and out of the rule by these ambitious empires. Significantly, the Chinese military presence in Kucha did not lead to any immediate cultural assimilation. In fact, it was not until the mid-8th century when Tang-style artistic elements became detectable at Kucha cave temples. Compositions depicting the Western Pure Land, the Buddha's life story recast in Chinese cities and buildings, as well as the Thousand Buddhas, appeared in several caves in the Northern Section of Kumtura, including Caves 14, 16, and 45.[34] Their arrival was a clear indicator of artistic influences from Dunhuang, the gateway to China and a bastion of Mahāyāna Buddhism about 600 kilometers east of Kucha. Cartouches identifying motifs and donors in Chinese were also found at the site.[35]

The Mogao Caves. More than a century before Chinese donors became active in Kucha, painters in Dunhuang were consciously imitating wall painting styles from that region. The Mogao Caves, among the world's most important repositories of Buddhist art, began modestly sometime in the 4th century after the monk Yuezun experienced a vision at the Sanwei Mountain and subsequently received sponsorship from local elites to create cave temples there. Of the 40 extant units dating to the period before the 7th century, quite a few boast unmistakable similarities with Kucha wall painting in terms of figural style, color palette, framing décor, and compositional scheme. Mogao Cave 285 provides by far the most significant example with which to consider the intraregional ties between Dunhuang and Kucha through the practice of wall painting. Two aspects are of particular relevance to the present discussion. The first pertains to the motif of individual monks meditating inside caves, which is commonly depicted in the ceilings of Kizil caves. In Mogao Cave 285, images of thirty-six meditating monks appear in a row that wraps around the lower parts of the four ceiling slopes. Their collective presence symbolically echoes the function of the cave's vihara design, which was intended for monastic practices as seen at Ajanta and other sites in India. However, only a few such structures were created in Dunhuang during its earliest phase of development, thus underscoring the site's overall orientation toward lay devotional practices. The second connection to Kucha concerns the painting style of over a dozen Hindu deities on the west wall. Vishnu, who was the supreme protector of the universe in Hinduism and who was appropriated to be part of the Buddhist pantheon, appears to the right of the main buddha statue as if serving as his guardian warrior (figure 8). Depicted with an intense expression on his face, Vishnu is in a dynamic pose that features multiple heads and arms in coordinated movements. The figural style is similar to that of the Vajrapāṇī from Kizil Cave 77 (see figure 4), whereas his hair style mimics the head of a male figure in wood from the same unit at Kizil.[36]

Figure 8. Vishnu, west wall, Cave 285, Mogao, Dunhuang, Gansu Province, China, 538–539.
Source: Reprinted from Dunhuang wenwu yanjiusuo, ed. *Dunhuang Mogaoku* (Mogao Caves of Dunhuang) (Beijing: Wenwu chubanshe, 1987), Vol. 1, plate 118.

The conscious attempt at imitating the Kuchean prototypes in Dunhuang points to the likelihood that the painters at Mogao learned of the earlier examples from pattern books and then carried out their work using local materials and techniques. It is also possible that the murals were painted by itinerary workshop artisans who traveled from one oasis to another for work. Regardless, upon comparison with the superb handling of color in creating the Vajrapāṇī from Kizil Cave 77, the less refined execution by the painters at Mogao suggests that they were rather new to the Kuchean artistic idiom and hence lacked experience in capturing the subtleties of this particular style. Furthermore, the dated inscriptions from 538 and 539 found on the south wall of Mogao Cave 285 confirm that the painting style associated with Kizil Cave 77 was known in Dunhuang by the first half of the 6th century. This in turn means that Style I in wall painting of Kizil existed with Style II at the same site, not earlier in a temporal sequence as frequently construed in studies that follow the German style-based chronology.[37]

By the 8th century, painters in Dunhuang had managed to develop artistic styles of their own out of materials coming from the Western Regions as well as central China. The emergence of Dunhuang art coincided with the Tang state's outward-looking foreign relations strategy that sought to achieve security in its vast northwestern frontiers by maintaining strongholds at strategic locations like Dunhuang. This in turn had directed tremendous human and material resources from central China to the frontier garrison. The embrace of cultural pluralism by the local ruling elite further facilitated adaptation of ideas and practices brought in from afar. The resulting cosmopolitanism clearly manifested in the iconographic repertoire of the Mogao Caves, which encompassed a far greater range than any other Buddhist sites in Eurasia. The many themes that emerged in the Tang period were based on Mahāyāna scriptures popular at the time. Pictorial compositions based on certain aspects of a particular text, be they narrative elements or abstract doctrines, were referred to in Chinese records as *jingbian* or *bianxiang*, terms commonly translated as "sutra tableau" or "transformation tableau."[38] Interestingly, a significant number of these works incorporated people, goods, and activities deemed exotic by the Chinese into Buddhist paradises that were modeled more or less after architectural spaces of Tang China.

In the debate between the householder Vimalakirti and Manjushri Bodhisattva, a memorable episode from the *Vimalakīrti Sūtra* that constituted the most recognizable feature of the transformation tableau named after the scripture, the lively event was attended by a large audience that included the Chinese emperor as well as dignitaries from numerous states near and far.[39] One of the most celebrated examples from the 8th century is painted inside Cave 103, where the two main protagonists face each other on two sides of the cave's entrance (figure 9). The colorful emissaries from South and Central Asia that fill up the audience space in the lower part of the wall are balanced with the two imposing debaters who were deftly created by firm, elegant brushwork, a hallmark of Chinese painting. The mural offers a tantalizing glimpse into what contemporary Tang painters such as Wu Daozi might have created in the Chinese capitals during the 8th century, as the legendary artist is known to have rendered wall paintings entirely in ink at several Buddhist temples there.[40] Those who witnessed the artist at work reported that Wu would raise his brush and sweep it around with the force of a whirlwind as if aided by a divinity.[41]

Another notable theme at the Mogao Caves that had fully captured the spirit of Tang cosmopolitanism was the Amitāyus transformation tableau based on the *Sūtra of the Meditation*

Figure 9. Vimalakīrt in a debate with Manjushri Bodhisattva, east wall, Cave 103, Mogao, Dunhuang, 8th cent.
Source: Reprinted from Dunhuang wenwu yanjiusuo, ed. *Dunhuang Mogaoku* (Mogao Caves of Dunhuang) (Beijing: Wenwu chubanshe, 1987), Vol. 3, plate 154.

on the Buddha of Immeasurable Life (or the *Meditation Sūtra*). It was one of the three key scriptures in the Pure Land school that promoted the devotional worship of Amitābha and the practice of visualization.[42] Adherents of the teachings presented therein believed that this Buddha's Pure Land offers a particularly viable path to enlightenment, for nirvana is ensured to all born there. To attain rebirth in the Pure Land, one would follow a set of practices spelled out in the texts, chief among which is the dedication to Amitābha by chanting his name and contemplating his radiance and Pure Land's splendors. Visual images have played a crucial role in helping devotees understand the underlying concepts and carry out the related practices. The pertinent murals in Dunhuang, for example, fleshed out an otherworldly realm that is within reach for all who are willing, with utmost sincerity, to make a vow to attain rebirth there. In the Amitāyus murals, in particular, the seeming paradox was presented and then solved purely in pictorial terms through two main components that define the composition: a large preaching assemblage in the middle representing the Western Pure Land; and clusters of narrative vignettes relating the story of Ajātaśatru and Lady Vaidehi's meditations that frame the preaching assemblage. Cave 172 at the Mogao Caves boasts two magnificent murals of the same theme exemplifying this unique compositional design (figure 10). The addition of the storytelling elements to a standalone preaching scene was what distinguished the Amitāyus transformation tableau from a preaching scene featuring Amitābha. The latter appeared in Dunhuang and elsewhere in China in earlier times largely as a fantastical yet distant place.[43] The story of Ajātaśatru provided the necessary human touch to bridge the divide between imagination and reality, thus allowing the viewers in Tang-dynasty Mogao to imagine themselves entering the Western Pure Land with ease.

Constituting a narrative preface to the Meditation Sūtra, the story of Ajātaśatru relates how this evil prince attempted a palace coup by imprisoning his father (King Bimbisara) and threatening to kill his mother (Lady Vaidehi). Her subsequent dialogue with Śākyamuni Buddha forms the bulk of the text in which a meditation process called the "Sixteen Meditations" was introduced as a path for sentient beings to free themselves from sufferings

Figure 10. Western Pure Land of Amitābha, south wall, Cave 172, Mogao, Dunhuang, 8th cent.
Source: Reprinted from Dunhuang wenwu yanjiusuo, ed. *Dunhuang Mogaoku* (Mogao Caves of Dunhuang) (Beijing: Wenwu chubanshe, 1987), Vol. 4, plate 9.

by gaining access to the Western Pure Land of Amitābha. The last three of the Sixteen Meditations spell out a rebirth system called the "Nine Grades of Rebirth." In Cave 172, both the story and the meditations appear sequentially within the vertical bands on two sides of the wall flanking the main preaching scene or occasionally in the space underneath it. Although the story was set in a foreign land ages ago, all characters in the tableau were dressed in Chinese-style garbs, just as all actions took place inside a Chinese-style courtyard comprised of various timber-framed structures.

The central preaching assemblage in the Amitāyus transformation tableau was likewise construed as a splendid imperial Chinese palatial complex. As seen in the two murals from Cave 172, it featured the Amitābha triad, with the Buddha in the middle and Bodhisattvas Avalokiteśvara and Mahāsthāmaprāpta on his two sides. Together, the three presided over a large assembly of attendants surrounding them. Unlike other preaching assemblages in Buddhist art, those representing the Western Pure Land typically include a pond of seven treasures in the lower foreground, out of which those attaining rebirth in the Pure Land emerge on lotus petals. There is also a large ensemble of musicians and dancers performing on large platforms above the water; additional musicians are flying above the assembly with musical instruments in hand. The music being performed must have come from the Western Regions, as indicated by a variety of instruments not known in China before Tang times. The same can be said about the dances. Indeed, one of the most memorable images from Dunhuang shows dancers gyrating while playing the lute on their back. One such pair can be seen in action at the center of the foreground in the Amitāyus mural on the south wall.

It is no surprise that the Amitāyus transformation tableau, with its alluring depiction of the Western Pure Land and the compelling story of Lady Vaidehi, was one of the most popular motifs at the Mogao Caves ever. This is attested by seventy-six examples created during the Tang dynasty alone and the fact that the other most frequently depicted motifs at the site, such as the Eastern Pure Land of the Medicine Buddha and the *Maitreya Sūtra* transformation tableau, were closely related in theme, often appearing with the Amitāyus mural inside the same cave unit. The widespread distribution of Pure Land imageries across China, Korea, and Japan certainly underscores the tremendous popularity that the teachings of the Pure Land school had attained from the 8th century onward. The situation also points to the use of a greater range of techniques and media for the production of a shared repertoire of iconographic motifs and compositional schemes on a scale not seen before. Dunhuang provides an exceptional resource for understanding this crucial aspect of Buddhist material culture in East Asia, filling the lacuna created by the lack of surviving evidence in central China. The Amitāyus transformation tableau, for example, was the subject of wall paintings in cave units as well as hanging scrolls on silk that were found inside the Library Cave, a hidden cache of thousands of ancient manuscripts and artifacts discovered inside a side chamber in Mogao Cave 16 in the early 20th century; there were related images of Amitābha and the Western Pure Land preserved as woodblock prints and paintings on paper too.[44]

FURTHER READING

Bussagli, Mario. *Central Asian Painting: From Afghanistan to Sinkiang*. Translated by Lothian Small. New York: Rizzoli International Publications, 1979.

Fraser, Sarah E. *Performing the Visual: The Practice of Buddhist Wall Painting in China and Central Asia, 618–960*. Stanford, CA: Stanford University Press, 2004.

Hansen, Valerie. *The Silk Road: A New History*. Oxford and New York: Oxford University Press, 2012.

Howard, Angela F., and Giuseppe Vignato. *Archaeological and Visual Sources of Meditation in the Ancient Monasteries of Kuča*. Leiden, The Netherlands, and Boston: Brill, 2015.

Huntington, Susan, and John C. Huntington. *The Art of Ancient India: Buddhist, Hindu, Jain*. New York: Weatherhill, 1985.

Klimburg-Salter, Deborah E. *The Kingdom of Bamiyan: Buddhist Art and Culture of the Hindu Kush*. Naples, Italy: Istituto Universitario Orientale, 1989.

Konczak-Nagel, Ines, and Monika Zin. *Essays and Studies in the Art of Kucha*. Leipzig Kucha Studies 1. New Delhi: Dev Publishers & Distributors, 2020.

Lee, Sonya S. "Buddhist Art and Architecture." *Oxford Research Encyclopedia of Asian History*, 2020. https://doi.org/10.1093/acrefore/9780190277727.013.398.

Leidy, Denise. *Art of Buddhism: An Introduction to Its History and Meaning*. Boston: Shambhala Publications, 2008.

Luczanits, Christian, ed. *Gandhara: Das Buddhistische Erbe Pakistans; Legenden, Klöster und Paradiese*. Bonn, Deutschland: Kunst- und Ausstellungshalle der Bundesrepublik Deutschland, 2008.

Rhie, Marylin Martin. *Early Buddhist Art of China and Central Asia*. Volume 2: The Eastern Chin and Sixteen Kingdoms Period in China and Tumshuk, Kucha and Karashahr in Central Asia. Leiden, The Netherlands: E.J. Brill, 2002.

Rowland, Benjamin, Jr. *Wall-Paintings of India, Central Asia, and Ceylon: A Comparative Study*. Boston: Merrymount Press, 1938.

Spink, Walter. *Ajanta: History and Development*. 7 vols. Leiden, The Netherlands: Brill, 2005.

Stein, Aurel. *Serindia: Detailed Report on Explorations in Central Asia and Westernmost China*. 5 vols. London: Clarendon Press, 1921.

Whitfield, Roderick. *The Art of Central Asia: The Stein Collection in the British Museum*. 2 vols. Tokyo: Kodansha, 1982.

Whitfield, Roderick, Susan Whitfield, and Neville Agnew. *Cave Temples of Mogao: Art and History on the Silk Road*. Los Angeles: Getty Conservation Institute, 2000.

Whitfield, Susan, ed. *The Silk Road: Trade, Travel, War, and Faith*. Chicago: Serindia, 2004.

Yaldiz, Marianne, Raffael Dedo Gadebusch, Regina Hickmann, Friederike Weis, and Rajeshwari Ghose. *Magische Götterwelten: Werke aus dem Museum für Indische Kunst Berlin*. Berlin: Staaliche Museen zu Berlin––Preußischer Kulturbesitz Museum für Indische Kunst, 2000.

Yamauchi, Kazuya, Yoko Taniguchi, and Tomoko Uno, eds. *Mural Paintings of the Silk Road: Cultural Exchange between East and West*. Tokyo: Archetype Publications, 2007.

NOTES

1. See the "Discussion of the Literature" in Sonya S. Lee, "Buddhist Art and Architecture," *Oxford Research Encyclopedia of Asian History*.
2. Justin M. Jacobs, "The Concept of the Silk Road in the 19th and 20th Centuries," *Oxford Research Encyclopedia of Asian History*.
3. Archaeological excavations were carried out at Jinnan Wali Dheri from 2002 to 2008 as well as in 2017 and 2018. Four fragments are illustrated in Muammad Ashraf Khan and Mahmood-ul-Hasan, "Eine neue Entdeckung im Taxilatal," in *Gandhara: Das Buddhistische Erbe Pakistans; Legenden, Klöster und Paradiese*, ed. Christian Luczanits (Bonn, Germany: Kunst- und Ausstellungshalle der Bundesrepublik Deutschland, 2008), 302–307.

4. See the discussion on Caves 1, 2, 16, and 17 in Walter Spink, *Ajanta: History and Development,* Volume 5: Cave by Cave (Leiden: Brill, 2007), 17–55, 179–229.
5. Comparative analyses of key features shared by Bamiayan and Kizil, such as the motif depicting the Buddha's parinirvana and the creation of colossal Buddhas, have shown that these practices likely originated in Kucha before being introduced to Bamiyan. See Shumpei Iwai, "Radiocarbon Dating and Art-Historical Studies in Central Asian Mural Paintings," in *Mural Paintings of the Silk Road: Cultural Exchange between East and West,* ed. Kazuya Yamauchi, Yoko Taniguchi, and Tomoko Uno (Tokyo: Archetype Publications, 2007), 54–59.
6. Valerie Hansen, *The Silk Road: A New History* (Oxford and New York: Oxford University Press, 2012), 26–27, 44–47, 207–209. Linguistic evidence also shows that the Kushans descended from the Lesser Yuezhi, a Tokharian-speaking people who, according to Chinese sources, originated in an area between Kroraina and Kucha and later migrated to Bactria. See Christopher I. Beckwith, *Empires of the Silk Road: A History of Central Eurasia from the Bronze Age to the Present* (Princeton, NJ: Princeton University Press, 2009), 380–383.
7. Shrine V and other Buddhist temples in Miran were discovered by Sir Aurel Stein, who visited the site in three expeditions to the Tarim Basin (in 1900–1901, 1906–1908, and 1913–1916, respectively). He carried out excavation during the second expedition and reported his findings at Shrine V in Aurel Stein, *Serindia: Detailed Report on Explorations in Central Asia and Westernmost China* (London: Clarendon Press, 1921), vol. 1, 512–523.
8. Marianne Yaldiz et al., *Magische Götterwelten: Werke aus dem Museum für Indische Kunst Berlin* (Berlin: Staaliche Museen zu Berlin–Preußischer Kulturbesitz Museum für Indische Kunst, 2000), entry no. 49 (I 58).
9. Yumiko Nakanishi, "The Art of Miran: A Buddhist Site in the Kingdom of Shanshan" (PhD diss., University of California, 2000), 264–265. A photograph of the inscription was published in Stein, *Serindia,* vol. 1, figure 144, 527.
10. Nakanishi, "Art of Miran," 225.
11. Gen'ichi Yamazaki, "The Legend of the Foundation of Khotan," *Memoirs of the Research Department of the Toyo Bunko,* 48 (1990): 69–70; and Ronald E. Emmerick, *A Guide to the Literature of Khotan* (Tokyo: Reiyukai Library, 1979), 3.
12. The legend was recorded by the Chinese monk Xuanzang (*c.* 596–664) in his *The Great Tang Record of the Western Regions,* English translation by Rongxi Li (Berkeley, CA: Numata Center for Buddhist Translation & Research, 1996), 331–332.
13. These fragments are in the Museum of Damago Buddhist Sites in Qira County, having been confiscated by local authorities from looters in 2011. They likely came from a Buddhist temple in Huyangdun. See Shanghai bowuguan, ed., *Silu fanxiang: Xinjiang Hetian Damagou fojiao yizhi chutu bihua yishu* [Buddhist Vestiges along the Silk Road: Mural Art from the Damago Site, Hotan, Xinjiang] (Shanghai: Shanghai bowuguan, 2014), 118–127.
14. M. Nasim Khan, "Fresco Paintings from Yakatoot (Peshawar) Gandhara," in *Annual Report of the International Research Institute for Advanced Buddhology at Soka University for the Academic Year 2015,* vol. XIX (Tokyo, 2016), 47–56.
15. Specifically, the decorative band is painted on the east wall of the main chamber in Kumtura Cave 21.
16. A local dealer named Badreddin Khan had sold mural fragments from Khotan to various foreign visitors, including Emil Trinkler, who headed an expedition to the area in 1928. There are 162 mural fragments from Balawaste alone in different museum collections worldwide. See Gerd Gropp, *Archäologische Funde aus Khotan Chinesisch-Ostturkestan: Die Trinkler-Sammlung im Übersee-Museum* (Bremen, Germany: Rover, 1974), 105–106.
17. The temple in Dandan-Oilik was labeled CD_4 by excavators in a joint Chinese-Japanese expedition, located in the northwest part of the site; see Zhang Yuzhong, Qu Tao, and Liu Guorui, "A Newly Discovered

Buddhist Temple and Wall Paintings at Dandan-Uiliq in Xinjiang," *Journal of Inner Asian Art and Archaeology* 3 (2008): 157–170 and figure 8. The example from Topulukdong came from No. 2 Temple Site; see Shanghai bowuguan, *Silu fanxiang*, entry no. 7, 68–69.

18. Matteo Compareti, "The 'Eight Divinities' in Khotanese Paintings: Local Deities or Sogdian Importation?" in *Proceedings of the Eighth European Conference on Iranian Studies*, ed. Pavel B. Lurje, vol. 1 (Saint Petersburg, Russia: State Hermitage, 2019), 117–132.
19. This wooden votive panel, along with a dozen others, was acquired by Claremont Skrine from Keraken Moldovack and Baddruddin Khan during Skrine's visit to Khotan as the British consul-general in Chinese Turkistan in 1922–1924. See his *Chinese Central Asia* (London: Methuen, 1926), 170–171. It is in the British Museum (1925,0619.35) (https://www.britishmuseum.org/collection/image/1132758001).
20. Albert Grünwedel was the first to discuss the artistic development in Kucha in terms of three distinct wall painting styles in cave temples: Style I was based on Gandharan models, Style II on Sasanian precedents, and Style III on Chinese tradition. The scheme was further developed by Albert von Le Coq and Ernst Waldschmidt, who periodized the three styles by assigning the Gandhara-related material to before the 6th century, Sasanian phase to 600–650, and Chinese phase to 650–800. See Albert von Le Coq and Ernst Waldschmidt, *Die Buddhistische Spätantike in Mittelasien*, Bd. 7: Neue Bildwerke (Berlin: Dietrich Reimer, 1933), 24–31. Scholars in Germany have adhered to the same chronology since then but with some changes in period names.
21. Angela F. Howard and Giuseppe Vignato, *Archaeological and Visual Sources of Meditation in the Ancient Monasteries of Kuča* (Leiden, The Netherlands, and Boston: Brill, 2015), 26, 39.
22. Monks from the Dharmagupta School were also active in Kucha, probably before the arrival of the Kushans and the Sarvastivadins, but they left few material traces in local cave temples, Howard and Vignato, *Archaeological and Visual Sources*, 163–164.
23. For a more extensive discussion of these types of cave architecture, see Howard and Vignato, *Archaeological and Visual Sources*, 63–68.
24. Seven distinct clusters of caves are evident at Kizil. These groupings of caves provide evidence for a relative chronology that can complement dating based on stylistic analysis of wall paintings, see Howard and Vignato, *Archaeological and Visual Sources*, 98.
25. Miyaji Akira, *Nehan to Miroku no zuzōgaku: Indo kara chūō ajia e* [Iconology of Parinirvana and Maitreya: From India to Central Asia] (Tokyo: Yoshikawa Kobunkan, 1992), 512–517.
26. Monika Zin, "Reflections on the Purpose of the Kucha Paintings," *Journal of the International Association of Buddhist Studies* 38 (2015): 373–390.
27. Examples are found in Caves 77, 110, 116, and 212. See the illustrations and discussion in Eric M. Greene, "Death in a Cave: Meditation, Death Bed Ritual, and Skeletal Imagery at Tape Shotor," *Artibus Asiae* 73, no. 2 (2013), 265–294.
28. Howard and Vignato, *Archaeological and Visual Sources*, 108–123.
29. See an analysis of the story in John S. Strong, *The Buddha: A Short Biography* (Oxford: Oneworld, 2001), 107–112.
30. See the examples in Kurita Isao, ed., *Gandhara bijutsu* [Gandharan Art], vol. 1 (Tokyo: Nigensha, 2003), 194.
31. Yaldiz et al., *Magische Götterwelten*, entry no. 289 (III 9061–9066), 198.
32. The test was performed during 1989–1990. See results in Xinjiang Qiuci shiku yanjiusuo, ed., *Kezier shiku neirong zonglu* [Content Catalogue for Kizil Caves] (Urumqi, China: Xinjiang meishu hying chubanshe, 2000), 304.
33. Howard and Vignato, *Archaeological and Visual Sources*, 37–38.
34. Xinjiang Weiwuer Zizhiqu wenwu guanli weiyuanhui et al., *Kumutula shiku* [Kumtura Caves] (Beijing: Wenwu chubanshe, 1992), plates 25–37, 43–47, 84–97.

35. These inscriptions are found in and around Cave 45, Xinjiang Qiuci shiku yanjiusuo, ed., *Kumutula shiku neirong zonglu* [Content Catalogue for Kumtura Caves] (Beijing: Wenwu chubanshe, 2008), 172–173.
36. See Yaldiz et al., *Magische Götterwelten*, entry no. 354 (III 7920), 242.
37. Howard and Vignato, *Archaeological and Visual Sources*, 5.
38. See the discussion of these terms in Wu Hung, "What Is Bianxiang?—On the Relationship between Dunhuang Art and Dunhuang Literature," *Harvard Journal of Asiatic Studies* 52, no. 1 (June 1992): 111–192.
39. There are numerous examples based on the *Vimalakirti Sutra* at the Mogao Caves, including over two dozen from the Tang dynasty.
40. Susan Bush and Hsio-yen Shih, *Early Chinese Texts on Painting* (Cambridge, MA: Harvard University Press, 1985), 64.
41. Bush and Shih, *Early Chinese Texts*, 56.
42. The other two texts are the shorter and longer versions of the *Sukhavativyuha Sutra*: the *Amitabha Sutra* and the *Amitayurdhyana Sutra*, respectively. For a concise discussion of these texts, see David Quinter, "Visualization/Contemplation Sutras (Guan Jing)," *Oxford Research Encyclopedia of Religion*.
43. For a brief introduction to the topic, see Eugene Y. Wang, "Pure Land Art," in *Encyclopedia of Buddhism*, ed. Robert Buswell (New York: Macmillan, 2004), 693–698. See also Shi Pingting, ed., *Dunhuang shiku quanji* [Complete Works of Dunhuang Caves], Vol. 5: *Amituo jinghua juan* [Amitabha Transformation Images] (Hong Kong: Shangwu yinshuguan, 2002).
44. See illustrations of these works from Dunhuang in Tokyo National Museum, ed., *The Grand Exhibition on Silk Road Buddhist Art* (Tokyo: Yuri Shimbunsha, 1996), entry nos. 196–200 on pp. 183-186. For an account of the discovery of the Library Cave and its contents, see Roderick Whitfield, Susan Whitfield, and Neville Agnew, *Cave Temples of Mogao: Art and History on the Silk Road* (Los Angeles: Getty Conservation Institute, 2000), 32–49.

Sonya S. Lee

BUDDHIST WIZARDS (*VIDHYADHĀRA/WEIZZĀ/WEIKZA*): CONTEMPORARY BURMA/MYANMAR

STUDYING "BUDDHISM-AS-LIVED"

The study of "lived religion" is interested in religion as people practice it in their everyday lives. This study of religion was first identified and schematized by David Hall and Robert Orsi to refer to "an approach to the study of religion that foregrounds practice: 'lived' in the sense of the performed or enacted" in order to examine the religious lives of individuals and the experiences they consider central to their lives—along with the varied rituals and practices that make up their personal religious expressions.[1] Situated "within the field of religious studies," it intentionally adopts "methods and interpretative paradigms from the discipline of anthropology."[2] Lived religion considers religion at the level of the individual and takes seriously his or her fluid, variegated—and at times contradictory—beliefs and practices.

It is valuable to grapple with the complexities, apparent inconsistencies, heterogeneity, and untidiness of the range of religious practices that people in any given culture partake in and find meaningful and useful. It reveals important things that we may not otherwise recognize about religious traditions and the ways people incorporate them into their daily lives. For the purposes of this article, such an interpretive strategy will help to situate narratives, practices, and ritual works within a broader landscape of Buddhist traditions and contemporary social dynamics in Myanmar. This analytical framework highlights the Buddhist wizards' function as "a symbolic agent mediating individual bodies and experiences and conventional discourses" within Myanmar society about religion, healing, politics, and significantly advances our understanding of Myanmar Buddhist religious culture.[3] To put it in slightly different terms, the religious tradition of the wizards can be approached as a "form of social discourse: a conceptual and experiential frame for the expression of various disjunctive experiences, interpersonal conflicts, perceived threats to life and happiness, or other stresses."[4]

For such an endeavor, we will not look at religion as something *sui generis* nor as an abstract system. Religion should be viewed as a social phenomenon that dynamically comes into being as a result of the tensions that develop out of what is perceivable, achievable, and imaginable in one's world and its social structures.[5] Timothy Fitzgerald, for instance, has argued that religion is a scholarly construct with a conceptual history and that using the concept of religion to analyze those traditions scholars recognize as "religious" is often ineffective: this is because it implies distinctiveness from the social or secular.[6] Indeed, the modern category of "religion" is a result of Enlightenment presuppositions and preoccupations with defining the essence of a phenomenon such as "religion." The word "religion" can be problematic when it is used to refer to a folk category used by scholars to refer to something that has no equivalent term or concept to many of the groups religious scholars study. However, while this may have been the case at the time when European scholars first encountered non-Christian peoples, with regard to Myanmar and Buddhism in Asia, the concept of "religion" has become deeply embedded in many, if not most, of the cultures throughout the world in this post-Enlightenment, postcolonial era. Despite attempts of non-Western peoples to define the nature of religion often resulting in definitions tainted with Western presuppositions, it is no longer fair to say that those peoples and groups studied by religious scholars do not now have an equivalent term for what scholars mean by "religion."[7]

From this position, then, we can begin to form a view of religion as it is actually lived in people's everyday lives. For example, when examining the beneficial, supernatural healing capabilities of certain wizards in an ongoing, dynamic relation with the realities and structures of everyday life in particular times and places, we realize that people in these situations do not simply act: "They attempt to understand and narrate themselves as actors," and the "lived religions" approach recognizes that the stories they narrate and interpret are, as Orsi writes, "ideas, gestures, and imaginings, all as media of engagement with the world . . . [for] it is pointless to study particular beliefs and practices apart from the people who use these ideas in the definite circumstances of their lives."[8] This allows us to understand how the practices, stories, and beliefs shared by informants are described and understood by them while also considering the circumstances of their experiences and the cultural structures and conditions from which these elements emerge.

In a sense, then, the object of study can be referred to as "popular religion" but not without first problematizing such a term. The term "popular religion" is

> badly in need of definition. Among detractors of the idea, popular religion means all those crazy religious things that people do and all the crazy ideas they have outside the structures of an organized and properly ordered church. Among its defenders, popular

religion too often means the nostalgic evocation of peasant spirituality or the angry defense of magic and folk practices.[9]

Such a term often gives the impression that it is mostly the uneducated, non-monastic legions of laity who engage in such practices. But this idea only perpetuates monastic/lay, educated/uneducated, sophisticated/unsophisticated, pure/impure dualities that imply a binary of right/wrong. Good scholarship has been undertaken in the field of Buddhist studies to help overturn such a bifurcated way of viewing Buddhism in Asia. Buddhism Richard Gombrich makes the salient point that the term is misleading because it implies a decline "from an ideal standard which is maintained by a few spiritual aristocrats, a relationship analogous to that between 'popular' and 'classical' music."[10] So if we use the term, it seems better to use it in the everyday sense: that is, with reference to those beliefs and practices that are "widely followed" or "prevalent."[11]

Furthermore, terms, such as "popular," "syncretic," and "hybridized" continue to perpetuate an imaginary stratification of religious elements that is not self-consciously reflected upon by the Buddhists engaging in many of the practices included in this article. When engaging in a variety of rituals, Buddhists in Myanmar do not attempt to unravel the many threads of their religious practices.[12] Take, for instance, U Kyaw, a Burmese Buddhist who chants the *Heart Sutra* (in Sanskrit) while seated in front of a statue of Sarasvati. The Sarasvati statue is placed next to a statue of the Buddha that is enveloped in smoke from a cigarette offered to a laminated picture of a revered wizard saint as a way of in hopes of finding success in a new business venture. U Kyaw is not saying to himself throughout this ritual, "Ok, this is Mahāyāna Buddhist, this is Hindu, this is a smattering of animism from my ancestors, and this is just some stuff I came up with on my own." It can be argued that such individuals, unless pressed to create such distinctions (i.e., if they even have knowledge of such constructs of "Hindu" "animism" and so on, in the first place) live their religious lives and practices as a dynamic, ever-changing, amalgamation of thoughts, feelings, and actions. People like U Kyaw draw on what they regard as coherent, well-formed practices of potency: our attempts to dissect them would be fruitless and perhaps disrespectful. We should be wary of terms such as "hybridization" and especially "syncretism" because of their historical uses and residual connotations.[13] Toward the end of the Long Reformation (1500–1800 CE), theologians gave the term "syncretism" a pejorative connotation in that it referred to the blending of non-Christian elements with supposed authentic Christian beliefs and practices. About two hundred years later, historians of religion tried to reframe syncretism as any mixing of elements from diverse religious traditions. They did not think there was anything problematic about the boundaries between those traditions: they saw those definitive features separating the religions as qualities essential to the religions themselves rather than as social constructions.[14]

It is important to point out that the term "lived religion" is not a simple substitution for "popular religion" or any of the above-mentioned terms. That would just be reifying the stratified view of religion that we are trying to transcend here. On the contrary, borrowing folklorist and religious studies scholar Leonard Primiano's words, the term "lived religion" is used to represent "a theoretical definition of another term, not just a terminological substitution for an older concept."[15] Approaching Buddhism from the perspective of a lived religion in order to shift our focus to the people (in this case, Buddhist wizards and their devotees), whether they be monastics or laypeople, elite or commoners, rich or poor, and so on.

Since the early 1990s there has been a growing body of research done by scholars of religion whose work focuses on the everyday practices, thoughts, and beliefs of lay Christians in various parts of the Western world.[16] Such scholars of religion have approached their subjects through history, sociology, ethnography, and close reading of texts to help expand our ways of thinking about the daily life of lived religious practices. Buddhist scholarship, however, has not kept up, and only recently have we begun to see a handful of studies done by scholars of Theravāda Buddhism whose work comes close to what one might think of as religion-as-lived.[17] The methodologies and interpretative strategies employed in the lived religions approach build upon and borrow from work done on Buddhism in South and Southeast Asia from the fields of Buddhist studies and history and anthropology of religion. And although few lived-religion studies of Buddhism have been undertaken, important works that were published over the past several decades have greatly influenced and informed how lived-religion approaches to the study of Buddhism have been adapted.

THE *WEIZZĀ* PHENOMENON AS LIVED RELIGION

Before continuing with the remainder of the article, an explanation of what, exactly, constitutes a "Buddhist wizard" is in order. A wizard, or *weizzā*, in Burmese language, is any human being—monastic, hermit, or lay—who has gained supernatural powers and transformed him/herself into a semi-divine being through specific practices and rituals. The wizards who are understood to possess such power are thought to manipulate the natural world around them to enact changes for the benefit of their followers and buddha's *sāsana*. At the time of death, the *weizzā* exits this world to remain in an otherworldly abode helping those in need and continuing to guard the *sāsana*. *Weizzā* are also known in Burmese as "htwet yat pauk" beings, and according to how one interprets this phrase, the compound *htwet yat pauk* can be understood and explained in two ways. For some, *htwet yat pauk* means "to reach (*pauk*) the place (*yat*) of exit (*htwet*)," in reference to the "exit" both from the cycle of rebirths and toward nirvana. A second gloss is "to exit (*htwet*)" from the cycle of rebirths—"to stop" (*yat*) rounds of rebirths—"to break out" (*pauk*) from the current earthly state. Such transformation is done in one of two ways: leaving dead (B. *athey-htwet*) or leaving alive (B. *ashin-htwet*). Those who attain *weizzā*-hood by the first method undergo a dying process similar to what an ordinary human being would experience, except that person's spirit (B. *nān*) leaves the body to dwell where it wishes. Those who become *weizzā* by the other way, however, leave this world with their physical bodies intact, and they disappear from this realm to dwell in a non-human abode.

Becoming a *weizzā* requires years of rigorous and disciplined training to master a specific form of technical knowledge aimed at gaining supernatural powers for manipulating the physical and psychical world around them. Ideally this is to help others, propagate the Buddha's religion, and eventually attain *nibbāna*. *Weizzā* achieve this state through any number of methods, including alchemy, meditation, recitation of sacred spells, or drawing magical diagrams. The literal translation of the Pāli word ("vijjādhara") from which "*weizzā*" ("vijjā) derives gives us an accurate idea of a *weizzā*: "A bearer of wisdom" or even "master of spells." Those who aspire to this mastery are said to traverse the "*weizzā* path" (B. *weizzā lam*) and systems for classifying and ranking *weizzā* can be found in the writings of famous monks, popular magazines, and websites. There is no ecclesiastical governing body that dictates and oversees the *weizzā* and their devotees, which leads to substantial innovation and regional difference on the behalf of *weizzā* path followers and the associations they belong to. Niklas Foxeus says that due to "its eclecticism there is no authoritative version of *weizzā* path systems/cosmology/practices, etc., and it is difficult to point to a discrete set of beliefs or practices common to all practitioners. Nevertheless, some general ideas seem to be shared widely."[18] One such general idea is the *weizzā* hierarchy. At the bottom of this ranking is the "common (P. *janapada*) *weizzā*" who uses knowledge of alchemy, sacred diagrams, spells, Vedic knowledge (among other methods) to obtain supernormal powers to be used for mundane (P. *lokiya*) affairs, especially pertaining to matters involving finance, love, and prognostication. Next is the "Small (P. *cūḷa*) *Gandhārī Weizzā*"—a middling level *weizzā* who has mastery over the same arts as the Common (P. *janapada*) *Weizzā* but who uses his powers for supramundane (P. *lokuttara*) affairs. Such *weizzā* include the mercury and iron *weizzā* who have devoted their practices to alchemy; the medicine *weizzā* whose practices involve the creation and mastering of various indigenous medicines and elemental properties; the sacred diagram *weizzā* whose practice in centered on the creation and manipulation of cabbalistic squares and other diagrams made up of syllables and quintessence of holy text; and the mantra *weizzā* who, like the sacred diagram *weizzā*, creates and adapts sacred verses. Perhaps the most widely known "Small" *weizzā* in Myanmar is in the form of the *zawgyi* figure (see figure 1). Dressed in red robes and turban, carrying a long walking stick used as a magic wand of sorts, and proficient in alchemy and magic, the *zawgyi* is often considered synonymous with the *weizzā* path, even though he is not considered as the highest power. This highest authority is reserved for the "Great (P: *Mahā*) *Gandhārī Weizzā*"

This *Mahā Gandhārī Weizzā* is a high-level *weizzā* who engages in concentration (P: *samatha*) and insight (P: *vipassanā*) meditation and who has fulfilled *pāramī* (perfection of certain virtues) thus allowing him to become a chief disciple of the future buddha or even a buddha himself. Such *weizzā* usually have some mastery of one or more techniques of the lower *weizzā*, as a mastery of one such technique is what elevates him to the state of *Mahā Gandhārī weizzā*, imbued with the complete set of ten superpowers: freedom from illnesses; youthful body; longevity of life; invincible from weapons; loved by all; able to find money easily; capable of traveling long distances quickly; and having the abilities to walk on water, fly in the air, and perform miracles. The most revered and popular *weizzā* of contemporary Myanmar fall under this category. Such *weizzā* include Bo Min Gaung, Yatkansin Taung Sayadaw, and Bo Pauk Sein Sayadaw, among many others (See figure 1, figure 2, and figure 3).[19]

Buddhist wizards have been a staple of the Myanmar Buddhist landscape since at least the 19th century, but their prominence has waxed and waned depending the sociopolitical nature of the times. For instance, after the deposition of Burmese Buddhist King Thibaw by the British in 1885, small bands of diverse, loosely connected networks of *weizzā* groups began to develop throughout the country with many of them professing anticolonial, nationalist agendas. None of these groups, however, were systematically organized or widely influential. This most likely had to do with the British criminalizing such groups by associating them with rebellious activities. It is, therefore, not surprising that we find the systematization of large-scale

Figure 1. Bo Min Gaung. Black-and-white laminated photograph.
Source: From author's personal collection.

weizzā groups immediately after independence in 1948. What separated *weizzā* associations from other Buddhist associations, however, was the strong emphasis they placed on not only saving the *sāsana* but also in saving all human beings by exposing them to this *sāsana*.

The postindependence period was the high point for the formation of *weizzā* associations whose primary aim was to strengthen the *sāsana* throughout the country. Groups of *weizzā* devotees that had advanced to some degree of institutionalization were referred to as *gaing*, a word that had a range of synonymous meanings that include "community," "congregation," and "association." They were often exclusive associations organized around a set of tenets and headed by a charismatic leader—with devotion centered on one or more *weizzā*. Members were given esoteric teachings aimed at developing supernatural powers through the practices of meditation, alchemy, reciting of mantras and magical incantations, ingesting sacred diagrams, and studying cabbalistic squares. These associations were often made up of members who came from a wide range of socioeconomic backgrounds. Merchants, office workers, taxicab drivers, booksellers, housewives, and monastics all joined these *gaing* to varying degrees of involvement and engaged in activities that included pagoda construction, healing ceremonies, sermonizing, and general Buddhist missionary work throughout the country, all of which was understood by members to be part of strengthening the *sāsana*. Regardless of *weizzā*

Figure 2. Yatkansin Taung Sayadaw. Laminated photograph.
Source: From author's personal collection.

affiliation with these associations and the activities they chose to focus on, they all had one thing in common: to defend and propagate the buddha *sāsana* at all costs.

Authors of *weizzā* publications at this time proclaimed that the country was on the threshold of a new era—an era governed by the *weizzā*—and provided step-by-step instructions for what members needed to accomplish so that a *weizzā* emperor could arise to unite all the continents under Buddhist rule. Most of the *weizzā* associations had disbanded or were absorbed into non-*weizzā* organizations during the 1980s. As a consequence of General Ne Win's purge of the religious landscape in the early 1980s, *weizzā* associations, especially those concerned with practices that could be interpreted as black magic or sorcery, were more closely monitored.[20] By the late 1970s, when these issues were under control, Ne Win turned his attention to religion and undertook a mission to purge the *sāsana* from elements he perceived as deviating from orthodox Buddhism. In a speech delivered in December of 1979, Ne Win likened these *weizzā* associations to the Jim Jones Peoples Temple cult and warned that such groups only seek to exploit their members for their own self-interests.[21] A series of restrictions were then placed upon the *weizzā* associations, and those considered illegal, like the Shwe-yin-kyaw Association (which was popular among soldiers and civil servants) were banned. Others such as the Mano-citta-pada Association were heavily monitored. During this period, Ne Win also banned magazines, printed

Figure 3. Bo Pauk Sein Sayadaw. Laminated photograph.
Source: From author's personal collection.

books, and other forms of media that were created by *weizzā* associations and even had portrayals of *weizzā* and their supernatural powers censored from written works and films.

When the associations dissolved, however, *weizzā* members did not simply stop engaging in activities defending and bolstering the *sāsana*. A further trickle-down effect seems to have occurred: instead of being in the hands of larger groups of organized *weizzā* factions, *sāsana* responsibility fell to individual *weizzā* devotees. Whereas previously the power and responsibility for the care of *sāsana* was in the hands of organized lay associations, it spread to a wider swath of individual Buddhists, both lay and monastic, who believed themselves to be sought out by the *weizzā* to carry out their *sāsana* propagation missions. Japanese scholar of *weizzā* associations, Keiko Tosa, discovered during her fieldwork in the late 1980s and early 1990s that although *weizzā* beliefs and practices among individual devotees were still widely popular (and were becoming increasingly so in the years she was in Myanmar), no one was particularly interested in forming new associations or joining the few remaining ones. Instead, they were devoted to personal, direct relationships with *weizzā* saints and carrying out *sāsana* propagation activities as directed to them by their patron *weizzā* saints.

This has all changed with the recent political developments in Myanmar. Within weeks of the government abolishing the Censor Board in February 2013, publishers began putting *weizzā* books back into circulation. Publications, general news stories, and websites and Facebook groups dedicated to the *weizzā* are reaching a much wider public sphere. Whereas previously there was only a handful of government-approved monographs dedicated to the *weizzā*, the 21st century has witnessed an explosion of *weizzā*-related publications, articles on devotees' experiences featured in long-running popular religious magazines, and even YouTube videos. Coupled with this are the newly established daily journals and online video news clips that began to carry stories about the *weizzā*.[22] This is enabling the swift dissemination of ideas to many parts of the country where *weizzā* associations may not have had local chapters established.

Take, for instance, the most revered wizard in contemporary Myanmar. Named Bo Min Gaung (b. 1885–d.1952), this *weizzā* has risen to the rank of "Chief Wizard" and is thought of to be second only to the Buddha in terms of inspiring strong faith and devotion among people from various religious traditions in Myanmar (see figure 1). Drawing from biographies of Bo Min Gaung, interviews with people who knew him personally, and the experiences of his devotees, it is clear that the biographic process through which the figure of Bo Min Gaung has been created for devotees. In publicly circulating oral and written sources, Bo Min Gaung's devotees add to his biography through their own experiences of him. His elevation to the status of wizard-saint, for example, was tied up with the events of World War II when Allied planes bombed his village, Japanese soldiers attempted to assassinate him, and Burmese Communist insurgents imprisoned and interrogated him. From these events, his devotees began to transform his biography after the war into something personalized and linked to their understanding of their own experiences, karmic biography, and aspirations.

Wizards such as Bo Min Gaung figure prominently in episodes of spirit possession among *weizzā* devotees in Myanmar and throughout the world. Monthly published religious magazines, devotional tracts, and other forms of popular media devote considerable attention to the *weizzā*'s role in spirit possession ritual activity, especially with regard to the healing that allegedly takes place during these episodes. Indeed, one way to interpret this phenomenon from a lived religions perspective is to examine how the cultural atmosphere in which magazines, devotional literature, and other forms of popular media all recognize, endorse, and publicize the ways these wizards interact with their spirit mediums and devotees to heal specific illnesses. For instance, female devotees being possessed by a wizard to carry out his bidding can be seen as a creative yet culturally sanctioned response to restrictive gender roles, a means for expressing otherwise illicit thoughts or feelings, and an economic strategy for women who have few options beyond traditional wifely or daughter roles. Young women who can channel the spirit of a powerful male wizard are able to renegotiate the often silent and passive roles assigned to them by the religious and medical culture by setting the experience of sickness into a new narrative framework—one where the wizards are the source of all healing. Women express their own needs and desires, and through their relationship with the saints, they find the conviction to have these needs met. On another level, illness is recast as a sacred drama in which the healing power is understood to come ultimately from the wizard-saints, whether they are entreated or not. Though never directly challenging the social structures that oppress them, these women are able to enact significant and positive changes in their lives and those around them through the power of their wishes and within the flexible parameters of devotional practice.

Despite the popularity of, and reverence for, these wizards, there is still hostility and mistrust toward the wizard phenomenon from segments of Myanmar's governmental and ecclesiastical authorities. This is due mainly to the belief that the most powerful Buddhist wizards have used their supernatural powers to manipulate the recent political and societal turn of events that have taken place in Myanmar in the past. Like a Myanmar-styled Illuminati, the wizards are thought to have clandestinely orchestrated a series of events starting with the 1988 nationwide pro-democracy uprising and continuing with the opening up of Myanmar in the 21st century. They are ultimately responsible for the political and socioeconomic transformations that have taken place in Myanmar in the 2010s, which has led to a renewed interest in the wizard-saints throughout the country.

Clearly, then, studying the lived religious landscape of Buddhist wizards in Myanmar requires drawing upon a variety of primary sources: interviews, conversations, and correspondences with the devotees; hundreds of *weizzā* related periodicals, private diaries, and *weizzā* associations' manuals and handbooks; videos and songs; two- and three-dimensional images; and websites. "The interpretative challenge of the study of lived religion," Robert Orsi stresses, "is to develop the practice of disciplined attention to people's signs and practices as they describe, understand, and use them, in the circumstances of their experiences, and to the structures and conditions within which these signs and practices emerge."[23] Such a model for undertaking a study of lived religion in Myanmar takes seriously the devotees' beliefs and practices on their own terms and for their own sake. In attempting to approximate the worldview of the people whose lives are enriched by the *weizzā*, one may wish to offer a synoptic narrative, which is "a comprehensive view of events pieced together from disparate and varied perspectives [where] multiple voices, including scholarly ones" are allowed to flesh out the lives and practices of *weizzā* devotees.[24] In other words, reiterating the primacy given to informants as a primary source, scholars can try whenever possible to give the devotees the last word, for their relationship with the *weizzā* saints makes them an authority on all matters pertaining to them. It is not because of a belief that they somehow possess some direct and unmediated access to divine forces but rather, "it is this very contingency that makes theirs the privileged voice."[25] One need not acknowledge the reality of these *weizzā*, but weaving the apparatus of anthropology, history, religious and cultural studies—and at times, psychology—in a nonintrusive manner while allowing the lives and voices of the devotees to remain in the foreground, one can come up with a study that does not reduce informants' religious experiences to merely mental fabrications. The resulting narrative then becomes polyphonic, sometimes relying heavily on the voices of informants or building analysis around their words. At other times, their voices recede into the background as sociological, historical, or theoretical issues come to the fore.

From this approach, we have been able to understand contemporary patterns of religiosity in the lives of *weizzā* devotees, and one cannot understand Buddhist practice in contemporary Myanmar more generally without knowledge of such widespread *weizzā* practice. Exploring the world of Buddhist wizards in Myanmar through the lens of lived religion helps drive home the reality that such phenomena are not as exotic and esoteric as they seem. Those unfamiliar with the *weizzā* phenomenon tend to characterize it as occult, otherworldly, even bizarre. But investigation shows us that people who belong to such associations lead quite ordinary lives. They go to work in the morning, return home, and perhaps attend *weizzā* activities in their spare time or simply incorporate their practices into their daily devotions. This form of lived religion in contemporary Myanmar is commonplace. It is not a sect consisting of select members of secret societies concerned with obtaining supernatural powers and awaiting the appearance of a millenarian savior. While this is certainly the case for some, the vast majority of *weizzā* devotees incorporate practices and beliefs associated with the *weizzā* path into their everyday lives. One cannot understand Buddhist practice in contemporary Myanmar without knowledge of such widespread *weizzā* practice.

Far from being confined to darkened corners of their lives, these *weizzā* and the roles they play are out in the open. For such individuals who have had astonishing encounters with *weizzā*, there may have been some initial uncertainty about which particular saint it was who came to visit. However, there was never any doubt about the kind of being it was. Although one may have been encountering a *weizzā* for the first time, there was a familiarity with the wizard-saint, and one knew immediately that it was a special being that had come bearing an important message. The devout themselves explicitly made the connection between a particular event in their life and the timing of the *weizzā*'s appearance, and there was almost always the feeling that the *weizzā* acted as something akin to an invisible guide helping the devotee through life. Such experiences are, to borrow Robert Orsi's terminology, "abundant events."[26] In other words, even though Myanmar Buddhist culture primes a person for an encounter with a wizard-saint, the person having such an encounter considers it highly unusual. Second, those having such experiences are certain that they are not delusions or hallucinations. Even those instances when the *weizzā* appear in dreams, devotees consider them real. Third, such events do not take place in a vacuum. They "arise at the intersection of past/present/future (as these really are or as they are dreaded or feared or hoped for). At the moment of such an event we have a new experience of the past while at the same time the horizon of the future is fundamentally altered."[27] These wizard-saints enter into peoples' lives often when they least expect it: through visionary apparitions, auditory voices, dreams, spirit mediums, flesh-and-blood persons, and two- and three-dimensional images and objects. These encounters have such significant impacts on the person having such an experience that he or she often wishes to deepen the bonds with the saints who visited them. In essence, such encounters are so significant for the person as to have a long-lasting and predominantly beneficial impact on the person's life.

REVIEW OF LITERATURE

With the United States' steadily increased involvement in Southeast Asia during the volatile years following World War II, several universities—with the help of funds from the State Department and Rockefeller Foundation—established programs dedicated to the study of Southeast Asia. It was at this time that, as Juliane Schober notes, "the Second World War disrupted both colonial rules as well as the episteme of colonial scholarship in Southeast Asia and elsewhere."[28] Whereas previous scholarship on Buddhism was dominated by historians, Indologists, and philologists, the 1950s and 1960s saw the intervention of a growing number of anthropologists who also wished to be part of this venerable field of Buddhist studies with the hopes of studying "Buddhism" as the object of an overtly social and cultural inquiry. One can get a sense of this newly emerging field and the problems anthropologists of Buddhism were preoccupied with by looking at the volume, *Anthropological Studies in Theravāda Buddhism*, which grew out of a conference of a similar name at the University of Chicago in 1962.[29] The works included in this volume express the specific set of assumptions brought by European and North American scholars of Buddhism to their anthropological work. Such presuppositions were highly influential and went on to inform both the academic study of Theravāda Buddhism as well as the Buddhism(s) of South and Southeast Asia for years to come. Most notable, however, were their ideas surrounding "text and context" and "the relations between the ongoing behavior of the ordinary Buddhist (both monk and laity) and voluminous canonical (in the *Tipiṭaka*) and semicanonical literature of *Theravāda* Buddhism."[30]

In the field of anthropology, scholars tended to view Buddhism in South and Southeast Asia through the Redfieldian distinction between great and little traditions, which came to dominate the way ethnographic inquiries were carried out during the Cold War period.[31] This binary differentiates between those religions shaped by elite groups of virtuosi on the one hand and village traditions composed mainly of the masses of nonliterate peasants on the other. The works of anthropologists such as Melford Spiro, Gananath Obeyesekere, and Manning Nash were largely predicated on such a view and "transformed in that way the epistemic focus of their orientalist predecessors." They failed to take seriously those beliefs and practices that did not correlate with what they read in Buddhist texts.[32]

Such work was not to be found solely in the fields of anthropology and sociology, however. In the 1971 classic, *Precept and Practice,* one can see that the anthropological spirit of the day even influenced the philologically trained Richard Gombrich to leave the confines of Oxford University and travel to Sri Lanka to conduct fieldwork for his dissertation. Upon his arrival, he was quickly confronted with the problem of how one could reconcile the practice of "actual" Buddhists he observed in a Sri Lankan village with the information he learned from the texts. Borrowing an idea from Gananath Obeyesekere's essay that was included in the previously mentioned *Anthropological Studies in Theravāda Buddhism,* Gombrich suggests that a fruitful way of looking at this seeming disconnect of "what people say they believe and say they do, and what they really believe and do" is to develop a cognitive/affective dichotomy: cognitively, Buddhists will attest to believing in such normative doctrines as *anicca, dukkha,* and *anatta,* while their actions indicate a supposed affective acceptance of, for example, an unchanging soul. In other words, Buddhists "cognitively" know the Buddha is dead and gone but "affectively" or "psychologically" feel his presence and power working in their lives.[33]

Writing in a similar vein as those scholars whose work is included in the seminal *Anthropological Studies in Theravāda Buddhism,* B. J. Terwiel, in his work on Buddhist magic in rural Thailand, discloses that when he first entered Thailand in the late 1960s to do anthropological work, he arrived with knowledge of Buddhism gained only from translated works from the Pāli texts. And, like Gombrich, he was thus surprised to find that the practices and beliefs of those in the Thai villages seldom, if at all, agreed with the texts. When Terwiel began to interview people about the relationship between Buddhist and "non-Buddhist" elements of their religious lives, he quickly realized that such categories had little relevance to his informants.[34] He struggles in his book with the issue of whether the Buddhism of his village is a harmonious blend of Buddhism and local creeds or whether an attempt should be made to delineate the two or more distinct strata found within it. The former view he terms "syncretist" and the latter "compartmentalized."[35] Those who adhere to a syncretistic model, he says, usually come to such a conclusion based on observations of the lesser educated members of one's field site. The scholars who tend to compartmentalize their findings often base their opinions upon data drawn from informants of the educated classes. These two groups of scholars would have avoided such "apparent controversies had they made clear that their description of

Buddhism does not encompass the whole Buddhist population, but refers only to certain sections of it."[36] It is necessary to point out that despite Terwiel's insistence that we view Buddhism in a more holistic manner (à la Tambiah), he nonetheless fails to recognize that his admission that the two groups of scholars are referring to different classes of Buddhists in Thailand places him in the company of those who differentiate between the distinct strata of Thai Buddhism. Such two-tiered models can be problematic because they "residualize" the religious lives of some Buddhists while simultaneously reifying an imagined Buddhist authenticity.[37]

Writing at least partially in response to Gombrich's work, Stanley Tambiah argued for a more holistic approach when encountering apparent inconsistencies in precept and practice. Dismissing Gombrich's affective/cognitive thesis as a "simpleminded proposition,"[38] Tambiah sees it as an arbitrarily imposed dichotomy that is "theoretically untenable."[39] Tambiah even goes as far as saying that this dichotomous way of looking at Buddhism is an "invention of the anthropologist dictated not so much by the reality he studies as by his professional perspective."[40] He feels the need to "rightly repudiate" such a bifurcated notion because "as far as the villagers are concerned there are not two traditions but simply one, 'which is their life'; for them village tradition is not conceptually separable into different elements."[41] Tambiah concludes that

> Buddhism is a shorthand expression for a total social phenomenon, civilizational in breadth and depth, which encompasses the lives of Buddhist monks and laymen, and which cannot be disaggregated in a facile way into its religious, political, and economic realms as these are currently understood in the West.[42]

Foreshadowing important work that would be undertaken by a new generation of scholars in the 1990s, Tambiah in 1984 offered prescient remarks when he wrote:

> I have found that those who espouse the narrow-minded view of religion . . . also frequently have a linear view of the development of Buddhism, from a pure, pristine, philosophical, salvation-search-oriented beginning, unstained and unsullied by the character and concerns of the social milieu in which it arose, to the later states of ever-widening popularization and vulgarization and deviation from the initial purity, in which are at play all the human passions and this-worldly concerned of the masses. This posture can be baptized as 'the Pāli Text Society mentality' . . . which is not only portrayed by some Western scholars of a puritanical bent but also by some Sri Lankan scholars who have not emancipated themselves from the presuppositions of that 'reformist Buddhism.'[43]

As if heeding Tambiah's words, the 1990s saw the emergence of a kind of scholarship undertaken primarily by scholars who wished to supply a dialectical counterweight to the theoretical study of Theravāda Buddhism evident in the scholarship discussed in the first part of this article under Studying "Buddhism-as-Lived." Scholars, most notably Steven Collins, Charles Hallisey, and Anne Blackburn, have suggested new ways of conceptualizing the relationships among Buddhist textual, ethnographic, and historical evidence in relation to one another while studying Theravāda Buddhism and Buddhist practice in South and Southeast Asia.

In his influential essay, "Roads Taken and Not Taken in the Study of Theravāda Buddhism," Hallisey pushes us to uncover the assumptions and cultural and academic practices that have shaped the course of Buddhist studies since the early part of the twentieth century. Most notable is his idea of "intercultural mimesis," which Hallisey uses to describe the participation of both European philologists and Sri Lankan Buddhists themselves in the processes of delineating the parameters of "Buddhism."[44] Exploring the connections between colonialism and Orientalism in the academic study of Buddhism, his essay explores precolonial constructions of what it meant to be a "Buddhist" in Asia while also helping to shape colonial European understandings of Buddhist thought and practice.

Anne M. Blackburn's careful study of the role of the Siyam Nikaya of Sri Lanka questions the common colonial/postcolonial view that prior to the intensification of colonial influence, "traditional" Theravāda Buddhism was essentially a stable and monolithic entity. Blackburn argues, on the contrary, that "pre- and early-colonial Lankan Buddhism was shifting, multiplex, and human."[45] In a related and equally important work, Blackburn, building on Keyes, Collins and Hallisey, proposes that we nuance our notions of the Theravāda Buddhist "canon" by distinguishing between two different types: what she refers to as a "formal" canon and a "practical" canon. The former include those texts that serve as "the ultimate locus of interpretive authority in the Theravāda" and the latter as "those portions of the *tipiṭaka* with their commentaries as well as texts understood by their authors and audience as consistent with, but perhaps not explicitly related to, the *tipiṭaka* and its commentaries."[46] Of the two, the practical canon, defined further as "the units of text actually employed in the practices of collecting manuscripts, copying them, reading them, commenting on them, listening to them, and preaching sermons based upon them that are understood by their users as part of a *tipiṭaka*-based tradition," plays a more central role in the lives of Buddhists.[47]

Other scholars such as Steven Collins revisit the discussion of how to reconcile the seeming Weberian contradiction of a radical ascetic discourse of otherworldly salvation on the one hand and a this-worldly gratification on the other. The most nuanced and suggestive thinking on this has been provided in Collins's *Nirvāna and Other Buddhist Felicities*. On first glance, one may think Collins is reiterating what anthropologists such as Keyes concluded at least ten years earlier.[48] Indeed, as Blackburn and Hansen rightly point out, Collins has certainly been influenced by anthropological studies of South and Southeast Asia, especially by Keyes's ethnographic data of illuminating the use and makeup of "canons" in modern-day Southeast Asia.[49] Collins, however, does not focus on Buddhist beliefs and practices and how they fit with those found in canonical texts. He concerns himself, rather, with looking at varieties of textual imagery and shifts in narrative to reveal what he calls a "Pāli imaginaire."

Collins's innovative notion of the "Pāli imaginaire," a cultural and ideological system he abstracts from premodern South Asian Buddhist civilizations, challenges the idea that nirvana, and the ascetic, world-renouncing practices that lead to it, was the primary goal for Buddhists. This involves a very different history of Buddhist ideas that looks at both philosophical and literary perspectives to understand how the *summum bonum* of nirvana fitted into a wider discourse of "felicities." Integrating more worldly felicities allows long-overdue attention to such often-overlooked elements such as heavenly rebirth, and health, wealth, and other life-enhancing merit-making rituals.

Another related perspective is found in the work of François Bizot. Bizot has given particular consideration to texts composed in South and Southeast Asian vernacular languages. Such texts highlight the idea that such vernacular sources, and not those solely from the Pāli *tipiṭaka*, were what Buddhists in South and Southeast Asia had access to and that played an integral role in informing their ideas about Buddhist practices and beliefs. The texts include diagrams and sacred formulae used to create the Buddha within one's body through the performance of ritual, thus indicating that the Buddha and his power are very much present and can be accessed via certain practices (see McGovern's "Esoteric Buddhism in Southeast Asia.").

Donald Swearer's work on Thai Buddhist statue consecration rituals, although the result of decades of research in Thailand, was nonetheless informed by Collins's and Bizot's work. Swearer's work goes a long way in discrediting long-held notions of Theravāda Buddhism as a rational, nontheistic, philosophical religion by broadening our understanding of Buddhism "on the ground." He sums up the spirit of this period of scholarship when he writes:

> Are we then, witness to two oppositional forms of Buddhism—an 'original' monastic worldview of high moral philosophy and spiritual practice versus a thoroughly compromised, if not debased, popular tradition of magical expectation? Such a dichotomy is the projection of the logical mind uncomfortable with the incongruities within religious thought and practice, and the creation of Buddhist apologists whose relatively narrow view of a non-theistic, rationalistic Buddhism appeals to the modern mind. But the lived tradition of Buddhism—like all classical religions—is not so tidy.[50]

Giving attention to the "lived tradition of Buddhism" as it is played out "on the ground" has becoming increasingly voguish among scholars trained as Buddhologists in the early 21st century. Recent monographs such as *Buddhism in Practice* (1997), *Sacred Biography in the Buddhist Traditions of South and Southeast Asia* (1997), *Life of Buddhism* (2000), *Critical Terms for the Study of Buddhism* (2005), and to a certain extent *Constituting Communities* (2003), comprised essays focusing mainly on pushing beyond elite representations of Buddhism to popular expressions that often include lives of the laity and/or the wider arena of Buddhist communities at large. Reynolds and Hallisey astutely observed back in 1987 that the field of Buddhist studies was slowly beginning to shift its focus from elements of Buddhism inside the monastic walls and of monks' elite lives to the cultural surroundings and ordinary people who inhabited local monasteries and villages. It was not until the mid- to late 1990s, however, that we really began to see a spate of works that, as Reynolds notes, moves away from "doctrinal issues toward a much greater emphasis on many various forms of Buddhist expression, including especially those that have been most deeply implicated in the everyday life of ordinary Buddhist practitioners."[51]

The essays in the aforementioned volumes give much attention to what Buddhists do rather than to what their texts say. The works direct our attention away from de-historicized discussions of philosophy to that of contextualized activities and practices by Buddhists. As Carl Bielfeldt says, these studies focus on "practices of what we might call the Buddhist silent majority: the men and women on the streets and in the rice paddies whose voices speak outside the canon."[52] Although such a project is certainly laudable and long overdue, it is still not without its problems. One may worry that such studies still portray the image of a bifurcated Buddhist world of elites and non-elites—little and big people. It is not clear to whom Reynolds was referring to, or what he had in mind, when he mentioned "ordinary Buddhist practitioners" in the quote cited in the previous paragraph. But one may see it as giving the false impression that those Buddhists who do not live within the monastery walls are somehow unconcerned with notions of liberation, and conversely, that monastics do not engage in any worldly (P. *lokiya*) practices. For example, we see such notions of "ordinary Buddhists" and "Buddhist silent majority" lose meaning in Southeast Asia, where the line between monastic and lay is blurred. This ambiguity is due to the fluid movement of men, and now women, in and out of the monastery walls as they undergo temporary ordination, sometimes several times a year and for only days at a time.

Recalling the earlier discussion of popular, syncretic, and hybridized forms of religion at the beginning of this article, the reader should resist the temptation to explain away these *weizzā*-related practices as a degenerative syncretism comprising Buddhist and non-Buddhist elements. Such outdated analytical frameworks, although attractive in their simplicity, are unhelpful.[53] Nonetheless, such a bifurcated way of looking at Buddhism, especially with regard to studies of the *weizzā* phenomenon, has had a lasting durability among scholars of religion in Myanmar. This is due in part, perhaps, to the way scholars have (and, in many cases, have not) dealt with certain source material, as well as the ways certain data collected in ethnographic research has been interpreted.

Firstly, scholarship has tended to ignore Burmese sources concerned with those Buddhist elements that clash with notions of a non-theistic, rationalistic Buddhism that many scholars still seem to associate with as "authentic" Theravāda Buddhism.[54] As previously discussed, the lack of references to certain Burmese Buddhist beliefs and practices is connected with the way scholars of Buddhism in Southeast Asia continue to address ahistorical and essentialist questions of what constitutes a "real" Buddhist and how one determines who is not. Such frameworks often consider such "magical" or "occult" practices as non-Buddhist in nature but are gradually incorporated into Buddhism by people who use them as tools to deal with the vicissitudes of everyday life.

Another reason why such practices are often ignored or, if addressed, are seen as later accretions to the Buddhist tradition may have to do with scholars' unfamiliarity with the extensive and complex histories of the beliefs and practices of modern-day *weizzā* path practitioners. There is a vast corpus of vernacular literature on the *weizzā* phenomenon that comprises published reference manuals, biographies, and histories; unpublished textbooks and pamphlets circulated among practitioners; monthly journals that focus specifically on the *weizzā* phenomenon; and paper-folding books (B. *parabaik*) and palm-leaf manuscripts that provide detailed information on practices used by those on the *weizzā* path. Scholars should make such valuable textual material an integral part of their research. They should do so because even anthropological studies of the religious developments of the *weizzā* phenomenon should integrate historically based comprehension of the complexities of how such phenomena developed, especially as contemporary Myanmar Buddhism and practice is strongly shaped by the literary vernacular print material and culture.

Descriptions and interpretations of Buddhist wizards in Myanmar have been few and varied. Michael Mendelson provided some of the first studies of the *weizzā*, especially as he observed the *weizzā* phenomenon during his research in Myanmar during the 1950s.[55] Melford Spiro, John Ferguson, and Juliane Schober offered updated accounts of the *weizzā* during their research in the country in the 1960s, 1970s, and 1980s, respectively.[56] In the 1990s, Patrick Pranke published the first English translation of a *weizzā* text, and Keiko Tosa provided the first in-depth anthropological study of *weizzā* gaing.[57] The 2000s saw a revival of *weizzā*-related research: Guillaume Rozenberg's work on *weizza* cults, saints, and alchemy, Niklas Foxeus's exhaustively in-depth historical and ethnographic analysis of an esoteric *weizzā* organization in upper Myanmar, Brac de la Perrière's work on spirit mediumship among *weizzā* path followers, and Celine Coderey's research on medicine *weizzā*.[58] A publication that resulted from the first academic panel dedicated to the study of the *weizzā* was also published at this time.[59] Most recently, Thomas Patton has published works on Burmese Buddhists' relationships with *weizzā*.[60]

FURTHER READING

LIVED RELIGION

Brown, Karen McCarthy. *Mama Lola: A Vodou Priestess in Brooklyn*. Berkeley: University of California Press, 2001.

Hall, David D., ed. *Lived Religion in America: Toward a History of Practice*. Princeton, NJ: Princeton University Press, 1997.

Hughes, Jennifer Scheper. *Biography of a Mexican Crucifix: Lived Religion and Local Faith from the Conquest to the Present*. Oxford, UK: Oxford University Press, 2010.

McGuire, Meredith B. *Lived Religion: Faith and Practice in Everyday Life*. Oxford, UK: Oxford University Press, 2008.

Orsi, Robert A. *History and Presence*. Cambridge, MA: Harvard University Press, 2016.

Orsi, Robert A. *Between Heaven and Earth: The Religious Worlds People Make and the Scholars Who Study Them*. Princeton, NJ: Princeton University Press, 2005.

Orsi, Robert A. *Thank You, St. Jude: Women's Devotion to the Patron Saint of Hopeless Causes*. New Haven, CT: Yale University Press, 1996.

WEIZZĀ IN MYANMAR

Brac de la Perrière, Bénédicte. "Being a Spirit Medium in Contemporary Burma." In *Engaging the Spirit World in Modern Southeast Asia*. Edited by Kirsten Endres and Andrea Lauser, 163–184. New York Berghahn Books, 2012.

La Perrière, Bénédicte Brac de, Guillaume Rozenberg, and Alicia Marie Turner, eds. *Champions of Buddhism: Weikza Cults in Contemporary Burma*. Burma-Myanmar Studies Conference. Singapore: National University of Singapore Press, 2014.

Foxeus, Niklas. "'I am the Buddha, the Buddha is Me': Concentration Meditation and Esoteric Modern Buddhism in Burma/Myanmar." *NUMEN* 63 (2016): 411–445.

Foxeus, Niklas. *The Buddhist World Emperor's Mission: Millenarian Buddhism in Postcolonial Burma*. Stockholm, Sweden: Department of Ethnology, History of Religions and Gender Studies, Stockholm University, 2011.

Mendelson, Michael. "Observations on a Tour in the Region of Mount Popa, Central Burma." *France-Asie* 19 (1963): 780–807.

Mendelson, Michael. "The King of the Weaving Mountain." *Journal of the Royal Central Asian Society* 48 (1961a): 229–237.

Mendelson, Michael. "A Messianic Buddhist Association in Upper Burma." *Bulletin of the School of Oriental and African Studies* 24, no. 3 (1961b): 560–580.

Patton, Thomas. *The Buddha's Wizards: Magic, Healing and Protection in Burmese Buddhism*. New York Columbia University Press, 2018.

Patton, Thomas. "Buddhist Salvation Armies as Vanguards of the *Sāsana*: Sorcerer Societies of Burma's Liberation Era." *Journal of Asian Studies* 75, no. 4 (2016a): 1083–1104.

Patton, Thomas. "The Wizard King's Granddaughters: Burmese Buddhist Female Mediums, Healers, and Dreamers." *Journal of the American Academy of Religion* 84, no. 2 (2016b): 430–465.

Patton, Thomas. "In Pursuit of the Sorcerer's Power: Sacred Diagrams as Technologies of Potency." *Contemporary Buddhism* 13, no. 2 (2012): 213–231.

Pranke, Patrick. "On Becoming a Buddhist Wizard." In *Buddhism in Practice*, Edited by Donald S. Lopez Jr., 343–358. Princeton, NJ: Princeton University Press, 1995.

Pranke, Patrick. "On Saints and Wizards—Ideals of Human Perfection and Power in Contemporary Burmese Buddhism." *Journal of the International Association of Buddhist Studies* 33, no. 1–2 (2010): 453–488.

Rozenberg, Guillaume. *Renunciation and Power: The Quest for Sainthood in Contemporary Burma*. Monograph 59, Yale Southeast Asia Studies. New Haven, CT: Yale University Southeast Asia Studies, 2010a.

Rozenberg, Guillaume. "The Alchemist and His Ball." *Journal of Burma Studies* 14 (2010b): 187–228.

Rozenberg, Guillaume. *The Immortals: Faces of the Incredible in Buddhist Burma*. Honolulu: University of Hawai'i Press, 2015.

NOTES

1. David Hall, "Lived Religion." *Encyclopedia of Religion in America*, eds. Charles H. Lippy and Peter W. Williams (Washington: CQ Press, 2010), 2182.
2. Jennifer Scheper Hughes, *Biography of a Mexican Crucifix: Lived Religion and Local Faith from the Conquest to the Present* (Oxford, UK: Oxford University Press, 2010), 14–15.
3. Kelly Hayes, *Holy Harlots: Femininity, Sexuality, and Black Magic in Brazil* (Berkeley: University of California Press, 2010), 9.
4. Hayes, *Holy Harlots*, 9.
5. Phenomenological anthropologists, such as Michael Jackson, refer to this as the "life-world": "that domain of everyday, immediate social existence and practical activity, with all its habituality, its crises, its vernacular and idiomatic character, its biographical particularities, its decisive events and indecisive strategies, which theoretical knowledge addresses but does not determine, from which conceptual understanding arises but on which it does not primarily depend." See Michael Jackson, ed., *Things as They Are: New Directions in Phenomenological Anthropology* (Bloomington: Indiana University Press, 1996), 7–8.
6. Timothy Fitzgerald, "Problems with 'Religion' as a Category for Understanding Hinduism," in *Defining Hinduism: A Reader*, ed. J. E. Llewellyn (New York, NY: Routledge, 2005), 171–201.
7. For example, in precolonial Myanmar there was no word in the Burmese language for what we would describe as "religion." The closest term they had was the Pāli word *sāsana*. As time went on, however, a word for religion (B. *bhātha* from the Pāli "bhāsa") came into existence and eventually referred to any subject of academic study, especially religion.
8. Robert Orsi, *The Madonna of 115th Street: Faith and Community in Italian Harlem, 1880–1950* (New Haven, CT: Yale University Press, 2010), xx–xxi.
9. Orsi, *The Madonna of 115th Street*, xiv.
10. Richard F. Gombrich, *Precept and Practice: Traditional Buddhism in the Rural Highlands of Ceylon* (Oxford, UK: Clarendon Press, 1971), 319.
11. Hall, "Lived Religion," 1284.

12. We still see such terms employed in works on Buddhism. In *Mediums, Monks, and Magic: Thai Popular Religion*, for example, anthropologist of religion Pattana Kitiarsa begins by showing that supernatural elements within what he considers contemporary "Popular Buddhism" are not a symptom of the decline of Buddhism. Unfortunately, such an approach still presents an image of Buddhism that consists of different layers, with those at the top being more authentic. Moreover, the danger of such a study is that the author becomes the arbiter of what constitutes these strands.
13. A sample of works on Buddhism in Southeast Asia that have employed such terminology include: Pattana Kitiarsa, "Beyond Syncretism: Hybridization of Popular Religion in Contemporary Thailand." *Journal of Southeast Asian Studies* 36, no. 3 (October 2005): 461–487 October 2005; and Jim Taylor, *Buddhism and Postmodern Imaginings in Thailand: The Religiosity of Urban Space* (Farnham, UK: Ashgate, 2008).
14. There is a large body of work that addresses the use of syncretism as a category for the study of religions. See, for example, Anita Leopold and Jeppe Jensen, eds., *Syncretism in Religion*, and Rosalind Shaw and Charles Stewart, *Syncretism/Anti-Syncretism*, for thorough discussions of the use of syncretism.
15. Leonard Primiano, "Afterword," in *Vernacular Religion in Everyday Life*, eds. Marion Bowman and Ulo Valk (Sheffield, UK and Bristol, CT: Equinox Publishers, 2012), 384.
16. David Hall (1997) notes that the concept of "lived religion" and its application to studying religious history has long been in use among French scholars of sociology of religion.
17. Recent books that provide excellent examples of works that focus on religion as lived in everyday lives of the Theravāda Buddhists include: Samuels, Jeffrey, *Attracting the Heart: Social Relations and the Aesthetics of Emotion in Sri Lankan Monastic Culture* (Honolulu: University of Hawai'i Press, 2010); McDaniel, Justin Thomas. *The Lovelorn Ghost and the Magical Monk: Practicing Buddhism in Modern Thailand* (New York: Columbia University Press, 2011); Turner, Alicia Marie. *Saving Buddhism: The Impermanence of Religion in Colonial Burma* (Honolulu: University of Hawaii Press, 2014); and Cassaniti, Julia. *Living Buddhism: Mind, Self, and Emotion in a Thai Community* (Ithaca, NY: Cornell University Press, 2015).
18. Niklas Foxeus, *The Buddhist World Emperor's Mission: Millenarian Buddhism in Postcolonial Burma* (Stockholm, Sweden: Department of Ethnology, History of Religions and Gender Studies, Stockholm University, 2011), 21.
19. See under "Further Reading" to learn more about these specific *weizzā*.
20. Foxeus, *The Buddhist World Emperor's Mission*, 176.
21. Foxeus, *The Buddhist World Emperor's Mission*, 81.
22. For two such examples in English language, see: Athens Zaw Zaw, "Magic in the Air: Myanmar Wizardy Flourishes," *Agence France-Presse* (AFP), March 9, 2017; and Fanny Potkin, "In Search of Burma's Wizard-Saints." BBC News, October 6, 2016.
23. Orsi, *The Madonna of 115th Street*, xx.
24. Jennifer Hughes, *Biography of a Mexican Crucifix: Lived Religion and Local Faith from the Conquest to the Present* (Oxford: Oxford University Press, 2010), x.
25. Hughes, *Biography of a Mexican Crucifix*, x.
26. Robert Orsi, "2+2 = 5, Can We Begin to Think about Unexplained Religious Experiences in Ways That Acknowledge Their Existence?" *The American Scholar* (Spring 2007). Available online.
27. Orsi, "2+2 = 5, Can We Begin to Think about Unexplained Religious Experiences in Ways That Acknowledge Their Existence?," (Spring 2007).
28. Juliane Schober, "Communities of Interpretation in the Study of Religion in Burma," *Journal of Southeast Asian Studies* 39, no. 2 (2008): 255–267, 258.
29. Manning Nash, *Anthropological Studies in Theravāda Buddhism* (New Haven, CT: Yale University Press, 1966).
30. Manning Nash hoped that such a work would help foster cooperation between "field anthropologists (sometimes accused of 'seeing everything and reading nothing') and historians of Buddhism and textual

scholars of Sanskrit and Pāli (sometimes maligned by anthropologists as 'reading everything and understanding nothing')." See Nash, *Anthropological Studies in Theravāda Buddhism*, ix.

31. Robert Redfield, *The Folk Culture of Yucutan* (Chicago, IL: University of Chicago Press, 1941).
32. Schober, "Communities of Interpretation in the Study of Religion in Burma," 258.
33. Richard F. Gombrich, *Precept and Practice: Traditional Buddhism in the Rural Highlands of Ceylon.* (Oxford, UK: Clarendon Press, 1971), 9. For a more recent reworking of the ideas put forth in earlier works by Gombrich, see his monograph, co-authored with Obeyesekere, *Buddhism Transformed.* In this work, their conceptual framework for what they term "Sinhala Buddhism" rests on the by now familiar bifurcated idea that there is, on the one hand, a Theravāda Buddhism that is rooted in Pāli canonical sources, and on the other, a "spirit religion" that is made up of those practices and beliefs that, if adhered to, make it difficult for Obeyesekere and Gombrich to "claim that they remain Theravāda Buddhists in any meaningful sense" (Gombrich, Richard, and Obeyesekere, Gananath. *Buddhism Transformed: Religious Change in Sri Lanka* (Princeton, N.J.: Princeton University Press, 1988), 29. One can glean from such statements that Obeyesekere and Gombrich have strong convictions in their views of what constitutes "real" Buddhism.
34. B. J. Terwiel, *Monks and Magic: An Analysis of Religious Ceremonies in Central Thailand* (Lund, Sweden: Studentlitteratur, 1975), 3.
35. Terwiel, *Monks and Magic*, 5.
36. Terwiel, *Monks and Magic*, 1.
37. L. N. Primiano, "Vernacular Religion and the Search for Method in Religious Folklife," *Western Folklore* 54, no. 1 (1995): 39.
38. Stanley Jeyaraja Tambiah, *The Buddhist Saints of the Forest and the Cult of Amulets: A Study in Charisma, Hagiography, Sectarianism, and Millennial Buddhism* (Cambridge, UK: Cambridge University Press, 1984), 5.
39. Tambiah, *The Buddhist Saints of the Forest and the Cult of Amulets*, 375.
40. Tambiah, *The Buddhist Saints of the Forest and the Cult of Amulets*, 371.
41. Tambiah, *The Buddhist Saints of the Forest and the Cult of Amulets*, 369.
42. Tambiah, *The Buddhist Saints of the Forest and the Cult of Amulets*, 7.
43. Tambiah, *The Buddhist Saints of the Forest and the Cult of Amulets*, 7.
44. Charles Hallisey, "Roads Taken and Not Taken in the Study of *Theravāda* Buddhism," *Curators of the Buddha: The Study of Buddhism Under Colonialism*, ed. Donald S. Lopez Jr. (Chicago, IL: University of Chicago Press, 1995), 33.
45. Blackburn, Anne. *Buddhist Learning and Textual Practice in Eighteenth-Century Lankan Monastic Culture* (Princeton, NJ: Princeton University Press, 2001), 139.
46. Blackburn, Anne. "Looking for the Vinaya: Monastic Discipline in the Practical Canons of the Theravāda," *Journal of the International Association of Buddhist Studies*, 22.2 (1999), 281–309.
47. Blackburn, "Looking for the Vinaya: Monastic Discipline in the Practical Canons of the Theravāda," 284.
48. Keyes, Charles F., "Merit-Transference in the Karmic Theory of Popular Theravāda Buddhism," in *Karma: An Anthropological Inquiry*, Charles F. Keyes and E. Valentine Daniel, eds. (Berkeley: University of California Press, 1983).
49. "Looking for the Vinaya: Monastic Discipline in the Practical Canons of the Theravāda," 283; and Hansen, Anne R., *How to Behave: Buddhism and Modernity in Colonial Cambodia 1860–1930* (Honolulu: University of Hawai'i Press, 2007), 9.
50. Swearer, Donald. *Becoming the Buddha: The Ritual of Image Consecration in Thailand* (Princeton, NJ: Princeton University Press, 2004), 10.
51. Frank E. Reynolds, "Coming of Age: Buddhist Studies in the United States from 1972 to 1997." *Journal of the International Association of Buddhist Studies* 22.2 (1999): 457–483.

52. Carl Bielefeldt."*Practice*." In Donald Lopez, ed., *Critical Terms for the Study of Buddhism*, pp. 229–244 (Chicago: University of Chicago Press, 2005), 243.
53. Tambiah, *The Buddhist Saints of the Forest and the Cult of Amulets*, 316.
54. Especially, as Peter Skilling points out, what is meant by the term, "Theravāda," is far from clear Skilling, Peter. "The Advent of Theravāda Buddhism to Mainland South-East Asia." *Journal of the International Association of Buddhist Studies* 20(1) (1997): 93–108.
55. Michael Mendelson, "Observations on a Tour in the Region of Mount Popa, Central Burma," *France-Asie* 19 (1963): 780–807; Michael Mendelson, "The King of the Weaving Mountain," *Journal of the Royal Central Asian Society* 48 (1961a): 229–237; and Michael Mendelson, "A Messianic Buddhist Association in Upper Burma," *Bulletin of the School of Oriental and African Studies* 24, no. 3 (1961b): 560–580.
56. Melford E. Spiro, *Burmese Supernaturalism: A Study in the Explanation and Reduction of Suffering* (Englewood Cliffs, NJ: Prentice-Hall, 1967); Melford E. Spiro, *Buddhism and Society: A Great Tradition and its Burmese Vicissitudes* (Berkeley: University of California Press, 1970); John P. Ferguson and Michael E. Mendelson, "Masters of the Buddhist Occult: The Burmese Weikzas," *Contributions to Asian Studies: Essays on Burma*, ed. John P. Ferguson, vol. 16 (Leiden, The Netherlands: Brill, 1981), 62–80; and Schober, Juliane, "The Path to Buddhahood: The Spiritual Mission and Social Organization of Mysticism in Contemporary Burma." *Crossroads* 4(1): 13–30.
57. Patrick Pranke, "On Becoming a Buddhist Wizard," *Buddhism in Practice*, ed. Donald S. Lopez Jr. (Princeton, NJ: Princeton University Press, 1995), 343–358; Keiko Tosa, "Biruma niokeru weikza shinko no ichikosatsu: gaing nitotteno Lawki and Lawkoktara," *The Japanese Journal of Ethnology* 61, no. 2 (1996): 215–242; and Keiko Tosa, *Biruma no weikza shinko* (Study on Weikza Belief in Myanmar). Tokyo, Japan: Keiso Syobo, 2000.
58. Guillaume Rozenberg, *The Immortals: Faces of the Incredible in Buddhist Burma* (Honolulu: University of Hawai'i Press, 2015); Bénédicte Brac de la Perrière, "Spirits Versus Weikza: Two Competing Ways of Mediation," in *Champions of Buddhism:* Weikza *Cults in Contemporary Burma*, ed. B. Brac de la Perrière, G. Rozenberg, and A. Turner (Singapore: National University of Singapore Press, 2014); and Coderey, Celine. "Healing through *Weikza*: Therapeutic Cults in the Arakanese Context," in *Champions of Buddhism:* Weikza *Cults in Contemporary Burma*, ed. B. Brac de la Perrière, G. Rozenberg, and A. Turner (Singapore: National University of Singapore Press, 2014).
59. Burma-Myanmar Studies Conference, *Champions of Buddhism: Weikza Cults in Contemporary Burma*, ed. B. Brac de La Perrière, G. Rozenberg, and A. M. Turner (Singapore: National University of Singapore Press, 2014).
60. Thomas Patton, *The Buddha's Wizards: Magic, Healing and Protection in Burmese Buddhism* (New York: Columbia University Press, 2018); Thomas Patton, "Buddhist Salvation Armies as Vanguards of the *Sāsana*: Sorcerer Societies of Burma's Liberation Era," *Journal of Asian Studies* 75, no. 4 (2016a): 1083–1104; Thomas Patton, "The Wizard King's Granddaughters: Burmese Buddhist Female Mediums, Healers, and Dreamers," *Journal of the American Academy of Religion* 84, no. 2 (2016b): 430–465; and Thomas Patton, "In Pursuit of the Sorcerer's Power: Sacred Diagrams as Technologies of Potency," *Contemporary Buddhism* 13, no. 2 (2012), 213–231.

Thomas Patton

BUDDHIST WIZARDS (*VIDHYADHĀRA/WEIZZĀ/ WEIKZA*): ORIGINS AND HISTORY

This article will provide a historical, ethnographic, and sociological examination of the Burmese cults of *weizzās* or *weizzādhours* (Sanskrit *vidyādhara*). It will focus on soteriological aspects; how authority is acquired by these cults; the institutional dimension; the political implications; the relationship between the state and the *weizzā* cults; and, finally, how these cults have become integral to prosperity Buddhism since the 1990s.[1]

VIDYĀDHARAS IN INDIAN AND TIBETAN BUDDHISM

The concept of *vidyādhara* originated in India and it was prevalent within all the institutionalized forms of religion—Buddhism, Hinduism, and Jainism.[2] In an earlier phase, the *vidyādhara*, "bearer of wisdom/practical knowledge/ritual lore," was known as a semidivine, youthful, beautiful, and amorous being flying about in the atmosphere between heaven and earth, possessing supernormal powers, usually holding a sword and being proficient in the art of mantras. This portrayal of the *vidyādhara* appeared in early Hindu, Jain, and Buddhist texts in India, including the Buddhist Pāli canon and its commentaries.[3] In these texts, the *vidyādhara* (P. *vijjādhara*) is not depicted as a soteriological state that the practitioners should seek to attain themselves. In later Indian texts, the goal of becoming a *vidyādhara* was especially linked to late Mahāyāna texts and tantric Buddhism (Vajrayāna), Hinduism, and Jainism. In these texts, a *vidyādhara* refers also to human beings that have transcended their human limitations. The *vidyādhara* could acquire an almost immortal life and supernormal powers (Sanskrit *siddhi* or *ṛddhi*), especially the ability to fly. In this sense, the *vidyādhara* was regarded as a soteriological state, a transformed spiritual and bodily condition, possible for humans to achieve in their present lives through their own efforts by strenuously performing certain practices, whereby they could transform from men to superhuman, god-like beings.[4] Although the *vidyā* in which the *vidyādhara* excels was usually understood to consist of spells or mantras in various Indian traditions, including the Pāli canon and its commentaries, the state of *vidyādhara* could also, in tantric traditions, be attained by cremation ground practices, external alchemy, asceticism, ritualized sexual practices, yoga, or *haṭha* yoga.[5] The path of the *vidyādhara* was rather common within a variety of Indian traditions in the first millennium CE; the *vidyādhara* were later replaced by other figures.[6]

In Buddhist texts belonging to Mahāyāna and Vajrayāna traditions (8th century onwards), the aim of becoming a *vidyādhara* in the present life figured in various texts, in which even the Buddha was identified with such a figure. Later, it became associated with a new religious ideal within tantric Buddhist traditions, namely the peripatetic lay *siddha*, the "perfected" or "accomplished one." Having made bodhisattva vows, the *siddha* should seek to become a *vidyādhara* and a lord of these beings on the path to buddhahood.[7] The notion of the *vidyādhara* spread with Buddhism and texts belonging to other Indian religions (Hinduism and Jainism) to other parts of South Asia, East Asia (e.g., Tibet), and to Southeast Asia, where the concept became localized and vernacularized. The significance of the concept of a *vidyādhara* as a soteriological ideal for humans to realize in their present lives has especially been emphasized in Indian, Tibetan, and Burmese traditions.

In Tibetan Buddhism, the ideal of becoming a *vidyādhara* (Tibetan *rig'dzin*) is mainly linked to the Nyingma school, and its legends of the quasi-historical Indian 8th-century yogi Padmasaṃbhāva, early Indian tantric texts, and hidden "treasure" texts (Tibetan *gter ma*).[8] In that school, as shown by Gyurme Dorje, the attainment of *vidyādhara*hood is achieved by the recitation of mantras on the path to buddhahood. There are, he explains, three kinds of mundane and four (or seven) kinds of supramundane *vidyādharas*.[9] The tantric Buddhist treatise *Mañjuśrīmūlakalpa* (8th century) and its outline of a Buddhist path of the *vidyādhara* leading to buddhahood was important both in Indian and Tibetan Buddhism. According to this text, a yogin transformed into a *vidyādhara*, acquiring supernormal powers and near immortality; he could then enter hidden worlds such as the underground *asura* caves in the paradise Pātāla, where bodhisattvas, *asuras*, and *nāgas* dwell, in order to have sexual intercourse with *asura* maidens (semi-divine beings), acquire treasures of gems and jewels, and dwell there until Buddha Maitreya arrives.[10]

As for Indian alchemical traditions, David Gordon White explores "magical alchemy" and "tantric alchemy" both within Hindu and Buddhist traditions, in which the goal was transmutation and bodily immortality, and to become a semidivine *siddha*, *vidyādhara*, or a second Śiva.[11] In the Indian Middle Ages, alchemical legends were transmitted orally, and there were also alchemical treatises (especially the 11th-century *Rasārṇava*) that prescribed how a human practitioner of alchemy could transform into a semidivine, immortal, and invincible person. That transformation should be effectuated by the alchemist plunging into a cauldron of boiling oil. An assistant should, after the alchemist plunged into the oil, throw substances or drugs into the boiling oil that could effectuate his transformation into an immortal one.[12] A comparable alchemical legend is found in Burmese royal chronicles of a *weizzādhour-zawgyī* and in Burmese folklore recorded by Maung Htin Aung in the mid-20th century.[13] The local narratives retold by Htin Aung, who does not reveal his sources, describe ordeals by earth and fire that *weizzā* practitioners must undergo, supported by assistants who threw in medicine balls to protect the would-be *weizzā* in his vulnerable liminal state of the ordeal, so that he could transform into a semi-immortal *weizzā* with supernatural powers that is ready to depart from the human realm. Similar descriptions of transmutation through ordeals can be encountered in contemporary Burma.

The legend of the *weizzādhour-zawgyī* (that could be interpreted as a *zawgyī* who has become a *weizzādhour*) is found in U Kalā's chronicle *Mahā-yāzā-win-daw-gyī* from the early 18th century.[14] The same description is repeated almost verbatim in later chronicles. In these texts, the narrative seems to be of a failed attempt to become a fully-fledged *weizzā* through an ordeal. A *zawgyī* is usually depicted as a red-robed figure holding a wand; he is mostly understood to be an alchemist and frequently appears in Burmese puppet shows. The word *zawgyī*, sometimes written *zawgī* (spelled *jogī* in the Indian-derived Burmese script), is likely a Burmanized pronunciation of the Hindi word *jogī*. The latter is a possessive adjective (*jogin*) that corresponds to the Sanskrit *yogī* (*yogin*) and refers to a practitioner of yoga. In medieval India, the word *jogī* frequently referred to Nāth Siddhas, followers of Gorakhnāth (sometimes claimed to be a *vidyādhara*), and other deviant forms of Śaiva ascetics that were considered heretical by the Hindu orthodox establishment. The term came largely to supplant older related words like *tāntrika* in Hindu medieval discourse.[15] Other themes from the Indian but also the Tibetan traditions that resonate with the Burmese ones are the motif of the *vidyādhara* and his sword; *vidyādhara*hood as a soteriological state that can be attained by human beings; the use of alchemy or mantras to become a *vidyādhara*; hidden realms to which the *vidyādhara* departs wherein *bodhisattvas* and *vidyādhara*s dwell waiting for the appearance of the next buddha, Maitreya; and the path of the *vidyādhara* as a path to awakening, nirvana, and buddhahood.[16]

BURMA/MYANMAR: A LOCALIZATION AND HYBRIDIZATION OF AN INDIAN CONCEPT AND RELATED PRACTICES

The early history of the cult of semi-immortal *weizzās* in Burma, representing a state that human beings can attain, is still unknown. The cult of *weizzās* or *weizzādhours* (P. *vijjādhara*) has been widespread since the colonial period in Burma/Myanmar (1826–1948), and became especially prominent in the postindependence period, around which time many esoteric congregations and cult groups emerged.[17] Some scholars have regarded the contemporary cults that began in the colonial period as an intrinsically modern phenomenon.[18] Although many aspects of the contemporary Burmese cults are clearly marked by modernity and the colonial encounter, some of their salient features resonate with certain Indian and Tibetan versions of this phenomenon and go back to earlier periods in Burma.[19] While the precolonial—and also the early colonial—practices and notions related to *weizzās* are unknown, there are, as Dietrich Christian Lammerts has pointed out, thousands of extant Burmese manuscripts from the precolonial period related to *vijjādhara* practices that have yet to be explored, mainly in the fields of indigenous medicine and alchemy.[20] Many relevant texts were also imported from India and translated into Burmese at the beginning of King Bodawhpaya's reign (1782–1819).[21] All these texts have still to be investigated. Given this lacuna within scholarship, it would be a hazardous enterprise to compare superficial similarities between contemporary Burmese traditions with medieval Indian texts, as such similarities could be the result of local Burmese, historical, contingent developments. Jonathan Z. Smith points out the inherent dangers in comparative studies based on superficial similarities and ahistorical juxtapositions of material from different historical periods. In the present state of scholarship on this Burmese phenomenon, issues pertaining to the premodern period must therefore be postponed.[22]

If historical documents were investigated, scholars would be in a better position to explore the ways in which the Indian cultural materials were transformed and adapted to a Burmese context. Oliver William Wolters criticized George Coedés's older concept of Indianization, because it implied that there were "monolithic and uniform characteristics" of Southeast Asian cultures.[23] The adoption of Indian cultural materials in Southeast Asia, he explains, "tended to be fractured and restated and therefore drained of their original significance." In that way, these cultural materials, he maintains, "had to be localized in various ways before they could fit into various local complexes of religious, social, and political systems."[24] Wolter refers to this process as "localization." The notion of *vidyādharas* and related practices have undoubtedly also undergone a localization in Burma, the specific features and the genealogies of which have yet to be investigated. As in many other Buddhist traditions, a recurrent way in which local cults and novel notions and practices have been absorbed in Burmese Buddhism has been to integrate them within a hierarchical Buddhist framework.[25] Thereby, they are provided with a Buddhist interpretation, and competing notions and practices are situated in a hierarchy with buddha, dhamma, and sangha, as well as the Pāli canon and its commentaries, at the apex.[26]

As a consequence of the colonization and modernization of Burma, legendary material—mostly oral traditions like folklore and other practices—were transformed in the 19th century into new cults in the modern era. According to John Ferguson and Michael Mendelson, such modern *weizzā* cults, although based on older traditions and notions, should be understood as a "symbolic reaction to the shock of colonization" and modernization.[27] In the precolonial sources that Ferguson and Mendelson examined (monastic and royal chronicles), they were unable to find references to clear-cut *weizzā* figures. As they demonstrated, *weizzā* path proponents refashioned, in *weizzā* literature from the late colonial period and the postindependence period, some historical figures mentioned in local chronicles—mostly monks—as being *weizzās*. According to Ferguson and Mendelson, the modern configuration of the *weizzā* phenomenon going back to the 19th century consisted of that "ad hoc" collection of premodern personages that were reconstituted as *weizzās*; the 19th-century legend of the *weizzā* Bo Bo Aung—the "archetype" for modern *weizzās*—and the organizational form (*gaiṇ*) of *weizzā* cults. (For more on Bo Bo Aung, see the section entitled "Political Imaginary in the Late Colonial and Early Postindependence Period"; for more on the organizational form, see the section on "Esoteric Congregations and Cult Groups.") Ferguson and Mendelson did not claim that the practices and notions related to *weizzās* as such can be dated to the 19th century but only that the distinctive modern form emerged in that period, with certain premodern people identified as *weizzās*, etc.[28] Since that modern configuration was depicted as being ancient, it thus represents a kind of invented tradition.[29] Therefore, Ferguson and Mendelson's thesis does not necessarily contradict Lammerts's statement about the existence of many premodern manuscripts about *vijjādhara* practices that have remained unexamined.

In the colonial period, *weizzā* cults developed into a predominantly lay-dominated movement with practitioners seeking to attain *weizzā*hood, acquiring supernormal powers and semi-immortality.[30] According to the historian Patrick Pranke, *weizzā* cults as a lay movement emerged along with the insight (P. *vipassanā*) meditation movement, as responses to colonization and the introduction of modernity in the 19th century. They represent two modern, soteriological lay-dominated movements.[31]

It was not until the postindependence period that these two tendencies within urban Buddhism turned into mass movements emphasizing practice and imminent success.[32] The members of both movements constituted moral communities embodying the Buddha's dispensation. Doctrinal Buddhism and *abhidhammic* categories were favored not merely by the *vipassanā* movement and large portions of the urban middle classes but also by some supramundane (*lawkuttara*) esoteric congregations (see the section on "Esoteric Congregations and Cult Groups"). In contrast to the insight meditation movement, the esoteric congregations mainly disseminated concentration meditation (P. *samatha*) that is generally attributed a lower status, combined with esoteric lore and the observance of Buddhist moral precepts. By this practice, the practitioners sought to acquire supernormal powers and to attain *weizzā*hood and, ultimately, to achieve awakening and nirvana.

In the premodern period in Burma and other Buddhist countries in South and Southeast Asia, it was held that it was no longer possible to attain awakening and nirvana due to the gradual decline of the Buddha's dispensation. Monks and laypeople therefore practiced the ritualistic karmic path of merit-making to avoid suffering and unfavorable rebirths, and to attain awakening and nirvana in a remote future, typically through the salvific power of the dispensation of the next buddha, Metteyya. Around the mid-19th century, following a scripturalist trend, there began to be a gradual shift in the view of the possibility of making soteriological progress on the path to awakening (*bodhi*) and nirvana (from *sotāpanna* to *arahant*) in the present life by means of *vipassanā* meditation. This development paved the way for the lay-meditation movement of the 20th century that stressed soteriological benefits in the here and now.[33] The evolving view of the possibility to attain *weizzā*hood in the present life on the path to awakening and nirvana should therefore be understood against the background of these historical developments.

THE *WEIZZĀ* PATH AS A BUDDHIST SOTERIOLOGICAL PATH

In the modern period, initiated by the British colonization of Burma in three stages (1824–1826, 1852, and 1885), and particularly in the postindependence period (starting in 1948), the esoteric *weizzā* path represented both a devotional and a soteriological hybridized form of Buddhism that incorporated a variety of practices that originated outside what is more generally labeled as Theravāda Buddhist traditions since the mid-20th century.[34] The *weizzā* path is frequently understood as a path to awakening and nirvana as an *arahant*, and in some cases as a buddha. Becoming an accomplished *weizzā* is a two-stage process: (a) a lower-state of *weizzā*hood is achieved by engaging in a variety of practices; it is a condition attained in the present life (a human *weizzā*), and (b) an ontological transformation (*htwek-yap-pauk*) takes place at death or through an ordeal. First, a human *weizzā* (*lū-weizzā*) is understood as a man who has acquired the ten (or thirteen) supernormal powers (S. *siddhi*) by means of practicing and achieving success in esoteric lore—consisting in mundane practices, such as yantras or magical squares (*in*), syllabic figures (*sama*), esoteric indigenous medicine (*hsay*), alchemy (*eggiyat*), or mantras—combined with the practice of concentration meditation (P. *samatha*), often involving visualization practices, and the observance of Buddhist moral precepts (P. *sīla*), as well as vegetarianism.[35] The concentration meditation frequently refers to counting beads on a rosary while reciting mantras or incantations. The magical squares or yantras (*in*) consist of a geometrical grid into which numbers or syllables are inscribed that are considered to produce power. The supernormal power is regarded as inhering in the yantras, syllabic figures, and alchemical substrates, that is, in devices that are external to the practitioner. These substances therefore must be transferred to the body by ingesting them. Yantras and syllabic figures are drawn on paper and the like, and either burnt into ash, mixed with water and drunk, or crumpled into small balls that are swallowed. Likewise, "golden ash" (*shwe-pyā*), which is produced by alchemical processes through heating crucibles in fire, is either mixed with honey and eaten or mixed with water and drunk. The goal of the alchemist is to produce a living mercury alchemic ball (*pyā-dā-shin-loun*) by which he can produce gold and attain *weizzā*hood. Traditionally, it was also regarded as necessary to undergo a dangerous ordeal in order for these external substances to be completely assimilated with the practitioner's body. The power inhering in the external devices (yantras, syllabic figures, alchemy) is mostly combined with the practitioner's own power, generated by the combination of concentration meditation and observance of Buddhist morality.

The mantra path is somewhat different. The practitioner should recite mantras or verses (*gāthās*) while counting beads on a rosary and combine these practices with astrological calculations, through which it is assumed that supernormal powers and *weizzā*hood can be attained. The practice is based on a system of correlations between the macro- and micro-cosmos that are derived from a traditional Burmese system of correlations (partly based on astrology) between weekdays, cardinal directions, numbers, syllables, planets, guardian animals, years, etc. In this way, calculations can be made for how many rounds the practitioner should count on beads while seated in different directions around a pagoda, on which day, and so forth. Frequently, a huge number or rounds should be counted on a rosary while reciting mantras. In some practices, aiming to control the four elements, the numbers are related to Buddhist cosmography and the mythic extent of the four elements. For instance, the earth is 240,000 *yojanas* thick (according to Buddhist commentarial literature), and therefore one should count beads and recite mantras for 240,000 rounds on the rosary to gain control of the earth element (480,000 rounds for the water element, etc.).[36]

Second, a person that has become a semi-immortal and superhuman god-like being is called a *htwek-yap-pauk-puggoul*, a "person who has reached the exit" (from samsara but has not yet attained awakening and nirvana), thereby halting the rebirth process. To attain that state, an ontological transformation (*htwek-yap-pauk*) is required, of which there are two kinds—either "going out" alive (*ashin-htwek*) or apparently dead (*athay-htwek*). In the latter case, it is sometimes thought that after "death," a *weizzā* will acquire a "subtle body" (*thukhuma-youp*; P. *sukhumarūpa*) before leaving for a hidden world.[37] In other cases, it is assumed that only the *weizzā*'s mind (*nān*; P. *nāma*) will depart for the hidden realm.[38] The *weizzā* who goes out alive, keeps his body intact and then departs for the hidden *weizzā* realm. Some would say that their gross bodies transform into bodies similar to those of the gods.[39] The most famous *weizzā* claimed to have gone out alive is Bo Bo Aung, who is believed to have attained such an ontological transformation during King Bodawhpaya's reign (1782–1819), and a famous one known to have gone out apparently dead is Bo Min Gaung, who passed away in 1952. Sometimes the culmination of this state occurs through an ordeal (*htoun-kū*) by fire, water, earth, or oil, involving a kind of death-and-rebirth symbolism, but it is (mostly) not considered necessary in the modern period. A common idea is that only practitioners who have undergone success in *gandhārī* practices (magical squares, syllabic figures, medicine, or alchemy) must undergo an ordeal. The underlying assumption is that the power of these practices is inherent in the devices. For the power to be fully assimilated by the body, an ordeal is therefore traditionally considered necessary.[40] In the final stages of practice, the would-be *weizzā* should be sunk down into water, should sit on a bonfire, should be dug down into the earth, or sunk down into a cauldron of boiling oil while meditating. An assistant should throw "medicine balls" (*hsay-loun*) that will protect him from the elements and evil spirits. In contemporary Burma, some *weizzā* practitioners still claim they will undergo such ordeals when the time is ripe. One alchemist explained that he had already attained success in alchemy, and that he only needed to swallow some more magical squares. Thereafter, he would undergo an ordeal by water and then by fire. Finally, he would leave for the mystical forest Mahāmyaing.[41] A spectacular cult in this respect is the one dedicated to four *weizzās* in the village of Mebaygon. Between the 1970s and the 1990s, a number of ordeals were held for these *weizzās*. In special temples, bonfires were lit on which the *weizzās* sat down meditating while assistants threw in medicine balls.[42]

The successful *weizzā* leaves his *samsāric* existence by means of an ontological transformation (but without attaining nirvana), thereby attaining semi-immortality and departs for a hidden *weizzā* realm from where he can communicate with his devotees in the human world through supernormal "hearing and seeing" (*akyā-amyin*), send messages through dreams, or possess them or transfer power to them (*dhāt-sī*). In contemporary Burma, a popular *weizzā* country is Mahāmyaing, "the great forest"—it is understood to be a hidden realm that mainly fully-fledged *weizzā*s can enter and see. However, it is also assumed that some advanced practitioners on the *weizzā* path, or people believed to be human *weizzā*s (like cult leaders), can temporarily be taken there during meditation while their bodies remain lifeless.[43] A common notion is that *weizzā*s occasionally hold conferences in such hidden *weizzā* realms to discuss how to protect and promote the Buddha's dispensation whenever it is perceived to be in danger. One such hidden realm, with stronger links to text-based Buddhist cosmology, is the cave at the eastern side of Mt. Meru, where thousands of *weizzā*s are assumed to dwell. Another hidden *weizzā* realm is the Nagāma Mountain, which is important in the *weizzā* cult at Mebaygon village in central Burma.[44]

By attaining ontological transformation, it is assumed that the *weizzā*s can remain in one and the same existence until attaining awakening and nirvana as Buddhist saints (P. *arahant*) or as buddhas on the bodhisatta path in the remote future, mostly at the end of the Sāsana era, when the Phantom Buddha will emerge from the relics of the Buddha and will thereby attain nirvana; or at the appearance of the next buddha, Metteyya.[45] Until the attainment of awakening and nirvana, the main purpose of the *weizzā*s is to defend and maintain the Buddha's dispensation in society and to save the suffering sentient beings by healing, exorcism, and disseminating teachings about the esoteric path (*weizzā-lan*) to them. In other words, these practices are intended for both mundane and supramundane (P. *lokiya* and *lokuttara*) objectives.

As a soteriological practice with the aim of acquiring supernormal powers—*weizzā*hood—and, ultimately, awakening and nirvana, the practice on the *weizzā* path resembles that of forest monks or hermits.[46] This practice should ideally be performed in the woods, in the mountains, in caves, or in famous pagodas. When periodically performing austere *weizzā* practices, which are usually for a limited period (like forty-five days, corresponding to the number of years the Buddha preached), the practitioners should make a vow (*adheiṭṭhān*) to adhere to the terms of their practice (for example, for how long time they should observe an ascetic regimen; how many Buddhist precepts (five, eight, or nine) they should observe; how many rounds they should count on a rosary each day, for how long time they should meditate, and/or whether they should observe vegetarianism, etc.). While performing such a practice, practitioners may wear brown robes, which are associated with austere practices in woods (it is also the color of hermits in Burma). While performing meditation, it is assumed that *weizzā*s can give them instructions for practice through supernormal "hearing and seeing," that is, they can receive messages in their minds or visually encounter a *weizzā* (as an apparition), whereby they can receive instructions for their practice; or they can acquire power from *weizzā*s through power-transfer (*dhāt-sī*); they can also, if they are spiritually mature, be taken temporarily to hidden realms by *weizzā*s during such practices. To some degree, the *weizzā* path is modeled upon that of the monk. Cult leaders, founders of esoteric congregations, and others who are regarded as having attained a lower level of *weizzā*hood are mostly expected to lead an ascetic life like monks, including the observance of celibacy.

LEDĪ HSAYĀDAW'S TAXONOMICAL SCHEME FOR VARIETIES OF *VIJJĀ* (*WEIZZĀ*)

Through the famous monk Ledī Hsayādaw (Ledi Sayadaw, 1846–1923) and his taxonomical scheme of various *weizzā*, "knowledge," the esoteric *weizzā* path became integrated into a legitimate Pāli Buddhist framework. In contemporary Burma, the *weizzā* path has been denigrated by many well-educated urban Buddhists as representing a kind of corrupt practice deviating from the doctrinal Theravāda Buddhism.[47] Since the colonial period, children and young adults have learned a doctrinal form of Buddhism in schools, and many adults have learned simplified versions of insight (*vipassanā*) meditation and scholastic *abhidhamma* philosophy that were popularized by monks like Ledī Hsayādaw from the beginning of the 20th century.[48] This tendency came to be emphasized in the postindependence period under Prime Minister U Nu, at which time the state organized courses on Buddhist doctrines and scholastic *abhidhamma* for young people and adults. Such education projects continued during the Ne Win period (1962–1988) and the SLORC-SPDC period (1988–2011).[49] Since the late Ne Win period and his *sāsana* reforms in the early 1980s, a scripturalist and doctrinal form of Theravāda Buddhism has become hegemonic in society. For that reason, religious practices must be provided a Buddhist identity to be viewed as legitimate.

In his treatise *Weizzā-megga-dīpanī*, "Explanation of the Path to Knowledge/Wisdom," published in 1898, Ledī Hsayādaw made a fivefold classification of *weizzā* (P. *vijjā*), "knowledge," "wisdom," "practice," that has exerted a major impact on the later developments by providing a Buddhist framework into which the esoteric *weizzā* practices could be integrated:

1. *wayda-weizzā* (P. *vedavijjā*), "Veda knowledge," referring to the four Vedas;
2. *manta-weizzā*, "knowledge about mantras," comprising mundane knowledge, not merely about mantras and verses but also treatises on astrology (*nekkhat*), omens (*nimeit*), and properties (*lekkhana*);
3. *gandhārī-weizzā*, "*gandhārī* knowledge," referring to abilities, supernormal powers, and supernormal cognition acquired from success in the practice of magical squares (*in*), esoteric medicine (*hsay*), and alchemy based on mercury and iron;
4. *lawkīya-weizzā* (P. *lokiyavijjā*), "mundane knowledge," referring to supernormal powers (P. *iddhi*) and supernormal cognitions (P. *abhiññā*) acquired by hermits, buddhas, solitary buddhas (P. *paccekabuddha*), and others through absorption meditation (P. *jhāna*) using circular meditation objects (P. *kaṭhina*); and
5. *ariyā-weizzā* (P. *ariyavijjā*), "noble knowledge/wisdom," referring to the doctrine on the three characteristics of all existence (impermanence, suffering, and no-self), the path to nirvana and the fruits of that path, and the Four Noble Truths.[50]

On a practical level, the main dichotomy in contemporary Burma is that between mundane knowledge/practice (P. *lokiya*) corresponding to points 2–4 in Ledī Hsayādaw's classification, on the one hand, and supramundane (P. *lokuttara*) knowledge and practices (*ariyā-weizzā*), on the other. Although Ledī Hsayādaw's aim was not to provide legitimacy to the esoteric *weizzā* knowledge that he outlined in his classification, it has later been used for that purpose. His intention was to differentiate the variety of *weizzā* (P. *vijjā*) prevalent in his time, and to arrange that in a hierarchy with the supramundane at the apex and the mundane at lower rungs of the ladder. Thereby, he identified the supramundane with *ariyā-weizzā*, "noble knowledge," that is, *vipassanā* meditation, the Four Noble Truths, etc., as the superior form of knowledge that alone can lead to awakening and nirvana, and all other forms of *weizzā* as mundane, with varying degrees of proximity to core Buddhist teachings.[51] In the religious field, his hierarchy has also been translated into a social hierarchy (see the section entitled "Hierarchies within the Religious Field"). As Patrick Pranke has pointed out, Ledī

Hsayādaw thereby also presented the mundane knowledge that is associated with the esoteric *weizzā* path in an authoritative *abhidhamma* idiom, something that has provided the *weizzā* path apologists with a theoretical structure and vocabulary with which they can defend their practices against criticism.[52] His scheme and definitions have been reproduced almost verbatim in many subsequent manuals and books about the *weizzā* path, as well as in interviews by the author (2005–2008).[53] This traditional kind of intertextuality probably resonates with many readers; and because Ledī Hsayādaw is famous, his writings are well known and are highly respected in Burma.

Ledī Hsayādaw's presentation of the five categories probably reflected a common Burmese understanding of them. For instance, in the commentarial literature, *gandhārī vijjā* mainly refers to mantras (P. *manta*), but in Burma it mostly comprises magical squares (*in*), medicine, and alchemy based on mercury and iron. The categories in Ledī Hsayādaw's scheme can thus nominally be attested to in Buddhist Pāli canonical texts and commentaries, but some of them are imbued with a local meaning derived from Burmese esoteric *weizzā* traditions. In this way, Ledī Hsayādaw's taxonomy could be employed as a legitimating strategy for integrating the Burmese *weizzā* practices within a Buddhist framework.

HIERARCHIES WITHIN THE RELIGIOUS FIELD: HYBRIDITY, SOCIAL STATUS, AND SOCIAL PRESTIGE

Throughout time in India, the notion of *vidyādhara* appeared in a variety of guises, a plasticity that it seems to have retained in Burmese traditions. In Burma, the *weizzā* field has remained a changing terrain with fluid, fuzzy boundaries. It has been the segment of the Burmese religious field most liable to change, adopting practices and notions seemingly external to Buddhism. Rather eccentric cult leaders, who are attributed charismatic authority, have been able to invent novel notions and practices, mostly under the pretext of receiving instructions from invisible *weizzā*s through dreams or during meditation.

Burmese Buddhism has long absorbed a variety of notions and practices and provided them with a Buddhist interpretation and arranged them into a hierarchy.[54] Although characterized by hybridity, as many of the esoteric practices and notions were incorporated from exogenous sources, the soteriological and social aims of the *weizzā* cults and their religious imaginary are framed in a specifically Buddhist manner. As for the aims, the practitioners on this path seek to attain *weizzā*hood and semi-immortality on the long path to awakening and nirvana as a Buddhist saint (P. *arahant*) or a buddha in one and the same existence. The attainment of sainthood is usually expected to occur at the end of the Sāsana era with the parinirvana of the Buddha's relics, or when Metteyya Buddha appears (see the section entitled "Weizzā Path as a Buddhist Soteriological Path"). Moreover, they should seek to save the sentient beings from suffering (for instance, by exorcism), and they should promote and maintain the Buddha's dispensation in society. Both of these senses are encapsulated by the Burmese phrase *thāthanā-pyu*, "looking after the Buddha's dispensation." In other words, practitioners should not merely seek to benefit themselves but also others, and they should maintain Buddhist morality and the materiality of Buddhism (by building pagodas, temples, and other edifices).

Some esoteric congregations have created a synthesis of the *weizzā* path and the long *bodhisatta* path modeled on the hagiography of Gotama Buddha as narrated in *Nidāna-kathā* (the introduction to the *jātakas*) and in the *jātakas*, the Buddha's birth-stories, etc. The achievement of *weizzā*hood is therefore merely a stage on the long path to *buddha*hood in one and the same existence.[55] For instance, in the Ariyā-Weizzā Organization (for its full name, see the section on "Esoteric Congregations and Cult Groups"), most of the members make *bodhisatta* vows at the initiation ceremony, and they perform visualization meditation in which they visualize themselves as the Buddha, and are even imagined to temporarily turn into buddhas.[56] Some people held to be *weizzā*s are thought to be among the ten future buddhas.[57] For instance, Bo Min Gaung (Bho Min Khaung) is widely believed to be the *bodhisatta* who will become Metteyya Buddha; and the founder of the Ariyā-Weizzā Organization (see the section on "Esoteric Congregations and Cult Groups") is thought to be the future Rāma Buddha.[58] In these ways, the *weizzā* path has been integrated within a Buddhist cosmology, soteriology, and eschatology. In premodern Burma and other Theravāda Buddhist South and Southeast Asian countries, it was mostly the king, as well as some other people from the elite (the nobility and some monks), who claimed to be *bodhisatta*s and who had embarked on the path to buddhahood.[59] After the abolishment of the monarchy in 1885 in Burma, this path came to be embarked upon by commoners as well.[60]

Michael Mendelson has suggested that the Burmese religious field should be analyzed not as compartmentalized sectors but as a continuum between "Buddhism," *weizzā* cults, and the *nat* cult of the Thirty-Seven Lords. These segments are arranged hierarchically, reflecting varying degrees of religious authority based on claims to Buddhist orthodoxy.[61] Largely following that model, the hierarchical social field of religion of the first decades of the 21st century could be analyzed as constituting a continuum between a scripturalist, doctrinal, rationalist discourse on Theravāda Buddhism at one end, the *weizzā* cults somewhere in the middle, and the *nat* cult of the Thirty-Seven Lords, which is a spirit cult, at the other end. The *weizzā* cults are perceived by devotees to be close to the doctrinal form of Theravāda Buddhism and to be very different from the denigrated cult of the Thirty-Seven Lords. For that reason, *weizzā* cults are attributed higher status and authority than spirit cults, but blend features from the entire spectrum. Like the spirit cults, a form of possession (*dhāt-sī*) is common in *weizzā* cults, but it is different from the possession within the spirit cults.[62]

In this way, *weizzā* practices and cults occupy an intermediate space with fuzzy boundaries, and represent something betwixt and between the extreme ends of the continuum. They are neither fully-fledged spirit cults nor something belonging solely to scripturalist, doctrinal Buddhism. *Weizzā* cults blend identities from both. Therefore, this field of practice and knowledge has become something ambiguous and contested, toward which many people, especially men from the educated middle classes, have tended to be ambivalent. They frequently reject these cults because they consider them to be incompatible with doctrinal, scripturalist Buddhism. Although the cult of *weizzā*s is denigrated by some, they are attributed superior authority within the religious field comprising the cult of *weizzā*s, the novel spirit cult of the guardians of the treasure trove (*thaik*), and the cult of the Thirty-Seven Lords.[63] While all three cults offer and emphasize protection and material gratification for the devotees, the *weizzā* cults have retained a soteriological dimension (see the section entitled "Weizzā Path as a Buddhist Soteriological Path"), as they seek to conform to the doctrinal, scripturalist Buddhism. They tend to emphasize—depending on the nature of the group—Buddhist doctrines, *abhidhamma* categories, and Buddhist precepts.

In many religious traditions all over the world, men tend to dominate religious roles and professions that are attributed high social and religious status and prestige, while women take precedence within cults that are attributed lower religious and social status.[64] The Burmese *weizzā* cults are not an exception. In general, women are not acknowledged to have the ability to attain *weizzā*hood, as that is perceived to be a male prerogative.[65] Although some cult leaders and writers might acknowledge this possibility, there are no cults of female *weizzās*. Women—insofar as they are accorded any authority at all—may serve as mediums of *weizzās*, mostly Bo Min Gaung. However, their ability to be vehicles for such elevated beings is widely questioned.[66] The number of women serving as mediums for Bo Min Gaung has increased since the late 1980s and the early 1990s.[67] This role has provided women with an alternative path for higher social and religious authority than the denigrated cult of the Thirty-Seven Lords.

ESOTERIC CONGREGATIONS AND CULT GROUPS: A COLLECTIVE PROJECT

Since the colonial period onwards, esoteric *weizzā* congregations and cult groups have been founded by charismatic individuals and have become an institutionalized phenomenon. A recurrent theme since that period is the aim to protect and promote the Buddha's dispensation. In 1885 the British annexed the entire Burma, abolished the monarchy, and incorporated Burma as a colony into British India. The king had been the foremost patron and defender of the Buddha's dispensation. In this context, the responsibility of promoting Buddhism shifted to the laypeople. Hundreds of Buddhist lay associations were founded between 1890 and 1920, with the aim of saving the Buddha's dispensation against the perceived threat posed by colonialism and modernity. The most influential association was the Young Men's Buddhist Association (YMBA) that was founded in Rangoon in 1906 by a Burmese Western-educated elite. These associations had a bureaucratic organizational structure (with a chairman, secretary, treasurer, etc.). The members constituted a Buddhist moral community (making pledges to observe the Buddhist precepts and signing a document in that regard) and were united in a common Buddhist cause of promoting the Buddha's dispensation.[68]

A few Buddhist esoteric congregations modeled some of their activities on these Buddhist lay associations and had similar aims, namely to promote the Buddha's dispensation in a time of perceived danger, and they constituted Buddhist moral communities.[69] Some also had a comparable bureaucratic organizational structure but were more hierarchical, and tended to be led by charismatic leaders. However, there were many important differences, and the comparison should not be taken too far. Besides the *weizzā* path and related practices, an important aim of the esoteric congregations was to provide exorcism and healing to people. The British colonization of Burma brought about a dramatic social, economic, and political transformation of society, especially in urban areas where most of the congregations had their headquarters. Rapid social change, modernization, urbanization, and social dislocation tend to bring about a sense of social anomie, social distress, and psychosocial problems, as attested by an increase of possession cases (and exorcisms).[70] The "medicine" the congregations provided were a variety of Buddhist-framed practices and remedies and observance of Buddhist precepts. Clients were encouraged to observe Buddhist morality, and this was also a means to support Buddhist practice at a time when it was felt to be endangered.

Although it remains to be investigated when semi-secretive, hierarchical, and initiatory esoteric congregations began to evolve in Burma, it is known that some congregations existed in the late 19th century and emerged throughout the colonial period, and that a large number of congregations were founded during the 1940s and especially in the early postindependence period. A distinction should be made between fairly well-organized initiatory "congregations"—with hundreds up to thousands of members who served as exorcists and healers, frequently with local branches or, at least, representatives throughout the country—and loosely organized, noninitiatory "cult groups," usually without any local branches. Both the congregations and the cult groups aim to save the suffering sentient beings and to promote and maintain the Buddha's dispensation (*thāthanā-pyu*). The esoteric congregations, in particular, represented a collectivistic trend to promote and strengthen the Buddha's dispensation in society. Since they had pledged to observe some or all the Buddhist precepts, these congregations constituted moral communities.

The most common word for an esoteric *weizzā* congregation is *gain* (P. *gaṇa*). Such congregations are founded by a charismatic leader (a *bodaw*, a *hsayā*, a monk, etc.), but after the founder dies, leadership can mostly be transferred to a successor, thereby maintaining the congregation through routinization of charisma, sometimes through the superior disciple.[71] A congregation requires initiation; it offers exorcism and healing to afflicted people; and provides teachings of semi-secret practices on the esoteric *weizzā* path. Healing and exorcism represent ways of both saving the sentient beings (*thatta-wā-keh*) and of promoting the Buddha's dispensation (*thāthanā-pyu*).[72] The exorcists and healers typically do not ask for a fee, although most clients give a voluntary donation. Moreover, clients must make a pledge to observe a few or all of the five Buddhist precepts (P. *pañcasīla*) for the exorcism to be efficacious. Asking the clients to observe Buddhist precepts is also part of the missionary work of the esoteric congregations. As for the exorcists, the esoteric congregations do not provide them with any power, but merely with a powerful repertoire of rituals, devices, procedures, elixirs, and incantations, and the exorcists speak as representatives of the founding and supporting *weizzā*s of the congregation, as well as other supernatural beings, when driving out evil spirits.[73]

The oldest esoteric congregation that can be attested to is the Bouddha-yāzā-hsay Gain, the "Medicine Congregation of the Buddha King," which was apparently established in Prome (Pyi) in central Burma. It is not yet known when this congregation was founded, but the extant manuscript seems to have been composed in the 1880s.[74] It used exorcism to treat clients suffering from problems caused by evil spirits and sorcery. Other organizations from the beginning of the 20th century have yet to be attested to by historical sources.[75] The Manaw-mayeiddhi Weizzādhour Gain, the "Congregation of the Weizzādhours with Supernatural Mind-Powers," was founded by Hsayāgyī Pyi-loun-kyanthā Hsayā Kyaw-gyī in the early 1920s. Another congregation, the Ariyā-Weizzā Manaw-Mayeiddhi Weizzādhour Pyinnyā Khwin Gyī, the "Great Field of Knowledge of the Accomplished Esoteric Masters, Who Have Supernormal Mind-Powers and Noble Esoteric Knowledge" (hereafter the Ariyā-Weizzā Organization), was founded in the late 1940s. It has branches throughout the country, where a local leader takes charge of the local ritual activities (including initiation rituals), the collection of donations, and the branch's administration, reporting everything back to the headquarters.[76] This organization also organizes courses to teach its doctrines and practices to new members (using a blackboard and textbooks in a modern manner).[77] Such organizations, albeit few, were comparable to the Buddhist lay associations that emerged in the colonial period. In most cases, however, these esoteric congregations constituted a loose network of individual exorcists—monks and laypeople—who were subordinated to a headquarters where an annual gathering took place, mostly in Yangon.[78] In these hierarchical congregations, members were initiated into a varying set of levels, providing them with increasing authority and influence within their congregations and enabling them to serve as exorcists; women were sometimes barred from the higher initiation levels.[79]

Members of esoteric congregations were recruited from all social strata, including businesspeople, rich merchants, civil servants, politicians, traditional healers, military officers, soldiers, monks, and workers, but also peasants. In the socialist period of General Ne Win (1962–1988)—at which time the country suffered from economic hardship and offered few venues for social mobility and roles of social authority and influence—the Buddhist esoteric congregations reached their peak of popularity and influence. The same holds for the *vipassanā* movement that became a Buddhist lay mass movement during the same period.[80]

A loosely organized, noninitiatory cult group with a low degree of institutionalization is usually centered on a charismatic cult leader (a *bodaw, hsayā*, a monk, etc.), but his charisma cannot be routinized, probably due to an absence of an organizational structure of the cult group with branches throughout the country.[81] A cult group does not require initiation; it may or may not offer exorcism and healing, and the like. It basically consists of a charismatic leader and his followers, and there is no formal membership. The cult leader offers consultation, gives advice and instructions for practice, collects donations for Buddhist ends, and performs rituals and ceremonies to save the sentient beings and to promote the Buddha's dispensation. The cult leader may also serve as a medium for *weizzā*s. After he passes away, the cult group mostly dissolves, the area becomes desolate, and it is soon forgotten.[82]

Those serving as mediums for *weizzā*s are mostly leaders of cult groups, or more entrepreneurial mediums that have become more common since the 1990s. Regarding the ability to communicate and interact with *weizzā*s, a recurrent assumption is that a devotee is thought to have a "karmic connection" (*paṭṭhān-hsek*) to the *weizzā* in previous lives, at which time they had a social relationship (e.g., a friend, a relative, son, or daughter, etc.). It is often claimed that *weizzā*s approach human beings for the sake of promoting the Buddha's dispensation—thereby giving instructions for building pagodas or shrines, to hold a certain ceremony, or for how to attain *weizzā*hood—or to provide healing to save the living beings.

When mediums are stated to be possessed by *weizzā*s (*dhāt-sī*), it is believed that the latter can speak, act, and perform healing and the like through their human vessels.[83] For someone to serve as such a vessel, he or she must be morally pure and constantly observe the five Buddhist precepts for laypeople (periodically extended to eight or nine), and continuously perform Buddhist meditation practices, mostly in the form of counting beads on a rosary while reciting Buddhist verses or mantras. This emphasis of Buddhist morality and practice stresses the Buddhist nature of these cults. It is a common idea that the medium must be elected by the *weizzā*, which tends to be linked to the karmic connection, to serve as his human mouthpiece and vessel. That could happen through dreams, apparitions (an encounter with the *weizzā* in visual form that is described as a physical manifestation of the *weizzā*), or while meditating.[84]

Miracles and displays of supernormal powers are depicted in early and later Buddhist texts as an integral feature of Buddhist practice, and they are employed to convince outsiders of the greatness of the Buddha's teaching and as a means of conversion.[85] In a similar manner, an important aspect of establishing charismatic authority by Buddhist leaders within *weizzā* cults in Burma is the display of supernormal powers (*dago-pya*), and this serves to recruit new members or to attract clients. Some congregations and cult groups are founded and led by people believed to be human *weizzā*s. Narratives and displays of feats like flying, materializing objects in one's hands, making objects disappear, being visible at two places at the same time constitute ways of building authority.[86] For instance, one hermit living on the top of a mountain outside Mandalay claimed that for twenty years he had not been sick, had not slept, had hardly eaten anything; his body had stopped producing excrements and all his wishes tended to be fulfilled. These abnormalities served as evidence for his followers that he was an accomplished *weizzā* possessing supernormal powers.[87]

Moreover, there has been competition over status and prestige between esoteric congregations. Some congregations have sought to establish themselves as hierarchically superior to other congregations, which they perceive to represent a lower kind of practice, labeled *gandhārī-weizzā* (see the section entitled "Ledī Hsayādaw's Taxonomical Scheme for Varieties of *Vijjā* (*Weizzā*)"). These allegedly superior congregations seek to incorporate more of Buddhist doctrinal discourses derived from the Pāli canon and its commentaries, labeled "supramundane" (*lawkuttara*) or "noble" (*ariyā*), and downplay putative lower mundane (*lawkī*) practices.[88] In Burma, the dichotomy of supramundane and mundane practices has thus been deployed as a strategy to gain superior authority, prestige, and status in the competition between esoteric congregations for members and clients.

POLITICAL IMAGINARY IN THE LATE COLONIAL AND EARLY POSTINDEPENDENCE PERIOD

Since the 1960s onwards, a common idea within scholarship is that there were militant nationalist *weizzā* groups and congregations during the colonial period that were opposed to the colonial government. These groups were supposed to be engaged in violent opposition using real weapons in combination with a variety of practices that tend to be associated (especially by Western scholars) with the *weizzā* path. These assumptions seem to have become naturalized and taken for granted by some scholars, although historical evidence appears to be lacking. Before presenting historical evidence for claims about the existence of such militant *weizzā* congregations, scholars should be cautious.[89] When the available documentation from the colonial period is examined, these militant groups seem to have been related to *nat*s (local spirits) rather than to the cult of *weizzā*s.[90]

However, the notion of *weizzā*s has played a prominent role in the political and nationalist imagination in Burma since the late colonial period into the 21st century. During the colonial period, it shaped an anticolonial imaginary (within *weizzā* congregations, cult groups, and elsewhere). These powerful figures have been imagined to intervene in political developments by means of their supernormal powers (for examples from the postindependence period, see the section on the "Liberation Era").[91] In the colonial period, Burmese people looked for a savior who could free them from the yoke of colonialism. During the independence struggle, the *weizzā* Bo Bo Aung was invoked as a future liberator of Burma from colonialism.[92] Developments in the 1930s contributed to the political significance of the *weizzās*. An old legend of Bo Bo Aung caught the popular imagination, and people hoped that his miraculous power would free them from British domination, and songs about Bo Bo Aung were popularized.[93] By the end of the 1930s, the politician Ba Maw, founding a coalition of nationalist political parties, drew instrumentally on this legend as a political strategy to gain the support of the masses, thereby suggesting that the Burmese people would receive support from Bo Bo Aung and his miraculous power to gain independence.[94]

The legend of Sekyā Min (P. *cakkavattin*), the would-be world emperor, was important in the resistance against the British colonizers and later became linked to Bo Bo Aung. The Sekyā prince was the crown prince and the only son of King Bagyidaw (r. 1819–1837). During his reign, Burma suffered a humiliating defeat in the First Anglo–Burmese War (1824–1826). In the Yandabo Treaty of February 1826, Burma had to cede Tenasserim and Arakan to the British in what was later designated Lower Burma. Thereafter, hopes became focused upon his son, Sekyā Min. After a coup by his uncle, the king was deposed and his son was executed by drowning, but rumors spread saying that he had survived.[95] It was hoped that Sekyā Min would drive out the British and usher in a prosperous era for Burma and Buddhism.[96] Several rebellions were led by people claiming to be that figure.[97] Later, various political leaders were identified with Sekyā Min, mostly by rumors.[98]

According to a popular legend, Bo Bo Aung miraculously saved Sekyā Min from drowning. In books from the 1930s and 1940s, Sekyā Min is portrayed as a pious personage engaged in esoteric practices on the *weizzā* path.[99] In his pamphlet *Bo Bo Aung and Hitler*, the monk U Nyāna even claimed that Adolf Hitler was an incarnation of Sekyā Min, and that Bo Bo Aung would later make him convert to Buddhism to work for the propagation and dissemination of Buddhism in the world.[100] In the late colonial period and the early postindependence period, prophecies about the imminent arrival of a righteous Buddhist king and/or of Sekyā Min circulated. In books and pamphlets published from the late 1930s, there were several discourses on Sekyā Min, only a few of which were framed by *weizzā* notions and Bo Bo Aung. The expectations and prophecies of the arrival of Sekyā Min in the postcolonial era were linked to the 2,500-year anniversary of Gotama Buddha's parinirvana in 1956. This year marked the midpoint of the Sāsana era, which has been prophesized to last for 5,000 years. For the Burmese, this represented a kind of turn of the millennium that evoked millenarian expectations.[101]

The Liberation Era: Soteriological Optimism. In the late 1940s, there was a conjunction of factors that contributed to the millennial expectations of a glorious new era. Burma had achieved independence from Britain in 1948, which entailed uncertainty about the future; Burma had a democratically elected government led by Prime Minister U Nu that promoted Buddhism; and this government organized the Sixth Buddhist Synod in 1954–1956 in Rangoon (later renamed Yangon). This seemingly favorable situation nourished optimistic imaginations that a so-called "Liberation era" would be inaugurated in the mid-1950s. The 2,500-year anniversary was also associated with millennial expectations in other Buddhist countries, including Sri Lanka.[102]

The U Nu government and many Buddhist lay associations assumed that the collective observance of Buddhist morality would bring peace and prosperity to the civil war-plagued union.[103] Some esoteric congregations likewise attempted to attain peace by making people in the villages and urban areas observe Buddhist morality and by conducting missionary work. A few had proselytizing "armies" (*tap*), and within the Ariyā-Weizzā Organization, the leaders were given military titles, such as the "Brave and Righteous Commanders-in-Chief of the Propagation of the Sāsana." Bodaw Myanmar Aye's organization and the Pathaman Congregation also had such "armies" and provided titles to their leaders.[104] The missionary fervor that characterized both U Nu's government and some esoteric congregations was related to widely held millenarian expectations of the advent of a glorious era for the newly independent Burma and Buddhism, as foretold by prophecies that were linked to the 2,500-year anniversary of the Buddhist era in 1956. The millenarianism of the esoteric congregations rested on the idea that the new era could be achieved by ritual means, morality, supernormal powers, and proselytizing.[105] Related to this millenarianism was a soteriological optimism of expectation that practice would yield immediate results, which was articulated in the novel concept of *wimoutti-yuga-khayt*, the "Liberation era." It would begin in the second half of the Buddhist era, starting in 1956–1957, and it was interpreted by some as the "Weizzā era," while others understood it as the "Vipassanā era," in which it would be easier to attain *weizzā*hood or make spiritual progress by means of insight meditation.[106] Still others imagined that period as the "Sekyā era," at which time Sekyā Min would reappear to inaugurate the new era and promote Buddhism.[107] While a democratization of awakening and nirvana characterized the insight meditation movement, and the cults of living Buddhist saints reached its peak in the 1950s, a democratization of *bodhisatta*hood was found in some esoteric congregations.[108]

The earliest evidence of esoteric congregations framed by Sekyā Min imagery seems to be from the 1940s, and these congregations were mostly linked to Bo Min Gaung. Many held him to be Sekyā Min and the future Metteyya Buddha. After Bo Min Gaung passed away in 1952, some cult leaders claimed that they had become his vessels and were therefore also Sekyā Min.[109] Other congregations were likewise led by Sekyā Min claimants but were not concerned with Bo Min Gaung. Congregations led by Sekyā Min claimaints could be labeled "royal esoteric congregations" because the leaders portrayed themselves as "kings" of the supernatural world and employed royal imagery and symbolism. The aims of these congregations were the same as other esoteric congregations (see the section on "Esoteric Congregations and Cult Groups").[110] Some also added rituals by which conditions in society, including political conditions and processes, would be improved to benefit the Buddha's dispensation. Followers of Bo Min Gaung built a number of "magic pagodas," and the Ariyā-Weizzā Organization performed rituals with the aim of removing the enemies of Buddhism and to change political processes, including ensuring that the leadership of the country is Buddhist, by means of the combined supernormal power of the members and the *weizzās*.[111] One related aspect of the political imaginary is that *weizzā*s are sometimes assumed to be the real agents behind events. In Sekyā Min's royal orders from the Ariyā-Weizzā Organization, Sekyā Min is depicted as the invisible agent behind the nationalist movement and the achievement of independence from Britain.[112] One cult leader of a Bo Min Gaung temple claimed that Bo Min Gaung caused some political leaders—including General Than Shwe during the SLORC-SPDC period (1988–2011)—to perform good deeds for Buddhism by temporarily possessing them.[113]

THE RELATIONSHIP TO THE STATE IN THE 1980S

General Ne Win suppressed a variety of religions that he regarded as being incompatible with a modern socialist state, such as the cult of the Thirty-Seven Lords, the esoteric congregations, and allegedly deviant forms of monastic Buddhism. In 1980, the state sought to unify and centralize the divided Sangha with a new ruling body called the State Sangha Mahā Nāyaka Committee to gain control of the monastic community. An ecclesiastic court system was established to deal with *Vinaya* infractions and doctrinal deviations. Hundreds of monks were disrobed in the purge, and some were linked to the esoteric movement. Ne Win's *sāsana* reforms in the 1980s created a more intolerant religious climate, which continued throughout the SLORC-SPDC period (1988–2011). Ne Win's promotion of doctrinal, scriptural Buddhism has contributed to the establishment of this interpretation of Buddhism as a hegemonic, normative discourse on pure Theravāda Buddhism in Burma.[114] Ne Win also cracked down on the esoteric congregations. The distinctive practices of the esoteric congregations have long been ridiculed and criticized, especially by those representatives of the middle classes who espouse insight meditation, scholastic *abhidhamma* philosophy, and doctrinal Buddhism.[115] In a speech delivered in December 1979, General Ne Win brought up the issue of the esoteric congregations and maintained that such deceitful congregations did not merely exist in Burma but could be found throughout the world. He cited Jim Jones and his Peoples Temple cult and the mass suicide of its members in the United States as a warning example. Constituting social and economic bases of influence and power, the esoteric congregations represented potential sources of opposition to the state and were therefore viewed with suspicion by the government and put under surveillance.[116]

The esoteric congregations never fully recovered after this purge, and the interest in such congregations has dwindled for various reasons. As a result of Ne Win's new policy, the esoteric congregations were harassed; some were banned and declared almost illegal; some went underground, and others vanished. However, many congregations still exist. The state imposed restrictions on the congregations to gain control over them, and since then their activities have been more circumscribed.[117] For instance, the Ariyā-Weizzā Organization ceased its large-scale and fervent proselytizing work in the early 1980s; it discontinued certain practices and changed its name.[118] One reason why these congregations did not fully regain their popularity was that the conditions in society had changed. As a result of the shift to a new military dictatorship—SLORC-SPDC in 1988—and its implementation of a limited market economy, various forms of individualistic prosperity Buddhism emerged, and people tended to focus more on their private economy in their religious practices rather than on the collective *sāsana*-preserving projects of the esoteric congregations. Since then, the *weizzā* phenomenon has gradually become more and more deinstitutionalized.

DEVOTIONAL *WEIZZĀ* CULTS AS PROSPERITY BUDDHISM: BUDDHISM AND CAPITALISM

For the majority of people, turning to *weizzā*s is a devotional practice resembling the cult of spirits, gods, or saints in other religions. Popular accomplished esoteric masters (*weizzā*) are the laypeople Bo Min Gaung and Bo Bo Aung, and the monk Yekkansin Taung Hsayādaw.

Other *weizzā*s appear in images and at altars, but they are mostly not the subject of devotional cults. However, some *weizzā*s enjoy cult status mainly within specific congregations or cult groups. Bo Min Gaung (1880–1952) was the most popular accomplished esoteric master in the 1940s and the early postindependence period and remains so into the 21st century. Devotees prostrate and pay obeisance in front of statues or images of *weizzā*s in a temple, at a shrine, or in their homes. They make a wish (*hsu-taung*), a vow (*adheiṭṭhān*) where they specify what they will give in return if their wish is granted. Usually, they present an offering consisting of a plate with bananas and coconuts (*kadaw-pwe*), a traditional token of respect in Burmese culture, and perform activities to promote the Buddha's dispensation (*thāthanā-pyu*). This entails, for instance, giving donations for Buddhist ends, alms to monks, contributing to building or renovating a pagoda, or building a pagoda oneself. This form of Buddhist devotionalism has increased since the early 1990s and has become part of "prosperity Buddhism."[119] Although wishes for material gratification, including wishing for economic success and health, have long been part of the *weizzā* traditions, since the 1990s this dimension has become the dominant one within the *weizzā* cults. At the same time, the soteriological dimension has been downplayed. The collective projects of promoting and maintaining the Buddha's dispensation in society that characterized the esoteric congregations, has been replaced by a kind of individualist trend with nonaffiliated ritual specialists serving as entrepreneurial mediums for Bo Min Gaung and the guardians of the treasure trove, and with devotees seeking to benefit their private economy while also promoting the Buddha's dispensation.

In 1988, the planned economy of the socialist Ne Win period (1962–1988) collapsed, and a new military government under SLORC-SPDC (1988–2011) seized power and implemented economic reforms with a limited market economy. In interplay with these economic changes, a variety of cults of "prosperity Buddhism" emerged in the early 1990s, especially the cult of Bo Min Gaung and other *weizzā*s and the cult of the guardians of the treasure trove (*thaik*).[120] Devotees turn to these beings to become wealthy, to gain success in business, to get a better job, to be able to buy a house, or to receive the winning lottery numbers, but also for better health. Among urban people belonging to especially the middle classes, the popularity of these cults has grown since the mid-2000s and came to virtually explode after 2011, when Burma/Myanmar opened up. That entailed a further liberalization of the capitalist economy, with a mushrooming of new cults, shrines, and temples throughout the country. From around the mid-2000s, Bo Min Gaung enjoys a nationwide cult. After 2011, the annual celebration, in September, of Bo Min Gaung's "exit" (*htwek-pwe*) at Mt. Popa in central Burma—that is, his attainment of ontological transformation in 1952—began to attract hundreds of thousands of devotees from mainly urban areas, especially Yangon and Mandalay, coming to present an offering before a statue of Bo Min Gaung, to make a wish and vow, before returning home.

REVIEW OF LITERATURE

In Western scholarship, the ethnographic investigation of *weizzā* congregations and cult groups began with Michael E. Mendelson, who conducted fieldwork in 1958–1959 and published some articles in the early 1960s. He was followed slightly later by Melford E. Spiro, who conducted fieldwork in the Mandalay area in 1961–1962 and published two monographs

(1967 and 1970) related to that subject.[121] Due to the political situation in the country, the field—with a few singular and noteworthy exceptions—did not attract many scholars between 1962 and the early 2000s. In the early postindependence period, many *weizzā* cults were devoted to Sekyā Min (the world emperor) and Bo Min Gaung. Based on fieldwork in the late 1950s, Michael Mendelson's articles constitute the first ethnographic accounts of *weizzā* congregations and cult groups. One article documents and analyzes a congregation founded and led by Bodaw Setkya (Sekyā), who was believed to be an incarnation of Bo Min Gaung held to be Sekyā Min.[122] This is a seminal article that examines a *weizzā* congregation in Mandalay and provides a unique portrait of a congregation in the late 1950s. Spiro's second monograph discusses the same congregation that Mendelson examined. Based on fieldwork in 1961–1962, that monograph is the only comprehensive study of various facets of Burmese Buddhism, including one chapter on *weizzā* cults.[123] Juliane Schober conducted fieldwork in the early 1980s, mainly in the Mandalay area. She investigated esoteric congregations, cult groups, and compared their practices with forest monks.[124] Guillaume Rozenberg made an ethnographic study of a cult group founded in the 1950s that was situated in Mebaygon in central Burma dedicated to four *weizzās*. This study explores how "believing" is established through the performance of miracles.[125] In several publications, Niklas Foxeus examined a supramundane esoteric congregation, in which the members had embarked on the path to buddhahood. It was founded in the late 1940s by an individual held to be an incarnation of Sekyā Min. This is the first study of a congregation founded by an individual believed to be an incarnation of that figure since Mendelson's and Spiro's pioneering studies in the early postindependence period.[126]

In the scholarship, there have been two main approaches to how the relationship between the *weizzā* cults and other cults and religious institutions should be analyzed, namely those of Michael Mendelson and Melford Spiro. Mendelson applied a kind of field approach to analyze the variety of aspects of religion and their internal relationships as constituting a hierarchy determined by religious authority based on claims to Buddhist orthodoxy (a discourse on doctrinal Buddhism). Instead of compartmentalizing the religious field, he viewed its various segments as a continuum, comprising doctrinal Buddhism and the denigrated spirit cult of the Thirty-Seven Lords as its extreme ends, with *weizzā* cults situated somewhere in the middle.[127] His approach is similar to Stanley Tambiah's holistic approach for analyzing Thai Buddhism as a field.[128] Melford Spiro's two influential monographs on Burmese religion are shaped by an Orientalist approach distinguishing between a "normative Buddhism"—located in a narrow selection of canonical texts—from what he perceived to be a "nonnormative Buddhism."[129] Being biased by such a normative textualist approach, Spiro compartmentalized the religious field into isolated, disconnected segments. Based on his textualist understanding of doctrinal "normative Buddhism," he tended to essentialize what, in his view, should be categorized as truly belonging to "Buddhism" and what failed to meet his criteria for inclusion. He was probably not merely under the influence of Orientalism but also of the views among well-educated Burmese Buddhists from the urban middle classes. Turning the emic normative categories of the urban middle classes (that were similar to the orientalist textualist view) into analytical categories cannot be seen as methodologically sound. Since he did not examine the interrelationships between the different segments of the religious field, he failed to analyze what power dynamics operated behind such normative divisions. In that way, he—probably unwittingly—provided support and justification of the views of the elite. Although referring to the *weizzā* cults as "esoteric Buddhism," he stamped the phenomenon as being "anti-Buddhist."

Later, most Burma scholars adopted approaches that are more in line with that of Mendelson. They have emphasized the social dynamic of establishing authority and creating hierarchies within Burmese religion, perceived as constituting a field with different segments. Highlighting the analytical theme of hierarchy, status, and authority in the religious field, Brac de la Perrière conducted research on the *weizzā* cults exploring the social dynamics between various cults. She compared the "higher" possession (*dhāt-sī*) within the *weizzā* cults and the "lower" form of possession within the *nat* cult of the Thirty-Seven Lords.[130] Patrick Pranke examined how esoteric congregations have employed the famous monk Ledī Hsayādaw's fivefold taxonomic scheme of mundane and supramundane *vijjās* (*weizzā*) as a legitimation strategy to defend their notions and practices against criticism (see also the section entitled "Ledī Hsayādaw's Taxonomical Scheme for Varieties of *Vijjā* (*Weizzā*)").[131] Keiko Tosa made a useful exploration of how the concepts of supramundane (*lawkuttara*) and mundane (*lawkī*) were employed to create social hierarchies between esoteric congregations.[132] Based on fieldwork in the early 1980s, Gustaaf Houtman made an important ethnographic study of the insight meditation movement in Burma, and he compared that movement with the esoteric congregations and their practice of concentration meditation, thereby demonstrating how the latter was denigrated and criticized by the former.[133] Patrick Pranke claimed that these two meditation movements emerged during the colonial period in response to colonization and the introduction of modernity.[134] Developing the focus on the relationship between the two soteriological meditation movements, Niklas Foxeus explored another aspect, namely how both movements were concerned with national identity and how they evolved in contradistinction to one another in their quest for Buddhist identity, but with different meditation techniques as their emblems. Moreover, he demonstrated how the Ariyā-Weizzā Organization has sought to establish itself as a supramundane esoteric congregation by emphasizing the "*ariyā* discourse" to claim itself to be superior to allegedly inferior mundane congregations.[135] In a different manner, Thomas Patton examined the practice of esoteric diagrams or yantras (*in*) in Burma. While briefly discussing the criticism of *weizzā* practices by some Buddhists espousing a more doctrinal form of Buddhism; he also situated these and other *weizzā* practices into the wider context of Burmese Buddhism, analyzing them on the basis of Steven Collin's concept of the "Pāli imaginaire" and the variety of Buddhist felicities ranging from the mundane to the supramundane ones.[136]

FURTHER READING

Brac de la Perrière, Bénédicte. "Ritual Tattooing and the Creation of New Buddhist Identities: An Inquiry into the Initiation Process in a Burmese Organization of Exorcists." *Religion and Society* 8, no. 1 (2017): 129–144.

Brac de la Perrière, Bénédicte. "Spirits versus Weikza: Two Competing Ways of Mediation." *Journal of Burma Studies* 16, no. 2 (2012): 149–179.

Coderey, Céline. "The Weikza's Role in Arakanese Healing Practices." *Journal of Burma Studies* 16, no. 2 (2012): 181–211.

Ferguson, John P., and Michael E. Mendelson. "Masters of the Buddhist Occult: The Burmese Weikzas." In *Contributions to Asian Studies* 16. Edited by John P. Ferguson, 62–80. Leiden, the Netherlands: Brill, 1981.

Foxeus, Niklas. "The Buddhist World Emperor's Mission: Millenarian Buddhism in Postcolonial Burma." PhD diss., Stockholm University, 2011.

Foxeus, Niklas. "'I Am the Buddha, the Buddha Is Me!' Concentration Meditation and Esoteric Modern Buddhism in Burma/Myanmar." *Numen* 63, no. 4 (2016): 411–445. https://www.diva-portal.org/smash/get/diva2:608940/FULLTEXT01.pdf.

Foxeus, Niklas. "Mimicking the State: Royal, Nationalist and Militant Ideology in a New Buddhist Movement in Burma/Myanmar." *Bijdragen tot de Taal-, Land- en Volkenkunde/Journal of the Humanities and Social Sciences of Southeast Asia* 172, no. 2–3 (2016): 197–224.

Foxeus, Niklas. "Possessed for Success: Prosperity Buddhism and the Cult of the Guardians of the Treasure Trove in Upper Burma." *Contemporary Buddhism* 18, no. 1 (2017): 108–139.

Foxeus, Niklas. "Vidyādhara (Weizzā/Weikza)." In *Oxford Bibliographies in Buddhism*. Edited by Michael Payne. New York: Oxford University Press, 2016.

Mendelson, Michael. "The King of the Weaving Mountain." *Journal of the Royal Central Asian Society* 48, no. 3–4 (1961): 229–237.

Mendelson, Michael. "A Messianic Buddhist Association in Upper Burma." *Bulletin of the School of Oriental and African Studies* 24, no. 3 (1961): 560–580.

Mendelson, Michael. "Observations on a Tour in the Region of Mount Popa, Central Burma." *France-Asie* 19 (1963): 780–807.

Patton, Thomas N. *The Buddha's Wizards: Magic, Protection, and Healing in Burmese Buddhism*. New York: Columbia University Press, 2018.

Patton, Thomas N. "In Pursuit of the Sorcerer's Power: Sacred Diagrams as Technologies of Potency." *Contemporary Buddhism* 13, no. 2 (2012): 213–231.

Pranke, Patrick. "On Becoming a Buddhist Wizard." In *Buddhism in Practice*. Edited by Donald S. Lopez Jr., 343–358. Princeton, NJ: Princeton University Press, 1995.

Pranke, Patrick. "On Saints and Wizards: Ideals of Human Perfection and Power in Contemporary Burmese Buddhism." *Journal of the International Association of Buddhist Studies* 33, no. 1–2 (2011): 453–488.

Rozenberg, Guillaume. "The Alchemist and His Ball." *Journal of Burma Studies* 14 (2010): 187–228.

Rozenberg, Guillaume. *The Immortals: Faces of the Incredible in Buddhist Burma*. Translated by Ward Keeler. Honolulu: University of Hawai'i Press, 2015.

Rozenberg, Guillaume. "Powerful yet Powerless, Powerless yet Powerful: The Burmese Exorcist." *Journal of Burma Studies* 16, no. 2 (2012): 251–282.

Rozenberg, Guillaume. *Renunciation and Power: The Quest for Sainthood in Contemporary Burma*. Translated by Jessica Hackett. New Haven, CT: Yale University Southeast Asian Studies, 2010.

Schober, Juliane. "The Path to Buddhahood: The Spiritual Mission and Social Organization of Mysticism in Contemporary Burma." *Crossroads* 4, no. 1 (1988): 13–30.

Spiro, Melford E. *Buddhism and Society: A Great Tradition and Its Burmese Vicissitudes*. Berkeley: University of California Press, [1970] 1982.

Spiro, Melford E. *Burmese Supernaturalism*. Expanded Edition. New Brunswick, NJ: Transaction, [1967] 1996.

Tosa, Keiko. "A Consideration of Weikza Belief in Burma: The Meaning of Làwki and Làwkoktara for the Gaing." *Mizokugaku Kenkyu* 61, no. 2 (1996): 215–242.

NOTES

1. In this article, "P." is an abbreviation for Pāli and "S." for Sanskrit. All foreign words are Burmese, unless otherwise indicated. The term "nirvana" will be used instead of the Pāli *nibbāna*, since the former has been adopted into English. The research for this article was mainly conducted when the author was a

Royal Swedish Academy of Letters, History and Antiquities Research Fellow. It was also supported by the Swedish Research Council under Grant number 2019–02601.

2. The Sanskrit word *vidyādhara* literally means a "bearer" or someone "proficient" (*dhara*) in "knowledge," "wisdom," or a certain "practice" (*vidyā*). It corresponds to the Pāli word *vijjādhara* which, in a Burmanized version, can be rendered "*weizzādhour*," or "*weikzado*." Frequently, the shorthand form *weizzā* or *weikza* has been used by Burmese people and scholars alike to refer to a person proficient in a certain knowledge or practices that have achieved a superhuman status endowed with supernormal powers. In the following, *weizzā*, unless otherwise indicated, is used in that respect. Since there is no word in English that corresponds to the meaning and role of this figure within Burmese traditions, I leave the word untranslated.
3. See Otto von Hinüber, "The Vidyādhara's Sword," in *Selected Papers on Pāli Studies*, ed. Otto von Hinüber (Oxford: The Pali Text Society, 1994); Jörg Grafe, *Vidyādharas: früheste Zeit bis zur kaschmirischen Bṛhatkathā* (Frankfurt am Main: Peter Lang, 2001); and Hans van Buitenen, "The Indian Hero as Vidyādhara," *Journal of American Folklore* 71, no. 281 (1958): 305–311.
4. David Gordon White, "Mountains of Wisdom: On the Interface between Siddha and Vidyādhara Cults and the Siddha Orders in Medieval India," *International Journal of Hindu Studies* 1, no. 1 (1997): 73–95; and Ronald M. Davidson, *Indian Esoteric Buddhism: A Social History of the Tantric Movement* (New York: Columbia University Press, 2002).
5. See David Gordon White, *The Alchemical Body: Siddha Traditions in Medieval India* (Chicago: Chicago University Press, 1996); White, "Mountains of Wisdom"; David Gordon White, *Kiss of the Yoginī: "Tantric Sex" in Its South Asian Contexts* (Chicago: University of Chicago Press, 2003); and Davidson, *Indian Esoteric Buddhism.*
6. Davidson, *Indian Esoteric Buddhism.*
7. Davidson, *Indian Esoteric Buddhism.*
8. Gyurme Dorje, "Introduction," in *The Nyingma School of Tibetan Buddhism: Its Fundamentals and History*, ed. Dudjom Rinpoche and Jikdrel Yeshe Dorje. Vol. 1: *The Translations*, trans. Gyurme Dorje, with the collaboration of Matthew Kapstein (Boston, MA: Wisdom Publications, 1991), 11–42.
9. Dorje, "Introduction," 31–34.
10. The *yogin* here is thus not an ascetic figure observing celibacy. In Burmese folklore, *zawgyīs* (derived from the Sanskrit word *yogin*) were believed to be alchemists who have sexual intercourse with "fruit maidens." See Maung Htin Aung, *Folk Elements in Burmese Buddhism* (London: Oxford University Press, 1962). In the later Burmese tradition, these figures came to be viewed as ascetics. See Phyllis Granoff, "Other People's Rituals: Ritual Eclecticism in Early Medieval Indian Religious," *Journal of Indian Philosophy* 28 (2000): 399–424; Robert Mayer, "The Importance of the Underworlds: Asuras' Caves in Buddhism, and Some Other Themes in Early Buddhist Tantras Reminiscent of the Later Padmasambhava Legends," *Journal of the International Association of Tibetan Studies* 3 (2007): 1–31; and Glenn Wallis, *Mediating the Power of Buddhas: Ritual in the Mañjuśrīmūlakalpa* (Albany, NY: State University of New York Press, 2002).
11. White, *Alchemical Body.*
12. White, "Mountains of Wisdom," 83–84.
13. Htin Aung, *Folk Elements.*
14. U Kala, *Mahā-yāzawin-gyī*, Vol. 3, ed. U Khin Soe (Yangon, Myanmar: Hanthāwatī Piṭakat Press, 1961), 178–180.
15. White, *Alchemical Body*, 8.
16. See von Hinüber, "The Vidyādhara's Sword." This standardized iconographic feature can be found in apocryphal Southeast Asian *jātaka* tales. See Isaline B. Horner and Padmanabh S. Jaini, trans., *Apocryphal Birth-Stories (Paññāsa-Jātaka)*, Vol. 1 (Oxford: The Pali Text Society, [1985] 2003); and in Burmese

manuscripts of the late 19th century until recently, see Niklas Foxeus, "The Buddhist World Emperor's Mission: Millenarian Buddhism in Postcolonial Burma," PhD diss., Stockholm University, 2011.

17. The *weizzā* cults and their related practices could be described as esoteric in a loose sense, as referring to social aspects, ritual features, and certain practices, as well as to organizations within which such features are salient. A core meaning of the word "esoteric" is that it is something pertaining to a circle of initiated disciples, that is, a knowledge that is communicated to, or that is intelligible by the initiated alone (see "esoteric," *Oxford English Dictionary* [Oxford: Oxford University Press, 2021]). This sense of the "esoteric" as a knowledge reserved for initiated disciples characterizes so-called esoteric Buddhism or tantric Buddhism (Vajrayāna Buddhism) that originated in India. It is also apparent to some degree in some Burmese *weizzā* congregations requiring initiation. In some congregations, it is required that what takes place in the ritual room (*dhāt-khan*) and certain practices must not be revealed to outsiders. However, the "esoteric" could be understood in a wider sense as comprising social features (a dynamic of the rhetoric of secrecy, and a master-disciple relationship); ritual aspects (initiation rituals); and certain practices that are labelled "esoteric" in both Western and Asian traditions—for instance, magical squares, alchemy, mantras, and the like (see Foxeus, "Buddhist World Emperor's Mission," 3–10).
18. See John P. Ferguson and Michael E. Mendelson, "Masters of the Buddhist Occult: The Burmese Weikzas," in *Contributions to Asian Studies* 16, ed. John P. Ferguson (Leiden, the Netherlands: Brill, 1981), 62–80; Patrick Pranke, "On Saints and Wizards: Ideals of Human Perfection and Power in Contemporary Burmese Buddhism," *Journal of the International Association of Buddhist Studies* 33, no. 1–2 (2011): 453–488; Foxeus, "Buddhist World Emperor's Mission"; and Thomas Patton, "Bearers of Wisdom, Sources of Power: Sorcerer-Saints and Burmese Buddhism," PhD diss., Cornell University, 2014.
19. Niklas Foxeus, "Vidyādhara (Weizzā/Weikza)," in *Oxford Bibliographies in Buddhism*, ed. Michael Payne (New York: Oxford University Press, 2016).
20. Christian Dietrich Lammerts, "Buddhism and Written Law: Dhammasattha Manuscripts and Texts in Premodern Burma," PhD diss., Cornell University, 2010, 22.
21. See Patrick Pranke, "On Becoming a Buddhist Wizard," in *Buddhism in Practice*, ed. Donald S. Lopez Jr. (Princeton, NJ: Princeton University Press, 1995), 343–358; and Pranke, "On Saints and Wizards."
22. Jonathan Z. Smith, *Imagining Religion: From Babylon to Jonestown* (Chicago: University of Chicago Press, 1982).
23. Oliver Williams Wolters, *History, Culture, and Region in Southeast Asian Perspectives*, rev. ed. (Ithaca, NY: Southeast Asia Program Publications, [1982] 1999), 49.
24. Wolters, *History, Culture, and Region*, 55.
25. Robert DeCaroli, *Haunting the Buddha: Indian Popular Religions and the Formation of Buddhism* (Oxford: Oxford University Press, 2004).
26. Ferguson and Mendelson, "Masters of the Buddhist Occult," 62.
27. Ferguson and Mendelson, "Masters of the Buddhist Occult," 68, 74.
28. One example of older evidence is the *weizzādhour-zawgyī* from U Kāla's 18th-century chronicle (see the section entitled "*Vidyādharas* in Indian and Tibetan Buddhism") that was clearly related to *weizzā* practices.
29. See Eric Hobsbawm, "Introduction: Inventing Traditions," in *The Invention of Tradition*, ed. Eric Hobsbawm and Terrence Ranger (Cambridge, UK: Cambridge University Press, [1983] 2000), 1–14.
30. See Ferguson and Mendelson, "Masters of the Buddhist Occult."
31. See Pranke, "On Saints and Wizards"; Ferguson and Mendelson, "Masters of the Buddhist Occult"; and Niklas Foxeus, "'I Am the Buddha, the Buddha Is Me!' Concentration Meditation and Esoteric Modern Buddhism in Burma/Myanmar," *Numen* 63, no. 4 (2016): 441–445.
32. See Gustaaf Houtman, "Traditions of Buddhist Practice in Burma," PhD diss., London University, SOAS, 1990; and Foxeus, "Buddhist World Emperor's Mission."

33. Pranke, "On Saints and Wizards"; Alexey Kirichenko, "From Thathanadaw to Theravāda Buddhism: Constructions of Religion and Religious Identity in Nineteenth- and Early Twentieth-Century Myanmar," in *Casting Faiths: Imperialism and the Transformation of Religion in East and Southeast Asia*, ed. Thomas David DuBois (Hampshire, UK: Palgrave Macmillan, 2009), 23–39; and Erik Braun, *The Birth of Insight: Meditation, Modern Buddhism, and the Burmese Monk Ledi Sayadaw* (Chicago: University of Chicago Press, 2013).
34. The term "Theravāda" was rarely used in premodern South and Southeast Asia. It became popular after 1950 in these regions and was linked to issues of Buddhist and national identity in nation-building projects. See Todd LeRoy Perreira, "Whence Theravāda? The Modern Genealogy of an Ancient Term," in *How Theravāda Is Theravāda*, ed. Peter Skilling et al. (Chiang Mai, Thailand: Silkworm Books, 2012), 443–571; and Kirichenko, "From Thathanadaw to Theravāda Buddhism."
35. The use of the word *siddhi* for supernormal powers suggests that this teaching of supernormal powers is derived from Indian treatises (probably Hindu) where the word used in that sense is common. In Pāli texts, the word *siddhi*, "accomplished," does not refer to supernormal powers. Words for supernormal powers are *iddhi* (S. *ṛddhi*) referring to ten kinds of supernormal powers (different from the ten *siddhis*) and *abhiññā* referring to five or six supernormal cognitions.
36. A *yojana* is a measurement found in Pāli Buddhist texts. Especially U Wāyāmā Bhiwuntha (aka the seventh Kyaw Aung San Htā Hsayādaw) living in Amarapura has systematized this mantra path. He has many disciples and followers and has written many books. His followers believe that he is a human *weizzā*.
37. Hsayā U Htoun Shein, *Weizzā-pyinnyā-nidān* (Yangon, Myanmar: Thā-mā-yū-nī-yan-sa-pay, 1967), 81–83. Some informants provided a similar explanation (interviews, Mandalay, December 2006).
38. These notions and practices are similar to those described by Gordon White about what he calls "tantric alchemy." The terminology and procedures of Burmese alchemy suggests that it is derived from Indian alchemy of the Middle Ages. For instance, the idea of "killing" (S. *māraṇa*) the mercury is found in Indian alchemy (see White, *Alchemical Body*, 159, 167, 281, *passim*), and it is also common in Burmese alchemy (see Guillaume Rozenberg, "The Alchemist and His Ball," *Journal of Burma Studies* 14 (2010): 187–228).
39. Htoun Shein, *Weizzā-pyinnyā-nidān*, 80–81.
40. See Htin Aung, *Folk Elements*; Michael Mendelson, "A Messianic Buddhist Association in Upper Burma," *Bulletin of the School of Oriental and African Studies* 24, no. 3 (1961): 560–580; Michael Mendelson, "Observations on a Tour in the Region of Mount Popa, Central Burma," *France-Asie* 19 (1963): 780–807; and Thomas Patton, "In Pursuit of the Sorcerer's Power: Sacred Diagrams as Technologies of Potency," *Contemporary Buddhism* 13, no. 2 (2012): 213–231.
41. Interview by the author, Mandalay, 2007.
42. For an ethnographic study of this cult, see Guillaume Rozenberg, *The Immortals: Faces of the Incredible in Buddhist Burma*, trans. Ward Keeler (Honolulu: University of Hawai'i Press, 2015).
43. See Foxeus, "Buddhist World Emperor's Mission."
44. Foxeus, "Buddhist World Emperor's Mission"; and Rozenberg, *Immortals*.
45. See Mendelson, "Messianic Buddhist Association," 560–580; Melford E. Spiro, *Buddhism and Society: A Great Tradition and Its Burmese Vicissitudes* (Berkeley: University of California Press, [1970] 1982); Pranke, "On Becoming a Buddhist Wizard"; and Foxeus, "Buddhist World Emperor's Mission."
46. Guillaume Rozenberg, *Renunciation and Power: The Quest for Sainthood in Contemporary Burma*, trans. Jessica Hackett (New Haven, CT: Yale University Southeast Asian Studies, 2010); Foxeus, "Buddhist World Emperor's Mission"; and Foxeus, "I Am the Buddha."
47. See Patton, "Bearers of Wisdom"; Patton, "In Pursuit of the Sorcerer's Power"; and Niklas Foxeus, "Mimicking the State: Royal, Nationalist and Militant Ideology in a New Buddhist Movement in

Burma/Myanmar," *Bijdragen tot de Taal-, Land- en Volkenkunde/Journal of the Humanities and Social Sciences of Southeast Asia* 172, no. 2–3 (2016): 197–224.

48. Braun, *Birth of Insight*; and Alicia Turner, *Saving Buddhism: Moral Community and the Impermanence of Colonial Religion* (Honolulu: Hawai'i University Press, 2014).
49. Donald Eugene Smith, *Religion and Politics in Burma* (Princeton, NJ: Princeton University Press, 1965); Michael Mendelson, *Sangha and State in Burma: A Study of Monastic Sectarianism and Leadership*, ed. John P. Ferguson (Ithaca, NY: Cornell University Press, 1975); and Gustaaf Houtman, *Mental Culture in Burmese Crisis Politics: Aung San Suu Kyi and the National League for Democracy* (Tokyo: Tokyo University of Foreign Studies, 1999).
50. Ledī Hsayādaw, *Weizzā-megga-dīpanī-paung-khyoup*, Vol. 2 (Yangon, Myanmar: Thāthanā-yay-usī-hṭāna, [1898] 1985), 261–263.
51. See also Pranke, "On Saints and Wizards."
52. Pranke, "On Becoming a Buddhist Wizard"; and Pranke, "On Saints and Wizards," 480.
53. In many books and manuals from esoteric congregations from the 1940s to the 1970s that I have examined, the esoteric *weizzā* practices are presented within this scheme.
54. See Ferguson and Mendelson, "Masters of the Buddhist Occult," 62.
55. See Juliane Schober, "The Path to Buddhahood: The Spiritual Mission and Social Organization of Mysticism in Contemporary Burma," *Crossroads* 4, no. 1 (1988): 13–30; Juliane Schober, "Paths to Enlightenment: Theravāda Buddhism in Upper Burma," PhD diss., University of Illinois, 1989; Pranke, "On Becoming a Buddhist Wizard"; Foxeus, "Buddhist World Emperor's Mission"; and Pranke, "I Am the Buddha."
56. Foxeus, "Buddhist World Emperor's Mission"; and Pranke, "I Am the Buddha."
57. The narratives of the ten *bodhisattas* who are future buddhas is derived from the late medieval Pāli treatise *Dasabodhisattuppattikathā*. See H. Saddhatissa, trans., *The Birth-Stories of the Ten Bodhisattas and the Dasabodhisattuppattikathā* (London: The Pali Text Society, 1975).
58. See Mendelson, "Messianic Buddhist Association"; Foxeus, "Mimicking the State"; and Foxeus, "Buddhist World Emperor's Mission."
59. See Jeffrey Samuels, "The Bodhisattva Ideal in Theravāda Buddhist Theory and Practice: A Reevaluation of the Bodhisattva-Sravaka Opposition," *Philosophy East and West* 47, no. 3 (1997): 399–415; Foxeus, "Buddhist World Emperor's Mission"; and Foxeus, "I Am the Buddha."
60. Foxeus, "I Am the Buddha"; and Spiro, *Buddhism and Society*.
61. Michael Mendelson, "The King of the Weaving Mountain," *Journal of the Royal Central Asian Society* 48, no. 3–4 (1961): 229–237; Mendelson, "Messianic Buddhist Association"; Michael Mendelson, "The Uses of Religious Skepticism in Modern Burma," *Diogenes* 11, no. 41 (1963): 94–116; Mendelson, "Observations on a Tour"; and Ferguson and Mendelson, "Masters of the Buddhist Occult."
62. See also Bénédicte Brac de la Perrière, "Spirits versus Weikza: Two Competing Ways of Mediation," *Journal of Burma Studies* 16, no. 2 (2012): 149–179; and Patton, "Bearers of Wisdom."
63. See Niklas Foxeus, "Possessed for Success: Prosperity Buddhism and the Cult of the Guardians of the Treasure Trove in Upper Burma," *Contemporary Buddhism* 18, no. 1 (2017): 108–139.
64. See Ioan M. Lewis, *Ecstatic Religion: A Study of Shamanism and Spirit Possession*, 3rd ed. (London: Routledge, [1971] 2003); and Meredith McGuire, *Lived Religion: Faith and Practice in Everyday Life* (Oxford: Oxford University Press, 2008).
65. See also Ferguson and Mendelson, "Masters of the Buddhist Occult"; and Rozenberg, *Renunciation and Power*.
66. That observation was made by the author during fieldwork in Burma; see also Brac de la Perrière, "Spirits versus Weikza," 175.
67. See Patton, "Bearers of Wisdom."

68. See Turner, *Saving Buddhism*.
69. See Foxeus, "Buddhist World Emperor's Mission"; and Foxeus, "Mimicking the State."
70. See Louis Golomb, "The Relativity of Magical Malevolence in Urban Thailand," in *Understanding Witchcraft and Sorcery in Southeast Asia*, ed. C. W. Watson and Roy Ellen (Honolulu: University of Hawai'i Press, 1993), 27–45.
71. See Keiko Tosa, "A Consideration of Weikza Belief in Burma: The Meaning of Làwki and Làwkoktara for the Gaing," *Mizokugaku Kenkyu* 61, no. 2 (1996): 215–242.
72. If clients are freed from afflictions, they are better equipped to practice Buddhism and advance on the Buddhist path.
73. See Foxeus, "Buddhist World Emperor's Mission"; and Guillaume Rozenberg, "Powerful yet Powerless, Powerless yet Powerful: The Burmese Exorcist," *Journal of Burma Studies* 16, no. 2 (2012): 251–282.
74. See the manuscript Cod.birm. 286, Cod.sim. 324, Bayerische Staatsbibliothek.
75. See Foxeus, "Buddhist World Emperor's Mission."
76. It has twenty-five buildings, and a few monasteries, as well as informal centers in the private homes of members (fieldwork, Mandalay and Yangon, 2007 and 2008).
77. Foxeus, "Buddhist World Emperor's Mission"; and Foxeus, "Mimicking the State."
78. Examples of such loose networks include Shwe Yin Kyaw Gain (see Rozenberg, "Powerful yet Powerless") and Manaw-seittouppād Gain-daw-gyī. See Bénédicte Brac de la Perrière, "Ritual Tattooing and the Creation of New Buddhist Identities: An Inquiry into the Initiation Process in a Burmese Organization of Exorcists," *Religion and Society* 8, no. 1 (2017): 129–144; and Tosa, "Consideration of Weikza Belief in Burma."
79. The number of initiation grades vary among the congregations. Shway Yin Kyaw Gain had nine grades and the Ariyā-Weizzā Organization had six (Foxeus, "Buddhist World Emperor's Mission"; and Rozenberg, "Powerful yet Powerless"). For Mano-seittouppād Gain, see Brac de la Perrière, "Ritual Tattooing and the Creation of New Buddhist Identities." This practice may have been influenced by the Freemasons, Golden Dawn, and other esoteric groups that were established in Yangon during the colonial period.
80. See Houtman, "Traditions of Buddhist Practice"; and Houtman, *Mental Culture*.
81. For examples of cult groups, see Rozenberg, *Immortals*; and Brac de la Perrière, "Spirits versus Weikza."
82. One example of such a cult group is that of Bha Bha Min, who had a large compound at Yankin Hill outside Mandalay, and attracted many followers (see Schober, "Paths to Enlightenment"). When I was there in 2005–2006, after he had passed away, the area was deserted, and many buildings had become dilapidated.
83. The word *dhāt* (P. *dhātu*) refers to the four elements, the properties of these elements, or it can mean "essence." In the context of *weizzā* cults, the word refers to the power or energy of *weizzā*s through which they can possess or enter human beings, for instance, through mediums. That is a form of possession called *dhāt-sī*, the "power [of the *weizzā*] rides" a human being or "flows" into him/her. It is not the *weizzā* himself that enters the human being but his *dhāt* "power" or "energy." For a detailed analysis of these words and possession practices, see Brac de La Perrière, "Spirits versus Weikza"; Patton, "Bearers of Wisdom," 61–72; Rozenberg, *Immortals*; and Foxeus, "Buddhist World Emperor's Mission."
84. For more on mediums and encounters with *weizzā*s, see Patton, "Bearers of Wisdom"; Rozenberg, *Immortals*; and Brac de la Perrière, "Spirits versus Weikza." For an analysis of the difference between this Buddhist form of possession and that of the cult of the Thirty-Seven Lords, see Brac de la Perrière, "Spirits versus Weikza."
85. Phyllis Granoff, "The Ambiguity of Miracles: Buddhist Understandings of Supernatural Power," *East and West* 46, no. 1–2 (1996): 79–96; for Burma, see especially Rozenberg, *Immortals*.
86. See Rozenberg, *Power and Renunciation*; Rozenberg, *Immortals*; Foxeus, "Buddhist World Emperor's Mission"; and Foxeus, "Mimicking the State."

87. Interviews by the author, Mandalay, 2005–2007.
88. The best examples of supramundane esoteric congregations are the Manaw-mayeiddhi Weizzādhour Gain and the Ariyā-Weizzā Organization. See Tosa, "Consideration of Weikza Belief in Burma"; Foxeus, "Buddhist World Emperor's Mission"; and Foxeus, "I Am the Buddha."
89. For instance, see Mendelson, "King of the Weaving Mountain"; Mendelson, "Messianic Buddhist Association"; Mendelson, *Sangha and State in Burma*; Susanne Prager, "The Coming of the 'Future King': Burmese *Minlaung* Expectations before and during the Second World War," *Journal of Burma Studies* 8 (2003): 1–32; and E. Sarkisyanz, *Buddhist Backgrounds of the Burmese Revolution* (The Hague: Martinus Nijhoff, 1965). For more on this issue, see Foxeus, "The World Emperor's Battle against the Evil Forces," *Journal of Burma Studies* 16, no. 2 (2012): 213–250; Foxeus, "Buddhist World Emperor's Mission"; and Patricia Herbert, "The Hsaya San Rebellion (1930–1932): Reappraised," *Centre of Southeast Asian Studies*, Working Papers No. 27 (1982): 1–16.
90. A frequently cited example of a militant *weizzā* group during the colonial period is Saya San and his Galon Army, the instigator of the "Saya San rebellion" (1930–1932) (see Mendelson, *Sangha and State in Burma*; Mendelson, "Messianic Buddhist Association"; and Mendelson, "King of the Weaving Mountain." However, in the scanty extant documentation of this rebellion, there seems to be nothing that confirms his alleged connection to the *weizzā* path. In his famous rebel oath, only a variety of local *nat* spirits and the Thirty-Seven Lords (*nats*) were invoked to protect Buddhism (see C. V. Warren, *Burmese Interlude* [London: Skeffington & Son, 1937], 92–94). In the early 1970s, Herbert ("The Hsaya San Rebellion") interviewed people who had participated in the Saya San rebellion. None of them saw any connection between the Saya San rebellion, and *weizzā* notions and practices (see also Ferguson and Mendelson, "Masters of the Buddhist Occult"; and Foxeus, "Buddhist World Emperor's Mission").
91. For examples, see Mendelson, "Messianic Buddhist Association," 573; Foxeus, "Buddhist World Emperor's Mission"; Foxeus, "Mimicking the State"; and Foxeus, "World Emperor's Battle."
92. Ba Maw, *Breakthrough in Burma: Memoirs of a Revolution, 1939–1946* (New Haven, CT: Yale University Press, 1968); Houtman, *Mental Culture*; and Foxeus, "Buddhist World Emperor's Mission."
93. Maw, *Breakthrough*; and Houtman, *Mental Culture*.
94. Maw, *Breakthrough*, 92–94.
95. Maung Htin Aung, *A History of Burma* (New York: Columbia University Press, 1967), 214, 221; and Aurore Candier, "Imagination and Knowledge: Some Comments on Rumours in the Mid-Nineteenth Century Konbaung Court," in *Traditions of Knowledge in Southeast Asia*, Part 1 (Yangon, Myanmar: Myanmar Historical Commission, 2004), 165–191.
96. See Ferguson and Mendelson, "Masters of the Buddhist Occult"; and Foxeus, "Buddhist World Emperor's Mission."
97. The first rebellion took place in 1839 and several more transpired after the whole of Burma was annexed in 1885–1886 (see Candier, "Imagination and Knowledge"; and Htin Aung, *History of Burma*).
98. Among political leaders identified with Sekyā Min were Saya San and General Aung San. The latter has been regarded as the father of Burma's army and nation. In the postindependence period, some held Prime Minister U Nu to be Sekyā Min (see Sarkisyanz, *Buddhist Backgrounds*, 161, 178; and Houtman, *Mental Culture*, 41).
99. Foxeus, "Buddhist World Emperor's Mission"; and Ferguson and Mendelson, "Masters of the Buddhist Occult."
100. U Nyāna, *Bho-bho-aung-hnin-hic-ta-lā* (Yangon, Myanmar: Lawkadhan Press, 1938).
101. See Sarkisyanz, *Buddhist Backgrounds*; and Foxeus, "Buddhist World Emperor's Mission."
102. See Sarkisyanz, *Buddhist Backgrounds*; and George D. Bond, *The Buddhist Revival in Sri Lanka: Religious Tradition, Reinterpretation and Response* (Columbia: University of South Carolina Press, 1988).

103. See Smith, *Religion and Politics*; and Mendelson, *Sangha and State in Burma.*
104. See Foxeus, "Buddhist World Emperor's Mission"; Foxeus, "Mimicking the State"; and Patton, "Bearers of Wisdom."
105. Foxeus, "Buddhist World Emperor's Mission"; and Foxeus, "Mimicking the State."
106. See Houtman, "Traditions of Buddhist Practice"; Pranke, "On Saints and Wizards"; Foxeus, "Buddhist World Emperor's Mission"; and Foxeus, "I Am the Buddha."
107. Foxeus, "Buddhist World Emperor's Mission."
108. Houtman, *Mental Culture*; Pranke, "On Saints and Wizards"; and Foxeus, "I Am the Buddha."
109. Mendelson, "King of the Weaving Mountain"; Mendelson, "Messianic Buddhist Association"; Mendelson, "Observations on a Tour"; and Foxeus, "Buddhist World Emperor's Mission."
110. Foxeus, "Buddhist World Emperor's Mission"; and Foxeus, "Mimicking the State."
111. Foxeus, "Buddhist World Emperor's Mission"; Foxeus, "World Emperor's Battle"; and Foxeus, "Mimicking the State."
112. Foxeus, "Buddhist World Emperor's Mission."
113. Interviews by the author, Mandalay area, December 2014. For an intriguing example from the late 1950s of how *weizzās*, gods (P. *deva*), and spirits intermingle in the political imagination, see Mendelson, "Messianic Buddhist Association," 573–574.
114. Tin Maung Maung Than, "*Sangha* Reforms and Renewal of Sasana in Myanmar: Historical Trends and Contemporary Practice," in *Buddhist Trends in Southeast Asia*, ed. Trevor Ling (Singapore: Institute of Southeast Asian Studies, 1993), 7–63; Juliane Schober, *Modern Buddhist Conjunctures in Myanmar: Cultural Narratives, Colonial Legacies, and Civil Society* (Honolulu: University of Hawai'i Press, 2011); Foxeus, "Mimicking the State"; and Foxeus, "I Am the Buddha."
115. Maung Than, "*Sangha* Reforms"; Schober, "Modern Buddhist Conjunctures"; Tosa, "Consideration of Weikza Belief in Burma"; Pranke, "On Saints and Wizards"; Foxeus, "Buddhist World Emperor's Mission"; Foxeus, "I Am the Buddha"; Foxeus, "Mimicking the State"; and Patton, "Bearers of Wisdom."
116. Foxeus, "Mimicking the State"; and Foxeus, "Buddhist World Emperor's Mission."
117. Tosa, "Consideration of Weikza Belief in Burma"; Pranke, "On Saints and Wizards"; and Foxeus, "Buddhist World Emperor's Mission."
118. Foxeus, "Buddhist World Emperor's Mission"; and Foxeus, "Mimicking the State."
119. See Niklas Foxeus, "Spirits, Mortal Dread, and Ontological Security: Prosperity and Saving Buddhism in Burma/Myanmar," *Journal of the American Academy of Religion* 86, no. 4 (2018): 1107–1147; and Foxeus, "Possessed for Success."
120. Foxeus, "Spirits, Mortal Dread"; Foxeus, "Possessed for Success"; Brac de la Perrière, "Spirits versus Weikza"; and Bénédicte Brac de la Perrière, "Being a Spirit Medium in Contemporary Burma," in *Engaging the Spirit World: Popular Beliefs and Practices in Modern Southeast Asia*, ed. Kirsten W. Endres and Andrea Lauser (New York: Berghahn Books, 2011), 163–183.
121. For a comprehensive overview of the literature on the *weizzā* phenomenon in Burma, see Foxeus, "Vidyādhara."
122. Mendelson, "Messianic Buddhist Association."
123. Spiro, *Buddhism and Society.*
124. Schober, "Paths to Enlightenment"; and Schober, "Path to Buddhahood."
125. Rozenberg, *Immortals.*
126. Foxeus, "Buddhist World Emperor's Mission"; Foxeus, "World Emperor's Battle"; Foxeus, "I Am the Buddha"; and Foxeus, "Mimicking the State."
127. Mendelson, "King of the Weaving Mountain"; Mendelson, "Messianic Buddhist Association"; Mendelson, "Observations on a Tour"; and Mendelson, "Uses of Religious Skepticism."

128. Stanley Jeyaraja Tambiah, *Buddhism and the Spirit Cults in North-East Thailand* (London: Cambridge University Press, 1970), 337–340.
129. Melford E. Spiro, *Burmese Supernaturalism*, exp. ed. (New Brunswick, NJ: Transaction, [1967] 1996); and Spiro, *Buddhism and Society*.
130. Brac de la Perrière, "Spirits versus Weikza."
131. Pranke, "On Becoming a Buddhist Wizard"; and Pranke, "On Saints and Wizards."
132. Tosa, "Consideration of Weikza Belief in Burma."
133. Houtman, "Traditions of Buddhist Practice."
134. Pranke, "On Saints and Wizards."
135. Foxeus, "I Am the Buddha."
136. Patton, "In Pursuit of the Sorcerer's Power."

Niklas Foxeus

C

CANDRAKĪRTI'S MIDDLE WAY PHILOSOPHY

CANDRAKĪRTI'S LITERARY AMBITIONS

Candrakīrti's textual output focuses on the works of the two figures held to be the founders of the Madhyamaka tradition, Nāgārjuna and Āryadeva. The great majority of his literary output takes the form of commentaries on their texts. This is how philosophy works in the Buddhist, and broader Indian, tradition: a commentary offers a spelling out of what the "root text" truly means and yet serves as a vehicle for doctrinal and philosophical innovation that takes the guise of venerated tradition. Candrakīrti wrote commentaries on three of Nāgārjuna's works—the *Fundamental Stanzas on the Middle Way* (*Mūlamadhyamakakārikās*), *Sixty Stanzas on Reasoning* (*Yuktiṣaṣṭikā*), and *Seventy Stanzas on Emptiness* (*Śūnyatāsaptati*)—and Āryadeva's major work, the *Four Hundred Stanzas* (*Catuḥśataka*). His is the only known Indian commentary (*vṛtti*) on *Sixty Stanzas on Reasoning* and, other than Nāgārjuna's autocommentary, the only Indian commentary on *Seventy Stanzas on Emptiness* until Parahitabhadra's in the 11th century. His *Clear Words* (*Prasannapadā*) is the only commentary on the *Fundamental Stanzas on the Middle Way* to survive in its entirety in Sanskrit, a fact that contributed to its importance in the eyes of Western interpreters of Madhyamaka and may also indicate its centrality to at least some Mādhyamikas who continued to preserve and copy it. *Clear Words* spends ample space arguing against rival interpreters of Madhyamaka as well as against the founder of the Buddhist epistemological tradition, Dignāga. Further, Candrakīrti's commentary to Āryadeva's *Four Hundred Stanzas* takes to task Dharmapāla's Yogācāra interpretation of the second half of that work. Candrakīrti's major independent treatise, *Entrance to the Middle Way* (*Madhyamakāvatāra*), and its autocommentary (*bhāṣyā*) likewise argue at length against the Yogācāra position (Vasubandhu, Dignāga, and Dharmapāla are singled out for criticism at the text's conclusion), in addition to holding forth on a range of central Madhyamaka issues. One can fairly say, then, that Candrakīrti worked to define a Madhyamaka textual corpus and to distinguish it from the Yogācāra school and the epistemological tradition.

Further, Candrakīrti's corpus reveals a deep concern with distinguishing a Madhyamaka orientation for the Mahāyāna Buddhist path. As the full title of Āryadeva's work reveals—*Four Hundred Stanzas on the Bodhisattva's Contemplative Cultivations* (*Bodhisattvayogācāraśāstracatuḥśataka*)—Candrakīrti did not initiate this process (depending on just which of the many texts attributed to Nāgārjuna one takes as authentic, one might argue that he began this endeavor). His commentary to Āryadeva and his major independent treatise, *Entrance to the Middle Way*, both take the bodhisattva path as their narrative structure, with the latter using the bodhisattva's ten "stages" (*bhūmi*) as chapters. Candrakīrti's interpretation of the central Madhyamaka doctrine of emptiness presents difficult problems for the Mahāyāna path, which he is only partially able to resolve. His Tibetan interpreters offer a range of solutions, advocating for his version of emptiness as definitive and essential to the completion of the bodhisattva path.

CANDRAKĪRTI'S MADHYAMAKA

Candrakīrti's *Entrance to the Middle Way* serves as a good introduction to his central Madhyamaka concerns; indeed, *-avatāra* could just as fairly be translated "Introduction," while the title's *Madhyamaka-* is frequently read as referring to Nāgārjuna's *Fundamental Stanzas on the Middle Way* (Candrakīrti often refers to Nāgārjuna's text simply as *Madhyamaka* or *Madhyamaka Treatise* [śāstra]). *Entrance to the Middle Way* may have been Candrakīrti's first major composition. It certainly predates his *Clear Words* and his commentary to the *Four Hundred Stanzas*, as he refers to this work in both those commentaries. The text's structure of the ten "stages" of the bodhisattva path gains support from the autocommentary, which refers throughout to the *Sutra on the Ten Stages* (*Daśabhūmikasūtra*). Each of the first six stages corresponds to mastery of a "perfection" (*pāramitā*), which Candrakīrti discusses in the first six chapters of his work. Some of these chapters are very short: the fourth chapter, on the perfection of effort (*vīrya*), is only two stanzas, while the fifth on meditation (*dhyāna*) contains only one stanza. The first five chapters offer a general Mahāyāna presentation of the bodhisattva's progress. The sixth chapter, on the perfection of wisdom (*prajñā*), is by far the longest (226 stanzas), as Candrakīrti takes great care to explain his Madhyamaka view of the object of wisdom, emptiness.

Entrance to the Middle Way's wisdom chapter argues first for universal emptiness and then turns to the "selflessness of persons" (*pudgalanairātmya*), a doctrine held in common with non-Mahāyāna Buddhists. The latter arguments present a sevenfold analysis of the person that will lead to realization of selflessness and liberation from samsara. Becoming a buddha, however, requires realization of emptiness, which Candrakīrti explains at length in the first half of the chapter. This half (stanzas 8–116) takes as its organizing structure Nāgārjuna's famous opening to his *Fundamental Stanzas on the Middle Way*: "Not from self, not from other, not from both, and not causelessly do any things ever, anywhere arise."[1] Candrakīrti (in his introduction to stanza VI.8) explains that Nāgārjuna begins his text by negating arising from the four alternatives (*catuṣkoti*) because understanding "non-arising" is the key to understanding all ten "samenesses" (*samatā*) of phenomena (according to the *Sutra on the Ten Stages*, non-arising is the third of the ten), which marks perfect wisdom. Candrakīrti's arguments against "arising from self"—which is Nāgārjuna's shorthand for referring to the Sāṃkhya "doctrine of effects existing [in their causes]" (*satkāryavāda*)—points out several consequences (*prasaṅga*) of this doctrine that the Sāṃkhya could not accept, including the problems that production of an effect that already exists would render production pointless or, if one understood already existent things to require further production, would make the process endless. He concludes that arising from self neither stands up to reasoning nor is accepted in the world.

Candrakīrti gives far greater attention to refuting "arising from other," as this perspective is accepted in one form or another by most Buddhists and—it would seem—is the commonsense perspective of the world. He will dismiss "arising from both [self and other]" summarily, reasoning that since "arising from self" and "arising from other" have both been defeated, "arising from both" could not possibly be. "Arising causelessly" receives a brief disproof, with Candrakīrti appealing to commonsensical notions: if things arose without cause, a farmer planting seeds could not expect any crops. He also rejects the materialist philosophy of the Cārvāka school as a form of causeless production. Candrakīrti has a broad range of concerns that constitute varieties of "arising from other." These include a lengthy argument against the Yogācāra idealist philosophy and a consideration of valid knowledge that is further fleshed out in his *Clear Words* (see "World Is Not Mind-Only" and "Authority, Knowledge, and the World"); in this section, his understanding of the "two truths" (*satyadvaya*) and his distinctive portrayal of emptiness take center stage.

Candrakīrti begins his arguments against "arising from other" by pointing out some problems with the non-Mahāyāna Abhidharma perspective on causality, in which (according to him) cause and effect are other. He points out that a proponent of this perspective would need to explain how any two things that are "other" could not equally be thought to be in a causal relationship: why would darkness not arise from flame, since darkness and light alike would be other from flame? He next considers the objection that the world understands that one thing arises from another and should be accepted as authoritative (*pramāṇa*) on the matter. His response explicates the "two truths," a central topic in Buddhist philosophy that was developed in the Abhidharma tradition but redefined by Mādhyamikas. Candrakīrti explains the two truths as two natures (*rūpa*) possessed by all entities (*bhāva*), natures that are seen respectively by false and correct vision: ignorance perceives conventional things (*saṃvṛtisatya*), while purified vision sees emptiness, the ultimate truth (*paramārthsatya*). The word "truth" (*satya*) has two senses. In English, "true" is typically predicated of statements or mental events: one makes a true statement that might express a true understanding. The Sanskrit has this sense and additionally denotes the objects of these statements and thoughts as existent (*sat*). Candrakīrti utilizes both senses in his portrayal of the two truths, as the entities that constitute conventional and ultimate truths are indexed to the types of minds that cognize them.

In his *Clear Words*, Candrakīrti explains that "conventional" (*saṃvṛti*) has three intertwined meanings: concealing (*varaṇa*), interdependent (*parasparasaṃbhavana*), and worldly conventional (*lokavyavahāra*). Although he utilizes all three, in his *Entrance to the Middle Way* explication of the two truths (oft repeated by his followers), he emphasizes the first sense. Conventional things are constituted by ordinary beings' ignorance, which thoroughly veils their minds and conceals the way things really are. This ignorance causes fabricated entities to appear to be true. One can more accurately (but less fluidly) express these as "things that are true for concealers" or "things that are true for ignorance." Candrakīrti does allow that false vision has gradations: entities perceived by those with well-functioning sense faculties are considered true within the world, while the perceptual illusions that appear to those with damaged senses and the wrong views of non-Buddhists are considered false in the world—Candrakīrti and his earliest commentators make clear that these false things fall outside "conventional truth" and instead constitute "mere conventions" (a second sense of "mere convention" will pertain to what is seen by those who know emptiness). The world may agree that some things are true and others false; yet all conventionalities are constituted by ignorance and prevent seeing the ultimate.

Ultimate (*paramārtha*) truth is the "object" of "the wisdom of purified vision." Candrakīrti explains that the ultimate surpasses ordinary beings' verbal and cognitive capacities and so can only be pointed at by way of analogy: just as the floating hairs that appear to those with the visual ailment *timira* (myodesopsia) do not appear to those with well-functioning eyes, so the fabrications that ordinary beings take as conventionally true vanish for the wise.[2] This absence is emptiness, which alone is nondeceptive (*bslu ba med pa, avisaṃvāda*). Emptiness is not really seen, but is "seen in the manner of not seeing," owing to the fact that it exceeds any form of consciousness. The absence that is emptiness is called the "highest object" (*paramārtha*), even though it is not really an object, because it is soteriologically essential: it overcomes the ignorance that binds one in cyclic existence (samsara). It is the ultimate truth not because it truly exists—emptiness itself is empty of true existence—but because those who have rooted out ignorance "see" it.

Candrakīrti's interpreters read his portrayal of emptiness in two different ways. Some take his analogy at face value: if the everyday objects that the world takes to be true are, for the realized, really like visual hallucinations, emptiness would seem to eliminate conventional things. Candrakīrti points out that when a normal sighted person tells one suffering from myodesopsia, who is busily attempting to sweep away the floating hairs, that there truly are no floating hairs present, this negation does not constitute a "deprecation" (along with "superimposition," one of the two "extremes" between which Madhyamaka presents itself as a "middle way"); the negation did not destroy the hairs—they never existed to begin with. And so, the elimination of conventionalities from the visual field of a realized being likewise would not destroy a previously existing world, but would only make clear what was always the case. However, Candrakīrti offers some evidence for those who read him as eliminating not conventional entities but an erroneous aspect of those things that ordinary people falsely believe them to have. In his discussion of the *timira* analogy, Candrakīrti explains that those who suffer from the disease of ignorance perceive a "self-nature" (*rang gi ngo bo*) of things like the five aggregates (*skandha*) and the six sense spheres (*ayatana*), which is the conventional nature of those things, suggesting that emptiness overcomes the perception of this false nature but leaves ordinary things unharmed.

The less austere interpretation of Candrakīrti's emptiness faces a significant challenge from his elaboration of the constitutive role ignorance plays in everyday experience. He distinguishes between the afflictive ignorance that binds sentient beings in cyclic existence from a "mere ignorance" that is responsible for appearances themselves. Realized beings—he lists Hearers (*śravaka*), Solitary Buddhas (*pratyekabuddha*), and Bodhisattvas—have overcome afflictive ignorance and so see conventional phenomena as being like reflections, as having a fabricated, rather than true, nature. This is the second sense in which Candrakīrti employs "mere conventions": appearances to these realized beings are not conventionally true because they know them to be false. The "mere ignorance" that perpetuates "mere conventions" will, however, be overcome by buddhas: "Due to the operation of the mere ignorance that has the character of obstructing what is to be known [that is, emptiness], [mere conventions] appear to those Āryas whose sphere of activities has appearances but do not [appear] to those lords whose sphere of activities is without appearance. For Buddhas alone, due to their being completely, manifestly awakened to all phenomena in all aspects, we assert that the movement of mind and mental factors has entirely stopped" (*Madhyamakāvatārabhāṣyā* ad stanza VI.28).

Buddhas eliminate all forms of ignorance and, consequently, all appearances. Candrakīrti's stark vision of the awakened state strongly suggests that emptiness eradicates not simply an aspect of ordinary entities but those entities themselves.

Candrakīrti's version of emptiness poses significant problems for his model of spiritual progress, as his claim of mental cessation shows. If a subtle form of ignorance is responsible for all appearances, Candrakīrti would have it that consciousness itself is imbued with it: overcoming ignorance entails the elimination of mind itself. All Buddhists understand ignorance to be the central problem that leads to lifetimes of suffering; all Mādhyamikas understand that ignorance to perceive an "intrinsic nature" of things, whereas things are empty of nature. The questions here concern what remains following the negation of intrinsic nature (a reformed conventional world or a simple absence) and whether consciousness can be rehabilitated. If consciousness can be cleansed of its propensity to superimpose real natures, awakening can be understood as (among other things) a purified mind. If, however, ignorance constitutes all consciousness, consciousness must—as Candrakīrti stated—cease upon awakening. Candrakīrti's model leaves a gap: how does awakening arise when consciousness has stopped?

The remaining chapters of *Entrance to the Middle Way* make clear that Candrakīrti does not discard the standard Mahāyāna vision of a Buddha. Chapters seven through ten briefly treat the final four stages of the bodhisattva's progress, covering those stages in a total of five stanzas, with an eleventh chapter devoting nine stanzas to the bodhisattva's attainment of miraculous "qualities" (*guṇa*) along the ten stages. The twelfth and final chapter offers a substantial and, for the most part, quite standard presentation of buddhahood, describing a buddha's three bodies (*kāya*) and ten powers (*bala*). Candrakīrti does, however, attempt to resolve the problem his model of mental cessation poses to the Mahāyāna vision of awakening. On one hand, he notes, "Conquerors attain omniscient wisdom in a single moment of knowledge" (in his comments to stanza XII.2) and goes on to detail a buddha's ten "wisdom powers" (*jñānabala*), describing just what each of these know in subject–object fashion (in stanzas XII.22–31). For instance, the eighth wisdom power enables a buddha to see one's own and others' past lives, which Candrakīrti explicitly speaks of as the object of this knowledge. And yet he undercuts all this seeming cognitive activity with reminders that buddhas have no mind. Addressing the question of how a buddha could know anything in the absence of consciousness, Candrakīrti explains that a buddha's knowledge is only metaphorical: when a cognition arises taking the aspect (*ākāra*) of a particular object, one says one has cognized that object; since cognition and its object are alike not produced, one can say that a buddha knows reality. A buddha's lack of mind "knows" the absence of nature that is emptiness.

Candrakīrti offers the three bodies as a solution for how a buddha continues to operate, or at least seems to ordinary beings to operate, in the world despite these absences. A buddha's collection of merit creates a "body of bliss" (saṃbhogakāya) that, from the power of both a buddha's previous vows to attain awakening for the sake of aiding all sentient beings and those sentient beings' ongoing desires to be helped, produces "emanation bodies" (*nirmaṇakāya*) that come to the assistance of others. In truth, a buddha remains in the "reality body" (dharmakāya): "This body having a nature of wisdom, having burned all the dry kindling of objects of knowledge, is non-produced due to the non-production of objects of knowledge" (autocommentary to stanza XII.8). The reality body, then, represents the absence of all cognition and cognitive objects. It cannot be known, as mind has stopped. If it is a buddha's true "state," how exactly does it come to be? Candrakīrti cryptically tells the reader (in stanza XII.8), "Since mind has stopped, it is realized by the body."[3] Jayānanda (fl. 12th century), the only known Indic commentator on *Entrance to the Middle Way*, writing hundreds of years after Candrakīrti and at a great distance from South Asia in the Tangut kingdom, understands this as a new kind of subject–object relationship: it is the enjoyment body that realizes the reality body. The enjoyment body, which itself arises from a bodhisattva's collection of merit, serves as a new kind of "subject" that does not know its object in dualistic fashion as consciousness would; that "object," the culmination of a bodhisattva's wisdom, is (for Jayānanda) "the essence of reality, having the nature of naturelessness." Whatever one makes of Jayānanda's fidelity to Candrakīrti's text, one must laud his attempt: Candrakīrti's model of mental cessation must somehow be reconciled with Mahāyāna awakening.

THE WORLD IS NOT MIND-ONLY

Candrakīrti's chief target in his *Entrance to the Middle Way*'s arguments against "arising from other" is the Mahāyāna Buddhist Yogācāra ("Yogic Practice") school, often labeled the "Mind-Only" (*cittamātra*) or "Percept-Only" (*vijñaptimātra*) school owing to its signature teaching that seemingly physical objects external to cognition do not exist. Although scholarly debate continues over whether and which proponents of this school actually argued for a radical idealism, Candrakīrti's arguments against it assume this view, as he makes clear in his presentation of the opponent's opening gambit (in stanza VI.45d): "The triple world is understood to be only consciousness." Candrakīrti considers the common Yogācāra dream analogy, which supporters use to suggest how cognition can function without an object external to it: as fully mental dreams appear to a dreamer to have objects external to cognition (and, as Vasubandhu notes in his *Twenty Stanzas* [*Viṃśatikākārikā*], can even have seemingly physical effects, as in the case of nocturnal emission), so, too, waking cognition appears to be of external objects but is in fact fully explained by the workings of consciousness. Candrakīrti offers a very different interpretation of the relevance of dreams to waking life, arguing that just as (for his opponent) a dream cognition has no external object, so (for him) a waking cognition—as well as the sense faculty and object that produced it—is false (*alīka*). He compares a dreamer to his trusty *timira*-sufferer: when cured of an eye affliction, one no longer sees floating hairs; when awoken, a dream vanishes; so, too, all waking life—upon waking from the sleep of ignorance, ordinary cognitions vanish. Candrakīrti does not here deny the absence of external objects, but extends this absence to sense organs and cognition. His approach here would allow later interpreters to read a kind of progression of philosophical views, in which Yogācāra arguments teach the bodhisattva the unreality of objects external to cognition, upon which Madhyamaka teaches the unreality of mind itself. Although without quite this sense of progression, Candrakīrti states (in stanza VI.71d), "Just as objects of cognition do not exist, so it is with mind."

Among his arguments against Yogācāra, Candrakīrti takes up the topic of "reflexive awareness" (*svasaṃvedana* or *svasaṃvitti*), a central piece of Dignāga's (*c.* 480–540) epistemology that explains how a moment of cognition could be established in the absence of an external object. Candrakīrti and his Buddhist interlocutors commonly assume that to exist is to be cognized—if something is not cognized, how would one know that it exists? What, then, cognizes a cognition that—the opponent claims—arises in the absence of an object? For Yogācāra, this would be one function of "reflexive awareness": a cognition knows itself. Candrakīrti's arguments against this possibility largely take a commonsensical perspective. Nowhere does one see an agent, an object, and an action being identical: a carpenter, wood, and cutting are obviously different. More simply, a sword cannot cut itself, fire does not burn itself, an eye cannot see itself. Candrakīrti concludes that the nonsensical nature of his opponents' proposed "reflexive awareness" leaves them without any way to prove the existence of a cognition arising without an external object. Where Candrakīrti initially takes the Yogācāra rejection of external objects even further, rejecting even mind, here he endorses the worldly perspective of distinct subjects and objects, valid only in the world. The later Mādhyamika Śāntarakṣita (725–788) would substantially revise Dignāga's conception of reflexive awareness and incorporate it in his Madhyamaka view.

Having to his satisfaction shown that "Mind-Only" accounts for neither ultimate truth nor the conventional world, all that remains is for Candrakīrti to explain why some Buddhist sutras—including the *Sutra on the Ten Stages* and the *Descent to Laṅka Sutra* (*Laṅkāvatārasūtra*)—do, in fact, teach it. He tells the reader that the Buddha intended to counter the false view that a permanent self (*nityātma*) or "person" (*pudgala*) serves as the agent of actions; instead, "mind alone" serves as the agent. The buddha underscored the mind's preeminent role in directing one's actions and the volitional nature of karma—given that (according to Buddhists) karma creates worlds and is determined by one's volition, mind can be considered to create the universe. Candrakīrti is quick to point out that this does not mean that physical matter does not exist; it simply is not an agent of action. One must either accept the nonexistence of both mind and external objects, in keeping with the Perfection of Wisdom Sutras, or accept the existence of them both, in accordance with Abhidharma and the world. Any sutra that speaks to the sole existence of mind cannot be taken as definitive (*nītārtha*), but must instead be read as "leading" (*neyārtha*) disciples toward a better view.

AUTHORITY, KNOWLEDGE, AND THE WORLD

Candrakīrti launched his discussion of the two truths in answer to the claim that the world, whose authority should be acknowledged, knows that one thing is produced from another; further, he offers "worldly convention" as one meaning of "conventional" (*saṃvṛti*). These points intertwine to create what one contemporary interpreter labels "framework relativity," in which conventional truths are "true" only within the framework of the world.[4] One outflow of this is that conventional truths are determined by those with well-functioning senses, while the hallucinations of those with defective senses are considered false within the worldly framework. One might expect, then, that Candrakīrti would accept his opponent's point that "production from other" is the way of the world—that it is conventionally true. However, he claims (in stanza VI.32) that production from other is not accepted even in the world, where people simply make statements such as "I produced this child" or "I planted that tree." Although these might seem to be cases of production from other, Candrakīrti supports his contention by telling the reader that "worldly conventional truths" are not to be examined. His point seems to be that any analysis of "from self" or "from other" would move consideration of causality beyond worldly conventions, into the realm of ultimate analysis, and that the world remains content to rest on superficial claims without considering notions like "same" and "different."

Candrakīrti additionally tells the reader that the world is not authoritative (*pramāṇa*), that an ignorant person (*mūḍha*) cannot be authoritative, and consequently, the claims of the world have no bearing on reality. Again, worldly cognition is shot through with ignorance; although that ignorance comes in gradations—enabling those with good senses to declare that some things (visual hallucinations, rival philosophical claims) are false—no worldly cognition can be trusted in matters of ultimate significance. Worldly claims of production have no bearing on the Madhyamaka denial of production in any of the four possible ways, just as the claim of one suffering from *timira* to see floating hairs carries no weight for those with good vision. Instead, the wise who see emptiness are to be considered authoritative. Candrakīrti holds up Nāgārjuna as the chief exemplar (one suspects that Candrakīrti wants his reader to hold *him* as trustworthy).

Candrakīrti's support of Nāgārjuna's authority and denial of the world's own in *Entrance to the Middle Way* can well be read alongside his later *Clear Words* rejection of Dignāga's system of "valid cognition," a more common translation of *pramāṇa*. Dignāga, and all Buddhists following him, famously accepted only two forms of valid cognition, perception (*pratyakṣa*) and inference (*anumāna*). Each knows a specific kind of object: perception knows "particular characters" (*svalakṣaṇa*), the momentary sense data of the cause-and-effect world; inference knows "general characters" (*sāmānyalakṣaṇa*), the changeless images assembled from sense data that one may fairly call "concepts." Perception is valid due to being reliably caused by its momentary objects. Unlike other concepts one might have, whether it be the memory of an elephant one once saw or the imagination of a pink elephant, inference provides trustworthy knowledge in virtue of the manner of its formation; it is reasoned knowledge that arises from particular relationships between a given locus, a property of that locus that will serve as "reason," and a property of that locus that can be inferred from the reason. The classical Indian example is "On a distant hill (the locus), there is fire (the inferred property) because there is smoke (the reason property)." The three factors that guarantee valid inferential cognition are

(a) the reason being a property of the locus (smoke is a property of the distant hill); (b) the reason entailing the inferred property (wherever there is smoke, there is fire); and (c) the negative of the inferred property entailing the negative of the reason property (wherever there is no fire, there is no smoke).

Candrakīrti launches a broad attack on Dignāga's epistemology, objecting both to the substance–property relationship he detects in it and to its foundationalist tendency, and a more targeted rejection of the applicability of his inferential schema to Madhyamaka emptiness. If, as Dignāga claims, the object of perception is the "particular character" and the object of inference is the "general character," this suggests that these must be characters, or properties, of something. Candrakīrti proceeds to deny any permutation of the character–characterized (property–substance) relationship, pointing to the fault that all ways of describing such a relationship must present "character" and "characterized" as inherently other, rather than as dependently arisen phenomena. Further, Dignāga's two forms of valid cognition position perception and inference as the ultimate arbiters of truth and place the objects of perception, momentary discreet sense data, as the building blocks of the world. In Candrakīrti's analysis, Dignāga's system represents a foundationalist epistemology and a foundationalist metaphysics, both of which he sees as running counter to the emptiness of all things.[5]

After dispensing with Dignāga's epistemology, Candrakīrti makes the surprising assertion that perception, inference, testimony (*āgama*), and comparison (*upamāna*) are the means by which "the world knows things" (*lokasyārthādhigama*). This fourfold model of valid cognition can be found in the Sarvāstivāda Abhidharma and is espoused by the Brahmanical Nyāya school. Why, after arguing against the validity of perception and inference, would Candrakīrti expand the list of valid forms of knowing? His very brief discussion of these four methods makes clear that each is simply a label for worldly practices: the form of knowing and the object known arise in mutual dependence, with only the world considering these to be valid knowledge. The world being not authoritative—one could also say the world not having valid cognition—renders Candrakīrti's admission of four forms of knowledge as nothing more than a description of what passes for knowledge among the benighted. The conclusions of these four forms of knowledge might be considered true within the framework of the world, but cannot reach the ultimate, emptiness.

FORMS OF ARGUMENT, SCHOOLS OF MADHYAMAKA

Candrakīrti frequently garners credit, along with Buddhapālita (*c.* 470–540), for founding the Prāsaṅgika ("Consequentialist") branch of Madhyamaka, which most Tibetan interpreters would regard as the highest interpretation of the Buddha's teaching, singularly offering the correct philosophical view necessary to attain nirvana. Although this attribution is certainly anachronistic, as evidenced by Candrakīrti's muted influence in his own time, his advocacy of argument by logical "consequence" (*prasaṅga*) and his denigration of inferential logic "in support of one's own" (*svatantra*) position would eventually serve as the key to dividing Madhyamaka into the Prāsaṅgika and Svātantrika subschools.

In *Entrance to the Middle Way*, Candrakīrti touched on the proper way to argue for Nāgārjuna's view of emptiness. His extensive comments in *Clear Words* to the opening stanza of Nāgārjuna's *Fundamental Stanzas on the Middle Way* serve as the locus classicus for this issue and engage the earlier commentators, Buddhapālita and Bhāviveka (*c.* 500–570), at length. In support of Nāgārjuna's claim that things do not arise from self, Buddhapālita offered two absurd consequences (*prasaṅga*) that would eventuate from "arising from self": production would be senseless—if a thing existed already, there would be no point in it producing itself again; and production would be endless inasmuch as a thing that could produce itself would never cease producing itself.[6] These absurd consequences intend to force the opponent to give up the false view of "arising from self" by pointing out the logical problems the view entails. Bhāviveka, in his *Lamp for Wisdom* (*Prajñāpradīpa*), critiqued Buddhapālita's argument, faulting it for "not stating a reason and example." One can certainly render Buddhapālita's words as reasons for Nāgārjuna's denial of arising from self; Bhāviveka, however, here alludes to Dignāga's formulation of "inference for the sake of others" (*parārthānumāna*), in which a logical reason must be a property of the inferential subject (*pakṣadharmatā*) and an example demonstrating the logical entailments between the reason and property predicated of that subject must be given. Bhāviveka provides his own inference, which demonstrates these procedures: "Ultimately, the inner sense spheres do not arise from self because they exist, like consciousness (*caitanya*)." The reason, "exist," is a property of the subject, the inner sense spheres (put more simply, both parties agree that "the inner sense spheres exist"). Bhāviveka's example of an existent that entails "not arising from self" is valid for both the Buddhist and the Sāṃkhya opponent: for the Buddhist, a moment of consciousness arises from a previous moment of consciousness, as well as from its object, neither of which are "self"; for Sāṃkhya, *caitanya* is the nature of *puruṣa*, the always existent "spirit" or "self," and so does not require "arising from self." Bhāviveka's statement provides a reason and example that are valid both for the opponent—the opponent would have to accept them—and for himself. In contrast, in a simplified version of Buddhapālita's statement, "things do not arise from self because their production would be senseless and endless," "senseless and endless production" are not properties of "things" for either party. Bhāviveka's critique of Buddhapālita revolves around the latter's failing to adopt Dignāga-style inference and, consequently, his failure to put forward an effective argument.[7]

Candrakīrti rejected Bhāviveka's insistence on Dignāga's method, labeling Bhāviveka's argument "inference in support of one's own [position]" (*svatantrānumāna*; Bhāviveka himself uses this expression a handful of times, but not in the present discussion). Explaining why this form of logic is not only unnecessary but inappropriate, he states, "It is not reasonable for Mādhyamikas themselves to compose inferences in support of one's own [position] due to not asserting other positions."[8] In the context of Nāgārjuna's opening stanza that denies arising from any of the four alternatives, Candrakīrti's implication would seem to be that if Bhāviveka wished to argue for, say, "arising from other," an inference supporting that position would be appropriate, but since Nāgārjuna rejected all four possibilities, such an inference remains out of place. The problem, of course, is that Bhāviveka did not offer an inference in support of another of the four possibilities, but in support of the denial of "arising from self." Candrakīrti, then, understands Bhāviveka to hold, problematically, the position "things (or, 'the inner sense spheres,' as an example of 'things') do not arise from self." What could be wrong with holding this position given that it seems to come directly from Nāgārjuna?

In his *Dispeller of Disputes* (*Vigrahavyāvartanī*), Nāgārjuna famously denied holding any "thesis" (*pratijñā*), a term synonymous with the "position" (*pakṣa*) Candrakīrti rejected.

Candrakīrti quotes Nāgārjuna's denial in his rejection of "inference in support of one's own [position]." So, Candrakīrti might offer a blanket statement of Madhyamaka procedure: Mādhyamikas simply do not hold any position, but merely refute their opponent's views; having no position to prove obviates an inference to prove it. However, both Bhāviveka and Candrakīrti label Nāgārjuna's rejection of the four possible manners of production "theses"; for Bhāviveka, Nāgārjuna stated the thesis of an inference, to which a commentator should provide reason and example. And so one must follow Candrakīrti's push further into the structure of Dignāga-style inference to grasp just what it is about inferential theses he finds objectionable. His objections, in turn, allow later interpreters to uncover a problem deeper than argumentative method: they see Candrakīrti criticizing Bhāviveka's understanding of emptiness and so relegate "Svātantrika Madhyamaka" (as Bhāviveka's view, in which *svatantra* inference is utilized, came to be known) to second-class status.

Candrakīrti leveled against Bhāviveka the charge of using an inference that has an "unestablished basis" (*āśrayāsiddha*), in which the predicate and reason are "based" on a subject that does not exist. This problem is well known to Buddhist logicians and must be faced whenever attempting to prove to an opponent the nonexistence of some entity the opponent accepts. A Buddhist might state, "A permanent creator god does not exist because of being unable to change." The logic here points out that "creation" implies change—bringing into existence things that once did not exist—while "permanence" implies changelessness, and so the opponent must give up the idea of a permanent creator god. The problem for the Buddhist, however, is that the reason "being unable to change" is attributed to a nonexistent entity, a permanent creator god. Does the Buddhist have to attribute existence to this god in order to speak of such a god's attributes? Buddhist logicians after Candrakīrti's time found a variety of solutions, with the most common being that it is perfectly fine to attribute *negations* as qualities of nonexistent entities—so long as the Buddhist does not make positive statements about the nonexistent "basis" of an inference, all is well. The important thing to recognize here is that Candrakīrti makes this same accusation against Bhāviveka's inferential subject, "the internal sense spheres," which, it would seem, do in fact exist. Candrakīrti explains that a Mādhyamika and non-Mādhyamika opponent will never agree on how such an inferential subject exists: for the Mādhyamika, internal sense spheres exist imputedly (*prajñaptisat*), while for the opponent, they exist substantially (*dravyasat*). If the subject is understood according to the views of one party, it will be unestablished for the other.

Dignāga stipulated that an inferential subject and reason must be established for both parties in a debate. Why not, then, acknowledge that both sides can know the subject pre-reflectively, without consideration of either side's views of *how* it is established? Candrakīrti rejects this solution, claiming that when the negation of arising is the predicate, the subject—which is constituted only by ignorance (*viparyāsa*)—"degenerates" (*pracyuti*). The negation of arising establishes the naturelessness of all phenomena, which—in Candrakīrti's interpretation—makes all phenomena like permanent creator gods. One might understand Candrakīrti here as reminding Bhāviveka of a shared Madhyamaka understanding of emptiness: as a Mādhyamika, Bhāviveka should know that any inference attempting to prove emptiness will cause the inferential subject to disappear, and so inference should not be used for this purpose. Or, one could see Candrakīrti as espousing a unique view of emptiness, one in which ordinary things are constituted only by ignorance and so vanish when realization of emptiness overcomes that ignorance. In this latter interpretation, Bhāviveka's use of inference (as well as the many Mādhyamikas who continued to employ inference to demonstrate emptiness following Candrakīrti's critique) implies a stronger conception of everyday objects and a weaker conception of emptiness: users of *svatantra* inference must, in this line of thought, falsely believe conventional truths to have some real establishment that emptiness does not negate. On this point, an argument over the proper way to argue becomes an argument over how to understand soteriologically essential emptiness.

CANDRAKĪRTI'S ASCENSION

The great significance his later interpreters, primarily in Tibet, would attribute to Candrakīrti's critique of inference—seeing in it the establishment of a lineage of Madhyamaka that alone espouses the correct view of emptiness—obscures the fact that his success in these pursuits seems to have been limited for hundreds of years. The integration of epistemological concerns within the Madhyamaka view only strengthened after his critiques of Dignāga and Bhāviveka. The dominant figures of 8th-century Indian Madhyamaka—Jñānagarbha, Śāntarakṣita, and Kamalaśīla—more closely wove Dharmakīrti's developments of Dignāga into their presentations of conventional truth and the method to cultivate inferential understanding of emptiness, all without discernable response to Candrakīrti's critiques. Further, Śāntarakṣita and Kamalaśīla adopted Yogācāra perspectives in their presentations of conventional truth, coming to be known as Yogācāra-Mādhyamikas, without answering Candrakīrti's objections to Yogācāra. Even Avalokitavrata, who wrote a massive subcommentary to Bhāviveka's *Lamp for Wisdom*, only includes Candrakīrti in a list of commentators to the *Fundamental Stanzas on the Middle Way* but does not take up any of Candrakīrti's criticisms or make any attempt to defend Bhāviveka from them. When Tibetans, working with Indian masters, translated a substantial body of Sanskrit Buddhist texts in the 8th and 9th centuries, a great number of Madhyamaka works were chosen, including those of Nāgārjuna, Buddhapālita, Bhāviveka, Jñānagarbha, Śāntarakṣita, and Kamalaśīla; only one of Candrakīrti's compositions, his commentary to *Sixty Stanzas on Reasoning*, was translated during this period (Āryadeva's *Four Hundred Stanzas* is another notable omission). In short, Candrakīrti appears to have had little impact in the two centuries after his death.

Candrakīrti's status in India rose around the year 1000 and was soon elevated in Tibet. Perhaps the earliest quotations of his work, from *Entrance to the Middle Way*, appear in Prajñākaramati's (*c.* 950–1030) commentary to Śāntideva's *Engaging the Practices of Enlightenment* (*Bodhicaryāvatāra*). Atiśa Dipaṅkaraśrījñāna (982–1054) approvingly references Candrakīrti's views, influencing a number of his Tibetan disciples in the Kadampa (*bka' gdams pa*) tradition. Most strikingly, around this same time two authors adopt Candrakīrti's name. The more important of the two wrote the influential *Illuminating Lamp* (*Pradīpoddyotana*) commentary on the *Secret Union Tantra* (*Guhyasamājatantra*) and was a key figure in the "Noble" (*ārya*) lineage of interpretation of this tantra that included a Nāgārjuna and an Āryadeva. That a tantric author would adopt the name of a Mādhyamika would seem to be in deference to that Mādhyamika's principles. In the case of Candrakīrti, it doubtlessly contributed to the rise of the Mādhyamika author from largely ignored commentator to upholder of the preeminent philosophical view. In some instances, this was a case of identity confusion: Atiśa praised Candrakīrti, calling him

Nāgārjuna's disciple, a relationship that obtained between the tantric authors, but not the Mādhyamikas; Abhayākaragupta (*c.* 1100) speaks of Candrakīrti's Madhyamaka and tantric writings as two phases of one author's works. Ratnākaraśānti (*c.* 1000), however, distinguished these two Candrakīrtis, praising the tantric author and criticizing the Mādhyamika. A third Candrakīrti in the 11th century wrote the brief *Entrance to Middle Way Wisdom* (*Madhyamakaprajñāvatāra*). Collectively, these figures evince a resurgence of interest in the Mādhyamika author.

Renewed Indian attention to Candrakīrti contributed to his rise in Tibet, as Tibetan translators and Indian paṇḍits again journeyed across the Himalayas. Atiśa initiated the Tibetan translation of the stanzas of (but seemingly not the autocommentary to) *Entrance to the Middle Way* that Naktso Lotsawa Tsültrim Gyelwa (*nag tsho lo tsā ba tshul khrims rgyal ba,* 1011–1064) produced. Patsap Nyimadrak's (*pa tshab nyi ma grags*) Tibetan translations of the complete *Entrance to the Middle Way* and *Clear Words,* along with Āryadeva's *Four Hundred Stanzas* and Candrakīrti's commentary on it, which he made in Kaśmir with Tilakakalaśa, Mahāsumati, and Sūkṣmajana, respectively, in the last decades of the 11th century, constitute a watershed in Tibetan Madhyamaka studies. Patsap's translations gave Tibetans access to the full spectrum of Candrakīrti's views for the first time, while his commentaries to Nāgārjuna's *Fundamental Stanzas on the Middle Way* and Candrakīrti's *Clear Words* were the earliest known texts to speak of Prāsaṅgika and Svātantrika subschools of Madhyamaka. Patsap's disciples expanded the influence of this new Prāsaṅgika tradition, as did Jayānanda, who sojourned in Tibet prior to his departure for the Tangut kingdom, where he wrote his commentary to *Entrance to the Middle Way.* Candrakīrti's influence met with substantial resistance from Tibetans steeped in the Madhyamaka of Jñānagarbha, Śāntarakṣita, and Kamalaśīla that had long been established in Tibet and that embraced Dignāga's and Dharmakīrti's epistemology. Chapa Chökyi Senggé (*phya pa chos kyi seng ge,* 1109–1169) composed a lengthy refutation of Candrakīrti's views. However, some of Chapa's disciples became supporters of Prāsaṅgika, as did many Tibetan scholars.

By the 15th century, Candrakīrti had become widely accepted across the Tibetan Buddhist world as offering the most refined perspective on the buddha's teachings. Tsongkhapa (*tsong kha pa blo bzang grags pa,* 1357–1419), founder of the Gélukpa (*dge lugs pa*) school, esteemed Candrakīrti as expressing the final view of emptiness, with the Svātantrika Madhyamaka of Bhāviveka, Jñānagarbha, Śāntarakṣita, and Kamalaśīla representing a flawed view. Tsongkhapa also integrated Dharmakīrti's epistemology with Candrakīrti's Madhyamaka and argued at length against one of the few Tibetans of this period to reject Candrakīrti, Dölpopa Shérab Gyeltsen (1292–1361). Scholars of the Sakyapa (*sa skya pa*) tradition argued against many of the details of Tsongkhapa's positions, portraying the Prāsaṅgika–Svātantrika divide as a distinction of logical method rather than as a dispute over emptiness and rejecting the importation of Dharmakīrti's epistemology into Prāsaṅgika. Tibetans would argue over how to interpret Candrakīrti's views, but very few would challenge the notion that his was the pinnacle of philosophical positions.

REVIEW OF LITERATURE

The heroic work of the great Belgian scholar Louis de La Vallée Poussin brought Candrakīrti's major works, *Entrance to the Middle Way* and *Clear Words,* to scholarly attention well over a century ago. La Vallée Poussin produced critical editions of the Sanskrit *Clear Words* and the Tibetan *Entrance to the Middle Way* in the Bibliotheca Buddhica series and made a French translation of the latter through stanza 165 of its sixth chapter.[9] Huntington's English translation of the stanzas of *Entrance to the Middle* Way remains the only complete translation of the work.[10] With the 2008 commencement of research on a rediscovered Sanskrit manuscript of this text, there likely will be new editions and translations; Li Xuezhu has published an edition of the stanzas of chapter six.[11] On the strength of La Vallée Poussin's edition, *Clear Words* has been incrementally translated into European languages. However, the discovery of Sanskrit manuscripts unknown to La Vallée Poussin calls for a new edition and translation of this foundational work. Anne MacDonald's magnificent two-volume treatment of the first chapter of *Clear Words* is a monumental accomplishment of Madhyamaka studies and yet represents only approximately 15 percent of the total work.[12] Cristina Scherrer-Schaub produced a critical edition of the Tibetan text of Candrakīrti's *Commentary to Sixty Stanzas on Reasoning* as well as a French translation of it.[13] Felix Erb produced a partial critical edition of the Tibetan text of Candrakīrti's *Commentary to Seventy Stanzas on Emptiness*, as well as a German translation, covering Candrakīrti's comments to the first fourteen stanzas.[14] Karen Lang translated into English the first four chapters of Candrakīrti's *Commentary to the Four Hundred Stanzas*, while Tom Tillemans has translated chapters twelve and thirteen.[15]

Lang additionally wrote an overview of Candrakīrti for volume 21 of Karl Potter's *Encyclopedia of Indian Philosophy*.[16] Western interpreters have engaged Candrakīrti's views with a range of philosophical viewpoints, extending back to La Vallée Poussin's mistaken notion that Madhyamaka espoused a radical nihilism and Stcherbatsky's equally confused portrayal of it as an absolute monism. Although mainly focused on Nāgārjuna, chapter two of Tuck's *Comparative Philosophy and the Philosophy of Scholarship* is an excellent analysis of the biases of these two early interpreters.[17] Other scholarship portrays Candrakīrti in much tamer terms. Siderits has treated Candrakīrti's understanding of emptiness, particularly his emphasis on the emptiness of emptiness, as a kind of "semantic non-dualism," a "deflationist" approach to truth, in which the ultimate truth is simply that there is no ultimate truth.[18] This interpretation must be found lacking when held up to the light of Candrakīrti's broader concerns with the Mahāyāna path: the ultimate, for Candrakīrti, remains radically transformative. Scholars have additionally tried to make sense of Candrakīrti's conception of the conventional and his purported alignment with "the world." Several of the essays in the *Moonshadows* collection portray Candrakīrti as offering a redescription of worldly practice, with Jay Garfield and Georges Dreyfus seeing strong parallels with Greek Pyrrhonian skepticism.[19] These accounts are strongly influenced by Tsongkhapa's rehabilitation of Candrakīrti and fail to account for the stark divide Candrakīrti places between worldly ignorance and appearance-free buddhahood. Arnold's analysis of Candrakīrti's rejection of Dignāga's epistemology suggests that scholars should understand Candrakīrti as offering transcendental arguments predicated on the fact that emptiness serves as the necessary precondition of a functioning world.[20] Arnold's work makes promising use of Candrakīrti's (and Nāgārjuna's) equation of emptiness with dependent arising (*pratītyasamutpāda*) and dependent designation (*upādāya prajñapti*); just where it would leave one who has realized emptiness remains unclear. Tillemans's analyses of Madhyamaka and its contemporary interpreters constitute philosophically and philologically astute insights into a variety of thinkers, including Candrakīrti.[21] Apple's work on the

Madhyamaka of the early Kadampa tradition offers insights into how Candrakīrti was understood by his earliest Tibetan interpreters.[22] Vose offers an account of the philosophical disputes that Candrakīrti's views engendered in 12th-century Tibet.[23] Hopkins presents Tsongkhapa's reading of several key points of Candrakīrti and elucidates Dölpopa's perspectives that served as Tsongkhapa's target.[24] Cabezón and Dargyay translate and analyze an important Sakyapa rebuttal to Tsongkhapa.[25] Finally, Wedemeyer offers insight into the "Noble" lineage of tantric interpretation, to which the latter Candrakīrti contributed, while Campbell and Thurman translate the first twelve chapters of his *Illuminating Lamp*.[26]

PRIMARY SOURCES

Erb, Felix. *Śūnyatāsaptativṛtti Candrakīrtis Kommentar zu den "Siebzig Versen über die Leerheit" des Nāgārjuna (Kārikās 1–14)*. Stuttgart: Steiner, 1997.

Huntington, C. W. *The Emptiness of Emptiness: An Introduction to Early Indian Mādhyamika*. Honolulu: University of Hawai'i Press, 1989.

Lang, Karen C. *Four Illusions: Candrakīrti's Advice to Travelers on the Bodhisattva Path*. Oxford: Oxford University Press, 2003.

La Vallée Poussin, Louis de. "Madhyamakāvatāra: Introduction au Traite du Milieu de l'Ācārya Candrakīrti avec le Commentaire de l'Auteur; Traduit d'après la Version Tibétaine." *Muséon* 8 (1907): 249–317; 11 (1910): 271–358; and 12 (1911): 236–328.

La Vallée Poussin, Louis de. *Madhyamakāvatāra par Candrakīrti*. Bibliotheca Buddhica 9. Osnabrück, Germany: Biblio Verlag, 1970.

La Vallée Poussin, Louis de. *Mūlamadhyamakakārikās de Nāgārjuna avec la Prasannapadā Commentaire de Candrakīrti*. Bibliotheca Buddhica 4. Osnabrück, Germany: Biblio Verlag, 1970.

MacDonald, Anne. *In Clear Words: The Prasannapadā, Chapter One*. 2 vols. Vienna: Österreichischen Akademie der Wissenschaften, 2015.

Scherrer-Schaub, Cristina. *Yuktiṣaṣṭikāvṛtti: Commentaire à la soixantaine sur le raisonnement ou Du vrai enseignement de la causalité par le Maître indien Candrakīrti*. Brussels: Institut Belge Des Hautes Études Chinoises, 1991.

Tillemans, Tom J. F. *Materials for the Study of Āryadeva, Dharmapāla and Candrakīrti: The Catuḥśataka of Āryadeva, chapters XII and XIII, with the Commentaries of Dharmapāla and Candrakīrti*. 2 vols. Vienna: Arbeitskreis für Tibetische und Buddhistische Studien Universität Wien, 1990.

Xuezhu, Li. "Madhyamakāvatāra-kārikā Chapter 6." *Journal of Indian Philosophy* 43 (2015): 1–30.

FURTHER READING

Apple, James. *Jewels of the Middle Way: The Madhyamaka Legacy of Atiśa and His Early Tibetan Followers*. Somerville, MA: Wisdom Publications, 2018.

Arnold, Dan. *Buddhists, Brahmins, and Belief: Epistemology in South Asian Philosophy of Religion*. New York: Columbia University Press, 2005.

Cabezón, Jose Ignacio, and Geshe Lobsang Dargyay. *Freedom from Extremes: Gorampa's "Distinguishing the Views" and the Polemics of Emptiness*. Somerville, MA: Wisdom Publications, 2007.

Campbell, John R. B., and Robert A. F. Thurman. *The Esoteric Community Tantra with the Illuminating Lamp*, vol. 1. Somerville, MA: Wisdom Publications, 2020.

The Cowherds. *Moonshadows: Conventional Truth in Buddhist Philosophy*. Oxford: Oxford University Press, 2011.

Hopkins, Jeffrey. *Tsong-kha-pa's Final Exposition of Wisdom*. Ithaca, NY: Snow Lion Publications, 2008.
Lang, Karen. "Candrakīrti." In *Encyclopedia of Indian Philosophy*. Vol. 21. Edited by Karl Popper, 15–50. Delhi: Motilal Banarsidass, 2017.
Siderits, Mark. *Personal Identity and Buddhist Philosophy: Empty Persons*. Hampshire, UK: Ashgate Publishing, 2003.
Tillemans, Tom J. F. *How Do Mādhyamikas Think?* Somerville, MA: Wisdom Publications, 2016.
Tuck, Andrew. *Comparative Philosophy and the Philosophy of Scholarship: On the Western Interpretation of Nāgārjuna*. Oxford: Oxford University Press, 1990.
Vose, Kevin A. *Resurrecting Candrakīrti: Disputes in the Tibetan Creation of Prāsaṅgika*. Somerville, MA: Wisdom Publications, 2009.
Wedemeyer, Christian K. *Āryadeva's Lamp That Integrates the Practices (*Caryāmelāpakapradīpa*): The Gradual Path of Vajrayāna Buddhism According to the Esoteric Community Noble Tradition*. New York: American Institute of Buddhist Studies at Columbia University, 2007.

NOTES

1. *Mūlamadhyamakakārikā* I.1 (Shaoyong Ye, *Zhunglunsong: Fanzanghan Hejiao, Daodu, Yizhu* [Mūlamadhyamakakārikā: New editions of the Sanskrit, Tibetan and Chinese versions, with commentary and a modern Chinese translation] [Shanghai: Zhongxi Book Company, 2011], 12): *na svato nāpi parato na dvābhyāṃ nāpy ahetutaḥ|utpannā jātu vidyante bhāvāḥ kvacana kecana||*.
2. Candrakīrti (*Entrance to the Middle Way*, stanza VI.29 and autocommentary) describes *timira* as causing one (a *taimirika*) to see floating hairs or a mass of hair in one's visual field. On the medical basis of this condition, see Anne MacDonald, *In Clear Words*, vol. 2 (Vienna: Österreichischen Akademie der Wissenschaften, 2015), 111–112n228; and David Higgins, *The Philosophical Foundations of Classical rDzogs chen in Tibet: Investigating the Distinction between Dualist Mind (*sems*) and Primordial Knowing (*ye shes*)* (Vienna: Arbeitskreis für Tibetische und Buddhistische Studien Universität Wien, 2013), 125n318. The author thanks an anonymous reviewer of this article for correcting my use of a common, but incorrect, translation of *timira*, "ophthamalia."
3. The author thanks an anonymous reviewer of this article for pointing me to the sutra and Abhidharma use of the phrase "realize with the body" (*kāyena sākṣātkaraṇa/sku yis mngon sum mdzad*), particularly Yaśomitra's *Clear Meaning* (*Sphuṭārthā*) commentary on the *Treasury of Abhidharma* (*Abhidharmakośa*), where Yaśomitra quotes an unidentified sutra describing the attainment of *parinirvāṇa*. These older sources would seem to be struggling with the same problem as Candrakīrti: explaining the direct experience of nirvana that entails the cessation of all five aggregates (*skandha*), including consciousness.
4. See Tom J. F. Tillemans, "Deflating the Two Images and the Two Truths: Bons baisers du Tibet," in *Wilfrid Sellars and Buddhist Philosophy: Freedom from Foundations*, ed. Jay L. Garfield (New York: Routledge, 2019), 80–96. Tillemans ultimately finds Candrakīrti's and Wilfred Sellars's framework truths dissatisfying.
5. At the close of his comments on *Mūlamadhyamakakārikā* I.1's denial of production from self, Candrakīrti considers the character–characterized (or definition–definiendum) relationship in terms of a definition of valid cognition, the objects of valid cognition, and perception; for an English translation, see MacDonald, *In Clear Words*, 2:224–294. Dan Arnold, *Buddhists, Brahmins, and Belief* (New York: Columbia University Press, 2005), 152–162, provides insightful analysis of Candrakīrti's *Prasannapadā* critique of Dignāga.
6. The second criticism, *skye ba thug pa med par 'gyur ba'i phyir*, can also be understood as "because production [would entail] an infinite regress." However, given that Buddhapālita explains that if something existent were produced, it would never not be produced (*gal te yod kyang skye na nam yang mi skye bar mi 'gyur bas de yang mi 'dod de |*), "endless" better fits his meaning. Candrakīrti's *Prasannapadā* understood

Buddhapālita's second criticism as "the fault of over-extension" (*atiprasaṅgadoṣa*); see MacDonald, *In Clear Words*, 2:53n17, for a discussion of this complexity.

7. For a translation of Buddhapālita's comments, see Akiro Saito, "A Study of the *Buddhapālita-mūlamadhyamaka-vṛtti*, volume two" (PhD diss., Australian National University, 1984). For a translation of Bhāviveka's comments, see William L. Ames, "Bhāvaviveka's *Prajñāpradīpa*: A Translation of Chapter One: 'Examination of Causal Conditions' (*pratyaya*)," *Journal of Indian Philosophy* 21, no. 3 (1993): 209–259.
8. MacDonald, *In Clear Words*, 1:145.4–145.146.1: *na ca mādhyamikasya svataḥ svatantram anumānaṃ kartuṃ yuktaṃ pakṣāntarābhyupagamābhāvāt*||.
9. Louis de La Vallée Poussin, "Madhyamakāvatāra: Introduction au Traite du Milieu de l'Ācārya Candrakīrti avec le Commentaire de l'Auteur; Traduit d'après la Version Tibétaine," *Muséon* 8 (1907): 249–317; 11 (1910): 271–358; and 12 (1911): 236–328; Louis de La Vallée Poussin, *Madhyamakāvatāra par Candrakīrti*, Bibliotheca Buddhica 9 (Osnabrück, Germany: Biblio Verlag, 1970); and Louis de La Vallée Poussin, *Mūlamadhyamakakārikās de Nāgārjuna avec la Prasannapadā Commentaire de Candrakīrti*, Bibliotheca Buddhica 4 (Osnabrück, Germany: Biblio Verlag, 1970).
10. Clair W. Huntington, *The Emptiness of Emptiness: An Introduction to Early Indian Mādhyamika* (Honolulu: University of Hawai'i Press, 1989).
11. Li Xuezhu, "Madhyamakāvatāra-kārikā Chapter 6," *Journal of Indian Philosophy* 43 (2015): 1–30.
12. MacDonald, *In Clear Words*.
13. Cristina Scherrer-Schaub, *Yuktiṣaṣṭikāvṛtti: Commentaire à la soixantaine sur le raisonnement ou Du vrai enseignement de la causalité par le Maître indien Candrakīrti* (Brussels: Institut Belge Des Hautes Études Chinoises, 1991).
14. Felix Erb, *Śūnyatāsaptativṛtti Candrakīrtis Kommentar zu den "Siebzig Versen über die Leerheit" des Nāgārjuna (Kārikās 1–14)* (Stuttgart: Steiner, 1997).
15. Karen C. Lang, *Four Illusions: Candrakīrti's Advice to Travelers on the Bodhisattva Path* (Oxford: Oxford University Press, 2003); and Tom J. F. Tillemans, *Materials for the Study of Āryadeva, Dharmapāla and Candrakīrti: The Catuḥśataka of Āryadeva, chapters XII and XIII, with the Commentaries of Dharmapāla and Candrakīrti*, 2 vols. (Vienna: Arbeitskreis für Tibetische und Buddhistische Studien Universität Wien, 1990).
16. Karen Lang, "Candrakīrti," in *Encyclopedia of Indian Philosophy*, ed. Karl Popper (Delhi: Motilal Banarsidass, 2017), 21:15–50.
17. Andrew Tuck, *Comparative Philosophy and the Philosophy of Scholarship: On the Western Interpretation of Nāgārjuna* (Oxford: Oxford University Press, 1990).
18. Mark Siderits, *Personal Identity and Buddhist Philosophy: Empty Persons* (Hampshire, UK: Ashgate Publishing, 2003).
19. The Cowherds, *Moonshadows: Conventional Truth in Buddhist Philosophy* (Oxford: Oxford University Press, 2011).
20. Dan Arnold, *Buddhists, Brahmins, and Belief: Epistemology in South Asian Philosophy of Religion* (New York: Columbia University Press, 2005).
21. Tom J. F. Tillemans, *How Do Mādhyamikas Think?* (Somerville, MA: Wisdom Publications, 2016).
22. James Apple, *Jewels of the Middle Way: The Madhyamaka Legacy of Atiśa and His Early Tibetan Followers* (Somerville, MA: Wisdom Publications, 2018).
23. Kevin A. Vose, *Resurrecting Candrakīrti: Disputes in the Tibetan Creation of Prāsaṅgika* (Somerville, MA: Wisdom Publications, 2009).
24. Jeffrey Hopkins, *Tsong-kha-pa's Final Exposition of Wisdom* (Ithaca, NY: Snow Lion Publications, 2008).
25. Jose Ignacio Cabezón and Geshe Lobsang Dargyay, *Freedom from Extremes: Gorampa's "Distinguishing the Views" and the Polemics of Emptiness* (Somerville, MA: Wisdom Publications, 2007).

26. Christian K. Wedemeyer, *Āryadeva's Lamp That Integrates the Practices* (Caryāmelāpakapradīpa): *The Gradual Path of Vajrayāna Buddhism According to the Esoteric Community Noble Tradition* (New York: American Institute of Buddhist Studies at Columbia University, 2007); and John R. B. Campbell and Robert A. F. Thurman, *The Esoteric Community Tantra with the Illuminating Lamp*, vol. 1 (Somerville, MA: Wisdom Publications, 2020).

Kevin Vose

CANON AND COMMENTARY IN THE EARLIEST BUDDHIST MANUSCRIPTS

HISTORY OF RESEARCH

The earliest Buddhist manuscripts, written on birchbark scrolls, were found in modern-day Pakistan and Afghanistan—the ancient region of Gandhāra—and, in one case, in western China.[1] They date as far back as the 1st century BCE and are written in the local Middle Indo-Aryan language Gāndhārī and the local Kharoṣṭhī script. In the 3rd and 4th centuries CE, a Buddhist community at Bamiyan in Afghanistan produced Sanskrit manuscripts in the pan-Indian Brāhmī script in parallel with Gāndhārī manuscripts, using palm leaves and the pothi format or a bound or wrapped folio for both. By the 5th century CE, the pothi, Sanskrit, and Brāhmī had completely taken over from the Gāndhārī manuscript tradition.[2] This earliest Buddhist manuscript tradition, thus spanning a period of approximately 500 years, provides unique insights into the early development of Buddhist canonical and commentarial literature.

The first discovery of a Gāndhārī manuscript was made in 1892 near the city of Khotan on the southern Silk Road in the form of an exceptionally long birchbark scroll containing a previously unknown version of the Dharmapada.[3] The manuscript was apparently complete on discovery, but was divided, with one-third each reaching Paris and St. Petersburg and the third third now lost. The discovery prompted a long scholarly discussion about a then-hypothetical Gāndhārī canon.[4] Gāndhārī language and Kharoṣṭhī script were used around the 3rd century CE for administrative purposes in the neighboring Kroraina kingdom, but only very few and small literary fragments are preserved among these documents.[5] In contrast, the earliest Chinese translations of Indian Buddhist texts showed signs of having been made from Gāndhārī originals, and the school affiliation of the Chinese Dīrghāgama (T 1) in particular pointed to the Dharmaguptakas as the most likely producers of such Gāndhārī texts.[6]

Throughout the 20th century, finds of Gāndhārī inscriptions from Pakistan, Afghanistan, and Uzbekistan accumulated, providing evidence of widespread literacy in the Gandhāran Buddhist milieu, and eventually a series of substantial new manuscript discoveries laid to rest any doubt about the existence of an extensive written Gāndhārī Buddhist literature. Unfortunately, none of these recent discoveries is the result of proper archaeological excavation, and the findspots of the vast majority of manuscripts—including all the earlier ones on birchbark—remain unknown, depriving scholarship of invaluable information about their geography and use contexts. The first new collection of twenty-nine Gāndhārī manuscripts was acquired by the British Library in 1994 from the private collector Robert Senior, who retained another collection of twenty-four scrolls in his personal possession.[7] Each of these two collections appears to represent an original manuscript deposit made in a clay pot with a dedicatory inscription, in the case of the British Library collection naming the Dharmaguptaka school and in that of the Senior collection providing a date around the year 140 CE.

Next, a large number of early palm-leaf and later birchbark folio fragments from Bamiyan came to light; these are now scattered across several collections, the majority being held by the private collector Martin Schøyen in Norway.[8] Two further collections of birchbark scrolls—the Bajaur collection of nineteen scrolls and the so-called split collection of five scrolls—came to light in Pakistan, where they remain.[9] The Bajaur collection was allegedly found in a stone chest in a monastery, while the find context of the split collection remains entirely unknown. Most recently, a large number of further privately held scrolls that appear to be connected (at least in terms of collecting if not deposit) to the split collection have become accessible to scholars; little is as yet known about the extent and contents of this group of manuscripts.[10] Altogether, approximately 150 birchbark scrolls and about the same number of small palm-leaf fragments in the Gāndhārī language are now known and have been discussed in at least a preliminary fashion in publications.[11]

HISTORICAL OVERVIEW

While a history of Gāndhārī literature cannot yet be written, three phases may be distinguished in terms of their textuality: (1) written and oral Buddhist literature in Gandhāra preceding the earliest preserved manuscripts (3rd–2nd centuries BCE), (2) an increasing body of written Buddhist texts without a written canon (1st century BCE to 2nd century CE), and (3) the incipient formation of written canons and transition to a new writing culture. Throughout these phases, there occurred three distinct but interlocked processes of the writing down of texts, the production of commentaries on them and scholastic treatises, and the delimitation of canons of texts.[12]

The first specimen of writing from Gandhāra are the two sets of Major Rock Edicts of the Emperor Aśoka at Shahbazgarhi and Mansehra (3rd century BCE).[13] The Aśokan epigraphic corpus can be subdivided into more and less explicitly Buddhist inscriptions, and the Major Rock Edicts belong to the latter group. Nonetheless, the later tradition does see Aśoka as the original spreader of Buddhism to Gandhāra, as evidenced by elements such as Mauryan pillars in the artistic production and references to the Mauryas and Aśoka in the epigraphic record.[14] The precise point in time when the technology of writing was first applied by Buddhist patrons and institutions to Buddhist literature in Gandhāra remains unknown, but the tradition of Buddhist relic donation inscriptions starting under Indo-Greek rulers in the 2nd century BCE suggests a likely terminus ad quem.[15] The fact that an already flourishing literature is encountered in the finds from the 1st century BCE, while the preceding stages are lost, can be attributed to the new custom of depositing manuscripts in a kind of burial or dharma relic installation in sealed clay pots at this time.[16] One can only speculate about the first genres of Buddhist literature committed to writing in Gandhāra; canonical sutras and verses, commentaries, and story collections all seem likely candidates.

The second phase of Gāndhārī literature (1st century BCE to 2nd century CE) is characterized by a continued oral transmission as the primary vehicle for the four main canonical text collections (*āgamas*).[17] The manuscript record contains copies of only select Dīrgha,

Madhyama, and Kṣudraka texts, as well as of small subgroups of sutras from the Ekottarikā and Saṃyukta collections. This state of affairs is mirrored by the earliest Chinese translations, presumably based on Gāndhārī originals, among which one also finds selections of Ekottarikā and Saṃyukta sūtras of the same type. Some originally incomplete copies of canonical texts may have had a symbolic rather than practical function as physical instantiations of the word of the buddha.[18] The existence of complete canonical text collections outside the written record is confirmed by the expression *ekotaria* in a 1st-century CE manuscript, as well as the epithet *trepiḍaga* (roughly, "sacred canon") for a learned monk in a donative inscription.[19] Commentaries and independent scholastic texts are richly attested among the manuscript finds of this phase, and judging from their way of expression as well as traces of damage and repair, these were very much intended for practical use. (A relief of three monks in debate holding manuscripts illustrates just such a use.[20]) Individual, uncollected Mahāyānasūtras, including a Prajñāpāramitā, also form an integral part of this phase, as do original poetical compositions.

The third phase of Gāndhārī Buddhist literature (3rd and 4th centuries CE) sees a transition in manuscript formats from the scroll to the pothi, which appears to have enabled the production of more extensive written texts and their efficient use.[21] This innovation can first be observed in the finds from Bamiyan and eventually spread over the entire northwest of the subcontinent, though it remains unclear when exactly it reached the heartland of Gandhāra. On the part of the canonical collections, fragments of an originally complete Ekottarikā manuscript have been found at Bamiyan, and this is mirrored by the appearance of complete Dīrgha, Madhyama, Ekottarikā, and Saṃyukta collections in Chinese translations at the same time.[22] In parallel with this development, a new category of very extensive Mahāyānasūtras developed, exemplified most clearly by fragments of a Bhadrakalpikasūtra manuscript from Bamiyan.[23] The assembly of several Mahāyānasūtras into larger collections is, however, not yet in evidence in this period.

ORAL AND WRITTEN CANONS

The definition of "canon" in Buddhism (as in other religions) is a complex matter. One first has to distinguish between orally transmitted canons and those given physical form in writing. The very act of putting a body of texts in writing implies organization and selection of material and can thus contribute to the clearer definition and potential narrowing of a canon. In parallel with this transition from oral to written form, exegetical activity in commentaries and independent scholastic treatises further shapes the form and arrangement of canonical texts. While selection, abridgement, and anthologization were at work on what has been called the "practical canons" of Buddhist communities, at the same time a "notional canon" (the totality of the teachings of the Buddha, the *buddhavacana*) remained authoritative, whether or not it was available in its entirety in a given place and time.[24] Eventually, the scriptures of the new Mahāyāna movement began to undergo similar processes of collection and authentication as the old Buddhist canon and to form canons of their own, even though the eventual results are outside the scope of the period covered here. Finally, one has to exercise caution when considering the institutional frames and scopes of the canons in question. Buddhist schools such as the Dharmaguptakas, the Sarvāstivādins, and the several others known to have operated in

Gandhāra may have shaped at least partly distinctive canons, but regional factors certainly also played a role in the availability and form of canonical texts. Bearing all this in mind, the following will give an overview of the Gāndhārī literature now known that may be considered canonical, following for convenience the traditional divisions of the Pali canon.

Sutra Dīrghāgama. Two manuscripts are extant containing texts belonging to the Dīrghāgama. One manuscript of the Senior collection preserves the beginning of the Śrāmaṇyaphalasūtra, a dialog between King Ajātaśatru and the Buddha;[25] this remains unpublished except for two small samples from six lines.[26] Among the Bamiyan palm-leaf fragments, there are several of a manuscript of the Mahāparinirvāṇasūtra, recounting the last days of the buddha.[27] It is likely that the Śrāmaṇyaphalasūtra scroll contained only this text (or part of this text), whereas the palm-leaf manuscript of the Mahāpariṇirvāṇasūtra may have contained additional texts. A third Dīrghāgama text, the Saṃgītisūtra, is preserved embedded in a commentary on it.[28]

Madhyamāgama. Five Madhyamāgama texts are preserved in whole or part in Gāndhārī versions. The most extensive is a version of the Dakṣiṇāvibhaṅgasūtra in the Bajaur collection.[29] The Senior collection contains the remains of probably four Madhyamāgama texts: a parallel to the Pali Dhammacetiyasutta;[30] probably a version of the Shìzhě jīng 侍者經;[31] probably the Saṃkhāruppattisutta;[32] and the Cūḷagosiṅgasutta.[33] Only the last of these has been published in its entirety. In addition, a list of text keywords that was found as part of the Senior collection suggests the presence in its milieu of a further ten Madhyamāgama texts.[34] The Dhātuvibhaṅgasūtra of the Madhyamāgama is attested in the form of a commentary on it.[35] Both the Dīrghāgama and the Madhyamāgama sutra manuscripts currently known from the Gāndhārī finds contain one single text each, and there is no evidence of multiple texts of these classes having been physically collected together.

Ekottarikāgama. One scroll of the British Library collection contains, on its recto, three short thematically connected texts (the "Droṇa," "Buddhavacana," and "Pradhāna" sutras), two of which have parallels in the Section of Fours of the Pali Aṅguttaranikāya, and all three of which thus appear to be an extract from an otherwise orally transmitted Ekottarikāgama of the second phase of Gāndhārī Buddhist literature.[36] The existence of such a collection is independently confirmed by the reference *yasa ekotariae* in a commentarial text of the period.[37] Among the Bamiyan palm-leaf fragments of the third phase are small remains of at least twelve sutras from the Sections of the Sixes, maybe the Sevens, the Nines, Tens, and Elevens of an apparently originally complete Ekottarikāgama manuscript.[38] These two different kinds of remains from within the Gāndhārī tradition illustrate neatly how a change of manuscript format went hand in hand with a different, more extensive written textuality.

Saṃyuktāgama. Saṃyuktāgama sutras are so far only attested in seven scrolls of the Senior collection. One of them contains a group of fourteen or more short sutras that correspond (though in different order) to the first fourteen sutras of the Pali Vanasaṃyutta.[39] Two further manuscripts contain a total of six sutras corresponding to six noncontiguous sutras in the Pali Khandhasaṃyutta.[40] The texts of another two manuscripts are, judging from the Pali, sourced from a number of different Saṃyuttas (Opamma-, Khandha-, Sacca-, and maybe Saḷāyatanasaṃyutta).[41]

Finally, two manuscripts contain one sutra each, from the Sotāpatti- and Saḷāyatanasaṃyuttas.[42] The Saṃyuktāgama manuscripts in the Senior collection thus illustrate several different patterns of selection and anthologization in putting material from a still primarily oral Saṃyuktāgama collection in writing. Among the three Chinese Saṃyuktāgama translations, that of Ān Shìgāo (T 101, made around 148–168 CE), containing a selection of twenty-five sutras, reflects this situation most closely and may well have been based on a Gāndhārī original. The two later translations (T 100, 350–430 CE, two divisions, and T 99, 435–426 CE, complete) appear to reflect, with about a hundred years' delay, the later type of textuality that is seen at Bamiyan.

Kṣudraka. The so-called minor texts (Kṣudraka) of early Buddhism entered the canons of various Buddhist schools in widely different places, and the Gāndhārī evidence confirms that in the first centuries of the written tradition, they were transmitted separately.[43] Three Kṣudraka texts are preserved in early manuscripts: the Dharmapada, the Arthapada, and the Khaḍgaviṣāṇasūtra. Of these, the Dharmapada is attested three times. The Khotan Dharmapada manuscript contains a recension of the text distinct from the Pali and other known versions and must have encompassed approximately 500 lines when it was complete, starting with a Brāhmaṇavarga followed by a Bhikṣuvarga.[44] The British Library collection contains a fragmentary scroll preserving the end of the Bhikṣuvarga, which may have formed part of a multiscroll set of the Brāhmaṇavarga with the Bhikṣuvarga.[45] One scroll of the split collection contains a collection of Dharmapada verses that can be tentatively grouped into five chapters, but without precise agreement with any of the other versions.[46] Another fragmentary scroll of the split collection preserves approximately one-quarter of a version of the Arthapada, corresponding to the Māgandiyasutta up to the Sāriputtasutta in the Pali version integrated into the Suttanipāta.[47] Another part of the Pāli Suttanipāta collection that is still separately transmitted among the Gāndhārī manuscripts is the Khaḍgaviṣāṇasūtra.[48] From a reference in a commentary to a *posalo parayaṇio*, it is clear that a version of the Pārāyaṇa also formed a part of early Gandhāran Buddhist literature, and likely that a written version (apparently lost) also existed.[49] Finally, one of the Gāndhārī wooden documents from Niya contains the introductory verse of the Udānavarga, attesting to the presence of this text (whether in Gāndhārī or Sanskrit) in Central Asia during the latter part of the Gāndhārī period.[50] It is unclear whether any other prominent Kṣudraka texts known from other traditions, such as an Udāna proper or a Sthavira- or Sthavirīgāthā, were transmitted in a written Gāndhārī version, but quotations from them in the Gāndhārī verse commentaries attest at least to their oral presence in the tradition.[51] A text whose position in the canon is unclear, but that has connections with the Kṣudraka class, are the Anavataptagāthā. They are preserved in two Gāndhārī manuscript remains in the British Library and Senior collections.[52]

Mahāyānasūtra. Scriptures of the Mahāyāna movement are also well represented among the early manuscript finds from Gandhāra with at least nine different texts. The split collection contains one scroll that preserves part of the first and fifth chapters of a Prajñāpāramitā corresponding closely to the Aṣṭasāhasrikā.[53] Next to this foundational Mahāyāna text, small fragments of three other early Mahāyānasūtras are preserved among the recent discoveries related to the split collection: namely, the Pratyutpannabuddhasaṃmukhāvasthitasamādhi;[54] a text that resembles the Samādhirājasūtra;[55] and what has been termed the *Sucintisūtra.[56] At the other end of the scale, the Bajaur collection contains a very extensive and well-preserved unknown Mahāyānasūtra describing a buddha paradise and comparing it to that of the Buddha Akṣobhya.[57] The same collection contains a group of related short scrolls with a scholastic discussion touching on Mahāyāna issues such as the bodhisattva path.[58]

Not a Mahāyāna text proper, but laying the ground for later Mahāyāna developments, is the Bahubuddhasūtra contained in a Gāndhārī scroll in the Library of Congress, detailing the relationships of our Buddha Śākyamuni with fourteen other buddhas of the past and future.[59] A much more developed example of this genre is the Bhadrakalpikasūtra, describing 1,004 buddhas of our present world age, which is preserved in a number of small fragments from what must have been a pothi manuscript of approximately 400 folios at Bamiyan.[60] Also at Bamiyan were found small pothi fragments of the Bodhisattvapiṭakasūtra;[61] the Sarvapuṇyasamuccayasamādhi;[62] and a further, unidentified Mahāyānasūtra.[63] Even in the later phase of Gāndhārī literature at Bamiyan, all of these Mahāyānasūtras appear to have been transmitted individually; the earliest example of a Mahāyānasūtra anthology occurs among the Sanskrit fragments from Bamiyan and dates to the 5th century CE.[64]

Vinaya. Examples of Vinaya texts have come to light in the Bajaur collection. One manuscript unites two different versions of the Prātimokṣasūtra, and another contains a set of Karmavācanā rules.[65] It is unclear whether three scrolls containing episodes from the life of the buddha in the Senior collection were embedded in a Vinaya context.[66]

COMMENTARY AND ABHIDHARMA

While most of the canonical Gāndhārī literature is known from parallel versions in other languages, the situation is entirely the opposite when it comes to commentarial and scholastic texts. There are numerous examples of the genre, but not a single one of them could yet be identified with a text known from other traditions; rather, we seem to have to do with original productions of Gandhāran Buddhism. This presents special challenges for the decipherment and understanding of these manuscripts, but also provides a unique glimpse into a living early Buddhist exegetical community. At the level of commentarial building blocks and exegetical techniques, some parallels, however, can be identified with Pali and Chinese Buddhist texts, revealing connections between Gandhāra and other regions and currents of early Buddhism. Commentaries proper and independent scholastic texts appear at the same time in the manuscript record, and there is no reason to assume that the latter evolved from the former. Rather, the systematic scholastic discussion of doctrinal topics occurs in canonical discourses already, and both commentaries and independent scholastic texts can be seen as evolving on this shared basis. In the case of commentaries, this happened in dialog with a (or several) root texts, while the development of other scholastic texts was driven more immediately by the doctrinal topics of concern.

Only four commentaries proper are currently known from the Gāndhārī tradition, all belonging to its second phase (1st to 2nd centuries CE). One is a commentary on a complete version of the Saṃgītisūtra on a scroll in the British Library collection.[67] In the arrangement of the sections of the root text, this commentary agrees almost perfectly with the translation of the Saṃgītisūtra in the Chinese Dīrghāgama (T 1), differing markedly from the Pali and Sanskrit versions of the root text. This suggests that the Chinese translation goes back to an original from the Gandhāran tradition, and possibly that this original, like the Chinese translation, should be attributed to the Dharmaguptaka school. The main exegetical services of the Saṃgītisūtra commentary are the explanation of the root terms, often by way of etymology (*nirvacana*), their illustration using similes (*aupamya*), and their mapping to other doctrinal sets (such that for example the four *saṃjñā* are equated with the three *dhātu*). This kind of mapping, or "categorial reduction," is also applied to the larger structure of the text in special summary (*uddāna*) sections that, in effect, reduce the entire doctrinal edifice covered in the Saṃgītisūtra to the four truths (*satya*) and the three courses (of dependent arising; *vartman*).[68] This procedure of categorial reduction as well as some of the technical terminology associated with it has close parallels in the Pali Peṭakopadesa and Nettippakaraṇa as well as in Ān Shìgāo's Yīnchírù jīng 陰持入經 (T 604), pointing to Gandhāra as the origin of this exegetical procedure.[69]

The other three Gāndhārī commentaries are closely related texts on at least four separate scrolls of the British Library collection that explain selections of verses from the Dharmapada, the Arthapada, and the Pārāyaṇa as well as some other Kṣudraka texts.[70] Commentaries such as these may thus have been instrumental in defining the class of Kṣudraka texts that eventually found a home in different locations in the different Buddhist schools' canons. The rationale for the particular selection of verses made in these commentaries as well as their order is not apparent, other than that they are generally speaking popular and well-known verses in early Buddhism, and it is likely that an unknown context of use (maybe pedagogical or ritual) lay behind the production of these texts. The three verse commentaries share with the Saṃgītisūtra commentary the procedure of categorial reduction and additionally employ word explanations with parallels in the Pali Suttaniddesa that are best considered a shared inheritance from the earliest period of Buddhist exegesis. Also, like the Saṃgītisūtra commentary, the verse commentaries contain references to and quotations from other canonical texts, attesting, for instance, to the notion of an Ekottarikā collection of sutras. Both the Saṃgītisūta commentary and the verse commentaries frequently introduce multiple alternative explanations of their root text without expressing a preference.

In addition to these clear commentaries, a manuscript in the University of Washington Libraries contains a discussion of the Dhātuvibhaṅgasūtra of the Madhyamāgama, but the fragmentary state of the text does not allow a decision as to whether it is a straightforward commentary on this sutra or another type of text introducing this discussion in a different context.[71]

In contrast, a scholastic text that is clearly not a commentary is preserved in a 1st-century CE manuscript in the British Library collection.[72] It discusses, apparently in a practice-oriented context concerned with defilements, the existence of past and future factors. The form of this discussion is polemical, with an unidentified proponent engaging with Kāśyapīya and Sarvāstivāda opponents. The closest literary parallel to this type of text is the Pali Kathāvatthu.

Very little can be said at the current stage of research about the other scholastic texts that are preserved in the British Library and Bajaur collections other than general indications of their concerns based on the employed vocabulary. Thus, in the former collection, CKM 12 discusses the Buddhist path in relation to defilements and CKM 19 dependent arising and a variety of topics related to religious practice. CKM 22 likewise appears to cover a broad range of topics related to practice, but does so in a catechetical format. In addition, the British Library contains several minor scholastic fragments that remain even more poorly understood.[73] In the Bajaur collection, manuscript CKM 272 discusses the character of types of thought (*citta*); fragments CKM 277, 279, and 281 appear to form a group, but it has not been possible to determine their content or that of fragment CKM 275 more precisely.[74] The Bajaur collection contains several Mahāyāna-related scholastic fragments.[75]

MISCELLANEOUS TEXTS

Canonical and scholastic early Buddhist texts coexisted with texts of other genres used in Gandhāran Buddhist monasteries. These include a number of original poetic compositions in praise of the buddha, Buddhist story collections and story outlines, an apotropaic text, and even a non-Buddhist treatise on statecraft written in Kharoṣṭhī script and Sanskrit language that caught the interest of a Gandhāran Buddhist monk.[76]

REVIEW OF LITERATURE

The earliest accounts of Gandhāran Buddhist manuscript finds, now lost, are owed to 19th-century Western travelers in the northwestern Indian borderlands, especially Charles Masson in 1841 and Martin Honigberger in 1851.[77] First sample editions of the two preserved portions of the Khotan Dharmapada by Émile Senart and Sergeĭ Ol'denburg", both published in 1891, gave rise to several decades of intensive detailed scholarship on this text by Senart, Heinrich Lüders, Sten Konow, Benimadhab Barua, and Sailendranath Mitra and H. W. Bailey and, eventually, a definitive edition by John Brough in 1962.[78] The "Gāndhārī hypothesis" concerning the existence of a written Gāndhārī Buddhist canon was summarized by Franz Bernhard in 1970.[79] Gérard Fussman published a synthesis of the state of Gāndhārī studies in 1989.[80] The first set of the manuscripts newly discovered since the 1990s reached the British Library in 1994, while another stayed with the private collector Robert Senior.[81] These two collections and the subsequent discoveries of Gāndhārī birch-bark manuscripts are gradually being published in the Gandhāran Buddhist Texts series starting in the year 2000.[82] Also since 2000, the palm-leaf fragments from Bamiyan are being edited in the Buddhist manuscripts in the Schøyen Collection series.[83] The progress of the editorial and interpretive work on the Gāndhārī manuscripts and related epigraphic material has been charted by Stefan Baums and Andrew Glass.[84] Concurrently with the editorial activities, a first *Dictionary of Gāndhārī* is being compiled by Baums and Glass.[85] Provisional summaries of the manuscript culture and literature of ancient Gandhāra have been published by Baums and Richard Salomon, as well as discussions of the development of Gāndhārī canonical literature by Salomon and Mark Allon and that of scholastic literature by Baums and Collett Cox.[86] In addition to the complete publication of the known manuscripts, a comprehensive study of the connections of Gāndhārī with Pali and Sanskrit Buddhist literature remains a desideratum.

FURTHER READING

Allon, Mark. "The Formation of Canons in the Early Indian Nikāyas or Schools in the Light of the New Gāndhārī Manuscript Finds." *Buddhist Studies Review* 35 (2018): 225–244.

Baums, Stefan. "Gandhāran Scrolls: Rediscovering an Ancient Manuscript Type." In *Manuscript Cultures: Mapping the Field*. Edited by Jörg B. Quenzer, Dmitry Bondarev, and Jan-Ulrich Sobisch, 183–225. Berlin: De Gruyter, 2014.

Baums, Stefan. "Truth and Scripture in Early Buddhism: Categorial Reduction as Exegetical Method in Ancient Gandhāra and Beyond." In *Buddhism across Asia: Networks of Material, Intellectual and Cultural Exchange, Volume I*. Edited by Tansen Sen, 19–38. Singapore: Institute of Southeast Asian Studies, 2014.

Baums, Stefan. "Commentary: Overview." In *Brill's Encyclopedia of Buddhism, I*. Edited by Jonathan A. Silk, 409–418. Leiden, The Netherlands: Brill, 2015.

Brough, John. *The Gāndhārī Dharmapada*. London: Oxford University Press, 1963.

Cox, Collett. "Gāndhārī Kharoṣṭhī Manuscripts: Exegetical Texts." In *From Birch-Bark to Digital Data: Recent Advances in Buddhist Manuscript Research: Papers Presented at the Conference "Indic Buddhist Manuscripts: The State of the Field," Stanford, June 15–19, 2009*. Edited by Paul Harrison and Jens-Uwe Hartmann, 35–49. Vienna: Verlag der Österreichischen Akademie der Wissenschaften, 2014.

Fussman, Gérard. "Gāndhārī écrite, gāndhārī parlée." In *Dialectes dans les littératures indo-aryennes*. Edited by Colette Caillat, 433–501. Paris: Institut de civilisation indienne, 1989.

Salomon, Richard. *Ancient Buddhist Scrolls from Gandhāra: The British Library Kharoṣṭhī Fragments*. Seattle: University of Washington Press, 1999.

Salomon, Richard. "Recent Discoveries of Early Buddhist Manuscripts and Their Implications for the History of Buddhist Texts and Canons." In *Between the Empires: Society in India 300 BCE to 400 CE*. Edited by Patrick Olivelle, 349–382. New York: Oxford University Press, 2006.

Salomon, Richard. "An Unwieldy Canon: Observations on Some Distinctive Features of Canon Formation in Buddhism." In *Kanonisierung und Kanonbildung in der asiatischen Religionsgeschichte*. Edited by Max Deeg, Oliver Freiberger, and Christoph Kleine, 161–207. Vienna: Verlag der Österreichischen Akademie der Wissenschaften, 2011.

Salomon, Richard. *The Buddhist Literature of Ancient Gandhāra: An Introduction with Selected Translations*. Somerville, MA: Wisdom Publications, 2018.

Salomon, Richard. "Where Are the Gandharan Sūtras? Some Reflections on the Contents of the Gandhari Manuscript Collections." In *Research on the Saṃyukta-Āgama*. Edited by Dhammadinnā, 179–181. Taipei: Dharma Drum, 2020.

NOTES

1. Richard Salomon, *Ancient Buddhist Scrolls from Gandhāra: The British Library Kharoṣṭhī Fragments* (Seattle: University of Washington Press, 1999); and Stefan Baums, "Gandhāran Scrolls: Rediscovering an Ancient Manuscript Type," in *Manuscript Cultures: Mapping the Field*, ed. Jörg B. Quenzer, Dmitry Bondarev, and Jan-Ulrich Sobisch (Berlin: De Gruyter, 2014), 183–225.
2. Stefan Baums, "Inventing the Pothi: The Adoption and Spread of a New Manuscript Format in Indian Buddhism," in *Body and Cosmos: Studies in Early Indian Medical and Astral Sciences in Honor of Kenneth G. Zysk*, ed. Toke Lindegaard Knudsen, Jacob Schmidt-Maxxdsen, and Sara Speyer (Leiden, The Netherlands: Brill, 2021), 343–362.
3. John Brough, *The Gāndhārī Dharmapada* (London: Oxford University Press, 1963).
4. Franz Bernhard, "Gāndhārī and the Buddhist Mission in Central Asia," in *Añjali: Papers on Indology and Buddhism: A Felicitation Volume Presented to Oliver Hector de Alwis Wijesekera on His Sixtieth Birthday*, ed.

J. Tilakasiri (Peradeniya, Sri Lanka: The Felicitation Volume Editorial Committee, University of Ceylon, 1970), 55–62.

5. Auguste M. Boyer et al., *Kharoṣṭhī Inscriptions Discovered by Sir Aurel Stein in Chinese Turkestan* (Oxford: Clarendon Press, 1920–29) and Christopher Atwood, "Life in Third–Fourth Century Cadh'ota: A Survey of Information Gathered from the Prakrit Documents Found North of Minfeng (Niyä)," *Central Asiatic Journal* 35 (1991): 161–199.
6. Boucher, "Gāndhārī and the Early Chinese Buddhist Translations Reconsidered"; and Seishi, 辛嶋静志, 「長阿含経」の原語の研究.
7. Salomon, *Ancient Buddhist Scrolls*; and Allon, "The Senior Kharoṣṭhī Manuscripts".
8. Jens Braarvig, ed., *Buddhist Manuscripts in the Schøyen Collection*, vol. I (Oslo, Norway: Hermes, 2000).
9. Harry Falk and Ingo Strauch, "The Bajaur and Split Collections of Kharoṣṭhī Manuscripts within the Context of Buddhist Gāndhārī Literature," in Harrison and Hartmann, ed. *From Birch-Bark to Digital Data*, 51–78.
10. Richard Salomon, "Where Are the Gandharan Sūtras? Some Reflections on the Contents of the Gandhari Manuscript Collections," in *Research on the Saṃyukta-Āgama*, ed. Dhammadinnā (Taipei: Dharma Drum, 2020), 179–181.
11. These are cataloged and collected in Stefan Baums and Andrew Glass, *Catalog of Gāndhārī Texts*, 2002–.
12. Richard Salomon, "Recent Discoveries of Early Buddhist Manuscripts and Their Implications for the History of Buddhist Texts and Canons," in *Between the Empires: Society in India 300 BCE to 400 CE*, ed. Patrick Olivelle (New York: Oxford University Press, 2006), 373.
13. Eugen Hultzsch, *Inscriptions of Asoka* (Oxford: Clarendon Press, 1925).
14. The sigla CKD, CKI, and CKM refer to items in Baums and Glass, *Catalog*. See CKI 242 and 256.
15. Stefan Baums, "Catalog and Revised Texts and Translations of Gandharan Reliquary Inscriptions," in *Gandharan Buddhist Reliquaries*, ed. David Jongeward, Elizabeth Errington, Richard Salomon, and Stefan Baums (Seattle, WA: Early Buddhist Manuscripts Project, 2012), 200–251.
16. Richard Salomon, "Why Did the Gandhāran Buddhists Bury Their Manuscripts?," in *Buddhist Manuscript Cultures: Knowledge, Ritual, and Art*, ed. Stephen C. Berkwitz, Juliane Schober, and Claudia Brown (London: Routledge, 2009), 19–34.
17. Salomon, "Recent Discoveries," 365.
18. Salomon, "Recent Discoveries," 369.
19. For the 1st-century CE manuscript, see CKM 9; for the epithet *trepiḍaga*, see CKI 232.
20. Maurizio Taddei, "Addenda to the Story of the Buddha and the Skull-Tapper (AION, 39, 1979, 3)," *Annali dell'Istituto Universitario Orientale* 43 (1983): 333–339.
21. Baums, "Inventing the Pothi."
22. Chanida Jantrasrisalai et al., "Fragments of an Ekottarikāgama Manuscript in Gāndhārī," in *Buddhist Manuscripts*, vol. IV, ed. Jens Braarvig (Oslo, Norway: Hermes, 2016), 1–122.
23. Stefan Baums, Andrew Glass, and Kazunobu Matsuda, "Fragments of a Gāndhārī Version of the Bhadrakalpikasūtra," in Braarvig, *Buddhist Manuscripts*, 183–266.
24. Salomon, "Recent Discoveries," 365.
25. See CKM 233.
26. Mark Allon, "A Gāndhārī Version of the Story of the Merchants Tapussa and Bhallika," *Bulletin of the Asia Institute* 23 (2009): 9–19.
27. See CKM 66; Mark Allon and Richard Salomon, "Kharoṣṭhī Fragments of a Gāndhārī Version of the Mahāparinirvāṇasūtra," in Braarvig, *Buddhist Manuscripts*, 243–273.
28. See CKM 17.
29. See CKM 264; Ingo Strauch, "The Bajaur Collection of Kharoṣṭhī Manuscripts: Mahāprajāpatī Gautamī and the Order of Nuns in a Gandhāran Version of the Dakṣiṇāvibhaṅgasūtra," in *Women in Early Indian Buddhism: Comparative Textual Studies*, ed. Alice Collett (Oxford: Oxford University Press, 2014), 17–45.

30. CKM 232; Mark Allon and Blair Silverlock, "Sūtras in the Senior Kharoṣṭhī Manuscript Collection with Parallels in the Majjhima-nikāya and/or the Madhyama-āgama," in *Research on the Madhyama-āgama*, ed. Dhammadinnā (Taipei: Dharma Drum, 2017), 12–14.
31. CKM 232; Allon and Silverlock, "Sūtras," 14.
32. CKM 242; Allon and Silverlock, "Sūtras," 15.
33. CKM 244; Blair Silverlock, "An Edition and Study of the Goṣiga-sutra, the Cow-Horn Discourse (Senior Collection Scroll No. 12): An Account of the Harmonious Aṇarudha Monks" (PhD diss., University of Sydney, 2015).
34. Allon and Silverlock, "Sūtras," 18–39.
35. See CKM 260.
36. See CKM 14; Allon, *Three Gāndhārī Ekottarikāgama-Type Sūtras.*
37. See CKM 4; Stefan Baums, "A Gāndhārī Commentary on Early Buddhist Verses: British Library Kharoṣṭhī Fragments 7, 9, 13, and 18" (PhD diss., University of Washington, 2009), 513.
38. See CKM 99; Jantrasrisalai et al., "Ekottarikāgama."
39. CKM 243.
40. CKM 237 and 249; Glass, *Four Gāndhārī Saṃyuktāgama Sūtras.*
41. CKM 252: Marino, "Metaphor and Pedagogy in Early Buddhist Literature"; and Marino, "The Gandhari 'Discourse on Pleasure and Pain,'" 254; Allon, "A Gāndhārī Version of the Simile"; and Allon, "A Gandhari Saṃyukta-Āgama Version."
42. CKM 245 and 251; Lee, "A Study of the Gāndhārī Dārukkhandhopamasutta."
43. Lamotte, "Problèmes concernant les textes canoniques 'mineurs' and Lamotte, "Khuddakanikāya and Kṣudrakapiṭaka."
44. See CKM 77; Brough, *Gāndhārī Dharmapada.*
45. See CKM 18; Lenz, *A New Version of the Gāndhārī Dharmapada*; and Baums, "Gandhāran Scrolls," 186.
46. CKM 369; Falk, "A New Gāndhārī Dharmapada," 23–62, 26–29.
47. CKM 293; Falk, "The 'Split' Collection of Kharoṣṭhī Texts; and Salomon, "Gandharan Sūtras," 178–179.
48. CKM 7; Richard Salomon, *A Gāndhārī Version of the Rhinoceros Sūtra: British Library Kharoṣṭhī Fragment 5B* (Seattle: University of Washington Press, 2000).
49. For the reference in a commentary, see CKM 9.
50. CKD 204; Baums, "Gāndhārī Commentary," 45–46.
51. See CKM 9.
52. CKM 1 and 246; Richard Salomon, *Two Gāndhārī Manuscripts of the Songs of Lake Anavatapta (Anavatapta-gāthā): British Library Kharoṣṭhī Fragment 1 and Senior Scroll 14* (Seattle: University of Washington Press, 2008).
53. CKM 371; Harry Falk and Seishi Karashima, "A First-Century Prajñāpāramitā Manuscript from Gandhāra–Parivarta 1 (Texts from the Split Collection 1)," 創価大学国際仏教学高等研究所年報 15 (2012): 19–61; and Harry Falk and Seishi Karashima, "A First-Century Prajñāpāramitā Manuscript from Gandhāra–Parivarta 5 (Texts from the Split Collection 2)," 創価大学国際仏教学高等研究所年報 16 (2013): 97–169.
54. CKM 294; Paul Harrison, Timothy Lenz, and Richard Salomon, "Fragments of a Gāndhārī Manuscript of the Pratyutpannabuddhasaṃmukhāvasthitasamādhisūtra (Studies in Gāndhārī Manuscripts 1)," *Journal of the International Association of Buddhist Studies* 41 (2018): 117–143.
55. CKM 296; Harrison, Lenz, and Salomon, "Fragments," 118.
56. CKM 292; Harrison, Lenz, and Salomon, "Fragments," 118, 120.
57. CKM 265; Ingo Strauch, "More Missing Pieces of Early Pure Land Buddhism: New Evidence for Akṣobhya and Abhirati in an Early Mahayana Sutra from Gandhāra," *The Eastern Buddhist* 41 (2010):

23–66; Andrea Schlosser and Ingo Strauch, "Abhidharmic Elements in Gandhāran Mahāyāna Buddhism: Groups of Four and the Abhedyaprasādas in the Bajaur Mahāyāna Sūtra," in *Text, History, and Philosophy: Abhidharma across Buddhist Scholastic Traditions*, ed. Bart Dessein and Weijen Teng (Leiden, The Netherlands: Brill, 2016), 47–107; Andrea Schlosser and Ingo Strauch, "The Bajaur Mahāyāna Sūtra: A Preliminary Analysis of Its Contents," *Journal of the International Association of Buddhist Studies* 39 (2016): 309–335; and Ingo Strauch, "Early Mahāyāna in Gandhāra: New Evidence from the Bajaur Mahāyāna Sūtra," in *Setting Out on the Great Way: Essays on Early Mahāyāna Buddhism*, ed. Paul Harrison (Sheffield, UK: Equinox, 2018), 207–242.

58. CKM 267, 269, 274, and 366; Andrea Schlosser, "On the Bodhisattva Path in Gandhāra: Edition of Fragment 4 and 11 from the Bajaur Collection of Kharoṣṭhī Manuscripts" (PhD diss., Freie Universität Berlin, 2016).
59. CKM 261; Richard Salomon and Stefan Baums, "Sanskrit Ikṣvāku, Pali Okkāka, and Gāndhārī Iṣmaho," *Journal of the Pali Text Society* 29 (2007): 201–227.
60. CKM 128; Baums, Glass, and Matsuda, "Bhadrakalpikasūtra."
61. CKM 114; Stefan Baums et al., "The Bodhisattvapiṭakasūtra in Gāndhārī," in Braarvig, *Buddhist Manuscripts*, 267–282.
62. CKM 186; Paul Harrison et al., "A Gāndhārī Fragment of the Sarvapuṇyasamuccayasamādhisūtra," in Braarvig, *Buddhist Manuscripts*, 311–319.
63. CKM 57; Matsuda Kazunobu, 松田 和信, "平山コレクションのガンダーラ語貝葉写本断簡について," 印度學佛教學研究 62 (2013): 354–346.
64. Braarvig, *Buddhist Manuscripts*, 63–218.
65. CKM 276 and CKM 270, respectively; Ingo Strauch, "Looking into Water-Pots and over a Buddhist Scribe's Shoulder: On the Deposition and the Use of Manuscripts in Early Buddhism," *Asiatische Studien* 68 (2014): 817–825.
66. CKM 248, 250, and 257; Allon, "A Gāndhārī Version of the Story of the Merchants Tapussa and Bhallika."
67. CKM 17; Stefan Baums, "Truth and Scripture in Early Buddhism: Categorial Reduction as Exegetical Method in Ancient Gandhāra and Beyond," in *Buddhism across Asia: Networks of Material, Intellectual and Cultural Exchange*, vol. I, ed. Tansen Sen (Singapore: Institute of Southeast Asian Studies, 2014), 19–38.
68. Baums, "Truth and Scripture."
69. Stefano Zacchetti, "An Early Chinese Translation Corresponding to Chapter 6 of the Peṭakopadesa: An Shigao's Yin chi ru jing T 603 and Its Indian Original: A Preliminary Survey," *Bulletin of the School of Oriental and African Studies* 65 (2002): 74–98.
70. CKM 5 and 9; Baums, "Gāndhārī Commentary."
71. CKM 260.
72. CKM 30; Salomon, *Ancient Buddhist Scrolls*, 29–30.
73. Collett Cox, "Gāndhārī Kharoṣṭhī Manuscripts: Exegetical Texts," in Harrison and Hartmann, *From Birch-Bark to Digital Data*, 35–49.
74. Ingo Strauch, "The Bajaur Collection of Kharoṣṭhī Manuscripts: A Preliminary Survey," *Studien zur Indologie und Iranistik* 25 (2008): 119.
75. These fragments are CKM 267, 269, 274, and 366.
76. For original poetic compositions in praise of the Buddha, see CKM 8, 268, 271, 273, 280, and 368; for Buddhist story collections and story outlines, see CKM 1, 2, 3, 5, 14, 18, 23, and 370; for an apotropaic text, see CKM 266; and for a non-Buddhist treatise on statecraft, see CKM 272; Harry Falk and Elisabeth Steinbrückner, "A Metrical Version from Gandhāra of the 'Miracle at Śrāvastī' (Texts from the Split Collection 4)," 創価大学国際仏教学高等研究所年報 23 (2020): 3–42; Timothy Lenz, *Gandhāran Avadānas: British Library Kharoṣṭhī Fragments 1–3 and 21 and Supplementary Fragments A–C*

(Seattle: University of Washington Press, 2010); Lenz, *A New Version of the Gāndhārī Dharmapada and a Collection of Previous-Birth Stories*; Ingo Strauch, "The Evolution of the Buddhist Rakṣā Genre in the Light of New Evidence from Gandhāra: The *Manasvi-nāgarāja-sūtra from the Bajaur Collection of Kharoṣṭhī Manuscripts," *Bulletin of the School of Oriental and African Studies* 77 (2014): 63–84; Strauch, "Bajaur Collection," 125–127; and Ingo Strauch, "The Character of the Indian Kharoṣṭhī Script and the 'Sanskrit Revolution': A Writing System between Identity and Assimilation," in *The Idea of Writing: Writing across Borders*, ed. Alex de Voogt and Joachim Friedrich Quack (Leiden, The Netherlands: Brill, 2012), 131–168.

77. Horace Hayman Wilson, *Ariana Antiqua: A Descriptive Account of the Antiquities and Coins of Afghanistan: With a Memoir on the Buildings Called Topes, by C. Masson, Esq.* (London: Honourable Court of Directors of the East India Company, 1841); and Johann Martin Honigberger, *Früchte aus dem Morgenlande oder Reise-Erlebnisse, nebst naturhistorisch-medizinischen Erfahrungen, einigen hundert erprobten Arzneimitteln und einer neuen Heilart dem Medial-Systeme* (Vienna, Austria: Carl Gerold und Sohn, 1851).
78. Émile Senart, "Le manuscrit Dutreuil de Rhins," in *Actes du onzième Congrès international des orientalistes: Paris-1897, première section: langues et archéologie des pays ariens* (Paris: Imprimerie nationale, 1897), 1–7; Сергей Федорович Ольденбургъ, *Предварительная замѣтка о буддійской рукописи, написанной письменами kharoṣṭhī* (Санктпетербургъ, Russia: Типографія Императорской Академіи Наукъ, 1897); Émile Senart, "Le manuscrit kharoṣṭhī du Dhammapada: Les fragments Dutreuil de Rhins," *Journal Asiatique* 12 (1898): 193–308; Heinrich Lüders, "Bemerkungen zu dem Kharoṣṭhī Manuscript des Dhammapada (MS. Dutreuil de Rhins)," *Nachrichten der Königlichen Gesellschaft der Wissenschaften zu Göttingen* 4 (1899): 474–494; Sten Konow, "Bemerkungen über die Kharoṣṭhī-Handschrift des Dhammapada," in *Festschrift Ernst Windisch zum siebzigsten Geburtstag am 4. September 1914 dargebracht von Freunden und Schülern* (Leipzig: Otto Harrassowitz, 1914), 85–97; Benimadhab Barua and Sailendranath Mitra, *Prakrit Dhammapada: Based upon M. Senart's Kharoṣṭhī Manuscript: With Text, Translation & Notes* (Calcutta: University of Calcutta, 1921); Sten Konow, "The Oldenburg Folio of the Kharoṣṭhī Dhammapada," *Acta Orientalia* 19 (1943): 7–20; Harold Walder Bailey, "The Khotan Dharmapada," *Bulletin of the School of Oriental and African Studies* 11 (1945): 488–512; and Brough, *Gāndhārī Dharmapada*.
79. Bernhard, "Gāndhārī and the Buddhist Mission in Central Asia."
80. Gérard Fussman, "Gāndhārī écrite, gāndhārī parlée," in *Dialectes dans les littératures indo-aryennes*, ed. Colette Caillat (Paris: Institut de civilisation indienne, 1989), 433–501.
81. Fussman, "Gāndhārī écrite, gāndhārī parlée"; and Salomon, *Ancient Buddhist Scrolls*.
82. Allon, "Senior Kharoṣṭhī Manuscripts"; Salomon, *Rhinoceros Sūtra*; Allon, *Ekottarikāgama-Type Sūtras*; Lenz, *Dharmapada and Previous-Birth* Stories; Glass, *Saṃyuktāgama Sūtras*; Salomon, *Songs of Lake Anavatapta*; and Lenz, *Avadānas*.
83. Braarvig, *Buddhist Manuscripts*; and Braarvig, *Buddhist Manuscripts*, 311–319.
84. Baums and Glass, *Catalog*; and Stefan Baums and Andrew Glass, *Bibliography of Gāndhārī Studies*, 2002.
85. Baums and Glass, *Dictionary of Gāndhārī*.
86. Baums, "Gandhāran Scrolls"; Baums, "Inventing the Pothi"; Salomon, *The Buddhist Literature of Ancient Gandhāra*; Salomon, "Recent Discoveries"; Richard Salomon, "An Unwieldy Canon: Observations on Some Distinctive Features of Canon Formation in Buddhism," in *Kanonisierung und Kanonbildung in der asiatischen Religionsgeschichte*, ed. Max Deeg, Oliver Freiberger, and Christoph Kleine (Vienna: Verlag der Österreichischen Akademie der Wissenschaften, 2011), 161–207; Richard Salomon, "On the Evolution of Written Āgama Collections in Northern Buddhist Traditions," in Dhammadinnā, *Research on the Madhyama-āgama*, 239–268; Mark Allon, "The Formation of Canons in the Early Indian Nikāyas or Schools in the Light of the New Gāndhārī Manuscript Finds," *Buddhist Studies Review* 35 (2018):

225–244; Salomon, "Gandharan Sūtras," 179–181; Baums, "Truth and Scripture"; Cox, "Exegetical Texts"; and Stefan Baums, "Commentary: Overview," in *Brill's Encyclopedia of Buddhism, I*, ed. Jonathan A. Silk (Leiden, The Netherlands: Brill, 2015), 409–418.

Stefan Baums

CHAN LITERATURE

TEXTS, GENRES, AND LANGUAGE

Chan literature is vast and enchanting. In the Song dynasty (960–1279), an extensive printed Chan literature came into wide circulation, including more or less intact Tang (618–907) and Five-Dynasties (907–960) Chan texts, Tang and Five-Dynasties Chan texts heavily reworked by Song editors, and a vast newly created set of Song Chan texts. Printed Chan literature was very important in the spread of Chan among the educated elite during the Song period.[1] Between the late 11th century and the beginning of the 15th at least several hundred Chan texts of Chinese origin were published by woodblock printing in China, Japan, and Korea (Chan texts in Chinese composed by Koreans and Japanese are excluded from this study). For example, Shiina Kōyū's *Sō-Genban zenseki no kenkyū* (*Studies in Song and Yuan Editions of Chan Books*) gives 205 titles in a list of extant Song–Yuan editions and medieval Japanese Gozan (Five Mountains) reprints of Song–Yuan editions.[2] Thirty titles from Shiina's list are considered in this article.[3] Notably, twenty-one of these thirty titles appear in Shiina's twelve-volume series entitled *Gozanban Chūgoku zenseki sōkan* (*Collection of Five-Mountains Editions of Chinese Chan Books*), showing the importance of Gozan editions for any comprehensive study of Chan literature.[4] Six Dunhuang-manuscript Chan texts dating to Tang times, which were rediscovered in the major Dunhuang collections in the early 20th century, and the *Patriarchal Hall Collection* (*Zutangji*), a Five-Dynasties text lost in China and rediscovered in a Korean monastery in the 20th century, have been added to the thirty titles.[5] Three further additions, two Ming-dynasty Chan texts (providing coverage of Ming Chan, which is often neglected in Western scholarship) and one title missing in Shiina's list, brings the total number of titles in this article to forty.[6]

A database of forty texts admittedly is quite small. This treatment of a small but representative sample of Chan books focuses on genres, language matters, literary aspects, and buddhological contents. Attention to the large secondary literature on the subject is not stressed. The focus is the presentation of snippets of translated material from many of the texts to suggest, at least to some small degree, the "taste" of Chan literature, which is perhaps ironic because many Chan texts speak of reaching a state of "no taste" or "no flavor" (*mei ziwei* 沒滋味). There are eight genres (the *rules-of-purity/qinggui* genre of monastic codes has been omitted as too technical):

1. Sayings records (*yulu*).[7]
2. Flame-of-the-lamp records (*denglu*).
3. *Gāthā* and *shi* poetry, etc. (*jisong* and *shi*).
4. Standards (*ze* 則) with poetry/prose comments.

5. Compendia (*gangyao*).
6. Letters (*shu*).
7. Pretend dialogues.
8. Glossaries.

Much of the language in the Chan records (both *yulu* and flame-of-the-lamp records) is a hybrid, a mixture of the written elegant language (*wenyan wen*) and a type of written Chinese based on spoken language. In prior ages, the latter was called "unrefined language" (*suyu; suhua*). The matter is complicated by the fact that certain vernacular elements from the Song onward "became 'frozen' and were also used when composing subsequent texts (instead of using the contemporary vernacular elements)."[8] Eventually, the language of the Chan records became a sacerdotal language for Chan insiders. In Song times, members of the elite (the *shidafu* or scholar-official class) with an interest in Chan practice or even just an interest in a "good read" could probably read the Chan records with ease, but they are not easy reading for the modern reader.

In tackling the sacerdotal language of the Chan records, one of many possible pitfalls is vainly trying to interpret a vernacular expression as if it were literary Chinese. Fortunately, in recent times a number of vernacular Chinese and Chan/Zen dictionaries and glossaries have been published in China and Japan, and these publications are of great assistance.[9] An example is the phrase *bangjia* (傍家). One may be tempted reflexively to render it into English as something like *nearby the home*. In fact, Japanese Edo-period Zen commentators made precisely this error when they glossed this phrase as *one who is nearby other family gates loses his own family treasure* or *other families*.[10] They mistakenly read the *jia* (家) as *family* or *home*, its usual meaning, unaware that here the *jia* is an "empty" adverbial suffix. This adverb *bangjia* means *straying off onto a byway, digression, going astray off onto a side street*, or *divorced from the correct path*. It appears in numerous Chan records.

Throughout the Chan records, ordinary, everyday words and expressions sometimes stand in for more imposing Buddhist-sounding equivalents. An example is the vernacular *yumo* 與麼 (with orthographical variants), which ordinarily means *in this way* or *in that way*. However, *yumo* can suggest the Sanskrit Buddhist term *tathatā*: *reality as it truly is* or, in what is sometimes humorously dubbed Buddhist Hybrid English, *suchness/thusness*. A problem is sorting out the instances in the Chan records when *yumo* carries only its everyday meaning (*in that way*) and the instances when it carries added buddhological weight of *tathatā*. The phrase *zhe ge tiandi* (者箇田地) has the everyday meaning *this rice/vegetable field*. But in the Chan records it often means *this state*, i.e., the *mind ground* (*xindi*), *the original face* (*benlai mianmu*), and so forth. The phrase *ci shi* (此事) in everyday usage simply means *this matter*, but in the Chan records it often stands for one's *original true nature* (*benfen*). The third-person pronoun *qu* (渠) in the Chan records often refers to *Mr. Man-in-charge* (*zhuren gong*), the person with no characteristics or form. The phrase *na bian* (那邊) in everyday language means *over there* or *yonder*, but there are cases in the Chan records where it means one's *original hometown* (*benlai jiaxiang*) or *original face* (*benlai mianmu*). *This person* (*ge ren* 箇人) can mean the *proper/accomplished Chan person*, and so on.

In the Chan records, one frequently encounters two lines concerned with the very Chan custom of tea drinking: *qie zuo chi cha* (且坐喫茶) and *chi cha qu* (喫茶去). At first glance, they look similar. However, they are drastically different in thrust. The first indicates approval: "Well, sit down and have a cup of tea." The second has a pronounced dismissive tone: "After you've gone and had a cup of tea in the hall, come back and start all over again!" If the reader misses the sarcastic tone inherent in the second, the whole import of the passage in the Chan record is lost. Compare:

> Suddenly someone asked the Master a question: "What if an extra-superior person were to come to you?" I'd say: "*Well, why don't you sit down and have a cup of tea!*"[11]
>
> . . .
>
> Question: "An ancient had a saying: 'If on the road you encounter someone who has awakened to the Way, do not respond with verbalization or with silence.' I don't know what to respond with." The Master said: "*Well, go have a cup of tea [and come back and start all over again]!*"[12]

These sorts of language patterns account for some of the power and beauty of Chan literature—its ability to enchant the reader.

Yulu. In fully developed Song-dynasty examples of the *yulu* (*sayings record*; 語錄) genre, which sometimes can run to ten or even thirty fascicles, the term *yulu* appears in two locations.[13] The first is at the very beginning of the text as the general title of the *yulu* compilation as a whole: *Such-and-Such Chan Master Yulu*. The second is in the titles of "abbacy *yulu*," discrete records for each monastery or hermitage at which the master in question served as abbot: *Such-and-Such Mountain/Superior Prefecture Such-and-Such Monastery Yulu*. The abbacy *yulu* are always placed at the very beginning of a Song *yulu* compilation. The sayings material in an abbacy *yulu* centers on formal talks of the master. These abbacy *yulu* are in turn followed by a mass of literary material of different genres—verses on old standards, *gāthā*, encomia, prefaces, colophons, stupa inscriptions, letters, and so forth. The first three texts in the following list, all from the Tang, could be dubbed "proto-*yulu*" or something of the sort. They provide only a small hint of what is to come. Here is a short list (with convenient abbreviations):

1. *Records* II and III (part of the *Bodhidharma Anthology*).
2. *Platform Talks* (*Tanyu*) of Heze Shenhui (荷澤神會; 684–758): Shenhui's *Platform*.
3. *Essentials of Mind Transmission* (*Chuanxin fa yao*) and *Wanling Record* (*Wanling lu*): *Huangbo Records*.
4. *Chan Master Linji Huizhao's Yulu* (*Linji Huizhao chanshi yulu*): *Linjilu*.
5. *Chan Master Yunmen Kuangzhen's Extended Record* (*Yunmen Kuangzhen chanshi guanglu*): *Yunmen guanglu*.
6. *Chan Master Dahui Pujue's Yulu* (*Dahui Pujue chanshi yulu*): *Dahui yulu*.
7. *Chan Master Hongzhi's Extended Record* (*Hongzhi chanshi guanglu*): *Hongzhi guanglu*.
8. *Chan Master Wuzhun Shifan's Yulu* (*Wuzhun Shifan yulu* = *Fojian chanshi yulu*): *Wuzhun yulu*.
9. *Chan Master Shixi Xinyue's Yulu* (*Shixi Xinyue chanshi yulu* = *Fohai chanshi yulu*): *Shixi yulu*.
10. *Preceptor Yanxi's Yulu* (*Yanxi heshang yulu*): *Yanxi yulu*.

11. *Preceptor Xutang's Yulu* (*Xutang heshang yulu*): *Xutang yulu.*
12. *Great Teacher Gaofeng's Yulu* (*Gaofeng dashi yulu*) and *Preceptor Gaofeng's Chan Essentials* (*Gaofeng heshang chanyao*): *Gaofeng yulu* and *Gaofeng chanyao.*
13. *Chan Master Dufeng Shan of Tianzhen's Essential Sayings* (*Tianzhen Dufeng Shan chanshi yaoyu*).

Records II and III of the *Bodhidharma Anthology* (a provisional English title for a text sometimes called the *Bodhidharma Treatise*) and Shenhui's *Platform Talks* constitute an embryonic phase. Portions of the *Bodhidharma Anthology* are excerpted in traditional sources, but pieces on Dunhuang manuscripts allow the assembly of a more or less complete anthology. It is one of ten texts attributed to Bodhidharma or claiming to present his teaching. There are seven separate texts of the anthology: a biography of Bodhidharma, an exposition his teaching of two entrances (*er ru* 二入), two literary-style letters, and three records (Records I, II, and III). Record II is cast in question-and-answer format; Record III is a set of sayings—these two records are a long way from a Song *yulu,* but they are a first step in terms of style and format.

Record II breaks down into three parts: the opening portion centers on an unknown figure called Master Yuan (*Yuan shi* 緣師); sections following that center on Bodhidharma's successor Huike; and the final sections are miscellaneous dialogues. Here are some sayings of Master Yuan:

> Dharma Master Yuan also says: "When you have vital energy, you will avoid being discombobulated by other people, and your spirit will be okay. Why? Because when you esteem knowledge, you will be deceived by other people and by dharmas. If you esteem even a single person as 'correct,' you will not avoid being discombobulated and confused by this person." . . . Dharma Master Zhi saw Dharma Master Yuan on the street of the butchers and asked: "Did you see the butchers slaughtering the sheep?" Dharma Master Yuan said: "I'm not blind! How could I not see them?" Dharma Master Zhi said: "Master Yuan—you're saying you've witnessed a sight [forbidden by the disciplinary code]!" Master Yuan said: "You've witnessed it on top of witnessing it!"[14]

Shenhui's *Platform,* a Dunhuang-manuscript text, is a record of talks given by the "evangelist" Shenhui sometime after 718. Although this text has a rather pronounced doctrinal cast, and thus is very far from a Song *yulu,* there is still a hint of the atmosphere of those *yulu* in the way Shenhui forcefully addresses his audience: "Good friends!" (*zhishi* 知識).[15] This "everyone!" or "all of you!" form of address conveys much the same feeling as the vocative "Chan worthies!" (*zhu chande* 諸禪德) found so often in the Song *yulu.* Shenhui's most basic doctrinal assertion involves the "clear and constant Knowing" that Bodhidharma silently pointed to as the very substance of mind:

> The original substance [of mind] is empty and calm. From this empty and quiescent substance there arises "Knowing." Correctly discriminating the greens, yellows, reds, and whites of the world as they are really is wisdom. But not conforming to that discrimination and thereby activating [false thought] is *samādhi.* Anything like congealing

mind to enter *samādhi* is falling into a dark emptiness. After exiting from *samādhi*, to activate mind to discriminate conditioned things—[in the world] this is called wisdom, but in the sutras it is called false thought.[16]

The two *Huangbo Records* dealing with the teachings of Huangbo Xiyun (黄檗希運; d. 850) were compiled by Pei Xiu (裴休; 797–870), the eminent Tang statesman, illustrious calligrapher, and fervent (some said eccentric) Buddhist practitioner. The *Chuanxin fa yao* portion of the *Huangbo Records* consists of lengthy sermons, some of which are dated ("on the first day of the ninth month the Master said to Xiu"[17]), and records of question-and-answer sessions between Pei Xiu and the Master Huangbo. The sermons have the flavor of "dharma talks" (*fayu*) in a Song *yulu*. The *Wanling lu* portion is mostly the record of question-and-answer sessions, but concludes with a formal "dharma-convocation talk" (*shangtang*) by Huangbo.[18] There is a relatively high density of vernacular elements in the *Huangbo Records*, though vernacular elements do appear in even earlier Tang texts such as Shenhui's *Platform*. These characteristics mark the *Huangbo Records* as a kind of precursor phase to the true *yulu* of the Song.

Pei Xiu's preface, which is dated to the day as "Dazhong 11, first eight days of the eleventh month" (October 22–29, 857), provides a detailed account of the genesis of the text:

In Huichang 2 [842] I was stationed as Surveillance Commissioner in Zhongling, and I welcomed the Master Huangbo Xiyun from [Huangbo] Mountain [in Gao'an county, Jiangxi] to [Hong]zhou [northwest of Zhongling] to take repose [i.e., become abbot] at Longxing Monastery. Day and night I inquired of him about the path. In Dazhong 2 [848] when I was stationed as Surveillance Commissioner at Wanling [in Jiangxi] I again went to do obeisance in welcoming him to the administrative department and had him dwell peacefully at the Kaiyuan Monastery, day and night receiving his dharma. I withdrew to record it [i.e., his talks], but I only obtained ten or twenty percent of it. I "wore it at my waist as a mind-seal pendant," not daring to publish it. But now I have come to fear that its divine, pure meaning may be lost to the future, so at last I took it out and handed it over to his monk disciples Taizhou and Fajian. They took it back to Guangtang Monastery on the old mountain [i.e., Xiyun's original Mt. Huangbo in coastal Fuzhou] and asked the venerables and dharma assembly whether it differed from what they had personally heard constantly in the past.[19]

Here is a snippet of the *Chuanxin fa yao*:

Question: "How can one not fall into the steps [of the bodhisattva practice]?" The Master said: "All day long eat your food without ever chewing a single grain. All day long walk about without ever treading on a bit of ground. If things are that way, there will be no [grasping of] the characteristics of self and other. Even though all day long you're never apart from events, you're not deluded by sense objects. This is called the 'free person.' And from moment to moment you never see any characteristics—don't recognize the three times of before and after. The past hasn't gone; the present doesn't abide; and the future doesn't come."[20]

The *yulu* described herein are but a small sampling of the enormous mature *yulu* literature of the Song, Yuan, and Ming. Let us first look at the *Linjilu*, the *yulu* of Linji Yixuan (臨濟義玄; d. 866). Although Linji is a Tang-dynasty master, his *yulu* is really the product of Song editorial work; it is undeniably one of the most influential of all Chan records. Teachings, motifs, expressions, and so forth found in the *Linjilu* are repeated in innumerable later Chan records. Key themes and phrases from the *Linjilu* include the following:

1. Do not be passively rotated by the sense fields—everywhere *use* the sense fields (*bu bei jing zhuan chuchu yong jing*).
2. Stop the mind that rushes around and around searching (*xiede niannian chi qiu xin*).
3. Do not dither or hesitate (*niyi*).
4. Do not be bewildered or deluded by other people (*mo shou renhuo*).
5. A realized practitioner brings to bear everything he's got, i.e., exhibits the nonverbal, unconstrained embodiment of the spontaneity of the buddha nature (*quanti zuoyong*).
6. In one's current venue of activities (*ni jin yongchu*), nothing is lacking.[21]

Yunmen Wenyan (雲門文偃; 864–949) and his lineage were very important in the development of Chan literature. The Yunmen-school figure Yuanjue Zongyan (圓覺宗演) of Mt. Gu in coastal Fuzhou edited both the *Linjilu* and the *Yunmen guanglu* in the early 1100s. Yuanjue's editing of these two *yulu* is noteworthy—the vibrant Linji persona of the standard edition of the *Linjilu* produced by Yuanje becomes a presence in subsequent Chan records, and the standards (*ze* 則) collections drew more standards from Yuanjue's edition of the *Yunmen guanglu* than from any other *yulu*. Yuanjue's shaping of the materials at his disposal may account for the fact that these two *yulu* show elements in common. For instance, both have sections labeled "calibrating and adjudicating" (*kanbian* 勘辨) and "record of the master's activities" (*xinglu* 行錄). Although scatological phrasing is common in Chan texts (the word *shit* [*shi* 屎] appears hundreds and hundreds of times), Yuanjue's *Yunmen guanglu* edition is particularly noteworthy in this respect, with almost thirty examples:

> The Master was drinking tea in the Sangha Hall. He held up a plate and said: "I'll let you eat steamed buns. What do you say this is?" He substituted for them: "Dried dog shit."[22]
>
> . . .
>
> Spoken at a Dharma convocation: "When I offer for consideration the words of an old standard and cause you to immediately accept it, I am already spreading shit on top of your heads. Even if I were to hold up a single hair and you were to thereby understand the whole world, it would already be gouging out a wound in perfectly good flesh. At any rate, you must really arrive at *this state* [*zhe ge tiandi* 者箇田地]. If you're not there yet, well, you mustn't filch empty names. Instead, you must take a step back and try and search for what is right there under your own feet: what is the principle here? In reality, there isn't the slightest thing that could constitute understanding for you or that could constitute hesitation for you. Each one of you persons on duty has *the one matter, the great function* that appears right in front of you. And you needn't trouble yourself about expending a single iota of energy. You are no different from the patriarchs and buddhas. From the outset, in the case of all you people, your confidence roots have been meager

and your bad karma thick. Suddenly you've sprouted so many [beast] horns. You shoulder your bowl bags as you make pilgrimage through thousands upon thousands of villages—why trouble yourselves? Well, what is it that all of you are lacking? Who among you great persons doesn't have his portion? You understand all by your lonesome, but still your luck isn't holding. You should not be deceived by others and do as others tell you. As soon as you see an old preceptor open his mouth, you'd better immediately stuff his mouth with a stone, then he'll be just like a green fly on top of shit!"[23]

Perhaps Yuanjue enhanced his *Linjilu* by inserting a bit of the outré style:

> Spoken at a Dharma convocation: "Beyond the red-meatball [i.e., the body-and-mind of the five *skandhas*] there is the one true person [i.e., true mind] without rank. [That true person] is constantly exiting and entering from the face-gates of all of you people. Those who have not seen with their own eyes: Look! Look! At one point there was a monk who emerged [from the standing assembly] to ask: 'What is the true person without rank?' The Master got down from his chair and grabbed him by the collar, saying: 'C'mon! C'mon!' The monk dithered. The Master, thrusting him back, said: 'This true person without rank—what a magnificent piece of dried shit!' And he at once returned to his room."[24]
>
> . . .
>
> "Venerables! You shoulder such traveling gear as your bowl bag and sack of shit [i.e., physical body], running around byways [*bangjia* 傍家] seeking 'the Buddha' and seeking 'the dharma.' The one [true person] rushing around right now in that way—just who do you think *he* [*qu* 渠] is? He is lively like a fish—he has no base. Try to round him up—he doesn't coalesce. Prod him—he doesn't disperse. Seek him—the further away he is. Don't seek him—he's right in front of you. The divine sound [of that true person] is filling your ears. If you don't have confidence in him, then even a century's toil is futile."[25]

Our next *yulu* is the *Dahui yulu* in thirty fascicles. Dahui Zonggao (大慧宗杲; 1089–1163) is *the* representative Chan master of the Song period. Due to his association with certain scholar-officials who advocated retaking the North from the Jin/Jurchen (some were his students), Dahui was exiled to the South for sixteen years, but finally was restored to the abbotship of the premier monastery of the day, Jingshan. This enormous thirty-fascicle text contains his abbacy *yulu* for seven Chan monasteries; a stupa inscription; master–student interactions in the master's room; verses on old standards; *gāthā*; encomia for the buddhas and patriarchs; self-encomia; "holding the torch" pieces (used in a type of funerary practice that symbolizes cremation); general sermons; dharma talks to named individuals; and letters (the last also circulated independently). The *Dahui yulu* was presented to the imperial court in 1171 and entered the canon the following year, less than a decade after Dahui's death. Here is a talk:

> Spoken at a Dharma convocation: "The Master picked up his stick and showed it to the sangha, saying: 'Do you see this?' Also, he hit the desk once, saying: 'Do you hear it? If you say you *really* saw it and *really* heard it, you're merely a fellow who follows sounds and pursues forms!' He once again raised it, saying: 'Do you see it?' Also, he hit the desk

once, saying: 'Do you hear it? If you say you *did not* see it and *did not* hear it, you're merely a fellow who avoids forms and evades sounds! When all is said and done, how about it?' He flung the stick down, saying: 'When the egret has nine marshes [to choose from], it finds it difficult to take flight freely; when the horse doesn't have a thousand miles to roam in, it futilely chases after the wind.' "[26]

Next is the *Hongzhi guanglu*. Hongzhi Zhengjue (宏智正覺; 1091–1157), the representative figure of the Song-dynasty revival of the Caodong school, was a monk of great literary talent. The *Hongzhi guanglu* consists of eight fascicles: his abbacy *yulu* for five Chan monasteries; verses on old standards; prose comments on old standards; another abbacy *yulu* for Mt. Tiantong; talks at small, impromptu gatherings; dharma talks for named individuals; praises; and verses and inscriptions, including the *Inscription on Silence-and-Illumination* (*Mozhao ming*) of seventy-two four-character lines.[27] Here are two of Hongzhi's talks, followed by the opening lines of his *Inscription on Silence-and-Illumination*:

> Spoken at a Dharma convocation: "Stand alone without changing—walk all around without risk. Don't be averse to the sense objects that fill up your eyes—just have confidence in the fact that the three realms are mind-only. Array the thousand peaks and face toward the commanding mountain—bring together the hundred rivers so they reach the sea. Chan worthies! If you are able to understand this, you'll roll up the drop-curtain and eliminate obstructions. If you are not able to understand this, you'll close the door and produce blockages. When you haggle over understanding vis-à-vis not understanding, the pail of black lacquer [i.e., nescience] remains the same, and you are uneasy."[28]
>
> . . .
>
> At a small [impromptu] gathering a monk asked: "What saying do you have, Preceptor, that can strike people like me personally and teach them?" The Master said: "I have no trace of elegant literary style—the initial *state of being* is impossible to transmit." The monk said: "Should we then say that Chan is a matter of empty and spontaneous illumination requiring no expenditure of mental effort?" The Master said: "Loom above things while relying on nothing; be ethereal while wading through sense objects." The monk said: "Isn't that the *100-percent time*?" The Master said: "Try to pass through to *yonder* [*na bian* 那邊 i.e., your *original hometown* or *original face*]—then you'll have a path to jettisoning self!" The monk said: "I open the golden bolt [on the mystery gate to this *yonder*] and try to get a look at what's inside, but it's an indistinct and strange scene." The Master said: "That's not the *yonder* [I'm talking about]!" The monk said: "What is this *yonder*?" The Master said: "[*Yonder* is,] when walking about the lapis lazuli hall, you fall forward and are surely pulverized into little bits."[29]
>
> . . .

Silence-and-Illumination Inscription:

> Complete silence—forget words; complete radiance—right in front of you.
> When reflecting, vast; the body-locus numinous.

Numinous in solitary illumination; within illumination a return to the miraculous.
The dew-laden moon in the Milky Way; the snowy pines on the cloudy peak.[30]

Wuzhun Shifan (無準師範; 1177–1249) belonged to the Yangqi-Po'an wing of the Linji lineage. At the invitation of the Song Emperor Lizong, he ascended the seat and gave a dharma talk in the Hall of Compassionate Brightness at the imperial court. His five-fascicle *Wuzhun yulu* contains the following: preface; abbacy *yulu* for five Chan monasteries; talks at small, impromptu gatherings; dharma talks for named individuals; general sermons; prose comments on old standards; verses on old standards; verses; praises of the buddhas and Chan patriarchs; requests for praises; remarks at minor functions; and prefaces and colophons. Here is one of his talks:

> Spoken at a Dharma convocation: The Master beckoned the great sangha, saying: "Chan. Chan. The sublime and high summit. In front of the thousand-foot cliff—how could there be an ancient pine tree? Strange and odd; strange and odd! Crooked and bent; crooked and bent! Twisting and slippery; twisting and slippery!' If any of you people understand in this manner, you were born in the [nonexistent] donkey year [i.e., you're so stupid that, no matter how many aeons you pass through, you'll never reach understanding]."[31]

Shixi Xinyue (石溪心月; d. 1254) was in the Yangqi–Songyuan branch of the Linji lineage. His *Shixi yulu* consists of three fascicles: a preface; abbacy *yulu* for six Chan monasteries; take-the-flywhisk talks; small, impromptu talks; general sermons; dharma talks for named individuals; prefaces and colophons; verses; praises on the buddhas and Chan patriarchs; requests for praises; and remarks at minor functions. Here are two talks:

> Spoken at a Dharma convocation: "Before the aeon of nothingness, continuous and tightly meshed. That's already gone—don't chase after it. After the aeon of nothingness, tightly meshed and continuous. That hasn't yet come—well, put it aside. Just when it's the aeon of nothingness—the continuous rests in the tightly meshed, and the tightly meshed rests in the continuous. How do you go about realizing this? A gnarled and withered tree—the message of springtime lies within it."[32]
>
> ...
>
> Spoken at a Dharma convocation: The Master picked up his stick, hit the desk once, and said: "Before the seven buddhas of the past, it was such." Again, he hit the desk once and said: "After the seven buddhas of the past, it's also such." He hit the desk once more: "A cloud arises—evening in the valley; a solitary crane descends—the distant sky."[33]

Yanxi Guangwen (偃溪廣聞; 1189–1263) was in the Yangqi–Dahui branch of the Linji lineage. His two-fascicle *Yanxi yulu* contains the following: abbacy *yulu* for eight Chan monasteries; general sermons; dharma talks for named individuals; verses; praises of the buddhas and Chan patriarchs; requests for praises; remarks at minor functions; prefaces and colophons; a memorial; stupa inscriptions; and a colophon. Here are two short talks:

Spoken at a Dharma convocation: " 'Complete silence—unexcelled awakening is gotten from this. Complete understanding—a smack on the golden pheasant, and one sees the light.' Chan disciples! Both of these [high-falutin' lines] are for the senile!"[34]

. . .

Spoken at a Dharma convocation: "Chan is non-thinking—the Way abjures any sense of meritorious accomplishment. Get rid of these two avenues, and it will be like the time of "Great Peace": You'll drive your buoyant carriage over deeply familiar roads and be able to go anywhere. You want to look off at Deshan's [stick] and Linji's [shout]—they are very far off! How so? Before [Confucius wrote down a single] stroke [of the commentaries on the *Classic of Changes* called the *Ten Wings*] there had always been [the sixty-four hexagrams of] the *Classic of Changes*; after [Confucius] edited [3,000 poems] down [to 305] there was no *Classic of Poetry*."[35]

Xutang Zhiyu (虚堂智愚; 1185–1269), also known by the sobriquet "the old man who has ceased plowing" (Xigengsou 息耕叟), belonged to the Yangqi–Songyuan branch of the Linji lineage. He was honored by two emperors. His ten-fascicle *Xutang yulu* contains the following: abbacy *yulu* for ten Chan monasteries; dharma talks for named individuals; prefaces and colophons; requests for praises; general sermons; verses on old standards; substitution comments (i.e., comments in the ancient's stead when the ancient is silent) and additional comments (i.e., comments as alternatives for the ancient's comment) for 100 old standards; praises for the buddhas and patriarchs; obeisance at the stupas of Chan patriarchs; remarks at rituals; verses; a "continued collection"; two "later records" of Dharma convocations at Chan monasteries; verses; remarks at functions; remarks at "holding-the-torch ceremonies" (a funerary practice symbolizing cremation); dharma talks for named individuals; requests for praises; and a farewell-to-the-world verse. Here is one of his talks and his farewell poem:

Spoken at a Dharma convocation: "Every day while doing cross-legged sitting on your cushions you people are immersed in delusive thoughts, idly looking on with folded arms. The result is you bolt to the south and run to the north. You are like ducks gulping down snails. Today I shall betray nothing in my tone of voice, so as to allow all of you to have a clue for entering awakening." After a long while he clapped his hands, saying: "One-half can enter; one-half cannot."[36]

Xutang's poem at death:

For eight-five years
I've known neither buddhas nor patriarchs.
I pay no attention and walk off,
Vanishing into the immense sky.[37]

The Yuan-dynasty Chan master Gaofeng Yuanmiao (高峰原妙; 1238–1295) was in the Yangqi–Po'an wing of the Linji lineage. Two records exist for Gaofeng, the *Gaofeng yulu* and the *Gaofeng chanyao*, and they show an enormous overlap—almost three-quarters of the *Gaofeng chanyao* text appears in the *Gaofeng yulu*. Gaofeng's "three essentials" (*san yao* 三要), which is found in both records, became well known throughout East Asian Chan/Sŏn/Zen. Yunqi Zhuhong of the Ming treasured the *Gaofeng yulu* and carried it on his person. The *Gaofeng chanyao* was printed numerous times in Korea and became an integral part of the monastic curriculum in Korea as one of the four books of the *Fourfold Collection* (*Sajip*), and, in Japan, Gaofeng's "three essentials" became a favorite Zen formulation of Hakuin Ekaku (1685–1768). Here are two Gaofeng talks, the first on zeal (for which he is justly known) and the second on his "three essentials":

> In the practice of Chan, if you want to achieve success within a set time limit, it is like falling to the bottom of a thousand-foot well. From morning till evening and from evening to morning all your myriad ruminations and reflections will be solely the thought of seeking a way out. In the end, you will have absolutely no thought beyond this. Truly, if you can accumulate results of practice in this way, it will take perhaps three days, perhaps five days, perhaps seven days. If you don't penetrate to awakening, then today I have committed a grave violation of the injunction against lying and for eternity will fall into the hell of the ox-plow that pulls out the tongues of oral-karma sinners.[38]
>
> . . .
>
> If you are thinking of making a genuine hands-on investigation of Chan, you absolutely must possess three essentials. The first essential is having the faculty of great confidence. You know perfectly well that there is *this matter* [*ci shi* 此事]—it is as if you are leaning against an unshakeable Mt. Sumeru. The second essential is having the determination of great fury—it is as if you have encountered the scoundrel who killed your father, and immediately you want to cut him in two with one thrust of your sword. The third essential is the sensation of great uncertainty or doubt—it is as if you have in secret committed an atrocious act, and the very moment has come when you are about to be exposed, but you are not yet exposed. Indeed, if you can come to possess these three essentials, certainly on that very day you will achieve success.[39]

The Ming Linji Chan master Dufeng Benshan (毒峰本善; 1419–1482) exhibited both the Dahui style of *huatou* practice found in *Letters of Dahui* (text no. 37) and the sort of extreme zeal for practice of the Yuan master Gaofeng (text no. 12). This amalgam was a powerful current in Ming Chan and into the Qing. Here are two excerpts from Dufeng's *yulu*, *Chan Master Dufeng Shan of Tianzhen's Essential Sayings*:

> Spoken at a Dharma convocation: A monk asked: "Preceptor Gaofeng instructed the assembly:
>
> 'The clay ox in the sea runs clenching the moon in his teeth.
> The stone tiger on the cliff ledge sleeps embracing her cub.
> The iron snake bores right into the *vajra* eye.
> Mounted on an elephant in the Kunlun Mountains, the egret guides it along.
>
> Within these four lines there is *the single line* [i.e., the *huatou*]. [The *huatou*] can both kill and bring to life, can both unleash and snatch up. If you can investigate [the *huatou*] thoroughly, it will permit your finishing your entire life's Chan training.' But I don't know *that single line*." The Master said: "Wait until you awaken, and then I'll tell you. Understand?" The monk said: "I don't understand." The Master said: "Haven't you heard it said: 'If you

have a staff, I'll give you a staff; if you don't have a staff, I'll snatch away your staff.' " He got down from the high seat.[40]

. . .

If you wish to achieve liberation from samsara, first you must produce the mind of great confidence and make the four great vows. Stake your life on it. Before you have awakened, don't retreat from the aspiration for awakening. Don't alter your integrity concerning practice. If you haven't smashed the case you are probing, seen clearly, and severed even the tiniest activation of samsara, then you must make a vow not to break off midway and let go of your *huatou* [i.e., the phrase *your face before your father and mother conceived you*], not to separate yourself from a real teacher. If on purpose you contravene this vow, you will fall into a bad rebirth path and suffer immeasurable suffering. If you produce this great vow and protect this mind-set, only then will you be able to grasp the case as *my thing*.[41]

FLAME-OF-THE-LAMP RECORDS

Flame-of-the-lamp records (*denglu* 燈錄) focus on sequences of inheritors of the Chan dharma. The root metaphor is the flame of one lamp igniting the next lamp in an endless series of lamps, a metaphor that appears in the sutras. For instance, the "Entrance into the *Dharmadhātu* Chapter" of the *Avataṃsaka Sūtra* says: "It is like a single lamp that lights hundreds and thousands of lamps—this single original lamp never decreases and never goes out."[42] These texts are not really "histories" like Sima Qian's *Shiji* and the standard histories of China. They are more accurately described as collections of Chan "standards" (*ze* 則) arranged as a series of heirs of the flame of the lamp (a genealogy). Here is the short list of texts:

1. *Record of the Transmission of the Dharma Treasure* (*Chuan fabao ji*): *Chuanfa*.
2. *Record of the Lanka Masters and Disciples* (*Lengqie shizi ji*): *Lanka*.
3. *Record of the Dharma Treasure down through the Generations* (*Lidai fabao ji*): *Lidai*.
4. *Precious-Forest Traditions* (*Baolin zhuan*): *Baolin*.
5. *Patriarchal Hall Collection* (*Zutangji*): *Zutang*.
6. *Jingde Era Record of the Transmission of the Flame-of-the-Lamp* (*Jingde chuandeng lu*): *Jingde*.
7. *Tiansheng Era Extended Flame-of-the-Lamp Record* (*Tiansheng guang denglu*): *Tiansheng*.
8. *Jianzhong Jingguo Era Continued Flame-of-the-Lamp Record* (*Jianzhong Jingguo xu denglu*): *Jianzhong*.
9. *Program of the Linked Lamp-Flames of the Chan School* (*Zongmen liandeng huiyao*): *Liandeng*.
10. *Jiatai Era Universal Flame-of-the-Lamp Record* (*Jiatai pu denglu*): *Jiatai*.

The *Chuanfa* and the *Lanka* are flame-of-the-lamp records produced in the "Metropolitan school" of Chan, the East Mountain school that migrated from rural Hubei Province to the region of the imperial capitals in the North beginning in the 680s.[43] Both are Dunhuang-manuscript texts with compilation dates in the early 8th century, making them the earliest extant examples of the genre. The *Lidai*, a Dunhuang-manuscript flame-of-the-lamp record with a late-8th-century compilation date, is the transmission record of the Baotang house of

Chan.[44] Baotong was located in Sichuan (and had considerable influence on the emerging Tibetan Chan tradition). The *Lidai* contains an extensive set of the sayings of Baotang Wuzhu (保唐無住; 714–774).

The *Chuanfa* gives us an excellent description of the genre:

> Therefore, I have now compiled a brief record. Those who have transmitted the dharma in succession down from Bodhidharma are recorded in sequence as the *Record of the Transmission of the Treasure* in one roll. I will merely continue the names and deeds which are known of them, the locations where they transformed beings [i.e., taught disciples], that which has come to the attention of the ears and eyes of people [i.e., oral traditions], and that which can be ascertained from books. Since they were fused with the unconditioned and the biographical records are themselves simple, when it comes to their realization of the sagely purport, it will not be possible to express it in words. Apart from this there are also "icon charts" used in the composition of this record.[45]

The *Chuanfa* begins with Bodhidharma, not Śākyamuni or Indian patriarchs, but it does quote Huiyuan's preface to Buddhabhadra's translation of the *Dhyāna Sūtra* in an attempt to make the connection backward to the most recent buddha in this world system, Śākyamuni:

> "The *Preface to the Dhyāna Sūtra* of the superior man Huiyuan of Mt. Lu of old says: 'The Buddha handed over to Ānanda. Ānanda transmitted to Madhyāntika, and Madhyāntika transmitted to Śaṇavāsa.' We know that after that it did not fall to the ground, but was preserved in someone. Wonderful!"[46]

Thus, the connection to the buddhas of the past is found in the earliest extant example of the flame-of-the-lamp genre.

This genre can be divided into three phases:

1. The three Dunhuang manuscript texts (*Chuanfa*; *Lanka*; and *Lidai*) of the 8th century (prototype phase; corresponding to the Dunhuang-manuscript text *Bodhidharma Anthology*).
2. The *Baolin* and *Zutang*, which were, to a certain extent, lost to the Chinese tradition (developing phase).
3. The five lamps (*wu deng*) of the Song dynasty (mature phase; corresponding to mature Song *yulu* compendia).

There is an enormous growth in size over time: from a single fascicle in the case of the *Chuanfa* of the early 8th century to thirty fascicles in the case of the five lamps of the Song. This inheritor genre from the beginning included material that was not genealogical or biographical, such as sayings and poetry. By the time of the five lamps of the Song dynasty, the inheritor genre had become a repository for all sorts of miscellaneous material, such as praises, letters, etc.

The *Baolin* of 801 is the flame-of-the-lamp record of the Hongzhou house of Chan.[47] Of the original ten fascicles, only seven are extant. The sequence of buddhas and patriarchs in the *Baolin* became the standard in later records. The *Zutang*, which is usually assigned a compilation date of 952, inherits the *Baolin* and becomes the basis of the later flame-of-the-lamp literature.[48] The *Zutang* seems to have circulated in China until the end of the 11th century, but its transmission after that is unclear. It was rediscovered in Korea at the beginning of the 20th century. There are several theories concerning the stages of development of this text; here is that of Christoph Anderl:

1. A short 952 version consisting of a collection of dialogues and comments on the southern lineage of Xuefeng Icun (822–908) and related lineages—this incarnation was one fascicle.
2. Between 952 and about 1000 additions were made—during this period the text came to be divided into ten fascicles.
3. After appearance of *Jingde* (1004), interest in *Zutang* faded.
4. Once the *Zutang* reached Korea more additions were made (Korean preface; table of contents; and entries on Korean monks).
5. Entries on the seven buddhas of the past, Śākyamuni, the Indian patriarchs and possibly even the Chinese patriarchs *may have been added in Korea*.[49]

The length of the *Zutang* entries varies a great deal—important lineage figures have long entries. Other entries are very short, with little or no biographical information—just mention of the succession (with the formula "*Y* succeeds *X*") and inclusion of sayings. This emphasis on sayings materials continues through the later five lamps of the Song.

The *Jingde* is the core of the five lamps of the Song. The original compilation of 1004 was the work of Daoyuan (道原), a little-known member of the Fayan school of Chan, successor to Tiantai Deshao (891–972). The Fayan school was oriented to the Zongmi–Yanshou advocacy of the harmony of Chan and teachings. Daoyuan's compilation was subsequently reedited by a group of scholar-officials led by Yang Yi (楊億; 974–1020), a major political figure at the Song court and a fervent partisan of the Linji school. Yang Yi's revised *Jingde* was presented to the Emperor Zhenzong and entered into the canon. Yang Yi's preface states:

> There was a monk of the Eastern Wu named Daoyuan. With tranquillized mind and the joy of having deeply entered *dhyāna*, he sought out the hidden principle of emptiness. He spread out the [genealogical] charts of the [Chan] patriarchs circulating in the world, made extracts from the *yulu* of all the regions, put in proper sequence the origins and developments of the [Chan] lineages, and reworked complexities of phrasing. From the seven buddhas down to the successors of the great Fayan [Wenyi; 885–958], altogether it encompasses fifty-two generations and 1701 people. Consisting of thirty fascicles, he called it *Jingde Era Record of the Transmission of the Flame-of-the-Lamp*.[50]

Note that Daoyuan, the original compiler, is said to have worked from "charts," just as in the case of the *Chuanfa* (where it is "icon charts"), and that he included extracts from *yulu*. *Yulu* material is found throughout the *Jingde*—in fact, like the *Zutang*, not a few entries lack any biographical information whatsoever and consist solely of sayings. The opening entries in the *Jingde* are entries for the seven *tathāgatas* of the past, the first of the seven being Vipaśyin Buddha. This material is parallel to several Indian Buddhist sources. The *Jingde* begins as follows:

> Vipaśyin Buddha: the 998th honored buddha of the past adorned eon. Verse: "The body receives birth in the midst of no-characteristics; it is like an illusionist's producing various forms. The illusionist and the mind have never existed; sin and good fortune are both empty and unfixed." The *Dirghāgama* says: "Human life-span was 80,000 years at the time this buddha emerged into the world. He was of the warrior-noble class, and his family name was Kolita. His father's name was Bandhumant; his mother's name was Bandhumatī. He lived in the city of Bandhumatī. [At the time of his awakening] he sat beneath a *pātali* tree. He spoke dharma at three assemblies [of arhat disciples]. He crossed over to nirvana 348,000 people. His two chief monk disciples were named Khaṇḍa and Tiṣya. His attendant was Aśoka, his son Susaṃvṛttaskandha.[51]

For each of the subsequent buddhas leading up to Śākyamuni, exactly the same categories are covered. Although each set of details is different, the life stories are identical, utterly stereotyped. This Indian formulaic approach sets the tone for the remainder of the 1,701 entries of the *Jingde* and, in fact, for the flame-of-the-lamp genre as whole. It is sometimes said the format of this genre is indebted to the arranged biographies (*lie zhuan*) format of the Sima Qian's *Shiji* and the subsequent standard histories of China, but it is at least arguable that the flame-of-the-lamp format owes a great deal to Indian traditions concerning the myriad buddhas of the past, such as the accounts found in the *Buddhavaṃsa* and *Dirghāgama*. The life-story trajectory in the flame-of-the-lamp entries (implicit when there really is no life story but only dialogues and sayings) is always the same as that of the seven *tathāgatas* of the past: awakening, speaking dharma, and teaching disciples. This is not the trajectory of the arranged biographies of the standard histories. Those entries emphasize "an individual's official career, contributions to orthodox learning, or outstanding moral qualities or lack of them."[52] Other aspects are left unmentioned.

The first actual date mentioned in the *Jingde* is at the end of the entry for the twenty-seventh patriarch Prajñātāra: it is stated that his cremation and stupa correspond to the date of "first year of the Daming era of Emperor Xiaowu of the Song dynasty" (i.e., 457). Chinese-style dating is now applicable. Following Bodhidharma is the "twenty-ninth patriarch Great Master Huike" and his successors. The entry for Huike, the first Chinese to appear, and subsequent entries use biographical material, sayings, and verse in the manner of Lego blocks. Sometimes, when nothing is known of the details of a master's life, there is only a name and a set of dialogues. Here is a typical entry:

> Chan Master Zongche of Luohan Temple in Hangzhou was a man of Wuxing district in Huzhou [Zhejiang]. His family name was Wu. When young he left home and at twenty received the full precepts. He made the rounds of various regions probing Chan with various teachers. He became a disciple of Chan Master Huangbo Xiyun [d. 850]. Huangbo with one glance assessed him as of high capacity. He entered Huangbo's room and understood the purport. Later, upon his arrival in Hangzhou, the Metropolitan Governor Liu Yan came to admire his Way and erected a monastery for him west of the Superior Prefecture. It was called *Arhat Temple*. He instructed three-hundred followers there. One time the Master had a Dharma convocation: A monk asked: "What is the meaning of Bodhidharma's coming from the West?" The Master said: "Bone breaker!"

(The Master often used this phrase in teaching students, and so people of the time called him "Preceptor Bone Breaker.") Question: "What is the southern lineage/northern lineage?" The Master said: "Mind is lineage." A monk said: "Do you still read the teachings?" The Master said: "The teachings are mind." Question: "My natural endowment is mostly dark—how can I awaken?" The Master said: "The clouds of the defilements are curled up by the wind [of emptiness]; the great sky is vast and clear." A monk said: "How does one attain brightness?" The Master said: "The lunar disk is gleaming and immaculate; its light rays bound over ten-thousand miles." The Master later showed illness and transmigrated. His disciples erected a stupa at the northern corner of the temple. In Zhenming 5 of the Liang [919] King Qian enlarged his temple into *Arhat Monastery for the Protection of the Country* and moved the Master's stupa to the escarpment of Mt. Daci. Today the monastery and the stupa both exist.[53]

Indian designations of cosmological time such as the "ornament" aeon (when a thousand buddhas appear) and the "auspicious" aeon (the present aeon) give way to historical dates according to reign titles of Chinese emperors, and fabulously imaginative Indian place names yield to the names of actual prefectures, cities, and so forth in China, but nothing really changes. In a sense, one *tathāgata* is all *tathāgatas*, one Chan master all Chan masters.

The *Tiansheng* (completed in 1036), which has a distinct Linji orientation, is a direct continuation of the *Jingde*, extending the Nanyue Huairang line (leading to Mazu and Linji) down to the ninth generation and the Qingyuan Xingsi line (leading to Dongshan Liangjie) down to the twelfth.[54] Its compiler Li Zunxu (李遵勖; 988–1038), a Linji layman, was on close terms with Yang Yi, who revised the *Jingde*. The *Jianzhong* of the Yunmen-line master Foguo Weibo (佛國惟白; d. unknown), which was completed in 1101, shows a different sort of structure from the *Jingde* and *Tiansheng* and a Yunmen orientation in its materials. It is divided into five gates and tips the scale even further away from biographical material towards sayings:

1. Gate of the correct lineage (*zhengzong men*).
2. Gate of responding to karmic trigger mechanisms (*duiji men*). This is by far the biggest section, containing a large number of dialogues and Dharma-convocation talks.
3. Gate of prose comments on old standards (*niangu men*).
4. Gate of verse comments on old standards (*songgu men*).
5. Gate of verses (*jisong men*) on Śākyamuni to Huineng (the 33rd Chan patriarch) and then miscellaneous poetry.[55]

The *Liandeng* of Huiweng Wuming (晦翁悟明; d. unknown), who was in the Dahui line of Linji Chan, was completed in 1183.[56] This work begins with Vipaśyin Buddha like the *Jingde* (giving the same verse for this buddha) and goes through the seven *tathāgata*s of the past, the twenty-eight Indian patriarchs and six patriarchs of China, before splitting into the Nanyue and Qingyuan lines. This flame-of-the-lamp record covers more than 600 figures. It, too, is strong on sayings and gives short shrift to biographical material. Perhaps most revealing of the increasing emphasis on sayings over biographical details is the fact that the *Liandeng* incorporates the whole of Dahui Zonggao's *Correct Dharma-Eye Depository* (*Zheng fayan zang*), a collection of old standards with Dahui's occasional comments. The last fascicle of the *Liandeng* consists of verse.

The *Jiatai* of Lei'an Zhengshou (雷庵正受; d. unknown) of the Yunmen school was completed in 1204.[57] It supplements gaps in the *Jingde, Tiansheng,* and *Jianzhong.* Beyond covering Chan monks as the previous flame-of-the-lamp records do, it incorporates entries on emperors and "worthy subjects" (*xian chen*). The last four fascicles include verses on old standards, praises, and miscellaneous writings (songs and inscriptions).

The overall development of the five lamps is in the direction of reduction of the quantity of biographical data and an increase in the number of sayings—sometimes to the point where there is only the name of the master in question followed by his sayings. However, the arrangement of entries always remains that of a genealogical tree—the presentation is always in terms of "dharma heirs" (*fasi* 法嗣).

POETRY

1. *Verses of the Patriarchs and Masters of the Chan School* (*Chanmen zhu zushi jisong*): *Verses of the Chan School.*
2. *Chan Monks of All Regions Chant of the Wind and Moon Collection* (*Jianghu fengyue ji*): *Wind and Moon.*
3. *Hanshan's Poems Collection* (*Hanshanzi shi ji*): *Hanshan.*

The two poles of Chan poetry run from occasionally pedestrian "religious verse" (*gāthā* = *ji/jisong*) sprinkled liberally with Buddhist terms to suggestive *shi* poetry in the style of the mainstream Chinese poetry tradition, which often aims for the classic goal of "fusion of feeling and scene" (*qingjing jiaorong*). Two Song-dynasty collections illustrate these two poles: *Verses of the Chan School* (the religious-verse pole) and *Wind and Moon* (the suggestive *shi* poetry pole).

Verses of the Chan School is a four-fascicle Song collection compiled jointly by two unknown monks named Zisheng (子昇) and Ruyou (如祐). It contains eighty-four pieces labeled variously as inscriptions; chants; *gāthās*; songs; warning whips; guidebooks; instructions; warnings; admonitions, and so forth. Such distinctions are quite imprecise. Titles include *Transmission of the Dharma Verses of the Buddhas and Patriarchs*; *Third Patriarch Chan Master Jianzhi's Trust-in-Mind Inscription*; several *Inscriptions on Cross-legged Sitting*; *Chan Master Fadeng's Imitations of Hanshan's Poems*; *Great Master Yongjia Zhenjue's Song of Realizing the Way*; *Guishan's Warning Whip*; *Preceptor Shitou's Verifying-Sameness Tally*; *Ten-Oxen Verses*; and *Six-Oxen Verses.*

The *Trust-in-Mind Inscription* (*Xinxin ming*) found in *Verses of the Chan School,* which consists of four-syllable lines, is attributed to the shadowy third Chan patriarch Sengcan. Here is the opening portion:

> The ultimate Way entails nothing hard, but hates selecting and choosing. Just have nothing to do with hatred and love, and you will have penetrating clarity.
>
> If there is the slightest differentiation, it will be as far apart as heaven and earth. Should you want to have the Way manifest itself right in front of you, don't preserve [the two poles of] *going along with me* and *going against me.*

When *going against me* and *going along with me* struggle with each other, this is mind illness. Without knowing the profound purport, you will strive in vain to still your thoughts.

The Way is a perfect sameness like the sky, with no deficit and no surplus. Because you seize and reject, it's not like this.

Don't pursue the karmically conditioned and don't fixate in awakening to emptiness. It's the *single taste* of steady-and-calm mind—without a trace everything spontaneously disappears.

If you insist mind is moving and force it to return to a stop position, the more you try to stop it, the more it will move. You'll just stagnate in the two extremes—how will you come to know the *single taste*?

If you don't comprehend the *single taste*, you'll be at a loss in the two extremes. Expel existence, and you'll sink into existence; follow after emptiness, and you'll turn your back on emptiness.

The more you engage in a lot of talk and deliberative thought, the more you won't be yoked to things as they really are. Cut off talk and deliberative thought, and you'll pass through every situation.[58]

The *Song of Realizing the Way* (*Zhengdao ge*) found in *Verses of the Chan School*, which consists mostly of seven-syllable lines, is attributed to a disciple of the sixth patriarch Huineng. Both this song and the *Trust-in-Mind Inscription* began drawing interest in the Chan community around the early 9th century, and by the Song period the *Song of Realizing the Way* had become one of the most well-known Chan texts. Here are its opening lines:

Why don't you take a look at . . .
The idle person of the Way who has cut off practice and is doing nothing?
He isn't trying to eliminate false thought, nor is he seeking the real.
Avidyā intrinsically is the buddha-nature.
The empty physical body of illusionary magical-creation is the *dharmakāya*.
When you've awakened to the *dharmakāya*, there is not a single thing.
The original source by its very nature is the buddha of the heavenly real.
The five *skandhas* are just clouds floating about in the sky.
The three poisons [greed, anger, and stupidity] rise and submerge like bubbles on water.[59]

Given their liberal use of Buddhist terminology in the service of a straightforward presentation of Buddhist truths, both the *Trust-in-Mind Inscription* and the *Song of Realizing the Way* show a strong affinity to the *gāthā* style and hence are far removed from the style of classical *shi* poetry.

Wind and Moon is a collection of 270 heptasyllabic *jueju* quatrains by seventy-nine Chan poet-monks. These quatrains observe the technical rules of the mainstream poetic tradition and are quite the equal of those of accomplished scholar-official poets. This Yuan-dynasty collection was compiled (for the most part) by Songpo Zongqi 松坡宗憩, who was in the Linji line of Wuzhun Shifan. Many of the poets included were disciples of Wuzhun Shifan, Xutang Zhiyu, Shixi Xinyue, and Yanxi Guangwen (all included in the *yulu* section). Here are four quatrains:

Listening to the Snow by Xutang Zhiyu
Though it's a cold, windless night, the bamboo is making a sound.
Few and far between and subtle, it passes through the window eaves beneath the pines.
Hearing with the ears is not as good as [the *Śūraṃgama Sūtra's*] *hearing with mind.*
So I stop chanting the sutra and sit before the lamp with a half-open sutra scroll.[60]

...

Listening to a Frog by Mozong Deben
A frog in the bluish moss makes the sound *ribbit, ribbit.*
In the mountains an empty stillness, in the sky a bright moon.
A karmic trigger mechanism is suddenly produced by the frog's croaking: [Layman Pang's final words] *empty the existent.*
The *Greater Court Odes* or wind in the pines are not the equal of this sound.[61]

...

Opening Printing Blocks for an Edition of the Canon by Zhitang Biao
Gautama was intricately adaptable and for the sake of beings spoke *upāyic* words.
Having it printed down through the generations has been a never-ending catastrophe.
Who said: *I'll do one circumambulation of the Chan platform*?
There's not even a single character to carve on the printing blocks.[62]

...

For a Chan Monk Seeking Instructive Sayings by Qianfeng Ruwan
This far and distant peak—has it deceived you into coming?
You mistakenly thought that I would skillfully tailor [rare and profound sayings] like the spring breeze [making flowers bloom].
But my sayings [were *tasteless*], not profound, the karmic triggering mechanism not miraculous.
Now [students will cease coming, and] my ten-foot square room will certainly become overgrown with moss.[63]

These quatrains from *Wind and Moon,* which are very imagistic with few grammatical function ("empty") words, offer a striking contrast to the vernacular poems of *Hanshan,* which have been characterized as "talky" because of extensive use of personal pronouns and function words.[64] The origins of *Hanshan* lie outside Chan, but by Song-Yuan times this collection had been thoroughly assimilated to the Chan tradition—Chan masters even wrote imitations. These *Hanshan* poems by and large do not follow the rules of classical *shi* poetry. The following pentasyllabic *shi* poem from the *Hanshan* collection not only disregards the technical rules of tonal regulation but makes the failure to observe those rules the topic of the poem:

> Take Cultivated-Talent Scholar Wang,
> He laughs at my poems for their many technical errors.
> He says: "You don't know about the tonal violation called 'wasp's waist,'
> And you still don't get the tonal violation called 'crane's knee.' "
> Level and oblique tones—I am unable to compel them to fit.
> I just haphazardly employ any old word.
> I laugh at the poems you compose, Wang.
> You're like a blind man singing of the sun.[65]

In general, Chan people have avidly read *Hanshan* (the Yuan-dynasty Chan master Zhongfeng Mingben and others even wrote poems in imitation of Hanshan's), but literary critics of the mainstream poetic tradition have looked askance at them. Western scholars in turn have paid much attention to Hanshan and little to the large corpus of classical *shi* poems composed by Song and Yuan Chan poet-monks. They are, however, an integral part of Chan literature and worthy of study.

STANDARDS-WITH-COMMENTS COLLECTIONS

1. *Collection of Preceptor Xuedou Xian's Verses on Old Standards* (*Xuedou Xian heshang songgu ji*): *Xuedou's Verses.*
2. *Blue Cliff Collection* (*Biyan ji*): *Blue Cliff.*
3. *Collection of Preceptor Hongzhi Jue of Tiantong's Verses on Old Standards* (*Tiantong Jue heshang songgu ji*): *Hongzhi's Verses.*
4. *Calm-and-Unhurried Hermitage Record of Old Man Wansong's Chants Appraising Preceptor Tiantong Hongzhi Zhengjue's Verses on Old Standards* (*Wansong laoren pingchang Tiantong Jue heshang songgu congrong an lu*): *Calm-and-Unhurried Hermitage.*
5. *Wumen's Checkpoint* (*Wumen guan*): *Wumen.*
6. *Correct Dharma-Eye Depository* (*Zheng fayan zang*): *Correct Dharma-Eye.*

The next genre in modern scholarship is customarily called "*gong'an* collections" (*gong'an ji*) or "case collections." However, this genre name does not appear in any of the Chan texts in the major collections, indicating that it is not a traditional term for the genre. Japanese Zen scholars coined the term "*kōan* collections" (*kōan shū*), leading to its eventual adoption by Western scholarship. A synonym of *gong'an*, much employed in Chan literature, is *ze* (則) (*standard; norm; precept; rule; example*). The most famous of Song dynasty transmission records, the *Jingde*, has 1,701 entries, beginning with the seven buddhas of the past. This has led to the assertion, which is found, for example, in the *yulu* of Xueyan Zuqin (d. 1287), that there are "1,700 *standards* or *gong'ans*."[66] In other words, each of the 1,701 entries constitutes material for a "standard," which can then be commented upon, either in verse or prose format. Such standards are perhaps comparable to the "American standards" of the Great American Songbook (not a real book), songs from the 1920s to 1950 or so to which singers and jazz musicians add "comments," i.e., do renditions. Thus, a rendering along the lines of "standards-with-comments collections" would perhaps be a more helpful genre name than "case-with-comments collections," shifting the metaphor from the legal precedents recorded in the tomes in the wall bookcase of a lawyer's office to the performance of a standard by a singer or jazz player.

The first collection, *Xuedou Verses*, by Xuedou Chongxian (雪竇重顯; 980–1052), who was in the Yunmen lineage, states in its preface that Xuedou "will now select 100 standards from the miraculous stories of the ancient sages, display language to compose verses, by means of the verses diffuse the purport, and by means of the purport bequeath abundance to those of later times."[67] Each standard is introduced with the word *ju* (舉; *lift up; raise; offer up for consideration*), followed by Xuedou's verse (introduced by *song yue*). Subsequently, Yuanwu Keqin (圜悟克勤; 1063–1135), who belonged to the Yangqi wing of the Linji lineage, added more levels of commentary—bequeathed instructions, brief comments, and chants of appraisal (*chuishi; zhuoyu;* and *pingchang*)—to Xuedou's 100-standard text, creating the *Blue Cliff Collection* (*Biyan ji*).[68]

Xuedou drew upon three types of sources for his standards: flame-of-the-lamp records; *yulu;* and sutras. The *Jingde* accounts for at least twenty-three of his 100 standards. Two other flame-of-the-lamp records are also sources: *Zutang* and *Tiansheng*. The *Yunmen guanglu* serves as the source for seventeen standards, but there are a significant number drawn from the *Zhaozhou yulu*, as well as a few from such texts as *Muzhou yulu, Zhimen yulu, Linjilu*, and *Pang jushi yulu*.[69] Finally, two standards are based on the *Śūraṃgama Sūtra*, a perennial favorite in Song, Yuan, and Ming Chan circles, and one on the *Vimalakīrti Sūtra*.

Let us examine the seventy-ninth standard in *Xuedou Verses*:

> Offered up for consideration: The World-honored-one one day ascended the seat. Mañjuśrī struck the mallet and said: "Carefully examine the dharma of the dharma king—the dharma of the dharma king is *thus*." [These words are usually said at the end of a dharma talk.] The World-honored-one immediately got down from the seat. Verse:
>
> The expert Chan monks arranged in rows [standing at a Dharma convocation]
> Know that the dharma rule of the dharma king is not like this.
> Were there in the assembly a realized person capable of correctly judging,
> What need would there be for a Mañjuśrī to perform a striking of the mallet?[70]

Blue Cliff makes this snippet into its ninety-second standard and adds the following: bequeathed instructions (*chuishi*) of a few lines at the beginning; three brief interlinear comments (*zhuoyu*) within the case itself; a lengthy chant of appraisal (*pingchang*); four brief comments (*zhuoyu*) at the end of each line of the verse; and finally another lengthy chant of appraisal (*pingchang*).[71] Xuedou's original case and verse totals fifty-seven characters. Yuanwu adds commentarial layers to this core for a total of 735 characters—the *Blue Cliff* standard is over twelve times the size of Xuedou's original!

The next collection is *Hongzhi's Verses*, which is included in the *Hongzhi guanglu* under the title *Preceptor Sizhou Puzhao's Verses on Old Standards* (*Sizhou Puzhao heshang song gu*).[72] During the Shaoxing era of the Southern Song (1131–1162) Hongzhi Zhengjue 宏智正覺 selected 100 cases from the flame-of-the-lamp records and *yulu*, adding a verse to each. In 1223 of the Southern Song Wansong Xingxiu (萬松行秀; 1166–1246), a teacher in the Caodong line, built a "Calm-and-Unhurried Hermitage" within the Bao'en Monastery of Yanjing (Beijing) and went into seclusion. The layman Yelü Chucai (Layman Zhanran; 1190–1244) was a Khitan, and, when the Jin/Jurchen extinguished the Liao dynasty (Qidan/Khitan), he came over to the Jin. Yelü Chucai asked Old Man Wansong to attach comments to *Hongzhi's Verses*, and Wansong added instructions to the sangha (*shi zhong*), chants of appraisal (*pingchang*), and brief comments (*zhuoyu*). The resulting work was labeled with the somewhat cumbersome title: *Calm-and-Unhurried Hermitage Record of Old Man Wansong's Chants of Appraisal on Preceptor Tiantong Hongzhi Zhengjue's Verses on Old Standards*.[73] The structural similarity between *Blue Cliff* and *Calm-and-Unhurried Hermitage* is very striking: the primary commentator Hongzhi is to his secondary commentator Wansong as the primary commentator Xuedou is to his secondary commentator Yuanwu.

The opening of each standard in *Calm-and-Unhurried Hermitage* is Wansong's instructions to the sangha (*shi zhong*). This opening is followed by Hongzhi's standard introduced by the phrase "offered up for consideration" (*ju*), which has short interlinear comments by Wansong. Next is a lengthy comment by Wansong introduced by the phrase *the Master says* (*shi yun*); then comes Hongzhi's verse (*song yun*) with short interlinear comments by Wansong. The conclusion is a lengthy comment by Wansong also introduced by the phrase "the Master says."

Here is the thirty-first standard in *Hongzhi's Verses*:

> Offered up for consideration: Yunmen bequeathed the saying: "When the old buddhas have [sexual] relations with an open-air pillar, what karmic trigger mechanism is this?" The sangha said not a word. He substituted for them: "On South Mountain rising clouds; on North Mountain falling rain" [note that "clouds and rain" carry a sexual overtone]. Verse:
>
> The one road, the divine light, from the outset has never been concealed.
> Transcending views and objective supports—so and yet not so.
> Outside of discriminative calculation—on point and yet not on point.
> Pollen of flowers on the cliff's ledge—the bees in their hives make honey from it.
> Juice from wild plants—the musk-deer produces an aromatic glandular secretion from it.
> Some things are three feet, some ten feet, and some sixty feet.
> Whatever you butt into, it's revealed as broad and limitless.[74]

The next collection is *Wumen* by the Linji master Wumen Huikai (無門慧開; 1183–1260). *Wumen* consists of forty-eight standards without the introductory phrase "raised for consideration" (*ju*), followed by "Wumen says" (*Wumen yue*) and "verse says" (*song yue*). In China the transmission of this text was cut off, but Muhon Kakushin (無本覺心; 1207–1298), a successor of the compiler Wumen Huikai, brought it to Japan, and there were printings from the late 13th century onward. There was not much interest in it in medieval Japan, but during the Edo period, it was rediscovered and became the object of countless commentaries. In comparison to the previous two collections, *Wumen* selects new, that is, contemporary materials. Several of the masters in Wumen Huikai's standards are close to his own time. But the most important difference with the previous two standards collections is that *Wumen* shows a direct link to Dahui Zonggao's style of *huatou* (話頭) practice as laid out in *Letters of Dahui*. Wumen's comment to the first standard, certainly the most famous standard of all, is a paraphrase of lines in *Letters of Dahui*:

> Well, tell me: What is the checkpoint of the patriarchal masters? Nothing other than this single *wu* 無 character [i.e., the *huatou*] is the single checkpoint of the Chan gate. . . . With the 360 bones and 84,000 hair follicles of your whole body produce the ball of uncertainty or doubt. Probe this *wu* 無 character. Day and night raise it to awareness. Don't understand it as an empty sort of non-existence. Don't understand it as the polarity exist/not exist. It will be like having a hot iron ball in your mouth—you won't be able to swallow it, and you won't be able to spit it out. All previous pernicious knowing and awareness will be washed away completely. Over a long period of time you will ripen, and spontaneously internal and external will unify.[75]

The previous three collections are compact (100 or 48 cases). The next collection, Dahui Zonggao's *Correct Dharma-Eye*, does not fit this pattern. It is voluminous, with 661 unnumbered standards. The 661 excerpts derive from many Chan records and are introduced by the phrases "instructions to the sangha" (*shi zhong*) and "dharma-convocation talk" (*shangtang*), as well as by markers for quotation. The most common introduction to the excerpts is the first of these three. Many (but not all) extracts are followed by Dahui's brief comments (*zhuoyu*), which begin with the phrase "Miaoxi says." The final excerpt is *Miaoxi's Instruction to the Assembly*.

Here is a very short standard with comment:

> Preceptor Langxie instructed the assembly: "Advancing forwards is death; retreating backwards is death. If you neither advance nor retreat, you fall into the parochial hometown of *nothing-to-do*. Why so? Though the capital Chang'an is a joyful place, it's not one to stay in very long."
>
> Miaoxi says: "Weeping aloud with blood flowing—that's useless. It's not as good as holding one's tongue and passing the last days of spring."[76]

COMPENDIA

1. *Prolegomenon to the Collection of Expressions of the Chan Source* (*Chanyuan zhuquan ji duxu*): *Chan Prolegomenon.*
2. *Eye for Humans and Gods* (*Rentian yanmu*): *Humans and Gods.*
3. *Record of [Clear Talks] in the Forest* (*Linjianlu*): *Forest.*
4. *Brief Compilation of Famous Monks of the Ming Dynasty* (*Huang Ming mingseng jilue*): *Ming Chan Masters.*

Chan compendia, which flourished in the Song, consist of extracts of materials drawn from various sources. The Song, of course, is the age of "brush notes" (*biji*) and encyclopedias of also sorts in non-Chan circles. Chan compendia are usually divided into sections (sometimes with rubrics for sections and with the source listed at the end of a section) . The greatest compendium of all Chan literature, the *Chan Canon/Chan zang* 禪藏 of Guifeng Zongmi (圭峰宗密; 780–841), was lost after the Tang, but we do have Zongmi's introduction to this treasure trove of Chan materials: the *Chan Prolegomenon* of around 833. The *Prolegomenon* is a good example of a Chan manuscript text of the Tang that was transmitted intact into Song times and printed. An 857 manuscript copy in the hand of the illustrious calligrapher Pei Xiu just over a century later wound up in the possession of a layman in the Hangzhou area, who arranged for a woodblock printing.[77] From the *Prolegomenon* we can reconstruct an image of the lost *Chan Canon*.

Both the *Chan Prolegomenon* and the *Chan Canon* are characterized by an all-inclusive attitude toward Chan—all the Chan houses of the 8th and early 9th centuries are accepted as valid expressions of Chan. The overarching theme of the *Prolegomenon* is the interlocking relationship between varieties of Chan and Indian Mahāyāna teachings. The master metaphor is the tally (*fu* 符), a two-halved bamboo or wooden segment, one half given to each of two individuals as a credential for legitimating proper transmission of military or official orders:

> Originally, the Buddha spoke both the all-at-once teaching and the step-by-step teaching, while Chan opens both the all-at-once gate and the step-by-step gate. These two teachings and the two gates fit together like the notches of a tally. At present, exegetes in a biased manner display the step-by-step principles, and Chan adepts in a biased manner encourage the all-at-once axiom-realization. When a Chan adept and an exegete meet, the distance between them is that between a Central Asian barbarian and a barbarian from the South. I do not know what they have done in past births to perfume their minds in this way.[78]

In total the *Chan Prolegomenon* mentions eight pairs of tally halves, and each pair fits together seamlessly to form a whole:

> Three types of canonical *teachings* ↔ three axiom-realizations [*zong* 宗] of Chan
> All-at-once teaching ↔ Chan all-at-once gate
> Step-by-step teaching ↔ Chan step-by-step gate
> Chan sayings ↔ the buddha's intention
> Intention of the Chan patriarchs ↔ buddha mind
> Chan records ↔ buddha sutras
> All-at-once awakening ↔ step-by-step practice
> Original awakening/real ↔ non-awakening/unreal

There are three scriptural teachings (three classes of sutras and treatises): mind-only (*cittamātra*); emptiness (*śūnyatā*); and dharma nature or nature (*dharmatā*). There are three Chan axiom-realizations: stopping unreal thought and cultivating mind-only (*xiwang xiuxin zong*); cutting off without relying on anything (*minjue wuji zong*); and directly revealing the mind nature (*zhixian xinxing zong*).[79] Into these three Chan axiom-realizations, the *Chan Prolegomenon* distributes eight Chan houses: the Jingzhong, Northern, Baotang, and South Mountain *Nianfo* (*Nembutsu*) Gate lineages are in the first axiom-realization; Shitou and Niutou are in the second; and Heze (Zongmi's own lineage) and Hongzhou are in the third, the highest rung.[80] Zongmi is not asserting the existence of historical connections between individual Chan houses and the text-based schools of Chinese Buddhism. This is taxonomy (*panjiao/dividing up teachings and texts* and *panchan/dividing up Chan axiom-realizations and houses*). The lost compendium, the *Chan Canon*, which is said to have been about one hundred fascicles in length, surely contained an enormous number of pieces produced by these Chan houses. There indeed was a "Chan corpus" in the Tang dynasty—Zongmi devoted much energy to collecting it.

The preface of *Humans and Gods* states that it is an "compendium of the five lineages of Chan": Linji; Yunmen; Caodong; Guiyang; and Fayan.[81] It was compiled by Huiyan Zhizhao (晦巖智昭; d. unknown) of the Dahui line and published in 1188. For each of these five, a brief biography of the founder is followed by sayings, verses, and statements of various masters of the lineage. The last section, entitled *Miscellaneous Record of the Chan School* (*Zongmen za lu*), is a mélange of materials. Typical of its contents is the following, an attempt to poetically encapsulate each of the five lineages (often using extracts from the *yulu* of the founders without much context) entitled *Essentials of the Five Houses of Perfect Awakening* (*Yuanwu wu jia zongyao*):

> An all-out manifestation of the capability of one's whole personality; the stick and the shout come and go continuously; seeking people with the sword; getting it hands down inside a lightning bolt (Linji).
>
> The Big Dipper exercises control over all the constellations; the gold wind is disclosed in its entirety; [Yunmen's] three phrases [i.e., "what is it that stops the flow of sentient beings?"; "what contains and covers heaven and earth?"; and "one wave following after another—what is this?"] should be distinguished; an arrowhead in the distant sky (Yunmen).
>
> Sovereign and court official unite in the Way; the *inclined* and the *straight* aid each other [i.e., the five ranks of Caodong]; a precipitous path on the mystery journey; a golden needle and jade thread (Caodong).
>
> Master and disciples sing the song in a chorus; fathers and sons are of one family; brightness and darkness come and go continuously; verbalization and silence are not revealed (Guiyang).
>
> Hear the voice and awaken to the Way; see forms and enlighten mind; in the phrases a sharp point is concealed; within the words there is an echo (Fayan).[82]

Forest of the Northern Song Chan master Juefan Huihong (覺範慧洪; 1071–1128) is a compendium of more than 300 sayings and anecdotes having to do with Chan masters, sutras and treatises, scholar-officials, and so forth. Huihong was in the Huanglong wing of the Linji lineage. The preface of *Forest* indicates that the work embraces the "harmony of Chan and the teachings" in the manner of Yongming Yanshou and Guifeng Zongmi. Some of the entries have a bit of the flavor of the Japanese *zuihitsu* (random essay) *Tsurezuregusa* (1330–1331) of Yoshida Kenkō. Here are two entries:

> Once with several monks I visited the stupa of Chan Master Yunfeng Yue. Bowing and rising, I comforted him, saying: "Are you alive or are you dead?" After a long while Yue

> himself answered: "You mustn't topple my stupa!" The monk next to me said: "Today an upright person has spoken his story of the working out of karma!" Thereupon I composed a verse: "Not knowing, I asked; not seeing, I inquired. He fully manifested right in front of me; what more need be said? Verily, his firm body experienced samsaric illness and aging. The stupa I am facing must not be toppled!"[83]
>
> . . .
>
> In "drunkard's hamlet" there was a crazy monk named "Precepts Way," who depended on the support of the village. He was drunk every single day, but he spat out strange, eccentric utterances. People of the time couldn't determine whether he was a common person or a sage. Once, when there was a bout of wine drinking, they had him compose an elegiac address. Monk "Precepts" responded with: "I'm only a numinous spirit born into this world of Jambudvīpa. Devoid of anger and envy, I love to drink wine, falling down in the streets of town. I'll end up being reborn in the Tuṣita Heaven of Maitreya Bodhisattva. *Then* I won't drink wine anymore. Why? In such a 'pure land' there's no wine to be bought."[84]

Ming Chan Masters by Yunqi Zhuhong (雲棲袾宏; 1535–1615) is compendium of extracts drawn from the *yulu* of ten Ming-dynasty Chan masters (with eight more as an appendix), to which Zhuhong has appended comments. This text serves as a convenient introduction to the *yulu* literature of Ming Chan, which is little known in the West. Since the arrival of the Ming Linji master Yinyuan Longqi (隱元隆琦; 1592–1673) in Nagasaki in 1654, Ming Chan has been scorned in some (but not all) Japanese Rinzai Zen circles as "*nembutsu* Zen." (This charge, to some degree, may well have been a "cover" for objections to lifestyle and cultural aspects of these immigrant Chinese Linji monks, who did not shave their heads often enough for Japanese tastes and insisted on Chinese ways in daily monastic life.) The negative Japanese reaction ultimately influenced Western attitudes. *Ming Chan Masters* contains a saying by the Linji master Chushan Shaoqi (楚山紹琦; 1403–1473), also known as "Old Man Illusion" (Huansou 幻叟), that illustrates the use of the *nianfo/nembutsu*, the mantra *Obeisance to Amitābha Buddha* (*Nanwu Amituofo*), as a *huatou* in the Dahui style of *huatou* practice found in *Letters of Dahui* (text no. 37):

> Merely raise to awareness the single phrase *Obeisance to Amitābha Buddha* [i.e., the *nianfo/nembutsu*] and install it in your heart. Silently engage in personal investigation of this phrase and at all times with a whip produce the sensation of uncertainty about: *the one doing this* nianfo—*in the end, who is it*? Over and over again investigate. You should make no conjectures about existence/non-existence, and you must not have your mind wait for awakening. Just the slightest false thought in your mind will constitute an obstruction. You must make it so that in your breast there is an empty vastness devoid of even a single thing, and, in walking, standing, sitting, and lying down, in those situations that are still or noisy, leisurely or busy, there is no need at all to employ discrimination or calculation. All that is necessary is that moment after moment be a continuum, that thought after thought be uninterrupted. After a long period of time your practice will be of a pure oneness, naturally still and peaceful. Then *dhyāna* will appear to you.[85]

LETTERS

1. *Letters of Chan Master Dahui Pujue* (*Dahui Pujue chanshi shu*): *Letters of Dahui.*

There are several famous stand-alone collections of letters in Chan literature, and some *yulu* compendia contain selections from letters of the master to fellow monks and laypeople. By far the most renowned letter collection in Chan literature is *Letters of Dahui*, a compilation of sixty-two letters of the Southern Song Linji Chan teacher Dahui Zonggao (大慧宗杲; 1089–1163) to forty members of the scholar-official class (*shidafu*), the elite class in Chinese society. There are also two letters to Linji Chan masters at the end of the collection. Both consist of advice on how to navigate a teaching career. These sixty-two letters, of course, represent only a fraction of Dahui's epistolary output over his teaching career. In only three cases is Dahui's letter preceded by the scholar-official's question letter, though quite often Dahui quotes or paraphrases passages from the question letter. Each of the sixty letters to laymen is fascinating as a document directed at a specific scholar-official with his distinctive niche, high or low, in the social-political landscape of Song-dynasty China and his relative level of development on the Buddhist path. When viewed in this light, the personality of the recipient and Dahui's response to that particular personality holds the foreground. But at the same time, Dahui in many cases regarded letters as a means to reach students beyond the recipient—they were not always crafted for the recipient alone, but for a wider audience of the recipient's friends and peers. Dahui assumed at least some of his letters would be copied, circulated, and studied as small essays, "dharma talks," explicating his style of Chan practice, which rather quickly became a dominant style of practice throughout East Asia.

Dahui's analysis of the main problem of the scholar-official class in the study of Chan is that they are too intellectually "sharp" and rely far too much on their hard-earned stock of intellectual knowledge, earned through grueling years of study of classical texts and the highly demanding examination system. He argues that they take great pride in their intellect, but, in fact, it constitutes a blockage for them on the Buddhist path. They all too frequently show "know-it-all" tendencies. Effective Chan practice, however, requires a *certain kind* of "dull-wittedness" or "obtuseness." As he says in a letter to a scholar-official very familiar with the demanding examination system, "taking a 'first' in the 'dull-wittedness examination' is no bad thing!" And in another letter he says:

> The reason most of today's members of the scholar-official class are incapable of comprehending *this matter* [*ci shi* 此事] and decisively attaining release is simply because their disposition is too intellectually sharp and their knowledge excessive. As soon as they see the Chan master open his mouth and begin to move his tongue, they immediately come to a snap understanding. Therefore, if anything, this is inferior to the dull-witted person who, free of a lot of pernicious knowing and perverse awareness, in a headlong fashion without expectations dashes against each skillful method and each gesture, each word and each phrase, [of the teacher].[86]

Dahui is famous (some would say notorious) for his vigorous polemic against "perverse teachers" in the *Letters*:

> In recent years there has been a type of perverse teacher who speaks "silence-and-illumination" Chan. They teach people: twenty-four hours a day pay no attention whatsoever to anything, and go on stopping-to-rest. They do not permit students to voice even a sound [i.e., the silence of "silence-and-illumination"]. They fear falling into the present epoch [as opposed to what they approvingly call "before the aeon of nothingness," i.e., before a single thought arose]. Frequently members of the scholar-official class, who are "used" by their own cleverness and sharp faculties, are apt to detest noisiness. When all of a sudden they are made to do stillness-sitting by this party of perverse teachers, and it's seems to them that they are saving on the expenditure of energy, they immediately think they've got it right. They do not seek further for wonderful awakening—they simply take this silence as the *ultimate standard*. I don't stint on oral karma [in deprecating these false teachers] and try my utmost to save people from this fraud.[87]

Dahui never cites the perverse Chan teachers by name, but one of the usual suspects in modern scholarship is Hongzhi Zhengjue—his *Silence-and-Illumination Inscription* does seem to fit the bill. The focal point of Dahui's polemic is actually very simple: how much emphasis should be accorded to cross-legged sitting. Dahui is fervently against absolutizing cross-legged sitting and thinks the perverse teachers are doing just that. The antidote for the perverse teachings, according to Dahui, is what he calls "doing *gongfu* (工夫) in this way," that is, "practicing in this way." Western scholarship generally contrasts Dahui's "new" *gongfu* style with an "older" literary or commentarial style. It should be remembered that Dahui himself engaged heavily in the commentarial style in his *Correct Dharma-Eye*. Dahui's *gongfu* consists of "rallying to awareness/lifting to awareness/keeping an eye on" the *huatou* (*phrase*). Though in the *Letters* Dahui mentions in passing quite a few *huatou*, he especially recommends two to his correspondents: *wu* 無 and *dried turd* (*ganshijue* 乾屎橛). Both of these phrases are tiny extracts from standards or cases, but in his "doing *gongfu* in this way" the standard from which the *huatou* has been extracted utterly falls away. No mental operation whatsoever is to be performed upon the *huatou*; one is not to attempt to "process" the *huatou* in any way. One lifts the *huatou* to awareness constantly, doing it twenty-four hours a day in all four postures: walking, standing, sitting, and lying down. One does it during everyday activities while responding to sense objects. One does it both during stillness and in the midst of noisiness. Nothing else counts.

PRETEND DIALOGUES

1. *Cutting-Off Examining Treatise* (*Jueguan lun*): *Cutting-Off*.
2. *Family Precepts of Illusory-Abiding Hermitage* (*Huanzhu jiaxun*) contained in *Preceptor Tianmu Zhongfeng's Extended Record* (*Tianmu Zhongfeng heshang guanglu*): *Family Precepts*.

A pretend dialogue sets up a discussion of typical Chan topics between imaginary figures (often with Buddhist-sounding names). This genre, well represented in the Dunhuang Chan manuscript corpus, did not thrive in the long run of Chan literature.[88] Let us begin with the Dunhuang-manuscript text *Cutting-Off*, a discussion between a master named Entered-into-Principle (Ruli) and his disciple Gate-of-the-Conditioned (Yuanmen). The disciple submits a series of questions for judgments by the master. The initial question is how does one "quiet mind" (*anxin* 安心), and this is the matrix from which the remainder of the text emerges. One could say that "quieting mind" is the theme of Chan literature as a whole.

Both the name of the master and the topic of quieting mind point to a link between this dialogue and the *Bodhidharma Anthology*, and, within the seven texts of that anthology, to the *Two Entrances* and Record I, which was known as the *Dharma Gate of Quieting Mind* (*Anxin famen*). It is even possible that the name of the disciple here, Gate-of-the-Conditioned, is connected somehow to the most important figure in the *Records* of the *Bodhidharma Anthology*, Master Yuan. The opening lines of *Cutting-Off* run as follows:

> Well, let us now provisionally set up two characters, who talk together about truth. The Master's name is Entered-into-Principle, the disciple's Gate-of-the-Conditioned. At the time, Teacher Entered-into-Principle was quiet and said nothing. Gate-of-the-Conditioned suddenly arose [as "thoughts" are said to do in the treatise *Awakening of Faith*] and asked Teacher Entered-into-Principle: "What is mind, and how does one quiet mind?" Answer: "You mustn't suppose such a thing as mind, and you mustn't force the issue of quieting it. You could call that 'quieting.' "[89]

However, the pretend-dialogue genre did not completely die out in later periods. For example, *Preceptor Tianmu Zhongfeng's Extended Record*, the *yulu* collection of the Yuan dynasty Chan master Zhongfeng Mingben (中峯明本; 1263–1323), contains a piece entitled *Family Precepts of Illusory-Abiding Hermitage* (*Huanzhu jiaxun*). *Family Precepts* is one of the "five leaves" or five key texts of Mingben, two others being his *Some Questions on the Śūraṃgama Sūtra* and *Imitations of Hanshan's Poems*. In this essay, illusory man speaks dharma to his illusory disciples. *Family Precepts* fuses the teachings of the *Perfect Awakening Sutra* (*Yuanjue jing*, a Chan favorite) on illusion with Dahui's *huatou* practice.

> When on a certain day *māyā* [illusion] man was at his *māyā* seat in his *māyā* room and holding his *māyā* flywhisk, his *māyā* disciples came in and assembled. They had questions: "Why is the pine straight?" "Why are thorns crooked?" "Why is the swan white?" "Why are birds dark in color?" *Māyā* man held his flywhisk upright and announced to the great sangha: "This *māyā* flywhisk of mine, it's not upright on its own—it's upright in conformity with *māyā*. When horizontal, it's not horizontal on its own—it's horizontal in conformity with *māyā*. When picked up, the picking up is not on its own—the picking up is in conformity with *māyā*. When released, the releasing is not on its own—the releasing is in conformity with *māyā*. . . . Well, there's no need to be bustling about in a hurried state. Just recognize your single iron-and-stone body-mind, risk your life for one or two births, and, at the "tasteless" *huatou* that you have been probing, be like a palm-tapping blind man who stands his ground and is furious in his mind. Keep on pressing hard with it [i.e., the *huatou*]![90]

A GLOSSARY OF TERMS AND EXPRESSIONS IN CHAN BOOKS

1. *Glossary of the Patriarchal Courtyard* (*Zuting shiyuan*): *Patriarchal Courtyard.*

The last genre is not "literary" but "philological." Mu'an Shanqing's (睦庵善卿; d. unknown) *Patriarchal Courtyard* (1108) is a glossary for certain *yulu*, Chan poems, and so forth.[91] It was compiled by Mu'an Shanqing because at the time some Chan students could not understand certain vocabulary items employed in these Chan books and used in Chan instruction. (One can only imagine how much grueling difficulty Koreans and Japanese experienced in reading Chinese Chan texts.) He selected more than 2,400 items from the Chan records (the *yulu* of Yunmen and Xuedou, the *Song of Realizing the Way*, and so forth) and provided glosses for them one by one, citing a wide range of Buddhist and secular sources. Although from the point of view of modern Chan studies there are quite a few errors in the entries, it is still a remarkable text, the earliest such glossary and the precursor of much modern scholarly work on the Chan records. Editions of the *Patriarchal Courtyard* were produced in Muromachi and Edo-period Japan, and, in fact, one can posit a line running from these editions to the Chan glossary *Notes on Chan Kudzu-Words* (*Kattōgo sen*) of Mujaku Dōchū (1653–1744), the "sage" of Chan/Zen scholarship. Mujaku's works, of course, are to this day of enormous use in reading the Chan texts laid out in this article.

THE CHAN RECORDS AND THE STYLE OF CHINESE POETRY

Guifeng Zongmi speaks of the difference between the Buddhist canonical teachings and Chan in his *Chan Prolegomenon*:

> The teachings are the sutras and treatises left behind by the buddhas and bodhisattvas. *Chan is lines of verse rehearsed by good friends on the path.* It is just that the buddha sutras open outward, ensnaring thousands of beings of the eight classes, and *Chan verse scoops up an epitome, being oriented to the karmic trigger mechanisms of a single category of being found in this land of China.*[92]

Chan, according to Zongmi, consists of the poetic utterances of Chan good friends on the path (*kalyāṇa-mitra*). Zongmi was writing in the Tang of the 9th century, but what he wrote is applicable to the Chan records of later eras. Much of the material in these Chan records is poetic in its sustained suggestiveness, compression, propensity for balanced couplets, and so forth and does indeed "scoop up an epitome." However, suggestiveness and compression in poetic expression is not uniquely Chinese by any means. The *Dohākoṣas* (*Treasuries of Couplets*) of the great siddhas of late Indian Buddhism, Saraha, Kāṇha, and Tilopa, certainly are suggestive and do "scoop up an epitome," but they are unequivocally Indian in their lampooning of brahmans and Jains; positive evaluation of the body and sexuality; concern with tantric "physiology," and so forth.[93] The *Dohākoṣas* and the Chan record do share an important language feature: both utilize written vernacular language (*Apabhraṃśa*, the forerunner of the North Indian vernaculars, in the case of the tantric couplets).

What makes Chan oriented to Chinese sensibilities and tastes? One answer may lie in the stylistic convergence of the Chan records and classical Chinese poetry. Many of the sayings found in the Chan records contain couplets. Both the sayings and the couplets often embody aesthetic ideals of Chinese poetry: "lexical economy, maximization of imagistic appeal, and minimal use of nonimagistic words."[94] The aim is to convey what lies beyond language with minimal use of abstractions. Thus, the Chan records (with the exception of *gāthā*-style pieces) make relatively scanty use of the technical terms of Buddhism, which often tend toward the abstract, and frequent employment of such vivid images as "red-meatball" (*pañca-skandha* or five aggregates), "green flies on top of shit" (*abhiniveṣa* or attachment to words), "egret with nine marshes to choose from" (*vikalpa* or discrimination), "pail of black lacquer" (*avidyā* or nescience), "solitary crane descending in the distant sky" (*tathatā* or thusness), and so forth.

REVIEW OF LITERATURE

The center of scholarship on Chan literature since the end of World War II has been Japan, and Western scholarship has been heavily influenced by Japanese research down to the present. The Chinese scholar Hu Shi began publishing on Chan literature as early as the 1930s, and the French scholar Jacques Genet followed his lead some years later.[95] A key development for both Japanese and Western research was the American Ruth Fuller Sasaki's assembling of a small team of researchers within the Zen monastery of Daitoku-ji in Kyoto in 1956. The core of this group was Iriya Yoshitaka and Yanagida Seizan. Iriya was a specialist in vernacular Chinese literature, particularly the vernacular found in the Chan records. He assumed that much of the vocabulary and rhetoric of the Chan records was originally ordinary spoken Chinese, and hence he collected examples of vocabulary and grammatical constructions from Yuan-dynasty plays, the classical novels, Dunhuang popular literature, etc., as an aid to understanding their meanings in the Chan records.[96] Yanagida came to occupy a unique position in the study of Chan literature. He stressed that it is necessary to carry out a "value critique" of the documents of Chan literature, to correctly "sort them."[97] The work of Iriya and Yanagida has, to a great degree, molded the field in Japan and still lingers. Philip B. Yampolsky, an American member of the Sasaki group, brought their work to America in the 1960s. Iriya and Yanagida, who were associated with the Rinzai Zen hub in Kyoto, were the driving force behind the *Zen no goroku* (*Sayings Records of Zen*) series of the 1960s and 1970s.[98] It was conceived as a set of twenty volumes with modern Japanese translations of key Chan texts. Despite its Rinzai Zen orientation and the fact that the title is not entirely accurate as a description of the volumes (many are not *yulu*), it still stands as a must-have series for students of Chan literature. Scholars associated with the Soto Zen hub of Komazawa University in Tokyo produced in the 1970s the greatest encyclopedia of Zen studies, the *Zengaku daijiten* (*Great Dictionary of Zen Studies*).[99] They have also produced other invaluable research tools, such as *Shinsan Zenseki mokuroku* (*Newly Edited Catalogue of Zen Books*) and Shiina *Kōyū's Sō-Genban zenseki no kenkyū* (*Studies in Song and Yuan Editions of Chan Books*).[100] Chinese scholarship took off in the 1980s (some of it concerned more with historical linguistics than the Buddhist side of the study of Chan literature) and continues to grow. Examples include the work of Cao Guangshun (曹广順) and Liu Xunning (劉勛寧) on the *Zutangji*. Western scholarship initially focused on the literature of Tang-dynasty Chan—the preeminent example being Yampolsky's *The Platform Sutra of the Sixth Patriarch*.[101] Also, Paul Demiéville's *Entretiens de Lin-tsi*, an annotated translation of the *Linjilu* (*Record of Linji*), which was much influenced by the work of Iriya and Yanagida, was a milestone in the production of solid translations into Western languages.[102] Another great stride forward was John R. McRae's *The Northern School and the Formation of Early Ch'an Buddhism.*[103] Eventually Western scholars turned their attention from the "golden age" of Tang (a much-criticized idealization) to Song-dynasty Chan literature. Two key publications in this area have been Albert Welter's *Yongming Yanshou's Conception of Chan in the* Zongjing lu and Morten Schlütter's *How Zen Became Zen.*[104] Song developments have taken on more and more prominence in recent decades. Eventually research on Chan literature is likely to overturn the usual simplistic picture of the resurgence of Neo-Confucianism in the Song. The study of some aspects of Chan literature could serve as a much-needed corrective to the assumption that Chan praxis and Confucian moral action in the world were mutually exclusive. Also, at some point in the indefinite future some of Chan literature may even take its rightful place within the field of Chinese literature.

PRIMARY SOURCES

Primary sources are found in (1) canonical collections and (2) in published series:

Many Chan texts are found in the canonical collections *Taishō Shinshū daizōkyō* (always abbreviated T) and *Dai Nihon zokuzōkyō* (*Manji zokuzō*). *Taishō* volumes 47 and 48 contain forty Chan texts. Volume 85 contains about ten Dunhuang-manuscript Chan texts. The *Manji zokuzō* (2.15 to 2.32) contains an enormous number of Chan texts. The *Taishō* is available online both from the Chinese Buddhist Electronic Text Association (CBETA) and the SAT Daizōkyō Database. CBETA also includes the *Manji zokuzō.*

The most important published series are listed here:

App, Urs, ed. *Hanazono University Concordance Series.* 21 vols. Kyoto: International Research Institute for Zen Buddhism, 1993–1995.

Some of these concordances are accompanied by newly punctuated texts. This series has been leapfrogged by the CBETA and SAT electronic texts.

Shiina Kōyū, ed. *Gozanban Chūgoku zenseki sōkan.* 12 vols. Kyoto: Rinsen shoten, 2012–.

Upon completion, this series will contain about 100 Chinese Chan texts printed in Japan during the Gozan (Five Mountains) period (*c.* 1300–1500). By October 2017, eleven volumes were published. The heritage of Chan literature from Japan's greatest era of printing Chinese Chan texts.

Yanagida Seizan, ed. *Zengaku sōsho.* 10 vols. Kyoto: Chūbun shuppansha, 1973–1979.

Contains various Chan records.

Yanagida Seizan and Shiina Kōyū, eds. *Zengaku tenseki sōkan.* 12 vols. Kyoto: Rinsen shoten, 1999–2001.

Facsimiles of rare and important editions of Chan texts: Five-Mountains editions, Song editions, and Korean editions.

Zen no goroku. 17 vols. Tokyo: Chikuma shobō, 1969–1976.

Conceived as a series of twenty volumes with Chinese text, modern Japanese translations, and notes, but only seventeen were published. Reissued in 20 volumes in 2016.

FURTHER READING

Adamek, Wendy L. *The Mystique of Transmission: On an Early Chan History and Its Contexts.* New York: Columbia University Press, 2007.

Anderl, Christoph. *Studies in the Language of Zu-tang ji*. 2 vols. Oslo: Unipub AS, 2004.

Broughton, Jeffrey L., and Elise Yoko Watanabe. *The Letters of Chan Master Dahui Pujue*. New York: Oxford University Press, 2017.

Collected Works of Korean Buddhism. 13 vols. Seoul: Jogye Order of Korean Buddhism, 2012. (Vols. 2, 3, 7.1, 7.2, 8, and 9 are useful for a comparison of the texts in this article with Chan/Sŏn texts in Chinese composed by Koreans.)

Egan, Charles, trans. *Clouds Thick, Whereabouts Unknown: Poems by Zen Monks of China*. New York: Columbia University Press, 2010.

Heine, Steven, and Dale S. Wright, eds. *The Zen Canon: Understanding the Classic Texts*. Oxford: Oxford University Press, 2004.

Henricks, Robert G. *The Poetry of Han-shan: A Complete, Annotated Translation of Cold Mountain*. Albany: State University of New York Press, 1990.

Keyworth, George Albert, III. "Transmitting the Lamp of Learning in Classical Chan Buddhism: Juefan Huihong (1071–1128) and Literary Chan." PhD diss., University of California, Los Angeles, 2001.

Kirchner, Thomas Yuho, ed. *The Record of Linji*. Translated by Ruth Fuller Sasaki. Honolulu: University of Hawai'i Press, 2009.

Mair, Victor H. "Buddhism and the Rise of the Written Vernacular in East Asia: The Making of National Languages." *Journal of Asian Studies* 53, no. 3 (August 1994): 707–751.

Poceski, Mario. *The Records of Mazu and the Making of Classical Chan Literature*. Oxford: Oxford University Press, 2015.

Schlütter, Morten. *How Zen Became Zen: The Dispute over Enlightenment and the Formation of Chan Buddhism in Song-Dynasty China*. Honolulu: University of Hawai'i Press, 2008.

Yampolsky, Philip B. *The Platform Sutra of the Sixth Patriarch*. New York: Columbia University Press, 1967.

NOTES

1. Morten Schlütter, *How Zen Became Zen: The Dispute over Enlightenment and the Formation of Chan Buddhism in Song-Dynasty China* (Honolulu: University of Hawai'i Press, 2008), 8 and 73–74.
2. Shiina Kōyū, *Sō-Genban zenseki no kenkyū* (Tokyo: Daitō shuppansha, 1993), 93–100.
3. However, for the purposes of this article, the editions found in CBETA (T and *Shinsan Zokuzōkyō/Xuzangjing*) were used.
4. As of October 2017, eleven volumes of this series have been published: Shiina Kōyū, ed., *Gozanban Chūgoku zenseki sōkan*, 12 vols. (Kyoto: Rinsen shoten, 2012–).
5. The Dunhuang-manuscript texts are nos. 1, 2, 14, 15, 16, and 38. The *Patriarchal Hall Collection* is no. 8. For these texts, see Yanagida Seizan, "Zenseki kaidai," in *Zenke goroku* 2, ed. Nishitani Keiji and Yanagida Seizan (Tokyo: Chikuma shobō, 1974), 453–466 and 507–508.
6. The two Ming texts are nos. 13 and 36. The title missing in Shiina's list is *Calm-and-Unhurried Hermitage* (text no. 30).
7. For a discussion of the *yulu* genre and the term *yulu*, see Mario Poceski, *The Records of Mazu and the Making of Classical Chan Literature* (Oxford: Oxford University Press, 2015), 111–118. Poceski (111) points out: "In its fully developed form, this genre was a product of the early Song period, although . . . it earlier origins can be traced back to the Tang and Five Dynasties eras." The earliest use of the term in the context of Chan literature dates to the beginning of the Song dynasty.
8. Christoph Anderl, *Studies in the Language of Zu-tang ji* (Oslo: Unipub AS, 2004), 1.xxvi.
9. See, for example, Iriya Yoshitaka and Koga Hidehiko, *Zengo jiten* (Kyoto: Shibunkaku shuppan, 1991); and Xu Shaofeng, ed., *Jindai Hanyu da cidian*, 2 vols. (Beijing: Zhonghua shuju, 2008). The former dictionary of Zen words is small, but the best for words and expressions (some of the following examples are taken from this dictionary). The latter is a dictionary of colloquial words and phrases in old books from

the Tang to the Qing, containing more than 50,000 entries. Sources are mainly drama, novels, Chan and Neo-Confucian records, Dunhuang transformation texts, and poetry (with many quotations).

10. These glosses are found in commentaries on the *Linjilu* by the Japanese commentators Kassan (夾山; d. 1654) and Kōunshi (耕雲子; d. 1698). Kassan glosses *bangjia* as "one who is nearby other family gates loses his own family treasure" (傍他門戶者失却自家珍); Kōunshi says: "*Bangjia* is like saying 'other families'" (傍家者猶言他家也). Rinzairoku *shōsho shūsei*, ed. Yanagida Seizan (Kyoto: Chūbun shuppansha, 1980), 484 and 1143.
11. *Yanxi Guangwen chanshi yulu* 偃溪廣聞禪師語錄: 忽有人問。上上機人來時如何。且坐喫茶。(CBETA, X69, no. 1368, p. 738, c12–13//Z 2:26, p. 140, c18–d1//R121, p. 280, a18–b1).
12. *Xuefeng Yicun chanshi yulu* 雪峰義存禪師語錄: 問。古人有言。路逢達道人。莫將語默對。未審將什麼對。師云。且喫茶去。(CBETA, X69, no. 1333, p. 73, c3–4//Z 2:24, p. 474, d11–12//R119, p. 948, b11–12).
13. For examples, see *Dahui yulu* (text no. 6) and *Xutang yulu* (text no. 11) below.
14. 緣法師曰。. . . 又曰。若有體氣時。免人法誑惑。精神亦可。何以故。貴智故。被人法誑。若重一人爲是者。即不免此人惑亂。. . . 志法師屠児行上見緣法師問。見屠児殺羊不。緣法師曰。我眼不盲。何以不見。志法師曰。緣公乃言見之。緣師曰。更乃見之。*Daruma no goroku*, Zen no goroku 1, ed. and trans. Yanagida Seizan (Tokyo: Chikuma shobō, 1969), 200–204.
15. *Jinne no goroku*: *Dango*, ed. Tōdai goroku kenkyūhan (Kyoto: Zenbunka kenkyūjo, 2006), 13, 51, 62, and 110. This is the equivalent of Sanskrit *kalyāṇa-mitra* and is similar to the Japanese *minasan* or *minasama* (皆さん/皆様).
16. *Tanyu* 壇語: 本體空寂。從空寂體上起知。善分別世間青黃赤白。是惠。不隨分別起。是定。只如凝心入定。墮無記空。出定已後。起心分別一切世間有爲。喚此爲惠。經中名爲妄心。*Jinne no goroku*: *Dango*, 84.
17. *Chuanxin fa yao* 傳心法要: 九月一日師謂休曰。(T2012A.48.381b17)
18. *Wanling lu* 宛陵錄: 上堂云。即心是佛。上至諸佛。下至蠢動含靈。皆有佛性。. . . (T2012B.48.386b2–3).
19. *Chuanxin fa yao* 黃檗山斷際禪師傳心法要: 予會昌二年。廉于鍾陵。自山迎至州。憩龍興寺。旦夕問道。大中二年。廉于宛陵。復去禮迎至所部。安居開元寺。旦夕受法。退而紀之。十得一二。佩爲心印。不敢發揚。今恐入神精義。不聞於未來。遂出之。授門下僧太舟法建。歸舊山之廣唐寺。問長老法衆與往日常所親聞同異如何也。唐大中十一年十一月初八日序 (T2012A.48.379c5–13).
20. *Chuanxin fa yao* 傳心法要: 問如何得不落階級。師云。終日喫飯未曾咬著一粒米。終日行未曾踏著一片地。與摩時無人我等相。終日不離一切事。不被諸境惑。方名自在人。更時時念念不見一切相。莫認前後三際。前際無去今際無住後際無來。(T2012A.48.384a12–16).
21. 不被境轉處處用境; 歇得念念馳求心; 擬議; 莫受人惑; 全體作用; and 伱今用處.
22. *Yunmen Kuangzhen chanshi guanglu* 雲門匡真禪師廣錄: 師在僧堂中喫茶。拈起托子云。蒸餅饅頭一任汝喫。爾道這箇是什麼。代云。乾狗屎。(T1988.47.565c9–11).
23. *Yunmen Kuangzhen chanshi guanglu* 雲門匡真禪師廣錄: 上堂云。舉一則語。教汝直下承當。早是撒屎著爾頭上也。直饒拈一毛頭。盡大地一時明得。也是剜肉作瘡。雖然如此。也須是實到者箇田地始得。若未且不得掠虛。却須退步向自己根脚下推尋看。是什麼道理。實無絲髮許與汝作解會。與汝作疑惑。況汝等且各各當人。有一段事。大用現前。更不煩汝一毫頭氣力。便與祖佛無別。自是汝諸人信根淺薄惡業濃厚。突然起得如許多頭角。擔鉢囊千鄉萬里受屈作麼。且汝諸人有什麼不足處。大丈夫漢阿誰無分。獨自承當。尚猶不著便。不可受人欺瞞取人處分。纔見老和尚開口。便好把特[持]石驀口塞。便似屎上青蠅相似。(T1988.47.546b28–c11).

24. *Zhenzhou Linji Huizhao chanshi yulu* 鎮州臨濟慧照禪師語錄: 上堂云。赤肉團上有一無位真人。常從汝等諸人面門出入。未證據者看看。時有僧出問。如何是無位真人。師下禪床把住云。道道。其僧擬議。師托開云。無位真人是什麼乾屎橛。便歸方丈。(T1985.47.496c10–14).
25. *Zhenzhou Linji Huizhao chanshi yulu* 鎮州臨濟慧照禪師語錄: 大德。爾檐鉢囊屎檐子。傍家走求佛求法。即今與麼馳求底。爾還識渠麼。活撥撥地。秖是勿根株。擁不聚撥不散。求著即轉遠。不求還在目前。靈音屬耳。若人不信。徒勞百年。(T1985.47.501b10–14).
26. *Dahui Pujue chanshi yulu* 大慧普覺禪師語錄: 上堂。拈起拄杖示衆云。還見麼。又卓一下云。還聞麼。若道實見實聞。正是隨聲逐色漢。復舉起云。還見麼。又卓一下云。還聞麼。若道不見不聞。正是避色逃聲漢。畢竟如何。擲下云。鶴有九皐難翥翼。馬無千里謾追風。(T1998A.47.820b2–6).
27. This summary is based on the T edition, which has a rearrangement of the contents. A Song edition has been found in Japan: *Wanshi roku*, ed. Ishii Shūdō, 3 vols. (Tokyo: Meicho fukuyūkai, 1984).
28. *Hongzhi chanshi guanglu* 宏智禪師廣錄: 上堂云。獨立不改。周行不殆。莫嫌滿眼諸塵。須信唯心三界。列千峯而向嶽。會百川而到海。諸禪德。恁麼會得也。卷簾除却障。恁麼不會也。閉戶生得礙。會與不會商量。漆桶依前不快。(T2001.48.12a13–17).
29. *Hongzhi chanshi guanglu* 宏智禪師廣錄: 小參僧問。如何是和尚親切爲人底句。師云。文彩未痕。初消息難傳際。僧云。可謂虛明自照。不勞心力。師云。卓卓不倚物。靈靈那涉緣。僧云。莫便是十成底時節也無。師云。透過那邊看。方有出身路。僧云。揭開金鎖裏頭看。隱隱風光元自異。師云。不是那邊事。僧云。如何是那邊事。師云。瑠璃殿上行。撲倒須粉碎。(T2001.48.58a3–10).
30. *Hongzhi chanshi guanglu* 宏智禪師廣錄: *Mozhao ming* 默照銘: 默默忘言。昭昭現前。鑒時廓爾。體處靈然。靈然獨照。照中還妙。露月星河。雪松雲嶠。(T2001.48.100a25–27).
31. *Wuzhun Shifan chanshi yulu* 無準師範禪師語錄 (= *Fojian chanshi yulu* 佛鑑禪師語錄): 上堂。召大衆云。禪。禪。妙高峯頂。千丈巖前。作麼生有箇古松樹。奇奇怪怪。屈屈曲曲。拳拳攣攣。諸人若恁麼會。驢年。(CBETA, X70, no. 1382, p. 227, c6–8//Z 2:26, p. 434, a12–14//R121, p. 867, a12–14).
32. *Shixi Xinyue chanshi yulu* 石溪心月禪師語錄 (= *Fohai chanshi yulu* 佛海禪師語錄): 上堂。空劫已前。綿綿密密。既往莫追。空劫已後。密密綿綿。未來且置。正當空劫。綿綿處密密。密密處綿綿。以何爲證。攣卷枯樹子。春信在其中。(CBETA, X71, no. 1405, p. 27, a6–8//Z 2:28, p. 26, c14–16//R123, p. 52, a14–16).
33. *Shixi Xinyue chanshi yulu* 石溪心月禪師語錄 (= *Fohai chanshi yulu* 佛海禪師語錄): 上堂。拈主丈。卓一下云。七佛已前只與麼。又卓一下云。七佛之後亦復然。卓一下。片雲生晚谷。孤鶴下遼天。(CBETA, X71, no. 1405, p. 33, a1–3//Z 2:28, p. 32, c9–11//R123, p. 64, a9–11).
34. *Yanxi Guangwen chanshi yulu* 偃溪廣聞禪師語錄: 上堂。默默。無上菩提從此得。了了。金雞一拍扶桑曉。衲僧門下。二俱漏逗。(CBETA, X69, no. 1368, p. 732, a10–11//Z 2:26, p. 134, a4–5//R121, p. 267, a4–5). Yanxi is following in the footsteps of Dahui in criticizing the "silence-and-illumination" of "perverse" Chan teachers.
35. *Yanxi Guangwen chanshi yulu* 偃溪廣聞禪師語錄: 上堂。禪非意想。道絕功勳。去此二途。比如太平時節。駕輕車行熟路。無往不可。要望德山臨濟門下遠矣。何也。畫前元有易。刪後更無詩。(CBETA, X69, no. 1368, p. 736, a16–18//Z 2:26, p. 138, a10–12//R121, p. 275, a10–12).
36. *Xutang heshang yulu* 虛堂和尚語錄: 上堂。每日蒲團上妄想。無爾插手處。以致奔南走北。如鴨吞螺螄。山僧今日不動聲氣。教爾諸人有箇入處。良久拍手云。一半入得。一半入不得。(T2000.47.996a1–4).
37. *Xutang heshang yulu* 虛堂和尚語錄: 辭世頌: 八十五年。佛祖不識。掉臂便行。太虛絕跡。(T2000.47.1063b14–16).

38. *Gaofeng Yuanmiao chanshi yulu* 高峰原妙禪師語錄: 參禪若要剋日成功。如墮千尺井底相似。從朝至暮。從暮至朝。千思想。萬思想。單單則是箇求出之心。究竟決無二念。誠能如是施功。或三日。或五日。或七日。若不徹去。西峰今日犯大妄語。永墮拔舌犂耕。(CBETA, X70, no. 1400, p. 696, c6–9//Z 2:27, p. 346, c3–6//R122, p. 692, a3–6). For the parallel passage in the *Gaofeng chanyao* 高峰禪要, see CBETA, X70, no. 1401, p. 706, b2–5//Z 2:27, p. 355, c14–17//R122, p. 710, a14–17.
39. *Gaofeng Yuanmiao chanshi yulu* 高峰原妙禪師語錄: 若謂著實參禪。決須具足三要。第一要有大信根。明知此事。如靠一座須彌山。第二要有大憤志。如遇殺父冤讐。直欲便與一刀兩段。第三要有大疑情。如暗他做了一件極事。正在欲露未露之時。十二時中。果能具此三要。管取剋日成功。(CBETA, X70, no. 1400, p. 687, b5–9//Z 2:27, p. 337, a17–b3//R122, p. 673, a17–b3). For the parallel passage in the *Gaofeng chanyao* 高峰禪要, see CBETA, X70, no. 1401, p. 708, b5–9//Z 2:27, p. 357, c17–d3//R122, p. 714, a17–b3.
40. *Tianzhen Dufeng Shan chanshi yaoyu* 天真毒峰善禪師要語: 上堂。僧問。昔高峰和尚示眾云。海底泥牛啣[嗡]月走。岩[巖]前石虎抱兒眠。鐵蛇鑽人[入]金剛眼。崑崙騎象鷺鷥牽。此四句內有一句。能殺能活。能縱能奪。若人檢點得出。許你一生參學事畢。不知是那一句。師云。待你悟即向你道。會麼。僧云。不會。師云。不見道。你有拄杖子。我與你拄杖子。你無拄杖子。我奪卻你拄杖子。下座。(CBETA, J25, no. B159, p. 137, a20–25). The Gaofeng saying is found in both *Gaofeng yulu* (CBETA, X70, no. 1400, p. 680, a1–3//Z 2:27, p. 329, d7–9//R122, p. 658, b7–9) and *Gaofeng chanyao* (CBETA, X70, no. 1401, p. 705, b7–9//Z 2:27, p. 354, d1–3//R122, p. 708, b1–3).
41. *Tianzhen Dufeng Shan chanshi yaoyu* 天真毒峰善禪師要語: 果欲脫生死輪迴。先須發大信心。立弘誓願。拼從今身。未悟之先。莫退菩提道心。莫改修行節操。若不打破這則所參公案。洞見父母未生已前面目。坐斷微細現行生死。誓不中途而廢放捨本參話頭。遠離真善知識。若故違此願。當墮惡道。受無量苦。發此大願。防護其心。然後方堪領荷公案。(CBETA, J25, no. B159, p. 137, b5–10). In this article *huatou* are in italics and bold font.
42. *Da fangguang fo huayan jing* 大方廣佛華嚴經: 譬如一燈。然百千燈。其本一燈。無減無盡。(T279.10.432c1–2).
43. For editions of these two Chan records, see *Shoki no zenshi* I, Zen no goroku 2, ed. and trans. Yanagida Seizan (Tokyo: Chikma shobō, 1976).
44. For an edition of this Chan record, see *Shoki no zenshi* II, Zen no goroku 3, ed. and trans. Yanagida Seizan (Tokyo: Chikma shobō, 1971).
45. *Chuan fabao ji* 傳法寶紀: 是故今修略紀。自達摩後。相承傳法者。著之於次。以爲傳寶紀一卷。維當綴其所見名迹。所化方處。耳目所取。書紀可明者。既而與無爲泯合。而傳記自簡。至於覺證聖趣。靡得甄言也。亦別有貌圖。將爲記。(Yanagida, *Shoki no zenshi* I, 346; T2838.85.1291b18–22).
46. *Chuan fabao ji* 傳法寶紀: 昔廬山遠上人禪經序云。佛付阿難。阿難傳末田地。末田地傳舍那婆斯。則知爾後不墜於地。存乎其人。至矣。(Yanagida, *Shoki no zenshi* I, 336–337; T2838.85.1291a20–22). The *Preface to the Dhyāna Sūtra* quotation is T618.15.301a7–10.
47. For a facsimile of the extant fascicles of the Hongzhou 洪州 school's *Baolin zhuan* 寶林傳, see *Sōzō ichin: Hōrinden, Dentō gyokuei shū*, Zengaku sōsho 5, ed. Yanagida Seizan (Kyoto: Chūbun shuppansha, 1983).
48. For a reprinted copy of the original Korean text of the *Zutangji* 祖堂集, see *Sodōshū*, ed. Yoshizawa Katsuhiro and Onishi Shirō (Kyoto: Zenbunka kenkyūjo, 1984).
49. Anderl, *Studies in the Language of Zu-tang ji*, 1.35–36.
50. *Jingde chuandeng lu* 景德傳燈錄: 有東吳僧道原者。冥心禪悅。索隱空宗。披弈世之祖圖。采諸方之語錄。次序其源派。錯綜其辭句。由七佛以至大法眼之嗣。凡五十二世。一千七百一人。成三十卷。目之曰景德傳燈錄。(T2076.51.196c1–5).

51. *Jingde chuandeng lu* 景德傳燈錄: 毘婆尸佛(過去莊嚴劫第九百九十八尊)偈曰。身從無相中受生。猶如幻出諸形象。幻人心識本來無。罪福皆空無所住。長阿含經云。人壽八萬歲時此佛出世。種刹利。姓拘利若。父槃頭。母槃頭婆提。居槃頭婆提城。坐波波羅樹下。說法三會。度人三十四萬八千人。神足二。一名騫茶。二名提舍。侍者無憂。子方膺。(T2076.51.204d1–8). The *Dirghāgama* reference is T.1.1.3b7–10.
52. Endymion Wilkinson, *Chinese History: A New Manual*, 4th ed. (Cambridge, MA: Harvard University Asia Center, 2015), 151.
53. *Jingde chuandeng lu* 景德傳燈錄: 杭州羅漢院宗徹禪師。湖州吳興縣人也。姓吳氏。幼歲出家。依年受具。巡方參禮。依黃檗希運禪師法席。黃檗一見便深器之。入室領旨。後至杭州。州牧劉彥慕其道。立精舍於府西。號羅漢院。化徒三百。師有時上堂。僧問。如何是西來意。師曰。骨剉也。(師對機多用此語。故時人因號骨剉和尚。) 問。如何是南宗北宗。師曰。心爲宗。僧曰。還看教也無。師曰。教是心。問。性地多昏。如何了悟。師曰。煩雲風卷。太虛廓清。曰。如何得明去。師曰。一輪皎潔。萬里騰光。師後示疾遷化。門人塔于院之北隅。梁貞明五年。錢王廣其院爲安國羅漢寺。移師塔於大慈山塢。今寺與塔並存。(T2076.51.293a15–27).
54. For text of the *Tiansheng guang denglu* 天聖廣燈錄, see CBETA, X78, no. 1553.
55. 正宗門; 對機門; 拈古門; 頌古門; and 偈頌門. *Jianzhong Jingguo xu deng lu* 建中靖國續燈錄: CBETA, X78, no. 1555, p. 622, a7–11//Z 2B:9, p. 1, a4–8//R136, p. 1, a4–8.
56. For text of the *Zongmen liandeng huiyao* 宗門聯燈會要, see CBETA, X79, no. 1557.
57. For text of the *Jiatai pu denglu* 嘉泰普燈錄, see CBETA, X79, no. 1559.
58. *Chanmen zhu zushi jisong* 禪門諸祖師偈頌: *Sanzu dashi Xinxin ming* 三祖大師信心銘: 至道無難。唯嫌揀擇。但莫憎愛。洞然明白。毫釐有差。天地懸隔。欲得現前。莫存順逆。違順相爭。是爲心病。不識玄旨。徒勞念靜。圓同太虛。無欠無餘。良由取捨。所以不如。莫逐有緣。勿住空忍。一種平懷。泯然自盡。止動歸止。止更彌動。唯滯兩邊。寧知一種。一種不通。兩處失功。遣有沒有。從空背空。多言多慮。轉不相應。絕言絕慮。無處不通。(CBETA, X66, no. 1298, p. 722, c17–p. 723, a2//Z 2:21, p. 457, b3–12//R116, p. 913, b3–12).
59. *Chanmen zhu zushi jisong* 禪門諸祖師偈頌: *Yongjia Zhenjue dashi Zhengdao ge* 永嘉真覺大師證道歌: 君不見。絕學無爲閑道人。不除妄想不求真。無明實性即佛性。幻化空身即法身。法身覺了無一物。本源自性天真佛。五陰浮雲空去來。三毒水泡虛出沒。(CBETA, X66, no. 1298, p. 731, c4–7//Z 2:21, p. 466, a10–13//R116, p. 931, a10–13).
60. *Jianghu fengyue ji* 江湖風月集: 聽雪: 寒夜無風竹有聲。踈踈密密透松櫺。耳聞不似心聞好。歇却燈前半卷經。 *Gōko fugetsushū yakuchū*, ed. Yoshizawa Katsuhiro (Kyoto: Zenbunka kenkyūjo, 2003), 76–77. The *Śūraṃgama* reference is T945.19.126c15–16.
61. 聽蛙:頭戴青苔咄咄鳴。千山虛寂月初明。一機頓發空諸有。太雅松風無此聲。 Yoshizawa, *Gōko fugetsushū yakuchū*, 131–132. These are the words of Layman Pang at death. *Pang jushi yulu* 龐居士語錄: "The Metropolitan Governor Yu Di came to inquire about the Layman's illness. Layman Pang said to him: 'Vow to empty the existent. Don't reify the non-existent.'" [州牧于頔問疾。士謂之曰。但願空諸所有。慎勿實諸所無。] (CBETA, X69, no. 1336, p. 134, b10–11//Z 2:25, p. 31, b10–11//R120, p. 61, b10–11). Mozong Deben (末宗德本) was a successor of Duanqiao Miaolun (斷橋妙倫; 1201–1261) of the Yangqi-Po'an wing of the Linji lineage.
62. 開藏經板:瞿曇曲爲說來由。遆代雕鐫禍未休。誰道邊禪牀一匝。更無一字落刀頭。 Yoshizawa, *Gōko fugetsushū yakuchū*, 177–178. An old woman sent money to Zhaozhou Congshen (趙州從諗; 778–897) with a request to "turn the canon" (*zhuan zang* 轉藏), and this was his response. Turning the canon means both reading the canon (not necessarily word by word) and spinning the revolving bookcase that contains the canon. Zhitang Biao (指堂摽; d. unknown) was in the Songyuan wing of the Linji lineage.

63. 禪者求語：迢迢峯頂賺伊來。將爲春風巧剪裁。語又不玄機不妙。方方丈地定生苔。Yoshizawa, *Gōko fugetsushū yakuchū*, 401–402. Qianfeng Ruwan (千峰如琬; d. unknown) was in the Linji line (Yanqi branch) of Yuanwu Keqin.
64. Charles Egan, *Clouds Thick, Whereabouts Unknown: Poems by Zen Monks of China* (New York: Columbia University Press, 2010), 45–47.
65. *Hanshanzi shi ji* 寒山子詩集: 有箇王秀才。笑我詩多失。云不識蜂腰。仍不會鶴膝。平側不解壓。凡言取次出。我笑你作詩。如盲徒詠日。(CBETA, J20, no. B103, p. 663, a9–11).
66. *Xueyan Zuqin chanshi yulu* 雪巖祖欽禪師語錄: 一千七百則公案 (CBETA, X70, no. 1397, p. 616, c16//Z 2:27, p. 267, b5//R122, p. 533, b5).
67. *Xuedou Xian heshang songgu ji* 雪竇顯和尚頌古集: 今又採古聖機緣之妙者凡百則。發言以爲頌。由頌以宣義。由義以垂裕。Iriya Yoshitaka, Kajitani Sōnin, and Yanagida Seizan, *Secchō juko*, Zen no goroku 15 (Tokyo: Chikuma shobō, 1981), 3.
68. 垂示; 著語; and 評唱. For text of the *Biyan ji* 碧巖集, see T2003.48.
69. 趙州語錄; 睦州語錄; 智門語; 臨濟錄; and 龐居士語錄.
70. *Xuedou Xian heshang songgu ji*雪竇顯和尚頌古集: 舉。世尊一日陞座。文殊白槌云。諦觀法王法。法王法如是。 世尊便下座。頌曰。列聖叢中作者知。法王法令不如斯。會中若有仙陀客。何必文殊下一槌。Iriya, Kajitani, and Yanagida, *Secchō juko*, 221–222.
71. 垂示; 著語; 評唱; 著語; and評唱. *Foguo Yuanwu chanshi biyan lu* 佛果圜悟禪師碧巖錄, T2003.48.216b18–c29.
72. 泗州普照和尚頌古. *Hongzhi chanshi guanglu* 宏智禪師廣錄, T2001.48.18b27–27c1.
73. For text of the *Wansong laoren pingchang Tiantong Jue heshang song gu congrong an lu* 萬松老人評唱天童覺和尚頌古從容庵錄, see T2004.48.
74. *Hongzhi chanshi guanglu* 宏智禪師廣錄: *Sizhou Puzhao heshang song gu*泗州普照覺和尚頌古: 舉雲門垂語云。古佛與露柱相交。是第幾機衆無語。自代云。南山起雲北山下雨。頌曰。一道神光。初不覆藏。超見緣也。是而無是。出情量也。當而無當。巖花之粉兮蜂房成蜜。野草之滋兮麝臍作香。隨類三尺一丈六。明明觸處露堂堂。(T2001.48.21b6–12).
75. *Wumen guan* 無門關: 且道。如何是祖師關。只者一箇無字。乃宗門一關也。遂目之曰禪宗無門關。透得過者。非但親見趙州。便可與歷代祖師。把手共行。眉毛廝結。同一眼見。同一耳聞。豈不慶快。莫有要透關底麼。將三百六十骨節八萬四千毫竅。通身起箇疑團。參箇無字。晝夜提撕。莫作虛無會。莫作有無會。如吞了箇熱鐵丸。相似吐又吐不出。蕩盡從前惡知惡覺。久久純熟。自然內外打成。(T2005.48.292c27–293a6).
76. *Zheng fayan zang* 正法眼藏: 琅邪覺和尚示衆曰。進前即死。退後即亡。不進不退落在無事之鄉。何故如此。長安雖樂。不是久居。妙喜曰。啼得血流無用處。不如緘口過殘春。(CBETA, X67, no. 1309, p. 578, a23–b1//Z 2:23, p. 23, a14–16//R118, p. 45, a14–16).
77. Jeffrey Lyle Broughton, *Zongmi on Chan* (New York: Columbia University Press, 2009), 214 (n. 54).
78. *Chanyuan zhuquan ji duxu* 禪源諸詮集都序: 原夫佛說頓教漸教禪開頓門漸門。二教二門各相符契。今講者偏彰漸義。禪者偏播頓宗。禪講相逢胡越之隔。宗密不知宿生何作熏得此心。(T2015.48.399c2–5).
79. 息妄修心宗; 泯絕無寄宗; and 直顯心性宗.
80. 淨衆宗; 北宗; 保唐宗; 南山念佛門禪宗; 石頭宗; 牛頭宗; 荷澤宗; and 洪州宗.
81. *Rentian yanmu* 人天眼目: 凡是五宗綱要者。即筆而藏諸。(T2006.48.300a10–11) 臨濟宗; 雲門宗; 曹洞宗; 潙仰宗; and 法眼宗.
82. *Rentian yanmu* 人天眼目: *Yuanwu wu jia zongyao* 圜悟五家宗要: 全機大用。棒喝交馳。劍刃上求人。電光中垂手(臨濟)。北斗藏身。金風體露。三句可辨。一鏃遼空(雲門)。君臣合道。偏正相資。鳥道玄途。金針玉線(曹洞)。師資唱和。父子一家。明暗交馳。語默不露(潙仰)。聞聲悟道。見色明心。句裏藏鋒。言中有響(法眼)。(T2006.48.331a14–24).

83. *Linjianlu* 林間錄: 予嘗與數僧謁雲峰悅禪師塔。拜起。拊之曰。生耶。死耶。久之。自答曰。不可推倒塔子去也。旁僧曰。今日時節正類道吾因緣。因作偈示之曰。不知即問。不見即討。圓滿現前。何須更道。維堅密身。生死病老。面前塔子。不可推倒。(CBETA, X87, no. 1624, p. 275, a22–b2//Z 2B:21, p. 323, a14–18//R148, p. 645, a14–18).
84. *Linjianlu* 林間錄: 醉里有狂僧。號戒道者。依止聚落。無日不醉。然吐詞恠奇。世莫能凡聖之。有飲以酒者。使自爲祭文。戒應聲曰。惟靈生在閻浮。不嗔不妬。愛喫酒子。倒街臥路。直得生兜率陀天。爾時方不喫酒故。何以故。淨土之中。無酒得沽。(CBETA, X87, no. 1624, p. 275, c21–p. 276, a1//Z 2B:21, p. 323, d7–11//R148, p. 646, b7–11).
85. *Huang Ming mingseng jilue* 皇明名僧輯略: 單單提起一句阿彌陀佛。置之懷抱。默然體究。常時鞭起疑情。這箇念佛的畢竟是誰。返復參究。不可作有無卜度。又不得將心待悟。但有微塵許妄念存心。皆為障礙。直須打併教胷中空蕩蕩無一物。而於行住坐臥之中。乃至靜鬧閒忙之處。都不用分別計較。但要念念相續。心心無間。久久工夫純一。自然寂靜輕安。便有禪定現前。(CBETA, X84, no. 1581, p. 370, a8–15//Z 2B:17, p. 213, c8–15//R144, p. 426, a8–15).
86. *Dahui Pujue chanshi shu* 大慧普覺禪師書: 今時士大夫。多於此事不能百了千當直下透脫者。只爲根性太利知見太多。見宗師纔開口動舌。早一時會了也。以故返不如鈍根者。無許多惡知惡覺。驀地於一機一境上一言一句下撞發。(T1998A.47.922c5–9). *Letters of Dahui* circulated as both an independent text and as a section of his *yulu*.
87. *Dahui Pujue chanshi shu* 大慧普覺禪師書: 近年以來有一種邪師。說默照禪。教人十二時中是事莫管。休去歇去。不得做聲。恐落今時。往往士大夫。爲聰明利根所使者。多是厭惡鬧處。乍被邪師輩指令靜坐。却見省力。便以爲是。更不求妙悟。只以默然爲極則。某不惜口業。力救此弊。(T1998A.47.923a5–11).
88. Examples in the Dunhuang Chan corpus beyond *Cutting-off* are: *No-Mind Treatise* (*Wuxinlun* 無心論), which says at the beginning it will "now hypothetically set up two people who together discuss the topic of no-mind" (今且假立二人共談無心之論矣 [T2831.85.1269a24–25]); the *Treatise on the Mahāyāna Opening Mind Revealing the Nature All-at Once Awakening to the True Axiom-Realization* (*Dasheng kaixin xianxing dunwu zhenzong lun* 大乘開心顯性頓悟真宗論; T no.2835), a dialogue between two aspects of the same person (Li Huiguang 李惠光and Chan Master Dazhao 大照) on "mind not arising" (*xin bu qi* 心不起); and the *Essential Judgments on the Dharma Gate of All at-Once Awakening to the True Thesis and Arriving at the Other Shore by the Practice of Thunderbolt Wisdom* (*Dunwu zhenzong jingang bore xiuxing da bi'an famen yaojue* 頓悟真宗金剛般若修行達彼岸法門要决), a *dhyāna* manual cast in the format of a dialogue between Chan Master Zhida 智達and Layman Houmochen Yan 候莫陳琰居士, two aspects of the same person. The last was translated into Tibetan (*Yang dag pa'i phyi mo cig car tshor ba'i chos kyi sgo mo = Dunwu zhenzong famen*) during Tibet's first dissemination of Buddhism. For an edition, see Ueyama Daishun, "Chibetto-yaku *Tongo shinshū yōketsu* no kenkyū," *Zen bunka kenkyūjo kiyō* 8 (1976): 33–103.
89. *Jueguan lun* 絕觀論: 今且立二人。共談真實。師主名入立。弟子號緣門。於是入立先生寂無言說。緣門忽起。問入立先生曰。云何名心。云何安心。答曰。汝不須立心。亦不須強安。可謂安矣。Yanagida Seizan and Tokiwa Gishin, ed. and trans., *Zekkanron* (Kyoto: Zenbunka kenkyūjo, 1973), 87.
90. *Tianmu Zhongfeng heshang guanglu* 天目中峯和尚廣錄: *Huanzhu jiaxun* 幻住家訓: 幻人一日據幻室依幻座執幻拂時。諸幻弟子俱來雲集。有問。松緣何直。棘緣何曲。鵠緣何白。烏緣何玄。幻人豎起拂子。召大衆曰。我此幻拂。豎不自豎。依幻而豎。橫不自橫。依幻而橫。拈不自拈。依幻而拈。放不自放。依幻而放。...且不要忽忽草草。但辦取一片鐵石身心。拌取一生兩生。尚所參底無義味話頭上。拍盲立定丁字脚頭。心憤憤地。與之抵捱將取。*Gozanban Chūgoku zenseki sōkan* 9, *Goroku* 4, ed. Shiina Kōyū (Kyoto: Rinsen shoten, 2013), 350 and 353.

91. For text of the *Zuting shiyuan* 祖庭事苑, see CBETA, X64, no. 1261.
92. *Chanyuan zhuquan ji duxu* 禪源諸詮集都序: 教也者。諸佛菩薩所留經論也。禪也者。諸善知識所述句偈也。但佛經開張。羅大千八部之衆。禪偈撮略。就此方一類之機。(T2015.399c18–22).
93. Roger R. Jackson, *Tantric Treasures: Three Collections of Mystical Verse from Buddhist India* (Oxford: Oxford University Press, 2004), 16–40.
94. Zong-qi Cai, ed., *How to Read Chinese Poetry: A Guided Anthology* (New York: Columbia University Press, 2008), 161–164.
95. See Hu Shi, *Shenhui heshang yiji* (1930; repr., Taipei: Hu Shi jinian guan, 1970); and Jacques Gernet, *Les entretiens du maître de dhyâna Chen-houei du Ho-tsö (668–760)* (Hanoi: École Française d'Extrême-Orient, 1949).
96. Two publications emblematic of Iriya's work are Iriya Yoshitaka and Koga Hidehiko, *Zengo jiten* (Kyoto: Shibunkaku shuppan, 1991); and Iriya Yoshitaka, trans., *Rinzairoku* (Tokyo: Iwanami shoten, 1989). The former is an invaluable dictionary of Chan words and expressions; the latter is a fluid and nuanced translation of the *Linjilu* (*Record of Linji*) into modern Japanese.
97. Two publications emblematic of Yanagida's work are Yanagida Seizan, *Shoki zenshū shisho no kenkyū* (Kyoto: Hōzōkan, 1967); and Yanagida Seizan, "Zenseki kaidai," in *Zenke goroku* 2, ed. Nishitani Keiji and Yanagida Seizan (Tokyo: Chikuma shōbo, 1974), 445–514. The former is a monumental study of early Chan literature that has had enormous influence on the field; the latter is an annotated list of over 300 Chan texts, giving a brief textual history for each.
98. *Zen no goroku*, 17 vols. (Tokyo: Chikuma shobō, 1969–1976). Reissued in 20 volumes in 2016.
99. *Zengaku daijiten*, ed. Komazawa daigaku nai zengaku daijiten hensanjo (1978; repr., Tokyo: Taishūkan shoten, 1985).
100. *Shinsan zenseki mokuroku*, ed. Komazawa daigaku toshokan (Tokyo: Komazawa daigaku toshokan, 1962); and Shiina Kōyū, *Sō-Genban zenseki no kenkyū* (Tokyo: Daitō shuppansha, 1993).
101. Philip B. Yampolsky, *The Platform Sutra of the Sixth Patriarch* (New York: Columbia University Press, 1967).
102. *Entretiens de Lin-tsi*, trans. Paul Demiéville (Paris: Fayard, 1972).
103. John R. McRae, *The Northern School and Formation of Early Ch'an Buddhism* (Honolulu: University of Hawaii Press, 1986).
104. Albert Welter, *Yongming Yanshou's Conception of Chan in the* Zongjing lu (Oxford: Oxford University Press, 2011); and Morten Schlütter, *How Zen Became Zen: The Dispute over Enlightenment and the Formation of Chan Buddhism in Song-Dynasty China* (Honolulu: University of Hawai'i Press, 2008).

Jeffrey L. Broughton

CHÖD: A TIBETAN BUDDHIST PRACTICE

HISTORICAL BACKGROUND OF CHÖD

According to the historical accounts, Indian Buddhism spread into Tibet during two main periods. The earlier dissemination of the teaching from the 7th to 9th centuries occurred during the Imperial period with the patronage from the royal courts of the Yarlung dynasty in a succession of sympathetic rulers, known as dharma kings. The second wave followed a period of persecution by the last king, Langdarma. With his assassination in 906 and the later re-emergence of Buddhist-inclined regional rulers and patrons, Buddhist teachers from India were invited to revive and realign the practices. The start of this second spread is often marked by the invitation of Atiśa (982–1054) in 1042 from Vikramaśīla, one of the great Buddhist universities of northern India. This was followed by a kind of renaissance, with many Tibetans making the arduous trip over the Himalayas to India carrying gold to offer to Indian masters, and in turn Indian teachers visiting and staying in Tibet. This period is known as the later or new translation period in contrast to the ancient translation period (*snga 'gyur snying ma*), due to the new influx of a vast amount of texts—sutras, tantras, *śastras*, and *upadeśas*—and the intense translation activity that followed. The result was the establishment of various lineages or schools, most of which still exist. The followers of those practices that had developed in the early dissemination became known as Nyingma (*snying ma*), or the "ancient ones," while all the others are collectively called Sarma (*gsar ma*), "new ones." These consist of the well-known schools such as Sakya, Kagyu, and Kadam, with its later descendant, the Geluk.

EIGHT PRACTICE LINEAGES

The less well-known lineages were added in a doxographical scheme first suggested by Sherap Özer (Skt. Prajñārasmi, 1518–1584) to account for the main streams flowing from India, either through Indian masters coming to Tibet or Tibetan masters returning from India.[1] The scheme, known as Eight Great Chariots of the Practice Lineages, or eight lineages that are vehicles of attainment in Tibet, was picked up by Jamgön Kongtrul Lodrö Tayé (1813–1900) and Jamyang Khyentsé Wangpo (1820–1892) as an organizational rubric in the vast preservation project of text collection, undertaken as part of what became known as rimé (*ris med*), meaning "nonsectarian" or "inclusive." The four lineages added in this eightfold scheme were Shangpa, Orgyenpa, Jordruk, and Zhijé. Chöd was added as a branch of Zhijé.[2]

ZHIJÉ

One of those masters who arrived during the early days of the second dissemination was the south Indian Dampa Sangyé ("Holy Buddha") (d. 1117), also known in Tibet as Pha Dampa ("Father Dampa,"), Dampa Gyagar ("Indian Dampa"), and Dampa Nakpo ("Black Dampa"). He would also sign his name as Mipam Gönpo. The Tibetans seemed to prefer these epithets to his actual name; but most Indian teachers were known by Tibetan names, perhaps for ease of pronunciation and recollection. His Indian name, Kamalaśrī or Kamalaśīla, created a good deal of confusion when his identity was conflated with that of the Indian scholar Kamalaśīla (*c.* 740–795). He was also identified with Bodhidharma (late 4th to early 5th centuries), the patriarch of Chinese Ch'an Buddhism, after his twelve-year sojourn in that country. This would give him a life span of some 570 years, which was attributed to a special practice called "taking the essence" (*bcud len*). In any case, he is said to have stayed in Tibet anywhere from three to seven times, during which he imparted a vast array of esoteric or tantric teachings, including several tantras.[3] These teachings are traditionally counted in three transmissions of early, middle, and last, with the middle transmission further divided into three successions, making five main lineages holding separate teachings, as well as minor ones. Collectively, all these varied teachings became known as *Dukngel Zhijé*, the Pacification of Suffering, a general term identified with a similar phrase in the *Heart Sutra*. Dampa himself said, "To beings tormented by suffering, explain immaculate, comforting pacification."[4] Kongtrul elaborates on its distinctive approach:

> Other teachings first refine away the cause [of suffering]—afflictive emotions—thus averting the consequence of suffering. In this system, the result—suffering—is directly refined and afflictive emotions are uprooted as a natural consequence of that. These are extraordinarily profound methods.[5]

Dampa Sangyé was also instrumental in bringing a large collection of pith instructions from the great adepts (*mahāsiddha*) of India, now contained in the Tengyur.[6] Despite this vast activity and his popularity as a brilliant master, it is difficult to find modern Zhijé practitioners as the lineage has barely survived. That it has at all was largely due to the early work of the Nyingma master Lochen Dharmasrī (1654–1718) and later Kongtrul and Khyentsé's preservation project. By contrast, the spread of its subsidiary, Chöd, and the proliferation of texts on that subject can hardly be imagined.

CHÖD

Sources of Machik's Chöd. The text usually cited as the Indian source for Chöd was imported to Tibet and translated by Dampa Sangyé himself. It is a short poem by his maternal uncle, Āryadeva the Brahmin (not to be confused with the famous Indian disciple of Nāgārjuna). Called *The Fifty Verse Poem* or, in its shorter version, *The Grand Poem*, it is found in several editions of the Tengyur and in many collections of Chöd texts.[7] Making the Indian connection was very important for the authentication of a line of Buddhist teachings in Tibet, and all the more so when those teachings are attributed to a woman. It is unclear if Machik Lapdrön ever actually saw this composition by Āryadeva the Brahmin. Nevertheless, it contains teachings reminiscent of hers, primarily on the perfection of wisdom, as it announces right at the start: "The essence of the subject matter is the meaning of nondual perfection of wisdom without root . . ." As methods of implementation, it recommends the six perfections and offers advice on dealing with devils (*māra*), gods and demons (*lha 'dre*), and their apparitions.[8] The text mentions three of the four *māra*s that later became characteristic of Chöd. Probably the earliest definition of the name may be found here as well:

> Since it severs the root of mind itself
> and severs the five toxic emotions,
> extremes of view, meditational formations,
> conduct anxiety, and hopes and fears;
> since it severs all inflation,
> it is called "severance" by semantic explanation.[9]

Semantics of the Name. In most explanations of the term *chöd* (*gcod*), its use in this context is said to derive from its homonym *chöd* (*spyod*), meaning conduct or practice, as it is used throughout the *prajñāpāramitā* literature, for example, in the line: "In this way one should train in performing the activity of the profound perfection of wisdom." The Tibetan word *chöd* means "to decide" as well as "to cut" or "to sever." The meanings converge, for instance in the common term *thag gcod pa* ("decide, resolve, put an end to, determine"). The two terms (*gcod* and *spyod*) are often used interchangeably in Chöd texts and both point to the original intent of putting one's understanding of the perfection of wisdom into practice. In Chöd visualizations, the verb *chöd* is rarely used for cutting up the body, which is *tubpa* (*stub pa*).

Relation to the Perfection of Wisdom. From the inception of the Chöd tradition in Tibet, the connections with the perfection of wisdom teachings are apparent on multiple levels, and not just because of its self-identification with that philosophy. One might say that Chöd *is* that wisdom embodied. The ancient personification of *prajñāpāramitā* as the Great Mother of all the buddhas manifests perfectly in Machik, the "One Mother," who was also an actual mother. Machik's own visionary revelations of the Great Mother only add to this relationship. The twin tenets of emptiness and compassion play out in the ritual itself as the realization that there is no "self" to be found in one's body (or anywhere else), and compassionately releasing one's body for the benefit of others. And the identification of the term "severance" with the *prajñāpāramitā* term "practice" mentioned above exactly reveals its intent—to act out (*spyod*) in a decisive way (*gcod*) one's own integration of that perfect wisdom. To study severance is to study the perfection of wisdom. There is a great deal more to be said on this subject.[10]

Transmission of Chöd to Machik Lapdrön. Machik Lapdrön's exposure to these instructions was apparently through a teaching by Dampa Sangyé called *The Six Pieces of Instruction*, identified by Kongtrul as an elucidation of Āryadeva's poem.[11] (Elsewhere, it is identified either as six parts of the perfection of wisdom or six parts of the *Magical Net*.) This happened during the middle transmission of Zhijé. Though no early text by this name is found in the Zhijé corpus, a later text similarly titled recounts that Dampa Sangyé bestowed a potent healing doctrine called Chöd to four people: Geshé Kyo Shakya Yeshé, Mara Serpochen, and two boys with leprosy.[12] Geshé Kyo secretly gave the instructions only to his nephew, known as Kyo Sönam Lama. This was Machik's principal guru and the likely source of her early encounter with some form of Chöd, though it is recorded that she was present, though tardy, at this same event with Dampa. It is said that Machik received four of these six "pieces," pertaining to the practice called Opening the Sky Door, which was sufficient for her to attain profound realization. There is no record of which four pieces she received.[13] And, importantly, no text on the subject of Chöd has come to light in the works of Dampa Sangyé or in the early Zhijé corpus.

Although Āryadeva's poem and Dampa's transmission provide the indispensable Indian connection, they fall far short of explaining the real development of the Chöd tradition. Most accounts include other inspirations, such as Machik's own understanding of the perfection of wisdom teachings and her visionary encounters with the *bodhisattva*-goddess Tārā. These very subjective sources require an overview of the life of the remarkable woman behind this successful practice tradition. There are a number of biographies and innumerable short accounts, mostly copied from each other, or else discovered as revealed treasure. One popular version is known as *Machik's Complete Explanation* (*Machik Namshé; ma gcig rnam bshad*), with two of its ten chapters recounting her life. These chapters were written by Namkhai Gyaltsen in the late

14th century. The entire compilation, however, is claimed as Machik's own words. The important events of her life reported in the various biographies are similar to those recounted here.

Machik Lapdrön. Machik was born in a sheep year, specifically the full moon day of the third month. The most reasonable guess in later Tibetan scholarship is 1031 according to the Western calendar, though many other dates have been suggested. The date 1055 has somehow gained a footing in the 21st-century publishing world. She lived for either 95 or 99 years, so it is safe to say that her life spanned the mid-11th to mid-12th centuries.[14] This was the heyday of the second dissemination, and her close contemporaries included other lineage founders such as the Kagyu master Marpa Lotsāwa (1022–1096), the Shangpa master Khyungpo Naljor (978–1079), and the Sakya patriarch Khön Könchok Gyalpo (1034–1102). But most accounts of Machik's life begin well before her birth, whenever that may have been, in her previous incarnation as the Indian yogi called, in Tibetan, Mönlam Drup (Praṇidhāna Siddhi) and later his ordination name Döndrup Zangpo (Arthasiddhi Bhadra).

The backstory of Döndrup Zangpo carries great significance for the Chöd tradition. First, it is yet another connection to the male Indian tradition. Additionally, in contrast to the many stories throughout Buddhist history in which female practitioners pray to be born as male to attain enlightenment, Döndrup Zangpo chooses to be born as female, in order to benefit beings. In this, he was following the instructions received in his visionary encounter with Tārā, the important bodhisattva who, legend has it, also made a similar wish to be born forever in female form.[15] Furthermore, his death is described in a way that foreshadows the actual Chöd practices: a wrathful black *ḍākinī* appears while he is resting in a charnel ground and becomes his guide as he intensifies his practice in Bhadra Cave. She then appears to cut out his heart with a flaying knife, while he dissolves his consciousness into her heart and is thus "carried" to Tibet. His corpse is preserved, so that later when Machik needs verification of her authenticity (as an Indian male), it is still there in the cave.

Transported in this way to Tibet, his consciousness enters the womb of Bumcham, the wife of the village head and Buddhist patron named Chökyi Dawa, in a village called Tsomer in lower Tamshö in Ei Gangwa, in the Lapchi region.[16] Many marvelous events occur during gestation and birth, as is usual in Tibetan hagiographies. The local king witnesses Machik's amazing abilities at a young age and bestows the name Light of Lap (Lapkyi Drönma or Lapdrön). At the age of sixteen she and her sister, a nun, meet Lama Drapa Ngönshechen (1012/1033–1090), a treasure revealer (*tertön*) and Lapdrön's earliest master. Her sister meditates for three years and travels to the celestial realm, leaving no remains; a feat as remarkable as Lapdrön's achievements, though seldom remembered. It is during some four years studying with Lama Drapa that Lapdrön masters both the reading and comprehension of the *prajñāpāramitā sūtra*, as well as many other teachings. This is time spent in a monastery, and probably the reason that some later accounts have her taking monastic ordination, although that has not been established. In recognition of her achievements, Lama Drapa enthrones her and presents her with resplendent robes and her iconic hat. It is also during this time that she first encounters Dampa Sangyé, who, according to the story in this biography, is there searching for Döndrup Zangpo's reincarnation. On meeting her, Dampa bestows this prophetic advice:

> Girl, expose your hidden faults. Overcome hesitation. Carry what you dare not. Cut your fetters. Give up attachments. Keep to haunted places. Know that beings are as vast as the sky. In haunted places, seek the buddha within yourself. Your doctrine will arise like the sun in the sky.[17]

After Lapdrön's training with Kyotön, and with his encouragement, she meets Sönam Lama, also of the Kyo clan, and requests empowerment (*abhiṣeka*). In the middle of the conferral she has remarkable experiences of levitating, passing through walls, encountering *nāgas*, and so forth. She returns nearly naked and tells the lama, "No neurosis, no clothes, naked I prostrate without modesty or shame, in homage to the sublime lama who truly removes all coverings." The empowerment event proves to be a pivotal moment in her spiritual career, with many visible changes in behavior and deep inner realizations occurring from this point on. She also receives many other specific teachings from other masters.

Lapdrön's skill in recitation of the *prajñāpāramitā sūtras* leads to employment as a local house chaplain, where she meets her future partner, an Indian named Töpa Bhadra. Despite seemingly auspicious circumstances of their union, Machik herself expresses doubt and even shame, until she receives assurance from her teachers. This might be a way of explaining the difficulty of her situation as a female teacher, for even if she were not a nun she would be expected to behave as one. In any case, Machik Lapdrön maintains a long relationship with this yogi from India and together they have a number of children; two boys and one girl are mentioned in this biography. Though there are conflicting accounts on which of Machik's descendants are biological and which are spiritual, many of them play crucial roles in the continuation of the lineage, and their instructive stories are often recounted in the hagiographies. For example, her second son Drupsé, later called Tönyön Samdrup (some say this is her grandson's name), had a difficult mental illness (thus the *nyön*, "crazy," in his name), which was later cured through spiritual practices by Machik and Dampa.[18] Her daughter was called Duma, but four other (spiritual?) daughters who all have "Gyen" in their names are referred to as the four Gyens and play a significant role in the narratives. What is remarkable is the image created of a woman with a full-time teaching career and at the same time dealing with various familial issues in what appears to be a very successful integration. Indeed, all the teachings on Chöd in the *Complete Explanation* are framed within a context of her children's queries during this home-schooling.

Around the age of thirty-seven Machik settles in a cave at Zangri Kangmar, "Red House of Copper Mountain," and a large community gathers around her. A crucial visionary encounter with Tārā occurs around this time (aged forty-one). She receives many teachings and empowerments and is told that she is both an emanation of Tārā herself as well as of the Great Mother (Yum Chenmo). This confirms both her female lineage and her connection with the perfection of wisdom teachings, which are personified as Prajñāpāramitā-ma, the Great Mother. Tārā explains:

> The one known as the Great Mother is emptiness, the true nature of all phenomena. She is the transcendent wisdom of nonself, the immaculate essence of the realm of emptiness, the absolute reality free of all veils and obscurations. Thus she is called the mother who gives birth to all the buddhas of the three times.[19]

So it is that in the practice of Chöd, the lineage is depicted and visualized with the Great Mother and Tārā as the sources. Not long after this visionary verification, however, Machik's credentials are again put to the text. By now her fame had spread back to India, and there were some very skeptical scholars who found it hard to believe that there was a woman of this stature. They must come to check if she is not actually a demon. In their presence and before a great crowd, she speaks in an Indian tongue that she remembers from her last life, describes the whereabouts of her previous corpse (which Dampa Sangyé quickly goes to check up on), and gives teachings that confirm the authenticity of her Buddhist connections. These teachings are contained in the text *Katsom Chenmo*, "The Great Bundle of Precepts" or "Great Collection of Buddha's Words." The Indian *paṇḍitas* are thoroughly convinced and return to India with the news. Thus begins the very distinctive reputation afforded to the Chöd of Machik, that it was the only doctrine that spread from Tibet to India in a reverse trajectory from all other lineages.

Early Development of Chöd. *The Great Bundle of Precepts* appears to be one of the earliest texts that is most likely to originate with Machik herself, though many are attributed to her. In this text, as in the poem by Āryadeva, the perfection of wisdom teachings dominate. However, there is plenty of mention, if not obsession, with the idea of *māra*, devil or negative influence, throughout the text:

> The root devilry is one's own mind.
> The devil lays hold through clinging and attachment
> in the cognition of whatever objects appear.
> Grasping mind as an object is corruption.

It is said that Machik's spiritual epiphany occurred specifically during her reading on the passages concerning *māra* in a *prajñāpāramitā sūtra*, in statements such as, "Know that clinging to anything, from form to omniscience, is the work of the devil."[20] The range of the word *māra* (Tib. *bdud*) covers everything from the buddha's original antagonist to hordes of ugly demons sweeping down the foothills of Tibet. But the particular meaning that Machik understood in the context of the perfection of wisdom was that the devil is anything that causes an interruption or "death" (the Sanskrit root of *māra* is *mṛ-*, "to die") of spiritual progress, such as the four *māras* of the sutras: that of the five aggregates, afflictive emotions, complacency, and actual death. Eventually Machik would develop another set of four devils to confront in the practice of Chöd:

(1) The tangible devil—attachment to actual things, visible phenomena.
(2) The intangible devil—attachment to thoughts and emotions, as well as invisible beings.
(3) The devil of exaltation—falling into the trap of delighting in the results of meditation practice.
(4) The devil of inflation—the belief or feeling that there exists a permanent, independent, singular *self*; a kind of ego-clinging or ego-inflation.

All of them come down to this last one—the lack of personal identity ubiquitous in all Buddhist teachings—but in Machik's nuanced treatment of it, the devil that causes inflation is intrinsic awareness itself, which of course is not to be eliminated.

The focus on these obstacles to spiritual realization also gives us the full name of the practice: Düdkyi Chöd Yul (*bdud kyi gcod yul*), "the devil/evil that is the object to sever." It is not only the personification of evil as so many demons that is to be severed, but rather any reification of objective reality (*yul*: "object") as intrinsically existing—the most salient point of all perfection of wisdom teachings, or even of all Buddhist teachings. In this quotation, "the cognition of whatever objects appear . . ." gestures to this important point. Inflation or reification of a self goes along with that self's response to objective phenomena as truly existent, creating the fundamental dualism at the root of all ignorance.

Although such ideas are presented in *The Great Bundle* and the other early works attributed to Machik, there is only one mention of casting out of the body as food:

Awareness carries the corpse of one's body;
cast it out in an unattached way
in haunted grounds and other frightful places.[21]

Based on such early statements, the elaborate visualizations of body sacrifice developed later from unknown sources, possibly absorbed from the surrounding culture of non-Buddhist practices and incorporated by Machik's immediate disciples. This is not to say that the full range of teachings were not given as oral instructions by Machik herself, only that there has not been a verifiable paper trail. The distinctive "motherly" nature of nurturing all beings, including one's worst enemies, and using one's own body to do so, would seem to suggest this actual mother as the source. Shamanic-type practices that deal with demonic possession and sickness usually aim to destroy those spirits, not help or feed them. The Chöd of Machik was eventually coopted for these purposes as well, and in that sense became more aligned with non-Buddhist practice. It would seem that this was not the original intention. She herself reportedly said so in a reference to the famous story of the bodhisattva, Buddha in a previous existence, offering his body to a hungry tigress and other examples of body offering as the supreme act of virtue (*dehadāna*).

Offering the Body to Spirits. By the time of the earliest known written commentaries—those by Jamyang Gönpo (1208–?) and the third Karmapa, Rangjung Dorjé (1284–1339)—the body offerings were in full swing and nearly eclipsed the main practice. Several characteristics developed that gave Chöd some of its most distinguishing aspects. The recommended locales in which to practice are haunted or wild places ("*nyensa*," from a species of particularly noxious spirits, *gnyan*); places that will test the practitioner's resolve. These are not new in Chöd; the *Hevajra Tantra* is often cited as a scriptural source:

Lone trees, graveyards,
abodes of the *mamo*, at night,
or in isolated outskirts,
there it is said to be excellent to meditate.[22]

Traveling to such places necessitates an unsettled lifestyle and specific equipment that give the *chödpa*—the practitioners of Chöd—their distinctive and exotic appearance. There is a special tent, called a *chokpu*, just big enough for one. Other required items are a thighbone horn, skull cup, skin seat, and an eye veil (*domra*) so that the spirits will not take fright at the sight of the human face. In *Machik's Complete Explanation*, there is a lengthy scene where Machik regales some poorly dressed yogins on what and what not to wear, the main offending item being dog skin.[23]

The musical instruments to accompany the haunting melodies of the Chöd liturgies are crucial, specifically the large two-headed drum known as the *chödam* and the tantric bell or *drilbu*, as well as the human thigh bone or *kangling* used as a horn to summon the spirits.[24] Many distinctive tunes and instrumentation developed over the centuries in Tibet, with each monastery and lineage having its own tunes. A tradition of movement and dance also developed in some lineages; one such dance system is preserved in the Zurmang Kagyu monasteries of eastern Tibet.

Gods and Demons. Perhaps another distinguishing development was the extensive categorization of spirits, collectively referred to as "gods and demons" or "god-demons" (*lha dre*). These are not new to Tibet; in fact they were already animating the Tibetan landscape long before Buddhism came along. Because the conduct of Chöd aims to challenge one's meditational experiences of tranquility and insight, the most disturbing situations are purposefully pursued. In this case, it is the unseen forces conceived of as benevolent or malicious gods and demons, the helpers and harmers of negotiated existence. The gods and demons are a separate category from the *māra*s of Buddhist scriptures and early Chöd texts. Some Chöd literature devotes much space to this demonology, describing the unseen beings in great detail—their types, colors, clothes, implements, mounts, servants, and so on. The prolific details seem to bely the final goal of recognizing their lack of true existence.

The Spread of Chöd in Tibet. A general methodology emerged that adhered to the tantric rituals and *sādhana* practices prevalent in Tibetan Buddhism, but with innumerable minor variations. The tradition is famous for the vast and unruly extent of literature that spread throughout the Himalayan region, such that tracing its development proves very challenging. This is compounded by the ubiquitous recycling of prayers and visualizations with no attribution as to source. A great complex of monasteries was never established to house the Chöd tradition, and its practices were gradually incorporated into the other sects, including the non-Buddhist Bön tradition in its modern form.[25] Though most of them trace to Machik Lapdrön's system, the Nyingma and Bön traditions developed practices based on revealed treasures that took on some distinctive forms, focusing on the wrathful black *ḍākinī* Tröma Nakmo. In the Gelukpa school, the practice was particularly upheld by the Second Dalai Lama.[26]

Chöd has been widely supported in all the Kagyu traditions, ever since it was promoted by the work of the third Karmapa hierarch, Rangjung Dorjé. He received the complete Zhijé transmission at the age of eighteen and the Chöd teachings from several sources, primarily Namtso Dopa Mikyö Dorjé, at the Karmapa seat in Tsurpu Monastery.[27] It was also apparently Rangjung Dorjé who appropriated the name of the highest Kagyu practice system, "Great Seal" (*mahāmudrā*), which had already been used since the time of Gampopa (1079–1153) for the teachings of the perfection of wisdom. Thus, it is often known as Mahāmudrā Chöd.[28]

Ritual Practice of Chöd. *Machik's Complete Explanation* provides an outline of the practice sequence that is more or less typical:

1. Arousing the resolve for enlightenment and gathering the guests.
2. Meditating on the objects of refuge, training the mind in the four immeasurables, and inviting the field of accumulation.
3. Paying homage with the eight branches and making offerings.
4. Separating body and mind, and offering the mandala.
5. Supplicating and bringing down blessings.
6. Offering the body and giving it in charity.
7. Concluding with the dedication, prayers, and dissolution.[29]

1. Many of these elements are common to all Vajrayāna (tantric) practices in Tibet that begin with the preliminaries of going for refuge, arousing the aspiration to attain enlightenment, called *bodhicitta,* and accumulation of merit. In a slight deviation from the norm, Chöd liturgies almost always begin with *bodhicitta* first. This is accompanied by inviting all the "guests," so that they can be present when the officiate leads them in going for refuge to the three jewels buddha, dharma, and sangha—and to the deities and holders of the Chöd lineage. Eight main kinds of guests are invoked: antagonizing enemies, harmful obstructers, disruptive spirit conditions, karmic bad spirits, body bad spirits, and bad spirits of the haunted places, plus one's mother and father. They are summoned by means of blowing a human thighbone horn. The spirits cannot resist the sound and gather from far and wide.

2. The practitioner imagines everyone going for refuge together. Generating the aspiration for enlightenment again is facilitated by recalling the four immeasurables: compassion, love, joy, and equanimity. Then the main visualization, called the field of accumulation, is created in more detail. This centers around the figure of Machik Lapdrön herself (or the wrathful Tröma Nakmo). She is described in glowing and otherworldly terms, as befits her now extremely elevated status: pure white, wearing minimal silks and jewels, standing in dancing posture with one leg up, and playing the bell and large drum. The Great Mother, Tārā, Dampa Sangyé, Vajrayoginī, and other deities and holy figures associated with the particular lineage surround her, as is depicted in the Tibetan art of scroll painting (*thangka*).

3. At this point the offering liturgies and supplications are chanted with the lilting tunes and musical accompaniment that has become the hallmark of this practice. The large Chöd drum and hand bell keep rhythm and evoke an altered state to enhance the visualizations.

4. Separating the mind from the body may be considered the main practice. Consciousness is visualized as a radiant drop of light and ejected out through the cranial aperture in a practice known as transference ("*powa*," *pho ba*) in other contexts, but here is called "Opening the Sky Door." This practice is aided by the powerful utterances of the Sanskrit seed syllable "*pé*" (*phaṭ*), which is also used throughout Chöd practice and is another of its notable characteristics. The consciousness, once ejected, takes the form of a *ḍākinī* who turns around to offer the now-abandoned corpse as a mandala. Mandala offering is a staple in Vajrayāna practice and is considered the greatest accumulation of merit because one can visualize and offer the entire universe and everything precious within it. A standard visualization had developed based on a symmetrical depiction of the Indian world cosmology. In this case, the parts of the body are visualized as that mandala: the four limbs are the four continents, the head is the central mountain, the eyes the sun and the moon, and so on. The standard pattern of liturgical practice in Vajrayāna is employed, but with the special emphasis on the corpse offering.

5. Supplicating and bringing down blessings is also standard practice, here supplemented by the beautiful tunes and musical instrumentation.

6. Offering the body up to the enlightened beings and then down to all others is the "post-meditation conduct" that constitutes the most involved aspect of Chöd. Far from feeding only so-called demons, there are usually four categories of special guests that are invoked to receive this offering: (1) the rare and sublime guests of honor are all manner of enlightened beings, from buddhas to deities to enlightened masters of the past; (2) the lordly guests of qualities are all the dharma protectors, both the wise and the worldly; (3) the guests of compassion are all six kinds of sentient beings: gods, demigods, humans, animals, hungry ghosts, and hell beings; (4) the malicious spirit guests are all the obstructing forces and those to whom one owes a karmic debt, such as from having eaten their flesh. The officiant imagines preparing the corpse in particular recipes according to the preferences of these four types of guests in what are called "distributions" (*'gyed*) or "feasts" (*tshogs*). For example, in a "white distribution" that is appropriate for the enlightened beings, the body is transformed into pure white elixir of awareness. In a "red distribution" it is imagined as "mountains of flesh, oceans of blood, and stacks of bones—bloody, greasy, and steaming,"[30] offered to various malicious spirits. Innumerable graphic variations have been developed by the creative masters in the lineage. This often stands in the place of the important communal feast circle (*gaṇacakra*) found in most Vajrayāna liturgies, except that here it involves one's body.

7. As with all Tibetan practice, it concludes with the dedication of the merit to all beings, directed by the subsequent aspiration prayers, and the dissolution of all visualization back into the emptiness from which it emerged.

Chöd in the Modern World. Chöd continues to be popular throughout the world, primarily as a practice more than a subject of study. In Bhutan, for instance, a movement in the early 21st century led by Garab Dorjé Rinpoché was reported to draw "hundreds of women" out to the hills for group practice.[31] In Mongolia, some women's temples feature daily day-long Chöd rituals, drawing many faithful laypeople to receive the blessings of shared merit. In Europe and the Americas, most visiting lamas have taught the practice to the students in their dharma centers, while others have performed the ritual as a healing or exorcism. Western Buddhist teachers have taken it up as well, modernizing it by applying Western psychological theory and methods. Tsultrim Allione, for instance, has developed an entire program based on Chöd at her remote center in Colorado, where it is the primary practice. She has published several books on her methods, such as *Feeding Your Demons: Ancient Wisdom for Resolving Inner Conflict*, a title that epitomizes modern Chöd. A quick search on the Internet turns up more hits than one could possibly investigate. However, investigation would be the first necessity to determine their authenticity. The continuing lure of a system based on such radical methods in modern cultures that have long been skeptical of anything unproven by science is quite interesting. Even the attempts to psychologize and demythologize have not stripped the practice of its roots in ancient Tibet.

REVIEW OF LITERATURE

The primary scholarly research on the subject of Chöd outside of the traditional Tibetan context has been textual in nature, although ethnographic, ethno-musical, and art-historical studies have played a minor role that could be expanded upon. Despite the fascination of the graphic ritual and female source of the lineage, the 21st-century scholarly literature is still relatively small. Initially it was restricted to translations of liturgies and commentaries for "in-house" use and curious descriptions, such as W. Y. Evans-Wenz's "The Path of Mystic Sacrifice: The Yoga of Subduing the Lower Self" in *Tibetan Yoga and Secret Doctrines* (1935) and Alexandra David-Neel's "Dreadful Mystic Banquet" in *Magic and Mystery in Tibet* (1967), that have tended to sensationalize and by the same token promote its popularity.[32] Brief summaries of Chöd have appeared within chapters of more general books, such as Tucci's *The Religions of Tibet* (1980), but they did not particularly further its study. The Chöd succession history translated by Roerich in *The Blue Annals* (1976) has been universally consulted due to its early appearance on the scene. On the popular front, the life of Machik Lapdrön recounted in Allione's *Women of Wisdom* (1984) generated considerable interest in the founding mother of Chöd.[33]

A turning point occurred in the scholarly study of the tradition with Janet Gyato's "The Development of the Gcod Tradition" in *Soundings in Tibetan Civilization* (1985), an excellent and still pertinent article that has hardly been surpassed. Around this time, numerous other monographs, masters theses, and PhD dissertations began to appear on campuses, at conferences, and in scholarly journals.[34] But it wasn't until Karénina Kollmar-Paulenz translated an important history into German in 1993 and Jérôme Edou published *Machig Labdrön and the Foundations of Chöd* in 1996 that book-length studies became available, combining research-based analysis with translation of Tibetan source material.[35] *Machik's Complete Explanation: Clarifying the Meaning of Chöd* was published in 2003 and expanded in 2013, offering an important biography of Machik together with extensive commentary that could be used by both practitioners and scholars.

The Tibetan 19th-century master scholar Jamgön Kongtrul Lodrö Tayé was instrumental in collecting texts of all the early Tibetan traditions. The Tsadra Foundation, a US-based nonprofit organization dedicated to the combined study and practice of Tibetan Buddhism, has paid particular attention to the translation of these collections, resulting in much more available material for study. In the translation of *The Treasury of Knowledge*, Kongtrul's comprehensive exposition of Indo-Tibetan Buddhism, his authoritative description of the Chöd practice can be found in *Book 8, Part 4: Esoteric Instructions* and a brief history of it in *Books 2, 3, and 4: Buddhism's Journey to Tibet*. This series has been followed up by the ongoing work of translating Kongtrul's *Treasury of Precious Instructions*, a collection of actual texts from the eight practice lineages. Harding's translations and introductions of volumes 13 and 14, devoted to Zhijé and Chöd, respectively, are now available. Volume 18 also contains a treatment of Chöd in *Jonang: The One Hundred and Eight Teaching Manuals*, translated by Gyurme Dorje.[36] On one hand, the translation of anthologies of repetitive ritual material and their instructions may not contribute enough in and of themselves to the field of theorizing and historical contextualization of the tradition. On the other hand, the recurring patterns that emerge from such broad collections reveal the actual enactments of a practice whose study might otherwise remain purely theoretical. It lends itself to the ethnographic studies that may follow into this living and still thriving popular tradition.

At present, in place of ethnographic studies, there have been numerous teachers from various lineages who have continued to teach students around the world and have produced publications, usually transcripts of their oral teachings. To name a few, Tenga Rinpoche's *Chö: The Garden of All Joy and Generosity of the Body* and Tsering Wangdu Rinpoché's *The Chöd Practice: Instructions, Commentaries and Texts*. Many more appear online, such as Khenchen Thrangu Rinpoché, "Chod: The Introduction and a Few Practices."[37] Innumerable liturgies have been translated as well. In addition, many of the actual rituals may be observed on YouTube videos. These works are intended primarily for use within a particular community or dharma center under the guidance of qualified lamas. They are important for the continuation of the lineage because, as with all Buddhist practice, Chöd is based on personal realization and experience arising from meditation. Their appearance on the scene has now been joined by the research coming out of academia that delves into the context and background of the practice. Together, these two streams provide ample support for everyone's interest.

PRIMARY SOURCES

The largest available collection of Tibetan source material at present is the "Dingri Volumes," a new digital collection of Zhijé and Chöd from the library of Trulshik Rinpoché, available in twelve volumes, plus one just for the titles.[38] The collection in volumes 13 and 14 of Kongtrul's *Treasury of Precious Instructions* (Shechen edition), now also published in English, is easily accessible and searchable in both Tibetan font and Wylie transliteration on the Tsadra Foundation website (https://dnz.tsadra.org). Similarly, revealed treasure texts on Chöd from Kongtrul's *Great Treasury of Rediscovered Teachings* can also be accessed on the Tsadra Foundation website (https://rtz.tsadra.org/index.php/Main_Page). There are several smaller collections available on the indispensable Buddhist Digital Research Center (BDRC), such as *Gcod tshogs kyi lag len sogs* from Limi, Nepal, and innumerable single texts that one can find by just searching under "*gcod*." The Tibetan of *Machik's Complete Explanation* and *The Religious History of Pacification and Severance* by Khamnyön Dharma Sengé (aka Jikdral Chökyi Sengé) was published as *Gcod kyi chos skor* in Delhi (Tibet House, 1974). Then there are many important sources in the collected works of various Tibetan masters, mostly available on BDRC, such as that of Karmapa Rangjung Dorjé (vol. 11), Karma Chakmé (vols. 52–53), and Minling Terchen (vols. 6 and 12). Tāranātha's Chöd compositions are in volume 20 of his collected works, and Gelukpa texts are in *The Collected Gcod Teachings of the Dge lugs pa Tradition* by Ma-ti Bhadra-Kīrti, Blo bzaṅ don-ldan, and others.[39] Volume 131 of a 2007 digital printing of Longchen Rabjam's collected works has editions (some incomplete) of important Chöd texts, although they are not actually connected with Longchenpa.[40] In short, there are almost innumerable versions and collections of older material, large sections of which reappear again and again; continuous revealed texts from treasures and visions; new compositions regularly cropping up; and even unsubstantiated rumors repeated as history. The literature itself is a challenge for any serious researcher.

FURTHER READING

Chaoul, Alejandro. *Chöd Practice in the Bön Tradition*. Ithaca, NY: Snow Lion, 2009.

Edou, Jérôme. *Machig Labdrön and the Foundations of Chöd*. Ithaca, NY: Snow Lion, 1996.

Gyatso, Janet. "The Development of the gCod Tradition." In *Soundings in Tibetan Civilization*. Edited by Barbara Aziz and Matthew Kapstein, 320–341. New Delhi: Manohar, 1985.

Harding, Sarah. *T'hröma Nagmo: A Practice Cycle for Realization of the Wrathful Black Ḍākinī, a Treasure of Dudjom Lingpa*. Junction City, CA: Padma, 1990.
Harding, Sarah. "Did Machik Lapdrön Really Teach Chöd? A Survey of the Early Sources." Tsadra Blog, Tsadra Foundation, 2013. https://www.tsadra.org/2014/04/28/did-machik-really-teach-chod/.
Harding, Sarah. *Machik's Complete Explanation: Clarifying the Meaning of Chöd*. Exp. ed. Boston and London: Snow Lion, 2013.
Jamgön Kongtrul Lodrö Tayé. *The Treasury of Knowledge: Book 8, Part 4: Esoteric Instructions*. Translated by Sarah Harding. Ithaca, NY: Snow Lion, 2007.
Jamgön Kongtrul Lodrö Tayé. *The Treasury of Precious Instructions: Essential Teachings of the Eight Practice Lineages of Tibet*. Vol. 14, *Chöd: The Sacred Teachings on Severance*. Translated by Sarah Harding. Boulder, CO: Snow Lion, 2016.
Jamgön Kongtrul Lodrö Tayé. *The Treasury of Precious Instructions: Essential Teachings of the Eight Practice Lineages of Tibet*. Vol. 13, *Zhije: The Pacification of Suffering*. Translated by Sarah Harding. Boulder, CO: Snow Lion, 2019.
Savvas, Carol Diane. *A Study of the Profound Path of Gcod: The Mahāyāna Buddhist Tradition of Tibet's Great Woman Saint Machig Labdron*. PhD diss., University of Wisconsin–Madison, 1990.
Tenga Rinpoche. *Chö: The Garden of All Joy and Generosity of the Body*. Auckland, New Zealand: Zhyisil Chokyi Ghatsal Charitable Trust, 2008.

NOTES

1. Shes rab 'od zer, *Meditation's Ambrosia of Immortality* (*sGom pa 'chi med kyi bdud rtsi*). See Marc-Henri Deroche, "Phreng po gter ston Shes rab 'od zer (1518–1584) on the Eight Lineages of Attainment," in *Contemporary Visions in Tibetan Studies: Proceedings of the First International Seminar of Young Tibetologists* ed. Brandon Dotson, Kalsang Norbu Gurung, Georios Halkias, and Tim Myatt (Chicago: Serindia Publications, 2009), 328–335.
2. See Sarah Harding, "Introduction," in *The Treasury of Knowledge, Book 8, Part 4: Esoteric Instructions* by Jamgön Kongtrul Lodrö Tayé (Ithaca, NY: Snow Lion, 2007).
3. Two *tantras* may have been composed by Dampa Sangyé. See Sarah Harding, "Pha Dampa Sangye and the Alphabet Goddess: A Preliminary Study of the Sources of the Zhije Tradition," paper presented at International Association of Tibetan Studies (IATS) meeting, Bergen, Norway, 2016, and Sarah Harding, "Introduction," in *The Treasury of Precious Instructions*. Vol. 13, *Zhijé*, by Jamgön Kongtrul Lodrö Tayé (Boulder, CO: Snow Lion, 2019).
4. Kamalasīla (Dampa Sangyé), *The Lamp of Enlightened Conduct: Bodhicaryāpradīpa: Byang chub spyod pa'i sgron ma* (Toh. 2321), f. 264a.
5. Jamgön Kongtrul Lodrö Tayé, *Treasury of Knowledge, Books Two/Three/Four: Buddhism's Journey to Tibet*, 357. Ithaca, NY: Snow Lion, 2010. Also, see George N. Roerich, trans., *The Blue Annals*, 2nd ed., Calcutta, 1949 (Delhi: Motilal Banarsidass, 1976/1988), 866.
6. See Kurtis Schaeffer, "Crystal Orbs and Arcane Treasuries: Tibetan Anthologies of Buddhist Tantric Songs from the Tradition of Pha Dam pa sangs rgyas," *Acta Orientalia* 68 (2007), 4–73. Also, for everything Zhijé, visit Dan Martin's blog.
7. *Tshigs su bcad pa lnga bcu pa* or *Tshigs bcad chen mo*. The longer title is *Esoteric Instructions on the Noble Perfection of Wisdom*. Translation in Jamgön Kongtrul Lodrö Tayé, *The Treasury of Precious Instructions*. Vol. 14, *Chöd: The Sacred Teachings on the Object of Severance*, trans. Sarah Harding (Boulder, CO: Snow Lion, 2016), 3–11.

8. Jamgön Kongtrul, *The Treasury of Precious Instructions*. Vol. 14, *Chöd*, 4.
9. Jamgön Kongtrul, *The Treasury of Precious Instructions*. Vol. 14, *Chöd*, 8.
10. See, for instance, "Prajñāpāramitā: The Great Mother," as mentioned in Sarah Harding, "Introduction," in *Machik's Complete Explanation*, trans. and ed. Sarah Harding (Boston and London: Snow Lion, 2013), 25–30.
11. Jamgön Kongtrul Lodrö Tayé, *The Catalog of The Treasury of Precious Instructions*, trans. Richard Barron (New York: Tsadra Foundation, 2013), 48.
12. *gDam ngag 'brul tsho drug* (New Delhi: Dingri Langkor Tsuglang Khang, 2013). The detailed story of this event is on pages 57 to 61. A shorter, somewhat different version is in Khamnyön Dharma Sengé, *The Religious History of Pacification and Severance* (Delhi: Tibet House, 1974), 436–439.
13. This text, called *Six Pieces*, continues to recount its history up to the time that it was received by Rok Bendhé Sherap Ö (1166–1244), which is of considerable interest for the Zhijé lineage. All other accounts of the story veer off at this point into the history of Machik Lapdrön.
14. The best discussions of Machik's dates are by Dan Martin, who does not commit to a date. See also Janet Gyatso, ed., *Women in Tibet* (New York: Columbia University Press, 2005), 52; and Khetsun Sangpo, who supports 1031, following Dudjom Rinpoche (Khetsun Sangpo, *Biographical Dictionary of Tibet and Tibetan Buddhism*, vol. 12 [in Tibetan] (Kathmandu: Nyingmapa Wishfulfilling Centre for Study and Practice, 1990), 331.).
15. See Jo Nang Tāranātha, *The Origin of Tārā Tantra*, trans. David Templeman (Dharamsala, India: Library of Tibetan Works & Archives, 1995), 2.
16. This may be present-day Tsome, administered from the capital of Tamzhol (Gyurme Dorje, *Footprint Tibet*, Bath, UK: Footprint, 3rd ed., 2004), 215–216. See an attempt to unravel the prevailing confusion regarding Lapdrön's birthplace in Jamgön Kongtrul, *The Treasury of Precious Instructions*, vol. 14, *Chöd*, 540n8.
17. Sarah Harding, *Machik's Complete Explanation: Clarifying the Meaning of Chöd*, Tsadra Foundation Series, exp. ed. (Boston: Snow Lion, 2013), 67.
18. Harding, *Machik's Complete Explanation*, 89–92.
19. Harding, *Machik's Complete Explanation*, 87.
20. Harding, *Machik's Complete Explanation*, 97.
21. Jamgön Kongtrul, *The Treasury of Precious Instructions*, vol. 14, *Chöd*, 22.
22. *Two Part Hevajra Tantra: Hevajratantrarājanāma*, Lhasa Kangyur, rgyud, f. 342b. See George W. Farrow and Indira Menon, *The Concealed Essence of the Hevajra Tantra* (Delhi: Motilal Banarsidass, 1992), Part 1, ch. 6, v. 5, p. 63.
23. See "Dress Styles of Chöd" in Harding, *Machik's Complete Explanation*, 207–212.
24. For more on the *gcod ḍamaru* and other music theory, see Rinjing Dorje and Ter Ellingson, "Explanation of the Secret gCod Ḍamaru: An Exploration of Musical Instrumental Symbolism," *Asian Music* 10, no. 2 (1979): 63–91, and other articles by Ellingson. Also Jeffrey W. Cupchik, "The Tibetan gCod Ḍamaru—A Reprise: Symbolism, Function, and Difference in a Tibetan Adept's Interpretive Community," *Journal of the Society for Asian Music* (January 2013), and other papers by Cupchik, including *The Sound of Vultures' Wings: The Tibetan Buddhist Chod Ritual Practice of the Female Buddha Machik Labdron*, SUNY Series in Religious Studies (Albany: SUNY Press, 2017).
25. See Alejandro Chaoul, *Chöd Practice in the Bön Tradition* (Ithaca, NY: Snow Lion, 2009).
26. See E. de Rossi-Filibeck, "The Transmission Lineage of the Gcod Teaching according to the 2nd Dalai Lama," in *Contributions on Tibetan and Buddhist Religion and Philosophy*, ed. E. Steinkellner and H. Tauscher (Vienna: University of Vienna Press, 1983).
27. *Collected Histories of the Glorious Zurmang Kagyu* (rdo dgon gna' deb srung skyob tshogs pa, n.d. BDRC W4CZ), 376.

28. See Michelle J. Sorensen, "Mahāmudrā Chöd? Rangjung Dorje's Commentary on the Great Speech Chapter of Machik Labdrön," in *Wading into the Stream of Wisdom: Essays in Honor of Leslie Kawamura*, ed. Sarah F. Haynes and Michelle J. Sorensen (Berkeley, CA: Institute of Buddhist Studies and BDK America, 2013), 129–160.
29. Harding, *Machik's Complete Explanation*, 140–212.
30. Jamgön Kongtrul Lodrö Tayé, "Beloved Garden," in Jamgön Kongtrul, *The Treasury of Precious Instructions*, vol. 14, *Chöd*, 492.
31. Oral communication to the author in Bhutan. The text used by this group is "Comprehensive Throema Tshok Recitation" (Trashigang, Bhutan: Kahling Karma, Ugyen Kha Choet Ling, Khaling, 2007).
32. *Tibetan Yoga and Secret Doctrines* includes an early translation by Lama Kazi Dawa-Samdup of the Jigmé Lingpa treasure text called "The Ḍākinīs' Laughter" (London: Oxford University Press, 1935). *Magic and Mystery in Tibet* was originally published in French as *Mystiques et magiciens du Tibet* (Paris: Plon, 1929).
33. Tsultrim Allione, *Women of Wisdom* (Ithaca, NY: Snow Lion, 2000).
34. Some examples: Michael Andrew Azzato, *Mother of Tibetan Buddhism: An Introduction to the Life and Teaching of Ma-cig Lab-kyi Sgron-ma*. MA thesis, University of Saskatchewan, 1981; Rossi-Filibeck, "The Transmission Lineage"; Giacomella Orofino, *Contributo allo studio dell' insegnamento di Ma gcig Lab sgron*, vol. 47, Supplemento n. 53 agli Annali (Naples, Italy: Istituto Universitario Orientale, 1987); David Stott, "Offering the Body: The Practice of Gcod in Tibetan Buddhism," *Religion* 19 (1989): 221–226; Carol D. Savvas, *A Study of the Profound Path of Gcod: The Mahāyāna Buddhist Meditation Tradition of Tibet's Great Woman Saint Machig Labdron*, PhD diss., University of Wisconsin–Madison, 1990; Michael R. Sheehy, "Severing the Source of Fear: Contemplative Dynamics of the Tibetan Buddhist gCod Tradition," *Contemporary Buddhism: An Interdisciplinary Journal* 6, no. 1 (2005): 37–52; and Michelle J. Sorensen, *Making the Old New Again and Again: Legitimation and Innovation in the Tibetan Buddhist Chöd Tradition*, PhD diss., Columbia University, 2013.
35. Karénina Kollmar-Paulenz, *"Der Scmuck der Befreiung": Die Geschichte der Zhi byed und gCod-Schule des tibetischen Buddhismus* ("The Ornament of Liberation: the history of the Zhi byed and gCod schools of Tibetan Buddhism") (Wiesbaden, Germany: Harrowitz Verlag, 1993). Includes translation of Khamnyön Dharma Sengé, *The Religious History*.
36. Jamgön Kongtrul Lodrö Tayé, *The Treasury of Precious Instructions*, vol. 18, *Jonang*, trans. Gyurme Dorje (Boulder, CO: Snow Lion, 2020).
37. "Most Venerable Khenchen Thrangu Rinpoche Chod: The Introduction and a Few Practices."
38. Published in 2013 by Dingri Langkor Tsuglang Khang, New Delhi. Sponsored by the Tsadra Foundation.
39. Dzamthang edition; published in 1986 by Library of Tibetan Works and Archives, Dharamsala, India.
40. The Collected Works of Omniscient Longchen Rabjam [*Kun mkhyen klong chen rab 'byams kyi gsung 'bum*]. Volume 26 (Beijing: Krung go'i bod rig pa dpe skrun khang, 2007).

Sarah Harding

D

D. T. SUZUKI: A BIOGRAPHY

SUZUKI'S CHILDHOOD AND YOUTH

Suzuki Daisetsu [Daisetz] Teitarō 鈴木大拙貞太郎 (1870–1966), more commonly known as D. T. Suzuki, was born as the youngest of five children into an educated family in the regional city of Kanazawa 金沢 in Japan. His father had been a member of the samurai class before the Meiji 明治 Restoration of 1868, serving as a physician to the ruling samurai house of the Kaga 加賀 domain. The Suzuki family was nominally affiliated with a local Rinzai Zen 臨済禅 temple, but his father was attracted more to the Chinese classics, Confucian thought, and Western learning than to Buddhism. When Suzuki was only six years old, his father passed away, and a year later one of his brothers died. From that time he and his mother lived in financial straits. Soon afterward his mother joined a small, insular group of Pure Land Buddhists that espoused "secret teachings" (*hiji bōmon* 秘事法門), which was not officially recognized by the Jōdo Shinshū 浄土真宗, or Shin Buddhist, ecclesiastical authorities. Suzuki too was initiated into this group when he was seven or eight years old. His earliest personal experience of Buddhism was thus with Pure Land rather than Zen.[1]

Though lacking financial resources, Suzuki was bright and industrious and excelled at school. He was accepted into the elite middle- and upper-level schools in Kanazawa and exposed to

Japan's new style of education based on Western models, emphasizing math, science, foreign languages, and Western approaches to history, literature, philosophy, and society. There, he was a classmate of Nishida Kitarō 西田幾多郎 (1870–1945), the future philosopher, who would become a lifelong friend. Suzuki distinguished himself in English in a way that few other Japanese of his generation did. Notwithstanding his success in school, in 1888 he was forced for financial reasons to withdraw before graduating and to take a job as an English teaching assistant at an elementary school on the remote Noto 能登 peninsula and, later, in the town of Mikawa 美川 near Kanazawa. In 1890, however, Suzuki's mother died, which was a great blow to him. But in the wake of this tragedy, he turned his attention once more to pursuing higher education, this time far from his hometown.[2]

UNIVERSITY STUDY AND ZEN TRAINING

With modest support from his second brother, Suzuki enrolled first at Waseda University in Tokyo in 1891 and then transferred the following year to Tokyo Imperial University as a special student. There he was exposed to a broad range of Western subjects. During this period he also took up Zen meditation, inspired by his math teacher in Kanazawa who had practiced meditation at the Engakuji 円覚寺 Monastery in Kamakura 鎌倉. Suzuki first visited the monastery two months after arriving in Tokyo, and in 1892, when Shaku Sōen 釈宗演 (1860–1919) was installed as the new abbot, Suzuki came under his instruction. Over the next three years, he spent so much time there that he withdrew from university altogether in 1895. Sōen, though a fully certified Rinzai Zen master, was an internationally minded Buddhist cleric who had lived in Sri Lanka as a Theravada monk from 1887 to 1889 and who attended the World's Parliament of Religions in Chicago in 1893. Suzuki, as a lay Zen disciple, became Sōen's close and devoted protégé, both in religious training and in the development of a new, Pan-Asian understanding of Buddhism that would have credibility not only in modern Japan but also in the West. Suzuki was well suited to this enterprise because his English was excellent (better than Sōen's, who asked him to translate his address for the Parliament of Religions) and because Suzuki was well read in Western philosophy, transcendentalist literature, psychology, and religious theory.[3]

At the Engakuji, Suzuki divided his time between Zen monastic training (including meditation and koan—specifically, the Nothingness, or *Mu* 無, koan, which Sōen assigned to him) and scholarly activities to promote Buddhism, making reference to Western concepts where apt. He also served as the English correspondent in Sōen's behalf with Paul Carus (1852–1919), who had befriended Sōen in the United States at the Parliament. Carus was the edited in chief at Open Court Publishing in LaSalle, Illinois, and an important scholar of religion with a particular interest in Buddhism. Suzuki was recruited to produce a Japanese translation of Carus's popular work, *The Gospel of Buddha* (*Budda no fukuin* 仏陀の福音), which appeared in 1895.[4] The following year Suzuki published his own extensive theoretical work on religion, *Shin Shūkyō ron* 新宗教論 (A New Interpretation of Religion), influenced in part by Carus's ideas.[5] These activities demonstrate the international scope of Suzuki's thinking at this early stage in his life, even as he undertook fairly traditional Rinzai Zen training at the Engakuji.

Through Sōen's connection to Carus, Suzuki was offered the opportunity to travel to the United States and assist him with an English translation project. But before departing, Suzuki redoubled his efforts in monastic practice in the hope of experiencing his first Zen awakening or *satori* 悟り. After months of effort, during Engakuji's intensive meditation retreat of December 1896, and only two months before he sailed for the United States, Suzuki finally had that *satori*. His account of it several years later did not focus on his engagement with the koan but rather described a feeling of being inseparable from the trees all around him as he walked from the meditation hall back to his quarters in the moonlight. That experience made a lasting impression on Suzuki and became a personal reference point for him throughout his life.[6]

LIFE IN THE UNITED STATES

When Suzuki departed Japan in 1897, little did he know he would spend twelve years abroad, eleven in the United States and one in Europe. Ostensibly, the reason for this trip was to assist Carus in a translation of the Daoist classic, *Daodejing* 道德経 (published as *The Canon of Reason and Virtue* in 1898). But once in the United States, Suzuki looked for other ways to extend his stay. As it turned out, few opportunities presented themselves, but assignments at Open Court Publishing, one after another, came his way so that he was able to piece together a living by translating, proofreading, editing, writing, answering correspondence, and doing many other tasks, both important and menial. Open Court produced a wide variety of publications that focused on philosophy and religion. The entire operation was financed by Paul Carus's father-in-law, Edward Hegeler (1835–1910), a wealthy industrialist who had an interest in monistic philosophy. In addition to books and translations of foreign texts, it published two well-respected journals: *The Open Court,* which featured high-quality and popularly accessible articles written by experts, and *The Monist,* which contained more specialized philosophical studies. Working at Open Court was a great boon to Suzuki, for it exposed him to the latest scholarship in the West on philosophy and religion.[7] Perhaps the most influential work that he encountered at this stage of his life was *The Varieties of Religious Experience* by the well-known psychologist and philosopher William James (1842–1910). It inspired Suzuki to explain Buddhism and especially Zen in terms of religious experience in all his subsequent writings.[8] This on-the-job education at Open Court endowed Suzuki with a vocabulary and a conceptual framework that became invaluable to him in interpreting Buddhism to the West.

During his long residency in the United States, Suzuki began to publish articles, translations, and books in English as he came to understand what topics Westerners were interested in and how they comprehended Asian religions. Some of his works were on Chinese philosophy, written mostly in response to the demands of the intellectual marketplace. But Suzuki's primary concern was to present the Mahayana Buddhism of East Asia in the best possible light.[9] There was a widespread assumption among Western readers that Theravada was the original and authentic Buddhism of Asia and that Mahayana was a later and inferior form. Suzuki strove to reverse this impression and to portray the Buddhism of Japan and China as a more advanced understanding of the religion. His translation of *Aśvaghoṣa's Discourse on the Awakening of Faith in the Mahayana* (1900) and his book *Outlines of Mahayana Buddhism* (1907) were both produced with this goal in mind.[10] It is noteworthy that during his long stay in the United States, Suzuki published very few works in English about Zen. It became the focus of his writings mostly in the middle of his career and the post–World War II years. At this early stage, the defense of Mahayana in East Asia was Suzuki's primary objective.

Though based somewhat remotely in LaSalle, Illinois, Suzuki developed contacts with a wide variety of people in the United States who influenced his thinking. For instance, he became acquainted with Albert J. Edmunds (1857–1941), the cataloger of the Historical Society of Pennsylvania, who was a strong promoter of Swedenborgianism, the 19th-century theological and mystical movement inspired by Emanuel Swedenborg (1688–1772). Suzuki was attracted to this nonmainstream spiritual movement because of its universalism and its acknowledgment of the truth of various religions, and he subsequently published translations of Swedenborg's major works in Japan.[11] Suzuki also spent ten months between 1905 and 1906 as the personal interpreter and guide of Shaku Sōen, his Zen master, who was invited to give lectures and talks in the United States. This tour not only deepened Suzuki's relationship with Sōen but also exposed him to influential groups and spiritually curious Westerners who were open to Buddhism. Among them was Beatrice Erskine Lane (1875–1939), a brilliant and highly educated individual who would later become Suzuki's wife. She attended a lecture by Sōen in New York in April 1906 and afterward developed an enthusiastic correspondence with Suzuki while he was editing Sōen's talks, published in 1906 as *Sermons of a Buddhist Abbot*. In the following year Suzuki visited her and her mother for several weeks in Connecticut, about the time he gave talks on Buddhism at the annual Greenacre summer religious retreat in Eliot, Maine. After Suzuki finally departed the United States in February 1908, he spent a year in Europe, mostly in London, sponsored by the Swedenborg Society, translating Swedenborg's *Heaven and Hell* into Japanese.[12]

NEW CAREER IN TOKYO

When Suzuki arrived back in Japan in April 1909, he did not have any means of support, and he was not well positioned to seek a teaching job, since he lacked the credential of a university degree. But he did have twelve years of experience living abroad and a strong command of English. Moreover, he had published high-level scholarship in both Japanese and English. With the recommendation of a former Kanazawa classmate who taught Japanese literature at Tokyo Imperial University, Suzuki managed to get a position as an English professor in the preparatory division of Gakushūin 学習院, the Peers School, in Tokyo.[13] At this early point in his career, he was recognized more for his English expertise than for his knowledge of Buddhism. Gakushūin became a good setting for Suzuki to embed himself in Japan's academic network, providing him with financial security in Japan even as he remained engaged with scholarship in the United States and Europe.

During his twelve years in Tokyo, Suzuki developed as a scholar in a variety of ways. First, he continued his writing and research on Emanuel Swedenborg, publishing four book-length Japanese translations of his works, producing an intellectual biography of him, and presenting a paper, "Swedenborg in Japan," at the annual Swedenborg conference in London in 1912.[14] His marriage to Beatrice Lane, who joined him in Japan in 1911, reinforced his interest in popular religious movements in the West, though she was attracted more to Theosophy, Hinduism, New Thought, Bahá'í, and Buddhism than to Swedenborgianism. Second, Suzuki became interested in Pure Land Buddhist thought after meeting Sasaki Gesshō 佐々木月樵 (1875–1926), a professor at Shinshū 真宗 University in Tokyo (which was later renamed Ōtani 大谷 University after its move to Kyoto). Though earlier Suzuki was somewhat disdainful of Pure

Land, through Sasaki he was exposed to modern interpretations that appealed to him, as he assisted Sasaki with English translations of two Pure Land works in 1910. These activities foreshadowed Suzuki's new interpretations of Pure Land in later decades.[15] Third, Suzuki reimmersed himself in Zen from the time he arrived back in Japan until the death of his master, Shaku Sōen, in 1919. Tokyo, where Suzuki worked, was only a short train ride away from Kamakura, so he would retreat there on weekends and school breaks and stay at the Shōden'an 正伝庵 cottage in the Engakuji monastic complex. He not only practiced meditation and koan training but also resumed his study of Zen's vast textual corpus, all under Sōen's direction. Together they launched a monthly journal entitled *Zendō* 禅道, or "Zen Way," in 1910, aimed at a general readership in which Suzuki published about sixty short articles over the next decade.[16] This period of intense study and training, more than his earlier practice at Engakuji, equipped Suzuki to become a world-class authority on Zen.

PROFESSORSHIP AT ŌTANI UNIVERSITY

In 1921 Suzuki resigned his position at Gakushūin to accept an appointment at Ōtani University in Kyoto as professor of English and Buddhist studies. This was the first position Suzuki held in Buddhist studies per se, even though he was already fifty years old. Sasaki Gesshō, who would become Ōtani's president in 1924, was the motivating force behind this appointment, and Suzuki's close friend Nishida Kitarō, who by then was a professor of philosophy at Kyoto Imperial University, also encouraged him to accept it. At Ōtani, Suzuki's prolific scholarly activities over the next two decades earned him a national and international reputation. One important venue in which he published many of his famous essays was the English journal *The Eastern Buddhist*, which Suzuki established at Ōtani in 1921 with the financial support of the Higashi Honganji 東本願寺 denomination of Shin Buddhism.[17] His publications in this period ranged across many topics in Mahayana, Zen, and Pure Land, delineating themes that he would continue to elucidate in later years. Some of his most famous books in English were written at this time.

One person who contributed to Suzuki's success was his wife, Beatrice Lane Suzuki. She had academic degrees from top institutions in the United States—Radcliffe College (the women's school affiliated with Harvard) and Columbia University. She was widely read and proficient in classical and modern European languages and had worked as a journalist, writer, and teacher. Hence, when Suzuki was appointed at Ōtani, she was simultaneously offered a position as an instructor of English in its preparatory division. Beatrice was also named coeditor of *The Eastern Buddhist* where her erudition and writing skills no doubt enhanced the quality of the journal. Most of Suzuki's English publications were reviewed, polished, and edited by her, up to the time of her death in 1939. She produced her own publications as well: articles, essays, and a few books on Japanese literature, culture, and Buddhism aimed mostly at general readers.[18] She was also a great proponent of animal welfare and became a relentless rescuer of stray cats and dogs in Japan, a commitment that spread to Suzuki resulting in their establishment of a Buddhist animal shelter.[19] Also, in 1916, early in their marriage, they adopted a baby, Alan Masaru Suzuki (1916–1971), in whom they had high hopes. But he became a problem child in his teenage years and ultimately gravitated toward Japan's glittering entertainment and music industry and away from their world of scholarship.[20] Nonetheless, together

Suzuki and Beatrice formed a powerful and productive partnership that successfully spread Buddhism to the English-reading public.

Another long-term contributor to Suzuki's success was his friend and fellow Kanazawa native Ataka Yakichi 安宅弥吉 (1873–1949), a wealthy entrepreneur in the import–export business. They originally met in Tokyo when both were lowly students, but once Ataka became rich he emerged as Suzuki's most generous, long-term patron. He provided subventions for Suzuki's English publications, produced in London and distributed worldwide. He also built a grand residence for Suzuki and his family near Ōtani University. And he was the primary donor for the construction of Suzuki's research library, Matsugaoka Bunko 松ヶ岡文庫, in Kamakura in the 1940s. Without Ataka's aid, it is doubtful that Suzuki could have attained such renown or undertaken as many projects as he did.[21]

During his two decades of active teaching at Ōtani, Suzuki published widely in both Japanese and English, mainly in three areas: Mahayana, Zen, and Pure Land. His best-known publications on Mahayana were his study, translation, and index of the *Lankavatara Sutra* (1930–1934), for which Suzuki was granted the doctor of letters degree in 1934, the first advanced degree that he ever received. On Zen, he published his three-volume classic, *Essays in Zen Buddhism* (1927–1934), followed by perhaps his most famous book, *Introduction to Zen Buddhism* (1934), all of which elevated Zen in the minds of Western readers. On Pure Land, he wrote a variety of innovative articles that appeared in *The Eastern Buddhist*, the longest of which was his monograph-length work, "The Shin Sect of Buddhism" (1939). Ōtani was a Shin Buddhist university with many progressive scholars. Suzuki sympathized with their this-worldly interpretation of Pure Land Buddhism, which from this time became a recurring topic of Suzuki's research and writing. Based on all these activities Suzuki gained recognition both in Japan and abroad, especially after his participation in the World Congress of Faiths in London in 1936.[22]

WARTIME AND POSTWAR YEARS IN JAPAN

After Suzuki's wife Beatrice died in 1939, he largely curtailed his teaching at Ōtani and began living in semiretirement at Engakuji's Shōden'an cottage in Kamakura. Publication of *The Eastern Buddhist* was suspended (perhaps indicating Beatrice's crucial editorial role) and did not resume fully until 1965. While living in Kamakura, Suzuki remained a productive scholar over the next decade even though he was in his seventies. During the war years, almost all of his publications were written in Japanese, since he was largely cut off from his English readership. But he explored new topics, including the idea of "unborn Zen" (*fushō Zen* 不生禅) of the little-known master Bankei 盤珪 (1622–1693) and the Pure Land teachings of Shinran 親鸞 (1173–1262), the founder of Shin Buddhism, in his *Tannishō* 歎異抄 collection of aphorisms and his magnum opus *Kyōgyōshinshō* 教行信証. Suzuki also published *Nihon teki reisei* 日本的霊性 (Japanese Spirituality) in 1944, a major work in which he extolled Japan's religious consciousness, particularly that of Zen and Shin Buddhism.[23] Such cultural aggrandizement of Japan seemed compatible with wartime nationalism though Suzuki considered others responsible for the war.[24] Nonetheless, his views on Japanese imperialism during this period became a point of controversy in later decades, pitting critics and defenders of Suzuki against each other.[25]

After World War II ended, when Suzuki was seventy-five years old, he emerged during the American occupation of Japan with a higher public profile than before, perhaps because of his newly voiced criticisms of Japan's war effort and his long-standing ties to the West. He was frequently treated as a spokesman for a new Japan, and in several publications he recast his idea of "Japanese Spirituality" into a symbol of this new consciousness. Suzuki also became aware of the burgeoning interest in Zen among Americans and Europeans who were posted to Japan during the occupation—some of whom visited him frequently in Kamakura for Buddhist guidance—and he produced a new introductory text for their benefit, *Living by Zen* (1949). In addition, Suzuki's ideas gained renewed attention overseas after Christmas Humphreys (1901–1983), a well-known British barrister and Buddhist convert who headed the Buddhist Society of London, received permission to republish Suzuki's earlier books on Zen. Under these circumstances he began to look for opportunities to go abroad.[26]

RISE TO FAME IN THE UNITED STATES

In June 1949, Suzuki traveled to Honolulu to attend the Second East–West Philosophers' Conference and to teach a one-semester course at the University of Hawai'i. This was the beginning of a series of appointments that resulted in his living in the United States until 1958. Most of the time he was affiliated with universities: Hawai'i, Claremont Graduate School in Southern California, and, most prominently, Columbia University in New York. The 1950s were precisely the period when interest in Buddhism, and especially Zen, skyrocketed in the United States and Europe. Suzuki was the right person to respond to this demand. He gave public lectures widely, offered university courses, and produced new publications, many aimed at general readers. In this context Suzuki quickly rose to fame as a public intellectual and popularizer of Buddhism. He was invited to the Eranos Conferences of 1953 and 1954, an annual summer gathering of world-class thinkers in Ascona, Switzerland, and he was a featured speaker at the Brussels World's Fair in Belgium in May 1958. Suzuki also became well known beyond elite circles, as he appeared in popular magazines—*The New Yorker, Vogue, Time, Mademoiselle,* and *Harper's Weekly*—and even in an NBC television series. All of these helped make him a celebrity intellectual. He was seen as the preeminent transmitter of Zen to the West and an expert on Buddhism.[27]

The major works that Suzuki wrote while in the United States were *Mysticism: Christian and Buddhist* (1957), *Zen and Japanese Culture* (1959, a revised and expanded version of his 1938 book on this topic), and *Zen Buddhism and Psychoanalysis* (1960, coauthored with Erich Fromm and Richard DeMartino). All were written in response to requests from various publishers, scholars, and foundations in the West. Apart from them, Suzuki's greatest hope and goal was to produce authoritative works on Zen philosophy and English translations of Chinese classics in order to place Zen on solid footing in the English-reading world. To support him in this effort, the multimillionaire Cornelius Crane (1905–1962), who was fascinated by Zen and became Suzuki's new patron, provided funds for the creation of the so-called Zen Studies Society, which guaranteed Suzuki a handsome salary for five years, thereby allowing him to step down from his Columbia University faculty position in 1957. Despite this support it was difficult for Suzuki to bring his proposed Zen publications to completion because of the incessant requests for public talks and popular writings and because of his advanced age.

By this time Suzuki was well into his eighties and was receiving the help of a young Japanese American woman, Mihoko Okamura (b. 1935), as his personal assistant. It was in these circumstances, amid Suzuki's meteoric rise to fame and his many projects on Zen, that he decided to return to Japan.[28]

OLD AGE IN JAPAN

When Suzuki arrived back in Japan in November 1958, accompanied by Okamura, he was eighty-eight years old. With renown in the United States came renown in Japan. He was showered with attention surpassing anything he had experienced previously and was inundated with requests for writings, interviews, and public appearances. Instead of returning to the Shōden'an cottage at the Engakuji, Suzuki took up residence at his Matsugaoka Bunko research library across the road from the monastery after the living facilities had been expanded. There he was cared for by Okamura and by his grandniece, Hayashida Kumino 林田久美野 (1918–2011), and her family, who were all in residence. The research library was in an inconvenient location for a person his age: at the top of a hill with a long stone stairway, without access by car. Nonetheless, with research materials, work space, living quarters, and caretakers all close at hand, he had everything he needed to proceed with his projects. Whenever he had invitations for appearances or other commitments in nearby Tokyo or in other parts of Japan, he would often group them together, traveling with the assistance of Okamura and staying in hotels along the way. Otherwise, scholars, journalists, and all manner of visitors would come to him, climbing the hill at Matsugaoka to meet him.[29]

During his years back in Japan, Suzuki organized various projects to continue his work on translations and foundational studies of Zen, just as he had planned in the United States. He recruited younger Japanese scholars, such as Furuta Shōkin 古田紹欽 (1911–2001) and Akizuki Ryōmin 秋月龍珉 (1921–1999), to collaborate with him on textual studies, and he enlisted younger English-speaking scholars, such as Richard DeMartino (1922–2013), to assist with translations. Despite his plans, his work was constantly interrupted by requests. The most noteworthy one was to translate the Pure Land classic *Kyōgyōshinshō* by Shinran, at the behest of the Higashi Honganji. Suzuki dedicated many months to it between 1959 and 1961 and continued to polish it until the time of his death. The translation was eventually published posthumously, in 1973.[30] Another project that Suzuki spent considerable time on was an illustrated and annotated edition of the simple, playful ink drawings by the Zen priest Sengai 仙厓 (1750–1837), at the behest of Idemitsu Sazō 出光佐三 (1885–1981). Idemitsu, who was a wealthy businessman in the petroleum industry, became a new benefactor of Suzuki after he returned to Japan and would regularly offer him his mountain villa at Karuizawa 軽井沢 in the summer to escape the city heat. He owned an extensive collection of Sengai's original drawings, which Suzuki admired, and urged Suzuki to write a book providing insights into the pictures—which was also published posthumously, in 1971.[31] These projects, while worthwhile, disrupted Suzuki's primary agenda to produce major, authoritative works on Zen. In the end he was able to publish only a few of the ones that he had planned.

In Suzuki's twilight years, he managed to make three more trips overseas. The first one was to Honolulu for two months in the summer of 1959, to attend the Third East–West Philosophers' Conference at the University Hawai'i. He was recognized as a leading figure at these conferences and was awarded an honorary doctorate degree by the university. The second trip was to India for four weeks in December 1960 and January 1961. There, Suzuki was received as a state guest by Vice President Sarvepalli Radhakrishnan (1888–1975), who had previously served as professor of Eastern religion and ethics at Oxford University. As part of the trip he visited important Buddhist pilgrimage sites in India, fulfilling a lifelong dream. The third trip was in the summer of 1964, first to New York, where Suzuki renewed acquaintances and had a now-famous meeting and intellectual exchange with the well-known Catholic monk and theologian Thomas Merton (1915–1968), and then to Honolulu for three weeks to join the Fourth East-West Philosophers' Conference (though his failing hearing limited his participation). This was his last trip abroad, at the age of ninety-three.[32]

In the last year of Suzuki's long life, he continued to work on projects—the *Kyōgyōshinshō* translation, the book on Sengai, and various Zen texts—and to give talks and interviews on occasion. He was surprisingly energetic for a nonagenarian, and his known health problems—high blood pressure, vitamin deficiency, and worsening eyesight and hearing—seemed to be managed adequately. But in July 1966, on the morning when he was scheduled to leave for his annual summer retreat at the mountain villa of Idemitsu Sazō, Suzuki fell acutely ill. Doctors were called in and, after examining him, decided to transfer Suzuki by ambulance to St. Luke's Hospital in Tokyo. After an arduous journey from Kamakura, he arrived about 5:00 p.m. and was immediately admitted to the hospital. His doctors surmised that Suzuki was suffering from an intestinal stricture or obstruction of some type, but they were hesitant to perform surgery in his state. Throughout the night, Mihoko Okamura and Hayashida Kumino attended to him. At the same time, a large number of friends, colleagues, acquaintances, protégés, and relatives gathered at the hospital in a vigil of sorts, as word of his grave condition spread. Finally, the next morning between 5:00 and 5:30 a.m., July 12, Suzuki quietly passed away. He was ninety-five years old. After his death a grand funeral was held at the Tōkeiji 東慶寺 Zen temple adjacent to Matsugaoka, and the next week a huge memorial service was organized by the Higashi Honganji and Ōtani University at the Asakusa Honganji 浅草本願寺 temple in Tokyo. Suzuki's ashes were divided into three parts and interred alongside Beatrice's at the Tōkeiji cemetery, at the Suzuki family gravesite in Kanazawa, and at the Okunoin 奥之院 cemetery on Mount Kōya 高野.[33] In death, Suzuki was celebrated as one of Japan's greatest Buddhist thinkers, and an aura of adulation settled around him. Though some scholars in later decades have raised questions about his portrayal of Buddhism, Suzuki still ranks as a seminal figure in the emergence of Buddhism worldwide during the 20th century.

REVIEW OF LITERATURE

There is no comprehensive biography of Suzuki in English. Moreover, the vast majority of important sources are written in Japanese. These include Suzuki's own writings, the most extensive collection of which is his so-called "Complete Works," *Suzuki Daisetsu zenshū*, comprising forty volumes. Four of these volumes contain letters by Suzuki written in both Japanese and English, providing insight into his activities, acquaintances, and influences. But the "Complete Works" does not include any of his major English writings. Those are published elsewhere in a wide variety of formats, outlets, and venues, some of which are out of print. One convenient English collection is the four-volume *Selected Works of D. T. Suzuki*, edited by Richard M. Jaffe.

Concerning Suzuki's daily life and activities, the tersely written but richest source of information, in addition to his letters, is "D. T. Suzuki's English Diaries," covering the period from 1920 to 1962 (with a few years missing).

The great majority of the secondary literature on Suzuki is likewise written in Japanese. An invaluable resource is Kirita Kiyohide, *Suzuki Daisetsu kenkyū kiso shiryō*, which contains a comprehensive chronology of Suzuki's life and a near-exhaustive list of his publications. More than one hundred brief remembrances and tributes to Suzuki—written by colleagues, former students, friends, relatives, and acquaintances—are assembled in *Suzuki Daisetsu: Hito to shisō*, by Hisamatsu Shin'ichi, all in Japanese. Two parallel collections of tributes in English are found in Nishitani Keiji and Hiroshi Sakamoto, *Special Issue: In Memoriam—Daisetz Teitaro Suzuki, 1870–1966*; and Masao Abe, *A Zen Life: D. T. Suzuki Remembered*. The most noteworthy accounts of Suzuki's life, all in Japanese, are the works by Nishimura, Okamura and Ueda, Hayashida, and Akizuki. In English, Winthrop Sargeant's "Great Simplicity" offers a popular profile of Suzuki during the Zen boom of the 1950s. Michael Goldberg's documentary video, *A Zen Life: D. T. Suzuki*, presents him sympathetically and appreciatively through interviews with people who knew him.

PRIMARY SOURCES

Suzuki, Daisetz (Daisetsu) Teitarō 鈴木大拙貞太郎. *Essays in Zen Buddhism: First, Second, and Third Series*. London: Rider, 1949–1953.

Suzuki, Daisetsu (Daisetz) Teitarō. *Suzuki Daisetsu zenshū* 鈴木大拙全集. 40 vols. Edited by Hisamatsu Shin'ichi 久松真一, Yamaguchi Susumu 山口益, and Furuta Shōkin 古田紹欽. Tokyo: Iwanami Shoten, 1999–2003.

Suzuki, Daisetsu (Daisetz) Teitarō. "D. T. Suzuki's English Diaries." In *Matsugaoka Bunko kenkyū nenpō*. Edited by Kirita Kiyohide, 19–29. Archived at Stanford University's library, 2005–2015.

Suzuki, Daisetz (Daisetsu) Teitarō. *Selected Works of D. T. Suzuki*. 4 vols. Edited by Richard M. Jaffe. Oakland: University of California Press, 2014–2021.

RESEARCH RESOURCES

Abe, Masao, ed. *A Zen Life: D. T. Suzuki Remembered*. New York and Tokyo: Weatherhill, 1986.

Hisamatsu Shin'ichi 久松真一, Yamaguchi Susumu 山口益, and Furuta Shōkin 古田紹欽, eds. *Suzuki Daisetsu: Hito to shisō* 鈴木大拙: 人と思想. Tokyo: Iwanami Shoten, 1971.

Kirita Kiyohide 桐田清秀, comp. *Suzuki Daisetsu kenkyū kiso shiryō* 鈴木大拙研究基礎資料. Kamakura: Matsugaoka Bunko, 2005.

Nishitani, Keiji, and Hiroshi Sakamoto, eds. *Special Issue: In Memoriam—Daisetz Teitaro Suzuki, 1870–1966*. *Eastern Buddhist* (New Series) 2, no. 1 (1967).

SECONDARY SOURCES

Akizuki Ryōmin 秋月龍珉. *Suzuki Daisetsu* 鈴木大拙. Tokyo: Kōdansha, 2004.

Hayashida Kumino 林田久美野. *Ōoji Suzuki Daisetsu kara no tegami* 大叔父鈴木大拙からの手紙. Kyoto: Hōzōkan, 1995.

Iwakura Masaji 岩倉政治. *Shinnin Suzuki Daisetsu* 真人鈴木大拙. Kyoto: Hōzōkan, 1986.

Nishimura Eshin 西村恵信. *Suzuki Daisetsu no genfūkei* 鈴木大拙の原風景. Tokyo: Daitō Shuppan, 1993.

Okamura Mihoko 岡村美穂子 and Ueda Shizuteru 上田閑照. *Daisetsu no fūkei: Suzuki Daisetsu to wa dare ka* 大拙の風景: 鈴木大拙とは誰か. Kyoto: Tōeisha, 1999.

Okamura Mihoko and Ueda Shizuteru. *Omoide no kobako kara: Suzuki Daisetsu no koto* 思い出の小箱から: 鈴木大拙のこと. Kyoto: Tōeisha, 1997.

Yamada Shōji 山田奨治. *Tōkyō bugiugi to Suzuki Daisetsu* 東京ブギウギと鈴木大拙. Kyoto: Jinbun Shoin, 2015.

FURTHER READINGS

Breen, John, Sueki Fumihiko, and Yamada Shōji, eds. *Beyond Zen: D. T. Suzuki and the Modern Transformation of Buddhism.* Honolulu: University of Hawai'i Press, 2022.

Dobbins, James C. "D. T. Suzuki: A Brief Account of His Life." *Eastern Buddhist* (Third Series) 2, no. 2 (2022).

Dobbins, James C. "D. T. Suzuki in Transition, 1949–53." *Matsugaoka Bunko kenkyū nenpō* 30 (2016): 47–61.

Dobbins, James C. "*Oxford Bibliographies.*" In Buddhism. Edited by Courtney Bruntz. New York: Oxford University Press, 2018. https://www.oxfordbibliographies.com/view/document/obo-9780195393521/obo-9780195393521-0257.xml?rskey=JA1Ovb&result=61.

Dobbins, James C. "The Life of Emma Erskine Lane Hahn: D. T. Suzuki's Mother-in-Law." *Matsugaoka Bunko kenkyū nenpō* 35 (2021): 11–65.

Henderson, Harold. *Catalyst for Controversy: Paul Carus of Open Court.* Carbondale: Southern Illinois University Press, 1993.

Hu Shih. "Ch'an (Zen) Buddhism in China: Its History and Method." *Philosophy East and West* 3, no. 1 (1953): 3–24.

Jaffe, Richard M. "Introduction to the 2010 Edition." In *Zen and Japanese Culture.* By Daisetz T. Suzuki, vii–xxviii. Princeton, NJ: Princeton University Press, 2010.

Jaffe, Richard M. "D. T. Suzuki and the Two Cranes: American Philanthropy and Suzuki's Global Agenda." *Matsugaoka Bunko kenkyū nenpō* 32 (2018): 29–58.

Mohr, Michel. "The Use of Traps and Snares: Shaku Sōen Revisited." In *Zen Masters.* Edited by Steven Heine and Dale Wright, 183–216. Oxford and New York: Oxford University Press, 2010.

Moriya Tomoe. "Social Ethics of 'New Buddhists' at the Turn of the Twentieth Century: A Comparative Study of Suzuki Daisetsu and Inoue Shūten." *Japanese Journal of Religious Studies* 32, no. 2 (2005): 283–304.

Moriya Tomoe. " 'A Note from a Rural Town in America': The Young Suzuki Daisetsu and the Significance of Religious Experience." *Eastern Buddhist* (New Series) 38, nos. 1–2 (2007): 58–68.

Sargeant, Winthrop. "Great Simplicity." *New Yorker*, August 31, 1957, 34–53.

Satō, Kemmyō Taira. "D. T. Suzuki and the Question of War." *Eastern Buddhist* (New Series) 39, no. 1 (2008): 61–120.

Sharf, Robert H. "The Zen of Japanese Nationalism." In *Curators of the Buddha.* Edited by Donald S. Lopez Jr., 107–160. Chicago: University of Chicago Press, 1995.

Snodgrass, Judith. *Presenting Japanese Buddhism to the West: Orientalism, Occidentalism, and the Columbian Exposition.* Chapel Hill: University of North Carolina Press, 2003.

Stunkard, Albert. "Suzuki Daisetz: An Appreciation." *Eastern Buddhist* (New Series) 36, nos. 1–2 (2004): 192–228.

Suzuki, Daisetz Teitaro. *Outlines of Mahayana Buddhism.* London: Luzac, 1907.

Suzuki, Daisetz T. *Swedenborg, Buddha of the North.* Translated by Andrew Bernstein. West Chester, PA: Swedenborg Foundation, 1996.

Suzuki, Daisetz T. *Sengai: The Zen of Ink and Paper*. Boston and London: Shambhala, 1999.

Suzuki, Daisetz T. *Zen and Japanese Culture*. Princeton, NJ: Princeton University Press, 2010.

Suzuki, Daisetz Teitarō, trans. *Shinran's Kyōgyōshinshō: The Collection of Passages Expounding the True Teaching, Living, Faith, and Realizing of the Pure Land*. Edited by the Center for Shin Buddhist Studies. Oxford and New York: Oxford University Press, 2012.

Suzuki, Teitaro, trans., *Aśvaghoṣa's Discourse on the Awakening of Faith in the Mahayana*. Chicago: Open Court, 1900.

Suzuki, Daisetz T., Erich Fromm, and Richard DeMartino. *Zen Buddhism and Psychoanalysis*. New York: Harper, 1960.

Switzer, A. Irwin, III. *D. T. Suzuki: A Biography*. Edited and enlarged by John Snelling. London: Buddhist Society, 1985.

Tweed, Thomas A. "American Occultism and Japanese Buddhism: Albert J. Edmunds, D. T. Suzuki, and Translocative History." *Japanese Journal of Religious Studies* 32, no. 2 (2005): 249–281.

Victoria, Brian. *Zen at War*. 2nd ed. Oxford: Rowman & Littlefield, 2006.

Yoshinaga Shin'ichi. "Suzuki Daisetsu and Swedenborg: A Historical Background." In *Modern Buddhism in Japan*. Edited by Hayashi Makoto, Ōtani Eiichi, and Paul L. Swanson, 112–143. Nagoya: Nanzan Institute of Religion and Culture, 2014.

Yusa, Michiko. *Zen and Philosophy: An Intellectual Biography of Nishida Kitarō*. Honolulu: University of Hawai'i Press, 2002.

VIDEO

Goldberg, Michael, prod. and dir. *A Zen Life: D. T. Suzuki*. DVD. Tokyo: Japan Inter-Culture Foundation, 2006.

NOTES

1. Daisetz T. Suzuki, "Early Memories," in *A Zen Life: D. T. Suzuki Remembered*, ed. Masao Abe (New York and Tokyo: Weatherhill, 1986), 3; Akizuki Ryōmin 秋月龍珉, *Suzuki Daisetsu* 鈴木大拙 (Tokyo: Kōdansha, 2004), 21–22; and "Yafūryūan jiden" 也風流庵自傳, in Suzuki Daisetsu 鈴木大拙, *Suzuki Daisetsu zenshū* 鈴木大拙全集, 40 vols., ed. Hisamatsu Shin'ichi 久松真一, Yamaguchi Susumu 山口晋, and Furuta Shōkin 古田紹欽 (Tokyo: Iwanami Shoten, 1999–2003), 29:147–150 (hereafter, *Suzuki Daisetsu zenshū* is cited as *SDZ*). A loose English translation of "Yafūryūan jiden," entitled "An Autobiographical Account," can be found in Abe, *A Zen Life: D. T. Suzuki Remembered*, 13–26.
2. Kirita Kiyohide 桐田清秀, *Suzuki Daisetsu kenkyū kiso shiryō* 鈴木大拙研究基礎資料 (Kamakura: Matsugaoka Bunko, 2005), "Nenpu" 年譜, 14–15; "Watakushi no rirekisho" 私の履歴書, *SDZ* 26:504–507; and Suzuki, "Early Memories," 5–6.
3. Akizuki, *Suzuki Daisetsu*, 28–36; "Yafūryūan jiden," *SDZ* 29:152–155; "Watakushi no rirekisho," *SDZ* 26:519–520, 524–526; and Suzuki, "Early Memories," 6–9.
4. Harold Henderson, *Catalyst for Controversy: Paul Carus of Open Court* (Carbondale: Southern Illinois University Press, 1993), 64–65, 69, 96–97; and *Budda no fukuin* 仏陀の福音, *SDZ* 25:275–509.
5. *Shin shūkyō ron* 新宗教論, *SDZ* 23:1–147; and two Suzuki letters to Paul Carus: Letter 36 (1895.6.3), *SDZ* 36:57–59; and Letter 49 (1896.5.14), *SDZ* 36:75–76.
6. Letter 141 (1902.9.23), *SDZ* 36:222; Akizuki, *Suzuki Daisetsu*, 36–37; and Suzuki, "Early Memories," 11–12.
7. Henderson, *Catalyst for Controversy*, 100–107; and "Yafūryūan jiden," *SDZ* 29:155–157.

8. Letter 141 (1902.9.23), *SDZ* 36:222.
9. For a list of Suzuki's publications in this period, see Kirita, *Suzuki Daisetsu kenkyū kiso shiryō*, "Chosaku nenpyō" 著作年表, 7–16.
10. Teitaro Suzuki, trans., *Aśvaghoṣa's Discourse on the Awakening of Faith in the Mahayana* (Chicago: Open Court, 1900); and Daisetz Teitaro Suzuki, *Outlines of Mahayana Buddhism* (London: Luzac, 1907).
11. Thomas A. Tweed, "American Occultism and Japanese Buddhism: Albert J. Edmunds, D. T. Suzuki, and Translocative History," *Japanese Journal of Religious Studies* 32, no. 2 (2005): 249–281; and Yoshinaga Shin'ichi, "Suzuki Daisetsu and Swedenborg: A Historical Background," in *Modern Buddhism in Japan*, ed. Hayashi Makoto, Ōtani Eiichi, and Paul L. Swanson (Nagoya: Nanzan Institute of Religion and Culture, 2014), 112–143.
12. Kirita, *Suzuki Daisetsu kenkyū kiso shiryō*, "Nenpu," 20–26; and James C. Dobbins, "The Life of Emma Erskine Lane Hahn: D. T. Suzuki's Mother-in-Law," *Matsugaoka Bunko kenkyū nenpō* 35 (2021): 41–43.
13. "Watakushi no rirekisho," *SDZ* 26:529; and "Yafūryūan jiden," *SDZ* 29:157.
14. Daisetz T. Suzuki, *Swedenborg, Buddha of the North*, trans. Andrew Bernstein (West Chester, PA: Swedenborg Foundation, 1996).
15. James C. Dobbins, ed., *Selected Works of D. T. Suzuki, Volume II: Pure Land* (Oakland: University of California Press, 2015), xvi.
16. "Yafūryūan jiden," *SDZ* 29:157–158; and Richard M. Jaffe, ed., *Selected Works of D. T. Suzuki, Volume I: Zen* (Oakland: University of California Press, 2014), xxiii–xxiv, xxviii–xxix.
17. Dobbins, *Selected Works of D. T. Suzuki, Volume II: Pure Land*, xi, xvi–xvii.
18. Dobbins, *Selected Works of D. T. Suzuki, Volume II: Pure Land*, xv–xvi.
19. James C. Dobbins, "D. T. Suzuki and the Welfare of Animals," in *Beyond Zen: D. T. Suzuki and the Modern Transformation of Buddhism*, ed. John Breen, Sueki Fumihiko, and Yamada Shōji (Honolulu: University of Hawai'i Press, 2022).
20. Yamada Shōji 山田奨治, *Tōkyō bugiugi to Suzuki Daisetsu* 東京ブギウギと鈴木大拙 (Kyoto: Jinbun Shoin, 2015), 19–23, 51–78.
21. "Watakushi no rirekisho," *SDZ* 26:521; and Nishiki Saburō 西木三郎, "Ataka Yakichi Ō shōtokuhi to Suzuki Daisetsu Sensei" 安宅弥吉翁頌徳碑と鈴木大拙先生, in *Suzuki Daisetsu: Hito to shisō* 鈴木大拙: 人と思想, ed. Hisamatsu Shin'ichi 久松真一, Yamaguchi Susumu 山口益, and Furuta Shōkin 古田紹欽 (Tokyo: Iwanami Shoten, 1971), 458–460.
22. Jaffe, *Selected Works of D. T. Suzuki, Volume I: Zen*, xxix–xxxii; and Richard M. Jaffe, "D. T. Suzuki and the Two Cranes: American Philanthropy and Suzuki's Global Agenda," *Matsugaoka Bunko kenkyū nenpō* 32 (2018): 30–44.
23. Kirita, *Suzuki Daisetsu kenkyū kiso shiryō*, "Chosaku nenpyō," 54–65; and Jaffe, *Selected Works of D. T. Suzuki, Volume I: Zen*, xxxi–xxxiv.
24. In the preface to the 1949 postwar reprint of *Nihon teki reisei* 日本的霊性, *SDZ* 8:9, Suzuki blamed the war on the military regime and on nationalism, totalitarianism, and nationalistic Shinto.
25. Brian Victoria, *Zen at War*, 2nd ed. (Oxford: Rowman & Littlefield, 2006), 22–29, 105–112, 147–152, 177–178, 208–209; and Kemmyō Taira Satō, "D. T. Suzuki and the Question of War," *Eastern Buddhist* (New Series) 39, no. 1 (2008): 61–120.
26. Kirita, *Suzuki Daisetsu kenkyū kiso shiryō*, "Nenpu," 138–154; "Chosaku nenpyō," 54–65; and Jaffe, *Selected Works of D. T. Suzuki, Volume I: Zen*, xxxv.
27. James C. Dobbins, "D. T. Suzuki in Transition, 1949–53," *Matsugaoka Bunko kenkyū nenpō* 30 (2016): 47–61.
28. Jaffe, "D. T. Suzuki and the Two Cranes," 44–53.
29. Hayashida Kumino 林田久美野, *Ōoji Suzuki Daisetsu kara no tegami* 大叔父鈴木大拙からの手紙 (Kyoto: Hōzōkan, 1995), 58–64; and Akizuki, *Suzuki Daisetsu*, 43–53.

30. Daisetz Teitarō Suzuki, trans., *Shinran's Kyōgyōshinshō, The Collection of Passages Expounding the True Teaching, Living, Faith, and Realizing of the Pure Land*, ed. Center for Shin Buddhist Studies (Oxford and New York: Oxford University Press, 2012), ix–xxiii.
31. Daisetz T. Suzuki, *Sengai: The Zen of Ink and Paper* (Boston and London: Shambhala, 1999), xii–xiv.
32. Kirita, *Suzuki Daisetsu kenkyū kiso shiryō*, "Nenpu," 213–214, 216–217, 224; Charles A. Moore, "Suzuki: The Man and the Scholar," *Eastern Buddhist* (New Series) 2, no. 1 (1967): 17–18; and Thomas Merton, "D. T. Suzuki: The Man and his Work," in *A Zen Life: D. T. Suzuki Remembered*, ed. Masao Abe (New York and Tokyo: Weatherhill, 1986), 121–126.
33. Hayashida Kumino, *Ōoji Suzuki Daisetsu kara no tegami*, 130–142; and Okamura Mihoko 岡村美穂子 and Ueda Shizuteru 上田閑照, *Daisetsu no fūkei: Suzuki Daisetsu to wa dare ka* 大拙の風景: 鈴木大拙とは誰か (Kyoto: Tōeisha, 1999), 89–90.

James C. Dobbins

D. T. SUZUKI: IDEAS AND INFLUENCES

ZEN BUDDHISM

Of all the forms of Buddhism propounded by Suzuki Daisetsu (Daisetz) Teitarō 鈴木大拙貞太郎 (1870–1966)—or, more commonly, D. T. Suzuki—he is best known for his writings on Zen 禅. It is the type of Buddhism he himself practiced and the one that made the deepest impression on him. His primary exposure to it occurred at the Engakuji 円覚寺 Monastery in Kamakura 鎌倉 after he came to Tokyo as a university student in the early 1890s. He practiced meditation and koan there assiduously for five years and, shortly before departing for America in 1897, had a Zen *satori* 悟り awakening. Throughout this period Suzuki also studied religion and Buddhism in a scholarly way and received not only Zen training but also intellectual mentoring from his master, Shaku Sōen 釈宗演 (1859–1919), who had his own views on how Buddhism should be presented and received in modern educated circles. The fruit of their collaboration was Suzuki's English translation of Sōen's address to the 1893 World's Parliament of Religions in Chicago and Suzuki's 1895 Japanese translation of *The Gospel of Buddha* (*Budda no fukuin* 仏陀の福音) by Paul Carus (1852–1919)—an acquaintance of Sōen's from the parliament who was an important scholar of religion and the editor in chief of Open Court Publishing in LaSalle, Illinois, under whom Suzuki would work for over a decade.[1] Simultaneously, in 1896, Suzuki published his own long theoretical work on religion. Ultimately Suzuki became famous as a thinker, scholar, and author, producing hundreds of essays, books, and translations over his career. But it was his original practice of Zen and the personal meaning he derived from it that triggered this lifelong intellectual outpouring.

Suzuki's most momentous works on Zen appeared in the 1920s and 1930s after he became a professor at Ōtani 大谷 University in Kyoto. His three-volume *Essays in Zen Buddhism, Series One, Two, and Three* were published in London in 1927, 1933, and 1934 successively. Some of their chapters were revised articles that had appeared in *The Eastern Buddhist*, the scholarly journal that he launched at Ōtani, but others were original to these volumes. In them he covered standard Zen topics—meditation, *satori*, koan, sayings of Zen masters, monastery life—all presented according to Suzuki's distinctive interpretation, which was shaped as much by Western scholarship as by traditional Japanese sectarian dogmatics. Some essays were not about Zen per se, but on themes and texts in Mahayana Buddhism that Suzuki related to Zen. In 1934 he followed these volumes with *An Introduction to Zen Buddhism*, arguably his most widely read publication, and *The Training of the Zen Buddhist Monk*, offering an idealized portrait of Zen monastic life. In 1935, he added the *Manual of Zen Buddhism*, providing English renderings of texts, verses, chants, sutra excerpts, and sayings of masters used in Zen monasteries. Finally, in 1938, he published *Zen and Its Influence on Japanese Culture*, attributing a Zen meaning to many of Japan's artistic and literary traditions.[2] This profusion of works, appearing in just over a decade, played a monumental role in introducing Zen in an accessible way to English readers and in establishing Suzuki as Zen's foremost authority in their eyes. Suzuki continued to publish on Zen in both Japanese and English during the next thirty years, and he sought to elucidate new topics and themes—for instance, the ideas of obscure Zen masters such as Bankei 盤珪 (1622–1693) and Sengai 仙厓 (1750–1837), and Zen texts discovered in Dunhuang 敦煌, China, which he did not have access to previously. But the main contours of Suzuki's teachings on Zen were set in this early wave of publications.

The key to Suzuki's presentation of Zen is his emphasis on *satori*, Zen awakening or enlightenment. He tended to interpret it using the language and conceptualizations of early-20th-century scholarship on religious experience, particularly that of the psychologist and philosopher William James (1842–1910) in *The Varieties of Religious Experience* published in 1902. Just as James sought to uncouple religious experience from doctrine and ecclesiastical organizations, likewise Suzuki portrayed *satori* as transcending sectarian structures and divisions.[3] He identified it as an intuitive and spiritual breakthrough resulting in a changed awareness or consciousness where things that were unseen before become clear and where discontents, perplexities, and dichotomies are resolved. This awakening has a noetic quality to it but does not lend itself easily to verbal description or rational explanation. Suzuki considered *satori* to be the essence of Zen, so that even if Zen texts, monasteries, and rituals all disappeared, Zen would endure as long as enlightenment could be found.[4] He also extended this rationale to claim that wherever such an enlightened awareness arises—even in the transcendentalism of Ralph Waldo Emerson (1803–1882)—Zen is present.[5] By defining Zen in this way, Suzuki detached it from its historical moorings and elevated it to a universal and ideal state of human consciousness.

Within this framework, Suzuki went on to explain the particular characteristics most commonly associated with Zen. First, he argued that Zen meditation is not merely to calm or pacify the mind, nor is it to induce visions of the Buddha. Rather, it is simply the activity wherein Zen monks wrestle with their koan. It is thus the koan that gives Zen meditation its value. Suzuki wrote extensively on koan, the perplexing phrases and vignettes—such as "nothingness" (*mu* 無) or "the sound of one hand" (*sekishu no onjō* 隻手音声) or "one's original face" (*honrai no menmoku* 本来面目)—that, when engaged intensively under the guidance of a Zen master and especially in the context of meditation, have the capacity to trigger a *satori* experience. Suzuki considered the koan's illogical and enigmatic quality to be a catalyst for disrupting dualistic and rational thinking and thereby provoking a profound and sudden awakening. Although he described koan as an expedient mechanism devised by Chinese masters for this purpose, and although he regretted that *satori* might be less spontaneous within this regimen, Suzuki nonetheless embraced and endorsed the koan path to *satori*. In the abstract, however, he believed enlightenment to be independent of all causal conditions and therefore possible anytime and anywhere—whether situated in meditation and koan and Zen monasteries or not.[6]

Suzuki likewise construed the vast body of sayings of Zen masters, all Zen literature and imagery, and life in a Zen monastery to be geared toward the actualization of *satori*. And, once actualized, continued practice of koan and monastery life were thought to heighten or deepen it. In fact, one could reside in a steady state of enlightened living—inured to dichotomies and conflict, egoless, harmonious with the world, and living in suchness or "as-it-is-ness" (*sono mama* そのまま or *kono mama* このまま).[7] In this way Suzuki wedded traditional Zen ideas about practice and enlightenment—especially drawn from the teachings of Linji 臨済 (d. 866) and Dahui 大慧 (1089–1163) in China and Hakuin 白隠 (1685–1768) in Japan—with modern analyses of religious experience to portray Zen *satori* as a profound and even mystical experience with a transformational effect on one's life. Critics of Suzuki have pointed out that his model of Zen is based almost exclusively on the Rinzai tradition in Japan, replete with koan practice, and that it virtually ignores the Sōtō 曹洞 tradition of the master Dōgen 道元 (1200–1253), which emphasizes quiet sitting in meditation as the embodiment of *satori*.[8] Critics also argue that Suzuki's Zen is overly dependent on Western concepts of religious experience, thereby recasting the old and complex Zen tradition to fit a Western model.[9] Whatever the case, Suzuki's interpretation has emerged as a dominant view of Zen in the West and has widely influenced the Japanese view as well.

MAHAYANA BUDDHISM

Mahayana (*Daijō* 大乗) is the branch of Buddhism most prevalent in Japan and East Asia. It coalesced around a host of sutras and other texts originating in India and Central Asia that were transmitted to China, translated into Chinese, and dispersed throughout East Asia. There, in contrast to India, Mahayana became the banner under which the vast majority of Buddhist traditions, philosophies, institutions, and systems of practice defined themselves. These included the Zen and Pure Land traditions of Japan. As academic research on Buddhism emerged among Western scholars in the 19th century, they tended to treat the Buddhism of Sri Lanka and Southeast Asia, specifically Theravada, as the earliest and most authoritative form of the religion, whereas they considered the Mahayana traditions in other parts of Asia to be later derivations and a corrupted form. This was the state of Western scholarship on Buddhism when Suzuki first encountered it in the 1890s. Under Shaku Sōen's influence and in step with other young Buddhists of the period, Suzuki committed himself not only to reforming Buddhism in Japan but also to enhancing Mahayana's reputation abroad and introducing Westerners to its sophisticated systems of thought.[10] Many of his early publications while living for eleven years in America at the turn of the 20th century should be understood in that context, and even his founding of *The Eastern Buddhist* journal at Ōtani University in 1921 was inspired by that goal. Although Zen is what Suzuki is best remembered for, Mahayana was the focus of his early writings.

Suzuki's presentation of Mahayana to the English-reading public was done through translations, essays, and books. Soon after he finished assisting Paul Carus with a translation of the Daoist classic *Daodejing* 道徳経, he translated the *Daijō kishinron* 大乗起信論, published in

1900 as *Aśvaghoṣa's Discourse on the Awakening of Faith in the Mahayana*. This text, although obscure in origins, had wide circulation in East Asia. Suzuki considered it an excellent introduction for Westerners to the grand vision and philosophical subtleties of Mahayana thought. The text is built around a Buddhist exegesis of mind (*shin* 心), which Suzuki translated as "soul" (perhaps under the influence of Carus). This "soul" does not refer to that of an individual person but to something ontological and all-encompassing. It is said to have two aspects, "suchness" and "birth-and-death" (i.e., samsara), and hence, it spans both the oneness of all things and their separate individuated existence, that is, their unity and their plurality. At the level of "birth-and-death," the text indicates that the "soul" emerges from the so-called Tathāgata womb (*Tathāgatagarbha*), and it introduces elements of Yogācāra philosophy to explain how the so-called all-conserving mind (*ālaya-vijñāna*), considered synonymous with the Dharmakāya of all the buddhas, is the oceanic base on which the waves of confused subjective thinking occur, manifested in the form of "ego-consciousness" (*manovijñāna*). There can be a two-way "perfuming" effect whereby, on the one hand, confused assumptions may perpetuate confusion but, on the other, enlightening thoughts may attenuate confusion. In all these states, the mind is the same whether it is in an enlightened or disturbed mode.[11] Suzuki's explanations of classical Buddhist texts and Yogācāra philosophy at this early stage in his career were tenuous, derived fragmentarily from both Western and Japanese scholarship and intermixed with Western philosophical terminology. He also had an insufficient knowledge of the latest text-criticism of the *Awakening of Faith*, which suggested it might be a Chinese compilation rather than an Indian work. But an important theme that Suzuki distilled from this text was that enlightenment is both a timeless pervasive reality and an experiential this-worldly process. Over the years, Suzuki never abandoned this formula and sought to apply it to Zen, Pure Land, Kegon 華厳, and all other forms of Buddhism that he explicated.

Suzuki sought to promote Mahayana in yet other publications during his early years in America. He wrote short essays on Mādhyamika (1898) and Yogācāra (1904), which were published in India and Europe, respectively. But his treatment of these topics was cursory and not completely reliable—especially Sanskrit references—for he did not have in-depth training in them and relied on limited sources.[12] Subsequently, the publication of Suzuki's *Outlines of Mahayana Buddhism* in 1907 had a great impact on Western readers. It introduced them, first of all, to the classification of Buddhism into the Mahayana and Hinayana branches, polemical categories that had originated in Mahayana texts. This division was roughly parallel to the prevailing classification of Northern and Southern Buddhism, although Suzuki argued that the Mahayana/Hinayana designation conveyed better the nature of the two. He further subdivided Mahayana into Northern and Eastern branches, thereby giving a separate and special place to China and Japan as major sites of Buddhism's efflorescence. This new classification familiarized and acclimatized readers to East Asia's view of its Buddhist identity and legitimacy. Second, Suzuki situated his discussion of Mahayana within the general issues about religion that were debated in the West at the beginning of the 20th century: questions about intellect versus feeling, reason versus faith, and philosophy versus religion. Moreover, he occasionally cited well-known thinkers or literary figures such as Immanuel Kant (1724–1804) and Alfred Lord Tennyson (1809-92) to make his points, thereby drawing on idioms and a vocabulary that English readers were accustomed to. Third, Suzuki explained an extensive array of Mahayana themes in easy-to-understand summaries: absolute and relative knowledge, suchness, Tathāgatagarbha, emptiness, Dharmakāya, three-body theory of the buddha, bodhisattvas and their ten stages, and the nonduality of nirvana and samsara. These succinct explanations made Suzuki's work a virtual handbook for novices interested in Mahayana.[13] As in the case of his other publications of this period, various points in the book were not quite accurate. In later decades, Suzuki never produced a revised edition and was hesitant to allow the work to be translated into Japanese.[14] But because there were no other introductions to Mahayana of this type in English and because of its readability, Suzuki's book had a strong impact on the image of Buddhism in the West and helped enhance the reputation of Mahayana and East Asian Buddhism.

Suzuki's promotion of Mahayana Buddhism extended well beyond his early career. In the 1920s and 1930s, after becoming a professor at Ōtani University and after Mahayana had received recognition among many Western readers, he continued to produce important works to make its extensive literature and systems of thought better known. In the first issues of *The Eastern Buddhist*, for instance, he presented a digest in excerpts of the *Kegon* or *Avatamsaka Sutra* in four installments, as well as his own brief explanation of the idea of the interpenetration of all things, a theme that he emphasized repeatedly in his writings.[15] More important, he published his widely praised *Studies in the Lankavatara Sutra* in 1930 and an English translation of the Sanskrit scripture, *The Lankavatara Sutra, A Mahayana Text*, in 1932. In it, Suzuki focused on themes and concepts that were closely associated with Yogācāra philosophy (illusory, conventional, and enlightened knowledge; dimensions of thought, consciousness, and mind; the theory of mind-only), with Prajñāparamitā thought (no-birth, emptiness, nonduality, no-substance), and with the Mahayana ideal (three-body theory of the buddha, the meaning of Tathāgata). He sought in particular to apply the *Lankavatara*'s ideas to Zen, since the two had a semilegendary connection through the Zen patriarch Bodhidharma.[16] Although Suzuki was never proficient as a Sanskritist (relying on the help of others such as his colleague at Ōtani, Izumi Hōkei 泉芳環 [1884–1947]), he made available in English a large selection of Mahayana texts from Sanskrit.[17]

In old age, Suzuki focused his attention on the presentation and explication of Zen, since interest in it was soaring in the West. But in doing so he frequently drew from his previous Mahayana studies to frame Zen philosophically and to offer a more intellectual interpretation of it. The primary setting in which this occurred was the lectures and seminars he gave as a professor at Columbia University in the 1950s. While in America, he began assembling and editing these presentations in the hope of publishing a major interpretive work on Zen, drawing from Buddhist thought, Mahayana philosophy, and Western religious comparisons. Unfortunately, Suzuki died before this project was complete, but his unfinished manuscript was eventually published in 2016 by the Matsugaoka Bunko 松ヶ岡文庫, the research library he had established in Kamakura. It consists of revised versions of his Columbia lectures from the fall of 1952 and the spring of 1953. In content, this work is wide-ranging and full of digressions, representing a kind of free-form Buddhist theologizing about Zen. It is noteworthy, however, that there are many references to Mahayana texts in it: *Awakening of Faith, Lankavatara, Prajñāparamitā, Kegon*, and other materials that Suzuki had presented in earlier publications. But unlike the work at the beginning of his career when his goal was to defend and legitimize Mahayana Buddhism, he treated Mahayana at this point as a philosophical mirror of Zen and as an intellectual articulation of its wordless teaching.[18]

PURE LAND BUDDHISM

It is a commonplace belief that Pure Land Buddhism (*jōdokyō* 浄土教), most notably the Shin 真 tradition of Japan, is the diametric opposite of Zen. For its part, Zen is considered a rigorous religious path involving meditation, monastic discipline, and inner struggle culminating in the realization that one's true nature is identical to the buddha's. Individuals must exert great effort in their practices and take responsibility for their religious fate. Pure Land Buddhism, on the other hand, entails relying on the buddha, specifically the all-pervasive Buddha Amida 阿弥陀, for the power, wisdom, and compassion whereby enlightenment occurs. Traditionally, it has been regarded as an otherworldly religious path in which people put their faith (*shinjin* 信心) in Amida during this life and intone his name earnestly with the words *Namu Amida Butsu* 南無阿弥陀仏, which, known as the *nenbutsu* 念仏, is its principal practice. Then after death, they are reborn in Amida's transcendent and resplendent paradise called the Pure Land (*jōdo* 浄土) or "Ultimate Bliss" (*Gokuraku* 極楽, Skt. Sukhāvatī), which is considered synonymous with and tantamount to enlightenment. Frequently, Pure Land Buddhism has been likened to traditional Christianity—structured around an all-powerful God, a life of faith, and salvation in heaven after death. Suzuki, however, beginning in mid-career, came to regard Pure Land as an important form of Mahayana and as a this-worldly Buddhist path parallel to, though different from, Zen.[19]

Suzuki was exposed to Pure Land Buddhism as a child through initiation into a secret *nenbutsu* group that his mother belonged to, but he turned his back on it as a young adult once he was exposed to Western thought and Zen Buddhism, treating it as an inferior and superstitious religion.[20] Two decades later, when appointed as an English professor in the preparatory division of Gakushūin 学習院, the Peers School, in Tokyo, he began to reconsider it after meeting Sasaki Gesshō 佐々木月樵 (1875–1926), a prominent figure in the Seishinshugi 精神主義 ("Spirituality") intellectual movement of Shin Buddhism and a professor at Shinshū (soon to be Ōtani) University. He had been introduced to Sasaki by his close friend, philosopher Nishida Kitarō 西田幾多郎 (1870–1945), who himself had great respect for this movement. Sasaki and his fellow Seishinshugi proponents sought to highlight people's inner subjective encounter with Amida Buddha in the present life instead of their aspiration for salvation in Pure Land after death.[21] Suzuki's reassessment of Pure Land Buddhism resulted in a few short articles in the 1910s but led to a steady, lifelong stream of publications after he became a professor at Ōtani in 1921. There he found sympathetic and like-minded colleagues from the Seishinshugi movement, especially members of *The Eastern Buddhist* editorial board. The presuppositions of Suzuki's interpretation of Pure Land, however, did not originate in Seishinshugi but rather came from the modern theories of religious experience that he used to explain Zen. Nonetheless, his innovative approach to Pure Land had strong resonances with Seishinshugi in that both emphasized religious life in the here and now.

Suzuki published several long and important articles on Pure Land in *The Eastern Buddhist* during his active years at Ōtani, most notably "The Development of the Pure Land Doctrine in Buddhism" (1925) and "The Shin Sect of Buddhism" (1939).[22] In them, he introduced English readers to the basic concepts and vocabulary of Pure Land and portrayed it as an expression of the spirit of Śākyamuni Buddha and as the type of mystical awakening found in other forms of Buddhism. He also interpreted the Pure Land paradise as an immanent reality in this world rather than as a separate realm encountered after death. Then during the war years he published his book *Jōdokei shisōron* 浄土系思想論 (Interpretations of Pure Land thought, 1942) and discussed Shin Buddhism extensively in his next book *Nihon teki reisei* 日本的霊性 (Japanese spirituality, 1944).[23] In those works, Suzuki explicated the ideas of Shinran 親鸞 (1173–1262), the founder of Shin Buddhism, from his *Tannishō* 歎異抄 collection of sayings and from his doctrinal masterpiece *Kyōgyōshinshō* 教行信証. In particular, Suzuki highlighted Shinran's conviction that Amida made his vow of bringing sentient beings to enlightenment specifically for one individual person, Shinran himself—thereby treating Shinran's belief as a personal existential realization.[24] In addition, Suzuki elucidated Shinran's idea of faith—referred to also in the *Kyōgyōshinshō* as the "one mind" (*isshin* 一心) and the "diamond-like true mind" (*kongō no shinshin* 金剛の真心)—to be an experience of oneness with Amida.[25] This interpretation suggests a parallel between the Pure Land experience and Zen's realization of one's own nature as the buddha's nature. Overall the major themes found in Suzuki's writings on Shin Buddhism revolve around (a) the present world—that Pure Land's true meaning is found in this life, not the next; (b) religious experience—that the place where religious meaning arises is an internal and personal experience often described as faith or relying on Amida's "other-power" (*tariki* 他力); and (c) nonduality—that in this experience the differentiation between oneself and Amida and between this world and the Pure Land falls away.[26] With these interpretations, Suzuki helped recast the image of Pure Land Buddhism from a religion preaching salvation in the afterlife to an experience of religious fulfillment in this life.

Another subject that Suzuki explored extensively in Pure Land Buddhism was the religious life of *myōkōnin* 妙好人, which he sometimes translated as the "wondrous good man." This term refers to lowly and sometimes illiterate believers who came to be seen as models of Shin Buddhist religiosity based on the feelings and convictions they expressed in popular sayings. Suzuki first encountered stories about them in the 1920s and published essays and translations on various *myōkōnin* from that time on. Some of the figures he presented expressed the full range of Shin Buddhist beliefs—from immediate fulfillment in the here and now to anticipation of birth in the Pure Land after death, as well as platitudes about conventional morality. But the sayings of one particular *myōkōnin*, Asahara Saichi 浅原才市 (1850–1932), introduced to Suzuki by the Kyoto philosopher Nishitani Keiji 西谷啓治 (1900–1990), fit perfectly with Suzuki's exposition of Shin Buddhism. Saichi's sayings, preserved mostly in short pithy verses, focus on his personal practice of the *nenbutsu*, chanting the Buddha's name with the words *Namu Amida Butsu*. His verses express in one way or another Saichi's feeling of oneness with the Buddha as he intoned the *nenbutsu*—in which his identity, as an unworthy sentient being, merges with the Buddha's identity, as the true embodiment of enlightenment. This sense of nonduality was one of Suzuki's signature themes in interpreting Shin Buddhism. As a result of his decades-long work on *myōkōnin*, Suzuki almost singlehandedly lifted their collections of sayings from the realm of popular Shin homilies to the plane of great religious literature. Suzuki no doubt found a power in their simplicity, perhaps akin to the earthy sayings of fabled Zen masters in China.[27]

Suzuki's final contribution to the study of Pure Land Buddhism, undertaken near the end of his life, was the English translation of Shinran's longest work, *Kyōgyōshinshō*. This was a project that Suzuki had not intended to undertake. In fact, earlier in his career he considered the text too abstract and obtuse to convey Shinran's ideas effectively, and less representative of his thinking than the *Tannishō*.[28] But the Higashi Honganji 東本願寺 branch of Shin Buddhism, to which Ōtani University belonged, urged Suzuki to do the translation. In the end, he managed to complete the first four of the work's six fascicles, which contain the crux of Shinran's teachings. In his translation, Suzuki presupposed the basic themes that he attributed to Shin Buddhism in his earlier writings—an emphasis on fulfillment in this life, the primacy of religious experience, and nonduality—but he also introduced new and innovative translations of some key Pure Land terms. Specifically, he rendered *gyō* 行, which is typically translated "religious practice," as "living," suggesting that a person's day-to-day life with Amida is tantamount to religious practice. He also translated the term *gan* 願, which usually refers to Amida's vow to bring all living beings to enlightenment, as "prayer," intimating that the primordial will of the Buddha and the religious hopes of ordinary beings are inseparable from each other.[29] Thus, Suzuki's parting gift to the international community of Shinran scholars was these interpretive brainteasers, challenging them to a more immanental and nondualistic understanding of Shinran's teachings.

THEORY OF RELIGION

Suzuki is usually remembered as a transmitter of Buddhism to the West, particularly Zen, and as an interpreter of Buddhism for modern living. In his own day, he was also considered an insightful observer and theorist of religion generally. Suzuki's interest in theoretical questions began early in his career with the publication of his *Shin shūkyō ron* 新宗教論 (A new interpretation of religion) in 1896, before he ever traveled abroad.[30] It was written only decades after the term *religion* (*shūkyō* 宗教) entered the Japanese vocabulary and while its meaning and semantic boundaries were still unstable.[31] By then Suzuki had read various works by 18th- and 19th-century Western philosophers and literary figures while attending university, and he was in correspondence with the Open Court editor Paul Carus, a noted turn-of-the-century proponent of the "religion of science," that is, of a rational religion compatible with science. Suzuki in his book adopted a similar rationalist stance, exploring religions with a critical eye, East and West, to discern what in them was empirically plausible and what problematic. A subtext to his study was the belief that, among the various religions of the world, Buddhism could easily be reconciled to reason and science, a view that Carus and other Western scholars had previously advanced. Although this rational depiction of Buddhism was important to Suzuki in his early thinking, and although he continued to apply a rational analysis to aspects of religion throughout his career, his interpretation of Buddhism began to shift after he traveled to America and encountered other theories.[32]

The interpretation of religion that Suzuki soon embraced in America revolved around the idea of religious experience. The underlying assumption was that religion arises from an inner, personal "feeling" rather than from the "intellect."[33] This emphasis on nonrational spirituality had roots in European Romanticism and American transcendentalism, which Suzuki was familiar with, and had parallels in Zen's idealization of "sudden awakening." For Suzuki, the most insightful articulation of this approach was found in William James's *The Varieties of Religious Experience*, which Suzuki read soon after it was published in 1902. By focusing on a person's internal psychological state, which itself is a real phenomenon, James reoriented the idea of religion away from external texts, doctrines, rituals, moral injunctions, and institutions that were typically considered the locus of religion.[34] From this time, Suzuki also used the concept of religious experience to elucidate Buddhism in all its forms—Zen, Pure Land, Mahayana, and Hinayana—and to make comparisons to religions worldwide.

In conjunction with the idea of religious experience Suzuki also adopted the widely recognized category of mysticism to explain Buddhism and other religions. He was influenced, first of all, by William James's analysis of mystical experience—which he characterized as ineffable, noetic, transient, and passive.[35] Suzuki himself maintained an interest in mysticism throughout his life. During his early years in America, he was attracted, for instance, to Swedenborgianism, the 19th-century theological and mystical movement inspired by Emanuel Swedenborg (1688–1772), partly because of its mystical visions. He also applied the idea of mysticism to the Shin Buddhist *myōkōnin* Shichiri Gōjun 七里恒順 (1835–1900) in his early article, "Sayings of a Modern Tariki Mystic," published in 1924.[36] Suzuki's explanation of Zen *satori*, or enlightenment experience, likewise bore a resemblance to William James's analysis of mysticism; specifically, Suzuki identified its characteristics as irrationality, intuitive insight, authoritativeness, affirmation, sense of the beyond, impersonal tone, feelings of exaltation, and momentariness (and added passivity in other writings).[37] Suzuki's most sustained treatment of mysticism appeared late in life in his book *Mysticism: Christian and Buddhist* (1957), in which he juxtaposed the Christian theologian and mystic Meister Eckhart (*c.* 1260–1328) and the Shin Buddhist *myōkōnin* Asahara Saichi. Thus, the themes of mysticism and religious experience provided Suzuki with a vocabulary to analyze Buddhism in a modern conceptual framework, to convey it intelligibly to Western readers, and to discuss religion as a phenomenon with Western scholars.[38] Although near the end of his life he expressed misgivings about describing Buddhism in terms of mysticism, the idea was so pervasive in all his writings that such regret in old age could hardly invalidate his lifelong use of it.[39]

Suzuki's scholarly engagement with Buddhism and the interpretation of religion gave him high visibility in many scholarly venues throughout his life. His early model for such venues was the 1893 World's Parliament of Religions in Chicago, which his Zen master and mentor Shaku Sōen had attended. Suzuki himself participated in the World Congress of Faiths in London in 1936 to great acclaim, and from that time, his international profile steadily rose. Soon afterward, he was invited to the First East–West Philosophers' Conference in Honolulu in 1939 (which he could not attend because of his wife's illness and death) and then to each subsequent East–West Conference—the second in 1949, the third in 1959, and the fourth in 1964—all of which he attended as a featured speaker. One other prestigious venue in which Suzuki appeared was the Eranos Conferences of 1953 and 1954 in Switzerland, an assembly of world-class scholars who presented and discussed their latest humanistic scholarship. Finally, two years before his death Suzuki participated in a famous interreligious dialogue with the Catholic monk Thomas Merton in New York, exchanging views about continuities and discontinuities between Buddhism and Christianity. By this time, Suzuki's reputation as an international expert on Buddhism was at its zenith. Although Suzuki always felt a particular affinity to philosophy, ironically his ideas did not gain traction with many philosophers in America, perhaps because analytic philosophy was well established at that point—the very type of logical thought that Suzuki often criticized. Instead, his ideas drew a positive response more from psychoanalysts, poets, writers, musicians, artists, religionists, theologians, clerics, and spiritual seekers of all types.

POPULAR INFLUENCES

With the emergence of Suzuki as a public intellectual in 1950s America, his celebrity soon crossed over to the popular domain as well. Because he was willing to give talks and presentations to all kinds of groups and to receive casual auditors into his lectures at Columbia University, his reputation began to spread beyond academic and professional circles. His congenial air and his habit of speaking in paradoxes only amplified people's curiosity. Moreover, he seemed to fit, both visually and behaviorally, the pervasive Western stereotype of the "wise old Oriental sage"—weathered, enigmatic, lively, gentle, and sporting flamboyant eyebrows and a balding pate.[40] All these factors converged to make Suzuki the talk of the town within a few years of moving to New York. His fame is best exemplified in a twenty-page feature article about him published in the mass-circulation magazine *The New Yorker* in 1957, which profiled him in the following way:

> Dr. Suzuki is as impressive personally as he is through the medium of his writing and scholarship. As a personality, he radiates not only the general glamour that attaches to aging Oriental men of wisdom but a special serenity that makes him a magnificent living example of the doctrine he preaches . . . even the most skeptical visitor, when under the spell of Dr. Suzuki's words, is apt to find himself believing—for a moment, at least—that zero is in fact equal to infinity, that the timeless and eternal instant of perception is all there is to the real world, and that "emptiness" is a thing.[41]

Suzuki's spell, described here, swept over countless people, both mainstream and marginal, who read his works or saw him in person.

It is difficult to enumerate all the people in popular culture that Suzuki inspired, but a few will demonstrate the range of his influence. The first is Erich Fromm (1900–1980), the well-known psychoanalyst of the Neo-Freudian school. He invited Suzuki to a weeklong workshop in Mexico for psychoanalysts and psychologists in August 1957 and, based on it, coauthored with him the book *Zen Buddhism and Psychoanalysis* (1960).[42] The second is Alan Watts (1915–1973), the mass-market author and speaker on Asian religions. Born in England and familiar with Suzuki's writings from his teenage years, he helped integrate Buddhism, Daoism, and Hinduism into the emerging counterculture of California. In the 1960s and 1970s, his writings—which were always dependent on Suzuki's scholarship—became for a time the most widely read works on Zen.[43] The third figure is the experimental music composer John Cage (1912–1992). After dropping out of college, he explored the arts widely in Europe, California, and Seattle and aligned himself mostly with the avant-garde Dada movement. By the time he moved to New York in 1942, he had established a reputation in experimental music. There he attended Suzuki's lectures on Zen at Columbia University and, from that time, cited Zen as an important influence on his work. He is famous for his 1952 piece titled *4′33″* (a three-movement, four-and-a-half-minute work consisting of silence by a musician on stage, which was inspired in part by Robert Rauschenberg's "White Paintings") and for introducing the idea of "indeterminacy" into his compositions derived from the Chinese divination classic *Yijing* 易經. Cage paid courtesy visits to Suzuki when he traveled to Japan in 1962 and 1964.[44] The fourth person is Jack Kerouac (1922–1969), the counterculture novelist who became a clarion voice for the Beat generation. He, along with such friends as poets Allen Ginsberg (1926–1997) and Gary Snyder (b. 1930), was proactively exploring Buddhism in the 1950s, including the writings of Suzuki. As a fictionalized account of these explorations, Kerouac published the novel *Dharma Bums* in 1958—permanently enshrining a place for Buddhism in the beatnik movement alongside anti-consumerism, itinerant life, sexual promiscuity, alcohol, and drugs. Kerouac had great admiration for Suzuki, and in October 1958, the very month that *Dharma Bums* was published (and just weeks before Suzuki moved back to Japan), he, Ginsberg, and their friend Peter Orlovsky (1933–2010) made an impromptu visit to Suzuki's residence in New York. He welcomed them in and served them thick, green *matcha* tea, urging them not to forget it. Upon leaving, Kerouac professed his desire to spend the rest of his life with Suzuki, to which Suzuki cryptically replied, "Sometime."[45]

Suzuki was fully aware of the ways his ideas were being appropriated, combined with other trends, and integrated into American culture. It is true that he had personal contact with all these figures—Fromm, Watts, Cage, and Kerouac—and that his interactions with them were cordial. But at the same time, Suzuki had questions or misgivings about their interpretations, and he particularly lamented that Zen might be blamed for the beatnik craze and the Beat generation.[46] In contrast to these developments in America, Suzuki's reputation in Japan was generally more dignified and mainstream. He frequently interacted, for instance, with the philosopher Nishitani Keiji, perhaps the most prominent intellectual heir of Nishida Kitarō in the Kyoto School of philosophy; and with the aesthetician Yanagi Sōetsu 柳宗悦 (1889–1961), the cofounder of the *mingei* 民芸 folk crafts movement in Japan. Suzuki also was a major influence on Ruth Fuller Everett Sasaki (1892–1967), teaching her the rudiments of Buddhist meditation when she traveled through Japan with her family in 1930 and later introducing her to the abbot of Nanzenji 南禅寺 Monastery in Kyoto, where she underwent four months of intensive Zen training in 1932. Sasaki went on to become an important bridge figure between America and Japan in the formation of American Buddhism. She headed the First Zen Institute in New York in the late 1940s and then established an outpost for it at the Daitokuji 大徳寺 Monastery in Kyoto where Americans could receive Rinzai training and study Zen texts. During the 1950s and 1960s, Sasaki lived mostly in Japan and developed a reputation as a Zen traditionalist with little sympathy for America's indulgent modifications of Zen. Suzuki maintained warm ties with Sasaki throughout his career.[47] From these examples, it is clear Suzuki's influence ran wide and deep, far beyond the Zen boom of the 1950s.

For all his celebrity and scholarly stature, Suzuki was not without his critics. Perhaps the most noteworthy one during his lifetime was the renowned Chinese scholar and thinker Hu Shih 胡適 (1891–1962), who expressed reservations about the historical objectivity of Suzuki's work on Chinese Zen.[48] Another harsh critic was the popular Hungarian British author Arthur Koestler (1905–1983), who treated Suzuki's Zen as the abandonment of reason and moral values in favor of a vague and elusive religious ideal.[49] In addition, another important wave of criticism occurred in the 1990s long after Suzuki's death. Robert Sharf depicted him as a Japanese cultural chauvinist who simply recast Buddhism by applying Western ideas of religious experience to it.[50] Bernard Faure, for his part, faulted Suzuki for his skewed image of Zen—championing Rinzai over Sōtō—and for deploying orientalist stereotypes to claim, inversely, Asia's spiritual superiority over the West.[51] Finally, Brian Victoria characterized Suzuki as a nationalistic supporter of Japan's military incursions in Asia prior to its war with the United States.[52]

These criticisms have done much to dim the glow that surrounded Suzuki after his death, but at the same time, they have inspired new rebuttals and defenses of him.[53] Whatever his shortcomings may have been, Suzuki's imprint was indelible on his generation and the construction of Buddhism then. Moreover, his ideas continue to reverberate among contemporary Buddhists through the enormous corpus of writings he left behind. Suzuki thus remains one of the most consequential thinkers and cultural icons of Buddhism in modern times.

REVIEW OF LITERATURE

The vast majority of writings by or about Suzuki are in Japanese. The most extensive collection of his own writings is his so-called complete works, *Suzuki Daisetsu zenshū*, comprising forty volumes. But it does not contain any of his major English works. Those are published elsewhere in a variety of formats, outlets, and venues, some of which are out of print. One representative collection is the four-volume *Selected Works of D. T. Suzuki*, edited by Jaffe. For Suzuki's best-known studies of Zen, see his three-volume *Essays in Zen Buddhism* and his *Introduction to Zen Buddhism*. For his most influential works on Mahayana Buddhism, see his *Outlines of Mahayana Buddhism* and his *Studies in the Lankavatara Sutra*. For his principal studies of Pure Land Buddhism, see his *Collected Writings on Shin Buddhism* and his translation of *Shinran's Kyōgyōshinshō*.

The majority of the secondary literature on Suzuki is also written in Japanese. An invaluable resource is Kirita, *Suzuki Daisetsu kenkyū kiso shiryō*, which contains a comprehensive chronology of Suzuki's life and a near-exhaustive list of his publications. Many studies of Suzuki's ideas and writings can be found in two journals: *The Eastern Buddhist* and *Matsugaoka Bunko kenkyū nenpō*. For a popular profile of Suzuki during the Zen boom of 1950s' America, see Sargeant, "Great Simplicity."

PRIMARY SOURCES

Suzuki, Daisetz (Daisetsu) Teitarō, trans. *Aśvaghoṣa's Discourse on the Awakening of Faith in the Mahayana*. Chicago: Open Court, 1900.

Suzuki, Daisetz (Daisetsu) Teitarō. *Studies in the Lankavatara Sutra*. London: Routledge & Sons, 1930.

Suzuki, Daisetz (Daisetsu) Teitarō. *Essays in Zen Buddhism, First, Second, and Third Series*. London: Rider, 1949–1953.

Suzuki, Daisetz (Daisetsu) Teitarō, Erich Fromm, and Richard DeMartino. *Zen Buddhism and Psychoanalysis*. New York: Harper, 1960.

Suzuki, Daisetz (Daisetsu) Teitarō. *Outlines of Mahayana Buddhism*. New York: Schocken, 1963.

Suzuki, Daisetz (Daisetsu) Teitarō. *Introduction to Zen Buddhism*. New York: Grove, 1964.

Suzuki, Daisetz (Daisetsu) Teitarō. *The Field of Zen*. New York: Perennial Library, Harper & Row, 1970.

Suzuki, Daisetz (Daisetsu) Teitarō. *Japanese Spirituality*. Translated by Norman Waddell. Tokyo: Japanese Society for the Promotion of Science, 1972.

Suzuki, Daisetz (Daisetsu) Teitarō. *Collected Writings on Shin Buddhism*. Edited by the Eastern Buddhist Society. Kyoto: Shinshū Ōtaniha, 1973.

Suzuki, Daisetz (Daisetsu) Teitarō. *Swedenborg, Buddha of the North*. Translated by Andrew Bernstein. West Chester, PA: Swedenborg Foundation, 1996.
Suzuki, Daisetz (Daisetsu) Teitarō. *Sengai: The Zen of Ink and Paper*. Boston and London: Shambhala, 1999.
Suzuki, Daisetsu (Daisetz) Teitarō 鈴木大拙貞太郎. *Suzuki Daisetsu zenshū* 鈴木大拙全集. 40 vols. Edited by Hisamatsu Shin'ichi 久松真一, Yamaguchi Susumu 山口益, and Furuta Shōkin 古田紹欽. Tokyo: Iwanami Shoten, 1999–2003.
Suzuki, Daisetz (Daisetsu) Teitarō. *Zen and Japanese Culture*. Princeton, NJ: Princeton University Press, 2010.
Suzuki, Daisetz (Daisetsu) Teitarō, trans., *Shinran's Kyōgyōshinshō, The Collection of Passages Expounding the True Teaching, Living, Faith, and Realizing of the Pure Land*. Edited by the Center for Shin Buddhist Studies. Oxford and New York: Oxford University Press, 2012.
Suzuki, Daisetz (Daisetsu) Teitarō. *Selected Works of D. T. Suzuki*. 4 vols. Edited by Richard M. Jaffe. Oakland: University of California Press, 2014–2021.
Suzuki, Daisetz (Daisetsu) Teitarō. *Daisetz Teitaro Suzuki's Columbia University Seminar Lectures*. Edited by Sōiku Shigematsu and Gishin Tokiwa. Kamakura: Matsugaoka Bunko, 2016.

SECONDARY SOURCES

Akizuki Ryōmin 秋月龍珉. *Suzuki Daisetsu* 鈴木大拙. Tokyo: Kōdansha, 2004.
The Eastern Buddhist, First Series. Kyoto: Eastern Buddhist Society, Otani University, 1921–1958; and New Series. Kyoto: Eastern Buddhist Society, Otani University, 1965–2018.
Hisamatsu Shin'ichi 久松真一, Yamaguchi Susumu 山口益, and Furuta Shōkin 古田紹欽, eds. *Suzuki Daisetsu: Hito to shisō* 鈴木大拙: 人と思想. Tokyo: Iwanami Shoten, 1971.
Kirita Kiyohide 桐田清秀, comp. *Suzuki Daisetsu kenkyū kiso shiryō* 鈴木大拙研究基礎資料. Kamakura, Japan: Matsugaoka Bunko, 2005.
Matsugaoka Bunko kenkyū nenpō 松ヶ岡文庫研究年報. Kamakura, Japan: Matsugaoka Bunko, 1987–.
Nishimura Eshin 西村恵信. *Suzuki Daisetsu no genfūkei* 鈴木大拙の原風景. Tokyo: Daitō Shuppan, 1993.
Sargeant, Winthrop. "Great Simplicity." *New Yorker*, August 31, 1957, 34–53.

FURTHER READINGS

Breen, John, Sueki Fumihiko, and Yamada Shōji, eds. *Beyond Zen: D. T. Suzuki and the Modern Transformation of Buddhism*. Honolulu: University of Hawai'i Press, 2022.
Dobbins, James C. "D. T. Suzuki in Transition, 1949–53." *Matsugaoka Bunko kenkyū nenpō* 30 (2016): 47–61.
Dobbins, James C. "D. T. Suzuki." In *Oxford Bibliographies*. Oxford: Oxford University Press, 2022. http://www.oxfordbibliographies.com/.
Dobbins, James C. "D. T. Suzuki: A Brief Account of His Life." *Eastern Buddhist* (Third Series) 2, no. 2 (2022).
Faure, Bernard. *Chan Insights and Oversights: An Epistemological Critique of the Chan Tradition*. Princeton, NJ: Princeton University Press, 1993.
Fields, Rick. *How the Swans Came to the Lake: A Narrative History of Buddhism in America*. Boston: Shambhala, 1992.
Hu Shih. "Ch'an (Zen) Buddhism in China: Its History and Method." *Philosophy East and West* 3, no. 1 (1953): 3–24.
Iwamura, Jane Naomi. *Virtual Orientalism: Asian Religions and American Popular Culture*. Oxford and New York: Oxford University Press, 2011.

Jaffe, Richard M. "Introduction to the 2010 Edition." In *Zen and Japanese Culture*. Edited by Daisetz T. Suzuki, vii–xxviii. Princeton, NJ: Princeton University Press, 2010.
Koestler, Arthur. *The Lotus and the Robot*. London: Hutchinson & Co., 1960.
Moriya Tomoe 守屋友江, ed. and trans. *Zen ni ikiru: Suzuki Daisetsu korekushon* 禅に生きる：鈴木大拙コレクション. Tokyo: Chikuma Shobō, 2012.
Satō, Kemmyō Taira. "D. T. Suzuki and the Question of War." *Eastern Buddhist* (New Series) 39, no. 1 (2008): 61–120.
Sharf, Robert H. "The Zen of Japanese Nationalism." In *Curators of the Buddha*. Edited by Donald S. Lopez Jr., 107–160. Chicago: Chicago University Press, 1995.
Snodgrass, Judith. *Presenting Japanese Buddhism to the West: Orientalism, Occidentalism, and the Columbian Exposition*. Chapel Hill: University of North Carolina Press, 2003.
Tweed, Thomas A. "American Occultism and Japanese Buddhism: Albert J. Edmunds, D. T. Suzuki, and Translocative History." *Japanese Journal of Religious Studies* 32, no. 2 (2005): 249–281.
Victoria, Brian. *Zen at War*. 2nd ed. Oxford: Rowman & Littlefield, 2006.

NOTES

1. Suzuki Daisetsu 鈴木大拙, trans., "*Budda no fukuin* 仏陀の福音*Budda no fukuin* 仏陀の福音," in Suzuki Daisetsu 鈴木大拙, *Suzuki Daisetsu zenshū* 鈴木大拙全集, 40 vols., ed. Hisamatsu Shin'ichi 久松真一, Yamaguchi Susumu 山口晋, and Furuta Shōkin 古田紹欽 (Tokyo: Iwanami Shoten, 1999–2003), 25:275–509. Hereafter, *Suzuki Daisetsu zenshū* is cited as *SDZ*.
2. Daisetz Teitaro Suzuki, *Essays in Zen Buddhism, Series One, Two, and Three* (London: Rider, 1949–1953); *Introduction to Zen Buddhism* (New York: Grove Press, 1964); *The Training of the Zen Buddhist Monk* (New York: Grove Press, 1962); *Manual of Zen Buddhism* (New York: Grove Press, 1960); and *Zen and Its Influence on Japanese Culture* (Kyoto: Eastern Buddhist Society, 1938).
3. William James, *The Varieties of Religious Experience* (London: Longmans, Green, 1902), 31.
4. Daisetz T. Suzuki, "On Satori—The Revelation of a New Truth in Zen Buddhism," in *Selected Works of D. T. Suzuki, Volume 1: Zen*, ed. Richard M. Jaffe (Oakland: University of California Press, 2014), 14–38.
5. Richard M. Jaffe, ed., *Selected Works of D. T. Suzuki, Volume I: Zen*, xxvi (Oakland: University of California Press, 2014), 113; Jeff Wilson and Tomoe Moriya, eds., *Selected Works of D. T. Suzuki, Volume III: Comparative Religion* (Oakland: University of California Press, 2016), 4; and "Emaason no Zengakuron" エマーソンの禅学論, *SDZ* 30:42–50.
6. Daisetz T. Suzuki, "The Koan and The Five Steps," in *Selected Works of D. T. Suzuki, Volume I*, ed. Richard M. Jaffe, 164–188.
7. Daisetz T. Suzuki, "Dōgen, Hakuin, Bankei: Three Types of Thought in Japanese Zen," in *Selected Works of D. T. Suzuki, Volume I*, ed. Richard M. Jaffe, 71–72; and Daisetz T. Suzuki, *Mysticism: Christian and Buddhist* (New York: Macmillan, 1957), 109–119.
8. Bernard Faure, "Suzuki's Zen," in *Chan Insights and Oversights: An Epistemological Critique of the Chan Tradition* (Princeton, NJ: Princeton University Press, 1993), 53–74.
9. Robert H. Sharf, "The Zen of Japanese Nationalism," in *Curators of the Buddha*, ed. Donald S. Lopez Jr. (Chicago: University of Chicago Press, 1995), 112–131, 139–146.
10. Daisetz Teitaro Suzuki, trans., *Aśvaghoṣa's Discourse on the Awakening of Faith in the Mahayana* (Chicago: Open Court, 1900), x–xiv; and Daisetz Teitaro Suzuki, *Outlines of Mahayana Buddhism* (London: Luzac and Company, 1907), v–vii, 16–22.
11. Suzuki, trans., *Aśvaghoṣa's Discourse on the Awakening of Faith in the Mahayana*, 55–106.
12. Daisetz T. Suzuki, "The Mādhyamika School in China" and "Philosophy of the Yogācāra," in *Selected Works of D. T. Suzuki, Volume IV: Buddhist Studies*, ed. Mark L. Blum (Oakland: University of California Press, 2021), 3–10, 44–57.
13. Suzuki, *Outlines of Mahayana Buddhism*.

14. Sasaki Shizuka 佐々木閑, "Yakusha kōki" 訳者後記, in *Daijō Bukkyō gairon* 大乗仏教概論, ed. Suzuki Daisetsu 鈴木大拙 (Tokyo: Iwanami Shoten, 2004), 419–437.
15. Blum, *Selected Works of D. T. Suzuki, Volume IV*, xv, 88–91.
16. Daisetz Teitaro Suzuki, *Studies in the Lankavatara Sutra* (London: Routledge & Sons, 1930).
17. Blum, *Selected Works of D. T. Suzuki, Volume IV*, xx–xxii.
18. Daisetz Teitaro Suzuki, *Daisetz Teitaro Suzuki's Columbia University Seminar Lectures*, ed. Sōiku Shigematsu and Gishin Tokiwa (Kamakura, Japan: Matsugaoka Bunko, 2016).
19. James C. Dobbins, ed., *Selected Works of D. T. Suzuki, Volume II: Pure Land* (Oakland: University of California Press, 2015), ix–x, xx–xxi.
20. Dobbins, *Selected Works of D. T. Suzuki, Volume II*, xxi–xxii.
21. Concerning the Seishinshugi movement, see Mark L. Blum and Robert F. Rhodes, eds., *Cultivating Spirituality: A Modern Shin Buddhist Anthology* (Albany, NY: SUNY Press, 2011).
22. Dobbins, *Selected Works of D. T. Suzuki, Volume II*, xx–xxvii, 1–27, 48–114.
23. *Jōdokei shisōron* 浄土系思想論, *SDZ* 6:1–320; and *Nihon teki reisei* 日本的霊性, *SDZ* 8:1–223.
24. Daisetz T. Suzuki, "Selections from *Japanese Spirituality*," in *Selected Works of D. T. Suzuki, Volume II*, ed. James C. Dobbins, 126–127.
25. *Jōdokei shisōron*, *SDZ* 6:213, 225, 228.
26. Dobbins, *Selected Works of D. T. Suzuki, Volume II*, xxiii–xxiv.
27. Dobbins, *Selected Works of D. T. Suzuki, Volume II*, xx, xxiv–xxv, xxvii–xxviii, 130–146, 147–185, 186–213.
28. Dobbins, *Selected Works of D. T. Suzuki, Volume II*, xxiii, 117, 127–129; and "Shinshū zakkan" 真宗雑観, *SDZ* 31:385–388.
29. Daisetz Teitarō Suzuki, trans., *Gutoku Shaku Shinran, The Kyōgyōshinshō, The Collection of Passages Expounding the True Teaching, Living, Faith, and Realizing of the Pure Land*, ed. Eastern Buddhist Society (Kyoto: Shinshū Ōtaniha, 1973). See also Mark L. Blum, "Standing Alone in the Faith of Non-obedience: Suzuki Daisetsu and Pure Land Buddhism," *Eastern Buddhist* (New Series) 39, no. 2 (2008): 27–68.
30. *Shin shūkyō ron* 新宗教論, *SDZ* 23:1–147.
31. Jason Ananda Josephson, *The Invention of Religion in Japan* (Chicago: University of Chicago Press, 2012).
32. *Shin shūkyō ron*, *SDZ* 23:1–147; and Wilson and Moriya, *Selected Works of D. T. Suzuki, Volume III*, xv–xxi, 3–28.
33. Letter 141 (1902.9.23), *SDZ* 36:222.
34. James, *The Varieties of Religious Experience*, 31.
35. James, *The Varieties of Religious Experience*, 379–382.
36. Daisetz T. Suzuki, "Sayings of a Modern Tariki Mystic," in *Selected Works of D. T. Suzuki, Volume II*, ed. James C. Dobbins, 130–146.
37. Daisetz T. Suzuki, "The Koan Exercise," in *Essays in Zen Buddhism, Second Series*, 28–34; and "Passivity in the Buddhist Life," 267–276.
38. Dobbins, *Selected Works of D. T. Suzuki, Volume II*, xviii–xix; and Wilson and Moriya, *Selected Works of D. T. Suzuki, Volume III*, xxi–xxvi.
39. Daisetz T. Suzuki, "Book Review: *A History of Zen Buddhism* by Heinrich Dumoulin," *Eastern Buddhist* (New Series) 1, no. 1 (1965): 123–126.
40. Jane Naomi Iwamura, *Virtual Orientalism: Asian Religions and American Popular Culture* (Oxford and New York: Oxford University Press, 2011), 23–62.
41. Winthrop Sargeant, "Great Simplicity," *The New Yorker*, August 31, 1957, 34–53.
42. Daisetz T. Suzuki, Erich Fromm, and Richard DeMartino, *Zen Buddhism and Psychoanalysis* (New York: Harper, 1960).

43. Monica Furlong, *Zen Effects: The Life of Alan Watts* (Woodstock, VT: Skylight Paths, 2001); Alan Watts, *The Spirit of Zen* (New York: Grove Press, 1958), and Alan Watts, *The Way of Zen* (New York: Vintage Books, 1989).
44. John Cage, "An Autobiographical Statement"; Kay Larson, *Where the Heart Beats: John Cage, Zen Buddhism, and the Inner Life of Artists* (New York: Penguin, 2012); and Allan Kozinn, "John Cage, 79, a Minimalist Enchanted with Sound, Dies," *New York Times*, August 13, 1992.
45. Jack Kerouac, *Dharma Bums* (New York: Viking Press, 1958); Jack Kerouac, "I rang Mr. Suzuki's door . . . ," in *Berkeley Bussei* (Berkeley, CA: Berkeley Young Buddhist Association, 1960), n.p. Ann Charters, *Kerouac—A Biography* (New York: St. Martin's Press, 1994); and Ellis Amburn, *Subterranean Kerouac—The Hidden Life of Jack Kerouac* (New York: St. Martin's Griffin Press, 1998).
46. Letter 1743 (1956.4.3), *SDZ* 38:330–331; Letter 1971 (1957.6.8), *SDZ* 38:533–534; Letter 2278 (1959.12.16), *SDZ* 39:183–184; Letter 2285 (1960.1.29), *SDZ* 39:190–192; Letter 2286 (1960.1.29), *SDZ* 39:192–194; and Letter 2437 (1962.3.25), *SDZ* 39:304–306.
47. Isabel Stirling, *Zen Pioneer: The Life and Works of Ruth Fuller Sasaki* (Emeryville, CA: Shoemaker and Hoard, 2006); and Janica Anderson and Steven Zahavi Schwartz, *Zen Odyssey: The Story of Sokei-an, Ruth Fuller Sasaki, and the Birth of Zen in America* (Somerville, MA: Wisdom Publications, 2018).
48. Hu Shih, "Ch'an (Zen) Buddhism in China: Its History and Method," *Philosophy East and West* 3, no. 1 (1953): 3–24.
49. Arthur Koestler, *The Lotus and the Robot* (London: Hutchinson & Co., 1960), 227–275.
50. Sharf, "The Zen of Japanese Nationalism," 112–131, 139–146.
51. Faure, "Suzuki's Zen," 53–74.
52. Brian Victoria, *Zen at War*, 2nd ed. (Oxford: Rowman & Littlefield, 2006), 22–29, 105–112, 147–152, 177–178, 208–209.
53. Kemmyō Taira Satō, "D. T. Suzuki and the Question of War," *Eastern Buddhist* (New Series) 39, no. 1 (2008): 61–120; and Nelson Foster and Gary Snyder, "The Fog of World War II: Setting the Record Straight on D. T. Suzuki," *Tricycle* 19, no. 4 (Summer 2010).

James C. Dobbins

DEBATE IN THE TIBETAN TRADITION

INTRODUCTION

In the sense that religious groups and identities are largely defined by differences on matters of doctrine, philosophy, and practice, it is unsurprising that the pages of religious history are replete with accounts of clashes on such matters. Terms such as "debate," "dispute," and "controversy" feature regularly in such accounts, primarily in reference to the substantive *content* of the exchanges. Less attention is generally given to the means by which exchanges have been conducted. And while such exchanges may always have been regulated by sets of customs, it should be recognized that only in certain times and places (and perhaps relatively rarely) have religious traditions developed strict rules and formalized practices regarding the medium and form of exchanges. Such was the case in Tibet.

The generic quality of a term such as "debate" and the wide spectrum of interactions that it could be said to encompass mean that even in the context of Tibetan religion, where there is a clearly identifiable practice, with a name translatable as "debate" (i.e., *rtsod pa*), discussion may lack focus. Hazy notions regarding a Buddhist "tradition" of questioning and inquiry, which some may assert that such a practice of argumentation either reflects or belongs to, can result in confusion regarding categories and history. To develop a clearer understanding, it is necessary to distinguish between different domains (e.g., the written and spoken; content and format) and to tease apart elements within these, which are usually bundled together. Here, therefore, the term "debate" is used specifically in a *technical* sense, to refer to this formalized practice of rules-based, public exchange, denoted by the aforesaid Tibetan term. In order to separate some constituents of the bundle, we turn first to consideration of the practice's history in Tibet.

ORIGIN AND HISTORICAL EVOLUTION

The claim of tradition is that Tibetan monastic debate has its origins in the great Buddhist monastic centers of India, particularly Nālandā and Vikramaśilā, which thrived during medieval times.[1] Events such as the late-8th-century "Samyé debate" are cited in support of assertions about a long history of religious public debate in Tibet. But the evolution of practices in Tibet has been subject to little historical research. Aspects of the traditional narrative of continuity also seem unreliable. Greater clarity, with respect to both the nature of practices and what is known about them, is gained by differentiating between three broad periods of history: (a) the Tibetan imperial era (7th–9th centuries); (b) the postimperial, medieval era (11th–15th centuries); and (c) the late medieval to the modern day.[2] Each appears to be associated with a different stage relating to the practice's evolution, describable, respectively, as the phases of informal practice, formal disputation, and debate.

Regarding the first, we encounter questions about transmission and the relation between Indian and Tibetan practices. Formal debate was undoubtedly practiced in Nālandā and Vikramaśilā.[3] But it cannot be seen as the creation of such Buddhist centers. The philosophical ideas on which this debate facilitated discourse, the procedures of that debate, and the literature concerning itself with both of these were all products of a wider culture of intellectual exchange. The contribution of non-Buddhist philosophical schools, most notably the Nyāya, must be acknowledged. However, despite the clear importance of formal debate to these great Buddhist centers, historical details about how it was actually practiced are scarce. Certain intrepid Tibetans, a number of whom went on to be major translators, gained exposure to these practices during their time at these institutions, but there are no specific accounts of attempts to introduce debate modeled on Indian practices into Tibet. Potentially more significant with regard to transmission were the activities of celebrated monastic figures from the subcontinent, such as Śāntarakṣita (725–788) and Kamalaśīla (740–795). They took up residence in Tibet, had strong ties with the Indian centers, and promoted the analytical brand of Buddhism prevalent in them at the time. This brand made inroads in central Tibet and enjoyed imperial support. *Samyé* (*bSam yas*), Tibet's first monastery, became the early center of intellectual activity and also hosted the so-called Samyé debate, one of the most important subjects of Tibetan religious narrative, between Kamalaśīla and a Chinese opponent (Moheyan). The event is often evoked by those who claim that the practice of religious debate in Tibet has a long and unbroken tradition. But this conflates Indian-origin monastic practices with what could more accurately be characterized as *court debate*, a category to which this encounter more properly belongs. The latter involved representatives of different traditions (chiefly religious) who were summoned to engage in public argumentation for the benefit of a ruler, with outcomes invariably having implications in terms of imperial/royal patronage.[4]

The Samyé discourse was not an isolated event in Tibet. Other court encounters, such as those between representatives of Buddhist and Bön (Bon) traditions, are reported to have occurred during Imperial times. Other confrontations involving Tibetan religious figures were also organized much later, during the Yuan dynasty, when, for instance, Chögyel Pakpa (Chos rgyal 'Phags pa, 1235–1280) was called upon to argue against Daoist representatives before Kublai Khan. The *discourse* element to such public events necessarily involved some formalization, but such accounts as exist suggest a straightforward, question–answer format, with basic adjudication. Nothing indicates the deployment of formalized procedures, strict rules, or technical practices, as probably existed in the Indian centers. Such a specialized format also seems unfeasible, given the nonscholastic backgrounds of most participants and attendees.

Looking beyond such court debates, there is no credible historical evidence that during Imperial times Tibetans either adopted or sought to develop formalized practices for structuring religious discourse within a public context. More specifically, there is no obvious sign of a precursor or antecedent for the later, *highly technical, rules-based* monastic activity. Debate *practice*, however, must be distinguished from other elements with Imperial-era origins that shaped the later scholastic tradition within which debate functioned. The brand of Buddhism promoted by the likes of Śāntarakṣita and Kamalaśīla left a legacy of conceptual frameworks, taxonomies, translated terminology, and a portion of the literature that would eventually be regarded as part of a scholastic canon. Certain other aspects of religious activity during Imperial times, particularly the methodical manner in which translation was approached within a state-sponsored project, also seem influenced by the analytical, scholastic brand of Buddhism. It should also be noted that several, mainly shorter works relating to Buddhist logic were translated into Tibetan during the Imperial period. But in the sphere of monastic *learning*, evidence of systematization and the enshrinement of institutional practices is more tenuous.

The second phase, during which formalized practices appear to have emerged, coincides with the start of the so-called later dissemination (*phyi dar*) of Buddhism in Tibet, during which, from the 11th century onward, there was an upsurge in translation activity, a fresh influx of teachings and teachers, and a series of major intellectual and artistic developments, particularly evident in the central and western regions. Perhaps most significantly, concerted efforts were made to create a solid institutional basis for monastic Buddhism. Here, the role played by the monastery of Sangpu (gSang phu ne'u thog), close to Lhasa, proved vital. This was founded in 1073 by Ngok Lekpé shérap (rNgogs Legs pa'i shes rab, fl. 11th century), an immediate disciple of Dīpaṃkara Śrījñāna (982–1054), the Bengali teacher (popularly known as Atiśa), who evolved (both in reality and in the imagination) into perhaps the preeminent figure of the Tibetan later dissemination. Atiśa's Tibetan followers developed a religious tradition they referred to as *Kadam* (*bKa' gdams*). But Sangpu's alignment with the tradition was loose, and with the accession of the second abbot, Ngok Loden shérap (rNgogs Blo ldan shes rab, 1059–1109), "nephew" of the monastery's founder, activities there took a distinctive intellectual turn. Loden shérap was a major translator, who had earlier spent time in Kashmir and took a keen interest in logic.

In terms of theory (as already advanced in Tibet by Śāntarakṣita and Kamalaśīla), the Buddhist practitioner should strive for perception of higher truths through meditation, but the initial route to these, and knowledge beyond the mundane, was inference. Reliable inference depended on logical principles and the ability to recognize whether particular proofs met stipulated criteria. An interest in logic, and specifically the treatises of the Indian *pramāṇa* (logico-epistemological) tradition, could therefore be justified in terms of spiritual goals. The importance of the *pramāṇa* tradition, and the works of its two chief thinkers, Dignāga and Dharmakīrti (5th/6th and 7th centuries CE, respectively), had already been recognized in other Buddhist monastic traditions in Japan, China, and Korea. In some of these, *logic*, as presented in the *pramāṇa* works, was studied as a separate branch of Buddhist learning. In Tibet, Loden shérap was the first to translate certain major works of Dharmakīrti, thereby bringing the *pramāṇa* system to wider Tibetan attention within an *institutional setting*.

Crucially, at Sangpu, rather than merely being considered a distinct topic, logic began to inform the approach to other areas of study and galvanized the organization of learning. It was at Sangpu that, apparently for the first time in Tibet, an institutional model for monastic education was successfully developed, eventually resulting in the formation of a scholastic curriculum, innovations in the field of educational materials, and the creation of a system of examinations and titles.[5] Convinced of the efficacy of the analytical approach and the place of logic within it, Sangpu scholars seem to have developed a logical method, designed to achieve not so much the more distant goals of spiritual realization already alluded to, but the more immediate ones, of structuring discourse. Logical structure, it was believed, should guide and inform dialectical discourse, something that was realized in the creation of a rules-based form of exchange, suiting employment in public situations. Popular tradition identifies Sangpu's sixth abbot, Chapa Chökyi sengé (Phwya pa Chos kyi seng ge, 1109–1169), with certain significant changes to practices (to be discussed later). The formalized practices appear to have spread widely through central Tibet, the main area of medieval Tibetan scholastic activity, as the Sangpu model gained in popularity, and seem largely to have been embraced by major monastic centers entirely independent of Sangpu, such as Sakya (Sa skya), despite some early misgivings.[6] By the late 13th or early 14th century, reliance on the characteristic "language," the formalized medium of dialectical discourse (to be discussed in the section "Tibetan Innovation: Shifting Discourse"), was standard. As will become clear in the section "Debate Session: Form and Structure," certain features of logic and content link medieval practices with those of subsequent times (i.e., the third phase, encompassing the present). And although much remains to be discovered about the exact nature of the medieval ones, aspects of their form, and more importantly their context and purpose, distinguished them from later ones. In recognition of this distinction, and in acknowledgment of certain correspondences with contemporaneous practices of European scholasticism, it seems appropriate to use the term "disputation" to denote the medieval Tibetan practice. Such disputation, as a method and practice, was employed during that era both in an educational context and for public confrontations between established scholars.

The differences between medieval disputation and the debate of the later, third phase are not discussed further here.[7] The exact process of transition from one to the other requires further research. But the rise of the Geluk school (from the 15th century onward) and its eventual dominance within the Tibetan state (from the 17th century) are heavily implicated in changes that occurred within the realm of practice. Geluk power (stretching far beyond the religious sphere) became concentrated in its major monastic institutions, especially the "three seats" near Lhasa.[8] As scholastic centers, these adopted a Sangpu-inspired model, emphasizing the importance of dialectical learning. Burgeoning institutional power, combined with growing insularity, contributed to an increased emphasis on debate, which established itself as the primary medium for learning and examination. Debate also became invested with substantial symbolic power. During the Mönlam or Great Prayer Festival (sMon lam chen mo) in Lhasa, an annual event, originally created in 1409 by Tsong kha pa (commonly described as the founder of the Geluk school), debate eventually formed a centerpiece, with those seeking the highest scholastic degree subjected to public examination. This huge gathering of monks from the three seats served as a showcase for Geluk power, the prominence of debate within the spectacle impressing upon the wider consciousness its importance within the Geluk order.

While this power nexus only took its ultimate form in the 19th and 20th centuries, evidence of continuity in debate practice itself comes to us in a rare account by an outsider, the Jesuit missionary Ippolito Desideri (1684–1733), who was resident in Tibet between 1717 and 1721. Desideri set out to master the Tibetan scholastic system, and the debate practices that he describes closely correspond with those of today.[9]

LOGICAL UNDERPINNINGS

The chief inspiration behind the structure of discourse in Tibetan debate is a system of logic that originated in India. Tibetan scholars identified this system with the Indian Buddhist *pramāṇa* tradition, as expounded by its chief exponents, Dignāga and his principal commentator, Dharmakīrti. The writings of these two have served as the main sources for the Tibetan debate tradition. Tibetan scholars have tended to depict this system of logic as exclusively Buddhist. More correctly, many elements within it should be seen as belonging to a shared Indian tradition. Buddhist logicians such as Dignāga and Dharmakīrti built upon centuries of earlier work. It is in Nyāya and Vaiśeṣika literature that we see the first moves toward the formulation of logic and the structuring of discourse through rules. In this section, the emphasis is on the Tibetan interpretation of that Indian heritage, but there is much here that would be entirely recognizable to logicians of the Nyāya, Vaiśeṣika, and Jain traditions. Certain similarities with Aristotelian logic may also seem apparent. The logic of the Indian system is, however, quite distinct. Trying to understand its formulations through the prism of the Western syllogism is misleading, and where terms such as "proof" are used here, they refer to the system's own concepts, not those familiar from the Western context.

A stock exemplar used in the tradition, for the purposes of analysis and demonstration, is:

On the smoky mountain (*A*)
There is fire (*B*),
Because there is smoke (*C*),
As in a kitchen hearth (*D*).

That is, according to the Tibetan understanding of Dignāga and Dharmakīrti's system, a correct logical assertion should take the following form:

A is *B* because of being *C*, as is the case with *D*.

The constituents are the subject (*A*), the predicate (*B*), the reason (*C*), and the example (*D*). The combination of the first two ("*A* is *B*") forms the probandum, that which needs to be proved. The reason is used to establish the probandum, and the example is cited in support. The copula "is" can indicate various forms of relationship, such as, in the exemplar, that in location *A*, there is *B*. The whole formulation constitutes a logical proof. Such proofs may be either correct or flawed. A correct proof rests on two bases: first, that C is a property of *A* (in the exemplar, that there is smoke on the mountain in question), and second, that where there is C there is *B* (i.e., that where there is smoke there is fire). The second, *C*'s concomitant relationship with *B*, is known as the "pervasion" (Sanskrit: *vyāpti*; Tibetan: *khyab pa*). Thus, the proof combines the particular (the specific smoke) with the general (that smoke is always related to fire). It is by means of logical proofs that one can move from the domain of perceptual to inferential knowledge; that is, one can *know* something beyond the realm of immediate experience. The cornerstone of this *pramāṇa* theory is that an inference arising from correct logic constitutes certain and indisputable knowledge—*pramāṇa*. In the Buddhist context, *pramāṇa* refers, primarily, to the epistemic instrument through which such knowledge is gained. Hence, *pramāṇa* is generally translated as "valid cognition" (*tshad ma*). Logical principles, once understood in terms of mundane phenomena, such as smoke and fire, are then supposed to be applied to inferences about more obscure phenomena, including technical and abstract features of the Buddhist spiritual path.

The *pramāṇa* tradition is concerned with not only how the individual can use logic to gain inferential knowledge personally, but also how an individual can bring about inferences (i.e., correct inferential knowledge) in another party. The state of that party's knowledge is a factor here. Our exemplar is generally regarded as a correct proof, but if it was presented to a second party who was unable to perceive the smoke in question or did not know that where there is smoke there is fire, it would not yield a correct inference. Moreover, a second party may not be amenable to generating a correct inference if that second party trenchantly believes in a contrary position. Much *pramāṇa* literature is devoted to identifying spurious philosophical views, which it attributes to various non-Buddhist and Buddhist schools. But it also expounds an argumentation theory. Here we encounter a crucial variant of the earlier logical form, known as the "consequence" (Sanskrit: *prasaṅga*; Tibetan: *thal 'gyur*), which is especially relevant to debate. Secondary literature frequently describes the consequence as a *reductio ad absurdum* argument. As such, it is most regularly associated with the method employed in Madhyamaka Buddhist philosophy, particularly by its most celebrated proponent, Nāgārjuna. To Tibetan scholars, the consequence seemed critical to distinguishing divergent positions among Nāgārjuna's commentators and had a central role in discussions on Madhyamaka philosophy and soteriology. In the *pramāṇa* writings (especially those of Tibet), the consequence is not linked to any such single issue, and its treatment, within argumentation theory, is more systematic.

The consequence largely dispenses with the example (*D*). But aside from this, the constituents are the same as those of the logical proof. The consequence is supposed to be deployed during a structured exchange between two parties, when one party wants to expose a flaw in the second party's position and to demonstrate, thereby, that the position is unsustainable. The consequence's basic form is:

It follows (therefore) that *A* is *B*, because of being *C*.

The consequence coopts a position held by the second party to reach a conclusion that the same party is unable to accept. That party must be someone who, elsewhere, has asserted that *A* is *C*. It must also be the case, for the same party, that if something is *C*, it is necessarily also *B* (or, in many cases, simply that *C* entails *B*). But the conclusion, that *A* is *B*, is one that contradicts another of the second party's positions. A correct logical proof must be rooted in fact; *A* actually is *C*, and so on. This is not a requirement of a correct consequence. It need only be the case that its conclusion derives from the second party's own assertion. The consequence is not designed to lead to an "absurd" conclusion. Instead, it is intended to leave the second party with no means of response, save that of relinquishing one of the positions held by that party. Hence, the consequence's frame of reference differs markedly from that of the logical proof. Consequences are conceived of within a framework of argumentation theory. Discussions about their usage necessarily concern themselves more with errant views than with correct ones. They also put greater emphasis on interaction and outcome than on striving for the truth. What has been set out in this section, it should be stressed, relates mainly to the theory behind employment of the consequence. Let us next consider the consequence's relevance to the evolution of debate in Tibet.

TIBETAN INNOVATION: SHIFTING DISCOURSE

Despite proclaimed loyalty to the *pramāṇa* tradition, as historical writings attest, Tibetan thinkers put their own slant on that tradition's writings and, with regard to logic, made their own contributions. The topic of these Tibetan variations is well represented in academic literature. But here, focusing on debate *practice*, our attention is drawn to Chapa Chökyi sengé (the sixth abbot of Sangpu) and the various important changes that popular tradition attributes to him. He is particularly associated with the introduction of the consequence format and, according to some, even the creation of the distinctive physical gestures that accompany debate (to be discussed in the section "Debate Session: Form and Structure"). Chapa Chökyi sengé was undoubtedly a significant figure and important writer.[10] But in terms of historical documentation, the precise nature of his innovations remains unclear. Nevertheless, it is at least consistent with current evidence that by the mid- to late 12th century a set of formalized practices was being used at Sangpu to structure dialectical discourse.

From the 12th century, we see the emergence in literature of the *debate language*. A lexicon of technical terms, useful for certain classificatory and descriptive purposes, can be thought of as one component of the language. But it is chiefly to be understood as a standardized medium, by means of which arguments (and responses) could be formulated and communicated. The language has various features, including an idiosyncratic use of personal pronouns in place of demonstratives.[11] But its most significant trait is its clear marking of the individual portions that the proof or consequence comprises. These elements are, respectively, the subject (*A*), predicate (*B*), and reason (*C*). The language distinguishes each by means of separate affixes—*chos can* (*A*), *te* and so forth (*B*–proof), *thal* (*B*–consequence), and *phyir* (*C*). In addition to clearly identifying and delineating each portion, these markers also largely determine the order in which they are to be presented (here implied by the *A*–*B*–*C* formulation). Although certain components of the language existed earlier, by the 12th century it had essentially reached its final form and began to be applied systematically and prescriptively. Although it is easy to see the language as ancillary to content, the extent to which its application shaped discourse, transforming it into a highly formulaic affair, is difficult to exaggerate. The introduction of the language (i.e., primarily the standardized form of the "marked" consequence) must be seen as the seminal event in terms of the Tibetan debate tradition. Several observations can be made about this introduction, all of which are relevant to understanding the direction and form of later practice:

1. Whether employed in the written or verbal domain, the language was intended to bring greater clarity to the positions held by individuals and whatever criticism others might wish to make of them. In this regard the introduction was largely a success, creating both a tool of analysis, by means of which the merits and implications of various positions and arguments could be subjected to scrutiny, and a medium of communication between two parties seeking exchange on these matters.
2. Analysis or discourse structured around the consequence format necessarily lends itself primarily to critiquing. It is neither designed, nor particularly able, to accommodate the *presentation* of an argument.
3. Not only does the language serve as the vehicle for the formulation and delivery of a criticism, structurally, it also dictates the form that the answer to it must take. The only effective means of responding to a consequence is to do so directly, *in its own terms*. This limits the options of response to three. An individual can either (a) accept the conclusion, (b) deny the relationship of C to *A* (that the reason is true of the subject), or (c) deny the pervasion (that C entails *B*). Expressed in terms of the debate language, these are reduced to three terse replies: (a) "(I) accept" (*'dod*), (b) "Reason not established" (*rtags ma grub*), or (c) "No pervasion" (*ma khyab* or *khyab pa ma byung*). Reference is occasionally made to a fourth answer, but this is simply a demand that the reason be stated where it has temporarily been withheld—something expressed as "For what reason?" (*ci'i phyir*).
4. The challenge–response structure helps define two distinct roles within the exchange. But, particularly through the restrictions it places on responses, it creates an asymmetrical dynamic between the two participants.
5. The language's introduction clearly pushes exchanges into a more technical sphere. Quite apart from knowledge of the content, participation in discourse requires mastery of the language and, by implication, some form of training. A new dimension to exchanges is also necessarily opened up, with questions about whether the language has been employed correctly, further contestation about how correct usage is to be defined, and so forth.

While insufficient to *explain* the direction that dialectical discourse in Tibet took, highlighting these attributes helps us understand how decisive the introduction of the format was and how it appears to have launched practice on a particular trajectory. A format that may have been intended to bring greater precision to exchanges and purge them of extraneous content may seem, in its sparse, pared-down style, to lend itself to procedure and, if rigidly enforced, to have the potential to impede the free flow of discourse and ideas.

The language is regarded as characteristic of both dialectical literature and debate practice. The tendency has been to look to historical writings (commentaries and treatises) by Tibetan authors for clues about the introduction of such features as the consequence form. But the assumption that innovations would necessarily have originated or found their first expression in the literary sphere, only later to be introduced into that of practice, seems questionable. There are no manuals of instruction for the language, even in the recently rediscovered writings of Chapa Chökyi sengé. Furthermore, particularly given the general Tibetan literary compulsion toward elaboration and ornamentation, the terse, repetitious style of the language is far more reminiscent of a verbal formulation, designed to encourage rapid interactions, rather than a literary one.

CURRENT PRACTICE

Debate within the Context of Monastic Education. In recent years, especially in Tibetan exile communities, the range of those introduced to debate has expanded to include nuns, lay college students, and even schoolchildren.

Traditionally, however, debate has overwhelmingly been regarded as the province of monks, pursuing a particular style of learning, culminating in the awarding of a scholastic degree and title. The best-known scholastic title, that of *geshé* (*dge bshes*), is now especially associated with the Geluk school. Debate also plays a significant role in other monastic educational programs, all of which have a scholastic dimension, even though their curricula and the titles they lead to—including *kachen* (*dka' chen*), *rapjampa* (*rab 'byams pa*), and *khenpo* (*mkhan po*)—differ. One or more of such programs and titles are found in every school of Tibetan Buddhism and also in the Bön tradition, despite varied and sometimes complex relations with the scholastic approach. The growing appreciation of its rigor and uniqueness has, in recent years, resulted in debate's becoming a more pervasive feature of Tibetan learning. The profile of debate within religious schools and monastic institutions differs, but it is in the main scholastic centers of the Geluk that debate and the culture surrounding it are at their most robust.[12] The remainder of this article focuses on debate within the Geluk educational system, although much of what is set out here is extendable far beyond the Geluk centers.

The scholastic curriculum is divided into two branches: topics of preliminary study and the principal, core topics. The five core topics (*Prajñāpāramitā, Pramāṇa, Madhyamaka, Abhidharma*, and *Vinaya*) are not individual texts, as suggested by their collective designation, "the five major tomes" (*gzhung chen po ti lnga*), but rather *areas* of study, albeit each organized around a single "root" text, of Indian origin, which has spawned a sizeable corpus of Indian and Tibetan commentarial writings. Study of both preliminary and core topics is organized into classes, through which the student progresses annually, following examination. Students who complete the classes on the curriculum and pass the examinations are eligible for final testing, by means of which they can gain the title of *geshé*. Previously, the whole process in Tibet, which might take twenty or more years, was regularly protracted in its latter stages, with candidates obliged to wait for final examination. The time required for completion is now shorter but can still be expected to be twelve or more years, with an average of one or two years spent on the preliminaries and the remainder on the core topics.

Debate, it is essential to note, is the key pedagogical method within this scholastic system, *not* a separate field of study, and the approach to it is entirely heuristic. Students receive no classes or separate instructions on debate, or on the theory and technique of argumentation.

The debate method is one they must learn through observation and imitation, somewhat akin to the process of informal language acquisition, the initial challenge simply being to grasp the basics of comprehension and communication. The model of learning involves three mutually dependent educational activities, performed in discrete locations. These are (a) memorization, (b) class learning, and (c) debate. Memorization is not organized formally but engaged in, like text reading, during self-study time, usually in or around the student's room or some accommodating open space. Students are required to equip themselves for participation in class and debate sessions. The system's great emphasis on committing material to memory, rendering it instantly retrievable in the appropriate public setting, without the support of the physical text, places great demands on the memory. In addition to numerous definitions, divisions, and individual fragments of quotation, the students must memorize the root texts, large portions of their manuals (which are discussed in the following section, "Materials and Topics of Debate"), and other relevant commentarial writings. The prodigious ability they develop to acquire material, in terms of both amount and speed, derives not from complex techniques but from daily practice and rhythmic recitation. Memorization is never a silent exercise, and there is no notion of reciting with excessive volume.

The second activity, performed in a classroom or some other indoor venue, is generally confined to a single daily session. As reflected in the activity's name (*dpe khrid*), which literally means "leading (through the) text," this is not a lecture, but a session during which a teacher walks the students through that section of the prescribed work the class has reached. Students receive instruction on the basic import of the words and the issues being addressed. But the session, like the texts themselves, is largely structured dialectically. The teacher's role is that of stimulating discussion and not of offering definitive answers. As various arguments and counterarguments are considered, the teacher can usually be relied on to adopt the position contrary to that of the students. The whole process thereby supplies food for the day's debate sessions. The final component (which is discussed at more length in the section "Debate Session: Form and Structure") is the debate session itself. In terms of both duration and frequency, debate sessions exceed class sessions roughly on a ratio of three to one. Debate sessions are long (rarely less than a couple of hours each) and are conducted in an open, dedicated space. This is the "debate ground" (*chos ra/grwa*)—an unenclosed area, usually paved, and loosely surrounded or interspersed with trees—from which the debate session itself derives its name.

As debate has constituted the central method of learning, unsurprisingly it has also served as the medium for examination during both annual and final testing. Only in recent decades, in a trend that began in exile, has a written component been added to examination procedures. Examination by debate has always been public, in the sense of having been conducted before the monastic assembly. But the Mönlam in Lhasa created an additional dimension to public testing. There are different subcategories of *geshé*, the highest being the *lha-ram* (*lha rams*). Those in the *lha-ram* class have also been ranked, based on their performance in the annual public debates, traditionally performed at the festival. Hence, a great deal of prestige has been attached to the titles, especially linked with these public performances.[13]

Materials and Topics of Debate. The written materials that serve as the direct basis for the classes and which students are expected to have the most intimate knowledge of favor a debate format. Although, as already mentioned, the core topics are each associated with a root text, the curriculum's preliminary subjects are not drawn directly from Indian works. They are based on Tibetan writings that condense and codify information, mainly from the *pramāṇa* tradition. These works, in terms of both their genre and content, have their origins in Sangpu and have principally been developed as educational materials, supporting the scholastic model's style of knowledge transmission. The first and most important of the primer materials is the "Collected Topics" (*bsDus grwa*). This is followed by two more (*Blo rig/rigs* and *rTags rig/rigs*) dealing respectively with fundamentals of epistemology and logical reasons (categories, definitions, etc.). The Collected Topics writings comprise almost exclusively paradigmatic debates. While providing no direct explanation or instruction, they help beginners become acquainted with debate through their organization and gradual introduction of topics. The first chapter begins with relatively straightforward material (starting with categories of colors and shapes). However, much in the Collected Topics is highly abstruse and is evidently intended to fuel debate, rather than provide any simple lessons.

For study of the core topics, although materials are organized around and always refer back to their respective Indian roots, students primarily learn from what are often described as "manuals" (*yig cha*). Individual monasteries or colleges within them have their own manuals, generally a collection of works by a single author (the majority hailing from the 15th and 16th centuries). The manual has two main genres, which are employed in tandem. Those of the first type (entitled *spyi don*) are more structured and present the divisions, definitions, debates, and passages of commentary that are understood to delineate a particular topic. Works of the second genre (*mtha' dpyod*) contain only debates. The topic is, therefore, predominantly explored through a series of debates or dialectically structured discourses, which generally present the responses of "our own system" to challenges mounted to it by various anonymous opponents. Thus, debates regularly begin with the phrase "someone says" (*kha cig*).

While debates clearly identify "incorrect" interpretations and stances, they do not always end with clear-cut conclusions or unambiguous statements about what constitutes the correct one. An understanding of what represents "our own system" emerges gradually, largely *through negation*, and is subject to increasing refinement. Despite the tradition's professed commitment to reasoned analysis, "our system" is underpinned by numerous implicit and largely unquestioned articles of faith. However, it is difficult to characterize it as a doctrine, and the scholastic approach, if it were intended to transmit such a thing, could well be deemed a colossal failure. Instead, the system is more concerned with inculcating a correct way of thinking, which could, theoretically, be applied to the analysis and understanding of matters on which textbooks offer only limited clarity or guidance.

The material covered in the program of scholastic classes follows, somewhat loosely, the order of their presentation in the chosen root texts. But it is commentarial writings that organize the material into distinct topics. The manuals have a special role in processing this material, identifying points of contention, bringing greater clarity to the issues, and implicitly determining what is, from the scholastic perspective, significant and worthy of interest. In this sense, with regard to the realm of debate, the manuals and their authors perform gatekeeper roles.

The range of topics debated during the course of the long education can only be dealt with cursorily here. But outlined generally, the commentarial tradition is preoccupied with the exact meaning of terms, phrases, and statements in the root texts, scriptures, and so forth. Correct understanding of these is supposed to reveal the actual intent of their authors, and ultimately the buddha. Because of this proclaimed goal, debates, like the commentarial writings, begin in specific sections of the source materials (a point elaborated on in the section "Debate Session: Form and Structure"). The areas and issues seen as debate's natural territory relate to the philosophical, hermeneutical, logical, and epistemological. In terms of material, no real divide is acknowledged between content and form: technical matters regarding an argument's formulation and criteria pertaining to it are of as much interest as what the argument conveys. Definitions, correct and incorrect, are a favorite topic of debate, and the term roughly translatable as "definition" (*mtshan nyid*) at least partly informs the name of the scholastic approach.

Related to its interest in meaning and import (inside the textual domain), debate is concerned with principles and generalities; its concern with particulars is only to the extent that they may instantiate these. Conversely, *specific* individuals, events, and circumstances, in all their unpredictability and unrepresentativeness, are seen as deficient in abstract value. Accordingly, debate is disinterested in such things as history, current affairs, and popular issues. It is also closed to new interpretations. The tradition projects a notion of debate-worthiness that does not simply inform discourse but verges on the proscriptive. It is also notable that debate practice appears always to have been confined to the scholastic domain: its techniques seem never to have been extended to other fields. Even within the monastic setting, it has also been restricted to the *scholastic* rather than the broader curriculum. Ritual, liturgy, grammar, poetry, tantra, and meditation, among others, have generally been seen as areas worthy of monastic attention and learning. Several also have corpuses of scholarly writing (e.g., commentarial) associated with them, which monks may receive teachings on. But these are generally not seen as territory for debate. Even in terms of the core curriculum, during study of *Abhidharma* and *Vinaya* (the latter two of the five areas), debate is a more muted, "senior" affair, devoted to sedentary reckoning and enumeration. It is in the study of the first three areas that the real energy and passion of debate are truly evident.

The Debate Session: Form and Structure. We return to the debate ground for a more detailed look at practice there.[14] This description contains few Tibetan terms (technical or otherwise), it being a curious fact that some of the most basic and important elements within the domain of practice lack names. Those who enter the ground for the session carry only a cushion/mat (*gdan*) and a string of religious beads (*phreng ba*). Reflecting the emphasis on memory and orality, the texts (e.g., manuals) are not permitted in the space. Debate sessions are convened at the same times each day, and all monk students, from complete beginners to the most senior, participate. Debate has only two forms of configuration: paired and group encounters. All participants on the debate ground are generally arranged, *simultaneously*, in either the first or the second configuration. Daily debate is principally between classmates, who mainly work in pairs. Individuals choose their partners for the session at its commencement. A debate has two distinct roles, those of *challenger* and *respondent*, most commonly referred to simply as "the one who debates" and "the one who answers" (with phrases such as *rtags gsal gtong mkhan* and *lan rgyag mkhan*).[15] Hence, it is also decided, by the participants, which of the roles each will adopt, although these may be switched later in the session. As is implied by the English terms used here for these roles, the debate is not an open discourse, but neither is it conducted in the style of a simple interrogation. Every aspect of the interaction is governed by the assigned roles. On the physical level, this manifests in the respondent being required to sit cross-legged on his cushion/mat, while the challenger must stand. The debate language is the required medium of communication, with arguments presented in consequence form and responses limited to the three/four outlined earlier. Only the challenger, whose role is dominant, may present arguments, choose what is debated, and generally steer the course of the interaction. The respondent should, upon the challenger's signal, answer sparsely, without elaboration (unless invited to do otherwise). The overriding duty of the participants is to perform their assigned roles well. These roles are oppositional and there are various resonances with those performed by parties arguing for the prosecution and defense in an adversarial legal system, as there are with aspects of procedure and various contrived features of the exercise.

Neither the session nor the individual encounters within them has any predetermined topic, although daily debates are expected to explore material covered in recent classes. The debate generally begins with the challenger citing a few words of text, then calling on the respondent to identify their source, locate them within the textual scheme, and explain their meaning. Even these "questions" must be formulated, verbally, as consequences, despite the empty meaning of the phrase "it follows." During these opening exchanges, in what is effectively the debate's orientation stage, the scheme of the root and commentarial overlay are partially rehearsed and mapped out, something essential both to the learning process and to situating the discussion. But this stage is only preparatory to the real debate. The challenger is either seeking or leading toward an entry point, through which an attack can be launched.

Thus, the challenger tries to find an identifiable position attributable to the respondent, which it can be argued leads to an unwanted consequence. The presentation of an unwanted consequence, followed by the response to it, is the basic pattern of exchange between the two parties. But as the respondent is essentially limited to either conceding or denying the fault, an exchange structured around a single consequence-criticism (and response) would be a short-lived one, resulting in immediate submission or stalemate. There would be nothing to sustain the process or any benefit to derive from it. Hence, the respondent inevitably rebuts the criticism, at which point the challenger presents a new consequence. If, for example, the challenger's argument, "It follows that *A* is *B* because of *C*," is met with the respondent denying the reason (that C is true of *A*), the challenger would commonly present another consequence, centering on the relationship between *C* and *A*, and so forth. Thus, the interaction is made up of the challenger constantly reconfiguring critical consequences, based on the responses. Each new consequence is meant to be related to and in some way derive from what has preceded it. The challenger's approach is sometimes described as one that uses "chains of consequence" (*thal phreng*). Although the process is represented as "logical," the progress from one consequence to the next is not always linear, nor is debate so systematic as to deal with and settle each individual issue before moving to the next.

In more general terms, the method employed by the challenger can be characterized as one that employs *dissonance* as procedure. He introduces passages of text or lines of reasoning that seem to conflict with the respondent's answers. The task of the respondent is, ostensibly, to resolve the apparent contradictions. But the other aspect of the challenger's role is more affirmative, since he must constantly search for potential links between textual passages, lines of reason, and the respondent's answers, hoping to discover new avenues of attack. As part of the daily grind, especially for those with insufficient familiarity or motivation, debate can sometimes be a meandering and unproductive affair, in which the challenges lack strategy and the responses are evasive. However, in the hands of keen and conversant interlocutors, the process is far more constructive. Although the debate does not begin with a stated position or thesis from either side, the challenger may follow a well-considered plan, structured around the answers expected of the respondent. The respondent may either choose or be pushed into adopting a particular line, and occasionally, a clearly defined stance may emerge through the exchange. This "basic thesis" (*rtsa ba'i dam bca'*) will henceforth serve as the challenger's main target. While more generally the challenger aims to entangle the respondent within a web of conflicting and unsustainable positions, ultimately he will attempt to assert chains of entailment, leading back to the basic thesis. As the respondent's role is to resist the challenger, he cannot afford to relinquish this thesis and must try to block potential routes back to it. Debate can, therefore, develop into a highly sophisticated contest, with each participant anticipating the likely moves of the opponent and seeking to thwart them by taking appropriate measures.

One of debate's most striking features, which further emphasizes the dominance of the challenger's role, is the use of physical gestures and movement. As the challenger is about to finish his point, he raises his left foot above the ground, projecting it forward. He also extends the left arm forward and bends the right arm back, above his head. Coinciding with the final words of his articulation, he simultaneously brings the left foot and the right arm down, both stamping on the ground and clapping in the respondent's direction. The clapping motion is a stylish one, which ends with the string of beads being gripped by the right hand and drawn up the left arm, around which they are wrapped. The two further gestures at the challenger's disposal involve him hitting the back of the right hand against the palm of his left, while calling out *tsha* (the exact spelling and etymology of which is not agreed upon) and that in which he circles the beads around the head of the respondent while uttering a phrase that literally means "three spheres" (*'khor gsum*). The first indicates the challenger asserting that the respondent has lost the point, the second that he has, in some way, contradicted himself. Various explanations have been advanced about what is denoted by the "three spheres." But none of them is entirely consistent with usage on the debate ground or in historical debate literature. While the basic pattern of these movements is fixed, there is a considerable range of expression within them. As the debate begins, the challenger's gestures are more restrained. But having dispensed with the procedural niceties, he binds the upper part of his robes around his waist, creating a more workmanlike and imposing impression. And as discussion continues and grows more heated, gestures and movements become more animated. The challenger may also pace and prowl around the respondent. As the general noise of the debate ground grows, voices are necessarily raised, the clapping becomes more audible, and the stamping more vigorous. Displays of exuberance are common and the gestures, which become more exaggerated, are clearly used in an intimidatory fashion. This, combined with the growing rapidity of the exchanges, creates further pressure on the respondent, increasing the likelihood of errors.

The group debate (popularly referred to as *dam bca'*) is largely an extension of the paired exchange. Generally, there are two respondents, seated beside each other, referred to as "those who sit for the group debate" (*dam bca' la sdod mkhan*, shortened to *dam bca'*).

Other monks sit in parallel opposing ranks, at right angles to the respondents, so that an empty aisle is formed in front of them, in which the challenger(s) move. Each debate begins with a single challenger, who will soon be joined by companions. The respondents may, therefore, be faced by a relatively large group of assailants. The audience members also generally act in support of the challenge. If they feel that the respondent has taken too long to answer, they will clap and shout the final word of the consequence formula (*phyir*) in unison three times (or, more occasionally, once).[16] Predictably, serving as respondent in a group debate (sometimes referred to as "defense") is regarded as the most testing of roles.

Another remarkable feature of debate, distinguishing it from the adversarial contests of courtrooms and medieval universities, is the absence of any third-party role. Debate is generally an unsupervised affair. Teachers, senior scholars, and those serving in a disciplinary role are prone to wandering around the debate ground and may stop to listen and occasionally intervene—the debate ground setup, generally, encourages such circulation and interaction between those of different levels. But students are largely left to their own devices. Most strikingly, there is nothing equivalent to a moderator or adjudicator. Hence, while the audience and participants have their own perceptions regarding the quality of performances, there are no rulings or judgments about which individual or position has prevailed.

Debate clearly benefits its practitioners, increasing their knowledge of and familiarity with the material, but also allowing them to venture into and test new waters. It also greatly develops verbal skills, dexterity of thinking, and powers of reasoning, and even fosters some degree of creativity. But as a process it is not designed to reach any outcomes, final decisions, or resolutions. And the only conclusions it reaches are those imposed by time. This aspect can prove perplexing to outside observers. Other features of debate, especially its physicality, volubility, provocative gesturing, and generally confrontational nature, have also regularly attracted criticism from those favoring more quiescent approaches to Buddhism. And those explaining debate regularly find themselves having to defend the practice, which itself represents an interesting comment on cultural interfaces and stereotypes of religious expression.

Despite the undeniable rigidity of the debate structure, exemplified by reliance on the language, exchanges can be more expansive than the format might immediately suggest.

Discussion frequently strays outside the prescribed parameters, giving way to bursts of more open discourse and exploration of the topic—"digressions," which it is the challenger's prerogative to allow. There are also other dimensions to the practice beyond those relating to religion and logic. The quickfire nature of the exchanges is, for instance, ideal for sharpening the wits, and humor is a prized feature of exchanges.[17] The verbal jousting and performative aspects of debate have only rarely been touched on. Only more recently have anthropological perspectives on debate been taken more seriously. Given debate's resilience and longevity, its centrality to a dominant religious system, and the fact that it remains the main daily practice for thousands of those within the Tibetan cultural sphere, it is perhaps surprising that it has not been the subject of more extensive and varied research.

DISCUSSION OF THE LITERATURE

Academic understanding of debate relies heavily on the Collected Topics writings. Notable early studies include those of Goldberg, Onoda, and Perdue.[18] These studies focus on the works' contents, that is, their topics and individual debates, with particular interest given to the logic employed and the theory behind it.

Although Goldberg's analysis has been criticized for being overly etic, all these studies are informative and help convey the sense of a characteristically Tibetan tradition. Some more recent significant work, such as Tillemans, exploring relations with Indian *pramāṇa* writings, and Hugon, on Chapa Chökyi sengé's use of consequences, help us to better understand the intellectual progression of logic and theory within a tradition of interpretation.[19]

The heft and title of Perdue's 1992 volume, *Debate in Tibetan Buddhism*, leads some to assume that it represents a comprehensive and even definitive study on Tibetan debate. This clearly misunderstands the work's scope. It deals only with the first portion of a text on the Collected Topics, which, it must be remembered, are primer works. Analyzing the content of such works may be essential to fathoming the logic and its theory, but it does not constitute an investigation of the whole tradition. This points to the main shortcoming with much of the academic writing on Tibetan debate: namely, its overreliance on the Collected Topics. Many academics seem to equate Tibetan Buddhist debate with the contents of these works. References to "practice" are, therefore, somewhat unreliable, as they seem to denote the customs among authors rather than those of individuals engaged in face-to-face encounters. The debates that serve as the basis of academic analysis are, in their original formulation, intended to be instructive and do not purport to be records of practice. But the academic writings on them do not sufficiently convey their artificiality. Readers turning to analysis of these debates to learn about the activity could justifiably feel confused. What, they may wonder, would be the point of two individuals engaging in a debate if its outcome was a foregone conclusion and one of them, apparently from the outset, was understood to be in the wrong?

When it comes to learning about the actual practice of debate, there is evidently a need to move outside the spheres of logic and theory. Despite its age and the fact that it is based on interviews with a single informant, Sierksma's 1964 article can be fully recommended as a starting point. It is an early attempt to approach debate anthropologically.[20] And, despite the author's limited grasp of Tibetan, it offers a more accurate guide to the terminology of debate than most later studies, which privilege literary sources. Although Sierksma's approach was not immediately followed up, being largely replaced with the sort of textual analysis referred to earlier, some more recent studies have brought us much closer to aspects of the practice itself. The studies of Dreyfus, Lempert, and Samuels explore debate within educational, sociocultural, and historical contexts, respectively.[21] They have the added advantage of bringing the perspective of those who have trained in the practice or observed it at close quarters.

Several of the studies cited earlier include portions of script from genuine debates. At least one sustained attempt has also been made to translate and analyze recorded exchanges.[22] But analyzing individual debates is a daunting prospect, due to not only their technical nature but also the convoluted and unpredictable course they take. When the help of the original participants is enlisted in deciphering such debates, they are rarely content with their performance and find it difficult to resist the urge to edit the script, somewhat undermining the exercise. The results to date, therefore, leave something to be desired. Notwithstanding the challenges relating to individual exchanges, in terms of demystifying the practice of debate, more could be done to explain its general structure, rather than presenting artificial samples. Some comparative analysis is offered in Samuels, but far more is needed.[23] It is also curious that some of the really characteristic features of the practice, such as the absence of any third-party role or clear outcomes, barely seem to warrant mention in most academic writings.

PRIMARY SOURCES

Chos kyi rgyal mtshan (1469–1546). *rGyan 'grel spyi don rol mtsho*. Beijing: Krung go bod kyi shes rig dpe skrun khang, 1989.

'Jam dbyangs mchog lha 'od zer (1429–1500). *Rwa stod bsdus grwa—Tshad ma rnam 'grel gyi bsdus gzhung shes bya'i sgo 'byed rgol ngan glang po 'joms pa gdong lnga'i gad rgyangs rgyu rig lde mig*. Dharamsala: Damchoe Sangpo, 1980.

Paṇ chen bsod nams grags pa (1478–1554). *Phar phyin mtha' dpyod yum don yang gsal sgron me*. Lhasa: Gangs can khyad nor dpe tshogs, 2009.

Sa skya Paṇḍita (1182–1251). *mKhas pa la 'jug pa'i sgo*. In *Sa paṇ Kun dga' rgyal mtshan gyi gsung 'bum*, Vol. 1, 459–501. Lhasa, 1992.

FURTHER READING

Dreyfus, Georges. *The Sound of Two Hands Clapping: The Education of a Tibetan Buddhist Monk*. Berkeley: University of California Press, 2003.

Dreyfus, Georges. "What Is Debate For? The Rationality of Tibetan Debates and the Role of Humor." *Argumentation* 22, no. 1 (2008): 43–58.

Goldberg, Margaret. "Entity and Antimony in Tibetan Bsdus grwa Logic (Parts 1 & 2)." *Journal of Indian Philosophy* 13 (1985): 153–199 and 273–304.

Hugon, Pascale. "Phya pa Chos kyi seng ge and His Successors on the Classification of Arguments by Consequence (thal 'gyur) Based on the Type of the Logical Reason." *Journal of Indian Philosophy* 44 (2016): 883–938.

Hugon, Pascale. "Phya pa Chos kyi seng ge on Argumentation by Consequence (thal 'gyur) (2): The Analysis of the Correspondence between a Consequence and Its Reverse Form and the Thirteenfold Typology of Consequences." *Journal of the International Association of Buddhist Studies* 39 (2016): 51–113.

Jackson, David. *The Entrance Gate for the Wise (Section III): Sa skya Paṇḍita on Indian and Tibetan Traditions of Pramāṇa and Philosophical Debate*. Vienna: Universität Wien, 1987.

Lempert, Michael. *Discipline and Debate: The Language of Violence in a Tibetan Buddhist Monastery*. Berkeley: University of California Press, 2012.

Onoda, Shunzo. *Monastic Debate in Tibet: A Study on the History and Structures of Bsdus Grwa Logic*. Vienna: Universität Wien, 1992.

Perdue, Daniel. *Debate in Tibetan Buddhism*. Ithaca, NY: Snow Lion Publications, 1992.

Perdue, Daniel. *The Course in Buddhist Reasoning and Debate*. Boston: Snow Lion, 2014.

Samuels, Jonathan. "The Tibetan Institutionalisation of Disputation: Understanding a Medieval Monastic Practice." *Medieval Worlds* 12 (2020): 96–120.

Samuels, Jonathan. "Tours, Titles, and Tests: Issues of Scholastic Standardisation in Medieval Tibet." *Journal for the International Association of Buddhist Studies* 43 (2020): 181–213.

Sierksma, Fokke. "Rstod-pa: The Monachal Disputations in Tibet." *Indo-Iranian Journal* 8, no. 2 (1964): 130–152.

Tillemans, Tom. *Scripture, Logic, Language: Essays on Dharmakīrti and His Tibetan Successors*. Boston: Wisdom Publications, 1999.

NOTES

1. As remarked by Georges Dreyfus, *The Sound of Two Hands Clapping: The Education of a Tibetan Buddhist Monk* (Berkeley: University of California Press, 2003), 5. The Indian centers survived until the 12th or 13th century. For more on them, see Hartmut Scharfe, *Education in Ancient India* (Leiden: Brill, 2002), 131–165.
2. It should be noted, more generally, that objections have been raised to usage of the term "medieval" in the Tibetan context. See Bryan Cuevas, "Some Reflections on the Periodization of Tibetan History," *Revue d'Etudes Tibétaines* 10 (2006): 44–55.
3. As attested by the accounts of Chinese pilgrims; Hartmut Scharfe, *Education in Ancient India*, 162.
4. On the phenomenon of court debate in India during the same era, see Johannes Bronkhorst, "Modes of Debate and Refutation of Adversaries in Classical and Medieval India: A Preliminary Investigation," *Atinqvorvm Philosophia* 1 (2007): 270–271.
5. For more on the medieval institutions of monastic learning, see Jonathan Samuels, "Tours, Titles, and Tests: Issues of Scholastic Standardisation in Medieval Tibet," *Journal for the International Association of Buddhist Studies* 43 (2020): 181–213.
6. In his treatise "Entrance to Scholarship" (*mKhas pa la 'jug pa'i sgo*), Sakya Pandita (Sa skya Paṇḍita Kun dga' rgyal mtshan, 1182–1251) voiced what appear to be objections to Sangpu practices. For a translation of the portion of this text relating to debate, see David Jackson, *The Entrance Gate for the Wise (Section III): Sa skya Paṇḍita on Indian and Tibetan Traditions of Pramāṇa and Philosophical Debate* (Vienna: Universität Wien, 1987), 249–462.
7. For more on this, see Jonathan Samuels, "The Tibetan Institutionalisation of Disputation: Understanding a Medieval Monastic Practice," *Medieval Worlds* 12 (2020): 96–120.
8. Ganden, Drepung, and Sera (*dGa' ldan*, *'Bras spungs*, and *Se ra*), which were for centuries the largest monasteries in the world.
9. See Filippo de Filippi, ed., *An Account of Tibet, The Travels of Ippolito Desideri of Pistoia, S.J., 1712–1727* (London: George Routledge & Sons, 1937 [1932]), 185–186.
10. A large number of his writings have only recently resurfaced and have been published in the *bKa' gdams gsung 'bum* (Sichuan: Si khron mi rigs dpe skrun khang, 2006).
11. For more on some of these features, see Samuels, "The Tibetan Institutionalisation of Disputation"; and Tom Tillemans, "Formal and Semantic Aspects of Tibetan Buddhist Logic," in *Scripture, Logic, Language: Essays on Dharmakīrti and His Tibetan Successors* (Boston: Wisdom Publications, 1999), 117–149.
12. The contrasting place of debate, and contemporary monastic education more generally, have been dealt with most extensively in Dreyfus, *The Sound of Two Hands Clapping*, especially 229–266.
13. Footage of the Fourteenth Dalai Lama's debate examinations, from Lhasa in 1958, survives.
14. The following description is based on personal experience. As such, it represents debate in the Geluk system, as practiced between monks. But it is worth observing that no significant variations relating to religious affiliation, institution, region, or indeed gender have yet been reported with regard to the way that debate is conducted.
15. This is a prime example of one of the flaws of previous studies, most of which include "technical" terms for these two roles, which are not those used by debaters but derive from literary sources and belong to other contexts.
16. The gesture is clearly the same one referred to by Desideri, *An Account of Tibet*, 185.
17. For more on this feature, see Georges Dreyfus, "What Is Debate For? The Rationality of Tibetan Debates and the Role of Humor," *Argumentation* 22, no. 1 (2008): 43–58.
18. Margaret Goldberg, "Entity and Antimony in Tibetan Bsdus grwa Logic (Parts 1 & 2)," *Journal of Indian Philosophy* 13 (1985): 153–199 and 273–304; Shunzo Onoda, *Monastic Debate in Tibet: A Study on the*

History and Structures of Bsdus Grwa Logic (Vienna: Universität Wien, 1992); and Daniel Perdue, *Debate in Tibetan Buddhism* (Ithaca, NY: Snow Lion, 1992).

19. Tom Tillemans, *Scripture, Logic, Language: Essays on Dharmakīrti and His Tibetan Successors* (Boston: Wisdom Publications, 1999); Pascale Hugon, "Phya pa Chos kyi seng ge and His Successors on the Classification of Arguments by Consequence (thal 'gyur) Based on the Type of the Logical Reason," *Journal of Indian Philosophy* 44 (2016): 883–938; Pascale Hugon, "Phya pa Chos kyi seng ge on Argumentation by Consequence (thal 'gyur) (2): The Analysis of the Correspondence between a Consequence and Its Reverse Form and the Thirteenfold Typology of Consequences," *Journal of the International Association of Buddhist Studies* 39 (2016): 51–113.
20. Fokke Sierksma, "Rstod-pa: The Monachal Disputations in Tibet," *Indo-Iranian Journal* 8, no. 2 (1964): 130–152.
21. Dreyfus, *The Sound of Two Hands Clapping*, 195–228; Dreyfus, "What Is Debate For?"; Michael Lempert, *Discipline and Debate: The Language of Violence in a Tibetan Buddhist Monastery* (Berkeley: University of California Press, 2012); Samuels, "Tours, Titles, and Tests"; and Samuels, "The Tibetan Institutionalisation of Disputation."
22. Kenneth Liberman, *Dialectical Practice in Tibetan Philosophical Culture: An Ethnomethodological Inquiry into Formal Reasoning* (Lanham, MD: Rowman & Littlefield, 2007).
23. Samuels, "The Tibetan Institutionalisation of Disputation."

Jonathan Samuels

DEBATE TRADITIONS IN PREMODERN JAPAN

WHAT IS DEBATE?

In premodern Japan, debate, or *rongi* 論義, was a formal discussion of a topic in which different (usually oppositional) arguments were submitted and examined. The term *rongi* literally means "discussing meanings." Its broadest definition includes a variety of activities, ranging from oral examinations and group discussions to formal debates and lecture and answer sessions. Some debates were meant to test candidates for monastic promotion, while others facilitated a free exchange of ideas. Some were formal and sponsored by the court, while others were informal, held in a teacher's private living quarters. Some were specialized and targeted toward elite scholars in the Confucian or Buddhist traditions, while others were performed to entertain a secular audience. Some were written, while others were performed as oral debates. Indeed, in discussing *rongi* in Japanese Buddhism, Tomabechi Seiichi has argued that the term has been used to refer to so many Buddhist scholarly practices that it has created great confusion among modern scholars.[1]

Although Tomabechi is correct to hope for a more precise definition of *rongi*, this article does not focus on providing one. Rather, by bracketing the terminological difficulties and using "debate" or *rongi* as a heuristic category, it seeks a broader perspective on the bewildering variety of debate practices as manifested in the different cultural and intellectual traditions of premodern Japan. While the main focus is on Buddhism, debate within Confucianism is also considered, as well as performance traditions such as *noh*, in order to illustrate the rich and diverse debate traditions of Japan and how they encompassed the realms of religion, politics, and the performing arts.

THE ORIGINS OF DEBATE IN ANCIENT JAPAN

Debate first developed in ancient Japan within the intellectual traditions of Buddhism and Confucianism. While Confucian debate came to Japan from China, its Buddhist counterpart originated in India. In Buddhism, *anumāna*, or "inference," included both internal reasoning processes and their public presentation, the latter of which is the focus of this article.[2] In East Asia, debate originally developed as part of a sutra lecture (*kōkyō* 講経 or *kōsetsu* 講説), which was popularized during China's Southern dynasties (420–589) as a means of teaching and learning Buddhist principles.[3] Tibet also enjoyed a strong tradition of Buddhist debate.[4]

Both Confucian and Buddhist debates began to appear in Japanese sources in the 7th and 8th centuries. The records of early debate performances, however, are scarce, and it was not until the Heian period (794–1185) that debates became firmly institutionalized, thus leaving abundant textual traces for modern scholars to study.

To better understand debate's development, it is important to consider the larger institutional framework of the ancient Japanese state within which it evolved. In the Confucian learning tradition of this era, debate was a component of the Sekiten 釈奠 ceremony organized by the University (Daigakuryō 大学寮), which was part of the Ministry of Ceremonial (Shikibushō 式部省), one of eight ministries placed under the leadership of the highest organ of the government, the Council of State (*Daijōkan* 太政官). The study of the Confucian classics (*myōgyōdō* 明経道) constituted one of the disciplines in the university's curriculum. The university was an elite institution of higher learning; only the sons of courtiers of the fifth rank or higher who were between thirteen and sixteen years of age were eligible to apply (an exception was made for the sons of *fuhitobe* 史部, or immigrant-descended scribal houses). Thus, in principle, the university provided relatively low-ranking courtiers with opportunities to advance their social position.[5]

The university thereby administered a series of examinations to determine the advancement of students to higher levels. Throughout their careers, students were regularly tested by the faculty and staff of the bureau as well as officials of the Ministry of Ceremonial, with a minor exam every ten days (*junshi* 旬試) and a major one at the end of each year (*nenshūshi* 年終試 or *saishi* 歳試). After completing all requirements, students took civil service examinations, the results of which determined their appointments in the government. The minor exam tested students' ability to recite from memory and explicate Confucian texts, while the major and civil service exams focused on explication. Thus, the curriculum of the university was designed to help students advance from basic to higher-order academic skills.[6]

None of these exams required oral discussion, but it became the focus of the Sekiten ritual, the purpose of which was to venerate Confucius and other great Confucian figures and to celebrate the cultural and political authority of the Confucian canons.[7] The program of "lecture-and-debate" (*kōron* 講論) was preceded by sacrificial offerings (*kikyō* 饋享), and the entire ceremony concluded with a banquet (*ennoza* 宴座). Held in the university's lecture hall (Todōin 都堂院), the program included recitation of a Confucian canonical text followed by a lecture and debate on the text.[8]

Buddhist monks did not have a centralized educational institution comparable to the Confucian university. Instead, the imperial state's efforts to standardize and ensure the academic qualifications of monks materialized in the yearly ordinands system (*nenbun dosha*

年分度者). Originating in the late 7th century, this system further developed in the 8th century to define the official qualifications for Buddhist ordination, such as an applicant's ability to recite (*dokyō* 読経) Buddhist scriptures or recite them from memory (*jukyō* 誦経).[9] The system, however, initially failed to administer a fair and equitable examination, which led to reform efforts during the early Heian period. Particularly prominent were the reforms of Emperor Kanmu 桓武 (r. 781–806). During his reign, Kanmu issued a series of decrees to change the nature of the system to one based on an applicant's academic attainments rather than on personal recommendations from senior monks and powerful aristocrats. For example, an age requirement and examinations were introduced to eliminate unqualified applicants. Kanmu's intention was not only to control the monastic population more strictly but also to support the different schools of Buddhism equally. In his decree dated 803, he lamented that increasingly more monks were studying the teachings of the Hossō 法相 school (Ch. Faxiang), causing the number of those studying the Sanron 三論 school (Ch. Sanlun) to decline. Hossō was the East Asian counterpart of the Yogācāra school, whereas Sanron focused on the three philosophical treatises written by the Indian Buddhist monk Nāgārjuna (ca. 150–250) and his disciple Āryadeva (*c.* 3rd century). To address this concern, Kanmu issued a decree in the year 804 to designate five ordinands per year to each of the two schools so that they could both prosper—thus marking the first attempt to consider an applicant's doctrinal school (*shū* 宗) in the yearly ordinands system.

Emphasis on sectarian qualities further increased as the system was modified in 806 in response to a proposal of the monk Saichō 最澄 (767–822), founder of the Tendai 天台 school, the Japanese counterpart of the Chinese Tiantai school.[10] The new system assigned a set number of applicants to each school while delineating their required fields of specialization. For example, the Hossō school was assigned three applicants, two of whom were required to study the *Jōyuishiki ron* 成唯識論 (*Vijñaptimātratāsiddhi*).[11] In this manner, the modified yearly ordinands system helped solidify sectarian boundaries between schools. Saichō's system included the major schools of Buddhism at that time—such as the Hossō, Sanron, and Kegon 華厳 (Ch. Huayan), which were established during the 6th and 7th centuries, and his own school, Tendai, established at the beginning of the Heian era. Although Saichō's proposal did not mention the Shingon 真言, founded by his contemporary Kūkai 空海 (774–835) and based on Indo-Chinese esoteric Buddhism, its applicants were later added to the system of yearly ordinands.[12]

Curiously, Kanmu's court does not appear to have shown a parallel enthusiasm for promoting the Confucian Sekiten. In his study of the history of the Sekiten in Japan, James McMullen observed that "there is no evidence that Kanmu saw the *sekiten* as a resource to dignify and sacralize the role of Confucian learning in his realm," and that extant documentation about the Sekiten receded at this time. This stands in contrast to the number of decrees issued during his reign for reforming the Buddhist yearly ordinands system.[13] Thus, the court's leadership and investment in this reform are undeniable; it would, however, be a mistake to describe Buddhist monks merely as the passive recipients of the court's policy, as exemplified by Saichō's proposal.

Kanmu's successors in the 9th century continued his efforts by organizing a series of lectures and debates as requirements for monastic promotion, thus marking the formal institutionalization of Buddhist debate. Under this system, a monk was required to participate in the three Nara assemblies (*nankyō sanne* 南京三会): the Yuima-e 維摩会 held at Kōfukuji 興福寺, the

Saishō-e 最勝会 held at Yakushiji 薬師寺, and the Misai-e 御斎会 held in the imperial palace. Upon completing the lectureship at these three assemblies, a monk would be promoted to the Sōgō 僧綱, the main ecclesiastical office comprising the highest-ranking monks. Placed under the Bureau of Buddhism and Aliens (Genbaryō 玄蕃寮), the Sōgō was in charge of managing temple resources and the registry of monks and nuns, as well as their ordination. To the original ritual triad were later added new ones, such as the three Heian assemblies (*hokkyō sanne* 北京三会) and the THREE LECTURES (*sankō* 三講). All these assemblies provided lectures and debates about Buddhist scriptures.[14] For example, the Yuima-e focused on the *Vimalakīrti Sūtra*, while the Saishō-e and the Misai-e dealt with the *Golden Light Sutra*.[15] Many debate questions were based on quotations from these scriptures.

When the Golden Light Lecture (Saishōkō 最勝講), one of the Three Lectures, was held in 1192, the following was a question raised in the evening session of the second day:

> [The Questioner of this debate session] asks about a sentence in the *sūtra* [i.e., the *Golden Light Sūtra*]. The founder [i.e., Tendai master Chigi; Ch. Zhiyi, 538–597] discusses that one terminates one's afflictions in the path of insight. Now, [according to Chigi,] how does a person of dull capacity terminate his afflictions?[16]

Although debate records (*mondōki* 問答記) such as this would often omit a quotation without explaining what the "sentence in the *sūtra*" was, this particular debate topic was referring to the sentence in the *Golden Light Sutra* as follows: "[A good son] swiftly and completely eliminates afflictions to be terminated in the path of insight and the path of cultivation."[17]

In addition to the quotation-driven debates, other debates focused on important doctrinal topics for each school. For example, the topic of the "attainment of Buddhahood by grasses and trees" (*sōmoku jōbutsu* 草木成仏)—the idea that not only humans but even plants possess innate buddhahood—was an important debate topic in the Tendai school.[18] In the Tendai and Hossō schools, compendiums of debate topics developed such as the *Tendaishū rongi nihyakudai* 天台宗論義二百題 (published in the 18th century) and the *Yuishikiron dōgakushō* 唯識論同学鈔 (compiled in the late 12th and early 13th centuries). The latter contains more than 1,100 debate topics, whereas the former includes 200 essential topics selected from more than 3,700.[19]

Those invited to these lectures and debates were known as "scholar monks" (variably called *gakuryo* 学侶, *gakuto* 学徒, *gakushō* 学生, or *gakusō* 学僧). The institutionalization of the yearly ordinands system and state-sponsored lectures and debates in the early Heian period contributed to delineating these monks' unique identity as scholars. As Nagamura Makoto has made clear using Tōdaiji as an example, there were monks even before the Heian period whose official responsibilities were deemed the study of Buddhist scriptures.[20] Then during the Heian period, scholar monks came to be differentiated as an elite population from the other monks. While both were legitimate members of their temples, the scholar monks' identity was tied to their scholarly activities, especially their participation in the assemblies. By the late Heian period, the monastic community in general had become stratified, with scholar monks becoming a distinct social class.[21]

In addition to state-sponsored debates, scholar monks also participated in debates held at their own temples, as evidenced by the case of the Tōdaiji scholar monk Sōshō 宗性

(1202–1278). Joining Tōdaiji in 1214 at age thirteen (according to the traditional system of counting age, which counts birth as one year old), Sōshō regularly attended the Kusha Sanjikkō 倶舎三十講, or lectures on and debates about the *Abidatsuma kusharon* 阿毘達磨倶舎論 (*Abhidharmakośa-bhāṣya*) held within Tōdaiji to train its monks.[22] The *Abidatsuma kusharon*, considered one of the foundational texts of Buddhist philosophy, was commonly referenced in state-sponsored debates. In 1219, at age eighteen, Sōshō's scholarship was recognized by the senior monks of Tōdaiji, who then recommended him for the examination debate (*ryūgi* 竪義) of the Yuima-e, one of the three Nara assemblies.[23] Thus, these debates trained burgeoning scholar monks and screened candidates for the state-sponsored ones.

Indeed, by Sōshō's time, debate had become an integral part of doctrinal training for monks regardless of their temple or school affiliation. That said, the reception of debate took a different course in each school. The Nara and Tendai schools were heavily invested in debate from the very beginning and were collectively called the exoteric schools (*kengyō* 顕教). Meanwhile, monks of the esoteric school (*mikkyō* 密教) of Shingon were not invited to the state-sponsored debates that developed in the early Heian period. Although Shingon temples did hold the Denbō-e 伝法会, where the central scriptures of this school were discussed, this assembly was discontinued in the early 10th century. Thus, the Shingon debate tradition did not fully mature until the late Heian period.[24]

The new schools established after the Heian era also incorporated debate into their traditions. For example, the Sōtō 曹洞 school developed its own debate tradition called *hōmon* 法問 (also *hōza* 法座 or *hossen* 法戦), which was an exchange of questions and answers about the canonical Zen riddles (*kosoku* 古則). Among its variants, the most famous *hōmon* is the so-called *shuso hossen shiki* 首座法戦式, which originated in medieval Japan but is still practiced. In this exchange, a monk in the position of the head seat (*shuso*) debates with other monks in attendance. Although today Sōtō Zen is famous primarily for its emphasis on sitting meditation and the study of the writings of its founder Dōgen 道元 (1200–1253), in premodern Japan *hōmon* was a major Sōtō practice, attended not only by monks of elite Sōtō temples but also by those from the samurai warrior class, most famously the shogun (*gozen hōmon* 御前法問; i.e., "*hōmon* debate in the presence of the shogun"). Thus, *hōmon* played an important role in establishing a close connection between the Sōtō Zen school and the secular authority.[25]

The example of *hōmon* debate points to an important aspect of the history of debate traditions in ancient Japan—that power and knowledge were intimately connected. Indeed, the interplay between the two was a driving engine for the development of *rongi* in Confucianism and Buddhism in the early Heian period. Both the Confucian University's examinations and the Buddhist yearly ordinands' system and state-sponsored debates were attempts by the imperial court to authenticate certain forms of knowledge over others and to dignify its rule by displaying its control over and support for these intellectual traditions. For scholars, debate was both a means of upward social mobility and doctrinal training.

DEBATE FORMATS AND TEXTS

The format of Confucian debate used in the Sekiten ritual, as recorded in Heian-period official histories and court ritual manuals, required the participation of a doctor (*hakase* 博士), who would recite a Confucian canon in Chinese; a director and lecturer (*zasu jikikō* 座主直講), who would render the canon into Japanese *kundoku* 訓読; and a questioner (*monja* 問者), who would raise questions to which the director and lecturer would respond. This format of debate was most likely introduced into Japan by Kibi no Makibi 吉備真備 (695–775), who studied in China for seventeen years as part of Japan's mission to Tang China (*kentōshi* 遣唐使).[26]

In the 9th century, a Japanese variation called the palace debate (*uchirongi* 内論義) was added to this Chinese format. This debate was held every year in the emperor's presence the day after the university's autumn Sekiten ceremony. Although the concept of a debate held in the imperial presence itself originated in China, what was new in Japan was staging it in connection with the Sekiten.[27] It was also likely inspired by its Buddhist counterpart, that is, the palace debate performed on the last day of the Misai-e, one of the three Nara assemblies.

Buddhist debate had many different formats. Three common ones were *ryūgi* 竪義, *kōmon* 講問, and *banrongi* 番論義 (also called *tsugai rongi*). *Ryūgi* can be likened to today's university oral examination, where a doctoral candidate is tested orally by a group of examiners. As Paul Groner has discussed, the main officiants of the examination debate included the questioner (*monja* 問者), who prepared and raised questions initiating the debate; the candidate (*rissha* 竪者 or *ryūgi* 竪義), or examinee, who answered the questions; and the examiner (*shōgi* 精義, 證義, or *shōsei* 証誠), who evaluated and graded the candidate's debate performance. The examination debate also served as a social debut for the young scholar monk who was serving as candidate.[28]

In the *kōmon*, or lecture-and-question format, the lecture master (*kōji* 講師) rather than the candidate took center stage by delivering a lecture on a Buddhist sutra and then responding to the questioner's questions. This format also required an examiner, whose role was that of a presider who sometimes intervened to provide comments, correct mistakes, or stop discussion when inappropriate, rather than officially evaluate the debaters' performance.[29] Finally, *banrongi* or *tsugai rongi* referred to a paired debate in which two debaters (*ronshō* or *ronjō* 論匠) would pair up (*tsugai*) to ask a question and respond.[30]

While preparing to participate in these debates, scholar monks produced a vast body of texts: notations and commentaries (*shoshaku* 疏釈), debate scripts (*rongisō* 論義草), records of debate performances (*mondōki* 問答記), excerpts (*shōmotsu* or *shōmono* 抄物), and written records of oral transmission (*kikigaki* 聞書).[31] These debate texts were part of the so-called *shōgyō* 聖教 ("sacred manuscript collection" or "sacred works"), which was a massive body of texts produced by medieval Japanese monks and preserved in archives and Buddhist temples.[32]

Shōgyō, including these debate texts, were transmitted from a teacher to his disciples. The immediate purpose of such transmission was to train one's disciples and ensure their academic success. More broadly, limiting *shōgō* transmission to one's disciples was a means of establishing a master–disciple succession (*shishi sōjō* 師資相承), on the basis of which lineages were formulated.[33]

The *shōgyō* texts of the previously mentioned Sōshō are a case in point. The Tōdaiji Library (Tōdaiji Toshokan 東大寺図書館) in Nara possesses the original copies of Sōshō's *shōgyō*, most of which concern his academic work, and especially those he produced to participate in state-sponsored debates. One of these works is a copy of the *Myōhonshō* 明本抄, composed by the Hossō monk Jōkei 貞慶 (1155–1213) and known among medieval scholar monks as a central writing on the topic of *inmyō* 因明, or Buddhist logic. Sōshō had studied *inmyō* under the tutelage of Jōkei's disciple Kakuhen 覚遍 (dates unknown), who, in 1225, finally gave Sōshō permission to copy all thirteen volumes of the *Myōhonshō*. Sōshō subsequently limited the transmission of this text to the "monks of my lineage," by which he meant those belonging to Sonshōin 尊勝院, the subtemple of Tōdaiji that he headed.[34] For Sōshō, the secret transmission of the *Myōhonshō* distinguished this subtemple from others and created a lineage of succession from Jōkei to Kakuhen to Sōshō to his disciples.[35]

In addition to such social formation, the production and transmission of debate texts also helped to develop doctrinal knowledge. In discussing debates in the Nanto and Tendai schools, Minowa Kenryō has observed a shift in Buddhist doctrinal formation toward the late Heian period. In the early Heian period, doctrinal texts were written as treatises of sizable length, but around the 11th century, texts called *tanjaku* 短釈 (literally, "short commentary"; also 短尺) began increasing. Focused on a specific debate topic, these *tanjaku* were short commentaries written in a question-and-answer format; after multiple rounds of questions and answers, they listed the relevant Buddhist sutras and commentaries at the end.[36]

Scholar monks' efforts to organize and systematize these *tanjaku* topics in turn led to the development of debate compendiums.[37] For example, the *Yuishikiron dōgakushō* 唯識論同学鈔 was a compendium of debate topics compiled by Jōkei's disciples in the late 12th and early 13th centuries.[38] The *Dōgakushō* contains more than 1,100 debate topics (*kamon* 科文) concerning the *Jōyuishiki ron*, one of the central texts for the Hossō school.[39] Each entry had a three-part structure: the first introduced the topic, the second recorded the discussion (*dangi* 談義) from a study group meeting, and the third added the compiler's personal views. The *Dōgakushō* was thus meant to be an introductory study allowing the reader to explore different interpretations, rather than conclusively establishing orthodox Hossō doctrine. Such debate compendiums were compiled in the Tendai and Shingon schools as well.[40]

Thus, both the acts and the texts of debate were mutually generative. As the number of new debates continued to grow, the production of debate texts increased proportionately, and these in turn were used by scholar monks to prepare for further debates. This interpenetration of the oral and written aspects of debate constituted Buddhist doctrinal formation. Debate was an embodied cognition, which represented Buddhist philosophy in the making.

THE POLITICIZATION OF DEBATE

Over the course of the Heian era, as the number of Buddhist debates drastically increased, the system of debate-based monastic promotion also grew—a development not seen in its Confucian counterpart. The proliferation of debates and debate texts was one consequence of this institutional expansion. The politicization of debate was another.

In principle, state-sponsored debates held as part of the various assemblies were open to monks of all schools. Yet, monastic appointment records such as the *Sōgō bunin* 僧綱補任 (Appointments to the Sōgō Office) attest otherwise. For example, the *Sōgō bunin* records more than 2,000 appointments to the Sōgō between the 7th and 12th centuries. Among those who completed the lectureship of the three Nara assemblies and entered the Sōgō, the percentage of those of the Hossō school was highest (over 60%), whereas those of the Tendai school were underrepresented (less than 5%).[41]

In 963, the Tendai school's efforts to challenge Hossō domination led to the famous Ōwa debate (*Ōwa no shūron* 応和の宗論). Unlike the three Nara assemblies, this was not an annual debate. It was convened by Emperor Murakami 村上 (r. 946–967) in response to an appeal by the Tendai monk Ryōgen 良源 (912–985). Murakami thereupon invited monks from the Tendai and Nara schools (mostly Hossō monks) to the imperial palace to debate doctrinal points of the *Lotus Sutra*, the central scripture of the Tendai school. Although several sources describe this debate, they disagree on details, and especially on who won.[42]

In addition to initiating the Ōwa debate, Ryōgen was responsible for instituting the debate called the examination on broad learning (the Kōgaku Ryūgi 広学竪義) at the main Tendai temple, Enryakuji 延暦寺. As Paul Groner has rightly pointed out, this was a strategy to combat Hossō dominance by creating a debate favorable to the promotion of Tendai monks.[43] Ryōgen's and his successors' efforts eventually yielded fruit in the 11th century, in the course of which the three Heian assemblies were created. Thus, although Tendai monks were severely underrepresented in the three Nara assemblies, they now dominated the Heian assemblies.

This whole system of debate-based monastic promotion, as represented by the Nara and Heian assemblies, was not, however, the only avenue of promotion available for monks. Indeed, what is said to have in fact caused the decline of the system was a new form of promotion; namely, the phenomenon of "bypass promotion" (*kandō no shōshin* 閑道之昇進).[44]

In his *Shakke kanpanki* 釈家官班記 (Arrangement of ecclesiastic positions), Cloistered Imperial Prince Sonnen 尊円 (1298–1356) deplored the fact that members of the imperial and aristocratic families, or those who received rewards (*shō* 賞) on certain occasions, were being promoted above their experienced seniors.[45] This describes the practice of bypass promotion, in which monks were promoted to the office of Sōgō without having completed the lectureship in the assemblies.

Prince Sonnen mentioned two alternative forms of promotion in particular—by transfer and based on pedigree—both of which became important in the late Heian period. Promotion by transfer meant that a monk would transfer a reward or compensation for his own ritual service to another monk. The recipient thus reaped the benefit through a promotion. A transferor was often the master of the transferee. Thus, "transfer" was a way to accelerate a disciple's promotion and was connected to the principle of the master–disciple succession. This method of bypass promotion was frequently used by monks of noble birth. In the late Heian period, members of the imperial family and of powerful aristocratic families began joining the monastic community in increasing numbers. In the race for promotion, they thereby enjoyed a significant advantage over ordinary monks.[46]

These forms of bypass promotion do not necessarily indicate a breach of the originally meritocratic system of monastic promotion. From the beginning, both leaders of the imperial state and monastic elites appropriated the system to control access to knowledge, thereby producing and reproducing the social classes of the monastic population. While the master–disciple lineage tended to solidify social stratification within the same school, temple, or subtemple, there also existed a temple hierarchy (*jikaku* 寺格) that organized temples into different classes, with each enjoying a different set of privileges.[47] Factors such as a monk's pedigree, temple affiliation, or school of thought he had studied intertwined to determine his access to power and knowledge. Bypass promotion reflected this complex social reality, but it did not immediately cause the total collapse of the assemblies. In the 14th century, during

Prince Sonnen's time, the system declined, and by the 15th century, with the exception of the Yuima-e, the assemblies had been discontinued.[48]

This did not bring about the death of the Buddhist debate tradition, however, since temples continued to organize a variety of lectures and discussions. Especially important was *dangi* 談義, described by Tomabechi as "a lecture followed by a free discussion by multiple scholars."[49] Watanabe Mariko further explained the primacy purpose of *dangi* as "explicating Buddhist scriptures and clarifying the teachings of Buddhism."[50] Although *dangi* was practiced in every school of Buddhism, in the late Kamakura period there emerged *dangi* centers (*dangisho* 談義所), which were Tendai, Shingon, Jōdo, and Nichiren temples specializing in *dangi*; these lasted until the Tokugawa period (1603–1867).[51] The Sendanrin of the Sōtō Zen school, the eight centers of the Tendai school, and the eighteen centers of the Pure Land school in the Kantō region were particularly active and well known.[52]

A further consequence of the close interplay between power and knowledge that had earlier driven the development of debate was its politicization. Kanmu's reform of the yearly ordinands system and his successors' efforts to organize the assemblies were meant to introduce a meritocratic principle into monastic ordination and promotion. Their blueprint was never fully implemented, however, allowing the Hossō to gain dominance, which in turn further intensified the rivalry among monks of different schools in competing for invitation to the assemblies. The increase in the number of noble monks and their bypass promotion then further increased the politicization of debates and the sectarian rivalry over them.

Indeed, the system of monastic promotion was an integral part of the whole social and political order of medieval Japan, which was based on shared rulership and Buddhist *kenmitsu* 顕密 ideology. Shared rulership was the medieval system of power wherein the highest authority was shared among court nobles (*kōke* or *kuge* 公家), a warrior aristocracy (*buke* 武家), and the temples and shrines (*jisha* 寺社). Emerging in the late Heian period and the Kamakura period (1185–1333) that followed, the system's ideological foundation was Buddhist *kenmitsu* ideology. *Kenmitsu* is an umbrella term for the views and practices that permeated the various schools and lineages of medieval Buddhism—more specifically, "the exoteric (*ken*) scriptures and the esoteric (*mitsu*), orally transmitted, rituals that dominated the religious world."[53] Debates supported this system by encouraging intersectarian studies (*kengaku* 兼学) through which various *kenmitsu* doctrines were transmitted. Therefore, the decline of the medieval *kenmitsu* system in the 14th and 15th centuries marked the end of most of the assemblies.[54]

This was not, however, the end of the interplay between power and knowledge, as exemplified by the Sōtō school's *hōmon* debate held in the presence of the shogun. In the Tokugawa period, monks were gathered for *gozen rongi* 御前論義 (debate in the presence of the shogun). According to Gaétan Rappo, the first Tokugawa shogun, Tokugawa Ieyasu 徳川家康 (r. 1603–1605), and his successor, Hidetada 秀忠 (r. 1605–1623), convened *gozen rongi* inviting monks of different schools, especially the Tendai, Shingon, Hossō, and Kegon. On the one hand, these debates helped their participants gain the shogun's backing in advancing their social positions. On the other hand, supporting their promotion was a way for the shogun to increase his own influence over their temples—a strategy comparable to that employed by the Heian court in using debates to both support and control the monastic community.

Interestingly, Rappo has pointed out that new debate topics emerged in the *gozen rongi* to address questions important for the samurai class, such as loyalty to one's master. This indicates that the shogun showed interest not only in the political aspects of *rongi* but also in its content.[55] In other words, a *rongi* was no mere pompous show; its secular audience—whether court nobles or the shogun himself—showed an interest in and enjoyed these performances of debate.

DEBATE AS A PERFORMANCE TRADITION

Debate was not only a means of scholarly learning but also a form of entertainment. Ishii Kōsei has presented examples from the late Six dynasties, Sui, and Tang periods in China (from about the 6th century BCE to the 10th century CE), where Buddhist debate was enjoyed as public entertainment and people enjoyed a monk's eloquence or humorous interjections by lay participants. In the Tang period (618–907), debate was performed outside Buddhist temples as a humorous art while influencing other performing arts and literature. In Japan, Ishii finds the earliest examples of Buddhist debate as public entertainment in the 8th century. In the subsequent Heian era, courtiers enjoyed the performance of debate just as they enjoyed *waka* 和歌 poetry and *kangen* 管弦 music.[56]

One can, in fact, argue that the close proximity of prayer and play in debate was part of the larger Buddhist culture, as evident in the development of the *ennen* 延年 tradition. According to Matsuo Kōichi, the term *ennen* began to be used in the late Heian period to refer to various performing arts (*geinō* 芸能) offered at the conclusion of Buddhist rituals, including debates. In medieval Japan, a variety of *ennen* performances were developed, not all of which were connected with Buddhist rituals. Buddhist *ennen* were most often offered as entertainment during a banquet following the performance of lectures or debates.[57]

An *ennen* performance was typically facilitated not by the scholar monks, however, but by their fellow *shuto* monks (衆徒; also called *shūto*). In the late Heian and Kamakura periods, as the socioeconomic power of Buddhist temples grew and the monastic population greatly increased, monastic society became more stratified. Scholar monks came to be clearly distinguished from the lower-ranking *shuto* monks. Although scholar monks usually served as debaters and *shuto* monks did not, the latter often observed debate sessions and helped facilitate the *ennen* performance at the end. Often, *shuto* monks were not quiet, passive observers; sources indicate they would respond to an unsatisfactory debate performance by hitting the floor and laughing aloud and applaud excellent debaters by waving their fans.[58]

The way *shuto* monks expressed their appreciation for or dissatisfaction with debaters indicates that debate inspired not only intellectual but also aesthetic appreciation—or more precisely, that the two were inseparable, as suggested by Fujiwara Akihira 藤原明衡 (d. 1066). His *Shin sarugaku ki* 新猿楽記 (An account of the new monkey music) describes various performing arts (*sarugaku* 猿楽; literally, "monkey music") as well as different occupations found in the then-emerging urban life of the Heian capital. He describes a Tendai scholar monk, commenting not only on the monk's academic prowess, such as his deep and encyclopedic knowledge of Buddhist scriptures, clear lectures, and eloquence in debate, but also on the beautiful quality of his voice and his eye-pleasing physical traits: his shoulders, wrists, and hips "resembling those of Ānanda," one of the Buddha's most important disciples.[59]

One feature of the *Shin sarugaku ki* that literary scholars have explored is its exhaustive listing of things (*mono zukushi* 物尽し), in this case, details of life in the Heian capital. As Ashton Lazarus has demonstrated, the list made up a significant portion of the work, not necessarily to provide realistic, detailed accounts of what life was like at the time in the city but rather to present commoners in different professions and performers of various arts "not as individuals but as archetypes."[60] Thus, Akihira's description of "the Tendai scholar monk," encompassing his intellectual, vocal, and physical qualities, should be read as such.

This archetypal description of debate performance is evidenced by a component of *ennen* called *kaikō* 開口, that is, the opening speech offered at the beginning. Ishii discusses a 13th-century example of humorous *kaikō* as one of its earliest instances. The *kaikō* subsequently developed into a type of performing art, characterized by "exhaustive listing, full of play on words," comparable to the *Shin sarugaku ki*.[61] The quintessential example of such a *kaikō* performance is recorded in the 16th-century *Tōnomine ennen shishō* 多武峰延年詞章, where anthropomorphized birds discuss what sorts of performance should be offered to entertain the deities who protect Buddhism.[62] Ishii has argued that *kaikō* as a speech-based performing art can in fact be understood as a parody of scholarly *rongi*.

The *ennen* tradition, such as *kaikō* performances, also influenced Japanese literature and performing arts traditions at large, including the theater art known as *noh*, performed from the 14th century to the present day. In fact, *rongi* became one of the so-called *shōdan* 小段, the fundamental building blocks of the *noh* plays (as a *noh* term, it is often transcribed in *katakana* as ロンギ). *Noh* music consists of vocal music (*utai* 謡) and instrumental ensembles (*hayashi* 囃子); the vocal music is performed by actors such as *shite* シテ and *waki* ワキ (the main and supporting actors), as well as by a chorus (*jiutai* 地謡).[63] In *noh rongi* the main actor is paired with the chorus or with another actor, singing by turns—a format similar to the pair debate.

The *rongi* in *noh* starts with the question-and-answer format and eventually shifts to the chorus in the latter half. Various techniques are used to make the *rongi* enjoyable as a theater performance. For example, it is usually written as a verse in the seven- and five-syllable meter (*shichi-go chō* 七五調), which is rhythmical and pleasing to the ear. Each pair uses a contrasting vocal tone, and as the *rongi* progresses, the number of phrases each party speaks decreases, quickening the pace of the dialogue and heightening the tension.[64]

Rongi is often used in a *noh* play where a character reveals his or her true identity in the middle of the play (*nakairi* 中入り). The *Nonomiya* 野宮 is a good example. In this play, *rongi* takes the form of an exchange between the main and supporting actors, namely, a Buddhist monk and a village woman. The monk initiates the *rongi* by asking the woman to reveal her name, to which she responds that she is, in fact, the spirit of Lady Rokujō (Rokujō-no-miyasudokoro 六条御息所), one of Genji's lovers in *The Tale of Genji* 源氏物語.[65]

As this example makes clear, the *rongi* in *noh* is not a scholarly discussion, but rather a stylized dialogue between two parties, which represents the aesthetic, entertainment aspect of debate. Although the *noh rongi*'s direct connection with its Buddhist counterpart is hard to establish, it is worth noting that the Buddhist *ennen* tradition included theater performances such as *furyū* 風流 and *renji* 連事, which developed during the Kamakura era under the influence of the earlier *sarugaku* performing arts. This in turn was based on Buddhist theater performances as well as the overall *sarugaku* tradition, from which the actor and playwright Kan'ami 観阿弥 (1333–1384) and his son and successor, Zeami 世阿弥 (dates unknown), drew to establish the *noh* tradition.[66] It is possible that Kan'ami and Zeami developed the *noh rongi* format after having observed Buddhist *rongi*, although they themselves did not attest to a direct connection between the two.

The debate format that most likely inspired the *noh rongi* is the pair debate. One of the three Nara assemblies, the Yuima-e, included the pair debate on its last day to entertain the imperial messenger (*chokushi* 勅使). Analyzing the format of this pair debate, which was always accompanied by drinking and eating, Takayama Yuki concluded that the debate suggested the nature of a "drinking banquet to entertain the imperial messenger as a sign of appreciation for his attendance."[67]

Divine guests were also entertained. Elizabeth Tinsley, analyzing Buddhist doctrinal debates at Mt. Kōya (Kōyasan 高野山) in the medieval period, demonstrates that they were considered offerings to *kami*, or local deities (*hōraku* 法楽). She further points out that *kami* were not merely passive recipients of Buddhist teachings; rather, they were expected to protect Buddhism while authenticating the doctrinal interpretations presented at debates.[68] Matsuo Kōichi has also revealed the central role played by the Kasuga 春日 deity in the Jion-e 慈恩会 of the Hosso school, especially in the dream ceremony (*yumemi no gi* 夢見の儀). Originally developed in the late medieval period, this ceremony occurs prior to the assembly to give a debate topic to a questioner. As Matsuo explains, this is a "ceremonial expression of the idea that the Kasuga deity reveals the debate topic in a dream."[69] The role of *kami* in Buddhist debates thus exemplifies the then widespread paradigm of *honji suijaku* 本地垂迹, according to which "the local, native deities (*kami*) are emanations of universal, Buddhist divinities."[70]

Finally, a performance of debate was also incorporated into the tradition of *shōmyō* 声明 (Skt. *śabda-vidyā*), or Buddhist vocal music. Originating in India as one of the five sciences (*gomyō* 五明; Skt. *pañca-vidyā*), in medieval Japan *shōmyō* was performed during Buddhist rituals and was transmitted through different lineages.[71] There were different types of *shōmyō*, of which *rongi* was one.[72] A modern recording and musical notation of *rongi* provide clues to what the vocal aspects of debate performance might have sounded like in medieval Japan.[73]

As Ōuchi Fumi has made clear, *shōmyō* is one of many Buddhist "vocal arts" (*koe no waza* 声の技) that were widespread in medieval Japan. Ōuchi argues that these vocal arts were closely connected to medieval Buddhist discourses about the importance of the body as a vehicle for enlightenment and that these discourses were theoretically grounded in original enlightenment thought (*hongaku shisō* 本覚思想).[74] Jacqueline Stone has also pointed out the influence of such thought on the Tendai *shōmyō* tradition.[75] Thus, the vocal arts of *rongi* exemplify the medieval Buddhist episteme and its larger influence in Japanese culture. The clear presence of these aesthetic, entertainment aspects in the Buddhist debate tradition in turn raises serious questions about the premise of knowledge as a being purely intellectual (and not a physical) property, suggesting instead the concept of embodied knowledge.

Thus, although the origins of *rongi* are to be found in the Buddhist and Confucian scholarly traditions, the world of *rongi* grew well beyond the scholastic. From this perspective, *rongi* came to belong to the speech-based performing arts that entertained people from all walks of life—from the shogun to commoners—thus traversing the realms of culture, politics, and religion.

REVIEW OF LITERATURE

Among the different debate traditions examined here, Buddhist debate is by far the most studied, with abundant attention given to it in Japanese-language scholarship.[76] Of particular note is Chisan Kangaku-kai's *Rongi no kenkyū*, published in 2000, which is an important attempt to bring together both Japanese academic and sectarian scholarship covering the Hossō, Tendai, and Shingon schools.[77]

Academic scholarship on Buddhist debate has tended to present two major methodological orientations: the historical and the philosophical. Uejima Susumu's *Nihon Chūsei shakai no keisei to ōken* is representative of the historical approach, in which historians, investigating the social and political aspects of Buddhist debate, describe the politicization of debate as part of the mechanism of the medieval system of power.[78]

This means that, as Mikaël Bauer's study of the Yuima-e illustrates, the performance of a state-sponsored debate was an extremely complex political event involving the conflict between different schools as well as the mutually dependent and yet competitive relationship between the secular and religious authorities.[79]

While the historical study of debate thus reveals the interplay between power and knowledge, the philosophical approach complements this by examining its intellectual content. Buddhist philosophy scholars have argued that, in addition to providing opportunities for promotion, state-sponsored debates advanced doctrinal studies. For example, Minowa Kenryō, examining the records of state-sponsored debates, revealed their rigorous academic nature. Studies have also been carried out on the debate tradition within a specific school: for instance, Kusunoki Junshō's study of the Hosso debate tradition or Tomabechi Seiichi's study of its Shingon counterpart.[80] Within English-language scholarship, Paul Groner's pioneering work has revealed the central role played by *rongi* in monastic education in the Tendai school and in the Seizan-ha of the Jōdo school in Heian and medieval Japan.[81]

To this rich debate tradition in the history of Japanese Buddhism, the Confucian Sekiten provides an important comparison. James McMullen's *The Worship of Confucius in Japan* is a comprehensive study of the history of the Sekiten in Japan from ancient to modern times.[82] Detailed studies have also been made of the Sekiten as a court ceremony in ancient Japan and of its revival under the Tokugawa shogunate in the early modern period.[83] In addition, Matsuo Kōichi and Elizabeth Tinsley have separately demonstrated how the interaction between Buddhism and *kami* worship manifested in Buddhist *rongi*.[84]

Finally, debate as a performance tradition can be approached from different methodological perspectives, presenting great potential for interdisciplinary research. One could argue that the examination of debate is ultimately incomplete without considering its embodied aspects. The study of *shōmyō* performances of debate, the Buddhist *ennen* tradition, and the mutual influence between the entertainment aspects of debate and other performing arts of medieval Japan such as *noh* provide a glimpse into the larger cultural impact that *rongi* had on the various religious and cultural traditions of premodern Japan.

PRIMARY SOURCES

Those interested in the content of state-sponsored Buddhist debates may consult the *Kuge Saishōkō chōmonshū* 公家最勝講聴聞集. A photographic copy as well as a transcription have been published as part of Kokubungaku Kenkyū Shiryōkan's *Kōsetsu Rongishū*.[85] The *Chōmonshū* is a collection of the records of debate sessions that took place during the Saishōkō 最勝講 (lectures on and debates about the *Golden Light Sutra*), covering more than 200 years.

While the Saishōkō invited participation from monks of different schools, debates were also held within a particular school to train its monks and advance their doctrinal studies, for which the *Jōyuishiki ron dōgakushō* 成唯識論同学鈔 provides valuable sources. Originally compiled in the late 12th and early 13th centuries, the *Dōgakushō* offers a collection of study notes that Hossō monks of Kōfukuji produced in discussing the *Jōyuishiki ron* and debate topics concerning this text. A sixty-six-volume version is included in the *Taishō shinshū daizōkyō* and a forty-eight-volume version is in the *Dai Nihon Bukkyō zensho*.[86] Kusunoki Junshō led the collaborative study of the *Dōgakushō*, which resulted in publication of the annotations of some of the debate topics included in this text.[87] For the Tendai school, *Wayaku Tendaishū rongi nihyakudai* provides an overview of the Tendai debate tradition as well as the 200 debate topics of the Tendai school included in the 18th-century *Tendaishū rongi nihyakudai* 天台宗論義二百題.[88]

NOTES

1. Seiichi Tomabechi, "Rongi no rekishi to shingon," in *Nihon Bukkyō to Rongi*, Ryūkoku Daigaku Ajia Bukkyō bunka kenkyū sōsho 13, ed. Junshō Kusunoki, Sei Noro, and Takahiko Kameyama (Kyoto: Hōzōkan, 2020), 271–314.
2. Tom J. F. Tillemans, "Introduction: Buddhist Argumentation," *Argumentation* 22, no. 1 (2008): 1–14.
3. Minowa Kenryō, *Nihon Bukkyō no kyōri keisei: Hōe ni okeru shōdō to rongi no kenkyū* (Tokyo: Daizō Shuppan, 2009), 20–49, chap. 1.
4. For representative studies of Buddhist debate in Tibet, see Shunzō Onoda, *Monastic Debate in Tibet: A Study on the History and Structures of Bsdus Grwa Logic*, Wiener Studien zur Tibetologie und Buddhismuskunde 27 (Vienna: Arbeitskreis für Tibetische und Buddhistische Studien Universität Wien, 1992); Daniel E. Perdue, *Debate in Tibetan Buddhism* (Ithaca, NY: Snow Lion Publications, 1992); Georges B. J. Dreyfus, *The Sound of Two Hands Clapping: The Education of a Tibetan Buddhist Monk* (Berkeley: University of California Press, 2003); and Katherine Rogers, *Tibetan Logic* (Ithaca, NY: Snow Lion Publications, 2009).
5. James McMullen, *The Worship of Confucius in Japan*, Harvard East Asian Monographs 421 (Cambridge, MA: Harvard University Asia Center, 2020), esp. pp. 66–67.
6. Hisaki Yukio, *Nihon kodai gakkō no kenkyū* (Tokyo: Tamagawa Daigaku Shuppanbu, 1990); Momo Hiroyuki, *Jōdai gakusei no kenkyū* (Kyoto: Shibunkaku Shuppan, 1994); and Satō Fumiko, "Kodai no tokudo ni kansuru kihon gainen no saikentō," *Bukkyō shigaku kenkyū* 48, no. 2 (2006): 1–24.
7. McMullen, *Worship of Confucius*, 2.
8. Kurabayashi Shōji, "Sekiten no Momodo-no-za," *Kokugakuin zasshi* 86, no. 2 (1985): 1–14.
9. Kanchū Ogami, "Nenbun dosha ni mirareru kashi seido (jō)," *Nihon Bukkyō* 8 (1960): 14–27.
10. In East Asia, Buddhist schools are often identified by particular texts or sets of texts and do not necessarily constitute a strict continuity from India. In addition, there are schools that were established in China and subsequently introduced to Japan.
11. Takakusu Junjirō and Watanabe Kaigyoku, eds. *Taishō shinshu daizōkyō*, 85 vols. Tokyo: Taishō Issaikyō Kankōkai, 1924–34. No. 1585, 31.
12. Ogami "Nenbun dosha ni mirareru kashi seido (jō)"; Asuka Sango, *The Halo of Golden Light: Imperial Authority and Buddhist Ritual in Heian Japan (794–1185)* (Honolulu: University of Hawai'i Press, 2015), 24–42, chap. 2.
13. McMullen, *Worship of Confucius*, 60–61.
14. Sango, *Halo of Golden Light*.
15. *Yuima kitsushosetsu kyo* (*T* no. 475, 14:537a–557b) and *Konkōmyō saishō ō kyō* (*T* no. 665, 16:403a–456c).
16. Asuka Sango, "Buddhist Debate and the Production and Transmission of Shōgyō in Medieval Japan," *Japanese Journal of Religious Studies* 39, no. 2 (2012): 241–273 (see pp. 259–268 for a discussion of this particular question). The original text is the *Records of Questions and Answers Discussed at the Saishōkō*

(*Saishōkō mondōki*) and Tōdaiji Toshokan in Nara has the original copy, and the Shiryō Hensanjo at the University of Tokyo has a photographed copy.
17. *T* no. 665, 16: 419c.
18. For the discussion of this debate topic, see Kakujō Nomoto, "Tendai no rongi: Sōmoku jōbutsu," in *Rongi no kenkyū*, ed. Chisan Kangaku-kai (Tokyo: Seishi Shuppan, 2000), 110–155.
19. See the "Primary Sources" section of this article for more information about these two debate compendiums.
20. Makoto Nagamura, *Chūsei Tōdaiji no soshiki to keiei* (Kyoto: Hanawa Shobō, 1989), 431–543, chap. 3.
21. See Nagamura, *Chūsei Tōdaiji no soshiki to keiei*, 431–543; Kikuchi Hiroki, "Kyōshu to tonse," in *Jiten Nihon no Bukkyō*, ed. Minowa Kenryō (Tokyo: Yoshikawa Kōbunkan, 2014), 238–241; and William E. Deal and Brian Ruppert, *A Cultural History of Japanese Buddhism* (Hoboken, NJ: Wiley, 2015), 121.
22. *T* no. 1558, 29.
23. Sango, "Buddhist Debate," 241–273.
24. Seiichi Tomabechi, *Heianki Shingon Mikkyō no kenkyū* (Tokyo: Nonburu, 2008), 675–76; Tomabechi, "Rongi no rekishi to shingon"; and Elizabeth Tinsley, "Hōraku no mondō: Chūsei Kōyasan ni okeru kōkyō rongi to jingi shinkō," *Ōtani Daigaku Daigakuin kenkyū kiyō* 27 (2010): 141–172.
25. Andō Yoshinori, *Chūsei Zenshū bunken no kenkyū* (Tokyo: Kokusho Kankōkai, 2000), 381–439 and Ozaki Masayoshi, "Hossenshiki ni tsuite," *Shūgaku kenkyū* 45 (2003): 103–108.
26. Teizō Iyanaga, "Kodai no Sekiten ni tsuite," in *Nihon kodai No Seiji to Shiryō* (Tōkyō: Takashina Shoten, 1988), 142–145; and McMullen, *Worship of Confucius*, 56–57.
27. McMullen, *Worship of Confucius*, 73–74.
28. Paul Groner, *Ryōgen and Mount Hiei: Japanese Tendai in the Tenth Century* (Honolulu: University of Hawai'i Press, 2002), 128–166.
29. Sango, "Buddhist Debate," 247.
30. Tomabechi, "Rongi no rekishi to shingon," 281.
31. Nagamura Makoto, *Chūsei jiin shiryō ron* (Tokyo: Yoshikawa Kōbunkan, 2000), 56.
32. As translated by Brian Ruppert, "A Tale of Catalogs and Colophons: The Scope of the Lineage, the Touch of the Master and Discourses of Authenticity in Medieval Shingon Buddhism," in *Scholars of Buddhism in Japan: Buddhist Studies in the 21st Century*, ed. James Baskind and Symposium for Scholars Resident in Japan (Kyoto: International Research Center for Japanese Studies, 2008), 49–66.
33. Kamikawa Michio, *Nihon chūsei Bukkyō keisei shiron* (Tokyo: Azekura Shobō, 2007), 291–336.
34. Hiraoka Jōkai, *Tōdaiji Sōshō Shōnin no kenkyū narabi ni shiryō*, vol. 2:460, 465 (Tokyo: Nihon Gakujutsu Shinkōkai, 1959).
35. Sango, "Buddhist Debate," 252–256.
36. Minowa, *Nihon Bukkyō no kyōri keisei*, 12–13, 176.
37. Minowa, *Nihon Bukkyō no kyōri keisei*, 12–13, 176.
38. James L. Ford, *Jōkei and Buddhist Devotion in Early Medieval Japan* (Oxford: Oxford University Press, 2006), 222n11.
39. Kusunoki Junshō, "Hossō no rongi," in Chisan Kangaku-kai, ed., *Rongi no kenkyū*, 35, 50.
40. Mariko Watanabe, "Tendai no rongisho to dangisho: 'Hokekyō,' 'Saidaibu' o chūshin ni," in Kusunoki, Noro, and Kameyama, ed., *Nihon Bukkyō to Rongi*, 219–245; Nomoto, "Tendai no rongi: Sōmoku jōbutsu," 110–155; Sakaki Gikō, "Shingi Shingon no rongi," in Chisan Kangaku-kai, ed., *Rongi no kenkyū*, 185–222; and Katsumata Shunkyō, *Shingon no kyōgaku: Daisho hyakujō daisnjū no kenkyū* (Tokyo: Kokusho Kankōkai, 1981).
41. Sango, *Halo of Golden Light*, 43–59.
42. Miyoshi Toshinori, "Bukkyō shi jojutsu no naka no shūron: Ōwa no shūron ni kanren suru tekusuto o megutte," *Nihon shūkyō bunka shi kenkyū* 12, no. 1 (2008): 63–80; and Groner, *Ryōgen and Mount Hiei*, 94–117.

43. Groner, *Ryōgen and Mount Hiei*, 141–42; and Okano Kōji, *Heian jidai no kokka to jiin* (Tokyo: Hanawa Shobō, 2009), 255–265.
44. Shunpō Horiike, "Yuima-e to kandō no shōshin," in *Chūsei jiinshi no kenkyū*, ed. Chūsei Jiinshi Kenkyūkai (Kyoto: Hōzōkan, 1988), 2:193–230; and Sango, *Halo of Golden Light*, 43–59, chap. 3.
45. *Shakke kanpanki*; reprint in *Shinkō gunsho ruijū* 18, ed. Ueda Kazutoshi, Mikami Sanji, and Kuroita Katsumi(Tokyo: Naigai Shoseki, 1932), 595.
46. Horiike , "Yuima-e to kandō no shōshin"; and Sango, *Halo of Golden Light*, 43–59.
47. Nagamura Makoto, "Chūsei jiin no chitsujo ishiki," *Nihon shūkyō bunkashi kenkyū* 10, no. 1 (2006): 1–23.
48. Susumu Uejima, "Kenmitsu taisei no shūen," in *Nihon Chūsei shakai no keisei to ōken* (Nagoya, Japan: Nagoya Daigaku Shuppankai, 2010), 456–461.
49. Tomabechi, "Rongi no rekishi to shingon," 272.
50. Watanabe, "Tendai no rongisho to dangisho."
51. Kōjun Yamaguchi, "*Dangi*," in *Jiten Nihon no Bukkyō*, ed. Minowa Kenryō (Tokyo: Yoshikawa Kōbunkan, 2014), 252.
52. Yamaguchi, "*Dangi*," 252–253; and Minowa Kenryō, *Nihon Bukkyōshi* (Tokyo: Shunjūsha, 2015), 190–191.
53. Mikael S. Adolphson, *The Gates of Power: Monks, Courtiers, and Warriors in Premodern Japan* (Honolulu: University of Hawai'i Press, 2000), 10–11.
54. Uejima, *Nihon chūsei shakai no keisei to ōken*.
55. Gaétan Rappo, "Edo jidai shoki no gozen rongi no shosō," in Kusunoki , Noro, and Kameyama, eds., *Nihon Bukkyō to Rongi*, 513–545.
56. Kōsei Ishii, "Rongi no geinōka to sono tenkai," in Kusunoki, Noro, and Kameyama, eds., *Nihon Bukkyō to Rongi*, 495–512.
57. Kōichi Matsuo, *Ennen no geinōshi teki kenkyū* (Tokyo: Iwata Shoin, 1997).
58. Matsuo , *Ennen no geinōshi teki kenkyū*, 37.
59. *Shin sarugaku ki*; reprint in Tōyō Bunko 424, *Shin sarugaku ki*, ed. Kawaguchi Hisao (Tokyo: Heibonsha, 1983), 254–265.
60. Ashton Lazarus, "Envisioning Difference: Social Typology and Exhaustive Listing in Fujiwara no Akihira's *An Account of the New Monkey Music*," *Proceedings of the Association for Japanese Literary Studies* 15 (2014): 95.
61. Ishii , "Rongi no geinōka to sono tenkai," 504, 505.
62. Shida Nobuyoshi, ed., *Zoku Nihon Kayō Shūsei 2: Chūsei hen* (Tokyo: Tōkyōdō Shuppan, 1961), 52–53 and Ishii, "Rongi no geinōka to sono tenkai," 506–507.
63. Susan Blakeley Klein, *Dancing the Dharma: Religious and Political Allegory in Japanese Noh Theater* (Cambridge, MA: Harvard University Asia Center, 2021), 6–8.
64. Nakatsukasa Yukiko, "Shōdan tte nani?: Nō no kōzō o kangaeru: rongi 1," *Kanze* 78, no. 9 (2011): 40–43.
65. *Nonomiya*; reprint in *Nihon koten bungaku taikei* 41, *Yōkyōkushū* 2, ed. Yokomichi Mariko and Omote Akira (Tokyo: Iwanami Shoten, 1963), 319–322.
66. Omote Akira and Amano Fumio, *Nōgaku no rekishi*, Iwanami Kōza: Nōgaku to kyōgen 1 (Tokyo: Iwanami Shoten, 1987), 12.
67. Takayama Yuki, *Chūsei Kōfukuji Yuima-e no kenkyū* (Tokyo: Benseisha, 1997), 348.
68. Tinsley, "Hōraku no mondō," 141–172.
69. Matsuo Kōichi, "Nanto Jion-e ni okeru yumemi no gi: Denshō to keisei," *Setsuwa Denshōgaku* 5 (1997): 34–47.
70. Fabio Rambelli and Mark Teeuwen, eds., *Buddhas and Kami in Japan: Honji Suijaku as a Combinatory Paradigm* (New York: RoutledgeCurzon, 2003), 1.

71. Alison Tokita and David W. Hughes, *The Ashgate Research Companion to Japanese Music*, SOAS Musicology Series (Aldershot, UK: Ashgate, 2008), 37–38; and see also Kōjun Ōyama, *Bukkyō ongaku to shōmyō* (Osaka, Japan: Tōhō Shuppan, 1989), 57–278.
72. Ōyama , *Bukkyō ongaku to shōmyō*, 4–5.
73. *Kōyasan no shōmyō: Iidate rongi, Sannōin tsukinami monkō*, performed by NPO Hōjin Saṃgha: Shingon Shōmyō no Kai, Nihon Dentō Bunka Shinkō Zaidan (Japan Traditional Cultures Foundation), 2007, compact disc; and Taki Dōnin and Yoshida Tsunezō, eds., *Tendai shōmyō taisei* (Sakamoto, Japan: Tendai Shūmuchō, 1935), 2:172–198.
74. Ōuchi Fumi, *Bukkyō no koe no waza: Satori no shintai sei* (Kyoto: Hōzōkan, 2016).
75. Jacqueline I. Stone, *Original Enlightenment and the Transformation of Medieval Japanese Buddhism* (Honolulu: University of Hawai'i Press, 1999), 129–130.
76. For a review of literature on the topic of Japanese Buddhist debate, see Asuka Sango, "Buddhist Debate in Medieval Japan," *Religion Compass* 9, no. 7 (2015): 216–225.
77. Chisan Kangaku-kai, *Rongi no kenkyū*.
78. Uejima, *Nihon chūsei shakai no keisei to ōken*.
79. Mikaël Bauer, "The Yuima-e as Theater of the State," *Japanese Journal of Religious Studies* 38, no. 1 (2011): 161–179.
80. Kusunoki's scholarly publications on Buddhist debate are too numerous to cite all of them here. For some examples, see Kusunoki Junshō, "Nihon Bukkyō no tenkai: Hossō yuishiki ni tsuite," *Bukkyōgaku kenkyū* 50 (1994): 156–190; and "Hossō rongi to butsudō: 'Jō yuishiki ron dōgakushō' ni miru fujōbutsu shujō no etsū," in Kusunoki, Noro, and Kameyama, ed., *Nihon Bukkyō to Rongi*, 5–32; see also, Tomabechi, *Heianki Shingon Mikkyō no kenkyū*; and Tomabechi , "Rongi no rekishi to shingon," 271–314.
81. Groner, *Ryōgen and Mount Hiei*, 128–166; and Groner, "Training through Debates in Medieval Tendai and Seizan-Ha Temples," *Japanese Journal of Religious Studies* 38, no. 2 (2011): 233–261.
82. McMullen, *Worship of Confucius in Japan*.
83. For example, Iyanaga, "Kodai no Sekiten ni tsuite," 99–206; Kurabayashi , "Sekiten no Momodo-no-za," 1–14; and Sudō Toshio, *Kinsei Nihon Sekiten no kenkyū* (Kyoto: Shibunkaku Shuppan, 2001).
84. Matsuo, , "Nanto Jion-e ni okeru yumemi no gi," 34–47; and Tinsley, "Hōraku no mondō," 141–172.
85. Kokubungaku Kenkyū Shiryōkan, ed., *Kōsetsu Rongishū*, Shinpukuji Zenpon Sōkan (Kyoto: Rinsen Shoten, 2011); and Shinpukuji Zenpon Sōkan, dai-2 ki, vol. 2, ed. Abe Yasurō and Yamazaki Makoto (Kyoto: Rinsen Shoten, 2011), 67–289 and 333–390.
86. *T* no. 2263, 66: 1a–595b; as well as in *Yuishikiron dōgakushō*; reprint in *Dai Nihon Bukkyō zensho* 76, ed. Bussho Kankōkai (Tokyo: Bussho Kankōkai, 1934); and *Dai Nihon Bukkyō zensho* 77 (Tokyo: Bussho Kankōkai, 1937).
87. For more information, see the three-part study of the *Dōgakushō*, for which Kusunoki Junshō served as the chief editor: Kusunoki Junshō, Kitabatake Tensei, Kenchū Jōjun, Gotō Yasuo, Ninagawa Sachiyoshi, and Miyama Reichi, eds., "'Jō yuishikiron dōgakushō' no kenkyū," *Ryūkoku Daigaku Bukkyō Bunka Kenkyūjo kiyō* 36 (1997): 33–162; Kusunoki Junshō, Kitabatake Tensei, Gotō Yasuo, Ninagawa Sachiyoshi, Miyama Reichi, Kenchū Jōjun, Fujimaru Kaname, and Morimoto Kōjō, eds., "'Jō yuishikiron dōgakushō' no kenkyū (2)," *Ryūkoku Daigaku Bukkyō Bunka Kenkyūjo kiyō* 37 (1998): 67–153; and Kusunoki Junshō, Gotō Yasuo, Miyama Reichi, Nishimura Ryō, Moro Shigeki, and Ninagawa Sachiyoshi, eds., "'Jō yuishikiron dōgakushō' no kenkyū (3)," *Ryūkoku Daigaku Bukkyō Bunka Kenkyūjo kiyō* 39 (2000): 11–124.
88. Kouda Ryōsen, ed., *Wayaku Tendaishū rongi nihyakudai: Denkyō daishi goseitan sennihyakunen kinen shuppan* (Tōkyō: Ryūbunkan, 1966).

Asuka Sango

DOMESTIC DHARMA IN JAPAN

Domestic dharma in Japan embodies the creative complexity and fluidity of lived religious experience. It aspires to the ideals of lived wisdom and embodied compassion even as it flourishes in the mundane messiness of everyday activities, life-cycle challenges, and efforts to support familial comfort and contentment. In what ways do domestic dharma practices encourage moral behavior? Can daily activities and simple conversations help people heal? Are there Buddhist resources to support overwhelmed and exhausted mothers and fathers? Is there a domestic dharma practice that can get you through the midnight crying of a feverish child or a terminal diagnosis? Are there practices that support caring for an elder with increasing cognitive and physical decline? What practices can help one grieve and integrate loss into one's life? Responses to these questions drive the ongoing stream of dharma activity in the home.

The present exposition begins with a brief overview of familial relationships in historical context. It is followed by a discussion of five modes of religious activity that characterize the dynamics of domestic dharma. Each of the subsequent eight sections explores different dimensions that collectively illuminate domestic dharma in Japan. In order of occurrence, they are: "Creativity and Adaptability of Home Practice," "Dharma of Daily Life," "Securing Protection," "Home Altars," "Mothering, Elder Care, and Healing," "Living with Ancestors as Personal Buddhas," "Recent Developments," and "Discussion of the Literature."

Although the contours of domestic dharma can be drawn, domestic dharma thrives in a context where sharp delineations between impulses emerging from a sinuous interplay between Buddhist, Shinto, and folk traditions are elusive. Moreover, the Sino-Buddhist tradition that was transmitted to Japan had already integrated Confucian and Taoist influences. To try and extricate the shores of Buddhist dharma out of this malleable and fluctuating dynamic would distort the phenomenon of domestic dharma. The category of "domestic dharma" is a conceptual lens that focuses on everyday lived phenomenon in order for scholars to see Buddhist activity occurring in the privacy of people's homes.

Domestic dharma in Japan frames domestic activity as dharma activity. Families' primary concerns are more pragmatic than ideological, giving rise to a highly flexible relationship with Buddhist teachings and practices. Although the domestic dimension of the Buddhist tradition is a robust and ubiquitous stream, it has not received much scholarly attention. Researchers can gain reasonably ready access to texts, temples, and monastic institutions, while the practices done by families in their homes are by their very nature hidden from public view. Domestic dharma practices are transmitted orally and bodily through largely informal networks of personal relationships and are not recorded in the written documents that researchers typically examine. The Buddhist teachings are mostly so deeply integrated into daily life that many people are not consciously aware that their thinking or behavior is based on Buddhist assumptions about the nature of the world.

Historically, family units were affiliated with a particular sect of Buddhism during the Tokugawa period (1603–1867) for political expedience. Families were compelled to register with their local temple as a means for the government to collect and transmit information. To which sect a family reported affiliation was not a matter of people seeking out which Buddhist teachings and practices were most meaningful and appealing, much less an individual spiritual choice. Family units conformed to the external structures used to organize society, but the predominantly nondoctrinal approach to matters of religiosity in Japanese culture gave rise to families not being constrained by institutional dictates in the intimacy of their own homes.

The domestic sphere includes extended family members, traditionally living in multigenerational households. Due to numerous ancestral rituals centered on the home Buddhist altar, the number of generations actively in interplay is extended to include deceased members. Though increasingly families live in nuclear units, cultivating a sense of family that includes more than one generation occurs by interlacing ancestral rituals into daily life. A common example of how it happens is to ask a child to take a cup of tea to the home altar to offer to their deceased grandpa. Pets are also increasingly woven into the family unit and they, too, are offered Buddhist rituals after they pass away.[1]

Traditionally the eldest son stayed in the natal home and his wife would move into the home with his parents. Younger brothers and sisters would usually move away upon marriage. Sometimes, however, a daughter would stay in the natal home and a groom would be adopted into the family. The family Buddhist altar is located in the main household, though some family branches choose to have their own altar, too. Once married, the majority of women become part of their husband's family unit and often eventually become caretakers of the home Buddhist altar where his ancestors are commemorated. In addition to this, some women have also established a separate altar for their natal family.

Not all Japanese people identify as Buddhist, especially since it is not a membership-based tradition. It is not uncommon, however, for a person who has not actively engaged in Buddhist practices to invoke them when a parent passes away. Those who are actively engaged in Buddhist communities, though, do not necessarily do all of the activities outlined here. People engage the practices that suit their concerns. There are also a range of practices that people turn to during different phases of their life span. These dynamics underscore the nondoctrinal and adaptive character of domestic Dharma practices.

Domestic Dharma practices fall under five broad overlapping modes of religious activity: ritualized, scriptural, communicative, materially interactive, and aesthetic.

1. Ritualized activities involve moving the body-mind in ways that actualize/perform the ideals of a tradition or community. They include a diverse swath of activities ranging from elaborate and intricate ceremonies to brushing teeth. Ritualizing activities in a Buddhist mode facilitates being in touch with the interrelated nature of existence and provides a stabilizing foundation of calm clarity in the midst of constant change.
2. Scriptural activities include a spectrum from chanting texts to reading silently. Dimensions of orality (vocalizing), aurality (listening), and information acquisition (thinking) come into play through this category.
3. Communicative activities focus on verbal interaction. They occur upon entering and leaving the home, beginning and ending a meal, or prayerfully talking with a deceased loved one—person or pet—at the home altar. A deep sense of interdependence, trust, and vulnerability undergird these interactions.
4. Materially interactive activities treat objects respectfully. Suffused with humble gratitude, people animate material objects with honor by placing a ceramic bowl down on a wood surface without making a sound, arranging shoes by the door so they are not in

anyone's way, yet are easy to put on when leaving, and arranging food offerings at the home altar before the family begins eating.

5. Aesthetic activities emerge out of awareness that an experience of beauty can give rise to peaceful relationships, expanded perspectives, and healing insights. They include gracefully serving tea to express warm affection, positioning an arrangement of flowers where people can readily relax into a view of the natural treasures of the season, and writing a poem of forgiveness on the death anniversary of a loved one.

These five modes of activity are not discrete. They often converge in a given activity. For example, a meal often includes treating the ingredients with respect (materially interactive) and arranging the food artfully on dishes chosen to highlight the season (aesthetic). The meal is framed by uttering ritualized words at the beginning and end. "*Itadakimasu*" is said before eating. It expresses humble gratitude for receiving the bounty of the earth and appreciation for the one who prepared the meal. "*Gochisōsamadeshita*" is said after eating. It expresses humble gratitude for the feast that was eaten (communicative). Both phrases are accompanied by physical gestures: palms together while making a slight bow (ritualizing). Analysis of these modes in other everyday events illuminate dharma implicit in a range of domestic activities.

Domestic dharma practices aim for *genze riyaku* (現世利益), practical benefits in present life. Daily life concerns are implicitly framed as matters of ultimate importance for they are undergirded by a cosmological orientation that does not demarcate sacred and profane realms. Family interactions are where most members expect to receive support for fundamental needs, including health, safety, childrearing, education and employment issues, assistance in aging, and succor when dying. A nonbifurcated approach to body-mind drives these life concerns, which are animated by specific factors in each given moment and location. The core dynamics of domestic dharma involve a field of adaptable practices, including ritualization of daily life, rites and objects for protection, offerings and chanting at a home altar, healing activities, mothering as locus of transmission of teachings and practices, and engagement with ancestors.

CREATIVITY AND ADAPTABILITY OF HOME PRACTICE

The hallmarks of dharma in the home are creativity and adaptability. Families customize received practices from a spectrum of sources to meet their specific needs and circumstances. Though sometimes informed by sectarian practices, rarely do families concern themselves with accurately observing or maintaining doctrinal and institutional boundaries of a sect or even of Mahāyāna Buddhism. Many of the practices are seamlessly woven into daily life. Practitioners sometimes do not identify them as religious activities, in part due to the fact that the concept of "religion" is not an indigenous Japanese category. Moreover, familial activities do not fit neatly into abstract categories and institutional frames, for they are complex, concrete, and ever-changing.

Even though domestic dharma dynamics are predominantly nonsectarian, the teachings and practices of Pure Land (Jōdoshū and Jōdo Shinshū), Nichiren (Nichiren-shū, Risshō Kōseikai, Sōka Gakkai, and Nichiren Shōshū), and Zen (Rinzai and Sōtō) sects are prevalent. The Pure Land and Nichiren traditions respectively entwine *nembutsu* and *daimoku* practice into daily home life. Chanting or focusing the heart-mind on entrusting "*Namu Amida Butsu*"

(Praise to Amida Buddha 南無阿弥陀仏) or "*Namu Myōhō Rengekyō*" (Praise to the Wondrous Lotus Sutra 南無妙法蓮華経) serve as ubiquitous conduits to the deepest values and aims of their distinct teachings. They elicit a humble, grateful, and expansive posture with which a person can respond to personal challenges regarding education, employment, and relationships. They quietly ground and connect people during tense situations, including intergenerational differences. Invoking the familiar and respected power of their distinct chants quells fears regarding health and calms anxieties of aging. It provides strength to face things one step at a time, all the while knowing one is not alone. The Zen traditions also integrate their teachings into everyday home life. The two Zen sects have different understandings of the relationship between practice and enlightenment. Rinzai approaches practice as what you do to attain enlightenment. Sōtō understands when you practice you are enlightened. This difference is subtle when the teachings are practiced in the home, for enlightenment is rarely a conscious aim. Zen practice in the home is manifest in impulses that animate aesthetic sensibilities when arranging flowers or serving tea. Precision and intricate care in cleaning and cooking are also marks of a Zen approach. Practitioners of Zen practice at home rarely engage in Zen meditation; rather, they focus on being respectful, practical, and efficient in the present moment, whatever the activity. Sōtō Zen has had a pervasive influence on Japanese domestic practices regarding ancestors, for it developed the funerary rite that recognizes the deceased as enlightened.[2] (More is written about this in the "Living with Ancestors as Personal Buddhas" section.)

In order to skillfully respond to issues as they arise, domestic dharma practices are typically simple, accessible, inexpensive, portable, direct, and immediate. Families do not need to engage in years of disciplined practice to perform or participate in most of these practices. A field of practices helps them navigate a broad range of familial concerns, difficulties, and crises. Some are individual practices and some are done as a family. Many seek peace and clarity in daily life through explicit practices such as chanting, sutra copying, and the contemplative practices of flower arranging and tea ceremony. Dealing with the challenges of conceiving and raising children, many turn to chanting certain *dhāraṇī* (sacred phrase) mantras, or sutras. Parents commonly pray for support and guidance. Mothers often clutch a protective amulet (*omamori*) during childbirth. Cooks add ingredients imbued with nutritious and healing powers, especially if someone in the family is sick or facing a difficult issue. Primary caretakers of elders, especially when caring for those who are completely dependent and/or exhibit dementia, include approaching daily tasks such as laundry and cleaning with meditative attentiveness, chanting and praying for strength and patience, and centering themselves with sutra copying. When facing intractable circumstances or traumatic events, offering incense, listening to the toning of the home altar bell, and talking with a trusted ordained Buddhist or temple wife are regularly invoked. Effects of a practice are often immediate and direct—from calming down in a moment of crisis to feeling compassionately heard—despite a steady stream or sudden avalanche of anxiety. Domestic dharma is a vital sphere in which harmonious and resilient responses to the vicissitudes of life are cultivated.

DHARMA OF DAILY LIFE

Daily life offers numerous opportunities to transmit dharma teachings. Due to the nature of how Buddhist observances are engaged in the home, accessing and understanding them largely depend on ethnographic research. It must be deeply qualitative research, for most of the people you are trying to understand do not perceive their actions in terms of the category "domestic dharma." Noticing the values that are encoded in daily activities and conversations is one way to see how dharma teachings are integrated into people's lives. The primary values that animate domestic dharma include respect, gratitude, harmony, hard work, mindfulness, cleanliness, sincerity, and awareness of nature.

Many dharma teachings are delivered to children through folk tales and pithy phrases. A common theme stressed in folk tales is be kind and generous, not greedy. The tale *Straw Hat Jizō* (*Kasa Jizō* 笠地蔵) is a popular example. The main character is poor, and he is rewarded with good fortune for his thoughtful acts. A commonly heard pithy phrase is: "It is bad to have likes and dislikes" (*Suki kirai wa dame* 好き嫌いはダメ。). Children are told this especially in reference to food. These are practical and concrete teachings that capture two of the three Buddhist poisons (desire and aversion).

Ritualized phrases encoded with Buddhist teachings are replete in adult daily conversation. Some examples are "*okage-samade*," "*otagai-sama*," and "*shikataganai*." The first phrase expresses humble gratitude for the undergirding support of others, which is a way of experiencing interdependence. The second phrase also invokes the interdependent nature of experience for it conveys respectful acknowledgment that we are in this together and dependent on each other. The third phrase is used to express awareness that there are causes and conditions beyond individual control, intimating the vast flux in which we live. A common proverb invoked when someone is having a difficult time encourages perseverance and resilience: "Seven times down, eight times up" (*Nana korobi, ya oki* 七転び八起き). Effort is one of the actions on the Buddhist Eightfold Path of "best practices" to stop suffering.

Many people approach the everyday activities of laundering, cooking, and cleaning as opportunities to practice the dharma. By doing household chores with conscious and singular focus on the task at hand, not only do you get food to eat, a tidy home, and clean clothes to wear, you can experience respite from emotional intensity that arises while tending to the varying needs of family members. Many women say that hanging laundry on a sunny day becomes a meditation on the causes and conditions required to dry a sheet and can be a palpable experience of interdependence. They feel refreshed and keenly grateful as a breeze flutters through clothes that had piled up over several days of rain. Touching the cotton that rose from the earth, nourished by the rain, thriving under the sun that now dries the plant fibers that a multitude of hands have gathered, woven, sewn, and transported to their own hands is a tactile meditation that invites gratitude for the connective web of support for their lives. One woman exclaimed how when she saw a butterfly land on a garment she had just hung out to dry, she was deeply moved by how light and joyfully they live on the earth. Then she realized that maybe flapping those big wings might require tremendous effort and it might be a difficult life being a butterfly. She reflected on how she was seeing from her personal human perspective and had no idea what the butterfly's life was like. It humbled her and she committed to being more respectful of others' perspectives. The depth of dharma that can be drawn from hanging laundry can likewise be drawn from cooking, cleaning, or any domestic activity.

Ritualizing a household chore is a rich vein for dharma activity, because it emerges out of immediate needs. Practitioners of domestic dharma become skillful in imbuing daily actions with meaning and moral import.

SECURING PROTECTION

Families want protection from illness, fires, natural disasters, and accidents. In addition to measures taken to mitigate or ameliorate such events, families also turn to a range of ritualized, scriptural, and materially interactive modes of action.

One of the most ubiquitous protection practices is having an *omamori* (お守り) protective talisman (see figure 1). They are ritually empowered objects that people quietly carry or grasp in times of need. They come in a range of forms that specify the type of protection or support sought. Traditionally, calligraphy of the protective words, often an excerpt from a sutra, were brushed on wood or paper. The most common *omamori* is made of a brocade cloth pouch that identifies the specific power of the amulet woven into the cloth. Innovative 21st-century talismans include decals, miniature *juzu* prayer beads, and keychains. *Omamori* are tucked into a wallet, affixed to a cell phone, and strung onto a school bag, purse, or briefcase. They are also placed in cars. *Omamori* can be purchased at Buddhist temples for a host of concerns: home safety (*kanai anzen* 家内安全), health (*kenkō* 健康), traffic safety (*kōtsū anzen* 交通安全), good fortune (*kaiun* 開運), education (*gakugyōjyōju* 学業成就), marital connection (*en-musubi* 縁結び), safe childbirth (*anzan* 安産), and even protection for pets (ペットお守り). They are customarily replaced around the new year to start the year off fresh without negative residue from the prior year.

Figure 1. *Omamori* protective talisman.
Source: Photograph © Paula Arai

Numerous ritualized activities also invoke protective power for a family. Two common ones are the *Daihannya-e* ("Great Wisdom Scripture" 大般若會) ceremony at temples and a *Setsubun* (節分) ceremony that marks the end of winter and the beginning of spring.[3] These rituals are for generalized protection of family members and the home. Ancestors also provide protection to a family, which will be discussed more fully in the "Living with Ancestors as Personal Buddhas" section.

The *Daihannya-e* is mostly done shortly after ringing in the new year. The ritual focuses on a core Mahāyāna Buddhist scripture, the *Mahāprajñāparamitā Sūtra*. The ritualized engagement with the scripture does not involve reading or reflecting on the meaning of its contents. The voluminous scripture is ceremoniously brought into the main worship hall of the temple. The 600 accordion-style sutra books (*kyōbon* 経本) are divided among the ordained clergy seated in orderly fashion along the sides of the worship hall. Dramatic rhythmic pounding of a large taiko drum fills the air as each cleric opens the *kyōbon* in their stack one at a time in practiced ritual form. They release the scripture's power by fanning open the scripture in the cardinal directions while chanting a *dhāraṇī* The lead celebrant has a special section of the sutra dressed in silk brocade covers. Each person in attendance can approach and receive the direct power from this special *kyōbon*. In order to transfer the healing power from the text to the person, some lead celebrants actually tap the large scripture on one's shoulder and some press the corner of the text into a pressure point at the base of the neck. It is understood that after exposure to the protective powers of the text, when a person goes home they are a vehicle for the power to protect the home and all its inhabitants. Most of the participants in the ritual are women. Laity then bring home and strategically place the paper *ofuda* お札 infused with the protective power of the sutra (see figure 2). Typically the *ofuda* is placed in the front entrance area (*genkan*) or in the home altar, but people can place them wherever they want protection.

The *Setsubun* ceremony is performed on February 3. It is commonly a ritual a family does at home, although Shinto shrines and some Buddhist temples also host ceremonies. The ritual is quite loud and playful. Each person cups some roasted soybeans in their hands and stands at a door or window for a bean-throwing ritual (*mamemaki* 豆まき). While throwing the beans, everyone shouts, "*Fuku wa uchi. Oni wa soto.*" 「福は内。鬼は外。」 "Fortune in. Devils out." After the bean throwing, people are to eat the number of roasted soybeans commensurate with their age. The ritualized activity offers agency to families who seek support and protection from forces that impact daily life.

HOME ALTARS

The home Buddhist altar is a pivotal locus of domestic dharma. The altar can occupy a specifically designated room or just a portion of a surface where offerings can be placed. Some altars are pristinely formal and others are endearingly adorned with generations of meaningful items, including amulets, poems, children's drawings, and traces of travels (see figure 3). A buddha statue or Buddhist calligraphy is enshrined, usually in accord with the sectarian practices with which the family became affiliated during the Tokugawa period. It is more common for women to be the primary caretakers of a family's home altar. Assuming responsibility for the home altar is sometimes a personal choice, but often done out of obligation to

Figure 2. *Ofuda.*
Source: Photograph © Paula Arai

perform the duty to maintain the altar of her husband's natal family. Although from the structure of the ritual it can appear that women are subservient to their husband's family, it is not merely that males place themselves structurally in a higher status. The women who perform the rites at the altar experience the calmness, clarity, strength, and support that accrue from the practice. Filial daughters and dedicated wives reap the benefits of praying and chanting for themselves as they are serving others. Although not common, women sometimes create a less formal altar for their own family in another room.

Practices at the altar usually begin with a bow. Prayer beads (*juzu* 数珠) are often draped on the left wrist or held in both hands. Fresh flowers are placed on the altar. Tea or water, rice, and sometimes other food, such as fruit, is offered in the morning and evenings, too, for more devout households. A candle is lit and stick or granular incense is burned. A singing bowl is rung with a mallet before chanting and prayers commence. The simple act of offering involves movement of the body and expands the mind beyond the self.

The daily chants (*mainichi otsutome* 毎日お勤め) done at the home altar range from short mantra-like phrases to long sutras. Families will usually chant the texts from the daily liturgy of the sect with which the family has traditionally been affiliated. Jōdo and Jōdoshin sects of Pure Land stress chanting the *nembutsu*: "*Namu Amida Butsu.*" Jōdoshin followers commonly

Figure 3. Traditional home altar.
Source: Photograph © Paula Arai

add the *Shōshinge* ("Hymn in Praise of Buddha" 正信偈). Those affiliated with Nichiren-based traditions repeat the *daimoku*: "*Namu Myōhō Rengekyō*." The *Heart Sutra* is chanted by those in Tendai, Shingon, Jōdo, and the Zen sects. The *Jikku Kannon-gyo* 十句観音経 is also commonly chanted, reflecting an affinity for the bodhisattva of compassion. The *Kannon-gyo* 観音経 from the twenty-fourth chapter of the *Lotus Sutra* is chanted when there is a special occasion, such as the seasonal equinox rite or a familial rite honoring the death of a loved one.

Chanting is often punctuated by periodic toning of a singing bell (りん) and the beat is kept by the thumping of the wood-fish drum (*mokugyō* 木魚). Chanting expands the person by filling the mind and body with sounds that pulsate through the surrounding space. Reflecting on the meaning of the words is not a notable focus in Japan's domestic dharma. Neither is chanting done with explicit intent to directly address emotional needs. Rather, the deep breathing and regular and rhythmic sounds facilitate an experience that serves as a break from the push and pull of emotions. After such a break, rejuvenation and clarity are gained through the expanded perspective of the chanting experience.

Offerings and chanting are ritualized activities that support a person in the kind of transformation sought in domestic dharma. Ritualizing activities helps a person direct their focus onto meaningful actions, which often eases the intensity of afflictive emotions. The home altar is a place that both reminds a person that there is a way that helps and that there is a space where an enlarged perspective on matters of the heart can be experienced. These ritual practices interrupt, stop, and change the flow of thought and surges of emotion. These practices function as an anchor for the household, providing stability and safety that allow a person to face heart-wrenching and intractable situations.

MOTHERING, ELDER CARE, AND HEALING

Domestic dharma is propelled by nurturing. Both women and men engage in activities that support family. Men often take the role of protectors, though much of their effort is financial support and occurs outside the home. Learning more about their attitudes, motivations, and practices is a ripe area for future research that will deepen our understanding of domestic dharma. Women predominantly tend to the physical, emotional, and spiritual needs of themselves and their families. They skillfully embed meaning and value into daily life tasks, responding to crises and offering healing ministrations. Amid the sounds of water running for the laundry, dishes, and baths, they embody wisdom. With the aroma of food cooking—sometimes adding spiritually purified water from a temple or a sanctified waterfall—they manifest steady, corporeal awareness that they are connected to and supported by an interrelated whole. Female practitioners of domestic dharma are also often the ones to perform the daily rituals at the home altar. Some deliberately light incense when family members will smell its calming fragrance and chant when they will hear the Buddhist scriptures and prayers, imbuing the home with wafts of healing and protective ethos.

Mothering is a locus of a woman's practice of domestic dharma. Transmission of teachings and practices occurs through a mother's actions. Preparing and eating a balanced meal is a lesson on how our bodies are aggregates of planetary nutrients and cosmic elements. Cleaning clothes, linens, dishes, floors, and bodies are practicums on caring for health and well-being. Listening to fears and dreams are master classes on understanding that one is not alone.

Tending to cuts and fevers is a tutorial on compassion in action. To fortify their efforts, many mothers invoke support from the bodhisattva of compassion. They quietly intone a *Lotus Sutra* passage that functions as a maternal mantra: "Namu Kannon Riki" ("Praise to the Power of Kannon" 南無観音力). Repeated utterances can help a mother gather focus and not be overwhelmed by midnight fever spikes, injuries, and upsetting incidents and interactions. As mothers do this practice, they serve as role models on how to regulate emotions and ameliorate intense situations.

Considering elder care as dharma activity helps family members navigate the challenges with more calm, respect, understanding, and strength. Women constitute a preponderance of the caretakers of elderly family members. Being a caretaker is highly stressful and demanding. When caring for an elder, there is no formal ritual to acknowledge the shift in power when the younger generation takes the lead. The nebulous shift is often a process fraught with frustration, for it requires each person to cultivate a new identity. In the shuffle, dignity, pride, and confidence are often lost to the elder, while patience is lost to the caregiver. Ritualizing household chores and performing rites at the home altar are the mainstays of practitioners of domestic dharma. These practices are known to provide grounding and rejuvenation from the emotional strains of caretaking and aging.

The quintessentially personal and creative nature of homemade healing rituals replete in domestic dharma is strikingly illustrated in the following example. A common household item, a *tenugui* (手ぬぐい) cleaning cloth, is the ritualized material object at the center of this invented dharma practice. The one depicted in figure 4 had the calligraphy of the highly respected Zen abbess, Aoyama Shundō Rōshi (青山俊董), and the image of a figure with hands held in prayer (*Gasshō Dōji* 合掌童子) printed on it (see figure 4). The abbess had commissioned these traditional cleaning cloths, so she would have something useful to give to people. She thought that many might not actually clean with it, but might use it for special occasions handling special dishes. She did not imagine that they would be used for healing. A lay woman, who frequented rituals and teachings of Aoyama Rōshi, received one of these cloths. When diagnosed with a terminal cancer, she believed that the *tenugui* cloth had the power to heal her. She lay in bed with one cloth on her pillow and one on her legs, the location of the cancer. She lived for more than a dozen years; the doctors could not find traces of cancer in her body. In this case, the method of healing was not "traditional." It was not even intended by the maker and giver of the cloth. An observable conclusion is that the meaning with which the receiver of the cloth endowed the cloth had an efficacious power when it was placed on her body. Regardless of the mechanics of this ritualized use of the unpretentious *tenugui*, the gratitude and joy that this woman experienced is genuine. After learning of this occurrence, others in the small community have used the cloth in a similar way. If someone did not have their own cloth and became sick, others would gift them in support of their healing. They report positive results. This new ritual practice initiated by a devout Zen Buddhist laywoman exemplifies the homemade nature of domestic dharma.

Healing is a central priority in domestic dharma. Healing sometimes results in a cure of a medical condition, but healing in the domestic context has a broader latitude of meaning. The spectrum of healing encompasses acute disease, approaching death, grieving loss, living with cognitive decline, caring for those with cognitive decline, depression, and the messiness and misery of a plethora of mild to intense life situations. How to live with chronic conditions,

Figure 4. *Tenugui* cleaning cloth used for healing.
Source: Photograph © Paula Arai

integrate unwelcome events, and adapt to changes in familial and social dynamics are matters for which a healing response is sought. Healing involves wholesome support and empowerment. Domestic dharma draws upon a vast array of activities to tailor ways to fortify healing responses to a host of life challenges. The ultimate aim of healing is to dissolve the poisonous root causes of suffering: delusion, greed, and aversion. The poisons appear in the home in incidents such as complaints about eating vegetables, insecurities or exhaustion that erupts in anger, and jealousy and misunderstanding among siblings that drive family dysfunction. Domestic dharma enlists ritualized, scriptural, communicative, materially interactive, and aesthetic activities to engage the conditions of life as fuel for burning away poisons.

Domestic dharma healing practices support people in facing infertility, crippling chronic pain, death through disease, untimely loss of family members, experiencing equanimity, cultivating harmonious relationships, and creating beauty in daily life. Disruptive events often generate powerful emotional responses, including paralytic fear, agonizing heartache, depression over the loss of dreams, and anxiety about not being able to perform daily tasks. Doing daily tasks with the intention of diffusing afflictive emotions helps people compose themselves with calm dignity. A measure of healing is evident when refined aesthetic sensibility and acts of kindness do not betray inner suffering. Healing is palpable when a person has descended into a kind of hell realm and emerged without cynicism, bitterness, or anger. Healing is also manifest when a person is quick to notice beauty in their midst. Healing is amplified by gratitude. The ritual practices of making offerings, chanting, and praying on a regular basis are the resources that fuel resilience and strength. Though they appear to be simple rituals, requiring no officiant and done in the privacy of their own crowded homes, these rituals form the framework within which tremendous challenges to the human spirit are faced and compelling tapestries are woven that empower and inspire. One laywoman encapsulates the core of healing in domestic dharma: "I know I am healed when I am kind."[4]

LIVING WITH ANCESTORS AS PERSONAL BUDDHAS

The domestic sphere includes continued connection with deceased family members, especially through ritual activities done at the home Buddhist altar. When a family loses a member, it is common for a family to intensify its association with Buddhist practices and rituals. Many in modern Japan admit to not knowing to which sect of Buddhism their family belongs until there is a funeral. When a family member passes away, they are referred to as "Hotoke-sama" (Honorable Buddha). Most families place a picture of the deceased near the altar. The altar becomes a conduit for families to maintain interactions with the deceased in a number of ways. Placing flowers, lighting candles and incense, making food offerings, especially rice and tea, and chanting scriptures at the altar are common daily activities. Many also enjoy offering things such as the deceased's favorite fruit when it is in season. The family will then eat the offerings with a sense of enjoying the food with the deceased family member.

As a gesture of respect, it is common to share a gift with a deceased loved one by placing it on the altar before the gift is opened. Verbal communication is quite natural, including providing updates such as report cards, new jobs, marriages, and births. The person addressing the altar utters the same appellation as when alive, such as "*Obāchan*" (Grandma). In this way, grandchildren can sense that they are nurtured in a multigenerational family.

While seated at the altar, it is also common for people to confide in their loved one through prayerful "conversation." Such interaction is safe for expressing vulnerabilities, pains, and fears, for the deceased—having been recognized as a Buddha upon death—is often understood to be compassionately listening and supporting the family. I devised the term "personal Buddha" to describe this distinctly domestic dharma phenomenon in Japan.[5]

A home altar ritual for one's personal Buddha provides an occasion for monks and nuns to come into the home to offer chants for death anniversaries. The date of the month someone passed away is called the *meinichi* (monthly death anniversary 命日). On this date each month, ideally, a monk or nun visits, usually from the temple with whom they have a relationship. After the chanting is complete, tea is served. In the privacy of their own home, the family members present are then able to open up to receive wise counsel about a matter. It is often just the wife, though men agree that they, too, are generally more comfortable speaking with a nun about a troubling matter than with a monk.[6] In this quiet way families receive spiritual and emotional support. Seeking mental health support is still stigmatized in Japan, so this domestic dharma practice serves a critical function in modern Japan.

The most elaborate ritual regarding ancestors is Obon. Depending on region, a range of activities occur in mid-July (solar calendar) or mid-August (lunar calendar). The rituals occur in the home, at gravestones, and at temples. They welcome ancestors home for a few days. Lanterns are lit to guide them home (*mukae-bi* 迎え火). Special foods are offered for the festive occasion. Monks and nuns visit homes to offer chants at that home's altar. The family visits the family gravestone to tend to it with extra cleaning and offerings. A community dance is held. At the end, the special offerings at the home altar are bundled up like a boat and traditionally released into a body of water with a lit candle to guide the way (*okuri-bi* 送り火). Due to environmental concerns, many temples have a bonfire where the offerings can be burned and thereby send off the ancestors for another year.

Pure Land teachings are distinctive in terms of home altar practices. Traditionally, True Pure Land followers do not have a mortuary tablet (*o-ihai* お位牌) with the deceased dharma name engraved on it. Neither is it encouraged to place a picture of the deceased on the altar. The altar is for Amida Buddha, who vows to help the deceased be reborn in the Pure Land. Therefore, offerings to ancestors at the home altar are not common. The offerings are given respectfully to Amida Buddha. Despite these sectarian concerns, however, many families in a Pure Land tradition engage with the deceased with the kind of intimacy found in the personal Buddha practices. This underscores the nondoctrinal and fluid boundaries of domestic dharma.

The practice of treating an ancestor like a "personal Buddha" developed through the lived practice of the tradition as people created ways to meet their needs and concerns. It is not based upon a scriptural text. Moreover, the understanding of karma in domestic dharma in Japan is extratextual. Confucian concern to respect ancestors gave rise to a domestic Buddhist practice that deflects potential rebirth of a family member into a lower realm. Karma comes to be interpreted in intergenerational terms. Out of filial piety, gratitude is accorded to ancestors for the positive life conditions a family has. This understanding intimates that karma flows forward in a family line. Karma, thus, also affects one's progeny. It fosters moral behavior and a sense of responsibility, for future family members' life conditions are understood to be shaped by one's present actions. A focus on how the present depends on the past and affects the future underscores the interconnections of a family.

RECENT DEVELOPMENTS

Another healing activity that has become increasingly popular in domestic dharma is sutra-copying practice (*shakyō* 写経). Although it had long been a practice among elite Buddhists, in the 21st century it is becoming a favored practice to do at home or in a temple. Sutra-copying is a contemplative practice, not a reflective practice. Comprehending the content of the scripture being copied is not the objective. The quiet, calm, stable qualities of being required to do the practice are akin to seated meditation. Maintaining straight posture, breathing slow and deep, and focusing on the present moment are the foundation of both practices. Most copy the *Heart Sutra*, for it is short. It can fit on one sheet of paper. Most commonly people get a special sheet that has light traces of the characters of the sutra printed on it. Brushing the calligraphic characters of the sutra with dark *sumi* ink takes about an hour. The intent focus of tracing the characters, a number of which are not in common use, requires intent concentration. The delicate hairs of the brush are utterly responsive to the level of pressure, steadiness, trajectory, angle, and speed with which a stroke is executed, revealing the quality of one's body-mind on the page. Receiving immediate feedback enables a person to gradually become attuned to the rhythms of body-mind activity required to brush the beautifully balanced strokes presented on the sutra-copying sheet. People with chronic situations, such as painful ailments, long-term elder care, and complicated relational dynamics, report that engaging in this contemplative practice is restorative and refreshing. It relieves stress and pressure, which helps them be stronger and more patient and have a more open perspective to their situations.

Mass urbanization over the 20th century has fractured family units as people moved from multigenerational homes in villages to small dwellings in large cities. Dislocated from traditional Buddhist activities and pressed to work hard and educate children, families often felt that the Buddhist tradition was old-fashioned and not relevant to their lives except when someone dies. An entrepreneurial insight gave rise to the Yanagiken company designing home altars with modern and Western (Scandinavian, Italian) aesthetics. They made home altars fresh and expanded the appeal to those who do not have a strong conscious association with a particular traditional Buddhist sect. Eliciting the sense of an altar as a meaningful and important site in a home, they suggest how it can be a place for quiet reflection, not tethered to any particular religious tradition, where disciplining children can be more effective and even facilitate engaging in practices of loving family members (living and dead), which may help foster world peace.[7] These developments affirm the centrality a home altar has on a family, even when the "Buddhist" aspect of it is actively unmoored. It is an example of how flexible domestic dharma is in Japan. People can engage the dharma in sufficiently resilient ways so it maintains relevance in their modern lives. Such innovations and experiments are possible precisely because they do not have institutional or textual concerns directing their course. The absence of these markers, however, requires scholars to recognize dharmic impulses in subtle and not explicitly Buddhist phenomena.

Another significant aspect of changes in domestic dharma practice pertains to the rituals and material interactions of gravestones. Traditionally, a family has one gravestone in which all family members' ashes are interred. Monthly visits to the grave to pay respects and make offerings involve a donation of "incense money" to the temple. With families living geographically distant, shifting family identity, and the high expense of ritually maintaining a family grave, an increasing number of people are pursuing novel ways to have their remains respected. Temples are responding by establishing communal graves for people with shared values. These are especially appealing to those who do not have someone to care for their grave, including people with no children or who do not want to burden their children with care for a family grave. Notably women are choosing to be interred in their own gravesite, separate from their husband's family. Others find it meaningful to have their ashes scattered in the sea or a forest.[8] These practices are not without complications and controversy. Nonetheless, they affirm the creative and responsive character of dharma as practiced by everyday people. They adapt ways to meet their personal and familial needs.

DISCUSSION OF THE LITERATURE

Buddhism as practiced in the domestic sphere has only recently received scholarly attention, so the number of publications that engage the topic are few. Ethnographic field work undergirds all the research. Ian Reader and George Tanabe's *Practically Religious: Worldly Benefits and the Common Religion of Japan* implicitly addresses the theme of domestic dharma.[9] They discuss common practices in their complex contexts that span the spectrum of those that identify with and defy institutional and textual boundaries. They set in high relief the fluid nature of people's engagement with religious practices, which stresses people's concern for meeting concrete and current-day needs. Paula Arai's *Bringing Zen Home* delves into a specific community of lay Buddhist women who primarily draw on Zen teachings and practices.[10] These women are not focused on doctrinal matters, which aligns with Reader and Tanabe's research. They harmonize various currents in their creative healing activities, which they integrate into daily life. Noriko Kawahashi's articles, "Jizoku (Priest's Wives) in Sōtō Zen Buddhism" and "Women Challenging the 'Celibate' Buddhist Order," opened up the dynamics and perspectives of Sōtō Zen temple wives.[11] They inhabit a distinctive domestic space that is part of a temple. Jessica Starling's *Guardians of the Buddha's Home* explores the dynamics of temple wives in a Pure Land context.[12] Domestic dharma in temple households adheres more closely to sectarian teachings and practices; however, fluidity is still manifest in the particular ways teachings are integrated into daily life activities. John Nelson's article on "Household Altars in Contemporary Japan" explores how demographic changes and economic interests affected the practices revolving around home altars.[13] It was a company vision, not Buddhist temple leadership, that encouraged ways to adapt home altars into modern life. Mark Rowe's *Bonds of the Dead* reveals the changing landscape of burial practices.[14] Novel practices regarding remains reflect families' shifting locations and priorities. People are choosing communal burial sites and dispersing their ashes into natural terrain over maintaining family gravesites where everyone is interred together. Barbara Ambros's *Bones of Contention: Animals and Religion in Contemporary Japan* sheds light on the depth to which pets have become ingratiated into people's families.[15] Over the 20th century, the fulsome multigenerational family unit shrank down to isolated nuclear pods. With people marrying later, staying single, living longer, and many choosing not to have children, pets are buttressing families. This changing nature of family drives the development of funerary rites for pets. Collectively these works open the door into the rich realm of domestic dharma. Biographical, visual, and literary sources are potential areas of research that would likely augment and enrich our view of the dynamics of dharma as it is lived in the domestic sphere.

FURTHER READING

Ambros, Barbara. *Bones of Contention: Animals and Religion in Contemporary Japan*. Honolulu: University of Hawaii Press, 2012.

Arai, Paula. *Bringing Zen Home: Japanese Women's Healing Rituals*. Honolulu: University of Hawaii Press, 2011.

Joskovich, Erez. "Zen in a Secular Age: The Development of the Laypeople Zen Narrative." In *Buddhism in East Asia: Aspects of History's First Universal Religion Presented in the Modern Context*. Edited by Anita Sharma, 215–231. Delhi: Vidyanidhi Prakashan, 2012.

Kawahashi, Noriko. "Jizoku (Priest's Wives) in Soto Zen Buddhism: An Ambiguous Category." *Japanese Journal of Religious Studies* 22, no. 1–2 (1995): 161–183.

Kawahashi, Noriko. "Women Challenging the 'Celibate' Buddhist Order: Recent Cases of Progress and Regress in the Soto School." *Japanese Journal of Religious Studies* 44, no. 1 (2017): 55–74.

Nara, Yasuaki. "May the Deceased Get Enlightenment! An Aspect of the Enculturation of Buddhism in Japan." *Buddhist–Christian Studies* 15 (1995): 19–42.

Nelson, John. "Household Altars in Contemporary Japan: Rectifying Buddhist 'Ancestor Worship' with Home Décor and Consumer Choice." *Japanese Journal of Religious Studies* 35, no. 2 (2008): 305–330.

Reader, Ian and George Tanabe. *Practically Religious: Worldly Benefits and the Common Religion of Japan.* Honolulu: University of Hawaii Press, 1998.

Rowe, Mark. *Bonds of the Dead: Temples, Burial, and the Transformation of Japanese Buddhism.* Chicago: University of Chicago Press, 2011.

Starling, Jessica. *Guardians of the Buddha's Home: Domestic Religion in Contemporary Jōdo Shinshū.* Honolulu: University of Hawaii Press, 2019.

NOTES

1. See Barbara Ambros's research on Buddhist funerary pet practices (Barbara Ambros, *Bones of Contention: Animals and Religion in Contemporary Japan* (Honolulu: University of Hawaii Press, 2012)).
2. William Marvin Bodiford, "Zen in the Art of Funerals: Ritual Salvation in Japanese Buddhism," *History of Religions* 32, no. 2 (1992): 146–164.
3. For more information about this ritual in three different contexts, see William Bodiford, "Sōtō Zen in a Japanese Town: Field Notes on a Once-Every-Thirty-Three-Years Kannon Festival," *Japanese Journal of Religious Studies* 21, no. 1 (1994): 4–36; Gregory Schopen, "The Phrase *'saprthivipradesas des'as' caityabhutobhavet'* in the *Vajracchedika*: Notes on the Cult of the Book in Mahayana," *Indo-Iranian Journal* 17: 3–4 (1975): 147–181; and David Gellner, " 'The Perfection of Wisdom'—A Text and Its Uses in Kwa Baha Lalitpur," in *Change and Continuity: Studies in the Nepalese Culture of the Kathmandhu Valley*, ed. Siegfried Lienhard (Alessandria, Italy: Edizioni dell'Orso, 1996), 223–240.
4. Arai, *Bringing Zen Home: Japanese Women's Healing Rituals* (Honolulu: University of Hawaii Press, 2011), 29.
5. For more detailed information about the meaning and function of "personal Buddhas," see Arai, *Bringing Zen Home*, 65–107.
6. In 1991, as part of field research conducted in Nagoya for my volume *Women Living Zen* (New York: Oxford University Press, 1999), I did a survey of laymen. I wanted to understand their views about nuns. I specifically questioned whether they prefer confiding in monks or nuns regarding personal matters when a monastic comes into a layperson's home to chant as part of ancestral rites. I received 90 survey responses, and all of them preferred nuns. I have not yet published these results elsewhere.
7. John Nelson, "Household Altars in Contemporary Japan: Rectifying Buddhist 'Ancestor Worship' with Home Décor and Consumer Choice," *Japanese Journal of Religious Studies* 35, no. 2 (2008): 326.
8. For more information on these practices, see Mark Rowe's *Bonds of the Dead: Temples, Burial, and the Transformation of Japanese Buddhism* (Chicago: University of Chicago Press, 2011).
9. Ian Reader and George Tanabe, *Practically Religious: Worldly Benefits and the Common Religion of Japan* (Honolulu: University of Hawaii Press, 1998).
10. Arai, *Bringing Zen Home.*
11. Noriko Kawahashi, "Women Challenging the 'Celibate' Buddhist Order: Recent Cases of Progress and Regress in the Soto School," *Japanese Journal of Religious Studies* 44, no. 1 (2017): 55–74; and Noriko Kawahashi, "Jizoku (Priest's Wives) in Soto Zen Buddhism: An Ambiguous Category," *Japanese Journal of Religious Studies* 22, no. 1–2 (1995): 161–183.
12. Jessica Starling, *Guardians of the Buddha's Home: Domestic Religion in Contemporary Jōdo Shinshū* (Honolulu: University of Hawaii Press, 2019).
13. Nelson, "Household Altars in Contemporary Japan."
14. Rowe, *Bonds of the Dead.*
15. Ambros, *Bones of Contention.*

Paula Arai

DUNHUANG ART

CAVE SHRINE AS ARCHITECTURAL PROTOTYPE

According to a dedicatory stele titled "Stele for a Buddhist Shrine at the Mogao Caves by Mr. Li" (*Li Jun Mogaoku fokan bei* 李君莫高窟佛龕碑), which is dated 698, the first cave shrine at the Mogao site was established by a monk named Lezun 樂尊.[1] In this account, Lezun arrived at the eastern edge of Mount Mingsha in the year 366 and witnessed a golden light which manifested the form of a thousand buddhas. Thereafter, he excavated the first cave shrine as a meditation chamber and was followed shortly after by another monk, named Faliang 法良. Certain Dunhuang manuscripts place the date of Lezun's arrival even earlier, in the year 353.[2] These two caves, their locations unknown as of the early 21st century, inaugurated a thousand years of continuous activity at the site.

The carving of shrines from living rock was a practice that began in India and was transmitted to China along the Silk Routes. The excavation of cave shrines involved the participation of teams of laborers and artisans, each specializing in specific skills, and unfolded over multiple steps. To begin, caves were carved directly into the cliff face through the use of hammers and chisels. Wooden facades were attached to the cliff face, and most cave shrines were divided into smaller antechambers and larger main chambers connected by a corridor. After the excavation of a cave was complete, the walls were smoothed over with several layers of earthen plaster composed of clay, silt, sand, and plant fibers, beginning with a thicker plaster and finishing with a thinner, finer plaster. After the final plaster layer had dried, it was treated with an alum and glue sealant that prepared the wall for the application of paints by creating a smooth, watertight ground.[3]

The construction and decoration of cave shrines was facilitated by a modular process that favored certain architectural prototypes and resulted in the establishment of a local painting academy as well as the development of the standardized painting compositions known as transformation tableaux (*bianxiang* 變相). At the Mogao site, the most common cave types are the central pillar and hall caves. Central pillar caves take their name from the square pillar that connects the floor and ceiling of the main chamber, a distant descendant of the India stupa, or reliquary mound (figure 1). Sculptural icons could be installed in a niche carved into the east-facing wall of the pillar, or on all four sides. The hall cave, however, consisted of an open main chamber in which the icons were placed in a niche carved in the rear, or west wall (figure 2). Another important cave type was the great buddha cave in which a colossal buddha statue was built against the rear wall; four of these exist at Mogao: the standing buddhas in caves 96 and 130 and the reclining parinirvāṇa buddhas of caves 148 and 158. The monumental buddha statues were carved from living rock and covered with clay. The sculptural icons of ordinary Mogao cave shrines were built on a wooden armature stuffed with reeds and covered with a mixture of straw and clay. Left unfired, they were painted on the surface with bright pigments. Although many of these statues have not survived the centuries, extant works still remain, such as the intact sculptural ensemble in the Tang dynasty Mogao Cave 45 (figure 3).

The painting materials consisted of plant dyes such as indigo and lac, mineral pigments including azurite and malachite, as well as locally produced synthetic pigments such as carbon black, lead white, and vermilion.[4] During the 10th century, a well-organized painting academy

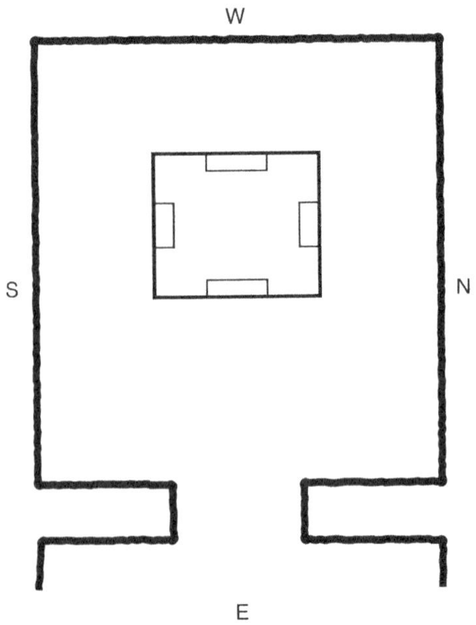

Figure 1. Plan of a central pillar cave.
Source: Drawing by Ernest Baroni

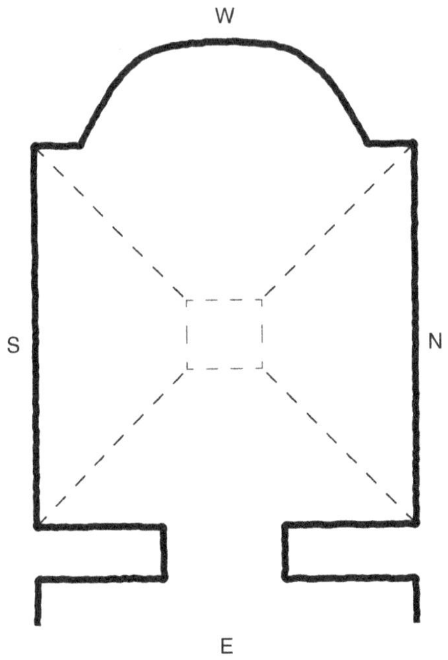

Figure 2. Plan of a hall cave.
Source: Drawing by Ernest Baroni

Figure 3. Sculptural ensemble. Tang dynasty (618–907). West wall niche, Mogao Cave 45, Dunhuang, Gansu Province.
Source: Reprinted from Dunhuang wenwu yanjiusuo, ed., *Zhongguo shiku: Dunhuang Mogaoku* 3 (Beijing: Wenwu chubanshe, 1987), plate 124

flourished under the patronage of the Cao 曹 clan, the local rulers of the Return to Allegiance Army (Guiyijun 歸義軍) between 914 and 1006. The hierarchical structure of this government-sponsored institution is attested in the Dunhuang manuscripts from the Stein and Pelliot collections. At the top of the hierarchy were the painting bureau commissioner and painting guild manager. Below them, the head of artisans oversaw specialists, painters, artisans, and apprentices possessing varying degrees of experience and skill.[5]

The general areas of mural paintings were laid down first by master painters in red, pale green, or black paints, after which they were painted over by subsequent layers of pigments by the artisans working under them.[6] Sketches and pounces from the Library Cave provide further insights into the artist's practice at Dunhuang. Sketches executed in monochrome black ink allowed artists to experiment with the visual formulae and compositions of large-scale murals. The greatest number of extant sketches pertain to the Magic Competition, a motif that appeared in fifteen cave shrines at the Mogao and Yulin sites. The theme of the Magic Competition was a contest between Buddhist devotees, led by the buddha's disciple Śāriputra, and the heretics, commanded by Raudrākṣa, with each side engaged in increasingly more elaborate feats of magic in order to demonstrate their supremacy over the opposing side. A close examination of the Magic Competition mural on the west wall of Mogao Cave 196, which dates to the period of the Return to Allegiance Army (848–1036), invites comparisons to sketches drawn onto three scrolls now in the Pelliot collection of the Bibliothèque nationale de France. The sketches pertain to individual characters and scenes of competition between the two sides.[7]

Due to differences between the dimensions of the cave shrines in which murals of the Magic Competition appeared, sketches could be employed as only a loose guide for the finished product, which necessitated the adjustment of proportions calibrated to different painting surfaces. Pounces, however, allowed painters to produce exact duplicates of certain motifs. A number of extant pounces pertain to the Thousand Buddhas motif, which was a repeating pattern of small seated buddhas commonly seen on the ceilings and walls of cave shrines (figure 4). Pounces are drawings in which the outlines are pricked with holes at regular intervals. After the pounce is laid against a wall, a colored powder is applied, which leaves behind an impression of the original drawing for the artists to fill in with line and color. Extant pounces of the Thousand Buddhas motif correspond to the dimensions of the Thousand Buddhas painted on the ceiling slopes of Mogao Caves 147 and 196. Along with red powder residue on the pounces and the remains of dotted lines on the south ceiling slope of Mogao Cave 98, this substantiates the use of pounces by artists at Dunhuang and demonstrates the variety of tools and methods that artists had at their disposal.[8]

Another intriguing aspect of painting production at Dunhuang is the use of stamps to produce standardized images of the Thouand Buddhas. In a 9th- to 10th-century scroll from Dunhuang (figure 5), repeated images of seated buddhas, similar to those seen on the ceilings and walls of the Mogao cave shrines, were impressed by stamps over which colored pigments were then applied. The buddhas' garments have been painted in alternating shades of red and brown. Beneath each figure is the expression "obeisance to" (*nanwu* 南無), followed by the buddha's name.

Lists of the names of the buddhas of the past, present, and future and ten directions are preserved in multiple versions of the *Sutra on the Names of the Buddha* (*Foshuo Foming jing* 佛說佛名經), of which there are numerous manuscript copies from Dunhuang. These formed the basis for repentance rites that were carried out in order to expiate the negative karma of devotees.[9] The repentance rites involved evoking the buddhas' presence by recalling their names and meditating upon their appearance.[10] Yet another scroll impressed with the seated Thousand Buddhas was marked with a date to the right of every twenty-first image; these dates coincided with the six fasting days of the Buddhist calendar, suggesting a possible ritual context for this practice of recalling the buddhas' names.[11]

COMMUNITIES OF DONORS AT DUNHUANG

Who were the donors who commissioned the construction of cave shrines, and what roles did they play in communicating with artists and monks? The patronage of caves could be attributed to multiple donors or to a single clan, from ordinary laypeople to monks to local rulers and social elites. Schematic images of male, female, and monastic donors were painted on the walls of cave shrines, recording the names and intentions of individual donors. Mogao Cave 428, which dates to the Northern Zhou dynasty (557–581), contains 1,189 donor images, the largest number of any cave shrine at the site. Of the donor images, 699 represented monks and nuns, demonstrating the joint patronage of laypeople and members of the monastic community.[12]

Figure 4. Pounce. Guiyijun period (848–1036), 926–975. Ink and color on paper with pricked outlines. Traces of powder remain on the paper's surface. 55.5 × 38 cm.
Source: From Dunhuang. British Museum, 1919,0101,0.73.2 (Ch.xli.004).

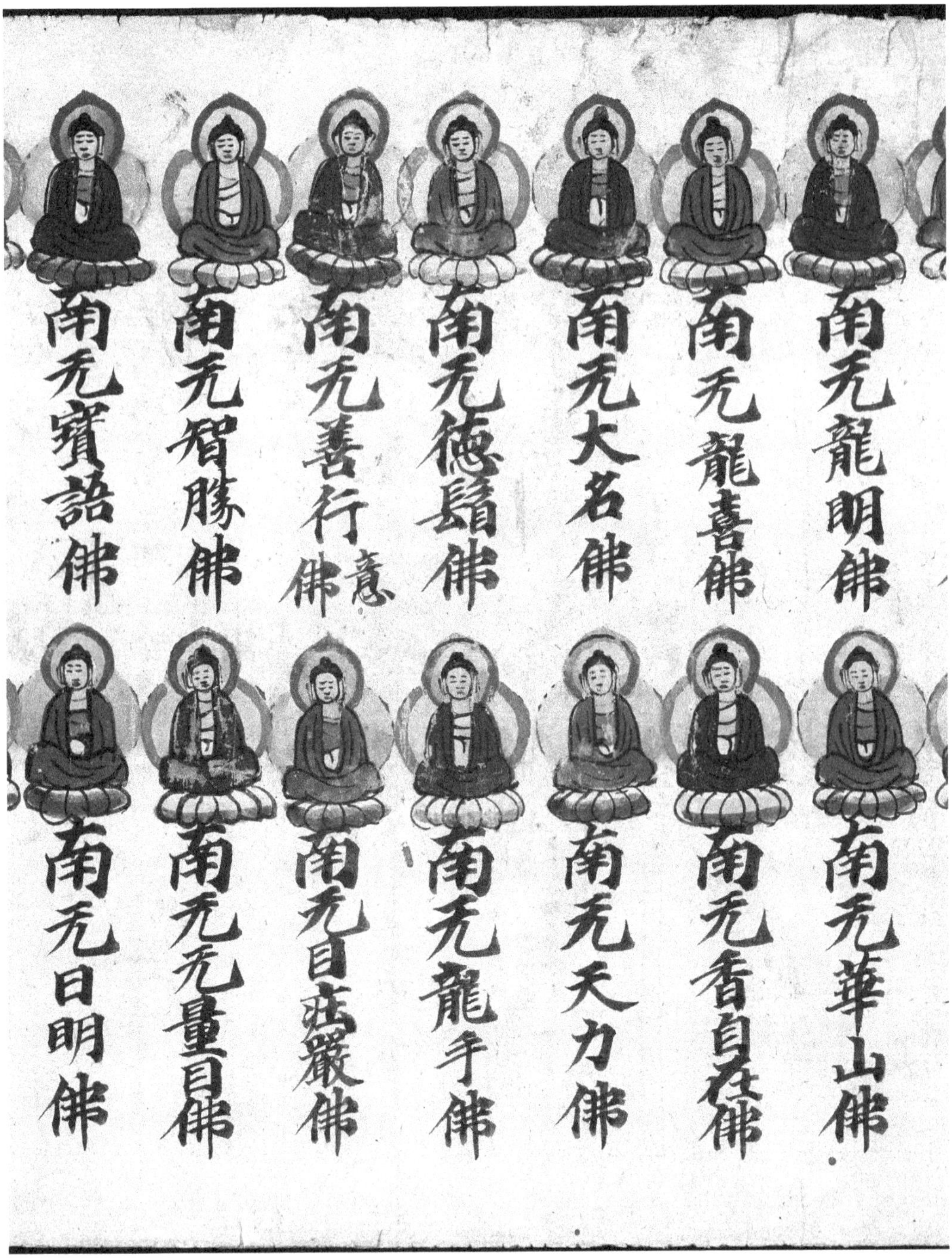

Figure 5. *Sutra on the Names of the Buddha* (section). Guiyijun period (848–1036), *c.* 9th–10th century. Ink and color on paper. 27.5 × 225 cm.
Source: From Dunhuang. The British Library, Or.8210/S.253

Yet other cave shrines, known as "family caves" (*jiaku* 家窟), resulted from the patronage of a single clan. The earliest identifiable family cave is the Tang dynasty (618–907) Mogao Cave 220, which was built under the patronage of the powerful Zhai 翟 clan. On the west wall, the words "Zhai family cave" (*Zhai jiaku* 翟家窟) were brushed. The cave shrine continued to be managed by the Zhai clan for three centuries after its initial construction, with later layers of paintings concealing the earlier ones.[13]

In family caves, it was a common practice for donor images of the living to be placed adjacent to those representing deceased family members, suggesting a clan united in devotion to the buddha in life and in death. In certain cases, the placement of donor images was purposeful and suggested reverence to elder family members and the accrual of merit for their benefit. In Mogao Cave 231, which is dated *c.* 839, images of the patron Yin Jiazheng's 陰嘉政 deceased parents are placed not along the lower walls or below the niche containing the main icon, as is typical for donor images, but rather above the doorway to the main chamber located on the east wall. Furthermore, they are markedly larger in size than the typical donor image. The prominence given to the images and their placement evokes the plaques erected above the gates and doorways of the temple building, as well as ancestor portraits that commemorated deceased family members.[14]

The continuity between generations of donors also extended to the very iconographic programs of cave shrines. Mogao Cave 61, which dates to *c.* 947–951, was built under the patronage of the Cao clan of the Return to Allegiance Army, specifically by Cao Yuanzhong 曹元忠 (r. 944–974). Intriguingly, eleven of the fifteen motifs that appear in the mural paintings of Mogao Cave 61 also appear in the earlier Mogao Cave 98, which dates a few decades earlier to *c.* 923–925. Mogao Cave 98 was the first family cave constructed under the Cao clan and the main patron was none other than Cao Yuanzhong's father, Cao Yijin 曹議金 (r. 914–935). The motivation for modeling his own cave shrine after that of his father might be attributed to Cao Yuanzhong's desire to firmly establish his political authority in the region; it is instructive to note that the construction of Mogao Cave 61 began only three years after Cao Yuanzhong assumed the position of military commissioner of the Return to Allegiance Army. As the fourth ruler, he followed after the relatively short reigns of his two elder brothers. Therefore, the appropriation of elements of the visual program of the earlier cave should be viewed as a purposeful borrowing and a visual evocation of the establishment of the Cao regime of the Return to Allegiance Army rather than as evidence of a lack of originality.[15]

In addition to untangling the visual cues that lay behind communicating religious devotion, political authority, and family lineage, another motivation for studying the patronage of the Mogao Caves is to gain a more robust picture of Dunhuang as a multiethnic and multicultural regional center. Comparisons between the visual programs of Tang dynasty cave shrines and literary records of Buddhist monasteries in the Tang capital of Chang'an reveal surprising overlaps in the choice of subject matter and their spatial arrangement.[16] This corroborates the presence of frequent cultural interchanges between the center and periphery of the Tang empire. However, the Tibetan occupation of Dunhuang (786–848) was marked by increased multiculturalism, and the period of the Return to Allegiance Army, which ruled after the fall of the Tibetans, was characterized by intermarriages with the neighboring Uyghurs and Khotanese.[17] Moreover, several dynasties that ruled in subsequent centuries, both in the central plains region of China and in the borderlands, were of non-Chinese origin, from the

Khitan Liao (907–1125) and Tangut Xixia (1038–1227) to the Jurchen Jin (1115–1234) and Mongol Yuan dynasties (1279–1368).

Extant paintings, manuscripts, and textiles from Dunhuang and present-day Xinjiang Uyghur Autonomous Region attest to the visibility of Uyghurs, a Turkic ethnic group, as donors and artists. Female donor figures wearing Uyghur dress can be seen in Mogao Caves 98 and 61, attributed, respectively, to the patronage of Cao Yijin and Cao Yuanzhong.[18] Comparisons between the religious iconography and artistic style of Dunhuang to images in the Bezeklik Caves and other sites of Xinjiang Uyghur Autonomous Region shed light on common features. Surprisingly, some of the most prominent stylistic traits of Uyghur Buddhist art, including the rendering of facial features and the use of dark backgrounds, bright primary colors, and gold leaf, are also shared with Uyghur Manichaean painting. Manichaeism was a monotheistic religion founded by the prophet Mani in Persia in the 3rd century CE. It seems likely that the Uyghurs began to convert from Manichaeism to Buddhism in the 10th century, yet still preserved the distinctive features of the older artistic tradition.[19]

DUNHUANG AS A MULTICULTURAL CENTER

A portable painting from Dunhuang, now in the collection of the British Museum represents an iconographic template known as the Maṇḍala of Eight Great Bodhisattvas (figure 6). A buddha wearing an elaborate crown is seated in the center under a jeweled canopy with his hands in the gesture of meditation, or *dhyāna mudrā*. On either side of the buddha is a row of four bodhisattva attendants. Their bodies turn to face the central buddha, and they are similarly adorned with jewelry and ornate crowns. According to horizontal cartouches bearing Tibetan inscriptions and the iconographic attributes of the deities, the identities of the bodhisattvas are, on the left, Maitreya, Kṣitigarbha, Mañjuśrī, and Ākāśagarbha; and on the right, Avalokiteśvara, Sarvanivāraṇaviṣkambhin, Samantabhadra, and Vajrapāṇi.[20] The elongated yet robust bodies of the deities suggest a Himalayan rather than Tang Chinese style of art.

The central buddha of the maṇḍala is understood to represent Vairocana Buddha. The identification of the buddha, in conjunction with the inscriptions from the painting, attests to the significance of Vairocana in early Tibetan Buddhism and the transmission of the iconography of this maṇḍala to the Dunhuang region, where it appears in Mogao Cave 14 and Yulin Caves 20, 25, and 38. The prominence of Vairocana as the main icon in Tibetan temples suggests that the cult of Vairocana had firmly taken root in Tibet by the 8th century.[21] During this period, Vairocana was associated with the foundation of the Tibetan empire, echoing the imperial associations of Vairocana that were present elsewhere in Asia, as in China and Japan, where important images of Vairocana at the Longmen Caves and Tōdaiji were sponsored through state patronage.[22]

Moreover, images of the Maṇḍala of Eight Great Bodhisattvas were commissioned in order to commemorate treaty negotiations between the Tibetans and Chinese in the early 9th century. Starting in the second half of the 7th century, the Tibetans and Chinese vied for control of the Tarim basin and the Chinese military garrisons in Central Asia, culminating in the fall of Dunhuang to the Tibetans in 786. Between 706 and 822, seven treaties were signed between the two parties.[23] The last of these was commemorated by a large stone carving of the Maṇḍala of Eight Great Bodhisattvas located in Denma Drak, Dagyab Province, in the Kham

Figure 6. *Maṇḍala of Eight Great Bodhisattvas*. Tibetan period (786–848), early 9th century. Ink and color on silk. 95 × 63.5 cm.
Source: From Dunhuang. British Museum, London, 1919,0101,0.50 (Ch.0074). © The Trustees of the British Museum

region of present-day Tibet Autonomous Region.[24] Sponsored by the abbot Yeshe Yang, the dedicatory inscription states that the sculpture was made in 816 at the beginning of treaty negotiations between the Tang and Tibetan courts. It also names the Tibetan ministers who led the treaty negotiations and the Tibetan and Chinese craftsmen who made the sculpture.[25] Furthermore, Tibetan language manuscripts from Dunhuang make note of a "treaty temple" named Dega Yutsel that was built to commemorate the same treaty. Importantly, its iconographic program too emphasized the Maṇḍala of Eight Great Bodhisattvas.[26]

Returning to the painting from Dunhuang, its relatively small size suggests that it might have been commissioned for the performance of a private ritual rather than to make a grand commemorative gesture. In the lowermost portion of the painting, beneath the pedestal supporting the buddha, the barely perceptible figures of two lay donors can be discerned. A dedicatory inscription was originally brushed adjacent to the female donor located in the lower right of the painting, although the fragmentary condition of the silk has rendered it illegible.

THE PATH TO THE PURE LAND

The motifs of Dunhuang paintings and donor inscriptions indicate that one motivation behind the sponsorship of paintings was the accrual of merit for deceased family members.[27] A 9th-century portable painting on silk depicts a bodhisattva with feet supported by opened lotus blossoms and holding an incense burner in one hand and a textile banner with trailing tassels in the other (figure 7). The bodhisattva's descent from a heavenly realm is suggested by the trailing red clouds behind him. His gaze is trained on a woman dressed in the characteristically voluminous Tang dynasty style; her face is turned downward in a reverential manner. As the title of the painting indicates, the deity is the "bodhisattva guide of souls" (*yinlu pu*[*sa*] 引路菩 [薩]). The woman represents the soul of a deceased devotee, and the Chinese-style buildings in the upper left corner convey the pure land toward which she is being led by the bodhisattva guide.[28]

A number of Dunhuang paintings and manuscripts articulate a belief in the bureaucracy of the afterlife, which was governed by the ten kings of hell. The earliest dated manuscript of the Sutra of the Ten Kings of Hell is from Dunhuang and was brushed in the year 908. The sutra itself was probably composed in China sometime between the 8th and 10th centuries.[29] An elaboration upon the Indic notion of the underworld, the ten kings were the judges of the afterlife in front of which the deceased would appear in sequence and have their deeds reported and evaluated. This liminal stage between death and rebirth lasted three years and was punctuated at regular intervals by the performance of memorial rituals directed toward the ten kings by monks who were engaged by the living relatives of the deceased family member in order to ease their loved one's progression through the prolonged process of judgment. In addition to the performance of ceremonies, the copying of the sutra was itself also a merit-making activity.[30]

One bodhisattva who was specifically charged with leading souls in the afterlife was Kṣitigarbha. A common formula of portable paintings from Dunhuang is the arrangement of the ten kings on either side of Kṣitigarbha, who is depicted in the center holding a staff that breaks open the gates of hell and a flaming jewel (figure 8). The prominence given to the bodhisattva in scale and position emphasizes his ability to intercede with the kings on behalf of

Figure 7. *Bodhisattva Guide of Souls*. Guiyijun period (848–1036), second half of 9th century. Ink and color on silk. 80.5 × 53.8 cm.
Source: From Dunhuang. British Museum, London, 1919,0101,0.47 (Ch.lvii.002). © The Trustees of the British Museum

the deceased. Each of the ten kings is shown seated in the manner of a court official behind a table upon which a scroll recording the deeds of the deceased is unrolled. Each king is attended in turn by petty bureaucrats. Below Kṣitigarbha is a jailor showing a deceased soul, his head locked in a wooden cangue, his sins as reflected in a round mirror. At the very bottom of the painting are images of the donors kneeling on either side of a blank central cartouche; this may have been a generic composition rather than one commissioned by a specific donor. Similar paintings in the Mogao Caves show the ten kings as an independent motif or joined with Kṣitigarbha.[31]

Figure 8. *Kṣitigarbha and the Ten Kings of Hell*. Guiyijun period (848–1036), *c*. 926–975. Ink and color on silk. 91 × 65.5 cm.
Source: From Dunhuang. British Museum, London, 1919,0101,0.23 (Ch.0021). © The Trustees of the British Museum

MAPPING PILGRIMAGE: MOUNT WUTAI AT DUNHUANG

The notion of a pure land was not restricted to buddhas alone. The most prominent of the bodhisattvas were also associated with their own realms that came to be identified with sacred mountains in China, allowing devotees the opportunity for direct encounters with bodhisattvas in these numinous realms. One of these was the bodhisattva Mañjuśrī, whose pure land was Mount Wutai 五台山, located in northern China in present-day Shanxi Province. His association with Mount Wutai had crystallized by the Tang dynasty. In the period of the decline of the dharma, it was believed that Mañjuśrī would reside on the "Mountain of Snows."[32] Although originally conceptualized as a mountain in the Himalayas, Chinese monks gradually came to identify Mañjuśrī with Mount Wutai in China, perhaps because the mountain was capped with snow even in the height of summer.[33]

Mount Wutai was indisputably an important pilgrimage site in its own right. Intriguingly, a number of Dunhuang mural and portable paintings pertaining to Mañjuśrī on Mount Wutai attest to the interconnectedness of these two sacred sites. The most well known of these is the celebrated mural painting on the west, or rear wall of Mogao Cave 61, in front of which originally stood a sculpture of Mañjuśrī seated atop his characteristic lion mount (figure 9). It provides a topographic view of Mount Wutai's five peaks and the western and eastern routes by which pilgrims accessed the many temples and stupas on the mountain, painted in fine detail and identified by the inscriptions brushed into cartouches. Although seemingly map-like in appearance, close examination of the painting reveals that its features do not accord strictly with the actual topography and architecture of the mountain peak but rather capture the experience of the pilgrim.[34]

Reinforcing such an interpretation of the mural painting, other motifs, particularly those in the upper register of the painting, depict the numinous sights and visions that were believed to be visited upon the pilgrim to the mountain. As a tenth-stage or advanced bodhisattva, Mañjuśrī could appear to devotees in a variety of forms distinct from his standard aspect as a young prince. These manifestations ranged from an old man to multicolored rays of light or clouds and mist; the bodhisattva was also associated with the imagery of auspicious birds or a lion, his mount. The manifestations of Mañjuśrī appear not only in the mural painting of Mount Wutai, but also in the corpus of Mount Wutai poems from the Dunhuang manuscripts.[35]

As a bodhisattva, Mañjuśrī frequently appeared as an attendant to a central buddha figure and was often paired in this respect with the bodhisattva Samantabhadra. Therefore, the representation of this bodhisattva in an independent guise as the "new-style Mañjuśrī" (*xinyang Wenshu* 新樣文殊) is noteworthy. This imagery, as seen in the north wall of the corridor of Mogao Cave 220 (figure 10), features Mañjuśrī seated frontally on his lion mount. Rather than flanking a central buddha, he is now treated as the central deity and is in turn flanked by his

Figure 9. *Panorama of Mount Wutai.* Guiyijun period (848–1036). Mural painting. West wall, Mogao Cave 61, Dunhuang, Gansu Province.
Source: Courtesy of Wei-cheng Lin, by permission of the Dunhuang Academy

Figure 10. *New-style Mañjuśrī.* Guiyijun period (848–1036), 925. Mural painting. North wall of corridor, Mogao Cave 220, Dunhuang, Gansu Province.
Source: Reprinted from Dunhuang wenwu yanjiusuo, ed., *Zhongguo shiku: Dunhuang Mogaoku* 5 (Beijing: Wenwu chubanshe, 1987), plate 20

own retinue, consisting of the young boy pilgrim Sudhana on the left and the king of Khotan on the right. Outside the thick outlines that encompass the painting, standing bodhisattva attendants have been painted on either side.

The large cartouche below Mañjuśrī not only identifies him as the new-style Mañjuśrī but further describes this representation as an auspicious image, or *ruixiang* 瑞様. This associates the new-style Mañjuśrī with a specific class of imagery that flourished at Dunhuang during the 9th and 10th centuries.[36] As recorded in numerous mural paintings and a large portable painting from the Stein collection divided between the British Museum and National Museum of India, certain famous icons were believed to have miraculously flown through the air from

India or Central Asia onward to China. The animation that these famous icons possessed had a twofold significance: first, this proved their authenticity and sacrality, and second, the fact that they chose to fly to China authenticated the latter as a Buddhist realm in its own right.[37]

DUNHUANG IN THE PRESENT TENSE: CONSERVATION AND CONTEMPORARY ART

The Mogao Caves were inscribed on the UNESCO World Heritage List in 1987. Even earlier, the site had been listed as one of the State Priority Protected Sites by the State Council in 1961 and was placed under the protection of national laws concerning the preservation of cultural relics.[38] Moreover, the formation of the Dunhuang Academy (then named the Dunhuang Art Institute) in 1943 has greatly facilitated the systematic study and conservation and digitization of the mural paintings and sculptures inside the cave shrines in the early 21st century.

In recent years, tourism at the Mogao Caves has boomed, due in no small part to the "One Belt, One Road" (OBOR) initiative promulgated by Chinese president Xi Jinping 習近平. Inaugurated in 2013, the goal of the OBOR policy is to foster economic development by recreating the premodern Silk Routes in two parts. The first is a land-based Silk Road economic belt that seeks to connect the interior provinces of China with Europe by establishing new infrastructure, particularly railroads, highways, and air routes that will cross Central Asia, Russia, the Middle East, and South and Southeast Asia. The second phase of the initiative is a maritime Silk Road that likewise seeks to increase connectivity between China and neighboring regions.

At Dunhuang, the economic impact of the OBOR initiative is felt most keenly in tourism.[39] In 2015 alone, over 1.1 million tourists visited the Mogao Caves, representing an increase of 40 percent in just one year. Interest in the Silk Routes has also led to the construction of a new conference center to accommodate an annual Silk Road Cultural Expo and the expansion of the small local airport.[40] The huge influx of visitors has the potential to disrupt the delicate balance of what is already a fairly complex microclimate inside the cave shrines. Under the best of circumstances, the mural paintings might potentially suffer from moisture and humidity, threats that are increased by the introduction of exterior air into the cave shrines as visitors enter and exit; visitors' bodies also carry moisture with them.[41] The resulting effects on mural paintings range from the detachment of paintings from the cave wall, the deterioration of paintings from flood damage, color degradation or alteration over time, and the flaking of paintings and upper layers of plaster.[42]

In order to better understand and combat these damaging effects, a long-term partnership was created in 1989 between the Dunhuang Academy and the Getty Conservation Institute. This resulted in the joint authorship of the *Principles for the Conservation of Heritage Sites in China* in 2002.[43] The next step in this partnership was the conservation of the Tang dynasty Mogao Cave 85 in 1997 through 2010 in order to develop a comprehensive conservation plan for this and other caves. Among the goals of the project were the investigation of the causes behind the deterioration of mural paintings, monitoring the condition of mural paintings, the conservation of mural paintings and sculpture without disrupting their original appearance, and training mural painting conservators and scientists.[44] The conservation regime for Mogao Cave 85 included establishing environmental control measures, stabilizing and readhering detached areas of plaster, and cleaning the surfaces of mural paintings.[45] The training of mural painting conservators has also been greatly facilitated by the establishment at the Courtauld Institute of a two-year master's degree program: Buddhist Art: History and Conservation.[46]

Yet another form of present-day engagement with the visual culture of the Mogao Caves lies in the realm of contemporary art. A 2013 special exhibition at the China Institute Gallery, "Inspired by Dunhuang: Re-Creation in Contemporary Chinese Art," presented the work of artists who have found inspiration in the figural and decorative motifs of Dunhuang mural paintings, as well as in the local desert landscape.[47] The artists featured in the exhibition were mostly born in China and are currently active in China, the United States, and Europe. Coming full circle, among this group of artists was the designer and educator Chang Shana 常沙娜 (b. 1931), the daughter of Chang Shuhong 常書鴻 (1904–1994), painter and founder of the Dunhuang Art Institute.

HISTORIOGRAPHY

One of the enduring concerns in the study of Dunhuang art, and indeed, of the artifacts from Dunhuang in general, is how to reconcile the mural paintings with the objects recovered from the Library Cave. Many questions still remain concerning the provenance of the manuscripts and paintings that were interred in the Library Cave. Moreover, the removal of such items from the cave in the early 20th century disturbed their original placement, complicating the process of reconstructing their original context yet further.

One of the most common compositional types is the transformation tableau, which refers loosely to a painting based upon a scriptural source. They frequently, though not exclusively, depict the buddha preaching in the center of a large composition that is flanked by narrative vignettes, conflating iconic and narrative modes of representation (figure 11). There may be additional panels of smaller images placed directly below that add further narrative details to the central composition. The term "transformation tableau" first appeared in Chinese literary sources in the 5th century and could refer variously to paintings, relief carvings, or sculpture. However, from the 8th century onward, the term began to be associated more closely with paintings based upon sutras of the type that we see in the Mogao Caves.[48] For this reason, such paintings have also been termed sutra paintings.[49] Compositions similar to these mural paintings are also noted among the portable paintings recovered from Dunhuang.

Some scholars have tried to establish a connection between transformation tableaux and the genre of Dunhuang literature known as transformation texts (*bianwen* 變文).[50] Transformation texts address both Buddhist and secular themes and may be defined as narratives that are written in semicolloquial Chinese in a prosimetric (alternating prose–verse) style. In drawing a connection between transformation texts and transformation tableaux, some scholars have looked toward South Asian prototypes for picture-storytelling and modern ethnographic data from throughout Asia in which narrative tales are recited or performed orally in front of portable illustrations, arguing that such a practice could have taken place in front of the Dunhuang mural paintings as well.[51]

A different perspective was introduced which posited that text and image mutually reinforced one another. A close study of Magic Competition murals showed that during the Tang dynasty, the mural paintings were composed for the first time in a manner that privileged spatial rather than narrative logic. Rather than following a linear narrative, the images were divided into two opposing groups: the Buddhist devotees and heretics. Furthermore, pairs of

Figure 11. *Amitābha Buddha in the Western Pure Land.* Tang dynasty (618–907). Mural painting. South wall, Mogao Cave 172, Dunhuang, Gansu Province.

Source: Reprinted from Dunhuang wenwu yanjiusuo, ed., *Zhongguo shiku: Dunhuang Mogaoku* 4 (Beijing: Wenwu chubanshe, 1987), plate 9

audience members that were absent from the textual source were added in order to create balance and underscore the compositional symmetry between the opposed figures.[52] By demonstrating that transformation tableaux were not merely aids to oral performance but rather had their own pictorial logic distinct from the logic of written tales or oral performance, this established the mutually constitutive relationship between text and image, rather than the dependence of image upon text.

Building on this, the concept of world-making has been applied to the study of transformation tableaux. Rather than treating images merely as illustrations of Buddhist texts, this approach posits that a particular sutra may give rise to a series of interrelated images unified by cues from the sutra that are shaped by concerns and agendas not necessarily present in the text itself. This is what is defined as the world of that sutra.[53] In the case of the Lotus Sutra, one of the most popular Buddhist sutras in East Asia and at Dunhuang, this approach explains why certain motifs were stressed in transformation tableaux over others and how artists grappled with the complexities of the sutra, which inevitably stymied a strictly linear approach.[54]

More recently, the issue of the text–image relationship has been revisited in consideration of the optical illusionism of cave shrines. It is argued that from the mid-8th century to the early 11th century, the interiors of Mogao cave shrines became more vernacular and therefore more immediate and immersive to their audiences. Illusionistic *trompe-l'oeil* effects are evident in the more lifelike treatment of furniture and textile elements of painted interiors. As a result, they elicited a type of viewer participation that was also characteristic of the interplay between the officiating monk and the audience during sutra lectures.[55]

PRIMARY SOURCES

The most important primary source for the study of Dunhuang art is the Mogao site. Open year-round, new policies were implemented in 2014 according to a visitor management plan developed by the Dunhuang Academy and Getty Conservation Institute that included the construction of a new visitor center located fifteen kilometers from the caves. Rather than proceeding directly to the caves, visitors first receive an orientation at the visitor center consisting of two films that address the history of Dunhuang and highlights of individual caves. Ticketing is managed via an online system, and the maximum capacity is six thousand visitors per day. In addition to tourist management, the Dunhuang Academy also responds to special requests from researchers.

The paintings and manuscripts from the Library Cave are now held in library and museum collections worldwide. The most prominent of these are the Stein collection in the British Museum, British Library, and National Museum of India, and the Pelliot collection in the Musée Guimet and Bibliothèque nationale de France. Those collections were assembled, respectively, by the Hungarian British archaeologist and explorer Aurel Stein (1862–1943), who came to Dunhuang in 1907, and the French sinologist Paul Pelliot (1878–1945), who followed one year later. In addition to these, the largest collection of Dunhuang materials in China is kept in the National Library of China in Beijing, where they were initially deposited in 1910 due to the intervention of Luo Zhenyu 羅振玉 (1866–1940) and other scholars to prevent their dispersal at the hands of foreign collectors. During the third Ōtani 大谷 expedition of 1910–1914, numerous Dunhuang manuscripts were collected by Tachibana Zuichō 橘瑞超 (1890–1968) and Yoshikawa Koichirō 吉川小一郎 (1885–1978). They are now divided among several institutions in Japan, including Ryūkoku University and Ōtani University.

Due to the absence of manuscripts in the Tangut script, the cave is believed to have been sealed up around the year 1035 for reasons which are still unknown.[56] Scholars have offered differing explanations for why these objects were secreted inside the cave. Given the fragmentary nature of some manuscripts, Aurel Stein hypothesized that the cave was used as a waste repository for items cast off from the local monasteries.[57] Yet another theory, put forth by Rong Xinjiang 荣新江, holds that the objects were stored in the cave by the Three Realms Monastery, which was located in front of the Mogao Caves. The monk Daozhen 道真 (916–987) had made a vow in 934 to repair manuscripts in the monastic library; the fragments may therefore have been used to patch damaged manuscripts.[58] Finally, noting the high number of Tibetan manuscripts in the cave and its location in the side wall of the memorial cave of Hongbian 洪辯, superintendent of monks during and after the period when Dunhuang was ruled by Tibetans (786–848), Imaeda Yoshirō has suggested that certain manuscripts may have constituted Hongbian's personal collection.[59]

The only major North American expedition to Dunhuang was the Fogg Expedition of 1923–1924, led by Harvard University art historian and curator Langdon Warner (1881–1955). The sculptures and mural fragments that he collected are how housed in the Harvard Art Museums. The Princeton University East Asian Library holds the Dunhuang and Turfan

Materials Collection. These items were collected by Guion M. Gest (1864–1948), the founder of the Gest Engineering Company and collector of Chinese rare books; the photographers James C. M. Lo 羅寄梅 (1902–1987) and Lucy Lo 羅先 (née 劉), who came to Dunhuang in 1943 and documented the site; as well as items gifted to the Los by the painter Zhang Daqian 張大千 (1899–1983), who was then also at Dunhuang, studying and copying the mural paintings.[60]

DIGITAL MATERIALS

Given the far-flung nature of the source material, digital resources are indispensable for the study of Dunhuang art and material culture. The newest of these is the impressive open-access Digital Dunhuang site (http://www.e-dunhuang.com/), developed by the Dunhuang Academy. The site currently provides 360-degree views of thirty cave shrines, enabling site users to engage in an entirely self-guided virtual visit and to examine specific murals closely. Still images of the mural paintings are also available for perusal, along with information regarding painting motifs. Users may select the English or Chinese language interface. The Dunhuang Academy's own homepage (http://en.dha.ac.cn/) provides useful information to visitors and links to other useful sites.

An important digital image resource is the Mellon International Dunhuang Archive on Artstor (http://www.artstor.org/content/mellon-international-dunhuang-archive), developed by Sarah E. Fraser of Heidelberg University. This collection of images is available only to users with an Artstor subscription. Digital images of mural paintings from more than forty cave shrines are available; in addition to two-dimensional images, three-dimensional visual representations may also be viewed using Quick Time Virtual Reality (QTVR) technology. A special capability of Artstor is the ability to zoom in and capture high-quality close-up details. This collection also includes objects from the Library Cave and digitized images from the Lo Archive, which consists of black and white photographs that were taken by James and Lucy Lo at the Mogao Caves. Beginning in 1943, they photographed the cave shrines for eighteen months using a system of mirrors and cloth screens in order to distribute natural light inside the caves. Their archive of 2,590 photographs is housed in Princeton University's Visual Resources Collection.

One of the most long-standing digital platforms for Dunhuang studies is the multilingual, open-access website of the International Dunhuang Project (http://idp.bl.uk). Founded in 1994 by Susan Whitfield and based at the British Library, the IDP is a partnership among libraries, museums, universities, and research institutes worldwide to preserve the archaeological legacy of Chinese Central Asia and to make this material accessible through online access and a program of research and education. The website offers over 470,000 high-resolution images and metadata pertaining to Silk Road artifacts from Dunhuang and other sites and is a veritable encyclopedia of Silk Road studies. Particularly helpful are the detailed entries on collections of Silk Road materials worldwide and downloadable PDF files of select publications on Dunhuang and Silk Road studies.

Digital Silk Road (http://dsr.nii.ac.jp/), a bilingual English–Japanese open-access website maintained by the National Institute of Informatics, is a valuable portal to a constellation of online resources. Among them are the Digital Archive of Toyo Bunko Rare Books, Database for Buddhist Temples in China, and Silk Road maps and photographs. The Toyo Bunko archive includes full-text and searchable access to over two hundred titles, including the Aurel Stein expedition reports mentioned earlier (see "Expedition Reports"), and nimble navigation functions.

The Silk Road Seattle site (http://depts.washington.edu/silkroad/), compiled by Daniel C. Waugh of the University of Washington, provides teaching and learning resources for Silk Road studies, including links to maps, historical texts, and curriculum materials. Particularly useful for the study of Dunhuang art, certain pages of the website highlight masterpieces of the Stein and Pelliot collections, as well as museums holding Silk Road artifacts. Finally, the Yale Silk Road website (https://web.library.yale.edu/digital-collections/yale-silk-road) presents an online database of over eleven thousand images of major Silk Road sites taken during faculty site seminars led by Mimi Hall Yiengpruksawan under the support of the Council on East Asian Studies at Yale University in the summers of 2006–2010. Among the sites documented are ones located in Gansu, Ningxia, and Xinjiang Uyghur Autonomous Region.

FURTHER READING

GENERAL READING

For general reading, the following titles provide accessible and scholarly introductions to the art and history of Dunhuang. *Eighteen Lectures on Dunhuang*, authored by one of the preeminent Chinese scholars of Dunhuang history, provides a historiographical overview of Dunhuang studies in tandem with a comprehensive introduction to the cultural, social, and political history of Dunhuang. Great attention is given to the discovery and dispersal of manuscripts from the Library Cave, as well as their potential for research. Though a slim volume, *Cave Temples of Mogao at Dunhuang: Art and History on the Silk Road* deftly addresses the history of Dunhuang and explores certain caves in detail in order to illuminate major themes in Dunhuang art. Authored by the former director of the Dunhuang Academy, *The Caves of Dunhuang* systematically surveys the history, religions, and art of Dunhuang, paying close attention to mural paintings and their chronological development, objects from the Library Cave, and conservation. Finally, *Foreign Devils on the Silk Road* is a classic study of the Western exploration of Silk Road sites and collecting of Silk Road artifacts.

Fan, Jinshi. *The Caves of Dunhuang*. Translated by Susan Whitfield. Hong Kong: Dunhuang Academy in collaboration with London Editions, 2010.

Hopkirk, Peter. *Foreign Devils on the Silk Road: The Search for the Lost Treasures of Central Asia*. London: John Murray, 2006.

Rong Xinjiang, *Eighteen Lectures on Dunhuang*. Translated by Imre Galambos. Leiden, The Netherlands, and Boston: Brill, 2013. Originally published as Rong Xinjiang 荣新江, *Dunhuangxue shiba jiang* 敦煌学十八講. Beijing: Beijing daxue chubanshe, 2001.

Whitfield, Roderick. *Cave Temples of Mogao at Dunhuang: Art and History on the Silk Road*. Rev. ed. Los Angeles: Getty Trust Publications, 2015.

SECONDARY LITERATURE

The secondary literature on the art of Dunhuang employs a broad range of disciplinary approaches. The most important source for Chinese-language scholarship on Dunhuang art and related topics is the journal *Dunhuang yanjiu*, which is edited by the Dunhuang Academy. Increasingly, the work of international scholars appears in the journal as well. Of the remaining four titles, the first two place Dunhuang art in conversation with the art of central plains China, and the latter two examine Dunhuang as a multicultural center for art production. *Performing the Visual: The Practice of Buddhist Wall Painting in China and Central Asia, 618–960* examines mural and portable paintings in light of painting workshops and the artist's practice and evaluates aesthetic theories of monochrome ink painting in Tang China. *Shaping the Lotus Sutra: Buddhist Visual Culture in Medieval China* reconstructs the visual worlds and cognitive model of the Lotus Sutra in Dunhuang and central plains China. *Uyghur Patronage in Dunhuang: Regional Art Centres on the Northern Silk Road in the Tenth and Eleventh Centuries* centers upon the impact of Uyghur donors on Dunhuang art during a period of the region's increasing independence from the central Chinese court. In a similar manner, *Maṇḍalas in the Making: The Visual Culture of Esoteric Buddhism at Dunhuang* explores the religious and artistic dialogue between Chinese and Tibetan communities at Dunhuang.

Dunhuang yanjiu 敦煌研究, 1981–present.

Fraser, Sarah E. *Performing the Visual: The Practice of Buddhist Wall Painting in China and Central Asia, 618–960*. Stanford, CA: Stanford University Press, 2004.

Russell-Smith, Lilla. *Uyghur Patronage in Dunhuang: Regional Art Centres on the Northern Silk Road in the Tenth and Eleventh Centuries*. Leiden, The Netherlands, and Boston: Brill, 2005.

Wang, Eugene Y. *Shaping the Lotus Sutra: Buddhist Visual Culture in Medieval China*. Seattle: University of Washington Press, 2005.

Wang, Michelle C. *Maṇḍalas in the Making: The Visual Culture of Esoteric Buddhism at Dunhuang*. Leiden, The Netherlands, and Boston: Brill, 2018.

REFERENCE SOURCES

Any research project on Dunhuang art will by necessity begin with the following volumes. The first three are publications by the Dunhuang Academy. *Dunhuang shiku neirong zonglu* is a comprehensive index to the contents of the Mogao, Western Thousand Buddhas, and Yulin Caves and the Five Temples site and offers detailed information concerning the numbers, placement, and motifs of mural paintings. This volume supersedes the earlier *Dunhuang Mogao ku neirong zonglu*, which focused solely on the Mogao Caves. *Dunhuang Mogao ku gongyangren tiji* provides transcriptions of extant donor inscriptions in the Mogao Caves. Shi Zhangru's *Mogaoku xing* records the dimensions of the Mogao Caves and was the product of a 1942 Academia Sinica expedition to the site.

Dunhuang yanjiuyuan 敦煌研究院, ed. *Dunhuang Mogao ku neirong zonglu* 敦煌莫高窟內總錄. Beijing: Wenwu chubanshe, 1982.

Dunhuang yanjiuyuan 敦煌研究院, ed. *Dunhuang Mogao ku gongyangren tiji* 敦煌莫高窟供人題記. Beijing: Wenwu chubanshe, 1986.

Dunhuang yanjiuyuan 敦煌研究院, ed. *Dunhuang shiku neirong zonglu* 敦煌石窟內容總錄. Beijing: Wenwu chubanshe, 1996.

Shi Zhangru 石璋如. *Mogaoku xing* 莫高窟形. Taibei: Zhongyang yanjiuyuan lishi yuyan yanjiusuo, 1996.

ILLUSTRATED CATALOGS

The following volumes offer high-quality color illustrations of mural paintings and items from the Library Cave, a great boon as photography is not permitted inside the Dunhuang Caves. The five volumes in *Zhongguo shiku: Dunhuang shiku* are organized chronologically and feature a selection of images from specific caves. The titles in the Dunhuang shiku yishu series, however, focus upon an individual or a few Mogao and Yulin cave shrines and present introductory essays. Individual volumes in the Dunhuang shiku quanji series focus upon specific iconographical or visual motifs in the Mogao and Yulin Caves. *Art of Central Asia: The Stein Collection in the British Museum* and *Les Arts de l'Asie Centrale* focus on paintings, drawings, and textiles in the Stein and Pelliot collections, respectively. Bridging the mural paintings and material from the Library Cave, Matsumoto Eiichi's *Tonkōga no kenkyū* is organized according to iconographic motif and treats Dunhuang mural and portable paintings in the Stein and Pelliot collections.

Dunhuang shiku quanji 敦煌石窟全集 series. Hong Kong: Commercial Press, 1999–present.

Dunhuang shiku yishu 敦煌石窟藝術 series. Nanjing: Jiangsu meishu chubanshe, 1993–present.

Dunhuang wenwu yanjiusuo 敦煌文物研究所, ed. *Zhongguo shiku: Dunhuang shiku* 中國石窟：敦煌石窟. 5 vols. Beijing: Wenwu chubanshe, 1982–1987.

Eiichi, Matsumoto 松本栄一. *Tonkōga no kenkyū* 敦煌畫の研究. 2 vols. Tokyo: Tōhō bunka gakuin, 1937.

Giès, Jacques, ed. *Les Arts de l'Asie Centrale*. 2 vols. London: Serindia, 1994–1996.

Whitfield, Roderick. *Art of Central Asia: The Stein Collection in the British Museum*. 3 vols. Tokyo: Kodansha International, in cooperation with the Trustees of the British Museum, 1982–1985.

EXHIBITION CATALOGS

In the past few years, the number of exhibitions on Dunhuang art has grown rapidly throughout the United States, Europe, and Asia. Four particularly outstanding exhibition catalogs are given here that are characterized both by their framing of Dunhuang as a religious and artistic center as well as the scope of catalog essays and object entries. The most recent of these is *Cave Temples of Dunhuang: Buddhist Art of China's Silk Road*, produced for a 2016 exhibition at the Getty Center in Los Angeles. Separate exhibition spaces featured portable paintings and drawings from the Library Cave, three full-size replica caves produced by artists from the Dunhuang Academy, and a three-dimensional virtual immersive experience. Particularly noteworthy was the emphasis on the multicultural nature of Dunhuang. *Inspired by Dunhuang: Re-creation in Contemporary Chinese Art* was authored for a 2013 exhibition at the China Institute in New York City. This exhibition took a novel approach to the art of Dunhuang by featuring the work of contemporary artists inspired by the cave shrines and the desert landscape of Dunhuang. *The Silk Road: Trade, Travel, War, and Faith* situated Dunhuang in the larger context of the Silk Routes, featuring portable objects from Dunhuang alongside artifacts from Khotan, Dandan Uiliq, Niya, Miran, and Gaochang. Organized at the British Library in 2004, the essays in this catalog, several of which were authored by International Dunhuang Project scholars, set a new standard for museum exhibition writing. Finally, *The Silk Route and the Diamond Path: Esoteric Buddhist Art on the Trans-Himalayan Trade Routes*, authored for a 1982 exhibition at UCLA's Frederick S. Wight Art Gallery, focused specifically on esoteric Buddhist art and addressed Dunhuang art in conjunction with Himalayan art, focusing on cross-cultural transmission.

Agnew, Neville, Marcia Reed, and Tevvy Ball. *Cave Temples of Dunhuang: Buddhist Art of China's Silk Road.* Los Angeles: J. Paul Getty Trust, 2016.

Hai, Willow Weilan, and Jerome Silbergeld, *Inspired by Dunhuang: Re-creation in Contemporary Chinese Art.* Edited by Willow Weilan Hai and J. May Lee Barrett. New York: China Institute Gallery, 2013.

Klimburg-Salter, Deborah E. *The Silk Route and the Diamond Path: Esoteric Buddhist Art on the Trans-Himalayan Trade Routes.* Los Angeles: UCLA Art Council, 1982.

Whitfield, Susan, and Ursula Sims Williams, eds. *The Silk Road: Trade, Travel, War, and Faith.* London: British Library, 2004.

EXPEDITION REPORTS

The government-sponsored expeditions led by Aurel Stein and Paul Pelliot emerged in the wake of the Great Game and resulted in the transportation of thousands of paintings, drawings, textiles, and sculptural fragments to London, New Delhi, and Paris. Aurel Stein's standard practice was to first publish popular accounts of his expeditions, followed by more scientific expedition reports. *Serindia: Detailed Report of Explorations in Central Asia and Westernmost China* was based on Stein's second expedition to Central Asia (1906–1908), during which he went to Dunhuang for the first time in 1907 and purchased manuscripts from Wang Yuanlu. His third expedition to Central Asia (1913–1916) brought him back to Dunhuang in 1914 and is recorded in *Innermost Asia: Detailed Report of Explorations in Central Asia, Kan-su and Eastern Īrān.* Paul Pelliot did not publish formal expedition reports, but the travel notebooks from his 1906–1908 expedition, during which he visited the Library Cave in 1908, were transcribed and published in 2008. They provide detailed insights into his itinerary, day-to-day movements, and personal reactions to the people and places that he encountered.

Pelliot, Paul. *Carnets de route: 1906–1908.* Edited by Jérôme Ghesquière and Francis Macouin. Paris: Indes savants, 2008.

Stein, Aurel. *Serindia: Detailed Report of Explorations in Central Asia and Westernmost China.* 5 vols. Oxford: Clarendon Press, 1921.

Stein, Aurel. *Innermost Asia: Detailed Report of Explorations in Central Asia, Kan-su and Eastern Īrān.* 4 vols. Oxford: Clarendon Press, 1928.

NOTES

1. See a transcription of this stele in Sonya S. Lee, *Surviving Nirvana: Death of the Buddha in Chinese Visual Culture* (Hong Kong: Hong Kong University Press, 2010), 278–281.
2. Rong Xinjiang, *Eighteen Lectures on Dunhuang*, trans. Imre Galambos (Leiden, The Netherlands, and Boston: Brill: 2013), 58–59. This was originally published as Rong Xinjiang 荣新江, *Dunhuangxue shiba jiang* 敦煌学十八講 (Beijing: Beijing daxue chubanshe, 2001).
3. Lori Wong and Neville Agnew, eds., *The Conservation of Cave 85 at the Mogao Grottoes, Dunhuang: A Collaborative Project of the Getty Conservation Institute and the Dunhuang Academy* (Los Angeles: Getty Conservation Institute, 2013), 156–163.
4. Wong and Agnew, eds., *Conservation of Cave 85*, 169–173.
5. Sarah E. Fraser, *Performing the Visual: The Practice of Buddhist Wall Painting in China and Central Asia, 618–960* (Stanford, CA: Stanford University Press, 2004), 34.
6. Wong and Agnew, eds., *Conservation of Cave 85*, 177–181.
7. Fraser, *Performing the Visual*, 71–86.

8. Fraser, *Performing the Visual*, 102–108; and Sha Wutian 沙武田, *Dunhuang huagao yanjiu* 敦煌畫稿研究 (Beijing: Minzu chubanshe, 2006), 266.
9. Kuo Liying, *Confession et contrition dans le bouddhisme chinois du Ve au Xe siècle* (Paris: Publications de l'École Française d'Extrême-Orient, 1994), 230–231; and Stanley K. Abe, "Art and Practice in a Fifth-Century Chinese Buddhist Cave Temple," *Ars Orientalis* 20 (1990): 1–31, 9–10.
10. See Paul Harrison, "Commemoration and Identification in Buddhanusmrti," in *The Mirror of Memory: Reflections of Mindfulness and Remembrance in Indian and Tibetan Buddhism*, ed. Janet Gyatso (Albany: State University of New York Press, 1992), 215–238.
11. Hou Ching-lang, "La Cérémonie du Yin-cha-fo d'après les manuscrits de Touen-houang," in *Contributions aux études de Touen-houang*, vol. 3, ed. Michel Soymié, 206–235 (Paris: École française d'Extrême-Orient, 1984), 229–230.
12. "Mogao Cave 428 (Northern Zhou 557–581AD)," Dunhuang Research Academy.
13. Ning Qiang, *Art, Religion, and Politics in Medieval China: The Dunhuang Cave of the Zhai Family* (Honolulu: University of Hawaii Press, 2004), 5–6.
14. Winston Kyan, "Family Space: Buddhist Materiality and Ancestral Fashioning in Mogao Cave 231," *Art Bulletin* 92, no. 1–2 (2010): 61–82, 71–74.
15. Sonya S. Lee, "Repository of Ingenuity: Cave 61 and Artistic Appropriation in Tenth-Century Dunhuang," *Art Bulletin* 94, no. 2 (2012): 199–225, esp. 217–218.
16. See Eugene Wang, "Pictorial Program in the Making of Monastic Space: From Jing'aisi of Luoyang to Cave 217 at Dunhuang," in *Buddhist Monasticism in East Asia: Places of Practice*, ed. James A. Benn, Lori Meeks, and James Robson (London: Routledge, 2010), 65–106.
17. Parallel developments at Dunhuang in Chinese and Tibetan Buddhist praxis and visual culture are the focus of Michelle C. Wang, *Maṇḍalas in the Making: The Visual Culture of Esoteric Buddhism at Dunhuang* (Leiden, The Netherlands, and Boston: Brill, 2018).
18. Lilla Russell-Smith, *Uyghur Patronage in Dunhuang: Regional Art Centres on the Northern Silk Road in the Tenth and Eleventh Centuries* (Leiden, The Netherlands, and Boston: Brill, 2005), 23–24.
19. Russell-Smith, *Uyghur Patronage in Dunhuang*, 77–172.
20. Jacob Dalton, "Amitābha with the Eight Bodhisattvas," in *The Silk Road: Trade, Travel, War and Faith*, ed. Susan Whitfield and Ursula Sims-Williams (London: British Library, 2004), 202–203.
21. H. E. Richardson, "The Cult of Vairocana in Early Tibet," in *Indo-Tibetan Studies: Papers in Honour and Appreciation of Professor David L. Snellgrove's Contribution to Indo-Tibetan Studies*, ed. Tadeusz Skorupski (Tring: Institute of Buddhist Studies, 1990), 271–274; see also Matthew T. Kapstein, *Tibetan Assimilation of Buddhism: Conversion, Contestation, and Memory* (Oxford: Oxford University Press, 2000), 58–65.
22. Kapstein, *Tibetan Assimilation of Buddhism*, 60.
23. See Yihong Pan, "The Sino-Tibetan Treaties in the Tang Dynasty," *T'oung Pao*, 2nd ser., 78, no. 1–3 (1992): 116–161.
24. For a close study of the carvings and a transcription and translation of the inscriptions, see Amy Heller, "Ninth Century Buddhist Images Carved at Ldan Ma Brag to Commemorate Tibeto-Chinese Negotiations," in *Tibetan Studies: Proceedings of the 6th Seminar of the International Association for Tibetan Studies, Fagernes, 1992*, ed. Per Kvaerne (Oslo: Institute for Comparative Research in Human Culture, 1994), 335–349.
25. Heller, "Ninth Century Buddhist Images," 12–14.
26. Matthew Kapstein provides a detailed study of the manuscripts Pelliot tibétain 16 and IOL Tib J 751 and their description of the "treaty temple" in Matthew T. Kapstein, "The Treaty Temple of the Turquoise Grove," in *Buddhism between Tibet and China*, ed. Matthew T. Kapstein (Boston: Wisdom Publications, 2009), 21–72. In this article, Kapstein identifies the temple with Yulin Cave 25, although more recently, he has revised his thinking on this issue. See Matthew T. Kapstein, "The Treaty Temple of De ga g.yu tshal: Reconsiderations," downloaded from the author's Academia.edu page.

27. This has caused Robert Sharf to suggest that cave shrines are best thought of as mortuary shrines; see his "Art in the Dark: The Ritual Context of Buddhist Caves in Western China," in *Art of Merit: Studies in Buddhist Art and Its Conservation*, ed. David Park, Kuenga Wangmo, and Sharon Cather (London: Archetype Publications, Courtauld Institute of Art, 2013), 38–65.
28. Whitfield and Sims-Williams, eds., *Silk Road*, 241 (plate 178), 243.
29. Stephen F. Teiser, *The Scripture on the Ten Kings and the Making of Purgatory in Medieval Chinese Buddhism* (Honolulu: University of Hawaii Press, 1994), 8–9.
30. Teiser, *Scripture on the Ten Kings*, 20–30.
31. Teiser, *Scripture on the Ten Kings*, 35–40.
32. For the prophecy concerning Mañjuśrī's arrival at the "Mountain of Snows," see David Quinter, "Visualizing the *Mañjuśrī Parinirvāṇa Sūtra* as a Contemplation Sūtra," *Asia Major*, 3rd ser., 23, no. 2 (2010): 97–128, esp. 109.
33. See Mary Anne Cartelli, *The Five-Colored Clouds of Mount Wutai: Poems from Dunhuang* (Leiden, The Netherlands, and Boston: Brill, 2013), 39.
34. Dorothy C. Wong, "A Reassessment of the Representation of Mt. Wutai from Dunhuang Cave 61," *Archives of Asian Art* 46 (1993): 27–52, esp. 46.
35. See Cartelli, *Five-Colored Clouds of Mount Wutai*, 65, 68–69, 78; it was believed that Mañjuśrī appeared as five-colored clouds to pilgrims who had less of a karmic affinity than those who were able to see him in his true form, seated atop his lion mount (116). One of the more unusual manifestations of Mañjuśrī was his thousand-armed form in which he holds a thousand begging bowls, from each of which a small Śākyamuni Buddha emerges. This form of the bodhisattva may also have been associated with Mount Wutai; see Michelle C. Wang, "The Thousand-Armed Mañjuśrī at Dunhuang and Paired Images in Buddhist Visual Culture," *Archives of Asian Art* 66, no. 1 (2016): 81–105.
36. Wei-cheng Lin, *Building a Sacred Mountain: The Buddhist Architecture of China's Mount Wutai* (Seattle: University of Washington Press, 2014), 172–178.
37. For other examples of auspicious icons at Dunhuang, see Wu Hung, "Rethinking Liu Sahe: The Creation of a Buddhist Saint and the Invention of a 'Miraculous Image'," *Orientations* 27, no. 10 (1996): 32–43; and Roderick Whitfield, "Ruixiang at Dunhuang," in *Function and Meaning in Buddhist Art*, ed. K. R. Kooij and H. van der Veere (Groningen, The Netherlands: Egbert Forsten, 1995), 149–156.
38. "Mogao Caves," UNESCO World Heritage Centre.
39. Tourism and the arts are topics that receive emphasis in the official English-language website for the OBOR initiative; see "The Belt and Road Initiative."
40. Simon Denyer, "China's Ancient Buddhist Grottoes Face a New Threat—Tourists," *The Washington Post*, May 16, 2016, https://www.washingtonpost.com/world/asia_pacific/chinas-ancient-buddhist-grottoes-face-a-new-threat--tourists/2016/05/16/4f31b68e-184e-11e6-8329-f3767b06317f_story.html.
41. Wong and Agnew, eds., *Conservation of Cave 85*, 191–213.
42. Wong and Agnew, eds., *Conservation of Cave 85*, 215–235.
43. Neville Agnew and Martha Demas, eds., *Principles for the Conservation of Heritage Sites in China* (Los Angeles: Getty Conservation Institute, 2002).
44. Wong and Agnew, eds., *Conservation of Cave 85*, 9–13.
45. Wong and Agnew, eds., *Conservation of Cave 85*, 259–293.
46. See the program website: "MA Buddhist Art: History and Conservation," The Courtauld Institute of Art.
47. Willow Weilan Hai and Jerome Silbergeld, *Inspired by Dunhuang: Re-creation in Contemporary Chinese Art*, ed. Willow Weilan Hai and J. May Lee Barrett (New York: China Institute Gallery, 2013).
48. Wu Hung, "What Is Bianxiang 變相?—On the Relationship between Dunhuang Art and Dunhuang Literature," *Harvard Journal of Asiatic Studies* 52, no. 1 (1992): 111–192, esp. 116–123.
49. Wu Hung, "Reborn in Paradise: A Case Study of Dunhuang Sutra Painting and Its Religious, Ritual and Artistic Context," *Orientations* 23, no. 5 (1992): 52–60. In this article, Wu notes the popularity of sutra

lectures delivered by eminent monks at Dunhuang, but observes that the relatively small and dark spaces of cave shrines would have ruled out the performance of such lectures within; see Wu, "Reborn in Paradise," 55–56.

50. The first publication to establish a direct connection between transformation texts and transformation tableaux was Pai Hua-wen and Victor H. Mair, trans., "What is Pien-wen 變文?," *Harvard Journal of Asiatic Studies* 44, no. 2 (1984): 493–514, originally published in Chinese in 1982. For investigations into "transformation" (*bian*), see Victor H. Mair, *Tun-huang Popular Narratives* (Cambridge, UK: Cambridge University Press, 1983).
51. On this point, see Victor H. Mair, *Painting and Performance: Chinese Picture Recitation and Its Indian Genesis* (Honolulu: University of Hawaii Press, 1988); and Victor H. Mair, *T'ang Transformation Texts: A Study of the Buddhist Contribution to the Rise of Vernacular Fiction and Drama in China* (Cambridge, MA: Council on East Asian Studies, Harvard University, 1989).
52. Wu, "What Is Bianxiang," 160–166.
53. Eugene Y. Wang, *Shaping the Lotus Sutra: Buddhist Visual Culture in Medieval China* (Seattle: University of Washington Press, 2005), xx–xxii.
54. Wang, *Shaping the Lotus Sutra*, 67–121.
55. Neil Schmid, "The Material Culture of Exegesis and Liturgy and a Change in the Artistic Representations in Dunhuang Caves, ca. 700–1000," *Asia Major*, 3rd ser., 19, no. 1–2 (2006): 171–210, esp. 197–199.
56. Rong Xinjiang, "The Nature of the Dunhuang Library Cave and the Reasons for Its Sealing," trans. Valerie Hansen, *Cahiers d'Extrême-Asie* 11 (1999): 247–275, esp. 247–248.
57. Rong, "Nature of the Dunhuang Library Cave," 250–257.
58. Rong, "Nature of the Dunhuang Library Cave," 257–266.
59. Imaeda Yoshirō, "The Provenance and Character of the Dunhuang Documents," *The Memoirs of the Toyo Bunko* 66 (2008): 81–102, esp. 86–92.
60. See Huaiyu Chen and Nancy Norton Tomasko, "Chinese-Language Texts from Dunhuang and Turfan in the Princeton University East Asian Library," *East Asian Library Journal* 14, no. 2 (2010): 1–13; and Huaiyu Chen and Nancy Norton Tomasko, "A Descriptive Catalogue of the Dunhuang and Turfan Materials," *East Asian Library Journal* 14, no. 2 (2010): 13–208.

Michelle C. Wang

DUNHUANG TEXTS

LANGUAGES AND SCRIPTS REPRESENTED

Dunhuang was an important hub on the Silk Road and home to peoples from diverse ethnic backgrounds. The manuscripts from Dunhuang Cave 17 were written in over twelve languages. Chinese and Tibetan are the most frequent, followed by smaller groups of Khotanese, Sogdian, Old Turkic, and Sanskrit texts. This diversity is a testimony to the cosmopolitan nature of the region.

Chinese-Language Materials. The documents in Chinese are, by far, the most numerous. They range from the 4th to the 11th century, right up to the probable sealing of the Library Cave.

The Chinese Buddhist scriptures form the largest corpus for the period and are crucial to understanding the early transmission of Buddhism. Most numerous among them are several key Mahayana sutras, some of which traveled to Dunhuang shortly after being translated. With its emphasis on the role of compassionate bodhisattvas, the *Lotus Sutra* proved extremely popular, especially in the translation by Kumārajīva (*Miaofa lianhua jing* 妙法蓮華經). Cave 17 yielded thousands of copies of the sutra, mostly from the Tang dynasty.[1]

The many Chinese copies of the *Sutra of Infinite Life* (*Fo shuo wuliang shou jing* 佛說無量壽經) found inside the Library Cave testify to the rise of Pure Land practices.[2] Chan Buddhism is another tradition that enjoyed a high status in Dunhuang.[3] Two complete copies of the *Platform Sutra of the Sixth Southern Patriarch* (*Liuzu Tanjing* 六祖壇經) by Huineng 慧能 survived: one is now at the British Library, Or.8210/S.5475; the other is at Dunhuang City Museum as part of the Ren Ziyi 任子宜 collection. This is the earliest known version of the text.

Scriptures like the *Text of a Prayer Made by the Great Master Zizhe of Tiantai* (*Tiantai zhizhe dashi fayuan wen* 天台智者大師發願文), which is contained in Pelliot chinois 3183, and the *Chart of the Doctrinal Points in Tiantai* (*Tiantai fenmen tu* 天台分門圖), which can be found in scroll Or.8210/S.2131, are connected to the Tiantai school. The substantial material relating to Chinese Vajrayana, also called Mijiao or esoteric Buddhism, demonstrates that it was practiced in the region of Dunhuang.[4] Chinese Yogācāra is also prominently featured in texts such as the *Record of Doctrinal Points of the Yogācārabhūmi-Śāstra* (*Yujia shidi lun fenmen ji* 瑜伽師地論分門記), a noncanonical text from Dunhuang.[5] Finally, an extensive amount of manuscripts are associated with the controversial Three Stages school, including ritual manuals and rules for monastic training.[6]

Apocryphal sutras in the form of scrolls and booklets abounded in cave 17. These indigenous compositions did not survive as transmitted texts. The ones most commonly seen include the *Sutra of the Ten Kings* (*Shi Wang jing* 十王經), the *Sutra on the Great Kindness of Parents* (*Fumu enzhong jing* 父母恩重經), the *Sutra on Causes and Effects* (*Shan'e yinguo jing* 善惡因果經), and the *Kṣitigarbha Sutra* (*Dizang pusa jing* 地藏菩薩經).[7] Several of the copies bear dedicatory lines that reveal their importance to the local population.

The Library Cave contained some extremely diverse secular texts, which is discussed in further detail in the section "Character of the Manuscripts." Among these are archives from Dunhuang monasteries and nunneries, such as ordination acts, accounts, contracts, and Buddhist rules, as well as personal archives in the form of correspondence, lay circulars, loan receipts, and contracts. There are also official documents, shedding light on the economic, political, and legal history of medieval China in a remote yet strategic location in its territory. They include imperial orders, decrees, certificates, petitions, and so on.[8]

Tibetan-Language Materials. Tibetan is the second most represented language among the materials from the Library Cave. According to Aurel Stein's report, which is the earliest description of the original contents of the secret repository, there were about eighty bundles of Tibetan scrolls when he was first given access in 1907. He also saw eleven large volumes of Tibetan *pothi* pages, as well as several "miscellaneous bundles" that contained, among other things, some smaller-sized Tibetan *pothis*.[9]

These thousands of Tibetan manuscripts are estimated to date from the 8th to the 10th centuries, but most of them were actually written down after the Tibetan rule of Dunhuang (786–848 CE), from the second half of the 10th century. Both Old Tibetan and classical Tibetan languages are found in the manuscripts, which also represent some of the earliest examples of Tibetan writing. As such, they constitute an unparalleled resource for the study of early Tibetan language and script, religion, history, and culture.

The majority of the Tibetan documents relate to Buddhism, offering an insight into the early phase of Tibetan Buddhism when the Tibetans were drawing upon Indic and Chinese Buddhist teachings to develop their own tradition. There are many translations of Buddhist sutras, primarily the *Perfection of Wisdom Sutras* (*Prajñāpāramitā-sūtra*) and the *Homage to Aparamitāyus Sūtra* (*Aparamitāyur-nāma-sūtra*). There are also Tibetan treatises on Madhyamaka and Yogacara that represent some of the earliest Tibetan writings on Buddhist philosophy.[10] Of particular significance are some of the only surviving Tibetan Chan materials, proving that the Tibetans in Dunhuang practiced Chan Buddhism.[11]

Materials from cave 17 also comprised a substantial number of Tibetan Vajrayana works. There are manuscripts of the *Guhyasamājatantra* (IOL Tib J 438 and IOL Tib J 481) and the commentary on the *Upāyapāśatantra* (IOL Tib J 321) attributed to Padmasambhava. In addition, several meditation texts (*sādhana*) are dedicated to a variety of deities like Avalokiteśvara, Vajrasattva, and Heruka. Ritual manuals and treatises on the subjects of tantric views, practices, and vows further inform knowledge of Tibetan Buddhism for the period. Most of these exemplify the approach preserved in the present-day Nyingma school, especially in the vehicles of Yoga, Mahāyoga, and Atiyoga.[12]

The manuscripts include unique sources for the early history of the Tibetan empire. The *Old Tibetan Annals* (Pelliot tibétain 1288 and IOL Tib J 750 and Or.8212/187) are a year-to-year account of important events, including alliances, military campaigns, hunting expeditions, and tax collections. Of particular significance are two fragments of the *Testament of Ba*, Or.8210/S.9498(A) and Or.8210/S.13683, recounting the establishment of Buddhism in Tibet during the reign of Trisong Detsen (r. 755–797/804). The *Tuyuhun Annals* (IOL Tib J 1368) record the activities of the king of the neighboring Tuyuhun tribes, affiliated with the Tibetans.

Other Tibetan official works provide information on clan divisions, administrative posts, appointment decrees, land, taxation, and military administration. Finally, the Library Cave yielded Tibetan translations of Chinese classical texts, philosophical writings as teaching material, and texts on divination, medicine, and other subjects.[13]

Khotanese-Language Materials. Khotanese was a Middle Iranian language used from approximately 200 BCE to 1000 CE by people inhabiting the southern edge of the Tarim basin. During the 10th century, the kingdom of Khotan had a strong diplomatic relationship with the local rulers of Dunhuang that fostered economic and cultural interactions. Cave 17 is the single largest source of Khotanese manuscripts. It yielded a sizeable group of items, dating mostly to the end of the 10th century.[14]

Many of these documents were transcribed on the verso of Chinese scrolls, but a significant number of copies entirely written in Khotanese can also be found in the form of booklets, *pothi* leaves, and rolls. The Khotanese manuscripts from the Library Cave were generally copied locally, with only a couple of exceptions. Among the latter is one official letter sent by the Khotanese king Viśa' Śūra. Dated to 970, it is addressed to Cao Yuanzhong, the ruler of Shazhou (Pelliot chinois 5538 recto).

Almost all the Khotanese Buddhist texts are translations from Sanskrit and Prakrit. They range from Mahayana scriptures, such as the *Sutra of Golden Light* (*Suvarṇabhāsa-sūtra*) or the *Lotus Sutra* (*Saddharmapuṇḍarīka-sūtra*), to 10th-century Vajrayana sutras. These copies, produced to accrue merit and dedicated to the local temples, often contain dates and colophons. IOL Khot S 46, a twenty-one-meter-long scroll at the British Library, contains six Mahayana and tantric texts and has been possibly dated to 943 thanks to its three colophons.

Few indigenous compositions, based on Indic sources, are extant. The so-called *Book of Vimalakirti* is a compendium of Mahayana doctrinal texts in the form of questions and answers. It is contained in two manuscripts from Dunhuang: on the verso of IOL Khot S 10, or Ch.00266 verso, lines 224–386; and on the verso of Pelliot chinois 2026, lines 1–60. Another scripture worth mentioning is the *Jātakastava*, a collection of stories about the Buddha's former births preserved in a British Library *pothi* (IOL Khot 65/1 to IOL Khot 74/3; or Ch.00274).

The manuscripts suggest the presence of an established Khotanese community in Dunhuang. Narratives like the *Rāmāyaṇa*[15] and *Sudhanāvadāna*[16] and literary works, such as lyric poems, were probably copied for entertainment, while alphabet exercises and conversation manuals must have served practical purposes like learning for the local Khotanese population. Medical texts are also represented.

Sogdian-Language Materials. Sogdian was a Middle Iranian language spoken in the Central Asian region of Sogdiana, in present-day Tajikistan and Uzbekistan. From the 4th to the 10th centuries, the Sogdians played a major role as international traders along the Silk Road. This led to the establishment of Sogdian communities at various staging posts, including Dunhuang. A number of manuscripts from the 8th to 10th centuries written in Sogdian were deposited in the Library Cave. Made of paper, they are either books of the *poṭhi* type or scrolls.[17]

The bulk of the Sogdian texts are Buddhist scriptures. Most are translated from Chinese, including both canonical and apocryphal sutras popular in contemporary China. There are also a few items whose direct prototypes are not yet identified but might be Sanskrit or Tocharian, as well as a few Chinese Buddhist texts transliterated in Sogdian. This indicates that the Sogdians based in Dunhuang, whose original faith was Zoroastrianism, must have converted to Buddhism over time. Almost all the Buddhist texts are transcribed in the Sogdian formal script, which is often referred to as sutra script.

The manuscripts are predominantly dated to around the 8th century. Only one of them, the so-called *Sutra of the Condemnation of Intoxicating Drink*, bears the date when it was translated in Luoyang (728 CE). The longest Buddhist text recovered is a copy of the *Vessantara Jātaka*. It is split between the Bibliothèque nationale de France (Pelliot sogdien 1) and the British Library (Or.8212/80(A)). The Bibliothèque nationale de France also holds a scroll of the *Sutra on Causes and Effects*, Pelliot sogdien 4, which survived intact.

A few miscellaneous fragments relate to Zoroastrianism, Manichaeism, and Christianity. Pelliot sogdien 25, for instance, was identified as an exercise copy of the Manichean *Wazargān āfrīwan*, or *Psalm of the Great*. Once part of the same 9th-century manuscript, Pelliot sogdien 13 and Or.8212/81 are two fragments of a Sogdian version of the story of Rustam and the demons. Among the Sogdian documents are also a unique text of rain-making magic (Pelliot sogdien 3 and Or.8212/80(B)), one fragment of a medical treatise (Pelliot sogdien 19), and the section of an omen text (Pelliot sogdien 22).

Old Turkic–Language Materials. Old Turkic language, which is also called Old Uighur, often refers not to a single language but collectively to the closely related stages of various Common Turkic dialects that were spoken during the first millennium and transcribed using many different writing systems. One of the scripts first attested was the Old Uighur alphabet, which was borrowed from Sogdian. Others include the Turkic runes and Manichean, Brahmi, and Perso-Arabic scripts.

The Old Turkic materials from Dunhuang chiefly contain Buddhist scriptures and Manichaean texts.[18] The latter are prevalent, possibly reflecting a shift in religious beliefs due to the close contact with Turfan, where Manichaeism remained a state religion until the 11th century. A version of the *Xuāstvānīft* was preserved in a scroll written in the Manichean script (Or.8212/178), and several fragments in Old Uighur script have also been identified in the Pelliot collection.

There are also a smaller number of secular writings and letters, perhaps brought or sent to Dunhuang from the Xizhou or Ganzhou Uighur Khaganates. One of the most significant finds in Old Turkic is the *Irk Bitig*, or *Book of Omens*, a text on omen divination possibly dated to the 9th century (Or.8212/161). Consisting of fifty-two folios, it is the only known booklet written in Old Turkic runes.

Sanskrit-Language Materials. Primarily used in Buddhist monasteries across Asia during the first millennium CE, Sanskrit is another one of the languages represented. Most of the few documents from Dunhuang are Buddhist scriptures preserved on paper. Interestingly, they are similar to the Sanskrit documents excavated along other northern Silk Road sites.[19]

The identified fragments include *vinaya* texts; sutras; *dhāraṇīs*, such as printed prayer sheets (Pelliot sanscrit 1– to 13) and a spell against snakebites (IOL San 378); the *Udānavarga*, which is the early collection of Buddha's sayings (IOL San 379–381); and a poem in praise of the Buddha (IOL San 416–418). The British Library also holds sixty-nine leaves of a *pothi* manuscript of the *Perfection of Wisdom in 100,000 Sections* (*Śatasāhasrikā Prajñāpāramitā Sūtra*) written on palm leaves (IOL San 1492). It is dated to the 6th to 8th centuries and possibly traveled to Dunhuang from northern India, where it is thought to have originated.

Finally, a few manuscripts feature Sanskrit with another language or script. On the recto of the British Library's concertina Or.8212/195, the *Heart Sutra* (*Prajñāpāramitāhṛdayasūtra*) is transcribed in alternating columns containing the actual scripture in Gupta script and a transliteration in Chinese characters.

CHARACTER OF THE MANUSCRIPTS

The majority of cave 17's documents are Buddhist scriptures or have an association with Buddhism, confirming the dominance of Buddhism in Dunhuang during the first millennium CE. But there are also a considerable number of other religious and secular texts, often written on the back of Buddhist texts, repurposed to mend Buddhist scriptures.

Buddhist Texts. The texts show a world pervaded by Buddhism at all levels of society in both public and private spheres. They roughly date to the period when Buddhism had already spread from India and gained popularity in Central Asia and China. Most of the documents from the Library Cave belong to one of the three categories that form the Buddhist canon, or *Tripitaka*: the sutras, the *abhidharma*, and the *vinaya*.

The largest group is composed of the sutras, which were at the center of Buddhist practice. Among these are thousands of copies in different languages of popular scriptures like the *Perfection of Wisdom* class of sutras, the *Lotus Sutra*, and the *Sutra of Golden Light*. In the Mahayana, producing or commissioning sutra copies, thereby encouraging the dissemination of sacred scriptures, was a way to accrue merit. Many colophons evidence the widespread belief in the efficacy of such activity. Some rulers, like the Tibetan emperor Tri Tsug Detsen (r. 815–841), even sponsored mass sutra-copying projects.[20]

A significant number of so-called apocryphal sutras compiled in China also found their way into the tradition.[21] Several discontinued or lost Buddhist texts were preserved in cave 17, including some Chinese and Tibetan Chan teachings,[22] as well as scriptures of the Three Stages school that have otherwise vanished.[23] Moreover, many texts of a more local nature survived and speak of a wide range of practices. There are collections of prayers to be recited, instructions on meditation, rituals for funerals and other important occasions, notes from lectures, and so on. For example, the Tibetan manuscript IOL Tib J 331 provides instructions for tantric meditation practice.

Several accounts by Buddhist pilgrims who journeyed to the holy Buddhist land of India were also deposited in cave 17. One of the most important ones is Xuanzang's *Great Tang Records on the Western Regions* (*Datang Xiyu ji* 大唐西域記), preserved in four copies: Pelliot chinois 2700 bis, Pelliot chinois 3814, Or.8210/S.2659 verso, and Or.8210/S.958. Another extraordinary discovery was that of an incomplete manuscript containing the travelogue of Hyecho 慧超, a Korean monk from the kingdom of Silla, for the years 723 to 727–728 (Pelliot chinois 3532). There is also a bilingual Sino-Tibetan record of pilgrimage with letters of introduction for a 10th-century monk (IOL Tib J 754).[24]

Documents from the Library Cave cast light on other aspects of early Buddhist culture, such as the development of local monasteries and nunneries. In addition to serving as centers of worship, these also played a key role in the life of the community. They received support from the local laity and, in return, performed various kinds of rituals for them. Moreover, they were key actors in scholarship and learning. For instance, monks and nuns set up clubs for laymen and women practitioners, whose activities included discussing sutras. Monastic accounts preserve information about various Buddhist festivities, recording how the ceremonies were conducted and what people aspired to achieve through them.[25]

Over a hundred manuscripts have been identified as the popular narratives known as "transformation texts," or *bianwen* (變文). They combine elements from Buddhism with historical and contemporary anecdotes, as well as other folk traditions. Some quote sutras to explain their meanings, while others retell stories from the life of the buddha or report a dispute about Buddhist teachings by his disciples. Closely related to oral and visual performance, they are designed to attract a wider public to the contents of Buddhist teachings.[26]

Other Religions. The Library Cave's contents attest to the presence of other religions in Dunhuang. In many cases there are clear links between these religions and the dominant Buddhist tradition. The mixture of Buddhist and Daoist traditions is apparent in a large number of manuscripts. Pelliot chinois 2153, for instance, is a scroll with an apocryphal Buddhist text containing numerous seals and talismans. Not only have copies of the *Daodejing* 道德經 been preserved but also six commentaries, including the previously lost *Laozi Xiang'er zhu* 老子想爾注 (Or.8210/S.6825). Several chapters of the *Classic of the Conversion of the Barbarians* (*Huahujing* 化胡經), attributed to Laozi, were also rediscovered in cave 17. See, for example, scrolls Or.8210/S.1857, Pelliot chinois 2004, and Pelliot chinois 2007.

There are sources relating to Zoroastrianism. Or.8212/84, a 9th-century fragment in Sogdian script, contains a short text concerning the prophet Zarathustra and a phonetic transcription of the *Ashem vohū*, one of the holiest Zoroastrian prayers. Several Chinese texts also refer to Zoroastrians, like the *Shazhou Dunhuang ershi yong* 沙洲敦煌二十詠, a poem in praise of the historical sites around Dunhuang that is contained in manuscript Pelliot chinois 2748.[27] Some records of expenditure of the Guiyijun authorities, like Pelliot chinois 4640, include offerings to a Zoroastrian deity.

Among the Chinese manuscripts from the Library Cave are some key Manichaean texts, including the National Library of China's *Manichaean Treatise on the Light-Nous* (BD08470) and the 731 CE *Compendium of the Teachings of Mani, the Buddha of Light* (*Moni guangfo jiaofa yilüe* 摩尼光佛教法儀略), which is split between the British Library and the Bibliothèque nationale de France (Or.8210/S.3969 + Pelliot chinois 3884). Moreover, several Manichean texts in Old Turkic and Sogdian have been identified. One of the most important is a scroll containing a well-preserved Old Turkic version of a confession book called the *Xuāstvānīft* (Or.8212/178).

Christianity is also in evidence in the materials retrieved from cave 17. The 8th- or 9th-century scroll Pelliot chinois 3847 comprises a translation of the *Gloria in Excelsis Deo*, as well as a list of saints and sacred books. A few more Christian manuscripts in Chinese can be found in Japanese collections, like the *The Sutra of Ultimate and Mysterious Happiness* (*Zhixuan anle jing* 志玄安樂經) and the *Sutra on the Origin of Origins* (*Xuanyuan ben jing* 宣元本經).[28]

Finally, Judaism is represented in a single manuscript: a Jewish prayer written in Hebrew script and roughly dated from the 7th to 9th centuries (Pelliot hébreu 1 or hébreu 1412).

Secular Documents. Thousands of manuscripts from the Library Cave preserve a great variety of secular texts ranging from economic, legal, and official documents to works on art, folk songs, and dance. Due to the scarcity of materials surviving from this period in China, they are almost the only primary sources available. They are often written on the back of Buddhist texts or seem to have come into the possession of Buddhist practitioners and to have been reused in the production of Buddhist scriptures. Secular texts also appear as writing practice in students' primers, textbooks, and notebooks.

Economic, Legal, and Historical Documents. The wide range of administrative documents produced by rulers, officials, monasteries, and private individuals cast light on the economic, legal, and social history of the Hexi corridor. It would be impossible to be exhaustive here, but the texts include imperial orders and decrees, official letters, land and tax registries, lists of administrative units and military garrisons of Dunhuang, reports about corvée labor, contracts, loan agreements, testaments, and so forth.[29] Family registers like the *Xinji tianxia xingwang shizu pu* 新集天下姓望氏族譜 (Or.8210/S.2052), for instance, provide important information about the Tang dynasty's local administration and its relation with neighboring countries.

The expansion of the Tibetan empire across Central Asia is documented through the *Old Tibetan Annals* (Pelliot tibétain 1288 + IOL Tib J 750 and Or.8212/187) and the *Old Tibetan Chronicle* (Pelliot tibétain 1287) that contains legendary narratives from the period of the mythical Nyatri Tsenpo until Trisong Detsen. The *Catalogue of the Ancient Principalities* refers to various tribes and territories on the Tibetan plateau, listing the names of rulers and ministers. It is followed, on the same scroll, by a list titled the *Royal Genealogy* (Pelliot tibétain 1286).

Chinese official histories found in Dunhuang comprise works like the *Records of the Grand Historian* (*Shiji* 史記)[30] and the *Book of Han* (*Hanshu* 漢書).[31] There are also a relatively large number of copies of Kong Yan's 孔衍 *Later Comments on the Spring and Autumn Annals* (*Chunqiu Houyu* 春秋後語), such as Or.8210/S.713 or Pelliot chinois 2589. Finally, local compositions on the history of Dunhuang that had been lost in transmission constitute valuable sources. See, for example, Pelliot chinois 2625, which is a history of the leading families of Dunhuang.

Geography. Equally remarkable are the geographical works discovered in the Library Cave. In addition to the pilgrimage accounts by monks that contain a wealth of geographic and topographic information, there are rare geographical treatises that deal with entire China. The *Tianbao shidao lu* 天寶十道錄 is a gazetteer kept at the Dunhuang City Museum (shelf mark 10–76). The *Zhenyuan shidao lu* 貞元十道錄 (Pelliot chinois 2522) discusses the provinces and commanderies in the twelve provinces of the Jiannan circuit and occasionally local historical sites.

Some local gazetteers, mainly dealing with Dunhuang and surrounding areas, were also deposited in cave 17. Sections 1, 3, and 5 of the *Shazhou tujing* 沙州圖經 are preserved in manuscripts Or.8210/S.2593, Pelliot chinois 2005 and Pelliot chinois 2695, and Pelliot chinois 5034. All of these gazetteers date to the late Tang, Five Dynasties, and early Song periods.

Literary and Philosophical Works. Due to the preponderance of Chinese materials found in cave 17, the literary and philosophical works in the Chinese language are the most numerous. Classical poetry, for instance, is represented by Or.8210/S.2717 and Pelliot chinois 3771, which are fragmentary copies of the *Zhuying ji* 珠英集, also known as the *Collection of Precious Glories*. There are Confucian classics, including Pelliot chinois 3573, an ancient edition of the *Analects* commented by Huang Kan 皇侃, as well as copies of the *Book of Documents* (*Shangshu* 尚書).[32]

Yet, the most important discoveries consist of works of previously unknown popular literature in vernacular language, including ballads, folk songs, and lyric forms of poetry. If the earliest transformation texts (*bianwen* 變文) focus on Buddhist subjects, wholly secular themes, both historical and contemporary in nature, were gradually added and narrated in a similar style.[33] Another genre is that of model letters, such as condolence letters or the entertaining apology for getting drunk (Or.8210/S.2200).

One example of literary work in Tibetan language is the *Rāmāyaṇa*, which is featured in manuscripts IOL Tib J 737.1, IOL Tib J 737.2, IOL Tib J 737.3, Pelliot tibétain 981, and Pelliot tibétain 983. This retelling of the Indian epic tale is more condensed than the original story.[34] The same narrative is also found in extant Khotanese texts, including the verso of Pelliot chinois 2801, Pelliot chinois 2781, and Pelliot chinois 2783.

Scientific Texts. Especially numerous among the Dunhuang manuscripts are writings related to the healing arts. Several are scattered throughout the Buddhist and Daoist scriptures, but there are also a variety of medical texts such as diagnostic methods, remedies, acupuncture, and *materia medica*.[35] This includes Ryokoku University Library's fragment of the *Bencaojing jizhu* 本草經記住, one of the earliest Chinese pharmacological texts, and some Tibetan treatises on moxibustion, such as Pelliot tibétain 1058.[36] There is also literature that belongs to the realm of Indian Ayurvedic medicine, like the Khotanese copy of Ravigupta's *Siddhasāra* (IOL Khot 116/1 to 137/2; or Ch.ii.002) and the incomplete Sanskrit Khotanese version of the *Jīvaka-Pustaka* (IOL Khot 87/1 to 110/2; or Ch.ii.003).

Cave 17 yielded a small number of arithmetic manuals, designed for practical use, and arithmetic treatises that were probably intended for teaching. For instance, there are three copies of the *Sunzi Suanjing* 孫子算經 (Pelliot chinois 3349, Or.8210/S.19, and Or.8210/S.5779), a mathematical treatise compiled during the Southern and Northern dynasties. A manuscript of the *Licheng Suanjing* 立成算經 (Or.8210/S.930), an unknown work on applied mathematics, was also discovered at Dunhuang.

The Library Cave's treasures comprised some valuable texts relating to astronomy, often closely linked to divination and religion. In addition to several almanacs, a fragment of an astrology manual written in 621, the *Xingzhanshu* 星占書 (Pelliot chinois 2512), was identified among the finds. The British Library also holds an 8th-century star chart, which is the earliest map of the skies known for any civilization (Or.8210/S.3326).

Other Works. Materials relating to divination are abundant in the manuscripts from cave 17. They can be found across all languages. Ranging from dice divination and auguromancy to topomancy, oneiromancy, or physiognomy, divinatory practices often appear to be linked to Confucian, Daoist, and Buddhist traditions.[37] There are also dictionaries, such as the *Qieyun*,[38] and phrasebooks.[39] The Library Cave also contained music scores, dance notations, and writings about recreational games like the *Classic of Go* (*Dunhuang Qijing* 敦煌碁經), which is the earliest surviving manual on the strategic board game (Or.8210/S.5574).

FORMATS, MATERIALS, AND TECHNIQUES

The forms, materials, and techniques represented in the manuscripts from the Library Cave are almost as diverse as their contents. They provide a wealth of information about the production, circulation, and use of Buddhist and non-Buddhist manuscripts as physical objects.

Book Formats. The most commonly found format is the scroll, a book form that prevailed in China for more than a thousand years. A scroll is a long roll generally made of paper and created by gluing together rectangular sheets. It was a fairly adaptable format insofar as more sheets could be added to augment or supplement books. It was also portable and could be easily stored. Scrolls were grouped and wrapped together in paper, cloth, silk, or bamboo strips tied with silk thread. Wrappers were often reinforced with layers of paper taken from old manuscripts.[40]

Another popular form, the *pothi*, was based on the shape of the long and slim palm leaves used for the production of ancient Indian books. The individual leaves were inscribed on both sides and bound together with a thread going through one or two central string holes. *Pothi* pages made from paper seem to have originated from Central Asia and then to have been adapted for Tibetan and Chinese Buddhist texts. They were produced in various sizes as shown by Dunhuang exemplars. A manuscript kept at the National Library of China (BD15001) shows how wooden boards could act as a cover to protect the text inside.[41]

A later development, derived from both the scroll and the *pothi*, was the concertina. This hybrid book form is based on rectangular sheets of paper pasted together and then folded over to form an accordion-shaped document whose folios are the same size as *pothi* leaves. The concertina probably emerged from the 9th century onward and is often considered to be the precursor of the booklet or codex, which is one of the latest stages of bookbinding found in the Dunhuang manuscripts. This is also a format that seems more frequent among the Tibetan texts from cave 17.[42]

Providing easy access to the text at various points, codices maybe appeared in Dunhuang in the late 9th to 10th centuries and became the dominant form in China by the Song dynasty (960–1127 CE). They were bound at the spine either by gluing the folded edge of the folios or by stitching several sheets of paper stacked together and folded over. About 400 such booklets, used to record Buddhist and non-Buddhist texts, are extant across the various Dunhuang manuscript collections.[43]

Materials and Techniques. Paper was the most commonly used material for the manuscripts from cave 17. Regarded as objects capable of generating merit and benefits to donors, sutras were often transcribed on the finest paper, much of which came from central China. A small group of official copies of the *Diamond Sutra* and *Lotus Sutra* in Chinese were made in the capital, Chang'an, using pounded fibers from the bark of the mulberry trees, hemp, and other plants. Like Or.8210/S.5318, which is dated to 671, they represent the highest standard of Tang sutra production and possess colophons detailing the elaborate process of making them.[44]

There were also other paper-making centers in Central Asia, including one in Khotan. Paper analysis of some Tibetan manuscripts at the British Library revealed fibers from the Daphne plant, indicating that the paper was perhaps made on the Tibetan plateau, where this species is available. Many of the manuscripts also seem to have been produced in or near Dunhuang, using paper composed of ramie and hemp rags.[45]

Before receiving ink, the sheets of paper had to be sized, using substances like starch, gypsum, talc, lime, and kaolin. They were then often dyed yellow. This was the most frequently encountered color of Buddhist sutras, obtained from the bark of Amur cork tree (*Phellodendron amurense*), known as *huangbo* 黃檗 in China.[46] In the scroll of the *Diamond Sutra*, Or.8210/S.4324, different shades of yellow, blue, and green were combined for a striking visual effect. By the late 9th to 10th centuries, some sutra copies were transcribed on indigo paper in gold or silver. The aesthetic qualities of colored paper were equally sought after in high-quality secular documents. Pelliot chinois 4642 and Or.8210/S.3753, which are respectively made of light blue and pink paper, contain texts based on the calligraphy of Wang Xizhi 王羲之.

A few Dunhuang scrolls and booklets bear illustrations. These tend to be drawn by hand in carbon ink and painted with pigments. Sometimes they precede or follow the text, and they are also displayed in a band above the written content or sandwiched inside it. In some instances they fulfill a purely decorative purpose, but they can be linked to the ritual use of certain manuscripts, as in the *Sutra of the Buddha's Names* (*Fo ming jing* 佛明經), or serve a more practical function. In Pelliot chinois 4513, which is a scroll of the *Guanyin Sutra* (*Guanyin Jing* 觀音經), the pictures complement the narrative structure of the scripture. This is also the case in illustrated copies of the *Sutra of the Ten Kings* (*Shi wang jing* 十王經), such as Or.8210/S.3691. Text and image can also be completely interdependent, especially in technical works like divination treatises or medical charts (Or.8210/S.6168).[47]

A significant number of printed items, which are among the earliest ones in China, were found in the Library Cave. They include prayer sheets, rows of buddha figures, and popular Buddhist sutras.[48] Because the replication of the buddha's word and image was considered a meritorious act, Buddhism possibly encouraged the development of woodblock printing as a means to do so faster, with accuracy, and on a larger scale. Nevertheless, laypeople also used printing, as shown by the presence of several almanacs. While some of cave 17's printed documents were produced locally, others were possibly printed in Sichuan, the then center of a thriving printing industry.[49] This might be the case of the British Library's printed copy of the *Diamond Sutra* that is dated to 868 (Or.8210/P.2).

Silk was seldom used in Dunhuang and reserved to particularly luxurious textual editions. A scroll of the *Sutra of the Golden Light* (Pelliot chinois 4506) is made of one piece of silk of approximately ten meters long and is dated to 471. It is one of the oldest existing Chinese Buddhist sutras on silk found in the Library Cave, together with the *Sutra of the Buddha of Infinite Life* (Pelliot chinois 4506 bis), probably commissioned by the same individual. Another apocryphal sutra (Pelliot chinois 4500) comprises two sheets of blue silk embroidered with the characters of the scripture.

PRIMARY SOURCES

Wang Yuanlu, the discoverer of the Library Cave, was famously convinced by Stein and Pelliot to part with a large portion of the manuscripts. Later visits by Japanese, Russian, and Danish explorers and the clearing of the cave by the Chinese government resulted in its contents being scattered around many public and private institutions across the world.

The British Library. Hungarian-born, naturalized British archaeologist and explorer Sir Marc Aurel Stein (1862–1943) visited Dunhuang in 1907, during his second Central Asian expedition (1906–1908). After lengthy negotiations with Wang Yuanlu, he purchased twenty-four cases of manuscripts and five cases of silk paintings, silk fabrics, and other artifacts. Stein returned to Dunhuang during his third expedition (1913–1916) and obtained 570 more manuscripts.

His finds were divided between London (the British Museum and the India Office Library) and India, whose government had also sponsored Stein's expeditions. By 1982, the majority of the London manuscripts had been transferred to the British Library. The British Library's Stein collection from cave 17 principally comprises about 14,000 scrolls, booklets, and fragments in Chinese, as well as over 3,000 items in Tibetan. The pressmarks given to the manuscripts reflect their institutional history.

The texts written in Chinese, Sogdian, and Old Turkic were originally deposited at the British Museum's Department of oriental manuscripts. They were cataloged under the prefix "Or," followed by a number that reflects some basic classification according to languages and archaeological sites:

- "Or.8210" was mostly assigned to the texts in Chinese language that came from the Dunhuang Library Cave.[50] Within this sequence, the letter S (possibly standing for "scroll") denotes manuscripts and is followed by the numbers 1 to 13677 that designate particular items; printed texts use the letter P (i.e., "print") and the numbers 1 to 20.
- "Or.8212" contains manuscripts in various languages. A small number of them are from Dunhuang. Written in Chinese, Tibetan, Sanskrit, Old Turkic, and Sogdian, they quite often bear multiple languages.

Texts in Khotanese and Tibetan were deposited at the India Office Library. Their pressmark is a combination of the acronym "IOL," which stands for their original hosting institution, with the language represented: "IOL Tib J" corresponds to the materials in Tibetan found in Dunhuang, "IOL Khot" was used for manuscripts in Khotanese language, and "IOL San" was attributed to the Sanskrit texts.

The Bibliothèque nationale de France. The Bibliothèque nationale de France has a rich collection of Dunhuang manuscripts, which were collected by the French Sinologist Paul Pelliot (1878–1945) in the course of the Central Asian expedition that he led from 1906 to 1908. Pelliot arrived at Dunhuang in February 1908 and was allowed by Wang Yuanlu to spend a full three weeks in the Library Cave.

Pelliot selected a range of religious and secular texts that he judged to contain new information or to be of linguistic interest, as well as a few statues and paintings. The many secular texts that he brought back have been one of the primary resources for research on the economic, social, and legal history of medieval Central Asia and China. The bulk of Dunhuang manuscripts in the Pelliot collection at the Bibliothèque nationale de France are in Chinese and Tibetan languages, with respectively over 4,000 items and around 3,000 pieces.

The collection has been divided and cataloged in subcollections or fonds that reflect the language of the materials:

- "Pelliot chinois" is for Chinese manuscripts. The numbering runs from 2001 to 4099, 4500 to 5043, and 5522 to 6038. The missing numbers at the beginning and in between were reserved for texts in Tibetan and other languages. Some of these remained unused and are still empty (e.g., 4100–4499, 5044–5521).
- "Pelliot tibétain" is for Tibetan manuscripts.
- "Pelliot sanskrit" is for Sanskrit manuscripts.
- "Pelliot sogdien" is for Sogdian manuscripts. Some were transferred here from Pelliot chinois 2511–3521.

- "Pelliot ouïgour" is for Uighur texts. Several were also moved from the Chinese and Sogdian fonds (e.g., Pelliot ouïgour 12 used to be Pelliot chinois 4637, and Pelliot ouïgour 11 used to be Pelliot sogdien 28).

Only the Khotanese manuscripts and the single Hebrew manuscript are not grouped separately.

Institute of Oriental Manuscripts. The manuscripts collected by Russian diplomats and explorers in northwest China at the end of the 19th century and beginning of the 20th century are kept at the Institute of Oriental Manuscripts (IOM), in St Petersburg. This institution holds one of the largest collections of Dunhuang manuscripts in the world. These are, for the most part, Buddhist scriptures, with less than 5 percent of secular texts.

Sergei Fedorovich Oldenburg (1863–1934) was the first director of the Institute of Oriental Studies, formerly the Asiatic Museum. The 19,000 manuscript fragments and 365 scrolls acquired by him during his second expedition in Russian Turkestan, from 1914 to 1915, constitute the largest part of the Dunhuang collection. The Khotanese expedition that Sergei Efimovich Malov (1880–1957) led in 1909 and 1910 contributed about 30 manuscripts, while the Russian Consul N. N. Krotkov collected a further 183 items in Uighur.

The shelf marks of the Russian collection of Chinese manuscripts from Dunhuang have a total of 366 Ф numbers, where the letter Ф refers to the initial in Kostantin K. Flug's surname, the man who was in charge of the manuscript collections at the Asiatic Museum and started to catalog and study the Dunhuang materials in the 1930s. The letters Дх are an acronym for "Dunhuang," and the overall majority of the manuscripts use these letters. The letters Ф and Дх are also sometimes romanized as F. and Dx (or Dh).

Chinese Collections. As news of the discovery of cave 17 was brought to the attention of scholars, a special committee was formed to convince the Chinese government to remove the remaining manuscripts and prevent their dispersal. By 1910, over 8,000 manuscripts had been transported to the capital and deposited at the Metropolitan Library, which later became the National Library of China. They form the core of the National Library of China's Dunhuang collection, which now amounts to 16,000 items, having been supplemented over the years by various donations and acquisitions. They all have shelf marks beginning with 北 or BD.

No attempt was made to look for the manuscripts that had come into the possession of the local population, nor were any excavations carried out in the caves themselves. In addition, several thousands of Tibetan items were left in Dunhuang and were subsequently relocated in local museums and libraries. With almost 400 items, the largest collection is currently held at the Dunhuang Academy. Other significant collections in the region include those of the Gansu Provincial Museum, the Dunhuang City Museum, and the Gansu Provincial Library. Several Chinese institutions, such as the Tianjin Museum, the Beijing University Library, and the Shanghai Library, also hold Dunhuang manuscripts.

Other Collections. During the third Central Asian expedition carried under the leadership of Count Ōtani Kozui 大谷 between 1910 and 1914, batches of Dunhuang manuscripts were acquired on several occasions by Tachibana Zuichō 橘瑞超 (1890–1968) and Yoshikawa

Koichirō 吉川小一郎 (1885–1978). They are now divided among several institutions in Japan, including Ryūkoku University, Kyoto National Museum, and Tokyo National Museum.

Besides these collections, institutions holding smaller collections of Dunhuang manuscripts and paintings include the National Museum of India in New Delhi; the Royal Library of Denmark and the Bavarian State Library in Europe; the Taipei National Central Library and the Academia Sinica in Taiwan; and the Fogg Art Museum of Harvard University, the Library of Congress, the Gest Library at Princeton University, and the Freer Gallery of Art in the United States.

REVIEW OF LITERATURE

The diversity of the materials from the Library Cave is mirrored by the multifaceted research built around them. Not only did they contribute to virtually every area of study connected to medieval China and Central Asia, they are also at the heart of a whole separate field established in the 20th century: Dunhuangology, or Dunhuang studies.

Catalogs. In Britain, Russia, France, and China, the focus was initially on cataloging the collections derived from cave 17. Given the breadth of the Dunhuang manuscript holdings, contemporary scholars are still actively engaged in this task, which is greatly contributing to the study of these resources. The cataloges themselves tend to focus on one language and sometimes on one specific genre.

Chinese-Language Materials. Most of the early research work undertaken by the Chinese scholars was devoted to collecting data and cataloging collections abroad. Nonetheless, the first large catalog of the National Library of China's Dunhuang manuscripts was published in 1931. In 2000, Shi and Tai wrote a catalog of the Chinese manuscripts from cave 17 covering several different collections. In 1957, Giles published a catalog of the Chinese manuscripts in the Stein collection. His work, which omitted most of the secular texts, was supplemented by Rong's catalog in 1994. In France, Pelliot started cataloging the Chinese manuscripts, a task that was continued by several French scholars after him, with the results published between 1970 and 2001. In Russia, Menshikov finished the annotated catalog of the Chinese Dunhuang manuscripts in St Petersburg's Institute of Oriental Studies in the 1960s.

Chen Yuan 陳垣 and Yu Zezhen 俞澤箴. *Dunhuang jieyu lu* 敦煌劫餘錄. Institute of History and Philology at Academia Sinica, 1931.

Bibliothèque nationale de France, Paul Pelliot, Michel Soymié, and Françoise Wang-Toutain. *Catalogue des manuscrits chinois de Touen-houang: Fonds Pelliot chinois*. Paris: Bibliothèque nationale, 1970–2001.

Giles, Lionel. *Descriptive Catalogue of the Chinese Manuscripts from Tunhuang in the British Museum*. London: Trustees of the British Museum, 1957.

Rong Xinjiang 荣新江. *Yingguo tushuguan cang Dunhuang hanwen fei fojiao wenxian canjuan mulu* 英國圖書館藏敦煌漢文非佛教文獻殘卷目錄. Taipei: Xinwenfeng Chuban Gongsi, 1994.

Shi Pingting 施萍婷, and Tai Huili 邰惠莉. *Dunhuang yishu zongmu suoyin xinbian* 敦煌遺書總目索引新編. Beijing: Zhonghua Shuju, 2000.

Vorob'eva-Desiatovskaia, Margarita I., et al. *Opisanie kitaiskikh rukopisei Dun'khuanskogo fonda Instituta narodov Azii*. 2 vols, Edited by Lev Nikolaevich Men'shikov. Moscow: Nauka/Izd-vo Vostochnoi Literatury, 1963–1967.

Tibetan-Language Materials. The Belgian scholar La Vallée Poussin compiled a partial catalog of the Tibetan Buddhist manuscripts that he finished before his death in 1939 but only came out in 1962. In 2006, Dalton and Schaik published a catalog of the tantric manuscripts among this material. The results of Thomas's research on Tibetan secular texts from the Stein collection were presented in a partial catalog in 1951. In France, Lalou and other contributors released the three-volume catalog of the Pelliot Tibetan collection between 1939 and 1961.

Dalton, Jacob, and Sam van Schaik. *Tibetan Tantric Manuscripts from Dunhuang: A Descriptive Catalogue of the Stein Collection at the British Library*. Leiden and Boston: Brill, 2006.

Lalou, Marcelle. *Inventaire des manuscrits tibétains de Touen-houang: Conservés à la bibliothèque nationale (Fonds Pelliot tibétain)*. 3 vols. Paris: Librairie d'Amérique et d'Orient, A. Maisonneuve, 1939–1961.

La Vallée Poussin, Louis. *Catalogue of the Tibetan Manuscripts from Tun-Huang in the India Office Library*, with an appendix on the Chinese manuscripts by Kazuo Enoki. Oxford: Oxford University Press, 1962.

Thomas, Frederick William. *Tibetan Literary Texts and Documents Concerning Chinese Turkestan, Part II: Documents*. London: Royal Asiatic Society, 1951.

Khotanese and Other Central Asian Materials. Bailey and Emmerick made significant contributions to Khotanese studies, while Skjærvø's 2002 volume on the British Library manuscripts is the first comprehensive catalog of Khotanese manuscripts in any collection. In 2008, Maggi also published an updated overview of Khotanese literature. Hamilton illustrated himself with his 1986 study of the Uighur manuscripts from cave 17. Together with Sims-Williams, he also helped catalog the Sogdian manuscripts in 1990. Yoshida's 2009 introduction and 2015 handlist are also extremely useful references with regard to Sogdian Buddhist texts.

Bailey, Harold Walter. *Khotanese Texts*, I–III, V. Cambridge, UK: Cambridge University Press, 1969, 1980.

Bailey, Harold Walter. *Khotanese Buddhist Texts*. Rev. ed. Cambridge, UK: Cambridge University Press, 1981.

Emmerick, Ronald Eric. *A Guide to the Literature of Khotan*. 2nd ed. Tokyo: International Institute for Buddhist Studies, 1992.

Hamilton, James Russell. *Manuscrits ouïgours du IXe–Xe siècle de Touen-houang, I–II*. Paris: Fondation Singer-polignac, 1986.

Maggi, Mauro. "Khotanese Literature." In *The Literature of Pre-Islamic Iran: Companion Volume I to a History of Persian Literature*. Edited by Ronald Erick Emmerick and Maria

Macuch. *A History of Persian Literature* XVII, 330–417. London and New York: I. B. Tauris, 2009.

Sims-Williams, Nicholas, and James Hamilton. *Documents turco-sogdiens du IXe–Xe siècle de Touen-houang*. Corpus inscriptionum Iranicarum, Part 2, *Inscriptions of the Seleucid and Parthian Periods and of Eastern Iran and Central Asia*, vol. 3. London: School of Oriental and African Studies, 1990.

Skjærvø, Prods Oktor. *Khotanese Manuscripts from Chinese Turkestan in the British Library: A Complete Catalogue with Texts and Translations*. With contributions by Ursula Sims-Williams. London: British Library, 2002.

Yoshida, Yutaka. "Buddhist Literature in Sogdian." In *The Literature of Pre-Islamic Iran: Companion Volume I to a History of Persian Literature*, edited by Ronald Eric Emmerick and Maria Macuch. *A History of Persian Literature* XVII, 288–329. London and New York: I. B. Tauris, 2009.

Yoshida, Yutaka. "A Handlist of Buddhist Sogdian Texts." *Memoirs of the Faculty of Letters, Kyoto University*, 54 (2015): 167–180.

Monographs and Reference Works

On Buddhist Texts. Originally, the Buddhist manuscripts from the Library Cave seemed to have triggered less scholarly interest than their secular counterparts, but the field of Dunhuang studies is currently moving in new directions, with a stronger emphasis on Buddhism.

Early Chan Buddhism, which was first brought to the attention of the Sinological world by Hu Shi 胡適 in the 1930s, remains one of the main areas of research. The French scholar Demiéville also realized the importance of Chan texts in the Dunhuang corpus fairly early on, relying on these sources in *Le Concile de Lhasa*, which he published in 1952. This resulted in a rich vein of scholarship in Japan and the United States, epitomized by the research of Tanaka and McRae. Recent contributions include monographs by Wang and Yang in 2006, Adamek in 2007, and Van Schaik in 2015.

Gernet's 1957 book on the economic aspects of Buddhism and their complex interplay with Chinese society opened a new line of questioning around the Dunhuang manuscripts. Leading scholars, such as Jiang Boqin 姜伯勤, also further explored the organizational structure and the economy of local Buddhist communities. In 1998, Hao Chunwen's book paved the way for research in the social life of Buddhist monks and nuns at Dunhuang. One of the recent studies reflecting a similar interest in the practical aspects relating to Buddhist institutions is Shi Xiaoying's 2013 monograph on the lives of nuns. Cuilan Liu has been investigating the legal practices of the Buddhist clergy in Dunhuang.[51]

In the 1980s, the American scholar Mair wrote a seminal book on Buddhist transformation texts. In recent years, the scope of studies on Buddhist-related popular literature has expanded thanks to contributions from Cartelli in 2013, Wang in 2009, and Huangjian in 2010. Teiser's 1994 book on the *Sutra of the Ten Kings* equally marked a significant shift toward reconstructing the liturgical background of Buddhist scriptures. This approach has led to exciting new research on the functionality and use(s) of Dunhuang manuscripts, as reflected by the research of Copp on *dhāraṇīs* which was published in 2014, or that of Van Schaik on Buddhist magic (2020).[52]

Finally, Vajrayana Buddhism has known some remarkable developments. Cantwell and Mayer's 2008 book on the Tibetan tantric texts connected to the ritual dagger, as well as the volume edited in 2010 by Kapstein and Van Schaik, best illustrate the mature scholarship in the field. Bentor and Shahar's publication looks at Tibetan tantric Buddhism and Chinese esoteric Buddhism side by side, with a whole section devoted to materials from cave 17.[53] Wang's 2018 monograph, which draws also on both the textual and art historical sources from Dunhuang, joins this growing body of scholarship.

Adamek, Wendi Leigh. *The Mystique of Transmission: On an Early Chan History and Its Context*. New York: Columbia University Press, 2007.

Bentor, Yael, and Meir Shahar. *Chinese and Tibetan Esoteric Buddhism*. Leiden and Boston: Brill, 2017.

Brooks, Phyllis, and Bernard Faure. *The Will to Orthodoxy: A Critical Genealogy of Northern Chan Buddhism*. Redwood City, CA: Stanford University Press, 1997.

Cantwell, Cathy, and Robert Mayer. *Early Tibetan Documents on Phur pa from Dunhuang*. Vienna: Verlag der Österreichischen Akademie der Wissenschaften, 2008.

Cartelli, Mary Anne. *The Five-Colored Clouds of Mount Wutai: Poems from Dunhuang*. Leiden and Boston: Brill, 2013.

Copp, Paul. *The Body Incantatory: Spells and the Ritual Imagination in Medieval Chinese Buddhism*. New York: Columbia University Press, 2014.

Demiéville, Paul. *Le Concile de Lhasa: Une Controverse sur le Quiétisme entre Bouddhistes de l'Inde et de la Chine au VIII siècle de l'ère Chrétienne*. Paris: Imprimerie nationale de France, 1952.

Gernet, Jacques. *Les aspects économiques du bouddhisme dans la société chinoise du Ve au Xe siècle*. Saigon: École française d'Extrême-Orient, 1956.

Hao, Chunwen 郝春文. *Tang houqi Wudai Songchu Dunhuang sengni de shehui shenghuo* 唐後期五代宋初敦煌僧尼的社會生活. Beijing: Zhongguo shehui kexue chubanshe, 1998.

Huangjian Taishi [Arami Hiroshi] 荒見泰史. *Dunhuang bianwen xieben de yanjiu* 敦煌變文寫本的研究. Beijing: Zhonghua Shuju, 2010.

Jiang, Boqin姜伯勤. *Tang Wudai Dunhuang sihu zhidu* 唐五代敦煌寺戶制. Beijing: Zhonghua shuju, 1987.

Kapstein, Matthew T., and Sam van Schaik. *Esoteric Buddhism at Dunhuang: Rites and Teachings for This Life and Beyond*. Leiden and Boston: Brill, 2010.

Mair, Victor Henry. *T'ang Transformation Texts: A Study of the Buddhist Contribution to the Rise of Vernacular Fiction and Drama in China*. Cambridge, MA: Harvard University Press, 1989.

McRae, John. *The Northern School and the Formation of Early Ch'an Buddhism*. Honolulu: University of Hawai'i Press, 1986.

Shi, Xiaoying石小英. *Ba zhi shi shiji Dunhuang niseng yanjiu* 八至十世紀敦煌尼僧研究. Beijing: Renmin Chubanshe, 2013.

Sueki, Yasuhiro. 大正蔵·敦煌出土仏典対照目録 [A concordance to the Taishō canon and Dunhuang Buddhist manuscripts]. Tokyo International College for Postgraduate Buddhist Studies Library, 2015.

Tanaka, Ryōshō. *Tonko Zenshū bunken no kenkyū*. Tokyo: Daitō Shuppansha, 1983.

Teiser, Stephen F. *The Scripture of the Ten Kings and the Making of Purgatory in Medieval Chinese Buddhism*. Honolulu: University of Hawaii Press, 1994.

Van Schaik, Sam. *Tibetan Zen: Discovering a Lost Tradition*. Boulder, CO: Shambhala, 2015.

Van Schaik, Sam. *Buddhist Magic: Divination, Healing, and Enchantment through the Ages*. Boulder, CO: Shambhala, 2020.

Wang, Michelle C. *Maṇḍalas in the Making: The Visual Culture of Esoteric Buddhism at Dunhuang*. Leiden and Boston: Brill, 2018.

Wang, Sanqing王三慶. *Dunhuang fojiao zhaiyuan wenben yanjiu* 敦煌佛教齋願文本研究. Taipei: Xinwenfeng, 2009.

Wang, Shuqin 王書慶 and Yang Fuxue 楊富學. *Dunhuang fojiao yu chanzong yanjiu lunji* 敦煌佛教與禪宗研究論集. Hong Kong: Tianma Chubanshe, 2006.

Zieme, Peter. *Fragmenta Buddhica Uigurica: Ausgewählte Schriften*. Edited by Simone Raschmann and Jens Wilkens. Berlin: Klaus Schwarz Verlag, 2009.

Other Religious and Secular Texts. As early as 1913, Pelliot and Chavannes wrote an article on the Manichaean treatise found in cave 17. Lin's 1997 monograph also draws on Dunhuang sources and remains one of the outstanding studies on this religion. Recent examples of the scholarly interest for the Western religions represented in the Library Cave manuscripts include Tang's 2002 book with English translations of some Christian texts.[54] Meanwhile, the French scholar Mollier explored the interchange between Buddhism and Daoism in her 2008 monograph.

Traditionally, studies on Dunhuang manuscripts have been skewed toward the secular texts. The Library Cave's important economic, social, and historical sources in Chinese and other languages, in particular, continue to generate much research, as shown by Dotson's 2009 overview of the *Old Tibetan Annals*. There is also an increasing number of publications looking at interactions with other Central Asian peoples, such as the book on Dunhuang and Khotan published by Rong and Zhu in 2013.

Finally, since the beginning of the 21st century, scholars have been examining the manuscripts from the standpoint of science and technology. For instance, Lo and Cullen's 2005 edited volume and Despeux's 2010 publication deal with medicine, while astronomy is the topic addressed in the article cowritten by Bonnet-Bidaux, Praderie, and Whitfied in 2009.

Chavannes, Édouard, and Paul Pelliot. "Un traité manichéen retrouvé en Chine." *Journal Asiatique*, Xe série 18 (1911): 499–617.

Bonnet-Bidaud, Jean-Marc, Françoise Praderie, and Susan Whitfield. "The Dunhuang Chinese Sky: A Comprehensive Study of the Oldest Known Star Atlas." *Journal of Astronomical History and Heritage* 12, no. 1 (2009): 39–59.

Despeux, Catherine, ed. *Médecine, religion et société dans la Chine médiévale: Étude de manuscrits chinois de Dunhuang et de Turfan*. Collège de France, Institut des hautes études chinoises, 2010.

Dotson, Brandon. *The Old Tibetan Annals: An Annotated Translation of Tibet's First History*. Vienna: Österreichische Akademie der Wissenschaften, 2009.

Lin, Wushu 林悟殊. *Monijiao ji qi dongjian* 摩尼教及其東漸. Taibei: Shuxin chubanshe, 1997.

Lo, Vivienne, and Christopher Cullen, eds. *Medieval Chinese Medicine: The Dunhuang Medical Manuscripts*. London and New York: RoutledgeCurzon, 2005.

Mollier, Christine. *Buddhism and Taoism Fact to Face: Scripture, Ritual, and Iconographic Exchange in Medieval China*. Honolulu: University of Hawaii Press, 2008.

Rong, Xinjiang. "The Relation of Dunhuang with the Uigur Kingdom." In *De Dunhuang à Istanbul: Hommage à J. R. Hamilton*, edited by Louis Bazin and Peter Zieme, 275–298. Turnhout: Brepols, 2001.

Rong, Xinjiang 荣新江 and Zhu Lishuang 朱丽双. *Yutian yu Dunhuang* 于阗与敦煌. Lanzhou: Gansu jiaoyu chubanshe, 2013.

Tang, Li. *A Study of the History of Nestorian Christianity and Its Literature in Chinese, Together with a New English Translation of the Dunhuang Nestorian Documents*. 2nd rev. ed. Frankfurt am Main and Oxford: Peter Lang, 2004.

Manuscript Studies. Researchers are paying more and more attention to the manuscripts as physical objects, taking into consideration their codicological and paleographic features, including the book formats, layout, punctuation and ornamental marks, and variant characters. French scholars have been among the most active, the latest example of this line of research being the 2014 volume by Drège and Moretti. The materiality of manuscripts has also been an integral part of a number of recent English language publications, including the book by Van Schaik and Galambos in 2011.[55] This is facilitating contributions to related areas of study such as the history of the book in Central and East Asia.

Drège, Jean-Pierre, and Costantino Moretti, eds. *La fabrique du lisible: La mise en texte des manuscrits de la Chine ancienne et médiévale*. Paris: Collège de France, Institut des hautes études chinoises, 2014.

Whitfield, Susan, ed. *Dunhuang Manuscript Forgeries*. London: British Library, 2002.

Van Schaik, Sam, and Imre Galambos. *Manuscripts and Travellers: The Sino-Tibetan Documents of a Tenth-Century Buddhist Pilgrim*. Vol. 2. Berlin: Walter de Gruyter, 2012.

DIGITAL MATERIALS

An aspect of increased accessibility is that images of manuscripts are being made available in digital form. On the website of the International Dunhuang Project (http://idp.bl.uk), they can be viewed alongside photographs of silk paintings and other artifacts from Dunhuang and several other Silk Road sites. In addition, this platform brings together images and catalog and bibliographical data on almost all worldwide collections of manuscripts. Another important online resource is the Artsor Digital Library (artstor.org), which offers a few images of manuscripts. Gallica, the digital library site of the Bibliothèque nationale de France (gallica.bnf.fr) includes images of the Dunhuang manuscripts from the Pelliot collection. The Digital Archive of Toyo Bunko Rare Books (National Institute of Informatics—Digital Silk Road Project) includes digital versions of Stein's reports from Central Asia.

FURTHER READING

GENERAL OVERVIEW

Aimed at a general audience, *Foreign Devils on the Silk Road* is an introduction to the exploration of Silk Road sites, including Dunhuang Cave 17. Rong's *Eighteen Lectures on Dunhuang* also provides a thorough summary of the discovery and dispersal of the Dunhuang manuscripts, while giving an overview of the history of Dunhuang studies and the contribution of this field to scholarship. The article by Imaeda focuses on the reasons behind the creation and sealing of the Library Cave, as well as the way it was possibly used. Ji's work is a general reference tool for Dunhuang studies, although it only represents the field up to 1994. Galambos's article is a summary of the field of Dunhuang studies in 2016. Sørensen's 2000 article is a clear introduction to the Buddhist materials, while his 2019 essay lists key sources pertaining to Buddhism in Dunhuang during the 9th–10th centuries. For a useful discussion of the different cultural and linguistic communities at Dunhuang, see Takata's article. Huang's dictionary lists variant character forms extracted from Dunhuang Chinese manuscripts.

Galambos, Imre. "A Snapshot of Dunhuang Studies, circa 2016." *Orientations* 47, no. 4 (May 2016): 33–38.

Hopkirk, Peter. *Foreign Devils on the Silk Road: The Search for the Lost Treasures of Central Asia*. London: John Murray, 2006.

Huang, Zheng 黃征. *Dunhuang suzidian* 敦煌俗字典. Shanghai: Shanghai jiaoyu chubanshe, 2005.

Imaeda, Yoshiro. "The Provenance and Character of the Dunhuang Documents." *Memoirs of the Toyo Bunko* 66 (2008): 81–102.

Ji, Xianlin 季羨林, ed. *Dunhuangxue daxidian* 敦煌學大辭典. Shanghai: Cishu chubanshe, 1998.

Rong, Xinjiang. *Eighteen Lectures on Dunhuang*. Translated by Imre Galambos. Leiden and Boston: Brill, 2013. Originally published as Rong Xinjiang 荣新江, *Dunhuangxue shiba jiang* 敦煌学十八講. Beijing: Beijing daxue chubanshe, 2001.

Sørensen, Henrik H. "Perspectives on Buddhism at Dunhuang during the Tang and Five Dynasties Period." In *The Silk Roads: Highways of Culture and Commerce*, edited by Vadime Elisseeff, 27–48. New York: Berghahn, 2000.

Sørensen, Henrik H. "Guiyijun and Buddhism at Dunhuang: A Year by Year Chronicle." *BuddhistRoad Paper* 4, no. 2 (2019). https://doi.org/10.13154/rub.br.125.111.

Takata, Tokio 高田時雄. "Multilingualism at Tun-huang." *Bulletin of the Institute of Eastern Culture* 78 (2000): 49–70.

EXHIBITION CATALOGS

The catalog of the 2004 exhibition *The Silk Road: Trade, Travel, War, and Faith*, edited by Susan Whitfield and Ursula Sims-Williams, places Dunhuang in the larger context of the Silk Road. It includes photographs and catalog entries for hundreds of items, as well as articles by renowned scholars in the field. Framing Dunhuang as a religious and artistic center, the 2016 Getty exhibition was accompanied by an important publication, which puts together excellent essays coauthored by a multinational team of scholars, along with detailed and well-researched object entries.

Agnew, Neville, Marcia Reed, and Tevvy Ball. *Cave Temples of Dunhuang: Buddhist Art of China's Silk Road*. Los Angeles: J. Paul Getty Trust, 2016.

Whitfield, Susan, and Ursula Sims Williams, eds. *The Silk Road: Trade, Travel, War, and Faith*. London: British Library, 2004.

EXPEDITION REPORTS

Pelliot, Paul. *Carnets de route: 1906–1908*. Edited by Jérôme Ghesquière and Francis Macouin. Paris: Indes savants, 2008.

Stein, Aurel. *Serindia: Detailed Report of Explorations in Central Asia and Westernmost China*. 5 vols. Oxford: Clarendon Press, 1921.

Stein, Aurel. *Innermost Asia: Detailed Report of Explorations in Central Asia, Kan-su and Eastern Iran*. 4 vols. Oxford: Clarendon Press, 1928.

JOURNALS

In recent decades, China has grown to be the dominant player in the field of Dunhuang studies. The most important source for Chinese-language scholarship on Dunhuang art and related topics is the journal *Dunhuang yanjiu* 敦煌研究, which is edited by the Dunhuang Academy and increasingly features the work of international scholars. It is published every other month. The *Dunhuangxue jikan* 敦煌學季刊 comes out four times a year.

NOTES

1. Sueki, Yasuhiro 大正蔵, 敦煌出土仏典対照目録 [A concordance to the Taishō canon and Dunhuang Buddhist manuscripts] (Tokyo: International College for Postgraduate Buddhist Studies Library, 2015).
2. Sueki, 敦煌出土仏典対照目録.
3. Wang Shuqin 王書慶 and Yang Fuxue 楊富學, *Dunhuang fojiao yu chanzong yanjiu lunji* 敦煌佛教與禪宗研究論集 (Hong Kong: Tianma Chubanshe, 2006). See also the major study by John McRae, *The Northern School and the Formation of Early Ch'an Buddhism* (Honolulu: University of Hawai'i Press, 1986).
4. Neil Schmid, "Dunhuang and Central Asia (With an Appendix on Dunhuang Manuscript Resources)," in *Esoteric Buddhism and the Tantras in East Asia*, ed. Charles D. Orzech, Richard K. Payne, and Henrik H. Sørensen (Leiden and Boston: Brill, 2011), 365–378.
5. Sueki, 敦煌出土仏典対照目録.
6. Jamie Hubbard, *Absolute Delusion, Perfect Buddhahood: The Rise and Fall of a Chinese Heresy* (Honolulu: University of Hawai'i Press, 2001).
7. Sueki, 敦煌出土仏典対照目録. See also Robert E. Buswell, ed., *Chinese Buddhist Apocrypha* (Honolulu: University of Hawaii Press, 1990).
8. For an overview of the secular texts found in Dunhuang, see Jacques Gernet, *Les aspects économiques du bouddhisme dans la société chinoise du Ve au Xe siècle* (Saigon: École française d'Extrême-Orient, 1956). Also refer to Lionel Giles, *Descriptive Catalogue of the Chinese Manuscripts from Tunhuang in the British Museum* (London: Trustees of the British Museum, 1957), 229–278.
9. Aurel Stein, *Serindia: Detailed Report of Explorations in Central Asia and Westernmost China*, vol. 2 (Oxford: Clarendon Press, 1921), 822–823.
10. For an overview of Tibetan Buddhist texts, see Louis La Vallée Poussin, *Catalogue of the Tibetan Manuscripts from Tun-Huang in the India Office Library* (Oxford: Oxford University Press, 1962). Marcelle Lalou, *Inventaire des manuscrits tibétains de Touen-houang: Conservés à la bibliothèque nationale (Fonds Pelliot tibétain)* (Paris: Librairie d'Amérique et d'Orient, 1939–1961).
11. Sam van Schaik, *Tibetan Zen: Discovering a Lost Tradition* (Boulder, CO: Shambhala, 2015).
12. Jacob Dalton and Sam van Schaik, *Tibetan Tantric Manuscripts from Dunhuang: A Descriptive Catalogue of the Stein Collection at the British Library* (Leiden and Boston: Brill, 2006). Also Matthew T. Kapstein

and Sam van Schaik, *Esoteric Buddhism at Dunhuang: Rites and Teachings for This Life and Beyond* (Leiden and Boston: Brill, 2010).

13. Gertraud Taenzer, *The Dunhuang Region during Tibetan Rule (787–848): A Study of the Secular Manuscripts Discovered in the Mogao Caves* (Wiesbaden: Harrassowitz, 2012). Secular Tibetan texts from the Stein collection are also covered in Frederick William Thomas, *Tibetan Literary Texts and Documents Concerning Chinese Turkestan, Part II: Documents* (London: Royal Asiatic Society, 1951).
14. For an overview of Khotanese literature, refer to Ronald Eric Emmerick, *A Guide to the Literature of Khotan* (Tokyo: International Institute for Buddhist Studies, 1992); and Mauro Maggi, "Khotanese Literature," in *The Literature of Pre-Islamic Iran: Companion Volume I to A History of Persian Literature*, ed. Ronald Eric Emmerick and Maria Macuch (New York: I. B. Tauris, 2009), 330–417. For official documents and letters in Khotanese, see Hiroshi Kumamoto, "The Khotanese in Dunhuang," in *Cina e Iran: Da Alessandro Magno alla dinastia Tang*, ed. Alfredo Cadonna and Lionello Lanciotti (Florence: Leo S Olschiki Editore, 1996), 79–101.
15. This narrative can be found on the verso of scrolls Pelliot chinois 2801, Pelliot chinois 2781, and Pelliot chinois 2783 at the Bibliothèque nationale de France.
16. Verso of Pelliot chinois 2957, lines 3–161; verso of IOL Khot S 10, lines 44–223.
17. For an overview of the Buddhist manuscripts in Sogdian language, refer to Yutaka Yoshida, "A Handlist of Buddhist Sogdian Texts," in *Memoirs of the Faculty of Letters, Kyoto University*, 54 (2015): 167–180. See also from the same author "Buddhist Literature in Sogdian," in *The Literature of Pre-Islamic Iran*, Companion Volume I, ed. Ronald Eric Emmerick and Maria Macuch (New York: I. B. Tauris, 2009), 288–329.
18. James Russell Hamilton, *Manuscrits ouïgours du IXe–Xe siècle de Touen-houang, I–II* (Paris: Fondation Singer-polignac, 1986).
19. Klaus Wille, "Survey of the Identified Sanskrit Manuscripts in the Hoernle, Stein, and Skrine Collections of the British Library (London)," in *From Birch Bark to Digital Data: Recent Advances in Buddhist Manuscript Research: Papers Presented at the Conference Indic Buddhist Manuscripts: The State of the Field. Stanford, June 15–19 2009*, ed. Paul Harrison and Jens-Uwe Hartmann (Vienna: Austrian Academy of Sciences Press, 2014), 187–212. In the same volume see also Jens-Uwe Hartmann and Klaus Wille, "The Central Asian Sanskrit Fragments in the Pelliot Collection (Paris)," 213–222.
20. See Pelliot tibétain 999, which states that the *Aparamitayus Sutra* was professionally mass copied along with the *Perfection of Wisdom Sutra*.
21. Buswell, *Chinese Buddhist Apocrypha*.
22. For a recent contribution on the topic of Chinese Chan texts, see Wendi Leigh Adamek, *The Mystique of Transmission: On an Early Chan History and Its Context* (New York: Columbia University Press, 2007). For a study of Tibetan Zen Buddhist texts from Dunhuang, see Schaik, *Tibetan Zen*, 2015.
23. Hubbard, *Absolute Delusion, Perfect Buddhahood*, 2001.
24. Sam Van Schaik and Imre Galambos, *Manuscripts and Travellers: The Sino-Tibetan Documents of a Tenth-Century Pilgrim* (Berlin: De Gruyter, 2012).
25. For a systematic analysis of the social life of the Dunhuang clergy, refer to Hao Chunwen 郝春文, *Tang houqi Wudai Songchu Dunhuang sengni de shehui shenghuo* 唐後期五代宋初敦煌僧尼的社會生活 (Beijing: Zhongguo shehui kexue chubanshe, 1998).
26. Victor Henry Mair, *T'ang Transformation Texts: A Study of the Buddhist Contribution to the Rise of Vernacular Fiction and Drama in China* (Cambridge, MA: Harvard University Press, 1989).
27. For more detail on this particular text and additional references to specific Dunhuang manuscripts, see Arthur Waley, "Some References to Iranian Temples in the Tun-huang Region," *Bulletin of the Institute of History and Philology, Academia Sinica* 28, no. 1 (1956): 123–128.
28. Matteo Nicolini-Zani, "The Dunhuang *Jingjiao* Documents in Japan: A Report of Their Reappearance," in *Winds of Jingjiao: Studies on Syriac Christianity in China and Central Asia*, ed. Li Tang and Dietmar W. Winkler (Vienna: LIT, 2016), 15–26.

29. On contracts, see Valerie Hansen, *Negotiating Daily Life in Traditional China: How Ordinary People Used Contracts, 600–1400* (New Haven, CT: Yale University Press, 1995). See also Gernet, *Les aspects économiques du bouddhisme*, 1956; and Giles, *Catalogue of the Chinese Manuscripts from Tunhuang*, 229–278.
30. Examples include Pelliot chinois 2627 at the Bibliothèque nationale de France, Ch 734 and Ch 938, at the Berlin-Brandenburgische Akademie der Wissenschaften. Five fragments have also been identified at the Institute of Oriental Manuscripts: Дх.02670, Дх.2663, Дх.2724, Дх.5341, and Дх.04666.
31. Fragments include Or.8210/S.2053 (verso) and Or.8210/S.20 in the British Library's Stein collection, and Pelliot chinois 2973A at the Bibliothèque nationale de France.
32. Gu Jiegang 顧頡剛 and Gu Tinglong 顧廷龍, *Shangshu wenzi hebian* 尚書文字合編 (Shanghai: Shanghai guji chubanshe, 1996).
33. Mair, *T'ang Transformation Texts*.
34. Matthew Kapstein, "The Indian Literary Identity in Tibet," in *Literary Cultures in History: Reconstructions from South Asia*, ed. Sheldon Pollock (Berkeley: University of California Press, 2003).
35. Vivienne Lo and Christopher Cullen, eds., *Medieval Chinese Medicine: The Dunhuang Medical Manuscripts* (London and New York: RoutledgeCurzon, 2005). Also Catherine Despeux, *Médecine, religion et société dans la Chine médiévale: Étude de manuscrits chinois de Dunhuang et de Turfan* (Paris: Collège de France, Institut des hautes études chinoises, 2010).
36. Ronit Yoeli-Tlalim and Vivienne Lo, "Travelling Light: Sino-Tibetan Moxa-cautery from Dunhuang," in *Imagining Chinese Medicine*, ed. Vivienne Lo and Penelope Barrett (Leiden: Brill, 2018), 271–290.
37. Mark Kalinowski, *Divination et société dans la Chine médiévale: Étude des manuscrits de Dunhuang de la Bibliothèque nationale de France et de la British Library* (Paris: Bibliothèque nationale de France, 2003).
38. Françoise Bottéro, "The *Qièyùn* manuscripts from Dūnhuáng," in *Studies in Chinese Manuscripts: From the Warring States Period to the 20th Century*, ed. Imre Galambos (Budapest: Eötvös Loránd University, 2013), 33–48.
39. Schaik and Galambos, *Manuscripts and Travellers*. See also Frederick William Thomas and Lionel Giles, "A Tibeto-Chinese Word-and-Phrase Book," *Bulletin of the School of Oriental and African Studies* 12, nos. 3–4 (1948): 753–769.
40. Jean-Pierre Drège, "Les Rouleaux de Papier," in *La Fabrique du Lisible: La Mise en Texte des Manuscrits de la Chine ancienne et médiévale*, ed. Jean-Pierre Drège et Costantino Moretti (Paris: Collège de France, 2014), 355–360.
41. Drège, "Les Ôles chinoises," in *La Fabrique du Lisible*, 361–364.
42. Drège, "Les Reliures en Sutra," in *La Fabrique du Lisible*, 365–367.
43. Drège, "Les Codices," in *La Fabrique du Lisible*, 373–376.
44. There are twenty-four manuscripts with tabulated colophons in the Stein collection. See Giles, *Descriptive Catalogue of the Chinese Manuscripts from Tunhuang*, xv.
45. Enami Kazuyuki and Okada Yoshihiko, eds., *Scientific Analysis, Conservation and Digitization of Central Asian Cultural Properties* (Kyoto: Ryukoku University, 2005).
46. Other yellow dyes included *chuanghuangbai* 川黃柏 (*Phellodendron sacchalinense*) and *cihuang* 雌黃 (orpiment). See Peter J. Gibb and Kenneth R. Seddon, *Berberine and Huangbo: Ancient Chinese Colourants and Dyes* (London: British Library, 1998).
47. Jean-Pierre Drège, ed., *Images de Dunhuang: Dessins et peintures sur papier des fonds Pelliot et Stein* (Paris: Ecole française d'Extrême Orient, 1999).
48. Several examples of well-preserved prayers sheets can be found in the British Library's Stein collection: Or.8210/P.9, Or.8210/14, and Or.8210/P.20. For a scroll printed with repeated buddha images, see 1919,0101,0.254 (Ch.00421) at the British Museum. Among the popular Buddhist sutras to have been printed were the *Lotus Sutra* (see Or.8210/P.13) and the *Diamond Sutra*, as illustrated by Or.8210/P.2, the famous copy dated to 868, and the booklet Or.8210/P.11.

49. From 972 to 983 the whole Buddhist canon was printed from woodblocks in Chengdu, Sichuan. See Thomas Francis Carter and Luther Carrington Goodrich, *The Invention of Printing in China and Its Spread Westward* (New York: Ronald Press, 1955).
50. Some of the manuscripts Stein obtained on his first and third trips in Khotan, Turfan, and other places have been intermixed with this material. Rong Xinjiang, "The Nature of the Dunhuang Library Cave and the Reasons for Its Sealing," in *Eighteen Lectures on Dunhuang* (Leiden and Boston: Brill, 2013), 139.
51. Cuilan Liu, "Buddhist Litigants in Public Court: A Case Study of Legal Practices in Tibetan-Ruled Dunhuang (786–848)," *Journal of the American Oriental Society* 139, no. 1 (2019): 91–114; Cuilan Liu, "Merit-Making or Financial Fraud? Litigating Buddhist Nuns in Early 10th Century Dunhuang," *Journal of the International Association of Buddhist Studies* 41 (2018): 169–208.
52. Articles examining Buddhist practices on the ground equally abound. It would be almost impossible to give an exhaustive list of articles, but recent publications include Jonathan A. Silk, "The Ten Virtues of Loudly Invoking the Name of Amitābha: Stein Tibetan 724 and an Aspect of Chinese Nianfo Practice in Tibetan Dunhuang," *Journal of the American Oriental Society* 137, no. 3 (2017): 473–482; Paul Copp, "Seals as Conceptual and Ritual Tools in Chinese Buddhism, CA. 600–1000 CE," *The Medieval Globe* 4, no. 1 (2018): 15–48. Ding Yi, "'By the Power of the Perfection of Wisdom': The 'Sūtra-Rotation' Liturgy of the Mahāprajñāpāramitā at Dunhuang," *Journal of the American Oriental Society* 139, no. 3 (2019): 661–679.
53. The scholar Henrik H. Sørensen has also been particularly active in this area of research. See, for instance, Sørensen, "A Padmapāṇi Spell-Amulet from Dunhuang: Observation on OA 1919,0101,0.18," *BuddhistRoad Paper* 2, no. 1 (2019): 1–26; Sørensen, "Tibetan Tantra and Chinese Esoteric Buddhism in the Melting Pot: A Study of a Chinese Recension of the Twenty-Eight Vajra Precepts," *BuddhistRoad Paper* 2, no. 2 (2019): 1–33.
54. Wang Chuan recently looked at the interplay between Buddhism and Christianity in Dunhuang texts in "The Adaptation of Buddhist Rituals and Liturgical Texts in the Chinese Christian Manuscripts from Dunhuang," *Bulletin of the Institute of History and Philology Academia Sinica* 89 (2018): 631–661.
55. See also articles by Imre Galambos, "Non-Chinese Influences in Medieval Chinese Manuscript Culture," in *Frontiers and Boundaries: Encounters on China's Margins*, ed. Zsombor Rajkai and Ildikó Bellér-Hann, 71–86 (Wiesbaden: Harrassowitz, 2012); Galambos, "Punctuation Marks in Medieval Chinese Manuscripts," *Manuscript Cultures: Mapping the Field* 1 (2014): 341–358; and Galambos, "Composite Manuscripts in Medieval China: The Case of Scroll P. 3720 from Dunhuang," *One-Volume Libraries: Composite Manuscripts and Multiple-Text Manuscripts* 9 (2016): 355–378.

Mélodie Doumy

DZOGCHEN

Dzogchen is a tradition of meditation practice and poetic literary expression in Tibetan Buddhism. Though it derives from Indic Buddhism, Dzogchen developed a distinct form of practice and literary expression only in Tibet, where it was particularly associated with the Nyingma and Bonpo traditions. The Tibetan word Dzogchen (*rdzogs chen*) is most commonly translated into English as "the great perfection."

Within the Nyingma school, Dzogchen is at the top of a ninefold categorization of Buddhist practice. Known in this context as *atiyoga*, "the utmost yoga," it is the highest of the three inner yogas, the other two being *mahāyoga* and *anuyoga*. Dzogchen is also at the pinnacle of the teachings of Tibet's Bonpo religion, which shares much of its doctrine with the Nyingma school and has in recent years been formally identified as one of the Buddhist schools of Tibet.

In general, Dzogchen texts evoke and discuss a state of awareness present in all living beings that transcends dualities and conceptual elaboration. Common terms for this kind of awareness are "mind itself" (*sems nyid*) and "awareness" (*rig pa*). Dzogchen literature often states that in the presence of this awareness, religious practice oriented toward enlightenment is dualistic and, therefore, not only unnecessary, but also obstructive.

However, Dzogchen also teaches meditative practices of a specific kind, and these are usually performed in the context of a graduated path (*lam rim*), which involves a wide variety of contemplative and ritual practices. Therefore the rejection of meditative and ritual practice in Dzogchen texts should be read as a rhetorical device aimed at attachment to the forms of these practices and at any concept of a cause–effect link between these practices and the state of enlightenment.

The integration of this understanding that the state of enlightenment is already present with a dedication to the Buddhist path is expressed in the following verse from a prayer by the 18th-century Dzogchen teacher Jigme Lingpa:

> In my own essence, stainless, unborn, and ever-pure,
> The radiance of unconditioned spontaneous presence rises up.
> This as the union of awareness and emptiness;
> Realizing this without looking for it elsewhere,
> And thus arriving at the full realization of the ground,
> May I not stray from the essential points of the path.[1]

The Dzogchen tradition encompasses a variety of literature and practice; the standard traditional way of categorizing this is a division into three classes, the mind series (*sems sde*), the space series (*klong sde*), and the instruction series (*man ngag sde*). The three series are defined as different approaches to the true nature of mind: in the mind series, one's own mind is established as the basis of all appearances, and then this mind is recognized as an empty and luminous awareness, mind itself; in the space series, one approaches mind itself by recognizing it as empty; and in the instruction series, mind itself is approached directly by the meditator, without any need to establish its character as the basis of all appearance or to recognize its emptiness.

The mind series contains most of the early Dzogchen literature and more recent material in the same style. The space series enjoyed only limited popularity and is little known today. The instruction series, by contrast, increased in popularity from its appearance in the 11th century and ultimately became the preeminent form of the Great Perfection.

Dzogchen is a living tradition of practice, taught within all of the main Buddhist schools, though most closely associated with the Nyingma and Bon schools. The practice of Dzogchen requires an authorized teacher and the ritual transmission of key texts, as well as an "introduction" to the nature of the mind given by the teacher to the student. The main sources of Dzogchen practice are texts held to be translations, collected in semicanonical compendia, treatises by scholar meditators such as Longchenpa (Klong chen pa, 1308–64), and revealed texts known as *terma* (*gter ma*), usually believed to have been concealed in the 8th century by the tantric master Padmasambhava.

ORIGINS

Both the Nyingma and the Bonpo traditions of Dzogchen trace its origin to an ancient kingdom to the west of Tibet. For the Nyingma, this is Oḍḍiyana, which is usually identified with the Swat Valley in modern Pakistan. The traditional lineage for the transmission of Dzogchen originates with a figure called Garab Dorje, who has not been identified with a historical person. For the Bonpo, Dzogchen originated in the kingdom of Zhangzhung in western Tibet. On the other hand, recent historical research into the origins of Dzogchen has turned instead to the Buddhist traditions of tantric practice of northern India.[2]

The term "Dzogchen" itself (*rdzogs chen* or *rdzogs pa chen po*) can be traced back into Indian tantric literature, in particular a group of tantras classified as *mahāyoga*. The earliest datable appearance of the term being used in a similar way to the later Tibetan tradition is in the *Guhyagarbha Tantra*. The Indian origins of this tantra were questioned in Tibet, but it is generally thought that this and other texts of a group known as the *Māyājāla Tantras* were circulating in some form by the mid-8th century, and by the 770s, commentaries were being written on them.

The practices described in *mahāyoga* tantras such as the *Guhyagarbha* involve the visualization of Buddhist deities and their entourage in a *maṇḍala*. These practices have a twofold structure, the "development stage" (*bskyed rim*) and the "perfection stage" (*rdzogs rim*). The term "Dzogchen" seems to be used in these tantras in association with a specific ritual moment, the state of being at the climax of the yoga of the perfection stage. In this context, the term *rdzogs chen* was used to refer to the great (*chen*) culmination of the perfection (*rdzogs*) stage.

In the *Guhyagarbha Tantra*, the meaning of Dzogchen is similar to what one finds in the later tradition: all enlightened qualities and activities—that is, the aims of the Buddhist practitioner—are perfected from the very beginning. The tantra also discusses the transcendence of concepts in a state beyond the reach of thought (*bsam gyis mi khyab*), and another phrase that frequently appears in the tantra, that everything is already accomplished (*lhun kyis grub*), is also characteristic of Dzogchen literature.

An early treatise on the practices based on these tantras, *Rosary of Views on the Instructions* (*man ngag lta ba'i 'phreng ba*), attributed to the 8th-century tantric master Padmasambhava, confirms that Dzogchen was understood in this way, as the culmination of deity yoga, which was structured in the trio of development, perfection, and great perfection. However, this relatively limited role for Dzogchen was already changing by the 9th century.

DUNHUANG MANUSCRIPTS

Dzogchen texts as such exist only in the Tibetan language. Early Dzogchen literature is available from two kinds of source: texts from semicanonical collections, available in manuscript and printed editions, and texts from manuscripts found in a sealed cave in Dunhuang, Central Asia.

The earliest surviving manuscripts containing Dzogchen texts were found in this cave, along with thousands of other manuscripts in Chinese, Tibetan, Sanskrit, and other languages. The cave was sealed at the beginning of the 11th century, and the Tibetan manuscripts containing Dzogchen texts were probably written during the 9th and 10th centuries. The majority of the Tibetan manuscripts are now held at the British Library, London, and the Bibliothèque nationale de Paris.

The British Library manuscript IOL Tib J 647 contains a brief Dzogchen text called *The Cuckoo of Awareness* (*Rig pa'i khu byug*) and a commentary upon it.

> The variety of things is non-dual in nature,
> And each one is free from elaboration.
> What we call "reality" is beyond concepts,
> And yet it still appears—all is good.
> Since you already have it, give up the sickness of effort,
> And since it is already present, leave it as it is.[3]

These six lines, also known as "the six vajra verses," are of great importance in the early Dzogchen tradition, featuring also among the canonical five early translations of Dzogchen texts and incorporated into the quasi-scriptural text *The All-Creating King* (see section "Early Canonical Literature"). These six lines state the basic themes of Dzogchen: non-duality, freedom from conceptual elaboration, and the pointlessness of attempting to reach the state of enlightenment when it is already present.

The Cuckoo of Awareness also references tantric Buddhist practice through a pun; the fourth line can be read as the names of two tantric deities, Vairocana and Samantabhadra. Furthermore, the commentary on the text in the manuscript IOL Tib J 647 specifically links the text to tantric Buddhist practice, by providing an interpretation of the practices of "union and liberation" (*sbyor sgrol*) according to the principle of non-duality and the conviction that enlightenment is already accomplished.

This role for Dzogchen, as a way of contextualizing the practices of the tantras, is also seen in the treatise attributed to Padmasambhava, and other texts from Dunhuang, which cannot easily be classified either as Dzogchen texts or as straightforward treatises on tantric practice, such as *The Questions and Answers on Vajrasattva (Rdo rje sems dpa'i zhus lan)* by Nyen Palyang (Gnyan dpal dbyangs, early 9th century). In these texts, Dzogchen is a "mode" (*tshul*) of tantric practice. This means, to put it simply, the state of mind in which one engages in the practice of deity yoga.[4]

Another Dunhuang manuscript, IOL Tib J 594, contains a text called *The Little Grains of Buddhagupta* (Sbas pa'i sgum chung), along with a commentary. The text is on the theme of the pointlessness of intellectual analysis or formal sitting meditation. Here there is no overt reference to tantric practices, and the context is clearly the Buddhism of the sutras, especially the *Prajñāpāramitā* sutras.

These Dunhuang manuscripts exemplify two divergent trends in early Dzogchen literature: first, texts that interpret and contextualize deity yoga practices from the perspective of non-duality, and second, poetic meditations on the enlightened state, dealing with practices only in terms of the general criticism of the idea that any formal practice could result in the state of enlightenment. In any case, in the larger context of the Dunhuang manuscript collections, these few Dzogchen texts are accompanied by many more texts on tantric meditation practice, as well as texts clearly intended for other forms of practice such as reciting prayers, sermons, and teaching.

This context allows us to understand how these Dzogchen texts with their radical reformulation or rejection of formal practice coexisted with the variety of Buddhist practices. Formal practice is not abandoned; instead it is informed by an understanding that there is no essential difference between an ordinary sentient being and a buddha, and that enlightenment is already present, and not to be brought into being by meditation. Among the new tantric traditions that flourished in Tibet from the 11th century onward, the tantric literary genre of "the great seal" (*phyag rgya chen po*, Skt. *mahāmudrā*) performed a similar function, describing the state of enlightened awareness that both precedes and arises out of the practice of deity yoga.

EARLY CANONICAL LITERATURE

The majority of early Dzogchen texts are available in the *Collected Tantras of the Nyingma* (*rnying ma'i rgyud 'bum*), which survive in several different manuscript and printed editions of Nyingma tantras. Another, overlapping collection of Dzogchen texts is the *Collected Tantras of Vairocana* (*bai ro rgyud 'bum*).[5] Among these, the texts that are traditionally held to have been the first to be introduced into Tibet are a group of eighteen, the "five earlier" and "thirteen later" translations. The five earlier translations are said to have been done by the Tibetan scholar Vairocana in the 8th century. The traditional histories also relate that, owing to intrigues at the Tibetan court, Vairocana was sent into exile in eastern Tibet; thus the next thirteen translations of Dzogchen texts were done by another Tibetan, Vimalamitra.

The five earlier translations include *The Cuckoo of Awareness*; this and three of the other texts in the group have an indefinite status as scriptures, sometimes being presented as sutras, sometimes as tantras. Only one of the five, a treatise titled *Gold Refined from Ore (Rdo la gser zhun)*, is attributed to an author, the Indian tantric scholar Mañjuśrīmitra. This text differs from the other seventeen in its more scholastic tone, its frequent explicit references to tantric practice, and its references to competing non-Buddhist schools of thought in India. It is also the only one of these texts that is attested in a source close to the time when it is meant to have been translated: an early-9th-century catalog of the holdings of the Denkar (*ldan dkar*) palace.[6]

Lists of the thirteen later translations are presented differently by different Tibetan authors and in the various editions of the *Collected Tantras of the Nyingma*. Several were considered lost for centuries, until recent textual scholarship identified them under other names, or embedded in other texts. Like the five earlier translations (except *Gold Refined from Ore*), these texts have an indeterminate status; though they are not attributed to authors, they are also not directly presented as the speech of the buddha or another divine being, as Buddhist scriptures generally are.[7]

Another highly influential text associated with these eighteen is a much longer work called *The Sutra of the All-Creating King* (*Kun byed rgyal po'i mdo*). Though it is considered to be the primary tantra of the mind series of Dzogchen, it appears to be a compilation of already-existing texts including the five earlier translations, presenting them as the speech of a buddha and thereby giving them full scriptural status.[8]

The dating of this early literature, preserved only in much later editions of semicanonical collections, remains elusive. A terminus ad quem is provided by a treatise written in the early 10th century, the *Lamp for the Eyes of Contemplation* (*Bsam gtan mig sgron*) by Nub Sangye Yeshe. This text was written to show the distinctions between four different approaches to the Buddhist path: (i) the gradual approach based on the sutras, (ii) the instantaneous approach of Chan, (iii) the practices of the *mahāyoga* tantras, and (iv) the approach of Dzogchen. In each section the author quotes numerous texts, and the Dzogchen section contains quotes from many of the eighteen translations (though not from *The All-Creating King*).[9]

Thus it remains a matter of debate whether there were Dzogchen texts in circulation during the initial phase of Buddhist translation in Tibet, and indeed whether they are really translations from Indic or other sources or original Tibetan compositions. It is notable that the one text that is attested in the early period, *Gold Refined from Ore*, is different in several ways from the others. The available evidence points to the conclusions that the discourse of Dzogchen is present in certain tantras and their commentarial literature circulating in the 8th century, and that brief poetic texts based on these may have been written in Sanskrit or other Indic languages.

The eighteen translations and *The All-Creating King* comprise only a fraction of the Dzogchen texts in the *Collected Tantras of the Nyingma*: around 370 texts in most editions. There are many other texts categorized as mind series or texts in the space and instruction series categories, as well as two other, rarely discussed, categories of "peak essence" (*spyi ti*) and "utter essence" (*yang ti*) However, the great majority of these, which are not quoted in the *Lamp for the Eyes of Contemplation*, probably date from the 11th century onward.[10]

Apparent similarities between early Dzogchen and the Chan literature written in China during the same period has evoked comment and comparison ever since the *Lamp for the Eyes of Contemplation*. While that work found a place in the Buddhist path for both Dzogchen and Chan, the later Tibetan tradition tended to reject Chan entirely as a false path, justifying this position through a story set in the Tibetan imperial period of a debate between a Chinese Chan monk and an Indian Buddhist scholar, in which Chan was defeated and rejected. Tibetan polemical critiques of Dzogchen, mainly from the Gelug school, have attempted to associate Dzogchen with a meditation that involves the suppression of all mental activity, which is how Chan meditation was presented in the Tibetan polemical accounts.

There have also been attempts in modern academic writing to link Dzogchen historically with Chan, but such links remain difficult to substantiate. Most similarities in the language of Dzogchen and Chan are likely to be due to their being based on similar scriptural sources, such as the *Laṅkāvatāra sūtra*, and the adoption of the language of these sutras in the tantric sources for Dzogchen. On the other hand, it is clear from the Dunhuang manuscripts that Chan meditation practices were combined with the deity yoga of the *mahāyoga* tantras. In this way, they occupied the same role as early Dzogchen. However, the popularity of Chan practices began to decline in Tibet during the 11th century, and they had all but disappeared by the 14th century.[11]

THE VEHICLE OF ATIYOGA

In the 11th and 12th centuries there was a great increase in translation activity in Tibet, and the transmission of these new texts and practices stimulated the development of new schools, which came to be known as the "new schools" (*gsar ma*). This was in contrast to the lineages of texts and practices that were considered to derive from the first major period of transmission of Buddhism to Tibet, known as the "old ones," or Nyingma. Despite this appellation, Nyingma lineages did in fact involve many new developments.

Nyingma scholars such as Rongzom Chokyi Zangpo (Rong zom chos kyi bzang po, 1012–1088) wrote new interpretations of the texts of their tradition, while others, such as Nyangral Nyima Ozer (Nyang ral nyi ma 'od zer, 1124–1192), wrote histories of the early period of transmission of Buddhism to Tibet. Most significant was the activity of *terton* (*gter ston*) or "treasure revealers," who presented new collections of texts said to have been concealed in the 8th century and rediscovered in rocks, pillars, or other hiding places.[12]

Drawing on earlier systems of classification, Nyingma authors of this period developed a classification of the Buddha's teachings into nine vehicles, comprising the non-tantric vehicles of hearers, solitary buddhas, and bodhisattvas; the lower tantric vehicles of *kriyā*, *ubhaya*, and yoga; and the higher tantric vehicles of *mahāyoga*, *anuyoga*, and atiyoga. With atiyoga being a synonym for Dzogchen, this system definitively placed these teachings at the top of the hierarchy of Buddhist practice.[13]

The question whether atiyoga should be considered a vehicle in itself was disputed by some Tibetans, including Sakya Paṇḍita (Sa skya paṇḍita, 1182–1251), one of the most eminent scholars of the 13th century. At this point, atiyoga was well established as a scriptural category in the Nyingma school, yet Sakya Paṇḍita considered this an inauthentic innovation, arguing that "the view of Atiyoga is wisdom, not a vehicle." This continued to be the view in the Sakya school, though since the 19th century at least, Dzogchen has been practiced to a limited extent in this school.[14]

The term "atiyoga" does appear in Indian tantras, perhaps the earliest of which is the *Sarvabuddhasamāyoga* (8th century). Much like "Dzogchen," the term is used to refer to a way of practicing deity yoga. It was only in Tibet that the term came to signify a specific class of practices and then a vehicle. However, the use of the term "vehicle" in the Nyingma system seems to be looser than in its Indian antecedents, where the vehicles of hearers (Skt. *śrāvaka*), solitary buddhas (Skt. *pratyekabuddha*), and bodhisattvas were treated as self-contained paths. On the other hand, there is no evidence that any of the six tantric vehicles out of the Nyingma nine vehicles were ever intended or practiced in isolation from the others.

In any case, the increasing acceptance in the Nyingma traditions of atiyoga as a distinct vehicle allowed for the development of a new scriptural literature of atiyoga. This occurred through the repurposing of the early literature of Dzogchen as sutras or tantras and through the appearance of new Dzogchen tantras through revelation. The practice of presenting new texts as *terma* (*gter ma*), "hidden treasures," began in Tibet in the 11th century, though it has precedents in the Indic Buddhist tradition.

Early *terma* were presented as works written or translated by famous figures from Tibet's past, such as the 8th-century translator Vimalamitra; later, almost all *terma*, particularly from the 14th century onward, were attributed to a single figure, Padmasambhava, in the 8th and early 9th centuries. While some *terma* may have included material that had been concealed and rediscovered, in general these were visionary revelations, and their acceptance depended on the reputation of the treasure revealer. For the Nyingma and Bonpo schools, treasure revelation was a means by which the tradition could evolve, while still retaining its connection to the first period of transmission of Buddhism to Tibet.[15]

BONPO DZOGCHEN

This period also saw the emergence of the Bonpo tradition of practice in Tibet (distinct from the Tibetan non-Buddhist rituals sometimes also referred to as "Bon," although incorporating some of them). This tradition took literary form through the means of *terma* revelation, and the collections attributed to the earliest treasure revealer, Shenchen Luga (Gshen chen klu dga', 996–1035), include Dzogchen texts. Later in the 11th century, other treasure revealers expanded the scope of Bonpo literature, resulting in three distinct lineages of practice with close similarities to Buddhist Dzogchen: the meditation instructions on *a* (*a khrid*), the aural lineage of Zhangzhung (*zhang zhung snyan rgyud*), and a Bonpo lineage that also bears the name Dzogchen.[16]

Close textual study of individual works among these Bonpo texts has shown that some are clearly based on earlier Buddhist Dzogchen texts, while others are quite different in approach. Among the latter is the *Authenticity of Awareness* (*rig pa'i tshad ma*), an influential work in which the methods of logical analysis (*tshad ma*, Skt. *pramāṇa*) are applied to the nonconceptual awareness of Dzogchen. This text remains part of the curriculum of study for the Paṇḍita qualification in the Bonpo school.[17]

In the 13th century, Drugom Yungdrung (Bru sgom rgyal ba g.yung drung, 1242–1290) composed works in the tradition of the "aural lineage of Zhangzhung," including *Advice on the Six Lamps*, teaching practices that are very similar to those of the leap-over practices of Buddhist Dzogchen. In the early 20th century, Bonpo Dzogchen was revitalized by Shardza Tashi Gyeltsen (Shar rdza bkra shis rgyal mtshan, 1859–1934), whose writings are now standard reference works for the tradition.[18]

THE INSTRUCTION SERIES

The instruction series built a complex system upon the basis of earlier Dzogchen literature, partly through the adaptation of material from Indic sutra and tantra sources, and in part through distinctive doctrines and practices of its own. By this stage, the Great Perfection had developed beyond its role as an interpretative approach to deity yoga (although it did not lose that role) and had developed a philosophical approach and meditation techniques of its own.

The philosophical vocabulary of instruction series Dzogchen is clearly based on previous Buddhist literature, yet turned to a new purpose. Among the many words used in the instruction series to denote the state of enlightenment, two are particularly significant: "awareness" (*rig pa*) and "the ground" (*gzhi*). Awareness, in this special sense, refers to the mind in the state of enlightenment, which does not distinguish between subject and object, self and other, and is free from all other kinds of conceptual elaboration. Awareness became increasingly distinguished from mind (*sems*), which refers to our ordinary state of consciousness, defined by subject and object and other conceptual constructions. In this sense, Dzogchen practice in the instruction series is aimed at being able to distinguish awareness from mind.

The ground has three aspects: essence (*ngo bo*), nature (*rang bzhin*), and compassion (*thugs rje*). The essence of the ground is defined as ever pure (*ka dag*), a concept that is closely related to the emptiness in the Prajñāpāramitā literature and the writings of Madhyamaka scholars. The ground's second aspect, its nature, is defined as spontaneous accomplishment (*lhun grub*), a term already in use in early Dzogchen texts and their tantric antecedants. The ground's nature is its experiential presence, often described as luminosity (*'od gsal* or *gsal ba*). Compassion, the third aspect of the ground, signifies more in this context than its literal meaning; it is the dynamic energy that is the manifestation of the ground. These three aspects of the ground are clearly based to some extent on the three bodies (Skt. *kāya*) of a buddha.

Whether one experiences reality as samsara or nirvana depends on what happens during dynamic manifestation of the ground. This manifestation is basic experience (*shes pa*). This experience becomes delusion when it does not recognize its own nature, and instead operates according to the false duality of self and other. This fall into delusion is sometimes called "experience moving away from the ground" (*shes pa gzhi las g.yo ba*). Nevertheless, non-dualistic awareness (*rig pa*) always remains present, and the catalyst that switches the practitioner's mode of being from delusion to realization is the recognition of this awareness (*rig pa'i ngo sprod*), which may be more simply called self-recognition (*rang ngo sprod*).[19]

The practices taught to actualize this state of self-recognition in the instruction series are twofold, "breakthrough" (*khregs chod*) and "leap-over" (*thod rgal*). Instructions on breakthrough practice, which has much in common with other Dzogchen literature, tell the practitioner to renounce the idea of meditation as causing the state of enlightenment, and in meditation to avoid straining to attain a state of enlightened awareness. A simple practice of sitting with one's eyes open and remaining in the present moment of awareness is taught. In leap-over, a more complex series of practices is involved, with special postures, breathing practices, and gazing at the sky or into darkness. These allow for the spontaneous emergence of luminous visions. While these practices are clearly similar to those of the perfection stage of later tantric literature, especially the *Kālacakra tantra*, they are distinguished in Dzogchen treatises by the fact that they are to be practiced without effort.[20]

THE SEMINAL HEART

The popularity of the instruction series owes much to a corpus of literature known as the Seminal Heart (*snying thig*). Although the term suggests an essential and condensed teaching, in fact the most elaborate discussions of the Great Perfection occur in Seminal Heart texts. Some doxographies identify the Seminal Heart with the instruction series, some place it at the pinnacle of various subdivisions of the instruction series, and some place it outside all the three series, as the very essence of them all.

The earliest known Seminal Heart texts are the collection of tantras known as *The Seventeen Tantras* (*rgyud bcu bdun*) and a collection of miscellaneous texts attributed to six Indian figures, named *Bima Nyingtig* (*bi ma snying thig*) after one of those figures, Vimalamitra. Both collections were circulating in Tibet from around the mid-11th century onward. The Indian masters, who also figure in other Great Perfection lineages, are Garab Dorje (Dga' rab rdo rje), Mañjuśrımitra, Śrī Siṃha, Jñānasūtra, Vimalamitra, and Padmasambhava. Several of these are also authors of *mahāyoga* treatises that were translated in the 8th and early 9th centuries and included in Tibetan canonical collections of Indian-authored treatises and commentaries, the Tengyur (*bstan 'gyur*). Garab Dorje and Śrī Siṃha are not attested elsewhere, but their names may be compared with the authors of influential commentaries on the *Guhyagarbha Tantra*, Vilāsavajra (*Sgeg pa'i rdo rje*) and Sūryaprabhāsasiṃha.

The key figure in the establishment of the Seminal Heart, and indeed of Dzogchen in general, as a coherent system of philosophy and practice was Longchen Rabjampa (Klong chen rab byams pa, 1308–1364. Longchenpa, as he is usually called, produced a monumental work, the *Fourfold Seminal Heart*, incorporating the *Bima Nyintig*, a new *terma* collection called *Khandro Nyingtig* (*mkha' 'gro snying tig*), and his own compositions: works based on the former collected under the title *Lama Yangtig* (*bla ma yang tig*) and works based on the latter collected under the title *Khandro Yangtig* (*mkha' 'gro yang tig*). The endurance of this cycle ensured that the great variety of meditation practices and doctrines contained in the Seminal Heart rubric would not be lost.

Longchenpa wrote many other texts, the most famous of which are known as his "seven treasuries." Among these, two lengthy prose works, the *Treasury of the Supreme Vehicle* (*theg mchog mdzod*) and the *Treasury of Topics* (*tshig don mdzod*), created a coherent system for the miscellaneous and heterogeneous doctrines and practices contained in the Seminal Heart collections. These materials are established as the supreme method of Buddhist practice, not only for the Nyingma, but for all of the Tibetan schools. The Seminal Heart is also given full Buddhist legitimacy by relating it to the Indic Buddhist tradition (especially the philosophical works of the Madhyamaka and Yogācāra) and to the interpretations of the tantras found in the new schools, thus giving the Great Perfection an acceptable place in the Tibetan Buddhist milieu of the 14th century.[21]

TERMA COLLECTIONS

Though Longchenpa's works are justly famous for their synthesis of the various practice traditions of Dzogchen and for their elegant, poetic style, they offer only a partial picture of the context in which Dzogchen was practiced. By the 14th century, *terma* collections had evolved into compendia of texts for all aspects of the practice of the Buddhist path. The *Embodiment of the Guru's Realization* (*bla ma dgongs 'dus*), revealed by Sangye Lingpa (Sangs rgyas gling pa, 1340–1396), is one of the largest and most influential of these compendia. Here we see Dzogchen (generally in the Seminal Heart category) texts alongside practice texts such as introductory tantric practices (*sngon 'gro*), deity yoga, and a host of manuals for ritual practices such as the making of *torma* (*gtor ma*) or effigies and the transmission of texts from master to student (*po ti'i lung*). In general, here, as in subsequent *terma* collections, Dzogchen was presented as part of a graduated path, in the ethical framework of Mahāyāna Buddhism, practiced in the context of tantric deity yoga and other ritual practices.

Over the following centuries, compendia of *terma* texts like these continued to be the way that new Dzogchen texts came into circulation, and Dzogchen was practiced in the context of graduated paths set out in these compendia. Other *terma* collections containing Dzogchen texts and practices include the *Northern Treasures* (*byang gter*) of Godem Ngodrup Gyaltsen (Rgod ldem dngos grub rgyal mtshan, 1337–1408), the *Union of the Three Jewels* (*kon mchog spyi 'dus*) by Jatson Nyingpo ("Ja" tshon snying po, 1595–1656), and the *Seminal Heart of the Vast Expanse* (*klong chen snying thig*) by Jigme Lingpa ('Jigs med gling pa, 1730–1799). These collections continue to serve as the source of practice traditions through to the present day. The *Union of the Three Jewels* has, since its appearance, been practiced within the Kagyu school as well as the Nyingma.

The *Seminal Heart of the Vast Expanse* is the most popular of these collections, and none of the *terma* collections from the following centuries has eclipsed this popularity. This collection evokes the influence of Longchenpa in its very name, as well as in the visions that Jigme Lingpa linked to its revelation. However, the heterogeneous contents of the collection have more in common with the *Embodiment of the Guru's Realization*, which was the source of many of Jigme Lingpa's own meditation practices. Thus though the sources of the practice of Dzogchen have evolved over the centuries, they continue to follow a model that was in place by the 14th century.

Dzogchen was also incorporated into Tibetan funerary traditions, including the *Liberation through Hearing in the Bardo* (*bar do thos grol*) by Karma Lingpa (Karma gling pa, 14th century), better known in the West as *The Tibetan Book of the Dead*. Funerary practices in which the spirit of the dead person is guided on the journey to the afterlife existed in pre-Buddhist Tibetan practices. Buddhist versions of these funerary rituals were in circulation from at least the 10th century, and from the 11th century onward there was a strong influence from Dzogchen, and the Seminal Heart in particular, on these rituals.[22]

From at least the 14th century, Dzogchen has been practiced alongside the similar contemplative tradition of Mahāmudrā, which is mainly transmitted through the lineages of the Kagyu schools. The 14th-century *terma* collection *Embodiment of the Guru's Realization* contains both genres of text. Equally, Dzogchen has also been an important part of the Kagyu schools, usually through Nyingma teachers of Kagyu students; for example, the *Union of the Three Jewels* is practiced in the Karma Kagyu school because Jatson Nyingpo was a teacher of Karmapa Choying Dorje (Karma pa chos dbyings rdo rje, 1610–1674). Also in the 17th century, Karma Chagme (Karma chags med, 1613–1678) merged Dzogchen with Mahāmudrā in his works.[23] Though they remain distinct genres, internally Dzogchen and Mahāmudrā texts show some mutual influence.

THE MODERN PERIOD

In Tibet before the mid-20th century, Dzogchen was not taught to large groups; instead, instructions were given by teachers to students in small sessions. As with other tantric practices, the students do not read the texts or put them into practice before receiving the reading transmission (*lung*) and, in the case of leap-over practices of the Seminal Heart, an initiation ritual. Dzogchen was taught and practiced in monasteries, especially after the establishment of large Nyingma monasteries in the 17th and 18th centuries. Yet it has been equally if not more often practiced outside the monastic context, among lay practitioners living as ordinary householders or in meditation communities. As with all tantric practices, meditators usually have a daily meditation practice and may also engage in meditation retreats for a fixed amount of time, sometimes as long as three years.[24]

In the mid-20th century, many Nyingma and Bonpo lamas left Tibet and settled elsewhere. This led to the introduction of Dzogchen, as part of the complex of Tibetan Buddhist practices, to the West. Most Tibetan lamas taught Dzogchen practices in a relatively traditional way, as part of a wider Buddhist path. An exception was Namkhai Norbu (Nam mkha'i nor bu, b. 1938), who was educated in Tibet in the Nyingma and Sakya traditions and moved to Italy in 1962 to take up a position at the University of Naples. Here he taught students and published influential works on Dzogchen for a general audience. In his writings, Norbu emphasizes that Dzogchen is found in both Buddhist and Bon traditions but is not defined by either.

Perhaps partially as a result of the success of Namkhai Norbu's books and the Dzogchen communities he established, the idea of Dzogchen as something that may be distinguished from other aspects of the Buddhist path and practiced without reference to them has entered popular culture. This may be compared to the Western appropriation of Japanese Zen Buddhism in the 20th century, though Dzogchen has not yet achieved the same level of penetration into popular culture. On the other hand, Tibetan Buddhist teachers, especially those from a Nyingma and Kagyu school background, continue to incorporate instruction in Dzogchen in a graduated path of practice. In Tibet, Dzogchen has continued to be taught and practiced by Nyingma teachers who chose to stay, the most influential of whom has been Jigme Puntsog ('Jigs med phun tshogs, 1933–2004), who established the Larung Gar (Bla rung sgar) Buddhist community in Sichuan. This community has been hugely successful, comprising an estimated forty thousand monks, nuns, and laypeople as of 2015.[25]

REVIEW OF LITERATURE

The study of Dzogchen outside the traditional Tibetan context is still relatively young. The key figure in the early stages of this study is Herbert Guenther (1917–2006), who published many translations and studies of Dzogchen literature from the 1970s to the early 2000s. However, Guenther's translations and discussions of this material were strongly influenced by his belief that it could be assimilated into the Western philosophical tradition, and a different, historicist path has been taken by the next generation of scholars.

Two Tibetan scholars who studied in Europe produced groundbreaking work on Dzogchen literature, in quite different ways. In books for a general audience, Namkhai Norbu has published translations and discussions of Dzogchen texts and from the 1980 onward has written about his firsthand experience of Dzogchen practitioners in Tibet. His works have sometimes synthesized the Nyingma and Bonpo Dzogchen traditions, and he also writes on Tibetan ritual practices, including Tibetan medicine, and astrology. Primarily a religious teacher, rather than an academic, Norbu is highly respected but remains on the margins of academic discourse.

Samten Karmay (b. 1936) has published extensively in English on Tibetan history, ritual, and religious practice. His book *The Great Perfection*, published in 1988, was the first major text-historical study of Dzogchen, dealing with its origins and early history, its later developments, and criticism within Tibet, including comparisons with Chan. Coming from a Bonpo background, Karmay compared Buddhist and Bonpo traditions of Dzogchen, showing where the traditions had borrowed from each other. Thus Karmay's interests overlap considerably with Norbu's, but his approach has situated him at the center of academic discourse on Dzogchen.

Several scholars have followed the historicist approach established by Karmay, most significantly David Germano, who has written a series of influential articles on Dzogchen, especially Longchenpa and the Seminal Heart tradition. The complex philosophical Dzogchen of Longchenpa has also been the subject of several articles and monographs by Jean-Luc Achard, whose work has moved from Buddhist to Bonpo Dzogchen. Further work on the origins and early development of Dzogchen has been published by Sam van Schaik, based mainly on the Dunhuang manuscript sources, and by Karen Liljenberg, based on the early canonical sources. The 10th-century syncretic treatise *Lamp for the Eyes of Contemplation*, one of the key sources for early Dzogchen, also continues to generate new research (see "Further Reading").

A number of Tibetan religious teachers and their students have published translations and discussions of Dzogchen literature and history, some of which are valuable resources. Notable Tibetan authors include Tulku Thondup, who has published translation anthologies, traditional histories, and a useful traditional account of the *terma* tradition. Some of the key early texts of Dzogchen have been reliably translated into English by John Myrdhin Reyonds, while Richard Barron's ongoing project of translating the works of Longchenpa into English is providing high-quality renditions of these key texts. In addition, Karen Liljenberg has published translations of key texts of early Dzogchen on her website (see "Digital Materials").

PRIMARY SOURCES

Dunhuang manuscripts containing early Dzogchen texts are held at the British Library, London (BL), and the Bibliothèque nationale de Paris (BnF). The key manuscripts are *The Cuckoo of Awareness,*[26] *The Little Grains of Buddhagupta,*[27] and *The Questions and Answers of Vajrasattva.*[28] Digital images of all are available at the website of the International Dunhuang Project (see "Digital Materials").

Dzogchen texts are found in the canonical collections *Collected Tantras of the Nyingma* (*rnying ma'i rgyud 'bum*) and *Collected Tantras of Vairocana* (*bai ro'i rgyud 'bum*). There are several editions of the *Collected Tantras of the Nyingma* available. See, for example, *Collected Tantras of the Ancients of the Tshamdrak Monastery.*[29] For the *Collected Tantras of Vairocana* see *The Rgyud 'bum of Vairocana.*[30] Scans are available from the website of the Tibetan and Himayalan Digital Library (see "Digital Materials").

For the works of Longchenpa and other authors and treasure revealers, the best source for bibliographical information and scans is the website of the Tibetan Buddhist Resource Centre (see "Digital Materials").

DIGITAL MATERIALS

International Dunhuang Project (http://idp.bl.uk/).
Tibetan Buddhist Resource Center (http://www.tbrc.org/).
Tibetan and Himalayan Digital Library (http://thlib.org/).
Zangthal—Translations of Tibetan texts into English (http://www.zangthal.co.uk/).

FURTHER READING

Dudjom Rinpoche. *The Nyingma School of Tibetan Buddhism: Its Fundamentals and History.* Translated by Gyurme Dorje and Matthew Kapstein. Boston: Wisdom, 2005.

Esler, Dylan. "The Exposition of Atiyoga in gNubs-chen Sangs-rgyas ye-shes' bSam-gtan mig-sgron." *Revue d'Etudes Tibétaines* 24, no. 4 (2012): 81–136.

Germano, David. "Architecture and Absence in the Secret Tantric History of the Great Perfection (*rdzogs chen*)." *Journal of the International Association of Buddhist Studies* 17, no. 2 (1994): 203–335.

Germano, David. "The Funerary Transformation of the Great Perfection (*Rdzogs chen*)." *Journal of the International Association of Tibetan Studies* 1 (2005): 1–54.

Hatchell, Christopher. *Naked Seeing: The Great Perfection, the Wheel of Time, and Visionary Buddhism in Renaissance Tibet.* New York: Oxford University Press, 2014.

Karmay, S. *The Great Perfection*. 2nd ed. Leiden, The Netherlands: Brill, 2007.
Liljenberg, Karen. "On the History and Identification of Two of the Thirteen Later Translation of the Dzogchen Mind Series." *Revue d'études tibétaines* 17 (2009): 137–156.
Longchen Rabjampa. *Precious Treasury of the Way of Abiding*. Translated by Richard Barron. Junction City, CA: Padma Publishing, 1998.
Longchen Rabjampa. *The Practice of Dzogchen: Longchen Rabjam's Writings on the Great Perfection*. Translated by Harold Talbott and Tulku Thondup. 2nd ed. Boston: Snow Lion, 2014.
Namkhai Norbu. *The Crystal and the Way of Light: Sutra, Tantra and Dzogchen*. 2nd ed. Boston: Snow Lion, 2000.
Pettit, John. *Mipham's Beacon of Certainty: Illuminating the View of Dzochen, the Great Perfection*. Boston: Wisdom, 1999.
Rossi, Donatella. *The Philosophical View of the Great Perfection in the Tibetan Bon Religion*. Boston: Snow Lion, 2000.
van Schaik, Sam. *Approaching the Great Perfection: Simultaneous and Gradual Approaches to Dzogchen Practice in Jigme Lingpa's Longchen Nyingtig*. Boston: Wisdom, 2004.
van Schaik, Sam. "The Early Days of the Great Perfection." *Journal of the International Association of Buddhist Studies* 27, no. 1 (2004): 165–206.

NOTES

1. Jigme Lingpa, *Aspirational Prayer for the Ground, Path and Result*, trans. Sam van Schaik, *Approaching the Great Perfection: Simultaneous and Gradual Approaches to Dzogchen Practice in Jigme Lingpa's Longchen Nyingtig* (Boston: Wisdom, 2004), 168.
2. See Samten Karmay, *The Great Perfection* (Leiden, The Netherlands: Brill, 2007), 137–144; and David Germano, "Architecture and Absence in the Secret Tantric History of the Great Perfection (*rdzogs chen*)," *Journal of the International Association of Buddhist Studies* 17, no. 2 (1994): 209–219.
3. Translation by the author from IOL Tib J 647, British Library, London (BL), fol. 1r.
4. Sam van Schaik, "The Early Days of the Great Perfection," *Journal of the International Association of Buddhist Studies* 27, no. 1 (2004): 171–175; for a translation of the *The Questions and Answers on Vajrasattva* see Jacob Dalton, "The Questions and Answers of Vajrasattva," in *Yoga in Practice*, ed. David White (Princeton, NJ: Princeton University Press, 2011), 185–203.
5. On the *Collected Tantras of the Nyingma* see Cathy Cantwell and Robert Mayer, *The Kīlaya Nirvāṇa Tantra and the Vajra Wrath Tantra: Two Texts from the Ancient Tantra Collection* (Vienna: Österreichische Akademie der Wissenschaften, 2006), 1–19. On the *Collected Tantras of Vairocana*, see Matthew Kapstein, "The Sun of the Heart and the Bai-ro-rgyud-'bum." *Revue d'études tibetaines* 15 (2008): 275–288.
6. On *Gold Refined from Ore* and its references to tantric practice, and probably antiquity, see Sam van Schaik, "Dzogchen, Chan and the Question of Influence," *Revue d'études tibetaines* 24 (2012): 15.
7. Karen Liljenberg, "A Critical Study of the Thirteen Later Translations of the Dzogchen Mind Series" (PhD diss., SOAS, University of London, 2012).
8. For a translation of the *Sūtra of the All-Creating King*, see Namkai Norbu and Adriana Clemente, trans., *The Supreme Source* (Ithaca, NY: Snow Lion, 1999).
9. See Dylan Esler, "The Exposition of Atiyoga in gNubs-chen Sangs-rgyas ye-shes' bSam-gtan mig-sgron," *Revue d'Etudes Tibétaines* 24, no. 4 (2012): 81–136.
10. See David Germano, "The Funerary Transformation of the Great Perfection (*Rdzogs chen*)," *Journal of the International Association of Tibetan Studies* 1 (2005): 1–54.
11. Van Schaik, "Dzogchen, Chan and the Question of Influence," 5–20.
12. On the activities of early treasure revealers and their role in the development of Dzogchen, see Ronald Davidson, *Tibetan Renaissance: Tantric Buddhism in the Rebirth of Tibetan Culture* (New York: Columbia University Press, 2005), 210–243.

13. On Nyingma lineages in the 11th and 12th centuries and the development of the nine vehicle system, see Jacob Dalton, *The Gathering of Intentions: A History of Tibetan Tantra* (New York: Columbia University Press, 2016), 30–47.
14. Sa skya paṇḍita, *Sdom pa gsum gyi rab tu dbye ba*, in *Sa skya bka' 'bum* (Dehradun, India: Sakya Centre, 1992–1993), 12:61.
15. For an insightful discussion of the nature of *terma*, see Robert Mayer, "gTer ston and Tradent: Innovation and Conservation in Tibetan Treasure Literature," *Journal of the International Association of Buddhist Studies* 36/37 (2015): 227–242.
16. See Donatella Rossi, *The Philosophical View of the Great Perfection in the Tibetan Bon Religion* (Boston: Snow Lion, 2000).
17. This text is discussed and translated in Anne Klein and Tenzin Wangyal, *Unbounded Wholeness: Dzogchen, Bon and the Logic of the Nonconceptual* (Oxford: Oxford University Press, 2006).
18. See Jean-Luc Achard, *Enlightened Rainbows: The Life and Works of Shardza Tashi Gyeltsen* (Leiden, The Netherlands: Brill, 2008).
19. Key concepts of the instruction series are discussed in van Schaik, *Approaching the Great Perfection*, 51–62; see also Jean-Luc Achard, "La Base et ses sept interprétations dans la tradition rDzogs chen," *Revue d'études tibetaines* 1 (2002): 44–60.
20. On the links between Dzogchen and the Kālacakra Tantra, see Christopher Hatchell, *Naked Seeing: The Great Perfection, the Wheel of Time, and Visionary Buddhism in Renaissance Tibet* (New York: Oxford University Press, 2014). See also Germano, "Architecture and Absence," 267–291.
21. A good anthology of Longchenpa's works is Longchen Rabjampa, *The Practice of Dzogchen: Longchen Rabjam's Writings on the Great Perfection*, trans. Harold Talbott and Tulku Thondup (Boston: Snow Lion, 2014). For a biography see Jampa MacKenzie Stewart, *The Life of Longchenpa: The Omniscient Dharma King of the Vast Expanse* (Boston: Shambhala, 2014).
22. On the Tibetan Book of the Dead and related traditions in Tibet, see Bryan Cuevas, *The Hidden History of the Tibetan Book of the Dead* (New York: Oxford University Press, 2003).
23. See for example Chokyi Nyima Rinpoche, *The Union of Mahamudra and Dzogchen*, trans. Erik Pema (Kunzang, Kathmandu: Rangjung Yeshe, 1989).
24. On meditation communities, with specific reference to Longchenpa's community, see David Germano and Janet Gyatso, "Longchenpa and the Possession of the Ḍākinīs," in *Tantra in Practice*, ed. David White (Princeton, NJ: Princeton University Press, 2000), 241–265.
25. On the teaching and treasure-revealing activities of Jigme Puntsog, see David Germano, "Re-membering the Dismembered Body of Tibet: Contemporary Tibetan Visionary Movements in the People's Republic of China," in *Defining Buddhism(s): A Reader*, ed. Karen Dennis and Natalie Gummer (Oakville, CT: Equinox, 2007), 176–213. On the community at Larung Gar, see Alan Taylor, "The Spectacular Seda Monastery," *The Atlantic*, May 21, 2015.
26. *The Cuckoo of Awareness*, IOL Tib J 647.
27. *The Little Grains of Buddhagupta*, IOL Tib J 594, BL.
28. *The Questions and Answers of Vajrasattva*, IOL Tib J 470, BL; Pelliot tibétain 819, Bibliothèque nationale de Paris.
29. *Collected Tantras of the Ancients of the Tshamdrak Monastery* (Thimphu, Bhutan: National Library, Royal Government of Bhutan, 1982).
30. *The Rgyud 'bum of Vairocana* (Leh, Ladakh: S. W. Tashigangpa Smanrtsis Shesrig Spendzod, 1971).

Sam van Schaik

E

EARLY HISTORY OF THE DRUKPA KAGYÜ SCHOOL

THE INCEPTION OF THE DRUKPA KAGYÜ SCHOOL BASED UPON HAGIOGRAPHIES AND DHARMA CHRONICLES

The Drukpa Kagyü ('Brug pa bka' brgyud) school is one of the main subschools within the Kagyü (Bka' brgyud) school, which is one of the four chief schools of Tibetan Buddhism, along with the Nyingma (Rnying ma), Sakya (Sa skya), and Geluk (Dge lugs). Mostly known for its role in the foundation of Bhutan in the 17th century, in the early 21st century, it has a strong presence in Himalayan enclaves like Ladakh, and has the second largest number of devotees within the entire Kagyü school.

The history of the Drukpa Kagyü school has been surveyed by several modern historians, including John Ardussi, Michael Aris, Yoshiro Imaeda, and Karma Phuntsho.[1] These historical studies enable us to grasp the outline of its general history. There are also detailed research works, translations, and commentaries on biographies of popular Drukpa Kagyü masters, such as Shabdrung Ngawang Nyamgyal (Zhabs drung Ngag dbang rnam rgyal, 1594–1651), who was the seventeenth chief abbot of the Drukpa Kagyü school and also the founder of Bhutan ('Brug yul),[2] the divine madman Drukpa Kunley ('Brug pa Kun legs, 1455–1529),[3] and Phajo Drugom Zhigpo (Pha jo 'Brug sgom zhig po, 1184–1251),[4] who was the first to be sent as a Drukpa Kagyü master to the current land of Bhutan.

If this literature has been helpful in providing a general overview, it is lacking in detail and nuance, particularly regarding the school's inception. The era of the school's founder Tsangpa Gyare (Gtsang pa rgya ras Ye shes rdo rje, 1161–1211) and his disciples has not been studied exhaustively, despite the existence of a few partial studies.[5]

Fortunately, more primary sources have become available, enabling the author of this article to reexamine the life of Tsangpa Gyare.[6] Comparing and analyzing available biographies (*rnam thar*) and dharma annals (*chos 'byung*) referring to Tsangpa Gyare, this research has revealed essential information about the school's founder, including basic data concerning the year and background of the foundation of head monasteries such as the Ralung monastery (Ra lung dgon pa).[7]

As a next step, this article reexamines the early history of the Drukpa Kagyü school, focusing especially on the relationship between Tsangpa Gyare, his master Ling Repa, and his disciples.

This article uses religious biographies and dharma annals as primary sources. Since both genres weave together mythological episodes and historical facts, they need to be employed critically and objectively compared to different historical sources. Contemporary studies of Tibetan hagiographies tend to make extensive use of historiographic literature, focusing not only on the individual lives of saints but also on the groups to which they belonged and the sociohistorical contexts they inhabited. American Tibetologist Andrew Quintman's approach, inspired by medieval historian Patrick Geary, is an example in this regard.[8] Likewise, this article uses biographies and dharma annals to both examine saints as individual figures and better comprehend their social relationships, especially their relationships with two collective entities, the Lingre Kagyü and the Drukpa Kagyü schools.

Figure 1. Tsangpa Gyare.
Source: Photo by Seiji Kumagai.

Figure 2. Statue of Ling Repa.
Source: Photo by Seiji Kumagai.

DIFFERENCES BETWEEN THE LINGRE KAGYÜ SCHOOL AND THE DRUKPA KAGYÜ SCHOOL

Here we first overview the lineage of the Kagyü school from its beginning until the founding of the Drukpa Kagyü school. Proponents of the Drukpa Kagyü school cite several precedents: the Lingre Kagyü (Ling ras bka' brgyud) school, the Phakdru Kagyü school, and more generally the Dakpo Kagyü (Dwags po bka' brgyud) school. The lineage tree of the Kagyü school is often listed like this:

1. Marpa Chökyi Lodrö (Mar pa Chos kyi blo gros, 1012–1097)
2. Milarepa (Mi la ras pa, 1052–1135)
3. Gampopa Sonam Rinchen (Sgam po pa Bsod nams rin chen or Dwags po lha rje, 1079–1153)
4. Phakmo Drupa Dorje Gyälpo (Phag mo gru pa Rdo rje rgyal po, 1110–1170)
5. Ling Repa Pema Dorje (Gling ras pa Padma rdo rje, 1128–1188)
6. Tsangpa Gyare Yeshe Dorje (Gtsang pa rgya ras Ye shes rdo rje, 1161–1211)

Tsangpa Gyare's biographies note his strong relationship of reciprocal trust with Ling Repa. On one hand, he respectfully regarded Ling Repa as his root master (*rtsa ba'i bla ma*). On the other, Ling Repa appreciated Tsangpa Gyare's impressive skills and capacities.[9] Many later historians thus came to regard Tsangpa Gyare as the direct successor of Ling Repa and generally identified the Lingre Kagyü school with the Drukpa Kagyü school.[10]

In currently available biographies of Ling Repa and Tsangpa Gyare, there is no source describing Ling Repa as the founder of the Drukpa Kagyü school. In the oldest annal referring to both lives, the *Lho rong chos 'byung* (Dharma history of the Kagyü tradition composed in Lhorong), composed in 1446 by Tatsag Tsewanggyal (Rta tshag Tshe dbang rgyal, b. 15th century), Ling Repa and Tsangpa Gyare were respectively called Je Naphuwa (Rje sna phu ba, master of Naphu monastery) and Chöje Drukpa (Chos rje 'brug pa, dharma master of Druk monastery),[11] so the former was not regarded as the founder of the Drukpa Kagyü school.

Interestingly, in *Deb ther sngon po* (*The Blue Annals*), composed in 1476 by Gö Lotsawa Zhönnupel ('Gos lo tsa ba Gzhon nu dpal, 1392–1481), Ling Repa is characterized as the root master of the Drukpa Kagyü school.[12] The Third Tukwan (Thu'u bkwan Blo bzang chos kyi nyi ma, 1737–1802), master of the Geluk school, included a chapter on the Drukpa Kagyü school in his doxography *Thu'u bkwan grub mtha'* (Buddhist doxography composed by Thuken). Therein he claimed, "The Drukpa Kagyü school is attributed to both Tsangpa Gyare and [his master] Ling Repa Pema Dorje, who is the disciple of Phakmo Drupa."[13] According to the sources referenced in this article, Gö Lotsawa seems to be the first person to regard Ling Repa as the origin of the Drukpa Kagyü school.

Modern Western historians tend to regard Ling Repa as the (co-)founder of the Drukpa Kagyü school (with Tsangpa Gyare).[14] Dan Martin, for example, cites Gö Lotsawa's explanation in claiming Ling Repa as a founder.[15] However, citing Gö Lotsawa only proves that some later historians regarded Ling Repa as the origin of the Drukpa Kagyü school. It does not prove that Ling Repa was regarded as the founder of the Drukpa Kagyü school before them. Martin also identifies the foundation of the Ralung monastery with the foundation of the Drukpa Kagyü school and insists that Ling Repa and his followers were responsible for founding the monastery. In support of this claim, Martin dates the foundation of the monastery to 1180, eight years before Ling Repa's death. In fact, the monastery was built in 1196, eight years after his death, so it could not have been founded by Ling Repa.[16]

Against historians like Martin, this article argues that the Lingre Kagyü school and the Drukpa Kagyü school were not identical, and that Ling Repa should not be regarded as a co-founder of the Drukpa Kagyü school. The argument is based on the following evidence:

- Tsangpa Gyare did not succeed to the abbotship of the Naphu (Sna phu) monastery, which was the head monastery of the Lingre Kagyü school built by Ling Repa. Instead, Tsangpa Gyare founded the Ralung monastery and the Druk monastery ('Brug gi dgon pa) as his head monasteries outside of Naphu.[17]
- Tsangpa Gyare only became a fully ordained monk five years after Ling Repa's death. It is implausible that such a novice monk would have succeeded to a head monastery of the Lingre Kagyü school. It is even more implausible that he would do so in the middle of his religious training.
- Tsangpa Gyare stayed with Ling Repa as his disciple for approximately five years at the very end of Ling Repa's life. When Ling Repa died, Tsangpa Gyare was temporally absent for a meditation retreat that his master had not sanctioned. Even if Tsangpa

Gyare had an unusually strong relationship with his master, other senior disciples who had accompanied Ling Repa for several decades would have been better positioned to assume the abbotship upon his death.

- Tsangpa Gyare, whose debating skills surpassed those of his master Ling Repa, was prohibited by him from debating other senior disciples in order to avoid troubles.[18] This suggests that he was not a person, at least at that time, who could direct senior disciples on behalf of Ling Repa.

In short, it would have been difficult for such a young novice monk to succeed to the abbotship of the head monastery of Naphu and direct senior disciples there. It is more reasonable to think that he continued the dharma lineage of Ling Repa but did not directly succeed him as the head of the Lingre Kagyü school. If so, who succeeded to the abbotship of the Naphu monastery?

In all likelihood, it was one of Ling Repa's senior disciples. First, after Ling Repa's death, a shrine containing his memorial stupa (*gdung khang*) was founded. Tsangpa Gyare met the head (*mkhan po*) of its consecration ceremony (*rab gnas*), who presumably was also the head (*mkhan po*) of the Naphu monastery.[19] Second, Tsangpa Gyare was prohibited by Ling Repa from debating his other disciples. If Ling Repa had really admitted him as a future head of the school, he would have let him instruct the other disciples through debates, but this was instead prohibited. This suggests that Ling Repa did not approve of him as an instructor of the other disciples or as a direct successor as head of the Lingre Kagyü school, even if he appreciated him as a future successor of his dharma lineage.

Here we need to clearly differentiate between successor in a religious organization and successor in a dharma lineage. The latter does not imply the former. For example, Ling Repa was one of many disciples who succeeded the dharma lineage from Phakmo Drupa. This does not mean that he became a direct successor of the Phakmodru Kagyü school after him.

When Ling Repa passed away, Tsangpa Gyare was absent for a meditation retreat that he had undertaken despite his master's initial opposition.[20] Many other disciples, in contrast, had stayed in Naphu to receive Ling Repa's final teachings and testimony.[21] These disciples founded a shrine containing Ling Repa's memorial stupa after his death, but Tsangpa Gyare was not involved in its construction. (He later expressed regret at having been absent when his master passed away and entered into meditation to visualize a shrine to honor him).[22] Given these facts, it is difficult to imagine that the senior disciples would have accepted this young novice monk, who was absent during the transcendent final stage of their master's life, as their new abbot. It seems more reasonable to assume that Tsangpa Gyare was excluded from the position of direct successor to the head of the Lingre Kagyü school after Ling Repa.

Tsangpa Gyare finally became a fully ordained monk five years after Ling Repa's death. This was his starting point as a senior monk. He became successful thereafter, founding the Ralung monastery eight years after Ling Repa's death (1196) and founding the Druk monastery nine years later.[23] He ultimately became a great and famous master who was surrounded by a large number of disciples, and who succeeded the dharma lineage from Ling Repa. But his fame and success came many years after Ling Repa's death.

What happened in the Lingre Kagyü school as Tsangpa Gyare's star was rising? Presumably, a lack of influential disciples other than Tsangpa Gyare in the school resulted in a gradual decline. Various dharma annals (*chos 'byung*) refer to the names of Ling Repa's masters but not those of his disciples, other than Tsangpa Gyare.

However, it is worth noting that Tsangpa Gyare himself had a close relationship with the Naphu monastery during his life. He sent many of the offerings he received to the Naphu monastery, which means he supported the monastery financially. According to Mangala Bhadra's biography,[24] Tsangpa Gyare is said to have become a caretaker (*gnyel*) of the Naphu monastery during the winter of 1193. Thereafter he founded the Longdol (Klong dol) monastery and moved there.

The facts analyzed in this section point to the conclusion that the Naphu monastery's abbotship passed from Ling Repa to his senior disciples other than Tsangpa Gyare, and that these senior disciples established the Lingre Kagyü school. The dharma lineage itself was succeeded to by Tsangpa Gyare and his disciples in the Ralung monastery and the Druk monastery of the Drukpa Kagyü school. Thus, it seems more appropriate to consider Ling Repa and Tsangpa Gyare to be the founders of the Lingre Kagyü school and the Drukpa Kagyü school, respectively, rather than cofounders of the Drukpa Kagyü school.

LIFE OF LING REPA

According to Marco Walther's list, there are eight traditional biographies and four dharma annals referring to the life of Ling Repa.[25] This section draws from the various dharma annals to give a brief outline of his life.[26]

Ling Repa was born in 1128 into a family belonging to the lineage of Lower Ling (Gling smad pa). Along with Upper Ling (Gling stod), this was one of two lineages existing at the time in the village of Langpona (Glang po sna), located in Zheng (Gzhengs) in the Upper Nyang area (Myang stod)[27] of the Eastern Tsang region.

His father was Gyälpo Kyoppa (Rgyal po skyob pa), who was skilled in the practices of mantra, medicine, and astrology. His mother was Sümo Darchung (Gzus mo dar chung). He was given the name Pema Dorje (Padma rdo rje).

In his childhood, Ling Repa excelled at reading and writing, and he started to learn medicine at around age nine (1136).[28] At seventeen (1144), he became a novice monk (*dge bsnyen*) under the direction of his uncle Ling (Gling), who was a Tibetan Buddhist scholar monk (*dge bshes*).

Thereafter he met Ra Lotsawa (Rwa lo tsa' ba) and studied with him the practices of Kālacakra, Cakrasaṃvara, and Vajravārāhi in Sekpalung (Sreg pa lung), located in the region of Western Yeru (G.yas ru nub).

Later on, he met Khyung Tsangpa Yeshe Lama (Khyung tshang pa Ye shes bla ma, 1115–1176) and received from him oral instructions on the doctrine of Nāropa. Thanks to Khyung Tsangpa's encouragement, Ling Repa became a fully ordained monk under the direction of the scholar monk Omthangpa ('Om thang pa) and studied the doctrine of the Kadam (Bka' gdams) school with him for one year.

At the age of thirty-five (1162), he met Sumpa (Sum pa) and Lo (Lo), both of whom were direct disciples of Rechungpa (Ras chung rdo rje grags pa, 1084–1161).

Sometime between 1164 and 1168, he met Phakmo Drupa and developed strong faith in him.[29] He was ordered by Phakmo Drupa to meditate on the genuine object (i.e., the absolute truth), and is said to have finally attained the state of meditation beyond the two extremes of subject and object of meditation. Phakmo Drupa passed away in 1170. It is said that more than one thousand disciples participated in his funeral.

After his teacher's death, Ling Repa founded the Naphu monastery in Chölung (Chos lung), located in Naphu in the region of Ü. Although the primary sources do not give the year of its foundation, fortunately, the biographies of Tsangpa Gyare describe how Ling Repa built a monastery in Naphu sometime between 1181 and 1183.[30] This means the monastery was built during the last years of Ling Repa's life.

At the age of sixty-one (1188), in the afternoon of the first month of summer, Ling Repa passed away.

LIFE OF TSANGPA GYARE

This section outlines Tsangpa Gyare's life.[31] Tsangpa Gyare was born in the village of the Gya (Rgya) clan in Saral (Sa ral), located in Khule (Khu le) at the bottom of the Hawo Kangzang mountain (Ha 'o gangs bzang) in the upper Nyang area (Myang stod) of the Eastern Tsang region in Central Tibet, on the morning of the 15th in the first month of summer in 1161.[32] His father Gyazurpo Tsape (Rgya zur po tshab pe) is said to have had Chinese ancestors, as indicated by his name; his mother Marza Tarki (Mar za dar skyid) is said to have come from Saral.[33] He was born the youngest of seven sons.

Figure 3. Tsangpa Gyare's birthplace.
Source: Photo by Seiji Kumagai.

Tsangpa Gyare is said to have been noble, handsome, and wise, with the right personality to become a monk. At around age twelve, working under the direction of the master Tathangpa (Rta thang pa), he renounced the secular world and received the dharma name Sherab Dutsi Korlo (Shes rab bdud rtsi 'khor lo).[34] After becoming a monk, he studied both sutras and tantras with many scholars and masters.

The tradition insists that he started to study with Ling Repa when he was between twenty-one and twenty-three years old, and continued to study with him intensively until the age of twenty-eight (1168).

At the age 33 (1193), he became a fully ordained monk under the direction of multiple masters, the most significant being Zhang (Zhang G.yu brag pa Brtson 'gru brags pa, 1122–1193) and Zepa (Bzad pa).[35]

He is said to have founded his first monastery some time between 1189 and 1194 in Longdol (Klong rdol dgon pa), near Nyethang, apparently in fulfilment of master Zhang's prophecy.[36]

He seems to have founded the Ralung monastery, located in the east end of upper Nyang near the boundary between the regions of Tsang and Lhokha, following the prophecy of a deity (*yidam*). Only the biography composed by Gyaltangpa gives the year 1196 for its foundation, while the other biographies do not mention its foundation year.[37]

The Druk Monastery ('Brug gi dgon pa or 'Brug Se ba byang chub chos gling), from which the Drukpa Kagyü school draws its name, was founded in 1205, toward the end of Tsangpa

Figure 4. Current Ralung Monastery.
Source: Photo by Seiji Kumagai.

Figure 5. Current Druk Monastery.
Source: Photo by Seiji Kumagai.

Gyare's life. Located to the southwest of Lhasa, the newly established monastery fulfilled Ling Repa's prophecy.[38]

Tsangpa Gyare continued to edify and educate his disciples and left many testaments as oral instructions into his later years. He died in 1211, at age 51. Biographies mention that tens of thousands of disciples and adherents gathered to attend his funeral. He thus seems to have gradually become successful and gained a substantial following.

LIFE AND ROLE OF THE SECOND ABBOT DARMA SENGE

Late in Tsangpa Gyare's life, he seems to have had a large number of disciples. Both the *Lho rong chos 'byung*, composed by Tatsag Tsewanggyal, and the dharma annals, composed in 1581 by Pema Karpo Ngawang Norbu (Padma dkar po Nga dbang nor bu, 1527–1592), mention that Tsangpa Gyare had 2,800 great disciples. His disciples can be classified into two groups: (a) those surrounding his nephew Darma Senge Sangye Wonre (Darma seng ge Sangs rgyas dbon ras, 1177–1237), who belonged to the Gya clan and became the second chief abbot of the Drukpa Kagyü school; and (b) the other disciples who did not belong to the Gya clan. Until the period of the seventeenth chief abbot Shabdrung Ngawang Namgyel, there was a big gap between the masters belonging to the Gya clan, who continued to hold the main monasteries, and those not belonging to this clan.

Figure 6. Statue of Darma Senge.
Source: Photo by Seiji Kumagai.

Darma Senge was a direct disciple of Tsangpa Gyare and became the chief abbot directing his dharma brothers after his death. Darma Senge succeeded to the abbotship of the Druk monastery and Ralung monastery at age thirty-five (1211). As mentioned in the *Deb ther sngon po* and Khetsun Sangpo's annal,[39] he was given offerings and served by Tsangpa Gyare's leading disciples, such as Götshangpa Gönpo Dorje (Rgos tshang pa Mgon po rdo rje, 1189–1258) and Lorepa Wangchug Tsöndru (Lo ras pa Dbang phyug brtson 'grus, 1187–1250). He also gave teachings on the "[six types of] equal taste" (*ro snyoms*) to disciples such as Götshangpa.

Darma Senge sent Phajo Drugom Zhigpo to the current land of Bhutan to convert local inhabitants to his school. Phajo's descendants in Bhutan later became strong supporters and protectors of Shabdrung Ngawang Namgyel, who moved from Tibet to Western Bhutan at the beginning of the 17th century, and who finally unified the land of Bhutan. In this regard, Darma Senge was an important political figure.

He also established a large stupa called Trashi Gomang (Bkra shis sgo mang) at the Ralung monastery and a statue of the buddha (Byang chub chen po) at the Druk monastery, thus developing and expanding the head monasteries.

Therefore, Darma Senge can be characterized as follows:

Figure 7. Statue of Götshangpa.
Source: Photo by Seiji Kumagai.

Figure 8. Statue of Lorepa.
Source: Photo by Seiji Kumagai.

Figure 9. Wall-painting of the Tashi Gomang Stupa and former Ralung Monastery.
Source: Photo by Seiji Kumagai.

- He succeeded to the abbotship of both the Druk monastery and the Ralung monastery following Tsangpa Gyare.
- He took over the role of teacher for a large number of Tsangpa Gyare's disciples.
- He expanded the headquarters of the Drukpa Kagyü school, constructing a large stupa and other monastic buildings.
- He expanded the territories in which the school operated by sending some of his disciples (e.g., Phajo) to new lands such as Bhutan.

CLASSIFICATION OF TSANGPA GYARE'S DISCIPLES

The dharma annal *Lho rong chos 'byung* classified the most relevant among Tsangpa Gyare's many disciples into three categories according to their monastic careers:[40]

1. First great disciples (*dang por che ba*): Pariwa Yeshe Gönpo (Spa ri ba Ye shes mgon po) and Kyangmo Khapa (Rkyang mo kha pa);
2. Middle great disciple (*bar du che ba*): Dremowa [Sangyebum] ('Bras mo ba [Sangs rgyas 'bum])
3. Last great disciples (*tha mar che ba*): Lorepa Wangchug Tsöndru and Götshangpa Gönpo Dorje

The *Deb ther sngon po* later added Gyayakpa (Rgya yags pa) to the category of "middle great disciples."[41]

We should note here that the category of "middle great disciples" is absolutely different from the category of "Middle Drukpa Kagyü school" (Bar 'brug). The concept of the "Middle Drukpa Kagyü school" may have been first attested in the dharma annals composed by Pema Karpo in 1581.[42] Pema Karpo gave the name "Middle Drukpa Kagyü school" to the "first great disciples," "middle great disciples," and the rest of the 2,800 disciples other than Götshangpa and Lorepa, who were called the founders of the "Upper Drukpa Kagyü school" (Stod 'brug) and the "Lower Drukpa Kagyü school" (Smad 'brug), respectively.

The classification system dividing the Drukpa Kagyü school into upper, middle, and lower subschools thereafter became common among Tibetan historians (and also modern historians). But it is necessary to note that it emerged in a relatively later period.

OVERVIEW OF THE EARLY HISTORY OF THE DRUKPA KAGYÜ SCHOOL

This article overviewed the early history of the Drukpa Kagyü school, focusing especially on Ling Repa, Tsangpa Gyare, and his direct disciples.

It is necessary to clearly differentiate the Lingre Kagyü school and the Drukpa Kagyü school. Several historians, both traditional and modern, have regarded Ling Repa and Tsangpa Gyare to be cofounders of the Drukpa Kagyü school. In so doing, they have considered the Lingre Kagyü and Drukpa Kagyü schools to be identical.

However, it should be noted that Tsangpa Gyare did not succeed the Naphu monastery founded by Ling Repa. Instead, he built his own head monasteries, such as the Ralung monastery and the Druk monastery, in places different from Naphu. It is also difficult to imagine that Tsangpa Gyare succeeded to the head monastery of the Lingre Kagyü school when Ling Repa died, since he was only a young novice monk at that time and there were many senior disciples other than him. Tsangpa Gyare was also forbidden by Ling Repa from debating with other disciples, so he was not regarded as a master directing other disciples within the Lingre Kagyü school. On the other hand, even after Ling Repa's death, Tsangpa Gyare financially supported Naphu monastery by sending many of the offerings he received, and he maintained a good relationship with the Naphu monastery and Ling Repa's disciples there.

We can therefore presume that Tsangpa Gyare did not directly succeed Ling Repa as the head of the Lingre Kagyü school; rather, he continued his doctrine and developed it in his new school of Drukpa Kagyü. Neither can Ling Repa be considered the cofounder of the Drukpa Kagyü school, because he had already died in 1188, well before Tsangpa Gyare founded the Ralung monastery in 1196 and the Druk monastery in 1205.[43]

Tsangpa Gyare studied with Ling Repa roughly during the last five years of his life, and became a fully ordained monk five years after his death. He subsequently educated monks and lay people in the Ü, Tsang, and Lhokha regions, finally gaining a large number of disciples (traditionally estimated at 2,800). The Drukpa Kagyü school thus became a large Buddhist school.

The school was succeeded to by his nephew Darma Senge. He succeeded to both the Druk monastery and the Ralung monastery, where he directed the other disciples of Tsangpa Gyare. He also expanded the head monasteries, building a gigantic stupa in the Ralung monastery and a buddha statue in the Druk monastery. He further tried to expand the territories of the school by sending disciples (e.g., Phajo) to new lands such as Bhutan.

The disciples of Tsangpa Gyare were later classified into three groups, according to their careers: the "first great disciples," the "middle great disciples," and the "last great disciples." Among them, the last two great disciples, Götshangpa and Lorepa, were respectively called the founders of the "Upper Drukpa Kagyü school" and the "Lower Drukpa Kagyü school." Both Tibetan and modern historians add a third category, the "Middle Drukpa Kagyü school," to the other two. However, we need to note that the label "Middle Drukpa Kagyü school" may have been first attested in the dharma annal composed by Pema Karpo in 1581.

The reason that so many subdivisions appeared within the Drukpa Kagyü school is that Tsangpa Gyare had many capable and influential disciples. Unfortunately, since his master Ling Repa probably did not have influential disciples other than Tsangpa Gyare, the Lingre Kagyü school did not survive as an independent entity into later periods. Instead, the doctrine of Ling Repa continued in the Drukpa Kagyü school through Tsangpa Gyare. The Drukpa Kagyü school produced capable masters, both belonging to the Gya clan, who succeeded to the abbotship. The Gya clan continued to control the main monasteries until the abbotship of Shabdrung Ngawang Namgyel. The school has maintained its presence in the Himalayan Buddhist world until the early 21st century.

REVIEW OF LITERATURE

The first Western academic article providing in-depth information about the life of Ling Repa was published by Dan Martin in 1979.[44] It was a pioneering study which outlined the life of Ling Repa, who was still unknown in the West at the time.

To that point, Western academics had generally regarded Tsangpa Gyare as the founder of the Drukpa Kagyü school, as he had built the Druk monastery and the Ralung monastery. Martin, on the other hand, attempted to identify Ling Repa as the founder of the school. Martin pointed out that there were also Tibetan historians such as Gö Lotsawa, who compiled the *Deb ther sngon po*, who regarded Ling Repa as the founder of the Drukpa Kagyü school. This information was academically valuable.

Martin believed that the Ralung monastery and the Drukpa Kagyü school were founded in 1180. The year 1180 was first presented by David Snellgrove in a paper published in 1968 without referring to any primary sources.[45] W. Blythe Miller's paper, published in 2005, and Walther's doctoral dissertation, published in 2017, also refer the same year, positioning Ling Repa as the (co-)founder of the Drukpa Kagyü school (with Tsangpa Gyare).[46] In particular, Walther's dissertation provide comprehensive information about the life and works of Ling Repa.

However, as Kumagai points out in his article published in 2018, the Ralung monastery was not built in 1180 but in 1196, as stated by Gyalthangpa Dechen Dorje.[47] It was founded by Tsangpa Gyare eight years after Ling Repa's death. Therefore, it is not possible to regard Ling Repa as the founder of the Drukpa Kagyü school. Considering the chronology of Tsangpa Gyare's relationship with Ling Repa, his relationship with Ling Repa's senior disciples, and the ownership of Naphu monastery, this article pointed out that a person other than Tsangpa Gyare likely became the head of the Lingre Kagyü school after Ling Repa's death. In other words, the article insisted that the Lingre Kagyü school, based in the Naphu monastery, and the Drukpa Kagyü school, based in the Ralung monastery, were distinct institutions. Therefore, the founder of the Drukpa Kagyü school was not Ling Repa but Tsangpa Gyare.

The articles of Martin and Miller also outline Tsangpa Gyare's life, but they provide incorrect dates for the founding of the Ralung and Druk monasteries. In a paper published in 2018, Seiji Kumagai draws from various dharma annals and seven different biographies of Tsangpa Gyare to correct the erroneous information given by previous researchers and to reexamine Tsangpa Gyare's life.[48] In another work, Kumagai reports his discovery of ruins associated with Tsangpa Gyare, including his birthplace.[49] Kumagai, Thupten, and Yasuda also list all the collected works of Tsangpa Gyare and explain their characteristics.[50] The latest information about Tsangpa Gyare's life and works is summarized in a paper published by Kumagai in 2020.[51]

Finally, there is no comprehensive study of the direct disciples of Tsangpa Gyare, a gap this article attempts to fill. This article offers an overview of Darma Senge, nephew of Tsangpa Gyare and the successor of the Drukpa Kagyü school. It also introduces a threefold division of Tsangpa Gyare's senior disciples: the first great disciples, the middle great disciples, and the last great disciples. Lastly, the article presents a threefold internal division by identifying the three types of Drukpa Kagyü schools: Upper, Lower, and Middle Drukpa Kagyü schools.

PRIMARY SOURCES

Chos 'byung bstan pa'i Padma rgyas pas'i nyin byed. Compiled by Padma dkar po Nga dbang nor bu (1527–1592) in 1581. In *Tibetan Chronicle of Padma-dkar-po*, edited by Lokesh Chandra, Śata-piṭaka Series, Indo-Asian Literatures, vol. 75, 1–619. New Delhi: International Academy of Indian Culture, 1968.

Deb ther sngon po (*Bod kyi yul du chos dang chos smra ba ji ltar byung ba'i rim pa*). Compiled by 'Gos lo twa wa gzhon nu dpal (1392–1481) between 1476–1478. Reproduced in *The Blue Annals*, edited by Lokesh Chandra. New Delhi: International Academy of Indian Culture, 1974.

Lho 'brug chos 'byung (*Lho phyogs nags mo'i ljongs kyi chos 'byung*). Compiled by Dge 'dun Rin chen (1926–1997) in 1972. Reprint, Thimphu, Bhutan: KMT, 2004.

Lho rong chos 'byung (*Dam pa'i chos kyi byung ba'i legs bshad lho rong chos 'byung*). Compiled by Rta tshag Tshe dbang rgyal (b. 15th century) in 1446. Reprint, Lhasa, Tibet: Bod ljongs bod yig dpe rnying dpe skrun khang, 1994.

Lho'i chos 'byung (*Lho'i chos 'byung 'phro mthud 'jam mgon smon mtha'i 'phreng ba*). Compiled by Bstan 'dzin chos rgyal (d. 1761) in 1759. Thimphu, Bhutan: KMT, 2004.

Mgur gi rim pa (*'Gro mgon rin po che'i gsung mgur gyi rim pa*). Composed by Gtsang pa rgya re Ye shes rdo rje (1161–1211).

(Bhutanese edition) *'Gro mgon rin po che'i gsung mgur gyi rim pa*, in *'Brug lugs gsung rab phyogs bsdebs las chos rje gtsang pa rgya ras kyi bka' 'bum*, vol. 1 (Ka), 265.1–438.3. Thimphu, Bhutan: Bhutanese Monastic Body, 2011.

(Nepalese edition) *'Gro mgon rin po che'i gsung mgur gyi rim pa*, in *'Gro-ba'i mgon-po chos-rjer tsang-pa rgya-ras ye-shes rdo-rje mchog-gi gsun-'bum rin-po-che*, 5–185. Kathmandu, Nepal: Shri Gautama Buddha Vihara, 1998. (TBRC: 23782)

Thu'u bkwan grub mtha' (*Grub mtha' thams cad kyi khungs dang 'dod tshul ston pa legs bshad shel gyi me long*). Compiled by Thu'u bkwan Blo bzang chos kyi nyi ma (1737–1802) in 1802. Gansu, China: Kun su'i mi rigs dpe krun khang, 1984.

FURTHER READING

Ardussi, John. "Bhutan Before the British: A Historical Study." PhD diss., Australian National University, 1977.

Aris, Michael. *Bhutan: The Early History of a Himalayan Kingdom*. Warminster, UK: Aris & Phillips, 1979.

Dargye, Yonten, and Per K. Sørensen. *The Biography of Pha 'Brug-sgom zhig-po Called the Current of Compassion*. Thimphu, Bhutan: National Library, 2001.

Dorji, Sangay. *The Biography of Shabdrung Ngawang Namgyal: Pal Drukpa Rinpoche*. Translated by Sonam Kinga. Thimphu, Bhutan: KMT Publications, 2008.

Dowman, Keith, and Sonam Paljor. *The Divine Madman: The Sublime Life and Songs of Drukpa Kunley*. 3rd ed. Scotts Valley, CA: CreateSpace, 2014. First published 1980 by Dawn Horse Press (Clearlake, CA).

Geary, Patrick. "Saints, Scholars, and Society: The Elusive Goal." In *Saints: Studies in Hagiography*, edited by Sandro Sticca, 1–22. Binghamton, NY: Medieval and Renaissance Texts and Studies, 1996.

Imaeda, Yoshiro. *Histoire médiévale du Bhoutan*. Tokyo: Toyo Bunko, 2011.

Kumagai, Seiji. "Introduction to the Biographies of Tsangpa Gyare (1161–1211), Founder of the Drukpa Kagyü School." In *Buddhism, Culture and Society in Bhutan*, edited by Seiji Kumagai, 9–34. Kathmandu, Nepal: Vajra, 2018.

Kumagai, Seiji. "Life and Works of Tsangpa Gyare (1161–1211), Founder of the Drukpa Kagyü School." In *Oxford Research Encyclopedia of Religion*. Oxford: Oxford University Press, 2020. https://doi.org/10.1093/acrefore/9780199340378.013.663.

Kumagai, Seiji. "A Report on Some Physical Evidences and Oral Transmission about Tsangpa Gyare (1161–1211) Collected at the Ralung Monastery and the Druk Monastery in Tibet." In *Vajrayana Buddhism in the Modern World: Proceedings of the Second Vajrayana Conference, 28–30 March 2018, Thimphu*, 34–48. Thimphu, Bhutan: Centre for Bhutan Studies & GNH 2018.

Kumagai, Seiji, Gawa Thupten, and Akinori Yasuda. "Introduction to the Collected Works of the Founder of the Drukpa Kagyü ('Brug pa bKa' brgyud) School: Tsangpa Gyare (gTsang pa rgya ras, 1161–1211)." In *Buddhism Without Borders: Proceedings of the International Conference on Globalized Buddhism, Bumthang, Bhutan, May 21–23, 2012*, edited by Karma Ura and Dendup Chophel, 36–52. Thimphu, Bhutan: Centre for Bhutan Studies, 2012.

Martin, Dan. "Gling-ras-pa and the Founding of the 'Brug-pa School." *The Tibet Society Bulletin* 13 (1979): 56–69.

Miller, W. Blythe. "The Vagrant Poet and the Reluctant Scholar: A Study of the Balance of Iconoclasm and Civility in the Biographical Accounts of Two Founders of the 'Brug pa bka' brgyud Lineages." *The Journal of the International Association of Buddhist Studies* 28, no. 2 (2005): 369–410.

Miller, W. Blythe. "'Brug pa'i lo rgyus zur tsam: An Analysis of a Thirteenth Century Tibetan Buddhist Lineage History." *Tibet Journal* 31, no. 3 (2006): 17–42.

Phuntsho, Karma. *History of Bhutan*. Noida, India: Random House India, 2013.

Quintman, Andrew. *The Yogin and the Madman*. New York: Columbia University Press, 2014.

Roerich, George. *The Blue Annals*. 2nd ed. Delhi: Motilal Banarsidas, 1996.

Smith, E. Gene. "Foreword." In *Tibetan Chronicle of Padma-dkar-po*, edited by Lokesh Chandra, 1–8. New Delhi: International Academy of Indian Culture, 1968.

Walther, Marco. *Gling-ras-pa Padma rdo-rje (1128–1188): Leben und Werk unter besonderer Berücksichtigung des Werkes. Eine Fackel, die das Wesentliche bündelt*. Munich: Ludwig Maximilian University of Munich, 2017.

NOTES

1. See John Ardussi, "Bhutan Before the British: A Historical Study" (PhD diss., Australian National University, 1977); Michael Aris, *Bhutan: The Early History of a Himalayan Kingdom* (Warminster, UK:

Aris & Phillips, 1979); Yoshiro Imaeda, *Histoire médiévale du Bhoutan* (Tokyo, Japan: Toyo Bunko, 2011); and Karma Phuntsho, *History of Bhutan* (Noida, India: Random House India, 2013).

2. See Ardussi, "Bhutan Before the British," 191–278; Aris, *Bhutan*, 201–254; Sangay Dorji, *The Biography of Shabdrung Ngawang Namgyal: Pal Drukpa Rinpoche*, trans. Sonam Kinga (Thimphu, Bhutan: KMT, 2008); Imaeda, *Histoire médiévale du Bhoutan*, 39–94; and Phuntsho, *History of Bhutan*, 207–254.
3. See Keith Dowman and Sonam Paljor, *The Divine Madman: The Sublime Life and Songs of Drukpa Kunley*, 3rd ed, (1980; repr., Scotts Valley, CA: CreateSpace, 2014).
4. See Yonten Dargye and Per K. Sørensen, *The Biography of Pha 'Brug-sgom zhig-po called The Current of Compassion* (Thimphu, Bhutan: National Library, 2001).
5. See Dan Martin, "Gling-ras-pa and the Founding of the 'Brug-pa School," *The Tibet Society Bulletin* 13 (1979): 56–69; and W. Blythe Miller, "The Vagrant Poet and the Reluctant Scholar: A Study of the Balance of Iconoclasm and Civility in the Biographical Accounts of Two Founders of the 'Brug pa bka' brgyud Lineages," *The Journal of the International Association of Buddhist Studies* 28, no. 2 (2005): 369–410. Both of these articles examine the relationship between Ling Repa and Tsangpa Gyare. The historical research on Bhutan and the Drukpa Kagyü school cited in note 1 also refers to some information about its early history. However, this research uses only limited number of primary sources and omits relevant variance between the information given in different sources.
6. See Seiji Kumagai, "Introduction to the Biographies of Tsangpa Gyare (1161–1211), Founder of the Drukpa Kagyü School," in *Buddhism, Culture and Society in Bhutan*, ed. Seiji Kumagai (Kathmandu, Nepal: Vajra, 2018), 9–34; and Seiji Kumagai, "A Report on Some Physical Evidences and Oral Transmission about Tsangpa Gyare (1161–1211) Collected at the Ralung Monastery and the Druk Monastery in Tibet," in *Vajrayana Buddhism in the Modern World: Proceedings of the Second Vajrayana Conference, 28–30 March 2018, Thimphu* (Thimphu, Bhutan: Centre for Bhutan Studies & GNH, 2018), 34–48.
7. For more details about Tsangpa Gyare's life, see Kumagai, "Biographies of Tsangpa Gyare"; and Kumagai, "Physical Evidences." Concerning his collected works, see Seiji Kumagai, Gawa Thupten, and Akinori Yasuda, "Introduction to the Collected Works of the Founder of the Drukpa Kagyü (*'Brug pa bKa' brgyud*) School: Tsangpa Gyare (*gTsang pa rgya ras*, 1161–1211)," in *Buddhism Without Borders: Proceedings of the International Conference on Globalized Buddhism, Bumthang, Bhutan May 21–23, 2012*, ed. Karma Ura and Dendup Chophel (Thimphu, Bhutan: Centre for Bhutan Studies, 2012), 36–52.
8. See Patrick Geary, "Saints, Scholars, and Society: The Elusive Goal," in *Saints: Studies in Hagiography*, ed. Sandro Sticca (Binghamton, NY: Medieval and Renaissance Texts and Studies, 1996), 1–22; and Andrew Quintman, *The Yogin and the Madman* (New York: Columbia University Press, 2014). Quintman also notes several prominent studies of Tibetan life writing literatures that partially accord with Geary's approach, such as Janet Gyatso, *Apparitions of the Self: The Secret Autobiographies of a Tibetan Cisionary* (Princeton, NJ: Princeton University Press, 1998); Kurtis Schaeffer, *Himalayan Hermitess: The Life of a Tibetan Buddhist Nun* (Oxford: Oxford University Press, 2004); and Hildegard Diemberger, *When a Woman Becomes a Religious Dynasty: The Samding Dorje Phagmo of Tibet* (New York: Columbia University Press, 2007).
9. As mentioned in Kumagai, "Biographies of Tsangpa Gyare," 25–27, Tsangpa Gyare won a debate with Ling Repa and was evaluated highly by him.
10. See Martin, "Gling-ras-pa and the Founding of the 'Brug-pa School," 62–64; Miller, "Vagrant Poet," 373; and Marco Walther, *Gling-ras-pa Padma rdo-rje (1128–1188): Leben und Werk unter besonderer Berücksichtigung des Werkes. Eine Fackel, die das Wesentliche bündelt* (München, Germany: Ludwig Maximilian University of Munich, 2017), 1–4.
11. See Rta tshag Tshe dbang rgyal, comp., *Lho rong chos 'byung* (*Dam pa'i chos kyi byung ba'i legs bshad lho rong chos 'byung*) (1446; repr. Lhasa, Tibet: Bod ljongs bod yig dpe rnying dpe skrun khang, 1994), 649 (line 5), 663 (line 20).

12. See Lokesh Chandra, ed., *The Blue Annals* (New Delhi: International Academy of Indian Culture, 1974), 491.2; and George Roerich, *The Blue Annals*, 2nd ed. (Delhi: Motilal Banarsidas, 1996), 564. Both are modern editions of 'Gos lo twa wa gzhon nu dpal, comp., *Deb ther sngon po* (*Bod kyi yul du chos dang chos smra ba ji ltar byung ba'i rim pa*) (1476–1478).
13. "lnga pa 'brug pa ni/rgyal ba phag mo grub pa'i slob ma gling ras padma rdo rje dang/chos rje gtsang pa rgya ras pa las brgyud pa ste/." Thu'u bkwan Blo bzang chos kyi nyi ma, comp., *Thu'u bkwan grub mtha* (*Grub mtha' thams cad kyi khungs dang 'dod tshul ston pa legs bshad shel gyi me long*) (1802; repr., Gansu, China: Kun su'i mi rigs dpe krun khang, 1984), 127.11–13.
14. See Martin, "Gling-ras-pa and the Founding of the 'Brug-pa School," 62–64; Miller, "Vagrant Poet," 373; and Walther, *Gling-ras-pa Padma rdo-rje*, 1–4.
15. See Martin, "Founding of the 'Brug-pa School," 62–64.
16. Regarding the year of foundation of the Ralung monastery, see Kumagai, "Biographies of Tsangpa Gyare," 28.
17. According to Alfonsa Ferrari, *Mk'yen brtse's Guide to the Holy Places of Central Tibet* (Rome: ISMEO, 1958), 46, Naphu is located near the Thub-bstan rdo-rje grags monastery, which is along the Tsangpo (Gtsang po) river, to the south of Lhasa in the Ü region. The Ralung monastery is located to the east of Gyantse (Rgyal rtse) in the Tsang region. The Druk monastery is located in Nyethang (Mnyes thang) to the east of Lhasa in the Ü region.
18. See Kumagai, "Biographies of Tsangpa Gyare," 25–26.
19. *'Gro mgon rin po che'i gsung mgur gyi rim pa*, in *'Brug lugs gsung rab phyogs bsdebs las chos rje gtsang pa rgya ras kyi bka' 'bum* (Thimphu, Bhutan: Bhutanese Monastic Body, 2011), 1 (Ka):282.1; *'Gro mgon rin po che'i gsung mgur gyi rim pa*, in *'Gro-ba'i mgon-po chos-rjer tsang-pa rgya-ras ye-shes rdo-rje mchog-gi gsun-'bum rin-po-che* (Kathmandu, Nepal: Shri Gautama Buddha Vihara, 1998), 22.4; both are modern editions of Gtsang pa rgya re Ye shes rdo rje, comp., *Mgur gi rim pa* (*'Gro mgon rin po che'i gsung mgur gyi rim pa*) (n.d.).
20. See Kumagai, "Biographies of Tsangpa Gyare," 26–27.
21. Regarding Ling Repa's testimony, see the *Lho rong chos 'byung*, 644.9–645.10; and Chandra, *Blue Annals*, 580.4–6.
22. *Mgur gi rim pa* (Bhutanese edition), 280.4–5; (Nepalese edition), 21.2.
23. Regarding the years of foundation of both monasteries, see Kumagai, "Biographies of Tsangpa Gyare," 28–29.
24. See *'Brug lugs gsung rab phyogs bsdebs las chos rje gtsang pa rgya ras kyi bka' 'bum glegs bam kha pa bzhugs so* (Thimphu: Bhutanese Monastic Body, 2011), 2 (Kha):24.5–6.
25. See Walther, *Gling-ras-pa Padma rdo-rje*, 9–17.
26. Regarding the life of Ling Repa, see Martin, "Founding of the 'Brug-pa School"; Miller, "Vagrant Poet"; and Walther, *Gling-ras-pa Padma rdo-rje*. Walther, in particular, offers full-scale information about Ling Repa's life and works.
27. Some have claimed Ling Repa's birthplace to be the Lower Nyang area(*Myang smad*). See, e.g., Dge 'dun Rin chen, comp., *Lho 'brug chos 'byung* (*Lho phyogs nags mo'i ljongs kyi chos 'byung*) (1972; repr. Thimphu, Bhutan: KMT, 2004), 94 (lines 11–12). But it seems better to follow the other older primary sources which insist on the Upper Nyang area as the location.
28. *Lho rong chos 'byung*, 630.10–11; and an anonymous biography of Ling Repa: *Grub thob chen po gling chen ras pa pad ma rdo rje'i rnam par thar pa*, in *Bka' brgyud gser phreng chen mo: Biographies of Eminent Gurus in the Transmission Lineage of Teachings of the 'Ba'-ra dkar-brgyud-pa sect* (Dehradun, India, published by Ngawang gyaltsen and Ngawang lungtok, 1970), 1 (Ka):372.6, give the age of nine (1136). Chandra, *Blue Annals*, 576.2, a relatively more recent dharma annal, gives the age of eight (1135). Yet another source, the biography of Ling Repa, gives the age of ten (1137). Gyelthangpa Dechen Dorje,

comp., *Grub thob kyi rgyal po gling chen ras pa'i rnam par thar pa*, in *Dkar brgyud gser 'phren: A Thirteenth-Century Collection of Verse Hagiographies of the Succession of Eminent Masters of the 'Brug-pa dKar-brgyud-pa Tradition* (Palampur, India: Sungrab Nyamso Gyunphel Parkhang, 1973), 443.5. This article takes the average from these sources and suggests that Ling Repa began learning medicine at "around age nine."

29. Different sources give different years. The biography of Ling Repa composed by Gyelthangpa, 448.5, gives the age of 37 (1164); Chandra, *Blue Annals*, 578.2–3, gives the age of 38 (1165); and the *Lho rong chos 'byung*, 632.19–633.3, gives the age of 41 (1168).
30. See Kumagai, "Biographies of Tsangpa Gyare," 26.
31. For information about Tsangpa Gyare's life including bibliographical information, see Kumagai, "Biographies of Tsangpa Gyare"; and Kumagai, "Physical Evidences."
32. See Kumagai, "Biographies of Tsangpa Gyare," 22.
33. See Kumagai, "Physical Evidences," 36–37.
34. See Kumagai, "Biographies of Tsangpa Gyare," 24.
35. Carl Yamamoto, *Vision and Violence: Lama Zhang and the Politics of Charisma in Twelfth-Century central Tibet* (Leiden, Netherlands: Brill, 2012) gives in-depth information on the life and writings of Lama Zhang.
36. Regarding the foundation of the Longdol monastery, see Kumagai, "Biographies of Tsangpa Gyare," 27–28.
37. Modern scholars give the year "1180" (at age 20) for the foundation of the Ralung monastery but they do not refer any primary sources. See, for example, David Snellgrove, *A Cultural History of Tibet* (New York: F. A. Praeger, 1968), 137; Martin "Founding of the 'Brug-pa School," 67n34; and Phuntsho, *History of Bhutan*, 210. However, the year 1180 is not reasonable because Tsangpa Gyare had not met Ling Repa at that time. Most of the monasteries founded by Tsangpa Gyare were built after 1193, when he had already received full ordination.
38. Regarding the foundation of the Druk monastery, see Kumagai, "Biographies of Tsangpa Gyare," 28.
39. See Chandra, *Blue Annals*, 586.1–2; and *Biographical Dictionary of Tibet and Tibetan Buddhism*, ed. Khetsun Sangpo Rinbochay (Dharamsala, India: Library of Tibetan Works and Archives, 1973) 8: 138.
40. *Lho rong chos 'byung*, 664.5–6.
41. Chandra, *Blue Annals*, 585.3–4.
42. Padma dkar po Nga dbang nor bu, comp., *Chos 'byung bstan pa'i Padma rgyas pas'i nyin byed* (1581), in *Tibetan Chronicle of Padma-dkar-po*, ed. Lokesh Chandra (New Delhi, India: International Academy of Indian Culture, 1968), 581.3–583.4.
43. As mentioned in Kumagai, "Biographies of Tsangpa Gyare," 28n47, some modern scholars state that the Ralung monastery was built jointly by both Ling Repa and Tsangpa Gyare. The statement is chronologically wrong, as pointed out here.
44. See Martin, "Founding of the 'Brug-pa School."
45. See Snellgrove, *Cultural History of Tibet*, 137.
46. See Miller, "Vagrant Poet," and Walther, *Gling-ras-pa Padma rdo-rje*.
47. Kumagai, "Biographies of Tsangpa Gyare," 28.
48. Kumagai, "Biographies of Tsangpa Gyare."
49. Kumagai, "Physical Evidences."
50. Kumagai et al., "Collected Works."
51. Seiji Kumagai, "Life and Works of Tsangpa Gyare (1161–1211), Founder of the Drukpa Kagyü School," in *Oxford Research Encyclopedia of Religion* (Oxford: Oxford University Press, 2020).

Seiji Kumagai

EARLY MODERN EUROPEAN ENCOUNTERS WITH BUDDHISM

INTRODUCTION

Although scholars in the field of Buddhist studies have been hesitant to adopt new methodologies and theoretical perspectives, the introduction of postcolonial theory and methodology into the field has been productive. The corpus of historical and genealogical studies has grown since the publication of Donald S. Lopez, Jr.'s *Curators of the Buddha: The Study of Buddhism under Colonialism* in 1995, a collection of essays on the origins of the field as an outgrowth of and justification for European colonialism.[1] Historian Urs App has also contributed greatly to our understanding of the European encounter with Buddhist peoples in Asia.[2] App has challenged the claims of others in the field, Tomoko Masuzawa and Roger-Pol Droit specifically, who contend that the 19th-century "discovery" or "invention" of Buddhism as a "world religion" by means of modern philology constituted a definitive break from the earlier study of Buddhism by Jesuit missionaries.[3] App argues that as early as the 16th century, the Jesuit missionaries had recognized Buddhism as a religion composed of an "inner" and an "outer" doctrine, the former being an atheistic, materialist philosophy reserved for elite disciples and the latter being moral and theistic teaching tailored for lesser disciples and the laity.

More recently, Martino Dibeltulo Concu advanced App's thesis against Masuzawa and Droit by looking at the delineation between "philosophy" and "religion" in Eugène Burnouf's 1844 *Introduction to the History of Indian Buddhism*, a study considered to be a watershed moment in the European "discovery" of Buddhism by a figure regarded as the "founding father" of Buddhist studies.[4] Dibeltulo Concu argues that this delineation in Burnouf's study is a rearticulation of the inner–outer distinction from Jesuit sources in a scientific, philological language. While App and Dibeltulo Concu have provided valuable insights into the genealogy of the field, this article defends the view put forward by Masuzawa and Droit: that the 19th-century European "discovery" of Buddhism by means of the science of philology constitutes a break from the earlier Jesuit accounts of Buddhism. It is a break precisely as far as the distinction between philosophy and religion found in Burnouf's *Introduction* neither matches the inner–outer Jesuit distinction nor does Burnouf draw on any Jesuit sources for this distinction. Rather, Burnouf's distinction between philosophy and religion is premised on his presumption to delineate between the "facts" of the buddha's life and the "beliefs" of Asian Buddhists. This approach is influenced by the work of Bruno Latour, particularly his essay "On the Modern Cult of Factish Gods," in which he identifies the fact–belief distinction as a key means for modern people (i.e., Europeans) to set themselves apart from nonmodern, non-European "Others."[5]

The first section of this article explores the Jesuit missionary encounters with Buddhists in Japan and China in the 16th century and emphasizes the construction of the inner–outer distinction in their earliest accounts. The next section turns to the adoption of this distinction in the 17th and 18th centuries and its confluence with the "African hypothesis" regarding the provenance of the buddha. The final section turns to the 19th century, with attention to figures such as Michel-Jean-François Ozeray, Brian Houghton Hodgson, Jean-Pierre Abel-Rémusat, and Eugène Burnouf, providing a new interpretation of the "epistemological" break that occurred among these authors. The conclusion returns to contemporary Buddhist studies scholarship and discusses the implications of the defense made for the view of Masuzawa and Droit.

SIXTEENTH-CENTURY BEGINNINGS

Through the approval of Pope Paul III (1468–1549), the Society of Jesus, or the Jesuits (derived from the Latin *Iesuitas*), was founded in 1540 by Ignatius of Loyola (1491–1556), Francis Xavier (1506–1552), and four of their fellow priests as a religious order within the Catholic Church engaged in evangelization of Christian doctrine. The aim of the Jesuits was, at least in part, to disseminate Christian teachings across the world, which was in accord with the Counter-Reformation of the Catholic Church and its effort to stem the spread of Protestant Christianity. As early as 1541, Francis Xavier and a team of Jesuits had landed in Goa, and by 1547 the group had claimed it as Portuguese Malacca. While there, Xavier encountered a Japanese man by the name of Anjirō (born *c.* 1511), who had fled Japan after committing murder. Anjirō converted to Christianity and traveled with Xavier back to Goa, where he studied at the College of St. Paul.

Anjirō regaled the Jesuits with stories of the religion of his homeland, which, based on his description, was remarkably similar to Catholic Christianity: belief in a single creator God, veneration of saints and angels, a divine feminine character who holds her child in her arms, and scheduled and calendrical chanting in a language only known by the literate elite.[6] Given Anjirō's knowledge of Japanese religious practices and beliefs, Xavier employed him as his translator. According to App, what would ensue when the Jesuits arrived in Japan in 1549 would set the stage for the first European awareness of Buddhism and the construction of so-called Oriental philosophy, that is, the atheistic, materialistic doctrine at the core of all the philosophies and religions found from Greece and Egypt to India, China, Tibet, and Japan.[7]

Initially, the Jesuits were received warmly by the Japanese, as Anjirō had introduced them as being from Tenjiku—the Japanese term for India.[8] As a result, the Japanese thought the Jesuits were Indian Buddhists bringing news of the tradition from the motherland. Further, Anjirō had translated *Deus* as "Dainichi," which is the Japanese translation for Mahāvairocana Buddha—the principal buddha for Shingon Buddhism. According to Jason Ānanda Josephson, Anjirō's choice of terms in translating *Deus* has a history in the Shingon tradition, to which Anjirō formerly belonged. On Josephson's reading, Anjirō's translation assumes *Deus* is simply Dainichi by another name, as the latter is the ultimate reality that manifests itself in numerous names to benefit all beings. Josephson calls this "hierarchical inclusion."[9] When the Jesuits preached to the Japanese, they urged them to pray to Dainichi and, to the missionaries' confusion, their audience was unfazed by this.

It quickly dawned on Xavier and his companions that Anjirō's translation work had caused some serious misunderstandings, which led them to question the veracity of what Anjirō had told them about Japanese religion. The Jesuits quickly did an about-face, telling their audiences they should *not* worship Dainichi, whose law was a diabolical invention. Whereas before they were eager to identify themselves as Buddhists and avail themselves of the resources provided by the Buddhists, the Jesuits now strongly asserted they were *not* Buddhists. Further, whereas they had been open to translating Christian ideas into Buddhist terms, Xavier and the Jesuits now proclaimed that *Deus*, in both name and essence, could not be translated into such terms.[10]

The remaining years of the Jesuit mission in Japan, which ended in 1587, were dedicated to acquiring a proper understanding of Japanese religion so it could be refuted from a Christian perspective. The Jesuits were primarily interested in understanding the teachings of Zen, as they understood that the elite mostly followed this tradition. They thought that if they could convert the elite to Christianity, the masses would soon follow. Fortunately, the Jesuits encountered two priests who could help them in this effort: Paulo Chōzen, a former high-ranking priest in the Tendai school, and Vincente Tōin, the son of a convert who was well-read on Zen.[11] Despite having the expertise of Chōzen and Tōin at their disposal there appears to have been a serious misunderstanding of Buddhist teachings among the Jesuits.

According to the earliest Jesuit accounts of Buddhism in Japan, such as the 1556 *Summary of Errors* (*Sumario dos erros*) by Cosme de Torres (1510–1570) and the 1586 *Catechism of the Christian Faith* (*Catechismus Christianae fidei*) by Alessandro Valignano (1539–1606), the buddha had initially taught a doctrine advocating moral virtue, endorsing postmortem retribution for good and bad actions, positing the existence of divine beings, and promoting ritual practices of making offerings. Yet, on his deathbed, the buddha recanted this teaching and proclaimed to his closest disciples that there was nothing after death and that only the four elements (Skt. *Mahābhuta*; Jp. *shidai*) exist. These elements, it was believed, emerged from a chaotic and formless *materia prima*—an elaborate translation of the Japanese Zen concept of "the fundamental part" or the "gist of the matter" (*honbun*). These accounts also describe the buddha teaching a series of successive doctrines, claiming each prior one to be untrue, and recanting all of them in his final moments and asserting the doctrine of the materia prima.

What we now understand as the doctrine of "skillful" or "expedient" means (Skt. *upāyakauśalya*; Jp. *hōben*) in Mahāyāna Buddhism appeared to the Jesuits as kind of "holy lie" (*mentira virtuosa*), which split the buddha's teachings into an exoteric doctrine of heavens and hells and an esoteric doctrine of atheistic materialism.[12] The account of the buddha's successive teachings derives from the "doctrinal classification" (*kyōsō hanjaku*) scheme of arranging the sutras according to when they were taught in the Buddha's lifetime as well as reflecting their proximity to the ultimate truth. These systems originated in China, where the Tiantai and Huayan schools developed their own unique approaches. The Japanese iterations of these schools held to these classifications, and the new schools that emerged in the Kamakura period (1192–1333), such as the Pure Land and Nichiren schools, developed their own means of classifying the sutras based on skillful means and proximity to the truth.

In their accounts, the Jesuit missionaries sought to portray Buddhist thought through the lens of the Catholic scholastic philosophy their authors had studied in Europe. As App states, in their ignorance of God's creation of the universe ex nihilo, Japanese Buddhists appeared to the Jesuits

> exactly like the heathen Greek and Roman philosophers that were criticized by the Christian commentators of Aristotle ... [who] blindly assert that everything must have arisen by chance from a *materia prima* or 'chaos' that is seen as eternal.[13]

From the perspective of the Jesuits encountering Buddhism,

> Shaka's ultimate teaching thus fits the pattern that students of scholastic philosophy had learned to identify as typical of ancient Greek and Roman atheism: the denial of an omnipotent and omniscient creator God in favor of an eternal chaos or materia prima from which all beings, like waves in water, arise only by chance only to eventually dissolve again into chaos in an endless cycle of birth and death.[14]

What App is pointing to here is that the Jesuits had at their disposal a ready-made category by which they understood the buddha's teachings: namely, the "heathen" Greek and Roman philosophers who did not acknowledge the divine creation of the universe. Alongside their understanding of *upāya* as a "holy lie," this profile of the Greco-Roman philosopher, it seems, provided the rationale for the Jesuit's construal of Buddhism as having an "inner" philosophy of nothingness and an "outer" religion of morality, elaborate rituals, heavens, hells, miracles, celestial beings, and so on.

For whatever garbled version of Buddhist thought these texts contain, App attempts to give their authors credit for introducing such thought to Europe. Of the *Summary of Errors*, App notes, "the fact that this 'law' [Buddhadharma, *buppō*] is said to have a number of sects, a founder, a founding scripture, and clergy in several Asian countries proves that Europeans already in 1556 regarded *buppō* (Buddhism) as a religion."[15] The overarching argument of App's *Cult of Emptiness* is that the European "discovery" of Buddhism as a "world religion" occurred not in the 19th century, as posited by Masuzawa, but in the 16th, when Francis Xavier and his Jesuit companions encountered Zen Buddhism in Japan. While it cannot be denied that the Jesuits were the first Europeans to have a prolonged engagement with Buddhists and their teachings, App's overarching argument is tenuous on two counts: (a) the notion of a religion as an institution with a founder, sacred scripture, clergy, and a series of sects had yet to be established in European thought; and (b) their means of registering what they encountered in Japan relied on other frameworks.

According to Peter Harrison, our contemporary notion of "religion," both in the singular and the plural, which App appeals to in his claim regarding the Jesuits in Japan, was first formed in the mid-16th century. Harrison points to the 1555 Peace of Augsburg between Charles V (1500–1558) of the Holy Roman Empire and the Schmalkaldic League, an alliance of Lutheran princes in the Holy Roman Empire, as an early example of a document recognizing plural religions. "The settlement was momentous," Harrison states, "because it provided the permanent division of the Holy Roman Empire, premised on the idea that religious differences could be given objective formulation and that the inhabitants of particular territories could be identified on the basis of their religion."[16] The Augsburg settlement recognized two "religions" (*Religionen*): the "old religion" (*alten Religion*, Catholicism) and the "Augsburg Confession," the latter of which is articulated in twenty-eight articles.[17] Furthermore, the settlement established the legal principle "whose land, his religion," which designates the religion of the sovereign as that of the territory. The settlement also allowed its two acknowledged "religions" to be understood not only as a set of codified beliefs but as a political and legal construct.[18]

The early modern period in Europe was marked by "wars of religion." The conventional view of these events holds that,

> the inadequacies of the Augsburg settlement led to the disastrous "wars of religion" that ravaged Europe for decades. In this version of events, religiously fueled violence was only brought to an end by the formation of the modern state, which banished religion to the private sphere, limiting its capacity to promote a sectarian violence based on irrational and mutually incompatible beliefs.[19]

While not dismissive of the role "religion" played in these conflicts or the emergence of the modern, secular state from them, Harrison notes that these conflicts were about the territorial disputes between the rival Bourbons and Hapsburgs, and Protestants and Catholics found themselves on the same side of a conflict as much as on opposing sides. Nevertheless,

> the idea of plural religions as codified sets of beliefs and specific practices that can exist independently of political considerations and are capable of relegation to a 'private sphere' was one of the end products of this process of state building.[20]

The development of "religion" seems to have involved some contradictory moves: First, it was newly *internalized* as belonging to the "private" conscience of individuals, outside of the realm of the public. Second, it was *externalized* as articles of belief and territorial designations. Religion both defines the boundaries of a secularized public space (territory) and transcends it as private belief. This contradictory construction of religion would set the groundwork for understanding it as a consciously held set of beliefs that inform publicly observable behaviors and practices. This understanding itself is the precondition for the "scientific" study of religion, which would come into its own in the 19th century. As Europe was being territorialized along lines of religious identity, Europeans were beginning to colonize the Americas, Africa, and Asia and were encountering other religious traditions in the process. "In much the same way that religious difference was now a feature of geography in Europe," Harrison states, "an analogous religious differentiation was thought to characterize the whole of the globe."[21] The earliest schema or taxonomy for the religions of the world held that there were four categories: Christians; Jews; Muslims; and heathens, idolators, or pagans.

According to Masuzawa, this fourfold schema recurs "in book after book with little variation from at least the seventeenth century up to the first half of the nineteenth century."[22] She provides two frameworks for understanding this schema: (a) that it presents us "three individually distinct religions and one generic type, under which all the rest are subsumed"; and (b) that it recognizes only one religion,

> alongside it were two forms of deviance; and as for the rest, they were nations bereft of religion altogether. . . . In sum, either there were countless religions or there was only one, yet, somehow both were true. The elasticity of the taxonomic system variously and flexibly enabled the demarcation of "our" sanctified domain from "their" state of perdition, but it enabled little else.[23]

Harrison and Masuzawa both point out how this taxonomy did not identify the four "religions" of the world as systems of belief but as nations, territories, or peoples. As Masuzawa puts it, this taxonomy "recognizes 'Christians,' 'Jews,' 'Mohammedans,' and 'heathens,' rather than different 'isms' that supposedly prescribe different spiritual cosmologies and so-called worldviews particular to each of these different peoples."[24] Furthermore, both of them stress the empirical and haphazard way in which the numerous accounts of the four "religions" were composed. On the one hand, Harrison contends that such accounts of "religions" reverse-engineered the beliefs from observation of the practices, and thus served to bolster the notion that "religions" were to be identified through observable behaviors that are related to beliefs.[25] On the other hand, Masuzawa argues that the authors of such works during this period seem "far more interested in collecting and enumerating empirical particularities and material details than in discovering any organizational principle that might help to synthesize these particulars and details."[26] According to Masuzawa, the aim of encyclopedic collections on religion, such as *The Ceremonies and Religious Customs of the Various Nations of the World*, edited by Bernard Picart (1673–1733) and Jean Frédéric Bernard (1683–1744), was neither to contribute to a "science of religion" nor to "offer practical intelligence considered efficacious for the vocational training of future missionaries."[27]

Rather, Masuzawa conjectures that this work and others like it were composed with the leisure class mind:

> Readers of these books expected above all else to be amused and diverted by the narratives of exotic lore, travels, and adventures abroad, and to be charmed and transported by the exquisite plates and engravings that often lavishly accompanied such accounts.[28]

Masuzawa alludes to the fact that these early modern encyclopedic works on the "religions" of the world drew their information on the non-Christian "religions" predominantly from the writings of Christian missionaries. Here we come to a reprise of the Jesuits in the 16th century. Regarding App's claim that the *Summary of Errors* identifies *buppō* as a "religion," we can see issues with this claim from App in what Harrison has presented. According to Harrison, the notion of plural "religions" as codified sets of beliefs and practices that correspond to various territories was only beginning to form in the mid-16th century, at the very time the *Summary of Errors* was being written halfway across the globe—and without news of such developments from Europe.[29] Further, as we saw with Masuzawa, the fourfold categorization of "religions" prevalent from the 17th century to the early 19th century presents non-Abrahamic traditions; that is, the "pagan/heathen/idolator" as either a generic type of religion or as the lack of religion altogether. This is to say, "religions" here are not defined in terms of institutions that include sacred texts, numerous sects, and founders but in terms of the beliefs and practices found in various territories of the world. The Jesuits perceived Buddhism as the devil's invention—the outward presentation of true religion without its content. If Buddhism counted as a "religion" at all for these 16th-century Jesuits, it was in a profoundly different sense than it was for Burnouf and the others involved in the European "discovery" of Buddhism nearly three centuries later.

The Jesuits found Japanese Buddhists, however clever they seemed, to be living in a world of benighted ignorance. Buddhism, for whatever outward similarities it presented with the true religion, Christianity, was to their minds clearly a devil's trick that the Japanese had been fooled by for many centuries. Contrary to what App claims, the earliest accounts of Buddhism from the Jesuits who landed in Japan did not portray it as a "religion" in our familiar sense. The

Jesuits would not have been aware of the concept because it was just being developed, and their schemes of categorization would not admit Buddhism as a "religion" but as heathen idolatry to be vigorously refuted.

DEVELOPMENTS IN THE 17TH AND 18TH CENTURIES

The Jesuit records of Japanese religions mentioned in the previous section, particularly Valignano's *Catechism of the Christian Faith*, were made available to the European public in the 17th century and were met with tremendous interest. The *Catechism* and its explanation of the atheistic, materialistic philosophy at the core of Buddhism was fodder for the speculations of Jesuit figures such as João Rodrigues (1561–1633) and Athanasius Kircher (1602–1680).[30] Rodrigues attempted to identify Valignano's writings on Buddhism an "oriental ur-philosophy," which he attributed to the biblical Ham and Zoroaster, who he thought were identical. According to Rodrigues, this oriental ur-philosophy had its origins in Chaldea, Persia, and India, and spread out both eastward to China and westward to Egypt and Greece. Kircher similarly offered a theory of "pan-Asian religion," as App puts it. According to Kircher, Egypt is the cradle of this religion and the buddha was an Egyptian priest of Ethiopian extraction who fled his homeland and traveled to India, spreading Buddhism across Asia. Despite differences in their theories, App claims that "both Rodrigues and Kircher saw Asian religions and philosophies as branches of a single root-heresy. . . . both posited a fundamental unity of doctrine not only embracing much of Asia but also the Greek and Roman world."[31]

In 1615, Nicolas Trigault published a Latin translation of the journals of Matteo Ricci (1552–1610) entitled *De Christiana expeditione apud Sinas*. Ricci, a Jesuit missionary, had traveled extensively in China from 1582 to 1610 and had studied Buddhist teachings during his time there. Ricci's journals describe his astonishment at what he deemed the idolatry practiced by Chinese Buddhists. He referred to Buddhism as "unnatural and hideous fiction of idol worship" and viewed Buddhist monastics as "vile and abject."[32] Taoism, according to Ricci, due to its similarities with certain Christian doctrines, was the work of the devil.[33] Ricci considered Confucianism as a moral philosophy and deemed it compatible with if not complementary to Christianity.[34] Ricci's journals would provide more material for the speculations of Europeans in the centuries to follow, particularly on the subjects of comparative religion, philosophy, and linguistics.[35]

Non-Jesuit sources also played a role in presenting Buddhism and Buddhists to Europeans at this time. One prominent example from this category is *The History of Japan* by Engelbert Kaempfer (1651–1716), a Westphalian-born Dutch doctor. Kaempfer traveled throughout Asia, first with a Swedish envoy to Persia and then with the Dutch East India Company, landing in Japan in 1690 where he remained for two years. Assisted by his servant, Imamura Gen'emon Eisei (1671–1736), Kaempfer was able to compile an extensive history of Japan, which was published posthumously in 1727. His account includes a description Buddhism, which he calls "Budsdo, or Foreign Pagan Worship."[36] Much like Kircher, he was convinced that there was not one but two buddhas: the first one of these buddhas was an ancient god not unlike those of Greece or Egypt; and the other was "some new Impostor who set up but about five hundred years before Christ's nativity."[37] This conclusion from Kaempfer comes from his experiences in India, where he would have noticed the buddha included as an *avatara* of

Vishnu. For Kaempfer, Hinduism is Egyptian in origin, as the two central tenets of the Egyptian religion—"the Transmigration of Souls and a Veneration for Cows"—were present in the beliefs and practices of the Hindus he encountered.[38]

Further, Kaempfer concludes that the buddha was a priest from Memphis who escaped Persian emperor Cambyses II's campaign of slaughter, fled to India, and taught his Egyptian doctrines. Kaempfer based this on sources he consulted in Ceylon, Siam, and Japan that described Cambyses II (559–522 BCE) conquering Egypt and subverting the Egyptians' religion by killing their holy cow and their priests around the time the buddha emerged in India.[39] Kaempfer was confident in his claim about the African provenance of the buddha due to the superficial similarities among Indian and Egyptian religious beliefs and the regular depiction of the buddha with dark, kinky hair. "This saint," Kaempfer claims, "being represented with curled Hairs, like a Negro, there is room to conclude, that he was no native of India, but was born under the hot Climate of Africa."[40] This conjecture has come to be known as the "African hypothesis" regarding the buddha's origins, which would be taken as definitive by European savants for a century.

We should note that Kaempfer was not the only one to suppose there were two Buddhas. Another figure to make this claim was the Augustinian friar Antonio Agostino Giorgi (1711–1797) in his 1762 Latin work *Alphabetum Tibetanum*, which chronicled the Capuchin mission to Tibet of 1708–1745. Donald S. Lopez, Jr. describes Giorgi's work as "a huge and vexing text, filled with some accurate information and much fanciful theorizing, with words in Greek, Hebrew, Arabic, Devanagari, and Tibetan script appearing on many of the work's more than nine hundred pages."[41] According to Giorgi, the two buddhas were named *Butta* and *Xaca*. The former was in Giorgi's estimation a fabrication of "heathen myths," by which he means that this Buddha was derived from the ancient Egyptian god Osiris. The latter was "invented by Gnostic, Basilidian, Manichean, and sacrilegious legends of the Pseudo-Christians."[42] Giorgi believed that the second Buddha, *Xaca*, was a confabulation of heretical Christians and the Manicheans introduced to India, China, and Tibet in late antiquity. While this theory strikes the contemporary reader as strange, Giorgi's work was once considered authoritative. Immanuel Kant (1724–1804), for example, cited it in his own studies of religion and geography.[43]

Two works introduced accounts of Buddhism from Jesuits and colonial travelogues to new audiences eager to learn about foreign curiosities: Bernard and Picart's *The Ceremonies and Religious Customs of the Various Nations of the World*, published in French between 1723 and 1742 and in English between 1733 and 1739, and the *Encyclopédie* (1751–1772) by Jean le Rond d'Alembert (1717–1783) and Denis Diderot (1713–1774). *Ceremonies* is still considered a valuable resource for information on religions during the Enlightenment, and Volume 4, which covers religion in Laos, Vietnam, Sri Lanka, Siam, Japan, and China, includes descriptions of Buddhism. Here Bernard and Picart explain, among other things, the Buddha's teachings, which include atheism, nothingness, the transmigration of souls, and the annihilation of the body and soul as the *desideratum* of the life of virtuous practice. They also speculate on his African origins, his biography, his meditative pose, and his relationship, historically and spiritually, to Jesus.[44]

In a similar fashion, the *Encyclopédie* includes an entry on "*Siaka*," which identifies this character with the *budso* of Japan, with *foë* of China, *visnou* or *buda* of India, and *sommonacodum* of Siam.[45] The entry notes that as the Buddha was dying, he told his many disciples that his teachings were all wrapped in a "veil of metaphors," and his true teaching was that: "there is . . . nothing real in the world, but nothingness and the void: this is the principle of all things; do not seek anything beyond, and do not place your confidence in anything else."[46] The entry further states that, following the buddha's death, his disciples divided his teachings into the "nothingness" view just expressed and an esoteric form, which taught the immortality and transmigration of the soul; the reward of good deeds by rebirth in *gokurakf* (Jp. *gokuraku*), which is presided over by Amida (Amitābha Buddha); punishment for misdeeds in *dsigokf* (Jp. *jigoku*), presided over by Jemma (Jp. Enma Ō); and a moral code that forbade "killing any living creature, committing adultery, lying, and using strong drink."[47] In both the *Encyclopédie* and *Ceremonies*, we can see that the buddha is understood to have taught an inner, esoteric materialistic doctrine *as well as* an outer, exoteric moral philosophy; that is, they do little more than parrot the accounts found in the *Summary* and the *Catechism* of de Torres and Valignano, respectively.

The latter half of the 18th century marked a turning point in European history, which began with the Seven Years' War (1756–1763) and the establishment of British colonial rule of India in 1765. Whereas the former event set the stage for the American, French, and Haitian revolutions; the latter event had implications for the European study of Asian language, literature, and religions. Each of these events had a reciprocal relationship with the Enlightenment, both influencing and being influenced by the *philosophes* and savants of the period. Chinese language and philosophy were of particular interest among the early Enlightenment thinkers. Lopez notes that the German polymath Gottlieb Wilhelm Friedrich von Leibniz (1646–1716) "was among many European thinkers of the 17th century who admired China for their rationality, and so condemned the introduction of idolatry into the realm, blaming it on the Buddha."[48] However, as the 18th century went on, Enlightened minds would turn their curiosity more and more to India; away from Chinese rationality and toward Indian mysticism.

Abraham Hyacinthe Anquetil-Duperron (1731–1805) returned to his native France as the Seven Years' War was ending. Anquetil-Duperron had spent the previous six years studying with Zoroastrian priests in India, known as "Parsis," under whose guidance he acquired "a working knowledge of Sanskrit, modern Persian, and its ancient ancestors Avestan and Middle Persian—plus scores of manuscripts in all these tongues."[49] In 1771, Anquetil-Duperron published a partial translation of the *Zend-Avesta*, becoming, as James Turner notes, "the first European to decipher an ancient language of Asia no longer in use . . . cracking open a window that would vastly widen Europe's view of the past."[50] However, Anquetil-Duperron's translation and the very authenticity of the *Zend-Avesta* were called into question by a young Sir William Jones (1746–1794), who was then still a student at Oxford studying Arabic, Persian, and Hebrew.

In an anonymous letter composed in French and published as a pamphlet, Jones voiced his suspicion that Anquetil-Duperron did not have the skills in modern Persian to properly understand his Parsi teachers and his teachers did not have enough facility in the Zend language to relay its contents clearly to Anquetil-Duperron. Based on his expectations of what an ancient religious text *should* contain, Jones thought the content of the *Zend-Avesta* was too fanciful and repetitive to be authentic.[51] Others, including Voltaire (1698–1778) and Diderot, joined the chorus against Anquetil-Duperron. Despite the fact that Jones later recanted his attacks against Anquetil-Duperron, the latter's reputation never recovered from these accusations in his lifetime, but his efforts were eventually validated by Burnouf's translation of a commentary on the *Yasna*, a Zoroastrian liturgical text, in the 1830s.

Less than a decade into its governance of India, the British East India Company (EIC) had faced a severe financial crisis due to a series of faulty trading decisions, which led to parliamentary action to regulate it. In order to curb corruption and make the EIC answerable to Parliament, the Regulating Act of 1773 established the position of Governor-General of India and a Supreme Court, with offices located in Calcutta. Warren Hastings (1732–1811), who was Governor of Bengal, was appointed to the position of Governor-General in 1774. During his time in India, Hastings is said to have gained proficiency in Bengali, Hindustani, and Persian, and was known to be in possession of Bernard and Picart's *Ceremonies*. As General of Bengal, Hastings had attempted to create a singular judicial system that incorporated Hindu and Muslim legal codes in matters pertaining to religious observance and customs; he also drafted a proposal for a professorship of Persian to be installed at Oxford. Neither initiative was met with enthusiasm. In his new role as Governor-General, he had the means and ability to put his plans into action.

His plan for a singular legal system for India involved the translation of Hindu and Muslim legal codes into English. While the Brahmins were not at all forthcoming when it came to letting foreigners study their sacred texts, it was nothing a little money could not solve. Hastings offered generous inducements to British civil servants, Brahmin pandits, and Muslim maulavis willing to be involved in translation efforts, producing considerable results. Among the first generation of civil servant orientalists involved in Hastings's translation projects were Nathaniel Brassy Halhed (1751–1830) and Charles Wilkins (1749–1836). Bengali pandits, such as Baneshvara Vidyalankara, Radhakanta Tarkavagisha, and Jagannatha Tarkapañcanana (1694–1807), were employed by the EIC to aid them in their work.[52]

By 1776, Halhed had, with the help of some eleven Bengali pandits, composed his *Code of Gentoo Laws*, which included a full translation of the Persian version of the Sanskrit *Vivadarnavasetu* (Bridge of the sea of litigation), a digest of Hindu law codes, and excerpts from *Bhagavad Gita*, the *Bhagavata Purana*, and other Sanskrit texts;. He also produced a Bengali grammar in 1788.[53] Wilkins created a type set for Bengali by 1778, established the first vernacular printing press in India, and most importantly produced the first English translations of the *Bhagavat Gita* and the *Hitopadesha* in 1785 and 1787, respectively.[54]

We now return to Jones, who began the months-long voyage to Bengal in 1783, arriving there in early 1784. Having abandoned a career as an Oxford-educated orientalist solely for the reason that it did not pay well—and it is true that he struggled to find work—he studied law and assumed work as a jurist. Jones was appointed to a position on the Supreme Court of Calcutta. The difficulties he encountered working with the Brahmin pandits prompted Jones to study Sanskrit, first with the Vaidya scholar Ramalocana Kanthavarna and then with Radhakanta Tarkavagisha. As a curious person and avid learner, Jones also established the Asiatic Society of Bengal, whose membership included those interested in learning about Asia and its civilizations. His efforts in studying Sanskrit and cultivating knowledge through the Asiatic Society would prove fruitful. Between 1784 and his untimely death in 1794, Jones would translate a number of Hindu Sanskrit texts into English. His most widely known work was *Sacontalá, or the Fatal Ring*, a 1789 translation of the *Abhijñanashakuntala* by the dramatist Kalidasa (ca. 4th–5th century CE). This work, Jones's translation of the *Manavadharmashastra*, and the *Bhagavat Gita* by Wilkins sparked a "sudden rage for ancient Indian culture" in Europe.[55]

Besides his translations, Jones is noteworthy for his contribution to the history of modern philology. His studies of the Sanskrit language led him to the conclusion that it shared roots with Persian and European languages, such as Greek, Latin, German, and the Celtic languages, identifying a language family we now refer to as Indo-European.[56] This observation, found in his presidential address to the Asiatic Society of Bengal of February 2, 1786, has come to be referred to as the "philologer's passage." As Turner notes,

> Jones in effect invented a new *kind* of philology. The concept of language families formed by genealogical descent gave students of language a novel way to classify languages and track their development. This fresh approach retained philology's central dogma of historical comparison. But it radically changed what to compare and the kind of conclusions to be drawn from the comparison.[57]

Although Jones helped to reinvent philology in an age of revolutions, he did little for European knowledge of Buddhism.

Like Kaempfer before him, Jones had noticed the curious status of the buddha in India.

> The Brahmans universally speak of the Bauddhas [Buddhists] with all the malignity of an intolerant spirit . . . yet the most orthodox among them consider Buddha himself as an incarnation of Vishnu: this is a contradiction hard to be reconciled.[58]

In several passages, Jones refers to the buddha as a reformer of the Brahmin tradition, but he is also unclear as to whether the buddha is a historical or mythological figure.[59] Following Giorgi's lead, Jones chooses to split the knot and suppose there were two buddhas: one mythical, one historical. According to Jones, the first buddha is the mythical *avatara* of Vishnu. The second, historical buddha is of African origin. He claims that the people living in the Bengal and Bihar regions of India were originally from the African continent, particularly Ethiopia, and that the buddha images seen in the region are evidence of this.[60]

Jones even consults the *Amarakosha* by Amarasimha (ca. 4th century CE) to justify his supposition that there were two buddhas. According to Jones, the *Amarakośa* provides eighteen names of "Buddha-in-general," such as "*Muni, Sastri, Munindra, Vinacaya, Samantabhadra, Dhermaraja, Sugata* and the like," and the names of a "particular-Buddha-*Muni*-who-descended-in-the-family-of-Sacya," such as "*Sacyamuni, Sacyasinha, Servarthasiddha, Saudhodani, Gautama, Arcabandhu*, or kinsman of the sun, and *Mayadevisuta*, or child of Maya."[61] Finding no resolution in the *Amarakosha*, Jones turns to his teachers, Radhakanta and Ramalocana, for answers. Radhakanta explained that the first set of names includes general epithets and the second set lists proper names, or patronymics, of one person. Rāmalocana noted that "Buddha might mean a sage or a philosopher, though *Budha* was the word commonly used for a mere wise man without supernatural powers."[62] Jones concludes that the *Sacyasinha* Buddha, whom the Brahmins praised, was the *avatara* of Vishnu, and the *other* Buddha was a latter-day follower of the first, who assumed "his name and character, attempted to oversee the whole system of the Brahmans, and was the cause of that persecution, from which the Bauddhas are known to have fled into very distant regions."[63] Locating the two buddhas historically was, for Jones, a lynchpin for providing an accurate chronology of Indian civilization from its earliest moments to his present. Yet to do so, Jones relies on figures such as Giorgi, who were working entirely from secondhand information.

The early works of de Torres, Valignano, Rodrigues, Kircher, Giorgi, and Kaempfer were the main sources of information for Europeans' knowledge of Buddhism and its various iterations across Asia. The claims of these figures—particularly the notion that the buddha taught an inner materialist and outer moralist doctrine, the idea that there were "two buddhas," and the so-called African hypothesis—remained influential throughout the 18th century, with works by Bernard and Picart, Diderot, D'Alambert, and Jones. The next section investigates the 19th-century "discovery" of Buddhism as an artifact of modern philology, with particular attention to Burnouf's 1844 *Introduction to the History of Indian Buddhism.*

THE "DISCOVERY" OF BUDDHISM IN THE 19TH CENTURY

The efforts of Jones, Halhed, and Wilkins, as well as Alexander Hamilton (1762–1824; a cousin of the American statesman by the same name), and Henry Thomas Colebrooke (1765–1837) would be influential in the establishment of a new subfield in modern philology: Indology. Typically, histories of Indology draw a line from the British civil servants trained in India, such as Wilkins, Hamilton, and Colebrooke; to their French and German students; and onward through successive generations of scholars through the 19th century. However, since that historical line is focused on Hindu Sanskrit literature, a detailed recounting of it is not necessary here. Suffice it to say that Indologists in Europe benefited from a productive tension—both in terms of professional appointments and intellectual resources—with classical philologists. Though obscure in its time, Michel-Jean-François Ozeray's (1764–1859) *Research on Buddou or Bouddou, Religious Teacher of East Asia* has been described as the "First Western Book on Buddhism and Buddha."[64]

Ozeray's approach and the conclusions he reached were ahead of their time, but only by a few decades. Ozeray did not rely on missionary sources, only on travelogues; and unlike his contemporaries, he supposed there was only *one* buddha who had *one* teaching (the exoteric moral one).[65] Further, Ozeray was unique in supposing that the Buddha was a human being who was later deified. "It is a fact that cannot be contested," Ozeray claims:

> Buddha is a famous personage who has not been wrested from oblivion by an industrial annalist or an able antiquarian. He has not become known through an inscription or a medallion but rather through his life and his morals. Removed from the altar on which blindness and superstition had placed him, Buddha is a distinguished philosopher (*un philosophe distingué*), a sage born for the happiness of his fellow creatures and for the good of humanity.[66]

But why *was* the Buddha placed upon that vaunted altar? Why was he not remembered simply as a distinguished philosopher? For Ozeray, the answer lies in the character of Asian peoples as uniquely superstitious. In Ozeray's view, people of all civilizations "appear hungry for marvels," but it is only Asia that "lacks all spirit of critique and analysis, [and] adopts with extreme ease the most extravagant fables." Ozeray firmly believed that the divinization of the buddha simply could not have taken place in Europe.[67]

Ozeray was just one of several voices challenging the consensus of the previous century. Two key figures who joined in during the 1820s were the French Sinologist Jean-Pierre Abel-Rémusat (1788–1832) and Brian Houghton Hodgson (1801–1894), an EIC Resident based in Kathmandu, Nepal. Abel-Rémusat was deeply critical of the African hypothesis, and he published an essay entitled "On Some Epithets of the Buddha, which Show that Buddha Did Not Belong to the Black Race" not once but twice, first in the *Journal des savans* in 1819 and again in *Mélanges asiatiques* in 1826. In his essay, Abel-Rémusat looks to the descriptions of the thirty-two *mahāpuruṣa lakṣaṇa*, or "marks of a great person," and *anuvyañjana*, or eighty minor attributes of the buddha found in the *Amarakosha* to demonstrate that the buddha's traits "belong obviously to the Indian race, and that it is impossible to apply to that of the blacks of Africa."[68] Three traits, according to Abel-Rémusat, clearly betray the Indian provenance of the Buddha: his *suvarṇavarṇā*, or golden complexion, his *urdhvagoroma*, or bluish-black hair, and his *tunganasah*, or "prominent" nose.[69]

Abel-Rémusat also points to the unanimous agreement among the Buddhist traditions regarding the Indian character of the buddha as further evidence for his claim:

> His [i.e., the Buddha's] birth once admitted as a historical fact, all traditions, without exception, agree to place it in kingdoms of central India: it is a fact established by too many testimonies, all agree together, independent of each other, so that it is necessary to stop there.[70]

Unfortunately, Abel-Rémusat's life was cut short by cholera in 1832. At the time of his passing, he was working on a translation of the *Foguoji* (Record of Buddhist kingdoms) by the Chinese Buddhist pilgrim Faxian (337– ca. 422 CE). While the text itself was fairly short, Abel-Rémusat compiled effusive notes on the places mentioned in the record to elucidate their importance for the chronology of the Buddha's life and for the early history of Indian Buddhism. Abel-Rémusat's translation, entitled *Foe kuoe ki; ou, relations de royaumes bouddhique*, was published posthumously in 1836 with the help of fellow Sinologists Julius von Klaproth (1783–1835) and Ernest Augustin Xavier Clerc de Landresse (1800–1862). As noted by Lopez, "Until 1844, the *Foe kuoe ki* was the most detailed study of Buddhism to be produced in Europe, and it remains a lasting testimony to how much of the Indian Buddhist tradition can be accurately understood from Chinese sources."[71] Max Deeg shows, however, that Abel-Rémusat's studies and translations did little to move the needle away from the African hypothesis or convince others of the utility of Chinese Buddhist travelogues for historical research.[72] Deeg points out that it was only at the turn of the 20th century that the travelogues by Faxian and other Chinese Buddhist pilgrims would be embraced as a trove of valuable information on early Indian Buddhism.[73]

Hodgson also contributed to the conversation challenging the consensus view of the previous century. Hodgson was educated at the EIC College at Haileybury, where he excelled in his studies of Bengali, political economy, and the classics. He graduated in 1817 and arrived in Calcutta the following year. The climate of Bengal did not suit Hodgson, and between that, his active lifestyle as a young civil servant, and his studies at the College of Fort William, he quickly faced a breakdown in his health. Upon examining Hodgson, his medical adviser gave him this choice: "six feet underground, resign the service, or get a hill-appointment";[74] Hodgson opted for a hill-appointment. This first sent him to Kumaon (present-day Uttarakhand, India) and then to the EIC residency in Kathmandu, where he arrived in October 1820. Hodgson would attempt another assignment in Bengal in 1822, but he fell ill again and returned to Kathmandu. By early 1824, Hodgson was a Resident in Kathmandu, where he would remain for more than two decades. He returned there with a mandate from a superior, Henry Thoby Prinsep (1792–1878), who helped him secure another position at the residency, to "go back to Nepal and master the subject in all its phases."[75]

In the ensuing years, Hodgson would begin to make a name for himself as an orientalist and naturalist. He collected artifacts and texts from Bhotiyan and Tibetan migrants whom he had befriended; he also commissioned local chitrakars, members of the Newar Buddhist artist caste, to draw portraits of the indigenous wildlife and the architecture of various temples. It was through his employment of the chitrakars that he was introduced to the Newar Buddhist pandit and Vajracarya Amritananda (ca. 1774–1835). Amritananda acted as Hodgson's principal informant and supplier of Buddhist manuscripts until his passing in the 1830s. One of Hodgson's earliest studies of Buddhism was his 1828 "Sketch of Buddhism, Derived from the *Bauddha* Scriptures of Nipál," which provides an enumeration of numerous Buddhist texts extant in Sanskrit as well as a set of questions posed to Amritananda on articles of Buddhist thought. Hodgson asks such questions as "How and when was the world conceived?" "What is matter, and what is spirit?" "Is the pleasure of God derived from action or repose?"[76] Amritananda tries to answer these slanted questions to the best of his ability.

Although Hodgson's "Sketch" is better remembered for its erroneous positing of a system of four Buddhist schools—the Svabhavika, Aishvarika, Karmika, and Yatnika—it also contains criticism of the African hypothesis.[77] Question 8 of Hodgson's "Sketch" asks: "What is the reason for the buddha being represented with curled locks?" In Hodgson's rendering, Amritananda notes that the Buddha is said to have had "thirty-two points of beauty (*lakshanas*)," one of which is his curled locks; and "there is no other reason for Buddha's being represented with curled locks."[78] Similar to Abel-Rémusat, Hodgson points out that there is unanimous agreement among the testimony of Buddhists regarding the Indian heritage of the Buddha.

> The Chinese, the Mongols, the Tibetans, the Indo-Chinese, the Japanese, Ceylonese, and other Indian Islanders, all point to India as the father-land of their creed. . . . The records of Buddhism in Nepaul and in Tibet, in both of which countries the people and their mother-tongues are of the Mongol stock, are still either Sanskrit or avowed translations from it by Indian pandits. Nor is there a single record or monument of this faith in existence which bears intrinsic or extrinsic evidence of an extra Indian origin.[79]

For Hodgson and Abel-Rémusat, the unanimity of the Buddhist traditions of Asia on this matter provide sufficient evidence of the Buddha's Indian provenance.

Despite having a learned pandit at his side, Hodgson seems to have gotten several things wrong regarding Buddhism, such as Pali being used prior to Sanskrit for the inscription of Buddhist sutras.[80] However, Hodgson did make some enduring contributions. First, he took a quasi-historicist approach to matters of textual authority—meaning, he presumed that the older a text was, the more authentic it was. Second, he distinguished between Buddhism "*as it is*" and "*as it ought to be*," with the most ancient sources providing the normative account.[81] Third, "Hodgson was convinced . . . that beneath the sundry local manifestations across the continent of Asia, there was indeed something called Buddhism, a view unusual for a colonial official situated amid the particular manifestations of the local religion."[82] In his 1834 essay "European Speculations on Buddhism," Hodgson claims that if Asian Buddhists still "possess and consult the primitive scriptures of their faith, either in their original language, or in careful translations, made in the best age of their church," how can "Buddhism in several countries where it is practically used as the rule of life and of faith, fail to exhibit a common character as to essentials at least?"[83] To the supposition of his time that there is no "common character" to the diversity of Buddhist traditions, Hodgson thought it would be as if to claim that "the Hebrew Old, or Greek New Testament was composed in and for Italy, France, or Spain exclusively."[84] For better or for worse, the notion that there is an original or "primitive" Indian Buddhism, encapsulated in the oldest sources and against which we can compare local traditions, has been a powerful one in the field of Buddhist studies.

Finally, Hodgson's engagement with Amritananda allowed him access to a large corpus of Buddhist texts thought to be lost in their original language, Sanskrit. Hodgson was able to procure copies of these texts and distribute them to archives, Asiatic societies, and university libraries in England, France, and India. Between 1827 and 1845, Hodgson distributed 423 manuscripts. Lopez notes that among them were several foundational texts of the Mahāyāna and Vajrayana Buddhist traditions.[85] The manuscripts Hodgson sent to England and India remained fairly untouched; those that went to the Collège de France in Paris, however, would be put to great use in Burnouf's *Introduction to the History of Indian Buddhism*. It is important to note that we find in neither Ozeray nor Abel-Rémusat nor Hodgson a continuation of the Jesuit claim that the buddha taught two different doctrines. What we find is an emphasis on what can be verified in Buddhist sources and empirical accounts and a crystallization of the notion of the Buddha as a singular person with one teaching.

The finer details of Burnouf's biography and intellectual background have been covered elsewhere.[86] The focus here is on his *Introduction* and its relationship to the Jesuit claim that the buddha taught an inner philosophy of atheistic materialism and an outer doctrine of rebirth and karma. It will have to suffice to state that Burnouf, as a philologist coming up in the early 19th century, saw his task as a philosophical one, tracing out the earliest history of the human mind through critical examination of ancient texts. This orientation landed him on the "philology of facts" (*Sachphilologie*) side of the *Methodenstreit* with August Wilhelm von Schlegel (1767–1845) and Friedrich August Rosen (1805–1837), against the "philology of words" (*Wortphilologie*) represented perhaps best by the work of Franz Bopp (1791–1867).[87]

As noted previously, Burnouf's *Introduction* was based on his study of the Sanskrit manuscripts Hodgson had sent to Paris. It should be noted that Burnouf also consulted texts found in the Tibetan Kanjur collected by the Transylvanian scholar Alexander Csoma de Kőrös (1784–1842), the Pali manuscripts collected by George Turnour (1799–1843), Abel-Rémusat's Chinese translations, and Mongolian texts translated by the Moravian missionary Isaac Jacob Schmidt (1779–1847), among other sources. One clue to his approach is found in the "Preliminary Observations" section of his work, where he points out that many of the texts found in the Tibetan, Mongolian, Burmese, and Chinese canons are translations of Sanskrit and Pali originals; thus, the purpose they serve for his study is to render intelligible the original texts they reproduce.[88] Burnouf's method was to work from primary sources in their original language as much as possible, with the use of translations to cover the places where no original was available. This method, empirical and positivist in its orientation, resembles Hodgson's quasi-historicist supposition of Buddhism *as it is* and *as it ought to be* far more than it resembles the 16th-century Jesuit suppositions regarding Buddhism.

At the close of the "General Description" of his text, Burnouf relays the difficulties he faced in producing it. Burnouf mentions the presence of a small cadre of scholars, resistant to the authority of texts and proudly immovable in their opinions founded on "common sense."[89] Such scholars had not read any texts, but they had already figured out all they needed to know. They claimed Buddhism "a venerable cult born in Central Asia" or "a miserable counterfeit of Nestorianism"; they made the buddha "a Negro, because he had frizzy hair; a Mongol, because he had slanted eyes; a Scythe, because he was called Śākya."[90] What we see here is Burnouf strongly delineating his own approach from that of this small cadre; he is dismissing their speculations about the Buddha as an African (Kaempfer, Kircher) and his teaching as a cult born in Central Asia (Rodrigues, Kircher) or a counterfeit of Nestorianism (Giorgi). Burnouf is *not* relying on the premises found in the Jesuit sources like Rodrigues, Kircher, and Giorgi and is attempting *to do away with them.*

In the rare instances that Burnouf does rely on Jesuit sources, we find that his use of them is critical. The one Jesuit source Burnouf cites with some frequency is Giorgi's *Alphabetum Tibetanum,* which he describes as a compilation that "contains curious information that would merit being verified and extracts of hodgepodge in the middle of which he [Giorgi] has embedded it."[91] Throughout the *Introduction,* one finds Burnouf citing Giorgi only to correct him, especially in the appendix entitled "On the Names of the Gods among the Buddhists."[92] As Lopez observes, "Burnouf's anticlerical sentiments occasionally overwhelm his usually charitable attitude toward the work of other scholars."[93] Notwithstanding his citation of Giorgi, Burnouf's sources for his study are composed in English, French, and German rather than Portuguese, Spanish, or Latin.

Lopez notes that we find four novel approaches in Burnouf's *Introduction*: Indianization, Sanskritization, Textualization, and Humanization. Lopez claims that humanization placed the Buddha "not in a pantheon of idols or even gods, but in a pantheon of philosophers."[94] We might ask how it is that Burnouf humanizes the Buddha to understand him as a philosopher? If he is not relying on the Jesuit sources for his understanding, what resources might he have at his disposal? This is where we turn our attention to the recent study of Burnouf's work by Martino Dibeltulo Concu.

In Section 2 of the *Introduction,* "Discourses of Śākya," Burnouf looks at the literature of the sutras, attempting to understand their content historically and philosophically. He identifies two basic groups of sutras: the group he calls "simply *sutras*" (*simplement* Sûtras), or "ordinary *sutras*" (Sûtras *ordinaire*), and another group he refers to as the sutras of "great development," his translation of the term *mahavaipulya.*[95] It is the ordinary sutras, according to Burnouf, that provide a glimpse into the historical realities of the Buddha's life and time: "the scene of the first [ordinary sutras] is India, the actors are humans and some inferior divinities; and save for the power to make miracles that Śākya and his foremost disciples possess, *what occurs there seems natural and plausible.*"[96] This is to say, the delineation between the two is premised on the plausibility for Burnouf of what is contained in the ordinary sutras, in contrast to the more mythical sutras of great development.

According to Dibeltulo Concu, "The issue of the simple sūtras, then, concerned the definition of Śākyamuni's human life. This definition issued from what Burnouf doubted and what he believed."[97] His primary example of this is Burnouf's gloss on the *Mandhatavadana* of the *Divyavadana*, which recounts the buddha's relinquishment of his psychic powers (*siddhi*), which led to his immanent *parinirvāṇa*, and the karmic roots of this in his previous life as the power-hungry prince Mandhatri. While Dibeltulo Concu notes that Burnouf seriously misunderstands the nature of the buddha's psychic powers due to a translation error, what is important is that Burnouf claims that the buddha's powers are not *plausible* and are therefore a matter of belief. On this basis, Dibeltulo Concu claims that "the relation between Buddhism [as a religion] and philosophy is empowered by what it excludes"; that is, magic, expressed as the buddha's psychic powers.[98] At this point, Dibeltulo Concu argues that the very condition for identifying Buddhism as a philosophy arises from the Jesuit sources of the 16th and 17th centuries.

Whereas Dibeltulo Concu supposes the *tertium quid* in transformation of Buddhism from a religion into a philosophy is magic, this entry proposes that it is "belief"—not just what Burnouf believed but what he presumed Buddhists believe as well. Dibeltulo Concu is correct to point out that the distinction between ordinary sutras and those of great development for Burnouf is founded on what he believed and what he doubted, but it seems that he does not interrogate this distinction in the first place. Bruno Latour has considered the character of "belief" in modern society at some length. According to Latour, "belief" was and is the means by which people who call themselves *modern* delineate themselves from *others*.[99] Not only is belief something *they* do, but we moderns *know* the difference between "fact" and "belief"; *others* are not capable of this distinction. Against the fetish objects of the *other*, the moderns cast themselves as antifetishists; against foreign idolatry, the moderns describe themselves as iconoclasts. We precisely saw this with Ozeray, who stated in his *Research on Buddou* that the Buddha was only deified due to the credulity of Asian people. Much the same logic is at play in Burnouf's *Introduction*.

One example from the *Introduction* illustrates Burnouf's point of view. In discussing the worship of *stupas* and whether the Buddha requested a funeral in the manner of a *cakravartin*, Burnouf is skeptical that *stupa* worship dated back to the Buddha's lifetime. To justify his position, he responds to an objection a Buddhist might make against the "impious doubts of the European skeptic."[100] Speaking as this hypothetical Buddhist, Burnouf notes that record of the Buddha giving away his hair and nail clippings provides a rationale for supposing he wished for his relics to be venerated. Replying as the impious critic, Burnouf finds the objection from his Buddhist plausible, though he notes that the accounts mentioned "are ordinarily mingled with fantastic circumstances," meaning they should be met with more suspicion. Here, he points to Tibetan Buddhist veneration of *lamas* and *tülkus* as an example of worship gone horribly wrong: the "stupid respect they have for their lamas has them prostrating before the most disgusting relics that human superstition has invented."[101]

To Burnouf, it is inconceivable that the "pure and chaste Śākya" could give way to the "ignoble cult" of the Tibetans. It was only by way of a "succession of pitiable analogies" that lead from Shakya to the Tibetan Buddhists, and this itself was due to the "fervor of adoration that has never been lacking in India."[102] Either the facts are true, and one cannot hold that the buddha recommended the veneration of his relics, or they were invented, and one must conclude that "Buddhism, like all human institutions, has been subjected over the course of time to modifications easy to understand, and that the books the tradition has preserved for us have followed this movement and have been modified under its influence."[103] Burnouf can differentiate between the plausible facts of the buddha's life and the inventions of the tradition that followed, but in his view, the Buddhists' "fervor of adoration" keeps them from clearly seeing this delineation—that is, where the European critic is capable, the *other* is not.

This section has shown how figures such as Ozeray, Abel-Rémusat, and Hodgson in the early 19th century sought to challenge the consensus view of the prior century, particularly the African hypothesis. They adopted an empirical and historicist orientation to the study of Buddhism, eschewing the speculative conclusions that were popular at the time. It also considered Burnouf's work in light of the claims made by App and Dibeltulo Concu. Burnouf's statements on his method speak to his decisive break from the assumptions found in the Jesuit sources. His use of Jesuit sources, such as Giorgi, is thoroughly critical; and his identification of the buddha as a human philosopher is premised not on the Jesuit distinction between an inner and outer doctrine, but on his presumption that he could differentiate fact from belief.

CONCLUSION

This article has explored the Jesuit missionary accounts of Buddhism composed in the 16th century, with a focus on the construction of the inner–outer doctrine, and described how these sources were taken up and parroted by others in the 17th and 18th centuries. In the 19th century, Buddhism was "discovered" by European scholars, including Eugène Burnouf, whose work presented a decisive break from the Jesuit sources and their premises. Burnouf's portrayal of the buddha as a human philosopher hinged on his own presumption that he could differentiate fact from belief.

This entry has not focused on Burnouf's *Introduction* and the break it represents to portray Burnouf in a heroic or triumphant manner. Rather, the intention is to shed light on the cultural assumptions that serve as the foundation for the field of Buddhist studies, namely, the assumption by Burnouf, as a modern person, to be able to delineate between facts and belief and the inability of Asian Buddhists to do the same. In defending the position taken by Masuzawa and Droit, this entry has endeavored to show that the "scientific" study of Buddhism that began in the 19th century, while indeed a break from the approach of prior centuries and a step toward more accurate portrayals of Buddhism in Western scholarship, works on deep-seated Eurocentric premises about who is capable of critical thinking and who is not. Of course, there is not much new here, as Masuzawa's study on "world religions" sought to demonstrate the Eurocentric patterns of thought baked into the very concept. What this entry can offer in conclusion, by way of Latour's analysis of "belief" mentioned earlier, is another way to interrogate the distorting efforts of the term itself and how these play out in the field of Buddhist studies.

According to Latour, belief is not a characteristic of nonmodern *others* but is something we suppose they do; thus, the only belief to be found on the scene is our own—"belief in belief" as he calls it. For us moderns, belief in belief depends on and reinforces "the distinction between knowledge and illusion, or rather . . . on the separation of practical life—which does not maintain this distinction—and theoretical life, which maintains it."[104] Just like the *others*, we have our own fetishes—what Latour, playing on the shared etymology of "fact" and "fetish," calls "factishes" (in French it is far more clever wordplay). His example of a factish is Louis Pasteur's observations of and experiments on microbes—something of human manufacture that nonetheless is capable of transcending its maker and gaining an agency of its own. "Whereas we fabricate them [scientific objects such as Pasteur's microbes] in our laboratories with our colleagues, our instruments, and our hands," Latour states, "facts are supposed to become, by some magical effort of reversal, something that no one has ever fabricated."[105] Likewise, we can understand Burnouf's portrayal of the buddha as a human philosopher as a factish; that is, something fabricated at the philologer's desk, which, "by some magical reversal," is taken never to have been fabricated at all. Yet one might be tempted to wonder what the implications of this are for the field and what does the factish tell us about our methodologies?

It means breaking with our antifetishism in theory and recognizing it in our practices. We see this in the act of writing, when we are carried away by what we have written. "In all our activities," Latour states, "what we fabricate goes beyond us. On the same basis as novelists, researchers, or sorcerers, so too politicians are challenged to lie on the Procrustean bed, unless they wish to be called liars."[106] Beginning to recognize this tendency in our practices will help to loosen the grip of the four coordinates of the modern repertoire: subjects, objects, theory, and practice. Recognition of how factishes pass through us can align theory with practice. What is more daunting, however, is working through the subject–object break.

This break between subjects and objects establishes two discrete domains of activity: interiority and exteriority. According to Latour, the interior domain is "filled with hollow dreams, having no reference whatsoever to the reality known only to the exact or social sciences"; this is the domain of beliefs, affects, and fantasies, which have no connection to the facts. The exterior domain is that of intransigent things "out there," the stuff of facts to be discovered by the sciences. Previous attempts to break this down have only sought to render one domain in the terms of the other. For example, the moderns have sought to describe the subject domain as "the temporary capacitance emerging from a neural network; a phenotype of a genotype; the conscious of the unconscious; the 'cultural idiot' of a social structure; a consumer of world markets."[107] Neither is it a matter of *believing with others*, for as far as belief is at play it stands in contradistinction to facts and thereby gets in the way. Rather, following the Chinese adage to look where the finger points and not at the finger itself, Latour suggests that we follow where one's actions go, to pay attention to what our actions produce and how what is produced is capable of transcending the particulars of its fabrication. Following actions and what passes through an action can serve to de-interiorize both ourselves and the *others* we study. While the adoption of postcolonial theory has been quite productive for the field of Buddhist studies, there is more to be done when it comes to grappling with the methodological foundations of the field. I believe Latour's analysis of belief and his notion of the factish, key to his "anthropology of the moderns," can provide direction for this methodological work.

FURTHER READING

Allen, Charles. *The Prisoner of Kathmandu: Brian Hodgson in Nepal, 1820–1843*. London: Haus Publishing, 2015.

Almond, Philip C. *The British Discovery of Buddhism*. New York: Cambridge University Press, 1988.

Amstutz, Galen. *Interpreting Amida: History and Orientalism in the Study of Pure Land Buddhism*. Buddhist Studies Series. Albany: State University of New York Press, 1997.

Berwitz, Stephen C. *Buddhist Poetry and Colonialism: Alagiyavanna and the Portuguese in Sri Lanka*. New York: Oxford University Press, 2013.

Hallisey, Charles. "Roads Not Taken in the Study of Theravāda Buddhism." In *Curators of the Buddha: The Study of Buddhism under Colonialism*. Edited by Donald S. Lopez, Jr., 31–62. Chicago: University of Chicago Press, 1995.

Hösle, Vittorio. "The Search for the Orient in German Idealism." *Zeitschrift der Deutschen Morgenländischen Gesellschaft* 163, no. 2 (2013): 431–454.

Lopez, Donald S., Jr., and Thupten Jinpa. *Dispelling the Darkness: A Jesuit's Quest for the Soul of Tibet*. Cambridge, MA: Harvard University Press, 2017.

Rocher, Rosane, and Ludo Rocher. *The Making of Western Indology: Henry Thomas Colebrooke and the East India Company*. London: Routledge for the Royal Asiatic Society, 2011.

Subrahmanyam, Sanjay. *Europe's India: Words, People, Empires, 1500–1800*. Cambridge, MA: Harvard University Press, 2017.

Waterhouse, David M. "Brian Hodgson: A Biographical Sketch." In *The Origin of Himalayan Studies: Brian Houghton Hodgson in Nepal and Darjeeling, 1820–1858*. Royal Asiatic Society Books Series. Edited by David M. Waterhouse, 1–24. New York, NY: Routledge Curzon, 2004.

NOTES

1. Donald S. Lopez Jr., ed., *Curators of the Buddha: The Study of Buddhism Under Colonialism* (Chicago: University of Chicago Press, 1995).
2. Urs App, *The Birth of Orientalism* (Philadelphia: University of Pennsylvania Press, 2010); and App, *The Cult of Emptiness: The Western Discovery of Buddhism and the Invention of Oriental Philosophy* (Wil, Switzerland: UniversityMedia, 2012.
3. Tomoko Masuzawa, *The Invention of World Religions; Or How European Universalism was Preserved in the Language of Pluralism* (Chicago: University of Chicago Press, 2005); and Roger-Pol Droit, *The Cult of Nothingness: The Philosophers of the Buddha*, trans. David Streight and Pamela Vohnson (Chapel Hill: University of North Carolina Press, 2003).
4. Martino Dibeltulo Concu, "Buddhism, Philosophy, History: On Eugène Burnouf's Simple Sūtras," *Journal of Indian Philosophy* 45 (2017): 473–511; and Donald S. Lopez Jr., "Burnouf and the Birth of Buddhist Studies," *The Eastern Buddhist* 43, nos. 1–2 (2012): 25–34.
5. Bruno Latour, *On the Modern Cult of the Factish Gods*, trans. Heather McLean and Catherine Porter (Durham, NC: Duke University Press, 2010).
6. Urs App, *The Cult of Emptiness*, 12–13.
7. App, *Cult of Emptiness*, 11–77.
8. App, *Cult of Emptiness*, 13.
9. Jason Ānanda Josephson, *The Invention of Religion in Japan* (Chicago: University of Chicago Press, 2012), 26.
10. Josephson, *Invention of Religion in Japan*, 25.
11. App, *Cult of Emptiness*, 34, 53.
12. App, *Cult of Emptiness*, 36.

13. App, *Cult of Emptiness*, 45.
14. App, *Cult of Emptiness*, 45.
15. App, *Cult of Emptiness*, 35.
16. Peter Harrison, *The Territories of Science and Religion* (Chicago: University of Chicago Press, 2015), 97.
17. Eric Lund, ed., *Documents in the History of Lutheranism, 1517–1750* (Minneapolis: Fortress Press, 2002), 170.
18. Harrison, *Territories of Science and Religion*, 97.
19. Harrison, *Territories of Science and Religion*, 98.
20. Harrison, *Territories of Science and Religion*, 98.
21. Harrison, *Territories of Science and Religion*, 99.
22. Masuzawa, *Invention of World Religions*, 59.
23. Masuzawa, *Invention of World Religions*, 60–61.
24. Masuzawa, *Invention of World Religions*, 61.
25. Masuzawa, *Invention of World Religions*, 101–102.
26. Masuzawa, *Invention of World Religions*, 61.
27. Masuzawa, *Invention of World Religions*, 62.
28. Masuzawa, *Invention of World Religions*, 62–63.
29. Harrison, *Territories of Science and Religion.*
30. App, *Cult of Emptiness*, 91–110, 111–128.
31. App, *Cult of Emptiness*, 127.
32. Louis J. Gallagher, trans., *China in the Sixteenth Century: The Journals of Matteo Ricci, 1583–1610*, 2nd ed. (New York: Random House, 1953), 98–99, 101.
33. Gallagher, *China in the Sixteenth Century*, 103.
34. Gallagher, *China in the Sixteenth Century*, 93–98.
35. Gerhard Strasser, "The Impact on the European Humanities of Early Reports from Catholic Missionaries from China, Tibet and Japan Between 1600 and 1700," in *Making of the Humanities, Vol. II: From Early Modern to Modern Disciplines*, ed. Rens Bod, Jaap Maat and Thijs Westeijn (Amsterdam: Amsterdam University Press, 2012), 192.
36. Engelbert Kaempfer, *The History of Japan: Together with a Description of the Kingdom of Siam*, vol. 3 trans. J. G. Scheuchzer (Glasgow: J. Maclehose and Sons, 1906), 2:56.
37. Kaempfer, *History of Japan*, 1:66.
38. Donald S. Lopez Jr., ed., *From Stone to Flesh: A Short History of the Buddha* (Chicago: Chicago University Press, 2013), 66–67.
39. Lopez, *From Stone to Flesh*, 145.
40. Kaempfer, *History of Japan*, 1:66.
41. Donald S. Lopez Jr., ed., *Strange Tales of an Oriental Idol: An Anthology of Early Modern Portrayals of the Buddha* (Chicago: University of Chicago Press, 2016), 142.
42. Lopez, *Strange Tales of an Oriental Idol*, 142.
43. Urs App, "The Tibet of the Philosophers: Kant, Hegel, and Schopenhauer," in *Images of Tibet in the 19th and 20th Centuries*, ed. Monica Esposito (Paris: EFEO, 2008), 18–22.
44. Lopez, *Strange Tales of an Oriental Idol*, 130–138.
45. Lopez, *Strange Tales of an Oriental Idol*, 143.
46. Lopez, *Strange Tales of an Oriental Idol*, 143.
47. Lopez, *Strange Tales of an Oriental Idol*, 143–144.
48. Lopez, *From Stone to Flesh*, 39.
49. James Turner, *Philology: The Forgotten Origins of the Modern Humanities* (Princeton, NJ: Princeton University Press, 2014), 92–93.

50. Turner, *Philology*, 93.
51. William Jones, "Lettre à Monsieur A*** de P***, dans laquelle et compris l'examen de sa traduction des livres attribuées à Zoroastre" (London: Elmisly, 1771).
52. Michael S. Dodson, *Orientalism, Empire, and National Culture: India 1770–1880* (New York: Palgrave Macmillan, 2007), 48–49.
53. Dodson, *Orientalism, Empire, and National Culture*, 23; and Rocher (1983): 48–73.
54. Om Prakash Kejariwal, *The Asiatic Society of Bengal and the Discovery of India's Past* (Delhi: Oxford University Press, 1988), 21.
55. Turner, *Philology*, 99.
56. William Jones, "On the Hindus," *Asiatic Researches* 1 (1788): 415–431. While Jones is often given credit for being the first to identify the Indo-European family of languages, Anquetil-Duperron and others had stumbled on the same conclusion around the same time as Jones, if not prior to him, in their own analyses. See Rosane Rocher, "Lord Monboddo, Sanskrit and Comparative Linguistics," *Journal of the American Oriental Society* 100, no. 1 (1980): 12–17; and Siep Stuurman, "Cosmopolitan Egalitarianism in the Enlightenment: Anquetil Duperron on India and America," *Journal of the History of Ideas* 68, no. 2 (2007): 255–278.
57. Turner, *Philology*, 99 (emphasis in original).
58. William Jones, "On the Chronology of the Hindus," *Asiatic Researches* 2 (1789): 97.
59. William Jones, "On the Gods of Greece, Italy, and India." *Asiatic Researches* 1 (1788b): 221–275.
60. Jones, "On the Hindus," 427–428.
61. Jones, "On the Chronology of the Hindus," 97.
62. Jones, "On the Chronology of the Hindus," 97.
63. Jones, "On the Chronology of the Hindus," 98.
64. Urs App and Michel-Jean-François Ozeray, *The First Western Book on Buddhism and Buddha* (Wil & Paris: UniversityMedia, 2017).
65. App and Ozeray, *First Western Book on Buddhism and Buddha*, 2017.
66. App and Ozeray, *First Western Book on Buddhism and Buddha*, 278–279.
67. App and Ozeray, *First Western Book on Buddhism and Buddha*, 146–147. As noted later, Burnouf's approach bears a striking resemblance to that of Ozeray.
68. Jean-Pierre Abel-Rémusat, "Sur quelques épithètes descriptives de Bouddha, qui font voir que Bouddha n'appartenant pas la race nègre," *Mélanges asiatique*, 1 (1825): 104.
69. Abel-Rémusat, "*Sur quelques épithètes descriptives de Bouddha*," 104–110.
70. Abel-Rémusat, "*Sur quelques épithètes descriptives de Bouddha*," 110.
71. Lopez, *From Stone to Flesh*, 180.
72. Max Deeg, "The Historical Turn: How Chinese Buddhist Travelogues Changed Western Perception of Buddhism," *Hualin International Journal of Buddhist Studies* 1, no. 1 (2018): 49–52.
73. Deeg, "Historical Turn," 62–67.
74. William Wilson Hunter, *Life of Brian Houghton Hodgson, British Resident at the Court of Nepal* (London: John Murray, 1896), 31.
75. Hunter, *Life of Brian Houghton Hodgson*, 84.
76. Brian H. Hodgson, "Sketch of Buddhism, Derived from the Bauddha Scriptures of Nipál," *Transactions of the Royal Asiatic Society of Great Britain and Ireland* 2, no. 1 (1828): 232, 235, 237.
77. David N. Gellner, "Hodgson's Blind Alley? On the So-Called Schools of Nepalese Buddhism," *Journal of the International Association of Buddhist Studies* 12, no. 1 (1989): 7–18; and Donald S. Lopez Jr., ed., "The Ambivalent Exegete: Hodgson's Contribution to the Study of Buddhism," in *The Origin of Himalayan Studies: Brian Houghton Hodgson in Nepal and Darjeeling, 1820–1858*, ed. David M. Waterhouse (New York: Routledge Curzon, 2004), 49–76.

78. Brian H. Hodgson, *Essays on the Language, Literature, and Religion in Nepál and Tibet* (London: Trübner, 1874), 46–47.
79. Hodgson, *Essays on the Language, Literature, and Religion in Nepál and Tibet*, 67.
80. Lopez, "Ambivalent Exegete," 62–63.
81. Hodgson, *Essays on the Language, Literature, and Religion in Nepál and Tibet*, 41.
82. Lopez, "Ambivalent Exegete," 64.
83. Hodgson, *Essays on the Language, Literature, and Religion in Nepál and Tibet*, 100.
84. Hodgson, *Essays on the Language, Literature, and Religion in Nepál and Tibet*, 100.
85. Lopez, "Ambivalent Exegete," 55.
86. See Thomas Calobrisi, "Beyond Belief: How a French Text on Indian Buddhism Changed American Culture," (PhD diss., Graduate Theological Union, 2021), ProQuest no. 28411633, 56–71; Lopez, "Burnouf and the Birth of Buddhist Studies"; Lopez, *From Stone to Flesh*, 195–211; Pascale Rabault-Feuerhahn, *Archive of Origins: Sanskrit, Philology, Anthropology in the 19th Century*, trans. Dominique Bach and Richard Willet (Baden, Germany: Waxmann Verlag, 2013), 114–118; and Akira Yuyama, *"Eugène Burnouf: The Background to his Research into the Lotus Sutra," Bibliotheca Philologica et Philosophica Buddhica Series*, vol. III (Tokyo: International Research Institute for Advanced Buddhology, Soka University, 2000).
87. For more on the *Methodenstreit*, see Henning Trüper, *Orientalism, Philology, and the Illegibility of the Modern World* (New York: Bloomsbury Academic, 2020), 39–44; Constanze Güthenke, "Enthusiasm Dwells Only in Specialization: Classical Philology and Disciplinarity in Nineteenth Germany," in *World Philology*, ed. Sheldon Pollock, Benjamin A. Elman, and Ku-ming Kevin Chang (Cambridge, MA: Harvard University Press, 2014), 276–284; and Anthony Grafton, "From Polyhistor to *Philolog*: Notes on the Transformation of German Classical Scholarship, 1780–1850," *History of Universities* 3 (1983): 171–185.
88. Eugène Burnouf, *Introduction to the History of Indian Buddhism*, trans. Katia Buffetrille and Donald S. Lopez Jr. (Chicago: Chicago University Press, 2010), 62.
89. Burnouf, *Introduction to the History of Indian Buddhism*, 112.
90. Burnouf, *Introduction to the History of Indian Buddhism*, 112–113.
91. Burnouf, *Introduction to the History of Indian Buddhism*, 333n188.
92. Burnouf, *Introduction to the History of Indian Buddhism*, 547–568.
93. Donald S. Lopez, "Introduction to the Translation," in *Introduction to the History of Indian Buddhism*, ed. Burnouf, 20.
94. Lopez, "Burnouf and the Birth of Buddhist Studies," 33.
95. Burnouf, *Introduction to the History of Indian Buddhism*, 117.
96. Burnouf, *Introduction to the History of Indian Buddhism*, 125.
97. Concu, "Buddhism, Philosophy, and History," 489.
98. Concu, "Buddhism, Philosophy, and History," 474n2.
99. Latour, *On the Modern Cult of the Factish Gods*, 2.
100. Burnouf, *Introduction to the History of Indian Buddhism*, 343.
101. Burnouf, *Introduction to the History of Indian Buddhism*, 344.
102. Burnouf, *Introduction to the History of Indian Buddhism*, 344.
103. Burnouf, *Introduction to the History of Indian Buddhism*, 344.
104. Latour, *On the Modern Cult of the Factish Gods*, 11–12.
105. Latour, *On the Modern Cult of the Factish Gods*, 18.
106. Latour, *On the Modern Cult of the Factish Gods*, 22–23.
107. Latour, *On the Modern Cult of the Factish Gods*, 41.

Thomas Calobrisi

THE ECONOMICS OF BUDDHISM

BUDDHIST ECONOMIC RELATIONS

The economics of Buddhism may seem like a paradox at first. If Buddhism propounds nonattachment to materiality and wealth, how is it that Buddhism and economics are even related in the first place? In Buddhist texts, wealth is disparaged, emphasizing how money and material goods are mere traps that seduce and "pollute the mind."[1] Even in the life story of Śākyamuni Buddha, he leaves behind a wealthy lifestyle in favor of the life of a renunciant. As John Kieschnick points out, "few religions have attacked the material world with the intellectual rigor of Buddhism. From the earliest strata of Buddhist texts to the present day, Buddhist monks have espoused an austere ideal of renunciation of the world of things."[2] Monks and nuns are only allowed very few personal and necessary items, including their robes, a bowl, sandals, a sewing needle, and so forth, and they are not to touch money. The image of a Buddhist monk or nun pursuing a simple lifestyle in a state of contentment while sitting deep in meditation on the top of a mountain or in a cave exemplifies a religion that focuses more on otherworldly striving than on this-worldly endeavors. The path toward release from suffering (*dukkha*) caused by craving (*taṇhā*) and attachment (*upādāna*) is the stated goal of a Buddhist monk or nun, whose very terms *bhikkhu* and *bhikkhuṇī* (monk and nun) denote a person who has renounced domestic, social, economic, and political engagement.[3] The material world is a mere distraction from the more lofty goal of attaining enlightenment. How then do Buddhists even engage in economic activity? How do monks and nuns support their austere lifestyles? If Buddhist canonical texts espouse the virtues of nonmateriality and nonattachment to wealth and material objects, how then do large, wealthy monasteries appear in the history of Buddhism? This could only be possible due to a dependence on the lay community for donations or *dāna*. Throughout the history of Buddhism, the lay community has supported monks and nuns though their donations of money, material, and labor, helping to build large, illustrious monasteries filled with monks and nuns who subsist on these donations.

The economics of Buddhism highlights the social relational exchanges between clerical and lay communities that have helped build and expand Buddhist institutions. By looking at economic relations that are based in social networks and exchange, the economics of Buddhism highlights how Buddhism, while eschewing attachment to wealth and material goods, at the same time is necessarily dependent on money and materiality. As Fabio Rambelli succinctly points out, "it is a fact, indeed, that the relation between materiality and spirituality has always been problematic and conflictual within the Buddhist tradition."[4] On the one hand, a focus on materiality and the use of material objects is encouraged in Buddhist practice; on the other hand, attachment to material objects in Buddhist practice is understood to be a grave degeneration leading to the end of Buddhism.[5] Countless *suttas* and canonical texts proclaim the benefits of religious objects for advancing along the Buddhist spiritual path, even while proclaiming that a reliance on sacred objects is associated with an "inauthentic religious experience" and "opposed to a spiritual experience."[6] As Rambelli and Eric Reinders point out, this ambivalence stems from the centrality of merit-making in Buddhism, which entails the practice of *dāna* as essential for accumulating good karma.[7] Within the Buddhist practice of *dāna*, material and economic donations to Buddhist institutions generate spiritual benefits, even though a focus on materiality in Buddhist texts is eschewed.[8]

The conception that Buddhists are necessarily apart from this-worldly concerns, especially when it comes to money and materiality, has been substantiated not only by consulting Buddhist texts, but also by the work of scholars. With the rise of the study of religion, an emphasis on understanding religion through what has been written in sacred texts has permeated the study of Buddhism, going back to the inception of Buddhist studies and the orientalist discovery of Buddhism. These studies emphasize text-based readings of Buddhism, while at the same time they disparage the ways in which Buddhists engage with Buddhism as a form of corruption of "authentic Buddhism."[9] These text-based studies pursue a type of Protestant reading of Buddhism and emphasize how Buddhists should lead a life apart from economic, social, and political spheres while pursuing "salvation," rather than "this-worldly" pleasures.[10] Max Weber, the influential German scholar best known for his book *The Protestant Ethic and the Spirit of Capitalism*, uses Buddhism in his writing as a comparison with which to show how some religions have more influence in the economic sphere than others.[11] Buddhism, he asserts, is a "salvation" religion that "conceals" monks from economic action, as well as from political and social engagement.[12] While in his aforementioned book he examines the link between the growth of modern capitalism and Protestant religious beliefs, in other works he delinks Buddhism and economic developments.[13]

An understanding of Buddhists as somehow apart from economic exchange relations, however, does not withstand scrutiny when one looks closely at early Buddhist texts, as well as historical and contemporary sources on Buddhist economic endeavors. The economics of Buddhism, hence, works to debunk the common misperception that Buddhists are somehow "noneconomic" and live apart from economic as well as material, social, and political realms. While the austere monastic lifestyle may be emphasized in Buddhist texts, when examining how Buddhists engage economically a different picture emerges. Even in Buddhist canonical texts, one sees that while attachment to material wealth can be problematic, material wealth in itself is not. What matters is how the wealth is made, how it is used, and to what extent this material wealth may be excessive. Even in the teachings of the buddha, there are instructions on how one should best generate wealth—by bringing no harm to living beings.[14] Once this wealth is accumulated, the best manner in which to use this wealth is to avoid accumulating too much wealth and to give it away to benefit other living beings, without attachment, greed, or longing. In the *Aṅguttara Nikāya*, the buddha recommended five ways to give away wealth, including providing for one's family and servants, sharing with friends and associates, saving for future need, spending on the performance of oblations, and making offerings to spiritual teachers and monks.[15] A life of poverty is also not the ideal, since poor living conditions make it more difficult to pursue the moral and spiritual path. In the *Cakkavattisīhanāda Sutta*, poverty is recognized as the source of social vices and crime; in the *Kūṭadanta Sutta*, the Buddha suggests economic development as a way to reduce crime.[16] In essence, the Buddha encouraged a middle way approach to wealth—pursuing neither a life of poverty, nor wealth for one's own sake. According to the Buddhist *suttas*, when accumulating wealth, one should not exploit sentient beings, and one should not deal with five types of trade: weapons, living beings, meat, intoxicants, and poisons.[17] Hence, it is not how much material wealth is procured that is problematic, but rather how one obtains this wealth, how it is spent, and how extravagant the accumulation of wealth appears that is questioned.[18]

From the very beginning, interpretations of Buddhism have posited a generally positive view toward wealth. Śākyamuni Buddha himself was born into a wealthy family, which was a sign of great merit (*puñña*) accumulated through his previous lifetimes. Furthermore, as Rachel Scott emphasizes, "one of the greatest ironies of the Buddhist path is that renunciation requires economic prosperity."[19] One of the only ways in which a monk or nun can abandon their economic role in the family is if the family can sustain itself without them, and a monk or nun can live an austere life through receiving surplus economic resources from the lay community. Hence, the entwinement of Buddhism and economics is necessarily a crucial part of Buddhism, as it has been since the time of the buddha.

THE ECONOMICS OF EARLY BUDDHISM

Accounts of early Buddhism show how the monastic communities were deeply enmeshed in economic activities, and the traditions inaugurated by the buddha were attempts not at rejecting worldly affairs, but rather supplementing them by providing an alternative.[20] As Gustavo Benavides and others argue, it was due to the rise of the monetary economy in India and the shift to an agrarian society that Buddhism could be established and spread since the 5th century BCE.[21] The early period in India was full of trading caravans, the development of market towns, and urbanization, including new modes of production leading to economic surplus. These developments led to social change, thus creating the conditions in which Buddhism was able to take root in India in the first place.

Furthermore, in looking at historical sources there is evidence that from very early on in the history of Buddhism, monks owned personal property and used money. Gregory Schopen contributed greatly to the field of the economics of Buddhism through his examination of archeological evidence and looking closely at the *vinaya*, the code of moral conduct for the *saṅgha*.[22] In the *vinaya*, there are clear guidelines as to how monks should deal with money and private property. These include instructions on how to pay debts and tolls, how to own furniture, and how to pay for damages incurred on other monks' property. They also instruct monks on how to pay for medicine, borrow money from laymen, inherit property, accept endowments, make loans and charge interest, and care for sick laymen, with the expectation that when the layman dies his wealth will be transferred to the monk. Further instructions include how to receive gold, accept money, sell the property of deceased monks, hire laborers, buy food, and so forth.[23] The *vinaya* acknowledges that monks owned individual private property, as there are rules for how to distribute the wealth owned by monks at the time of their death.[24] To prevent this wealth from being transferred to the state or the king, the *vinaya* states specifically that the wealth should be transferred among the monks and not be renounced or disposed of.[25] The image that appears when examining historical sources does not substantiate the ideal of the austere monk with few personal items who lives apart from worldly affairs in pursuit of otherworldly and spiritual benefits. Not only in India, but also in China, monks owned personal property including animals, slaves, and large estates.[26] Moreover, this seeming ideal of the austere Buddhist monk who spends his time deep in meditation and contemplation was not always an ideal in historical times. Schopen points out that in the *vinaya* texts, monks who spent too much time engaged in asceticism, meditation, and doctrinal learning were spoken of with ambivalence and sometimes ridiculed. These ascetic monks appear as "ridiculous characters" in funny stories or as "nasty customers" that monks do not want to spend time with.[27]

Furthermore, while individual monks may have been encouraged to avoid amassing personal wealth, there were no limits or restrictions on the wealth procured by monasteries. Descriptions of Buddhist art and architecture paint a picture of opulence and wealth, not of austerity and simplicity.[28] In the *Lotus Sutra*, lay followers are encouraged by the buddha to make offerings of gold, silver, crystal, clamshell, and agate.[29] Historical Buddhist inscriptions on monastic sites and Buddhist monuments state explicitly who the donors were, and not all of them were Brahmin elite householders. In fact, the largest group of donors were monks and nuns.[30] Buddhist monastics were not only recipients of material wealth, but also patrons in that they gave their accumulated wealth to the monastery. Monastics and monasteries relied on donations from the laity and repeated teachings on how giving to the monastic community reaps benefits through merit (*puñña*), relating stories about generous donors from the past.[31]

Merit Economy. Merit (*puñña*) has played a pivotal role in the spread, survival, and expansion of Buddhism throughout history.[32] Within Buddhism, there is a symbiotic economic exchange system in which *puñña*, religious merit, is exchanged for *dāna*, material donations. Monks and nuns are dependent on material donations from the lay community, and in exchange, the lay community receives *puñña*, which helps to improve their spiritual conditions in this life and the next. Monks and nuns offer services to lay supporters, such as religious instruction and performing of rituals. In giving to monasteries, monks, and nuns, this benefits lay supporters in that they not only receive merit, but they practice generosity and selfless renunciation of material wealth when having the right intention.[33] *Puñña* is an important aspect in Buddhist thought and practice, in that it is through the accumulation of merit that one may be reborn in a better rebirth or even liberated from rebirth and become awakened. In addition, once merit has been obtained, it can be transferred to someone else, for example during death rites, without diminishment and even multiplying in effect.[34]

However, the practice of *dāna* is not merely that of gift exchange. Material and monetary donations are not gifts to the monastery since there is no expectation or obligation to reciprocate the gift; in fact, the gift should not be reciprocated.[35] Nicolas Sihlé argues for making a distinction between gifts and transactions, suggesting instead that one considers the practice of *dāna* as remuneration. When lay supporters request the services of a religious specialist, there is an implicitly made mutual agreement: in exchange for a particular service, the layperson will offer money or material goods, such as food, precious metals, and so forth.[36] Hence, there is a symmetrical, symbiotic exchange system upon which Buddhist institutions are dependent for their survival and expansion. What is important to point out is that the recipients of these material offerings, the monks and nuns, are not producers of merit but merely help to create the conditions upon which the lay giver accumulates merit.[37]

For the laity in Buddhist societies, charity and giving to monastic institutions is an important part of lay Buddhist practice. For example, in Burma, spending money on religion is in many ways more effective in satisfying material desires than saving this money.[38] As Melford Spiro observes, "religious spending is the Burman's soundest financial investment."[39] Giving money to a monastery brings material rewards in that the giver receives not only immediate gratification, but also prestige in the surrounding social environment. Religious spending offers the immediate pleasure in the present, for example enjoying lavish meals accompanying Buddhist ritual ceremonies. Religious spending also helps to provide pleasure in the future through the workings of karma and the accumulation of merit (*puñña*). Saving money can be risky, moreover, and does not offer the enjoyment of pleasures in the present or the future.[40]

Hence, it is through the economy of merit that Buddhist monasteries, which were founded on the teachings of the buddha emphasizing nonattachment to material wealth, have amassed great material wealth in the past and continue to do so in the early 21st century. The laity are encouraged to give money and material goods and to offer their labor to the monastery in order to sustain these Buddhist institutions, secure their survival, and aid in their expansion. Without the support of the laity, monks and nuns could not lead their lifestyles in pursuit of spiritual development not weighted down by householder duties. Furthermore, for monastic communities to become established and survive there must be surplus resources in the material conditions of the surrounding lay community. Without this economy of merit, Buddhism and Buddhist institutions would not have been able to take root and spread across Asia. Instead, what one sees is the rise of large monastic institutions that have become centers of economic exchange.

Monasteries as Economic Epicenters. Due to the merit economy, monasteries were built across Asia, some of which became large, wealthy landowners at the center of economic, political, and cultural exchange. Monasteries acquired large parcels of land through donations and in this way procured economic capital in order to secure their social standing and survival. As Michael Walsh argues, land was the primary economic foundation of the sangha or monastic community by which the monastery could survive.[41] Land provided food for the monastery, as well as opportunities for the lay community to offer their labor in exchange for *puñña*, such as through agricultural work on monastery-owned land.

Monasteries formed a complex network of commerce, often established near agricultural and commercial centers and along central trading routes. Buddhist texts mention the necessity of receiving donations from wealthy patrons, relating stories about trade, merchant caravans, and maritime journeys in order to promote donation practices among the laity.[42] In fact, monasteries were some of the "most powerful economic forces in society."[43] In China, early Yuan emperors built large temples and gave large endowments in order to legitimize their rule and gain support.[44] In the 13th century, the largest monasteries were also the largest landholders, owning property and running various business ventures, such as grain mills, hydraulic mills and presses, pawn shops, storehouses, money lending, and so forth, becoming centers of commerce and usury.[45] Buddhist monastic networks helped to promote the exchange of high-value commodities between South Asia and Central Asia along trade routes through the complex exchange networks of patronage, conversion, migration, and institutional expansion.[46] The dependence on lay support connected monasteries to commercial networks and long-distance trade networks, especially since merchants and wealthy donors donated their profits to monasteries. Buddhist itinerant monks traveled along similar routes as traders, sometimes together with them, soliciting donations from them along the way.[47]

Monasteries became attractive places to join and receive ordination, especially among poor families who wished to avoid hunger and hard labor for their children. Monks and nuns were often exempt from paying taxes or corvée, unpaid labor. Monasteries, in some cases, provided social welfare where governments could not. In addition to food and housing, they offered an education to families who could not afford the expensive fees of private tutors.[48] But this did not apply only to the poor. Wealthy families were also drawn to the monastery to avoid paying taxes and avoid being recruited into hard labor or the military.[49]

Monasteries relied on the lay community to provide labor for their economic activities. Due to the mechanisms of the merit economy, labor done for the sake of Buddhism and Buddhist institutions is performed voluntarily. However, with the range of commercial activities at monasteries, monastic labor is also needed to fill all the roles. While one may think of monastic labor as entailing ritual services and teaching dharma, in reality, running a monastery requires a large labor force supplied by monks and nuns.[50] This form of work includes the administrative and managerial functions of the monastery, as well as the hard labor necessary for taking care of the land owned by monasteries. For large monasteries, the managerial duties can be cumbersome. Maintaining the buildings and the land of the monasteries is a large task, occupying the time and energy of monks instead of them focusing on study and practice.[51] Hundreds, even thousands, of monks need to be fed, along with the tenants and laborers who work in the fields and paddies. Even when engaged in these forms of more mundane or "this-worldly" activities, this is meritorious in that it supports the monastery, hence prolonging the survival of Buddhism.[52] In this sense, material action is also a religious undertaking.[53]

Monasteries, due to their large land holdings and storehouses of material wealth, as well as access to free labor, have been at the forefront of economic change. Monasteries have had an advantage for production in that they owned large tracts of land, and monastics have not been bound by patrimonial households and personal relations. In this way, monasteries have been freer to invest in new forms of production and exchange. Randall Collins considers Buddhist monasteries as the "first entrepreneurs" in Asia, due to their role in spurring economic growth in traditional societies.[54] Collins points out that the capitalist economy in Japan and China was ushered in through monastic institutions paving the way for new economic modes of expansion and production, spearheading a growing market economy. Due to the Buddhist "religious economy," the "secular market economy" was sparked, he argues, similar to the way in which Christianity aided in the capitalist transformation of medieval Europe.[55]

Hence, Buddhist monasteries represent a socioeconomic institution that engages in commercial activity to support the religious undertakings of the monks and nuns. Considering monasteries as institutions includes both the physical structure and the compound, as well as the social structure that "defines, imposes, and maintains sets of values and seeks to acquire and distribute capital—economic, cultural, or otherwise—in a competitive manner."[56] Since monasteries consist of a corporation of interests, some scholars consider monasteries as corporations.[57] In Tibet, for example, monks have had to do business to provide their own income, and monasteries have owned vast estates, loaned money with interest, and engaged in trade.[58] Berthe Jansen suggests that Tibetan Buddhist monasteries have been primarily concerned with continuation and preservation.[59] As such, she argues, the monastery is a corporate entity, since as an institution it creates a notion of belonging to a larger community and has the corporate features of social and economic objectives.[60]

In contrast to how Weber portrayed Buddhist monastic endeavors as noneconomic, the economics of Buddhism is based on a system of symbiotic exchange in which the lay community donates surplus material resources in exchange for merit, thus aiding the establishment and spread of Buddhist institutions. Monasteries as centers of not only economic exchange, but also social and cultural exchange, are tied into an expansive network of people and ideas. As Jason Neelis emphasizes, "the intertwining of religious and economic networks stimulated material and ideological exchanges and processes of cross-cultural mobility."[61] Buddhist monasteries, rather than being apart from social and economic spheres, have been highly influential in affecting these spheres, helping to usher in new ideas and new economic models as centers of religious as well as social, economic, and political power.

CHANGING BUDDHIST ECONOMIC CONDITIONS

Since the early 20th century, changes incurred by the forces of colonialism, modernization, and globalization have meant that monastic institutions have had to adapt to shifting economic conditions in order to survive. For example, changes in land tenure acts have threatened to take land, and hence their economic foundation, away from monasteries, as was the case in China during the Cultural Revolution (1966–1976). With the rise and spread of global capitalism, an economic transition from land-based societies dependent on agriculture and animal husbandry, to cash-based societies with formal wage employment and access to surplus cash, has ushered in a new consumer society, especially in Asia. With the impact of modernization and capitalism, especially in Asia, societies have transformed swiftly, with market forces affecting every aspect of social life. Since the mid-1980s, a "new spirit of capitalism" has transformed social relations in which the consumer market has become an increasingly important site for identity formation.[62] Consumers increasingly shape their identities based on the goods they consume, rather than a particular community or a particular religion.[63] Where monasteries once held the position of having utmost social prestige, new education opportunities, along with an expanding bureaucracy, have ushered in new pathways for social prestige, thus threatening the social standing of monasteries and temples in Asia. As a result, a deep concern among monastic leaders as to the state and survival of Buddhism can be found across Asia. Accompanying modernization processes, such as industrialization, urbanization, expanding bureaucracies, and globalization, not to mention impending processes of secularization, have meant that monasteries and temples have had to make adjustments in order to secure their survival and hold on to their economic viability and positions of social prestige.

Changes in economic exchange relations have affected the ways in which Buddhist institutions raise the money needed to maintain and secure their economic survival.[64] A common way to raise funds for temples is through tourism, leading to heightened commercial activity surrounding the pilgrimage practices to these locations.[65] While the local government may be interested in promoting tourism because of the economic development that tourism brings, monks are also interested in promoting tourism in order to promote their institution and procure the survival of Buddhism.[66] Monastery leaders often play an active role in promoting tourism at their monasteries and in the commodification of these sites, a process that is not necessarily new, as monasteries have frequently been popular pilgrimage and travel destinations.[67] The commodification of Buddhist sites has provided economic support, and hence the survival of these Buddhist sites and institutions. In China and Japan, a revival of Buddhism has taken place due to new ways of generating economic income for monasteries, especially due to tourism. Some Buddhist temples have become so filled with tourists that it has become difficult to visit these sites as places for Buddhist worship.[68]

On a slightly different note, Buddhism has also become a conduit for generating economic wealth in the global capitalist economy—what some scholars have termed "prosperity Buddhism."[69] Buddhist practice and affiliation with a Buddhist organization has become a way to generate material wealth and prestige. According to Pattana Kitiarsa, prosperity Buddhism entails a religious movement that emphasizes wealth more than salvation, and "a religio-cultural space where popular Buddhism has converged with market economy, consumers' practices, and the quest for personal and cultural identities."[70] Prosperity Buddhism points toward a conjunction of religion and capitalism, in which wealth and success in business is a main motivation for participating in these organizations.[71] Some examples include Buddhist spirit cults in Burma, Dhammakaya, and Luang Phor Khoon in Thailand, and Soka Gakkai and Happy Science in Japan.[72] These Buddhist groups have amassed great fortunes and wield tremendous influence in the wider community, at times through social and political engagement.[73]

With the rise of global capitalism, moreover, there has been a concurrent resurgence of religion.[74] Buddhism has spread to all corners of the globe, mostly due to the technological and economic advances of global capitalism. As Kitiarsa, in his work on religion and commodification, argues, "the more society is rationally modernized, scientifically educated, technologically advanced, and economically prosperous, the more people tend to be enchanted or re-enchanted by their committed faiths."[75] Market dynamics such as marketing and branding have become useful ways to spread Buddhism, as well as to generate income. For example, the marketing of blessed amulets and other religious objects has become a multibillion-dollar industry.[76] The goods and services marketed by dharma centers, such as through teachings, seminars, meditation retreats, books, ritual paraphernalia, meditation cushions, incense, pilgrimages, and so forth, have become an essential part of the economics of Buddhism in the global world. As Cecile Campergue recognized, the "commercialization and commodification dynamic pervades the whole of Western Buddhism."[77] Economic norms from consumer societies have had an increasing impact on religious values and behavior, in which religions compete in a spiritual marketplace, offering their goods and services in the consumer market.

Taking a closer look at the commodification of religion helps to narrow down how religions are being redefined as market commodities in the spiritual marketplace and exchanged through transnational connections.[78] Kitiarsa defines religious commodification as an "emerging multifaceted and multidimensional marketized process, which turns a religious faith or tradition into a consumable and marketable good."[79] Merit (*puñña*) can also be considered a commodity, in that it is a "commodified object of exchange."[80] The spread of global capitalism has affected how Buddhist images, goods, and services have been adopted and altered in new environments. For instance, the global trend of mindfulness as a panacea for the hectic, modern life has transformed a Buddhist meditation practice into something not immediately recognizable as Buddhist.[81] Global sentiments regarding Buddhism as a philosophy or a spirituality that is beneficial to everyone regardless of their religious background due to its peaceful and calming aspects has led to the proliferation of Buddhist-inspired objects for sale in the mass consumer society. Marketing firms have taken up the positive brand image of Buddhism to advertise various goods, from cars and mobile phones, to beer and bars.[82] As a result, mass-produced buddha heads in supermarket aisles is no longer an uncommon sight.

When considering the commodification of Buddhism, it is important to keep in mind that Buddhist goods and services have always been on the marketplace.[83] The sale of statues, ritual implements, paintings, and so forth is not a new phenomenon. Perhaps what one can pinpoint as necessarily new in the global capitalist market is the mass production of Buddhist-inspired goods, which are proliferating and spreading to all corners of the global market. However, as Kitiarsa points out, when Buddhism is commodified, this does not mean that it loses its symbolic power and efficacy.[84] Trine Brox has recognized how labor transforms the aura of mass-produced Buddhist goods into having spiritual efficacy through the three processes of spiritual labor, packaging, and claims of authenticity.[85] The marketing and branding of Buddhism, and selling Buddhist commodities and services, can also be a form of *upāya*, skillful means, to help spread global awareness of Buddhism.[86] Hence, it is through the marketization of Buddhism that Buddhism has spread, and it is through consumer markets that Buddhism has taken root in new contexts.

Morality of Buddhist Economics. Protests against the ways in which Buddhism has been commodified, and the ways in which Buddhist monks have acquired too much wealth and power, moreover, are not uncommon and were also heard in the past. Buddhist adepts must walk a fine line between acquiring and eschewing material wealth. In many cases, material wealth is a sign of previous good deeds and spiritual progress.[87] However, having too much wealth is problematic, such as when Dhammakaya monks from Thailand fly on private jets, wearing designer sunglasses and bags, spurring widespread protest.[88] The decline of Buddhism in Mongolia, furthermore, has been attributed to the criticism of Buddhist monasteries for having too much wealth and political power.[89] As Rambelli and Reinders have pointed out in the case of Japan, so-called anti-Buddhists have specifically targeted Buddhist wealth accumulation as a waste of valuable resources and manpower.[90]

The commercialization of Buddhism in Thailand, moreover, has been a significant point of contention, as have the ways in which Buddhist goods appear in the marketplace.[91] The Knowing Buddha Organization has been highly vocal in protesting the ways in which Buddhist symbols appear in the market, charging specific companies with blasphemy.[92] Criticisms directed at the ways in which Buddhism has become injected into the global capitalist economy have given rise to new Buddhist organizations and new Buddhist models. For example, in Thailand, Phra Phothirak established Santi Ashok as an alternative community that promotes moderation and a "back to the basics" ideology that is critical of materialism.[93]

Buddhist Economics. Similarly, a subfield of what has been termed "Buddhist economics" has arisen that offers Buddhist alternatives to global capitalism as a more ethical way to engage with the global market economy. The term "Buddhist economics" first appeared in the work of Ernst F. Schumacher as a response to mass production, market competition, and the unequal distribution of wealth.[94] Buddhist leaders have since employed the term Buddhist economics in their search for ways to substantiate a Buddhist economic model as an alternative to both capitalism and socialism. For example, Jigme Singye Wangchuk, a former monarch of Bhutan, coined the term "Gross National Happiness" as an alternative to "Gross Domestic Product" (GDP) and the continual focus on economic and material growth and prosperity.[95] In the Gross National Happiness paradigm, the focus is on spiritual and mental development rather than material and economic development, in which well-being instead of consumption is the parameter of development. Various movements forged by Buddhist leaders across Asia, such as Buddhadāsa Bhikkhu, A. T. Ariyaratne, Sulak Sivaraksa, Padmasiri De Silva, H. N. S. Karunatilake, Ananda W. P. Guruge, and Venerable Payutto, have positioned Buddhism in contrast to Western development and global capitalism. Buddhism has become an opponent and antidote to global capitalism and an example of antimaterialism, which is reminiscent of the widespread assumptions that Buddhists are and should be antimaterialist and noneconomic.

CONCLUSION

The economics of Buddhism is a wide and growing field that examines Buddhist engagements with material and economic exchanges deeply embedded in social relations. In contrast to Buddhist economics, which offers economic models inspired by Buddhist tenets for how one *should* engage economically, the economics of Buddhism examines how Buddhists necessarily *must* engage economically. In order to support the lifestyles of monks and nuns who do not seek gainful employment or extend family relations through the household, the lay community provides for their livelihoods through donations, or *dāna*. Through an economy of merit, or *puñña*, monks and nuns can pursue their monastic lifestyles, and Buddhist institutions can be established, maintained, and expanded. The building of large monasteries could only be managed through the material support of the lay community. In exchange for religious services, monks and nuns receive material donations, and in some cases, monasteries have acquired large tracts of land and accumulated vast material wealth, at times seen as excessive and overly extravagant. Monasteries in Asia, due to the patronage of kings, political leaders, merchant traders, and wealthy patrons, have been deeply entwined in local economies, even paving the way for new economic models, such as creating pathways for establishing capitalism and market economies in Asia. Like the Christian monasteries in Europe during the ushering in of capitalism, Buddhist monasteries have played a significant role in aiding the foundation of the capitalist market economy as well as the global consumer market.

When taking a close look at how Buddhists and Buddhist institutions engage in economic relations, the social and political aspects of Buddhist life are brought to light. Instead of seeing Buddhist economic action and the marketing of Buddhism as somehow degraded and forwarding an inauthentic form of Buddhism, what one instead sees is how Buddhists adapt to and shape economic environments wherever they land. Buddhists have always been economically engaged, even while pursuing austere lifestyles and teaching about the benefits of nonattachment to materiality and wealth. The only way that large monasteries could materialize is through Buddhist influence in the social, political, and economic realms. Moreover, with the global capitalist economy, Buddhists have taken advantage of these changing economic conditions and found opportunities to start new Buddhist institutions and spread Buddhism worldwide. As Lionel Obadia asserts, "the economics of Buddhism—by which it is seen as 'commodity' and 'corporation'... opens a new perspective, considering economy as a model of reality."[96] In this sense, when considering the economics of Buddhism, new perspectives on economic realities shed light on contemporary developments in which religion and economics are necessarily entwined. Ian Reader and George Tanabe have previously made the essential point that "economics, marketing, and commercialization are part of the religious process."[97] There is nothing new in this process. Buddhists have always been intricately engaged in economic relations and have used market dynamics through tapping into trade and selling Buddhist commodities. The subfield of the economics of Buddhism plays an important role in debunking the myth that Buddhists are somehow "noneconomic" and points to the power and influence that Buddhists have had in the past and continue to wield in the contemporary global world.

REVIEW OF LITERATURE

The economics of Buddhism has benefitted immensely from the work that historians have done to reveal how Buddhists have always been engaged in economic relations. From looking at Buddhist texts and archeological remains, scholars have gleaned the ways in which Buddhist monastics have in fact owned personal property and had access to material wealth.[98] Through family ties and work done to procure material and economic donations, monks and nuns have acquired the resources needed to pursue their austere lifestyles and spread Buddhism across Asia. Historians have examined how Buddhist monasteries became economic epicenters, tapping into extensive trade networks and relying on royal patronage. As a result, scholars have shown how Buddhist monasteries attained enormous social, political, and economic influence throughout Asia.[99]

Furthermore, scholars of contemporary Buddhism have shown how changing economic conditions, including the impact of modernization and global capitalism, have affected the ways in which Buddhists engage in economic relations. In some cases, scholars have shown how the economic foundations upon which Buddhist monasteries have rested for centuries have become uprooted due to political and economic changes.[100] Other scholars have pointed out that new economic opportunities have opened for Buddhist institutions. Some scholars have paid attention to how tourism has become a significant source of income for Buddhist monasteries, which otherwise faced challenges in procuring the economic support needed to survive.[101]

The ways in which Buddhism has spread globally cannot ignore how changing economic conditions have also created pathways for expanding Buddhist institutions. Global capitalism has played a crucial role in the spread of Buddhism to newer contexts, such as Europe and North America. While some scholars criticize the ways in which Buddhism has become marketed and commercialized, others examine the ways in which Buddhism has transformed under these conditions by utilizing market dynamics of branding and commodification.[102] This work shows the ways in which the global marketplace has influenced the spread and survival of Buddhist institutions.[103]

The field of the economics of Buddhism has attracted a great deal of interest in the early 21st century, with multiple collaborative research projects approaching the ways in which Buddhists and Buddhism engage in economic relations. Work done to theorize how Buddhism and economics are necessarily entwined, along with the ways in which to analyze and conceptualize these Buddhist economic relations, has shown the great potential that lies in expanding the field of the economics of Buddhism.[104] This work offers new insights not only into the field of Buddhist studies, but also into the field of religion and economy more generally. Buddhist economic relations pinpoint how Buddhists engage with an economic model, bringing to the fore the social and moral contexts within which these Buddhist economic relations take place.[105] The economics of Buddhism, moreover, provides a point of comparison for other religions, improving on the since debunked theories by Max Weber and others that Buddhists are somehow noneconomic and "concealed" from the economy.

FURTHER READING

ADDITIONAL OVERVIEWS OF THE FIELD OF THE ECONOMICS OF BUDDHISM

Benavides, Gustavo. "Economy." In *Critical Terms for the Study of Buddhism*. Edited by Donald S. Lopez, Jr., 77–102. Chicago and London: University of Chicago Press, 2005.

Brox, Trine, and Elizabeth Williams-Oerberg. "Buddhism, Business, and Economics." In *Oxford Handbook of Contemporary Buddhism*. Edited by Michael Jerryson, 504–517. Oxford: Oxford University Press, 2016.

Williams-Oerberg, Elizabeth. "Introduction: Buddhism and Economics." *Journal of Global Buddhism* 20 (2019): 19–29.

HISTORICAL STUDIES OF BUDDHIST ECONOMIC RELATIONS

Amstutz, Galen. "Materiality and Spiritual Economies in Premodern Japanese Buddhism: A Problem in Historical Change." *Journal of Religion in Japan* 1, no. 2 (2012): 142–167.

Gernet, Jacques. *Buddhism in Chinese Society: An Economic History From the Fifth to the Tenth Centuries*. New York: Columbia University Press, 1995.

Kieschnick, John. *The Impact of Buddhism on Chinese Material Culture*. Princeton, NJ: Princeton University Press, 2003.

Neelis, Jason. *Early Buddhist Transmission and Trade Networks: Mobility and Exchange Within and Beyond the Northwestern Borderlands of South Asia*. Leiden, The Netherlands: Brill, 2017.

Schopen, Gregory. *Buddhist Monks and Business Matters: Still More Papers on Monastic Buddhism in India*. Vol. 2. Honolulu: University of Hawai'i Press, 2004.

Walsh, Michael J. *Sacred Economies: Buddhist Monasticism and Territoriality in Medieval China*. New York: Columbia University Press, 2010.

CONTEMPORARY STUDIES OF BUDDHIST ECONOMIC RELATIONS

Brox, Trine, and Elizabeth Williams-Oerberg, eds. *Buddhism and Business: Merit, Material Wealth and Morality in the Global Market Economy*. Honolulu: University of Hawai'i Press, 2020.

Caple, Jane. "Monastic Economic Reform at Rong-Bo Monastery: Towards an Understanding of Contemporary Tibetan Monastic Revival and Development in a-Mdo." *Buddhist Studies Review* 27 (2010): 197–219.

Covell, Stephen G. *Japanese Temple Buddhism: Worldliness in a Religion of Renunciation*. Honolulu: University of Hawai'i Press, 2005.

Foxeus, Niklas. "Spirits, Mortal Dread, and Ontological Security: Prosperity and Saving Buddhism in Burma/Myanmar." *Journal of the American Academy of Religion* 86, no. 4 (2018): 1107–1147.

Jackson, Peter A. "The Enchanting Spirit of Thai Capitalism: The Cult of Luang Phor Khoon and the Post-Modernization of Thai Buddhism." *South East Asia Research* 7, no. 1 (1999): 5–60.

Scott, Rachelle M. *Nirvana for Sale? Buddhism, Wealth, and the DhammakāYa Temple in Contemporary Thailand.* Albany: State University of New York Press, 2009.

Sizemore, Russell F., and Donald K. Swearer. *Ethics, Wealth, and Salvation: A Study in Buddhist Social Ethics.* Columbia: University of South Carolina Press, 1990.

THEORETICAL APPROACHES TO THE ECONOMICS OF BUDDHISM

Borup, Jørn. "Spiritual Capital and Religious Evolution: Buddhist Values and Transactions in Historical and Contemporary Perspective." *Journal of Global Buddhism* 20 (2019): 49–68.

Brox, Trine. "The Aura of Buddhist Material Objects in the Age of Mass-Production." *Journal of Global Buddhism* 20 (2019): 105–125.

Obadia, Lionel. "Is Buddhism Like a Hamburger? Buddhism and the Market Economy in a Globalized World." *Research in Economic Anthropology* 31 (2011): 99–120.

Payne, Richard. "Religion, Self-Help, Science: Three Economies of Western/ized Buddhism." *Journal of Global Buddhism* 20 (2019): 69–86.

Schedneck, Brooke. "An Entangled Relationship: A Lived Religion Approach to Theravāda Buddhism and Economics." *Journal of Global Buddhism* 20 (2019): 31–48.

Wilson, Jeff. "Buddhism Without Merit: Theorizing Buddhist Religio-Economic Activity in the Contemporary World." *Journal of Global Buddhism* 20 (2019): 87–104.

NOTES

1. John Kieschnick, *The Impact of Buddhism on Chinese Material Culture*, Vol. 5 (Princeton, NJ: Princeton University Press, 2003).
2. Kieschnick, *The Impact of Buddhism on Chinese Material Culture*, 3.
3. James Mark Shields, "Buddhist Economics: Problems and Possibilities," in *The Oxford Handbook of Buddhist Ethics*, ed. Daniel Cozort and James Mark Shields (Oxford: Oxford University Press, 2018), 407–431, 409.
4. Fabio Rambelli, *Buddhist Materiality: A Cultural History of Objects in Japanese Buddhism* (Stanford, CA: Stanford University Press, 2007), 3.
5. Fabio Rambelli and Eric Robert Reinders, *Buddhism and Iconoclasm in East Asia: A History* (New York: Bloomsbury, 2012), 22.
6. Rambelli and Reinders, *Buddhism and Iconoclasm in East Asia*, 22, 41–42.
7. Rambelli and Reinders, *Buddhism and Iconoclasm in East Asia*, 24.
8. Rambelli and Reinders, *Buddhism and Iconoclasm in East Asia*, 24.
9. See Charles Hallisey, "Roads Taken and Not Taken in the Study of Theravāda Buddhism," in *Curators of the Buddha*, ed. Donald S. Lopez, Jr. (Chicago: University of Chicago Press, 1995), 31–62.
10. See, for example, Frederic L. Pryor, "A Buddhist Economic System—in Principle: Non-attachment to Worldly Things Is Dominant But the Way of the Law Is Held Profitable," *American Journal of Economics and Sociology* 49, no. 3 (1990): 339–349.
11. Max Weber, *The Protestant Ethic and the Spirit of Capitalism*, ed. Max Weber, Talcott Parsons and R. H. Tawney (London: George Allen & Unwin, 1930).
12. Max Weber, *The Religion of India: The Sociology of Hinduism and Buddhism* (Glencoe, IL: The Free Press, 1958), 233, 343; see also Elizabeth Williams-Oerberg, "Introduction: Buddhism and Economics," *Journal of Global Buddhism* 20 (2019): 19–29; and Matthew King, "Buddhist Economics: Scales of Value in Global Exchange," *Oxford Handbooks Online* (2016), 1–29, 2.
13. Weber, *The Religion of India*, 1958.

14. Peter Harvey, "Buddhist Reflections on 'Consumer' and 'Consumerism'," *Journal of Buddhist Ethics* 20 (2013): 334–357, 339.
15. Georgios T. Halkias, "The Enlightened Sovereign: Buddhism and Kingship in India and Tibet," in *A Companion to Buddhist Philosophy*, ed. Steven M. Emmanuel (Hoboken, NJ: John Wiley & Sons, Inc., 2013), 491–511, 495.
16. Halkias, "The Enlightened Sovereign," 494.
17. Halkias, "The Enlightened Sovereign," 495.
18. Harvey, "Buddhist Reflections," 340; see also Russell F. Sizemore and Donald K. Swearer, *Ethics, Wealth, and Salvation: A Study in Buddhist Social Ethics* (Columbia: University of South Carolina Press, 1990), 17.
19. Rachelle M. Scott, *Nirvana for Sale? Buddhism, Wealth, and the Dhammakāya Temple in Contemporary Thailand* (Albany: State University of New York Press, 2009), 33.
20. Shields, "Buddhist Economics," 3.
21. Gustavo Benavides, "Economy," in *Critical Terms for the Study of Buddhism*, ed. Donald S. Lopez, Jr. (Chicago and London: University of Chicago Press, 2005), 77–102.; Greg Bailey and Ian Mabbett, *The Sociology of Early Buddhism* (Cambridge, UK: Cambridge University Press, 2003), 63; and King, "Buddhist Economics," 1.
22. Gregory Schopen, *Buddhist Monks and Business Matters: Still More Papers on Monastic Buddhism in India*, Vol. 2 (Honolulu: University of Hawai'i Press, 2004); Gregory Schopen, "The Good Monk and His Money in a Buddhist Monasticism of 'The Mahāyāna Period'," *The Eastern Buddhist* 32, no. 1 (2000): 85–105.
23. Schopen, *Buddhist Monks and Business Matters*, 14; see also Jason Neelis, *Early Buddhist Transmission and Trade Networks: Mobility and Exchange within and beyond the Northwestern Borderlands of South Asia* (Leiden, The Netherlands: Brill, 2017), 34–35.
24. Schopen, *Buddhist Monks and Business Matters*, 5.
25. Schopen, *Buddhist Monks and Business Matters*, 6.
26. Kieschnick, *The Impact of Buddhism on Chinese Material Culture*, 5.
27. Schopen, *Buddhist Monks and Business Matters*, 15.
28. Kieschnick, *The Impact of Buddhism on Chinese Material Culture*, 11.
29. Kieschnick, *The Impact of Buddhism on Chinese Material Culture*, 7.
30. Neelis, *Early Buddhist Transmission and Trade Networks*, 24.
31. Kieschnick, *The Impact of Buddhism on Chinese Material Culture*, 6.
32. See Galen Amstutz, "Materiality and Spiritual Economies in Premodern Japanese Buddhism: A Problem in Historical Change," *Journal of Religion in Japan* 1, no. 2 (2012): 142–167, 153.
33. Neelis, *Early Buddhist Transmission and Trade Networks*, 18.
34. Benavides, "Economy," 89.
35. Nicolas Sihlé, "Towards a Comparative Anthropology of the Buddhist Gift (and Other Transfers)," *Religion Compass* 9, no. 11 (2015): 352–385, 352.
36. Sihlé, "Towards a Comparative Anthropology," 355.
37. Sihlé, "Towards a Comparative Anthropology," 367.
38. Melford E. Spiro, "Buddhism and Economic Action in Burma," *American Anthropologist* 68, no. 5 (1966): 1163–1173, 1166.
39. Spiro, "Buddhism and Economic Action in Burma," 1167.
40. Spiro, "Buddhism and Economic Action in Burma," 1168.
41. For an in-depth discussion of *saṅgha*, see Thomas Borchert, "The Sangha as an Institution," in *Oxford Research Encyclopedia of Religion* (2017); and Michael J. Walsh, *Sacred Economies: Buddhist Monasticism and Territoriality in Medieval China* (New York: Columbia University Press, 2010), 4.

42. For an in-depth discussion of the influence of maritime travel on the spread of Buddhism, see Andrea Acri, "Maritime Buddhism," in *Oxford Research Encyclopedia of Religion* (2018); and Neelis, *Early Buddhist Transmission and Trade Networks*, 28, 34.
43. Walsh, *Sacred Economies*, 6.
44. Claudia Fritz, "An Interpretation of the Relationship Between Chan-Buddhism and the State With Reference to the Monastic Code at the End of the Yuan Era," *Schweizerische Gesellschaft für Asienkunde. Asiatische Studien* 70, no. 1 (2016): 13–74.
45. Amstutz, "Materiality and Spiritual Economies," 154; Fritz, "An Interpretation of the Relationship," 53; and Jacques Gernet, *Buddhism in Chinese Society: An Economic History from the Fifth to the Tenth Centuries* (New York: Columbia University Press, 1995).
46. Neelis, *Early Buddhist Transmission and Trade Networks*, 10.
47. Neelis, *Early Buddhist Transmission and Trade Networks*, 37.
48. Fritz, "An Interpretation of the Relationship," 58.
49. Fritz, "An Interpretation of the Relationship," 57.
50. See Thomas Borchert, "Monastic Labor: Thinking About the Work of Monks in Contemporary Theravāda Communities," *Journal of the American Academy of Religion* 79, no. 1 (2010): 162–192.
51. Fritz, "An Interpretation of the Relationship," 63.
52. See Borchert, "Monastic Labor," 171.
53. Walsh, *Sacred Economies*; Michael J. Walsh, "The Economics of Salvation: Toward a Theory of Exchange in Chinese Buddhism," *Journal of the American Academy of Religion* 75, no. 2 (2007): 353–382.
54. Randall Collins, "An Asian Route to Capitalism: Religious Economy and the Origins of Self-Transforming Growth in Japan," *American Sociological Review* 62 (1997): 843–865, 848.
55. Collins, "An Asian Route to Capitalism," 850.
56. Walsh, *Sacred Economies*, 9.
57. Walsh, *Sacred Economies*; Berthe Jansen, *The Monastery Rules* (Oakland: University of California Press, 2018); and Collins, "An Asian Route to Capitalism."
58. Jansen, *The Monastery Rules*, 10.
59. Jansen, *The Monastery Rules*, 41.
60. Jansen, *The Monastery Rules*, 59.
61. Neelis, *Early Buddhist Transmission and Trade Networks*, 38.
62. Luc Boltanski and Eve Chiapello, "The New Spirit of Capitalism," *International Journal of Politics, Culture, and Society* 18, nos. 3–4 (2005): 161–188; see also Elizabeth Williams-Oerberg and Trine Brox, "Introduction: Buddhist Encounters With the Global Market Economy and Consumer Society," in *Buddhism and Business: Merit, Material Wealth and Morality in the Global Market Economy*, ed. Trine Brox and Elizabeth Williams-Oerberg (Honolulu: University of Hawai'i Press, 2020), 1–22; for an in-depth discussion on the impact of the consumer society on identity formation and religions, see François Gauthier, Linda Woodhead, and Tuomas Martikainen, "Introduction: Consumerism as the Ethos of Consumer Society," in *Religion in Consumer Society: Brands, Consumers and Markets*, ed. François Gauthier and Tuomas Martikainen (Surrey: Ashgate, 2013), 1–24.
63. Niklas Foxeus, "Spirits, Mortal Dread, and Ontological Security: Prosperity and Saving Buddhism in Burma/Myanmar," *Journal of the American Academy of Religion* 86, no. 4 (2018): 1107–1147, 1134.
64. See Trine Brox and Elizabeth Williams-Oerberg, eds., *Buddhism and Business: Merit, Material Wealth and Morality in the Global Market Economy* (Honolulu: University of Hawai'i Press, 2020).
65. See Courtney Bruntz and Brooke Schedneck, eds., *Buddhist Tourism in Asia: Global Networks Within Sacred Sites* (Honolulu: University of Hawai'i Press, 2020).
66. See Thomas Borchert, "Of Temples and Tourists: The Effects of the Tourist Political Economy on a Minority Buddhist Community in Southwest China," in *State, Market, and Religions in Chinese Socieites*,

ed. Yang Fenggang and Joseph B. Tamney (Leiden, The Netherlands: Brill, 2005), 87–111; Elizabeth Williams-Oerberg, "Buddhism: A Unique Selling Point in Ladakh," in *Buddhist Tourism in Asia: Global Networks Within Sacred Sites*, ed. Courtney Bruntz and Brooke Schedneck (Honolulu: University of Hawaiʻi Press, 2020), 227–246; and David Geary, "Destination Enlightenment: Branding Buddhism and Spiritual Tourism in Bodhgaya, Bihar," *Anthropology Today* 24, no. 3 (2008): 11–14.

67. Amstutz, "Materiality and Spiritual Economies," 157.
68. See Gareth Fisher, "In the Footsteps of the Tourists: Buddhist Revival at Museum/Temple Sites in Beijing," *Social Compass* 58, no. 4 (2011): 511–524.
69. Niklas Foxeus, "Possessed for Success: Prosperity Buddhism and the Cult of the Guardians of the Treasure Trove in Upper Burma," *Contemporary Buddhism* 18, no. 1 (2017): 108–139; Scott, *Nirvana for Sale?*; Jørn Borup, "Prosperous Buddhism, Prosperity Buddhism, and Religious Capital," *Numen* 65, nos. 2–3 (2018): 256–288; Pattana Kitiarsa, "Introduction: Asia's Commodified Sacred Canopies," in *Religious Commodifications in Asia: Marketing Gods*, ed. Pattana Kitiarsa (London: Routledge, 2008), 1–13; and Peter A. Jackson, "The Enchanting Spirit of Thai Capitalism: The Cult of Luang Phor Khoon and the Post-Modernization of Thai Buddhism," *South East Asia Research* 7, no. 1 (1999): 5–60.
70. Kitiarsa, "Introduction," 121; see also Foxeus, "Spirits, Mortal Dread, and Ontological Security," 1134.
71. Foxeus, "Possessed for Success," 108.
72. See Foxeus, "Possessed for Success"; Borup, "Prosperous Buddhism"; Jackson, "The Enchanting Spirit of Thai Capitalism"; and Scott, *Nirvana for Sale?*
73. See Levi McLaughlin, *Soka Gakkai's Human Revolution: The Rise of a Mimetic Nation in Modern Japan* (Honolulu: University of Hawaiʻi Press, 2018).
74. See also Juliette Koning and Gwenaël Njoto-Feillard, "Introduction: New Religiosities, Modern Capitalism, and Moral Complexities in Southeast Asia," in *New Religiosities, Modern Capitalism, and Moral Complexities in Southeast Asia*, ed. Juliette Koning and Gwenaël Njoto-Feillard (New York: Springer, 2017), 1–15.
75. Kitiarsa, "Introduction," 4.
76. Jackson, "The Enchanting Spirit of Thai Capitalism," 18.
77. Cecile Campergue, "Gifts and the Selfless Work Ethic in Tibetan Buddhist Centres in France," *Religion Compass* 9, no. 11 (2015): 443–461, 459.
78. Kitiarsa, "Introduction," 6.
79. Pattana Kitiarsa, "Buddha-izing a Global City-State: Transnational Religious Mobilities, Spiritual Marketplace, and Thai Migrant Monks in Singapore," *Mobilities* 5, no. 2 (2010): 257–275; see also Koning and Njoto-Feillard, "Introduction," 2.
80. Walsh, *Sacred Economies*.
81. Jeff Wilson, "Selling Mindfulness: Commodity Lineages and the Marketing of Mindful Products," in *Handbook of Mindfulness: Culture, Contexts, and Social Engagement*, ed. Ronald E. Purser, David Forbes, and Adam Burke (New York: Springer, 2016), 109–119.
82. Jørn Borup, "Branding Buddha—Mediatized and Commodified Buddhism as Cultural Narrative," *Journal of Global Buddhism* 17 (2016): 41–55.
83. See Neelis, *Early Buddhist Transmission and Trade Networks*, 22.
84. Kitiarsa, "Introduction," 7.
85. Trine Brox, "The Aura of Buddhist Material Objects in the Age of Mass-Production," *Journal of Global Buddhism* 20 (2019): 105–125.
86. Campergue, "Gifts and the Selfless Work Ethic," 451.
87. Jane Caple, "The Ethics of Collective Sponsorship: Virtuous Action and Obligation in Contemporary Tibet," *Religion and Society* 8, no. 1 (2017): 145–157.
88. See also Shawn W. Crispin, "Money and Monks," *Far Eastern Economic Review* 166, no. 42 (2003): 54–56.

89. Michael K. Jerryson, *Mongolian Buddhism: The Rise and Fall of the Sangha* (Seattle: University of Washington Press, 2008).
90. Rambelli and Reinders, *Buddhism and Iconoclasm in East Asia*, 42; see also Rambelli, *Buddhist Materiality*, 261–262.
91. Jackson, "The Enchanting Spirit of Thai Capitalism," 41.
92. Michael Jerryson, *If You Meet the Buddha on the Road: Buddhism, Politics, and Violence* (Oxford: Oxford University Press, 2018).
93. Scott, *Nirvana for Sale?*, 40.
94. Ernst Friedrich Schumacher, *Small Is Beautiful: A Study of Economics as if People Mattered* (London: Blond & Briggs, 1973); see also Lionel Obadia, "Is Buddhism Like a Hamburger? Buddhism and the Market Economy in a Globalized World," *Research in Economic Anthropology* 31 (2011): 99–120, 105.
95. Sander G. Tideman, "Gross National Happiness," in *Ethical Principles and Economic Transformation: A Buddhist Approach*, ed. Laszlo Zsolnai (New York: Springer 2011), 133–154.
96. Obadia, "Is Buddhism Like a Hamburger?," 114.
97. Ian Reader and George Joji Tanabe, *Practically Religious: Worldly Benefits and the Common Religion of Japan* (Honolulu: University of Hawai'i Press, 1998), 229.
98. Schopen, *Buddhist Monks and Business Matters*, 2; Schopen, "The Good Monk and His Money"; and Matthew D. Milligan, "Corporate Bodies in Early South Asian Buddhism: Some Relics and Their Sponsors According to Epigraphy," *Religions* 10, no. 4 (2019), 1–22.
99. Neelis, *Early Buddhist Transmission and Trade Networks*; Walsh "The Economics of Salvation"; Walsh, *Sacred Economies*; Amstutz, "Materiality and Spiritual Economies"; Kieschnick, *The Impact of Buddhism on Chinese Material Culture*, 5; Gernet, *Buddhism in Chinese Society*; Bailey and Mabbett, *The Sociology of Early Buddhism*; Jansen, *The Monastery Rules*; Gregory K. Ornatowski, "Continuity and Change in the Economic Ethics of Buddhism: Evidence From the History of Buddhism in India, China and Japan," *Journal of Buddhist Ethics* 2 (1996): 198–240; and Uma Chakravarti, *The Social Dimensions of Early Buddhism* (New York: Oxford University Press, 1988).
100. Stephen G. Covell, *Japanese Temple Buddhism: Worldliness in a Religion of Renunciation* (Honolulu: University of Hawai'i Press, 2005); and Jane Caple, "Monastic Economic Reform at Rong-bo Monastery: Towards an Understanding of Contemporary Tibetan Monastic Revival and Development in A-mdo," *Buddhist Studies Review* 27 (2010): 197–219.
101. Borchert, "Of Temples and Tourists"; Bruntz and Schedneck, *Buddhist Tourism in Asia*; and Fisher, "In the Footsteps of the Tourists."
102. Jeremy Carrette and Richard King, *Selling Spirituality: The Silent Takeover of Religion* (London: Routledge, 2005); Todd Lorentz, "The Dharma and the West: Can Buddhism Survive Consumerism?," *Contemporary Buddhism: An Interdisciplinary Journal* 2, no. 2 (2001): 191–199; David Bubna-Litic, "Buddhism Returns to the Market-Place," in *Contemporary Buddhist Ethics*, ed. Damien Keown (Richmond, Surrey: Curzon 2000), 183–212; Borup, "Branding Buddha"; and Wilson, "Selling Mindfulness."
103. Williams-Oerberg, "Buddhism: A Unique Selling Point in Ladakh."
104. See special issue on "Buddhism and Economics" in the *Journal of Global Buddhism* 20 (2019).
105. Caple, "The Ethics of Collective Sponsorship"; Jane Eluned Caple, *Morality and Monastic Revival in Post-Mao Tibet* (Honolulu: University of Hawai'i Press, 2019); Jeff Wilson, "Buddhism Without Merit: Theorizing Buddhist Religio-Economic Activity in the Contemporary World," *Journal of Global Buddhism* 20 (2019): 87–104; Brox, "The Aura of Buddhist Material Objects"; and Brox and Williams-Oerberg, *Buddhism and Business*.

Elizabeth Williams-Oerberg

ENGAGED BUDDHISM

INTRODUCTION

In August 2014, the Buddhist Peace Fellowship hosted its first national gathering since 2004. It opened with a dialogue between two keynote speakers: Thai activist and founder of the International Engaged Buddhist Network Sulak Sivaraksa, and American environmentalist Joanna Macy. Over the next three days, four hundred attendees participated in workshops on longstanding engaged Buddhist concerns such as environmental justice and caste discrimination in India and new areas of focus such as the erasure of Asian Americans in American Buddhism and the ethics of the secular mindfulness movement.[1] These workshops were held at the East Bay Meditation Center in Oakland, California, a nonsectarian Buddhist community, which was founded on the principles of multiculturalism, radical inclusivity, and social engagement.[2] After the gathering, a small group formed a meditation blockage outside a nearby Marriott hotel in protest of the Urban Shield conference, a weapons expo and militarized police training event, it was hosting.[3]

In bringing together engaged Buddhist pioneers such as Sivaraksa and Macy with an emerging generation of millennial Buddhist activists and interweaving global and local concerns, the 2014 Buddhist Peace Fellowship Gathering offered a glimpse into the trajectory of engaged Buddhism since its emergence as a loosely related wave of Buddhist social and political movements in Asia in the mid-20th century. This article will survey the ever expanding landscape of engaged Buddhism by mapping four major areas: (a) engaged Buddhist activism across the globe, (b) engaged Buddhist hermeneutics, (c) engaged Buddhism as an academic category, and (d) ongoing debates and new directions in engaged Buddhism.

GLOBAL ENGAGED BUDDHISM: ESTABLISHED AND EMERGING FIGURES AND COMMUNITIES

The term "engaged Buddhism" was coined not by a scholar but by the Vietnamese monastic peace activist Thich Nhat Hanh in the 1960s to describe social activism based on Buddhist principles.[4] While it has been dated to 1963, Hanh dates it to 1964 when he used it as the English translation for a book composed of previously written essays that he published on his return to Vietnam after lecturing at Columbia University in 1963–1964.[5] The extended term "socially engaged Buddhism" was taken up in the 1980s by Asian and Western engaged Buddhist activists on the ground and in print.[6] Since its emergence in Asia in the 20th century, engaged Buddhist individuals, organizations, and ideas have emerged and traveled via the transnational routes forged by Buddhist modernism. While not comprehensive, the following offers a glimpse at both established and emerging figures and communities with attention to demographic and generational diversity. Many of the newer organizations have not been studied academically so information comes from primary material that must be treated with caution. Similarly, there remains a lacuna of critical historical analyses of established engaged Buddhist figures or communities, with most studies produced by engaged Buddhist advocates or insiders from the communities.

While engaged Buddhist activism spans a wide range of projects, there are central areas of focus across the international landscape: militarism, anticapitalist developmental work, ethnic violence and oppressions, environmental concerns, women and gender rights, and poverty relief. Engaged Buddhist priorities have shifted, however, in response to historical developments, cultural shifts, and urgent societal needs. Whereas early engaged Buddhism, which emerged in the shadow of World War II, the Vietnam War, and the nuclear threat, focused heavily on peace activism, the pressing climate and ecological crisis has become a major current concern.[7] Alongside work on caste oppression against the Dalits in India and the burakumin in Japan, in the context of #BlackLivesMatter engaged Buddhism in the United States has turned more fully to addressing structural racism.[8] A further development is the emergence of an intersectional and decolonizing engaged Buddhist sensibility that links feminism, environmental activism, and indigenous rights together as a force of resistance to the interlocking systems of patriarchy, racism, capitalism, and the military-industrial complex.[9]

Engaged Buddhism in South and Southeast Asia. Most engaged Buddhist narratives begin with Vietnamese Thien (Zen) monk Thich Nhat Hanh (b. 1926), who coined the term engaged Buddhism. Hanh gained international prominence due to his Buddhist-based peace activism during the Vietnam War in the 1960s. He studied comparative religion at Columbia University and Princeton University in the 1960s and became inspired by Dr. Martin Luther King, Jr. He returned to Vietnam in 1963 and in 1964 founded the Order of Interbeing (Tiep Hien), which centered on extending Buddhist thought and practice to promote peace and social responsibility. Sister Chan Kong (b. 1938) was one of the original members of the Order. He also cofounded the School of Youth for Social Services (SYSS), which applied Buddhist principles to a range of activities included leading antiwar demonstrations, rebuilding bombed villages, and providing medical treatment. Each week, the SYSS practiced a day of mindfulness in which they would recite the Fourteen Mindfulness trainings and chant the Heart Sutra.

Due to his antiwar work, Hanh came under fire from both the American-controlled South Vietnam and the communist-controlled North Vietnam and many of his supporters were jailed or killed. In 1967, he was exiled from Vietnam by the Vietnamese government and Nhat Chi Mai, one of the first six Order of Interbeing members, immolated herself as a peace protest. In the same year, Hanh was nominated for a Noble Peace Prize by Dr. King. Hanh, Sister Kong, and other community members were granted asylum in France where they focused their efforts on helping Vietnamese refugees. The community eventually grew into a thriving monastic and lay community know as Plum Village Buddhist Center, which has branch monasteries in the United States, an international community, and its own printing press. Through a series of books and international tours, Hahn has promoted engaged Buddhist ideals through the practice of mindfulness. At the very center of his mindfulness work is the conviction that "peace is the way" and that individual and societal transformation are inseparable. He presents his engaged Buddhism as continuous with the tradition rather than signaling a new or radical break.[10]

Dr. A. T. Ariyaratne (b. 1931), the founder and president of the Sarvodaya Shramadana movement, has been at the forefront of engaged Buddhism in Sri Lanka. Trained as a teacher, Ariyaratne first developed a "service-learning program" to help rural villagers in Kanatoluwa in 1958. Sarvodaya Shramadana works on a "bottom-up" self-governance model by collectively identifying basic community needs such as systems of clean water, sanitation, housing, or education and then collectively meeting those needs through combining the skill sets of Sarvodaya Shramadana volunteers and village members. Its success is indicated by the fact that it has grown into the largest nongovernmental organization in the country. Ariyaratne bases his work on what he calls a "Buddhist economics" model, which combines secular post-colonial development principles with Buddhist values of generosity. The word *sarva* means "all" and *udaya* means "awakening," signifying Ariyaratne's engaged Buddhist conviction that the Buddhist soteriological goal of liberation can be expressed in all activities including social and economic development.[11] Since the 1990s, Ariyaratne has expanded his efforts to nonviolent peace activism to aid the ethnic violence between the Sinhala Buddhist majority and the Tamil Hindu minority. He has been the recipient of a number of international peace prizes including the Gandhi Peace Prize in 1996 from the government of India. He founded Vishva Niketan International Peace and Meditation Centre, which is centered in the core engaged Buddhist belief that "enduring peace can only be attained when individuals achieve inner peace—cessation of conflict—within themselves."[12]

In Thailand, both monastics and lay Buddhists have been active in forging engaged Buddhist movements. Modern reformist monk Buddhadasa Bhikku (1906–1993) developed what he called a "Dhammic Socialism," which rejected the traditional Theravadin distinction between the mundane and supramundane and placed the nonviolent reform of society, politics, and economics at the center of Buddhist practice.[13] Alongside Thich Nhat Hahn and Mohandas Gandhi, Buddhadasa was one of the inspirations behind the International Network of Engaged Buddhists (INEB), which was cofounded in 1989 by fellow Thai Buddhist Sulak Sivaraksa (b. 1933).[14] Sivaraksa is a lay Buddhist social critic, lawyer, prolific author, and grassroots activist who has been a major force in engaged Buddhism across the globe. Combining Buddhist thought and values with a Marxist systemic critique, his activities span rural development projects, nonviolent peace activism and reconciliation, developing Buddhist economic models, environmental activism, advocating for women's rights, and promoting interfaith work. A vocal critic of the Thai government and Buddhist monastic orthodoxy, he has faced exile and imprisonment and was nominated for a Noble Peace Prize in both 1993 and 1994.[15] Since the 1980s, Thai monastics led by Phrakhru Pitak Nanthakhun have wrapped orange clerical robes around trees in an innovative "tree ordination movement" to protect them from deforestation and its resultant environmental harms.[16]

Efforts to reestablish the Theravāda bhikkhuni movement have been led by Thai and Sri Lankan nuns. On the face of much opposition, Bhikkhuni Dhammananda became Thailand's first fully ordained bhikkhuni in 2003 and is the abbess of Songdhammakalyani Monastery, the country's first all-female Buddhist monastery. Former director for the Women and Gender program at INEB, Buddhist feminist activist Ouyporn Khuankaew leads trauma-informed retreats and workshops for women dealing with domestic violence, retreats for activists suffering from burnout, and leadership training to empower Buddhist nuns and laywomen. Founded in 2002, her organization, the International Women's Partnership for Peace and Justice (IPPJ), is rooted in Buddhism and intersectional feminism and offers programs for Buddhist peace-building, nonviolent resistance, and social change for women.[17] In Cambodia, Maha Ghosananda (1913–2007) led an annual Dhammayietra, or peace walk, which has come to signify the revival of Buddhism, which was all but wiped out during the brutal reign of the Khmer Rouge and the following Vietnamese communist occupation, as well as an international expression of engaged Buddhism. Ghosananda had been living in Thailand for a decade when refugees began forming camps along the Thai–Cambodia border. He distributed thousands of booklets on the *Mettā Sutta* on loving-kindness from the Pali canon and began to work in the camps, eventually becoming a consultant to the UN Economic and Social Council and co-founder of the Inter-religious Mission for Peace in Cambodia. Influenced by Nipponzan Myohoji, a Japanese Buddhist organization dedicated to world peace, and Thich Nhat Hanh's mindfulness, Ghosananda began the Dhammayietra in 1992 when he led 350 refugees on foot back to Cambodia with the teaching that "each step is a meditation." This was the first of what became an annual pilgrimage taken by Buddhist monastics and laity and organized around pressing social themes: repatriation, elections, the Khmer Rouge/government conflict, land mines ban, and illegal logging. Ghosananda was honored as the Supreme Patriarch of Cambodian Buddhism and nominated six times for the Noble Peace Prize.[18]

In Myanmar, formerly Burma, the 1991 Nobel Peace Prize laureate Aung San Suu Kyi was heralded as an icon of engaged Buddhism for her opposition to the country's military regime and her advocacy for democratic government and human rights. She was born in 1945, while Burma was under British colonial rule; her father, Aung San, secured independence from the British empire in 1947 but was assassinated the same year. Educated at Oxford University, Suu Kyi returned to Myanmar to oppose the repressive military regime that had seized power in 1962. In 1988, she cofounded the National League for Democracy and in 1989 she was placed under house arrest, which would last until 2010. During this time, Suu Kyi developed a political rhetoric of resistance that drew heavily on Buddhism, particularly the teachings of metta or lovingkindness, and emphasized the compatibility of Buddhism with liberal democracy.[19] In 2015, Suu Kyi was elected head of government, but not only has the expected democratic revolution failed to materialize, her government has been accused of jailing opponents, silencing the press, and, most damagingly, ethnic cleansing against the Rohingya, Myanmar's minority Muslim population. Suu Kyi's failure to denounce the attempted genocide of the 700,000 Rohingya who have been forced to flee the country after a brutal military campaign has led to her being stripped of a number of human rights awards. Many engaged Buddhists, including the INEB and Sister Kong from the Order of Interbeing, have written public letters to Suu Kyi pleading with her to denounce the ethnic cleansing and support the Rohingya.[20]

Engaged Buddhism in South Asia. Bhimrao Ramji Ambedkar (1891–1956), who led the mass conversion of the Dalits (also historically referred to as outcastes and Untouchables) to Buddhism in India to liberate them from the oppressive hierarchical social and religious caste system, was a pioneer of engaged Buddhism in India. Ambedkar was born into a Dalit Hindu family and became one of the first Dalits to attend college in India before studying at both Columbia University and the London School of Economics. There he trained in Western liberal thought, pragmatic philosophy, and the Protestant social gospel, all of which shaped his political vision and interpretation of Buddhism. He played a major role in the Indian independence movement and became a dedicated activist for Dalit rights under the slogans "Liberty, Equality and Fraternity" and "Educate, Agitate, Organize." He became India's first Law and Justice minister and was the chairman of the constitution drafting committee in Jawaharlal Nehru's first government.[21] After suffering at first hand the relentless discrimination against Dalits, Ambedkar concluded that the Hindu caste system could not be reformed and had to be rejected. He converted to Buddhism in 1956 and immediately initiated a mass conversion of his fellow Dalits to Buddhism, which led to a revival of the tradition in India. Ambedkar's book *The Buddha and His Dhamma* (1957), which was published posthumously, is a seminal engaged Buddhist text and remains the foundation of Ambedkarite Buddhism today. It radically reinterprets the individual liberation from suffering found in traditional Buddhism through a progressive, pragmatic social lens. Recognizing his departure from tradition, Ambedkar framed his socially liberative Buddhism as a *navayāna* or "new vehicle" in the history of the *buddhadharma*.[22] The conversion of Dalits to Buddhism continued after Ambedkar's death and the growth of his community was nurtured by the English monastic Sangharakshita (1925–2018), formerly Dennis Lingwood, who played an important role in Ambedkar's conversion to Buddhism. Sangharakshita founded Trailokya Bauddha Mahasangha Sahayaka Gana (TBMSG), which is the Indian branch of Triratna, the organization Sangharakshita founded on his return to the United Kingdom.[23] TBMSG runs a number of social justice programs combatting poverty, promoting education, and fighting against caste discrimination.[24] Another engaged Buddhist organization that focuses on empowering women and children from the lower caste is the Bodhicitta Foundation. Founded by Ayya Yeshe, an Australian Tibetan Buddhist nun, who is an outspoken critic of the patriarchy in Buddhism, it provides food, healthcare, housing, education, and job skills training as well as legal support for victims of domestic abuse.[25]

Tibetan Buddhist spiritual and political head the Fourteenth Dalai Lama Tenzin Gyatso is also considered a key representative of engaged Buddhism because of his leadership in the Tibetans' nonviolent struggle for self-determination. In his early twenties, he was forced to flee Tibet in 1959 after it was invaded by the Chinese and has since resided in Dharamshala in India, which is the seat of the Tibetan administration in exile. Since 1966, the Chinese occupation has resulted in the systematic destruction of Buddhist communities, monasteries, libraries, and cultural artifacts. The nonviolent resistance Free Tibet Movement emerged in the Tibetan refugee camps in India in the 1970s, with the Tibetan Youth Congress and the Tibetan People's Freedom Movement at its center and the Dalai Lama as its international face. Through a series of world tours and books, he has drawn on Buddhist principles and practice to promote world peace through inner peace as well as advocating for the development of a transnational secular ethics of peace and kindness. In 1989, the Dalai Lama won the Noble Peace Prize in recognition of his nonviolent campaign to end the Chinese occupation. Other major Tibetan Buddhist leaders who have embraced engaged Buddhism include His Holiness Ogyen Trinley Dorje, the seventeenth Karmapa, who is the head of the Kagyü lineage and has foregrounded environmental concerns and promoted vegetarianism in his teachings and activities framed through the Buddhist principles of nonharm and compassion.[26]

There has also been an embrace of socially engaged Buddhist initiatives in the Northwest Indian region of Ladakh, which have taken place as part of wider resistance to secularization processes in the region and have involved both monastic and lay communities. Buddhist monastic and political leader Bakula Rinpoche (1917–2003) set the stage by promoting a "social work ethos" as a key part of Buddhist practice. Bhikku Sanghasena, an internationally renowned Ladakhi monk within the Theravāda Buddhist tradition, founded the Mahabodhi International Meditation Centre (MIMC), which runs a number of educational, health, and service programs under the mantra "Compassion in action. Meditation in action."[27]

Engaged Buddhism in East Asia. While most engaged Buddhist narratives start with Thich Nhat Hanh, scholars have shown that Hanh was influenced by the Chinese monastic Taixu (1890–1947), who spearheaded a modern reform of Buddhism in China in the 1920s. Taixu taught "*renjian fojiao*," translated as "Buddhism for this world" or "Buddhism for this human life," which emphasized the importance of education, publishing, social work, and lay Buddhism for Buddhism to remain relevant in the modern world. In service of "creating the Pure Land in the human realm," his reforms shaped the Chinese Buddhist Revival and initiated the emergence of "humanistic Buddhism," which saw innovations such as Buddhist clinics, orphanages, and schools as well as teaching in prisons. Taixu traveled to Vietnam in 1928 and 1940 and his teachings significantly shaped the climate in which Hanh's engaged Buddhism emerged.[28] Recent scholarship has established that Taixu was deeply involved in radical anarchist and socialist political movements in his formative years and this greatly influenced his interpretations of Pure Land Buddhism and the Maitreya school he founded in 1924.[29] While scholars disagree on whether Chinee Buddhist modernizers such as Taixu, Daxing (1900–1950), and Fafang (1904–1951) are best labeled humanistic Buddhists, engaged Buddhists, or "activist Buddhists," the close historical and structural relationships between them and normative engaged Buddhists such as Hanh requires attention.[30] Against the backdrop of the 1949 Chinese Communist Party victory, humanistic Buddhism migrated to Taiwan, where Yinshun (1906–2005) played a major role in establishing it. Since Taiwan's democratization there has been a remarkable growth in humanistic Buddhist groups, with six major organizations emerging: the Buddhist Compassion Relief Tzu Chi Foundation, Fo Guang Shan, Dharma Drum Mountain, Chung Tai Chan Tzu, Ling Jiou Shan, and Fu-chih. While each group differs in its approach and services, common to all is the commitment to the concept of *renjian fojiao* and establishing a Pure Land on earth through social improvement. For instance, Dharma Drum Mountain was started by the Chan Buddhist monastic Master Sheng Yen. It has a robust social welfare and education program, which it promotes under "the Pure Land on Earth" movement. It runs an extensive meditation retreat program and refers to students who have attended retreats as "Ambassadors of Peace."[31]

Aided by a combination of financial resources, improved education, transportation, and communications, Taiwanese *bhiksunis* or nuns have been particularly active in Buddhist social service since the 1970s.[32] *Bhiksuni* activism includes both radical social and political activism and mainstream humanitarian activities. On one end of the spectrum is Bhiksuni Chao Hwei (b. 1957), who is actively involved in the political arena with a focus on human rights, particularly women's rights. Trained as an academic, her work is explicitly feminist, seeking to dismantle expressions of the hierarchical, oppressive "gender order" in both Buddhist institutions and society. On the other end is the Venerable Cheng Yen (b. 1937), who founded the Tzu Chi Foundation in 1966, an organization with more than 4 million members.[33] The Tzu Chi Foundation leads emergency relief efforts across the world and funds national and international projects focused on free medical care, providing education, and environment. Tzu Chi has been careful not to align with an explicit political agenda, and Venerable Cheng Yen has presented her work as an expression of traditional Buddhist values and traditional feminine gender roles of self-sacrifice and nurturing.[34]

Just as Pure Land Buddhism has been at the heart of engaged Buddhist efforts in Taiwan, so have new interpretations of Nichiren Buddhism been at the center of engaged Buddhism in

Japan. Nichiren (1222–1282) believed the world had entered a degenerate age in which liberation was only possible through the recitation and chanting of the title (*daimoku*) of the *Lotus Sutra*. In the 20th century, three new Nichiren groups emerged that are typically viewed as examples of socially engaged Buddhism: Soka Gakkai, Rissho Kosei-kai, and Nipponzan Myohoji.[35] While all three groups direct their Buddhist practice toward world peace and believe that social improvement can only come about through individual transformation, each group interprets Nichiren distinctively and each pursues a particular style of social activism. Soka Gakkai was founded in the early 1930s and through intense proselytizing has grown into one of Japan's largest new religions, with an international membership of 12 million. Since its early years it has equated the spread of Buddhism with world peace. In 1938 Niwano Nikkyo (1916–1999) and Naganuma Myoko (1889–1957) founded Rissho Kosei-Kai, and since the 1960s, when Nikkyo became involved with the nuclear disarmament movement, the group has framed the Lotus Sutra as expressing "an ideology of peace." Nipponzan Myohoji is a much smaller sect that was founded in 1924 by monastic Nichidatsu Fujii (1885–1995), who was deeply influenced by Mahatma Gandhi. It became active in the Japanese antinuclear war movements in the 1950s. It is much smaller than the other two but has gained international prominence through its peace marches, which influenced Maha Ghosanda's Dhammayietra, and its peace pagodas.

Engaged Buddhism in the United States. Engaged Buddhism in the United States is typically traced back to beat poet, Zen Buddhist, and environmentalist Gary Snyder.[36] His 1961 essay "Buddhist Anarchism," which calls for the union of the "social revolution" of the West and the "individual insight into the basic self/void" of the East, set the analytic framework for much of engaged Buddhism in the West.[37] The nonsectarian Buddhist Peace Fellowship (BPF) was the first engaged Buddhist organization in the United States. It was started by Robert Aitkin Roshi, Anne Aitkin, and Nelson Foster in 1978 after the Vietnamese antiwar movement and had a strong peacemaking focus.[38] In 1983, BPF and the San Francisco Zen Center coorganized Thich Nhat Hanh's first retreat for Western Buddhists in the United States and sponsored some of his subsequent North American tours. Among BPF's many initiatives are the training program Buddhist Alliance for Social Engagement (BASE), which ran from 1990 to 2005, and its *Turning Wheel Journal*, which has featured the work of many engaged Buddhist leaders.[39]

Among BPF's directors and board members are the most prominent first-generation engaged American Buddhists. Sōtō Zen priest Alan Senauke established BPF's international presence and founded the Clear View Project, which is a partner of the INEB, with a focus on Burma and India.[40] Donald Rothberg has been a leading voice of engaged Buddhism in the Insight community with a specialization in conflict resolution.[41] Author and activist Joanna Macy has developed "The Work That Reconnects," a training program that unites Buddhism, deep ecology, and systems thinking.[42] Soto Zen priest Zenju Earthlyn Manuel has confronted the suffering of racial, gender, sexual orientation, and class oppressions in her writings.[43] Representing a second generation of engaged Buddhists, in 2013 Katie Loncke and Dawn Haney launched the "radical rebirth" of BPF on a social media platform and expanded its focus to address antiblackness, racism against Asian American Buddhists, and indigenous rights.[44]

In 1996, American Zen teacher Bernie Glassman (1939–2018) and his wife Sandra Jishu Holmes founded the Zen Peacemaker Order to expand the work they had been doing with the Greyston Foundation, which served homeless populations including those living with HIV/AIDS, through providing housing, child care, and healthcare. Zen Peacemakers has grown into an international community that includes many prominent Buddhist teachers such as Joan Halifax, whose Upaya Institute has developed Buddhist chaplaincy programs.[45] Glassman and the Peacemakers are particularly known for their creative approaches to socially engaged Buddhism based on their three tenets of not knowing, bearing witness, and taking action. These include Bearing Witness retreats at Auschwitz-Birkenau and the Native American Bearing Witness Plunge.[46]

In 2007, American Theravadin monastic Bhikkhu Bodhi (b. 1944) and a group of his students founded Buddhist Global Relief, an engaged Buddhist organization focused on ending world hunger and promoting equitable and ecologically sustainable food systems.[47] Bodhi is also a prolific translator of Pali texts, and he has provided a foundation for engaged Buddhism by drawing attention to the often neglected communal and social teachings of the buddha.[48]

In 2014, at the first White House–US Buddhist Leadership Conference, engaged Buddhists presented two letters—one on climate change and one on racial justice—indicating current pressing concerns. Alongside Joanna Macy's pioneering work, David Loy started the Rocky Mountain Ecodharma Retreat Center as a geographical base for his focus on developing Buddhist practices to respond to the ecological crisis.[49] Kritee Kanko, a co-founder of Rocky Mountain, is a climate scientist and Zen teacher who interlinks climate justice, racial justice, and decolonization.[50] Similarly, One Earth Sangha, a Buddhist climate justice group, cofounded by Insight practitioners Kristin Barker and Lou Leonard, that has blended ecology with the Buddhist concept of the bodhisattva to develop an "Ecosattva training".[51] Dekila Chungyalpa brings Tibetan Buddhist resources to Buddhist environmental activism. She is the director of the Loka Initiative at the Center for Healthy Minds, at the University of Wisconsin-Madison, which promotes interfaith environmental, climate, and sustainability work.[52]

In 2007, the East Bay Meditation Center (EBMC) in Oakland, California, opened to unite the wisdom teachings of Buddhism with social justice. It operates on the principles of radical inclusivity, gift economics, and environmental sustainability.[53] EBMC teachers such as Larry Yang and Mushim Patricia Ikeda have been at the forefront of racial justice initiatives within American Buddhism and have developed spiritual activist programs. Rev. Angel Kyodo Williams, Lama Rod Owen, and Jasmine Syedullah have developed Radical Dharma, a teaching and community that puts Buddhism into conversation with the Black Lives Matter movement.[54] Led by scholar-practitioner Duncan Ryuken Williams, Japanese American community leaders have formed Tsuru for Solidarity, a nonviolent and direct-action project to protest the inhumane treatment of immigrants detained in the United States.[55] One can also see the adoption of engaged Buddhist values, particularly diversity, inclusion, and equity values and ecologically sound practices, across a number of American Buddhists communities that do not explicitly identify as engaged Buddhists. An example is the "statement of repentance and recognition" ritually delivered at the 2018 Soto Zen Buddhist Association conference, which acknowledged the "collective karma" of participating in colonialism, racism, and capitalism.[56]

While engaged Buddhist efforts have been mostly tracked in meditation-based convert communities, other convert and heritage Buddhists have also made significant contributions to engaged Buddhism in the United States.[57] Unlike meditation-based convert communities, Soka Gakkai International (SGI) is marked by significant racial and class diversity and was a lead organization for the First White House–US Buddhist Leadership Conference in 2015. This continued SGI's established history of engagement with racial justice issues. For instance, in 1993, SGI's president, Daisaku Ikeda, met with civil rights pioneer Rosa Parks and she accepted his invitation to visit Soka University in Japan the following year.[58]

Shin Buddhists have also been engaged in a variety of social activism programs.[59] One such initiative is Project Dana, which was founded by Shimeji Kanazawa and Rose Nakamura, two members of Mo'ili'ili Hongwanji Mission, a Shin Buddhist temple in Hawai'i.[60] It provides services to the elderly and vulnerable as an expression of the Buddhist practice of *dana* or selfless giving.[61] Jodo Shinshu Buddhists have also been at the forefront of Buddhist LGBTQI inclusion efforts. In the 1970s, Rev. Koshin Ogui officiated the first same-sex wedding in the Buddhist Church of San Francisco and the Buddhist Church of America officially stated supported for same-sex marriage in 2004.[62]

Myokei Caine-Barret, the first African American and Western woman to be ordained as a priest and bishop in the Nichiren Order, has led social justice efforts in her community such as developing a diversity program for the Nichiren Shu Order of North America, being a leader in racial justice work in American Buddhism, and working with incarcerated populations in Texas.[63]

Engaged Buddhism in Europe. While Buddhism in North America is often considered synonymous with Western Buddhism, and many US-based engaged Buddhist organizations have branches in Europe, it is important to recognize the particularities of Buddhism in Europe.[64] The Amida Trust has been at the forefront of engaged Buddhist efforts in the United Kingdom.[65] Founded in 1998 by the then married couple David and Caroline Brazier, the Amida Trust is a Pure Land Buddhist organization that developed with an explicit engaged Buddhist agenda. Framing their work as an expression of devotion to the "other-power" of Amida Buddhism, members have participated in a range of activities such as antiwar protests and developing Buddhist alternatives to neoliberal economics. Triratna, formerly Friends of the Western Buddhist Order, was founded in 1969 by Sangharakshita, a Briton who had trained as a Buddhist monastic in Asia. It is a nonsectarian international Buddhist modernist organization that has focused on socially beneficial forms of "right livelihood," including sustainable living and social activism. The Community of Interbeing, the UK sangha that follows Thich Nhat Hanh's teaching, began to grow in the 1980s and was registered formally as a charity in 1994. Centered around the practice of mindfulness, their focus has been on transforming society through transforming the individual.[66]

Welsh Chan Buddhist activist and author Ken Jones (1930–2015) cofounded the UK Network of Socially Engaged Buddhists (1983–2014) and developed a model of a "socially radical culture of awakening."[67] Insight teacher Christopher Titmuss has also taken a prominent role in developing a Buddhist social critique and organizing engaged Buddhist responses to environmental harms.[68] An emerging force is Extinction Rebel Buddhists (XRBuddhists), which functions as a Buddhist subgroup of Extinction Rebellion, a global movement using nonviolent civil disobedience to combat the global climate emergency.[69] It shares many members, goals, and strategies with the Dharma Action Network for Climate Engagement (DANCE).[70]

A similar environmental focus is shared by the Ecodharma Center in Catalonia, which runs engaged Buddhist meditation retreats, study seminars, and training camps focused on healing climate change, economic precarity, and social injustice.[71] The Ecodharma Center and its sister secular group the Ulex Project are marked by intersectional and decolonizing sensibilities that characterize generational shifts in engaged Buddhist communities in the West.[72] They center sustainable activism, self-care, understanding power and privilege, and trauma-informed approaches and have trained activists across Europe. These newer approaches are circulated across and beyond more established networks such as the German Network of Engaged Buddhists, which has long been active in peace work, providing emergency aid to Asia, women's liberation, and human rights movements.[73]

Australia, South Africa, and International Groups. The emerging intersectional and decolonizing ethos in engaged Buddhism is fully demonstrated at Dharmagiri: Sacred Mountain Retreat on the border of South Africa and Lesotho. This center was started by former Theravadin monastics Thanissaro and Kittisaro, who have been active in initiating and supporting responses to HIV in South Africa. Under the ethos of the bodhisattva ideal, it combines insight meditation, Buddhist dharma, indigenous wisdom, and permaculture in service of an "equitable, just and sustainable world."[74] Bhante Buddharakkhita is the founder and abbot of the Uganda Buddhist Center, which runs a number of engaged Buddhist initiatives ranging from using meditation to heal the intergenerational trauma of colonialism to female empowerment.[75] In Australia, engaged Buddhist efforts include international aid as well as a range of social welfare activities.[76] The Association of Engaged Buddhists, which was started in 1993, is a monastic and lay organization focused on active social service.[77]

Many of the figures and organizations mentioned previously have international reach and some are part of wider engaged Buddhist networks. One example of an engaged Buddhist organization that began as an international collaboration is Sakyadhītā: International Association for Buddhist Women, which was formed in 1987 after the first international gathering of Buddhist women in Bodhgaya, India, by the German nun Ayya Khema, the American nun Karma Lekshe Tsomo, and the Thai professor Chatsumarn Kabilsingh (now Bhikkhuni Dhammananda). Sakyadhitā translates as "Daughters of the Buddha," and its focus is on advancing the spiritual and secular welfare of women as well as working for gender equity in Buddhism. It hosts biannual conferences across the world that bring together Buddhist nuns and laywomen, many of whom are academically trained, to collaborate on a range of initiatives from providing education and health services for vulnerable women to promoting female ordination and leadership.[78] In response to sexual abuse in Buddhism, Sakyadhita members have launched "The Alliance for Buddhist Ethics," an organization that aims to develop codes of ethics for safe teacher–student relationships and produce educational material for monastic and lay Buddhists on what constitutes abuse and what organizations can do to reduce the risk of harm.[79]

ENGAGED BUDDHIST HERMENEUTICS

While engaged Buddhists see the core teachings of Buddhism as congruent with their social and political activism, they acknowledge that key Buddhist doctrines have not always been taught in a beneficial way and, in some cases, have been used to justify and reproduce social inequities. They see this as due to the wider conservative religious, social, and political context of traditional Buddhism. Some engaged Buddhists argue, for instance, that the teachings of the historic buddha have been distorted by the gender bias and social class privilege of the monastic elites who controlled canonical texts. These monastic elites were also materially supported by the ruling classes and so they reinforced rather than questioned oppressive social hierarchies.[80] Others emphasize the encounter with Western modernity as the key factor in actualizing the progressive social potency of key Buddhist doctrines.[81]

Common to engaged Buddhist hermeneutics is a shift from thinking about core Buddhist doctrines from an individual/existential level to a collective/structural level.[82] For instance, engaged Buddhists consider how the three poisons of greed, ill will, and delusion manifest on a social and institutional level through exploitative labor practices and racist ideologies. In some cases, engaged Buddhists explicitly identify alternative systems of knowledge that have influenced their reading of Buddhist doctrines, such as feminism or systems theory.[83] For others, the emphasis is on how their lived experience with different forms of suffering inspired their interpretations. One emerging pattern within engaged Buddhist hermeneutics is an emphasis on the social context in which a doctrine is taught, for instance, how Buddhist teachings on no-self and anger have a different impact on marginalized populations than they do on those from dominant cultures.[84] A brief glimpse at how engaged Buddhists have interpreted key concepts demonstrates both continuity and innovation within engaged Buddhist hermeneutics and reflects generational and demographic shifts currently underway in engaged Buddhist communities.[85]

Just as the encounter with *dukkha* or suffering forms the core of Buddhism, so the encounter with social suffering lie at the heart of engaged Buddhism. As Paul Fuller notes, "engaged Buddhism is simply a form of Buddhism with a wider discourse of suffering, with types of suffering, with the causes of suffering, with the origination of suffering, and with overcoming and eradicating suffering."[86] The signature doctrine of engaged Buddhism is dependent-arising, which refers to a cosmic web of causes and conditions that constitutes samsara. Whereas early Buddhist readings cast the chain of dependent-arising as something to be liberated from, engaged Buddhists draw on the Mahāyāna concept of Indra's net and embrace dependence-arising as the sustaining network between all sentient beings. Renaming dependent-arising as "interbeing"—being with others and the world—Thich Nhat Hanh has placed it at the very center of his work to denote the mutual dependency between humans, animals, and the ecological systems of which they are part. Similarly, Joanna Macy's "Work That Reconnects" interweaves dependent-arising, systems theory, and deep ecology to forge an ecological Buddhism.[87] Extending the work of both, scholar-practitioner Hsiao-Lan Hu grounds the ethics of socially engaged Buddhism in interdependent co-arising, feminist theories and peace studies.[88]

A similar revision occurs with the teachings on karma. Engaged Buddhists acknowledge that the traditional teachings on karma perpetuate oppressive social conditions in Southeast Asia by encouraging passivity and placing the blame on individuals for their own suffering rather than on social structures. For this reason, Ambedkar reinterpreted the teaching of karma from his new Buddhist community *Navayāna* composed of former Dalits.[89] Others have similarly reinterpreted karma on a social level. Thai Buddhist feminist Khuankaew, for instance, notes that the violence against women is not a fruition of their "bad" individual karma but a result of oppressive gender conditioning and sexism. Engaged Buddhists have forwarded a way of thinking about karma on a societal level in which working to counter unjust systems is viewed as taking responsibility for collective karma.[90]

The Five Precepts (*pañca-śīla*) are the foundational ethics for lay Buddhists. Engaged Buddhism extends these precepts to social, collective, and institutional levels. For instance, the first precept of nonharm is commonly extended to promoting nonharm by actively supporting peace movements, resisting militarization processes, protesting the weapons industry, and adopting a vegetarian diet. The second precept of not taking what is not freely offered is commonly interpreted to include not overusing the earth's natural resources or engaging in consumerist behavior that supports unjust economic systems and protesting against capitalism and unjust labor practices. The third precept of refraining from sexual misconduct is commonly interpreted to protest against exploitative sexual labor and has been recently extended to include forms of gender or sexual discrimination. The fourth precept of refraining from false speech is commonly interpreted to include engaging in racist or discriminatory language against vulnerable minorities. The fifth precept of not using intoxicants includes reflecting on the precarious conditions under which intoxicants such as coffee are produced and being caught up in the consumer culture that produces new intoxicating technologies.[91] Thich Nhat Hahn developed the Fourteen Precepts of Engaged Buddhism, which include speaking out in situations of injustice and not accumulating wealth in the face of global poverty.[92]

The Mahāyāna figure of the bodhisattva, and the bodhisattva vow to save all sentient beings from samsara, figure prominently in engaged Buddhist hermeneutics. Tzu Chi, a Taiwanese Mahāyāna Buddhist organization, frames its social service work as part of the bodhisattva path and describes bodhisattvas as those who take voluntary action to help relieve the suffering of others.[93] Engaged Buddhist scholars have provided canonical support by turning to Mahāyāna sutras that depict bodhisattvas being called upon to relieve material suffering as a prerequisite for teaching the dharma.[94] Similarly, much of the work done by engaged Buddhists, be it feeding the hungry or protesting environmental exploitation, is framed as an expression of the wide range of *upāya* or skillful means at the bodhisattvas' disposal.

The Two Truths doctrine in Mahāyāna Buddhism, which differentiates between absolute truth (paramārtha) the ontological ultimate nature of reality, and relative truth (saṃvṛti) or conventional daily existence, has been harnessed by engaged American Buddhists to legitimate attending to suffering in the relative realm. Zenju Earthlyn Manuel offers a sophisticated hermeneutic of the two truths to work with the embodied differences of race, gender, and sexuality that often lead to systemic discrimination.[95] The Mahāyāna doctrine of Buddhanature, that all beings have the potential for awakening, has been adopted by engaged Buddhists working in prisons who report it as a powerful antidote for inmates who feel they are innately ethically defective. Buddhist narratives of ethical transformation have also been taken up in prison work. One Buddhist chaplaincy organization is named after Angulimala, a fearsome mass murderer whose killing spree came to an end after his encounter with the buddha and who eventually became an *arhant*.[96]

For early proponents, it is the absence of anger that marks engaged Buddhism as a uniquely Buddhist form of social activism.[97] For some Gen X and millennial Buddhists, however, anger is considered an appropriate response to an unjust situation and they warn against its premature dismissal. Lama Rod Owens offers a tantric approach to anger, which liberates its wisdom energy in the service of racial justice.[98] Similar generational differences can be seen in approaches to right speech. While Sallie King turns to a close reading of the Pali suttas to show that right speech does not always involve being gentle and can include sharp rebuke, Edwin Ng draws on critical race theory to deliver a much more provocative reading of how right speech is weaponized to shut down conversations about white privilege and racism in Buddhist communities and beyond.[99] Central to racial justice work in American Buddhism is the revisioning of the traditional fourfold sangha into the "beloved community" in which the building of diverse and inclusive sanghas is offered as a corrective to the individualism that has historically marked meditation-based convert Buddhism.[100] Similarly, Asian American Buddhists have reformulated the Buddhist practice of "taking refuge" to "be the refuge" to signify the creation of safe spaces for practitioners who have been harmed and marginalized in majority white Buddhist and wider cultural spaces.[101]

ENGAGED BUDDHISM AS AN ACADEMIC CATEGORY

The first wave of academic scholarship on engaged Buddhism appeared in the 1990s and was produced by Buddhist scholar-practitioners who were advocates as well as analysts of the phenomenon. Pioneers of the subfield of engaged Buddhism Christopher Queen and Sallie King adopted the term to describe Buddhist social movements such as Hanh's peace activism, Ambedkar's challenge to caste discrimination in India, A. T. Ariyaratne's alleviation of rural poverty in Sri Lanka, and the Tibetan fight for self-determination that emerged after World War II in Asia against the backdrop of militarism, nationalism, and colonialism. Their coedited *Engaged Buddhism: Buddhist Liberation Movements in Asia* (1996) was the first academic scholarship on the topic and set the normative parameters for its study: identifying its historical parameters, its modern Western influences, main characteristics, and relationship to traditional Buddhism.

First, it set the historical parameters for engaged Buddhism by starting the narrative in Vietnam in the 1960s with the antiwar movement of Thich Nhat Hanh, but it asserted that the groundwork for engaged Buddhism began in the late 19th century with reforms resulting from the encounter between Buddhism and Western modernity under the conditions of colonialism. Queen dates these reforms to 1880 with the arrival of American Henry Steel Olcott (1832–1907) in Sri Lanka, then Ceylon. Olcott and his protégé Anagarika Dharmapala (1864–1933) produced an ecumenical vison of Buddhism that blended Buddhist and Western thought and has since been identified as Buddhist modernism.[102]

Second, it highlighted the modern Western philosophical, cultural, and theological discourses that shaped engaged Buddhism: Christian liberation theology rooted in the Hebrew Prophetic tradition and the modern Euro-American Enlightenment discourses of individual rights, democracy, and social reform. Third, it identified the main characteristics of engaged Buddhism, with the most significant being (a) a commitment to nonviolence, (b) a grassroots movement around a charismatic leader, and (c), signifying a shift from a transcendent to a mundane liberation, "we may conclude that a profound change in Buddhist soteriology—from a highly personal and other-worldly notion of liberation to a social, economic, this-worldly liberation—distinguishes the Buddhist movements in our study."[103] Fourth, in relationship to traditional Buddhism, it noted that while engaged Buddhism was a new phenomenon in the history of the tradition, it was a legitimate innovation and an authentic expression of its core ideals that was well captured by the Buddhist hermeneutical framework of *upaya* or skillful means.[104]

Just a few years after this groundbreaking collection marked the beginning of engaged Buddhism as a subfield within the larger field of Buddhist studies, a number of academic books, journals, and conferences on the topic appeared.[105] The scholarship produced through these early networks has generally remained faithful to the historical, analytical, and evaluative parameters set in Queen and King's seminal collection, although its geographical scope has extended to North America and Europe.[106] While some have sought to emphasize the traditional "Buddhist" side of engaged Buddhism, either by drawing historic parallels with early Buddhist reformers such as Indian King Ashoka (304–232 BCE) and Japanese Buddhist reformer Nichiren (1222–1282) or by highlighting canonical contributions, the scholarly consensus is that engaged Buddhism is an Asian and Western culturally hybrid form of Buddhism that falls under the theoretical category of Buddhist modernism.[107] A number of studies identify key characteristics of engaged Buddhism, and while there are minor differences, nonviolence, critique of the nation-state, and collective liberation remain foundational principles.[108]

Evaluations of engaged Buddhism reflect wider debates on the legitimacy of Buddhist modernism, with the main area of dispute revolving around its relationship to traditional Buddhism.[109] On the one side, scholars have emphasized its historical precedents and canonical Buddhist foundations and its valid and necessary extension of Buddhist ideals for modern political and social contexts.[110] On the other side, scholars have argued that the profound shift from individual suffering and liberation to structural suffering and collective liberation marks it as historically discontinuous with classical Buddhism but have stressed its soteriological validity as a "new vehicle" or a "fourth yana in the evolution of the Dharma."[111] Less vocal but not absent were scholars who concluded it was only nominally Buddhist.[112]

Another area of debate is what counts as "engaged" action.[113] Some suggest a widely inclusive understanding of engagement that includes mindful actions in all areas of life.[114] Others push for a more specific definition of actions marked by systemic analysis and social engagement. Ken Jones offers the categories of "soft" engagement for those Buddhists primarily committed to practicing "mindfulness in daily life," who tend to be more interested in personal practice, and "hard" engagement for those committed to social analysis and institutional transformation.[115] The mainstreaming of mindfulness in areas such as business, medicine, and education rendered by the secular mindfulness movement has reignited this debate.[116] Despite differences about what counts as engagement, however, the consensus was that engaged Buddhism referred to liberal and progressive Buddhist figures or groups rather than conservative and reactionary ones.[117]

Finally, another notable characteristic is that the majority of the first generation of scholars of engaged Buddhism are also engaged Buddhist activists and, in many cases, have produced both academic and popular literature on the topic.[118] This crossover between the study and practice of engaged Buddhism has undoubtedly contributed to an overwhelmingly positive portrayal of it and the theoretical dominance of a critical-constructivist approach in the academic subfield of engaged Buddhism.[119] Engaged Buddhist scholar-practitioners have brought

Buddhism into conversation with not just modern but also postmodern, poststructural, and postcolonial thought. Reflecting generational and demographic shifts, new scholarship sees an increasing attention to intersectional feminism and critical race theory.[120] In the field of Buddhist studies, engaged Buddhism has been closely aligned with Buddhist ethics and American Buddhism.[121] Other methodological and theoretical approaches include the anthropology and sociology of religion.[122]

New Directions in the Academic Study of Engaged Buddhism. While the term "engaged Buddhism" has been commonly used to describe and celebrate movements emerging in the mid-20th century that extend Buddhist principles to nonviolent social activism such as peacemaking, environmental justice, and women's rights, more recently, scholars have questioned the historical, structural, and ethical range of the term as normatively employed. These scholars make two major interventions: first, they demonstrate connections between engaged Buddhists of the mid-20th century and Buddhists who were active in the pre-World War II period, thereby extending the term's historical range. Second, they question the structural features of the term, particularly nonviolence and critique of the nation-state, thereby extending the category to include Buddhists whose social actions include nationalism and violence.

Jessica Main and Rongdao Lai offer a revised version of the analytic category of socially engaged Buddhism, which they ground in their respective scholarship of Buddhist movements in China and Japan occurring in the first half of the 20th century.[123] They problematize the normative definition on two grounds: first, they argue that it locates engaged Buddhism with a particular form—pacifist and independence from the nation-state—of Buddhist activism; and second, they question the moral praise bestowed on these groups. For Main and Lai, the academic category of engaged Buddhism should be detached from both moral evaluation and particular forms and be understood more broadly as the performance of action—typically collective or group action—that is characterized by a type of moral reasoning, soteriology, and resistance to secularism. They explain:

> We argue that Buddhist social engagement is a modern phenomenon that relies on a particular form of modern reasoning, which resonates with some of the axioms of liberation theology: this reasoning depicts society as fundamentally unjust and in need of change, social ills as systemic and in need of systematic solutions, social activity itself as Buddhist practice, and positions religious modern action within the putatively "secular" sphere of the modern nation-state.[124]

According to Main and Lai, socially engaged Buddhism arose primarily in response to secularization, which relegated religion to the private sphere, thereby reducing its societal and political impact. Rejecting the secular insistence on the distinction between public and private, certain Asian Buddhist groups began to view social action occurring within public spheres as essentially soteriological in nature. They point to the religious-social activism of the Chinese monastic reformer Taixu (1890–1947) and his student monks in the 1930s and 1940s and the efforts of Japanese Shin Buddhist priest Takeuchi Ryo'on (1891–1967) from the 1920s to the 1950s. Not only do such prewar figures expand the historical range of engaged Buddhism, they also undermine core ethical characteristics because they were nationalistic and not pacifist.[125]

Paul Fuller has also exerted analytic pressure on the normative definition of engaged Buddhism.[126] He returns to Hanh's definition of engaged Buddhism as Buddhism "entering into life," and he delineates between two meanings of engaged Buddhism: (a) the prevailing nonviolent and progressive form and (b) a more general meaning that allows for a wider perspective on the multiple ways in which Buddhists engage with issues in society. As he notes,

> engaged Buddhism in this sense can get messy, because it is involved, it is a Buddhism which has a social, ethical, political, ecological and even ethnic voice. It can tackle issues of identity, whether national or sexual, and can lend its voice to support liberal or conservative agendas.[127]

Employed in this wider sense, Fuller includes the Burmese Buddhist monk Ashin Wirathu (b. 1968), the leader of the ethnocentric nationalistic 969 movement, which has incited violence against the Burmese Muslim population, alongside renowned pacifists such as A. T. Ariyaratne (b. 1931), who has attempted to reconcile the Sinhala Buddhist majority and the Tamil Hindu minority in Sri Lanka in his survey of engaged Buddhism.

As noted, there have been debates within normative engaged Buddhist studies on what engagement signifies—with some scholars emphasizing "soft" and others "hard" engagement; however, these new studies go much further by undermining two core characteristics: nonviolence and critical distance from the nation-state. In interrogating core assumptions of what constitutes engaged Buddhism, the work of these scholars not only expands the historical and ideological parameters of the field of engaged Buddhism but also raises serious questions about the utility of the category itself. What kind of modifiers are needed to delineate between the structurally similar but radically different agendas of Buddhist radicals and Buddhist conservatives, nationalistic Buddhists and cosmopolitan Buddhists? Should one, for instance, discriminate between "progressive" engaged Buddhism and "ethnocentric" engaged Buddhism? Or do the radically different agendas and activities of these forms render the category itself limited and in need of replacement?

ONGOING DEBATES AND NEW DIRECTIONS IN ENGAGED BUDDHISM

Relationship to Tradition and Questions of Legitimacy. Since the emergence of engaged Buddhism, there has been much debate over its relationship to traditional Buddhism and its legitimacy as a Buddhist movement. This is often framed as a debate between "traditionalists" and "modernizers," with the former arguing for its continuity with traditional Buddhism and the latter emphasizing its distinctiveness.[128] Some traditionalists argue that Buddhism has always been socially engaged but this engagement was neglected or ignored in modern representations of the tradition because it served Christian missionaries and the colonial enterprise to depict it as an apolitical and asocial religion. Others stress that the misrepresentation of Buddhism as apolitical is due to limited scholarship that relied too heavily on Max Weber's flawed categorization of Buddhism as "other-worldly asceticism."

Traditionalists look for precursors of social action in Buddhist texts such as enlightened Buddhist monarchs and government, or Buddhist reformers. They also stress engaged Buddhist activities as contemporary expressions of classical Buddhist ethics such as compassion and altruism.[129] Others go even further by looking beyond both modernity and tradition to early Buddhist doctrines and practices and argue that the radical social potency of these teachings was thwarted by both male monastic elites and modern orientalist scholars.[130]

Modernizers acknowledge the historic and ethical distinctiveness of engaged Buddhism. They suggest that traditional Buddhism has either had little interest in social engagement or that the type of social actions it has conducted are categorically distinct from modern engaged Buddhism. In terms of the former position, they suggest that the soteriological focus of Buddhism on freedom from samsara rendered the social and political landscape as largely irrelevant to its ultimate aims. Those who hold the latter perspective argue that unlike earlier Buddhist elite leadership, engaged Buddhism is rooted in grassroots, nongovernmental movements and has an explicit political critique absent in socially beneficent Buddhist monarchs. Most significantly, they recognize that the shift from the classical focus on individual suffering and liberation to the engaged Buddhist focus on collective and structural suffering and liberation marks it as a significant departure from the classical tradition. They propose that the radical social and political potency of Buddhism has only been ignited by its encounter with Western modernity. In recognition of its uniqueness, they have developed signifiers that recognize its innovations, such as Ambedkar's *Navayāna* or "new vehicle" or Queen's "fourth yana" and "action dharma."[131]

Some seek to destabilize or delegitimize engaged Buddhism by arguing that it is an entirely modern phenomenon that represents modern values such as human rights that have been imposed onto the tradition. Drawing on Buddhist texts from the 7th and 8th centuries, for instance, Amod Lele identifies "disengaged Buddhists," who explicitly "look with suspicion on, or even actively reject, engagement with social and political problems." He argues that scholar-practitioners of engaged Buddhism have failed to attend to the significant doctrinal challenge posed by disengaged Buddhism.[132] On a similar note, others have argued for maintaining the distinctive Buddhist canonical focus on wisdom rather than blending or replacing it with Western concerns of justice.[133]

Others accept the legitimacy of engaged Buddhism as a Buddhist movement but disagree on its relationship to canonical Buddhism.[134] For traditionalists, this legitimacy is ultimately rooted in relationship to tradition; for modernizers it is rooted in a necessary extension of Buddhist individual ethics to the social and political realm, an extension only made possible by the encounter with Western modernity. Later scholarship, however, has troubled certain assumptions in both modernist and traditionalist perspectives. One critique suggests that modernists reproduce colonialist and orientalist textual approaches to Buddhism by exclusively focusing on Buddhist texts and not paying sufficient attention to the ways in which those texts have been put to use by Asian Buddhists in service of sociopolitical goals. This lack of attention is undergirded by the orientalist binary of a mystical/passive East and a rational/active West and a "Western savior" model in which modernity rescues Buddhism from its supposed apolitical, asocial slumber.[135]

THE MAINSTREAMING OF MINDFULNESS

The first round of academic scholarship on engaged Buddhism was produced at the turn of the millennium, when mindfulness was little known outside Buddhist circles. The 2010s, however, saw the growth of the secular mindfulness movement and the mainstreaming of mindfulness practice across education, health, business, and other secular domains.[136] The mainstreaming of mindfulness raises new questions and challenges for what counts as "engagement" in engaged Buddhism: what conditions are necessary to make mindfulness an engaged practice? In what ways does the individualism, self-help, and commodification that mark sectors of the secular mindfulness movement threaten its force as a tool of engaged Buddhism? How can one differentiate between engaged and nonengaged mindfulness practice when it has been decontextualized from its Buddhist context and recontextualized in various domains of public life including the military and capitalism?[137] How can engaged Buddhists resist what has been dubbed "McMindfulness"—the commodification of mindfulness in service of neoliberalism and capitalism?[138]

One useful typology in assessing different types of engagement is the delineation between "assimilative" and "radical" currents in the adoption of mindfulness as a force of social change.[139] The assimilative current is based on the assumption that individual mindfulness practice will naturally lead to social transformation and underlies the incorporation of meditation into established institutions such as schools and hospitals, capitalist business enterprises, and the political arena. An example here is US Congressman Tim Ryan's book *The Mindful Nation: How a Simple Practice Can Help Reduce Stress, Improve Performance, and Recapture the American Spirit,* which inspired "The Mindful Nation Foundation," a nonprofit organization begun in 2013 with the mission of building a "national grassroots, ambassador-led community" to support mindful living for "veterans, children, teachers, leaders and healthcare professionals."[140] The radical current shifts focus from individual practice to radical structural change and collective liberation and is most visible in progressive social activist communities, which have adopted meditation as a strategy of self-care and a creative tool of protest. An example here is the mass meditations organized by the Interdependence Project, a secular Buddhist organization in New York City, organized in Zuccotti Park, the site of the anticapitalist Occupy Wall Street protests in downtown Manhattan.

ETHNOCENTRIC "ENGAGED" BUDDHISM

Early scholarship on engaged Buddhism insisted on a fundamental distinction between nonviolent grassroots movements and violent nationalist forms. As Sallie King notes,

> not every activist engagement of Buddhism with social and political issues can be considered Engaged Buddhism, however. Certainly, the chauvinist Buddhist nationalism of contemporary Sri Lanka is not Engaged Buddhism in as much as its stance is based on opposition and ill-will towards the other—in this case, non-Buddhist Sri Lankan minorities—a stance that easily escalates into acts of violence, as has frequently occurred in recent decades.[141]

New definitions proposed by Main and Lai and by Fuller, however, reopen the question of who can be considered an engaged Buddhist.[142] Their respective broader definitions of engaged Buddhism open the door to a whole new cast of engaged Buddhist figures and concerns including those whose overt agendas stand in direct opposition to normative engaged

Buddhism. Whether one thinks engaged Buddhism is a legitimate signifier for these movements will depend upon what definition of engaged Buddhism is accepted.

The most controversial new movements to be considered as engaged Buddhism are those that promote what Fuller has called "ethnocentric Buddhism," Buddhist forms of identity that collapse religious and national identity and result in violent social and political action against those deemed to be a threat to Buddhist nationalism.[143] Fundamental to such groups is the idea that the teachings of the Buddha are under threat and need to be protected through action in the social and political realm. Here the collective preservation and defense of the *sāsana*, a term used to denote the Buddhist order, teachings, and practices, takes precedence over the individual goal of liberation, signifying a shift in concern from the supramundane to the mundane. A prominent example is the Buddhist monk Ashin Wirathu, famous for his association with the nationalistic 969 movement and leader of the "Organization to Protect Race and Religion" (*amyo barthar thathanar*), commonly known as the Ma Ba Tha movement, which has been at the forefront of violence against Burmese Muslims. Similar sentiments are also displayed in Burmese Buddhist monastic reactions to what is perceived as the misuse of images of the buddha, which have resulted in the public denouncement, fines, and imprisonment of Burmese citizens and foreign nationals.[144]

GENERATIONAL SHIFTS, INTERSECTIONALITY, AND DECOLONIZATION

New generations and demographics of Buddhists drawn from Generation X and millennial populations are emerging and reshaping the landscape of engaged Buddhism in America.[145] Such shifts have been amplified by the impact of new social medias and technology that enable easy flows of information and the development of new formats and modalities with which to practice engaged Buddhism. One characteristic of the generational shift has been an increased focus on the lack of racial diversity, white privilege, and racism within American convert Buddhism and the wider American culture. While African American Zen teacher Zenju Earthlyn Manuel served as a director of the BPF, and an early initiative of the BPF was the development of antiracist training programs, the first generation of engaged Buddhists in the United States comprised an overwhelmingly white middle-class demographic. BPF's millennial director Katie Loncke, and her former Generation X codirector Dawn Haney, have prioritized addressing structural racism, healing antiblackness, and countering the erasure of Asian Americans in convert Buddhist circles.[146] BPF's membership is marked by significant race, class, gender, and sexual orientation demographic diversity, including a new generation of Asian American engaged Buddhist activists.[147] BPF members are drawing on critical race theory and postcolonial thought to foster an intersectional engaged Buddhist hermeneutics. One characteristic of this hermeneutic is to center marginalized experience and draw attention to the troubling ways in which Buddhist doctrines can be weaponized in ways that shut down conversations about oppression in Buddhist circles.[148] A similar intersectional and marginalized lived experience commitment is found in *The Arrow*, a virtual journal produced by second-generation Shambhala students, which explores the relationship between contemplative practice, activism, and politics.[149] Scholar-activist Rima Vesely-Flad demonstrates the ways in which Black Buddhists expand the parameters of engaged Buddhism with their focus on the particular suffering generated from racialized bodies.[150]

A related development has been increasing connections between engaged Buddhist and Native American indigenous communities and more attention to the ongoing harms of colonialism in the United States. In 2014, the Zen Peacemakers, after twenty-five years of witnessing retreats, held their first Native American Bearing Witness (NABW) retreat in the Black Hills of South Dakota. One of the largest environmental protests in the history of the United States was the Dakota Access Pipeline protests that began at the start of 2016 at Standing Rock reservation in North Dakota. A number of different indigenous groups came together as "water protectors" to stop the construction of an oil pipeline project that posed a serious threat to the ecological safety of the land and the treaty rights and well-being of the Standing Rock Sioux. A number of engaged Buddhist groups and individuals such as the BPF, One Earth Sangha, and the Zen Peacemakers set up a Buddhist camp and protested alongside indigenous activists.[151] This reflects growing connections between engaged Buddhism, environmental justice, and indigenous activism.[152] The encounter with indigenous communities has also impacted engaged Buddhism on a theoretical level. For instance, Joanna Macy's *Deep Times: A Journal of the Work that Reconnects*" contains a new section, "Evolving Edge," which attempts to decolonize certain assumptions and practices within the Work that Connects.[153] Recent scholarship has also recovered some of the anticolonial roots of early Buddhist modernism, which links contemporary turns with earlier engaged Buddhist expressions.[154]

Another development reflecting a decolonial turn is the strengthening of ties between marginalized Asian and Western communities, which is taking place in a global context in which boundaries between engaged Buddhists in Asia and the West are being crossed and blurred due to the transnational flow of information, organizations, and activism. One example here is the presentation by Lama Choyin Rangdrol, an African American Tibetan Buddhist teacher, at the 2017 B. R. Ambedkar International Conference in Bangalore, India, where he drew a parallel between the sufferings of African Americans and the Dalits in India.[155] Given ongoing generational and demographical shifts within engaged Buddhist scholarship and activism, one can expect further developments along intersectional and decolonial lines.[156]

DIGITAL MATERIALS

The Alliance for Buddhist Ethics (https://allianceforbuddhistethics.com) is a collective to promote ethical behavior in Buddhist communities particularly related to sexual abuse in Buddhism.

The Arrow: A Journal of Wakeful Society, Politics and Culture (https://arrow-journal.org) is an online journal that explores the relationship between contemplative practice, politics, and activism.

Buddhistdoor Global (BDG) (https://www.buddhistdoor.net) is an online nonsectarian Buddhist media platform that includes a focus on engaged Buddhists and Buddhist progressive action.

International Network of Engaged Buddhists (http://inebnetwork.org) is the website and journal of the International Network of Engaged Buddhists.

The Mindfulness Bell: Journal of the Community of Mindful Living (https://www.mindfulnessbell.org) is the online journal of Thich Nhat Hanh's Interbeing community.

Donald Rothberg's website (http://www.donaldrothberg.com/resources/resources-on-socially-engaged-buddhism) contains a comprehensive list of resources on socially engaged Buddhism; dharma and climate change; and race, whiteness, and dharma.

North American Buddhist Alliance (https://www.northamericanbuddhistalliance.org) is the website of a network of North American Buddhist communities that hosts a "Justice Resource" section including the "Buddhists for Racial Justice" initiative.

Sakyadhītā: International Association for Buddhist Women (https://www.sakyadhita.org) is a hub for resources on women and gender in Buddhism.

Turning Wheel Media Buddhist Peace Fellowship (http://www.buddhistpeacefellowship.org/our-work/turning-wheel-media/) is the online journal of the Buddhist Peace Fellowship.

Trans Buddhists (https://transbuddhists.org) is a collective of Buddhist practitioners who seek to address systemic exclusion of transgender and gender nonconforming people from Buddhist spaces.

Tsuru for Solidarity (https://tsuruforsolidarity.org) is a nonviolent, direct action project of Japanese American social justice advocates working to end detention sites and support frontline immigrant and refugee communities.

FURTHER READING

Chandler, Stuart. *Establishing a Pure Land on Earth: The Foguang Buddhist Perspective on Modernization and Globalization.* Honolulu: University of Hawaii Press, 2004.

Fuller, Paul. *An Introduction to Engaged Buddhism.* London: Bloomsbury, 2021.

Gleig, Ann. *American Dharma: Buddhism Beyond Modernity.* New Haven, CT: Yale University Press, 2019.

Gleig, Ann. "Enacting Social Change Through Meditation." In *Oxford Handbook of Meditation*, Oxford Handbooks Online, edited by Miguel Farias, David Brazier, and Mansur Lalljee. London and New York: Oxford University Press, 2020.

Harris, Ian, ed. *Buddhism and Politics in Twentieth-Century Asia.* London: Cassell Academic, 2001.

Henry, Phil. *Adaption and Developments in Western Buddhism: Socially Engaged Buddhism in the U.K.* London: Bloomsbury, 2013.

Hu, Hsiao-Lan. *This-Worldly Nibbana: A Buddhist-Feminist Social Ethic for Peacemaking in the Global Community.* Albany: State University of New York Press, 2011.

Ip, Hung-yok. "Buddhist Activism and Chinese Modernity." Special Issue, *Journal of Global Buddhism* 10 (2009).

Jondhale, Surendra, and Johannes Beltz, eds. *Reconstructing the World: B. R. Ambedkar and Buddhism in India.* New Delhi: Oxford University Press, 2004.

Keown, Damien, ed. *Contemporary Buddhist Ethics.* Richmond, UK: Curzon Press, 2000.

King, Sallie. *Being Benevolence: The Social Ethics of Engaged Buddhism.* Honolulu: University of Hawaii Press, 2005.

King, Sallie. *Socially Engaged Buddhism.* Honolulu: University of Hawaii Press, 2009.

Kraft, Kenneth, ed. *Inner Peace, World Peace: Essays on Buddhism and Nonviolence.* Albany: State University of New York Press, 1992.

Lele, Amod. "Disengaged Buddhism." *Journal of Buddhist Ethics* 26 (2019): 240–289.

Le Hoang Anh Thu, "Doing Bodhisattva's Work: Charity, Class and Selfhood of Petty Traders in Hồ Chí Minh City." *Journal of Vietnamese Studies*, Vol. 15, Issue 4, pps. 4–32.

Loy, David. *Money, Sex, War, Karma: Notes for a Buddhist Revolution.* Somerville, MA: Wisdom, 2008.

McMahan, David. *The Making of Buddhist Modernism*. Oxford: Oxford University Press, 2008.

Macy, Joanna. *Mutual Causality in Buddhism and General Systems Theory*. Albany: State University of New York Press, 1991.

Macy, Joanna, and Stephanie Kaza. *A Wild Love for the World: Joanna Macy and the Work for Our Time*. Boulder, CO: Shambhala, 2020.

Main, Jessica L., and Rongdao Lai. "Introduction: Reformulating 'Socially Engaged Buddhism' as an Analytical Category." *The Eastern Buddhist* 44, no. 2 (2013): 1–34.

Prebish, Charles S., and Martin Baumann, eds. *Westward Dharma: Buddhism Beyond Asia*. Berkeley: University of California Press, 2002.

Prothero, Stephen. *The White Buddhist: The Asian Odyssey of Henry Steel Olcott*. Bloomington: Indiana University Press, 1996.

Queen, Christopher S. *Engaged Buddhism in the West*. Somerville, MA: Wisdom, 2000.

Queen, Christopher S., and Sallie B. King, eds. *Engaged Buddhism: Buddhist Liberation Movements in Asia*. Albany: State University of New York Press, 1996.

Queen, Christopher S., Charles Prebish, and Damien Keown, eds. *Action Dharma: New Studies in Engaged Buddhism*. Surrey, UK: RoutledgeCurzon, 2003.

Sara Swenson, "The Affective Politics of Karma among Buddhist Cancer Charities in Vietnam." *Journal of Vietnamese Studies*, Vol. 15, Issue 4, pps. 33–62.

Tsomo, Lekshe, ed. *Buddhist Feminisms and Femininities*. Albany: State University of New York Press, 1992.

Yancy, George, and Emily McRae, eds. *Buddhism and Whiteness: Critical Reflections*. Lanham, MD: Lexington Books, 2019.

Yao, Yu-Shuang. *Taiwan's Tzu Chi As Engaged Buddhism: Origins, Organization, Appeal and Social Impact*. Leiden: Global International, 2012.

Zu, Jessica Xiaomin, "A Spiritual Evolutionism: Lü Cheng, Aesthetic Revolution, and the Rise of a Buddhism-Inflected Social Ontology in Modern China." *Journal of Global Buddhism, Journal of Global Buddhism* 2021, Vol.22 (1): 49–75.

NOTES

1. "BPF Summer Gathering Schedule," Buddhist Peace Fellowship.
2. Ann Gleig, "East Bay Meditation Center," World Religions and Spirituality.
3. Richard Eskow, "Don't Just Sit There, Do Something," *Tricycle: The Buddhist Review*, November 10, 2014.
4. Damien Keown suggests that the term "engaged Buddhism" was coined by Thich Nhat Hanh in 1963 but that he did not reference this claim; see Damien Keown, *A Dictionary of Buddhism* (London: Oxford University Press, 2003), 86. Paul Fuller updates this to 1964 with a direct reference from Hanh; see Paul Fuller, *An Introduction to Engaged Buddhism* (London: Bloomsbury, 2021); and Thich Nhat Hanh, "Dharma Talk: History of Engaged Buddhism," *Mindfulness Bell*, May 6–7, 2008.
5. Hanh, "Dharma Talk."
6. Sulak Sivaraksa, *Socially Engaged Buddhism* (Bangkok: Thai Inter-Religious Commission for Development, 1988). The history of the term is discussed in Christopher S. Queen and Sallie B. King, eds., *Engaged Buddhism: Buddhist Liberation Movements in Asia* (Albany: State University of New York Press, 2016), 34, note 6.
7. Stephanie Kaza offers a timeline of Buddhism and environmentalist activism that spans more than fifty years; Stephanie Kaza, *Green Buddhism: Practice and Compassionate Action in Uncertain Times* (Boston: Shambhala, 2019). For an example of an international collaboration, see Dharma Teachers International Collaborative on Climate Change.

8. In 2003, Sharon Smith noted that apart from the efforts of Soka Gakkai, race has not featured prominently in engaged Buddhism; Sharon Smith, "Widening the Circle: Communities of Color and Western Buddhist Convert Sanghas," in *Action Dharma: New Studies in Engaged Buddhism*, ed. Christopher Queen, Charles Prebish, and Damien Keown (Surrey, UK: RoutledgeCurzon, 2003), 220–236.
9. An example is Thanissara, *Time to Stand Up: An Engaged Buddhist Manifesto for Our Earth; The Buddha's Life and Message Through Feminine Eyes* (Berkeley, CA: North Atlantic Books, 2015).
10. Patricia Hunt-Perry and Lyn Fine, "All Buddhism Is Engaged: Thich Nhat Hanh and the Order of Interbeing," in *Action Dharma: New Studies in Engaged Buddhism*, ed. Christopher Queen, Charles Prebish, and Damien Keown (Surrey, UK: RoutledgeCurzon, 2003), 35–66.
11. George Bond, "A. T. Ariyaratne and the Sarvodaya Shramadana Movement in Sri Lanka," in *Engaged Buddhism: Buddhist Liberation Movements in Asia*, ed. Christopher S. Queen and Sallie B. King (Albany: State University of New York Press, 2016), 121–147; George Bond, "Sarvodaya Shramadana's Quest for Peace," in *Action Dharma: New Studies in Engaged Buddhism*, ed. Christopher Queen, Charles Prebish, and Damien Keown (Surrey, UK: RoutledgeCurzon, 2003), 126–133; Ahangamage Tudor Ariyaratne, *The Power Pyramid and the Dharmic Cycle* (Moratuwa: Sarvodaya Vishva Lekha, 1998); and Ahangamage Tudor. Ariyaratne, *Peace Making in the Buddhist Context* (Moratuwa: Sarvodaya Vishva Lekha, 1987).
12. Vishva Niketan, International Peace and Meditation Centre.
13. Santikaro Bhikku, "Buddhadasa Bhikku: Life and Society Through the Natural Eyes of Voidness," in *Engaged Buddhism: Buddhist Liberation Movements in Asia*, ed. Christopher S. Queen and Sallie B. King (Albany: State University of New York Press, 2016), 147–193.
14. See International Network of Engaged Buddhists.
15. Donald K. Swearer, "Sulak Sivaraksa's Buddhist Vision for Renewing Society," in *Engaged Buddhism: Buddhist Liberation Movements in Asia*, ed. Christopher S. Queen and Sallie B. King (Albany: State University of New York Press, 2016), 195–235; and Matteo Pistono, *Roar: Sulak Sivaraksa and the Path of Socially-Engaged Buddhism* (Berkeley, CA: North Atlantic Books, 2019).
16. Sue Darlington, *The Ordination of a Tree: The Thai Buddhist Environmental Movement* (Albany: State University of New York Press, 2012).
17. See the International Women's Partnership for Peace and Justice.
18. Kathryn Poethig, "Moveable Peace: Engaging the Transnational in Cambodia's Dhammayietra," *Journal for the Scientific Study of Religion* 41, no. 1 (2002): 19–28.
19. Stephen McCarthy, "The Buddhist Political Rhetoric of Aung San Suu Kyi," *Contemporary Buddhism: An Interdisciplinary Journal* 5, no. 2 (2004): 67–81.
20. "Buddhist Response to Rohingya Crisis," Buddhist Humanitarian Project; "Drops of Compassion: A Letter from Sister Chan Kong," Plum Village; and Hozan Alan Senauke, "Myanmar's Buddhist Leaders Must Stand Against Ethnic Cleansing," *Lion's Roar: Buddhist Wisdom for Our Times*, September 21, 2017.
21. Christopher Queen, "Dr. Ambedkar and the Hermeneutics of Buddhist Liberation," in *Engaged Buddhism: Buddhist Liberation Movements in Asia*, ed. Christopher S. Queen and Sallie B. King (Albany: State University of New York Press, 2016), 1–44.
22. Bhimrao Ramji Ambedkar, *The Buddha and His Dhamma* (Bombay: Siddharth, 1984).
23. Alan Sponberg, "TBMSG: A Dhamma Revolution in Contemporary India," in *Engaged Buddhism: Buddhist Liberation Movements in Asia*, ed. Christopher S. Queen and Sallie B. King (Albany: State University of New York Press, 2016), 73–120.
24. See Nagaloka: A Major Center of the Buddhist Revival in India.
25. See the Bodhicitta Foundation.
26. "The Karmapa's Environmental Activity," Khoryug.
27. Elizabeth Williams-Oerberg, "Buddhist Business and Benevolence in Leh, Ladakh," *Journal of Human Values* 27, no. 1 (2021): 60–71.

28. Elise A. Devido, "The Influence of Chinese Master Taixu on Vietnamese Buddhism," Special Issue on "Buddhist Activism and Chinese Modernity," *Journal of Global Buddhism* 10 (2009): 413–458.
29. Justin R. Ritzinger, *Anarchy in the Pure Land: Reinventing the Cult of Maitreya in Modern Chinese Buddhism* (Oxford: Oxford University Press, 2017).
30. Hung-yok Ip, "Buddhist Activism and Chinese Modernity," Special Issue on "Buddhist Activism and Chinese Modernity," *Journal of Global Buddhism* 10 (2009): 145–192.
31. David Schack and Hsin-Huang Michael Hsiao, "Taiwan's Socially-Engaged Buddhist Groups," *China Perspectives* 59 (2005): 1–19.
32. Karma Lekshe Tsomo, "Socially-Engaged Buddhist Nuns: Activism in Taiwan and North America," Special Issue on "Buddhist Activism and Chinese Modernity," *Journal of Global Buddhism* 10 (2009): 459–485.
33. Yu- Shuang Yao, *Taiwan's Tzu Chi as Engaged Buddhism: Origins, Organization, Appeal and Social Impact* (Leiden: Global International, 2012).
34. Yao, *Taiwan's Tzu Chi*, 468.
35. Jacqulyn L. Stone, "Nichiren's Activist Heirs: Soka Gakkai, Rissho Kosei-kai, Nipponzan Myohoji," in *Action Dharma: New Studies in Engaged Buddhism*, ed. Christopher Queen, Charles Prebish, and Damien Keown (Surrey, UK: RoutledgeCurzon, 2003), 63–94.
36. Forthcoming scholarship on the formative but neglected role that Shin Buddhism played in the construction of American Buddhist modernism is likely to also change the current narrative of engaged Buddhism in the U.S. See Scott Mitchell, "Mid-Century Modern Jōdo Shinshū and the Making of American Buddhism."
37. Gary Snyder, "Buddhist Anarchism," *Journal for the Protection of All Beings* 1 (1961).
38. Judith Simmer-Brown, "Speaking Truth to Power: The Buddhist Peace Fellowship," in *Engaged Buddhism in the West*, 67–94.
39. For a selection of *Turning Wheel* writings, see Susan Moon, ed., *Not Turning Away: The Practice of Engaged Buddhism* (Boston: Shambhala, 2004).
40. See Clear View Project.
41. Donald Rothberg, *The Engaged Spiritual Life: A Buddhist Approach to Transforming Self and the World* (Boston: Beacon Press, 2006).
42. See Work That Reconnects Network.
43. Zenju Earthlyn Manuel, *The Way of Tenderness: Awakening Through Race, Sexuality and Gender* (Somerville, MA: Wisdom, 2018).
44. Ann Gleig, *American Dharma: Buddhism Beyond Modernity* (New Haven, CT: Yale University Press, 2019), 250–258.
45. Christopher Queen, "Glassman Roshi and the Peacemaker Order: Three Encounters," in *Engaged Buddhism in the West*, (Boston: Wisdom, 2000), 95–127.
46. Bernie Glassman, *Bearing Witness: A Zen Master's Lessons in Making Peace* (Boston: Blue Rider Press, 2013).
47. See Buddhist Global Relief.
48. Bhikku Bodhi, *The Buddha's Teaching on Social and Communal Harmony: An Anthology of Discourses from the Pali Canon* (Somerville, MA: Wisdom, 2016).
49. See Rocky Mountain Ecodharma Retreat Center.
50. Boundless in Motion-Zen Meditation, Grief Rituals and Strategic Activism.
51. See One Earth Sangha.
52. Dekila Chungyalpa, "Human-Earth Connection" Mind & Life Podcast May 21 2021 https://podcast.mindandlife.org/dekila-chungyalpa/
53. Ann Gleig, "Dharma Diversity and Deep Inclusivity at the East Bay Meditation Center: From Buddhist Modernism to Buddhist Postmodernism?" *Contemporary Buddhism: An Interdisciplinary Journal* 15, no. 2 (2014), 312–331.

54. Angel Kyodo Williams and Jasmine Syedullah, *Radical Dharma: Talking Life, Love and Liberation* (Berkeley, CA: North Atlantic Books, 2018).
55. Duncan Ryuken Williams and Asoka Mukpo, "Tsuru for Solidarity: Never Again," *Tricycle* Summer 2020 (Cambridge: Harvard University Press, 2019).
56. Hayleigh Atwood, "Soto Zen Buddhist Association Conference Examines Diversity and Privilege," *Lion's Roar: Buddhist Wisdom for Our Times*, September 25, 2018.
57. The neglect and erasure of heritage Buddhists in the United States is addressed by Funie Hsu, "We've Been Here All Along," *Lion's Roar: Buddhist Wisdom for Our Times*, May 17, 2017.
58. Daisaku Ikeda, "Rosa Parks: Just One Word," Daisaku Ikeda.
59. Alfred Bloom, "Engaged Buddhism in Shin."
60. For information on Shimeji Kanazawa sand Rose Nakamura see *Japanese Eyes, American Hearts: Learning to Live in Hawai'i* Volume III Tendai Educational Foundation, 2013. The author wishes to thank the Engaged Jodo Shinshu Buddhism Twitter Account (https://twitter.com/EngagedPureLand) for their help in providing source material on Jodo Shinshu.
61. See Project Dana.
62. Jeff Wilson, "All Beings are Equally Embraced by Amida Buddha," Jodo Shinshu Buddhism and Same-Sex Marriage in the United States, *Journal of Global Buddhism* Vol 13 (2012): 31-59. See also, Kiyonobu Joshin Kuwahara, "Is My Sangha Inclusive?" *Lion's Roar* June 2 2017 https://www.lionsroar.com/lets-talk-is-my-sangha-inclusive/ and the 2021 special series run by the Institute for Buddhist Studies, "Queering Buddhism for Pride Month" http://blog.shin-ibs.edu/desire-lines-queering-buddhism-for-pride-month/
63. Zen T. C. Zheng, "A Spiritual Quest," *Houston Chronicle*, November 13, 2009; and Meet A Teacher: Myokei Caine-Barret, Shonin," *Lion's Roar: Buddhist Wisdom for Our Times*, July 4, 2017.
64. Laurence Cox, "European Buddhist Traditions," in *Oxford Handbook of Contemporary Buddhism*, ed. Michael Jerryson (Oxford: Oxford University Press, 2016), 332–345.
65. For a review of engaged Buddhism in Britain, see Sandra Bell, "A Survey of Engaged Buddhism in Britain," in *Engaged Buddhism in the West*, 397–422.
66. Phil Henry, *Adaption and Developments in Western Buddhism: Socially Engaged Buddhism in the U.K.* (London: Bloomsbury, 2013).
67. Ken Jones, *The New Social Face of Buddhism: An Alternative Sociopolitical Perspective* (Somerville, MA: Wisdom, 2003).
68. See Christopher Titmuss.
69. In April 2020, Extinction Rebellion U.K. Buddhist Facebook private group had 208 members; Yogaratna, "Extinction Rebellion as Spiritual Practice: Some Thoughts, Triratna.
70. See Dharma Action Network for Climate Engagement.
71. See Ecodharma Center: Radical Ecology, Radical Dharma.
72. See the Ulex Project.
73. Franz-Johannes Litsch, "Engaged Buddhism in German-Speaking Europe," in *Engaged Buddhism in the West*, 423–445.
74. See Dharmagiri: Sacred Mountain Retreat.
75. Uganda Buddhist Centre.
76. Roderick S. Bucknell, "Engaged Buddhism in Australia," in *Engaged Buddhism in the West*, 468–481, was the first article on engaged Buddhism in Australia. Its findings are disputed in Patricia Sherwood, "Buddhist Contribution to Social Welfare in Australia," *Journal of Buddhist Ethics* 8 (2001): 61–74.
77. See the Association of Engaged Buddhists.
78. See Sakyadhītā: International Association for Buddhist Women.
79. See the Alliance for Buddhist Ethics.

80. Hsiao-Lan Hu, *This-Worldly Nibbana: A Buddhist-Feminist Social Ethic for Peacemaking in the Global Community* (Albany: State University of New York Press, 2011), 2–3; and Kenneth Kraft, "Wellsprings of Engaged Buddhism," in *Not Turning Away: The Practice of Engaged Buddhism*, ed. Susan Moon (Boston: Shambhala, 2004), 154–161.
81. See Queen, *Action Dharma*; and David Loy, *The Great Awakening: A Buddhist Social Theory* (Boston: Wisdom, 2003).
82. For an overview of some traditional Buddhist concepts used in engaged Buddhism, see Sallie King, *Socially Engaged Buddhism* (Honolulu: University of Hawaii Press, 2009), 13–38.
83. Hu, *This-Worldly Nibbana*; and Loy, *The Great Awakening*.
84. Gleig, *American Dharma*, 139–175.
85. Gleig, *American Dharma*, 209–248.
86. Fuller, *An Introduction to Engaged Buddhism*.
87. Hui Ling Lim, "Environmental Revolution in Contemporary Buddhism: The Interbeing of Individual and Collective Consciousness in Ecology," *Religions* 10, no. 2 (2019): 120; and Joanna Macy, *World as Lover, World as Self: Courage for Global Justice and Ecological Renewal* (Berkeley, CA: Parallax Press, 2003).
88. Hu, *This-Worldly Nibbana*.
89. Ambedkar, *The Buddha and His Dhamma*.
90. Jonathan S. Watts, ed., *Rethinking Karma: The Dharma of Social Justice* (Chiang Mia: Silkworm Books, 2009). Joy Brennan, "Deconstructing Whiteness," Lion's Roar June 18 2021.
91. Loy, *The Great Awakening*, 37–40; and Sulak Sivaraksa, *Seeds of Peace: A Buddhist Vision for Renewing Society* (Berkeley, CA: Parallax Press, 1992), 73–78.
92. Thich Nhat Hanh, *Interbeing: Fourteen Guidelines for Engaged Buddhism* (Berkeley, CA: Parallax Press, 1987).
93. "The Bodhisattva Path," Tzu Chi USA.
94. Stephen Jenkins, "Do Bodhisattvas Relieve Poverty?" in *Action Dharma: New Studies in Engaged Buddhism*, ed. Christopher Queen, Charles Prebish, and Damien Keown (Surrey, UK: RoutledgeCurzon, 2003), 38–49.
95. Zenju Earthlyn Manuel, *The Way of Tenderness: Awakening Through Race, Gender and Sexuality* (Somerville, MA: Wisdom, 2015).
96. Angulimala: The Buddhist Prison Chaplaincy; and Virginia Cohn Parkum and John Anthony Stultz, "Symbol and Narration in Buddhist Prison Ministry," in *Action Dharma: New Studies in Engaged Buddhism*, ed. Christopher Queen, Charles Prebish, and Damien Keown (Surrey, UK: RoutledgeCurzon, 2003), 237–249.
97. King, *Socially Engaged Buddhism*.
98. Lama Rod Owens, *Love and Rage: The Path of Liberation Through Anger* (Berkeley, CA: North Atlantic Books, 2020).
99. Sallie King, "Right Speech Is Not Always Gentle: The Buddha's Authorization of Sharp Criticism, Its Rationale, Limits, and Possible Applications," *Journal of Buddhist Ethics* 24 (2017): 347–367; and Edwin Ng, "Fuck Your Right Speech (Are You Listening?)," Buddhist Peace Fellowship.
100. Larry Yang, *Awakening Together: The Spiritual Practice of Awakening and Community* (Somerville, MA: Wisdom, 2017). For contextualization of this work, see Ann Gleig, "Undoing Whiteness in American Buddhist Modernism: Critical, Collective, and Contextual Turns," in *Buddhism and Whiteness*, ed. George Yancy and Emily McRae, Philosophy of Race Series (Lanham, MD: Lexington Books, 2019), 21–42.
101. "In Memory of Aaron J. Lee," Angry Asian Buddhist, November 11, 2019; and Chenxing Han, *Be the Refuge: Raising the Voices of Asian American Buddhists* (Berkeley, CA: North Atlantic Books, 2020).

102. Christopher S. Queen, "Introduction," in *Engaged Buddhism: Buddhist Liberation Movements in Asia*, ed. Christopher S. Queen and Sallie B. King (Albany: State University of New York Press, 2016), 22–28. For a study of Olcott, see Stephen Prothero, *The White Buddhist: The Asian Odyssey of Henry Steel Olcott* (Bloomington: Indiana University Press, 1996).
103. Queen, "Introduction," 10.
104. Queen, "Introduction," 29.
105. For details, see Kenneth Kraft, "New Voices in Engaged Buddhist Studies," in *Engaged Buddhism in the West*, ed. Christopher S. Queen (Somerville, MA: Wisdom, 2000), 485–511.
106. Christopher S. Queen, ed. *Engaged Buddhism in the West* (Somerville, MA: Wisdom, 2000).
107. King, *Socially Engaged Buddhism*. For an historical and theoretical examination of Buddhist modernism, see David McMahan, *The Making of Buddhist Modernism* (Oxford: Oxford University Press, 2008).
108. Queen, *Engaged Buddhism in the West*, 6–11.
109. For a critique of Buddhist modernism, see Donald S. Lopez, *The Scientific Buddha: His Short and Happy Life* (New Haven, CT: Yale University Press, 2012).
110. King, *Socially Engaged Buddhism*, 2.
111. Queen, *Engaged Buddhism in the West*, 1–2.
112. James E. Dietrick, "Engaged Buddhist Ethics: Mistaking the Boat for the Shore," in *Action Dharma: New Studies in Engaged Buddhism*, ed. Christopher Queen, Charles Prebish, and Damien Keown (Surrey, UK: RoutledgeCurzon, 2003), 252–269.
113. For a summary of the debate, see Queen, *Engaged Buddhism in the West*, 8–11.
114. Hunt-Perry and Fine, "All Buddhism Is Engaged."
115. Jones, *The New Social Face of Buddhism*.
116. Christopher S. Queen, "The Ethics of Engaged Buddhism in the West," *Oxford Handbook of Buddhist Ethics*, ed. Daniel Cozort and James Mark Shields (Oxford: Oxford University Press, 2018), 501–529.
117. King, *Socially Engaged Buddhism*, 3.
118. See, for instance, Kaza, *Green Buddhism*.
119. For a discussion of Buddhist critical-constructivism, see Roger R. Jackson and John Markransky, eds., *Buddhist Theology: Critical Reflections by Contemporary Buddhist Scholars* (Richmond, UK: Curzon, 2000).
120. Representative of earlier approaches are David Loy and Ken Jones; see Loy, *The Great Awakening*; and Jones, *The New Social Face of Buddhism*. Later work nuances these approaches by bringing intersectional feminism and critical race theory into the conversation. See Hu, *This-Worldly Nibbana*; and Edwin Ng and Zack Walsh, "Vulnerability, Response-Ability, and the Promise of Making Refuge," *Religions* 10, no. 2 (2019): 80.
121. The *Journal of Buddhist Ethics* has been a major site for the exploration of engaged Buddhism. Damien Keown has written extensively on engaged Buddhism and Buddhist ethics; see, for instance, Damien Keown, ed., *Contemporary Buddhist Ethics* (Richmond, UK: Curzon Press, 2000). See also Queen, "The Ethics of Engaged Buddhism in the West." For a discussion of the relationship of engaged Buddhist scholarship to the study of American Buddhism, see Kenneth Kraft, "New Voices in Engaged Buddhist Studies," in *Engaged Buddhism in the West*, ed. Christopher S. Queen (Somerville, MA: Wisdom, 2000), 485–511.
122. For an anthropological approach, see Darlington, *The Ordination of a Tree*; for a sociological approach, see Henry, *Adaption and Developments in Western Buddhism*.
123. Jessica L. Main and Rongdao Lai, "Introduction: Reformulating 'Socially Engaged Buddhism' as an Analytical Category," *The Eastern Buddhist* 44, no. 2 (2013): 1–34.
124. Main and Lai, "Introduction," 5.

125. Main and Lai, "Introduction," 18–24.
126. Fuller, *An Introduction to Engaged Buddhism.*
127. Fuller, *An Introduction to Engaged Buddhism.*
128. A summary of the traditionalist vs. modernist debate is provided by Thomas Freeman Yarnall, "Engaged Buddhism: New and Improved? Made in the USA of Asian Materials," in *Action Dharma: New Studies in Engaged Buddhism*, ed. Christopher Queen, Charles Prebish, and Damien Keown (Surrey, UK: RoutledgeCurzon, 2003), 286–343.
129. An example here is Jenkins, "Do Bodhisattvas Relieve Poverty?"
130. This is the perspective taken by many feminist engaged Buddhist scholar-practitioners. See Rita M. Gross, *Buddhism After Patriarchy: A Feminist Analysis, History and Reconstruction of Buddhism* (Albany: State University of New York Press, 1992); and Hu, *This-Worldly Nibbana.*
131. Queen, *Engaged Buddhism in the West*, 22–26.
132. Amod Lele, "Disengaged Buddhism," *Journal of Buddhist Ethics* 26 (2019): 240–89, at 258.
133. Thanissaro Bhikku, "Wisdom Over Justice," *Lion's Roar: Buddhist Wisdom for Our Times*, November 3, 2017.
134. James Dietrick concludes that socially engaged Buddhist ethics are only "nominally" Buddhist. See Dietrick, "Engaged Buddhist Ethics."
135. Yarnall, "Engaged Buddhism," 303–331.
136. For a history of the secular mindfulness movement, see Jeff Wilson, *Mindful America: The Mutual Transformation of Buddhist Meditation and American Culture* (Oxford: Oxford University Press, 2014.) For critiques of secular mindfulness from an engaged Buddhist perspective and socially engaged forms of mindfulness, see Gleig, *American Dharma*, 50–83.
137. Queen, "The Ethics of Engaged Buddhism in the West," 501–529.
138. David Loy and Ron Purser, "Beyond McMindfulness," *Huffpost*, August 13 2013.
139. Ann Gleig, "Enacting Social Change Through Buddhist Meditation," in *Oxford Handbook of Meditation*, ed. Miguel Farias, David Brazier, and Mansur Lalljee, Oxford Handbooks Online, 2020.
140. See Mindful Nation.
141. King, *Socially Engaged Buddhism*, 3.
142. Main and Lai (2013), Introduction; and Fuller, *An Introduction to Engaged Buddhism.*
143. Paul Fuller, "The Narratives of Ethnocentric Buddhist Identity," *Journal of the British Association for the Study of Religion* 20 (2018): 19–44.
144. Paul Fuller, "The Idea of 'Blasphemy' in the Pali Canon and Modern Myanmar," *Journal of Religion and Violence* 4, no. 2 (2016): 159–181.
145. Gleig, *American Dharma*, 209–248.
146. Gleig, *American Dharma*, 250–258.
147. Han, *Be the Refuge.*
148. Ng, "Fuck Your Right Speech"; and Ng and Walsh, "Vulnerability, Response-Ability, and the Promise of Making Refuge."
149. *The Arrow: A Journal of Wakeful Society, Culture, and Politics.*
150. Rima Vesely-Flad, "Black Buddhists and the Body: New Approaches to Socially Engaged Buddhism," *Religions* 8, no. 11 (2017): 239.
151. James K. Rowe, "Micropolitics and Collective Liberation: Mind/Body Practices and Left Social Practices," *New Political Science* 38, no. 2 (2016): 206–222; and James K. Rowe and Mike Simpson, "Lessons From the Front Lines of Anti-Colonial Pipeline Resistance," *Waging Nonviolence*, October 9, 2017.
152. Rod Meade Sperry, "Among the Bodhisattvas at Standing Rock," *Lion's Roar: Buddhist Wisdom for Our Times*, December 4, 2016.

153. "Evolving Edge," *Deep Times: A Journal of the Work That Reconnects.*
154. Alice Marie Turner, Brian Booking, and Laurence Cox, *The Irish Buddhist: The Forgotten Monk Who Faced Down the British Empire* (Oxford: Oxford University Press, 2020).
155. Sharyn Skeeter, "In India, Seattle Lama Presents on Links Between African Americans' and Untouchables' Experience," *Northwest Dharma Association* 30, no. 3 (2017).
156. Turner, Bocking, and Taylor, *The Irish Buddhist.*

Ann Gleig

EPIGRAPHY AND THE STUDY OF BUDDHISM: SOUTH ASIA'S NORTHERN CORRIDOR

INTRODUCTION

Inscriptions are a fundamental and essential source for the study of Buddhism in India. By revealing the beliefs, practices, and aspirations of their composers or sponsors that were current at the time and place of their composition, they both balance and supplement the depictions provided by canonical and other normative texts. Inscriptions also provide abundant historical evidence of the institutional structures of Buddhist communities, which in Buddhist literature are typically described only in ideal or theoretical terms.

Moreover, because of the extreme paucity of historical literature in pre-Islamic Indian literature in general, inscriptional records constitute the primary source of information about the chronology and historical context of Indian Buddhism throughout its history. Scholars' understanding of such fundamental developments in the history of Buddhism as the origin of the buddha image, the origin and growth of the Mahāyāna, the development of the major monastic centers, and even the date of the buddha itself are largely dependent, directly or indirectly, on epigraphic material. For inscriptions by their very nature—unlike literary texts—provide at least an approximate chronological context, whether from explicit dates or, in their absence, in the form of estimates based on the script or language.

Indian Buddhist inscriptions are extremely numerous, numbering more than four thousand from their first appearance during the reign of King Aśoka in the 3rd century BCE through Buddhism's final decline in the 12th and 13th centuries CE. They are, as might be expected, especially concentrated in major cultic sites and stūpa complexes, most notably Sanchi (925 inscriptions), Bharhut (225), Sarnath (231), and Kasia (ancient Kuśinagara; 126), but are scattered virtually all over north India at various periods.[1]

TYPES OF INSCRIPTIONS

By far the most numerous class of inscriptions consists of those that record various kinds of donations. Typical of this class in earlier centuries are donations of stūpas or components thereof, relics of the buddha, and images of the buddha (or buddhas) or other venerable individuals. Short donative inscriptions are also sometimes found on practical objects such as lamps, pots, and kitchen utensils. Inscriptions on seals, found in large numbers at some sites such as Kasia, can provide useful information about administrative structures of monastic institutions. Prominent among later inscriptions are copperplate charters recording royal grants of land or villages to monastic institutions, and eulogistic texts (*praśasti*) on stone slabs.

Less numerous but also useful are inscriptions containing citations of Buddhist texts, either independently or embedded in donative records. Another important class is label inscriptions that identify the accompanying sculptural or painted scenes.

LANGUAGES AND SCRIPTS

Over the millennium and a half of northern Indian Buddhist epigraphy, the preferred languages evolved gradually from Prakrit to Sanskrit. All early inscriptions, from the 3rd century BCE until about the 2nd century CE, were composed in Prakrit, either in a nonregionally specific general epigraphical dialect or in a regional Prakrit, most notably the Gāndhārī Prakrit of the northwestern part of the subcontinent. Between the 2nd and 4th centuries CE, the language of Buddhist inscriptions gradually evolved into a language intermediate between Prakrit and Sanskrit, known as "Epigraphical Hybrid Sanskrit," which mirrors the "Buddhist Hybrid Sanskrit" of literature of the corresponding period. Then, from about the 4th century, north Indian Buddhists adopted Sanskrit—once again paralleling the development of their literary styles—as the main epigraphic language. In succeeding centuries, the vocabulary and style of Buddhist inscriptions is gradually assimilated to the high classical of Brahmanical Hindu *kāvya* literature. Throughout the history of Buddhist epigraphy in north India, as elsewhere in the Indian subcontinent, Pali is extremely rare as an epigraphic language, attested only in the form of a handful of inscriptions whose dialect approximates canonical Pali.

The scripts of Buddhist inscriptions follow the general pattern of the history of writing in historic India as a whole. That is to say, everywhere except in the northwest the early inscriptions are written in Brāhmī script, while later ones are recorded in the various local varieties and derivatives of Brāhmī. But in the region of Gandhāra and adjoining areas of the northwest, until around the 3rd century CE, the dominant script was Kharoṣṭhī, used to record the local Gāndhārī language, or a Sanskritized variety thereof. Although not Buddhist in origin, Kharoṣṭhī in effect became a Buddhist script in that nearly all inscriptions and manuscript texts that use it reflect a Buddhist environment.

CHRONOLOGICAL AND TYPOLOGICAL SURVEY

The First Buddhist Inscriptions: Aśoka and the Mauryan Period (3rd Century BCE). The inscriptions of Aśoka Maurya (reigned *c* 272–232 BCE) can be divided into the nonsectarian category, comprising the major rock edicts and the major pillar edicts, and the explicitly Buddhist inscriptions, namely the minor rock and minor pillar edicts.[2] In the minor rock edicts, which are reproduced in similar form in eighteen different sites around north, central, and south India, Aśoka explicitly describes himself as a Buddhist lay-follower (*upāsaka*) and expresses his determination to practice more zealously in the future. In the "schism edict," recorded on pillars at Sanchi, Sarnath, and Kausambi, he warns against schism in the monastic communities (sangha) and prescribes a penalty of banishment for monks or nuns who promote disharmony. The minor pillar edicts at Rummindei (Lumbini) and Niglīvā (Nigāli Sāgar) celebrate, respectively, the birthplace of the Buddha Śākyamuni and Aśoka's expansion of the stūpa of the earlier Buddha Konāgamana, as well as noting Aśoka's personal visit to both sites. Finally, in the Calcutta-Bairāṭ (or "Bhābrā") rock inscription, Aśoka, after declaring his reverence and devotion to the three jewels of Buddhism, recommends seven canonical texts that he considers to be particularly worthy of the attention of the local monks and nuns as conducive to the long survival of the dharma.

These inscriptions show scholars Aśoka in his role as an enthusiastic sponsor and propagator of Buddhism who was personally involved in monastic affairs, both in giving advice and in wielding authority. Particularly significant is the list of seven preferred texts in the Bairāṭ edict; although their identification with specific texts of the Pali and other Buddhist canons as now known is difficult in several respects, the edict is the earliest direct documentary reference to any canonical texts.[3]

The only other Buddhist inscription that clearly dates back to the period of the Mauryan dynasty (*ca.* 324–187 BCE) is on the reliquary vase found at Piprāwā (Basti District, Uttar Pradesh), which bears an inscription labeling it as the "receptacle for the bodily relics of Buddha, Lord of the Śākyas" (*salila-nidhane budhasa bhagavate sakiyānaṃ*).[4] It is a uniquely early precursor of the relic cult inscriptions, large numbers of which were produced, especially in the northwest, in succeeding centuries.

The Śuṅga Period: Stūpas and Inscriptions (2nd–1st Centuries BCE). In the succeeding period of north Indian history, conventionally referred to as the Śuṅga period, Buddhist epigraphy takes entirely new forms, with the dominant types being donative records memorializing the contribution by devotees of individual components of stūpas, and label inscriptions (particularly at Bharhut) explaining the content of the accompanying sculpted image. Two stūpa sites in particular dominate the corpus in this phase, namely Bharhut in northeast central India (Satna District, Madhya Pradesh) with 225 inscriptions, and Sanchi in north central India (Raisen District, Madhya Pradesh) with 925.[5] None of the inscriptions of this period are specifically dated, but one Bharhut inscription (no. A 1) is recorded as "during the reign [or 'in the kingdom'] of the Śuṅgas" (*suganaṃ raje*), presumably placing them in or around the 2nd and 1st centuries BCE, a dating that is consistent with their paleographic and linguistic features.[6] The Bharhut and Sanchi inscriptions are roughly contemporary, but their relative dating is a matter of controversy.

Of the 225 inscriptions at Bharhut, 141 are donative, recording the gifts of individuals, both lay and monastic, and male and female (in a ratio of about three to two). The objects donated are components of the elaborately decorated circumambulatory railing around the stūpa proper. The donative inscriptions are written directly on the object donated, sometimes specifying it as "pillar" (*thabha-*) or "railing" (*suci-*), but often simply referring to it as "gift" (*dāna-*). The simple formula may contain only the donor's name, the type of object, and the word "gift," as in "[This] railing [is] the gift of Dhuta" (*dhutasa suci dāno*).[7] About one-third of the donative inscriptions mention the donor's place of origin or residence, for example, "[This railing is] the gift of Bhutarakhita from Vidiśā (*vedisāto Bhutarakhitasa dānaṃ*).[8] Such inscriptions indicate that the Bharhut stūpa drew visitors and donors from a considerable distance.

The remaining 84 Bharhut inscriptions are labels explaining the accompanying scenes sculpted into the pillars and railings. Twenty-seven of the labels refer to *jātakas* and *avadānas*, for example, *chadaṃtiya jātakaṃ*, "the jātaka of the six-tusked [elephant]," referring to a story corresponding to Pali Jātaka no. 514 (see figure 1).[9] Other inscriptions label the bodhi trees of the buddhas (B 13-17), scenes from the life of the buddha (B 18-40), and images of yakṣas and other local deities (B 1-12), some of them not otherwise known.

The early inscriptions at Sanchi generally resemble those at Bharhut, with the important difference that they are virtually all donative. There are no label inscriptions at Sanchi, but the reason for the difference remains to be convincingly explained. The donative formulas are similar to those seen at Bharhut, typically recording at least the donor's name and the word "gift" (*dānaṃ*), often with additional information such as place of origin or profession—most frequently "merchant," as in "Gift of the merchant Nāgila" (*nāgilasa seṭhino dānaṃ*).[10] An example of a donation by a feminine donor is "Gift of Devabhāgā, [wife and] mother of son(s) of the merchant from Kandaḍigāma" (*kaṃdaḍigāmiyasa seṭhino pajāvatiyā devabhāgāya dānaṃ*).[11] As at Bharhut, donations by monks and nuns are common, but unlike Bharhut the nature of the object donated (usually a pillar or railing) is usually not specified. Besides the many donative inscriptions, stūpas 2 and 3 at Sanchi have also yielded six inscribed reliquaries and one stone box, declared to contain the remains of the buddha's primary disciples Śāriputra and Mahāmaudgalyāyana as well as of several local masters.[12]

Unlike Bharhut, where all of the inscriptions date from the Śuṅga period, the Sanchi stūpa was in use both before—as attested by the aforementioned Aśokan schism edict—and after that time. Several significant later inscriptions have been found there, including donations of images of the Buddha Śākyamuni and the Bodhisattva Maitreya dating from the Kuṣāṇa

Figure 1. Bharhut: The *jātaka* of the six-tusked [elephant] (*chadaṃtiya jātakaṃ*).
Source: From Alexander Cunningham, *The Stûpa of Bharhut: A Buddhist Monument Ornamented with Numerous Sculptures Illustrative of Buddhist Legend and History in the Third Century* B.C. (London: W. H. Allen, 1879), pl. XXVI.6.

period (1st–2nd century CE) and grants of land and cash and other gifts to the sangha during the Gupta Empire (5th–6th century CE).[13]

Similar short donative inscriptions of this period are found in smaller numbers at other sites, notably Pauni (Bhandara District, Maharashtra) with thirty inscriptions; for example, on a railing, "Gift of Yakhadinā, a renunciant (*yakhadināya pavajitāya dānaṃ*).[14] Of particular interest is inscription 8, recording a gift of one Nāga, with the title "[Master] of the five *nikāya*s" (*pacanikāyakasa*).[15] This honorific title, also attested at Bharhut and Sanchi, refers to a person who has mastered the five divisions (*nikāya*) of the Sutta Pitaka, indicating that this arrangement of the sūtras, matching that of the surviving Pali canon, was already current in north India at a relatively early period.

Similar short donative inscriptions appear in smaller numbers at sites such as Sarnath and Bodh Gaya, which became major epigraphic sites in succeeding centuries.[16] At Bodh Gaya, a woman named Kuraṃgī, wife of King Iṃdāgimita (Skt. Indrāgnimitra), figures as a particularly prominent donor, mentioned in seventeen inscriptions on pillars and coping stones.[17] One of the early inscriptions records a gift by one Bodhirakhita who hailed from Sri Lanka (*tabapanakasa*).[18] This early record prefigures Bodh Gaya's ongoing role as the foremost Buddhist place of pilgrimage, which is richly attested by inscriptions there from later centuries recording visitors not only from various parts of India and Sri Lanka but also from Burma and China.[19]

An important discovery of this period are the two inscriptions from the stūpa at Deorkothar (Rewa District, Madhya Pradesh), which uniquely record lineages of the donor monks going back to the buddha and his disciple Anuruddha.[20] One of the inscriptions also contains the earliest epigraphic reference to the donor's school affiliation (*nikāya*), the Kaukkuṭika-Bahuśrutika school. In later centuries, *nikāya* affiliations are more frequently mentioned, serving as an important source of information about the history of Buddhist scholastic lineages.[21]

The Period of the Sātavāhanas, Western Kṣatrapas, Indo-Scythians, and Kuṣāṇas (1st–3rd Centuries CE). During this period, Buddhist inscriptions become more common and more widespread in northern and northwestern India, particularly in three regions: in the rock-cut cave monuments in the Western Ghats in Maharashtra, around Mathura in central north India, and in Gandhāra and adjoining areas in the northwest.

The Western Cave Complexes. In the western caves, large numbers of inscriptions from about the first two centuries CE are found at sites such as Ajanta, Bedsa, Bhaja, Junnar, Kanheri, Karle, Kuda, Nasik, and Pitalkhora, all of which lay along or near trade routes between the ports on the west coast and the cities and towns of the interior. Their location along the passes through the Ghats provided convenient rest sites at which travelers and traders would stop and pay their respects to the resident monks.

These inscriptions—more than two hundred in all—were edited by Bhagwanlal Indraji in 1881.[22] Most of them were re-edited in 1883 by Georg Bühler.[23] A comprehensive modern edition of this corpus is still lacking, although newer editions for some of the sites are available, and they have all been conveniently collected by S. Nagaraju on the basis of previous editions.[24] Most of these inscriptions are short records in Prakrit of gifts by various individuals of caves, cells, stūpas, columns, doors, images, and other components or decorative elements of the cave complexes. They often mention the donors' place of origin or profession; for example,

Karle no. 9 reads "[This] pillar with relics is the gift of the reciter Sātimita of the venerable Dhamuttarīyas, from Sopāraka" (*sopārakā bhayaṃtānaṃ dharmutariyānaṃ bhāṇakasa sātimitasa sasariro thabho dānaṃ*), and Kuda, "[This] cistern is the pious gift of the merchant Vasulaṇaka" (*seṭhiṇo vasulaṇakasa deyadhaṃma poḍhi*).[25]

But there also begin to appear in this period longer and more ornate inscriptions recording donations by members of the Western Kṣatrapa and Sātavāhana dynasties, which during this period were engaged in a struggle for the control of this lucrative territory. These dynastic inscriptions record the assignment of revenue from designated villages or agricultural lands or from permanent cash endowments (*akṣaya-nīvi*) for the maintenance of the monastic communities, marking a shift away from piecemeal donation campaigns among individual donors and toward direct royal patronage. Particularly noteworthy is the lengthy Nasik inscription 12, in which Uṣavadāta, son-in-law of the Western Kṣatrapa ruler Nahapāna, enumerates various agricultural and financial endowments to members of the Buddhist dwelling in the cave where it is recorded.[26] Nasik inscription 4 was issued by the Sātavāhana king Gautamīputra Śrīsātakarṇi to confirm a previous grant by Uṣavadāta, showing how the Sātavāhanas continued the patronage policies of their Kṣatrapa predecessors.[27]

The shifts in donative practices are manifested in more formal epigraphic styles, with some inscriptions, notably Nasik 10, recorded in large calligraphic characters, and with the longer Kṣatrapa inscriptions in hybrid Sanskrit or in one case (Nasik 10) partly in correct Sanskrit.[28] In this linguistic flux can be seen the forerunners of the wholesale adoption of classical Sanskrit by the Buddhists in the succeeding period. The Sātavāhanas continued to use Prakrit, but the long memorial inscription of Gautamī Bālaśrī (Nasik 2), mother of the deceased Gautamīputra, is composed in literary form with long sentences and rhythmically patterned nominal compounding, foreshadowing the ornate poetic style of later Buddhist inscriptions.[29]

The Mathura Region. Mathura and the surrounding villages became a major site of Buddhist inscriptions, about 150 in all, during the period of the Saka Kṣatrapas in and around the 1st century CE, and especially in the 2nd century under Kaniṣka and the succeeding Kuṣāṇa rulers who made Mathura the southern capital of their vast Indo-Central Asian empire. The majority of these inscriptions are collected in Heinrich Lüders's definitive posthumous collection, but several important discoveries have been made since then.[30] Numerous donative inscriptions on the pedestals of statues of the buddhas, bodhisattvas, and other venerable figures testify to the early prevalence of image worship in the Mathura region. Donative inscriptions on other types of objects such as pillar and pillar bases, stone slabs, and utensils are also well attested.

Most of the inscriptions from this period are written in local forms of Brāhmī script and composed in Epigraphical Hybrid Sanskrit, with varying degrees of more Prakritic or more Sanskritic tendencies. An example of an image dedication in hybrid language is the Mathura inscription of Dhanavatī: "Year 33 of the Great King, Son of the Gods, Huviṣka, summer [month] 1, day 8: [This] bodhisattva was established in Madhuravaṇaka, together with her mother and father, by the nun Dhanavatī, maternal niece of the nun Buddhamitrā who knows the Tripiṭaka and who was the disciple of the monk Bala who knows the Tripiṭaka."[31] This inscription is particularly important in what it reveals about the Buddhist patronage networks under the Kuṣāṇas. The donor Dhanavatī's aunt, the nun Buddhamitrā, is described as the disciple of the monk Bala. Bala's name is recorded in inscriptions of the third regnal year of

Kaniṣka as the sponsor of colossal inscribed bodhisattva images, carved in the distinctive red stone of Mathura, found at Sarnath and Saheth-Maheth (Śrāvastī), while Buddhamitrā herself was the donor of three similar images at Kausambi in Kaniṣka's second year. Thus these inscriptions reveal a program of establishment of images in four major Buddhist sites in north India under the auspices of a lineage of monks and nuns centered in Mathura, which may have been sponsored by or at least had the blessings of the Kuṣāṇa rulers.[32]

A recently discovered example of a pillar donation inscription (a type found in large numbers at sites around Mathura) reads, "In the year 33 of the Great King, Son of the Gods, Huveṣka, winter month 1, day 2: On this day [this] pillar is the gift of the lay followers, the brothers Buddharakṣita and Dharmarakṣita, sons of Soma, brahmans of the Aupamanyava gotra, from Taxila, in their own monastery at Toyī, in the possession of the Sarvāstivādin masters, for the benefit of their own good health, for honoring of their mother and father, for the long life of their sons and daughters, for the benefit and happiness of all beings."[33] This inscription is particularly rich in information on the social history of Buddhism in the Kuṣāṇa period, introducing two brothers, Buddharakṣita and Dharmarakṣita, who converted to Buddhism and took Buddhist names, yet proudly retained their identity as Brahmans, including citing their gotra affiliation. The brothers had emigrated from Taxila in the northwest to Mathura, illustrating the interregional contacts and Buddhist networks in operation at the time. The inscription also confirms the presence of the Sarvāstivādin *nikāya* at Mathura, which had previously been only weakly attested compared to the better attested Mahāsāṃghikas (with thirteen Mathura inscriptions), as well as of the Dharmaguptakas and Sāṃmitīyas.

The Sarvāstivādin school is, however, also attested in the unique and highly important but enigmatic Mathura lion capital inscription, datable to the early years of the period in question here. According to one interpretation, it announces that "the act of possession of the teacher Budhila, the city-dweller (and) Sarvāstivāda monk, should be announced to the Mahāsāṃghikas. In honor of the whole Sa̱kastana."[34] Although the interpretation of this passage—as of many in this inscription—is controversial, it is suggestive of conflicts over monastic territories between congregations belonging to different scholastic lineages. The reference to "Sakastana" and the occurrence of several personal names of clearly Iranian origin, as well as the fact that this inscription, almost uniquely at Mathura, is written in Kharoṣṭhī rather than Brāhmī script, show that it demonstrates the adoption of Buddhist beliefs and the patronage of local Buddhist establishments by recent invaders or immigrants from the northwest.

Particularly important for the history of Buddhism is the unique pedestal inscription recording the dedication of an image of the Buddha Amitābha, regardless of whether it is taken as indicative of the growing presence of the Mahāyāna in the early centuries of the Common Era, or rather is understood to show, in its isolation, the marginality of Mahāyāna at this period.[35]

Gandhāra and the Northwest. Between the 1st century BCE and the 3rd century CE, Buddhist inscriptions, nearly all in the local Gāndhārī language and Kharoṣṭhī script, become increasingly common in the northwestern edge of the Indian subcontinent, in and around the region of Gandhāra (the Peshawar Valley in modern northern Pakistan). The range of Gāndhārī and Kharoṣṭhī extends to the east and south into other parts of the Indian subcontinent, including

Punjab, Sindh, and Mathura, and to the north and west into eastern Afghanistan and southern Uzbekistan.

The corpus of these inscriptions has grown rapidly. Sten Konow's 1929 corpus of Kharoṣṭhī inscriptions contained only one hundred, whereas by 2020 more than one thousand were known.[36] These are now comprehensively and reliably cataloged in the online Catalog of Kharoṣṭhī Inscriptions.

Gandharan inscriptions typically record the foundation of stūpas and dedication of relics of the buddha; the dedication of images and wells; and the donation of pots, bowls, lamps, and other types of utensils to monastic institutions. Relic and stūpa inscriptions, of which some sixty examples have been published, are particularly useful in revealing contemporary Buddhist beliefs and ritual practices.[37] They are also of prime importance for reconstructing the dynastic history of the period, since they often provide the names and dates of otherwise unknown rulers of the northwest.

The abundance of Buddhist inscriptions in this period reflects the historical situation in which successive waves of invaders from eastern Iran and Central Asia were penetrating into the borderlands of India and setting up kingdoms, satrapies, and eventually empires centered in the northwest. Most of these newcomers enthusiastically embraced Buddhism, generously patronizing existing Buddhist institutions and establishing new ones. Particularly revealing is the reference in at least ten reliquary inscriptions to the belief, also attested in various Buddhist texts, in the special karmic reward called "Brahma-merit," which is gained by persons who establish a relic of the buddha in a place where one had not previously been established.[38] This evidently widespread doctrine, combined with the eagerness of new elites to Indianize themselves by adopting Buddhism, helped to promote the expansion of Buddhism in the northwest and beyond. As a result, the northwest became one of the most important centers of Buddhist culture in the subcontinent, and the connections established during this period with adjoining regions beyond India opened the door for Buddhism's spread beyond India into Central and eventually East Asia.

Gandharan reliquary inscriptions usually include, at the minimum, the donor's name, the object donated—typically bodily remains (*śarīra, dhātu*) of the buddha and/or a stūpa—and the appropriate form of the verb "establish" (Skt. *pratiṣṭhāpayati*). Additional information is frequently included such as the date, location, and the names of persons with whom the donor wished to share the benefits of the pious act. Thus the length of the inscriptions may vary from a single short sentence to several hundred words. The shorter inscriptions are usually inscribed on the reliquary itself, typically a small stone bowl, limiting the amount of space available. The longer relic inscriptions are written on surfaces that permitted longer texts, such as single or multiple sheets of metal (copper, silver, or gold) or stone slabs that covered the chamber inside the stūpa in which the relics were placed.

The earliest Gandharan Buddhist inscription is the Shinkot reliquary, originally dedicated during the reign of the Indo-Greek king Menander who ruled around the middle of the 2nd century BCE.[39] The reliquary was rededicated during the reign of the kings of Apraca (modern Bajaur) around the beginning of the Common Era, who also sponsored more than a dozen other reliquary donations, such as the ornate silver reliquary of Indravarma (see figure 2).[40]

Another example of a relatively early and brief relic donation inscription is the reliquary of Theodotos, which reads "this relic of the Lord Śākyamuni was dedicated by the meridarch

Figure 2. Inscribed silver reliquary of the Apraca Prince Indravarma, Miho Museum, Shigaraki, Japan. *Source*: Photograph courtesy of Los Angeles County Museum of Art.

Theodotos, for the benefit of many people."[41] Here is another example of a member of the non-Indian ruling elite, in this case a person of Greek or Hellenized ethnicity, who has fully adopted Buddhist practices.

The longest Gandharan inscription is the gold plate inscription of Senavarma (see figure 3), with more than five hundred words including numerous citations or paraphrases of Buddhist texts.[42] Senavarma belonged to a line of kings of Oḍi, ruling in the Swat Valley to the north of Gandhāra proper, who like the Apraca kings were of extra-Indian origin but who claimed to be descended, like the buddha himself, from the ancient lineage of Ikṣvāku.[43]

Donative inscriptions on pottery and other utensils are common in Gandhāra and adjoining regions of Afghanistan and Central Asia.[44] They typically record the type of vessel (e.g., "this water-jug," *aya paṇighaḍe*), the name of the donor, and the recipient community, usually identified with reference to its *nikāya* affiliation. A relatively rare example of a complete specimen is British Library pot D, reading, "this pot is for the universal community, in the keeping of the Sarvāstivādin masters in the Pūrṇaka monastery."[45] Here, as also in Gandharan reliquary inscriptions, the donation is theoretically made to the entire unitary "universal community," and is presented only "in the keeping" or "in the possession" (*parigrahe*) of this particular sangha of the Sarvāstivādin lineage.

Figure 3. The gold plate inscription of Senavarma.
Source: From David Jongeward, Elizabeth Errington, Richard Salomon and Stefan Baums, *Gandharan Buddhist Reliquaries* (Seattle WA: Early Buddhist Manuscripts Project, 2012), fig. 6.9, p. 228.

Such inscriptions are found in large numbers, though usually in fragments, at some archaeological sites, helping to establish the affiliation of institutions there. An outstanding case is the hundreds of inscriptions found at the sites of Kara Tepe and Faiz Tepe near modern Termez.[46] The Termez inscriptions in Gāndhārī are sometimes found in trilingual combinations with corresponding texts in the local Bactrian language and in hybrid Sanskrit written in Brāhmī script. These illustrate the multicultural character of the Termez monasteries, which were evidently populated by monks from Gandhāra and mainland India as well as by local people. The texts of the multilingual inscriptions are typically markers of personal property, rather than donative, as in "this pot is the personal property of the monk Buddhaśira."[47] The Termez potsherd inscriptions regularly cite the Mahāsāṃghika school, whereas potsherd inscriptions from Gandhāra itself and nearby regions most frequently mention the Dharmaguptaka *nikāya*, although other schools such as the Sarvāstivādins, Mahīśāsakas, Mahāsāṃghikas, and Kāśyapīyas are also attested.

Donative inscriptions on the pedestals of images of the buddha are of particular importance for their role in the study of the history of Gandharan sculpture. Particularly valuable are such inscriptions bearing dates, though these are unfortunately quite rare. Moreover, even when dates are present, their interpretation is often complicated and controversial, in part because several different eras were in use simultaneously and the era is not always explicitly identified.

A classic case is the so-called Brussels Buddha (see figure 4), which bears a complete text with a clearly legible date in "the year 5": "Year 5, on the fifth day of the month Phālguna: pious gift of Buddhananda, the Tripiṭaka master. May it be for the honor of his late mother and father."[48] Here the year 5 is generally agreed to be a date in the era of Kaniṣka, which probably began in 127 CE, but it may actually represent the year [10]5 of the Kaniṣka era, since it was apparently the practice in this era to begin the year numbers anew at the beginning of each century. So here, not untypically, the evidence of the inscription remains tantalizingly ambiguous for those trying to establish a stylistic chronology for Gandharan Buddhist art.

An important related corpus consists of thousands of brief inscriptions left by monks, pilgrims, traders, and other travelers over the routes along the Indus and Hunza Rivers by which

Figure 4. The "Brussels Buddha" of [Kaniṣka] year 5.
Source: The Huntington Archive, scan no. 56516.

they crossed the Karakoram Mountains en route between India and the lands to the north, ultimately leading to the Tarim Basin in western China. The vast majority of these are brief records containing the travelers' names, sometimes with additional information such as their titles or brief pious statements, such as "this pious gift was made by me, Devasiṅga," engraved in the local proto-Śāradā script.[49] Here the inscription is written below a rudimentary design representing a stūpa, this presumably being the "pious gift" (*devadharma*) referred to in the inscription itself (see figure 5).

The inscriptions, most of which date from between about the 3rd to the 7th century, are written in a wide variety of Indian and non-Indian languages and scripts, most commonly Brāhmī, Kharoṣṭhī, Sogdian, and other middle Iranian languages. These inscriptions have been scrupulously edited and analyzed in the eleven volumes of the series Materialien zur Archäologie der Nordgebiete Pakistans (1994–2013) and summarized (up to 2003) in the third volume of Tsukamoto's *Indo bukkyō himei no kenkyū* インド仏教碑銘の研究.[50] This massive corpus brings to life the individuals who carried Buddhist ideas and practices from their Indian homeland into adjoining lands to the north and east.

The Gupta-Vākāṭaka Period (4th–6th centuries CE). During the period in which the Gupta dynasty dominated much of northern India in alliance with the Vākāṭakas on their southern flank, Buddhist inscriptions continue to be plentiful, but their format and character change drastically, becoming increasingly assimilated to the styles and formats of Brahmanical epigraphy. Nearly all are in more or less formal Sanskrit, and to some extent they even imitate Brahmanical vocabulary with terms such as *mandira* (temple) and *agrahāra* (Brahman village). Copperplate grants and ornate stone inscriptions on pillars or stone slabs imitating Brahmanical

Figure 5. Hodar inscription 69.31: "The pious gift of Devasiṅga."
Source: From Ditte Bandini-König, *Die Felsbildstation Hodar* (Mainz, Germany: Philipp von Zabern, 1999), pl. 122.

formats become frequent among Buddhist inscriptions, although more distinctively Buddhist forms also survive, especially donative records on image pedestals and inscriptions containing Buddhist texts and formulas. References to Mahāyāna ideas and practices become much more frequent in this period.

Overall, Buddhist inscriptions are very abundant during this period, but compared to earlier centuries they are proportionally less common than non-Buddhist ones. In terms of geographical distribution, they are more widely distributed than before and less strongly concentrated in particular sites or areas, although they are still relatively numerous at major Buddhist centers and pilgrimage sites such as Nālandā, Sārnāth, and Bodh Gaya.

The copperplate inscriptions typically announce the assignment of the revenues from villages or agricultural lands to a monastic institution. In their format and content, inscriptions of this type are often virtually identical to the corresponding non-Buddhist inscriptions, except that the recipients are Buddhists rather than Brahmans. The issuing authority is typically the king, although the king is often not himself a Buddhist but may rather be acting to administer or approve requests by relatives or influential citizens who are Buddhists. Copperplates with Buddhist recipients are first known in south India in the late 3rd century, but become fairly common in the north from the 5th century onward.

A revealing corpus of some two dozen copperplates from the later Gupta period was issued by the Maitraka kings of Valabhī in Gujarat.[51] For example, a plate issued in Gupta year 248 (567–568 CE) by King Guhasena grants the income from the village of Bahumūlā to provide permanent funding for the requisites of monastic life to the congregation of a monastery of monks who "had come from far and wide and belonged to the eighteen schools," suggesting a situation in which members of different *nikāya* lineages dwelt together harmoniously.[52] In the same inscription, King Guhasena styles himself a "devoted Buddhist lay follower" (*paramopasāka*), but in another inscription issued only two years earlier, he is called "devoted worshipper of Viṣṇu" (*paramabhāgavata*), showing the typical flexibility in the religious affiliation of Indian kings.[53] This inscription concludes with imprecatory verses of the type constantly found in Brahmanical inscriptions, threatening violators of the contract with the five great sins and the associated sins, again a characteristically Brahmanical expression.[54]

An interesting example of a relatively early attestation of Mahāyāna institutions is presented in the Guṇaighar (Tippera District, Bangladesh) plate of Vainyagupta of 507 CE, recording the gift of eleven plots of land for the maintenance of Mahāyāna monks of the Avalokiteśvarāśrama-vihāra.[55] The approximately contemporary Jayarampur plate (Balasore District, Orissa) similarly refers to a monastery (*vihāra*) presided over by Avalokiteśvara, confirming the prevalence of his cult in eastern India during the Gupta era.[56] The issuing king of the Jayarampur plates, Gopacandra is styled as a "devoted worshipper of Śiva" (*paramamāheśvara*, line 9), and the inscription concludes with Brahmanical verses, including citations from the Mahābhārata as well as a verse invoking the Vedic Hindu deities Ādityas, Vasus, Rudras, Soma, Viṣṇu, Agni, and Yama (lines 43–44).

Buddhist stone inscriptions of this period mirror the Brahmanical *praśasti* genre not only in their physical form but also in containing large amounts of eulogistic praises of the donors. A classic example from the high imperial Gupta era is the Sanchi inscription of the time of Candragupta II (411–412 CE).[57] This is inscribed on a railing bar of the great stūpa in proximity to the inscriptions of the pre–Common Era, indicating the continuity of the epigraphic tradition at Sanchi as at other major Buddhist centers such as Bodh Gaya and Sarnath. The inscription records a donation by the otherwise unknown Āmrakārddava, a dependent of the emperor, of a village and a cash endowment for the feeding of monks and the maintenance of a ceremonial lamp. The text includes eulogistic descriptions of the donor, his patron the emperor, and of the Buddhist congregation at Kākanādaboṭa, that is, Sanchi, who "have developed their sensory faculties through the virtues of proper behavior, meditation, and wisdom."[58]

The Kura (Punjab) stone inscription of the time of the Hun king Toramāṇa (*c.* 500 CE) testifies to the ongoing presence of Buddhism in the northwest after its great efflorescence during the previous era.[59] The inscription records the dedication of a monastic residence (*vihāra*) by one Roṭasiddhavṛddhi, the son of Roṭṭajayavṛddhi who was himself the sponsor of "many *vihāras*." The text opens with lavish praises of the buddha and closes with the donor's wish for the attainment of supreme wisdom (*anuttarajñāna*) by his family, by members of King Toramāṇa's family, and by all beings. This is followed by a declaration that the equipment (*upakaraṇa*) of the *vihāra* is placed "in the keeping" (*parigrahe*) of the masters of the Mahīśāsaka lineage, following the usual pattern. But here the word "Mahīśāsakas" has clearly been altered from its original reading, apparently "Mahāsāṃghikas," suggesting that control of the *vihāra* had at some point changed hands between members of different *nikāyas*.[60] This reminds the reader of the hint of conflict between *nikāyas* implied in the Mathura lion capital inscription, and suggests that the rosy picture of inter-*nikāya* harmony suggested in the Waḷā inscription of Guhasena was by no means the whole story.

Several interesting inscriptions of this class (all of them unfortunately more or less incomplete) are found in the caves of Ajanta, dating from the reign of the Vākāṭaka dynasty around the late 5th century CE.[61] Notable among them is the inscription, composed in high *kāvya* style with thirty-two verses in various meters, that announces the dedication of cave 16 by the minister Varāhadeva in honor of his parents.[62] After a long genealogical profile, the text describes the excavated cave (*caityamandira*, line 20) in terms that, though hyperbolic, agree well with its architectural features. The inscription then concludes with a wish that the whole world attain "the place that is free of grief, without the fever (of desire), calm, and honorable" (i.e., nirvana; line 32).

The inscriptions at the Ajanta caves (ninety-nine in all according to Cohen) include several other interesting types. Many of the donative inscriptions, some of them dating back to before the Common Era period, are painted rather than incised, a very rare feature among surviving Indian inscriptions. A few inscriptions also provide labels to the accompanying painting, such as those in cave 22 listing the names of the eight depicted buddhas and their bodhi trees.[63] A different type of label inscription is found in cave 2, where scenes from the story of Kṣāntivādin are labeled with three verses from Āryaśūra's *Jātakamālā*.[64]

Such inscriptional quotations of non-canonical texts are rare in Buddhist epigraphy; more frequently seen are epigraphic citations or paraphrases of canonical literature. An early example, datable on paleographic grounds to the 2nd or 3rd century CE, is a presentation of the four noble truths in Pali on a fragment of a stone umbrella from Sarnath.[65] This is one of the very few Pali or Pali-like inscriptions found in India; another interesting specimen is the reliquary from Devnimori (Gujarat), which bears, besides a dedicatory inscription in metrical Sanskrit datable to the 3rd or 4th century CE, a text of the chain of dependent co-origination (*pratītya-samutpāda*) in Pali or a similar dialect.[66] A similar text is also cited in the Kurram inscription of Śveḍavarma, a Kharoṣṭhī Gāndhārī inscription on a stūpa model reliquary dating from the mid-2nd century CE.[67] Various *pratītya-samutpāda* texts datable to the Gupta period have been found at several other sites, including on a copperplate from Kasia, on several bricks at Gopalpur and Nalanda, and on stone slabs at Ratnagiri (Odisha).[68] Two such inscribed bricks from Nalanda include a lengthy additional section entitled "Analysis of dependent co-origination" (*pratītyasamutpādasya vibhaṅgaḥ*).[69] The text of such inscriptions typically closely resembles but does not agree exactly with the corresponding canonical presentations in Pali and other languages, exemplifying the characteristic variability and flexibility of Buddhist texts.

A donative inscription from about the same time on a copper scroll from the Hun kingdom of Toramāṇa in the northwest presents this familiar text in a different and unusual guise, and in an explicitly Mahāyāna context.[70] Here the dependent co-origination formula is embedded in an abbreviated citation of the Mahāyāna sūtra entitled "Questions of the Brahman Śrīmatī" (*Śrīmatībrāhmaṇīparipṛcchā*), which was previously known only in the form of Tibetan and Chinese translations. The sūtra quotation is then followed on the scroll by the first two verses of Nāgārjuna's *Mūlamādhyamakakarikā*. This unique inscription is a remarkable new contribution to the history of Mahāyāna literature and practice.

Exceedingly common in this period and in succeeding centuries is a wide variety of epigraphic presentations of the so-called Buddhist creed (or more properly, the *Pratītyasamutpāda-gāthā*), "the Tathāgata expounded the cause of those dharmas which arise from a cause, and the cessation of them; so speaks the great renouncer."[71] Such inscriptions are found in huge numbers in north India and throughout the Buddhist world from Afghanistan to Southeast Asia, often in the form of clay sealing or tokens, which were considered to be dharma-relics functionally equivalent to bodily relics of the buddha. The "creed" is also often inscribed on images, either by itself or incorporated into a longer donative inscription. An interesting example is an image inscription from Saheth-Maheth bearing an original dedicatory inscription of the 1st or 2nd century CE to which has been added the text of the "creed" in characters datable to the 8th or 9th century.[72] This piece reveals on the one hand the long-term preservation and use of the image itself, and on the other the changes in Buddhist epigraphical practices.

Another important source of information on Buddhist institutions in this and succeeding periods is monastic seals and sealings, which are found in large numbers at major sites such as Kasia, Kosam, Nalanda, and Sarnath.[73] Seal inscriptions can be important in confirming the archaeological identification of ancient sites such as Kosam (Kauśāmbī), Kasia (Kuśinagara), and Saheth-Maheth (Śrāvastī), and in providing information on the names and administrative structures of the monasteries there. Nalanda, for example, has yielded "thousands of seals and sealings," many of them containing only the "Buddhist creed," but others bearing the names and titles of monastic groups, especially "the community of noble monks of the

Nālandā-Mahāvihāra."[74] Other seals found there belonged to other sanghas, or to individual supervisory officials such as the "Mūla-navakarmmavārikas."[75] From seals found at Kasia, scholars learn that the congregation there was called "the congregation of monks at the monastery of the Great Parinirvāṇa" (*śrī-mahāparinirvāṇavihārīyabhikṣusaṅgha*).[76] Some seals bear besides an inscription an image appropriate to their location, such as a coffin between two trees representing the buddha's *parinirvāṇa* at Kasia.[77]

During and after the period in question here, Buddhist inscriptions began to appear in some numbers in Nepal, although they are overall much less common than Brahmanical Hindu records in this and succeeding periods. Buddhist inscriptions are typically on stone slabs or stelae or on the pedestals of images, and are nearly always donative in content. The stone inscriptions typically usually record royal donations of land and/or grants of special privileges to Buddhist institutions. Other inscriptions record the gift of images or of wells or other provisions for water supply. Several cultic inscriptions refer to Avalokiteśvara and other bodhisattvas, providing important information on the role of the Mahāyāna.[78]

Late Buddhist Inscriptions (7th–13th Centuries CE). During the last phase of Indian Buddhist epigraphy, the inscriptions are increasingly assimilated in format and style to Brahmanical norms. The predominant type are stone inscriptions containing lengthy eulogistic records (*praśasti*) in ornate verse, and elaborate copperplate land grant charters. Other important types are image dedications and monastic or cultic seals and sealings. Buddhist inscriptions in this period are generally less widely distributed than previously, tending to be concentrated in and around major pilgrimage sites such as Bodh Gaya, Sarnath, Saheth-Maheth, and Kasia. Inscriptions of this period increasingly reflect Mahāyāna as well as Vajrayāna beliefs and institutions.

An important example of a Mahāyāna inscription is the Nalanda inscription of Vipulaśrīmitra (*c.* 1200 CE), with references to Prajñāpārimitā, Tārā, Khasarpana, and Mañjurava (Mañjuśrī).[79] It is composed in thirteen Sanskrit verses in ornate *kāvya* style and engraved in highly calligraphic proto-Bengali script (see figure 6).

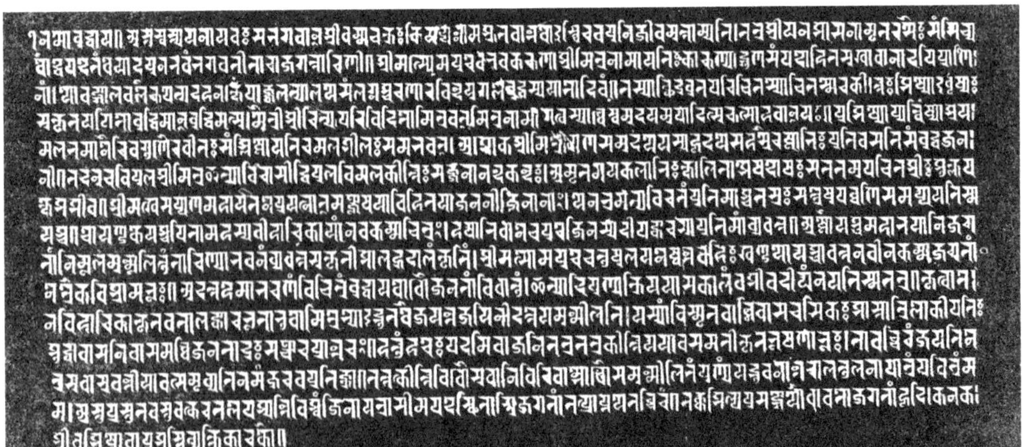

Figure 6. Nalanda inscription of Vipulaśrīmitra.
Source: From *Epigraphia Indica* 21 (1931–1932): plate facing p. 98.

The Vajrayāna is represented by the Hasra Kol stone inscription of the 12th century CE, containing a description of a self-visualization as the *tathāgata* and a dhāraṇī (see figure 7).[80]

Such dhāraṇī inscriptions are common throughout north India and beyond in this period; for example, Ratnagiri has yielded several examples dated between the 9th and 11th centuries.[81] Minor inscriptions with the *Pratītasamutpāda-gāthā* or "Buddhist creed" continue to be extremely common in this period.

During this later phase, several inscriptions testify to travel to sacred sites and monastic centers in the north from other parts of India and of Asia. The stone inscription from Ghosrawa near Nalanda, dating from the 9th century CE, describes the career of a monk, Vīradeva, who traveled from his homeland in Nagarahāra in eastern Afghanistan where he had initially been ordained, to Nalanda where he became the head monk.[82] This inscription testifies to the continuing presence of Buddhist institutions in the far northwest in later centuries despite the paucity of epigraphic testimony from the region.[83] The Saheth-Maheth copperplate inscription of 1128–1129 CE records a grant by the Hindu king Govindacandra of six villages to the sangha at the Jetavana, at the instigation of two monks who had come from Coḍa (Tamil Nadu) and Odisha (Utkala) and settled in Śrāvastī.[84] International contacts are attested by the long (sixty-six lines) Nalanda copperplate inscription of King Devapāla of the Pāla dynasty (9th century CE), recording the grant of four villages to a monastery, which had been founded in Nalanda by King Balaputradeva of the Śailendra dynasty of Sumatra and Java.[85] Between about the 8th and the 12th centuries, the Pāla dynasty dominated northeastern India and enthusiastically supported Buddhist institutions, as attested by large numbers of images with donative and/or cultic inscriptions.[86]

Similar patterns are discernible among the abundant inscribed images from the later centuries. A cache of ninety-three exquisite inscribed bronze images dating from around the 9th to

Figure 7. The Hasra Kol dhāraṇī inscription.
Source: From Arthur Venis, "Notes on a Buddhist Inscription from Hasra Kol, Gaya," *Journal & Proceedings of the Asiatic Society of Bengal* 4 (1908): 462.

the 11th century CE was found at Kurkihar near Bodh Gaya.[87] Thirteen of the dedicatory inscriptions mention donors from Kanchi and Kerala in distant southern India.[88]

The waning days of Buddhism in north India are attested in a handful of late stone inscriptions composed in ornate Sanskrit verse. The Bodh Gaya stone of the time of the last Gāhaḍavāla king Jayaccandradeva, dating from between 1183 and 1192 CE, memorializes in seventeen verses the construction of a cave and images of the Tārās by a monk, Śrīmitra, who is said to have initiated the king himself.[89] The latest dated Buddhist inscription from northern India is the Saheth-Maheth stone inscription of 1219–1220 CE, recording the dedication of a *vihāra* by one Vidyādhara, son of a royal minister.[90] Hereafter, there is no further record of the fate of such beneficiary institutions as Buddhism disappears from the epigraphic scene, marking its nearly complete disappearance from north India.

REVIEW OF LITERATURE

The study of Buddhist epigraphy is closely intertwined with that of Indian epigraphy in general, so that the two areas cannot be neatly separated; this is shown, for example, by the inscriptions of the Maitraka and Gāhaḍavāla dynasties, whose documents sometimes combine Buddhist and Hindu themes. The study of both areas began simultaneously with the decipherment by James Prinsep in 1837 of Brāhmī script on the basis of repeated patterns in the donative inscriptions at Sanchi.[91] In the following years, the Kharoṣṭhī script was gradually deciphered by Prinsep and others, and early editions of important Buddhist inscriptions from the northwest were published by Edward Thomas in 1858.[92]

After the initial decipherment period, the early phase of Indian Buddhist epigraphic studies was largely focused on the abundant material from the western caves. Various examples were published in articles by several scholars in the 1840s and 1850s, followed by the comprehensive editions by Bhagwanlal Indraji in 1881 and Georg Bühler in 1883.[93]

Meanwhile, Alexander Cunningham had undertaken his groundbreaking work on early Indian archaeology, history, and epigraphy. A landmark volume in Buddhist epigraphy was his *Bhilsa Topes; or, Buddhist Monuments of Central India*, with readings of more than two hundred of the Sanchi inscriptions with some improvements on Prinsep's original decipherments.[94] Another breakthrough by Cunningham was *The Stûpa of Bharhut: A Buddhist Monument Ornamented with Numerous Sculptures Illustrative of Buddhist Legend and History in the Third Century B.C.*, which provided reasonably accurate transcriptions and translations of many of the Bharhut inscriptions.[95] Then in 1892, he documented some of the inscriptions of Bodh Gaya in *Mahâbodhi, or the Great Buddhist Temple Under the Bodhi Tree at Buddha-Gaya.*[96]

Beginning in the later decades of the 19th century, a need began to be felt for comprehensive collections and systematic venues for publication of the ever-increasing epigraphic material then being discovered. This led to the establishment of the Corpus Inscriptionum Indicarum series, whose first volume was Cunningham's *Inscriptions of Aśoka* (1877), later supplanted by Eugen Hultzsch's entirely revised edition in 1925. Eventually, seven volumes of the Corpus were published, of which two consist entirely or mostly of Buddhist material: Sten Konow's *Kharoṣṭhī Inscriptions with the Exception of Those of Aśoka* (volume II, part I, 1929), and Heinrich Lüders's *Bharhut Inscriptions* (volume II, part II), published posthumously in 1963.[97] In the meantime, new epigraphically oriented journals were founded, including the

Indian Antiquary in 1872, which contains many original editions of important inscriptions, and above all *Epigraphia Indica* in 1888, dedicated entirely to inscriptions, including many Buddhist inscriptions. *Epigraphia Indica* was regularly published biennially through volume 42 (1977–1978); since then, volumes have been published only sporadically, including volume 43, part 1, published in 2011.

Excavations undertaken by the Archaeological Survey of India in the first two decades of the 20th century at major Buddhist sites such as Sarnath, Saheth-Maheth, and Kasia provided abundant and important new additions to the corpus of Buddhist inscriptions. These inscriptions were published in the survey's *Annual Reports* for this period, but much of this material has not been subsequently collected or studied in detail.

Buddhist and other Indian inscriptions continued to be published regularly, though less copiously and spectacularly, through the 20th century. Major achievements during this period in terms of definitive compilations of important corpora include N. G. Majumdar's definitive edition in 1940 of the massive corpus of Sanchi inscriptions, published as part 4 (chapters XVIII–XXII, pp. 261–396) of Marshall and Foucher's *The Monuments of Sāñchī*, and Heinrich Lüders's posthumous *Mathurā Inscriptions* (1961) and *Bharhut Inscriptions* (1963).[98]

In general, throughout the earlier phases of the study of Indian epigraphy in the 19th century and through most of the 20th century, the primary concern of epigraphic scholars with regard to both Buddhist and non-Buddhist materials tended to be on the reconstruction of dynastic histories. Dated inscriptions were particularly sought after, while cultic inscriptions of purely Buddhist content tended to be dismissed or ignored as "not of historical importance." This is not to say that Buddhologists during these periods did not make good use of inscriptions; a positive example was Étienne Lamotte's compilation of inscriptional data on the geographical distribution of Buddhist *nikāyas*.[99]

Nevertheless, Buddhist scholars did tend to share in the prevailing somewhat myopic view of epigraphic data, particularly in tending to interpret inscriptions in light of and with reference to canonical literature, rather than letting them speak for themselves. A revolutionary new attitude was introduced by Gregory Schopen in a series of articles in the 1980s and 1990s. By way of example, in his edition of the Bharhut inscriptions, Heinrich Lüders expressed surprise at the relatively large number of donations by monks and nuns, "as they were forbidden to own any personal property besides some ordinary requisites," and surmised that "probably we have to suppose that they collected the money required for some pious purpose by begging it from their relatives and acquaintances."[100] But Schopen has shown in several articles that sponsorship of monuments by monastics is very much the rule rather than the exception at early Buddhist sites generally, and that the image of the austere, ascetic monks and nuns removed from lay concerns and financial activities is an illusion derived from naive readings of textual sources and unconscious presuppositions about the nature of Buddhist monasticism. In short, Schopen concludes, "the ascriptions of primacy to textual sources in Buddhist studies not only effectively neutralizes the independence of archaeological and epigraphical sources as witnesses, it also effectively excludes what practicing Buddhists did and believed from the history of their own religion."[101]

Schopen's innovative ideas and methods have helped to raise the profile of epigraphic studies as a component of Buddhist studies, particularly in the North American academic community. At the same time, the publication and primary study of Buddhist inscriptions has continued to flourish since the late 20th century, and articles by established and younger epigraphists continue to appear regularly. Particularly notable are the very many new Gandharan inscriptions published since the 1970s by Gérard Fussman, Harry Falk, and Richard Salomon among others, while Stefan Baums's "Catalog and Revised Texts and Translations of Gandharan Reliquary Inscriptions" provides a definitive corpus of previously published material. A spectacular addition to the corpus of Indian Buddhist inscriptions (though falling outside the scope of this article; see Lammerts and Tournier's article on Buddhist inscriptions from South India) are the approximately 270 inscriptions from Kanaganahalli definitively published by Oskar von Hinüber.[102]

PRIMARY SOURCES

The indispensable resources for research in Indian Buddhist inscriptions are the two comprehensive Japanese catalogs. Shizutani Masao's 静谷 正雄 *Indo bukkyō himei mokuroku* インド仏教碑銘目録 (Catalog of Indian Buddhist inscriptions) provides summaries and bibliography for more than two thousand inscriptions.[103] More extensive is Tsukamoto Keishō's 塚本 啓祥 *Indo bukkyō himei no kenkyū* インド仏教碑銘の研究 (Comprehensive study of the Indian Buddhist inscriptions), published in three volumes between 1996 and 2003, which comprises more than four thousand inscriptions from nearly two hundred sites presented with full or partial transliterated texts, detailed commentary, and translation in Japanese. The first volume (1996) presents the main collection, while volume 2 (1998) contains indices and other supplementary information to volume 1, including a complete index and reverse index of words in the inscriptions as well as general maps and detailed maps of major sites, plus a general chronology of Indian Buddhism. Tsukamoto's third volume (2003) presents the discoveries of some fourteen hundred inscriptions in the Indus and Hunza valleys in northern Pakistan.[104] Although Shizutani and Tsukamoto's catalogs are in Japanese, they contain transcriptions in Roman script and a great deal of bibliographic information in English, making them largely accessible to non-Japanese readers.

Shizutani's and Tsukamoto's catalogs are, however, already somewhat outdated, as numerous important discoveries, particularly of inscriptions from the northwest, have appeared since then. The latter are comprehensively collected in Stefan Baums and Andrew Glass's online Catalog of Kharoṣṭhī Inscriptions (https://gandhari.org/catalog?section=inscriptions). Such comprehensive modern resources are, however, lacking for north Indian epigraphy generally; useful for south Indian inscriptions is the website of Arlo Griffiths and Vincent Tournier, Early Inscriptions of Āndhradeśa (http://hisoma.huma-num.fr/exist/apps/EIAD/index2.html).

Still convenient for general research, in the absence of more recent equivalents, are the old "lists" of Indian inscriptions published as appendices to *Epigraphia Indica*: Franz Kielhorn, *A List of the Inscriptions of Northern India from About a.d. 400*, appendix to volume 5 (1898–1899); Heinrich Lüders, *List of Brāhmī Inscriptions from the Earliest Times to About a.d. 400*, appendix to volume 10 (1912); and Devadatta Ramakrishna Bhandarkar, *A List of the Inscriptions of Northern India in Brahmi and its derivative Scripts, from about 200 A.C.*, appendix to volumes 19–23 (1927–1936).[105]

Still lacking, and an urgent desideratum, is a dedicated anthology of major or representative Buddhist inscriptions. The definitive anthology of Indian inscriptions in general is Dines Chandra Sircar's *Select Inscriptions Bearing on Indian History and Civilization*, which contains a large number of Buddhist inscriptions but does not sort them into a separate category.[106] Important collections of exclusively or primarily Buddhist inscriptions from major sites such as Sanchi, Bharhut, and Mathura have been mentioned in the Review of Literature section. To these may be added, for the Buddhist inscriptions of Aśoka, Paul Kent Andersen's *Studies in the Minor Rock Edicts of Aśoka I: Critical Edition*.[107]

DIGITAL MATERIALS

Catalog of Kharoṣṭhī Inscriptions (https://gandhari.org/a_inscriptions.php) (Stefan Baums and Andrew Glass).

Early Inscriptions of Āndhradeśa (http://hisoma.huma-num.fr/exist/apps/EIAD/index2.html) (Arlo Griffiths and Vincent Tournier).

Indian Epigraphy (http://indepigr.narod.ru/). "Collections of Early Indian Inscriptions systematized by findplaces" (D. N. Lielukhine).

Indoskript 2.0 (http://indoskript.org/). "Indoskript 2.0 is a paleographic database of Brahmi and Kharosthi that aims at covering the full historical development of these two Indic scripts."

Siddham: The Asia Inscriptions Database (https://siddham.network/). "An online resource for inscriptions in the languages of south, central, and south-east Asia."

FURTHER READING

The four introductory chapters of Tsukamoto's *Indo bukkyō himei kenkyū* (pp. 3–128) summarize the sites of Buddhist inscriptions, the attestation of the *nikāyas* in inscriptions, the origin and development of the Brāhmī and Kharoṣṭhī scripts, and the phonology and morphology of the epigraphic dialects. Much of this material is presented in transliterated or tabular form so that it is to a significant degree accessible to non-Japanese readers.[108]

Other than this, there is no convenient overall introduction to Indian Buddhist epigraphy. General guides to Indian epigraphy, including but not specific to Buddhist materials, include Sircar's *Indian Epigraphy*, part I of his "Introduction to Indian Epigraphy and Palaeography," and Richard Salomon's *Indian Epigraphy*, which includes a brief section (pp. 241–243) on Buddhist materials.[109] For a brief overall introduction of Indian epigraphy, see Richard Salomon, "Epigraphy."[110] Useful for technical terms and specialized vocabulary in inscriptions, including some Buddhist material, is Sircar's *Indian Epigraphical Glossary*.[111]

The indispensable essays by Gregory Schopen proposing the (re-)interpretation of early Buddhist inscriptions generally are conveniently collected and reprinted in three volumes in the University of Hawai'i's Studies in the Buddhist Traditions series.[112]

For the languages of Indian Buddhist inscriptions, see Tsukamoto's fourth introductory chapter. For Epigraphical Hybrid Sanskrit, see Th. Damsteegt, *Epigraphical Hybrid Sanskrit* and Salomon, *Indian Epigraphy* (pp. 81–86).[113]

On the scripts of Buddhist inscriptions, see Tsukamoto's third introductory chapter. For Indian scripts and the history of writing in the Indian world in general, recommended are part II (pp. 104–136) of Sircar's "Introduction to Indian Epigraphy and Paleography," Georges-Jean Pinault, "Écritures de l'Inde continentale," and Harry Falk, *Schrift im alten Indien: Ein Forschungsbericht mit Anmerkungen.*[114] Indispensable for paleographic studies is the Indoskript database.

NOTES

1. The numbers of inscriptions (except for recent inscriptions not recorded there) are cited according to Tsukamoto Keishō 塚本 啓祥, *Indo bukkyō himei no kenkyū* (インド仏教碑銘の研究) [{The English title page of this book has "A" at the beginning of the title: "A Comprehensive Study…" > }Comprehensive study of the Indian Buddhist inscriptions] 3 vols. (Kyoto: Heirakuji shoten, 1996–2003).
2. For general information on the Aśokan inscriptions, see Frank Raymond Allchin and Kenneth Roy Norman, "Guide to the Aśokan Inscriptions," *South Asian Studies* 1 (1985): 43–50. For further details, see Harry Falk, *Aśokan Sites and Artefacts: A Source-Book with Bibliography*, Monographien zur indischen Archäologie, Kunst und Philologie 18 (Mainz am Rhein, Germany: Philipp von Zabern, 2006).
3. See, for example, Étienne Lamotte, *History of Indian Buddhism from the Origins to the Śaka Era*, trans. Sara Webb-Boin, Publications de l'Institut Orientaliste de Louvain 36 (Louvain-la-Neuve, Belgium: Université Catholique de Louvain, Institut Orientaliste, 1988), 234–237. Originally published as *Histoire du bouddhisme indien: Des origines à l'ère Śaka*, Bibliothèque du Muséon 43 (Louvain, Belgium: Publications Universitaires [et] Institut Orientaliste, 1958), 256–259.
4. Tsukamoto IV Piprāhwā 1, pp. 696–697. Inscriptions are listed in Tsukamoto's catalog according to geographical region denoted by roman numeral (IV = Central India), site name or abbreviation, and inscription number.
5. This total includes 920 inscriptions recorded by Tsukamoto (1.707–895) plus five additional inscriptions from Sanchi stupa II presented in Matthew D. Milligan, "Five Unnoticed Inscriptions and the Relative Chronology of Sanchi Stūpa II," *Annual Report of the International Research Institute for Advanced Buddhology at Soka University* 18 (2015): 11–22.
6. The numbering and texts are given according to the definitive edition by Heinrich Lüders (revised posthumously by E. Waldschmidt and M. A. Mehendale), *Bharhut Inscriptions*, Corpus Inscriptionum Indicarum 2, part II (Ootacamund, India: Government Epigraphist for India, 1963).
7. A 96; Lüders, *Bharhut Inscriptions*, 50–51; and Tsukamoto IV Bhārhut 164, p. 594.
8. A 31; Lüders, *Bharhut Inscriptions*, 25; and Tsukamoto IV Bhārhut 154, pp. 591–592.
9. B 49; Lüders, *Bharhut Inscriptions*, 128–130; and Tsukamoto IV Bhārhut 100, p. 578.
10. Inscription no. 365 in John Marshall and Alfred Foucher [inscriptions edited by Nani Gopal Majumdar], *The Monuments of Sāñchī* (Kolkata: Government of India, 1940): 1.337; and Tsukamoto IV. Sāñcī 351, p. 782.
11. Marshall and Foucher, *Monuments of Sāñchī*, 1.303, no. 41; and Tsukamoto IV Sāñcī 27, pp. 714–715.
12. Marshall and Foucher, *Monuments of Sāñchī*, 1. 289–296, nos. 2–14; and Tsukamoto IV Sāñcī 678-688, pp. 845–847. See also Michael Willis, "Buddhist Saints in Ancient Vidisha," *Journal of the Royal Asiatic Society*, series 3, 11 (2001): 219–228.
13. Marshall and Foucher, *Monuments of Sāñchī*, 1.385–387, nos. 828–830; Tsukamoto IV Sāñcī 907–909, pp. 888–890; Marshall and Foucher, *Monuments of Sāñchī*, 1.388–393, nos. 833–839; and Tsukamoto IV Sāñcī 95, 103, 912–916, pp. 728–732, 890–892.
14. Shantaram Bhalchandra Deo and Jagat Pati Joshi, *Pauni Excavation (1969-70)* (Nagpur, India: Nagpur University, 1972): 40, no. 12; and Tsukamoto III Pauni 12, p. 518.
15. Deo and Joshi, *Pauni Excavation*, 39 (wrongly interpreted); and Tsukamoto III Pauni 8, p. 517.
16. Daya Ram Sahni, *Catalogue of the Museum of Archaeology at Sārnāth* (Calcutta: Superintendent Government Printing, India, 1914), 210–211, 214; and Tsukamoto IV Sārnāth 76–78, 80, 85, pp. 909–912.
17. T. Bloch, "Notes on Bōdh Gayā," *Archaeological Survey of India, Annual Report 1908-9*, 147.

18. Tsukamoto I Bodh-Gayā 10, p. 138.
19. Bloch, "Notes on Bōdh Gayā," 155–158.
20. Oskar von Hinüber and Peter Skilling, "Two Buddhist Inscriptions from Deorkothar (Dist. Rewa, Madhya Pradesh)," *Annual Report of the International Research Institute for Advanced Buddhology at Soka University* 16 (2013): 13–26; and Richard Salomon and Joseph Marino, "Observations on the Deorkothar Inscriptions and Their Significance for the Evaluation of Buddhist Historical Traditions," *Annual Report of the International Research Institute for Advanced Buddhology at Soka University* 17 (2014): 27–39.
21. See the further discussion of *nikāya* affiliations in "Review of Literature."
22. In Jas. Burgess, *Inscriptions from the Cave Temples of Western India with Descriptive Notes, &c.*, Archaeological Survey of Western India, Reports, Old Series 10 (Mumbai: Government Central Press, 1881).
23. In Jas. Burgess, *Report on the Buddhist Cave Temples and their Inscriptions . . .*, Archaeological Survey of Western India 4 (London: Trübner, 1883).
24. Karle: E. Senart, "The Inscriptions in the Caves at Karle," *Epigraphia Indica* 7 (1902–1903): 47–74; Nasik: Emile Senart, "The Inscriptions in the Caves at Nasik," *Epigraphia Indica* 8 (1905–1906): 59–96; and Kanheri: Shobhana Gokhale, *Kanheri Inscriptions* (Pune, India: Deccan College Post Graduate and Research Institute, 1991). See also Vasudev Vishnu Mirashi, *The History and Inscriptions of the Sātavāhanas and the Western Kshatrapas* (Mumbai: Maharashtra State Board for Literature and Culture, 1981); and *Buddhist Architecture of Western India (C. 250 B.C.–C. A.D. 300)* (Delhi: Agam Kala Prakashan, 1981), 328–346.
25. Senart, "Inscriptions in the Caves at Karle," 55; Tsukamoto III Kārli 9, pp. 458–459; Georg Bühler in Jas. Burgess, *Report on the Buddhist Cave Temples and their Inscriptions . . .*, Archaeological Survey of Western India 4 (London: Trübner, 1883), no. 26, p. 88; and Tsukamoto III Kuḍā 27, pp. 481–482.
26. Senart, "Inscriptions in the Caves at Nasik," 82–85; and Tsukamoto III Nāsik 12, pp. 500–502.
27. Senart, "Inscriptions in the Caves at Nasik," 71–73; and Tsukamoto III Nāsik 2, pp. 487–489.
28. Senart, "Inscriptions in the Caves at Nasik," 78–81; and Tsukamoto III Nāsik 10, pp. 498–500.
29. Senart, "Inscriptions in the Caves at Nasik," 60–65; and Tsukamoto III Nāsik 4, pp. 490–494. See also Andrew Ollett, *Language of the Snakes: Prakrit, Sanskrit, and the Language Order of Premodern India* (Berkeley: University of California Press, 2017), 35–38.
30. Heinrich Lüders, *Mathurā Inscriptions: Unpublished Papers Edited by Klaus L. Janert*, Abhandlungen der Akademie der Wissenschaften in Göttingen, philologisch-historische Klasse 3.47 (Göttingen, Germany: Vandenhoeck & Ruprecht, 1961); Richard Salomon, *Indian Epigraphy: A Guide to the Study of Inscriptions in Sanskrit, Prakrit, and the Other Indo-Aryan Languages*, South Asia Research Series (New York: Oxford University Press, 1998), 144; and R. C. Sharma, "New Inscriptions from Mathura," in *Mathurā: The Cultural Heritage*, ed. Doris Meth Srinivasan (New Delhi: American Institute of Indian Studies, 1989), 308–315.
31. Lüders, *Mathurā Inscriptions*, no. 24, pp. 54–55; and Tsukamoto IV Mathurā 11, p. 642; *mahārajasyadevaputrasya huveṣkasya saṃ 30 3 gr̥ 1 di 8 bhīkṣ usya balasya trepiṭakasya antevā sinīye bhikṣ uṇīye trepiṭ ikāye buddhamitrā ye bhāgineyī ye bhikhuṇiye dhanavatī ye bodhisatvo pratithāpito madhuravaṇ ake sahā mātāpitihi.*
32. Gregory Schopen, "On Monks, Nuns, and 'Vulgar' Practices: The Introduction of the Image Cult into Indian Buddhism," *Artibus Asiae* 49 (1988–1989): 153–168; reprinted in Gregory Schopen, *Bones, Stones, and Buddhist Monks: Collected Papers on the Archaeology, Epigraphy, and Texts of Monastic Buddhism in India*, Studies in the Buddhist Tradition (Honolulu, HI: University of Hawai'i Press, 1997), 238–257.
33. Harry Falk, "A Dedicatory Inscription of the Time of Huviṣka in the Mathura Museum," *Berliner Indologische Studien* 11/12 (1998): 109–121; *maharajasya devapūtrasya huveṣkasya saṃvatsare 30 3 hemaṃtamāse 1 divase 2 etasya pūrvayaṃ upāsakanaṃ buddharakṣitaddharmarakṣitanaṃ bhratr̥ṇaṃ*

somaputraṇaṃ brahmaṇanaṃ opavañasagotraṇaṃ takhaśīlakanaṃ dānaṃ kubhakaṃ svake vihare toyīyaṃ ācāryyanaṃ sarvastīvadīnaṃ parigrahe ātma-ārogadakṣiṇaya mātapitṛṇaṃ pujarttham darakanaṃ darikanaṃ ca dīrghāyūkataya sarvasatvanaṃ hitasūkharthaṃ.

34. Stefan Baums, "Catalog and Revised Texts and Translations of Gandharan Reliquary Inscriptions," in *Gandharan Buddhist Reliquaries*, by David Jongeward, Elizabeth Errington, Richard Salomon, and Stefan Baums, Gandharan Studies 1 (Seattle, WA: Early Buddhist Manuscripts Project, 2012), 221; *ayariasa budhilasa nakarakasa bhikhusa sarvastivatasa pa<*ri>grana mahasaghiana prañavitave sarvasa sakastanasa puyae.*
35. Gregory Schopen, "The Inscription on the Kuṣān Image of Amitābha and the Character of the Early Mahāyāna in India," *Journal of the International Association of Buddhist Studies* 10 (1987): 99–134; reprinted in Gregory Schopen, *Figments and Fragments of Mahāyāna Buddhism in India: More Collected Papers*, Studies in the Buddhist Tradition (Honolulu, HI: University of Hawai'i Press, 2005), 247–277.
36. Sten Konow, *Kharoṣhṭhī Inscriptions with the Exception of those of Aśoka*, Corpus Inscriptionum Indicarum 2, part I (Kolkata: Government of India, Central Publications Branch, 1929).
37. See Baums, "Catalog and Revised Texts and Translations of Gandharan Reliquary Inscriptions."
38. According to the Mūlasarvāstivāda-vinaya: *yaḥ pudgalaḥ apratiṣṭhitapūrve pṛthivīpradeśe tathāgatasya śāriraṃ stūpaṃ pratiṣṭhāpayati, ayaṃ prathamaḥ pudgalaḥ* [*sic*] *brāhmaṃ puṇyaṃ prasavati*. See Richard Salomon, "The Copper Plates of Helagupta: A New Edition and Study," *Indo-Iranian Journal* 63 (2020): 25–26.
39. *Catalog of Kharoṣṭhī Inscriptions* no. 176.
40. *Catalog of Kharoṣṭhī Inscriptions* no. 241.
41. *Catalog of Kharoṣṭhī Inscriptions* no. 32: *theudutena meridarkhena pratiṭhavida ime śarira śakamunisa bhagavato bahujaṇahitaye.*
42. *Catalog of Kharoṣṭhī Inscriptions* no. 249.
43. Richard Salomon and Stefan Baums, "Sanskrit *Ikṣvāku*, Pali *Okkāka*, and Gāndhārī *Iṣmaho*," *Journal of the Pali Text Society* 29 (2007): 201–227.
44. Summarized in Richard Salomon, *Ancient Buddhist Scrolls from Gandhāra: The British Library Kharoṣṭhī Fragments* (Seattle: University of Washington Press, 1999), 187–191.
45. *Aya panighaḍe saghe cadurdiśami acaryana sarvastivatana parigrahami purnagarañami*; Salomon, *Ancient Buddhist Scrolls*, 200.
46. Gérard Fussman, *Monuments bouddhiques de Termez/Termez Buddhist Monuments, 1: Catalogue des inscriptions sur poteries*, 2 vols., Collège de France, Publications de l'Institut de Civilisation Indienne, fasc. 79.2 (Paris: Édition-Diffusion de Boccard, Paris, 2011).
47. Kara Tepe 20, *ayo kuḍiya bhikṣusya budhaśirasya pugaligasya*; and Fussman, *Monuments bouddhiques*, 65–66.
48. *Sa[ṃ] 4 1 phagunasa masasa di paṃcami budhanadasa trepiḍakasa danamukhe madapidarana adhvadidana puyaya bhavatu* (*Catalog of Kharoṣṭhī Inscriptions* no. 232).
49. *Devadharmo yaṃ kṛtaṃ māyā devasiṅgena* (Hodar no. 69.31); Ditte Bandini-König, *Die Felsbildstation Hodar*, Materialien zur Archäologie der Nordgebiete Pakistans 3 (Mainz, Germany: Philipp von Zabern, 1999), 310–311 and pl. 122.
50. The broader historical and cultural context of this corpus is discussed, among other places, in Jason Neelis, *Early Buddhist Transmission and Trade Networks: Mobility and Exchange within and Beyond the Northwestern Borderlands of South Asia*, Dynamics in the History of Religion 2 (Leiden, The Netherlands: Brill, 2011).
51. Tsukamoto III Waḷā 1–23, pp. 526–542.
52. Tsukamoto III Waḷā 6, pp. 532–533; and *nānādigabhyāgatāṣṭādaśanikāyabhyantarāryyabhikṣusaṅghāya* (line 7).
53. Tsukamoto III Waḷā 5, pp. 530–532.

54. *Paṃcabhir mmahāpātakais sopapātakais saṃyukta* [*sic*] *syād;* Lionel D. Barnett, "Wala Plate of Guhasena: The Year 246," *Epigraphia Indica* 13 (1915–1916): 339, line 15.
55. Dinesh Chandra Bhattacharya, "A Newly Discovered Copperplate from Tippera (The Gunaighar Grant of Vainyagupta: The Year 188 Current [Gupta Era])," *Indian Historical Quarterly* 6 (1930): 45–60; and Tsukamoto I Guṇāighar 1, pp. 168–172.
56. P. R. Srinivasan, "Jayarampur Plate of Gopachandra," *Epigraphia Indica* 39 (1971–1972): 141–148 (not in Tsukamoto).
57. Devadatta Ramakrishna Bhandarkar, *Inscriptions of the Early Gupta Kings,* ed. Bahadurchand Chhabra and Govind Swamirao Gai, rev. ed., Corpus Inscriptionum Indicarum vol. III (New Delhi: Director General, Archaeological Survey of India, 1981), 247–252; and Tsukamoto IV Sāñcī 95, pp. 728–730.
58. *Śīlasamādhiprajñāguṇabhāvitendriya-,* line 1.
59. Georg Bühler, "The New Inscription of Toramana Shaha," *Epigraphia Indica* 1 (1892): 238–241; and Tsukamoto V Kura 1, pp. 976–978.
60. Richard Salomon, "Schism and Sectarian Conflicts as Revealed – and Concealed – in Indian Buddhist Inscriptions" (forthcoming).
61. The Ajanta inscriptions are collected in Richard S. Cohen, "Ajanta's Inscriptions," in *Ajanta: History and Development,* vol. 2, *Arguments about Ajanta,* by Walter M. Spink, Handbook of Oriental Studies 18/2 (Leiden, The Netherlands: Brill, 2006), 273–339.
62. Cohen, "Ajanta's Inscriptions," no. 67, pp. 311–313; and Tsukamoto III Ajaṇṭā 52, pp. 371–374.
63. Cohen, "Ajanta's Inscriptions," nos. 91 and 92, pp. 331–332; and Tsukamoto III Ajaṇṭā 67a–b, p. 381.
64. Heinrich Lüders, "Ārya-Śūras Jātakamālā und die Fresken von Ajaṇṭā," *Nachrichten von der königlichen Gesellschaft der Wissenschaften zu Göttingen,* philologisch-historische Klasse (1902): 758–762; reprinted in Heinrich Lüders, *Philologica Indica: Ausgewählte kleine Schriften von Heinrich Lüders; Festgabe zum siebstigsten Geburtstage am 25. Juni 1939 dargebracht von Kollegen, Freunden, und Schülern* (Göttingen, Germany: Vandenhoeck & Ruprecht, 1940), 73–77; and Cohen, "Ajanta's Inscriptions," nos. 4–6, pp. 276–277.
65. Sten Konow, "Two Buddhist Inscriptions from Sarnath," *Epigraphia Indica* 9 (1907–1908): 291–293; and Tsukamoto Sārnāth 94, p. 913.
66. Oskar von Hinüber, "Epigraphic Varieties of Continental Pāli from Devnimori and Ratnagiri," in *Buddhism and Its Relation to Other Religions: Essays in Honour of Dr. Shozen Kumoi on His Seventieth Birthday* (Kyoto: Heirakuji Shoten, 1985), 185–200; and Tsukamoto III Devnī Morī 1, pp. 394–396.
67. *Catalog of Kharoṣṭhī Inscriptions* no. 153.
68. Frederick Eden Pargiter, "The Kasia Copper-Plate," *Archaeological Survey of India, Annual Report 1910–11,* 73–77; Tsukamoto IV Kasiā 125, pp. 628–629; Edward Hamilton Johnston, "The Gopalpur Bricks," *Journal of the Royal Asiatic Society of Great Britain and Ireland* (1938): 547–543; Tsukamoto IV Gopālpur 1–5, p. 611; Debala Mitra, *Ratnagiri (1958–61),* 2 vols., Memoirs of the Archaeological Survey of India 80 (New Delhi: Director General, Archaeological Survey of India, 1981–1983), 411–422; and von Hinüber, "Epigraphic Varieties," 193–196.
69. Niranjan Prasad Chakravarti, "Two Brick Inscriptions from Nalanda," *Epigraphia Indica* 21 (1931–1932): 193–199; Probodh Chandra Bagchi, "A Note on the Pratitya Samutpada Sutra," *Epigraphia Indica* 21 (1931–32): 199–204; and Tsukamoto I Nālandā 2–3, pp. 197–198.
70. Gudrun Melzer and Lore Sander, "A Copper Scroll Inscription from the Time of the Alchon Huns," in *Manuscripts in the Schøyen Collection: Buddhist Manuscripts,* ed. Jens Braarvig (Oslo: Hermes Publishing, 2006), 3:251–278. See also Hans Bakker, "A Buddhist Foundation in Śārdīysa," *Indo-Iranian Journal* 61 (2018): 1–19; and Cristina Scherrer-Schaub, "The Quintessence of Mādhyamika Teachings Blossoms Again," *Journal Asiatique* 306 (2018): 115–146.
71. Daniel Boucher, "The *Pratītyasamutpādagāthā* and Its Role in the Medieval Cult of the Relics," *Journal of the International Association of Buddhist Studies* 14 (1991): 1–27; *Ye dharmā hetuprabhavā hetuṃ teṣāṃ*

tathāgato hy avadat/teṣāṃ ca yo nirodha evaṃvādī mahāśramaṇaḥ. The verse was said to have been originally uttered by the buddha's disciple Aśvajit, who uttered them to Śāriputra when asked to explain the buddha's dharma.

72. Daya Ram Sahni, "A Buddhist Image Inscription from Śrāvastī," *Archaeological Survey of India, Annual Report 1908–09*, 133–138; Boucher, "*Pratītyasamutpādagāthā*," 14–15; and Tsukamoto IV Saheṭh-Maheṭh 1, pp. 699–700.
73. This material is conveniently summarized in Kiran Kumar Thaplyal's *Studies in Ancient Indian Seals: A Study of North Indian Seals and Sealings from circa Third Century* B.C. *to Mid-seventh Century* A.D. (Lucknow, India: Akhila Bharatiya Sanskrit Parishad, 1972), 206–222.
74. Hirananda Sastri, *Nalanda and Its Epigraphic Materials*, Memoirs of the Archaeological Survey of India 66 (Delhi: Manager of Publications Delhi, 1942), 26; *Śrī-nālandā-mahāvihārīyāryabhikṣusaṅghasya*; and Sastri, *Nalanda*, 36.
75. Sastri, *Nalanda*, 37. On this problematic term, see Jonathan Silk, *Managing Monks: Administrators and Administrative Roles in Indian Buddhist Monasticism* (Oxford: Oxford University Press, 2008), 93. On related administrative terms in inscriptions and literature, see Silk, *Managing Monks*, 75–99 (ch. 4, "Navakarmika"); and Silk, *Managing Monks*, 101–125 (ch. 5, "*Vārika* and Specialization of Duties").
76. Jean Philippe Vogel, "Exacavations at Kasiā," *Archaeological Survey of India, Annual Report 1906-07*, 63; and Tsukamoto IV Kasiā 19–22, pp. 617–618.
77. Thaplyal, *Studies in Ancient Indian Seals*, 222.
78. See especially Diwakar Acharya, "Evidence for Mahāyāna Buddhism and Sukhāvatī Cult in India in the Middle Period: Early Fifth to Late Sixth Century Nepalese Inscriptions," *Journal of the International Association of Buddhist Studies* 31 (2008): 23–75.
79. Nani Gopal Majumdar, "Nalanda Inscription of Vipulasrimitra," *Epigraphia Indica* 21 (1931–32): 97–101; and Tsukamoto I Nālandā 9, pp. 199–202.
80. Arthur Venis, "Notes on a Buddhist Inscription from Hasra Kol, Gaya," *Journal & Proceedings of the Asiatic Society of Bengal* 4 (1908): 459–462; and Tsukamoto I Hasra Kol 1, pp. 173–174.
81. Mitra, *Ratnagiri*, 1.98–100, 229–232.
82. Franz Kielhorn, "A Buddhist Stone-Inscription from Ghosrawa," *Indian Antiquary* 17 (1888): 307–312; and Tsukamoto I Ghosrāwā 1, pp. 166–168.
83. A localized but important exception is the series of inscribed bronzes of the Palola dynasty (6th to 8th centuries ce) in the region of Gilgit in modern northern Pakistan; see Oskar von Hinüber, *Die Palola Ṣāhis: Ihre Steininschriften, Inschriften auf Bronzen, Handschriftenkolophone, und Schutzzauber; Materialien zur Geschichte von Gilgit und Chilas*, Antiquities of Northern Pakistan, Reports and Studies 5 (Mainz, Germany: Philipp von Zabern, 2004).
84. Daya Ram Sahni, "Saheth-Maheth Plate of Govindachandra; [Vikrama-]Samvat 1186," *Epigraphia Indica* 11 (1911–1912): 20–26; and Tsukamoto IV Saheṭh-Maheṭh 7, pp. 705–709.
85. Hirananda Shastri, "The Nalanda Copper-Plate of Devapaladeva," *Epigraphia Indica* 17 (1923–1924): 310–327; and Tsukamoto I Nālandā 10, pp. 202–204.
86. Seventy-seven examples of "inscribed dated sculptures" of this period are collected and summarized in Susan L. Huntington, *The "Pāla-Sena" Schools of Sculpture*, Studies in South Asian Culture 10 (Leiden, The Netherlands: E. J. Brill, 1984), 203–250. See also the readings of inscriptions by Gouriswar Bhattacharya in Claudine Bautze-Picron, *The Art of Eastern India in the Collection of the Museum für Indische Kunst, Berlin: Stone and Terracotta Sculptures*, Monographien zur indischen Archäologie Kunst und Philologie 12 (Berlin: Dietrich Riemer Verlag, 1998).
87. Anantaprasad Banerji-Sastri, "Ninety-Three Inscriptions on the Kurkihar Bronzes," *Journal of the Bihar and Orissa Research Society* 26 (1940): 236–251; and Tsukamoto I Kurkihar 1–81, pp. 178–192.

88. The donors from Kanchi are discussed in Gouriswar Bhattacharya, "Kāñcī Monks at Kukkuṭapāda-giri-vihāra," in *Eṭṭāvatu, 9th World Tamil Conference, Tanjavur, Souvenir Volume*, ed. I. Nagaswami (Thanjavur, India: 1995), 89–93 reprinted in Gouriswar Bhattacharya, *Essays on Buddhist Hindu and Jain Iconography and Epigraphy*, ed. Enamul Haque (Dhaka: International Centre for Study of Bengal Art, 2000), 91–96.
89. Niradbandhu Sanyal, "A Buddhist Inscription from Bodh-Gaya of the Reign of Jayaccandradeva – V. S. 124x," *Indian Historical Quarterly* 5 (1929): 14–30; and Tsukamoto I. Bodh Gaya 38, pp. 153–157.
90. Franz Kielhorn, "A Buddhist Stone-Inscription from Sravasti, of [Vikrama]-samvat 1276," *Indian Antiquary* 17 (1888): 61–64; and Tsukamoto IV Saheṭh-Maheṭh 6, pp. 702–705.
91. Salomon, *Indian Epigraphy*, 204–209.
92. Salomon, *Indian Epigraphy*, 209–215.
93. For references, see the section "The Period of the Sātavāhanas, Western Kṣatrapas, Indo-Scythians, and Kuṣāṇas" in this article.
94. Alexander Cunningham, *Bhilsa Topes; or, Buddhist Monuments of Central India* (London: Smith, Elder, 1854).
95. Alexander Cunningham, *The Stûpa of Bharhut: A Buddhist Monument Ornamented with Numerous Sculptures Illustrative of Buddhist Legend and History in the Third Century B.C.* (London: W. H. Allen, 1879).
96. Alexander Cunningham, *Mahâbodhi, or the Great Buddhist Temple Under the Bodhi Tree at Buddha-Gaya* (London: W. H. Allen, 1892).
97. Alexander Cunningham, *Inscriptions of Asoka* (1877); Eugen Hultzsch (1925); Konow, *Kharoṣhṭhī Inscriptions*; and Lüders, *Bharhut Inscriptions*.
98. Marshall and Foucher, *Monuments of Sāñchī*; Lüders, *Mathurā Inscriptions*; and Lüders, *Bharhut Inscriptions*.
99. Lamotte, *History of Indian Buddhism*, 578–583 = *Histoire du bouddhisme indien*, 523–528. Lamotte's material is, however, by now badly out of date, and is superseded by the second introductory chapter ("Tradition and Historical Evidence in Connection with the Formation of Nikāya-Buddhisms," 45–65) to Tsukamoto's *Indo bukkyō himei no kenkyū*, though this, too, is already considerably outdated.
100. Lüders, *Bharhut Inscriptions*, 2.
101. Gregory Schopen, "Archaeology and Protestant Presuppositions in the Study of Indian Buddhism," *History of Religions* 31 (1991): 14, reprinted in Schopen, *Bones, Stones, and Buddhist Monks*, 9. Schopen's innovative approaches have, however, not been universally or uncritically accepted. See, for example, the critique of this article in Richard Nance, *Speaking for Buddhas: Scriptural Commentary in Indian Buddhism* (New York: Columbia University Press, 2012), 7–12, calling for a methodology that strikes a balance between normative texts and inscriptional records rather than seeing them in terms of a dichotomy: "We need not draw a hard and fast line between the descriptive and the normative" (8).
102. Maiko Nakanishi and Oskar von Hinüber, "Kanaganahalli Inscriptions," *Annual Report of the International Research Institute for Advanced Buddhology at Soka University* 17, supplement (2014).
103. Shizutani Masao, 静谷 正雄, *Indo bukkyō himei mokuroku* (インド仏教碑銘目録), Catalog of Indian Buddhist Inscriptions (Kyoto: Heirakuji Shoten, 1979).
104. Tsukamoto, *Indo bukkyō himei no kenkyū*.
105. Franz Kielhorn, *A List of the Inscriptions of Northern India from About a.d. 400*, appendix to vol. 5 (1898–1899){Calcutta: Office of the Superintendent of Government Printing, India}; Heinrich Lüders, *List of Brāhmī Inscriptions from the Earliest Times to About a.d. 400*, appendix to vol. 10 (1912) {Calcutta: Superintendent of Government Printing, India}; and Devadatta Ramakrishna Bhandarkar, *A List of the Inscriptions of Northern India in Brahmi and its derivative Scripts, from about 200 A.C.*,

appendix to vols. 19–23 (1927–1936) {Calcutta: Manager, Government of India Central Publication Branch}.
106. *Select Inscriptions Bearing on Indian History and Civilization*, vol. 1, *From the Sixth Century B.C. to the Sixth Century A.D.*, 2nd ed. (Kolkata: University of Calcutta, 1965); and *Select Inscriptions Bearing on Indian History and Civilization*, vol. 2, *From the Sixth to the Eighteenth Century A.D.* (Delhi: Motilal Banarsidass, 1983).
107. Paul Kent Andersen, *Studies in the Minor Rock Edicts of Aśoka I: Critical Edition* (Freiburg, Germany: Hedwig Falk, 1990).
108. Tsukamoto, *Indo bukkyō himei no kenkyū*.
109. Dines Chandra Sircar, *Indian Epigraphy* (Delhi: Motilal Banarsidass, 1965); Dines Chandra Sircar, "Introduction to Indian Epigraphy and Palaeography," *Journal of Ancient Indian History* 4 (1970–1971): part I; and Salomon, *Indian Epigraphy*.
110. Richard Salomon, "Epigraphy," in *Art of India: Prehistory to the Present*, ed. Frederick M. Asher (New Delhi: Encyclopædia Britannica, 2003), 271–282.
111. Dines Chandra Sircar, *Indian Epigraphical Glossary* (Delhi: Motilal Banarsidass, 1966).
112. Gregory Schopen *Bones, Stones, and Buddhist Monks* (Honolulu: University of Hawai'i Press, 1997); Gregory Schopen, *Buddhist Monks and Business Matters: Still More Papers on Monastic Buddhism in India* (Honolulu: University of Hawai'i Press, 2004); and Gregory Schopen, *Figments and Fragments of Mahāyāna Buddhism in India: More Collected Papers* (Honolulu: University of Hawai'i Press (2005). A fourth volume by Gregory Schopen, *Buddhist Nuns, Monks, and Other Worldly Matters: Recent Papers on Monastic Buddhism in India* (Honolulu: University of Hawai'i Press (2014), is less concerned with epigraphical matters.
113. Th. Damsteegt, *Epigraphical Hybrid Sanskrit*, Orientalia Rheno-Traiectina 23 (Leiden, The Netherlands: E. J. Brill, 1978); and Salomon, *Indian Epigraphy*, 81–86.
114. Sircar, "Introduction to Indian Epigraphy and Paleography"; Georges-Jean Pinault, "Écritures de l'Inde continentale," in *Histoire de l'écriture: De l'idéogramme au multimedia*, ed. Anne-Marie Christin (Paris: Flammarion, 2001), 93–121; and Harry Falk, *Schrift im alten Indien: Ein Forschungsbericht mit Anmerkungen*, ScriptOralia 56 (Tübingen, Germany: Gunter Narr Verlag, 1993).

Richard Salomon

ESOTERIC BUDDHISM IN SOUTHEAST ASIA

Both possible applications of the category "esoteric Buddhism" to Southeast Asia—to refer to the *mantranaya* of the Mahāyāna or to a "Tantric Theravāda"—are problematic and contested, independently of one another and of the broader issues with the category "Buddhist Tantra" writ large. The historical application of the category "esoteric Buddhism," that is, the search for evidence of *mantranaya* within the Mahāyāna Buddhisms found in Southeast Asia in the past, is made problematic by a lack of evidence and the ambiguities involved in interpreting what evidence exists. While several scholars have seen extensive evidence of the *mantranaya* in Southeast Asian art historical evidence, their conclusions have not been universally accepted, as it is often difficult to determine whether a particular artifact is representative of the *mantranaya* specifically or the Mahāyāna more generally. On the other hand, while evidence for the so-called "Tantric Theravāda" is abundant, the very applicability of the categories "Tantra" and "esoteric" to Pali Buddhist contexts has been called into question. This is in large part because these categories are not emic to the tradition and are based on an implicit or explicit comparison to Mahāyāna Buddhist Tantra, with which there is no clear evidence of a historical connection.

This article will explore the application of the category "esoteric Buddhism" to Southeast Asia in both of these ways while highlighting the problematic and contested aspects of both applications. It should be noted that a further complicating factor is the relative lack of work, especially synthetic work, that has been done on Southeast Asian esoteric Buddhism, especially in comparison to esoteric Buddhism in India and Tibet. Nevertheless, a partial synthetic article covering Mahāyāna Buddhist Tantra in Southeast Asia has been published by Hiram Woodward, as has an analogous synthetic work on "Tantric Theravāda" by Kate Crosby;[1] given the lack of other broad coverages of esoteric Buddhism in the region, this article is particularly indebted to these two synthetic works.

MAHĀYĀNA BUDDHIST TANTRA (*MANTRANAYA*) IN HISTORICAL SOUTHEAST ASIA

The search for Mahāyāna Buddhist Tantra in Southeast Asia is immediately complicated by the broad issues that one faces in defining "Buddhist Tantra" (or "Tantra" for that matter) in general, additionally compounded by the nature of the Southeast Asian evidence. The term *tantra* has the advantage of being an emic term, referring to a genre of texts and, within the Tibetan context, to the systems of ritual based on those texts. The application of the term *tantra* to the earlier of these texts, however, is often retrospective. Likewise, the emic term Vajrayāna is fairly late, dating in India only to the late 7th century, and thus refers more specifically to the more developed rituals of the later *tantras*. An earlier term that has the advantage of being both emic to the (Indian) tradition and sufficiently broad to cover what scholars usually refer to as "Tantra" is *mantranaya* ("way of mantras"). This term is opposed to *pāramitānaya* ("way of perfections"), and together they refer to two paths within the Mahāyāna.[2]

When framed broadly in this manner, the search for Mahāyāna Buddhist Tantra in Southeast Asia consists essentially of searching for any evidence of Mahāyāna Buddhism that makes use of even the most basic technologies of Tantra, i.e., mantras and *maṇḍalas*, as opposed to the apparati of ordinary *bodhisattva*-path Mahāyāna Buddhism, oriented toward slow cultivation of the perfections in pursuit of buddhahood in the distant future. Unfortunately, the nature of the evidence leaves even such a broad search open to ambiguity and contestation. The Mahāyāna Buddhist traditions relevant to this search are for the most part not living traditions, and there are few historical records from which to gain insight into the extent to which Mahāyāna Buddhists in Southeast Asian history conceived of their practices as belonging to either the *mantranaya* or *pāramitānaya*. Indeed, even historical memory of Mahāyāna Buddhism was to a large extent obliterated by the rise of Pali Buddhism in the mainland and Islam in (pen)insular Southeast Asia in the early to mid-2nd millennium. This leaves modern researchers with little evidence to go on: for the most part, inscriptions, which are short and cryptic; art historical artifacts, whose doctrinal referents are generally ambiguous; and historical records of non-Southeast Asian tantric practitioners who traveled to Southeast Asia, from which one can do little more than make inferences about the state of affairs in Southeast Asia when they visited.

Politico-Historical Contexts. The religious landscape of what is often called "classical" Southeast Asia—referring to the second half of the first millennium and the very beginning of the second millennium, prior to the rise to dominance of Pali Buddhism on the mainland and the adoption of Islam in the archipelago—was variegated and lacked the sorts of rigid boundaries that characterize religion in the modern world. While earlier scholarship labeled such a religious landscape as "syncretistic," the model of syncretism has now fallen into disfavor as being premised on the existence of "pure" religions available for "mixing" that are completely hypothetical and have no referent in the real world. The earlier model of "Indianization" has likewise been replaced by an emphasis on "localization," the process whereby Southeast Asian actors adapted Indian cultural forms to local circumstances. From this perspective, the religious landscape of "classical" Southeast Asia can be described as one in which various rulers somewhat eclectically patronized and adapted Indian religious iconography, mythology, vocabulary, doctrine, and personnel in order to suit their particular local circumstances. In many cases, the sources of inspiration for Southeast Asian religious developments were what modern scholars might retrospectively label "Hindu," and often even more specifically Śaiva. Although other states, such as those of the Burmese in Pagan and the Mon in central mainland Southeast Asia, were more Buddhist in orientation, they tended to patronize Pali forms of Buddhism rather than Sanskritic Mahāyāna.

There are, however, three major contexts in which Mahāyāna Buddhism was a significant source of inspiration to local rulers and thus are possible contexts in which to find evidence of the *mantranaya* ("way of mantras"). The first and most long-lived was Śrī Vijaya, a maritime state based in Sumatra that was a significant power in the region from roughly the late 7th century to the early 11th century. This state is recognized as having, more than any other Southeast Asian state, been a patron of Mahāyāna Buddhism, and as such appears to have been a significant destination for Buddhist pilgrims from both South and East Asia. The second context is the relatively short-lived Śailendra dynasty, which ruled in central Java in the late 8th and early 9th centuries and like Śrī Vijaya tended to patronize Mahāyāna Buddhism. This dynasty was responsible for the construction of Barabudur, a giant *stūpa* in the form of a *maṇḍala* that represents the greatest Buddhist monument of classical Southeast Asia. Finally, a third Mahāyāna Buddhist context is the mainland Angkorean Empire. Although Angkor tended to be Śaiva in orientation throughout most of its history, its rulers also at times patronized Mahāyāna Buddhism, most significantly, Jayavarman VII (r. 1181–1216 CE), who built Angkor's largest Mahāyāna Buddhist monument, the Bayon. As we will see, most of the evidence for *mantranaya* in classical Southeast Asia clusters around these three contexts—Śrī Vijaya, the Śailendra dynasty of 8th/9th-century Java, and the late Angkorean Empire—but there are a few significant exceptions.

Inscriptions and Texts. Given that there are not many ordinary written texts preserved from the classical period in Southeast Asian history, inscriptions provide rare glimpses into the narrative worlds of that period. Unfortunately, inscriptions are relatively short, and chance references within them tantalize modern researchers without giving enough context to fully assess their significance. The earliest inscriptions containing references that might imply *mantranaya* influence are from Sumatra and were erected under the auspices of Śrī Vijaya. The Tulang Tuwo inscription of 684 makes use of various Sanskrit loanwords associated with the *pāramitānaya* but also uses the word *vajraśarīra*, which may or may not imply an acquaintance with Buddhist tantric thought in which the *vajra* (diamond/thunderbolt) took on great significance. Likewise, the Kota Kapur inscription of 686 and the Telaga Batu inscription refer, respectively, to the use of mantras in war and the use of a magical diagram (*yantra*) and blood-filled bowl to punish disloyalty.[3] Mantras and *yantras* are important technologies of Tantra in general, and blood is suggestive of the transgressive practices of Tantra, but again it is not clear if these references bespeak a specifically *mantranaya* context.

Slightly later inscriptions from Java are perhaps more specific in their *mantranaya* allusions but also remain ambiguous. The 782 Kelurak inscription, according to Woodward, "records the installation of an image of Mañjughoṣa, a form of the Bodhisattva Mañjuśrī, under the auspices of guru from Gauḍī, a section of Bengal." The inscription further refers to Mañjughoṣa as Vajradhara ("*vajra*-bearer"), Brahmā, Viṣṇu, and Maheśvara;[4] the use of the term Vajradhara and homologization with Hindu gods may imply a tantric context. The 792 Ratubaka inscription, on the other hand, includes the phrase "esoteric concerns" (*saṃgūḍārtha*) within a broader context discussing Buddhist themes.[5] This could be taken as a literal reference to "esoteric Buddhism," but it is not necessarily clear that this is what the term *saṃgūḍārtha* is intended to mean. By far the most compelling piece of evidence for the presence of the *mantranaya* in Java is an actual text, the Old Javanese *Sang Hyang Kamahāyānan Mantranaya*, which was compiled sometime between the 9th and 11th centuries. Aside from the fact that this text quite literally refers to the *mantranaya* in its title, it also includes verses in Sanskrit from several *mantranaya* texts, including the *Mahāvairocana Sūtra*, the *Vajraśekhara* or *Jāpa Sūtra*, the *Sarvadurgatipariśodhana Tantra*, the *Kriyāsaṃgrahapañjikā*, and the *Adhyardhaśatikā Prajñāpāramitā*.[6]

Inscriptions from Angkorean Cambodia, like those of Sumatra and Java, give reference to the possible presence of *mantranaya* Buddhism. Woodward cites two 10th-century inscriptions that refer to Avalokiteśvara and appear to imply knowledge of the *Kāraṇḍavyūha Sūtra*.[7] A bit less ambiguous are a 979 inscription that records the giving of gifts to an image of Trailokyavijaya and an 1108 inscription that records the installation of an image of the same deity. Trailokyavijaya is a wrathful deity who is mentioned in Buddhist tantric texts, including the *Mahāvairocana Sūtra*.[8] Finally, a 1041 inscription at Phimai (about which more below) refers to four bodies of the buddha corresponding to four Māras, which, according to Woodward, implies knowledge of certain *mantranaya maṇḍalas*.[9]

Although the inscriptions cited so far have all been clustered around the three major Mahāyāna Buddhist contexts of classical Southeast Asia discussed above, there are some inscriptions from other contexts that also might be construed as indicating *mantranaya* influence. One is the An Thai inscription of 902 in Champa. This inscription implies knowledge of the *Mahāvairocana Sūtra* insofar as it refers to the three buddha families of that text in the form of *dhātus*, or "realms."[10] Likewise, a 1442 inscription refers to the donation of a variety of texts to a monastery in Pagan, including what appear to be three works of Mahāyāna Buddhist Tantra: *Mṛtyavañcana*, *Kālacakra*, and *Kālacakraṭīkā*.[11] The fact that this last inscription represents the only reference whatsoever to Mahāyāna Buddhist tantric literature in premodern Burma, the religious context of which is known from the vast preponderance of evidence to have been dominated by Pali Buddhism, reminds us that inscriptional references to the *mantranaya*, whether ambiguous or not, should not be overinterpreted. Passing references to terms, texts, deities, and ideas associated with the *mantranaya* may or may not imply a broader *mantranaya* context and must be interpreted in light of other evidence.

Art Historical Evidence. Art historical evidence, while serving to complement inscriptional evidence in suggesting influence from esoteric Buddhism in Southeast Asia, faces perhaps even greater difficulties of interpretation. Given that iconography varied over time and space, scholars often do not agree on the identification of a particular *bodhisattva*/buddha/deity, and even if they do agree, the significance of that particular figure in a particular context can be contested. Most art historical evidence that has been identified as possibly reflecting the *mantranaya* is clustered in Java and greater Cambodia. The most contested piece of art historical evidence for *mantranaya* in all of Southeast Asia is undoubtedly Borobudur, the world-famous *stūpa* built in the 9th century by the Śailendras in central Java. Evidence for the influence of the *prajñāpāramitānaya* of the Mahāyāna on this monument is clear and uncontroversial: in addition to scenes from the life of the Buddha Śākyamuni and Jātaka tales, Borobudur also has reliefs that depict scenes from the story of Sudhana found in the Mahāyāna *Gaṇḍavyūha Sūtra*. Aside from the rather generic fact that the placement of buddha-images across the monument give it the appearance of a *maṇḍala*, however, evidence of *mantranaya* influence is less clear. Although some scholars have argued that certain aspects of Borobudur suggest a tantric interpretation, the evidence is sufficiently unclear that Jan Gonda stated baldly that Borobudur "cannot . . . be shown . . . [to be] a monument of the Tantric current in Buddhism."[12]

Other art historical evidence in Java besides Borobudur has been suggested to reflect *mantranaya* influence. The temple Chandi Mendut, built about the same time as Borobudur, has an arrangement of *bodhisattvas* and goddesses that suggests possible influence from the proto-*mantranaya Kāraṇḍavyūha Sūtra*. A group of 10th- to 11th-century bronze statues found at Nganjuk in East Java has been identified as depicting deities from the Vajradhātu *maṇḍala*; likewise, gold plates inscribed with the names of deities from the Vajradhātu *maṇḍala* have been found deposited at Chandi Gumpung.[13] Finally, a group of bronze statues discovered at Surocolo in East Java has been identified as coming from the *maṇḍala* of the *Adhyardhaśatikā Prajñāpāramitā* and the Hevajra *maṇḍala*.[14]

Angkor was dominated by Śaivism through most of its history but began to show influence from Mahāyāna Buddhism beginning around the 10th century, with fairly clear evidence of specifically *mantranaya* influence. Several bronze images of Hevajra, dating from the 11th to the 13th centuries, have been found in the sphere of Angkorean influence, although in most cases he is depicted without his female consort.[15] Of the Angkorean Buddhist monuments, Prasat Phimai, built in the late 11th or early 12th century by Jayavarman VI in what is now Thailand, is the one most generally accepted to reflect tantric influence. An inscription already discussed above refers to an image of the tantric deity Trailokyavijaya, and the lintels depict *yoginīs* and various male tantric deities, including possibly Cakrasaṃvara.[16] Esoteric interpretations of other Buddhist monuments, such as those found in Angkor itself, are less widely accepted. Woodward, for example, has argued that the iconic faces of the Bayon, built by Jayavarman VII in the late 12th or early 13th century, depict not Avalokiteśvara or Brahmā as often thought, but rather the tantric deity Hevajra.[17]

Travelers to Southeast Asia. Another form of evidence for esoteric Buddhism in classical Southeast Asia, somewhat more circumstantial, is the record of travelers who passed through Southeast Asia and are known to have been involved in the transmission of *mantranaya* Buddhism. For example, the Indian monks Vajrabodhi (670–741) and his disciple Amoghavajra (705–774), who were involved in the translation of *mantranaya* texts into Chinese and played a pivotal role in the foundation of the esoteric Zhenyan school in China, both passed through Southeast Asia during their travels and may have studied or transmitted *mantranaya* teachings there.[18] In addition, the Indian monk Atiśa, famous as a transmitter of Buddhism to Tibet, studied in Śrī Vijaya from 1012 to 1024 prior to going to Tibet. A commentarial text of the Tibetan Tengyur is attributed to Atiśa's teacher Dharmakīrti, who is specifically said to have resided in Śrī Vijaya. This raises the possibility, somewhat speculative, that Atiśa might have brought tantric teachings from Śrī Vijaya to Tibet as well.[19]

A Living Relic: Bali. In discussing the possible inclusion of *mantranaya* ideas and practices in the Mahāyāna Buddhism of "classical" Southeast Asia, a brief word should be said about Bali, which is unique in Southeast Asia in preserving religious practices that go back to the classical period without having been overwhelmed by the hegemonic influence of either Sinhala-oriented Pali Buddhism, Sinitic Mahāyāna Buddhism, or (as is specifically relevant in Indonesia) Islam. Although the religion of modern-day Bali is generally described as "Hindu," evidence of past Buddhist influence is found in the fact that the Brahman priests are divided into two groups: a majority known as *padanda Śiva* and a smaller number known as *padanda Buddha*. These latter, who have been studies by Hyookas, perform rituals that involve basic *mantranaya* technologies such as the use of mantras and *mudrās*.[20] *Mantranaya* influence can also be found in the Balinese *Nāgabāyu Sūtra*, which refers to wrathful deities corresponding to five cosmic buddhas.[21]

"TANTRIC THERAVĀDA" OR "ESOTERIC SOUTHERN BUDDHISM"

The second way in which the category "esoteric Buddhism" can be and has been applied to Southeast Asia is to refer to an aspect of Pali/Theravāda Buddhism, present throughout the second millennium (possibly even earlier in Burmese and Mon contexts) and continuing to the present day. The field of study for what is often called "Tantric Theravāda" was created almost single-handedly by François Bizot, who published a series of works, beginning in 1976 with *Le figuier a cinq branches*, making the case that Theravāda Buddhism has a "Tantric" aspect.[22] These publications are editions—with translations of and extensive commentary upon— of mostly Cambodian texts that Bizot obtained and likely saved from obliteration just prior to the devastation wreaked by the Khmer Rouge. Bizot argues that these texts are the products of an old tradition in Southeast Asian Theravāda Buddhism that can be described as "Tantric" and that is rapidly dying out due to the increasing hegemony of reformist orthodoxy and (in the case of Cambodia) socio-political upheaval.

The field of study of this "Tantric Theravāda" remains small and dominated by Bizot's pioneering work, but there have been a few scholars who have accepted and extended Bizot's basic argument for the existence of an esoteric tradition in Theravāda Buddhism. Lance Cousins, for example, coined the term "esoteric Southern Buddhism" to describe what he sees as a well-defined esoteric tradition in Theravāda Buddhism exemplified by the texts published by Bizot.[23] In 2000, Kate Crosby wrote a useful article summarizing in English the publications of Bizot and other French scholars working on similar materials.[24] There she prefers to refer to the tradition as *yogāvacara*, which, unlike "Tantra" and "esoteric," is an emic term. In her more up-to-date 2013 book on the tradition, she refers to it as *boran kammaṭṭhāna*, "old meditation," the term by which it came to be known in the early 20th century in contrast to the new forms of meditation increasing in popularity at that time. This phrase has been taken up by Choompolpaisal and Skilton, who have begun documenting detail of one of the remaining lineages in Bangkok.[25]

The application of the category "esoteric Buddhism" to Pali/Theravāda Buddhism in the manner followed by Bizot and his successors, however, is not uncontested. It has been criticized in particular by Justin McDaniel, who argues that, aside from the fact that categories like "Tantric Theravāda" and "esoteric Southern Buddhism" are completely foreign to the tradition they describe, they also obscure the fact that the practices they refer to are in fact the mainstream within Southeast Asian Buddhism, even today.[26] In her 2013 book, Kate Crosby looks at this aspect from a different perspective, namely the broader technologies of transformation that underpin South Indian tantra and esoteric Theravāda and explain their common features. She shows how esoteric Theravāda meditation shows close parallels with generative grammar, group theory mathematics, ayurvedic obstetrics, and the chemistry of mercury, and suggests that it is the commonality of these sciences to the cultures that hosted various forms of "Tantra" that explains the apparent similarities. Thus, while the remainder of this section will outline the key features of the tradition(s) described as "Tantric Theravāda" or "esoteric Southern Buddhism" and why some scholars have seen fit to describe them as such, particular attention will also be given to the problematics of the implicit comparison between these Pali traditions and more generally recognized tantric traditions of Mahāyāna Buddhism and Hinduism.

Defining a Useful "Esotericism" in Pali Buddhism. The traditions studied by Bizot and others bear several resemblances to the *mantranaya* of the Mahāyāna and tantric traditions more generally that have led them to refer to these traditions as "Tantric" or "esoteric Buddhism." Kate Crosby has provided a useful list of seven key features: (1) the ritual construction of a buddha within oneself; (2) the homologization of microcosm and macrocosm through the use of sacred language; (3) the principle that the *dhamma* arises out of Pali syllables as such; (4) a principle of (magical) substitution; (5) "Esoteric interpretations of words, objects and myths that otherwise have a standard exoteric meaning or purpose in Theravāda Buddhism"; (6) the practice of initiation; and (7) the use of the preceding six "methodologies" in pursuit of both mundane and supramundane goals.[27]

While these characteristics certainly bear a resemblance to those found in other tantric traditions, it is important to be clear about the exact extent of those resemblances in evaluating whether the traditions they describe can be usefully referred to as "Tantric" or "esoteric Buddhism." To begin with, the texts and practices studied by Bizot and his followers are completely within the Pali/Theravāda tradition. That is, while perhaps differing from a perceived or actual Theravāda "orthodoxy," they make use of only Pali, not Sanskrit, as a sacred language and refer only to canonical and extracanonical Pali texts, never Sanskrit texts of the Mahāyāna.

There is therefore no direct evidence that these traditions were influenced in any way by the *mantranaya* of the Mahāyāna. In addition, these traditions lack the sexual rituals that are found in some forms of Mahāyāna Buddhist and Śaiva Tantra. Given that many of the technologies of Tantra (e.g., mantras and *maṇḍalas*) are not unique to tantric traditions, David White has argued that sexual rituals are what give Tantra its specificity.[28] According to such a criterion, these Pali Buddhist traditions would not qualify as Tantra.

Another possible way to define the "specificity" of these Pali traditions so as to justify comparison to other traditions of Tantra is the use of characteristic ritual technologies in the pursuit of liberation. "Tantric Theravāda" would then be understood to draw from a range of practices that are somewhat continuous with the ordinary practices of Theravāda Buddhism, but the name would be justified insofar as these practices are summoned to the purpose of attaining *nibbāna* in a unique way. A comparison to the *mantranaya* of the Mahāyāna is illustrative. *Tantras* of the *kriyā* and *caryā* classes describe rituals that involve the use of "characteristic" tantric technologies such as mantras, *maṇḍalas,* and *mudrās,* but neither rituals per se nor the technologies used therein are unique to the *mantranaya.* When we move on to the *yoga, mahāyoga,* and *yoginī tantras,* however, these ritual technologies are applied to the pursuit of nirvana, which is unique and thus grants the *mantranaya* specificity vis-à-vis its other, the *pāramitānaya.*

A particular facet of the issue of specificity relates to the label "esoteric Buddhism." McDaniel has criticized the use of this term because, as he shows, many of the practices associated with it are completely mainstream and hardly secret.[29] However, this situation is not really different from the more widely recognized "esoteric" tradition of the Mahāyāna. After all, "esoteric Buddhism" is the mainstream tradition in Tibet and Mongolia, and there is no reason to believe that the situation was any different in certain contexts in India in the late first millennium when esoteric Buddhism was being transmitted to Tibet. The application of the label "esoteric" to the *mantranaya* is justified, in spite of the fact that the bulk of its practices are mainstream and therefore quite literally exoteric, by a rhetoric of secrecy and the use of initiation to limit access to particular advanced practices to select initiates. The same sort of situation appears operative in the traditions studied by Bizot and his followers. The next two sections will outline, first, those mainstream practices found in Southeast Asian Pali Buddhism that resemble the ritual technologies of other tantric traditions and, then, the evidence for a specific tradition of meditation that draw on these practices in pursuit of liberation.

Mainstream "Tantric" Practices in Southeast Asian Pali Buddhism. As is the case with any tantric tradition, many of the ritual technologies associated with "Tantric Theravāda" are actually quite mainstream and widely used. First and foremost among them can be counted mantras, the use of sacred syllables in Pali that may be understood to have an "esoteric," syllable-by-syllable meaning, but in any case are understood to have an intrinsic power of their own. The centrality of mantras to Pali Buddhist practice in Southeast Asia is so great, in fact, that in Thai the word for "pray" is *suatmon,* literally, "to recite mantras." Closely related to the concept of *mantra* in Pali Buddhism is the *gāthā,* which generally refers to a longer prayer dedicated to a particular sacred figure or purpose, such as the *Jinapañjara Gāthā* studied by McDaniel that is associated with the famous Thai monk Somdet To.[30] *Gāthās,* like mantras, are understood to have an intrinsic power.

Another "tantric" technology that is common throughout Southeast Asian Buddhism is the use of *yantras*, or sacred diagrams. *Yantras* are also associated with the tantric Mahāyāna and Śaiva traditions but are mostly overshadowed, especially in textbooks, by *maṇḍalas*, "circles" of deities arranged around a central deity in imitation of the political theory of Indian Arthaśāstra. As found in mainstream Pali Buddhist practice, *yantras* are more general sacred diagrams that may be of any shape and include pictures, shapes, and text. Like mantras, they are understood to have an intrinsic power, and often they incorporate mantras within them. Because of this intrinsic power, *yantras* are often used for protective purposes. It is very common, for example, to ask a monk to draw a *yantra* on the wall of a new house or building, or on the ceiling of a new car, to protect the structure/vehicle and those within it. There is also an extensive tattooing tradition in Southeast Asia, in which *yantras* are drawn permanently onto the skin of (usually) young men, including monks. While tattooed *yantras* have a general protective purpose, they have been popular especially with soldiers and criminals who seek their protection against being wounded or killed.

Lying behind the technologies of *mantra*, *gāthā*, and *yantra* is a general understanding that there exists sacred power, which can be generated, stored, and transmitted much like electricity, and which can be deployed with real effect in the ordinary world. The correct utterance of mantras is one of the most common ways of generating this sacred power, which can then be deposited in *yantras*, amulets, sacred images, and human beings. Monks, especially highly renowned monks, are also understood to be a source of sacred power, in part because they utter mantras, but also because of their heightened state of merit in the ordained state and, when applicable, because of their meditative attainments. Much of the everyday ritual of Pali/Theravāda Buddhism involves the generation and manipulation of sacred power. Even the simplest ritual will involve the transmission of sacred power to laypeople when monks chant in Pali. Slightly more complex rituals store this sacred power in *yantras* and amulets (which often incorporate *yantras*) and allow it to be carried off in portable form. The most complex rituals, such as the consecration of buddha images or *buddhābhiṣeka* studied by Donald Swearer,[31] deploy all technologies available, including mantras, *gāthās*, and *yantras*, as well as collective meditative power, in elaborate fashion to generate, transmit, and manipulate sacred power so as to ultimately infuse it in particular material objects that will then become sources of sacred power in their own right.

When viewed from the Protestant perspective of earlier Western scholarship, such practices can appear "unorthodox." That is, they do not find explicit sanction in the canonical texts of the *Tipiṭaka*. However, if one drops the Protestant antipathy to tradition as a methodological principle, it can be seen that these practices are a not unnatural extension of more normative ideas that do find sanction in the canonical texts. For example, the use of sacred language for protective purposes can easily be traced back to the canonical *paritta* texts, which are explicitly enjoined by the buddha for use as such. Likewise, the commentarial tradition regarded Pali (referred to as Māgadhī) as a "natural" language, clearly giving it a privileged role in the Pali *imaginaire* that lies at the basis of its use for the generation of sacred power. Finally and most importantly, the possibility of supranormal powers is not denied, but explicitly recognized, in the canonical texts, in the form of the six *abhiññās* ("higher knowledges") that can be attained by particularly skilled monks through meditation. Given that they are mainstream, widely practiced, and rooted in canonical concepts, the ritual practices described here, whether labelled "tantric" or not, should be understood as a natural development of the Pali tradition, rather than an aberration.

A Specific Tradition? What then gives specificity to certain traditions in Pali Buddhism such that they might be described as "Tantric Theravāda" or "southern esoteric Buddhism"? This specificity can be found in a tradition of meditation, or rather a conglomerate of related traditions of meditation, in Southeast Asia that, rather than deriving directly from the techniques found in the canon and in Buddhaghosa's *Visuddhimagga*, draw from the popular "tantric" technologies described above and, arguably, serve as their legitimizing source. When Bizot did his pioneering work on this tradition of meditation, he did so mostly on the basis of manuscripts from Cambodia. He described the tradition as a rural one that differed from, and was slowly being overtaken by, a reformist system of meditation more common in the cities that was promoted by the Siamese Thammayut sect. It has since become clear that this tradition, whatever one wishes to call it, was not limited to Cambodia and, until fairly recently, represented the mainstream of meditation practice in the Pali Buddhist world of Southeast Asia. Indeed, as Kate Crosby, Andrew Skilton, and Amal Gunasena have shown, this tradition of meditation was sufficiently mainstream as late as the 18th century that it was exported to Sri Lanka in the course of the formation of the Siyam Nikāya.[32]

The techniques of this system of meditation, while completely rooted in the Pali tradition and making no reference whatsoever to the Mahāyāna, are clearly reminiscent of certain meditative techniques in the Mahāyāna *mantranaya*. A practitioner must be initiated and guided by a qualified teacher, who may be either a monk or a layperson. The meditation itself involves the visualization of a buddha within and the placement of mantras within the body so as to gradually transform it into an enlightened *dhamma* body. This process of transformation has clearly delineated stages that are homologized to the development of a fetus in the womb. Underlying the entire system is a theory of correspondences, in particular between microcosm and between mantric syllables and categories of *dhamma*. The source of mantras is Pali, and there is a particular emphasis on the use of words and syllables derived from the Abhidhamma.

This tradition of meditation, since it does not draw from the Mahāyāna *imaginaire*, does not refer to Buddha-families arranged in *maṇḍala*s in the fashion of the higher *tantras* of the *mantranaya*. In other respects, however, it provides a soteriological system similar to that found in the Mahāyāna Yoga Tantras: a ritualized system of meditation making use of visualization and mantras to physically transform oneself into an enlightened being. Although the tradition appears to have been fairly mainstream prior to the onset of recent modernist reforms, this is no different from the soteriological *mantranaya* systems of the Mahāyāna, especially in Tibet, where Tantra is and always has been mainstream. "Esoteric" in such a context is a useful phenomenological category for comparative purposes; it refers not to actual secrecy and marginality so much as a rhetoric of secrecy and a program of assigning deeper "inner" meanings to outward forms. It should be noted, however, that even when understood in this way, the similarities between the Pali esoteric tradition and the Mahāyāna *mantranaya* are limited in one particular way. The former tradition simply does not go so far as to embrace in a systematic way transgressive practices, including but not limited to the use of sexual ritual in pursuit of liberation. It is most similar, therefore, to the Yoga Tantras and not to the transgressive

Mahāyoga and Yoginī Tantras. Even here, however, the difference is perhaps more a rhetorical than a practical one. Although the rhetoric of transgression has always allowed for the possibility of its practice in Vajrayāna contexts, in reality transgressive practices in the Vajrayāna have often been executed through the technique of visualization that is shared by the Yoga Tantras and the Pali esoteric tradition.[33]

"Esoteric Buddhism" as a Comparative Category Between the Sanskrit and Pali Cosmopolises. The history of Pali Buddhism in Southeast Asia is long and complex, especially in the Mon and Burmese cultural regions of the central and western mainland. Nevertheless, from the late 12th century when Southeast Asian monks began traveling to Lanka to be re-ordained in the Mahāvihāra lineage and then brought this "Sīhaḷa" lineage back to Southeast Asia, the Pali Buddhism of Southeast Asia has become increasingly intertwined with that of Lanka, in what can be characterized as an ongoing, dialectical, "reformist" project. Although the Mahāvihāra lineage in which these monks re-ordained is an ancient one going back to the earliest years of Buddhism in Lanka, throughout the first millennium it was not the only monastic fraternity on the island and was in fact often overshadowed by its rivals, particularly the Abhayagiri. The importation of the "Sīhaḷa" lineage to Southeast Asia coincided with the triumph of the Mahāvihāra over its rivals in Lanka itself: in the late 12th century, Parākramabāhu I "purified" the *saṅgha* by switching patronage exclusively to the Mahāvihāra, which he considered more orthodox/prax, and forcing monks in other orders to re-ordain in the Mahāvihāra.

As Jonathan Walters has shown, the key difference between the Abhayagiri and the Mahāvihāra in the first millennium was that the former was cosmopolitan, while the latter was not. The Abhayagiri was open to new developments in Buddhism on the mainland, including the Mahāyāna, but the Mahāvihāra was closed to such developments and valorized a Lanka-centric ideology and the exclusive use of Pali, the language of the canonical scriptures, as opposed to Sanskrit.[34] The 12th-century success of the Mahāvihāra in winning exclusive patronage in Lanka and the exportation of its lineage to Southeast Asia set in motion a slow and often incomplete process of "reforms" that led to the entrance of "Theravāda Buddhism" (albeit somewhat misnamed as such[35]) as a branch of Buddhism distinct from "Mahāyāna Buddhism" in the modern discourse of "world religions." Although Walters has emphasized the anti-cosmopolitan ethos of the Mahāvihāra in the first millennium, the fact that its Pali-centric ideology became hegemonic throughout both Lanka and mainland Southeast Asia in the second millennium indicates that, in the end, it led to the formation of a new cosmopolis. In parallel to the "Sanskrit cosmopolis" articulated by Sheldon Pollock,[36] in which the Abhayagiri partook and the Mahāvihāra did not, we might call this new cosmopolis the "Pali cosmopolis."[37] This Pali cosmopolis arose at a time when the Sanskrit cosmopolis was in decline and represents a major realignment that took place in the geopolitics of the Buddhist world as Islamic rule took hold in North India and Buddhism died out throughout most of the Indian subcontinent.

Whatever its shortcomings, the category "esoteric Buddhism" can serve as a useful phenomenological tool for comparison between the Sanskrit and Pali cosmopolises. On the one hand, Southeast Asia in the "classical" period was clearly participating in the Sanskrit cosmopolis, while the second millennium saw a shift either to the Pali cosmopolis (on the mainland) or to an Islamic cosmopolis (in the [pen]insular region). "Esoteric Buddhism" can thus serve as a useful comparative category for considering similar practices articulated in a (Sanskritic) Mahāyāna framework in the classical period and in a Pali "Theravāda" framework in the second (and now third) millennium, as this article has done. On the other hand, "esoteric Buddhism" is also a useful comparative tool insofar as it allows us to consider the ways in which Buddhism in the Pali cosmopolis, seemingly independently, developed ritual technologies parallel to the tantric ritual technologies (Buddhist or otherwise) of the Sanskrit cosmopolis. As Buddhist studies increasingly becomes aware of the ways in which Buddhism throughout its history has differed markedly from Buddhist Modernism,[38] the study of such parallel developments will surely prove crucial in mapping the structure and development of multiple Buddhisms in the premodern world, as well as in understanding the recent re-articulations of these Buddhisms under the hegemony of modern ideas.

REVIEW OF LITERATURE

The study of *mantranaya* Buddhism in Southeast Asia is unfortunately rather underdeveloped in comparison to the study Indian tantric traditions, Vajrayāna Buddhism in Tibet, and the Zhenyan/Shingon school of East Asia. Given the paucity of written sources, the majority of work that has been done is by art historians, while also drawing from the earlier work of historians studying epigraphical sources. Hiram Woodward has provided an extremely useful synopsis of the work that has been done on Southeast Asian *mantranaya* in a review of Ronald Davidson's *Indian Esoteric Buddhism*.[39] Woodward himself has made significant contributions to the study of *mantranaya* Buddhism in Angkor.[40] Also worthy of particular note is the work J. J. Boeles on Hevajra in Khmer art[41] and that of Pia Conti on Prasat Phimai, undoubtedly the foremost example of Buddhist tantric architecture in mainland Southeast Asia.[42] Within the context of what is now Indonesia, the work of two scholars particularly stands out: the comparative work on Sanskrit, Tibetan, and Old Javanese texts by Max Nihom[43] and the similarly comparative work, also taking into account art historical sources, of Lokesh Chandra.[44] The study of Borobudur and its possible tantric influences has become a contentious mini-industry in itself; Alex Wayman, for example, has argued that Borobudur should be read as a tantric *maṇḍala*,[45] while Jan Gonda has argued that tantric influence on the monument cannot be demonstrated at all.[46] In a sign of recent trends in Buddhist studies that emphasize transnational flows, a recent edited volume by Andrea Acri includes several contributions that situate the evidence for Southeast Asian *mantranaya* Buddhism within larger trans-Asian maritime networks.[47]

As explained above, the application of the category "esoteric Buddhism" to the more recent and contemporary practice of Pali/Theravāda Buddhism in Southeast Asia is due almost single-handedly to the work of François Bizot. Beginning with the publication of *Le figuier à cinq branches* in 1976, Bizot published with the *Ecole Française d'Extrême-Orient* several volumes containing editions and translations of mostly Cambodian texts represented what he argued was a country tradition differing from the "reform" tradition of the cities and displaying certain "tantric" features.[48] While Bizot's work was published in French, Lance Cousins published an article speculating on the possible origins of this tradition, in which he dubbed it "esoteric Southern Buddhism."[49] Kate Crosby has published a useful article in English as well summarizing the work that has been done on what she called the *yogāvacara* tradition (using an emic term), including Bizot's publications on the topic and those of other scholars.[50] More recently, Crosby and others have done important work on this tradition, which they now refer to with the more contemporary emic term *boran kamaṭṭhāna*, in particular showing that a tradition of meditation with certain esoteric/tantric-like features was mainstream in Southeast Asian Pali Buddhism prior to the spread of modern reform movements and the modern *vipassanā* method.[51]

The use of categories such as "Tantric Theravāda," "esoteric Southern Buddhism," and *yogāvacara* to refer to an esoteric current in Southeast Asian Pali Buddhism, however, has been called into question by Justin McDaniel. McDaniel's critique is simply that the traditions labeled "esoteric" or "tantric" are not confined to the "unlettered masses" but rather represent the mainstream of Buddhist practice, even today, in Southeast Asia.[52] This critique is situated within McDaniel's study of Thai traditions concerning the famous monk Somdet To and the associated *Jinapañjara Gāthā*, all of which bear "esoteric" features as defined by Kate Crosby, yet are completely mainstream. McDaniel's work can be seen as part of a fairly long line of writings by scholars who have shown that the mainstream practice of Buddhism in Southeast Asia differs markedly from the modern image of a purely "rational" form of Buddhism, including the work of Tambiah on forest monks and amulets,[53] Spiro on the supernatural elements of Burmese Buddhism,[54] Terwiel on "magical monks,"[55] and Donald Swearer on Thai Buddhist ritual.[56]

FURTHER READING

MANTRANAYA

Acri, Andrea, ed. *Esoteric Buddhism in Mediaeval Maritime Asia: Networks of Masters, Texts, Icons*. Singapore: ISEAS Publishing, 2016.

Chandra, Lokesh. *Cultural Horizons of India*. Vol. 4. New Delhi: International Academy of Indian Culture and Aditya Prakashan, 1995.

Hooykaas, C. *Balinese Bauddha Brahmans*. Amsterdam: Verhandelingen der Koninklijke Nederlandse Akademie der Wetenschappen, 1974.

Nihom, Max. *Studies in Indian and Indo-Indonesian Tantrism: The Kuñjarakarṇadharmakathana and the Yogatantra*. Vienna: Publications of the de Nobili Research Library, 1994.

Woodward, Hiram. "Esoteric Buddhism in Southeast Asia in the Light of Recent Scholarship." *Journal of Southeast Asian Studies* 35, no. 2 (June 2004): 329–354.

"TANTRIC THERAVĀDA"

Bizot, François. *Le figuier à cinq branches: Recherche sur le bouddhisme khmer*. Paris: Ecole Française d'Extrême-Orient, 1976.

Cousins, Lance. "Aspects of Esoteric Southern Buddhism." In *Indian Insights: Buddhism, Brahmanism and Bhakti. Papers from the Annual Spalding Symposium on Indian Religions*, edited by Peter Connolly and Sue Hamilton, 185–207. London: Luzac Oriental, 1997.

Crosby, Kate. "Tantric Theravāda: A Bibliographic Essay on the Writings of François Bizot and Others on the Yogāvacara Tradition." *Contemporary Buddhism* 1, no. 2 (2000): 141–198.

Crosby, Kate. *Traditional Theravāda Meditation and Its Modern-Era Suppression*. Hong Kong: Buddha-Dharma Centre of Hong Kong, 2013.

McDaniel, Justin Thomas. *The Lovelorn Ghost and the Magical Monk: Practicing Buddhism in Modern Thailand*. New York: Columbia University Press, 2011.

Skilton, Andrew Trevor, and Phibul Choompolpaisal. "The Ancient Theravāda Meditation System, Boran Kammatthana: Anapanasati or 'Mindfulness of the Breath' in Kammatthan Majjima Baeb Lamdub." *Buddhist Studies Review* 32, no. 2 (2015): 207–229.

Skilton, Andrew Trevor, and Phibul Choompolpaisal. "The Old Meditation (boran kammatthan), a Pre-Reform Theravāda Meditation System from Wat Ratchasittharam: The Piti Section of the Kammatthan Matchima Baep Lamdap." *Aséanie* 33 (2017), 83–116.

NOTES

1. Hiram Woodward, "Esoteric Buddhism in Southeast Asia in the Light of Recent Scholarship," *Journal of Southeast Asian Studies* 35, no. 2 (June 2004): 329–354; and Kate Crosby, "Tantric Theravāda: A Bibliographic Essay on the Writings of François Bizot and Others on the Yogāvacara Tradition," *Contemporary Buddhism* 1, no. 2 (2000): 141–198.
2. In adopting this terminology, I am following Paul Williams and Anthony Tribe, *Buddhist Thought: A Complete Introduction to the Indian Tradition* (London: Routledge, 2000), 196.
3. Woodward, "Esoteric Buddhism," 335.
4. Woodward, "Esoteric Buddhism," 340.
5. Woodward, "Esoteric Buddhism," 341.
6. Woodward, "Esoteric Buddhism," 339.
7. Woodward, "Esoteric Buddhism," 348.
8. Woodward, "Esoteric Buddhism," 349, 351.
9. Woodward, "Esoteric Buddhism," 351.
10. Woodward, "Esoteric Buddhism," 345.
11. D. Christian Lammerts, *Buddhist Law in Burma: A History of Dhammasattha Texts and Jurisprudence, c. 1250–1850 CE*, ch. 2 (Honolulu: University of Hawai'i Press, forthcoming).
12. Jan Gonda, "The Indian Religions in Pre-Islamic Indonesia and their Survival in Bali," *Handbuch der Orientalistik*, 3. Abteilung, 2. Band, Abschnitt 1 (1975), 10.
13. Woodward, "Esoteric Buddhism," 343–344. Max Nihom, however, has argued on textual grounds that the Vajradhātu *maṇḍala* was not present in Indonesia: Max Nihom, *Studies in Indian and Indo-Indonesian Tantrism: The Kuñjarakarṇadharmakathana and the Yogatantra* (Vienna: Publications of the de Nobili Research Library, 1994), 113–115.
14. Woodward, "Esoteric Buddhism," 344.
15. Woodward, "Esoteric Buddhism," 350.
16. Woodward, "Esoteric Buddhism," 350–351; and Pia Conti, "Tantric Buddhism at Prasat Hin Phimai: A New Reading of Its Iconographic Message," in *Before Siam: Essays in Art and Archaeology*, eds. Nicolas Revire and Stephen A. Murphy (Bangkok: River Books and The Siam Society, 2014), 375–395.
17. Hiram Woodward, "Tantric Buddhism at Angkor Thom," *Ars Orientalis* 12 (1981): 57–67.
18. Woodward, "Esoteric Buddhism," 338–339.
19. Woodward, "Esoteric Buddhism," 347; Alaka Chattopadhyaya, *Atīśa and Tibet* (Calcutta: Indian Studies Past and Present, 1967), 84–95; and Peter Skilling, "Dharmakīrti's *Durbodhāloka* and the Literature of Śrīvijaya," *Journal of the Siam Society* 85 (1997): 187–194.
20. C. Hooykaas, *Balinese Bauddha Brahmans* (Amsterdam: Verhandelingen der Koninklijke Nederlandse Akademie der Wetenschappen, 1974).

21. Woodward, "Esoteric Buddhism," 341–342.
22. François Bizot, *Le figuier à cinq branches: Recherche sur le bouddhisme khmer* (Paris: Ecole Française d'Extrême-Orient, 1976); François Bizot, *La grotte de la naissance: Recherche sur le bouddhisme khmer II* (Paris: Ecole Française d'Extrême-Orient, 1980); François Bizot, *Le don de soi-même: Recherche sur le bouddhisme khmer III* (Paris: Ecole Française d'Extrême-Orient, 1981); François Bizot, *Les traditions de la pabbajjā en Asie de Sud-Est: Recherche sur le bouddhisme khmer IV* (Göttingen, Germany: Vandenhoeck and Ruprecht, 1988); François Bizot, *Le chemin de Laṅkā* (Paris: Ecole Française d'Extrême-Orient, 1992); François Bizot and Oskar von Hinüber, *La guirlande de joyaux* (Paris: Ecole Française d'Extrême-Orient, 1994); and François Bizot and François Lagirarde, *La pureté par les mots* (Paris: Ecole Française d'Extrême-Orient, 1996).
23. Lance Cousins, "Aspects of Esoteric Southern Buddhism," in *Indian Insights: Buddhism, Brahmanism and Bhakti. Papers from the Annual Spalding Symposium on Indian Religions*, eds. Peter Connolly and Sue Hamilton (London: Luzac Oriental, 1997), 185–207.
24. Crosby, "Tantric Theravāda."
25. Andrew Trevor Skilton and Phibul Choompolpaisal, "*The Ancient Theravāda Meditation System, Boran Kammatthana: Anapanasati or 'Mindfulness of the Breath' in Kammatthan Majjima Baeb Lamdub,*" *Buddhist Studies Review* 32.2 (2015): 207–229; and Andrew Trevor Skilton and Phibul Choompolpaisal, "The Old Meditation (boran kammatthan), a Pre-Reform Theravāda Meditation System from Wat Ratchasittharam: The Piti Section of the Kammatthan Matchima Baep Lamdap," *Aséanie* 33 (2017): 83–116.
26. Justin Thomas McDaniel, *The Lovelorn Ghost and the Magical Monk: Practicing Buddhism in Modern Thailand* (New York: Columbia University Press, 2011), 100–109.
27. Crosby, "Tantric Theravāda," 141–142.
28. David Gordon White, *Kiss of the Yoginī: "Tantric Sex" in Its South Asian Contexts* (Chicago: University of Chicago Press, 2003), 7, 14.
29. McDaniel, *Lovelorn Ghost*, 100–109.
30. McDaniel, *Lovelorn Ghost*, 77–85.
31. Donald K. Swearer, *Becoming the Buddha: The Ritual of Image Consecration in Thailand* (Princeton, NJ: Princeton University Press, 2004).
32. Kate Crosby, Andrew Skilton, and Amal Gunasena, "The *Sutta on Understanding Death* in the Transmission of *Borān* Meditation from Siam to the Kandyan Court," *Journal of Indian Philosophy* 40 (2012): 177–198.
33. On the usefulness of "semiotics" for understanding the role of the rhetoric of transgression in Buddhist *tantras*, see Christian K. Wedemeyer, *Making Sense of Tantric Buddhism: History, Semiology, and Transgression in the Indian Traditions* (New York: Columbia University Press, 2013).
34. Jonathan S. Walters, "Buddhist History: The Sri Lankan Pāli Vaṃsas and Their Community," in *Querying the Medieval: Texts and the History of Practices in South Asia*, ed. Ronald Inden et al. (Oxford: Oxford University Press, 2000), 99–164.
35. Scholars of "Theravāda Buddhism" have increasingly come to realize that, aside from certain technical uses, "Theravāda" was not a common emic term for the religious system it refers to prior to the modern period. See Peter Skilling, "Theravāda in History," *Pacific World*, Third Series, no. 11 (Fall 2009): 61–93; and Peter Skilling et al., *How Theravāda is Theravāda? Exploring Buddhist Identities* (Chiang Mai: Silkworm Books, 2012), especially the Introduction by Peter Skilling and ch. 12 by Todd LeRoy Perreira.
36. Sheldon Pollock, *The Language of the Gods in the World of Men: Sanskrit, Culture, and Power in Premodern India* (Berkeley: University of California Press, 2006).
37. On the scholarly revolution that took place in Lanka leading to this new cosmopolitan formation in Pali, see Alastair M. Gornall, "Buddhism and Grammar: The Scholarly Cultivation of Pāli in Medieval Laṅkā" (unpublished PhD diss., Cambridge University, 2013).

38. On the use of the category "Buddhist Modernism" to refer to a new type of Buddhism that has arisen in the modern world, mainstream in the West but also increasingly popular in cosmopolitan parts of Asia, see David L. McMahan, *The Making of Buddhist Modernism* (Oxford: Oxford University Press, 2008).
39. Woodward, "Esoteric Buddhism in Southeast Asia."
40. Woodward, "Tantric Buddhism at Angkor Thom"; and Hiram Woodward, *The Art and Architecture of Thailand: From Prehistoric Times Through the Thirteenth Century* (Leiden, The Netherlands: Brill, 2003).
41. J. J. Boeles, "Two Yoginīs of Hevajra from Thailand," *Artibus Asiae. Supplementum* 23 (1966): 14–29.
42. Conti, "Tantric Buddhism at Prasat Hin Phimai."
43. Nihom, *Studies in Indian and Indo-Indonesian Tantrism.*
44. Lokesh Chandra, *Cultural Horizons of India*, Vol. 4 (New Delhi: International Academy of Indian Culture and Aditya Prakashan, 1995).
45. Alex Wayman, "Reflections on the Theory of Barabuḍur as a *Maṇḍala*," in *Barabudur: History and Significance of a Buddhism Monument*, eds. Luis Gomez and Hiram W. Woodward, Jr. (Berkeley, CA: Asian Humanities Press, 1981).
46. Gonda, "The Indian Religions."
47. Andrea Acri, ed., *Esoteric Buddhism in Mediaeval Maritime Asia: Networks of Masters, Texts, Icons* (Singapore: ISEAS Publishing, 2016).
48. See note 22.
49. Cousins, "Aspects of Esoteric Southern Buddhism."
50. Crosby, "Tantric Theravāda."
51. Crosby et al., "The *Sutta on Understanding Death*"; Kate Crosby, *Traditional Theravāda Meditation and Its Modern-Era Suppression* (Hong Kong: Buddha-Dharma Centre of Hong Kong, 2013); Skilton and Phibul, "*The Ancient Theravāda Meditation System*; and Skilton and Phibul, "The Old Meditation (boran kammatthan)."
52. McDaniel, *The Lovelorn Ghost*, 100–109.
53. Stanley Jeyaraja Tambiah, *The Buddhist Saints of the Forest and the Cult of Amulets: A Study in Charisma, Hagiography, Sectarianism, and Millennial Buddhism* (Cambridge, UK: Cambridge University Press, 1984).
54. Melford E. Spiro, *Burmese Supernaturalism: A Study in the Explanation and Reduction of Suffering* (Englewood Cliffs, NJ: Prentice-Hall, 1967).
55. Barend Jan Terwiel, *Monks and Magic: Revisiting a Classic Study of Religious Ceremonies in Thailand* (Copenhagen: NIAS Press, 2012).
56. Swearer, *Becoming the Buddha.*

Nathan McGovern

ETHICS AND BUDDHISM

INTRODUCTION

There is no technical, philosophical term in Buddhist canonical languages that straightforwardly translates as "ethics." The closest analogue is *śīla*, the Sanskrit word often translated as "moral discipline" or simply "discipline" (Pāli: *sīla*; Sanskrit: *śīla*; Tibetan: *tsül trim*; Chinese: jie; Japanese: kai 戒). While discussions of moral discipline do figure prominently in various Buddhist traditions, "ethics" itself as an object of systematic reflection has neither a robustly philological background nor a meta-philosophical treatment in Buddhist literature. This reflects the fact—sometimes surprising to readers who assume that the styles and conventions associated with

European and North American ethical traditions are universal to other global philosophical traditions—that in canonical Buddhist sources, there is no abstract, systematic theory justifying Buddhist moral principles as such, because ethics per se was not traditionally isolated as a discrete focus of the tradition.[1]

This is not to say, however, that Buddhism does not deal in any depth with ethics. Rather, from its inception, Buddhism has in many ways shown itself to be a profoundly ethical tradition. While there may not be a Buddhist meta-ethics, nonetheless, in Buddhist thought one finds soteriology grounded by the project of eradicating suffering, nuanced moral psychologies, instructions on ultimate flourishing, prescriptions for moral behavioral observances, prohibitions on ethically insalubrious behaviors, descriptions of moral exemplars, and expositions of virtue and other wholesome mental and emotional states to cultivate. In addition to these descriptively and prescriptively rich accounts of moral life, a diverse collection of Buddhist contemplative practices provide practical instructions on how to personally integrate the principles of Buddhist ethics and thereby enact them in the structure of one's consciousness, embodied rapport with the world, and sociohistorical context. Although Buddhist ethical theorizing does not necessarily pursue the style or structure of argumentation and conceptual manipulation that readers of Western moral theory might consider de rigueur, there is an abundance and diversity of ethical theorizing within traditional and contemporary Buddhist literature.

The ethical emphases and methods of Buddhist traditions vary, however. Furthermore, as a living tradition that is in an ongoing process of intercultural transmission, the reception and articulation of Buddhist ethics by Western scholars have been a remarkably active subfield for several decades. The academic study of Buddhist ethics by Western scholars includes competing interpretations of the structural features of Buddhist ethics, new developments within Buddhist ethics that seek to expand its scope in light of contemporary social and political issues, and applications of traditional Buddhist ethical theories and practices to novel theoretical problems and contexts.

ETHICAL FOUNDATIONS OF THE BUDDHIST TRADITION

Suffering and the Way Out of It: The Four Noble Truths. The basic ethical landscape that motivates the theory and practice of Buddhist ethics and, indeed, Buddhism generally, is the problem of suffering and the way out of it. This ethical mandate is therefore much broader than a strictly normative moral schema of, for example, generating rules for behavior. The problematization of suffering and the elaboration of a path that leads to liberation from suffering are ethically salient because they deal, most broadly, with the nature of human flourishing (and even the flourishing of all sentient beings). This line of ethical thinking on "the good life" is one to which many global philosophical traditions have turned time and again over millennia, and indeed questions about what conduces to happiness and relieves suffering reappear throughout Buddhist scriptures and constitute the centerpiece of Buddhist ethical theory. This ethical thrust of Buddhism was initiated by the historical Buddha Śakyamuni (5th century BCE) in his first discourse after attaining enlightenment. In this teaching, known as "The Discourse on Setting the Wheel of Dhamma in Motion" (Pāli: *Dhammacakkappavattana Sutta*), the buddha offers a diagnosis of the human condition as beset with suffering, together with a treatment that will eradicate that suffering, leading to total liberation (P: *nibbana*).[2] This diagnosis and regimen is the four noble truths: the truth of suffering, the truth of the origin of suffering, the truth of the cessation of suffering, and the truth of the path. Here the term *suffering* renders as the Pāli word *dukkha*, which admittedly is a slightly inadequate translation, as it can connote a more abject or dramatic malaise than the broader meaning of *dukkha*. Some translators therefore prefer the rather clunkier "dissatisfactoriness" or the possibly equally misleading term "stress" as translations for *dukkha*. Clearly there is no unproblematic translation for this singularly important term in Buddhist philosophy, so regarding these translations, it is up to the reader to appreciate that what the buddha has in mind in this diagnostic overview of the human condition. The dissatisfactory, stressful suffering of the human condition encompasses not only the pains of birth, old age, sickness, and death but also the subtler emotional and psychological experiences of anxiety, distress, instability, irritation, frustration, and disappointment with the ephemerality of satisfaction.

With the first of these truths, the truth of suffering, the buddha problematizes in a broad way the vicissitudes of human life. In his discourse, he glosses them as follows: "Birth is suffering, aging is suffering, illness is suffering, death is suffering; union with what is displeasing is suffering, separation from what is pleasing is suffering, not to get what one wants is suffering."[3] His list is meant to capture the range of challenges of human life, challenges that one may not even initially regard as worthy of ethical scrutiny but rather could ordinarily be taken as the unavoidably painful costs of being alive. Here the buddha-as-pathologist takes them up as the starting point of his existential "diagnosis," noting the presence of a disease—a disease that shows itself as suffering—that is to be treated in the patient.

With the second noble truth, the truth of the cause of suffering, the buddha explains that one can identify a distinct point of origin of this suffering that is endemic to the human condition: "this craving that leads to renewed existence, accompanied by delight and lust, seeking delight here and there; that is, craving for sensual pleasures, craving for existence, craving for extermination."[4] In other words, the suffering that one might assume is an inevitable feature of existence is actually brought about by a specific cause. That cause is the infelicitous moral-psychological habit of craving (P: *taṇhā*, alternatively translated as "desire," "longing," or "greed"). What this means is that, through their craving for both what they want and the eradication of what they do not want, beings become authors of their own suffering. This signals the stage of the Buddha's diagnosis in which he has identified the nature of the underlying disease causing the patient's symptoms.

With the third noble truth, the truth of the cessation of suffering, the Buddha introduces the possibility that this process of causation can be intervened on—that there is a mechanism by which a person can shift the trajectory of the human condition, signaling that the disease underlying the problem of suffering is treatable. Essentially, he puts forth the optimistic prognosis that "the remainderless fading away and cessation of that same craving, the giving up and relinquishing of it, freedom from it, nonattachment" is possible.[5] The cause of suffering can be extinguished by eradicating the problematic craving that fuels it.

With the fourth noble truth, the truth of the path, the Buddha lays out the treatment regimen that will realize that optimistic yet ambitious future to which the third noble truth gestures. In typical Buddhist fashion, the truth of the path, or the "way leading to the cessation of suffering," contains yet another list, the Noble Eightfold Path: right view, right intention, right speech, right action, right livelihood, right effort, right mindfulness, and right concentration.[6] Together, these eight principles enumerate the components of the kind of Buddhist life that accomplishes the cessation of suffering: a life of cultivating moral discipline (P: *sīla;* encompassing right speech, action, and livelihood), meditation (P: *samādhi;* encompassing right effort, mindfulness, and concentration), and wisdom (P: *pañña,* encompassing right view and intention). Collectively, moral discipline, meditation, and wisdom are known as the "three trainings." Altogether, this path adds up to a profound reorientation away from the problematic self-regarding orientation that gives rise to suffering. Although moral discipline has the most clearly ethical valence of these aspects of the Buddhist life, it is important to hold in mind that the cultivation of wisdom and mental discipline are also ethically salient in the Buddhist path, because the ability to see oneself and the world clearly and abide in mental equanimity are necessary conditions for liberating oneself from suffering and for being altruistically skillful in the world.[7]

Understanding Action and Its Fruition: Karma. Another foundation of the ethical worldview underwriting Buddhist traditions is the teaching of karma.[8] The Sanskrit word *karma* (Pāli: *kamma*) literally means "action," although the range of karmically relevant actions that the term covers goes beyond gross, physical behaviors to include speech and thought as well. Thought, speech, and deeds all have consequences, however subtle, in shaping a being's psychology as well as the conditions of their future rebirths. Karma is sometimes illustrated by way of a horticultural metaphor: any action plants a certain "karmic seed" in one's consciousness that will come to fruition in due time, under the specific causes and conditions that "water" or "cultivate" its maturation. What kinds of seeds one plants—and the causes and conditions that one puts in place that lead to their fruition—matter a great deal, as these choices end up dictating the very world that one inhabits, psychologically and practically. This is why the buddha taught in the early Buddhist *Upajjhatthana Sutta,*

> I am the owner of my actions, heir to my actions, born of my actions, related through my actions, and have my actions as my arbitrator. Whatever I do, for good or for evil, to that I will fall heir.[9]

All of this places an extraordinary amount of responsibility in the hands of the individual for shaping and transforming the conditions under which they live and experience their world. The karmic consequences for one's actions show themselves not only in the felicitous or infelicitous circumstances in which one finds oneself in a literal sense (inasmuch as karma determines the relative advantages or disadvantages of future rounds of rebirth) but also more subtly in the dispositions, qualities, and capacities through which the conditions of one's life are experientially inflected in real time. The doctrine of karma can be understood as highlighting how a person is in fact the author of the structure of their own life in the most profound sense possible. It points to the moral-psychological agency that a person holds, which allows them to shape the ongoing development of their ethical selfhood in the present and even for the kind of world they will inhabit—phenomenologically and literally—in the future. The promise of Buddhist soteriology rests on this deep understanding of karmic cause and effect.

The Practice of Self-Transformation: Moral Psychology and the Emotions. What becomes apparent from this is the therapeutic nature of much of Buddhist ethics. Oriented as it is by the problem of suffering and the path of practice that eradicates it, Buddhist ethics is tied to a way of life and a commitment to self-cultivation through contemplative practice that will liberate the practitioner from suffering. One way to understand the conceptual schema underwriting this approach to self-cultivation is as a form of moral psychology. Within philosophy, moral psychology is a domain of ethical reflection concerned with themes such as moral development, character, emotion, sensibility, and motivation. Although the finer particularities of how one should practice (and how the nature of the problem of suffering is articulated in the first place) differ across traditions, most generally the Buddhist moral-psychological project can be characterized as a task of extirpating oneself from suffering by correcting infelicitous affective, perceptual, and cognitive habits that keep sentient beings ensconced in suffering.

The human condition (and indeed the condition of all sentient beings) is characterized as wandering in the suffering of cyclic existence and continuous rebirth (Pāli, Sanskrit: *saṃsāra*). This suffering can only be interrupted once one comes to realize the karmic process of cause and effect that fuels it. From a moral-psychological standpoint, the basic fuel for saṃsāric wandering is ignorance (Pāli: *moha*, Sanskrit: *avīdya*), the most habitual manifestation of which is the reification of and identification with the self. The no-self doctrine (Pāli: *anatta*, Sanskrit: *anātman*) holds that there is no permanent, intrinsically existent "self" but rather a dynamic, impermanent set of psycho-physical constituents on which beings impute the notion of a "self." Beings hypostasize their own atomic, individualized selfhood, projecting on it a permanence and a substantial reality that it in fact lacks.[10]

The most immediate manifestation of ignorance is the experience of afflictive emotions (Pāli: *kilesa*, Sanskrit: *kleśa*). The afflictive emotions are most commonly categorized as threefold: ignorance (namely, the ignorance that shows itself in reification in the first place) and the desire (Pāli: *lobha*, Sanskrit: *rāga*) and aggression (Pāli: *dosa*, Sanksrit: *dveṣa*) in which beings become entangled on the basis of that ignorance. Pivoting between desire and aggression, beings are hostile toward whatever they regard as displeasing, fearful, or "other" while clinging to anything that appears as desirable, protective, or comfortingly familiar. Karmically speaking, with every thought, word, and deed to which a person commits themselves on the basis of their attachment to this "self," they are deepening the habitual force of the ignorance that motivates the afflictive emotions and underwrites attachment to the "self" and its interests.[11]

The Buddhist ethical approach to ending suffering and promoting human flourishing problematizes this conventional orientation of hypostasizing that keeps beings wandering in *saṃsāra*. The transformation of that orientation in the interest of liberation is the work of Buddhist contemplative practice, the style and particularities of which differ across Buddhist traditions.

NOT BUDDHISM BUT "BUDDHISMS"

In the two and a half millennia that have followed on the buddha's first problematization of suffering, various Buddhist traditions have refined distinct articulations of the nature and causes of suffering and liberation, as well as distinct moral theories and practices for realizing them. This is to say, there is no single, unified Buddhism but rather there are "Buddhisms," with distinctive doctrinal emphases that relate to their styles and foci of ethical concern. The doctrinal and philosophical distinctions of the various Buddhist schools are the result of thousands of years of philosophical and religious movements as well as intercultural transmissions. The most common classification of these schools currently in use divides them into three main groupings: the early Buddhist schools, the Mahāyāna (Sanskrit: "Great Vehicle," Tibetan: *tekpa chenpo*), and the tantric tradition of Vajrayāna (Sanskrit: "Indestructible Vehicle"; Tibetan: *dor jé tek pa*) Buddhism, which is considered a subset of the Mahāyāna.[12] While even within these groupings there is considerable sectarian debate, there are a few major thematic and doctrinal developments that characterize the ethical approaches of early Buddhism, the Mahāyāna and the Vajrayāna.

The Path of Liberation of Early Buddhist Ethics. As discussed in the section "Suffering and the Way Out of It: The Four Noble Truths," the ethical project that the buddha introduced was one that problematized suffering and proposed a path conducing to liberation from suffering. Although there are various doctrinal developments and philosophical commitments that characterize the early Buddhist schools, from the standpoint of ethics, the principal distinguishing feature of the ethical mandate of early Buddhism is the installation of the *arahant* ("accomplished one"; Sanskrit: *arhat*) as its moral exemplar. The *arahant* embodies moral and spiritual perfection. They achieve the goal of liberation from the cyclic suffering of rebirth in *saṃsāra* and attain the highest happiness, enlightenment. The primary objective orienting the ethics of the Pāli canon—the scriptures that form the doctrinal basis of early Buddhism—is therefore to become an *arahant*.

The Noble Eightfold Path spells out the training in moral discipline, meditation, and wisdom that lead to *arahantship*. What is at stake in following that path, however, is not simply rote adherence to its strictures as a "formula" for a Buddhist life. The personal training denoted by the Noble Eightfold Path requires an intensive practice of monitoring unwholesome behaviors and thoughts—anything motivated by passion, aggression, and ignorance—and replacing them with wholesome behaviors and thoughts. As Bhikkhu Bodhi, a commentator in the contemporary Theravāda school, which counts the early Buddhist Pāli canon as its source texts, puts it:

> The course of spiritual training taught by the Buddha is a double process of self-transformation and self-transcendence issuing in complete emancipation from suffering. . . . When this double process is brought to its culmination, suffering is extinguished, for with the awakening of wisdom the basic root of suffering—craving backed by blinding ignorance—falls away never to rise again.[13]

A common way of characterizing this early Buddhist path of eradicating unwholesomeness in thought, speech, and deed and cultivating wholesomeness on the way to *arahantship* is as a "path of purification."

This approach to ethical self-cultivation via purification finds an eloquent exponent in Buddhaghosa (5th century CE), one of the foremost early Buddhist commentators who remains a key lineage figure in the contemporary Theravāda tradition. Buddhaghosa's *Path of*

Purification (*Visuddhimagga*) is composed as a guide leading a monk through successive stages of practice that culminate in the attainment of absolute purification.[14] Buddhaghosa weaves together a meticulous exegesis of the practice and scholarly "view" of an ideal Buddhist life, moving the through seven stages of purification of the mind that are divided into three sections corresponding to three trainings of establishing moral discipline, the practice of concentration, and the attainment of understanding. What is at stake in this architectonic path of practice is a gradual transformation of the moral selfhood of the practitioner down to the very way in which they experience the world.

The first section of Buddhaghosa's text deals with the moral precepts undertaken by Buddhist monastics, which sets the foundation for further practice. Strict adherence to moral norms is literally just the beginning of the path; it is meant to create enough basic stability in the mind and life of the practitioner so that they may pursue the deeper and, in many respects, more rigorous work of transforming their consciousness. Buddhaghosa's subsequent chapters delve into that deeper work with intensive discussions of meditative practices that aim to challenge and radically transform the structure of the practitioner's consciousness, which ultimately conduces to a way of seeing and knowing the world "as it is" (Pāli: *ñaṇadassana*), undistorted by confusion, in the manner of complete liberation. Such is the culmination of the path of perfection.

An Expansive Vehicle: Mahāyāna Buddhism. Generally speaking, the foundational teachings of early Buddhism such as the Four Noble Truths, karma, and the no-self doctrine were agenda setting for the Buddhist traditions that followed. However, with the development of Mahāyāna Buddhism in India around the 1st century CE, the Buddhist soteriological and ethical mandate expanded considerably.[15] The most pronounced difference between the ethical aims of early Buddhism and that of the Mahāyāna was the emergence in the latter of the bodhisattva as an ethical exemplar in place of the *arahant*.

The bodhisattva ("awakening being") is the person defined by their compassionate aspiration to attain enlightenment for the benefit of all sentient beings, a wish known as *bodhicitta* ("awakening mind"). In this respect, the bodhisattva is the paragon of compassion (*karuṇā*). Taken together, the figure of the bodhisattva and their compassionate motivation signal a change in emphasis of the goal of Buddhist ethical self-cultivation. According to adherents of the Mahāyāna, in their commitment to attaining enlightenment not simply to liberate themselves but in order to liberate all sentient beings, the bodhisattva has the highest of motivations for their practice, a motivation that surpasses the goal of individual liberation of the *arahat*. Of course, this sectarian comparison is almost surely unfair to the early Buddhist schools, which also enshrined compassion and other altruistic virtues as important values of the *arahat*. Whether or not the bodhisattva's contradistinction with the *arahat* withstands scrutiny in actual fact, Mahāyāna ethical texts nonetheless repeatedly expound upon the superiority of a compassionate motivation as a starting point for the path.

Moreover, in the Mahāyāna, compassion works in tandem with wisdom (Sanskrit: *prajñā*, Tibetan: *she rab*). Here, "wisdom" denotes the profound realization of emptiness (Sanskrit: *śunyatā*; Tibetan: *tongpa nyi*)—seeing things "the way they truly are," as lacking any inherent, substantial existence as a separate self or phenomenon. Compassion and wisdom are complementary concepts, because practicing unbiased compassion toward all beings is the ethical expression of the wisdom that realizes the metaphysics of emptiness. If nothing exists separately but rather all beings and all phenomena are intimately interdependent, then a compassionate stance of other-centered altruism is not a moral norm to which the *bodhisattva* submits but rather a way of expressing through one's behaviors their realization of the truth of "the way things truly are."[16]

The complementarity of wisdom and compassion in the path of the *bodhisattva* is evinced by the highly influential *Introduction to the Practices of Awakening* (Bodhicaryāvatāra) by the 8th-century Indian scholar-monk Śāntideva.[17] In this text, Śāntideva praises the value of *bodhicitta* and gives instructions on the cultivation of the six perfections (Sanskrit: *pāramitā;* Tibetan: *pa röl tu chin pa*). These six transcendent excellences are generosity, moral discipline, patience, vigor, meditation, and wisdom. Together these six perfections describe the character of the *bodhisattva.*

Śāntideva's text blends philosophical argumentation with contemplative instruction, moving between expositions of topics such as compassion, emptiness, and the perfections and meditations for cultivating *bodhicitta* such as the practice known as "exchanging self with others." While some of the perfections—such as patience and generosity—have a straightforwardly moral valence, perfections such as meditation and wisdom still figure into Śāntideva's overall ethical project by fostering the mental discipline, personal stability, and clear understanding that define the *bodhisattva.* As the contemporary scholar of Indian Buddhism Amber Carpenter describes it, "the *Bodhicāryāvatāra* exemplifies the dialectic between phenomenology and metaphysics in the service of ethical praxis and development."[18] Even when he engages in lengthy philosophical argumentation, Śāntideva is not just indulging in Mahāyāna apologetics as a matter of intellectual jousting. What underwrites the text as a whole is the aspiration to truly perfect oneself in order to liberate others in the manner of the *bodhisattva.*

A subset of the Mahāyāna, Vajrayāna Buddhism maintains the bodhisattvic motivation of practicing for the benefit of sentient beings as its ethical impetus. However, Vajrayāna differs from other Mahāyāna traditions in its use of esoteric, tantric contemplative techniques as the method by which its practitioners pursue that goal. The Vajrayāna approach is characterized by a method of using tantric rituals to transmute unenlightened qualities into enlightened ones. These rituals use the powers of the imagination in a practice known as deity yoga, in which the practitioner engages in elaborate visualizations, the repetition of mantras, and the use of ritual objects to imagine themselves as an enlightened deity. Vajrayāna practices can involve antinomian behaviors that contravene other Buddhist monastic precepts, such as drinking alcohol, eating meat, or ritualized sexual intercourse. Often these antinomian behaviors are only visualized, but nonetheless, their use highlights an important stylistic feature of the Vajrayāna view of ethical development: that ignorance—symbolized by alcohol, meat, and sex—can be transmuted into wisdom. These tantric methods are considered extremely potent and possibly hazardous if not practiced under the right conditions, so the guidance and supervision of a *guru* (Tibetan: *lama*) are considered essential. The *guru* personally empowers the student to engage in tantric practice and administers specific tantric vows (Sanskrit: *samaya,* Tibetan: *dam tsik*). Many components of these vows may be quite similar to other Mahāyāna precepts, but others are more tailored to the tantric context, such as the commitment to maintain the secrecy of the esoteric teachings and practice of tantra.

SYSTEMATIC INTERPRETATIONS OF BUDDHIST ETHICS

Buddhist ethical thought is richly diverse and pluralistic. The primary difficulty with assigning any particular systematic identity to Buddhist ethics as a whole is that the multiplicity of Buddhist traditions does not readily submit to any single categorization.[19] Even within specific traditions, there is not the kind of meta-ethical grounding for moral reasoning that guides many ethical systems of European and North American traditions. Nonetheless, some contemporary Buddhist studies scholars have attempted to reconstruct Buddhist ethics comparatively, by drawing forth their structural similarities to Western paradigms such as virtue ethics or consequentialism. Alternatively, other theorists have thought it better to systematize Buddhist ethics on its own terms rather than through the lens of a Western tradition.

Virtue Ethics. One influential systematic reading of Buddhist ethics casts it as structurally similar to classical virtue ethics. Virtue ethics is a branch of Western moral philosophy that originated in ancient Greece and focuses on a description of the "good life"—the *summum bonum* of human life—as tied to the development of a virtuous character. The ancient Greek philosopher Aristotle, for example, argued that the best and happiest life—the life of *eudaimonia*, or flourishing—is made possible by the cultivation of character virtue as well as five intellectual virtues. Exponents of the reading of Buddhist ethics as a form of virtue ethics point out a number of affinities between them, beginning with the fact that in virtually all Buddhist traditions as well as in Western virtue ethics, moral development depends on the cultivation of specific virtues—personal qualities such as mental states, motivations, and capacities for action that enable well-being. They see the main ethical thrust of both traditions as the work of becoming a certain kind of person—a *virtuous* person—in order to live well. This requires not just theorizing what it means to "do the right thing" but also giving a psychologically complex account of what it means to *be* the person who does the right thing naturally and spontaneously, down to their dispositions, emotions, philosophical view of the world, and ethical perception.

The most widely commented-on advocate of this view is Damien Keown, who argues in *The Nature of Buddhist Ethics* that Buddhist ethics is structurally similar to the virtue ethics of Aristotle.[20] Keown makes the argument that "*eudaemonia* and nirvana are functionally and conceptually related in that both constitute that final goal, end and *summum bonum* of human endeavour."[21] Furthermore, he notes that it is specifically the cultivation virtues—for example, of what he calls Buddhist "cardinal virtues" of non-hatred, non-passion, and non-delusion—is what conduces to liberation in a way that is analogous to how the cultivation of character virtue and the five intellectual virtues conduce to complete happiness in Aristotle's system.[22] Finally, Keown also notes a common concern for cognitive dimensions of moral life in the moral psychologies underwriting Aristotle's ethics and Buddhist ethics. For example, he dedicates a fine-grained analysis to similarities between the Buddhist discussion of intention (Sanskrit: *cetanā*) and Aristotle's exposition of moral choice (*prohairesis*).

One criticism of the virtue-ethical interpretation of Buddhist ethics rests on the respective metaphysics of the ethical subject in Buddhism and in a system like Aristotle's. Mark Siderits, for example, points out that, in theorizing a *summum bonum* at all, virtue ethics must rely on some conception of a human essence that can best be realized through the perfection of virtue.

However, as Siderits puts it, "to believe in a human essence is . . . to believe in a self," which is incompatible with the Buddhist view of no-self.[23]

Consequentialism. Another interpretation of Buddhist ethics reads it as a form of consequentialism. Consequentialism names the view that the ethical value of an action should be evaluated according to the consequences that follow from it. A particularly well-known strand of consequentialist thinking is utilitarianism, which in its classical form holds that what matters most in moral life is the impartial maximization of happiness, informally summarized as "the greatest happiness for the greatest number." Proponents of the consequentialist reading of Buddhist ethics argue that the emphasis on the elimination of suffering and achieving the highest well-being possible in the form of liberation in Buddhist thought aligns with the utilitarian mandate of maximizing happiness. Although this affinity is especially obvious when one looks to the Mahāyāna and the unbiased compassion of the bodhisattva, one can also discern the utilitarian tendencies in the altruism and impartial care for all sentient beings evinced by teachings on ethical ideals such as loving-kindness and equanimity from the early Buddhist Pāli canon.

Among the most prominent theorists of the consequentialist reading of Buddhist ethics is Charles Goodman.[24] A major feature of Goodman's analysis is the distinction he draws between rule-consequentialism and act-consequentialism and how each of these manifests in Buddhist ethical traditions. Rule-consequentialism emphasizes adherence to specific rules that, when enforced, promote the greatest good. Goodman argues the ethics of the Theravāda school aligns with this view. He notes that even though much of the moral training and adherence to precepts put forth in the Theravāda's Pāli canon source texts seem prima facie concerned with personal self-cultivation and not with social action per se, there is still a consequentialist strand to the rigorous moral training required for those on the path of the *arahat*:

> If the main contributor to your well-being is the state of your mind, and if you have relatively little control over anyone else's mind but your own, then the way for you to promote the welfare of sentient beings is to cultivate your own mind.[25]

As a general rule, therefore, the pursuit of individual self-cultivation may be the best possible means by which the Theravāda practitioner can promote happiness in the world.

Meanwhile, Goodman views the ethics of the Mahāyāna as an instantiation of act-consequentialism. Act-consequentialism expresses the utilitarian method of evaluating the morality of actions depending how well they promote overall happiness in that specific situation. An act-consequentialist, therefore, would be less beholden to following strict rules if their occasional contravention stands to promote overall happiness. Such seems to be the recommendation in the *Bodhicaryāvatāra*, for example, when Śāntideva claims, "One should always strive for the benefit of others. Even that which is prohibited has been permitted for the compassionate one who sees benefit."[26] Moreover, in general, the bodhisattva's commitment to eradicating suffering wherever it occurs, not just for themselves, and practicing so that one may be capable to liberating others from suffering are goals that resonate with the utilitarian aim of maximizing universal well-being.

Critics of the consequentialist reading of Buddhist ethics have pointed out that this systematization necessarily requires emphasizing certain doctrinal points and themes while muting the importance of others in order to make a generalized theory work. For example, Stephen Harris points out that the ethics expounded by Śāntideva are more heterogeneous in their evaluation of moral development and action than would otherwise be indicated by the consequentialist reading.[27]

Moral Phenomenology. Jay Garfield argues that the primary concern of Buddhist ethics is not to theorize in a normative way obligations, consequences, actions, or human happiness per se but rather to problematize the structure of one's conscious encounter with ethical life. For this reason, Garfield characterizes Buddhist ethics as moral phenomenology.[28] Phenomenology is a philosophical field dedicated to the study of the structures of consciousness, the subjective factors that shape experience. Moral phenomenology, at least so far as Garfield approaches it, is concerned with reshaping the way one experiences oneself and the world in the interest of ethical growth. This is a matter of

> training people to *see* themselves and others in a better way, with the confidence that that experience will not only be more accurate, but also that it will yield more effective engagement with the world in a host of situations.[29]

Garfield's moral-phenomenological reading of Buddhist ethics takes as its starting point the basic claims of Buddhist psychology and its connection to the problem of suffering. Most beings experience the world through the lens of their ignorance, beset by the afflictive emotions that spring from that ignorance. This is what keeps them ensconced in cyclic suffering. Buddhist ethics qua moral phenomenology addresses this not by recommending changes in behavior per se but by advancing methods for understanding and revising the very structure of their consciousness, the conditions through which they experience the world in the first place. Garfield frames the ethical work of Buddhist moral phenomenology in this way:

> we are . . . called upon to work first to understand how we in fact see the world, then to correct for the distortions we know we impose upon our perception of ourselves and others, and finally, to transform the nature of that experience. For all else flows from our spontaneous experience.[30]

Evaluating the merits of this view of Buddhist ethics, Christopher Gowans has questioned whether a moral-phenomenological interpretation of the Buddhist answer to suffering necessarily precludes ascribing to it normative ethical commitments altogether.[31] That is, in his view, it may be the case that Buddhist ethics harbors a virtue-ethical or consequentialist bent, even if only implicitly, while at the same time addressing suffering through a path of deep self-transformation on the model of moral phenomenology.

Particularism. Moral particularism is a view critical of the reliance on universal, normative principles as the foundation of ethical life. Particularists hold the views that moral thought and action need not appeal to moral principles in order to be justified and that adherence to principles is an insufficient if not occasionally hazardous basis for moral decision-making. The scholar most closely associated with a reading of Buddhist ethics as particularist is Charles

Hallisey, although Hallisey does not ascribe to any Buddhist thinker a position that is explicitly critical of moral principles per se.[32] Rather, Hallisey argues, limiting his analysis to the philosophy of the Theravāda school, that there is simply no single moral theory that characterizes Theravāda ethics. When one looks to source texts of the Theravāda Buddhist tradition, such as commentaries on the influential *Maṅgalasutta*, he argues, they do not reveal a single underlying ethical theory but rather give the "impression that all sorts of things matter, but in a way that is not structured by systematic consistency."[33] Furthermore, Hallisey notes that in one of these commentaries, this multiplicity of these "things that matter"—and indeed the *way* in which they matter—is expressed through narrative. These narrative stories function as exercises in sensitizing readers to ethically charged situations and Buddhist responses to them without taking recourse to normative guidelines for behavior.

Jay Garfield affirms the basic substance of Hallisey's argument and even holds that its validity extends beyond the Theravāda, to all of Buddhist ethics generally. However, Garfield offers the qualification that what follows from Hallisey's particularist reading is that there is no universalist Buddhist moral theory but not that there is no Buddhist moral theory whatsoever.[34] That is, Garfield takes Hallisey's reading as largely affirmative of a broader project of training ethical perceptual skills, even if the rationale for those skills is not grounded in a set of metaethical principles.

CONTEMPORARY BUDDHIST ETHICS

Engaged Buddhism. Engaged Buddhism articulates a Buddhist-inspired activist stance on contemporary social and political issues. As a 20th-century Buddhist modernist movement, its beginnings are attributed both to the Indian politician and scholar B. R. Ambedkar, who founded the neo-Buddhist *Navayāna* movement, which reinterpreted key dimensions of Buddhist doctrine to emphasize social reform, as well as the Vietnamese Zen monk Thich Nhat Hanh, who coined the term "engaged Buddhism" in the 1960s at a time when he was deeply engaged in antiwar activism.

Exponents of engaged Buddhism generally see their work as an expansion of traditional Buddhist ethical, social, and political doctrines. In that sense, engaged Buddhist scholars find themselves often pressing the scope of Buddhist ethics into new territories, reinterpreting Buddhist soteriological principles to include questions such as environmentalism, economic and social development, and anti-racism. The objectives of engaged Buddhist scholar-activists generally coalesce around mobilizing Buddhist practitioners toward great social engagement on the basis of their religious commitments, on one hand, and offering the theoretical and practical resources of Buddhism to established social justice movements, on the other.

Applied Buddhist Ethics. In a fashion similar to that of engaged Buddhism, the subfield of contemporary applied Buddhist ethics aims to generate Buddhist-inspired responses to contemporary ethical issues such as human rights, abortion, euthanasia, and even business. Although in practice what distinguishes this body of literature from engaged Buddhism can be subtle (and may touch upon the same topic areas, as in Buddhist environmental philosophy), the main difference between these two streams of literature is the more commentarial approach of applied Buddhist ethics, which largely seeks to mine traditional Buddhist ethical sources to infer what the most consistent possible Buddhist response would be to ethical issues that are otherwise historiographically and socially foreign to canonical Buddhist thought.

Contemplative Science. One further dimension of contemporary Buddhist ethics concerns the secularization and scientific study of Buddhist contemplative practices such as mindfulness meditation and compassion cultivation, which have traditionally been integral to Buddhist frameworks for ethical self-cultivation. Deliberately repackaging these practices in secular (that is, non-Buddhist) trappings in order to make them more widely accessible, this process of secularization has, to a great extent, helped spur the contemporary Mindfulness Movement. The first wave of the secularizations of Buddhist practice as a foundational element of contemplative science began in the 1970s with the work of Jon Kabat-Zinn, the founder of the influential secular mindfulness protocol Mindfulness-Based Stress Reduction.

In the 21st century, a second wave of secularization of Buddhist practice began in the form of contemporary "compassion trainings" such as Stanford University's Compassion Cultivation Training and Emory University's Cognitively-Based Compassion Training. Derived from the Tibetan Buddhist Mind-Training (Tibetan: *lojong*) tradition, which is traditionally propagated as a method for cultivating *bodhicitta*, the ethical significance of secular compassion trainings is often framed according to more ecumenical ethical ideals, such as diminishing habitual perception of divisions between in-groups and out-groups and equipping participants to constructively relate with contemporary social justice problems.

REVIEW OF LITERATURE

The primary texts most closely associated with early Buddhism are known collectively as the Pāli canon, and several bodies of literature within it inform the early Buddhist ethical view. The Pāli *suttas* ("discourses") primarily recount teachings delivered by the historical buddha to a variety of interlocutors on a wide range of topics, many of them pertaining to ethical questions such as the four noble truths, suffering, the Buddhist path, and the no-self doctrine.[35] The collection of stories from the previous lifetimes of the buddha known as the *Jātaka* tales provide ethical instruction in the form of narrative illustrations of compassionate aspiration and examples of moral behavior.[36] The *Vinaya* enumerates the rules of training and discipline governing monastic and nun communities as well as guidelines for monastic governance.[37] The portion of the Pāli canon comprised of scholastic treatises on the buddha's teachings is known as the *abhidhamma* (Pāli: "supplementary teachings"). Buddhaghosa's *Visuddhimagga*, discussed in the section "The Path of Liberation of Early Buddhist Ethics," comes from this body of commentarial literature, culminating several centuries of development since the codification of the Pāli canon, and is considered one of the most prominent manuals expounding the early Buddhist view of the moral development of the *arahant*.[38]

As for primary Mahāyāna ethical texts, Śāntideva's two texts, the *Bodhicaryāvatāra*, discussed in the section "An Expansive Vehicle: Mahāyāna Buddhism," and the somewhat lesser-known *Śikṣā-samuccaya* (Sanskrit: "Training Anthology") are both extensive descriptions of the *bodhisattva* path, and the former is among the most widely read and commented-upon ethical texts in Buddhist philosophy.[39] The Indian Buddhist scholar-sage, Nāgārjuna composed the *Ratnāvalī* (Sanskrit: "Precious Garland") as a letter of advice to a king, in which he articulates not only a view of Buddhist governance but also Mahāyāna ethical values grounded in the view of emptiness.[40] The Indian Buddhist philosophers Candrakīrti, Āryadeva, and Asaṇga also wrote treatises on Mahāyāna ethics and the bodhisattva path, with Candrakīrti and Āryadeva representing the Madhyamaka school and Asaṇga writing from the perspective of the Yogācāra school.[41]

In the Vajrayāna tradition, expositions of the Mahāyāna path that express the particular style and forms of tantric Buddhism include Tsongkhapa's *Great Treatise on the Stages of the Path* (*lamrim chenmo*), Gampopa's *Jewel Ornament of Liberation* (Tibetan: *dam chö yi zhin nor bu tar pa rin po ché gyen*) and Patrul Rinpoche's *Words of My Perfect Teacher* (Tibetan: *kunzang lamé shyalung*).[42]

Because the relationship between Buddhism and ethics encompasses such a vast number of questions, approaches, and theories that span canonical texts and commentaries that may or may not be shared across Buddhist traditions; cross-cultural and systematic exegeses; and contemporary reinterpretations and expansions upon traditional Buddhist ethics, the secondary literature covering this ground is often quite fragmented by topic as well as by the Buddhist tradition(s) on which it draws. However, three unusually serviceable introductions to Buddhist ethics as a subfield that, to different degrees, reaches across these diverse subject areas are Harvey's introductory synthesis, *An Introduction to Buddhist Ethics*; Cozort and Shields's more up-to-date and comprehensive collection, *Oxford Handbook of Buddhist Ethics*; and Christopher Gowans' detailed yet readable survey, *Buddhist Moral Philosophy: An Introduction*.[43]

There is a large body of secondary literature performing exegeses of Buddhist ethics specific to major texts or Buddhist traditions. An influential contribution on the ethics found in the Pāli *suttas* is Kalupahana's *Ethics in Early Buddhism*.[44] Paul Williams's *Altruism and Reality* and Barbra Clayton's *Moral Theory in Śāntideva's Śikṣāsamuccaya* each provide analyses of Śāntideva's ethics.[45] The Cowherds' collection *Moonpaths* addresses different aspects of Mahāyāna ethics in light of the doctrine of emptiness.[46] Gareth Sparham's essay "Tantric Ethics" outlines the unique features of moral guidance in Indian and Tibetan tantric Buddhist texts.[47]

Debates on problem-oriented topics within and related to Buddhist ethics are active fields of Buddhist studies scholarship. Scholars of early Buddhism have examined the role of narrative in early Buddhist ethical texts.[48] A number of articles have analyzed the relationship between Buddhist metaphysics—particularly teachings on the no-self doctrine and emptiness—and their relationship to questions of agency and ethics.[49] William Edelglass outlines the methodological and metaethical challenges of interpreting Buddhist ethics systematically.[50]

Works in applied Buddhist ethics have explored the relationships between Buddhism and topics such as environmentalism, human rights, bioethics, and abortion.[51] Thinkers such as Thich Nhat Hanh, Sallie King, and David Loy have been key figures in the developing field of engaged Buddhism, applying Buddhist principles to social justice issues, while Christopher Ives and Amod Lele have criticized the doctrinal and methodological issues behind engaged Buddhism.[52] Edited volumes on Buddhism and science document the process of transformation and secularization to which Buddhism has been subjected in creating the field of contemplative science as well as the meta-philosophical issues that that transformation portends.[53]

FURTHER READING

Bodhi, Bhikkhu. "Nourishing the Roots: Essays on Buddhist Ethics." Access to Insight (BCBS Edition), 1995. https://accesstoinsight.org/lib/authors/bodhi/wheel259.html.

Carpenter, Amber. *Indian Buddhist Philosophy: Metaphysics as Ethics*. New York: Routledge, 2014.

Clayton, Barbra R. *Moral Theory in Śāntideva's Śikṣāsamuccaya: Cultivating the Fruits of Virtue*. London: Routledge, 2006.

Conze, Edward. *Buddhist Wisdom: The Diamond Sutra and the Heart Sutra*. New York: Vintage, 2001.

Cozort, Daniel, and James Mark Shields, eds. *The Oxford Handbook of Buddhist Ethics*. Oxford Handbooks. New York: Oxford University Press, 2018.

Davis, Jake H., ed. *A Mirror Is for Reflection: Understanding Buddhist Ethics*. New York: Oxford University Press, 2017.

Dodson-Lavelle, Brooke. "Compassion in Context: Tracing the Buddhist Roots of Secular, Compassion-Based Contemplative Programs." In *The Oxford Handbook of Compassion Science*. Edited by Emma M. Seppälä, Emiliana Simon-Thomas, Stephanie L. Brown, Monica C. Worline, C. Daryl Cameron, and James R. Doty, 44–54. New York: Oxford University Press, 2017.

Garfield, Jay L. *Buddhist Ethics: A Philosophical Exploration*. New York: Oxford University Press, 2021.

Gowans, Christopher W. *Buddhist Moral Philosophy: An Introduction*. New York: Routledge, 2015.

Gyatso, Tenzin. *Ethics for the New Millennium*. New York: Riverhead Books, 2001.

Hallisey, Charles. "Ethical Particularism in Theravāda Buddhism." *Journal of Buddhist Ethics* 3 (1996): 11.

Harvey, Peter. *An Introduction to Buddhist Ethics: Foundations, Values and Issues*. New York: Cambridge University Press, 2000.

Heim, Maria. *Voice of the Buddha: Buddhaghosa on the Immeasurable Words*. New York: Oxford University Press, 2018.

Kabat-Zinn, Jon. "Some Reflections on the Origins of MBSR, Skillful Means, and the Trouble with Maps." *Contemporary Buddhism* 12, no. 1 (May 1, 2011): 281–306.

Keown, Damien. *Contemporary Buddhist Ethics*. Richmond, Surrey, UK: Routledge Curzon, 2000.

Keown, Damien. *The Nature of Buddhist Ethics*. New York, NY: Palgrave Macmillan, 2001.

King, Sallie B., ed. *Socially Engaged Buddhism*. Honolulu: University of Hawaii Press, 2009.

McRae, Emily. "Buddhist Therapies of Emotion and the Psychology of Moral Improvement." *History of Philosophy Quarterly* 3, no. 32 (2015): 101–22.

The Cowherds. *Moonpaths: Ethics and Emptiness*. New York: Oxford University Press, 2015.

NOTES

1. For rehearsals of possible reasons why metaethics is not an emphasis of traditional Buddhist ethics, see Damien Keown, "Buddhism: Morality without Ethics?" in *Buddhist Studies from India to America: Essays in Honor of Charles S. Prebish*, ed. Damien Keown (London: Routledge, 2006), 40–48; and Christopher W. Gowans, *Buddhist Moral Philosophy: An Introduction* (New York: Routledge, 2015), 54–57.
2. Although the lifetime of the buddha is dated to around the 5th century BCE, this and the other early Buddhist discourses were transmitted as oral tradition for centuries after his lifetime and were only committed to written text in the Pāli language during the 1st century BCE; and Bhikkhu Bodhi, ed., *In the Buddha's Words: An Anthology of Discourses from the Pāli Canon* (Boston: Wisdom Publications, 2005), 75–78.
3. Bodhi, *Buddha's Words*, 76.
4. Bodhi, *Buddha's Words*, 76.
5. Bodhi, *Buddha's Words*, 76.

6. Bodhi, *Buddha's Words*, 76.
7. Amber Carpenter elaborates upon this point: "The description of the way to the cessation of suffering is not a list of commandments, duties or prescriptions for action. In fact, of the eight, only three have to do directly with action; the rest are concerned with our "inward" mental states. Thus we do not have, at least not at this level of description, anything like *rules* for living. What we have is rather a schema within which to reflect comprehensively on our lives, ourselves, and our conditions in all of its aspects"; Amber Carpenter, *Indian Buddhist Philosophy: Metaphysics as Ethics* (New York: Routledge, 2014), 11.
8. The doctrine of rebirth is not proprietary to Buddhism. In fact, karma was a more or less doxographical presumption of the cosmological worldview of the historical buddha's time and place. However, the Buddhist view of karma is not identical to that of other traditions, such as Hinduism and Jainism, nor is its style of presentation or emphasis uniform across Buddhist traditions. Furthermore, the views of karma of any of these traditions should be distinguished from the casual use of the term in contemporary culture, which often mistakenly identifies karma as an arbiter of cosmic justice that keeps a list of someone's good and bad actions and then metes out rewards or punishments via quotidian events like recovering one's lost wallet or getting a parking ticket.
9. Thanissaro Bhikkhu, trans., "Upajjhatthana Sutta: Subjects for Contemplation (https://www.accesstoinsight.org/tipitaka/an/an05/an05.057.than.html)," 1997.
10. The problematization of the self in early Buddhism undergoes a significant expansion in the later developments of Mahāyāna Buddhism. Briefly, beyond critiquing only the self as lacking intrinsic existence, the Mahāyāna doctrine of emptiness (*śunyatā*) similarly holds that not only the self but in fact all phenomena lack intrinsic existence as well. In this view, nothing whatsoever exists as a separate, inherently existing entity, and everything exists interdependently. The overcoming of hypostasization of the Mahāyānist therefore encompasses the content of all phenomenal experience: not only the sense of self but also the structure of subject–object duality through which the world and the apparent intrinsic reality of the objects appear.
11. See Peter Harvey, "Karma," in *The Oxford Handbook of Buddhist Ethics*, ed. Daniel Cozort and James Mark Shields (New York: Oxford University Press, 2018), 7–28; and Carpenter, *Indian Buddhist Philosophy*, 93–116. For a cross-cultural, syncretic elaboration of how beings shape themselves and their world through a reading of karma in conversation with the contemporary phenomenological "enactivist" paradigm of Varela, Thompson, and Rosch, see Matthew MacKenzie, "Enacting Selves, Enacting Worlds: On the Buddhist Theory of Karma," *Philosophy East and West* 63, no. 2 (2013): 194–212. However, this psychological reading of karma should not outstrip the cosmological understanding of karma and its role in determining rounds of rebirth, the centrality of which in canonical Buddhist doctrine commentators such as Gethin are careful to point out; Rupert Gethin, "Cosmology and Meditation: From the Agañña-Sutta to the Mahāyāna," *History of Religions* 36, no. 3 (1997): 183–217.
12. The nomenclature that should be applied to the early Buddhist schools is a source of scholarly contention. Some use the term *Theravāda* ("Doctrine of the Elders") loosely as a stand-in name, because the contemporary Theravāda school is the only extant non-Mahāyāna school that claims an unbroken lineage with one of these eighteen early Buddhist schools. However, the actual historical continuity of the contemporary Theravāda school and the early Buddhist schools is doubtful (Sven Bretfeld, "Theravāda Buddhism," in *Oxford Research Encyclopedia of Religion*, July 29, 2019). Some Mahāyāna practitioners use the name Hinayāna to refer to early Buddhism. *Hinayāna* means "narrow vehicle" in Sanskrit and is therefore obviously prejudicial. Other alternatives are Pāli Buddhism or pre-Mahāyāna Buddhism, but each of these is also problematic, as Pāli Buddhism suggests that all early Buddhist discourse was conducted in Pāli, which was not the case, or that these schools of Buddhism only existed or were developed prior to the emergence of the Mahāyāna, which is also not accurate. *Śrāvakayāna* ("Disciples Vehicle") has been advanced as a less politicized alternative to the earlier mentioned terms, although the

term is primarily used in Mahāyāna texts to refer (non-derisively) to early Buddhism, and it therefore is an exonym.

13. Bhikkhu Bodhi, "Nourishing the Roots: Essays on Buddhist Ethics (https://accesstoinsight.org/lib/authors/bodhi/wheel259.html)," 1995.
14. Buddhaghosa, *Path of Purification: Visuddhimaga*, trans. Bhikkhu Ñāṇamoli (Kandy, Sri Lanka: Buddhist, 1975).
15. Exponents of this new development of the Buddhist tradition did not put themselves forth as such but rather held that these teachings were indeed the "word of the Buddha," albeit from a specific subset of teachings that were not presented widely until conditions were appropriate and auspicious.
16. There is some scholarly disagreement about the relationship between practicing compassion and realizing emptiness and whether one is instrumental to the other. Stephen Harris rehearses the terms of the debate and advocates the view that, at least in the work of Śāntideva, understanding the no-self doctrine facilitates bodhisattvic compassion. See Stephen Harris, "Does Anātman Rationally Entail Altruism? On Bodhicaryāvatāra 8:101–103," *Journal of Buddhist Ethics* 18 (2011): 93–123.
17. Śāntideva, *A Guide to the Bodhisattva Way of Life*, trans. Vesna A. Wallace and B. Alan Wallace (Boston: Snow Lion Publications, 1997).
18. Carpenter, *Indian Buddhist Philosophy*, 226.
19. For these reasons, Mark Siderits even asks the question of whether "Buddhist ethics" even exists. See Mark Siderits, "Does Buddhist Ethics Exist?" in *Moonpaths: Ethics and Emptiness*, the Cowherds (New York: Oxford University Press, 2015), 119–139.
20. Damien Keown, *The Nature of Buddhist Ethics* (Basingstoke, UK; New York: Palgrave, 1992). Keown has further developed this view in Damien Keown, "Karma, Character and Consequentialism," *Journal of Religious Ethics* 24, no. 2 (Fall 1996): 329–350; and Damien Keown, *Buddhist Ethics: A Very Short Introduction* (New York: Oxford, 2005). For other articulations of Buddhist ethics as a form of virtue ethics, see David E. Cooper and Simon P. James, *Buddhism, Virtue and Environment* (Aldershot, UK: Ashgate, 2005); James Whitehill, "Buddhist Ethics in Western Context: The 'Virtues' Approach," *Journal of Buddhist Ethics* 1 (1994): 1–22; Charles Fink, "The Cultivation of Virtue in Buddhist Ethics," *Journal of Buddhist Ethics* 20 (2013): 668–701; and Abraham Vélez de Cea, "The Dalai Lama and the Nature of Buddhist Ethics," *Journal of Buddhist Ethics* 20 (2013): 499–540.
21. Keown, *Nature of Buddhist Ethics*, 195.
22. Keown, *Nature of Buddhist Ethics*, 116–118.
23. Mark Siderits, *Studies in Buddhist Philosophy*, ed. Westerhoff (New York: Oxford University Press, 2016), 272. For another critique of the virtue-ethical reading, see also Georges Dreyfus, "Meditation as Ethical Activity," *Journal of Buddhist Ethics* 2 (1995): 35.
24. Charles Goodman, *Consequences of Compassion: An Interpretation and Defense of Buddhist Ethics* (New York: Oxford University Press, 2009). He also elaborates this view in Charles Goodman, "Consequentialism, Agent-Neutrality, and Mahāyāna Ethics," *Philosophy East and West* 58, no. 1 (2008): 17–35. For another iteration of the consequentialist reading, see Mark Siderits, *Studies in Buddhist Philosophy*, ed. Jan Westerhoff (New York: Oxford University Press, 2016), 263–276.
25. Goodman, "Consequentialism, Agent-Neutrality," 59.
26. *Bodhicaryāvatāra* V.84 (Śāntideva, *Guide to the Bodhisattva Way of Life*, 57).
27. Stephen Harris, "On the Classification of Śāntideva's Ethics in the *Bodhicaryāvatāra*," *Philosophy East and West* 65, no. 1 (2015): 249–275. For a critique along similar lines but related instead to the Theravāda, see Peter Harvey, *An Introduction to Buddhist Ethics: Foundations, Values and Issues* (Cambridge, UK: Cambridge University Press, 2000), 49.
28. Jay L. Garfield, *Engaging Buddhism: Why It Matters to Philosophy* (New York: Oxford University Press, 2015); and Jay L. Garfield, *Buddhist Ethics: A Philosophical Exploration* (New York: Oxford University

Press, 2021). See also Colin Simonds, "Buddhist Ethics as Moral Phenomenology: A Defense and Development of the Theory," *Journal of Buddhist Ethics* 28 (2021): 339–402.

29. Garfield, *Buddhist Ethics*, 22.
30. Garfield, *Buddhist Ethics*, 42.
31. Gowans, *Buddhist Moral Philosophy*, 142.
32. Charles Hallisey, "Ethical Particularism in Theravāda Buddhism," *Journal of Buddhist Ethics* 3 (1996): 11. See also Harris, "On the Classification of Śāntideva." Although Harris does not explicitly condone a reading of Buddhist ethics as particularist, he argues that Śāntideva's ethics have more to do with the cultivation of certain perceptual skills than enacting a general moral theory.
33. Hallisey, "Ethical Particularism," 40.
34. Garfield, *Buddhist Ethics*, 23n9.
35. Bhikkhu Bodhi, trans., *The Connected Discourses of the Buddha: A New Translation of the Saṃyutta Nikāya*, 2 vols. (Boston: Wisdom Publications, 2000); Bhikkhu Bodhi, trans., *The Numerical Discourses of the Buddha: A Translation of the Aṅguttara Nikāya* (Boston: Wisdom Publications, 2012); Bhikkhu Ñanamoli, trans., *The Middle Length Discourses of the Buddha: A Translation of the Majjhima Nikāya* (Boston: Wisdom Publications, 2005); and Maurice Walsh, trans., *The Long Discourses of the Buddha: A Translation of the Digha Nikāya* (Boston: Wisdom Publications, 1995).
36. Sarah Shaw, *The Jātakas: Birth Stories of the Bodhisatta* (New Delhi: Penguin, 2006).
37. Charles Prebish, *A Survey of Vinaya Literature* (New York: Routledge, 1994).
38. Buddhaghosa, *Path of Purification*.
39. Śāntideva, *Guide to the Bodhisattva Way of Life*; and Śāntideva, *The Training Anthology of Śāntideva: A Translation of the Śikṣā-samuccaya*, trans. Charles Goodman (New York: Oxford, 2016).
40. Nāgārjuna, *Nāgārjuna's Precious Garland: Buddhist Advice for Living and Liberation*, trans. Jeffrey Hopkins (Ithaca, NY: Snow Lion Publications, 1988).
41. Karen Lang, trans., *Āryadeva's Catuḥśataka: On the Bodhisattva's Cultivation of Merit and Knowledge* (Copenhagen: Akademisk, 1986); Karen Lang, trans., *Four Illusions: Candrakīrti's Advice for Travelers on the Bodhisattva Path* (New York: Oxford University Press, 2003); and Mark Tatz, trans., *Asanga's Chapter on Ethics with the Commentary of TsongKha-Pa, The Basic Path to Awakening, The Complete Bodhisattva*, Studies in Asian Thought and Religion, vol. 4 (Lewiston, NY: Edwin Mellen Press, 1986).
42. Tsongkhapa, *The Great Treatise on the Stages of the Path to Enlightenment*, vol. 2, trans. The Lamrim Chenmo Translation Committee (Ithaca, NY: Snow Lion Publications, 2003); Gampopa, *Jewel Ornament of Liberation: The Wish-Fulfilling Gem of the Noble Teachings*, trans. Khenpo Konchog Gyaltsen Rinpoche (Ithaca, NY: Snow Lion Publications, 1998); and Patrul Rinpoche, *The Words of My Perfect Teacher: A Complete Translation of a Classic Introduction to Tibetan Buddhism* (New Haven, CT: Yale University Press, 1991).
43. Peter Harvey, *An Introduction to Buddhist Ethics: Foundations, Values and Issues* (New York: Cambridge University Press, 2000); Daniel Cozort and James Mark Shields, eds., *The Oxford Handbook of Buddhist Ethics*, Oxford Handbooks (New York: Oxford University Press, 2018); and Gowans, *Buddhist Moral Philosophy*.
44. David J. Kalupahana, *Ethics in Early Buddhism* (Honolulu: University of Hawai'i Press, 1995).
45. Paul Williams, *Altruism and Reality* (London: Curzon, 1998); and Barbra R. Clayton, *Moral Theory in Śāntideva's Śikṣāsamuccaya: Cultivating the Fruits of Virtue* (London: Routledge, 2006).
46. The Cowherds, *Moonpaths: Ethics and Emptiness* (New York: Oxford, 2015).
47. Gareth Sparham, "Tantric Ethics," in *The Oxford Handbook of Buddhist Ethics*, ed. Daniel Cozort and James Mark Shields (New York: Oxford, 2018), 246–259.
48. Charles Hallisey and Anne Hansen, "Narrative, Sub-Ethics and Moral Life: Some Evidence from Theravāda Buddhism," *Journal of Religious Ethics* 24, no. 2 (1996): 305–327; Martin Adam, "Moral

Development in the Jātakas, Avadānas, and Pāli Nikāyas," in *Oxford Handbook of Buddhist Ethics*, ed. Cozort and Shields (Oxford: Oxford University Press, 2018), 77–95; Amber Carpenter, "Transformative Vision: Coming to See the Buddha's Reality," in *Buddhist Literature as Philosophy, Buddhist Philosophy as Literature*, ed. Rafal Stepien (Albany, NY: SUNY Press, 2020); and Sarah Shaw, "*Jātakas* and the *Abhidhamma*: Practical Compassion and *Kusala Citta*," in *Buddhist Literature as Philosophy, Buddhist Philosophy as Literature*, ed. Rafal Stepien (Albany, NY: SUNY Press, 2020).

49. Martin Adam, "No Self, No Free Will, No Problem—Implications of the *Anattalakkhaṇa Sutta* for a Perennial Philosophical Issue," *Journal of the International Association of Buddhist Studies* 33, no. 1–2 (2010): 239–265; Karin L. Meyers, "Free Persons, Empty Selves: Freedom and Agency in Light of the Two Truths," in *Free Will, Agency, and Selfhood in Indian Philosophy*, ed. Dasti and Bryant (New York: Oxford University Press, 2014), 41–67; Paul Williams, "The Absence of Self and the Removal of Pain: How Śāntideva Destroyed the Bodhisattva Path," in *Altruism and Reality: Studies in the Philosophy of the Bodhicaryāvatāra* (Oxfordshire, UK: Routledge Curzon, 1998), 104–176; Barbra R. Clayton, "Compassion as a Matter of Fact: The Argument from No-Self to Selflessness in Śāntideva's *Śikṣāssamuccaya*," *Contemporary Buddhism* 2, no. 1 (2001): 83–97; and Harris, "Does Anātman Rationally Entail Altruism?" 93–123.
50. William Edelglass, "Buddhist Ethics and Western Moral Theory," in *A Companion to Buddhist Philosophy*, ed. Steven M. Emmanuel (Hoboken, NJ: John Wiley & Sons, 2014), 476–490.
51. Stephanie Kaza and Kenneth Kraft, eds., *Dharma Rain: Sources of Buddhist Environmentalism* (Boston: Shambhala Publications, 2000); Damien Keown, Charles Prebish, and Wayne Husted, eds., *Buddhism and Human Rights* (Richmond, Surrey, UK: Curzon Press, 1998); Damien Keown, *Buddhism and Bioethics* (New York: Palgrave, 2001); and Damien Keown, *Contemporary Buddhist Ethics* (Richmond, Surrey, UK: Curzon Press, 2000).
52. Thich Nhat Hanh, *Interbeing: Fourteen Guidelines for Engaged Buddhism*, 3rd ed. (Berkeley, CA: Parallax Press, 1998); Sallie King, *Being Benevolence: The Social Ethics of Engaged Buddhism* (Honolulu: University of Hawai'i Press, 2005); David Loy, *The Great Awakening: A Buddhist Social Theory* (Boston: Wisdom Publications, 2003); David Loy, *A New Buddhist Path: Enlightenment, Evolution, and Ethics in the Modern World* (Boston: Wisdom Publications, 2015); Christopher Ives, "Deploying the Dharma: Reflections on the Methodology of Constructive Buddhist Ethics," *Journal of Buddhist Ethics* 15 (2008): 22–44; and Amod Lele, "Disengaged Buddhism," *Journal of Buddhist Ethics* 26 (2019): 239–289.
53. Donald S. Lopez Jr., *Buddhism and Science: A Guide for the Perplexed* (Chicago: University of Chicago Press, 2008); and David McMahan and Erik Braun, *Meditation, Buddhism, and Science* (Oxford: Oxford University Press, 2017).

Jessica Locke

F

FILIAL PIETY IN CHINESE BUDDHISM

BRIEF REVIEW OF SCHOLARLY STUDIES ON THE TOPIC

Many people, even scholars like Kenneth Ch'en, have argued that filial piety is a special feature of Chinese Buddhism as it has been influenced by Confucianism, which considers filial piety as the foundation of its ethics and the root of moral teaching.[1] Later scholars such as Gregory Schopen and John Strong demonstrated in their studies that Indian Buddhists also practiced filial piety. But Schopen, who mainly used epigraphical material in his research, pointed out that he could not find definitive support from the early Buddhist textual sources, while John Strong used mainly Jātaka stories for his research. In fact, we find much evidence in the early Buddhist textual sources of both the Pāli Nikāya and Chinese Āgama that filial piety is not only taught and practiced in Indian Buddhism but also considered an essential moral good deed, although it is never taken as the foundation of Buddhist moral teaching. One of the most important suttas directly related to this issue in the early Buddhist resources in Pāli is the *Kataññu Sutta*, which teaches children to pay their debts to the parents who gave them birth and brought them up with much difficulty and hardship. When Buddhism was introduced in China during the Eastern Han dynasty (25–220), Confucianism already occupied the central position in Chinese philosophical thought, and it continued until the end of imperial rule in the beginning of the early 20th century, although its position was challenged by Buddhism and Daoism from time to time. In response to Confucian criticism of Buddhists being unfilial, the learned Chinese Buddhists responded in the following four ways: (1) providing translations of and references to Buddhist sutras that teach filial behavior; (2) writing scholarly refutations of the charges of unfilial practices, such as Mouzi's *Lihuolun*, also known as *Mouzi Lihuolun*, and Qisong's *Xiaolun*; (3) interpreting Buddhist precepts as equal to the Confucian concept of filial piety; and (4) teaching people to pay debts to four groups of people, that is, parents, sentient beings, kings, and Buddhists.[2] Ordinary Chinese Buddhists replied to the criticism by practice in (1) composing apocryphal scriptures, such as the *Fumu Enzhong Jing*, to teach filial piety and (2) popularizing stories and parables such as the *Pusa Shanzi Jing* (*Śyama Jātaka*) and the *Yulanpen Jing* (*Ullambana Sūtra*) by way of public lectures, painted illustrations called *Banxiang* or tableaus on walls and silk, and the annual celebration of the *Yulanpen* festival, popularly known as the ghost festival. Chinese Buddhism has become a religion that emphasizes the teaching and practice of filial piety with rich resources through such exchange and interaction with Confucianism and Daoism for the last two thousand years.

FILIAL PIETY IN EARLY BUDDHISM

Many people have a misconception about Buddhist teaching of filial piety and thinking that Buddhist monks or Buddhists in general should reject all family ties and social relationships in order to pursue nirvana. This misunderstanding of Buddhist practice is quite common. In fact, filial piety is a very important moral teaching in early Buddhism, and children are advised to respect and support their parents in their old age according to many early Buddhist scriptures.[3] First, filial piety is taught and practiced as the way to repay debts to parents. The *Kataññu Sutta* teaches children that they owe a great debt to the parents who gave them birth and have brought them up with many difficulties and introduced them into this world.[4] The counterpart of this sutta is found in the Chinese translation as the *Fumuen Nanbao Jing* (The Discourse on the Difficulty in Repaying the Debts to Parents) and according to which the apocryphal text *Fumu Enzhong Jing* (The Discourse on the Great Compassion of Parents) was created in China.[5] In the *Sabrahma Sutta* (Brahmā), the Buddha addresses the monks, saying that mother and father should be worshipped and venerated as Brahmā, first teachers, first deities, and that they are worthy of offering.[6] According to the early Buddhist teaching, parents should be respected with the greatest honor just like Brahmā, the god of creation in Hinduism. This is important because according to Confucianism, respect and veneration of parents are considered foremost in the practice of filial piety. The *Mahāyañña Sutta* (Great Sacrifice) addresses to a Brahmin of fire worshipper who asks the buddha how to conduct a good sacrifice for his welfare and happiness.[7] The buddha advises the fire Brahmin that instead of killing animals for sacrifice, he should happily maintain three fires: the first fire is mother and father, which is the fire of those worthy of gifts; the second is wife and children, which is the householder's fire; and the third is religious people, which is the fire of those worthy of offering. It will bring happiness to him for a long time when these three fires are maintained, esteemed, revered, venerated, and respected. In these three suttas, the audiences are different and include ordinary people, a fire Brahmin, and even monks who have left their parents for a homeless life, but the idea of respecting and supporting parents is articulated without ambiguity.

Second, filial piety is also taught as an important meritorious deed in early Buddhism. The *Mātuposaka Sutta* informs us that a Brahmin asks the buddha whether it is proper for him to support his mother and father by begging for alms food in a righteous way.[8] The buddha replies affirmatively to the Brahmin that it is not only proper but also a great meritorious deed if one can support his parents by seeking alms food after the normal manner of a mendicant. According to Indian tradition, people normally think that alms food obtained from begging by a mendicant is only for the mendicant himself or his fellow mendicants to consume. However, the buddha is quite open-minded and praises those mendicants who support their parents with alms food. The *Devā (sattavatapada) Sutta* tells us that supporting one's parents is the first of the seven ethical meritorious deeds performed by Sakka when he was a human being, and as a result, he was born in the heaven of Brahmā world and become the king of all gods.[9] The other good deeds are respecting elders, good words, no harsh words, no slandering talk, speaking the truth, and being generous. In the Chinese *Ekottarāgama*, it says that the merits of making offerings to parents are equal to that of making offerings to the bodhisattva, who has one more birth to bodhi.[10] The *Parābhava Sutta* of the *Suttanipāta* says that if one who is able does not support his mother or his father when they have grown old, their youth gone, that is a cause of downfall.[11] On the other hand, according to the Buddhist teaching, there are five kinds of the gravest bad karma with immediate rebirth in hell: taking the lives of one's mother and father are the first two, and others are taking the life of an arahant, shedding the Tathāgata's blood hatefully, and creating a schism in the Saṅgha.[12] So when Ajātasattu became his disciple, the buddha said that he was done for, with his fate sealed as he had killed his father.[13] Buddhaghosa further explained in his commentary to the *Dighanikāya* that no good karma can avert such a rebirth in the next life.[14] These suttas and passages from both the positive and negative aspects clearly demonstrate that filial piety is considered important ethical good conduct in early Buddhism.

Third, filial piety is also seen as dharma, the way things should be or the social order in early Buddhism. It is believed that the society and the world will be in peace and harmony if parents are respected and yet that there will be more bad things (e.g., fighting) if parents are not respected. According to the *Aṅguttaranikāya*, the four great heavenly kings observe the conduct of people in the world three times every half month.[15] The four great heavenly kings send their ministers and assembly members to the world to inspect whether many folk among men pay reverence to mother and father, to recluses and Brahmins, and show deference to the elders of the clan, and do good work on the eighth day of every half month. Then they send their sons to the world to make the same inspection on the fourteenth day of every half month, and at last they themselves come to the world and make the same inspection on the fifteenth day of every half month. The four great heavenly kings report the matter to Sakka, the ruler of the gods of the Thirty-Three as they sit in the hall of righteousness. The gods of the Thirty-Three are displeased and say the company of gods will decline but the company of asuras will flourish when they hear that people in the world do not respect mother and father, recluses, and Brahmins and do not do good deeds. But on the other hand, the gods of the Thirty-Three are pleased and say the company of gods will flourish, but the company of the asuras will decline, when they hear that people in the world do respect mother and father, recluses, and Brahmins and do good deeds.

Asuras are known for their fighting with gods in the Buddhist scriptures while gods represent righteousness. According to the *Pali–English Dictionary* of the Pali Text Society, "the fight between Gods & Asuras is also reflected in the oldest books of the Pāli Canon and occurs in identical description under the title of devāsura—sangāma" in many places.[16] So the above passage implies that if many folk do not pay reverence to mother and father, to recluses and Brahmins, there will be increasing of fighting since *asuras* love fighting while gods maintain peace. So according to this passage, whether human folk respect parents is the source of the ethical practices that directly affect the peace of the world.

It is clear from the above discussions that filial piety is indeed presented as an important ethical teaching in early Buddhism and includes all the important aspects of filial piety taught in Confucianism such as supporting and respecting parents.[17]

CHINESE BUDDHISM

When Buddhism was introduced in China during the Eastern Han dynasty (25–220), Confucianism already occupied the central position in Chinese philosophical thought, and the idea of "ruling the state by using filial piety" was conceived of and implemented by the state in this dynasty and continued until the end of the imperial rule in the 19th century because loyalty to the emperor was also considered the same as filial practice to father. In response to Confucian criticism of Buddhists being unfilial, the learned Chinese Buddhists retorted in theoretical argumentation in the following four ways: (1) translations of and references to Buddhist sutras that teach filial behavior; (2) writing scholarly refutations of the charges of unfilial practices, such as Mouzi's *Lihuolun* and Qisong's *Xiaolun*; (3) interpreting Buddhist precepts as equal to the Confucian concept of filial piety; and (4) teaching people to pay debts for four groups of people: parents, sentient beings, kings, and Buddhists. Ordinary Chinese Buddhists replied to the criticism through the (1) composition of apocryphal scriptures, such as the *Fumu Enzhong Jing*, to teach filial piety, and (2) popularizing such stories and parables as the *Śyama Jātaka* and the *Ullambana Sūtra* by way of public lectures, painted illustrations called *Banxiang* or tableaus on walls and silk, and annual celebration of the *Yulanpen* festival, popularly known as the ghost festival. Chinese Buddhism has become a religion that emphasizes the teaching and practice of filial piety with rich resources through such exchange and interaction with Confucianism and Daoism for the last two thousand years. Even today, ordinary Chinese Buddhists still teach and read the *Fumu Enzhong Jing* and celebrate the *Yulanpen* festival every year. This influenced Daoism such that they also created a similar text teaching filial piety, celebrate the festival on the same day, and perform the same activities of feeding the hungry ghosts, but they call it Zhongyuan.

TRANSLATIONS OF BUDDHIST SUTRAS RELATED TO FILIAL PIETY

The translation of Buddhist texts that directly teach filial piety was an important way to respond to criticism of Confucians. At least fourteen texts that focused on filial piety and thirty-one related texts were translated between the Han and Tang dynasties for nine centuries. After the Song dynasty, Buddhist translation virtually stopped so there was no new text that appeared after 13th century. The Chinese translation of Buddhist scriptures related to the issue of filial piety can be divided into two groups. The first group of scriptures teaches either directly or indirectly the theory of filial piety and discusses how and why filial piety should be practiced. The second group of scriptures tells stories of how Buddhists practiced filial piety.

The first group of Chinese translation started at the very beginning when Buddhism was introduced in China during the Eastern Han dynasty. Two important texts were introduced and translated by An Shigao in 148–170. The first is the *Fumuen nanbao jing* (The Discourse on the Difficulties in Repaying the Parents' Great Compassion), whose title could be restored as *Kṛtajña Sūtra,* same as the Pāli version of the *Kataññu Sutta* from the *Aṅguttaranikāya* as discussed above. This short text is quite important because it entirely focuses on the great compassion of the parents toward their children and how the children repay their debts.[18] The translator must have taken it from the *Ekottarāgama* and translated it independently for Chinese readers. Even today the sutra is still found in Gautama Saṅghadeva's Chinese translation of the *Zengyi ahan jing* (*Ekottarāgama*).[19] This text was translated on the demand of the Chinese readers, or the translator himself selected the text in order to show the Buddhist teaching of filial piety since he faced a challenging situation. This, of course, is already testified by the *Mouzi Lihuolun,* a text written in the 2nd century CE to refute the charges of Buddhists being unfilial. It is on the bases of this sutra that the popular text of the *Fumu Enzhong Jing* (The Discoure on the Great Compassion of Parents) was written by Chinese Buddhists in the late 7th century.

The second text translated by An Shigao is the *Shijialuoyue liufangli jing* (Śṛgāla's Worship of the Six Directions). This is an important text in which the buddha advises a layperson named Śṛgāla to pay his reverence to six groups of people in five ways instead of the six directions: the first group is his parents, and others are his teachers, wife, relatives, servants, and religious people. In general, it is a teaching on the importance of the proper observance of societal principles. This text is quite appropriate to the situation in the Han dynasty as the government started to implement the policy of selecting officials by looking into the person's practice of filial piety as well as good behaviors.[20] So we can infer that the text was translated because of the demand of the situation in China. This text in the Pāli version, entitled *Sigālaka Sutta,* is regarded as the ethics for laypeople in Theravāda tradition even today.

The *Dacheng bensheng xindi guan jing* (Mahāyāna Discourse on the Concentration of Mind Ground) translated by Prajña in 790 has a special chapter on "Repaying Debts." There is a long discussion on paying debts to four groups of people including parents, sentient beings, kings, and Buddhism, and this became a standard list and spread not only in China but also in other East Asian countries for teaching in monasteries. Here we can see a development in the theory of practice of filial piety from paying debts to parents to paying debts to four groups of people.

The second group of scriptures that tells the stories of the Buddhist practices of filial piety can be divided into three subgroups: (1) the stories of the buddha who practiced filial piety in the present life, (2) the stories of the buddha who practiced filial piety in his previous lives as a bodhisattva, and (3) the stories of his disciples who practiced filial piety.

The stories related to the buddha who practiced filial piety in this life include the following texts: the *Fosheng daolitian weimu shuofa jing* (佛昇忉利天為母說法經) (The Sutra of the Buddha's Ascension to the Trāyastriṃśa Heaven to Preach the Dharma to His Mother), also known as the *Mohe moye jing* (摩訶摩耶經) (*Mahāmāyā Sūtra*), translated by Tanjing in 479–502, is a perfect texts to show that the buddha not only taught but also did practice filial piety. According to the Buddhist tradition, Mahāmāyā, the mother of the buddha, died and was reborn in heaven after giving birth to the bodhisattva. The buddha ascended to heaven and preached to his mother a few years after his enlightenment, and as a result she attained *srotāpanna*, the stage of stream-enterer. This story is referred to in the Chinese translation of the *Saṃyuktāgama* (sutra no. 506) and the *Ekottarāgama* (section 36, sutra no. 5). This text is included in Daoshi's *Fayuan Zhulin* (法苑珠林) (compiled during the 7th century) under the section on "Repaying Debts" to show the Buddha's practice of filial piety.

The second text is the *Jinfanwang banniepan jing* (Suddhodana's Parinirvāṇa Sūtra), translated by Zhuqu Jingsheng in 455. The text tells the story of Suddhodana, the buddha's father, who was about to die and asked to see his son, and the buddha came back and attended the funeral as a way of practicing filial piety. This story is also found in the Theravāda tradition and according to which, in the fifth year after Gotama's enlightenment, Suddhodana died, having realized arahantship, and the buddha flew through the air, from the Kūtāgārasālā in Vesāli where he was staying, to preach to his father on his death bed.[21]

The third text is the *Foshuo Daaidao bannianhuan Jing* (*Mahāpajāpatī Gotami Parinirvāṇa Sūtra*), translated twice, first by Bai Fazhu in Western Jin dynasty (290–307 CE) and a second time by Huijian in 457. The story is also found in the Chinese translation of the *Ekottaraāgama*.[22] According to Buddhist tradition, Mahāpajāpatī Gotami was the younger sister of Mahāmāyā, and they both married King Suddhodana together. Mahāpajāpatī Gotami nursed Siddhartha Gautama when Māyā died after giving birth. The text describes how Mahāpajāpatī Gotami died and the buddha came and collected her ashes. However, in the Therāvada Vinaya, we find that the buddha had a great love for Pajāpatī, and when she lay ill, as there were no monks to visit her and preach to her because it was prohibited, the buddha went himself to preach to her and also amended the rule that a monk should not preach to a nun.[23]

The stories related to the buddha practicing filial piety in his previous lives as a bodhisattva are found in many collections. The first and most important story is the *Foshuo pusa shanzi jing* (*Śyāmakajātaka Sūtra*), which is the same as the *Sāma Jātaka* (no. 540) in the Theravāda tradition. This short sutra tells the story of the buddha in his former life as a filial son supporting his blind parents in their old age. In order to fulfill his objectives, Bodhisattva Śyāma led a bachelor's life and single-mindedly served his parents without any complaints. The sutra was twice translated into Chinese, and the extant version was translated by Shengjian in 388–409. This is a suitable text to teach filial piety, and there have been many versions with the Taisho edition of the Tripiṭaka containing four. This story became so popular in China that it was even included in the Confucian tradition of the twenty-four stories of filial piety. The *Zabaozang jing* (*Saṃyuktāratna Sūtra*) translated by Kekaya and Tanyao in 472 contains ten stories related to the teaching of filial piety, and they all tell the stories of the buddha practicing filial piety in his previous lives as a bodhisattva in different appearances, that is, that of ordinary people, animals such as birds, and so forth.

The third group of texts is the buddha's disciples who practiced filial piety. The *Foshuo yulanpen jing* (*Ullambana Sūtra*) translated by Dharmarakṣa in the 3rd century has influenced Chinese Buddhism tremendously.[24] It tells the story of how the buddha's disciple

Maudgalyāyana saves his mother from hell. According to this narrative, the mother of Maudgalyāyana was reborn into hell after death due to her bad deeds. Maudgalyāyana saw his mother suffering in hell through his magic power and tried to save her but failed. So he asked the buddha to help, and the latter told him that it was only through collective merit of Sangha that his mother could be saved. Thus, Maudgalyāyana made a great offering to the Sangha just after the raining retreat, and his mother was saved.

There is another Mahāyāna text named the *Dizang pusa benyuan jing* (Sutra on the Past Vows of Kṣitigarbha Bodhisattva), translated by Śikṣananda in 695–700. This text tells the story of the previous life of Dizang (Kṣitigarbha), a daughter of a Brahmin woman who saved her father from hell. This text is widely circulated and considered a sutra teaching filial piety by the East Asian Buddhists. Apart from the above scriptures related to either the buddha or his disciples, there are also texts containing passages teaching filial piety, such as Zhi Qian's translation of the *Foshuo weishengyuan jing* (*Sutra of King Ajātasatru*) in 222–280.

From the above survey of Chinese translations of Buddhist scriptures related to the issue of filial piety, we may come to a tentative conclusion that with such a large number of Buddhist texts either directly teaching or indirectly related to filial piety, Chinese Buddhists were able to (1) show the Confucian and Daoist scholars that Buddhists also taught and practiced filial piety and (2) refute unreasonable criticism by references to the above sutras.

WRITING SCHOLARLY REFUTATIONS

Learned Chinese Buddhists also wrote scholarly refutations to the Confucian criticism of Buddhists being unfilial. These scholarly refutations underwent three stages of development and finally reached a stage arguing that the Buddhist practice of filial piety is superior to that of Confucianism. The first stage is the explanation of Buddhist standpoints such as the *Mouzi Lihuolun* and the teachings of master Huiyuan 慧遠 (334–416). The second stage is more direct refutation by many Chinese Buddhists, both monks and laypeople. The third is comparing both Buddhist and Confucian concepts and practices of filial piety.

The first stage of refutation is from Mouzi 牟子 in the 2nd century, to Master Huiyuan in the beginning of the 5th century, where the questions asked by critics remained the same, but the answers given by the Chinese Buddhists got more refined and detailed with specific references to Buddhist texts and practices as more and more Buddhist scriptures had been translated into Chinese. During these two hundred years, Buddhism developed rapidly, and the differences between Buddhism and Confucianism and Daoism became clearer as people learned more Buddhist teachings, and the conflict between the former and the latter also became intense. Chinese Buddhists made great effort in explaining the Buddhist standpoint when criticisms on the practice of filial piety became more refined.

We find in the *Mouzi Lihuolun* that critics questioned three aspects on the issue of filial piety. Mouzi refuted the critics by quoting many historical precedents and references from both Confucian and Daoist classics and traditions arguing that all kinds of practices similar to those of the Buddhists were also found in China, where they were not condemned by Confucius and other people, but in fact praised as virtuous behavior.

The first criticism is that monks' cutting of their hair is an unfilial practice because the Confucian *Xiaojing* says that since body, limbs, hair, and skin are received from parents, one should not harm them. Mouzi refuted the critics by saying that virtue was more important than skin and hair, and he also quoted from the same Confucian classic that Confucius praised Taibo 泰伯 as a sage but also cut his hair. The second criticism is about monks' celibacy without posterity. Mouzi refuted this by giving examples that Confucius praised these Chinese Xu You 許由, Bo Yi 伯夷, and Shu Qi 叔齊 as sages but did not blame them for not having posterity. Of course, celibacy was not a recognized way of life in ancient China, and this is particularly true of Confucians, thus Confucian scholars would never be satisfied with the answers or reasons given by Chinese Buddhists. The third criticism concerns Buddhist customs as Buddhist monks from India wore one piece of red cloth that was considered by Chinese people as uncivilized, as the ancient Chinese wore cloth that fully covered one's body called *li* 禮, rites or propriety. They also were critical that Buddhist monks did not observe the proper obeisance to some personages, as monks do not bow to officers. Mouzi answered from two points of view. First, Mouzi argued that in the ancient time of the three emperors of sages, people even wore animal skins, but they were praised as having virtue. Second, Mouzi argued that Chinese and Buddhists led two different ways of life. The Chinese sages of Yao 堯, Shun 舜, Zhou 周, and Confucius 孔 practiced worldly affairs, while the Buddha and Laozi 老子set their minds on nonaction. These arguments are quite weak without the support of Buddhist teachings, and it was only Sun Chuo who gave a better answer.

Sun Chuo's 孫綽 (314–371) essay "Yu Dao Lun" (喻道論) is another important work after the *Mouzi Lihuolun* in defense of Buddhism.[25] We find only one question on filial piety, but it covers two of the three aspects found in the *Mouzi Lihuolun*: posterity and harming of physical appearance by cutting hair. Sun Chuo refuted the critics by referring to the highest form of filial piety according to the Confucian books of the *Xiaojing* and the *Li Ji* (禮記). According to the *Xiaojing*, the highest form of filial piety is to make the family name famous in future ages and glorify one's parents. While according to the *Li Ji*, the greatest filial piety is seen in widely disseminating the teaching of virtue to people and providing them with all things necessary. Sun Chuo argued that judging by Confucian standard, the buddha was a good example of the highest fulfillment of filial piety, because he made his father's name known to the world and also saved numerous people from suffering by tirelessly teaching virtue and morality. Sun Chuo's argument is better than Mouzi's because he used the Confucian theory of filial piety to argue that Buddhist monks also practiced it by establishing themselves in virtue and working for the good of society in promoting virtue.

The questions discussed in the above two essays later became the central points of contention in the form of issues such as "monks not paying homage to the ruler" and "Chinese and Barbarian," from the Wei and Jin, up to the Southern and Northern dynasties. In the Eastern Jin 東晉, there was a debate over whether monks should pay respect to rulers. Although the real issue behind it is a political power struggle between the two clans, it also demonstrates the tension between the authority and Buddhist Sangha.

After sixty years, when Huan Xuan came into power, he renewed the same argument and asked Buddhist monks to pay homage to the emperor. There were many officials as well as monks who rose against Huan Xuan. Among them, Wang Mi 王謐 represented the officials, and Huiyuan represented the clergy. As a Buddhist leader, Huiyuan explained in his letter to Huan Xuan that Buddhism supported imperial rule, and its doctrine was similar to Confucian teachings. Buddhist monks had different customs from secular people: it was only different in formality, yet the same in essence. Therefore, Buddhist monks did not discard their practice of filial piety and respect to the emperor; instead they supported imperial rule by way of promoting virtues. The debate came to a stop with Huiyuan's convincing arguments.

The debate on monks' not paying homage to the ruler is a precursor to the debate on "Chinese and Barbarians," which is also the second stage of refutation. During the Southern and Northern dynasties (420–577), Buddhism developed in China at an amazing speed. The conflict among Buddhism and Confucianism and Daoism took different forms in the Southern and Northern dynasties. In the north, it took the violent form of persecution: The first occurred in the time of the emperor Tai Wudi 太武帝 in the Northern Wei (386–534), and the second in the time of the emperor Zhou Wudi 周武帝 of the Northern Zhou (557–581). In the south it took on a milder form, through debate by writing essays that are recorded in books such as Sengyou's 僧祐 *Hongming ji* (弘明集).[26] According to the Chinese scholar Tang Yongtong 湯用彤, these scholarly writings can be classified into two main areas: (1) the Chinese and the barbarian and (2) form and spirit.[27] The former concerns the cultural differences between China and Central Asia (for instance, differences in filial piety, way of life, and rituals), whereas the latter focuses on philosophical discussions of the "imperishable spirit."

Our concern is the first kind of debate since it relates to filial piety. The entire debate was started by Gu Huan 顧歡, a Daoist, who wrote an essay *Yixia Lun* (夷夏論) (Barbarian and Chinese). There is nothing new in his essay, as the criticisms were already found in previous essays such as the *Mouzi Lihuolun*. But it represents a group of people who had the superior feeling of Chinese culture and despised other cultures. Although Gu Huan wrote the essay with an aim to conciliate the conflict between Daoism and Buddhism, he treated Buddhism as a barbarian culture from the traditional Chinese point of view. Gu Huan's *Yixia Lun* caused a huge reaction from the Buddhists, and at least six essays written by both Buddhist monks and laypeople to refute the charges are preserved in Sengyou's *Hongming Ji*.[28] First, the Chinese Buddhists refuted Gu Huan's idea of superiority of Chinese and uncivilized barbarians (Buddhists), saying that we (Chinese people) should have an open-minded attitude toward foreign people and their customs. Second, Chinese Buddhists argued that people should appreciate the value of the Buddhist theory and teaching rather than the custom and tradition of a religion or culture. Third, Chinese Buddhists distinguished philosophical Daoism from religious Daoism and praised the former, particularly Laozi's thought, as a teaching for self-cultivation and governing the state, and criticized the latter as a doctrine for longevity that could never be obtained.

Apart from Gu Huan, another Daoist wrote *Sanpo Lun* (三破論) (On Three Destructions) in the name of Zhang Rong 張融, a well-known person in the Southern and Northern dynasties (420–577). The author of the book attacks Buddhism from Confucian moral grounds as a teaching of destruction (1) to the nation, (2) to the family, and (3) to the person who believed in it, because the Confucian teaching is on state governing, family regulation, and personal cultivation. Liu Xie replied that it was not because of Buddhism that the state declined, and in fact the state became prosperous after the introduction of Buddhism.[29] Sengshun argued that Buddhism contributed to imperial rule by way of teaching people to cultivate virtue.[30] Concerning the second point, Liu Xie refuted that lay Buddhists practiced the Confucian teaching and performed filial piety accordingly, while Buddhist monks cultivated themselves in virtue and also performed filial piety by saving their departed relatives. With regard to the third point of cutting hairs, Liu Xie replied by saying that filial piety was not found in the hairs but in the mind. Buddhist monks practice great filial piety by abandoning minor filial acts because they worked to save their ancestors forever. Of course, the criticism on posterity was still not answered since Buddhist and Confucian ways of life are different.

The third stage of refutation is during the Tang and Song dynasties. Zongmi 宗密 in the Tang dynasty compared the Confucian and Buddhist concepts and practices of filial piety and came to the conclusion that both religions have filial piety as their foundation, in his commentary to the *Ullambana Sūtra*. He first quoted the Confucian *Xiao Jing* and said that filial piety is "a perfect virtue and all-embracing rule of conduct." And then he quoted the Buddhist *Fan Wang Jing* (梵網經) to show that filial piety is a teaching of the ultimate way to attain enlightenment and is same as Buddhist precepts.[31]

Later in the Song dynasty, Qisong 契嵩 in his *Xiao Lun* argued that Buddhist teaching on filial piety was even better than that of Confucianism. Qisong said that according Buddhist sutra, filial piety was called precepts. This meant that filial piety was the beginning of precepts because filial piety should be practiced before precepts and all virtues come from precepts. The five precepts of abstaining from killing, stealing, adultery, lying, and intoxicating drinks were the components of filial piety in Buddhism, and these were the same as the Confucian five virtues of benevolence, righteousness, propriety, fidelity, and wisdom. Qisong's *Xiaolun* discusses the concept and practice of filial piety from the following five points. (1) Filial piety is the source of human life and human nature. The greatest filial piety is in serving one's parents with sincerity as parents give one life. (2) Filial piety is the beginning of Buddhist precepts, and the five precepts are the components in the practice of filial piety. (3) The Buddhist concept of filial piety is greater than that of Confucianism because Buddhism advocates compassion to all sentient beings including animals, as they could be our past parents with the first of the five precepts of nonkilling. (4) Buddhism advocates repaying the debts to parents by leading a virtuous life and teaching the same virtue to all people because supporting and serving parents alone as advocated by Confucianism cannot repay their debts. (5) Buddhist monks should also participate in parents' funeral ceremonies and perform mourning rituals with an expression of deep remorse of loss in their hearts and minds. After its publication, Qisong's *Xiaolun* won the admiration from and influenced not only Buddhists but also Confucian scholars.

Table 1. Comparison between the Confucian Five Constants and Buddhist Five Precepts[32]

Confucianism: five constants 五常	**Buddhism: five precepts** 五戒
Benevolence 仁	Not to kill or harm any living being 不殺生
Righteousness 義	Not to steal anything from others 不偷盜
Propriety 禮	Not to commit adultery 不邪婬
Honesty 信	Not to tell lies 不妄語
Wisdom 智	Not to take intoxicating drinks 不飲酒

REINTERPRETING BUDDHIST PRECEPTS AS EQUAL TO THE CONFUCIAN CONCEPT OF FILIAL PIETY

The *Fanwang Jing* (梵網經) is a very important text in Chinese Buddhism as it is thought to lay a foundation for the Mahāyāna Bodhisattva precepts tradition. Many eminent Buddhist scholarly monks such as Zhiyi and Fazang wrote commentaries. In the second fascicle of the text, it says, "filial piety is called precepts," which is to say that filial piety and precepts are the same. It is based on this understanding that the Chinese scholarly Buddhists further developed the Buddhist concept of filial piety and reinterpreted it same as the precepts. Many modern Japanese and Chinese scholars think that the *Fanwang Jing* is an apocryphal work compiled in China through a selection of passages from other Buddhist scriptures in Chinese translations such as the *Bodhisattvabhūmi Sūtra* (菩薩地持經), the *Upāsakaśīla Sūtra* (優婆塞戒經), the *Mahāparinirvāṇa Sutra* (涅槃經), and the *Renwang Bore Boluomi Jing* (The Human King Perfection Wisdom Sutra) (仁王般若波羅蜜經), while only a few modern scholars think that it is a true translation of an Indian Buddhist text. However, the *Fanwang Jing* occupies an important place in the history of Chinese Buddhism and has deeply influenced Chinese Buddhists, as it is the text for bodhisattva precepts in bodhisattva ordination. Zhiyi (538–597), the founder of the Tiantai Buddhist school, explained and disseminated the teaching of the *Fanwang Jing* to his students, and Guanding, according to his teacher's lectures, compiled the *Commentary on the Meaning of the Bodhisattva Precepts* (菩薩戒義疏), which is still in extant.[33] As a result, the *Fanwang Jing* was and is still considered an important text for Mahāyāna precepts and has become the authoritative text for Mahāyāna ordination in Chinese Buddhist circles for all Chinese Buddhist schools. This text became so popular due to its teaching that "filial piety is called precepts," which is suited to Chinese society. Thus Chinese scholarly monks accepted the idea that "filial piety is called precepts" and further explained it.

Zhiyi believed that Buddhist precepts are the same as Confucian filial piety. He compared the Buddhist five precepts with the Confucian five constants, as shown in table 1.

Chinese Buddhists accepted Zhiyi's explanation and upheld the idea that Buddhist precepts and Confucian filial piety are the same. Zhongmi (780–841), the Tang dynasty scholarly monk and also a patriarch of the Huayan school, stated that both Buddhism and Confucianism have filial piety as their foundation because although the Buddhist precepts cover all wholesome practices, filial piety is fundamental in his commentary to the *Ullanbana Sūtra*.[34] It is on this basis that Qisong (1007–1072) in his *Treatise on Filial Piety* (孝論) further explained that filial piety precedes precepts and the five precepts are the constituents of filial piety. In other words, filial piety should be practiced before the observation of precepts, and the observation of the five precepts is the actual practice of filial piety.[35] Qisong further stated that the Buddhist practice of filial piety is greater than that of Confucianism.

TEACHING PEOPLE TO PAY DEBTS TO FOUR GROUPS OF PEOPLE

Paying debts to four groups of people is a special teaching in Chinese and East Asian Buddhism, as we do not have any reference to the Indian Buddhist practice of it. Although the *Zhengfa Nianchu Jing* (正法念處經) (*Saddharmasmṛtyupasthāna Sūtra*) mentions paying debts to a group of four (mother, father, Tathāgata, and the dharma teacher) without further explanation, this list never became popular. The *Dacheng ben shengxin di guan jing* (大乘本生心地觀經) (Mahāyāna Discourse on the Concentration of Mind Ground), translated into Chinese by Prajñā in 790, mentions paying debts to four groups of people (parents, sentient beings, rulers, and Buddhists) and devotes the entire second chapter to the detailed explanation of the four debts.[36] This list has become very popular, and the great Buddhist masters taught their disciples and lay devotees the teaching of paying debts to the four kinds of people. Thus it became a regular practice in monasteries throughout China in the Tang dynasty. The Chinese Buddhists since then started to recite a verse of dedication of merits at the end of the morning and evening chanting and also every ceremony, wishing, "May this merit and virtue adorn the Buddhas' Pure Lands, repay the four debts above, and rescue those in the three suffering realms below." As a consequence, in later dynasties there was no such a debate as to whether the monks should pay homage to the emperor.

CHINESE CREATION OF APOCRYPHAL TEXTS

As discussed above, there is a Chinese translation of the *Fumuen nanbao jing* (The Discourse on the Difficulties in Repaying the Debts to Parents) by An Shigao, which is same as the Pāli version of the *Kataññu Sutta*. However, the text mentions that one can repay parents' kindness by doing five things: establishing parents in faith, morality, knowledge, generosity, and wisdom. This idea opposes the Confucian way of practicing filial piety, particularly the idea of establishing immoral parents in morality. According to the Confucian concept of filial piety, a child can never disobey his parents even if they are wrong. The only thing children can do to their parents is to serve them and do whatever they ask for without any complaint. This is because the Confucians emphasize respect and reverence toward parents in the practice of filial piety as taught in the *Lunyu* (論語) (2.7). On the other hand, unfiliality was considered in antiquity the first of the five grave crimes to be punished. The idea of punishing the unfilial son started quite early, and it was implemented through law in the Han dynasty. This became a tradition and was inherited by the Southern and Northern dynasties and Sui and Tang dynasties until Ming and Qing. In such an environment, the Buddhist principle of repaying parents' kindness, especially to establish the immoral parents in morality as told in the *Fumuen Nanbao Jing*, could not be preached to Chinese audiences, particularly to the ordinary masses, without modification since it is in contradiction with the Confucian concept of filial piety, which emphasizes respect and reverence to parents. This probably also explains why the *Fumuen Nanbao Jing* has never been widely spread in China after its translation, and many people, especially ordinary masses, do not even know of its existence. As a result, the Chinese Buddhists created the apocryphal text entitled *Fumu Enzhong Jing* (The Discourse on the Great Compassion of Parents) by imitating the *Fumuen Nanbao Jing*, probably in late 8th century, in order to teach filial piety. It enjoyed such popularity among the common people that it was expressed in various ways and means such as popular preaching and lectures, mural and cave paintings, and stone carvings. By the early 9th century, the apocryphal text was even accepted by Buddhist scholarly monks such as Zongmi, who quoted from it in his commentary to the *Ullambana Sūtra*. This text was and is still quite popular in Buddhist monasteries in China, Korea, Japan, and Vietnam, and it is printed for free distribution to everyone who comes to a monastery.

The stories about parents bringing up their children discussed in the text are also presented in painting illustrations. We find six illustrations of the above text in Dunhuang: four mural paintings in caves numbers 156, 170, 238, and 449 and two silk paintings stored in the British and Gansu Museums, respectively.

POPULARIZATION OF STORIES AND PARABLES THAT TEACH FILIAL PIETY

The popularization of Buddhist stories related to the teaching of filial piety such as the *Pusa Shanzi Jing* (*Śyāma Jātaka*), the *Yulanpen Jing* (*Ullambana Sūtra*), and the *Fumu Enzhong Jing* among ordinary people in Chinese society took many different forms, such as establishing a festival, popular preaching and public lectures in monasteries, mural and cave paintings in temples such as Dunhuang, stone carvings in Dazu and Shandong, copying and printing of the sutras, and Mulian operas of saving his mother and precious scrolls of Dizang and Guanyin.

First, Chinese Buddhists established the so-called ghost festival according to the *Ullambana Sūtra* to practice filial piety. According to the sutra, Maudagalyāyana, a disciple of the buddha, rescues his mother from hell by making offering to monks on the fifteenth day of the seventh lunar month, the day on which the raining retreat ends. Chinese people celebrate it with ancestor worship, so it is seen as a filial practice. And this festival is still celebrated in the Chinese communities in mainland China and among overseas Chinese to this day.

Second, in the Dunhuang Caves, many transformation texts 變文 are found and were written on the basis of Buddhist sutras for preaching and public lectures with an aim to disseminate the Buddhist teachings. Many of these transformation texts are related to the theme of filial piety, such as the transformation texts of the *Fumu Enzhong Jing* and the ten kindnesses (of the mother) (十恩德). These transformation texts show the great effort of Buddhists in antiquity to promote the Buddhist teaching of filial piety and also served as texts for popular lectures in monasteries in the Tang dynasty.

Third, illustrations of the sutras, called *Bianxiang* 變相 or tableaus to teach ordinary people Buddhism, are found in Dunhuang and other places in China, and most of them were created in the Tang and Song dynasties. Filial piety is one of the popular themes in these illustrations. The central theme in these illustrations is the buddha's preaching, and the contents of the *Fumu Enzhong Jing* are painted around the central figure buddha.

Fourth is the hand copying and printing related scriptures to disseminate the teaching of filial piety. According to Ma Shicheng 馬世長, there are more than sixty hand-copied Dunhuang texts of the apocryphal *Fumu Enzhong Jing* found in libraries in Beijing, Paris, and London.[37] The text has even been transmitted to Korea and Japan and has been widely circulated there. After the invention of printing technology, the printing of Buddhist scriptures became one of the national events in China. So the *Fumu Enzhong Jing* was printed easily for mass distribution. Today, the title of this text is *Foshuo Fumu Enzhong Nanbao Jing* (佛說父母恩重難報經) (Discourse on the Great Compassion of Parents and the Difficulties in Repaying their Debts), a combination of both An Shigao's translation of the *Fumuen Nanbao Jing* and the apocryphal text *Fumu Enzhong Jing*. Other sutras on the theme of filial piety, such as the *Ullambana Sūtra*, have also been copied and printed in monasteries for free distribution.

Fifth, the story of Mulian (Maudgalyāyana) saving his mother was also put on stage as an opera as it is an appropriate topic for teaching filial piety and became popular in China from the Southern and Northern dynasties through the *Yulanpen* festival. The earliest record of the Mulian opera is found in Men Yuanliao's 孟元老 *Dongjing Menhua Lu* (東京夢華錄), from the Song dynasty, in which it says that during the *Yulanpen* festival, Mulian opera was put on stage from the seventh to the fifteenth day of the seventh month of the Chinese lunar calendar, and many people came to watch it. Later the Mulian opera was expanded with additions in the Ming and Qing dynasties. Today the Mulian opera is still a favorite drama in the countryside in China. It has become a living fossil in the history of Chinese opera and occupies an important place.

REVIEW OF LITERATURE

Most of the basic primary sources dealing with the teaching and practices of filial piety in Chinese Buddhism have been introduced and discussed in this article already, as they are vital for the study of this topic. The secondary sources and studies on the issue of filial piety in Buddhism in Western languages are not many, so I have listed nearly all of them in the further reading. There are many scholarly studies of this topic in Japanese, and they are not listed.

FURTHER READING

Ch'en, Kenneth. "Filial Piety in Chinese Buddhism." *Harvard Journal of Asiatic Studies* 28 (1968): 81–97.

Ch'en, Kenneth. *Chinese Transformation of Buddhism*. Princeton, NJ: Princeton University Press, 2015.

Guang, Xing. "Filial Piety in Early Buddhism." *Journal of Buddhist Ethics* 12 (2005): 82–106.

Guang, Xing. "A Study of the Apocryphal Sūtra: *Fumu Enzhong Jing*." *International Journal of Buddhist Thought and Culture* 11 (2008): 105–146.

Guang, Xing. "A Buddhist-Confucian Controversy on Filial Piety." *Journal of Chinese Philosophy* 37, no. 2 (2010): 248–260.

Guang, Xing. "Popularization of Stories and Parables on Filial Piety in China." *Journal of Buddhist Studies* 8 (2010): 129–137.

Guang, Xing. "Chinese Translation of Buddhist Sutras Related to Filial Piety as a Response to Confucian Criticism of Buddhists Being Unfilial." In *Buddhism in East Asia: Aspects of History's First Universal Religion Presented in the Modern Context*. Edited by Anita Sharma, 75–85. New Delhi: Vidyanidhi Prakashan Press, 2012.

Guang, Xing. "Early Buddhist and Confucian Concepts of Filial Piety: A Comparative Study." *Journal of the Oxford Centre for Buddhist Studies* 4 (2013): 846.

Guang, Xing. "Buddhist and Confucian Attitudes toward Life: A Comparative Study." *International Journal of Buddhist Thought and Culture* 23 (2014): 7–48.

Guang, Xing. "The Teaching and Practice of Filial Piety in Buddhism." *Journal of Law and Religion* 31, no. 2 (2016): 212–226.

Hu, Wenho. "A Re-study of the *Stone Carving of Parental Love* at Paoding, Dazu." *Chung-Hwa Buddhist Journal* 15 (2002): 115–140.

Jan, Yunhua. "The Role of Filial Piety in Chinese Buddhism." In *Buddhist Ethics and Modern Society: An International Symposium*. Edited by Charles Wei-hsun Fu and Sandra A. Wawrytko, 27–39. Contributions to the Study of Religion. Westport, CT: Greenwood Press, 1991.

Ohnuma, Reiko. "Debt to the Mother: A Neglected Aspect of the Founding of the Buddhist Nuns' Order." *Journal of the American Academy of Religion* 74, no. 4 (2006): 861–901.

Schopen, Gregory. "Filial Piety and the Monks in the Practices of Indian Buddhism: A Question of 'Sincization' Viewed from the Other Side." *T'oung Pao* 70, no. 1/3 (1984): 110–126.

Schopen, Gregory. "The Buddhist Bhikṣu's Obligation to Support His Parents in Two Vinaya Traditions." *Journal of the Pali Text Society* 29 (2007): 107–136.

Strong, John. "Filial Piety and Buddhism: The Indian Antecedents to a 'Chinese' Problem." In *Traditions in Contact and Change*. Edited by Peter Slater and Donald Wiebe, 171–186. Waterloo, UK: Wilfred Laurier University Press, 1983.

Teiser, Stephen. *The Ghost Festival in Medieval China*. Princeton, NJ: Princeton University Press, 1988.

NOTES

1. Kenneth Ch'en. "Filial Piety in Chinese Buddhism." *Harvard Journal of Asiatic Studies* 28 (1968): 81–97.
2. Hajjhime Nakamura mentions the Confucian criticism of Buddhist being unfilial in his book, *The Ways of Thinking of Eastern People* (Honolulu: University of Hawaii Press, 1964), 269–270.
3. The term "Early Buddhism" refers to the teachings found in the Pāli Nikāya and Chinese Āgama. These writings are considered by all modern Buddhist scholars to be the earliest Buddhist resources.
4. *Anguttaranikāya*, I, ed. R. Morris (Oxford: Pali Text Society, 1989), 61–62 (AN 2.33).
5. For detailed discussion read Guang Xing, "A Study of the Apocryphal Sutra: *Fumu Enzhong Jing*," in *International Journal of Buddhist Thought and Culture* 11 (2008): 105–146.
6. The sutta is found in the *Aṅguttaranikāya* twice: I, 132 (AN 3.31); II, 70 (AN 4.63).
7. *Aṅguttaranikāya* IV, ed. E. Hardy (Oxford: Pali Text Society, 1979), 44 (AN 7.47).
8. *Saṃyuttanikāya* I, ed. L. Feer (Oxford: Pali Text Society, 2006), 181–182 (SN 7.19).
9. *Saṃyuttanikāya* I, 228 (SN 11.11).
10. *Taishō Shinshū Daizōkyō* [(大正新脩大藏經)], ed. Takakusu Junjirō [高楠順次郎] and Watanabe Kaigyoku [渡邊海旭], 100 vols. (Tokyo: Taishō Issaikyō Kankōkai, 1924–1932), vol. 2, no. 125 (20.11), 600c. (hereafter references to the works within the *Taishō Shinshū Daizōkyō* [Taishō Tripitaka] will be in the standard abbreviated form of T [volume], no. [sutra number], [page and column], e.g., the *Dīrghāgama*, T1, no. 1 [27], 107a).
11. *Suttanipāta*, ed. Dines Andersen and Helmer Smith (Oxford: Pali Text Society, 1990), no. 97.
12. *Aṅguttaranikāya* III. 146 (AN 5.129). *Vibhaṅga*, ed. C. A. F. Rhys Davids (Oxford: Pali Text Society, 1978), 378.
13. *Dīghanikāya* I, ed. T. W. Rhys Davids and J. E. Carpenter (Oxford: Pali Text Society, 2007), 85 (DN, 2).
14. *Aṭṭhasālinī*, ed. E. Müller (1897, revised reprint with indexes by L. S. Cousins (Oxford: Pali Text Society, 1979), 358.
15. *Aṅguttaranikāya* I. 142 (A.3.37).
16. PTS *Pali-English Dictionary* (p. 89); the fighting of gods with asuras is mentioned in the following passages: *Dīghanikāya* II. 285; *Saṃyuttanikāya* I. 222, IV. 201, V. 447; *Majjhimanikāya* I. 253; *Aṅguttaranikāya* IV. 432.
17. See Guang Xing, "Early Buddhist and Confucian Concepts of Filial Piety: A Comparative Study," *Journal of the Oxford Centre for Buddhist Studies* 4 (2013): 8–46.
18. An Shigao's translation is found in Taisho edition of Tripiṭaka as no. 684.
19. It is found as the eleventh sutra in the eleventh Juan of the Chinese *Ekottarāgama* (CBETA, T02, no. 125, 600c–601a).
20. The text was again translated twice by Dharmarakṣa (active in China during 266–313) and Zhi Fadu, in 301, respectively.

21. Cited from the entry "Gotama" in the *Dictionary of Pali Proper Names*, ed. G. P. Malalasekera (1899–1973) (Oxford: Pali Text Society, 1960). The story is found in the Therīgāthā Commentary, ed. William Pruitt (Oxford: Pali Text Society, 1997), 141.
22. The first sutra of the 52th vagga or chapter of the *Ekottaraāgama* is about Mahāpajāpatī Gotami's *Parinirvāṇa*.
23. *The Book of Discipline*, trans. I. B. Horner, vol. 2 (Oxford: Pali Text Society, 1997), 277.
24. According to *The Korean Buddhist Canon*, ed. Lewis R. Lancaster in collaboration with Sung-bae Park (Berkeley: University of California Press, 1979), the *Ullambana Sūtra* was translated between the second year of Tai Shi and the first year of Jian Xing, Western Jin dynasty (266–313).
25. Sengyou's *Hong Ming Ji*, Fascicle three. T52, no. 2102, 16b–17c.
26. Other books in which these scholarly writings are preserved are Daoxuan's 道宣 *Guang Hongming ji* (廣弘明集) and *Ji gujin fodao lunheng* (集古今佛道論衡), and Zhisheng's 智昇 *Xuji gujin fodao lunheng* (續集古今佛道論衡).
27. Tang Yongtong, *Hanwei liang Jin Nanbeichao fojiao shi* (漢魏兩晉南北朝佛教史) (Beijing: Konglun Publication, 2006), vol. 1, 407.
28. T52, no. 2102.
29. T52, no. 2102, 50.
30. T52, no. 2102, 52.
31. T24, no. 1484, 1004.
32. T46, no. 1911, 77b. Table 1 was created according to Master Zhiyi's discussion and comparison of the Confucian Five Constants and Buddhist Five Precepts in his *Mohezhiguan* (摩訶止觀) in the 6th century.
33. T40, no. 1811.
34. T39, no. 1792, 505b.
35. T52, no. 2115, 660a–662c.
36. T3, no. 159, 297a.
37. Ma Shichang, "*Fumu Enzhong Jing* xianben yu bianxiang" [(父母恩重經) 寫本與變相], in *Zhongguo fojiao shiku kaogu wenji* (中國佛教石窟考古文集) (Taiwan: Jue Feng Buddhist Art and Culture Foundation, 2001), 467–480.

Guang Xing

FO GUANG SHAN

THE STRUCTURE OF FO GUANG SHAN

Starting in the late 1960s, Fo Guang Shan 佛光山 has grown into one of the largest Buddhist organizations in the world. Buddha's Light International Association 國際佛光會 (BLIA), the lay and monastic membership of Fo Guang Shan, supports over 200 Fo Guang Shan affiliate branches around the world. BLIA is headquartered in Hacienda Heights, a suburb of Los Angeles, in the Hsi Lai Temple 西来寺, the largest Chinese Buddhist temple in North America. Master Hsing Yun 星云大师 (b. 1927; Pinyin: Xingyun) founded Fo Guang Shan in 1967 and has overseen its rise in Taiwan and around the world. This section includes an overview of the structure of Fo Guang Shan and BLIA.

Institutional Structure of Fo Guang Shan. Fo Guang Shan is headquartered at its main monastery in Kaohsiung, Taiwan. Hsing Yun has lived at the monastery since its construction and served as the head abbot, the de facto president of the organization until 1985. Four head abbots, all males, have followed Hsing Yun, each serving around a decade. The current head abbot is Hsin Bao 心保, who took over in 2013. Although each of the subsequent head abbots has been a popular teacher and leader, none has been able to match the venerated status of Hsing Yun, who remains the face and heart of Fo Guang Shan.

Unfortunately, most research on the institutional structure of Fo Guang Shan is quite dated, as it appeared in the early 2000s. Stuart Chandler provides a detailed examination of the 1997 election for the Religious Affairs Committee (RAC), the ultimate governing body of Fo Guang Shan.[1] The committee is made up of nine members, usually highly respected senior monastics, who are responsible for policymaking for the institution. Another major RAC responsibility is the election of the committee chair, who also serves as the head abbot of Fo Guang Shan.[2] Hsing Yun sees two benefits to the RAC elections: however, Fo Guang Shan gets to demonstrate that it is an advocate for and practitioner of democracy, an especially important value for Hsing Yun and, on the other hand, it is clear that Hsing Yun heavily influenced the RAC elections, giving strong hints to voters about his preferred candidates.[3] Due to Hsing Yun's advanced age, poor health, and the fact that no other Fo Guang Shan leader has emerged to take his position, it is likely that the RAC election process has become more democratic. The second reason that Hsing Yun espoused the democratic election for the RAC is so that the institution would remain up to date with the times as younger candidates were elected to the committee.

Research on Fo Guang Shan often points out that females dominantly outnumber males, both in total monastics and lay members. In a somewhat dated chapter on Fo Guang Shan, André Laliberté notes that the monastic community includes 1,000 nuns to only 300 monks.[4] A more recent article goes even further in its claim that about 90 percent of Fo Guang Shan monastics are female and also indicates that it is likely that women lay members outnumber men.[5] Thus, it is no surprise that nuns do serve on the RAC and in other positions of power (i.e., administrative and management roles) within the organization; however, no woman has ever served as the head abbot of Fo Guang Shan. At the same time, Fo Guang Shan has removed many of the traditional patriarchal monastic codes for nuns (e.g., nuns do not have to bow to monks of equal rank), and Hsing Yun has supported and promoted many nuns throughout his tenure with Fo Guang Shan.[6] Nevertheless, it remains notable that the RAC has never elected a female head abbot, especially given the first female president of the Republic of China, Tsai Ing-wen 蔡英文, was elected in 2016.

Buddha's Light International Association. Buddha's Light International Association (BLIA) is Fo Guang Shan's voluntary lay organization. BLIA gives lay members opportunities to serve alongside Fo Guang Shan monastics and helps decide and plan the future programs and services Fo Guang Shan offers. Hsing Yun founded BLIA in 1992 and three years later claimed that the membership had reached one million members.[7] More recent estimates have suggested around six million members within the total Fo Guang Shan community.[8] BLIA is currently headquartered at Hsi Lai Temple, and there are more than 200 chapters around the world.[9] The United Nations officially recognized BLIA as a nongovernmental organization in 2003.

Although BLIA is intended as a lay organization, it is common that Fo Guang Shan monastics serve in positions of power. According to at least one BLIA member who is officially recognized as a "Dharma Teacher" (i.e., allowed to give sermons at Fo Guang Shan temples), lay members clearly remain subordinate to monastics within the organization.[10] However, when looking at the members of the sixteen standing committees, it appears that lay members are very active participants.[11] There are thirty-three lay members on the sixteen different standing committees to just nine monastics. Including lay and monastics, there are twenty-seven women and fifteen men serving on the committees, which range in topics from social charity, scholarship, and international outreach to committees on the arts, children's education, and BLIA Scouts (a similar organization to the Boy Scouts of America). The organization holds an annual World Congress, and over 2,000 BLIA members attended in 2018 from nearly one hundred countries.[12]

Fo Guang Shan and BLIA are quick to advertise their global membership, but it is likely that the majority of BLIA members are located in Taiwan.[13] Because BLIA has not released any exact numbers, it is hard to determine exact totals and demographics of their members, but it is assumed that the largest BLIA chapter outside Taiwan is in Los Angeles and based out of Hsi Lai. That region accounts for twenty-three subchapters totaling around 1,800 BLIA members, the majority of which are Taiwanese Americans.[14]

According to the January 2019 BLIA Bulletin, worldwide entry fees for BLIA members are standardized at US$20, which includes a membership card and member handbook.[15] Each chapter determines their own annual dues, however, based on their own financial contexts. There are many FAQ pages for various BLIA chapters online, and all promote the BLIA mission to globalize the dharma, practice humaneness and compassion, and increase members' wisdom of Buddhist teachings. In addition, BLIA members receive privileges including special functions or rituals for birthdays, funerals, and weddings, and they may apply to reside on the main Fo Guang Shan campus to volunteer or apply for financial aid during periods of hardship.[16]

FO GUANG SHAN PROPERTIES

Fo Guang Shan boasts an impressive global network of temples and properties that places it among the largest Buddhist organizations in the world. There are over 200 temples, education centers, hostels, and monastic retreats around the globe in the Fo Guang Shan network. The organization is represented on every continent save Antarctica. The headquarters remain the main Fo Guang Shan campus in Kaohsiung, Taiwan, where leaders and the rest of the community regularly return for meetings, conferences, and retreats. This section will take a closer look at the main campus of Fo Guang Shan and its first chief temple in North America, Hsi Lai Temple.

Fo Guang Shan Main Campus. Fo Guang Shan Monastery is a sprawling property that features a wide array of religious buildings and offices providing services to support the monastery's humanistic missions. The monastery sponsors or operates schools, lodges and dormitories, retirement communities, columbariums, medical clinics, and more, both on and off its main campus. However, given its status as a working monastery, the majority of buildings are dedicated to facilitating the Fo Guang Shan monastics or hosting guests on retreat. Hsing Yun's own personal residence and office are also on the main campus. The main monastery began construction in 1967 in a rural area outside Kaohsiung, near where Hsing Yun had been working since his move to Taiwan. The land (originally close to seventy-five acres) he purchased for the project was completely undeveloped, and its hilly, densely overgrown landscape made the construction doubly difficult. In the fifty-plus years since then, the main campus of Fo Guang Shan has seen continual development to house its thousands of monastics and entertain its millions of visitors.

The main campus features several attractions to welcome visitors. Hsing Yun wants guests to experience the grounds as if they were a pure land on earth. Among its many shrines featuring a number of buddhas and bodhisattvas, the most notable for many tourists is the Great Buddha Land (*Dafo cheng* 大佛城). Four hundred eighty life-size buddha statues surround a 130-foot statue of a golden Amitabha. The statue faces the main highway leading to Fo Guang Shan and welcomes guests and blesses them as they travel past the monastery. It was completed in 1975 and was the largest standing Amitabha statue in the world at that time, though it has since been surpassed. Nevertheless, the statue was a central tourist attraction for Fo Guang Shan and Taiwan for decades. Like many notable buddha icons, the statue features in several miraculous tales that demonstrate its auspiciousness. The Pure Land Cave (*jingtu dongku* 淨土洞窟) is another long-lasting tourist attraction that has welcomed and entertained guests since its opening in 1981. The human-made "cave" treats guests to a show in which buddhas and bodhisattvas welcome them to Amitabha's Pure Land and illustrates the blessings they will receive upon their rebirth there. It is said that Hsing Yun's experience of Disney's "It's a Small World" ride inspired the attraction, which mimics its campy appeal.[17]

Although the Fo Guang Shan main campus became a tourist destination that brought development and tourist income into the region, the monastery and local area have not always had a positive relationship. Local residents have claimed that Fo Guang Shan is not as generous as it should be, while Fo Guang Shan has criticized residents for not being grateful for the services they provide to the area.[18] These tense relations came to a head in 1997 when Hsing Yun decided to close the monastery to outside guests. This decision was at least in part a result of the failed presidential campaign of Chen Lüan 陳履安, an outsider candidate who Fo Guang Shan openly supported. The organization's support rankled many Taiwanese, and Fo Guang Shan faced significant backlash after the 1996 election.[19] In addition, the shuttering of the monastery reminded both the public and the Fo Guang Shan monastics that the grounds were first and foremost a working monastery, perhaps a message that had been forgotten or made secondary in the three decades it had been welcoming tourists and local residents. Fo Guang Shan slowly reopened to the public three years later, in 2000, when it claims Taiwan's then president, Chen Shui-bian 陳水扁, on behalf of Taiwan's citizens, requested the monastery to reopen.[20] It was likely during this time that Hsing Yun began to envision a separate space that would allow the monastery to thrive while also welcoming tourists.

In 1998, a group of exiled Tibetan Buddhists gave Hsing Yun a tooth relic of the Buddha in thanks and celebration of Fo Guang Shan's efforts to spread the dharma. A series of massive celebrations welcomed the tooth relic to Taiwan and raised the profile of Hsing Yun and Fo

Guang Shan even higher. Irritated by the connection of Taiwan and the Tibetan Buddhists, Chinese authorities tried to undermine the authenticity of the relic. In response, Fo Guang Shan disassociated the gift from any connection with the Dalai Lama.[21] Undaunted, Hsing Yun wanted to create a special place to house the relic and initially considered constructing a large stupa in Yilan County.[22] It was ultimately decided to build a large museum and tourist center directly behind the main campus of Fo Guang Shan. The groundbreaking took place in 2003 and the Fo Guang Shan Buddha Museum opened fully in 2011. Since then, a major tourism campaign has directed guests to the museum, allowing the monastery more space to operate, though guests may still visit the grounds. According to the Tourism Bureau of Taiwan, over 7.4 million people visited the Fo Guang Shan main campus in 2017, significantly more than any other Buddhist site in Taiwan.[23] Despite over fifty years of existence, Fo Guang Shan remains a top tourist destination.

In true Fo Guang Shan fashion, the Buddha Museum is much more than a standard museum. In addition to housing the tooth relic and other Buddhist artifacts in its main hall, there are eight large pagodas on the grounds that lead guests toward the Fo Guang Big Buddha (*foguang dafo* 佛光大佛). The bronze Gautama Buddha sits on a lotus throne, and at over 350 feet, it easily surpasses the height of the original Amitabha statue on the main campus. There are also forty-eight "underground palaces" that Hsing Yun has envisioned as time capsules that store religious and culture relics. Guests can peruse the grounds and relax at one of the teahouses and pavilions, all while learning about Buddhism. In a *Taiwan Today* feature on the museum's inauguration, Miao Kai 妙開, a notable master in the Fo Guang Shan community, suggests "Visiting the center is the equivalent of reading a book on Buddhism and its development."[24]

The main campus in Kaohsiung is the heartbeat of Fo Guang Shan. The majority of its monastic population reside on the main campus, and many within its global community were trained there or visit regularly. The material resources that Fo Guang Shan has poured into its development are evident to any visitor. As Hsing Yun and Fo Guang Shan rapidly expanded in the latter half of the 20th century, however, a global ambition to spread the dharma emerged. Hsing Yun began to envision a truly transnational Fo Guang Shan that not only served the Chinese diaspora around the world, but also served and welcomed all humans.

Hsi Lai Temple. Hsing Yun first came to the United States as it celebrated its bicentennial in 1976. While spending time in California, Chinese immigrants who had settled in the area requested that he build a Fo Guang Shan branch there. Although initially reluctant, Hsing Yun decided to move forward and selected a group of monastics to search for property. They eventually purchased a church as the first meeting place for the California Fo Guang Shan community. Shortly after, however, Fo Guang Shan purchased fourteen acres in Hacienda Heights, an eastern suburb of Los Angeles.

As the land was cleared, and architects began to process Hsing Yun's vision for the temple, the project gained attention in the local community. After the locals expressed concern about the project, the local government held a number of public hearings and negotiations to allow representatives for the temple to answer questions and introduce themselves to the community. Local concerns about the project mostly stemmed from xenophobic fears about a foreign Buddhist community building a temple in a traditional

Chinese architectural style. The home of one Hsi Lai nun was firebombed within a year of the temple's opening in 1988.[25]

During temple construction, the growing Hsi Lai community tried to maintain a low profile in the community with the exception of a public relations campaign that sought to win over the locals. Hsing Yun went to work on a charm offensive that targeted local, state, and national political leaders. He was successful in this endeavor as he was welcomed to perform purifying rituals at the opening of the December 1988 California legislature session, and President Reagan sent representatives to the official opening of Hsi Lai Temple that same year. Hsing Yun's contacts with national political leaders came into the spotlight after Hsi Lai Temple hosted a fundraiser for Al Gore while he was running for president in 1996. What Hsing Yun viewed as politics as usual based on his experiences in Taiwan came under intense scrutiny in the United States. Due to Hsi Lai's status as a tax-exempt religious organization, the fundraiser was deemed to have violated campaign finance laws. Moreover, an investigation performed by the United States Department of Justice debated whether the People's Republic of China was trying to influence US elections through events like the Hsi Lai fundraiser, which was ultimately inconclusive. Hsing Yun, Hsi Lai Temple, and Al Gore all denied any wrongdoing. The story received widespread media attention and still emerges as a top result on internet searches for "Hsi Lai Temple."

The construction of the temple reportedly cost US$30 million. The design of the temple emulated Fo Guang Shan's classic Chinese architectural style. Although some locals remained suspicious of the temple after its opening, it soon became a tourist attraction that economically benefited the area, not unlike the original Fo Guang Shan temple in Kaohsiung. The temple remains among the largest Buddhist temples in North America and welcomes hundreds of thousands visitors annually. Like Fo Guang Shan, Hsi Lai Temple has many points of interest. Its notable gateway welcomes visitors as they enter the property. The Arhat and Avalokitesvara Gardens are reminiscent of the Great Buddha Land and Pure Land Cave on the Fo Guang Shan campus. There are also similar shrines, halls, meditation centers, and teahouses on the property.

Hsi Lai, which translates as "Coming [to the] West," has succeeded in bringing Hsing Yun's humanistic Buddhism to North America. In addition to Hsi Lai, there are more than twenty other branches of Fo Guang Shan in North America. As of 2019, Hsi Lai Temple claims it has around 12,000 members and the temple offers a variety of programming to accommodate its membership.[26] Like temples throughout Asia, Hsi Lai is busiest during the Lunar New Year, when families visit en masse to participate in the numerous services the temple hosts. According to the temple, over 230,000 guests visit Hsi Lai each year. Although temple visitors come from all backgrounds, the majority of the members are first-generation immigrants who speak Mandarin.[27] One Hsi Lai official estimated that 90 percent of their members speak Chinese, indicating that the temple is largely supported by the robust Asian American community in Hacienda Heights and the surrounding area.[28]

Increasingly, Fo Guang Shan branch temples like Hsi Lai are growing more diverse than the temples in Taiwan. Although the majority of these branch temples are Taiwanese, increasingly emigrants from other nations are joining Fo Guang Shan. Chinese from the People's Republic of China are the second-largest group of members at Hsi Lai, and their numbers continue to rise in other Fo Guang Shan branches.[29] The rise of PRC Chinese membership might be a result of Hsing Yun's friendly affiliation with the Chinese Communist Party and controversial statements that seem to suggest reunification of Taiwan and China. Despite the political tension between Taiwan and China, these diaspora communities choose to put aside those differences in the temple setting.

Lay members of Hsi Lai participate in the community through social community outreach programs and volunteering at the temple. Many of the largest services and rituals happen during weekends, and around one hundred volunteers help operate the temple, suggesting a strong base of relatively affluent members. Many of these members appreciate the "orthodoxy" of Fo Guang Shan temples in contrast to folk religious practices that both the early Kuomintang (KMT) and Communist Party of China (CPC) often labeled as superstition.[30]

Fo Guang Shan has emulated the success of Hsi Lai Temple on other continents. Two other notable chief temples that serve as the continental headquarters for Fo Guang Shan and their affiliated BLIA groups are Nan Tien Temple 南天寺 in Wollongong, Australia, and Nan Hua Temple 南華寺 in Bronkhorstspruit, South Africa, which features more lay members from China than Taiwan.[31] Nan Tien opened in 1995 and Nan Hua opened a decade later. Like Hsi Lai Temple, the construction costs for these temples were well into the tens of millions of dollars. Their locations—just outside major destination cities—and traditional Chinese architectural designs have ensured their status as tourist landmarks that attract large crowds. These temples, including Hsi Lai, enjoy strong reputations on online tourism sites like Tripadvisor that encourage and perpetuate more tourism.

EDUCATION ENDEAVORS AND TECHNOLOGY

Education, technology, and entertainment are three main methods that Fo Guang Shan has focused on in order to expand their reach in Taiwan and abroad. It is no coincidence that Fo Guang Shan uses these methods: many of Hsing Yun's early jobs on the mainland and in Taiwan positioned him in schools as an educator or administrator. He was also among the first monastics to accept and use many of the emerging technologies during his lifetime. As a result, educational facilities and media outlets make up a significant portion of the Fo Guang Shan empire.

Education. Fo Guang Shan supports or operates educational facilities at every level of education, from primary to graduate studies. Many of its primary schools are located in Taiwan, though it is also common for the chief temples to be affiliated with a primary school that offers elementary through high school education. For example, Buddha's Light Hsi Lai High School is an affiliate of Hsi Lai Temple in Hacienda Heights. Although these schools have secular curricula, many of the schools supplement it with afterschool programs that focus on traditional Chinese and Buddhist culture. Even where there are no Fo Guang Shan–affiliated schools, branch temples often offer these afterschool services or youth groups that are attractive to Chinese immigrants in that community who want their children to be exposed to their ancestral cultures. It is also common for schools and temples to host traditional Chinese festivals and summer camps that attract the local community and encourage them to support additional temple and school programming.

Hsi Lai University, Fo Guang Shan's first university, opened in 1990, just a few years after the opening of Hsi Lai Temple. In 2004, its name was changed to the University of the West. The Western Association of Schools and Colleges granted the university accreditation in 2006. The university campus eventually settled in Rosemead, California, near Hsi Lai Temple in Hacienda Heights, where its first courses were held. Hsing Yun served as president of the university for several years after its opening, before eventually passing on the title to traditionally qualified candidates. According to the National Center for Education Statistics, the enrollment for the college is often below 500 students, and a significant number of those students are Fo Guang Shan monastics seeking to gain an education.[32] Two reports published by the University of the West indicate that the graduate student population outnumbers the undergraduate population and that over 70 percent of graduate students are of Asian ethnicity.[33]

University of the West is part of the Fo Guang Shan University Consortium, which is the collective body of all Fo Guang Shan institutions of higher learning. The consortium consists of four other colleges in addition to University of the West: Fo Guang University in Yilan County in northern Taiwan, Nan Hua University in Chiayi County in central Taiwan, Guan Ming College in Manila of The Philippines, and Nan Tien Graduate Institute in Wollongong, Australia. Like University of the West, the Nan Tien Graduate Institute is affiliated with the chief temple in the Oceania region. Guan Ming College opened in 2014 and offers free tuition to students who want to pursue a Bachelor of Arts in Buddhist Studies or a Bachelor of Performing Arts in Dance or Theater. Despite being the eponymous university, Fo Guang University opened in 2000, four years after Nan Hua University in 1996. Nan Hua's enrollment—reportedly around 5,500 students—outpaces FGU by close to 2,000 students and accordingly offers more degrees to its larger student body.[34]

Fo Guang Shan also operates a number of monastic academies for monastics who want serious training and preparation for joining the Fo Guang Shan monastic community and rising up its monastic ranks. Like monastic life, these academies separate monks and nuns. In addition to their highly organized and demanding monastic education, academy students often have chores around campus or the affiliated temples and monasteries. As a result, attrition is somewhat common, the quality of the education is sometimes questioned, and critics have suggested that the academies exploit student labor.[35]

Entertainment and Technology. Hsing Yun and many of the branch temples of Fo Guang Shan have a significant presence on the Internet and various social media platforms. Even a cursory review of the online posts of these institutions would reveal that there are a number of entertaining festivals and shows that the local community hosts in order to bring in both members and visitors. Throughout Fo Guang Shan history, Hsing Yun has often combined entertainment with the latest technologies in order to propagate the dharma and increase membership.

Fo Guang Shan owns and operates a media empire that instantly connects its global membership. Even before the rise of digital and instant media, Hsing Yun was an early adopter of media platforms in order to spread his message. He frequently appeared on radio programs during his early days in Taiwan. In addition to his radio presence, he was a prolific author. From 1994 to 2013, he commonly authored multiple books each year; several of these books have been translated into multiple languages to serve Fo Guang Shan's global community. Fo Guang Shan's own publishing houses release these books, often run out of the major temples. Hsi Lai Temple hosts Buddha's Light Publications in the United States, which produces Fo Guang Shan literature in English. Buddhist reference works including encyclopedias and dictionaries are published regularly. Hsing Yun has launched a number of periodicals as well. *Universal Gate* (*pumen* 普门) began in 1980 and features scholarly work about Buddhism. The *Merit Times* (*renjian fubao* 人間福報) is a daily newspaper that updates Fo Guang Shan members on the most recent happenings around the global community. Several different kinds of literature are featured in the Fo Guang Publishing House offerings, from scholarly translations and commentaries of Buddhist scriptures to comic books and children's literature.

Fo Guang Shan's media output is not limited to print media, however. Hsing Yun began *Buddha's Light TV* in 1997, a station dedicated to propagating the dharma to its television audience. The station was renamed *Beautiful Live TV* (*renjian weishi* 人間衛視) in 2002. The programming consists of uplifting news programming and recordings of dharma talks, and even features a digitally animated child monk (who strongly resembles Hsing Yun) cartoon to entertain its younger viewers. Although the station only airs in Taiwan, it is increasingly available due to satellite and Internet capability. Much of the programming has been available on the station's app, iBLTV, which was released in December 2017. Another phone app is *Fo Guang Go!*, an augmented reality app that visitors to Fo Guang Shan can use to tour and interact with the main campus. The app features the digitally animated child monk from the cartoon who guides users around Fo Guang Shan while giving them facts about each stop along the tour.

Like their physical facilities, Fo Guang Shan's media output is impressive in scale. Not all of Fo Guang Shan's entertainment programming uses technology, however. Youth and community choirs are a common feature at many Fo Guang Shan temples. Their performances are a staple at many of the festivals hosted at the temples. In one notable case, members of the Fo Guang Shan temple in Manila created and performed a musical based on Hsing Yun's biography of the Buddha entitled *Siddhartha: A Musical Journey to Enlightenment.* Like many religious communities, the Fo Guang Shan community engages its members and attracts visitors using entertainment, though the degree to which Fo Guang Shan produces entertainment through its publishing house, cable-satellite channel, phone apps, and seasonal festivals is far beyond the capabilities of many religious communities.

REVIEW OF LITERATURE

Several scholarly studies of Fo Guang Shan were released in the early 2000s, but very few have been published since then. The recent scarcity is likely due to the wide scope and high quality of studies released during that earlier period. Many of the studies profile Fo Guang Shan as a central part of the Buddhist revival in the late 20th century. Others note the organization's connection to the nation-state as it negotiated tense relations with the mainland. There are only a couple of ethnographic accounts of Fo Guang Shan, which provide the most complete study of Fo Guang Shan to date. This section will briefly review these scholarly contributions.

Stuart Chandler has conducted the most thorough research on Fo Guang Shan. His work emerged out of his ethnographic research that took place in the mid-1990s, an especially booming period for Fo Guang Shan. He conducted dozens of interviews and used them to create the seminal work on the organization, *Establishing a Pure Land on Earth: The Foguang Buddhist Perspective on Modernization and Globalization*. The book was a major information source for this entry and provides great detail on many of the points mentioned. Chandler has authored a few articles on Fo Guang Shan as well, though they are mostly woven into his book. In a 2018 article, "Sacred Secularities: Ritual and Social Engagement in a Global Buddhist China," Jens Reinke shares his ethnographic research of Hsi Lai Temple. The article highlights how the temple's ritual service and social programming connect the Chinese diaspora community it serves.

Richard Madsen profiles Fo Guang Shan comparatively alongside the other Buddhist organizations that emerged in Taiwan in the mid-20th century. In the third chapter of his book, *Democracy's Dharma: Religious Renaissance and Political Development in Taiwan*, he notes how Fo Guang Shan helped contribute a civic cultural identity to the emerging nation-state through its popular programs and temples. Echoing Max Weber, Madsen notes how Fo Guang Shan has grown and expanded in conjunction with the growth of the Taiwan's new middle class. This reciprocal relationship supplies both the organization and the people with economic and spiritual needs, respectively, and how that relationship benefits Taiwan as a whole. The strength of Madsen's work is his contextualization of Fo Guang Shan amid the other Buddhist groups that emerged in Taiwan over the same period.

In the same vein to Madsen's point about how organizations like Fo Guang Shan interact with the state, other researchers have highlighted that connection. André Laliberté's work considers how the politics of Buddhist organizations including Fo Guang Shan aligns or contrasts with the state. Laliberté suggests that these moments of dissent with the government are remonstrant demonstrations. Although Hsing Yun has mostly sided with the KMT since his time in Taiwan, there have been a few notable instances where he opposed their candidates for political office. Charles B. Jones provided one of the earliest profiles of Fo Guang Shan in his *Buddhism in Taiwan: Religion and the State, 1660–1990*. He focuses on the interactions between Fo Guang Shan and the Buddhist Association of the Republic of China (BAROC), a conservative group of Buddhists in Taiwan that sometimes clashed with Hsing Yun's progressive humanistic Buddhism. Although scholarly studies of Fo Guang Shan are currently adequate, several are beginning to show their age. It will soon be necessary to revisit and initiate new studies of the organization. Their growth has slowed significantly since the 2000s, which is likely due to the recent global recession as well as Hsing Yun's advancing age. As Hsing Yun nears the end of his life and Fo Guang Shan moves on after his passing, it will be interesting to see what the future holds for the organization. It will be necessary for scholars to highlight that transitional phase and document the changes likely to take place. The reform and opening of mainland China has led many scholars to study modern religion there, resulting in far more research on Chinese Buddhism that profiles mainland sects. However, given Taiwan's quick economic rise and recent stagnation, studies that chronicle how organizations like Fo Guang Shan have handled the last two decades would be welcomed.

PRIMARY SOURCES

As noted in the main essay, Hsing Yun's catalog is prolific, and many of his works have been translated in various languages. The majority of these are available in libraries and online. This section highlights three selections from Hsing Yun's recent publications. The first introduces the reader to Buddhist thought as taught and understood by Hsing Yun. The next book is a beginner's guide to practicing Buddhism. The last book sees Hsing Yun modeling Thich Nhat Hanh's style, in which Buddhism is disguised as a self-help book for those seeking a more fulfilling life. Lastly, Hsing Yun's biography published through the official Fo Guang Shan organ is essential reading. Additionally, anyone interested in the Fo Guang Shan published print materials should visit the University of the West Library.

Fu Chi-ying. *Handing Down the Light: The Biography of Venerable Master Hsing Yun*. Translated by Amy Lui-ma. Hacienda Heights, CA: Buddha's Light Publishing, 2003.

Hsing Yun. *The Core Teachings*. Hacienda Heights, CA: Buddha's Light Publishing, 2016.

Hsing Yun. *For All Living Beings: A Guide to Buddhist Practice*. Hacienda Heights, CA: Buddha's Light Publishing, 2010.

Hsing Yun. *The Carefree Life*. Hacienda Heights, CA: Buddha's Light Publishing, 2004.

DIGITAL MATERIAL

FoGuangPedia is a digital archive for resources associated with Fo Guang Shan. The site grants access to the latest news and publications from Fo Guang Shan. It also hosts a relevant wiki that users can edit, learn, and share. Additionally, the site collects translated excerpts of many of Hsing Yun's works.

FURTHER READING

Chandler, Stuart. *Establishing a Pure Land on Earth: The Foguang Buddhist Perspective on Modernization and Globalization*. Honolulu: University of Hawai'i Press, 2004.

Chung, Oscar. "Buddha's Light Shines Brighter." *Taiwan Today*, April 1, 2012.

Clart, Philip, and Charles B. Jones. *Religion in Modern Taiwan: Tradition and Innovation in a Changing Society*. Honolulu: University of Hawai'i Press, 2003.

Johnson, Ian. "Is a Buddhist Group Changing China? Or Is China Changing It?" *The New York Times*, June 24, 2017.

Jones, Charles B. *Buddhism in Taiwan: Religion and the State, 1660–1990*. Honolulu: University of Hawai'i Press, 1999.

Kuo, Cheng-Tian. *Religion and Democracy in Taiwan*. Albany: State University of New York Press, 2008.

Laliberté, André. *The Politics of Buddhist Organizations in Taiwan: 1989–2003*. New York: Routledge Curzon, 2004.

Madsen, Richard. *Democracy's Dharma: Religious Renaissance and Political Development in Taiwan*. Berkeley: University of California Press, 2007.

Reinke, Jens. "Sacred Secularities: Ritual and Social Engagement in a Global Buddhist China." *Religions* 9, no. 11 (2018): 338.

Yao, Yu-Shuang, and Richard Gombrich. "Christianity as Model and Analogue in the Formation of the 'Humanistic' Buddhism of Tai Xu and Hsing Yun." *Buddhist Studies Review* 34, no. 2 (2017): 205–237.

NOTES

1. Stuart Chandler, *Establishing a Pure Land on Earth: The Foguang Buddhist Perspective on Modernization and Globalization* (Honolulu: University of Hawai'i Press, 2004), 213–220.
2. Chandler, *Pure Land*, 213.
3. Chandler, *Pure Land*, 217–218.
4. André Laliberté, *The Politics of Buddhist Organizations in Taiwan: 1989–2003* (New York: Routledge Curzon, 2004), 84.
5. Yu-Shuang Yao and Richard Gombrich, "Christianity as Model and Analogue in the Formation of the 'Humanistic' Buddhism of Tai Xu and Hsing Yun." *Buddhist Studies Review* 34, no. 2 (2017): 205–237, 216.
6. Laliberté, *Buddhist Organizations*, 84.
7. Laliberté, *Buddhist Organizations*, 82.
8. Yao and Gombrich, "Christianity as Model": 215.
9. http://www.bliango.org.
10. Cheng-Tian Kuo, *Religion and Democracy in Taiwan* (Albany: State University of New York Press, 2008), 24.
11. BLIA.org.
12. BLIA.org, "The 2018 BLIA World Conference Opening Ceremony Displays 'We Are One' Spirit."
13. Laliberté, *Buddhist Organizations*, 82.
14. Jens Reinke, "Sacred Secularities: Ritual and Social Engagement in a Global Buddhist China." *Religions* 9, no. 11 (2018): 3.
15. BLIA.org, "BLIA World Headquarters December 2018-January 2019 Bulletin."
16. Chandler, *Pure Land*, 193.
17. Chandler, *Pure Land*, 11.
18. Chandler, *Pure Land*, 18–20.
19. Laliberté, *Buddhist Organizations*, 75–77.
20. Laliberté, *Buddhist Organizations*, 71.
21. Zhenggao Su 蘇正國, "'兩岸' 星雲大師：佛牙源自貢噶多傑" ("'Two coasts' Master Hsing Yun: Buddha tooth came from Kunga Rinpoche"). *新新聞* (*The Journalist*). August 17, 2011.
22. Richard Madsen. *Democracy's Dharma: Religious Renaissance and Political Development in Taiwan*. (Berkeley: University of California Press, 2007), 56.
23. Tourism Bureau MOTC Republic of China, "106年1至12月國內主要觀光遊憩據點遊客人數統計" ("2017 January–December visitors to main scenic spots in Taiwan").
24. Oscar Chung, "Buddha's Light Shines Brighter." *Taiwan Today*, April 1, 2012.
25. *Los Angeles Times*, "Local: Buddhist Priest Home Fire-Bombed," July 3, 1989.
26. Email correspondence with Hsi Lai Clergy. April 2019.
27. Reinke, "Sacred Secularities," 3.
28. Email correspondence with Hsi Lai Clergy. April 2019.
29. Reinke, "Sacred Secularities," 3.
30. Reinke, "Sacred Secularities," 7–8.
31. Reinke, "Sacred Secularities," 10.
32. National Center for Education Statistics.
33. University of the West, "Fall Student Headcount 7 Year Trend" and "Student Population by Ethnicity November 2013."
34. Nanhua University. Fo Guang University. "近 5 年學校學生人數與變動趨勢圖" ("Five year student enrollment trends report").
35. Chandler, *Pure Land*, 122–123.

Kendall Marchman

FOUR NOBLE TRUTHS

THE FOUR NOBLE TRUTHS AS A FUNDAMENTAL TEACHING

The four noble truths are one of the key teachings of the buddha's first talk after his enlightenment, according to the *vinaya* and sutta/sutra literature of the early Hinayana schools, preserved in the Pali Buddhist canon. This narrative that identifies the four noble truths as the first talk of the buddha belongs to the early Hinayana tradition, and recent scholarship suggests that the primacy of this teaching was not shared by all Buddhist schools as Buddhism spread throughout India and the rest of Asia.[1] The story of Gautama Buddha's enlightenment and first talk on dhamma/dharma is found in the Pali, Mahīśāsaka, and Dharmaguptaka canons, the latter two of which we have in Chinese.[2] When the four noble truths are said to be a fundamental teaching of the buddha and thus of all of Buddhism, this is one answer that early Buddhists gave to the question "What did the Buddha teach?" As European scholarship has traced the spread of Buddhism with greater accuracy since the late 20th century, scholars have begun to trace the historical emergence of Buddhist teachings with greater precision. The buddha's talk on "The Turning of the Dhamma Wheel" is one such teaching. Contrary to assumptions that locate the buddha's teaching on the four noble truths at the heart of all schools of Buddhism, Dessein has demonstrated that there is a range of interpretations in the early schools of Buddhism. The narrative found in the *vinaya* and sutta portions of the Pali canon, however, is the one widely recognized to be the first talk of the buddha (*Vin* I.1 and *S* V.420).

The story of Gautama Buddha's first talk on dhamma/dharma (Pali/Sanskrit) after his enlightenment is well known throughout Buddhist literature, primarily from the "Talk on the Turning of the Dhamma Wheel" (*Dhammacakkappavattana Sutta*) in the Pali Buddhist canon: five companions of the buddha were gathered in Deer Park in Sarnath, outside of ancient Bārāṇasi (now Varanasi), and the buddha approached them to tell them of his awakening.[3] The buddha began his talk on dhamma (*dhammakathā*) by explaining that there are two extremes to be avoided: devotion to sensual pleasures and devotion to ascetic practices. Between these two poles, the buddha continues, lies the middle way, which consists of the noble eightfold path: right view, right intent, right speech, right action, right living, right effort, right mindfulness, and right concentration. The buddha explains that this path leads to "insight, knowledge, calm, higher knowledge, enlightenment, and *nibbāna*"—in short, the eightfold path leads to enlightenment. With the next sentence the buddha begins explain to the first noble truth: "this is pain" (*idaṃ dukkhaṃ*), and continues with the second, third, and fourth truths. Each truth is laid out in three ways: the buddha states that he, first, came to know that he had to realize the truth that was the truth of pain (future). Secondly, he states that he realizes the truth that was the truth of pain (present), and, third, he declares that he had realized the truth that was the truth of pain (past). These three tenses are the three ways in which the Buddha understood the four noble truths, and when they are multiplied by the four truths, we see the twelvefold way in which the buddha realized the four noble truths.

The buddha explains to his companions that once he realized and knew the fourth noble truths in the twelve ways, he realized that this life was his last rebirth and that he had no more births in the future. At that moment, inspired by this Dhamma Talk, one of his companions by the name of Aññā Koṇḍañña (i.e., "One among the Koṇḍañña clan who knows") cultivated a knowledge of the four noble truths and thereby became an enterer into the stream, or the first of four stages on the path to full awakening. At the end of this Dhamma Talk, the gods in the heavens and all beings throughout the cosmos proclaim that the wheel of dhamma has turned and that no one may turn it back. With this setting for the four noble truths in the "Talk on the Turning of the Dhamma Wheel," we see how the Buddhist traditions remembered the integral relationship between the buddha's own autobiographical experience of enlightenment and the act of teaching the four noble truths. As soon as one of the buddha's companions realized the truth of what the buddha had learned in his own enlightenment and taught in the "Talk on the Turning of the Dhamma Wheel," the wheel of dhamma was turned in the world and could not be turned back. Put differently, the wheel of dhamma was not turned when the buddha himself was enlightened: the wheel of dhamma was turned in the world only when Koṇḍañña, the first awakened follower of the buddha, experienced enlightenment. At the moment when Koṇḍañña became a stream-enterer, the "Talk on the Turning of the Dhamma Wheel" declares that a cosmological "noise or sound" (*saddaṃ*) was let loose throughout the heavens and echoed from one heaven to the next. This is how all Buddhist traditions remember that the wheel of dhamma was turned. Dessein points out that the version of this talk that appears in the *Dharmaguptakavinaya* (T.1428) does not refer to a wheel but does say "that when the World-honoured One [the Buddha] cannot make someone else awaken for the four noble truths, he does not set the wheel of the doctrine in motion."[4] The four noble truths are the most fundamental teaching of Buddhism because that teaching was the means by which Koṇḍaññā realized the path and thus the way that the buddha set the wheel of dhamma in motion for all humanity.

The symbol of the dhamma/dharma wheel is found throughout all of Buddhism and refers to the teachings of the buddha(s). The dhamma wheel is the wheel with four (rare), eight (common), and ten (unusual) spokes found on top of monasteries and temples throughout Buddhist cultures and as images on countless websites for a symbol of Buddhism; the eight spokes refer to the eightfold path and the wheel represents the Buddha's teachings, recalling the moment at which the wheel was turned. The symbol of the wheel turning was used by Buddhists to symbolize subsequent momentous points in Buddhist teachings. For example, as the biography of the buddha expanded to include the lives of past buddhas, each buddha turned the wheel of dhamma to spread the teachings for that buddha.[5] So, too, the teachings of the second turning of the wheel are recognized as articulated in the early Prajñāpāramitā sutras and in the commentarial tradition of the Madhyamaka.[6] The third turning of the wheel refers to the celestial setting of the *Saṃdhinirmocana Sūtra*, an Indian text that dates to the second century CE.[7] From the point of view of the second and third turnings of the wheel, each provides a different teaching on *śūnatā* or emptiness. There are occasional references to four and five turnings of the wheel, the latter usually in relation to the *Avataṁsaka-Sūtra*. In short, the first, second, and third turnings of the wheel of dhamma/dharma are powerful images and textual metaphors found throughout Mahayana literature. The actual physical symbol, as well as the textual metaphor of the turning of the dhamma/dharma wheel, is a powerful image that runs throughout Buddhist teachings and beyond.[8] Dessein suggests that a comparison of the different versions of the *Dharmacakrapravartana Sūtra/Dhammacakkappavattana-Sutta* reveals a far more complex history of the turning of the dharma wheel.[9] The earliest strata, relatively speaking, within the Buddhist canons included the teachings on the middle path

(Dessein translates this as the "middle mode of progress") that were connected to the four noble truths as the content of the first dharma talk of the Buddha. He suggests that the element of the "five companion monks" was introduced into the narrative as a link between this first sermon and the portion of the buddha's life as an ascetic, prior to his enlightenment. "Further philosophical development," Dessein continues, "led to the interpretation of these four noble truths in terms of 'three cycles' and 'twelve constituent parts.'"[10] From this point on, however, different schools differ in what they record as the setting for the first talk on dharma, and the content. The major difference between the schools, according to Dessein, lies in the point at which the schools consider the wheel of dharma to be turned. Briefly, Dessein demonstrates that the Vaibhāṣika and Sautrāntika schools of the Sarvāstivāda have different opinions about when the wheel first turned that set them apart from the Mahāsāṃghikas; while the Mahāsāṃghikas disagreed, the Vaibhāṣika and Sautrāntika claimed that the Mahāsāṃghika taught that the wheel was turned when the buddha gave his first talk under the bodhi tree immediately after his enlightenment.[11] Thoughout this excursion into the disagreements about when the dharma wheel was turned, however, the four noble truths remain a stable element in all of these variations.

WHAT THE FOUR NOBLE TRUTHS MEAN

When we read statements by such eminent Buddhist teachers as the Dalai Lama and Thich Nat Hahn describing the four noble truths as the most fundamental teaching of Buddhism, those declarations read like unequivocal and unproblematic assertions. And they are correct: seen from the point of view of the *Sutta on the Turning of the Dhamma Wheel*, the four noble truths are, indeed, the most important teaching of the historical buddha because they were the substance of his first talk on dharma to his five companions. In a much broader sense, too, the four noble truths are among the thirty-seven factors of enlightenment, another crucial category of Buddhist teachings. In terms of Buddhist pedagogy, to say that the four noble truths are a fundamental teaching is, again, an accurate statement: they are the substance of the buddha's first "*dhamma kathā*," or talk on Buddhism. *Kathā*, in this sense, often gets translated as "sermon," so we often see references to the four noble truths as the buddha's first sermon on the four noble truths. We also need to recognize that many would claim that the four noble truths must be the most important doctrine of Buddhism. And here we run into some difficulties: the category of doctrine, usually in Christianity, is not the same thing as a "talk on dhamma" (*dhamma kathā*) in the Buddhist literature.[12] So when we begin to answer the question of what the four noble truths are, we need to use categories found in Buddhist sources, not categories such as doctrine (which come primarily from Christianity). According to the Pali canon, then, the four noble truths should be understood as right views (*sammā diṭṭhi*).

There are, according to scholar Steven Collins, three types of right views.[13] The first is a generalized sense of a positive attitude toward the basic ideas of karma and samsara within Buddhism. A practitioner at this stage has not experienced the truth of karma and samsara but is willing to consider that these are true teachings. The second type of right view means recognizing right view as the first "limb" of the eightfold path, along with such fundamental teachings as the four noble truths and the teachings on dependent origination (*paṭiccasamupāda*). The third type of right view, according to Collins, is that of full, liberating insight, which is the highest realization of right view: the wisdom and insight that lead to an experience of *nibbāna*. To know what the four noble truths are, then, we need to know that the four noble truths are, according to Buddhist frameworks of knowledge, true statements in the sense that they are taught by the buddha but whose truth is recognized gradually by individuals striving to understand the truth of the four noble truths, along with other key teachings of the buddha (including the eightfold path and dependent origination). At the first stage, we should regard the four noble truths with a generally positive attitude. At the second stage, we recognize the truth of the teaching on the four noble truths as a key component of all of the buddha's teachings. At the third stage, followers recognize the liberating insight of the four noble truths for themselves, as Koṇḍañña was enlightened upon hearing the buddha's first "Talk on the Turning of the Dhamma Wheel."

The Four Noble Truths in the Pali Canon. There is little to no debate in the Pali tradition about how we should understand the four noble truths. There is a strong agreement throughout the canonical texts and commentaries that carries through to contemporary teachings. One noteworthy observation is that the Pali explanations of each of the truths are rather brief. In many contemporary works on the four noble truths, however, the four noble truths become the framework by which other teachings of the buddha are taught. The buddha taught for forty-five years, and within that period, there is no single teaching that emerges as unquestionably more central than others—including the four noble truths. At the same time, learning the entirety of the buddha's teachings is a difficult task; even memorizing the thirty-seven factors of enlightenment is a challenge. It is natural, then, to use the four noble truths as a scaffold, if you will, to understand the central teachings of the buddha. The canonical explanations of each truth, however, are relatively brief, as we will see. Elsewhere in the canon and commentaries the individual truths are occasionally the subject of single *dhamma* talks, and in those talks, they are often explained with other teachings of the buddha not discussed in the explanations of the four noble truths as a set.

The four noble truths are often discussed as a medical diagnosis. Professor Gethin's introduction of the teaching follows this model: the subheading for his chapter on the four noble truths is "The Disease, the Cause, the Cure, the Medicine."[14] This is a very common metaphor that we find throughout contemporary writings on the four noble truths. At the same time, it is not a metaphor or an image that we find in the actual canonical teachings. The buddha uses the simile of a physician in such suttas as the *Cula-Malumkyovada Sutta* (M I 426), in which the buddha says that someone who asks questions about how the cosmos came to be (the ten unanswerable questions) is like a man shot with a poisoned arrow who refuses the attention of a surgeon or a doctor until he knows all details of how he was shot—both will die before they find the answers to their questions. Bhikkhu Thanissaro has assembled a study guide for the buddha's teachings on birth, illness, old age, and death under the title "Beyond Coping: The Buddha's Teachings on Aging, Illness, Death, and Separation," in which he includes the references to the buddha as a physician.[15] As persuasive as this image of the buddha as a physician is, we need to be cautious about drawing any conclusions from this metaphor about the relationship between Indian medical traditions and the actual practices of Buddhist medicine. The *vinaya* has extensive discussions about which medicines should be used for how long and by whom within the monasteries and nunneries. Kenneth Zysk's study of Buddhist medicine is the classic study on this topic; Wezler suggests that the teaching on the four noble truths may actually have influenced Hindu medical teachings.[16] Thus, the logical model of the buddha as a physician who diagnoses the problem of pain (*dukkha*), determines its cause (taṅhā or craving), and offers a cure (*nirodho* or stopping) and medicine (*magga* or *paṭipadā*, path or way) is a very compelling metaphor. It is not one, however, that we see closely tied to the four noble truths in the Pali canon or commentaries themselves, although we do see references to diagnosis in other canonical passages.

***The First Truth:* Dukkhaṃ.** In the *Sutta on the Turning of the Wheel of Dhamma*, the buddha explained the first truth at greater length than at other points in the Pali canon:

> This, monks, is the noble truth that is pain. Birth is pain, old age is pain, illness is pain, death is pain, sorrow and grief, physical and mental suffering, and disturbance are pain. Association with things not liked is pain, separation from desired things is pain, not getting what one wants is pain; in short, the five aggregates of grasping are pain.
> (*Vin* I.5–12; M I 55; D II 290; S V 420; commentary on *Vin* I.5–12 = *Sp* V.962–965)

This is the most expansive description of the first truth of the noble ones: the truth that is pain is birth, old age, illness, death, and so on. An important distinction should be made here: the first truth is not pain in and of itself, but rather the pain that is associated with all of the following conditions: birth is pain, death is pain, not getting what we want is pain, and so on. All of these conditions are characteristic of human life, and thus the first truth is often understood to mean that Buddhism claims that human life is associated with pain, or to use a term from the Abrahamic religions, human life is suffering. The Pāli term *dukkha* is most often translated as "suffering." However, it is more accurately construed as pain: *dukkha* refers to those things that hurt, that are painful. The four truths should be understood descriptively: the buddha was simply describing the truths—the ultimate and real truths—that he realized while sitting under the bodhi tree during his experience of enlightenment. The first truth, then, is not an argument or a debate about the fact that human life is painful. The first truth is an observation that human life is full of pain. What is painful? All of these things: birth, death, old age, illness, not getting what we want, having to deal with things that we don't want to deal with, and so on—all of these things are painful. And the truth of that pain, the fact of that pain, is the first truth. The passage in the Pali canon continues: "in short, the five aggregates of grasping are pain." The five aggregates are the aggregates of grasping or holding onto one's body, one's feelings, one's perceptions, one's formations, and one's consciousness. Taken together, these five aggregates of grasping represent the various ways that people come to the conclusion that there is an independent and permanent self or an "I." And all of these ways (grasping the body, feelings, perceptions, formations, and consciousness) are *dukkha*: pain or suffering.[17]

The teaching on pain is occasionally the subject of an independent talk on *dhamma* in the Pali canon, as in the short talk in the *Saṃyutta-nikāya* called the *Dukkha Sutta*. In that talk, Bhikkhu Thanissaro translates *dukkha* as "stress" and as "pain," which gives us a slightly different connotation: "there are three kinds of stress (*dukkhatā*): the stressfulness of fabrication (*dukkhadukkhatā*), the stressfulness of formations (*saṅkhāradukkhatā*), and the stressfulness of change (*vipariṇāmadukkhatā*)."[18] The *Acela Sutta* ("The Naked Ascetic") contains an exchange in which Kassapa approaches the buddha, asking him how *dukkha* is created: "Is stress self-made? . . . Is stress other-made? . . . Then is it both self-made and other made? . . . Then is it the case that stress, being neither self-made nor other made, arises spontaneously?" The buddha's answer to each of these questions is "Don't say that, Kassapa." Frustrated, Kassapa asks the buddha if *dukkha* exists; yes, the buddha replies. "Well, in that case, does Master Gotama not know or see stress?" "I know stress, I see stress," the buddha answers. The buddha finally gives a longer explanation, which is the twelvefold chain of dependent arising or origination (*paṭiccasamuppāda*).

> "The one who acts is the one who experiences [the result of the act]" amounts to the eternalist statement, "Existing from the very beginning, stress is self-made." "The one who acts is someone other than the one who experiences" amounts to the annihilationist statement, "For one existing harassed by feeling, stress is other-made." Avoiding these two extremes, the Tathagata teaches the dhamma via the middle:
>
> From ignorance as a requisite condition come fabrications.
> From fabrications as a requisite condition comes consciousness.
> From consciousness as a requisite condition comes name-and-form.
> From name-and-form as a requisite condition come the six sense media.
> From the six sense media as a requisite condition comes contact.
> From contact as a requisite condition comes feeling.
> From feeling as a requisite condition comes craving.
> From craving as a requisite condition comes clinging/sustenance.
> From clinging/sustenance as a requisite condition comes becoming.
> From becoming as a requisite condition comes birth.
> From birth as a requisite condition, then aging & death, sorrow, lamentation, pain, distress, and despair come into play. Such is the origination of this entire mass of stress and suffering. (S II.18)[19]

This sutta is an example of how the buddha's teachings intersect with each other. In this *dhamma* talk to Kassapa, the clothesless (or naked) ascetic, *dukkha* is explained in terms of the teaching on dependent arising. This is a teaching that is widely represented with paintings and images, each stage of the twelve steps represented as an equal segment of a circle. Moving forward, each step is one movement to another that traces the origins or causes that result in rebirth. Moving in reverse order, we learn how to deconstruct the chain of arising in order to be freed from the cycle of rebirth, or to attain enlightenment. This pairing of the analysis of arising and the analysis of ending is the same as that of the second and third truths and is often found as an independent explanation for the difference between the direct and reverse order of this teaching on dependent arising: all that arises, passes away.

The Second Truth:* Samudayo *(Arising). The second truth of the four noble truths is *samudayo*, or arising. In the *Sutta on the Turning of the Dhamma Wheel*, it reads: "This, monks, is the noble truth that is the arising of pain. This is craving that leads to rebirth, is connected with pleasure and passion and finds pleasure in this or that; that is, craving for desire, craving for existence, and craving for existence to fade away." This second truth is most often understood as laying out the causation of pain, the first truth. In short, what is the arising of pain? Craving is the short answer—human attachment to things that we want, to things that feel good in a mundane or daily sense as well as the fundamental human craving for desire, existence, or the fading away of existence. The second truth lays out these three kinds of craving: "craving for desire, existence, and the craving for existence to fade away." The first, craving for desire or "sense pleasures" (kāma), is familiar to all of us: one way of putting it is that we all want to love, we want to be in love, we want to desire life itself in a profound sense. We want things that make us feel good. The second kind of craving is equally straightforward: we want to live, we want to exist in the world, and we often want to exist permanently—we want to renew and continue our existence in the world or even in the heavens. But permanent existence is simply not part of the cosmos, according to Buddhist traditions. Nothing exists permanently, and to become attached to the idea of any kind of permanence is to sow the seeds of craving for existence and thus opens the door to the arising of pain.

The third kind of craving is perhaps more challenging to understand: we want our existence to ultimately fade away. Bhikkhu Thanissaro translates the term as "craving for our annihilation after death."[20] The compound itself "annihilation-craving" (*vibhava-taṇhā*) can be interpreted in a variety of ways, as one can readily determine by typing the word into any search engine. Classical interpretations of the craving for annihilation refer to the desire, the thirst, or the craving for nonexistence or annihilation, usually referring to the self. In this framework, the second and third types of craving are two poles that represent wrong thinking: the craving for permanent and renewable existence and the craving for nonexistence. The Buddhist response to these two kinds of craving is to say that we need to recognize our attachment or our thirst for both permanent existence and nonexistence, and to be attached to neither. Contemporary interpretations of craving for annihilation take the term as applicable to certain states, such as wanting certain emotional states to be annihilated. We can readily understand this type of craving in this contemporary sense, when we want our embarrassing or debilitating emotions to permanently disappear. Regardless of how the third type of craving is interpreted, the point in all Buddhist interpretations is to recognize the force of such craving in life, to watch, and to observe the force and the role of craving or thirst to better understand how pain arises on a daily basis.

The Third Truth:* Nirodho *(Ending). The third truth is *nirodho*, or ending. It is explained in the *Sutta on the Turning of the Dhamma Wheel*: "This, monks is the noble truth that is the ending of pain. This is the complete fading away and ending of that very craving, giving it up, renouncing it, releasing it, and letting go." This is a natural movement in the sequence of the truths thus far: the first is to recognize the truth "this is pain" or "this is suffering." The second step is to know why "this is pain." The three types of thirst or craving lead to things that cause us pain in this life. We stop that pain, we stop that hurting or suffering by stopping craving or thirst: "the complete fading away and ending of that very craving, giving it up, renouncing it, releasing it, and letting it go." This truth is just a simple fact: to end things that cause us pain, we need to end their arising. The pair of the second and third truths is often extracted into a separate formula in the Buddhist texts, as in the saying that Koṇḍañña uttered when he became a stream winner: "Whatever has the nature of arising, all that has the nature of ending."

Buddhaghosa was a late-4th- and early-5th-century commentator on the Pali canon who synthesized the buddha's teaching into a compendium of teachings known today by its popular translation as the *Path of Purification*. In that work, Buddhaghosa offers the following commentary on the third truth: "[*Nirodha* (cessation):] the word *ni* denotes absence, and the word *rodha*, a prison. Now, the third truth is void of all destinies [by rebirth] and so there is no constraint (*rodha*) of suffering here reckoned as the prison of the round of rebirths; or when that cessation has been arrived at, there is no more constraint of suffering reckoned as the prison of the round of rebirths. And being the opposite of that prison, it is called *dukkha-nirodha* (cessation of suffering). Or alternatively, it is called 'cessation of suffering' because it is a condition for the cessation of suffering consisting in non-arising."[21] Briefly, Buddhaghosa is explaining just how the third truth (*nirodho*) means "stopping" or "cessation." The key for Buddhaghosa is the term *rodho*, or prison. The prison of future births is simply stopped according to this third truth. When pain is stopped, or when suffering is ended, there is no more rebirth and there will be no more arising of pain or suffering.

The Fourth Truth:* Paṭipadā *(Way). The fourth truth, the way, according to the *Sutta on the Turning of the Dhamma Wheel*, reads:

> This, monks, is the noble truth that is the way leading to the ending of pain. This is the eightfold path of the noble ones: right view, right intention, right speech, right action, right livelihood, right effort, right mindfulness, and right concentration.

The fourth truth, again, follows logically after the first three: pain, arising, ending, and the way—or the how. The eightfold path is always found as the explanation of the fourth truth, and is often taken as the buddha's teaching of "the" path to enlightenment. It is more accurate to say that the eightfold path is one path among many that the buddha taught, although it is foundational within the Pali Buddhist tradition, often serving as a synonym for the word *path* (*maggo* or more commonly, *magga*). Each of the eight steps is explained at different points in the Pali canon and commentaries.[22] Buddhaghosa followed one particular explanatory framework found in the Middle Length Sayings collection in the Suttapiṭaka that classified the eightfold path into three stages: virtue or ethics (*silaṃ*), concentration (*samādhi*), and wisdom (*paññā*). Right speech, right action, and right livelihood are grouped under the heading of virtue or ethics. Right effort, right mindfulness, and right concentration are gathered under concentration, and right view and right intention are classified under wisdom. It is vital to understand that this is not a linear "path." Each of these steps is interdependent. For example, right concentration is sometimes explained in terms of the other seven stages of the eightfold path. The fourth truth is not always explained in Buddhist literature, but when it is, it is always laid out in terms of the eightfold path. So, too, the eightfold path often appears independent of the other three truths, as in the *Maggavibhaṅga Sutta* (Analysis of the Path) in the *Saṃyutta-nikāya* (S V.2).

There is a broader point to make here in relationship to the fourth truth. While the set of the four noble truths consistently teaches the eightfold path as the path to achieve the cessation of pain—that is, an experience of the state of nirvana—the concept of the "path" is far more expansive than the fourth truth. There are many paths in Buddhism, and while the fourth truth and the eightfold path are among the most common, the concept of *magga/mārga* is one of the most generative concepts in all of Buddhist thought. Perhaps it would be accurate to say that there are overlapping definitions of the "path leading to the ending of pain." Where the fourth truth is explained within the set of the four noble truths, it is consistently explained as the eightfold path. But the teachings on *magga/mārga* in the whole of Buddhism are far greater. The best volume on this point is now a classic, *Paths to Liberation: The Mārga and Its Transformations in Buddhist Thought*. Buswell Jr. and Gimello, the editors, provide a list to illustrate precisely the point under scrutiny here. They sketch out a list of the various kinds of "*mārga* schemes" found in Buddhist teachings: the noble eightfold path, the four approaches or paths (stream-winners, etc.), the thirty-seven factors of awakening, the five paths, the six or ten stages of the bodhisattva's career, the six or ten perfections, the bodhisattva path in fifty-three stages (Huayan traditions), and the "five ranks" of different Chan or Zen schools.[23] When the "way leading to the ending of pain" is explained *as the fourth truth* it should be understood as the eightfold path. But when "the way leading to the ending of pain" is simply identified as "path" (*magga*), we need to specify which path, in which Buddhist tradition, and according to whom.

VARIATIONS ON THE FOUR NOBLE TRUTHS

The teaching on the four noble truths is almost ubiquitous within Buddhist literature. References to the four noble truths are found everywhere that the Buddha's biography appears, because the teachings are remembered as the substance of the Buddha's first talk on dhamma, according to the *Sutta on the Turning of the Dhamma Wheel*. This scene appears in the Buddhist Sanskrit versions of the *vinaya* in the *Mahāvastu*, the *Saṅghabhedavastu*, the *Catuṣpariṣatsūtra*, and the *vinaya* collections of the *Mahīśāsaka*, and the Dharmaguptaka schools found in the Chinese Tripitaka.[24] The four noble truths sometimes appear in some accounts of the buddha's departure from earth, when he enters the state of *parinibbāna*. The four noble truths also appear in the Buddhist Sanskrit *Avadāna* literature. In short, there is no question about the significance of the four noble truths within the Buddhist tradition. For example, Nāgārjuna deconstructs the four noble truths in the *Mūlamadhyamakakārikaḥ*—he demonstrates neatly how they exist conventionally but how they are ultimately empty. Similarly, the four noble truths are recognized as ultimately empty in the *Heart Sutra*. The four noble truths are found woven throughout the schools and teachings of Hinayana and Mahayana Buddhism.

In looking more closely at these canonical collections, however, the four noble truths are missing from certain narratives of the buddha's life story where they should be present if they were as universally central as presumed to be. Using the Pali Canon, K. R. Norman identified different "grammatical sets" of how the four noble truths are introduced within this body of Pali literature. Each of these grammatical sets for the four noble truths is found in different points in the canon, and thus the presence and absence of the four noble truths can be traced within the narrative structures of the Buddha's biography. The result of this analysis demonstrates that the four noble truths were gradually integrated into the buddha's life story as the textual tradition unfolded within the history of Pali Buddhism, as can be seen by looking at Norman's argument in more detail.

Grammatical Inconsistencies. In the *Sutta on the Turning of the Dhamma Wheel*, the Buddha explains the four noble truths as the content of what he realized during his own enlightenment. His audience is the five former companions who left him when he decided to break his fast. The Buddha introduces the concept of the middle path and then immediately leaps into the first truth, that is, the truth of pain. However, there is a grammatical error in this sutta. Norman first identified this slip, and in doing so, discovered that the "four noble truths" are not written with the same terms and grammar throughout the Pali canon. Norman translates the first lines that declare each truth: "Monks, the noble truth that 'this is pain'; [and,] monks, the noble truth that 'this is the origin of pain'; [and,] monks, the noble truth that 'this is the ending of pain'; [and,] monks, the noble truth that 'this is the way leading to the ending of pain.' "[25] The inconsistency in grammatical gender for the four truths within the *Sutta on the Turning of the Dhamma Wheel* is as follows. The first truth, "pain," is *dukkha* in Pali. The grammatical ending of *dukkha* is singular in number, neuter in gender, and in the nominative case. That ending matches up with the pronoun "this" (*idaṃ*), which is also in the nominative or accusative case, singular in number, and neuter in gender. The second and third truths, "arising" (*samudayo*) and "ending" (*nirodho*), are masculine in gender, singular in number, and are declined in the accusative case (or mistakenly declined in the nominative neuter). The fourth truth, "way or practice" (*paṭipadā*), is singular in number, nominative, and singular. The same pronoun, "this" (*idaṃ*), is used to refer to *each* of these terms. But Norman asks a critical question: How can a neuter pronoun refer to masculine and feminine nouns, as occurs with the second, third, and fourth truths? The expected form would be the pronoun "this" declined in the masculine or feminine singular, which is not the form that is actually found in the *Sutta on the Turning of the Dhamma Wheel*.

Grammatical Inconsistencies Resolved. Norman has found the four noble truths introduced elsewhere in the canon that do *not* have these grammatical errors. In particular, there are no errors in the genders of the pronouns and nouns in a sutta called the "Talk on Fear and Terror" (*Bhayabherava Sutta*).[26] The audience for this talk is a Brahmin by the name of Jāṇussoni, who has asked the buddha whether it is a distraction to meditate in the midst of a jungle, with all of its wild animals and noises. The Buddha replies that those who are not properly purified are, in fact, scared when they are meditating in the jungle. The buddha explains that he did not walk alone in the thick of the jungle until he was calm in mind and body. The sutta ends with the Buddha explaining how he came to be enlightened, but it is a different version of the enlightenment story than is found in the *Sutta on the Turning of the Dhamma Wheel*. The four noble truths appear toward the end of the "Talk on Fear and Terror," but they are not called "four" or "noble," or even "truths." They simply appear with the properly gendered pronouns "this": " 'I understood as it really is' 'this is pain (*idaṃ dukkhaṃ*),' 'this is the arising of pain (*ayaṃ dukkha-samudayo*),' 'this is the ending of pain (*ayaṃ dukkha-nirodho*),' and 'this is the way leading to the ending of pain (*ayaṃ dukkha-nirodho-gāminī-paṭipadā*).' " Using the appearance of the four noble truths in the *Sutta on Fear and Terror*, then, Norman suggests that this form, with the properly declined pronouns and nouns, is the accurate and thus the relatively earlier form for the four noble truths. It is worth noting that the truths are not identified as "four," "noble," or "truths"—they simply appear in the sentence above as the content of what the Buddha realized during his enlightenment.

Absence of the Four Noble Truths. There is another version of the Buddha's enlightenment where the four noble truths do not appear at all, in the "Talk on the Noble Quest" (*Ariyapariyesana Sutta*).[27] The buddha gave a talk to a group of monks on the difference between the noble quest and the quest that is not noble. Put a bit differently, the buddha gave a talk on the difference between the quest of those who are noble and the quest of those who are not. The search of those who are noble is the quest of "one who is subject to birth, who knows the danger in that which is equally subject to birth, who searches for *nibbāna* where there is no birth [and is] the greatest respite from effort." This person knows the dangers of aging, illness, death, grief, and stain, and looks for *nibbāna* where there is no old age, no illness, no death, no grief, and no stain. The description of the goal of the quest of the noble ones is the same as the first truth found in the *Sutta on the Turning of the Dhamma Wheel*, but no mention is made of "the truth that 'this is pain,'" or the second, third, or fourth truths. "Noble ones" should look for the *nibbāna* that is characterized by an absence of all of those things that are defined in the *Sutta on the Turning of the Dhamma Wheel* as "pain," but the words *pain, arising, ending,* or *the way* are not found in the canonical version of the story—but the commentator Buddhaghosa, in his discussion of this sutta, inserts the four noble truths and says that this is what the story means.[28] The absence of the four noble truths in this sutta is significant because the framework for this sutta is the story of how the Buddha came to be enlightened. After the Buddha distinguishes between the quest (or search) that is noble and that which is not, he explains how he came to this realization during his own search for enlightenment. Based on the appearance of the four noble truths in the *Sutta of the Turning of the Dhamma Wheel*, this *Sutta on the Noble Quest* would be expected to contain the four noble truths as the content of what the Buddha realized—but they are not found there. What the *Sutta on the Noble Quest* offers instead is the quest described previously: he sought, and realized, the "*nibbāna* where there is no birth [and is] the greatest respite from effort." The passage continues, and the buddha declares that he is now enlightened: "Knowledge and vision arose in me: release is unshakeable for me, this is the last birth, there is no more becoming." Thus, there is a different story of the buddha's enlightenment from which the four noble truths are missing.[29]

These variations on the pattern of the four noble truths require a reassessment of the assumption that the four noble truths are the most important teaching of the Buddha in Buddhism because they are the content of the *Sutta on the Turning of the Dhamma Wheel*. The grammatical inconsistencies identified by Norman illustrate that the four noble truths were not always written and recited with the same grammatical forms. Norman suggests that the grammatical inconsistencies for the four noble truths in the *Sutta on the Turning of the Dhamma Wheel* lead to the conclusion that they were a later addition to the canon, although Cousins disagrees. However, by identifying a relative sequence for "earlier" and "later" versions of the truths, scholars are trying to identify a relative chronology for the different grammatical versions of the truths. Other scholars have recognized that the pattern of presence and absence of the four noble truths in the buddha's biography indicates a more complex narrative structure for the development of the life story of the Buddha and the question of precisely how the Buddha became enlightened. At the least, this evidence demonstrates that the early Buddhist tradition had multiple answers to the question of how the Buddha was enlightened, and the fact that the four noble truths were written into the *Sutta on the Turning of the Dhamma Wheel* illustrates that the four noble truths emerged at an early period in the history of Buddhism as a compelling and thus fundamental teaching of the buddha.

TRANSLATING THE "FOUR NOBLE TRUTHS"

The translation of the Pali phrase *catur-ariya-saccāni* as the "four noble truths" is probably not the most accurate translation of this phrase, according to recent scholarship. There are several reasons for this, the first of which reflects the ways in which the phrase was remembered in Buddhist canons, the Pali Buddhist canon in particular. In 1982, K. R. Norman published an article in which he observed that the Pali canon records the teachings on the four noble truths with different linguistic formulas. Briefly, Norman finds that the grammatical form of the truths in the *Sutta on the Turning of Dhamma Wheel* is different from the truths found elsewhere in the Pali canon, and suggests that the appearance of the truths in that sutta is later than the simpler form found at other locations in the Pali canon. Norman also points out that the term *ariya-sacca-* (noble truths) was probably not used to describe the four truths themselves (*dukkha* [pain], *samudaya* [arising], *nirodha* [ending], and *mārga/magga* [path] or *dukkhanirodhagāminī paṭipadā* [way leading to the ending of pain]) in the earliest versions of the truths. In other words, in the earliest strata of the teachings, there was likely only this fourfold formulaic analysis: pain, arising, ending, and the path. But that fourfold analysis came to be identified as the "*catur-ariya-sacca*" ("four-noble-truths") at some unspecified later point in the development of the tradition. Bhikkhu Anālayo offers a parallel reading of one of the suttas in which the four truths appear in the Chinese and Pali versions of the canon, suggesting that the adjective "noble" (*ariya*) was not always found in association with the four truths. In conclusion, then, it is probable that the teachings that we know now as the "four noble truths" were, in their earliest formulation in the Pali and Chinese canons, not recognized as either "noble" or even as "noble truths."

In a book review essay, Lance Cousins reassessed Norman's claims about twenty years after Norman's first article on the four noble truths. Cousins pointed out that Norman's arguments do not necessarily require the positing of an earlier version of the *Sutta on the Turning of the Dhamma Wheel* without the "(noble) truths."[30] Cousins also suggested that while it is reasonable to argue that the *Sutta on the Turning of the Dhamma Wheel* was a later addition to the Pali canon or that the four noble truths were a later addition to the sutta, definitive proof is unlikely to be found at present. At the same time, scholars are in agreement that the translation of the Pali compound "catur-ariya-sacca-" as "four noble truths" is rather unsatisfactory. Norman laid out the possible translations of the compound *ariya-saccāni* in Pali and concluded that the translation of "four noble truths" is the least accurate of all possible translations because it is the only translation that calls the truths themselves noble. Other possible translations, discussed following, refer to the noble ones.[31] Other possible translations include "the truths of the four noble ones," referring to the four paths of the stream-enterer, once-returner, non-returner, and arhat. Peter Harvey has synthesized much of the scholarship on the four *ariya-sacca*s and argues that *sacca* in Pali (Sanskrit *satya*) should be understood as referring to four crucial true or genuine realities, with "*ariya*" as not an adjective qualifying these, but as referring to the noble or spiritually ennobled people with the insight to directly see them.

These questions of grammar and syntax are central to the ways in which the teachings of the four noble truths are understood. They are also entirely in keeping with the explanations found in the commentaries on the Pali canon. There is a rich commentarial tradition for the Pali canon, and while there has been no comprehensive examination of the commentaries on the four noble truths, Norman discusses the key commentaries on the four noble truths.[32] In the commentary on the *Dīgha-nikāya*, Buddhaghosa offers only one definition for "noble truth," which is "the truths which cause nobleness." Buddhaghosa gives two definitions in his commentary on the *Aṅguttara-nikāya*: "the truths which cause nobleness or are penetrated by the noble one[s]." Finally, Norman lays out Buddhaghosa's longer discussion of the compound in the *Visuddhimagga*, which includes these possible meanings:

- "because the noble ones, the Buddhas, etc. penetrate, therefore they are called 'the noble ones' truths'"
- "they are the truths of the Noble One, 'the Noble One's [the Buddha's] truths'"
- "because of the attainment of nobleness arising from their discovery, the ennobling truths"

These possible translations of the Pali compound *ariya-saccāni* in Buddhaghosa's commentaries from the late 4th and early 5th century in Sri Lanka demonstrate that these questions about why the truths were called noble rest at the heart of the tradition. These questions about what "four," "noble," and "truths" mean should be understood as the most recent scholarly consensus on this central teaching. My own choice to retain the traditional "four noble truths" in this article reflects contemporary use, while alerting readers to the fundamental questions of translation. These questions about whether the teachings of pain, arising, ending, and the way were *always* identified as "the four noble truths," the "truths of the four noble ones," or the "four genuine realities of the spiritually ennobled ones" should not divert from the fact that the four noble truths are a central teaching of the Buddhist canon and commentaries. Norman points out that those scholars who first translated the compound *ariya-saccāni* as "the four noble truths" could have translated the compound as "the noble's truths," "the nobles' truths," "the truths for nobles," or "the nobilising truths." He ends that sentence with the observation that "they could only have one of them."[33]

REVIEW OF LITERATURE

Examinations of the four noble truths first appeared in European scholarship in the mid-19th century, and several of these early studies remain useful for their attention to the different texts in which the four truths appeared. These early studies also provide us with a glimpse of the changing ways in which the four truths have been interpreted throughout the last two centuries of colonial encounters with Buddhism. Two relatively recent books address the four noble truths in colonial scholarship on Buddhism: Elizabeth Harris provides consistent attention to the four noble truths in her history of British scholarship and Theravada Buddhism, and Anderson offers a chapter on the topic.[34]

Throughout these early studies, there is increasing attention given to the teaching of the four noble truths throughout the 19th and early 20th centuries as *the* most important teaching of the buddha, as Anderson and Harris both illustrate. Spence Hardy and Rhys Davids were the two most outstanding examples of many scholars to eventually focus on the four noble truths as the most significant teaching of the buddha.[35] T. W. Rhys Davids served in the Civil Service in Sri Lanka (then Ceylon) between 1866 and 1874 and returned to England to found the Pāli Text Society. The talk in which he argues for the centrality of the four noble truths was written for a popular audience in 1879. Other classical European studies that located the four noble truths at the center of Buddhist thought include those of Professor Feer, who traced different versions of the *Sutta/Sutra on the Turning of the Dhamma Wheel*, identifying the four truths in different Buddhist schools and offering parallel translations of the sutra (in French).[36] Feer's work remains the best for parallel translations of the *Sutta on the Turning of the Dhamma Wheel*, in that he traced Sanskrit, Pali, and Chinese versions. La Vallée Poussin offered a different interpretation of the four truths, drawing attention to the relationship between the four noble truths and what he saw as the path itself, instead of the person of the buddha.[37] E. J. Thomas continued to emphasize that the four noble truths are most significant because they were discovered by the person of the buddha.[38] The classical scholars of Indian religions Louis Renou and Étienne Lamotte both identified the four noble truths as the most comprehensive way to organize Buddhist teachings.[39]

The most pressing issue surrounding the teaching of the four noble truths today remains the linguistic and grammatical analyses of the late 20th and early 21st centuries, as introduced in the work of Professors Norman, Cousins, and Harvey. Without additional textual sources, however, the question of whether or not the buddha himself conceptualized the four noble truths as "*the* four noble truths" in the way that the *Sutta on the Turning of the Dhamma Wheel* remembers must remain unanswered. Most scholars today are satisfied to recognize the linguistic puzzles that characterize the teaching on the four noble truths in the various Buddhist canons. Work that may lie ahead would involve a more extensive analysis of the parallel versions of the teaching, not so distant from the work of Feer in the 1870s. At present, the teaching on the four noble truths remains one of the most widely studied by Buddhists and scholars of Buddhism throughout the world.

FURTHER READING

Anālayo, Bhikkhu. "The *Ekottarika-āgama* Parallel to the *Saccavibhaṅga-sutta* and the Four (Noble) Truths." *Buddhist Studies Review* 23, no. 2 (2006): 145–153.

Anderson, Carol S. *Pain and Its Ending: The Four Noble Truths in the Theravāda Buddhist Canon*. Curzon Critical Studies in Buddhism Series. Edited by Charles S. Prebish and Damien Keown. Richmond, UK: Curzon Press, 1999.

Bodhi, Bhikkhu, trans. "Dhammacakkappavattana Sutta (Setting in Motion the Wheel of the Dhamma)." In *The Connected Discourses of the Buddha: A New Translation of the Samyutta Nikaya*. Edited by Bhikkhu Bodhi, 1843–1847. Boston: Wisdom Press, 2000.

Bstan-'dzin-rgya-mtsho, Dalai Lama XIV. *The Four Noble Truths: Fundamentals of Buddhist Teachings*. London: Thorsons, 1997.

Buswell, Robert E., Jr., and Robert M. Gimello, eds. *Paths to Liberation: The Mārga and Its Transformations in Buddhist Thought*. Kuroda Institute Studies in East Asian Buddhism 7. Honolulu: University of Hawai'i Press, 1992.

Cousins, L. S. "Review of Anderson, *Pain and Its Ending*." *Journal of Buddhist Ethics* 8 (2001): 36–41.

Cousins, L. S. "Buddhism." In *New Penguin Handbook of Living Religions*. 2nd ed. Edited by John R. Hinnells, 369–444. London: Penguin, 2003.

Gethin, Rupert M. L. *The Foundations of Buddhism*. Oxford: Oxford University Press, 1998.

Harvey, Peter. "The Four *Ariya-saccas* as 'True Realities for the Spiritually Ennobled'—the Painful, Its Origin, Its Cessation, and the Way Going to This—Rather than 'Noble Truths' Concerning These." *Buddhist Studies Review* 26, no. 2 (2009): 197–222.

Harvey, Peter. *An Introduction to Buddhism: Teachings, History and Practices*. 2nd ed. Cambridge, UK: Cambridge University Press, 2013.

Harvey, Peter. "*Dukkha*, Non-Self, and the Teaching on the Four 'Noble Truths.'" In *Blackwell Companions to Philosophy: A Companion to Buddhist Philosophy*. Edited by Steven M. Emmanuel, 26–45. Somerset, NJ: John Wiley, 2013.

Horner, I. B., trans. *Book of Discipline*. Vol. 4 (*Mahāvagga*). Oxford: Pali Text Society, 1982. Reprint 2000, see pages 1–19.

Nanayakkara, S. "Four Noble Truths." In *Encyclopedia of Buddhism (Sri Lanka)*. Edited by G. P. Malasekera. 8 vols. Colombo: Government of Sri Lanka, 1961–2008.

Nhat Hanh, Thích. *The Heart of the Buddha's Teaching: Transforming Suffering into Peace, Joy and Liberation—The Four Noble Truths, The Noble Eightfold Path, and Other Basic Buddhist Teachings*. New York: Broadway, 1999.

Norman, K. R. "The Four Noble Truths: A Problem of Pāli Syntax." In *Indological and Buddhist Studies (Volume in Honour of Professor J. W. de Jong)*. Edited by L. A. Hercus, 377–391. Canberra: Australian National University, Faculty of Asian Studies, 1982. Republished in 1984 and reprinted in K. R. Norman, *Collected Papers*, Vol. II. Oxford: Pali Text Society, 1991. See especially, pp. 210–223.

Norman, K. R. "Why Are the Four Noble Truths Called 'Noble'?" In *Ānanda: Essays in Honour of Ananda W. P. Guruge*. Edited by Y. Karunadasa, 11–13. Colombo, Sri Lanka: Vision House, 1990.

Reprinted in K. R. Norman, *Collected Papers*, Vol. IV. Oxford: Pali Text Society, 1993. See especially pp. 171–174.

Payutto, Phra Prayudh, and Grant A. Olson, trans. *Buddhadhamma: Natural Laws and Values for Life*. Albany: SUNY Press, 1995. See especially pp. 158–168.

Tsering, Geshe Tashi. *The Four Noble Truths*. Translated by Gordon McDougall. Boston: Wisdom, 2005.

Wezler, Albrecht. "On the Quadruple Division of the Yogaśāstra, the Caturvyūhatva of the Cikitasāśāstra and the 'Four Noble Truths' of the Buddha." *Indologica Taurinensia* 12 (1984): 291–337.

NOTES

1. Ann Heirman and Stephan Peter Bumbacher, eds., *The Spread of Buddhism* (Leiden, The Netherlands: Brill, 2012), 5.
2. Bart Dessein, "The First Turning of the Wheel of the Doctrine: Sārvastivāda and Mahāsāṃghika Controversy," in *The Spread of Buddhism*, ed. A. Heirman and S. P. Bumbacher, 15–48 (Leiden, The Netherlands: Brill, 2012), 16. The versions of the *Dhammacakkappavattana-sutta/Dharmacakrapravartana-sūtra* are found in the *vinaya* collections of these canons as follows: the Pali in *Vinaya-piṭaka* I.1 (translated in), the *Mahīśāsakavinaya* "Mishasai bu hexi wufen lü" (T.1421) and the *Dharmaguptakavinaya* "Sifen lü" (T.1428).
3. In Pali, see "*Dhammacakkappavattana Sutta (Sutta on the Turning of the Dhamma Wheel)*," *Saṃyutta-nikāya* volume V, 420–423 (Oxford: Pali Text Society, 1991). See the translation in *The Connected Discourses of the Buddha: A New Translation of the Samyutta Nikaya* (Boston: Wisdom Publications, 2000); and *The Book of the Kindred Sayings* (by C. A. F. Rhys Davids and F. L. Woodward, 1917–1930). For online access, the Access to Insight website by John Bullit offers different translations by leading scholars of the *Talk on the Turning of the Dhamma Wheel*.
4. Bart Dessein, "The First Turning of the Wheel of the Doctrine: Sārvastivāda and Mahāsāṃghika Controversy," in *The Spread of Buddhism*, ed. A. Heirman and S. P. Bumbacher, 15–48 (Leiden, The Netherlands: Brill, 2012), 17n8.

5. Jonathan S. Walters, "Stupa, Story and Empire: Constructions of the Buddha Biography in Early Post-Asokan India," in *Sacred Biography in the Buddhist Traditions of South and Southeast Asia*, ed. J. Schober (Honolulu: University of Hawai'i Press, 1997), 160–192.
6. Abraham Vélez de Cea, "Emptiness in the Pāli Suttas and the Question of Nāgārjun a's Orthodoxy," *Philosophy East and West* 55, no. 4 (October 2005): 507–528.
7. Reginald Ray, "Response to John Cobb," *Buddhist Christian Studies* 8 (1988): 86, 83–109. While the title of this article is obscure, this is a succinct and useful introduction to the three turnings of the dharma wheel. See also Tsepag Ngawang, "Traditional Cataloguing and Classification of Tibetan Literature," *Tibet Journal* 30, no. 2 (Summer 2005): 55, 49–60.
8. John Ross Carter, *Dhamma: Western Academic and Sinhalese Buddhist Interpretations—A Study of a Religious Concept* (Tokyo: Hokuseido Press, 1978), 74n44.
9. Dessein, "First Turning," 41–42.
10. Ibid.
11. Ibid.
12. Carol S. Anderson, *Pain and Its Ending: The Four Noble Truths in the Theravāda Buddhist Canon*, Curzon Critical Studies in Buddhism Series, ed. C. S. Prebish and D. Keown (Richmond, UK: Curzon Press, 1999), 32–33.
13. Steven Collins, *Selfless Persons: Imagery and Thought in Theravāda Buddhism* (Cambridge, UK: Cambridge University Press, 1982), 90.
14. Rupert M. L. Gethin, *The Foundations of Buddhism* (Oxford: Oxford University Press, 1998), 59.
15. *Access to Insight.*
16. Kenneth G. Zysk, *Asceticism and Healing in Ancient India: Medicine in the Buddhist Monastery* (New York: Oxford University Press, 1991), 48–49; and Albrecht Wezler, "On the Quadruple Division of the Yogaśāstra, the Caturvyūhatva of the Cikitasāśāstra and the 'Four Noble Truths' of the Buddha," *Indologica Taurinensia* 12 (1984): 291–337.
17. For a very good introduction to this, see Peter Harvey, *An Introduction to Buddhism: Teachings, History and Practices*, 2nd ed. (Cambridge, UK: Cambridge University Press, 2013), 50–87. This chapter forms the bulk of his essay in the Blackwell *Companion to Buddhist Philosophy*: Peter Harvey, "Dukkha, Non-Self, and the Teaching on the Four 'Noble Truths,'" in *A Companion to Buddhist Philosophy*, ed. Steven M. Emmanuel (London: Blackwell, 2013).
18. The *Dukkha Sutta*, found at S IV.259 and Bhikkhu Thanissaro, trans., "*Dukkha Sutta*: Stress," Access to Insight.
19. Translation found at Access to Insight and other standard translations of the *Saṃyutta-nikāya*.
20. M I.55–63; Bhikkhu Thanissaro, "The Foundations of Mindfulness: *Satipatthana Sutta*," Access to Insight.
21. Bhikkhu Ñāṇamoli, trans., *The Path of Purification by Bhadantácariya Buddhaghosa*, 4th ed. (Kandy, Sri Lanka: Buddhist Publication Society, 1975 and 2010), 507. This passage is found in Chapter XVI, "The Faculties and Truths."
22. Harvey, *Introduction to Buddhism*, 83–84.
23. Robert E. Buswell Jr. and Robert M. Gimello, eds. *Paths to Liberation: The Mārga and Its Transformations in Buddhist Thought* (Honolulu: University of Hawai'i Press, 1992), 7–8.
24. Anderson, *Pain and Its Ending*, 16.
25. K. R. Norman, "The Four Noble Truths: A Problem of Pāli Syntax," *Collected Papers*, Vol. II (Oxford: Pali Text Society, 1991), 212.
26. M I.16–24; Bhikkhu Ñāṇamoli, trans., and Bhikkhu Bodhi, ed., "Bhayabherava Sutta: Fear and Dread," in *Middle Length Discourses of the Buddha: A New Translation of the Majjhima Nikāya* (Boston: Wisdom Publications, 1995), 102–107; and Bhikkhu Thanissaro, trans., "Bhayabherava Sutta or Sutta on Fear and Terror," Access to Insight.

27. M I.160–175; Bhikkhu Ñāṇamoli, trans. and Bhikkhu Bodhi, ed., "Ariyapariyesanā Sutta: The Noble Search," in *Middle Length Discourses of the Buddha: A New Translation of the Majjhima Nikāya* (Boston: Wisdom Publications, 1995), 253–265; and Bhikkhu Thanissaro, trans., "Ariyapariyesana Sutta or Sutta on the Noble Search," Access to Insight.
28. *Samantapāsādikā*, Buddhaghosa's Commentary on the Vinaya Piṭaka, ed. J. Takakusu and M. Nagai (Oxford: Pali Text Society, 1969), 2:174.
29. Bhikkhu Thanissaro, introduction, "Ariyapariyesana or Sutta on the Noble Search," Access to Insight.
30. L. S. Cousins, "Review of Anderson, *Pain and Its Ending*," *Journal of Buddhist Ethics* 8 (2001): 36–41.
31. Norman, K. R., "Why Are the Four Noble Truths Called 'Noble'?," in *Ānanda: Essays in Honour of Ananda W. P. Guruge*, ed. Y. Karunadasa (Colombo, Sri Lanka: Vision House, 1990), 11–13.
32. Norman, *Ānanda: Essays in Honour of Ananda W. P. Guruge*, 171–172. The commentary on the *Dīgha-nikāya* is found at Sv 542, line 33; the commentary on the *Aṅguttara-nikāya* is Mp II.281, lines 1–2.
33. Norman, "Why Are the Four Noble Truths Called 'Noble?' " 174.
34. Elizabeth J. Harris, *Theravāda Buddhism and the British Encounter: Religious, Missionary and Colonial Experience in Nineteenth-century Sri Lanka* (London and New York: Routledge, 2006); and Anderson, *Pain and Its Ending*
35. Robert Spence Hardy, *The Legends and Theories of the Buddhists Compared with History and Science* (London: Williams and Norgate, 1866); and T. W. Rhys Davids, "Buddha's First Sermon," *Fortnightly Review* 39 (1879): 899–912.
36. Léon Feer, "Études bouddhiques: Les quatre vérité et la predication de Bénarès (*Dharma-cakra-pravartanaṃ*)," *Journal Asiatique* 6.15 (May–June 1870): 345–472.
37. Louis de La Vallée Poussin, *The Way to Nirvana: Six Lectures on Ancient Buddhism as a Way to Salvation* (Cambridge, UK: Cambridge University Press, 1917).
38. Edward J. Thomas, *The Life of the Buddha as Legend and History* (London: Routledge & Kegan Paul, 1927).
39. Louis Renou and Jean Filliozat, *L'Inde classique: Manuel des Études indiennes*, 2 vols. (Paris: École Française d'Extrême Orient, 1953); and Étienne Lamotte, *Histoire du bouddhisme indien, des origins à l'ère Śaka*, Bibliotèque du Muséon, vol. 43 (Louvain: Publications Universitaires, 1958). English translation by Sara Webb Boin, *History of Indian Buddhism from the Origins to the Śaka Era*, Publications de l'Instiut Orientaliste de Louvain 36 (Louvain-la-Neuve: Institut Orientaliste, 1988).

Carol S. Anderson

FROM MANUSCRIPT TO PRINT IN SOUTH AND SOUTHEAST ASIA

HISTORIOGRAPHICAL CONSIDERATIONS

What is referred to as a manuscript—a text written by hand—may be self-evident. The reference to print is more ambiguous. Print has generally been taken to mean products, practices, and regimes historically connected to the European printing press, involving the use of movable types dating from the 15th century and, by implication, modernity, the emergence of the nation-state, capitalism, and colonialism, as well as specific forms of historiography. Authors such as Marshall McLuhan, Elizabeth Eisenstein, and Benedict Anderson have shaped our understanding of the emergence of print as a revolutionary, epoch-making event with irreversible consequences. It has been explained as an event that led to the creation not only of new forms of knowledge but also of new means of production, new social classes, new societies, to emancipation and democratization, but also to homogenization and estrangement on a global and unprecedented level. The background against which the concept of print developed was scribal culture, which has tended to be defined by what print culture was not: limited, cumbersome, expensive, elitist, and premodern, to name just a few, but also preparing and facilitating the emergence of print. This understanding of print prioritizes the modern over the premodern by framing the relationship between manuscript and print through a narrative of subsequence (manuscript before print), rupture (manuscripts replaced by print), and teleology (manuscript leading to print). All these features do indeed play a role in the introduction to Buddhist countries of the European printing press, but they are disproportionally highlighted, if the inception of print is indeed reduced to this particular event. A printing press–centered historiography, further, creates a before-and-after the introduction of this specific form of technology to Buddhist countries and thus prioritizes print as a historiographical category, foreclosing an understanding of more intimate interactions of writing and printing. In these interactions, writing, on the one hand, may retain control over the processes of mediatic change, whereas print, on the other, may submit to these processes or help initiate parallel, if intertwined, developments. These historical movements can only be properly recognized if one understands manuscript and print not as criteria for periodization but as partners in a relationship.

Print understood primarily from the perspective of the European printing press may also suggest that something called Buddhism always preexisted print, may make believe that an entity called Buddhism would be indeed be made to move "from manuscript to print," or that print may stand for a more recent phase in an ancient tradition mostly transmitted in ways other than print. Buddhism is seen either as itself antecedent or foreign to and independent of the conditions of its own production and reproduction or, even more problematically, as an entity to which print attaches itself like an external accoutrement rather than helping to create what Buddhism historically becomes, in the first place. A more inclusive and relational understanding of print, however, would allow us to see that in some parts of the Buddhist world, print stood at the beginning and not at the end of Buddhist textual production, just as print, under other historical circumstances, particularly those of modernity, also allowed forms of Buddhism to emerge that indeed saw themselves as different, later, and better. The historical "rhetoric" of print carries as its baggage the idea of involving a "revolution" and thus invokes the uniqueness, novelty, and irreversibility of an imagined event and the supposed radical and comprehensive changes it wrought.[1] Relativizing the paradigmatic character of the European printing press and instead contextualizing it as one of the most recent and consequential forms of "pattern reproduction," to use a term coined by Timothy H. Barrett, helps to break down the monolithic and discrete character suggested by a historically specific and contingent form of print culture when taken as normative, as well as the binaries it forces upon the historiography of texts.[2] It allows us to recover the manuscript as a historical protagonist in its own right, with all its inherent resilience and as a condition for human inventiveness. But it also helps us avoid revisionist and confrontational proposals, such as opposing "script-mercantilism" to "print-capitalism," that intend to, reversely, stress the revolutionary stature of the manuscript in order to minimize the epistemic impact of print.[3] According to this view, it is manuscript, not print culture, that is "truly historic for literary cultures in India," its historicity being attached to the outdated character of the economic model by which it is defined. Just as with the "print revolution," here the manuscript is turned into the historiographical tool, now to deny historical depth and extension to what is termed "middle class book consumption" and the "culture of private reading."[4] Such an approach is only possible on the basis of a fundamentally apologetic stance, a reductive identification of print culture with the Western printing press, a conscribed and ultimately conservative view of both Asia and manuscript culture, and, most importantly, an abstraction from the historically productive relation between various forms of print and manuscript practices through time. Manuscript and print culture reinvented their relationship not once but at least twice and in fundamentally different ways in the history of Buddhism. Their relationship was mediated by South Asian language and religion transferring from South Asia into Central and East Asia around the 1st century BCE leading to the development and spread of block print in East Asia in the middle of the first millennium CE, and then again, including other parts of Asia where that relationship did not exist, around the middle of the 19th century with the introduction of the movable-type printing press from Europe.

PRINTING AND THE SPREAD OF SOUTH ASIAN BUDDHISM

Barrett points at "pattern reproduction" as the prehistory and context of the printed book that should not be seen as the apex but as merely one particularly prominent variant of practice that ranges from coinage, cord pottery, textile prints, seal culture, or the forming of clay *caityas* from molds. Many of these practices preceded and continued long after the emergence of the printed text in China and beyond.[5] The printing, if not of books but of texts, in Barrett's more extended sense, starts as a Buddhist project and gets off to a very early start in South Asia, with *dhāraṇīs* printed on clay tablets beginning in the 1st century BCE. The number of "print runs" of these texts is likely to have been elevated, as the items onto which the texts were imprinted in a seal-like fashion were repeatedly and persistently required for ritual purposes.[6] The printed texts were not expected to be read as one would read book-length texts but were produced with the intention of being ritually effective by their mere production and ritualized deployment.[7] At this point in time in South Asia, print effected the reliable and economic reproduction of the same efficacious ritual object and not the enhanced communication between readers or the building of archives, as in later times. Early South Asian–inspired print seems to have been as equally text- as image-oriented, as the earliest record of a buddha image and Sanskrit text dating from 5th-century China shows.[8] It was South Asian Buddhism and its deployment of iconography and language that drove the unfolding of print culture to new forms north to Central Asia and east to Southeast Asia, both beyond the modern geographic boundaries of South Asia and then, through Tibetan Buddhism, back south into and across the Himalayas.

Print is as closely connected to the rise of Buddhism as paper, suiting both the cosmology of a Mahāyāna world pervaded by innumerable iterations of the buddha, his nature, and his word, exemplified by the Thousand Buddha pattern as well as its strategies of proselytizing that included the book as a new center of ritual practice.[9] In both cases, "multiplication becomes the norm."[10] It was the development of paper, however, that made possible a vast new array of reproductive practices such as pounces and rubbings, allowing for the creation of two-dimensional copies of Buddhist objects, images, and inscriptions and opening up new avenues for the differentiation of pattern reproduction. In Sanskritized Central Asia and Buddhist East Asia, books transitioned from sewn-together thin bamboo and wood strips to the paper scroll (*juan*), which would remain the dominant book form for East Asian Buddhist texts. Other formats were the concertina codex, in which long sheets, or short single folios after having been attached to each other, are folded leporello-like, and the South Asian *poṭhi*, which stacks single, loose, horizontally oriented, long folios, tied together with a string or skewered on thin sticks that run through usually two perforations parallel to the long sides of the folio and located in its middle section. In *poṭhi*s, text and illuminations run parallel to the long sides of the folio. For reading, pages are lifted, turned, and piled in reverse order on the other side of the remaining stack, facing the reader. The method of inscription depends on the material: applying of ink with a brush or pen in the case of paper, carving with a metal stylus of grooves to be filled with pigment in the case of palm leaf. In East Asia, concertina and *poṭhi* appeared in the 8th century but remained marginal and were used mostly for non-Chinese language texts.[11] In China, paper, which spread parallel to Buddhism around the 1st or 2nd century, opened up opportunities in equal measure for both manuscript (calligraphy) and print culture.[12] Later, woodblock printing relied on wet calligraphies on paper being pressed against the wood, letting the pigment seep in and creating the pattern in which then to carve the wood.[13] Barrett has argued that the dynastic politics of the Chinese royal reproduction of relics or talismanic material in the form of *dhāraṇī*s under Empress Wu Zetian (624–705, r. from 690), stamped on paper and distributed over vast areas, initiated a development that eventually led to the printing of Buddhist books.[14] The Dunhuang corpus contains relatively little printed material, and it is only in 858 that we find the oldest known dated xylograph, the famous printed Chinese version of the *Vajracchedikā-prajñāpāramitāsūtra* scroll from the Stein collection in the British Library. It documents the technological progress made in printing by that time insofar as the numbered slabs had been produced expressly for stamping the entire text on the basis of a calligraphy of the text dated 824.[15]

VIETNAM BETWEEN CHINESE AND EUROPEAN COHABITATIONS

Recent scholarship has shown that far from being a region dominated by Chinese language and Confucian literature, Vietnamese print and book culture was from the beginning driven by Buddhists, and much of its production involved the regional vernacular.[16] In Southeast Asia, the year 1007 marked the beginning of a history of high-level orders of the Tripiṭaka (Đại tạng kinh) from Northern Song dynasty China by King Lê Long Đĩnh (986–1009, r. from 1005) of Jiāozhōu, as the area of present-day northern Vietnam was called until then. The first copy arrived in 1009, leading to the establishment of the first prominent archives. Lý Thái *Tổ* (1010–1028, r. from 1009), followed up by a second order in 1018, which he received in Thăng Long (now Hanoi) in 1020 and had copied in 1023 and 1027.[17] From early on in Vietnam, the ordering and producing of print and manuscript material went hand in hand: The 12th-century monk Bảo Giám is recorded to have copied by hand the entire Tripiṭaka.[18] The Trần dynasty (1225–1400) saw the development of the demotic Vietnamese Nôm script and the establishment of the Thắng Nghiêm temple as an important press and print and manuscript repository in connection with the mid-13th-century emergence of the Trúc Lâm tradition initiated by

Trần Nhân Tông (1258–1308).[19] Nhân Tông's successor Pháp Loa (1284–1330) led another important initiative to print the canon in 1295–1319, reportedly inked by the blood collected from particularly dedicated donors, followed by the printing of a key Vietnamese Vinaya text, the *Tứ Phần Luật*, in 1322.[20] Samples of book printing in Vietnam are preserved from the 16th century, the *Avataṃsakasūtra* (*Đại phương quảng Phật hoa nghiêm kinh*) preserved in the Thắng Nghiêm temple being the most prominent example.[21] Among the other early preserved woodblock book prints are that of the 1665 version of the original 1479 manuscript version of the *Đại Việt sử ký toàn thư* ("Complete Annals of Đại Việt"), printed in Hong Lieu, Hai Duon Province, in 1697.

The Red River delta, but eventually all of present-day Vietnam, became an important market for Chinese print products as soon as Chinese book trade networks started expanding south more dynamically in the 17th century and remained robust until the late 19th century. That means that at that point in time, although a print culture backwater compared to China and Japan, Vietnam was by far the most print-oriented country in South and Southeast Asia.[22] Buddhist scriptures kept being imported at low cost, while the more expensive locally printed texts covered specialized fields such as lineage history, ritual, medicine, and Chinese reading guides.[23] Kathlene Baldanza's study of a sample of old temple libraries around Hanoi shows that in the 19th century, manuscripts were abundantly found next to prints, with many popular printed books extant in several manuscript versions, demonstrating that the demand for certain texts far exceeded the supply of print copies, which was then met by copying by hand.[24] But it was only certain genres that were transmitted in manuscript form and not in print. They included Buddhist manuals dealing with monastery management or medicine, literary compendia, and local lineage lists, as well as books with glosses in Nôm or Hán-Nôm bilingual texts.[25] The Chinese presses, however, were well aware of the demand for texts featuring Hán-Nôm bilingual content and ensured a regular supply.[26]

It was only with the abolition of civil service examinations in Vietnam in 1919 and following the introduction of the Roman quốc ngữ script by the French colonial authorities that the book market moved more decisively from Chinese to Western print technology, weakening the book trade networks between Vietnam and China, with mostly Buddhist and medicinal circles maintaining old ties and continuing traditional forms of book making and circulation, thus becoming increasingly detached from the readership of a modernist, urban literature emerging in the early 20th century.[27] The quốc ngữ script had been connected to the colonial printing press culture since its introduction by the Jesuit missionaries in the 16th century and the publication of the *Dictionarium Annamiticum Lustianum et Latinum* in Rome in 1651 and had served a medium for the Christian communities among which the Western printing press had been in use ever since.[28] As Shawn McHale points out, both print and manuscript cultures in Vietnam, as in most other manuscript cultures in South and Southeast Asia, were restricted to very small literate communities, in this case Confucian and Buddhist, later Christian elites, representing the script-oriented fringes of what were mostly oral textual communities.[29] It was only the move from one much older print culture, more intimately enmeshed with manuscript culture, to a relatively new print culture much less involved with manuscripts that allowed for widespread literacy and for the development of a more broadly defined public sphere.[30] Yet in Vietnamese Buddhism, the relation between manuscript and print remains complex. Within traditional Buddhist circles, sutra copying as meritorious activity has been uninterrupted since the days of Bảo Giám and the emergence of a modern movement on the fringe of Buddhism,[31] like the Hòa Hảo tradition from the western Mekong delta, was only possible within a print culture environment.[32]

TIBETAN MEDIATIC MIMESIS

Chinese-style woodblock printing in the Tibetan script is likely to have developed in the Tangut Kingdom in an environment where the printing of Tangut and Chinese scripts was also common. Earliest finds at Kharakhoto in western Inner Mongolia date back to the 12th and 13th centuries, the earliest known being a print from 1153.[33] Three forms are found: the *dpe cha* or *poṭhi* format for Buddhist scriptures, codices containing *dhārāṇīs*, and single sheets displaying ritual diagrams.[34] Mongol rule over Tibet and China (1271–1368) saw a proliferation of printed texts, sponsored by Mongol queens and produced in the Yuan capital Dadu/ Khanbalik, near present-day Beijing, as part of merit-accumulating practices. As part of the Mongol efforts to consolidate the empire, facilitated by the wide-flung infrastructure, many of the texts were later circulated to central Tibet and found their home there, most of them in Drepung. Under the sponsorship of Kublai Khan's queens, Tibetan copyists had the texts "put down in letters" (*yig ger bkod*) that were then carved by Chinese artisans, the first text of this corpus being Sa skya Paṇḍita Kun dga' rgyal mtshan's (1182–1251) *Tshad ma ris pa'i gter* ("The Treasury of Valid Reasoning"), engraved and printed in 1284, not long after its author's death.[35] Though we have no remaining textual evidence, Gansu province seems to have been another site of printing in Tibetan script as early as 1207 in the Mongol period and we have remains from Central Asia.[36] It is in the 15th century, after the collapse of Yuan rule, that printing took off in Tibet as a field of merit making not only in royal circles but across informal lay and monastic networks.[37] The first preserved printed book from central Tibet, Haribhadra's commentary on the *Abhisamayālaṃkāra*, hails from Shel dkar and dates to 1407, printed by the local ruler of the La stod Lho region, Situ Lha btsan skyabs, in honor of his father, who in the colophon is compared to Kublai Khan and thus seems to have followed the Mongol tradition of print sponsorship.[38] The work mimics the manuscript format not only in its *poṭhi* shape but also by including circles representing, *ad modum antiquum*, the rings of paper manuscripts, themselves carryovers from the string holes found in palm leaf manuscripts and retained for aesthetic and apotropaic reasons, representing transformations of the material memory of the Southern provenance of Buddhist sacred texts.[39] The fixed woodblock was chosen over movable types, as the diacritics and stacked consonants, different from Chinese types, required widely differing line spacing.[40] In 1410, there was the printing of the Yongle Kanjur, the first print version of the Tibetan canon, in Beijing.[41] These were followed by the print edition of the works of the recently deceased Tsong kha pa (1357–1419) in the 1420s and 1430s.[42]

In the 15th century, production relied on small printing establishments (*par khang*) and it was only in the 17th and 18th centuries that larger printing houses emerged and printing was organized more strongly along sectarian lines.[43] What preceded the rise of the printed text as dominating in Tibet was the 11th-century establishment of the *poṭhi* or *dpe cha* as the standard format for Buddhist books and the marginalization of others such as leporello and codex, which kept being used for less high-prestige works such as manuals and generally for texts more frequently and personally used, as well as the scroll used for documents.[44] The emergence of print culture in this period also favored a differentiation of domains. The 13th century, in fact, also saw the rise of lavishly ornamented and illustrated manuscripts of high-status texts such as the Kanjur and the Tanjur, as well as of sectarian canons.[45] Print also led, as elsewhere, to an explosion in the number of texts produced, standardization, and attitudes critiquing the conflation of knowledge and textuality. However, and in spite of the technological opportunities offered by woodblock printing, manuscripts still exceeded printed texts right up to the early 20th century.[46] The move from manuscript to print potentially involved redactorial interventions on texts such as creating new textual units in terms of layout and paratextual additions, linguistic editing, and the fashioning of unified texts from miscellaneous collations.[47] The peculiarities of the woodblock, however, still required the skills of copyists and calligraphers. Letters, layouts, and ornamentation, not to speak of illuminations, had to be transferred from manuscripts in mirror-reverse by re-inking templates for imprinting onto woodblocks, which would then need to be carved by woodworkers skilled in the intricacies of script, line arrangement, and flourishes shared with artisans specializing in the visual arts. The printing, stacking, binding, and cataloging process too would need to be supervised by those familiar with the constitution and organizing books and archives, practices that would have emerged from expertise in handling manuscripts. Unlike practices entirely based on movable types, inscribed beyond the realm of the manuscript handwriting, nonnormative orthography, and even errors, thus enabling a parallel life of manuscript culture in the world of print. Tibetan print culture was certainly a transregional phenomenon, extending from East Asia as far west as Ladakh and from Mongolia as far south as Bhutan, Sikkim, and Nepal, relativizing claims that forms of print predating the Western printing press were not present in South Asia.[48]

RELUCTANT SHIFTS IN SOUTH ASIA AND THE KATHMANDU VALLEY

Although, as we have seen, printing technology was something South Asians had been familiar with from early on, one may ask why south of the Himalayan region printing on paper emerged only very slowly and unevenly. With the earliest extant Sanskrit *dhāraṇīs* printed on paper dating from 10th-century Dunhuang, we have the first appearance of a South Asian language printed on paper, even if outside the geographical borders of what would be considered South Asia today. It is only in the 13th–14th centuries that we find the first xylographs of works in Sanskrit in the Turfan area, coinciding with the Uighur occupation of the city of Qočo.[49] Camillo Formigatti, reflecting on possible forces that withstood the transfer of print technology from East and Central Asia beyond the Himalayas or a development of print culture out of the early clay sealings, points out that paper, the medium best-suited for printing, began to be produced in the region on a larger scale only in 13th century in western and in the 15th century in eastern South Asia.[50] This is a period that, as Formigatti points out, in large parts of northern South Asia coincides with the period of decline of Buddhism, the driving force behind print culture in East and Central Asia Buddhism.[51] The consistent dissolution of the large Buddhist monastic complexes in places ranging from what today are Afghanistan, Pakistan, the Punjab, Gujarat, and Maharashtra to Bihar, Orissa, and Bangladesh and all the way south to present-day Andhra cut short the possibility of an expansion of librarian networks that may have exposed more Buddhist readers to technologies that held sway in the north. Climatic conditions inimical to paper preservation and the greater availability of palm leaf, particularly in southern South Asia and in Southeast Asia, may have been further factors in the successful resistance of manuscript culture to the advent of print until the 19th century. Graham Shaw points at aesthetic considerations, to which one should add the importance of religious tradition and cultural prestige, that led missionaries in the Tamil- and Oriya-speaking regions to have printed texts transposed onto palm leaf manuscripts and made particularly Muslim literati favor lithography, a technique which was able to reproduce the manuscript more faithfully, over movable letter print.[52] But Shaw also points out that the comparably late influx of paper and printing technology into South Asia also went hand in hand with the control of the supply of these tools and materials by the colonial powers, protracting further the appropriation of the technology by indigenous producers of books.[53] However, in regions such as Nepal and northern Southeast Asia, paper had been readily available through trade and technology transfer with Tibet and southern East Asia from much earlier, demonstrating that proximity with print culture Buddhism and independence from colonial material and technological flows did not necessarily lead to precolonial print cultures.[54] One further possible explanation for retention of manuscript technologies in this part of the world is the absence of large, central, state-sponsored institutions as part of imperial enterprises that involved proselytizing, comparable to those in East Asia and Western Europe, which aimed at homogenizing far-flung communities of readers through print.

The whole South Asian Himalayan region is likely to have been part of the world of Tibetan print culture from very early on. First records of Tibetan scholars frequenting the Kathmandu Valley, attractive for both its scholarly and its wood-carving traditions, the latter of interest for the manufacturing of woodblocks, are recorded from the 11th century onward. The 14th century marks a period of intensified Nepalese–Tibetan interaction, suggesting that the Kathmandu Valley Newars would have been familiar with materials and technologies and may have played a role in their development, with Tibetanized non-Newar communities too taking part in this new economy. The mostly paper-based book production for Newar consumption, however, remained staunchly manuscript-oriented, and the only domain wood print technology came to be used in, among Buddhist and Hindu Newars, was the paper-based manufacturing of deity images and ornamental paraphernalia for ritual use. The manuscript remained the exclusive form of Newar Buddhist book culture right up to the first decade of the 20th century. The first European movable-type printing press arrived in Nepal in 1815 when Prime Minister Jaṅga Bāhadur Rāṇa brought one from England, and this was kept under government control. This meant that the first center of private Nepalese printing turned out to be Benares, where the Nepali elites went to study.[55] Both pulp fiction and what would soon become the literary canon in Nepali emerged from what was primarily a Sanskrit-oriented Hindu and predominantly ritual center of textual production.[56] The first movable-type printed book was a translation into Newar of the twenty-one verses of the goddess Prajñāpāramitā (*Śrī prajñāpāramitā devīyāgu ekaviṃśati ślokayā bhāṣā sahita*) in 1909, followed by Newar versions of the *Lalitavistara*, printed in the *poṭhi* format, and the *Svayambhūpurāṇa*, both in 1914, all by Paṇḍit Niṣṭhānanda Vajrācārya (1858–1935), who procured a press from Calcutta and in Kathmandu, using wooden print blocks, took care of the printing himself.[57] One of the most important consequences of this import of types from India was the shift in Newar texts from the traditional variety of scripts in use, including Pracalit, Rañjanā, Bhujimol, *and* Devanāgarī, to Devanāgarī as the exclusive print script for Newar. Newar activists soon saw the adoption of this script, used for Nepali manuscript and print texts and established as the dominant script across Nepal by the politically dominant Nepali-speaking Parbatiyā elites, as an act of relinquishing Newar distinctiveness. Ironically, it was the Devanāgarī-centric print culture that, after decades of language-based ethnic repression by the state, contributed to the modernist "re-awakeing of Newar" (*nepālbhāṣāyā punarjagaraṇ*) as a language of Newar literary culture and Theravāda and Vajrayāna Newar activism. Although traditional scholars have until today resisted converting particularly the local tantric manuscript tradition into print, these reservations have from early on been consistently undermined by more progressive religious leaders through the curation of print versions, the reliance on print editions of Buddhist tantric or other texts produced in India, and the eventual microfilming and more recent digitization of entire manuscript holdings in collaboration with foreign research institutions.

Large-scale manuscript production came to an end in the 1920s, with the production of ritual manuals (*vidhi*s or *paddhati*s) in manuscript form surviving the longest. In fact, most *vajrācārya*s today still carry with them manuscript copies of the handbooks for the rituals they are in charge of performing and keep an archive of them at home, as for most liturgies there are no printed versions. Ritual variants tied to place and lineage still rely on manuscripts handed on from father to son and resist the homogenizing tendencies that come with the moderately large print runs of printed manuals that allow for proselytizing in favor of specific ritual traditions. Those copies of family-owned manual manuscripts, one or two priestly generations old, that have deteriorated beyond practicality are nowadays replaced either by the inheritors hastily scribbling the manuals' contents into exercise books and notebooks with ballpoint pens or carefully calligraphing them in black and red ink onto paper dyed yellow, to resemble traditional folios and to produce a "cleaned-up copy" (*śuddha gāreko kāpi*) to replace the rundown one. Early print editions of ritual texts appeared in the typical South Asian glued and string-bound, later stapled, paperback quarto format following colonial models from south of the border. Only more recently have publishers of ritual texts moved toward printing in the *poṭhi* format on yellow, user-friendly laminated paper with spiral binding, in order to both appeal to traditional aesthetics and respond to the needs that come with their repeated use in the ritual arena. A prominent case that illustrates well not so much manuscript surviving print or the afterlife of manuscript in print but rather the intricate ways in which both media keep being tied to each other is the serial renovations of a 14th-century manuscript of the *Aṣṭasāhasrikāprajñāpāramitā* held and worshipped at Kvābāhāḥ (or the Golden Temple) in Lalitpur studied by Christoph Emmrich. The renovations of the manuscript involve not only the physical consistency of the book covers and folios or the illuminations but the wording of the text itself, which is "corrected" or "restored" on the basis of a 1960 printed edition of the text produced by the Indian scholar P. L. Vaidya.[58] The direction from manuscript to print is here inverted: The print version, which comes with all the help and prestige modern and foreign philological technology has to offer, is deployed for the upgrade and re-establishment of a text perceived of as decayed and preserved in a charismatic manuscript as part of the overall restorative project. This effort is made in order to allow the book, which stands at the center of the local temple cult, to serve as the field of merit and for it to have a beneficial effect on the lives of all those involved in its worship. Here print is not used to historically freeze and preserve medium, form, and content from a bygone era, as in the academic study of manuscripts, but is ritualized, subordinated, and integrated in order to contribute to the life of a ritual world in which the manuscript still rules supreme. This movement from print to manuscript, however, as sporadic and striking as it may be, is not confined to the ritual context, to Nepal, or to Buddhism: Producing the manuscript of a text entirely on the basis of a printed edition has been documented and for *Jinālaṅkāraṭīkā* and *Milindapañhaṭīkā* palm leaf manuscripts at the U Po Thi Library in Thaton, Mon State, as well as for Vedic material in contemporary Maharashtra.[59]

PHILOLOGICAL DEPARTURES IN SRI LANKA

The relation between manuscript and print has been no less intricate in Sri Lanka. With paper, print culture's preferred medium, having been produced and circulated in the Arabic-speaking regions on a large scale already since the 9th century at the latest.[60] Muslims in the western coastal regions are likely to have been exposed to paper much earlier. The Portuguese brought it with them in the early 16th century, yet the first recorded paper manuscript dates only from the 18th century.[61] Until Buddhists themselves took control of the printing press in the second half of the 19th century, the palmyra palm leaf (*ola*), readily available, time-honored, beautiful, and resistant to climate and animals, was regarded as the most appropriate medium for texts produced in monasteries, at the court, and by village scribes.[62] Although the Portuguese imported religious and other print material from their press in Goa, it was the Dutch who established the first press in Colombo in 1736 and who were able to build on a local elite print literacy already established by the Portuguese.[63] The first Sinhala type in woodcuts goes back to Joannes Ruell's *Grammatica of Singaleesche Taal-kunst*, published in Amsterdam in 1708. The first Sinhala movable type was cast by Gabriel Schade in Colombo sometime between 1725 and 1729 and probably used between 1736 and 1737 for the first printed texts in Sinhala: a Lord's Prayer and a plakkat.[64] The Sinhala versions of the plakkaten, regulatory announcements for public display printed by the Dutch press in Colombo on single sheets, embodied the relation between manuscript and print in that period, as they mimicked manuscript (or epigraphic) formatting by using punctuation (e.g., the use of the *kuṇdaliya*, "ear drop") and adhering to the manuscript format of *scriptio continua*.[65] Print products for a Sri Lankan audience were seen to need to adapt to a preexisting tradition of textual representation in order to reach as large an audience as possible, be recognized, and possible carry some of the authority held by traditional formats. It is, however, only with the British takeover that printing began to affect Sri Lankan society in a comprehensive fashion. Both the abolishment of the monarchy as the main sponsor of palm leaf manuscript production and the breaking of the monopoly on education of monastic schools, the main producers and users of manuscripts for instruction and ritual practice, deeply affected the status of Sri Lankan manuscript culture. Greatly expanding the Dutch instrumentalization of print for the securing of colonial power, the British pursued a missionary and government takeover of institutions that removed the manuscript as the main medium of record-keeping, official communication, and instruction. The manuscript became more confined to religious spaces and practice, covering, as in the past, monastic scholarship, archiving, and preaching, as well as lay donative activity and worship. Referring to lay book culture in Sri Lanka and speaking from the perspective of later mass readership,

Kularatne points out that "before the establishment of the missionary presses and the vernacular and bilingual schools and the printing of tracts and Scriptures, the Sinhala society had no actual reading public," and, referring to the practice of attending readings from manuscripts by monks, speaks of a "listening (*śrāvaka*) public."[66] However, even the transition of reading practices from manuscript to paper seems to have been a leap, at least for manuscript-trained readers, as an observation by Sir Emerson Tennent, writing at the end of the 19th century and quoted by Kularatne, shows: "Many who can read with comparative ease their own books, which are written with an iron stylus upon *olas*, are embarrassed by the same letters when impressed upon paper."[67] It appears that the rise in literacy of larger parts of Sri Lankan society during the 19th and 20th century occurred through printed government textbooks, missionary print products, and later Buddhist publications rather than through traditional monastic manuscript-based education.

It was in the engagement of Buddhists with anti-Buddhist Christian proselytizing, in the imitation of and reaction to Christian forms of textual practice, and in the emergence of new forms of Sri Lankan Buddhist awareness and activism that Sri Lankan producers and consumers of Buddhist texts moved from manuscript to print.[68] Comparable to early-20th-century Nepal, only about half a century earlier, in Sri Lanka print technology became the avenue for the modernist "Buddhist revival," which continued earlier reform movements and was to radically change the face of Sri Lankan Buddhism.[69] Though an anti-Christian apologetic literature had emerged on palm leaf, it lacked the reach, the modernist appeal, and the participatory role that print offered to lay Buddhists.[70] The first Buddhist-run press, called Laṃkopakāra, was established close to the Paramānanda Vihāra in Galle in 1862 by the Amarapura Nikāya monk Bulatgama Dhammālaṅkara Sumanatissa (1795–1891). Its equipment had been imported on purpose from England and it was financially supported first by community donations, then by the Thai king and a wealthy donor from Kandy. Different from Nepal, its first main products were not print versions of scripture but periodicals, featuring contributions by scholar-activists like Hikkaḍuvē Sumaṅgala (1826–1911) and others.[71] In the same year, following this first success, scholar and orator Mohoṭṭivattē Guṇānanda (1823–1890), supported by the Śāsanābhivṛddhidāyaka Samāgama (the Society for the Propagation of the *Śāsana*) and using a printing press bought by a Sinhalese from a local church mission, established the Sarvajña Śāsanābhivṛddhidāyaka Press at the Dīpaduttārāma Vihāraya in Koṭahena, Colombo, which started using this name by 1863 and by 1867 had begun printing the periodical *Satyamarga*.[72] Also in 1863, disrobed scholar-monk Don Andris de Silva Baṭuvantudāve (1819–1892) initiated the establishment of the Laṅkābhinava Viśruta Press at Māligākanda, Colombo, focusing on literary works in Sinhala and Pali.[73]

The road through which older Sri Lankan Buddhist texts found their way into print was paved by pioneers such as George Turnour (1799–1843), who was the first to have a complete Pali Buddhist text printed in Roman characters, the *Mahāvaṃsa*, translated and edited by him in Ceylon in 1837.[74] It would take until the 1870s for a surge in print versions of Pali works, as an increased support for indological projects by the administration of British governor Henry Gregory (in office 1872–1877) dovetailed with the increased political stature of Sinhalese intellectual leaders in the colony, and the general enthusiasm among the activists after the victory of Guṇānanda over David de Silva in the Great Debate of Pānadura in 1873. One of the first examples of scripture going from manuscript to print in that period was the 18th-century *Milindapraśnaya* by Hīnaṭikumburē Sumaṅgala, a Sinhalese version of the *Milindapañha*, published by Gunānaṇda's press in Kotahena in 1877.[75] On the part of the colonial authorities, the opening salvo fired in the same direction as in 1876 when the Government Press under acting government printer George J. A. Skeen published the *Varṇarītiya*, a grammar by Hikkaduve Sumaṅgala, a Sinhala translation of the *Mahāvaṃsa* produced by Sumaṅgala and Don Andris de Silva Baṭuvantudāve, the grammatical Pali work *Nāmamālā*, and the *Catalogue of Pali, Sinhalese and Sanskrit Manuscripts*.[76] The printed manuscript catalog that emerged as a new genre in Sri Lanka is a good example of the relationship between manuscript and print. The printed catalog was a novel metatextual genre imported from Europe through which the manuscript became subjected more than with handwritten catalogs to technologies of accounting, recording, and access and were thereby produced, in the first place, as a category in opposition to print, very similarly to how modernity creates tradition. Data concerning the location, content, material features, and ownership of a manuscript, formerly known to merely a few, mostly firsthand users or scholarly lineage members, became evenly distributed across the colonial community of investigators. Its members ranged from archivists, conservators, sellers, collectors, and editors, including their various assistants, but also sponsors—in other words, those involved in building and maintaining collections, authoring catalogs, and controlling the access to the sources, on the one hand, and on the other, the users, the readers, the editors of text editions from manuscripts, and their translators. All these would have included, first and foremost, academic administrators or more generally academically trained Europeans (later also Americans), based either in the colony or in the metropole. But from the very beginning, they included the growing Sri Lankan and other Buddhist countries' elites who had grown up under the colonial regime. In most cases, it was these local elites who, at least in the preacquisition phase, controlled the access to sources that mediated the transfer, possessed the required linguistic and cultural expertise, and thus played key roles in the creation of this new genre. The printed manuscript catalog helped to increase, at least theoretically, availability and conservation and also to amplify institutional claims to ownership, giving objects, traditionally used, worshipped, or simply stashed away, the additional identity of musealized artifacts and hierarchically producing and reinforcing the difference in kind between the soft, singular handwritten object in need of protection, on the one hand, and the hard, universalizing printed instrument to which it is made to surrender for its own good, on the other. Copious editions and translations of canonical and noncanonical Pali works followed in the years and decades to come. The entire Sinhala Pali canon, including the *aṭṭhakathā*s and the *Visuddhimagga*, was printed between 1917 and 1940 in the Simon Hewawitarne Bequest Series.[77] "Between 1880 and 1924 every major classical Sinhala work had been edited and published."[78] As a consequence, large-scale production of palm leaf manuscripts decreased rapidly and had dwindled to an all-time low by the second half of the 20th century. Though there are still institutions like the Traditional Palm Leaf Manuscripts Preservation Project, Rangiri Technical Centre, in Dambulla, northeast of Colombo, which keep producing books the traditional way, the only domain worth mentioning in which palm leaf manuscript culture is still thriving in Sri Lanka and in parts of continental Southeast Asia is astrology, palm leaves being the most popular medium through which to record and circulate horoscopes.

BURMESE VICISSITUDES IN PRINT AND STONE

European print arrived in Burma later than in Vietnam and Sri Lanka and in fits and starts. In 1740, the Italo-French Giuseppe Expilly, assisted by the Barnabite Father Melchiorre Carpani (1726–1797), designed Burmese types, which, however, were destroyed during the fire of Thalyin during the reign of King Singu (1756–1782, r. from 1776) in 1776 together with the two presses that were brought along. Only a Burmese abecedary, the *Alphabetum barmanorum seu regni avensis*, the first printed book printed with Burmese script, produced in Rome in 1776, survives from that period, but a second edition came off the press of the Sacra Congregatio de Progapanda Fide in Rome in 1787 with recast types and a new text by Cajetanus Mantegatius and Johannes Percotius.[79] It was a press from Serampore that was used to produce the first printed texts: The second known set of Burmese movable types was created by Felix Carey (1786–1822), son of William Carey of the British Baptist mission, who was granted permission by King Bodawpaya to establish a missionary press in Yangon in 1813.[80] The equipment served Baptist missionary Adoniram Judson (1788–1850) in his publication of the first book ever printed in Burma, his pamphlet *The Way to Heaven*, and in his translation into Burmese of the Gospel of Matthew.[81] They were followed by Judson's *Burmese Grammar* and his *Burmese-English Dictionary*, published in the Baptist Mission Press in Rangoon, which became a remarkable print enterprise, extending to the cities of Mawlamyine, Bathein, Sittway, and Taungoo. Both the scholarly and missionarizing transfer of Buddhist literature into the new medium began in Lower Burma with the printing of the first Pali text, Kaccāyana's grammar, by the Baptist missionary Francis Mason as a *Pali Grammar on the Basis of Kachchayano, with Chrestomathy and Vocabulary*, printed by Karen technicians with Burmese, Aśokan Brahmi, Devanāgarī, and Roman types sponsored by the Asiatic Society of Bengal in 1864 and published in 1868.[82]

Burmese kings from Bodawpaya (1745–1819, r. from 1782) to Bagan (1811–1880, r. 1846–1853), as Yan Naing Lin points out, failed to realize the potential of the new medium until it was too late.[83] It was only after the British occupation of Lower Burma during the Second Anglo-Burmese War in 1852, which split the country in two halves, that the modernizing King Mindon (1808–1878, r. from 1853) imported a printing press through the Catholic Bishop Paul Ambroise Bigandet (1813–1894) and established three printing houses in Mandalay with the explicit purpose of propagating Buddhism, focusing on publications covering religion and law, published in two separate presses, as well as a newspaper.[84] A divergent but analogous initiative of Mindon was the engraving of the Burmese Pali canon onto 729 marble stelae, today popularly known as "the world's largest book," with the engravings originally filled with gold ink, at the Kuthodaw Paya following the convocation of the 5th Council, the Pañcamasaṃgāyanā, in Mandalay in 1871. Although the manuscript–inscription relation is indeed very old, this particular move, marking the transfer of the Buddha's word as a whole to a different medium, was unprecedented and may be connected to the impact print was beginning to have. The possible connections to Mindon's print effort hold even further as the implicit effects of a transfer of the canon onto stone were similar to those highlighted by Elizabeth Eisenstein for print: display of technological and economic investment, heightened long-term durability, the greater public accessibility of the texts so far only available orally or on manuscript, the effect of stressing the status of this particular edition of the canon as the, at the time, definitive one, and, to conclude with a very Buddhist rationale, sending a widely visible sign of royal piety and responsibility.[85] The text was then copied on palm leaf manuscripts, an example of a shift from epigraphy to manuscript,[86] and eventually transferred to the third medium (i.e., print) by Philip H. Ripley's Haṃsavatī Press thirty-eight-volume edition in 1900.[87] Apart from probably inspiring a comparable project in Thailand in 1957,[88] Mindon's project was emulated across Burma for various kinds of text, either canonical and from manuscript or authored by influential Burmese scholars and from print. Prominent examples are the controversial *Milindapañha-aṭṭhakathā* by the Ū Nārada Jetavana Sayadaw, which was carved onto stone slabs set up at a site in Yangon, and the works of Ledi Sayadaw (1846–1923), which were immortalized in the same fashion and preserved in Monywa, Pyinmana, and Windwin.[89] In this case, print comes to share the status of source medium with manuscript during Mindon's reign vis-à-vis the epigraphical target medium: Stone is meant to achieve what both palm leaf and paper cannot.

Mindon's successor Thibaw (1859–1916, r. 1878–1885) did not reign long enough to successfully continue the court's energetic media policy. Following his abdication in 1885, the British authorities had the formerly royal presses auctioned off to Burmese service- and businessmen.[90] This fed into an emerging private Mandalay print market, fueled by an increased interest by the *saṃgha* and affiliated learning centers to have Buddhist and classical literary texts transferred from manuscript to print. Until the 1920s, print publications remained overwhelmingly Buddhist, which only changed in the Wunthanu Period (1921–1930). Just as in British-occupied Lower Burma, decades earlier, now in Upper Burma too print was not only deployed by the colonizers for missionarizing, educational, scholarly, and administrative purposes but also led to the development of popular and lay-oriented Burmese print culture that, similarly to developments in Sri Lanka, with an absent royal center, increasingly delinked literary production from the monasteries' control over the manuscript economy and allowed for an unprecedented production and range of circulation of literary vernacular Burmese texts. The persistence of manuscript culture in Burma through these mediatic shifts cannot be more visible than in the fact that until today "literature," belles lettres, *cā pe* in Burmese, refers back to the palm leaf text (*pe cā*). One of the most spectacular moves from manuscript to print was the most recent comprehensive edition of the canon, including commentaries and subcommentaries, printed on the occasion of the Sixth Council, the Chaṭṭhasaṅgāyana, which opened in Rangoon in 1956 to commemorate the 2500th anniversary of the Buddha's parinirvāṇa. It comprises 117 volumes and can be found in digital form as *Dhammagiripāliganthamālā*, published by the Vipassana Research Institute, Igatpuri, India.

THAI SCRIPTURAL NATION-BUILDING

In Thailand, palm leaf (*bai lan*) and paper manuscripts (*samut khoi*), coexisting for centuries, were joined by printed books in Thai script only a few decades later than in Sri Lanka, by the late 18th century. The Roman Catholic missionary Arnaud-Antoine Garnault reported from Pondicherry, India, to have printed a catechism in Romanized Thai. The first printing press arrived in Ayutthaya in 1796, initiating a trickle of further missionary publications, also in Romanized Thai. The first book in Thai script, *Cathechism of Religion* by the American Baptist missionary Ann Hasseltine Judson, intended for a group of Thai prisoners of war in Burma, was printed not in Thailand but, as with the first Burmese prints, in Serampore, India, in 1819, and the types were eventually shipped to Singapore. It was only in 1831 that the first books printed in Thai script, a catechism and excerpts from the New Testament, made their way to Thailand.[91] The first text printed by Thais was a proclamation of King Nangklao Rama III (1788–1851, r. from 1824) against the opium trade in 1839. His successor, King Monkut Rama IV (1804–1868, r. from 1851), experimented with lithography in the context of his own attempts to develop a new script for printing Pali. Printing caught on with Thai elites in the urban centers and quickly became a medium through which the status of books and readership was redefined. Rural monastics seem to have resisted the use of printed books. They were associated with missionaries, were believed to contain Christian doctrines, and were discredited for this by policymakers such as Prince Patriarch Wachirayan.[92] In 1880, Thai script was first used in print for the production of a collection of Pali chants, the *Nangsu suan mon*, commissioned by Chulalongkorn, King Rama V (1853–1910, r. from 1868), and distributed to shrines throughout the realm, together with instructions on how to read the printed Thai script now used for the Pali that was previously written in Khmer script, or *khorm*. Texts in other northern Thai and Lao scripts too had to be transliterated into the central region's Thai script on the basis of which the new and normative typesets had been cast.[93] One important divergence was the Pak Lat Mon Press, which started printing books in Mon orthography in Paklat in 1902 and became the precursor to monastery-based Mon printing efforts in the early decades of the 20th century.[94]

Building on earlier attempts by Rama IV and similar to the deployment of Devanāgarī in Nepal, the introduction of print was seen by the elites as an opportunity to intervene at a liturgical level and create a national Buddhist script that would attempt to linguistically homogenize and sever historical literary ties that reached beyond the boundaries of the emerging nation-state. The first printed paper edition of the Tipiṭaka, also in Thai script, was produced in 1893 for the king's twenty-fifth jubilee. An edition of the commentaries was only initiated in 1920.[95] Manuscripts began to be associated with the old and traditional, representing either the respected tradition of scripture or the to-be-discredited repositories of the local, the obscure, or the insubordinate, in any case foreign to a colonizing Thai metropole, which would take what was useful for nation-building and discard what did not fit the model of what a modern and Thai nation should look like.[96] The printing of books and, just as in Sri Lanka, the compiling of printed catalogs became part of a larger project of nation-building. Manuscripts were attributed a precarious status of both lacking and requiring attention, care, and systematic collection lest their content, viewed as crucial for the Thai nation, remain unknown or eventually be lost. Prince Damrong Rajanubhab (1862–1943), responsible for the development of the National Library, urged the collection of manuscripts and their transfer into print medium as part of the Wachirayan Library Editions and their distribution for the benefit of the country.[97] The National Library either carried out these print projects itself or collaborated with private printers for a profit. But the largest part of the publication effort went toward the production of cremation volumes (*nangsu ngan sop*), which were printed and distributed as *dhammadāna* (*thammathan*), "the gift of the dhamma," on occasion of death rites and played a key role in the development of Thai print culture.[98] First in the urban centers, but soon also beyond, and right into Lao territory, which became part of the Thai Buddhist print universe, print allowed for a much larger participation in the ritual of book gifting, which was previously bound to the more labor-intensive production of palm leaf manuscripts.[99] By selecting specific works deemed to have particular importance for knowledge related to Buddhism or Thai national historiography in cremation volumes, *thammathan* was reinterpreted as *vidyādān* (*witthayathan*), "the gift of knowledge," stressing its cognitive, intellectual, and educational import.[100] It was the sale of cremation volumes by the National Library that allowed for the costly upkeep of its ambitious printing project. The introduction of print and of the textbook in the monastic teaching environment dramatically changed both classroom interaction and the student–teacher relationship. The teacher was no longer in the privileged position to be the only one to hold the book, but students could use their own copies and study on their own, leading to the current practice in which "a teacher refers to passages and page numbers in student textbooks, rather than orally describing the content of his own manuscript,"[101] a change that led to the disappearance of entire genres of commentary (*nissaya*, *vohāra*, *nāmasadda*) linked to manuscript-centered forms of education.[102] The sense that manuscripts, particularly palm leaf manuscripts, are endangered and require particular attention still persists in Thailand and beyond, the "Fragile Palm Manuscript" project bearing such concern in its very name. That printed matter, particularly from the first century of its appearance, requires equal attention, and that its materials are most often even more fragile than palm leaves has also been increasingly acknowledged throughout the scholarly world in recent decades. It was only in 1922, when printed books too began to be systematically collected, that print production in Thailand exploded. As Coedès notes, in 1920 manuscripts outnumbered printed texts held in the National Library by far.[103] The selection of which recension or version of a particular work to print; its presentation in a new, prestigious format; the range of distribution; and the regimes necessary for the production, consumption, and appreciation of these books all contributed to the formation of a new kind of canon and has shaped Thai Buddhist literature up to the present.

CAMBODIAN RESISTANCE AND CURATORSHIP

In Cambodia, Buddhist palm leaf manuscript culture ruled right up to the second decade of the 20th century. Though the first Khmer types were cut in Vienna in 1847, only those produced in Paris in 1877, fourteen years after Cambodia had become a French protectorate, were actually put to use for books published in Paris, Saigon, and Hanoi.[104] Printing in Khmer, initiated officially through the establishment of the Imprimerie du Protectorat in Phnom Penh in 1886, responded to the double French colonial need of building a Khmer administrative class through educational and bureaucratic structures, on the one hand, and the documentation, archiving, and study of the country's historical data on the other.[105] The development of the Khmer types had to contend with the fact that Khmer manuscript culture deployed two types of script styles: the *mul* or "round" style, in which Buddhist works were written, and the *chrieng*, the "singing" or "inclined" style, which was used for all other writing.[106] The move from carving or painting to printing on paper involved decisions regarding the script design, but although in Thailand those decisions were made by the Thais themselves, in Cambodia this was in the hands of the colonial scholars and administrators. In the early 1940s, the joint dynamic of technology and foreign rule also led to attempts to change the script for Khmer altogether, a project similar to the royal project in Thailand in terms of envisioned rupture but reversed in terms of moving the colonized closer to the French metropole rather than building an ethnocentric nation-state—a project which, however, was soon abandoned. In 1905, the French established a curriculum that included a Buddhist primer and also covered Khmer script, morality tales, didactic poems (*chbap*), and historiography.[107]

The resistance to print and particularly printing Buddhist texts among the *saṃgha* was fierce, motivated by the reluctance to relinquish control over the production of books and the monopoly on education. In 1918–1919, two progressive Mahānikāy monks, Chuon Nath and Huot That, filed a request with the Ministry of Education to have two works on Vinaya matters published, print editions of the *Pāṭimokkha* and the *Kaṭhinakkhandhaka*. The request was rejected due to the resistance by traditionalist monastics, who insisted that works regulating monastic practice should be transmitted only on palm leaf. The rejection led to a wave of clandestine printing activities of these and other works, most prominently, Huot That's *Sāmaṇera-vinaya*, which eventually paved the way to a Buddhist-run printing culture in Cambodia.[108] By 1929, modernizing monastic activists such Chuon Nath and Huot Tath themselves, who had been collaborating with the French scholar Louis Finot in acquiring and promoting Western academic textual expertise, had come to play leading roles in the Cambodian saṃgha. Earlier, the establishment of the École superieure de pâli d'Angkor Vatt in 1909, an attempt to build a counterweight to the Buddhist institutions in Bangkok that both empowered Cambodians and kept control with the colonizers, included the plan to reproduce scriptures on palm leaf and in print, which never materialized.[109] It was through the more successful École de pâli (or Sālā Pāli) in Phnom Penh, founded in 1914, and the activity of Suzanne Karpelès at the Bibliothèque nationale beginning in the mid-1920s, however, that the shift of Cambodian Buddhist textual practice from manuscript to print gained pace. Similar to the nation-building Thai initiatives, the library's mission was to collect manuscripts from across the country and, in collaboration with the scholars produced by the Sālā Pāli, to publish and sell print editions in Khmer script on the basis of manuscripts that, due to the strong dependence of Khmer libraries on the Thai supply chain, were often in Thai script.[110] The transition from manuscript to print appeared instrumental for creating a national form of Khmer Buddhism attractive to both French colonizers and Khmer Buddhist religious reformers. The production of printed books met a growing demand, with Chuon Nath's tract on lay conduct *Gihipaṭipatti* reaching bestseller status in 1926–1927 and individual donors initiating the printing of texts with the intention of the production and transfer of merit.[111] Karpelès also promoted the copying from palm leaf to palm leaf, but, at least in the view of Jacqueline Filliozat, "copies produced by Karpelès' scribes were often hurriedly executed, lacking the meticulousness and aesthetic beauty of earlier texts, more like mass-produced printed books" that "undermined rather than preserved the sacred dimensions of these texts."[112] More than the quality of its execution, however, is its ritual environment, including the conditions of production, donors' and recipients' roles, formalized handling, and storage conditions that mark the difference between print and manuscript culture and which, no doubt, were crucial for the relative status of the books in question. The crowning piece of this joint French–Khmer project, led, among others, by the early Cambodian Buddhist print pioneers Chuon Nath and Huot Tath, was the production of a Pali–Khmer version of the Tipiṭaka on both palm leaf and paper, including a translation into Khmer, initiated in 1929, with the first volume out in print in 1931 being the Vinaya, and the edition completed only in 1968, by which time Chuon Nath had taken over the leadership of the Cambodian *saṃgha*.[113] Within less than a decade from the completion of the first Khmer Buddhist canon, however, not only Huot That, the other hero of Cambodian Buddhism's shift from manuscript to print, but many other monastics too would meet a violent death at the hands of the Khmer Rouge regime. All over Cambodia, Buddhist texts in both media would jointly go through their darkest period.

20TH-CENTURY PRINT-BORN BUDDHIST TRADITIONS AND THE ELEMENTARY MANUSCRIPT

Print was crucial for the emergence of the historically younger traditions of Theravada Buddhism, as we have seen, in Vietnam and Nepal, but also in Indonesia and Malaysia, in the early 20th century. The textual production of these traditions emerged from existing Theravada print literatures in historically older Theravada communities abroad, such as in Sri Lanka, Burma, and Thailand, or from modern academic publications dealing with ancient Buddhism. No independent manuscript culture to speak of was ever developed in these cases, particularly because most activists and scholars could not rely on older local manuscript-producing institutions and because unpredictable economic conditions of emerging and sometimes disenfranchised communities required the most economic solutions. More recent traditions on the fringe of Theravada Buddhism, particularly Dalit Buddhism or the Insight Meditation or Vipassana movement, similarly developed within print environments. Additionally, the distance to traditional monastic institutions, older forms of learning and archiving, and specific manuscript-centered ritual practices such as donating or reciting proclaimed by these traditions meant that there was no place for manuscripts in the communities they created. For K. Ayōttitācar (C. Iyothee Thass, 1845–1914) and B. R. Ambedkar (1891–1956), print, not manuscript, culture was the media through which they presented their vision of Buddhism to urban progressive and oppressed parts of colonial Indian society, using books, pamphlets, and magazines and encouraging print literacy as forms of subaltern empowerment. *The Buddha and His Dhamma*, the most important foundational text of a novel and modernist South Asian form of Buddhism, was the first Buddhist scripture-like text that, including its source material, was entirely a product of print culture.[114] However, not much attention has been given to the fact that most 20th-century print products were based on handwritten manuscripts, with the machine-written typescript being the version progressively used for typesetting right up to the digital era. In fact, in his preface Ambedkar thanks his collaborators "for the burden they have taken upon themselves to type out the manuscript."[115] Although the author failed to see his magnum opus appear in print, right up to his death Ambedkar worked on typescript proofs, inserting marginalia and interlinear interventions by hand; correcting, upgrading, and completing a printed text through the technology of the manuscript; and leaving it to the editor to give the Dalit Buddhist scripture its final printed form. Just as that of any other modernist Buddhist author working toward print publications, much of the posthumous publication of Ambedkar's work relied on typescripts or manuscripts that never did, or were never meant to, find their way into print.

Scholarship with an eye on the interface of manuscript and print needs to become more aware of this other manuscript culture, which is both modern in its relation to being seen as preliminary or marginal to print and at the same time continuing a premodern strand of functional writing, reading, and circulation practices. In the modern sense, a manuscript is not defined by its material form or its technological means of production (a typescript or a printed-out digital document file is still called "a manuscript") but by its relation to its serially printed-and-published form (the poem, the novel, the article, the monograph) and its editorial curatorship and distribution through a publishing platform, in other words, by its status vis-à-vis its wider readership. The premodern form of the manuscript defined by status, in turn, is embodied in the scrapbook type prevalent in South and Southeast Asia for centuries, known particularly from the Burmese black parabaik with their erasable and reusable surfaces inscribed with a soapstone or chalk, which were, similar to their print-lined bound notebook or loose sheet counterparts emerging in the 19th-century colonial worlds, regarded as marginal to the more prestigious, expensive, cherished, and better preserved media of textual production and publication in palm leaf or ornately lacquered cloth.[116] As the resilience of contemporary ritual manuals from Nepal proves, the production and use of handwritten documents in South and Southeast Asia reaches right into the age of desktops, laptops, tablets, and smartphones. Prominent examples of the continuing use of handwriting on paper are ink marginalia and interlinear annotations copiously added every day by monastic and lay students of Buddhism to printed editions of scripture, commentary, or other genres used in monasteries, nunneries, and meditation centers, not to speak of test answers and handwritten essays produced in the exam-oriented monastic education systems not well-funded enough to afford computers or printers. A more highly visible genre are tables drawn with ballpoint pen on notebook paper to schedule and assign to individual monks the reading of particular sections of scriptures during large public events for the recitation of the Tipiṭaka organized in Theravada Buddhist venues, as well as announcements of the times and places of daily routines in nunneries or monasteries, stuck against walls and pillars. Another ubiquitous continuation of manuscript practices is the production of lists by monks, nuns, priests, and people in charge of domestic ritual, mostly women, on scraps of paper on which they record items to be purchased for Buddhist events, or their counterpart, the handwritten receipts or filled-out receipt forms shopkeepers hand out to Buddhist customers in the absence of electric cash registers. These "minor" yet in their quantity and pervasiveness massive and persistently surviving forms of manuscript culture, produced, owned, and handled by Buddhists throughout South and Southeast Asia, just as by almost all literate or semiliterate communities around the world (including those of us who stick post-its to their refrigerator doors), tell us more about Buddhism in practice than most of the surviving prestigious manifestations of manuscript culture, and they certainly tell different stories than the more visible (and, admittedly, more easily readable) articulations in print. Due to the still prevalent historiographical models circumscribing our view on the relation between manuscript and print, they will continue to refuse to find a place in an archive, but in a world which is fast moving from print to digital, they may continue to exist, opaquely and for quite a while longer, thanks to their very enduring impermanence.

FURTHER READING

Ambhanwong, Suthilak. "Major Periods in Thai Printing." *The Journal of Library History* 1, no. 4 (1966): 242–247.

Bretfeld-Wolf, Ann-Kathrin. "Hoisted by Their Own Petard. The Emergence of Sril Lankan Buddhist Printing and Counter-Christian Activities." *Kervan—International Journal of Afro-Asiatic Studies* 21 (2017): 339–356.

Chi, Dinh Minh, Ly Kim Hoa, Ha Thuc Minh, Ha Van Tan, and Nguyen Tai Thu. *The History of Buddhism in Vietnam.* Edited by Nguyen Tai Thu. Washington, DC: Council of Research Values and Philosophy, 2008.

Diemberger, Hildegard, Franz-Karl Ehrhard, and Peter Kornicki, eds. *Tibetan Printing: Comparison, Continuities, and Change.* Leiden, The Netherlands: Brill, 2016.

Shaw, Graham. "South Asia." In *A Companion to the History of the Book.* Edited by Simon Eliot and Jonathan Rose (pp. 269–281). Oxford: Wiley Blackwell, 2007.

Vaidya, P. L., ed. *Aṣṭasāhasrikā Prajñāpāramitā With Haribhadra's Commentary Called Āloka.* Buddhist Sanskrit Texts. 4. Darbhanga, India: The Mithila Institute, 1960.

Welch, Michael W. "Fa-tsang, Pure Light and Printing: An Enquiry into the Origins of Textual Xylography." PhD diss., University of Minnesota, 1981.

NOTES

1. Cristina Scherrer-Schaub, "Printing versus Manuscript: History or Rhetoric? A Short Note Inspired by Pelliot DIC," in *Tibetan Printing: Comparison, Continuities, and Change,* ed. Hildegard Diemberger, Franz-Karl Ehrhard, and Peter Kornicki (Leiden, The Netherlands: Brill, 2016), 153–170; Aleix Ruiz-Falqués, "Notes on Printing Press and Pali Literature in Burma," *Kervan—International Journal of Afro-Asiatic Studies,* 21 (2017): 357–371, 358–359.
2. Timothy H. Barrett, "Pattern Reproduction Possibilities and the Alpha and Omega of Tibetan Printing," in *Tibetan Printing: Comparison, Continuities, and Change,* ed. Hildegard Diemberger, Franz-Karl Ehrhard, and Peter Kornick (Leiden, The Netherlands: Brill, 2016), 560–574.
3. Sheldon Pollock, "Literary Culture and Manuscript Culture in Precolonial India," in *Literary Cultures and the Material Book,* ed. Simon Eliot, Andrew Nash, and I. R. Willison (London: British Library, 2007), 77–94, esp. 77–78.
4. Pollock, "Literary Culture and Manuscript Culture in Precolonial India," 78.
5. Barrett, "Pattern Reproduction Possibilities," 560–568.
6. S. D. Lawson, "A Catalogue of Indian Buddhist Clay Sealings in British Museums," PhD diss. (Oxford University, 1982).
7. (Kornicki 2012, 52) Peter Kornicki, "The *Hyakumantō darani* and the Origins of Printing in Japan," *International Journal of Asian Studies* 9 (2012): 43–70.
8. Timothy H. Barrett. *The Woman Who Discovered Printing* (New Haven, CT: Yale University Press, 2008), 67.
9. Jean-Pierre Drège, "Les premières impressions des dhāranī de Mahāpratisarā," *Cahiers d'Extrême Asie* 11 (1999): 25–44, 25–26.
10. Barrett, "Pattern Reproduction Possibilities," 568.
11. Imre Galambos, "Manuscripts and Printing: East Asia," in *Brill's Encyclopedia of Buddhism,* vol. I, ed. Jonathan A. Silk, Vincent Eltschinger, and Oskar von Hinüber (Leiden, The Netherlands: Koniglijke Brill NV, 2015), 968–978, esp. 972.
12. Tsuen-Hsuin Tsien, *Written on Bamboo and Silk: The Beginnings of Chinese Books and Inscriptions* (Chicago: University of Chicago Press, 1962), 38.
13. Helmut Eimer, "The Tibetan Kanjur Printed in China," *Zentralasiatische Studien* 36 (2007): 35–60, 38–39, incl. n. 23.
14. Barrett, *Woman Who Discovered Printing.*

15. Scherrer-Schaub, "Printing versus Manuscript," 157.
16. John D. Phan, "Introduction: Considering 'Buddhist Literacy' in Early Modern Vietnamese Print Culture," *Journal of Vietnamese Studies* 13, no. 3 (2018): 2–8.
17. Cuong Tu Nguyen, *Zen in Medieval Vietnam: A Study and Translation of the Thien Uyen Tap Anh* (Honolulu: University of Hawaii Press, 1997), 341n41; Dinh Minh Chi et al., *The History of Buddhism in Vietnam*, ed. Nguyen Tai Thu (Washington, DC: The Council of Research Values and Philosophy, 2008), 95–96.
18. Nguyen, *Zen in Medieval Vietnam*, 92.
19. Chi et al., *History of Buddhism in Vietnam*, 125, 129.
20. Chi et al., *History of Buddhism in Vietnam*, 154–155.
21. Li Tana, "The Imported Book Trade and Confucian Learning in Seventeenth and Eighteenth-Century Vietnam," in *New Perspectives on the History and Historiography of Southeast Asia: Continuing Explorations*, ed. Michael Arthur Aung-Thwin and Kenneth R. Hall (New York: Routledge, 2011), 169.
22. Shawn F. McHale, *Print and Power. Confucianism, Communism, and Buddhism in the Making of Modern Vietnam* (Honolulu: University of Hawaii Press, 2004), 12.
23. Kathlene Baldanza, "Publishing, Book Culture, and Reading Practices in Vietnam: The View from Thắng Nghiêm and Phổ Nhân Temples," *Journal of Vietnamese Studies* 13, no. 3 (2018): 9–28, esp. 10–13.
24. Baldanza, "Publishing, Book Culture, and Reading Practices in Vietnam," 16.
25. Baldanza, "Publishing, Book Culture, and Reading Practices in Vietnam," 23–24.
26. Baldanza, "Publishing, Book Culture, and Reading Practices in Vietnam," 13.
27. John D. Phan, "The Twentieth-Century Secularization of the Sinograph in Vietnam, and Its Demotion from the Cosmological to the Aesthetic," *Journal of World Literature* 1 (2016): 275–293.
28. Jacques Roland, *Portuguese Pioneers of Vietnamese Linguistics Prior to 1650* [Pionniers portugais de la linguistique vietnamienne jusqu'en 1650] (Bangkok: Orchid Press, 2002).
29. McHale, *Print and Power*, 14.
30. McHale, *Print and Power*, 7–11.
31. Nguyen, *Zen in Medieval Vietnam*, 92.
32. McHale, *Print and Power*, 150–156.
33. Kurtis Schaeffer, *The Culture of the Book in Tibet* (New York: Columbia University Press, 2009), 9 and n. 48.
34. Shi Jinbo, "Zuizao de zangwen mukeben kaolue" [A Study of the Earliest Printed Tibetan Woodcut Texts], *China Tibetology* [Zhongguo Zangxue] 4 (2005): 33–49, cited in Sam van Schaik, "Manuscripts and Printing: Tibet," in *Brill's Encyclopedia of Buddhism*, vol. I, ed. Jonathan A. Silk, Vincent Eltschinger, and Oskar von Hinüber (Leiden, The Netherlands: Koniglijke Brill NV, 2015), 961.
35. Scherrer-Schaub, "Printing versus Manuscript," 161–162.
36. Leonard van der Kuijp, "Faulty Transmissions: Some Notes on Tibetan Textual Criticism and the Impact of Xylography," in *Edition, editions: L'écrit au Tibet, évolution et devenir*, ed. Anne Chayet et al. (Munich: Indus, 2010), 441–442.
37. Hildegard Diemberger, "Patronage and Printing Innovation in 15th century Tibet," in *Patronage as Politics in South Asia*, ed. Anastasia Piliavsky (New York: Cambridge University Press, 2016), 362. See also Michaela Clemente, "From Manuscript to Block Printing: In the Search of Stylistic Models for the Identification of Tibetan Xylographs," *Rivista Degli Studi Orientali. Nuova Serie* 84, no. 1/4 (2011): 51–66.
38. Diemberger, "Patronage and Printing Innovation," 356, 362.
39. Diemberger, "Patronage and Printing Innovation," 350–351; Hildegard Diemberger, "Quand le livre devient relique: Les textes tibétains entre culture bouddhique et transformations technologiques," *Terrain* 59 (2012): 18–39, esp. 24; Scherrer-Schaub, "Printing versus Manuscript," 163–166.

40. Eimer, "Tibetan Kanjur," 35–60.
41. Jonathan Silk, "Notes on the History of the Yongle Kanjur," in *Suhṛllekhāḥ. Festgabe für Helmut Eimer*, ed. Michael Hahn, Jens-Uwe Hartmann, and Roland Steiner (Indica et Tibetica: Swisstal-Odendorf, 1996), 153–200.
42. Franz-Karl Erhard, *Early Buddhist Block-Prints From Mang-yul Gung-thang* (Lumbini, Nepal: LIRI, 2000), 11.
43. van Schaik, "Manuscripts and Printing: Tibet," 961.
44. van Schaik, "Manuscripts and Printing: Tibet," 960.
45. Cristina Scherrer-Schaub and George Bonami. "Establishing a Typology of the Old Tibetan Manuscripts: A Multidisciplinary Approach," in *Dunhuang Manuscript Forgeries*, ed Susan Whitfield (London: British Library, 2002), 184–215; Agnieszka Helman-Ważny, *The Archaeology of Tibetan Books* (Leiden, The Netherlands: Brill, 2014), 76–94.
46. Helman-Ważny, *Archaeology of Tibetan Books*, 64–75.
47. Ulrich Timme Kragh, "The Significant Leap from Writing to Print: Editorial Modifications in the First Printed Edition of the Collected Works of Sgam po pa Bsod nams rin chen," *Journal of the International Association of Tibetan Studies* 7 (2013): 365–425, esp. 400.
48. Scherrer-Schaub, "Printing versus Manuscript," 166.
49. Camillo A. Formigatti, "A Forgotten Chapter in South Asian Book History? A Bird's Eye View of Sanskrit Print Culture," in *Tibetan Printing: Comparison, Continuities, and Change*, ed. Hildegard Diemberger, Franz-Karl Ehrhard, and Peter Kornick (Leiden, The Netherlands: Brill, 2016), 86–87.
50. Klaus Ludwig Janert, *Von der Art und den Mitteln der indischen Textweitergabe: Bericht über mündliche und schriftliche Tradierungsmethoden sowie die Schreibmaterialien in Indien* (Cologne: Bibliothekar-Lehrinstitut, 1955), 60.
51. Formigatti, "A Forgotten Chapter in South Asian Book History?" 118.
52. Graham Shaw, "South Asia." In *A Companion to the History of the Book*, edited by Simon Eliot and Jonathan Rose (Oxford: Wiley Blackwell, 2007), 125.
53. Shaw, "South Asia," 132.
54. Formigatti, "A Forgotten Chapter in South Asian Book History?" 115.
55. John Whelpton, *A History of Nepal* (Cambridge, UK: Cambridge University Press, 2005), 81.
56. Roderick A. M. Chalmers, "Pandits and Pulp Fiction: Popular Publishing and the Birth of Nepali Print-Capitalism in Banaras," *Studies in Nepali History and Society* 7, no. 1 (2002): 35–97.
57. Premśānti Tulādhar,. *Nepālbhāṣā sāhityayā itihās* [A History of Newar Literature] (Kathmandu: Nepālbhāṣā ekedami, NS 1120, 1999), 81–82; Sarah LeVine and David N. Gellner, *Rebuilding Buddhism: The Theravada Movement in Twentieth-Century Nepal* (Cambridge, MA: Harvard University Press, 2007), 38.
58. Christoph Emmrich, "Emending Perfection: Prescript, Postscript and Practice in Newar Buddhist Manuscript Culture," in *Buddhist Manuscript Cultures: Knowledge, Ritual and Art*, ed. Stephen Berkwitz, Juliane Schober, and Claudia Brown, 140–156 (London: Routledge, 2008); see also Alexander O'Neill, "Textual Manifestations: The Use and Significance of Mahāyāna Literature in Newar Buddhism," *European Bulletin of Himalayan Research* 54 (2020): 36–65.
59. William Pruitt et al., *To Digitize Myanmar Manuscripts, Manuscript List and Digital Book Protection* (Tokyo: Chuo Academic Research Institute, 2017), 2.
60. R. H. Clapperton, *Paper: An Historical Account of Its Making by Hand from the Earliest Times down to the Present* (Oxford: The Shakespeare Head Press, 1934), 61; and Dard Hunter, *Papermaking: The History and Technique of an Ancient Craft* (New York: Alfred A. Knopf, 1943).
61. Ove K. Nordstrand, "The Introduction of Paper to Ceylon," *Ceylon Today* 10 (1961): 15–18; Ananda Kentish Coomaraswamy, *Mediaeval Sinhalese Art* (Broad Campden, UK: n.p, 1908).

62. Tilak Kularatne, *History of Printing and Publishing in Ceylon, 1736–1912* (Dehiwala, Sri Lanka: Tilak Kularatne, 2006), 7.
63. Kularatne, *History of Printing and Publishing in Ceylon*, 9.
64. Kularatne, *History of Printing and Publishing in Ceylon*, 15–17.
65. Kularatne, *History of Printing and Publishing in Ceylon*, 8.
66. Kularatne, *History of Printing and Publishing in Ceylon*, 232.
67. Sir James Emerson Tennent, *Christianity in Ceylon: Its Introduction and Progress under the Portuguese, the Dutch, the British, and American Missions; With an Historical Sketch of the Brahmanical and Buddhist Superstitions* (London: John Murray, 1850), quoted in Kularatne, *History of Printing and Publishing in Ceylon*, 233.
68. Anne M. Blackburn, *Locations of Buddhism. Colonialism & Modernity in Sri Lanka* (Chicago: University of Chicago Press, 2010), 199.
69. Anne M. Blackburn, *Buddhist Learning and Textual Practice in Eighteenth-Century Lankan Monastic Culture* (Princeton, NJ: Princeton University Press, 2001).
70. Richard Fox Young and G. P. V. Somaratna. *Vain Debates. The Buddhist–Christian Controversies of Nineteenth-Century Ceylon* (Vienna: Sammlung de Nobili, 1996), 113.
71. Kularatne, *History of Printing and Publishing in Ceylon*, 158–160; Blackburn, *Locations of Buddhism*, 15.
72. Kularatne, *History of Printing and Publishing in Ceylon*, 160.
73. Kularatne, *History of Printing and Publishing in Ceylon*, 165.
74. Oskar von Hinüber, "Manuscripts and Printing: South, Southeast, and Central Asia," in *Brill's Encyclopedia of Buddhism*, vol. I, ed. Jonathan A. Silk, Vincent Eltschinger, and Oskar von Hinüber (Leiden, The Netherlands: Koniglijke Brill NV, 2015), 954.
75. G. P. Malalasekera, *The Pāli Literatur of Ceylon* (Kandy, Sri Lanka: Buddhist Publication Society, 1928), 303–304; Young and Somaratna, *Vain Debates*, 210.
76. Kularatne, *History of Printing and Publishing in Ceylon*, 45.
77. Von Hinüber, "Manuscripts and Printing," 954.
78. Mark Frost, "'Wider Opportunities.' Religious Revival, Nationalist Awakening and the Global Dimension in Colombo, 1870–1920," *Modern Asian Studies* 36, no. 4 (2002): 937–967, esp. 945.
79. Yan Naing Lin, "Mandalay and the Printing Industry," *Mandalay University Research Journal* 7 (2016): 2–26, esp. 5.
80. Lin, "Mandalay and the Printing Industry," 5–6.
81. Maung Shwe Wa, Genevieve Sowards, and Erville Sowards, *Burma Baptist Chronicle* (Rangoon: Board of Publications, Burma Baptist Convention, 1963).
82. Ruiz Falqués, "Notes on Printing Press and Pali Literature in Burma," 365.
83. Lin, "Mandalay and the Printing Industry," 6.
84. Lin, "Mandalay and the Printing Industry," 8–9.
85. Elizabeth L. Eisenstein, *The Printing Press as an Agent of Change: Communications and Cultural Transformations in Early-Modern Europe* (Cambridge, UK: Cambridge University Press, 1979).
86. Willem B. Bollée, "Some Lesser Known Burmese Pali Texts," in *Pratidānam. Indian, Iranian and Indo-European Studies Presented to Franciscus Bernardus Jacobus Kuiper on His Sixtieth Birthday*, ed. Jan C. Heesterman, G. H. Schokker, and V. I. Subramoniam (The Hague, The Netherlands: Mouton, 1968), 495.
87. Ludu Daw Ahmar, *The World's Biggest Book* (2nd ed.) (Than Tun, Trans.) (Mandalay, Myanmar: Kyipwayay Press, 1980).
88. Mark Allon et al., "The Kuthodaw Pagoda Marble-stelae Inscriptions, Mandalay, Myanmar: Conservation, Photographing, and Study of a Neglected Recension of the Pali Buddhist Canon," *Bulletin of the Chuo Academic Research Institute (Chūō Gakujutsu Kenkyūjo Kiyō)* 45 (2016): 222–249, esp. 223.

89. Bollée, "Some Lesser Known Burmese Pali Texts," 495; Ahmar, *World's Biggest Book*, 42–45; Pa Pa Aung, "A Study of Engraved Buddhist Texts by Ledi Sayadaw," *Yangon University of Distance Education Research Journal* 4, no. 1 (2012): 1–7.
90. Lin, "Mandalay and the Printing Industry," 10.
91. Michael Winship, "Early Thai Printing: The Beginnings to 1851," *Crossroads: An Interdisciplinary Journal of Southeast Asian Studies* 3 (1986): 45–61; Michael Winship, "The Printing Press as an Agent of Change? Early Missionary Printing in Thailand," *Common-Place* 8, no. 2 (2008).
92. Patrick Jory, "Books and the Nation: The Making of Thailand's National Library," *Journal of Southeast Asian Studies* 31, no. 2 (2000): 351–373, esp. 365 and n. 71.
93. Jory, "Books and the Nation," 372.
94. Robert Halliday and Christian Bauer, eds., *The Mons of Burma and Thailand, Volume 1. The Talaings* (Bangkok: White Lotus Press, 2000), 143.
95. Von Hinüber, "Manuscripts and Printing," 954.
96. Jory, "Books and the Nation," 365–366.
97. Jory, "Books and the Nation," 362, 369.
98. Grant A. Olson, "Thai Cremation Volumes: A Brief History of a Unique Genre of Literature," *Asian Folklore Studies* 51 (1992): 279–294.
99. Justin McDaniel, *Gathering Leaves and Lifting Words. Histories of Buddhist Monastic Education in Laos and Thailand* (Seattle: University of Washington Press, 2008), 163.
100. Jory, "Books and the Nation," 369–370.
101. McDaniel, *Gathering Leaves and Lifting Words*, 163.
102. McDaniel, *Gathering Leaves and Lifting Words*.
103. Georges Coedès, *The Vajirañana National Library of Siam* (Bangkok: Authority of the Council of the National Library, 1924), 8, quoted by Jory, "Books and the Nation," 19.
104. Zachary Quinn Scheuren, "Khmer Printing Types and the Introduction of Print in Cambodia 1877–1977," Magisterial thesis (Department Typeface Design, University of Reading, 2010), 21.
105. Penny Edwards, *Cambodge: The Cultivation of a Nation, 1860–1945* (Honolulu: University of Hawaii Press, 2007), 105; Scheuren, "Khmer Printing Types and Introduction of Print."
106. Jacques Nepote, "Introduction à une histoire de la presse au Cambodge," *Présence indochinoise* 2 (1979): 96–129; Jacques Nepote, "La presse au Cambodge: Des consensus traditionnels aux expressions divergentes de l'opinion publique modern," *Péninsule* 53, no. 2 (2006): 27–80.
107. Edwards, *Cambodge*, 173.
108. Anne R. Hansen, *How to Behave. Buddhism and Modernity in Colonial Cambodia, 1860–1930* (Honolulu: University of Hawaii Press, 2007), 106–107; Edwards, *Cambodge*, 121.
109. Hansen, *How to Behave*, 132.
110. Hansen, *How to Behave*, 143.
111. Hansen, *How to Behave*, 145.
112. Personal communication, in Hansen, *How to Behave*, 144, 221n216.
113. Hansen, *How to Behave*, 144–146.
114. B. R. Ambedkar, *The Buddha and His Dhamma: A Critical Edition* (Aakash Singh Rathore and Ajay Verma, Eds.) (Oxford: Oxford University Press, 2011).
115. Ambedkar, *Buddha and His Dhamma*, xxvii.
116. Christian Lammerts, "Notes on Burmese Manuscripts: Text and Images," *Journal of Burma Studies* 14 (2010): 229–253, esp. 242.

Christoph Emmrich